AF516049

Proceedings of the Indian National Congress

Vol.1:1885-1889

Edited and Introduced by

Mushirul Hasan

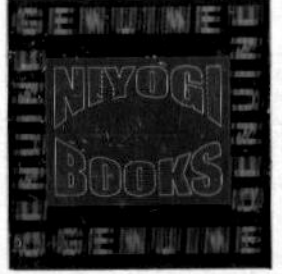

Published by

NIYOGI BOOKS

D-78, Okhla Industrial Area, Phase-I
New Delhi-110 020, India
Tel: 91-11-26816301, 49327000
Fax: 91-11-26810483, 26813830
email: niyogibooks@gmail.com
www.niyogibooks.com

ISBN: 978-93-81523-14-8
Year of Publication: 2012

Printed at: Niyogi Offset Pvt. Ltd., New Delhi, India

EDITOR'S NOTE

The first Indian National Congress was held in 1885, one year after the Marquess of Ripon left India: 'in that world of high mortality among political parties, for India's Congress party to have survived for a century is in itself no small achievement. But the party has done much more than survive. It successfully transformed itself from movement to party in order to change from protest to governance ...,'[1]

The same year, Henry Cotton, a British civil servant, published a book, *New India, or India in Transition*. This book created quite a stir, and was highly spoken of by the *Times* newspaper. It discussed 'the future that attends the Indian races and of the great Indian movement upon which, after the lapse of a quarter of a century, public attention has been fixed, but to which at that time men's eyes were blind.'[2]

These volumes are not just a record of Congress speeches and resolutions, but they also capture the mental, emotional, and political life of late-nineteenth century India. They are, furthermore, a gallery of some leading individuals who contributed, with infinite patience and tenacity, to the evolution of an Indian nationality. I hope the readers will, besides enjoying their endearing company, capture the cross-currents at a time when 'New India' was being unveiled.

Scores of books exist on the Indian National Congress. We have taken a different route to illuminate the birth of an idea that has captured the imagination of millions. This is probably the first authentic version of the Congress proceedings; earlier printed texts were either abridged or tampered with. I hope to publish the rest until we reach the year of Independence. Some reports were torn in parts; we have left those portions as they are. In some places the missing words have been added to make the text intelligible to the reader.

I thank Bikash Niyogi and his team for agreeing to support this venture.

Mushirul Hasan
New Delhi, April 2012

1. R.A.M Joshi & R.K. Hebsur, Eds. *Congress in Indian Politics: A Centenary Perspective*, Bombay, 1987, p. 1.
2. Henry Cotton. *Indian and Home Memories*, London, 1911, p. 197.

Lord Ripon (1827-1909) was a popular Governor General and Viceroy of India (1880-1884). The controversial Ilbert Bill issue marked Ripon's administration. The controversy arose out of the question of jurisdiction of native judges over European subjects. The Law member introduced a bill banning the protected status of the white and seeking equality of all subjects in the eyes of the law. The Anglo-Indian community forced the government to enact the bill bringing substantial amendments to its original spirit and letter. The Vernacular Act (1878) was also opposed by the Anglo-Indian press. However, Ripon's idea about granting freedom of press to all without showing any racial discrimination prevailed. Ripon left India in 1884.

Dadbhai Naoroji was one of the major organisers of a Ripon Memorial Fund. He organised a packed town hall meeting on 29 November 1884 for sending off Ripon. One other Parsi, H.A. Wadiyar, had collected funds from princes in Kathiawar.

Introduction

Unveiling New India 1885-89: The Congress in History[3]

In nineteenth-century Europe, nationalism became associated with popular sovereignty and with the idea that loyalty to the people came before loyalty to the ruler. These were the ideas of Mazzini and the Irish patriots, who influenced India and other Asian countries as prophets of nationalism. As a student in London, Surendranath Banerjea learnt of Mazzini's work and lectured on him. Lala Lajpat Rai considered himself to be one of his disciples and wrote Mazzini's biography in Urdu. Today, the word nationalism is understood to be an umbrella term under which are subsumed the related phenomena of national identity and consciousness, and collectivities based on them—nations; occasionally, it is employed to refer to the articulate ideology on which national identity and consciousness rest.

Is nationalism an idea imported into Asia from Europe? Some people think that in China and Japan, and to a lesser extent in India, the sense of patriotism was strong and deeply imbedded in people. According to them, nationalism in Asia grew alongside the same movement in Europe and arose out of similar circumstances; that is, resistance to foreign rule. The provincial associations and the Congress thereafter expressed this sentiment in different ways but their common refrain was to petition the government to reform the legislative council and give a greater share of public office to Indians.[4] This resolution, according to Allan Octavion Hume—who the *Hindi Punch* described as the 'political rishi of Modern Bharat'—'indicated the very essence of the great task which the people of India, at last a nation, one and indivisible henceforth and forever, was soberly and deliberately girding up their loins to undertake.'[5] The struggle lasted long; ultimately this prayer for popular representation was conceded by the Morley-Minto reforms of 1909.

---

3. See S.R. Mehrotra, *The Emergence of the Indian National Congress* (Delhi, 1971), for a detailed history of associations; Briton Martin, Jr, *New India, 1885*: *British Official Policy and the Emergence of the Indian National Congress* (Bombay, 1970) and John R. McLane, *Indian Nationalism and the Early Congress* (Princeton, 1987), for early Congress History; John Gallagher, Gordon Johnson and Anil Seal (eds.), *Locality, Province and Nation* (Cambridge, 1973); Bipin Chandra, *Rise and Growth of Economic Nationalism in India: Economic Policies of Indian National Leadership 1880-1905* (New Delhi, 1966); D.A. Low (ed.), *Soundings in Modern South Asian History* (Berkeley, 1968); D.A. Low (ed), *Congress and the Raj: Facets of the Indian Struggle* (London, 1977) and *Indian National Congress Centenary Hindsights;* Richard Sisson and Stanley Wolpert (ed.) *Congress and Indian Nationalism: The Pre-independence Phase* (Berkeley, 1988), for essays covering various themes in different regions.

4. 'This Congress considers the reform and expansion of the Supreme and existing Local Legislative Councils, by the admission of a considerable proportion of elected members (and the creation of similar Councils for the North-West Provinces and Oudh, and also for the Punjab) essential; and holds that all Budgets should be referred to those Councils for consideration, their members being moreover empowered to interpolate the Executive in regard to all branches of the administration; and that a Standing Committee of the House of Commons should be constituted to receive and consider any formal protest that may be recorded by majorities of such Councils against the exercise by the Executive of the power which would be vested in it, of over-ruling the decisions of such majorities.'

5. In 1905, Gokhale summed up the Congress demands: securing for the people a larger share in administration, including a reform of the legislative councils, the appointment of Indians to the Secretary of State's council and the executive councils in India; improving the methods of administration, such as the separation of judicial from executive functions; reduction of the tax burden and military expenditure; reducing the indebtedness of the peasantry, extension of primary education, and facilities for industrial land technical training.

Sal-i nau ki mubarakbad! Lady Congress-khelo! Beta khelo! Aur is se taraqqi ka khush-aind gana gao.

'Happy New Year,' 8 January 1891. This illustration by Lal Bahadur shows a mother urging a child to play the bugle (marked taraqqi or progress) and sing the song of progress. The 'Lady Congress' has 'Congress' written on her band; the little boy '1891.' The trishul here is symbolic of power, strength and confidence.

The British Indian Association had been formed in Calcutta as early as 1851, the Bombay Association less than a year later. Madras merchants formed a local branch of the British Indian Association in February 1852, replacing it six months later by an independent body, the Madras Native Association. It aimed to amend the Company charter, revise the taxation system, and curb missionary activity. The association was active for a decade, but with the transfer of British India from the East India Company to the Crown in 1858, one of its principal grievances had vanished. By July 1862, it had become virtually defunct. This had been the fate of several associations, and yet they reflected the political disenchantment in several regions. Surendranath Banerjea, a life-long educationist and publicist, convened the first Indian National Conference in December 1883 as the response of educated India to the Ilbert Bill agitation. It was followed by the founding of the Madras Mahajana Sabha in May 1885 and the Bombay Presidency Association in January 1885. They acted in concert to launch a National Conference in Poona, a city associated with the leading reformers in Maharashtra. The Peshwa's Pace of Heerbagh was the chosen venue, but the outbreak of cholera compelled them to move to the Goculdas Tejpal Boarding school, Sanskrit College and Library, situated at Gowalia Tank in Bombay.

On December 28, 1885, some eighty-three odd participants gave birth to a historic movement. They belonged to different social and economic strata, and their differences in wealth, caste, region and religion did sometimes turn sour, even where there was no real class struggle. Yet, they were men of unusual vision, courage and commitment. Dadabhai Naoroji, whose intellectual prestige was guaranteed by his learned contacts within the Parsis in Bombay, successfully steered the Congress through difficulties of every kind and watched its growth vigilantly but with anxiety; Pherozeshah Mehta, assured of a strong social position in the legal profession, was in full flow; Surendranath Banerjea, a brilliant lawyer representing the best of the Bengal renaissance, walked up and down acquainting fellow-delegates with his campaigns; Lal Mohun Ghose, another brilliant orator whose eloquence excited the admiration of John Bright; Rash Behari Ghose, a lawyer of unrivalled reputation who also became the President of the Congress; Kashinath T. Telang lobbied for his resolution; Ananda Charlu, one of the founders of the Madras Mahajana Sabha, and the turbaned Subramaniya Iyer, editor of *Hindu* (1878-98), lent the Congress a more representative character; W.C. Bonnerjee, the President, enjoyed being in the thick of things. When his turn came to speak, he enumerated the government's good deeds and tried to dispel the image of the Congress as 'a nest of conspirators and disloyalists.' He provided, so William Wedderburn believed, 'the wise head and firm hand, and took the helm when the good ship was launched.'[6]

Allan Octavian Hume, a former civil servant, occupied centre stage. Somebody who always felt a warm attachment to the Indian people, he recognised the Bombay gathering as a truly momentous occasion, much as the first sitting of the Continental Congress at Philadelphia in 1774 was for the United States. Badruddin Tyabji of the President of the Bombay Presidency Association was conspicuously absent, but he joined the second Congress along with Camruddin Tyabji, Dharansi, a Bombay corporator, and R.M. Sayani, who had served as Sheriff of Bombay.

'All these men', the Congress boasted in 1885, 'assembled in the same hall, presented such a variety of costumes and complexions, that a similar scene can scarcely be witnessed anywhere except at a fancy ball.' According to the official report, 'Not only were all parts of India thus represented, but also most classes; there were barristers, solicitors, pleaders, merchants, landowners, bankers, medical men, newspaper editors and proprietors, principals and professors of independent colleges ... It is difficult to conceive any gathering of this restricted number more thoroughly representative of the entire nation....'

'The National Congresses, the second of which has just concluded its session in Calcutta, are visible symbols of this unmistakable tendency towards nationality,' commented H.J.S. Cotton, who kept a warm heart for India and Indians. Both in India and in England he played the part of patron to those of his friends who were involved in Congress activities. He attended the Congress meeting in the Town Hall, along with Charles Elliott, a senior government servant, and George Yule, a leading Calcutta merchant. Dufferin, the Viceroy, invited the delegates to a garden party at Government House. 'Never, I suppose,' Cotton noted in his second book, 'was a more interesting and picturesque assemblage collected there, from all parts of India, from Lahore and Sind to Travancore.'[7]

Slowly, the Congress began to reveal the intricate relationship between different groups. Consider, for example, the 1887 Congress where each of the leading activists belonged to a tiny group of the Western-educated from Madras city. Among the commercial groups was the millionaire-industrialist A. Sabhapaati Mudaliar of Bellary, who had close contracts with the city

6. William Wedderburn, *Allan Octavian Hume* (London, 1913), p. 58.

7. Henry Cotton, *Indian and Home Memories*, p. 199.

through his litigation and social reform activities. The list included the Indian mercantile elite of Madras city, a number of wealthy zamindars, and religious leaders like the Sankaracharya of Kumbakonam and the Pandarasanidhi of Dharmapuram. There were, finally, some 67 Muslims, including the prominent Madras city Persian family of Badsha, and the Maracair Muslims of Negapatam, the official Congress agents for eastern Tanjore. The communal division, which later emerged to tear apart provincial and national politics, were as irrelevant to the Congress of the late 1880s as they were to most aspects of local politics all the time.

The 1887 Congress at Madras provides us with political map of the presidency in which were drawn both the boundaries of local political constituencies and the threads that connected these constituencies in the capital. It represented most of the important political elements against growing governmental interference. As virtually every indigenous political power felt the prodding of government, so virtually every major political interest backed the Congress demands.[8]

By the time the Congress travelled to Allahabad in 1888, the city where the confluence of the two sacred rivers takes place, the *Gham Khwar-i-Hind* (Lahore) of 15 December 1888 reported that 200 tents had been pitched for the reception of delegates at Allahabad in addition to a considerable number of *shouldaris*. It was said that a bazaar would be opened in the midst of the camp for the delegates. Chairs were provided for delegates and galleries erected for about 5,000 visitors.[9] George Yule, Sheriff of Calcutta, presided over the Congress.

In Allahabad, the Congress was essentially a secondary organisation for many local leaders. Their association with it derived from the need to pursue within the regional and all-India skeletal organisation and aspiration the much more circumscribed local and sectional aims that derived from lower levels of politics. C.A. Bayly reminds us of the vitality of patron-client relationship and the corresponding weakness of other forms of political associations. The most powerful patrons in Allahabad were, according to his erudite study, wealthy bankers and traders, while amongst their clients were priests, lawyers and others who worked to maintain the family's ritual, social and political status. In addition, publicists and literati attached themselves to the connections of town magnates as hagiographers and propagandists, or in the hope of gaining support for wider religious or political projects.[10]

The *Oudh Punch* (Lucknow) of 3 January contains a picture in which a native lady called the Jumna, and a European lady called the Ganges, are represented as standing on high pedestals, and pouring water from vessels held in their hands into a reservoir, to water a garden marked the Indian Empire. The stream of water poured by the Jumna is marked loyalty, wealth and greatness, and that poured by the Ganges, education, protection and peace; and the union of the two streams is called the National Congress. The letterpress below is: "The new year's presents. The auspicious conjunction of Jupiter and Venus at Allahabad."[11]

The *Taj-ul-Akhbar* (Rawalpindi) of 4 January 1890 reported the success of the Congress meeting that year, in spite of the efforts of its opponents to bring it into discredit. It felt that the detractors, following the lead of Syed Ahmad Khan, made a great mistake in opposing the movement, since there was no harm in making the requirements of the country known to the Government. The writer wanted the British Parliament and the people of England generally to pay greater attention to the affairs of this country.

---

8. This and the preceding paragraphs are based on Washbrook, *Emergence of Provincial Politics*.
9. Report on the Native Newspapers, Punjab, Jan-Dec 1889, p. 21-22.
10. C.A. Bayly, *The Local Roots of Indian Politics – Allahabad 1880-1920* (Oxford, 1975).
11. Report on the Native Newspapers, Punjab, Jan-Dec 1888.

Aananki khak ra banazar-i keemiya kunand, Aaya buwad ki, gosha-i chashm-i bima kunand.

'Fifth Congress; Those who with our glance turn dust into the Philosopher's stone, is it possible that they will cast an oblique glance towards us too?' 2 January 1890. Congress representatives submit their complaints and grievances (shikayat). The word 'Azadi' or freedom is written below the tiger-like figure, while an anxious-looking eagle looks on. With education (talim) written on a burning flame and the roll of complaints lying on the floor, the Viceroy, with Ingilistan (England) inscribed on his chest, looks on in total discomfort.

To sum up, regional and local perspectives offer a different and, indeed, a more complex perspective.[12] They facilitate, moreover, our understanding of the points of contact between greater and lesser institutions and hence our understanding of the processes and politics and of political change. As British colonial and Indian history has so many points of contact between larger and smaller socio-political structures, it must aid our appreciation of them.[13]

What was the Congress all about in its early years? The apparent strong cohesion which existed between the first generation leaders doesn't mean that the leaders were always united in thought or in mutual confidence. They were not. There was, moreover, a great divergence between demands and values. The first five years do not give the impression of a full-fledged political party. There were no paying members, there was no permanent organisation, no official other than the general secretary, no central office and no funds. Dadabhai Naoroji clarified that the Congress wasn't a nursery for sedition and rebellion. Many of its members were, in fact, educated and enlightened and equipped to be a source of infinite strength to British rule. They were on good terms with the Viceroy, despite the occasional tiff, and were united among

12. Rajat Ray, *Urban Roots of Indian Nationalism: Pressure Groups and Conflict of Interests in Calcutta City Politics, 1875-1939* (Calcutta, 1979).
13. D.A. Washbrook, *Emergence of Provincial Politics*, p. 6.

themselves. They did their best to convince the government that the Congress was much more than the handmaiden of English-educated and professional men drawn principally from the higher, literate Hindu castes of the maritime presidencies, and that Lord Dufferin, the Viceroy, should engage with them and heed their administrative, agrarian, and social grievances. Their sentiments were expressed in the following words:

It is the British Government in their noble enthusiasm for the emancipation of this great people—God's trust to them—from the letters of ignorance, who by the broadest dissemination of Western education and Western ideas of liberty, the rights of subjects, public spirit and patriotism, have let loose forces which, unless wisely guided and controlled, might, nay sooner or later certainly must, involve consequences which are too disastrous to contemplate. And it is precisely to limit and control these forces and direct them, while there is yet time, into channels along which they can flow auspiciously, bearing safely the agonies of progress and prosperity on their heaving waves, that this Congress movement was designed. The Government has, broadly speaking, never realised the vast proportions of the coming flood which is being engendered by the noble policy of which in 1833 Lord Macaulay was so prominent an exponent; and it is we of the Congress, who through good repute and ill repute, careless what men say of us if only haply God may bless our efforts, who standing between the country and the coming development, are labouring—labouring almost frantically—to provide in time channels through which this surging tide may flow, not to ravage and destroy but to fertilise and regenerate.

A newspaper from Punjab explained that the object of the Congress was not that the British should abdicate India, or that all powers of government should be vested in the hands of the Natives, for which they are totally unfit, but that government should, in the first instance, take the opinions of the representatives of the people while enacting laws, or while imposing taxes or incurring any expenditure. Government officials may or may not follow the suggestions, but the one thing needed was to consult them in matters of administration; and if this rule was established, it will not always be easy for them to go against the people's wishes.[14]

The vernacular press, which increased its numbers from 599 to 1,107 from 1885 to 1905 and circulation from 299,000 to 817,000, aided the Congress cause. New ideas spread also because of the improved transport and communication. In the first five years, therefore, attendance grew steadily, rising from 72 delegates in 1885 to almost two thousand in 1889. The third Congress in Madras was, thanks to the efforts of the Madras Mahajana Sabha, a great success. Eighty-three Muslims, led by Badruddin Tyabji, were present to refute charges of Muslim apathy. The Anglo-Indian press, despite its intransigence, sensed that the potential of the new political force of drawing together all-India interests, classes, and religions.[15] Thus, what was little more than an experiment in 1885 bore every appearance of becoming a permanent national institution.

II

Not quite, argued Anil Seal, formerly of Trinity College, Cambridge.[16] In the late-1960s, his thesis triggered a major debate; it centred on a detailed description, some said caricaturing, of Indian nationalism. Arguing against the then dominant Marxian aand nationalist interpretations, he insisted that the Congress movement wasn't formed through the promptness of any class demand or as a consequence of any sharp economic changes. Instead, he vociferously argued

14. *Swadeshamitran*, 17 December 1887

15. Martin, *New India*, pp. 325.

16. Anil Seal, *The Emergence of Indian Nationalism: Competition and Collaboration in the Later Nineteenth Century* (Cambridge, 1968).

keen internal rivalries between caste and caste, community and community, and not between class and class. This became the preoccupation of the 'Cambridge school' for at least two more decades.

Anil Seal talked of the educated men in the three coastal presidencies and their efforts to conserve or improve the position of their prescriptive groups—caste and community. As these groups were usually caste, and since caste is unknown outside South Asia, he regarded this elite to be of a special kind. Some years later, he dealt with the race for influence, status, and resources to be critical in deciding political choices in the localities. In the pursuit of these aims, patrons regimented their clients into factions, which jockeyed for positions. Rather than partnerships between fellows, these were usually associations of bigwigs and followers. In other words, they were vertical rather than horizontal alliances. Indeed, local struggles were seldom marked by the alliance of landlord with landlord, peasant with peasant, educated with educated, Muslim with Muslim, and Brahmin with Brahmin. More frequently, Hindus worked with Muslims and Brahmins were hand to glove with non-Brahmins; and notables organised their dependants as supporters, commissioned professional men and spokesmen, and turned government servants into aides. In the everyday decisions of life taken in many localities, the social dockets devised by the administrator and adopted by the historian had little meaning.

By the end of the nineteenth century, India was no more than a shapeless, jumbled, bundle of societies. The idea of nation was non-existent. If so, what was India? Seal's answer is: nothing more than a graveyard of old nationalities and the mother of new nationalism struggling to be born. Thus, the Cambridge historian didn't find it credible to write about a movement grounded in common aims, led by men with similar backgrounds, and recruited from widening groups with compatible interests. That movement appeared more like a ramshackle coalition throughout its long career. Its unity seems illusory, its power as hollow as that of the imperial authority it was supposedly challenging. Its history was the rivalry between Indian and Indian, its relationship with imperialism that of the mutual clinging of two unseemly men of straw. For these reasons, modern Indian history, Seal concluded, couldn't be organised around the old notions of imperialism and nationalism.

True, the Congress leaders lived in the presidency towns. It is also true that they belonged to the upper layers of the caste hierarchy, and were in some cases, if not all, tied to each other by friendship, family and patronage, these being sometimes accompanied by links of land, commerce and wealth. But it is also true that the Congress proved to be the meeting-point of all these inter-connections. It is also true that occasional signs of superficial tensions between the different groups surfaced, but that could not jeopardise the fundamental unity of their cause. The top leadership consistently devoted itself to helping the party in the difficult circumstances that accompanied the founding of the Congress.

C.A. Bayly, also from Cambridge, argues that the national movement drew up and recast some patterns of social relations, sentiments, doctrines, and embodied memories that had come into existence before British rule was established in the subcontinent in the late eighteenth century.[17] Sentiments against the Raj had been violently expressed in 1857, and they stayed, without being coherently expressed, in public conscience. In the following two decades, there was no great outburst of public anger, but there was, nonetheless, criticism of the government's total disregard of what was being put together as the collective interests and goals of 'Indians'. In each town and locality, local alignments and antagonisms largely shaped the nature and character of opposition to the Congress movement.

17. C.A. Bayly, *Origins of Nationality*, p. 1.

Muft me yun khaak uraana koi hamse seekhe.

'Somebody should learn the futility of raising the dust from me,' 17 April 1890. This cartoon illustrates the futility of the anti-Congress movement symbolized by the bewildered man sweeping the floor, i.e., signifying the gathering opposition (read, dust) against the Congress. The three men dressed in Western clothes—termed as 'sympathisers of the Congress'—indicate utter contempt for their detractors.

Long before M.K. Gandhi's *Hind Swaraj* (1908), vernacular newspapers, notably the *Awadh Punch* from Lucknow, critiqued British famine policy that let many regions prey to economic stagnation and even social disintegration. They dwelt on famine, military expenditure and drain of wealth to illustrate Great Britain's exploitation of India and the impoverishment of its people. Naoroji and Romesh Chunder Dutt worked out how India paid annually to Britain, though all kinds of direct or devious channels, a ruinously heavy tribute, and how India was drained of its wealth. The drain in 1882 amounted to 1,355 million rupees—at 1946-7 prices, over 5 per cent of the national income that year. Thus the *Colonel* of Moradabad in UP carried a picture in which the Viceroy is represented as holding a money bag, marked as saving a million rupees from the rise in exchange, in his hand, and is surrounded by a number of hungry dogs, one of which is called the Hazara Expedition, another, the Zhob Valley Expedition, another, the Lushai Expedition, another the Commission. The letter-press is as follows:

One man's mouth can be filled with sugar, but those of ten men not even with dust. There will be a saving of a million rupees from the rise in exchange, but while saving is sure to be absorbed by these strange expeditions and commissions, and the country will again have poverty staring it in the face, as before.[18]

18. Reports on Native Newspapers, Punjab, 8 January 1891, p. 41.

Anokhi meharbani, khane ki jagah pani.

'Unusual generosity: Only water instead of food,' 13 July 1893. A typical but powerful depiction of a starved family being offered clean water when there is no food. The children of the weeping mother stand behind her—the daughter consoles her. The artist is Lal Bahadur. The glass has 'clean water' written on it.

III

The plea for rewriting the histories of Indian nationalism is accompanied by a critique of the 'modest' Congress demands and the neglect of the poverty-stricken masses of India.[19] The Congress leaders suffered from a disjunction between their individual economic situations and their intellectual understanding of the causes of poverty. Hence, R.P. Dutt, the London-based Marxist historian, offered insights on the indigenous Indian capitalist industry and its links with some of the Congress leaders and focused on the lack of empathy for or sense of common interest with the many millions of peasants who lived on the verge of starvation. Indeed, an important feature of the Congress's organisational activity was the absence of any specific programme and slogans of appeals to the mass of the rural and urban poor and an ambivalence in the position vis-à-vis agrarian issues. This was reflected in the language of the propaganda and appeals that emanated from the Congress leaders. That's why the social depth of their movement diminished, though the organisation, strength, and the scale of their campaign widened. Jawaharlal Nehru had made the following observations in *Glimpses of World History*:

This organisation, which you and every boy and girl in India know well, has become in recent years great and powerful. It took up the cause of the masses and became, to some extent, their

19. Sanjay Seth 'Rewriting Histories of Nationalism', in Sekhar Bandyaopadhyay, *Nationalist Movement in India: A Reader* (Delhi, 2009), p. 39.

champion. It challenged the very basis of British rule in India, and led great mass movements against it. It raised the banner of independence and fought for freedom manfully. And today it is still carrying on the fight. But all this is subsequent history. The National Congress when it was first founded was a very moderate and cautious body, affirming its loyalty to the British and asking, very politely, for some petty reforms. It represented the richer *bourgeoisie*; even the poorer middle classes were not in it. As for the masses, the peasants and workers, they had nothing to do with it. It was the organ of the English-educated classes chiefly, and it carried on its activities in our step-mother tongue—English language. Its demands were the demands of the landlords and Indian capitalists and the educated unemployed seeking for jobs. Little attention was paid to the grinding poverty of the masses or their needs. It demanded the "Indianisation" of the services—that is to say, the greater employment of Indians in government service in place of Englishmen. It did not see that what was wrong with India was the machine which exploited the people, and that it made no difference who had charge of the machine, Indian or foreigner.

A scholarly attempt has been underway by the 'subaltern school' to offer an alternative discourse based on the rejection of the spurious and unhistorical monism characteristic of its view of Indian nationalism and on the recognition of the coexistence and interaction of the elite and subaltern domains of politics. The arguments of the subaltern historians are simple enough: the historiography of nationalism has been dominated by elitism: colonialist elitism and bourgeois-nationalist elitism. Both these varieties of elitism argue that the development of national consciousness and the making of Indian nationalism is, thus, written up as a sort of spiritual biography of the Indian elite. As a consequence, the contribution made by the people on their own, that is, independently of the elite to the making and development of this nationalism, is ignored. What, therefore, needs to be done is to explore the role of the subaltern classes and groups who operated in an autonomous domain.[20]

IV

'Muslim spokesmen' vigorously contested the Congress claims. Ameer Ali and Abdul Latif in Calcutta had harsh words to say against the Congress. The theologians did not think differently; they issued religious decrees against the ungodly Hindus who were out to destroy the foundations of Islam in India. They were naive and short-sighted in their assessment. Syed Ahmad Khan, the Aligarh reformer, thundered against the Congress demands. He maintained that the 'backward' Muslim community would lose out to the empowered Bengali Hindus. This was a false assumption. Moreover, he was uncomfortable with the language of sedition; it reminded him of the year 1857, when the Muslims of upper India faced reprisals for instigating a revolt against their British rulers. He accepted the need to reconcile changes in the modern world with the immutability of religion, yet he did not propose the reformulation of political doctrines. On religious matters, he accepted the inevitability of change but not when it came to political disputations.

20. Ranajit Guha. 'Preface', and 'On Some Aspects of the Historiography of Colonial India' in Ranajit Guha (ed.), *Subaltern Studies I* (New Delhi, 1982), for the 'subaltern' perspective and critique of elitist interpretations; C.A. Bayly, 'Rallying Around the Subaltern', *Journal of Peasant Studies*, vol. 16, no. 1, Oct. 1989; Gyan Prakash, 'Writing Post-Orientalist Histories of the Third World: Perspectives from Indian Historiography', *Comparative Studies in Society and History*, 32, 1990. For critiques of the subaltern view, see Rosalind O'Hanlon, 'Recovering the Subject: Subaltern studies and Histories of Resistance in Colonial South Asia', *Modern Asian Studies*, 22, I, 1988, and Sumit Sarkar, *Writing Social History*, Ch. 3 (New Delhi, 1997).

Syed Ahmad was not, however, the only one to shun the Congress. In UP, the Maharaja of Benaras, Raja Siva Prasad and the Raja of Bhinga and the Anglo-Indian editors were his allies. In Bombay and Madras, some groups of untouchables, identified with the non-Brahmin movements, treated the Congress as an adversary, fearing that the high caste Congress elite would dominate any Indian representative body. The landowning classes and the government servants fulminated against the Congress. Very soon they were going to see 'red' in everything the Congress said or did. It was the fear of a class endangered by political change.

At first, Dufferin tried to discount the role of the Congress. Lord Lansdowne, Viceroy from December 1888 to December 1893, did the same. But their hostility had no great impression on the Congress and its trajectory. As a matter of fact, the pressure mounted for reforms yielded a major result: in 1892, the Indian Councils Act was passed through Parliament. Then, the government tried to play one side off against another in a masterly manner, but it did not work with Badruddin Tyabji. Nationalism was the primary focus and reference point for him. The shift in orientation was evident in the recasting of his intellectual framework as well as activism. He told Tyabji that there was no such thing as the general progress of India or India as one nation. The different castes and creeds didn't belong to a nation and their aims and aspirations weren't the same. He believed the doings of the misnamed National Congress were not only injurious to Muslims but also to India at large.

Indeed, the Muslims were not, however, all cut out of the same cloth. Out of 1,620 individuals who signed the roll as delegates from 1885 to 1901, 596, or slightly over one-third, were Muslims from UP. Their strength increased steadily from 8 per cent in 1886 to high points of 42 per cent in 1889 and 55 per cent in 1890. And six-tenths of all Muslim delegates from 1886 to 1901 were from Lucknow alone. When the Congress met at Allahabad in 1888 and 1892, it had more Muslim delegates in attendance than the host city. There were 313 Muslims at the 1889 Congress; 288 were from Lucknow itself. Maulvi Mohammad Hidayet Rasul boasted:

Now you can say how so many able and distinguished delegates have come to be returned from Oudh and especially from Lucknow? ... The truth of it is, that this good result is due to the kindness of one brethren in the Aligarh College—the opponents of the Congress. (*Loud cheers*). ... To my mind, the National Congress is like the vine, which, the more it is pruned, the more it flourishes.[21]

Muslims always had an important place in the agenda of the associations and Surendranath Banerjea and Syed Ahmad had cooperated with each other, but now enlisting minority support became Congress' organising principle. To woo them they decided, in 1887-88, not to discuss issues that were unanimously or nearly unanimously opposed either by Hindus or Muslims. Later, they bowed to mounting pressure from the Muslim delegates and eschewed discussion on the Punjab Alienation Bill (1900). As a concession to minority sensibilities, they also refrained from debating social issues in order to articulate political aspirations and eschew debates on religious and social matters. As a result, in 1895, the National Social Conference, the brainchild of Mahadeo Govind Ranade and R. Raghunath Rao, which used to hold its annual conference at the same place and about the same time as the Congress, had to meet separately.

The Congress sheltered all and sundry, accommodating a wide variety of regional, caste and communitarian concerns. At times, this coalition was strained by the moderate-extremist divide, but instead of disintegrating into pieces, the Congress managed to harness its resources to put up a united front. A house divided would have invited nothing but ridicule from the government.

21. Report of the Fourth Indian National Congress, Allahabad, 1888, p. iii.

V

Beyond a fleeting interest in the annual sessions, the colonial government found no room for the Congress.[22] Dufferin had contempt for the 'microscopic minority', whereas Landsowne and Elgin, who were fed with biased reports by their officer, had no reason to think differently. Curzon, of course, was determined, like his predecessors, to 'reduce the Congress to impotence. Clearly, the 'safety-valve' thesis, which some expounded, did not work.

Lord Curzon's partition of the undivided province of Bengal, Bihar and Orissa was the last straw. His ill-advised decision, for which there were many motives, illustrated the worst features of bureaucratic rule—its arrogant pretensions to superior wisdom, its reckless disregard of public opinion. It stirred people to come out on the streets and their leaders to organise swadeshi and boycott. The Congress grew, as Jawaharlal observed in his *Glimpses of World History*, but even faster than the Congress drew the idea of nationality and the desire for freedom. Tilak had expressed contempt for annual sessions, which he thought, were 'like the croaking of frogs in the rain', although reports of his own activities, as indeed his conviction, spread far and wide. 'Almost without an exception', noted Jawaharlal, then studying in England, 'we were Tilakites or Extremists...'[23]

The line of cleavage in the Congress, to which Jawaharlal and others alluded to, was drawn between those who wanted to tread warily in the volatile political world and those advocating militancy. There was no love lost between them. Tilak exploited a great volume of anti-British feeling; Gokhale, on the other hand, pinned his faith in the justice of British democracy and was reconciled to foreign domination as a transitional arrangement. Aurobindo Ghose, who secured a senior classical scholarship at Cambridge, was embittered after his return to India. The Home Rule Leagues and the Servants of India Society widened the arena of conflict within the Congress. They were the nucleus of significant mobilisation, and left behind structures and networks which M.K. Gandhi harnessed in his bitter encounters with the Raj which unfolded in the decades leading up to Independence in 1947.

22. Martin, *New India*, pp. 335-6.

23. Jawaharlal Nehru, *An Autobiography* (London, 1936), p. 21.

PROCEEDINGS

OF THE

FIRST INDIAN

NATIONAL CONGRESS.

HELD AT

BOMBAY,

ON

The 28th, 29th and 30th December,

1885

CONTENTS.

—:o:—

SECOND DAY, 29TH DECEMBER 1885.—*(Continued.)* PAGE

THIRD DAY, 30TH DECEMBER 1885.—*(Continued.)* PAGE

APPENDICES :—

THE FIRST

INDIAN NATIONAL CONGRESS,

HELD AT BOMBAY,

On the 28th, 29th and 30th December, 1885.

SUMMARY OF RESOLUTIONS passed at the Indian National Congress, composed of Representatives from Calcutta, Madras, Bombay, Poona, Allahabad, Lahore, Lucknow, Agra, Benares, Ahmedabad, Kurrachee, Surat, Veerumgaum, Ganjam, Masulipatam, Chingleput, Tanjore, Combaconum, Madura, Tinnevelly, Coimbatore, Cuddapah, Anantapoor, Bellary, and Umballa, held in Bombay on the 28th, 29th, and 30th December, 1885.

RESOLUTIONS.

I.—Proposed by Mr. G. Subramania Iyer (Madras), seconded by Mr. P. M. Mehta (Bombay), and supported by Mr. Norendronath Sen (Calcutta): "That this Congress "earnestly recommends that the promised inquiry "into the working of Indian Administration, here and "in England, should be entrusted to a Royal Com-"mission, the people of India being adequately "represented thereon, and evidence taken both in "India and in England."

II.—Proposed by Mr. S. H. Chiplonkar (Poona), seconded by Mr. P. Ananda Charlu (Madras), and supported by Mr. J. Ghosal (Allahabad): "That this Congress con-"siders the abolition of the Council of the Secretary "of State for India, as at present constituted, the "necessary preliminary to all other reforms."

III.—Proposed by the Hon. K. T. Telang C.I.E. (Bombay) seconded by the Hon. S. Subramania Iyer (Madras), and supported by the Hon. Dadabhai Naoroji (Bombay) "That this Congress considers the reform and expan-"sion of the Supreme and existing Local Legislative "Councils, by the admission of a considerable pro-"portion of elected members (and the creation of "similar Councils for the N. W. Provinces and Oudh, "and also for the Punjab) essential and holds that "all Budgets should be referred to these Councils for "consideration, their members being moreover em-"powered to interpellate the Executive in regard to "all branches of the administration; and that a "Standing Committee of the House of Commons "should be constituted to receive and consider any "formal protests that may be recorded by majorities "of such Councils against the exercise by the "Executive of the power, which would be vested in "it, of overruling the decisions of such majorities."

IV.—Proposed by the Hon. Dadabhai Naoroji (Bombay) "seconded by Mr. Vira Raghavacharyar (Madras) "and supported by Mr. D. S. White (Madras) "That in the opinion of this Congress the competitive "examinations now held in England, for first appoint-"ments in various civil departments of the public "service, should henceforth, in accordance with the "views of the India Office Committee of 1860, 'be "held simultaneously, one in England and one in "India, both being as far as practicable identical in "their nature, and those who compete in both coun-"tries being finally classified in one list according to "merit,' and that the successful candidates in India "should be sent to England for further study, and "subjected there to such further examinations as may "seem needful. Further, that all other first appoint- "ments (excluding peonships, and the like) should be "filled by competitive examinations held in India, "under conditions calculated to secure such intellec- "tual, moral, and physical qualifications as may be "decided by Government to be necessary. Lastly, "that the maximum age of candidates for entrance "into the Covenanted Civil Service be raised to not "less then 23 years."

V. Proposed by Mr. Rangaya Nayadu (Madras), seconded "by Mr. Dinsha Edaljee Wacha (Bombay), and sup- "ported by Mr. Dayaram Jethmul (Karachi) :— "That in the opinion of this Congress the proposed "increase in the military expenditure of the empire is "unnecessary, and regard being had to the revenues "of the empire and the existing circumstances of the "country, excessive."

VI.—Proposed by Mr. J. U. Yajnik (Bombay), seconded by Mr. S. A. Swaminath Iyer (Tanjore), supported by Rao Saheb S. Venkata Subbarayudu Pantulu (Masulipatam) : "That in the opinion of this Congress, if the "increased demands for military expenditure are not "to be, as they ought to be, met by retrenchment, "they ought to be met, firstly, by the re-imposition "of the Customs duties ; and, secondly, by the exten "sion of the license-tax to those classes of the com- "munity, official and non-official, at present exempted "from it, care being taken that in the case of all "classes a sufficiently high taxable minimum be "maintained. And further, that this Congress is of "opinion that Great Britain should extend an imperial guarantee to the Indian debt."

VII.—Proposed by Mr. P. M. Mehta (Bombay), seconded by Rao Bahadur Krishnaji Laxman Nulkar (Poona):—
"That this Congress deprecates the annexation of "Upper-Burmah and considers that if the Government "unfortunately decide on annexation, the entire "country of Burmah should be separated from the "Indian Viceroyalty and constituted a Crown Colony "as distinct in all matters from the government of "this country as is Ceylon."

VIII.—Proposed by Mr. Murlidhar (Umballa), seconded by Mr. H. H. Dhruva (Surat): "That the resolutions "passed by this Congress be communicated to the "political Associations in each province, and that "these Associations be requested with the help of "similar bodies and other agencies within their res "pective provinces to adopt such measures as they "may consider calculated to advance the settlement "of the various questions dealt with in these resolu "tions.

IX.—Proposed by Mr. A. O. Hume (Bengal), seconded by "the Hon. S. Subramania Iyer (Madras): "That "the Indian National Congress re-assemble next year "in Calcutta, and sit on Tuesday, the 28th of Decem "ber 1886, and the next succeeding days."

Origin and Composition of the Congress.

In March 1885 it was decided to hold a meeting of Representatives from all parts of India at the then coming Christmas. Poona was considered the most central and therefore suitable place and the following circular was issued.

"A Conference of the Indian National Union will be held at Poona from the 25th to the 31st of December 1885..

"The Conference will be composed of Delegates—leading politicians well acquainted with the English language—from all parts of the Bengal, Bombay and Madras Presidencies.

"The direct objects of the Conference will be:—(1) to enable all the most earnest labourers in the cause of national progress to become personally known to each other; (2) to discuss and decide upon the political operations to be undertaken during the ensuing year.

"Indirectly this Conference will form the germ of a Native Parliament and, if properly conducted, will constitute in a few years an unanswerable reply to the assertion that India is still wholly unfit for any form of representative institutions. The first Conference will decide whether the next shall be again held at Poona, or whether following the precedent of the British Association, the Conferences shall be held year by year at different important centres.

"This year the Conference being in Poona, Mr. Chiplonkar ard others of the Sarvajanik Sabha, have consented to form a Reception Committee, in whose hands will rest the whole of the local arrangements. The Peshwah's Garden near the Parbati Hill will be untilized both as a place of meeting (it contains a fine Hall, like the garden, the property of the Sabha) and as a residence for the delegates, each of whom will be there provided with suitable quarters. Much importance is attached to this since when all thus reside *together* for a week, far greater opportunities for friendly intercourse will be afforded than if the delegates were (as at the time of the late Bombay demonstrations) scattered about in dozens of private lodging houses all over the town.

" Delegates are expected to find their own way to and from Poona—but from the time they reach the Poona Railway Station until they again leave it, everything that they can need, carriage, accommodation, food, &c., will be provided for them gratuitously.

" The cost thus involved will be defrayed from the Reception Fund, which the Poona Association most liberally offers to provide in the first instance, but to which all delegates, whose means warrant their incurring this further expense, will be at liberty to contribute any sum they please. Any unutilized balance of such donations will be carried forward as a nucleus for next year's Reception fund.

" It is believed that exclusive of our Poona friends, the Bombay Presidency, including Sindh and the Berars, will furnish about 20 delegates, Madras and Lower Bengal each about the same number, and the N. W. Provinces Oudh, and the Punjaub together about half this number."

A few days, however, before the time fixed for the assemblage, and after the Sarvajanik Sabha had completed all their preparations at Poona, several cases of cholera occurred there. These cases might or might not be the commencement of a severe outbreak, travellers arriving tired at a station where there is cholera are notoriously proved to take the disease, and it was therefore considered prudent despite the difficulties attendant on any change at so late a period, to hold the Conference, (which it had in the meantime been decided to call the CONGRESS) at Bombay.

Thanks to the exertions of the Bombay Presidency Association and the liberality of the Managers of the Goculdas Tejpal Sanscrit College and Boarding Trust (who not only placed the grand buildings above the Gowalia Tank at the Association's disposal, but also supervised the furbishing up, furnishing and lighting of these large premises on behalf of he Association), everything was ready by the morning of the 27th when the REPRESENTATIVES (as it was determined to designate them to distinguish them from the *Delegates*, the title by which the Indian Representatives *sent to England* had become popularly known) began to arrive.

During the whole day and far into the night of the 27th, informal discussions were carried on between the Representatives and the order of the proceedings for the next three days was thus settled.

It should, however, be noted that about two hours in the evening were devoted to receiving the Hon'ble Sir W. Wedderburn Bart, the Hon'ble Mr. Justice Jardine, Colonel Phelps, Professor Wordsworth and a large number of the leading citizens of Bombay who most kindly came to the Goculdas Tejpal College, to welcome the Representatives and express their sympathy with the work on which these were about to enter.

The first meeting took place the next day, on the 28th December. Very close on one hundred gentlemen attended, but a considerable number of these being Government servants like Mr. D. S. White, President of the Eurasian Association, Dewan Bahadur Rubgande Rugonath Row, Collector of Madras, the Hon'ble Mahadeo G. Ranade, Member of the Legislative Council and Small Cause Court Judge of Poona, Lalla Baijnath of Agra, Professor Abaji Vishnoo Kattawatha of Ahmedabad, Professor Kadambi Sundararaman, M. A. of Arcot, Mr. T. Narasemina Iyer of Tiruvellur, Professor R. G. Bhandarkar of the Deccan College and many others did not (with one exception) take any direct part in the discussions, but attended only as

Amici curiæ, to listen and advise, so that the actual number of *Representatives* was, only so far as the records go, (though it is feared some few names have been omitted from the Register) 72, *viz*:—

From Karrachi, 2; Viramgam, 1; Surat, 6; Poona, 8; Calcutta, 3; Agra, 2; Benares, 1; Simla, 1; Lucknow, 3; Allahabad, 1; Lahore, 1,; Amballa, 1; Ahmedabad, 3; Bombay, 18; Madras, 8; Berhampore, 1; Masulipatam, 1; Chinglipat, 1; Tanjore, 2; Kumbakonum, 1; Madura, 1,; Tinnevelly, 1; Coimbatore, 1; Salem, 1; Cuddahpa; Anantapore, 1; Bellary, 1.

The following is a nominal list of these Representatives so far as they entered their names in the Register.

Karachi.—Messrs. Dayaram Jethmal and Ooderam Moolchund, Pleaders.

Viramgaum.—Mr. Harilal Mayaram Vakil and Municipal Commissioner and representative of the Loka Somgraha Sabha.

Surat.—Messrs. H. H. Dhruva, B.A., L.L.B., Pleader and Municipal Commissioner, member, managing committee Praja Hitwardhak Sabha; Mancharshaw Pallanji Kaikobad Honorary Secretary, Praja Hitwardhak Sabha; Gokuldas Bhaidass Vakil, Municipal Commissioner, Pleader; Manch hashankar Jiwanram, B.A., L.L.B.; Hosangji Burjorji, B.A L.L.B., Pleader; Narandass Parshotamdass, merchant and Vice-President, Praja Hitwardhak Sabha.

Poona.—Rao Bahadoor Krishnaji Laxaman Nulkar Chairman, Poona Sarvajanik Sabha; Messrs. Gangaram Bhan Mashke, Pleader, District Court; Ramchandra Moreshwar Sane, Marathi editor, *Dnyan Prakash*; Sitaram Hari Chiplonkar, Honorary Secretary, Poona Sarvajanik Sabha and edito the *Quarterly Journal* of the P. S. Sabha ; Shivaram Hari .e, Secretary Poona Sarvajanik Sabha ; Dr. Pandurang l, G. G. M. C.; Mr. Waman Shivaram Apte, M. A., Principal, Fergusson College and Superintendent, New English school ; Ramchandra Keshaw Limagi, Pleader, District court ; Gopal Ganesh Agarkar, M. A., Professor, Fergusson college, and editor of the *Maratha* and *Kesari*.

Calcutta.—Messrs. W. C. Bonnerji, Barrister-at-law, standing Counsel ; G. B. Mookerji, editor of the *Nababibhakar*, Pleader, High Court ; Norendranath Sen, Proprietor and editor, *Indian Mirror*.

Agra.—Messrs. Babu Jamandas, Pleader, Municipal Commissioner, and editor of the *Nassim* ; Babu Prabhu Daya Chowdhry, Pleader.

Benares.—Mr. Ram Kali Chowdry, pensioned Sub-Judge.

Simla.—Mr. A. O. Hume.

Lucknow.—Messrs. Munshi Gangaprasad Varma, proprietor of the *Hindusthani* ; Pranauth Pandit, teacher, Lord canning College ; Munshi Jawala Prasad, Pleader,

Amballa.—Babu Murlidhar, Pleader, representing *the tribune*

Lahore.—Satyanand Agnithori, Brahmo missionary.

Allahabad.—Mr. J. Ghosal, editor of the *Indian Union*.

Ahmedabad.—Messrs. Keshawlal Motilal, Vakil, Municipal Commissioner, and Manockjee P. Mody, Vakil, Secretry of the Gujerat Sabha.

Bombay.—The Hon. Dadabhai Naoroji, Member of the Legislative Council ; the Hon. Kashinath T. Telang, C. I. E., Member of the Legislatiye Council, Messrs Pherozeshaw Merwanji Mehta, Barrister-at-law, Chairman of the Municipal

Corporation; Dinshaw Edalji Wacha, Secretary Bom' Presidency Association; Dinshaw Pestonji Kanga, Solici Ghanasham Nilkanth Nadkarni, Vakil, High Court.: M Bhowanidas Barbhaya, Solicitor; Tribhuwandas Mungai Nathubhoy; Jehangir B. Wacha, merchant; Rahimtula Sayani, Solicitor; Bal Mungesh Wagle, Barrister-at-law; K. Sethna. Barrister-at-law: Behramji M. Malabari, propric tor & editor *Indian Spectator*; Ganesh Ramchandra Kirloskai Vakil, High Court; Shamrao Vithal, Vakil High Court Abdalla Mehrali Dharamsi, Solicitor: Javerilal Umiashankar Yajnik, Merchant; N. G. Chandavarkar. editor of the *Indu Prakash*, and Bombay Delegate to England.

Madras.—Messrs. P. Rungiah Naidu, President of the Madras Mahajana Sabha, Municipal Commissioner, and Vakil, High Court, Madras; the Hon'ble S. Subramania Aiyar. B.L., Member of the Legislative Council and Vakil, High Court, Madras; P. Ananda Charlu. B.L., Vakil. High Court; and Municipal Commissioner, Madras; G. Subramania Aiyar, B.A., editor of the *Hindu*, Madras; M. Viraraghava Charriar, B A, Sub-Editor of the *Hindu*, Madras and Secretary, Madras Mahajanah Sabha; C. Singarvelloo Moodeliar, Municipal Commissioner, Madras, Merchant and Trustee of the Patchappa charity; M. E. Shriranga Charriar, B.A., B.L., High Court Madras; Dr. S. V. Athalye, Medical Practitioner, Madras

Berhampore.—Mr. M. Vishwanath Aiyar, B. A., Pleader District Court Ganjam, and Municipal Commissioner Berhampore.

Masulipatam.—Mr. S. Venkata Subba Royadu, B.L. Vakil of the High Court. and Pleader, District Court, Masupi patam.

Chingleput.—Mr. M. Y. Ramanuja Charriar, Pleader Chingleput.

Tanjore.—Messrs. S. A. Swaminath Aiyar, Public Prosecutor and President, People's Association, Tanjore; N. Narayanswami Aiyar, Landholder, Tanjore,

Kumbakonum.—Mr. K. Pattabirama Aiyar, Landholder, Kumbakonum

Madura.—Mr. P. Subramania Aiyar, Madura.

Tinevelly.—Mr. Peter Paul Pillay, landholder and schoolmaster, Tinnevelly.

Coimbatore.—Mr. S. P. Narasimhulu Naidu, editor, *Crescent*, and member of the Local Board, Coimbatore.

Salem.—Mr. Kristnaswamy Rout, Salem.

Caddapah.—Mr. M. Nageswara Row, Pleader, Caddapah.

Anantapore.—Mr. P. Kesava Pillay, Pleader and member of the Local Board, Anantapore.

Bellary.—Mr. A. Sabapathy Moodeliyar, merchant, landholder, and chairman of the Municipality, Bellary.

Not only were all parts of India thus represented, but also most classes; there were barristers, solicitors, pleaders, merchants, landowners, bankers, medical men, newspaper editors and proprietors; principals and professors of independent colleges, headmasters of schools, religious teachers and reformers. There were Hindus of many castes, high and low, Mahomedans (though owing to certain unfortunate accidents far fewer than were expected) and Christians, both native, Eurasian and European. All the leading Native political Associations and the principal Anglo-native newspapers were represented; there were members of Legislative Councils, Presidents and members of Municipal Committees and Local Boards, and it is difficult to conceive any gathering of this restricted number more thoroughly representative of the entire nation than was this Congress of which the *Bombay Gazette* had the following interesting notice:—"A new era is marked in the political history of this Presidency with the organisation of what is called a National Conference which held on Monday its first sitting in Bombay. Poona was at first selected for this meeting, and Delegates from all parts of India had already assembled there; but owing to the prevalence of cholera in the capital of the Deccan, the Delegates had to be brought down to this city, and here they have been accommodated in the spacious building of the institution which is known as "The Goculdas Tejpal Boarding-school, Sanscrit College, and Library," situated at Gowalia Tank. Before commencing the serious work for which the Conference is held, an opportunity was given at an informal gathering on Sunday afternoon to those who are strangers to this city to be introduced to some of the representative men belonging to the native community of Bombay. And the spectacle which presented itself of men representing the various races and communities, castes and sub-divisions of caste, religions and sub-divisions of religions, met together in one place to form themselves, if possible, into one political whole, was most unique and interesting. For they had come not from the Presidency towns alone, but from all parts of India, and their presence afforded a most interesting study of the heads and head-dresses typical of the numerous variety of castes and communities inhabiting this country. There were men from Madras, the blackness of whose complexion seemed to be made blacker by spotless white turbans which some of them wore. A few others hailing from that Presidency were bare-headed and barefooted, and otherwise lightly clad, their bodies from the waist upwards being only partially protected by muslin shawls. It may fairly be presumed that they are the leading lights of the towns which they represent, and as such it may be supposed that they are well educated. But they have preferred to retain their national dress and manners, and in this respect they presented a marked contrast to the Delegates from Bengal. Some of these appeared in entirely European costume, while others could be easily recognised as Babus by the peculiar cap with a cap behind which they donned. None of them wore the gold rings or diamond pendents which adorned the ears of come of the Madrasees; nor had they their foreheads painted like their more orthodox and more conservative brethren from the Southern Presidency. Then there were Hindus-Tanis from such places as Delhi, Agra, Lucknow and Benares some of whom wore muslin skull-caps and dresses chiefly made of the same fine cloth. On the other hand, there were Delegates from the North-West—bearded, bulky, and large-limbed men—in their coats and flowing robes of different hues and in turbans like those worn by Sikh soldiers. There were stalwart Sindhees from Kurrachee, wearing their own tall hat surmounted by a broad brim at the top. In this strange group were to be observed the familiar figures of Banyas from Gujarat, of Marathas in their "cart-wheel" turbans, and of Parsees in their not very elegant head-dress, which they themselves have likened to a slanting roof. Some members of this community had, however, appeared in their "phenta," which is now largely patronised by the younger generation of Parsees, and which threatens in course of time to supersede the time-honoured turban. All these men, assembled in the same hall, presented such a variety of costumes and complexions, that a similar scene can scarcely be witnessed anywhere except at a fancy ball. After the ceremony of introduction had been concluded, the Delegates freely exchanged with one another their views upon things in general and politics in particular.

They included a large number of lawyers and conductors newspapers, and they all appeared to have agreed in th opinion that they had some political aspiration which could by no possibility clash with opposing interests, and that for the promotion of their common object there was a necessity for concerted action. It may be easily imagined that there were some enthusiasts in their number, one of whom was profuse in the expression of his unbounded joy at seeing in flesh and blood good men and true working for the public weal, whom he had formerly known only by name.

Report of the Proceedings of the Congress.
First Day—28th December 1885.

The first formal meeting of the Congress took place at 12, noon, of the 28th of December, in the great Hall of the Gokuldas Tejpal Sanscrit College. All the Representatives &c., having assembled,

It was proposed by Mr. A. O. Hume (Bengal), seconded by the Hon'ble Subramania Iyer (Madras), supported by the Hon'ble K. T. Telang (Bombay), and unanimously carried, that Mr. W. C. Bonerjee, Standing Counsel, Bengal, be invited to assume the office of the President of the Congress.

The President-elect, in rising to acknowledge the honour done him, said he might well be proud of being thus called on to preside over the first National Assembly ever yet convened in India. Looking round he saw the representatives of all the important centres of the Bombay Presdency, Karrachi, Ahmedabad, Surat, Poona, Bombay itse and other less populous though still important towns; almos every district in the Madras Presidency was represented, as well as the towns of Madras, Salem, Coimbatore and others. Of Bengal his friends and himself might to a certain extent be accepted as representatives, since although owing to a series of misfortunes, deaths, illnesses and the like, of which the meeting were already aware, Bengal was very inadequately represented so far as the numbers actually present were concerned, though as the delegated exponents of educated native thought in Bengal, they might claim a consideration to which their numerical strength would hardly entitle them. Then there were the representatives of Lahore, Lucknow, Agra, Allahabad, Benares, each representing political Associations collectively of very widespread influence. Besides these representatives who would take an actual part in the proceedings, he rejoiced to see present, as it were as *amici curiæ*, several of the most distinguished native officials of this country, whose presence would materially enhance the weight and the dignity of the proceedings. It was not merely provinces that were represented, almost all the political Associations in the Empire were represented by one or more of the gentlemen present, while as regards the Press, the proprietors, editors or delegates of the *Mirror*, the *Hindu*, the *Indian Spectator*, the *Tribune*, and others showed, conclusively, the universality of the feelings which had culminated in this great and memorable gathering. Surely never had so important and comprehensive an assemblage occurred within historical times on the soil of India. He claimed for it an entirely representative character. It was true that, judged from the standard of the House of Commons, they were not representatives of the people of India in the sense the members of the House were representatives of the constituencies. But if community of sentiments, community of feelings and community of wants enabled any one to speak on behalf of others, then assuredly they might justly claim to be the representatives of the people of India. It might be said that they were self-elected, but that was not so. The news that this Congress would be held had been known throughout the year in the different provinces of India, and they all knew that everywhere the news had been received with great satisfaction by the people at large, and though no formal elections had been held, the representatives had been selected by all the different Associations and bodies, and he only wished that all thus selected had been able to attend, instead of their having now to lament the absence of many valued coadjutors, whose attendance had been unhappily barred by various unfortunate circumstances.

And now it seemed a fitting occasion for answering a question that had continually been asked in the world outside during the past few weeks, viz., what the objects and aims of this great National Congress really were. He would not pretend to reply to this question exhaustively. The ensuing proceedings would, he believed, do this more effectually than any single speaker could hope to do; but he might say briefly, that the objects of the Congress could for the most part be classed under the following heads:—

(*a*) The promotion of personal intimacy and friendship amongst all the more earnest workers in our country's cause in the parts of the Empire.

(*b*) The eradication by direct friendly personal intercourse of all possible race, creed, or provincial prejudices amongst all lovers of our country, and the fuller development and consolidation of those sentiments of national unity that had their origin in their beloved Lord Ripon's ever memorable reign.

(*c*) The authoritative record after this has been carefully elicited by the fullest discussion of the matured opinions of the educated classes in India on some of the more important and pressing of the social questions of the day.

(*d*) The determination of the lines upon and methods by which during the next twelve months it is desirable for native politicians to labour in the public interests.

Surely there was nothing in these objects to which any sensible and unprejudiced man could possibly take exception, and yet on more than one occasion remarks had been made by gentlemen, who should have been wiser, condemning the proposed Congress, as if it were a nest of conspirators and disloyalists. Let him say once for all, and in this he knew well after the long informal discussions that they had all had amongst themselves on the previous day, that he was only expressing the sentiments of every gentleman present, that there were no more thoroughly loyal and consistent well-wishers of the British Government than were himself and the friends around him. In meeting to discuss in an orderly and peaceable manner questions of vital importance affecting their well being, they were following the only course by which the constitution of England enabled them to represent their views to the ruling authority. Much had been done by Great Britain for the benefit of India, and the whole country was truly grateful to her for it. She had given them order, she had given them railways, and above all she had given them the inestimable blessing of Western education. But a great deal still remained to be done. The more progress the people made in education and material prosperity, the greater would be the insight into political matters and the keener their desire for political advancement. He thought that their desire to be governed according to the ideas of government prevalent in Europe was in no way incompatible with their thorough loyalty to the British Government. All that they desired was that the basis of the government should be widened and that the people should have their proper and legitimate share in it. The discussions that would take place in this Congress would, he believed, be as advantageous to the ruling anthorities as he was sure it would be to the people at large.

Telegrams of sympathy with the objects of the Congress were then read from the British Indian Association, from the Provincial Conference recently held at Calcutta, from a Public Meeting held in Assam under the presidency of the Hon. Mr. Ananda Mohun Bose, &c, &c.

The Chairman then having formally declared the Congress open, Mr. G. Subramania Iyer (Madras) rose and spoke to the First Resolution as follows:—

GENTLEMEN,

The proposition which I have been asked to move relates to a subject of the utmost importance to the country it relates to a periodical enquiry into the material and moral progress of our people by the Imperial Parliament, the final arbiters of our destiny. By a merciful dispensation of Providence, India, which was for centuries the victim of external aggression and plunder, of internecine wars and general confusion, has been brought under the dominion of the great English power. Gentlemen, i need not tell you how that event introduced a great change in the destiny of her people, how the inestimable good that has flown from it has been appreciated by them, and how profoundly grateful they fed for it. The rule of Great Britain has given India peace an security, and, on the whole, has been better in its results and direction than any former rule. At home that rule is directed by forces which the whole history of the world shows are the most conducive to high material and moral prosperity

It has for ages developed and fostered individual liberty and social freedom which have made the English people what they are at present——the most prosperous, the most pushing and the most enlightened nation in the world, enjoying sovereignty over nearly one-seventh of the globe with control over millions of divers races and creeds. And how have *we* fared under a rule animated by the spirit of such a nationality ? Without descanting at length upon the benefits of that rule, I can summarize them in one remarkable fact, namely, that for the first time in the history of the Indian populations there is to be beheld the phenomenon of national unity among them, of a sense of national existence, and of a common solicitude for the well-being and honour of their common country. This large and influential meeting that I have the honour of addressing to-day, this assemblage in Bombay of my chosen countrymen from Calcutta and Lahore, from Madras and Sind, from places wide apart and difficult of intercommunication, indicates the beginning of a national political life, destined to produce a profound change in the immediate future. From to-day forward we can with greater propriety than heretofore speak of an Indian nation, of national opinion and national aspirations. Gentlemen, to what do we owe this marvellous change over the people ? Do we not owe it to that spirit of justice and generosity, to that spirit of progressiveness, so remarkable in the English political character ? Well then, it is our duty to watch jealously, so that the contact of that influence with the Government of this country is regular and constant and does not suffer prolonged intermission. It is a matter of the deepest concern to us that the affairs of our country should be periodically, if not continuously, brought to the notice of the Parliament and people of England, and be subjected to the healthy influences of a free and open inquiry conducted by the best of English politicians.

Such an inquiry was regularly made in the days of the East India Company. In 1773, 1793, 1813, 1833, and 1853, which were the years when the Charter of that Company came up for renewal, searching and elaborate investigations were made into the results of the administration ot the Company as represented by the financial condition of the Government and by the general progress of the people. Each time that the investigation took place, valuable information was collected and was utilized in the legislation that followed. Parliament was jealous of the political power that a Company of merchants was permitted to exercise over the government of a country, which, in area as well as in population, was a continent in itself, and which gave early promise of proving to England a prolific source of moral and material advantages. While the domestic and foreign policy of the Company was closely watched and subjected to periodical criticism and reform, these inquiries furnished wholesome checks and safeguards, particularly in the administration of finance.

Since the abolition of the East India Company those checks and safeguards have mostly disappeared, because although Parliament exercises in theory the ultimate and responsible control over the Indian Government, it has practically surrendered it to the India Council. This Council, you are aware, is only a resuscitation, in a slightly modified shape, of the body of mercantile rulers which Parliament, after deep and prolonged consideration, abolished as being inconsistent with the good government of a dependency like that of India. It is wonderful that the great statesmen of England should abolish the Company, vexed at its incompetency and its mal-administration, and in the same breath should bless it with fresh life in the shape of an even more incompetent and more despotic ruling body. Be it as it may, it is a fact that the power that Parliament assumed in theory and the direct responsibility it undertook have been seldom exercised, and on those rare occasions when Parliament exercised them, it was not to save Indian interests not to save them from the effects of a spirit of irresponsible and ambitious enterprise or of reckless innovation, but to sacrifice them to the exigencies of English politics. In many respects India has been a loser by the transfer of the Government to the Crown instead of a gainer. Since that time, the condition of the people has undergone a most distressing deterioration. They have been subjected to a tighter and less sympathetic despotism, and the expenditure and indebtedness of their Government have increased in a ratio utterly disproportionate to all improvement in its financial resources.

I said that since the abolition of the East India Company the ultimate control and responsibility of the Indian Government that was transferred to the Crown had been seldom exercised disinterestedly or for the benefit of the Indian people. There is, however, fair reason to believe that a change is coming over Parliament and the English public generally in this respect, and that if they be placed in possession of correct facts they will be better able to comprehend their duty and responsibility and their interference will result in substantial good. Well, gentlemen, are Parliament and the people in England in possession of such correct facts? Do they possess accurate evidence to convince them that the delegates of their power in India have properly discharged their trust hitherto? Are they certain that the policy that they have deliberately laid down for the government of their dependency is carried out in a liberal and fair spirit? Do they know that the just, the generous, and the noble pledges of Her Majesty, pledges made deliberately on a most solemn occasion, have not been ignored, aye, have often been assumed to be mere meaningless protestations prompted by a ceremonial necessity? Yet the Proclamation of the Queen, containing these pledges, is cherished by the Indian people as the great charter of their privileges and rights, as their guarantee against the vagaries of irresponsible alien administration, as the basis, in fact, of their future progress. About the feelings and opinions of the populations of India as well as about the manner in which the declared policy of the Sovereign, Parliament and Ministers of England are practically carried out, the great Legislature of England is utterly ignorant. It cannot for obvious reasons attend to Indian matters as a portion of its regular business; nor has it done anything during the past twenty-five years to take stock of the results of the change made in 1858. In future years the internal and external interests of the United Kingdom will demand, in view of their growing dimensions and complications, even more exclusive attention, more devotion and talent than hitherto, while Indian problems themselves will assume increased gravity and require deliberate and cautious handling.

At present, on almost every important Indian question, there is extreme difference of opinion. I do not know whether there is any other country in the world of which such contradictory opinions are held regarding the most vital questions by men whose opinions are entitled to respectful attention. While one set of very esteemable men assert that India is growing happier and more prosperous under the effects of British rule, another set hold just the contrary opinion and state on very plausible evidence that India is sinking in exhaussion, and, unless prompt and radical remedies are adopted by Parliament, her complete ruin is only a matter of time. Again, while officials and their advocates say that the system of the Indian Government is the most perfect and the most benevolent system in the world, almost the whole body of non-official critics declare that under the alien and unsympthetic bureaucracy which holds itself responsible to no higher authority, to no public opinion, and to no moral principles in political relations, it is impossible that the regeneration of the country can be accomplished. So, too regarding other questions, such as the true financial condition of the country, the system of our land administration, the employment of Natives in the higher branches of the civil and the military administration, the most divergent views are held. How long can such an uncertain state of things continue ? How does England mean to do justice to her responsibility and the well-being of 250 millions of human beings, if her best men remain bewildered at the contradictory views put forth on some of the first problems of good government in India and otherwise continue ignorant of the facts relating to their most obvious duties and obligations? I do not forget that in official reports and in the utterances of official apologists facts of a certain description are placed before the English public. But I believe, gentlemen, there is common sense enough in England which refuses to accept as incontrovertible truths the account given by the bureaucracy of its own conduct and doings. The members of the bureaucracy must be heaven-sent indeed, not in any ironical sense, if they ever in public documents speak ill of themselves and deliberately go about to deprive themselves of their occupation. It ought to strike every person possessing common sense that the one-sided and flattering account given by the Civil Service of its own performances should not be accepted without extraneous corroborative evidence. The necessity for this extraneous evidence would be felt all the more in the face of the perplexing contradictions with which Indian controversial literature abounds.

Well, gentlemen, in soliciting an inquiry into the affairs of our country, our object is nothing more than to see that correct and full evidence relating to the real wants of the country and to the requirements of its future well-being is placed before the English public. The inquiry, we may hope, will be entrusted to men of the highest rank among English politicians, to men who represent what is best in the instincts and character of the English nation, who uphold and cherish the progressive element in their political system. and to men whose principles of statesmanship have made England what she is among the modern countries of the world. We want in the body, which may be entrusted with the inquiry, men of broad principles and liberal training rather than men of local and special knowledge. Under the direction of such men, the inquiry will be full and impartial, and will lead, as similar inquries have led in the past, to the emphasising or to the fresh application in the government of this country of those great first principles of political progress which it is the glory of England to have discovered. Gentlemen, all of us have the utmost confidence in the justice and fairness of the English people, and we have only to solicit an inquiry into facts, being content to leave the issue in the hands of their great political leaders, be they of one party or the other, of the Conservative or the Liberal party.

Gentlemen, I have confined myself to very general remarks, and have refrained from saying anything about the scope and constitution of the Committee of inquiry we pray for. These are matters of detail and may be safely left for future consideration. With these remarks I beg to recommend to your favourable consideration the proposition that has been placed in my hands, namely, "That this Congress earnestly approves of the promised Committee to inquire into the working of the Indian administration."

Mr. Pherozeshah M. Mehta, in seconding the above proposition, remarked:—

That it was not needful to prove the desirability or necessity of an enquiry into Indian affairs, since the leading men of both English parties have joined in admitting it. But while it was satisfactory to find both parties of one mind on this point, that circumstance itself rendered it extremely requisite to watch carefully the composition of the body to whom such an enquiry would be entrusted. The conditions under which the old Parliamentary Committees were appointed to enquire into the administration of the E. I. Company had altered and it was necessary to adopt a mode of enquiry suited to the altered state of things. Three considerations had, therefore, to be borne in mind. The body entrusted with the enquiry should be of a character that would enablo it to pursue its investigations in India itself. Secondly, it was essential that the natives of this country should be represented on it, and thirdly, that the Commission or Committee should take evidence in India. Mr. Mehta was strongly of opinion that unless the enquiry was granted in the manner pointed out, it would be almost better to have no enquiry at all. Parliamentary Committees and Royal Com missions were not to be had within short intervals and it would be disastrous to have a body composed mainly of Anglo-Indians sitting in judgment upon themselves. They could well imagine beforehand the conclusions to which such a body would arrive—superficially plausible, but essentially unsound. These conclusions would be accepted for guiding principles for at least another twenty years, and the mischief thus ensuing would be incalculable. He trusted that the enquiry would be of such a character as to ensure confidence on all sides. Fairly conducted and properly constituted, such an enquiry would be of immense service to the future government of this country by allaying many alarms, correcting many prejudices, exposing many fallacies and establishing sound principles in harmony with the healthy progress of time.

Babu Norendronath Sen said :- It would be the height of absurdity for any sane person, European or Native, at this hour of the day, to think of denying the importance of a Parliamentary enquiry into Indian affairs after the experience that we have had, for nearly twenty-seven years, of the working of the system of direct government of India by the Queen without any enquiry at all during that long period. The neglect of such an enquiry which had been previously of regular recurrence, though at varying intervals of time has been most disastrous in its consequences to the Indian people. The transfer of the Government of India from the Company to the Crown has been almost, if not altogether, nominal, since it carried with it, and still retains the worst features of the old system of administration—the present Indian Council merely taking the place of the old Court of Directors, with this further disadvantage that the Board of Control which looked after, and supervised, the action of the Court of Directors, was abolished, and that the wholesome check of a liability to the loss of their charter—in case of proved misrule—under which the East India Company always governed this country, was destroyed. The remedy has thus proved worse than the disease. Whatever may have been the defects of the old East India Company, this much can be said in their favour, that acting

Under the restraints I have mentioned, they took very good care to see that India was governed, so as not to cause grave discontent in the Native population. Their efforts were directed generally to the promotion of measures, which did not bear harshly on the people; and the main ground on which they generally claimed a renewal of their Charter, on each expiry of its term, was that they governed the country in the interests of its Native population. Whatever great advantages we enjoy at the present day are due entirely to the reforms which were introduced during the East India Company's rule on each renewal of the charter, which they obtained. No particular reforms, worth mentioning, have been introduced into the country since the direct assumption of its government by the Queen-Empress, beeause of the abolition of the good old system of enquiring into Indian affairs with the abolition of the East India Company themselves. Twenty-seven years is a long time; and the changes those years have wrought are almost marvellous. But no corresponding change has been made in the administration of the country to keep pace with the progress of the people. Great reforms in the present administrative svstem are urgently called for. We want a Parliamentary enquiry into Indian affairs with the view that the urgent necessity for such reforms may be made as clear as the sun at noon day. A close and constant Parliamentary control over Indian affairs is the one thing essentially needed to satisfy the feelings of the people, and to improve the condition of the country. If it had not been for even such occasional control. as the Parliament does exercise. our lot would have heen simply intolerable. But no such cou-tiol can be advantageously exercised by Parliament, without a searching enquiry into Indian affairs. There is very much ignorance in Parliament in regard to Indian questions. Not only is Indis not represented in Parliament, but it wants also a party that would identify itself with Indian interests.

The truth as regards this country hardly ever reaches Parliament. It is certainly not the interest, though it is undoubtedly the duty, of the Indian Council to make it known to Parliament; for that body, under its present constitution, is the greatest obstruction to all Indian reforms. As a matter of fact, there is no actual or even approximate representation of India in any of the great Councils of the State, whether in India or in England. Our Legislative Councils in this country are merely shams. The truth is always burked. It is never allowed to rise to the surface and good care is always taken by the official classes to seo that a true representation of Indian views and feelings never goes to the British public and the British Parliament. The Anglo-Indian or official view of every Indian question is always placed before the British public, whether through the Press or the platform or in Parliament. Thus India is allowed to be governed from England in entire ignorance of the wants and wishes of the Indian people. But ignorance is excusable. What is even worse is that when Native public opinion on any question of importance is known, it is completely ignored and disregarded. It is this that we most bitterly complain of, and that almost breaks our hearts. We therefore, want a searching and independent Parliamentary enquiry into Indian affairs, in order that the truth, the whole truth and nothing but the truth may come out, as the result of such enquiry, and that Indian reforms may be introduced on the lines suggested by such enquiry. And in order that the truth may be got at, we wish to see a Parliamentary Committee of enquiry come out to this country and take the evidence of the best and most independent portion of the Indian community—I mean the Native community of India, who will bear testimony without fear or favour, and who will conceal nothing. A Parliamentary enquiry, held and carried out in England, will not be as complete and effectual, as it will be if it is directed to be held by a Royal Commission, sent to India. Such an enquiry will not only be most interesting, but most useful as a sort of stock-taking after the trial that the system of direct Government of India by the Queen has passed through uninterruptedly during the long lapse of twenty-seven years.

Mr. Dayaram Jethmal* rose to propose an amendment which was seconded by Mr. Oodharam Moolchund and was as follows :—

That the following words be added to the proposition as moved :—"and hopes that such enquiry will be by a Royal Commission which should be fairly constituted and which should have instructions to take evidence both in England and in India." Speaking in support of his amendment Mr. Dayaram pointed out that the Resolution as proposed was lame and would show that the Congress had arrived at a lame conclusion. It did not express the national wish: it expressed a mere approval of the proposed enquiry and did not ask for any thing further. He reminded the meeting that the Resolution did not state what the constitution of the Commission of Inquiry should be, and where evidence should be taken, which were the points on which an expression of the national wish was very necessary, if the proposed enquiry was to be of much practical good. He laid stress upon the difference between an inquiry by a Parliamentary Committee and a Royal Commission, and said that whereas the former would take evidence in England and would be composed of some members of Parliament, the

---

* Since appointed a Member of the Bombay Legislative Council.

latter would be of a different character as it would be competent to take evidence in India and could be composed of well informed men who understood Indian affairs better than members of Parliament. If the Resolution as proposed was adopted, India would have no right to complain if the inquiry was not satisfactorily carried on, whereas if his amendment were embodied in the Resolution and the proposed inquiry were conducted by a Parliamentary Committee without evidenee being taken in India we should not be in a position to say that we did not get what we wanted

Mr. P. M. Mehta observed that he had no objection to adopt Mr. Dayaram's amendment.

Mr. J. U. Yajnik said that the constitution of a Roya Commission rested entirely with the Ministry in power at the time of its appointment. It was by no means possible to say whether a Liberal or a Conservative Ministry would be in office when the Committee came to be appointed. And therefore there would be much chance of men being appoint ed who would not take impartial views of the matters that would come before them. He thought, therefore, that the proposition should remain as it was, couched in genera terms.

Mr. K. T. Telang believed that a Parliamentary Com mittee could not take evidence in India—a most importan consideration.

Mr. K. L. Nulkar would support Mr. Dayaram's sugges tion. It was absolutely necessary that evidence should be taken in India. A Royal Conunission would do that, and would also be independent of English political parties

Mr. D. E. Wacha said that the Congress should ask for a Royal Commission. The Parliamentary Committee on India Finance broke off by dissolution of Parliament without mak ing any final report, though a mass of valuable evidence was collected. That might occur again.

Mr. V. Subrayadu was not in favour of the proposed amendment. Let the authorities consider the course proper to be adopted. It might look like dictation to Parliament, if the Congress adopted the proposed amendment. Details as to place of examining witnesses, &c., might be considered hereafter.

Mr. Sabapathy Mudliar dissented from the last speaker's view about the amendment looking like dictation.

Mr. J. Ghosal thought that evidence must be taken in India, but perhaps they might try a Select Committee, and afterwards ask for a Royal Commission if that was found necessary.

Mr. A. O. Hume suggested the omission of the phrase "fairly constituted," and Dr. S. V. Athalye having supported the suggestion, the proposer and seconder of the Resolution agreed to its omission.

Mr. Sabapathy Mudaliar of Bellary said the Royal Commission, like the Famine Commission, should go about travelling in the country and enquire into the nature of the administration of the country and personally examine witnesses.

Mr. P. Peter Pillai, from Tinnevelly District, said :—
I would support the proposed amendment to the resolution so that the Royal Commission or Parliamentary Committee might be a great and real success. Unless there is some good organisation or system of working such Commissions and Committees, they will not be of much use. Mr. Sabapathy Mudaliar of Bellary alluded to the Famine Commission. I came in contact with the Commission and I

closely studied its various questions and system of working. I had anticipated the failure of the Commission and I published a reveiw of the working of it in a public journal. When I met Mr. William Digby, who took great interest in famine matters, I told him that nothing would come out of it productive of much good to the country. My remark has been fully verified. Though the Commission had a great deal to do with questions affecting the general interests of the country, we find the condition of the ryots growing worse than before—in certain respects worse than what it was at the time of the Commission and the famine—for instance the forest laws, the salt laws, the re-organisation of the village establishment &c., which are all very oppressive to the people. Lately, there was the Education Commission. That is also a great failure. I say this from personal experience, being connected with the Educational Department. We have now some new difficulties in addition to the difficulties which the Commission professed to remove. I do not say any thing disparagingly of the gentlemen that were in these Commissions. They were all men of superior attainments and character. But the defect lies in the working and organisation of these Commissions, which were not of a sufficiently representative character and in which the wants of the people were not sufficiently represented. Unless the Committee or Commission to be asked for be thoroughly representative in character, and unless a portion of the Commission is composed of members chosen by the people, either among Europeans or Indians, I do not entertain great hopes of the success of the Commission. So I strongly support the amendment proposed.

Mr. Dadabhai Naoroji said :—I had no thought of speaking on this resolution, but I see I must say something.

There is a notion running under some remarks that if a Conservative Government appoints a Committee it will not be a good one. I do not think there is any good reason for that assumption. The Conservatives are not so bad as that they will never do a good thing, nor are the Liberals so good that they never did a bad thing. In fact we owe good to both, and we have nothing to do with them yet as parties We are thankful to either party that does us good. The Proclamation is the gift of a Conservative Government I have some experience of a Parliamentary Committee, and that Committee, a Liberal one; and yet under the Chairmanship of a gentleman like Mr. Ayrton, you cannot be sure of a fair hearing. On the other hand, a fair minded Chairman and similar members, be they Conservatives or Liberals, would make a good Committee, and give a fair inquiry. Much depends upon the Secretary of State for India. If he is a fair minded person and not biassed in any particular way, you will have a fair Committee. If we are asking for a Parliamentary Committee, we need not be afraid of asking one from a Conservative Government. A Secretary of State like Sir Stafford Northcote (Lord Iddesleigh) will give a fair one, and we should not assume that the present Secretary will not give a good one. We should only desire that Anglo-Indians may not be put in it, or only a few such in whom Natives have confidence. In such an enquiry Anglo-Indian officials are on their trial, and they should not be allowed to sit in judgment upon themselves.

From the remarks already made, there appears to be an undecidedness, whether to ask for a Committee, or for a Royal Commission. And there seems also a notion underneath, that if we were not satisfied with the one we could ask for the other. Now we must bear in mind that it is not an easy thing to get a Parliamentary Committee or a Royal

Commission, and that you cannot have either whenever you like. Do not suppose that if we have a Committee or a Commission and if we say we are dissatisfied with its results. we would at onco get another for the asking. We must mako up our minds definitively as to what we want and what would be the best thing for us. You should not leave it open whether there should be a Committee or Commission. Whichever you want, say it out once for all. In dealing with Englishmen, make up your minds deliberately, speak clearly, and work perseveringly. Then and then only can you hope to be listened to, and get your wishes. You must not show that you do not know your own mind. Therefore, know your own mind, and say clearly whether you desire a Parliamentary Committec, or a Royal Commission. It is evidently the desire here, that a full and impartial enquiry by fair and high minded English statesmen, with an adequate number of Natives on the enquiring body. should be earried on in India itself. If so, then we must remember that a Parliamentary Committee can consist only of members of Parliament, and can sit in the Parliament House only. For our parpose to lay bare the actual conditions of India, an inquiry in India, in all departments and in the whole condition of India—material and moral—is absolutely necessary. No enquiry in England, and that with the evidence of Anglo-Indians chiefly—who themselves are on trial, and who would not naturally condemn their own doings and work—can ever bring out the truth about India's true condition and wants, and necessary reforms. We, then, irresistibly come to one conclusion that an enquiry in India itself is absolutely necessary and that such an enquiry can be conducted, by a Royal Commission. Only let us clearly say our mind that we ask for a Royal Commission. Do not let there be any doubt about what we do really waht. If I am right in interpreting your desire, then I say let there be no vague general resolution, but say clearly and distinctly that we require a Royal Commission.

After some further discussion in which Mr. S. Agnihotri, Mr. Ananda Charlu, Mr. Rangayya Naidu, and Mr. B. M. Malabari took part, Mr. P. M. Mehta explained that then was no insinuation contained in the words "fairly constituted" They were intended to emphasize the necessity for a Commission about which no room should be left for dissatisfaction, as a second Commission would not be granted soon after the first.

The President in summing up the debate pointed out that every one wanted an inquiry in India as well as in England and that that really would be best secured by adopting a resolution asking for a Royal Commisssion.

The Resolution was then unanimously carried in the following form :—" That this Congress earnestly recommends that the promised inquiry into the working of the Indian administration here and in England, should be entrusted to a Royal Commission, the people of India being adequately represented thereon. and evidence taken both in India and in England."

The Congress was then adjourned to 8 A. M. of the following day.

PROCEEDINGS

OF THE

2nd Day, 29th December 1885

The Congress having assembled at 8 A. M. Mr. S. H. Chiplonkar (of Poona) rose to move the 2nd Resolution in the following speech :—

Mr. Chairman and Members of the National Congress :— The Resolution which I have to propose for your acceptance relates to the India Council of the Secretary of State for India. This Council is a remnant, though in another shape, of the form of goverment that prevailed in the days of the East India Company; and, in my humble opinion, the time has arrived when the necessity or otherwise of the existence of such an institution as the India Council should be considered. It was perhaps inevitable when the government of this country was vested in a commercial corporation that that corporation should have delegated its trust to a Managing Board; but it seems to me to be very strange that the same device should be perpetuated after the goverment of this country has been transferred to the Crown. The practical result of this state of things is that though nominally we are said to be directly governed by the British Crown and Parliament, we are still virtually under the government of the Company; nay more, for in some respects, Sir, we may be said to be worse off than before. Unlike the old Court of Directors, the India Council is composed almost exclusively of retired Anglo-Indian officials who as a class are naturally prone, often from force of habit and sometimes from force of conviction, to hand down to their successors the British Indian Empire in pretty nearly the same condition in which they found it and who from the operation of the same causes are incapable of being struck by the abuses of that system which gave them birth, though such abuses might at first sight strike any superficial independent observer. Sir, even the authors of the Government of India Act of 1858 did not contemplate such a consummation with equanimity or without misgivings; for we find the late Lord Beaconsfield even then confessing that "with such men (*i. e.* retired Anglo-Indian officials) exercising supreme authority you could not feel sure that you would be able to obtain for tho inhabitants of India that redress from the grievances under which they suffered that English protection ought to secure." The question, therefore, naturally arises what is it that English protection ought to secure to the people of India? I think you will all agree with me in holding that English protection ought to secure the gradual and progressive advance of this country in its political status. and indirectly also in its social status, for it may, I trust. afford some consolation to those of my brethren within these walls as well as outside who have the cause of social reform in India at heart to know—and I may be permitted here to passingly observe that English history strikingly emphasizes this lesson—that political progress must bring social progress also in its train; for I hold that a nation which is politically forward cannot long afford to be socially backward and that a nation which is politically backward can never hope to be socially forward. It thus follows that the constitution of the Government of India in England must be framed primarily with a view to this object. It is necessary to draw a distinction between the Government of India in England and the Government of India in India. The former should be constituted with a view to bring to bear upon the latter the opinion of the Parliament and people of England, and to make the latter realize their responsibility to that opinion. To enable the former to discharge these functions adequately a knowledge of local details is not absolutely necessary ; nay, I would go further and say that such a knowledge of local detailswould decidedly constitute a positive disqualification in the controlling authority for the simple reason that such intimate knowledge of local details leads its possessors to sacrifice general principles of good government to local prejudices, engendered by bureaucratic selfishness, and to rely almost exclusively upon those prejudices in their conduct of Indian affairs. What we should look for and have a right to expect in any authority constituted in England and invested with the power of controlling the actions of the Government of India in India is an intimate acquaintance with the general principles of human nature and of good government, uncontaminated by local and bureaucratic prejudices. In the India Council, constituted as it now is, you have nothing but an intimate knowledge of local details; and, consequently it is no wonder that the India Council ever since its establishment in 1858 has been developing an ever increasing desire for interference in all manner of details. It possesses no substantive power which at one time the advocates of its continued existence believed it to possess, and to my mind this circumstance accounts for its increasing desire to interfere in all the details of local administration, being of course naturally anxious to justify the wisdom of its original creation and of its continued maintenance. Here, Sir, with your permission I wish to invite the attention of the Congress to the testimony of the late John Stuart Mill, than whom none worked harder for averting the fate which at last overtook the East India Company, and for establishing the India Council exactly on the lines of the old Court of Directors. During the course of the discussions on the Bill of 1869, which amended the Act of 1858 in a few details, Mr.

Mill, who was then a Member of Parliament, said that it was most important that India should be governed in India and confessed that of late owing to the increasing facilities of communication there was a great tendency to over-interference on the part of the Home Government. Mr. Mill held the same views in 1869, as he did in 1858, as regards the necessity of surrounding the Indian Minister by a Council of experts, but he proceeded to add that "if the Council did not possess some substantive power, if they were made a consultative body only, they would never have that degree of weight which they ought to possess; they would be a mere superfluous wheel in the machinery; if they had only the power of giving their opinions, they would never be so powerful with the Secretary of State as his own subordinates in office." It was, however, conclusively shown in 1880 by the Duke of Argyll and the Law Officers of the Crown, that the Act of 1859 did not vest in the India Council any substantive power whatever. In 1869 the Conservatives were in opposition and they thought for a time that under the Act of 1858 the Indian Council possessed a substantive power in reference to the financial administration; but it should be borne in mind that the Conservative leaders wished even then to deprive the India Council of that power of financial control. It will be thus seen, Sir, that neither Liberals nor Conservatives wanted the India Council to be anything more than a mere consultative body. Under such circumstances, I believe, I am fully justified in citing the testimony of the late John Stuart Mill in favour of the Resolution I am submitting for your acceptance.

At the very commencement of my observations I have stated my belief, that though we are nominally under the direct government of the Crown and Parliament of England, yet we are still virtually under the government of the East India Company; nay, I might go further and add that while the existing constitution of the English portion of the Indian administration possesses to the fullest extent all the vices or shortcomings of its predecessor, it possesses none of its redeeming features. It is unnecessary to go into details, and it will be sufficient for the purposes of my argument if I notice here briefly the striking results of British administration in India and Ceylon which are, each of them, governed on separate principles, it being of course well-known that Ceylon is governed on Colonial principles. Firstly, then, the race disqualification, which was sought to be removed by the Ilbert Bill, does not exist in Ceylon, where the Native and European Magistrates and Judges enjoy similar powers as regards their jurisdiction over European British-born subjects. Secondly, as regards the maximum limit of age for candidates competing for the Civil Service Examination of Ceylon it is even now fixed at 24, while for India the maximum limit is fixed at 19, thus practically shutting the door of public competition to the natives of India. Thirdly, as regards the disestablishment of the English Church, Ceylon has already obtained what it wanted, while we in India can hardly be said to have entered upon even the first stage of the question. And fourthly and lastly, the Ceylon Legislative Council has for several years past been representative in its character, inasmuch as the independent or non-official members of that Legislature are elected by the respective communities which they represent, and not nominated by Government as in India. In this connection it has also to be borne in mind, that the independent members of the Ceylon Legislature have the privilege of interpellating the official members of the body on executive matters—a privilege whieh is entirely denied to us in India. But by far the most important feature in connection with the powers and privileges of the Ceylon Legislature has yet to be noticed That feature consists in the fact that that Legislature possesses a complete control over the finances, in that the annual budget must be discussed and sanctioned by it. In India it is different. The Indian Budget is never presented to the Indian Legislature for approval and sanction except upon those occasions when new taxation is contemplated. Thus it comes to pass that so long as the Indian Government can manage to pull on without additional taxation, the Indian Legislature has no opportunity afforded to it of examining and criticizing the budget. Mr. Chairman and gentlemen, you will all, I dare say, agree with me in holding that the extreme importance of this last mentioned privilege cannot be exaggerated; for it cannot for a moment be denied that that privilege alone has enabled Ceylon to enjoy an immunity, which we in India might well envy, from having to bear oppressive burdens which do not rightly belong to it. Ceylon has never had to bear, for instance, the cost of the Abyssinian War, of the Egyptian Expedition, or of the entertainment of the Sultan of Turkey when in London. The question, therefore, naturally arises, what is the cause of this difference in the treatment which India and Ceylon receive at the hands of one common mistress? It surely cannot be found in the character of the people of the two countries; for as a race the Cinghalese or the natives of Ceylon are not only not superior to the Hindus in intelligence, political capacity, or civilization, but on the contrary are admittedly their inferiors. The late Sir Erskine Perry, who knew both the countries well, bore such a testimony to our superiority over the natives of Ceylon. In his speech during the course of the debate in the House of Commons on Lord Palmerston's motion for leave to introduce his India Bill, Sir Erskine Perry said that :—"he knew the island (Ceylon) well, and was able to say, that notwithstanding the inferiority of the Cinghalese to the Hindus as a race, the improvement, the progress and the civilization, that had taken place there, under the Queen's Government, were infinitely greater than could be boasted of in India." Since 1858, India too, like, Ceylon, has been direct under the Queen's Government for nearly one whole generation, and yet it must be sorrowfully confessed that we have not been able to overtake our cousins of the neighbouring island in the race of progress and civilization. That island still maintains its superiority over the main continent as intact as ever. And this fact necessarily suggests the question, what is the prime cause of this sad and sorry spectacle? To my mind it appears that only one answer is possible to the question formulated above. Abolish the Indian Council, and let the Indian Secretary of State direct the Government of this country on the some principles on which the Secretary of State for the Colonies governs Ceylon and the other Colonies; and you will soon observe a change for the better coming over India. The monstrous fiction that in the Indian Council India would and did find an institution to represent her and to jealously and efficiently watch her interests did at no time, and does not even now, deceive any one in India; and I am loth to believe that, though such a fiction might have deceived the English nation in days long gone by, it can deceive that nation any longer. It is this fiction which is primarily and principally responsible for the great body of the evils this country is labouringunder; and unless it receives its death-blow, which, I firmly believe, it will receive when it is next put upon its trial, India can never hope to obtain that measure of justice which is her due. With these observations I beg to move for your acceptance the Resolution with which I have been charged, namely, "That this Congress considers the abolition of the Council of the Secretary of State for India, as at present constituted, the necessary preliminary to all other reforms."

In seconding the Resolution Mr. P. Ananda Charlu addressed the Congress as follows:—I rise to do a duty that has an unpleasant feature about it. It consists in proposing that we should turn undertakers. There is, however, one circumstance that relieves it of much of its disagreeableness. The proposal is made under the call of our mother-country and in her best interests. Under such a call and in such interests I take it that we shall not hesitate to turn undertakers, and even worse, within constitutional limits. What, then, is the thing the extinction of which we have to propose? It is what is quaintly designated "The India Council"—not any Indian Council, or any Council doing duty *in* India. How was it composed? How is it composed? What is its history? In its inception, it was little better than a relic of the discredited John Company; for when the whole body of the East India Company was found to be inefficient, a part of that very inefficient body was considered fitter to do what the entire body was incapable of doing. This method of procedure is, *prima facie*, queer. But, perhaps, nothing better was feasible under the circumstances, consistently with the conflicting interests that had then to be taken into account. Be that as it may, the institution at its formation was a mere relic, kept alive, I must assume, as the best makeshift then possible. In its next stage of development it was no better, for it was mainly little else than an oligarchy of fossilised Indian administrators, presided over by the Secretary of State—a member of the British Cabinet. Nearly every vacancy, as it occurred, was filled by such as had been declared superannuated for service *in* India, and it is difficult to see how a body of such men could fulfil the functions of a Council, which is virtually the final arbiter of India's destinies and which has to grapple with far more weighty problems than call for solution *in* India. I do not forget that there is a transit to a far more propitious climate. But that does not count for very much. The change might put off dissolution or might diminish the rate of decline ; but it is inconceivable that, after the meridian of life had long been passed, the change could restore the mental and physical energy of vigorous manhood. Then, again, the Indian experience of these men is not abreast of the times, as they have long been removed from, and are, for all practical purposes, beyond the reach of the influences and forces actually' in operation *in* India. It is not, in the nature of things, possible for these and such as these to do justice to growing Indian requirements. The evil effects of these manifestly infirmatory features in the members are aggravated by the absolute supremacy which is reserved to the Secretary of State for India, as the President of the Council. In practice, as well as by the letter of the law, this tremendous authority is reserved to the President, and it does not require much effort of imagination to realize the utter helplessness of the Council when its views are overridden by the dictator. No machinery exists for an appeal to Parliament at the instance of the Indian Council as against the decision of the Secretary of State, and I think this is after all not a matter of regret ; for, suppose such a machinery existed, the result would be no better, as the Secretary of State for India, possessing the ear of his fellow-Cabinet-ministers, enjoys by that circumstance the command of a Parliamentary majority as a matter of course. Without at all imputing to the British Cabinet a wanton desire to injure India, it may well be predicated that, when opposed to purely British interests, Indian interests will always give way. Thus we find, by an examination of its constitution and by calculation of probabilities, that the India Council contains no elements of usefulness, but contains a great many elements tending to do harm. One of the previous speakers said that the British Parliament, conscious of its powerlessness to do justice to the claims of India, abdicated its right as a final Court of appeal in favour of the India Council, which was evidently instituted as an experiment. The experiment has failed, according to the universal verdict, and we wish that an institution which has luckily not existed for quite a generation yet, but which having been weighed in the balance has been found wanting, may cease to exist. What is proposed to take its place as a more effectual body to dispose of Indian matters does not fall within my province. The proposition to be next moved will contain the provision for its substitute. The true scope of my duty is to indicate the inefficiency of the existing Council and the necessity of its abolition as a primary condition of all other reforms. For the purposes of the proposal which I am seconding, it is enough to say that no improvement is possible till this Council is abolished, without at all implying that, by itself, such a step will at once right every thing. To adopt the Rev. Sidney Smith's happy way of putting a like case, "the medical man does not tell you, you will be all right, *when* the bile is got rid of, but he tells you that you will *not* be right, *till after* the bile is got rid of." With these remarks I beg to second the proposition before you.

Mr. J. Ghosal (of Allahabad) made the following speech in support of the Resolution :—Mr. Chairman and gentlemen: The subject of the resolution which I am called upon to support has for some time past occupied so much the attention of thoughtful men, who take any interest in the good administration of the Indian Government both here and in England, and it has been so lucidly and ably discussed by the two previous speakers, that I have little or nothing to say in support of it.

Regarding the necessity of abolishing, or at least re-constituting, the India Council no two persons who have given the least thought to the subject have any difference of opinion. There exists such a general agreement on the subject that no arguments are necessary to convince those who care to pay any attention to the subject, that steps must be taken to effect a change in or to abolish the Council altogether without further loss of time, not only for the good of the people of this country, but also for that of the Government itself, because I consider what is good for the one is also good for the other.

The India Council was no doubt instituted at first to serve a good and useful purpose ; but practically it has proved otherwise, as is often found to be the case with many administrative arrangements made in different countries at different times. Our best intended schemes are often found in practice to prove the contrary. When the administration of this country was transferred from the East India Company to the Crown it was virtually transferred to the Secretary of State for India. Owing to the very constitution of the British Government and the frequent changes of party government in England there was, and still there is, no knowing who might become the Secretary of State for India and at what moment. As a rule, persons having no previous connection with this country and possessing no knowledge of its affairs are selected to fill the post. For such men to carry on properly the administration of this vast country, and that while sitting in England, was considered almost an impossibility unless helped with information and advice by men who had real knowledge of this country and its people. Under the circumstances the English statesmen then in power thought it necessary to provide the Secretary of State with a Council whose members might not only help him, but also to a certain extent serve as a check on his vagaries and high-handedness. No one could at that time find fault with such an arrangement. Let us see, however, what have been its practical results and why. For reasons already stated no single individual holds the office of Secretary of State for a long time, but the fifteen members of his Council, are almost permanent fixtures there. It is true that they are not now appointed to hold office during good behaviour, which meant almost for life, still the ten years for which they are now appointed is a pretty long time, and they are all considered great authorities on all questions concerning India. The Secretary of State having no such pretensions cannot but be guided more or less by the views, opinions and advice of these members; consequently, it is these members who virtually control and guide the administration of this country. I may say the Secretary of State is almost bound to act according to their views. Even the general impression, that in matters concerning the expenditure of public funds, the Secretary of State possesses the power of acting without the concurrence of his Council, has no real foundation. This is apparent from what has just been so ably explained by my friend, Mr. Chiplonkar. In fact, if the Secretary of State possessed the power, placed as he is, he would be most reluctant to use it except on rare occasions, when backed or guided by a much stronger force, the policy of his party in Parliament, or the decision of the Cabinet Ministers. Knowing all these circumstances we look up to those fifteen members of the India Council as the most important personages in deciding the fate of our country. This brings us to a consideration of their qualifications for exercising such powers. Are they really fit to govern India or to control, give shape to, supervise, and to find out the defects in the policy of those who carry on the actual work of administration in this country? Almost all of them are retired Anglo-Indian officials. Owing to the peculiar circumstances and surroundings of their position while in this country, some of these Anglo-Indian officials have in them less of an Englishman than of an Oriental despot. Consider also, gentlemen, the value of their knowledge of this country and its people. India is now passing through a rapid, very rapid, transition. Look at the changes that have taken place within the last twenty, or say ten, years. The India of today is very different even from the India of 1880. Five years ago who could have foreseen or believed that all classes of people, Hindoos, Mahomedans, Parsis, and others, in every part of this vast country—Madras, Bombay, Bengal, Punjab, North West Provinces, Oudh, &c,—would, without any pre-arrangement or intercommunication, simultaneously become so enthusiastic in manifesting their grateful feelings for a single individual, as they did in their demonstrations towards our late beloved Viceroy, Lord Ripon, on the occasion of his retirement from the country. Again, five years ago the very idea of such a national gathering as this of delegates from every part of India, belonging to different castes and creeds, uniting for common objects, and travelling long distances almost at a moment's notice—because it is not yet a month since the time and place of this Congress were fixed and notified—the very idea of a National Congress would have been considered utopian or impossible. The members of the India Council would be the very last persons to believe that since their departure from India the country has undergone such a mighty change. The knowledge possessed by these members regarding India is of very little use at the present moment. Their ideas and notions of the India of their days and its people have become almost ancient. As men grow in age, their opinions and convictions as well as their prejudices are liable to become fixed and stereotyped, and their capability to understand and realise the effects of the changes daily taking place around them is proportionately diminished. Even when they understand them they feel disinclined to adapt themselves to the altered state of things. For this reason the conclusions arrived at by these members of the India Council are often formed on a wrong basis, and, therefore, sometimes they do us harm even in wishing to do us good. It is a well known fact that the generality of Anglo-Indian officials conduct the administration of this country in a manner which best ensures the preservation of their interests and of the services to which they belong. Their policy is always opposed to our advancement. And as the India Council is regularly recruited from the very same class of officials its members are the perennial representatives of Anglo-Indian prejudice, policy, and interest. Honourable exceptions are occasionally found among them, but these only prove the rule. Members of the India Council are, however, not always to be blamed for all the mischief that is done to Indian interests. They are but human. In many cases they have to uphold the policy they themselves had been carrying on while in this country, and sometimes they have to sit in judgment upon their own acts during their official careers. At other times they have to judge of the acts done by those whom they personally know well, of whose abilities they have high opinions and for whose judgment they have respect. It is but natural that under such circumstances they should do as they have been doing. If we had a different class of men as members of the India Council, men free from local and party prejudices and having no real or imaginary interest in upholding this, that or the other policy, men who would understand and could take cognizance of the real state of affairs as they are now, or happen to be from time to time, and had sympathy with our just aspirations, such a Council would be a great boon to our country. As it is at present constituted it has become an anachronism—more a source of mischief than good. The proceedings of the India Council are not made public. The public can never know who is really responsible for the decision which a Secretary of State may have given on any particular question. It is almost an open secret that in the question of raising the age of the Indian Civil Service candidates the late Secretary of State arrived at the decision not according to his own lights, but according to those of the members of his Council; but no one can fix the responsibility on them. In fact, the mouthpieces of the Anglo-Indian bureaucracy, the newspapers conducted in this country to represent their views, have already done their best to fix the responsibility on the Secretary of State alone, because Lord Kimberley, who was then holding that office, happened to belong to the Liberal party. Divided responsibility by itself is a sure source of mischief, but the members of the India Council, though the real arbiters of our fate, are irresponsible, and the exercise of irresponsible power is always most mischievous and dangerous. Is it not, gentlemen, then high time that these irresponsible dignitaries should cease to take such supreme part in the administration of our country? Considering these, as well as a few other points which the limited time allowed to each speaker will not permit me to touch upon, we cannot help asking for the abolition of the India Council. When we think of this question, another naturally occurs to us, that is, by what other agency or agencies that useful purpose could be served for which the India Council was originally created, and how the work that is now done by that body should be conducted. The question is so important and vast that I don't think this is the proper time and place to go into its details. Much of the work could be easily performed by Under-Secretaries as is the case with the office of the Secretary of State for the

Colonies. But there would still remain a good portion which it is desirable, nay necessary, should be disposed of by a tribunal composed of men who are duly qualified to deal with it. We have also to consider whether such a tribunal should be located in England or in India, or partly there and partly here. Should the much wished for Royal Commission for enquiring into the administration of India be soon appointed, much light will also be thrown on this subject during the course of that enquiry. Whatever that enquiry may lead to one thing is certain. The reconstitution or the abolition of the India Council is particularly necessary as a preliminary to all other much needed reforms in the administration of this country. We no longer wish to be blessed with the so-called wisdom and experience of the members of the India Council nor with the fruits of their brain and pen. At the same time we want some other body to take not only their functions, but also some additional ones and in the deliberations of that body wish to have the views and the wants of the people of this country represented by our own countrymen, and those selected not from the class favoured by the Anglo-Indian bureaucracy, but from a different one. We want our interests represented by such of our countrymen as are more anxious to do good to our country than to please the big officials and secure titles for themselves and lucrative appointments for their relations—we want men who are in real sympathy with the educated classes and the people at large. To speak plainly, we, who suffer most on account of the shortcomings of our administrators, wish to have a real share in the administration of our own affairs. We want to take the work of administration more and more into our own hands so far as it is compatible with the imperial policy of the British Government. We cannot, however, expect this reform and a change in the fiscal policy of the country, until the India Council is abolished and the India Act of 1858 amended.

With these observations, gentlemen, I beg to recommend to your favourable consideration the Resolution which I have been called upon to support.

Mr. Sayani said he did not wish to oppose the Resolution, but rather to make an inquiry. The India Council had existed for many years and we ought to be cautious in asking for its total abolition. Would not the Secretary of State become a perfect autocrat without the Council? And would it not be better to wait for the result of the inquiry that the Congress were asking for, as that inquiry must necessarily embrace this question of the existence and powers of the Indian Council.?

Mr. V. Subrayadu said that fears had been expressed that if the India Council was abolished, the Secretary of State would become a perfect autocrat. He thought the Secretary of State was an autocrat now. The Councillors are worthy men of antiquated notions and obsolete knowledge. They are not representative, and it is difficult to arrange for a representative Council. The system we should have is that which exists in the Colonies.

Mr. P. M. Mehta in reference to Mr. Sayani's doubts pointed out that the inquiry asked for was not so much for the purpose of their making up their minds as for testing the conclusions they had come to. The case as regards the India Council seemed to him complete. The other doubt of Mr. Sayani had been answered by the late speaker. [A member: But the Colonies have Parliaments of their own.] That is true, but I don't believe in secret irresponsible conclaves. We must have a government carried out in open day-light. And here, continued Mr. P. M. Mehta, I would ask leave to make a remark about a matter on which there is a great deal of misapprehension. I wish all our countrymen to consider how far we can get on without the aid of what is called party government. The system of English administration is based on party and our fortunes being bound up with England, we must resort to that system for our wants also. In the English system, truth cannot be brought out except by the concussion of debate when each case is explained from both sides. Returning to the main subject of debate, Mr. P. M. Mehta said, Indian officers of Government were supposed to be unfit for work at the age of 55. Could it, then, be reasonably supposed that the effete Anglo-Indian officials who are appointed to the India Council are less unfit? Further it must be remembered that these bureaucrats must always be partial to what their brother bureaucrats do out here, as they have themselves done similar things in their time. They are, therefore, an exceedingly unsatisfactory appellate tribunal over the local officers.

Mr. Sabapathi Mudaliar said that the abolition of the India Council is necessary not only for the sake of the efficient administration of the country, but it is also necessary, in point of economy. The poverty of India is such as not to be able to afford to pay heavily for the double government when there is nothing to recommend it. By the abolition of the Council we shall obtain a large saving to the public revenue, and we shall have the further advantage of making the government more local than now.

The Resolution was then put to the vote and carried unanimously.

In proposing the next resolution, the Hon'ble K. T. Telang observed: Mr. President, I confess I feel a certain amount of embarrassment, because I happen just now to be a member of one of those bodies, the reform of which is insisted on in the Resolution that has been entrusted to me

However, I will endeavour to do my best in placing that Resolution before you. It runs as follows:—"That this Congress considers the reform and expansion of the Supreme and existing Legislative Councils, by the admission of a considerable proportion of elected members (and the creation of similar Councils for the North West Provinces and Oudh, and also for the Punjaub) essential; and holds that all Budgets should be referred to these Councils for consideration, their members being moreover empowered to interpellate the Executive in regard to all branches of the administration; and that a standing committee of the House of Commons should be constituted to receive and consider any formal protests that may be recorded by majorities of such Councils against the exercise by the Executive of the power, which would be vested in it, of overruling the decisions of such majorities." I think it will be convenient if I say a few words on each of the important points embraced in the Resolution I have now read. In the first place there can be little doubt that the two great division of the Empire, viz, the Punjaub, and the North West Provinces and Oudh, ought to have Legislative Councils of their own. It is unnecessary now to consider the question whether they should have had their own local Councils before. We have got now to deal with the future, and I do not anticipate that there will be any difference of opinion among ourselves on this point, that in future those Provinces should have Local Legislative Councils constituted like those which the other Provinces possess or may hereafter possess. How should those Councils, then, be constituted? At present they are almost entirely under the system of nomination. I say almost entirely, because in the reign of our late beloved Viceroy, Lord Ripon, what may be called in some sense a new departure was made in the mode of nomination when our late distinguished countryman, Babu Kristodas Pal, was called into the Supreme Legislative Council. And that mode has been followed in the appointment of the successor of Kristodas Pal—my friend Mr. Pyari Mohan Mukarji. Barring these exceptions, however, which may be said to prove the rule, our Legislative Councils have always been recruited by nominations. Now I do not know whether I am estopped, as we lawyers phrase it, from saying that the practical working of this system has not always been satisfactory. But however that may be, there can be no doubt that that system is now, at all events, unsatisfactory in principle. Under the excellent scheme of Local Self-government elaborated during the viceroyalty of Lord Ripon we shall have a complete network of Municipal and Rural Boards, which shall to a greater or less extent be manned by representatives of the people elected by the people themselves. And that being so, it seems quite manifest, that as a keystone, so to say, to this arch of local elective bodies in each Presidency you must have elected Legislative Council at the capital city of each Presidency. This seems obviously so appropriate that it is unnecessary to further labour the point.

It will be noticed, that the phrase used in the Resolution is "a considerable proportion of elected members." This phrase has been used advisedly, as it does not seem to be desirable that we should now pledge ourselves to any specific proportion to be observed throughout the Empire. Local conditions, the laws enacted to effectuate local self-government in different Provinces, will have to be looked to in fixing the proportion in each case. But it seems to me, personally, that in order to give the principle of election a fair scope, at least one half of each Council should be elected. In our Local Boards and Municipalities' Acts in this

Presidency that is the proportion fixed, and it would not be a very revolutionary demand to ask for that proportion in the highest Council in each Presidency. There is one important question in connection with this point as to election, which, as being one of detail and depending to a very large extent on local conditions, has not been dealt with in the Resolution itself. But it is desirable that I should now refer to it. We may be asked, what is your electoral constituency? How are you going to get your members elected? Well, as I say, I am not going to ask the Congress to come to any formal resolution on these points, but I think it is right that I should indicate some modes by which the thing can be done, if it is determined to do it. For each Presidency Town, then, there are several well organised bodies to which the right of election may be given. There are, for instance, the Municipal Corporations of each of our Presidency Towns, which can be asked to return one or more members. Then there are the Chambers of Commerce, and the Universities to which also such a right may properly be given. Again, well-established political Associations—such as the one whose aid the Government of India recently resorted to on the two occasions I have just named—might fairly be asked to return some members. Thus we can get a satisfactory electoral body within the Presidency Towns. But this is, of course, very far from enough. The Mofussil Districts must also be represented. And for this purpose, too, well-established political Associations in the Districts might be utilized as well as the bodies which naturally present themselves as suitable for the purpose, namely, the various Rural and Municipal Boards established in each Province. It will be understood that I am making these remarks, not as showing what in my opinion should be done at once, but as showing rather, that while we leave open these questions touching the working out of the details of our scheme we have bestowed some thought upon those questions, and can, when the time comes, suggest some feasible modes for their solution.

So much for the constitution of the Councils. Now as to their functions. And the first additional function which this Resolution points out is one connected with finance. Under the existing law and practice, financial Budgets have to be submitted to the Legislative Councils, whenever new measures of taxation have to be passed. But according to a ruling of Lord Northbrook's, about the correctness of which it is not needful now to inquire, Budgets *cannot* be submitted to the Legislative Councils when new measures of taxation are not proposed by the Executive Government. And we know, accordingly, that such Budgets have only been published for many years as part of Government Resolutions. Well, we propose that the practice prevailing in cases where new taxation is called for should be made the universal practice and be prescribed by law. It will be noticed that at present we only ask for the Budget being brought forward for consideration in the Councils. We do not propose what would probably be a too radical measure just now—namely, that the Councils should have power to reject the Budgets of the Executive Government. But even without this power, which might conceivably hamper the work of Government, it must do some good, and can do no harm to allow non-official views of Government measures to be publicly proclaimed by responsible persons, in recognised modes, and in such a way that the constituted authorities must necessarily be informed about them, and feel themselves called upon, in some sense, to answer such views. It seems to me quite obvious, that as I have said before, our proposal on this point may fairly be expected to do some good and cannot possibly do any harm.

Well, then, the next point is in reference to the power of interpellation. This, again, appears to me to be a very moderate modicum of reform, the concession of which cannot lead to any mischief. I had occasion a few months ago to speak on this subject to an eminent authority in this Presidency, who must for the present be nameless, and an objection was then somewhat faintly, I may say, suggested to this reform. It was suggested that this power of interpellation may be abused, as it has been by Mr. Ashmead Bartlett in the House of Commons. I quite accepted then, as I accept now, the view that the power of interpellation is susceptible of being abused, like any other power, but I ventured to point that there was no reason to anticipate any such abuse of the power here, at all events for many years after it was first conceded. And when the time comes, it will be quite open to the authorities then to deal with the evil as may seem most fitting. But until that time comes, I think we may very fairly and reasonably consider the objection as beyond the pale of practical politics. And now let us see what will be the advantages of giving such a power to our Councils. In the first place, we all know that at present the responsible authorities of Government have very few unexceptionable modes of quieting discontent, by explanations of the motives and actions of Government. There is no official journal, and therefore no way which the officials consider to be consistent with their dignity for offering any information that may dispel dissatisfaction. A power of interpellation vested in the Council affords a most unobjectionable remedy for this state of things. Again, matters are always cropping up, which do not attract attention at headquarters in time to avert mischief. To these matters attention could be drawn in Council effectively and without much difficulty, and, at the same time, with the best results. The whole administration will thus be popularised, and friction between the rulers and the ruled minimised. In questions like those which have arisen in connection with the Forest, the Abkari, or the Land Revenue administration in this Presidency, the existence of a general power of interpellation must be productive of great good.

Lastly, we come to the point how differences of opinion in Council should be dealt with. On unimportant points, of course, the Executive Government on the spot must decide finally — the responsibility for the administration being vested in them. But on important points, where also, of course the Government on the spot must decide for the same reason, it need not be allowed to decide *finally*. If the point is important enough for a majority of the Council, thus overruled by the Executive to record their protests, such protests ought to go up for final decision to the great and Supreme Council of the British Empire —the House of Commons. These protests would deal, almost necessarily one may say, with great and fundamental questions of policy, and upon them, even under present arrangements, the ultimate authority now rests with the House of Commons. On that point also, therefore, our proposals cannot be fairly regarded as either impracticable or revolutionary.

I do not know, Mr. President, that I need say more on the present occasion. The subject is one which has been frequently discussed by our countrymen, and there is a general consensus of opinion amongst us. The remarks, therefore, which I have ventured to address you really embody the main reasons upon which we have generally arrived at the conclusion that the reforms mentioned in this Resolution ought now to be undertaken. Those reforms I venture to think are in themselves quite reasonable ; they are thoroughly practicable and not in the least revolutionary ; and they are calculated, on the one hand, to facilitate the work of the Government, and, on the other, to afford a fair scope for the aspirations of the people in the direction of public usefulness. I therefore confidently commend this Resolution to the acceptance of the Congress.

The Hon'ble S. Subramania Iyer (Madras) :— Mr. Chairman and Gentlemen—I rise with great pleasure to second the proposition just proposed to you by my Hon'ble friend Mr. Telang, especially as I see that there is no need to make a speech in support of it. Gentlemen, my friend has so well exhausted all that could be said on the subject and has so completely anticipated me that I really have nothing to add to what he has already told you in such elegant and convincing language, unless I mean to paraphrase to you what he has been saying and thus mar the effect of his speech. He has pointed out to you the defects in the present constitution of these Councils and has indicated to you the nature of the remedy to be applied and the lines on which reformation should proceed. He has sketched out to you a scheme which is perfect in its details so far as it goes and withal so feasible, that if we but succeed in getting Government to recognise it as practicable, we need not yet despair of a bright future. As he has himself admitted the scheme is not put forward as a panacea for all the evils, but I have no hesitation whatever in saying that it would go very far indeed to minimise the evils to a considerable degree. Håvıng said this, I am almost tempted to sit down and make over the balance of my ten minutes to my friend Mr. Naoroji, whom I am sure you will all be anxious to hear at some length. But before I sit down, I think I may say a few words which will enable you to judge to what opinion I myself incline. Though my connection with the Madras Legislative Council has not been quite as long as Mr. Telang's in Bombay—I have been only a year in it—I think I may fairly claim to have had sufficient experience of its working to enable me to form an opinion as to their utility. I should not fail to admit, however, that the actual working of these Councils is enveloped in somewhat of a mystery and to one outside it, it is a puzzle how it is that the non-official members are so little able to do good of any kind. Naturally enough they come in for a good round of abuses. I myself on many an occasion, when bad laws were enacted, laid the whole blame on their shoulders, and indulged in rather severe criticism of their actions. It was not till I myself became a member of the Madras Council that I saw how unjustly our friends in the Council were censured in the majority of instances and what little influence they possessed in the Council either for good or for evil. With the best intentions in the world, I may assure you gentlemen, they find themselves in the wrong place, and so long as the present constitution of these Councils remain unchanged it is idle to expect that these non-official members will prove of any great use to the country. The misfortune is that these non-official members are not allowed to feel any responsibility, and, even if some of them assume it, no opportunity is given them to render themselves useful. I do not say this in any captious spirit and I disclaim all intention of giving any offence Somehow or other, these local Councils have become so altered in their constitution that they have altogether lost their original character and I do not think that they now answer the purpose for which they were originally designed. Whatever may have been the intention with which these

Councils were constituted at first and whatever doubts may be entertained now as to their present constitution, I do not suppose, there can be any doubt that they at no time possessed a representative character. For some time past these Councils have been so worked as to render them by no means afficient even as exponents of non-official opinion. If one carefully noted the successive laws that are enacted by these Councils, one would plainly see that the functions of these Councils are limited to registering the decrees of the Executive Government and stamp them with Legislative sanction. I am willing to agree with Mr. Telang that there is an element of usefulness in these Councils which might yet be utilized to our advantage. Admitting that, I am sceptical whether any material good will result from these Councils, so long as the present system of the Executive settling beforehand for all practical purposes in an irrevocable manner the principle of all measures that are introduced into these Councils is maintained. It appears to me that I might say without any breach of confidence, that during the short time that I have been in the Council, I have not experienced any difficulty in getting my suggestions adopted if only they related to details. Every suggestion that I made was received with great consideration so long as it did not trench on the principle already determined upon by the Government. So far as that goes, I must do the Government the justice to say that they are not only anxious te hear non-official opinion, but they also try to adopt it as far as possible consistent with the principle of the measure. The drawback then, as I just now pointed out, is that the principles of the measures that are introduced into the Councils are previously determined by the Government, behind the back of the Legislative Councils as it were, and the difficulty of the non-official members consists in their not being able to modify them in any manner. The difficulty lies in this and I am glad that Mr. Telang has thrown light on this aspect of the question. I must concede that it may be difficult to counsel Government of the real extent of this evil and whatever difficulties there may be in convincing Government that the scheme that is now put forward is practicable, I do not think that there is any difficulty in bringing home to them the necessity of reconstituting these Councils on a popular and a representative basis. I am afraid I have taken more of your time than I properly ought, especially as my good friend Mr. Dadabhai Naoroji, whom I feel no doubt you are all impatient to hear, is to follow me. I will not therefore take any more of your time and I do not believe that, before I sit down, it is necessary that I should formally commend the proposition moved by Mr. Telang for your acceptance, as I do not think there can possibly be two opinions on the subject.

The Hon'ble Dadabhai Naoroji (Bombay) :—I am glad my friends, the Hon'ble Mr. Telang and the Hon'ble Mr. S. Iyer have relieved me of much trouble, as they have anticipated a deal of what I had to say, which I need not repeat.

We ask for representation in the Legislative Councils of India. It is not for us to teach the English people how necessary representation is for good government. We have learnt the lesson from them, and knowing from them how great a blessing it is to those nations who enjoy it, and how utterly unEnglish it is for the English nation to withhold it from us, we can, with confidence and trust, ask them to give us this. I do not want to complain of the past. It is past and gone. It cannot be said now that the time is not come to give us representation. Thanks to our rulers themselves, we have now sufficiently advanced to know the value of representation and to understand the necessity that representation must go with taxation, that the taxed must have a voice in the taxation that is imposed on them. We are British subjects, and I say we can demand what we are entitled to and expect still at British hands as their greatest and most noble institution and heritage. It is our inheritance also and we should not be kept out of it. Why, if we are to be denied Britiain's best institutions, what good is it to India to be under the British sway? It will be simply another Asiatic despotism. What makes us proud to be British subjects, what attaches us to this foreign rule with deeper loyalty than even our own past Native rule, is the fact that Britain is the parent of free and representative Government, and, that we, as her subjects and children, are entitled to inherit the great blessing of freedom and representation. We claim the inheritance. If not, we are not the British subjects which the Proclamation proclaims us to be—equal in rights and privileges with the rest of Her Majesty's subjects. We are only British drudges or slaves. Let us persevere. Britain would never *be* a slave and could not, in her very nature and instinct, *make* a slave. Her greatest glory is freedom and representation, and, as her subjects, we shall have these blessed gifts.

Coming to the immediate and practical part of our demand I may say that it will be to Government itself a great advantage and relief—advantage, inasmuch as it will have the help of those who know the true wants of the Natives, and in whom the Natives have confidence, and relief so far that the responsibility of legislation will not be upon the head of Government only, but upon that of the representatives of the people also. And the people will have to blame themselves if they fail to send the right sort of men to represent themselves. I think Government has now reason rather to thank than repel us for demanding this boon which, if granted, will, on the one hand, make government easier and more effective, and on the other, attach the people to British rule more deeply than before.

Our first reform should be to have the power to tax ourselves. With that and another reform for which I shall move hereafter, India will advance in material and moral prosperity, and bless and benefit England. The proposal about the right of interpellation is very important,—as important and useful to Government itself as to the people. The very fact, that questions will be put in the Council, will prevent in a measure that evil which at present is beyond Government's reach to rodress. Government will be relieved of the odium and inconvenience which it at present suffers from misunderstanding and want of opportunities of giving explanation. The British Parliament and public, and the British Government in all its departments, benefit largely by this power of putting questions in Parliament and the same will be the result here. There will be, in the circumstances of India, one essential difference between the British Parliament and the Indian Legislative Councils. In Parliament, the Government, if defeated, resigns, and the Opposition comes into power. That cannot be done in India. Whether defeated or not, Government will remain in power. Moreover, the Secretary of State for India will have the power to veto, and no harm can happen. If the Government, either Provincial or Supreme, disregard the vote against it, and if the Secretary of State support the disregarding Government, there will be, as a last remedy, the standing Committe of Parliament as the ultimate appellate body to decide on the point of disagreement; and thus Parliament will truly, and not merely nominally as at present, become the final controlling authority.

We are British subjects, and subjects of the same gracious sovereign who has pledged her royal word that we are to her as all her other subjects, and we have a right to all British institutions. If we are true to ourselves, and perseveringly ask what we desire, the British people are the very people on earth who will give what is right and just From what has already been done in the past we have ample reason to indulge in this belief. Let us for the future equally rely on that character and instinct of the British. *They* have taught us our wants and they will supply them.

Mr. Venkat Subarayadu in supporting the Resolution pointed out that the Indian Council's Act was now nearly twenty-five years old and that it was time it should be amended.

Mr. Dayaram Jethmal said :—That there was no representation of the country in these Councils in the proper sense of the word. Although the Councils contained some official members who could boast of past acquaintance with certain provinces in the course of their official duties, these gentlemen were in no sense representatives of those provinces. To speak of them as representatives would be as correct as to speak of Mr. Maclean as a representative of the Presidency of Bombay in the British Parliament. He urged the meeting to consider whether the views and wishes of the people could be represented in any sense by the official members. There were several measures vitally affecting the inhabitants of vast tracts of country as to the passage of which through the Councils those inhabitants knew absolutely nothing. And yet the speaker and every one could say that in respect of such measures the proceedings of the Councils showed that the people affected by them had made no objections, though the several Bills had been duly published. As a matter of fact sufficient publicity was never given to the Bills and proceedings of the Legislative Councils. The chief defect lay in the fact that these proceedings and Bills were not published in the languages or characters or in papers which the people understood or read, and were not accessible to all. Take the instance of the Sind Encumbered Estates' Act and the Sind Village Cess Act which had not come to the knowledge of the people of Sind until after they actually became law. The few who heard or read about the former were those who were least affected by them. These Acts had not the approval of the people and were being continually complained of in Sind, and yet in the Council it seemed to have been assumed that the people wanted them because, though duly published, no objections to them had been received by Government! Would this happen if the provinces were represented in the Councils? If nothing else the representatives would at least inform their constituents of the introduction of measures into the Councils even if they were unable to successfully oppose their passing or bring about their passing in the form acceptable to the people.

Mr. K. L. Nulkar (Poona) said that this was the first constructive Resolution, so to speak, that the Congress would be adopting. He therefore desired to know what it was proposed to do in regard to this class of Resolutions after the Congress had passed them. He also thought that the Resolution might go further and ask for the right of election to the Secretary of State's Council.

In reply to Mr. Nulkar's question the President stated that it was intended to bring up before the Congress a formal resolution in regard to the point raised, and that the matter could then be most properly discussed.

Mr. Murlidhar (Punjaub) said that previous speakers had spoken of the existing Legislative Councils as "shams," but in the N. W. Provinces and the Punjaub; even these "shams" had no existence. There, it is supposed, that officials, not mixing with the people, knowing little of their wants and wishes, were nevertheless representatives of the people. This will not do. We must have real direct representation and then we shall be able to minimise the influence of the men who are not true representatives of the people.

The Hon'ble M. G. Ranade remarked that the Congress ought to put forward a scheme complete in itself. The provision in the proposed Resolution about differences of opinion was not enough. The Secretary of State alone would be almost powerless before the War Department and the Treasury Department of the United Kingdom, and it was, therefore, necessary to have something instead of his Council, if that Council was to be abolished. He had hoped that such a substitute would be proposed in this Resolution, but he did not see any such substitute. He pointed to the repeal of the Cotton Duties, the Vernacular Press Act, the introduction of a Permanent Settlement of the Land Revenue into the whole empire, and the expenditure in the Military Department as instances of matters in which it was necessary to strengthen the hands of the Secretary of State by a Council well constituted. After referring to Fox's and Pitt's India Bills, Mr. Ranade suggested for consideration the point whether it was not desirable to ask that the Council of the Secretary of State should be composed partly of elected and partly of nominated members.

Mr. Hume pointed out that a substitute for the Indian Council as regards extravagant expenditure was provided in the scheme proposed by the Resolution—in the power of interpellation and the financial power.

Mr. G. Subrahmanya Iyer said that it would never do to trust to a Council for escaping from the settled policy of the

Ministry and of Parliament. The question of the permanent settlement was a vital one in Madras. Sir Louis Malet helped Madras there, but it was the Council of the Secretary of State which was obstructive in that matter.

Divan Bahadur R. Raghunath Rao thought that a Council would be unnecessary only if the Secretary of State was like the Colonial Secretary, but not otherwise. He thought the reference to a Parliamentary Committee would expose India to the risk of government by English political parties.

Mr. P. M. Mehta thought that no doubt there were evils in both courses, but, on a choice of evils, he thought a substitute for the India Council unnecessary. That Council is a continuously existing evil ; the other would be only an occasional one. As to a Parliamentary Committee landing us in party politics, he thought the publicity of the discussions of the Committee would be a very great advantage.

Mr. Norendranath Sen thought that a Standing Committee of the House of Commons would be good, if we had representatives of our own in the House. As an alternative proposal there might be a small Parliament in India with many Indian members. Indian political bodies should be asked to name such members and also have a voice in the formation of the existing Executive Councils.

Messrs. Sundara Rama and Ananda Charlu having spoken in support of the Resolution, Mr. Dadabhai Naoroji said :

Before the Hon'ble Mr. Telang replies I may ask to be allowed to say a few words. I may just explain what an important thing this Standing Committee will be. During the East India Company's time, Parliament was entirely independent of it. Parliament was then truly an effective appellate body. It tool up Indian questions quite freely and judged fairly, without the circumstance of parties ever interfering with its deliberations. If there was a complaint against the Company, Parliament was free to sit in judgment on it. What is the position since the transfer of the government to the Crown? The Secretary of State for India is the Parliament. Every question in which he is concerned becomes a Cabinet question. His majority is at his back. This majority has no concern in Indian matters further than to back the Government, *i.e.* the Secretary of State for India. All appeals, therefore, to Parliament against the Secretary of State become a mere farce. M. P.'s are utterly discouraged from their inability to do any thing. And the Secretary of State becomes the true Great Mogul of India—a despotic monarch. His will is his law. Nor can the people of India influence him, as their voice is not represented in Parliament. Thus, that tribunal can scarcely exercise any effectual check over his despotism. The present legislative machinery, from the Local Councils upwards, is simply a device to legalise despotism and give it the false mask of constitutionalism. The taxpayers have no voice in the imposition of the taxes they pay and Parliament has not the ability to prevent the levy of unfair or oppressive taxation. The ultimate controlling authority seems helpless to control anything! Now if we have complete representative legislation here, and if we have a Standing Committee in Parliament, we shall have both the voice of the taxed on the one side and effectual control of Parliament on the other. Such a Standing Committee will naturally be independent of all parties. Its decision will be no defeat of Government. It will be simply a final decision on the point of difference that may have arisen between the representatives of the people in India on the one hand, and the Government on the other, on any particular question. India will thus have an effectual parliamentary control.

It is said we hould propose something as a substitute for the present India Office Council. The resolution now before the Congress makes this unnecessary. The Council, when it was established, was considered to be protective of Indian interests. It has not proved so. When it suits the Secretary of State, he screens himself behind that Council. When it does not suit him, he flings the Council aside. We have no means of knowing what good at all is done by the Council. Its irresponsibility and its secrecy are fatal objections to its continuance. Such a thing in the government of an empire of 200 millions of people and under the British is an utter and an inexplicable anachronism. Moreover, the majority of the Council consists of Anglo-Indians. These, sitting in judgment on their own handiwork, naturally regard it as perfect. Having left India years ago they fail to realise the rapid changes that are taking place here in our circumstances, lose touch with us and offer resistance to all progress. Times are now changed. The natives, I may say, have come of age. They can represent directly their wishes and views to the Government here, and to the Secretary of State. They do not require the aid of this Council at the India Office for their so called representation or protection.

I may here remark, that the chief work of this the first National Congress of India is to enunciate clearly and boldly our highest and ultimate wishes. Whether we get them or not immediately, let our rulers know what our highest aspirations are. And if we are true to ourselves, the work of each delegate present here will be to make the part of India where he happens to live devote itself earnestly to carrying out the objects resolved upon at this Congress with all due deliberation. If, then, we lay down clearly that we desire to have the actual government of India transferred from England to India under the simple controlling power of the Secretary of State, and of Parliament, through its Standing Committee, and that we further desire that all taxation and legislation shall be imposed here by representative Councils, we say what we are aiming at. And that under such an arrangement no Council to advise the Secretary of State is necessary. Neither is a Council needed to attend to the appellate executive work. There is a permanent Under-Secretary of State who will be able to keep up continuity of knowledge and transact all current business. There are, besides, Secretaries at the head of the different departments as experts. I do not deny that at times the India Office Council has done good service. But this was owing to the personality and sympathy of individual—men like Sir E. Perry. The constitution of the body as a body is objectionable and anomalous. When the whole power of imposing taxation and legislation is transferred here, the work of the Secretary of State will be largely diminished. It will only be confined to general supervision of important matters. Whatever comes before him for disposal will be set forth by the Government from here fully and fairly in all its bearings. No Council will be needed to aid him in forming his judgment. Thus no substitute is required for the India Office Council. It is enough for us to formulate the scheme, now submitted for your consideration, as one which India needs and desires, viz, representative Legislative Councils in India, wih full financial control and interpellatory powers. And we shall not need to trouble much the authorities in England.

The President here observed that as it was arranged that the members should visit the Elephanta caves in the course of the afternoon he would postpone the Congress till 10 A.M. of the following day.

The Congress accordingly adjourned.

controlling power of the Secretary of State and of Parliament, through a Standing Committee, and that we further desire that all taxation and legislation shall be imposed here by representative Councils, we say what we are aiming at. And that order such an arrangement no Council to advise the Secretary of State is necessary. Neither is a Council needed to attend to the appellate executive work. There is a permanent Under-Secretary of State who will be able to keep up continuity of knowledge and transact all current business. There are, besides, Secretaries at the head of the different departments as experts. I do not deny that at times the India Office Council has done good service. But this was owing to the personality and sympathy of individual men like Sir E. Perry. The constitution of the body as a body is objectionable and anomalous. When the whole power of imposing taxation and legislation is transferred here, the works of the Secretary of State will be largely diminished. It will only be confined to general supervision of important matters. Whatever comes before him for disposal will be set forth by the Government from here fully and fairly in all its bearings. No Council will be needed to aid him in forming his judgment. Thus no substitute is required for the India Office Council. It is enough for us to formulate the scheme, now submitted for your consideration, as one which India needs and desires, viz., representative Legislative Councils in India, with full financial control and interpellatory powers. And we shall not need to trouble much the authorities in England.

The President here observed that as it was arranged that the members should visit the Elephanta caves in the course of the afternoon he would postpone the Congress till 10 A.M. of the following day.

The Congress accordingly adjourned.

PROCEEDINGS

OF THE

3rd Day, 30th December 1885.

The Hon'ble K. T. Telang :—I should like to say a few words in reply to the criticisms that have been made in this debate. I am glad that those criticisms have been made because it enables me to offer some explanations which will probably be even more necessary for outsiders than for those who have assembled here. The first, and most important, point to deal with is that the Resolution now before the Congress does not provide, as it was expected to provide, some substitute for the India Council—which I should prefer to call by an apter title, the Council of the Secretary of State for India. I am afraid I must take some blame to myself for not having made this point clear in my opening remarks. And as I did not do this then, I must dwell on the point now somewhat more fully than I had thought would be necessary. Well, in my view, then, the centre of the practical work of Indian administration should be shifted from London to India. That, it seems to me, is a most urgently wanted reform. It ought not to be necessary in matters of practical administration to appeal against well-informed local officers on the spot, to what has been not inappropriately designated a conclave of "effete officers" hundreds of miles away. This being my view, I am not prepared to accept one of the suggestions thrown out by our friend Mr. Norendranath, that we should work for representation of our country in Parliament. I do not think that that ought to be the goal towards which we should work. What I prefer is that we should have a properly and liberally framed constitution, affording due scope for local knowledge and capacity, under a general supervision in matters involving important general principles vested in the great authority which governs the whole empire, namely, the Imperial Parliament. This object appears to me to be served by the constitution proposed in this resolution for representative Councils in the country, supplemented by the Standing Committee of the House of Commons. Such bodies will also serve the purpose which some of the speakers in the debate have in view. If we want, as we do want, the hands of the Secretary of State to be strengthened against the unfair demands of the English departments of War, &c., it seems to me obvious that such strength will be better and more effectively supplied by such Councils as are here proposed than by any substitute that we could devise for the present constitution of the India Council. On the one hand, these Councils being representative, and presumably well informed in consequence of the councillors being themselves able personally to examine the matter to be adjudicated on, will necessarily have great weight attached to their opinions. And, on the other hand, there will be great difficulties in carrying out the only proposed modification in the constitution of the India Council, namely, making it a partly representative body. In the first place, we shall not always be able to secure the services of our best men for working upon a Council sitting in London. In the second place, if we did secure them, they would be very far removed from the field of actual administrative work, and also from that influence of public opinion to which they must always be open if they are to give the fullest satisfaction in the performance of their high trusts. Thirdly, an individual member, or even more than one individual member, of such a Council sitting in London, will be quite unable to make his influence felt in all departments of administration. For, I believe, in the India Council there is specialization of functions and work in the same way as we know there is in the

Executive Councils in the country. Therefore, my scheme is that the India Council should go and leave not a wrack behind, while the useful portion of work which it is supposed to discharge ought to be performed by the proposed Councils in India. It will thus be seen that our scheme is not a merely destructive one. We propose a substitute, and what I venture to think will be a very good substitute, for that which we recommend for abolition.

And having said this, let me now ask whether this India Council as it has existed—this Council the abolition of which we are asked to be so cautious in recommending—whether it has done any real good during the period for which it has already existed. In the first place, most of its deliberations and acts are done in secret conclave—in itself, according to my humble judgment, a strong reason for condemnation in such a case as this. The result is that its work, whether for good or for evil, is not easy to survey and judge. But portions of it necessarily see the light from time to time, and we may form some sort of provisional opinion from these materials. My friends, Mr. Chiplonkar and Mr. G. Subahmanya Iyer, have told us of one or two items of this work. That referred to by the latter may be examined in the pages of the Famine Commission's Report. And there can be no doubt that in several of these matters, the India Council has fairly earned the epithet which has recently been bestowed upon it, and which has, if I may so say, become almost classical in Bombay—namely, "abominably obstructive." But then some specific matters have been brought forward in favour of the Council. As regards the permanent settlement of the land revenue, whatever the Council may or may not have done, it has certainly failed to give that to those Provinces which have been asking for it. As to the cotton duties, again, what influence has the India Council had on actual administrative measures? The duties *have* been abolished, in supposed obedience to a resolution of the House of Commons which was contingent on the fulfilment of conditions that we all know were not satisfied—and the Council has been impotent to prevent the abolition. As to the Vernacular Press Act, the Act was passed and *not* vetoed by the Secretary of State. It was the law of the land until, *not* the India Council, but Lord Ripon's Council, repealed it. There were doubtless some most vigorous and excellent protests by the late Sir Erskine Perry and other members of the India Council, against that precious piece of legislation. But then those protests in actual fact went for nothing, and furthermore you cannot count upon the presence of more than one Sir Erskine Perry in the Council, or even one Sir Erskine Perry always and continuously. Lastly, as to war expenditure, if the India Council has said anything about it, it has certainly not succeeded in doing anything at all. Therefore, upon the whole, I must say that in my opinion the matters brought forward in favour of the India Council show nothing more than this, if they show so much, that in that Council you have now and then had members who have fought our battles valiantly and well, as valiantly and as well—I will add if you like—as probably any elected representative of ours would have done. But this does not really afford any argument in favour of the system, which is vicious in itself, and which in actual working has failed to influence the administration for good.

There is one other objection, which I must now advert to. It is said that to trust to a Parliamentary Committee in the last resort as is here proposed is to throw Indian affairs into the party politics of England. I beg to say in reference to this objection, that in the first place I am not very much afaid of the result, at all events, in this particular matter—because the points which will be sent up before the Parliamentary Committee must be points relating to general principles of Government. But I go further, and I say that the intervention of Parliament in our affairs asked for by the present Resolution will not throw us more into English party strife than we are already under present circumstan ces. Parliament is now our final tribunal, and now govern all our affairs in the last resort. And a Starding Committ of Parliament, such as we propose, is really and truly the same tribunal. We are not asking for any very serious innovation in this respect.

Upon all these grounds, Sir, I recommend the Congress to pass the Resolution as it now stands. It seems to me to be not open to the objections made ; to be free from the particular defects and imperfections pointed out ; to constitute really a step and an important step in the direction of progress, while at the same time it is by no means revolutionary, and involves no risk wha tever.

The President in summing up the debate said that it was not necessary for the Congress to frame a complete scheme. He thought their function was to state and record what improvements were in their opinion desirable, and having done that to leave to the authorities the duty of formulating a scheme. The argument in favour of the Council seemed to him weak. It might as well be argued that the whole of the Indian system of administration should be preserved intact because such gentlemen as Wordsworth, Hume and Wedderburn held office under that system. The Council of India was from the beginning a sham. Passing on to another point the President said, it was not at all unreasonable to look forward to a time when in the Government of India there should be Ministries and changes of Ministeries as in the Colonies. This is not, of course, provided for just now, but it is not inconsistent with what is asked for. As regards the Supreme Council, that, the President said, ought to be representative of the whole country and of every great province in it. Every member will thus be able to understand what is going on in all the provinces of the Empire and they will be able to tcompare notes with great advantage to themselves and to the whole country.

The Resolution was then put and carried unanimously.

The President introduced Mr. N. G. Chandavarkar, one of the Indian Delegates to England, who had on the preceding day returned to Bombay.

The Congress thereupon passed by acclamation a vote of thanks to Mr. Chandavarkar and the other Delegates for the valuable services they rendered to the country during their stay in England.

Mr. Chandavarkar in acknowledging gratefully on behalf of himself and his colleagues the vote of thanks passed by the Congress said that while in England he had taken the opportunity of calling on Lord and Lady Ripon, and explaining what the Delegates had done. Lord Ripon said, "tell your countrymen not to despair. If the friends of your country have been defeated at the elections, they have not been defeated on any Indian question, but on the Church and Irish question."

The resolution was then put to the vote and carried unanimously.

The Hon'ble Dadabhai Naoroji in moving the 4th Resolution said :—The Resolution which I am proposing does not in any way involve the question whether the distinction between the covenanted and uncovenanted services should be abolished or not. That is a separate question altogether, and in fact, if my resolution is adopted that question will become unnecessary or very subordinate. The resolution which I propose to you is of the utmost possible importance to India. It is the most important key to our material and moral advancement. All our other political reforms will benefit us but very little indeed if this reform of all reforms is not made. It is the question of poverty or prosperity. It is the question of life and death to India. It is the question of questions. Fortunately, it is not necessary for me on this occasion to go into all its merits as I hope you are all already well aware of my views and their reasons or it would have been very difficult for me to lay before you all I should have had to say without speaking for hours. There is an additional good fortune for me that what I want to propose was already proposed a quarter of a century ago by no less an authority than a Committee of the India Office itself The report of this Committee gives the whole matter in a nutshell from the point of view of justice, right, expediency and honest fulfilment of promises. And the reasons given by it for the covenanted civil service apply equally to all the other services in the civil department. I do not refer to the military service in this resolution, as that is a matter requiring special consideration and treatment. To make my remarks as brief as possible, as we are much pressed for time, I shall first at once read to you the extract from the report of the Committee consisting of Sir J. P. Willoughby, Mr. Mangles, Mr. Arbuthnot, Mr. Macnaughten, and Sir Erskine Perry. The report, dated 20th January 1860, says:—

"2. We are, in the first place, unanimously of opinion that it is not only just but expedient that the Natives of India shall be employed in the administration of India to as large an extent as possible, consistently with the maintenance of British supremacy, and have considered whether any increased facilities can be given in this direction.

"3. It is true that, even at present, no positive disqualification exists. By Act 3 and 4 Wm. 4 C. 85 S. 87, it is enacted "that no Native of the said territories, nor any natural born subject of His Majesty resident therein, shall, by reason only of his religion, place of birth, descent, colour or any of them, be disabled from holding any place, office or employment under the said. Company." It is obvious therefore that when the competitive system was adopted it could not have been intended to exclude Natives of India from the Civil Service of India.

"4. Practically, however, they are excluded. The law declares them eligible, but the difficulties opposed to a Native leaving India, and residing in England for a time, are so great, that as a general rule, it is almost impossible for a Native sucessfully to compete at the periodical examination held in England. Were this inequality removed we should no longer be exposed to the charge of keeping promise to the ear and breaking it to the hope.

"5. Two modes have been suggested by which the object in view might be attained. The first is by allotting a certain portion of the total number of appointments declared in each year to be competed for in India by Natives and by other natural-born subjects of Her Majesty's residents in India. The second is, to hold simultaneously two examinations, one in England and one in India, both being, as far as practicable, identical in their nature and those who compete in both countries being finally classified in one list according to merit by the Civil Service Commissioners. The Committee have no hesitation in giving the preference to the second scheme, as being the fairest, and the most in accordance with the principles of a general competition for a common object."

Now according to strict right and justice the examination for services in India ought to take place in India alone. The people of Australia, Canada and the Cape do not go to England for their services. Why should Indians be compelled to go to England to compete for the services, unless it be England's despotic will. But I am content to propose the resolution according to the views of the Committee for simultaneous examinations, both in England and India, and the reasons that apply to the Civil Service apply equally well to the other services in the Civil Department, viz., Engineering, Medical, Telegraph, Forest and so on.

I may here remind you that in addition to the Act of 1833 referred to by the Committee we have the solemn promises contained in the Proclamation of our gracious Sovereign. The fact is told to us in unmistakable language:—"We hold ourselves bound to the Natives of our Indian territories by the same obligations, of duty which bind us to all our other subjects; and those obligations, by the blessing of Almighty God, we shall faithfully and conscientiously fulfil." And then they declared her gracious promise specifically on this very part of the services:—"And it is our further will that, so far as may be our subjects, of whatever race or creed, be freely and impartially admitted to offices in our service, the duties of which they may be qualified, by their education, ability and integrity, duly to discharge." This gracious proclamation and the promises contained therein were made known in 1858. And the India Office Committee showed, in 1860, in what way these promises could be fulfilled, so as to relieve the English nation from "the charge of keeping promise to the ear and breaking it to the hope." With the Act of Parliament of 1833, the solemn promises, of 1858, of our Sovereign before God and man, and the declaration by the India Office of the mode of fulfilling those promises in 1860, it is hardly necessary for me to say more. Our case for the resolution proposed by me is complete. As a matter of justice, solemn promises and even expediency I would have ended my speech here, but my object in proposing this resolution rests upon a far higher and a most important consideration. The question of the extreme poverty of India is now no more a controversial point. Viceroys and Finance Ministers have admitted it. The last official declaration by Sir E. Baring is complete and unequivocal. In his budget speech of 18th March 1882 he said :—"It has been calculated that the average income per head of population in India is not more than Rs. 27 a year ; and though I am not prepared to pledge myself to the absolute accuracy of a calculation of this sort, it is sufficiently accurate to justify the conclusion that the taxpaying community is exceedingly poor. To derive any very large increase of revenue from so poor a population as this is obviously impossible, and, if it were possible, would be unjustifiable." Again, in the discussion on the budget, after repeating the above statement regarding the income of Rs. 27 per head per annum, he said :—"But he thought it was quite sufficient to show the extreme poverty of the mass of the people. In England the average income per head of population was £33 per head ; in France it was £23 ; in Turkey, which was the poorest country in Europe, it was £4 per head. He would ask Honorable members to think what Rs. 27 per annum was to support a person and then he would ask whether a few annas was nothing to such poor people." With this emphatic and clear opinion before you, I need not say more. The question is what is the cause of this poverty ? I have shown in my papers on the poverty of India, and in my correspondence with the Secretary of State for India, that the sole cause of this extreme poverty and wretchedness of the mass of the people is the inordinate employment of foreign agency in the government of the country and the consequent material loss to and drain from the country. I request those who have not already seen these papers to read them, for it is utterly impossible for me to go through the whole argument here. It will be, therefore, now clear to you that the employment of Native agency is not merely a matter of justice and expediency, according to the views of the India Office Committee, but a most absolute necessity for the poor, suffering, and starving millions of India. It is a question of life and death to the country. The present English rule is no doubt the greatest blessing India has ever had, but this *one evil* of it nullifies completely all the good it has achieved. Remove but this one evil, and India will be blessed in every way and will be a blessing to England also in every way. The commerce between England and India will increase so that England will then be able to benefit herself ten timesmore by India's prosperity than what she does now. There will be none of the constant struggle that is at present to be witnessed between the rulers and the ruled—the one screwing out more and more taxes, like squeezing a squeezed orange—inflicting suffering and distress, and the other always crying itself hoarse about its inability to provide them owing to extreme poverty. By the removal of the evil—India will be able not merely to supply a revenue £70,000,000, but £170,000,000, with ease and comfort. England takes over 50 shillings a head for her revenue, why may not India under the same rule be able to take even 20 a head? Indians would easily pay £200,000,000. I should stop now. I hope you will see that this resolution is of the greatest possible importance to India and I implore every one of you present here to-day to strain every nerve and work perseveringly in your respective localities to attain this object. With regard to the second part of the resolution, the uncovenanted services, the same reasoning and necessity apply. A fair system of competition, testing all necessary qualifications—

mental, moral and physical—will be the most suitable mode of supplying the services with the best and most eligible servants and relieve Government of all the pressure of back door and private influences, and jobbery.

The subject of the age of candidates for the Civil Service examination needs no lengthened remarks from me. It has been only lately threshed out, and it has been established beyond all doubt that the higher age will give you a superior class of men, whether English or Native. I conclude, therefore, with the earnest exhortation that you will all apply yourselves vigorously to free poor India from the great evil of the drain on her resources.

If the British will once understand our true condition, their conscientious desire to rule India for India's and humanity's good, will never allow the evil to continue any longer. Lastly, I hope and trust that our rulers will receive our representations in their proper spirit. We sincerely believe that the good we propose for ourselves is also a good for them. Whatever good they will do to us cannot but in the very nature of things be good to them also. The better we are in material and moral prosperity the more grateful, attached and loyal we shall be; the worse we are the less our gratitude and loyalty shall naturally be. The more prosperous we are, the larger shall be their custom, the worse we are the condition will be the reverse. The question of our prosperity is as much the question of the prosperity of England and her working man. England's trade would be enriched by £250,000,000, if with our prosperity each unit of the Indian population is ever able to buy from England goods worth only £1 per annum.

What is wanted is the fructification in our own pocket of our annual produce. I repeat that it is my hope and trust that our rulers may receive our prayers in their right spirit and do us all the good in their power, for it will redound to their good name, honour and everlasting glory. Let us have the Royal Proclamation fulfilled in its true spirit and integrity, and both England and India will be benefitted and blessed.

With these observations I beg to propose the Fourth Resolution :—

"That in the opinion of this Congress the competitive examinations now held in England, for first appointments in various Civil departments of the public service, should hence forth, in accordance with the views of the India Office Committee of 1860, 'be held simultaneously, one in England and one in India, both being as far as practicable identical in their nature, and those who compete in both countries being finally classified in one list according to merit,' and that the successful candidates in India should be sent to England for further study, and subjected there to such further examinations as may seem needful. Further, that all other first appointments (excluding peonships and the like) should be filled by competitive examinations held in India, under conditions calculated to secure such intellectual, moral, and physical qualifications as may be decided by Government to be necessary. Lastly, that the maximum age of candidates for entrance into the covenanted Civil Service be raised to not less than 23 years."

M. Vira Raghavachariar (Madras) seconded the resolution in the following speech :—

Mr. President and gentlemen :—

In rising to second the proposition so well explained by our veteran statesman, Mr. Dadabhai Naoroji, I have to make a few observations. Individually, gentlemen, my opinion about this question is, that the distinction between the Covenanted Civil Service and Uncovenanted Civil Service must be done away with, and Native gentlemen, of approved ability and integrity, found in the Uncovenanted department, should be drawn into the ranks of the former. My reasons for the abolition of that service are numerous. Firstly, such a coveted service is no longer required. Education has made considerable progress in this country and the character of educated Natives for integrity and honesty of purpose is established beyond all doubt. Secondly, you must all admit that the members of that service are overpaid and overrated. The scale of their pay was fixed at a time when the patronage as regards those appointments was in the hands of the Directors of the East India Company and those genlemen had to provide for their sons, cousins, and dependants. It was also the general impression of men in England, then, that India was the land of pagodas and mohurs. Circumstances have changed now and we see no reason why we should continue to get men for that service from England, at such an enormous cost. Now, again, let us see whether they are not overrated. The work that they do is not of a high order; most of it is trivial, and even this they perform negligently and inefficiently. The Collectors are, in fact, respectable Head Clerks and the Assistants are in training for that respectable position. Is it right, I ask gentlemen, that Collectors should be paid 2,500 Rupees a month for uprooting prickly pear and for karkunlike criticism of subordinate Magistrates' returns? Again, I ask gentlemen, is it fair that Assistants should get about Rs. 1,000 for going about the country in tents? You know, gentlemen, that that service, to maintain which the lifeblood of the nation is sucked, has degenerated. Many Anglo-Indians have admitted this fact. Who will venture to gainsay my statement that the Civil Service has degenerated when we see that the service which has produced a Hume, a Wedderburn, and a Cotton, now holds among its ranks Macleans, Laidmans, and

Atkinson and Machiavockes? Gentlemen, the fact is that we are now getting men of inferior order from England. The men we get are mere boys distinguished for their mental rawness and immaturity of character. They are generally minutely instructed rather than highly educated. The nobility of England does not care to take office in India. But, gentlemen, Mr. Dadabhai has said that that service should be retained at least for some time to come and we must all yield to his wiser counsels. The proposition moved by my honourable friend, is so modest and reasonable, that I am sure it will command the attention of the British public. By demanding these reforms, gentlemen, we must all bear in mind that we are clamouring for no special indulgence. We condemn the existing rules that are so framed as to secure all advantages to English competitors and to throw considerable impediments and difficulties in the way of competitors from India. While professing to treat all competitors with impartiality, the rules are so framed as to practically shut out the children of the soil from competition. We say, let these inequalities be removed, let Natives and Englishmen be allowed to compete on equal terms. If it be remembered that our youths join an English school and begin the English alphabet when they are eight or nine years old, that on an average they spend about six years in acquiring the English language, that it is about their fifteenth year that they begin to construe English books for themselves and that it is after that that they can devote their time to the study of English literature, history, science, philosophy, will it be considered unreasonable, gentlemen, if we demand that our youths should be permitted to compete for the examination upto the age of 23? If, again, it be remembered, that under existing rules our youths are compelled to quit these shores at a very early age to go to England and put themselves under tuition of somebody for a year or two, will it be considered unreasonable if we demand that the examinations should be held in some Indian centres, simultaneously with the examination in London? Again, gentlemen, as for numerous other appointments in the Salt, Forest, and other departments, supposed to be reserved exclusively for the Natives of this country, I need not tell you that the relations of influential members of the Civil Service are put in. I hold in my hand a list of such appointments in the Presidency of Madras, and you will see from it that only three Natives hold employments in the Settlement Department. The truth of the whole matter is that at the cost of Indian money English youths are fed, clothed, and patted to the detriment of the interests of the Natives. These facts have been repeatedly brought to the notice of the Secretary of State and Parliament by several philanthropists in England and India, and now the voice of the nation loudly demands a reform. It remains to be seen how long the authorities will choose to walk in the old way. Though our demands may be put off for a short time, they cannot be indefinitely postponed. The progress of education throughout the different provinces of the Indian Empire is so great, and the facilities for intercommunication so various, that we, who were hitherto strangers to each other as the Sikhs, the Mahrattas, the Bengalees and the Madrasees, consider ourselves as one people with the same grievances, and with the same aspirations. We now begin to perceive that notwithstanding the existence of differences in our mother tongue, social habits, and manners, we possess the true elements of a nationality about us, we possess the talent for organization, and we possess too many things in common to permit of our living apart for ever as strangers. Is it not time for us now to sink our minor differences and concentrate our forces for the attainment of grand national objects? With these observations, I heartily second the propositior so ably moved by our illustrious countryman Mr. Dadabhai Naoroji.

Mr. D. S. White (Madras) :—I do not rise to oppose the Hon. Mr. Dadabhai Naoroji's Resolution, nor to propose an amendment. I desire merely to submit some observations which I think the members of this Congress should hear and take into serious consideration. The proposition contemplates an application for raising the competitive age in England of candidates for the Civil Service, and for holding examinations simultaneously in India. On both points I differ. I do not think the remedy is in raising age but in procuring the gradual abolition of the Civil Service. What we need I think is that the future importation of boys should be put a stop to. The real education of these boys takes place in India and the State is put to enormous expense in connection therewith, while there is no need for the expenditure. The State now has at hand indigenous talent, educated at its own expense, either locally or in England, and should take advantage of it, and if it requires special talent from England it may import it just as men ready made are imported for the Educational Department. For the Judicial Service, the Bar in India offers itself, and why boy Civilians should be paid for years to learn to become Judges is a matter not easily understood. I do not think that any one in India would grudge paying for anything which would add to the stock of knowledge in it, and therefore it seems to me that the competitive system should be abolished and that men of eminence and skill alone, in any profession, should be brought out on limited covenants. On the same or rather stronger grounds I do not approve of holding examinations in India. All that we will get will be boys again, boys to be trained at the expense of the State, boys whose views of life will be limited to Indian experience. Either from England or India, we want men of experience and istablished reputation, and it is by such men that the New India will be moulded to higher and better things. I must not be understood as desiring that existing appointments should be interfered with, but only as enuniciating the view that the present system should gradually die out and give place to a better one. I do not approve of the Resolution for another reason. I have always maintained that the present law and the orders of the Secretary of State give us as much as we want; and I think it will be more profitable if we try to secure what is ours instead of raising fresh issues, the determination of which none of us perhaps will live to see. The age and local examination questions involve fresh legislation and the extinction of that which exists. While therefore we are waiting for the fresh legisration we shall lose what we have. Fifteen years have elapsed and the Statute of 33 Victoria Chapter III. is still being violated; that is fifteen years have not proved sufficient for the mere carrying out of a well-defined piece of legislation. What will be the time needed for fresh legislation and for securing honest compliance with it? In the recent Blue Book, Lord Kimberley, on the very points I am referring to, says that the Statutory Civil Service was expressly designed to remedy any disadvantages arising out of the age restriction in England and that before Parliament is again resorted to, the remedy already prescribed should be thoroughly exhausted. It is our primary duty therefore to press for the enforcement of the boons already granted to us. The Statute 33 Victoria Chapter III. has never had a chance, and it cannot be condemned as bad law when it has never been tried. I will go very lightly over the ground to show how disappointment after disappointment was caused to the Natives of India. The Act distinctly said that Natives of India of proved merit and ability were to be selected as Statutory Civilians. This was an admirable measure and a wiser one could not possibly have been provided. If carried out it would have rewarded the best men, secured them for the higher administration of the country, and acted as the most powerful lever for training subordinates into officials of the highest character. But respect for vested interests and prejudices prevailed. The word "proved" was thrust out for "approved" in the rules framed, and any one "*approved*, though not of *proved* merit and ability, was appointed. The nominations of *approved* persons turned out most unfortunate as they were bound to do, and on a protest to the Secretary of State, an examination of candidates was ordered. At last, however, the Act has some chance of being carried out honestly, for a person of proved merit and ability has been appointed in Madras. But even in this case the Statutory Civilian has been compelled to go into one of the lowest grades, the object apparently being that no Statutory Civilian should have influence or power for the space of 15 or 20 years. If the Hon'ble gentleman's proposition is carried I wish it to be understood that I do not object to it. I have merely taken the opportunity of expressing my views which have been arrived at after a very long and careful consideration.

During the progress of this Conference the necessity for union among all Natives of India for the purpose of securing their common rights and privileges has been much pressed on our attention. My own belief is that withont such union we will never accomplish what we desire. I am willing to do my best, but I trust this Congress will help me by giving some assurance that it is serious in desiring unity. I have just come from a Conference of the Eurasian and Anglo-Indian Associations held at Jubbulpore. It was decided by the Delegates that a memorial be sent to the Viceroy, praying that on the next occasion a Eurasian or

Anglo-Indian Native of India be appointed to the Statutory Civil Service. I shall be delighted to know that this Conference is prepared to ask the bodies it is associated with to support such a memorial. (Loud Applause.)

Mr. Girijabhusan Mookerjee (Bengal) in rising to support the Resolution said:—It was unnecessary that he should speak at any length, even if he were permitted to do so, upon a subject which had engaged the attention of the country for some years and with regard to which the country had pretty emphatically expressed its opinion. They were asked simply to record the unanimous opinion of the country on the subject. The government of the country was practically in the hands of the Civil Service and the exclusion of the Natives from that Service meant their practical exclusion from the administration of their own country. Then, again, from a long employment of the monopoly of power, privilege and prestige these Civilian rulers here had become, if his Bombay friends would permit him to borrow an expression from them, "abominably obstructive" in the way of national progress. That being so, if they could secure for their countrymen additional facilities te enter the service they would not only succeed in obtaining a larger and fairer share in the administration of their own country, but would also succeed in materially weakening the force of that obstructive opposition which was so heavily felt now. They would not only do this, they would do something else. They would succeed in removing a stain from the honour of England. For although the principle, that the Natives like the Europeans were eligible to all posts without distinction of race, creed or colour, had been affirmed in successive Acts of Parliament since 1833, although this principle had been reiterated in the Royal Proclamation, although for half a century the Crown as well as the people of England had been pledged to this just and liberal policy, the position of their countrymen with regard to the Civil Service had not materially altered. The rule of holding examinations in England, the reduction of marks assigned to oriental classics and the reduction of the maximum age for competition had pratically put competition out of their reach. Lord Monteagle, in the debates in the House of Lords in 1853, when the renewal of the Charter was under the consideration of Lord Aberdeen's Government, truly observed that "if the only door of admission to the Civil Service of India is a competitive examination carried on in London, what chance or what possibility is there of Natives of India acquiring that fair share in the admistration of their own country which their education and abilities would enable them to fulfil, and therefore entitle them to possess," They all know how the observations of Lord Monteagle had been verified by subsequent experience. It was unnecessary that he should dilate upon these almost insurmountable difficulties, for they all felt them. But he regretted with his countrymen that these difficulties had been created with the deliberate object of keeping them out of the Civil Service. This was no doubt a serious charge against an enlightened Government and an enlightened people and he would be the last person to bring this charge if he were not armed with unimpeachable evidence to support it To convict an accused person what better evidence could the jury expect than the confession of the culprit himself. Here they had the confession of Government by the mouth of its executive head, one who was certainly not over friendly towards the Natives of this country. Need he mention the name—Lord Lytton. The speaker then read the following extracts from a confidential minute of Lord Lytton's :—

"The Act of Parliament is so undefined and indefinite obligations on the part of the Government of India towards its Native subjects are so obviously dangerous that no sooner was the Act passed than the Government began to devise means for practically evading the fulfilment of it. Under the terms of the Act, which are studied and laid to heart by that increasing class of educated Natives whose development the Government encourages, without being able to satisfy the aspirations of its existing members, every such Native, if once admitted to Government employment in posts previously reserved to the Covenanted Service, is entitled to expect and claim appointment in the fair course of promotion to the highest posts in that service. We all know that these claims and expectations never can, or will, be fulfilled. We have had to choose between prohibiting them and cheating them : and we have chosen the least straightforward course. The application to Natives of the competitive examination system as conducted in England, and the recent reduction in the age at which candidates can compete, are all so many deliberate and transparent subterfuges for stultifying the Act, and reducing it to a dead letter. Since I am writing confidentially, I do not hesitate to say that both the Governments of England and of India appear to me, up to the present moment, unable to answer satisfactorily the charge of having taken every means in their power of breaking to the heart the words of promise they had uttered to the ear."

The speaker then went on and said no language could be plainer or stronger than this. Would the English people allow such ugly charges to be brought against them, simply because the Civilian bureaucracy here as well as at the India Office had taken upon themselves to question the wisdom of the Imperial Legislature, and to think that the stability and maintenance of the British rule required the exclusion of the Natives from the higher administrative posts. He would not waste time in exposing the unsoundness of these views. They had yet to learn that a generous and liberal policy of trust and confidence in a subject race ever endangered the maintenance of a foreign rule. The teachings of history had always pointed to a different conclusion. The events which took place in the different parts of this vast empire, on the eve of Lord Ripon's departure from India, amply showed how a liberal policy could evoke the loyalty of a conquered people. Amidst a conquered population, alien in race and religion, and largely exceeding the number of their conquerors, with education spreading fast and wide among them, with a public opinion ever growing stronger and with powers of organisation rapidly developing, if there was any danger to a foreign rule it must proceed not from a liberal policy founded on natural justice and expediency, but from a policy of repression and exclusion founded on narrow prejudice and unmerited distrust. The speaker then pointed out that their claims to extended employment in the higher service, were not only based upon the ground of national justice to the people, but upon the ground of the plainest political expediency. Economy also required it. If goods were available in their own market, why should they, poor as they were, go to a foreign country and pay a much higher price for imported goods. Then again, the high salaries and pensions enjoyed by their Civilian rulers were mostly spent out of the country. The experience bought at such a high price was not also retained in the country for its future use, but was shipped out of the country and pretty often employed against its interest.

What justice the Indians to the honour of the English people loudly demanded, what expediency plainly required, what economy distinctly sanctioned, should they not have that simply because Lord Kimberley, evidently under some evil influence, said *no* to the earnest prayers of the united people of India and to the wise recommendation of the Government of India. No. they ought not to despair. They had ample confidence in the justice of the English people. They must agitate and earnestly and perseveringly agitate till they got what they wanted. Let them not simply pass this resolution, but let them resolve further that they should not rest satisfied till they got all that they wanted.

The Hon'ble Dadabhai Naoroji :—I am glad I have not much to reply to. The appreciation of the importance of the resolution is clear. My remarks will be more as explanations of a few matters. I had much to do with the passing of the clause for granting to us the Statutory Civil Service. It is an important concession, and we have to be very grateful for it I need not here go into its history. The statesmen in England who gave us this were sincere and explicit in the matter. Whatever complaint we have it is with the authorities here. First of all, after the clause was passed, the Government of India entirely ignored it and did nothing to give it effect for 6 years! It was only when pressure was applied to it from England, into the details of which this is not the time or place for me to enter, that the necessary rules were at last prepared and published. These rules have been so drafted that they may be carried out in a way to bring discredit on the Service. And whether this is done intentionally or not, whether the subsequent objectionable action upon it was also intentional or not, I cannot say. But the most important element in the carrying out of this clause was partially or wholly ignored, and that has been the real cause of its so-called failure,—I mean educational competence, ascertained either by suitable competition, or proved ability, was an absolutely indispensible condition for admitting candidates to this Service. It is just this essential condition that has been several times ignored or forgotten. Let therefore your efforts be devoted trenuously, not against the clause itself, but against the objectionable mode in which the nominations are made. The Bengal Government has moved in a satisfactory direction, and its example should be followed by all the Governments. It will be the height of folly on our part to wish for the abolition of this Statutory civil service—excepting only when simultaneous examinations are held in England and India giving a fair field to all, as proposed in the present resolution. In this fair competition, Eurasians, or domiciled Englishmen, in fact all subjects of Her Imperial Majesty, will have equal justice. I understand that the Eurasians and domiciled Anglo-Indians come under the definition of what is called "statutory Natives." It is only right that those whose country is India should be considered as Natives, and should enjoy all the rights and privileges of Natives. United action between the Natives and Eurasians and domiciled Anglo-Indians will be good for all. What is objectionable is, that Eurasians and domiciled Anglo-Indians blow hot and cold at the same time. At one moment they claim to be Natives, and at another they spurn the Natives and claim to be Englishmen! Common sense must tell them that this is an absurd position to take up and must ultimately do them more harm than good. I desire that there should be cordial union between all whose country is, or who make their country, India. One of the speakers remarked that the employment of Natives will be economical. This is a point which I am afraid is not clearly understood. The fact is that the employment of a Native is not only economy, but *complete gain* to the whole extent of his salary. When a European is employed, he displaces a Native whom nature intended to fill the place. The Native coming in his place, is natural. Every pie he eats is therefore a gain to the country, and every pie he saves is so much saved to the country for the use of all its children. Every pie paid to a foreigner is a *complete material loss* to the country. Every pie paid to a Native is a *complete material saving* to the country. In fact, as I have already endeavoured to impress upon you as earnestly as possible, it is the whole question of the poverty or prosperity of the country. We should of course pay a reasonable price for English rule, so that we may have the highest power of control and supervision in English hands, but beyond that is simply ruin to India and not such a benefit to England as she would otherwise have, were India a prosperous country. Our friend there expressed some doubt about the necessity of going to England. I say without the least hesitation that the candidate himself as well as the service will be vastly benefitted by a visit to England. The atmosphere of freedom and high civilization which he will breathe will make him an altered man—in character, in intelligence, in experience, in self respect and in appreciation of due respect for others. In short he will largely increase his fitness and command more respect in his responsible service. I mean, of course, in the resolution that the expenses of such visits to England by the candidates who have successfully passed the different examinations for the different services in India, should be paid from the public revenue. It may be made clear in the resolution, by adding "at the public expense."

I conclude with my most anxious and earnest exhortation to this Congress, and to every individual member of it, that they should perseveringly strain every nerve to secure the all important object of this resolution as early as possible. Once this foreign drain, this "bleeding to death," is stopped, India will be capable by reason of its land, labour and it vast resources to become as prosperous as England, with benefit to England also and to mankind, and with eternal glory to the English name and nation.

Mr. M. P. Modi (Surat) inquired with reference to the proposition put by Mr. Dadabhai Naoroji regarding the Indian Civil Service and other Services, whether that part of the proposition, which said that after passing the examinations in India, the successful candidates should be made to spend two years in England, applied to all Services. He said all could see the desirableness of those who wanted to enter the Civil Service and return administrators of this country being made to spend that time in England. But if that requirement was extended to other Services such as Medical and Engineering, the speaker wished to know what necessity there was for that.

Mr. Dadabhai said that the words were intended to apply to the "Civil Service" only.

Mr. G. Subrahmanya asked whether Lord Kimberley's last Despatch should not be specifically referred to.

The President pointed out that the last clause of the proposed Resolution was in truth a reply to that Despatch. In putting the proposition to the vote, the President said, that there was a little difficulty about recommending a residence in England as a compulsory measure. He thought it would not be acceptable to the country at large, but the Congress might, perhaps, accept it as a provisional compromise for the present.

The Resolution was then put to the vote and passed.

Mr. P. Rung'ah Naidu (Madras) moved the 5th Resolution as follows :—

Mr. Chairman and Gentlemen,

You are aware that while the poverty of India is daily increasing the limits of taxation have been reached and almost all resources of revenue exhausted. British Administration has unfortunately not been economical, either from ignorance, inability, unwillingness, or some other cause or motive unknown. Nay, it has been extremely extravagant, so extravagant that it is not able to make the two ends meet. Our rulers have often recourse to another, and a very disastrous, expedient, of raising loans to maintain equilibrium between income and expenditure. This is generally a method to which spendthrifts and reckless speculators resort, but fortunately for them, at the last stage, when they are no longer able to raise loans, they have a ready relief at hand, viz., either the Bankruptcy or the Insolvent Court; but, I do not think, our Government, has such an institution to give it relief.

That the above is not an overdrawn picture but a real representation of the embarrassed condition of Indian finance, has been borne testimony to by several financiers of great and tried ability and by several humane, able and far seeing Viceroys, the true representatives of our Queen-Empress and the true sons of the land of liberty and philanthropy,—representatives who have unanimously declared that India is not capable of enduring further taxation and that the only remedy is to rigidly enforce retrenchment and economy in all directions. Moreover, experts in military affairs as well as the members of the Simla Army Commission have, after fair discussion and mature deliberation, pronounced their opinion that the military expenditure has grown very excessive and that there is absolute necessity to curtail it.

In 1857 the Indian Military expenditure was			11,463,000
64	do.	do.	14,510,247
66	do.	do.	16,748,220
70	do.	do.	16,329,739
72	do.	do.	15,678,112
76	do.	do.	15,308,460
77	do.	do.	15,792,112
80	do.	do.	21,712,862
84	do.	do.	16,975,750

Thus the military expenditure has increased by five millions. While, therefore, the cry is for reduction, to our surprise, disappointment and misfortune, the Ministry of the day have resolved to increase the expenditure already unbearable by an additional charge of 2 millions for adding 30,000 men to the existing army without proving the necessity for such an increase.

Gentlemen, let us, first of all, see whether there is any necessity for this increase. Peace and order have been restored to the country and there is no fear of internal disquietude. It is true that the scare of foreign invasion, caused by the recent action of the Russian Government, created some apprehension. It is more the bad feeling evinced by some of our Anglo-Indian fellow-subjects than anything else that made the Russians believe that the Natives were ready to assist them in subverting the British Indian Empire. Was not Russia sufficiently undeceived when, on the occasion of her threat, all the inhabitants of India, from the prince down to the peasant, vied with one another in placing the entire resources of their several States and their hard earned private fortunes, at the disposal of our Government? Did not many native gentlemen also apply, on the same occasion, to the Governor

General to give them permission to enlist themselves as Volunteers so that they might by action also, and not only by mere word of mouth, display their loyalty by fighting for their country and for their Sovereign? Did not the whole body of Native Princes and the entire mass of the population all over this country evince well and spontaneously similar loyalty to our Queen-Empress on the occasion of the departure of our late and most beloved Viceroy, Lord Ripon? And if it were not quite superfluous, I should, once more, declare, and I am perfectly certain that all of you will join me in that declaration, that no Native of India will ever be guilty of want of gratitude and loyalty to our Queen-Empress for the innumerable and inestimable blessings conferred on us by British rule. Gentlemen, had it not been for English education and Western civilisation, persons inhabiting different parts of this vast country, speaking diverse languages and professing diverse religions, would not have this day met together in this Hall to interchange thoughts, give expression to their common grievances and aspirations, and discuss in a most constitutional manner the means for redressing those grievances and fulfilling those aspirations.

Under these circumstances, it is to be hoped that our rulers will change their present policy of suspicion and distrust for a generous and confiding one. Let them moderately encourage rather than rudely damp the martial spirit of our martial races, by improving the status of the Native army, treating it, not as a mere mercenary force but, as part of the national army, accepting the offers of the people to enrol themselves as Volunteers, systematically utilising the armies of the Native States by giving them better arms and better discipline and making them an integral and efficient part of the army of the Empire and by admitting Native gentlemen as officers in the Indian army A generous policy that will introduce these changes will vastly strengthen the military position of the British in this country, backed as it will be by the whole moral force of the people. It will be seen that we therefore do not require more troops. But if, in spite of these facts, more European soldiers be required for the purposes of war, should it actually break out on any future occasion, they could be called from England very easily, and at an exceedingly short notice, because of the existence, at present, of greater facilities of communication between the two countries. But I believe that there is no present necessity of increasing the military expenditure of this country by adding 30,000 men to its army at a cost of 2 millions to overburdened India.

With these remarks, I propose the Fifth Resolution:—

"That in the opinion of the Congress the proposed increase in the military expenditure of the empire is unnecessary, and regard being had to the revenue of the empire and the existing circumstances of the country, excessive."

Mr. Dinsha Edulji Wacha (Bombay) seconded the Resolution in the following speech:—

GENTLEMEN.— Our Madras friend, the mover of the Resolution, has just pointed out to you in general terms the alarming growth of the military expenditure during the last few years. And I would now endeavour to place before you the causes and nature of that growth in details. The particulars I am about to bring to your notice will, I am sure, convince you how burdensome, and even partially unjust, is the present expenditure of 17 millions sterling per annum, and how great is the necessity of reducing it to the figure of 14½ to 15 millions which was with little fluctuation maintained till 1871-2. It is superfluous to say

8

that the net increase during the last twenty years has been 3 millions sterling or an annual average growth of £150,000. Contrast, gentlemen, for a moment the 17 millions expended in 1884 on an army of 189,000 men, British and Native, with 11½ millions in 1856 on an army of 254,000 men. Admitting all that has been urged as to the organic changes that have been introduced into the British army for better efficiency, the rise in prices of food and forage and clothing, and the dearness of recruits—admitting all these facts, none who has impartially studied the question and given some thought to the cost of the various armies maintained by the great military monarchies on the Continent of Europe can fail to acknowledge the extravagance of the army services as maintained in India. No subject demands greater attention than the cost of the army at this juncture when the Indian revenues are threatened with a further charge of 2 millions sterling per annum on account of the 30,000 more soldiers who are now being rapidly enlisted. I trace the root of the continuous growth in the military expenditure to the amalgamation scheme of 1859. It has been the main cause of financial embarrassment to the Government of India. Sir George Balfour regretted that he took a part in that scheme. Sir Charles Trevelyan observed that it was based on a principle which has been found to be extravagant and crushing in practice. It is in the nature of a one-sided partnership in which India was not allowed freedom of contract. What the exact nature of this partnership is may be best stated in the words of the late Mr. Fawcett:—"A few years after the abolition of the East India Company what is known as the Army amalgamation scheme was carried out in direct opposition to the advice of the most experienced Indian statesmen. India was thus, as it were, bound hand and foot, to our own costly system of army administration, without any regard apparently being had to the fact that various schemes of military organisation, which may be perfectly suited to a country, so wealthy as England, may be altogether unsuited to a country so poor as India. . . . A partnership has been established between England and India, and as one of these countries is extremely rich, and the other extremely poor, much of the same incongruity and many of the same inconveniences arise as if two individuals were to join in house-keeping, one of whom had £ 20,000 a year and the other only £1,000. An expenditure which may be quite appropriate to the one whose income is £20,000 would bring nothing but embarrassment to the one whose income is only £1,000. The money which is expended may be judiciously laid out, but if the man with the smaller income finds that he is gradually becoming embarrassed with debt because he has to live beyond his means, it is no compensation to him to be told that he is only called to contribute his proper share of the expenses. His position would be the more intolerable if like India, after having been compelled against his wish to join the partnership, he is forced to continue in whether he desires to do so or not." This, gentlemen, is the precise condition to which India has been reduced by the amalgamation scheme. No doubt, it has certain advantages but these are greatly overbalanced by the many disadvantages India has to put up with.

So far, I have dealt with what I may call *the* cause of the present costliness of the Indian army. I hope you will be good enough to give me a patient hearing for a few minutes while I briefly dilate on the broad *results* of that one sided contract to which I have referred. They are deduced from official facts and statements. Indeed, I shall try throughout to support my observations byplacing before you overwhelming official testimony to convince you beyond the shadow of a doubt how excessive is this expenditure and how far is it incurred without due regard to the interests of the country. In their report, the Simla Army Commissioners state (p. 185):—"We think that the portion of the army employed in this country should be organised and administered with due regard to the interests of the people of India, and not for the purpose of supplying defects in the system of home defence, and, above all, that it should not be made the means of obtaining, at the cost of India, advantages for the army at home which do not entirely affect the interests of the country." I do not think the justice of this principle can be impugned. But to give a fair idea of how the process of increasing the charges on the European forces in India has been carried on, it is needful to cite the testimony of the Government of India itself. It should be remembered that in the aggregate these charges have thrown an additional permanent burden of £800,000 per annum—charges in levying which the Indian Government has had no voice. In the 45th paragraph of their despatch of 21st November 1884, it is stated:—

"In 1864-65 increased rates of pay were granted to medical officers of the British service in India, amounting to £20,000 a year; and a revised scale of clothing and compensation to the British army was introduced costing £20,000 a year.

"In 1865-66 increased rates of pay were granted to veterinary surgeons, amounting to £3,500 a year.

"In 1866-67 gymnastic instruction was introduced for British troops at a cost of £15,000 a year.

"In 1867-68 an increase of 2d. a day was made to the pay of British soldiers, and an additional penny on re-engagement, the cost being £250,000 a year.

"In the same year skeleton companies of Royal Engineers were formed in India, at a cost of £2,500 a year.

"In 1868-69 increased pay was given to paymasters, quarter-masters, and riding-masters of British regiments, amounting to £15,000 a year.

"In 1870-71 the grant of good-conduct pay, at earlier periods, to British soldiers, increased our Army estimates by £35,000.

"In 1871-72 instruction in army signalling and telegraphy was introduced at an annual cost of £4,000.

"In 1871-74 garrison instruction was introduced, at a cost of £20,000 a year.

"In 1871-74 the appointment of additional subalterns to regiments in India, to allow others to attend the course of garrison instruction, formed a new charge of £5,000 a year.

"In 1873-74 improvements in the regimental schools of British regiments in India by the application of Home regulations, increased the estimates by £7,000 a year; the grant of band allowance to British regiments in India by £14,720; and the readjustment of ranks of the British Medical Service in India by £18,000.

"In 1874-75 the raised rates of pay of British troops in India added to the estimates £64,000 a year.

"In 1875-76 the grant of pay of rank to majors of Royal Artillery and engineers in India created a new annual charge of £27,000.

"In 1876-77 the increased pay of non-commissioned officers and lance ranks amounted to £40,000 a year.

"In the same year prospective charges for deferred pay were introduced, the maximum to be reached in 1890 being £165,000.

"In 1876-77 also the promotion of British medical officers after 12 years' service, and non-effective charges by changes in the rules for compulsory retirement, introduced a new item of £29,000.

"In 1879-80 the readjustment of veterinary surgeons' pay cost £1,900 a year.

"In 1880-81 a reorganisation of the army Medical Department non-effective charges involved a new annual charge of £13,320.

"In 1881 the Royal Pay Warrant of 25th June 1881 raised a fresh charge for the pay of non-commissioned officers and men of £30,000 a year,"

The Despatch goes on to say that "these additional charges amount to more than £800,000 a year. Some of them were necessary for improvements; others were imposed with little or no reference to Indian wants, and in most cases without the Indian Government having any voice in the matter." It will be seen from the above facts and figures how costly and how ruinously one-sided is the partnership, which the Imperial Government has obliged India to enter into, in the matter of military administration, without giving her the smallest voice in the conduct of that partnership.

I hope I have made it clear to you from the extract just quoted the fact that almost all the charges were fastened on this country in consequence of the exigencies of the organisation of the British army in England. Home demands for payments have been steady and persistent. In their Military Despatch (No. 168, dated Simla, 22nd May 1879) the Government of India observed:—"A large part of the Home expenditure is for pensions, furlough allowances, the overland troop transport service, and stores. The remainder is for payments to the Imperial Government on account of Imperial troops which have been repeatedly investigated, but with results we have not been able to accept as satisfactory.........Justice to India requires the reduction of these payments to a consolidated yearly payment of £850,000." Two years later, the Government of Lord Ripon remonstrated on the burden of these charges in a manner so telling that I would best make you understand their gravity by quoting the paragraph on the subject (44, Despatch No. 401 of 1881). "It has to be observed that whereas the British garrison in India has practically remained unaltered in respect of numbers and efficiency for many years past, its cost has been in course of constant increase from the various changes which have been made in the organisation of the British army, *changes made entirely, it may be said, from imperial considerations in which Indian interests have not been consulted or advanced*......It has to be remembered that charges which do not cause any very serious addition to the English estimates, and which are carried on without the least reference to India involve very much larger charges on the Indian revenues by reason of the much more liberal allowance enjoyed by officers in this country. The conversion for example of the first Captains of the Royal Artillery into Majors gives the officer so promoted an increase of only 5 shillings a day in England: in this country the difference between the pay of a Major and a Captain of artillery is Rs. 342 a month." Gentlemen, look at the immense difference in this one item of military charges alone. Fancy, a poor country like India being screwed by a wealthy country like England to pay Rs. 292 more per month for the promotion of officers in *one grade only of one branch* of the army! But, the enormity of the heavy charges thrown upon this country in the matter (*a*) of home depôts, (*b*) of recruits, (*c*) of non-effective services, (*d*) of transports, and (*e*) of short service will be perceived at its full from the sequel. As to Home Depôts, the *Westminster Review* observed for as back as 1866 or 1867 :—"England bears the expense of maintaining an army for the use of India whereas the truth is that India is maintaining a vast army which, though paid by India, is available at any moment for the service of England. Of these troops paid from the revenues of India, no less than 10,000 on the average are stationed in the Home Depots and form a part of the defences of England at all times. Now, India is not merely required to pay for the transport of troops both to and from India but is made to pay a consolidated charge of £10 per annum to the Horse Guards for *every British soldier serving in the country upon the pretext* that it is necessary to keep these depots in England to maintain the force. This charge of late years has amounted to nearly £700,000 a year, and must be held to be a most *unwarrantable exaction* when it is remembered that these depôts form an important part of the garrison required for the defence of the United Kingdom......At the very time the Colonels of the French army were threatening the nation with invasion (1859) on account of the Orsini plot, the Ministers and publicists of England were congratulating themselves upon the presence in England of some 20,000 to 22,000 soldiers in depot the cost of whom was being defrayed *by the Indian tax-payer* on the ground that the regiments to which the men belonged were serving in India. *The pretext was true, but the exaction was surely disgraceful*.......Thus was the defence of the richest country in the world *shabbily* devolved upon the very poorest." Gentlemen, this is the true history of the cost of home depôts. After the vigorous manner in which the reviewer has criticised the gross injustice of the burdensome charge, an injustice which, I regret to say, they have done but little to repair even now, it is unnecessary for me to further comment upon it.

As to the extravagant cost of recruits, I may mention that a continued controversy has gone on during the last 25 years as to the mode of calculating on a fair and equitable basis the charge for their enlistment and maintenance prior to their embarkation for India. And though one method after another has been adopted and discarded, they have not yet come to any satisfactory arrangement so far as this country is concerned. Meanwhile, it would not be uninstructive to quote here the reports of General Jamieson and Mr. (now Sir Thomas) Seccombe on the extraordinary dearness of a recruit, as supplied by England to India. "We feel it to be our duty again to refer to the fact that the East India Company were able to send efficient artillery and infantry recruits to India at a cost of £26-7-5 per man, instead of £136-13-11 for cavalry and £63-8-5 for infantry recruits as now proposed. We are fully aware that the changes made in the terms of enlistment, pay, clothing, would have increased the charge, as incurred by the East India Company, but the proposed establishments for, and the period of training which have formed the basis of this Third Report of the Committee, appear to us to be *enormously in excess* of what can possibly be required for the purpose of properly recruiting the British Army in India." According to Colonel Sykes the maximum in one particular year was as much as £376 ! So strongly impressed were General Jamieson and Mr. Seccombe with the "enormously" excessive charge of recruits per man, that they raised the serious question why India should bear the whole burden of maintaining depôts which virtually form a part of England's home defences, and why should that burden be increased by the long periods of training enforced on recruits for service in this country ? For further particulars I would refer members to the evidence taken by the Parliamentary Select Committee which sat from 1871 to 1874 to inquire into the questions relating to the finances of India. Suffice to say that the experts who were examined and cross examined on the subject failed to give any satisfactory explanation.

Coming now to the burden of the non-effective services, I would ask you to refer to the blue-book on the subject published by order of the House of Commons, on 12th August 1884. It gives a succinct account of how the charges have grown year after year and how vigorously the Government of India has been fighting for years past to bring these charges within a reasonable limit. I would not, therefore, tax your patience further on this head beyond informing you in a few words how alarming is the growth. "Prior to 1822 India paid nothing for non-effective charges; that from 1822 to 1861 the principle which governed the division of non-effective charges between England and India was one of a fixed payment by India to England of £ 60,000 a year; that from 1861 to 1870 this latter principle was abandoned in favour of a capitation payment; and finally, that in 1870 the principle of capitation was abandoned in favour of a system under which the capitalised value of the pensions was paid by the Indian to the English Treasury. This latter is the system which is still in force. Gentlemen, here are the figures of the enhanced charges between 1871 and 1884. In the former year they amounted to £1,775,133, in the latter to £4,158,780. The increase has amounted to £ 2,383,647 in 14 years or 134 per cent. In others words, the charges on account of non-effective services have steadily increased at an annual average of

£ 170,260! The iniquity of the charges however does not rest here. While disputes as to the fairness of the demand by the War Office for charges from year to year have gone on, during which the Government of India continued to pay large sums in part, a claim for arrears was made for a million sterling and more which, as you all know, has had to be paid only last year by the Indian Treasury. Nay you will have some idea of the gross injustice of their demand when I tell you that £100,000 were claimed for interest alone—interest on arrears which remained unadjusted on account of the delay at the War Office alone! This is the treatment which India has to suffer from the military authorities at home. Moreover, the injustice of the charge is greatly enhanced when it is considered that *the Crown Colonies are never charged a six-pence for non-effective services.* I will just read what the Government of India has said on the point." We believe also that we are correct in saying that Crown Colonies pay nothing towards the non-effective charges." It is one of the heaviest items of Army charges, and entails besides a large loss byexchange.

Coming to the overland transport service, it may be mentioned that the East India Company incurred on an average £70,000 per annum, net. Of course, the troops came via the Cape in ships. But though the opening of the Suez Canal has revolutionised the whole transit trade between Europe and Asia, though freights have in consequence been lower than they were prior to 1870, and though immense facilities of communication now exist, the charges are indeed very extravagant. In 1864-65 they came to £182,244; in 1883 to £365,000 or fully double! Besides, it must be remembered that India has been saddled with the cost of five transport vessels amounting to £1,200,000. Some years ago public feeling on the subject was very vigorously expressed in the columns of the *Englishman.* "There is one item of military expenditure touched upon in General Norman's excellent financial analysis of the Indian Army Bill for the past year which deserves instant attention and correction. As a bit of senseless extravagance, it is solely chargeable against the home authorities who make India pay for the patronage and political capital it affords to the Admiralty. We allude to the transport charge of £400,000 for the carriage of, let us say at hazard, some 4,000 soldiers ......being at the rate of £100 per man.........Nor is the exorbitant nature of the charge its only objection. The ordinary carrying and other trade is injured by it. It is in the nature of competition without containing one of the elements of competition." Another veteran journalist of great experience observed :—" the truth seems to be that the Home Government is utterly reckless what it spends on Indian account. That the building of this fleet was an act of extravagant folly when the circumstances of the country are remembered who can doubt? India is not in circumstances to afford *this wanton outlay of public money.*" Gentlemen, it is again needful to remember that England *never charges a sixpence for the transport of her troops to her foreign possessions* in every part of the civilised world. In a minute on this subject, Sir Charles Wingate recorded as far back as 1859 as follows :—" The cost of transporting British troops to India, is also charged upon the British shipowners, and as it is made for the maintenance of British authority in India it would clearly be reasonable and fair that the charge, as in the case of troops sent to any of our foreign dependencies, should be borne by the British Exchequer." It may be fairly admitted that public criticism has had the effect of getting the expenditure somewhat reduced of late under this head. Still it is not all that is desirable. The Simla Army Commission recommend in their report, (para 210) " that the system whereby all reliefs and drafts of British troops are sent by British troopships to Bombay, should be revised......We advise that steps be taken to ascertain at what rates the great English Steam Companies would convey troops regularly to the several ports of Calcutta, Madras, Kurrachee and Rangoon. We believe, that, if a contract were made for a considerable number of troops, and for a term of years, private companies would convey troops regularly and comfortably to and fro from the several ports nearest their stations, at considerably below the cost of transport by the troopships."

I now come to the last of those charges fastened on India in consequence of the changes in the organisation of the British Army nearly, the short service system. It would be presumptuous for me as a layman to pronounce on the merit or demerit of the system. I would, therefore, content myself by again quoting the testimony of experts. The Simla Army Commission (paragraph 209) state :—" It has been already mentioned that the short service system recently introduced into the British Army has increased the cost, and has materially reduced the efficiency of the British troops in India. *We cannot resist the feeling that, in the introduction of this system, the interest of the Indian taxpayer was entirely left out of consideration.*"

Gentlemen, I fear, I have already trespassed too much on your time by referring to the several details of the army charges which have increased the total cost to 17 millions sterling. But I trust you will bear with me a few minutes longer before I sit down. I ask you, to remember that the Home Military Charges are divided into two parts—the one includes the expenditure under the control of the Indian Government, and the other the expenditure not under such control and regulated by the

War Office. While the former has been steadily maintained at an average of £2,500,000 since 1874-5, the latter, that is the expenditure controlled by the War Office, has risen since that year from £800,000 to about £1,400,000 and there is no saying how rapidly it may swell to £2,000,000.

View, then, this expenditure of 17 millions sterling as you may from every point, you cannot help admitting its appalling enormity. It means 39¼ per cent of the net revenue of 43 millions. In other words the Army service charges absorb the whole of the net land revenue save a million. While the normal growth of the latter is estimated at about £57,000 per annum, the growth of the former is more, £150,000—that is to say, one year's growth of military expenditure absorbs the growth of the net land revenue for nearly 2¾ years. Consider the weight of this burden on so poor a country as ours—a country which has no true surplus of revenue to fall back upon and has no ordinary means to provide for unforeseen contingencies like war or famine. Consider the burden from another point also. Out of the total expenditure of 17 millions, 4 millions on an average are annually disbursed in England. The amount has to be paid in gold. So that, we have to pay nearly one crore of Rupees more to meet the loss by exchange, under this one head only. I will not detain you with the economic aspect of this fact. But I may mention that every million sterling that is expended in England on account of India involves a loss by exchange of about 25 lakhs of Rupees at the present rate The larger the amount annually of the bills drawn by the Secretary of State on the Indian treasury for Home Charges, especially military, the larger the exports of the products of this country. In other words, India has to grow more and part with more products in exchange for home remittances. The significance of this economic fact I leave it to you to realise. But while this military expenditure is growing apace, while all India to a man has been loud in denouncing its crushing burden, the authorities have determined to add 10,000 more British and 20,000 more Native troops at an estimated cost of 2 millions sterling per annum, and that, too, without any cogent reasons. How is this additional permanent expenditure to be provided for? For months past the air has been rife with rumours of the imposition of an Income Tax. Indeed statements have lately been freely made on authentic sources that we may very soon expect a bill being introduced into the Viceregal Legislative Council for the purpose. As, however, another member of this Congress will speak to the general question of revenue and taxation I will refrain from dwelling on this subject.

But I hope, gentlemen, I have made it quite clear to you how great is the strain on Indian finance on account of the maintenance of a small army of 1,89,000 men—an army which, I unhesitatingly say, costs twice as much and a little over as any army in any part of the civilised world. In fact there is no parallel to its extravagant cost. The growing charges on the army services are a source of perpetual embarrassment to the Government of India. Viceroy after Viceroy and Finance Minister after Finance Minister have remonstrated with successive Secretaries of State for India on the urgent necessity of curtailing the expenditure but they seem to have remonstrated to little purpose hitherto. In fact, the evidence taken before the Select Committee on Indian Finance in 1872-3, conclusively shows that the Secretary of State himself is almost powerless to prevent the War Office perpetually making inroads under one pretext or another on the revenues of India.

That part of the expenditure which is not under the control of the India Office, needs to be brought under control by a Parliamentary statute, apart from an honest retrenchment all round in the various branches of the army administration. I cannot help believing that Mr. Laing was perfectly correct when he said that "India is the milchcow of England" and that Indian revenues are encroached upon "to suit the exigencies of English estimates."

The Select Committee to which I have referred, stated in their Report that they "could not lay down too strongly, the position that the English estimates ought not to be relieved at the expense of the Indian revenues, but that the Secretary of State for India in Council has the constitutional right of refusing to pay for objects in which he considers that India has no interest." In this respect it has been admitted that India was better situated during the administration of the late East India Company, though, it has been observed, that even then the authorities at the Horse Guards did not fail in spite of the most formidable opposition offered by the Court of Directors, to saddle 10 millions sterling of the cost of the first Afghan War on the revenues of this country. Mr. Fawcett observed:—" It should, however, never be forgotten that when the East India Company was abolished, the English people became directly responsible for the Government of India. It cannot, I think, be denied that this responsibility has been so imperfectly discharged that in many respects the new system of Government compares unfavourably with the old . . . . There was at that time an independent control of expenditure which now seems to be almost entirely wanting. It was no doubt, intended, when the Government of India by the Act of 1858 was transferred from the Company to the Crown, that the Council of the Secretary of State should exercise, the same control over Indian expenditure, as had formerly been exercised by the Directors of the Company and by the Court of proprietors. But gradually the influence and control of the Council have been so completely whittled away that it is now openly declared by the Secretary of State that he can spend the revenues of India, beyond her frontiers, without obtaining the consent, or even bringing the subject under the notice of his Council. . . . . Nothing can be more unsatisfactory than the present state of things. When the Secretary of state desires to avoid responsibility he can shelter himself behind his Council, when he desires to act untrammelled by their control and unhampered by their advice, he can ignore them as completely as if they did not exist." The root of the evil lies here and active steps must sooner or later be taken, the sooner the better, to bring an end to it, highly injurious as it is to the material interests of the country and its people. It is to be earnestly hoped, therefore, that the Resolution which this Congress will now be asked to adopt will be turned to practical account by the various political organisations. For unless a vigorous remonstrance is sent up to the authorities against the burdensome character of the total charge, and the injustice of a portion of the charges, I am humbly of conviction that this growth of the military expenditure alarming, and in certain matters uncontrolled as it has been in the past, will grow more burdensome and uncontrolled and seriously embarass the finances of the country in future. This contingency our united efforts must at all hazards legitimately attempt to avert—relying on that stern sense of justice which preeminently distinguishes the British among the great nations of the civilised world.

The Resolution was supported by Mr. Dayaram Jethmal (Kurrachee) who began by suggesting an earnest and careful consideration of this question. The pith of the matter he said was :—Had the Government made out the necessity for the proposed increase? If it was justifiable there was of course nothing to be said against it. So far as the people of India were aware the reasons for it were totally wanting. This was certainly a fit case for enquiry. Had the people given cause for it? No. Surely no mutinous spirit had been exhibited by the Natives of India. Had the inhabitants in the interior assumed a warlike attitude towards the ruling power? Loyalty was the ruling spirit that moved the nation from one end of the country to the other. The only excuse which the speaker had heard of for the proposed increase was the bugbear of a Russian invasion. Well, with regard to this plausible excuse, whatever the fears might be, there were facts important and patent which should be borne in mind. It had been acknowledged by competent authorities that the existence of a neutral zone on the North West of India was a factor in the problem which should always be considered by the British Government. With friendly Afghanistan, between Indian and Russian territory, there was no necessity of a very large Indian Army. And was not Afghanistan friendly? What chance had a warlike foreign power like Russia of doing harm to India in the immediate present or in the near future? The expenditure was quite unjustifiable. Even if the frontier required to be strengthened with larger troops there was no need of increasing the Indian Army. It could not be said that sufficient troops were not available in the interior of the country for frontier purposes. Regiment after regiment remained unemployed from year's end to year's end and kept in cities and provinces where they were not required. He instanced the regiments in Sind, in the cities of Karachee and Hydrabad, the men of which found their time hang heavy on their hands. They were absolutely idle. If there was any agreeable occupation for them, they, or rather some of the members of these regiments, found it in annoying the harmless civil population and in insulting the modesty of respectable Native women innocently walking in the streets. The meeting also knew well the enormous number of cases of running amuck on the part of Native sepoys which had occured and which were occurring almost everywhere, in India—wherever, in fact, Native regiments were stationed. These occurrences, he thought, were inevitable and natural, as the causes were well known, as the men had nothing to do. Hardly any evidence was required to prove what the Native regiments in India were doing. If there was anything more than another for which they were required, it was to guard the frontier. They were not required to guard the population. There was enough police in the districts and cities of India for the protection of the people and for preserving peace and order. The whole of the present Native army was not required for ordinary garrison duty. Then it might be said that sudden emergencies might arise and to be prepared was half the battle. But it was absurd to think that large bodies of troops should be scattered thickly in and about the country. For emergencies in towns we have large bodies of volunteers. The volunteers cost the State something. There was no reason why their services should not be utilized in cases of emergency. The volunteers, at least the European and Eurasian volunteers, were dispersed in all important centres. Why should not volunteering become still more general? It was a matter of extreme regret that the Native volunteer movement had not received encouragement. The representations of the people had not been granted. The feelings of loyalty did not always meet with the response which they deserved. It was devoutly to be wished that Natives should be admitted as volunteers. There was no doubt that the movement would spread. There would then be no necessity for increasing the army even if increased fighting strength was required. Every one understood that the foundation of the British Empire rested on the loyalty of the people. The people were remarkably peaceful. The proposal to increase the army, instead of utilizing the available troops in British India and the troops of the Native Princes and Chiefs and admitting Natives as volunteers, was calculated to create an impression in the minds of the inhabitants of India that our rulers had no confidence in us. This policy of distrust must cease. What did the recent Central Asian crisis prove? Did it not prove completely the loyalty of the educated Natives? That they rallied round their rulers was a truth now acknowledged far and wide. The example of the educated Natives spread and spread till the whole country resounded with echoes of loyalty and enthusiasm. The Government would be pursuing the safest policy in trusting to the education of the people. Education must spread. If the reasons for the increase were of any value such reasons could be urged in every country and in every age. Where would the British Government stop? Two millions would in course of time be increased to four millions if the present policy and present apprehensions continued. After all the increased cost would have to be met from the pockets of the people. It would be raised by grinding taxation. This increased burden was a serious affair. The good-will of the people was the one thing which was all important. Going back to history, the speaker referred to the Mogul Emperors and reminded the hearers that the best allies, the best friends, the best supporters of the Mogul rulers were the Hindus, the Rajputs. He strongly recommended the adoption of the proposed Resolution.

The Resolution was then put to the vote and carried.

Mr. Javerilal Umiashankar Yajnik (Bombay) proposed the Sixth Resolution as under:—Mr. Chairman and gentlemen of the Congress, the proposition to which I solicit your attention is: "That, in the opinion of this Congress, if the increased demands for military expenditure are not to be, as they ought to be, met by retrenchment, they ought to be met, firstly, by the re-imposition of the Customs Duties; and, secondly, by the extension of the License-tax to those classes of the community, official and non-official, which are at present exempted from it, care being taken that in the case of all classes a sufficiently high taxable minimum be maintained." So far, gentlemen, the topics which have engaged your attention have had for their object the reform of the administrative and consultative departments of the State; but the subject of the Resolution you have just passed, and that to which I have now the honour of addressing you, are of an eminently practical character. They directly touch your pockets. Three months hence, you will have before you the Financial Statement of the Government of India. That Statement will lay bare the matured proposals of Government arising out of the balance sheet of the year. Already the air is thick with rumours in regard to fresh taxation, as to the probable imposition of an Income Tax in place of the existing License-tax. The time is opportune, therefore, for this Congress to formulate its own views as to the best means of raising a maximum of revenue with a minimum of annoyance. For this purpose it is needful to recall what Sir Auckland Colvin said at the conclusion of the last Financial Statement (for 1885-86, para. 139):—'If during the ensuing year (1886-87), we are not called upon to submit to any material increase of expenditure, the estimates, based as they are on a very low rate of exchange and a very moderate calculation as to the revenue of our trade, may, I think, be trusted to bear the test of trial. Should trade revive or exchange become more favourable, we shall have resources ample enough to meet our estimated expenditure. On the other hand, it is impossible to say whether additional expenditure may not in the course of the year have to be provided for, exceeding the limits of any addition which our revenues may reasonably hope to derive from the strengthening of our railway receipts or from the improvement in our exchange.' The worst forebodings herein pointed out have been realised. Our expenditure on account of the military operations during the year and on account of the proposal made in Lord Randolph Churchill's statement to add a permanent burden of 2 millions a year for the cost of 30,000 troops to the Indian army, has exceeded 'the limits of any addition which our revenues may reasonably hope to derive from the railway receipts or from the improvement in our exchange.' No doubt there has been an increase in railway receipts but it has been more than counterbalanced by other circumstances. There has been an increase of expenditure over and above the estimated amount. Exchange has suffered a serious fall since the date of the last budget. It has touched a limit below 1s. 6*d*. and may, for aught we know, go down still further. Mr. Westland has calculated that for every fall of a farthing in exchange, the Government of India suffers a loss amounting to somewhere about a quarter of a million sterling. On this basis we must be prepared for a loss of at least a million sterling in exchange. To this add the two millions of permanent charge for additions to the army of India. Against this it is possible you may have a set-off in the shape of a surplus over estimated revenue. In bad times Indian financiers are apt to estimate revenues under several heads at a much lower level than they do ordinarily. This plan no doubt strengthens their contention for elasticity' of revenue, and enables them to claim credit for prudent management of finances. Trade, again, has been dull. Perhaps this has been a year of the most depressed trade in India during a very long period. As a set-off against these adverse influences, the Government of India issued, some months back, a Circular letter directing 'all optional expenditure, whether from Provincial or Imperial Revenues, to be suspended,' 'all proposals for increases of salaries, or of establishments or for additional expenditure of any kind should be narrowly scrutinized'. Particular attention was directed to the Public Works Department as offering perhaps the readiest scope for the use of shears. It seems to me that considerable relief would be given to the finances, if retrenchments were carried out in a thorough and rigorous manner, without impairing the effeciency of the public service. But what has been the fact? A retrenchment Circular from the Government of India is no new thing. In 1879 a similar Resolution from the Govern- of India was issued. But the relief afforded by it was hardly appreciable. Generally the plan adopted by Heads of Departments for the purpose of showing what reduction is or can be made by them is to dispense with the services of a clerk here and a clerk there, to dismis a *paniwala* or water-bearer who supplies water to the thirsty members of a public establishment, or a *Chapprasi* on perhaps Rs. 8 or Rs. 10 a month. Until retrenchment, to be effectual, goes up higher, until it touches the pockets of those who receive very high salaries, any cheeseparing policy of the kind at present pursued can surely impart no sensible relief. Retrenchment must begin at the top, with the salary of the Viceroy, with the salaries of the members of the Supreme Government, and of the highly paid Secretaries to the Government of India. Shears should next be applied to the salaries of Presidency Governors and to those of the Members of their Councils, including the salaries of the Commanders-in-Chief of the different Presidencies. Then there is the Civil Service—the most highly paid service in the world. Time was when this service needed to be remunerated on the present extravagant scale. Thirty years ago the Covenanted Civil Servant was looked upon as living as an exile in a foreign land. But circumstances have immensely changed. The Civil Servant of the present day can run back to his native land, meet his relations and friends, and rejoin his post in India within a period of eight or ten weeks. Again, some of the over-grown departments called into being to meet special emergencies may very well stand a clipping. Of this we have a notable instance in the revenue Commissionership for the Central Division of this Presidency. The office was created to meet a famine emergency. That emergency has long passed away but the Commissionership still remains and is a drag on the revenues of this Presidency to the extent of about half a lakh of rupees a year. It is not, however, the salaries which are alone to be considered. Increase of salaries carries with them increase of pensions. It is not intended by these remarks to urge that there should be a sudden cutting down of all salaries. The retrenchment policy of Government, to be of any permanent benefit, should aim at reductions for the future. The reduced scale must be made applicable to new incumbents. This will remove grounds of ill-treatment or injustice in the case of existing holders of appointments. The new comers will know what they are to expect. And thus the working of the retrenchment policy will be sensibly felt not only in the amount of salaries, but in the amount ot pensions which are periodically payable. No doubt much courage and firmness are needed to carry out a policy of rigorous retrenchment: much odium and unpopularity have to be incurred. But if this is faced in the exigencies of Indian finance, and if the war policy of the Government of India in the sacred name of the security of the country gives way, there can be no doubt of a substantial relief being imparted to the Indian Exchequer.

Turning now to the proposals for obtaining increased revenue allow me in the first place, to point out that in the re-imposition of the Customs Duties the Government of India possess a source of revenue the burden of which will be *least* felt by the people. Its expediency will be recognised at a time of great financial pressure. We have instances in the past financial history of this country which show that as heavy a duty as 10 per cent. at one time, and 7½ per cent. at another, was imposed on imports into this country by Mr. James Wilson in the interests of revenue. It has been urged that the abolition of import duties was necessary in the interests of free trade; but it must be remembered that import duties here were never laid with a view to protection; that its levy has had no protective effect, and that even in the best free-trade country in the world, we have it on the highest financial authority, on the authority of Mr. Gladstone, that the state of the revenue should be the guiding consideration in all such impositions. The abolition of customs duties means that while India is to be made a free port for the benefit of the English and of the European manufacturer, Indian tea and Indian silver ware must continue to be handicapped by customs duties in the English and European markets. Is this fair? Is this just? Is it because India has no voice powerful enough to influence the policy which governs the fiscal relations of India and England that she should be thus unfairly treated? It shows that the British manufacturer, or the British trader is to enjoy all the benefit arising from the protection of the country, from the construction of strategic railways and from frontier fortifications, while the Indian taxpayer is to bear the burden of them. The customs revenue can be collected at the least expense and with the least annoyance to the people. I trust, therefore, that in considering the expediency of the re-imposition of import duties, the Government of India will give a fresh proof of their solicitude for the welfare of the people. I now come to the second expedient, namely, the re-adjustment of the License-tax, this re-adjustment to consist chiefly in its extension to classes who have hitherto escaped from its burden, and in the maintenance of a sufficiently high taxable minimum. Gentlemen, the unfair and unsatisfactory manner in which the License-tax has worked has, as a rule, been admitted by successive Finance Ministers. It was admitted by Sir John Strachey and it was admitted by Sir Evelyn Baring. And I do not think that Sir Auckland Colvin has been an exception to the rule. But Sir John Strachey did not like to be unpopular with the official and professional classes who are able to make their voices heard. It was the voiceless millions therefore that he preferred to operate upon. Sir Evelyn Baring fared no better in this respect. The License-tax has worked unfairly in this way. Officials from the Viceroy with his 2½ lakhs or £25,000 a year and Governors with their £12,000 a year, Lieut-Governors with their £8,000 a year, and successful lawyers like barristers, and attorneys or solicitors, and medical men, who, after a successful practice of some years in this country, retire with fortunes to their native land, are left untaxed while a poor, wretched trader, with his 4s. a week, has to bear the brunt of it. The Act has worked unfairly in three ways. In the first place, it has left untouched, as I said just now, the richer and more influential classes. Secondly, the incidence of the tax has varied in different places. In Bengal, and the N. W. Provinces, the limit of taxable minimum has been Rs. 700 a year. In Madras it is Rs. 500. In Bombay it is Rs. 200. And thirdly, the limit of taxable minimum put is very low. Having regard to the condition of the masses from whom the tax is levied, it would be a relief to most of those whose income is below Rs. 1,000 a year to be exempted from its operation. But with the extension of the taxable limit and the extension of the tax to those classes who can pay it more easily, not only will much of the inequality in its incidence and much of the unfairness in its levy be removed, but those classes will be brought under its operation who can pay it without reminding one of 'much cry and little wool,' Besides these, there is of course the Income Tax, but its general unsuitableness to this country, coupled with the inquisitorial character of the proceedings in which the practical working of the Act results, has made it to be regarded with disfavour though it is just possible to take away the sting from it. With these remarks I trust the Resolution I hold in my hand will commend itself to your approval.

Mr. S. A. Swaminath Iyer (Tanjore), seconded the proposition, He said :—

Mr. Chairman and Gentlemen,

In rising to second the proposition moved by my friend opposite, I may point out that the subject of this Resolution is one that immediately concerns the well-being of the teeming millions of this vast continent. The very mention of the words " fresh taxation" is enough to strike horror into the hearts of the people. It must be clear to all who have the interest of the dumb millions of the poor of the country, that additional taxation means their complete ruin. It has been admitted by successive Viceroys and Finance Ministers that all sources of taxation have been fully exhausted and that India, poor as it is acknowledged to be, can ill afford to bear any fresh burdens. The present subject is one which is immediately connected with the

Resolution we have just now passed, viz., increase of military expenditure. In discussing that subject our attention was chiefly directed to the proposed additional expenditure. But in dealing with the question now on hand, we have to go further and consider whethen the existing military establishments are required for the preservation of the British empire in India. Gentlemen, I may without much fear of contradiction safely answer this question in the negative. At present the military strength of the country consists of (in round numbers) 64,000 European soldiers and 126,000 Native soldiers maintained at a cost of 17 millions sterling. I see, Gentlemen, you are surprised to find that the military expenditure of the country almost covers the whole of the Land Tax raised in this purely agricultural country. But let us pause and enquire how this extravagant expenditure has come to exist. It is the outcome of the policy of *distrust* of Natives which of late years characterises the administration of this country. Gentlemen, I must appeal to your feelings of loyalty and devotion to the British Crown and ask you if we, in any way, deserve this treatment at our rulers' hands. Who was it that conquered India for the British? Who was it that fought the battles of Plassey, Assaye, and Sobraon? Is it possible to forget that it was the Native soldiery and not a handful of Europeans that won those brilliant victories by which the British Empire in India was formed and consolidated. Surely, nothing has since happened to change this policy of *trust* into one of *distrust*. I ask you, Gentlemen, if, at the present moment, the one thousand and one races that inhabit this vast continent of India do not all join together in praying for the stability and continuance of the benign rule of Her Gracious Majesty, our Queen-Empress. When, a few months back, Russia threatened to invade India, what was the conduct of the Natives? The Native States throughout this vast Empire and Native noblemen stood firmly by the British Supremacy and offered to place all their available forces and resources at the disposal of the Government of India. Did not the Indians of all creeds and colours join together and offer to form Volunteer Corps? It is superfluous to multiply instances of Native fidelity and attachment to British rule. If, therefore, our rulers will only change their policy of *distrust* into one of *confidence*, if they will utilize the martial spirit of the country, there can be no doubt that a very considerable reduction in expenditure can be effected. Even if the bugbear of a Russian invasion should become a reality, the Imperial army formed on the lines above indicated, assisted by the armies of Native States will be able effectually not only to repel the invaders but also to maintain peace and order in the country. Consistently, therefore, with the efficiency of our army, I would urge very strongly upon the attention of this Congress the necessity of curtailing our present military expenditure by more largely utilising the martial spirit of the country.

The next quarter where the shears may be applied with advantage is the favoured heaven-born Civil Service. When any financial pressure is felt, the Government of India sends circulars to all heads of Departments to make retrenchments to meet the financial crisis. What do the Departmental heads do? They forthwith proceed to dismiss a Musalji, a peon and one or two underpaid clerks and show a saving of a few thousands of Rupees. This is not what will satisfy the exigencies of the State. The high salaries paid to Civil Servants require closer attention. These high salaries were fixed at a time, when a voyage to India was a matter of six months and more, to induce good men to accept service in India. But times are altered. Steamers and telegraphs have placed England almost next door to India. A voyage to India now occupies of less than 3 weeks. Now, therefore, in the changed circumstances of the case, it cannot for a moment be seriously contended that those inducements in the shape of princely salaries are any longer required. There is a general complaint that the quality of the material we now get for the price paid has deteriorated very considerably. These officials are now too expensive, seeing that all they do could be accomplished by the Indians themselves. They have now become a luxury too costly for the means of the governed. Judged by our means, there can be no difference of opinion as to the necessity there is of reducing the salaries of the highly-paid public servants. The number of Civil Servants must be reduced. The Natives of the country should be more largely employed in the different branches of the public service on less pay than is given to Europeans. It is then and then alone that the cry of financial embarrassment will gradually cease to be heard. If additional expenditure be after all found absolutely necessary, if by judicious retrenchment and strict economy, it should be found impossible to provide ways and means for meeting the additional expenditure then the only course left open is to have recourse to taxation. We have now to consider which of the three courses now open to us is to be adopted :—(1) increase of Salt Duty, (2) reimposition of the Customs Duties, (3) and extension of the License Tax. In dealing with this part of the question, I may begin by stating that direct taxation is at present impossible, the highest limits having been already reached.

As regards the increase of *Salt Duty.* It would be unjust and unrighteous if the tax on salt should be increased. It is a necessary article both for human as well as animal well-being. It was but recently that the tax on this article of consumption was reduced and equalized. Since then there has been a steady increase in the income from salt and it would be bad policy and a retrograde movement to raise the tax, especially at a time when the poor millions of India are anxiously looking forward for a further reduction of the tax. It must be conceded on all hands that, in the interests of the poor of India, the price of salt cannot be too much cheapened. As any increase, therefore, of this tax will fall heavily upon the masses of the people of the land, I would strongly urge upon the attention of this Congress the necessity of its entering its strong protest against any attempt on the part of Government to raise the tax on salt.

Next comes '*The Import Duties.*' The Customs Duties, you will remember, were partially abolished by Lord Lytton's Government in 1878, and the rest, those on finer cottons, by its successors—entailing upon India the enormous loss in the aggregate of a little over a million pounds. This large sum was taken from the half-starved people of India and given away to the millionaires of Great Britain to secure to the party in power the votes of Lancashire. The duties on the coarser cottons were abolished, as the mover of the proposition stated, not at a time when the finances of the country were in a flourishing condition, but at a crisis when the country could ill-afford to lose such a revenue. It must be borne in mind that of all modes of taxation indirect taxation is the least offensive and the least oppressive. The Import Duties on Cotton goods have scarcely been ever felt and much less have been complained of. It was an act of gross injustice to poor India that, under the plea of extending Free Trade, English manufactures should be exempted from Customs Duties, when imported into India, while Indian products imported into England are still held liable to the same duties. Government would have acted fairly by

India if it had prepared India to compete successfully in the market with the machine-made articles of England, before it proceeded to do away with the above duties raised for revenue purposes only. The re-imposition of the cotton duties, therefore, would not only meet in a great measure the additional expenditure thrown on the Government of India but repair the fiscal injustice inflicted on this country. Furthermore, it would not be oppressive to the people and could be collected unseen and unfelt. If the amount thus raised be insufficient to meet the cost thrown upon the Government, then, I would suggest the extreme desirability of remodelling the License Tax, so as to bring the official and professional classes within the scope of its operation. It is the official and professional classes that benefit by the peace and security of the British rule in India and it is they that contribute the least to the revenues of the country. If the License Tax were so extended as to reach the official and professional classes and if a judicious gradation of the tax were adopted much of the odium now attaching to this tax would be removed.

Gentlemen, I have already trespassed upon your patience and exceeded the time allotted to me. I shall now leave the rest in the hands of Mr. Venkata Subbarayudu Garu, the supporter of this proposition, who I believe has devoted much time and attention to the study of this question.

With these few observations I have great pleasure in seconding the Resolution moved by my friend Mr. J. U. Yajnik.

Rao Saheb Singarajee Venkata Subbarayudu Pantulu Garu (Masulipatam) supported the Resolution in the following speech :—

The subject is one of paramount importance. If there is one subject which affects us most it is taxation. We admit that a goverment cannot be carried on without taxing its subjects. This is but a truism. It is equally true that heavy taxation impoverishes the people and defeats its object. Taxation, therefore, cannot proceed beyond a certain point. That we have reached this point has been admitted on all hands. The recent expression of a strong opinion on this matter by Lord Randolph Churchill in his budget speech obviates all necessity for giving reasons for this view. According to Dr. Hunter, a great authority on Indian statistics, forty millions of our countrymen go through life upon insufficient food. This number is gradually increasing. Unquestionably India is one of the poorest countries on the face of the earth. We are subject to periodical famines, and each famine carries away three or four million souls; while it reduces to a state of utter destitution fifty or sixty millions. The average income per head has been ascertained to be Rs. 27 per annum. This will not give one wholesome meal a day. Eighty per cent. of the population live by holding or tilling land. That land has been most heavily taxed has been proved to demonstration by the miserable condition of the agricultural classes who form the backbone of our country. Additional taxation in this direction is out of the question. But even granting that this is an overdrawn picture of the country, and that the country is fairly prosperous and wealthy, it will occur to one when additional taxation is proposed what is the necessity for it? The answer to this question is furnished by the present Secretary of State for India and other Russophobists. It is this—Russia wants to invade India which must be defended. The best way to defend India is to fortify the North-West frontier by building a chain of forts from Karachi to Peshawar and by increasing the standing army. Is it likely that Russia will invade India? Is the proposed method of defence absolutely indispensable for safeguarding India against Russian aggression? Russia is far away from us. Strong natural barriers and independent kingdoms lie between us. Russia's finances are not in a solvent condition. These circumstances alone will suffice to dispel from the minds of all reasonable men all delusions of Russian advance against India.

As to the second question, the proposed method of defending India is utterly uncalled for and useless. It has its advantages. I do not deny them. It will provide employment for large numbers of Europeans and Indians. It will create a large demand for materials of various descriptions in English and Indian markets. Apart from these, I see no advantages derivable from it. This step convinces Russia that the British Government is very nervous about its position in India and that that Government has begun to feel that it is not sufficiently strong to resist her at least with the existing means of defence. We have about 1,000 Native States small and large. They maintain an armed force of 381,000 men. The British Indian army is by no means small. We have 60,000 British soldiers in our service, and nearly double that number of sepoys. We have, therefore, a total force of 180,000. Discipline and train the Native armies, give them arms of precision. You can withdraw from the Native States 250,000 out of their 381,000 men and utilise them. You will have then a united force of about 500,000 men. The ternal peace of the country can very well be preserved by the Police and Volunteer Corps. Oppose this united army to Russia not in Afghanistan but on our North-West frontier. You will be able to annihilate the Russians. If our paternal and benevolent Government will adopt the policy of 'trust and fear not,' not a pie need be spent on defensive military preparations. Gentlemen, we are a grateful nation. We feel grateful to the British Government, for the immense benefits it has conferred upon us. We know that that Government is the only one in the world that could do us good. We know that the British nation is the richest nation in the world. We know that it is to our advantage to continue to be ruled by a nation, which possesses at once the best form of constitutional Government and the greatest wealth on the face of the globe and that Government has made us what we are and has given us all the best institutions we have at present. Therefore, there is no motive to be disloyal. Disloyalty is foreign to our nature. The history of the country proves it beyond all doubt. We consider a king as a god on earth. Have we ever as a nation tried to oust the established Government in this country? Have we not crushed those deluded people, who under an erroneous conception supposed that their religion was intentionally attacked by the introduction of greased cartridges? Has it not been admitted by impartial and enlightened Englishmen that their Government in this country is one by sufferance? If this has been so for nearly a century, what is there then to make us disloyal now? Every English knowing Indian is a patriotic soldier in the British cause. There are some Anglo-Indians who say that English education has awakened in us wishes and aspirations which are inconsistent with existing Government. There cannot be a more malicious and unfounded calumny than this. It is the interest of some of them to say so while others are led away by ignorance. The generous English nation knows that we are peaceful, loyal and law abiding. Gentlemen, our position is this: we are the children of our beloved mother Empress. We have been passing through a long minority. Some of us at least have arrived at majority. We solicit that those may in administrative matters be consulted by the servants of our mother. Our affectionate mother has most graciously promised to grant our prayer, but our elder brothers, to whose care that good mother has committed us, continue to misrepresent, that we are not fit to participate with them in the management of our affairs. We say this ought to be set right. For saying this, we are called disloyal. In the speech of Lord R. Churchill, there is a passage which we should protest against. In proposing to increase the Indian Army, he said he would require 20,000 sepoys and 10,000 British soldiers, to keep the sepoys down. Bearing in mind that it is the Indian sepoy who is the main-stay of British power here, it is a serious slur on his loyalty, I say to my English brethren, that utterance of Lord Randolph Churchill. You take the sepoy to Egypt, to Malta, Afghanistan and what not. He renders most praiseworthy services. He has placed his country at your feet and he has destroyed his countrymen, under your orders. You say you cannot do without him. But, you declare that he ought not to be trusted! Is this fair? Is this just? Can this be British fair play? I believe England and India would not approve of that rash observation. What pains an Indian most is to see that this policy of distrust has been growing. In the early days of the Company's rule, we had five sepoys to one British soldier. Just before the mutiny we had three sepoys to one British soldier. We have now two sepoys to one British soldier. Gentlemen, this state of things is grievous to us and discreditable to our rulers. In the matter of volunteering, the most loyal, patriotic and most respectable children of the soil have not been trusted. There is no cause for alarm. There is no real necessity for augmenting the strength of our army or for fortifying the frontier. You know, and know it only too well, that our views are not the views of our rulers. I would, therefore, say a few words as to what should be done if additional expenditure is unavoidable in the defence of the country. The first effort of a wise and benevolent Government, such as the one we have, should be to see if savings cannot be effected by curtailing current expenditure. The wisdom of this is admitted and printed circulars are constantly issued by our rulers on the subject. A chaprasee here, and a sweeper there, and an attendant or a dufter-bund in a third place have been dispensed with. This is not satisfactory. In spite of these orders, existing departments have been overgrowing and new ones are brought into being. I would ask that expenditure in certain branches of the administration may be retrenched at once. I will enumerate them if you will permit me.

1. Carry out the recommendations of the Simla Army Commission. Abolish the Presidency military commands and carry out the other suggestions mada by that Commision. This will effect a saving of Rs. 1,00,00,000.

2. Put a stop to gubernatorial migrations to olympian heights.

3. Don't undertake unremunerative public works, unless they are intended as protection against famine.

4. Abolish the system of purchasing stores required for India in England.

5. Cut down the salaries of the Civil Service. Employ Natives largely. Deputy Collectors can fairly do the work of Head Assistant Collectors and Sub-Collectors.

6. Discontinue payment of subsidy to Afghanistan and stop entertainments and durbars.

If extravagance of expenditure be put a stop to, enough money will be found for useful and necessary expenditure. Otherwise, we shall never be free from want. If ways and means should be devised, I would say re-impose the cotton duties. The unwise step of abolition was taken by a Conservative Viceroy and reluctantly completed by his Liberal successor. The free-trade principle urged in support of that step was a threadbare pretext. If more revenue is wanted—I don't think it will be—I say, extend the licence tax to the official and professional classes and to incomes derived from stocks or public debt irrespective of the fact whether the holder thereof lives in England or India.

Additional taxation and extravagant expenditure proceeding simultaneously would involve the British Indian Government in financial embarrassment from which the Government will find it difficult to extricate itself. These financial difficulties and additional taxes will create an enemy in the shape of a canker within the bosom of our paternal Government, and you know what it will do. The country will be impoverished; cultivators will abandon their lands and Government will follow their example and relinquish India. May heaven forbid this dire calamity. This will be worse than an invasion by Russia; therefore, the remedy proposed is worse than the disease. As for raising the salt tax, it is out of the question. We are paying Salt Tax at a rate varying from 500 to 2500 per cent on the cost of production. Men and live-stock cannot live without it. We vegetarian Indians absolutely need salt. The average income of an Indian ryot is a half pence per diem. Why not Lancashire and Birmingham and York and others, who are benefitted by India, contribute to our defence fund? Why cannot this be done by reviving the import duties?

I will, with your permission, quote from Ransome's work on "India and how we keep it:—'

"Now suppose for a moment that we were expelled from India or abandoned it; what would happen? Would things go on as they are? Certainly not. In the first case, a terrible blow to the purchasing power of India would be struck in the desperate struggle that would certainly ensue before we are defeated; and after we were gone, Russia would certainly endeavour by hostile tariffs, to cut us and our colonies out of all share of what trade might be left. In the second case, our abandonment of India would certainly be followed by an anarchy such as on a small scale followed the withdrawal of the Romans from Britain 1,400 years ago. In it all the work we have done for the material prosperity of the country would disappear; capital would fly before its attacks; the commercial prosperity of India, built up with so much toil, would perish like a dream."

"I need not picture to you the terrible results to England of such a catastrophe. We know something of bad times. No bad times that we have ever known would be even a shadow of what would ensue. Lancashire would be utterly ruined; Yorkshire would feel a terrible blow, and I hope you will agree with me that when we think of what value India is to us in the present, and what a mine of wealth it will be to our children and grand-children, that any one who for a moment suggests indifference to its fate, or stints his hand in doing what is needful for its maintainance, is trifling with the well being, not only of his fellow citizens, but of millions yet unborn."

Gentlemen the time alloted to me has been exceeded. I cannot detain you any longer. So I will close with these words that I would cordially support the resolution moved by Mr. Javerilal.

Mr. S. H. Chiplonkar proposed that a rider in the following words should be added to the resolution asking for an Imperial guarantee to the Indian debt:—"and, further that the Congress is of opinion that Great Britain should extend an imperial gurantee to the Indian debt."

The Hon'ble K. T. Telang seconded the proposal, observing that the arguments in support of this view have been collected together in one of the "Indian Leaflets" issued during the last English Elections.

The rider was accepted as part of the Resolution by the proposer and seconder.

Mr. Dayaram Jethmal proposed as an amendment that the words "secondly by the extension of the License Tax to the official and professional classes &c" be omitted. He said the extension of the License Tax in the proposed manner meant virtually the imposition of an Income Tax which he said was very unpopular and distasteful. He said he did not mean that the present License Tax should be retained as it is. He was no advocate of the License Tax. He thought the License Tax which affected the mercantile classes at present was equally bad. He objected on principle most strongly to any increase of taxation. The Resolution as worded would have the effect of proving to Government an unobjectionable way of raising a tax in this country. It could be understood very well how advantage would be taken of the expression of such views by the Congress. The Government does not sometimes mind acting on the principle, "give an inch and take an ell." The "if" in the Resolution was not enough. The Resolution pointed out the ways and means to carry out the proposal for an increased army expenditure, and was inconsistent with the Resolution on that question. The Government would necessarily impose an Income Tax and increase the army. That would be the effect of the Resolution.

The amendment was seconded by Mr. Oodharam but on being put to the vote was lost.

The original Resolution then with the rider was put to the vote and carried.

Mr. P. M. Mehta asked leave to bring in a motion about the Burman question, and in doing so said that he would not go into the question of the annexation which he thought was unwise, unjust and immoral. But he would only look at the matter from the Indian point of view. Lord Dufferin has said that the weakness of our North West Frontier disables him from giving as much attention as he would like to give to home affairs. What will be the result, when we have similar trouble on our North East Frontier also? He would say that if annexation was decided upon, they should make Burmah a Crown Colony; and then with Ceylon in the South and Burmah in the East, they could ask with greater strength and reason far more liberal institutions in India than she now possesses.

These remarks were received with so much applause that the President said he would take the applause as equivalent to a grant of leave to make the motion which was:— "That this Congress deprecates the annexation of Upper Burmah and considers that if the Government unfortunately decide on annexation, the entire country of Burmah should be separated from the Indian Viceroyalty and constituted a Crown Colony, as distinct in all matters from the Government of this country, as Ceylon."

Rao Bahadur Krishnaji Luxman Nulkar (Poona) seconded the motion made by Mr. P. M. Mehta. He said he was glad the Congress was taking up this burning subject, as he thought it was the duty of the Congress to do so. The financial burdens under which India is groaning are due in a most serious measure to the First Afghan war. The annexations of Sindh and the Punjaub were the outcome of that war— and the aggressions of Russia might be said to be traceable to those early aggressions of our own British Government. We must, therefore, raise our voice against these aggressions which are in character precisely similar. The difficulties occasioned will be such as will defy any remedy being applied. There will be increased taxation, for the necessity of fortifications at the North East frontier will arise much earlier than it did in the case of the N. W. Frontier. The course of this Burman business shows indifference in the first instance, and then all of a sudden a change, and a declaration of war for the interests of trade. If the annexation is in the interests of trade, let the country be made a Colony, and add British Burmah to that Colony, if that is thought expedient.

[A member] Burmah is a paying province.

I doubt that. It was similarly said that the Punjaub was a paying province, but the accounts show a very different result. For it must be remembered that in consequence of the annexation of the Punjaub the frontier military expenditure had to be increased. This sort of increased expenditure is generally omitted from the calculation when the remunerative character of annexed provinces is talked of.

The Hon'ble S. Subrahmanya Iyer asked whether it was desirable to retain the earlier part of the resolution. Might not the Congress merely content itself with saying that if unfortunately the decision of the authorities is to be as threatened, India ought not to be affected or disturbed by the effects of such a decision ?

Mr. Swaminath Iyer and Professor Sundadara Ramana spoke in support of this suggestion.

Mr. P. M. Mehta pointed out that the adoption of this suggestion might exhibit the force of the opposition to the annexation policy as being weaker than it really was. This view being then accepted by The Hon'ble Subrahmanya Iyer and others the Resolution was passed unanimously.

Mr.. Murlidhar (Umballa) then rose to propose the Eighth Resolution:—"That the Resolutions proposed by this Congress be communicated to the political associations in each province, and that these associations be requested with the help of similar bodies and other agencies within their respective provinces to adopt such measures as they may consider calculated to advance the settlement of the various questions dealt with in these Resolutions"

Mr. Murlidhar said that the Congress must take some steps to give effect to the Resolutions passed. Their opponents were sure to misrepresent and perhaps vilify them. And, therefore, it was necessary that the opinion of the intelligent classes among their countrymen should be brought out upon all the subjects discussed by the Congress.

Mr. H. H. Dhurva (Surat) seconded this resolution and it was carried unanimously.

It was next proposed by Mr. Hume and seconded by The Hon'ble S. Subrahmanya Iyer:—"That the Indian National Congress reassemble next year in Calcutta, and sit on Tuesday, the 28th of December 1886, and the succeeding days."

The Hon'ble Subrahmanya Iyer in seconding the Resolution said that Madras would be most ready to welcome the Congress, if they were pleased to fix Madras at their next place of meeting. But he thought Calcutta was the appropriate place for the purpose.

The Resolution was carried unanimously.

The President said he could say on behalf of his brethren of Bengal that though owing to various unfortunate and accidental circumstances Bengal was not largely represented at this Congress as was to be desired, that the

Congress had the warm sympathy of that Presidency which would give them a cordial welcome when they met there next year.

Mr. G. Subramanya Iyer then proposed and Mr. S. Agnihotri seconded the proposition:—"That the thanks of the Congress be offered to the Managing Committee and officers of the Gokuldas Tejpal Charities for their kindness in allowing the use of the Gowalia Tank House to the Congrass, and in rendering other valuable assistance to the Members, as also to the Secretaries of the Bombay Presidency Association and those associated with them." Mr. Murlidhar in supporting the proposition said he had one complaint to make against his Bombay friends. He charged them with theft. They had robbed him of his heart.

The Resolution was carried by acclamation.

The Hon'ble K. T. Telang in responding said, that it had been a great disappointment to Poona that owing to untoward circumstances the place of the meeting had to be changed after their preparations had made considerable progress. The Trustees of the Gokuldas Charities also deserved special thanks for their help in the matter rendered at excessively short notice.

A cordial vote of thanks to the President for his very-able conduct in the chair was then proposed by Mr. P. M. Mehta and carried by acclamation. Three cheers were next called for Mr. A. O. Hume which having been given.

Mr. Hume, after acknowledging the honour done him, said that as the giving of cheers had been entered on he must be allowed to propose, on the principle of better late than never, the giving of cheers, and that not only three, but three times three, and if possible thrice that for one the latchet of whose shoes he was unworthy to loose, one to whom they were all dear, to whom they were all as children—need he say Her Most Gracious Majesty, the Queen-Empress.

The rest of the speaker's remarks were lost in the storm of applause that instantly burst out and the asked for cheers were given over and over again with a vehemence and enthusiasm rarely equalled.

The Congress was then dissolved.

latchet of whose shoes he was unworthy to loose, one to whom they were all dear, to whom they were all as children—need he say Her Most Gracious Majesty, the Queen-Empress.

The rest of the speaker's remarks were lost in the storm of applause that instantly burst out and the asked-for cheers were given over and over again with a vehemence and enthusiasm rarely equalled.

The Congress was then dissolved.

APPENDIX A.

Adoption of the foregoing Resolutions in all parts of the country.

The foregoing Resolutions were widely circulated in the larger towns in all parts of the country and new public meetings or meetings of existing Associations were held for the purpose of considering them. In most places all the Resolutions were unanimously adopted ; in one or two, there was a difference of opinion as regards the total abolition of the " India Council", and as regards the necessity of a stay in England on the part of selected candidates for the Civil Service. Both these points were referred to in the debates of the Congress (see pp. 53, 69, 101, supra). And it is probable that with the explanations afforded by the debates, which of course were not generally available at the time, these differences of opinion may be found to be smaller than they are at present.

Communications have been received from the following places, showing the acceptance of the Resolutions of the Congress.

Bengal.—Berhanpur, Bhagalpur, Balasore, Cuttack, Mymensing, Dacca, Rajshaye, Bankipore.

Bombay.—Ahmadabad, Ahmadnagar, Alibag, Belgaum, Carwar, Dhulia, Hydrabad (Sindh), Karachi, Poona, Ratnagiri, Satara, Solapur, Surat, Thana.

N. W. Provinces and Oudh.—Allahabad, Benares, Bulandshahar, Fyzabad, Lucknow.

Madras.—Adoni, Anantapur, Ariyahir, Bapatlal Bezvada, Calicut, Chintalpudi, Coconada, Coimbatore, Cuddalore, Cuddappah, Erode, Gooty, Guntur, Kulitilai, Kumbakonam, Madras, Madura, Manargudi Masulipatam, Melur, Mettapollium, Mylapore, Negapatam, Palabur, Panruti, Rajahimandry, Sattur, Srirangam Sinckerrydoorg, Tanjore, Tinnevelly, Tiruchangad, Trinchinopolly, Triplicane, Trivellore, Vellore.

At Bapatla, the majority of the meeting resolved:— "That there ought to be a Council with enlarged powers to check the action of the Secretary of State, or, in case of this not being possible, the present Council should stand as it is."

At Ahmedabad, Anantapur, Calicut Guntur, and Masulipatam, there was a difference of opinion as to the necessity of selected candidates for the Civil Service staying in England. At Anantapur, the following proposal was carried:—"That the successful candidates in India may be sent to England, for further study, and allowed there to appear for such further examinations as may seem needful, provided, however, that being sent to England should not be compulsory, and those who prefer going to England should be entitled to full pay, and those that do not only two-thirds pay of the post to which they are appointed." At Calicut, the following resolution was proposed but rejected by a majority. "And that the successful candidates in England should be sent to India for further study, and subjected here to such further examinations as may seem needful."

At Calicut, two members dissented from the Resolution about Military Expenditure.

At Masulipatam, the resolution to extend the License Tax to the legal profession was objected to by a majority of the meeting on the ground that the Government already levied an entrance fee from members of the Profession and that there was a Municipal Tax imposed upon them.

APPENDIX B.

Political progress in India.

(From the "Times's" Bombay Correspondent.)
Times's Weekly Edition, Feb. 5th 1886.

Bombay, Dec. 31.

The people of Bombay claim as the motto for their city "*Urbs prima in Indis*," and it is really not without reason. When the agitation over the Ilbert Bill was at white heat, and in Calcutta not only race division, but even division between English and English rendered social intercourse almost impossible, still the natives in Bombay kept their heads cool and discussed the question at a great representative meeting in the Town-hall with a discretion and moderation that left nothing to be desired. At the time of Lord Ripon's departure they showed themselves capable of organizing an ovation which not merely delighted the sympathizers with the recent benignant rule, but still more startled the great mass of Anglo-Indians as the first proof that the natives of India are really capable of a national movement.

This last week the Bombay leaders have again given proof of their organizing power. They brought together a national congress composed of delegates from every political society of any importance throughout the country. Seventy-one members met together; 29 great districts sent spokesmen. The whole of India was represented from Madras to Lahore, from Bombay to Calcutta. For the first time, perhaps, since the world began India as a nation met together. Its congeries of races, its diversity of castes, all seemed to find common ground in their political aspirations. Only one great race was conspicuous by its absence; the Mahomedans of India were not there. They remained steadfast in their habitual separation. They certainly do not yield to either

Hindu or Parsee in their capacity for development, but they persistently refuse to act in common with the rest of the Indian subjects of the Queen-Empress. Not only in their religion, but in their schools, and almost all their colleges, and all their daily life they maintain an almost haughty reserve. The reason is not hard to find. They cannot forget that less than two centuries ago they were the dominant race, while their present rivals in progress only counted as so many millions of taxpaying units who contributed each his mite to swell the glory of Islam.

But, in spite of the absence of the followers of the Prophet, this was a great representative meeting last week. The delegates were mostly lawyers, schoolmasters, and newspaper editons, but there were some notable exceptions. Even supposing those three professions alone provided the delegates, the meeting would fairly represent the education and intellectual power of India. And now let us see what they did, what was the outcome of this important gathering. They discussed politics alone; not a word was said of social reform. They evidently had a firm belief that a nation could be made happy by Acts of Parliament, for all they discussed and all they demanded was political power and political changes. A tone of most absolute loyalty pervaded all the proceedings; the Empress was rapturously applauded, and many nice things were said of the beneficent effect of British rule. Education and material prosperity, order, security, and good government were all incidentally mentioned as causes of gratitude towards the present rulers. But such allusions were only by the way. Every desire was concentrated on political advancement and an immense increase of the share at present given to the natives of India in the government of their own country. The question of their ability to govern themselves was never even touched by the wisest of the speakers. The major premiss of all the arguments seemed to be "Every Hindoo is a born administrator. It is mere Western folly to think that representative government is an act which only comes by long political training in all the lower stages of a citizen life and the patient selection of the fittest." Much stress was laid on the need of a monster Commission of Inquiry into the whole existing administrative fabric. The vials of patriotic wrath were opened on the Indian Council, and a Standing Committee of the House of Commons was thought a panacea for all evils. But though there was much crude talk, much of that haste which only makes delay, and that ignorance which demands premature concessions, there was also much of most noble aspiration and a sense of patriotism and national unity which is a new departure in the races of the East.

even touched by the wisest of the speakers. The major premise of all the arguments seemed to be: "Every Hindu is a born administrator. It is mere Western folly to think that representative government is an art which only comes by long political training in all the lower stages of a citizen life and the patient selection of the fittest." Much stress was laid on the need of a monster Commission of Inquiry into the whole existing administrative fabric. The vials of patriotic wrath were opened on the Indian Council, and a Standing Committee of the House of Commons was thought a panacea for all evils. But though there was much crude talk, much of that haste which only makes delay, and that ignorance which demands premature concessions, there was also much of most noble aspiration and a sense of patriotism and national unity which is a new departure in the races of the East.

APPENDIX C

The Indian Congress.

(EDITORIAL OF THE *Times* ON THE ABOVE.)

Bombay' has been making, a noteworthy effort to substantiate its claim to be the leading city of India. At the end of last year it was the gathering-place of a National Congress, brought together from all parts of the country for the discussion of public affairs. It is at Bombay, therefore, that India has for the first time given proof of the existence of a national life and spirit. In India, as elsewhere, there is abundant room for improvement, not altogether, perhaps, in the directions to which the Congress points, nor by the methods in which it chiefly trusts. The resolutions cover a wide ground. Some of them we very heartily approve. Others appear to us something more than questionable. But from first to last there is one common idea running through them. The Congress is not satisfied with the slender political power which the Natives of India possess. It demands for them a larger share in the deliberative and executive functions of government. The memory of Lord Ripon's administration is still held in honour at Bombay, and the Congress there met has given utterance to aspirations which Lord Ripon has had no small share in encouraging. On the representive character of the late Congress our information is not precise Our correspondent tells us who were there and who were not there. Every important political society in India sent its delegates to Bombay, but of whom these political societies consist and for whom they can claim a right to speak we are not told. One great section of the Native population was conspicuously not there. No Mahomedan took any part in the proceedings. The members present were drawn, for the most part, from three orders—native lawyers, native schoolmasters and native newspaper editors. There were some notable exceptions, but the rule was as we have said. It is what we might have expected beforehand. The work of the Congress has certainly been intrusted to the hands most likely to be found capable of performing it and most forward in offering themselves for it. A more mixed assembly would have been less competent, perhaps, but its claim to be representatives all round might have been admitted with less doubt.

The first resolution of the Congress was in favour of a Royal Commission of Inquiry into the working of the Indian Administration. There is good ground for the request. It is now nearly thirty years since the government of the country was transferred from the East India Company to the Crown, and for so long a time no such inquiry has been held. In former days it was of regular periodical recurrence as often as the time came for a renewal of the Company's charter. The need for it has been now recognized. The Commission for which the Congress asks was mentioned in the Queen's Speech, and, since Mr. Gladstone has signified his strong approval of it, we may expect that it will be issued whatever political party may be in power. It is a matter of course that the people of India will be represented upon it, and that all available evidence will be taken to guide the Commissioners to a judgment upon the whole case. How far the results of the inquiry will correspond with the hopes of the Congress is a wholly different question. The delegates have sketched in advance a scheme of reforms or changes which they wish to see carried into effect. First and foremost, and as a necessary preliminary to all other reforms, the Indian Council is to be abolished, and its place to be taken by a Standing Committee of the House of Commons. In India itself the Supreme Legislative Council and the several provincial Councils are to be expanded by the admission of a considerable number of elected members. Thus reformed, they are to have a necessary voice on all questions of finance, and a right to interpellate the executive on all points of administration. If protests are raised and overruled, the protesting members are to have a right of appeal to the Standing Committee by which the present Indian Council is to be replaced. Changes are next proposed in the rules for the examinations of candidates for the Indian Civil Service. The Congress asks, *inter alia*, that these examinations should be held in England and in India simultaneously, and that the admissible age of competing candidates should be 23 at least. As regards finance, the Congress holds that the increased and, as it believes, the needless demands for more military expenditure are most properly to be met by retrenchment in other branches. But if this is not done, and if more money must be raised, the Congress looks in the first place to a re-imposition of the customs duties, and secondly to extension of the licence tax. This second demand has been granted. The Income Tax Bill was passed after a short debate, in the course of which the various restricting amendments proposed to it were lost. The final demand of the Congress that Great Britain should extend a guarantee to the Indian debt has not been granted in terms, and is not likely to be. But while the English rule exists in India, there is enough of a practical guarantee to give absolute safety to the bondholders. The Congress is further prepared to offer advice on the Burmese question. Its objection to the annexation of Upper Burmah comes a little too late. Its claim that all Burmah should in any case be separated from India and should be constituted a Crown colony includes matter on which it has an imperfect right to speak. The separation of Burmah and the consequent loss of the Burmah surplus revenue it may very properly ask. But what is to be done with the country afterwards it is for England rather than for India to determine. The approaching visit of the Indian Viceroy to Mandalay will put him in a position to give advice on this matter.

The first question which this series of resolutions will suggest is whether India is ripe for the transformation which they involve. If this can be answered in the affirmative, the days of English rule are numbered. If India can govern itself, our stay in the country is no longer called for. All we have to do is to preside over the construction of the new system and then to leave it to work. The lawyers and schoolmasters and newspaper editors will step into the vacant place and will conduct affairs with no help from us. Those who know India best will be the first to recognize the absurd impracticability of such a change. But it is to nothing less than this that the resolutions of the Congress point. If they were carried out, the result would soon be that very little would remain to England except the liability which we should have assumed for the entire Indian debt. Then, however, would be the time at which the representative character of the late Congress would be subjected to a crucial test. Our correspondent tells us that the delegates fairly represent the education and intellectual power of India. That they can talk, and that they can write, we are in no doubt at all. The whole business of their lives has been a training for such work as this. But that they can govern wisely, or that they can enforce submission to their rule, wise or unwise, we are not equally sure. That the entire Mahomedan population of India has steadily refused to have anything to do with them is a sufficiently ominous fact. Even if the proposed changes were to stop short of the goal to which they obviously tend, they would certainly serve to weaken the vigour of the Executive and to make the good government of the country a more difficult business than it has ever been. The Viceroy's Council already includes some nominated native members. To throw it open to elected members, and to give minorities a statutable right to be heard before a Parliamentary Committee, would be an introduction of Home Rule for India in about as troublesome a form as could be devised. Do what we will the government of India cannot be made constitutional. If it works well, neither England nor India can have any reason to be dissatisfied with it. The educated classes may find fault with their exclusion from full political rights. Political privileges they can obtain in the degree in which they prove themselves deserving of them. But it was by force that India was won, and it is by force that India must be governed, in whatever hands the government of the country may be vested. If we were to withdraw, it would be in favour not of the most fluent tongue or of the most ready pen, but the strongest arm and the sharpest sword. It would, perhaps, be well for the members of the late Congress to reconsider their position from this very practical point of view.

APPENDIX D.

The Hon'ble K. T. Telang's Letter to "The Times" dated 9th March 1886, touching the remarks made in the foregoing correspondence about the Mahomedan community and Social Reform.

TO THE EDITOR OF "THE TIMES."

Sir.—The letter of your Bombay correspondent, dated 31st December last, regarding the Indian National Congress, together with your editorial article based upon it, has been read here with much interest. The members of the Congress have not much reason to complain of the account of their work given by your correspondent, and they must feel grateful to you for the amount of sympathy manifested in your remarks upon it. At the same time it seems probable that some of the conclusions arrived at in your article would have been modified, if some further details of the proceedings of the Congress had been brought to your notice. As one of the Secretaries of the Congress, therefore, and with the approval of the President, I beg to send you some particulars regarding two important points made in your article.

The first point is in reference to your remark that the Mahomedans of India were conspicuous by their absence at the Congress. Although it must be admitted that the Mahomedan community was not adequately represented at our meeting, your remark is not altogether an accurate one. Two leading Mahomedan gentlemen did attend the Congress, *viz.*, Mr. R. M. Sayani and Mr. A. M. Dharamsi. Both of these gentlemen are graduates of the University and attorneys of standing at the High Court of Bombay. Mr. Sayani held the office of Sheriff of Bombay last year; was a member of the Khoja Law Commission appointed by Government some years ago; and has for many years past been a member of the Municipal Corporation and Town Council of Bombay. Mr. Dharamsi, also, is a member of the Municipal Corporation of Bombay. Further, the Hon. Mr. Badroodin Tyabji, a member of the Legislative Council at Bombay, and Mr. Cumroodin Tyabji would have attended the Congress, had they not been absent from Bombay at the time the Congress was sitting. Mr. Badroodin is Chairman of the Managing Committee and Mr. Cumroodin one of the vice-presidents of the Bombay Presidency Association, which, in concert with the Poona Sarvajanik Sabha, convened the Congress. As regards the other provinces, causes similar to the above indicated must doubtless have operated with greater force. And it must be remembered that this Congress was the first of its kind, and naturally, therefore, there were some shortcomings. But we feel confident that next year, when the assemblage will be at Calcutta, the Mahomedan community will be represented as it befits its numbers and importance. The second point relates to the omission of social reform from the proceedings of the Congress. As regards this, it is to be observed that the main object of the Congress was a political one. But when the programme of business was informally discussed by the members, they decided that after the subjects for which they had specially assembled were disposed of, questions of social reform should be considered if there was time. As it happened there was no time to do this, because several of our members were obliged to leave for their respective homes on the third day of our meeting. But on that day, a very earnest social reformer, Divan Bahadur Raghunath Rao, of Madras, gave an eloquent address on social questions, and he was followed by another eminent reformer, the Hon. M. G. Ranade, of this Presidency. You will probably consider that the importance of social reform is even more powerfully recognised when it is eagerly discussed by persons avowedly assembled for another purpose than when it is taken up in ordinary course as part of a formal programme. I hope you will give insertion to this in your journal.

I am, &c.,

K. T. TELANG.

High Court, Bombay, 9th March.

APPENDIX E.

Telegrams despatched by the Indian National Telegraph Union to London.

(To the Daily News.)

1885.

No. 1. *On 15th April:*—The Association* during the present political crisis has received from all parts of the country strong and universal assurances of sympathy with England. The feeling of the Indian Princes and people was never more loyal. All the principal Indian Princes including Cashmere, Holkar, Mysore, Scindia, Gaikawad, Nizam, have voluntarily offered their cordial co-operation. People everywhere showing enthusiasm with British rule against Russian aggression. Native volunteering advocated everywhere and by the whole of the Native Press. Offers have been made to the Viceroy by 400 principal Natives of the Bengal Presidency consisting of Zemindars, barristers, officials, graduates, to enlist. In the Madras Presidency enlistment has already commenced. A similar feeling is manifested in Bombay, Poona and elsewhere. This unprecedented manifestation is everywhere regarded as a striking justification of the policy of the Royal Proclamation as carried out and brought home to the people during Lord Ripon's Administration. This Association gave Lord Reay an address of welcome which while pointing out the necessity of various internal reforms unreservedly expressed confidence in and attachment to the British Government.

2. *On 7th May:*—Great satisfaction felt at determination of Government to avoid war, if possible. Every confidence in the Gladstone Ministry on this point. No danger of Native loyalty being impaired by peace with Russia. War would retard internal reforms happily commenced by Lord

* This telegram was despatched by the Bombay Presidency Association on behalf of the I. N. T. Union.

Ripon which have evoked such marked good-will throughout the country. The desire to support Government by Volunteering becoming stronger and more general.

3. *On 30th July* :—Native Community view with great alarm rumoured establishment British Cantonment Kandahar, because it will paralyse peace negociations and suggest forward movement on part of Russia, because even though Amir may consent it will involve complications with Afghan people, because it will entail serious and useless extra expenditure. Country already suffering from retrenchments necessitated by recent preparations for war. Many useful and popular schemes checked for wants of funds.

Great satisfaction at Lord Churchill's renewed declaration in favour of inquiry into Government of India Act, 1858. Strong feeling in favour of reform or alterations of Indian Council. Fresh nominations to Council deprecated.

(To Mr. John Slagg, M.P.)

4. *On 8th June* :—Great satisfaction here at your motion for inquiry into Government of India Act, 1858. Subject much discussed by Native Press. Steps being taken to hold meetings and petition Parliament thereon. Fawcett's opinion strongly upheld, namely, Parliamentary inquiry into Act. extremely important work for new Parliament.

5. *On 5th August* :—On Indian Budget Debate please bring on motion for Parliamentary inquiry into Government of India Act. Feeling against Indian Council unanimous.

(To The Daily News.)

6. *On 27th August* :—Telegraphic summary Lord Randolph's Budget Speech widely discussed by Native Press. Full text anxiously awaited now received. Attack on Ripon's frontier and financial policy unanimously condemned by Native public opinion. *Bombay Gazette*, influential and impartial exponent of Anglo-Indian opinion, elaborately exposes exaggerations and misstatements of speech which it calls thoroughly partisan. Between frontier policies adopted by Beaconsfield and Gladstone Governments, no hesitation here. Thoroughly understood that former policy chimerical, dangerous, designed rather to gratify army and portion of official hierarchy than safeguard interests of India. Situation not really changed by advance of Russia long foreseen on Merv. Leading sentiment of Afghans fear of losing independence now threatened by Russian advance. Thus their present friendly temper towards English alliance furnishes remarkable confirmation of wisdom of resolution to evacuate Kandahar and abandon forward policy. Similarly, present disposition of Indian people so radically different from what it was under Lytton undeniable fruit of Ripon's farsighted and liberal domestic policy. Such policy best preparation for securing safety of Empire by developing resources, conciliating affection of all classes, and avoiding costly aggressive enterprises.

Additional permanent military expenditure of two millions viewed with great anxiety. Increased military strength should be sought in preparations within Indian frontier, utilising support of Native volunteers, and help cordially offered by Native Princes.

Promised inquiry into system of Indian Government and declared readiness to listen to enlightened Indian opinion regarded with satisfaction ; but all feel that promised boons but empty shadows if disastrous policy of Lytton Strachey regime adopted by present Government and forced on Indian people.

7. *On 4th September* :—Large enthusiastic meeting last Wednesday for Fawcett Memorial. Lord Reay presided, all classes joined. Great stress laid on Fawcett's advocacy of economy in Indian finance. Gratitude expressed for his disinterested and distinguished services to India. Influential representative Committee appointed to collect funds and determine form of Memorial. Sympathy expressed and support promised by Provincial centres. Nawab of Junaghad subscribed £100. One speaker remarked amidst vociferous applause that if India and England united as Fawcett wished, they might defy 100 Russias.

8. *On 11th September:*—Government proposal to add 30,000 men to peace effective Indian army, besides large expenses on frontier defences and Railways, has created general alarm. Necessity of this expenditure disputed, and generally felt that burden will be unendurable. Thoroughly understood that domestic reform and developing country's resources must be laid aside. Also, general fear that present Government in permanent power may under military influences be tempted or driven into wasteful perilous foreign policy from which Elections of 1880 delivered India. Lord Randolph's recent speeches grieved and surprised people as not showing independence expected from one having personal experience of Indian opinion. He now appears as mouthpiece of small official clique hostile to Ripon.

9. *On 17th September* :—Active movement in India to bring Indian topics before Electors of United Kingdom. Delegates already left.

Dadabhai Naoroji nominated to Legislative Council. Lord Reay's nomination of him and Madhev Govind Ranade highly approved everywhere.

10. *On 17th September* :—British Indian Association, Indian Association of Calcutta, Mahajan Sabha of Madras, Poona Sarvajanik Sabha, Sind Sabha have joined this Association* in united movement to bring Indian topics before British Electors. This Association held important meeting and adopted General Appeal to Electors urging fulfilment of Parliamentary and Royal pledges with Parliamentary inquiry how far

* Bombay Presidency Association.

already redeemed. Confirmed appointment of Delegates to London from Calcutta. Madras and Bombay. Gratitude expressed to Bright and Hartington and goodwill for candidature of Slagg, Ghose, Digby, Phear and others. Temple and others not recognised to represent Indian interests.

11. *On 7th October* :—Madras Mahajan Sabha held meeting, to bring Indian questions before British Electors, adopted Rajah Sir Madhevrao's instructions to Indian Delegates: to gratefully acknowledge benefits of British rule ; solicit greater attention to Indian affairs, sympathy for Indian feelings and aspirations ; plead for moderate taxation necessaries of life, and security of land tenure : explain material benefits from connection of India and England placing reliance on British wisdom, justice and generosity.

12. *On 14th October* :—Native Press intelligently discusses and condemns proposed increased Military expenditure. No evidence showing increase required for necessary effective strength.

13. *On 26th September* :—Public warned against telegrams tending promote war with Burmah. Alleged provocation disputed between Bombay Burmah Trading Company and Burmah Government about sale of timber. Indian tax payers' interest not sufficient justify war. Shareholders accepted risk to profit by monopoly.

14. *On 5th November* :—*Times's* Calcutta Correspondent misinformed in ascribing partisan motives to Indian Delegates' Mission. Objects fully explained in this Association's proceedings and reply to Sir Jamshedji Jeejeebhoy's resignation. Printed copies now in Delegates' hands for distribution. Native Press condemns Sir Jamshedji's action.

Sir Charles Aitchison's appointment of Native Judge, Punjaub Chief Court, given great satisfaction in Punjaub and generally approved.

Public feeling against appointment of Resident at Kashmir.

Late Maharaja opposed it as affecting his position New Maharaja assiduous at administrative reforms.

15. *On 20th November* :—Indian public expresses hearty gratitude at sympathetic receptions Indian Delegates in England. Large audiences assembled to hear them very gratifying as showing readiness of British people to hear India's appeal even during election turmoils.

Burmah War viewed with disfavour by Indian opinion and annexation protested against as causing complications. King Theebaw's misconduct insufficient ground for depriving Burmese people of independence.

(To the Manager Press Association.)

16. *On 31st December* :—Indian National Congress, embracing nearly hundred distinguished representatives from all parts of Empire, concluded after three days' continuous debate. Mr. W. C. Bonnerji, Standing Counsel, Calcutta, presiding. Honourables S. Subramania Iyer, Dadabhai Naoroji, Kashinath Trimbuk Telang, M. G. Ranade ; Messrs. P. M. Mehta, Rao R. Raghunathrao, Satyanand Agnihotri, A. O. Hume, S. D. White, present. Passed Resolution urging that promised inquiry into Indian affairs should be by Royal Commission on which Natives should be represented—evidence being taken in India and England ; proposing abolition of the India Council, introduction of representative element into Supreme and Local Legislative Councils, including additional Councils for North West Provinces and Punjaub, with general right of interpellation, and power to discuss financial questions, provision being made to refer to a Standing Committee of the House of Commons any formal protests of such Councils ; opening of all civil departments to all Statutory natives with simultaneous examinations in England and India, raising of maximum age of Civil Service examination to 23 ; objecting to increased military experditure; demanding Imperial guarantee to Indian Debt and extension License tax to professions and officials, and reimposition of Import Duties, if additional taxation absolutely indispensable ; deprecating annexation Upper Burmah and suggesting, if annexation determined, making whole Burmah Crown Colony entirely distinct from Government of India. Congress closed with enthusiastic cheers for Queen Empress. After Congress, Delegates and large Bombay gathering discussed questions Hindu Social Reform.

1886.

17. *On 14th January* :—Great public meeting held here, welcome Indian Delegates returned from England. Delegates acknowledged gratefully interest and sympathy evinced, by British public, specially working men. Delegates' work enthusiastically approved as wholy successful.

18. *On 22nd January*:—People of India appeal to people of England to instruct representatives to support Hunter's intended motion condemning annexation of Upper Burmah to India, and earnestly trust this question may be decided solely on principles of right and justice. Annexation under pretext of opening new markets condemned as unworthy of England and deprecated as strengthening Military and despotic tendencies in Government.

19. *On 28th January*:—Influential crowded Meeting at Madras to welcome Delegate returned from England. Rajas Nilambore, Calicut, Ramnad present and took part. Telegrams of sympathy received from public meetings at 21 provincial centres. Delegate enlarged on sympathy of British and expressed admiration of English home-life. Thanks voted to all Delegates. Meeting separated with cheers for Queen.

20. *On 4th February*:—Bombay Association forwarded detailed Memorial to Indian Secretary against necessity two millions permanent additional annual military charge. For imperial defence England should bear equitable share. Each Indian Finance Minister has vainly protested against unjust encroachments of War Office of Indian revenues. Laing, Balfour held fourteen millions army charge sufficient. Now seventeen millions without increased number or efficiency. Salisbury, Northbrook, Argyll, Sandhurst, Lytton, quoted. Memorial recommends provide additional strength by reducing noneffective military charges, and Native Volunteers to keep internal order. Should avoid taxation on population with average yearly income forty shillings.

Chief Justice Garth proceeding on leave. Rumoured English junior supersedes Native Justice Mitter who acted, 1883. Much indignation, Calcutta, supposed reversal Ripon policy.

Popular demonstration Krishnaghur. Welcomed Manmohan Ghose returned Indian Delegate. Crowd gave cheers for Deptford Liberal Electors.

21. *On 12th February*:—Much satisfaction felt at Lord Ripon's joining Cabinet. Indian opinion had hoped he would be Indian Secretary.

General disapproval of haste passing Income Tax Bill.

Financial Committee appointed does not command confidence. Members official with one exception.

22. *On 22nd February* :—Much disappointment and regret at the proposal of Ministry to throw Burman War expenses on India. Adverse opinion strong. Whole Burman question exciting keen criticism and much feeling.

23. *On 6th March* :—Requisition to Sheriff, Bombay, largely and influentially signed by Europeans, and Natives for Public Meeting to ask for Royal Commission on Indian affairs. Lord Dufferin's declaration of Ministry preferring Parliamentary Committee over Royal Commission, not considered satisfactory. Old precedents relied on not applicable as circumstances changed and Indian public opinion grown stronger. Local Meetings being held throughout India, ratifying resolution of Indian National Congress regarding Royal Commission.

(To the Right Hon'ble W. E. Gladstone, Prime Minister.)

24. *On 23rd February* :—United Associations Bengal, Madras, Bombay, earnestly pray inquiry into Indian affairs should be by Royal Commission containing English statesmen and competent Indians. No Anglo-Indian official as already telegraphed by Bengal Chamber of Commerce. Commission would take evidence here. This essential. Parliamentary Committee of 1871 on Indian Finance rendered fruitless by dissolution.

25. *On 26th March* :—General disappointment expressed at Parliamentary Committee instead of Royal Commission. Little hope Indian witnesses of age, experience, position visiting England. Peers nomination well received. Commons' nomination inspire no confidence as Anglo-Indian official element strong. Independent Indian interest weak.

(To the Manager Press Association.)

26. *On 9th April* :—Monster meeting of agriculturists in Jessore district of Bengal. Confirmed resolutions of National Congress. Other public affairs, like administration of criminal law and taxation, discussed. Right of representation in government desired. Honourable Tyabji, Mahomedan Member of Council, publicly declared Indian Mahomedans cordially sympathising with other sections of nations in Congress resolutions and political movements generally.

27. *On 21st April* :—Anglo-Indian and Native Press condemns Grant Duff's Government for mode of disposing of charges brought by Crole, Collector of Madura, against Thomas, Senior Member of Council. On ex-parte report twenty Native officers recently dismissed or degraded for recommending remission Land Revenue on account of disastrous flood. No opportunity for explanation afforded. Report kept confidential. Public feeling much excited. Numerous meetings to protest being held..

28. *On 25th June* :—Deep grief felt at the death of two great Maratha Princes, Holkar and Sindhia. They were two of the most loyal friends of British Power among Indian Princes. Holkar's son adult and was invested with powers during father's lifetime. Sindhia's son minor. Arrangement for government of the States believed satisfactory.

Ensuing elections watched with keen interest, especially candidature of Hon'ble Dadabhai Naoroji and Lalmohan Ghose. Desire keenly felt and universally expressed for their success. Much gratitude felt to Holborn and Deptford for supporting Indian candidates. Public meetings to express confidence will soon be held.

Much anxiety felt about Thibet mission. Misgivings entertained about fresh developments of activity on frontier.

No regret felt at collapse of Parliamentary Committee on India. Preference for Royal Commission confirmed. Proposed Indian Civil Service Committee not regarded with satisfaction.

Correspondence touching Sullivan—Crole case of Madras partially published. Much adverse comment on Grant Duff and his government. Independent investigation insisted upon as indispensable.

29. *On 30th June* :—Crowded Public Meeting held here, 29th. All communities represented. Dinshaw Petit presided, opened proceedings, eulogising worth Lal Mohun Ghose and invaluable patriotic public services of Dadabhai Naoroji. Resolution expressing confidence in both and gratitude to electors, Holborn and Deptford, passed amid enthusiastic cheers. Sympathising telegrams received from public meetings held at all principal stations in Presidency.

30. *On 30th July* :—A very crowded influential Meeting held at Calcutta last week, protesting against Simla Exodus. All classes of people, European and Native, fairly represented. Eloquent speeches made showing financial and political mischief consequent on migration of Government.

Practice shown to be recent. Meeting received telegrams of sympathy from all quarters.

31. *On 13th August* :—Regret widely expressed at Ilbert s approaching departure from country. His sympathy with Indian people and support of beneficent measures of Lord Ripon's Viceroyalty and absence of morbid activity of Legislative Department under him generally appreciated.

Aitchison's approaching departure from Punjaub Government also viewed with regret in Punjaub. Meetings held asking for extension of his term of office.

Abandonment of intended Thibet mission viewed with satisfaction as avoiding frontier complications.

Continued disturbances in Burmah regarded as auguring graver difficulties. Fears entertained that overgrown Military expenditure will grow still further.

32. *On 28th August* :—Much satisfaction felt at Samuel Smith's proposed amendment to address regarding Burman War operations and expenses.

33. *On 4th September* :—Secretary of State's decision in Crole case generally considered somewhat disappointing.

Rumour at Madras that Sullivan retires forthwith. Thomas's appointment of at least questionable wisdom. His recent proceedings at Madura and Tanjore most unpopular.

Vote on Samuel Smith's amendment and Hunter's received with regret but the strength of minority considered hopeful sign.

Gorst's reply to Lethbridge about exodus thought unsatisfactory. Provincial exodus not so important as Supreme Government's Simla migration for seven months.

34. *On 1st October* :—Lord Harris's reference to reimposition of Cotton duties considered here more practical than seems to be supposed. Increase of Salt duty clearly less defensible than imposition of Cotton duties.

Ministerial declaration regarding Parliamentary Committee on Indian affairs not thoroughly satisfactory. Opinion respecting necessity of Royal Commission unchanged. Committee's scope narrower than Lord Randolph Churchill had proposed in last Parliament. India Government Committee on Civil Service not looked forward to with confidence.

Anxiety felt about proposed Bonerwal Expedition and Badekshan affairs. These military movements considered objectionable financially and otherwise.

REPORT

OF THE

SECOND

Indian National Congress,

HELD AT

CALCUTTA

On the 27th, 28th, 29th and 30th December,

1886.

Contents.

THE CONGRESS.

THE LEADING CHARACTERISTIC of the Congress of 1886 was, that it was the whole country's Congress. The Congress of 1885 had been got together with some difficulty by the exertions of a few leading reforms, and included less than one hundred of the more advanced thinkers blonging to the most prominent centres of political activity. The Congress of 1886 may be said to have grown, almost spontaneously, out of the unanimous resolve of the educated and semi-educated classes, throughout the Empire, to take a decisive step towards the attainment of that political enfranchisement to which they have come, of late years, to attach so much importance.

In all the more advanced provinces action commenced early in the autumn, and it very soon became apparent that the second Congress was destined to be, in many essential respects, a decided advance on the first.

The delegates or representatives who attended the first Congress, though representatives of the highest culture of the land, and fully qualified to speak as to the wants and wishes of the nation, yet appeared as volunteers in the good cause, uncommissioned, as a rule, by any constituencies, local or general, to appear on their behalf. Very early it seems to have occurred, simultaneously, to all those most interested in the renewed movement, that something more than this was requisite and that the gentlemen who were to take part in the second Congress ought to receive some public authorization from the bodies and communities (or leading members of these latter) whom they were to represent. Accordingly, at the time of the Congress drew near, the leading Associations at all the more important towns and cities procceded to elect delegates, and great public meetings, [illegible] all classes of the community, who were in any way interested in the matter, are also held, almost throughout the country, at which representatives were designated.

It has not been possible to collect the records of all these elections, but a sufficient number of notices of these, gleaned from papers of different presidencies and provinces, have been placed on record in Appendix II, to show how thoroughly and systematically this new feature in the arrangements was developed.

Another point, that grew to be generally insisted on, was that the representatives ought to be made aware, beforehand, of the principal subjects likely to come under discussion at the Congress, and so be in a position to ascertain, in advance, the views there on. of their constituencies.

Accordingly, printed suggestions as to subjects for the consideration of the Congress were issued from several of the provinces and circulated to all the others. The first was issued from Calcutta (where the general feeling on the subject first took a tangible form), and is reproduced in Appendix III as sufficiently indicating the nature of these preliminary steps. Unfortunately, admirable as the idea was, the necessary machinery (now provided by the Standing Congress

Committees, Resolution XIII of 1886) did not exist for carrying in out in its integrity, and a considerable proportion or the delegates never saw, or even if they saw, never properly considered, in consultation with their constituents, these important papers of suggestions, which constituted the foundation stones of the subsequent Congressional deliberations. Still, although rot as fully circulated as they should have been, a majority, of the delegates come "forewarned and forearmed," and even this was a great advance on the procedure of the previous year.

But the greatest advance lay, perhaps, in the total change in the character of the Congress. In the previous year people had to be pressed and entreated to come ; to the late Congress everybody *wanted* to come of their own accord. The first Congress was created by the labour of a few who had to nurse carefully the young plant ; the second Congress burst into vigorous growth on its own account, with a luxuriance that demanded careful pruning From some provinces double, or more than double, the numbers actually delegated would have been sent, but for inter-provincial communications as to the numbers other provinces contemplated sending, and remonstrances against one province swamping the others.

For the first Congress there was no enthusiasm until after it was over and its results had been announced (though then indeed the entire country endorsed those results and warmly approved the new departure) ; but, in regard to the second Congress, the greatest enthusiasm prevailed, especially throughout Bengal. Bengal alone could have furnished a thousand delegates, and not only did a great many more people desire to attend than could possibly have been admitted, but hundreds, certainly, of persons (some say over a thousand) came down from distant parts of the country merely to *see* the Assemblage ; and when at the close of the first meeting at the Town Hall, where the delegates were almost stifled in a crowd of from 2,000 to 3,000 lookers-on, it was decided to hold subsequent meetings elsewhere, where real business might be possible, the gravest dissatisfaction was expressed by the Indian public and the proposed arrangements had to subsequently modified.

Nor was this all : at many places, large crowds accompanied the delegates to the ships or railway stations on their departure for the Congress giving them ovations, as if they were great conquerors returning laden with the spoils of victory, rather than humble soldiers, departing to share in one of the little preliminary skirmishes of Freedom's great battle. Perhaps they truly felt that that battle—

> "Once begun
> Bequeathed from wearied sire to son,
> Tho' baffled oft, *is* ever won ;"

and that the feeble advanced guard whom they were sending forth to MAKE that beginning, more lacked their support and more truly deserved their gratitude, than would the laurel-crowned victors of a later time.

But, perhaps, the best evidence of the widespread enthusiasm that pervaded the country is to be gathered from a study of the list of the delegates (Appendix I), together with only " a small scale map " of this vast empire.

When we reflect that (excluding the people of Calcutta, and those within comparatively easy reach of the capital) 300 men left their homes, many of them men who had scarcely ever before crossed the boundaries of the districts in which they were born, to make long journeys (in the case of nearly 30 of them exceeding 2,000 miles in length) into, to them, unknown provinces, inhabited by populations speaking unknown languages; that the average distance travelled to the Congress by *each* of these 300 gentlemen (by no means as a rule over rich) was no less than 903 miles: that high caste Brahmins, from Madras, boldly ventured on and crossed those dark waters so full of nameless dread and solemnity to most of them, we may begin to realize a little the growing strength of the idea, of which this late National Congress was the embodiment.

Altogether about 500 gentlemen were elected either at public meetings, or by Societies, Associations and Sabhas (Literary, Political, Agricultural and the like), representing each of them considerable (and some of them *very* large) bodies of intelligent, if not, according to European notions, fully educated, persons. Deaths—deaths of near relatives (which in the case of Hindus prevent a participation for from ten to thirty days in such an undertaking)—sickness, urgent private affairs or professional calls, and accidents of travel, somewhat thinned the numbers, and only about 440 actually attended the Meetings of the Congress. In Appendix I will be found a list, as complete as circumstances have permitted us to compile, of 434 of these, but some four or five gentlemen, it is believed, left Calcutta without recording their names, or depositing any credentials of their delegateship, whose names, from want of the necessary particulars, have consequently been omitted.

These numbers, however, by no means represent the real deliberative strength of the Assembly, since, besides these delegates, a considerable number of more or less eminent members of the Government Services visited Calcutta at the time of the Congress; and, although taking no part in the Public Proceedings, privately afforded the delegates of their own provinces advice at many of those friendly informal consultations, at which much of the real work of the Congress was practically disposed of.

Taking, however, the list as it stands, the geographical completeness of the representation will be apparent at a glance. Not only were all the presidencies, provinces and natural sub-divisions of the country, Madras, the Deccan, the Konkan, Guzerat, Sindh, the Panjab, Oudh, the N. W. Provinces, Rohilkhand, the Central Provinces, Behar, Assam, Lower Bengal, Chota Nagpore and Orissa, represented by natives of these territorial divisions, but most of the smaller sub-divisions included in these provinces were equally represented by people belonging to *them*.

From Madras, where the representative system received great attention, delegates were sent from almost every single district, and duly constituted representatives appeared from Madras city, from Berhampur, Vizagapatam, Bimlipatam, Rajamundry, Masulipatam, Bezwada, Gudiveda, Nellore, Ongole, Bellary, Gooty, Anantpore, Penukondah, Kurnool, Walajanaggar, Chittore, Chingleput, Combaconum, Mayaveram, Cuddalore, Coimbatore, Calicut, and Raichore. From the Konkan delegates came from Bombay and Bassein; from the Deccan, from Sangli, Poona, Sattara, and Belgaum; from Guzerat, from

Ahmedabad, Surat, Broach, Viragaum, Nariad and Baroda ; and from Sindh from Sukkur, Kotri, Hyderabad, and Kurrachee. From the Punjab, Lahore, Amritsur, Ambala, Gurdaspur, and Dehra Ismail Khan sent delegates ; from the N. W. Provinces, Allahabad, Ballia, Tajpore (Bijnore), Ghazipur, Agra, Mynpooree, Benares, Almora, Mirzapur, Aligarh, Farukhabad, Meerut, Kankhal (Hurdwar), Azimgarh, Basti and Muradabad were represented. Oudh furnished contingents from Lucknow, Unao, Partabgarh, Barabanki and Fyzabad, and the Central Provinces from Nagpur, Khandwa, Jubbulpore and Hoshungabad. Every district of Behar furnished its quota, and representatives came from Patna, Bankipore, Behar, Shahabad, Doomraon, Chupra, Gya, Mozufferpore and Bhagulpore. The list of the places represented in Lower Bengal is almostoreist of all the districts. Chota Nagpore sent delegates from Hazaribagh, Ranchi and Purulia ; Orissa from Balasore ; and Assam from Sylhet, Cachar, Shillong Nowgong and Debrugarh.

Limited as the number was (and had it not been limited probably two thousand, instead of five hundred delegates, would have been elelcted) it is not easy to conceive a more complete representation from a merely geographical point of view than the Congress provided.

Taking the populations of the British portions only, of the presidencies and provinces represented, the total may be stated in round numbers at 196 millions, and the 431 delegates (excluding three from places in Native States) were therefore in the ratio of 2·2 per million of the population. But this ratio, as will be seen, was not maintained in the several provinces.

Presidency or Province.	Number of Delegates.	Population in millions of British terri- tories only.	Number of Delegates per million.
Madras	47	31	5
Bombay	47	17	7
Punjab	17	19	9
North-Western Provinces and Oudh	74	44	7
Central Provinces	8	10	8
Bengal	230	70	8
Assam	8	5	6

No great objection need be taken to the figures of Madras, Assam or the North-Western Provinces and Oudh, though the delegates from these were less numerous than they should have been ; but the two backward provinces the Punjab and the Central Provinces, were inadequately represented, while Bombay, always zealous to be to the front, and with three strong centres of political activity, Poona, Bombay and Surat, was, perhaps, over-represented, and Bengal (to large portions of which the place of assemblage was temptingly near) was very decidedly so.

But in order to realize how fairly catholic, on the whole the representationg was, and on the other hand to distinguish clearly the points in which it was defective, it is necessary to analyse more closely the composition of the Assemblage. Unfortunately the list of representatives, as explained in the final footnote to Appendix I, is by no means complete in regard to those particulars of station, profession and the like, so essential to a really exhaustive analysis ; and only a little additional information has been obtained since this list was published.

Nevertheless the facts available are quite sufficient to enable us to form a fairly correct idea of the composition of the Congress as a whole.

The first thing that strikes one, in going through the list, is the entire absence of the old aristocracy, the so-called natural leaders of the people, and who, were they capable of understanding their own interests, would have been foremost in this movement. Several more or less distinguished gentlemen, like Sirdar Uttam Singh, Nawab Reza Ali Khan, Raja Rampal Sing, Maharajah Sir Jotendro Mohun Tagore, Rajah Rajendra Narain Deb, Maharaj Kumar Nilkrishna, Nawab Gholam Rubbani and others, graced the Congress with their presence ; but of the hundreds of the old hereditary aristocracy, who are still to be found scattered over the whole country, not one leading member was to be found amongst the delegates. The reason is obvious ; the policy of the Government has excluded these gentlemen persistently from all positions worthy of their rank, whether in the army or in the civil administration of the country, and they have consequently, as a rule, entirely lost the desire, if not the capacity, for personally exerting themselves or taking any direct active interest in public affairs.

The next point that attracts attention is the absence of the shop-keeping class. The British rule has been called the Bunya's Raj. Shop-keepers by millions swarm over every part of the country, many of them rich, most of them fairly well-to-do, yet only one single man of this class was to be found in the ranks of the delegates. The higher commercial classes, bankers, merchants, were fairly represented ; but petty money-lenders and shop-keepers were conspicuous by their absence. In the first place, these classes are, broadly speaking, grossly ignorant and entirely immersed in their own personal concerns ; and in the second place they, naturally enough, do not care for any change in a form of Government, which, while it prevents others from robbing *them*, furnishes, in its system of civil jurisprudence, ample facilities to *them*, for enriching *themselves!*

Lastly, the ryots and cultivating classes were insufficiently represented ; five ryots came as representatives, and six other gentlemen came as the elected representatives of different Ryots' Associations, and over and above this from several parts of the country, the Deccan, Madras and Lower Bengal, came representatives, known champions of the ryot, and, in their own parts of the country, trusted and looked up to by these ; but, for all this, considering the vast magnitude of the class and of the aggregate interests involved, it cannot be denied that the cultivating classes were inadequately represented.

For this of course there were two obvious reasons : The first is that the great bulk of the ryots, intelligent worthy men as so many of them are, have as yet but a very imperfect knowledge of political matters. A great number of them realize that the times are somehow out of joint, but they have not learnt to rise from particular instances to generalizations, and they neither understand exactly what is wrong nor have they, as a class, any clear and definite ideas as so what could, or ought, to be done to lighten somewhat their lot in life. To educate the intelligent members of the cultivating classes (and these are immensely more numerous than those who have not dealt directly with them suppose) in all such matters, is one of our most pressing duties. In some comparatively limited tracts the work has already been undertaken, but it has to be extended to *all* parts of the country, and persevered in for years, before we can hope to see this, the most important of all classes, fitly and fairly represented in our Councils.

The second reason is the comparative poverty of the class, which must always debar all, but a very few, of them from themselves making long journeys to attend such gatherings, though not, of course, from electing others, more favoured by fortune, to represent their views and wishes at these.

Excluding then the old aristocracy and the shop-keepers and petty money-lenders, who were in no way represented, and the cultivating classes who were inadequately represented, all other important classes and interests were satisfactorily represented. It may be thought that the artizans too were left somewhat out in the cold, as no artizan appeared as a delegate ; but under British rule the old artizan class has almost disappeared ; skilled artizans, of the modern type, are few in number and form as yet but a comparatively small class, and where at all numerous have begun to join and are members of People's and other Associations which did send representatives, so that thus far it cannot be said that they were inadequately represented. Doubtless, as technical education gains ground and India develops, as all hope it gradually may, into a manufacturing country, this class will require and obtain more direct representation.

The higher landed interests were well represented, as about 130 of the delegates were talukdars, zemindars, or landed proprietors of one kind or another.

The legal profession, as in the English House of Commons, mustered very strong, since no less than 166 delegates belonged to it. But in this large number are included not only barristers, solicitors, attorneys, vaquils and pleaders, but also retired judges, and amongst the vaquils and pleaders several are gentlemen who, although they have qualified, do not practise, but are landholders, editors of newspapers, principals of colleges and the like, so that some deduction has to be made from the gross total given above if the real strength of the legal profession in the Congress is to be gauged. None the less the legal profession is the one path to distinction, position and wealth (outside Government service) open to Indians of ability and moderate means, and so, everywhere, a majority of the cleverest men, who are unable to secure or unwilling to take Government service, enter the legal profession ; and as the bulk of the ablest and cleverest men in the whole country, outside the Government services, appeared at this late Congress, necessarily the lawyers *were* strong in it.

It is curious to note, as illustrating the stimulus afforded by high education to rational conceptions of individual and national rights and to political aspirations generally, that more than one-fourth of the delegates were graduates, mostly of Indian Universities, but a few of European ones, and one or two of both.

Of course the Indian Press was well represented, some forty editors, sub-editors and proprietors of newspapers appearing as delegates. Amongst the papers so represented may be mentioned the "Hindu," the "Andhra Prakasika," the "Crescent" and the "Kerala Patrika" (all of the Madras Presidency) ; the "Indu Prakash," the "Dhyan Prakash," the "Journal of the Sarvajanik Sabha" the "Gujerati," "Sindh Sudhar" and "Sindh Times" (of the Bombay Presidency) ; the "Tribune" and "Kohinoor" (of the Punjab) ; the "Prayag Sumachar," the "Naseem Agra," the "Sitara Hind," the "Miratul Hind," the "Hindustani," the "Rozana Akhbar," the "Indian Union" and the "Indian Courier" (of the N. W.

Provinces and Oudh) ; and the "Behar Herald" and "Indian Chronicle," the "Hindu Patriot," the "Bengali," the "Mirror," the "Suravi," the "Sar Sudhanidhi," the "Bharatbasi," the "Sanjivani," the "Reis and Rayyet," the "Indian Nation," the "Amrita Bazar Patrika," the "Ahmedi" and the "Christian Herald," all of Bengal.

There were two dozen of principals, professors and masters of Indian Schools and Colleges, but as yet the great bulk of those engaged in the work of higher education are Government servants, and hence did not appear as delegates.

Then there were some twenty merchants, nearly the same number of bankers, sixteen medical men, a small group of mill-owners, manufacturers, tea and indigo planters, a couple of contractors, a single engineer and three ministers and missionaries.

About 70 of the delegates were presidents, vice-presidents or elected members of the Municipalities in which they reside, and some 30 held similar positions in their local district or sub-divisional Boards.

We had not many members of the Governor-General's or local Legislative Councils, because until quite of late years the gentlemen selected for these responsible positions were, as a rule, hardly up to the intellectual standard required for delegates. But a great improvement has taken place in these matters in recent times, and we were able to show seven "Honorables" second in ability to none of their colleagues at the Congress.

Only fifteen Honorary and Presidency Magistrates appear in the list, though there were two or three more who, though not recorded as such, hold, it is believed, one or other of these offices. But even if we say 20, this is an extraordinarily small number, considering the multitude of these dignitaries spread all over the country, and the fact that so many of the delegates were far better qualified for this position than the bulk of those gentlemen who occupy it in the mofussil. The explanation, however, is simple. As a broad rule, gentlemen are created Honorary Magistrates on the recommendations of local officials, and also as a broad rule these local officials recommend gentlemen for the post, not on account of any special qualifications therefor, but because they are well-to-do, and study obsequiously the wishes of the district authorities in all they say and do. Of course this was not a class likely to furnish many delegates, when the impression prevailed that the European officials, as a body, were hostile to the Congress. It is to be hoped that this impression was an erroneous one, and certainly His Excellency the Viceroy set the example of maintaining a most kindly attitude towards the assemblage, but, well or ill-founded, the impression was almost universal, and it must be taken into consideration when estimating the earnestness which animated the delegates. It was not merely the loss of time, the expense, the discomforts of the long journey that had to be faced, but the fact, as so many of the delegates from the mofussil believed, that from the day they started for the Congress they would be marked men, and their names recorded in the blackest of the district official's black books.

We have said nothing yet of religious distinctions, because we consider that it is a community of temporal interests and not of spiritual convictions that qualify men to represent each other in the vast majority of political questions. We hold that, their general interests in this country being identical, Hindus, Christians, Mahomedans and Parsees may, as fitly as members of their respective communities, represent each other in the discussion of public secular affairs. We contend that, as regards the universal feeling that the people of India are not altogether getting fair play under the existing form of the administration, and as regards the equally universal desire for a reform in this latter, the aspirations of every loyal, honest and educated man, no matter what his creed, so long as he be an Indian, *must* be identical on all general principles. There will be differences of opinion as to details, but these differences will hinge, not on differences of creed, but on differences in social position, profession, occupation, and the like. As regards the great general outlines of the leading reforms at which these Congresses aim, and with which alone they pretend to deal, there can be no difference of opinion between good and capable Indians (be their creed what it may) arising out of, or in any way dependent on, religious differences.

Therefore we utterly deprecate the introduction of any religious sentiment, or any reference to gentlemen's religious beliefs into political movements of the nature of these Congresses, and on the present occasion should have considered it sufficient merely to record that Hindus, Mahomedans, Sikhs, Christians, Brahmos and Parsees, took part in the Conference.

But unfortunately an effort has been made to detract from the national character of the late assemblage, by pointing out that numerically, according to the proportion observable in the population, the Mahomedans were inadequately represented; which is just as if the nationality of the House of Commons in England were denied, because it contained a smaller proportion than the population of Great Britain as a whole, of Methodists or Roman Catholics. Of course as every one knows, even in Ireland, where the religious antagonism of Protestants and Roman Catholics far exceeds that anywhere existing in India between Mahomedans and Hindus, a Protestant like Mr. Parnell. represents a Catholic constituency.

The objection raised is of course frivolous in the extreme, but let us see what it amounts to. In the population of India as a whole, the Mahomedans constitute less than one-fifth,* but out of our 196 millions, 44 millions, or exactly $\frac{11}{49}$ths are Mahomedans, so that if the exact arithmetical proportion were maintained, a thing no sane man could ever dream of in an assemblage constituted to deal with secular matters only, 97 (and a *fraction*) of our 431 delegates should have been Mahomedans, whereas as a fact only 33 of the representatives were Mussulmen. Now, considering how very backward as regards education the great bulk of the Mahomedans are in the present day, and the consequent apathy to all large political questions that characterizes them, this comparatively small number of Mahomedan delegates might have been accepted as the natural result of the present lack of higher education† amongst our Mahomedan brethren. But in reality a special cause operated to restrain the Mahomedans of Calcutta and its neighbourhood, whence many representatives were expected, from joining the Congress.

Three prominent Calcutta Mahomedans, two of them the leaders of the only local Mahomedan Associations of any note, under some misapprehension, into which

* Plowden says 1,974 in every 10,000.

† Bengal alone contains 22 out of the 44 millions of Mahomedans inhabiting the Provinces which the Congress was supposed to represent. In Bengal, of males of 10 years and upwards only 0·6 per cent.; in the case of Mahomedans are "persons engaged in the learned professions and in literature, art and science," while in the case of the Hindus no less than 1·78 per cent. were so engaged. Unfortunately these details were not worked out at the Census in any other Province (*V. Indian Empire, Census*, 1881, *I. pp.* 374, 375).

it is too late now to enquire, saw fit at the last moment to declare publicly against the Congress, to which they were pleased to prefer what one of them styled "a policy of confidence in the Government," and no time being left for threshing out the question, the Mahomedans of Calcutta and its neighbourhood, not knowing what might lie behind these manifestos, almost as a body abstained from taking part in the movement.

This short-sighted action has not commended itself to the Mahomedans of India as a body.* Mahomedan speakers at the Congress, one after the other,† from Dacca, Patna, Lucknow and other centres, denounced it as unjustifiable and unpatriotic, and declared that where they came from Mahomedans and Hindus ever worked, in all such matters, shoulder to shoulder, and were too wise not to understand that their interests, where the political enfranchisement of the country was concerned, were identical. Even in Calcutta itself, a certain reaction has taken place, and some, at any rate of the Mahomedans feel and admit that a mistake has been made.

The matter was of no importance and need not have been noticed but for the absurd prominence given to it by some of the Anglo-Indian journals, who vainly sought to attach to it a grave political significance. Having, however, noticed it, it may be well, before dismissing the subject, to quote from his annual address to the Positivists, what Mr. H. J. S. Cotton, one of the clearest-sighted of the European officials in India, has felt constrained to say on the subject. He says (not being of course aware of the real circumstances, and judging only as a spectator) :—

"The National Congresses, the second of which has just concluded its session in Calcutta, are visible symbols of this unmistakable tendency towards nationality. The meetings of this Congress, while they are distinctly political in character, have been marked

* Take, for instance, the speech of Sheikh Reza Hossain (a gentleman who is not to be confounded with Nawab Reza Ali Khan), the President of the Rifa-i-am (the most important Association in Upper India), on the occasion of the visit, on their tour through the N. W. Provinces, of certain of the Madras delegates, a few days after the close of the Congress.

Gentlemen,—I thank you heartily for having taken the trouble to come to this city after your recent deliberations at Calcutta. I welcome you, gentlemen of Bellary, from the bottom of my heart to this ancient capital. If political Congresses are not likely, as some Anglo-Indian friends allege, to end in anything great, they have done so much at least, that to-day we find the nobility and gentry of Lucknow welcoming the inhabitants of other parts of the country. (*Cheers.*) Gentlemen, I have read in the papers that, some, apparently very narrow minded men, call this Congress a Hindu Congress. But I will not resume my seat to-day without denying this unfounded allegation. (*Cheers.*) I do not think that the Mahomedans, who have kept aloof, are all absolutely devoid of reason, but it seems to me that their actions have rather been the result of prejudice and selfishness than of principle and reason. (*Loud cheers.*) It is a calumny to say that Mahomedans have no sympathy with this great national movement. In every community there are some gentlemen of fault-finding tendencies, and when these gentlemen found that they had no other way of justifying their conduct, they took upon themselves to misrepresent the objects of the Congress. But, as in every other case, truth prevailed, and all attempts to discredit the promoters of the good movement have been laid bare. (*Cheers.*) I tell you, gentlemen here present, that the Mahomedans have full sympathy with the Congress. If need were, I could take upon myself to furnish the signatures of 50,000 Mahomedans (*loud cheers*) in support of my assertion. In the by-gone days of Mahomedan power, though the great sections of the Indian community differed in respect of religion and customs, the Hindus never lacked in their fidelity towards the ruling powers; and, in return, the Mahomedans took them into their confidence, and gave them a share in the administration of their country. (*Hear, hear.*) In my opinion no country can prosper in which there is not a national unity. We may differ in religous views, but in our aspirations I hold that we are one. We have a common goal before us; and in every other respect, we are, in reality, one nation. (*Loud cheers.*) When, unfortunately, there is any famine or plague or misfortune among us, there is no distinction made between the various communities. So, in respect of laws, should they all be treated alike. (*Applause.*) I do not think those gentlemen wise who say that there is no necessity for a Conference of this kind, inasmuch as the Government will themselves consider our needs, and grant us all we desire and ought to receive. I never knew any Government taking any people into its confidence unless the latter showed that they were fit for such a distinction; and I should like to know what better way exists for proving our fitness than the holding of Congresses and Conferences? (*Cheers.*) This nationaldemonstration has shown, to a great extent, the moderation of our demands. It has clearly shown that these demands are not the demands of a handful of interested and self-seeking agitators. Nobody can raise any question as to the representative character of the meeting, which numbered among its delegates the greatest and best of our patriots—men who are not for doing away with law and order, but who and actuated by the purest of principles. In honoring such men all Hindus and Mahomedans ought to be, and I be lieve, are united. (*Long and continued cheers.*)

† *Vide* the detailed Report of the Proceedings, pages 51, 105, 106, 107, 109.

by order and sobriety, by firmness and persistence. The meetings at the Town Hall, of which I was myself an eye-witness, are among the most remarkable assemblages ever gathered together in this or any country. The ablest and most competent representatives from all the provinces in India have taken part in the discussions. The prospect opened out to us is in the highest degree satisfactory. The only incident that clouds our hopes is the unwise reluctance which the Mahomedans of Bengal have shown in co-operating with their Hindu brethren in the movement. It appears, indeed, to be limited to the Mahomedans of Bengal, and not to be shared in by their co-religionists of North-Western, Western, Central and Southern India. But in any case it is unwise on their part to stand aloof, and I can only hope that their reluctance, which under all the circumstances of the case, historic and otherwise, is perhaps not unnatural, may yield to time. Hindus and Mahomedans, Parsees and Sikhs, Armenians and Eurasians, are all Indians alike with their home in India, and it is both their interest and their duty, suppressing as far as possible all differences and personal jealousies, to combine and work together in the same fold, and in the same direction, and with the one object of their own national advancement."

Early in September a Committee to arrange for the reception and entertainment of the 250 delegates expected from Northern, Western and Southern India, was established at Calcutta under the presidency of Sir Jotendro Mohun Tagore. It is an understanding that, while delegates from any part of the province in which a Congress may be held, make their own arrangements for their sojourn thereat, the delegates from other provinces shall be, during the Congress, the guests of the province where the assemblage is held.

A good deal of money had therefore to be raised, the Maharajahs of Cooch Behar, Durbangah, Hutwa and Dumraon, Sir Jotendro Mohun Tagore and other leading gentlemen of the British Indian Association, the Venerable Debendro Nath Tagore and many other distinguished members of our community heading the list with great liberality, and several large houses (Mr. W. C. Bonnerjee and Baboo Hem Chunder Gossain giving up their fine houses amongst others for the purpose) had to be secured* for the accommodation of the expected delegates. The work of receiving and entertaining so large a body of guests belonging to so many different castes and creeds was necessarily very arduous. Many helped in one way or another, or success would have been impossible, but the bulk of the actual labour practically devolved on three gentlemen, Messrs. J. Ghosal, Girija Bhusan Mookerjee, and Kumud Chunder Mookerjee, whose unwearying assiduity and thoughtful kindness have been gracefully and gratefully acknowledged by all our visitors.

Great stress was laid in the circular issued in March 1885,† to which these Congresses owe their origin, on the expediency of *all* the delegates living *together* throughout the Congress week; partly to enable them to become personally well acquainted with each other, and thus cement the union between the most earnest reformers of all parts of the Empire, and partly to secure ample opportunities for the thorough threshing out of all important questions in friendly, informal committees, prior to their formal consideration at the public sittings of the Congress. The number of these public sittings. owing to the shortness of the holidays, during which alone the Congress can be held, and the huge distances so many of the delegates must always have to travel, are necessarily limited to three or four, and it was felt that these could never suffice to dispose satisfactorily of the great subjects that would be sure, yearly, to demand the attention of the Congress, unless

---

* All the houses so occupied were in Park Street and close to one another.

† See page 4 of the Report of the Proceedings of the FIRST Indian National Congress.

they were thoroughly worked out beforehand, in informal consultations of far longer duration than could be allotted to any formal public sitting. From the first the idea in regard to these public sittings has always been that they should do little more than formally and publicly record the conclusions arrived at "in committee," and set forth authoritatively the more important of the grounds on which these conclusions were based.

At the first Congress at Bombay, this idea was thoroughly worked up to, but at the late Congress, in Calcutta, local circumstances prevented, to some extent, a strict adherence to this system. Bengal sent some 230 delegates, and the majority of these were scattered here and there over the immense area of this great capital and its widely extending suburbs (including Howrah, &c). It was impossible for these gentlemen, as a body, both to attend at the public sittings and also spend the rest of the day, their mornings and evenings, at the guest houses, at one or other of which (they being close together) consultations and discussions were going on from sunrise till late at night, joined in sometimes by many, sometimes by few, sometimes carried on in provincial groups, sometimes by the leading spirits only of several such groups. Fortunately Messrs. Ananda Mohun Bose and Surendra Nath Bannerjee managed to get together, elsewhere, informal committees of over a hundred of the Bengal delegates, ascertain their views and communicate them to, and discuss them on behalf of their provincial colleagues with, the leaders of some of the other provincial groups at the guest houses. But it must be conceded, we fear, that after making all allowances, nearly one-fourth of the delegates never had the opportunity of discussing the many important subjects disposed of by the Congress, either directly or through those who knew and shared their views, with their colleagues of *other* provinces, until they met at the public sittings, which were no more favourable, than is the House of Commons, to the calm arguing out of individual views. This acknowledged defect in the practical working of our late Congress will, it is hoped and believed, be rem edied at all subsequent ones.

The delegates began to arrive on the 25th of December, and on the 26th several of the Bengal leaders, and one or two of the most distinguished of the delegates of most of the other provinces, met at the rooms of the British Indian Association, and talked over certain draft resolutions, which had been prepared in consultation with certain of the delegates who had arrived, mainly on the lines of the "suggestions" already circulated, to serve as a preliminary basis for discussion. Some of these resolutions were modified, others were added, and the result was the establishment of a somewhat more definite series of proposals to place in the hands of the now fast arriving delegates. These proposals again were modified and added to day by day, as they were discussed and criticised at the friendly conferences already referred to, and some again were further altered at the public sittings ; but it is needless now to say more about these, as a complete summary of all the resolutions, as finally passed, will be found at the close of this introductory notice.

The first public sitting of the Congress took place on Monday, the 27th, at the Town Hall. Despite the enormous size of the hall, it was everywhere crowded to excess ; but, as was remarked by one of the Anglo-Indian papers—*

---

* *The Daily News*, December 28th, 1886.

"The utmost unanimity, enthusiasm, and sympathy prevailed among all present, numbering some 2,000* or more, representing all classes of the community in India, from the four points of the compass."

No one who witnessed this vast gathering, one of the greatest ever known in Calcutta, will ever forget it. To not a few, in startling contrast with the present scene, arose a remembrance of another vast gathering of representative men from all parts of the Empire—the Delhi Assemblage. But how different the two scenes! There, crowds of Princes, girt with all the glamour of martial glory, the blare of trumpets, the thunder of artillery—there, the richest robes that the looms of Asia and Europe could evolve, a blaze of jewels, countless and priceless, set in a gorgeous amphitheatre;—here only the ringing, heart-wrung cheers of honest citizens, soberly clad, amid the squalid surroundings of a dingy, barn-like hall. There, the representatives dragged together, grumbling, by an Imperial ukase, here spontaneously hurrying up from the most distant provinces in eager mutual rivalry in the good work. There the object of the gathering, the celebration of an addition to the titles of our Gracious Sovereign, here the inauguration of a new era and the public assertion of the claims of two hundred millions of that Sovereign's subjects, to some, at least, of those rights and privileges which are the indefeasible birthright of every free-born British citizen.

Posterity will lightly put aside all remembrance of Delhi's somewhat theatrical *tableau*, but will dwell with ever-increasing reverence, as the years roll by, on the record of this great Congress, as marking a distinct step in the progress of a mighty, though still infant, nationality.

Preparatory to the election of a president, the world-known archæologist and scholar, Dr. Rajendralala Mittra, was unanimously voted to the Chair. In a long and able speech† Dr. Mittra cordially welcomed the assembled delegates in the name of the citizens of Calcutta; it had been, he said, the dream of his life that the scattered units of his race might some day re-unite, and that instead of living merely as individuals they might some day grow to live as a nation, and he beheld in this Congress the dawn of that better and happier day for India. He vindicated the Congress from the foolish attempts that had been made to fix upon it charges, of indicating a distrust of the Government, or of seeking to force its hand, and rebuked those who for selfish ends had endeavoured, though vainly, to mar the success of the gathering. He insisted on the reconstitution and reformation of the Legislative Councils as the most important of all the subjects to which the Congress could direct its attention, dwelt upon the notorious incapacity of too large a proportion of the selected Indian Members of these Councils, showed that already in the past the Government itself had made two distinct steps in advance in its system of enacting laws, and that there could not possibly therefore now be anything disloyal or unbecoming in urging Government to make, now that the country was fully ripe for it, yet a further reform in that system.

"At present," he said—

"We want only one step forward: for nomination by the authorities, nomination in any case of an irresponsible character, we want election by those whom the elected are

* As subsequent calculations have shown fully 3,000 not 2,000 persons must have been present.

† This and all the other speeches will be found reported at length in the detailed report of the proceedings of the Congress, *infra* pages 47-50.

to represent. This is the primary object of our agitation with regard to the Legislative Councils. Let the representatives be elected. Let the system be whatever the Government in its wisdom may think proper, but let the policy be a policy of representation, and let there be a sufficient number of representatives to make the feelings and wants of the people fully heard by the Government. We live, not under a National Government, but under a foreign bureaucracy; our foreign rulers are foreigners by birth, religion, language, habits, by everything that divides humanity into different sections. They cannot possibly dive into our hearts; they cannot ascertain our wants, our feelings, our aspirations. They may try their best, and I have no reason to doubt that many of our Governors have tried hard to ascertain our feelings and our wants; but owing to their peculiar position, they have failed to ascertain them. Therefore, what we want is to have a sufficient number of men to represent the people, each bringing his quota of knowledge of the requirements of a particular section of the community."

He went on to insist on the concession to such elected councillors of the right of interpellation; and after glancing at the Public Service Commission concluded by urging moderation, alike in speeches and in projects, and calling on the assembly to elect a President.

This speech was received throughout, as it deserved to be, with great applause, and the enthusiasm of the meeting grew more and more marked when the great landed proprietor Baboo Joykissen Mookerjee rose to propose the Hon'ble Dadabhai Naoroji as President. Baboo Joykissen had ever had the reputation of being a strict landlord, a man of great ability and independence of character, but a typical Conservative, and that he, an old man, blind and trembling with age, should have come forth from his retirement to head and encourage this new liberal movement was a sign of the changed times in which we are living that could not escape even the dullest-witted of the spectators. The Anglo-Indian papers had been crying down the Congress as a group of Radical schoolboys and needy political adventurers, and here was the Nestor of the Bengal Conservatives, beside whose broad acres many a ducal heritage sinks into pettiness, supported by the millionaires of India's metropolis, Baboos Doorga Charan Law, Juddoo Lall Mullick and many others, actually foremost in this demonstration, that British rule and British education have, thus far, nobly performed the task allotted to them by Providence, and have wakened in a slumbering people the instinct of nationality and the aspiration for political enfranchisement.

No wonder that the old man's trembling form and feeble accents were greeted with a tempest of cheers, or that (to anticipate) when later at the close of the President's inaugural address, he concluded a second short speech—

"Standing as I do, one of the few remaining links between the old India of the past and the new India of to-day, I can scarcely hope to see or enjoy the fruit of those labours on which this Congress and the nation it represents is entering, but I am glad to have lived to see this new departure, and if an old man's sympathy and good wishes can aid or encourage you in the noble work you are undertaking, I can say from the bottom of my heart that that sympathy and those good wishes are already yours. Be wise, be moderate and above all be persevering, and the success that you will then deserve will assuredly be yours" no wonder, we say, that the enthusiasm of the vast crowd rose to a pitch never before witnessed, it is believed, even in that hall of a thousand meetings.

To return: The Nawab Reza Ali Khan, Bahadur, of Lucknow, speaking in *Urdu*, seconded* Baboo Joykissen's nomination of Mr. Dadabhai as President, and proceeded indignantly and eloquently to deny that the Mahomedans were holding aloof from, or lacked sympathy with, the Congress, concluding his speech amidst vociferous cheering with the following words: "The Association that has done us the honour of deputing us is largely composed of leading Mahomedans, Nawabs, Wasekadars, Political Pensioners, and scions of the once Royal House of Oudh, and I assure you that our Association and my brother Mahomedans, generally, of Oudh, will utterly repudiate and condemn any unworthy attempt to create dissensions in our ranks by unfounded statements as to our supposed want of sympathy with the present movement. Hindus or Mahomedans, Parsees or Sikhs, we are one people *now*, whatever our ancestors six or eight hundred years ago may have been, and our public interests are indivisible and identical. Gentlemen, I pray you disregard any such slanders; we Mahomedans (at least such of us as can think at all) think just as all thinking Hindus do on these public questions, and believe me when I say that you will ever find us side by side with you in every legal constitutional endeavour to raise the political status of the people of our common home and country."

Mr. Hamid Ali Khan, Barrister-at-Law, briefly rendered in English the purport of this eloquent speech, and on his own behalf emphatically denied† the existence of any want of sympathy with the National Reform Party on the part of the Mahomedans of Upper India.

Mr. Dadabhai's election as President having then been carried by acclamation, that gentleman took the chair, and then rising addressed the meeting.

Thanking‡ the delegates for the honor done him, he dwelt upon the immense importance of the assemblage, pointed out how impracticable any such representative and all class-and-creed-embracing meeting would have been under *any* previous *régime*, Hindu or Mahomedan, and asserted that it was under British rule, and British rule alone, that such a national gathering was possible. He dwelt upon the many and great blessings for which India is indebted to British rule, and ridiculed the idea of an assemblage, every member of which vividly realized the greatness of those blessings, harbouring any purpose inimical to that rule, and showed that (however irresponsible persons might misrepresent the case) our rulers here and in England do appreciate and rely on our loyalty and common sense, and neither resent, nor take alarm at, our growing political activity. Then referring to the Jubilee year, and speaking, amidst rapturous applause, in terms of the most affectionate devotion to our Gracious Queen-Empress, he proceeded to vindicate the Congress from the reproaches hurled at it from certain quarters, for not including in its discussions questions of Social Reform. He pointed out that these reproaches were absolutely groundless; that there were times and places for everything; that the Congress was a political body met together to represent to our rulers our political aspirations, and that you might as well blame the House of Commons for not discussing the abstruser problems of metaphysics as this Congress for not discussing social problems. He went on to show that, composed as the Congress was of men

* *Vide* detailed Report, page 51.
† *Vide* detailed Report, page 51.
‡ *Vide* detailed Report, page 52.

of all castes and creeds, it was simply impossible for it to pretend to handle such topics.

"How," he said, "can this gathering of *all* classes discuss the Social Reforms needed in each individual class? What do any of us know of the internal home-life, of the traditions, customs, feelings, prejudices of any class but his own? How could a cosmopolitan gathering like this discuss to any purpose the reforms needed in any one class? Only the members, of that class can effectively deal with the reforms therein needed. A National Congress must confine itself to questions in which the entire nation has a direct participation, and it must leave the adjustment of Social Reforms, and other class questions, to class Congresses. But it does not follow because this National Political body, as such, does not presume to discuss Social Reforms, that the delegates here present are not just as deeply, nay, in many cases far *more* deeply, interested in those questions, than in those political questions which we *do* discuss, or that those several communities, which these delegates represent, are not doing their utmost to solve those complicated problems on which hinge the practical introduction of those reforms. Any man who has eyes and ears open must know what struggles, towards higher and better things, are going on in every community. And it could not be otherwise with the noble education we are receiving. Once you begin to think about your own actions, your duties and responsibilities to yourself, your neighbour and your nation, you cannot avoid looking round and discerning much that is wrong amongst you. And we know, as a fact, that each community is now doing its best according to its lights and the progress that it has made in education. The Mahomedans know how much is being done by persons of their community to push on the education their brethren so much need; the Hindus are everywhere doing what they can to reform those social institutions which they think require improvement. There is not a single community, here represented, of which the best and ablest men do not feel that much has to be done to improve the social, moral and religious status of their brethren, and in which, as a fact, they are not striving to effect gradually those needful improvements; but these are essentially matters too delicate for a stranger's handling—matters which must be left to the guidance of those who alone fully understand them in all their bearings, and which are wholly unsuited to discussion in an assemblage like this, in which men of all classes, creeds and castes are intermingled."

He then glanced at the resolutions passed at the first Congress and showed that some progress had been made.

"We should therefore," he said, "persevere, having confidence in the conscience of England and resting assured that the English nation will grudge no sacrifice to prove the sincerity of their desire to do whatever is just and right."

He deprecated any distrust of Lord Dufferin's intentions (which he believed to be in the highest degree noble, and in sympathy with our aspirations), or of the results of the Public Service Commission.

Recalling the noble words of the Act of 1833:—

"That no Native of the said territories (India) nor any natural-born subject of His Majesty, resident therein shall, by reason only of his religion, place of birth, descent, colour or any of them, be disabled from holding any place, office, or employment under the said Company." (*Act 3 and 4 Wm. 4, c. 85, s. 87*) he said :—

"We do not, we *could* not, ask for more than this, and all we have to press upon the Commission and Government is, that they should now honestly grant us in practice here, what Great Britain freely conceded to us 50 years ago, when we, ourselves, were too little enlightened even to *ask* for it."

He went on to refer to the proclamation of 1858, granted of free grace in the hour of triumph "which we should for ever prize and reverence as *our Magna Charta*," which he did not repeat, "for it is engraven on all your hearts," and which "embodied the germs of all that we aim at now, of all that we can desire hereafter." "We had only," he said, "to go before the Government, and the Commission now sitting, and repeat that proclamation and say that all we *want* is only what has already been granted to us in set terms by that proclamation, and that all we now *ask* for is, that the great and generous concessions therein made to us, in words, shall now actually be made ours by deeds."

He touched lightly on the question of representative institutions so fully dealt with by Dr. Mittra, only insisting that they had become necessary as much, or more, in the interests of our rulers themselves, as in those of their subjects. Then he referred to the great poverty of our immense population, which he contended no longer could be, or was, denied by competent authorities, and pointed out that if a proper system of representation was granted to us, we should be in a position to bring about the necessary remedies for this most terrible of all evils, the poverty of the masses.

"All the benefits," he said, "that we have derived from British rule, all the noble projects of our British rulers, will go for nothing if after all the country is to continue sinking deeper and deeper into this abyss of destitution." "It has become," he went on a little later to say, "the right as well as the duty of this Congress to set forth its convictions, both as to this widespread destitution and the primary steps needful for its alleviation. Nothing is more dear to the heart of England, and I speak from actual knowledge, than India's welfare ; and if we only speak out loud enough and persistently enough to reach that busy heart, we shall not speak in vain." Then with a caution as to moderation he resumed his seat. Throughout, the speech was interrupted, at the close of almost every period, by the most enthusiastic cheers, showing how thoroughly the speaker's words were going home to the hearts, not only of his brother delegates, but of the vast crowd of educated listeners that thronged every portion of the great Hall.

Baboo Joy Kissen Mookerjee, as already noticed, then made a second brief speech.* And after a large number of telegrams of sympathy and congratulation from all parts of the Empire (Appendix IV) had been laid on the table and one from the Mahomedans of Hyderabad read, a vote of thanks to the Chair was proposed by Maharajah Sir Jotendro Mohun Tagore and responded to by the entire meeting, which, rising, gave a prolonged succession of cheers for the Queen-Empress, and also cheers for the Viceroy, and then separated.

In the evening a large party was given at the Town Hall to welcome the delegates. It was largely attended and included many of the ablest and most distinguished members of the Indian community ; but although invitations

* *Vide* page 57 of detailed Report.

had been sent to the majority of the leading official and non-official Europeans, only Messrs. H. L. Harrison, H. J. S. Cotton, J. Wilson, and at most a dozen more or less well known gentlemen graced the party with their presence. The apparent want of sympathy exhibited by the bulk of the Europeans of Calcutta (so different to what is the case at Bombay) with the noble efforts now being made by the Indian community to secure, by constitutional means, their political enfranchisement—efforts which cannot but earn the respect and support of every true British heart, uncontaminated by the traditions of the despotic system under which we here live,—is greatly to be regretted, though, perhaps—the ordinary run of men being so entirely the creatures of their environment as they are—scarcely to be wondered at.

The Congress re-assembled the next day (28th December, 1886) at the Rooms of the British Indian Association.

The transaction of real business in the Town Hall, where the delegates were pressed in, on all sides, by a crowd of some 2,500 deeply sympathising listeners, seemed impossible. With such huge numbers in a bare stone-walled hall, even the involuntary movements and mutual whisperings of the audience produced a dull continuous hum like that of waves on a shingly beach, while every moment, when any sentiment they approved caught their ears, and often apparently in sheer exuberance of sympathy, their applause rolled through the hall, literally drowning everything. This might do for an inaugural meeting with a short-hand writer sitting at the speaker's feet, but for anything approaching to real discussion it was not to be thought of. Hence it had been decided, at the close of the first meeting, to hold the next at some place where only a limited number of spectators (as in the Strangers' Gallery of the House of Commons) could accommodate themselves. Again, the only other hall available, that of the British Indian Association, barely afforded space in the body of the hall, for the delegates, packed with a closeness that set all sanitary laws at defiance, and it was simply impossible to make room for any table at which the many reporters for the Press could sit, except in the side passage to which the public were admitted, a place quite unsuited to their purposes, and so only one reporter, the best short-hand writer available, was admitted, who was placed at the President's small table, touching which, all round, the delegates, as elsewhere in the hall, were closely crowded.

These seem trivial details to notice, but on the one hand the local Indian public were a good deal dissatisfied at being deprived of what they looked upon as their legitimate share in the proceedings, and on the other some of the leading Anglo-Indian newspapers seized upon the occasion to declare that the Congress was sitting with closed doors; that it was afraid to have its sayings and doings made public and the like; whereas, throughout, the meetings were open to the public, and as many admitted as could find standing room, and every word spoken was being recorded, so far as one short-hand writer (who did his work extremely well) could succeed in accomplishing this.

The first business taken up was a resolution whereby the Congress offered "its dutiful and loyal congratulations" to Her Majesty "on the approaching completion of the first half century of her memorable, beneficent and glorious reign" and heartily wished her "many, many more, and happy, years of rule over the great British Empire." The unmistakably genuine enthusiasm and delight with which this motion was received and carried, and the prolonged and resounding cheers for the Queen-Empress with which the announcement of this latter fact by the President was greeted, indicated at the very outset those strong feelings of loyalty to, and love for, our Sovereign which pervaded the entire proceedings from first to last.

The next resolution touched upon that most momentous question,—which, in the present day, agitates the minds of all thinking men in India—the growing impoverishment of the population. It set forth the deep sympathy and grave apprehension with which the Congress regarded this sad fact; and, while acknowledging that the Government was not overlooking the matter and was contemplating certain palliative measures, recorded the fixed conviction of the country that one of the most important practical steps that could be taken towards the amelioration of the condition of the people was the introduction of representative institutions.

A long and very interesting discussion ensued ; no single delegate doubted or questioned in any way the fact of the extreme poverty of the masses; delegate after delegate from every single province and sub-province of the Empire testified to the great destitution which prevailed amongst the lower classes in their own portions of the country. A few, a very few, contended that there was no sufficient evidence that this poverty was at the present time *increasing*, and desired to omit this word from the resolution, but this view was scouted by the assembly, and the amendment rejected by an overwhelming majority. But there were an appreciable number who desired to set forth other reforms as practical steps towards the amelioration of the condition of the people, which should be taken in conjunction with the introduction of representative institutions.

One of these was a permanent settlement, but the proposal was negatived; not because there were not a large number present who favoured such a settlement, but because most of these understood that this and all special remedies were beside the purpose of the resolution, which insisted on a change in the form of the administration as the only measure which would render it possible for the country to insist, effectively, on the application of all the various remedies necessary.

For the same reason an amendment, proposing that the wider employment of the natives of India and the encouragement of indigenous trade and manufactures, be included along with the introduction of representative institutions as important steps towards the amelioration of the condition of the people, was rejected by a large majority. The whole discussion deserves perusal, but certain of the remarks of some of the speakers may be specially referred to here. The proposer, Mr. Edulji Watcha, after glancing at the condition of the peasantry in the various Presidencies, said :* " Thus on all sides and in all provinces we seem to be met with the sad fact of the impoverished condition of the masses, and the one question is how to improve this condition. Of course there are exceptionally favoured tracts, but broadly speaking, and taking the Empire as a whole, the produce of the land is scarcely sufficient to enable those who till it, and they

* *Vide* page 61 of detailed Report.

constitute the bulk of the population, to meet the assessment (whether this be assessed by Government or some intermediate landholder) and eke out the barest existence, leaving no margin for carrying out any agricultural improvements or developments, all of which require an outlay of capital. It is said that the ryots themselves are partly to blame; that they are ignorant and improvident and spend whatever little money they chance, in good seasons, to acquire in marriage ceremonies and *tamashas* (merry-makings). This may be true, to some slight extent, but as a cause of the widespread destitution that exists, this want of thrift is insignificant as compared with the real cause, *viz.*, the extremely small share of the produce of their labours left to the actual tillers of the soil either by Government, or by superior holders, under the existing Government revenue systems. The mainstay of Indian Finance, however, is the Land Revenue. No material reduction in this can be contemplated. Landholders, too, have vested rights which cannot be confiscated or their existing rents materially cut down. The only alternative lies in increasing the produce of the soil, and this is only possible by the expenditure everywhere of capital on the land, in minute fractions doubtless in each case, but in large masses in the aggregate. But how is this possible when year by year the bulk of the profits of the entire population are drained away in the tribute to Great Britain? Exported to fructify there and swell further the unparalleled wealth of those distant isles, never in any shape to return here to bless the country from whose soil it was extracted, or the people, the sweat of whose brows it represents. Here is the essence of the question: this tribute must be reduced—if we had it, we would not grudge Great Britain her profit on the connection between us, to which we owe so much. But we have it not; the masses here, to nearly double the number of the entire population of Great Britain, are starving, or nearly so, for the want of that capital which we have not, and she must not thus, for ever, go on despoiling us, year by year, of that small capital which our toiling millions succeed in creating during the twelve months of ceaseless labour. One of the very first and most important of remedies is to minimize the foreign agency now employed in the administration and defence of the country, so that the money, spent unavoidably for these purposes, shall remain in it to grow and multiply and bless the land, and not, as now, to a very large extent, be drafted away to England. Unless and until this question of foreign agency is solved, the question of the poverty of our masses will not be solved either." Then, after pointing out that, so far from decreasing, the home charges, military and civil, were year by year increasing, that the tribute included not only all these but all the savings annually remitted by Europeans in service in India, merchants' profits, loss by exchange, &c., amounting, according to Sir R. Temple, to something like 30 millions a year, he went on to say:—

"Whatever may be the difference between the cost of tilling and the value of the producc of the soil, no country can prosper, so long as such an enormous annual drain on that difference, which ought to be accumulating in the country, is going on. This is what gives such enormous importance to the question of foreign agency. But, of course, immensely important as it is, this reduction of foreign agency is not the only reform in the administration necessary if the people are to be lifted out of the slough of poverty into which they are sinking, and placed once more on the firm ground of comfort and prosperity. But neither this reduction of foreign agency nor, indeed, any of those other needful reforms do we see the slightest hopes of getting carried out, until we succeed in attaining a position whence our protests and appeals must be respectfully listened to, and either fairly met or practically yielded to, and it is in this sense that our resolution sets forth our "fixed conviction that the introduction of representative institutions will prove one of the most important practical steps towards the amelioration of the condition of the people."

Then, after insisting further on this point, he went on :—

"Where representative institutions are once established there the Government, even though a Government of foreigners, can be drawn into the right track, but so long as a purely autocratic system prevails, and the autocrats are foreigners, the case seems hopeless."

Following and supporting him, the Hon'ble S. Subramania Iyer incidentally deprecated the ryotwari system, saying :* "It may be that the zemindars, as is believed by some, do, in some cases, screw out every farthing that they can from their tenants, but the zemindars, as we have seen, can be reached by a Tenancy Act, whereas in the Presidency of Madras it is impossible to control by any Tenancy Act the extortions of the revenue authorities. I should like to see a Government servant on our side of India, who is prepared to admit that the right of enhancement ought to be defined and limited by legislative enactment as against the Government."

Pandit Pran Nath of Lucknow, after dwelling on the poverty of the masses in that province, "which has been called the Garden of India, where no famine has ever been known," went on to say† : "If the Governments, local and supreme, included some substantial representative element—if they were thus in a position to have any real knowledge of the actual state of affairs amongst us—perhaps the country would not be so poor as it actually is. I do not mean that the mere fact of our having representatives in the Council would work any direct miracle, but that the pressure that these would then be in a position to put upon Government would incline it to mend its ways and adopt those reforms which can alone arrest the impoverishment of the land."

"It is only reasonable to suppose that the educated natives of India know the ins and outs of their own country better than foreigners, who visit it only for a short time, and that they are alike more competent, than these, to suggest, more anxious to discover, and more capable of applying the remedies demanded for that poverty, which has in fact been admitted by the Government, which is patent to every one of us here and to every Indian capable of observation, and which, as matters now stand, bids fair, in the course of one or two generations more, utterly and hopelessly to destroy the country."

Munshi Sadho Lall, a Banker and Reis of Benares, very strongly supported the resolution in a most eloquent Urdu speech,‡ some passages of which deserve special notice.

"I know," he said, "that this growing poverty depends upon many causes, but the most important of these have a common source, and that is what the papers call loss of touch between the Government and the people. I am not one of those who run down the Government. I am sure the Government does its best

* *Vide* page 62 of detailed Report.
† *Vide* page 63 of detailed Report.
‡ *Vide* page 63 of detailed Report.

—but its best, even though better in many ways than the best of all preceding Governments, is yet not good enough for the age in which we live. And this is only because the Government, being composed of Europeans, is unable thoroughly to understand the circumstances of India, and never knows, nor can know, what really wants doing, and above all how best to do what has to be done. We, who do know, are not taken into Council, not because the Government does not wish to do right, not because it desires to oppress us, but because it is not the practice at present to associate us in the administration."

* * * * * * *

"That the poverty of the masses is increasing every day cannot be disputed by any man past middle age, who has for only 20 years, even, been watching such matters, and certainly one cause of this increasing poverty is the manner in which the production of most of the manufactured necessaries of life, clothing, tools, implements, &c., has been diverted from the hands of our countrymen into those of foreign manufacturers. I do think that, with a considerable body of our own people in the several councils, means would be found to revive our ancient and establish new industries, so that as time went on all our requirements in this line should be supplied to us by our own artizans, and the enormous profits of this gigantic work reaped by our own people. I am aware that this is a difficult matter, and it is therefore that I pick it out, and say that, granting this is the most difficult of all the causes of our growing poverty to grapple with, even this would be able to be more or less successfully dealt with, if only we were so placed as to be able to guide rightly and wisely the action of Government."

Another speaker,* Lalla Hukum Chand, of Lahore, while declaring that the decay of indigenous industries was "not so much the fault of the English as our own fault" put the case for representative Government very tersely. "No doubt," he said, "some form of representative Government *is* required on all grounds. In every case before a Court of Justice both sides are heard, and each side has the opportunity of proving to the Judge the justice of his own cause. Here it is a Court of injustice. Government has it all its own way, and we have no one to plead for us and controvert the arbitrary claims of the Government. They surround themselves with people who just repeat their opinions, and so nothing can be done for the good of the country and its people, who suffer in every way because they are never heard before the Court."

Row Bahadur A. Subapathy Mudaliar, a Madras merchant, while supporting the demand for representative institutions, remarked†: "We all attribute the poverty of India to the mismanagement of our Rulers, and no doubt it is to a considerable extent due to that cause, but much blame also attaches to ourselves. We allow the English to beat us in competition in everything that we use; from a toothpick to a steamer, every branch of trade is, through our want of energy, monopolized by Europeans." And he concluded his speech by saying: "Our late beloved Viceroy, Lord Ripon, ordered the purchase of country-made in preference to European goods, and yet, on account of the greater energy of the Europeans, many articles can be obtained more cheaply and of better quality from Europe than they can be at present produced here. Even if we had the

* *Vide* page 64 of detailed Report.
† *Vide* page 65 of detailed Report.

complete control of everything in our own hands, we could not desire Indian manufactures to be purchased by the State at a higher price than is demanded for equally good English articles of the same kind. That would not be just to the interests of our nation. It is, therefore, necessary and desirable that, in addition to all political reforms, we should devote our best attention to the improvement of the industries of the country. It is true that this has nothing directly to do with the immediate objects of this Congress, but I think it ought to be clearly understood that too much must not be expected from representative institutions, and that the improvement of our national industries and the development of our commerce and trade, by our own exertions, are amongst the greatest necessities of India of the present day."

Pundit Jwalanath Sarma, in pressing the necessity of representation, urged* that "representative institutions will give due scope for the exercise of our own energies, and whatever we achieve by their means, will satisfy us. It is not the wish to have representative institutions merely to obtain power, but to put us in the way of doing good for ourselves and to foster habits of thinking and acting for ourselves."

The various amendments already referred to were then proposed, and more or less discussed, but their want of relevancy was strongly insisted on by Baboo Guru Prasad Sen of Patna who said† : "But if I have understood the real meaning of the resolution, it does not mean to say that the larger employment of natives, the encouragement of trade, or, I may add, the reduction of military expenditure and the revision of existing revenue systems, are not, one and all, important reforms which will greatly tend to improve the condition of the people, *but it signifies that we have little chance of securing these or any other reforms, until we can bring the lever of representative institutions to bear on the bureaucracy that now holds everything in its hands*." Mr. S. K. Chatterjee of Meerut emphasized the position saying‡ : "We don't say that that (representative Government) is the only thing required, but we do know that, if we get that, it will not be long before we get those other reforms that are necessary." And after a little further discussion the original resolution was carried by a very large majority.

The next resolution emphatically re-affirmed the third resolution of the Congress of 1885, and declared that the reforms therein suggested had "now become essential alike in the interests of India and England." The resolution thus re-affirmed ran as follows :—

"That this Congress considers the reform and expansion of the Supreme and existing local Legislative Councils, by the admission of a considerable proportion of elected members (and the creation of similar Councils for the N. W. Provinces and Oudh, and also for the Punjab) essential ; and holds that all Budgets should be referred to these Councils for consideration, their members being moreover empowered to interpellate the Executive in regard to all branches of the administration ; and that a Standing Committee of the House of Commons should be constituted to receive and consider any formal protests that may be recorded by majorities of such Councils against the exercise by the Executive

* *Vide* page 66 of detailed Report.
† *Vide* page 68 of detailed Report.
‡ *Vide* page 68 of detailed Report.

of the power, which would be vested in it, of overruling the decisions of such majorities."

The most absolute unanimity prevailed on this subject. It was pointed out that, since that Congress, this resolution had "been placed before and adopted by all the Associations throughout the country, while literally hundreds of public meetings in every portion of the Empire have declared it to represent correctly the views of the entire nation.*" Again it was said: "The voice of India has already declared that this resolution must be re-affirmed, and re-affirmed until its substance becomes the law of the land. There is no backward step here, now possible, for any of us. All the Associations, I may say the entire population from one end of India to the other, have been consulted on the subject, and all our countrymen, high and low, have declared that these are their wishes, this the goal at which they aim. This resolution has been accepted throughout India, and not one single Indian voice in the entire Empire has been raised against it; * * * it is simply formally re-affirming in words a resolution that the entire country has already engraved upon its heart.† Pundit Thakur Prasad (of Agra) in an Urdu speech, the whole of which merits careful consideration, said‡: "There is not a corner in the country where folks have not talked over that resolution, and said it was good. Every man who knows anything, whether he be an English speaker, or like myself knows only Indian languages, knows at least this, that if the country is to prosper, we its children who understand its ways and wants must be allowed a share, and a good share, in the management of its public affairs."

A very effective Urdu speech§ was delivered by Malik Bhugwan Dass, from Dera Ismail Khan, a stalwart frontier man whose eloquence little needed his opening apology that he came from a land where men handled the sword more readily than the pen. He ridiculed the idea that the Congress was the work of Bengali Baboos; he had come 1,600 miles to join the Congress, and proud as he should be of being a Bengali Baboo, the most highly educated class in India, did *he* look like a Bengali Baboo? He said that the Anglo-Indian papers, like the *Pioneer* and the *Civil and Military Gazette*, wanted to persuade people that the martial races of the frontier had no interest in political questions. "Backward," he said, "we may be, but it is absurd to suppose that we Punjabis, even we frontier people, are altogether ignorant of such matters, or fail to sympathize in the work which this Congress is endeavouring to get done. What, gentlemen, would they make out that God, the Almighty Father, has not endowed us with human reason, but has left us incapable of knowing what is good for us and what is bad, of feeling how unjust to us are many things in existing arrangements, of realizing that the first thing necessary if that injustice is to be done away with, is that we should have a strong voice in the management of our country's, of our own, affairs?" Later he enumerated several distinguished men whom his own little town had produced, the last of whom, he said, was utterly opposed to the late Cabul war and prophesied accurately its results; twenty crores spent and spent for nothing. "There is not," he went on to say, "a district, not a town, that does not contain many such or better men, and do

* Speech of Mr. Ganasham Nilkanth (*Bombay. No. 53*), page 70 of detailed Report.
† Speech of Row Sahib S. Narayana Swami Chetty (*Nellore, No. 19*), page 71 of detailed Report.
‡ Page 71 of detailed Report.
§ Page 72 of detailed Report.

you suppose that many of them are greatly pleased with a form of administration which denies to ninety-nine out of every hundred of them any career; or that any of them fail to see that representative institutions and a much larger employment of Indians in the higher offices of State would be important steps towards the opening they want?" When later he wound up with the words "and while I say may God prosper British rule in India for ever, I also say may he give our rulers wisdom to understand the reasonableness of our demands for reform and the magnanimity to concede what we ask for," he received a perfect ovation.

Not a dissentient voice was raised, not the faintest hint of any difference of opinion was expressed, and the resolution was carried unanimously amidst enthusiastic cheering.

The next business before the Congress was the appointment of a Committee to consider the Public Service Question. A long and very animated discussion took place. Some delegates seemed to be of opinion that as a Government Commission was investigating the matter, the case was, as it were, *sub-judice*, and should not, therefore, be touched by the Congress. Others held that, as the Commission required evidence, no better evidence of the views generally entertained could be anywhere procured than the conclusions of such a large and truely representative body as the Congress. Again, differences of opinion existed as to whether the Committee, if appointed, should report direct to the Commission in the name of the Congress, or to the Congress for the consideration, and if approved, confirmation by this latter. To the first alternative Dr. Rajendralala Mittra objected, and in an amusing speech protested against the Congress appointing a set of *akulbardars* (or wisdom-bearers) like certain imbecile princes and nobles, who, besides their *hookhabardars* (or pipe-bearers) are always accompanied by some shrewd person (ironically termed an *akulbardar*) who replies or suggests the answers to any remarks addressed to their chief. He said that if that was to be the way they did their work of thinking by deputy, the delegates might have saved themselves their long journey and might have merely written from their homes to say: Do whatever you like and we will say ditto. *Per contra*, Pundit Satyanand Agnihotri, the well-known Brahmo missionary of Lahore, argued that the question had been discussed in all circles for years; that on most points perfect unanimity existed; that the men selected were those, for the most part, known to be specially versed in the subject; and that if the Congress could not place confidence in the doings of such a Committee there was an end of representative Government. "For," said he, "what is representation if we may not have a number of *akulbardars* in whom we have confidence. Any one who pleases may make a joke of *akulbardars*, but what are the members of the English House of Commons but the *akulbardars* of the people of England."

Ultimately it was resolved to appoint a Committee that should report upon the question to the Congress at its last sitting, and the Congress adjourned until the next day.

The British Indian Association Rooms having proved too small to contain, with any degree of comfort, the large body of delegates, the meeting of the 29th took place at the Town Hall, but the sitting being an early morning one, and the public not having generally heard of the change in the place of meeting, only between four and five hundred spectators were present, and the majority of these only arrived towards the close of the proceedings, so that no inconvenience of any kind was experienced, and business was proceeded with under most satisfactory conditions.

Four important resolutions, relating to reforms in the administration of criminal justice were discussed and passed, and, as a large proportion of the delegates were lawyers, many of them with a large amount of criminal business, the conclusions arrived at are deserving of attention. The first was that the time had arrived for giving a great extension to the jury system, which as yet has been only applied to a limited number of districts. The excellent character of the verdicts given, as a rule, was testified to by gentlemen who were public prosecutors, barristers, pleaders and attorneys. It was pointed out that the jury system was indigenous in India and had been in force there from time immemorial, and that the spread of education had now almost everywhere provided an abundance of qualified jurors. One speaker* instanced the number of gentlemen sitting on Municipal Committees, local and district boards, as a proof of this fact, and went on to say: "But this Congress seems to me to furnish a conclusive reply to this pretence of a paucity of qualified jurors. Here we are gathered together to the number of nearly five hundred men from almost every single district in the Empire, each of us elected, at least, by hundreds, in many cases by thousands, in some few cases by tens of thousands, of our countrymen, one and all sufficiently enlightened to take the keenest interest in public affairs, and sufficiently independent to make a public avowal of that interest, notwithstanding the frowns of many in authority. Is there here any want of materials for good juries? Manifestly these old objections have melted away; they may have had weight in the past, but in the present day they are only official fictions." By all speakers a distrust of the manner in which justice was administered by district officials of the present day was manifested, and the political aspect of the question was touched upon. Rao Sahib Singaraju V. Subboroyudu remarked†: "Some political life is now becoming manifest amongst us. In political discussions expressions are unavoidably used which give offence to political opponents—in our case mainly the bureaucracy. We desire to obtain certain rights, as we consider them, and declare it monstrous that these should be withheld from us; on the other hand those who now enjoy what we wish to secure, consider our attempts to get their places and oust them, monstrous, and out of such natural differences of view, a tendency grows up for the existence of strained relations between the non-official public and the district authorities. Hence, on this ground as on others, it is highly necessary that our rights, our privileges, our personal liberty, should be carefully safe-guarded by the general adoption of the system of trial by jury."

One gentleman only, from the Punjab, deprecated the extension of the jury system there, saying‡: "Trial by jury as a system is a double-edged thing. It is very useful where you have honest and independent jurors, but a curse where the contrary is the case. For the verdict of a jury, however unjust, if in consonance with the views of the local bureaucracy, is final. There is no getting behind a conviction thus obtained. Where the local official passes an

* Rao Sahib M. B. Namjoshi (*Poona, No. 69*). Page 82 of detailed Report.
† *Vide* detailed Report, page 81.
‡ Lala Kunhya Lal (*Punjab, No. 104*). Detailed Report, page 79.

unjust sentence there is a chance of obtaining redress from higher authorities, but where such sentence is based upon a verdict of ignorant and obsequious jurors there is no hope of justice. Now I do not think that the Punjab can furnish many of the right stamp of jurors ; the district officers are too powerful and overbearing, and therefore I submit that our province is not ripe for the general extension of trial by jury. The jurymen will be selected by the local officials, and they will choose the *ap ke wastes*,* and bad as things are now, they will be worse I fear under the jury system." But another gentleman† from the same province strongly opposed this view saying: " I came to attend this Congress, released, on bail, from a jail by the chief court, to which jail I had been sent by an unjust decision of a magistrate who could never have got any jury to convict me. You are most of you familiar with the case, through the public prints. The charge against me was utterly frivolous and false, that of attending an unlawful assembly, the facts being, first that the assembly was *not* unlawful‡ ; and, second, that, whether lawful or the reverse, I had not attended it, but, simply, because I am considered a political agitator, because I have my own opinions and speak without fear, I was as a matter of—call it what you like—convicted, not on weak evidence, but on absolutely no evidence at all." Later he went on to say that he neither understood the arguments nor concurred in the facts of his friend who opposed the extension of the jury system in the Punjab. "I doubt," he said, " whether there are many, if any, districts in the Punjab, where excellent materials for juries do not exist. I can only say that, in all the parts of the province with which I am acquainted, I would far rather be tried by any jury that could be got together, than by most of the local magistrates of whom I have had any experience. From my own experience—and I have been practising for more than 12 years—I can say that accused persons do not get that fair and impartial trial before magistrates which they would get in a trial by jury." This seemed to be the unanimous view of the Congress, and the resolution was passed without a dissentient voice.

The second resolution advanced this question one step further, and urged the introduction into the Criminal Procedure Code of a provision (similar to that contained in the Summary Jurisdiction Act of England), enabling accused persons, in warrant cases, to demand that, instead of being tried by the magistrate, they be committed to the Court of Sessions. The resolution was proposed by Mr. Mano Mohan Ghose, a Barrister, with probably the largest practice in all India in criminal cases. There was only one opinion as to the absolute necessity of this reform. Both, during the discussion of this and the previous resolution, the youth and inexperience of many of the officers invested with first class magisterial powers, by whom three-fourths of the more serious cases are disposed of, were pointed out, and the grievous failures of justice that occurred from this cause and from the fact of district officers taking advantage of their judicial powers to punish persons who had given them offence in their executive capacities, were insisted on.

Mr. T. Chidambara Row said§ : "Magistrates of the first class, often

---

* People who say " ditto" to whatever those in authority say.
† Lala Murlidhur (*Punjab, No. 107*). Detailed Report, page 81.
‡ Since these lines were in type Lala Murlidhur has been declared innocent, and honourably acquitted by the Chief Court of the Punjab, which held the recent assembly at Umballa, to have been peaceful, and the dispersing order illegal.
§ *Vide* page 83 of detailed Report.

quite young and inexperienced officers, are invested with extraordinary powers: they can sentence to imprisonment for two years and to a fine of Rs. 1,000; and unless those powers are restricted in some way, and we are given some protection against their arbitrary misuse, our liberties will remain, as now, at the mercy of men often far from competent, from a legal point of view, to exercise these great powers, and occasionally devoid even of that conscientiousness that in former days was the characteristic of British officers. Moreover, in many cases of imprisonment (in all below a certain term), there is no appeal, and some magistrates take advantage of this and pass minor sentences in order that the unfortunate persons they desire to punish may not have a chance of justice." Mr. M. Ramanuja Charriar pointed out* how great a boon respectable persons always felt it even now, when their cases were committed to the Sessions, "because they feel and know that they will then have a trial by jury or by the aid of assessors, as well as before far more experienced and (in consequence of their having no executive functions) far more impartial Judges." Other delegates vindicated the personal character of the district officers, saying they did not think that they willingly did injustice,† but that the lamentable failures of justice, in which all concurred, was due to bias insensibly acquired in the exercise of executive functions.

The proposer, it may be added, pointed out that European British subjects, by the Criminal Procedure Act of 1882, already enjoyed the right, and that all this resolution proposed was that natives of India should be placed on a similar footing. The subject was very fully discussed, and finally the resolution was unanimously passed.

The third resolution, proposed by Mr. W. C. Bonnerjee, late Standing Counsel to the Government of India, referred to the innovation made in India in 1872 in the jury system, and urged "that the powers then for the first time vested in Sessions Judges and High Courts of setting aside verdicts of acquittal should be at once withdrawn." As the law at present stands, whether a jury acquit or convict, it is open to the Sessions Judge, if he differs from the jury, to refer the case to the High Court, and then to the High Court to convict and sentence the acquitted person, or acquit the convicted person, and this merely on the papers and without the parties being even represented before them. The proposer urged‡ that this was at variance with a fundamental axiom of jurisprudence that the prisoner is entitled to the benefit of any reasonable doubt, as to his guilt, that may exist in the mind of any person trying him. While, therefore, retaining the power of acquitting persons convicted by a jury, he would withdraw that of convicting acquitted persons, so "that where a doubt exists as to his guilt, be it in the minds of jury or judge, the accused shall have the benefit of that doubt."

This resolution was at first very strongly opposed by Assamese and many Bengal delegates. The fact was that, in a recent case, an European had been acquitted by an European jury, but (his case having been referred by the Sessions Judge) convicted and sentenced by the High Court, as the native community considered most righteously, and there was therefore in Assam and parts of

* *Vide* page 83 of detailed Report.
† Khajeh Abdool Aleem (*Dacca. No. 351*). *Vide* detailed Report, page 84.
‡ *Vide* detailed Report, page 85.

Lower Bengal (where there are many planters, and where unfortunately race-feeling is still strong) a grave disinclination to give up what was considered a possible protection against the escape, by the verdicts of European jurors, of European offenders who had committed crimes against Indians. Baboo Kali Sunkur Sukul remarked in his speech*: "We ought to remember that we are unfortunately a subject race, and if there are certain provisions in the existing code of laws which guard us against the oppression of the dominant race, we should cling to those safeguards which afford us some chance at least of having justice done to us. You are aware that every Anglo-Indian has, at the present moment, the right to be tried by jury, and you know that, in too many cases, where Europeans are the culprits, this trial by jury is followed by results which are not consistent with justice It is a matter of very great regret, but nevertheless it is a fact, that we do not get justice done in such cases. Under these circumstances, if we pass this resolution, and if the Government accept it and carry out our views, I think it will be productive of very great wrong. A case occurred some time ago, to which I shall only make the faintest allusion, where the voice of the country was unanimously raised against a grave miscarriage of justice—a miscarriage which was remedied by the interference of the High Court, although unfortunately the Government, to a great extent, rendered that interference of no avail. The country has, with one voice, declared against the action of Government, and Government will probably be more careful henceforth how it interferes with the deliberate judgments of the High Court. But if we pass this resolution we shall be placing ourselves at the mercy of juries, strong in class bias and far more intent on screening even a disreputable member of their own community than on protecting us from the oppression of the culprit and others like him, and we shall have deprived those higher-minded and less-prejudiced Europeans, our High Court and Sessions Judges, of all power of interposing to prevent such miscarriages of justice": But the other view of the case was equally strongly put by Baboo Koylash Chunder Sen who had practised he said for 16 years in Assam and Backergunj—"a district remarkable for criminal accusations": "A previous speaker," he said,† "has dwelt upon the danger of depriving higher authorities of the power of rectifying the injustice done by European juries in acquitting European prisoners, especially in Assam. I know something of Assam, and I want to ask you in how many cases has that power ever been exercised? There have been many cases in which, were not this power a mere legal fiction, where Europeans are concerned, it ought certainly to have been exercised. But has it ever been so? Never, I say, never until this recent case to which that speaker referred, and in which two Judges of the High Court, one of them a native, mark that, tried to do justice and to punish as he deserved an European transgressor of the law, wrongfully, as the High Court held, acquitted by a jury of his fellow-countrymen. And what was the result? The Government nullifying the work of the Judges releases the offender. So in fourteen years there has been one case in which the High Court has tried to do justice under this provision in the case of an European, and in that one case the Government undid their work. It is foolish then to talk of this provision being any protection to us, any safeguard

* *Vide* detailed Report, page 85.

† *Vide* page 86 of detailed Report.

against the escape of guilty Europeans. So far as this is concerned it is a mere sham. But, on the other hand, during these fourteen years numbers—I dare say I should be correct in saying hundreds (but I speak only from my own experience)—of natives acquitted by juries, who had all the parties before them, have been under this provision, as I believe wrongfully, punished on paper evidence. There is no sham about this ; it is a stern and terrible reality, and there are scores and scores of desolate homes and hundreds of men working in chains or lying dead in dishonored graves in the Andamans by reason of this unconstitutional and objectionable provision. To cling to it is indeed to grasp a shadow and let go a reality."

Baboo Kalicharan Bannerjee* dwelt very strongly on the fact that there were perverse verdicts, that this power which it was proposed to withdraw was a valuable safeguard against such, and that High Courts would not interfere except in cases in which the verdicts were perverse. But Pundit Jwalanath Sarma urged† in reply that, " in this country the judging persons and the judged persons do not, in the mass of these cases, belong to the same class. Native juries trying native prisoners are far more likely to be right in the conclusions at which they arrive than is the English Judge. Native juries know a great many things that European Judges do not ; they understand how false cases are got up. A thousand insignificant matters may transpire in the course of a case, which have no significance to the Judge, but which at once carry a conviction of the innocence of the prisoner to the better-informed minds of the jurors. As Mr. Bonnerjee pointed out, it is only right that in all cases the prisoners should have the benefit of any doubt as to his guilt, but it is doubly essential that he should receive this benefit when the persons in whose minds that doubt exists are people who understand him and his ways and customs and thoughts, and those of all the parties concerned in the case, while the only persons who do not doubt his guilt are foreign Judges, who are more or less ignorant of all these things. Of course I understand the feeling that underlies the opposition that this resolution is meeting with. The fear is that some English planter criminals, wrongfully acquitted by juries of their own countrymen, will, in the absence of this provision, escape their merited punishment. Now there are three answers to this argument which, taken together, are absolutely conclusive. In the first place, as I assume that native juries are the best judges of native criminals, so I think it not unreasonable to suppose that European juries are the best judges of the guilt of European prisoners. I refuse to believe that European juries, anywhere, habitually betray their trust. I think it quite possible that in some cases in which we think that they have done so, they, with their better knowledge of what Europeans are, may be right.

"Again, if fifty Europeans thus escaped, it would be better, if our authorities are correct, than that one man should be wrongfully convicted. But what is the fact ? Why, as has already been pointed out, for one European who may possibly thus escape his merited punishment, hundreds of innocent natives are, under this provision, wrongfully convicted.

" But, lastly, as has also been pointed out, the power is never used to prevent

---

* *Vide* detailed Report, page 87.
† *Vide* detailed Report, page 87.

that one European escaping ; it is only, and very freely, used to prevent the escape of innocent natives.

"Baboo Kalicharan Bannerjee is very strong about perverse verdicts. Well, as to perverse verdicts of European juries, I venture to hope I have disposed of these, and I would ask you all, and I suppose nearly one-fourth of you belong, like myself, to the legal profession, how many perverse verdicts of native juries have you met with ? I believe you will agree with me that these are quite exceptional. Now we have to look to the bulk of the cases not the exceptions, and here I say, as I said before, better ten men escape in such cases than one man be punished where it is not the verdict of the jury but the opinion of the Judge that is perverse, or at any rate erroneous, and, as a fact, this latter is ten times more common than any perversity in verdicts of native juries."

The question was very vigorously argued out from various points of view, but enough has been said to show the earnestness and ability with which the subject was treated, and referring those who may care to go more closely into the debate to the detailed report of the speeches, it may suffice now to add that the resolution was ultimately carried by a very large majority.

The fourth resolution declared the urgent necessity of a complete separation of executive and judicial functions, even though this should (which was denied by many speakers) involve some extra expenditure. The proposer Mr. Daji Abaji Khare in the course of his speech remarked*: "The existing system violates the very first principles of jurisprudence, for if you invest the executive, as now, with judicial powers, you in fact make that executive, prosecutor as well as judge ; nay, as a large number of offences are mere transgressions of rules and regulations of the executive, you go further, and in such cases make this executive the Judge, as it were, in its own cause. It is not wholly the fault of the executive but, somehow or another, it has often occurred, indeed it seems to be almost a general rule, that executive officers work up a sort of personal interest in carrying certain measures into operation, and consequently insensibly generate a certain bias in their minds against particular people who disapprove those measures, and this bias clearly makes them unfit judges in cases relating to those measures or those people. Secondly, executive officers, burthened with a vast variety of miscellaneous business, have not and cannot by any effort make sufficient time to dispose calmly, systematically and with due deliberation of the judicial work that comes before them. It has been found in Bombay that the Collector of the District, although invested with full judicial powers, very seldom, if ever, tries any cases in which he has no personal concern, and that simply because he has not sufficient time. Yet, every now and then, he takes it into his head to try some particular person whose conviction he wants to make sure of, and it is needless to say that such trials are characterized, as a rule, throughout, by the exhibition, on the part of the presiding officer, of a spirit more befitting a public prosecutor than an impartial Judge. He may be right in the main ; the accused may be a great rascal, the presiding officer's *animus* against him may be based on the purest concern for the public welfare ; the Collector may know the ins and outs of the case better than any one else ; he may be the fittest possible person to be public prosecutor, but it

* *Vide* detailed Report, page 90.

is a mere mockery of justice to allow such a person to be also the Judge. Moreover, in order that a person may be safely entrusted with large judicial powers, he must lead the life of a Judge,—a life apart from, and uncolored by, those conflicting interests out of which so many cases arise, and he must have besides ample opportunities for mastering the spirit as well as the letter of the law, and for becoming saturated with the fundamental principles of jurisprudence. It will not be gainsaid that, as matters now stand, the executive, in all but the highest grades, is unfortunately almost normally in opposition to the people, and as a necessity the conduct of cases—and they are very numerous—in which the opposing parties are the executive and the people, by that executive, is far from being impartial." After giving a typical instance of such miscarriages of justice from his own recent personal experience, he concluded his speech with the following words : "There is not, I venture to say, a single delegate here present who could not, from his own personal knowledge, give similar instances of the untoward results of the present objectionable system; and it is really, therefore, useless for me to say more in favour of a resolution which aims, solely, at superseding that system by a better and more rational one." Other speakers supported the resolution, adducing instances from their own knowledge of the defective character of the existing system, but the discussion was not prolonged, as the whole assemblage was of one mind, and the resolution was passed unanimously.

The next resolution was an important one, *viz.*, "that in view to the unsettled state of public affairs in Europe, and the immense assistance that the people of this country, if duly prepared therefor, are capable of rendering to Great Britain in the event of any serious complications arising, this Congress do earnestly appeal to the Government to authorise (under such rules and restrictions as may to it seem fitting) a system of Volunteering for the Indian inhabitants of the country, such as may qualify them to support the Government, effectively, in any crisis."

It may be, as has been often asserted, a mere matter of sentiment, but there is no subject on which the intelligent classes, throughout India, feel more keenly than this, and looking to the immense importance which the assemblage clearly attached to it, to the absolute unanimity with which they regarded it, and the enthusiasm with which they greeted its introduction, it may be desirable to quote at length from the proposer, Rajah Rampal's speech, which put the case, apparently, to the entire satisfaction of his audience. He said* :— "The spirit of this meeting has been so uniformly loyal and conciliatory that I hope no one will blame us if we now proceed to deal with a matter in regard to which we are distinctly at variance with Government. Every one knows that, for a variety of reasons, the whole country is of opinion that Native Volunteer Corps ought to be organised. Every one knows that the entire country memorialised and endeavoured to move Government in this matter, and every one further knows that, to our great regret and disappointment, the Government—and that not over-graciously—distinctly refused to pay any attention to the unanimous voice of the country. None the less, however, do we now feel it our duty to reiterate those representations which are based on a consideration of the highest interests of Great Britain as well as of India.

---

* *Vide* detailed Report, page 92.

"We are deeply grateful to the Government for all the good that it has done us, but we cannot be grateful to it, when it is, no matter with what best of intentions, doing us a terrible and irreparable injury.

"We are grateful to it for the peace and order which it has diffused over the land—for the education that it has so nobly and unselfishly imparted to us—for its promise of admitting us to every post and office in the administration for which we prove our fitness—for the share that it has given us in the comforts and conveniences provided by the triumphs of Western science, railways, telegraphs, telephones—we are grateful to it, in a word, for all the innumerable boons and blessings that it has conferred on us; but we cannot be grateful to it for degrading our natures, for systematically crushing out of us all martial spirit, for converting a race of soldiers and heroes into a timid flock of quill-driving sheep.

"Thank God, things have not yet gone quite so far as this; there are some of us yet, everywhere, who would be willing to draw swords, and, if needful, lay down our lives, for hearths and homes, aye and for the support and maintenance of that Government to which we owe so much. But this is what we are coming to; and when we once come to that, then I think that, despite the glories of the Pax Britannica, despite the noble intentions of Great Britain, despite all the good that she may have done or tried to do us, the balance will be against her, and India will have to regret rather than rejoice that she has ever had anything to do with England.

"This may be strong language, but it is the truth. Nothing can ever make amends to a nation for the destruction of its national spirit and of its capacity to defend itself, and the soil from which it springs.

"Nor is it only we who shall have to regret and suffer for the mistaken policy that our Government is unhappily pursuing in this matter. Look where you will around you in the world, and you will see gigantic armies and armaments. There is trouble in store for the whole civilised world, and sooner or later a tremendous military struggle will commence, in which assuredly, before it terminates, Great Britain will be involved. Great Britain with all her wealth cannot put one hundred men into the field for every thousand that several Continental powers can. England herself is isolated, and by her insular position to a certain extent protected. But no friendly sea rolls between Europe and Asia, the landward path to India is known and open. India is not isolated, and it will be India, on whose possession half Great Britain's wealth and status depends, that will be the scene of any serious attack by any Continental powers on Great Britain. Then will England regret that, instead of having millions of brave Indians trained to arms to fling back the invaders, she has only her scanty legions to oppose to them, and from her timid subjects can only look, at most, for good wishes—Good wishes—truly good things in their way, but poor bulwarks against Berdan rifles and steel ordnance.

"But, on our own account, we deprecate the existing policy. High and low, we are losing all knowledge of the use of arms, and with this that spirit of self-reliance which enables a man to dare, which makes men brave, which makes them worthy of the name of men. When I was only five years of age my grandfather made me begin to learn all physical exercises in vogue amongst us, and I was trained to the use of all arms and in all martial exercises.

"But what man now sends his son for such training ? What young man now-a-days knows anything of these things ? Fifty years ago, without desiring warfare, every young man's heart glowed within him at the thought of some day showing his prowess in a fair field. Now most young men would, I fear, contemplate any such possible contingency with very—let me say—mixed feelings. If men are to be fit for soldiers—fit to fight to any purpose when the time of trial comes, and come it must for every country—then they must be trained in the use of arms, they must from their childhood see their parents, their elders, using arms and participating in those martial exercises which only 35 years ago, in Oudh at least, were part of every gentleman's occupation.

"And there is another very important point. India is practically being impoverished to a great extent by the enormous expense of her standing army. Sooner or later the crushing weight of this (for her resources) enormous expenditure will break down either the country or the Government. Now, by a judicious encouragement of Indian Volunteers, it would be possible to reduce very greatly this military expenditure and yet leave the country far stronger for *defensive purposes than it now is.*

"But I might go on for hours. I might dwell on the fact that, in the way the Arms Act is now worked in many localities, the people, their herds, their crops, are wholly at the mercy of wild beasts. I might dwell on the insult, the injustice, the violation of the most sacred and solemn pledges by England to India, that are involved in the rules that permit Indian Christians, but do not permit Indian Hindus or Mahomedans, to volunteer. But I have said enough, and, indeed, being, as we are, all of one mind, too much already, I fear, on this subject, in which I am deeply interested ; and I will only now add that we do not ask Government to put arms blindly into all men's hands, but only to permit, under such rules and restrictions as it sees fit, the better and more educated classes of its loyal Indian subjects to qualify themselves to defend, when occasion may require, their homes, their country, and their Government."

It is perhaps needless to say, the subject being, as the President remarked, one of those few in regard to which there is absolutely no difference of opinion throughout the length and breadth of the land, that this resolution was passed by acclamation, amidst the most enthusiastic cheering.

The Congress then adjourned, but a little later in the morning a number of the leading delegates—Rao Sahib P. Rangiah Naidu (*Madras, No.* 1) ; The Hon'ble. S. Subramania Iyer, B.L. (*Madras, No.* 2) ; Rao Sahib S. A. Saminada Iyer (*Tanjore, No.* 41) ; The Hon'ble Dadabhai Naoroji (*Bombay, No.* 48) ; Mr. N. G. Chandavarkar, B.A., L.L.B. (*Bombay, No.* 49) ; Mr. Daji Abaji Khare, B.A., L.L.B. (*Bombay, No.* 56) ; Mr. S. H. Chiplunkar (*Poona, No.* 65) ; Rao Sahib Harilal Harshadrai Dhruva, B.A., L.L.B. (*Surat, No.* 88) ; Lala Ramcharan Das (*Allahabad, No.* 114) ; Baboo Charoo Chunder Mittra (*Allahabad, No.* 119) ; Nawab Reza Ali Khan Bahadur (*Lucknow, No.* 167) ; Mr. Hamid Ali Khan (*Lucknow, No.* 168) ; Mr. Gungadhar

Rao Madhaw Chitnavis (*Nagpur, No.* 187); Baboo Doorga Charan Law, C.I.E. (*Calcutta, No.* 231); The Hon'ble Peary Mohun Mookerjee, M.A., B.L. (*Calcutta, No.* 233); and a few others—had the honour of private interviews with His Excellency the Viceroy. Lord Dufferin received his visitors with his usual kindness, and showed much interest in the work of the Congress, but, as he specially informed all, that he received them, not as delegates or representatives, they having no legal status as such, but, only as distinguished visitors to the capital whose views on public matters he was glad to learn, the reception must be held to have been private, and nothing need be said further as to the conversations that occurred.

In the afternoon, a large steamer being provided by the kindness of Baboo Mohes Chandra Chowdhry, the majority of the delegates made a most pleasant trip up the river. There was no time to waste, so the Public Service Committee held their conference on the steamer's deck, with all their brother delegates round them to consult at each step, and by dusk, when all landed, a perfect unanimity had been arrived at, in regard to all those questions, relating to admission into the public service, which it was found possible to discuss thoroughly.

The next day, Thursday, the 30th of December, the Congress re-assembled for its fourth and last sitting, and the first business dealt with was the report of the Public Service Committee. This was duly read out to the assemblage and entirely approved. Although very brief, it really covered every important point, except one, in regard to which the Congress was greatly divided in opinion, and that was whether successful candidates for the Civil Service, at the proposed examinations in India, should or should not be required to proceed thereafter to Europe to complete their training. A great many delegates considered this to be a *sine qua non,* if these candidates were, later in life, to do the fullest credit, and be of the greatest possible service, to their country; but an equally large number, probably, held that it should remain optional, maintaining with Dr. Rajendralala Mitra, that, however desirable such a visit to England might be, it was monstrous and without any precedent in modern times, that, before a man could serve his own country in any of the higher grades of the public service, he should be compelled to proceed to another country, five thousand miles or more distant, and reside there for two or three years, and especially monstrous in the case of Hindus, to the orthodox amongst whom such journey and residence involved, it was asserted, loss of caste and other social and religious disabilities. On this question the difference of opinion was notoriously fundamental and radical in its character, and it was, therefore, excluded from the report, which, dealing as it did with every other important point connected with the subject, was, by a resolution, formally accepted and unanimously adopted as correctly representing the views of the entire Congress.

Then followed the most important resolution, perhaps, passed by the Congress. On the second day, as will be remembered, a resolution had been passed re-affirming the third resolution of the Congress of 1885, and declaring that the introduction of a representative element into the Government of the country had become a necessity. This present resolution (*IV of the Summary, page* 41) went a step further and indicated "(subject to such modifications as on a more detailed examination of the subject may commend themselves to the Government)" the principles to which, in the opinion of the Congress, regard should be had "in giving practical effect to this essential reform."

The scheme (if nothing else, at least a modest and practical one) is too long to reproduce here, but may be referred to *loc. cit. sup.* The discussion that followed was of the highest interest. Mr. Surendranath Banerjee (*Bengal*) proposed, and Mr. N. G. Chandavarkar (*Bombay*) seconded the resolution, in speeches of great eloquence and cogency which *must be read.** For they are long, and especially Mr. Chandavarkar's, closely argued, and could not be fairly represented by any mere extracts. But passages illustrating well the character of the discussion may be cited from other speeches. Of the representation, so eagerly desired by the whole country, Mr. Ananda Charlu of Madras said†: "After all, dispassionately considered, what is it but the embodiment of an ancient, fundamental, political aphorism, in its juster, truer and nobler acceptation? What is the prayer we lay before Government? It is nothing more and nothing less than a petition to our rulers, to act, in practice, on the well known advice to rulers, DIVIDE and GOVERN; not in its sinister interpretation which prompts men to set class against class, section against section, in a body politic in which perfect concord should prevail, but (as I said) in its juster, truer and nobler interpretation of dividing *with* the subjects the responsibilities and labours of the administration and thereby establishing their rule immutably, on the broad basis of the national concurrence."

Moulvi Syed Shurfuddin (a Barrister-at-law and Landholder) remarked‡: "It is almost needless to say that, as natives of India, we are better versed in the manners and customs, the ideas and convictions, the wants and wishes of our people than any Englishman can be. How then can it be otherwise than reasonable that, after having been educated by the magnanimity of the people of England, we should ask from them that share in the administration of our country which they have taught us to desire and have qualified us to deserve?"

"We want to be legislated for by people who have a real knowledge of our habits and customs; by people who understand us, who are of us, not by foreigners and strangers, who, however good their will, lack that intimate sympathy with, and participation in, our views and aspirations, which is essential if their measures are to command anything like the approval and unanimous assent of the country."

He pointed out that Government had already tacitly admitted the necessity of representation, and concluded his speech with these words: "And many other instances might be cited to show that they (the Government), themselves, are aware of the dangers of the present blindfold system of legislating for people of whom they know little and understand less. So that this great reform is already well within the sphere of practical politics, and all we have to do is to press, and press for it earnestly, energetically, steadily and perseveringly until we get it, and in getting it, crown our rulers, teachers,

* *Vide* pp. 98 and 100 of detailed Report.
† *Vide* detailed Report page 103.
‡ *Vide* page 105 of detailed Report.

friends and guides with new and imperishable laurels. I have heard a Roman apothegm '*Finis coronat opus,*' and in no way can Great Britain more gloriously crown her noble work in India than by the introduction here of representative institutions."

Sheikh Kadir Buksh, a merchant, ridiculed the idea that any differences between Hindus and Mahomedans would in any way vitiate the scheme before them, and said he had been some time on an elected Municipal Board. "We* are Hindus and Mahomedans alike on our Board; never has there been any difference between us arising out of religious feelings, and how should there be? We are not Molvis and Pandits meeting to argue on religious topics, but business men, meeting to arrange for keeping the town clean and healthy and for levying the funds, required for these purposes, equitably and with as little expense and worry to the rate-payers as may be. If we keep the place dirty and cholera comes, will it not kill us Mahomedans as well as the Hindus? If we get pure good water to drink, shall we not drink it as well as they? And so it will be with the proposed elected Legislative Councils. Will it not be all our objects to keep the Government out of useless wars; to make them economize; to reduce taxation; to give fair play to native talent; to encourage native industries? Religión is one thing and business another, and only very foolish or ill-disposed persons mix the two together, and try to set any sect against a work which is equally for the good of all sects."

Malik Bhugwandas of Dera Ismail Khan, a born orator, pointed out that "this† system of representation and Government by Councils composed of our own people is indigenous in the Punjab, and from time immemorial the frontier tribes, though wanting in education, have always possessed sufficient intelligence to manage matters admirably for themselves. We had regular representative Legislative Councils long before we had even heard the name of England; and those Councils made laws which, though not compiled in bulky, statute books, were none the less binding and obeyed; and to this day the independent frontier tribes, in our neighbourhood, are governed by just such Councils; and these Councils have made laws from time to time, and if a man commit adultery or other offence, he is tried by those Councils, and convicted and sentenced according to those laws, which the whole tribe unites to uphold, because they are home-made and commend themselves to all minds as just and right." And he went on to argue, very fairly, that if representative institutions answered so well amongst the ignorant *pushtunis* (or tribes outside the frontier) how much better would they succeed amongst the comparatively educated populations inside the frontier. His brief peroration too pointed well the moral of his eloquent speech. "Great," he said, "are the benefits that have been conferred on us by the British Government. May it prosper for ever and ever, and a third time I say ever, but that this may be so, let it never forget that its real strength lies, not in its artillery but, in the hold it has, and I pray God may ever retain on the hearts of its subjects."

But perhaps the speech that was most enthusiastically received was one made by Pandit Madan Mohun Malavia, a high caste Brahmin, whose fair

* He spoke in Urdu; this is a translation. *Vide* detailed Report, page 105.
† He spoke in Urdu; this is a translation. *Vide* detailed Report, page 106.

complexion and delicately chiseled features, instinct with intellectuality, at once impressed every eye, and who, suddenly, jumping up on a chair beside the President, poured forth a manifestly impromptu speech with an energy and eloquence that carried everything before them.

"It is not to the great British Government," he said,* "that we need demonstrate the utility, the expediency, the necessity of this great reform. It might have been necessary to support our petition for this boon by some such demonstration were we governed by some despotic monarch, jealous of the duties, but ignorant and careless of the rights of subjects. But it is surely unnecessary to say one word in support of such a cause to the British Government, or to the British Nation—to the descendants of those brave and great men who fought and died to obtain for themselves, and preserve intact for their children those very institutions that, taught by their example, we now crave; who spent their whole lives and shed their hearts' blood so freely in maintaining and developing this cherished principle? What is an Englishman without representative institutions? Why not an Englishman at all—a mere sham—a base imitation, and I often wonder, as I look round at our nominally English magnates, how they have the face to call themselves Englishmen, and yet deny us representative institutions and struggle to maintain despotic ones. Representative institutions are as much a part of the true Briton as his language and his literature. Will any one tell me that Great Britain will in cold blood deny us, her free-born subjects, the first of these, when, by the gift of the two latter, she has qualified us to appreciate and has incited us to desire it?

"No taxation without representation! That is the first commandment in the Englishman's Political Bible; how can he palter with his conscience and tax us here, his free and educated fellow-subjects, as if we were dumb sheep or cattle?

"But we are not dumb any longer. India has found a voice at last, in this great Congress, and through it we call on England to be true to her traditions, her instincts and herself, and grant us our rights as free-born British citizens." Then after acknowledging enthusiastically all India has owed to England, he went on: "But while we are thus deeply grateful for the blessings we enjoy, we cannot but feel that there are still many points in which our condition can be, and ought to be, improved; and we see, first and foremost, that the system of administration that now obtains is despotic and is deficient in the principle of representation—the fundamental characteristic of a free Government. There is not a true born Englishman who would not be horrified if told that the Government of India dealt with the whole people of India as slaves, and yet, if any such man will fairly face the facts of the case, he will be compelled to admit that, despite all other good gifts, in this matter of excluding us from all share in the Government of our own country, the Government is really treating us as mere slaves. The right to be represented is inherent in every educated, free-born British subject." He urged that the Queen's Proclamation solemnly promised that her Indian subjects should be treated like all her other subjects, and

* *Vide* detailed Report, page 107.

he showed that they were not so treated, and concluded: "Surely it is the desire of every generous-hearted Englishman, who loves liberty, to confer the freedom he himself enjoys on all?"

"For he," as an English poet says, "that values liberty, confines
"His zeal for her predominance within
"No narrow bounds; her cause engages him
"Wherever pleaded. 'Tis the cause of Man."

"But our President signs that I am exceeding the allotted period, and I will only add, may the cause of the people of India, the cause of liberty and right, engage the attention, heart and soul, of every honest Englishman in India and in England, and may each true Briton, who values the rights, the privileges, the freedom which have made him and his country what they are, aid us *like* true Britons to the fruition of our aspirations, for equal rights, equal privileges and equal freedom."

An Assam delegate concluded his speech with the remark*: "Allowing freely that our rulers, foreigners and strangers as they are to all that most intimately affects us, are actuated by the highest motives and do their best for us, the present state of the country and the universal feeling that pervades it, sufficiently show that neither the purity of their intentions nor the conscientiousness of their efforts can compensate for that want of practical sympathy and detailed knowledge of the circumstances of our case which only our own people, carefully selected by ourselves, can supply."

These extracts and a perusal of the proposer's and seconder's speech will give some idea of the earnestness, ability and enthusiasm with which this discussion was carried on. It is needless to say that the resolution was carried, but it may be added that it was carried without a dissentient voice, although it was known that some few of the delegates, including two or three gentlemen of great distinction, were doubtful of the expediency of entering so much into details as the scheme put forth by the resolution does.

This completed the more important work of the Congress, but a few other resolutions, more or less formal (one, calling upon all public bodies and associations, throughout the country, to entreat the Viceroy to move the Secretary of State to appoint a Commission to enquire into the best practical methods of introducing representative institutions into India; another, for the submission of the resolutions to the Government of India and Her Majesty's Secretary of State for India; a third, for the constitution of permanent Congress Committees at all important centres), and the usual votes of thanks were passed. Still some passages from the closing speech† of the President demand notice. "I am only speaking tamely I fear," he said, "when I say that from first to last nothing could possibly have been more honorable to our country than the conduct of all concerned, or than the spirit that has pervaded the entire assemblage. In the heat of argument, under that greatest of all stimuli, patriotic enthusiasm, not one word, I believe, has escaped a single speaker, that he need wish unspoken. Kindness, courtesy, a spirit of cheerful mutual concession have pervaded our proceedings which, but for this, could never have reached this happy and success-

* Mr. Devi Charan Barua (*Debrughur, No.* 429). *Vide* page 109 of detailed Report.

† *Vide* page 112 of detailed Report.

ful termination." Thanking the assemblage for the uniform support they had accorded to him, he went on to say : "There is, however, just one point to which I ought perhaps to refer more particularly, and that is to the spirit of fairness and moderation and respect towards the Government which has characterized your proceedings from the beginning to the end. I need not say how gratified I have been to observe how thoroughly all have seemed to be imbued with that spirit; not only is it our interest that it should be so, but it is what the Government, after all they have done for us, have a just right to expect from us, and I only hope that the example which this great assemblage has set, in this respect, will be followed, not only at all future meetings of the Congress, not only by all and every Association throughout the country, but also by the entire Indian Press, some members of which, under the influence of the bad example too often set to them by a portion of the Anglo-Indian Press, have at times, it must be confessed, transgressed in this respect. If we really desire to be respected, if we wish our requests to be attended to, if we honestly expect that the English nation will do its duty towards us, we must prove ourselves worthy by showing that we are never unreasonable, never violent, never uncharitable; we must show that we are earnest, but temperate; cognizant of our own rights, but respectful of those of others; expecting the fairest construction of our own acts and motives, and conceding this to those of others ; that, in a word, whatever our *status* in life, high or low, rich or poor, we have become gentlemen, in the highest sense of the word. Unless we are and can prove ourselves gentlemen in this highest, noblest sense, I do not know that we are worthy to receive the concessions for which we are pressing." And he concluded : "I thank you, for myself, for the honour you have done me in choosing me as President and for the generous kindness with which you have upheld me in the performance of the responsible duties of that high position, and I thank you on behalf of all your countrymen—on behalf of posterity—for the noble manner in which at this great Congress—which history will not readily forget—you have upheld the credit, the character, the dignity of our beloved India."

Then, as the storm of cheers, which followed on this peroration, somewhat subsided, volleys of cheers were given for the Queen-Empress, the Viceroy and others, and the Congress of 1886 dissolved.

That night some of the delegates started homewards, but many remained to be present next day (Friday) at a garden party given by His Excellency the Viceroy, to which all the delegates, on the Government House lists of their respective provinces and presidencies, had been kindly invited, not, as His Excellency was careful to explain, in their capacities of representatives, but as gentlemen of more or less distinction and culture whom he was pleased to be able thus to honour.

Another couple of days and only a few stragglers remained of that great assemblage. It had melted away as rapidly as it had gathered. Is it to bear no fruit, to have no results? Well, even if no concrete results should proximately flow from this memorable Congress, if the Government, here and in England, should unhappily remain deaf to the unanimous reclamations of the country, this assemblage will, at any rate, have demonstrated our loyalty to our Sovereign, our gratitude for all the blessings conferred on us, our abiding faith in the innate sense of justice of the British nation, our profound dissatisfaction with the existing form of the administration, and our entire fitness, from every point of view, for those representative institutions, on which the Congress so strongly insisted and on which the entire mass of the educated and intelligent classes, throughout the Empire, have now set their hearts.

These things has this Congress demonstrated, and it must now leave to time, to justice, and to God, the fruition of the national aspirations.

SUMMARY
OF
Resolutions passed at the SECOND INDIAN NATIONAL CONGRESS, held in Calcutta on the 27th, 28th, 29th and 30th December 1886.

RESOLUTION I.

Resolved.—That this Congress of Delegates from all parts of India do humbly offer its dutiful and loyal congratulations to Her Most Gracious Majesty, the Queen Empress, on the approaching completion of the first half century of her memorable, beneficent and glorious reign, and heartily wish her many, many more, and happy, years of rule, over the great British Empire.

[Proposed by Mr. Rahimatulla M. Sayani *(Bombay)*; seconded by Lala Murlidhur, *(Ambala)*; supported by Mr. G. Subramania Iyer *(Madras)* and carried by acclamation.]

RESOLUTION II.

Resolved.—That this Congress regards with the deepest sympathy, and views with grave apprehension, the increasing poverty of vast numbers of the population of India, and (although aware that the Government is not overlooking this matter and is contemplating certain palliatives) desires to record its fixed conviction that the introduction of Representative Institutions will prove one of the most important practical steps towards the amelioration of the condition of the people.

[Proposed by Mr. Dinshaw Edulji Watcha (*Bombay*); seconded by the Hon'ble S. Subramania Iyer (*Madras*); supported by Pandit Prannath (*Lucknow*) and carried by a very large majority.]

RESOLUTION III.

Resolved.—That this Congress do, emphatically, reaffirm the 3rd Resolution of the Congress of 1885, and distinctly declare its belief that the reform and expansion of the Council of the Governor-General for making Laws and of the Provincial Legislative Councils, therein suggested, have now become essential alike in the interests of India and England.

[Proposed by Rai Kunja Lall Banerjee, Bahadur (*Calcutta*); seconded by Mr. P. Rangiah Naidu (*Madras*); supported by Mr. Ghanasham Nilkanth (*Bombay*) and carried unanimously.]

RESOLUTION IV.

Resolved.—That this Congress is of opinion that in giving practical effect to this essential reform, regard should be had (subject to such modifications as, on a more detailed examination of the question, may commend themselves to the Government) to the principles embodied in the following tentative suggestions :—

(I.)—The number of persons composing the Legislative Councils, both Provincial and of the Governor-General, to be materially increased. Not less than one-half the Members of such enlarged Councils to be elected. Not more than one-fourth to be officials having seats *ex-officio* in such Councils, and not more than one-fourth to be Members, official or non-official, nominated by Government.

(2.)—The right to elect members to the Provincial Councils to be conferred only on those classes and members of the community, *primâ facie*, capable of exercising it wisely and independently. In Bengal and Bombay the Councillors may be elected by the members of Municipalities, District Boards, Chambers of Commerce and the Universities, or an electorate may be constituted of all persons possessing such qualifications, educational and pecuniary, as may be deemed necessary. In Madras, the Councillors may be elected either by District Boards, Municipalities, Chambers of Commerce and the University, or by Electoral colleges composed of members partly elected by these bodies and partly nominated by Government. In the North-West Provinces and Oudh and in the Punjab, Councillors may be elected by an Electoral College composed of members elected by Municipal and District Boards and nominated, to an extent not exceeding one-sixth of the total number, by Government, it being understood that the same elective system now in force where Municipal Boards are concerned will be applied to District Boards, and the right of electing members to these latter extended to the cultivating class. But whatever system be adopted (and the details must be worked out separately for each province) care must be taken that all sections of the community, and all great interests, are adequately represented.

(3.)—The elected Members of the Council of the Governor-General for making Laws, to be elected by the elected Members of the several Provincial Councils.

(4.)—No elected or nominated Member of any Council, to receive any salary or remuneration in virtue of such membership, but any such Member, already in receipt of any Government salary or allowance, to continue to draw the same unchanged during membership, and all Members to be entitled to be reimbursed any expenses incurred in travelling in connection with their membership.

(5.)—All persons, resident in India, to be eligible for seats in Council, whether as electees or nominees, without distinction of race, creed, caste or colour.

(6.)—All legislative measures and all financial questions, including all budgets, whether these involve new or enhanced taxation or not, to be necessarily submitted to and dealt with by these Councils. In the case of all other branches of the administration, any Member to be at liberty, after due notice, to put any question he sees fit to the *ex-officio* Members (or such one of these as may be specially charged with the supervision of the particular branch concerned) and to be entitled (except as hereinafter provided) to receive a reply to his question, together with copies of any papers requisite for the thorough comprehension of the subject, and on this reply the Council to be at liberty to consider and discuss the question and record thereon such resolution as may appear fitting to the majority. Provided that, if the subject in regard to which the inquiry is made involves matters of Foreign policy, Military dispositions or strategy, or is otherwise of such a nature that, in the opinion of the Executive, the Public interests would be materially imperilled by the communication of the information asked for, it shall be competent for them to instruct the *ex-officio* Members, or one of them, to reply accordingly, and decline to furnish the information asked for.

(7.)—The Executive Government shall possess the power of overruling the decision arrived at by the majority of the Council, in every case in which, in its opinion, the public interests would suffer by the acceptance of such decision; but whenever this power is exercised, a full exposition of the grounds on which this has been considered necessary, shall be published within one month, and in the case of local Governments they shall report the circumstances and explain their action to the Government of India, and in the case of this latter, it shall report and explain to the Secretary of State; and in any such case on a representation made through the Government of India and the Secretary of State by the overruled majority, it shall be competent to the Standing Committee of the House of Commons (recommended in the 3rd Resolution of last year's Congress which this present Congress has affirmed) to consider the matter, and call for any and all papers or information, and hear any persons on behalf of such majority or otherwise, and thereafter, if needful, report thereon to the full House.

[Proposed by Mr. Surendra Nath Banerjee (*Calcutta*); seconded by Mr. N. G. Chandavarkar (*Bombay*); supported by Mr. Sharfuddin (*Behar*) and carried without a dissentient voice.]

RESOLUTION V.

Resolved.—That this Congress do invite all Public Bodies and all Associations throughout the Country, humbly and earnestly, to entreat His Excellency the Viceroy to obtain the sanction of Her Majesty's Secretary of State for India, to the appointment of a Commission, to enquire exhaustively into the best method of introducing such a tentative form of Representative Institutions into India, as has been indicated in Resolutions III of the past, and IV of the present year's Congress.

[Proposed by Mr. N. N. Gupta (*Karrachi*); seconded by Mr. M. B. Namjoshi (*Poona*); supported by Kumar Binay Krishna (*Calcutta*) and carried unanimously.]

RESOLUTION VI.

Resolved.—That a Committee composed of the gentlemen named in the margin* be appointed to consider the Public Service Question and report thereon to this Congress.

Hon'ble Dadabhai Naoroji (*Bombay*).
,, S. Subramania Iyer (*Madras*).
,, Peary Mohan Mookerjee (*Calcutta*).
Mr. G. Subramania Iyer (*Madras*).
Babu Matilal Ghose (*Calcutta*).
Mr. Surendra Nath Banerjee (*Calcutta*).
,, Gangapershad Varma (*Lucknow*).
,, Ramkali Chaudhuri (*Benares*).
,, Guru Prasad Sen (*Patna*).
Pundit Prannath (*Lucknow*).
Munshi Kashipershad (*Allahabad*).
Nawab Reza Ali Khan (*Lucknow*).
Mr. Hamid Ali (*Lucknow*).
Lala Kanhyalal (*Amritsar*).
Rao Sahib Gungadhar Rao Madhaw Chitnavis (*Nagpur*).
Mr. Rahimatulla M. Sayani (*Bombay*).

[Proposed by Mr. Surendra Nath Banerjee (*Calcutta*); seconded by Mr. M. B. Namjoshi (*Poona*); supported by Pandit S. Agnihotri (*Lahore*) and carried unanimously.]

RESOLUTION VII.

Resolved.—That this Congress approves and adopts the report* submitted by the Committee appointed by Resolution VI.

[Proposed by Mr. Surendra Nath Banerjee (*Calcutta*); seconded by the Hon'ble S. Subramania Iyer (*Madras*) and carried unanimously.]

RESOLUTION VIII.

Resolved.—That, in the opinion of this Congress, the time has now arrived when the system of trial by jury may be safely extended into many parts of the Country where it is not at present in force.

[Proposed by Mr. S. A. Saminada Iyer (*Tanjore*); seconded by Mr. H. H. Dhruva (*Surat*); supported by Dr. Trailokyanath Mitter (*Calcutta*) and carried unanimously.]

RESOLUTION IX.

Resolved.—That, in the opinion of this Congress, the innovation made in 1872 in the system of trial by jury, depriving the verdicts of juries of all finality, has proved injurious to the Country, and that the powers then, for the first time, vested in Sessions Judges and High Courts, of setting aside verdicts of acquittal, should be at once withdrawn.

[Proposed by Mr. W. C. Bonnerjee (*Calcutta*); seconded by the Hon'ble Peary Mohan Mookerjee (*Calcutta*); supported by Munshi Sadho Lal (*Benares*) and carried by a very large majority.]

RESOLUTION X.

Resolved.—That, in the opinion of this Congress, a provision, similar to that contained in the Summary Jurisdiction Act of England (under which accused persons in serious cases have the option of demanding a committal to the Sessions Court), should be introduced into the Indian Code of Criminal

---

* REPORT.

We, the Members of the Committee appointed by the Congress to submit a statement in connection with the Public Service Question, have the honour to report that the following resolutions were unanimously adopted by us at a meeting held yesterday :—

1.—That the open Competitive Examination be held simultaneously both in India and in England.

2.—That the simultaneous examinations thus held be equally open to all classes of Her Majesty's subjects.

3.—That the classified list be prepared according to merit.

4.—That the Congress express the hope that the Civil Service Commissioners will give fair consideration to Sanskrit and Arabic among the subjects of examination.

5.—That the age of candidates eligible for admission to the open Competitive Examination be not less than 19, or, as recommended by Sir C. Aitchison, more than 23 years.

6.—That simultaneous examinations being granted, the Statutory Civil Service be closed for first appointments.

7.—That the appointments in the Statutory Civil Service, under the existing rules, be still left open to the Members of the Uncovenanted Service and to professional men of proved merit and ability.

8.—That all appointments requiring educational qualifications, other than covenanted first appointments, be filled by Competitive Examinations held in the different Provinces, and open in each Province to such natural-born subjects of H. M. only as are residents thereof.

These Resolutions it is hoped, cover the main principles which underlie the questions set by the Public Service Commission. For a more detailed consideration there was no time.

(Sd.) DADABHAI NAOROJI,
President of the Committee.

30th December 1886.

Procedure, enabling accused persons, in warrant cases, to demand that, instead of being tried by the Magistrate, they be committed to the Court of Sessions.

[Proposed by Mr. Mano Mohan Ghose *(Calcutta)*; seconded by Mr. T. Chidambara Row *(Bellary)*; supported by Khajeh Abdul Aleem *(Dacca)* and carried unanimously.]

RESOLUTION XI.

Resolved.—That this Congress do place on record an expression of the universal conviction, that a complete separation of executive and judicial functions (such that in no case the two functions shall be combined in the same officer) has become an urgent necessity, and that, in its opinion, it behoves the Government to effect this separation without further delay, even though this should, in some Provinces, involve some extra expenditure.

[Proposed by Mr. Daji Abaji Khare *(Bombay)*; seconded by Munshi Kashipershad *(Allahabad)*; supported by Mr. Sri Ram *(Lucknow)* and carried unanimously.]

RESOLUTION XII.

Resolved.—That in view to the unsettled state of public affairs in Europe, and the immense assistance that the people of this country, if duly prepared therefor, is capable of rendering to Great Britain in the event of any serious complications arising, this Congress do earnestly appeal to the Government to authorise (under such rules and restrictions as may to it seem fitting) a system of Volunteering for the Indian inhabitants of the country, such as may qualify them to support the Government, effectively, in any crisis.

[Proposed by Rajah Rampal Singh *(Oudh)*; seconded by Mr. R. D. Mehta *(Calcutta)* and carried by acclamation.]

RESOLUTION XIII.

Resolved.—That Standing Congress-Committees be constituted at all important centres.

[Proposed by Mr. W. C. Bonnerjee *(Calcutta)*; seconded by Mr. N. G. Chandavarkar *(Bombay)* and carried unanimously.]

RESOLUTION XIV.

Resolved.—That the Third Indian National Congress assemble at Madras on the 27th of December 1887.

[Proposed by Mr. A. O. Hume *(Punjab)*; seconded by the Hon'ble S. Subramania Iyer *(Madras)* and carried by acclamation.]

RESOLUTION XV.

Resolved.—That copies of these Resolutions be forwarded to His Excellency the Viceroy in Council, with the humble requests, that he will cause the 1st Resolution to be submitted in due course to Her Majesty the Queen Empress, that he will cause all the Resolutions to be laid before Her Majesty's Secretary of State for India, and that he himself will be graciously pleased, in consultation with his colleagues, to accord them his best consideration.

[Proposed by Mr. Rangiah Naidu *(Madras)* ; and seconded by Mr. Sorabjee Framjee Patel *(Bombay)* and carried unanimously.]

(*Signed*) DADABHAI NAOROJI,

President of the Second Indian National Congress.

DETAILED
REPORT OF THE PROCEEDINGS
OF
THE SECOND INDIAN NATIONAL CONGRESS
HELD AT
CALCUTTA
On the 27th, 28th, 29th and 30th of December 1886.

FIRST DAY'S PROCEEDINGS.

THE INAUGURAL MEETING of the Congress was held on the 27th December at the Town Hall.

"We never remember to have seen the Hall more densely packed, and what was a striking feature of the meeting, was its undoubtedly cosmopolitan character. It was, in short, a vast gathering of the Indian people. Every race and every sect was there represented, and the proceedings, exceedingly earnest and enthusiastic, were remarkable for their expressions of loyalty to the Crown. At the time (3 P.M.) appointed for the commencement of the proceedings, Mr. Dadabhai Naoroji was conducted to the platform amidst loud and deafening cheers, which again resounded through the Hall on the appearance of Raja Rampal Singn and Mr. Cotton.*"

The Hon'ble S. SUBRAMANIA IYER (*Madras, No.* 2 *of List*) then proposed, and Mr. N. G. CHANDAVARKAR (*Bombay, No.* 49) seconded the proposal, that, pending the election of a President, Dr. Rajendralala Mitra (*Bengal, No.* 229) do take the Chair. The proposition having been carried by acclamation, Dr. Rajendralala assumed the Chair amidst enthusiastic cheering, and then again rising addressed the assemblage.

DR. RAJENDRALALA MITRA said: "Gentlemen,—The duty I have to perform on the present occasion is to receive the delegates who have come from the various Provinces of the Empire to take part in our deliberations. It is a very agreeable duty, and I most heartily welcome the gentlemen to this assemblage. In the name of my colleagues who have organized this Congress, I express my welcome to them. In the name of the citizens of Calcutta, I beg to tender them our most cordial greetings. I receive them with my extended hands; I offer them the right hand of fellowship for the cordial manner in which they have responded to our invitation. It is not for me on the present occasion to dwell at length upon the subjects which will be brought forward for consideration here. But I cannot rest content with the few words I have already said. It has been the dream of my life that the scattered units of my race may some day coalesce and come together; that instead of living merely as individuals, we may some day so combine as to be able to live as a nation. In this meeting, I behold the commencement of such coalescence. (*Cheers.*) I hope the union will not be very distant. It may not be left to me to realize the sight, but it is highly gratifying to me that we are here assembled together, delegates from the North and from the South, from the East and from the West, all anxious to join as members of one nation for the good of our country. Addressing those of my own race, I can tell you that there was a time when our forefathers lived as one single race. Circumstances led to their dispersion, and parochial hedges of various kinds kept them apart. It is therefore not a matter of small rejoicing that we should have surmounted those difficulties and come together. The Aryan blood that courses in my veins is the same which vivifies you, and as blood is thicker than water, I take the highest delight in being able to welcome my long separated brethren. (*Loud cheers.*) Pardon me, gentlemen, if in the exuberance of my emotion I have forgotten for one moment only the Mahomedan gentlemen who have graced this meeting with their presence. They are as much welcome as the people of my own race. I welcome them with all my heart, and I look upon their presence here to-day as a guarantee of this being truly a National Congress. Without them we might have felt that we were at a marriage party without the bride. Diverse we are in origin, in religion, in language, and in our manners and customs, but we are not the

---

* "Statesman and Friend of India," December 28th, 1886. For more detailed notices of and remarks of the Press on the Congress see Appendix V.

less members of the same nation. *(Cheers.)* We live in the same country, we are subjects of the same Sovereign, and our good and evil depends entirely on the state of the Government and the laws passed in this country. Whatever is beneficial to the Hindus is equally beneficial to the Mahomedans, and whatever is injurious to the Hindus is equally injurious to the followers of Mahomed. Nations are not made of sects but of tribes bound together in one political bond. *(Loud and prolonged cheering.)* We are all bound by the same political bond, and therefore we constitute one nation. I behold in this Congress the dawn of a better and a happier day for India. I look upon it as the quickening of a new life. For long, our fathers lived and we have lived as individuals only, or as families, but henceforward I hope we shall be living as a nation, united one and all to promote our welfare and the welfare of our mother country. *(Cheers.)* That is the great object of this Congress, and if you bear that in mind, I am sure there will be no difference of opinion as to the propriety of our receiving each other in brotherly love and trying our best to secure the utmost union possible. It would be absurd to suppose that we can for one moment secure perfect union. We know that Jesus Christ failed to secure perfect union in the body of his disciples, and out of 250 millions of people, you must find that we have many more than one disciple who is opposed to us.

"There has been a good deal written lately about the impropriety of this Congress, about the injustice we do to the Government by holding these meetings. *(Here Mr. A. O. Hume entered the Hall amidst loud and deafening applause.)* I shall not stop to refer to the scandalous and absurd charges which have been hurled against us about our being a discontented people, a band of wire-pullers and professional agitators. I would not say one word against those who complain of our being disloyal; for such charges are beneath contempt. But there are others who are more moderate in their tone and in the charges they bring against us and therefore are more injurious in their action. For instance, we have been told that we are trying to force the hand of Government. What is meant by that, I must confess, I do not clearly understand. As an old man, it has been my habit occasionally to cut in for a hand at whist. I know that in this position it is an object with the players to force the hand of their opponents. But are we really forcing the hand of our opponent, the Government? Do we really look upon the Government as an opponent? It is understood in the game that my opponent has some card, some honour, some trumps, which he is not at all disposed to let me know. Has the Government any such thing? Does the Government desire that there should be something kept secret and away from the public, and which we are trying to force the Government to disclose? No. Those who say so libel the Government. It is altogether wrong to suppose that the Government is holding anything away from us; and we cannot try therefore to force the hands of the Government, when they contain nothing that would not be given to us freely. Again, we have been told, we must have a policy of confidence in the Government. I would say at once, away with such nonsense. I will never have a policy of confidence. A policy of confidence implies the simulation of a merit which we do not possess; it is the simulation of a feeling which we do not really feel. If we really have confidence in the Government, we need not adopt any policy or semblance of it. We have perfect confidence in the Government, and therefore it is absurd to talk of 'adopting a policy of confidence.' Let those who have no confidence in the Government, but who have their own purposes to serve, say they have 'a policy of confidence.' We shall have none of it. *(Loud cheers.)*

"We have again been told that the Government should not be obliged to precipitate their action; that they have already adopted a resolution for enquiry, and that we should not oblige them to come to a conclusion without such enquiry. But are we doing so? Do you for a moment believe that by assembling here to-day and taking into consideration all those subjects which concern us most, we are forestalling the decision of the Government? The Government has itself said that the Public Service Commission is of a judicial character, and that the whole business depends on the evidence produced before it. Who is to produce the evidence for the whole people of the country if the men of light and leading, who are our leaders in every respect, should keep away and be prevented from joining together and deliberating in the manner in which they can put forth the most reliable evidence? We are only preparing the evidence, and not forestalling the action of the Government. If you were to say, as they have said, that we force resolutions instead of allowing time for consideration, the same may be said of those gentlemen of the long robe who take up so much of the time of our judges in discussing matters before the judges have made up their minds. There is no pretence whatever to say we have not the utmost confidence in the judges of the High Court, and the other great Courts of the country. We all have the utmost confidence in the judges. Still we deem it necessary, for the interest of our cause, that we should employ the gentlemen of the long robe to explain matters to the judges; we desire that our cases shall be put rightly before them. This is an analogous case, and we want our delegates of mature judgment to consider the evidence and put it in ship-shape, so that it may be laid before the Government with perfect confidence of success, and may enable the Government to see through our cause much better. *(Cheers.)* If it be true that the Government is superseded, by such action, the same may be said of the judges, and the consequence would be that if the gentlemen of the long robe insisted on not interfering with the discretion of the judges during trial, they would very soon find their green bags to be empty. There are some other charges made, but they are all of the same stamp, and I shall not take up your time by dwelling on them, for I must leave ample time to my successor to deliver his inaugural address. I will, however, in this connexion tell you a thing which occurred to me two years ago. As President of the British Indian Association, I took a deep interest in organizing the opposition to the Bengal Tenancy Bill, and I asked a Hindu gentleman,—I am particular to say a Hindu gentleman,—to join the opposition. He said, no, he would not. And why so? 'Because my Collector won't like it.' 'But what do you care about your Collector; your interests are involved?' 'But you require a subscription from me, and if I join you, I shall lose my money and I shall lose the good graces of my Collector. You will not lose your case, because I keep back; if you win, I shall derive the full benefit and I shall retain the friendship of the Collector and my money; if you lose, you lose all, but I shall still have the benefit of the Collector's good graces and my money.' Is there anything like this feeling somewhere which makes people keep away from this conference? It is not for me to attribute motives, but I found that in one case, and it is not out of my way to bring it to the notice of the Congress.

"The subjects which you will have to consider are so varied and so diverse in character, and they will be expatiated upon so fully by my friend who will soon occupy this chair, that I shall not take up time by going through them *seriatim*. The most important of them is the reconstitution of the Legislative Councils. I look upon that as the corner-stone of all the topics of political condition. *(Loud cheers.)* Nothing can be done, nothing will be advantageous, as long as our legislatures are in their present condition. All other things dwindle into very little, when you place beside them this primary consideration, the reconstitution and reformation of the Legislative Councils. Nor is this a matter in which we have for the first time conceived any idea. Time was when our laws were passed *in camera*, in the Council Chamber, with closed doors, and when nobody knew anything of how our laws were fashioned, until they were read, passed, and published in the Gazette. The Government itself felt that that was not a very fair way of doing business. The Government itself wanted co-operation from without, and the first step taken was to appoint a native gentleman of vast experience and illimitable judicial lore to lend his aid to the maturing of bills. This was, however, a very poor substitute for better representation; it was a procedure which was felt to be utterly worthless, and in a few years it was set aside. The Councils' Act under which we now live is a great improvement on the past. It has given you several persons in the Council instead of only one adviser, but the evil arose from the several persons who were appointed not being representatives of anybody but themselves (*cheers*); they represented no one but their own good interests (*cheers*); they were selected, I will not say how or with what motive, but we know that they were selected so as to produce more ornament than usefulness. *(Cheers.)* We have heard with reference to ladies what Mrs. Grundy sometimes calls heaps of millinery, and we had several such; there were others who acted with perfection as dummies; others who had taken up the role of *ap ke waste's*. (*Cheers.*) But whether as *ap ke wastes*, as dummies, or as heaps of millinery, they were just the men not wanted. When I say this, I must not forget that there were some who were my personal friends, and better men India did not produce. But they were few. They were not able to cope with the overwhelming dead weight of the official majority that rested upon them, and their usefulness was minimised. If by the action of Government at three different stages you see that it has been felt expedient to alter the constitution of the Councils for the preparation of our laws, there is nothing disloyal or improper if we once more say 'let us take another step forward.' The goal may not be reached for some time, but our grand children might come to it. At present, we want only one step forward: for nomination by the authorities, nomination in any case of an irresponsible character, we want election by those whom the elected are to represent. This is the primary object of our agitation with regard to the Legislative Councils. Let the representatives be elected. (*Cheers.*) Let the system be whatever the Government in its wisdom may think proper, but let the policy be a policy of representation, and let there be a sufficient number of representatives to make the feelings and wants of the people fully heard by the Government. We live not under a National Government, we live under a foreign bureaucracy (*cheers*); our foreign rulers under the peculiar circumstances of the case are foreigners by birth, religion, language, habits—everything that divides humanity into different sections. They cannot possibly dive into our hearts; they cannot ascertain our wants and feelings and aspirations. (*Cheers.*) It is impossible for them to do so. They may try their best, and I have no reason to doubt that many of our Governors have tried hard to ascertain our feelings and our wants; but owing to their peculiar position, they have failed to ascertain them. Therefore, what we want is to have a sufficient number of men to represent the people, each bringing his quota of knowledge of the requirements of a particular section of the community. (*Cheers.*) Perhaps it is not for this Congress to decide the number of such representatives; it would be for the Government to decide. But this much is clear, that in all honesty we do want a much larger number than at present.

"There is one point in connection with the Legislative Councils which I must not forget, and that is the right of interpellation. (*Cheers.*) At present, owing to the peculiar circumstances of the Government, there is no interchange of opinion, each party having the right to express its views. We have thus to make our guesses as to what others think, and many Acts which are most useful in their way, many orders of an administrative kind which are most necessary and judicious, are announced in the pages of the Gazette without a single word of explanation, and the people cannot help doubting the good faith of those who pass them. A single question in the Council Chamber would at once explain the matter; and therefore we think that as a matter of justice it is extremely important that whatever might be the constitution of the Legislative Councils, we should have the right of interpellation. (*Loud cheering.*)

"With regard to the other subjects before the Congress there is one only to which I shall refer, and that is the Public Service question. It is not so important, not nearly so vitally important, as the question of the reconstitution of the Councils; it is rather a narrow question and has a bad stamp on its face, an anxiety on our part to get the loaves and fishes; but still it is a very important question; because, without taking into account the money point of view, the nation have a right to demand that they shall have the privilege of serving their own country. (*Cheers.*) This is a right inalienable from the people in all other parts of the world. It has been conceded even by the Czar of Russia, and I hold that the keeping it away from us is a grave injustice. (*Loud cheers.*) That this deprivation should be done away with is a matter which should occupy your foremost attention. True, it may be said that at present the people can go to England and enter into the Civil Service, but it is such a mockery that the man who tells it is either joking with me or actually insulting me. The question is, that we should send our children, at the age of 16, five thousand miles away for three years together for the purpose of passing an examination of the strictest possible kind. The odds are against them, the prizes are few, and the blanks numerous, and the risks of sojourn by youths without guardians in a large metropolis, teeming with temptation, are most serious. As a matter of fact, several Indian youths have returned from England as raving maniacs. Parents must be foolhardy indeed who, in the face of these facts, will venture to send their children to England at the age of 16. But suppose the age is raised by two years. Would that satisfy all your demand? I say, nay. For the service of one's country, in no part of the world is a person called away from his native land to pass an examination. (*Cheers.*) Canada is under the British Government. But Her Majesty the Queen-Empress does not require that every French subject there shall go to England to pass an examination before being admitted into the Canadian service. Nothing of the kind is required in the Cape Colonies, nor in Australia, nor in Ceylon. And what is true of them is true of any other country which is a foreign dependency. Why should then the case be different in India alone? The rule here is that no man should be allowed to serve the country without running the great risks which await them in England, without having to expatriate himself for three years, and come home to be excluded from caste. This is a great grievance too and it is one regarding which every Hindu and every Mahomedan gentleman has a right to make a strong protest. I do not deny for a moment that there are advantages in going to England, intellectual and moral, of a very high order (*loud cheers*), and I would be the last to put an embargo on any one going to England. But I hold that it should not be made a *sine qua non* for appointment under the Government. It is just as bad as the Czar's mandate which will allow no man to become a high officer unless a Mahomedan Ali Khan changes his name to Alikhanoff. Our Sovereign, Her Gracious Majesty the Empress, would be the last to show that she is in this respect on a par with the Czar of Russia, and I hope therefore that those who will take the subject into consideration will not lose sight of this important point.

"I shall say nothing further with regard to the subjects which will come before you, and I shall close by simply urging that whatever you do and say, and whatever policy you mature, bear in mind that of all things moderation is of the utmost importance. (*Cheers.*) Let your speakers speak moderately; let your schemes be moderate; and let your resolutions be so framed that *no* Government can have any occasion to complain of want of moderation. That is what I am particularly anxious to ensure, and I hope your Committee and your Congress men will bear this fact prominently in mind.

"I shall say nothing more, but repeat our welcome to the gentlemen here assembled and leave the matter to your consideration." (*Prolonged cheering.*)

BABOO JOYKISSEN MOOKERJEE (*Bengal No.* 230) then rose and said: "I have the honour to move that Mr. Naoroji be elected President of this Congress. I do not think that because our Bombay friends did us the high honour of electing our distinguished countryman, Mr. W. C. Bonnerjee, as President of the Congress held last year at Bombay, we are therefore bound to return the compliment by electing a Bombay gentleman to the chair at the present Congress. But happily we have, in Mr. Naoroji, a gentleman who would do honour to any assembly over which he might be called upon to preside. (*Cheers.*) Warm devotedness to his country, a life spent in active participation of every public movement for her welfare, distinguished abilities, and singular moderation both in aspirations and expressions,—what more could be desired in one whom we wish to guide the deliberations of the Congress. (*Vociferous sheering.*) The task before him is far from a difficult or disagreeable one. The assembly over which we are about to request him to preside, is not one composed of village Parnells, met together for the purpose of giving vent to disloyal feelings, or expressing their discontent with the Government of the country (*loud cheers*), but to take advantage of the Jubilee year for giving expression to their feelings of loyalty to the Throne (*loud cheers*), to offer thanksgiving and prayer for the incalculable benefits which have been conferred on them by Her Gracious Majesty's Government (*cheers*), and to lay at the foot of the Throne their humble suggestions for such improvements in the administration of the country as they humbly think are required if that administration is to keep pace with the spread of education and enlightenment, and with the progress of the country. (*Loud and continued cheers.*) It is no wonder that objects such as these should have drawn together distinguished gentlemen from all parts of the country, when you find a blind old man like myself of 79 years of age bending under the infirmities of age, taking a part in the deliberations." (*Loud and enthusiastic cheers.*)

NAWAB REZA ALI KHAN BAHADUR (*Lucknow, No.* 167) then rose and seconded Baboo Joy Kissen Mookerjee's proposition. He said (*speaking in Urdu*): "Mr. Chairman and Gentlemen,—It is with the greatest pleasure that I rise to second the proposal just made by my venerable colleague, that the Honourable Dadabhai Naoroji should be the President of this National Congress, and I think I express only the universal opinion of the entire assemblage, when I assert that no fitter President could possibly be found than our veteran patriot whose entire life has been spent in advocating the cause and endeavouring to improve the condition of the people of India. (*Cheers.*)

"This, gentleman, is a subject on which I need not enlarge. You all know as well as myself, indeed many of you better, what strong claims Mr. Naoroji has established on the gratitude of his country. To dilate on the subject would be sheer waste of time. But there is one subject on which I must entreat you to permit me to say a few words before I close. I find to my astonishment that some people here in Calcutta are going about saying, and even printing in the newspapers, if these have been correctly translated to me, that the Mahomedans of India have no interest in this Congress, and have no intention of joining their Hindu brethren in the efforts, of which this Congress is one result, to obtain for the nation at large some instalment of their rights as free subjects. No assertions, gentlemen, could be more baseless, more false, more utterly preposterous than these. (*Loud and prolonged cheers.*) In the part of the country whence I have come, where we Musselmen number some millions, Hindus and Mahomedans have ever lived together in amity so far as differences of creed is concerned. We have had plenty of fighting in past times amongst ourselves no doubt, but it has not been over religious matters. There have been parties, but these parties have not been Mahomedans against Hindus, but *one* set of Mahomedans *and* Hindus against *another* set of Mahomedans *and* Hindus. For hundreds of years, as history shows, we have worked together without ever dreaming that there could be any differences in our worldly interests, because some of us worship one way and some of us another. We are not educated —more the pity—and hence it is that I am unable to address you this day in English; but yet you see, though fully aware that in consequence of this ignorance of mine I should understand but little of the proceedings, I have travelled 700 miles to this Congress to show on my own behalf, and on that of my co-religionists, how real our interest, how deep our sympathy, is in this great National movement. (*Enthusiastic cheering.*) To all of you I say, without distinction of race or creed, in this endeavour to secure their rights for the people of India, we Mahomedans are with you with our whole hearts. The Association that has done us the honour of deputing us is largely composed of leading Mahomedans, Nawabs, Wasikadars, political pensioners, and scions of the once Royal House of Oudh, and I assure you that our Association and my brother Mahomedans, generally, of Oudh, will utterly repudiate and condemn any unworthy attempt to create dissensions in our ranks by unfounded statements as to our supposed want of sympathy with the present movement. Hindus or Mahomedans, Parsees or Sikhs, we are one people *now* (whatever our ancestors 800 years ago may have been), and our public interests are indivisible and identical. Gentlemen, I pray you disregard any such slanders. We Mahomedans (at least those of us in any way capable of thinking at all) think just as all thinking Hindus do on these public questions, and believe me when I say that you will ever find us side by side with you in every legal constitutional endeavour to raise the political status of the people of our common home and country." (*Prolonged cheering.*)

MR. HAMID ALI KHAN (*Oudh, No.* 168) gave a brief summary of this eloquent speech in English for the benefit of those few delegates who did not understand Urdu; and he went on to say: "On my own part I desire to say that I endorse every word of my friend Nawab Reza Ali's speech. I can assure you that whatever individuals may do, we Mahomedans are not going as a body to exclude ourselves from the national councils. (*Cheers.*) We are one with our fellow countrymen, we are one with all, be they of what country they may, who desire the glory and freedom of India and the welfare and prosperity of her people. (*Loud cheering.*) If any Mahomedans do keep aloof from these political movements, it is not on account of any antagonism to persons of other religious persuasions, but on account of their want of education and necessary failure to understand the importance of these movements. (*Cheers.*) I can assure you that, though there may be individual exceptions, and you cannot expect everybody to be of precisely the same opinion on all points, the great bulk of the, in any degree, educated Mahomedans throughout the country are with you and for you in all you aim at, and will always be glad and proud to be associated with you in your efforts to benefit our common country and to afford you ever fresh and fresh proofs of our sincere desire to assist and co-operate with you in all your undertakings."

The proposition was then put and carried with the greatest enthusiasm, loud and persistent cheers being given for Mr. Naoroji and then "one cheer more," a hurricane of cheers, was given "for the Mahomedan community and the National Unity."

Dr. Rajendralala Mitra then amidst tumultuous applause declared Mr. Naoroji elected by acclamation and installed him in the chair.

THE HON. DADABHAI NAOROJI (*Bombay, No.* 48), President of the Congress, said: "I need not tell you how sincerely thankful I am to you for placing me in this position of honour. I at first thought that I was to be elevated to this proud position as a return for what might be considered as a compliment paid by us to Bengal when Mr. Bonnerjee was elected President of the first Congress last year at Bombay. I can assure you however that that election was no mere compliment to Bengal, but arose out of the simple fact that we regarded Mr. Bonnerjee as a gentleman eminently qualified to take the place of President, and we installed him in that position in all sincerity as the proper man in the proper place. I now see, however, that this election of my humble self is not intended as a return of compliment, but that, as both proposer and seconder have said, you have been kind enough to select me because I am supposed to be really qualified to undertake the task. I hope it may prove so and that I may be found really worthy of all the kind things said of me; but whether this be so, or not, when such kind things are said by those who occupy such high positions amongst us, I must say I feel exceedingly proud and am very grateful to all for the honour thus done me. (*Loud cheering.*)

"Your late Chairman has heartily welcomed all the delegates who come from different parts of India, and with the same heartiness I return to him, and all our Bengal friends on my own behalf and on that of all the delegates from other Provinces, the most sincere thanks for the cordial manner in which we have been received. From what has been done already, and from what is in store for us during our short stay here, I have no doubt we shall carry away with us many and most pleasant reminiscences of our visit to Calcutta. (*Cheers.*)

"You will pardon me, and I beg your indulgence when I say that when I was asked only two days ago to become your President and to give an inaugural address, it was with no small trepidation that I agreed to undertake the task; and I hope that you will extend to me all that indulgence which my shortcomings may need. (*Loud cheers.*)

"The assemblage of such a Congress is an event of the utmost importance in Indian history. I ask whether in the most glorious days of Hindu rule, in the days of Rajahs like the great Vikram, you could imagine the possibility of a meeting of this kind, where even Hindus of all different provinces of the kingdom could have collected and spoken as one nation. Coming down to the later Empire of our friends, the Mahomedans, who probably ruled over a larger territory at one time than any Hindu monarch, would it have been, even in the days of the great Akbar himself, possible for a meeting like this to assemble composed of all classes and communities, all speaking one language, and all having uniform and high aspirations of their own.

"Well, then what is it for which we are now met on this occasion? We have assembled to consider questions upon which depend our future, whether glorious or inglorious. It is our good fortune that we are under a rule which makes it possible for us to meet in this manner. (*Cheers.*) It is under the civilizing rule of the Queen and people of England that we meet here together, hindered by none, and are freely allowed to speak our minds without the least fear and without the least hesitation. Such a thing is possible under British rule and British rule only (*Loud cheers.*) Then I put the *question* plainly: Is this Congress a nursery for sedition and rebellion against the British Government (*cries of no, no*); or is it another stone in the foundation of the stability of that Government (*cries of yes, yes*)? There could be but one answer, and that you have already given, because we are thoroughly sensible of the numberless blessings conferred upon us, of which the very existence of this Congress is a proof in a nutshell. (*Cheers.*) Were it not for these blessings of British rule I could not have come here, as I have done, without the least hesitation and without the least fear that my children might be robbed and killed in my absence; nor could you have come from every corner of the land, having performed, within a few days, journeys which in former days would have occupied as many months. (*Cheers.*) These simple facts bring home to all of us at once some of those great and numberless blessings which British rule has conferred upon us. But there remain even greater blessings for which we have to be grateful. It is to British rule that we owe the education we possess; the people of England were sincere in the declarations made more than half a century ago that India was a sacred charge entrusted to their care by Providence, and that they were bound to administer it for the good of India, to the glory of their own name, and the satisfaction of God. (*Prolonged cheering.*) When we have to acknowledge so many blessings as flowing from British rule—and

I could descant on them for hours, because it would simply be recounting to you the history of the British Empire in India—is it possible that an assembly like this, every one of whose members is fully impressed with the knowledge of these blessings, could meet for any purpose inimical to that rule to which we owe so much? (*Cheers.*)

"The thing is absurd. Let us speak out like men and proclaim that we are loyal to the backbone (*cheers*); that we understand the benefits English rule has conferred upon us; that we thoroughly appreciate the education that has been given to us, the new light which has been poured upon us, turning us from darkness into light and teaching us the new lesson that kings are made for the people, not peoples for their kings; and this new lesson we have learned amidst the darkness of Asiatic despotism only by the light of free English civilization. (*Loud cheers.*) But the question is, do the Government believe us? Do they believe that we are really loyal to them; that we do truly appreciate and rely on British rule; that we veritably desire its permanent continuance; that our reason is satisfied and our sentimental feelings gratified as well as our self interest? It would be a great gratification to us if we could see in the inauguration of a great movement like this Congress, that what we do really mean and desire is thoroughly and truly so understood by our rulers. I have the good fortune to be able to place before you testimony which cannot be questioned, from which you will see that some at least of the most distinguished of our rulers do believe that what we say is sincere; and that we do *not* want to subvert British rule; that our outspoken utterances are as much for their good as for our good. They do believe, as Lord Ripon said, that what is good for India is good for England. I will give you first the testimony as regards the educated classes which was given 25 years ago by Sir Bartle Frere. He possessed an intimate knowledge of the people of this country, and with regard to the educated portion of them he gave this testimony. He said: 'And now wherever I go I find the best exponents of the policy of the English Government, and the most able co-adjutors in adjusting that policy to the peculiarities of the natives of India, among the ranks of the educated natives.' This much at least is testimony to our sincerity, and strongly corroborates our assertion that we, the educated classes, have become the true interpreters and mediators between the masses of our countrymen and our rulers. I shall now place before you the declaration of the Government of India itself, that they have confidence in the loyalty of the whole people, and do appreciate the sentiments of the educated classes in particular. I will read their very words. They say in a despatch addressed to the Secretary of State (8th June 1880): 'But the people of India accept British rule without any need for appeal to arms, because we keep the peace and do justice, because we have done and are doing much material good to the country and the people, and because there is not inside or outside India any power that can adequately occupy our place.' Then they distinctly understand that we do believe the British power to be the only power that can, under existing circumstances, really keep the peace, and advance our future progress. This is testimony as to the feeling of the whole people. But of the educated classes this despatch says: 'To the minds of at least the educated among the people of India—and the number is rapidly increasing—any idea of the subversion of British power is abhorrent, from the consciousness that it must result in the wildest anarchy and confusion. (*Loud cheers.*)

"We can, therefore, proceed with the utmost serenity and with every confidence that our rulers do understand us; that they do understand our motives, and give credit to our expressions of loyalty, and we need not in the least care for any impeachment of disloyalty or any charge of harbouring wild ideas of subverting the British power that may be put forth by ignorant, irresponsible or ill-disposed individuals or cliques. (*Loud cheers.*) We can therefore quietly, calmly and with entire confidence in our rulers, speak as freely as we please, but of course in that spirit of fairness and moderation which becomes wise and honest men, and in the tone which every gentleman, every reasonable being, would adopt when urging his rulers to make him some concession. (*Hear, hear.*) Now although, as I have said, the British Government have done much, very much for us, there is still a great deal more to be done if their noble work is to be fitly completed. They say this themselves; they show a desire to do what more may be required, and it is for us to ask for whatsoever, after due deliberation, we think that we ought to have. (*Cheers.*)

"Therefore, having said thus much, and having cleared the ground so that we may proceed freely and in all confidence with the work of our Congress, I must at once come to the matter with which I should have commenced had I not purposely postponed it until I had explained the relations between ourselves and our rulers; and that is the most happy and auspicious occasion which the coming year is to bring us, *viz.*, the Jubilee of our good Queen-Empress' reign. (*Loud cheers.*) I am exceedingly glad that the Congress has thought it right to select this as the subject of the initial resolution, and in this to express, in humble but hearty terms, their congratulations to our Gracious Empress. (*Cheers.*) There is even more reason for us to congratulate ourselves on having for half a century enjoyed the rule of a Sovereign graced with every virtue, and truly worthy to reign over that vast Empire on which the sun never sets. (*Loud cheers.*) That she may live long, honoured and beloved, to continue for yet many years that beneficial and enlightened rule with which she has so long reigned, must be the heartfelt prayer of every soul in India. (*Prolonged cheering.*)

"And here you must pardon me if I digress a moment from those subjects which this Congress proposes to discuss to one of those which we do not consider to fall within the legitimate sphere of its deliberations.

"It has been asserted that this Congress ought to take up questions of social reforms (*cheers and cries of yes, yes*) and our failure to do this has been urged as a reproach against us. Certainly no member of this National Congress is more alive to the necessity of social reforms than I am; but, gentlemen, for everything there are proper times, proper circumstances, proper parties and proper places (*cheers*); we are met together as a political body to represent to our rulers our political aspirations, not do discuss social reforms, and if you blame us for ignoring these you should equally blame the House of Commons for not discussing the abstruser problems of mathematics or metaphysics. But, besides this, there are here Hindus of every caste, amongst whom, even in the same provinces, customs and social arrangements differ widely,—there are Mahomedans and Christians of various denominations, Parsees, Sikhs, Brahmos and what not—men indeed of each and all of those numerous classes which constitute in the aggregate the people of India. (*Loud cheers.*) How can this gathering of *all* classes discuss the social reforms needed in each individual class? What do any of us know of the internal home life, of the customs, traditions, feelings, prejudices of any class but our own? How could a gathering, a cosmopolitan gathering like this, discuss to any purpose the reforms needed in any one class? Only the members of that class can effectively deal with the reforms therein needed. A National Congress must confine itself to questions in which the entire nation has a direct participation, and it must leave the adjustment of social reforms and other class questions to class Congresses. But it does not follow that, because this national, political body does not presume to discuss social reforms, the delegates here present are not just as deeply, nay, in many cases far more deeply, interested in these questions than in those political questions we do discuss, or that those several communities whom those delegates represent are not doing their utmost to solve those complicated problems on which hinge the practical introduction of those reforms. Any man who has eyes and ears open must know what struggles towards higher and better things are going on in every community: and it could not be otherwise with the noble education we are receiving. Once you begin to think about your own actions, your duties and responsibilities to yourself, your neighbours and your nation, you cannot avoid looking round and observing much that is wrong amongst you; and we know as a fact that each community is now doing its best according to its lights, and the progress that it has made in education. I need rot I think particularise. The Mahomedans know what is being done by persons of their community to push on the education their brethren so much need; the Hindus are everywhere doing what they *can* to reform those social institutions which they think require improvement. There is not one single community here represented of which the best and ablest men do not feel that much has to be done to improve the social, moral, religious status of their brethren, and in which, as a fact, they are not striving to effect, gradually, those needful improvements; but these are essentially matters too delicate for a stranger's handling—matters which must be left to the guidance of those who alone fully understand them in all their bearings, and which are wholly unsuited to discussion in an assemblage like this in which all classes are intermingled. (*Loud cheers.*)

"I shall now refer briefly to the work of the former Congress. Since it met last year, about this time, some progress, I am glad to say, has been made, and that is an encouragement and a proof that, if we do really ask what is right and reasonable, we may be sure that, sooner or later, the British Government will actually give what we ask for. We should therefore persevere, having confidence in the conscience of England, and resting assured that the English nation will grudge no sacrifice to prove the sincerity of their desire to do whatever is just and right. (*Cheers.*)

"Our first request at the last Congress was for the constitution of a Royal Commission. Unfortunately the authorities in England have not seen their way to grant a Royal Commission. They say it will upset the authorities here; that it will interfere with the prestige and control of the Government here. I think that this is a very poor compliment to our rulers on this side. If I understand a man like Lord Dufferin, of such vast experience in administration, knowing, as he does, what it is to rule an empire, it would be impossible for him to be daunted and frightened by a commission making enquiries here. I think this argument a very poor one, and we must once more say that to the inhabitants of India a Parliamentary Committee taking evidence in England alone can never be satisfactory, for the simple reason that what the Committee will learn by the ear will never enable them to understand what they ought to see with their eyes if they are to realize what the evidence of the witnesses really means. Still, however, it is so far satisfactory that, notwithstanding the change of Government and the vicissitudes which this poor Parliamentary Committee has undergone, it is the intention of Parliament that under any and all circumstances a Committee shall be appointed At the same time this Committee *in futuro* ties the hands of the authorities here to a large extent and prevents us from saying all we do really want.

"Another resolution on which we must report some progress was to the effect that the N. W. Provinces and the Punjab ought also to have Legislative Councils of their own. We know that the Government has just given a Legislative Council to the N. W. Provinces, and we hope that this progress may extend further and satisfy our wishes as to other provinces also.

"The fourth resolution had regard to the Service question. In this matter we really seem to have made some distinct progress. The Public Service Commission is now sitting, and if one thing more than another can prove that the Government is sincere in its desire to do something for us, this appointment of such a Commission is that thing. You perhaps remember the words which our noble Viceroy used at Poona. He said: 'However, I will say that from first to last I have been a strong advocate for the appointment of a Committee or Commission of this sort, and that when succeeding Governments in England changed, I have on each occasion warmly impressed upon the Secretary of State the necessity of persevering in the nomination of a Commission. I am happy to think that in response to my earnest representations on the subject, Her Majesty's present Ministers have determined to take action. I consequently do not really see what more during the short period I have been amongst you, the Government of India could have done for that most important and burning question which was perpetually agitating your mind, and was being put forward by the natives as an alleged injustice done to the educated native classes of this country in not allowing them adequate employment in the Public Service. I do not think you can point out to me any other question which so occupied public attention or was nearer to the hearts of your people. Now the door to inquiry has been opened, and it only remains for you, by the force of logic of your representations and of the evidence you may be able to submit, to make good your case; if you succeed in doing so, all I can say is, that nobody will be better pleased than myself. In regard to other matters, which have been equally prominent in your newspapers and your addresses, and which have been so constantly discussed by your associations, I have also done my best to secure for you an ample investigation.'

"There we haven is own words as to his intentions and the efforts he made to get this Commission. This should convince us of his good faith and sympathy with us. When I think of Lord Dufferin, not only as our present Viceroy, but bearing in mind all we know of him in his past career, I should hesitate to believe that he could be a man devoid of the deepest sympathy with any people struggling to advance and improve their political condition. Some of you may remember one or two extracts which I gave in my Holborn Town Hall speech from Lord Dufferin's letters to the *Times*, and I cannot conceive that a person of such warm sympathies could fail to sympathise with us. But I may say this much that, feeling as I naturally do some interest about the views and intentions of our Viceroys and Governors, I have had the opportunity of getting some information from friends on whom I can rely and who are in a position to know the truth; and I am able to say in the words of one of these friends that 'the Viceroy's instincts are eminently liberal, and he regards with neither jealousy nor alarm the desire of the educated classes to be allowed a larger share in the administration of their own affairs. Indeed he considers it very creditable to them that they should do so.' As Viceroy he has to consider all sides of a question from the ruler's point of view, and to act as he thinks safe and proper. But we may be sure that we have his deep and very genuine sympathy, and we may fairly claim and expect much good at his hands.

"But yet further I would enquire whether the intentions of the Secretary of State for India and of the other home authorities are equally favourable to our claims. The resolution on its very face tells us what the intention of the Secretary of State is. It says: 'In regard to its object the Commission would, broadly speaking, be required to devise a scheme which may reasonably be hoped to possess the necessary elements of finality, and to do full justice to the claims of natives of India to a higher and more extensive employment in the Public Service.'

"There we have the highest authority making a declaration that he desires to do full justice to the claims of the natives of India. Now our only reply is that we are thankful for the enquiry, and we hope that we may be able to satisfy all, that what we ask is both reasonable and right.

"As another proof of the intentions of our British rulers, as far back as 53 years ago, when the natives of India did not themselves fully understand their rights, the statesmen of England of their own free will decided what the policy of England ought to be towards India. Long and important was the debate; the question was discussed from all points of view; the danger of giving political power to the people, the insufficiency of their capacity and other considerations were all fully weighed, and the conclusion was come to in unmistakable and unambiguous terms, that the policy of British rule should be a policy of justice (*cheers*), the policy of the advancement of one-sixth of the human race. (*Cheers.*) India was to be regarded as a trust placed by God in their hands, and in the due discharge of that trust they resolved that they would follow the 'plain path of duty,' as Mr. Macaulay called it; on that occasion he said, virtually, that he would rather see the people of India free and able to govern themselves, than that they should remain the bondsmen of Great Britain and the obsequious toadies of British officials. (*Cheers.*) This was the essence of the policy of 1833, and in the Act of that year it was laid down, 'That no native of the said territories, nor any natural-born subject of His Majesty resident therein shall, by reason only of his religion, place of birth, descent, color or any of them be disabled from holding any place, office or employment under the said Company.' (*Prolonged cheering.*)

"We do not, we could not, ask for more than this; and all we have to press upon the Commission and Government is that they should now honestly grant us in practice here what Great Britain freely conceded to us 50 years ago, when we ourselves were too little enlightened even to ask for it. (*Loud cheers.*)

"We next passed through a time of trouble, and the British arms were triumphant. When they had completely surmounted all their difficulties, and completely vanquished all their adversaries, the English nation came forward, animated by the same high and noble resolves as before, and gave us that glorious proclamation which we should for ever prize and reverence as our Magna Charta—greater even than the Charter of 1833. I need not repeat that glorious proclamation now, for it is engraven on all your hearts (*loud cheers*); but it constitutes such a grand and glorious charter of our liberties that I think every child as it begins to gather intelligence and to lisp its mother-tongue, ought to be made to commit it to memory (*Cheers.*) In that proclamation we have again a confirmation of the policy of 1833 and something more. In it are embodied the germs of all that we aim at now, of all that we can desire hereafter. (*Cheers.*) We have only to go before the Government and the Commission now sitting and repeat it, and say that all we want is only what has already been granted to us in set terms by that proclamation, and that all we now ask for is that the great and generous concessions therein made to us in words shall actually be made ours by deeds. (*Loud cheers.*) I will not, however, enter into further details, for it is a subject on which I should be led into speaking for hours, and even then I should fail to convey to you an adequate idea of all that is in my heart. I have said enough to show our rulers that our case is complete and has been made out by themselves. (*Cheers.*) It is enough for me therefore to stop at this point.

"Another resolution is the improvement and enlargement of the Legislative Councils, and the introduction into them of an elective element, but that is one on which my predecessor in the chair has so ably descanted that I do not think I should take up more of your time with it. I need only say that in this matter we hope to make a further advance, and shall try to place before our rulers what we consider a possible scheme for the introduction of an elective element into the Legislative Councils. I need not say that if this representation is introduced, the greatest benefit will be conferred upon the Government itself, because at present whatever Acts they pass that do not quite please us, we, whether rightly or wrongly, grumble and grumble against the Government, and the Government only. It is true that we have some of our own people in the Councils. But we have no right to demand any explanation, even from them; they are not our representatives, and the Government cannot relieve themselves from any dissatisfaction we may feel against any law we don't like. If our own representatives make a mistake and get a law passed which we do not want, the Government at any rate will escape the greater portion of the consequent unpopularity. They will say—here are your own representatives; we believed that they represented your wishes, and we passed the law. On the other hand with all the intelligence, all the superior knowledge of the English officials, let them come as angels from heaven, it is impossible for them to enter into the feelings of the people, and feel as they feel, and enter into their minds. (*Cheers.*) It is not any disparagement of them, but in the nature of things it cannot be otherwise. If you have therefore your representatives to represent your feelings, you will then have an opportunity of getting something which is congenial and satisfactory to yourselves; and what will be satisfactory to you must also be satisfactory to and good for the Government itself (*Cheers.*)

"This brings me also to the point of representation in Parliament. All the most fundamental questions on which hinge the entire form and character of the administration here are decided by Parliament. No matter what it is, Legislative Councils, the Services,—nothing can be reformed until Parliament moves and enacts modifications of the existing Acts. Not one single genuine Indian voice is there in Parliament to tell at least what the native view is on any question. This was most forcibly urged upon me by English gentlemen who are in Parliament themselves; they said they always felt it to be a great defect in Parliament, that it did not contain one single genuine representative of the people of India.

"One of the questions which will be placed before this Congress and will be discussed by them, is the deep sympathy which this Congress feels for the poverty of the people. It is often understood and thought that when we struggle for admission into the Services it is simply to gratify the aspirations of the few educated. But if you examine this question thoroughly, you will find that this matter of the Public Services will go far to settle the problem of the poverty of the Indian people. One thing I congratulate myself upon. I don't trouble you with any testimony about the poverty of India. You have the testimony of Sir Evelyn Baring given only a couple of years ago, who told us in plain terms that the people of India were extremely poor, and also of the present Finance Minister who repeats those words. But amongst the several causes which are at the bottom of our sufferings, this one, and that the most important cause, is beginning to be realized by our rulers, and that is a step of the most hopeful and promising kind. In the discussion about the currency, the Secretary of State for India, in a letter to the Treasury of the 26th January 1886, makes certain remarks which show that our rulers now begin to understand and to try to grapple with the problem ; and are not, ostrich-like, shutting their eyes to it. I was laughed at when I first mooted the question of the poverty of India, and assigned as one of its causes the employment of an expensive foreign agency. But now the highest authority emphasizes this view. The Secretary of State, in the letter just referred to, said : 'The position of India in relation to taxation and the sources of the public revenues is very peculiar, not merely from the habits of the people and their strong aversion to change, which is more specially exhibited towards new forms of taxation, but likewise from the character of the Government, which is in the hands of foreigners, who hold all the principal administrative offices, and form so large a part of the Army. The impatience of new taxation which would have to be borne, wholly as a consequence of the foreign rule imposed on the country and virtually to meet additions to charges arising outside of the country, would constitute a political danger, the real magnitude of which, it is to be feared, is not at all appreciated by persons who have no knowledge of, or concern in, the Government of India, but which those responsible for that Government have long regarded as of the most serious order.'

"We may be sure that the public conscience of England will ask why the natives of India, after a hundred years of British rule, are so poor ; and as John Bull, in a cartoon in *Punch* is represented as doing, will wonder that India is a beggar when he thought she had a mint of money.

"Unfortunately this idea of India's wealth is utterly delusive, and if a proper system of representation in the Councils be conceded, our representatives will then be able to make clear to these Councils and to our rulers those causes which are operating to undermine our wealth and prosperity, and guide the Government to the proper remedies for the greatest of all evils—the poverty of the masses. All the benefits we have derived from British rule, all the noble projects of our British rulers, will go for nothing if after all the country is to continue sinking deeper and deeper into the abyss of destitution. At one time I was denounced as a Pessimist, but now that we have it on the authority of our rulers themselves that we are *very* poor, it has become the right, as well as the duty, of this Congress to set forth its convictions, both as to this widespread destitution and the primary steps needful for its alleviation. Nothing is more dear to the heart of England—and I speak from actual knowledge—than India's welfare ; and if we only speak out loud enough, and persistently enough, to reach that busy heart, we shall not speak in vain. (*Prolonged cheering.*) There will be several other questions brought before the Congress at their Committee meetings during the next three days, and I am sure from the names of the delegates, as far as I am informed, that they will prosecute their deliberations with all possible moderation. I am sure that they will fully appreciate the benefits of the rule under which they live, while the fact that our rulers are willing to do whatever we can show them to be necessary for our welfare, should be enough to encourage all in the work. I do not know that I need now detain you with any further remarks. You have now some idea of what progress has been made in respect of the matters which were discussed last year. I hope we may congratulate ourselves next year that we have made further progress in attaining the objects alike of the past year's resolutions and those we may this year pass. I for one am hopeful that, if we are only true to ourselves, if we only do justice to ourselves and the noble education which has been given to us by our rulers and speak freely, with the freedom of speech which has been granted to us, we may fairly expect our Government to listen to us and to grant us our reasonable demands. (*Loud cheers.*)

"I will conclude this short address by repeating my sincere thanks to all of you for having placed me in this honourable position and by again returning thanks to our Bengal brethren on behalf of all the delegates whom they have so cordially welcomed here."

On the President resuming his seat, amidst the most energetic and prolonged cheering, BABOO JOY KISSEN MOOKERJEE (*Bengal, No.* 230) again rose and said : "It is I am sure with great pleasure that we have all listened to the impressive inaugural address of our President. If our proceedings are conducted with that moderation and dignity which have characterised his eloquent address, I have no doubt that we shall disarm all adverse criticism. Some of the schemes for administrative reform sketched out by the Honourable Mr. Dadabhai might appear almost too ambitious, but we must bear in mind that to a subject people, on whom has been conferred the inestimable boon of a Free Press, there are few privileges, that a governing nation can grant, which can be fairly characterized as too ambitious for us to crave.

"The India of to-day is very different from the India of 1835. And yet the boon of a Free Press was conceded in that distant past more than half a century ago, when our rulers were comparatively new to the country, when the very loyalty of the people was problematical, when the Government had but just recovered from the effects of the Mahratta war, when hostilities with the Afghans seemed inevitable, and when several of the Native Chiefs were anything but friendly to the British Crown. The Court of Directors expressed a strong apprehension that the concession of this privilege would imperil the very existence of their Government, but Sir Charles Metcalfe was firm, and the wisdom of the English people allowed him to render his short term of office as Governor-General memorable in the annals of Indian Administration by the emancipation of the Press From a people who showed such liberality and magnanimity at a time of danger and unrest, we can hardly ask too much, in the way of administrative reforms, in these days of profound peace, when India is daily becoming more and more an integral part of Great Britain, and her people more and more devoted to the principles (though they may object to some of the methods) of British rule. Standing as I do, one of the few remaining links between the Old India of the past and the New India of to-day, I can scarcely hope to see or enjoy the fruit of those labours on which this Congress and the nation it represents is entering ; but I am glad to have lived to see this new departure, and if an old man's sympathy and good wishes can aid or encourage you in the noble work you are undertaking, I can say from the bottom of my heart that that sympathy and those good wishes are already yours. Be wise, be moderate and above all be persevering, and the success that you will then deserve will assuredly be yours." *(Loud and prolonged cheering.)*

A very large number* of telegrams and other communications from all parts of the Empire (excluding Burmah), conveying congratulations to, or expressing sympathy with, the Congress were laid on the table, and one telegram from Hyderabad, which ran as follows, was read by the President :—

"The Mahomedans of Upper† and Southern India fully sympathise with the objects of the Congress, and wish it Godspeed. They deeply regret their Calcutta brethren keeping off, and trust they will still join." *(Loud cheers.)*

The crowd and the heat had been very trying, and the President announced that next day the Congress would sit in Committee in the rooms of the British Indian Association.

THE MAHARAJAH SIR JOTENDRO MOHUN TAGORE, K.C.S.I. (*Bengal, No.* 228) then rose and proposed a vote of thanks to the Chair, which was seconded and carried with prolonged cheering.

After this gentlemen rose simultaneously in all parts of the Hall, allotted to the delegates, and proposed "three cheers for the Queen-Empress and God bless her," which elicited such a prolonged storm of cheers, renewed and renewed over and over again, that only some of the delegates were aware that cheers were also, just at the close, given for His Excellency the Viceroy.

The Congress then adjourned till the next day.

---

* A selection of these will be found in Appendix IV.

† A mistake, as it appeared for *Deccan*.

SECOND DAY'S PROCEEDINGS.

Tuesday, 28th December, 1886,

AT THE ROOMS OF THE BRITISH INDIAN ASSOCIATION.

THE delegates having assembled, the HON. DADABHAI NAOROJI (*Bombay, No.* 48), the President, said: Brother delegates, let me first thank you once more for having assigned to me this post of honor. We now meet here 'in Committee,' as I might say, to go on with our business, which we must transact in a proper manner, and not expect long speeches. I hope that every speaker will limit his speech to a duration of five minutes, but in no case should this exceed ten. In that way only can we hope to get through all the business on the list which has been prepared. We are here, as you are aware, delegates from different parts of the country—Bengal, the North-West Provinces, Oudh, the Punjab, Bombay, Madras; so we can congratulate ourselves on the progress which has now been made, and I hope and pray it may be the beginning of the political union of the whole nation in order to the advance of the whole nation. I shall set an example of brevity myself by being satisfied with the one minute for which I have detained you, and begin the business at once."

MR. R. M. SAYANI (*Bombay, No.* 54) then rose and said: "I have great pleasure in moving the first resolution, *viz.*, "that this Congress of Delegates from all parts of India do humbly offer its dutiful and loyal congratulations to Her Most Gracious Majesty the Queen-Empress on the approaching completion of the first half century of her memorable, beneficent and glorious reign, and heartily wish her many, many more and happy, years of rule over the great British Empire." (*Resolution I of the Summary, page* 41.) I can assure you that no task could be more congenial, no honor more acceptable, than that of being allowed to move this resolution. The worth, the virtues of the great Sovereign, who rules over us, are too well known to, and too gratefully realized by, all of you to need much talking about, and I shall therefore confine myself to a very few remarks. Gentlemen, all the subjects of Her Majesty the Queen-Empress are well aware of the very noble and excellent qualities which adorn Her Majesty. (*Loud cheers.*) Her solicitude for all her subjects, including her Indian subjects, is so well understood that her sacred name is revered throughout the country. (*Cheers.*) I shall therefore now make only a few suggestions as to how, on the coming auspicious occasion of Her Majesty's year of Jubilee, the country might practically give proof of the love and reverence that they bear her. I would suggest that one and the same day be fixed for celebrating the Jubilee of the Queen-Empress all over the country, and that at one and the same time there should be illuminations all over the country and that subscriptions should be limited to some small sum, say Rs. 10, or even less, so that all but the very poorest of Her Majesty's subjects may be able to testify, by a contribution to the fund, the earnest and deep feelings of loyalty and love which animate one and all of us. (*Cheers.*) But I see that I am travelling somewhat from the scope of the resolution which I rose to move, and which, all unnecessary as I feel this to be, I now commend to your most hearty acceptance." (*Prolonged cheering.*)

LALA MURLIDHUR (*Punjab, No.* 107), in seconding the motion, said: "A great many Anglo-Indians charge the natives of India with being seditious and mutinous, and I admit that, in one sense, we are all that. But how are we that? We are seditious and mutinous against false imputations. But I go further and confess myself guilty of a more terrible thing. I admit that I am a murderer of the blackest dye. But perhaps you are startled. But you should not be, for after all I am only a murderer of the Queen's English. (*Cheers and laughter.*) There is, I believe, no true-born Indian who is a more disloyal subject of Her Majesty than myself; and yet, even I, that most disloyal of all men, that worse than disloyal, that murderer as I have confessed, even I am loyal to our blessed Empress to the backbone. (*Loud cheers.*) She has given us peace and order, she has taught us in her colleges, she has given us all a common language, she has enabled me to come to Calcutta now, to go to Bombay last year, and she has done all these things for a man guilty of the horrible crime of murdering her noble language. Then think of what good nature she must be—a Queen who reigns over half the globe, whose subjects are of a hundred different races, creeds and colour; this Queen, this noble-hearted woman, this kindly lady who shields now her elder sister in her dotage, poor old India, who in olden time gave birth to heroes like Rama, Krishna and the like, but who now is unable to rear any but puny children like ourselves, and so has sought the protection of her younger sister, England. She has given us innumerable blessings, and we are grateful to her, and let us show our gratitude by shouts of congratulations that will resound even to the precincts of her far-off palace, and sink even deeper the foundations of a reverence for her reign into the hearts of the whole of India. (*Loud cheers.*) How is this Jubilee to be celebrated in India? I am not for founding magnificent buildings or anything of that sort: nothing should be done for the higher classes, but rather some tangible good work should be done for those who really need it. I am not an advocate for building palatial houses. I recommend that something should be done for the poor man, who lives on the soil of India, so that even the poor man in his hut may long joyfully remember the Jubilee of Her Gracious Majesty's reign. (*Cheers.*) If the money which is collected—and you all know that in India every event is, now-a-days, an occasion for collecting money (*laughter*)—if, I say, the money collected is thrown away in illuminations and fireworks at a few centres, or devoted (I will not *say* wasted, though I have my own ideas on this subject) to grand buildings or Institutes or the like, the people, the masses, will know little and feel nothing about the matter: the few who see the fireworks will consider the affair a treat for a single night, and to the country it will all be nothing. But if they see that some tangible good is done for them, which reaches the masses, then they will feel that the Queen Mother has been kind to them, and they will pray for the permanence of her reign. However, this is perhaps beyond what need now be said, and I will close by again heartily seconding the resolution."

MR. G. SUBRAMANIA IYER (*Madras, No. 5*) said: "Most heartily and with the greatest pleasure do I rise to support the proposition which has been made and seconded, but having said so much, the subject is one on which all of us here, the entire country, is so completely of one mind (*cheers*), that I do not think I should be justified in detaining this meeting with any further remarks." (*Cheers.*)

RAJAH RAMPAL SINGH (*Oudh, No.* 178), Talukdar of Partabgarh, said: "As regards the loyal and grateful feelings towards Her Majesty, with which the whole country is animated, there can be no doubt; and as to the necessity of testifying in some practical and unmistakable manner, now, on the occasion of her Jubilee, to the depth and sincerity of that loyalty and love, there can be no two opinions (*hear, hear*); but as to the manner in which this should be done, and as to how the funds collected for this purpose should be, and can be best, utilized, I am not sure that I altogether concur in what has fallen from previous speakers. I am disposed to think that something worthy of the occasion should be done. I do not know what is meant by doing something for each poor man. Is anything of the kind really practicable with any subscriptions (mere drops in the ocean) that we can possibly hope to collect? I venture rather to suggest—"

Here the speaker was interrupted by

MR. MANO MOHAN GHOSE (*Bengal, No.* 270), who said: "The object of the first resolution is simply to offer our congratulations to the Queen, and it is surely not necessary now to go into details as to how the Jubilee is to be celebrated. That must be left for future consideration." (*Cheers and cries of "yes," "yes," "put the resolution."*)

THE PRESIDENT accordingly, in response to the loudly expressed wishes of the Congress, formally put the resolution, which was carried by acclamation; three cheers for the Queen-Empress being called for and given with great emphasis.

MR. DINSHAW EDULJI WATCHA (*Bombay, No.* 51) said: "I have been asked to move the following resolution:—

"That this Congress regards with the deepest sympathy, and views with grave apprehension, the increasing poverty of vast numbers of the population of India, and (although aware that the Government is not overlooking this matter and is contemplating certain palliatives) desires to record its fixed conviction that the introduction of Representative Institutions will prove one of the most important practical steps towards the amelioration of the condition of the people. (*Resolution II of the Summary, page* 41.")

"*Mr. President and Gentlemen,*—The question of the poverty of the people of India is now so well understood, so thoroughly realized, that it hardly requires any words, especially from me, to elucidate or substantiate it. It is our President alone who could really have done justice to this great subject, to the exposition of which he has devoted half a lifetime, and in regard to which I am but, as it were a pupil, of his. (*Cheers.*) However, since the task has been assigned to me I will endeavour, within the limited space of time allotted to me, to touch on some few of the causes of this lamentable poverty. The root of the evil lies in the condition of the ryots. The peasantry in all parts of the country are very poor and they have grown markedly poorer since 1848. (*Hear, hear.*) There have been now and then periods of prosperity, as for instance, the prosperity of Bombay during the American war, when cotton became very dear, and the peasantry benefited by this rise in price. But, as a general rule, the condition of the peasantry, whether in the Deccan, in Madras, or in other places, has deteriorated steadily since 1848, so much so that it is now generally admitted that something like 40 millions of people (and many authorities say more) are going with only one meal a day, and sometimes do not even get that. To take, first, that part of the country with which I am personally best acquainted, we may note that the commission which sat to investigate the causes of the Deccan riots established the fact that, in consequence of the scarcity of the rainfall in the Deccan, and the high fixed rate at which the assessment was pitched, the condition of the peasantry in the Deccan had been steadily going from bad to worse. I admit that, since the Commission made its report, very laudable attempts have been made by the Bombay Government to remedy this state of affairs, but the most sanguine will not pretend that the lowest classes in the Deccan are at this day other than poor, and very poor. Again, from the information given in the Report of the Famine Commission, and the evidence of the Collector of Cuddapah and others, it would appear that the condition of the Madras peasantry is hardly better than that of their fellows in the Deccan. The Upper Provinces of India are outside my experience, but we all know, from the very admirable analysis that has been published, the whole history of the population there, and taking one division only as a type, the way in which Jhansi, a country as large as some of the smaller European kingdoms, has been ground into the dust by injudicious revenue arrangements, was very ably set forth by Mr. Robert Knight in the *London Statesman*, in papers reproduced largely in India, and doubtless familiar to you all. I am not in a position to speak much about the Bengal peasantry, but there are many here who are well acquainted with their condition, and will, doubtless, speak to it, but we may safely say this much that it is not materially better than that of their brethren elsewhere. Thus on all sides and in all provinces we seem to be met with the sad fact of the impoverished condition of the masses, and the one question is how to improve this condition Of course there are exceptionally favoured tracts, but, broadly speaking, and taking the Empire as a whole, the produce of the land is scarcely sufficient to enable those who till it, and they constitute the bulk of the population, to meet the assessment, whether that be assessed by Government or some intermediate landholders, and eke out the barest existence, leaving no margin for carrying out any agricultural improvements or developments, all of which require an outlay of capital. It is said that the ryots themselves are partly to blame; that they are ignorant and improvident and spend whatever little money they chance, in good seasons, to acquire in marriage ceremonies and *tamashas*. This may be true to some slight extent, but, as a cause of the widespread destitution that exists, this want of thrift is insignificant as compared with the real cause, *viz.*, the extremely small share of the produce of their labours left to the actual tillers of the soil, either by Government or by superior holders under the existing Government revenue systems.

"The mainstay of Indian finance, however, is the land revenue. No material reduction in this can be contemplated. Landholders too have vested rights which cannot be confiscated, or their existing rents materially cut down. The only alternative lies in increasing the produce of the soil, and this is only possible by the expenditure everywhere of capital on the land, in minute fractions doubtless in each case, but in large masses in the aggregate. But how is this possible when year by year the bulk of the profits of the entire population are drained away in the tribute to Great Britain, exported to fructify there, and swell still further the unparalleled wealth of those distant Isles, never in any shape to return here to bless the country from whose soil it was wrung, or the people, the sweat of whose brows it represents? (*Loud cheers.*) Here is the very essence of the question; this tribute must be reduced; if we had it, we would not grudge Great Britain her profits on the connection between us, to which we owe so much. But we have it not—the masses here, to nearly double the number of the entire population of Great Britain, are starving, or nearly, so for want of that capital which we have not, and she must not thus, for ever, go on despoiling us, year by year, of that small capital which our toiling millions succeed in creating during the twelve months of ceaseless labour.

"One of the very first and most important remedies is to minimise the foreign agency, now employed in the administration and defence of the country, so that the money spent unavoidably for these purposes shall remain in it to grow and multiply and bless the land, and not as now, to a very large extent, be drafted away to England. Unless and until this question of foreign agency is solved, the question of the poverty of our masses will not be solved either. But the worst points of the case are that the Government knows these facts, and that yet, yet from year to year, that tribute is allowed to grow. As to knowing how the case stands, only in 1881, when the House of Commons was discussing the question of the incidence of the cost of the Egyptian war, Lord Ripon and Sir E. Baring and others remonstrated against saddling India with even a single pie of that expenditure on account of the poverty of India, and the utter inability of the people to bear further fiscal burthens. Again, the average annual income per head of the population was stated by the Government of India at Rs. 27 per head. Mr. Dadabhai Naoroji, as we know, put it lower at only Rs. 20 per head, but even taking the figures of the Financial Department, it will be seen that the Government itself is fully aware of the extreme poverty of the people. Some four shillings a month to live upon—think of that! And there are millions who spend far more than this, and therefore probably tens of millions who do not get even these miserable four shillings a month. Then, as to increase of the tribute, it is one endless growth. As to military home charges they have grown and grown by little and little until, last year, the addition of 11,000 European troops to our army made them grow further by a big jump. The civil expenditure which is diverted to England is something like 11 millions, of which 7 millions, I believe, go towards payment of pensions and the like. It has been calculated by Sir Richard Temple that the permanent loss to India in the shape of pensions, salaries, private remittances, merchants' profits and loss by exchange, amounts to something like 30 millions a year, and whatever may be the difference between the cost of tilling and the value of the produce of the soil, no country can prosper as long as such an enormous annual drain on that difference, which ought to be accumulating as the capital of the country, is going on. This is what gives such enormous importance to the question of foreign agency. But, of course, immensely important as it is, this reduction of foreign agency is not the only reform in the administration necessary if the people are to be lifted out of the slough of poverty, into which they are sinking, and placed once more upon the firm ground of comfort and prosperity. But neither this reduction of foreign agency nor, indeed, any of those other needful reforms, do we see the smallest hopes of getting carried out, until we succeed in attaining a position whence our protests and appeals must be respectfully listened to, and either fairly met, or practically yielded to, and it is in this sense that our resolution sets forth our "fixed conviction that the introduction of representative institutions will prove one of the most important practical steps towards the amelioration of the condition of the people." (*Loud and prolonged cheering.*)

If we have representative institutions, if we have elected, or partly elected, assemblies in every province, and also constituting an integral part of the Government of India—assemblies in which the representatives of the people can secure the notice of their rulers to their views on all those questions most intimately affecting the interests of their province and the country as a whole, and where such views must be respectfully listened to and thoroughly canvassed and discussed—then we do not doubt that, within a decade or so, we shall be able to ensure the adoption of those essential reforms on which a renewed lease of the prosperity of the country in a great measure depend. (*Loud cheers.*) Where representative institutions are once established there the Government, even though a Government of foreigners, *can* be drawn into the right track; but so long as a purely autocratic system prevails, and the autocrats are foreigners, the case seems hopeless. (*Cheers.*)

No doubt, even without full blown representative institutions every step which admits natives to a larger share in the administration of the country, will tend to improve the position of affairs, and in this way, if we obtain even that tentative form of those institutions at which we are now aiming, we may fairly hope for a beginning of renewed prosperity. I will only add this more: foreigners are apt to underrate the extreme poverty of the country because there are a few rich, even though there are many poor; and it is very easy for them, coming in contact only with the well-to-do, to imagine that India is prosperous. But when they really take the trouble of going into the question they learn better. Quite recently, Mr. Samuel Smith, a member of Parliament, came out here and personally inquired somewhat into the condition of the country, and he, little as he saw, saw enough to be convinced that the country was indeed very poor, and he had the courage to bring the subject before Parliament. May we have many such men who will come and see for themselves, and having seen, dare to tell the people of England the truth, and the whole truth, about our poor pauperized India." (*Prolonged cheering*)

THE HON. S. SUBRAMANIA IYER (*Madras, No.* 2) said: "Mr. President and Gentlemen,—It is my pleasant duty to second the proposition which has just been moved, and to my mind it seems to be very fitting that Mr. Watcha should propose, and I should second, this resolution, for we come respectively from opposite sides of India. Certainly the poverty of India, if it can be demonstrated at all, to my mind seems to be capable of demonstration in respect of the Madras Presidency. At one time it was the boast of administrators in my part of the country that it was administered under the ryotwari system and not the zemindari system. I believe the history of the ryotwari administration has led to the conclusion that it is better to have a system of zemindari administration, with all its faults, than the ryotwari system. It may be that the zemindars, as is believed by some, do, in some cases, screw out every farthing that they can from their tenants; but the zemindars, as we have seen, can be reached by a Tenancy Act, whereas in the Presidency of Madras it is impossible to control by any Tenancy Act the extortions of the revenue authorities. (*Loud cheers.*) I should like to see a Government servant, on our side of India, who is prepared to admit that the right of enhancement ought to be defined and limited by legislative enactment as against the Government. (*Cheers.*) Then, with reference to the ryotwari districts in the Madras Presidency, there is this to be said: I constantly talk to my friends and ask their opinion as to the question of poverty. Our worthy Chairman has proved it, as far as possible, to an unbiassed public, and the Government itself has admitted, that the country is poor. But there are some, nevertheless, who affirm that the country is growing richer, and the other day I asked one of them why they thought so: he referred to the enormous exports of rice, jute, oil-seeds and an infinite variety of other raw produce. As far as Madras is concerned we do not profit by exports and the high rate of exchange; we have no cotton and no jute to export; at all events, therefore, so far as the thirty millions of people and more of the Madras Presidency are concerned, the question of poverty is exactly where our President left it, and the Government, as a fact, have admitted it. It is, therefore, fitting that I should rise to support this proposition, and assert that my part of the country is certainly entitled to be described as a poor country. Now, how is this poverty to be got rid of. I do not say directly and immediately by representative institutions, but if there is one system more than another under which we are more likely to be able to improve the administration of the country and to devise and ensure the adoption of measures to get rid of poverty, it is under a system of representation. Our worthy President has demonstrated, long ago, the poverty of the land, and has done his best to keep this matter before the public in and out of India, and we, the representatives here of all India, endorse his views, but at present with no apparent results; and what we are now aiming at is to obtain, for this voice of India, a legal status. (*Loud cheering.*) Very often it is said that we ask for things for which we are not fit, but that seems to me to be altogether begging the question. It is not any particular kind of representation for which we ask; we do not claim representative institutions in the fully developed form now enjoyed in England. All that we want is the recognition of the principle of representation. (*Cheers.*) To that extent, therefore, it seems to me that there is hardly any question, unless it be said that we are not fit to receive representation in any form whatever. This very assembly completely proves that we are (*loud cheers*), since no one would, I presume, pretend that, when the required privilege was granted to us by the State, we should deteriorate and prove less competent to discuss public affairs wisely than we now are. It cannot be said that the people are not sufficiently advanced to receive the boon of representation in some form or other; for that would be inconsistent with what has already been given to us in the existing local councils, in which there is, at any rate, a pretence of representing the Indian community by two or three Indian members. Unless it can be said that that was a mistake, it seems difficult to contend that we are not also entitled to representation in some form or other, in the larger matter of administrative Government. With these observations I have much pleasure in supporting the proposition." (*Cheers.*)

PANDIT PRANNATH (*Oudh, No.* 172) said: "I rise to support this resolution; although what was required to be said in support of it has already been well and ably stated by those gentlemen from Bombay and Madras who have preceded me, still I at least can add my testimony, from a widely distant part of the country, that our people are now extremely poor, and that they are much poorer now than they were a quarter of a century only ago. There are many other gentlemen here from Oudh, which has been called the Garden of India, and where no famine has ever been known, and yet you will not find one of them who doubts that the masses of Oudh are cruelly poor, are pressed by poverty, and feel every day and hour the burthen of that poverty. (*Loud and prolonged cheering.*) There can be no question, it seems to me, as to the poverty of India. It has been felt by all who have really worked amongst us; it has been admitted by the most intelligent of those who have governed the State; and if there is any doubt at all it is simply with respect to the causes of that poverty and not with regard to the poverty itself. If the Governments, local and supreme, included some substantial representative element—if they were thus in a position to have any real knowledge of the actual state of affairs amongst us—perhaps the country would not be so poor as it actually is. I do not mean that the mere fact of our having representatives in the councils would work any direct miracle, but that the pressure that these would then be in a position to put up on Government, would incline it to mend its ways and adopt those reforms which can alone arrest the impoverishment of the land. (*Cheers.*) Those representative institutions which have done so much for England and for every country where they have been fairly tried, cannot fail to do equal good to India also. It is only reasonable to suppose that the educated natives of India know the ins-and-outs of their own country better than foreigners, who visit it only for a short time, and that they are alike more competent than these to suggest, more anxious to discover, and more capable of applying the remedies demanded for that poverty, which has, in fact, been already admitted by the Government, which is patent to every one of us here and to every Indian capable of observation, and which, as matters now stand, bids fair, in the course of one or two generations more, utterly and hopelessly and absolutely to destroy the country." (*Prolonged cheering.*)

ROW SAHIB S. V. SUBBOROYUDU PANTULU (*Madras, No.* 18) said: "I am a ryot amongst other things, and hold several acres of land in the Madras Presidency, and I tell you from my experience of many years that the people's poverty, in our part, is due, to a great extent, to high assessments. It has become a settled practice to increase the assessment at every periodical revision, and I believe that, so far as ryotwary tracts are concerned, the true remedy lies in a permanent settlement, and this is the thing we want, and this is what all our representatives, if we ever get these, will recommend and struggle for if the poverty of the ryots of Southern India is to be remedied; permanent settlements ought to be concluded throughout that portion of the country." (*Cheers.*)

MUNSHI SADHO LALL (*Benares, No.* 146) said, speaking in Urdu: "I strongly support this resolution. (*Cheers.*) I say that the most important practical step towards improving the circumstances of this country and preventing the increasing poverty of the masses is most assuredly the introduction of representative institutions amongst us, and I agree with those who think that the only way that these institutions can be introduced, at the present time, is by enlarging the councils and allowing these to consist largely of members selected or chosen by ourselves. (*Cheers.*) I know that this growing poverty depends upon many causes, but the most important of these have a common source, and that is, what the papers call, loss of touch between the Government and the people. I am not one of those who run down the Government. I am sure the Government does its best *(hear, hear)*; but its best, even though better in many ways than the best of all preceding Governments, is yet not good enough for the age in which we live *(cheers)*; and this is only because the Government, being composed of Europeans, is unable thoroughly to understand the circumstances of India, and never knows or can know what really wants doing, and above all *how* best to do what has to be done. (*Cheers.*) We, who do know, are not taken into council—not because the Government does not wish to do right—not because it desires to oppress us, but because it is not at present the practice to associate us in the administration. Of course that practice had its origin in times when we were quite children, quite incapable of seriously helping the Government. But now we are growing up. (*Loud cheers.*) There are a great many of us—tens of thousands—both those who have had an English education, and those who like myself can speak English only imperfectly—who understand and take an interest in public matters, and who can and would help in such matters, and therefore now while thanking Government for all they have done for us, and confessing all their good intentions towards us, we yet want that old unsuitable practice to be changed (*cheers*); and I say that until it is changed, and until we Hindustanis are joined in the management of affairs, it will be impossible to bring about those changes on which depend the improvement of the condition of the people. *(Loud cheering.)* As matters stand the wants, the grievances, the sufferings of the people, do not really become thoroughly known to, or appreciated by, the Government; and whilst this remains the case, how can legislation be conducted appropriately to our requirements, and, if it be inappropriate, is it not worse than no legislation at all? (*Hear, hear.*) That the poverty of the masses is increasing every day cannot be disputed by any man past middle age, who has for only 20 years, even, been watching such matters (*cheers*); and certainly one cause of this increasing poverty is the manner in which the production of most of the manufactured necessaries of life, clothing, tools, implements, &c., &c., has been diverted from the hands of our countrymen into those of foreign manufacturers. I do think that, with a considerable body of our people in the several councils, means would be found to revive our ancient and establish new industries, so that as time went on all our requirements in this line should be supplied to us by our own artizans, and the enormous profit of this gigantic work reaped by our own people. (*Loud cheers.*) I am aware that this is a difficult matter, and it is therefore that I pick it out, and say that, granting that this is the most difficult of all the causes of our growing poverty to grapple with, even this would be able to be more or less successfully dealt with if only we were so placed as to be able to guide rightly and wisely the action of Government. As matters now stand, if the prevailing impoverishment is to be allowed to grow on, as it has been growing during the last quarter of a century, the Government revenue will, at no distant period, despite income taxes and all other possible novel and obnoxious forms of taxation, begin to decline, and nothing but National Bankruptcy will lie before us. (*Prolonged cheering.*)

"Therefore the time has now fully come, when those who really understand and feel the condition of affairs should have a powerful voice in managing them, and this is the first and only practical step that I can see towards ameliorating that sad condition." (*Loud cheers.*)

BABOO KESHUB CHUNDER ACHARJEE CHOWDHRY (*Bengal, No.* 394*a*) said: "The Committee have already heard from delegates from different parts of the country that the people of India are poor, and that may truly be taken as an undoubted fact. You have heard, however, a great deal of the curse of poverty in Bombay, Madras, Oudh and the N. W. Provinces, but you have not heard anything about Bengal. If you enquire into our secrets you will discover that Bengal is as much a poor province as any other part of the country. To take one special case: look at the condition of the weavers whose occupation has been ruined by competition from without. I know, from my own experience, that weavers have became *Boishtobs*, a people who were originally indigenous to Bengal. Everywhere and in every place you will see that Englishmen are depriving us of our bread, and appropriating all the loaves and fishes, and if you do not make an united effort the only result will be that we shall be driven out from every occupation and every branch of industry (*cries of No! No!*) and our people left to starve." (*Cheers and laughter*).

LALA HUKM CHAND (*Punjab, No.* 96) said: "We have not come here to air our eloquence but simply to express our heart-felt feelings, to make our wants known, and to set forth alike our sufferings and the remedies for these. The resolution has been ably moved and seconded, and gentlemen from Madras and Bombay, Oudh, the N. W. Provinces and Bengal, have commented upon it; but as I am a Punjabee it is necessary for me also to support the resolution and to show that for us in the Punjab also it is necessary. The poor are not able to express their own wants, and if questions are decided by hearing only one side of the question, they cannot be rightly decided; therefore it is necessary that representative institutions should be adopted in all parts of the country. Various causes have been mentioned for the great poverty of our people. It has been said that the artisans have been driven away, and our indigenous industries ruined, but this is not so much the fault of the English as our own fault. (*Hear, hear.*) We should try to compete with England by establishing such institutions as would support our own artisans, and by purchasing things from them. The object aimed at by the resolution is, no doubt, of primary importance, but it must be supported on its true grounds, and certain things which have been said, as for instance, in regard to the weavers of Bengal, hardly bear upon the resolution. I think it is possible or us to establish institutions for the improvement of art, and to take measures to support the artisans of the country quite independently of any representation. One question connected with the poverty of India, on which representation has a distinct bearing, is the question of Exchange. That question has not been touched upon by any of the Associations, either in Bengal or the Punjab; but it is a question of no little importance. We are the subjects of the British Government, and constitute an integral part of the British Empire; why should there be two currencies? Why should there not be one and the same set of standard coins for the whole Empire, and thus the existing loss on Exchange be avoided? I know I shall be told that all existing engagements of the Government are in terms of rupees, and that the change I advocate would involve great difficulties. All changes involve difficulties—this one as far as I can see no greater difficulties than any other. Here is one step that could be taken at once if we had representatives and they urged the question properly—pending that very distant time which the proposer seemed to think of when by the reduction of foreign agency, and consequently of expenditure in England, loss by Exchange would become of less consequence. No doubt some formal representative government is required on all grounds. In every case before a Court of Justice both sides are heard, and each has the opportunity of proving to the Judge the justice of his own cause. Here it is a Court of injustice. Government has it all its own way, and we have no one to plead for us, and controvert the arbitrary claims of the Government. They surround themselves with people who just repeat their opinions, and so nothing can be done for the good of the country and its people, who suffer in every way, just because they are never heard before the Court." (*Cheers.*)

Row Bahadur A. Sabapathy Mudaliar (*Madras, No.* 23) said: "I will not occupy your time beyond what the necessities of the case require. The previous speakers have scarcely even touched upon one of the chief causes of the poverty of the country, *viz.*, the want of commercial enterprise in the community. As I, myself, am engaged in commerce, naturally I take much interest in this subject, and I shall take some other opportunity of giving a lecture on the subject; but as I shall not have the pleasure of meeting all the gentlemen who are now present on that occasion, I will just say a few words now about the matter: We all attribute the poverty of India to the mismanagement of our rulers, and, no doubt, it is to a considerable extent due to that cause, but much blame also attaches to ourselves. (*Cheers.*) We allow the English to beat us in competition in everything which we use, from a tooth-pick to a steamer; every branch of trade is, through our want of energy, monopolized by Europeans. (*Hear, hear.*) This Congress has devoted its attention to purely political questions, and of these the most important is undoubtedly that of representative government, and I am certainly entirely in favor of this great reform; but even when we have that representative government, the people will have to realize that the chief causes which have brought about the great poverty of India are not all political. No doubt, with representative government, we may have the means of impressing upon the Government the propriety of encouraging the trade and industry of the country in many ways, as, for instance, by purchasing in the country all articles necessary for the use of the troops, and all other public departments. But we have to do something ourselves. (*Loud cheers.*) Our late beloved Viceroy, Lord Ripon, ordered the purchase of country-made in preference to European goods; and yet, on account of the greater energy of the Europeans, many articles can be obtained more cheaply and of better quality from Europe than they can be at present produced here. Even if we had the complete control of everything in our own hands, we could not desire Indian manufactures to be purchased by the State at a higher price than is demanded for equally good English articles of the same kind: that would not be just to the interests of our nation. It is, therefore, necessary, and desirable that, in addition to all political reforms, we should devote our best attention to the improvement of the industries of the country. It is true that this has nothing directly to do with the immediate objects of this Congress, but I think it ought to be clearly understood that too much must not be expected from representative institutions, and that the improvement of our national industries and the development of our commerce and trade by our own exertions are amongst the greatest necessities of India of the present day." (*Prolonged cheering.*)

Rajah Rampal Singh (*Oudh, No.* 178) said: "I only wish to say that we should not forget the question of the usurer. If the Government would protect the people from the usurer they would help the people in despite of themselves. There are millions of ignorant people who are living truly from hand-to-mouth, and these should be protected from the oppression of the usurer."

PANDIT JWALANATH SARMA (*Calcutta, No.* 251) said: "The proposition before the meeting asserts that this Congress views with grave apprehension the increasing poverty of India. The wants of the people are not large, and therefore their poverty can scarcely be owing to a deficiency in the production of the necessities of life. The proposition also asserts that we not only view the poverty of the masses of the people with grave apprehension, but we also sympathise with them, and as this poverty is increasing we view it with grave apprehension. Happily it is the case that we find deep sympathy with the sufferings of the people, and sympathy looks for the removal of the causes of this poverty, and this resolution affirms that the introduction of representative institutions is one of the measures for removing this evil. I admit that poverty is a relative term, and relative poverty we cannot ever remove from the land; but what we want to remove is the want of the necessaries of life, and that want makes the people discontented. If people succeed in anything they congratulate themselves in their success; but if the thing is done for them by other people, they have not the same satisfaction as if they do it for themselves. Representative institutions will give due scope for the exercise of our own energies, and whatever we achieve by their means will satisfy us. It is not the wish to have representative institutions merely to obtain power, but to put us in the way of doing good for ourselves and to foster habits of thinking and acting for ourselves. I humbly suggest that all of us should habituate ourselves to the habit of really thinking out questions for ourselves, for that of itself will enable us to remove many evils, not only the evil of poverty, but the causes of disease, and so on. We should look at the question all round; we should see whether it is any undue increase in the population which prevents their being supplied with food, or the scantiness of the production due to imperfect agriculture or the neglect of industrial arts that makes us poor. We must look into all causes; we must realize the fact not of a single cause but of a great many causes. We should constantly endeavour to find out all the causes. Let us compare and generalize, let us see what are the differences between one Presidency and another, one district and another, one class and another, and so on, and then only shall we be able to realize all the many causes which tend to keep India so poor. No foreigners can make this detailed investigation, and I heartily support the resolution now before the Congress, because representative institutions will give the greatest conceivable stimulus to an exhaustive and scientific treatment of this great problem—the growing poverty of the masses." (*Loud cheers.*)

MR. SATYANATH BORAH (*Assam, No.* 431), who was indistinctly heard, was understood to say that the condition of Assam was generally unknown to the public of India, but there was no doubt that it was the very poorest province in all India.

THE PRESIDENT then rose and said: "Now that delegates from all the different provinces of India have spoken, unless any one has any objection to offer to the resolution, we must try to expedite the business of the Congress. I have not the slightest wish to prevent any one from speaking, but we must consider whether there is any practical utility in going on speaking on the same subject in the same tone indefinitely. I believe that one or more gentlemen from every province have already spoken—gentlemen from Bombay, Madras, Bengal, Oudh, the North-Western Provinces, the Punjab and Assam—and I should like to know whether, in the opinion of the meeting, it is desirable to continue the discussion, because, thus far, there appears to have been no difference of opinion so far as the resolution before us goes. But I believe that, despite this apparent unanimity, some of the gentlemen from Bengal contemplated proposing some amendment and, if so, I think the time has come for this to be brought forward."

MR. SURENDRA NATH BANERJEE (*Bengal, No.* 239) said: "On behalf of the Bengal delegates I wish to offer a few remarks.

"There was a preliminary meeting of Bengal delegates yesterday at the Ripon College, under the presidency of Baboo Sambhu Chunder Mookerjee, at which the draft resolutions were fully considered and certain alterations suggested, and on behalf of that large body of representatives I desire now to propose an amendment. The Bengal delegates propose to substitute for the last three lines of the resolution, as it now stands (after the words "fixed conviction that"), the following: 'the wider employment of natives of India, the encouragement of indigenous trade and manufactures are among the circumstances which, along with the introduction of representative institutions, would palliate the poverty of the masses.'

"They do not, in the slightest degree, depreciate the value of representative institutions; they know that re resentative institutions will be an unspeakable blessing, and they also allow that the passing of this resolution is a fitting introduction to the resolutions which follow. At the same time it seems to them that the poverty of the masses would not be remedied simply by the introduction of representative institutions; and that being so, it becomes necessary to refer, at least incidentally, to those other important reforms which might equally tend to remove the poverty of the masses. Therefore on behalf of the Bengal delegates I move this amendment." (*Cheers.*)

Baboo Kalicharan Banerjee (*Bengal, No.* 273) seconded the amendment.

Baboo Ambica Charan Mazumdar (*Furreedpur, No.* 316) said: "I rise to join my feeble voice with the earnest and solemn utterances which are still ringing within the walls of this great hall. The prominence given to the subject, under discussion, by this Congress, is of itself an unmistakable proof of both its importance and urgency at the present moment. Indeed the problem of the increasing poverty of the people has become a matter of so deep a concern to the intellectual portion of the various communities in the country and such a harassing trouble to the whole nation, that a practical solution of it admits of neither delay nor shuffling. In spite of all the intellectual advancements of its people with its dying energies and mouldering industries, the land of once fabulous wealth, the gorgeous Ind, is but hastening on to decay. Not a year passes without some cry of famine or distress in some quarters. You, who live amidst the grandeur and foreign opulence of the provincial capital cities, cannot adequately comprehend the abject poverty and wretchedness of the unhappy people inhabiting the rural tracts of this vast Empire. (*Loud cheers.*) Not a few of these places are desolate, and many are being covered with dense jungles, with a mixed population of wild beasts and still wilder beggars and vagabonds. Those who exultingly see nothing but submission and security in this state of things have not the foresight to perceive the great danger that underlies this great evil. It has a deep political significance which it will require a true statesmanship to discover. The evil is portentous, and its signs and demonstrations ominous. The universal discontent of the masses has its real origin in their growing wants and increasing poverty, and if this strong down-current is not promptly tided up I know not in what disastrous consequences it may terminate. (*Loud cheers.*) As to the palliative suggested in the resolution, I am humbly of opinion that it may hereafter act as a strong invigorative; but the immediate remedy for the evil lies in some other phial. The connection between the poverty of the people on the one hand and representative institutions on the other seems to me to be somewhat remote; and I hope this Congress will not, in its eagerness to emphasise the third resolution of the Congress' of 1885, mar the effect and potency of the second resolution of the Congress of 1886. I would, therefore, humbly entreat you gentlemen of the Congress to accept the amendments of the Bengal delegates, as far as the remedial portion of the resolution is concerned, and incorporate therein the two clauses regarding technical education and encouragement of native industries, which have been so clearly explained to you by one of their leaders. In other respects the proposition of Mr. Edulji Watcha has my fullest support." (*Loud cheers.*)

Row Sahib M. B. Namjoshi (*Poona, No.* 69) said: "Before rising to suggest an amendment I thought it necessary to consult the President of this Congress. From what has fallen from gentlemen, representing different provinces, I gather that the supposed remedies for the poverty of India are several, whereas only one single remedy is set forth in the resolution. Baboo Surendra Nath Banerjee has now suggested two other remedies. When consulting the President on this matter, I was told that I ought to have considered the matter earlier, and like our Bengal friends have given due notice of an amendment; but with due deference I would submit that I only got these resolutions, as it were, at the eleventh hour. The Bengal delegates had previous opportunities of considering the resolutions, but some, at any rate, of us from Bombay have had none. I would suggest that it would be better if all the resolutions were read, and if some time were now given to those of us who have not yet had sufficient time for this to consider the questions involved in all their aspects and prepare such amendments as any of us may wish to propose. Anyhow as regards this particular resolution the amendments which I have to propose are: First, that the word "increasing" in the resolution be omitted; and second, that the introduction of a permanent settlement throughout the ryotwari-settled provinces be included as one of the most important steps towards the alleviation of the poverty of the masses.'

Munshi Sadho Lall (*North-Western Provinces, No.* 146) seconded this latter amendment.

Mr. Sorabji F. Patell (*Bombay, No.* 50) said: "I think the subject of the introduction of a permanent settlement is far too vast and complicated a question to introduce thus at the tail of a resolution. (*Loud cheers.*) It is one which should be discussed by itself, if discussed at all. It is a matter which has been discussed for the last fifty years, and in regard to which the greatest diversity of opinion prevails. By lumping up a number of different matters in one resolution, many of us will be prevented from voting for the resolution; therefore I would suggest that the question of the permanent settlement should be left alone, and that we confine ourselves to the 'one practical' step about which we are all agreed." (*Cheers and cries of yes, yes.*)

Baboo Guru Prasad Sen (*Behar, No.* 198) said : ' As I understand the second resolution it does not profess to give an exhaustive list of all the causes which lead to the poverty of the people. It does not even enumerate a single cause of that poverty, neither does it go into all the remedies or profess to do so. It merely states that the introduction of representative institutions will prove one of the most important steps towards the amelioration of the condition of the people. Now does any one deny this ? No. Baboo Surendra Nath Banerjee, on behalf of a large number of my Bengal friends, desires to add to this reform two others which he and they think will also be efficacious in the same direction. But if I have understood the real meaning of the resolution, it does not mean to say that the larger employment of natives, the encouragement of trade, or I may add the reduction of military expenditure and the revision of existing revenue systems are not one and all important reforms which will greatly tend to improve the condition of people ; but it signifies that we have little chance of securing these, or any other, reforms until we can bring the lever of representative institutions to bear on the bureaucracy that now holds everything in its hands. (*Enthusiastic and prolonged cheering.*) That being so, I do not see any need for this amendment. Everybody knows that many causes contribute to the poverty of India ; but that is not the substantive resolution before the meeting. For our view is that, until we get representation, it is hopeless to deal effectively with any of those causes. (*Loud cheers.*) As to Mr. Namjoshi's amendments, I personally object to omit the word increasing, but that is for the Congress to decide. His other amendment I have practically already disposed of ; therefore I oppose all the amendments." (*Cheers.*)

Pandit Jwalanath Sarma (*Calcutta, No.* 251) said : " It has been suggested that this single fact of the poverty of the people has a plurality of causes, and this is undoubtedly the case, but we are still only on the threshold of our work and need not trouble ourselves at present with an exhaustive catalogue of these causes. It is better that we should first try and secure representative institutions ; then we shall be in a position and have strength enough to deal with all these complicated questions. If we are only able to secure the first, it will be one real and, as I think, the most important step. Then we shall have a certain combined strength, and shall not, as now, have to speak unlistened to. (*Hear, hear.*) It is better to deal with one point at a time." (*Yes, yes.*)

Mr. Hume (*Punjab, No.* 112) said : " We find here gentlemen who come from Bombay and Madras, who have never had any practical experience of a permanent settlement, strongly insisting on it as a remedy for the poverty of the masses. But we, here, have had it in full play for nearly one hundred years, and I am sure there is no province in India where the masses are poorer than in Bengal."

Mr. Sitalakanta Chatterjee (*Meerut, No.* 155) said : " I will speak only one word upon what has been said. The resolution for consideration at this moment deals with the question of the poverty of the people. The delegates from Meerut do not understand that the Congress is dealing with all the causes of, or remedies for, this poverty. The resolution before the meeting only suggests one of the great remedies for that poverty. There are a hundred other measures of course which will tend to remove it ; but we are dealing at present simply with the question of representative government, not with the question of the permanent settlement, or anything else. A permanent settlement may be a good thing, but what we are now insisting upon is that representative government ought to be conceded to us, and we say that, if representative government be conceded, it will be a most important step towards improving the condition of the people. We don't say that that is the only thing required, but we do know that, if we get that, it will not be long before we get those other reforms that are needful. (*Loud cheers.*) I think we ought not to mix up other questions with this one in our resolution ; they will only tend to weaken its force and the cause which we are supporting."

Mr. R. M. Sayani (*Bombay, No.* 54) said : " I rise to a point of order, and with due deference to my friends and the judgment of the President, I desire to point out that most of these amendments are not amendments at all. The resolution points out one of the most important remedies for removing the poverty of the people. If you say there are other remedies that is not an amendment. We don't dispute that there *are* other remedies, but your statement of this fact is no amendment to our proposition that this particular measure is *one* important remedy. I ask you, Sir, as President, to rule that these are not amendments."

Rao Sahib S. A. Saminada Iyer (*Tanjore, No.* 41) said : "The resolution contains these words : 'The Government is not overlooking the matter, and is contemplating certain palliatives.' These words include the Public Service Commission which is insisted on, in order to enable the Government to introduce more of the native element into the services, and the question of technical education also is under the consideration of Government ; therefore, I think, this resolution is wide enough to embrace all forms of remedies for the removal of the poverty of the people."

Baboo Mati Lal Ghose (*Bengal, No.* 335) said: "I must give an unqualified denial to the statement made by my friend, Mr. Hume, that the peasantry of lower Bengal, at any rate, is in as impoverished condition as in any other province of the Empire."

The President said: "I think the discussion shows that, in mixing up other matters with this resolution, we are really doing injustice to the particular subject which is mentioned in this resolution. The question of a permanent settlement, for instance, is so important a matter that it requires separate consideration. I would ask the Congress to consider whether it is not proper to go on with this resolution as indicating one of the most important remedies for the poverty of the people, and if other remedies be considered sufficiently important to require prominent notice at this time, to consider whether other distinct resolutions should not be proposed in regard to these. If, in dealing with one resolution, we endeavour to embrace in it all the various questions which have been raised by the different speakers who have discussed it, we shall be involved in complete chaos, and there will be absolutely no end to the matter. With regard to my friend Mr. Sayani's suggestion I have consulted some of the gentlemen around who are competent to advise me, and they doubt whether the additions proposed to be made by Mr. Banerjee can be included in the category of amendments. They are questions which ought to be discussed by themselves and are really not amendments; and I am also advised that the second of the so-called amendments made by Mr. Namjoshi should not be admitted as an amendment. I am willing to take the opinion of the meeting upon the question of order; or if I am allowed to rule (*cries of yes, you are,*) then I say that we are not competent to regard these as amendments."

Baboo Surendra Nath Banerjee (*Bengal, No.* 239) asked whether his amendment was in order.

The President said he could not admit it as an amendment.

Baboo Surendra Nath Banerjee said that if it was not considered to be an amendment, he would ask it to be taken as a substantive proposition substituted for a part of the resolution. (*Cheers.*)

Mr. Mano Mohan Ghose (*Bengal, No.* 270) said: "It seems to me that the object of the resolution is not to enumerate either the different causes of the poverty of India or the several necessary remedies for this, but the object is simply to point out that the introduction of representative institutions will be one of the most important remedies. (*Loud cheers.*) That being so, if the amendments or amplifications, or whatever they are called, were relevant to the main purport of the resolution, I should have voted for them; but they are not relevant, and I would therefore ask Baboo Surendra Nath Banerjee to consider whether he ought to press the point."

Baboo Kalicharan Banerjee (*Bengal, No.* 273) said: "Some of us may be of opinion that if only one of the remedies for ameliorating the condition of the people be mentioned, this one stated in the resolution is not the one remedy which should be specified. When, therefore, the Bengal delegates suggested the idea of certain remedies, it was out of deference to the resolution as it stood. We did not want to take it upon ourselves to expunge the remedy therein specified, *viz.*, representative institutions, but we suggested, as additions, certain other remedies that to us appeared the true ones. But if the ruling be that these particular remedies cannot be considered by way of amendment, and if the resolution must contain only one of the remedies, then it may be that we would prefer these other remedies to the remedy now embodied in the resolution."

The President then put the question whether Mr. Namjoshi's proposal as to the permanent settlement should be considered as an amendment, and by counting of hands it was ascertained that an immense majority were against it.

The President also put the question whether Baboo Surendra Nath Banerjee's proposition should be considered as an amendment, and ascertained that a very large majority were against it also.

Mr. Namjoshi (*Poona, No.* 69) then formally moved that the word "increasing" be omitted from the resolution.

Mr. Sorabjee F. Patell (*Bombay, No.* 50) seconded the amendment, which was, however, negatived by an overwhelming majority.

The original motion was then put to the vote and carried by a very large majority.

The President then called on Rai Kunja Lall to move the next resolution.

S

RAI KUNJA LALL BANNERJEE, BAHADUR (*Calcutta, No.* 234), said : "I have never in my life been a speaker, and as brevity is the soul of wit I shall be as brief as possible. The resolution which has been entrusted to me to move for your acceptance runs thus :—

"That this Congress do, emphatically, reaffirm the third resolution of the Congress of 1885, and distinctly declare its belief that the reform and expansion of the Council of the Governor-General for making Laws and of the Provincial Legislative Councils, therein suggested, have now become essential alike in the interests of India and England." (*Resolution III of the Summary, page* 41.)

"As some of those present may have forgotten exactly how the third resolution, which the Congress passed last year, runs, I shall read it :

"That this Congress considers the reform and expansion of the Supreme and existing Local Legislative Councils, by the admission of a considerable proportion of elected members (and the creation of similar Councils for the N. W. Provinces and Oudh, and also for the Punjab), essential ; and holds that all Budgets should be referred to these Councils for consideration, their members being moreover empowered to interpellate the Executive in regard to all branches of the administration ; and that a Standing Committee of the House of Commons should be constituted to receive and consider any formal protests that may be recorded by majorities of such Councils against the exercise by the Executive of the power, which would be vested in it, of overruling the decision of such majorities."

"The object of the resolution before you now is to affirm the resolution passed last year : that is the object with which the promoters of this meeting have put this on record, and the question is whether it will meet with your approval. I therefore move this resolution."

ROW SAHIB P. RUNGIAH NAIDU (*Madras, No.* 1) said : "It is with great pleasure that I second this resolution that we should re-assert, here, what we set forth last year at Bombay. (*Cheers.*) At Bombay the facts and arguments in favour of that proposition were ably and eloquently placed before the delegates there assembled, and after the fullest discussion the Congress, unanimously and enthusiastically, adopted that resolution. But we have got both friends and enemies in our country, and our enemies averred that the resolutions passed at Bombay were the resolutions of a few intelligent English-educated native gentlemen and were not the opinions of the native public, and were, therefore, not worthy of consideration by the Government or by anybody else. But now, having ascertained the views of the entire native community in every part of India, we can re-assert the proposition with additional force, and can challenge our opponents to deny that the whole population of India agrees with us in this resolution (*loud cheers*) ; and we must re-assert it now, and it may be many times more before we achieve our end. Even in a country like Great Britain, which is said to be the home of liberty and where the voice of the people is talked of as the voice of the Deity, no important reform is ever carried out in a single day or secured without a persistent struggle. When Wilberforce moved for the abolition of slavery, he did not succeed in a day, but he succeeded only after many years of constant agitation. (*Cheers.*) And Cobden, the apostle of free trade, when he and the strong party of radicals, who worked with him, made up their minds that the Corn Laws ought to be repealed, even in his own free country and with a Parliament of his own race to appeal to, he was not at once successful ; he, and those who worked with him, had to hold thousands of meetings and distribute millions of pamphlets and leaflets and canvass unceasingly for support, for years, throughout the country. And even coming to the present day we have a number of instances of this sort. There is, for instance, the question of the legalization of marriage with a deceased wife's sister. When it was first brought before Parliament there was a large majority against it, but although the proposition was lost for the time, its advocates did not give it up, but brought it forward again and again, the majority decreasing year by year, until it was carried in the House of Commons and only defeated in the Lords ; and in course of time, I think, it will pass the Lords, even, and the movement will be successful. Therefore, I think, we should now re-assert the views we asserted at the Congress at Bombay, and be prepared to re-assert and re-assert, and insist and enlarge on it, until our rulers accept it and act on it. (*Loud cheers.*)

"It is our duty, by dint of perseverance, to overcome all opposition, to struggle and labour unceasingly till we win the day, although not we, but our children, should be those who reap the fruits of that victory." (*Prolonged cheering.*)

MR. GHANASHAM NILKANTH (*Bombay, No.* 53) : **I support the proposition. As previous** speakers have explained, it was most fully discussed at Bombay, and has subsequently been placed before, and adopted by, all the Associations throughout the country, while literally hundreds of public meetings in every portion of the Empire have declared it to represent correctly the views of the entire nation (*loud cheers*) ; and there can consequently be no hesitation, this day, in emphatically re-affirming that now famous Resolution III of 1885.

Row Sahib S. Narayana Swami Chetty (*Nellore, No.* 19) said : "The voice of India has already declared that this resolution must be re-affirmed and re-affirmed until its substance becomes the law of the land. There is no backward step here now possible for any of us. (*Loud cheers.*) All the Associations, I may say the entire population, from one end of India to the other, have been consulted on the subject, and all our countrymen, high and low, have declared that these are their wishes, this the goal at which they aim. (*Cheers.*) This resolution has been accepted throughout India, and not one single Indian voice in the entire Empire has been raised against it. I think, therefore, that there need not be any long discussion upon the subject. It is simply formally re-affirming in words a resolution that the entire country has already engraved upon its heart. (*Loud cheers.*)

Pundit Thakur Prosad (*Agra, No.* 137) spoke in Urdu, and said : "Certainly there can be no hesitation in affirming the resolution last year passed at Bombay. Since then there is not a corner in the country where folks have not talked over that resolution and said it was good. Every man who knows anything, whether he be an English speaker, or, like myself, knows only Indian languages, knows at least this : that if the country is to prosper, we, its children, who understand its ways and wants, must be allowed a share, and a good share, in the management of its public affairs. (*Cheers.*) And it is only by some system of representation that we can hope to secure, and that only gradually, this power in the State. But we must do more than re-affirm this resolution. We must bring the whole power of the country to support and join with us in insisting on the concession of our demand. In my part of the country barely half the inhabitants yet understand this matter. Every man of any education, of any marked intelligence, is agreed upon this matter, but then half the people have neither education nor intelligence. We must teach them, we must prepare and publish and distribute, in vast numbers, small simple tracts in village language, that even the lowest and most ignorant can understand, explaining what it is that we are trying to get, and why we are so trying, and how this matter will, in the long run, affect their interests as much as ours, and why, therefore, they ought to join with us and help us. It will not be until we put the entire weight of the country into the scale that we shall outweigh the opposition which confronts all attempts at elevating our political position. Let us not merely join, as I do, most heartily in re-affirming this resolution, but let us each, in his own fashion, work with all our power at getting it carried into effect, and then perhaps in time something will come of it." (*Loud cheers.*)

Rajah Rampal Singh (*Oudh, No.* 178) said : "As I come from a Province which has already affirmed this proposition at numerous public meetings, and as I am the Chairman of a Board in which the elective system has been adopted and has proved a great success, far greater than even I could have expected, I most heartily support this resolution." (*Cheers.*)

Lala Kanhya Lal (*Punjab, No.* 104) said : "I come from the Punjab ; there from sheer necessity we affirm this resolution inasmuch as, since the time of Lord Lawrence, who invited Rajah Sahib Dyal to sit in the Legislative Council, we have never had the favour of even one member being appointed from our own country. The members who have been since appointed have been the Chief Commissioner, and the Financial Commissioner of the Province—not one member chosen out of the people, much less elected by themselves. We, therefore, thank our colleagues and brethren of other Provinces for pressing this resolution, which is even more vitally important to us than to any other Province. Elsewhere (now even in the N. W. Provinces) there is a show of representation, since there are councils, and Indian gentlemen, no matter how little qualified effectively to represent their Provinces, still Indian gentlemen, sitting on those Councils ; but, as for us, we have no council, no pretence even of representation."

Baboo Kakumul (*Fyzabad, No.* 180) said : "The system of election of Municipal Commissioners is working very well in Fyzabad. Only one-fourth of the Commissioners are nominated by the Government, of the Municipality of which I am the Chairman, and if those gentlemen who are nominated had not been nominated, they would certainly have been elected ; and we have an Honorary Secretary, selected by ourselves, who does the work very well and controls the expenditure of two lakhs of rupees annually. It is a petty matter you will say, but the perfect manner in which the system now actually works, on a small scale, should encourage the Government to try it on that larger scale, which the entire country desires, and the resolution we are about to affirm contemplates. It may be true that, where the system has not been introduced, nearly half the population know nothing of the representative system ; but in Fyzabad, where it is in force, everybody understands it and everybody approves it." (*Loud cheers.*)

The President rose and said : "I would particularly ask speakers to stick to the resolution under discussion; if we are to wander off into analogies and illustrations, the discussion will be indefinitely prolonged. I am much inclined to say that, if any gentleman has anything to say against the resolution, he should say it; but that otherwise it is scarcely necessary to speak further in its favour."

MALIK BHUGWAN DASS (*Dehra Ismail Khan, No.* 110) spoke in Urdu (with an eloquence to which the translation scarcely does justice), and said: "Though our President does not want us to go on speaking always to the same tune, and though, being what I am, I shall not be able to give any better or stronger reasons for re-affirming the resolution than have been given by the abler and more eloquent speakers who have addressed you; still having coine sixteen hundred miles to tell you what we think in our part of the country, I should be unworthy of the trust reposed in me did I not say, at least, a few words on this most important subject. Gentlemen, let me say before I proceed further, that I come from the western frontier of the British dominion, from a land where men handle the sword more readily than the pen, where none of us are scholars, none of us orators, and therefore whose representatives need every indulgence in coming before an assembly like this. Well, I have managed to pick up a little education, and though I do not venture to speak in English, I can read and understand it, and I do read it, and the papers a good deal; and by reading the *Civil and Military Gazette* and the *Pioneer* I have learned that the persons who desire a change in the present form of the administration and want representative institutions and a larger share in the Government of the country, are only the Bengali Baboos, and that the public in India generally do not care for, and do not understand, such things. Now, gentlemen, I should be very proud of being a Bengali Baboo (the most highly educated class in India), but do *I* look like a Bengali Baboo? (*The speaker was a stalwart frontier man, wearing the frontier dress.*) (*Loud cheers and cries of no, no.*) Let me tell the editors of those Anglo-Indian papers that it is *not* only the Bengali Baboos who desire these things, but the more intelligent persons in every class and caste of people in every part of the country in which I have been. Even in our Dera Ismail Khan there are plenty who know all about these matters, and in other districts of the Punjab a still greater number. Backward we may be, but it is absurd to suppose that we Punjabis, even we frontier people, are altogether ignorant of such matters or fail to sympathize in the work which this Congress is endeavouring to get done. What, gentlemen, would they make out that God, the Almighty Father, has not endowed us with human reason, but has left us incapable of knowing what is good for us and what is bad, of feeling how unjust to us are many things in existing arrangements, of realizing that the first thing necessary, if that injustice .is to be done away with, is that we should have a strong voice in the management of our country's, of our own, affairs? During the last few years the Punjab has been making progress in education. There may not be the huge number of educated men that you have here, but there are yet a good number, and these have learnt how things stand and have explained them in their own way to all their brethren. There are tens of thousands of, what you may call, ignorant men, who yet know very well what the great defect in the Government's administration of affairs is. You must not overlook the fact that our people in the Punjab have a natural intelligence that, quite independent of education, makes them capable and, therefore, desirous of administering public affairs. In my own little town of Dera Ismail Khan, I can give many instances of this. Take Nawab Mohamed Faujdar, whom you must have heard of as British representative at Cabul, an almost illiterate man, of a not very high position, who simply by force of character and natural intelligence so distinguished himself in political administration as to be made a Nawab, C.S.I., &c. Or Nawab Gholam Hossein Khan, a K.C.S.I., I believe, who similarly won distinction as a diplomatist; or again Nawab Ata Mahomed Khan, who was the British representative at Cabul for many years, who induced the Amir Shere Ali to attend the Amballa Durbar (a wonderful achievement to those who understand how affairs really stood then in Cabul), but who was utterly opposed to the late war in Cabul and prophesied accurately its results—twenty crores spent and spent for nothing. There is not a district, not a town, that does not contain many such or better men; and do you suppose that any of them are greatly pleased with a form of administration which denies, to ninety-nine out of every hundred of them, any career; or that any of them fail to see that representative institutions, and a much larger employment of Indians in the higher offices of State, would be important steps towards the opening they want? (*Loud cheers.*) I will not detain you longer, I will only repeat that this Congress and the objects it aims at have the sympathy of every thinking man in India, be he educated or uneducated; and though the newspapers may misunderstand the subject, I think the Government knows better, and as, despite mistakes that it makes, the Government is a generous Government, I hope, and *think* too, that coming to realize how universal is the feeling, it will yield to our desire, and concede, if not at once, yet piece by piece, all we ask for. If I speak plainly it is not that I am opposed to British rule—far from it; that rule has no more earnest supporter than myself. But good as it is, there are many things yet that should be improved, and amongst them the matters dealt with by this Congress, and while I say may God prosper British rule in India for ever, I also say may He give our rulers wisdom to understand the reasonableness of our demands for reform and the magnanimity to concede what we ask for." (*Loud and prolonged cheers.*)

THE PRESIDENT said : "I really think we must now put this resolution to the vote. The subject is one of such vast and far-reaching importance, that a hundred more speeches might be made on the subject without exhausting it. But to what end ? If, as it seems, we are all entirely of one mind on this matter, further discussion is surely not wanted, and we have so much other work to do." (*Cries of vote, vote.*)

The resolution was then formally put and carried unanimously with loud cheers.

THE PRESIDENT then said : "The matter of appointing a Committee to consider the Public Service Question is an important one, and should, I venture to think, be given priority over other subjects, because the Committee, if one be appointed, will have to complete its work within the next two days. Last year we passed a resolution calling for a Public Service Commission : that Commission is now sitting. The question for consideration is whether we should now enter into any discussion of the subject, or whether we should not rather let the Commission finish their work, and then see what the public have to say to it. That is one view of the question. But it is said, on the other hand, that it is important that this Congress should say what they think in regard to the matters before the Commission, and make any suggestions which they think fit. A third proposition is that a Committee be appointed to consider this question and submit their report to the Congress, and a further proposition is that this Committee be authorized to exercise their own judgment in preparing and publishing such a series of expositions of the principles involved in the various questions published by the Commission as should enable witnesses to give consistent and appropriate answers on all points.

"This subject must be dealt with in one way or another. To open the discussion it would be well if some one, who is of this opinion, would definitely propose that we should abstain from dealing with the matter at the present Congress, and allow the Commission to finish its work before attempting to touch the question."

RAJAH RAMPAL SINGH (*Oudh, No.* 178) said : "As the whole question is under the consideration of the Government, I think the Congress should not pass any resolution in regard to it, or interfere in the matter at all. When a case is under trial in a Court of Justice the press does not offer any opinion. This question is now, as it were, *sub-judice* before the Commission, and we should certainly not, in any way, directly or indirectly, suggest to the witnesses, that are going to be examined, what we happen to consider the proper replies to give to the several questions put by the Commission. I therefore move that all consideration of the Public Service Question, so far as this Congress is concerned, be deferred until the completion of the Public Service Commission's labours."

BABOO KAKUMUL (*Fyzabad, No.* 180) said : "I second the motion. This is not, it seems to me, the time to affirm any principles: the question should be postponed until there is sufficient information upon which to frame a resolution. At present, we don't know what the Commission will do; we should wait and see what they decide and what reasons they are able to assign for their decisions."

BABOO SALIGRAM SINGH (*Calcutta, No.* 235) said : "I am also of opinion that this question should not be considered at present. It should be omitted from the list of business before the Congress."

LALA KANHYA LAL (*Punjab, No.* 104) said : "I am against this motion, as I think a Committee should be appointed to consider the question and submit its report before the Congress is dissolved. As far as I have seen of the proceedings of the Commission, I observe that, whenever a witness gave evidence which was unacceptable to the Commission, another witness from a different class of society (some old-fashioned sycophant) was immediately procured to rebut that evidence. There was a considerable diversity of evidence, and in some cases evidence was given against the interests of India, and the result was unintelligible. I submit that this Congress should distinctly record its views with reference to the more important questions which are before the Commission and which are really very few in number."

MR. SURENDRA NATH BANERJEE (*Bengal, No.* 239) said : "It seems to me that we ought to be guided, to a considerable extent, by the experienced observations of my friend who comes from the Punjab, and has had the opportunity of personally coming into contact with the evidence which has been given; he speaks, therefore, with weight and authority. That is one point. Those who have been reading this evidence, from day to day, might have been impressed with one striking fact, namely, the perfect chaos, confusion and anarchy which prevails. A says something, B supports it, C strikes out another proposition, D is brought forward to rebut it, and the whole becomes a perfect chaos. Mark the importance of the matter. Lord Dufferin, in reply to the Poona address, said that it was not so much on the Government as on the witnesses that the result depends.

Therefore the question is whether the evidence, which is to be tendered, is to be, or not to be, in accordance with our highest and most cherished wishes, and whether we ought not, if possible, to formulate the principles which should guide the evidence of the witnesses. In my humble opinion we ought to try to evolve something like order out of the chaos. I don't wish that this Congress should answer the 184 questions which have been propounded by the Commission, or their secretary. That is quite impossible. But there are certain principles which underlie most of these questions, and it is for this Congress to consider these principles and to formulate the decisions they arrive at in relation to those principles, so that the final verdict may be in some sort guided by the verdict which this Congress may pronounce. It is a life and death struggle. You have considered these questions for the last forty years, and if you make this self-sacrifice and leave the matter alone now, it is too much to suppose that advantage will not be taken of your silence. That being so, I do think that we ought to appoint a Committee to-day. We do not bind ourselves by the judgment of that Committee; we do not seek to tie you down to the names, provisionally suggested, in the draft resolution.* Let the men, whom you may appoint on the Committee, be men in whom you have confidence, and who have the confidence of the inhabitants of every town and station in the country. You do not pledge yourselves to the report that they may make. But still as these gentlemen will have your confidence they will have the confidence of your constituents, and the views they enunciate will everywhere be studied and carefully considered, and will certainly aid many hazy-minded persons to arrive, not necessarily at these same, but at any rate at some definite conclusions. It is a matter of the highest importance that we should so distinctly place the principles, on which we desire action, before the Commission, and so aid our witnesses to furnish definite and consistent replies, that the Commission may be able to come to soine definite conclusions."

Pandit Satyanand Agnihotri (*Lahore, No.* 98) said: "I agree word for word with what has been said by Baboo Surendra Nath Banerjee. There are certain witnesses being examined by the Commission, and their depositions are not such as to be quite satisfactory to the public and to the whole of India, and it is, therefore, necessary for this Congress to appoint a Committee for the purpose which has just been stated. If we neglect this opportunity we shall lose a most important chance and one which we shall all, for ever, regret losing."

Row Sahib M. B. Namjoshi (*Poona, No.* 69) said: "After the eloquent speech of Baboo Surendra Nath Banerjee it will be superfluous to urge the same points as he has done, though I must say that if after all we have been so persistently urging in the papers we now, when we have the chance, fail to submit some practical suggestions, we shall scarcely be doing our duty—nay we shall, it seems to me, expose ourselves to well-merited ridicule. But there are two special points scarcely touched upon as yet on which I desire to say a few words. The idea of appointing a Committee originated, I believe, with myself, and two of the reasons which influenced me in advocating this course differ from those which have been mainly relied upon by Baboo Surendranath. The first of these is, that this seems to me the best opportunity of authoritatively controverting the assertion made in influential quarters as to the action taken by the leaders of Native Society in this matter. They have been stigmatised as being wire-pullers, and it has been gravely maintained that a dozen or so of educated men alone care about this Service Question. It is partly as a means of emphatically contradicting this absurd assertion that I suggest this formal consideration of the question by the Congress. If the Congress ignored the question, no matter on what grounds they might really do this, there would be an opening to pretend that the Congress does not really care about it. But if the Congress take it up and show how deeply interested it is in the matter,—we are here some four hundred and fifty in number and we cannot all be wire-pullers,—and the first step towards proving that anxiety, since we cannot discuss in detail all the 184 questions propounded, is to appoint a Committee, composed of all the men whom all of us rely on, to look into and reply, so far as time may permit, to the more important of these questions.

---

* The draft resolution, which was at the time in every delegate's hands, and which, though it had not been formally proposed, was what was under consideration, is subjoined. It differs materially from the resolution ultimately passed.

Draft Resolution.

VI. That this Congress congratulate the Government and the people of the country upon the appointment of a Public Service Commission, and taking the deepest interest in the labours of that body, deems it expedient (although, the question being *sub-judice*, it refrains from re-affirming its last year's fourth resolution) to appoint a Committee* to prepare and submit to the Commission an expression of the opinions of the Congress on all those points, connected with the Civil Service Question, on which a general unanimity exists amongst the delegates.

* The Hon'ble M. G. Ranade (*Bombay*).
" Dadabhai Naoroji (*Bombay*).
" S. Subramania Iyer (*Madras*).
" Peary Mohun Mukerjee (*Bengal*).
Mr. G. Subramania Iyer (*Madras*).
" Motilal Ghose (*Bengal*).
" Surendranath Banerji (*Bengal*).
" Pran Nath (*Lucknow*).
" Gangapershad Varma (*Lucknow*).
" Murlidhur (*Amballa*).
" Ramkali Chowdhry (*Benares*).
" Guruprasad Sen (*Patna*).
Rajah Lutchman Singh (*N. W. Provinces*).

"The Sub-Committee, who have been charged with drafting the rosolutions, have entered the names as proposed members of the suggested Committee, of persons in whom the Congress, I believe, has full confidence. They are persons who, many of them, have devoted their lives to India's cause, who have studied the question thoroughly; but there may be others as well qualified. It is for the Congress to decide upon the names. I am only insisting on the appointment of a Committee."

RAJAH RAMPAL SINGH (*Oudh, No.* 178) said: "I rise to a point of order. I made a substantive motion that all consideration of the Public Service Question, so far as this Congress is concerned, be deferred until the completion of the Public Service Commission's labours. I am not aware that any substantive amendment has been proposed, but it seems to me we are beginning to consider the Public Service Question. I think a vote should be taken on my motion, or a distinct amendment moved."

THE PRESIDENT said: "I do not think that at present we need interrupt the discussion; considering the terms in which I introduced the subject to the notice of the Congress, and that thus far Mr. Namjoshi is merely arguing, in opposition to Rajah Rampal's motion that no notice be taken, that, on the contrary, notice ought to be and must be taken, I think we should allow Mr. Namjoshi to continue."

MR. NAMJOSHI (*resumed*): "The second point that I desire to urge is this. Those who propose to drop the question have not given their reasons for so doing. But the only reason, I anticipate, is that they are afraid that the Congress may not come to an unanimous finding on all points: that there may be points in regard to which differences of opinion will arise. If this be so, then this is one of the very reasons for appointing a Committee. I admit that there may be differences of opinion (though I believe on one-single point only). I welcome the fact. The members of this Congress have severally studied the question in their own way, and in reference to their own provinces; they may well have something to say, irrespective of what others say, with regard to their own provinces. They may be perfectly justified in their views, so far as their own province is concerned, but they possibly fail to realize what other provinces are doing in the matter, and what they wish should be done for the future. And, therefore, some organized attempt should be made to formulate the principles upon which the matured views of all should be based, and there is no surer method of doing this than that now proposed of setting a limited number of the best men of every province to work out, so far as may be possible, unanimous solutions of the problems set before us. Moreover, by this resolution, we declare to the world, and to the official world in particular, the persons whom we select, as it were, as our witnesses in whom we have the fullest confidence, and whose evidence will represent the views of the entire Congress. Therefore, for the reasons given by Baboo Surendra Nath Banerjee, and for the additional reasons that I have given, I think it inexpedient to defer consideration of the question, and think it necessary that a Committee should be appointed; and I shall be glad if the question is placed in their hands."

MUNSHI KASHI PROSAD (*Allahabad, No.* 113) said: "After so much has been written and said on this subject for some years past the opportunity should not be lost of considering what replies should be placed before the Commission. I believe that one reason why some gentlemen shrink from the proposal to appoint a Committee is the necessity which they think this will impose on them of considering the enormous number of questions put forward by the Commission and the voluminous literature on the subject. But this could not be a reason for shirking our duty, and, as has been explained by Baboo Surendra Nath Banerjee, the Committee need not go into all these intricate questions, but only formulate and give expression to the general views of the Congress. I can assure you that it has not been in the majority of cases any fault of the witnesses who have been examined that has led to the conviction that some authoritative exposition, of the principles on which all replies should be based, is needed.

"If simple questions had been asked, plain answers would have been given to them, but when the questions are so complex as not to be within the comprehension of many of the witnesses, naturally they cannot elicit clear answers; and I think it very necessary that a Committee of chosen men, selected by the whole Congress, should help to clear the matter up, for all future witnesses, by enunciating the simple principles, in which we are really all agreed, which underlie the ridiculous mass of answers expected from every witness."

DR. RAJENDRALALA MITRA (*Calcutta, No.* 229) said: "I wish I could induce the supporters of this draft resolution, the adoption of which I understand Baboo Surendranath and others to advocate, to drop it. I wish it had not been brought before the meeting. I am afraid it is very indiscreet, under any circumstances, to delegate your power of consideration and judgment to a dozen men, most of whom are utterly unknown (*cries of no, no*) to the gentlemen here present. Have you such a knowledge of their business qualifications and their capacities that you are sure they will do as you would do yourself? Even if you were convinced of this it would not be proper to delegate your authority to them. Some 450 gentlemen here present are ready, it would seem, to act as a flock of sheep and to be guided by twelve unknown men. (*Cries of well-known, well-known.*) Could anything be more injurious to the interests of this Congress than the delegation of their entire power to such a small minority. If you had laid down the principles upon which they should make their representations, and limited their discretion, it would be a different thing. But here no principle is laid down, no directions are laid down, and these twelve men are told to do something for the Congress, and the draft resolution concludes by saying that a general unanimity exists amongst the delegates. What that unanimity is I presume I can guess. There may be, for aught I know, very strong differences of opinion with regard to the Public Service Question, and can they say let these twelve men do what they think proper and so rid us of the trouble? Have you travelled here hundreds of miles to say, let A, B and C do everything for us? This is a scandal upon our common sense. If that was all you had to do you might have written from your homes to say that you would subscribe to whatever was done. That is exactly what you are going to do, and it is most inconsistent and irrational to do so. I object to any man playing the part of *akulbardar* for me, and this Congress should be ashamed of itself if it cannot do for itself what it ought to do."

Mr. Surendra Nath Banerjee (*Calcutta, No.* 239) said: "I think there is some misunderstanding: I have not formally moved the draft resolution that stands on the printed list of business for to-day, though I took it as a text from which to set forth my dissent to Rajah Rampal's motion that this Congress should take no notice of the Service Question, and press my own view that it should take effective notice, and for that purpose appoint a Committee of picked representative men to deal with it, it being impossible, with the very short time available, for the Congress, as a body, to do this. But I quite admit that there may be objections to the course proposed in the draft, and as I omitted to move a formal amendment to Rajah Rampal's motion I now move—

"That a Committee composed of gentlemen, to be hereafter named, be appointed to consider the Public Service Question and report thereon to this Congress." (*Resolution VI of the Summary, page* 43.)

Row Sahib M. B. Namjoshi (*Poona, No.* 69) said: "I second the amendment."

Pandit Satyanand Agnihotri (*Lahore, No.* 98) said: "I support the amendment moved by Baboo Surendra Nath Banerjee and seconded by Mr. Namjoshi. You must be well aware that this question has been discussed for a long time, and it has been considered in every place in which a branch of the Indian Association or any other political Association has been formed, and has been a burning question in every province. Such a large assembly like this cannot deal with this question in the first instance, and I see no reason why a well-selected representative Committee should not be appointed to formulate principles. If we cannot give our confidence to the members of a Committee selected from amongst ourselves, then I say that there can be no representative government at all. For what is representation if we cannot have a number of *akulburdars* in whom we have confidence. Any one who pleases may make a joke of *akulburdars*, but what are the members of the English House of Commons but the *akulburdars* of the people of England? (*Loud cheers.*) Since the Commission is taking evidence all over India, why should not such a Congress as this give its own evidence to the Commission. We are not prepared to consider all the questions, so liberally propounded by the Commission, but we can lay down some broad lines and principles upon which all the replies of witnesses can be based. Such questions, for instance, as the simultaneous examination of candidates in England and in India can be discussed as well by a committee of experts, on whom we all rely, as here in Congress. The Committee, if there be any doubts in any case, can easily ascertain our views and might, it seems to me, for any possible harm it could do, submit its report direct to the Commission."

Mr. Daji Abaji Khare (*Bombay, No.* 56) said: "I wish to say a few words on the question which seems to have given rise to so much difference of opinion. Certain important points seem to me to run a chance of being overlooked, or I should not thus trespass on your time. We know that the Civil Service Question has been agitated for the last half century; several of our ablest men have devoted their lives to its consideration, and its importance cannot be made more manifest to you than by recalling your attention to the reply made by the Viceroy to the deputation at Poona, in which he said that the settlement of this question would be a settlement for a considerable time. When, therefore, the Government once takes action on the report of the Commission, we need not hope to effect any change in the course it may adopt for some time to come; surely therefore now is our time. It is no use waiting until the Commission has completed its labours—that will be too late. It is now that we must take whatever steps we can to secure our long-cherished object. The Government has appointed a Commission, and has asked us to prove our case; we must show that we are prepared to take a larger share in the government of the country, and show how we propose that this be brought about. In selecting the witnesses to be examined by the Commission the choice is given, to a great extent, to the local authorities; and if we remain silent, for aught we know, the majority of the gentlemen, whom this representative Congress know to be best qualified to reply on our behalf, and whom it is proposed to name as a Committee, may be left out in the cold, and the local authorities will, in place of these, call upon certain other people whose views they know to be in accord with their own, and thus with a packed witness box our cause will go by default. It is, therefore, our duty to appoint certain gentlemen from amongst ourselves, whom we look upon as our leading experts in these matters, to formulate certain principles; to educate the people as to the real bearings of the questions; and generally represent the Congress before the Commission. It seems to me to be clearly our business to help the less educated and less well-informed witnesses to arrive at sound conclusions in regard to every question that may arise. I propose that Dr. Rajendralala Mitra and Mr. Sayani be added to the Committee."

The President then rose and said: "Rajah Rampal Singh's motion is that the Public Service Question shall not be taken into consideration by this present Congress. To this an amendment is proposed that a Committee should be at once appointed to consider this question, with instructions to report thereon to this Congress before it dissolves. If no other gentlemen has anything further to say for or against these counter-propositions they might now, I think, be put to the vote.'

Dr. Gurudas Banerjee (*Calcutta, No.* 271) said: "I suggest that the Committee be authorized to submit its report direct to the Commission without laying it before the Congress, and that the Committee should also be empowered to name witnesses.

"I will move this as an amendment of Mr. Surendra Nath Banerjee's motion, that is if I am in order. I leave the matter in our President's hands, but I desire that, in some way, the sense of the meeting be taken as to the points I have suggested."

The President said: "I am afraid that matters are getting a little mixed with amendments on amendments. But, after all, we need not be sticklers for form, overmuch. What we really want to get at is the opinion of the majority of this Congress, and now as it seems to me that the matter has been pretty well threshed out, I propose, with your approval, to try and clear the ground by a few votes. I will put to you the several more important proposals that have been made, and you can by your votes decide which is to be accepted and which are to be rejected." (*Cries of yes, yes, vote, vote.*)

Rajah Rampal Singh's motion that all consideration of the Public Service Question, so far as this Congress is concerned, be deferred, etc., was put to the vote and negatived by a very large majority. The proposal that a Committee be appointed to frame a report and submit it direct to the Commission without laying it before the Congress, was also put and negatived by an overwhelming majority.

Baboo Surendra Nath Banerjee's amendment that a Committee be appointed for the purpose of considering the Public Service Question and reporting thereon to the Congress on the last day of its sitting, was then put by the President; but

Dr. Gurudas Banerjee (*Calcutta, No.* 271) rose and said: "I move as a rider to this motion that the Committee be also instructed to name witnesses."

Baboo Kali Charan Banerjee (*Calcutta, No.* 273) said: "In seconding this amendment, or rider, I wish to point out that the Congress has no right or authority to submit to the Public Service Commission any report which a committee of this Congress may make to it. The Commission has been appointed to take evidence, and not to take into consideration reports that may be submitted to them, no matter whence originating; therefore, the report of our Committee can be of no particular use to our cause, and we shall have done nothing unless we name certain witnesses who will be prepared to give evidence according to the conclusions contained in any report which we may adopt. That is my reason for seconding the amendment."

The President said. "I really do not think that Dr. Gurudas Banerjee's proposition, which is an amendment of an amendment, and which in fact starts a fresh hare, can be accepted. It is all very well, in the Hitopodesa and Alif Leila, to start a new story in the middle of every preceding story, so as to prevent coming too soon to the end of the matter, but our object *is* to come to an end of our work as soon as we reasonably can. Of course I leave it to you, but my counsel would be that, if he desires to press the matter, Dr. Gurudas Banerjee be requested to move a separate resolution on the subject another day, and that now, it being very late, we proceed at once to vote on Baboo Surendra Nath's amendment." (*General cries of vote, vote.*)

Baboo Surendra Nath Banerjee's motion was then put and carried unanimously.

The whole Congress then sitting as a Committee proceeded to discuss the composition of the Committee, the appointment of which had just been agreed to. It was pointed out that the Hon'ble Mahadeo Govind Ranade, and Rajah Lutchman Singh, being Government servants, and not being delegates, would certainly not consent to sit on the Committee. Dr. Rajendralala Mitra said that he did not feel disposed to sit on the Committee either.

After much conversation the names of the following gentlemen were unanimously agreed to :—

Hon'ble Dadabhai Naoroji (*Bombay, No.* 48).
" S. Subramania Iyer (*Madras, No.* 2).
" Peary Mohun Mookerjee (*Calcutta, No.* 233).
Mr. G. Subramania Iyer (*Madras No.* 5).
Baboo Matilal Ghose (*Calcutta, No.* 335).
Mr. Surendra Nath Banerjee (*Calcutta, No.* 239).
" Gungapershad Varma (*Lucknow, No.* 174).
" Ramkali Chowdhry (*Benares, No.* 149).
" Guru Prasad Sen (*Patna, No.* 198).
Pundit Prannath (*Lucknow, No.* 172).
Munshi Kashipershad (*Allahabad, No* 113).
Nawab Reza Ali Khan (*Lucknow, No.* 167).
Mr. Hamid Ali (*Lucknow, No.* 168).
Lala Kanhya Lal (*Amritsur, No.* 104).
Rao Sahib Gungadhur Row Madheo Chitnavis (*Nagpur, No.* 187).
Mr. Rahimatulla M. Sayani (*Bombay, No.* 54).

THE PRESIDENT then declared the Congress adjourned till the next day.

THIRD DAY'S PROCEEDINGS.

Wednesday, 29th December, 1886.

AT THE TOWN HALL.

THE PRESIDENT said : "We begin to-day with a resolution which Mr. Saminada Iyer will kindly lay before you."

ROW SAHIB S. A SAMINADA IYER (*Tanjore, No.* 41) said : "The resolution, which I have the honor to move, is one which calls for but few remarks from me. It runs as follows: That, in the opinion of this Congress, the time has now arrived when the system of trial by jury may be safely extended into many parts of the country where it is not at present in force. (*Resolution VIII of Summary, page* 44.)

"The gentlemen here assembled are aware that the natural intelligence of their countrymen, sharpened as it has been by the education which has been given to them during the last fifty years, has qualified them to weigh evidence and arrive at just conclusions in the trial of cases before the Court of Sessions. I have myself been a public prosecutor and a Government pleader for 16 years, and I have found during this lengthened experience that the verdicts of juries and of assessors have been in 99 cases out of 100 just and reasonable, and in the vast majority of cases in harmony with the opinion of the Judge himself. I have, therefore, the greatest pleasure in moving this resolution, which should, I think, be accepted by this Congress without the slightest hesitation." (*Cheers.*)

ROW SAHIB HARILAL HARSHADRAI DHRUVA (*Surat, No.* 88) said : "Trial by jury has been tried in many parts of the country, and wherever it has been tried it has been found successful. We have abundant testimony, with which I need not here trouble you, to this fact, and a pleader myself, I can heartily endorse what has fallen from the proposer, himself, a public prosecutor of long standing. Education has now sufficiently advanced in many other parts of the country to render desirable the extension to these also of the jury system. I, therefore, cordially second this resolution, and recommend to your most favorable consideration this most important subject. We have advanced not only in general but also in political education, and this is, if rightly considered, an additional reason for pressing for the extension of trial by jury. It is the proud privilege, I might almost say the indefeasible right, of every free-born subject of Her Gracious Majesty." (*Loud cheers.*)

DR. TRAILOKYANATH MITTER (*Bengal, No.* 269) supported the motion. He said : "It is unnecessary to dilate upon the benefits of trial by jury, which are very well known to all of us. The question we are considering is whether it should not be much more widely extended ; in fact, broadly speaking (though there are exceptions), to all parts of the country. I suppose it is now well known, and generally admitted, that by the progress of education throughout the country, provinces which were at one time backward have now come forward and are ready to accept, and desirous of obtaining, the boon of trial by jury. To those districts, or at any rate to many of them which hitherto have not enjoyed the benefit of trial by jury, it is now the desire of this Congress that it should be extended. It will, of course, remain for the Executive Government to exclude certain districts as, even now, not fit for trial by jury. There are some such, and we do not propose in this resolution of ours to presume to dictate such matters of detail to the Government, or formulate a list of those districts to which an immediate extension is necessary. All we say is, that the time has now come when a very material extension of the system of trial by jury has become alike desirable and practicable. I think no further remarks are necessary from me to commend this resolution to your acceptance."

LALA KANHYA LAL (*Punjab, No.* 104) said : "It is my duty to say something of the circumstances of the province from which I come. When the jury system is once introduced in any place all cases must be tried by a jury, and it will not be left to the option of the accused to refuse or demand trial by jury. That being so, I fear that the Punjab, as a whole, by no means ripe for such a reform, and therefore I think that in the Punjab we should be reluctant to accept the jury system. The fact is we have not yet a sufficient number of dependent educated men from whom jurymen could be selected, and there would always be complaints of the jurors being under the thumb of the officials and the ruling powers of the district. Trial by jury, as a system, is a double-edged thing. It is very useful where you have honest and independent jurors, but a curse where the contrary is the case ; for the verdict of a jury, however unjust, if in consonance with the views of the local bureaucracy, is final. There is no getting behind a conviction thus obtained. Where the local official passes an unjust sentence, there is a chance of obtaining redress from higher authorities, but where such sentence is based upon a verdict of ignorant and obsequious jurors, there is no hope of justice. Now I do not think that the Punjab can furnish many of the right stamp of jurors; the district officers are too powerful and overbearing and therefore I submit that our province is not ripe for the general extension of trial by jury. The jurymen will be selected by the local officials, and they will choose the *ap-ke-wastes,* and bad as things are now they will be worse, I fear, under the jury system. Therefore, in my opinion, in the Punjab, trial by jury should only be at the option of the accused and not in every case, as otherwise I fear it may too often result in a lamentable failure of justice."

MR. K. VENKATA ROW (*Bellary, No.* 24) said: "I beg to propose an amendment, by the addition of a rider to the resolution before us, to the effect 'that in presidencies or provinces, where the system of trial by jury has been partially tried and has proved successful, it should be extended to all cases tried by Courts of Sessions; and that the system should also be introduced in trials of all warrant cases before magistrates of all grades, the prisoner having the right, before going into his defence, to demand committal to the Court of Sessions, in cases where, in the opinion of the presiding magistrate, a jury cannot be empanelled before him.'

"My reasons for moving this amendment are that so far as the Madras Presidency, of which I can speak with some experience, is concerned, the system has been in vogue for more than three years in respect of offences against property, and it has worked well and to the satisfaction of the presiding Judges and the public. Very rarely the Judges have differed from the verdict of the jury, and in the majority of such cases, where differences of opinion have existed, the High Court have upheld the jury's verdict. Surely then it is high time to extend the system to all cases coming before the Courts of Sessions.

"With reference to the remaining portion of the proposed amendment, it is in my opinion a very essential and necessary one. The reasons in support thereof are numerous and weighty, but as the gentlemen of the Congress are fully aware of them, some by their bitter personal experience, I will not dilate much upon the subject but shall confine myself to the time allowed by the President. The Sessions Judges are generally, on our side of India, officers of sound judicial education and of long experience, and yet in cases coming before them trial by jury is considered necessary; more necessary must the aid of juries be in cases tried before magistrates. These officers are generally young men of imperfect legal knowledge, and of little experience of the customs and manners of the people over whose destinies they preside. Civilians, within a year or two of their arrival in India, are given second and even first class criminal powers with jurisdiction over large territories and over zemindars, merchants, and all classes of men. As to magistrates of the Uncovenanted Service, these are, at present, with us in Madras, recruited from the lower ranks of the service and as such they have had no good education and their official morality has not been tried and approved. Most of them do not belong to high or respectable families. Their appointments generally go by favoritism, and, in some cases, directly counter to public opinion. Liberty, property, honor, and everything dear to the nation are at the tender mercies of young magistrates, and I need not say that honor, like chastity, once lost is lost for ever. (*Cheers.*) Of the crimes arising in the country 90 per cent. are disposed of by these gentlemen, practically, without any check. The District Magistrate is, no doubt, authorised by law to supervise their duties, but, his hands being full of administrative work, he rarely exercises his revisional powers. There is, therefore, a great necessity of safe-guarding the exercise of the all-too-large and practically-uncontrolled powers vested in these officers, alike in the interests of justice and for the good of the country, by extending the system of trial by jury to all serious cases tried by them. This proposal of mine will, I believe, be approved by Englishmen in general, as even in England, where elderly men of high family, long experience, tried merit, approved morality and good legal knowledge are given criminal powers, all serious offences of the kind known in India under the denomination of warrant cases are tried by jury, and in other summary cases the prisoner has the right of demanding trial by jury. By granting this boon, criminal work will not be unnecessarily enlarged or delayed, as the trial will be only in warrant cases, and even in such cases the magistrate would have the option of, and the prisoner the right of demanding, committal to the Sessions a proper jury cannot be empanelled, or if the magistrate think such trial should take place before the higher Court. The prisoner is not likely to exercise this right vexatiously or without reasonable cause, unless he fears that the magistrate is likely to be carried away by prejudices or unworthy motives, as he has to take the chance of getting a severer punishment if convicted by the Court of Sessions. The Judge's work will not be much increased by the adoption of this scheme, as the Sessions Judge will be saved the time and trouble required for hearing appeals in such cases. Even, if it be otherwise, the time spent in such cases is not wasted, as nothing is more precious to the nation, or more essential to the highest interests of Government, than the effective protection of the liberty and honor of the subject. (*Loud cheers.*)

"I, therefore ,earnestly pray that the Congress will heartily support me in this amendment."

Row Sahib S. A. Saminada Iyer (*Tanjore, No.* 41), the proposer, said: "I am quite willing to accept this amendment if it be considered appropriate by the President. I entirely concur in it but it seems to me to go somewhat beyond the scope of the resolution I was asked to move."

Lala Murlidhur (*Punjab, No.* 107) said: "I support this proposal. I came to attend this Congress, released, on bail, from a jail, by the Chief Court (*loud cheers*), to which jail I had been sent by an unjust decision of a magistrate who could never have got any jury to convict me. You are most of you familiar with the case through the public prints. The charge against me was utterly frivolous and false, but simply because I am considered a political agitator, because I have my own opinions and speak what I think without fear (*cheers*), I was as a matter of—call it what you like—convicted, not on weak evidence, but on absolutely no evidence at all. (*Loud cheers.*) There is a great deal of this abuse of power in the Punjab, and I certainly support this amendment as offering us a means of protecting ourselves against official oppression." (*Prolonged cheering.*)

The President said: "Here we have a new proposition which embraces an important principle and involves a large number of details. It is one, I think, that demands a separate and full discussion. I submit that the resolution before us is intended merely to embody the general proposition that the jury system, at present existing in only some parts of India, ought now to be extended to other parts of India which are fitted to receive it, and it will be better to stick at present to this proposition and dispose of it. I may add that Mr. Mano Mohan Ghose has given notice of a separate resolution which he intends to propose to-day, which very nearly covers, I think, the proposed amendment; but if after the discussion of that resolution there still remain any important point, which our friend Mr. Venkata Row desires to press, I would ask him then to draft a separate resolution and place it in my hands for submission to the Congress."

Mr. R. Venkata Row (*Bellary, No.* 24) then withdrew his amendment.

Row Sahib Singaraju V. Subboroyudu (*Madras, No.* 18) said: "The system of trial by jury is not a novelty in India, as some seem to suppose that it is; it had been in force in India for countless ages before we ever heard of the name of Great Britain, in the shape of village punchayets and the like. (*Cheers.*) In my own province there are communities consisting of aboriginal tribes, and even amongst them all their disputes are disposed of by juries. We Hindus are not new emigrants into this country, but it would seem that, even before our advent, the ruder races that preceded us were fully alive to the merits of trial by jury. (*Cheers.*) I must say, I think, that the time has come for extending the system of trial by jury to all criminal cases all over India. Some political life is now becoming manifest amongst us. In political discussions expressions are unavoidably used, which give offence to political opponents—in our case mainly the bureaucracy. We desire to obtain certain rights, as we consider them, and declare it monstrous that these should be withheld from us; on the other hand those who now enjoy what we wish to secure, consider our attempts to get their places and oust them as monstrous, and out of such natural differences of view a tendency grows up for the existence of strained relations between the non-official public and the district authorities. Hence, on this ground as on others, it is highly necessary that our rights, our privileges, and our personal liberty should be carefully safeguarded by the general adoption of the system of trial by jury."

Lala Murlidhur (*Punjab, No.* 107) said: "Ever since it has been enacted by certain wiseacres in certain parts of the province from which I come—'the Punjab'—that to join an assembly of five or more persons is an offence under section 141 of the Penal Code, I have been afraid (as you must all have observed) to take part in any proceedings of this Congress, lest I should be sent to the Presidency Jail. One gentleman from the Punjab has already spoken on the subject of juries, but he has not undergone the trial which I myself have undergone, or his views might perhaps have been different. But, whether or not a trial by one man is better than a trial by a number of gentlemen combined as a jury—whether one man's judgment is always likely to be sound and a number of persons always likely to be such duffers as to be unable to decide a case with at least as much discretion and judgment as the one man now exhibits—this much I must say that, in that part of the province from which I come, the Government has been very unhappy in its choice of magistrates. From my own experience—and I have been practising for more than 12 years in Ambala—I can say that accused persons do not get that fair and impartial trial before magistrates which they would get in a trial by jury. If one thing has been found to work well in one...[Illegible] this country, why should it not work well in other very similarly circumstanced nation. Certainly it does not follow that what has been found good for England should be good for India, the two countries differ so very much in their conditions; but jury has been successful, as we know it has wherever it has been introduced should it not be successful in others and not in India.

introduction was so deprecated by my friend Lala Kanhya Lal. I confess I neither understand his arguments nor concur in his facts. I doubt whether there are many, if any, districts in the Punjab where the materials for excellent juries do not exist. I can only say that in all the parts of the province with which I am acquainted I would far rather be tried by any jury that could be got together than by most of the local magistrates of whom I have had any experience. So far from deprecating the introduction of the system of trial by jury into the Punjab, I advocate it most strongly, and I feel sure that it would be a success. It must necessarily be successful; it is not an exotic plant. India has known it from time immemorial; it is not a new system in the Punjab as it exists in every village and every community, and even amongst the lowest classes of the people, who, I must say, are wiser than we are in certain respects, as they manage their own affairs by their own juries and seldom go before the Courts. They have their own magistrates sitting with juries who dispose practically of all cases that can be kept from the knowledge of the police. This system is very popular for under it justice is done, the criminal is punished, and the injured party gets redress instead of being further punished by the extortions of the police; and when a man is found guilty he gladly accepts any punishment which his countrymen may inflict upon him. I say that this indigenous system is the best for our countrymen, and I wish that it was universal instead of prevailing only amongst some of the lower classes; and since the system of trial by jury is the nearest approach to this, now practicable, and is well known to the people, and thoroughly believed in by them, even by those classes in which a resort to it has become more or less obsolete, I have no hesitation in advocating the general introduction of this system even into the 'backward' Punjab."

Row Sahib M. B. Namjoshi (*Poona, No.* 69) said: "The question of the extension of the system of trial by jury to other provinces has come up at a very opportune time: firstly, inasmuch as the Government of India has at present before it the question of amending the Criminal Procedure Code; and, secondly, by reason of its being placed before this National Congress, the importance of which latter fact will be gathered from my subsequent remarks. The reasons given by the several local Governments for not extending the system of trial by jury may be gathered from the papers relating to the past history of the question. It was introduced in 1862, it was modified in 1872, and again further modified in 1882. The discussions that took place on these several occasions show sufficiently the reasons which have been urged against the extension of the jury system. They are practically only two in number, *viz.*, first, that the people are not fit to enjoy this privilege, and, secondly, that, even if the Government were to concede it, there would be, in most places, a difficulty in finding a sufficient number of men capable of acting as jurors. As far as I have been able to study the question neither of these two reasons possess now-a-days any real cogency so far as the great majority of British districts are concerned. There is, however, a third reason which has been urged by certain local Governments, and that is the danger of a miscarriage of justice. There may indeed be a danger of this in the one province of India, the most backward of all, into every district of which (I refer of course to Assam) the Government have, with praiseworthy consistency, extended the jury system, but elsewhere, so far as I can judge there is no such danger. But even if there were any such danger elsewhere, which I deny, if you only examine the change introduced into the Act of 1872, you will find that it provides, theoretically, against the possible miscarriage of justice by investing the High Courts with revisional powers, so that this supposed possible miscarriage of justice can no longer be urged by any one as a bar to that further extension of the system which we advocate. But to return to the point of the number of persons capable of serving, to good purpose, on juries. Probably the objection based on the supposed paucity of these is also one that can no longer be urged by any reasonable man. The facts of the spread of English education, of the extension of local self-government, of so many persons taking an intelligent interest in public matters, are sufficient to prove that this ground is not now tenable. By the several resolutions which various local Governments have passed they have admitted that, in several parts of the country, we are fitted to exercise the right of self-government. This is a political privilege, higher than that of trial by jury; and if the Government have thought us sufficiently advanced to be entitled to the former, it can scarcely be pleaded that we are still unfit to enjoy the latter—a privilege of a lower degree. But this Congress seems to me to furnish a conclusive reply to this pretence of a paucity of qualified jurors. Here we are gathered together to the number of nearly five hundred men, from almost every single district in the Empire, each of us elected, at least, by hundreds, in many cases by thousands, in some few cases by tens of thousands, of our countrymen, one all sufficiently enlightened to take the keenest interest in public affairs, and sufficiently independent to make a public avowal of that interest, notwithstanding the frowns of many rity. Is there here any want of materials for good juries? Manifestly these old have melted away; they may have had weight in the past; but in the present day ly official fictions. (*Loud cheers.*) Therefore, on all the three grounds that the or and desires the extension of the system of trial by jury, that almost most abundant materials exist for excellent juries, and that, except in Assam (where the juries are not Indian), no danger of any miscarriage of justice as a result of trials by jury exists, I uphold and support the resolution now before this Congress."

The President said: "As far as I can judge this assemblage is pretty unanimous in favour of the adoption of this resolution, and, if so, we ought I think to put it to the vote, for we have a great amount of business to get through, and unless we restrain ourselves somewhat and forego the pleasure of ventilating our special views—'I don't speak in any spirit of disparagement—we shall really, as perhaps I may have casually hinted before, never come to an end of our labours. One gentleman did deprecate the extension of the jury system to his province, but his views do not appear to be shared by other delegates from the Punjab. Now, if there is any other gentleman who is opposed to the extension anywhere else, by all means let him speak; but if all the rest of us are agreed, I think we should proceed to the vote." (*Cries of vote, vote.*)

After waiting a minute the motion was then put by the President and carried unanimously.

The President said: "In connection with the resolution which has just been passed, it has been the opinion of many gentlemen that there is one very important further step which requires to be taken. A resolution has accordingly been drafted, which is not in the printed list (to which I referred when asking Mr. Venkata Row recently to withdraw his proposed amendment), and I will ask Mr. Mano Mohan Ghose to introduce it."

Mr. Mano Mohan Ghose (*Bengal, No.* 270) said: "The forcible observations which have fallen from Mr. Venkata Row of Bellary would alone suffice to justify and support the resolution that I have considered it my duty, in the interests of the country at large, to frame, and now desire to urge upon your consideration. We have just passed a resolution asking for the extension of the jury system in parts of India where it has not hitherto been in force. But our object will be defeated if the policy of 1872 is further extended and certain powers of the Court of Sessions are to be taken away from them and made over to first class magistrates. I speak from personal experience of the criminal administration of the country when I say that there is a large class of cases where, by reason of the combination of the magisterial and judicial functions, a failure of justice results. In 1882, by the Summary Jurisdiction Act, every European accused became entitled to demand that, in serious cases, *viz.*, cases which are punishable by imprisonment of more than two for three months, he should be tried by a jury. I propose a similar provision whereby every accused person may demand, in serious cases, to be tried by the Court of Sessions. A suggestion of this character was made to the Government in 1882, and met with the cordial approval of Mr. Ilbert, but it was then too late as the Bill was ready for passing, and we were advised to submit the suggestion when the Act was next revised. It is now probably soon to be again revised, and if you now pass a resolution of the character I propose, it will no doubt have great weight with the Government. (*Cheers.*) Therefore I move the following resolution, *viz.*, that, in the opinion of this Congress, a provision, similar to that contained in the Summary Jurisdiction Act of England (under which accused persons in serious cases have the option of demanding a committal to the Sessions Court), should be introduced into the Indian Code of Criminal Procedure, enabling accused persons, in warrant cases, to demand that, instead of being tried by the magistrate, they be committed to the Court of Sessions." (*Resolution X of Summary, page* 44.)

Mr. T. Chidambara Row (*Bellary, No.* 26) said: "In seconding this resolution I have to offer a few remarks. Magistrates of the first class, often quite young and inexperienced officers, are invested with extraordinary powers; they can sentence to imprisonment for two years and to a fine of Rs. 1,000; and unless those powers are restricted in some way, and we are given some protection against their arbitrary misuse, our liberties will remain, as now, at the mercy of men often far from competent, from a legal point of view, to exercise these great powers, and occasionally devoid even of that conscientiousness that in former days was the characteristic of British officers. Moreover, in many cases of imprisonment (in all below a certain term), there is no appeal, and some magistrates take advantage of this and pass minor sentences in order that the unfortunate persons, they desire to punish, may not have a chance of justice. (*Cheers.*) It is for these and other reasons that my learned friend proposes to give this option of trial before a Sessions Court and a jury to the accused, in all warrant cases, and I have no hesitation in saying that this is most desirable, not only in the interests of the people, but even in that of the Governme if they are to maintain the character of their Courts for justice." (*Loud cheers.*)

Mr. M. Ramanuja Chariar (*Chingleput, No.* 39) said: "In rising to sur resolution I will only say a very few words. I have known of many cases respectable men have been tried by magistrates for serious offences. In thes parties have had to employ counsel at great expense, to induce magistrates to cor Sessions Court, even if the case is one of concurrent jurisdiction, but in th which the Sessions Court has no jurisdiction the accused has no option, but submit to trial by the magistrate. Where, however, the Sessions Court has concurrent jurisdiction, the parties think it a great boon to have their cases transferred because they feel and know that they will then have a trial by jury, or by the aid of assessors, as well as before far more experienced and, in consequence of their having no executive functions, far more impartial Judges. (*Loud cheers.*) I, therefore, submit that it is desirable to pass this resolution."

Khajeh Abdool Aleem (*Dacca, No.* 351), who spoke in Urdu, said: "I do not know and I do not think that our British officers willingly do injustice, but certainly when an officer working as head policeman has for a long time been trying to find out who committed a crime, and then, consulting with the superintendent of police, gradually gets what he thinks is a clue, and then day by day the police send in evidence, and at last on this a man is arrested, it is no disparagement to that officer to say that the supposed criminal cannot get as impartial a trial before that officer as he would before one who had never heard anything of the case before, and had formed no opinion as to who the guilty persons were. No one ever has to find fault with our Calcutta magistrates; and why? Because those magistrates are quite separate from the police, and they are as ready to find fault with the police if they have done wrong as to punish the accused if he is found guilty, and no one will blame them if there are acquittals in many cases coming before them, and they come, quite without prejudice against the prisoner, to the case of which they know nothing. But all this is quite different with our mofussil magistrates. Now we want all our mofussil magistrates to be just like our Calcutta magistrates, and we hope this will be some day; but till we get this, at least let accused persons, in all warrant cases, have the right to demand a trial before the Sessions Judge, who must necessarily be a more experienced officer, and who will not be at all likely, or at any rate so likely, to be biassed in any way in the case, as the magistrates almost necessarily in the mofussil must be. I say warrant cases, because imprisonment, however unjust, and even though the sentence be later reversed, is with us the destruction of a gentleman's position (*izzut*), and once destroyed, like a mango tree cut down, it can never grow again. I do not want to waste the time of this assembly, but I have known so many and cruel cases of irreparable injury thus done that I have no hesitation in most earnestly advocating this resolution."

Munshi Sadho Lal (*Benares, No.* 146) said: "The system of summary trials is altogether injurious to the public, and it should be, I think, abolished altogether."

Mr. Devi Charan Barua (*Assam, No.* 429) said: "All the districts in Assam are jury districts, and the introduction of the jury system there has been injurious. It is not so of course universally, but chiefly in cases in which Europeans are involved, because the majority on the jury list are Europeans, and they are selected from a class of men strong in race prejudices and ignorant of the first principles of jurisprudence—I mean the class of tea planters. They are generally a class greatly wanting not only in culture but in that sense of fair play (where natives of India are concerned) wrongly supposed to be inherent in all Britons, and their verdict is not always in conformity with the evidence or the dictates of justice; and in my opinion—and I speak from personal experience—the jury system has proved injurious to Assam, and this very system is one of the reasons why our poor coolies are so oppressed in Assam. I know little of other parts of the country, and knowing what the results had been in Assam, I hesitated to support the extension of the system to other provinces. If, however, even in the jury system, we got fair play—if the European members of the jury were reduced to one half and the remaining half were taken from the native community—even in Assam there would not be any great probability of injustice to the poorer classes. So I say the jury system in itself is no doubt good, but if dishonestly worked—and if in Assam, why not elsewhere?—it becomes a curse instead of a blessing."

Mr. Mano Mohan Ghose (*Calcutta, No.* 270) here rose and explained that this objection to the extension of the system of trial by jury was scarcely in order, since the question of its extension had already been disposed of by the previous resolution. The speaker (Mr. Barua) concluded by saying that, on the whole, he was in favour of the jury system, and he hoped it would be extended to all the provinces of the Empire, and more honestly worked there than it ever had been in Assam.

Row Sahib Raghunath Pandurang Karandikar (*Sattara, No.* 78) said: "It is
sed that in warrant cases the accused person should be able to claim a trial by
This is quite right and proper, but there seem to be practical difficulties. Take the
lookas, in which 3rd class magistrates have to try such cases—I mean warrant
hich at present the accused cannot claim trial by jury. This side of the question
be considered. We have 2nd and 3rd class magistrates before whom
es are daily taken; there ought to be one rule, and it is very necessary that in
s well as in those coming before a 1st class magistrate, the accused should
ion of trial by jury; therefore, unless we wish that our reform should remain

imperfect, our resolution should recommend that these magistrates also should be empowered to commit to the Court of Sessions."

MR. MANO MOHAN GHOSE (*Calcutta, No.* 270) said: "I have to make one observation in explanation. This privilege would only be claimed in extreme cases where the accused felt that he was very unlikely to receive a fair trial before the magistrate, for he must know that by demanding a trial by the Sessions Court he runs the risk of a severer punishment, and that would prevent his insisting on the privilege frivolously. It will not be necessary to empower 2nd and 3rd class magistrates to commit to the Sessions. It even now happens that 2nd and 3rd class magistrates often have before them cases which they cannot punish adequately, and consequently send them on to 1st class magistrates, who have power to commit to the Sessions. Similarly the few warrant cases coming before 2nd and 3rd class magistrates, in which the right to be tried by jury was insisted on, would be sent on by these magistrates to some 1st class magistrate who would commit. There is no difficulty in this."

The resolution was then put to the vote and carried unanimously.

MR. W. C. BONNERJEE (*Calcutta, No.* 275) said: "The resolution which has been entrusted to me is a corollary of the two resolutions which you have just passed. It runs as follows:—

"'That, in the opinion of this Congress, the innovation made in 1872 in the system of trial by jury, depriving the verdicts of juries of all finality, has proved injurious to the country, and that the powers then, for the first time, vested in Sessions Judges and High Courts, of setting aside verdicts of acquittal, should be at once withdrawn.' (*Resolution IX of Summary, page* 44).

"I shall explain in a few words what is meant by this resolution. If we are to have trials by jury it is absurd to suppose that when a verdict of acquittal has been passed by a jury it is to be left to the Sessions Judge to say whether he will accept the verdict or not, or whether he will send the case to the High Court to be tried by them on paper evidence, without, in the case of a poor person, the accused being represented before them. Trials by jury will become a dead letter if this power continue to be vested in Sessions Judges. As I have always understood, the prisoner is entitled to the benefit of any reasonable doubt as to his guilt that may exist in the mind of any person trying him. How can it be said, if 5 or 7 or 9 persons are of opinion that a man is not guilty, that there is no doubt as to his guilt, to which he is entitled to have the benefit? A jury acquits, but the Sessions Judge says, I think the jury are wrong, and the High Court, looking at the evidence on paper, agrees with him, and therefore the man must be convicted. In such a case the man does not really get the benefit of trial by jury or the benefit of the doubt which must have existed in the minds of the jury, or they would not have acquitted him. If a verdict of acquittal is pronounced that verdict should be final. It used to be so until the year 1872. The law which existed up to that time was first drafted by the Indian Law Commission sitting in England. It was very carefully revised by such distinguished jurists as Sir B. Peacock, Sir Mordaunt Wells, Sir C. Jackson and others; and they concurred in the wisdom of treating verdicts of acquittal as final. But Sir James Stephen and Sir George Campbell thought otherwise, and though we did all we could to prevent this being done, unfortunately our voice did not prevail. I have purposely confined myself to the verdicts of acquittal by juries. Where a jury convicts, and the Judge is of opinion that the verdict is wrong, I would allow the Sessions Judge to refer the case to the High Court; and I would do so on the same principle that I oppose convictions where a jury thinks the accused is not guilty, *viz.*, that where a doubt exists as to his guilt, be it in the minds of jury or Judge, the accused ought to have the benefit of that doubt. So far as acquittals are concerned, we say that this power which was given to the Sessions Judges in 1872 was in violation of a fundamental principle of jurisprudence and has proved injurious to the country, and we, who are in the practice of the law, see the immense wrong that has been done under this provision of the law."

THE HON. PEARY MOHAN MOOKERJEE (*Calcutta, No.* 233) said: "I second the motion.

BABOO KALI SUNKUR SUKUL (*Calcutta, No.* 258) said: "I beg leave to oppose the motion. It is with great diffidence that I rise to measure lances, and especially as to a point of law, with so redoubted a champion as Mr. W. C. Bonnerjee; but I think the proposal is likely to be fraught with great inconvenience and injustice, in Bengal at any rate. This is a corollary to other resolutions, no doubt, but suppose our other proposals are not accepted by the Government, surely great injustice will result if only this proposal is accepted and others ignored. We ought to remember that we are unfortunately a subject race, and if there are certain provisions in the existing code of laws, which guard us against the oppression of the ominant race, we should cling to those safeguards which afford us some chance, at least o having justice done to us. You are aware that every Anglo-Indian has at the present mo hent the right to be tried by jury, and you know that in too many cases, where Europeans are the culprits, this trial by jury is followed by results which are not consistent with justice. (*Cheers.*) It is a matter of very great regret, but, nevertheless, it is a fact that we do not get justice done in such cases. (*Cheers from Bengal and Assam delegates.*) Under these circumstances, if we pass this resolution, and if the Government accept it and carry out our views, I think it will be productive of very great wrong. (*Cheers.*) Under present circumstances especially in Bengal, the proposal to introduce this change into the law, just at this present time, is scarcely a happy one. If the other resolutions before the Congress are accepted by Government, I would certainly not oppose this one, but standing, as it possibly may, alone, I cannot approve it. (*Cheers.*)

"A case occurred some time ago, to which I shall only make the faintest allusion, where the voice of the country was unanimously raised against a grave miscarriage of justice—a miscarriage which was remedied by the interference of the High Court, although unfortunately the Government has, to a great extent, rendered that interference of no avail. The country has, with one voice declared against the action of Government, and Government will probably be more careful, henceforth, how it interferes with the deliberate judgments of the High Court; but, if we pass this resolution, we shall be placing ourselves at the mercy of juries, strong in class bias, and far more intent on screening even a disreputable member of their own community than on protecting us from the oppression of the culprit and others like him, and we shall have deprived those higher-minded and less-prejudiced Europeans, our High Court and Sessions Judges, of all powers of interposing to prevent such miscarriages of justice. (*Loud cheers.*)

"Under these circumstances, however desirable a resolution of this description may be after the main propositions to which this is a corollary have been adopted, I must contend that, under present circumstances, especially in Bengal, the adoption of this proposition will be fraught with grievous injustice to the people of Bengal and Assam. (*Cheers.*)

Baboo Kailash Chandra Sen (*Dacca*, *No.* 350) said: "I support the resolution. Within the course of my experience, extending over a period of 16 years as a pleader in Assam, and for some time in Backergunge, a district remarkable for criminal accusations, I can testify to the fact that the power given to the Sessions Judges of interfering with the verdicts of juries and ignoring the opinion of assessors has been fraught with great evil. Only the other day there was a case in Dacca in which the verdict of a jury, supported by public opinion of a very strong character, was for acquitting the prisoners; the Judge opposed the verdict and referred the matter to the High Court; and although the Dacca public were convinced that the prisoners, one and all, were innocent, they were sentenced to transportation for life. Other cases have come within the range of my own experience—and I can speak with authority when I say that this power, exercised by the Sessions Court, is most injurious, so much so that whenever there is a sensational case against any native prisoners and the jury acquits the prisoners, the Sessions Judge generally refers the case to the High Court, and the High Court, without having the prisoners before them, are required to pass an opinion upon evidence manufactured by the police. A previous speaker has dwelt upon the danger of depriving higher authorities of the power of rectifying the injustice done by European juries in acquitting European prisoners, especially in Assam. I know something of Assam, and I want to ask you in how many cases has that power ever been exercised? There have been many cases in which, were not this power a mere legal fiction where Europeans are concerned, it ought certainly to have been exercised. But has it ever been so? Never, I say; never until this recent case to which that speaker referred and in which two Judges of the High Court, one of them a native—mark that—tried to do justice and to punish as he deserved, an European transgressor of the law, wrongfully, as the High Court held, acquitted by a jury of his fellow countrymen. And what was the result? The Government nullifying the work of the Judges, releases the offender. So, in fourteen years, there has been one case in which the High Court has tried to do justice under this provision, in the case of an European, and in that one case Government undid their work. It is foolish then to talk of this provision being any protection to us, any safeguard against the escape of guilty Europeans. So far as this is concerned it is mere sham. But on the other hand, during these fourteen years, numbers—I dare say it would be more correct to say hundreds, but I speak only from my own experience—of natives, acquitted by juries who had all the parties before them, have been under this provision, as I believe, wrongfully punished on paper evidence. There is no sham about *this*—it is a stern and terrible reality, and there are scores and scores of desolate homes and hundreds of men working in chains or lying dead in dishonoured graves in the Andamans, by reason of this unconstitutional and objectionable provision. To cling to it is indeed to grasp a shadow and let go the reality.

"I therefore, beg to support this resolution, and hope that the amendment of the law, which has been very isely proposed by Mr. W. C. Bonnerjee, will be accepted; and that in cases of acquittal the verdict of juries will be final, while in cases of conviction by juries the existing power of interference will be allowed to continue, so that the prisoner may have the benefit of the doubt, in all cases, be that doubt one in the minds of jurors or Judges."

Munshi Sadho Lal (*Benares, No.* 146), speaking in Urdu, said: "I desire to endorse what has been said by the last speaker. As a matter of practice, great injustice and cruelty results from the exercise of this power of punishing in defiance of the verdicts of juries, who understand the way cases are got up better than English Judges, and I have never known *any* good of any kind come of it."

Baboo Kalicharan Banerjee (*Calcutta, No.* 273) said: "This is a matter in which we are in danger of being carried away by sentiment. Two arguments appear to have been adduced in support of this proposed resolution. One is the desirability of carrying out the system of trial by jury in its integrity—of having, in fact, a perfect jury system. Now, gentlemen, a perfect jury system is only adapted to a perfect condition of society. If we were certain of always getting juries who would give the right verdict, I should be the first to desire absolute finality for those verdicts. But the learned mover of the resolution has admitted that we are not likely to be blessed with any such infallible aud immaculate juries, inasmuch as he is prepared, and desires, to allow a reference to the High Court in cases in which the jury bring in a verdict of guilty and the Judge disagrees. The second argument in favour of the resolution is that, when a jury arrives at a verdict of acquittal, that verdict implies that there is a doubt in the case, and inasmuch as the benefit of the doubt should always be given to the accused, there should be no reference to the High Court and, consequently, no conviction. But we must take into account a certain class of verdicts of acquittal wherein the acquittal is not based on the principle of giving the benefit of a doubt to the prisoner: these verdicts are known as perverse verdicts, where doubt or no doubt the jurors make up their minds to acquit. If juries sometimes do, as is well known, give perverse verdicts, the argument that the benefit of the doubt should be given to the accused clearly does not apply to all cases; and, although the Code provides for reference in such cases to the High Court, this latter never interferes with a verdict of acquital unless it considers it a perverse verdict. I consider this provision a substantial safeguard against perverse verdicts, and I must, therefore, oppose any proposal for its removal."

Mr. Sitala Kanta Chatterjee (*Meerut, No.* 155) said: "I rise to support what has been said by Baboo Kali Sunkur Sukul. I am of opinion that the two previous resolutions must first be accepted by the Government before this present resolution can be supported by this Congress. You have heard of cases of murder and outrage of women in Assam, which is the most backward province in India, and yet it is the only province in which every district is a jury district, and what is the reason? In Bengal, which is one of the most advanced provinces, there are very few jury districts. In most districts Sessions cases are tried with the aid of assessors. The reason is that, in every district of Assam, there are planters, and the result is that, when any outrage is committed and the case is tried by a jury, the accused is generally acquitted. If the jury system was extended to all parts of India—if the natives could claim to be tried by juries of their own countrymen, as Europeans can—in that case we might support this resolution."

Pandit Jwalanath Sarma (*Calcutta, No.* 251) said: "I have something to say in reply to the observations made by Baboo Kalicharan Banerjee. In this country the judging persons and the judged persons do not, in the mass of these cases, belong to the same class. Native jurors, trying native prisoners, are far more likely to be right in the conclusion at which they arrive than is the English Judge. Native juries know a great many things that European Judges do not; they understand how false cases are got up; a thousand insignificant matters may transpire in the course of a case, which have no significance to the Judge, but which at once carry a conviction of the innocence of the prisoner to the better informed minds of the jurors. As Mr. Bonnerjee pointed out, it is only right that, in all cases, the prisoner should have the benefit of any doubt as to his guilt, but it is doubly essential that he should receive this benefit when the persons, in whose minds that doubt exists, are people who understand him and his ways and customs and thoughts, and those of all parties concerned in the case, while the only persons who do not doubt his guilt, are foreign Judges who are more or less ignorant of all these things.

"Of course I understand the feeling that underlies the opposition that this resolution is meeting with. The fear is that some English planter criminals, wrongfully acquitted by juries of their countrymen, will, in the absence of this provision, thus escape all punishment. Now there are three answers to this argument which, taken together, are absolutely conclusive. In the first place, as I assume that native juries are the best judges of native criminals, so I think it not unreasonable to suppose that European juries are the best judges of the guilt of European prisoners. I refuse to believe that European juries anywhere habitually betray their trust. (*Cheers.*) I think it quite possible that in some cases in which we think that they have done so, they, with their better knowledge of what Europeans are, may be right. (*Hear, hear.*)

"Again, if fifty Europeans thus escaped, it would be better, if our authorities are correct, than that one man should be wrongfully convicted; but what is the fact? Why, as has been already pointed out, for one European, who may possibly thus escape his merited punishment, hundreds of innocent natives are, under this provision, wrongfully convicted.

"But, lastly, as has also been pointed out, the power is *never* used to prevent that one European escaping; it is only, and very freely, used to prevent the escape of innocent natives.

"Baboo Kalicharan Banerjee is very strong about perverse verdicts. Well, as to perverse verdicts of European juries, I venture to hope I have disposed of these, and I would ask you all—and I suppose nearly one-fourth of you belong, like myself, to the legal profession—how many perverse verdicts of native juries have you met with? I believe you will agree with me that these are quite exceptional. Now we have to look to the bulk of the cases, not the exceptions, and here I say, as I said before, better ten men escape, in such cases, than one man be punished where it is not the verdict of jury but the opinion of the Judge that is perverse (*cheers*), or at any rate erroneous; and, as a fact, this latter is ten times more common than any perversity in verdicts of native juries. I do not know whether I have succeeded in convincing any of those opposed to this resolution, but I know that I, at any rate, shall heartily support it."

Baboo Bepin Chunder Pal (*Assam, No.* 432) said. "I want to say a few words to our brethren from Madras and Bombay. Some of our Bengal delegates at any rate know sufficiently well the state of things here. I should like to ask the delegates from Madras and Bombay to go over the files of cases that have occurred in the Bengal Presidency, as for instance the case of Webb and other similiar cases to which I don't wish to refer, and to say whether under the system of trial by jury in Assam there has not been a very serious miscarriage of justice. Sylhet is a district in Assam which has not the privilege of trial by jury, because it is not a planting district. Therefore, in the name of the coolies in Assam, I ask you not to pass this resolution. There will be ample time when the previous resolution has been accepted by Government to have this resolution passed."

Mr. W. C. Bonnerjee (*Calcutta, No.* 275) said: "I wish to say a few words in explanation. In reference to the speeches delivered by two of our delegates from Assam I wish to point out that they have lost sight of the fact that, as far as European British subjects are concerned, they may claim trial by jury in districts where ordinary cases are triable with the aid of assessors. A European British subject must be so tried as a matter of right, and probably by a jury consisting of his own countrymen anywhere and everywhere in British India. There is nothing to prevent that being done. Let us assume that five persons improperly escape the punishment due to their offences. Is that any reason why hundreds, nay thousands, of your countrymen should be wrongfully punished? Is it not the admitted principle, as Pandit Jwalanath has rightly insisted, that ten guilty persons should escape rather than that one innocent person should suffer? We must not surely say that because, if we pass this resolution, injustice may possibly be done at some future day in some one or two isolated cases, therefore we will not pass this resolution which will get rid of a system under which injustice is actually being done daily, is actually done in hundreds of cases yearly. We must not allow the race-feeling that underlies the present opposition to lead us into misstatements and misrepresentations. The prevalence of the jury system in Assam, its absence in Sylhet, have nothing earthly to do with the planters, or planters' interests. Sylhet is truly the only district in Assam where the system of trial by jury does not exist; but that is simply, because at one time Sylhet was a part of Bengal in which trial by jury did not exist, and has only recently been made a part of Assam. In Assam proper, long before any planters went there, the whole province had trial by jury. We have many legitimate grounds for complaint, but we must not injure a good cause by misstatements."

Baboo Ambica Charan Mazumdar (*Furreedpore, No.* 316) said: "Having heard what has been said by Mr. W. C. Bonnerjee in explanation of his proposition and by previous eloquent speakers, I am still far from convinced that this proposed measure is free from serious disadvantages. The hypothesis is I believe that it is practically only native prisoners who are punished by High Courts after acquittal by juries and not any other persons; and this belief is strengthened by the explanation which has just been offered by Mr. Bonnerjee, in which he said that we must consider rather the cases of the thousands of natives of India and not of the five or ten Europeans who might stand as accused persons. But, if you look at the principle of the thing and the state of the country also, you must admit that these five or ten persons may do more injustice and harm than 5,000 other men can do. And in fact, I believe, that this proposition is premature, and as our eloquent countryman Baboo Kalicharan Banerjee has virtually suggested, it is better to postpone the consideration of this proposition to the next Congress. It is not perhaps in my power to convince you of the reasonableness of my objection, but you must all feel and understand that it will be a serious step to take at the present moment. In principle it may be a very good thing. It may sound very well. But look at the condition of the country and then pronounce your verdict. You are all delegates here from various parts of the Empire, but before raising your hands in favour of this proposition, pause and consider whether your verdict will be supported by the verdict of those whom you represent. Do not in the excitement of the moment accept this principle."

Baboo Keshub Chunder Acharjee Chowdhry (*Mymensing, No.* 394a) said: "If I at all understand the argument of the gentleman who has just sat down it is that these Europeans are such terrible beings that it is better for 5,000 natives to be wrongfully convicted than for five or ten of these Europeans to escape the punishment of their crimes. That is what his argument comes to if it means anything. Ho said that if we looked round the country we must admit that these five or ten Europeans may do more harm and injustice than 5,000 other men can, and that therefore he would oppose the resolution, which I may summarise as doing away with a power under which theoretically these five or ten might receive their deserts, but under which practically thousands of innocent men are wrongfully punished. But it has been pointed out again and again in this discussion that this theoretical power is *never* exercised where Europeans are concerned. Therefore, merely for the sake of being able to feel that a power exists which theoretically might be, though it never is, used to punish rightly five or ten Europeans wrongfully acquitted by juries, you will maintain that power which is only practically used to punish wrongfully thousands of natives rightly acquitted by juries. This, gentlemen, is a height of sentiment to which I am unable to rise. But leaving this for a moment there is another aspect of the case which seems to me to have been wholly overlooked. Suppose, for an instant, that a complaint is brought by a planter against a coolie; suppose he charges him with having tried to kill him and that the native jury pronounce a verdict of acquittal. What is likely to be the fate of that poor coolie if the Judge retains the power of sending the case to the High Court? Mr. Bonnerjee has been accused of being influenced by sentiment, but I rather think that it is those who oppose this resolution who are so influenced. There are, say, 500 planters and 5 millions of natives in Assam. It is not a new or unheard-of thing, I regret to say, for planters to bring false cases against their coolies. What Judge will believe that an apparently respectable planter with respectable surroundings will swear falsely to ruin a poor native. The native jury may know better and they may rightfully acquit, but if the existing power remains in the Judge's hands, I would not give much for the chance of that innocent man's escape when his case is sent up with a recommendation for conviction by the Judge to the High Court. But those who oppose this resolution would rather leave the 5 millions of Assam, nay the 200 millions of India, liable to such wrongful convictions, than forego the vast privilege of feeling that there does exist theoretically a power, never exercised in practice, whereby some five or ten planters, wrongfully acquitted by their countrymen, might, if the Government chose (which it does not), be punished as they deserve. This view of the case is beyond my comprehension and I support most strongly Mr. Bonnerjee's motion."

Baboo Krishna Kumar Mitra (*Calcutta, No.* 260) said: "In Bengal there are 42 districts, and out of these only five or six districts enjoy the right of trial by jury. If this resolution is passed only one section of the community will be benefited—I mean Englishmen—and therefore I object to this proposition, and I appeal to the delegates who have come from Madras and Bombay to think twice before they express any opinion on this proposal. We in Bengal shall be the principal sufferers if this proposal is passed.'

Row Sahib P. Ananda Charlu (*Madras, No.* 6) said: "From the beginning of this discussion I was willing to be a listener, because this is a resolution which I was not prepared for. All the grounds which can be urged against it have been put forward in a very masterly way by Baboo Kalicharan Banerjee, and I, at any rate, feel that I have to thank him greatly for having put his side of the question so clearly before me. I am inclined to think there is an undue assumption involved in this resolution, and that assumption is an utter want of confidence in the highest tribunals of the land. I could never be a party to any resolution which assumes that the highest Court of the land has a tendency to prove perverse. It has been said that thousands of cases have to be considered, that in hundreds, if not thousands, of cases prisoners rightly acquitted by juries have on reference been wrongly convicted by High Courts. I coming from Madras (and speaking from an experience there of 15 years in the legal profession) am prepared to say that, as far as my experience is concerned, the desire of the High Court is not to differ from the verdicts of juries, but if possible to sustain them. If the state of things is altogether different in Bengal that may be a proper reason for a movement in connection with Bengal but it is not a sufficient ground for passing a resolution by a National Congress. In Madras the complaint is rather that the High Court is not sufficiently inclined to interfere with the verdicts of juries, and I have known several cases in which the High Court has refused to do this. I look upon the section of the Code to which objection is taken as a safeguard; and I look upon the highest Court of the land as an additional safeguard. If it goes wrong in any case it is a misfortune, but I could not be brought to take part in any resolution if the effect of it be, as in this case it *prima facie* seems to be, to show a want of confidence in the High Courts. I speak, however, under correction, and I should be glad to hear more on this point."

Baboo Norendro Nath Sen (*Calcutta, No.* 243) said: "I think the best person to speak upon this subject would be Mr. Mano Mohan Ghose, who has had very great experience in criminal proceedings, especially in the mofussil, and I should like to hear what he has to say on the subject."

Mr. Mano Mohan Ghose (*Calcutta, No.* 270) said: "There has been a great deal of misunderstanding and misapprehension on this subject. As far as European British subjects are concerned they had, in all cases before 1872, the right to be tried by the High Court only and before a jury of their own countrymen, but in 1872 it was enacted that, in certain specified classes of cases, European British subjects could be tried in the mofussil, but even then only before a jury composed of a majority of their own countrymen. Therefore, as far as European British subjects are concerned, this resolution does not practically make any appreciable difference. It is intended only to protect the native population of the country, and there is great force in what Baboo Keshub Chunder Chowdhry so forcibly urged, that Mr. Bonnerjee's resolution could only operate to provide a safeguard for the native races. I yield to no one in my respect for the High Court; it is the great bulwark of the liberties of the people in the present state of the country, and I have watched with great regret and pain the operation of that section of the Code which enables the High Court to interfere with the verdicts of juries. I know of many cases where, on paper evidence, men have been hanged contrary to the verdict of juries, and where in my judgment they ought not to have been even committed. I am not prepared to say that two Judges, even of the High Court, however eminent, are better qualified with only the papers of a case before them to judge of its merits than five intelligent natives of the country who have had before them all the parties and witnesses.

"The present Chief Justice of Bengal has declared that he would be very sorry, as a foreigner, to disturb the verdict of five men of the country. If now you understand this resolution correctly, and are able to realize that it does not confer any new privilege practically upon European British subjects, but that it only helps the natives and puts them to a great extent in the same position that the Europeans now occupy, a good deal of the misapprehension that seems to have existed will I hope disappear. A recent case has probably had a great deal to do with the reluctance felt by some of you to accept this resolution; but, as a matter of fact, if a man is convicted by the Sessions Court on a charge which, under the Criminal Procedure Code, could not be tried before such Court, and if that point were taken, he could not be tried by jury in Assam at all, but must be tried by the High Court here by a jury of Europeans whose verdict is even now final. Therefore I advise you not to be led away by sentiment, but to take the matter properly into consideration.

"You will find that, in the immense majority of mofussil cases, natives will be the accused persons, and it is specially to meet their cases that Mr. Bonnerjee has wisely suggested this resolution. It may be that a few European offenders may escape, but that happens even now, and will happen no oftener even if you agree to this resolution. At present what we aim at is to place natives in the same position in these matters that Europeans already practically occupy."

The Honorable S. Subramania Iyer (*Madras, No.* 2) said: "I cannot discover that this resolution involves, as my friend Mr. Ananda Charlu seems to suppose, any assumption derogatory to the dignity, or in any way impugning the integrity of our High Courts. As pointed out at the outset by the proposer, the one vital principle that underlies the resolution is that the accused is entitled to the benefit of any doubt as to his guilt that may arise in the minds of any of the parties whose office, whether as judge or juror, it is to try him. A great deal of irrelevant matter, if I may presume to say so, has, I think, been introduced into the discussion, but I would now ask does any one doubt the correctness of that principle, and if no one does, why should we not pass a resolution which simply embodies this principle, neither more nor less." (*Loud cheers.*)

The President said: "Although considerable differences of opinion appear to exist in regard to this resolution, it has been so exhaustively and ably discussed that I do not think any further light is likely to be thrown on the subject, and therefore with your approval I will now put it to the vote." (*Cries of yes, yes.*)

The resolution was then put to the vote and carried by a very large majority.

Mr. Daji Abaji Khare (*Bombay, No.* 56) said: "The resolution which I have to submit for your consideration is one dealing with a matter in which all are interested, and with which all are well acquainted, and I am quite sure that very little need be said to commend it to your approval.

"This resolution runs as follows: 'That this Congress do place on record an expression of the universal conviction, that a complete separation of executive and judicial functions (such that in no case the two functions shall be combined in the same officer) has become an urgent necessity, and that, in its opinion, it behoves the Government to effect this separation without further delay, even though this should, in some provinces, involve some extra expenditure.' (*Resolution XI of Summary, page* 45.)

"The principle embodied in this resolution has not only been accepted by all of us, throughout the country, but it has been accepted by the Government of India, and by almost all the local Governments, who have agreed that the separation of the executive and judicial functions is a necessary condition of really satisfactory administration. The only doubt that is felt, in this matter, is as regards the additional expenditure that will be incurred, in consequence of effecting this separation. But even as regards expenditure, alike in Bengal, in the North-Western Provinces, and in Madras, it has been made pretty clear that no considerable increase of expenditure will, under a proper scheme of reconstruction, be entailed. In Bombay also I am confident that, if proper enquiries are made and proper methods adopted, it will be found that the necessary extra expenditure is by no means large, and certainly not so large as to outweigh the great advantages which the entire population will derive from this fundamental reform.

"How desirable this reform is in the interests alike of the Government and the people it is almost superfluous to explain. The existing system violates the very first principles of jurisprudence (*cheers*), for if you invest the executive, as now, with judicial powers, you in fact make that executive prosecutor as well as judge; nay, as a large number of offences are mere transgressions of rules and regulations of the executive, you go further in such cases and make this executive the judge, as it were, in its own cause. (*Loud cheers.*) It is not wholly the fault of the executive, but somehow or another it has often occurred, indeed it seems to be almost a general rule, that executive officers work up a sort of personal interest in carrying certain measures into operation, and consequently insensibly generate a certain bias in their minds against particular people, who disapprove these measures, and this bias clearly makes them unfit judges in cases relating to those measures or those people. (*Cheers.*) Again, executive officers, burthened with a vast variety of miscellaneous business, have not, and cannot by any effort *make*, sufficient time to dispose calmly, systematically and with due deliberation of the judicial work that comes before them.

"It has been found in Bombay that the Collector of the District, although invested with full judicial powers, very seldom if ever tries any cases in which he has no personal concern, and that simply because he has not sufficient time. Yet, every now and then, he takes it into his head to try some particular person whose conviction he wants to make sure of, and it is needless to say that such trials are characterized, as a rule throughout, by the exhibition, on the part of the presiding officer, of a spirit more befitting a public prosecutor than an impartial judge. (*Cheers.*)

"He may be right in the main, the accused may be a great rascal, the presiding officer's *animus* against him may be based on the purest concern for the public welfare; the Collector may know the ins and outs of the case better than any one else; he may be the fittest possible person to be public prosecutor, but it is a mere mockery of justice to allow such a person to be *also* the judge. (*Prolonged cheers.*)

"Moreover, in order that a person may be safely entrusted with large judicial powers, he must lead the life of a judge—a life apart from and uncoloured by those conflicting interests out of which so many cases arise, and he must have besides ample opportunities for mastering the spirit as well as the letter of the law, and for becoming saturated with the fundamental principles of jurisprudence. It will not be gainsaid that, as matters now stand, the executive, in all but the highest grades, is unfortunately almost normally in opposition to the people, and as a necessity the trial of cases—and they are very numerous—in which really the opposing parties are the executive and the people, by that executive, is far from being impartial. (*Loud cheers.*) I will give a recent example that occurred in the Canara district. There, there is an association, a sabha constituted for the protection locally of public interests—a perfectly legal, constitutional and well-managed association. All know how cruelly our forest laws have of late years pressed upon the people of our presidency, and, in discharge of its legitimate functions, this association commenced an agitation in this matter of forest administration. Uufortunately the unpleasant truths that had to be told wounded the feelings of the executive officers of the district, and they having judicial powers in their hands set to work to persecute that association, and very nearly succeeded in bringing its leading members into a disastrous prosecution. But I need not dwell upon these matters; such cases are occurring in one province or another daily: there is not, I venture to say, a single delegate here present who could not, from his own personal knowledge, give similar instances of the untoward results of the present objectionable system, and it is really, therefore, useless for me to say more in favour of a resolution, which solely aims at superseding that system by a better and more rational one." (*Loud cheers.*)

MUNSHI KASHI PERSHAD (*Allahabad, No.* 113) said: "I think there can be no two opinions on the point that it is absolutely necessary that a separation of judicial and executive functions should take place without a moment's delay. Wherever these two functions are combined in the same individual, there is a very great probability, to say the least, of a miscarriage of justice. The same man dismisses your civil suit and then tries you criminally for making a false verification or bringing a false suit. In some provinces these functions are already to a great extent separate, and wherever such is the case, the advantage of that separation to all parties is no longer a matter of question. What we now want is that this separation should be made absolute and universal. With these observations I gladly second the resolution."

Baboo Chandi Kishore Kushari (*Calcutta, No.* 256) said: "I move as an amendment that the words at the end of the resolution 'even though this should in some provinces involve some extra expenditure' be omitted.

"We know perfectly well that it won't really cost any extra money. If six men giving only half time to each can get through two works, certainly these can be done, and better done, by allotting one work entirely to three men, who would give it their whole time and thought, and the other work to the other three who would similarly give their undivided attention to that work. It is a mere division of labour, which is supposed to cheapen not augment the cost of operations, then why put it into the head of Government to spend more money?"

The President remarked that this was really no amendment; as in fact the words proposed to be omitted only emphasized the resolution. He suggested that the motion should not be pressed and it was accordingly withdrawn.

Baboo Sriram (*Oudh, No.* 169) said: "I come from a province in which, until very lately, *all* judicial (civil as well as criminal) and executive powers were centred in the same officials, and it is only lately judicial powers in civil matters have been withdrawn from the district officers who are now only invested with judicial powers in criminal cases, and general executive powers in revenue and all other matters. Yet even now miscarriages of justice often take place in consequence of this combination of functions. I come, I may explain, from Oudh, which is what is called a non-regulation province, and I am the public prosecutor in the Judicial Commissioner's Court. Very lately several cases came up for revision in which the district officers in their executive capacities served writs of demand against revenue defaulters, and on these failing to pay up on the fixed date, these revenue officers taking advantage of their powers as magistrates, arraigned the defaulters under section 188 and in their judicial capacities fined them. Naturally when the cases came up before the highest Court the fines were remitted, but it is needless to explain that this was a poor consolation to the accused for all the expense, trouble, and waste of time to which they had been subjected by the injustice of the local officials. This is a single case. I could give many others; every one of us could give any number of similar illustrations of the defective and injurious character of the existing combination of functions. But I will allude to one more case with which you are all familiar, and I will say that, had not both judicial and executive functions centred in the same officer, the case of our universally respected friend Munshi Murlidhar would have been impossible. But I fear I am needlessly occupying your time; no rational being can doubt that the separation of the judicial and executive functions is essential if any regard is to be had either to the comfort of the people or the good name of the Government."

The resolution was then put to the assembly by the President and carried unanimously.

Rajah Rampal Singh (*Oudh, No.* 178) said: "The resolution which I am to submit for your acceptance runs as follows:—

"'That in view to the unsettled state of public affairs in Europe, and the immense assistance that the people of this country, if duly prepared therefor, is capable of rendering to Great Britain in the event of any serious complications arising, this Congress do earnestly appeal to the Government to authorise (under such rules and restrictions as may to it seem fitting) a system of Volunteering for the Indian inhabitants of the country, such as may qualify them to support the Government, effectively, in any crisis.' (*Resolution XII of Summary, page* 45.) (*Loud and prolonged cheering.*)

"But I really doubt whether there is sufficient time for the discussion of this important resolution, and if I might be allowed to propose such a thing I would suggest that we should adjourn to-day and resume the discussion to-morrow."

The President took the sense of the meeting, and then announced that it was the general desire that the discussion of the question should be proceeded with.

Rajah Rampal Singh then said: "The spirit of this meeting has been so uniformly loyal and conciliatory that I hope no one will blame us if we now proceed to deal with a matter, in regard to which, we are distinctly at variance with Government. Every one knows that, for a variety of reasons, the whole country is of opinion that native Volunteer Corps ought to be organized. Every one knows that the entire country memoralized and endeavoured to move Government in this matter, and every one further knows that, to our great regret and disappointment, the Government, and that not over-graciously, distinctly refused to pay any attention to the unanimous voice of the country. None the less, however, do we now feel it our duty to reiterate those representations—representations which are based on a consideration of the highest interests of Great Britain as well as India.

"We are deeply grateful to Government for all the good that it has done us, but we cannot be grateful to it when it is, no matter with what best of intentions, doing us a terrible and irreparable injury. (*Loud cheers.*)

"We are grateful to it for the peace and order which it has diffused over the land (*cheers*); for the education that it has so nobly and unselfishly imparted to us (*cheers*); for its promise of admitting us to every post and office in the administration for which we prove our fitness (*cheers*); for the share that it has given us in the comforts and conveniences provided by the triumphs of Western science, railways, telegraphs, telephones—we are grateful to it in a word for all the innumerable boons and blessings that it has conferred on us (*cheers*); but we cannot be grateful to it for degrading our natures, for systematically crushing out of us all martial spirit, for converting a race of soldiers and heroes into a timid flock of quill-driving sheep. (*Prolonged shouts.*) Thank God, things have not yet gone quite so far as this. There are some of us yet, everywhere, who, would be willing to draw sword, and if needful lay down our lives, for hearth and homes, aye and for the support and maintenance of that Government to which we owe so much. (*Cheers.*) But this is what we are coming to—and when we once come to that, then I think that, despite the glories of the Pax Britannica, despite the noble intentions of Great Britain, despite all the good she may have done or tried to do us, the balance will be against her, and India will have to regret rather than rejoice that she has ever had anything to do with England. (*Hear, hear.*)

"This may be strong language,.but it is the truth; nothing can ever make amends to a nation for the destruction of its national spirit, and of the capacity to defend itself and the soil from which it springs. (*Loud cheers.*)

"Nor is it only we who shall have to regret and suffer for the mistaken policy that our Government is unhappily pursuing in this matter. Look where you will around you in the world, and you will see gigantic armies and armaments. There is trouble in store for the whole civilized world, and sooner or later a tremendous military struggle will commence in which assuredly, before it terminates, Great Britain will be involved. Great Britain with all her wealth cannot put one hundred men into the field for every thousand that several Continental powers can. England herself is isolated, and by her insular position to a certain extent protected, but no friendly sea rolls between Europe and Asia, the landward path to India is known and open; India is not isolated, and it will be India, on whose possession half Great Britain's wealth and status depends, that will be the scene of any serious attack by any Continental powers on Great Britain. (*Hear hear.*)

"Then will England regret that, instead of having millions of brave Indians trained to arms to fling back invaders she has only her scanty legions to oppose to them, and from her timid subjects can only look at most for good wishes—good wishes, truly good things in their way, but poor bulwarks against Berdan rifles and steel ordnance. (*Hear, hear.*)

"But on our own accounts we deprecate the existing policy. High and low we are losing all knowledge of the use of arms, and with this that spirit of self-reliance which enables a man to dare, which makes men brave, which makes them worthy of the name of men. (*Loud cheers.*) When I was only five years of age my grandfather made me begin to learn all physical exercises in vogue amongst us, and I was trained to the use of all arms and in all martial exercises. (*Cheers.*) But what man now sends his son for such training? What young man now-a-days knows anything of these things? Fifty years ago, without desiring warfare, every young man's heart glowed within him at the thought of some day showing his prowess in a fair field. Now most young men would, I fear, contemplate any such possible contingency with very, let me say, mixed feelings. If men are to be fit for soldiers, fit to fight to any purpose when the time of trial comes, and come it must for every country, then they must be trained in the use of arms, they must from their childhood see their parents, their elders, using arms and participating in those martial exercises which only 35 years ago, in Oudh at least, were part of every gentleman's occupation.

"And there is another very important point—India is practically being impoverished, to a great extent, by the enormous expense of her standing army. Sooner or later the crushing weight of this (for her resources) enormous expenditure will break down either the country or the Government. Now by a judicious encouragement of Indian Volunteers, it would be possible to reduce very greatly this military expenditure, and yet leave the country far stronger for defensive purposes than it now is. (*Prolonged cheering.*)

"But I might go on for hours. I might dwell on the fact that in the way the Arms Act is now worked in many localities, the people, their herds, their crops are wholly at the mercy of wild beasts. I might dwell on the insult, the injustice, the violation of the most sacred and solemn pledges by England to India, that are involved in the rules that permit Indian Christians but do not permit Indian Hindus or Mahomedans to volunteer. (*Loud cheers.*) But I have said enough, and indeed being, as we are, all of one mind, too much already I fear on this subject in which I am deeply interested, I will only now add that we do not ask Government to put arms blindly into all men's hands, but only to permit under such rules and restrictions as it sees fit, the better and more educated classes of its loyal Indian subjects to qualify themselves to defend, when occasion may require, their homes, their country and their Government." (*Enthusiastic cheers.*)

MR. R. D. MEHTA (*Calcutta, No.* 272) said: "This resolution is so unanimously acquiesced in, and has been so eloquently expounded by Rajah Rampal Singh, that it needs no words of recommendation from me. I may, therefore, content myself with saying, and that from the bottom of my heart, that I not only second this resolution, but on your behalf, and on behalf of my own community, venture to assert that we are all loyal to the core (*cheers*); and that if the Government will try us and prove us, make us volunteers and try to curtail their military expenditure, they will never regret it, but will find in us always good men and true, ready to assist in times of peace, in maintaining civil order and upholding their authority, and in times of war willing to stand by them to the last." (*Loud cheers.*)

THE PRESIDENT said: "Unless any one is opposed in any way to this resolution, I think that it might be put to the vote without further discussion. The fact is, this is just one of those few questions in regard to which no difference of opinion exists, throughout the whole of India, and we need not say one single word more on the subject."

The resolution was then put to the vote amidst prolonged cheering and carried by acclamation.

The Congress then adjourned until the next day.

FOURTH DAY'S PROCEEDINGS.

Thursday, 30th December, 1886,

AT THE TOWN HALL.

THE PRESIDENT said: "Gentlemen,—Before we commence our proceedings I wish to say a few words on one subject. I have received several proposals for the introduction of new subjects for discussion. I think it would be very embarrassing, as well as be bad in principle, to spring upon the Congress new subjects for which the majority of our delegates are not prepared. I therefore appeal to those gentlemen from whom those proposals have originated not to insist on them, but to reflect that to do so would be unjust to the majority of the delegates, embarrassing to the Congress as a whole, and likely to create a bad precedent and a deal of confusion. So far as my experience goes, I do not think that in any Congress the programme which has once been settled is materially departed from except with the unanimous consent of all the delegates. I shall not, therefore, I think, be able to allow any entirely new subject to be brought forward, unless such prove to be the unanimous wish in any case of the entire meeting."

MR. SURENDRA NATH BANERJEE (*Calcutta, No.* 239) said: "Mr. President, bowing to your ruling as to entirely new subjects, I yet venture to enquire whether it would be possible for you to allow me to call attention to the operation of the Assam Emigration Act, considering that I duly gave notice of my intention to raise this question."

THE PRESIDENT said: "I fear that I cannot allow this; the notice you refer to was only given at a very late stage of the proceedings, and many delegates I find are of opinion that this is rather a question for discussion in the Bengal Provincial Congress than in this present National Assemblage. I would therefore ask you to drop that subject and kindly put before the Congress the Report of the Committee on the Public Service Question."

MR. SURENDRA NATH BANERJEE (*Calcutta, No.* 239) said: "It will be remembered that at a previous meeting a motion was carried at my instance appointing a Committee for the purpose of submitting a report on the questions which the Public Service Commission have prepared. The Committee met yesterday, and I hold in my hand the report of the Committee. We have not been able to answer the 184 questions which were originally propounded by the Commission, nor even the reduced number which they subsequently issued. But we have been able to formulate certain general principles which, we believe, cover almost the entire ground in regard to which the Commission have been putting forward these questions; and the report, except in one unimportant detail, is a perfectly unanimous report. I will therefore, with the leave of the Congress, read the Report :—

REPORT.

We, the Members of the Committee appointed by the Congress to submit a statement in connection with the Public Service Question, have the honor to report that the following resolutions were unanimously adopted by us at a meeting held yesterday :—

1. That the open Competitive Examination be held simultaneously both in India and in England.
2. That the simultaneous examinations thus held be equally open to all classes of Her Majesty's subjects.
3. That the classified list be prepared according to merit.
4. That the Congress express the hope that the Civil Service Commissioners will give fair consideration to Sanskrit and Arabic among the subjects of examination.
5. That the age of candidates eligible for admission to the open Competitive Examination be not less than 19, or, as recommended by Sir C. Aitchison, more than 23 years.
6. That simultaneous examinations being granted, the Statutory Civil Service be closed for first appointments.
7. That the appointments in the Statutory Civil Service, under the existing rules, be still left open to the members of the Uncovenanted Service and to professional men of proved merit and ability.
8. That all appointments requiring educational qualifications, other than covenanted first appointments, be filled by Competitive Examinations held in the different provinces, and open in each province to such natural-born subjects of H. M. only as are residents thereof.

These resolutions, it is hoped, cover the main principles which underlie the questions set by the Public Service Commission. For a more detailed consideration there was no time.

Sd.) DADABHAI NAOROJI,

President of the Committee.

30th December, 1886.

"On behalf of the Committee which has been appointed by this Congress, I now venture to move that this Congress approves and adopts the report submitted by the Committee appointed by Resolution VI." (*Resolution VII of Summary, page* 44.)

THE HON'BLE S. SUBRAMANIA IYER (*Madras, No.* 2) said: "I beg to second the motion."

THE PRESIDENT said: "I hope, having regard to the confidence which the Congress was pleased to place in the Committee, and the careful consideration which has been bestowed by the Committee (most of the members of which were already familiar with the subject) on each of those several points with which they found time to deal, that no discussion by way merely of affirming the report will be considered necessary. If any gentleman specially desires to make any remarks he can of course do so, or if any delegate desires to express his dissent from anything embodied in the Committee's report, we shall, I am sure, all gladly hear him; but if we are all agreed, and if it be the unanimous opinion that the report should be adopted, I will put Mr. Banerjee's motion and pass on to other work."

BABOO AMBICA CHARAN MAZUMDAR (*Furreedpore, No.* 316) said: "What has been done with regard to the question of going to England for a certain term after having passed the examination in this country? Is it proposed to make this compulsory or not?"

THE PRESIDENT said: "This is a difficult question, and the Committee had no time to discuss it fully and conclusively, and they therefore recorded no opinion in regard to it. We did our best, but in the limited time at our disposal necessarily left some points untouched."

DR. ANNADA CHARAN KASTAGIRI (*Chittagong, No.* 389) said: "Perhaps gentlemen you are aware that Chittagong, whence I come as a delegate, is a Mahomedan district, and that three-fourths of the people there are Mahomedans. A meeting which was held there was well attended by Mahomedans, and they appointed four delegates, two Mahomedans and two Hindus, and of the two Hindus I am one. We all duly reached Calcutta. The two Mahomedans purposed to attend the Congress with me, and it was arranged that I should give them a lift in my carriage. That was before the Congress met. On the following day they did not join me. The next morning they came to me and said that, although they were desirous of attending, pressure which, from their circumstances, they could not resist, had been put on them to prevent their so doing by certain influential gentlemen of their own persuasion whose names I will not mention. I say this now to explain to you all here, as I shall have to explain later to our constituents, how and why Chittagong is so imperfectly represented. With regard to the subject before the Congress, the meeting held at Chittagong specifically instructed us to press one particular point on the attention of the Congress, and I trust you will bear with me while I carry out my instructions. They said that when the Marquis of Wellesley was in India in 1801, there was an institution called the Fort William College in which all gentlemen appointed to fill vacancies in the Civil Service were educated, and it was not until after they had spent at least two years in this College that they were sent into the country to administer justice. That College only remained in existence for a few years; it was abolished and replaced by Haileybury College; the Fort William College of later days had nothing to do with that College. Sir Charles Metcalfe was brought up in that College, and the success with which he, and others similarly trained, administered the several departments of which they had charge, seems to show that the system was a good one, and they desire to suggest that as Indian civilians appointed in India ought to pass their period of probation in England, so English civilians, appointed in England, might advantageously pass a time of probation in India and there learn, in a way they never do now, the language, manners, and customs of the country, before having any official duties thrust upon them, and our Chittagong people consider that thus alone can Europeans become really successful administrators. The Chittagong Association desires that all the Europeans appointed to any branch of the civil administration, whether in England or in India, should pass a probationary period in India so as to learn the customs and habits and manners of the people before they are invested with any authority. I therefore suggest that some provision giving effect to these views be added to the report."

THE PRESIDENT said: "This is one among several other points which, as I have already explained, the Committee have had no sufficient time to examine closely and consider. There is no time now to go back upon points which they have been compelled to leave untouched. The question before the meeting is either to adopt or reject the Committee's report, or to discuss in view to its modification any particular points mentioned in it. The suggestion which has just been made is a very good one. It was discussed at great length in 1853 when the revision of the Charter was being considered, and certain conclusions were come to, but that is not a subject which can now be discussed."

BABOO DWARKANATH GANGULI (*Calcutta, No.* 253) said: "I will make one suggestion. We know that our Mahomedan friends, so far as Bengal is concerned, are not duly represented. So in justice to them I wish to point out that the report should state that a certain proportion of the appointments should be reserved for Mahomedans who are qualified."

The President remarked that this question was considered very carefully, and the third of the Committee's conclusions showed the Committee's views; neither for Indians in general, nor for Mahomedans in particular, was it deemed expedient to reserve any appointments. The interests of the country demanded that the best men should get the appointments irrespective of nationality, caste or creed.

The resolution was then put to the vote and carried unanimously.

Mr. Surendra Nath Banerjee (*Calcutta, No.* 239) then rose and said: "The resolution that has been confided to my charge is a rather lengthy one, and I will, with your permission, read it through to you before offering any remarks in regard to its subject. The resolution runs as follows :—

"'That this Congress is of opinion that, in giving practical effect to this essential reform, regard should be had (subject to such modifications as, on a more detailed examination of the question, may commend themselves to the Government) to the principles embodied in the following tentative suggestions :—

(1.)—The number of persons composing the Legislative Councils, both Provincial and of the Governor-General, to be materially increased. Not less than one-half the Members of such enlarged Councils to be elected. Not more than one-fourth to be officials having seats *ex-officio* in such Councils, and not more than one-fourth to be Members, official or non-official, nominated by Government.

(2.)—The right to elect Members to the Provincial Councils to be conferred only on those classes and members of the community *primâ facie* capable of exercising it wisely and independently. In Bengal and Bombay the Councillors may be elected by the Members of Municipalities, District Boards, Chambers of Commerce and the Universities, or an electorate may be constituted of all persons possessing such qualifications, educational and pecuniary, as may be deemed necessary. In Madras, the Councillors may be elected either by District Boards, Municipalities, Chambers of Commerce and the University, or by Electoral Colleges composed of Members partly elected by these bodies and partly nominated by Government. In the North-West Provinces and Oudh and in the Punjab, Councillors may be elected by an Electoral College composed of Members elected by Municipal and District Boards and nominated, to an extent not exceeding one-sixth of the total number, by Government, it being understood that the same elective system now in force where Municipal Boards are concerned will be applied to District Boards, and the right of electing Members to these latter extended to the cultivating class. But whatever system be adopted (and the details must be worked out separately for each province) care must be taken that all sections of the community, and all great interests, are adequately represented.

(3.)—The elected Members of the Council of the Governor-General for making Laws to be elected by the elected Members of the several Provincial Councils.

(4.)—No elected or nominated Member of any Council to receive any salary or remuneration in virtue of such membership, but any such Member, already in receipt of any Government salary or allowance, to continue to draw the same, unchanged, during membership, and all Members to be entitled to be reimbursed any expenses incurred in travelling in connection with their membership.

(5.)—All persons, resident in India, to be eligible for seats in Council, whether as electees or nominees, without distinction of race, creed, caste or colour.

(6.)—All legislative measures and all financial questions, including all budgets, whether these involve new or enhanced taxation or not, to be necessarily submitted to and dealt with by these Councils. In the case of all other branches of the administration, any Member to be at liberty, after due notice, to put any question he sees fit to the *ex-officio* Members (or such one of these as may be specially charged with the supervision of the particular branch concerned) and to be entitled (except as hereinafter provided) to receive a reply to his question, together with copies of any papers requisite for the thorough comprehension of the subject, and on this reply the Council to be at liberty to consider and discuss the question and record thereon such resolution as may appear fitting to the majority. Provided that, if the subject in regard to which the inquiry is made involves matters of Foreign policy, Military dispositions or strategy, or is otherwise of such a nature that, in the opinion of the Executive, the Public interests would be materially imperilled by the communication of the information asked for, it shall be competent for them to instruct the *ex-officio* Members, or one of them, to reply accordingly, and decline to furnish the information asked for.

(7.)—The Executive Government shall possess the power of overruling the decision arrived at by the majority of the Council, in every case in which, in its opinion, the public interests would suffer by the acceptance of such decision; but whenever this power is exercised, a full exposition of the grounds on which this has been considered necessary shall be published within one month, and in the case of local Governments they shall report the circumstances and explain their action to the Government of India, and in the case of this latter, it shall report and explain to the Secretary of State; and in any such case on a representation made through the Government of India and the Secretary of State by the overruled majority, it shall be competent to the Standing Committee of the House of Commons (recommended in the 3rd Resolution of last year's Congress which this present Congress has affirmed) to consider the matter, and call for any and all papers, or information, and hear any persons on behalf of such majority or otherwise, and thereafter, if needful, report thereon to the full House. (*Resolution IV of Summary, page 41.*)

"Gentlemen, I should have preferred if somebody else—some one unconnected with our province—had been entrusted with the duty of proposing this resolution. We, the people of Bengal, occupy a peculiar position with reference to this Congress. We have invited the rest of India—the culture, the intelligence and the public spirit of this great Empire—to our city and to this great conference for the discussion of public questions. We are the hosts and you are our guests, and as hosts it best befits us to restrain our tongues and (standing by while you speak) to listen to the words of wisdom—the collective wisdom of united India—that may fall from your lips. (*Cheers.*) The scene of to-day and the scenes which we have been witnessing for the last two days (pardon me for the digression) remind me of those spectacles in ancient India when the lord of Aryavarta would summon his feudatory chiefs to his capital to celebrate the most imposing of Aryan rites—the Rajsuya Jagya. But those were gatherings of princes, not the gatherings of peoples. (*Cheers.*) Here we have before us personified the incarnate majesty of the nation. (*Cheers.*) What visions of glory, what prospects of rapturous joy unfold themselves before the imagination of the poet, the historian and the philosopher. I will not indulge in them. I will not allow myself to be carried away by the inspiration of the moment. But this I will say—I may be permitted to indulge in this hope—that this feeling of sympathy and brotherhood between the different Indian races may grow and deepen, that it may draw together the most distant parts of the Empire and bind all races, all creeds, and all nationalities that inhabit this great country, in one golden chain of brotherly love and affection. (*Cheers.*) But there is another reason why I should have preferred that some one, not a native of Bengal, had taken up this resolution. Whatever agitation takes place, whatever wave of national feeling surges from one part of the country to the other, whatever upheaval of the national mind is observable, manifesting itself in great and imposing popular demonstrations, is ascribed to the instrumentality of the people of Bengal. (*Cheers and laughter.*) But I am unwilling that Bengal should take the credit, or the discredit, as it may seem to some, of having originated the agitation in connection with this movement. The truth is that all India, with all her races and creeds, is united in making this one common, universal prayer for the introduction of representative Government. (*Cheers.*)

"Self-government is the ordering of nature, the will of Divine Providence. Every nation must be the arbiter of its own destinies—such is the omnipotent fiat inscribed by Nature with her own hands and in her own eternal book. But do we govern ourselves? The answer is no. Are we then living in an unnatural state? Yes, in the same state in which the patient lives under the ministrations of the physician. We are passing through a period of probation and a period of trial under the auspices of one of the most freedom-loving nations in the world. And we claim that the period of probation may now fairly terminate, that the leading-strings may be taken off, and the child having emerged into the dawn of mature manhood may at any rate be partially entrusted with the management of his own affairs. (*Loud cheers.*) If it were otherwise, the circumstance would imply the gravest slur upon the character of British rule in India; for it would mean that after more than a century of British rule and of English education, we are still unfit to appreciate the principles and to practise the art of self-government. (*Cheers.*) But I have no fears on this score. In our own province, local self-government has been remarkably successful. We have it on the highest authority; for no less a personage than His Honor the Lieutenant-Governor has declared that in Bengal local self-government has on the whole been a success; and I am quite sure similar testimony would be forthcoming in reference to the other provinces of India. It would indeed be a marvel if it were otherwise. Our Punchayet system is as old as the hills and is graven on the hearts and the instincts of the people. Self-government is therefore nothing new to the habits or the ways of thought of the people of India. (*Cheers.*)

"The resolution with which I am entrusted follows as a matter of course from the third resolution which you have already adopted. Having affirmed that the reconstitution of the Legislative Councils has become necessary alike in the interests of the people of India and for the honor of English rule, it becomes necessary for us to determine how the reform should be carried out—what are the lines which should be followed—what are to be the principles upon which it should be based? It will not do to appear before Government, to quote the expressive language of my friend opposite, as the Great Mr. Blank We must make it clear that we are not mere talkers, that we are not mere brawlers and charlatans, but that we have devoted some of the most precious moments of our lifetime, moments of anxious thought and of patient consideration, to the solution of this great problem. Our proposals may be rejected. We put them forward as only tentative suggestions. But that is no concern of ours. The responsibility lies with the Government. And at the very threshold of the enquiry, I desire to remove a difficulty which some may feel in connection with this resolution. To some, it may appear that we are entering too much into details. But I am prepared to show, and I hope to be able to make it clear as I proceed, that we are dealing with broad general principles, and that the details, such as they may appear to the superficial observer, are necessary to the elucidation of the principles involved. They may be said to form part and parcel of an integral structure, every stone of which has been laid with the utmost care and precision. The principles which may be said to underlie the resolution are these: We desire that a fair proportion of the members of the reconstituted Councils should be elected. We have not the remotest idea that the Government should vacate its position in favour of our worthy president and his following. We do not desire that our rulers "should mount guard while we handled the monies." Yesterday we passed a resolution in favour of our mounting guard, if the Government would let us do so, by enrolling us as volunteers. It is not indeed a question of the abdication of the Government. It is much more a question of the association of the people, in a partial and modified form, in the government of the country.

"Having decided that a proportion of the members should be elected, the next question we have to consider is—how are they to be elected—what are to be the constituencies? We say the members are to be elected by local bodies, Chambers of Commerce, Trades' Associations, Universities and other similar bodies of established repute. I can however conceive of a possible objection to this scheme, aud I am anxious to meet this objection before I proceed further. It may be said that our local bodies are untried, and that the elective Municipalities were created only the other day. But the Municipalities in Bengal, in one form or other, have now been in existence and have had a trial for nearly a quarter of a century; and the District Boards of to-day are the Road Cess Committees which were established about the year 1871. This objection must therefore fall to the ground. But admitting that the local bodies are untried, admitting the force of the objection which has been raised, we reply that we pin our faith upon no particular system, no creed, no dogma. Representation is our motto, our watch-word, our battle-cry, the gospel of our political redemption. (*Cheers.*) We give the Government a *carte blanche*. We tell them that if our programme does not please them, let them devise any system of their own—let it be a system of direct representation or any other form or system which may please them best. But we say at the same time—mark the moderation of our views—that whatever may be your scheme of representative government, the interests of all classes of the community, Hindus, Mahomedans, Parsees, Sikhs, Eurasians, of all races and of all creeds, should be adequately cared for. We desire to exclude none. All are alike welcome to the holiest of holies—the temple of representative government. We do not desire that the majority should swamp the minority, or that any particular class should have any preponderance, except such as may belong to superior devotion, courage and self-sacrifice. These are the qualities which have governed humanity in the past; and they will continue to govern the representative institutions of New India. (*Loud cheers.*)

"Such being the constitution of our Councils, the next question which we have to consider is—what are to be their powers aud functions? These powers are to be of a limited character. They are not such as will displace or supersede the authority of the Executive Government; on the contrary, their exercise will be a source of material help to the Government. In the first place, the Councils should have the right of interpellation; secondly, they should be vested with some power of control over the finances. The right of interpellation would be an advantage to the Government as it would be an advantage to the people. It is a constant complaint, which we hear repeated on all sides, that there are frequent misinterpretations and misconceptions of the motives and objects of the Government in the Public Press. Now if this is so, explanations with regard to the policy and the conduct of the Government made by official members from their place in Council, and upon their personal responsibility, would be received with implicit confidence and would go far to remove the misconceptions from which, under existing circumstances, the Government no doubt must occasionally suffer. From this point of view the right of interpellation would be an immense gain to the Government. It would likewise be the safeguard of popular liberty. It is a right which if carefully exercised will enable the popular representatives to bring many an erratic magistrate to book. In the worst days of imperial rule in France, Louis Napoleon deprived the Legislative Chamber of this important right, lest it should be a source of embarrassment to his Government.

"With reference to the control over finance, with which we suggest that the Councils should be invested, the present rule is that the Budget must be laid before the Supreme Council only when new taxes have to be levied. We advocate a further extension, and upon the same lines, of this concession which has already been made. We propose that whether the Budget concerns the Province or the Empire, whether a new tax has to be levied or not, in all cases and under all circumstances, the Budget should be laid before the Council—Provincial or Imperial—that those who pay the taxes may have some voice in the expenditure.

"Such is to be the constitution of the Councils—such are to be the powers with which they should be vested. But are the Councils to be left in the unfettered exercise of these powers? Is the Government to abdicate all powers in favour of the President and his followers? Not at all. Mark how moderate our demands are. We propose that the Government should have the right of vetoing the decisions of the Council. If any measure passed by the Council seems inconsistent with the public interests, the Government may disallow it, stating of course its reasons within a reasonable limit of time, the power of appeal in such cases being vested in a standing committee of the House of Commons. Some may say—why introduce this question—why talk about this right of veto at all? I think it would be wise on our part to do so. You may depend upon it that the Government will reserve to itself some power of control over bodies which are thus reconstituted and invested with these new powers. You are familiar with the sections relating to control in your Local Self-Government Acts, and you may be sure that when the experiment of self-government is carried to a higher stage, a similar power will be reserved by the Government. Such being the case, it seems to me that it would be as wise as it would be moderate to suggest from our point of view what the nature of the control should be.

"Such are the principles which underlie the scheme which has been tentatively suggested. But whether this or any other scheme is adopted, I trust we shall continue to press upon the Government, in season and out of season, that the time has come when, alike in the interests of the people and for the honor of English rule, the representative element should be recognised in the Government of the country. I have a profound faith in the ultimate success of our cause. Faith can remove mountains were the memorable words uttered eighteen hundred years ago by the illustrious founder of Christianity. If we are true to ourselves, and if we have faith and patience, the victory will assuredly be ours. I have abundant confidence in the justice and generosity of the English people. Britain, the august mother of free nations, cannot refuse to us a boon which is in such entire accord with her own traditions and the instincts of her great people. But I have yet an appeal to make to the assembled representatives of all India. We should begin the agitation at once. The struggle must now commence. We are on the threshold of a new age. We are witnessing a new birth. The darkness of midnight has disappeared; and the faint grey streaks of dawn are distinctly visible in the distant horizon. Grave and solemn are our responsibilities; and I hope and trust that the voice which has been raised in this hall will be re-echoed in every town, in every district, and in every province, and will be wafted across seas and mountains and deserts to the footsteps of that throne, from whose beneficence and justice and liberality we anticipate the fulfilment of our hopes and the redemption of our people."

MR. N. G. CHANDAVARKAR (*Bombay, No.* 49), in seconding the resolution, said: "Mr. Chairman and Gentlemen,—In rising to second this resolution I confess I feel a certain amount of difficulty. Considering the vast importance of the subject—and, if I may be permitted to say so, next to the question of religious and social reform there is no other subject to which I attach greater importance—considering, I say, the vast importance of the subject and that the time allowed to every speaker in this assembly is very limited, I am afraid I shall not be able to do that justice to it which its nature demands. I hope, however, I shall receive indulgent treatment at your hands, as I propose to lay before you certain facts which seem to me to deserve your careful attention in connection with this demand for representative government. I propose to show by means of those facts that this demand of ours is based not on mere sentiment, and that it is due to ourselves and the Government we live under that, having affirmed at the last Congress the principle of representation, we should go one stage further and point out that the principle is capable of being worked out in practice. I am aware that our hostile critics are finding fault with the scheme now placed before you for your approval. But recent events encourage me in thinking that these critics will gradually come round. They are in fact already coming round. One of them has admitted that India is poor; and only the other day you passed a resolution declaring the poverty of India to be an evil which required to be remedied. Another, who would not admit last year that the Congress represented any one but those who took part in its debates, has come round this year so far as to say that the present Congress is a Hindu Congress, which, I take it, means, according to the critic, that it represents at all events the Hindus. Next year I doubt not our critic will, if he goes on improving at this rate, feel the force of facts so strong that he will admit the Congress to be national. (*Cheers.*)

"Now, coming to the subject before us, the line I propose following is shortly this :—

"*Firstly*—I shall answer the objection that the political soil of India is not congenial to the growth of representative institutions.

"*Secondly*—I shall go on to show that the British Government in India is founded on the principle of representation.

"*Thirdly*—I shall point out why I venture to think that the time has come for an expansion of that principle.

"*Fourthly*—I shall lay before you schemes of representative government suggested (before the present Congress was even thought of) by experienced Anglo-Indian administrators and writers.

" *Lastly*—I shall wind up with a few observations on the scheme which has just been submitted for your consideration.

" Let us take the first of the five points I have indicated above. We now and then hear it said that the people of India are not fit for representative institutions—that India is not England, and that it would not do to introduce here systems of Government which have worked well in a self-governing country like Great Britain. Let us examine this statement by the light of history. History tells us that India was, down to a recent period, known for her village municipalities and *punchayets*, both based and worked on the elective principle. We have it on the authority of an eminent Anglo-Indian writer that these institutions 'exercised a great and beneficial influence over the people.' I am quoting these words from Mr. Greig's Life of Sir Thomas Munro. Well I shall cite another authority. I daresay you have heard the name of Sir John Malcolm. Now, his testimony is important, because he was both a soldier and statesman—one, of whom, borrowing the language of Lord Rosebery, I might say, that he knew both how to conquer and maintain an empire. His testimony is also valuable for another reason, *namely*, that he has distinctly declared that as India was conquered by the English with the assistance of the natives, it can be maintained with their assistance alone. To quote his own words: 'We could never have conquered India without the assistance of the natives of the country, and by them alone can we preserve it. Our actual condition makes this necessity more imperative.' Now Sir John, speaking of the *punchayet* system as it prevailed in India, says: 'A recent instance occurred of a respected president of a *punchayet* determining, from his sense of an unjust measure, to leave a town; and between two or three hundred of its wealthiest citizens so decidedly followed his example that oppression was stopped in its career and compelled to conciliate, by concession, an offended judge.' And this occurred in Sir John Malcolm's time—not very long ago. Then, again, some one has said that 'the East is the parent of municipalities,' and I have seen cited in illustration of that saying the following fact. When, on the conquest of the Twenty-four Pergunnahs, the old municipal system was abolished great calamities befel that country, so much so that Mr. Butterworth Bayley, then in charge of the district, had to restore the old system, and trust to the people themselves. The consequence of this revival of the municipal system has been stated in an official paper to have been that in nine months the crime sheet presented a blank. I shall adduce one more authority in support of the view I am now presenting for your consideration. Sir Bartle Frere, you all know, was an experienced Anglo-Indian administrator. He was by no means inclined to be partial to the natives of this country. His testimony, must therefore, carry some weight with those who cry from the house-tops that India is not, and can never be, fit for representative institutions. Sir Bartle read a paper in 1871 at a meeting of the East India Association in London on 'Public Opinion in India,' and here is what he said on the occasion: 'Any one who has watched the working of Indian society will see that its genius is one to represent, not merely by election under Reform Acts, but represent generally by provisions, every class of the community, and when there is any difficulty respectively any matter to be laid before Government, it should be discussed among themselves. When there is any fellow-citizen to be rewarded or punished, there is always a caste meeting, and this is an expression, it seems to me, of the genius of the people, as it was of the old Saxons, to gather together in assemblies of different tribes to vote by tribes or hundreds.' I think all these are clear authorities and expressions of opinion in support of the view that the Indian soil is congenial to the growth of representative institutions—that, in other words, the genius of the Indian people is of a representative character, and under proper guidance and with proper encouragement that genius is capable of gradual development. (*Loud cheers.*)

" But then, it is said, if representative institutions be conceded to India, the concession will be inconsistent with the principles on which the British rule in this country is founded. That is, those who are opposed to the grant of a representative form of government to India are known to argue that the British Government is a despotism—a despotism, which is tempered by justice but is nevertheless a despotism, that, in the interests of good government in this country, does, as it ought to do, everything for the people instead of having it done by the people. I seriously join issue with those who maintain this view, which I now propose to show is based on a total disregard of the history of the growth of the British Government in India. Mr. Bosworth Smith, in his excellent biography of the late Lord Lawrence, has told us that the ideal set before themselves by the two Lawrences when they were placed in charge of the Punjab was this—to have everything done by the people. 'The English Magistrate was naturally the moving spirit in each city, but associated with him there was to be a Town Council elected by the natives from their own body.' And that, I say, may be regarded as the ideal set before it by the British Government. If that Government were a despotism, having nothing to do with the principle of representation, how happens it that you cannot be taxed unless the Legislature has passed a law sanctioning the tax sought to be imposed on you? And as to the Legislature itself, mark this fact. Men who are nominated its members are selected not as nominees of the Government but true *representatives of the people.* It is true that the people do not select them; the members are nominated, not elected. But that makes no difference, so far as the principle is concerned. The difference only lies in the practical application of the principle, which is that no act shall be done by any public officer unless the Legislature has sanctioned it. Here you see the *germs* of representation. Note again this. Before a law is passed, it is published as a bill for public information and translated into the vernaculars. This further shows that our Legislative Councils, without which no act of any officer would be legal, are founded upon the principle of representation. It does not matter for the purposes of my present point that the laws are often passed in utter disregard of public opinion. We are not concerned with the practice now, for practice grows slowly out of principle, and it is, therefore, that I ask you to look at the principle only and to say whether the basis of the Government is not one of representation. Indeed, even looking to the practice, I may say that on several occasions the Secretary of State has refused to sanction Acts passed by the Indian Legislature on the ground that the people had not been consulted in the matter. For instance, when the Viceroy's Legislative Council had before it in 1873 the Punjab Canals Bill, the Punjab Government objected to its provisions on the ground that they were 'unfair to the agricultural interest, which is not consulted in the making of the canal, and ought not, therefore, to be saddled with its cost.' And the Secretary of State vetoed the measure on that very ground. Mark again what occurred immediately on the introduction of the Legislative Councils system into India in 1861. Sir George Clerk was then Governor of Bombay, and he inaugurated the opening ceremony of the Bombay Legislative Council on the 22nd January, 1862, by addressing the nominated members, among whom were several native gentlemen, in these memorable words: 'You will remember that you owe to those whom you represent a strict account of the fulfilment of your duties—to a people who reasonably desire your protection of their acknowledged rights to live in peace.'

"'An assembly on this scale has naturally a tendency to expand, and seeing it has pleased Her Majesty's Government to consider that the time has arrived for conferring this privilege on you, it will doubtless in due time be enlarged.'

"Now, these are very important words—important, because they were addressed on a memorable occasion by a responsible representative of Her Majesty. They conveyed a sacred promise. They make two things clear—one, that members were appointed to the Council as popular representatives; the other, that in due time the principle on which the Council was founded would be gradually expanded. And it is this expansion we now ask for in putting forward the scheme embodied in the resolution before you. (*Cheers.*)

"This brings me to my third point, which is this—has the time come for such an expansion? Or rather, where is the necessity of asking Government to reconstitute the Legislative Councils on a popular basis? The necessity, I answer, is clearly indicated by the difficulty of making the rulers understand the ruled. What the late Lord Halifax, then Sir Charles Wood, said in 1853 from his place in the House of Commons stands true of the present time. He then said: 'There is no mixture of the English population with the Native population. We go, we govern, and we return.' The result is that misunderstandings frequently arise. Government contemplates a certain measure; and the people interpret its act and motive, sometimes rightly, sometimes wrongly. The Native Press no doubt speaks for the people, but its position is anomalous. It has often no means of obtaining correct information; and it is apt to misunderstand and be misunderstood. Well, if the people gather in public meetings or in a Congress like this and tell Government what the wants and grievances of the people are, they are likely to be told in return by captious critics that they do not represent the masses. In other words, these critics would allow none to be representatives of the people but the Government, and the Government is foreign and practically bureaucratic. Is it then to be wondered at that measures passed without the consent or advice of the people should often give rise to misunderstandings? Is it not necessary that such a Government as ours should seek every means of consulting the people on important questions and of taking them into its confidence? 'It is the despotic ruler who most requires to know public opinion,' wrote Sir Bartle Frere. What is the means adopted by the Government for duly ascertaining such opinion in India? The necessity of ascertaining it was pointed out by Sir Donald McLeod, formerly Lieutenant-Governor of Punjab, in his evidence before the East India Finance Committee of 1871. Asked whether he would recommend an increase of the duty on salt, he answered,—'before expressing a decided opinion, I would consult the Natives more than wo do generally.' Questioned again, he said: 'I would be very cautious about expressing a definite opinion about any tax until I had had the opportunity of discussing with the Natives regarding them.' He was further asked: 'Do you think it would be unwise generally to impose any new tax or increase of existing taxes till the Natives have been consulted?' He answered: 'I think myself it is most desirable before anything is done, for we really do not know what would be the result unless we consulted them.' And yet are the people consulted in matters of taxation? Now, in quoting these answers of Sir Donald in support of the view that a system of representative government is necessary for India, Sir Bartle Frere in the paper already referred to said: 'They are the mature opinions of his (Sir Donald's) lifetime, and I think they are shared by many of those who worked with him, before him, about him, and below him.' These 'mature opinions' were expressed fifteen years ago, when public opinion was not so strong and enlightened as it now is. Now you have an intelligent class of educated Natives who occupy the position of interpreters between the rulers and ruled. That the masses on the whole accept their educated countrymen as their leaders was proved to demonstration on the eve of Lord Ripon's departure from this country, when they joined the latter in bearing their testimony to the popularity of his Lordship's Indian policy. And in every country, even in England, it is the educated classes who represent the feelings of and lead the people. It follows, I think, from what I have said and quoted that the Government should devise some means whereby the people may be enabled to express their opinions on administrative questions affecting their weal or woe.

"Dealing with my fourth point, I wish it to be clearly understood that the demand for an expansion of our Legislative Councils and for a system of representative government had been made for us by such men as Sir Bartle Frere long before the present Congress was so much as thought of. In his paper, to which I have repeatedly referred, Sir Bartle sketched out a scheme somewhat, if not exactly, similar to the one now before you. Another scheme, having the same object in view, was suggested by an able Anglo-Indian writer in the pages of the *Calcutta Review* of the year 1873. That article, which is headed 'Provincial Councils,' will amply repay perusal. A third scheme was that proposed some years ago by Mr. M. J. Shaw Stewart, lately of the Bombay Civil Service, who was for many years a District Collector and for some time Chief Secretary to the Government of Bombay. I bring these schemes to your notice to show that our demand was anticipated by experienced administrators and officials, who had no reason to take an exaggerated view of either our capacities or requirements. This alone ought to serve as a refutation of the charge that we are asking for revolutionary measures in praying for an expansion of the representative principle in the case of our Legislative Councils.

"As to the scheme now submitted for your approval, I shall not say more than this, that it is merely of a suggestive character. I do not claim freedom from error for it. My own opinion is that all we are called upon to do is to prove that the time has come for expanding the principle of representation, and to show, generally, how it is capable of being expanded. In the scheme before you we have attempted to show that and that only. A perfect scheme can be formulated only after you have fully consulted both officials and non-officials. At present we do not go beyond generally indicating the lines on which the Legislative Councils may be reconstituted. Bear this in mind in determining whether you should vote for or against the scheme. And now, before concluding, let me impress upon you one circumstance. Whatever some of our captious critics may say, I am firm in the faith that as long as we are under British rule, so long the development of the representative principle is secured. That development may be and ought to be gradual. You may not have the Councils expanded as you wish to-day or to-morrow. But sooner or later the expansion must come, for the very foundation of the rule is, as I hope to have already shown, *representation*. There is a saying which I have seen oft quoted that the Englishman carries representative institutions with him wherever he goes. He took them to America, to Canada, and the Colonies. And he has brought them to India too. This was evidently in Mr. Gladstone's mind, when, in 1883, addressing the British public through the House of Commons, he said: 'You will go on; you will be compelled to go on; and what is more, I hope, you will be inclined to go on in this noble and upright and blessed work of gradually enlarging the Indian franchise.' It is only a question of time when and how the institution is to grow. The solution of that question will depend not so much on Government as on yourselves—that is, on the people of this country. You must advance in all directions; you must be true to yourselves and show that you deserve the privileges and rights which you seek. The large numbers in which you have met at this Congress—the long distances many of you have travelled—and the sobriety and sound judgment your deliberations have shown, are in themselves promising, for they prove that you are prepared to serve your country; that its welfare occupies a prominent place in your heart; and that you have begun to see that, though speaking different languages and separated by social distinctions, your interests are identical and you must learn to be united. You have begun well, and if you go on as you have begun, depend upon it you will succeed in obtaining the boon of representative Government for your country. You have only to persevere. 'If the English,' says Sydney Smith, 'were in a paradise of spontaneous productions, they would continue to dig and plough, though there were never a peach nor a pine-apple the better for it.' You must work at these questions in this spirit of the Englishman and then success will, I assure you, be yours." (*Loud and prolonged cheering.*)

ROW SAHIB P. ANANDA CHARLU (*Madras, No* 6) said: "Mr. Chairman, Gentlemen and Brethren,—I rise to support the proposition now before you, and I am sorry that the time allowed me is ten minutes—not that it is too little, but that it is too much. I am sure you will realize my embarrassment when you remember that the two speakers who have preceded me—two of our best speakers—have done such full justice to the task they undertook and I may add to themselves also) that they have been compelled to do me the cruel injustice of practically leaving me next to nothing to say on the main points at issue. (*Cheers.*) It is fortunate, however, that the accident of my coming from Madras enables me to say just a fow words relevant to the proposal before you, which have not been already said.

"It is too much the fashion to represent the scheme of reform, which our resolution embodies, as the hasty conception of a few ardent spirits—revolutionary in its aim and radical in its character—taken in hand in a haphazard sort of way, and advocated without due reference to practical possibilities. Such an accusation is most unfounded, and most gratuitous. (*Loud cheers.*) Speaking for the presidency from which I come, I am bound to state that the subject has been regarded as one of primary importance from the very first, and this long before the National Congress became an accomplished fact. (*Cheers.*) You all know, I take it, that before even the first National Congress was held, we in Madras held two Conferences of native gentlemen from the different parts of our presidency at an interval of a twelve-month. At the first conference this subject of representative institutions was earnestly taken up and thoroughly discussed. We then laid down the main lines of a scheme for the introduction of a representative element into the. Government, and decided to entrust the Mahajana Sabha with the task of maturing that scheme, and submitting it to the opinion of the ablest and most advanced thinkers—the men who might be expected to take a real and permanent interest in the subject, and to be abreast of the times. The scheme was accordingly fully elaborated, and sent round for consideration and advice as had been contemplated. Finally, it was submitted in the form of a draft memorial to the second of our conferences, and, having been, with minor modifications, accepted, it was submitted to, and is, I believe, now lying before the authorities for disposal. It is a matter of genuine and unfeigned satisfacton to us, the so-called benighted citizens of Madras, that the National Congress of both this present year and of the last should so entirely endorse our views, and single out, as we had already done, the question of the reconstitution of our Legislative Councils as one of the first importance. (*Cheers.*) The two conferences in Madras, the equally early discussions of the question in Poona, Bombay, Bengal, and finally the two National Congresses, stamp the proposal that awaits your verdict with the character of a long and carefully considered reform, universally desired, in the best interests of the people of this country. (*Loud cheers.*) Is universality of acceptance the only merit of this proposed reform? Most assuredly not. Whatever our amiable critics may say to the contrary, the system contended for is, to my thinking, one essentially practical and urgently demanded by the condition of the country. After all, dispassionately considered, what is it but the embodiment of an ancient fundamental political aphorism, in its juster, truer and nobler acceptation? What is the prayer we lay before Government? It is nothing more and nothing less than a petition to our rulers to act, in practice, on the well known advice to rulers, 'DIVIDE AND GOVERN,' not in its sinister interpretation which prompts men to set class against class, section against section, in a body politic in which perfect concord should prevail, but (as I said) in its juster, truer and nobler interpretation of dividing *with* the subjects the responsibilities and labours of the administration, and thereby establishing their rule, immutably, on the broad basis of the national concurrence. (*Loud cheers.*)

"Not only policy, however, but common justice should lead our rulers to concede our claim, and there are many who, unable to realize the policy of including us in the Government of the country, admit the theoretical justice of our claim, and yet fancy they can meet it by the statement that we cannot back our demand with the argument of force. It is simply impossible to approve the logic of such a contention; and it further implies a gross ignorance of the genius of our people, the teachings of our revered scriptures, and the traditions of our country. Our ancestors, of whom we cannot cease to be proud, their writings which we cannot forget, the traditions which have for ages dominated the national sentiments—all alike teach us to put *reason*—moral pressure—*the art of persuasion*—in the foremost place in the order of methods by which it is wise and right to endeavour to secure anything that may be desired. You are all aware of the methods, known as *Shama*, *Dana*, *Bheda* and *Danda* which mean respectively the policy of persuasion, of compromise, of breaking up the adversaries solidarity, and of resorting to force of arms. It is manifest that this is the order that sterling good sense and sturdy sentiments of justice dictate; and the people of this country will not reverse the order enjoined by this time-honored and no less solidly wise teaching and tradition. They will certainly not make any show of force—whatever force they may possess—they will certainly never resort to force until all other methods have failed. No! our countrymen will adhere to this wise counsel of trusting first to reason, despite Anglo-Indian gibes, and despite evil examples elsewhere to the contrary. I blush for those who, in the latter end of this boasted century of high civilisation, talk still as if might were right, and not right might. Let them for once banish from their minds false logic, and the unmerited apotheosis of the *animal* part of man, and let our rulers raise the worth of their sway by dividing and governing in that higher, nobler and truer sense that the ancient Aryan mind conceived, formulated, and enforced by precept and practice, for ages together." (*Prolonged cheering.*)

Molvi Syud Sharfuddin (*Behar, No.* 197) said: "Mr. President and Brother Delegates,—In rising to support this resolution I have the honor at the same time of informing you that I am a Mahomedan. I am one of the delegates from a place which has been recognized by the Government as a great centre of Mahomedan activity. On reading one of the daily papers of Calcutta I find, as has already been said by one of the speakers, that this Congress has been characterized as a Hindu Congress, but I venture to submit that this designation is erroneous, and that this assemblage constitutes not a Hindu Congress but a National Congress—it is a Congress of all nationalities. If you look to races, you have only to consider attentively the costumes of the members to discover that all Indian Aryan races are represented. If you look to religions, you will find Mahomedans, Christians, Hindus, Parsees, Sikhs, Brahmos and, I believe, small as these communities are, even one Jain and one Jew. As for my own co-religionists I find in this hall Mahomedans from almost every part of this vast Empire. I need not inform you that besides the four Mahomedan delegates from Patna, Messrs. Sayani and Chilmai from Bombay, and Syud Jawad Hosein from Rohilkhund, we have from the province of Oudh Nawab Reza Ally and Mr. Hamid Ally, Haji Mahomed Tegh Bahadur, and Sheikh Kadir Buksh; Syud Abdul Aziz from Nagpur, and Sheikh Wazir Ally from Sarun; there are also Mahomedan gentlemen from Dacca, Howrah, Rungpore, Khulna, Nuddea, Tipperah, Julpiguri, Mymensing, Benares and other places, and with all these is it possible for any one to say truly that this is merely a Hindu Congress? (*Loud cheers.*) I may also inform you, before I come to the subject before the meeting, that I have found the greatest sympathy with the objects of this Congress amongst the Mahomedans of Behar. (*Cheers*). There may be a few isolated exceptions; there may be some few gentlemen, either good conservatives of the old school who hold that whatever is, is best, or who have not been correctly informed of the objects of this Congress, and who therefore hang back; but these I can truly assure you are only the exceptions that prove the rule. (*Cheers.*) No doubt there are not so many Mahomedans here as in proportion to their numbers we might have expected, but in the first place our people are backward; and in the second place this schism of the Calcutta Mahomedan leaders was quite unexpected. I conversed yesterday with some Mahomedan gentlemen from Oudh who informed me that if they had had any knowledge of the unhappy differences which exist amongst the Mahomedans of Calcutta, leading many of these to abstain from participating in the Congress, they could have brought down any number of Mahomedans of the highest ranks, talookdars and rajahs, from Oudh, and I mention this circumstance as another evidence that this Congress is not a Hindu Congress only but a National Indian Congress, in which, broadly speaking, all the races and creeds of India are equally interested and equally sympathise. (*Loud cheers.*)

"With respect to the resolution which is now before us I need not take up much of your time, as the three gentlemen who have preceded me have already demonstrated its essential character at great length. Let me simply say that, on behalf of my brother delegates from Behar, I fully support this resolution. (*Loud cheers.*) It is almost needless to say that as natives of India we are better versed in the manners and customs, the ideas and convictions, the wants and wishes of our people than any Englishman can be. How then can it be otherwise than reasonable that, after having been educated by the magnanimity of the people of England, we should ask from them that share in the administration of our country which they have taught us to desire and have qualified us to deserve? (*Cheers.*) They have already given us a liberal first instalment of local self-government; they have accepted the elective system in many Municipalities; everybody knows that these reforms have worked admirably in practice, and no unprejudiced person can doubt that if the principle of representation be introduced into the Legislative Councils the results will be even more conspicuously advantageous to all parties. (*Cheers.*) And is not our desire natural? We want to be legislated for by people who have a real knowledge of our habits and customs; by people who understand us, who are of us, not by foreigners and strangers, who, however good their will, lack that intimate sympathy with, and participation in, our views and aspirations which is essential if their measures are to command anything like the approval and unanimous assent of the country. (*Prolonged cheering.*) The Government has already recognised to some extent the reasonableness of our claim, and has given us grounds for hoping that they are not unwilling gradually to concede it. Everybody here remembers, during the controversy about the Bengal Tenancy Act, the laudable desire of the Government to secure some sort of representation in the Council, of both the zemindar and the ryot classes; and many other instances might be cited to show that they themselves are aware of the dangers of the present blindfold system of legislating for people of whom they know little and understand less. So that this great reform is already well within the sphere of practical politics, and all we have to do is to press, and press for it earnestly, energetically, steadily and perseveringly until we *get* it, and in getting it crown our rulers, teachers, friends and guides with new and imperishable laurels. I have heard a Roman apothegm, *Finis coronat opus,* and in no way can Great Britain more gloriously crown her noble work in India than by the introduction here of representative institutions." (*Loud and enthusiastic cheers.*)

Sheik Kadir Buksh (*Fyzabad, No.* 185) said, speaking in Urdu: "After the eloquent speeches to which we have all listened with so much pride and pleasure, it may seem almost an impertinence for me, a mere merchant and, compared with so many of our distinguished fellow-countrymen that I see around me, an uneducated man, to presume to trespass on your time. But I have to say that in mv province our people are quite fit for and thoroughly appreciate representative institutions. Those co-religionists of mine, and I am happy to say that their number is limited in the extreme, (*cheers*) who pretend that the introduction of a representative element in the councils will do our community no good, simply talk nonsense. I have now sat some time on an elected Municipal Board, and I wish they would ask any Mahomedan of my district how he appreciates this boon of local self-government that we already possess. We are Hindus and Mahomedans alike on our Board. Never has there been anv difference between us arising out of religious feelings, and how should there be? We are not Moulvis and Pundits meeting to argue on religious topics, but business-men meeting to arrange for keeping the town clean and healthy, and for levying the funds, required for these purposes, equitably and with as little expense and worry to the rate-payers as may be. If we keep the place dirty and cholera comes, will it not kill us Mahomedans as well as the Hindus? If we get pure good water, shall we not drink it as well as they? And so it will be with the proposed elected Legislative Councils. Will it not be all our object to keep the Government out of useless wars, to make them economize, to reduce taxation, to give fair play to native talent, to encourage Indian industries? Religion is one thing and business another, and only very foolish or ill-disposed persons mix the two together and try to set any sect against a work which is equally for the good of all sects." (*Vociferous cheering.*)

MALIK BHUGWAN DAS (*Dera Ismail Khan, No.* 110), speaking in Urdu, said: "We ought really to congratulate ourselves on having brought together in one assemblage so many delegates from so many parts of the country. (*Cheers.*) It is only when one goes about amongst them, and has the pleasure of making their acquaintance and finding out who and what they are and whence they come, that one begins to understand how truly national is this meeting. (*Cheers.*) What profession or occupation, what class, what race, what creed is not represented? It is wonderful (*cheers*), and nothing in my whole life has pleased me so much as having been able to take part in this Congress, and so actually to see gentlemen living in all those wonderful distant parts whose names even I had previously scarcely heard. Certainly I thought they would be altogether different, and so their dress is, but when I come to talk to them I find they are much the same as I am; and when I speak of our grievances, I find that theirs are much the same, and when I tell them of our aspirations, why they are theirs also. Yes they may differ in dress, in mother tongue, in customs, in place of birth, but I find that in all essentials they are one with me, for they are all fellow-countrymen. (*Loud and prolonged cheers.*) And what is this I see in one of the English papers, that they call this a Hindu Congress? Why Hindu? Why not Mahomedan? Does it follow because a man is a Hindu that he does not represent Mahomedans as well as Hindus? (*Loud cheers.*) I am a Hindu, perhaps people fancy I only represent Hindus, but that is far from the case. Malik Nebraj and I are delegates from an Association composed both of Hindus and Mahomedans (*cheers*), and these Hindus and Mahomedans meeting jointly appointed us two to represent them. The Mahomedans did not say let us appoint a Mahomedan, let us not appoint a Hindu, but they said let us have the best men to represent us, and they never troubled to think whether those men belonged to this faith or that faith, because there is none of that nonsense there in these public matters; and we feel that in these we are all one, all brethren. Of course we are *not* the best men, but we were, they were kind enough to think, the best men who could conveniently come, and so they sent us. So even if there were only Hindus like us, but sent by Mahomedans, it could not be a Hindu Congress (*cheers*); but I look round and I see many Mahomedans, and I see Sikhs and I see Christians and Parsees, and I do not understand this foolishness of calling us a Hindu Congress. (*Cheers.*) Either the editor of that paper is a very ignorant man, and it is the ignorance on all Indian matters of Europeans which is doing India so much harm, and to provide against which our present resolution is partly intended, or he must be a sort of British Afghan (*loud cheers*), who to gain some end says what he knows is not a fact. But to turn to the resolution before the Congress, and I do so asking pardon for having to long detained you. I do not think that, as to the general question, the previous eloquent speakers have left me anything to say. But there are some local details to which I wish to draw your attention. The first is that this system of representation and of Government by councils composed of our own people is indigenous in the Punjab, and from time immemorial the frontier tribes, though wanting in education, have always possessed sufficient intelligence to manage matters admirably for themselves. We had regular representative legislative councils long before we had even heard the name of England, and those councils made laws, which, though not compiled in bulky statute books, were none the less binding and obeyed, and to this day the independent frontier tribes in our neighbourhood are governed by just such councils, and these councils have made laws from time to time, and if a man commit adultery or other offence he is tried by those councils and convicted and sentenced according to those laws, which the whole tribe unites to uphold, because they are home-made and commend themselves to all minds as right and just. (*Cheers.*)

"Now we people inside the frontier were never at any time behind the *Pushtunis*—I mean the frontier tribes outside the frontier—in wisdom or capacity for managing our own affairs. And if they, still ignorant and unenlightened, get on so well under representative institutions. how much better may we be expected to thrive under them, now that, by reason of the widespread, though not as yet what you call high, education which the British Government has given us, we are so much more advanced in all such matters than our *Pushtuni* neighbours.

"And as a matter of fact there is a strong desire throughout all parts of the Punjab for a local council—above all a local council largely composed of gentlemen of the province to make the laws and manage the public affairs of the province, and as there never was and never will be, as I have, on a former occasion, explained, any want of thoroughly capable men to sit in that council, I do not see why the British Government, that has done so much for us and, as we believe, where I come from, so honestly wishes to do us good, should not, in compliance with the universal desire, grant us all, that this resolution, which I support with all my heart, advocates and prays for.

"Great are the benefits that have been conferred on us by the British Government. May it prosper for ever and ever, and a third time I say ever, but that this may be so let it never forget that its real strength lies, not in its artillery, but in the hold it has, and I pray God may ever retain, on the hearts of its subjects." (*Prolonged cheering.*)

KHAJEH ABDOOL ALEEM (*Dacca, No.* 351), speaking in Urdu, said : "This gentleman comes from the far west, I from the east. I can only say that with us, as with him, Hindus and Mahomedans united to elect delegates. He is a Hindu representing Mahomedans as well as Hindus. I am a Mahomedan representing Hindus as well as Mahomedans. As my Hindu brother from the Western frontier sees no difference between Mahomedans and Hindus in questions relating to the administration of public affairs, so neither do I a Mahomedan from the east see any difference either. We are all subjects of the same Sovereign, all children of the same soil, our more important public interests are the same, our disabilities, grievances and desires identical, and in the name of the great community I came to represent, and of all the Mahomedans of Eastern Bengal I heartily support, and I know they will endorse that support, the resolution that is now before this Congress."

PANDIT MADAN MOHAN MALAVYA (*Allahabad, No.* 118) said : "After the very able and eloquent speeches to which you have already listened, it may seem almost superfluous to add anything as to the expediency, as to the necessity, of the reform contemplated in the fourth resolution. It seems, however, necessary to show to the Government and to the public at large that it is not only by the people of a certain limited portion of the country that the principle of representative government is understood and approved, but that in every presidency and province, of this vast Indian continent, the people equally appreciate it and are equally anxious for its introduction into the administration. Delegates from Calcutta, Bombay, Madras, Patna, Fyzabad, Dera Ismail Khan, Dacca, have already endorsed this fact. Let me a humble delegate from Allahabad confirm their testimony. (*Cheers.*) It is not to the great British Government that we need demonstrate the utility, the expediency, the necessity of this great reform. (*Cheers.*) It might have been necessary to support our petition for this boon with such a demonstration were we governed by some despotic monarch, jealous of the duties, but ignorant and careless of the rights of subjects ; but it is surely unnecessary to say one word in support of such a cause to the British Government or the British nation—to the descendants of those brave and great men who fought and died to obtain for themselves and preserve intact for their children those very institutions which, taught by their example, we now crave *cheers*), who spent their whole lives and shed their hearts blood so freely in maintaining and developing this cherished principle. (*Loud and prolonged cheers.*)

"What is an Englishman without representative institutions? Why not an Englishman at all (*cheers*), a mere sham (*cheers*), a base imitation (*cheers*), and I often wonder as I look round at our nominally English magnates how they have the face to call themselves Englishmen and yet deny us representative institutions, and struggle to maintain despotic ones. (*Loud cheers.*) Representative institutions are as much a part of the true Briton as his language and his literature. Will any one tell me that Great Britain will, in cold blood, deny us, her free-born subjects, the first of these when, by the gift of the two latter, she has qualified us to appreciate and incited us to desire it? (*Cheers.*)

"No taxation without representation. That is the first commandment in the Englishman's Political Bible; how can he palter with his conscience and tax us here, his free and educated fellow-subjects, as if we were dumb sheep or cattle? But we are not dumb any longer. India has found a voice at last in this great Congress, and in it, and through it, we call on England to be true to her traditions, her instincts, and herself, and grant us our rights as free-born British citizens. (*Prolonged cheering.*) Representation is a thing required in every part of the world, as soon as a nation emerges from barbarism, even where rulers and ruled are one people, having one common language, domicile, religion, literature, and what not, and how much more so is it needful in this country? We know that the English people, true to their higher instincts, have introduced here so much that is good, that to them we owe many and great blessings. (*Cheers.*) We acknowledge these blessings with gratitude; we owe a heavy debt of gratitude to the English people, and there is no fear of our ever forgetting our obligations to them. (*Loud cheers.*) But while we are thus deeply grateful for the blessings we enjoy we cannot but feel that there are still many points in which our condition can be and ought to be improved, and we see first and foremost that the system of administration, that now obtains, is despotic (*loud cheers*), and is deficient in the principle of representation, the fundamental characteristic of a free government. (*Cheers.*) There is not a true-born Englishman who would not be horrified if told that the Government of India dealt with the whole people of India as slaves, and yet, if any such man will fairly face the facts of the case, he will be compelled to admit that, despite all other good gifts, in this matter of excluding us from all share in the government of our own country, the government is really treating us as mere slaves. The right to be represented is inherent in every educated free-born British subject. (*Loud cheers.*) Gentlemen, we all recognize the great Proclamation of 1858 as our Magna Charta, and in that Proclamation Her Gracious Majesty was pleased to assure us solemnly that she would regard all her subjects of whatever race, creed or colour with an equal eye, and consider the welfare of all equally. Her Majesty's Indian subjects were therefore to be regarded in the same light as her subjects in any of her other colonies and possessions. But how can it be said that we are treated in the same way when we are not allowed the slightest voice in the administration (*Cheers*), when we are not allowed the opportunity of saying one word as to our sentiments in regard to the laws and edicts which year by year are flung forth over the land, and under which we have to live and suffer? (*Cheers.*) I ask you if that is regarding us with an equal eye, if that is treating us as those of the English race in other possessions of Her Majesty are treated? (*Cheers.*)

"I am sorry that time does not allow me to speak fully and freely on this great subject, but after all in the present day it is almost a waste of time to prove either the reasonable character or the justice of our claim. Every cultured mind admits this, at any rate as an abstract proposition. It is always imaginary practical difficulties, or our supposed incapacity, that is urged. But when you see Indians competing with Englishmen in every walk of life to which they can find or force an entrance, and not unfrequently emerging triumphant from the friendly contest (*loud cheers*), it is extremely inconsistent to say that they are unfitted to assist in the consideration and preparation of laws for their own people, and incapable of joining in that great work of administration, which has, or should have, for its sole object the prosperity of their native land (*cheers*); and I ask every generous English mind to say whether we have not a strong ground for complaining against this exclusion as a piece of un-English injustice. Surely it is the desire of every generous-hearted Englishman who loves liberty to confer the freedom, he himself enjoys, on all—

> "For he," as an English Poet says, "that values liberty, confines
> "His zeal for her predominance within
> "No narrow bounds; her cause engages him
> "Wherever pleaded. 'Tis the cause of man." (*Loud cheering.*)

"But our President signs that I am exceeding the allotted period, and I will only add may the cause of the people of India, the cause of liberty and right, engage the attention, heart and soul, of every honest Englishman in India and in England, and may each true Briton, who values the rights, the privileges, the freedom which have made him and his country what they are, aid us, like true Britons, to the fruition of our aspirations for equal rights, equal privileges and equal freedom." (*Loud cheers.*)

LALA KANHYA LAL (*Punjab, No.* 104) said: "The second clause of the resolution makes mention of the several provinces in which legislative councils of the reformed type should be established, but it omits to mention* the Punjab. I presume that this is an oversight, as the Punjab is, as Malik Bhugwan Das has already told you, quite prepared and fitted for such representative institutions. The amount of confidence which was placed by the people in their own representative institutions before the introduction of British rule into the Punjab is well known: the decisions pronounced by punchayets were looked upon as oracles proceeding from the deity, as the people said, *panch panch mil, khuda míl* (*cheers*), and this shows what implicit confidence was placed by the people in the decisions of their own representatives. The present system of appointing members to the Legislative Councils is by nomination: the Government nominate their own officials and sometimes other men having personal influence with leading officials and ready to vote as they are told. The officials are paid heavy salaries and have an interest in maintaining heavy taxation upon the people and keeping up all the many official abuses, and therefore, I think, I am justified in saying that the Government is not at present acting fairly by us. It may seem churlish in us to cast such an imputation upon a nation which has in the past done so much for us in the way of civilizing this country; but it is their present persistency in not giving us fair play, and not granting us that representation that we ask for, and that, as I maintain, we are entitled to, that leads us to cast such imputations upon them: if they fairly concede to us a proper system of representation our mouths will be shut for ever, and they will become, once more to us, what we used to believe them to be."

* This was a typographical error in one set of the printed draft resolutions,

Munshi Syud Abdul Aziz (*Nagpur, No.* 190), speaking in Urdu, said : "I wish to say a word or two only. First I want to explain that, backwards as our province is, all those of us who are at all educated deeply sympathize in the objects of this Congress, and most especially in this resolution now under consideration, and we look forward hopefully to having a council of our own at Nagpur with elected members. Even now such a council would be a great boon to us, and every year it will grow more and more of a necessity. Secondly, as my co-religionists from Dacca, Fyzabad, and other places have told you, it is quite ridiculous to pretend that the Mahomedans who have any sort of education are wanting in interest in this Congress, or consider that their interests differ from those of their Hindu brethren where these administrative reforms are concerned. Our numbers are not large in the Central Provinces, but so far as we go, we are as heartily with you as the rest of the community."

Pandit Jwala Datt Joshi (*Kumaon, No.* 150) said : "This subject has been so exhaustively discussed by the gentlemen who have preceded me that it really leaves nothing for me to say as to the matter of the resolution. I only rise to say before the Congress that I am a delegate from a province where Hindus and Mahomedans live together in perfect harmony, and that I represent both communities—that both sympathize in all the work of the Congress, and both have at heart (I mean those amongst them at all educated) the reform in the administration which is asked for in the resolution under discussion. There has been a good deal of writing in some of the papers about this demand for representation, now not denied to be widespread, being the result of wire pulling, and I want to say that so far from this, if no one else in the whole country even had taken up the matter, we in Kumaon should have independently worked for it. No one who knows us will believe that there are any men living who can wire pull us." (*Cheers.*)

Pandit Shyam Narain (*Lucknow, No.* 173), speaking in Urdu, said: "Mr. Chairman and Gentlemen,—I am unable to express my joy when I see before me so many patriotic men taking part in the deliberations of this great National Congress. It is a mistake to suppose that only English-knowing natives sympathize with the objects of this Congress or that our Mahomedan brethren do not quite as well appreciate them as ourselves. (*Cheers.*) I come from Lucknow which stands third or fourth in respect to population, though in English education it is far behind other Indian cities, and stands the first city in India in respect to the number of Mahomedan Princes and Nawabs who have made it their home. (*Cheers.*) Oudh was annexed only some 30 years ago. The Riaf-i-Am Association which has sent me here as one of its delegates has been established for some ten years. It counts among its members many Princes, Nawabs and Talukdars. The majority of its members are Mahomedans. It responded to the call of our countrymen most enthusiastically. (*Cheers.*) It elected more delegates than those that have joined the Congress. Its President, Shaikh Reza Hosain, on his way down to Calcutta, fell ill at Cawnpore. The ill-founded rumour of cholera kept some back. Among those that have come from Lucknow, Nawab Reza Ali Khan represents the Shia nobility; Mr. Hamid Ali represents the English-educated Mahomedans, and Haji Mahomed Tegh Bahadur, Proprietors of *Rozana* (an Urdu Daily), represents the Sunni sect of Lucknow Mahomedan. There are also Kashmiri Pundits, Khatri, Kayasth and Bengalees, all representative men among the Lucknow delegates. One of our brother delegates had received a letter from a Doctor advising him not to go to Calcutta, but sympathy with the noble objects of this Congress prevailed against the fear of cholera.

"In support of this fourth resolution I beg to say that I consider it essential to the true progress of my country. (*Cheers.*) So long as some representative element be not introduced into the several Legislative Councils of India, so long this country will not be able to get over its present difficulties. Unless the right to elect members to our Legislative Councils be conferred upon us the true interests of neither the government of this country nor of its people will ever be secured. (*Cheers.*) It is a common saying among us that God manifests Himself in the Punchayet. Unless we have, in our Legislative Councils, men elected by us and conversant with our inner life, no suitable laws to promote our true happiness can ever be enacted. As the Government of our country is the most civilized Government in the world and our true well-wisher, I confidently expect that it will grant our request. I have every reason to expect nothing but kindness from our most merciful mother, the Queen Empress, and the most enlightened British Parliament, if only our humble petition and the true state of our case be laid before them." (*Loud cheers.*)

Mr. Devi Charan Barua (*Debrughur, Assam, No.* 429) said : "I speak on behalf of the Province of Assam when I say that we are quite in accord with you on the question of representation. The introduction of a representative system in some form is as urgently required in Assam as it is in all the other provinces of the whole Empire of India. Unless a representative system is introduced the real wants of the country can scarcely be met. Allowing freely that our rulers, foreigners and strangers as they are to all that most intimately affects us, are actuated by the highest motives and do their best for us, the present state of the country, and the universal feeling that pervades it, sufficiently show that neither the purity of their intentions nor the conscientiousness of their efforts can compensate for that want of practical sympathy with and detailed knowledge of the circumstances of our case, which only our own people, carefully selected by ourselves, can supply. (*Loud cheers.*) I support this resolution most strenuously and on behalf of the whole of the Assam people."

Munshi Sadho Lal (*Benares, No.* 146), speaking in Urdu, said: "No one seems yet to have spoken on behalf of Benares, India's most sacred and one of her largest cities. Perhaps it is not needful. From North to South, from East to West, one feeling pervades the country, and Benares, you may be sure, a stronghold of education, though not as yet English education, is not behind the rest of the country in its aspirations after representative institutions. On behalf then of my brother delegates, and the holy city of Kashi, I declare our entire concurrence in this resolution." (*Cheers.*)

The President then said: "We have seen that there is but one opinion in regard to this resolution. We have heard representatives from every portion of the Empire testifying on its behalf, and it is time now that I put it to you for your formal acceptance."

The resolution was then put and carried by acclamation without a dissentient voice.

Mr. N. N. Gupta (*Sind, No.* 95) said: "I will now, with your permission, move the following resolution: 'That this Congress do invite all public bodies and all Associations throughout the country, humbly and earnestly, to entreat His Excellency the Viceroy to obtain the sanction of Her Majesty's Secretary of State for India, to the appointment of a Commission, to enquire exhaustively into the best method of introducing such a tentative form of representative institutions into India as has been indicated in Resolutions III of the past and IV of the present year's Congress.' (*Resolution V of the Summary, page* 43.) This is a necessary corollary of the resolution just so enthusiastically passed. The whole nation has made up its mind upon the subject, and having done so the next thing is to endeavour to bring home this fact to the authorities here and in England, and induce them, if possible, to take the initial steps necessary for giving practical effect to the universal wish."

Row Sahib M. B. Namjoshi (*Bombay, No.* 69) said: "I have been asked to second this resolution and I gladly do so. The only remark I think necessary is that, after having passed the fourth resolution, it becomes absolutely necessary to make this prayer to the Government. We have affirmed the proposition that the several provinces of the Empire are prepared for representative Legislative Councils, and this would naturally follow with the progress we have been making since the passing of the Indian Council's Act of 1861. We have been saying for several years past that we are prepared for the introduction of representative Legislative Councils, that we are fit for the privilege of representation; we have unanimously moreover now decided that the grant of this privilege has become a necessity from all points of view whether our own or that of our rulers (if only they can realise their own highest interests), and now we invite the Government to make inquiry and ascertain whether all things are not exactly in accordance with what we have said, and whether the present condition of the country does, or does not, render the proposed reform desirable and expedient." (*Cheers.*)

Kumar Binay Krishna (*Calcutta, No.* 242) said: "I support the resolution, and I do so with my whole heart, but will not take up the time of the Congress with further discussion at this late hour."

The President said: "This proposition, I dare say, requires no further discussion. It is only an appeal to the Government to satisfy themselves by the appointment of a Commission or otherwise, that what we ask is reasonable."

The motion was then put and carried unanimously.

Row Sahib P. Rangiah Naidu (*Madras, No.* 1) said: "I beg to move the following resolution: 'That copies of these resolutions be forwarded to His Excellency the Viceroy in Council, with the humble requests, that he will cause the first resolution to be submitted in due course to Her Majesty the Queen Empress; that he will cause all the resolutions to be laid before Her Majesty's Secretary of State for India; and that he himself will be graciously pleased, in consultation with his colleagues, to accord them his best consideration.' (*Resolution XV of Summary, page* 45.) I don't think I need detain you longer. The resolution speaks for itself and must commend itself to every one."

Mr. Sorabjee F. Patell (*Bombay, No.* 50) said: "I have great pleasure in seconding this resolution. You will remember the object of our first resolution. It was in connection with the Jubilee, a memorable event which we could not more appropriately celebrate. Our second request is that H. E. the Viceroy will honor us by sending all the resolutions at which this National Congress has arrived officially to Her Majesty's Secretary of State for India, and our third that he will himself in consultation with his colleagues accord them his best consideration, and I am sure you will agree with me that, knowing what we do of His Excellency, we have every reason to hope and believe that in these, and all other matters, he will do the best he can for us and our country." (*Cheers.*)

THE PRESIDENT said: "I may now I suppose put the resolution."

The resolution was then put and passed unanimously.

MR. W. C. BONNERJEE (*Calcutta, No.* 275) said: "I am afraid I am transgressing the rule our President laid down this morning that no new subject should be introduced at this Congress. But I have no doubt you will agree that an exception should be made in favor of the subject that I am about to propose. My opinion is that permanent Committees of this Congress ought to be constituted in all the provinces of India. (*Loud cheers.*) Each province will, no doubt fix the number of its own Committee, and appoint its own Committee men, but a Committee, small or large, is absolutely requisite in every province. Without such Committees it is quite impossible to keep up a regular correspondence between all the different parts of the country, and so to arrive in due time at a general agreement as to the various questions on which action is to be taken at the Congress.

"I propose, therefore, that Standing Congress-Committees be constituted at all important centres." (*Resolution XIII of Summary, page* 45.)

MR. N. G. CHANDAVARKAR (*Bombay, No.* 49) said: "I beg to second the resolution. We are all agreed as to the necessity of that arrangement, and I need say no more on the subject."

The resolution was then put to the vote, and unanimously agreed to.

MR. A. O. HUME (*Punjab, No.* 112) said: "I also, like my friend Mr. Bonnerjee, am about to venture to transgress the ruling of the President by introducing a subject not included in the list of business. But my excuse is that, if the resolution I have to propose be a new one, it is at any rate a very little one, and when you hear what it is, you will, I am sure, pardon my transgression, and cordially assent to my proposition. I now propose that the Third Indian National Congress assemble at Madras on the 27th of December, 1887. (*Resolution XIV of Summary, page* 45.) (*Loud and prolonged cheering.*) It is, I see, quite needless for me to commend this resolution to your acceptance or to say a single word more."

THE HON'BLE S. SUBRAMANIA IYER (*Madras, No.* 2) said: "It is my pleasant duty to second this resolution, and first I desire to say that words fail me in expressing our heartfelt thanks to our Calcutta brethren for the hospitable, nay noble, manner in which they have received the delegates from all parts of India. I am not speaking the language of exaggeration when I say that they have imposed upon us a weighty and lasting debt of gratitude. In the next place it is my duty—and I speak the feeling of my brethren here—to convey our warmest and heartiest thanks to the Reception Committee for the excellent reception they have accorded us and to say how deeply we feel the persistent and patient kindness with which Mr. Ghosal, Baboos Girija Bhusan and Kumud Chunder Mookerjee, not to mention other gentlemen whose names I have not yet learned to pronounce, have provided for all our wants and anticipated all our wishes. (*Cheers.*) I can assure you that our most sanguine expectations of the character of the reception which we were to receive in Calcutta have been exceeded by the reality. (*Cheers.*) Gentlemen, the proposal to hold this Congress next year at Madras was made by me last year at Bombay, but I did not press it for reasons which I then explained. The reception which we have received here makes my heart falter as to whether I should press it at this time, but my brethren insist on our undertaking the duty, and asking you to hold the Congress next year at Madras. (*Loud cheers.*) If the invitation which I now make to you is accepted, I can only assure that we shall give you the best, the most cordial, the most loving reception which lies in our power, though it may not be so princely as that which our Calcutta brethren have here accorded to us. (*Cheers.*) Therefore, in the name of my Madras colleagues who are here assembled, and in the name of our Madras brethren, whose representatives we are, I invite you to meet us next December in the Capital of the Presidency which terminates with Cape Comorin, and I hope that you will accept this invitation in the hearty and brotherly spirit in which, despite all our misgivings as to our possible shortcomings, we now give it." (*Loud cheers.*)

MR. SORABJEE F. PATELL (*Bombay, No.* 50) said: "I am glad to be allowed to join in thanking the Reception Committee, their able secretaries, and all our Bengal friends who have taken part in the kind work of receiving us. They have not only provided most completely for the accommodation of all the delegates, but have also in a thousand ways promoted their comfort, and we are all, in common gratitude, bound to, and *do*, most heartily thank them for having so cordially welcomed us and so kindly cared for us."

THE PRESIDENT, in putting the resolution, said: "I am sure all here present will respond to the kind invitation of our Madras friends with the utmost enthusiasm."

The motion was then carried by acclamation.

THE HONORABLE PEARY MOHUN MOOKERJEE (*Calcutta*, [*No.* 233) said: "It only remains for me to propose a vote of thanks to the President, which I have, accordingly, the greatest pleasure in now doing."

MR. S. H. CHIPLUNKAR (*Poona*, *No.* 65) seconded the motion, which was carried by acclamation.

MR. SURENDRA NATH BANERJEE (*Calcutta*, *No.* 239) said: "I propose a vote of thanks to the delegates for having come from all parts of India to this capital. And in doing so I will only make one remark. There are a great many Mahomedan gentlemen of Upper India amongst us here. I would ask them to go back and exercise their influence in preventing, in future, those fratricidal tumults and *emeutes* between Hindus and Mahomedans, which have occurred so frequently in recent times, and which we all so deeply deplore. I only hope their efforts will be crowned with that complete success which the righteousness of the cause deserves." (*Long cheers.*)

The motion was then put and carried by acclamation.

THE PRESIDENT said: "In responding to the vote of thanks, which you have so kindly accorded to me, I hope the meeting will allow me to say that my expectations as to the admirable conduct of this large assembly have been thoroughly fulfilled and more than fulfilled. I am only speaking tamely I fear when I say that from first to last nothing could possibly have been more honourable to our country than the conduct of all concerned or than the spirit that has pervaded the entire assemblage. In the heat of argument, under that greatest of all stimuli, patriotic enthusiasm, not one word, I believe, has escaped a single speaker that he need wish unspoken. Kindness, courtesy and a spirit of cheerful mutual concession have pervaded our proceedings, which, but for this, could never have reached this happy and successful termination. (*Loud cheers.*) You are pleased to thank me, but it is for me rather to thank you, for had it not been for the noble spirit in which each and all of you have co-operated in the work and for the support which you have so heartily afforded me in respect of every proposition, which has come before the Congress, I could never have succeeded in thus bringing to a successful close the important business that devolved upon us. (*Cheers.*) I heartily, therefore, thank you one and all for having enabled me to perform my duty and for having made it so easy for me to do it. (*Loud cheers.*)

"There is, however, just one point to which I ought perhaps to refer more particularly, and that is to the spirit of fairness and moderation and respect towards the Government which has characterized your proceedings from the beginning to the end. I need hardly say how gratified I have been to observe how thoroughly all have seemed to be imbued with that spirit. Not only is it to our interest that it should be so, but it is what the Government, after all they have done for us, have a just right to expect from us. (*Cheers.*) And I only hope that the example which this great assemblage has set in this respect will be followed not only at all future meetings of the Congress, not only by all and every Association throughout the country, but also by the entire Indian Press, some members of which, under the influence of the bad example too often set to them by a portion of the Anglo-Indian Press, have at times, it must be confessed, transgressed in this respect. (*Hear, hear.*) If we really desire to be respected, if we wish our requests to be attended to, if we honestly expect that the English nation will do its duty toward us, we must prove ourselves worthy by showing that we are never unreasonable, never violent, never uncharitable. We must show that we are earnest, but temperate, cognizant of our own rights, but respectful of those of others; expecting the fairest constructions of our own acts and motives, and conceding these to those of others; that, in a word, whatever our status in life, high or low, rich or poor, we have become gentlemen in the highest sense of the word. Unless we are and can prove ourselves gentlemen in this highest, noblest sense, I do not know that we are worthy to receive the concessions for which we are pressing. (*Loud cheers.*) I do not think I need trouble the Congress with any further remarks. I will simply say once more: I thank you. I thank you, for myself, for the honour you have done me in choosing me as President, and for the generous kindness with which you have upheld me in the performance of the responsible duties of that high position, and I thank you on behalf of all your countrymen—on behalf of posterity—for the noble manner in which, at this great Congress—which history will not readily forget—you have upheld the credit, the character, the dignity of our beloved India." (*Long and enthusiastic cheering.*)

Three cheers were next called for, for Her Most Gracious Majesty the Queen-Empress; three for His Excellency the Viceroy; three for the Provincial Governors and Lieutenant-Governors, and three more for Mr. A O. Hume, which were all given most warmly and vehemently.

The Congress was then dissolved.

APPENDIX I.

LIST OF DELEGATES.

WHO ATTENDED* THE

SECOND INDIAN NATIONAL CONGRESS,

HELD AT CALCUTTA, DECEMBER 1886.

Number.	Presidency.	Province.	District or City.	Names of the Delegates.	Place or Association which they represent.	Remarks.
1	Madras		Madras	Rao Sahib P. Rangiah Naidu...	Madras Mahajana Sabha and Triplicane Literary Society.	Landed Proprietor, Ml. Councillor, Dist. Board Member, President, Mahajana Sabha.
2	"		"	Hon. S. Subramania Iyer, B.L.	Mahajana Sabha.	Vakil, High Court, and Member, Madras Legislative Council.
3	"		"	Mr. T. Numberumal Chettiar, B.A.	"	Merchant.
4	"		"	Rao Sahib A. Danakoti Mudaliar Avl.	"	Zemindar of Malepankum, Municipal Councillor, Wandiwash.
5	"		"	Mr. G. Subramania Iyer, B.A.	"	Editor of the "Hindu."
6	"		"	Rao Sahib P. Anunda Charlu, B.L.	"	Vakil, High Court, Ml. Councillor and Secretary, Mahajana Sabha.
7	"		"	Mr. P. Subramania Iyer ...	"	Articled Clerk.
8	"		"	Mr. M. Ramasawmy Naidu ...	"	Merchant and Contractor.
9	"		"	Mr. M. Veeraraghava Chariar, B.A.	Mahajana Sabha and Trip. Lit. Society.	Joint-Editor of the "Hindu," and Secy., Mahajana Sabha.
10	"		"	Mr. M. G. Sriranga Chariar, B.A., B.L.	Madras M. Sabha.	Vakil, High Court.
11	"		"	Mr. N. Radhakrishna Iyer ...	Madras	

* Many more delegates were nominated or elected, but were prevented by sickness, business, &c., from attending.

LIST OF DELEGATES.

Number.	Presidency.	Province.	District or City.	Names of the Delegates.	Place or Association which they represent.	REMARKS.
12	Madras		Madras	Mr. M. Aguppah Mudaliar ...	Madras	Municipal Commr., Burmah.
13	"		"	Mr. N. Kristnasawmy Naidu, B.A., B.L.	The Hindu Excelsior Reading Rooms.	
14	"		"	Mr. A. C. Parthasaradhi Naidu	Madras	Editor of the "Andhraprakasika."
15	"		Ganjam Dt.	Rao Sahib Pakala Gopal Row, B.A.	Berhampore	Pleader, District Court, Landholder and Municipal Councillor.
16	"		Vizagapatam Dist.	Mr. Vepa Kristna Moorthy Pantulu Garu, M.A.	Vizagapatam and Bimlipatam.	Pleader, Dist. Court.
17	"		"	Mr. P. Venkannah Pantulu Garu.	"	Ditto ditto.
18	"		Godavery District.	Rao Sahib Singaraju V. Subboroyudu Pantulu Garu, B.L.	Rajamundry and Masulipatam.	Vakil, High Court, Masulipatam, and Ml. Councillor.
	"		Kristna Dt.	Do. Do. ...	Bezwada, Gudiveda and Kristna	Ditto ditto.
19	"		Nellore Dt.	Rao Sahib S. Narayana Sawmy Chetty, B.A.	Nellore and Ongole.	Pleader, District Court, and Municipal Councillor and Dist. Board Member.
20	"		"	Mr. M. Venkata Subba Row ...	"	Pleader, Munsiff's Court.
21	"		"	Mr. Anchoor Subbanaidu ...	"	Merchant and Landed Proprietor.
22	"		"	Mr. Kalanakur Vencata Reddy	"	Contractor.
23	"		Bellary Dt.	Rao Bahadur A Sabapathy Mudaliar Avl.	Bellary	Merchant, Chairman, Municipal Council.

LIST OF DELEGATES.

Number.	Presidency.	Province.	District or City.	Names of the Delegates.	Place or Association which they represent.	REMARKS.
24	Madras		Bellary Dt.	Mr. K. Venkata Rao Garu ...	Hospett, Bellary	1st Grade Pleader and Landholder.
25	„		„	Khan Sahib Kurnool Abdool Kareem Saheb.	Bellary.	Municipal Councillor and Merchant.
26	„		„	Mr. T. Chidambara Row Garu, B.A.	„	1st Grade Pleader.
27	„		„	Mr. L. Rama Row ...	„	District Registrar. President, Rate-payers' Association, Bellary.
28	„		„	Mr. C. E. Ranganatham Mudaliar.	„	Medical Officer.
29	„		Anantpur District.	Mr. Y. Choudappa Garu ...	Gooty	Pleader and Ryot and Chairman of the Gooty Union.
30	„		„	Mr. N. Nagesa Row Garu ...	Penukondah and Gooty.	Do. do. and member of the Gooty Taluqa Board.
31	„		„	Rao Sahib P. Kesava Pillai Avl	Anantpore and Gooty	Pleader and Ryot and Member of the District Board. Secy, Gooty People's Association.
32	„		„	Mr. P. Venketachella Pillai ...	„	Landholder.
33	„		Kurnool.	Rao Sahib V. Soonki Reddy Garu.	Kurnool.	Local Fund Member, Municipal Councillor, Landholder.
34	„		„	Rao Sahib P. Chenchi Reddy Garu.	„	Ditto
35	„		„	Rao Sahib M. Govinda Reddy Garu.	„	Ditto.
36	„		North Arcot D strict	Mr. Chedambadi Subbiah Naidu Garu.	Walajanaggar	1st Grade Pleader.
37	„		„	Mr. V. Gopala Chariar Avl, B.A.	Chittore	1st Grade Pleader
38	„		„	Mr. C. V. Srinivasa Chariar Avl, B.A.	„	Ditto.

LIST OF DELEGATES.

Number.	Presidency.	Province.	District or City.	Names of the Delegates.	Place or Association which they represent.	REMARKS.
39	Madras		Chingleput District	Mr. M. Ramanuja Chariar Avl.	Chingleput	Pleader, District Court.
40	„		„	Mr. Shummugarvya Modaliur Avergal.	„	Zemindar.
41	„		Tanjore Dt.	Rao Sahib S. A. Saminada Iyer Avl	Combaconam.	Pleader, District Court, District Board Member, and the President of the Tanjore People's Association.
42	„		„	Mr. P. Krishnaswamy Aiyar Avl.	Mayaveram.	Mirasdar.
43	„		South Arcot District.	Mr. S. Devanayaga Mudaliar Avl.	Cuddalore	Landed Proprietor and Chairman, Municipal Council.
44	„		„	Mr. T. Govindaswamy Naidoo	„	Landed Proprietor.
45	„		Coimbatore District.	Rao Sahib S. P. Narasimha Naidoo.	Coimbatore	Editor and Proprietor of the "Crescent," Member of the District Board and Director of the Mercantile Bank.
46	„		Raichore	Mr. P. Nagapa Moodaliar ...	Raichore	Cotton Merchant.
47	„		Malabar Dist.	Rao Sahib C. Kunhi Raman Menon Avl., B. A.	Calicut ...	Editor and Managing Proprietor of the "Kerala Patrika" and Municipal Councillor.
48	Bombay	The Concan	Bombay.	Hon. Dadabhai Naoroji ...	Bom. City	Merchant, Member, Legislative Council.
49	„	„	„	Mr. N. G. Chandavarkar, B.A., L.L.B.	„	Editor of the "Induprakash," Pleader, High Court.
50	„	„	„	Mr. Sorabjee F. Patell ...	„	Merchant.

LIST OF DELEGATES.

Numbre.	Presidency.	Province.	District or City.	Names of the Delegates.	Place or Association which they represent.	REMARKS.
51	Bombay	The Concan	Bombay	Mr. Dinshaw E. Watcha ...	Bom. City	Hon. Secretary, Bombay Presidency Association.
52	,,	,,	,,	Mr. Shamrao Vithul ...	,,	Pleader, High Court.
53	,,	,,	,,	Mr. Ghanasham Nilkanth ...	,,	Ditto.
54	,,	,,	,,	Mr. R. M. Sayani ...	,,	Solicitor, High Court, Late Sheriff of Bombay.
55	,,	,,	,,	Kazi Mahomed Ismail Chilmai	,,	Translator and Interpreter, High Court.
56	,,	,,	,,	Mr. Daji Abaji Khare, B.A., L.L.B.	,,	High Court, Pleader.
57	,,	,,	,,	Mr. Chunilal Laloobhai Parekh	Bom. Arya Dnyan Vardhak Sabha.	Vice-President of the A. D. V. Sabha and Merchant.
58	,,	,,	,,	Mr. Gordhandas Khattan ...	Bom. City	Agent, Khattan Makanji Mills.
59	,,	,,	,,	Mr. Mathuradas Lilladhar ...	,,	Mill Owner, Agent, N. G. Eastern Mills.
60	,,	,,	,,	Mr. Bamanji Phirozesha ...	,,	Solicitor, High Court.
61	,,	,,	Tanna.	Rao Sahib Gangadhar Kashinath.	Bassein.	Pleader, Vice-President of the Taluqa Board.
62	,,	,,	,,	Rao Sahib Laxuman Narayan	,,	Landholder and Municipal Commissioner.
63	,,	Deccan	Sangli ...	Mr. Krishnarao Vinayak Khadilkar.	Sangli ...	Landholder.
64	,,	,,	Poona ...	Rao Sahib T. N. Ragmachikar	Poona Sarvajanik Sabha.	Sirdar, Landholder and Ml. Commissioner.
65	,,	,,	,,	Mr. S. H. Chiplunkar ...	,,	Hon. Secretary, Poona Sarvajanik Sabha, and Editor, P. S. S.'s Quarterly Journal.

LIST OF DELEGATES.

Number.	Presidency.	Province.	District or City.	Names of the Delegates.	Place or Association which they represent.	REMARKS.
66	Bombay	Deccan	Poona ...	Mr. S. H. Sathe ...	Poona Sarvajanik Sabha.	Secy., Poona S. Sabha.
67	"	"	"	Mr. Vaman Prabhakar Bhave...	"	Member, P. S. S., and Principal, Poona Native Institution.
68	"	"	"	Mr. M. V. Natu ...		Member, P. S. S. and Landholder.
69	"	"	"	Rao Sahib M. B. Namjoshi ...	"	Municipal Commissioner, and Life Member, Deccan Education Society.
70	"	"	"	Mr. Venkatesh Govind Lailey	"	Pleader and Member, P. S. S.
71	"	"	"	Mr. N. B. Kanitkar ...	Poona ...	Ditto.
72	"	"	"	Rao Sahib Raghunath Daji Nagarkar.	"	Municipal Commissioner, Landholder and Member, P. S. S., Pleader.
73	"	"	"	Rao Sahib Damodar Vidyadhar Gokhie.	"	M. Commissioner and Member, Poona S. S., Assistant Public Prosecutor.
74	"	"	"	Rao Sahib A. Moodookrishna Moodliar.	"	Landholder, Municipal Commissioner and Member, P. S. S.
75	"	"	"	Mr. B. V. Moodliar ...	"	Landholder, M., P. S. S.
76	"	"	Sattara ...	Rao Bahadoor Ganesh Pandurang Agte.	Sattara ...	Vice-President, District Local Board.
77	"	"	"	Rao Sahib Govind Vishnoo Ranade.	"	Ml. C., District Court Pleader.
78	"	"	"	Rao Sahib Ragrunath Pandurang Karandikah.	"	Pleader, Ml. Councillor.

LIST OF DELEGATES.

Number	Presidency.	Province.	District or City.	Names of the Delegates.	Place or Association which they represent.	REMARKS.
79	Bombay	Deccan	Sattara ...	Rao Sahib Balvant Shridhar Sahasrabudhe.	Sattara ...	District Court Pleader, M. Commissioner, Sattara.
80	„	„	„	Rao Sahib Ganesh Gopal Kuber	„	Pleader, District Court, and Ml. Commissioner.
81	„	„	„	Rao Sahib Mahadaji Gopal Kuber	„	Pleader, Member, District Board.
82	„	„	Belgaum	Rao Sahib Sadashiv Balkrishna Bhate.	Belgaum Branch of the Bo. Pres. Assn.	Pleader and M. C., Secy. of Belgaum Branch of Bo. Pres. Assn. Proprietor, New English School.
83	„	Baroda	Baroda ...	Mr. Vithal Luxuman Kavathekar, B.A.		
84	„	Gujrat	Ahmedabad	Mr. Manilal Govind Rai ...	Gujrat Sabha	Vakil.
85	„	„	„	Rao Sahib Kesavlal Motilal ...	„	Vakil and Municipal Commissioner.
86	„	„	„	Mr. Lallubhai Nanabhai Bhat...	„	
87	„	„	Surat ...	Mr. Hoshangji Barjorji, B.A., L.L.B.	Prajahit Vardhak Sabha.	Pleader, High Court.
88	„	„	„	Rao Sahib Harilal Harshadrai Dhruva, B.A., L.L.B.	Do. and Broach, Viragaum & Nariad.	High Court Pleader, Municipal Commissioner, Hon. Secretary, Prajahit Vardhak Sabha.
89	„	„	„	Mr. Manchhashankar Jivanram, B.A., L.L.B.	Surat ...	High Court, Pleader.
90	„	„	„	Mr. Ratiram Durgaram Dave, B.A.	„	Articled Clerk to Messrs. Payne, Gilbert and Sayani, Solicitors, Bombay, Editor of the "Gujarati."
91	„	„	„	Mr. Manchersha Pallonji Kaikobad.	„	Head Master, Mission High School, and Hon. Secy., Prajahit Vardhak Sabha.

LIST OF DELEGATES.

Number.	Presidency.	Province.	District or City.	Names of the Delegates.	Place or Association which they represent.	REMARKS.
92	Bombay	Sind	Sukkur	Rao Sahib Gobind Buksh Awatrai.	Sind Sabha, Sukkur and Hyderabad.	Zemindar, Pleader, Municipal Commissioner and Member, District Board.
93	„	„	Hyderabad	Mr. Hiranand Showkiram Advani.	Sind Sabha, Kurrachi.	Editor of the "Sind Sudhar."
94	„	„	Kurrachi	Seth Vishindas Nihal Chand ...	Kotri and Kurrachi.	Zemindar, Municipal Commissioner and District Board Member.
95	„	„	„	Mr. N. N. Gupta ...	Sind Sabha.	Editor of the "Sind Times."
96	Bengal	Punjab	Lahore	Lala Hukm Chand ...	Indian Association, Lahore	Pleader, Member, Anjumani, Punjab.
97	„	„	„	Sirdar Uttam Singh Sud ...	Lahore ...	Rais, Political Pensioner.
98	„	„	„	Pundit Satyanand Agnihotri ...	„	Brahmo Missionary.
99	„	„	„	Mr. C. Goloknath ...	Indian Association, Lahore	Barrister-at-law, Secy., Indian Association, Lahore.
100	„	„	„	Mr. G. N. Chatterjee ...	„	Asst. Professor, Government College.
101	„	„	„	Baboo Jogendra Chunder Bose, M.A., B.L.	Lahore ...	Pleader, Chief Court, Punjab.
102	„	„	„	Mr. Jagat Narain ...	„	Son of Munshi Hursook Rai, Reis and Proprietor of the "Kohinoor." Manager of the Kohinoor and Member, Unjumani, Punjab.
103	„	„	„	Pundit Din Dayal ...	„	Editor of the "Kohinoor."
104	„	„	„	Lala Kanhya Lal ...	„	Pleader, Chief Court.
105	„	„	Amritsar	Sirdar Bhai Atma Singh ...	Amritsar	Municipal Commissioner.
106	„	„	Ambala	Pundit Shahzada Ram ...	Ambala	Pleader, Chief Court and Municipal Commr.

LIST OF DELEGATES.

Number.	Presidency.	Province.	District or City.	Names of the Delegates.	Place or Association which they represent.	REMARKS.
107	Bengal	Punjab	Ambala.	Lala Murlidhar ...	Ambala.	Pleader.
108	"	"	"	Pundit Tailoo Ram ...	"	
109	"	"	Gurdaspur	Lala Ram Saran Das ...	Gurdaspur	Pleader.
110	"	"	Dera Ismail Khan	Malik Bhugwan Das ...	Dera Ismail Khan	Pleader and Vice-President, Bhratri Sabha.
111	"	"	"	Malik Nebraj ...	"	Fellow B. Sabha.
112	"	"	Simla	A. O. Hume ...		Late of Bengal Civil Service.
113	"	N. W. P.	Allahabad.	Munshi Kashi Prosad ...	Allahabad.	Vakil, High Court, Hon. Secretary of Hindu Samaj and of N. W. P. and Oudh Association. President, Arya Samaj.
114	"	"	"	Lala Ramchurn Dass ...	"	Rais, Banker, Junior Vice-Chairman, Municipal Board and Hony. Magistrate.
115	"	"	"	Konr Sivanath Sinha ...	"	Barrister-at-law, and Vice-President, N. W. P. and Oudh Association.
116	"	"	"	Mr. T. N. Ghose ...	"	Municipal Commissioner.
117	"	"	"	Pundit Newal Behary Bajpaye...	"	Vakil.
118	"	"	"	Pundit Madan Mohan Malavya, B.A.	"	Teacher.
119	"	"	"	Baboo Charoo Chunder Mittra...	"	Senior Vice-Chairman, Municipal Board, Secy., N. W. P. and Oudh Association.
120	"	"	"	Babu Bholanath Chatterjea ...	Hindu Samaj, Allahabad.	
121	"	"	"	Pundit Deokinandan ...	"	Editor of the "Prayag Samachar."
122	"	"	"	Mr. Satyendraprosad Sannyal...	"	
123	"	"	"	Munshi Taraprosad, M.A. ...	"	Vakil.

LIST OF DELEGATES.

Number.	Presidency.	Province	District or City.	Names of the Delegates.	Place or Association which they represent.	REMARKS.
124	Bengal	N. W. P.	Allahabad.	Dr. Brojendranath Banerjea ...	Hindu Samaj, Allahabad.	Medical Practitioner.
125	„	„	„	Baboo Shama Churn Mookerjee	„	Pleader.
126	„	„	„	Pundit Mourgunnesh ...	„	Asst. Secy., Hindu Samaj.
127	„	„	„	Pundit Gobind Rao Goray ...	„	
128	„	„	Brindaban	Pundit Radha Charan Gosvami	„	Municipal Commissioner, Brindaban.
129	„	„	Ballia	Pundit Indira Datta Upadhyaya, M.A.	Ballia Institute	Secy. of Ballia Arya Desopkarini Sabha, and Asst. Secy., Ballia Institute.
130	„	„	„	Baboo Deo Narain Singh ...	„	Talukdar of Mainya.
131	„	„	„	Munshi Devi Prasada ...	Ballia	Pleader and Secy. to the Ballia Municipality.
132	„	„	„	Pundit Bhugwandin Rai ...	„	
133	„	„	Bijnour	Konr Syam Sinha ...	Tajpore	Rais.
134	„	„	Ghazipur	Baboo Sukdeva Narayan Sinha	Ghazipur	
135	„	„	Agra	Konr Kanhi Singh ...	Agra Association	Rais, Municipal Commissioner, Honorary Magistrate, Member, Agra Association.
136	„	„	„	Baboo Jumna Das Biswas ...	„	Editor, Nasim Agra, Chairman "Arya Samaj," Secretary, Agra Association and Municipal Commissioner.
137	„	„	„	Pundit Thakur Prosad ...	„	Assistant Professor of Sanskrit, Agra College.
138	„	„	„	Thakur Umrao Singh ...	„	Rais of Jatow.
139	„	„	Mynpuri	Thakur Zahir Singh ...	Mynpuri	Reis.

LIST OF DELEGATES.

Number.	Presidency.	Province.	District or City.	Names of the Delegates.	Place or Association which they represent.	Remarks.
140	Bengal	N. W. P.	Benares	Baboo Madho Dass ...	Benares.	Rais, Zemindar, Banker, Hon. Magistrate.
141	"	"	"	Baboo Madhusudan Dass ...	"	Rais, Zemindar and Banker.
142	"	"	"	Mirza Mahomed Rahmutullah Beg.	"	Landholder & Pleader.
143	"	"	"	Baboo Abnasi Lall ...	"	Landholder, Rais and Banker.
144	"	"	"	Munshi Rughunandan Prasad, B.A.	"	Pleader & Landholder, Hon. Secy., District Board.
145	"	"	"	Rai Shyam Krishna Das ...	"	Rais, Zemindar and Banker.
146	"	"	"	Munshi Sadho Lal ...	"	Rais, Zemindar and Banker.
147	"	"	"	Baboo Luchman Das ...	"	Rais and Banker.
148	"	"	"	Dr. Chhunnoo Loll ...	"	Medical Practitioner.
149	"	"	"	Baboo Ram Kali Chaudhuri ...	"	Govt. Pensioner, late Subordinate Judge, Benares.
150	"	"	Kumaon	Pundit Jwala Datt Joshi ...	Almora	Vakil, High Court, N. W. P.
151	"	"	Mirzapur	Munshi Bindeswari Prasada ...	Mirzapur Institute	Pleader.
152	"	"	Aligarh	Baboo Bhowanee Chandra Chakravarti, B.A. ...	Aligarh	Vakil.
153	"	"	Farukhabad	Mr. Gopal Hari ...	Vaidik Samaj, Farukhabad.	
154	"	"	"	Mr. Thakur Das ...	Farukhabad	

LIST OF DELEGATES.

Number.	Presidency.	Province.	District or City.	Names of the Delegates.	Place or Association which they represent.	REMARKS.
155	Bengal	N. W. P.	Meerut	Mr. Sitalakant Chatterjee ...	Meerut Association	Pleader.
156	,,	,,	,,	Mr. Mullu Mal ...	,,	Pleader.
157	,,	,,	,,	Mr. Pralhad Singh ...	,,	Rais, Pleader, Hon. Secy., Meerut Association.
158	,,	,,	,,	Mr. Raghobir Saran ...	Meerut	Pleader and Rais.
159	,,	,,	,,	Choudhree Durga Singh ...	,,	
160	,,	,,	Hurdwar	Mr. Binayakant Dat ...	Kankhal	
161	,,	,,	Azimgurh	Mr. Dhunput Lal ...	Azimgurh	Sadar Kanungo.
162	,,	,,	,,	Mr. Basdeo Sahay ...	,,	Head Master, Mission School.
163	,,	,,	Basti	Ramnath Shukla Ballabhay Kabi	Basti	
164	,,	(Rohilkhand)	Muradabad	Pundit Bunwari Lall ...	Muradabad	Proprietor, Sitarahind Newspaper.
165	,,	,,	,,	Moulivi Sayad Jawad Hosein...	British In. Association, Muradabad.	Government Pleader.
166	,,	,,	,,	Baboo Baijnath ...	,,	Pleader, Ml. Commissioner, Assistant Secretary British In. Association Muradabad.
167	,,	Oudh	Lucknow	Nawab Reza Ali Khan Bahadoor	Rifah-Am-Association.	Wasika Holder and Municipal Commissioner.
168	,,	,,	,,	Mr. Hamid Ali Khan ...	,,	Barrister-at-law.
169	,,	,,	,,	Baboo Sri Ram, M.A., B.L. ...	,,	Public Prosecutor, Municipal Commissioner.
170	,,	,,	,,	Baboo Avinash Chunder Ghose, B.L.	,,	Pleader and Municipal Commissioner.

LIST OF DELEGATES.

Number.	Presidency.	Province.	District or City.	Names of the Delegates.	Place or Association which they represent.	Remarks
171	Bengal	Oudh	Lucknow	Baboo Bepin Behari Bose, M.A.	Rifah-Am-Association.	High Court Pleader.
172	„	„	„	Pundit Prannath ...	„	Teacher, Canning College, and Hon. Secretary to the Jalsai Tehzib.
173	„	„	„	Pundit Shyam Narain ...	Lucknow	Rais and Proprietor, Miratul Hind Newspaper.
174	„	„	„	Baboo Gangaprasad Varma ...	„	Editor and Proprietor of the "Hindustani" Newspaper.
175	„	„	„	Haji Mahomed Tegh Bahadur	„	Proprietor of the Rozana Akhbar.
176	„	„	„	Mr. B. M. Ray ...	„	Merchant and Proprietor of the firm of Messrs. H. C. Ray & Co.
177	„	„	Unao	Baboo Hargovind Dyal, M.A.	Unao and Lucknow	Government Pleader.
178	„	„	Partabgurh	Raja Rampal Singh ...	Partabgurh	Talukdar of Kala Kankur.
179	„	„	Bara Banki	Munshi Lalta Pershad ...	Bara Banki & Fyzabad.	Pensioner and Grant Holder.
180	„	„	Fyzabad	Baboo Kakkumul ...	Unjuman-i-Tehzib	Pleader, Chairman, Municipal Board.
181	„	„	„	Munshi Balak Ram ...	„	Pleader, Muncpl. Comr., Member, Dist. Board, Landed Proprietor.
182	„	„	„	Munshi Salagram, B.A., ..	„	Pleader and Member, Municipal Board.
183	„	„	„	Baboo Bepin Behary Dutt, B.L.	„	Ditto.
184	„	„	„	Baboo Gokul Chand ...	„	Pleader, Zemindar and President Unjuman Tehzib.
185	„	„	„	Sheikh Kadir Baksh ...	Fyzabad	Merchant Municipal Commissioner, Hony. Magistrate.

LIST OF DELEGATES.

Number.	Presidency.	Province.	District or City.	Names of the Delegates.	Place or Association which they represent.	REMARKS.
186	Bengal	Oudh	Fyzabad	Baboo Raghunandan ...	Fyzabad	Govt. Pensioner and Mahajan.
187	„	Central Provinces	Nagpur	Mr. Gungadhar Rao Madhaw Chitnavis	Nagpur and Loka Sabha.	Zemindar, son of the late Finance Minister of the late independent Raja of Nagpur, and President of the "Loka Sabha."
188	„	„	„	Rao Sahib Gopal Hurry Bhiday	Nagpur	Pleader, Municipal Commissioner, and Member of the District Council.
189	„	„	„	Rao Sahib Bapoo Rao Dada Tinkheria, M.A.	„	Ditto.
190	„	„	„	Munshi Syud Abdul Aziz ...	„	Pleader.
191	„	„	Khandwa	Baboo Haridas Chatterjee, M.A., B.L.	Khandwa	Pleader.
192	„	„	Jubbulpore	Mr. Behari Lal	Jubbulpore	
193	„	„	Hoshangabad	Baboo Behari Lall Basu ...	Hoshangabad.	Pleader.
194	„	„	„	Baboo Khetra Mohan Bose ...	„	Pleader.
195	„	Central India Agency	Indore	Mr. N. M. Khory ...	Indore	Pleader, Central India Courts, and Law Lecturer, Rajkumar College.
196	„	„	Mhow	Mohendra Nath Chatterjie ...	Central India Association	Pleader.
197	„	Behar	Patna	Moulvi Syud Sharfuddin ...	Bankipore	Barrister-at-law and Zemindar.
198	„	„	„	Baboo Guruprasad Sen M.A., B.L.	„	Pleader, Joint-Editor, "Behar Herald and Indian Chronicle," President, People's Association, and Secretary, Behar Landholder's Association.
199	„	„	„	Baboo Gajadhar Prasad ...	„	Pleader and Municipal Commissioner.

LIST OF DELEGATES.

Number.	Presidency.	Province.	District or City.	Names of the Delegates.	Place or Association which they represent.	Remarks.
200	Bengal	Behar	Patna	Moulavi Ahsan-uttowhid *alias* Wali ul-Hassan.	Bankipore	Zemindar.
201	"	"	"	Baboo Bisseswar Sing ...	"	Ditto and Pleader.
202	"	"	"	Baboo Jai Narayan Bajpaye ...	"	Merchant and Banker.
203	"	"	"	Baboo Buldeo Ram ...	"	Banker.
204	"	"	"	Baboo Govinda Charan, M.A., B.L.	"	Pleader.
205	"	"	"	Baboo PurnenduNarayan Singh, M.A., B.L.	"	Ditto.
206	"	"	"	Baboo Kuldip Sahay ...	"	Ditto.
207	"	"	"	Baboo Narayan Prashad, B.L.	"	Ditto.
208	"	"	"	Rai Ishree Pershad ...	"	Zemindar.
209	"	"	"	Rai Radha Kissen ...	"	Zemindar and Banker.
210	"	"	"	Shah Reza Hossein ...	Behar ...	Zemindar.
211	"	"	"	Shaik Allyool Hossein ...	"	
212	"	"	"	Baboo Raja Ram ..	Patna ...	Banker.
213	"	"	Shahabad	Baboo Baijnath Sing ...	Shahabad	Zemindar of Kulharia.
214	"	"	"	Baboo Raj Rajeswary Pershad Singh	"	Zemindar of Surajpoora.
215	"	"	"	Baboo Shyamalanand ...	"	Pleader and Zemindar.
216	"	"	"	Baboo Rughoobans Sahay, B.A., B.L.	"	Ditto.
217	"	"	"	Baboo KandhjiSahay, B.A., B.L.	"	Ditto.

LIST OF DELEGATES.

Number.	Presidency.	Province	District or City.	Names of the Delegates.	Place or Association which they represent.	REMARKS.
218	Bengal	Behar	Shahabad	Baboo Kishoree Lal Haldar, M.A., B.L.	Shahabad	Pleader.
219	„	„	„	Rai Jaiprakash Lall Bahadur...	Doomraon	Dewan of the Maharaja of Doomraon, late Member, Bengal Legislative Council.
220	„	„	Sarun	Syud Mahomed Naki ...	Chupra ...	Zemindar.
221	„	„	„	Baboo Bansidhar Gupta ...	„	Pleader.
222	„	„	„	Sheikh Waris Ali ...	„	Do.
223	„	„	Gya	Baboo Shew Shunkur Sahay ...	Gya	Zemindar and Pleader.
224	„	„	„	Baboo Nand Kishore Lal, M.A.	„	Zemindar.
225	„	„	Muzuffer-pore.	Baboo Ramdhare Sahay ...	Muzuffer-pore.	Zemindar and Secretary to Tirhoot Landholders' Association.
226	„	„	„	Baboo Parmeshwar Narayan Mahta.	„	Banker and Zemindar.
227	„	„	Bhagulpore	Baboo Tejnarain Singh ...	Bhagulpore	Zemindar.
228	„	Bengal	Calcutta	Maharaja Sir Jotendro Mohan Tagore, K.C.S.I.	British Indian Association.	Zemindar, President of the Bengal National League, late Member of the Supreme Legislative Council, &c., &c., &c.
229	„	„	„	Dr. Rajendralala Mitra, LL.D., C.I.E.	„	President, British Indian Association, late President, Bengal Asiatic Society, &c., &c.
230	„	„	„	Baboo Joykissen Mookerjee ...	„	Zemindar.
231	„	„	„	Baboo Doorga Churn Law, C.I.E.	„	Merchant, Zemindar, late Member, Supreme Legislative Council, &c., &c.
232	„	„	„	Baboo Syama Charan Law ...	„	Zemindar and Merchant.
233	„	„	„	Hon. Peary Mohan Mookerjee, M.A., B.L.	„	Zemindar, Member, Supreme Legislative Council, Honorary Secretary, British Indian Association, &c., &c.
234	„	„	„	Rai Kunja Lal Banerjee Bahadoor.	„	Late Small Cause Court Judge, Calcutta.
235	„	„	„	Baboo Saligram Singh, B.L. ...	„	Zemindar, Vakil, High Court, Presidency Magistrate.

LIST OF DELEGATES.

Number.	Presidency.	Province.	District or City.	Names of the Delegates.	Place or Association which they represent.	REMARKS.
236	Bengal	Bengal	Calcutta	Baboo Rajkumar Sarvadhikari, M.A., B.L.	British Ind. Association.	Editor of the "Hindu Patriot."
237	"	"	"	Rajah Rajendra Narain Deb Bahadoor.	Indian Association and British Indian Association.	Zemindar and President, Indian Association.
238	"	"	"	Hon. A. M. Bose, M.A. ...	I. A. and Assam and Noakhally.	Barrister-at-Law, Member, Bengal Legislative Council, Hon. Magistrate, &c., &c.
239	"	"	"	Mr. Surendra Nath Banerjee, B.A.	Indian Association.	Editor of the "Bengallee," Hon. Secretary, Indian Association and Bengal National League, Municipal Commissioner, Presidency Magistrate, &c., &c., &c.
240	"	"	"	Baboo Mohesh Chunder Chowdhry.	"	Zemindar, Vakil, High Court.
241	"	"	"	Maharaj Kumar Neel Krishna Bahadoor.	"	Zemindar, Municipal Commissioner, Presidency Magistrate.
242	"	"	"	Maharaj Kumar Binay Krishna Bahadoor.	Indian Association, Calcutta, and Khirpai and Ghatal Associations (Midnapore).	Zemindar.
243	"	"	"	Baboo Narendra Nath Sen ...	Indian Association.	Editor of the "Indian Mirror," Municipal Commissioner, Presidency Magistrate, Attorney-at-Law.
244	"	"	"	Baboo Jagarnath Khannah ...	"	Merchant, Municipal Commissioner, Presidency Magistrate.
245	"	"	"	Kumar Satyabadi Ghosal ...	"	Zemindar.
246	"	"	"	Hon. Kali Nath Mitter ...	"	Attorney-at-Law, Member, Bengal Legislative Council, Municipal Commissioner, Presidency Magistrate.
247	"	"	"	Baboo Jogendra Chandra Ghosh, M.A., B.L.	"	Vakil, High Court.

LIST OF DELEGATES.

Number.	Presidency.	Province.	District or City	Names of the Delegates.	Place or Association which they represent.	REMARKS.
248	Bengal	Bengal	Calcutta.	Baboo Neelkamal Mookerjee ...	Indian Association.	Zemindar.
249	"	"	"	Baboo Upendra Nath Mookerjee, B.L.	"	Pleader.
250	"	"	"	Baboo Jogendra Chandra Bose, B.A.	Indian Association and Tumlook Indian Association.	Editor of the "Suravi."
251	"	"	"	Pundit Jwala Nath Sarma ...	Burrabazar Political Association.	Pleader, Small Cause Court, Calcutta, and Secretary, Bharat Maitri Mandal.
252	"	"	"	Pundit Sadanand Misser ...	"	Editor of the "Sar Sudhanidhi."
253	"	"	"	Baboo Dvaraka Nath Ganguli	Indian Association and Nowgong Ryots' Association.	Assistant Secretary, Indian Association, Cal.
254	"	"	"	Baboo Devaprasad Sarvadhikari, M.A., B.L.	Indian Association.	Articled Clerk.
255	"	"	"	Baboo Satyaprasad Sarvadhikari	"	Joint-Editor of the "Bharatbasi," & Medical Practitioner.
256	"	"	"	Baboo Chandi Kishore Kushari	"	
257	"	"	"	Dr. Mohini Mohan Bose, M.D., L.R.C.P., &c., &c.	"	Medical Practitioner.
258	"	"	"	Baboo Kali Sunkur Sukul, M.A.	"	Professor, City College.
259	"	"	"	Baboo Heramba Chandra Maitra, M.A.	Indian A., Br. I. A., Krishnagar and Comercolly.	Professor, City College.
260	"	"	"	Baboo Krishna Kumar Mitra, B.A.	Indian A., Paschim, Mymensing, Sammilani, and Tangail Br. Ind. A.	Chief Editor of the "Sanjivani."
261	"	"	"	Pundit Siva Nath Shastri ...	Ind. Association.	Brahmo Missionary.

LIST OF DELEGATES.

Number.	Presidency.	Province.	District or City.	Names of the Delegates.	Place or Association which they represent.	REMARKS.
262	Bengal	Bengal	Calcutta	Baboo Umesh Chandra Dutt, B.A.	Indian Association, and Orissa People's Association.	Principal, City College, Calcutta.
263	"	"	"	Baboo Shambhuchandra Mukerjee	Indian Union and Baranagore Rate-payers' Association.	Editor, "Reis and Rayyet."
264	"	"	"	Baboo Jaygobind Law ...	Indian Union.	Merchant, Zemindar, Presidency Magistrate and Mun. Commissioner.
265	"	"	"	Baboo Prannath Datta ...	"	Merchant and Municipal Commissioner.
266	"	"	"	Baboo Surendranath Das, M.A.	"	Attorney-at-Law and Ml. Commissioner.
267	"	"	"	Baboo Pashupatinath Bose ...	"	Zemindar.
268	"	"	"	Baboo Jyotirindranath Tagore	"	Zemindar.
269	"	"	"	Baboo Trailokyanath Mitter, M.A., D.L.	"	Vakil, High Court, Hony. Secy. I. Union, Chairman, Serampore Municipality.
270	"	"	"	Mr. M. Ghose ...	Indian Union and Ind. Association.	Barrister-at-Law, Zemindar, Hony., Secy. I. Union.
271	"	"	"	Baboo Gurudas Banerjee, M.A., D.L.	"	Vakil, High Court and Mun. Commissioner.
272	"	"	"	Mr. R. D. Mehta ...	"	Merchant.
273	"	"	"	Baboo Kalicharan Banerjea, M.A., B.L.	"	Vakil, High Court.
274	"	"	"	Mr. N. N. Ghosh ...	Ind. Union	Barrister-at-Law, Editor of the "Indian Nation" and Mun. Commissioner.
275	"	"	"	Mr. W. C. Bonnerjee ...	Bengal National League.	Barrister-at-law and Vice-President, B. N. League.
276	"	"	"	Baboo Girijabhusan Mookerjee, M.A., B.L.	Do. and Siliguri.	Hon. Secy., Bengal National League, Vakil, High Court, late Premchand R. Scholar.
277	"	"	"	Mr. J. Ghosal ...	B. N. League	Landholder.

LIST OF DELEGATES.

Number.	Presidency.	Province.	District or City.	Names of the Delegates	Place or Association which they represent.	REMARKS.
278	Bengal	Bengal	Midnapore	Baboo Debendra Nath Ghose, M.A., B.L.	Midnapore Branch, In. Association.	Pleader.
279	"	"	"	Dr. Jogendra Nath Mitra, M.R. C.P., (London.)	Moysadal Branch, Indian Association	Medical Practitioner.
280	"	"	"	Baboo Jogendra Nath Chatterjee	"	Head Master, Moysadul, H. E. School.
281	"	"	"	Baboo Jadu Nath Chakravarti, B.A.	"	Teacher.
282	"	"	"	Baboo Kailas Chandra Samanta	Natshal Gramya Samiti.	Landholder.
283	"	"	"	" Mahendra Nath Samanta		Do.
284	"	"	"	" Priya Nath Das ...		Do.
285	"	"	"	Baboo Kunja Behary Dass ...	Chandrakona	
286	"	"	"	Baboo Adhar Chunder Ghose...	"	
287	"	"	"	Baboo Tara Prasanna Banerjee	Branch I. Association, Ghatal.	
288	"	"	Contai-Midnapore.	Baboo Baikanta Nath Hazra ...	Parulya Gramya Samiti.	Pleader, Contai.
289	"	"	Hoogly	Baboo Gunga Churn Sircar ...	Hoogly & Chinsura...	Government Pensioner, Late Subordinate Judge.
290	"	"	"	Baboo Mohendra Lal Bose ...	"	Zemindar.
291	"	"	"	Baboo Sidessur Ghosh ...	"	
292	"	"	"	Baboo Jogendra Chunder Mukerjee.	Chinsura Well-wishing Club.	
293	"	"	"	Baboo Ananda Kumar Dutta...	"	
294	"	"	"	Baboo Hem Kumar Dutta ...	"	
295	"	"	"	Baboo Gokul Chunder Mandal	"	
296	"	"	"	Baboo Jogendra Krishna Shome	"	
297	"	"	"	Baboo Bepin Behary Ghosal ...	Hora Branch I. Association.	
298	"	"	"	Baboo Pares Nath Biswas ...	"	Tradesman.

LIST OF DELEGATES.

Number.	Presidency.	Province.	District or City.	Names of the Delegates.	Place or Association which they represent.	REMARKS.
299	Bengal	Bengal	Serampore (Hoogly)	Baboo Kisari Mohan Ganguli, B.L.	Serampore Moffussil Association and also Seebpur Rep. Rate payers' Association.	Pleader.
300	„	„	Hoogly	Baboo Umakali Mookerji, B.L.	Serampore M. Association.	H. C. Pleader.
301	„	„	„	Baboo Lakshmi Kanta Mullick	Singur Branch Indian Association.	Landholder.
302	„	„	„	Baboo Upendra Nath Roy ...	Panishehala Br. I. Association.	Zemindar.
303	„	„	Howrah...	Baboo Jatadhari Haldar ...	Howrah People's Association.	
304	„	„	„	Baboo Kangali Churn Haldar...	Seebpur Association.	
305	„	„	„	Baboo Taranga Nath Rai Choudhuri.	Utterparah Union.	Practical Agriculturist.
306	„	„	„	Baboo Shib Narain Mookerjee	„	Zemindar.
307	„	„	„	Baboo Chundra Kumar Mookerjee, L.M.S.	„	Medical Practitioner.
308	„	„	„	Baboo Jyot Kumar Mookerjee	„	Zemindar.
309	„	„	„	Baboo Hriday Krishna Samanta	Guzurpur Ind. Association.	
310	„	„	„	Baboo Umes Chundra Baitalik	„	
311	„	„	„	Baboo Asutosh Maiti ...	„	
312	„	„	„	Munshi Nurul Huq ...	Ulubaria Branch In. Association.	Pleader.
313	„	„	„	Moulavi Soughat Ali ...	„	Merchant.
314	„	„	„	Baboo Ambika Churn Bose ...	„	Vakil, High Court and Zemindar.
315	„	„	„	Baboo Sripati Bose, B.A. ...	„	
316	„	„	Furreedpore.	Baboo Ambica Charan Mazumdar, B.L.	Furreedpore People's Association.	Pleader and Chairman, Furreedpore Municipality.
317	„	„	„	Baboo Jaladhar Sen ...	Goalundo Branch In. Association.	Landholder.

LIST OF DELEGATES.

Number.	Presidency.	Province.	District or City	Names of the Delegates.	Place or Association which they represent.	Remarks.
318	Bengal	Bengal	Rungpore	Baboo Mohini Mohun Chakravarti, M.A., B.L.	Rungpore	Pleader.
319	"	"	"	Baboo Prasanna Nath Chowdhry.	"	Do.
320	"	"	"	Mr. Samiruddin Ahmed, B.A. ...	"	Zemindar.
321	"	"	Nelphamari (Rungpore.)	Munshi Rajab Ali Ahmed ...	Nelphamari Association	Pleader.
322	"	"	Dinagepore.	Baboo Debendra Nath Palit, M.A., B.L.	Dinagepore I. A.	Do.
323	"	"	Moorshedabad.	Baboo Baikant Nath Sen ...	Moorshedabad Association.	Pleader, President, Moorshedabad Association.
324	"	"	"	Baboo Gopal Chunder Mookerjee, M.A., B.L.	"	Vakil, Vice President, Moorshedabad Association.
325	"	"	"	Baboo Srish Chunder Basu Sarvadhikari.	"	Zemindar.
326	"	"	"	Baboo Barada Prasad Bagchi...	"	Secretary, Moorshedabad Association and Pleader.
327	"	"	"	Dr. Ram Das Sen ...	"	Zemindar.
328	"	"	"	Baboo Sri Nath Pal ...	"	Do.
329	"	"	"	Mr. K. C. Rai ...	"	
330	"	"	Jangipur (Moorshedabad.)	Baboo Asutosh Ghosh ...	Jangipur Br. I. A.	Pleader.
331	"	"	Jessore ...	Baboo Kali Nath Mookerjee, B.A.	Jessore Indian Association.	Pleader and Landholder.
332	"	"	"	Baboo Jogendra Nath Sen, M.A.	Narail	Principal, Narail College.
333	"	"	"	Baboo Sura Nath Chowdhuri.	Jessore	Zemindar and Member, District Board, Jessore.
334	"	"	"	Baboo Kishori Lal Sarkar, M.A., B.L.	Jhinkergacha Ryots' Association & Jhenida	Vakil, High Court.
335	"	"	"	Baboo Mati Lal Ghose ...	Jhinkergacha Ryots' Association	Joint-Editor, "Amrita Bazar Patrika." Member, District Board, Jessore.

LIST OF DELEGATES.

Number.	Presidency.	Province.	District or City.	Names of the Delegates.	Place or Association which they represent.	Remarks.
336	Bengal	Bengal	Jessore.	Baboo Nilkamal Dass ...	Jhinkergacha Ryots' Association	Auditor, E. I. Railway.
337	"	"	"	Baboo Amrita Lal Roy ...	"	
338	"	"	Kalia-Jessore.	Baboo Sivendra Nath Gupta, M.A.	Kalia Young Men's Association.	
339	"	"	Khulna ...	Baboo Triguna Charan Sen, M.A.	Senhati People's Association.	Head Master, Ripon Collegiate School, Kidderpore.
340	"	"	"	Baboo Manomohan Sen ...	"	Medical Practitioner.
341	"	"	"	Baboo Indu Bhusan Mazumdar, B.A.	Maheswarpasha.	
342	"	"	"	Baboo Jadu Nath Kanjilal ...	Bagirhat People's Association.	Pleader.
343	"	"	"	Molvi Syud Basaratullah ...	"	Talookdar, Member Local Board.
344	"	"	"	Baboo Beepin Behary Ray ...	"	Pleader.
345	"	"	Backergunge.	Munshi Saududdin Mohamed ...	Barisal People's Association.	Pleader and Zemindar.
346	"	"	"	Baboo Rakhal Chunder Roy ...	"	Zemindar.
347	"	"	"	Mr. P. L. Roy ...	"	Barrister-at-law and Zemindar.
348	"	"	"	Baboo Chandra Kanta Sen, M.A., B.L.	"	Vakil, High Court.
349	"	"	Dacca ...	Baboo Rama Kant Nundy ...	Dacca People's Association.	Pleader, Vice-Chairman, Dacca Municipality.
350	"	"	"	Baboo Kailash Chandra Sen ...	"	Zemindar and Pleader.
351	"	"	"	Khajeh Abdool Aleem ...	"	Zemindar.
352	"	"	"	Syed Abdool Bari ...	"	Ditto.
353	"	"	"	Moulavi Rezauddin ...	"	Ditto.
354	"	"	Rajshaye	Baboo Bhuban Mohan Maitra...	Rajshaye Association.	Zemindar and Pleader, District Court.
355	"	"	"	Baboo Rajkumar Sarkar ...	Digapathia (Nattore)	Zemindar. Member, District Board, Rajshaye.
356	"	"	"	Baboo Mohendra Nath Sanyal, B L.	Rajshaye	Pleader.

LIST OF DELEGATES.

Number.	Presidency.	Province.	District or City.	Names of the Delegates.	Place or Association which they represent.	REMARKS.
357	Bengal	Bengal	Rajshahye	Baboo Syama Charan Roy, B.L.	Rajshaye	Pleader.
358	"	"	Nattore (Rajshahye)	Baboo Jadav Chandra Bishi ...	Nattore People's Association.	Zemindar of Juari (Nattore).
359	"	"	"	Sarat Chandra Bose, B.A.	"	Head Master, Nattore H. School.
360	"	"	"	Dr. Kedar Nath Pal ...	Agricultural Society, Tahirpur.	
361	"	"	Pubna	Baboo Giris Chandra Ray, B.L.	Pubna	Chairman, Pubna Municipality, and Pleader.
362	"	"	"	Mr. A. Chaudhuri M.A. (Cal.) B.A. (Cantab.) L.L.B.	"	Barrister-at-law.
363	"	"	"	Baboo Umagati Roy, B.A. ...	Khetupara Ryots' Association.	
364	"	"	"	Baboo Jadav Chandra Chakravarti, M.A.	Serajgunge British I. Association.	Professor, City College.
365	"	"	"	Baboo Jagadish Chandra Roy	Bagbati Branch I. Association. Serajgunge.	
366	"	"	"	Baboo Jadav Chandra Bhuttacharjee.	Chatmohar.	
367	"	"	"	Baboo Rajani Kant Bhuttacharji	Pechakola.	
368	"	"	Nuddea	Roy Jadu Nath Roy Bahadoor	Nuddea.	Chairman, Krishnagar, Municipality, Zemindar and Indigo-planter.
369	"	"	"	Baboo Jadu Nath Chatterjee ...	Branch I. Association, Krishnagar.	Pleader.
370	"	"	"	Baboo Surendra Nath Pal Chaudhuri.	Nuddea.	Zemindar, Chairman, Ranaghat Municipality.
371	"	"	"	Dr. Athar Ali ...	"	Medical Practitioner, Chuadanga.
372	"	"	"	Baboo Akhay Kumar Mookerjea	Branch I. Association, Krishnagar.	Pleader and Vice-Chairman, Krishnagar Municipality.
373	"	"	"	Baboo Nuffur Chunder Pal Chaudhuri.	Nuddea.	Zemindar, Member, District Board, Nuddea.

LIST OF DELEGATES.

Number.	Presidency.	Province.	District or City.	Names of the Delegates.	Place or Association which they represent.	Remarks.
374	Bengal	Bengal	Nuddea.	Mr. B. Pal Chaudhuri, M.I. & S.I. (Lond.)	Nuddea.	Engineer and Zemindar.
375	„	„	„	Baboo Basanta Kumar Chatterjee, B.L.	Katdah Association.	Pleader, Krishnagar, Member of the District Board of Nuddea.
376	„	„	„	Munshi Fakir Ali Miyah ...	„	Landholder.
377	„	„	Ranaghat (Nuddea.)	Baboo Krishna Chandra Ghatak	Branch I. Association, Ranaghat.	
378	„	„	„	„ Akhoy Kumar Ghosh ...	„	Municipal Commissioner.
379	„	„	„	„ Girija Bhusan Datta ...	„	Medical Practitioner.
380	„	„	Chogdah (Nuddea.)	„ Jogendra Narayan Mitra	Chogdah.	Teacher.
381	„	„	Kissen-gunge (Nuddea.)	„ Jagadischandra Lahiri ...	Kissen-gunge	Medical Practitioner.
382	„	„	„	„ Nandagopal Bhaduri ...	Mahajan Sabha, Majdia, Kissen-gunge.	
383	„	„	Bhajan-ghata (Nuddea.)	Baboo Suresh Chandra Roy, M.A.	Branch I. Association, Bhajan-ghata.	
384	„	„	Santipore (Nuddea.)	Baboo Bepin Behary Maitra, M.B.	Santipore	Medical Practitioner.
385	„	„	Joyrampore (Nuddea.)	„ Surendra Nath Rai ...	Joyrampore Jnan Pradayini Sabha.	
386	„	„	Tipperah	Baboo Gobind Chunder Das, M.A., B.L.	Tipperah People's Association.	Pleader.
387	„	„	„	Munshi Lateef Hossain ...	Shahbazpur	
388	„	„	„	Munshi Anayat Ali ...	Kansua.	
389	„	„	Chittagong	Dr. Annada Charan Kastagiri...	Chittagong	Medical Practitioner.
390	„	„	„	Baboo Akhil Chunder Sen, M.A., B.L.	„	Vakil, High Court.
391	„	„	Jalpaiguri	Baboo Hara Mohun Das ...	Jalpaiguri	Jotedar and Dewan to the Raikat of Jalpaiguri.

LIST OF DELEGATES.

Number.	Presidency.	Province	District or City.	Names of the Delegates.	Place or Association which they represent.	Remarks.
392	Bengal	Bengal	Jaipaiguri.	Dr. Tamizuddin Ahmed, M.B., C.M., B.Sc., L.S.A., (London.)	Jalpaiguri.	Medical Practitioner
393	„	„	„	Baboo Nirmal Chunder Sinha, M.A., B.L.	„	Pleader and Zemindar, Municipal Commissioner and Hon. Secy., Branch I. Association.
394	„	„	Mymensing	Moulavi Hamid Uddin Ahmed, B L.	Mymensing	Pleader.
395	„	„	„	Baboo Revati Mohan Guha, M.A., B L.	„	Pleader.
396	„	„	„	Baboo Isan Chandra Gupta ...	West Mymensing Association	Secretary, West M. Association.
397	„	„	Sherpur (Mymensing.)	Baboo Banwarilal Chaudhuri ...	Sherpur Land-holders' Association.	Zemindar.
398	„	„	„	Baboo Giris Chandra Bhattacharjee.	„	
399	„	„	Sakrail (Mymensing.)	Baboo Lalit Chandra Sen ...	Sakrail Hitasadhini Sabha.	
400	„	„	„	Baboo Umbika Prasad Sen ...	„	
401	„	„	„	Baboo Bhabani Kisor Majumdar, B. L.	Husainpore	Pleader.
402	„	„	„	Moulavi Nowshir Ali Khan ...	Tangail ...	Talookdar, Charan, Editor of the "Ahmedi."
403	„	„	„	Baboo Ram Narayan Agasti, B.A.	Kishoreganj	Teacher.
404	„	„	Malda	Baboo Madhu Sudan Sinha, B.A.	Malda Association.	
405	„	„	Burdwan	Baboo Mathura Nath Sanyal, B.A.	Purbasthali Br. I. Association.	
406	„	„	„	Baboo Pramatha Natha Raya...	Purbasthali Hitakari Sabha.	
407	„	„	„	„ Abinash Chandra Nundy	„	

LIST OF DELEGATES.

Number.	Presidency.	Province.	District or City.	Names of the Delegates.	Place or Association which they represent.	REMARKS.
408	Bengal.	Bengal.	24-Pergunnahs.	Baboo Asutosh Biswas, M.A., B.L.	Suburban Ratepayers' Association. Bhowanipore, and Indian Association. Calcutta.	Pleader, Municipal Commissioner.
409	„	„	„	Debender Chunder Ghosh, B.L.	Indian Union, Calcutta.	Pleader, Judge's Court, Alipore, Hon. Magistrate.
410	„	„	„	Revd. P. M. Mukerjea ...	Russapagla Improvement Association.	Missionary of S. P. G. Taliganj.
411	„	„	„	Nawab Gholam Rubbani ...	„	(Of the Mysore Princes Family.)
412	„	„	„	Baboo Mohendranath Sen ...	„	Teacher, Commissioner S., Suburban Municipality.
413	„	„	„	Baboo Siddeshur Bannerjee ...	Rohora Patriotic Association.	
414	„	„	„	Baboo Baiconto Nath Chowdhuri.		
415	„	„	„	Baboo Nibaran Chunder Chowdhuri.		
416	„	„	„	Baboo Gopal Chunder Mookerjee.		
417	„	„	„	Baboo Sarada Prasad Banerjee	Baranagore Local Committeeof the Ind. Association.	Chairman, Baranagore Municipality.
418	„	„	„	Baboo Sasipada Banerjee ...	Baranagore Workingmen's Club and Ratepayers' Association.	
419	„	„	„	Baboo Issury Charan Mookerjee	Baranagore Ratepayers' Association.	Zemindar.
420	„	„	„	Baboo Jogendra Nath Bose, M.A., B.L.	„	Vakil, High Court.
421	„	„	„	Baboo Bijay Lall Dutt ..	Arbalia J. V. Sabha.	
422	„	„	„	Baboo Surendra Chundra Basu		

LIST OF DELEGATES.

	Presidency.	Province.	District or City.	Names of the Delegates.	Place or Association which they represent.	Remarks.
423	Bengal.	Bengal.	24-Pergunnahs.	Roy Jotendra Nath Chowdhuri, B.A.	Taki Br. I. Association, Indian Association, Calcutta and Baranagore Local Committee of the I. Association.	Zemindar.
424	"	Chota Nagpore.	Hazaribagh	Rai Jadu Nath Mookerjee ...	Hazaribagh & Ranchi.	Government Pleader.
425	"	"	Purulia	Pundit Prannath Saraswati, M.A., B.L.	Purulia	Vakil, High Court.
426	"	Orissa	Balasore	Kumar Baikunta Nath Dey ...	Balasore National Society & British Indian A.	Zemindar, late Member, Bengal Legislative Council, &c. &c. &c.
427	"	Assam	Cachar ...	Baboo Deno Nath Dutta ...	Cachar	Manager of C. N. J. Stock Co., Ld.
428	"	"	Shillong...	Mr. Kali Kanta Barkagti, B.A.	Shillong A.	
429	"	"	Dibrugarh	Mr. Devi Charan Barua, B.A.	Upper Assam A.	
430	"	"	"	Mr. Gopi Nath Bardoloye, B.A.	"	
431	"	"	Nowgong	Mr. Satya Nath Borah, B.A. ...	Ryots' A. Nowgong.	Tea Planter.
432	"	"	Sylhet ...	Baboo Bepin Chunder Pal ...	Sylhet	Landholder.
433	"	"	"	Baboo Joygobind Shome, M.A., B.L.	"	Vakil, High Court. Editor, "Christian Herald."
434	"	"	Silchar ...	Baboo Kamini Kumar Chanda, M.A.	Habiganj People's A. Silchar.	Landholder.
			Names of Delegates omitted inadvertently from the foregoing List.			
394A	"	Bengal	Mymensing	Baboo Keshub Chander Acharjee Chowdhry.	Mymensing	Zemindar.
412A	"	"	24-Pergunnahs.	Baboo Sirish Chunder Basu ...	Russapagla Improvement Assn	Asst. Secy. of the Association.

(Besides these Delegates, several Visitors—the Honorable Mr. Ranade, Rajah Lutchman Singh, the Honorable Mr. Baij Nath (Chief Justice, Indore) and others—were present, and though taking no part in the Public Proceedings, assisted the Delegates at some of their informal committees with their advice.)

(N.B.—This list, it is feared, is not quite *complete as to names even, since it is believed that some few gentlemen left without recording their names. It is* certainly *incomplete as to many whose names* are *recorded, owing to gentlemen failing to note their academical degrees, professions, and other particulars opposite their names before leaving.)*

APPENDIX II.

PAPERS RELATING TO THE ELECTION OF DELEGATES.

(Extracts from Newspapers.)

ARRAH.

The 13th December, 1886.

A MEETING of the people of Shahabad was held here on Sunday, the 12th instant, for the purpose of electing delegates for the National Congress to be held at Calcutta. It was presided over by Mr. Shurfuddin, Barrister-at-Law. Great enthusiasm prevailed. Mahomedans took as much part as Hindus in its proceedings, and both showed the greatest earnestness. The mass, that had mustered two thousand strong, heard with rapt attention the proceedings of the day which were all conducted in Urdu.

The President opened the meeting with a brief but a succinct and clear statement of the aims and objects of the National Congress. He showed that, with the growth of free citizen ideas, corresponding alterations must be made in the mode of the Government to suit those ideas. Such ideas cannot be stifled, but must have a natural outlet. The National Congress purposes to attain those ends by constitutional agitation. He then called upon Baboo Rughubuns Sahai, B.A., B.L., to move the first resolution which runs thus :—

" I.—That this meeting entirely sympathises with the aims and objects of the National Congress to be held during Christmas holidays at Calcutta, and deems it desirable to send representatives to the said Congress."

The mover dwelt upon the advantages of representative Government, the establishment of which is one of the chief aims of the Congress. He said that a foreign Government, however strong and well-intentioned, could never enter into the real wants and wishes of the country, and that a representative Government would have the double advantage of removing popular grievances and satisfying the people.

Baboo Koilash Chunder Bannerji, M.A., B.L., in seconding the resolution, exhorted the people to see their ancient *punchayet* system re-established on a broader and more scientific basis in a representative form of Government. He likened district representation to feeders of a large river, which without them would dry up. The National Congress must be fed by district representation to be effective.

Baboo Chaturbhuj Sahai moved the second resolution which was as follows :—

" II.—That some gentlemen be sent as delegates to represent this District at the said Congress."

He said that the money of India is expended in pageants and shows and unprofitable wars, while millions of Indian people are starving for want of daily bread. Those millions who are not consulted or cared for would have to bear the burden of these departures from morality.

Moulvi Lukman Hyder was right glad to find that the time he had up to that time thought to be far distant was near at hand—the time which would see India governed for the Indians.

Baboo Kandhji Sahai, B.A., B.L., in support of the resolution, assured the meeting that the Congress was in the highest degree constitutional, and it would serve as a safety-valve to the State in times of trouble. He showed that it could never be considered dangerous to the State, in that it always had hopes of its objects being realized, while one destitute of such hopes could do worse out of utter desperation.

Baboo Jadu Nath Sahai moved that a Select Committee be formed of the following gentlemen for the purpose of selecting the delegates: Baboo Raj Rajeswari Prosad Singh, Rai Jaiperkash Lall Bahadur, Baboo Jadu Nath Sahai, Baboo Chaturbhuj Sahai, Baboo Symlanund, Baboo Kandhji Sahai, Baboo Bhagwan Dass, Baboo Udaichand, Baboo Baijnath Sahai, Baboo Baijnath Singh, Baboo Sikher Chand, Moulvi Lukman Haider, Moulvi Kazizohur Alum, Moulvi Mirza Ismail, Baboo Koilas Chunder Bannerji and Baboo Thakurpershad Singh.

Baboo Kandhji Sahai, B.A., B.L., was then authorized on behalf of the meeting to hold necessary communication with the Secretary to the National Congress on the subject of receiving representatives from this district.

In the end a telegram and a letter from Baboo Raj Rajeswari Prosad Singh of Surojpura were read out. He was to have attended the meeting, but was kept away owing to an unforeseen circumstance.

CONJEEVERAM.

A PUBLIC meeting was held here in the Cloth Bazar Choultry, Hodsenpett, for nominating delegates to be sent to the National Congress. Notices had been circulated by Mr. C. T. M. Appavo Mudaliar, Rao Sahib, Municipal Councillor. Precisely at the hour, 4 P.M., the proceedings of the meeting began, upwards of 500 people assembling in the Hall, while a greater number had to remain outside. The public kept good order, and the spectacle witnessed that day is without any precedent in the history of this town. Among those present were all the resident Municipal Councillors, inclusive of the Chairman, being 15 in number out of the whole body of 20 members, members of the District Board and the several Taluq Boards of the District, Zemindars, Shrotriemdars and other landholders, managers of temples and other orthodox Brahmins, influential merchants of the town and of the district, Schoolmasters, and, in fact, representatives of every section of the community were vieing with each other in the display of enthusiasm for what the whole assembly accepted as their one common and sole object. The proceedings began, the assembly voting unanimously with acclamations to the Chair our respected citizen M. R. Ry. Namasivaya Chettiar, Rao Sahib, Municipal Councillor, and Honorary Magistrate. The President [illegible] in a short speech, explained the object [illegible] and sat down amidst applause. T[illegible] Charriar, Chief Mirassidar of

of the Taluq Board of Chingleput spoke at considerable length about the object of the meeting, the subjects to be discussed at the Congress and the importance and necessity of sending delegates to represent the views of the public of the District at the Congress.

The next sperker P. B. Sumbanda Mudaliar Rao Bahadur, Chairman of the local Municipal Council and also Civil apothecary, impressed upon the meeting the importance of introducing technical education, one of the subjects to be discussed this year by the Congress, its useful effect upon the declining manufacturing industries of India in competition with English manufactures. He also convinced the meeting of the necessity of forming an Association in the town and other parts of the district calculated to train the people politically. Then Mr. Krishnasamy Thatha Chariar Rao Sahib, Dharmakarta of the Sri Dewarajaswamy's Temple, member of the District Board and of the Local Municipal Council, spoke also of the importance of the Congress and of the meeting sending its delegates. He suggested that the Congress should take up in hand the subject of the abolition of the income-tax, which he said operated very harshly as direct taxation, the deficit owing to such abolition being made up by means of indirect taxation. Then Mr. M. Y. Ranga Chariar, Vakil of the District Court, explained to the audience the necessity of the remodelling of the Legislative Council on the lines laid down in the third resolution of the last year's Congress at Bombay, and how it was practicable to elect such representatives. Then Mr. Kristnasamy Thathachary proposed that Mr. M. Y. Ranga Chariar be appointed delegate to represent the district at the Congress. As an amendment of this proposition Mr. C. M. Ranga Iyengar, Mirasidar, proposed the following gentlemen be also appointed delegates: M. Viraragava Chariar Avergal, a Mirasidar of the Taluq; M. Shunmuga Moodaliar, Zemindar of Nallatur; M. G. Sriranga Chariar, B.A. and B.L., Vakil, High Court; A. Ranga Chariar, of Damal. The last proposition as amended was seconded by S. Sreenivasa Iyer, Rao Sahib, Head Master of the Pacheappa's High School.

The last named Mr. A. Ranga Chariar of Damal, pleaded ill-health, but on the gentlemen then present expressing surprise that such a patriotic gentleman should now care more for his health than his country, he very willingly withdrew his plea and enthusiastically declared acceptance of his appointment. The whole proposition was carried unanimously.

It was next asked by M. R. Ry. Narasima Charriar if he will be allowed to propose the payment of the delegates' expenses by public subscription, but the delegates expressing for themselves and for their fellows their unwillingness to accept any such payment, the matter was dropped. The meeting then dispersed with a vote of thanks to the Chairman.

HOSPETT.

A PUBLIC meeting of the inhabitants of Hospett Taluq, Bellary District, was convened under the auspices of the "Ryots' Sabha," Hospett, in the Hospett Town Hall and Reading Room, on the 4th December, 1886, for the purpose of appointing delegates [illegible] represent Hospett Taluq at the [illegible]ss.

[illegible] Rau Garu, Row Saib, 1st Grade [illegible]ipal Councillor, Bellary, delivered an able address, and the following resolutions were passed by the meeting :—

I. Resolved that Mr. C. H. Goud Row Sahib, Member of the District Board, Mirasidar, and an Honorary Magistrate and Mr. K. Venkat Row, Garu Row Sahib, Landholder in the Taluq, and 1st Grade Pleader, Bellary, be nominated delegates of this Taluq at the ensuing National Congress to be held at Calcutta.

II. That a vote of thanks be given to the chairman and the lecturer.

VIZAGAPATAM.

A PUBLIC meeting was held at Vizagapatam on the 6th instant, and Mr. Krishna Murthi and Pudupeddi Venkannah were elected delegates.

BANKIPORE.

29th November, 1886.

A MOST crowded meeting of the residents of Bankipore and Patna, numbering probably nearly one thousand persons, called by the Behar People's Association, was held at Bankipore yesterday. Syed Tajammal Hossein Khan, son of Nawab Valayat Ali Khan Bahadur, C.I.E., presided. Resolutions were passed unanimously in favour of the introduction of a representative element into the government of this country. Delegates to the National Congress elected. Mr. Shurfuddin, Barrister-at-Law, moved the first resolution. A very large number of Mahomedan gentlemen were present. Great enthusiasm prevailed.

JUBBULPORE.

23rd December, 1886.

AN influential meeting of the residents of this town was held on the 21st instant, under the auspices of the Hitcarni Sabha, to consider what steps should be taken to represent the interest of the people of the Central Provinces in the various questions that are to be discussed in the National Congress to be held in Calcutta during Christmas. Among others we noticed the following gentlemen: Seth Bullubh Dass Rai Bahadur, Seth Behary Lal Khazanchi, Seth Gouri Dass, Seth Bhuban Mohun, Seth Omrao Singh Chowdhry, Gontia Aman Singh, Zemindar, Baboo Brojendra Nath, Pleader, Baboo Kailash Chunder, M.A., Baboo Nanhak Chand, B.A., Baboo Behary Lal, B.A., Baboo Janoki Prashad, Pleader, Baboo Gopal Prashad, B.A., and nearly all the other residents of the town, who command weight and influence. Seth Behari Lall Khazanchi opened the meeting by explaining the object which had brought them together, after which the following resolutions were moved :—

I.—That we fully sympathize with the object and proceedings of the National Congress to be held in Calcutta during the ensuing vacation. Proposed by Seth Behari Lal Khazanchi, and seconded by Chowdhry Omrao Singh and Mr. Abdul Gafur.

II.—That one or two delegates be sent to the National Congress to represent the interest of the people of the Central Provinces in the various important public questions that are are to be discussed there, and a Committee be formed of a few gentlemen to raise subscriptions and to arrange for sending delegates as early as possible. Proposed by Gontia Aman Singh and seconded by Mr. Gopal Swamy.

ALLAHABAD.

19th December, 1886.

A GREAT public meeting of the residents of Allahabad took place here to elect delegates to represent this ancient city in the forthcoming National Congress to be held in your city. The meeting was a crowded one, and attended by almost all the respectable and influential citizens. Seldom have I seen such an orderly and enthusiastic meeting. It was presided by the much respected vakil Pundit Bishambhar Nath. The meeting was addressed by the Chairman, Pundit Vyasji, the reputed Kaviraj, Mr. Crowley of Messrs. Crowley & Co., Dr. Brojendra Nath Bannerji, the late celebrated physician of this city, and now of your own town, who has lately come up here to treat a rich patient, Pundit Sunder Lal, Pleader, High Court, Pundit Madan Mohun Malavya, B.A., Munshi Kashi Pershad, Vakil, Mr. T. N. Ghose, Thakur Mahabir Pershad and others. The following delegates were unanimously elected: Lala Ram Charan Dass, the Rothschild of Allahabad, Baboos Charu Chunder Mitter and T. N. Ghose, Pundit Madan Mohun Malavya, B.A., Mr. Abdul Majid, Barrister-at-Law, Mr. Mahmud, Vakil, High Court, Mr. Newal Behary Bajpai and Munshi Kashi Proshad, Vakil. Mr. Crowley offered to pay the fare of any of the delegates who required pecuniary help. I am glad that two Mahomedan gentlemen are going to represent this city.

HOSHANGABAD.

21st December, 1886.

THE following is a report of the proceedings of an important meeting, held to-day at 8 A.M., in the hall of the Zillah School, Hoshangabad, to consider the propriety of sending delegates to represent the inhabitants of the district in the National Congress to be held at Calcutta on the 27th, 28th and 29th of this month:—

Present: The leading residents of the town of Hoshangabad, the members of the local Bar and many others.

I.—Proposed by Baboo Behary Lal Bose that Seth Dalchand do take the chair, seconded by Pundit Sukhdeo Prasad, and carried *nem con.* The object of the meeting being explained by Baboo Kalidas Chowdhry, it was resolved that delegates be sent to Calcutta to represent the District of Hoshangabad.

Proposed that Baboos Behary Lal Bose and Khetter Mohun Bose, Pleaders of the District, be selected as delegates to the National Congress.

II.—That these gentlemen be sent as delegates.

III.—That copies of the resolution be sent to the Secretary to the National Congress, to the *Indian Mirror*, and to the *Nyay Sudha*.

MYLAPORE.

IN pursuance of a notice issued by the Secretary to the People's Association of Mylapore there was a meeting of the public of Mylapore in the Athenæum Hall at 6 P.M., on Sunday, the 21st instant. There were present: Dewan Bahadoor R. Raghunatha Row; Messrs. R. Balajee Row, B.L.; C. Mahadeva Iyer, B.A. and B.L.; D. S. Runga Charriar, B.A. and B.L.; M. Sreenivasa Row, B.A. and B.L.,; T. R. Ramanatha Iyer, B.A.; M. Swaminatha Mudaliar; P. S. Sevaswami Iyer, B.A. and B.L.; S. Kalayna Rama Iyer, B.A. and B.L.; S. Ramasawmi Iyengar, B.A. and B.L.; K. Narayana Row, B.A. and B.L.; V. Kristnaswami Iyer, B.A. and B.L.; P. R. Sundarum Iyer, B.A. and B.L.; and many others. Mr. Swaminatha Mudaliar, the largest landholder in the Municipal Division, was voted to the chair. Mr. R. Balajee Row explained at considerable length the objects of the National Congress and proposed that the Honorable S. Subramania Iyer be requested to represent the public of Mylapore in the National Congress which meets in December at Calcutta. he proposition was seconded by Mr. P. S. Sevaswami Iyer. Several speakers dwelt upon the necessity for every town and village sending a delegate to the Congress. The proposition was then put to the vote and carried unanimously. It was resolved that the request be communicated to the Honorable S. Subramania Iyer. With a vote of thanks to the chairman, the meeting dispersed.

WALLAJANUGGUR.

IN accordance to a notice circulated by the Wallajanuggur Hindu Brethren Association, a public meeting was held on Sunday, the 21st instant, at 9 A.M., in the premises No. 26, Bhuvarna Chetty Street, for the purpose of electing a delegate to represent the people of Wallaja Taluq in the ensuing National Congress.

People of every description, namely, merchants, landholders, vakeels and several others were present. Mr. Canche Canganna Chetti Garu, a landholder at Wallajah, was unanimously voted to the chair. Mr. P. Govindarajulu Mudaliar explained in Tamil the object of the meeting. Mr. S. Etherajulu Naidu explained in full the object of the National Congress. Then the Chairman rose and asked the audience to elect a delegate, whereupon Palnati Etherajulu Chetty, a landholder, proposed that Mr. Chethambadi Subba Naidu Garu, 1st Grade Pleader, should be elected as a delegate to attend the National Congress. The proposition was seconded by Mr. Kulvaraya Pillai, the Head Master of the H. B. M. School, and supported by Mr. Ponnusawmi Mudaliar, a merchant, and unanimously carried.

It was suggested by S. Alwar Naidu to raise a fund for the defrayal of the expenses of the delegate. The suggestion thus made was objected to by Palnati Etherajulu Chetti who said that such a patriotic gentleman as Mr. C. Subba Naidu Garu would decline to accept any money for his expenses and offer his services for the public good gratuitously. It was then resolved that the name of the delegates should be communicated to the Secretary to the Madras Mahajana Sabha and that of the Indian National Congress. Thereon, the audience and the Chairman rose and prayed God for a few minutes for the happy success in the long journey* of our delegate and of all the delegates of the Presidency. The meeting dispersed with a vote of thanks to the delegate and the Chairman.

BALLIA.

THE *Indian Union* says: "A well-attended meeting, which included nearly all the *raises* and educated gentry of the town, was convened at Ballia in the N. W. P. on the evening of the 13th instant under the auspices of the Ballia Institute, to elect delegates for the Calcutta National Congress. Baboo Sribalabh Dutt, a leading member of the local Bar, was in the chair. Munshi Parmeshari Dayal explained to the audience at some length the objects of the National Congress He dwelt also on the blessings of the people of India enjoyed under the British Raj and on the

* A journey of 2,000 miles.

importance of constitutional agitation conducted in a moderate and loyal spirit. He was followed by Pundit Indira Dutt, Upadhyaya, M.A., who, in a short impressive speech, exhorted these present to call to mind the glories of the ancient *Aryavarta*, and to unite in the common bond of brotherhood for the furtherance of the best interests of their country. Five gentlemen were nominated by the unanimous vote of the meeting as delegates to be present at the conference, *viz.*, Baboo Sribullabh Dutt, Vakil and Chairman of the evening, Pundit Indira Dutt Upadhyaya, M.A., Baboo Bhugwan Din Ray and Baboo Padma Deva Narain Pande and Deo Narain Singh, well-known zemindars and *raises* of the district. The first three gentlemen have expressed their willingness to join the Congress as desired by the Committee; the other two, who were unavoidably absent from the station on the day the meeting was held, have been requested by letter to accept the invitation of the meeting. The proceedings were conducted entirely in the vernacular, and all present evinced the utmost interest and enthusiasm."

DACCA.

16th December, 1886.

A CROWDED and enthusiastic meeting of the Hindu and Mahomedan inhabitants, such as has rarely before been here seen, was held last evening at the Jagannath College Theatre, at the instance of the People's Association, Khajah Mahomed Azghur presiding. The following resolutions were unanimously adopted:—

I.—The reconstitution of the Indian and Bengal Legislative Councils on the elective basis.

II.—The examination of the Indian candidates for the Civil Service in India, and raising the maximum age to 23, leaving it optional with the successful candidates to proceed to England or not.

III.—The appointment of a Commission of Enquiry into the coolie grievances in Assam.

IV.—The separation of the Judicial from the Executive functions of the Magistrates.

V.—The appointment of delegates to the coming National Congress.

VI.—Sympathy was expressed with the aims of the Congress, and an entire approbation of the principles enunciated in the pamphlet entitled the *Star in the East*. The following gentlemen were appointed delegates: Syed Abdul Bari, Khajeh Abdul Alim, Moulvi Riajuddin, Baboos Ramakanta Nundy, Kailas Chunder Sen and Kaliprosunno Ghose.

SYLHET.

17th December, 1886.

AN influentially-attended meeting representing all sections of the native community was held here yesterday at the premises of the Murary Chand High School, to consider the desirability of sending delegates to the ensuing National Congress. Baboo Nova Krishna Roy, Dastidar, Zemindar, was in the Chair. Among those present we noticed Baboo Girish Chunder Roy, Zemindar, Tea-Planter and Proprietor of the Girish School and Murari Chand School; Baboo Loke Nath Surma, Zemindar, Tea-Planter and Honorary Magistrate; Baboo Dulal Chunder Dey, B.L., Vice-Chairman of the Municipality and Law Lecturer; Baboo Ananda Kiser Dutta Roy, B.L., Tara Kisore Chowdhry, M.A., B.L., Radha Binod Dass, Romes Chunder Bose, Sham Kisore Sen, Moulvi Masadar Ali, Pleaders, Judge's Court; Maulavi Abdul Zalil, Zemindar; Moulvi Abdul Karim, late a Sub-Registrar; Baboos Radha Govinda Dass and Mohendra Chunder Dass, landowners; Baboo Prosunno Kumar Guha, merchant; Baboo Radha Nath Chowdhry, Editor "*Paridasak*'; Baboo Janoki Nath Sen, Head Master, National Institution; Baboo Prosunno Kumar De, B.A., Teacher, Murari Chand School; Baboo Radha Nath Das, Nava Kisore Dass, Sarat Chunder Dutt, Sita Mohun Dass, Pleaders, Munsiff's Court; Baboos Sundari Mohun Dass, M.B., and Biseswar Sen, Medical Practitioner. After the objects of the meeting were explained by Baboo Dulal Chunder De, B.L., in a neat speech, resolutions to the following effect were passed unanimously amidst much enthusiasm:—

I.—That this meeting expresses its hearty sympathy with the National Congress. Moved by Moulvi Masadar, Ali, Pleader Judge's Court, seconded by Baboo Sundar Mohun Dass, M.B.

II.—That in view of the rapid progress of education and enlightenment in this country, this meeting is of opinion that it has now become necessary, alike in the interests of India and England, to reconstitute the Legislative Councils upon the following lines:—

(*a.*) That no less than two-thirds of the whole Council should be elected members chosen by local bodies.

(*b.*) That the Council thus formed should have the right of interpellation.

Moved by Moulvi Abdul Zalil, Zemindar, seconded by Moulvi Abdul Karim, and supported by Baboos Prosunno Kumar Guha and Radha Nath Chowdhry.

III.—That this meeting is of opinion that the maximum age of the Civil Service Examination should be raised to 23 years, and that the open competitive examination should be held in India, simultaneously with that in London.

Moved by Baboo Janoki Nath Sen, seconded by Babu Ananada Kisore Dutt Roy, and supported by Baboo Romes Chunder Bose.

IV.—That this meeting takes this opportunity of expressing its full confidence in the Bengal National League, and pledges itself to support it by every legitimate means that lies in its power.

Moved by Baboo Dulal Chunder De, seconded by Baboo Sarat Chunder Dutt, and supported by Baboo Sita Mohun Dass.

V.—Resolved that the following gentlemen be selected as delegates to represent the Sylhet public at the forthcoming National Congress: Baboo Prosunno Kumar Guha, Baboo Radha Nath Chowdhry, Baboo Joy Gobinda Shome, M.A., B.L., and Baboo Bipin Chunder Pal.

Moved by Baboo Tara Kisore Chowdhry, seconded by Moulvi Nasarullah, and supported by Baboo Prosunuo Kumar Dey.

VI.—Resolved that the proceedings of this meeting be sent to the Press for publication.

Moved by Baboo Loke Nath Sarma, and seconded by Baboo Nava Kisore Dass.

The meeting dispersed with a vote of thanks to the Chair.

CHITTAGONG.

25th December, 1886.

A PUBLIC meeting was held on Monday, the 13th instant, at 6 P.M., at the instance of the Chittagong Association, to elect delegates to the forthcoming National Congress, and to ascertain the views of the general public ou the reconstitution of the Legislative Councils and Covenanted Civil Service age question. Baboo Kamala Kanta Sen, B.L., High Court Pleader, President of the Chittagong Association, was unanimously voted to the Chair. He gave a succinct view of the questions to be discussed at the meeting, and in a short and neat speech, impressed upon the audience the necessity of the re-formation of the Legislative Councils as at present constituted, and the raising of the age of the candidates for the Covenanted Civil Service.

The following resolutions were passed and carried unanimously:—

I.—That having regard to the rapid progress of education and enlightenment, and the growth of public spirit in these provinces, this meeting is of opinion that it has now become urgently necessary, alike in the interests of the people of India and for the honor of English rule, that the Legislative Council of Bengal should be reconstituted in a manner more in harmony with the popular aspirations, the requirements of the time, and the necessities of the Government.

Proposed by Baboo Satis Chunder Sen, B.L., Pleader, seconded by Baboo Gagan Chand Chowdhry.

II.—That, in the opinion of this meeting, the Legislative Council of Bengal should be reconstituted upon the following lines:—

(*a.*) That the principle of representation should be recognised, and that the elected members of Council, being not less than two-thirds of the whole Council, should be chosen by local bodies, such as the Municipalities and the District Board of each district, to represent the different districts, and by the Chamber of Commerce, the Trades' Association, the British Indian Association, the University of Calcutta, the Calcutta Municipality and other established public bodies of similar reputation.

(*b.*) That the members of the Council thus formed should have the right of interpellation.

(*c.*) And, further, that the Provincial Budget should be laid before the Council and be discussed and passed by the Council.

Proposed by Baboo Romes Chunder Sen, B.L., Pleader, seconded by Moulvi Abdul Hossein, B.L., Pleader.

III.—That this meeting takes this opportunity of expressing its full confidence in the Bengal National League, and pledges itself to support it by every possible means in its power, and begs that the League will address the Government for the reconstitution of the Legislative Council according to the terms of the resolutions adopted by this meeting.

Proposed by Baboo Durga Das Dutt, Medical Practitioner, and seconded by Moulvi Ahmed Ulla.

IV.—That in the opinion of this meeting, it is resolved that the age of the candidates for the Covenanted Civil Service be raised at least to 21, and the examination be held simultaneously both in England and India.

Proposed by Baboo Raj Kumar Dutt, seconded by Baboo Kasi Chunder Gupta.

V.—That the meeting is of opinion that Chittagong should be represented in the forthcoming National Congress in Calcutta, and requests Baboo Aukhil Chunder Sen and Dr. A. C. Khastgir, Mahomed Ibrahim and Bodial Alam to go as delegates to the said Congress.

Proposed by Munshi Kajim Ali, and seconded by Baboo Aukhil Chunder Nundy.

The meeting was a grand success. Every one resent took a lively interest in the proceedings of the meeting. The meeting lasted for about two hours. The meeting was of a representative character. Hindus, Mahomedans, zemindars, merchants, in fact all sections of the commuuity, were fairly represented in the meeting.

COIMBATORE.

In pursuance of a notice circulated by the Secretaries of the Sudasa Darma Ratchani Sabha (The People's Association), a great public meeting was held on the 8th instant at the Native High School Hall, Coimbatore. M. R. Ry. V. Cooppoosawmy Iyer Avl., a well-known leading native gentleman, 1st Grade Pleader, and President of the 1st Bank having been voted to the Chair. Messrs. Kastury Ranga Iyengar, B.A., B.L., High Court Vakeel, Vigianthra Row Avl, Native High School, and others spoke in English, and S. P. Narasimulu Naidu spoke in Tamil of the objects of the Indian National Congress. Then the following gentlemen were elected to be deputed as delegates of Coimbatore to the Indian National Congress: Messrs. V. Cooppoosawmy Iyer, Kostury Ranga Iyengar, B.A., B.L., Annasowmy Row, Bujanja Row, B.A., Satagopa Charlu, M.A., Thiruvengadasamy Mudaliar, Vejiaranga Mudaliar, V. Krishna Row, H. Rama Row, Coottianna Mudaliar, Mahamed Kahan Sahib, Kunna Gounder, Mahamed Hosein Markair, S. P. Narasimmulu Naidu. After a vote of thanks to the Chairman and the Managers of the Native High School the meeting dispersed.

CALICUT.

A general public meeting of the citizens of Calicut was held at the Mananjara Municipal School House on Saturday, 6th November, 1886, for the purpose of delegating a gentleman to the forthcoming National Congress at Calcutta. There were present: Messrs. D. Manekjee, Koya Assu, Koya Haji, L. A. Rama Pattar (Merchants and Municipal Councillors), Kasturi Chund Ram Chund (Merchant), E. Subramanya Pillay (Merchant), S. Varadarajayyar (Pleader), Jum Saji Framji, Nanabai Bomanshah (Merchants), B. Ramunni Menon (Pleader and Municipal Councillor), Ismail Saheb, Chutra Choj Sett, M. Kadrli Koya, M. Abdulla Koya Haji (Merchants), C. M. Rarichan Muppan (landlord and Municipal Councillor), K. Choyikutti (landlord), H. Sankaranarayana Aiyar, P. A. Krishna Menon (Pleaders), C. Kunhiraman Menon, B.A. (Editor of the *Kerala Patrika* and Municipal Councillor), V. Karunakara Menon, Sivaramakrishnayyer, N. Subramanya Aiyar, K. R. Ramasawmy Aiyar, K. Krishna Menon, B.A. (Pleaders), S. Anantakrishnayyar, B.A. (Teacher), T. Kunhikutti Ali, M. Kunhamad (Merchants), D. Ganpat Rau, B.A., G. Appa Rau, N. G. Srinivasa Rau (Proprietors of the Native High School and Teachers), Visvanatha Aiyar, B.A., T. Panchapatesayyar, B.A. (Teachers), A. N. Anantaramayyar, B.A., B.E., T. Narayana Menon (Pleaders), and a great many more. M. R. Ry. L. A. Rama Pattar Avergal, a leading Brahmin merchant, having been voted to the Chair, opened the proceedings as usual. Mr. P. A. Krishna Menon, a 1st Grade Pleader, made an appropriate speech in Malayalam to explain to the audience the object of the National Congress and the urgent necessity there is for sending representatives to these annual Conferences from every part of India to make these Conferences thoroughly representative. Messrs. Varadaraja Ayyar and K. R. Ramasawmy Iyyar followed him with short speeches on the same subject.

(1.) It was proposed by Mr. P. A. Krishna Menon, seconded by Mr. S. Varadaraja Ayyar, and carried unanimously, that a delegate be sent to represent the citizens of Calicut at the National Congress to be held at Calcutta in December next.

(2.) Mr. C. Kunhiraman Menon, Editor and Proprietor of *Kerala Patrika's* offer to represent Calicut at the Congress, was accepted with thanks amid loud acclamations.

(3.) Proposed by Mr. H. Sankara Narayanayyar, seconded by Mr. K. Achutan Nayar, and carried unanimously, that Messrs. L. A. Ramayyar, Koya Assu, Koya Haji, Abdulla Koya, D. Manekji, C. M. Rarichan Muppan, and P. A. Krishna Menon, do form themselves into a Committee to give the necessary instructions to the delegate selected.

(4.) Proposed by Councillor Mr. B. Ramunni Menon, seconded by Mr. A. N. Anandaramayyar, and carried unanimously, that the expenses of the delegate be borne by public contributions.

A subscription list was at once pened, and a little over Rs. 100 were subscribed on the spot.

(5.) Resolved that a Sub-Committee composed of Messrs. L. A. Rama Pattar, C. M. Rarichan, Subramanya Pillay and P. A. Krishna Menon be appointed to collect the contributions.

A vote of thanks was then passed to the Chairman and the delegate Mr. Kunjiraman Menon. The meeting then terminated amidst shouts of applause.

NATTORE.

28th November, 1886.

AT a well attended general meeting of the People's Association, held this evening, resolutions for reconstructing the Legislative Councils on a representative basis, raising the limit of age to 23 years of candidates for the Civil Service and holding simultaneous examinations in India and England were unanimously adopted. Six delegates were elected to the National Congress.

GHATTAL.

26th December, 1886.

A MEETING of the people of Ghattal Sub-Division was held at Khirpie on the Friday, the 26th December. There were present Baboos Prosunno Kumar Bannerji, Zemindar; Girish Chunder Pahari, Zemindar; Priya Nath Roy; Peary Laul Ghose, Government Pleader; Grish Chunder Chatterji, Zemindar; Umesh Chunder Ghose, L. L., &c., &c. The following resolutions were passed:—

I.—That this meeting desires to place on record that the Legislative Council of this country, as at present constituted, does not suit the condition of this country, because its members generally come from a class who are absolutely ignorant of the wants and requirements of the general population of this country, therefore, this meeting earnestly entreats the Government to substitute election for nomination.

II.—That this meeting having heard with sincere delight that a National Congress will be held at Calcutta to advance the political rights, and to ameliorate the condition of the people of this country, this meeting gladly appoints Kumar Binoya Krishna Bahadur, the young patriotic and philanthropic zemindar, and a scion of a great family of Bengal, as delegate to represent the Association in the said National Congress.

III.—That a copy of the above resolutions be sent to the *Statesman* and the *Indian Mirror* for publication, and to Baboo Surendra Nath Banerjee, the Secretary of the Indian Association, and to Kumar Benoya Krishna Bahadur for information.

HALISHAHAR.

26th December, 1886.

THE following is an abstract of the proceedings of a general meeting of the Halishahar Good Will Fraternity in Sub-Division Baraset, held on the 25th instant for the purpose of expressing the sympathy of the whole community with the Bengal National League:—

I.—That this meeting considers the reform and expansion of the supreme and existing local Legislative Councils by the admission of a considerable proportion of elected members essential, and that such representative Councils should have some voice and control over the finance of the country.

II.—That this meeting has full confidence in, and sympathy with, the aims and objects of the Bengal National League.

III.—That this meeting is of opinion that the subjects to be discussed at the ensuing National Congress are of vital importance to the well-being of the country, and that the Halishahar Good Will Fraternity will, as far as it lies within its power, co-operate with the Bengal National League in furtherance of its objects.

IV.—That some delegates from the Fraternity be deputed to attend the National Congress.

V.—That copies of these resolutions be forwarded to the Local Government, Secretary to the Bengal National League, and the Editor of the *Indian Mirror*.

RANAGHAT.

1st December, 1886.

THE following is a copy of the resolutions, passed unanimously at a meeting of the Ranaghat Improvement Society, held at the Rivers Thompson Hall on the 28th November, 1886, Baboo Makhan Lal De, B A., in the Chair:—

I.—That in view of the necessity of combined agitation for political rights, the Association, hitherto known as the Ranaghat Improvement Society, be affiliated with the Indian Association, Calcutta, and be styled "Branch Indian Association, Ranaghat," and that the following gentlemen be appointed office bearers:—

Baboo Surendra Nath Pal Chowdhry, *President*; Makhun Lal De, B. A., and Baboo Ram Chunder Ghose, L.M.S., *Vice-Presidents*; Baboo Krishna Chunder Ghattak, *Secretary*; and Baboo Junendra Nath Pal Chowdhry, *Joint Secretary.*

II.—That a representative public meeting of this sub-division be convened at an early date to consider the desirability of addressing Government on the subject of the reconstitution of the Legislative Councils, as in the opinion of this meeting the introduction of a representative element into these Councils has become necessary.

III.—That Baboos Girija Prosunno Dutt, Aukhoy Kumar Ghose, (Municipal Commissioners), and Krishna Chander Ghattak be requested to represent this Association at the forthcoming National Congress to be held at Calcutta on the 28th proximo, and that the nominations made by the Krishnaghur Association for this district be approved.

IV.—That a copy of the foregoing resolutions be forwarded to the Secretary, Indian Association, Calcutta.

GUDIVADA.

At a public meeting held at Gudivada, Kistna District, on the evening of the 31st October, 1886, the following resolutions were unanimously passed :—

1. That the meeting fully sympathises with the working of the Mahajana Sabha at Madras, and with the objects of the National Congress held at Bombay last year.

2. That a Branch of the District Branch of the Mahajana Sabha be constituted here for furnishing the necessary information concerning the wants of this part of the district.

3. That M. R. Ry. Singaraju Venkata Subbarayadu Pantulu Garu be requested to represent them at the Anniversary of the Mahajana Sabha and at the National Congress to be held at Calcutta.

4. That M. R. Ry. Raja Kamadana Venkata Narasimharaogar, an ex-zemindar of this place, be thanked for his kindness in presiding on the occasion and for consenting to be the President of this branch in future.

GOOTY.

In pursuance of a notice issued by the Secretary of the Gooty People's Association, a large and influential meeting of Mahomedans, Hindus of all classes, and native Christians was held on the premises of the Sanscrit School, at 6-30 P.M., yesterday. Among those that were present there were Messrs. K. Runga Roa, Bujanga Roa, J. Yellappah Papasastrulu, N. Sreenivasa Roa, A. Ambajee Roa, Setharama Roa, T. Ramachendra Roa, B.A., B.L., District Munsiff, Kistamurthi Iyengar, B.A., Assistant Director of Revenue Settlement, K. Singaracharlar, Deputy Inspector of Schools, C. N. Subramania Iyer, Overseer, Angadi Karibasabha, Ambati Ramasawmy Chetty, Bara Sahib, Chandana Kasim Sahib, N. Sanna Reddy, R. Venkata Reddy, Belluli Iyanna, Lemboo Seshanna, Cheman Naik Sahib, Vahamia Sahib, B. Iyappah Reddy, Mr. I. J. Martin and Amhed Sahib, Native Doctor and many others.

On the motion of Mr. T. Ramachendra Row, B.A., B.L., seconded by Mr. Kistamurthi Iyengar, B.A., Mr. K. Runga Rad, 1st Grade Pleader and a ryot of this District, was unanimously voted to the Chair.

The Chairman opened the meeting with a short speech making allusions to the excellence and necessity of the National Congress, and calling upon the meeting to appoint a few delegates on behalf of Anantapur District to attend the Congress to be held this year in Calcutta. He said that the district that sent two delegates to the first Congress in Bombay should not fail to send delegates to the second Congress in Calcutta, and that he was happy to see that people of all classes and creeds of this small historical town should have met together, and taken the lead in appointing delegates on behalf of this district. He called upon the Secretary of the Local Association to read the letter received from Mr. J. Ghosal, Secretary to the Reception Committee, Calcutta.

The Secretary read the letter, and added that he had every reason to believe that the nominations made by the meeting would be approved by the people of Anantapur, Pennukondah and other towns in the district.

Mr. C. Madhva Row, Pleader, moved the following resolution in a short speech, remarking that the delegates they were appointing that day were worthy of their unqualified support and confidence, and that he knew that they would prove themselves to be their worthy representatives.

That Messrs. Y. Chondapah, Pleader, ryot, and the Chairman of the Gooty Union ; M. Nagesa Roa, Pleader, ryot, and a member of the Gooty Taluk Board ; and P. Kesava Pillai, Pleader, ryot, and a member of the Anantapur District Board, be appointed as the delegates of Anantapur District to the National Congress to be held in Calcutta in December next.

Mr. Cheman Naik Sahib, on behalf of the Mahomedans, seconded it in a Hindustani speech.

Mr. J. Yellappah, ryot, and an influential old member of the Gooty Bar, supported it in a Telugu speech.

It was also warmly supported by Messrs. Angadi Karibasappa in Canarese, Ramasawmy Chetty in Telugu on behalf of Comaties, and Mr. I. J. Martin in English on behalf of Native Christians.

Mr. P. Kesava Pillai moved a rider to the proposition " that Mr. Chenna Reddy, an influential ryot, and a member of the Taluk Board, be also appointed as a delegate from Anantapur District."

Mr. T. Ramchendra Rao seconded the rider.

The Chairman having put the proposition with the rider to the meeting, it was warmly and unanimously passed as the substantative resolution of the meeting. After several other gentlemen having passed a few remarks, Mr. T. Ramachendra Roa, B.A., B.L., proposed a vote of thanks to the Chairman in an eloquent Telugu speech, exhorting the people to take more interest in public matters, to form themselves into Associations, and to represent their wants and grievances to Government. He insisted that Government was not so much to blame as the people themselves, and assured them that Government will meet their wishes if only properly and constitutionally urged.

Mr. Singara Chariar having seconded the vote, the meeting dispersed in mutual good feeling and sympathy.

MHOW.

25th December, 1886.

The Central India Association held a public meeting to-day. They have delegated Mr. Mohendra Nath Chatterji and Seth Gungaram Chunilal to represent the Association at the National Congress. The delegates will start to-morrow.

DIBRUGHUR.

25th December, 1886.

The Council of the Upper Assam Association have appointed Baboos Gopinath Berdoloi, B.A., and Debi Churna Baru, B.A., delegates of the Association at the forthcoming National Congress.

MYSADUL, MIDNAPORE.

28th December, 1886.

At an influential meeting of the Branch Indian Association the following resolutions were unanimously adopted :—

I.—The reconstitution of the Legislative Councils in India on a representative basis is absolutely necessary.

II.—The Parliamentary enquiry into the working of the Indian Administration has become highly necessary for the better government of the Indians.

III.—The members of the Secretary of State's Council should not be taken largely from the returned Civilians from India. A reconstitution of that Council should immediately be effected, if it be not abolished altogether.

IV.—The examination of the Indian candidates for the Civil Service be held in India simultaneously with that held in England, and the maximum age of the candidates be raised to 23 years, leaving it optional with the successful candidates to proceed to England or not.

V.—That, considering the present financial condition of India, it is absolutely necessary that the military expenditure be reduced.

VI.—The Indians have given such tangible proofs of their loyalty so often that the Arms Act should immediately be repealed to increase the love for, and confidence of, the people in the British Government.

VII.—The sooner the old Theebaw is restored to his kingdom the better, or if it be found impracticable to do so some other Native Prince of Burmah should be invested with the government of Burmah under the British protection.

VIII.—In a country like India, the income-tax should never have been introduced. Besides the working of the tax is so oppressive to the people that the Government should try its best to put a stop to this crying evil.

IX.—Sympathy was expressed with the aims of the National Congress, and the following gentlemen were appointed delegates: Dr. J. N. Mitra, M.R.C.P. (Lond.), and Baboos Jogendra Nath Chatterji and Jodu Nath Chuckerbutty, B.A.

BAREILLY.

The following is an extract from the proceedings of the annual meeting of the Bareilly Institute, held on the 21st December, 1886:—

3. Read a letter from the Honorary Secretary, N. W. P. and Oudh Association, asking the Institute to send some members to join the National Congress, Calcutta. Resolved unanimously that Rai Durga Prosad Rai Bahadur, Munshi Bishen Lal M.A., Nawab Abdul Aziz Khan and Syed Mahomed Ashfak Hossein be deputed to represent the Bareilly community at the coming National Congress, and that a copy of this resolution be sent to the Secretary of the said Congress and the *Indian Mirror*.

TANJORE.

At a very large meeting of the Tanjore People's Association attended by representative Mirasidars of Combaconum, Mayavaram, Nannilam, Tiruturaipundi, Mannargudi and Negapatam, held in the Porter Town Hall, Combaconum, on 7th November, 1886, the following resolutions were passed:—

1. That the Association present an address of welcome to the Viceroy on his approaching visit to Tanjore.

2. That a memorial be drawn up and presented to His Excellency the Viceroy on the occasion of his visit to Tanjore on 7th December next on the subject of remission of kist for Fusly 1214 in this district.

3. That Messrs. S. A. Saminatha Iyer Avl., S. K. Annasami Iyer Avl., Sivaswami Odiar Avl., Rungaswamy Mudaliar Avl., Sinna Marakayarmalmiyar Avl., Vencatarama Iyer Avl., Kothandarama Iyer Avl., Pattamangalam Narayanasami Iyer Avl., Srinivasa Iyer Avl., Sambasiva Sastriar Avl., Thiruvangadam Pillai Avl., and the Chairmen of the Municipalities in the district, be requested to proceed to Calcutta and represent the Association at the National Congress to be held there on the 28th December next.

SHOLINGUR.

The Secretary writes: An enthusiastic meeting was held in the Reading-Room here on the 26th instant. Mr. E. Venkatasamy Raju was voted to the Chair. The objects of the Congress having been explained, it was proposed by the Chairman that Mr. C. Subbiah Naidu, a 1st Grade Pleader of the Munsiff's Court, should be requested to proceed to Calcutta to represent this Association. Mr. Subbaraya Pillay, Pleader, seconded this proposition, and this being supported by Mr. Tiruenkata Charyar, Head Master, was unanimously carried. Mr. N. Venkata Row, Vakil, then suggested that his expenses for going to and returning from Calcutta should be defrayed by the Association, but he, the chosen delegate, declined the offer with thanks. A vote of thanks to the Chairman concluded the proceedings.

BOMBAY.

At the meeting of the Bombay Presidency Association it was resolved that the following gentlemen be asked to attend the National Congress at Calcutta, which takes place on the 27th, 28th and 29th instant: The Hon. Dadabhai Naoroji, the Hon. V. N. Mundlik, C.S.I., the Hon. K. T. Telang, C.I.E., Messrs. Javerilal Umiashunker Yajnik, N. G. Chandavarkar, Sorabjee F. Patell, Dinshaw E. Vacha, Dinshaw P. Kanga, Shamrao Vithul, G. Nilkanth, R. M. Syani, Kazi Mahomed Ismail Chilmai, Lallubhai Ambalal Desai, Vizbhookandas Atmaram, Dajee Abajee Khare and Golabdas Bhaidas, Vakil.

CUDDALORE.

A public meeting was convened at the Government College at Cuddalore on the 1st November, 1886, in order to consider the steps to be taken to reconstruct the Gadilum Bridge, to send delegates to Calcutta in order to attend the National Congress to be held there in December, and to raise contributions in aid of the National Fund. The following gentlemen were present:—

M. Rajarathna Moodaliar, S. Devanayaga Moodaliar Avergal, M. Arumuga Pillay, T. Govindasawmy Naidu, S. Doroisawmy Aiyer, C. S. Sami Iyengar Avergal, B.A., B. Kristnaiyer Avergal, B.A., T. Ramasawmy Moodeliar Avergal, S. Manikam Moodaliar Avergal, O. Radhakristnaiyer Avergal, C. Kristnaiengar Avergal, E. Sivachidambara Chettiar Avergal, C. Dorasawmy Moodaliar Avergal, Subbarayalu Reddiar Avergal (Villapuram), V. M. Ramasawmy Iyer Avergal, P. Vadivalu Moodaliar Avergal, K. Bashyam Iyengar Avergal, B.A., M. Minakshisundra Siva Iyer Avl., B.A., A. Manika Moodaliar Avl., B.A., N. Paramasiva Iyer Avl., B.A., M. Ramasawmy Iyer Avl., B.A., K. Kandasawmy Moodaliar Avl., C. Munisawmy Moodaliar Avl., S. Palani Appa Moodaliar Avl., S. V. Cooppusawmy Sastriar Avl., B.A., K. Sambasiva Iyer Avl., B.A., P. T. Sadagopahcharriar Avl., M. Veerasawmy Moodaliar Avl., B. Ramalinga Iyer Avl., A. Ragavacharriar Avl., Sreenivasa Chettiar Avl., M. Arunachala Chettiar Avl., V. Cooppusawmy Naidu Avl., K. Krishnasawmi Moodaliar Avl., S. Ruthna Moodaliar Avl., C. Chinnasawmi Iyer Avl., T. Veerasawmy Naidu Avl., C. Kolandavalu Moodaliar Avl., Arumuga Moodaliar Avl., Sabapathy Chettiar

Avl., S. Rungasawmi Moodaliar Avl., C. Muthia Chettiar Avl., T. A. Hari Row Avl. and many more.

Mr. M. Rajarathna Moodaliar was unanimously voted to the Chair.

The Chairman opened the proceedings by stating that the gentlemen present were aware, from the notice circulated, of the purpose for which the meeting was convened. He would say a few words on each of the subjects under consideration. In the first place, the fall of the Gadilum Bridge is a public calamity. It has entailed on the people considerable inconvenience. Public traffic is much impeded and great difficulty is experienced in consequence. The Municipality with its limited resources can hardly maintain itself, and, therefore, cannot undertake such an expensive work. It is, therefore, necessary that application should be made to Government for the restoration of the Bridge. Going to the second subject, the National Congress is to be held at Calcutta in December, with the object of holding a conference in the interests of the country. In that Council the wants and requirements of the people will be fully discussed, with a view to their being communicated to the British Parliament. The advantages resulting therefrom cannot be overstated. It is, therefore, necessary that we should send delegates to represent this district in the Congress. Lastly a Fund has been set on foot at Madras for National purposes. So many things are done in furtherance of public objects, the Fund in question is applied towards defraying its expenses. It is, therefore, proper that we also do something in aid of the Fund. Everything will be stated at length in connection with the respective propositions for the consideration of the meeting.

Then Mr. Sadagopa Charriar, Editor of the Local Tamil paper, addressed the meeting at some length. He first dwelt on the measures adopted by the Mahajana Sabha at Madras in furtherance of the public cause, thereby pointing out the necessity of supporting the Institution in all possible ways. It was necessary also, he said, that delegates should attend the Congress at Calcutta.

Proposed by S. Manika Moodaliar Avergal, Town Councillor, seconded by M. Arumuga Pillay Avergal, Town Councillor, and carried unanimously that a memorial be addressed to Government on the subject of the re-construction of the Gadilum Bridge.

Proposed by B. Ramalinga Iyer Avl., District Court Pleader, seconded by T. Ramasawmy Moodaliar Avl., Manager, and carried unanimously that delegates be sent from this district to attend the National Congress at Calcutta.

Proposed by M. Arumuga Pillay Avl., seconded by M. Veerasawmy Moodaliar Avl., Town Councillor, and carried unanimously that S. Devenayaga Moodaliar Avl., B. Kristnaiyer Avl., Muthia Chettiar Avl., Mahomed Moral Merkayer Avl., T. Govindasawmy Naidu Avl., and M. Rajarathna Moodaliar Avl., be deputed to represent this district at the National Congress.

Proposed by S. Sawmy Aiyengar Avl., seconded by O. Rathakristna. Aiyer Avl., District Court Pleader, and carried unanimously that M. Arumuga Pillay Avl. be requested to join the delegates.

Proposed by M. Arumuga Pillay Avl., seconded by Govindasawmy Naidu Avl., and carried unanimously that contributions be made here in aid of the National Fund at Madras.

Proposed by S. Rungasawmy Mudaliar Avergal, seconded by B. Kristnaiyer Avergal, and carried unanimously that a Fund be raised for the purpose of this Sabha, and one-half of it be sent to Madras in aid of the National Fund.

Proposed by B. Kristnaiyer Avl., seconded by S. Dorasawmy Iyer Avergal, District Court Pleader, and carried unanimously that the Secretaries of this Sabha be Treasurers, and be authorized to take steps to co-operate with the heads of the community for this purpose.

After a vote of thanks to the Chairman, and the Head Master of the College for having allowed the meeting to be held in the College premises, the meeting dispersed.

BURRA BAZAR POLITICAL ASSOCIATION.

On the 24th December, 1886, the Burra Bazar Political Association, *i.e.*, the Raj Niti Sabha, was instituted by the leading members of the Burra Bazar. The enlightened and leading members of all the communities residing in Burra Bazar were present.

The main object of the meeting was to assist the National Congress in its deliberations, which cannot but be good both for the public and the Government, and to represent its own views on various subjects of general interest.

The meeting was held at 12 noon, and several subjects were discussed up to 2 P. M. Baboo Nahar Malji Lohia was elected Chairman, and the proposal for the establishment of the Sabha was made by Pundit Sadhanandji, seconded by Pundit Dhebi Sahaiaji, and supported by Baboos Siva Bukshiji, Surajmalji, Bilasiramji and other gentlemen present.

The objects of the Congress, the necessity of co-operation in politics and commerce in Burra Bazar, &c., were all carefully explained by Pundit Sadanandji. He further proposed the necessity of sending representatives to the Congress.

The Chairman then proposed Pundit Jwala Nath Sarma, Secretary, Bharata-maitra, Mandala, Burra Bazar, as their delegate to the Congress.

Pundit Gobind Naryanji commented upon the utility of this body, and lucidly pointed out that patience and perseverance were the true price of success. He further considered that the greater the strength of the representatives the better for the public. Thereupon the meeting proposed Pundit Sadanandji together with Pundit Jwala Nath Sarma as representatives for the Congress, and the proposition was carried with applause.

The meeting concluded with a vote of thanks to the Chair.

BELLARY.

In pursuance of a notice circulated by the Secretary of the " Native Club," a public meeting was held at 7 P.M., on the 13th instant, for the purpose of appointing delegates to represent the people of the Bellary District in the ensuing National Congress. All castes, trades and professions were fully represented. Mr. G. Ruthna Chennepah, a leading merchant of Bellary, was voted to the Chair. Mr. D. Kristna Charlu, 1st Grade Pleader, explained in Telugu the object of the meeting. Messrs. P. C. Ananta Charlu (High Court Vakil), M. Vasudeva Naidu and A. Sabbapathy Modelliar addressed the meeting on the object of the National Congress, its doings of the last year and the advantages to be derived therefrom in future. The Chairman then said that for a purpose like this, all patriotic gentlemen should offer their services without even a request from any quarter.

The following gentlemen were then elected as delegates of the Bellary District to the Congress, *viz.*, Mr. Vasudeva Naidu Garu Rao Sahib (1st Grade Pleader and Municipal Councillor), Sindigi Marisiddapah Garu (Merchant and Manager of the *Vizia Dhwaja*, a Canarese paper newly started), R. Venkata Narasiah Garu (Merchant), K. Venkata Rao Garu (1st Grade Pleader), Abdul Karim Saib Khan Sahib (Merchant and Municipal Councillor), A. Gopalswamy Naidu Garu (Contractor), Mollagavali Sunjeeva Reddi Garu (Landholder), Joharapuram Seetharama Reddi Garu (Landholder), C. E. Runganadam Modelliar Avl. (Medical officer), A. Sabbapathy Modelliar Avl., Rao Bahadur (Merchant, Landholder and Municipal Chairman). A suggestion was then made for raising subscriptions to meet the costs of the delegates, but the gentlemen delegates declined to accept any money for their expenses and offered their services gratuitously. Their offer was accepted with loud acclamation. It was resolved that the names of these delegates be communicated to the Secretaries of the Mahajana Sabha and the Bengal National League. The meeting was closed with a vote of thanks to the Chairman.

RUSSAPAGLA.

At a special meeting of the Russapagla Improvement Association, held on Friday, the 24th December, 1886, it was resolved :—

1.—That this Association expresses full sympathy with the National Congress which will meet in Calcutta during the Christmas holidays.

II.—That this meeting appoints the Rev. P. M. Mukerji, Nawab Golam Rubbani and Baboo Mohendra Nath Sen as its delegates to represent the Russapagla Improvement Association at the sittings of the Congress.

CALCUTTA.

There was an enthusiastic meeting of the Hindustanis of Calcutta at the Natmandir of the late Rajah Sír Radha Kant Deb Bahadur, K.C.S.I., on Saturday, the 25th instant, at 3 P.M., to select a delegate to the National Congress. Pundit Sada Nund Misra, Editor of *Sudhanidhi*, was unanimously elected delegate.

PENUKONDAH.

In pursuance of a notice circulated by the Penukondah Telugu Newspaper Club, a public meeting was held on the 13th instant in Ramasawmy Temple, when M. R. Ry. G. Narasinga Rao Garu, B.A , a popular Pleader and Vice-President of the Taluq Board, was unanimously voted to the Chair. There were present : Messrs. Chacravarthi Iyengar, Shrotriamdar, Pleader and a member of the Taluq Board ; Wahamiya Sahib, Jaghirdar ; Jagannayaculu Naidu, B.A., Clerk, Head Assistant Collector's office ; Sreenivasacharlu Garu, Pleader and Landlord ; Hanumayya Garu, Shrotriamdar and Abkari Contractor ; Bysani Subbiah Chetty Garu, Merchant ; V. Hanumantha Rao Garu, Taluq Sheristadar ; Vankatasamiah Garu, Pleader and ryot, Kristnamacharlu Garu, Darmakarta, Kocherum Temple ; M. Paupa Rao Naidu, ryot and Clerk of the Head Assistant Collector's office ; Jagannadahraju Garu, Hospital Assistant ; Ramanna Naidu Garu, Deputy Inspector of Vaccination ; Dasappa Garu, Pleader and Landlord ; Venkoba Rao Garu, Pleader and Landlord ; Hanumantha Reddi Garu, ryot and Village Munsiff, and others representing all sects and sections of the community. The Chairman opened the meeting by explaining the necessity and advantages of the National Congress, and called upon the audience to appoint delegates to represent Penukondah Division of Anantapur District. Mr. Paupa Rao Naidu then briefly touched upon the various grievances which are within the reach of the Congress. The following resolutions were unanimously passed :—

1. Resolved that Mr. V. R. Chacravarthi Iyengar be requested to represent this division of the district at the National Congress to be held at Calcutta and that the nominations made by the Gooty Association for this district be approved.

2. Resolved that this meeting fully sympathizes with the objects of the National Congress held last year at Bombay and the working of the Mahajana Sabha at Madras.

3. Resolved that a vote of thanks be given to Mr. Chacravarthy Iyengar for having accepted the honor of being a delegate to proceed to the National Congress and the meeting wish him a safe and happy journey.

4. Resolved that copies of proceedings of this meeting be communicated to the delegates appointed by the Gooty Association and to newspapers. A vote of thanks was then passed to the Chairman, and the meeting dissolved amidst shouts of applause.

NELLORE.

At 6 P.M., on the13th instant, a public meeting was held in the hall of the Nellore Reading Room. The attendance was large, Mr. S. Narayanasamy Chetty, B.A., was voted to the Chair. He explained in Telugu the object of the meeting ; Mr. M. Butchia Puntulu, the Editor of the *Hindu Reformer*, who is now here, addressed the meeting in Telugu for about an hour. The Chairman again delivered an enthusiastic speech. Then the assembly elected their delegates to represent them at the National Congress which is to meet at Calcutta on the 28th proximo.

Proposed and carried unanimously that Messrs. S. Narayanasamy Chetty, B.A., F. T. Ward, District Court Pleader, and M. Venkatasubba Row, Munsiff Court Pleader, be requested to represent the people of this district at the National Congress.

BERHAMPORE.

A public meeting was convened under the auspices of the Berhampore Association to select delegates to the Calcutta Congress. Proposed and carried unanimously that the following gentlemen be requested to attend the coming Congress : M. R. Ry. Pakula Gopala Rau Patrudi Garu, B.A., Pleader of the District Court of Ganjam, and Abdul Kareem Sahib Bahadoor, an influential merchant of Berhampore, both natives of the district, extensive Landholders and Town Councillors.

ROHORA.

16th December, 1886.

At a general meeting of the Rohora Patriotic Association at Rohora near Barrackpore, attended by the whole of the intelligent and educated portion of the community, the following resolution was passed :—

"That this Association, while expressing its cordial sympathy with the Calcutta National Congress, requests Baboo Gopal Chunder Mukerji, M. B., Baboo Nibaran Chunder Chowdhry, Baboo

Baikunto Nath Chowdhry and Baboo Siddessur Bannerji to attend the said Congress as delegates from this Association."

RAJAMUNDRY.

At a general meeting of the Literary and Debating Association, Rajamundry, held on the 7th November, 1886, resolved :—

1. That M. R. Ry. N. Subbarau Pantulu Garu, B.A. and B.L., be voted to the Chair.

2. That M. R. Ry. Singaraz Subbarayalu Garu, B.L., of Masulipatam, be requested to represent Rajamundry at the next National Congress, Calcutta, and that of the next Mahajana Sabba, Madras.

SURAT.

The following gentlemen have been elected by the *Surat Sabha*, at a general meeting, to attend the second National Congress to be held at Calcutta on the 27th December :—

Rao Saheb Dolatrai Surbhai Desai, B.A.., LL.B. (London), Barrister-at-Law, President of the Sabha and a Municipal Commissioner ; Messrs. Hosangji Burjorji, B.A., LL.B. ; Manchha Shankar Jinauram, B.A., LL.B., Rattiram Durgaram Dave, B.A., Chhaganlal Thakur Dass Modi, B.A., Narbheram Mansukhram, Abdul Reheman Ganibhai, and Messrs. Harilal, Harshadrai, Dhrum B.A., LL.B., Manchersha Palonji Kaikobad, Head Master, Mission School, Surat, Honorary Secretaries.

MADRAS.

A general meeting of the Mahajana Sabha was held at 6 P.M., on Saturday, the 27th instant, at the Mahajana Office for the purpose of appointing delegates to the National Congress to be held at Calcutta on the 28th, 29th and 30th December. There were present the Zemindar of Devacottah, Messrs. P. Rangiah Naidu, P. Somasundaram Chettiar, C. Etherajulu Naidu, K. Krishna Row, S. Biligiri Iyengar, P. Etialwar Naidu, P. Theagaraja Chetti, C. V. Sundaram Sastri, K. P. Sankara Menon, S. Ramasawmy Mudaliar, G. Subramania Iyer, Gopal Nair, C. Ponurangam Pillay, Gulam Dastagiri Saheb, Waljee Laljee Sait, Abdul Kareem Saheb and many others. Mr. P. Rungiah Naidu, the President of the Sabha, being voted to the Chair, Mr. P. Anunda Charlu explained briefly the object of the meeting. He said that some time in the month of October at the instance of the Central Committee at Calcutta a circular letter was addressed to all the affiliated Associations and to all the corresponding members of the Sabha by the Committee to send delegates to the Congress. In response to that letter, in some towns public meetings were held for the purpose, while in other places the local Associations held general meetings and delegates to represent them at the ensuing Congress were appointed. Now it is the business of the Sabha members to appoint delegates to the Congress. After some discussion among the members present, M. R. Ry. P. Somasundaram Chettiar proposed that Messrs. P. Rangiah Naidu, Hon'ble S. Subramania Iyer, P. Kottasawmy Dever, M. Jaga Raw Pillay, S. Ramasawmy Mudaliar, C. Singaravalu Mudaliar, T. Namberumal Chettiar, A. Danakoti Mudaliar, G. Subramania Iyer, P. Anundacharlu, R. P. Subramania Iyer, M. Samasawmy Naidu, M. E. Sriranga Chariar, Abdul Raiman Sett and Waljee Laljee Sait represent this Sabha from Madras as its delegates at the forthcoming National Congress. This proposition being seconded by Mr. K. P. Sankara Menon was put to vote and adopted. It was further resolved that the Central Committee at Calcutta be informed that the following gentlemen who were nominated at meetings held in several towns in the Presidency will also attend the Congress as delegates from their respective towns and Associations :

Ganjam District.—Berhampore—Mr. Pakala Gopal Row Patrudu Garu, B.A., Pleader, District Court and Landholder and Town Councillor, Berhampore ; Mr. Abdul Karim Saheb Bahadur, Influential Merchant, Landholder and Town Councillor, Berhampore. Chicacole—Mr. Makunda Row Naidoo Garu.

Urlam Estate.—Mr. Venkatasawmy Naidoo Garu.

Soudam Estate.—Mr. Jivaravyya Sastri Garu.

Vizagapatam District.—Vizagapatam Town—Mr. A. Surianarayana Row Pantulu Garu, B.A., Pleader.

Godavery District.—Rajamundry—Mr. Row Saheb Singaraju V. Subbaroyudu Garu, B.L., Vakil, High Court, Masulipatam.

Kristna District.—Bezwada, Gudiveda and Kristna—Mr. Row Saheb Singaraju Venkatasubboroyudu Garu, B.L., Vakil, High Court, Masulipatam.

Nellore District.—Nellore—Mr. S. Narayanasawmy Chetti Guru, B.A., Pleader, District Court, and Municipal Councillor, Nellore ; F. T. Ward, Esq., Pleader, District Court, Nellore ; Mr. M. Venkatasubba Row Garu, Pleader, Munsiff's Court.

Bellary District.—Bellary—Mr. Row Saheb ; A. Sabapathy Mudaliar Avl., Merchant, Chairman, Municipal Council, Bellary ; Mr. K. Venkata Row Garu, Pleader, 1st Grade, Bollary ; Mr. Kurnool Kareem Sahib Avl., Bellary ; Mr. Sindigi Marisiddappa Garu, Merchant, Bellary ; Mr. T. Chidambara Row Garu, B.A.

Anantapur District—Gooty—Mr. Y. Chondappa Garu, Pleader and Ryot and Chairman of the Gooty Union ; Mr. N. Negasa Row Garu, do. do. and Member of the Gooty Taluq Board ; Mr. P. Kesava Pillai Avl., Pleader and Ryot, and member of the District Board, Anantapur.

Kurnool District.—Penukonda—Mr. V. R. Chackravarthi Iyengar Avl., Pleader, Penukonda.

North Arcot Dt.—Walajanaggar—Mr. Chedambadi Subba Naidoo Garu, 1st Grade Pleader.

Chittore.—Mr. Gopala Chariar Avl., B.A., 1st Grade Pleader ; Mr. C. Srinivassa Chariar Avl., B.A.

Chingleput Dt.—Chingleput—Mr. M. Y. Ramanuja Chariar Avl., Pleader, Dt. Court.

South Arcot Dt.—Cuddalore—Mr. S. Devanayaga Mudaliar Avl., Landed Proprietor and Chairman, Municipal Council ; Mr. C. Kristna Iyyer Avl., Pleader, Dt. Court, and Municipal Councillor and Member of the Local Fund Board ; Mr. Muthayya Chettier Avl., Merchant and Municipal Councillor ; Mr. Mahomed Nairad Marocayar Avergal, Merchant and Municipal Councillor ; Mr. T. Govindasawmy Naidoo Garu, Landed Proprietor ; Mr. M. Rajarathna Mudaliar Avergal, late Railway Engineer ; Mr. M. Arumugam Pillai Avergal, Landholder and Municipal Councillor.

Tanjore Dt.—Combaconam—Mr. S. A. Saminatha Iyer Avl., Pleader, Dt. Court, and the President of the Tanjore People's Association.

Coimbatore Dt.—Coimbatore—Mr. S. P. Narasimhalu Naidoo Garu, Editor and Proprietor of the "Coimbatore Crescent."

Malabar Dt.—Calicut.—Mr. C. Kunhi Raman Menon Avl., B.A., Editor and Managing Proprietor of the "Kerala Patrika" and Municipal Councillor.

The next subject that was brought before the Sabha was the consideration of the subjects to be discussed at the Congress. Mr. P. Anunda Charlu said that the Committee of the Sabha some time ago met to consider the matter, and have resolved to send a list of subjects to be discussed at the Congress. He said that the Central Committee issued a circular to all the public bodies in India to suggest subjects for the consideration of the Congress, and the Committee of the Sabha have accordingly prepared a list. When all the members of the Congress meet at Calcutta, the subjects sent up by the several Associations in India will be considered, and the members present will decide what subjects should be omitted and what discussed at the Congress. After some discussion about the matter Mr. J. M. Nallaswami proposed that the subjects proposed by the Committee of the Sabha be approved by the general body. This being seconded by Mr. C. V. Sundaram Sastriar was passed.

With a vote of thanks to the Chairman the meeting was dissolved.

PUBNA.

19th December, 1886.

A PUBLIC meeting convened by the Pubna Branch Indian Association was held this day to elect delegates to the National Congress. After much discussion the following gentlemen were elected:—

1. Moulvi Mahomed Ahmed Chowdry.
2. Baboo Grish Chunder Roy, B.L.
3. „ Kally Charan Sen.
4. „ Jadav Chandra Chuckerbutty.
5. „ Mohini Mohan, Dr., M.A.
6. „ Parbati Nath Kar.
7. Munshi Amir Ally.
8. „ Rahimuddin.

The members of the Pubna Indian Association also appointed Mr. A. Chaudhri, B.A., LL.B. (Cantab.), Barrister-at-Law, as one of their delegates to the National Congress. Mr. Chaudhri is a member of an old zemindar family of that district, having considerable influence there.

LUCKNOW.

10th December, 1886.

THE following gentlemen have been formally elected as delegates from the Jalsai Tahzib, Lucknow, to the ensuing National Congress:—

1. Nawab Syed Raza Ali Khan.
2. Baboo Abinash Chunder, B.A., Pleader.
3. M. Hamid Ali Khan, Esq., Barrister-at-Law.
4. Baboo Sriram, M.A., Pleader.
5. Baboo Bansilal Singh, Pleader.
6. Pundit Pran Nath.

MIDNAPORE.

13th December, 1886.

A MEETING of the Executive Committee of the Local Indian Association was held yesterday at the Public Library Hall, when it was resolved to send the following gentlemen as delegates to represent the Association at the coming Congress:—

1. Baboo Bepin Behary Dutt, B.L., Chairman of the local Municipality.
2. Baboo Debendro Nath Ghose, M.A., B.L., Vakil.
3. Baboo Rughunath Dass, M.A., B.L., Municipal Commissioner.
4. Baboo Krishna Lal Mozumdar, Pleader and Municipal Commissioner.

KISSENGUNGE.

22nd December, 1886.

THE Mahajans' meeting was held here to-day to move the Government for the reconstitution of the Legislative Councils. Baboos Nunda Gopal Bhaduri and Jogodish Chunder Lahuri were appointed delegates to the National Congress. Great enthusiasm prevailed.

MR. CHUNILAL LULLUBHAI PAREKH, the Vice-President of the Arya Guyan Vardhak Sabha, having been elected its delegate to attend the ensuing Calcutta National Congress, left Bombay by last Monday's mail train.

AT a meeting of the Managing Committee of the Arbalia J. V. Sabha, held on the 19th December, the following resolutions were unanimously carried out:—

I.—That this meeting expresses cordial sympathy with the Second National Congress, which will meet in Calcutta during the Christmas holidays.

II.—That this meeting appoints Baboo Bejoy Lal Dutt as its delegate to represent the Arbalia J. V. Sabha at the sittings of the Congress.

NAGPORE.

23rd December, 1886.

MESSRS. GANGADHAR RAO CHITNAVIS, Gopal Hurry Bapu Rao Dada and Abdul Aziz, elected at the late public meeting, have left this station for Calcutta to attend the National Congress as delegates from Nagpore.

[*And a vast number of similar brief telegraphic notices, which it is useless to reproduce. A great number of meetings published no reports whatsoever of their proceedings, merely telegraphing to the Calcutta Committee: "To-day great public meeting, A. B. C. & D. elected delegates, arrive Calcutta, such an hour, such a date." Only in the Madras Presidency were full reports of all the meetings immediately published in the local Press; many of these Madras Reports have been reproduced above; the rest are similar.*]

APPENDIX III.

SUBJECTS FOR THE NATIONAL CONGRESS.

CALCUTTA NO. 1.

To

THE SECRETARY OF THE COMMITTEE.

DEAR SIR,

ONE of the most important subjects that will engage the attention of the National Congress this year will be the best system under which practical effect can be given to the third resolution of last year's Congress.

It is proposed to accept the eleven provisional rules, printed as an Appendix to the "Old Man's Hope," as a *basis for discussion*, and it is hoped that before joining the Congress at Calcutta, all delegates will consider carefully, in consultation with their constituents, the alterations in and additions to these rules necessary to convert them into a really satisfactory and sufficient code.

Since in each Province the circumstances differ, it will be specially necessary for all provincial delegates to make up their minds as to the exact bodies and classes to whom in their own province the Eranchise should be extended.

Although the unofficial Europeans and Eurasians have not, thus far, except perhaps in Southern India, joined the movement to any appreciable extent, we must not overlook their rights in propounding a national scheme, and must in any such scheme provide for the due election by these communities of fitting representatives.

Certain general principles may be suggested for consideration.

Probably no official should be allowed a vote, firstly, because the official element will be sufficiently represented ; and, secondly, because such persons could hardly exercise the Franchise with sufficient independence. This however will not exclude from the Franchise *quondam* officials who have left or have retired from Government service on pension.

So far as may be, our scheme should provide for the representation of the intellect and the wealth of the country.

It seems probable that in each province, or at any rate in some provinces, it will be best to constitute an "Electoral College" as it is termed, for the selection of members of the Provincial Councils. It might in some provinces be arranged, for instance, that the municipalities of every town of 25,000* inhabitants and upwards should elect one member for every 25,000 souls they represent, to sit in this college ; that all the graduates of its university should elect one member, for every 200* graduates still on its rolls; that all persons paying income-tax on an income of say Rs. 5,000 per annum and upwards should elect one member for every 100* such persons ; that all political associations containing not less than 100* members, each paying a subscription of not less than Rs 5* per annum, should elect one member for every 100* such members ; that the editors of all papers having a *bonâ fide* circulation of 500* copies and upwards, should amongst them elect one member ; that the Bar, including all native barristers and duly licensed vakeels and mooktears, should elect one or more members ; that the native chambers of commerce should elect one or more members. And other bodies and classes, according to the circumstances of each province, might equally obtain the Franchise. Persons qualified to be allowed to vote in two or more classes.

The Electoral College thus constituted would then proceed to elect, either from amongst themselves, or from outside, those men that appeared to them to be best qualified, irrespective of race, creed, colour or caste, to represent the Indian interests of the province in the local councils.

It must be left to the unofficial European and Eurasian communities, unless these should join in our deliberatians, to decide exactly how best the election of representatives of their communities could be managed, but it is clearly open to us to suggest with reference to the ability, wealth, and interests at stake, of each community, what numerical ratio should in our opinion obtain between Indian, Eurasian, and European elected representatives in each province.

The question of whether representatives in the local councils should or should not necessarily have a private income of not less than a certain monthly sum, either of their own in realized property or earned by them in some profession or business, or guaranteed to them by their constituents (if this be thought advisable), will also have to be considered.

The above remarks are submitted purely to illustrate, by the suggestions they embody, the nature of the questions connected with the all-important subject of representations that will require consideration and discussion.

But it may perhaps be affirmed with some confidence, that while one object of any scheme must necessarily be to secure as broad a basis for electoral operations as is consistent with excluding those unqualified by education and manner of life to share in the Government of the country, the main object of any scheme that we adopt must be to secure as our representatives the ablest, most independent and above all most public-spirited men available.

It is very possible that this primary object will not be attainable in any two provinces by precisely the same system, and delegates should beforehand carefully work out with the rest of the ablest men

* All figures are inserted purely tentatively to avoid blanks.

of their province, subdivision or city, the precise method by which under local conditions this primary object seems most likely to be attained.

In conclusion I am to remark that the time of the Congress will be limited, and that this question of representation is the pressing one of the day, and that it is not desirable to complicate it with a multitude of minor or secondary questions; but that at the same time if in your committee's opinion there be any other subjects of *pressing* national importance, the discussion of which at this coming Congress they consider essential, it is earnestly hoped that you will, with the least possible delay, set the same forth in a circular letter to all other committees so that all may be prepared to discuss the same. It would be well if in such circular you could conveniently sketch out the nature of the resolution which your committee would desire to see carried, as a basis for preliminary discussion by the delegates of other provinces with their constituencies.

It would be convenient if your circular could be printed, and sent in sufficient number of copies to each select committee to enable them to distribute copies to sub-committees and representatives.

Such circulars might be headed like this present one, and bear the town name of the committee as this does, with, if you issue more than one such circular, your own serial number,

November 5th, 1886. * * * * *

CALCUTTA NO. 2.

To

The SECRETARY of the COMMITTEE.

Dear Sir,

The great importance of securing for India, Indian representatives in Parliament, requires no demonstration now.

We consider that at the coming Congress the best means of securing funds to meet the expenses of Indian candidates in England should be carefully considered, and some definite scheme for the future adopted. The points, *inter alia*, to be considered are—

1*st*—How it is to be determined, whether any Indian proposing to stand for a seat in Parliament is or is not entitled to be considered a national candidate and therefore entitled to national support?

[This requires an immediate, *temporary* solution—later when representation has been introduced into India, it will probably be sufficient to require that three-fourths of the Indian representatives in the supreme council certify that the person is in all ways qualified and appears to have a reasonable prospect of success, but in the meantime some other scheme for approving candidates must be adopted.]

2*nd*.—Shall any but Indians be competent to become national candidates?

[It is to be suggested that Europeans non-domiciled, if fit to be members of Parliament, will almost necessarily possess sufficient means of their own to require no pecuniary assistance from us, and further, that any such assistance from us would lead to their being considered paid members greatly diminishing, in the case of Europeans, their power for good in the House. As regards domiciled Europeans and Eurasians, probably unless these communities join our movement, they should be left to make their own arrangements for their respective representatives should they desire to have such in the House.]

3*rd*.—What should be the nature and extent of assistance afforded to national candidates?

[For instance, should it be only a lump sum, of not exceeding say Rs. 5,000, or Rs. 10,000 towards preliminary and election expenses, given once for all, without demand for accounts, or requiring full accounts and the repayment of any balance; or should, besides this, a yearly allowance of say Rs. 2,000, or Rs. 4,000 be made so long as the candidate continued to sit in the House and retain the confidence of the country? Should passages to and fro be paid?

Again should the assistance to an approved national candidate be supposed to be all he will receive (except from his own personal friends and family), or should it be treated as a supplementary grant to one partly provided for by his province?]

4*th*.—How shall funds be raised for providing such grants, if any, as it may be decided to give to national candidates?

It is needless to press the matter further; numerous other minor questions will suggest themselves as soon as the matter is thoughtfully considered, and the above remarks are merely intended to suggest the nature of the points which ought, our committee believe, to be settled at the coming Congress.

* * * *

November 7th, 1886.

(*Many other similar suggestions, of subjects for discussion, were circulated, but the above will suffice to show the character of these pre-Congress inter-communications.*)

APPENDIX IV.

(*Selection of Telegrams and Communications expressive of Sympathy with the objects of Congress, laid on the table at the close of the First Day's Proceedings, vide ante, pp. 16 and 58*).

From President, Literary Association, Coconada.

Association regrets its inability to send delegates. Sympathizes warmly with movement.

From President of General Meeting at Santipore.

At a meeting of the people of Santipore, held yesterday, it was resolved that this meeting desires to convey to the National Congress its entire sympathy with the objects of the Congress.

From Chairman of Shillong Meeting.

Public Meeting, Shillong, express complete sympathy with National Congress.

From Secretary, Bulsar Arya Sabha.

Sabha entirely sympathizes in proceedings of National Congress at Calcutta.

From President, Central India Association.

We have delegated Messrs. Mohendranath Chatterjee and Gangaram Choonilall, and have fullest sympathy with objects of Congress.

From Desai Kahanrai Hukoomatrai, President, Broach Association.

Accept our sincerest sympathy in the cause the Congress has at heart. Broach wishes success to your patriotic labours.

From Secretary, Vidyabhivarkani Sabha, Vizianagram.

Sabha heartily sympathizes with National Congress.

From Secretary of Lok Sangraha Sabha, Veerumgaum.

General Meeting desires to express deep sympathy with Congress work. Empowers Dhruva to represent them.

From Honorary President, Baraset Association.

Express Association's hearty sympathy with the objects of the National Congress, and its desire to move Government for the several reforms in the administration which have become necessary.

From President of the Oriental Debating Society, Mombadevie.

The Oriental Debating Society heartily sympathizes with the Congress.

From the Secretary of the Patriotic Association, Trichinopoly.

Please convey to the Chairman of the Congress the deep regret we feel at our inability to be present, and kindly offer our warmest thanks to all the members of the Congress for the deep interest they have shown in meeting together to advocate the cause of the dumb millions of our countrymen. We heartily wish the Congress every success.

From Radhika Charan Mittra, Vaqueel, Dibrugarh.

Entire Indian community, Dibrugarh, have full sympathy with, and highly appreciate importance of, National Congress to be held at Calcutta on 27th December, and following days.

From (unintelligible) Sabha, Mangalore.

South Canara wishes success to endeavours of the National Congress. Long live India.

(And a number of similar Messages from minor Associations all over the country.)

From Maharajah of Durbhangah.

Regret very much my inability to attend the Meeting of the National Congress owing to ill-health, but wish it every success; hope some practical scheme will be resolved upon about the best way to develop the natural resources and utilize the dormant capital of the country. It is indeed a happy thing for natives to see representatives from all parts of the country assembled together to discuss the future advancement of India. Only a few years ago such a thing could not even be dreamt of, and sincerely hope something practical will be done to encourage trades and manufactures in the country.

From Eardley Norton, Esq., Barrister-at-Law, Madras.

Regret inability attend Meeting this year. Grateful for invitation. Accept assurance, warmest sympathy in your work.

From Bramhamoyi Debya, Sabrool, viâ Madhanagar.

Heard all about the National Congress. Accept the blessings of an old Hindu widow. I bless you and pray your this union might last for ever.

From Rajah of Nilambur, Mullaparam.

Regret notice received to late; anxious to share in the undertaking in which fully sympathize.

(And a great number of similar messages, from all kinds of people, expressing sympathy, sending good wishes or blessings, or explaining non-attendance in consequence of sickness, deaths of relatives, and a variety of causes.)

(Also numerous letters like the following.)

No. 1373.

PARJOAR ASSOCIATION OFFICE,
47, SANGATTOLA, DACCA.
The 26th December 1886.

To

THE SECRETARY TO THE NATIONAL CONGRESS COMMITTEE,
BRITISH INDIAN ASSOCIATION ROOMS,
Calcutta.

SIR,

I HAVE the honor, on behalf of the Parjoar Association, Dacca, to inform you that it expresses its cordial sympathy with the objects and the aspirations of the National Congress about to be held in Calcutta. The Association has entire confidence in the Congress, and hopes that the important question of the reconstitution of the Legislative Councils of this country, on a representative basis, will receive the greatest attention of the Congress. The Parjoar Association wishes the Congress a happy and successful issue.

I have the honor to be,
SIR,
Yours most faithfully,
SATIS CHANDRA GHOSE,
Honorary Secretary, P. A.

(Notices of Departure of Delegates.)

"The Tribune" of Lahore says :—

"Six Lahore delegates to the National Congress of Calcutta left this station by the evening mail of the 23rd instant. A large number of native gentlemen assembled on the Station platform to see them off; and the train carrying them left the station amidst loud and enthusiastic hurrahs."

Ex "Mirror."

An Ahmedabad telegram says: "The Guzerat delegates, representing the various towns and stations, started on the 22nd instant for the National Congress. There was a great demonstration at the railway station, where garlands and flowers were showered on them. Many people attended at the station to wish them a happy journey."

Ex "Mirror."

A telegram from Lucknow says :—

"A large and influential gathering of citizens of Lucknow of all classes accompanied the delegates notwithstanding the hour of their departure to the Railway Station, and despatched them with hearty good wishes and enthusiastic cheers.

(And many similar notices appeared in the various Indian papers.)

APPENDIX V.

COMMENTS OF THE PRESS.

THE NATIONAL CONGRESS.

[*" The Indian Mirror."*]

THE great demonstration which took place yesterday afternoon in the Town Hall will never be forgotten by the thousands who witnessed it. In the point of mere display of what may not inaptly be described as the national colors, the demonstration must have exceeded the most sanguine expectations of even the most ardent among its promoters. But the event was not only a mere display—it was a solid fact and proof positive of the welding together of the different communities into an animated, hope-inspired and self-sustained whole. It was a pleasure to watch the upturned faces, as they glowed with the enthusiasm caught from the speakers. Congratulations were flying from mouth to mouth, and every one was conveying the glad message to his neighbour that he had realized what he would not have dared even to hope for a very few years since. And the fact is, indeed, hard to realize. Just imagine numerous representatives of all Her Majesty's Indian subjects grouped together under one roof—Hindu, Parsi, Mahomedan, Eurasian, and even English,—and the still more numerous castes and creeds,—their hearts beating together, their feelings the same, their thoughts running to a common goal,—even their very language the same,—imagine all this, and then open your eyes, and you will feel the truth and force of the never trite simile of John Keats:—"Imagination is like Adam's dream, he woke and found it truth." And thus what we had so long dreamed while we slept the sleep of inaction, has become reality, when we have awakened to action.

The opening of the National Congress yesterday was, indeed, an event of which any country might be proud. It is also an event which will fill with undefined dread the enemies of Indian progress. It has been the fashion with these people to remind us ever and anon that all political agitation in this country has been in the hands of men who have made a profession of it, that it has been in the hands of men with no stake in the country, and that the aristocracy of the country, Rajahs, Zemindars, and men of wealth, if not of light, had no sympathy with it. Critics of this class must have been cruelly undeceived yesterday, when the large majority of the delegates were not only not professional agitators, but were actually men who must have made considerable sacrifice of time, comfort, and money for the cause. Again, the men who took part in yesterday's proceeding were not professional agitators whom school-boys had come to *encore*. Nor was it irresponsible youth that wakened the susceptible audience to ringing and reiterated applause. The speakers were men, whose hair had whitened with age. Old and young India had met to consider common objects. Dr. Rajendralala Mittra represented that aristocratic body, the British Indian Association; and as he spoke yesterday, one felt that that venerable figure represented something more than the aristocracy; he represented the wisdom and experience of age, and he represented the learning both of West and East. Then there was the first Native gentleman of Calcutta, Maharaja Sir Jotendro Mohun Tagore, the old man honored by his people and by his Sovereign. The Hon'ble Dadabhai Naoroji could not be considered young by any stretch of the imagination. But, perhaps, the most striking figure among the speakers was Baboo Joykissen Mookerjee. He spoke for some considerable time, and the old man's voice was very faint and low, yet infirmity and age had not prevented him from coming to the Town Hall, to speak encouraging words to the delegates and to the public who had come to welcome them. The sight was most impressive, and will be a great and useful lesson to much younger men. Now all these men have a stake and, some of them, a very large stake in the country, and are certainly not professional agitators. Among the delegates who spoke yesterday, and spoke with great effect, was Nawab Reza Ali Khan Bahadur, a nobleman of note in Lucknow. Tall and slim, as he rose from his seat on the platform, the spectators greeted him with ringing cheers. But the message of peace and good will he conveyed from the Mahomedans of the united provinces—the most important in India—to their Hindu and other fellow-subjects, was received with tumultuous enthusiasm. This nobleman repudiated the action of certain Bengal Mahomedans, and altogether his speech was a hearty and unstinted peace-offering; and as such it was received with satisfaction and gratitude. That the vast majority of the Indian Mahomedans fully sympathised with the objects of the Congress was proved later on when the President read the telegraphic congratulations of the Mahomedans of Hyderabad and of the whole of the Deccan. Indeed, there were Mahomedan delegates in the hall from all parts of India, not the least among whom was Mr. Rahmatullah Mahomed Syani, late Sheriff of Bombay. It will be seen that the Mahomedans have acquitted themselves most creditably on the day when the whole nation was on its trial, and its triumphant emergence from this most severe ordeal may be attributed to a very appreciable extent to the hearty co-operation of the Mahomedans.

The tone of yesterday's proceedings was unexceptionable. There was absolutely nothing in them to which the most pronounced Babu-phobist could object. Unalloyed and affectionate loyalty to the Throne, enthusiastic veneration for the Queen, these were displayed continuously throughout the afternoon. All the great virtues of Englishmen were freely admitted, and ungrudgingly extolled. And Mr. Dadabhai Naoroji managed to raise a cheer even for Lord Dufferin. This little fact abundantly testifies to the good temper and sense of the meeting, and the probable bias of the future deliberations of the Congress. The fact is that the people of India are loyal to the backbone. We take and give hard blows. Englishmen kiss and make friends with thrashed adversaries. We have learnt the genial lesson from our masters. And if we find it our duty, a little oftener than is agreeable to us, to say bitter things of English rule in some of its aspects, none the less do we love to dwell on its brighter side. The people of India had met yesterday to consider some of the darker aspects of this rule. But when asked by the

President if they were disloyal, because they made certain demands, an indignant thundering "no" rumbled for many seconds in the huge hall. And as for their loyalty, its depth may be judged when they cheered even Lord Dufferin.

THE SECOND NATIONAL CONGRESS.

[By a Bombay Delegate.]

Yesterday's monster meeting in the Town Hall ought to be registered in the annals of British India as unique of its kind. There may have been, perhaps, for all we know, more crowded meetings in that noble hall in times past, where the voice of wisdom and the charms of eloquence have united to make Native demonstrations for political objects a grand success. And it is possible to imagine that in times to come, equally successful meetings will be held for purposes the most beneficent for the weal of the State at large. But never, perhaps, for another half a century to come will there congregate an audience at once so intelligent, so instinct with moderation, so unbounded in its enthusiasm, so throbbing with the generous pulsations of national life, and withal so hopeful of the ultimate political emancipation of their race as the one that gathered yesterday afternoon in the hall of the metropolis of the Empire, under the presidency of a true and devoted son of India, and one of the most unselfish and honored patriots that the country has produced during the last fifty years. Whether we think of the various nationalities that were grouped in that hall, men of every caste and community, of every shade of opinion, or whether we take into consideration the representatives which each Town, District and Province sent forth to deliberate on questions of common weal, one cannot help remarking that the time and the occasion were unique. The meeting marks a distinct epoch in the history of our Indian communities. It is the herald of coming events—events still in the womb of time, but which are sure to take place at the proper moment, and with the happiest of results. The burning words in which Macaulay concluded his great speech, fifty-three years ago, have been verified. It is in reality the dawn of that "proud day," which he forecast with the instinct of the seer—a day to be proud of not only for India but for England. It is an event in which every genuine Englishman should rejoice. For it is the happy result of that beneficent policy of education which our rulers laid down in 1854. As the Hon'ble Mr. Dadabhai Naoroji reminded the meeting, India is a trust which Providence has reposed in the British for the benefit of the Indian races. And this meeting may fairly be pointed out as an example of the honest and liberal spirit in which that trust has been hitherto discharged. If we are now agitating for greater political freedom in the constitutional manner we are now doing, our rulers must remember how far we have falsified the alarmists in their own ranks, men of narrow vision and still narrower spirit, men steeped in selfishness and prejudices, men who are never tired of proclaiming on the house-top that by giving knowledge to the Indians they are giving them power which they will rather abuse than use. Have not Indians, guided by the knowledge, which English literature and English history impart, learned to make proper use of the freedom of speech so long granted to them? Who could deny, after hearing the words of moderation and wisdom, which fell from the lips of two such veteran politicians as Dr. Rajendralala Mittra and the Hon'ble Dadabhai Naoroji, that Indians of liberal education are in every way fit for greater political freedom? I am fully convinced that had there been present at the meeting those severe critics, who, in season and out of season, have been vainly vociferating that we are not yet far removed from our state of pupilage, and therefore, unfit for a larger political freedom, they would have found ample reason to modify their views. Nay, I go a step further, and say that they would have acknowledged with all the sterling honesty characteristic of Englishmen that we had fully made out our case to participate more largely in the government of the country, and to represent in the Councils of the Empire the true wants and wishes of our people. Thus, the reforms which the President enumerated as being now necessary for the better government of the country are reforms which would, if granted, tend rather to strengthen than undermine the British Indian Empire. As Sir Charles Trevelyan sagaciously observed half a century ago, of us Indians, "so far from having the idea of driving the English into the sea uppermost in their minds, they have no notion of any improvement, but such as rivets their connection with the English, and makes them dependent on English protection and instruction." Thus the reforms, which we are now advocating, have, for their foundation, mutual benefit and good will. These two points, I think, were very well brought out by Mr. Dadabhai in his speech; and it is to be hoped they will be read in the light and in the spirit in which he candidly placed them before the meeting. Altogether the two addresses were most admirable, and are sure to commend themselves to the judgment of every right-thinking Englishman, who has at heart the genuine welfare of our countrymen and his own. It is also to be hoped that the important and authentic information which Mr. Dadabhai communicated to the meeting with regard to the sentiments and feelings which the Viceroy cherished towards us, will tend to disabuse the mind of many a sceptic who has hitherto viewed all actions emanating from that exalted personage as retrogressive or distinctly injurious to the interests of the Indians. It is needful at this juncture that our people should disabuse their minds of erroneous impressions and prejudices—be these latter ill-founded or well-founded. Mutual toleration and confidence are most essential for a consummation of some of those pressing reforms which have been long since in the air. Without these we shall be able to achieve nothing; the second National Congress will, it is to be hoped, show by its deliberations during the next three days how far it is worthy of being respected by our rulers, and how far it is a duty on their part in return to comply with some of its most reasonable demands.

THE NEXT CALCUTTA CONGRESS.

[*"Native Opinion," Bombay.*]

The anniversary of the great national movement, which was inaugurated last year, and which first came to a head in this city has arrived, and the National Congress meets this year at Calcutta. The Bombay Presidency Association has chosen its delegates for the great assembly, and all the public bodies throughout the country will do the same, and there will assemble at Calcutta during the ensuing Christmas a gathering as remarkable for its representative character as for the capacity and ability of its collective members. The delegates from Bombay show names, which are not only representative of the Presidency, but some of whom would be gladly accepted as their representatives by any portion of the country. So, too, gentlemen from Madras, the Punjab, the North-West Provinces and from the other provinces of the Empire will assemble at the capital and discuss with the representatives of Bengal the grievances of the people of this vast country, and suggest to Government means of removing them. Bombay, it is said, sends 16 members only, but it is not by numbers that we should calculate the benefit of their presence. No doubt, if more could have been sent, the better it would have been. But even sixteen is not a very small number, and their presence will doubtless be as influential as that of the fifty-two delegates which Madras is going to send forth.

This institution of a National Congress, which is to meet once a year in one of the great cities of the Empire, speaks volumes for the silent progress the country has been achieving. It is an institution which is destined to play a very important part in the political history of our country, and is a very forcible exponent of the patriotism and the desire for progress which exists at present. It has long been asserted that there is no national feeling in the country, that the people are incapable of political thought like the people in the West, and that the Asiatic mind is a soil very unfavorable for the growth of free aspirations. No doubt, the past history of the continent has in some measure justified these assertions. But students of political history will not fail to mark in these Congresses the great lesson of time. Thanks to Western education, already the film that had spread over the vision of the people has been removed, and their eyes opened to ways of combination for the purpose of achieving political liberties by legitimate exertions. The rough and ready warlike spirit which characterised the different provinces of the country in by-gone times, and which arose to the surface by fits and starts, whenever oppression was to be repelled, has already given place to legitimate agitation by means of the Press and the platform. The exclusive feelings of difference between the inhabitants of different parts of the country, which made them as ready to fight with each other as with a common enemy, and which at times was intensified so much as to make one section side with the common enemy in order to accomplish the destruction of the other, has vanished, and under the wand of this great magician has turned into a feeling stronger than friendship, and has become a link to join all in the common understanding of a national brotherhood. These changes are really so very vast and glaring as to be read by all not wilfully blind. No doubt, several self-constituted judges still persist in thinking that national life in India is even yet not awakened. We may safely leave these people to the obscurity of their own ignorance, and looking for ourselves see in these Congresses and similar other institutions signs of the times which are pregnant with future efficacy. We at least regard these Congresses as landmarks which the future historian will take hold of as landmarks of the rapid progress of political thought.

THE NATIONAL CONGRESS.

[" *The Express.*"]

"Then as regards the National Congress now assembling in Calcutta. We are apprehensive that, unless the questions to be deliberated are approached in a very accommodating frame of mind, the whole affair will end in a *fiasco*. This would be a pity for many reasons. We think it indicates a healthy condition of the body politic, when any considerable section of the community is prepared to sacrifice time, money, and a not overabundant leisure, in order that its members may survey the political and social situation, and cast about to see in what respects the present lot and the future prospects of the people may be ameliorated. The pre ent Native Congress has many important subjects to deal with, and no true friend of India can, we think, in any just or right spirit either ridicule or condemn the convocation of such a representative assemblage. It cannot too frequently be borne in mind that the Indian Government is a quite despotic bureaucracy. There may not be manifest any special illiberality in its dealings with the people or public interests *en bloc*, but that it is anything but an enlightened despotism admits of no argument. Such being the case, it is a very wholesome sign indeed to find the intelligent members of the community fully alive to the fact that, if they ever expect to get anything of value in either an administrative or a representative connection, they must keep their demands well in the forefront of affairs, and make sure that the Government understand the nature of their requirements. It does not follow by any means, that such demands should be at all revolutionary or have a tendency to make the State suspicious of the loyalty of the people. As the providers of the *means* of administration, it is but reasonable that the people should be represented in the local Councils; it is not asking more than they are fully entitled to, that they should have a voice in the government of the country. At present they have neither. They are no more represented in the Councils of the Government than are the Russian peasants in the Great Council of the Czar; in a word, they are governed by a System and by Codes which they have no part or lot in formulating or framing. The people are very sensible of all this, and although they appreciate the honesty with which the laws are administered, and the fairness with which they are themselves governed, they *feel* and *know* that, were it otherwise, they would be practically as helpless as any other people who are subject to the personal whims of an irresponsible ruler and living under the most unmitigated despotism. It is not surprising, then, that the popular cry should be for representation in its real form,—not the hollow sham which now obtains in the Presidency and Supreme Legislative Councils; whilst their aspirations to be directly represented in the Imperial Parliament are altogether legitimate. At this conjuncture we think it is to be regretted that the National Mahomedan Association of Bengal should have resolved upon holding aloof from the Native Congress.

The reasons urged are *primâ facie*, substantial enough and sufficiently tenable; nevertheless, we think it is to be regretted that an influential Mahomedan section should separate itself from a Conference which, as we take it, is not convened for the purpose of embarrassing the Government, but rather to assist it with suggestions and advice, the outcome of deliberations shared in by popular representatives from every part of the country."

THE NATIONAL CONGRESS.

[" *Statesman.*"]

The most striking testimony to the character of the English rule of India that has yet presented itself to the world is, we believe, the assemblage of Native gentlemen therein, to whom the local commanity of Calcutta gave a welcome yesterday at the Town Hall. We have now gathered together for a few days in this city men to whom we can point with pride, as the outcome of a century of our rule. They have come here, not so much because they have grievancvs to represent to the Supreme Government, but that we ourselves have taught them to cherish honorable and healthful ambitions, the absence of which amongst any people stamps both them and their rulers with degradation and reproach. It is no assembly of ignorant and disaffected men to whom Calcutta has given this hearty welcome, but a body of distinguished men who acknowledge with almost passionate earnestness and gratitude what English rule has done for their country, and who simply ask the Government to complete the work and realise—both for itself and for them—the fruition of the hopes we have taught them to cherish, as essential to wise and healthful government.

The refusal of the National Mahomedan Association and of the Mahomedan Literary Society—represented respectively by Mr. Amir Ali and the Nawab Abdul Lutiff—to take part in the National Congress now assembled in this city does not, we are assured, command the sympathy or approval of the Mahomedan community generally, who have certainly a right to ask what steps were taken by these gentlemen to ascertain the views of the community, in writing these letters. The Mahomedan community at Madras have sent delegates to the Congress, and so have the Mahomedans of Bombay, the North-Western Provinces, Oudh, and the chief towns and cities of Bengal, and before taking so serious a step as that which Mr. Amir Ali and the Nawab have taken, they will themselves allow, we think, that they ought to have ascertained, beyond doubt, that the community which they are supposed to represent, desired them to take such action. We are not able to affirm that they did not take it, but there is, we fear, a strong presumption against their having done so. It is strong testimony to the character of the local Native Press that the subject has been dealt with in a spirit of extreme moderation, unusual in the public Press, and this moderation is of itself a most forcible reply to the charges that are so unjustly and commonly brought against our Native contemporaries. Let them but continue to show this self-command, and no one will be able, or even desire, to resist their representations and demands. The letters must have been a sharp trial to many of them, and the perfect self-command they have shown in their comments thereon is an honorable fact upon which we congratulate them very sincerely.

["*Indian Union.*"]

WHEN we cast back a glance at the history of our country during the last twelve hundred years; when we consider the various vicissitudes it has undergone, passing from the subjection of one foreign tyrant to that of another; when we recollect the invasions of Mahomed, the devastations of Taimur, and Ghangiz and Nadir Shah; when coming to still recent times, we think of the hordes of Pathan and Pindari free-booters who so fearfully disturbed the peace of the country and made life and property equally insecure; and compare it with the present condition of our country, where peace reigns, and life and property rest secure, where religious persecution is unknown, and the gift of free speech and writing is vouchsafed to the highest as well as to the lowest individual, our heart swells with gratitude for the people who, under Providence, have been instrumental in bringing about this happy change around us. It is most true that neither affluent prosperity, nor abject poverty, neither exalted freedom nor degraded servitude, is the eternal lot of nations, or of individuals. And though at periods of a nation's existence, when all its energies seem exhausted, its sacred fire burnt out, and the people steeped in indolence, selfishness, and corruption, sink lower and lower in the scale, the lover of his country might not unnaturally despair of its advancement, yet all history teaches us that "such a state of things is not eternal; that a remedy, an effectual remedy, is provided against its evils, in the rise of other States, the advent of fiercer passions, or the inroad of a brave people; and that, as certainly as the bursting vegetation of spring succeeds the torpid vitality of winter, so surely will the energy and power of mankind come to revive the decaying spirit of nations." And so has it been here. We have always regarded the advent of the English into this country as a clear providential arrangement meant to revive the decaying spirit of the Indian Nation,—a spirit so far decayed as to make people doubt the existence of the nation itself. The new life which English rule has infused into the country, the new spirit which English education has breathed into the hearts of the people, is too clearly visible in all the various movements set on foot all over the country for the moral and material, social and political advancement of the people. But it was nowhere seen so fully as in that ever-memorable assemblage, the National Congress, which met last year at Bombay, and which will meet next week again at Calcutta. To say that that phenomenon is unique in the political annals of India is to say very little of it. But it is one which, while it fills the heart of every Indian with the most cheering anticipations for his country, will also inspire a noble pride in the heart of every generous Englishman to think that that phenomenon was made possible only under England's rule in India. England is the land of freedom and the mother of free nations. And it would really have been a matter of not only surprise but shame if the close connection of above a century with England, such as India has known, had not revived the spirit of freedom among the Indian people, who yield to none in the glory of their past warlike traditions, and whose warlike instincts, though often suppressed, have never yet been extinguished. While, therefore, we rightly expect every honest Englishman, who has the uncontaminated blood of a free Briton running in his veins, to come forward cheerfully to help and encourage the movement in a loving spirit, we cannot at the same time help pitying those misguided men, who, calling themselves sons of free England, still, on account of perverse prejudices towards the Native people, show themselves hostile to such movements and speak in the most merciless and unjust manner of their promoters and doings. Still more do we pity those Indians who, unable to overcome the selfishness which enthrals them, catch the contagion from such comments, and not only hold themselves aloof from, but speak derogatingly of them. We sincerely trust that these may soon see the folly of their conduct, and instead of incurring the obloquy and the sin of being the detractors and opponents of such movements, may unite their efforts with those of the earnest patriots who are engaged in the arduous but glorious task of regenerating their country and restoring it to something like its pristine glory.

The spectale of hundreds of men of light and leading coming together from the remotest parts of this vast Indian Continent to consider their common grievances, and to formulate their common wants, cannot fail to create the deepest impression even on the most cynical minds. The meeting of the people of the Punjab, of Bombay, of Madras, of Bengal, of the N. W. Provinces and Oudh, will be a meeting of so many brethren after a separation of long, long years or rather centuries; and the thrill of hope and joy which will pass through the frame of those who will see them folding one another in their loving embraces, can only be felt and not described. Let no one have the impudence to say after this that the Indian people do not constitute a nation. A phenomenon like the one which will be witnessed in only five or six days in Calcutta, is impossible in the absence of strong national feeling and national sentiments.

It is unnecessary for us to say what impression the meeting of the Congress will make on the minds of those who have the actual reins of government in their hands; how it will dry up like a mighty sun the mist of wrong impressions which seem unhappily yet to bedim the vision of most people both here and in England with regard to the Indian people and their feelings. The very fact of such a Congress will go far to falsify all the foolish things which certain Anglo-Indians and their servile organs have been persistently dinning into the ears of English statesmen and the English people about the actual condition of India. It will demonstrate to them that India is now no longer what it was 20 years ago: that the spread of English education has changed the aspect of this country; that Indian youths drinking at that fountain-head of freedom—the glorious Literature of England—have been imbued now with an irrepressible desire for some share in the administration of their country's affairs; and that the system of government which might very well have been suited to the India of 1850, does not at all agree with the fitness of things in the India of to-day.

Not the most ardent of our reformers has ever said that the Congress will express the opinion—in the strict sense of the word—of the whole Indian population. The opinion of the *whole mass of the people* has never yet been fully represented in England itself, where representative Government has a proud history of above six hundred years. And the opinion which any representatives or delegates will express in India in any Council or Congress whatever, cannot, in the nature of things for many many years to come, make anything except a faint approach to even that imperfect representation which obtains in England at the present day. But there can be no manner of doubt that it will faithfully represent the views of the thoughtful portion of the Indian people, and these, as every man with a grain of common sense can easily understand, guide and control in all lands and climes the opinion of the people. To say that the delegates assembled at the Congress will give expression to their own individual views alone is to say the merest falsehood. Hundreds of public meetings, large and small, have been held all over the country to nominate delegates for the Congress, and the views which they will express will virtually be the views of those who have nominated them. The questions that are almost sure to come up for discussion thereat are discussed in these meetings; and though it would be foolish to expect that the views of the people on every little point could be obtained, the general drift of their views, especially on the more important and prevailing topics of the day, can, and we are sure will be known and faithfully represented by the delegates, and should, as such, command the serious consideration of the Government. We have already enumerated the subjects that are likely to be discussed at the Congress in a previous issue, and we need not, therefore, repeat them in this article again. We shall have to say a great deal more about them when the deliberations and resolutions of the Congress have been made known. In the meantime, we wish our readers a happy Christmas, and our delegates a safe and pleasant journey to and from Calcutta.

THE FIRST DAY'S WORK OF THE NATIONAL CONGRESS.

There can be no two opinions as to the complete success which the Congress has achieved during the first day's sitting of its delegates. No assembly of enlightened men in the world, bent upon honest hard work for the good of their country, could have proceeded to deliberate and resolve on matters the most momentous in a more business-like fashion. It was, indeed, a sight of which the representatives of any free nationality might be proud. There sat packed closely together in the not too commodious hall of *the Association*, which has been deservedly called *the parent* of all other like organisations in the country, nearly five hundred delegates, surrounded by a crowd of eager spectators, keenly intent, each in his own way, in taking some active part in the business submitted for transaction, and more or less burning with a desire to have his say on the resolution proposed and seconded. It seemed as if the genius of order and harmony had presided on the occasion, and guided the deliberations of the representative assembly. No doubt, a variety of opinions were expressed; but there was not a single speaker who did not feel the weight of his responsibility, and who was unmindful of the importance and gravity of the debate. All appeared to be animated by the sole desire of arriving at unanimity on questions which have more or less passed from the stage of controversy, and entered into the regions of the practical or the possible. Tolerance of each other's opinion and due deference to the wishes of the indefatigable and impartial President, these were the marked features of the proceedings. Nor were patience and good humour wanting. These, too, have had their sobering influence on the minds of the delegates. All went to work with such an amount of earnestness and cordiality as to leave nothing to be said by way of objection or criticism. Though the hour of business was fixed at 11 A. M., it was nearly noon before the President took the chair, and opened the proceedings. His speech was brief and to the point, and, on the whole, served well as a model for the various gentlemen who spoke to four of the resolutions that were passed. Mr. Dadabhai impressed on his brother delegates the importance of economising the limited time at their disposal by mildly hinting that each speaker should do his best to limit his speech to five or ten minutes at the utmost. And, like the stern disciplinarian that he is, he rigidly adhered to the ruling. This procedure in a great measure facilitated the business of the Congress, and the Honorable President certainly deserves the congratulations of the delegates for the admirable way in which the work was transacted.

* * * * *

Thus have ended the proceedings of the first day of the Congress. They amply bear out our repeated assertion in these columns that enlightened Natives are in every way qualified to discharge the higher duties of self-government. For a more satisfactory illustration of the practice of self-government could not have been found than the first day's work which the delegates transacted in the rooms of the British Indian Association under the presidency of a gentleman who has not only made his mark here but in England—that nursery of free thought and free action and the mother of constitutional Government. In this connection how prophetic seem to be the words of Sir Charles Trevelyan recorded forty-eight years ago: "They (the Natives) duly converse with the best and wisest Englishmen through the medium of their works......Admitted behind the scenes, they become acquainted with the principles which guide our proceedings; they see how sincerely we study the benefit of India in the measures of our administration. . . . They learn to make a proper use of the freedom of discussion, which exists under our Government, by observing how we use it ourselves; and they cease to think of violent remedies, because they are convinced that there is no indisposition on our part to satisfy every real want of the country." It is because Natives are convinced that there is, in reality, no indisposition on the part of Great Britain to gratify the real wants and wishes of the country that they have organised Congresses to give body and form to those wishes. This and this alone is the *rationale* of the Indian Congress.

PROCEEDINGS OF THE NATIONAL CONGRESS.

[By a Bombay Delegate.]

Now that the Congress is dissolved, after its arduous work during the last three days, it may not be uninteresting or uninstructive to give my own impressions with regard to the variety of business it has been able to transact. It may be safely acknowledged that this second National Indian Congress is a complete success. Nay, it is something more. It is a complete vindication of the enlightened and liberal policy which the British Crown and Parliament first laid down half a century ago. The Congress is the natural outcome of that slow but steady progress which English education has been making among our countrymen in all parts of this vast Empire. Unparalleled as is the British Indian Empire in the annals of the world, more unparalleled still is this phenomenon of picked men of the various communities of India, separated the one from the other by hundreds, or even in some cases thousands, of miles, differing in race, religion, and customs, who assemble on a common platform for a common purpose, and that, too, in the very heart of the capital of the Empire. For we should never forget the vast extent of India. Where each Province is almost as large as France, or Spain, or Austria, where, in fact, all the Provinces together, which, now constitute British India, are equal in area to Europe, excepting Russia, the political phenomenon which Calcutta has witnessed since Monday last, must be pronounced unprecedented. It is not only unprecedented in the history of India, but in the history of the world. For when, we may ask, has history recorded a single instance in times, ancient or modern, of whole nations, I mean picked men of the various communities of which India is made up, separated one from another by hundreds of miles and differing in race, religion, and customs, of whole nations having assembled on a common platform, animated by a common instinct to work for a common cause, and that cause nothing short of the political welfare of their fellow-men. I consider this event to be quite an epoch in the annals of our countrymen—an epoch of which not only we Indians should feel proud but every genuine Englishman also. As the Hon'ble Dadabhai Naoroji justly observed in his inaugural address, the Congress has been made possible only because of English rule. It is British freedom of speech and thought, British liberty, British institutions, British statesmanship, British sympathy, and British righteousness, that have all combined to evolve the present Congress. Never, even in the "halcyon" days of Vikramaditya, or in the palmiest days of Akbar, could such an assemblage have become possible. All honor and gratitude, therefore, to our rulers, who have so far helped us to emancipate ourselves from a degrading slavery, and to struggle for, nay ambitiously aspire to, these higher political aspirations, which, when realised, will add a greater glory to, and reflect a brighter lustre on, the British name. This I take to be the happy result of a century of British rule. Though I am not one of those "emotional" men who grow enthusiastic on any particular subject, I cannot help wishing that William Zachray Macaulay had been present to witness the political phenomenon now displayed to the entire civilized world. How it would have gladdened his heart to know that the whirligig of time had wrought out those changes which he had so sagaciously forecast half a century ago, sooner or immeasurably sooner than he had ever hoped or anticipated. In his own words it may be truly observed that "the public mind of India" has so far expanded under the English system that it has, in reality, "outgrown" it. That, "by good government," the statesmen of England have educated us, Indians, into a capacity for better government. Nay more, "that having become instructed in European knowledge," we have already arrived at that stage in the history of our political condition when we are able to "demand European institutions." The day of which he was not sure has come to pass. And I take it te be the proudest day in English history. And yet, with a strange want of apprehension, with a lamentable inability to grasp the real situation, there are among us a certain class of Anglo-Indian critics, official and non-official, who would still attempt to avert or retard it. But we can afford to pass by in silence the endeavours of such short-sighted critics. Who has ever succeeded in stopping a rising tide by his Partingtonian mop or, for that matter, with his tiny goosequill?

But to return to the proceedings of the Congress. Firstly, I must say that this second Congress has far surpassed the first in point of strength and publicity. We at Bombay sat more as a private conference, and shut out the public from witnessing our proceedings. Again, being the first of its kind, we were not so overpoweringly strong in numbers. Perhaps that was an advantage. All beginnings should be modest. The strength of the rivulet at its source is always feeble, but as it glides on in its onward course both its momentum and force increase till at last its power becomes irresistible. Not that the second Congress has arrived at such a stage, but it is certainly true that the demonstrations, which have accompanied its sittings here have attracted greater notice, and the work done had been of a more practical character. The first Congress formulated abstract principles of great pith and moment. The second Congress chalked out a line of action on those principles. This is exactly what is wanted. Unless you first lay down broad principles you can never proceed to details

THE THIRD AND LAST DAY'S WORK OF THE NATIONAL CONGRESS.

["*Indian Mirror.*"]

THE third and last day's sitting of the Congress was unusually interesting, as everyone who was present on the occasion will be able to testify. Whether for moderation, eloquence, earnestness, and unanimity, the speeches delivered by a large number of the delegates present at the Congress were unsurpassed. Those who are always having a tilt at the "Bengali Baboos" should have been present at the Congress yesterday to witness how the Native public sentiment outside Bengal is unanimous on some of the important public questions affecting Native interests. They should also have taken the opportunity of seeing for themselves how ur Mahomedan fellow-subjects, beyond the pale of a small coterie in Calcutta, are in perfect accord and sympathy with the objects of the, Congress There was a strong array of Mahomedan speakers from different parts of the country, who, one after another, got up and almost vied with each other in expressing their hearty concurrence in the aims and objects of the Congress, and their readiness to co-operate with their brethren of the Hindu community in promoting the common good of their common country. We are glad to learn that three distinguished European gentlemen, who were present on the occasion, bear witness to this fact; and these are the Marquis of Huntley, Mr. Elliot, the President of the Finance Committee, and Mr. H. J. S. Cotton. The spectacle that the Town Hall presented yesterday was one of such a rare character that it had never been witnessed on any previous occasion. It was probably only yesterday that one could fully realise the wholly representative character of the great national gathering that met in the chief public hall of the Metropolis. Delegates from Behar, the North-Western Provinces, the Punjab, Bombay, Madras, Sind, Assam, and the Central Provinces, came almost in swarms, and poured forth their sentiments, not only in English but in their respective provincial vernaculars with the utmost fervour and earnestness. One Mahomedan gentleman from the Central Provinces, Moulvi Abdul Aziz, quite astonished the audience by his sweet Persian diction. The delegates from the North-Western Provinces, Oudh, and the Punjab, such as Pundit Madan Mohan Malavya of Allahabad, Munshi Sadu Lall of Benares, Pundit Shyamnarain of Lucknow, Lalla Bhugwan Dass of Derah Ismail Khan, Lalla Kunhya Lall of Lahore, simply electrified the audience by their eloquent Urdu speeches. The truly earnest and impressive way in which Pundit Madan Mohan Malavya, Pundit Shyamnarain, Lalla Bhugwan Dass, and Lalla Kunhya Lall spoke formed a correct index to the truly patriotic spirit which animated them. It was difficult to repress the eloquence of some of the speakers from Upper India. But the gentleman who attracted a large share of attention, as much by his speech as by his striking figure and costume, was Lalla Bhugwan Dass. His very presence and his speech most unmistakably established the great fact of India having begun to think with one mind, from Calcutta to the remote border districts in the Punjab, and from the Himalayas to Cape Comorin. Those who are in the habit of charging the Bengalis with getting up all sorts of political agitation in the country should have been present to listen to the speech of Lalla Bhugwan Dass in order to judge for themselves how even some of the frontier tribes, who have received the benefit of English education, have begun to feel its elevating influence and to co-operate with their fellow-countrymen of the Provinces near the Presidency Towns in the constitutional agitation of all public questions of vital importance to the country at large. We wish that such of the Indian bureaucrats, and such of the Indian journalists, as try to ignore the fact of any germs of national life springing up among us had been present on the occasion, and seen in common with us how the educated and intelligent Indians in all parts of the country have begun to be closely identified in sentiment and in feeling, and to sympathise in each other's thoughts and ideas. One fact that Lalla Bhugwan Das brought forward was a most important one in support of our contention for the larger extension of the principle of local self-government and the gradual introduction of representative institutions, and, that is, that even the frontier tribes have their own tribally-made laws and their own tribal Councils, and that they have among them a complete system of tribal Government. And he very rightly held that if barbarous and unlettered tribes were fit to manage their own affairs, the civilised and educated Indians were still more capable of exercising the powers of self-government with great advantage to the country. It is always said that it is the Bengalis alone who claim political rights and privileges of all sorts, and that the other races do not. A visit to the several sittings of the Congress would have satisfied any of our Anglo-Indian friends that all the races of India, besides the Bengalis—and this though some of their number may not be scholars enough to make English speeches—hold views exactly similar to those held by the educated classes of the Gangetic Provinces of India. Many of the speakers would have been taken for Bengalis if it had not been for their distinctive costume and the language that they spoke; and we are sure that, after hearing all the speeches made by our brethren of other parts of India, many of our fellow-countrymen of Bengal have, by this time, come to be disabused of the notion that it is they alone who have a monopoly of the intelligence of India, and that the inhabitants of other Presidencies and Provinces have scarcely as much command over the English language as themselves. It was quite interesting to listen to Lalla Bhugwan Dass, as a representative of the frontier Hindu and Mahomedan tribes, and to the other speakers from the North-Western Provinces and the Punjab, and to realise for ourselves what rapid advancement India is making in these days of progress and enlightenment under the beneficent influence of the English Government. Another speaker, who made a most favorable impression on the audience, and who clearly showed how hollow is the abstention of a small section of the Mahomedans of Calcutta from the Congress, was Mr. Shurfuddin of Behar, Barrister-at-Law. He delivered an excellent speech, and drew forth repeated and loud applause. He pointed out, in the plainest terms possible, that, though Behar was a chief centre of the Mahomedans of the Lower Provinces of Bengal, the Mahomedan inhabitants of that Province were not at all in sympathy with such of their co-religionists as have held themselves aloof from the National Congress. He said in the most distinct terms that his co-religionists in Behar mostly sympathised with the objects of the Congress; and he very pertinently observed that he did not quite understand how the Congress had been called a "Hindu Congress," by an Anglo-Indian contemporary, when it was presided over by a Parsi gentleman. His speech did not leave the slightest doubt on the mind of anyone of those present at the assembly that, except a few Mahomedans, represented by the Central National Mahomedan Association, and the Mahomedan Literary Society of Calcutta, the rest of the Mahomedan inhabitants of Bengal, and especially of the province to which he belongs, were heartily in agreement with the aims and objects of the Congress. He was followed by other Mahomedan speakers, namely, Munshi Kadir Buksh of Fyzabad, Khajeh Abdul Alim of Dacca, and other Mahomedan gentlemen, who all regretted the conduct of their unsympathetic co-religionists in Calcutta.

The resolutions adopted yesterday will be found in our local column. Resolution IV was moved by Baboo Surendra Nath Bannerji in a stirring speech, which evoked loud cheers. He was followed by Mr. Chandavarkar of Bombay, who distinguished himself so much in England a short time ago as an Indian delegate. His speech was, as usual, a most practical one, and exactly to the point. It was very much admired for the large amount of information that he gave, and for the cogency of the arguments he used in seconding the resolutions. He spoke in a thoroughly honest, bold, and fearless spirit, and the audience evidently appreciated his speech much. The resolution was supported by the well-known Mr. Ananda Charlu of Madras, who represents the highest intellect of that Presidency, and who is distinguished as an orator. He also made an admirable speech. It was decided at the meeting that the next National Congress should be held at Madras on the 27th December, 1887. The meeting concluded with three cheers for the Queen, three for the Viceroy and the Provincial Governors, and three for Mr. A. O. Hume.

As regards the Civil Service question, the report of the Committee, which was appointed to consider it, was adopted. One gentleman, present at the Congress, enquired how the point had been settled as to going to England for study and competition for the Civil Service. The President replied that for want of time that and all other details had not been considered and decided upon. But whatever may be the present state of the question we hope that the Congress will insist on the necessity of Indians going for study and training in England as an indispensable condition of their admission to the Covenanted Civil Service.

Thus closed the second Indian National Congress in Calcutta, which will always form a historical event for our city, and mark a new epoch in the annals of the national progress of India. The delegates will disperse in a day or two. We cordially wish them Godspeed on their journey home.

The *Indian Daily News* says:—"The evening party at the Town Hall on Monday, in connection with the National Congress, was a peculiar gathering which we imagine would have been a study for Sir George Campbell. He is greatly interested in ethnological studies, and the occasion would have furnished specimens from all parts of what may be termed civilised India. There was, indeed, an absence of the border tribes, who represent the undeveloped "Native," and so far the collection was incomplete. Still it was a remarkable assembly, and different from any we have yet seen. In many gatherings of Natives there is to be seen a considerable admixture of "barbaric pearls and gold" that lend fictitious aid to the brilliance of the assembly. There was very little of these visible on Monday night. Indeed, it might be said that they were conspicuous by their absence. There was an apparent negligence of appearance as regards dress that is not often observable in Native social gatherings. There were, however, some Native gentlemen who appeared in "forked habiliments," swallow-tails and the orthodox waiters' tie. They were kept in countenance by a sprinkling of Europeans in like attire. There were others who, despising such things as swallow-tails and white ties, sported overcoats, and wore mufflers which concealed their identity except to their more immediate and familiar acquaintances · and there was every medium between these extremes. There were representatives of all points of the compass, differing in features, attire and language and yet they seemed, with exceptions, to have one common medium of communication not "Native" to any of them, namely, the English language. This was largely the common bond and means of overcoming strange speech, and the Babylonish confusion of tongues, that must otherwise have prevailed in the assembly. But on this score, there was no difficulty, or, if there were, it was not among the delegates proper, but with men who are mostly residents in Calcutta, occupying respectable positions in society, but who have not had the advantage of being educated in any language but their own. It was interesting to see the company group themselves into small parties, discussing with great animation topics of interest more or less germane to the subjects which the Congress would take in hand. But these were, by no means, exclusively the themes of discourse. There was a large amount of introductions and much hand-shaking, and everything seemed agreeable all round. Even some of the opponents of the Congress were present, probably to indicate that any difference of opinion on matters of policy should not interfere with the social amenities which should exist among all sections of the community. The President of the Congress, Mr. Dadabhoy Naoroji, was well occupied during the evening in making the acquaintance of the delegates and others; and the leading members of the League were similarly occupied. It was remarked by a Hindu gentleman that "their leaders" were not present. This, in a certain sense, was correct; but the remark does not recognize the change that has come over society, of which the speaker himself is an example. There was a time when Maharajahs, Rajahs, &c., were the leaders of Hindu society; and certainly they were conspicuous by their absence on Monday evening. But who are and who have ever been the leaders of men? No nobles by the mere fact of their position, though there have been occasions when *men* have held the position of noblemen and have been leaders. There have been leaders in all ranks of society. Wat Tyler was a leader of men, though only a blacksmith, Cavendish was a leader of men, when he and a few others, in a small house on Whittington Moor, arranged to bring about the Revolution that placed William of Orange on the throne of England. Cavendish, however, was a Duke, or became one, as well as a man, and would probably have been a leader in any rank of life. So it will be in India. It will not be the well-appointed wardrobe, or the lengthy title that will enable the wearer to be a leader of men. It will be the cultivated understanding, the active brain, the moral courage begotten of right, that will lead men and accomplish the revolution of the future. These are facts that are beginning to be realised, that will multiply themselves, as these remarks strength till their full purpose is accomplished the same work will not be done in a day or a generation, though it will be not the less certain in the end Those who are active now will not see the full fruition of their labours. There may be years or even generations of suffering and disappointment in India, as there have been in Europe and that are still before some of the struggling nationalities Patriots in all countries have had to endure much, to suffer much, and to wait for the result, which they have not always seen except by the eye of faith. There is no reason why Indian experience withdiffer from that of other nations; and those who are most burning with zeal will do well to accept the injunction of Longfellow, and while—

> "Still, achieving, still pursuing,
> Learn to labour and to wait."

["*The Statesman.*"]

THE National Congress, the delegates to which from all parts of India are now gathering themselves together in this city, will hold their first sitting, we believe, on Sunday next, the 26th instant. The Congress has been looked forward to with deep interest throughout the year. Our readers are no doubt aware that it is the second meeting of the same order. The first Congress was held at Bombay on the 28th, 29th and 30th December last. Before breaking up a resolution was unanimously passed that the Indian National Congress re-assemble "next year in Calcutta and sit on Tuesday, the 28th "December, 1886, and the next succeeding days." It was originally intended that the Congress of last year should assemble at Poona, but the appearance of cholera in that city, a few days before the time fixed for its opening, led to a decision to hold the Congress at Bombay. The first sitting was held, as appointed, on the 28th December, nearly one hundred gentlemen attending it from all parts of India. Many of these gentlemen being Government servants, took no direct part in the proceedings of the Congress, but were drawn thereto from strong and enlightened sympathy with its aims and a desire to assist by their advice in its counsels. The actual number of *representatives* properly so called was between 70 and 80, and on the eve of the first sitting Sir WILLIAM WEDDERBURN, Mr. JUSTICE JARDINE, Professor WORDSWORTH, and many other leading men of Bombay, met the representatives at the Goculdass Tejpal College, and welcomed them to the city.

The Congress was a very signal success. In commenting upon it the *Times* remarked that "it was at Bombay that India had, for the first time, given proof of the existence of a national life and spirit," but it remarked that no Mahomedan gentlemen took any part in the proceedings and that "its members "were for the most part drawn from three orders— "native lawyers, native school-masters and native "newspaper editors. There were some notable ex- "ceptions, but the rule was as we have said." It emphasized particularly the fact, that "the entire Mahomedan population of India had steadily refused to have anything to do with the Congress," and declared their abstention to be "a sufficiently ominous fact." The statement was far from being accurate, and the Hon'ble Mr. TELANG, of the Bombay High Court, pointed out, in a letter to the *Times*, that it had been misinformed, and that although but two Mahomedan gentlemen attended the Congress others would have been present had it been possible for them to be so. Mr. TELANG very properly reminded the paper that the Congress was the first of its [illegible] and he expressed a confident belief that [illegible]n community would be represented [illegible] at the Congress in this city, which is now [illegible]out to open. Whether that hope is realised or [illegible]t, it would be idle to conceal that the movement [illegible]es not command the sympathy of the Mahomedan community in by any means equal measure with [illegible]at of the great educated Hindu community. Our readers have seen, from the letter of Mr. AMIR ALI [illegible] our issue of Sunday last, and frem Mr. HUME's letter to that fine old man SYUD AHMED HOSSEIN of Alighur, that the movement has not taken such hold of the convictions, or the imagination, of the Mahomedan community as to awaken any very great sympathy therewith as a whole. Nor could any one have reasonably expected that it would do so. The *Times* itself, as we have seen, lays stress upon the fact that it is the educated classes who are the strength of the movement. The movement throughout is the direct, the anticipated and foreseen outcome of the high education that has been brought within the reach of the people. The Mahomedans, unhappily for themselves, but from motives which we can heartily respect, have hitherto stood aloof from the colleges and universities, which are the nursery of those honorable aspirations and ambitions, which are beginning to be so widely cherished in the country. High education would have done little for the people—we may properly say that it would have done nothing for them—if it had failed to produce the unrest, the uneasiness, and the distress, with which it has taught them to regard their exclusion from all share in the administration of their own country and the management of their own affairs. The indifference of the Mahomedan community as a body, to their present exclusion from these duties in common with their Hindu fellows, is as much and as directly the result of their self-enforced adherence to inadequate methods of education as is the almost passionate longing of the educated Hindu community to share responsibilities which they have been sedulously taught by ourselves that it is their duty and their privilege to bear in common with Englishmen. On their own account we regret the indifference which the Mahomedan community, as a whole, shows towards this great movement, but their children will be wiser than themselves. We suspect, moreover, that a far larger number of Mahomedan gentlemen will take part in the coming Congress than many suppose to be likely. Meanwhile we counsel the Congress to take the right view of their abstention, should it be ever so marked. It is a matter that affects the Mahomedan community itself, more than all others, and must of necessity come to be regretted by their children. It would have been wiser for them to have said nothing, and quietly abstained from all part in the Congress, than to have placed the evidence upon record that as a community they have no sympathy with the honorable ambitions of their fellow-subjects. They have made a mistake, but as the letter binds no one but the few who have concurred in, and adopted it, we advise the Mahomedan community to ignore it altogether.

We have received no communication of any kind from the gentlemen who are making arrangements for the holding of the Congress, nor do we know whether its "sittings" will be thrown open to the public. We believe, however, that their preparations were completed nearly a month ago, and that the "representatives," who will attend the assemblage, have been partly nominated by the branch political associations of the country, and partly elected by them. We understand, further, that the main subject of discussion at the Congress will be the necessity of strengthening the local Councils of the various Governments of the country by the election of members thereto, under some system of "representation." We think the Congress will certainly act wisely by concentrating its efforts in this way upon some special reform, directing its whole strength to its achievement. It would be doubtfully wise, we think, while the Public Service Commission is sitting, for the Congress to commit itself to any definite plan of reform in that direction until the Commission has produced its report. For ourselves we are not convinced, we confess, of the advantage of recruiting the higher appointments of the Service by competition. We doubt if "an open Civil Service" might not be the wisest step that could be taken in that direction, reserving "competition" for the recruiting of the subordinate services.

We were most glad to notice the prominence given at the Bombay Congress to the question of "the condition of the masses of the people" under British rule, and we hope very earnestly that the subject will be revived at this Calcutta assemblage. It will consist mainly of the representatives of those classes to whom British rule has proved an almost unmixed blessing. The Madras and Bombay members gave earnest and honorable prominence to this question at the Bombay Congress, and we indulge a hope that it will occupy the close attention of the coming assembly. What is it that occasions an almost universal deterioration in the condition of the masses of the people under British rule? "It is a question of life and death to the country," said one of the speakers (Mr. DADABHAI NAOROJI) "The present English rule is no doubt the greatest "blessing India has ever had, but this *one evil* of "it nullifies completely all the good it has achieved. "Remove but this one evil and India will be blessed "in every way, and will be a blessing to England in "every way" The speaker attributed it to the "foreign agency" under which British rule is carried on. Had, he said, the "foreign institutions" that our rule has introduced, we think we would have been nearer the root of the evil. What we all want is light, more light! The question is ever present to our own mind, and has never yet been solved by us. Let us hope that these assemblies will eventually prove the means of giving us the light we so sorely need.

THE COMING REFORM.

["*The Hindu.*"]

IT is satisfactory to observe how public opinion is rapidly forming itself regarding the subject of legislative reform. Among the Natives there is absolutely no difference of opinion. They are agreed as to the main outlines of the scheme as well as to its principle. They ask for a moderate but substantial measure of representation in the Councils of the Empire with a view to exercise a control, however limited, over the general and financial administration of the country. They are also ready with a scheme to give effect to this proposal. The members of the Councils, Supreme as well as Local, are to be increased in number according to the population, area and the general fitness of the Provinces, and not less than one-half the members of these Councils are to be elected. The election is to be made by the Municipal and other local institutions, by the Universities, Chambers of Commerce and political associations of a certain status; and the elective members of the Supreme Council are to be chosen by the elected members of the local Councils. These reformed Legislative Councils are to be given, in addition to their power of legislation, the privilege of interpellation and discussing the budget and passing upon it their own resolutions, which, however, are not intended to be absolutely binding upon the Government. In every case of dissent from the recorded decisions of the Council the Government is to publish its reasons. The members of the Council are further to be empowered to appeal against the veto of the Supreme Government to the Secretary of State, and to a standing Committee of Parliament, against the decisions of the Secretary of State. These are the outlines of the scheme agreed to by the Native community. The scheme may be susceptible of improvement; but it is a great advantage in discussions of this kind to have to start with a scheme, however defective, which will render further discussion definite and practical. This scheme will be subjected to further consideration at the Congress at Calcutta and then submitted for an early and favorable consideration to His Excellency Lord Dufferin, who is said to be inclined to approve of some such scheme. But irrespective of this unanimity among the leaders of the Native community, and the favorable inclination of the Viceroy, the gradual rallying of Anglo-Indian opinion on our side is to be welcomed with delight. During the past few days several Anglo-Indian officials and non-officials have expressed themselves favorably to the reform that is so prominent in the discussions of the Native press. Lord Dufferin himself has more than once drawn our attention to the great lesson of history, that a progressive Government must change its institutions according to the changes that occur in the spirit of every successive generation, and no one is more conscious of the changes that l come over India within the last thirty years than the present Viceroy. This opinion, valuable and encouraging as it is, has been supplemented by echoes, more or less distinct and audible, in quarters to which we are not accustomed to look with hope. Even the *Pioneer* has found itself unable to resist the influence of the change that is fast overtaking public opinion on this question. A few days back our contemporary wrote as follows: "The immense difficulties of adapting to India, with its immense population crossed and intersected everywhere by the dividing lines of caste, creed and race, a representative system, that was originally invented for and by small homogeneous European communities, may have before long to be faced; the complicated problem of the proper distribution of legislative powers between Imperial and local Councils may have soon to be solved for India. But these are questions for the wisdom of the sovereign Parliament to decide, and in such forward movements the older provinces of the Empire, with great commercial capitals and concentrated civilization, will probably be expected to show the way." Here will be perceived, amidst a studied vagueness of language, a clear admission of the inevitable character of the change that is demanded by the Native community; and, as a sign of surrender on the part of obstructive officialism, we welcome this admission in the columns of the *Pioneer*. A few days later, while speaking at St. Andrew's Dinner at Calcutta, the Lieutenant-Governor of Bengal, who, speaking about this time last year, ridiculed the Ten Commandments and called the educated Indians a small and uninfluential section of the Native community, admits that "it is well that the old order should change, giving place to the new." "It needs constantly fresh eyes to see," observed Sir Rivers Thompson, "and fresh hands and heads to work out the right solution of those ever-changing conditions and circumstances which a closer contact with England, facilities of communication, the growing extension of education, and a hundred other influences are pouring, like a perpetual torrent, upon the stagnation of Indian thought and character and social habits." Sir Rivers Thompson made after Mr. George Yule's suggestion on the occasion that the widening of the doors of on. Legislative Councils will be the next change in our present administrative arrangements. Mr. George Yule, who is the President of the Bengal Chamber of Commerce, approached this question in his speech with a fairness and breadth of view truly praiseworthy. He thought that in any new arrangement that might be made "it would be better if the Governor-General ceased to be a part of the legislative machinery, but should become its greaser or overseer with a veto more or less limited over its decisions." The reasons alleged by Mr. Yule in support of this suggestion deserve consideration. He said: "What I think I clearly perceive is that, under existing conditions of legislation, and more so under wider conditions, neither lofty reputation nor transcendant ability nor unspotted integrity will save our Governor-Generals, while members of the Council, from being dragged in the mud of angry reproach, first by one party and then by another, until their influence as representing the impartial attitude of the Crown is wholly gone; and they will be the subject of aspersion or praise according as they side with this or that kind of legislation. They will become partizans in spite of themselves, to the loss alike of their dignity and usefulness." The suggestion is an important one, and will receive the attention of the authorities when the change is introduced. But meanwhile it is worth noting by the leaders of Na[illegible] th[illegible]opinion as indicating the attitude of Anglo-Indian non-officials regarding the subject of legislative reform. If Mr. Yule represents to any degree the opinion of his class, it is evident that the mercantile community of Europeans agree with us in thinking that the re-organization of the Legislative Councils is a question ripe for early solution. In addition to the opinions that we have referred to in the preceding lines, to those of the *Pioneer*, Sir Rivers Thompson and Mr. George Yule, representing respectively the lower official class, the higher official class and the mercantile community, we have to note the valuable and renewed testimony of Professor Wordsworth of Bombay to the propriety of our demand. In his review of the *Star in the East* he expresses his opinion in the following passage: "We seem to be reaching a time when it will be impossible to govern this country altogether on the old lines, and yet the official conservatives in India and their spokesmen in the London Press seem to consider it the highest wisdom to ignore this fact and to rail at everybody as a revolutionist, or what is almost worse, a *doctrinaire*, who advocates the most moderate reform designed to lighten the strain of a situation which may become impossible before we are aware of it." This is the opinion of a known and esteemed friend of the people of this country; but it is nevertheless timely, for whatever inferior officials of the bureaucracy may think of Professor Wordsworth, with the higher officials and with the direct representatives of Her Majesty, the opinion of a man so respected for his learning and moderate views must command considerable weight. Nor are the generous sentiments of Lord Reay and Lord Rosebery towards the people of this country less opportune. The illustrious nobleman, now at the head of the Bombay Government, while presiding at St. Andrew's Dinner in Bombay, reminded all Englishmen and Scotchmen of the great claims that this land has upon them, and observed that "on an Englishman or Scotchman or an Irishman there cannot fall a happier lot than to devote his best energies to the prosperity of this great country;" and these words of wisdom and truth were supplemented by Lord Rosebery, who exhorted his hearers to "maintain the traditions of English justice and English strength, Scotch justice and Scotch strength, justice within and strength without." These are noble sentiments, and should be treasured up in the hearts of statesmen and administrators as their motto and guide in the discharge of their duties. Justice within leads to strength without, because no Government threatened by foreign aggression can have a worse foe than a people rendered discontented and unhappy by a sense of justice denied or postponed; but the people of India ask for nothing more than to be treated according to the ideals of English justice.

We have referred to the opinions of several representatives of the ruling race in different parts of the country as a proof that the unanimous appeal of the people for some measure of control over the administration of their country is not regarded after all as the revolutionary and impracticable demand that it is often asserted to be in the organs of the Anti-Native party. It is evident that a large section of the Anglo-Indian community, official as well as non-official, is in favor of the reform, and the Native community may reasonably look to its help in pressing on the public and Parliament in England its important and urgent nature. The Congress should carefully note these indications of Anglo-Indian sympathy and make the best use of them.

["*The Bombay Gazette*"]

THE Native politicians of Bombay have chosen their delegates for the forthcoming Congress at Calcutta. They are sixteen in number, and no exception can be taken to them on the score of either capacity or status. They will represent, as well as any company of men who could have been chosen from this side, the sobriety, the good sense, and the sweet reasonableness which characterize the political thought of Western India.

THE National Congress, which is an assembly of the representatives of the various races of the Empire, has, we see, proved too much for our Anglo-Indian friends. The Anglo-Indian journals all over the land look with jealous eyes on the Congress, and try their best to lower its importance. We do not exactly know what makes the Anglo-Indians assume an inimical attitude towards the Congress, unless they be opposed to the political progress of the Indians. The Anglo-Indians can hardly expect to gain anything by decrying every loyal and constitutional step the Natives may adopt in asserting their rights as British subjects, and in creating a strong public opinion on the questions of political reform. The wisest and most just policy the Anglo-Indian community could adopt is to encourage the Natives in their legitimate aspirations and to cultivate their friendship. The Anglo-Indians in this country will ever be in the small minority, and however great may be their influence they must sooner or later have to yield to Native claims. If they are wise in their generation, they should make common cause with the children of the soil, and live on the most amicable terms with them.

["*The Indian Mirror.*"]

MR. CROWLEY, of Allahabad, in his speech in support of the National Congress, declared that he knew that there were several European gentlemen in the country, nay in Allahabad too, who think of the Congress as well as he does, with the difference that they hesitate to come forward to have their say, lest they should be taunted in society. We are truly glad to be informed on the authority of a European gentleman that many of his countrymen out here are supporters of the National Congress, but we must say that it is not at all becoming on their part to keep themselves in the background. They ought to come forward boldly, and give out their minds on the Congress, and we have little doubt that many of their countrymen will gradually follow them.

ALL ABOUT THE CONGRESS AND CALCUTTA.

[By Mr. N. G. Chandavarkar.]

[" *Indu Prakash*."]

The second National Congress of India has come and gone, and it has been by all who either witnessed it in Calcutta or watched its proceedings from elsewhere declared a success. The general verdict seems to be that it passed off admirably well. Before it came off I confess I had serious misgivings about it. The attempt of the Hon. Mr. Amir Ali and Nawab Abdul Latif Khan to keep the Mahomedans away from it threatened at first sight to mar its success. Indeed, when Mahomedan delegates arrived from other parts of India, they were got at and asked not to put in their appearance at the Congress. " The Hindus are ahead of us. We are lagging behind them. We still want the patronage of Government; and shall gain nothing by joining them." This was, I understand, the plea urged for the conversion of our Mahomedan colleagues, but, to their credit be it said, like good men and true, they stood firmly by their cherished conviction that the best policy was to make common cause with the Hindus and Parsees. They regularly attended the meetings; watched the proceedings as closely as the other delegates; and in their speeches showed an amount of good will and confidence which might well afford an example to others. That feeling of theirs was duly reciprocated by delegates representing other sections of the community; and thus our misgiving on this head proved fortunately false. The second thing that contributed to the success of the Congress was the behaviour of the Bengal delegates. Some one—he was from Bengal itself—it appears had dinned into their ears, before the arrival of the delegates in Calcutta, *his* view that Bengalis had obtained in other parts of India a bad reputation for hospitality to strangers. But our Bengal friends surprised their delegate-guests by the splendid arrangements they had made for their reception. Every one seemed to be anxious that the delegates from other parts should return pleased with Calcutta and its people. Even Bengali students vied with one another to mark their desire to give the delegates a cordial greeting. For instance, after the formal sittings of the Congress were over, a lecture on Rajah Ram Mohun Roy, the greatest religious and social reformer modern India has produced, was delivered in the City College Hall by Mr. Kally Churn Banerji, one of the delegates. Long before the hour of the lecture, the hall was closely packed up by a crowded audience, mostly consisting of students. Many of the delegates attended the meeting just when the lecture was about to begin. As they neared the door of the hall, they found the place so full that they could hardly hope to get in. But the moment the students—and Bengal students, I was told by a Bengali friend, are not generally respectors of persons—found it was a delegate who was seeking admittance, the way was cleared, and he found himself in the hall welcomed by cheers which rung through it. Welcomed cordially, lodged comfortably, and treated everywhere hospitably, the delegates could not but carry favorable impressions of Bengal hospitality, to which, I say, part of the success I am speaking of is due. Add to all this the Chairman's suavity, patience, and urbanity, any deliberation held under such circumstances was bound to be a success. The mania for speechifying did not prevail largely; and where a man here or there showed an inclination to orate, Mr. Dadabhai managed him with admirable tact. I heard a delegate say that Mr. Dadabhai's venerable appearance was enough to disarm the most stubbornly, verbose speaker. One might well, looking to the harmony which characterised the proceedings throughout, and the tone of loyalty and moderation which marked all speeches, adopt for the Congress that has just passed away old Richard Baxter's motto: " In all things essential, union; in things non-essential, liberty; and in all things, charity."

And now arises the question—of what practical use is all this demonstration? Politically, some say, Congresses and their resolutions will carry no weight. Government, it is said, regard them as emanating from the educated minority of Natives in India. But no one amongst us is, I believe, so foolishly sanguine as to suppose that when we have met, spoken, and passed resolutions, we have done all. The Congress may or may not have the desired effect on the Government. The Government may or may not give wholly or partially what we have asked. It may not be *national* in the sense that the masses are still unable to sympathise fully with its political demands. These seem to me to be secondary questions altogether, and the highest value of the Congress seems to me to lie in this, that, quite apart from the fact that it is a present political force, it is a great social lever. It is *national* at all events in the sense that it is calculated to form us into a *nation*, by bringing us together, and making us by an interchange of views think, feel, and act alike. I care not whether the array of resolutions we have passed in the past and may pass in future are attended to or not by the Government as long as these Congress meetings develop the bond of union among the people. All things else are subsidiary, and its gain is not so much in the present as in the future.

The charge has been brought against the Congress, however, that while dealing boldly with political questions it quietly ignored the equally, if not more, important question of social reform. It is, indeed, to be regretted that social questions, on which the future of the country so greatly depends, should have been regarded as beyond the sphere of the Congress politics. But I do not think we can say that they were altogether ignored. Many of the delegates, I can say from my own personal knowledge, felt strongly on them, and had the question been *formally* placed before the Congress, I doubt not the advocates of social reform would have found a good number on their side. There were many practical reformers among the delegates; there were others who sympathised with Mr. Malabari's agitation. We all agreed that our primary object was *union*; that questions on which all felt alike ought alone to be taken up by the Congress; and by following such a course alone could we hope to unite all and make them see the necessity of social reform. The idea, therefore, of *formally* discussing the question was dropped. But that did not prevent us from taking it up informally. The Congress closed on Thursday. On Friday Mr. Kally Churn Bannerji delivered a lecture on the services rendered by Rajah Ram Mohun Roy to the cause of religious and social reform in India; on Saturday Pundit Shiva Nath Shastri, one of the missionaries of the Brahmo Somaj, held a religous service, which was attended by many of the delegates—more could not attend owing to the mournful news just then received from Madras about the fire in People's Park—and in the course of an eloquent discourse, he dwelt on the imperative necessity of controlling the present political fervour by means of faith in God and religion " Otherwise," said he, " all this excitement might lead to socialism, anarchy, and thoughtlessness, which would prove disastrous to India."

Indeed, in any other place it would have been possible to shut one's eyes to the question of religious and social reform, but in Calcutta, where such men as Rajah Ram Mohun Roy, Dwark Nath Tagore, Debendro Nath Tagore, and Keshub Chunder Sen, the leading lights of religious and social reform in India, have lived and worked, it was impossible. The influence of these men is not gone; and after what I have seen in Calcutta, I must say that there is good reason to think that the charge of being a mere *prattler* and *political agitator* would be unjust in the case of the Bengali, whatever might be said of the men of Bombay or Madras. There is, of course, a great deal yet to be accomplished in Bengal; men are complained of as being indifferent to religious and social questions as much as we are here. But something is being done to remove the evil. In a country, where custom rules as a tyrant, and men have the blind conservatism of ages to fight against, you cannot expect things to mend in a day; the test of progress is whether there is any movement which does for religious and social reform what most of our Associations do for political advancement, and whether that movement is moving onwards, moving slowly it may be but nevertheless moving and giving the country every year, say, half a dozen at least of men, having the courage of their convictions, and prepared to act and not merely talk. Judged by this test, Calcutta may safely expect a favorable verdict. And the Brahmo Somaj is doing yeoman's service in this respect. Those who do not sympathise with it make it a point to tell you that its influence is waning; and that made me all the more curious to know what its present condition and future propects are. Now the Brahmo students have what is called the Students' Weekly Service. Every Sunday morning a meeting is held, to which students of all classes are invited. After prayers are offered, a sermon or discourse is delivered. This Weekly Service is attended largely, and every year, I was informed, it brings a fresh accession of converts to the Brahmo Somaj. It happens in this way: A student attends the service for some weeks or months; he gradually shows leanings in favor of religious and social reform: his parents on discovering it propose marriage as an antidote; the student remains firm; refuses to marry; has his remittance stopped; is subjected to persecution. That leads to a crisis. He stands it all; becomes more devoted to the cause than ever; avows himself a Brahmo; and shows that he has the spirit of self-sacrifice in him. The parents find it useless to persecute the boy any longer. They leave him to his convictions, and thus *moral courage* wins the day. I came across many students who have passed and are passing through such a crisis, and their self-sacrificing spirit could not but rouse my sympathy and admiration. How many of us, said, I might well take a lesson from their example! Here are young men—whose number is slowly, very slowly, but steadily increasing—brave lads, of whom their country ought to be proud. This is a hopeful sign.

So much about the influence silently and slowly but steadily worked by the Brahmo Somaj among the student class. Equally hopeful is the work it is doing for women's emancipation. In Bengal the difficulties are greater than in any other part of India on account of the *zenana* system. Nevertheless, it has been the first to give the country female graduates, some of whom are Brahmos and others Christians. Besides, there are Brahmo ladies who have received excellent education, and are doing good work for religious and social reform. They have started a Sunday School, where children are given religious and moral instruction. Let no one say after this the Bengali is a mere political prattler. He has done yet very little; but he has done more than we have; and side by side with political activity you also see in Calcutta activity in the direction of religious and social reform.

THE NATIONAL CONGRESS AND THE RECONSTITUTION OF THE LEGISLATIVE COUNCILS.

["*The Bengalee.*"]

In our last issue we reproduced the resolution which the National Congress recorded on the all-important question of representative government. There has been some misconception in some quarters with regard to the scope and purport of this resolution. It has been remarked with more humour than good sense that the practical effect of the resolution was to invite the Government to vacate office in favor of Mr. Dadabhai Naoroji and his followers, and that what the Congress really asked for was that the English rulers of the country should mount guard and protect the country, but that all real power and authority should be vested in the people. Such a view of the matter would be amusing if it did not proceed from a journal of considerable influence with the Government and the Anglo-Indian community. It could only have proceeded from ignorance, coupled with a sense of uneasiness and impatience. If the terms of the resolution were carefully examined, it would be found that the Congress put forth a very modest demand for participation in the government of the country, which should disarm all opposition and enlist the sympathies of right-thinking men. The principles underlying the resolution are these: That a fair proportion of the members of the Legislative Councils should be elected, and that they should be elected by local bodies, Chambers of Commerce, Trades' Associations, Universities, &c., and other public bodies of established repute. But we pin our faith on no particular system. The resolution leaves a door wide open for the adoption of any system that may please the Government. If it should be said that these local bodies are untried, let the franchise be granted directly to such persons as in the opinion of the Government are capable of exercising it. We give the Government a *carte blanche.* Let the Government choose its own system and devise its own scheme. All that we care for is that the representative element should be recognised in the government of the country. But whatever may be the system that is introduced, we are anxious that the rights of all classes of the community should be respected. Mark the language of the resolution. "But whatever system be adopted (and the details must be worked out separately for each province) care must be taken that all sections of the community, Europeans, Eurasians, Mahomedans, Hindus, &c., and all great interests, the agricultural, mercantile, professional, &c., are adequately represented." We have heard a great deal quite recently about the interest of minorities. But we are solicitous—and the Congress was solicitous—that those interests should be cared for, that the majority should not swamp the minority, and that they should not have a preponderant influence, except such as may belong to superior devotion, courage and self-sacrifice. The Councils thus constituted and thus reformed should have the right of interpellation and some measure of control over finance. The right of interpellation would be as great a benefit to the people as it would be a gain to the Government. To the people it would be the safeguard of their rights; to the Government it would afford opportunities of removing many a misconception, many a mistake. It is said that the lips of the Government are closed against imputations which are sometimes made in the Native press. We are sorry that such imputations should be made. The Government, we think, has enough to answer for in the shape of actual defects in the administration, and for which it cannot escape responsibility. But if these imputations continue to be made, the remedy lies in the hands of the Government, and if the Government does not choose to make use of it, we do not think it has much right to complain. Be that as it may, the right of interpellation would be a distinct advantage both to the people and the Government. But it is not an unrestricted and illimitable right in this respect that is demanded. There is a certain use of this right which may embarrass the Government, but we are unwilling to embarrass the Government, and therefore we say in the resolution: "Provided that if the subject in regard to which the inquiry is made involves matters of foreign policy, military dispositions or strategy, or is otherwise of such a nature that, in the opinion of the Executive, the public interests would be materially imperilled by the communication of the information asked for, it shall be competent for them to instruct the *ex officio* Members, or one of them, to reply accordingly, and decline to furnish the information asked for."

What could be more moderate or more legitimate than this? What becomes of the charge that we want our rulers to vacate office in our favor? It is not Home Rule or Parliamentary institutions that we want. Our humble prayer is that we should be associated with our rulers, and only in a limited measure, in the government of the country. With reference to the consideration of the Budget, it is a right which is already conceded to the Supreme Council when new measures of taxation are introduced. We suggest a further extension of this right. We suggest that whether new taxes be imposed or not, whether the Budget concerns the Province or the Empire, it should in every case be laid before the Council and discussed. Now nothing is so well established as the financial solvency of the Corporations of Calcutta and Bombay, and the secret lies in the circumstance that those who pay the taxes and have the keenest personal interest in economy have a voice in the expenditure. We seek to give effect only partially and in a tentative manner to this principle which underlies the secret of successful government. If our suggestions with regard to the reconstitution of the Legislative Councils had stopped here, they would have been sufficiently moderate, and we are confident they would have challenged the assent of even responsible officials. But with a view to disarm all opposition, and to make it impossible to refuse our demands, we suggest that in the very first stage of this great experiment, "the Executive Government shall possess the power of overruling the decision arrived at by the majority of the Council," a full exposition of the grounds on which this is considered necessary being published. Our demands are thus very moderate, and we would earnestly call upon the Government to give effect to them, or at any rate to introduce some form of representative government which would be more acceptable to its views. Ten years hence the reform will be too late. It will fail to conciliate, and it will have the appearance of a concession made to popular agitation. The public mind has been deeply stirred, and the Congress has given volume and shape to our aspirations in this respect. In Bengal the agitation has already been commenced; and we may depend upon it that, as the result of the labours of the Congress, the agitation will now be taken up in other parts of the country. We would earnestly call upon the Government to anticipate all this agitation by spontaneously offering to the people of India, out of the abundance of its own good will and grace, the inestimable blessing of representative government And no gift would be more welcome in the Jubilee year of Her Gracious Majesty's reign. She has reigned long and she has reigned beneficently. Deep has been her concern in the welfare of her Indian people. May this feeling find expression in the emancipation of her Indian subjects, and may it form the proudest, as it will be the most durable, monument of her glorious reign!

THE BRITISH RAJ.

["*Reis and Rayyet.*"]

To whatever criticism of detail it may be open, the British Raj is—now at any rate—a political necessity for India. It might be extravagant to say that, without it, there can be no security of life, no protection of property in the country. It may, with better truth, be urged that when it came into existence in India there was little or none. If any fact is more patent than all others in the history of India, it is the invasions from without, and depredations from within, during the later period of the Mogul rule, when the sceptre of AKBAR and AURENZEBE fell into weaker hands, and when the imperial authority could hardly be maintained even in the provinces around the capital. The invasion of NADIR SHAH was a frightful calamity. It not only gave a death-blow to the Empire—*cet arbre séché jusque dans ses racines*—but also caused incalculable loss of life and property to the people. That descent was a signal for general revolt. The provinces of the Empire became independent, and the Mahrattas, who were struggling for the consolidation of their power since the days of AURENZEBE, appeared on the scene to measure their strength with any competitors for the sovereignty of India. The battle of Paniput, however, blasted their hopes for ever, and hastened the desolation of what remained of the once mighty Empire of the Moguls in India. In the scramble that followed among the provincial governors and daring adventurers, for power, there was neither protection of property nor security of life—neither rule nor order; all was dire confusion and chaos. In a word, a perfect anarchy prevailed, under which people were reduced to wretchedness in the extreme. It was under such circumstances that the English appeared on the scene and succeeded gradually in extending their sway over the fairest provinces. With the establishment of their Government, external inroads at once ceased and internal violence came to an end; until now, from one end of the country to the other, the *Pax Britannica* now reigns to the joy of the people. A peace so profound and so extensive India had never enjoyed before and she owes it all to the presence of the British. If the British Government has secured nothing more for our country than this profound peace, it has, to our thinking, established the highest claim to our earnest gratitude and earned a right for its existence among us.

Nor is this all. England has done more—much more. She has accomplished for India what none of her past rulers had ever dreamt, we mean of course the creation of a state of things in which the growth of a national political life has become possible. She has galvanized bones and put fresh blood into the arteries. She has opened up the country and drawn out the soul. She has given us eyes to see and ears to hear. By giving education and spreading knowledge, by diffusing a taste or a literature pre-eminent among the literatures to the world, as well as for European science, she has awakened new hopes and aspirations for a higher status. The signs are as clear as the broad daylight. The English language, which is the *lingua franca* among the educated classes, has become the vehicle of thought not only between rulers and rulers but also between provinces and provinces; and we verily believe our rulers feel in their heart of hearts a generous satisfaction, when they see the stalwart Punjabi open his mind to the lithe Bengali, and the astute Mahratta communicate his thoughts to the proud Moslem. This is indeed a unique sight, and the nation that has brought it about can well afford to be proud of it.

No country in the world contains so many discordant elements as India. You have the Hindu, the Moslem, the Parsee, the Christian,—representatives of four different religions characterized by distinct *cultes*. Nor are the ethnic, the social and the linguistic differences less considerable. To fuse these diverse elements into a harmonious whole, to make these varying interests subserve a common purpose, is one of the grandest problems of statesmanship. And such statesmanship was evinced by those who inaugurated the educational policy. After the lapse of half a century, the seed has begun to bring forth fruit. That education, which a TREVELYAN, a BENTINCK, and a MACAULAY introduced, at length bids fair to solve the almost insoluble problem of enlightened and successful foreign dominion. We think we see the first signs in the voluntary Congress to be held early next week in the metropolis of British India, whereat the delegates from the different parts of the Empire will meet to deliberate on matters connected with the welfare of their fatherland. The coming Congress will be a noble and grand sight; and if those statesmen could now be made to see the fruits of the tree, which they themselves planted, how glad they would be! But unfortunately for India, that race is now gone, leaving a rather miscellaneous lot, mostly of mere politicians and officials. Narrow in their views and unwilling or incapable of appreciating the moral grandeur of their predecessors' policy, these view the ensuing Congress with jealousy and seem prepared to attempt to frustrate its object. We have thought that Anglo-Indian statesmanship would rejoice to see a political spectacle which is only possible under their Government and which no other nation can show. But we must confess disappointment. Whatever, however, a certain section of nervous or misguided Anglo-Indians may do or say for disparaging the Congress, we still hope that the present head of the Indian Government—a statesman of mature experience and not ungenerous sympathies—will countenance the movement so far at least as to watch it, as the first Indian essay in constitutional existence, with indulgent forbearance, adding thereby a fresh laurel to the fair fame of his country, which has done so much for the elevation of nationalities and throughout the globe.

THE *TIMES* ON THE NATIONAL CONGRESS.

[*"Reis and Rayyet"*]

THE *Times* pours contempt upon the National Congress. It is an unreal imitation of the English Caucus, and merely an affair of discontented place-seekers—men of straw, with little or no stake in the country. It writes:—

"A 'National Indian Congress,' composed, it is said, of some three hundred delegates from all parts of the country, holds its first meeting in Calcutta to-day. It is organized, of course, upon the model of the societies which discuss social and political affairs in this country. Papers will be read, and debates will take place, while the necessary relief from that attractive but arduous labour will be found in excursions and evening parties. The subjects discussed are the representation of Natives in the Legislative Councils, the admission of Natives to more numerous and responsible posts in the Civil Service, and, generally, the objections to British administration which naturally occur to persons of considerable imitative powers, of great fluency of speech, and of total ignorance of the real problems of Government and the means by which they have to be overcome in practice. The Mahomedan community appear to hold aloof from this kind of thing, on the ground that they prefer not to hamper the Government at a time when it is doing its best for the Natives of India. This incidentally shows what the real aims and results of the 'National Indian Congress' are considered to be by the Natives of India themselves; at the same time, adding another to many proofs that we must look to our Mahomedan subjects for the most sensible and moderate estimate of our policy. These annual gatherings, held now in one great town and again in another, derive their significance from the fact that they represent a vast amount of continuous discussion by local societies. We have produced an extensive class of talkers, and equipped them with a great deal of second-hand knowledge of English history and literature. In every considerable town, these gentlemen form associations and discuss real or imaginary grievances with the confident dogmatism always displayed by people, whose pet theories work *in vacuo*. Such a Congress as that which sat last year in Bombay, or is now sitting in Calcutta, is composed of delegates from all these talking clubs who focus the valuable results of their perennial activity. Thus we have to deal with public opinion of a kind, but it is important to remember that it is the public opinion of a class whose aims and interests are not by any means identical with those of the great masses of the Indian populations for whom we have to care. It is a highly vocal class, which can repeat all the commonplaces of English political life with extraordinary facility, but which has very little stock-in-trade besides that aptitude. Such a class has only two congenial occupations after supplying a certain limited number of busy doctors and lawyers—one is to seek employment under Government, and the other to abuse the Government which does not give it employment enough. These societies and the newspapers they control represent a very trifling percentage of the people of India; it is much less certain than they probably imagine that their success would prove a benefit to any section of the Indian people except themselves. But they have learned from us, among other valuable lessons, how to throw dust in the eyes of the mob, and how to present their own ends under the guise of public benefits. Consequently they constitute a factor which has to be reckoned with, and which in certain circumstances might become a serious danger to public tranquillity."

The worth of this estimate may, however, be easily appraised. It is based neither upon an actual knowledge of what the Congress was and what it did—that being out of the question—nor even upon good hearsay evidence. The article from which we quote being written on the day of the Congress Meeting, the London journal could only evolve its facts and conclusions from the bowels of its inner consciousness. Not that it had not materials of some kind for a judgment. The newspapers of this country, not to say its own correspondents, had announced the coming event as well as the character of the discussions which were to take place. But that hardly afforded adequate grounds for an opinion so strong and so dogmatic upon a matter on which one could not speak with the weight of personal knowledge. The *Times* might, at the least, wait till after the Congress was over. Apparently, however, from its impatience of the very name of a National Congress, it could not command even that moderate degree of self-restraint. The very idea of a Congress was too abhorrent in its eyes—it was too great an impertinence for forbearance. So while here in Calcutta the Congress begins or has scarcely begun its sittings, and does its best to make itself a success, its result is pronounced to be a failure from another end of the world, before those on the spot are sure how it will terminate. Before those on the spot are aware of the extent and character of the gathering, the *Times* tells the world all about it to the exact number of the delegates, with their social position and other particulars. Could the spirit of wild assurance farther go? Is there any humbug (speaking in befitting vernacular) like to the humbug of leading journalism?

But the dodge—not to mince matters again—will not do. The Congress was too unequivocal a success to be put down by misrepresentation. We do not belong to that pronounced school of politics which identified itself with the Congress. Our moderate counsels on questions, which are generally discussed with enthusiasm, have exposed us to no little misunderstanding in that quarter. We are all the more free, therefore, to speak with impartiality on the subject. And we must say that the Congress was in reality something very different from what the *Times* would fain imagine. It is a grievous wrong to say that it was composed of men who had no stake in the country. A glance at the published list of delegates would show that the flower of every section of Indian society was there. Indeed, before we saw the thing in its consummation, we scarcely expected it would be so great a success. Zemindars, merchants, bankers, lawyers, doctors, editors, teachers, members of District and Municipal Boards, Honorary Magistrates, in a word, the leaders of thought in every community, were assembled, so that it would have been impossible for the Indian Congress to be more respectable, more influential, more representative, that is, more national. It is true all the best men of every section did not attend, but that is nowhere possible. It must be remembered that at such meetings it is only the leisured people who can take part. But, from the large numbers who came from remote parts of the continent, one may be justified in assuming that those whom their avocations or other obstacles prevented from coming were still present in spirit. The delegates were, for the most part, representatives of some Association or other, or elected at great public meetings, but that is all the more a proof of their representative character. In the absence of electoral institutions, it is these Associations and Meetings which best discharge elective functions, and the fact that these Associations are something better than talking clubs, was well proved by the sober and practical character of the entire proceedings. It may be all very well to pretend that the masses were not represented. That is the stock argument of cavillers, but does anybody seriously think that the masses of the Indian population have other thoughts and sentiments than those which found expression from the mouths of their leaders. Of the questions which occupied the attention of the Congress, none excited more earnest discussion than the growing poverty of the people, and if the representation of Natives in the Legislative Councils be altogether so extravagant a demand in the eyes of Englishmen that demand was urged in the interests of those masses themselves. It was thought that, with representation in the Councils, a check might gradually be placed on heedless expenditure which was at the root of much of the taxation and misery borne by the masses. Indeed, it is simply false to suggest that the masses, if they could think out on the problem, should be otherwise minded, not to say that they could possibly have any sympathy with the suggestions of such friends as the *Times*. It is idle to detract from the national character of the Congress by pointing to the absence of the masses. Their representation, except on rare occasions, as in every other country, is of an indirect kind, but, however indirect, it substantially serves all practical purposes. It is undeniable that some sections of the Mahomedan community have held aloof from the Congress, but the *Times* entirely misconceives their attitude. The truth is, notwithstanding their abstention, they have at heart the same objects as the rest of their countrymen. They desire no less keenly that the administration should be placed more largely in Native hands, that the people should have a more influential voice in legislation. And so with respect to the other things on which the Congress held its deliberations. They, of course, have their own ideas as to the method for gaining those objects, but there can be no mistake as to the direction of their real sympathies. It has now become a favorite game of some politicians to set the two great religious sections of the Indian people by the ears, but their interests are too identical for the game to succeed. As to the charge that the Congress meant to hamper the Government, no one who witnessed the moderation and perfect orderliness of the proceedings would listen to it for a moment. The Congress was indeed a great gathering; its demands, various as they were, were all urged with earnest emphasis, and so far it amounted to a strong proof that the people at large were far from satisfied with the ways of administration, and those ways must change to bring more contentment and happiness in the land. But fail to see that there can be anything at all with in the people respectfully telling their rulers what they feel to be grievances, instead of allowing them to rankle in their breast.

But it is vain to argue with those who would perforce be in the wrong. The *Times* is only true to its traditions in endeavouring to discredit this honest movement of the Indian people. With the leading humourist, the leading journal—no longer leading thank God, as COBDEN, in his famous literary duel with DELANE, demonstrated—has always been the champion of the stronger race against the weaker ones. It has ever lent itself to the unrighteous cause. We firmly believe that, between the savage caricature of Paddy in *Punch* and the truculent leaders of the *Times*, both continued through a generation, Ireland has been driven to its present irreconcilable attitude. Under the teaching of an equally unrighteous and blind press, England resisted every concession to that country until every one of those concessions could not well be withheld. When at last made, they lost their grace as free gifts and failed to secure peace for the land. With the blood of Ireland lying on its head, it is a wonder that leading journalism tries to play the same game in India.

REPORT OF THE PROCEEDINGS OF THE THIRD SESSION OF INDIAN NATIONAL CONGRESS

1887

INDIAN NATIONAL CONGRESS,
LONDON AGENCY.

25, CRAVEN STREET,
STRAND,
LONDON.

MAY, 1888.

beg your kind acceptance of the accompanying Record of Proceedings of the Third Indian National Congress and ask your most careful perusal of the various matters it contains.

The Resolutions submitted to and (in some cases after most detailed discussion of differences) unanimously adopted by the Congress, and the speeches in which those Resolutions were discussed, reveal, with a force and intensity which nothing can distort, these things, among others.—

1. That the Reforms loudly called for by the condition of the country & by the intelligence and law-abiding conduct of the people will be striven for by constitutional means only;
2. That the Indian people as a whole, and their leaders in particular, are dominated by a sincere loyalty to the British Government, and are convinced that the granting of their demands would not diminish—but, on the contrary, would greatly increase—the strength of the Government against external foes, while, at the same time, largely adding to the prosperity of the country; and
3. That Indian Reformers are, before all things, desirous, in the attainment of their objects, of establishing solidarity with their British fellow-subjects, being conscious that only through the sympathy & good-will of yourself, & of others like-minded with you, can the Reforms so urgently required be attained.

An examination of the particulars given on pp 16 & 17 and (especially) in Appendix I will show that the Congress, whose proceedings are placed before you, was fairly representative of the Indian peoples. The delegates were, in no single instance, self-elected, but were appointed, either at open public meetings or by a political or trade association. No part of India was unrepresented; no section of the varied communities inhabiting Britain's Eastern Empire failed of appropriate representation.

Side by side with the education and consolidation of opinion in India and the organization of the people to press their desires upon the Government it is intended to undertake like effort in this country. Every possible opportunity will be taken to impress upon the inhabitants of the

United Kingdom—(any single voter here has more direct control over the destinies of India than have the whole two hundred millions of British subjects in that Empire)—the absolute need existing for the reforms which the Congress advocates. We know that without your co-operation we are quite helpless. The only road to Indian Reform runs through the British Parliament. That Parliament you can make what you will. We implore you to acquaint yourself with the unfortunate circumstances in which so many of your fellow-subjects are placed. Having so acquainted yourself we ask you to render to this movement your most powerful assistance.

We venture to hope that your perusal of the accompanying statement of Indian needs and aspirations will lead you to wish for further information. Such information we shall be happy to supply. Communications addressed to Mr Dadabhai Naoroji, 25, Craven Street, Strand, London, will receive the most prompt attention and all possible information will be freely given. With the view of affording the maximum of information to our English friends at the least expenditure of trouble on their part arrangements are in progress which will, we hope, when fully matured, be of special service. Such action will be taken as may serve to maintain, to increase, & to completely inform that kindly disposition towards the well-being of India which we know dwells in the minds of your countrymen. This kindly disposition we regard as the most powerful weapon which can be used in our behalf.

Again commending the <u>most urgent</u> matters contained in the accompanying Record to your consideration.

We are, Sir,

Your obedient servants,

W. C. Bonnerjee
President of the First Congress,

Dadabhai Naoroji
President of the Second Congress,

Budrudin Tyabji
President of the Third Congress.

CONTENTS.

THE CONGRESS.

"The Soundest Triumph of British Administration, and a Crown of Glory to the British Nation."—

Introductory speech of RAJAH SIR T. MADAVA ROW, K.C.S.I.

THE THIRD INDIAN NATIONAL CONGRESS, which was held at Madras during the last week of the year 1887, was not inaptly described, by one of the speakers thereat, as "the Soundest Triumph of British Administration, and a Crown of Glory to the British Nation."

Exaggerated as these expressions may at first appear to those little conversant with the rule of the British in the East, a merely superficial examination of the circumstances of the case will show that this wonderful assemblage was, indeed, all that India's veteran statesman claimed for it in the memorable words that we have adopted as the motto of this article.

Little more than one hundred years ago, when the British first came practically as a growing Power on the scene, the entire country was sub-divided into innumerable warring clans and principalities, separated even less by physical obstacles, though these were great, than by mutual misconceptions and distrust. Here and there, from time to time, a more astute or able leader enabled this or that State to overflow and absorb its neighbours; to be in its turn broken up by internal dissensions or external foes; and so, from year to year, despite occasional oases of comparative peace and order, the tide of anarchy surged ceaselessly from North to South, from East to West, obliterating all the ancient landmarks of art and culture. There was little security for life or property. There were scarcely any means of communication between comparatively close neighbours, and men starting on pilgrimages to shrines a few hundreds of miles distant made all their dispositions, as though on their death-beds, ere they parted, too often for ever, from their weeping families. Lands were falling out of cultivation, the great hydraulic works of past generations were crumbling into disrepair, and a cloud of ignorance, black hopeless ignorance, was settling heavily, like a blight upon the entire country.

It had not always been thus. India had had brighter days, dim traditions of whose glories still clung round her people's hearts, but the country had disintegrated. It would be of no avail to question now how far the persistent and exclusive devotion of the intellect of the country, through long ages, to quietism and esotericism, and how far other causes, had contributed to this result, suffice it that the India of the time we speak of no more resembled the India of the days of her glory, than does the crumbling, though still glittering, debris, the adamantine granite peak it once combined to constitute.

And now, after a century of British rule in some parts, after less than half that period in others, what do we see? A mighty assemblage of men, gathered from every part of this vast continent, an assemblage such as India's proudest days never witnessed;—an assemblage rendered possible, primarily, only by British railways, post-offices, and telegraphs, and by the profound peace enjoyed under British rule;—an assemblage, composed of men of every race, of every creed, of every community that, in the aggregate, compose the population of India;—men chosen by their fellows to represent their views, and gathered in one spot and beneath the roof of one vast hall; gathered together at great personal sacrifice and much expense to discuss, in one common language, and that language English, matters not relating to their own petty, private, or sectional interests, but to the welfare of the entire country and the whole body of their fellow-countrymen. British education and British literature, instinct with the highest principles of civil and religious liberty; British history and the examples of Britain's noblest sons: these, the grandest gifts ever bestowed by conquerors on a subject nation, poured with an unselfish hand into the minds of a noble though fallen people alone rendered this great Congress a possibility. Where, but a few brief decades ago, ignorance alike of the rights and duties of citizens had reigned supreme, there a keen and growing appreciation of both had been substituted. The mutual hatred and scorn of rival creeds and clans, which rendered all contact but as enemies impossible, had been replaced by tolerance, a willingness to co-operate, and a growing sense of brotherhood. An exclusive devotion to family interests had been tempered by public spirit and a wider sense of duty; and, through the fading mists of local and sectarian prejudices, the outlines of a new-born nationality had become clearly distinguishable.

All this has been the work of British rule, and all that this has, thus far, accomplished towards the political regeneration of this vast empire was, as it were, focussed in the assemblage that Madras has just witnessed, and it was, therefore, with equal truth and appreciative insight that the Nestor of Indian statesmen deliberately declared the Congress to be "THE SOUNDEST TRIUMPH OF BRITISH ADMINISTRATION AND A CROWN OF GLORY TO THE BRITISH NATION."

Compared with the Congress of 1886 this last Congress was more numerously attended, was more thoroughly representative and national in its character, and, by the still more widely spread interest that it awakened throughout the empire, the more systematic manner in which all its arrangements and proceedings were conducted, and, above all, by the cordial support which it received from high-class English papers in every Presidency,* gave abundant proof of the great increase in the vitality of the movement of which it is one outward and visible sign. Indeed, what in 1885 was little more than an experiment, in 1887 bore every appearance of having become a permanent National Institution.

As this paper will necessarily be read by many who know but little of the India of to-day, it may be well to explain that the objects of the National movement, of which the Congress is one, and at the moment, the most prominent and tangible outcome, are threefold; the fusion into one national whole of all the different and, till recently, discordant elements that constitute the population of India; the gradual regeneration along all lines, mental, moral, social, and political, of the

* The *Bombay Gazette*, Bombay *The Mail*, Madras; the *Indian Daily News* and the *Statesman*, Calcutta, &c.

nation thus evolved; and the consolidation of the union between England and India by securing the modification of such of its conditions as may be unjust or injurious to the latter country.

A persistent and ungenerous effort has been made by a certain section of the Anglo-Indian Community, chiefly consisting of officials, and by the few newspapers * that are their mouth-pieces, to misrepresent the aims and objects of the national party and affix to them the stigma of disloyalty, because, in their public or political work (their work on other lines is necessarily more private in its character), they, naturally enough, devote more of their energies to pointing out and endeavouring to secure the reform of what is faulty in the existing administration, than to the more pleasing but profitless occupation of lauding its many undoubted merits; and, since the Calcutta correspondent of the London *Times*, from whose telegrams the British public appears to learn most of what little it hears of India, is a conspicuous member of this party and evinces as little regard for facts in his messages to England as others of the clique do in their utterances here, it may be right to make it quite clear that, from the very conditions of the case, loyalty to the British Crown and British Government is necessarily the basis and guiding principle of the national party.

Broadly speaking, the leaders of the national party include the entire culture, their followers the entire intelligence, of the country. There are, no doubt, a very few educated men of strongly conservative tendencies, who hold aloof because the thing is new, and a considerable number of half-educated selfish men who take no part in the movement, hoping thereby to ingratiate themselves with the official class; others there are, not a few, the advantage of whose overt co-operation is denied their country by reason of their official positions; but, broadly speaking, the national party embodies the entire culture and intelligence of the empire. Now, this culture is the direct offspring of the union with Great Britain, and Great Britain is, to all who share this culture, the parent of all that, to them, makes life worth living. From the conditions of the case, therefore, they are necessarily loyal to the backbone;—they could only be *dis*loyal, if the British Government were a very bad Government.

Mr. Budrudin Tyabji (till recently a member of the Bombay Council and President of this Congress) put this point clearly in his inaugural address. He said:—

"No, gentlemen, let our opponents say what they please, we, the educated natives, by the mere force of our education, must be the best appreciators of the blessings of a civilized and enlightened Government, and, therefore, in our own interests, the best and staunchest supporters of the British Government in India. (Applause.) But, gentlemen, do those who thus charge us with disloyalty, stop, for a moment, to consider the full meaning and effect of their argument,—do they realise the full import and significance of the assertion they make? Do they understand that in charging us with disloyalty they are in reality condemning and denouncing the very Government which it is their intention to support? (Hear, hear, loud and continued applause.) For, gentlemen, when they say that the educated natives of India are disloyal, what does

* The *Englishman*, Calcutta; the *Pioneer*, Allahabad; the *Civil and Military Gazette*, Lahore; and the *Times of India*, Bombay.—One of the speakers at the Congress, Malik Bhugwan Das, of Dera Ismail Khan (page 128 of detailed report), very neatly characterised these objecting journals. He said:—

"There is no doubt now, as to this Congress being truly representative of the entire country, and, though certain Anglo-Indian papers may still make a great show of disputing this point, their position is just like that of a certain class of barristers, who, well knowing that they have no case, still, to please their clients, storm and bluster as if they were sure of gaining their cause, and abuse and affect to despise the other side, well knowing that the latter are sure to win. It is not the best kind of barristers who do this; neither are our opponents the best kind of journalists."

it mean? It means this: that in the opinion of the educated natives,—that is to say, of all the men of light and leading, all those who have received a sound, liberal, and enlightened education, all those who are acquainted with the history of their own country and with the nature of the present and past Governments, that in the opinion of all these—the English Government is so bad that it has deserved to forfeit the confidence and the loyalty of the thinking part of the population. (Hear, hear, and applause.) Now, gentlemen, is it conceivable that a more frightful and unjust condemnation of the British Government can be pronounced than is implied in this charge of disloyalty against the educated natives of India? Gentlemen, if this charge were brought by some bitter enemies of Great Britain, if it were brought by the Russians, for example, I could understand it. (Hear, hear.) But it is almost beyond my comprehension that it should come not from enemies, but from the supposed friends of the British Government (loud laughter, and hear, hear), not from the Russians, but from Englishmen (hear, hear), who, presumably, want, not to destroy but, to support their Government! I say it surpasses my comprehension. (Loud applause.) Gentlemen, just consider for a moment the effect of this reckless allegation upon the uneducated millions of the inhabitants of this country, upon the hordes of the Russians in the North, and upon the enlightened nations of Europe! I say, therefore, that the conduct of those who thus recklessly charge us with disloyalty resembles the conduct of the foolish woodman who was lopping off the very branch of the tree upon which he was standing (hear, hear, loud applause and loud laughter), unconscious that the destruction of the branch meant the destruction of himself. (Applause and laughter.)"

Naturally, the more highly educated class have gathered round them, by the mere force of mental superiority, nearly the whole of the more intelligent though little educated classes, and the party thus formed in pursuance of their fundamental objects are gradually leavening the ignorant masses with (to say nothing of work on other lines) a sound and healthy, if rudimentary, political education, and, week by week, are adding thousands to their own party, and to the supporters of British rule. Every man who, with understanding, joins the movement, is one less possible enemy, in any crisis, to Great Britain. It is the National Party who are the true British Party; those who recklessly denounce it and wantonly misrepresent it, the real traitors to our common Queen and country.

Now, the objects with which the Congress, primarily, a political body, though calculated indirectly to subserve other purposes, was started by the National Party may be divined from a consideration of that party's threefold objects, already set forth.

The Congress was intended to bring face to face, and make thoroughly known to each other, all the men of light and leading of all portions of the empire. Thus far, there had been much correspondence, and, here and there, a single leader from one province, on his way to Europe or in the course of travel, found his way to the capital of another province, and there made the acquaintance of some of its leaders. But it was now intended to bring all such yearly together and establish the closer bonds of personal friendship between all the most earnest and eminent labourers in the work of India's political regeneration.

Of course, it was not overlooked that in this way would also be brought together men equally, or even more, interested in other branches of the national regeneration, and that these would equally profit indirectly from these gatherings; and that in conjunction with, though distinct from them, conferences, of groups of co-religionists or co-workers in the same branches thus met together, would be held, and some advance thus secured in all directions. But the primary and avowed objects are political, in the broadest sense of the word, and with these only, and not with the incidental advantages it brought in its train to other branches of the work, is it now proposed to deal.

Further, the Congress was intended to enable all interested in public questions to supplement their knowledge and correct their views in the light of the information possessed, and the opinions held, by others equally interested.

It was intended to eliminate provincial jealousies, prejudices, and misconceptions, by close personal intercourse, not only from the minds of the members of the Congress itself but from those of the leading inhabitants, and, so far as might be, the people generally, of all the presidencies and provinces, in each of which it was arranged that the Congress should in turn assemble.

It was intended to exorcise sectarian and class antipathies by associating in one common work, for the common good, leading professors of all creeds and leading members of all sects and classes.

It was intended—as no such gatherings could be accomplished, except at considerable cost in money, time, and personal convenience, not only to the members of the party in the province in which the assemblage took place, who were to act as hosts, but to all the members of the Congress delegated from other provinces, who had from one to two thousand miles to travel—to habituate all to personal sacrifices for the common good.

It was intended, by concentrating the most strenuous efforts on great national questions and diminishing the absorption in local or purely selfish interests, to foster a wider altruism and a more genuine public spirit.

It was intended to educate all who took part in it, not merely in the arts of public-speaking and debate, developing the faculty of thinking out clearly opinions and expressing them lucidly to others, not merely in habits of accuracy and research, but in the practice of self-control, moderation, and a willingness to give and take; to educate them, in fact, into what, but for the miserable displays of recent times, might fitly have been termed a genuine Parliamentary frame of mind.

It was intended to familiarise the country with the methods and working of Representative Institutions on a large scale, and, thus, as this familiarity grew, to demonstrate to the Government and People of England that India was already ripe for some measure of those Institutions to which the entire intelligence of the country so earnestly aspires.

It was intended to unify public opinion by the interfusion of the views held by all classes in all the various provinces, and, eliminating matters sectional and provincial, to arrive at definite and unanimous conclusions on all truly national questions, and to press these conclusions on the Government, not in the spirit of an Opposition but rather as *amici curiæ*.

It was intended to widen the basis of the National Party, the party of Progress and Order, the British Party in the truest sense of the word, until it became absolutely co-extensive with the entire population of the Empire, not solely by the awakening of the masses that follows in each province its assemblage there, but by the missionary labours of all the members of the Congress throughout the year, who, in and near their homes, as Standing Congress Committees and Sub-Committees, by lectures, public meetings, and the distribution of tens of thousands of simple tracts* in the local vernaculars, were expected to spread from mind to mind an elementary knowledge of the burning political questions of the day and, generally, of the rights and duties of all good citizens of a civilized State.

It is to the eternal honour alike of England, the beneficent teacher, and India, the docile pupil, that at the close of this the Third Congress, we are in a position to assert that there is not one of these objects that has not been already partially achieved, and not one single one of them of which the perfect accomplishment, in a not distant future, does not appear to be, humanly speaking, certain.

But, numerous and wide-reaching as the objects of the Congress, the more important of which we have now indicated, unquestionably are, "the carping crew of narrow brains," unable to find fault with what the Congress does, has never ceased to revile it for not aiming at something more. Boldly has the Congress taken the Ossa of Political Reform upon its shoulders, but this fault-finding party, who themselves will not extend a finger to lighten the burdens of the country, find no words, it would seem, too bitter in which to denounce it for not piling the Pelion of Social Reform also on its existing load. The National Party have undertaken through the Congress the political regeneration of two hundred millions of men; and these fatuous foes of progress revile it, because, through this same organization, it does not also attempt their social, moral, and religious regeneration! The National Party is as deeply interested, we may say more deeply interested, in these latter than even in the former, question, but it suits its means to its ends and applies in each case the proper mechanism. Throughout the country social and religious conferences, associations, and guilds are working at these deeper and more spiritual problems, and in many cases, men most prominent in the political work of the Congress will be found equally amongst the most prominent in the more spiritual work which other bodies are carrying on. But the methods and organization requisite for success in the one case would be fatal to success in the other; and it really seems impossible for any honest man, possessing any real knowledge of the country or its wants, to continue to find fault with the Congress because it refuses to overstep the bounds of its natural sphere, wherein it can work effectively, in order to plunge into other spheres in which it could only introduce confusion and discord.

The true state of the case was clearly put in his inaugural speech by Mr. Dadabhai Naoroji, the President of the 1886 Congress. He said:—

"It has been asserted that this Congress ought to take up questions of social reforms: (cheers, and cries of 'Yes, Yes,') and our failure to do this has been urged as a reproach against us. Certainly, no member of this National Congress is more alive to the necessity of social reforms than I am; but, gentlemen, for everything there are proper times, proper circumstances, proper parties, and proper places (cheers); we are met together as a political body to represent to our rulers our political aspirations, not to discuss social reforms, and, if you blame us for ignoring these, you should equally blame the House of Commons for not discussing the abstruser problems of mathematics or metaphysics. But, besides this, there are here Hindus of every caste, amongst whom, even in the same provinces, customs and social arrangements differ widely,—there are Mahomedans and Christians of various denominations, Parsis, Sikhs, Brahmos, and what not—men, indeed, of each and all of those numerous classes which constitute in the aggregate the people of India. (Loud cheers.) How can this gathering of all classes discuss the social reforms needed in each individual class? What do any of us know of the internal home-life, of the customs, traditions, feelings, prejudices of any class but our own? How could a gathering, a cosmopolitan gathering, like this, discuss to any

* Translations of two of these, "The Tamil Congress Catechism," of which 30,000 copies were circulated in Southern India, and of an Oordoo and Hindee tract on Representative Institutions, in the form of a conversation, o which 25,000 copies were circulated in Northern India, are given in Appendices II. and III.

purpose the reforms needed in any one class? Only the members of that class can effectively deal with the reforms therein needed. A National Congress must confine itself to questions in which the entire nation has a direct participation, and it must leave the adjustment of social reforms and other class questions to class Congresses. But it does not follow that, because this national political body does not presume to discuss social reforms the delegates here present are not just as deeply, nay, in many cases far more deeply, interested in these questions than in those political questions we do discuss, or that those several communities, whom those delegates represent, are not doing their utmost to solve those complicated problems on which hinges the practical introduction of those reforms. Any man who has eyes and ears open must know what struggles towards higher and better things are going on in every community: and it could not be otherwise with the noble education we are receiving. Once you begin to think about your own actions, your duties and responsibilities to yourself, your neighbours, and your nation, you cannot avoid looking round and observing much that is wrong amongst you; and we know, as a fact, that each community is now doing its best, according to its light and the progress that it has made in education. I need not, I think, particularise. The Mahomedans know what is being done by persons of their community to push on the education their brethren so much need; the Hindus are everywhere doing what they can to reform those social institutions which, they think, require improvement. There is not one single community here represented of which the best and ablest men do not feel that much has to be done to improve the social, moral, religious status of their brethren, and in which, as a fact, they are not striving to effect gradually those needful improvements; but these are essentially matters too delicate for a stranger's handling—matters which must be left to the guidance of those who alone fully understand them in all their bearings, and which are wholly unsuited to discussion in an assemblage like this, in which all classes are intermingled. (Loud cheers.)"

It might be thought that this authoritative exposition of the situation, not one single line of which can be traversed, would have sufficed to silence the cavillers; but they none the less, and for their sakes we deeply regret being compelled to say it, persisted in their attacks, and at this recent Congress the President, Mr. Budrudin Tyabji, felt compelled to allude once more briefly to the subject. He said:—

"Now, gentlemen, one word as to the scope of our action and deliberations. It has been urged—solemnly urged—as an objection against our proceedings, that this Congress does not discuss the question of social reform. But, gentlemen, this matter has already been fully dealt with by my friend, Mr. Dadabhai Naoroji, who presided over your deliberations last year. And I must confess that the objection seems to me strange, seeing that this Congress is composed of the representatives, not of any one class or community, not of one part of India, but of all the different parts, and of all the different classes, and of all the different communities, of India, whereas any question of social reform must of necessity affect some particular part, or some particular community, of India only; and, therefore, gentlemen, it seems to me, that although we Mussulmans have our own special problems to solve, just as our Hindu and Parsee friends have theirs, yet these questions can be best dealt with by the leaders of the particular communities to which they relate. (Applause.) I therefore think, gentlemen, that the only wise and, indeed, the only possible, course we can adopt is to confine our discussions to such questions as affect the whole of India at large and to abstain from the discussion of questions that affect a particular part or a particular community only. (Loud applause.)"

After explanations like these we can only conclude, of any who persist in denouncing our Political Congress because it is not also a Social Conference, that Divine Providence, in its inscrutable wisdom, has seen fit to withhold from them either integrity or intellect, or both.

But, though the Congress concerns itself mainly with political questions, the National Party aims at the regeneration, on all lines, of the people of India. Some years ago a gentleman who has always been an earnest worker in this party and a zealous supporter of the Congress gave expression in a letter to what he conceived to be the views on this question of the leaders, as opposed to the rank and file, of the National Party.

He said:—

"It is essential, I think, that we should all try to realise that, closely interwoven in humanity as are the physical, intellectual, and psychical factors, progress in any direction, to be real or permanent, postulates a corresponding progress in other directions—that though we may, and must, most specially devote our energies to overcoming the particular adversary that circumstances have most immediately opposed to us, we each form but one unit in a force contending against a common foe, whose defeat will depend as much on the success of each of our fellow-soldiers as on our own.

"At present the greatest obstacle to all progress here appears to me to consist in a general failure to realise the essential unity of the cause of reform. You find earnest men whose eyes appear to be closed to everything but the material wants of the people, and to whom the poverty of our population appears to be the one sole evil against which it is necessary to concentrate all efforts. You find equally devoted enthusiasts who see in the ignorance of the masses the source of all their sufferings and in their intellectual elevation a panacea for all woes. You find men of the purest and highest aspirations, careless to a great extent of both the material and mental wants of the nation, making their sole aim either its moral development or religious culture. There are your social reformers who hold that India is to be saved by the abolition or modification of some evil or obsolete custom or habit, and, nailing this flag to their own masts, are willing to see the rest of the fleet sink if only their ships forge somewhat ahead. And last, but not least, you have the strong practical men, who, Gallio-like, care for none of these things, but place all their hopes on the realisation of their aspirations for the political enfranchisement of their countrymen.

"What we want, it seems to me, at the present time most of all, is that all these good labourers should understand that they are comrades in one cause, that their aims, though diverse, are not only not antagonistic but are inextricably interlinked parts of one whole; that if you could multiply tenfold every peasant's means, you would serve the country's interests but little did you not simultaneously elevate the mental and moral faculties, so as to secure a wise, prudent, and good use of the money, root out old customs involving its rapid dissipation, and confer such a political status as would enable the owners to preserve and protect their newly-found wealth;—that no great development of brain-power is possible on empty stomachs, and where men's whole energies have to be devoted to simply satisfying the cravings of these, and that even, if possible, it would become a positive evil if unaccompanied by moral or spiritual evolution, and by means for gratifying the necessarily resulting political aspirations;—that moral culture is best fostered, mankind being what it is, by removing from men's paths those terrible temptations to evil engendered by poverty, hunger, and natural envy of those more fortunate, and that the hope of attaining to the exercise of political functions is often one of the strongest incitements to a higher morality; that the extinction of a few evil customs will avail little without a thorough recast of the social framework, a thing only possible as the result of a general advance along all the other lines—physical, intellectual, psychical, and political;—and that, lastly, nations in the long run always get precisely as good a Government as they deserve, and that no nominal political enfranchisement will, in practice, prove more than a change of evils unless such an advance has simultaneously or antecedently been made along all these other lines as shall render the country qualified to assimilate its improved political status."

This letter was published and widely circulated at the time, and was endorsed by the press throughout the country as embodying fairly the views of the National Party as a whole, and from innumerable workers, specially devoted to this or that branch of reform, came the assurance that the writer was in error, and that the real "unity" of the work, which all the different members of the party were carrying on, was fully recognised.

All, then, that it is needful to bear in mind is that the National Party, catholic in its aims, is one thing, the Congress only the instrument, by the help of which it seeks to promote those aims in one single direction, and that if more is heard of the Congress than of other efforts made by this party, it is because from its very nature it comes, necessarily, prominently before the general public; while the even more strenuous efforts that are being made in other directions, being sectional in character and, owing to the nature of the matters dealt with, to a great extent, private in their operation, are scarcely heard of, except in the minor groups they affect, and will only become slowly recognizable, by the public, in the results that they gradually evolve.

The first Congress assembled at Bombay during the last days of 1885. It comprised less than one hundred gentlemen (though there were at least one or two from each province in the empire), who, "though representatives of the highest culture of the land and fully qualified to speak as to the wants and wishes of the nation, yet appeared as volunteers in the good cause, uncommissioned, as a rule, by any constituencies, local or general, to appear on their behalf." They elected as their President Mr. W. C. Bonnerjee, a Bengali Brahmin, at that time Standing Counsel to the Government of India, and, as the result of their deliberations (to which no reporters were admitted), passed a series of Resolutions on important public questions which will be found recorded at the close of this volume. Later, a report of their formal proceedings relating to these Resolutions, and embodying the substance of the principal speeches delivered, was duly published.

Besides discussing these public questions, however, much consideration was given to the future development of the Congress, and it was decided that at the next gathering the Representatives, as they were at first called, or Delegates, as they are now styled, should not come self-appointed, but appear as the authorised representatives of some community or public body, or of the people of some locality. It was also resolved that an attempt should be made to settle by correspondence, beforehand, the leading subjects likely to be discussed, so as to enable the Representatives to ascertain, beforehand, the wishes and views thereon of their several constituencies.

The second Congress assembled in Calcutta during the Christmas week of 1886. But, in the meantime, the proceedings of the first Congress had become widely known; hundreds of public associations, and meetings in all parts of the empire, had endorsed its Resolutions, a strong general interest had been awakened, and the country had virtually taken the movement out of the hands of the original promoters, and, while adhering scrupulously to the lines laid down by them, had made the enterprise their own.

So it resulted that fully five hundred gentlemen, of whom some four hundred and forty actually put in an appearance, were elected all over India at public meetings of the inhabitants of large towns or groups of villages, or at general meetings of societies, associations, and sabhas, political, agricultural, and literary. But, although all the delegates, as the public now commenced to call them, were undoubtedly elected by some meeting or body of men, the elections had in some cases been hurried and were wanting in formal regularity. Many delegates failed to bring regular credentials of their delegation, and no materials were available for even an approximate estimate of the numbers of persons whom they directly represented.

Attempts had been made to fore-warn and fore-arm the delegates as to the subjects likely to be discussed, and several printed suggestions in regard to such were issued from several of the provinces and circulated to all the rest. But, "unfortunately, admirable as the idea was, the necessary machinery (since provided by the Standing Congress Committees—Resolution XIII. of 1886) did not exist for carrying it out in its integrity, and a considerable proportion of the delegates never saw, or, even if they saw, never properly considered, in consultation with their constituents, these important papers of suggestions, which constituted the foundation stones of the subsequent congressional deliberations."

Still the Congress met, electing as its President the Honourable Dadabhai Naoroji (a Parsee), at that time a member of the Bombay Council, a veteran reformer, whose name is a household word throughout the Empire. It met, and the moderation and eloquence that characterised its proceedings, the earnestness, order, and good temper that pervaded its discussions, and the widespread enthusiasm that it engendered, especially throughout Bengal, excited the admiration and surprise of all candid minds. Reporters for the Press were present on the first day, but, owing to changes in the place of meeting, no suitable place was found for these at subsequent sittings, and only the reporters employed by the Congress were present; this accident gave an opportunity to those opposed to the movement to declare that the reporters for the Press had been designedly excluded. After a prolonged series of debates, many of them contested with an acuteness, energy, and, above all, good sense, that would have done credit to any assembly in the world, the Second Congress passed a series of Resolutions of the highest importance, which, if accepted, along with those passed in 1885, would, in ten years, so improve the condition of the country and the relations between England and India as to leave only comparatively minor reforms for the time needful. These Resolutions also, to facilitate reference, will be found recorded on the closing pages of this Report.

But, besides their public discussions, the leaders of the several provincial circles had found time to arrange that the next Congress, which it had been settled should assemble at Madras, should be more systematically organized, and its arrangements still more methodically conducted than those of its Calcutta predecessor.

Accordingly, on the 1st of May, 1887, a great public meeting was held at Madras, and a very strong Reception Committee was formed, consisting of some 120 members, with Rajah Sir T. Madava Row, K.C.S.I., as Chairman, and including the Honourable Mir Humayun Jah Bahadur, C.I.E., Sir Savalai Ramasawmi Mudeliar, C.I.E., the Honourable S. Subramania Iyer, the Honourable Rajah T. Rama Row, the Honourable P. Chentsal Row Pantulu, C.I.E., Messrs. P. Somasundram Chettiar, Rungiah Nayudu, G. Mahadeva Chettiar, N. Subramaniem, Thavasi Moothoo Nadar, B. Lovery, B. H. Chester, Khan Bahadur Hajee Mahomed Abdulla Badshah Sahib Mahomed Nizamudeen Khan Bahadur, the Honourable Raja G. N. Gajapathi Row, Mr. P. Ananda Charlu, Dr. S. Pulney Andy, etc., etc., in fact, with few exceptions, all the leading men, Eurasians, Mahomedans, Native Christians, Hindus (both Brahmins and other castes) of the Madras Presidency. Out of this Commitee, again, an Executive Committee of about twenty-five members was constituted and the work commenced.

Arrangements were made for sub-committees in every town of 10,000 inhabitants and upwards in the Presidency. The uneducated masses of the province, now that the Congress was to be held at their very doors, had to be taught its nature and object, beforehand, so as to preclude the possibility of their being led away into any false notions of its scope or aims.* This was done partly

* That this was pretty well understood in Madras before the Congress actually assembled may be inferred from the fact that, out of the very large number of communications from the people of the Presidency addressed to the Congress, its President or the General Secretary, only a very small number were alien to its purposes. Still there were a few such. Three gentlemen requested the Congress to procure them good Government appointments. One referred to it a serious difference he had had with his father-in-law. Two or three prayed it to induce Government to restore jaghirs and pensions of which, they averred, that they had been unjustly deprived, and so on.

through the sub-committees, at public meetings and by lectures, and partly in the Tamil-speaking districts which comprised the more advanced portions of the population, by the broadcast circulation of a Tamil "Congress Catechism," by Mr. Viraraghava Chariar, one of the Secretaries to the Congress, of which 30,000 copies were distributed. How admirably this little work* fulfilled its object may be judged from the influence it had upon the subscriptions. The funds required for the expenses† of the two previous Congresses (about Rs.3,000 and Rs.16,000 respectively), were exclusively raised from the rich, or comparatively rich, members of the party residing in the province where the Congress took place, in sums varying from Rs.50 to Rs.2,500.‡ But of the large sum of Rs.30,000 required for the purposes of the Third Congress, no less than Rs.5,500 were contributed by over 8,000 petty subscribers in amounts varying of from 1 anna to Rs.1-8, and some Rs.8,000 by subscribers of from Rs.1-8 to Rs.30. Nay, to the surprise of the Reception Committee, unexpectedly and unsolicited, from the natives of India, mostly Tamil-speaking Madras people, clerks, hotel-keepers, traders, peons, medical men, artisans, Government servants, and even coolies, residing in Mandalay, Rangoon, Singapore, and the eastern Islands, to which the catechism had found its way,—how, it has been impossible to discover,—came purses of several hundreds of Rupees made up, spontaneously, out of pure love for their native land and an unselfish desire for its welfare, by these distant isolated communities. Nor was this all. From other places beyond the limits of the Presidency, where the catechism if even it ever reached them could not have been understood, came spontaneous gifts, showing how widely the impulse had spread, so that the Reception Committee (varying slightly the words of that good man who here closed his pure and beneficent life) might well have said with him:—

"From Kashmir's icy mountains,
From Cochin's coral strand,
Where Mysore's sunny fountains
Roll down their golden sand;
From many an ancient river,
From many a palmy plain,
They call us to deliver
Their land from error's chain."

For, there is not one man of the National Party who does not feel that the political chains in which we are now bound are the chains of error; error as to the condition of the country, error as to the wants and wishes of the people; error which before its persistent exposure, to which these Congresses cannot fail to contribute

But the most amusing was an enthusiast who desired the Congress (and his letter came a week after the Congress had dissolved!) to pass a vote of censure on the late Governor of Madras "for the false and malicious libels on the people of India, of which he has courageously delivered himself behind their backs"—men like Sir Grant Duff come, and create a general, but transitory, feeling of disapprobation, and then they go and are forgotten. Who now here cares even to read what Sir Grant Duff writes? No doubt the evil that men like Sir Grant Duff do lives after them awhile, but time rights all this, and anyhow it is not the ponderous hammer of the Congress that is to be set in motion to crush "a little shrivelled nut" of this kind.

* For translation of this, as now re-issued, brought up to date and including notice of Third Congress also, see Appendix II.

† All delegates from other provinces (and at Madras from anywhere outside the city itself) from the moment they land from board ship or step out of their railway or other carriage, are the guests of the province in which the Congress meets, until the latter closes and they depart. Food, servants, lights, furniture, medical treatment, and accommodation generally, in every case suitable to the creed, caste, and class of the several delegates, have to be provided, a task not only involving much expense, but, looking to the extraordinary differences in habits and customs that prevail amongst our people, demanding an amount of foresight and organization incredible to any one who has never taken part in the work. Then meeting halls, of the largest dimensions, have to be hired, or, as at Madras, erected. Carriages have to be hired in large numbers, a great deal of petty printing work has to be carried on during the Congress, shorthand reporters engaged, and finally the Report printed and distributed widely (7,000 copies in the case of the second, 12,500 copies in that of this late, Congress) in India and in England. All this involves what in a poor and excessively over-taxed country like India is, a very considerable expenditure for one province at one time.

‡ Given by H.H. the Maharajah of Durbungah to the Calcutta Congress.

largely, must dissolve peacefully away, leaving India no longer bound to England by chains but love-linked in flower garlands of gratitude and esteem.

Certainly one of the most encouraging and novel features of this last Congress was the extent to which the masses and dwellers in far distant lands spontaneously contributed to its support.

But all this only came gradually to light, and, in the meantime, the Reception Committee laboured on zealously, but a little despondingly. For it could not escape consideration that Madras was the worst situated capital in India for such a gathering. Two thousand miles distant by rail from Lahore, and farther still from more western portions of the Punjab; an equal distance from Calcutta by the same mode of conveyance, though only half this distance for those who were willing to brave the sea; fifteen hundred miles or thereabouts by rail, or rail and sea, a little more or less, one way or the other, from Lucknow, Allahabad, Benares, Patna, Agra; more than one thousand and thirteen hundred from Nagpore and Kurrachi, respectively; and close upon eight hundred even from Bombay; it seemed hopeless to expect that any province, except Madras itself, could furnish any large quota of representatives. Travelling such huge distances, in India as elsewhere, means considerable expenditure, especially for gentlemen holding the positions most of those elected do, who must at least travel second-class, and some of whom feel compelled to travel first-class to escape the disagreeables to which, unfortunately, native gentlemen, even travelling second-class, are, particularly on some lines of Railway, so constantly subjected. As it was, at least Rs.50,000 were expended by the delegates, many of whom necessarily brought servants of their own, merely in their journeys to and fro; but it was impossible to believe beforehand that so large a sum would, in so poor a country, be thus cheerfully sacrificed, not for any personal object but solely for what was believed to be the good of the country. One point in this connection, however, deserves notice. It came to light not only that, in many cases, constituencies had subscribed the travelling expenses of delegates, too poor to pay these themselves, but that, in several instances, gentlemen in high position, sympathizing in the movement but fearing to arouse official animosity,* and thus unable to take any personal part in it, had, unsolicited, sent sums of from Rs.50 to Rs.200 privately, to delegates who had been elected, but who were known to be not too well off, to assist them in their journey.

Nor was it money only, or time which, to the large contingent of professional men, Lawyers, Doctors, etc., was equally important, but the fatigues of these tremendous journeys, where travelling averages only about 17 miles an hour, and—above all—the great changes of climates, that had to be faced. The warm humid air

---

* It must be clearly understood that this animosity does not extend to the highest and most enlightened officials, nor is much heard of it outside the Bengal Presidency. Englishmen like Lords Dufferin, Connemara, and Reay, Sir Stewart Bayley, Sir Auckland Colvin, and many High Court Judges, have ever evinced a kindly feeling towards the Congress, and both the first-named took distinct steps to show this; indeed, at Madras, a large number of Government tents were kindly lent to supplement the Reception Committee's preparations when, at the last moment, the unexpectedly large proportions of the coming assembly began to develop themselves. Of course, they do not, and cannot, officially accept the delegates as the representatives of the country,—they have no legal status as such,—but they have all exhibited in one way or another sympathy in the movement. It is the great body of the district officers of Bengal, the North-West Provinces, Oudh, and the Punjab (though in all these provinces there are noble exceptions, and a good many neutrals) who have in a variety of ways endeavoured to obstruct the Congress. In more than one case, officers have actually sent for respectable and leading men and have warned them against taking any part in the movement in a way that amounted to threatening them with their displeasure and that of the Government if they did take part. But it is needless to dwell on this now, since any recurrence of such illegal action and such misuse of the name of Government will be promptly dealt with by future Congresses.

of Madras, was anticipated with no satisfaction by the dwellers in the cold dry north and the men who left Dera Ismail Khan and Banu, wrapped in furs and then almost died of cold in their first night's journey, found themselves, after six days' and nights' continuous churning, in a warm, steamy atmosphere in which muslin garments were the only suitable apparel. And, lastly, these protracted journeys which had to be made right off (for most men could hardly afford even the time thus absorbed, and very few, indeed, could loiter on the way), presented, and must always present, a most serious obstacle to high-caste Hindus, who can only take their meals under conditions not present in a Railway train.

So, the Madras Committee were by no means sanguine of the results, but still they set to work manfully, as if their work was certainly to culminate in the grand success which, in the end, crowned their unselfish labours.

First, they decided that every portion of their own Presidency, at any rate, and every class and creed and community that it contained, should be thoroughly represented. How successfully they accomplished this object, through the various central and local associations, and through their sub-committees, the sequel will show. All that can be said is, that compared with the rest of India, Madras was too well represented.

Then, they took the collection of funds in hand. To commence with, numbers of the leading men in the Presidency made handsome donations* in accordance with their respective means, as did also the Princes of Mysore. Travancore, Cochin, &c. Then, through their sub-committees they collected subscriptions from the humbler but intelligent classes, to whom their catechism, which they issued at the outset, had appealed. Madras boasts, moreover, of a host of petty Mutual Loan, Benefit, and Pension Funds such as are almost, if not quite, unknown elsewhere in India, which aggregate a capital or collected subscriptions of some £200,000, and in which, probably (for these are institutions for the comparatively poor, created amongst, and managed by, themselves), an almost equal number of persons are sharers. Not a few of these voted small donations towards the work, which, in the aggregate, constituted a not inconsiderable sum. Lastly, the priests of some of the great temples of Southern India were addressed and the high priests in response sent donations; and, in one case, at any rate, a representative also.

Having thus in their own case provided alike for the men and the money, the Reception Committee proceeded to stir up the Standing Congress Committees, all over the country, to set on foot the necessary elections in their several juris-

* The following are the principal of these donations :—

	Rs.	A.	P.
His Highness the Maharajah of Mysore	1,000	0	0
,, Maharajah of Travancore...	500	0	0
,, Rajah of Cochin	500	0	0
,, Maharajah of Vizianagaram	1,000	0	0
,, Rajah of Venkatagiri	500	0	0
Rajah of Bobili	200	0	0
Rajah G. N. Gajapathy Row	325	0	0
His Holiness the Mahant of Tripathy...	500	0	0
M.R.Ry. C. Moothoo Kumarasawmi Moodeliar	250	0	0
,, Shunmooga Roya Moodeliar	200	0	0
,, V. Thavaseemoothoo Nadar...	500	0	0

	Rs.	A.	P.
Rajah Sir T. Madava Row, K.C.S.I. ...	200	0	0
Sir S. Ramasamy Moodeliar, C.I.E. ...	200	0	0
Hon. S. Subramania Iyer ...	400	0	0
M.R.Ry. G. Mahadeva Chettiar ...	200	0	0
,, P. Thyaga Raya Chettiar ...	200	0	0
,, Ramakrishniah	200	0	0
,, A. Ramachendra Iyer ...	200	0	0
Khan Bahadur Haji Mahomed Abdulla Badshah Sahib	200	0	0
M.R.Ry. A. Sabapathy Moodeliar, Rai Bahadur	200	0	0
,, P. Anantha Charloo	200	0	0
,, A. Danakoti Moodeliar ...	300	0	0
,, P. Rangiah Nayudu	400	0	0

Besides these donations the Honourable Mir Humayun Jah Bahadur, C.I.E., to whose zealous co operation the ultimate success of the Congress was in no small measure due, lent no less than three of his fine houses towards the accommodation of the Delegates.

dictions and to ascertain and communicate to them the subjects that their people desired to be brought forward at the coming Congress.

A long list of subjects was thus collected and compiled, and, then, through the several committees, and through the medium of many of the native newspapers, circulated, about the middle of November, in the several Provinces. This list of proposed subjects, therefore, became known to all the delegates a month before they left, and all were thus in a far better position than in the previous year, to consider the questions that were to be discussed, maturely, with the assistance of the more intelligent of their constituents. But there were still two defects; the list was far too long, and though it gave the subjects (*e.g.*, "reduction of military expenditure,") it in no case formulated the Resolution that the proposers desired to have set forth in regard to them. Of course, the delegates were able to learn generally what their constituents' views were on the leading subjects, but, in many cases they did not know exactly what they thought upon the details of these or exactly how far they desired the Congress to go in regard to them. Moreover, it was apparent to the great bulk of them, that a very large proportion of these subjects (for everything that anybody had formally proposed had been honestly included) were, for one reason or another, unsuited to, or still unripe for, discussion by the National Congress. So, after much private discussion amongst the delegates who had assembled, as many did, before the Congress met, on the day of the inaugural sitting, the whole Congress formally appointed a very strong "Subject Committee," comprising representative men from every province, to weed the list, and to draft Resolutions on such of the subjects as all were agreed in retaining. Their report formed the basis of the subsequent proceedings (though several of the Resolutions were greatly modified and some subjects added during the course of the debates), and all this constituted a distinct advance on the procedure of former Congresses.

At the previous Congress the want of a sufficiently large and suitable meeting Hall had been much felt, and the Congress had had to shift its quarters from the Town Hall to the rooms of the British Indian Association and back again, involving, as we have seen, the involuntary exclusion of the Press reporters—and, as Madras had no Hall, in which speakers could be heard, capable of accommodating, say 1,500 persons besides the delegates, it was decided to erect a temporary Hall. This was nothing but a huge shed or "Pandal," as it is locally called, 130 feet long by 92 feet wide (of which a plan will be found facing the cover at the beginning), and open at the sides; but nicely lined with mats and coloured cloth, the interior when closely packed, as it was throughout the session, with delegates and spectators, constituted a sight that none there present will ever forget, and it moreover developed acoustic properties that were simply marvellous. At one period fully 3,000 persons, including the delegates, were crowded beneath its roof, and yet, every word of every speaker (all spoke from the President's platform) was distinctly heard by everybody. No doubt this was partly due to the very orderly character of the assemblage which, though making the whole structure vibrate at times, with cheers at the close of sentences and speeches, for the most part maintained the most perfect silence whilst these were in progress. Still, allowing for this, it may be safely said that there is not in India, at present, a single Hall where speakers could be equally well-heard by an equally large audience. And, then, proper accommodation was throughout provided for the large body of Press reporters who represented almost every paper of importance in the country. So, in all these matters too, the late Congress was a marked advance on its predecessors.

All through October, November, and December, elections were going on. So far as these went they were regularly and properly conducted, and the fact of the elections having been held and the names of the parties delegated were duly and regularly notified to the Reception Committee at Madras. There was no attempt, so far, to divide the country into definite electoral divisions, or restrict the number of delegates that might be sent from any particular locality; the one suggestion that was made was, that no province (other than that in which the Congress was held) should, as a whole, send more than two delegates per million of its total population. Any town, any of whose inabitants felt interested in the question, held a public meeting, often consisting of only one or two hundred people, but, in some cases, mustering several thousands, and thereat, after speeches explaining the nature and the objects of the Congress, elected as delegates those men who were generally looked up to as leaders. Again, any association, (no matter whether it numbered only fifty or five thousand members), that desired to be represented, called a general meeting and thereat elected one or more of its leading members. But, except in Madras, where they were only too successful, no persistent efforts were made to make all towns and all associations do their duty in this matter, or to get the smaller towns and villages to hold preliminary meetings and select thereat several of their number to represent them at the election meetings in the bigger towns. This was done in several cases, but only just where the people, of their own accord, saw fit to do it. Again, except in Madras, where the political organization is more advanced than in any other province, no regular system was adopted to ensure the adequate representation of all creeds, classes, castes, and interests; anyone who wanted to be represented could be represented, but no one troubled about those who did not themselves come forward, and if, after all, the representation was singularly exhaustive, it is due to the general interest in the Congress which pervades the community. In all these matters the idea has been to let the thing develop in its own fashion for a year or two before attempting to lay down any fixed rules.

Moreover, no sufficient materials were collected to show what the true extent of the constituencies that the delegates represented really was. No doubt they represented the entire population in this sense, that if the Resolutions they passed were translated and carefully explained in every town and village in the empire a large majority in every place would endorse and approve these Resolutions. But, so far as direct participation in the elections go, adding up the totals of the reported meetings and taking into account the preliminary out-station meetings held in some cases, and including (so far as this can be ascertained) every member on the rolls of the several associations that sent delegates, and making other necessary allowances, barely half a million men actually directly took part in the movement. Of course, each of these represent at least* four others of the population belonging to their own families, and a very much larger number of their fellows and their families. For, amongst this still very conservative, and, in guild matters, united population, if three Telees (oil-sellers) out of any bazaar attended and voted, it is quite certain that the great majority, if not every one, of the other Telees in that

* Considering what native families are, and that the men who had time to attend meetings, &c., must have belonged to the comparatively well-to-do classes, this average of five per family, including the heads, is probably far too low.

bazaar agreed to, and approved of, their so doing, and so on through all but the very highest and most enlightened classes and communities. But we are dealing with a population of nearly two hundred millions, and while we may confidently assert that, if the matter was carefully explained to them, ninety per cent. of the adult male members of the entire community would ratify and express concurrence in the conclusions of the Congress, we cannot, making all allowances, see grounds for supposing that more than ten* per cent. of these, at the utmost, even indirectly and passively supported the Congress. Very likely eighty out of the ninety non-participators, would, if brought face to face with the question, follow the ten participators. Not improbably the ten per cent. includes fully seventy-five per cent. of the in-any-degree awakened intelligence of the country, but, none the less, the statistics thus far available do not lead to the conclusion that, as yet, the Congress is by any means so "broad-based upon the people's will" as has been supposed and asserted; and we think, supposed without good reason, seeing that, however ripe the country may have been for this movement, it is still quite young and has been conducted by sober constitutional methods, conducive rather to steady growth than to sudden gourd-like developement.

On the 25th of December the delegates commenced to appear, and by the morning of the 27th, on which the inaugural sitting was held, all but a very few, who came by the early mail of the 28th, had arrived. Then, it was seen that out of some seven hundred and sixty delegates who had been elected, only six hundred and seven were present. The situation of Madras had told although (except in the case of the Panjab, whence only nine out of forty-two delegates actually appeared) not to to the extent anticipated. "Deaths—deaths of near relatives (which in the case of Hindus prevent a participation, for from ten to thirty days in such an undertaking),—sickness, urgent private affairs or professional calls, and accidents of travel," may always be expected to prevent some twelve per cent. of those elected actually attending. Thus, some ninety of the absentees were easily accounted for, but the rest of the truants, nearly seventy in number, were undoubtedly mainly deterred from appearing by the great length and expense of the journey; and these belonged almost exclusively to the Punjab, North-West Provinces and Oudh, and Behar.

Compared with the previous year the figures stand thus:

Presidency or Province.	Number of Delegates.	
	In 1886, at Calcutta.	In 1887, at Madras.
Madras	47	362
Bombay and Sindh	47	99
Punjab	17	9
North-West Provinces and Oudh	74	45
Central Provinces	8	13
Bengal, Behar, Orissa and Assam	238	79
Total ..	431	607

* The percentage is much higher in Madras, but, again, lower in other provinces.

And these figures illustrate the effect these huge distances have on the attendance. The Madras 47 have, at any rate partly, in consequence of contiguity, risen to 362; while Bengal's 238, when the Conference was held in Calcutta, has fallen to 78: The Punjab, very distant from Calcutta, but far more distant from Madras, has sunk from 17 to 9; and the N.-W. Provinces and Oudh from 74 to 45, while Bombay, not only nearer to Madras than to Calcutta but more akin to it, alike in people and in climate, has risen from 47 to 99. Still there was, on the whole, a clear gain, (much as is shown in the Central Provinces, to which Madras and Calcutta are about equally convenient and which had 13 delegates against 8 last year), for, if we deduct in each case the delegates belonging to the Province or Presidency in which the Congress was held, we find the out-province delegates 245 in 1887 against 193 in 1886.

But, though the representation was unequal and still far from perfect, yet, considering that this was only the second Congress for which any attempt at elections had been made, a glance at the list of delegates (Appendix I.) will show that it was such as no man could, even three years ago, have believed that the people could have spontaneously created for themselves, not only without Government assistance but, in many places, in the face of the opposition of the local officials. Every province, every sub-province, and, except in the Punjab, almost every large city was represented; while in Bombay and Madras every town, every district, and almost every association were represented. The representation, too, was more satisfactory than in 1886. There was this time no class of the community that had not spokesmen. This year not only were there two or three representatives of the old aristocracy amongst the delegates but, as already noticed, all the leaders of this class in the Madras Presidency, from the Maharajah of Vizianagram downwards, contributed to the work, and we may add, several of them attended and closely followed the debates. There were quite a number of shopkeepers, (last year, conspicuous by their absence,) and no less than ninety-five ryots or cultivators, against only five last year. Doubtless, Madras sent the bulk of these; for poor men cannot, unaided, travel these huge distances, but twelve came from the Bombay Presidency, one from the Central Provinces, four from lower Bengal, and three from the North-Western Provinces. Besides these, as in the previous year so in 1887, the higher landed interests, important Zemindars and Talookdars, were well represented from every Province. The legal profession again mustered very strong, and, while in 1885 there were only about 40 merchants and bankers, in 1886 these numbered 144. The principals, professors, and masters of Indian schools and colleges were far more numerous than on the previous occasion, and it may be noted that as in 1885 so in 1886 25 per cent. of all the delegates were graduates. There were the usual quotas of newspaper editors, 43 in number, of medical men, millowners, manufacturers, ministers and missionaries—and what was very satisfactory, 19 artizans, 2, 3, 4, 6 from every great province (except the Punjab), one of whom, be it noted, a carpenter by trade, made a most sensible speech, in Tamil, on the necessity of a regular system of technical education. (Vide pp. 146, 147 of Detailed Report.)

Amongst the delegates were, as before, members past and present of the Legislative Councils, Fellows of the Universities, Honorary Magistrates (some 31 this year) and no less than 160 of them were chairmen, vice-chairmen, or members of Municipal or Local Fund Boards.

So far as social grades and positions, professions and occupations were concerned, no assembly could possibly have been more truly representative of the entire community than was this last Congress; and although we attach less importance to this (since we hold "that it is a community of temporal interests and not of spiritual convictions that qualify men to represent each other in the vast majority of political questions") it was equally representative where creeds, sects, and castes were concerned. There were Christians, (Catholics and Protestants—Native, Eurasian and European,) Jains, Parsees, Brahmos, a Sikh, Hindoos of all castes, (except the very lowest or no-castes,) and Mussalmans.

Is it necessary to allude to the pretended defection of the Mussalman community from this national movement? With one of the very ablest men in India, a distinguished Mussalman, as President, with the Honourable Mir Humayun Jah Bahadur, and some eighty odd other Muslim delegates from all parts of the empire, with the great bulk of the Muslim Press * supporting or professing sympathy with the Congress, it may suffice to say that one veteran reformer of 70 years of age, whose past devoted services to the cause of education entitle him to universal respect, unable to keep abreast of the rapidly changing conditions of the age, has been displeased with the Congress, and has supplemented, by unusually forcible language, arguments against it, of the feebleness of which he seems himself not wholly unconscious. This worthy gentleman it is who constitutes the head and front of that so-called Mussalman opposition, of which we still hear from certain cliques of Anglo-Indian officials and their especial organs, and, if we regret his thus holding aloof, it is solely because we would fain see his latest days crowned with the regard and respect of his fellow-countrymen of whom, in the past, he has deserved so well.

To return, a marked feature in this late Congress was the presence, amongst the delegates, of some ten Eurasians and Europeans, all men of mark in their own communities, who took an active part in the debates. The Anglo-Indian and Eurasian Association of Southern India co-operated with the Reception Committee throughout and deputed their ablest members as delegates, Mr. D. S. White, their President, only failing to attend, because detained at Calcutta by the Public Service Commission of which he was a member. And, as regards Europeans, it was not only that men like Mr. Eardley Norton, a prominent Barrister, Mr. John Adam, the Principal of the great Pachiappa's Collegiate establishment, —with its 1,800 pupils—and founder in India of a "commercial education," attended as delegates, but that numerous independent Europeans in various parts of the country, including even Mr. F. T. Atkins, so well known for the vehement part he took against the Ilbert bill, sent telegraphic messages, regretting their inability to attend, and expressing their most cordial sympathy with the Congress and its objects. When to this we add the fact that leading English newspapers like Sir C. Lawson's *Madras Mail*, the first paper far and away in Madras; the *Bombay Gazette*, one of the two leading papers of Bombay; the *Daily News* and the *Statesman* of Calcutta; together with the entire Indian Press, English and Vernacular, warmly supported the Congress, all really interested in India's welfare may congratulate themselves that, despite the lamentably erroneous

* Only two, even nominally, Mahomedan papers at present, so far as we know, oppose the Congress, the *Aligurh Observer*, and the *Muslim Herald*, of Madras, edited by Europeans.

statements of the *Times'* Calcutta correspondent, the *Pioneer*, and one or two other similar papers here, the nature of the Congress is at last becoming clear to all classes, in India at any rate, and all are beginning to recognize that what it aims at are simply those changes in the existing form of the administration that the progress effected, along all lines, has rendered not only desirable but necessary in the interests of all classes of the inhabitants, be they European, Anglo-Indian, or Indian.

One word more and we proceed to review the proceedings of the Congress. Not only did many of the European Community here assume a distinct friendly attitude towards the delegates, His Excellency Lord Connemara inviting the President and all the gentlemen associated with him in the Congress to a garden-party, Mr. Eardley Norton organizing for them a grand evening entertainment,* which many Europeans attended, and so on, but, throughout the Session, besides the general body of Indian spectators, (varying in number, from time to time, from about 1,000 to close upon 2,500,) the reserve gallery behind the President's platform was occupied by a succession of visitors, the Maharajah of Vizianagram, Rajah Gajapathi Row, the Rajah of Bobbili, and many other native noblemen, European tourists, members of the civil and military services, and ladies, not only European and Eurasian, but Indian, and one or two of these from each Presidency, being amongst the number.

On the afternoon of the 27th of December, the inaugural sitting of the Congress was held in the great Hall, erected for the purpose. Rajah Sir Tanjore Madava Row, K.C.S.I., as Chairman of the Reception Committee, whose duty it was to welcome the delegates and call upon them to elect a President, took the chair. Independently of Sir Madava Row's great and just reputation as an experienced statesman, the prominent part he took in the proceedings is interesting because it has been the habit of the opponents of the Congress to declare that the older and abler leaders of the Indian community held aloof from it. This assertion received a strong contradiction last year, in the persons of Babu Joykissen Mookerjee and Dr. Rajendra Lalla Mitra, the Nestors of Bengali politicians, but our critics, nothing daunted, fell back on Sir Madava Row, saying that at least he was a statesman, the foremost of Indian statesmen, and he would have nothing to do with it, the fact being that the movement has no warmer or wiser friend than this very cautious politician, though the sadly enfeebled state of his health renders it no more possible for him to go to Bombay or Calcutta to attend Congresses than to go to the latter place to attend the Viceroy's Council, a seat in which he has recently declined.

Warmly Sir Madava Row welcomed all the delegates, and, in a brief but impressive address, he declared the movement, of which the Congress was an outcome, to be the inevitable result of contact with the British nation.

> "Contact with such a nation," he said, "is like the contact of iron with the magnet. It has the inevitable effect of the nation operated upon being, by insensible degrees, assimilated to the dominant type."

---

* Sir Savalai Ramasami Mudaliar, C.I.E., Sheriff of Madras, also, with his customary liberality, nobly entertained the delegates on another evening, His Excellency Lord Connemara being amongst the guests on this occasion.

He showed how British rule had created this intellectual uprising, and he went on :—

"Thus, then, it seems to me nothing strange, nothing phenomenal, that I should witness before me, in a vast and most influential assembly, the union of cultivated intelligence and patriotic ardour, and the confluence, so to speak, of many different streams of thought and of feeling. I see before me representatives from all parts of India, whose very personal appearance will bring home to the mind of the unprejudiced observer the conviction that, varied as are the castes and creeds and races of India, there is still a powerful bond of union which makes our hearts vibrate with sympathy and mutual love, and a common affection for our mother-country. (Loud and continued applause.) To well-balanced minds such a gathering must appear the soundest triumph of British administration, and a crown of glory to the great British nation. (Great applause.)

"Gentlemen, let us not mind too much, or too little, what unfriendly, or rather mistaken, critics may say against us.

"Let us stand firm in our conviction that these gatherings are useful and desirable for a multitude of reasons. Let our single aim be to justify ourselves by invariable loyalty, good sense, and moderation in our thoughts, words, and deeds. These great qualities we have not to acquire afresh. Innumerable antecedent generations have happily bequeathed them to us. Let us retain this inheritance, and trustfully place ourselves under the guidance of the great nation and the great Government which are providentially in charge of our destinies, and our future will be as satisfactory as it can possibly be.

"Now, that a splendid Empire has been constructed, completed, and consolidated, now that unbroken peace and order have been established beyond the dreams of Asiatic philosophy, this Congress represents that very factor which is necessary for the further development of India. (Applause.)

"Henceforth, let us, therefore, invariably act on the principle that the various populations of this extensive Empire are bound together by a common Government, by common interests, and by mutual sympathies. (Applause.)

"Judged, most unsparingly, the worst features of gatherings of this description might be superabundance of enthusiasm and youthful impetuosity. But, as a great thinker has said men learn to run before they learn to walk; they stagger and stumble before they acquire a steady use of their limbs. What is thus true of individuals is equally true of nations; and it is uncharitable to form a forecast of the future from the failings and weaknesses, if any such should exist, incidental to a nascent stage. The sentiments appropriate to such a condition of things are sympathy and kindly direction. An attitude of antagonism or of scorn only causes irritation and soreness, and it rouses, not unfrequently, a spirit of recrimination, if not also of answering disdain. This is almost a law of nature. I will, therefore, ask our critics to remember the early history of nations and to judge in a spirit of charity and magnanimity.

"When I ask this of our censors, permit me to advise you to be moderate and forbearing. It is the nature of vaulting ambition to overleap itself. It is the character of renovated youth to be carried away by excessive zeal. Steer clear of such shoals and quicksands. Discuss without prejudice; judge without bias; and submit your proposals with the diffidence that must necessarily mark suggestions that are tentative in their character. Much irritation and retaliation will be avoided if the mutual dependence of the rulers and the ruled is steadily kept in view. With the ruled it must be a postulate that rulers err from ignorance and in spite of their efforts to avoid mistakes. By the rulers it must be taken for granted that when subjects petition and expostulate it is not in a spirit of disputation or cavilling, much less of disaffection and disloyalty (hear, hear), but only to enlighten those holding sway over them, and in a peaceful and constitutional manner to have their wishes understood and their grievances made known. I intreat you to lay to heart these words of caution to all parties concerned—words which I ask you to accept out of regard for my long experience (applause), for my age (applause), and for my earnest desire to see my countrymen prosperous and happy." (Loud cheers.)

He then called upon the assembly to elect a president, when Mr. Budrudin Tyabji, the leading Mussalman Barrister of Bombay, (who, a few months ago, resigned his seat in the Bombay Council, when leaving India, in consequence of ill-health), was unanimously chosen. Naturally, as a Mussalman, Mr. Tyabji, at the very outset of his inaugural address, vindicated his co-religionists from the charge of holding aloof from the Congress.

"Gentlemen," he said, "it has been urged in derogation of our character as a representative national gathering that one great and important community—the Mussalman community—has kept aloof from the proceedings of the two last Congresses. Now, Gentlemen, in the first place, this is only partially true and applies only to one particular part of India, and, moreover, is due to certain special, local, and temporary causes (hear, hear, and applause), and in the second place, no such reproach can, I think, with any show of justice, be urged against this present Congress (applause); and, Gentlemen, I must honestly confess to you that one great motive which has induced me, in the present state of my health, to undertake the grave responsibilities of presiding over your deliberations, has been an earnest desire on my part to prove, as far as in my power lies, that I, at least, not merely in my individual capacity, but as representing the Anjuman-i-Islam of Bombay (loud applause), do not consider that there is anything whatever in the position or the relations of the different communities of India—be they Hindus, Mussulmans, Parsees, or Christians—which should induce the leaders of any one community to stand aloof from the others in their efforts to obtain those great general reforms, those great general rights which are for the common benefit of us all (hear, hear, and applause), and which, I feel assured, have only to be earnestly and unanimously pressed upon Government to be granted to us.

"Gentlemen, it is undonbtedly true that each one of our great Indian communities has its own peculiar social, moral, educational and even political difficulties to surmount, but so far as general political questions affecting the whole of India—such as those which alone are discussed by this Congress—are concerned I, for one, am utterly at a loss to understand why Mussulmans should not work shoulder to shoulder (hear, hear, and applause) with their fellow-countrymen of other races and creeds for the common benefit of all (Applause.) Gentlemen, this is the principle on which we, in the Bombay Presidency, have always acted, and from the number, the character, the position, and the attainments of Mussulman delegates from the Bengal Presidency and from the Presidency of Madras, as well as from the North-West and the Punjab, I have not the smallest doubt that this is also the view held, with but few, though, perhaps important, exceptions, by the leaders of the Mussulman communities throughout the whole of India. (Hear, hear, and applause.)"

Then he dealt with the charge of disloyalty so often, and so absolutely groundlessly, brought by the opposition clique against the movement and exposed its utter absurdity. But we have already (*ante p.* 3) quoted one passage from that portion of his address which refers to this subject, and need not further dwell upon it here.

Next he alluded to the ludicrous attacks persistently made by the same clique upon the Congress, because it is only a political assemblage and declines to interfere in other matters with which its constitution unfits it to deal; but, in this connection likewise, we have in previous pages (*ante p.* 7) reproduced some of his remarks, which will suffice to show the position he assumed.

He repudiated the idea that all Europeans were unsympathetic to "the just aspirations of the natives of India," affirming that he had—

"the good fortune to know many Europeans than whom truer or more devoted friends of India do not breathe on the face of the earth." (Hear, hear, and applause)—

and said that one of the greatest and most difficult problems of the day, was "how to persuade our European friends to look upon India, in some sense, as their own country even by adoption."—

"For, Gentlemen," he continued, "if we could but induce our retired Merchants, Engineers, Doctors, Solicitors, Barristers, Judges, and Civilians to make India permanently their home (hear, hear, and applause), what an amount of talent and ability, political experience and ripe judgment, we should retain in India for the benefit of us all. (Applause.) All those great questions in regard to the financial drain on India, and those questions arising from jealousy of races and the rivalry for public employment, would at once disappear. And when we speak of the poverty of India because of the draining away of vast sums of money from India to England, it has always seemed to me strange that so little thought should be bestowed upon the question of the poverty of our resources caused by the drain of so many men of public, political, and intellectual eminence from our shores every year." (Applause.)

He paid a fitting tribute to the memory of Messrs. Girija Bhusan Mookerjee, Dayaram Jethumal, and other active labourers at the previous Congresses, "who have now, all too soon for their country's sake, passed from amongst us," and concluded with the words:

"But, to all these gentlemen, of whose assistance and guidance we have been deprived, we must owe a lasting debt of gratitude. They, in their lifetime, spared no pains to make the Congress, either in Bombay or Calcutta, a success as far as their power lay, and it only remains for us, while cherishing their memories, to emulate their example." (Loud and continued applause.)

He then referred to the very large number of letters and telegrams, (the latter more than sixty in number, and many more were received subsequently) expressing sympathy, and said :—

"But, Gentlemen, there is one amongst those (telegrams) which I am particularly anxious to bring to your notice, and that is from our old and distinguished friend, Mr. Atkins (applause), whom by name, at least, I have not the smallest doubt every one of us here perfectly knows. (Applause.) Gentlemen, in his telegram he wishes this Congress and all future Congresses perfect success. (Applause.) He wishes that the unity of the different communities should be promoted and that the objects which we all have at heart should be attained. (Applause.) I think you will be of opinion that that is a very good omen. We want the assistance, not only of representative men of the Indian communities, but we also want the assistance of Europeans. (Applause.) Gentlemen, while we are attempting to learn some few lessons in the art of Self-Government, our European friends have inherited that art from their forefathers after centuries of experience, and it cannot be doubted that if we can induce our European friends to co-operate with us in these various political matters, which, in point of fact, affect them no less than they affect us, it cannot, I say, be doubted that it will conduce to the advantage, not only of ourselves, but of the European community also." (Loud applause.)

But really the letters and telegrams received deserve fuller notice than our President, in the waning evening light, was able to accord them, the more so that a very large number, in addition to those that he had before him, came to hand subsequent to the delivery of his speech. Telegrams and letters, expressive of sympathy and regret at not being able to attend, were received during the second Congress but in nothing like the numbers that poured in upon us on this third occasion. Setting aside communications asking for assistance in some way or another, and letters in all the vernaculars of India, which there has been no time to attempt to translate, there were over three hundred letters and telegrams of sympathy, mostly also expressing regret at not being able to attend. Of course, there are several telegrams, in some cases, from the same locality. Thus, from Hyderabad, Deccan, there are twenty-seven telegrams and letters from Rajah Padman Raj, on behalf of Shorapore Jaghirdars and other landowners; Rajah Sivaraj; Savoy Sankarama, "on behalf of my minor grandson, Rajah Ramasor Row, and other members of our family;" Rajah Murali Manohur; Mir Sarfarazi Ali Khan; Syed Abdulla Shah Quaderi; Quazi Ahmed; a whole number of Moulvies, and other Mussulmans and Hindus. Calcutta, Dacca, Patna, Allahabad, Lucknow, Delhi, all sent several telegrams and letters, but still very close upon two hundred places communicated with us—places separated as widely as Almora and Tuticorin, Bunnoo and Debrooghur. Many of the communicants were men of note, *e.g.*, Mr. R. M. Sayani, (Mussulman), late Sheriff of Bombay;

the Hon'ble Kashinath Trimbuck Telang,* the Hon'ble Ananda Mohun Bose, Messrs. Mano Mohan and Lal Mohan Ghose, Rai Jai Perkash Lall, H. H. the Maharajah of Durbungah, H. H. the Third Rajah of Calicut, Sri Mahant Bhaghan Dossji, of Tirupati; the Rev. T. J. Scott, of Bareilly; Rajah Mohina Ranjan Roy Chowdhuri, of Kakinarajbari; Mr. T. F. Atkins, and a host of others, four of them Europeans. There were telegrams from Presidents of all kinds of Associations—of the Arya Samaj, Yeola, and, again, Muttra; of the Bilgram Institute; of the Mombadevie Oriental Society; of the Anjumani Reayah; of the Society for the Prevention of Crime; of the Mahomedan Association, Rajahmundry; of the Bhratri Sabha, Dera Ismail Khan; of the Working Men's Club, Barnagore; of the Sukhdik Sabha, Bunnoo; of the Behar Landowners' Association; of the Prayag Najar Gnyan Vardhak Sabha; of the Sunbeam Library and Reading Room; besides others from regular political associations from whom such marks of sympathy might have been expected. Then there were letters and telegrams from chairmen of public meetings at the most out-of-the-way places—Verunkonda, Shillong, Sambhur, Ambasamudrum, Barisal—besides others at Bangalore, and a score of other well known places. It is really impossible to avoid the suspicion created by this mass of communications from all classes of men and all parts of the country that the interest in the Congress may, after all, be more widely diffused amongst the inhabitants of the country than on the figures and facts available to us we have felt justified in assuming.

To return, the President, then closing his address as it was growing dusk, called on the assembly to appoint a strong committee of men from each province, whom their brother delegates were willing to accept as their representatives, to work out a programme of subjects and resolutions as a basis for the discussions of the Congress at its coming sittings. This was done, the meeting dissolved, and the Committee, taking up their work then and there, were able, the matter having already been much discussed in most of the provincial groups, to complete their work that night, and to send the programme to the National Press, so that copies might be in every delegate's hands next morning.

Next day, the 28th, the Congress assembled a little after mid-day, and, in pursuance of the programme, prepared by the Committee just referred to, the first work brought forward was the appointment of a Committee to consider and report to the Congress what Rules, if any, might now usefully be framed in regard to the constitution and working of the Congress. In proposing this, Dr. Trailokya Nath Mitter † said:—

"We ought, it seems to me, to have some rules as to who our delegates are to be, how they are to be elected, and how certified to. We ought to have some rules as to the procedure to be followed in this assembly and as to other similar matters. The rules must, of course, in the beginning, be very simple indeed, embodying the existing practice, as far as possible, and giving, as it were, the force of Law to Custom. They must not be hard and fast rules that will prematurely bind us down to any special scheme; ours is a young and growing institution, and, if our constitution is really to fit us, it must grow with us; but there must be some very simple temporary rules as to the selection of delegates and as to the working of the Congress. That is all, I think, that we ought, at this very early stage of our career to attempt. We may avoid, by this, one serious objection that has been raised to this National Congress. It has been said that this National Congress is a sort of mutual admiration society (voices of 'No, No'), consisting of a number of self-constituted delegates, each one appointed by himself as his own delegate, without

* The Honourable Mr. G. M. Ranade was present, as usual, though not as a delegate but as an universally respected *amicus curiæ*.

† Page 77 of Detailed Report.

any sort of representation whatever. If, by our rules, we can show to our critics that the men whom we allow to take part in the deliberations of this assembly are, as we all know that they are, men duly elected, either by public bodies at general meetings, or by towns or groups of towns at public meetings, and if we can thus convince them that the delegates who take part in the deliberations of this great assembly are men who have the confidence of important groups of their countrymen all over this vast Empire, shall we not be sufficiently answering our unkindly critics? (Applause.)'

Mr. Hamid Ali, a Lucknow barrister, in seconding the proposition, remarked* that there could be hardly two opinions on the subject, and that "the necessity of crystallising existing practice, if only for a season, into tangible rules and regulations (that all who run may understand)" was, he believed, universally admitted. Mr. W. S. Gantz, a Madras barrister, who followed, said: †

"Gentlemen, it is not a figure of speech, it is no exaggeration to say, that this Congress is now a great national factor. (Applause.) Two years ago, when the son of one of the greatest statesmen the world then knew, happened to be travelling through this country, he visited one of these Congresses—the very first one, I think, and he went home and described it as a factor which every Government should hereafter take account of. (Applause.) Gentlemen, that was when this movement was not merely in its infancy, but, as it were, a mere babe of an hour old. (Applause.) Since then it has grown and grown apace at a rate which few could have anticipated, and, therefore, since the Congress has become, and will, year by year, increase and still more become, a great factor in the progress of this vast Empire, we are now bound not only to make clear to the world what it is and how it works, but further to consider carefully, all means and steps and ways whereby its business may be carried out, from year to year, more efficiently and effectively."

This seemed reasonable enough, but the assembly would not, at first, accept it. There was a strong feeling that nothing should be done to fetter the natural growth of the institution, that the thing was still too young and the practice of too recent introduction to warrant its "crystallisation," as yet, into "tangible rules." Moreover, the word constitution was a little misapprehended, and, on an amendment for its omission, a rather amusing episode occurred. As a rule, all persons who desired to speak were required to speak from the President's platform; no one was allowed to speak from their seats in the body of the hall; but—

"A Delegate (name not ascertained) here rose in his seat, and said: 'I want to know what a constitution is. Will somebody define it?' (Cries of 'Look in your Dictionary,' 'This is not a school,' and 'Sit down.')

"The President said: 'The amendment before the meeting must first be seconded, if anybody intends to second it, before any discussion on the subject can be allowed.

"A Delegate: 'But what's the use of talking about things one does not understand? I want a constitution defined—it may mean anything (cries of 'No, No'). But I say it may.'

"The President said: 'You will have full opportunity later on of saying whatever you wish to say, but I must now request you, Sir, to resume your seat,'—

which the offending delegate then did with perfect good humour. Well, an amendment was proposed by Mr. R. P. Karandikar for the omission of the words "if any" and "constitution and." As to the first, he submitted that it was for the Congress itself, and not for any Committee, however influential, to decide whether there should be any rules or not, and as to the second he said‡:—

"We have held a Congress in Bombay in 1885, and another more splendid one, no doubt, in Calcutta in 1886, and one still more splendid here in 1887, but, gentlemen, there are other Presidencies and Provinces

* Page 78 of Detailed Report.
† Pages 78, 79 of Detailed Report.
‡ Pages 79, 80 of Detailed Report.

which have yet to learn the needful lesson by the enlightening presence of the Congress—for instance, we may have a Congress in Allahabad next year and another in the Punjab in the following year,—and just as the people of the Madras Presidency have evinced an amount of interest and zeal, we may be able to observe further development in the interest from the people of the Punjab and the people of the North-West Provinces. I do not mean to say that they are lacking in that energy and spirit and zeal which is necessary and which marks the whole character of our National Congress. But what I mean is, that we ought to bring the Congress nearer home to the people of these other Presidencies, and to give them an opportunity of witnessing the working of such vast numbers of delegates as we have before us now, to learn in fact the lessons of the Congress by practical personal experience before we ask them, through their representatives, to join in framing any constitution."

Other speakers followed on the same lines. Mr. A. R. Jogalekar contended that —

"the populations of all the great Provinces must have been enabled to realise what these Congresses are, must have had an actual practical experience of their working, and must have become one with us of Bombay, Madras, and Calcutta in our knowledge of them, before it is expedient to set to work to establish a constitution. I do not, of course, object to the framing of rules for the working of the Congress when it has met, but all else I would leave to local discretion until the whole country really knows, by practical experience, what is needful, and I see no use in embodying existing practice, which we may hope to improve year by year, in anything so formal as a constitution."

Again, Mr. R. M. Sane remarked—

"If we take into consideration the very varied political and intellectual development of the different Provinces of India, I believe you will agree with me in thinking that we have not yet arrived at a stage at which uniform constitutional rules are possible or desirable. Let this annual gathering be held in all Provinces. Let the people of all Provinces grow into taking an equally absorbing interest in the movement, and then, perhaps, we may arrive at a stage when the laying down of definite rules would be proper; otherwise, if we have rules for working the Congress now, we shall continually have to make alterations in, and additions to, them as difficulties crop up and we gain experience. Is this worth while? I think not. We are proceeding on a certain system, but, until we completely elaborate it, why seek to codify it in a constitution?"

Ultimately the proposal was unanimously agreed to, but not before it had been made quite clear that the rules, if any, that the Committee might frame, would, in no way, bind the Congress, to which each and all of them would be submitted for discussion and approval, and not before the President had explained as follows, the meaning of that word "constitution" to which so many had taken objection.

"I think some one asked an explanation as to the meaning of the word constitution. Well, I think it is a word which, as here used, is not very difficult of comprehension. The Resolution, I think we all feel, does not contemplate any gigantic growth of ages like the British Constitution (laughter), or even any such grave comprehensive formal contract as the American Constitution—nay, I am not sure that the word "composition" might not, without injuring the sense of the Resolution, have been substituted for "constitution." What is intended is that there should be some rules framed as to who and what the delegates, who come up to the next Congress, should be; how and when they should be chosen, or elected, and which are the provinces or places from which they may be sent. And again the rules might lay down whether the number of the delegates should be in any way limited, whether the Congress is to consist of 700, 1,000, 1,500 or 3,000 delegates, or whether there should be no limit at all, and so on. These are matters, of course, which will have to be considered by the Committee. I merely allude to them to explain what I understand to be the meaning of the word constitution as used in the proposed resolution."*

We may add, to avoid the necessity of referring to the question again, that when on the last day of the Congress, the Committee submitted its report with a

* Page 81 of Detailed Report.

rather elaborate system of rules, it was generally felt that the matter was not ripe for decision, and a Resolution was unanimously passed,*—

"That the rules drafted by the Committee appointed under Resolution I. stand over for consideration till next Congress, but that, in the meantime, copies be circulated to all Standing Congress Committees with the request that they will, during the coming year, act in accordance with these rules, so far as this may seem to them possible and desirable, and report thereon to the next Congress with such further suggestions as to them may seem meet."

In itself the matter is not perhaps of much consequence, but it has been dwelt on as illustrating what every discussion in this late Congress made more and more clear, viz., the extreme care with which the delegates avoided being led into affirming anything that they did not fully apprehend and concur in. Last year it was more than once asserted by hostile critics that a score or so of men decided what was to be said and done, the rest following blindly like a flock of sheep, and the difference between this and real Parliamentary work was insisted on. But, as a matter of fact, it is ten times more difficult to get anything through the Congress (at least on which public opinion is not absolutely unanimous) than through the English House of Commons. There, if the leaders of both parties concur, the thing is done, while in the Congress, although the leading men of all the twelve great circles may be entirely of one mind, if one single delegate out of the six hundred is not satisfied or does not understand, up he gets and proposes an amendment, to which he adheres until convinced that he is in error. It is a great trouble no doubt, and delays work, but it ensures a very thorough consideration of every question, and certainly entitles the final unanimous conclusions of the Congress to a weight that they could in no other way acquire.

The next Resolution was the most important passed at the Congress, and as having been affirmed unanimously at three successive Congresses, and, intermediately, at several hundred public meetings and general meetings of an equal number of Associations, Institutes, and Societies throughout the length and breadth of the land, may be commended to the earnest consideration of all really interested in the welfare and progress of India. This Resolution ran as follows:—

"That this Congress re-affirms the necessity for the expansion and reform of the Council of the Governor-General for making Laws and the Provincial Legislative Councils, already set forth in Resolutions III.† of the Congresses of 1885 and 1886, and expresses the earnest hope that the Government will no longer delay action in the direction of this essential reform."

Mr. Surendra Nath Bannerjee opened the discussion in an eloquent speech‡ which should be read in its entirety. But we may extract a passage or two as illustrating the position he assumed. He said:—

"Gentlemen, we attach the utmost importance to this question of the reconstitution of the Legislative Councils. We accord to it the foremost place amongst the topics of discussion. We unfurl the banner of the Congress, and upon it are written, in characters of glittering gold which none may efface, the great words of this Resolution—'Representative Institutions for India.' (Applause.)

"Are we guided by mere sentimental considerations in making this act of deliberate choice? Ah! no! There are the strongest reasons why the reconstitution of the Legislative Councils should be placed in the forefront of topics to be discussed by the National Congress. It is impossible to think of a domestic grievance or a matter of domestic complaint which will not be remedied if the constitution of the Councils

* Page 162 Detailed Report.
† All these Resolutions will be found reprinted at the close of this volume.
‡ Pages 83, 86 of Detailed Report.

were changed and remodelled according to our programme. Talk of the separation of judicial from executive functions: why, the reform would be effected at once if we had a potential voice in the making of our laws. Talk of the wider employment of our countrymen in the public service: why, the Queen's Proclamation would be vindicated to the letter (applause) if we had some control over the management of our domestic concerns. (Applause.) You fret and fume under the rigours of an income-tax which touches even the necessaries of subsistence: why, the incidence of the tax would be altered, the minimum raised, if we had anything to do with the imposition of the tax, or if we were permitted to modify it. (Applause.) I might multiply instances, but that is not necessary. The reconstitution of the Legislative Councils would be a panacea for countless grievances in relation to the internal administration of the country. Gentlemen, by this Resolution we reaffirm the necessity for the expansion and reform of the Councils according to the programme laid down by the Congresses of 1885 and 1886.* We lay down the principles, but further elaboration is not needed and further elaboration would be unwise. It would be presenting a broader flank to the attack of our opponents. They would attack us in points of detail, and the great cardinal principles of the scheme would be lost sight of in this discussion. Therefore it has been wisely resolved that there should not be, at present, any further elaboration of details. We have suggested the principles; we have made it abundantly clear that we have thought—earnestly thought—out the subject; but we are not the Legislators of the country, though we hope to be so some day (hear, hear), when the Councils are reconstituted. The Government has highly-paid officials drawing thousands of Rupees a month (laughter), and it is for them to elaborate the Bill and settle the details upon principles which may find acceptance with the Government."

He pointed out in detail that all that was asked for was a moderate advance after twenty-five years' growth of the country on lines that more than a quarter of a century ago the British Government had approved. He quoted from a recent speech of Mr. Macaulay, Secretary to Government, in the Bengal Council, practically supporting our demands, as also a passage from Lord Dufferin's Jubilee speech, (reproduced on the inside of the cover of this vol.) expressing the gratification he would experience were he enabled during his term of office to concede them, and concluded with these words:—

"I have heard with feelings, I may say, of concern, the disappointment which has sometimes been expressed with regard to the work of the National Congress. It has been said, of course, by our opponents, that the labours of the National Congress have not yet been attended with any definite and marked results. But the Congress is an infant institution of only two or or three years' growth. What are two or three or even fifty years in the lifetime of a nation? We must go on working and agitating. The Goddess of Liberty is a jealous goddess, and she is exacting in her worship from her votaries. We should worship her with assiduity, sincere, sustained, and devoted, and then only can we expect to receive her smiles. It will not do to take part in this great national assembly on this particular occasion and then to go to sleep for the rest of the year. We must be steady and continuous in our work, and I am quite sure that when the whole country has, with one voice, expressed itself with reference to this question, England, the august mother of free nations, will not refuse to grant us a boon which is in such entire accord with her own traditions, and which will establish her Empire broad-based upon the affections of her people. (Applause.) To England we may appeal with confidence. When Italy was struggling for liberty England stretched forward the right hand of sympathy. When Greece was endeavouring to assert her place amongst the nationalities of the earth England was there, the foster-mother of freedom, responsive to the call. We are neither Italians nor Greeks. We are something better. We are British subjects. (Hear, hear, and applause.) England has taken us into her bosom and claims us as her own. We appeal to her by the sweetest, the gentlest, the tenderest and yet, with all, the most durable of all ties, that which binds the mother to her offspring, to confer upon us the inestimable boon of representative institutions, and, I am sure, we shall not appeal in vain. Let us go on, praying, asking, agitating, resting our hopes of success upon Divine Providence, and victory will assuredly crown our efforts." (Loud and continued cheering.)

To him succeeded Sir T. Madava Row in a speech,† brief, it is true, but one which no one acquainted with the position, attainments, and past history of this

---

* Vide Resolutions III. of the Congress of 1885 and III. and IV. of the Congress of 1886, reprinted at the close of this volume.

† Pages 86, 87 of Detailed Report.

extremely cautious statesman, can read without a deep conviction of the necesssity for early action in this matter.

"Gentlemen," he said, "I believe my friends, and the public generally, have given me some credit for prudence. (Laughter.) Gentlemen, I do claim some credit for prudence, and I believe most gentlemen here will agree with me in admitting my pretensions to this virtue.

"If they are doubtful about it, I will prove it to you beyond all doubt by the prudence I exercise in refraining, after the magnificent and enthusiastic speech to which we have all listened with so much admiration—(applause)—from attempting anything like a long or elaborate speech of my own. No, I shall simply confine myself to my duty upon this occasion. I have specially attended here not to make a speech, but simply to express a few sentiments of my own on this subject, and I have particularly attended here because I take a deep interest in this part of the proceedings of this Congress. (Hear, hear, and applause.) I have written out what I desired to say, partly because I am far from well, but chiefly in order to convince everybody that the sentiments I express, are the deliberate results of my most mature consideration, set forth, not in the enthusiasm engendered by such an address as we have listened to, but carefully written out beforehand in words as expressive and emphatic as I can command. I will now, with your kind permission, read out what I have written.—*(Reads.)* Gentlemen, I cordially second the important Resolution now before you. (Hear, hear.) I do so under a profound conviction of the necessity and good policy of the measure proposed. It is a profound conviction, I assure you, because, by temperament and training I am, to a great extent, conservative, and yet, having looked at the matter from every point of view, and having carefully considered it, I have a profound conviction that the measure proposed is a necessity, that it is quite consistent with good policy, and even required by good policy. (Hear, hear, and applause.) I further aver my conviction that it should not be long postponed." (Applause.)

Mr. P. Somasundram Chettiar, the "Doyen" of the Madras native mercantile community, a large and wealthy body, next supported the Resolution in a speech from which we may quote the following*:—

"We all know the objects with which these Councils" (the existing Legislative Councils) "were established. They were established after the direct assumption of the Government of India by Her Majesty the Queen, Government taking into consideration the expediency of rendering the laws good and safe so as to meet the wants and wishes of the people at large, and to suit the convenience of each sect and creed. They have undergone various changes and reforms in their constitution since their establishment, but, permit me to observe, the practical utility of these Councils has not been such as to merit the approbation of the people, owing to the limited number of non-officials constituting the Council, the ruling authorities taking precautionary measures to have the official element prevailing over the non-official, thereby retaining all legislative power in their hands, who are, in fact, the authorities in the Executive branches; thus the feelings of the Native community in regard to these Councils have not been satisfactory, and agitations for their reform were frequently and repeatedly made by local and other associations and institutions, by the Press, and through the channel of separate publications, but without success. The subject was, however, warmly taken up by the Congress meetings in the two last previous years on behalf of the nation, urging the necessity for a general reform in the constitution, showing the grounds and reasons for such reform, adding that the vitality of the Councils so reformed will be increased, and they will be better adapted and suited to the nation, which in these days of its education and progress is wanting better and sounder legislators. There are many instances, too numerous to enumerate here, where grave defects have been noticed and no remedial measures have been adopted to afford relief to the nation. Hasty steps are too generally taken, without mature consideration, when, under financial pressure, the thought of raising taxes occurs, without giving any reasonably satisfactory explanation for so doing. As education and culture advance, people naturally aspire to better forms of administration, which the Government is bound to provide for, as well as to receive and view favourably, liberally, and with equanimity, all suggestions for Reform. So long as the ruling authorities encroach in all manners possible upon the incomes of individuals, and tax them under one designation or other, in their resources, under pretext of the exigencies of the State, their mode of administrative procedure should be such as to satisfy the general feelings of the natives. I learn that the Chambers of Commerce in Calcutta and Madras, the representatives of the European mercantile community, have lately represented, rightly and justly, the necessity of the Imperial Budgets being laid before the public at an earlier time, with elaborate returns so as to

* Pages 87, 88 of Detailed Report.

enable that Public to know precisely how the financial administration is conducted, and thus to see the real wants of the country. Every individual before payment of additional taxes will be very desirous to know how the money is being spent, in a similar way as our household expenses are known, and the Government should be pleased to satisfy the reclamations of the people on this head. A large independent and representative element should be added to the Councils thus conferring on them a larger sphere of usefulness and respectability, and thereby winning the good will and affection of the people, soothing the feelings of the rulers and the ruled."

A series of so-called amendments were then proposed and seconded, but it was clear that these were in no sense amendments, but perfectly distinct substantive propositions, which could not be taken up in conjunction with the Resolution before the assemblage, on which, therefore, the discussion proceeded, Mr. Eardley Norton, a leading Madras Barrister, and Coroner of the place, who had been elected by two of the divisions of the city, and who was received with loud cheers, speaking next. The whole speech* should be read, but as the first considerable speech made by any European at any Congress we may be allowed to quote from it at some length:—

"Mr. President," he said, "and my Native Friends: Your warm welcome ringing in my ears enables me to face you in a spirit of glad exultation. I say, in a spirit of glad exultation, because in your greeting I taste, in the first place, something of the promise of that kindlier feeling and of that more cordial relationship between ourselves and our respective races, which shall make our connection in the future more harmonious than it is to-day, and cement our friendship with the solemn seal of a more perfected trust. (Cheers.) In the second place, I realise that your attitude to-day exhibits that earnestness of purpose which foreshadows triumph, a triumph that, I hope, I may share with you—(cheers)—and shows that you are alive to the privileges and responsibilities of being British subjects. (Cheers.) Your cordial welcome is a kindly compliment to my nationality. (Cheers.) Not infrequently, gentlemen, the illiberal reproach is cast in our teeth that the spirit of an unconquerable antagonism is abroad between the Europeans and the Natives, that there is a great gulf, which never can be bridged, between us, which must keep us each, for all time, apart from the other. And even more frequently is the reproach cast upon us, with greater particularity in the matter of the Congress, that your objects are confined exclusively to the Native communities of this vast continent, objects with which no Englishman can have any legitimate sympathy or tie. Let me in my own person refute that aspersion as unfounded; let your reception of me attest the complete concord of European and native aspiration. (Cheers.) I assure you, speaking from this platform to-day, that I feel sincerely how great is the honour of my position. I am not a "self-elected" delegate. I have not nominated myself. I have been sent here, without any solicitation on my part, to place before you not merely the sentiments with which my constituents—humble they may be, yet my constituents still (hear, hear)—are animated, but also to convince you into the belief that in all the great and fundamental principles of your political and social reforms, not only I, but thousands of Englishmen, whose voices are tied partly by reason of their official positions (applause) and partly by their generous but mistaken belief in a state of things which does not exist, are influenced by feelings of the deepest sympathy and by the most vivid desire to see you in the enjoyment of something of their own political freedom at home. (Cheers.) In my opinion there is no Resolution before you so important and far-reaching in its ultimate effects as that which touches the reconstitution of our Legislative Councils. (Cheers.) Act, therefore, gentlemen, on my advice. Cling to that reform. That is the key-stone of all your future triumph. And, when once you achieve it, you will find yourselves, at last, in an atmosphere in which you can breathe without effort, which will no longer stifle all your aspirations to regard yourselves as human beings of some intelligence with a right to have a voice in the administration of your own affairs. (Prolonged che .) Then shall you really be worthy of being England's children. (Cheers.)

"Frequently have I had many capacities thrust most unwillingly upon myself in Madras. Only last night I have been made to assume a new representative capacity. (Laughter.) I was told yesterday by one for whose character and educated qualities I cherish a great esteem, that, in joining myself with the labourers in this Congress, I have earned for myself the new title of a 'veiled seditionist.'† (Laughter.) If it be sedition, gentlemen, to rebel against all wrong, if it be sedition to insist that the people should have a fair share in the administration of their own country and affairs, if it be sedition to resist class-tyranny, to raise my voice against oppression, to mutiny against injustice, to insist upon a hearing before sentence, to

---

* Pages 89, 93 of Detailed Report.

† This was the appellation recently conferred by the *Pioneer* on another English gentleman who has always taken a lively interest in the Congress.

uphold the liberties of the individual, to vindicate our common right to gradual but ever-advancing reform—(cheers)—if this be sedition I am right glad to be called a 'seditionist'—(cheers)—and doubly, aye, trebly glad when I look around me to-day to know and feel I am ranked as one among such a magnificent array of 'seditionists.' (Loud cheers.)

"We have been told, again, that in this matter your aims are purely Hindu and Mahomedan. What can you conceive, gentlemen, more false than that? Have our critics forgotten that we, as Europeans, even for the limited portion of our sojourn in India, are as deeply affected by questions of taxation and of legislation as any of yourselves, Mahomedan or Hindu? (Cheers.) Have they forgotten that there are many important European interests in India eager to be represented upon the Legislative Councils so that their owners may have a voice in the formation and formulation of those laws which they are called upon themselves to obey—(cheers)—such interests, for example, as the planting, the mining, the mill-owning and the whole of the non-official interest throughout the length and breadth of this land? These, gentlemen, are among the persons who take a deep and anxious interest in the welfare of the Congress; and I am enabled honestly to assure you that if I speak with the feeble voice of a single individual I speak with the accumulated strength of many hundred Englishmen behind me." (Loud and continued applause.)

Then, after touching upon other branches of the question, he insisted on the importance of the right of interpellation,* and proceeded to refer to a recent lamentable outrage on decency by a high official, which Government have passed over, if not with approval, at any rate without the public censure it merited. He said:—

"Do you suppose, gentlemen, that the English Civilian in Central India, whose name I will presently mention, of high official rank, occupying a position of great trust and of grave responsibility—do you think that this officer of the Government would have delivered himself of the speech which we have all read—a speech, let me add, to the shame of his English birth and his official reputation—(loud cheers)—if we were, at this moment, possessed of the great right and weapon of a public interpellation of the Government? ('Shame, Shame.') The official, to whom I allude, instead of attempting to efface social mistrust, instead of endeavouring to allay religious fanaticism, to still animosity and to appease faction—although himself a representative of that great Power whose splendid mission in India it is to promote a cordial harmony among the various populations entrusted to its Rule—has thought fit to widen the breach that caste and religion have created in this land, to separate one part of India from the other, to foment sectarian hate, to excite the Mahratta against the people of Bengal, and thus to betray his trust to his conscience, his country, and his Queen. Loud cheers.) This official is Sir Lepel Griffin. (Groans and loud cries of 'Shame, Shame.') Had we the right of interpellation, do you think Sir Lepel Griffin would not have been more cautious before committing himself to a course which, so far as we have yet seen, has provoked not a word of official censure or rebuke? ('Shame, Shame.') If we might put questions, we should put some excessively unpleasant ones. We should ask, for instance, what action the Government of India intended to adopt towards one of their own servants who, in broad daylight and, apparently, under the ægis of their silence, has cast a slur upon the Government of the Queen and discredited the service of which he is a member." (Loud cheers.)

Then, again, later adverting to the necessity for continued agitation, and especially in England, he remarked,—

"I do not know of any measure which will more surely or more speedily effect the advancement and enlightenment of this country, than the measure for which I speak. I believe that the reconstitution of the Legislative Councils on the lines indicated, and the employment of a large number of the natives of the country upon those Councils, will tend, not merely towards political progress, but to create and foster and disseminate throughout this enormous Empire an increase of that sense of self-respect without which you can never hope to become a nation worthy of true political advancement. (Cheers.) These, surely, are aims worthy of achievement. These, surely, are objects worthy of some self-sacrifice. (Cheers.) You will not win them easily. I do not believe you will get them from the Government of India. You will have to reach the ears and touch the hearts of the great English people, as you have already done, to a limited extent, through the medium of such men as Messrs. Mano Mohun and Lal Mohun Ghose, Mr. Chandavarkar

* Vide Clause 6 of Resolution IV. of the Congress of 1886, printed at the close of this volume.

and Mr. Ramasamy Mudaliar. The people at Home know next to nothing about you. They are in absolute ignorance of our form of Government. They do not know your wants. They believe that our system of Government here is ever surely and beneficently carried on, and they believe it is carried on, more or less, upon the lines of their own freer rule. You must disturb that belief. You must continually agitate, both in India and in England. Words are not enough. You must be up and doing."

And, after pressing this point strongly, he concluded a speech that was rapturously received, with the words,—

"Boldly and constantly reaffirm your great resolution till you carry it in spite of all (cheers), carry it and by your indomitable courage and perseverance break down the barriers of suspicion, of ignorance, of indifference. (Loud cheers.) The time is fast coming when you shall enjoy that fuller political franchise which you are fit to enjoy even to-day. (Loud and continued cheering.) Its attainment needs, as I have told you, considerable self-sacrifice. You will not be reluctant, you, who have already shown so much self-sacrifice by attending here, some of you from such enormous distances, and all of you also at much personal inconvenience, for you will all recognise that the cause is worth your most devoted services. (Cheers.) Accord to it that ungrudging labour and single-mindedness of purpose of which you have not stinted it hitherto. (Cheers.) Even if we ourselves do not live to see the great reform carried out in our own time—though I am convinced the boon is not far distant (cheers)—there is not a little ennobling in the belief, not a little consoling in the reflection, that we are working, not merely selfishly for ourselves, but unselfishly, for the generations of our children yet unborn. (Loud cheers.) These, when we are dead, though not forgotten, shall bless us for our labours (cheers), and make grateful and reverent mention of our names who, meeting here to-day, and elsewhere year after year, with stubborn insistance (cheers), devote our lives with ready gladness and whatever of eloquence and of energy we may possess, to the triumph of a measure which we believe to be necessary for the national welfare (cheers), to be indispensable for the security and progress of ourselves and of our children. (Loud cheers.) Let us labour in a spirit of mutual brotherhood and forbearance, for the realisation of so grand a dream (loud cheers), patient in the trials we may have to endure to-day because we are secure in our belief that to-morrow will bring us consolation (cheers), and strong in the knowledge that, if we are capable of resolute self-sacrifice, we, too, may hope to--

"Stretch a hand through time to catch
The far-off interest of tears."

(Loud and continued cheering.)

Pandit Bishen Narayan Dar, was the next speaker, and from his address also we shall make lengthy excerpts. His speech * strongly contrasted in its calm argumentative tone with the fervid eloquence of the previous orator.

"Gentlemen," he said, "there are a great many advantages that we all know must accrue from the introduction of some, or any, real form of representative institutions into this country. I shall simply allude to one which I believe to be one of the greatest of all, viz., that such institutions constitute the best practical school for mental and moral discipline. Gentlemen, the very idea that you are citizens of a vast Empire, and that your actions and opinions have a permanent and substantial influence over the welfare of your country is in itself a restraining power of the highest moral value. Gentlemen, to be called upon, from time to time, to take part in the affairs of your country, to discuss, with the sense of responsibility that power gives, public questions, to have to employ your highest faculties in the management of affairs that have a direct bearing on your country's glory and on the happiness of her people, these things, I say, are all steps in the education necessary for the unfolding of all the speculative and practical faculties of a nation."

Without this education, he said, the genius of a people could never be fully developed.

"Such a nation may be temporarily glorified by the effulgence of the fine arts and the lustre of the more effeminate types of poetical genius, but it will lack that instinctive sense of liberty, that robustness of character which are essential to all healthy and, therefore, progressive, national life." . . . .

---

* Pages 93, 96 of Detailed Report.

"Gentleman, what is the strongest objection brought against our demand for Representative Government for this country? It is said that India is divided by petty sectarian differences, and that, moreover, she is divided into two great nationalities, Hindu and Mahomedan. It is alleged that in a country where there are so many sects and so many creeds and, above all, two such great rival parties, representative institutions are unworkable. Well, gentlemen, this argument has been answered and disposed of, time after time, so that it seems impossible that it can now-a-days be brought forward in earnest by people capable of thinking. Turn it over in our minds as we will, it is impossible to discover in it any of that cogency which people often profess to attach to it. There is one point, and only one point, on which there is not a perfect accord, a perfect sense of oneness, between Indian Hindus and Indian Mahomedans, and that is, of course, their religious beliefs. In social customs, in manner and languages, in their habits of thought, and I may say even in their prejudices and in their inclinations, there is no essential difference between them. Why, the whole past history of India shows how, when there was no British Government, Hindus and Mahomedans pulled on together, and how, if they fought, they fought about secular, and not religious, matters. It shows that Hindu Generals have led Mahomedan armies more than once, and that Mahomedan swords have been unsheathed on behalf of Hindus.

"But, gentleman, it has been urged that, as the larger portion of the population is Hindu, the introduction of Representative Government in India will place Mahomedans at the mercy of the Hindus, as they will form a great majority, and put their own interests before Mahomedan interests and do everything they like. Now, gentlemen, for my part I have never been able to understand what is meant by Mahomedan and Hindu interests. In Europe, there may be Catholic interests and Protestant interests, because there, there is a real connection between the Church and the State, and yet the existence of such interests have not prevented the success of representative institutions. But, in India, no such connection exists, and the objection seems to me wholly futile. In England, I could understand this objection having some specious appearance of validity. I could, I say, understand this, because there are two powerful parties, the Established Church and the Nonconformists, both of which might have their antagonistic political interests, but even in England we do not find these supposed antagonistic sectarian interests have, in any way, impaired the success of representative institutions; and how can it do so in India, where, fortunately, there is no connection between Church and State? The Government has wisely taken its stand upon the principle of religious neutrality, and, under these circumstances, to pretend that there are in matters of politics Mahomedan interests distinct from Hindu interests, is really mockery, delusion, and a snare. (Hear, hear.) Sir, I think, that if you look into this question dispassionately, you will find that, so far as India is concerned, Mahomedan interests and Hindu interests have no separate existence whatsoever.

"But, gentleman, there is yet another thing of which we hear as barring the way to the fruition of our aspirations. It is said that there is such hostility between Hinduism and Mahomedanism as to render it impossible. To this I first reply, that were this really so, it would be the strongest of all reasons why Representative Government should be introduced into this country. Why, gentlemen, supposing the Hindus and the Mahomedans were really divided by deep social and religious prejudices, are we to keep them apart and perpetuate that supposed hostility? Would not the question rather be, how to remove these prejudices, how to dissipate that hostility, and how to blend the two communities into one nation? Now, gentlemen, sectarian prejudices are the result of selfishness of the heart and patriotism is the best corrective of selfishness. A representative form of government is best calculated to eradicate all hostile race prejudices, by raising men above the cloud of selfishness into the purer regions of the wider and more enlarged sympathies of national feeling. By the more intimate intercourse it necessitates, by the juster mutual appreciation it engenders and in a thousand other ways it removes those prejudices and that sectarian bias which stand in the way of unity between the various communities which are combined in it.

"But I need not pursue this question further, because, though accepting them for the sake of argument, I deny the premises. I say if this terrible antagonism did exist, even then, representative institutions would do more than anything else to remove it. But I deny that it exists. There are low ignorant people of both communities—mostly, what the English papers call 'roughs'—who, at festivals, when intoxicated by religious zeal and, perhaps, something else, will fight, and there may be a Hindu or a Mahomedan leader here and there who, from selfish motives, tries to engender the hatred that does not exist, and speaks of it as if it were really so. But, gentlemen,—and I speak to several hundreds of both communities—is it true that we Hindus and Mahomedans hate each other in this way (cries of 'No, No,'), aud is it not a fact that we live as very good friends? (Cries of 'Yes, Yes.') We have our ways in minor matters, and you don't perhaps much like them, but we don't want you to follow them, and you have your ways, and they are not quite like ours—and we don't dine together or intermarry—neither do we Hindus of different castes amongst each other for that matter—but despite all this, the great mass of us are good friends, rejoicing in each other's good fortune and sympathizing in each other's troubles; and is this a state of affairs that precludes the introduction of representative institutions?" (Loud applause.)

Then the speaker quoted opinions expressed by Lord Lawrence, Mr. Gladstone, and Sir Richard Temple, in support of the claim made in the Resolution, and, after a few other remarks, concluded thus:—

"Now, gentlemen, all these things lead me to believe that it is by no means on a hopeless quest that they have embarked who are now, at this time, seeking to secure the expansion of our councils and the introduction of some tentative form of Representative Government in India. Gentlemen, that we all desire this the unanimous voice of the country here embodied declares, and it is a desire which has been created in us by the English Government itself and which is the greatest glory of that Government. England has moved us from our ancient anchorage. She has cast us adrift, against our will, upon the wide waters of a seething proletariat, and we turn back to England and ask her to grant us that compass of representative institutions by which, amid a thousand storms, she has steered her prosperous course to the safe haven of regulated political freedom. (Loud applause.)

"Gentlemen, the desire for greater freedom is not confined simply to the educated classes, but is shared also by the uneducated classes, by the masses who feel it as keenly as we do, but in whom it has not (and in this lies the danger) yet found an articulate utterance. Gentlemen, it is in truth a national demand that we are making this day, and it is the duty of every one of us, so far as in him lies, to bring home this fact to the British Government and the British public, and to open their eyes to the true character of the efforts that are being made to blind that Government and that public, to the universality of the desire of which the proposition, now before us, is a temperate expression.

"Two of the most eloquent speakers who preceded me have referred in very just terms to Sir Lepel Griffin, and to another person, a native gentleman of very high repute. One of them has been inciting the Mahrattas against the Bengalese, the other, whatever he may allege, has been, in practice, egging on the Mahomedans to be less friendly with the Hindus. (Cries of "Shame, Shame!") And this, gentlemen, is the class of man, and the only class, that denies, what we all so well know, the truly national character of our present demand. Well, things hidden from political sages have sometimes been revealed to the masses of the people, and, believe me, gentlemen, that they are no true statesmen who are blind to the dawning lights of the fires which Western civilization is kindling in our hearts, and who raise their puny arms to arrest the chariot of India's destined development. Gentlemen, the demand we are making is a national demand, and, strong in the consciousness that we are the honest mouthpieces of countless millions, too long dumb, I ask you not to take to heart too much the base insinuations or the idle clamours that may be raised against you and the sacred task you have in hand. These will all pass away; the rising tide—(loud cheers)—is with us; so let us unite together in the performance of this noble task, which is practically the political regeneration of India. Let us aim, not to do good to one community or to two communities, to Hindus or Mahomedans, but to all the communities and all the sects of India. That is undoubtedly the noble ideal, the national ideal, that we have set before us, the realisation of which will be the political Kingdom of Heaven. The various races, sects, and creeds of India will blend together into one imperial whole in which all a free-born British subject's privileges and rights will be obtained and enjoyed; not by one sect or creed but by all, and thereby the British Government, so far from being weakened, will be strengthened beyond measure. (Applause.) For the link which will then join a happy and united India to England will not be the link of fear, will not be the link of servility, but it will be the link of affection and gratitude which no misfortune can sever, and which no calamity can shatter." (Applause.)

At this stage of the proceedings the President, alarmed at the flood of eloquence which this subject (the depth of feeling in regard to which it is difficult to exaggerate) threatened to let loose upon the assembly, appealed to intending speakers, of whose names he held a portentous list in his hand, to limit their addresses to a period of five minutes each.

Then rose Pandit Madan Mohun Malaviya, a very young and enthusiastic labourer in the cause, and from his speech too we feel bound to extract largely; partly because, although over-fervid in expression towards its close, it embodies truths that merit careful consideration; but mainly because it was the only single speech during the whole Congress to the tone of which even hostile critics could possibly take objection, and we consider it only just, therefore, to place it before the reader.

Apologising for venturing to speak after the practised orators who had preceded him, he continued* :—

"Allow me to say this much, that, placed as we are in this country, under a foreign Government, however benevolent and generous its motives—the motives of those who take part in the administration—we stand in the greatest need of our own representatives in the Legislative Councils. Gentlemen, the whole of Europe, with the exception of Russia, has declared that the most efficient and best form of Government for any country which has made any advance in any civilization is a Government conducted not solely by the few for the many, but to a greater or less extent by the many for themselves—a Government, in fact, in which the representatives of the people have some potential share—and if this be expedient for European countries, where the rulers and the ruled are of the same nationality, and where they are of the same religion, I think it must be conceded that it is even more essential for India, which is inhabited by people whose habits, manners, customs, language, race and creed differ from those of their rulers. If we demand for India that there should be representatives of her people in the State Councils, we only ask for what, not simply Europe, but America, Australia, and almost the whole civilized world, have declared with one unanimous voice to be essential, for any Government that is to be suitable to any country, as it is only where the representatives of the people are allowed to take part in that administration that the wants and wishes, the aspirations and grievances, of the people can be adequately set forth, properly understood, or duly provided for.

"What is it that we see year after year? People assembling from all parts of India, from the Punjab, Sindh, Assam, Madras, Bengal, Bombay, the N.-W. Provinces, Oudh, the Central Provinces; from every province, from every town, coming together to implore Government humbly to grant this reform which is after all their birthright as free-born British subjects. (Loud cheers.) It is no desire or motive of self-ambition that brings these people together at such heavy cost and at such great personal inconvenience. There is no taint of self-interest in the matter. No. Their sole idea is that India, their country, of all things, stands badly in need of this fundamental reform, and they hope, and God grant that they may not hope in vain, that their unselfish persistence in asking may secure for their native land this great boon.

"The British Government has already made this concession to so many countries, so many colonies; so many British colonies enjoy it. Canada, the Cape, the Australian colonies, innumerable smaller places, even the so-called Crown colonies, except perhaps the Fiji Islands and some purely military posts, all enjoy some measure, and most of them the fullest measure, of representative Government. Britain has granted or conceded this concession to all these places. (Applause.) Why should she withhold it from the people of India? (Hear, hear.) Does she think that we are less loyal than her subjects in other lands? (Hear, hear, and applause.) Australia would break with her to-morrow if she ventured to prevent Australia from taxing British goods, while we in all good temper accept an odious income-tax, vilely administered, and imposed not to meet the expenses of our own Government, but to provide funds to enable Great Britain to annex Burmah or menace Russia. (Loud and continued applause.) Does she think we are not prepared for the privilege? I think this very Congress is proof positive of our ripeness for the task and of the intelligence and knowledge which would be brought to bear upon the affairs of the nation, if only the Government were kind enough to accede to our wishes. (Applause.) Gentlemen, I am sorry that, looking to the announcement our worthy President has made, I cannot venture to take up much more of your time, but if you will permit it I will go on for a few minutes more. (Voices, 'Go on.') I thank you, gentlemen, for this indulgence. This question of the reform of the Legislative Councils is one in regard to which too much can hardly be said. Something was said in speeches in Parliament about the Budget being introduced there at an earlier date, but what effective criticism can we hope for there if we do not supply the materials by our criticisms when the Budget is introduced here? But how can we, outside, criticise a thing of details, when those details are skilfully veiled from us? It is only when we have our own representatives inside the Government, who can get at those essential details, that we shall ever be able to control, or, at any rate, effectively protest against, financial mismanagement.

---

* Pages 96-99 of Detailed Report.

"The Indian Councils Act was passed when the Government was transferred from the East India Company to the Crown. According to the provisions of that Act, the expenditure of this country should be checked and controlled by the Secretary of State, assisted by the Council. But how has this been carried out? We see that provision was made for the Budget being presented to Parliament, with the object of securing some check. But we also know that no less a personage than Professor Fawcett, of lamented memory, speaking in Brighton in 1872, was compelled to confess that 'the most trumpery question ever brought before Parliament—a wrangling over the purchase of a picture, a road through a Park,—excited more interest than the welfare of 180,000,000 of our Indian fellow-subjects.' (Loud applause.) And as it was then, so it is now. It is not only Professor Fawcett, moreover, who has protested against this monstrous injustice. Year after year some honest independent politician has raised his voice against a state of things which, if it means our misery, means also England's shame. Even this last session, Mr. Bradlaugh rose to protest 'against the practice of bringing this subject (the Indian Budget) forward at so late a period of the 'Session. Last year the Budget was considered on June 21st and the year before on August 6th. It was 'not right to leave to the last moment of the Session the only opportunity that was afforded to Parliament 'of considering the wishes and the grievances of the 200,000,000 of people whom we rule. That any 'Parliamentary control should be exercised over the affairs of India was impossible when the Indian Budget 'figured upon paper as the eighth order upon one of the last days of an expiring Session.' (Applause.) Following him Mr. Reid said: 'How could Parliament do anything when these matters were only brought 'to its cognizance on one of the very last days of a weary Session, when only fifteen or sixteen gentlemen 'had sufficient energy left to watch the proceedings—the debate was almost reduced to a farce—the 'discussion was begun at about quarter-past six o'clock, and in four or five hours from that time they 'would have settled the affairs of 200,000,000 of their fellow-subjects and sanctioned the expenditure of 'between seventy and eighty millions of money. Surely it would be better to delegate these duties than to 'continue doing that which was a mere mockery. Would it not be possible to appoint a Committee to 'overlook the affairs of India, in order that the people of that country might know that their interests were 'being cared for adequately by the Imperial Parliament.' (Loud applause.)

"Then, again, Sir John Gorst, in connection with this matter, said: 'The regret which the Honourable 'Member expressed with regard to the late period of the session at which the affairs of India had come up 'for discussion was shared by the Government with those who sat on the opposite side of the House. He 'believed every one would be glad, if it were possible, to bring the affairs of India under consideration of the 'House at a time when more members were present, and when greater interest would be taken in the matter 'Although many promises to introduce Indian Financial Statements earlier in the session had been made, 'no Government had ever succeeded in fulfilling those promises, and ever since he had a seat in the House 'the Indian Budget had been one of the incidents of the Session that had immediately preceded the Prorogation.' (Applause.)

"Now, gentlemen, you see that Parliament will not or can not give that consideration even to our Budget, even to the expenditure of eighty millions of money, yearly wrung out of the country,—and none know better than you do with what hardships to the people,—that we have a right to expect from them—that common sense and justice demand—and, if this be the case with the Budget, what chance have the rest of our affairs of getting a hearing of any kind? I say, "None," and, therefore we ask Parliament to allow us to look after our own affairs. We say if you cannot or will not do your duty by us, at least put us in a position to do some portion of our duties to ourselves. We say, we entreat you in all fairness to allow us some control over our Budget, to put us in a position to say something through our representatives about it when it is brought into the Council (applause), to give us some voice here in the management of our domestic affairs. But it would seem as if our entreaties were vain. They will not do their duty by the country themselves, and they will not allow us to do it. (Applause.) Can anything be more cruel, or more unjust of the English nation, which professes to love freedom and justice, and boasts itself the founder of constitutional and free Government? Gentlemen, after this, I think, nothing need be said by England about justice and freedom, if this concession is not granted to us.

"Gentlemen, I must express my regret that the rapidly passing minutes debar me from speaking on this subject more fully, as I should wish to do, though I know it does not require much further illustration after the speeches you have heard. Allow me now to say in conclusion that we should continue to press this righteous demand on the Government, and, if all else fail, simply ask them to act according to their own Christian principles, which tell them to do unto others as they would be done by. Would the English nation like to have their affairs treated in this way; would they tolerate it for one instant? Would they even dare to treat us in this way did they not know that we are the most patient and law-abiding people on the face of the earth? Only twenty-six members present out of six hundred and seventy-five, or something like that, when the welfare of two hundred and fifty million souls is to be discussed and when a sum of seventy or eighty millions is to be disposed of.

(Loud applause.) How would they like their own affairs to be treated in that way? Would they, I repeat, stand it for one week? Would they dare thus to deal with only five millions of Irishmen? Gentlemen, I must leave them to reply, and that reply, if truthful, must be their own condemnation. No, gentlemen, let them allow us a gradually increasing liberty to look after and manage our own business, and they will find that we shall forget any temporary injustice that their negligence has caused us and always, always remember per contra all the good they have done us and be grateful to them for all this, and not least grateful for that concession we are now urging." (Applause.)

Now, fully admitting that there are expressions in this powerful appeal to Great Britain's sense of justice that might well have been toned down, we cannot believe that any impartial Englishman will read it without acknowledging that the present position of affairs is both unsatisfactory and unjust to India, and that the time has arrived when it is due to both countries that the administration of this vast Empire should be placed on a broader and sounder basis.

Many other speeches followed, for which we may refer the reader to the detailed Report. One gentleman, Mr. A. K. Dutt,* produced a petition in favour of this Resolution, signed by 25,000 persons in a single district, and gave numerous instances to prove how even the lowest classes everywhere, were becoming growingly interested in, and anxious for, this fundamental reform.

Rajah Rampal Singh, in a brief speech† that convulsed the assembly with laughter, exposed the utterly fictitious character of the representation now supposed to be embodied in the existing councils. He said:—

"Gentlemen,—I do not rise here to make any set speech, but I think I may touch on certain circumstances which will help to illustrate this question of reform in the Legislative Council. Gentlemen, we, the people of India, are permitted (nominally) to send a certain limited number of our countrymen, who are elected by the Viceroy and the Lieutenant-Governors, to these existing Councils. It is very kind of them to take this trouble off our shoulders (laughter), but with their permission we would rather elect them ourselves. Joking apart, the defect which lies in this present system is this: the natives who sit in Council are chosen by the Governors and Lieutenant-Governors, whom they look to as their constituents, and are not, therefore, likely to bring forward the views of the people, whom they in no way represent and on whose suffrages they are in no way dependent. Necessarily, these men, who are mostly the favourites of Governors and Lieutenant-Governors, think of nothing but pleasing their Patrons; there are noble exceptions, but this is the rule. (Hear, hear.) On one occasion, I was talking to a gentleman who had the honour of being a Member of the Council of the Governor-General for making laws, but who knew not one syllable of English. (Laughter.) He was one of the Maharajahs of the North-Western Provinces, and a relation of mine too. (Laughter.) I asked the Maharajah, 'How did you manage to vote and take part in the discussion?' (Laughter.) He told me, 'It was difficult for me at first, for I do not understand English, nor was I allowed to take anybody with me to explain what went on to me (laughter), but as I received it through the favour of the Viceroy, I raise my hand whenever the Viceroy raises his, and I hold down mine when he holds down his hand.'" (Loud laughter.)

Mr. Gantz followed on the same lines; he said,‡ appealing to delegates who were, or had been, members of the so-called Legislative Councils:—

"Let me put to them the simple question, whether it is not true that every public measure of any importance that comes before these Councils is practically framed and shaped and pushed through by Government, so that free and independent criticism is absolutely impossible? Have they, has any independent member, ever any potential voice in determining the outcome of their deliberations? So far as any real practical good comes of their labours, beyond perhaps the softening of some repugnant clause, might they not just as well remain at home? I throw out these as questions, and I should like to have definite replies. On what principle are gentlemen

---

* Page 102 of Detailed Report.
† Page 100 of Detailed Report.
‡ Pages 100, 101 of Detailed Report.

nominated to these Legislative Councils? (Voices, 'None, None.') That is the opinion, I see, of some gentlemen from Bengal. If it is the opinion in Bengal, I can assure you it is the opinion in Madras also. But, inasmuch as these institutions are considered to be representative institutions, we have a right to know who and what these men are. Are they to be the men who, in the eloquent and significant language of Rajah Rampal Singh, hold up their hands when the Viceroy holds up his, and keep theirs down when he keeps his down?" (Laughter.)

And he went on to show that in the absence of real representatives of the country in these councils, the local European officials were so strong as to render null and void, in many places, even that small measure of Local Self-Government which Lord Ripon endeavoured to confer on the country.

"I may say," he went on, "that I have had some experience of the working of self-government in the Mofussil, and I tell you that self-government as it exists in this Presidency is simply nothing more than a sham and a delusion. (Applause.) I can tell you that we cannot even raise the pay of an ordinary duffadar by one rupee without sanction. (Applause.) The Municipalities are called upon to spend large sums of money, year after year, in the maintenance and the support of educational, medical, and charitable institutions, and in regard to these also we have no real control, but have simply to find the money; we are over-ridden by some dominant official who takes us under his paternal wing. In one particular station there was the greatest dissension and the greatest dissatisfaction in regard to the working of one particular branch of that particular Municipality. His Excellency the Governor was expected to visit the place on his tour, and some of the members thought they would ventilate their grievances in an address. An address was duly prepared by the Official Chairman, which was to be merely an address of welcome to H.E. the Governor. The dissentient members, who wanted to ventilate their grievances, thereupon resolved to wait upon His Excellency by deputation with another address. A meeting was called, at which this second address was to be framed, and I may tell you this, that in one of those mysterious ways, familiar to most of us, the wires were pulled, and there was no quorum. His Excellency came, received the Chairman's address of welcome, and in his reply said, 'I am happy to find, gentlemen, that you have no wants and no grievances. (Laughter and applause.) That is an instance of the kind of self-government that we enjoy in the Madras Mofussil."

Of course, with the Councils reconstituted on a representative basis, cases like this, and they are of daily occurrence, would cease to be possible, and officials would cease to be able to defeat, in the interests of their own autocratic authority, the plain intentions of the Legislature and of the Governments both of India and of England.

Ultimately, as evening closed in, the entire assembly, to one man, being absolutely unanimous on the necessity for this great reform, the President suggested that the Resolution should be put, and this being done it was carried unanimously with loud acclamations, and the Congress adjourned.

We have dwelt, it may be thought, at excessive length on this debate, because this question of enlarging greatly the various Councils and reconstituting them on a partially representative basis, is really the question of the day in India. Tens of millions of men who, as yet, know little or nothing of the Congress, and cannot be said as yet to have supported it in any way, fully understand and are acquiring a lively interest in this matter of representation, which is one entirely in consonance with their traditions. As one of the speakers * remarked:—

"The principle of representation underlies Hindu society in all its various forms and phases. A Hindu, from his childhood, understands what representation is, nay, you will also find the principle of representation underlying the Hindu religious system."

It is no exotic plant: its original habitat is the village communities of India, and the nations of the West merely enjoy cultivated varieties of a stock which has travelled to them from the East. It is indispensable, we think, that all

* Babu Mohun Sadan Das, page 103 of Detailed Report.

should fully realise not only the justice of, but the enormous weight of public opinion which gives stability to this one demand, at any rate, of the National Congress.

The first Resolution brought before the Congress when it reassembled, about mid-day, on the 29th, was one re-affirming the necessity, strongly urged in 1886, for the complete separation of Judicial and Executive functions.

Of secondary questions there is probably none in which the educated classes throughout India feel a stronger interest than in this, because, every day of their lives, instances of injustice to their poorer and more ignorant countrymen, resulting from the combination of these functions, come to their notice. Mr. N. Subramaniem, a Native Christian barrister, in proposing* the Resolution, said that, as is undeniable, neither work was as well done as it would be by specialists in each branch, and he pointed out that, moreover, from the nature of the case, it was impossible for any one human being to do his duty properly in both capacities. He said :—

"The Magistrate must necessarily, if he is to be a just magistrate, shut his ears completely to everything said outside of his court, and yet, how can the same individual, who is a magistrate, shut his ears to everything he hears as an executive officer? As an executive officer, the Magistrate is bound to receive all sorts of information, and a great deal of information is sent to him by demi-official letters—I do not know whether you have any such document in other Provinces—(Voices, 'Yes, Yes')—and his mind is prejudiced, or, let me say, necessarily influenced, by the reports sent to him by the police officers. But he is to set aside all this information, all the bias, nay, all the conviction that is thus necessarily engendered, when he enters his court, where he must not be biased as a magistrate one way or the other in regard to the criminal, and he must know nothing of him or of the case but what comes up in evidence before him. Surely this is impossible! Again, the executive officer, to be successful, has to be in constant touch with the people. He has to know all the vagaries of the various men within his district, all the bad qualities of the men, and yet that is the very thing which would unfit him for the just performance of his duties as a magistrate. It is impossible for a man who is an executive officer to avoid forming his opinion for good or evil in regard to a person that he has to judge, in regard to a witness or criminal or complainant—it is impossible, I say, for him to avoid forming his opinion partly on knowledge acquired out of court, and, therefore, impossible for him to deal with them impartially—(hear, hear, and applause)—on the evidence before him, and on that evidence alone, as a magistrate is bound to do." (Hear, hear.)

Then he dwelt upon the practical drawbacks of the existing system; how, as a matter of fact, it is the good executive officers, and not the conscientious Magistrates who get promotion, and how, consequently, there is a strong temptation to men to devote all their energies to executive work and to scamp their judicial work; also how great the hardships are to which the system exposes accused persons, and he added that, although it was well known that the necessary re-arrangements could be effected without extra expenditure, he, and he believed every other man in the country, who understood the question, would gladly "pay an additional pie in the rupee, rather than allow my poorer fellow-countrymen to continue exposed to this constantly recurring failure of Justice." Babu Kalicharan Bannerjee, a pleader, but better known as an earnest and eloquent social and religious reformer, supported the Resolution. In the course of his speech† he remarked :—

"You will understand what the combination of these functions implies. It implies, in the first place, the combination of the Prosecutor and the Judge in the same person. (Applause.) It is

* Page 105 of Detailed Report.
† Page 108 of Detailed Report.

not necessary to be initiated into the mystery of law to understand that justice is in jeopardy if the prosecutor happens to be also the judge. If you have a case, in which there is a private complainant, there the prosecuting and persecuting energies of the private complainant are brought to bear upon you. Then you have, in addition, the Police machinery, with all its prosecuting and persecuting energies brought to bear upon you, and if, in addition to these two-fold prosecuting energies, you have brought to bear upon you all the prosecuting energies of a magistrate, why the poor defendant finds himself simply in a hopeless condition. (Applause.) We cannot avoid private complaints being, at any rate, preferred. We do not contemplate, here at any rate, any interference with the Police machinery. All that we pray for is, that the strong arm of the magistrate should not be, by anticipation, lent either to the private complainant or to the police machinery set on foot by him. (Applause.)

"Then, again, as you have already been told, the combination of these two functions sets aside all the safeguards which the rules of evidence have provided for the due administration of justice. There is the magistrate, listening attentively to the police papers read out to him by the Police officer early in the morning. The Police officer is in personal communication with the magistrate and instils into his mind his own ideas in respect to the case he has been kind enough to take into his own hands. And the magistrate listens to all sorts of things, and not only is much of the so-called evidence which is, at such times, laid before a magistrate no evidence at all, but he, as it were, has his judgment sketched out for him beforehand by the policeman. He listens to all this, and then, if it so happens, as it often does, that he places the case on his own file, when he sits to try it the conditions are all reversed, for the judicial function has been exercised by the policeman while the magistrate has been closeted with him, and when he comes into court, he is merely the executive who carries out that secret judicial decision. (Applause.) The judge has become the executive, while the executive has become the judge." (Loud applause.)

Other speakers followed, and the Resolution was unanimously adopted. No sane man can doubt that, as Mr. Ambica Charan Mozumdar remarked,* this is—

"one of the cardinal questions upon which the fair fame of the British administration of this country, not less than the happiness and contentment of the many millions of people who obey its sway, materially depend."

As Babu Kalicharan Bannerjee said towards the commencement of his speech,

"Gentlemen, this is another Resolution which we, as a Congress, find ourselves in a position to re-affirm to-day. In one sense, it is reassuring that the experience of a year enables us to re-affirm the position we took up last year. (Hear, hear, and applause.) In another sense, it is discouraging to realise that there should still be occasion so to reaffirm it." (Loud and continued applause.)

This is the real point: the whole thinking portion of the community is lost in astonishment at the inaction of Government in a matter at once so simple, and involving so grave a scandal. Instances of executive officers abusing their magisterial powers in furtherance of objects that they have in view in their executive capacities are, in some provinces, so frequent as hardly to attract sufficient notice. Certainly the Government do not approve such improprieties, as, especially of recent years, they have publicly marked their displeasure of some of them that have, by special efforts, been pressed upon their notice; but why do they allow a system to continue under which such abuses of power are possible? A considerable section of the community undoubtedly adopt the view embodied in the following passage from Mr. B. Narasime Swara Surma's speech† :—

"Our critics say: 'Well, if you separate the two functions, how are you to collect the revenue? How is the Collector to get the money out of the people if they do not fear him, knowing what he can do to them in his magisterial capacity?' We reply, that the present system defeats its own purposes—it does not strengthen authority; injustice never does, it only weakens it."

* Page 113 of Detailed Report.
† Page 114 of Detailed Report.

But the majority absolutely refuse to believe that Government deliberately winks at getting its work done by unlawful means. Why then does it persist in refusing a reform which every man in the country knows to be urgently required? "It cannot," they say, "be a matter of expense; in every one of the large Provinces the Associations have worked out detailed schemes proving that no extra expenditure is needed, though in some the substitution, in a few highly-paid appointments, of uncovenanted men on salaries of from one-half to two-thirds of what the existing covenanted* incumbents draw, may be needed. Besides, you are not usually so careful of our money; you have absolutely needlessly† increased military expenditure by two millions a year, besides wasting, none of us know how many, tens of millions on forts, fortifications, strategic railways and the like; so, if even you believe that this reform will cost money, it can hardly be that which deters you. But if it be this, the whole country has declared that it will cheerfully pay anything that is necessary on this account. So, why do you not move?"

There is no doubt that the inaction of Government in the case of this reform, which it has itself repeatedly declared to be desirable, is producing an unsatisfactory feeling amongst those classes capable of understanding the question, but, of course, this is not one that the masses, who chiefly suffer by it, have yet come as a rule to realize in the abstract. They feel that they do not get justice, and grumble, but they do not yet clearly perceive how and why this is so.

Next came a Resolution, urging the establishment of Military Colleges in India, whereat the sons of Indian noblemen and gentlemen might be trained as officers of the Indian Army.

"If it be England's divine mission," said Babu Norendra Nath Sen,‡ in proposing the Resolution,—

"that she should raise us as a nation in every respect, she should offer every facility for our admission into the higher ranks, not only of the civil, but equally of the military, services, in order that we may be equally qualified for Self-Government in times of peace, and Self-Defence in times of war. (Applause.) Our lessons in the art of Self-Government will be incomplete, if we are not trained in the art of Self-Defence. (Applause.) If England means to confer upon us the highest benefits in the present advanced stage of Indian progress—in the present turning-point in the national life,—both for the sake of herself and for the sake of India she cannot, consistently with her duty, withhold, any longer, opening out a military career to the higher classes, at least, of our countrymen, as officers of the Indian army. (Applause.) We claim nothing which is immoderate or unreasonable. If the sons of foreign noblemen, such as the

---

* Covenanted Civilians, as a rule, do not shine as Judges. If two thirds of the existing covenanted Civilian Judges on £2,500 a year were replaced by Barristers and Sub-Judges on £1,500 a year, the country would gain in every way, and High Courts would not be so often, as they now are, at their wits' ends as to how to deal with the vagaries and incompetence of District Judges. At this very moment three such cases are in the papers. In one of these a Judge, after deciding the case without hearing any evidence on the one point on which the matter turned, passed a decree that it was impossible to execute, of which Mr. Justice Straight (concurred in by Mr. Justice Tyrrell) pathetically remarked: "The decree of the Judge, therefore, is a most difficult one to deal with, and what our decision with regard to it hereafter may be I am at this moment unable to say, and find very great difficulty in imagining."

† It is necessary to understand that Native opinion throughout India is as nearly as possible unanimous as to the needlessness of this expenditure. No one doubts (or very few do) the good faith of Government: no one denies (though many doubt) the danger of Russian aggression; what all contend is, that a far smaller sum (expended on creating and rendering efficient powerful bodies of native militia and volunteers throughout the Sindh, the Punjab, Rajputana and the N.-W. Provinces and Oudh), would have strengthened the Empire far more than anything that has been done, and would, once for all, have won all hearts. No one believes that Russia will ever be able to get more than 50,000 regular troops across the Frontier; the danger, they think, lies in her bringing with her hundreds of thousands of Afghans, Turks, and what not, bribed by the hope of plundering all the, to their idea, rich cities of India. To meet the regular troops, the existing British army sufficed, while the native militia and volunteers would have promptly exterminated the robber vermin. Of course, from an English point of view arises the question, "*Quis custodiet ipsos custodias*"—Can we trust that militia? The country says, "You can,—we are not only just as interested as you are in keeping out these ruffians, but a great deal more so, and we can't turn against you because we know well that we can't do without you, and, really we like you, and if you would only be a little more reasonable in some matters, should downright love you." This is the crucial point—trust or no trust—and it was fully discussed when the modification of the Arms Act and the subject of native volunteering came up later before the Congress.

‡ Page 115 of Detailed Report.

Duc D'Orleans, can be admitted as officers of the British army, and as it was announced that he was to be admitted, I do not see why the scions of great houses of this country, eminent for their loyal services to the crown, and young gentlemen of good birth, good education, and high culture, should not be educated and trained as officers of the Indian army. (Applause.) . . . .

"The loyalty and devotion, the bravery and heroism I may say, of native soldiers are too well-known and have been too often recognised by Government to need any particular mention from me. (Hear, hear.) The native soldiery is the ultimate bulwark, the main body of the support of the empire. (Hear, hear.) The fine steel edge may be our gallant European troops, but the body of the sword is our native soldiery. . . . .

Well, then, gentlemen, if such be our experience—if such be our general experience of the native army of the past,—I fail to perceive why the Government should hesitate, in the least, to open military colleges, as we propose, for the education of the sons of Indian noblemen and gentlemen. They cannot certainly, as the result of higher education, nobler antecedents, loftier position or closer ties to Government, prove less devoted and less loyal, less faithful or less courageous in the discharge of their duties, when admitted into the commissioned ranks of the Indian army, than their humbler and more ignorant countrymen have proved as mere soldiers and non-commissioned officers. (Hear, hear.) If the present native troops, soldiers, havildars, jemadars, subadars of the Indian army are admitted to be bound by the strongest ties to Government—if, I contend, they have proved so faithful, brave and useful to Government and the country, as they have in many a hard-fought field—how much more may we not expect from the better born of these and from the scions of the higher classes still, who will not enter the army on the present footing, if they are admitted to the commissioned ranks of the army? (Hear, hear, and applause.) The inclusion in the army of those who necessarily keep aloof, at present, will only serve to identify their interests more closely with the interests of the British Government and lay deeper the foundations of the empire. (Applause.) As an addition to the physical defences of the empire, if for no other reason, I say that it should be the policy of Government to start military colleges for the education of the young noblemen and gentlemen of this country. (Applause.) But the indirect addition to what I may call the moral bulwarks of British rule will prove even more important. Gentlemen, we have had our losses and gains under the British Government—our gains have been many—but, one of our chief losses has been our exclusion from the higher ranks of the army (hear, hear), and that, in my opinion, has led to a rapid deterioration in the character of the natural leaders of the people, and so, indirectly, through their example, in our national character. (Hear, hear). The privilege we ask for is one which has not been denied to India by any previous dynasty. It is not even now denied to the many subject races in Central Asia by the less civilized Russians (applause), and I will not believe that it will long be denied to us by our British rulers and friends." (Cheers.)

A prolonged discussion took place in regard to this resolution, and amendments were brought forward and strongly supported. It was not that the principle of the Resolution was questioned—all were agreed as to this—but, because, in the first place, as originally worded, it only proposed the training of sons of noblemen and gentlemen, and, in the second place, because a small section of the Congress desired to append to the Resolution, a recommendation to Government to devote the large sums of money, recently offered by certain Native Princes for the defence of the country, to the purposes of the proposed colleges. As regards this latter proposition, after some speaking, the President remarked*:—

"I may say it does seem extraordinary for the delegates here to pray that any funds that had been offered by one party to another party for one purpose should be disposed of in a different manner according to the desire of a third party! If A gives some money to B for an express object, it is surely no business of C's to say that that money should be diverted to some other object or even to any particular purpose. (Laughter.) I have already appealed to the proposer of this amendment, but he does not see the absurdity into which we shall be led. He wishes to press his proposition, and, therefore, I shall allow the discussion to proceed. But I desire that it should be distinctly understood that what is really asked for is this, namely, that the

* Page 119 of Detailed Report.

money that has been offered by Native States to the British Government, for certain purposes. according to arrangements between the two parties of which we know nothing, and which, so far as we know has not yet been accepted, should be devoted by Government, on our advice, to the purposes of these military colleges." (Laughter.)

This view, however, was not allowed to pass altogether unchallenged. Some at least of the delegates declined to be considered third parties.

"With regard to the remarks made by the learned President," said one gentleman,* "I have to say that we are not third parties. A certain amount of money has been placed by a certain party in the hands of the British Indian Government. We are loyal subjects of the British Indian Government, and, being loyal subjects, we are identified with Government. I really think it is exceedingly to be regretted that any distinction should be made between Government and the subjects of Government. I think we, the representatives of the nation, can very properly advise and suggest how any sum of money which becomes part of the national funds should be expended by Government—the Government of the nation. The first part of the Resolution requires that Government should establish new institutions, and, therefore, if it is proper for us to suggest the establishment of the institutions it is equally proper for us, as subjects, to go on and advise Government how the requisite funds may be provided, and pray them to expend certain moneys that they have received, on our account, in a certain, viz., in this particular, way. I think, therefore, that as a matter of principle the second part of the amendment should remain. I really believe it would be mischievous to make any distinction between Government and the subjects of Her Majesty. They are one and the same. They have every right to advise Government to take any action as to the expenditure of any money or anything of that sort. I should be very sorry to know that the delegates of the people of India are to have no voice and no right to suggest anything they please as regards the expenditure of money in the hands of Government." (Applause, and a voice of "But it is not in the hands of Government yet, and you ought not to count your chickens before they are hatched." Laughter.)

All the same the proposal was generally opposed. Babu Bepin Chandra Pal said†:—

"It is a question of principle whether the money that has been offered to the Government of India for the defence of the Indian Empire by certain native princes should be accepted or not. Speaking on behalf of those whom I represent, I can assure you, gentlemen, that the native Press, with hardly any exception, has asked Government not to accept this money. I condemn the policy involved in the acceptance of such offerings (hear, hear), and I think the Congress would be going entirely out of its way if we took up this question, and, on a side-issue, affirmed that policy. We ought by no means to affirm it."

And Munshi Devi Prasad remarked:‡

"It has been suggested that the money which has been placed at the disposal of Government by certain native Princes should be spent in the construction of colleges for military education. Well, the first thing to be considered is this. This money has been given for purposes of defence. It is not known when the money will be required. We, however, are to ask that the money may be expended at once on these colleges. But even considering that the construction of these colleges can be held to be a step in the defence of the empire coming within the scope of the donors' instructions, which I doubt, complications on our frontier may become serious to-morrow, and we shall then not have our colleges nor our trained men to fight for us, nor shall we have our money for practical purposes of defence. It will take years to construct the colleges and to turn out officers, but, in the meantime, the money may be required at any moment for the defence of the empire. (Applause.) I therefore propose that this last part of the amendment be expunged." (Applause.

This portion of the amendment was then withdrawn, but the general sense of the assembly was that the original wording was too restricted. Mr. Norton objected§ to the combination of the words "noblemen and gentlemen," as he did

* Page 119 of Detailed Report.
† Page 119 of Detailed Report.
‡ Page 120 of Detailed Report.
§ Page 122 of Detailed Report.

"not see why a nobleman might not also be a gentleman!" Mr. Ganguli insisted that,*—

"The interests this Congress is intended to promote are not the interests of any special class of Her Majesty's subjects, but of all classes of Her Majesty's subjects,"—

and, therefore, protested against any reference to any special class. Moreover, it was pointed out that Eurasians, Anglo-Indians, and Domiciled Europeans might be excluded, whereas their inclusion was a *sine quâ non*.

Again, it was contended that the Resolution did not sufficiently prominently set forward the fact that, under the Queen's Proclamation, natives of India had a right to admission to the higher offices in the Military, as well as in the Civil, branches of the service. Ultimately, after a very long and animated discussion, the following Resolution was agreed to:—

"That in view of the loyalty of H.M.'s Indian subjects, this Congress considers it desirable that the Queen's Proclamation should be given effect to, that the Military service in its higher grades should be practically opened to the natives of this country, and that the Government of India should establish Military Colleges in this country whereat the natives of India, as defined by statute,† may be educated and trained for a military career as officers of the Indian Army."

The Volunteer question, on which so strong a feeling exists throughout the country, next came before the Congress. The Resolution proposed was couched in the same guarded language adopted in 1886, and ran as follows:—

"That, in view of the unsettled state of public affairs in Europe and the immense assistance that the people of this country, if duly prepared therefor, are capable of rendering to Great Britain in the event of any serious complications arising, this Congress do once again earnestly appeal to the Government to authorize (under such rules and restrictions as may to it seem fitting) a system of volunteering for the Indian inhabitants of the country such as may qualify them to support the Government, effectively, in any crisis."

The Resolution was proposed by Mr. Sankaran Nair, about as fine a specimen of one of India's fighting races as could be met with. This gentleman, himself a High Court Vakil, was one of four Indian gentlemen of the City of Madras, who, at the time of the last Russian scare, endeavoured to enter the Madras Artillery volunteers. They were received with open arms by the volunteers themselves, and duly admitted, but, by a piece of that lamentable want of perception that characterized Sir Grant Duff's entire administration, were, by his orders, removed from the corps. The whole case was explained by Mr. Adam,‡ one of the subalterns of the corps, and a delegate.

---

* Page 121 of Detailed Report.

† As one of the speakers remarked, page 122 of Detailed Report,
"All Hindus, all Mahomedans, all Parsees, all Eurasians, all East Indians, and all domiciled Europeans and *all* persons born in India of domiciled parents are in the eye of the law, '*natives of India*,' and are defined to be so by statute."

‡ Mr. Adam said, "Some time ago, about the time of the Russian scare, my friends, Mr. Sankara Nair, who proposed this motion, and Mr. Salem Ramasami Mudaliar, one of the delegates to England, and two or three other native gentlemen, applied to be admitted into our volunteer corps, and they were accepted at once. (Applause.) There was no difficulty at all as to their being accepted; we were all most happy to welcome them. But, unfortunately, and through a misunderstanding or misinterpretation of the order of the Government of India—a misinterpretation on the part of the Government of Madras, or the military authorities here—these gentlemen, although we desired it, were not allowed, at that time, to be admitted into the corps. Subsequently, and in fact, quite recently, it was discovered that a mistake had been made, and that the interpretation which the Government of Madras had put upon this order of the Government of India was not applicable to the Madras Presidency, but was applicable only to Burmah, which, at the time this order of the Government of India was issued, was considered a portion of the Madras military command; but the military authorities here and the Government extended the limitation—which

There was, therefore, a peculiar propriety in Mr. Sankaran Nair proposing the Resolution, and we may quote at some length from his temperate and sensible speech:—*

"There is this difference between this Resolution and the previous ones which have been carried In this case we have, if we are correctly informed, an expression of opinion by the Viceroy of India which is not very favourable to our views. The Viceroy has expressed his sympathy with our aspirations for a reform and expansion of our Legislative Councils, and also, to a certain extent, in regard to the separation of judicial from revenue functions. But in this case, I regret to say, it is understood that the Viceroy has stated that it is impossible to meet our views, and therefore, the task of moving this Resolution to one who entertains the highest respect for Lord Dufferin, both as our gracious Empress's representative and as a statesman of European reputation, is by no means an easy or pleasant one. But, gentlemen, though the Viceroy, in the discharge of his duty, as he views it, may have been compelled, peremptorily to negative our former prayer, this is no real reason why we of the country, who know more of its real needs and condition than any Viceroy can know, why we, the representatives of the thinking classes throughout the Empire, should not also do what we believe to be our duty, and persistently urge a prayer, the granting of which will, we know, conduce, in such a high degree, not only to our own safety, but to the stability and glory of the throne of that great Empress whose servant he is and whose loyal and loving subjects we are. (Loud cheers.) . . . .

"It is impossible to doubt that, sooner or later, we are sure to have a radical reform in the constitution of the Legislative Councils, but neither that blessing nor the separation of the judicial and executive functions, nor any other blessing that we enjoy under the British Government, can compensate us for the state of helplessness into which, as the result of the policy pursued by the British Government in this matter, we are rapidly drifting. Not only has it made us helpless, it has had also the effect of lowering and degrading the character of our countrymen. But this has already been pointed out by Baboo Norendra Nath Sen, and was dwelt upon so eloquently and fully by Rajah Rampal Singh last year, that I shall not take up your time by going over the same ground again, but I shall pass on at once to the next, though kindred, ground, which I have to adduce in support of this Resolution. Every mail that comes from England brings alarming news of the state of affairs in Europe, a state of affairs that can mean nothing but that war between mutually jealous neighbours, in which England must be involved, is sure to be proclaimed at some not distant date. Now, gentlemen, what is our state or position under these circumstances? Our ancient civilization—is that to be broken into and destroyed by Northern invaders? Of course, we have this much freedom, that we have full liberty to offer our prayers for the success of the British Government. But prayers, I fear, are not likely to be of much use to us or to them. Is the peace and tranquility, I say, which we now enjoy to be ravished from us, without our voices being heard, our arms being raised in the settlement of the dispute? It appears to me absurd to entertain such an idea. It appears to me intolerable, the more especially as even the English themselves cannot assert what the result of the struggle here is likely to be if India continues debarred from helping herself and them. It is impossible to foresee what will happen, if this policy of Government of refusing our co-operation is persisted in. It appears to be absolutely suicidal and we only hope, equally for our own and their sakes, that the English may not some day regret that she has refused, while there was yet time and we could have been trained into serviceable allies, those prayers which we have so repeatedly put up in regard to this matter. (Hear, hear, and applause.) The Russians have armed their foes of yesterday to fight on their own behalf to-day, and the result shows that they have been justified in their action. (Applause.) Have we been less loyal to the British than the Turkomans to the Russians, whom they fought with only yesterday? (Applause.) They lie who say that our loyalty cannot be depended upon in the hour of danger. (Applause.) It is in the highest degree probable that the fighting races of India will be required to have a voice in the settlement of that dispute if it is to end favourably for our empire, and, therefore, it is absolutely necessary now, while

---

should have been applicable only to Burmah—to the whole of the Madras Presidency. The mistake was afterwards discovered when the original Government order was republished a little time ago. But, subsequent to that, a short time ago, three of these gentlemen applied to be re-admitted into the corps under the conditions which were laid down in that order. Immediately on their application, steps were taken to give effect to their wishes, but it was necessary, under the Government order, that the consent and approval of all the existing members of the corps should be obtained, to the admission of these gentlemen as fellow-comrades with them in the corps. This consent is in process of being, and I believe has been practically and unanimously, given. (Applause.) Speaking for myself, I may say that, in that portion of the corps specially under my charge and which I had to consult upon the matter, both officers and men, were perfectly unanimous in agreeing most cordially to welcome them, and I believe the same is the case in various other detachments of the corps. I may also say that all the officers are perfectly unanimous in agreeing to receive these gentlemen into the corps." (Applause.) Naturally, however, an order which requires every single member of corps' assent—of a corps scattered over half a presidency—to the admission of a pure-blooded Hindu or Mahomedan gentleman as a volunteer, while every other race, full-blood and half-blood, that finds its way to India is admitted, as a matter of course, is not calculated to soothe the feelings of these excepted communities.

* Page 123 of Detailed Report.

there may be yet time, to train and educate them, so that they may be able to bear their share, the lion's share, in the defence of that portion of the empire which is their home and mother-land. (Applause.) I should have thought that no objection could reasonably be urged against this proposition, as worded both last year and this, but the Viceroy has expressed himself, it is said, unable, on account of race feelings that are alleged to exist between the various races in India, to grant our prayer to be enrolled as volunteers. He expressed that opinion, it appears, to some delegates from Madras, after this Resolution was passed last year It appears to me that if he did so, and my friend here assures me he did, he did so without carefully reading over the Resolution. I understood from a speaker yesterday that a journalist may review magazines without reading them and that hostile critics often criticise without knowing what they are criticising. But a man in the Viceroy's position, I take it, would surely have read the Resolution properly before he delivered himself of such an opinion. Now, gentlemen, under our proposals, it is in the Viceroy's power to make rules such that only those gentlemen whom he may consider unquestionably loyal, who he is convinced may be entirely relied upon, should be admitted as volunteers, as soldiers who, in the hour of danger, would stand beside the British.

"It is to me inconceivable that a representation thus carefully guarded should be summarily rejected by any reasonable man. Race feelings, indeed! The assertion cannot be challenged by anybody who at all understands the country, that in a corps of volunteers composed of men drawn from the Mahomedan and Hindu communities indifferently, we shall have the best, the only possible effective, safeguard against any collision between the lower classes of these races. In my own district, for instance, a part of the district has been disarmed on account of what was called the Moplah outbreak, and it is the opinion of many of us, both Hindus and Mahomedans, that a corps of volunteers, in which both of these races were represented, would be the best safeguard against the occurrence of any further ebullitions of fanaticism."

There was absolutely no dissentient voice in this discussion, the whole assembly, as one man, supported the Resolution. Malik Bhugwan Das, from Dera Ismail Khan, said *:—

"Now, I will bring certain facts to your notice which should lead every honest thinker to hope that this Resolution will be accepted by the Government. Just about the year 1849, Dewan Mulraj, the Governor of Mooltan, rebelled against the Sikh Government, which was practically the British Government, as the entire administration was guided by British officers, and the Gondapurs and afterwards the Pathans, who were well trained in the use of the arms, were collected in hundreds and thousands to help the British officer, Mr. Edwardes, Resident on the Derajat frontier, in those days. There was no Railway in those days, and it was a most critical time. It would have been in the utmost degree difficult, if not, as I believe, absolutely impossible, for the British officers to have put down that rebellion but for the help of the arms-trained Pathans of the country. Again, you well know, gentlemen, that it was a very critical time for our Government during the Mutiny of the year 1857. The British empire was in a most dangerous position, and it really was, for a time, a mere toss up (let British historians disguise it as they please), whether India would not be lost to it for ever. But, fortunately, the Panjab, especially the frontier part of that province, had been recently conquered, and there were, at that time, a great number of persons, in the frontier districts, especially, who had been trained in the use of the arms and had known what a soldier's life was and liked it.

"Col. Nicholson, who was then deputy commissioner of the Bunnu district (to whom the capture of Delhi was admittedly in a great measure due), collected thousands of such trained warriors and of the frontier Pathan tribes, and with these joined the attack on Delhi and the success attained, if the truth be told, was in a great measure due to these Pathans. I need not give you more examples, my brethren, as these two will suffice to inculcate the lesson that, in times of the extremest danger, it is on the natives trained to arms that the British Government and we, its loyal subjects, must, as a last resort, rely. Now, the past policy for the last thirty years of our Government, has been such as to kill out everywhere a knowledge of the use of arms and a willingness to accept the dangers and privations of a soldier's life. Even for the native army, recruits, untrained recruits, that take a couple of years to turn into anything like soldiers, are scarcely to be procured, and if, at this moment any crisis were to arise, the Government could not rely upon the assistance, in the field, of one hundredth of the men it could have commanded thirty years ago. I mean

* Page 127 of Detailed Report.

of course, in my part of India. Now this, to me, seems a grievous misfortune, and it is to remedy this state of affairs, and ensure Government having at its call in any crisis hundreds of thousands of partially trained soldiers, that I so strongly advocate as I do the volunteer movement. God forbid that the Russians, bribing the Afghans, should, with them, make a joint descent on the rich plains of India, but if they were to do so and the Government perseveres in its present policy of converting its bravest and most soldierly races into helpless pen-and-word men, the results would be the loss of India to the British and of all the blessings that we owe to them, of all we most prize and cherish, to us. (Applause.) Therefore, brethren, we have a right, the best of all rights, to claim, again and again from Government, that our young men shall be trained to arms, and made fit to defend us and our homes, our liberties and our lands. (Loud cheers.) The Government cannot be blind, they must see the contingencies lying before them and us, as we frontiermen see them, and, if so, it is cruel, it is unjust, for them to refuse us what we ask for in this Resolution—(cheers)—nay, it is a folly, a crime, for we ask it as much in their interests, as much in the interests of our empire and our Empress, as in those of our country, our families, and ourselves. (Loud cheers.) Gentlemen, I support this Resolution, and so does every man on our frontier, and so does every well-wisher of the British Government throughout the empire." (Continued applause.)

The debate was closed by a most powerful speech by Mr. Ali Mahomed Bhimjee, a Mill-owner from Mhow, which was received with a continuous and deafening applause, that showed only too clearly that the speaker's words were embodying the thoughts of all his hearers' hearts. The subject is becoming one of primary importance, and we need, therefore, scarcely apologise for reproducing the whole of this really remarkable speech, lengthy as it is.

He said* :—

"I appear before you to support a Resolution that has been proposed, as regards our admission into volunteer corps. Government ask us why we should be admitted into volunteer corps, and why we want to be admitted. I answer, 'For the simple reason that this is our home and we want to defend our hearths and homes.' (Applause.) It is their hearths and homes that Englishmen want to defend, and it is the same that we want to defend here in our own country. (Applause.) You have heard some speakers refer to Lord Canning's order, that natives of India may be admitted into volunteer corps if the members of the corps consent to their admission. I say, 'Why make that restriction? If you are honest, grant us the privilege. Why make the restriction? If you wish us to be admitted, then, why leave it to the members of any corps to decide whether they choose to admit us or not? Answer that question.' (Applause.) I say it is the authorities, and not the members of any corps (applause), who are competent to judge whether we are entitled or not to defend our hearths and homes. (Applause.) Our Government is perfectly mistaken. You will excuse my warmth. I am carried away, but I will cool down. (Laughter and applause.) I say that our Government is making a terrible mistake. Some fifty or sixty years ago, by a lavish expenditure of money they were able to raise as many German and other mercenaries as they desired, but they will never be able to do so in these days, and if they fancy they will be able to do so, they commit a great blunder which they will some day bitterly repent. Mercenaries are a class of people who are not to be had now. You all know that the different continental nations have not only their standing armies, but every male in their populations, between 18 and 45 or even 50 years of age, registered as soldiers in one class of reserve or other, which they had not about the time of Waterloo. Not one mercenary soldier can England now draw from any continental nation. Russia has some five millions, Germany four, Austria has got two or three millions, France three or four million soldiers of the line and reserves, and so on. Had they anything of all this when Waterloo was fought? Even in the Crimean war? (Voices of 'No, No.') They had not, and, consequently, our English Government, in virtue of their long purse—by their unbounded and unlimited expenditure of money—were able to procure mercenaries to help them to fight their battles. Where will they procure mercenaries now when the odds against England are three-fold what they were? (Hear, hear.) Supposing Russia does invade India, and we all know that from the time of Peter the Great, Russia's aim has been—India! India! India! It is not barren Central Asia she has been aiming at. She has been sending large armies into Central Asia and wasting untold millions there, but she has been aiming at India. She wants an outlet for commerce, and she must have it either here or on the Golden Horn, at the expense of the Turkish or the British Empire, and all

* Page 129 of Detailed Report.

those who have studied this question know this very well. Now Austria, Germany, and Italy bar the way to Constantinople, and it is much to be feared that it will be at our expense that the outlet of Russian commerce will be found.

"Gentlemen, if Russia realizes this desire to pounce upon India, she will first create serious complications in Europe, and when our English rulers' energies are perfectly absorbed in meeting the dangers that beset them there, when they have, as in the Crimean war, denuded India of European troops, and, probably, as has been her practice, even in petty wars in late years, of a strong contingent of her best native troops, then, I ask, how many men will England be able to throw into the field here to meet the million or so of soldiers and robbers of a hundred wild tribes that Russia will be able to tempt into making common cause with her, in plundering our towns and ravishing our women? The English Government may have millions and hundreds of millions of money, but money won't fight—it is men that will fight, and where will she get them when, by her present policy, she has (laughter and hear, hear) turned us all into women? (Laughter.) Are we to be for ever treated as if we cannot be trusted? Are we so low and degraded that we are not able to be trusted to defend our hearths and homes? (Hear, hear, and applause.) Are we such fools as not to realize the difference between British and Russian rule? (Cheers.) What then? Is it not mockery? Is it not idiotic to say to us, 'You may be enrolled as Volunteers with the consent of all the members of any existing corps;' and how many hundreds, should I not say thousands, will thus be able to obtain some military training? Some gentleman here told us, 'We are all unanimous in admitting native gentlemen.' Yes, you are at the moment all unanimous, but will this unanimity continue. Does it exist elsewhere? In one or two instances, corps may be unanimous; but, is that any guarantee that we shall be admitted generally throughout the country in anything like adequate numbers to defend our homes, our families? We have a perfect right to be admitted. Why make these conditions? What are you afraid of? We do not want to drive you away from the country. (Cries of 'No, no; certainly not.') We want to keep you, to help you, to support you. (Tremendous cheers.) Is there one here so false, so foolish, as to say, 'We want to drive the English away from this country'? (Loud cries of 'No, no, no.') No, we are not so base (applause); we are not such fools (loud applause); were we to drive you away from our country, what would become of us? Who should we have instead? We may go from one end of the earth to the other end, we shall not find one to come up to you. (Loud applause.) 'England, with all thy faults, we love thee still.' There is not one single Power in all the world to come up to England, or that would, on the whole, have dealt so nobly and generously with a subject nation as England has done. (Loud applause.) Whom shall we have instead of you? We must have a head here; a body without a head cannot live. (Applause.) If we get our Hindu friends here, who are so well educated, and after we have driven you away, we take them and put them into power, and give them the *gadi** (voices of 'No, No'), shall we get on well? Or are we fit to rule the whole empire? Or can we in our present state, even combined, produce a Government half as good as that of England? No. We must have the English. But they are treating us like mere children (applause): they are simply trifling with us. We do not want to drive you away from here; we cannot do without you; and if you give us all the liberty in the world, we shall still respect you and cling to you and keep you with us (a voice of 'And respect you all the more'); yes, and respect you all the more. Thank you, sir, for your correction. I did not want to speak to-day, but, when I saw this matter brought up I asked the President to allow me to speak. Who does not feel the degradation of not being allowed to become a volunteer? Who does not feel the humiliation of being debarred from the use and practice of arms? Who does not tremble for the day when unarmed, helpless, our martial spirit dead, we shall have to stand wailing like women to see our English friends massacred by Russian hordes, and ourselves, our fortunes and our families, the prey of their ruthless barbarities? (Applause.) I say this meeting speaks with one voice, and it is the voice of India, and no Government in the world can turn a deaf ear to such a voice or long refuse to permit us to qualify ourselves for defending it and ourselves, our hearths and homes, and the British empire." (Loud and prolonged applause, and cries of "Vote, vote." "We are all agreed.")

The resolution was then unanimously carried.

To those unfamiliar with the state of affairs in India, the persistent refusal of the Government of India to avail itself of the vast addition, it may so urgently need, to the defence resources of the empire, which a general, but

* Literally on "the cushion," *i.e.*, place them on the throne.

carefully regulated, system of volunteering would provide, must seem neither more nor less than an illustration of the oft-quoted line, "*Quem Deus vult perdere, prius dementat.*"

The matter is, however, by no means so simple as it may at first sight appear. In the first place, despite the enthusiasm on the subject that prevails in certain classes, to create a really powerful and effective body of, say, only a quarter of a million of Volunteers, would need time, a great deal of trouble, and (for the people are poor) no small expenditure. Ten, fifteen, or twenty thousand Volunteers might very probably appear spontaneously,—and there seems to us no really valid reason why their services should not be accepted and innumerable reasons why they should,—but to create a force of Volunteers that should constitute a real bulwark to the empire such as all the speakers contemplated, would be a work of much labour, involving not only the exercise of much tact and talents of a high order, but a kindly rapprochment between the rulers and the ruled to which the official classes, who, as a rule, pose as gods amongst their humble mortal subjects, are utterly unwilling to condescend. In every province there are noble gentlemen who would do it, but, to the bulk of the European officials any spirit of "*bon cameraderie*" with natives, such as the successful development of a general scheme of volunteering would involve, would be held to be a degradation.

This, however, might, in time, and by the exercise of judicious pressure on the part of the highest and unprejudiced functionaries, be surmounted; but then would arise the real difficulty—viz., that the development of such a body of volunteers would gradually involve a radical change, not in the principles but in the practice of the administration. "Undoubtedly," the Government may say, "such a body of volunteers, officered by the best amongst themselves and picked men of our own, would set at rest for ever all anxiety in regard to Russian aggression. There might be only a quarter of a million of actual volunteers at any moment, but there would be many times that number of men who had been, more or less, trained in the force in previous years, and brothers and other relatives of the volunteers ready to join them in any crisis, and the whole heart of the country would be with these volunteers and with us, and there need never then be any apprehension of troubles in our rear, even if we threw every soldier on to the frontier. We might then, doubtless, materially reduce the strength of the standing army, the taxation involved by the maintenance of which, at its present strength, is crushing the country (so that it is becoming almost a case of *propter vivendi causas perdere vitam*), and, we fear, somewhat alienating the affection of the people; and we might not only establish a financial equilibrium, despite the gradual loss of the opium revenue, which is now an assured fact, but even have money available for that internal development of the resources of the country which is what India so much needs. But, on the other hand, our position in the country would be altogether changed. We do not for a moment pretend that these volunteers would join the Russians, or any other foreign foe against us. Far from it; they know when they are well off, and they would, we doubt not, loyally and enthusiastically support us in any such crisis. But, for all that, the situation would be altogether altered. At present, we practically do what we like. If we want to take Egypt or Burmah, or threaten Russia, we do it,—use

Indian soldiers and make India pay for it;—if we desire, in violation of our Free Trade gospel, to tax your tea or your silver we do it;—if we want to prevent your taxing our cotton goods, no matter if it destroys your entire fiscal system, we do it;—in minor matters we do make some show of deferring to the wishes of the people, but in great matters we make no pretence of this, we do just what we think right, and we leave the people of India to like it or not, as they please. Our Government is absolutely despotic in all great matters, though in minor matters it is in a small degree constitutional. But, with a quarter of a million of volunteers, backed by the whole country, and with all our native troops necessarily more in sympathy with their fellow-countrymen than with us—our native troops that some of us have considered a possible danger, isolated as they are—the present system would be impossible. It is quite true that we do not now dread any recurrence of a mutiny; and, even in such a case, the volunteers would, we believe, stand by us. We do not for an instant say, and very few of us even think, that the volunteers would ever actually fight us; but the fact remains that such a body, supported as we have indicated above, would, from its potentiality of doing this, acquire a moral force that we could not disregard, and we should be compelled thenceforth, alike in great and small matters, to govern India with considerable regard to the views, wishes, and opinions of the country. This means a revolution—a noiseless, bloodless revolution, but none the less a complete revolution—in our existing system of Government for which we are not prepared, and which, if made at all, must be made deliberately by the people of England, and not slid into unwittingly by us out here, who, after all, are merely the servants of the English people. This is why we will not hear of volunteering on an extended, in fact, practical scale. As to the ten or twenty thousand purely spontaneous volunteers, they would, of course, be of little account, either as a protection or as disturbants of the present equilibrium, but we won't have them either, because, once allowed, it might be very difficult, if not impossible, to prevent further and, from our point of view, inexpedient developments."

This is an intelligible argument, and explains, we believe, what to the country at large is unaccountable in the present attitude of the Government of India towards the volunteering question. Not only are the people loyal, but the mass of them, we mean of those who do the thinking for the country, are convinced that the Government believes them to be so, and, in the face of this, its refusal to allow them to take the necessary steps to provide for their own and its defence, seems incomprehensible.

It remains for the English nation to decide, whether the principles it has laid down for the Administration of India shall really be acted up to or not, whether the pledges given, time after time, by the greatest statesmen of both parties shall continue persistently to be violated, and whether for the sake of being able to make poor patient India pay for her little wars and make other trumpery little profits out of her, Great Britain will persevere in keeping India only half-defended (as such she must ever remain until a system of a national defence be organised) when even that imperfect measure of defence entails taxation that is crushing the country, and if it continues to grow, as it has grown during the last three years, will, before many years are over, have absolutely ruined it.

To resume. The volunteering question was succeeded by one in regard to the income tax. The proposal was to raise the taxable minimum to Rs.1,000 (say £68 a year) and to provide for the loss of Revenue thus entailed either by retrenchment or the re-imposition of an import duty on the finer classes of cotton goods. The whole case was fairly enough put by the proposer, a leading pleader of Behar, Mr. Guru Prasad Sen, and we may quote what he said*:—

"Gentlemen,—When the first Congress met at Bombay we had to deal with the license tax, a tax so illogical and inconsistent that we could do nothing better than to propose that an income tax should be substituted in its stead. We did not approve either license tax or income tax. We said if more money be really wanted for military purposes and the Government will not provide this, as they ought to provide it, by retrenchment in other branches of the service, the required funds ought to be provided 'firstly, by the re-imposition of the customs duties: and secondly, by the extension of the license tax to those classes of the community, official and non-official, at present exempted from it, care being taken that, in the case of all classes a sufficiently high taxable minimum be maintained.' What we said then was, 'If you will have more money, if you won't retrench, as you ought to do, if you won't re-impose the customs duties, then, rather than devise new schemes of taxation, turn your illogical license tax into a logical income tax, only keep your taxable minimum high enough.' It was, in fact, the lesser of two evils which we chose. But we soon found that the taxable minimum had been struck too low, that the administration of the income tax, as it was worked when the income tax came to be introduced—we found, I say, that the practical administration of the tax was by no means so satisfactory as it ought to have been, especially with reference to the taxation of incomes below, or coming but little above, the minimum. Now, having given the matter a fair trial, we propose that the taxable minimum be raised to Rs.1,000, and we do this in the interest of the humbler classes of our countrymen. (Applause.) It is not in the interest of the distinguished delegates whom I see before me, not ten per cent. of whom, probably, have incomes of less than Rs.1,000 a year, but in the interests of the large body of our countrymen of the middle classes, that we desire that this relief should be granted, namely, the raising of the minimum from Rs.500 to Rs.1,000. (Applause.) Now, there are many reasons why this raising of the minimum has become a necessity. In the Act, we find the minimum Rs.500, and that, of course, you must admit is a very low limit. It means, at the present rate of exchange, that all incomes of £34 a year and upwards are liable to taxation. Well, prices have risen during the last twenty years enormously, and they have even risen within the last two years. Sir, the minimum, I submit, ought to be fixed with due regard to the necessities of life, and this limit of Rs.500 takes no account of these. Is it at all conceivable for a man, in our part of the country, a respectable householder, who lives on from Rs.500 to Rs.800 or 900 a year, which comes to from Rs.40 to 70, or say £2 15s. to less than £5, a month, to provide the mere necessaries of life and then have any margin to spare for income tax? (Loud applause.) Then there are not only his own necessities and those of his family to be supplied, but, in all Indian families there are a number of dependants to be clothed and fed. It is not a question of individuals, but a question of many dozens, in every case, depending upon individuals. In fact, as you all know, a man has not only to feed, clothe, and educate his own sons, but he has to feed, clothe, and educate those of his relatives, subordinates, and so on. This, of course, is inevitable; it may be a good or bad custom, but it is one hallowed by the traditions of thousands of years, and that we must still bow to. We cannot help ourselves, if we would, and for all its disadvantages, it is a good and kindly custom. It is not the question of the support of one individual and his family, but the support of a family and its connections and retainers. The income really belongs to half a dozen families. It is an aggregate of incomes here treated as one, but which would in other countries have stood divided. These points were not sufficiently taken into consideration when "the necessaries of life" for Indians were considered, or the taxable minimum, which is supposed to be fixed above necessities, would not have been placed so low. The necessities of life for Indian families are not to be measured with reference to the single individual requirements; but with reference to the requirements of his family and household, and if you measure necessary requirements with due regard to these you will all agree with me that the minimum of Rs. 40 a month is very much too low (applause), and, therefore, under these circumstances, we now propose that the taxable minimum be raised from Rs. 500 to Rs. 1,000. (Applause.) It was, I believe, originally under contemplation to fix the minimum at this figure for a certain class of people—I mean for officials in Government employ. Government thought this was a minimum exactly suited to the necessities of that class, but it was pointed out that, if that concession was made, a concession of a similar nature would be needed on behalf of every class, and that otherwise the tax would be inconsistent and illogical, and it was then, and then only, that the minimum, in their case, was reduced to Rs. 500; so that, according to the admission of Government, in regard to the only class of which it knows anything, the

* Page 131 of Detailed Report.

minimum ought to be fixed at Rs.1,000, and not at Rs.500; and we, who know all classes, can tell them that this is equally necessary in the case of all classes. (Applause.) Well, that being so, there can be no difference of opinion, it seems to me, with respect to the raising of the minimum. But, before I leave the question, I have one word more to say. In England, the minimum is, I am told, £150 a year, which would correspond, at the present rate of exchange, to something like Rs.2,250. (Hear, hear.) So that our present minimum is fixed at a very low figure, if you compare it with the English minimum, and especially if you take into consideration the fact that the one is for a single family, while in India, looking to the requirements of an Indian family with its dependants, it is really the income of a group of families, and you must admit that the minimum, if it is not to be Rs. 2,000, ought, at least, to be raised to Rs.1,000. (Applause.) Then, sir, we are confronted with this difficulty. If the minimum is raised from Rs. 500 to Rs. 1,000, how are we to meet the loss in revenue? I submit we can do it by reducing expenditure. In a household, where the expenditure is seventy millions of pounds sterling, do you not think it possible that a paltry reduction of, say, one-third of one of those millions (which, I suppose, would be the utmost loss that would be sustained), could be very well made up by the reduction of expenditure? A prudent householder, under such a contingency, would, in the first place, set about and reduce his expenditure, if he had no reasonable prospect of increasing his income, and if Government could at all be made to feel that the limit of taxation has already been reached, I think it would immediately set to work to bring about a reduction in expenditure, sufficient to meet the reduction our proposals involve in the outturn of the income-tax. . . .

"But we say further: 'Even if that is not possible, that is to say, if you persist in not seeing that it is possible,—and none are so blind as those who won't see,—if you insist that you cannot meet the lost by reduction of expenditure, do this,—as the present low minimum is telling so heavily on the well-being of the masses of our lower middle class people—do this, re-impose the import duty which has been given up (hear, hear), an import duty, not on the poor man's clothing but on the finer kinds of cloth, which only the comparatively rich—those really able to contribute to the necessities of the State—practically use.' Well, the only thing that can be said against this measure is, that it is a measure of protection. But it may be so low as to be practically inoperative in this direction. Even were it otherwise, I would still say it is not a protective measure at all; it is a fiscal measure, adopted solely in the interests of our finances. It would not be, nay, all the circumstances considered, no one can pretend that it could be opposed to the rules laid down by the best political economists, and, indeed, it is absurd to talk, in these days, of protection for our industries—our industries do not require protection—but so as to leave no handle for such an argument, let there be a corresponding excise duty on our own similar finer productions."

Babu Jogendra Chundra Ghose went further into the practical evils of the existing ridiculously low minimum. He pointed out* that—

"A man who has only three or four hundred rupees a year may easily be mistaken by the most honest assessing officer, misled by subordinates who want to make a name, for one who has five hundred rupees. But when you raise the minimum to Rs.1,000 a year, it is different. None of the mass of folks who have two, three, or four hundred a year can be assessed by mistake at Rs.1,000. Of course, there will be men on seven, eight, and nine hundred, in regard to whom such a mistake may be made, but there are ten of the former class to one of the latter; and it is not only mistakes that have to be guarded against—the hundreds of thousands of comparatively helpless ignorant persons who have between Rs. 200 and 500 a year are made to pay by rascals who threaten them that, if they do not bribe them, they will have them taxed, and you get rid of all this, which is the cause of half the discontent the income-tax brings about, by raising the limit to Rs.1,000, because the seven, eight, and nine hundred people are very, very much fewer in number, and are in a better position and know more, and are stronger and much less liable to be frightened by threats.

"I think, gentlemen, that our demand is very reasonable. All that we want is the exemption of the poor and the weak from the tax and its accompanying oppression. The classes that will thus be exempted will be the more poorly-paid servants of Government, and the great mass of small traders, shopkeepers, and artisans.

"As regards Government servants, you know, gentlemen, that they are mostly taken from the middle classes, the lower ranks of what we may call the gentry of the country. You know how, day by day,

* Page 133 of Detailed Report.

they are being reduced to poverty. Their wants are many and their means are small, and we know how keen their struggle for existence is, and the accident of birth has added to their misery. Rs. 25 is a large sum for them, for they can save nothing. If possible, as a matter of humanity only, they should be let alone; but the principal reason why this tax, so far as they are concerned, should be removed is that it diminishes the efficiency of the public service, because it still further, and materially, reduces the salaries of the poorest-paid and yet hardest-worked servants of the Government. In Bengal, we had the Salaries' Commission for the avowed purpose of increasing the pay of our ill-paid officials, and that purely in the interests of the public service. But nothing came out of it. The income tax, however, still remains. When the income tax bill was first framed, these servants of the State, drawing small salaries, were exempted from its operation. But our wise legislators thought that, by this, the principle of equality would be infringed; and, for once, equality was accepted to be a very important principle in the administration of the country,—indeed, more important than the efficiency of the public service. But I think I express the opinion of the Congress when I say, that the other classes would not, certainly, have grudged these officials this poor privilege.

"As for the other classes upon which the measure of this tax falls the heaviest, it is the class of small traders and shopkeepers, and these men, besides illegitimate extortions wrung from them by threats of getting them still more highly assessed, are always assessed at a great deal more than their actual incomes. Most of them are illiterate, many of them entirely so, and none of them keep, or can possibly keep, account-books that assessors will accept, and these poor men are always the least able to defend themselves, and least able to pay competent men to protect their interests. Many small tradesmen have been thus obliged to give up their trade, and many that have not done this yet, find it most difficult to keep up their business. I know one, a man who was literally obliged to close his shop on account of the heavy income-tax imposed upon him, and for no other reason—just absorbed his entire profits. As for the small artisans and manufacturers, English competition is daily driving them out of the market; and the income-tax has added to their difficulties and is absolutely crushing them. There is no encouragement for them anywhere, and they are dying out, to the great detriment of the prosperity of the country. That is a bad tax which benefits the Government financially far less than it oppresses and injures the people. And that is just what this income-tax does when imposed upon these classes. If the Government had only a conception of all the suffering caused and all the injury inflicted on the prosperity of the country by allowing the nominal taxable minimum to remain at its present low level, they would not hesitate one moment, cost what it might, to accept our recommendation."

Then, referring to the re-imposition of the Customs duties, he remarked :—

"We all know how, at the bidding of the merchants of Manchester, the cotton duties were abolished. The voice of a few English merchants was found more powerful than the voice of two hundred and fifty millions of Indians. We hope that, at last, the good sense and the keen sense of justice of the great English nation will awake to the injustice of adding to the burdens of a poor and already over-burdened people for the sake of a few merchants."

An amendment was then proposed by Mr. Daji Abaji Khare, which will be best explained in his own words* :—

"Gentlemen,—I am entirely at one with the proposer and seconder of the proposition now before you, but I desire to insert a few additional words in it. Gentlemen, if the Government refuse to raise the taxable minimum as we recommend, then our recommendation about the re-imposition of the Customs duties falls, as it were, to the ground; whereas, gentlemen, it should be our object never to allow this to fall to the ground, but to perpetually keep before the eyes of the British public and the British Government that, though we may forgive, we can never forget, the gross injustice that was done to us at the bidding of a small though powerful English mercantile clique, and that we will never rest, at any rate as long as other worse and far less productive taxes have to be borne by us, until we obtain redress. I may say, gentlemen, that I am told that, now that the true fiscal character of those duties have become known to them, now that they realise that they were in no degree practically protective—that it is advantages in situation and cheap labour, and not any duties

* Page 134 of Detailed Report.

that favour our mills, and that despite the abolition of these, our mills go on, year by year, absorbing more and more of the trade—now, I say, that they have come to realise this, I am told that the more enlightened members of the Manchester manufactuers themselves regret having had any indirect share in inflicting on this financially struggling country the terrible financial loss which the abolition of these duties involved (cheers), and I believe it, gentlemen, for though manufacturers, though Manchester manufacturers, they are Englishmen, and though they may be hasty for the moment they cannot help being just in the long run. (Loud cheers.) But be this as it may, it is essential, for us at any rate, to make clear that not only as a means of recouping any such reduction of revenue as is involved in our present recommendation, but in all and every case in which additional revenue may be required, the re-imposition of Customs duties on articles mainly used by the rich is, in our opinion, in the opinion of the entire country, the only legitimate course of action. We say the entire country says, If you at any time really need more money, you must not enhance the income tax, you must not raise the salt tax, you must not go devising any new fiscal instruments of torture, you must so re-impose the Customs duties that they shall be paid by the rich and not add to the burdens of the poor."

This amendment was universally accepted, and was followed by another which was as universally rejected, as will be seen from the proceedings which we quote.* Mr. Chackravarti rose and said:—

"At this late hour, I do not wish to try your patience too much. As the income tax is now administered it is working great injustice and is utterly iniquitous, so I beg to propose that the tax be abolished. The amended proposition which I suggest would run thus:—'That as the administration of the income tax has involved very great hardships, it is essential, in the opinion of this Congress, that the tax be abolished.' (Voices of 'No, No,' 'Withdraw,'; 'It is the only tax that reaches the rich'; 'We don't want to relieve ourselves of taxation'; 'We won't have it,' and 'Withdraw, Withdraw.') Well, gentlemen, of course, I bow to the general sense of the assembly, but I retain my own opinion, that the only thing to be done about the income tax is to abolish it *in toto*. What is the use of half measures? (Cries of 'Sit down,' 'Sit down.') Well, as you will have it, I withdraw my amendment." (Loud applause.)

Then came another amendment to the effect that besides raising the minimum to Rs.1,000, a rebate of Rs.300 should be granted. But this, too, was rejected on the grounds, firstly, that the object of the Resolution was to relieve the poorer middle classes, and not the comparatively rich who had incomes of Rs.1,000 and upwards; and secondly because, whether rightly or wrongly, the Government had definitely decided not to admit the principle of rebate in India, and it was inexpedient "to complicate our otherwise simple Resolution by pressing Government to reverse its mature and carefully considered procedure,"† in such a comparatively unimportant matter.

At last, the following Resolution was unanimously passed:—

"That as the administration of the income-tax, especially as regards incomes below Rs.1,000 a year, has proved extremely unsatisfactory, it is essential, in the opinion of the Congress, that the taxable minimum be raised to Rs. 1,000, the loss of revenue thus involved being made good and further financial difficulties, if any, met by reductions in the existing public expenditure, or, should this prove impossible, by the re-imposition of an import duty on the finer classes of cotton goods."

The meeting then adjourned till next day.

The Congress assembled for its last sitting at 11 a.m. on the 30th of December, and the first Resolution brought before it was the following:—

"That, having regard to the poverty of the people, it is desirable that the Government be moved to elaborate a system of Technical Education, suitable to the condition of the country, to encourage indigenous manufactures by a more strict observance of the orders already existing in regard to utilizing such manufactures for State purposes, and to employ more extensively than at present the skill and talents of the people of the country."

---

* Page 135 of Detailed Report.

† Mr. Guru Prasad Sen, page 135 of Detailed Report.

It was proposed by Sir Savalai Ramasawmi Mudeliar, C.I.E., now Sheriff of Madras, and renowned throughout the South of India for his munificent gifts for charitable and other public purposes. It was seconded by Mr. John Adam, to whom reference has already been made. (*Vide ante, pp.* 18, 43.) The main point brought out in regard to Technical Education was that, despite the facts that the educated classes throughout India took a deep interest in the matter, and that in various localities, Bombay, Madras, Patna, &c., really large sums of money had been subscribed for the purpose, these sums remained unexpended, because the various committees, composed of the most enlightened Europeans and Indians of the several localities, were unable to devise or propound any really suitable and practical plan for securing the required technical education for the people. It was therefore eminently a case in which the Government might justly be pressed to elaborate a suitable scheme. Given this, the country would soon have it in working order. Mr. Adam pointed out that here, as elsewhere, it is ignorance that bars progress. There is absolutely nothing of any value on record as to the actual existing condition of the several arts and industries. We do not know what they lack, wherein they fail, in what points they need aid and guidance. As Mr. Adam said, in a Minute laid before Government long ago, and which he quoted:—

"I have, in common with many other persons, a floating general idea that much can be done, but what inquiry I have been able to make into specific industries, for instance weaving, shows only how little we know, and the impossibility of framing on that scanty knowledge any practical scheme or suggestion. I think that a small Committee might be appointed, either by the Technical Institute Committee or by Government, to investigate the actual condition of native industries, *in esse* and *in posse*, not from the æsthetic, but from the practical and economic, point of view. The aim should not be to produce a renaissance in Indian industrial art, but to discover whether, by improved methods of working and increased technical skill, competition is possible between native manufactures and foreign imports. I cannot think of any way in which money, whether of the Institute or of Government, can be better expended than in payment of the expenses of such a preliminary inquiry."

The main point of the Resolution was to press Government to cause such inquiries to be made, and collect such detailed data as are necessary, and thereupon on the solid basis of facts, to elaborate and present the country with a really practical scheme. Mr. Adam commented humorously on "a portentous-looking blue book called a Note upon Technical Education," recently published by the Government of India, the sum and substance of which, despite its great volume, simply was that we are to establish technical schools, wherever an inquiry establishes the fact that these are wanted!

"This, then, is their suggestion—that we are to establish technical schools wherever an inquiry establishes the fact that technical schools are wanted. This inquiry is the very thing we have not got, and this is the very thing we want the Government of India to make for us, either by appointing a Commission, as the motion impliedly suggests, or by local committees or special officers. That is the outcome of this long Note, viz., that we are to aid and promote technical education by establishing technical schools in localities where they are required. It goes on further to state, very sympathetically, but not very practically, 'Natives of all castes are increasing in number looking to technical education as affording an honourable livelihood and career in life. It is submitted that it is desirable to assist and encourage this popular feeling; that room exists for improvement in almost every department of technical instruction in India, and that the time is ripe not only for calling on local Governments to take the matter up in earnest, but for indicating to them some of the directions in which improvement seems possible, and from which funds can be obtained for effecting it.' Thus, Sir, we see that the Government has admitted that the main point of difficulty in connection with the subject is an inquiry, and I think, therefore, that we are justified in going forward, in the strongest and in the most emphatic terms, to ask the Government of India to make some such inquiry."

The subsidiary points in the Resolution are akin to the main point. Time after time the Government of India has directed that, so far as possible, all stores required for the public service should be procured of local manufacture in the local market. But, as a fact, these directions are daily disregarded everywhere, and the Resolution suggests that the existing Orders on the subject should be more strictly enforced. That anything will result from this suggestion the Congress was far from sanguine. The greatest defect in British rule is the predominance in it of promise over performance. If practical effect had been given to all the noble sentiments in regards to India's Government enunciated by British Sovereigns, Statesmen, and Viceroys, and endorsed by the British Houses of Parliament and the British nation, India would at this day be the happiest and most prosperous, instead of one of the poorest, countries in the World. There is not a single grievance of which her people complain which cannot be shown to exist in defiance of solemn pledges given either by Great Britain's Sovereign or her most eminent Statesmen.

The whole secret of the matter is that between those high and enlightened authorities (whose honest aim and object, in most cases,* have been the welfare of our nation,) and our poor suffering people has ever stood the compact, all-powerful phalanx of the Indian Bureaucracy. Comprising as it has, at different times, men of the noblest characters and highest aspirations, consisting almost without exception of highly educated, and so far as pecuniary matters are concerned, rigidly upright† men, it has nevertheless steadily opposed a *non possumus* to all orders devised in England, and even by Viceroys here, for the elevation of the status of the Indian community. If you say to one of these gentlemen: "But the Queen's Proclamation distinctly lays down so and so," he either replies with Sir James Stephen, "Oh, the Queen's Proclamation don't count;—it was a mere kindly expression of her own private feelings, and has no legal or official status," or he says, "The Queen didn't know anything about it; it's all nonsense—mere talk—the thing is not possible and can't be done, and what's more, it won't be done." In other words, they won't do it. They are, the great bulk of them, very good men, mostly honest hard-workers, and willing to labour zealously for the good of India, as they understand it—but they will hear of nothing that tends towards curtailing their autocratic powers, nothing that will operate towards changing their position from that of kindly despots into that of responsible servants of the people. They believe that all knowledge of the people and the country (of which they often really know less than many unbiassed men who have spent only a couple of months in India mixing freely as equals with the best of the Indians) is centred in themselves, and they honestly consider all who desire to go beyond what they like, be they local reformers, Viceroys or Governors, the House of Commons, or even our gracious Queen-Empress, to be either very mischievous and designing, or unhappily ignorant, persons, and they are stedfast in preventing any real effect being given to what they are pleased to consider the seditious, or erroneous, views of these objectionable or mistaken parties. Until this all-powerful phalanx is weakened by the admission

* Of course, the cotton duties, and one or two "little war" bills are not forgotten, but they are distinctly exceptions.

† Madras ought perhaps to be excluded—but it is in that Presidency alone that any serious shortcomings in these respects have, during nearly fifty years, tarnished the fair fame of the public service.

of a large body of independent members into the Councils, and by the inclusion in itself of a large proportion of Indians, England's beneficent intentions in regard to India will always continue to be unrealised.

Akin to the question of utilizing local manufactures is that of utilizing indigenous skill and talent. Although something has been done in the way of substituting statutory natives as Postmasters, Engine-drivers, Guards, and the like, for Europeans,* there are still large numbers of these holding posts on salaries fully twice as large as would be needed to secure equally competent natives for the work, and it is against this abuse—which has a distinct, if not very considerable, bearing on the poverty of the country—that the last clause in the Resolution was directed.

The entire Congress was unanimous on all the points embodied in the Resolution though amendments for enlarging its scope were proposed and subsequently withdrawn. Mr. B. H. Chester, M.A., one of the ablest members of the Madras Eurasian community, made a speech† which should be read, but from which we may cull a couple of passages.

Explaining that he was one of the delegates elected by the large Eurasian community of Madras and authorised by their leader, Mr. D. S. White, at the moment detained in Calcutta on the Public Service Commission, of which he was a member, to express his entire sympathy with the movement, he said :—

> "I am happy to be able to stand here, and speak to you as one of yourselves. (Cheers.) Though I am proud, and justifiably so, I hope, of the English blood that flows in my veins, still I feel that by birth, by residence, by community of interests, I am as much entitled to the designation 'native of India' as any delegate now present."

He then went into the details of the main question, and showed that out of three millions and odd of scholars receiving education throughout the empire in colleges and schools of different classes, only some six thousand were receiving any technical training. This, he pointed out, was the crucial defect in the existing system of education in India.

> "The great fault has been that too many men have been trained in one single groove. At considerable cost thousands of youths have been highly educated, but only a very limited number of them are absorbed by the public service and the liberal professions. What the country needs is a radical change in the character of the training given in our public schools, so that, while some may qualify for the Government service and the various professions, others may turn their attention to the useful and necessary branches of trade, of commerce, and of manufacture."

After going further into the question of the kinds of industry to which attention might first be turned, he concluded with these words :—

> "When the young men of India know that this Congress views with favour the encouragement of industrial and technical pursuits, they will be more likely to shake off that false pride and shame which keeps so many of them from earning an honest livelihood by following trade. And, is it idle to say, that, just as the present educational system has produced brilliant scholars, thinkers and writers, and speakers such as we have heard during the past few days, so, in the near future, by the new scheme of education which, we hope, will soon be inaugurated, we shall have distinguished

* Non-domiciled Europeans, be it understood. No native objects to the domiciled European, who has become a countryman, and whose pay and pension alike remain in India. Nor if the truth be told, do they seriously object to even non-domiciled Europeans who are already here; what they protest against is the persistence, in getting out year after year, relays of fresh men when equally good men are available on better terms in the country already.

† Pages 144, 145 of the Detailed Report.

inventors and brilliant discoverers who will sow the seeds of gigantic manufacturing and com al enterprises originated and worked by India's sons, with India's money, and for India's good." (Loud cheers.)

But perhaps the most interesting feature in the debate was a long, sensible, matter-of-fact speech in Tamil, by Mr. Mookanasari,* of Tanjore, a working carpenter, who, with two other artisans, came here, as he said, "as the duly elected representatives of the whole industrial class in the Tanjore District." He maintained that the country was steadily growing poorer, and that only a revival and development of local industries could arrest the downward progress.

"We should pray," he said,† "the Government to establish and maintain throughout the country technical institutes, where the manufacture, by machinery, of all articles of Indian consumption should be carried on, and all facilities afforded to those who wish to learn and study the principles and modes of such manufactures. Should this, however, be found impossible, we should ask them to establish, experimentally at least, model factories in every one of the Presidency cities in India, the capital for which will be found either by Government, exclusively from its own funds, or by the raising of a private capital under Government guarantee and supported by Government aid. The management of these institutions should not be exclusively in the hands of Government like the Madras School of Arts, but should be left in the hands of a company formed of native capitalists, subject to the control and supervision of Government. Such institutions, if they prove to be flourishing, may be established again at important mofussil centres, and the Government should encourage such institutions, by purchasing from them all their supplies of such articles as are locally manufactured in this country. Besides, the Government should stimulate a desire for improvement and progress among the native artisans and the industrial classes, by the holding of periodical exhibitions in various local centres, of all local manufactures and industries, whereat the best design and the most excellent workmanship will be selected and encouraged, by the granting of prizes and certificates. All the Local and Municipal Boards should be made to contribute for a prize-fund, which will be necessary for this purpose. By the Congress working towards the achievement of this end, not only the dying industries of the country will be revived and receive a stimulus for improvement, but also, new industries will spring up everywhere, tending to the growth of material improvement in the country and to our independence of support as a nation, which will ultimately regain for us our lost place among the nations of the world. These factories and workshops, gentlemen, when they spring up, will be a source of gaining an honest livelihood to thousands of our countrymen who now, destitute of any means, are driven to despair how to keep body and soul together. And, gentlemen, how welcome will be the day for India when, by the immense and growing development of her arts and industries she will be able to find at least a wholesome morsel of food for her forty-five millions of completely destitute children who are now, by official admission, going without even one single full meal a day!"

Referring to Mr. Mookanasari's concluding words, it may not be amiss to explain, that it is due to no want of sympathy for the miserable half-starving millions of their fellow-countrymen that so little has been said during this last Congress of that cruel poverty which is year by year decimating the lowest classes, and as many, perhaps a majority, believe is surely, if slowly, creeping higher up the social scale. The fact simply is that since the resumption of the aggressive annexive policy and the enormous increases of taxation that have, thus far, been the chief features of Lord Dufferin's administration, the Indian community despair of obtaining any material alleviation of the misery they see around them until they can secure a potential voice in the administration, and, it is this conviction more than anything else, that is giving such an intense earnestness to their efforts in the direction of representation.

---

* An artisan, who never enjoyed anything which would be considered education in Europe; this gentleman is one of the most prominent citizens in Tanjore, a Municipal Commissioner, and member of the Local Board, devoting daily many hours to his private, so many to his public, work, and absolutely untiring in his exertions to do good to his neighbours. A monster meeting of the artizans of the entire District of Tanjore was held at Kumbakonam and this gentleman with two more were duly elected.

† Page 146 of Detailed Report.

The next Resolution referred to the existing Arms Act, under which no native of India may possess or carry arms without special license, whereas Europeans, Eurasians, Negroes, Hottentots or Fiji Islanders, any scum of the earth even that the ocean casts on India's shores, may bear arms unquestioned. Naturally this is a law (passed by Lord Lytton it may, perhaps, be needless to remark) which does not commend itself to the Indian public. Thousands and tens of thousands of men and cattle are killed by dacoits and wild beasts, and the crops of millions are ravaged by wild animals, owing to the defenceless state in which the community is thus left, but even this, bad as it is, is nowhere felt so deeply as the insult which the Indians consider is involved in the Act to every single one of them.

Every delegate present was of one mind as to the intolerable character of the existing arrangements, and yet the Resolution in regard to them gave rise to the most energetic debate of the whole session. How this came about was clearly set forth by the President when, after an animated, almost fiery, discussion, which lasted some hours, he was enabled to put a modified Resolution satisfying all parties. He said* :—

"The essence of this debate, I take it, has been this: the proposer of the original Resolution, fixing his attention mainly on the point that the Act presumes that everybody in the country not specially authorized to wear arms is unfit to be trusted with them, and feeling the slur thus implied on the loyalty of the nation keenly, proposed the abolition of the Act. He did not stop to consider that the Act embodied numerous necessary provisions; he saw what was galling to the national self-respect in the Act, and desired to get rid of it *in toto*. On the other hand, the proposer of the amendment, fully realising the necessity of an Arms Act, and the beneficial character of many portions of the existing Act, only thought to provide for such a liberal administration of the Act as should enable all persons, considered by their neighbours to be fit to have arms, to possess and wear them. He probably did not quite realise how strong the sentimental objection to the presumption involved in being required to take out licenses is throughout the country. The amendment, it is true, assumed that all people who were certified to be fit to wear arms, by their neighbours, were thus fit, but what the proposer of the original Resolution, and, as it would seem from the course of the debate, a very large number of other delegates, desired, was that all persons should be presumed to be fit to be trusted with arms who were not certified to be unfit. In practice, probably, the result would be much the same, but, under the latter scheme, the presumption of disloyalty or unworthiness to be trusted with arms, which even the first amendment, though to a limited extent, involves, would disappear. So, now, we have prepared a new Resolution, which gives full weight both to the objections of those who supported the amendment, and of those who objected to it, and this Resolution will run as follows:—

"RESOLVED,—That in view of the loyalty of the people, the hardships which it causes, and the unmerited slur which it casts upon the people of this country, the Government be moved so to modify the provisions of Chapter IV., and, if necessary, any other portions of Act XI. of 1878, as will enable all persons to bear arms, unless debarred therefrom, either as individuals or as members of particular communities or classes, by the order of the Government of India (or any local authority empowered by the Government of India, in that behalf) for reasons to be recorded in writing, and duly published."

This Resolution was carried unanimously and with acclamation, but the discussion was a very characteristic one, and passages from it may be here advantageously reproduced. The proposer, who advocated simply the entire repeal of the Act, was Rao Bahadur Sabapathy Mudaliar, a gentleman who carries much weight in the Southern Presidency, and whose sobriety of temperament and general cautiousness no one who knows him can question. He said†:

"Under the previous and present Act, no man can carry arms, whatever his position may be, without obtaining a license from the magistrate of the district, except, indeed, certain persons who

* Page 161 of Detailed Report.
† Pages 147, 148 of Detailed Report.

are exempted on account of their high position. I mean the magistrates and members of the Municipal Council and Local Board, and some few gentlemen, specially exempted. But this exemption is not of any great value; I mean that the exempting of such people means practically nothing where the country is concerned. It is no concession at all to the people as a whole. On the other hand, I consider the provisions of the Act degrading. Although I, personally, am exempted, in virtue of my official position, still I consider it a degradation—(hear, hear)—that so many of my worthy and loyal countrymen should be deprived of this privilege. (Applause.) Of course, the official view is that persons who want to get arms can apply to the magistrate and get them by payment of a license fee. But the slur which it casts upon us, and upon our loyalty, is the thing that has been preying upon my mind (Hear.) To the farmer, to which class I belong, to protect his crops and stores from the attacks of wild beasts as well as from the attacks of robbers, the possession of arms is a necessity: so much so that, in consequence of being deprived of them, the poor ryot has everywhere been a loser of much of his hard-earned produce. I may also say, that before the Mutiny of 1857 people enjoyed the privilege of carrying arms wherever and whenever they liked; and even after the Mutiny, even after, I say, that calamitous event, the Government never thought of imposing any restrictions as to the possession of arms; but recent events have induced the Government to frame this Act, to the great detriment of the people in general. Up to the Mutiny, during the Mutiny, and for years after the Mutiny, we possessed arms; what have we done since to deserve their forfeiture? If the Government find it necessary to keep any part or any parts of India, for political reasons, under the operation of this Act, it may be so enacted that the Governor-General may have the power of prolaiming that such districts shall not have the use of arms for a while. Beyond which, I do think it is necessary for the Government to possess any power in this matter, and I do not think it is right that there should be an Act of the present nature, entailing, as it does, the greatest hardships on the people, and involving, as it does, a slur on the entire nation."

Babu Bipin Chandra Pal seconded the original Resolution, and from his elaborate speech, which illustrates well alike the merits and defects of the Bengal school of oratory, we shall make a lengthy quotation, the more so that it puts very clearly an important feature of the case, scarcely touched upon by any of the many other speakers. He said,* after a very humorous and florid introduction:—

"I am loyal to the British Government, because, with me, loyalty to the British Government is identical with loyalty to my own people and my own country. I am loyal to the British Government, because I believe the British Government to be an instrument in the hand of God for the salvation of my people. (Applause.) I am loyal to the British Government because I love Self-Government. (Applause.) I am loyal to the British Government because I love this Congress. I confess, sir, that I am a radical and a democrat, but, strange to say, my radicalism and my democracy have both combined to make me a sincere well-wisher of the British Government. (Applause.) And gentlemen, the love that I bear to the British Government compels me to condemn strongly the suicidal policy enunciated in the Arms Act, and to call for its repeal. The Resolution which I am here to second seems, sir, to be slightly different from those that have gone before it. The supporters of those Resolutions appealed on behalf of the people to the Government, but I appeal on behalf of the Government to itself. It is not for me to say, sir, that this Act does not operate to the injury of the people. When I remember that year after year, ravages of wild beasts are increasing with alarming rapidity; when I remember that thousands of my countrymen and countrywomen are every year killed by tigers and leopards; when I find poor cultivators everywhere appealing to Government to protect their crops from the ravages of wild animals—for the Arms Act has deprived them of the means by which they could protect their crops themselves—when I say I look to all these facts, how can I say that this Act does not operate against the life and property of the people? But excuse me, gentlemen, for saying that the direct injury which this law does to the people simply dwindles into insignificance before the immense harm that it is doing to the Government itself. We are very frequently told, sir, that the Government must maintain its prestige. But I can never fully understand the meaning of the prestige of the British Government in the face of this obnoxious Act. If you have really any prestige, why, then, that ought in itself to be a tower of strength to you which needed no Arms Act, and the consequent disarming of a whole nation, to keep up. It appears to me, gentlemen, that like some low caste-men, suddenly grown rich and placed in honourable positions, who are ever anxious to keep up their position—because they ever suspect that they have really no solid basis for that position—our Government also, in their extreme anxiety to preserve their prestige, betray their weakness only. (Applause

* Pages 148, 149, 150 of Detailed Report.

and laughter.) I am not destined to be a military man, and it is not for me to say what injurious effect the disarming of the nation is exercising upon the people of the country by demartializing them. I am a peace-loving Bengalee, who is living in comfortable security under the protection of the British Government, and to my mind the most injurious effect of the Arms Act consists in the temptation that it is holding out to Russia to come and invade India. I am not a Russophobist, gentlemen; God save me from that dire disease! I do not believe that Russia's advance has been actuated by a policy which has the invasion and conquest of India as its ultimate aim. But if ever Russia comes and puts in her appearance at our North-Western frontier, she will be brought there by the Arms Act. What, I ask, are all our professions of loyalty worth in the face of the Arms Act? The Nizam may offer sixty crores instead of sixty lacs for the defence of the Empire; ten thousand Jubilee demonstrations may be organized, the Government may publicly acknowledge the sincerity of these loyal demonstrations, British newspapers may trumpet them forth to the whole world; but the question is, will foreigners believe, will Russia believe, in the truth and sincerity of these demonstrations in the face of the Arms Act? Would she not put the unpleasant question: If the people of India are loyal, and if you believe them to be so, why do you require the disarming of the entire population by an Arms Act to maintain your position there? So long as this Arms Act exists nothing will convince outside people that the British Government feel themselves strong in the loyalty of their subjects. You know, sir, that the Russian war party set considerable store by the supposed disaffection and disloyalty of the Indian people, and, if ever Russia makes bold to invade India, the Arms Act, I repeat, will be her chief temptation. Her Majesty has most solemnly declared that in our contentment she shall find her principal strength. Why then do her Indian Government ignore our loyalty and our contentment, and set up the flimsy bulwark of a disarming law for the safety of her Indian Empire? The policy of the Arms Act, sir, is wrong in principle, injurious in its effect, and is simply suicidal to the Government, and, as such, in the interest of that very Government, whose safety it seeks to secure, it should at once be repealed." (Loud and prolonged cheers.)

The debate, which was throughout most animated, and every step in which was followed by every member of the assembly, showing the vivid, if somewhat sentimental, interest taken by all in the question, may be read, but it does not seem necessary here to quote further from its pages.

The Arms Act question disposed of satisfactorily, and other formal Resolutions adopted (Detailed Report, p. 162, *et seq.*), the President delivered a brief parting address, from which we may reproduce the following passage*:—

"Gentlemen, if this Congress does no other good, it will still have achieved a very great good, if it brings the members of different provinces and the members of different communities into contact with each other. I have not the smallest doubt that you, gentlemen of the Madras Presidency, have now far kinder feelings for the defects of your brethren of Bengal and Bombay than you had before you had that intimate knowledge of us, which you have now obtained by coming in almost hourly contact with us during this past week. I say that this is a great good in itself. I trust we shall be able to obtain great political reforms in the administration of our own country, if we carry on a perfectly legitimate and constant agitation. At the same time, I do think that the social improvement we are introducing among ourselves by contact is in itself a very great good. (Applause.) Gentlemen, one of the best features of the Congress in Madras has been the hearty co-operation that we have received from the European members. (Hear, hear, and loud and continued applause.) It has, gentlemen, been alleged that the Europeans keep aloof from the natives, and that there is always a great deal of misunderstanding between the two communities. I took the liberty of addressing a few observations to you on that question. You will remember that I absolutely denied the universal application of that assertion. (Hear, hear.) Gentlemen, at that time my knowledge of the Madras Presidency was very limited, and I was not aware that my assertion would be completely borne out by what I have seen of the conduct of our European friends. (Applause.) Gentlemen, I for one am absolutely at a loss to understand why our European friends should not co-operate with us in the business that we have undertaken. As I have said, the limit and scope of our agitation and action are the good of the whole of India, not the good of any particular part of India, and not the good of any particular community, but, gentlemen, the good of the whole of India, and are not our European friends included? (Cheers.) The good of the one must

* Pages 163, 165 of Detailed Report.

necessarily re-act upon the good of the other. Therefore, I do heartily wish that the co-operation of all our European friends should go on increasing from year to year, till we find that the delegates are composed, not of six hundred natives and five or ten Europeans, but of a very large portion of Europeans, who should assist us by the experience—by the true political experience—which they have inherited for centuries from their forefathers. (Applause.) Gentlemen, I must ask our European friends, such of them as have honoured us with their presence, or such of them as may read the proceedings in the newspapers, if they find any expression or sentiment which may, perhaps, have been uttered in the heat of the discussion, to which they think objection may be justly taken, to remember that this Congress is only in its third year, and that no political association can achieve any great success till it has acquired a great deal of experience, which must take a very, very long time for us to get, who are entirely new to the art of self-government. (Applause.) I do trust that any defects which may have been found in the proceedings of this Congress will be pointed out to us, not in the spirit of cavil, not in the spirit of hostility, not in the spirit of antagonism, but in that spirit of consideration, conciliation, and assistance which I think our European friends are in a position to accord us." (Applause.)

Then the Congress (which it had been settled should reassemble at the close of December, 1888, at Allahabad) after venting its loyalty in an air-quake of hurrahs for our gracious Queen-Empress, and after subsequently delivering itself of batches of cheers for the President and others, peaceably dissolved, and it is not, we think, too much to say of them, that each one of the delegates returned to his home a wiser, better, and happier man than when he left it, at his country's call, to attend the late assemblage.

Looking back on the Congress, the characteristics that most impressed themselves on the minds of spectators, we found, and justly so, were the extreme earnestness and extraordinary good humour of the entire gathering.

Of the earnestness, the speeches embodied in the Detailed Report (from which we have given extracts), may convey some conception, but while they testify to the ardour of individual speakers, they can give no idea of that which was imprinted on the faces of that vast assemblage, or of the wrapt attention with which every turn in the debate, every speaker, and almost every word he uttered was followed, not only by the six hundred delegates, but by the very much larger body of spectators, several hundreds of whom had travelled from considerable, in a few cases huge, distances, merely to witness the proceedings.

But of the good humour that prevailed it seems impossible to convey to those not present any adequate notion. Amongst no body of educated men elsewhere in the world would such a combination of enthusiasm with imperturbable good temper have been, we believe, possible. Throughout the session every little joke and play of words, of which there were many, though these are lost in shorthand reporting, was instantly caught, and as warmly responded to by hearty laughter (even when the most animated discussions were proceeding) by the party against whom they were directed, as by the speaker's own friends. Not one cross or sour face was to be seen, not one harsh or unkind word was spoken by any one, even of that far from popular body—the Bureaucracy. Men vindicated their rights, or what they conceived to be such, with an outspoken energy that could not have been surpassed in England, but they did not abuse,—on the contrary, they dealt with—their opponents in a most brotherly spirit. All was so harmonious, despite vigorous differences of opinion, that one might have supposed the whole thing concerted beforehand, the result of a solemn compact. But there was nothing of the kind; it was only the normal kindly, charitable nature of the people shining out under favourable circumstances. Whether all would have been quite so *couleur de rose* had the Congress been a failure instead of the conspicuous success it was, or had its foes triumphed, instead of being, as they were, defeated along the whole line, we cannot presume to say; but, as a fact, the whole thing went off as though "envy, hatred, malice, and all uncharitableness" were unknown to the hearts of all who entered those portals.

And now we must take leave of the Congress, and the many speakers must, in the following pages, speak in their own words for themselves and their country, and it will remain for the great English nation, in whose abiding love of justice and freedom all here, as yet, rely implicitly, to bethink themselves seriously of the responsibilities which Providence has imposed upon them and which they have accepted, and to make up their minds that India, who loves and trusts them, shall henceforth have something like fair play, and that something like justice shall be, at last, the reward of Her patience and Her loyalty.

SUMMARY OF RESOLUTIONS

PASSED AT THE

THIRD INDIAN NATIONAL CONGRESS,

Held at Madras, on the 27th, 28th, 29th, and 30th December, 1887.

Resolution I.

Resolved.—That a Committee be appointed, consisting of the gentlemen, (marginally enumerated*) to consider what rules, if any, may now be usefully framed in regard to the constitution and working of the Congress, with instructions to report thereon to the Congress, on the 30th instant.

* Messrs. Nam Joshi, Chandavarkar, Mir Humayun Jah Bahadur, Hajee Mahomed Abdul Shakoor Badshaw Sahib, S. Subrahmania Iyer, W. S. Gantz, Rangiah Naidu, Surendra Nath Bannerjee, Trailokyanath Mitra, Kali Charan Bannerjee, Guru Prasad Sen, Saligram Singh, Ram Kali Chaudhuri, Hafiz Abdul Rahim, Rampal Singh, Pandit Madan Mohun, Ganga Prasad Varma, Bishan Narayen Dar, Hamid Ali, Murlidhur, Satyanand Agnihotri, H. H. Dhruva, W. C. Bonnerjee, Norendra Nath Sen, Eardley Norton, Joy Govind Shome, Iswari Lal Sircar, G. Subramania Iyer, D. A. Khare, S. A. Saminada Iyer, Sabapathy Mudaliar, A. O. Hume, C. Vijiya Raghava Chariar, Govind Buksh, and Karandikar.

[Proposed by Dr. Trailokyanath Mitra (Bengal), seconded by Mr. Hamid Ali (Oudh), supported by Mr. W. S. Gantz (Madras), and carried unanimously.]

Resolution II.

Resolved.—That this Congress re-affirms the necessity for the expansion and reform of the Council of the Governor-General for making Laws, and the Provincial Legislative Councils, already set forth in Resolutions III. of the Congresses of 1885 and 1886, and expresses the earnest hope that the Government will no longer delay action in the direction of this essential reform.

[Proposed by Mr. Surendra Nath Bannerjee (Bengal), seconded by Raja Sir T. Madhava Row, K.C.S.I. (Madras), supported by M.R.Ry. P. Somasundaram Chettiar (Madras), and carried unanimously.]

Resolution III.

Resolved.—That this Congress once again places on record an expression of the universal conviction, that a complete separation of the Executive and Judicial functions (such that in no case the two functions shall be combined in the same officer) has become an urgent necessity, and declares that, in its opinion, it behoves the Government to effect this separation without further delay, even though this should, in some Provinces, involve some extra expenditure.

[Proposed by Mr. N. Subramaniem (Madras), seconded by Babu Kali Charan Bannerjee (Bengal), supported by Mr. Hafiz Abdul Rahim (N.-W. Provinces), and carried unanimously.]

Resolution IV.

Resolved.—That in view of the loyalty of Her Majesty's Indian subjects, this Congress considers it desirable that the Queen's Proclamation should be given effect to; that the Military Service in its higher grades should be practically opened to the natives of this country, and that the Government of India should establish Military Colleges in this country, whereat the natives of India, as defined by Statute, may be educated and trained for a military career as officers of the Indian Army.

[Proposed by Babu Norendra Nath Sen (Bengal), seconded by Babu Saligram Singh (Behar), supported by Mr. Eardley Norton (Madras), and carried unanimously.]

Resolution V.

Resolved.—That in view of the unsettled state of public affairs in Europe, and the immense assistance that the people of this country, if duly prepared therefor, are capable of rendering to Great Britain in the event of any serious complications arising, this Congress once again earnestly appeals to the Government to authorize (under such rules and restrictions as may to it seem fitting) a system of volunteering for the Indian inhabitants of the country, such as may qualify them to support the Government effectively in any crisis.

[Proposed by C. Sankara Nair (Madras), seconded by Khan Bahadur Sheikh Ahmed Hussain Khan (Oudh), supported by Rajah Rampal Singh (N.-W. Provinces), and carried unanimously.]

Resolution VI.

Resolved.—That, as the administration of the Income Tax, especially as regards incomes below Rs.1,000, has proved extremely unsatisfactory, it is essential, in the opinion of the Congress, that the taxable minimum be raised to Rs.1,000, the loss of revenue thus involved being made good, and further financial difficulties, if any, met by reductions in the existing public expenditure, or, should this prove impossible, by the re-imposition of an import duty on the finer classes of cotton goods.

[Proposed by Babu Guru Prasad Sen (Behar), seconded by Babu Jogender Chander Ghose (Bengal), and carried unanimously.]

Resolution VII.

Resolved.—That having regard to the poverty of the people, it is desirable that the Government be moved to elaborate a system of Technical Education, suitable to the condition of the country, to encourage indigenous manufactures by a more strict observance of the orders already existing, in regard to utilizing such manufactures for State purposes, and to employ more extensively than at present the skill and talents of the people of the country.

[Proposed by Sir S. Ramaswami Mudaliar, C.I.E. (Madras), seconded by Mr. John Adam (Madras), supported by Sheikh Kadir Buksh (Oudh), and carried unanimously.]

Resolution VIII.

Resolved.—That in view of the loyalty of the people, the hardships which the present Arms Act (XI. of 1878) causes, and the unmerited slur which it casts upon the people of this country, the Government be moved so to modify the provisions of Chapter IV., and, if necessary, other portions of the said Act, as shall enable all persons to possess and wear arms, unless debarred therefrom, either as individuals or members of particular communities or classes, by the orders of the Government of India (or any local authority empowered by the Government of India on that behalf), for reasons to be recorded in writing and duly published.

[Proposed by Rao Bahadur Sabapathi Mudaliar (Madras), seconded by Babu Bipin Chandra Pal (Bengal), and carried unanimously.]

Resolution IX.

Resolved.—That the rules drafted by the Committee appointed under Resolution I. stand over for consideration till next Congress, but that, in the meantime, copies be circulated to all standing Congress Committees, with the request that they will, during the coming year, act in accordance with these rules, so far as this may seem to them possible and desirable, and report thereon to the next Congress, with such further suggestions as to them may seem meet.

[Proposed by Mr. A. O. Hume (Madras), seconded by Dr. Trailokya Nath Mitra (Bengal), and carried unanimously.]

Resolution X.

Resolved.—That the Fourth Indian National Congress assemble at Allahabad, on the 26th December, 1888.

[Proposed by Mr. A. O. Hume (Madras), seconded by Rajah Rampal Singh (N.-W. Provinces), and carried by acclamation.]

Resolution XI.

Resolved.—That copies of these Resolutions be forwarded to His Excelleucy the Viceroy in Council, with the humble request that he will cause all the Resolutions to be laid before Her Majesty's Secretary of State for India, and that he himself will be graciously pleased, in consultation with his colleagues, to accord them his best consideration.

[Proposed by Rajah Yatindra Nath Chaudhuri (Bengal), seconded by Babu Jotendra Nath Tagore (Bengal), and carried unanimously.]

(Signed) BUDRUDIN TYABJI,

President of the Third Indian National Congress.

DETAILED

REPORT OF THE PROCEEDINGS

OF THE

THIRD INDIAN NATIONAL CONGRESS,

HELD AT

MADRAS

On the 27th, 28th, 29th and 30th of December, 1887.

FIRST DAY'S PROCEEDINGS.

THE INAUGURAL MEETING of the Congress was held on the afternoon of the 27th December at the "Pandal," a vast temporary Hall, erected for the purpose in Mackay's Gardens, Madras.

The local enthusiasm was great, and from mid-day, or even before this, a huge crowd had assembled in the neighbourhood of the Hall. When the proceedings opened the Hall, which provided accommodation for about 1,500 spectators, besides the delegates, was closely packed, and probably almost an equal number of visitors were grouped round the Hall, which, being open at the sides. permitted most of the speeches to be fairly well heard, even by those outside.

The chair was taken by RAJAH SIR TANJORE MADHAVA ROW, K.C.S.I., &c., as Chairman of the Reception Committee, whose duty it was to welcome the Delegates and invite them to elect a President.

SIR T. MADHAVA ROW (Madras, No. 1 in List) rose and said :—Gentlemen,—The language of genuine pleasure is short. I am delighted to meet so many of my countrymen from so many parts of this extensive empire. (Applause.) The Congress, every one must now see, is a great success. In fact it seems, every time it meets, to outgrow its originally contemplated dimensions. My duty now is to offer a cordial welcome to the delegates assembled before me. (Loud applause.) It is a pleasant and a very agreeable duty, and I consider it a privilege—a great privilege—which has been conferred upon me by my colleagues of the Madras Congress Reception Committee, who have asked me to offer to you all, in their names, the warmest of welcomes. (Applause.)

Gentlemen, I am indeed glad that the state of my health,—of late, I regret to say, far from satisfactory,—has permitted my presence here to-day (applause) ; had it been otherwise, as I at one time feared, and had I been debarred from witnessing and aiding in this grand assemblage, I should have considered it one of the greatest misfortunes of my life. (Applause.) Owing to my feeble state of health I am unequal to the task of addressing, at any length, an assembly so very large as this. My failing voice, I fear, will reach but few of those thousands now assembled around me, as delegates and as earnest sympathisers in the work which those delegates have met to undertake, and yet, there are some things that I wish to say to all, and so, trusting to your indulgence to an old man, I have ventured to put on paper something of what I desire to lay before you, and, with your kind permission, I shall now hand this brief address to a younger and stronger friend, who will read it for me.

The following address was then read for SIR T. MADHAVA ROW by Mr. C. V. Sundaram Sastri, Madras, No. 77 in List :—

Gentlemen,—On behalf of the Congress Reception Committee, and on behalf of the citizens of Madras, I welcome you from the bottom of my heart.

Gentlemen, it is a matter of sincere congratulation that this city has been chosen for the meeting of the Congress this year: you may well imagine that Madras ardently coveted the honour which the sister cities of Bombay and Calcutta have already enjoyed. (Applause.)

Many of you have come down from very dist...t parts of the empire. We hope that your stay here will be comfortable, pleasant and interesting, and that when you have returned home you will retain a kindly remembrance of your brethren in this far-off part of India. (Applause.) It may be that we cannot compete with our Bombay brethren in the kindly care and the generous hospitality with which gentlemen from this part of the country were received at the first Congress. It may also be that we must despair of being able to imitate the princely character of the reception which was accorded to those who attended the second Congress, in the 'city of palaces. (Applause.) But if you are prepared to take the will for the deed,—as I trust you are,—you may rest assured that we gather you to our bosom with hearts as sympathetic as they are proud. (Loud cheers.)

That we should rejoice with pride to receive you, and that you should kindly consent to be our honoured guests is, gentlemen, I think, quite natural when we take into account the forces which have been at work among us, and the environment with which we have been surrounded by the wisdom, justice, and generosity of the British nation. (Applause.) Contact with such a nation is like the contact of iron with the magnet. It has the inevitable effect of the nation operated upon being, by insensible degrees, assimilated to the dominant type. Let cavillers at this view show me the people who, having been taught the lessons of liberty and enlightened statesmanship, did not, in due time, thirst for the blessings of freedom and good government. (Hear, hear.) Let them show me the community which, having been brought within the sphere of liberal education, did not wish and strive to secure a status consistent with such culture and necessitated by such discipline. Let them show me the land which is covered with a net-work of railways, spanned by telegraphic lines, and studded with post-offices, but which is not characterized by the dropping off, like autumn leaves, of local prejudices and home-bred idiosyncrasies. (Hear, hear.) Such a people and such a land can exist only in the reveries of a wild imagination,—at any rate, I cannot bring myself to believe that they could exist within the pale of that empire which has been beautifully described as the empire on which the sun never sets. (Hear, hear, and applause.) To a multitude of factors such as these the Indian community has been subjected for over fourscore years; and who can wonder that local differences are getting effaced, and that there is among us an earnest desire to recognise original identity of type and undoubted community of interests, and to fraternise and unite. Thus, then, it seems to me nothing strange, nothing phenomenal, that I should witness before me, in a vast and most influential assembly, the union of cultivated intelligence and patriotic ardour, and the confluence (so to speak) of many different streams of thought and of feeling. I see before me representatives from all parts of India, whose very personal appearance will bring home to the mind of the unprejudiced observer the conviction that, varied as are the castes and creeds and races of India, there is still a powerful bond of union which makes our hearts vibrate with sympathy and mutual love, and a common affection for our mother-country. (Loud and continued applause.) To well-balanced minds, such a gathering must appear the soundest triumph of British administration, and a crown of glory to the great British nation. (Great applause.)

Gentlemen, let us not mind too much, or too little, what unfriendly or rather mistaken critics may say against us.

Let us stand firm in our conviction that these gatherings are useful and desirable for a multitude of reasons. Let our single aim be to justify ourselves by invariable loyalty, good sense, and moderation in our thoughts, words, and deeds. These great qualities we have not to acquire afresh. Innumerable antecedent generations have happily bequeathed them to us. Let us retain this inheritance and trustfully place ourselves under the guidance of the great nation, and the great Government, which are providentially in charge of our destinies, and our future will be as satisfactory as it can possibly be.

Now that a splendid Empire has been constructed, completed and consolidated, now that unbroken peace and order have been established beyond the dreams of Asiatic philosophy, this Congress represents that very factor which is necessary for the further development of India. (Applause.)

From all that I have known of Englishmen, during half a century of intimate intercourse with the best of them, I have no hesitation in assuring you that your well-meant offer will not be superciliously rejected. (Hear, hear.)

Henceforth, let us therefore invariably act on the principle that the various populations of this extensive empire are bound together by a common Government, by common interests, and by mutual sympathies. (Applause.)

Judged most unsparingly, the worst features of gatherings of this description might be superabundance of enthusiasm and youthful impetuosity. But, as a great thinker has said, men learn to run before they learn to walk; they stagger and stumble before they acquire a steady use of their limbs. What is thus true of individuals is equally true of nations; and it is uncharitable to form a forecast of the future from the failings and weaknesses, if any such should exist, incidental to a nascent stage. The sentiments appropriate to such a condition of things are sympathy and kindly direction. An attitude of antagonism or of scorn only causes irritation and soreness; and it rouses, not unfrequently, a spirit of recrimination, if not also of answering disdain. This is almost a law of nature. I will, therefore, ask our critics to remember the early history of nations and to judge in a spirit of charity and magnanimity.

When I ask this of our censors, permit me to advise you to be moderate and forbearing. It is the nature of vaulting ambition to overleap itself. It is the character of renovated youth to be carried away by excessive zeal. Steer clear of such shoals and quicksands. Discuss without prejudice; judge without bias; and submit your proposals with the diffidence that must necessarily mark suggestions that are tentative in their character. Much irritation and retaliation will be avoided if the mutual dependence of the rulers and the ruled is steadily kept in view. With the ruled it must be a postulate that rulers err from ignorance and in spite of their efforts to avoid mistakes. By the rulers it must be taken for granted that when subjects petition and expostulate it is not in a spirit of disputation or cavilling, much less of disaffection and disloyalty—(hear, hear)—but only to enlighten those holding sway over them, and, in a peaceful and constitutional manner, to have their wishes understood and their grievances made known. I entreat you to lay to heart these words of caution to all parties concerned—words which I ask you to accept, out of regard for my long experience,—(applause)—for my age,—(applause)—and for my earnest desire to see my countrymen prosperous and happy.

Gentlemen, there are amongst you many men of distinguished attainments, of high culture, liberal views, sound judgment and sincere patriotism. The infirmities of age prevent me from enjoying the honour and discharging the duty of taking an active part in the discussions that you will enter upon. (Hear, hear.) Let me, therefore, call upon you to elect from among the multitude of wise and learned and earnest men that I see around me, a President, whose lead you may follow with perfect confidence, and whose force of character and sincere interest in the true well-being of the country, will lead to your deliberations being directed into such paths, and confined within such limits, as will secure to your conclusions the regard and attentive consideration of all right-minded men. I welcome you once again with a heart overflowing with joy and pride, and wish you "God-speed" in your generous and noble efforts to elevate the political and social condition of our common mother-land. (Loud and continued applause.) Proceed, then, to elect a President: and may the Almighty Disposer of all things grant that you command that success which you so richly deserve. (Loud applause.)

Mr. W. C. BONNERJEE (Calcutta, No. 546 in List) then rose and said:— Sir T. Madhava Row, and Gentlemen,—In response to the invitation of our honoured and worthy Chairman, I rise to propose that Mr. Budrudin Tyabji be elected—(loud applause)—the President of the National Congress for the year 1887, and I do so with peculiar pleasure—(applause)—both on personal and on public grounds. (Applause.) Mr. Tyabji is, I have no doubt, very well known to you as a distinguished member of the Bombay Bar—(hear, hear, and applause)—and a distinguished citizen of Bombay—a gentleman who has, in many trying circumstances, been of great service, not only to his own Presidency, but also to other parts of India. (Hear, hear and applause.)

I had the pleasure of being introduced to him as early as 1865—(applause)—when both he and I were students of the Middle Temple in England—(hear, hear)—trying to be called to the Bar, so that we might come back to our own country and do the best we could, both for ourselves and for that country. (Applause.) You see Mr. Tyabji before you, and I need hardly say that both in his public and private capacities the promise of his youth has been more than fulfilled. (Applause.) But, gentlemen, it is not simply upon personal grounds that I ask you to accept my nomination; Mr. Tyabji is, as I have told you, a well-known citizen of Bombay. (Applause.) But in this connection, it is necessary for me to remind you that he is also a Mahomedan gentleman. (Loud and continued applause.) I am very sorry indeed to have to say it, but there is no disguising the fact that in Bengal, in some quarters amongst our Mahomedan friends, some misapprehension as to the scope and objects of our National Congress still exists,—(hear, hear)—and it is absolutely necessary that that misapprehension should be removed,—(applause)—and that we should be in fact, as we are in thought, one community and one country, owing allegiance to one Sovereign. (Loud applause.) The misapprehension under which those Mahomedan gentlemen (some of them at least) labour who do not cordially sympathise with us, is due, I believe, to an apprehension that the question of "Representative Government" which was presented to the Congress of the year 1885, which was again pressed by the Congress of the year 1886, and which I believe will be once more urged by us here—(applause)—will not, if given effect to, practically prove to be conducive to the interests of the Mahomedan population of this country—(Voices of "No, No"). I am very glad to hear these murmurs of dissent from this assembly of delegates, a large number of whom, I see, are Mahomedans, because, I was just going to say that this apprehension was perfectly unfounded. There is nothing in the objects and scope of this National Congress which can, directly or indirectly, be in any way inimical to the interests of our Mahomedan fellow-countrymen, or of any other section of the community. (Prolonged applause.) We want a representative Government in its truest and best sense, and I for one—and I am speaking in this matter on behalf of, I believe, the whole of the Hindu delegates—(loud applause)—do not desire a hole-and-corner representation, but a representation of every community in the country—(hear, hear, and applause)—so that the whole of India may be perfectly represented to the governing authorities, so that their grievances may be remedied, so that everything necessary to make the nation contented and happy may be done by the governing authorities. (Applause.) It is not necessary for me to detain you at any length upon this subject as I see we are all agreed upon it. (Applause.) I have no doubt you will accept my nomination with the acclamation with which Mr. Tyabji's name was first received by you. (Loud and continued applause.)

THE HON. S. SUBRAHMANIA AIYAR (Madras, No. 5 in List) said:—Gentlemen,—It is my pleasant duty to second the proposition just moved by Mr. Bonnerjee. It is quite unnecessary, gentlemen, after his speech, for me to trouble you any further. I have only one word to say. You can easily conceive the pleasure and pride which I feel in having the honour of seconding the proposal that Mr. Tyabji be elected as our President when you remember that he is a distinguished ornament of the profession of one section of which I am an humble member. (Applause.)

RAJAH RAMPAL SINGH (N.-W. Prov., No. 484 in List,) said:—Gentlemen, I have been asked to speak as a delegate from the North-West Provinces on this subject, and to express my opinion. I have much pleasure in supporting—or I may say, speaking in favour of—this proposition. Mr. Bonnerjee has ably set forth Mr. Tyabji's public claims to our respect, and has feelingly dwelt on his long private acquaintance with that gentleman, whom you are going, as I hope, to elect as your President. Unfortunately for me, my acquaintance with the Hon. Mr. Tyabji has been but of short duration, but this one thing I can tell you in regard to him, and that is that all of us will be very pleased to see a Mahomedan gentleman presiding over us on this occasion—(applause)—as a Parsee gentleman did at the last Congress, and a Hindu at the first, so as to enable us to vindicate, even in this matter, the catholicity and nationality of our assemblage. The belief which has been expressed by some wise people (wise, at any rate, in their own conceits), and even, I may say, by some journals which I have read to-day, that Hindus and Mahomedans are not at one in this matter, is quite erroneous. (Hear, hear.) I can tell you, gentlemen, that Mahomedans and Hindus in my part of the country are so at one in this and all public matters, and so sympathising with each other, that during the Mohurrum we almost moved as one people, neglecting our own festivals, which happened at the same time. On the other hand, when small-pox and other epidemic diseases have afflicted the joint community, the Mahomedans sympathetically joined in the observances of the Hindus of their neighbourhood. (Hear, hear.) I might be contradicted here by some gentleman, who has acquired experience in places where either priesthood enjoys a marked predominance, but that does not alter the case that Hindus and Mahomedans, in parts of the country where there is no strong ecclesiastical element, live in perfect accord. (Hear, hear.) But I need not pursue the subject, and with the remark that Mr. Budrudin Tyabji is, I believe, the oldest and most distinguished of Indian Barristers, and his son, the youngest and most distinguished of Indian covenanted civilians, I urge you to adopt my friend Mr. W. C. Bonnerjee's proposal and elect Mr. Tyabji as President of this Congress. (Applause.)

SIR T. MADHAVA ROW, (Chairman), then asked if any one desired to propose any one else for President, and being answered in the negative by the whole assembly, put the proposal to the Congress, which was received and carried by acclamation amidst a perfect storm of cheers. The Chairman then declared Mr. Budrudin Tyabji duly elected, and, rising, led him and installed him in the Presidential chair.

MR. BUDRUDIN TYABJI, President, (Bombay, No. 361 in List), rose and said :—Rajah Sir T. Madhava Row and Gentlemen,—I thank you most sincerely for the very great honour you have done me by electing me President of this great national assembly. (Applause.) Gentlemen, it is impossible not to feel proud of the great distinction you have thus conferred upon me, the greatest distinction which it is in your power to confer upon any one of your countrymen. (Loud and continued applause.) Gentlemen, I have had the honour of witnessing great public meetings both in Bombay and elsewhere, but it is quite a novel sensation for me to appear before a meeting of this description—a meeting composed not merely of the representatives of any one city or even of one province—but of the whole of the vast continent of India, representing not any one class or interest but all classes (hear, hear, and applause) and all interests of the almost innumerable different communities that constitute the people of India. (Applause.)

Gentlemen, I had not the good fortune to be present at the proceedings of the first Congress, held in Bombay in 1885, nor had I the good fortune to take a part in the deliberations of the second Congress, held in Calcutta last year. But, gentlemen, I have carefully read the proceedings of both those Congresses, and I have no hesitation in declaring that they display an amount of talent, wisdom, and eloquence of which we have every reason to be proud. (Applause.)

Gentlemen, from the proceedings of the past two Congresses I think we are fairly entitled to hope that the proceedings of this present Congress will not only be marked by those virtues, but by that moderation and by that sobriety of judgment which is the offspring of political wisdom and political experience. (Applause.) Gentlemen, all the friends and well-wishers of India, and all those who take an interest in watching over the progress and prosperity of our people, have every reason to rejoice at the increasing success of each succeeding Congress. At the first Congress in Bombay, in 1885, we had less than 100 representatives from the different parts of India, in the second Congress, at Calcutta, in 1886, we had as many as 440 representatives, while at this Congress, I believe, we have over 600 delegates—(applause)—representing all the different parts and all the different communities of this great empire. I think, then, gentlemen, that we are fairly entitled to say that this is a truly representative national gathering. (Hear, hear, and applause.) Indeed, if that tentative form of representative institutions which has so often been asked for from Government were granted to us I have not the smallest doubt but that many of the gentlemen I now have the honour of addressing, would be elected by their respective constituencies to represent their interests. (Applause.)

Gentlemen, it has been urged in derogation of our character, as a representative national gathering, that one great and important community—the Mussulman community—has kept aloof from the proceedings of the two last Congresses. Now, gentlemen, in the first place, this is only partially true, and applies only to one particular part of India, and is moreover due to certain special, local, and temporary causes,—(hear, hear, and applause)—and in the second place, no such reproach can, I think, with any show of justice, be urged against this present Congress;—(applause) and gentlemen, I must honestly confess to you that one great motive which has induced me, in the present state of my health, to undertake the grave responsibilities of presiding over your deliberations, has been an earnest desire, on my part, to prove, as far as in my power lies, that I, at least, not merely in my individual capacity, but as representing the Anjuman-i-Islam of Bombay —(loud applause)—do not consider that there is anything whatever in the position or the relations of the different communities of India,—be they Hindus, Mussulmans, Parsees, or Christians—which should induce the leaders of any one community to stand aloof from the others in their efforts to obtain those great general reforms, those great general rights, which are for the common benefit of us all,—(hear, hear, and applause)—and which, I feel assured, have only to be earnestly and unanimously pressed upon Government to be granted to us.

Gentlemen, it is undoubtedly true that each one of our great Indian communities has its own peculiar social, moral, educational and even political difficulties to surmount, but so far as general political questions affecting the whole of India—such as those which alone are discussed by this Congress—are concerned, I, for one, am utterly at a loss to understand why Mussulmans should not work shoulder to shoulder—(hear, hear, and applause)—with their fellow-countrymen, of other races and creeds for the common benefit of all. (Applause.) Gentlemen, this is the principle on which we, in the Bombay Presidency, have always acted, and from the number, the character, the position, and the attainments of Mussulman delegates from the Bengal Presidency and from the Presidency of Madras, as well as from the North-West Provinces and the Punjab, I have not the smallest doubt that this is also the view held, with but few, though, perhaps, important, exceptions, by the leaders of the Mussulman communities throughout the whole of India. (Hear, hear and applause.)

Gentlemen, it has been urged as a slur upon our loyalty that this Congress is composed of what are called the educated natives of India. Now, if by this it is intended to be conveyed that we are merely a crowd of people with nothing but our education to commend us, if it is intended to be conveyed that the gentry, the nobility, and the aristocracy of the land have kept aloof from us, I can only meet that assertion by the most direct and the most absolute denial. (Hear, hear, and applause.) To any person who made that assertion I should feel inclined to say, Come with me into this Hall—(applause)—and look around you—(applause)—and tell me where you could wish to see a better representation of the aristocracy, not only of birth and of wealth, but of intellect, education, and position, than you see gathered within the walls of this Hall. (Applause.) But, gentlemen, if no such insinuation is intended to be made, I should only say that I am happy to think that this Congress does consist of the educated natives of India. (Hear, hear.)

Gentlemen, I, for one, am proud to be called not only educated but a "native" of this country. (Applause and hear, hear.) And, gentlemen, I should like to know, where among all the millions of Her Majesty's subjects in India are to be found more truly loyal, nay, more devoted friends, of the British empire than among these educated natives. (Loud and continued applause.) Gentlemen, to be a true and a sincere friend of the British Government, it is necessary that one should be in a position to appreciate the great blessings which that Government has conferred upon us, and I should like to know who is in a better position to appreciate these blessings—the ignorant peasants or the educated natives? Who, for instance, will better appreciate the advantages of good roads, railways, telegraphs and post offices, schools, colleges and universities, hospitals, good laws and impartial courts of justice?—the educated natives or the ignorant peasants of this country? (Applause.) Gentlemen, if there ever were to arise—which God forbid—any great struggle between Russia and Great Britain for supremacy in this country—who is more likely to judge better of the relative merits of the two empires? (Hear, hear.) Again I say, gentlemen, that in these matters it is the educated natives that are best qualified to judge, because it is we, who know and are best able to appreciate, for instance, the blessings of the right of public meeting, the liberty of action and of speech, and high education which we enjoy under Great Britain, whereas, probably, under Russia, we should have nothing but a haughty and despotic Government whose chief glory would consist in vast military organization, aggression upon our neighbours, and great military exploits. (Applause.)

No, gentlemen, let our opponents say what they please, we, the educated natives, by the mere force of our education, must be the best appreciators of the blessings of a civilized and enlightened Government, and therefore, in our own interests, the best and staunchest supporters of the British Government in India. (Applause.) But, gentlemen, do those who thus charge us with disloyalty stop for a moment to consider the full meaning and effect of their argument,—do they realise the full import and significance of the assertion they make? Do they understand that, in charging us with disloyalty, they are, in reality, condemning and denouncing the very Government which it is their intention to support. (Hear, hear, loud and continued applause.) For, gentlemen, when they say that the educated natives of India are disloyal, what does it mean? It means this: that in the opinion of the educated natives,—that is to say, of all the men of light and leading, all those who have received a sound, liberal and enlightened education, all those who are acquainted with the history of their own country and with the nature of the present and past governments, that in the opinion of all these—the English Government is so bad that it has deserved to forfeit the confidence and the loyalty of the thinking part of the population. (Hear, hear, and applause.) Now, gentlemen, is it conceivable that a more frightful and unjust condemnation of the British Government can be pronounced than is implied in this charge of disloyalty against the educated natives of India? Gentlemen, if this charge were brought by some bitter enemies of Great Britain, if it were brought by the Russians—for example—I could understand it. (Hear, hear). But it is almost beyond my comprehension that it should come, not from enemies, but from the supposed friends of the British Government,—(loud laughter, and hear, hear)—not from the Russians, but from Englishmen—(hear, hear)—who presumably want, not to destroy, but to support, their Government! I say it surpasses my comprehension. (Loud applause.) Gentlemen, just consider for a moment the effect of this reckless allegation upon the uneducated millions of the inhabitants of this country, upon the hordes of the Russians in the North, and upon the enlightened nations of Europe! I say, therefore, that the conduct of those who thus recklessly charge us with disloyalty resembles the conduct of the foolish woodman who was lopping off the very branch of the tree upon which he was standing,—(hear, hear, loud applause and loud laughter)—unconscious that the destruction of the branch meant the destruction of himself. (Applause and laughter.)

Happily, however, gentlemen, this allegation is as absurd as it is unfounded. It is as unjust to us as it is unjust to the Government it impeaches. But, though, gentlemen, I maintain that the educated natives, as a class, are loyal to the backbone, (hear, hear,) I must yet admit that some of our countrymen are not always guarded, not always cautious, in the language they employ. I must admit that some of them do sometimes afford openings for hostile criticisms, and I must say that I have myself observed in some of the Indian newspapers and in the speeches of public speakers, sentiments and expressions which are calculated to lead one to the conclusion that they have not fully realised the distinction between license and liberty; that they have not wholly grasped the lesson that freedom has its responsibilities no less than its privileges. (Hear, hear.) And, therefore, gentlemen, I trust that not only during the debates of this Congress, but on all occasions, we shall ever bear in mind and ever impress upon our countrymen that, if we are to enjoy the right of public discussion, the liberty of speech, and liberty of the press, we must so conduct ourselves as to demonstrate by our conduct, by our moderation, by the justness of our criticisms, that we fully deserve these—the greatest—blessings which an enlightened Government can confer upon its subjects. (Hear, hear, and applause.)

Gentlemen, it has been sometimes urged that Europeans in this country do not fully sympathize with the just aspirations of the natives of India. In the first place, this is not universally true, because I have the good fortune to know many Europeans than whom truer or more devoted friends of India do not breathe on the face of the earth. (Hear, hear, and applause.) And, in the second place, we must be prepared to make very considerable allowances for our European fellow-subjects, because their position in this country is surrounded by difficult and complicated questions not merely of a political but of a social character, which tend more or less to keep the two communities asunder in spite of the best efforts of the leaders of European no less than of native society. Gentlemen, so long as our European friends come to this country as merely temporary residents, so long as they come here merely for the purposes of trade, commerce, or of a profession, so long as they do not look upon India as a country in whose welfare they are permanently interested, so long it will be impossible for us to expect that the majority of the Europeans should fraternize with us upon all great public questions,—(hear, hear)—and it has, therefore, always seemed to me that one of the greatest, the most difficult, the most complicated, and, at the same time, one of the most important, problems to be solved is how to make our European friends look upon India as in some sense their own country, even by adoption. For, gentlemen, if we could but induce our retired merchants, engineers, doctors, solicitors, barristers, judges and civilians, to make India permanently their home,—(hear, hear, and applause)—what an amount of talent and ability, political experience and ripe judgment, we should retain in India for the benefit of us all. (Applause.) All those great questions in regard to the financial drain on India and those questions arising from jealousy of races and the rivalry for public employment would at once disappear. And when we speak of the poverty of India, because of the draining away of vast sums of money from India to England, it has always seemed to me strange, that so little thought should be bestowed upon the question of the poverty of our resources caused by the drain of so many men of public, political, and intellectual eminence from our shores every year. (Applause.)

Now, gentlemen, one word as to the scope of our action and deliberations. It has been urged—solemnly urged—as an objection against our proceedings that this Congress does not discuss the question of Social Reform. But gentlemen, this matter has already been fully dealt with by my friend, Mr. Dadabhai Naoroji,* who presided over your deliberations last year. And I must confess that the objection seems to me strange seeing that this Congress is composed of

* The passage alluded to in Mr. Dadabhai's presidential address for 1886, runs as follows :—

"It has been asserted that this Congress ought to take up questions of social reforms, (cheers and cries of 'Yes, Yes') and our failure to do this has been urged as a reproach against us. Certainly no member of this National Congress is more alive to the necessity of social reforms than I am ; but, gentlemen, for everything there are proper times, proper circumstances, proper parties and proper places ; (cheers)—we are met together as a political body to represent to our rulers our political aspirations, not to discuss social reforms, and if you blame us for ignoring these you should equally blame the House of Commons for not discussing the abstruser problems of mathematics or metaphysics. But, besides this, there are here Hindus of every caste, amongst whom, even in the same provinces, customs and social arrangements differ widely,—there are Mahomedans and Christians of various denominations, Parsis, Sikhs, Brahmos and what not—men indeed of each and all of those numerous classes which constitute in the aggregate the people of India. (Loud cheers.) How can this gathering of all classes discuss the social reforms needed in each individual class? What do any of us know of the internal home life, of the customs, traditions, feelings, prejudices of any class but our own? How could a gathering, a cosmopolitan gathering, like this, discuss to any purpose the reforms needed in any one class? Only the members of that class can effectively deal with the reforms therein needed. A National Congress must confine itself to questions in which the entire nation has a direct participation, and it must leave the adjustment of social reforms and other class questions to class Congresses. But it does not follow that, because this national, political body does not presume to discuss social reforms, the delegates here present are not just as deeply, nay, in many cases far more deeply, interested in these questions than in those political questions we do discuss, or that those several communities whom those delegates represent are not doing their utmost to solve those complicated problems on which hinge the practical introduction of those reforms. Any man who has eyes and ears open must know what struggles towards higher and better things are going on in every community: and it could not be otherwise with the noble education we are receiving. Once you begin to think about your own actions, your duties and responsibilities to yourself, your neighbours, and your nation, you cannot avoid looking round and observing much that is wrong amongst you ; and we know as a fact that each community is now doing its best according to its light, and the progress it has made in education. I need not, I think, particularize. The Mahomedans know what is being done by persons of their community to push on the education their brethren so much need ; the Hindus are everywhere doing what they can to reform those social institutions which they think require improvement. There is not one single community here represented of which the best and ablest men do not feel that much has to be done to improve the social, moral, religious status of their brethren, and in which, as a fact, they are not striving to effect, gradually, those needful improvements ; but these are essentially matters too delicate for a stranger's handling—matters which must be left to the guidance of those who alone fully understand them in all their bearings, and which are wholly unsuited to discussion in an assemblage like this, in which all classes are intermingled." (Loud cheers.)

the representatives, not of any one class or community, not of one part of India, but of all the different parts, and of all the different classes, and of all the different communities of India. Whereas any question of Social Reform must of necessity affect some particular part or some particular community of India only,—and, therefore, gentlemen, it seems to me that, although we Mussulmans have our own social problems to solve, just as our Hindu and Parsee friends have theirs, yet these questions can be best dealt with by the leaders of the particular communities to which they relate. (Applause.) I, therefore, think, gentlemen, that the only wise, and, indeed the only possible, course we can adopt is to confine our discussions to such questions as affect the whole of India at large, and to abstain from the discussion of questions that affect a particular part or a particular community only. (Loud applause.)

Gentlemen, I do not, at present at least, propose to say anything upon the various problems that will be submitted to you for your consideration. I have no doubt that the questions will be discussed in a manner and in a spirit that will reflect credit upon us all. I will only say this: be moderate in your demands, be just in your criticism, be accurate in your facts, be logical in your conclusions, and you may rest assured that any propositions you may make to our rulers will be received with that benign consideration which is the characteristic of a strong and enlightened Government. (Applause.) And now, gentlemen, I fear, I have already trespassed (voices of 'No, No,') too long upon your time. Before I sit down, I will once more offer to you my thanks from the very bottom of my heart for the very great honour you have done me, and I pray to God that I may be enabled, in some measure at least, to deserve your approbation and justify the choice you have made and the confidence you have reposed in me. (Loud applause.) Gentlemen, I wish this Congress and all succeeding Congresses every success and every prosperity. (Applause.)

I am very glad to see the representatives of so many different communities and parts of India gathered together this afternoon before us. This, in itself, gentlemen, is no small advantage that we, as representatives of the different parts of India, should have the opportunity of meeting and discussing together the various problems that affect us all. (Applause.) Gentlemen, I will not take up much more of your time. I say, as our chairman, Sir T. Madhava Row, has said, I welcome you here—but at the same time I cannot help expressing my deep regret, a regret that I know you all share, that on this occasion we are deprived of the aid and counsel of some of those gentlemen who laboured most earnestly for and who graced with their presence the Congress on previous occasions, and who have now, all too soon for their country's sake, passed from amongst us. Among the friends we have lost are Dr. Athalye of Bombay and Madras, who took such an energetic part in the first Congress, held in Bombay in the year 1885, and Mr. Girija Bhusan Mookerjee whom you all know, and whom all who knew, loved and respected, and who was one of the most active workers for the Congress held in Calcutta last year. Then, too, we have to mourn the loss of Mr. Dayaram Jethmall, the founder of the National Party in Sind, and a distinguished gentleman belonging to this Presidency, (though I fear I am not in a position to pronounce his name correctly), Mr. Singaraju Venkata Subbaroyudu, of Masulipatam. But, to all these gentlemen, of whose assistance and guidance we have been deprived, we must owe a lasting debt of gratitude. They in their lifetime spared no pains to make the Congress, either in Bombay or Calcutta, a success, as far as in their power lay, and it only remains for us, while cherishing their memories, to emulate their example. (Loud and continued applause.)

Gentlemen, in addition to those of you who have been able to come to Madras, we have received numerous letters and telegrams from associations of various kinds, and from a large number of representative men in other parts of India, who, for some reason or other, have been debarred from being represented at or attending this Congress. We have received telegrams from Hyderabad, from all kinds of places in the Madras Presidency,—the names of which I shall not venture to pronounce,—from Kurrachi, Calcutta, Dehra Dhun, Sambhur, Bangalore, Dacca, from His Highness the Maharaja of Durbungah, Messrs. Lal Mohun and Mano Mohan Ghose, Mr. Telang, and a vast number of other places and persons too numerous for me to pretend to recapitulate. There are no less than sixty odd telegrams alone placed before me. But, gentlemen, there is one among those which I am particularly anxious to bring to your notice, and that is from our old and distinguished friend, Mr. Atkins (laughter), whom by name, at least, I have not the smallest doubt every one of us here perfectly knows. (Applause.) Gentlemen, in his telegram, he wishes this

Congress and all future Congresses perfect success. (Applause.) He wishes that the unity of the different communities should be promoted, and that the objects which we all have at heart should be attained. (Applause.) I think you will be of opinion that that is a very good omen. We want the assistance not only of representative men of the Indian communities but we also want the assistance of Europeans. (Applause.) Gentlemen, while we are attempting to learn some few lessons in the art of Self-Government, our European friends have inherited that art from their forefathers after centuries of experience, and it cannot be doubted that if we can induce our European friends to co-operate with us in these various political matters, which in point of fact affect them no less than they affect us, it cannot, I say, be doubted that it will conduce to the advantage, not only of ourselves, but of the European community also. (Loud applause.)

Gentlemen, before we can actually proceed with our deliberations, it will be necessary to have a programme carefully prepared, and the best course we can adopt is to appoint a Committee, whose duty it will be to look over the various suggestions that have come from the different parts of India and to prepare a workable programme which will be laid before you for discussion and deliberation. I, therefore, propose that the gentlemen whose names I will presently read out to you do form themselves into a Committee in order to draw up a programme of the work which is to be first brought before the Congress. The names are :—

Bengal, Assam and Orissa.—Mr. W. C. Bonnerjee, Babus Trailokya Nath Mitra, Surendra Nath Bannerjee and Norendra Nath Sen.

Behar.—Babus Saligram Singh and Guru Prasad Sen.

Bombay and Sindh.—Messrs. Chandavarkar, Khare, Dhruva, Nam Joshi, and Gobind Buksh.

North-West Provinces and Oudh.—Moulvi Hamid Ali, Rajah Rampal Singh, Babu Ram Kali Chaudhuri and Pandit Madan Mohan Malaviya.

Punjab.—Pandit Satyanand Agnihotri and Lalla Murlidhur.

Madras.—Messrs. Hume, Sabapathi Mudaliar, Sankara Nair and W. S. Gantz. (Loud and continued applause)

These gentlemen, whom I see you have accepted for this duty, will frame the necessary programme, and it will be laid before you to-morrow, after which we shall proceed, at noon precisely, with our deliberations, and I hope I shall then have the pleasure of not only seeing you all again, but also those other delegates (and there are still some more to come from Bombay, and, perhaps, other parts of India) who have not as yet arrived. (Loud applause.) I think it is desirable that the gentlemen whose names I have read out, instead of dispersing, should at once meet together and proceed with the business that has been entrusted to them. (Loud and continued applause.)

Mr. W. C. Bonnerjee (Bengal, No. 546 in list) rose and said : Gentlemen, I wish to say one word to you before you disperse. Mr. Eardley Norton, one of our brother-delegates, has been good enough to organise an evening entertainment for us all on the 29th, and he wishes to ask you all to be good enough to honour this entertainment with your presence. (Loud applause.)

Loud and prolonged cheers were then given for the President, handkerchiefs and hats were waved, and gradually the great gathering dispersed and the Select Committee were left to their labours.

SECOND DAY'S PROCEEDINGS.

Wednesday, 28th December, 1887.

The delegates having assembled, and order having been established amidst the vast crowd of visitors, THE PRESIDENT, MR. BUDRUDIN TYABJI rose and said :—Gentlemen, since we rose last evening we have received several additional telegrams from various gentlemen from several parts of India, sympathising with us in our efforts and wishing success to this Congress. I need not read those telegrams, but I think it right to announce the fact to you. Another matter I wish to mention is that the Committee appointed yesterday to frame a programme of business for the Congress has completed its work. The programme has been sent to be printed, and as soon as it comes to hand, and we are expecting it every minute, it will be placed in the hands of all the delegates present. I think, therefore, we had better proceed in accordance with the programme, of which a few copies have already come to hand, and I will therefore call upon my friend on my left to move the first Resolution, in regard to the appointment of a certain Committee. (Applause.)

DR. TRAILOKYA NATH MITRA (Bengal, No. 549 in List) rose and said : Mr. President and Brother Delegates,—It is a very simple and, at the same time, a very agreeable duty that I have been called upon to perform. I have to move—

"That a Committee be appointed consisting of the following gentlemen to consider what rules, if any, may now be usefully framed in regard to the constitution and working of the Congress, with instructions to report thereon to the Congress on the 30th instant." The names of the proposed Committee men are :—*Messrs. Namjoshi, Chandavarkar, Mir Humayun Jah Bahadur, Hajee Mahomed Abdul Shakoor Badshaw Saheb, S. Subramania Iyer, W. S. Gantz, P. Rangiah Naidu, Surendra Nath Bannerjee, Kalicharan Bannerjee, Guru Prasad Sen, Saligram Singh, Ram Kali Chaudhuri, Hafiz Abdul Rahim, Rampal Singh, M. M. Malaviya, Ganga Persad Varma, Bishen Narayen Dar, Hamid Ali, Murlidhur, Satyanand Agnihotri, H. H. Dhruva, W. C. Bonnerjee, Norendra Nath Sen, Eardley Norton, Joy Gobind Shome, Iswari Lal Sircar, G. Subramania Iyer, D. A. Khare, S. A. Saminada Iyer, Sabapathi Mudaliar, A. O. Hume, Vijaya Raghava Chariar, and Gobind Buksh.*

Speaking for myself, gentlemen, I should say that we ought to have some sort of constitution for this great assembly. (Hear, hear, and applause.) A constitutional assembly without a constitution is a sort of misnomer and inconsistency, and it may be a logical absurdity. Therefore we ought, it seems to me, to have some rules as to who our delegates are to be, how they are to be elected, and how certified to. We ought to have some rules as to the procedure to be followed in this assembly, and as to other similar matters. The rules must, of course, in the beginning, be very simple indeed, embodying the existing practice as far as possible, and giving, as it were, the force of law to custom. They must not be hard and fast rules that will prematurely bind us down to any special scheme ; ours is a young and growing institution, and if our constitution is really to fit us it must grow with us ; but there must be some very simple temporary rules as to the selection of delegates and as to the working of the Congress. That is all, I think, that we ought, at this very early stage of our career, to attempt. We may avoid, by this, one serious objection that has been raised to this National Congress. It has been said that this National Congress is a sort of mutual admiration society (voices of "No, No"), consisting of a number of self-constituted delegates, each one appointed by himself as his own delegate without any sort of representation whatever. If, by our rules, we can show to our critics that the men whom we allow to take part in the deliberations of this assembly are, as we all know that they are, men duly elected either by public bodies at general meetings, or by towns or groups of towns at public meetings, and if we can thus convince them that the delegates who take part in the deliberations of this great assembly are men who have the confidence of important groups of their countrymen all over this vast empire, shall we not be sufficiently answering our unkindly critics? (Applause.)

If it be only for this purpose and for nothing else, I think we should have some rules defining and making public a knowledge of our constitution, such as it is, and the procedure which we really adopt. I have read to you the names of the gentlemen to whom it is proposed to entrust this work. These gentlemen have been carefully selected by the Committee that was appointed by you last evening to frame the programme for this Congress's proceedings. The names will, I hope, be accepted as those of really representative men, of people who are entitled to speak and advise in this matter with some authority, each one of them having already studied the question and having more or less discussed it with his fellow co-provincial delegates. You will therefore, I have little doubt, adopt this first Resolution which I have had the honour to propose to you.

Mr. Hamid Ali (Lucknow, No. 520 in List), in seconding the motion, said: Mr. President and brother delegates, I have much pleasure in seconding the Resolution, and the fact that I am a purely orthodox Mahomedan (applause), though I am afraid I look more like a Christian (applause), adds infinitely to the pleasure I feel in advocating the expediency and the wisdom of this Resolution. I really think that there can be hardly any two opinions on this subject. The necessity of crystalizing existing practice, if only for a season, into tangible rules and regulations (that all who read may understand) for the working and constitution of this Congress is, I believe, as generally admitted in the mis-called "benighted" Presidency of Madras, in the enlightened Presidency of Bombay, and in the eloquent and cultured Presidency of Bengal, as it is in the backward Provinces of the North-West Provinces, Oudh and other remote parts of India.

And, here I may say, on the part of the Mahomedans of Oudh, that we have felt this necessity in a peculiar and painful degree. For, in our out-of-the-way part of the country we hardly knew what was going on in the more advanced portions, and felt by no means sure that we were electing men properly and the like, and yet, having as near neighbours co-religionists by no means friendly to this movement, we were specially anxious to avoid any laches that might give them a handle for reviling us. And, here, I hope you will forgive me, if I digress for a moment, and say that to my mind the Mahomedans and Hindus are, as it were, the two eyes of India. (Applause.) The policy of such of our co-religionists as assume an unfriendly attitude towards the Congress has a tendency to make our dear India a poor one-eyed creature, while, on the other hand, the far-sighted policy of Mr. Budrudin Tyabji and the Bombay Mahomedans, of Mir Humayun Jah and the Madras Mahomedans, and of some, at any rate, of the ablest Mahomedan gentlemen of Bengal, Oudh, the North-West Provinces and the Punjab, is calculated to allow our mother-land to retain her vision unimpaired, and it is their example that has prevented the rest of us from blindly—as a poet, I am pursuing the metaphor—following the suicidal policy of those two or three able, but short-sighted, leaders, to whose unhappy defection from the national cause Mr. Budrudin Tyabji referred, in kindly and eloquent language, in his yesterday's speech. I hope I may say that, in regard to those great subjects upon which the mind of the country is already made up, in regard, in fact, to those subjects which have heretofore occupied the consideration of this Congress, there is absolutely no different platform for Hindus and Mahomedans, but one common platform where there is ample room for both. (Applause.)

But, to return, the time has arrived, it seems to me, for defining to a certain extent our constitution, and laying down some simple and definite, though not stringent, rules for regulating the representation at, and the methods of procedure in, the Congress. I have not the smallest doubt that most of you will concur in this view, and that without any further discussion you will adopt the proposition which has been laid before you by my able friend, Dr. Trailokya Nath Mitra.

Mr. W. S. Gantz (Madras, No. 52 in List) said: Mr. President and Gentlemen, I have very great pleasure in supporting this proposition, if indeed, after the two able speeches which you have heard, it can be said that any support is necessary. I think, gentlemen, that the most powerful argument that I can appeal to in support of this proposition is—this vast assembly that I see before me. Gentlemen, it is not a figure of speech, it is no exaggeration to say, that this Congress is now a great national factor. (Applause.) Two years ago, when the son of one of the greatest statesmen the world then knew happened to be travelling through this country, he visited one of these Congresses—the very first one, I think, and he went home and described it as a factor which every Government should hereafter take account of. (Applause.) Gentlemen, that was when this movement was not merely in its infancy, but, as it were, a mere babe of an hour old. (Applause.) Since then it has grown and grown apace at a rate which few could have anticipated, and therefore, since the Congress has become, and will, year by year, increase and still more become, a great factor in the progress of this vast empire, we are now bound not only to make clear to the world what it is and how it works, but, further, to consider carefully all means and steps and ways whereby its business may be carried out from year to year more efficiently and effectively. (Loud applause.) And, therefore, gentlemen, it seems to me that one of the first things we ought to do is to try to fix upon certain rules—not hard and fast, gentlemen, but necessarily at first somewhat elastic—by a general adherence to which we may hope to render the working of this movement more successful and efficient.

But, gentlemen, there are many other considerations which render the proposition now before you deserving of your acceptance. These large Congresses are simply annual, and they are held in different places at the very end of the year, and then the Congress disperses, and in most provinces (of course, I speak subject to correction) no very great amount of work is done between the dispersing of one and the meeting of another Congress. But if we can constitute ourselves into smaller Committees or Sub-divisions, so to speak, of this Congress, working under something like definite rules, and as such continue our work throughout the year, I am in great hopes that before we next meet we may be able to lay down our procedure and define our position in a much more satisfactory way than we are able to do at present, for we shall then have had a practical experience of our difficulties and requirements, far beyond what we now possess, and shall be in a position to begin building on the rough foundations that we are now asking you to lay. Gentlemen, I need not detain you longer, because the proposition is one which must, I think, commend itself to you as a deliberative assembly which is not intended to be merely a deliberative assembly, of which it may be said that beyond passing Resolutions it does nothing, but an assembly of which before long it will have to be conceded that throughout the year it labours to bring about those results that, at its great annual meeting, it decides to be desirable. (Applause.)

Babu Surendra Nath Bannerjee (Calcutta, No. 550 in list) said: Mr. President, I desire to supply one little omission. I think that the name of the mover should be included in the list of Committeemen, and I therefore propose that the name of Dr. Trailokya Nath be added to the list.

This proposal was received with loud acclamations, and, although never formally seconded or put, was accepted as carried.

The President then rose and said: Before any further discussion is allowed upon this general proposition it is necessary for me to inform you that a copy of an amendment has been handed to me, coming, apparently, from a delegate from the Bombay Presidency. I do not know whether the gentleman, whose name I find here, is now prepared to move the amendment, but I will call upon Mr. Karandikar to say what he has to say. The amendment runs thus: "That the words 'if any,' in line 2, and the words 'constitution and,' in line 3, be omitted."

Mr. Raghunath Pandurang Karandikar (Bombay, No. 409 in list) said: Mr. President and Gentlemen, Of course, it is no great wonder if I feel myself placed in a rather awkward position in having to propose an amendment on a Resolution which has been so ably proposed by Dr. Trailokya Nath, seconded by Mr. Hamid Ali, and supported by Mr. Gantz. But then, gentlemen, it is the business of every delegate who has been sent here by any constituency whatsoever, under our existing rules—rules not as yet laid down in black and white—it is the business, I say, of every delegate to speak up, and not be silent (hear, hear), when he has to say anything against a proposition before the assembly, and, with that view, and simply with that view (I am open to correction if I am wrong) I rise, though I do not rise without a considerable amount of hesitation, to address you. The amendment I have to move is this: That the words "if any," in line 2, and the words "constitution and," in line 3, be omitted.

Gentlemen, you will perhaps agree with me in thinking that such an important duty as the business of determining whether there ought to be a constitution for this National Congress or not, should not be entrusted to a mere Committee, however important its members may be in character and personage. I should like to have the sense of the whole meeting taken on the subject, whether the constitution of the Congress ought to be fixed upon by the Committee appointed or by the Congress itself. It is a difficult task, however, to have the opinion taken, and I believe if you are prepared to open that question, the question should not go to the Committee but should be answered either in the negative or affirmative by the Congress, and then I believe you will have done a great part of the business that will have to be entrusted to the Committee. Because the first part of the proposition, which provides for the consideration of the rules, carefully inserts the words "if any"; there, you will mark, a certain amount of diffidence in the mind of the person proposing this Resolution, and also, I may say, a corollary to this in the minds of the persons seconding and supporting the same Resolution. If it is fixed and resolved to have a constitution for the Congress, let us omit, for justice sake, the words "if any."

Well, gentlemen, we have again to think over another most important factor in this Resolution. It is whether we ought to accept, from the Committee appointed, I believe, of no less than forty personages—distinguished personages, no doubt,—a report upon such an important matter as the constitution in such a short space of time as three days. You will remember the Committee is to be appointed "to report thereon to the Congress on the 30th instant." I believe there is not a more important question affecting the cause than the constitution of the Congress, and I submit—with all due deference to the arguments offered in support of the Resolution and also in seconding it—I submit that more time and more thought ought to be devoted to such an important subject as the constitution of the Congress. (Applause.) It was especially because of this consideration that I have made myself bold enough to come forward, though it was not quite within my power to refute the arguments so ably set forth by Dr. Trailokya Nath Mitra and others. I trust you will, however, take into consideration the few sentences I have been able to offer for your consideration. Well, then, to proceed further about the constitution of the Congress. We have held a Congress in Bombay in 1885, and another more splendid one, no doubt, in Calcutta, in 1886, and one still more splendid here, in 1887. But, gentlemen, there are other presidencies and provinces which have yet to learn the needful lesson by the enlightening presence of the Congress—for instance, we may have a Congress in Allahabad next year, and another in the Punjab in the following year,—and just as the people of the Madras Presidency have evinced an amount of interest and zeal we may be able to observe further development in the interest from the people of the Punjab and the people of the North-West Provinces. I do not mean to say that they are lacking in that energy and spirit and zeal which is necessary and which marks the whole character of our National Congress. But what I mean is, that we ought to bring the Congress nearer home to the people of these other presidencies, and to give them an opportunity of witnessing the working of such vast numbers of delegates as we have before us now; to learn, in fact, the lessons of the Congress by practical personal experience before we ask them, through their representatives, to join in framing any constitution. Well, then, it was on this account that I have risen, with due deference to the arguments you have heard from previous speakers, to propose this amendment for your kind consideration.

A Delegate (name not ascertained) here rose in his seat and said: "I want to know what a constitution is. Will somebody define it?" (Cries of "Look in your Dictionary," "This is not a school," and "Sit down.")

The President said: The amendment before the meeting must first be seconded, if anybody intends to second it, before any discussion on the subject can be allowed.

A Delegate: But what's the use of talking about things one does not understand? I want a constitution defined; it may mean anything (cries of "No, No"). But I say it may.

The PRESIDENT said: You will have full opportunity, later, of saying whatever you wish to say, but I must now request you, Sir, to resume your seat.

Mr. A. RAMACHANDRA JOGLEKAR (Bombay, No. 430 in list) rose and said: Sir, I beg to second the amendment, and in seconding, I will only offer a single remark as to the necessity or otherwise of framing a constitution. We have as yet only made a beginning. We have had two Congresses, one in Bombay and one in Calcutta, within two years, and this is only the third Congress. No doubt, before long, we shall feel the necessity of a formal constitution. People will require to know exactly what our rules are and what the constitution of the Congress is. But my learned friend suggested the holding of Congresses in Allahabad and in the Punjab, and I must say I think that the populations of all the great provinces must have been enabled to realise what these Congresses are, must have had an actual practical experience of their working, and must have become one with us of Bombay, Madras, and Calcutta in our knowledge of them, before it is expedient to set to work to establish a constitution. I do not, of course, object to the framing of rules for the working of the Congress when it has met, but all else I would leave to local discretion until the whole country really knows, by practical experience, what is needful, and I see no use in embodying existing practice, which we may hope to improve year by year, in anything so formal as a constitution.

Mr. RAMACHANDRA MORESHWAR SANE (Bombay, No. 403 in list) then said: Mr. President, I rise to support the amendment which has just now been proposed by my friend, Mr. Karandikar. I do not wish to take up your time by advancing the same arguments that he has done. If we take into consideration the very varied political and intellectual development of the different Provinces of India, I believe you will agree with me in thinking that we have not yet arrived at a stage at which uniform constitutional rules are possible or desirable. Let this annual gathering be held in all provinces. Let the people of all provinces grow into taking an equally absorbing interest in the movement, and then perhaps we may arrive at a stage when the laying down of definite rules would be proper; otherwise if we have rules for working the Congress now, we shall continually have to make alterations in and additions to them, as difficulties crop up and we gain experience. Is this worth while? I think not. We are proceeding on a certain system, but, until we completely elaborate it, why seek to codify it in a constitution?

The PRESIDENT then rose and said: Gentlemen, Before we discuss the proposition before us any further, I trust you will bear with me if I venture to point out what seems to me a misapprehension on the part of the gentlemen who moved, seconded, and supported the amendment. I myself have not the smallest doubt that every one of the delegates here is prepared to welcome in the highest degree any and the fullest discussion on every proposition that may be brought forward. (Loud applause.) And, therefore, so far from deprecating any discussion or deprecating any amendment that may be brought forward, I welcome every amendment, and I desire the amplest discussion on every Resolution and amendment that comes up before the meeting. But before this amendment is pressed further,—and if it is pressed further, of course, it must be discussed,—before we proceed further, I would appeal to the gentlemen who have moved and seconded the amendment to consider whether the amendment has not been proposed under some misapprehension, and that misapprehension seems to be this:—they seem to suppose that, simply by the appointment of a Committee to consider whether any rules are necessary in regard to a constitution, this Congress at this present meeting binds itself to accept the rules, if any, that may be framed by that Committee. But this is not so. What is referred to the Committee is to consider whether any rules are necessary. (Hear, hear.) That will be the first thing. They may come to either conclusion;—they may agree with the proposer and seconder of this amendment that, in the present infantile stage of the Congress movements, it is not necessary to frame any rules in regard to its constitution. On the other hand, they may consider that some rules are necessary, and then, in that case, they will suggest the rules that they may think necessary. But ultimately, and before the rules can have any force, they must be submitted to the Congress itself. (Hear, hear, and applause.) And, therefore, I now appeal to the mover and seconder to inform me whether they still press their amendment, because if they do, then I must say, with reference to other speakers, that the discussion must proceed, both upon the original proposition and upon the amendment, and I will then take votes on the question. What do you say, Mr. Karandikar, do you press the amendment?

Mr. Karandikar (Bombay, No. 409 in list) said: In order to express myself fully, I shall have to take up a few minutes of your time. I should prefer to defer my remarks until the 30th instant.

The President: Either you must withdraw your amendment now, or press it.

Mr. Karandikar: Then I withdraw it. (Applause.)

The President: I hope it is not withdrawn under the impression that any pressure has been put on anybody? (Voices, "No, No," and applause.)

The President: If it is the sense of this meeting that the amendment should be withdrawn, as it apparently is from the acclamations I have heard, then there is no amendment now before the meeting upon which any speaking is necessary; but still it is open to any of you who desire to speak, if you still think it necessary to speak, upon the original proposition and point out anything in it which you think objectionable or susceptible of improvement. If you will allow me to say it—I think some one asked an explanation as to the meaning of the word constitution. Well, I think it is a word which, as here used, is not very difficult of comprehension. The Resolution, I think we all feel, does not contemplate any gigantic growth of ages, like the British constitution (laughter), or even any such grave comprehensive formal contract, as the American constitution—nay, I am not sure that the word "composition" might not, without injuring the sense of the Resolution, have been substituted for "constitution." What is intended is that there should be some rules framed as to who and what the delegates who come up to the next Congress should be; how and when they should be chosen or elected; and which are the provinces or places from which they may be sent. And, again, the rules might lay down whether the number of the delegates should be in any way limited, whether the Congress is to consist of 700, 1,000, 1,500 or 3,000 delegates, or whether there should be no limit at all, and so on. These are matters, of course, which will have to be considered by the Committee. I merely allude to them to explain what I understand to be the meaning of the word "constitution" as used in the proposed Resolution. Does anyone wish to say anything further? (Cries of "No, No.")

A Delegate: I have to make a proposal here that the name of the proposer of the amendment be added to the list of the Committee. (Voices, "No, No.")

The President: We have heard his views here, and I think it is important that this gentleman should have an opportunity of expressing his views before the Committee, and therefore, with your permission, I will include his name in the list. I take it that this Resolution, with this addition, is now generally agreed to. However, that there may not be any doubt upon the subject, I put it to the vote. It will now stand:—

Resolved,—That a Committee is appointed, consisting of the following gentlemen (marginally enumerated*), to consider what rules, if any, may now be usefully framed in regard to the constitution and working of the Congress, with instructions to report thereon to the Congress on the 30th instant.

* Messrs. Namjoshi, Chandavarkar, Mir Humayan Jah Bahadur, Hajee Mahomed Abdul Shakoor Badshaw Sahib, S. Subramania Aiyar, W. S. Gantz, Rangiah Naidu, Surendranath Bannerjee, Trailokyanath Mitra, Kalicharan Bannerjee, Guruprasad Sen, Saligram Singh, Ram Kali Chaudhuri, Hafiz Abdul Rahim, Rampal Singh, Madan Mohun, Ganga Prasad Varma, Bishen Narayen Dar, Hamid Ali, Murlidhur, Satyanand Agnihotri, H. H. Dhruva, W. C. Bonnerjee, Norendranath Sen, Eardley Norton, Joy Gobind Shome, Iswari Lal Sircar, G. Subramania Iyer, D. A. Khare, S. A. Saminada Iyer, Sabapathy Mudaliar, A. O. Hume, Vijaya Raghava Chariar, Gobind Buksh, and Karandikar.

The Resolution was then put and carried unanimously.

The President: The next Resolution which is proposed for your consideration by the Subject Committee, whom you appointed yesterday, runs as follows:—

"That this Congress do re-affirm the necessity for the expansion and reform of the Council of the Governor-General for making Laws and the Provincial Legislative Councils, already set forth in Resolutions III. of the Congresses of 1885 and 1886, and expresses the earnest hope that the Government will no longer delay action in the direction of this essential reform."

Babu Surendra Nath Bannerjee (Calcutta, No. 550 in list), who was received with an enthusiastic greeting, said: Gentlemen and Brother Delegates, I thank you for the cordial greeting which you have just accorded to me, and I shall endeavour, to the best of my ability, to discharge the very onerous and responsible duty which the proposer of this Resolution has to perform. I will not repeat the words of the Resolution, as they have already been read out to you by our distinguished President. But, before I proceed to make any remarks upon this Resolution, you will permit me, on my own behalf, and on behalf of my brother-delegates of Bengal (applause), and I may claim also, on behalf of my countrymen in Bengal in general, whose sympathies—whose watchful sympathies, I may add—will follow us through every part of these proceedings, to tender our obeisance, and the tribute of our heart-felt homage, to this great and representative national gathering. (Applause). Gentlemen, the dream of ages is about to be realised. The differences of generations are about to be forgotten (hear, hear), and a noble prospect is opening out to view, a prospect fraught with brilliance, with beauty, and untold happiness to the people. I will not dare to anticipate the future, nor will I indulge in the ecstacies of prophetic vision; but this I undertake to say, that whatever may be the future of this Congress, and with it of the country, we are on the right track—that track of light—leading to the destined goal (loud and continued applause), marked by the consolidation of British rule and the emancipation of our people. (Applause.) Gentlemen, in this connection it would ill become me not to refer for a moment to the magnificent hospitality which we are receiving at present from our countrymen of Madras—Madras, miscalled "benighted," but a source of living light to the sister Presidencies of India. (Hear, hear.) May the spirit of union and sympathy, of which this Congress is the highest expression and the noblest embodiment, grow and deepen to the eternal honour of English rule and to the manifold advantage of the people of India. (Applause.)

Gentlemen, we attach the utmost importance to this question of the reconstitution of the Legislative Councils. We accord to it the foremost place amongst the topics of discussion. We unfurl the banner of the Congress and upon it are written, in characters of glittering gold, which none may efface, the great words of this Resolution, "Representative Institutions for India." (Applause.)

Are we guided by mere sentimental considerations in making this act of deliberate choice? Ah! No! There are the strongest reasons why the reconstitution of the Legislative Councils should be placed in the forefront of topics to be discussed by the National Congress. It is impossible to think of a domestic grievance, or a matter of domestic complaint, which would not be remedied if the constitution of the Council were changed and remodelled according to our programme. Talk of the separation of judicial from executive functions: why, the reform would be effected at once if we had a potential voice in the making of our laws. Talk of the wider employment of our countrymen in the public service: why, the Queen's Proclamation would be vindicated to the letter (applause), if we had some control over the management of our domestic concerns. (Applause.) You fret and fume under the rigors of an income-tax which touches even the necessaries of subsistence: why, the incidence of the tax would be altered, the minimum raised, if we had anything to do with the imposition of the tax, or if we were permitted to modify it. (Applause.) I might multiply instances, but that is not necessary. The reconstitution of the Legislative Councils would be a panacea for countless grievances in relation to the internal administration of the country. Gentlemen, by this Resolution we reaffirm the necessity for the expansion and reform of the Councils, according to the programme laid down by the Congresses of 1885 and 1886.* We lay down the principles, but further elaboration is not needed, and further elaboration would be unwise. It would be presenting a broader flank to the attack of our opponents. They would attack us in points of detail; the great cardinal principles of the scheme would be lost sight of in this discussion. Therefore, it has been wisely resolved that there should not be at present any further elaboration of details. We have suggested the principles; we have made it abundantly clear that we have thought—earnestly thought—out the subject; but we are not the legislators of the country, though we hope to be so some day (hear, hear), when the Councils are reconstituted. The Government has highly-paid officials drawing thousands of

* See the Resolutions of these Congresses reprinted at the end of this volume.

rupees a month (laughter), and it is for them to elaborate the Bill and to settle the details upon principles which may find acceptance with the Government.

We did, as you will remember, submit at the last Congress a succinct scheme to prove to our rulers that we, at any rate, knew what we wanted and had fully considered how the concession we desired might be practically granted to us. But, gentlemen, succinct as our scheme was it did not escape criticism. Criticism we do not wish to avoid. Ah! No! The National Congress walks by the broad light of publicity. We court and solicit criticism; but it must be honest criticism. (Hear, hear, and applause.) What, then, are we to think of a critic who, forgetting what is due to his official position and the reserve which such position implies, tells the public upon a memorable occasion that this Congress is a sham Congress (voices, "Shame, Shame"), that it is a Hindu Congress (cries of "No, No"), and that it is a Congress of nobodies? (Voices, "No, no.") Sham Congress! In the midst of this illustrious array of delegates and of this stupendous spectacle of self-sacrifice, which the delegates have displayed in coming from their distant homes to attend the Congress! If ever there can be any true test of sincerity it lies in self-sacrifice. Tell me the measure of your self-sacrifice and I will tell you what is the measure of your patriotism. But we are told this Congress is a Hindu Congress, presided over, forsooth, by an illustrious Mahomedan gentleman! (Applause and laughter.) But it is also a Congress of nonentities, where there is Rajah Sir T. Madhava Row (laughter and applause), and where, last year, such men as Sir Maharaja Jotendro Mohun Tagore and Dr. Rajendra Lalla Mitra and others took a prominent part in the proceedings!

But, gentlemen, we will leave our official critic to reflect upon his own performance in the solitude of his official dignity. Let us pass on to another gentleman who has been criticising the Congress—not so much the Congress as the scheme of Representative Government propounded by that body. I suppose we expect our critics to read what we have been saying or what we have been writing. Gentlemen, I am a journalist, and I know that we sometimes depart from this principle (laughter) and criticise books without reading them (laughter), and possibly our friend who hails from Allyghur—(A voice, "Beneath notice.")—Yes, he is beneath notice, but one or two of his observations have to be noticed,—our friend who hails from Allyghur possibly acted on the principle of the journalist, and he was good enough to tell the public, in a letter which extended over twelve columns of a leading journal, that what we wanted was an oligarchy of educated natives, but that it was an impossibility to place the army under the control of this oligarchy. Now this was precisely what we did not want. (Loud laughter.) We neither wanted an oligarchy nor any other "archy." The dream of an oligarchy never entered into our remotest conceptions. As for the army, we specially excluded it from all control on the part of our reconstituted Legislative Councils. It was not even covered by the right of interpellation.

Gentlemen, such have been the criticisms which have been made with regard to the scheme. It is not from such critics that we can derive any light or leading; but it strikes me that the more we examine the scheme, the more we examine the principles underlying it, the deeper becomes the conviction that it is marked by a remarkable degree of moderation, and I am prepared to prove by reference to the existing state of things, by reference to the recorded views of the Government, and by reference to legislative enactments, that our scheme judged by them is moderation itself. (Applause.) The Legislative Councils were constituted under the India Councils Act of 1861. Let me read to you the 45th section of the Act which applies to the Provincial Legislative Councils: "Whenever such Proclamation as aforesaid shall have been issued regarding the said division or territories respectively, the Lieutenant-Governor thereof shall nominate for his assistance in making Laws and Regulations such number of Councillors as shall be in such Proclamation specified; provided that not less than one-third of such Councillors shall in every case be non-official persons."

Now, what do we want? What is our programme? We want that, instead of one-third, not less than one-half of the Council shall consist of non-official members, and that we should have the right of electing that half. The Government itself makes the concession that at least one-third of the members should be non-officials. After twenty-five years of trial and experience we want the Government to move a step farther and raise the third to a half. I do not think that we are making a very extravagant demand. On our side of the country (I am not prepared to speak of Bombay and Madras) the Municipal laws are revised every ten years. I hope it is the case here also. I am not competent to speak, nor do I hear any response from the Bombay or Madras delegates. If the Municipal Laws are revised once in every ten years, why should not the laws relating to the constitution of the Councils be revised at least, say, once in every twenty years? In 1861 these laws were passed, and now more than quarter of a century has elapsed, and great changes have taken place; therefore I think that upon the very foundations the Government have laid for us we have a very strong case to urge.

But this is not all. The second point which we insist upon is that the right of interpellation should be accorded to the Legislative Councils. Well, gentlemen, will it be believed that a right of this nature was actually enjoyed by the members of the Supreme Legislative Council at one time, but because some lawyers made the Council too hot for the officials,—they would drive a coach and four through the restrictions imposed upon the right,—the privilege was subsequently withdrawn. The first meeting of the Legislative Council of India was held on the 20th May, 1854, during the reign of Lord Dalhousie, who was not only vigorous in his foreign policy but was an ardent reformer in regard to domestic affairs. Let me read from the Standing Order of the first meeting. The order is as follows: "A member may ask a question of another member, but such questions must be confined to matters immediately connected with the business of the Legislative Council, and must be asked in a manner which does involve argument or inference."

Thus you see that the right of interpellation existed in regard to the items of business then pending before the Council. All that we now tell the Government is: "Go a step further, and give us the right of interpellation, but do not confine it merely to matters pending before the Council, but rather extend it to all matters of domestic concern." I think that is a reasonable request to make, and especially bearing in mind the great and rapid advance which the country has made within the last thirty years.

Well, gentlemen, there is a third prayer in connection with the reconstitution of the Legislative Councils, and that is, that the Budget should be discussed by the Councils. (Hear, hear.) Now, how does this matter stand at present? I suppose you are aware that the Budgets are discussed by the Supreme Legislative Council, but only when any fresh measure of taxation is proposed; otherwise the Budget is—shall I use the word?—burked; it is not laid before the Council at all. Well, now, it so happens, curiously enough, for truth must triumph, and it receives unexpected support from unexpected quarters, that the Chambers of Commerce of all the Presidencies have addresssed a memorial to the Government asking that the Parliamentary statute might be revised, so as to permit the discussion of the Budget by the Supreme Legislative Council in all cases, whether it is proposed to levy a new tax or not. (Hear, hear.) In this matter the Chambers of Commerce, the National Congress, and all India with its multitudinous races, creeds and sects, are unanimously agreed; this fact again points to the moderation of our demands.

Thus, then, gentlemen, you will see that, whether in regard to the addition of non-official members, or to the right of interpellation, or to the discussion of the Budget by the Legislative Council, we ask Government to proceed upon lines which the Government has either partially adopted or which meet with the unanimous support of public opinion. Gentlemen, it is with satisfaction we find that, our demands being so moderate, the question has come within the range of practical politics. It is no longer a dream, an Utopia, or the phantom of an excited imagination. In February, 1885, Mr. Macaulay, Secretary to the Bengal Government, thus wrote or rather spoke,—but it is all the same thing, for all their speeches are really written beforehand—(laughter)—: "We require critics and destroyers as well as authors and constructors. From this point of view I, for one, entirely agree with those who consider that our Council should be enlarged. It seems to me of the utmost importance that all views, all rights, all parties, should be properly represented, in order that the broad light of practical knowledge and experience, as well as the keener gleam of special interests, and it may even be of special prejudices, may be freely let in upon our deliberations."

This was what Mr. Macaulay said in February, 1885. But one greater than Mr. Macaulay, greater than all Indian civilians—His Excellency the Viceroy himself—has, upon a memorable occasion, expressed his warmest sympathy with our aspirations in this respect. This was what the Viceroy said in his speech on the Jubilee occasion: "Glad and happy should I be if, during my sojourn among them (the people of India), circumstances permitted me to extend and to place upon a wider and more logical footing the political status which was so wisely given a generation ago by that great statesman, Lord Halifax, to such Indian gentlemen as by their influence, their acquirements, and the confidence they inspired in their fellow-countrymen, were marked out as useful adjuncts to our Legislative Councils." Thus we are within measurable distance of victory. We are in view of the "promised land," so to speak. If we are true to ourselves, and if we go on affirming, re-affirming, and re-affirming again and again, the Resolution of to-day, God willing, it will soon be an accomplished reality. (Applause.)

I have heard with feelings, I may say, of concern, the disappointment which has sometimes been expressed with regard to the work of the National Congress. It has been said, of course, by our opponents that the labours of the National Congress have not yet been attended with any definite and marked results. But the Congress is an infant institution of only two or three years' growth. What are two or three or even fifty years in the lifetime of a nation? We must go on working and agitating. The goddess of Liberty is a jealous goddess, and she is exacting in her worship from her votaries. We should worship her with assiduity, sincere, sustained, and devoted, and then only can we expect to receive her smiles. It would not do to take part in this great national assembly on this particular occasion, and then to go to sleep for the rest of the year. We must be steady and continuous in our work, and I am quite sure that when the whole country has with one voice expressed itself with reference to this question, England, the august mother of free nations, will not refuse to grant us a boon which is in such entire accord with her own traditions, and which will establish her empire broad-based upon the affections of her people. (Applause.) To England we may appeal with confidence. When Italy was struggling for liberty England stretched forward the right hand of sympathy. When Greece was endeavouring to assert her place amongst the nationalities of the earth England was there, the foster-mother of freedom, responsive to the call. We are neither Italians nor Greeks. We are something better. We are British subjects. (Hear, hear, and applause.) England has taken us into her bosom and claims us as her own. We appeal to her by the sweetest, the gentlest, the tenderest and yet withal the most durable of all ties, that which binds the mother to her offspring, to confer upon us the inestimable boon of representative institutions, and, I am sure, we shall not appeal in vain. Let us go on, praying, asking, agitating, resting our hopes of success upon Divine Providence, and victory will assuredly crown our efforts. (Loud and continued cheering.)

Rajah Sir T. Madhava Row (Madras, No. 1 in list), in seconding the proposition, said: Mr. President and Gentlemen, I believe my friends and the public generally have given me some credit for prudence. (Laughter.) Gentlemen, I do claim some credit for prudence, and I believe most other gentlemen here will agree with me in admitting my pretensions to this virtue.

If they are doubtful about it I will prove it to you beyond all doubt, by the prudence I exercise in refraining, after the magnificent and enthusiastic speech to which we have all listened with so much admiration—(applause)—from attempting anything like a long or elaborate speech of my own. No, I shall simply confine myself to my duty upon this occasion. I have specially attended here, not to make a speech but simply to express a few sentiments of my own on this subject, and I have particularly attended here because I take a deep interest in this part of the proceedings of this Congress. (Hear, hear, and applause.) I have written out what I desired to say, partly because I am far from well, but chiefly, in order to convince everybody that the sentiments I express are the deliberate results of my most mature consideration, set forth not in the enthusiasm engendered by such an address as we have listened to, but carefully written out beforehand in words as expressive and emphatic as I can command. I will now, with your kind permission, read out what I have written. *(Reads.)* Gentlemen, I cordially second the important Resolution now before you. (Hear, hear.) I do so under a profound conviction of the necessity and good policy of the measure proposed. It is a profound conviction, I assure you, because by temperament and training I am to a great extent conservative, and yet, having looked at the matter from every point of view, and having carefully considered it,

I have a profound conviction that the measure proposed is a necessity that is quite consistent with good policy and even required by good policy. (Hear, hear, and applause.) I further aver my conviction that it should not be long postponed. (Applause.) The principle upon which the proposal rests, and which is embodied in the Resolution, is one which the British Government, I am sure, will not and cannot refuse to recognise. Gentlemen, English statesmen possess immense political knowledge and immense political experience, and they will not find it a difficult or an embarrassing problem to give effect to the principle once they recognise it. We already see, it seems to me, unmistakeable signs of their recognition of the principle, and I would only beg you to persevere for a year or two, patiently awaiting the results, and you will, believe me, receive a satisfactory response to our very reasonable recommendations. I need say no more, even did my present state of health permit it. The matter requires no further exposition. We are all convinced. We thoroughly know and understand the whole thing. It is a matter which, nowadays, requires no demonstration whatever. (Hear, hear, and applause.)

Mr. P. Somasundaram Chettiar (Madras, No. 6 in list) supported the resolution, and, in doing so, said: Mr. President and Gentlemen, In supporting the proposition moved by Mr. Surendra Nath Bannerjee, and seconded by Sir T. Madhava Row, in respect to the reform of the constitution of the present Legislative Council in different Provinces, my two able friends, whose speeches on the matter have so emphatically attracted the attention of the great assembly present in this pandal, have dwelt largely on the various aspects of the question, and it may seem, therefore, needless for me to enlarge on the subject, but being aware that many of my friends may be desirous of knowing my views, I rise to say a few words, and I will be as brief as possible, so as not to tire the patience of the assembly. We all know the objects with which these Councils were established. They were established after the direct assumption of the Government of India by Her Majesty the Queen, Government taking into consideration the expediency of rendering the laws good and safe, so as to meet the wants and wishes of the people at large, and to suit the convenience of each sect and creed. They have undergone various changes and reforms in their constitution since their establishment, but, permit me to observe that the practical utility of these Councils has not been such as to merit the approbation of the people, owing to the limited number of non-officials constituting the Council, the ruling authorities taking precautionary measures to have the official element prevailing over the non-official, thereby retaining all Legislative power in their hands, who are, in fact, the authorities in the Executive branches; thus the feelings of the Native community in regard to these Councils have not been satisfactory, and agitations for their reform were frequently and repeatedly made by local and other associations and institutions, by the Press and through the channel of separate publications, but without success. The subject was, however, warmly taken up by the Congress meetings in the two last previous years on behalf of the nation, urging the necessity for a general reform in the constitution, showing the grounds and reasons for such reform, adding that the vitality of the Councils so reformed will be increased, and they will be better adapted and suited to the nation which, in these days of its education and progress, is wanting better and sounder legislators. There are many instances, too numerous to enumerate here, where grave defects have been noticed and no remedial measures have been adopted to afford relief to the nation. Hasty steps are too generally taken without mature consideration, when, under financial pressure, the thought of raising taxes occurs, without giving any reasonably satisfactory explanation for so doing. As education and culture advance people naturally aspire to better forms of administration, which the Government is bound to provide for, as well as to receive and view favourably, liberally, and with equanimity all suggestions for reform. So long as the ruling authorities encroach in all manners possible upon the incomes of individuals, and tax them under one designation or other in their resources, under pretext of the exigencies of the State, their mode of administrative procedure should be such as to satisfy the general feelings of the natives. I learn that the Chambers of Commerce in Calcutta and Madras, the representatives of the European mercantile community, have lately represented, rightly and justly, the necessity of the Imperial Budgets being laid before the public at an earlier time, with elaborate returns, so as to enable that public to know precisely how the financial administration is conducted, and thus to see the real wants of the country. Every individual before payment of additional taxes will be very desirous to know how the money is being spent, in a similar way as our household expenses are known, and the Government should be pleased to satisfy the reclamations of the people on this head. A large, independent, and representative element should be added to the Councils, thus conferring on them a larger sphere of usefulness and respectability, and thereby winning the good-will and affection of the people, soothing the feelings of the rulers and the ruled. From this expression I do not mean to signify the existence of any dangerous discontent but to urge wise actions on Government for preventing differences. Though we may not meet with success in our efforts immediately, yet we should continue without any discouragement, agitating constitutionally till we gain the object, as we are told in an old adage, that the "mother will give milk to the child when it continues to cry." For the reasons stated, I warmly and gladly support the proposition just moved. I have only a few words to express in conclusion, being apprehensive that no further public opportunity will be given to me for addressing the meeting. I, on behalf of my community and myself, tender most heartily, sincerely, and cordially our humble thanks to our brethren in this Hall who have travelled from various distant countries at great inconvenience and expense to this city with the sole aim of assisting the work of this Congress, which has been the means of gathering so large a number as are now present, and I trust that the Almighty giver of all things will confer His benediction for the prosperity and happiness of us all and aid us in our efforts. (Loud cheers.)

The PRESIDENT: Gentlemen, Before the discussion proceeds further on this resolution, as I have received notice of certain amendments, I will call upon the gentleman who has given me that notice to move his amendments, and if those amendments are duly seconded, then the further discussion can proceed on both the resolution and the amendments.

Mr. NAM JOSHI (Bombay, No. 390 in list): Gentlemen, Our worthy President has just told us that we shall have a very good discussion both on the proposition submitted for acceptance and the amendments that I now propose. I would rather, therefore, reserve my observations both as regards the proposition and also as regards the amendments to some future time. I would only read the amendments, and then when the discussion is over it would be time for me to reply to such arguments as may be urged against my amendments. If no arguments are urged against them, and if they are found to be acceptable to my friends in other provinces, any remarks on my part would be unnecessary. I will, therefore, read the amendments for your acceptance, and then, with the permission of the President, discussion will take place, and then, if it is necessary for me to say anything, either in support of the amendments or against the proposition, I will do so. With these remarks, I will read the amendments:—

(1.) That this Congress views with satisfaction the establishment of a separate Legislative Council for the North-West Provinces, and is of opinion that the time has arrived when a similar concession may be extended to the Punjab, as prayed for in the Resolution of the Congress of 1885.

(2.) That in view of the fact that the amendment of the Indian Councils Act cannot be secured on the lines recommended by the Congress before the inquiry prayed for in the Resolution No. 5 of the Congress of last year, this Congress is of opinion that the Government of India should be moved to obtain sanction for a short amendment of the Act, authorising them to submit their annual Budget for scrutiny by the Select Committee of the Supreme Council.

(3.) That in the interests of the administration the Government of India should on all occasions on which the opinions of Local Governments and of influential gentlemen in the different parts of India are invited on matters of public interest, consult this Congress through the Standing Committees, lists of which will be submitted to the Government every year.

Mr. H. H. DHRUVA (Kaira, No. 451 in list) said: I beg to second the amendments proposed by my friend Mr. Nam Joshi, and I may tell you in connection with these amendments that they do not in any way clash with the original proposition that has been so ably moved by Mr. Surendra Nath Bannerjee. There is nothing new in them. They are intended simply to show that we are doing something. We have been questioned by many people, and even by friends, as to what the Congress has been actually doing from year to year, and so we should endeavour to show some practical results. We should show that since the first resolution that was proposed at the Congress of 1885 we have made some progress, and that that resolution has obtained a Legislative Council for the North-West Provinces. Further, we want to show to the different provinces, as well as to the people who do not take part in these meetings, that having secured a Council for the North-West Provinces, we are this time going to press for a similar concession, where the Punjab is concerned, and later, when this is made, as if we press it, it soon must be, we shall have another tangible piece of work to point to. The other amendments are clear in themselves, and by bringing these matters to the notice of Government, who will doubtless concur with us (especially as in the Budget matter we have all the European Chambers of Commerce with us), we shall have several tangible concessions to point to as the results of our labours, and fair grounds for all men to believe that we may expect further and even more important results in the future. It is with that view that I and my friend have brought these amendments before you for your consideration.

The PRESIDENT: I did not wish to stop the mover or the seconder of the amendments, because I was not exactly aware of the form in which these so-called amendments would be put before you. If they were really amendments, it would have been the proper thing to discuss them along with the resolution. But I did not know exactly what it was that these gentlemen wanted to put forward; now that we all know, I must say that it appears to me that these propositions are not really amendments of the original proposition (applause), but are rather distinct and independent Resolutions, which can in no way affect the original Resolution itself. The course, therefore, that I propose to adopt is this—I accept these propositions as having been duly proposed and seconded and as capable of being taken up independently, but not as in any shape amendments of the Resolution now before the assembly, to which the discussion should at present be confined. After that Resolution has been distinctly dealt with, and the rest of the work on the programme disposed of, we can go on to consider these Resolutions which have been duly proposed and seconded. I will now call upon Mr. Norton, whose name stands next on the list of gentlemen desirous of speaking on the original proposition, to proceed with the discussion.

Mr. EARDLEY NORTON (Madras, No. 43 in list) who was received with loud cheers, said: Mr. President, and my Native Friends, your warm welcome ringing in my ears enables me to face you in a spirit of glad exultation. I say, in a spirit of glad exultation, because in your greeting I taste, in the first place, something of the promise of that kindlier feeling and of that more cordial relationship between ourselves and our respective races which shall make our connection in the future more harmonious than it is to-day, and cement our friendship with the solemn seal of a more perfected trust. (Cheers.) In the second place, I realise that your attitude to-day exhibits that earnestness of purpose which foreshadows triumph, a triumph that I hope I may share with you (cheers), and shows that you are alive to the privileges and responsibilities of being British subjects. (Cheers.) Your cordial welcome is a kindly compliment to my nationality. (Cheers.) Not infrequently, gentlemen, the illiberal reproach is cast in our teeth that the spirit of an unconquerable antagonism is abroad between the Europeans and the Natives, that there is a great gulf, which never can be bridged between us, which must keep us each for all time apart from the other. And even more frequently is the reproach cast upon us, with greater particularity in the matter of this Congress, that your objects are confined exclusively to the Native communities of this vast continent, objects with which no Englishman can have any legitimate sympathy or tie. Let me, in my own person, refute that aspersion as unfounded; let your reception of me attest the complete concord of European and Native aspiration. (Cheers. I assure you, speaking from this platform to-day, that I feel sincerely how great is the honour of my position. I am not a "self-elected" delegate. I have not nominated myself. I have been sent here, without any solicitation on my part, to place before you, not merely the sentiments with which my constituents—humble they may be, yet my constituents still—(hear, hear)—are animated, but also to convince you into the belief that in all the great and fundamental principles of your political and social reforms, not only I, but thousands of Englishmen, whose voices are tied, partly by reason of their official positions (applause) and partly by their generous but mistaken belief in a state of things which does not exist, are influenced by feelings of the deepest sympathy, and by the most vivid desire to see you in the enjoyment of something of their own political freedom at home. (Cheers.) In my opinion there is no resolution before you so important and far-reaching in its ultimate effects as that which touches the re-constitution of our Legislative Councils. (Cheers.) Act, therefore, gentlemen, on my advice. Cling to that reform.

That is the key-stone of all your future triumph. And when once you achieve it, you will find yourselves at last in an atmosphere in which you can breathe without effort, which will no longer stifle all your aspirations to regard yourselves as human beings of some intelligence with a right to have a voice in the administration of your own affairs. (Prolonged cheers.) Then shall you really be worthy of being England's children. (Cheers.)

Frequently have I had many capacities thrust most unwillingly upon myself in Madras. Only last night I have been made to assume a new representative capacity. (Laughter.) I was told yesterday, by one for whose character and educated qualities I cherish a great esteem, that in joining myself with the labourers in this Congress I have earned for myself the new title of a "veiled seditionist." (Laughter.) If it be sedition, gentlemen, to rebel against all wrong; if it be sedition to insist that the people should have a fair share in the administration of their own country and affairs; if it be sedition to resist class-tyranny, to raise my voice against oppression, to mutiny against injustice, to insist upon a hearing before sentence, to uphold the liberties of the individual, to vindicate our common right to gradual but ever advancing reform—(cheers)—if this be sedition, I am right glad to be called a "seditionist," (cheers), and doubly, ay, trebly glad, when I look around me to-day to know and feel I am ranked as one among such a magnificent array of "seditionists." (Loud cheers.)

We have been told, again, that in this matter your aims are purely Hindu and Mahomedan. What can you conceive, gentlemen, more false than that? Have our critics forgotten that we, as Europeans, even for the limited portion of our sojourn in India, are as deeply affected by questions of taxation and of legislation as any of yourselves, Mahomedan or Hindu? (Cheers.) Have they forgotten that there are many important European interests in India worthy to be represented upon the Legislative Councils, so that their owners may have a voice in the formation and formulation of those laws which they are called upon themselves to obey (cheers), such interests, for example, as the planting, the mining, the mill-owning, and the whole of the non-official interest throughout the length and the breadth of this land? These gentlemen are among the persons who take a deep and anxious interest in the welfare of the Congress; and I am enabled honestly to assure you that if I speak with the feeble voice of a single individual, I speak with the accumulated strength of many hundred Englishmen behind me. (Loud and continued applause.)

Again, there is another reproach. It has been said that the native aristocracy of this country shows no interest in the affairs of this Congress, exhibits no concern in the political development of this country. I am glad to think that, at any rate, so far as Madras is concerned, the presence of His Highness the Maharajah of Vizianagram (loud applause) on this platform, himself one of the best educated and wealthiest of our native nobles, entitles me to say that that accusation is as untrue as is each one of those others to which I have already referred. (Loud applause.)

Let me reiterate my advice already given. Let me repeat my solemn warning. Cling to this resolution and its aims. Never let it go from you. It contains the richest germs of all your future political progress. (Cheers.) My eloquent friend, Mr. Surendra Nath Bannerjee, has told you, in language I would not venture to imitate because I could not (applause), although I envy him his happy gift (loud applause), of the liberty and freedom which must follow if only you are true to your conscience and your cause. (Cheers.) I have had much reason to look very carefully into the political condition of the people of this Presidency during the last five years, to scrutinize their liberties, and to ponder over the system under which they and I live. We urgently need the salutary reform for which we plead. (Cheers.) Therefore persevere as you have begun, and march ever onwards. Do not be cowed by opposition. Meet sneers and threats with a front of adamant. Adhere to your policy through all dangers, and through all doubts, and complete for yourselves the schemes of reform you have so admirably begun. The day will come when an infinitely larger and truer freedom will be yours, when the great question of taxation will be within your grasp, when you will in truth realise that you have got something more than mere potential power, when you shall place your hand upon the purse-strings of the country and the Government. (Loud and continued applause.) Money is power, whether it be in the hands of an individual or of a Government. He who has the dispensing of money is he who has the control of all ultimate authority. (Cheers.) Once you control the finances, you will taste the true meaning of power and of freedom. (Cheers.)

Gentlemen, with respect to this resolution, there are two points I would more particularly bring to your attention. The first is the body with whom is to rest the ultimate election of Representatives.* Madras differs somewhat upon this point from her sister Presidencies. I think our proposal a reasonable and a feasible one. It is that our various District and Municipal Boards, Chambers of Commerce, and Universities should elect a certain number of persons apiece, who shall form a so-called "Electoral College." Each of these bodies would send up, say, from two to twenty such individuals, who would number, let us say, between two hundred and four hundred. These, it is suggested, should choose the various members for the various districts and bodies who are to be represented upon the reconstituted Council. Local patriotism is apt to be somewhat short-sighted and perverse. The richest man of the district would, probably, apart from any other qualification, be elected to represent or misrepresent—(laughter)—his constituents' views. Whereas there is a distinct safeguard in the system which would transfer the power of election from the Districts themselves, which are scarcely equal as yet to such a responsibility, to a body of men who would practically represent the flower of the educated inhabitants of the Presidency. It is further suggested, and the suggestion seems a good one, that the Government should be empowered to scrutinise the list of the "Electoral College," and supplement any deficient representation thereon of any particular sect or interest by a nomination of a certain number of persons from such deficient interest or sect. You would thus have a large body of qualified and widely representative men to consult the best interests of the country at large in the choice of candidates for seats upon the Council. The scheme is, of course, only tentative, and I would gladly give way and advocate any better system which could be suggested. (Cheers.)

The second point is, in my opinion, even of greater importance than the first. I mean the right of interpellation. (Cheers.) That will be the beginning of great good. It will place in your hands, for your country's benefit, an engine of enormous power. It will furnish you with a check upon authority. (Cheers.) It will entitle you, in the public interests, to put questions to Government which they must either answer, or the refusal to answer which they must refer to a Standing Committee. I can picture nothing more desirable than that we should possess a real and substantial check upon the governing authorities, as they are at present constituted. (Cheers.) I speak with all respect when I maintain that it is not for the good of this country, or of Government themselves, that they should be allowed to rule unquestioned and unrestrained, exercising a discretion unfettered by public opinion—(cheers)—or by the knowledge that they are bound to account to the nation for any single legislative or executive action. (Cheers.) I speak after eight years' experience of such a state of things. (Cheers.) As an instance of the license to which I allude, let me refer you to what has happened quite lately, within the last ten days. Do you suppose, gentlemen, that the English Civilian in Central India, whose name I will presently mention, of high official rank, occupying a position of great trust and of grave responsibility—do you think that this officer of the Government would have delivered himself of the speech which we have all read—a speech, let me add, to the shame of his English birth and his official reputation —(loud cheers)—if we were, at this moment, possessed of the great right and weapon of a public interpellation of the Government. ("Shame, Shame.") The official to whom I allude, instead of attempting to efface social mistrust, instead of endeavouring to allay religious fanaticism, to still animosity and to appease faction—although himself a representative of that great Power whose splendid mission in India it is to promote a cordial harmony among the various populations entrusted to its rule—has thought fit to widen the breach that caste and religion have created in this land, to separate one part of India from the other, to foment sectarian hate, to excite the Mahrattas against the people of Bengal, and thus to betray his trust to his conscience, his country, and his Queen. (Loud cheers.) This official is Sir Lepel Griffin. (Groans, and loud cries of "Shame, Shame.") Had we the right of interpellation do you think Sir Lepel Griffin would not have been more cautious before committing himself to a course which, so far as we have yet seen, has provoked not a word of official censure or rebuke? ("Shame, Shame.") If we might put questions we should put some excessively unpleasant ones. We should ask, for instance, what

* *Vide* Clause 2 of Resolution IV. of 1886, reprinted at the end of this volume.

action the Government of India intended to adopt towards one of their own servants who, in broad daylight, and apparently under the ægis of their silence, has cast a slur upon the Government of the Queen and discredited the service of which he is a member. (Loud cheers.) Gentlemen, the right of interpellation has received considerable attention from a native statesman who has addressed you to-day. (Loud applause.) He has himself told you that he is remarkable for nothing if he is not remarkable for prudence. (Applause.) Never in the whole course of his career has Rajah Sir T. Madhava Row shown himself more prudent than he has to-day, in speaking on this resolution. (Cheers.) I recollect some four or five years ago, when he addressed the natives of this city in a popular institution, in the presence of many Englishmen, that he induced us all in Patcheappah's Hall to insist upon the right to interpellate the Government as being a fresh guarantee of national security and independence. (Loud cheers.) Sir T. Madhava Row spoke with all the prudent authority due to one who had himself for many years held the reins of government, and experienced something of the lust of power. (Laughter.) The suggestion of such a safeguard, coming from such prudential quarters may, therefore, fairly be accepted, not only with gratitude but also with safety. (Loud applause.) Once again, when Lord Ripon (loud and continued cheers), who has done so much for us all (renewed cheering), when Lord Ripon landed in Madras, he was met by a large section of our most highly-educated native gentlemen. In the petition that was presented to him by, I think, Sir T. Madhava Row, this very question of the interpellation of the Government was insisted upon with some force. (Cheers.) This shows that we are not straining after an empty chimera—(cheers)—but that we are demanding that practical and reasonable concession which has already received the approval of so moderate, so practical and so prudent a statesman as your fellow-countryman, Rajah Sir T. Madhava Row. (Loud cheers.)

I do not know of any measure which will more surely, or more speedily, effect the advancement and enlightenment of this country than the measure for which I speak. I believe that the reconstitution of the Legislative Councils on the lines indicated, and the employment of a large number of the natives of the country upon those Councils will tend, not merely towards political progress, but to create and foster and disseminate throughout this enormous empire an increase of that sense of self-respect without which you can never hope to become a nation worthy of true political advancement. (Cheers.) These surely are aims worthy of achievement; these surely are objects worthy of some self-sacrifice. (Cheers.) You will not win them easily. I do not believe you will get them from the Government of India. You will have to reach the ears and touch the hearts of the great English people, as you have already done, to a limited extent, through the medium of such men as Messrs. Manomohun and Lalmohun Ghose, Mr. Chandavarkar, and Mr. Ramasamy Mudaliar. The people at home know next to nothing about you. They are in absolute ignorance of our form of Government. They do not know your wants. They believe that our system of Government here is ever surely and beneficently carried on, and they believe it is carried on more or less upon the lines of their own freer rule. You must disturb that belief. You must continually agitate, both in India and in England. Words are not enough. You must be up and doing. You must act. We must not mind if we are sneered at as "agitators." We, in Madras, are accustomed to that of old. (Laughter.) Boldly and constantly re-affirm your great resolution, till you carry it in spite of all; (cheers)—carry it, and by your indomitable courage and perseverance break down the barriers of suspicion, of ignorance, of indifference. (Loud cheers.) The time is fast coming when you shall enjoy that fuller political franchise which you are fit to enjoy even to-day. (Loud and continued cheering.) Its attainment needs, as I have told you, considerable self-sacrifice. You will not be reluctant, you, who have already shown so much self-sacrifice by attending here, some of you from such enormous distances and all of you at much personal inconvenience, for you will all recognise that the cause is worth your most devoted services. (Cheers.) Accord to it that ungrudging labour and single-mindedness of purpose of which you have not stinted it hitherto. (Cheers.) Even if we ourselves do not live to see the great reform carried out in our time—though I am convinced the boon is not far distant—(cheers)—there is not a little ennobling in the belief, not a little consoling in the reflection, that we are working not merely selfishly for ourselves, but unselfishly for the generations of our children yet unborn. (Loud cheers.) These, when we are dead though not forgotten, shall bless us for our labours—(cheers)—and make grateful and reverent mention of our names who, meeting here to-day, and elsewhere, year after year, with stubborn insistance (cheers), devote our lives with ready gladness, and whatever of eloquence and of energy we may possess, to the triumph of a measure which we believe to be necessary for the national welfare (cheers), and to be indispensable for the security and progress of ourselves and of our children. (Loud cheers.) Let us labour, in a spirit of mutual brotherhood and forbearance, for the realisation of so grand a dream (loud cheers), patient in the trials we may have to endure to-day because we are secure in our belief that to-morrow will bring us consolation, (cheers) and strong in the knowledge that, if we are capable of resolute self sacrifice, we too may hope to

> " Stretch a hand through time to catch
> The far-off interest of tears."

(Loud and continued cheering.)

PANDIT BISHAN NARAYAN DAR (Bengal, No. 516 in list) next rose and said: Gentlemen, After the very eloquent speeches that have been made upon this resolution, in regard to the expansion and reform of the Legislative Councils, it well becomes a man of my poor ability to hide his diminished head, and it is only the sense of national duty that impels me to speak a few words instead of remaining silent. But this is a subject of the most vital importance to this country—indeed, I know no subject at all comparable, in its importance to all of us, with this subject of the inclusion of a representative element in the Government of India. (Loud applause.) Gentlemen, I am inclined to think with our eloquent proposer that, under existing circumstances, there is great wisdom at this hour of the day in laying less stress upon the details of the subject, and more upon the principle more especially, when we consider the state of public opinion in England. (Hear, hear.) Gentlemen, when Lord Salisbury, in his repudiation of Ireland's claim to Home Rule, groups us Indians and Hottentots together as equally outside the pale of political freedom; when Goldwin Smith says that to grant the Hindus any form of popular government would be to hand them over to a murderous anarchy; when the *Times* of London says that India has been conquered by the sword and by the sword it must be held; when the *Quarterly Review* says that we are unfit for freedom, because we are a nation of liars, (voices, " Shame, Shame "); when Mr. Froude, whose antipathy to democracy is well known, says that in case we show any signs of discontent he would send a contingent of Australians and pack us off to other scenes; when this is the state of public opinion in certain not altogether uninfluential quarters in England, I say it is necessary to discuss the principle itself, and thus, if possible, clear away the delusions which seem to stand in the way of its acceptance by a considerable section of the English nation. (Hear, hear.)

Gentlemen, there are a great many advantages that we all know must accrue from the introduction of some, or any, real form of representative institutions into this country. I shall simply allude to one which I believe to be one of the greatest of all, viz., that such institutions constitute the best practical school for mental and moral discipline. Gentlemen, the very idea that you are citizens of a vast Empire and that your actions and opinions have a permanent and substantial influence over the welfare of your country is in itself a restraining power of the highest moral value. Gentlemen, to be called upon from time to time to take part in the affairs of your country; to discuss, with the sense of responsibility that power gives, public questions; to have to employ your highest faculties in the management of affairs that have a direct bearing on your country's glory and on the happiness of her people,—these things, I say, are all steps in the education necessary for the unfolding of all the speculative and practical faculties of a nation.

Gentlemen, wherever a nation is debarred from this education, though there may be genius in it, it will wither undeveloped; and though there may still be certain kinds of literary and artistic activity; though there may be philosophers, metaphysicians and scientists, there will never be an intelligent public, or a nation really capable of judging or appreciating the policies of its rulers, or capable even of benefiting to the fullest extent by such experience and wisdom as their rulers may possess. Such a nation may be temporarily glorified by the effulgence of the fine arts and the lustre of the more effeminate types of poetical genius, but it will lack that instinctive sense of liberty, that robustness of character, which are essential to all healthy and therefore progressive national life.

Gentlemen, the sentiment of nationality is, perhaps, the grandest outcome of British Rule in India. But though it is to them we owe the seed, the plant is still in its infancy; it requires very careful fostering before it can grow up into a strong and stately tree, under the shadow of whose mighty branches the planters may repose. We must do, as we are doing this day, all we can, but it is to them, to whom we owe the inspiration, to foster, by conceding what we aspire to, what they have called into life.

Gentlemen, what is the strongest objection brought against our demand for Representative Government for this country? It is said that India is divided by petty sectarian differences and that, moreover, she is divided into two great rival nationalities, Hindu and Mahomedan. It is alleged that in a country where there are so many sects and so many creeds, and above all, two such great rival parties, representative institutions are unworkable. Well, gentlemen, this argument has been answered and disposed of time after time, so that it seems impossible that it can now-a-days be brought forward in earnest by people capable of thinking. Turn it over in our minds as we will, it is impossible to discover in it any of that cogency which people often profess to attach to it. There is one point and only one point on which there is not a perfect accord, a perfect sense of oneness, between Indian Hindus and Indian Mahomedans, and that is, of course, their religious beliefs. In social customs, in manners and languages, in their habits of thought, and I may say even in their prejudices and in their inclinations, there is no essential difference between them. Why, the whole past history of India shows how, when there was no British Government, Hindus and Mahomedans pulled on together, and how if they fought they fought about secular and not religious matters. It shows that Hindu generals have led Mahomedan armies more than once and that Mahomedan swords have been unsheathed on behalf of Hindus.

But, gentlemen, it has been urged that, as the larger portion of the population is Hindu, the introduction of Representative Government in India will place the Mahomedans at the mercy of the Hindus, as the latter will form a great majority, and put their own interests before Mahomedan interests and do everything they like. Now, gentlemen, for my part, I have never been able to understand what is meant by Mahomedan and Hindu interests. In Europe, there may be Catholic interests and Protestant interests, because there, there is a real connection between the Church and the State; and yet the existence of such interests have not prevented the success of representative institutions. But in India no such connection exists, and the objection seems to me wholly futile. In England, I could understand this objection having some specious appearance of validity. I could, I say, understand this, because there are two powerful parties, the Established Church and the Nonconformists, both of which might have their antagonistic political interests, but even in England we do not find that these supposed antagonistic sectarian interests have in any way impaired the success of representative institutions, and how can it do so in India where fortunately there is no connection between Church and State? The Government has wisely taken its stand upon the principle of religious neutrality, and under these circumstances to pretend that there are, in matters of politics, Mahomedan interests distinct from Hindu interests, is really mockery, delusion, and a snare. (Hear, hear.) Sir, I think that if you look into this question dispassionately, you will find that, so far as India is concerned, Mahomedan interests and Hindu interests have no separate existence whatsoever.

But, gentlemen, there is yet another thing of which we hear as barring the way to the fruition of our aspirations. It is said that there is such hostility between Hinduism and Mahomedanism as to render it impossible. To this I first reply that were this really so, it would be the strongest of all reasons why Representative Government should be introduced into this country. Why, gentlemen, supposing the Hindus and Mahomedans were really divided by deep social and religious prejudices, are we to keep them apart and perpetuate that supposed hostility? Would not the question rather be how to remove these prejudices, how to dissipate that hostility, and how to blend the two communities into one nation? Now, gentlemen, sectarian prejudices are the result of selfishness of the heart and patriotism is the best corrective of selfishness. A representative form of government is best calculated to eradicate all hostile race prejudices by raising men above the cloud of selfishness into the purer regions of the wider and more enlarged sympathies of national feeling. By the more intimate intercourse it necessitates, by the juster mutual appreciation it engenders and in a thousand other ways, it removes those prejudices and that sectarian bias which stand in the way of unity between the various communities which are combined in it.

But I need not pursue this question further, because, though accepting them for the sake of argument, I deny the premisses. I say if this terrible antagonism did exist, even then representative institutions would do more than anything else to remove it. But I deny that it exists. There are low, ignorant people of both communities—mostly what the English papers call "roughs"—who, at festivals, when intoxicated by religious zeal, and, perhaps, something else, will fight, and there may be a Hindu or a Mahomedan leader here and there who, from selfish motives, tries to engender the hatred that does not exist, and speaks of it as if it were really so. But, gentlemen—and I speak to several hundreds of both communities—is it true that we Hindus and Mahomedans hate each other in this way (cries of "No, No"), and is it not a fact that we live as very good friends? (Cries of "Yes, Yes!") We have our ways in minor matters, and you don't perhaps much like them, but we don't want you to follow them, and you have your ways, and they are not quite like ours—and we don't dine together, or intermarry—neither do we Hindus of different castes amongst each other, for that matter; but despite all this, the great mass of us are good friends, rejoicing in each other's good fortune and sympathising in each other's troubles; and is this a state of affairs that precludes the introduction of representative institutions? (Loud applause.)

But, gentlemen, there are the recorded views of some of the most eminent Englishmen who have held high offices in this country. But I am afraid I have taken too much of your time, and I shall not detain you with their views. (Cries of "No, No," "Go on, Go on.") Since you are so indulgent, I will venture to quote some of the views to which I referred. You all know Sir Richard Temple. He was not an enthusiastic advocate of the Hindus. What does he say about this demand for representative Government? He says:

"For all that it must be remembered that the elective principle is essential to that political training which every stable Government, like that of the British in India, must desire to see possessed by its subjects. . . . . Public spirit cannot be created without entrusting the people with a part of their own public business, a part limited at first but increasing as their fitness shall grow. Even if political risks should accrue they must be borne in performing the duty which the British Government owes to the people of India. In that country a trustful policy will be found a wise one, and that which is sound morally will prove to be the safest politically."

This is the view of Sir Richard Temple. The view of Sir John Lawrence, in 1864, was:—

"The people of India are quite capable of administering their own affairs, and the municipal feeling is deeply rooted in them. The village communities, each of which is a little republic, are the most abiding of Indian institutions. Holding the position we do in India, every view of duty and policy should induce us to leave as much as possible of the business of the country to be done by the people."

Now, gentlemen, here is the opinion of the greatest statesman this century has seen—the patriarch of British Liberalism. (Loud cheers.) Mr. Gladstone says:

"I hold that the capital agent in determining finally the question whether our power in India is or is not to continue, will be the will of the two hundred and forty millions of people who inhabit India. The question who shall have supreme rule in India is, by the laws of right, an Indian question; and those laws of right are from day to day growing into laws of fact. Our title to be there depends on a first condition, that our being there is profitable to the Indian nations; and on a second condition, that we can make them see and understand it to be profitable."

Now, gentlemen, all these things lead me to believe that it is by no means on a hopeless quest that they have embarked who are now at this time seeking to secure the expansion of our Councils and the introduction of some tentative form of representative Government in India. Gentlemen, that we all desire this the unanimous voice of the country here embodied declares, and it is a desire which has been created in us by the English Government itself, and which is the greatest glory of that Government. England has moved us from our ancient anchorage. She has cast us adrift, against our will, upon the wide waters of a seething proletariat, and we turn back to England and ask her to grant us that compass of representative institutions by which, amid a thousand storms, she has steered her prosperous course to the safe haven of regulated political freedom. (Loud applause.)

Gentlemen, the desire for greater freedom is not confined simply to the educated classes; it is shared also by the uneducated classes, by the masses who feel it as keenly as we do, but in whom it has not (and in this lies the danger) yet found an articulate utterance. Gentlemen, it is in truth a national demand that we are making this day, and it is the duty of every one of us, so far as in him lies, to bring home this fact to the British Government and the British public, and to open their eyes to the true character of the efforts that are being made to blind that Government and that public to the universality of the desire of which the proposition now before us is a temperate expression.

Two of the most eloquent speakers who preceded me have referred in very just terms to Sir Lepel Griffin, and to another person, a native gentleman of very high repute. One of them has been inciting the Mahrattas against the Bengalees, the other, whatever he may allege, has been in practice egging on the Mahomedans to be less friendly with the Hindus (cries of "Shame, Shame.") And this gentleman is the class of man, and the only class, that denies, what we all so well know, the truly national character of our present demand. Well, things hidden from political sages have sometimes been revealed to the masses of the people, and believe me, gentlemen, that those are no true statesmen who are blind to the dawning lights of the fires which Western civilization is kindling in our hearts, and who raise their puny arms to arrest the chariot of India's destined development. Gentlemen, the demand we are making is a national demand; and, strong in the consciousness that we are the honest mouthpieces of countless millions, too long dumb, I ask you not to take to heart too much the base insinuations or the idle clamours that may be raised against you and the sacred task you have in hand. These will all pass away; the rising tide (loud cheers) is with us; so let us unite together in the performance of this noble task, which is practically the political regeneration of India. Let us aim, not to do good to one community or to two communities, to Hindus or Mahomedans, but to all the communities and all the sects of India. That is undoubtedly the noble ideal, the national ideal that we have set before us, the realisation of which will be the political Kingdom of Heaven. The various races, sects, and creeds of India will blend together into one imperial whole, in which all a free-born British subject's privileges and rights will be obtained and enjoyed; not by one sect or creed, but by all, and thereby the British Government, so far from being weakened, will be strengthened beyond measure. (Applause.) For the link which will then join a happy and united India to England will not be the link of fear, will not be the link of servility, but it will be the link of affection and gratitude which no misfortune can sever and which no calamity can shatter. (Loud applause.)

The President: Before I call upon the next speaker, I think it is necessary, seeing the amount of work we have yet to get through, to say that I feel disposed to follow the rule which was laid down by my predecessors, viz., that speakers should try, if possible, to confine their speeches within the limit of five minutes.

Pandit Madan Mohan Malaviya (Allahabad, No. 485 in list) then said: Mr. President and Gentlemen, my heart beats high within me as I rise to speak on this great subject. You have listened to the weighty words of Sir T. Madhava Row and the eloquent appeals of Babu Surendra Nath Bannerjee, Mr. Eardley Norton, and others, and if after such speakers as these I venture to address you, it is with the hope that you will grant me that indulgence which, being placed in this position, I earnestly crave of you. Gentlemen, after what has been said, it would be difficult to advance further arguments, or to bring forward additional reasons, as to the expediency and necessity for this great reform. But allow me to say this much, that, placed as we are in this country under a foreign Government, however benevolent and generous its motives—the motives of those who take part in the administration,—we stand in the greatest need of our own representatives in the Legislative Councils. Gentlemen, the whole of Europe, with the exception of Russia, has declared that the most efficient and best form of government for any country which has made any advance in civilization is a government, conducted not solely by the few for the many, but to a greater or less extent by the many for themselves—a government, in fact, in which the representatives of the people have some potential share—and if this be expedient for European countries, where the rulers and the ruled are of the same nationality, and where they are of the same religion, I think it must be conceded that it is even more essential for India, which is inhabited by people whose habits, manners, customs, language, race and creed differ from those of their rulers. If we demand for India that there should be representatives of her people in the State Councils—we only ask for what, not simply Europe, but America, Australia, and almost the whole civilized world have declared with one unaminous voice to be essential for any Government that is to be suitable to any country, as it is only where the representatives of the people are allowed to take part in that administration that the wants and wishes, the aspirations and grievances, of the people can be adequately set forth, properly understood or duly provided for. That being so, gentlemen, I think there cannot possibly be two opinions on the point that the reform which we crave for from Government is one so essential for the well-being of this country that it should be conceded to us without the least avoidable delay. This is now the third time that we have thus been meeting at yearly intervals; we have come from every district, from the most distant portions of this Empire, and in many cases at the cost of great personal sacrifice. We have nothing personally to gain, no selfish aim to serve. We come together, chosen by our fellow-countrymen primarily to press upon Government the fact that the country stands badly in need of this reform, and that the entire nation prays for it. But, unhappily, Government has not yet listened to our people's prayer!

What is it that we see year after year? People assembling from all parts of India,—from the Punjab, Sindh, Assam, Madras, Bengal, Bombay, the N.-W. Provinces, Oudh, the Central Provinces, from every province, from every town,—coming together to implore Government humbly to grant this reform, which is after all their birthright as free-born British subjects. (Loud cheers.) It is no desire or motive of self-ambition that brings these people together at such heavy cost and at such great personal inconvenience. There is no taint of self-interest in the matter. No. Their sole idea is that India, their country, of all things stands badly in need of this fundamental reform, and they hope—and God grant that they may not hope in vain—that their unselfish persistence in asking may secure for their native land this great boon! I cannot possibly believe that there is one single educated Indian, who after studying this question can rest happy in his mind, without trying his very best to secure this reform. (Applause.) I cannot possibly believe that any good man who once really understands what this reform truly means for his country and his countrymen, for his kinsman, his children and himself, can remain indifferent to it. And, gentlemen, neither we nor any other intelligent Indians are indifferent to it; and though thus far success has not crowned our efforts, we must only go up to Government again and ask their earliest consideration of our demands, or of our prayers (call them which you will), and entreat them again and again to concede to us this reform. Gentlemen, it is nothing very great we are asking them to do. The British Government has already made this concession to so many countries. So many colonies, so many British colonies, enjoy it. Canada, the Cape, the Australian Colonies, innumerable smaller places, even the so-called Crown Colonies, except perhaps the Fiji Islands, and some purely military posts, all enjoy some measure, and most of them the fullest measure, of Representative Government. Britain has granted or conceded this concession to all these places. (Applause.) Why should she withhold it from the people of India? (Hear, hear.) Does she think that we are less loyal than her subjects in other lands? (Hear, hear, and applause). Australia would break with her to-morrow if she ventured to prevent Australia from taxing British goods, while we, in all good temper, accept an odious income tax, vilely administered, and imposed not to meet the expenses of our own Government, but to provide funds to enable Great Britain to annex Burmah or menace Russia. (Loud and continued applause.) Does she think we are not prepared for the privilege? I think this very Congress is proof positive of our ripeness for the task and of the intelligence and knowledge which would be brought to bear upon the affairs of the nation if only the Government were kind enough to accede to our wishes. (Applause.) Gentlemen, I am sorry that, looking to the announcement our worthy President has made, I cannot venture to take up much more of your time, but if you will permit it I will go on for a few minutes more. (Voices, "Go on.") I thank you, gentlemen, for this indulgence. This question of the reform of the Legislative Councils is one in regard to which too much can hardly be said. Something was said in speeches in Parliament about the Budget being introduced there at an earlier date, but what effective criticism can we hope for there if we do not supply the materials by our criticisms when the Budget is introduced here? But how can we outside criticise a thing of details when those details are skilfully veiled from us? It is only when we have our own representatives inside the Government, who can get at those essential details, that we shall ever be able to control, or at any rate effectively protest against, financial mismanagement.

The Indian Councils Act was passed when the Government was transferred from the East India Company to the Crown. According to the provisions of that Act the expenditure of this country should be checked and controlled by the Secretary of State assisted by a Council. But how has this been carried out? We see that provision was made for the Budget being presented to Parliament with the object of securing some check. But we also know that no less a personage than Professor Fawcett, of lamented memory, speaking in Brighton in 1872, was compelled to confess that "the most trumpery question ever brought before Parliament—a wrangling over the purchase of a picture, a road through a Park—excited more interest than the welfare of 180,000,000 of our Indian fellow-subjects." (Loud applause.) And as it was then, so it is now. It is not only Professor Fawcett, moreover, who has protested against this monstrous injustice. Year after year some honest independent politician has raised his voice against a state of things which if it means our misery means also England's shame. Even this last Session, Mr. Bradlaugh rose to protest against the practice of bringing this subject (the Indian Budget) forward at so late a period of the Session. Last year the Budget was considered on June 21st and the year before on August 6th. It was not right to leave to the last moments of the Session the only opportunity that was afforded to Parliament of considering the wishes and the grievances of the 200,000,000 of people whom we rule. That any Parliamentary control should be exercised over the affairs of India was impossible when the Indian Budget figured upon paper as the eighth order upon one of the last days of an expiring Session." (Applause.) Following him, Mr. Reid said: "How could Parliament do anything when these matters were only brought to its cognizance on one of the very last days of a weary session when only fifteen or sixteen gentlemen had sufficient energy left to watch the proceedings. The debate was almost reduced to a farce. The discussion was begun at about a quarter past six o'clock, and in four or five hours from that time they would have settled the affairs of 200,000,000 of their fellow-subjects and sanctioned the expenditure of between seventy and eighty millions of money. Surely it would be better to delegate these duties than to continue doing that which was a mere mockery. Would it not be possible to appoint a Committee to overlook the affairs of India, in order that the people of that country might know that their interests were being cared for adequately by the Imperial Parliament?" (Loud applause.)

Then, again, Sir John Gorst, in connection with this matter, said: "The regret which the Honourable Member expressed with regard to the late period of the session at which the affairs of India had come up for discussion was shared by the Government with those who sat on the opposite side of the House. He believed every one would be glad, if it were possible, to bring the affairs of India under consideration of the House at a time when more members were present and when greater interest would be taken in the matter. Although many promises to introduce Indian financial statements earlier in the session had been made, no Government had ever succeeded in fulfilling those promises, and ever since he had had a seat in the House the Indian Budget had been one of the incidents of the sessions that had immediately preceded the Prorogation." (Applause.)

Now, gentlemen, you see that Parliament will not or cannot give that consideration even to our Budget, even to the expenditure of eighty millions of money yearly wrung out of the country—and none know better than you do with what hardships to the people,—that we have a right to expect from them—that common sense and justice demand—and if this be the case with the Budget, what chance have the rest of our affairs of getting a hearing of any kind? I say none, and therefore we ask Parliament to allow us to look after our own affairs. We say if you cannot or will not do your duty by us, at least put us in a position to do some portion of our duties to ourselves. We say, we entreat you in all fairness to allow us some control over our Budget, to put us in a position to say something through our representatives about it when it is brought into the Council—(applause)—to give us some voice here in the management of our domestic affairs. But it would seem as if our entreaties were vain. They will not do their duty by the country themselves and they will not allow us to do it. (Applause.) Can anything be more cruel, or more unjust, of the English nation which professes to love freedom and justice and boasts itself the founder of constitutional and free Government? Gentlemen, after this, I think nothing need be said by England about justice and freedom if this concession is not granted to us.

Gentlemen, I must express my regret that the rapidly-passing minutes debar me from speaking on this subject more fully, as I should wish to do, though I know it does not require much further illustration after the speeches you have heard. Allow me now to say in conclusion that we should continue to press this righteous demand on the Government, and if all else fail simply ask them to act according to their own Christian principles which tell them to do unto others as they would be done by. (Applause.) Would the English nation like to have their affairs treated in this way; would they tolerate it for one instant? Would they even dare to treat us in this way did they not know that we are the most patient and law-abiding people on the face of the earth? Only twenty-nine members present out of six hundred and seventy-five or something like that, when the welfare of two hundred and fifty million souls is to be discussed, and when a sum of seventy or eighty millions is to be disposed of. (Loud applause.) How would they like their own affairs to be treated in that way? Would they, I repeat, stand it for one week? Would they dare thus to deal with only five millions of Irishmen? Gentlemen, I must leave them to reply, and that reply, if truthful, must be their own condemnation. No, gentlemen, let them allow us a gradually-increasing liberty to look after and manage our own business, and they will find that we shall forget any temporary injustice that their negligence has caused us, and always, always, remember per contra all the good they have done us, and be grateful to them for all this and not least grateful for that concession we are now urging. (Applause.)

Rao Saheb Raghunath Pandurang Karandikar (Satara, No. 409 in list) said: Gentlemen, it is hardly necessary for me to support the proposition now before this assembly, which is in itself so strong that it clearly needs no support from anybody, least of all, after the many speeches which have been delivered, support from an humble voice like mine. But I must add something as a representative from the Bombay Presidency, though I shall confine myself to only a few sentences. What we ought all to do is, to look to the practice of Government in passing Acts, which we will hope will give a clue to their practice in dealing with the requests of the people also. We have three times affirmed this proposition. We asserted it first in 1885, affirmed it in 1886, and reaffirmed it in 1887, and I venture to hope that this will be the last time, because we all know that Bills in the Legislative Councils are all read three times, and only three times. Now, this is the third reading of this National Bill, and I hope that it will now be passed, and that our efforts will be crowned this year with success and our requests will be fully granted. I need hardly say anything more. (Applause.)

Mr. Sabapathy Mudaliar (Bellary, No. 271 in list): Gentlemen, Before I commence the few words I am going to say, I hope you will not be disappointed if I say that I am not going to give a lecture, as my predecessors, who had the ability to do so, have done on representative Government. I mean to speak only of a few facts—facts that are, I think, convincing as to the mutual friendship that prevails in the Bellary district, where I and my colleagues are living, between Hindus and Mahomedans. (Applause.) During the Mohurrum festival for the last three years there were grave apprehensions entertained by the officials of the place, as well as by other people, as to some conflict between the ignorant mobs of both creeds, but to the great credit of the Mahomedans, as well as of the Hindus, they both cheerfully gave up some of their rights as to places through which their processions usually passed, when they saw that it would be a convenience to the members of the sister religion, and I can boldly say that, so far as my knowledge goes, the Hindus and Mahomedans of our place have no feeling of ill-will towards each other and that there is absolutely no disunion amongst them. (Applause.)

When the Municipal Bill was being enacted I was appointed one of the members of the Committee that sat to frame the present Madras Municipal Act. During the discussion of the provisions, I was strongly in favour of certain clauses being inserted which were excluded by official interference. I mean so far as the election of a chairman was concerned. I considered that such a matter should be left entirely in the hands of non-officials and not in the hands of the officials. One of my European colleagues feared that as they had had an unfortunate riot in the district of Salem, if that clause was inserted in the Act there would be riots all over India, although I pointed out to him that he was mistaken in his views, as my experience of the Bellary district—in fact of the whole of the Ceded Districts—was that Hindus and Mahomedans were very friendly with each other. (Applause.) As an instance, I had even gone the length of showing him that at the recent elections which had taken place a month or two previously the Hindus elected three leading inhabitants who were Mahomedans, as Councillors, and the voters were for the most part all Hindus. (Applause.) This itself was evidence that no spirit of rivalry or animosity existed as far as that province was concerned. (Applause.) But still this did not satisfy him—I mean my European colleague, who was an official of high standing. Then I told him in plain words that if he meant to bring forward this argument for not supporting my proposition, I should simply bring out the present state of Ireland where riots were always going on. They had no Mahomedans and Hindus there to cause all these riots. They were all one nation and professed one religion. I attributed the riots amongst Hindus and Mahomedans, firstly to bad administration, and secondly to the wretchedness and ignorance of the lower classes, which also are due to that bad administration, and when I mentioned these facts it was enough to shut his mouth and he had nothing more to say on the subject. It is very unfortunate that our critics seize upon this imaginary religious animosity whereby to blot our character and if possible defeat our hopes, and we must simply, it seems to me, point out persistently instances where Hindus and Mahomedans have been acting in perfect unison, which have come under our own personal notice, as I have just done. I have nothing more to say. I thank you for listening to me. (Applause.)

Rajah Rampal Singh (Allahabad, No. 494 in list): Gentlemen, I do not rise here to make any set speech, but I think I may touch on certain circumstances which will help to illustrate this question of reform in the Legislative Council. Gentlemen, we the people of India are permitted (nominally) to send a certain limited number of our countrymen, who are elected by the Viceroy and the Lieutenant-Governors, to these existing Councils. It is very kind of them to take this trouble off our shoulders, but with their permission we would rather elect them ourselves. Joking apart, the defect which lies in this present system is this: the natives who sit in Council are chosen by the Governors and Lieutenant-Governors, whom they look to as their constituents, and are not, therefore, likely to bring forward the views of the people, whom they in no way represent and on whose suffrages they are in no way dependent. Necessarily these men, who are mostly the favourites of Governors and Lieutenant-Governors, think of nothing but pleasing their patrons; there are noble exceptions, but this is the rule. (Hear, hear.) On one occasion I was talking to a gentleman who had the honour of being a member of the Council of the Governor-General for making laws, but who knew not one syllable of English. (Laughter.) He was one of the Maharajahs of the North-Western Provinces, and a relation of mine, too. (Laughter.) I asked the Maharajah, "How did you manage to vote and take part in the discussion?" (Laughter.) He told me. "It was difficult for me at first; for I do not understand English, nor was I allowed to take anybody with me to explain what went on to me (laughter), but as I received it through the favour of the Viceroy, I raise my hand whenever the Viceroy raises his, and I hold down mine when he holds down his hand." (Loud laughter.)

Mr. W. S. Gantz (Madras, No. 52 in list) rose and said: Mr. President and Gentlemen, I must ask your indulgence for five minutes, and for five minutes only. With the general principle underlying this proposition, I apprehend, we all agree, and, therefore, it is not necessary for me to follow, at any length, the previous speakers who have so eloquently addressed you. I did not intend to speak on this subject, until this morning I saw the last issue of the *Madras Mail*. But, since we have had, from one or two speakers, allusions to the utterances or writings of prominent men in the northern portion of India, which certainly are very decided opinions, I trust I may be permitted to refer to another and very different view. I find the Lieutenant-Governor of the North-West Provinces, Sir A. Colvin, speaking so lately as the

19th of this month, in regard to representative institutions, said that "the business of administration in India becomes more complex as years pass on and the wants of the country grow more numerous; and he went on to say that "it is impossible for Government, unaided by the people, either to know, or to supply, all these wants. It is to the co-operation of the people in the administration of certain branches of public business, that the Government must look to enable it to deal successfully with its difficulties. The assistance which may be thus rendered to Government has a two-fold advantage. It enables the Government to work more efficiently, and it trains those who assist it in those habits of exertion, of self-discipline, and of interesting themselves in the general welfare which lie at the root of all progress and improvement."

Gentlemen, I think these are very appropriate words, and I say they supplement in a most marked and significant degree the remarks culled from the speeches of others. Sir A. Colvin further says, "Nobody knows better than I how sound is the sense and how temperate the judgment of the Natives of this Province, and I look with great confidence to the ultimate success of the institutions that have been given us. But the best way of obtaining success is to look facts in the face. The fact is that all of us, both official and private, are at the commencement only of an effort which requires for many years to come all our energies, and which will need all the intelligence, patience, forbearance and goodwill which all of us can bring to it." I thought it was my duty, when I saw this extract, to lay it before the meeting, and you will pardon me for reciting it to you.

Gentlemen, I much regret that some members of these existing Councils whose constitution we have been criticising have not risen and spoken in regard to the work of these Councils. I see several gentlemen here who have been members of Council, and I see one very prominent member of the Madras Council, and I very much regret indeed that not one of these gentlemen has got up and said a word about these Legislative Councils. Let me ask them now to do so. Let me put to them the simple question whether it is not true that every public measure of any importance that comes before these Councils is practically framed and shaped and pushed through by Government, so that free and independent criticism is absolutely impossible? Have they, has any independent member, ever any potential voice in determining the outcome of their deliberations? So far as any real practical good comes of their labours, beyond, perhaps, the softening of some repugnant clause, might they not just as well remain at home? I throw out these as questions, and I should like to have definite replies. On what principle are gentlemen nominated to these Legislative Councils? (Voices, "None, None.") That is the opinion, I see, of some gentlemen from Bengal. If it is the opinion in Bengal I can assure you it is the opinion in Madras also. But, inasmuch as these institutions are considered to be representative institutions, we have a right to know who and what these men are. Are they to be the men who, in the eloquent and significant language of Rajah Rampal Singh, hold up their hands when the Viceroy holds up his and keep theirs down when he keeps his down? (Laughter.)

Gentlemen, in regard to the question of self-government (and the remarks of Sir A. Colvin, which I have quoted, originated in certain matters appertaining to this that came before him), I may say that I have had some experience of the working of self-government in the mofussil, and I tell you that self-government, as it exists in this Presidency is simply nothing more than a sham and a delusion. (Applause.) I can tell you that we cannot even raise the pay of an ordinary duffadar by one rupee without sanction. (Applause.) The Municipalities are called upon to spend large sums of money year after year in the maintenance and the support of educational, medical and charitable institutions, and in regard to these also we have no real control, but have simply to find the money; we are over-ridden by some dominant official who who takes us under his paternal wing. In one particular station there was the greatest dissension and the greatest dissatisfaction in regard to the working of one particular branch of that particular Municipality. His Excellency the Governor was expected to visit the place on his tour and some of the members thought they would ventilate their grievances in an address. An address was duly prepared by the official chairman which was to be merely an address of welcome to H. E. the Governor. The dissentient members, who wanted to ventilate their grievances thereupon resolved to wait upon his Excellency by deputation with another address. A meeting was called, at which this second address was to be framed, and I may tell you this, that in one of those mysterious ways, familiar to most of us, the wires were pulled, and there was no quorum. His Excellency came, received the Chairman's address of welcome, and in his reply said: "I am happy to find, gentlemen, that you have no wants and no grievances." (Laughter and applause.) That is an instance of the kind of self-government that we enjoy in the Madras mofussil.

Babu A. Kumar Dutt (Bengal, No. 582 in list) then ascended the platform bearing a huge bundle and said: Everybody may wish to know what is the meaning of this burden that I bear here. I have been instructed by Mr. Surendra Nath Bannerjee to place it on this table here. I am not going to inflict a long speech upon you. "Only five minutes," as our President is good enough to say. Now, then, gentlemen, I come from a district, which is considered one of the most backward districts in Bengal. If you only hear what I have to say as to the interest that the people of this backward district take in this question of Reform and Representation I am sure you will all be convinced that the time has already come when the Government should, and without further delay, grant us this concession. Considering the rapid progress the country has made, the genuine enlightenment that prevails on these matters, and the success that has, in Bengal at any rate, attended Local Self-Government, the country's demand that the electoral principle be duly embodied in the constitution of the Legislative Council is the reverse of premature. All honour to Lord Ripon. (Loud applause.) His Local Self-Government has been the chief educator of the people. I have sounded the people myself, gentlemen, in many parts of my province, and I have found even the common people, the lowest classes, taking great interest in this matter. The preceding speakers have spoken eloquently, but they have spoken little about the common people, and I am going to say something about them—something of what the people feel in my own district. I had to attend a mass-meeting and there I addressed the people on this question of the re-constitution of the Legislative Councils. It was drizzling then, and some people said "Better disperse." But the people of the lowest rank, who are called "chandalas," immediately held up their hands and raised the cry "Go on, Go on." We had to go on with that address. When it was finished, a chandala, a very low-caste man, came forward and said "We are going to have our own men to be our legislators, that is very good, that is very good." (Applause.) The man in his delight, actually forgot his position, the surroundings, everything, when he came before the meeting and thus addressed them, and that is how the common people think in one of our most backward districts about this subject.

It is not a very difficult question, and I have always been staggered by persons saying that these common people do not understand it, and that they look upon us as sedition-mongers who simply wish to kick up a row. They say that the common people do not understand one iota of what we are doing in regard to these things. Now, I have placed before you an example of what illiterate people do understand. I can recount many other instances. Another instance occurred in Backergunje. I was there addressing people on this very subject, and directly I finished my address a grim-looking Mussulman, poorly clad, stepped out and said: "Babu, I was dreadfully afraid that you had come to impose some new tax upon us. But after hearing what you have said, I have come forward to pay down this four-anna piece to help on your cause." That four-anna piece was more to that poor old pauper than lacs of rupees are to some of you. That, gentlemen, is how the common people feel about this question. Don't you believe that the common people have no common sense. I know plenty of cases in which, at Municipal elections, the common people voted for and elected the best men, though these were opposed by European candidates possessing great local interest or nominees backed by such influence. All kinds of pressure was brought to bear, but when the election took place the common people all voted straight. Gentlemen, I could tell you many instances of this sort. I have been going through the various parts of Bengal, and wherever I went, I met with an enthusiastic welcome directly I opened the question of the reconstitution of the Legislative Councils.

Now, here is this burden which I am now about to explain to you. It is a petition signed by more than forty-five thousand persons, praying for this reform. The number of people in Backerganje who can read and write is forty thousand. We have not taken signatures of minors or persons under age. Of these forty thousand some twenty-five thousand have come and put their names to that petition. I want you to work in this way, to bring in signatures from every district of every province and let us overwhelm the Government with petitions (laughter), and they will be bound to listen to our prayers. When we send in petitions to Government from our meetings, our adversaries say that we exaggerate the number of people who attend the meetings. But here you have got the chairman and vice-chairman, so that you can really know how many persons attended the meeting. If you put in signatures like this, there is no gainsaying signatures. If they doubt the signatures, let them send and inquire whether they are not all genuine. I know of one case—no, I am not going to take up your time. (Voices, 'Go on.') Thanks for the indulgence. Well, when I was getting these signatures, as I told you, there was one Mussulman—he is almost illiterate—he can barely sign his name. He asked me to explain what the question was about. But another Mussulman explained it all to him. You will be surprised how he got to the very pith and marrow of this matter. He said, "Look here, as we elect our arbitrators, and as we hold ourselves bound by the decisions of such people, so let us elect our own men to be our Legislators and they will pass laws by which we will gladly be bound." It is clear that the people really understand the question. They know what it is to put questions before arbitrators, to elect their own Panchayats. Now that is Local Self-Government in conjunction with the Panchayet system. But of twenty-five thousand signatures, there are many thousand signatures of Mahomedans in Backergunje. Here is a telegram that I received from a Mahomedan delegate. "Regret, unavoidable circumstances, express heartiest sympathy with the Mahomedan Community of Backergunje." We are there acting like friends and brothers whenever national questions arise, and we stand shoulder to shoulder, Hindus and Mahomedans, for the advancement of our national cause.

I have given you a picture of Backergunje life. Other districts give us a brighter picture. But now I will not take up your time. I want everybody else to go home, and to go about bestirring themselves, getting the people to sign petitions. (Hear, hear.) I feel as if the Almighty hand were outstretched for the helping of our cause. I begin to see that the Ruler of all the nations of the world has ordained that we should get representative institutions as soon as we sufficiently exert ourselves. So I want you all to bestir yourselves, this and nothing more, and go onwards! onwards!! onwards!!! Do not cease to agitate; as Mr. Norton has advised us, agitate, agitate, agitate. When we have once put our shoulders to the wheel, as we have done now, we must just push, push, push on, and on, and on, until we have achieved our end. Let us realise and act upon this, and we shall very soon attain that end, foreshadowed in the encouraging words of Lord Dufferin, uttered on that memorable occasion of the Jubilee, which have been already repeated to you by Babu Surendra Nath Bannerjee.

Babu Mohun Sudan Das (Bengal, No. 600 in list) next spoke as follows: Gentlemen and Brother Delegates, When I came here, I never thought of speaking, but I may assure you that I will not go beyond the limit of five minutes. I came to hear, and not to speak, as I think it is always easier to listen than to speak. But, by one or two remarks which have fallen from previous speakers, I am tempted to lay before you a few facts from my own personal experience. It was said by one of the speakers that in certain quarters we are alleged to be self-constituted delegates. I myself am a delegate, and I am proud to say that I come as a duly elected delegate, from a part of Bengal which is, perhaps, the most backward part of Bengal—I mean Orissa. I say I am proud, because the fact that I come from and was formally elected in that part of Bengal, shows that even the masses of a backward province do take an interest in this movement; and, sirs, not only was I elected, but I am sure you will be delighted to hear that two other gentlemen, who are present at this meeting, were also elected delegates from the same part of Bengal. One of them is a very wealthy Zamindar, Babu Romesh Chandra Mandle. He comes as a delegate from Chinsurah and Hugli, but he was also elected a delegate at Balasore. But even there the matter does not stop. That the people do really take an interest in a movement of this nature will be further evident from the fact that a brother delegate who has travelled with me to this place has had all the expenses of the journey paid by his constituents. If there is any measure for the interest which the people take in a cause it is in the pounds, shillings, and pence that they are willing to disburse to advance that cause. Of all measures, Englishmen, at least, ought to admit that this is the best. (Applause.) Again, it has been said by one of the speakers that the aristocracy of the nation are alleged not to take an interest in this national movement. I can mention one fact which will not only show that some of the aristocracy do take an interest, but that they take a very keen and active interest in it. My brother delegate, who has been putting up with me, has just received Rs.100 by telegram, sent unsolicited, by one of the Indian Chiefs, towards defraying his expenses, and this is certainly an active interest. Are we to be told that this assembly of delegates is an assembly of self-constituted delegates? (Voices, "No, No.") We are told that the masses of the people do not care for representative institutions, do not value representative institutions, and do not ask for representative institutions. To any person who makes these assertions I should reply, Look at this assembly, of which, at any rate, each delegate understands the principle on which he represents hundreds or thousands of people, each one of whom equally understood it, or they could not have elected their delegates. The principle of representation underlies Hindu society in all its various forms and phases. A Hindu from his childhood understands what representation is, nay, you will also find the principle of representation underlying the Hindu religious system—but I promised not to take more of your time than five minutes, and I have taken exactly five minutes. So, I will not pursue the subject as I might, but I thought it my duty to mention these two facts, coming within my personal knowledge, which tend to show that the aristocracy, the highest in the land, take a vivid interest in this matter, and that we delegates are not self-constituted delegates, but are the formally accredited representatives of hundreds and thousands of people, who elected us to speak for them and who take an active and keen interest in this great and growing national movement. (Applause.)

The President: I think, gentlemen, that this question of the reconstitution and expansion of the Legislative Councils has been thoroughly discussed from the affirmative point of view. So far as the speeches that have been delivered are concerned they are all in favour of it. It seems to me that it is hardly necessary to go on with any further discussion of the question, unless some one takes the opposite view. (Cries of "No, No.") I take it then that this Congress is practically unanimous upon the question. (Hear, hear, and applause.) Our time is limited and life is short, and we have other work to do. It is already 4.30 p.m., and I would ask you, by the indication of your hands, to show whether you desire that the Resolution should now be put to the vote. (All hands were raised with loud cries of "Vote, Vote.") Then I put the Resolution, which will stand as follows:—

Resolved.—That this Congress re-affirms the necessity for the expansion and reform of the Council of the Governor-General for making Laws and the Provincial Legislative Councils, already set forth in Resolutions III. of the Congresses of 1885 and 1886, and expresses the earnest hope that the Government will no longer delay action in the direction of this essential Reform.

The Resolution was then put and unanimously carried, and the meeting adjourned until 12 noon, next day.

THIRD DAY'S PROCEEDINGS.

Thursday, the 29th December, 1887.

The PRESIDENT: We proceed to-day to the further discussion of the subjects contained in our programme. The first now standing on the list is the proposal:—

"That this Congress do once again place on record an expression of the universal conviction that a complete separation of executive and judicial functions (such that in no case the two functions shall be combined in the same officer) has become an urgent necessity, and declare that in its opinion it behoves the Government to effect this separation without further delay, even though this should in some Provinces involve some extra expenditure."

This is the proposition which will be discussed first, but I must remind the delegates that we have a very great deal to do, and that the time we have at our disposal is exceedingly short, and that it is necessary that gentlemen should bear that in mind, and the proposers and seconders confine their speeches to a period of ten minutes each, and the other speakers to one of five minutes each, and I venture to hope that all will observe this rule without rendering any interference on my part necessary.

Mr. N. SUBRAMANIEM (Madras, No. 9 in list) rose and said: Mr. President and gentlemen, the sight of this vast assembly fills me with immense joy. I see gentlemen here from every part of this great country, speaking different languages and professing different faiths, but all come together with one desire—to consider and to discuss questions affecting the welfare of this common country, of our common motherland (applause), and with one heartfelt feeling of loyalty to one common sovereign. (Applause.) It is to me a source of the deepest joy to see such a huge gathering as this. If any man, twenty years ago, had prophesied that within a quarter of a century such a representative gathering from all the different parts of the country, would be possible, he would have been mistaken for a lunatic, and if he was possessed of any property coveted by his relatives, probably promptly walked off to an asylum. (Laughter.) Even if they did not go so far as that, his friends world certainly have winked at each other when he passed, and have pointed to his head and said that there was something wrong in his upper story. (Laughter.) But what has been the real cause or mainspring of such a gathering having been made possible? I answer without any hesitation that the English education—the higher education, which has been granted to this country—has made it possible. (Applause.) That what was before an impossibility has become a possibility—that men from all parts of the country should come and band together under one "Pandal" and discuss earnestly and lovingly the affairs of this, their common country: for this, gentlemen, we are indebted to the British Government. (Applause.) Mr. T. B. (later Lord) Macaulay, Sir Charles Trevelyan, and other eminent men realised long ago the wisdom of imparting a sound English education, and the principle for which they then fought, the dissemination of a sound English education, and whose cause they won, firmly established under the Government of Lord William Bentinck, was thenceforth carried out by Government and by Missionary Societies, of whose instruments Dr. Duff (applause), the prince of Indian missionaries, was the foremost—this principle, I say, continued to be given effect to by the Indian Government and by Missionaries, and lastly, in later times, by our own countrymen, will now be religiously adhered to, I doubt not, to the end of time. (Applause.) Gentlemen, because we here, forsooth, come and open our minds to Government in regard to the grievances which afflict our country, some people, we hear, say that we are not grateful for the blessings we already enjoy. Nothing is farther from the truth. (Applause.) A son who has received the larger portion of the share of that patrimony to which he is entitled would not go to his father and say, "I have already received from you this and that and the other thing." All that is already known to both of them, but, rather, he would go to his parent and say, "Now, father, that I have made a good use of what I have received give me that other estate to which I am entitled." Here we are together assembled under this "Pandal"; but we do not come merely to express gratitude for the blessings we already enjoy, but to prove our gratitude for the English education and railway communication and telegraphic communication, and the thousand other blessings we enjoy, (many of which have combined to make it possible for us, thus drawn from all parts of the empire, to meet during our brief holidays), by discussing all the more important questions that affect our country, and thus pointing out to our benefactors what is still lacking and how they may best complete their good work. (Applause.) There are critics who, instead of coming into our midst and seeing and hearing for themselves what we are, and what we are doing, and what we say, prejudge us and affect to disbelieve in the goodness of our motives, to disbelieve, as it were, in our loyalty, and then try to sow the seeds of dissension between one section of the community and another. (A voice, "Shame.") The English Government, the English nation, have given us the education and the physical facilities which have made it possible for us thus to come together and enlighten them as to our real condition and wants. But there are isolated Englishmen, some of them in high position even, who attempt to undo and nullify their country's noble work, and to sow the seeds of discord amongst our many races. Fortunately for us, these seeds have fallen, it would seem, upon a barren soil. (Loud applause.)

Now, gentlemen, the proposition I have been asked to move is one that was discussed at the last Congress at Calcutta, and it is one that seemed to demand on that occasion no great argument to convince all those present of the necessity of its adoption, and it will not be necessary, I take it, for me now to adduce arguments at any great length in its support. In moving the Resolution, I think it is nothing but right and proper to state some of the qualifications which warrant my presuming to speak upon this subject. Mr. President, while you are much my senior as a barrister-at-law and an advocate of the High Court, I may mention that, long before I became a Barrister, I had been in the practice of the law as a public prosecutor and a District Court pleader from as far back, indeed, as the beginning of 1867, and, although, Mr. President, I may not then have had the privilege of pleading before the High Court judges, it has been my lot to practise a great deal before the mofussil courts, and the conclusion that I have arrived at is the result of twenty or twenty-one years' experience before the lower courts, where the combination of the executive and the judicial functions are daily and hourly before one's eyes, and where the evil consequences that arise from that combination are constantly and lamentably apparent. Gentlemen, in principle every one will admit that it is not right and proper to join together two distinct functions of this nature in one and the same man. Every watchmaker, every manufacturer, every merchant will tell you that work is done the speediest and most satisfactorily when it is divided between different hands, each specially trained for and skilled in the part he undertakes. The principle of the division of labour is well understood even by a man who manufactures a hatchet. He gets one man to make the wooden handle, out of wood that other men have cut down and seasoned, and that others again have sawn into suitable scantlings, and he gets another man to shape and perhaps sharpen the iron portion out of metal that others have wrung from the stony ore, and then the two are put together in a shorter time, and prove more durable and effective, than if one person had attempted to do the whole work; and the same is true in the present case,—indeed, Government have themselves confessed the expediency of the separation of the executive and judicial functions—they have so far approved of it as to have carried out this principle in various Provinces. They have carried it out as far as they saw it could be done easily, but they have not carried it out in its entirety. In this Presidency the judicial work in the higher grades is entirely separated from the revenue work and other executive work. But the two are combined in the Magistrates and Collectors of districts. The District Magistrate and the Collector are rolled into one. The Subordinate Magistrates and the Subordinate Collectors are also rolled into one. The evil consequences arising from this combination are such—but before I come to that, I would say, first of all, that the kind of work the Magistrate has to perform is wholly different in character from that which the Collector or executive officer has to do. The Magistrate is a judge, and by instinct he ought to be a man thoroughly impartial; he ought never to be led away by reports and rumours or influenced by anything he hears outside. Whereas, the executive officer, in order to be a successful man, ought to have his ears open in order to turn all such reports and information as he can obtain to the benefit of his district. The Magistrate must necessarily, if he is to be a just magistrate, shut his ears completely to everything said outside his court, and yet, how can the same individual, who is a magistrate, shut his ears to everything he hears as an executive officer? As an executive officer the magistrate is bound to receive all sorts of information, and a great deal of information is sent to him by demi-official letters—I do not know whether you have any such document in other Provinces (voices, 'Yes, Yes')—and his mind is prejudiced, or, let me say, necessarily influenced, by the reports sent to him by the police officers. But he is to set aside all this information, all the bias, nay, all the conviction that is thus necessarily engendered, when he enters his court, where he must not be biased, as a magistrate, one way or the other in regard to the criminal; and he must know nothing of him or of the case but what comes up in evidence before him. Surely, this is impossible! Again, the executive officer to be successful has to be in constant touch with the people. He has to know all the vagaries of the various men within his district, all the bad qualities of the men, and yet that is the very thing which would unfit him for the just performance of his duties as a magistrate. It is impossible for a man who is an executive officer to avoid forming his opinion for good or evil in regard to a person that he has to judge, in regard to a witness or criminal or complainant, it is impossible, I say, for him to avoid forming his opinion partly on knowledge acquired out of court, and therefore impossible for him to deal with them impartially (hear, hear, and applause) on the evidence before him, and on that evidence alone, as a magistrate is bound to do. (Hear, hear.) Again, gentlemen, Government, in the selection it makes of these officers, has, I am sorry to say, to a great extent, to be influenced by the success of the man as an executive officer. If he turns out to be a good Collector, and shows a large revenue in the district, why Government does not, it seems to me, much care how he does his magisterial work, and the result is that, good, faithful and honest as the officers are, when there is work placed before them, magisterial and executive, the temptation to discharge the executive work in order to win the approbation of Government is far too great for any man to resist entirely, and he therefore sticks to the executive work and scamps the judicial work. (Hear, hear.) Therefore, only for this, if for no other reason, it is absolutely necessary that one man should be told off to do the executive work, which is no doubt very important, and that another man should be told off to do the magisterial work, which is, I submit, if the welfare of the people be regarded, quite equally important. (Hear, hear). Gentlemen, such cases are an every-day experience; but I may tell you of one particular instance where the combination of the two functions very nearly wrecked a client of mine. There was a case before the magistrate and I had to defend the prisoner. I successfully defended him and got him off, but the magistrate told me that if he only used the information he received, and which he received as an executive officer, he should have convicted my client. (Hear, hear.) He received information, which he believed to be true, that my client was guilty, but the evidence on paper was such that he could not convict him, and therefore he acquitted him. Well, he was one officer who realised the necessity of separating legal from illegal evidence; but, out of ten officers I believe that nine, under the like circumstances, would have convicted my client. Gentlemen, I will give you another instance, an instance of the manner in which magisterial work is shelved and takes the second place because of the pressure of executive work. There is a magistrate, a personal friend of mine, before whom a prisoner was being tried. He thought the vakils would take up time in arguing the case. He had a great deal of executive work to do, and so he said, "Gentlemen, I will not hear your case; I will not hear your arguments. Will you please put down on paper what you have to say and I will read it over at night?" (Hear, hear, and laughter.) The vakils did so and the man was convicted. There was another officer that I knew who was compelled to do these two kinds of work, and he said, "Let the other go to the wall," and he confined himself to executive work. Gentlemen, justice, in order to be effectual, must be speedy and sure; but, by reason of the combination of the two functions, the results are neither speedy nor sure. These are not imaginary cases. I have had hundreds of them. The magistrate receives a case and he posts the case for a certain day. The day arrives, the parties are there, but the magistrate has a lot of executive work that must be attended to. He, therefore, goes on with his letters. He has been at them from early morning, and he is at them till 10 or 11 o'clock. Even when the magistrate has had his breakfast, the unfortunate prisoner and witnesses and complainant have to wait till the magistrate is at liberty to take up the case. It often happens that at 3 or 4 or 5 o'clock in the afternoon the magistrate is not even then at liberty. He has still got other things to do, and so the case drags on. Sometimes, again, the executive work compels the magistrate to go away far into camp, some twenty miles or more, and there he holds court in his tent. The poor parties who come before him have to wait outside in the sun or rain, and then comes the difficulty of getting legal advisers; no legal adviser worth anything can afford to go out and hang about the tents, and if an unfortunate vakil does go out, he has to roam round about the tents for hours, wasting his time, with only his Penal Code and Criminal Procedure Code under his arm to amuse him. (Laughter.) He has to wait outside, and when he does go inside he finds a small camp-table and one single chair, on which latter the magistrate sits, and he has to sit down on the floor or stand where he is. (Laughter.) Vakils, therefore, do not care to go and hang about the tents or to go inside and be received in this manner. The magistrates, of course, try to accommodate the vakils; but the system is wrong, and unless you put an end to the system, this sort of inconvenience will arise, resulting in a great failure of justice, as the unfortunate prisoners can get no vakils to defend them. Gentlemen, very often the case is partly heard, and the magistrate then tells the parties: "The case is adjourned till the day after to-morrow." The parties accordingly appear. The magistrate looks over his diary and says, "I am off twenty miles away; I have got business there," and so on for the next week and the following week, and he adjourns the case for three weeks. He has more important and pressing executive work which occupies all his time. Gentlemen, there is one other observation, and that is—something has been said about the expenditure. I do not believe there will be extra expenditure, but if there is extra expenditure in the separation of the two functions, will you not pay for it? (Hear, hear, and applause.) Let them re-adjust the taxes. Let them throw away some other burden upon the State. Properly managed, there need not be any additional expenditure; but even were it necessary that an additional tax should be imposed, I, for one, would pay an additional pie in the rupee rather than allow my poorer fellow-countrymen to continue exposed to this constantly recurring failure of justice. Gentlemen, with these observations, I have great pleasure in moving the proposition that has already been read to you by our President, and which was adopted at our last Congress. One word more. This Congress has been a still greater success than the two previous Congresses. We have numerous representatives of the Mahomedans of all parts of India—a community that, to some extent, kept aloof before. (Applause.) We have also able representatives of the Eurasian community, who, also, to some extent, kept aloof (applause); and, lastly, we have even a few representatives of the European community, and I would venture to express the hope that the Europeans, as natives of India—those Europeans who come and settle down here, and consider themselves citizens of this vast empire—may now be induced to join us in larger numbers, and aid us by their superior knowledge of and experience in political matters. I must say that it is very unfair that anyone outside should refuse to come and look at us and hear what we have got to say, and yet, standing outside and knowing nothing of what we are humbly trying to effect, judge us in an uncharitable manner. I would only, humble though I am, give them a piece of advice, and for this advice I would charge no fee (laughter), and that is, that instead of finding fault with us from outside, they should themselves come in and see for themselves the proceedings that take place, and if we be wrong help us to do better; I give this advice, not only to our rulers, but also to all those other gentlemen who refuse to join us, and, receiving information second-hand, condemn us on hearsay evidence. (Cheers). Why, gentlemen, if these very functionaries wanted to judge of a dramatic performance, they would, if they wished to judge honestly of it, go and see it, and they would not abuse it on the strength of second-hand reports. Our performance may be very poor, but such as it is, let them come and see it, and see what kind of men we are, and whether we are preaching sedition or whether we are preaching loyalty; nay, if any of our rulers wish to come as delegates to represent the interests of their class, and make sure that these are not overlooked in our deliberations, I am certain that we shall all receive them with open arms and be only too thankful for their co-operation. (Cries of "Yes, Yes," and loud applause.)

Babu Kali Charan Bannerjee (Calcutta, No 557 in list) then said: Mr. President and Gentlemen, after the exposition and support which this resolution has received at the hands of my learned leader, I feel, especially as we are pressed for time, as if I ought not to venture to do more than formally second it. If I overcome the feeling, it is because I have another feeling; it is because there is such a tremendous reality about the question that it would be unpardonable trifling to approach it in a merely formal manner. (Applause.) Gentlemen, this is another Resolution which we, as a Congress, find ourselves in a position to reaffirm to-day. In one sense, it is reassuring that the experience of a year enables us to reaffirm the position we took up last year. (Hear, hear, and applause.) In another sense, it is discouraging to realise that there should still be occasion so to reaffirm it. (Loud and continued applause.) Gentlemen, if you compare the propositions recorded in the programme of business which is in your hands, if you consider the various demands made in these propositions, you will find, I think, that this proposition which I have now the honour to second, has, perhaps, on the whole, most to recommend it. (Applause.) Not only is it true of this Resolution, that it represents the concentrated voice of all India—(hear, hear)—but I feel that I am in a position to include in that concentration the voice of our rankest opponents. That the complete separation of executive from judicial functions will contribute in an important degree to the ends of justice, not one even of our opponents can decently gainsay. I have advisedly used the word "decently," for I feel that there is nothing to which rank opposition is not equal. There are no heights to which it could not rise. I should correct myself and say rather, that there are no depths to which it could not stoop. (Loud cheering.)

There is another recommendation which this Resolution carries with itself. If we could get the officers who would be affected by this Resolution, if we could get them to express their sincere convictions on the subject, I believe that they likewise would join us in pressing the Government for the boon we crave. (Hear, hear, and applause.) It could not be said, as far as this Resolution goes, that the country is not yet ripe for this concession: unhappily, the country is already too ripe for it. (Applause.)

There is another reason why we might go up to Government without hesitation with this prayer that is before the Congress, and that is, that if it contemplates a curtailment of power that curtailment will affect our own countrymen as well as Europeans. (Applause.) In fact, there are more of our own countrymen likely to be affected by this curtailment than European officers, for there are more sub-divisions than districts.

There is yet one other reason why this Resolution, as I have said, carries with it the greatest recommendation of all. In urging our prayer we need not imply any reflection whatever on the officers concerned. I say, we need not imply, because, if only they would be prepared to plead guilty to the soft impeachment, namely, that we charge them with being human beings, they would admit that the difficulty we have in view is a real difficulty. (Applause.) Man is man whether we be terrestrials or celestials. (Applause.) So long as we are all men we are open to the difficulty which this Resolution pre-supposes. Therefore, gentlemen, we see that the Resolution which we are now reaffirming is a Resolution that has about it many a recommendation, and we need feel no hesitation whatever in reaffirming it, and in asking further that effect may be given to it without any further delay. (Applause.) As far as the merits of the Resolution are concerned, they have received an exhaustive exposition at the hands of my learned leader. You will understand what the combination of these functions implies. It implies, in the first place, the combination of the Prosecutor and the Judge in the same person. (Applause.) It is not necessary to be initiated into the mystery of law to understand that justice is in jeopardy if the prosecutor happens to be also the judge. If you have a case in which there is a private complainant, there the prosecuting and persecuting energies of the private complainant are brought to bear upon you. Then, you have, in addition, the Police machinery, with all its prosecuting and persecuting energies brought to bear upon you, and if, in addition to these two-fold prosecuting energies, you have brought to bear upon you all the prosecuting energies of a magistrate, why, the poor defendant finds himself simply in a hopeless condition. (Applause.) We cannot avoid private complaints being, at any rate, preferred. We do not contemplate here, at any rate, any interference with the Police machinery. All that we pray for is that the strong arm of the magistrate should not be, by anticipation, lent either to the private complainant, or to the police machinery set on foot by him. (Applause.)

Then, again, as you have already been told, the combination of these two functions sets aside all the safeguards which the rules of evidence have provided for the due administration of justice. There is the magistrate listening attentively to the police papers read out to him by the police officer in the early morning. The police officer is in personal communication with the magistrate and instils into his mind his own ideas in respect to the case he has been kind enough to take into his own hands. And the magistrate listens to all sorts of things, and not only is much of the so-called evidence which is at such times laid before a magistrate no evidence at all, but he, as it were, has his judgment sketched out for him beforehand by the policeman. He listens to all this, and then, if it so happens, as it often does, that he places the case on his own file, when he sits to try it the conditions are all reversed for the judicial function has been exercised by the policeman while the magistrate has been closeted with him, and when he comes into court he is merely the executive who carries out that secret judicial decision. (Applause.) The judge has become the executive, while the executive has become the judge. (Loud applause.)

If you have such a reversal of conditions, how can you expect that justice should be properly administered? There comes the witness before him, the policeman has given him a certain version of the evidence of that witness. God alone knows whether the witness has made such a statement before the police. But the magistrate, having heard the police papers read out to him, has the idea that the witness has made such a statement. The witness, when he gives his evidence, does not, perhaps, say a word of what the police papers record him to have said. It is not easy for the magistrate, then and there, to disabuse himself of the impression produced by the police papers that have been read out to him. He fancies that the witness has been tampered with by the defendant; that he has stated the truth before the police; and that he is now contradicting himself, and, according to the amended Procedure Code, he must be prosecuted for perjury. (Laughter and applause.) He sees witness after witness coming, but his mind is made up, and, therefore, he is impatient of cross-examination. He has certain convictions, and he is not prepared to allow those convictions to be unsettled or disturbed in any way. His mind is made up, and that is the secret of his impatience. (Applause.) Gentlemen, if only we could get statistics on this point, we might prove that there have been failures of justice in simply countless cases, because of this unsound procedure.

I may tell you some facts connected with the working of this mode of procedure. Sometimes a case is made over by a magistrate who has had the benefit of the police papers to a magistrate who has not had the benefit of the police papers. I have a certain sub-division in view at the present moment. It happened that a number of cases "challaned," *i.e.* sent up, by the police, were dismissed by the magistrate who, as I have said, had not been in good time initiated into the mystery of the police machinery in respect to them. The police officer was impatient of such a result, and he could not brook the indignity of having cases "challaned" by him dismissed, and I may tell you that in this sub-division, for a time, at any rate (I do not know whether this practice continues to this day), it was so arranged that the cases "challaned" by the police officer were to be so arranged on the file that the sub-divisional officer might have the necessary morning whispers instilled into his ears by the police officer. If you compared the cases tried on the one hand by a magistrate who has had the benefit of police coaching, and, on the other hand, by a magistrate who has had nothing to do with the police, you would find that the magistrate who went solely by the evidence and his own convictions, constantly dismissed cases while the magistrate who had the benefit of police guidance seldom dismissed but frequently convicted. If we could only collect statistics, I say, they would prove beyond denial how constantly failures in the administration of justice have been brought about by this uncivilized method of procedure. No doubt there are difficulties in the way. When, in many cases, we go up to Government as one united India, and when we challenge the opinions of their own officers, I do not know whether the love of power—and all our reforms tend to render this less absolute—would not stand in the way of their owning the truth, but still we might challenge even their opinions on this particular point, and challenge the opinion of our opponents. When we thus go up to Government with this concentrated voice of all classes, no doubt the Government will admit the desirableness of the separation, but there is no doubt also that even the Government might find itself in difficulties as to how to carry out this separation. Now, in many cases, the separation might very easily be effected. In places where you have a magistrate and a joint-magistrate as well, it is a fact that the magistrate does only a small proportion of the judicial work and chiefly hears only appeals from the decisions of the second and third-class magistrates. Of original judicial work he has very little to do. If the magistrate of the district, who does little of judicial work except the hearing of appeals, is altogether relieved of judicial duties, and the joint-magistrate, who practically does the bulk of the judicial work, is required to do the whole judicial work, and nothing else, then the difficulty, in some measure at least, may be obviated. It may be less easy, no doubt, in sub-divisions where, in addition to one first-class magistrate, there is no other magistrate. But, as my learned leader has put it to you, if any extra expenditure is incurred for this purpose, each of us might be called upon to bear, and will cheerfully accept, his share of the burden. I would not detain you longer, but I would conclude by drawing your attention to the fact, that this measure, the desirableness of separating the judicial and executive functions was realized as an imperative necessity, by our great reformer Raja Ram Mohun Roy. (Cheers.) So far so that that great reformer, in the exercise of that keen fore-sight which he possessed, saw that a crisis in this matter must come sooner or later, and that he should be compelled to go up to Government and require at their hands this measure which is indispensable to the due administration of justice. (Applause.)

Pandit Jwala Dutta Joshi (Kumaon, No. 496 in list) was then called on by the President, and spoke as follows: After the speeches of the learned gentlemen who so ably proposed and seconded the Resolution, it seems, I confess, superfluous on my part to say anything further on the subject, but, since I have been called upon to speak, I cannot do better than give the substance of my own thoughts on the subject. The proposed separation has always appeared to me to be not only necessary on legal grounds, as essential to the right administration of justice, but to be so on economic grounds as well. According to the general principles of law, a man can not be a Prosecutor and a Judge in the same case, and Magistrates, who are the heads of the Executive Departments in their respective districts, are, as the representatives of Government, prosecutors in all cases in which the Queen-Empress is the complainant. The combination also is not justifiable, according to the generally accepted principle of the division of labour. We have also found in practice that officers, acting in these various capacities, can not and do not attain the excellence in any branch which they might, if allowed, to become specialists in any one. And the judicial work, especially, is apt to obtain less attention than executive, and men do not do it as well as they could do, even without becoming specialists, for want of time. With regard to the expenditure, it may be said that division of labour, as a rule, cheapens rather than enhances the cost of work, and even supposing that it does not, as it should, cheapen it, the same amount of money which is set apart for the salaries of the officers now performing both judicial and executive duties ought certainly to be sufficient for their salaries, even when each is confined to a single branch. Only the division of the officers into two classes will have to be made and the work re-arranged between the two, and in those parts of the country with which I am acquainted it certainly would not be a difficult task. But the subject of expenditure seems to be outside the pale of our discussion, inasmuch as we are prepared to have the separation effected even if it necessitates some extra expenditure in some parts of the country. (Applause.)

Mr. Syed Abdul Aziz (Nagpur, No. 463 in list) spoke in Hindustani. He said: I beg to be permitted to say a few words in support of Resolution No. III. My brother delegates who delivered their excellent speeches before me have completely shown the necessity of the separation of the executive from the judicial. It is not necessary for me to dilate upon the same subject again; but finding that executive and some criminal powers are invested in one person in the provinces from which my brother-delegates have come to this assembly, and civil, criminal, and revenue powers are centred in one and the same person in the Central Provinces from which I have the honour to attend here, I thought it better to add a few words myself with reference to the Central Provinces. It is absolutely necessary that a separation of the judicial and executive functions should take place without any further delay. Executive officers burdened with a variety of miscellaneous work have not and can not find sufficient time to dispose calmly, systematically, and with due deliberation, of the judicial work that comes before them. It is, moreover, the duration that prevents judicial business being done in the proper style. If a case is not gone through within the prescribed time, no matter what its nature, explanation has to be furnished, and want of time is not considered to be a sufficient excuse. Under these circumstances, a judge tries to get rid of the case anyhow, and the result is well known. I have always seen, as must be the experience of many others of my brothers in the profession to which I belong, that when there is a large number of witnesses in a case they are not examined on the same day, owing to the pressure of work or want of time, and the party on whose side witnesses have been examined loses the advantage of cross-examination because the opposite party gets an opportunity to tutor his witnesses. Wherever these two functions, executive and judicial, are combined in the same individual officer, there is a very great probability of a miscarriage of justice. With these observations I submit that the separation of the executive from the judicial has become a great desideratum in the Central Provinces.

Before resuming my seat, however, I cannot help making a few remarks regarding the feeling that prevails between the Mahomedans and the Hindus of the Central Provinces. To be brief, I may say it is one of complete cordiality and friendship. In all movements of general interest, whether set on foot by my co-religionists or the Hindus, one section of the community takes as much care to assist the other as is expected between Mahomedans or Hindus themselves. (Hear, hear.) I can speak with confidence with regard to my province that none of my sect, so far as I have been able to find out, have been dissatisfied with these Congress meetings. (Hear, hear.) The assertion of the Mahommedans who do not wish to take part in the Congress, that when the Hindus are in want of aid from the Mahomedans, they willingly join with them, but when the Mahomedans require any assistance from the Hindus, they decline to give it;—this assertion, I say, is without any truth whatsoever in it. In this Congress, several Mahomedan gentlemen have joined, and not only that, but one of them has been elected the President. Under these circumstances, this Congress can very well be designated "The Indian National Congress." You have already heard Mr. W. C. Bonnerjee say that the election of a Mahomedan gentleman to the presidential chair has been welcome to the Mahomedans and to the Hindus as well. I fully endorse this expression of Mr. Bonnerjee's. With these few remarks I beg to take my seat.

Rao Saheb K. Venkata Row (Madras, No. 272 in list), said: Worthy President and Gentlemen of the Congress, I have come here, not to repeat what has been set forth by previous speakers, but, limiting my remarks to the time allowed us by the President, to set forth a few simple facts. One fact is in connection with myself, *i.e.*, I had the pleasure, or rather, let me say the misfortune, to be myself formerly for some time a second-class magistrate and deputy tahsildar. In me the two functions were then combined, and I had to exercise those functions. With regret, I submit that I duly tasted the pleasures, or rather, I should say, the bitters, of these two-fold functions that I was supposed to exercise. With the greatest regret I tasted them, and within a very short time I perceived that this sphere of life would neither suit me nor any other man who desired to go in the straight path of justice, and I resigned the appointment of my own accord, and took up the more congenial profession of a lawyer, although born in the family of a land-holder. (Loud applause.) During the time those functions were combined in me, they had to be exercised in conscious conflict with each other, and conscience had its own conflict to overcome. Since then, *i.e.*, for the last five years, I have made it a rule of my life to keep a regular diary of what has been taking place in the different parts of this Presidency, so far as I could ascertain it from the papers and other sources illustrative of the mal-discharge by persons exercising these two functions of their duties in one or other branch, in consequence of their irreconcilable character, and of the injustice which they in consequence were led into doing when they were seated in the seat of justice. Of course, official decorum will not permit me to state in what manner external pressure was brought upon me continually by my superior officers, beginning from the District Magistrate and down to the Superintendent of Police, and how I was virtually threatened with dismissal, criminal prosecution, and what not, at one time or another, in order to induce me to divert the course of justice and modify the procedure that ought to have been followed according to the rules of law. But such was the sum of my experience, and I therefore submit that the combination of these two powers in one and the same person is the cause of immense mischief, especially to the ignorant ryots. In the case of mere labourers the consequence of this combination is, that in ninety-nine cases out of one hundred it is sheer injustice that is done in our so-called Courts of Criminal Justice.

Whenever there is an important crime committed some old offender is brought before the taluq Magistrate, or the sub-divisional Deputy Collector, or the sub-divisional Magistrate, and that man—for the purpose of clearing the file of heavy cases, such as dacoities, robberies, and showing convictions in them,—is too often convicted without any genuine evidence, merely for the purpose of pleasing the superior officials who always desire to show to the public at large in their administration report that they are highly efficient officers, having secured convictions in all important cases, and so have got a clean file. As regards the financial difficulty that is being urged constantly by the Government, since they have admitted the anomaly of combining these two functions in one and the same person, I may say that after attending the last Congress in Calcutta, in December, 1886, I travelled all over northern India, and I took special interest in this particular matter. I found that in Delhi, for instance, having a population of three and a half lacs, besides a number of honorary second and third-class magistrates, there was a pensioned extra assistant commissioner, exercising not the special first-class powers, but ordinary general first-class powers, to try all first-class cases (not the summary cases that have been noted down in chapter on "Summary Trials"), and I found that on three occasions the honorary magistrates had been placed in charge of an entire city division, to perform all the duties of the divisional magistrates, and I can quote numerous other instances both in northern and southern India, where honorary first-class magistrates have been appointed to the divisional magistracy, including the general duties of a first-class magistrate, and have proved fully qualified for the task; I maintain that if Government utilized properly the gentlemen of this class available the complete separation of the two functions need not cost one rupee extra. I remember—(Cries of "Time, time")—but I must bow to the judgment of the President and the gentlemen of the Congress, and I must not detain you longer than the five minutes which have been granted to me. (Applause.)

Babu Ambika Charan Muzumdar (Bengal, No. 572 in list), said: Mr. President and Gentlemen, the question of the separation of the judicial from the executive functions in this country must be admitted to be a question of vital importance. It is, indeed, one of the cardinal questions upon which the fair fame of the British administration of this country, not less than the happiness and contentment of many millions of people who obey its sway, materially depend. The agitation which we have been making for the separation of judicial from executive functions has not been the result of an effervescent display of cultivated taste, nor the effect of a momentary and feverish excitement. It has been the impulse, not of excitement but of a stern necessity, and therefore, as we see, the whole country from one end to the other, with one voice, joins us in asking for the separation of the two functions. It is an unhappy combination, and it is disastrous and mischievous in its application. As has been pointed out, it combines the prosecutor and the judge. It has brought untold misery upon many millions of British subjects. We all know of a recent infamous case in Assam and of the Salem riots in Madras. Gentlemen, we often hear of the Vernacular Press being charged with sedition, or rather that which is called the Vernacular Press of this country, for I do say, without fear of contradiction or challenge, that for many of the editors of the real Vernacular Press the jail is the proper place. (Voices of "No, No, No.") You must please understand what I mean by the Vernacular Press. I do not mean our leaders of thought, who write English, but the local Bengali papers, and certainly there is a kind of maniacal writing in many of the petty Vernacular papers that would qualify, and should qualify, the writers for prison diet. (Voices of "No, No.") It may be as you say, and I am glad you think so. But understand me, I do not withdraw my contention. (Voices of "No, No; Sit down.") As I said, you often hear our papers charged with sedition, the higher class groundlessly, the lower class not without cause, but this, at least, is a subject which both classes may discuss, and in regard to which both classes may paint in the most vivid colours the cruel injustice inherent in the existing system, without laying themselves open to this charge. False patriotism has nothing to do in a matter like this. (Voices of "Drop it," laughter, hisses, and voices again of "Time, time.")

(There was much noise during the remainder of this speech, which only lasted about two minutes more, the speaker concluding with "I do say, the time has come when we ought all to support this proposition.")

Mr. B. Narasimheswara Sarma (Vizagapatam, No. 113 in list), said: Mr. President and Gentlemen, With great diffidence I approach this august assembly to speak on a subject of such vital importance as the separation of the judicial and executive functions. The various arguments that can be adduced in favour of the reform have been most ably set forth by previous speakers. I shall touch on only two or three, as showing the necessity of the reform. There can be no two opinions as to the necessity of the immediate separation of the two functions, and I think it is a question that has distinctly come within the region of practical administration. One thing history seems to teach us is that no class or party should be entrusted with too much power, as human nature is liable to be corrupted by inordinate power being placed in its hands. Our critics say: "Well, if you separate the two functions how are you to collect the revenue? How is the Collector to get the money out of the people, if they do not fear him, knowing what he can do to them in his magisterial capacity?" We reply, that the present system defeats its own purposes—it does not strengthen authority, injustice never does, it only weakens it. No nation can be well governed for any length of time by simply striking terror into the hearts of the people. What can a poor unlettered man think of a system according to which the Magistrate is not only the head of the police but also the Judge? A fellow that is brought into court may be a great rascal and known to the Judge in his executive capacity to be such, and because of this, though quite innocent of the particular charge on which he is arraigned, the ends of justice may be perverted and the man convicted. This present system causes people to sympathise with the culprit when they see the great injustice done to him, not because of his known bad character, far from it, but because of the gross injustice done to him by the magistrate, who is at once the head of the judicial as well as the executive branch. Gentlemen, it is said that the Indians are notorious for servility. How can this system do anything else than make them servile, though, indeed, this present National Congress shows clearly of what even we servile Indians are capable when the chance is afforded us of speaking our minds freely?

Mr. Ali Mahomed Bhimjee (Indore, No. 472 in list) here stood up in his seat and said: I think sufficient time has been devoted to this question. Two hours have been taken up, and I submit that no further discussion is necessary. (Hear, hear.)

Mr. K. Subramanya Aiyar (Madras, No. 24 in list), who was on the platform at this time, said: I had come to make the same proposition that this Mahomedan gentleman, whose name I do not know, has suggested.

The President said: I understand that this gentleman has come forward to propose the same thing as Mr. Ali Mahomed Bhimjee. If that is the general sense of the meeting, I think, perhaps, it will not be necessary to proceed further with the discussion. (Hear, hear.) Those who are in favour of closing the discussion, kindly hold up their hands. (Voices of "All, all.") I do not think any gentlemen after this will have the courage to come up here. (Laughter.) Then, gentlemen, I put this Resolution :—

Resolved.—That this Congress once again places on record an expression of the universal conviction that a complete separation of Executive and Judicial functions (such that, in no case, the two functions shall be combined in the same officer), has become an urgent necessity, and declares that, in its opinion, it behoves the Government to effect this separation without further delay, even though this should, in some provinces, involve some extra expenditure.

The Resolution was then put and carried unanimously.

The President: The next proposition submitted to us by the Subject Committee is that the Congress should pass a Resolution to the effect :—

"That, in the opinion of this Congress, it is desirable that Government should establish military colleges in this country, whereat the sons of noblemen and gentlemen of all classes, permanently resident in India, may be educated and trained for a military career as officers of the Indian Army."

A complaint has been made to me that some of the delegates do not clearly understand the Resolutions, when they are read out in English, and, therefore, I have to request, that some gentleman will translate this Resolution into the languages of this Presidency, and some other gentleman will kindly translate it into the Urdu language.

(This was accordingly done, and the same procedure was followed in the case of subsequent Resolutions.)

Babu Norendra Nath Sen (24-Pergannahs, No. 561 in list), rose and said: Mr. President, Brother Delegates, The proposition which I have been asked to move is one which does not reaffirm the principle of any Resolution adopted at any previous Congress, but is a new Resolution altogether. It is new and it is important. It is impossible for me to exaggerate its importance. If it be England's divine mission that she should raise us as a nation in every respect, she should offer every facility for our admission into the higher ranks, not only of the civil but equally of the military services, in order that we may be equally qualified for Self-Government in times of peace and Self-Defence in times of war. (Applause.) Our lessons in the art of Self-Government will be incomplete, if we are not trained in the art of Self-Defence. (Applause.) If England means to confer upon us the highest benefits in the present advanced stage of Indian progress—in the present turning-point in the national life, both for the sake of herself and for the sake of India, she cannot, consistently with her duty, withhold any longer opening out a military career to the higher classes, at least, of our countrymen, as officers of the Indian army. (Applause.) We claim nothing which is immoderate or unreasonable. If the sons of foreign noblemen, such as the Duc D'Orleans, can be admitted as officers of the British army, and as it was announced that he was to be admitted, I do not see why the scions of the great houses of this country, eminent for their loyal services to the Crown, and young gentlemen of good birth, good education, and high culture, should not be educated and trained as officers of the Indian army. (Applause.) The concession that we are asking for is not one which is at all novel or unusual. The expediency of admitting a few noblemen as honorary officers of the Indian army has already been recognised by Government. I allude to the appointments of their Highnesses the late Maharajahs Scinda and of Kashmir, of Kuch Behar, and others. Besides, the privilege we claim is in accordance with the known views of Government; a scheme for establishing an Indian Sandhurst has been under consideration by Government for some time past. (Applause.) Indeed, we anxiously looked forward to the public announcement of that scheme on the occasion of the Jubilee celebration, but, unfortunately, only to be disappointed. Gentlemen, the desire amongst our high-bred youths, our *jeunesse dorée*, as they call them in Europe, to enter the commissioned ranks of the Indian army is quite as natural as that of the more advanced youths of the upper and middle classes to enter the higher ranks of the Civil Service, both in its so-called covenanted and uncovenanted branches, and such an aspiration amongst a people situated as we are to our rulers, should, alike in their interests and ours, no longer be kept unsatisfied. (Applause.) The loyalty and devotion, the bravery and heroism, I may say, of native soldiers are too well-known and have been too often recognised by Government to need any particular mention from me. (Hear, hear,) The native soldiery is the ultimate bulwark, the main body of the support, of the empire. (Hear, hear.) The fine steel edge may be our gallant European troops, but the body of the sword is our native soldiery. Their services to the State have been simply invaluable, and that they are justly prized may be judged from the fact that, on the occasion of the celebration of the Jubilee in England, our beloved Queen-Empress herself conferred special marks of favour on those native officers of the Indian army who had the honour of representing their brave comrades in the national rejoicings of Great Britain. (Hear, hear, and loud applause.) Well, then, gentleman, if such be our experience—if such be our general experience of the native army of the past—I fail to perceive why the Government should hesitate in the least to open military colleges, as we propose, for the education of the sons of Indian noblemen and gentlemen. They cannot, certainly—as the result of higher education, nobler antecedents, loftier position or closer ties to Government—prove less devoted and less loyal, less faithful or less courageous in the discharge of their duties, when admitted into the commissioned ranks of the Indian army, than their humbler and more ignorant countrymen have proved as mere soldiers and non-commissioned officers. (Hear, hear.) If the present native troops, soldiers, havildars, jemadars, subadars, of the Indian army are admitted to be bound by the strongest ties to Government—if, I contend, they have proved so faithful, brave, and useful to Government and the country, as they have, in many a hard-fought field—how much more may we not expect from the better-born of these, and from the scions of the still higher classes who will not enter the army on the present footing, if they are admitted to the commissioned ranks of the army? (Hear, hear, and applause.) The inclusion in the army of those who necessarily keep aloof at present, will only serve to identify their interests more closely with the interests of the British Government and lay deeper the foundations of the empire. (Applause.) As an addition to the physical defences of the empire, if for no other reason, I say that it should be the policy of Government to start military colleges for the education of the young noblemen and gentlemen of this country. (Applause.) But the indirect addition to what I may call the moral bulwarks of British rule will prove even more important. Gentlemen, we have had our losses and gains under the British Government,—our gains have been many,—but one of our chief losses has been our exclusion from the higher ranks of the army, (hear, hear,) and that, in my opinion, has led to a rapid deterioration in the character of the natural leaders of the people, and so, indirectly, through their example in our national character. (Hear, hear.) The privilege we ask for is one which has not been denied to India by any previous dynasty. It is not even now denied to the many subject races in Central Asia by the less-civilized Russians (applause), and I will not believe that it will long be denied to us by our British rulers and friends. (Cheers.) With these words, I beg to move the proposition which has already been read out to you by the President. (Applause.)

Babu Saligram Singh (Behar, No. 534 in list), said: Mr. President and Gentlemen, After the eloquent speech of the last speaker I am afraid I can say very little additional by way of commending this resolution to your acceptance. If it was for our joint benefit that Government established schools and colleges for the education of our countrymen in order to enable them to qualify for entrance into the Civil Service, it is equally expedient now in their and our interests that there should be military colleges established for the purpose of imparting a military training to the sons of noblemen and gentlemen of this country, so as to qualify them for entrance into the military service. A nation without trained military men in its midst is not a perfect nation. (Hear, hear.) It is an imperfect, one-armed, or one-legged thing, unfit to do its duty in this rough world. Moreover, it is desirable that such colleges should be instituted, as they will afford an honourable opening for the sons of people of good families, and it will also preserve and develop the martial spirit which still, to some extent, subsists in the sturdier races of the country. (Applause.) Gentlemen, it has already been mentioned to you by the last speaker that our native soldiers, drawn chiefly from the lower classes, have won golden opinions from all by their services in this country and abroad, in Mauritius, Burmah, Afghanistan, Egypt, and Abyssinia, and from this we may fairly infer that if the members of the higher classes be allowed to enter the military service, they also will win golden opinions from the authorities here as well as in England. (Applause.) With these few observations I beg to second the Resolution. (Applause.)

The President: Gentlemen, An amendment on this Resolution has been sent up to me, and I therefore now call upon Mr. Patshaha to move the same.

Mr. P. J. Patshaha (Ahmedabad, No. 450 in list), said: Mr. President and Delegates, It is not in any carping spirit, nor in any spirit of opposition, that I rise to address you and propose an amendment. It is not, I say, in any spirit of opposition to the original resolution that I venture to move an amendment. In so doing, all I seek is to evolve explicitly what has been implicitly involved in the proposition, moved and seconded by the preceding speakers. It seems to me that the original Resolution involves a principle, a principle which ought to be distinctly recognised. It has been implicitly asserted, silently moved, and silently recognised by the original speaker. What I intend to do is to bring out more clearly the principle of the absolute necessity of throwing open the higher branches of the military services to all the natives. The principle which I assert is a principle which makes no difference between native generally, and perhaps properly, so-called aristocracy, and the other natives of India. (Applause.) This principle I assert, and in support of this principle I argue that in demanding the recognition of this principle we assert no new privilege. It is a principle already directly recognised by the Act of Parliament of 1833, a clause from which I will, if you please, read out to you. "No native of the said territories, nor any natural born subject of Her Majesty shall, by reason only of his religion, place of birth, descent, or colour, be disabled from holding any place, office, or employment under the said Government." This principle has been recognised by the Act of Parliament. The same principle has been also recognised by the great Magna Charta of the Indians—the charter of 1858, the substance of which it is sufficient for me to recall to your memory. I say that the same principle has been ennunciated recently on the authority of the Duke of Connaught. No one questions it. No one denies it.

Where is the necessity of holding back when such an opportunity occurs? It seems to me that, instead of this limited proposal, we might rightly go up to Government and directly sue for the concession of this principle in its broad integrity. This principle, I contend, is one we should hold to and maintain.

The preceding speakers, in speaking as to the original proposition, adduced arguments which fully support my view. It has been argued that the present uneducated native officers, holding even the subordinate position they do, have been most useful; much more useful would be, therefore, the educated native officers, supplied by the native gentry and aristocracy, in higher positions. But if men drawn from the lower classes, as now, even the uneducated, have proved the veritable bulwarks of the empire, why should they not, when educated and trained, prove ten times more useful? It is on individual capacity and training that the usefulness mainly depends. Why talk of training the nobility and gentry only? The ability of the natives, as a body, is such as not to be denied. Where is the necessity for thrusting into the background that which we can boldly demand as a matter of right, military training for all ranks and classes that chose to avail themselves of it. I say this is the Jubilee year—the 50th year of the reign of Her Majesty the Queen-Empress. (Applause.) I say we may approach Her Majesty with the request that she may be pleased to recognise in practice the principle that the higher branches of military service are henceforth to be opened to all natives. This is the opinion of that portion of the delegates whom I represent. This principle being recognised, it follows as a consequence that military colleges must be established. I want only to give prominence to the principle, and I should, therefore, rather put in the fore-front what has been thrust into the background by the wording of the Resolution which has been proposed to you. I attach minor importance to the founding of colleges, and the greatest importance to the principle that has been suppressed, by confining to the native gentry or the aristocracy the proposed admission into the higher ranks of the army. It may not even be necessary to state anything about the colleges in the proposition. If the Government understand and recognise the general principle that henceforth the higher branches of the military service are to be opened to all natives of India, the creation of military colleges follows as a matter of logical necessity. The colleges will train up a body of men who will be drafted as officers into the native army when the Government has begun to recognise the real value of this native army. But it is absolutely necessary that the body of men whom the Government train up should be in complete sympathy—not partial sympathy, and not artificial sympathy—but in complete sympathy with the native army, and this would be doubtful if that body of men were drawn from a single class only. The colleges would turn out well-trained and well-educated officers, in perfect sympathy both with the Government they supported and the men they commanded. But if there are to be military colleges funds must be provided. Now the Government need exact no new tax from us for this purpose. There are actually funds available for this purpose. We all know that the native princes of India have offered liberal donations, large sums of money for the support and defence of the empire. This may well be utilised for the purpose of maintaining these colleges, thus securing a legitimate and righteous use of the funds. If, then, the utilization of these funds be considered legitimate and fair, then we might in our Resolution also pray the Government (I do not call upon the Government) that all such donations and contributions as have been or may be tendered by the native princes towards the defence of the empire may be utilised for the purposes of constructing these colleges and working them efficiently. Gentlemen, you see there is no cardinal difference between me and the original speakers, between my arguments and their arguments. The fact is that I intend to assert the principle which underlies the proposition originally moved. Yesterday a gentleman told us that in such cases we should rather discuss and assert principles, and need not in the present state of the case much mind the details. I take up that argument for my own purpose; and I say that we must get, first and foremost, the general principle recognised and accepted. This is the very thing we want to get. What is the special necessity of opening military colleges, if we do not get the broad principle recognised? My amendment, taken together with the proposition, stands thus:—"That, in view of the loyalty of Her Majesty's Indian subjects, this Congress considers it desirable that the military service, in its higher branches, should be opened to natives of this country, and that, for the training of native officers in the British service and in certain native States, it is desirable that the Government should establish military colleges in this country, whereat the sons of Indian noblemen and gentlemen, and all classes, permanently resident in India, may be educated and trained for a military career as officers of the Indian army, and that the funds loyally offered by Native States may be utilised in aid of the establishment of such colleges." My amendment does not materially differ from the original proposition. (Hear, hear.) It renders explicit what is implicitly involved; my proposition is of universal application. (Applause.)

The PRESIDENT: Does the amendment say, "sons of noblemen and gentlemen of all classes," or "and all classes"?

MR. PATSHAHA (Ahmedabad, No. 450 in list): "Sons of noblemen and gentlemen and all classes." My proposition is of universal application. The original proposition thrusts this essential principle into the background and renders null, or only timidly implies, what we boldly pray for as the matter for recognition.

BABU DWARAKA NATH GANGULI (Calcutta, No. 553 in list) said: I shall second the amendment. I am anxious that it should not be understood that this Congress is intended for the promotion of the interests of certain classes only; I am anxious that it should be known that this Congress is intended for the promotion of the interests of all classes. (Hear, hear.)

The PRESIDENT: There does not appear to be any very great or important difference between the original proposition and this amendment, though the latter is much wider in its scope, we might see if some sort of Resolution might not be drawn up that will meet the views of both parties.

The PRESIDENT (after some consultation with the proposer of the original proposition and the proposer of the amendment) said: So far as the first part of the Resolution is concerned, it seems to me, when I compare the amendment with the original Resolution, the difference resolves itself in a great measure into a question of language. Perhaps the language of the amendment is wider and brings out more clearly what I understand was intended by the original proposer, who now has no objection whatever to adopt the language of the amendment. (Hear, hear.) I will read the original Resolution, and you will see that practically there is not much difference. But there is one part of the amendment which seems to be an independent proposition in itself; namely, that Government should be prayed "that the funds loyally offered by Native States be utilised in aid of the establishment of such colleges." It seems to me that that refers to a very different question altogether, which will have to be very carefully considered before the delegates resolve upon it one way or the other. But, so far as the Resolution itself stands, I may take it that the proposer of the amendment and the proposer of the original Resolution are agreed, and therefore you need not discuss that part. The amended Resolution reads: "That in view of the loyalty of Her Majesty's Indian subjects, this Congress considers it desirable that the military service in its higher branches should be opened to the natives of this country, and that for the training of Native officers in the British service it is desirable." The original amendment added "and in certain Native States," but I am informed that the proposer drops these words, and I do not think we can make any Resolution as to what should take place in Native States. However, the Resolution goes on: "It is desirable that the Government should establish military colleges in this country whereat the sons of Indian noblemen and gentlemen of all classes, resident in India, may be educated and trained for a military career as officers of the Indian Army" So far, the proposer of the original Resolution and the proposer of the amendment are agreed, and then it goes on, "and that the funds loyally offered by various Native States may be utilised in aid of the establishment of such colleges." This latter portion, in point of fact, becomes a substantive Resolution in itself. I may say it does seem extraordinary for the delegates here to pray that any funds that have been offered by one party to another party for one purpose should be disposed of in a different manner according to the desire of a third party! If A gives some money to B for an express object, it is surely no business of C's to say that that money should be diverted to some other object, or even to any particular purpose. (Laughter.) I have already appealed to the proposer of this amendment, but he does not see the absurdity into which we shall be led. He wishes to press his proposition, and, therefore, I shall allow the discussion to proceed. But I desire that it should be distinctly understood that what is really asked for is this, namely, that the money which has been offered by Native States to the British Government for certain purposes, according to arrangements between the two parties of which we know nothing, and which, so far as we know, has not yet been accepted, should be devoted by Government, on our advice, to the purposes of these military colleges. (Laughter.)

The PRESIDENT (continuing): I may now mention that this last part of the proposition is not yet seconded, because the seconder of this last part asks permission to withdraw his concurrence in support of it, and therefore, unless it is duly seconded by some other gentleman, we need not discuss it, because there is really no proposition before us. (Applause.)

BABU ISWARI LAL SIRCAR (Hugli, No. 567 in list): As regards the second part, I beg to support it. With regard to the remarks made by the learned President, I have to say that we are not third parties. A certain amount of money has been placed by a certain party in the hands of the British Indian Government. We are loyal subjects of the British Indian Government, and, being loyal subjects, we are identified with Government. I really think it is exceedingly to be regretted that any distinction should be made between Government and the subjects of Government. I think we, the representatives of the nation, can very properly advise and suggest how any sum of money which becomes part of the national funds should be expended by Government —the Government of the nation. The first part of the Resolution requires that Government should establish new institutions, and, therefore, if it is proper for us to suggest the establishment of these institutions, it is equally proper for us, as subjects, to go on and advise Government how the requisite funds may be provided, and pray them to expend certain moneys that they have received on our account in a certain, viz., in this particular, way. I think, therefore, that, as a matter of principle, the second part of the amendment should remain. I really believe it would be mischievous to make any distinction between Government and the subjects of Her Majesty. They are one and the same. They have every right to advise Government to take any action as to the expenditure of any money or anything of that sort. I should be very sorry to know that the delegates of the people of India are to have no voice and no right to suggest anything they please as regards the expenditure of money in the hands of Government. (Applause, and a Voice: "But it is not in the hands of Government yet, and you ought not to count your chickens before they are hatched,"—laughter.)

BABU BIPIN CHANDRA PAL (Assam, No. 602 in list): Mr. President and Brother Delegates, I did not think that it would be my unpleasant duty to oppose the amendment that has been brought forward for our consideration. I had not the least idea that I should have been called upon to speak to-day. I oppose the amendment on two distinct questions of principle. The first is that it is a question of principle whether the money that has been offered to the Government of India for the defence of the Indian Empire by certain native princes should be accepted or not. Speaking on behalf of those whom I represent, I can assure you, gentlemen, that the Native Press, with hardly any exception, has asked Government not to accept this money. I condemn the policy involved in the acceptance of such offerings—(hear, hear)—and I think the Congress would be going entirely out of its way if we took up this question, and on a side issue affirmed that policy. We ought by no means to affirm it; and the second question of principle involved is that as yet we have only taken up those questions in regard to which we have had to some extent a lead from Government itself—leading us to hope that they were willing to receive our views. In regard to the reforming of the Legislative Councils, Government has been indirectly seeking our help, and, as Lord Dufferin said, in no way disapproves our aspirations. In the matter of the Arms Act, Government have shown indications that they are prepared to take us into their confidence and would like to place matters on a more satisfactory footing. But, in matters of their foreign policy, I think that on principle the Congress should not go out of its way to make suggestions of this nature.

MUNSHI DEVI PRASAD (Ballia, No. 487 in list) said: Gentlemen, it has been suggested that the money which has been placed at the disposal of Government by certain native princes should be spent in the construction of colleges for military education. Well, the first thing to be considered is this: This money has been given for purposes of defence. It is not known when the money will be required. We, however, are to ask that the money may be expended at once on these colleges. But even supposing that the construction of these colleges can be held to be a step in the defence of the empire coming within the scope of the donors' instructions, which I doubt, complications on our frontier may become serious to-morrow, and we shall then not have our colleges nor our trained men to fight for us, nor shall we have our money for practical purposes of defence. It will take years to construct the colleges and to turn out officers, but, in the meantime, the money may be required at any moment for the defence of the empire. (Applause.) I therefore propose that this last part of the amendment be expunged. (Applause.)

MR. PATSHAHA said: Mr. President, with your permission, I will not press that portion of the amendment, as it has caused so much opposition. (Applause.)

BABU NORENDRA NATH SEN (24-Pergannahs, No. 561 in list): As proposer of the original proposition I accept the first part of the amendment.

A DELEGATE (speaking from his seat) said: Gentlemen, in my opinion the Resolution, as now amended, destroys the very principle really embodied in the original Resolution. In the original Resolution, we assumed, and I suppose very rightly, that the higher appointments in the military department are actually open to us. This has been recognised by Act of Parliament, and also by the Queen's Proclamation. We are therefore bound to assume that the higher appointments in the military department are now open to us. But in accepting the Resolution in its amended form, we are distinctly assuming that the appointments are not open to us.

The PRESIDENT: This is a real difficulty, but what has suggested itself to the proposer of the original proposition and the proposer of the amendment is that the Resolution should run somewhat as follows, viz.: "That in view of the loyalty of Her Majesty's Indian subjects, this Congress considers it desirable that the Queen's Proclamation should be given effect to, whereby, among other concessions, the military service, in its higher branches, should be opened, &c." That assumes that the Queen's Proclamation should be given effect to, and that the military service, in its higher branches, should be open to us. (Applause.)

A DELEGATE: I would suggest the further slight modification, "should be practically opened to the natives of this country."

(Some consultation here took place on the platform between the President and the delegates who had been speaking on the subject.)

The PRESIDENT: Gentlemen, I am trying to see whether we cannot pour oil upon these troubled waters. (Laughter.)

The PRESIDENT: Gentlemen, we are all agreed as to what we desire, it is only a question of what language should be employed to prevent others misunderstanding what we all so perfectly realise. This is how it is now proposed that the Resolution should run: "That in view of the loyalty of Her Majesty's Indian subjects, this Congress considers it desirable that the Queen's Proclamation should be given effect to, and that the military service, in its higher grades, should be practically opened to the natives of this country." (Applause.)

The DELEGATE (who made the last suggestion) : I have nothing more to say.

The PRESIDENT : I am very glad that the insertion of the word "practically" has saved this gentleman the necessity of making a speech. (Laughter.) The Resolution goes on—"And that the Government of India should establish military colleges in this country, whereat the sons of noblemen and gentlemen of all classes, permanently resident in India, may be educated and trained for a military career as officers of the Indian army."

A DELEGATE : I would propose the substitution of the words "and all classes" instead of "of all classes."

The PRESIDENT : As the Resolution now stands, it is "of all classes." It is now proposed, gentlemen, to alter the word "of" into "and." That is not agreed to by the proposer of the original Resolution, and therefore I think it will still have to be debated. The point of difference seems to be that, on the one hand it is sought to include the sons of gentlemen of all classes, provided they are sons of gentlemen, and on the other hand it is intended, by the substitution of the word "and" for "of," that everybody—no matter what his position in life may be—should be allowed to become an officer in Her Majesty's service. Unless some arrangement is come to, the question will have to be discussed; but if this alteration is to be insisted on we must have it first formally proposed and seconded.

BABU DWARAKANATH GANGULI (Calcutta, No. 553 in list) said : Then, sir, I rise to propose formally that the word "and" be substituted for "of," and I repeat what I said before. I distinctly understood that the interests this Congress is intended to promote are not the interests of any special class of Her Majesty's subjects but of all classes of Her Majesty's subjects.

RAJAH RAMPAL SINGH (Allahabad, No. 484 in list) said : Gentlemen, I am not going to speak on this point at any length. I simply rise to second the motion, and to express my hearty concurrence in the proposition that this Conference is a representation, not of any particular class, but it is a representation of all creeds and classes, and that we should not, therefore, make any such invidious distinctions as is implied in the amended resolution. (Applause.) It is highly desirable that we should accept any candidate, if he is qualified, and if he is worthy of being a member of the military college. (Applause.)

BABU SURENDRA NATH BANNERJEE (Calcutta, No. 550 in list), then rose and said : Gentlemen, I would say : strike out the words "whereat the sons of noblemen and gentlemen of all classes, permanently resident in India, may be educated and trained for a military career." The question of the future organisation of the military colleges is a question of detail, and may very well be left to the judgment of Government. All we care for is the acceptance of the principle—the establishment of the colleges. How these colleges are to be governed, and who are to be educated there, and where funds are to come from,—all these are questions of detail which ought to be left to the Government te settle. I therefore propose that those words be struck out.

Mr. W. C. BONNERJEE (Calcutta, No. 546 in list) said : I propose that the words "natives of India" should be substituted for "the sons of noblemen and gentlemen of all classes."

Mr. W. S. GANTZ (Madras, No. 52 in list) said : I suggest a very slight alteration ; let it stand as "natives of India as defined by statute." (Loud applause, and cries of "Yes, Yes.")

The PRESIDENT : As now proposed to be altered, the latter part of the Resolution will stand thus : "and that the Government should establish military colleges in this country, whereat natives of India, as defined by statute, may be educated and trained for a military career as officers of the Indian army." (Loud applause.)

ANOTHER DELEGATE asked that the term "natives of India, as defined by statute" might be clearly explained to the Congress.

The PRESIDENT: Mr. W. C. Bonnerjee will, perhaps, kindly explain to the assembly exactly what is meant by the term "natives of India, as defined by statute."

Mr. W. C. BONNERJEE (Calcutta, No. 546 in list): Mr. President, You have imposed upon me a task of some magnitude if I were to take your instructions *au pied du lettre*—but really I thought everybody knew what the term "native of India" meant. I thought it was well known that all Hindus, all Mahomedans, all Parsees, all Eurasians, all East Indians, and all domiciled Europeans, and all persons born in India of domiciled parents are, in the eye of the law, "natives of India," and are defined to be so by statute. The words "as defined by statute" have to be introduced, because they will prevent misunderstanding on the part of such of our brethren as are Eurasians, East Indians, or domiciled Europeans, or the children of these, all of whom are really included in the legal term, "native of India." We are now perfectly agreed that these colleges should be for the benefit of the whole of India. Let it not be said that this Congress has put anything in such an uncertain way that it might hereafter be said that Eurasians and East Indians and domiciled Europeans were not included in the term "native of India." (Loud applause.)

Mr. EARDLEY NORTON (Madras, No. 43 in list): I rise merely to second formally the proposition which has been moved by my friend Mr. W. C. Bonnerjee, with the addition proposed by Mr. Gantz. I think it is far better that we should eliminate from the Resolution those words which stood there originally. The distinction between "gentlemen" and "noblemen" is a distinction which I, for one, fail to perceive, as I do not see why a "nobleman" may not also be a "gentleman." (Laughter.) And there is another reason why I think all specification of classes should disappear, namely, because its retention will be placing in the hands of the authorities another quantum of discriminating patronage. We all know what difficulties we have had to contend with, on that very account, in regard to that amphibious creature "the statutory civil servant." In accepting this amendment you at once make it so plain in its terms that no ambiguity can arise. You obviate the danger which has already arisen in other cases, and which may arise in this case, of the authorities misconstruing your meaning in such a way as to exclude from the operations of your proposition all those persons to whom India is, in fact, a fatherland. I trust you will accept the amendment in the same spirit in which it was moved—the spirit of universal sympathy with all classes whether they happen to be gentlemen by birth or whether they are not. (Applause, and cries of "Vote, Vote.")

The PRESIDENT: It seems to me, gentlemen, that, as the result of this long discussion, we have steered clear of some shoals. (Hear, hear.) It certainly would have been most undesirable if the impression went forth that the delegates had the interest of any particular class at heart. (Hear, hear.) Nothing could have been further from the intention of the proposer and seconder of the original Resolution. It was only a question of language, and I am glad we have now, at any rate, been able to discover language that apparently meets all objections. I am, I say, glad, but until this proposition is voted and carried, it is impossible to know whether some gentleman may not yet get up and drive a coach and four through it. I will therefore ask first, whether you are desirous that we should proceed further with the discussion. (Voices "No, No, No.") That being so, I will now put the Resolution in its latest, and I venture to hope, universally approved form.

RESOLVED: "That, in view of the loyalty of H. M.'s Indian subjects, this Congress considers it desirable that the Queen's Proclamation should be given effect to, that the military service in its higher grades should be practically opened to the natives of this country, and that the Government of India should establish military colleges in this country, whereat the natives of India, as defined by statute, may be educated and trained for a military career as officers of the Indian army."

The Resolution was carried unanimously and with loud acclamations.

The PRESIDENT: It is now carried beyond the power of anybody to amend further. (Laughter.)

The PRESIDENT: We proceed now to the fifth proposition in our programme, which runs as follows:—

"That, in view of the unsettled state of public affairs in Europe, and the immense assistance that the people of this country, if duly prepared therefor, are capable of rendering to Great Britain in the event of any serious complications arising, this Congress do once again earnestly appeal to the Government to authorise (under such rules and restrictions as may to it seem fitting) a system of Volunteering for the Indian inhabitants of the country such as may qualify them to support the Government effectively in any crisis."

Mr. SANKARA NAIR (Madras, No. 73 in list): Mr. President and Gentlemen, the President has already read out to you the Resolution which I have to submit for your acceptance, and I think, therefore, it is needless for me to read it again. There is this difference between this Resolution and the previous ones which have been carried. In this case we have, if we are correctly informed, an expression of opinion by the Viceroy of India which is not very favourable to our views. The Viceroy has expressed his sympathy with our aspirations for a reform and expansion of our legislative councils, and also, to a certain extent, in regard to the separation of judicial from revenue functions. But in this case, I regret to say it is understood that the Viceroy has stated that it is impossible to meet our views, and therefore the task of moving this Resolution to one who entertains the highest respect for Lord Dufferin, both as our gracious Empress's representative and as a statesman of European reputation, is by no means an easy or pleasant one. But, gentlemen, though the Viceroy, in the discharge of his duty, as he views it, may have felt compelled peremptorily to negative our former prayer, this is no real reason why we of the country, who know more of its real needs and condition than any Viceroy can know, why we, the representatives of the thinking classes throughout the empire, should not also do what we believe to be our duty, and persistently urge a prayer the granting of which will, we know, conduce in such a high degree, not only to our own safety, but to the stability and glory of the throne of that great Empress whose servant he is, and whose loyal and loving subjects we are. (Loud cheers.) I have not the magnificent eloquence, the persuasive powers of some of the speakers that have preceded me, and for that reason I shall simply confine myself to a statement of some of the grounds which may be adduced in support of this Resolution. After what has passed yesterday, and after what we know even of the Viceroy's views, it is impossible to doubt that, sooner or later, we are sure to have a radical reform in the constitution of the legislative councils, but neither that blessing nor the separation of the judicial and executive functions, nor any other blessing that we enjoy under the British Government, can compensate us for the state of helplessness into which, as the result of the policy pursued by the British Government in this matter, we are rapidly drifting. Not only has it made us helpless, it has had also the effect of lowering and degrading the character of our countrymen. But this has already been pointed out by Babu Norendra Nath Sen, and was dwelt upon so eloquently and fully by Rajah Rampal Singh last year, that I shall not take up your time by going over the same ground again, but I shall pass on at once to the next, though kindred, ground, which I have to adduce in support of this Resolution. Every mail that comes from England brings alarming news of the state of affairs in Europe, a state of affairs that can mean nothing but that war between mutually jealous neighbours, in which England must be involved, is sure to be proclaimed at some not distant date. Now, gentlemen, what is our state or position under these circumstances? Our ancient civilization,—is that to be broken into and destroyed by Northern invaders? Of course, we have this much freedom that we have full liberty to offer our prayers for the success of the British Government. But prayers, I fear, are not likely to be of much use to us or to them. Is the peace and tranquillity, I say, which we now enjoy to be ravished from us without our voices being heard, our arms being raised in the settlement of the dispute? It appears to me absurd to entertain such an idea. It appears to me intolerable, the more especially as even the English themselves cannot assert what the result of the struggle here is likely to be if India continues debarred from helping herself and them. It is impossible to foresee what will happen if this policy of Government, of refusing our co-operation, is persisted in. It appears to be absolutely suicidal, and we only hope, equally for our own and their sakes, that the English may not some day regret that she has refused, while there was yet time and we could have been trained into serviceable allies, those prayers which we have so repeatedly put up in regard to this matter. (Hear, hear, and applause.) The Russians have armed their foes of yesterday to fight on their own behalf to-day, and the result shows that they have been justified in their action. (Applause.) Have we been less loyal to the British than the Turkomans to the Russians, with whom they fought only yesterday? (Applause.) They lie who say that our loyalty cannot be depended upon in the hour of danger. (Applause.) It is in the highest degree probable that the fighting races of India will be required to have a voice in the settlement of that dispute if it is to end favourably for our empire, and therefore it is absolutely necessary now, while there may be yet time, to train and educate them, so that they may be able to bear their share, the lion's share, in the defence of that portion of the empire which is their home and mother-land. (Applause.) I should have thought that no objection could reasonably be urged against this proposition as worded both last year and this; but the Viceroy has expressed himself, it is said, unable, on account of race feelings that are alleged to exist between the various races in India, to grant our prayer to be enrolled as volunteers. He expressed that opinion, it appears, to some delegates from Madras, after this Resolution was passed last year. It appears to me that if he did so—and my friend here assures me he did—he did so without carefully reading over the Resolution. I understood from a speaker yesterday that a journalist may review magazines without reading them, and that hostile critics often criticise without knowing what they are criticising. But a man in the Viceroy's position, I take it, would surely have read over the Resolution properly before he delivered himself of such an opinion. Now, gentlemen, under our proposals it is in the Viceroy's power to make rules, such that only those gentlemen whom he may consider unquestionably loyal, whom he is convinced may be entirely relied upon, should be admitted as volunteers—as soldiers who, in the hour of danger, would stand beside the British.

It is to me inconceivable that a representation thus carefully guarded should be summarily rejected by any reasonable man. Race feelings, indeed! The assertion cannot be challenged by anybody who at all understands the country, that, in a corps of volunteers, composed of men drawn from the Mahomedan and Hindu communities indifferently, we shall have the best, the only possible effective, safeguard against any collision between the lower classes of these races. In my own district, for instance, a part of the district has been disarmed on account of what was called the Moplah outbreak, and it is the opinion of many of us, both Hindus and Mahomedans, that a corps of volunteers in which both of these races were represented would be the best safeguard against the occurrence of any further ebullitions of fanaticism. (Applause.) Now, gentlemen, I have very little to add to what I have already stated, and to what has already been stated by Rajah Rampal Singh,* when he moved this proposition last year, and it will be needless occupying your time by dilating upon the subject. Let us all be united, and let us ask Government to grant our prayer that all loyal inhabitants of the country may take their share in the defence of the country. We should be animated by a sense of the glory which will attach to us if we take our proper share in the defence of our country, and no doubt many of us will be found willing in an emergency, if it is necessary, to put ourselves

---

* Rajah Rampal Singh's speech delivered at the Congress of 1886, a speech that has been endorsed by the entire Indian Press, ran as follows:—

"The spirit of this meeting has been so uniformly loyal and conciliatory that I hope no one will blame us if we now proceed to deal with a matter in regard to which we are distinctly at variance with Government. Every one knows that, for a variety of reasons, the whole country is of opinion that native volunteer corps ought to be organised. Every one knows that the entire country memorialised and endeavoured to move Government in this matter, and every one further knows that, to our great regret and disappointment, the Government, and that not over-graciously, distinctly refused to pay any attention to the unanimous voice of the country. None the less, however, do we now feel it our duty to reiterate those representations—representations which are based on a consideration of the highest interests of Great Britain as well as India.

"We are deeply grateful to Government for all the good that it has done us, but we cannot be grateful to it when it is, no matter with what best of intentions, doing us a terrible and irreparable injury. (Loud cheers.)

"We are grateful to it for the peace and order which it has diffused over the land (cheers); for the education that it has so nobly and unselfishly imparted to us (cheers); for its promise of admitting us to every post and office in the administration for which we prove our fitness (cheers); for the share that it has given us in the comforts and conveniences provided by the triumphs of Western science, railways, telegraphs, telephones; we are grateful to it, in a word, for all the innumerable boons and blessings that it has conferred on us (cheers); but we cannot be grateful to it for degrading our natures, for systematically crushing out of us all martial spirit, for converting a race of soldiers and heroes into a timid flock of quill-driving sheep. (Prolonged shouts.) Thank God, things have not yet gone quite so far as this. There are some of us yet, everywhere, who would be willing to draw sword, and if needful

forward and avail ourselves of this advantage. (Applause.) Gentlemen, subsequent to the Resolution which we passed last year we received a Resolution from the Government of India giving us permission to enrol ourselves as volunteers, if all the members of any existing corps accepted us. But, gentlemen, that is hardly a concession. (Applause.) Of course, very few can expect admission with the consent of all those who compose such corps. Those corps were originated expressly for the purpose of training Europeans and East Indians alone, and they will not care to be outnumbered by natives. Further, gentlemen, I may tell you that though I and some others were admitted to the local corps, and then removed by the orders of the Local Government (this was before the promulgation of that Resolution by the Government of India to which I have referred) yet, subsequent to the receipt of that Resolution, we have not been re-admitted, though we appealed for such re-admission some months ago. With these observations, I propose for your acceptance the Resolution which has been read by the President. (Applause.)

Rajah Rampal Singh (Allahabad, No. 484 in list) said: Gentlemen, after hearing the speech of the mover of this Resolution, I rise with a very bad grace, and I feel almost in despair of being able to say anything further worth saying on this subject. But, gentlemen, as martial exercises, the martial calling, are so dear to me that they become a part and parcel of my life, I may be forgiven if I yet venture to say something on the subject, and I think that belief in your indulgence will give me strength to bring certain facts before you here on this occasion. Gentlemen, before I speak further on the subject, I must explain to you why I have been so discouraged by what I have heard from the last speaker. In the same way, gentlemen, as my friend has heard of His Excellency the Viceroy's speaking adversely to this concession, I had been in the same manner informed by one of my friends that he is disposed to regard it favourably. One of my friends told me while I was at Simla, or I have heard from some other source, which I cannot name to you directly, that while discussing the question with an Indian gentleman,

---

lay down our lives, for hearth and homes, aye, and for the support and maintenance of that Government to which we owe so much. (Cheers.) But this is what we are coming to; and when we once come to that, then I think that, despite the glories of the Pax Britannica, despite the noble intentions of Great Britain, despite all the good she may have done or tried to do us, the balance will be against her, and India will have to regret rather than rejoice that she has ever had anything to do with England. (Hear, hear.)

"This may be strong language, but it is the truth; nothing can ever make amends to a nation for the destruction of its national spirit and of the capacity to defend itself and the soil from which it springs. (Loud cheers.)

"Nor is it only we who will have to regret and suffer for the mistaken policy that our Government is unhappily pursuing in this matter. Look where you will around you in the world, and you will see gigantic armies and armaments. There is trouble in store for the whole civilized world, and sooner or later a tremendous military struggle will commence in which, assuredly, before it terminates, Great Britain will be involved. Great Britain, with all her wealth, cannot put one hundred men into the field for every thousand that several Continental Powers can. England herself is isolated, and by her insular position to a certain extent protected, but no friendly sea rolls between Europe and Asia: the landward path to India is known and open; India is not isolated, and it will be India, on whose possession half Great Britain's wealth and status depends, that will be the scene of any serious attack by any Continental Powers on Great Britain. (Hear, hear.)

"Then will England regret that, instead of having millions of brave Indians trained to arms to fling back invaders, she has only her scanty legions to oppose to them, and from her timid subjects can only look at most for good wishes—good wishes, truly good things in their way, but poor bulwarks against Berdan rifles and steel ordnance. (Hear, hear.)

"But on our own account we deprecate the existing policy. High and low we are losing all knowledge of the use of arms, and with this that spirit of self-reliance which enables a man to dare, which makes men brave, which makes them worthy of the name of men. (Loud cheers.) When I was only five years of age my grandfather made me begin to learn all physical exercises in vogue amongst us, and I was trained to the use of all arms, and in all martial exercises. (Cheers.) But what man now sends his son for such training? What young man nowadays knows anything of these things? Fifty years ago, without desiring warfare, every young man's heart glowed within him at the thought of some day showing his prowess in a fair field. Now most young men would, I fear, contemplate any such possible contingency with very, let me say, mixed feelings. If men are to be fit for soldiers, fit to fight to any purpose when the time of trial comes, and come it must for every country, then they must be trained in the use of arms, they must from their childhood see their parents, their elders, using arms and participating in those martial exercises which, only thirty-five years ago, in Oudh at least, were part of every gentleman's occupation.

"And there is another very important point—India is practically being impoverished, to a great extent, by the enormous expense of her standing army. Sooner or later the crushing weight of this (for her resources) enormous expenditure will break down either the country or the Government. Now, by a judicious encouragement of Indian volunteers, it would be possible to reduce very greatly this military expenditure, and yet leave the country far stronger for defensive purposes than it now is. (Prolonged cheering.)

"But I might go on for hours. I might dwell on the fact that in the way the Arms Act is now worked in many localities, the people, their herds, their crops, are wholly at the mercy of wild beasts. I might dwell on the insult, the injustice, the violation of the most sacred and solemn pledges by England to India, that are involved in the rules that permit Indian Christians, but do not permit Indian Hindus or Mahomedans, to volunteer. (Loud cheers.) But I have said enough, and indeed being, as we are, all of one mind, too much already, I fear, on this subject, in which I am deeply interested; I will only now add that we do not ask Government to put arms blindly into all men's hands, but only to permit, under such rules and restrictions as it sees fit, the better and more educated classes of its loyal Indian subjects to qualify themselves to defend, when occasion may require, their homes, their country, and their Government." (Enthusiastic cheers.)

His Excellency was asked to bestow the same boon on the North-West Provinces as he had been kind enough to confer on the Madras Pesidency, and that in answer he said: "Oh! I have nct, indeed, sanctioned it only for the Madras Presidency, but for the whole of India." Then the gentleman who was talking to him, asked his permission to give publicity to these facts in the papers. He said that this might be done, and that the recent Madras orders had been issued on the basis of Lord Canning's original Resolution. Gentlemen, I am not able to give you the purport of that Resolution, because, although we have heard a little about it we have not been able as yet to obtain a copy of it. I have heard something about it, viz., that it lays down that we cannot form separate purely native corps, but that we must be admitted into, and join, some of the existing European and Eurasian corps, and that we must conform to the rules and regulations of these existings corps. This is not much; these corps, as has been said, will, perhaps, not accept many of us, but still it is something, and we ought to show, I think, some gratification at this concession, because we were so unanimous on the former occasion in asking for this privilege. We now press this subject on the Government with the same vehemence and force as we did on the last occasion; ought we not at the same time to acknowledge this step, small though it may be, towards complying with our request? Gentlemen, undoubtedly, we have received many blessings from the English Government, such as immunity from anarchy, safety of our property and of our lives, education, railways, telegraphs, admirable postal arrangements, ice and soda-water—(laughter)—and a host of minor comforts and conveniences, but we have not yet received that highest privilege which we enjoyed under the former rulers of this country, I mean our Mahomedan friends. They, at least, trusted us, but this the British Government seems resolved not to do. Under the Mahomedans we were not only employed in all the civil departments, and in all posts from the highest to the lowest, but we were often the leaders and generals of their armies. Gentlemen, we might have many things to complain of as regards the treatment that we all, Hindus and Mahomedans, received at the hands of our Persian rulers, but they employed and trusted us Hindus as they did their own people. Once our people had been conquered they were always admitted by Akbar to the highest offices of State, and not only lieutenant-governorships, but also the leaderships of armies and the position of commanders-in-chief were conceded to Hindus. Maharajah Todar Mall, the famous financial minister, who was at one time the Governor of Madras, was almost the most distinguished man in the empire under the Mahomedan rule of the time. Maharajah Madin Singh was not only the Governor of Madras but also of Kabul Some of the Mahomedans may not have patronised this Congress as they ought to have done (laughter), still they showed in those days that they held us to be their countrymen, and our countrymen they irrevocably became, and are now sharing our destinies for good or evil; whether they are just or unjust to us, whether they aid or oppose us in these our efforts, they are still a part of ourselves, and with us they and their children and their property remain in the country. Gentlemen, our present rulers, with all their good works and all their even-handed justice, are still too much of foreigners who make of India their happy hunting grounds and treat it primarily as a place in which to make their fortune and leave with all their possessions at the earliest possible moment. I heartily endorse the remarks which fell from our worthy President the other day, when he opened the Congress, as to the extreme importance of welcoming with open arms any European gentlemen who may be persuaded to make our country their home, but ("Question, Question"), well, I think, perhaps, this is a digression (Voices: "Yes, Yes") and I will drop it. (Hear, hear.) I must not say much more now, gentlemen. This is a very grave question, and we none of us wish to press this question too far. We don't say that the privilege of volunteering should be conferred on everybody in India—far from it. We only make a very reasonable demand, viz., that the Government should just allow those it knows it can trust, and those only, to volunteer. Now, gentlemen, it has been said that several gentlemen in this Presidency who were admitted as volunteers on one occasion were dismissed from their corps by the orders of the Government of Madras; that this latter was set right by the Government of India and directed to act on Lord Canning's Resolution already referred to, but that despite this, and their having several months ago sought re-admission, this has not yet been conceded to them. It would therefore seem that the existing spirit is against us. For this reason I am ready to press a very small measure, and, if you concur, ask a very little favour only in order to make, at any rate, a beginning. Gentlemen, instead of the demand made in our Resolution, and which, moderate as it is, seems, from all we hear, hopeless, might we not begin by asking this: You know that under this famous Arms Act, although a great hue and cry is raised against it, very few of the more educated and reliable persons of our community are not exempted from its operation? I mean to say that members of district and local boards, municipal commissioners, honorary magistrates, rajahs, and most gentlemen of any position are exempted from its operation, and therefore what I propose is that, if the Government is opposed in granting us any more general permission, we might at least ask it to permit these people who are already exempted from the operation of the Arms Act to form themselves into volunteer corps. I think it very indiscreet on the part of the Government to give us arms and not allow us to know the proper way of using them. They should not stultify themselves so far. This at any rate they might and must concede to us. Now, might it not be wise this time to press only this minor point? (Cries of "No, no," "Shut up," and "Time, time.") Well, I see you won't have it, and I am exhausting your patience, so, although I am inclined to think that my very modest demand would be more likely to meet with a favourable reception, still, as I entirely agree in the sense of the Resolution before us, I am happy, in sitting down, to be able to say that I second it with the best possible goodwill. (Hear, hear, and loud applause.)

Mr. John Adam (Madras, No. 88 in list) said: Gentlemen, it has been suggested by one or two of my friends that, as I happen to be an officer of the volunteer corps to which Rajah Rampal Singh has referred, it would be well if I corrected a small misapprehension he has fallen into with respect to the conduct of the members of that corps, and I would do so by simply stating the facts as they occurred. Some time ago, about the time of the Russian scare, my friends, Mr. Sankara Nair, who proposed this motion, and Mr. Salem Ramaswami Mudaliar, one of the delegates to England, and two or three other native gentlemen, applied to be admitted into our volunteer corps, and they were accepted at once. (Applause.) There was no difficulty at all as to their being accepted; we were all most happy to welcome them. But, unfortunately, and through a misunderstanding or misinterpretation of the order of the Government of India—a misinterpretation on the part of the Government of Madras, or the military authorities here—these gentlemen, although we desired it, were not allowed at that time to be admitted into the corps. Subsequently, and in fact quite recently, it was discovered that a mistake had been made, and that the interpretation which the Government of Madras had put upon this order of the Government of India was not applicable to the Madras Presidency, but was applicable only to Burmah, which, at the time this order of the Government of India was issued, was considered a portion of the Madras military command; but the military authorities here and the Government extended the limitation which was applicable only to Burmah and made it apply to the whole of the Madras Presidency. The mistake was afterwards discovered when the original Government order was republished a little time ago. But, subsequent to that, a short time ago, three of these gentlemen applied to be re-admitted into the corps, under the conditions which were laid down in that order. Immediately on their application steps were taken to give effect to their wishes, but it was necessary, under the Government order, that the consent and approval of all the existing members of the corps should be obtained to the admission of these gentlemen as fellow-comrades with them in the corps. This consent is in process of being, and I believe has been practically and unanimously, given. (Applause.) Speaking for myself, I may say that, in that portion of the corps specially under my charge, and which I had to consult upon the matter, both officers and men were perfectly unanimous in agreeing most cordially to welcome them, and, I believe, the same is the case in the various other detachments of the corps. I may also say that all the officers are perfectly unanimous in agreeing to receive these gentlemen into the corps. (Applause.) I thought you would perhaps pardon me for simply offering this explanation, as otherwise a mistaken impression might have been carried away in regard to the action of the volunteer corps. Rajah Rampal Singh will also thank me, I am sure, for having given this explanation (applause), and having, as I hope, given him grounds for believing that here, at any rate, there is no disposition to exclude loyal native gentlemen from our ranks.

Malik Bhugwan Das (Dera Ismail Khan, No. 481 in list) then spoke in Urdu, and said: Mr. President and Brethren, I congratulate you on this, the third, National Congress, on my own behalf and on behalf of the Hindus and Mahomedans whom I represent. Brethren, I call you brethren because we are children of the same motherland and co-workers in the same common cause—the good of our nation. Though we may differ in respect of dress and religion, yet we are all none the less brothers collected here in Madras to-day under this vast roof to labour for one and the same cause—the cause of India. My brethren, there is no doubt now as to this Congress being truly representative of the entire country, and though certain Anglo-Indian papers may still make a great show of disputing this point, their position is just like that of a certain class of barristers who, well knowing that they have no case, still, to please their clients, storm and bluster as if they were sure of gaining their cause and abuse and affect to despise the other side, well knowing that the latter are sure to win. It is not the best kind of barristers who do this, but neither are our opponents the best kind of journalists. Of course, the barrister keeps up his bluster until the case is decided, and the opposition of certain journalists will not cease nor their falsehoods come to an end till the Government passes its final decision in our favour, but after that I am doubtful if we shall ever hear more of the matter unless, indeed, they be well fee'd to try and procure a review of judgment. (Laughter.) Well, gentlemen, I will read the Resolution which I have risen to support to-day (for, though I speak in Urdu, I both read and write English) in order that our opponents may not accuse me of not understanding what I am going to support. (He then read the Resolution in English.) Now, I will bring certain facts to your notice which should lead every honest thinker to hope that this Resolution will be accepted by the Government. Just about the year 1849, Dewan Mulraj, the Governor of Mooltan, rebelled against the Sikh Government, which was practically the British Government as the entire administration was guided by British officers, and the Gondapurs, and afterwards the Pathans, who were well trained in the use of the arms, were collected in hundreds and thousands to help the British officer, Mr. Edwardes, Resident in the Derajat frontier in those days. There was no railway in those days, and it was a most critical time. It would have been in the utmost degree difficult, if not, as I believe, absolutely impossible, for the British officers to have put down that rebellion but for the help of the arms-trained Pathans of the country.

Again, you well know, gentlemen, that it was a very critical time for our Government during the Mutiny of the year 1857. The British empire was in a most dangerous position, and it really was, for a time, a mere toss-up (let British historians disguise it as they please) whether India would not be lost to it for ever. But, fortunately, the Punjab, especially the frontier part of that province, had been recently conquered, and there were at that time a great number of persons, in the frontier districts especially, who had been trained in the use of the arms and had known what a soldier's life was and liked it.

Colonel Nicholson, who was then deputy commissioner of the Bunnu district (to whom the capture of Delhi was admittedly in a great measure due) collected thousands of such trained warriors and of the frontier Pathan tribes, and with these joined the attack on Delhi, and the success attained, if the truth be told, was in a great measure due to these Pathans. I need not give you more examples, my brethren, as these two will suffice to inculcate the lesson that in times of the extremest danger it is on the natives trained to arms that the British Government and we, its loyal subjects, must as a last resort rely. Now the past policy for the last thirty years of our Government has been such as to kill out everywhere a knowledge of the use of arms and a willingness to accept the dangers and privations of a soldier's life. Even for the native army, recruits, untrained recruits, that take a couple of years to turn into anything like soldiers, are scarcely to be procured, and if at this moment any crisis were to arise, the Government could not rely upon the assistance in the field of one-hundredth of the men it could have commanded thirty years ago. I mean, of course, in my part of India. Now this to me seems a grievous misfortune, and it is to remedy this state of affairs and ensure Government having at its call in any crisis hundreds of thousands of partially-trained soldiers that I so strongly advocate as I do the volunteer movement. God forbid that the Russians, bribing the Afghans, should with them make a joint descent on the rich plains of India; but if they were to do so, and the Government perseveres in its present policy of converting its bravest and most soldierly races into helpless pen and word men, the results would be the loss of India to the British and of all the blessings that we owe to them, of all we most prize and cherish to us. (Applause.) Therefore, brethren, we have a right, the best of all rights, to claim again and again from Government that our young men shall be trained to arms and made fit to defend us and our homes, our liberties and our lands. (Loud cheers.) The Government cannot be blind, they must see the contingencies lying before them and us, as we frontier men see them, and if so it is cruel, it is unjust, for them to refuse us what we ask for in this Resolution (cheers); nay, it is a folly, a crime, for we ask it as much in their interests, as much in the interests of our empire and our Empress, as in those of our country, our families, and ourselves. (Loud cheers.) Gentlemen, I support this resolution, and so does every man on our frontier, and so does every well-wisher of the British Government throughout the empire. (Continued applause.)

Mr. Ali Mahomed Bhimjee (Indore, No. 472 in list) said: Mr. President and Fellow-countrymen, I appear before you to support a Resolution that has been proposed as regards our admission into volunteer corps. Government ask us why we should be admitted into volunteer corps and why we want to be admitted. I answer, "For the simple reason that this is our home and we want to defend our hearths and homes." (Applause.) It is their hearths and homes that Englishmen want to defend, and it is the same that we want to defend here in our own country. (Applause.) You have heard some speakers refer to Lord Canning's order, that natives of India may be admitted into volunteer corps if the members of the corps consent to their admission. I say, "Why make that restriction? If you are honest, grant us the privilege. Why make the restriction? If you wish us to be admitted, then why leave it to the members of any corps to decide whether they choose to admit us or not? Answer that question." (Applause.) I say it is the authorities and not the members of any corps (applause) who are competent to judge whether we are entitled or not to defend our hearths and homes. (Applause.) Our Government is perfectly mistaken. You will excuse my warmth. I am carried away, but I will cool down. (Laughter and applause.) I say that our Government is making a terrible mistake. Some fifty or sixty years ago, by a lavish expenditure of money, they were able to raise as many German and other mercenaries as they desired, but they will never be able to do so in these days, and if they fancy that they will be able to do so they commit a great blunder which they will some day bitterly repent. Mercenaries are a class of people who are not to be had now. You all know that the different continental nations have not only their standing armies, but every male in their populations between eighteen and forty-five, or even fifty, years of age, registered as soldiers in one class of reserve or other, which they had not about the time of Waterloo. Not one mercenary soldier can England now draw from any continental nation. Russia has some five millions, Germany four, Austria has got two or three millions, France three or four million soldiers of the line and reserves and so on. Had they anything of all this when Waterloo was fought? Even in the Crimean War? (Voices 'No, No.') They had not, and consequently our English Government, in virtue of their long purse—by their unbounded and unlimited expenditure of money—were able to procure mercenaries to help them to fight their battles. Where will they procure mercenaries now when the odds against England are three-fold what they were? (Hear, hear.) Supposing Russia does invade India, and we all know that from the time of Peter the Great, Russia's aim has been—India! India! India! It is not barren Central Asia she has been aiming at. She has been sending large armies into Central Asia and wasting untold millions there, but she has been aiming at India. She wants an outlet for commerce and she must have it either here or on the Golden Horn at the expense of the Turkish or the British Empire, and all those who have studied this question know this very well. Now, Austria, Germany and Italy bar the way to Constantinople, and it is much to be feared that it will be at our expense that the outlet of Russian commerce will be found. Gentlemen, if Russia realizes this desire to pounce upon India, she will first create serious complications in Europe, and when our English rulers' energies are perfectly absorbed in meeting the dangers that beset them there, when they have, as in the Crimean war, denuded India of European troops, and probably, as has been her practice even in petty wars of late years, of a strong contingent of her best native troops, then, I ask, how many men will England be able to throw into the field here to meet the million or so of soldiers and robbers of a hundred wild tribes that Russia will be able to tempt into making common cause with her, in plundering our towns and ravishing our women? The English Government may have millions and hundreds of millions of money, but money won't fight—it is men that will fight and where will she get them, when, by her present policy, she has (laughter and hear, hear) turned us all into women? (Laughter.) Are we to be for ever treated as if we cannot be trusted? Are we so low and degraded that we are not able to be trusted to defend our hearths and homes? (Hear, hear, and applause.) Are we such fools as not to realise the difference between British and

Russian rule? (Cheers.) What then? Is it not mockery? Is it not idiotic to say to us, "You may be enrolled as volunteers with the consent of all the members of any existing corps?" And how many hundreds, should I not say thousands, will thus be able to obtain some military training? Some gentlemen here told us: "We are all unanimous in admitting native gentlemen." Yes, you are at the moment all unanimous, but will this unanimity continue? Does it exist elsewhere? In one or two instances corps may be unanimous; but is that any guarantee that we shall be admitted generally throughout the country in anything like adequate numbers to defend our homes, our families? We have a perfect right to be admitted. Why make these conditions? What are you afraid of? We do not want to drive you away from the country, (Voices of "No, No; Certainly not,") we want to keep you, to help you, to support you. (Tremendous cheers.) Is there one here so false, so foolish, as to say, "We want to drive the English away from this country?" (Loud cries of "No, No, No.") No, we are not so base (applause), we are not such fools. (Loud applause.) Were we to drive you away from our country, what would become of us? Who should we have instead? We may go from one end of the earth to the other end we shall not find one to come up to you. (Loud applause.) "England, with all thy faults we love thee still." There is not one single Power in all the world to come up to England, that would, on the whole, have dealt so nobly and generously with a subject nation as England has done. (Loud applause.) Whom shall we have instead of you? We must have a head here. A body without a head cannot live. (Applause.) If we get our Hindu friends here, who are so well educated, and, after we have driven you away, we take them and put them into power and give them the *gadi*, (voices of "No, No,") shall we get on well? Or are we fit to rule the whole empire? Or can we, in our present state, even combined, produce a Government half as good as that of England? No. We must have the English. But they are treating us like mere children (applause), they are simply trifling with us. We do not want to drive you away from here. We cannot do without you. If you give us all the liberty in the world we shall still respect you and cling to you and keep you with us—(A voice: "And respect you all the more,")—yes, and respect you all the more. Thank you, sir, for your correction. I did not want to speak to-day, but when I saw this matter brought up I asked the President to allow me to speak. Who does not feel the degradation of not being allowed to become a volunteer? Who does not feel the humiliation of being debarred from the use and practice of arms? Who does not tremble for the day when unarmed, helpless, our martial spirit dead, we shall have to stand wailing like women, to see our English friends massacred by Russian hordes, and ourselves, our fortunes and our families, the prey of their ruthless barbarities? (Applause.) I say this meeting speaks with one voice, and it is the voice of India, and no Government in the world can turn a deaf ear to such a voice or long refuse to permit us to qualify ourselves for defending it and ourselves, our hearths and homes, and the British empire. (Loud and prolonged applause, and cries of "Vote, Vote": "We are all agreed.")

The PRESIDENT: Gentlemen, if, as it seems, you are all of one mind and desire no further discussion, and I confess that I hardly see how there can be two opinions in regard to this present cautiously-worded Resolution, or, for that matter, that any more speaking in regard to it can be needed, I will now put it. (Cries of "Put it, Put it," "Vote, Vote.") The Resolution will stand thus:—

RESOLVED—That in view of the unsettled state of public affairs in Europe and the immense assistance that the people of this country, if duly prepared therefor, are capable of rendering to Great Britain, in the event of any serious complications arising, this Congress once again earnestly appeals to the Government to authorise (under such rules and restrictions as may to it seem fitting) a system of volunteering for the Indian inhabitants of the country such as may qualify them to support the Government effectively in any crisis.

The Resolution was then put and carried unanimously.

The PRESIDENT: The next proposition on the programme, gentlemen, is:—

That as the administration of the Income Tax, especially as regards incomes below Rs.1,000 a year, has proved extremely unsatisfactory, it is essential, in the opinion of the Congress, that the taxable minimum be raised to Rs.1,000, the loss of revenue thus involved being made good by reductions in the existing public expenditure, or, should this prove impossible, by the re-imposition of an import duty on the finer classes of cotton goods.

Babu Guru Prasad Sen (Behar, No. 532 in list) said: Gentlemen, when the first Congress met at Bombay we had to deal with the license-tax—a tax so illogical and inconsistent that we could do nothing better than to propose that an income-tax should be substituted in its stead. We did not approve either license-tax or income-tax. We said, if more money be really wanted for military purposes and the Government will not provide this, as they ought to provide it, by retrenchment in other branches of the service, the required funds ought to be provided, "firstly, by the re-imposition of the customs duties; and, secondly, by the extension of the license-tax to those classes of the community, official and non-official, at present exempted from it, care being taken that, in the case of all classes, a sufficiently high taxable minimum be maintained." What we said then was, "If you will have more money, if you won't retrench as you ought to do, if you won't re-impose the customs duties, then, rather than devise new schemes of taxation, turn your illogical license-tax into a logical income-tax, only keep your taxable minimum high enough." It was, in fact, the lesser of two evils which we chose. But we soon found that the taxable minimum had been struck too low, that the administration of the income-tax as it was worked when the income-tax came to be introduced—we found, I say, that the practical administration of the tax was by no means so satisfactory as it ought to have been, especially with reference to the taxation of incomes below, or coming but little above, the minimum. Now, having given the matter a fair trial, we propose that the taxable minimum be raised to Rs.1,000, and we do this in the interest of the humbler classes of our countrymen. (Applause.) It is not in the interest of the distinguished delegates whom I see before me, not ten per cent. of whom probably have incomes of less than Rs.1,000 a year, but in the interests of the large body of our countrymen of the middle classes, that we desire that this relief should be granted—namely, the raising of the minimum from Rs.500 to Rs.1,000. (Applause.) Now, there are many reasons why this raising of the minimum has become a necessity. In the Act we find the minimum Rs.500, and that, of course, you must admit, is a very low limit. It means, at the present rate of exchange, that all incomes of £24 a year and upwards are liable to taxation. Well, prices have risen during the last twenty years enormously, and they have even risen within the last two years. Sir, the minimum, I submit, ought to be fixed with due regard to the necessities of life, and this limit of Rs.500 takes no account of these. Is it at all conceivable for a man in our part of the country, a respectable householder, who lives on from Rs.500 to Rs.800 or Rs.900 a year, which comes to from Rs.40 to Rs.70, or say £2 15s. to less than £5 a month, to provide the mere necessaries of life, and then have any margin to spare for income-tax? (Loud applause.) Then there are not only his own necessities and those of his family to be supplied, but in all Indian families there are a number of dependants to be clothed and fed. It is not a question of one or two, but a question of many dozens, in every case, depending upon individuals. In fact, as you all know, a man has not only to feed, clothe, and educate his own sons, but he has to feed, clothe, and educate those of his relatives, subordinates, and so on. This, of course, is inevitable; it may be a good or bad custom, but it is one hallowed by the traditions of thousands of years, that we must still bow to. We cannot help ourselves if we would, and for all its disadvantages it is a good and kindly custom. It is not the question of the support of one individual and his family, but the support of a family and its connections and retainers. The income really belongs to half a dozen families; it is an aggregate of incomes here treated as one, but which would in other countries have stood divided. These points were not sufficiently taken into consideration when "the necessaries of life" for Indians were considered, or the taxable minimum which is supposed to be fixed above necessities would not have been placed so low. The necessities of life for Indian families are not to be measured with reference to the single individual requirements, but with reference to the requirements of his family and household, and if you measure necessary requirements with due regard to these, you will all agree with me that the minimum of Rs.40 a month is very much too low—(applause)—and, therefore, under these circumstances, we now propose that the taxable minimum be raised from Rs.500 to Rs.1,000. (Applause.) It was, I believe, originally under contemplation to fix the minimum at this figure for a certain class of people—I mean for officials in Government employ. Government thought this was a minimum exactly suited to the necessities of that class, but it was pointed out that if that concession was made a concession of a similar nature would be needed on behalf of every class, and that otherwise the tax would be inconsistent and illogical, and it was then, and then only, that the minimum in their case was reduced to Rs.500, so that, according to the admission of Government in regard to the only class of which it knows anything, the minimum ought to be fixed at Rs.1,000 and not at Rs.500, and we, who know all classes, can tell them that this is equally necessary in the case of all classes. (Applause.) Well, that being so, there can be no difference of opinion, it seems to me, with respect to the raising of the minimum. But, before I leave the question, I have one word more to say. In England the minimum is, I am told, £150 a year, which would correspond, at the present rate of exchange, to something like Rs.2,250. (Hear, hear.) So that our present minimum is fixed at a very low figure if you compare it with the English minimum, and especially if you take into consideration the fact that the one is for a single family while in India, looking to the requirements of an Indian family with its dependants, it is really the income of a group of families; and you must admit that the minimum, if it is not to be Rs.2,000, ought at least to be raised to Rs.1,000. (Applause.) Then, Sir, we are confronted with this difficulty: If the minimum is raised from Rs.500 to Rs.1,000, how are we to meet the loss in revenue? I submit, we can do it by reducing expenditure. In a household where the expenditure is seventy millions of pounds sterling, do you not think it possible that a paltry reduction of, say, one-third of one of those millions (which, I suppose, would be the utmost loss that would be sustained) could be very well made up by the reduction of expenditure? A prudent householder under such a contingency would, in the first place, set about and reduce his expenditure if he had no reasonable prospect of increasing his income, and if Government could at all be made to feel that the limit of taxation has already been reached, I think it would immediately set to work to bring about a reduction in expenditure sufficient to meet the reduction our proposals involve in the outturn of the income-tax. Government have, no doubt, instituted a finance committee; that committee has been making inquiries, and many suggestions have been made to it. Those suggestions, at least those likely to be accepted, though good only to a certain extent, would at any rate provide for this small reduction of thirty-five lacs in income, so that the deficit resulting from the relief we propose would and could be properly made up by reduction of expenditure. The report, it is true, is not before the public as yet, but there were many valuable suggestions made by those with whom the finance committee took counsel, and though I do not say that all the suggestions were good, or even if good likely to be acceptable to Government, still, if only one of these be accepted, the economy effected would make up for a loss of revenue which is simply represented by thirty-five lacs of rupees. I do not wish to name anybody, but I shall simply name the Board of Revenue of Bengal. If we simply give effect to the recommendations made from all quarters that this Board of Revenue should be abolished, we should at once get a reduction of expenditure to the tune of six lacs in Bengal, and thirty-five lacs would be half made up by similar reductions in other provinces. It is not, however, for us to specify reductions. We simply point out the fact that such a reduction is possible, and that if the taxable minimnm be raised as we advocate, and as the whole country demands, the loss of revenue thus involved can very well and ought to be made up by corresponding reductions in expenditure. But we say further. Even if that is not possible—that is to say, if you persist in not seeing that it is possible, and none are so blind as those who won't see—if you insist that you cannot meet the loss by reduction of expenditure, do this: as the present low minimum is telling so heavily on the well-being of the masses of our lower middle-class people—do this: re-impose the import duty which has been given up—(hear, hear)—an import duty, not on the poor man's clothing, but on the finer kinds of cloth, which only the comparatively rich—those really able to contribute to the necessities of the State—practically use. Well, the only thing that can be said against this measure is that it is a measure of protection. But it may be so low as to be practically inoperative in this direction. Even were it otherwise, I would still say it is not a protective measure at all; it is a fiscal measure, adopted solely in the interests of our finances. It would not be, nay, all the circumstances considered no one can pretend that it could be, opposed to the rules laid down by the best political economists, and, indeed, it is absurd to talk in these days of protection for our industries—our industries do not require protection; but, so as to leave no handle for such an argument, let there be a corresponding excise duty on our own similar finer productions. All we cry for is that, in the interest of our finances, if money be really needed to meet the deficit, the import duties should be re-imposed, and this our proposal contemplates. With these words I beg to propose for your acceptance the Resolution which the President has already read out to you. (Applause.)

Babu Jogender Chunder Ghose (Calcutta, No. 555 in list) said: Gentlemen, I, of all men here, should make some apology for speaking on this occasion; but apology takes time, and therefore I shall go on to my subject at once. The matter before us is one of great importance. There is no doubt that the administration of the income tax, especially as regards incomes below Rs.1,000 a year, has proved extremely unsatisfactory. It is well known that the income tax is a source of constant oppression and terror to the poorer people of this country. I know from my experience as a pleader—and you know that poor people only venture to come to men of little practice like myself—how the poor are oppressed. People are too frequently assessed at four times their actual income by those who desire to be considered *khairkhwah** servants of the Government. Poor people do not always keep proper accounts and are the least able to protect themselves, and then woe to the man who goes to collectors like Mr. Goodrich, of Calcutta, the *Zubberdust* the great, the great grinder of the poor. I know the clerk of a pleader was assessed at more than his master; and I still remember the look of terror of the man when he was told that his books were not regularly-kept account books. A man who has only three or four hundred rupees a year may easily be mistaken by the honestest assessing officer, misled by subordinates who want to make a name, for one who has five hundred rupees. But when you raise the minimum to Rs.1,000 a year it is different. None of the mass of folks who have two, three or four hundred a year can be assessed by mistake at Rs.1,000—of course there will be men on seven, eight and nine hundred, in regard to whom such a mistake may be made, but there are ten of the former class to one of the latter. It is not only mistakes that have to be guarded against. The hundreds of thousands of comparatively helpless ignorant persons who have between Rs.200 and Rs.500 a year are made to pay by rascals who threaten them that if they do not bribe them they will have them taxed. You get rid of all this, which is the cause of half the discontent the income-tax brings about, by raising the limit to Rs.1,000, because the seven, eight and nine hundred people are very, very much fewer in number, and are in a better position and know more, and are stronger and much less liable to be frightened by threats.

I think, gentlemen, that our demand is very reasonable. All that we want is the exemption of the poor and the weak from the tax and its accompanying oppression. The classes that will thus be exempted will be the more poorly-paid servants of Government, and the great mass of small traders, shop-keepers and artisans.

As regards Government servants, you know, gentlemen, that they are mostly taken from the middle classes, the lower ranks of what we may call the gentry of the country. You know how day by day they are being reduced to poverty. Their wants are many and their means are small, and we know how keen their struggle for existence is; the accident of birth has added to their misery. Rs.25 is a large sum for them, for they can save nothing. If possible, as a matter of humanity only, they should be let alone, but the principal reason why this tax, so far as they are concerned, should be removed is that it diminishes the efficiency of the public service because it still further and materially reduces the salaries of the poorest-paid and yet hardest-worked servants of the Government. In Bengal we had the Salaries Commission for the avowed purpose of increasing the pay of our ill-paid officials, and that purely in the interests of the public service. But nothing came out of it. The income tax, however, still remains. When the income-tax bill was first framed servants of the State drawing small salaries were exempted from its operation. But our wise legislators thought that by this the principle of equality would be infringed; and for once equality was accepted as a very important principle in the administration of the country—indeed, more important than the efficiency of the public service. But I think I express the opinion of the Congress when I say that the other classes would not certainly have grudged these officials this poor privilege.

As for the other classes upon which the measure of this tax falls the heaviest, it is the class of small traders and shop-keepers, and these men, besides illegitimate extortions wrung

* *i.e.*, well-wishing.

from them, by threats of getting them still more highly assessed, are always assessed at a great deal more than their actual incomes. Most of them are illiterate, many of them entirely so, and none of them keep or can possibly keep account books that assessors will accept; these poor men are always the least able to defend themselves, and least able to pay competent men to protect their interests. Many small tradesmen have been thus obliged to give up their trade, and many that have not done this yet, find it most difficult to keep up their business. I know one, a man who was literally obliged to close his shop on account of the heavy income-tax imposed upon him, and for no other reason—it just absorbed his entire profits. As for the small artisans and manufacturers, English competition is daily driving them out of the market; the income-tax has added to their difficulties, and is absolutely crushing them. There is no encouragement for them anywhere and they are dying out, to the great detriment of the prosperity of the country. . That is a bad tax which benefits the Government financially far less than it oppresses and injures the people. And that is just what this income-tax does when imposed upon these classes. If the Government had only a conception of all the suffering caused, and all the injury inflicted on the prosperity of the country, by allowing the nominal taxable minimum to remain at its present low level, they would not hesitate one moment, cost what it might, to accept our recommendation.

And how do we propose to make up the loss to the public revenue which will thus be caused? It is by the re-imposition of an import duty on the finer classes of cotton goods. We all know how, at the bidding of the merchants of Manchester, the cotton duties were abolished. The voice of a few English merchants was found more powerful than the voice of two hundred and fifty millions of Indians. We hope that, at last, the good sense and the keen sense of justice of the great English nation will awake to the injustice of adding to the burdens of a poor and already overburdened people for the sake of a few merchants. And we hope also that the great and just statesman who is now at the head of Government, a nobleman by nature as he is by birth, will accede to our prayers and redress this great grievance.

The PRESIDENT: Gentlemen, I have received notice in due form of an addition to the proposition before the assembly; a small but not unimportant amendment, and I will call upon the proposer, Mr. Khare, to submit it to you.

Mr. DAJI ABAJI KHARE (Bombay, No. 370 in list) said: Gentlemen, I am entirely at one with the proposer and seconder of the proposition now before you, but I desire to insert a few additional words in it. Gentlemen, if the Government refuse to raise the taxable minimum as we recommend, then our recommendation about the re-imposition of the customs duties falls as it were to the ground, whereas, gentlemen, it should be our object never to allow this to fall to the ground, but to perpetually keep before the eyes of the British public and the British Government that, though we may forgive, we can never forget, the gross injustice that was done to us at the bidding of a small though powerful English mercantile clique, and that we will never rest, at any rate as long as other worse and far less productive taxes have to be borne by us, until we obtain redress. I may say, gentlemen, that I am told that, now that the true fiscal character of those duties have become known to them, now that they realize that they were in no degree practically protective—that it is advantages in situation and cheap labour, and not any duties that favour our mills, and that, despite the abolition of these latter, our mills go on year by year absorbing more and more of the trade—now, I say, that they have come to realize this, I am told that the more enlightened members of the Manchester manufacturers themselves regret having had any indirect share in inflicting on this financially struggling country the terrible financial loss which the abolition of these duties involved (cheers). I believe it, gentlemen; for, though manufacturers, though Manchester manufacturers, they are Englishmen, and though they may be hasty for the moment, they cannot help being just in the long run. (Loud cheers.) But, be this as it may, it is essential for us at any rate to make clear that—not only as a means of recouping any such reduction of revenue as is involved in our present recommendation, but in all and every case in which additional revenue may be required—the re-imposition of customs duties on articles mainly used by the rich is, in our opinion, in the opinion of the entire country, the only legitimate course of action. We say—the entire country says—if you at any time really need more money you must not enhance the income tax, you must not raise the salt tax, you must not go devising any new fiscal instruments of torture, you must so re-impose the customs duties that they shall be paid by the rich and not add to the burdens of the poor. The proposition is not quite so generally put as I would have liked to see it in this resolution, but my main purpose will have been accomplished if you will agree to insert between the words, "made good" and "by reductions," these few words, "and further financial difficulties, if any, met." (Loud cheers, and cries of "Yes, Yes.")

BABU GURU PRASAD SEN (the proposer), said: Mr. President, I gladly accept this amendment, and so, I am sure, will this assembly, for Mr. Khare has most clearly and eloquently expressed what I, and I am sure every one here, think on this matter. (Loud applause, and cries of "Yes, Yes.")

The PRESIDENT: Then I am to understand that this addition is approved. ("Yes, Yes.") Does any one object to it? ("No, No.")

The PRESIDENT (continuing): Gentlemen, another amendment has been sent up to me, and I therefore call upon the proposer to expound it.

Mr. CHAKRAVARTI (Anantapur, No. 292 in list): At this late hour I do not wish to try your patience too much. As the income-tax is now administered it is working great injustice and is utterly iniquitous, so I beg to propose that the tax be abolished. The amended proposition which I suggest would run thus: "That as the administration of the income-tax has involved very great hardships, it is essential in the opinion of this Congress that the tax be abolished." (Voices of "No, No, Withdraw," "It is the only tax that reaches the rich," "We don't want to relieve ourselves of taxation," "We won't have it," and "Withdraw, Withdraw.") Well, gentlemen, of course I bow to the general sense of the assembly, but I retain my own opinion, that the only thing to be done about the income-tax is to abolish it *in toto*. What is the use of half measures? (Cries of "Sit down," and "Shut up.") Well, as you will have it, I withdraw my amendment. (Loud applause.)

The PRESIDENT: Gentlemen, I have to announce that I have received yet another amendment.

Mr. SUBRAMANIA SASTRI (Madras, No. 14 in list) rose and said: Gentlemen, I am not going to adduce arguments in favour of my amendment. I shall simply state the amendment and leave it in your hands. In the sixth resolution, after Rs.1,000, in line 3, I propose to add, "and that of taxable amounts, Rs.300 be exempted from taxation." I may pay income-tax on my salary. A man who receives Rs.500 per annum has to pay an income-tax of Rs.11, and he has Rs.489 nearly left for his expenses. On the other hand, a man who receives Rs.499 per annum has the whole Rs.499 left for his expenses, so that a man who receives Rupee 1 more is worse off by Rupees 10. In England it is customary to exempt a certain amount of a person's income from taxation. For instance, in the case of a person whose income is £500, £120 of that sum will be exempted from taxation. What I want is not to calculate on the whole Rs.1,000, but to subtract Rs.300 from this, and take the tax on the remainder.

RAJAH YATINDRA NATH CHAUDHURI (24-Pergannahs, No. 560 in list): I second this amendment.

BABU GURU PRASAD SEN: I have only two objections to the amendment. In the first place, in the resolution what was sought for was relief for the poorer middle class, and not, as is involved by the amendment, for the richer classes. In the second place, this question of rebate has been also discussed repeatedly in the Viceroy's Council, and it has been definitely decided that the principle shall not be admitted in India. Rightly or wrongly, this is so, and I am unwilling to complicate our otherwise simple resolution by pressing Government to reverse its entire and carefully-considered procedure in this matter.

(After some consultation with other delegates, this amendment was withdrawn by the proposer.)

The **President**: Gentlemen, I am happy to be able to inform you, though, perhaps, you will hardly yet credit the fact, but really there are no further amendments—(laughter and cheers)—and if you approve, I will now put the Resolution. (Cries of "Yes, Yes," "Vote, Vote.") Very good, gentlemen, then the Resolution, with Mr. Khare's emendation, will now stand :—

Resolved.—That as the administration of the income-tax, especially as regards incomes below Rs.1,000 a year, has proved extremely unsatisfactory, it is essential, in the opinion of the Congress, that the taxable minimum be raised to Rs.1,000, the loss of revenue thus involved being made good and further financial difficulties, if any, met by reductions in the existing public expenditure, or, should this prove impossible, by the re-imposition of an import duty on the finer classes of cotton goods.

The Resolution was then put and carried unanimously, and the assembly adjourned until 11 o'clock the next day.

FOURTH DAY'S PROCEEDINGS.

Friday, the 30th December, 1887.

The Congress re-assembled at 11 a.m., and the PRESIDENT, taking the chair, said: Gentlemen, this is the last day of our session; we have still a good deal of business to dispose of, and I hope that you will all remember how precious our time is, and not occupy one minute longer with your speeches than is necessary to express clearly what you desire to say. I trust you will excuse my making this appeal, but, unless discussion be confined within the narrowest practicable limits, we shall not, I fear, do all that we desire to do before separating. The first business before us to-day is the following proposed Resolution :—

"That, having regard to the poverty of the people, it is desirable that the Government be moved to elaborate a system of Technical Education, suitable to the condition of the country, to encourage indigenous manufactures by a more strict observance of the orders already existing in regard to utilizing such manufactures for State purposes, and to employ, more extensively than at present, the skill and talents of the people of the country."

I call now on Sir Savalai Ramaswami Mudaliar to move this proposition.

SIR SAVALAI RAMASWAMI MUDALIAR (Madras, No. 4 in list) said: Mr. President and Gentlemen, after having heard the brilliant speeches delivered during the last three days by gentlemen from various parts of India, I have thought it prudent, being myself no orator, to put down in writing and to read out to you what I have to say, and I beg that I may be excused for the liberty I have taken in doing so.

(He then read the following Address :)

Gentlemen,—I feel extremely thankful for the honour the executive committee have done me in placing this important Resolution in my hands. It gives me much pleasure to move it. Technical Education has been the dream of my life. It has ever been my earnest desire to do something to ameliorate the condition of the masses. And now, in God's good providence, this Congress has been organized for the good of the country. The poverty of India is becoming proverbial. Agriculture fails to satisfy the mouths of the fast-increasing population of India, while other industries, the only other sources of livelihood for the people, are fast falling into decay. The industrial classes, unable to compete with European manufacturers, are rapidly forgetting the cunning of their hands. The importance of a system of technical education cannot, therefore, be over-estimated. I look upon it as a rope of salvation let down to save our sinking population. Technical education commends itself to all classes and creeds of people. Unlike other movements which affect but certain sections of the community, the proposed movement, if once set agoing, would make its beneficial effects felt by every individual in the land. Our esteemed Mahomedan brethren are in full sympathy with us; and, as a token of this, their association in Madras has already established an Institute for Technical Education in some branches, and on a small scale, of which, together with Rajah Sir Madhava Row and other gentlemen, I have the honour of being a patron; I am happy to add that their Institute is thriving under the indefatigable superintendence of Colonel Underwood. My long mercantile experience convinces me that the elaboration by Government of an exhaustive system of Technical Education will prove an inestimable boon to the poorer millions of India. (Applause.) In course of conversation with many an honoured Government official, with reference to the Technical Institute which is now about to be organised in this city as an abiding result of Her Gracious Majesty's Jubilee, I have found that the Government do certainly look upon the movement with favour. His Excellency the Governor has more than once expressed his conviction of its desirability, and among others, the Hon. Mr. Hutchins, to whose superior tact and ability I need not refer here, views the idea with the greatest pleasure. We have, therefore, much reason to calculate on the sympathy and co-operation of the Government in this important undertaking. (Applause.) Even when looked at from a mercantile point of view, the movement commends itself to us in a high degree. We just passed a Resolution, part of which has reference to the re-imposition of an import duty on the finer classes of cotton goods. In my humble opinion, such an import duty would not only prove itself a source of additional revenue, but might also, by a reflex action, tend to a revival and rapid development of our slumbering local industries. (Cries of "No, No.") Anyhow, the development of a suitable and comprehensive scheme of technical education would effect this. Long neglected manufactures would receive a fresh lease of life, and ample scope would be afforded to native talent and native enterprise in this direction. Useful and honourable employment would be found for millions of Indians, while heads of departments, too, would then with greater facility meet local needs with local supplies. In connection with the establishment of the proposed Institute, I beg to express my firm conviction that a small technical school in every Taluq of India would be most beneficial—a school in which all classes might be taught one or more of the useful arts. And as such schools increase in number, and cover the length and breadth of the land, hundreds of available educated young men would find a fresh field of labour for their skill and talent. Now-a-days we are becoming familiar with the saying that industry is of far greater value than education. But I think that industry combined with at least a moderate degree of elementary education would prove far more useful than industry without any education at all. Moderately educated workmen would learn to appreciate such qualities as beauty, symmetry, etc., in the different kinds of work they turn out, and constantly endeavour to improve on their workmanship; and in this way remove from our working countrymen the long-standing reproach that they continue to weave, spin, and perform every other industrial work in exactly the same way as their fathers did thousands of years ago. (Applause.) Viewed, therefore, from a mercantile as well as a philanthropic standpoint, the elaboration of a system of technical education becomes a great necessity, a necessity which is, I am sure, as deeply felt by Government as by the people of India. Let us, therefore, persevere in pressing our claims in this direction on the attention of our benign Government who, according to their light and knowledge, are doing their very best to promote the welfare of the Indian nation, and I am fully convinced that what I have already remarked has been but the dream of my life will, at no distant future, become an accomplished fact, spreading its blessings far and wide like a mighty river, and making glad the hearts of the people. With these few remarks, I beg to propose the Resolution, which has been already read out to you by our respected President.

Mr. JOHN ADAM (Madras, No. 88 in list) said: Mr. President and Delegates, I must commence by expressing my appreciation of the very high honour which has been conferred upon me by asking me to second the resolution which has just been proposed by my friend Sir Savalai Ramaswami Mudaliar. It is a great honour to address an assemblage of this description upon any subject, and I consider it a still greater honour to address it upon a subject which is, I conceive, perhaps the most important of all the subjects which have to be brought before a national assembly like the present. (Applause.) I must at the same time ask your kind consideration when you remember the sad restrictions of time which are placed upon speakers on the present occasion, and all the more so as this subject is, from its very nature, a most complicated subject, and one which, if it were to be treated with any fulness, would necessitate my entering into many details. The subject of technical education is one which is exciting a great deal of attention, not only in this country but also at the present time in England, America, and various other countries, which are holding or endeavouring to hold the first rank in commerce and native industries. We find that this subject, even when treated and discussed by the wisest heads in these old countries, presents an extraordinary amount of difficulty in bringing to any reasonable settlement. We must not, therefore, be surprised or ashamed when we find here that we have to face similar serious difficulties in the practical treatment of the subject. It may, however, clear the ground if I point out in the first place, what has been very often overlooked, that there are two different branches, so to speak, which are popularly mixed up under the head of technical education. They are separate branches and they are very often confused in people's minds. The first of these branches is that description or kind of technical education which is auxiliary to, or ought to be auxiliary to, whatever comes under the head of general education. That is a part of the question which we may put very largely on one side; for I think it is fortunately in process of solution at present and does not present such extensive difficulties. The fact of the great advantage derivable from the addition of some practical education to ordinary general education has been brought home to all persons who are engaged, like myself, in educational pursuits in this country. It has been specially borne in upon me, because, as many of you know, I have the honour of being the head of the largest native institution in this Presidency, possessing no fewer than 1,800 pupils in its various branches. Now, my idea of a schoolmaster is not that of a man who sits in a high chair, with a book in one hand and a cane in the other, but of one who has the highest aims in teaching and who tries to teach, not simply what he himself learnt many years ago, but what he thinks most profitable to his pupils at the present day. It has consequently become a very serious question with me, what it really would be most profitable for these very large classes of pupils, who are usually trained to no practical work, to be taught. (Applause.) Remember, I do not say a word against university education; I should be the last man to say anything against university education. The difficulty is to decide how we can do the best for that large class of pupils who receive education up to a certain, and not very high, standard, and never hope to go further. In this Presidency we had, a fortnight ago, not fewer than 6,700 candidates for the matriculation examination. Of these 6,700, I think I am quite within the mark when I say that there are at least 5,000 that will never go beyond the matriculation examination, and out of these 5,000, a very large proportion will fail even in that. Now, here we have got 5,000 boys who are being educated up to this standard. Is it not better to educate them to some final standard and teach them something that will be directly and practically useful in their after-life, instead of educating them up to a standard which is really only the commencement of another type of education? At present, we have got these boys ending their school career with very little real education, to the disadvantage of both the parties. Now, this is a question which has struck a great many people. Amongst others, it engaged the very earnest attention of the Education Commission that sat some four years ago, and they in their report called attention to it in this Resolution,—"That in upper classes of high schools there be two divisions; one leading to the entrance examination of the universities, the other, of a more practical character, intended to fit youths for commercial or non-literary pursuits." On this recommendation, the Government of India passed the following most sympathetic order: "The bifurcation of studies suggested is of special importance at the present time. Every variety of study should be encouraged which may serve to direct the attention of native youths to industrial and commercial pursuits. To be of any value, the bifurcation should be carried out, as the Commission advise, in the High School course." That strong recommendation was not left there, but after having made it the Government of India communicated with the local Governments and asked these to report what steps were being taken to carry out those recommendations. Some at least (certainly this local Government, which, I am glad to say, in the persons of the Director of Public Instruction, and of the Hon. Mr. Hutchins, a member of Council, as also of His Excellency the Governor himself (applause), has shown the most hearty sympathy in the matter) took it up, and they have already sanctioned a scheme, for which, moreover, a certain sum of money has been already allotted in the educational budget, thus removing the difficulty which we previously felt. Instead of turning out a number of boys who have been taught a number of subjects which will be of little, if any, direct practical use to them, they will be taught subjects which will be of practical benefit and importance to them. I, therefore, think I need go no further upon this point. Now I come to the second part of technical education, whereby we should give an actual training in the various industries and try to promote the interests of those who are actually employed in these industries. I am bound to admit that this is a very difficult question. There are a great many schemes, but the problem is to get a feasible scheme—a workable scheme. We propose to have here an Institute called the Victoria Jubilee Technical Institute as a Jubilee memorial. We have got a certain amount of money, and we have got some expectation of Government assistance, and we have also hopes of additional assistance from subscribers when we can show a working scheme. But I am sorry to say that we are at present very far from having a feasible scheme to put before the public. I am almost ashamed to make such a confession, but I have the mournful satisfaction of knowing from the President that our friends in Bombay are in almost the same position. Having in hand a very large amount of subscriptions for the promotion of technical education, they are not yet in a position to bring forward any comprehensive and satisfactory working scheme. The great difficulty which I can see, the preliminary difficulty—the difficulty which is met to a very large extent by the Resolution which has been proposed—is the want of accurate, collected, and digested information upon the subject. When our local committee made the report upon the subject, I added a minute which was circulated to the members, and in which I put the point this way: "I have, in common with many other persons, a floating general idea that much can be done, but what inquiry I have been able to make into specific industries,—for instance, weaving,—shows only how little we know, and the impossibility of framing on that scanty knowledge any practical scheme or suggestion. I think that a small committee might be appointed, either by the Technical Institute Committee or by Government, to investigate the actual condition of native industries, *in esse* and *in posse*, not from the æsthetic but from the practical and economic point of view. The aim should not be to produce a renaissance in Indian industrial art, but to discover whether, by improved methods of working and increased technical skill, competition is possible between native manufactures and foreign imports. I cannot think of any way in which money, whether of the Institute or of Government, can be better expended than in payment of the expenses of such a preliminary inquiry." This was the recommendation which I made some time ago. I have met the reward of having made such a complete confession of my ignorance in having been asked by the Hon. Mr. Hutchins to assist the Director of Public Instruction in drawing up a practical scheme. We are now trying to draw up such a scheme, but I am afraid with very little success as yet. This proposal of a committee of inquiry to find out facts is, I find, supported in this pamphlet, published and circulated to the members of the Congress, by Dinshaw Ardeshar Taleyar Khan, who has also published another pamphlet on the subject, which is, I think, the most suggestive publication which has yet appeared in this country. He says: "I hold it a great misfortune that as yet we are unable to prevail upon the Government of India to appoint a high commission to report upon an imperial scheme for introducing suitable and widespread technical education in India. In a recent pamphlet of mine I have plainly explained the grave short-comings of our administration in this connection. This great problem, the fulfilment of which will be a sure remedy to the general poverty of India, needs a most comprehensive and masterly dealing. Any ultimately authoritative despatch on the subject, based on full and generous investigations of a Royal Commission, will live for centuries. The Congress ought to persevere and bring about this result. Real patriotism may take pride in the achievement of this one work a thousand times more than we need take in the nomination of a few natives in the councils or even in the House of Commons." There is no doubt this is one of the greatest and the noblest works which the Congress can undertake. Further, we find that not only local bodies, private individuals, and local Governments are trying their hand at working out something, but we find that the Government of India has been having a try in the matter. I have here a portentous-looking blue-book called a "Note upon Technical Education," which has recently been published. It is very exhaustive, so far as it goes, for it begins with the origin of technical education. This, I find, originated in the despatch of 1854. That despatch has been responsible for a great deal, and it has now been made resposible for the origin of technical education. The "Note" goes on to give what we already possess, or what we at least ought to be able to find out for ourselves, an account of various agricultural, engineering, medical and other colleges which exist in the various Presidencies in India at the present time, and that is the main part of this long document. It then goes on to make certain recommendations, which we may take to be the plan of the Government of India. Apart from various suggestions, as to teaching drawing in schools, etc., as far as technical education is concerned this is the sole suggestion it makes, viz., that to middle and high schools there should be attached technical branches wherever an inquiry brings to light the demand for technical training. This is their suggestion—that we are to establish technical schools wherever an inquiry establishes the fact that technical schools are wanted. This inquiry is the very thing we have not got; and this is the very thing we want the Government of India to make for us, either by appointing a commission, as the motion impliedly suggests, or by local committees or special officers. That is the outcome of this long note, viz., that we are to aid and promote technical education by establishing technical schools in localities where they are required. It goes on further to state, very sympathetically but not very practically, "Natives of all castes are increasing in number, looking to technical education as affording an honourable livelihood and career in life. It is submitted that it is desirable to assist and encourage this popular feeling; that room exists for improvement in almost every department of technical instruction in India; and that the time is ripe not only for calling on local Governments to take up the matter in earnest, but for indicating to them some of the directions in which improvement seems possible, and from which funds can be obtained for effecting it." Thus, Sir, we see that the Government has admitted that the main point of difficulty in connection with the subject is an inquiry, and I think, therefore, that we are justified in going forward in the strongest and in the most emphatic terms to ask the Government of India to make some such inquiry. And here I wish to make a suggestion which I think might well be carried out by this Congress, although it is not in the motion. In case the Government of India should not appoint a commission, or during the interval that may elapse in bringing the matter under public consideration, we might ourselves take the matter in hand. It is a very common course of proceeding in Congressef and associations such as this in other countries when they have a complicated and difficult subject, the principle of which is fully accepted and the details of which cannot be readily worked out, to appoint a sub-committee or a standing committee, which has to occupy itself during the year, as far as possible, in gathering information, in working out the various details and endeavouring to place itself in a position to submit to the succeeding Congress a report on the whole subject. So we might appoint a committee for the purpose of eliciting information and drawing up some working scheme in regard to technical education with which we might go to the Government os India. This Congress might very well, I say, appoint a small sub-committee, consisting of representative members of all the various districts who may be willing to undertake the duty, to collect information, by comparing and considering the needs of different districts in various industries, to try to evolve something like a practical scheme for general technical education, and to report results to the next Congress. We should thus be able to go up to the Government of India next year, not only, as now, with a request, but with a scheme for giving practical effect to our request.

I have, Sir, carefully avoided looking at the clock. I feel sure, however, it is now "time," and, therefore, it is not possible to deal with a great many interesting questions regarding the subject. I should be only taking an unfair advantage of your generosity if I went into them at length. As far as I have gone, I have necessarily touched upon only one part of the subject, the details of one point of those we have under consideration. Because I have not gone into the other parts of the question, you must not think that I am oblivious of the very large and important aspects of it connected with the improvement of the industrial status of the population of this country. I mention this simply to show you that I have not overlooked it. I hope that amongst the eloquent speakers to follow some will be found to enlarge upon this point.

Our Resolution acknowledges and recognises the poverty of the people of India, and we know that this statement has been questioned in some quarters. I need not infringe on the task that has been so ably undertaken by Mr. Dadabhai Nowrojee, who has made this question his own. I merely wish to point out that the poverty of the country is a poverty which is not irremediable, and it is simply because there is a remedy by which it may be alleviated, if only in the long future, that we bring forward this motion at the present time. Passing over all other advantages which this country possesses as an industrial and a trading community, I may point out that the one great main feature is the cheapness of labour in this country. When I say "cheapness" I do not wish you to suppose that I think labour here is sufficiently well-paid. When you take into consideration how in European countries many thousands die yearly simply because they are not able to purchase the heat which we get here for nothing; when you consider this you will readily understand how wages here might be raised fivefold—aye, tenfold—and that would be to many in this country a luxury beyond the dreams of avarice, and yet be far below the level of the wages of European labour. It is not merely that wages are actually low, but that they may with safety be raised to give people in this country every comfort, and even luxury, which they may desire, and still remain far below the rates prevailing in Europe. I do not for a moment say that pure labour, however cheap, unassisted by technical education and unassisted by machinery and all the improvements of science, will ever compete with educated labour however dear; but I do say that all these advantages being equal, the physical differences of the country will, and ought, to give an inestimable advantage to India in any competition which might ensue. There is only one further point to which I wish to call your attention before I sit down, and it is in the way of caution. This is, that we are very much inclined, when we are agitating for improvements, to expect that they can all be done in a hurry, and at once. Even if we had a system of technical education, the most perfect system in the world, and even if we had it introduced at the present moment, it must be very, very many years before any practical and lasting result could be seen from the working of the system. We talk about the real spread of education in the country, but consider that the general education of this country has really only touched the *élite* of the country, that it has hardly touched the lower classes who are to be reached by technical education. If this education, which has been found to reach the intellectual *élite* only, has taken more than fifty years to reach its present standard, you may consider how long the scheme of technical education would take to reach the masses in order to show any great or effective results. But, at the same time, we must not be disheartened by that. We are only sowing the seed which will remain for our children and grandchildren, and perhaps, future generations, to water, to watch its progress, and gather the fruits of it. If we are to delay putting our hands to the work, that will only postpone the doing of it to some future generation. We ought to rejoice that we are doing something which, though we do not find the full fruition of it in our own days, will be enjoyed at least by our descendants and future generations. If it is a great, as I believe it to be, a great and a laudable desire, so to work and live as to gain the applause and approbation of one's fellow-citizens, it is possibly a still greater and nobler life for a man to live so that, after he is gone, future generations shall rise up and call him blessed. If we look forward, future generations will look back to the present, and they will read the proceedings of this Congress and the history of the great intellectual activity which has characterised this present generation. I have no doubt that they will feel that, to us in the present generation, is due the honour of having sown the seed of which they are reaping the fruit. Therefore, I think we should not be disheartened by the feeling that the good work will be prolonged to some distant future. We should be all the more gratified and all the more honoured at being enabled to work, to some extent at least, for the generations that will come after us. (Loud and continued applause).

Sheik Kadir Buksh (Fyzabad, No. 527 in list) then spoke in Urdu, and said: Mr. Chairman and Brother Delegates, this Resolution, which is just before you, is far more important than the other Resolutions passed and carried by you, since it is intended for those poor people of India whom extreme poverty has nowadays reduced to a most miserable condition. (Cheers.) Before, however, I speak anything relating to the Resolution, I consider it my duty to enlighten you, gentlemen, with a description of those people who have done me the honour of sending me as their representative to take part in this Congress. I come from the city of Fyzabad, a city which stands second in rank to Lucknow in the Province of Oudh; the Hindus and Mahomedans of which place are in perfect and hearty sympathy with the National Congress movement, and cherish brotherly feelings among themselves, in testimony whereof I have been furnished with credentials duly signed by the representatives of both the communities. (Hear, hear.) Gentlemen, we are perfectly in accord that this Congress is neither a Bengali Congress nor the Congress of any particular nationality, nor the Congress representing the views of any particular society, as has been maliciously declared by the detractors of this institution; but it is truly and undeniably the Indian National Congress. Whether Hindus or Mahomedans, we are all the children of the same mother India, and as such are indissolubly bound in a fraternal tie. (Loud cheers.) Gentlemen, I would now request your earnest attention to the few words which I am going to speak in support of this Resolution. The greater portion of my countrymen are reduced to the lowest level of poverty, and I am grieved to say that this poverty is daily on the increase, so much so that even starvation has not become a very uncommon thing. This poverty, so far as I have been able to understand, is mainly attributable to the total absence of local industries and want of support to industrial arts and manufactures. All our necessaries of life are supplied from foreign countries; owing to their cheapness they insure a ready sale, displacing the native articles manufactured by manual labour, which for obvious reasons cannot compete in price with the machine-turned articles of foreign manufacture. Gentlemen, this influx and import of cheap foreign articles has virtually suppressed those indigenous manufactures for which our country was once famous. As a natural consequence of this, millions of rupees are monthly and annually drained away. Gentlemen, if you now turn your attention towards the departments of the public service, you will find that posts carrying high emoluments, whether in the military or the civil line, are, so to speak, the monopoly of the Europeans, while only the poorly-paid appointments fall to the lot of even those of us who have attained the highest educational qualifications, the consequence being that thousands of us of ordinary abilities are hopelessly in want of employment. Gentlemen, I need hardly say that an inquiry as to how this class of our countrymen manage to keep body and soul together, not to say of the thousand other requirements, would, however painful, be a fitting task for this august assembly. (Hear, hear.) In my opinion, the Resolution under reference should be prominently brought to the attention of the supreme Government, in view to the gradual amelioration of the condition of our countrymen, and in strongly supporting this Resolution I think I shall have fully acquitted myself of the onerous duty imposed on me by my constituents at Fyzabad. (Loud cheers.)

The President: Gentlemen, I have received a notice of a proposed amendment by the Hon'ble Mr. Ranade. He wants to add to the Resolution before us the words: "and that the concession of a permanent settlement be extended to those parts of the empire where such does not exist." But I do not consider this to be an amendment. (Cheers.) It may be proposed, however, as a separate Resolution, after the business before the Congress is disposed of. There is another amendment that I have received from Mr. Chackravarti, but that is not seconded, and I cannot take any notice of it. There is another amendment by Mr. Huckam Chand, of Lahore. The same observation applies to that amendment also, as I have no name of any seconder. Any amendment that any gentleman desires to propose should be sent up to me with the name of the proposer and also of the seconder. There is another amendment, in fact, several amendments, sent up by Mr. Peter Paul Pillai, but none of these gives the name of any seconder. But I have one amendment which bears the name of the proposer and the seconder, and this is that, in line 3, after the word "country," we should insert the words "to improve Indian agriculture." I call on the proposer of this amendment to lay it before the Congress.

Mr. Chackravarti (Anantapur, No. 292 in list): Gentlemen, I do not intend to make any elaborate speech. I shall confine myself to bringing to your kind notice that if, as proposed, it is essential to have an elaborate scheme of technical education, it is still more essential to elaborate a scheme for the improvement of our agriculture, which is a far more momentous question. I would also submit for your consideration that India has from time immemorial been known to be, first and foremost, an agricultural country. It is also well understood that agriculture is the backbone of India. Agriculture also supplies the wants of the people. By my amendment, I submit, there is no material alteration in the proposition itself. It only seeks to bring agricultural education in as part of technical education. I submit, if it is necessary to encourage Indian manufactures it is also necessary to encourage agriculture improvements, and, therefore, I submit for your consideration that the improvement of agriculture should be also included in the proposition.

Mr. J. Dharma Ranga Raju (Chingleput, No. 153 in list): Gentlemen, in heartily thanking you for the kindness with which you have greeted me (roars of laughter—the speaker not having been greeted at all), I am sorry to tell you that you will be greatly disappointed in listening to what I have to say upon this subject. I am only a farmer, and being such, you cannot expect me to talk correct English. I am still a student, and that in a technical institution, namely, the college of agriculture at Sydapet. (Laughter and applause.) That college consists of students from all parts of India—from Bengal, Bombay, Madras, Conjeveram, and other places, and they have selected me to come here as their representative before this august body (much laughter), and represent their views, and this I am able to do in seconding this amendment. (The student then began to read a paper, which was not properly heard or understood, being interrupted very frequently by roars of laughter and recommendations to the reader to return to school, and after a few minutes he resumed his seat, again thanking the audience, now perfectly convulsed with laughter, for the kindness with which they had received him.)

The President: Order, gentlemen, please. The amendment is, that the words "and to improve Indian agriculture" be added to the proposition. I would appeal to the proposer and seconder to consider whether, as a fact, the Resolution does not embrace the improvement of Indian agriculture. We are recommending the elaboration of a scheme of technical education, and necessarily one of the branches of technical education is education in the art of agriculture. We are now going into the details of technical education. It seems to me that we are really making a proposal to Government that some system of technical education should be introduced in this country; and if we specifically mention one branch we may as well go on to all the other branches. I would, therefore, appeal to the proposer and seconder of this amendment to reconsider their amendment.

The proposer and seconder then withdrew the amendment. (Applause.)

Mr. B. H. CHESTER, M.A. (Madras, No. 50 in list), then rose and said: I have much pleasure in supporting the proposition that has been moved by my esteemed friend the Sheriff of Madras, and seconded by that gentleman who is associated in this Presidency with commercial education, Mr. Adam. (Cheers.) Before offering a few remarks on the subject, permit me to make a personal observation. I appear here as a delegate from the Eurasian and Anglo-Indian Association of Southern India (cheers), an association founded by Mr. D. S. White, whose absence from Madras is due to his labours in Calcutta in connection with the Public Service Commission, and who, had he been here, would have rejoiced to take part in this movement. (Cheers.) I am authorized to state that he is in full sympathy with you, and had he been here, he would have been delighted to address you. (Cheers.) I am happy to be able to stand here, and speak to you as one of yourselves. (Cheers.) Though I am proud, and justifiably so, I hope, of the English blood that flows in my veins, still I feel that by birth, by residence, by community of interests, I am as much entitled to the designation "native of India" as any delegate now present. (Loud cheers.) When I consider who are before me, when I recall the eloquent utterances, the noble sentiments, the loyal words that have thrilled us during these memorable days, I am more than ever convinced of the wisdom of the movement inaugurated by Mr. White, which has brought me and other members of the community to which I belong to meet you on one common platform as "natives of India." (Prolonged cheers.) To return to the proposition before you. I have been asked by the mover and seconder of the Resolution to say that agricultural education is, of course, understood to be included in the general phrase "technical education," which appears in the resolution now before you. In the present century there have been three great periods in the educational history of this country. There was the period anterior to 1854, when the responsibility of the State for the education of the people was not acknowledged; then came the great despatch of 1854, admitting such responsibility, and, as a consequence, secondary and collegiate education made great strides. In 1871, the third period commenced, for since that year there has been a wonderful development of elementary education. Now, in consequence of these events, we have had remarkable results. Indeed, I doubt, if it were not for the educational advantages India has enjoyed whether such a Congress as this would have been possible. But, while we acknowledge the blessings of the present system of education, we must not shut our eyes to its defects. The great fault has been that too many men have been trained in one single groove. At considerable cost thousands of youths have been highly educated, but only a very limited number of them are absorbed by the public service and the liberal professions. What the country needs is a radical change in the character of the training given in our public schools, so that, while some may qualify for the Government service and the various professions, others may turn their attention to the useful and necessary branches of trade, of commerce, and of manufacture. (Cheers.) In 1884 the Viceroy published a Resolution saying that "every variety of study should be encouraged which may serve to direct the attention of native youths to industrial and commercial pursuits"; but how far has that laudable desire been realized? You will be able to judge from the following figures: 2,665,000 children are receiving elementary instruction; 430,000 pupils are being taught in colleges and High Schools, making a total of 3,095,000 scholars. But only 6,287 are in technical institutions. In this Presidency of Madras, out of a school-going population of 45,000 scholars, only 1,000 are students in technical schools. These figures, taken from recent official papers, are eloquent in themselves, and sufficient to prove the need for reform. I would suggest that the very high theoretical training given in our engineering colleges be supplemented by a thorough practical training in the great workshops of the country—the railway workshops, for instance. (Cheers.) We want drawing taught in all our schools, and with the remarkable advance that scientific education has recently been making in our midst, there ought to be no difficulty in filling to the utmost capacity institutions where the arts of glass manufacture, sugar refining, dyeing, pottery, and woodwork, for instance, may be practically and, therefore, successfully taught. (Cheers.) Much has been done during this year in getting up schemes for technical institutes to celebrate the Jubilee of our august and revered Sovereign, the Queen-Empress of India, to whom we all bow—(cheers)—but unless all these bodies co-operate with each other and acknowledge some central guiding authority their efforts will, I fear, be productive of very meagre results. Let us move Government, therefore, to establish a Department of Science and Art which will take the lead in this matter. (Cheers.) I have trespassed on your patience too long already, but I must make one more remark before I sit down. When the young men of India know that this Congress views with favour the encouragement of industrial and technical pursuits, they will be more likely to shake off that false pride and shame which keeps so many of them from earning an honest livelihood by following trade. And is it idle to say that, just as the present educational system has produced brilliant scholars, thinkers, and writers, and speakers such as we have heard during the past few days, so in the near future, by the new scheme of education which we hope will soon be inaugurated, we shall have distinguished inventors and brilliant discoverers who will sow the seeds of gigantic manufacturing and commercial enterprises originated and worked by India's sons, with India's money, and for India's good. (Loud cheers.)

Mr. Kashinath Trimbuck Khare (Bombay, No. 373 in list) then spoke in Hindustani as follows: Mr. President and Brother-Delegates, is India impoverished? and if so, what measures should be taken to better its position? These are the main points to be attended to in connection with this subject. The poverty of India is a patent fact. In my part of the country the Government of India found it necessary to have an Act passed, namely, Act XVII. of 1879, in aid of the agriculturists of four districts—Poona, Sholapore, Sattara, and Ahmednagar—and now it has been proposed to extend this Act to other districts. With the blessings of civilization conferred by the British Government, population is increasing by leaps and bounds. But, unfortunately, the doors of wealth have not been correspondingly opened by the establishment of productive manufactures. Agriculture and technical arts are the sources of wealth. Agriculture is not at all improved, notwithstanding considerable expenditure by Government in its agricultural department, and this source of the country's wealth will not be improved unless the aid of competent trained natives in adequate numbers be secured.

Our arts also are on the decline. No systematic attempts are being made to utilize the raw material which is produced in abundance in India itself. India is still suffering, so far as regards its commerce, from the evil effects arising from a multitude of causes, among which the change of Government may be mentioned. Two hundred years ago the state of India was quite different. It used to export manufactured articles to the value of many millions to the various countries of Europe, but at present the position is exactly the reverse. Notwithstanding their comparative barrenness in raw materials, European countries have struggled hard for the improvement of their manufactures on scientific principles. The same zeal has not been shown by our countrymen. India has been materially declining. Ignorance and poverty are the two great drawbacks to all the undertakings of the Indians. By the help of their improved arts and sciences, Europeans turn imported raw materials into finished articles of convenience and beauty, and under sell us even in our own markets. We need not go far to realise the fact. If we look around us in this stupendous hall, we shall be surprised to find that almost everbody in it is clothed in garments of European make. The same is the case with other things, for which we are obliged to depend on foreign countries.

It is, therefore, necessary to establish in this country factories of many and various kinds and importance, and Government may well be requested to devise a good scheme for technical education in all its branches. His Excellency Lord Reay, the Governor of Bombay, is earnestly trying his utmost in this direction, but nothing of importance has yet come out of it, partly because the demand for Indian-made articles is small. The Government should be, therefore, requested to enforce the order already existing in regard to the purchase of articles of indigenous production. The educated amongst us also must move in the matter. They should collect subscriptions and circulate small pamphlets amongst the people for their information. There are many small hand-machines in Europe, by the aid of which people there work with profit. Such machines should be imported here for the purpose of starting new industries. There should also be a small museum of such machines. The various tracts and books on the subject, published in Europe and America, should be kept within the reach of everybody. If people begin in this unostentatious way many labourers will find work, and things like stockings, nightcaps, pins, pens, and other articles of daily use, will be produced here, and new modes of subsistence will be opened to the poor people.

Mr. MOOKKANASARI (Tanjore, No. 211 in list), who spoke in Tamil, said: Mr. President and Gentlemen, in the last two Congresses held at Calcutta and Bombay, there was at least one very noteworthy defect to be found in its constitution. That was, that of the four important classes forming the population of India—namely, the official, the industrial, the trading, and the agricultural classes—the industrial class did not sufficiently bestir themselves for the occasion and send in some representatives of their own to attend the Congress. But it is a fact, gentlemen, which you all know, that that defect has been made up in the present Congress, which, fortunately for us, has met together in this city of Madras. Gentlemen, I am myself a direct representative of that class, and am one of the three delegates from Kumbakonum, who have come here as the duly elected representatives of the whole industrial class in the Tanjore district.

The question of Technical Education, which is now before this Assembly, is one of such vital importance to the country, and capable of being productive of such immense beneficial results to the class I directly represent, that, being present here as their delegate, I cannot forbear saying a few words on the subject.

There is no doubt that the Congress has deeply at heart, and is strongly impelled by the desire to promote, the welfare of this our common country. Gentlemen, though we may see thousands of our countrymen holding high and responsible positions in the State, and all of them distinguishing themselves, like our Rajah Sir T. Madhava Row and the Honourable Mr. Muthusamy Aiyar, as enlightened statesmen and impartial administrators of justice, it is impossible for us to expect that this alone will lead to our country's prosperity. Nor will trade and agriculture alone in a country devoid of any industries lead to a nation's prosperity. For it is industry alone that primarily gives an impulse to trade and agriculture; and who on earth will dare deny the fact that industry alone, over all others, is the prime cause of a nation's prosperity? It is to this cause the nations of Europe owe the prosperity which they at present so justly enjoy. It is, therefore, gentlemen, of the utmost importance for us to see that our arts and industries, which, as we have seen, form such a prime cause of national prosperity, are not allowed to die a languishing death. We should see that they are carefully cultivated in all the different parts of our country; and it is urgently necessary that our benign and gracious Government should, with a view to the industrial development of the country, lose no time in making a systematic effort at introducing and extending a suitable system of technical education among the masses of people. Our country now, gentlemen, is indeed in a critical state. Taxation has increased, the resources are scanty for want of proper development, and the wealth of the people is being continuously drained away from the country. If the Government persist in being still cold and indifferent to the state of the country, if they will not even now boldly grapple with the situation and come to the rescue of the country, then there need be no doubt that what little of wealth yet remains in the country will soon find its way to other and distant lands, leaving the country in a state of complete destitution. To prevent this deadly end towards which the country is now drifting, we should pray, gentlemen, to the Government to establish and maintain throughout the country technical institutes, where the manufacture by machinery of all articles of Indian consumption should be carried on, and all facilities afforded to those who wish to learn and study the principles and modes of such manufactures. Should this, however, be found impossible, we should ask them to establish, experimentally at least, model factories in every one of the Presidency cities in India, the capital for which will be found either by Government exclusively from its own funds, or by the raising of a private capital under Government guarantee and supported by Government aid. The management of these institutions should not be exclusively in the hands of Government like the Madras School of Arts, but should be left in the hands of a company formed of native capitalists, subject to the control and supervision of Government. Such institutions, if they prove to be flourishing, may be established again at important mofussil centres, and the Government should encourage such institutions by purchasing from them all their supplies of such articles as are locally manufactured in this country. Besides, the Government should stimulate a desire for improvement and progress among the native artisans and the industrial classes by the holding of periodical exhibitions in various local centres of all local manufactures and industries, whereat the best design and the most excellent workmanship will be selected and encouraged by the granting of prizes and certificates. All the Local and Municipal Boards should be made to contribute to a prize-fund which will be necessary for this purpose. By the Congress working towards the achievement of this end, not only the dying industries of the country will be revived and receive a stimulus for improvement, but, also, new industries will spring up everywhere, tending to the growth of material improvement in the country and to our independence of support as a nation, which will ultimately regain for us our lost place among the nations of the world. These factories and workshops, gentlemen, when they spring up, will be a source of gaining an honest livelihood to thousands of our countrymen who now, destitute of any means, are driven to despair how to keep body and soul together. And, gentlemen, how welcome will be the day for India when, by the immense and growing development of her arts and industries, she will be able to find at least a wholesome morsel of food for her forty-five millions of completely destitute children, who are now, by official admission, going without even one single full meal a day! And now, gentlemen, I have only to ask your excuse for having thus presumed to take up so much of your most precious time, and, trusting you will view with indulgence whatever trifling things I may have said in speaking before you, I beg to conclude.

The PRESIDENT: The sense of the assembly seems to be that we have had discussion enough on this subject, in regard to which there is no substantial difference of opinion; and, therefore, although perhaps the second clause of the Resolution might with advantage have received some attention, and the failure to utilize to the fullest possible extent existing indigenous products and manufactures for State purposes might, had time permitted, have been more explicitly dealt with, I shall proceed to put the Resolution, which will run as follows:

RESOLVED,—"That, having regard to the poverty of the people, it is desirable that the Government be moved to elaborate a system of Technical Education, suitable to the condition of the country, to encourage indigenous manufactures by a more strict observance of the orders already existing, in regard to utilizing such manufactures for State purposes, and to employ more extensively than at present the skill and talents of the people of the country."

The Resolution was then put and carried unanimously.

The PRESIDENT: The next proposed Resolution is worded as follows:—

"That in view of the loyalty of the people, the hardships which it causes, and the unmerited slur which it casts upon the people of this country, the Congress is of opinion that the present Arms Act should be repealed."

I call upon Rao Bahadur Sabapathy Mudaliar to open the discussion.

RAO BAHADUR SABAPATHY MUDALIAR (Bellary, No. 271 in list) rose and said: in proposing the Resolution which has just been read to you by the President, I have to say that, under the previous and present Acts, no man can carry arms, whatever his position may be, without obtaining a license from the magistrate of the district, except, indeed, certain persons who are exempted on account of their high position. I mean the magistrates and members of the municipal council and local board, and some few gentlemen specially exempted. But this exemption is not of any great value. I mean that the exempting of such people means practically nothing where the country is concerned. It is no concession at all to the people as a whole. On the other hand I consider the provisions of the Act degrading. Although I personally am exempted, in virtue of my official position, still I consider it a degradation (hear, hear) that so many of my worthy and loyal countrymen should be deprived of this privilege. (Applause.) Of course, the official view is that persons who want to get arms can apply to the magistrate and get them by payment of a license fee. But the slur which it casts upon us and upon our loyalty is the thing that has been preying upon my mind. (Hear.) To the farmer, to which class I belong, to protect his crops and stores from the attacks of wild beasts, as well as from the attacks of robbers, the possession of arms is a necessity; so much so, that in consequence of being deprived of them the poor ryot has everywhere been a loser of much of his hard-earned produce. I may also say that, before the Mutiny of 1857 people enjoyed the privilege of carrying arms wherever and whenever they liked; and even after the Mutiny, even after, I say, that calamitous event, the Government never thought of imposing any restrictions as to the posssession of arms, but recent events have induced the Government to frame this Act, to the great detriment of the people in general. Up to the Mutiny, during the Mutiny, and for years after the Mutiny, we possessed arms; what have we done since to deserve their forfeiture? If the Government find it necessary to keep any part or any parts of India, for political reasons, under the operation of this Act, it may be so enacted that the Governor-General may have the power of proclaiming that such districts shall not have the use of arms for a while, beyond which I do not think it is necessary for the Government to possess any power in this matter, and I do not think it is right that there should be an Act of the present nature, entailing as it does the greatest hardships on the people, and involving as it does a slur on the entire nation. With these few remarks, I beg to submit for your consideration the proposition which has been read to you, and I hope you will give your hearty approval to the same. (Applause.)

Babu Bipin Chandra Pal (Assam, No. 602 in list), being called upon to second the Resolution, said: Mr. President and Brother-Delegates, I thank you, sir, for the very great honour you have done me by calling upon me to second this Resolution, and I do so with very great pleasure. I know sir, that I have not the ability, the experience, and the weight of authority with which the seconders and supporters of the previous Resolutions have spoken, but if unselfish motives go for anything, then I do claim that I am the fittest person to second this Resolution. (Laughter and applause.) When my friends Babu Surendra Nath Bannerjee (applause) and Mr. Norton (applause) proposed the reconstitution of the Legislative Councils, evil-minded persons might impute some selfish motives to them. (Applause and laughter.) Because I am sure that if, during our lifetime and Mr. Bannerjee's, our dreams of a reformed and representative Legislature be ever realised, he will be about the first man that will be elected to it. (Laughter and applause.) And Mr. Norton has done so much for Madras and the Madrasees, and he is so very popular here, (applause) that I am sure that if our Madras friends have a representative Legislature of their own Mr. Norton will be as much welcome to a seat there as any native gentleman of equal qualifications. (Laughter.) When Rajah Rampal Singh proposed the Resolution regarding the volunteer question, I will not undertake to say that he could completely shut his eyes to the fact that if ever we had a corps we would vote him our captain, (laughter and applause), and when Mr. Subramaniem and Mr. Kali Charan Bannerjee proposed the divorce of the Judicial and Executive functions of magistrates, I am not sure that they were not aware of the fact that if they succeeded in that Resolution their professional duties would be made much easier and simpler than now. (Applause.) But, gentlemen, I do not think that even my rankest enemies could attribute such motives to me. (Cheers.) The Resolution which I now press for your acceptance, if accepted, not only by you all, but by the Government also, will bring me no especial good; for I am sure, gentlemen, that I shall never have the unpleasant necessity of using any arms in my life (laughter and applause), except my steel pen and my sharp tongue (laughter), which, I believe, are not included in the schedule of the Arms Act. Allow me to say, sir, that the admirable tact and judgment with which you have conducted this meeting (applause), under very difficult and trying circumstances, have been thrust entirely in the shade by the wonderful sagacity you have just displayed in calling upon me, a puny, a weak, Bengalee, to second the prayer of the Congress for the repeal of an Act which does not stand in the way of my personal ambition or enjoyment (applause), and which, if repealed, will serve me no personal ends. But there may be ladies and gentlemen present here who may not see my fitness to second this Resolution as clearly as the President does, and they may, therefore, like to know what right have I to second this Resolution? My right consists in my sincere loyalty to the British Government. (Applause.) My motives for seconding this Resolution are to be found in my earnest, ardent, and sincere desire for the welfare of the Government under which I live. I am one of those who believe in the workings of a benign Providence in human history; but never did I so plainly recognise the hand of the Divine Mother in the present history of my beloved country as when I entered this vast and sacred assembly and took my seat there as an humble delegate of this Congress. As I stand upon this platform, and, looking around me, see this immense crowd of men—the Mahratta, the Punjabi, the North-Westerner, the Parsi and the Bengalee—sitting in the midst of hospitable Madrasees, the beaming faces, the deafening cheers, the flow of brotherly love, the exchange of friendly greeting, the eloquent smile, the hearty hand-shake, the maddening enthusiasm, and the earnest patriotism of this vast assembly,—all combine to inspire me with a feeling of gratefulness, the like of which I could never experience elsewhere, and, when standing on this platform, and even while sitting there, in the midst of this vast assembly, many a time has my heart gone out to my God to offer Him its humble tribute of gratefulness for all the blessings which He has in store for my beloved fatherland, and the faintest indications of which are to be seen here in this Hall. (Applause.) And I thank Him for having brought the English Government to this country to work out our salvation. (Applause.) Such being my feelings, and I have not the slightest doubt that such are also the feelings of each and all of my brother delegates here (applause), is it anything strange that I should be loyal to the British Government? I utter the barest truth when I say that I am loyal to the British Government. It is not the language of dissimulation. I hate dissimulation. It is not the language of false diplomacy. I hate that diplomacy which is not based on truth. (Applause.) I am loyal to the British Government, because with me loyalty to the British Government is identical with loyalty to my own people and my own country. I am loyal to the British Government because I believe the British Government to be an instrument in the hand of God for the salvation of my people. (Applause.) I am loyal to the British Government because I love Self-Government. (Applause.) I am loyal to the British Government because I love this Congress. I confess, sir, that I am a radical and a democrat, but, strange to say, my radicalism and my democracy have both combined to make me a sincere well-wisher of the British Government. (Applause.) And, gentlemen, the love that I bear to the British Government compels me to condemn strongly the suicidal policy enunciated in the Arms Act and to call for its repeal. The Resolution which I am here to second seems, sir, to be slightly different from those that have gone before it. The supporters of those Resolutions appealed on behalf of the people to the Government, but I appeal on behalf of the Government to itself. It is not for me to say, sir, that this Act does not operate to the injury of the people. When I remember that, year after year, ravages of wild beasts are increasing with alarming rapidity; when I remember that thousands of my countrymen and countrywomen are every year killed by tigers and leopards; when I find poor cultivators everywhere appealing to Government to protect their crops from the ravages of wild animals—for the Arms Act has deprived them of the means by which they could protect their crops themselves,—when, I say, I look to all these facts, how can I say that this Act does not operate against the life and property of the people? But excuse me, gentlemen, for saying that the direct injury which the law does to the people simply dwindles into insignificance before the immense harm that it is doing to the Government itself. We are very frequently told, sir, that the Government must maintain its prestige. But I can never fully understand the meaning of the prestige of the British Government in the face of this obnoxious Act. If you have really any prestige, why, then, that ought in itself to be a tower of strength to you which needed no Arms Act, and the consequent disarming of a whole nation, to keep up. It appears to me, gentlemen, that like some low caste-men suddenly grown rich and placed in honourable position, who are ever anxious to keep up their position—because they ever suspect that they have really no solid basis for that position,—our Government also, in their extreme anxiety to preserve their prestige, betray their weakness only. (Applause and laughter.) I am not destined to be a military man, and it is not for me to say what injurious effect the disarming of the nation is exercising upon the people of the country by demartialising them. I am a peace-loving Bengalee who is living in comfortable security under the protection of the British Government, and to my mind the most injurious effect of the Arms Act consists in the temptation that it is holding out to Russia to come and invade India. I am not a Russophobist, gentlemen. God save me from that dire disease. I do not believe that Russia's advance has been actuated by a policy which has the invasion and conquest of India as its ultimate aim. But if ever Russia comes and puts in her appearance at our

North-Western frontier, she will be brought there by the Arms Act. What, I ask, are all our professions of loyalty worth in the face of the Arms Act? The Nizam may offer sixty crores instead of sixty lacs for the defence of the empire, ten thousand Jubilee demonstrations may be organised, the Government may publicly acknowledge the sincerity of these loyal demonstrations, British newspapers may trumpet them forth to the whole world: but the question is, will foreigners believe, will Russia believe in the truth and sincerity of these demonstrations in the face of the Arms Act? Would she not put the unpleasant question: if the people of India are loyal, and if you believe them to be so, why do you require the disarming of the entire population by an Arms Act to maintain your position there? So long as this Arms Act exists nothing will convince outside people that the British Government feel themselves strong in the loyalty of their subjects. You know, sir, that the Russian war party set considerable store by the supposed disaffection and disloyalty of the Indian people, and, if ever Russia makes bold to invade India, the Arms Act, I repeat, will be her chief temptation. Her Majesty has most solemnly declared that in our contentment she will find her principal strength. Why then do her Indian Government ignore our loyalty and our contentment and set up the flimsy bulwark of a disarming law for the safety of her Indian Empire? The policy of the Arms Act, sir, is wrong in principle, injurious in its effect, and is simply suicidal to the Government, and as such, in the interest of that very Government whose safety it seeks to secure, it should at once be repealed. (Loud and prolonged cheers.)

The President: There is a notice of an amendment sent up to me. It is an amendment which requires your careful consideration. The amendment is this:—Omit the last clause of the proposition now before you and substitute the following: "This Congress do move Government to administer the Arms Act in a liberal spirit, and so arrange that all persons whom the Local or Municipal Boards, within whose jurisdiction they reside, certify to be fit and proper persons to wear arms shall thereupon be authorised once for all by the proper authorities to wear arms until they, by some act or omission, in contravention of the criminal law of the country, prove themselves unfit to continue to enjoy that privilege." I call upon Dr. Trailokya Nath Mitra to move the amendment.

Dr. Trailokya Nath Mitra (Calcutta, No. 549 in list) said: I have a very disagreeable duty to perform, and that is to move an amendment. If I thought that the Resolution as it stands was one which we could in its entirety accept I certainly would not have inflicted the few words upon you that I now intend to do. I must tell you, gentlemen, that I yield to none as to the sentiments that have been expressed by my friend Rai Bahadur Sabapathy Mudaliar and my friend Babu Bipin Chandra Pal. These sentiments I fully approve of. But we must—I say must because I think it is our positive duty, assembled here as a National Congress,—we must, I say, recommend to Government only things which we know to be practicable, and which we feel to be wise. We must not forget that Government, having to administer and maintain peace in this country, has certain responsibilities. Supposing the Government of the country were handed over to us, which, I think, is a very remote contingency, we ought to think for ourselves, whether an Arms Act, not necessarily the precise one in the statute book now, but an Arms Act of some shape, embodying certain limitations, would not necessarily find a place in the statute book. I do put it to you as a practical suggestion. It is a matter open to discussion, but I put it to you, knowing well enough that there are many persons into whose hands to put arms promiscuously would be to endanger the peace of the country. For instance, one could not like to put arms in the hands of the criminal classes? There are many dangerous persons. (Voices of "No, No.") Well, we shall have to take the sense of the meeting upon that question. I am simply stating my own views. I do not wish to force them upon anybody. (A voice of "Quite welcome.") The amendment is in these words—remember, I am entirely at one with the sentiment expressed by the mover and seconder of the proposition,—"That this Congress do move Government to administer the Arms Act in a liberal spirit and so arrange that persons whom the local or municipal boards"—(I do not wish to have anything to do with the executive),—"within whose jurisdiction they reside"—(and I think it is well known that these boards are representative institutions)—"shall certify to be fit and proper persons to be allowed to possess and to wear arms shall thereupon, once for all, be authorised by the proper authority to bear arms." One of the grievances I have heard was the impossibility or rather the difficulty of always renewing the pass or license every year, or every six months, as is now required of those persons who are entitled to keep arms. Well, that I wish to provide for. The amendment says that if municipal or local boards within whose jurisdiction the man is residing shall certify that he is a fit and proper person to wear arms, he shall be thereupon entitled to wear and possess arms and the Executive shall give him a license for the same once for all until the end of his life, without his having to renew the license or anything of the kind, "until such time as he shall by some act or omission in contravention of the criminal law of the country prove himself unfit to continue to enjoy the privilege." I do think you will all agree with me that persons convicted of breaches of the criminal law of the country are not fit persons to be entrusted with arms. That is the only ground on which a man is to forfeit the privilege of carrying arms of which his respectable fellow-countrymen have declared him worthy, and when a man has once been convicted before the criminal authorities of any offence against the peace of the country, or any other breach of the criminal law, he ought, I submit, to forfeit that privilege. But all other respectable and peaceful citizens may enjoy the privilege to the end of their lives. I do think that if we go before Government, in whose hands the responsibility of administering and preserving the peace of the country is centered, with a proposal of this kind—not that the present Arms Act, stock and block, should be struck out of the statute book, but that it should be worked liberally and only those limitations that I have suggested imposed on the possession of arms—then, I do think that as wise and practical people putting forward a reasonable prayer we may be entitled to hope that our prayer may be accepted by Government. But if we go before Government with one of those utopian Resolutions, with a demand to wipe out the Arms Act *in toto*, then I think you will have very little chance of getting anything that you pray for. I do not want to inflict upon you anything like a speech. I am putting it before you as practical and wise men. Remember, I am quite at one as to the sentiments expressed by the mover and seconder of the original proposition. I agree that the way in which the Arms Act is now worked involves a grave slur, an unmerited slur, on our loyalty. I agree, the whole country agrees, that the people are suffering cruelly under the existing system. I am as eager as any of you for its immediate reform. It is only a question of methods that is at issue between us, and I venture to submit to you that, by the method I propose, you will practically obtain all you want, and that my method has a fair chance of meeting the acceptance of our rulers, whereas your method—forgive me for saying so, but it is true, for, if I was Viceroy myself, I would not accept it—has no earthly chance of being accepted. Well, I have said my say, and I only now ask you to exercise your own common sense as to whether we should not amend the Resolution in the way I have suggested.

Mr. Govind Buksh (Sindh, No. 449 in list): I do not at all feel equal to the task of addressing such an audience as this with many arguments and reasons, but as I have been called upon to second the amendment, in which I entirely concur, I will do my best to discharge the duty imposed upon me. After what we have heard from many able speakers during this session of the Congress, I am compelled to admit that even if we demand what may be called too much, viz., the total repeal of the Arms Act, we should not perhaps be wrong in principle, because Mr. Norton, amongst others, himself an Englishman, has assured us, and many others have already assured us, that the idea of the best and wisest Englishmen has always been that we should be made capable to govern, and if to govern, necessarily to defend, our own country; and, therefore, it might not, in principle, be too much to ask our English rulers, amongst other things, for the abolition of the Arms Act, so that we might qualify ourselves, so that the whole nation might qualify itself to defend the country. But, at the same time, when we remember that we have already asked for representative councils, which are the foundation of all reforms, and through which we shall ultimately be put in a position to secure, if it then be deemed necessary, all that we ask for in this Resolution, I confess that I am in favour of the more moderate prayer embodied in the amendment. Again, it will be remembered that we have asked for the establishment of military colleges. Will not these military colleges entitle our young men to carry arms when they are admitted as military students? In military colleges they would necessarily be taught to use arms, and by the institution of military colleges for our own youth the slur involved in the present Act would be to a certain extent removed. Then we have asked the Government to permit us to enrol ourselves as volunteers. If we are enrolled as volunteers shall we not carry arms? (Hear, hear.) Now, if these two Resolutions that you have already carried are accepted by the Government certainly the slur involved by the Arms Act will almost disappear, and we shall be placed in a better, far better, position than we should be by the abolition of the Act and the consequent permission to all men to carry arms without a license. To give that permission to the whole of India would not be a wise policy at the present time. There are many provinces where it should be the standing order that no one should carry arms without a license. It is only a wise and sensible amendment on the proposal to abolish the Act altogether, that, while throwing open the possession of arms to all respectable persons whom their neighbours can trust, you should yet require to have a license to exercise the privilege.

The question is one to be dealt with with some moderation. We have heard many speeches exhorting us to proceed with moderation and only put forward a reasonable request, and this is the course we have pursued throughout the sittings of the Congress, and now you want to put all this good sense, as it were, in a bag, and ask the Government straight off to abolish the Arms Act altogether, though we well know that some provisions about carrying arms are necessary. This may well be seized by hostile critics as a ground to show that we are demanding extravagant things, all in all. Although we may be deserving of every confidence as a people, and I am sure you will all join with me, with one voice, in confessing that we are true to Government and true to our Queen, though we may be entitled, without the shadow of doubt, to any and all privileges, yet the fact that being entitled to these privileges, and deserving of all these privileges so long as we are loyal, we still ask for only an instalment of these, will, if anything can, shut the mouths of hostile critics. It would be wise, then, to be moderate in this, as we have been in all other matters. Then, it being framed in that spirit of moderation, this amendment may be considered one that would not only shut the mouths of critics, hostile critics, but would obviate all those objections that may fairly be raised against some classes at any rate being authorised to carry arms without a license. Now, by this amendment which is proposed, you are not at all put in a worse position than you would obtain by the abolition of the Act. On the contrary, the amendment gives you a double power. The amendment entitles you to a double privilege. In the first place, it entitles you to give arms to whomsoever you deem fit. It will be your own boards and your own representatives, not a foreign executive, that will have to exercise the power. It will not then happen that the poor peasants who often most need them to protect their crops will be prevented from carrying arms. This right will be simply restricted to a certain extent, viz., to those whom their neighbours consider fit to exercise it, and the decision of this point will be within the jurisdiction of their own representatives. It is not, therefore, that any one fit to be trusted with arms will be deprived under our amendment of the use of arms. So you will get both things under this amendment; you will, all of you whom your fellow-countrymen think fit to be trusted with arms, have arms, and also, as you know the Act provides this permission will cover your servants, subordinates, and dependants of all kinds, and even the poor peasantry, as I have explained, will have the arms they need; and then you will have the further privilege of being yourself the authorities who decide who should and who should not enjoy this privilege or right—and all this by a measure the moderation of which no one can question. (Cries of "Time, Time," and "We want the Act repealed.")

Mr. N. G. Chandavarkar (Bombay, No. 372 in list) said: Gentlemen, you have so ably so wisely, and so sagaciously assisted the President in conducting the business of this Congress in a truly practical spirit that I hope you will all show a practical harmony on the question that is before you. I entreat you to give your most careful consideration to the question that is placed before you, to judge it and decide it, and to give your votes upon it, in a truly practical spirit, as men of business and as sensible men, and not in a spirit of sentimental bias. Gentlemen, I am no advocate of the Act, nor am I an advocate of the policy that led to its passing, nor am I an advocate of the *régime* under which it was passed. At the same time, let me tell you that it would be entirely impracticable, it would be simply utopian, on our part to ask the Government to repeal the Arms Act. If you ask for a repeal you might as well ask for the repeal of the Penal Code. It is true, there are many objectionable features in the Arms Act. If you go up at all to the Government, you must ask the Government to take the sting out of the Act, to deprive it of all its really objectionable features and make it acceptable to public feeling and to public opinion, but you must not ask it to repeal an Act many portions of which are necessary to the good government of the country. It is in this spirit that this amendment has been brought before you. The Resolution that is put before you has been proposed by Mr. Sabapathy and seconded by Bipin Chandra Pal, the rising orator. So far as the spirit that actuated those gentlemen is concerned, I admire it. But, if you go to the Government with this Resolution, it is sure to be rejected, and it would be simply said that you have not carefully thought out the question. Ask, I entreat you, for something tangible, and something practical, and do not go up to the Government like school boys asking for something that cannot be granted, that ought not to be granted. (Mingled cheers and cries of disapprobation, and of "We want the Act repealed.")

Mr. Sundaram Sastri (Madras, No. 77 in list), said: Though what I may say now may not be palatable to some, still I hope you will extend to me that courtesy for five minutes that you have accorded to all previous speakers. We have been asking Government to give us concessions of a political character—concessions which, if given, will enable us not only to improve our status but also to be true helpers of Government. We have carried these Resolutions with perfect unanimity; but now you want to pass a Resolution which many of us cannot agree to, and the passing of which would, in my opinion (I hope no one will be offended) show Government that we are mixing up good and bad things without being endowed with the power of discriminating what is good and what is bad. Nothing less than the total repeal of the Arms Act? Do you want, gentlemen, that the Arms Act should be repealed, and the country inundated with guns and pistols of every capacity and calibre? Every one having it in his power when fired by drink or maddened by rage or jealousy to shoot his neighbour down! Gentlemen, I say no Government in a country like this can afford to put arms in the hands of people without any consideration as to their antecedents, or as to their character or their fitness to be trusted to wear and possess weapons. I hope, gentlemen, you will save yourselves from the reproach—you, who are the educated *elite* of the three or four Presidencies here—of going up to Government and asking the Government to put weapons into the hands of every *budmash* in the land. The steel pen is my only weapon, though I write very little, and therefore do not carry even a steel-pen about me. I am only a vakil, and what am I to do, gentlemen, if I am attacked? I am very short-sighted, and probably some evening as I am quietly going home from office some blackguard will be amusing himself by having a pop at me, and then I shall have to thank some of my countrymen for arming, as you want to do, the criminal classes, if the shots hit me and I am shot down like a mad dog. There is another thing to be mentioned. There is perfect accord between the educated Mahomedans and educated Hindus—we are brethren owning one God. I was discussing religious questions the other day with a Mahomedan friend, and he said to me: "You are a Mahomedan!" I said that I was so far as the essential of believing in one Supreme Being is concerned. Gentlemen, most of us educated persons, be we Hindus or Mahomedans, will, if they see a man honourable, moral, and a believer in one God, extend to him the hand of friendship without considering the particular creed he professes. But, gentlemen, there are times when religious fanatacism will set half the lower classes of a district in a blaze, and you should not shut your eyes to that, I think. We should come to some agreement about modifying this Resolution, and not let it go forth to the world that we are pressing Government to do a thing so impossible as repealing the Arms Act. We can so modify the Resolution, I am sure, under the judicious guidance of our President, as will make it satisfactory to all, and will put arms into the hands of every Hindu and Mahomedan, every British subject, who can show credentials that he is a fit person to wear arms. It is the duty of Government to allow arms to all persons to whom it can safely give the privilege, but not necessarily to every one who pretends that he will clear the jungle of tigers and keep away dacoits, nor to every one who wants to go about on horseback with a brace of revolvers in his pocket. It will be a true test of loyalty if those who consider it a glory to wear arms qualify themselves for doing so, and prove that they are people fit to be trusted with arms and capable of bearing arms properly for the safety of the country and for the safety of the public and for their own safety. I will tell you a little story. When first I was enrolled as an attorney and took the oath of allegiance to Her Majesty the Queen, I had to go to Chitur, and had to travel for two or three nights. There were no tigers on the way except, perhaps, two-legged tigers, which are often the most dangerous; but I went to Messrs. Oakes and Co.'s and asked for a dozen cartridges. They asked me if I had a license. I was very angry, and thought it a great hardship that a person in my position should be treated in this way. All my property was in Government paper, and any indiscretion on my part might leave me a penniless beggar without even a steel-pen as a weapon. But, on second thoughts, I resolved to go to the Commissioner and pay my four annas and take out the license. I did so, and must now own that it was no real hardship, only a needful precautionary arrangement. Gentlemen, people in Europe have to take out passports. Is this construed there to be an insult? Is it thought to be a slur on their loyalty? It is a nuisance, perhaps, but it is, as those Governments think, a precautionary measure which they are bound to take for the public safety, and is there anything wrong in that? Gentlemen, we have thus far been making most reasonable requests, let us not spoil matters by an unreasonable demand. What is gained by asking Government to allow all India from the Himalayas to Cape Comorin to carry fire-arms? I submit that the country is too great, the population in many places too widely scattered, the organised police by no means sufficient, and crimes are committed every day. Men disappear, and it takes a very long time to discover, if it is discovered at all, how they disappear. Let us not aggravate matters by asking Government to repeal the Arms Act which was passed, no doubt too hastily, and has no doubt been worked in a way that has given just offence to many people, but which was passed with the best intentions, with the desire of promoting the peace and quiet of the country.

There has been a good deal said about wild beasts roaming about. I do not know how it may be in other Presidencies where there are many such. Let a sufficient number of people who are fit to use them receive arms—but, though, of course, I speak only for myself, I can only say that I have travelled a great deal in this Presidency and I have never come across one. But suppose we were all armed with double-barrelled guns, how many of us would face a tiger thirty yards off? (Hear, hear, and applause.) Gentlemen, pray be contented with the amendment ("No, No," and loud cheers), and do not press for what is impracticable. (Cheers and cries of "We want the Act got rid of.")

MIR ALI MAHOMED BHIMJEE (Indore, No. 472 in list), who ascended the platform amidst tumultuous cheers, said: Gentlemen, you are likely to flurry a young speaker like me if you go clapping your hands like that. (Laughter.) We have been hearing a good deal of special pleading here, but I come here to oppose the amendment that has been put forward. (Hear, hear, and loud cheers.) It is not so much that I wish to arm, as my friend the last speaker puts it, every budmash in the Madras Presidency with daggers and guns and rifles. No, no, it is not with that idea, but I come to oppose this amendment, because, in fact, it hampers us and ties our hands —(applause)—worse than the Arms Act itself. (Laughter and applause.) What does the amendment say? Will you kindly allow me to read it again. (Reads.) Remember, my friends, the local or municipal board—the whole local or the whole municipal board—they are to certify that a person is a fit and proper person to wear arms. ("Why not? Why not?") Supposing one of the members of the board takes it into his head to refuse the certificate—one member out of the whole board! (Voices of "No, No, No.") I go by the words written on this paper. (Voices, "No, No.") Do not obstruct me while I am speaking.

The PRESIDENT: That is not the meaning of the amendment. The local board or the municipal board means, in all cases, a majority of such board. The person is to be recommended by a board, and that means, in all cases, the majority of that board.

MIR ALI MAHOMED BHIMJEE (continuing): I thank you, sir, for the explanation. But what I read is "local or municipal boards," and I take it, that "local board" means all the members composing that board—(Voices, "No, No, No,")—and "municipal board" means all the members. (Voices—"No, No, No," and "It means the majority of the members.") Then, again, the amendment goes on to say: "Anyone authorised by these boards and certified to be a fit and proper person to be allowed to possess and carry arms shall, thereafter, once for all, be authorised to possess and wear arms until such time as they shall, by some act or omission in contravention of the criminal law of the country, prove themselves unfit to continue to enjoy the privilege." Now what is the criminal law? Not only is it a breach of the criminal law if you join or become a rebel. (A voice :—" Time.") The gentleman who said " Time," did he take out his watch and look at the time? (Laughter.) I say the criminal law includes not only rebellion, but everything else—perjury, forgery, and so forth. Does this amendment define what crime? Make it clear, gentlemen. If you want restrictions placed on our carrying arms make them clear. If you cannot trust us with arms after so many years' education, why do you trust England? Is there any test there? And yet there are murders in every English paper you take up. (Applause, and voices of " Sit down, Sit down.")

Mr. Daji Abaji Khare (Bombay, No. 370 in list) said : Gentlemen, I formed a resolve not to speak, unless it was absolutely necessary to do so, at this present Congress. But now that I find that the proposition and the proposed amendment have excited so much opposition in this vast assembly, I think it behoves every man who desires to perform his duties without fear or favour to come forward and say whatsoever he really feels on the subject from the bottom of his heart. I yield to none in my desire to wear arms. I yield to none in the feeling of degradation which I experience in consequence of my countrymen being prevented from wearing arms. Nor do I entertain a less opinion of the usefulness to the British Government and of the added prestige to that Government which will result from their allowing us to possess and to wear arms. I am at one in these matters with the mover, and although the gentleman who proposed the matter would not listen to the amendment, because the amendment was supported by pleaders, although I am a pleader myself I would still ask your indulgence and beg you to hear me a while and then decide according to the best of your judgment. (Hear, hear.) Gentlemen, the sting does not lie in the Arms Act having been passed and in all our countrymen being prevented from wearing arms. The sting is in the exemption of a certain class from the operation of the Act and the non-exemption of other classes. The sting lies in the Europeans and some other classes of the residents of the country being allowed to wear arms without license, while other classes are required to obtain licenses. If you realise this we shall very soon do away with the opposition that now prevails in this assembly. We do not want to give arms to those who would make a bad use of them. I know that there are certain classes of people who are sure to make a bad use of arms. There are professional robbers and great many other classes of people to whom to allow the wearing of arms without let or hindrance, would be to let loose upon the country a huge Pandora's box, so to speak. Therefore, I say, take away the sting, get rid of the slur; and in order to do this I will support the amendment, which I should explain in this way. The restriction which the amendment imposes will apply equally to all Her Majesty's subjects in India. Have a list of the natives who are fit to be entrusted with arms supplied by the district boards, and also have a list of the Europeans supplied, and then allow arms to all persons included in both lists. As I have pointed out to you some restrictions are necessary, and it would certainly be folly to relieve the badmashes of these restrictions. What I want you to do is to take away the sting and the slur and make the amendment applicable to all classes, though even as it is, if it is we who are entrusted with the responsibility of deciding who are to be trusted with arms, I cannot see that much sting or any slur on our loyalty, as a nation, can remain, If we are to pass the original proposition we are quite certain that what we pray for will never be granted. Do you really expect, do you really even desire in your hearts, whatever you may say, that the Arms Act should be altogether repealed? Do you expect that the British Government, constituted as at present, will or can repeal the Arms Act under present circumstances? If your hearts reply in the negative, why do you not confess it? Why ask for things that will never be granted? Then I would beg you, and I would invite you to consult your hearts, to look inside your hearts and see what is really there, and not be swayed by sentimental feelings. But rather show that you are and deserve to be real representatives of the people, and show that you are worthy of being listened to and consulted by the British Government. I would ask you to remember that we, professing ourselves to be the Congress of the country, a country which is of all countries reasonable, moderate, and conservative, are bound to submit moderate proposals to the Government. I have very little more to say, gentlemen, but I want to place one circumstance before you. We are virtually asking the British Government to consult us upon every question, to take our opinion, and to take our advice. Before we succeed in obtaining that proud position of assistants to our rulers in promoting the welfare of our fellow-countrymen, we must show that we are worthy of the position. We must show that we are not to be led away by every rush of sentiment, that we are not mere theorisers, but that we are practical statesmen, practical politicians. Every individual gentleman amongst us must learn to be practical; let us give whatever advice we have to offer to Government like practical men. (Applause.)

Babu Surendra Nath Bannerjee (Calcutta, No. 550 in list), said: Gentlemen and Brother Delegates, I come upon the platform as one of my friend Mr. Chandavarkar's schoolboys (laughter). I come here with the object of strongly protesting against the amendment, and supporting the original proposition, and adding a small rider to it, which, I trust, will be generally accepted by this great assembly of my countrymen. (Hear, hear, and applause.) Gentlemen, the Arms Act casts an unmerited slur upon the loyalty of my countrymen. (Hear, hear, and a voice of "No, no.") It does, sir. (Voices of "It does.") To the Englishmen, to Eurasians, we are quite willing to extend the right hand of friendship, and we are quite willing to accept from them the substantial tokens of their sympathy which have added lustre to this Congress. The European, the Eurasian, the American, the West-Indian, the Negro, all races, all creeds, and all nationalities may bear arms unrestricted, but not the loyal Indian subjects of our Queen-Empress. (Hear, hear, and loud and continued applause.) They, and they alone, must obtain a license from the constituted authority before they are in a position even to wear a dagger or a poinard. Gentlemen, is this a position of self-respect? Is this the position which we can contemplate with complaisance? I have been told that we should be practical. Ah! Yes. We ought to be practical politicians, and the greatest of practical politicians is Mr. Gladstone. (Applause.) What did he say in his Midlothian speech about the Arms Act? I am not prepared with the quotation, but I know he thought that it was a disgrace to the statute book that such an Arms Act should be made a part of the law of the land. (Applause.) Then, sir, we have passed the Resolution relating to the re-imposition of the import duties. Does any one of its most ardent supporters dream for a moment that the Resolution will be given effect to immediately, and at once. (Hear, hear, and a voice of "May be.") It may be, and so also this may be given effect to. (Applause, and a voice "At any rate it is a dream.") At any rate it is a dream, but our dreams at times become realities. Dreams become pregnant realities. Who would have dreamt twenty years ago that the question of representative government could have come within the range of practical politics in this country? Who would have dreamt twenty years ago that the *élite* of our community should have been honoured with seats in the highest courts in the land? (Applause.) Who would have dreamt, ten years ago, that a native of India would be made the Chief Justice of Bengal? (Applause.) These are dreams, utopian to the unthinking and to the unimaginative (hear, hear, and applause), but dreams that, like prophecies, often realize themselves. Who are those who, with the instinct of a prophet, see deep into the things of the future, and, exulting in what they feel must come, carry on their patriotic work, and endow with life and reality their visions? Yes, it may be a dream, but it is none the less a duty to cling to and to strive to make it a reality. We should go on protesting and protesting against this Act, until we have got rid of it from the statute book, and I think that this Congress will have been wanting in its duty if it does not, by an overwhelming majority, throw out the amendment which has been proposed. (Hear, hear.) I am also surprised at the logical inconsequence of that amendment. These gentlemen, who support the amendment,—and I desire to speak of them with the utmost possible respect,—these gentlemen, I say, seize hold of our premisses and quietly depart from our conclusions. (Voices of "Shame, shame.") "That in view of the unmerited slur which it casts, ... local boards are to certify, and the magistrates are to give passes." Does that remove the unmerited slur? ("Yes, yes;" "No, no.") It does not do so, unless, as Mr Khare contends, we are to include Europeans in that amendment. We know perfectly well that Europeans will never be included. I protest against the degradation to the country. I protest against the humiliation which is proposed to cast upon us. If we cannot rise to their heights are they to be pulled down to our depths? Against that policy, and against that principle, let this Congress raise its voice and protest. (Hear, hear, and applause.) Therefore, gentlemen, you will see at once that, accepting the premisses, this conclusion set forth in the amendment cannot follow at all, and that neither the slur, nor the hardship which is set forth in those premisses can be removed, if we accept that conclusion. For how, pray, to turn now to these, are the hardships to be removed? Local boards and municipalities will certify. There has been some little straining of legal technicalities here; and I am not a lawyer, but I am guided by my common sense, and I say that "municipality" means the chairman of the municipality. "Local board" means the chairman of the local board. Now, pray, who are the chairmen? Why, just these magistrates and sub-divisional magistrates in whom are now vested the powers of granting or refusing passes; I think it is flying from the frying-pan into the fire, only the agony is both intensified and prolonged. Instead of one appeal to the magistrate you will have to appeal to him twice—first, as chairman of the board; second, as the head of the district or the sub-division. Now, gentlemen, let me put these questions. Upon what ground of common sense, upon what ground of logic, upon what ground of sentiment, are we to accept the amendment? I say, with all the earnestness I can command, that it would be really unworthy of the national gathering if it did not, from year to year, protest, in the most emphatic terms, against an enactment which disgraces the statute book and which involves a national humiliation which is inconsistent with the Queen's proclamation. I trust, therefore, that with one voice you will reject the amendment. You may like to know what remedy I suggest. The remedy is this, that the Act of 1857 should be substituted in place of the present Act. Mark you, this was passed in the time of the Mutiny, when the Empire was trembling in the balance. We surely do not want a more stringent Act when peace and benevolence shine brightly over the land. Lord Canning's terms are substantially just. Suppose there are budmashes; suppose there are rebellions in one district, to those budmashes and to that district the Act was applied, and to none other. So far as that one district even was concerned good and true men were allowed to be supplied with arms. That legislation is singularly short-sighted which punishes good men for the faults of bad men, millions for the misdeeds of hundreds. Upon the highest grounds of common sense, upon the highest grounds of statesmanship, upon the highest grounds of patriotism, I appeal to this great Congress to reject the amendment and support the motion that I have laid before you, viz., that the original proposition be retained with the addition of the words, "and Lord Canning's Arms Act be re-enacted in place thereof." (Loud and tumultuous applause.)

Babu Kali Charan Bannerjee (Calcutta, No. 557 in list) said: Gentlemen, I feel it my duty to second the amendment which has been moved by my esteemed friend, Mr. Surenda Nath Bannerjee. In doing so, I would add a few remarks to those which he has submitted for your consideration. It seems to me that certain words in the original Resolution have been overlooked by those who considered it their duty to propose the amendment. The concluding words of the original Resolution are: "The Congress is of opinion that the present Arms Act should be repealed." In the remarks already submitted for your consideration the existence of the word "present" has been altogether overlooked. (Hear, hear.) In fact, the first amendment concedes that the present Arms Act is filled with stings and that it must be divested of its stings. Those who have introduced the first amendment before you have conceded that the original Resolution does not contemplate as my esteemed leader, the mover of the amendment, suggested, that we contemplate the abolition of the Arms Act in its totality, and that we contemplate not having the Arms Act at all. That is not what is contemplated in the original Resolution. (Hear, hear, and applause.) It does not say that we are not to have the Arms Act at all; but it says that the present Arms Act should be repealed. Is there any one in this august assembly that is prepared to stand up for the present Arms Act in its entirety? (Applause.) So far we see that the original Resolution carries with it the mind of the whole assembly. The present Arms Act must be repealed. Then, your attention has been drawn to the fact that the present Arms Act must be divested of its sting. What is the sting, pray? (Applause.) Does not the sting consist in this: that the possession of arms, without a license, is declared to be an offence? Is not that the sting? Are you not going to substitute one form of the sting for another? Is the amendment a stingless amendment? (Hear, hear, and applause.) Will the amendment secure an Arms Act which has no sting about it? No such thing. They have only put before you another sting, to express which it has been necessary to place before you, I believe, what would be some five lines of printed matter. (Laughter and applause.) You have the sting in five lines of printed matter. (Laughter.) Then again the great argument that has been adduced before you in support of the amendment is "if the present Arms Act is repealed, what are we to do with our budmashes?" Are there not budmashes in Europe? Then, we are told: "Are we to bring about a condition of affairs under which these budmashes might with impunity carry on their trade?" Well, I say, I am sorry to say, are we, as a National Congress, going to proclaim that India is the monopoly of budmashes? Are there no budmashes outside India? Are there no budmashes in England? Is there an Arms Act in England? (Cries of "Yes," and "You can't carry arms without a license.") Well, then, is there an Arms Act in England such as that which you pray Government to repeal? Is there such an Arms Act among the English nation? Would there not be a rising in the English nation from one end of the country to the other if the English Parliament sought to impose such an Arms Act on the people of England? (Hear, hear, and applause.) I am much mistaken if there would not be a general rising of the nation. Gentlemen, we speak from the national point of view and when we go up to Government affirming that we, as a country, are prepared to receive those liberal institutions which are enjoyed by the people of England, are we side by side with this to go up to the Government with a declaration that as far as the Arms Act is concerned, we are not yet ripe for such a liberal treatment of the question as is pursued in England? That, I say, is a suicidal position to take up. (Hear, hear, and applause.) Gentlemen, if you would not stultify yourselves, if you would not give a lie to all your declarations concerning the readiness of the Indian people to receive and enjoy as a blessing every institution which characterizes the present state of things in England; if you would not go before the Government and before the world with the declaration that India needs special legislation in view of the superabundance of budmashes in the various Presidencies of India; if you would not go up to Government and ask the Government to substitute one form of sting for another, and if you are all of one opinion as to the sting that lurks in the present Arms Act, then, I say, you will agree with the original Resolution so far as to pray Government to repeal the present Arms Act. (Loud and continued applause.) Contingencies there may be, contingencies are certainly to be provided for. The proposer of the proposition, which I have the honour to second, has met the contingency, *i.e.*, by substituting Lord Canning's Act for the existing one. (Loud and continued applause.)

Mr. A. O. Hume (Madras, No. 11 in list): Gentlemen, I am not come to support the original Resolution, which as it stands is an impossible one, nor to oppose my friend Babu Surendra Nath's amendment, because I do not know its exact value. What I come here for is to ascertain from him—and from all of you who are apparently ready to support him—exactly what the terms of that Act are which he and you propose to re-enact. Have you a copy of the Act? (Cries of "No.") Can any one repeat the sections? ("No.") I confess I am quite ignorant of the terms of the Act, but I do know that as a magistrate, many years ago, I worked Lord Canning's Arms Act, and my recollection of its operation is—of course, this was in the North-Western Provinces, where all the districts were proclaimed—that it was a great deal more stringent than the present Arms Act. Whatever we do let us not fall from the frying-pan into the fire. Let us at any rate, act like sensible and business men. I strongly recommend this assembly to see the Act before it comes to any conclusion, as to asking for its re-enaction.

Babu Trailokya Nath Mitra (Calcutta, No. 549 in list), turning to the proposer, said: Have you got a copy of the Act?

Babu Surendra Nath Bannerjee (Calcutta, No. 550 in list): No; but I have got something better than a copy of the Act. I have it here! (Touches his forehead.)

Mr. A. O. Hume: I insist on the necessity of our seeing the Act before we come to any conclusion, at least before we decide to ask Government to re-enact it.

Mr. Salem Ramaswami Mudaliar (Madras, No 64 in list), one of the delegates sent to England, then rose and said, amidst loud cheers: Mr. Chairman and Gentlemen, It is with very great regret that I appear before you on this occasion. I say it is with great regret that having hastened to the utmost of my powers to leave Calcutta, the moment my duties in connection with the Public Service Commission were over, so that I might take part in the proceedings of this Congress, I arrive here to-day only to find that, on an important question like this before us, which involves the safety and happiness of the country, there exists an apparently serious split amongst you. But, if you consider for a moment, both parties are agreed as to the principle. One party looks at the subject from one point of view, the other party looks at it from another point of view, but with all I say both parties are agreed in the conviction that this present Act has been worked in such a way as to create universal dissatisfaction. (Hear, hear, and applause.) If anybody told me on the one hand that I was in favour of the present Arms Act, or on the other wanted me to agree that it would not be for the interest of India that we should have some rules by which to regulate the possession of arms, I should reply that I am the last man to assent to either proposition. You must look at the Act as it is, and as it was, and you must realise clearly what the defects of the present Act are and in what way they can be remedied. Gentlemen, in an assembly like this, where we are met all of a sudden, as people drawn from all parts of India to take part in the proceedings, there must very often be a want of accurate knowledge and due consideration of details. If we do not possess accurate information as to details we can arrive at no conclusions satisfactory either to ourselves or to the Government. There is a feeling, I believe, existing in the minds of all, in the minds most certainly of those who proposed this amendment, and who proposed the original proposition, that this Act has been so worked as to give rise to nothing but dissatisfaction and great hardship. Now, I would put this feeling aside, and consider the question solely in the light of principle, and the principle I would accept in dealing with the question is this: if it be found that any man is, by his misconduct, rendered unworthy to exercise the important right of carrying arms, that right should be taken away from him. It may be that times will come when whole districts and even whole provinces will have to be disarmed. I do not for a moment deny the right which every Government ought to possess, the right of disarming any of its subjects or all its subjects for a time if it finds that it is necessary to do so in the general interests of the country. But it is one thing to use extreme remedies like these in emergencies, and it is another thing to be always applying them when the state of things is normal. That a man should be debarred from carrying arms, unless he takes out a license, simply because he happens to be a native of India—and that not one individual as a temporary measure, but the whole nation for all time—is an insult to every Indian subject, and is equivalent to saying that he is either disloyal or a bad character. I say I am a British subject, and unless you can show that I have been guilty of some misconduct or am disloyal you have no justification for taking away the right which is inherent in me. They tell me, "Unless you get the authority of a magistrate and pay a fee, and do this year by year, you shall not wear or possess arms." There must be a limit to such things as these, no doubt; but I do not know whether, in framing the original Resolution which proposes to sweep away the Act altogether, all the conditions of the case, all the details of the matter, were fully considered. I fear not. Unquestionably there is an universal feeling of dissatisfaction with the Act, and we are agreed on that point, viz., that the Act has produced universal dissatisfaction and is worked in a most unsatisfactory way; but would it not be sufficient to say this? If you persist in asking what is the remedy? I candidly say I am not prepared to suggest exactly what the remedy should be, and therefore I for one would only assert what I know, and not go on to tell Government what it ought to do in the matter. It seems to me that it is for the Government to suggest a remedy. We tell Government what a curse the thing is as it now stands. We pray Government to take this matter into their consideration and see—this Act being so unsatisfactory as it is—whether they cannot devise a better Act.

I cannot agree to, and I cannot accept, the proposal that we should fall back upon the original Act. There are serious defects in that Act, and it might prove in practice even a worse Act than the one we have. We must not run the risk, as Mr. Hume has said, of falling from the frying-pan into the fire. I do not think we as reasonable men, as men possessing common sense, should commit ourselves to a demand for the re-enactment of an Act having no accurate knowledge of it. I cannot support either the first or the second amendment, or the original Resolution. We feel that the way we are dealt with in the matter of arms is a grievance, and we know it is a grievance, but we are not in a position, I submit, after listening to the whole discussion, to suggest exactly what remedy can be most advantageously applied. All that we should ask the Government to do is to collect the opinions of officials—both European and Native—as to how the Act has worked, and in what way it has been felt to be a grievance, and take also the evidence of people all over the country. When such an inquiry is going on, each one of us will give his best attention to the matter, and if we take the present Act of this country and compare it with past Acts, and with those in force in other countries and thoroughly work up the question, we shall be able amongst us to suggest what form of enactment will both give satisfaction to the people and secure the peace and safety of the country. I admit that I every moment feel myself to be a degraded citizen so long as this Act or its working is not so modified as to remove the stigma now cast on every loyal Indian subject of Her Majesty. I say that the wearing of arms is a right which every man in every province should enjoy unless he is debarred from its exercise by some personal misconduct, or unless it can be shown that there are special grounds for believing that it is not safe that the people of some particular province of which he is an inhabitant should exercise that right; it is on these, and these, grounds alone, I say, that this inherent right can be justly held in abeyance; but if this Act be not repealed or modified, if the existing system be continued, it takes away the right unjustly from the many and it concedes it as a privilege to the few. That is in itself a great hardship. Europeans have been permitted to carry arms, and Eurasians are permitted to do so, as a body; but we, native subjects of Her Majesty, are not allowed to wear arms, unless we possess a license, or unless we are, as a special favour, exempted from the operation of the Act. Till two years ago I was a district Munsiff, and then I was exempted. But when I came to Madras I was told that I must obtain a license, and I had to apply to the Police Commissioner for one. Of course, there was a difficulty in getting it. But is it not a slur upon a man who was exempted two years ago when he was a district Munsiff, and who is now exempted because he is a municipal commissioner, to be called upon to produce a certificate of loyalty? I think it is a shame (hear, hear, and applause); but feeling all this as strongly as any one, I yet do not want to go up to Government with any specific advice as to how they should remedy this great national grievance, but I would tell them—and here I am expressing the feelings of every one present, aye, and every native of India not present likewise—that this Act has been worked in such a way as to give dissatisfaction to all men (applause), and that we look confidently to them to remove, in such manner as may seem best to them, the grounds for that just dissatisfaction. (Loud cheers, and cries of "They'll do nothing, then.")

Mr. Annasami Aiyar (Madras, No. 203 in list) rose and said: Gentlemen, in the amendment proposed by Dr. Mitra, the presumption seems to be that unless a person can obtain a certificate from the municipal or local boards as to his fitness to carry arms he cannot be fit to carry them. That presumption is alike degrading and derogatory to our national dignity and to our national interest. Every true native will therefore scout that presumption with scorn. But there is no doubt there are practical difficulties involved in the original proposition which ought to be looked into. In every nation, however highly cultured it may be, there must be certain classes whose wicked propensities ought to be curbed. How is that to be done in India? A very easy solution suggests itself to me. A slight alteration in the amendment proposed by Dr. Mitra will do it—leave the original Resolution as it stands, and add the words "provided that it be open to Government, on the recommendation of municipal or local boards, to restrict the use of arms to any such individuals or classes as they may deem necessary, for reasons to be stated in writing."

Mr. Surendra Nath Bannerjee: I would accept that amendment.

Mr. Annasami (continuing): Here there is an assembly of six or seven hundred persons from all parts of India, and it is our duty both to put things in a form that may be palatable to Government, and to look into our rights and find out what they are. These rights we shall obtain. Let me not lead you to suppose that while insisting upon our rights on one side I am blind and deaf to the practical difficulties in conferring those rights upon us. We should be really unworthy of the name of politicians if we did that. Let not any restriction you may impose for the purpose of keeping order in society involve a stigma on any respectable member of society. This appears to be the only solution of the difficulty. (Applause.)

The President: Gentlemen, it has always been my desire that any proposition which may be carried in this Congress should not only be carried by the votes of a very large majority, but should, as far as practicable, be carried with the unanimous consent of all (Applause.) If you find, for instance, in one particular part of India that there is opposition to a particular proposition, it will not do I think for this Congress of all parts of India to force upon that particular part of India a particular Resolution, and therefore I, as your President, am desirous of trying, as I have been always doing (hear, hear) to see whether it is not possible to throw oil on the troubled waters. (Hear, hear, and applause.) If you will allow me five minutes to consult with the proposers of the Resolution, the first amendment and the second amendment, and other leading delegates, I think I shall be able to get some such Resolution framed as shall meet with your unanimous approval. (Hear, hear, and applause.)

(A consultation was then held on the platform for about five minutes.)

The PRESIDENT (continuing) said: Gentlemen, I am extremely happy to announce to you that my prophecy has been fulfilled. (Applause.) The result of this conference of, I may say, the representative members of this Congress, has resulted in the production of a Resolution, which, I feel sure, will commend itself to every one present here. This new Resolution like all other similar Resolutions, involves a compromise, and retains the best features of the original Resolution and the best features of the amendment. (Hear, hear, and applause.) You will remember that the original Resolution was that the Arms Act should be repealed *in toto*. I am perfectly sure that the whole of the Arms Act cannot have been carefully read by the gentleman who proposed the Resolution, because there are many provisions to which that gentleman has in no way referred, and they are useful provisions also. The essence of this debate, I take it, has been this: The proposer of the original Resolution, fixing his attention mainly on the point that the Act presumes that everybody in the country not specially authorised to wear arms is unfit to be trusted with them, and feeling the slur thus implied on the loyalty of the nation keenly, proposed the abolition of the Act. He did not stop to consider that the Act embodied numerous necessary provisions; he saw what was galling to the national self-respect in the Act, and desired to get rid of it *in toto*. On the other hand the proposer of the amendment, fully realising the necessity of an Arms Act, and the beneficial character of many portions of the existing Act, only thought to provide for such a liberal administration of the Act as should enable all persons considered by their neighbours to be fit to have arms, to possess and wear them. He probably did not quite realise how strong the sentimental objection to the presumption involved in being required to take out licenses is throughout the country. The amendment, it is true, assumed that all people who were certified to be fit to wear arms by their neighbours, were thus fit, but what the proposer of the original Resolution, and, as it would seem from the course of the debate, a very large number of other delegates desired, was that all persons should be presumed to be fit to be trusted with arms who were not certified to be unfit. In practice, probably, the result would be much the same, but, under the latter scheme, the presumption of disloyalty or unworthiness to be trusted with arms, which even the first amendment, though to a limited extent, involves, would disappear. So now we have prepared a new Resolution, which gives full weight both to the objections of those who supported the amendment, and of those who objected to it, and this Resolution will run as follows:—

RESOLVED.—That in view of the loyalty of the people, the hardships which it causes, and the unmerited slur which it casts upon the people of this country, the Government be moved so to modify the provisions of Chapter IV. and, if necessary, any other portions of the Act XI. of 1878 as will enable all persons to bear arms, unless debarred therefrom, either as individuals or as members of particular communities or classes, by the order of the Government of India (or any local authority empowered by the Government of India in that behalf) for reasons to be recorded in writing and duly published."

The result will be this: whereas, now no one can be allowed to wear arms, unless he is expressly authorised to do so, under our present Resolution every man will be allowed to wear arms, unless he is expressly debarred from so doing. I think it is not necessary to discuss the point any further, unless you wish to do so. (Cries of "No, No," and "Vote, Vote.")

The proposition was then put to the vote, and was carried unanimously, with acclamation.

The PRESIDENT: We will now pass on to the consideration of a Resolution which is not on the printed programme, and which will be moved by my friend, Mr. Hume.

Mr. A. O. Hume (Madras, No. 11 in List) said: Gentlemen, You will remember that on the first day of the Congress, a committee was appointed to consider what rules, if any, could be at this present time, advantageously framed for the guidance and governance of this Congress in future. Well, gentlemen, that committee, as directed in the order constituting it, made its report, which I here present to you.

It includes a long series of tentative rules, and perhaps you will expect me to read it out to you. I hope, however, that you will take it as read, because it is not proposed to pass these rules or to make them binding upon you on the present occasion. These rules must, we think, stand over for the consideration of the next Congress; but, in the meantime, they ought to be circulated to all the standing committees to reconsider, at their leisure, and see how far they are workable. Next year they will be brought up again for final consideration, together with all such emendations and additions as may have, in the meantime, suggested themselves to the several standing committees. The rules, as they stand, practically embody existing practice, if not throughout the country, in one province or another, but an additional year's experience will enable all to judge better how far that practice should be accepted, and how far it may advantageously be modified. With this explanation, I shall venture, with your permission, to read to you at once the Resolution which I have been called on to propose. It runs thus :—

Resolved,—That the rules drafted by the Committee appointed under Resolution I. stand over for consideration till next Congress, but that in the meantime copies be circulated to all Standing Congress Committees, with the request that they will during the coming year act in accordance with these rules so far as this may seem to them possible and desirable, and report thereon to the next Congress, with such further suggestions as to them may seem meet.

Dr. Trailokya Nath Mitra: I second the proposition.

The President: Gentlemen, does any one object to this Resolution being put to the vote? (Cries of "No, No. Put it.") Then, without troubling you by reading it over again, I put it. The Resolution was then carried unanimously.

The President: I must now call upon Mr. Hume to move another Resolution that stands in his name.

Mr. A. O. Hume thereupon again rose and said: Gentlemen, I am ashamed to address you again immediately, but there is one Resolution that I have to propose, which will not detain you long, and that is: "That the fourth Indian National Congress assemble at Allahabad (applause) on the 26th December, 1888." (Tumultuous applause.) I say the 26th, because we should have a clear day before the Congress begins its public sittings in which to thresh out more thoroughly the subjects and Resolutions which are to be dealt with by the Congress at these sittings. (Loud cheers.) We were all practically agreed, the whole country was agreed, before we ever came here, about the arms question, but see how much time we lost to-day simply because we had not had time to thresh out, in the subject Committee beforehand, a Resolution so worded as to meet exactly all objections and embody all our views. (Hear, hear.)

Rajah Rampal Singh (Allahabad, No. 484 in list) said: Gentlemen, I rise with the greatest pleasure to second this Resolution. It has been our earnest desire that this Congress should be held next year at Allahabad, and we are very pleased to find from the kind manner in which you received my friend Mr. Hume's proposition, that you have been good enough to accept our invitation. (Applause.) I am afraid I cannot expresss in equally eloquent words the sentiments of gratification and gratitude at our being so honoured, which were expressed by the Hon. S. Subramania Aiyar on the last occasion at Calcutta when Madras was chosen as the next meeting-place, nor can I even do my duty in thanking the Madras committee in detail for the admirable work which they have done as he thanked the Calcutta committee, because he was furnished with the details of the working of that committee and he was able to tender to every member those special thanks that were his due. Unfortunately, I am not acquainted with the detailed working and arrangements of the committee here, and so I cannot do as he did, but can only thank you all for being willing to allow Allahabad the honour of welcoming the next Congress, and the Madras Committee, *en masse*, for all they have so kindly, so generously, done for all of us. I do not think that there will be one dissenting voice when I ask you all to express heartily, the deep and perfect satisfaction we have all experienced in the loving and brotherly reception all have met with from our brethren of Madras. (Loud and continued applause and tumultuous cheers for "Our Madras brethen.")

The PRESIDENT: We are all agreed? (Cries of "Yes, Yes," "Carried, Carried.")

Then the proposition was carried by acclamation.

The PRESIDENT: There is only one more Resolution, and that I will now ask you, sir, to propose.

RAJAH YATINDRA NATH CHAUDHURI (24-Pergannahs, No. 560 in list) then rose and said: The Resolution that I have to propose needs no comments from me—good wine, it is said, needs no bush; and this Resolution calls for no explanation or justification—it is this:

RESOLVED—"That copies of these Resolutions be forwarded to His Excellency the Viceroy-in-Council, with the humble request that he will cause all the Resolutions to be laid before Her Majesty's Secretary of State for India, and that he himself will be graciously pleased, in consultation with his colleagues, to accord them his best consideration.

BABU JOTENDRA NATH TAGORE (Calcutta, No. 548 in List) said:—I second the proposition. (Cheers and cries of "Put it, Put it.")

The PRESIDENT: I now put this resolution.

The Resolution was then put and carried unanimously.

The PRESIDENT then rose and said: Gentlemen, I am very glad to say that the business which brought us all together has now been completed. (Applause.) There is no proposition, and I am glad to say, no amendment to be laid before you. (Laughter.) We have carried all the Resolutions, and I am happy to say that we did so with perfect unanimity. (Applause.) Gentlemen, I may say, before I dissolve this Congress, that this is really the spirit in which I should desire to see all the future Congresses conduct themselves. (Applause.) If we are really to do the work of our nation, and if we are really to do good to India, we must learn not only to demand but when necessary to concede. (Applause.) If we ask that a certain proposition be accepted, and if there is an opposition to it from the delegates of any part of India, I think it would always be a wise policy for the gentleman who proposed the Resolution so to modify his proposal as to meet, if possible, the objection that is raised. For some time, indeed, we cannot expect to see every Resolution carried with perfect unanimity, but I do say that with a little patience and mutual forbearance practical unanimity may be arrived at in almost every case which it is essential to proceed with. For I feel perfectly sure that you will all agree with me that, on any future occasion, if the delegates from Bombay, for instance, desire to press a particular Resolution which is not acceptable to the delegates from Bengal or Madras, our Bombay friends will need to drop the Resolution when they cannot win over the Madras delegates or the Bengal delegates to their side.

Gentlemen, I thank you most sincerely for the very great honour you have done me by electing me as President of this Congress. (Applause.) I have already expressed to you my thanks for the honour you have done me, and I can only say that I am now thankful that our proceedings——(Mr. Rangiah Naidu, here interrupting, said: "I propose three cheers for the Empress." This suggestion from Mr. Rangiah Naidu resulted in some cheering.) That will be done before we part, with higher echoes and in far, far larger volumes than have yet reached my ears. (Laughter.) Well, gentlemen, it has been decided to hold our next National Congress at Allahabad. No doubt this step has been taken after great consideration, and it is certainly desirable that all the different capitals of India should have the honour of seeing the Congress assembled, and this honour should not be confined to presidency towns. I am extremely happy that we have resolved to assemble at Allahabad next year, and I trust that we shall go on assembling year after year in all the great centres of India. I have no doubt that this will be one of the means by which we can reach the feelings of those interested in the national welfare, and which we must reach before we can make our voices reach the ears of the Government of India. Gentlemen, before I sit down I would say that on my own part I desire to thank not only the Reception Committee of the Madras Presidency, but also all the people of Madras for their kind hospitality, not only to myself personally but to all the delegates who have come from distant parts of India. (Loud applause.) Gentlemen, if this Congress does no other good it will still have achieved a very great good if it brings the members of different provinces, and the members of different communities, into contact with each other. I have not the smallest doubt that you, gentlemen of the Madras Presidency, have now far kindlier feelings for the defects of your brethren of Bengal and Bombay than you had before you had that intimate knowledge of us which you have now obtained by coming in almost hourly contact with us during this past week. I say that this is a great good in itself. I trust we shall be able to obtain great political reforms in the administration of our own country if we carry on a perfectly legitimate and constant agitation. At the same time, I do think that the social improvement we are introducing among ourselves by contact is in itself a very great good. (Applause.) Gentlemen, one of the best features of the Congress in Madras has been the hearty co-operation that we have received from the European members. (Hear, hear, and loud and continued applause.) It has, gentlemen, been alleged that the Europeans keep aloof from the natives, and that there is always a great deal of misunderstanding between the two communities. I took the liberty of addressing a few observations to you on that question. You will remember that I absolutely denied the universal application of that assertion. (Hear, hear.) Gentlemen, at that time my knowledge of the Madras Presidency was very limited, and I was not aware that my assertion would be completely borne out by what I have seen of the conduct of our European friends. (Applause.) Gentlemen, I, for one, am absolutely at a loss to understand why our European friends should not co-operate with us in the business that we have undertaken. As I have said, the limits and scope of our agitation and action are the good of the whole of India, not the good of any particular part of India, and not the good of any particular community, but, gentlemen, the good of the whole of India, and are not our European friends included? (Cheers.) The good of the one must necessarily re-act upon the good of the other. Therefore, I do heartily wish that the co-operation of all our European friends should go on increasing from year to year, till we find that the delegates are composed, not of six hundred natives and five or ten Europeans, but of a very large portion of Europeans, who should assist us by the experience—by the true political experience—which they have inherited for centuries from their forefathers. (Applause.) Gentlemen, I must ask our European friends, such of them as have honoured us with their presence, or such of them as may read the proceedings in the newspapers, if they find any expression or sentiment which may, perhaps, have been uttered in the heat of the discussion, to which they think objection may be justly taken, to remember that this Congress is only in its third year, and that no political association can achieve any great success till it has acquired a great deal of experience, which must take a very, very long time for us to get, who are entirely new to the art of self-government. (Applause.) I do trust that any defects which may have been found in the proceedings of this Congress will be pointed out to us, not in the spirit of cavil, not in the spirit of hostility, not in the spirit of antagonism, but in that spirit of consideration, conciliation, and assistance, which I think our European friends are in a position to accord us. (Applause.) One word, gentlemen, about a Resolution that has been carried in regard to the constitutional working of the Congress. It is very wise, on our part, not to have absolutely bound ourselves hand and foot by any hard and fast rules that may be framed here. It will take months, I may say even years, before we understand what the various requirements of the different Provinces are and what the real elements which should be represented in this Congress are. Therefore, I am happy to find that our rules have been left in a somewhat indefinite form, so that they may be worked so far as this may be considered desirable and possible. That some rules are absolutely necessary, my little experience of the last three days has convinced me. Remember the responsibilities of any President. Resolutions after Resolutions of the most important character are thrust into his hands for discussion—Resolutions of which no notice has been given to any of the delegates, Resolutions which the President has not even had the time carefully to read over. Resolutions which are to be put forward before the Congress should be considered long before the Congress meets, and should be circulated among the delegates, in order that they may fully and carefully consider them. Again, gentlemen, look at the amendments proposed. The amendments were actually put into my hands during the debate, and some even after the Resolutions were carried. I am afraid that I may appear to some of my friends a tyrannical despot (Voices of "No, No"), most unwilling to allow the discussion to proceed (Voices: "No, No"); but I assure you that I acted on the one principle that no Resolution should be carried in this Congress unless it was a Resolution that would commend itself to the judgment of all reasonable and thinking men. (Hear, hear.) I would rather that the Resolution, even if it was desirable, and even if it was pressed, stood over for the next year to be fully discussed than that it should be moved and passed in five minutes (applause), by gentlemen holding up their hands before they knew what the full merits of the Resolution were. I would certainly suggest to the consideration of the standing committee, which may have the framing of these rules, that the Resolutions and amendments should reach the delegates before, at all events, the Congress assembles. Gentlemen, I fear I have already trespassed too long upon your patience. (Voices, "No, no.") It is time now, gentlemen, that I should declare that this Congress is dissolved. Before I do that, however, my attention has been drawn to a subject which I have not the smallest doubt, when the proper occasion arises, will meet with the approval not only of every one of the delegates assembled here, or any delegate who may be present on the occasion of any future Congress, but will approve itself to the judgment of every one of the two hundred and fifty millions of Her Majesty's subjects in India. Gentlemen, it has been suggested that in case of any complication arising on our North-Western frontier, in order that our loyalty should be placed beyond the reach of cavil, we, the Members of the National Congress, should undertake, for the purpose of enabling the Government of India to make a full and complete defence, to collect taxes, and that we should constitute ourselves tax-collectors, levying voluntary contributions (loud and continued applause) from our countrymen—not large sums of money like Rs.1,000 or Rs.100 or even one rupee, but four annas per head (applause) which, if contributed, will yield about a crore and a half. (Hear, hear.) I trust that there will be no occasion for any member of the Congress to convert himself into a collector of this voluntary contribution. But I feel perfectly certain that, if ever such an occasion arises, there will not be one who will not voluntarily and willingly undertake the otherwise unpleasant task. (Loud applause.) Now, gentlemen, I must thank you for the very great patience and courtesy with which you have heard me, and I trust I may be able to be present at the next Congress at Allahabad. I will then, if I am enabled to take part in the debates, at all events do my best to show that it is possible to make a speech of five minutes, and yet that that speech should contain a considerable amount of matter. (Loud and continued applause.)

Mr. SALEM RAMASWAMI MUDALIAR (Madras, No. 64 in list), said: The high privilege of proposing a vote of thanks to our worthy President has devolved upon me (hear, hear, and applause), and there is no task which could have been entrusted to me which could give me greater pleasure and greater satisfaction to fulfil. (Applause.) I thank him from the very bottom of my heart on my own behalf and on behalf of all the gentlemen assembled here. (Loud applause.) Not only in my own Presidency, but throughout India, our countrymen have been watching our proceedings with keen interest. The feelings that prompt all of us at this moment is one of deep gratitude for the able way in which our worthy President has fulfilled the duties entrusted to him. (Loud applause.) Gentlemen, if you simply look at it as a question of patience,—if you look at the way in which he has listened to speech after speech, sitting here from morning to evening day after day, I say as a question of patience he deserves our best thanks. (Loud applause.) But that was the least difficult portion of the task that he had to fulfil. Considering the great divergence of views that was to be expected in a body of men assembled from all parts of India, whose faces were more or less strange to each other at the time they came here (loud applause), I say considering the difficulties that one had to anticipate and which, as a matter of fact, were felt every moment whilst the work was proceeding, the way in which the whole thing has been brought to a satisfactory conclusion is quite a crown of glory to our President. (Loud cheers.) For the success we have achieved has been mainly due to the ability, tact, good judgment, and—above all—good temper which our President has shown in discharging his duties. (Loud and prolonged applause.) Gentlemen, when he leaves this pandal he will leave it with the proud consciousness of having discharged a great duty (loud applause), he will leave it carrying with him the respect, the regard, the sincerest good-wishes of all here assembled. (Loud cheers.) Gentlemen, he has taken a most important part in this great national movement. (Applause.) High honors may be in store for him. He may be rewarded as he deserves. His merits may be recognized by Government, but I am sure there is one feeling which he will cherish above all these honours, and that feeling will be one of satisfaction and gratification at the spontaneous outburst of gratitude and admiration with which you have greeted him. (Great applause.) I do not think I need add anything more, but I may as well take this opportunity of thanking many of the gentlemen who have rendered us valuable assistance in making this Congress a success. I do not refer to those who took part in our proceedings, but to others, and I thank them for the zeal with which they worked, and the way in which they placed their services at our disposal, and these deserve recognition at the hands of this assembly. (Hear, hear, and applause.) You will permit me to thank all those gentlemen on your behalf for the hearty way in which they placed their services at our disposal. (Loud and continued applause.)

Mr. Kumar Rameswar Maliah (Hugli, No. 566 in list) said: I second the proposal of the previous speaker.

Dr. Trailokya Nath Mitra said: Gentlemen, As our illustrious President refuses to put this Resolution to the vote, I, acting as his faithful lieutenant, do put it to the vote, and I am sure, gentlemen, you will carry it with acclamation. (The vote of thanks was then carried by acclamation.) (Cries of "Order, Order.")

The President: Surely those gentlemen who cry "Order, Order" do not want any more speeches. I thought they would have been quite satisfied and that their appetite would have been fully satiated by this time. I can only say that I thank you extremely from the very bottom of my heart for the manner in which the vote of thanks has been carried by the delegates. (Applause.) It is certainly true that I shall carry with me, beyond all other feelings, the feeling of the deepest satisfaction at the position I have been allowed to occupy here, and I shall remember it to the end of my days (loud applause) as the highest honour that it is possible on the part of my countrymen to bestow upon any one. I shall always prize, gentlemen, the honour of having presided over your deliberations, as the very greatest honour that has ever been, or that is ever likely to be, conferred on me in any future time. (Applause.) I must take care not to tax your patience any longer. I must dissolve this Congress, and I must once more thank you for the very great honour you have done me. I trust we shall meet again, not in the capacities of president and delegates but in the capacity of brother-delegates. (Loud and continued cheers.)

Mr. Rangiah Naidu (Madras, No. 7 in list) then again called for cheers for the Queen-Empress, and the call was responded to by vociferous and prolonged cheering. Then cheers were given for the President and others, and at last the assembly broke up.

List of Abbreviations used in Appendix I.

Agt.	*Agent.*
Asst.	*Assistant.*
Assn.	*Association.*
B. N. L.	*Bengal National League.*
B. P. Assn.	*Bombay Presidency Association.*
Cir.	*Circulation.*
Dist. Bd.	*District Board.*
F. C. M.	*Free Church Mission.*
F. Uni.	*Fellow of the University.*
Genl.	*General.*
Hd.	*Head.*
H. C.	*High Court.*
Hony.	*Honorary.*
L. F. Bd.	*Local Fund Board.*
L. Propr.	*Landed Proprietor.*
Magte.	*Magistrate.*
M. J. S.	*Maha Jana Sabha.*
Memb.	*Member.*
Mercht.	*Merchant.*
Ml. Cr.	*Municipal Commissioner.*
Presdt.	*President.*
Prof.	*Professor.*
Pub. Meetg.	*Public Meeting.*
R. P. Assn.	*Ratepayers' Association.*
R. Room	*Reading Room.*
S. J. S.	*Sarva Jana (or Janik) Sabha.*
Secy.	*Secretary.*
Tal.	*Taluq.*
Un.	*Union.*
1st Gd.	*First Grade.*

APPENDIX I.

LIST OF DELEGATES

WHO ATTENDED THE

THIRD INDIAN NATIONAL CONGRESS,

HELD AT MADRAS, DECEMBER, 1887.

Number.	Presidency.	Province.	District.	Name in full, with Honorary Titles, Scholastic Degrees, &c.	Religious denomination and caste, if any.	Occupation, Address, &c.	Place or Places or Association, &c., which they represent.	How and when elected.
1	Madras	Carnatic	Madras City.	Rajah Sir T. Madava Row, K.C.S.I.	Hindu Brahman.	Retired Dewan of Travancore, Indore and Baroda, F. Uni., Madras, Mylapore.	Madras and Graduates' Association.	Public meeting on the 18th Dec. at Mylapore, (Div. 8), and by the Committee of the Graduates' Association.
2	"	"	"	Hon'ble Mir Humayun Jah Bahadur, C.I.E.	Mussulman.	Landholder, President Central Mahomedan Association, Member Legislative Council, Municipal Councillor, and F., Uni. Madras, Adyar.	Madras.	Public meetings on the 18th Dec. at Mylapore, (Div. 8), and at Triplicane on the same date, (Dec. 7).
3	"	"	"	Hon'ble P. Chentsal Rao, C.I.E.	Hindu Brahman.	Retired Government Servant, Member Legislative Council, and F., Uni. Madras, Teynampet.	Madras and Graduates' Association.	Public meeting on the 18th Dec. at Mylapore (Div. 8), and by the Committee of the Graduates' Association.
4	"	"	"	Sir Savalai Ramaswami Mudaliar, Kt., C.I.E.	Hindu.	Merchant, Sheriff, Municipal Councillor, and Vice-President Mahajana Sabha, Poonamallee Road.	do.	Public meeting on the 5th Dec. at Pudupet (Div. 6), and at a general meeting of the Mahajana Sabha, on the 26th Dec.
5	"	"	"	Rai Bahadur Hon'ble S. Subramania Iyer, B.L.	Hindu Brahman.	Vakil, Member Legislative Council, Vice-President, Mahajana Sabha, and F., Uni. Madras, The Luz.	Madras, Graduates' Association and Mahajana Sabha.	Public meeting on the 18th Dec. at Mylapore (Div. 8), by the Committee of the Graduates' Association, and at a general meeting of the Mahajana Sabha, on the 26th Dec.
6	"	"	"	Mr. P. Somasundaram Chettiar	Hindu.	Merchant, Vice-President Mahajana Sabha, Tondiarpett.	Madras and Mahajana Sabha	At a general meeting of the Mahajana Sabha, on the 26th Dec., by the Madras Hindu Union Bank, and also at a public meeting at Black Town (Div. 3).
7	"	"	"	Rao Saheb P. Rangia Naidu Garu.	do	Zemindar, Vakil, Municipal Councillor L.F.&Tal. Bd. Memb. & President, Mahajana Sabha., Poonamallee Road.	Mahajana Sabha.	At a general meeting of the Mahajana Sabha, on the 26th Dec.
8	"	"	"	Khan Bahadur Hajee Mahomed Abdulla Badshaw Sahib.	Mussulman.	Merchant, Vice-President, Central Mahomedan Association, Member, Anjumani Mufid-i-Islam, and Mahajana Sabha, Triplicane.	Madras, and Mahajana Sabha.	Public meeting held on the 18th Dec. at Triplicane (Div. 7), and at a general meeting of the Mahajana Sabha, held on the 26th Dec.

LIST OF DELEGATES.

Number.	Presidency.	Province.	District.	Name in full, with Honorary Titles, Scholastic Degrees, &c.	Religious denomination and caste, if any.	Occupation, Address, &c.	Place or Places or Association, &c., which they represent.	How and when elected.
9	Madras.	Carnatic	Madras City.	Rao Saheb N. Subramaniem, B.A., B.L.	Native Christian.	Barrister-at-Law, and Municipal Councillor The Luz.	Madras, and Mahajana Sabha.	Public meeting on the 18th Dec. at Mylapore (Div. 8), and at a general meeting of the Mahajana Sabha, on the 26th Dec.
10	"	"	"	Mahomed Nizamuddin Khan Bahadur.	Mussulman.	Secy., Anjumani Mufid-i-Islam and Landowner, Mylapore.	Madras, and Anjumani Mufid-i-Islam.	Public meeting on the 18th Dec. at Mylapore, (Div. 8), and at a meeting of Anjumani Mufid-i-Islam, on 3rd Dec.
11	"	"	"	Mr. A. O. Hume.	Christian European.	Retired Civil Servant, Simla.	B.N.L. B. P. Assn. and M. J. S. Madras	General meetings on the 8th, 15th, and 26th Dec.
12	"	"	"	Mr. S. Appasami Chettiar.	Hindu.	Retired Public Servant, Tondiarpett.	Madras.	Pub. meeting on the 26th Dec. at Tondiarpett (Div. 1.)
13	"	"	"	Mr. P. Tiruvengadasawmy Pillai.	do	Attorney - at - Law, Tondiarpett.	do	do
14	"	"	"	Mr. C. V. Subramania Sastri.	Hindu Brahman.	do	do	do
15	"	"	"	Mr. P. Thiagaraya Chettiar.	Hindu.	Mercht., Tondiarpett.	do	do
16	"	"	"	Mr. Jaga Rao Pillai, B.A., B.L.	Native Christian.	Vakil, High Court, Vice - President, Mahajana Sabha, Tondiarpett.	Madras, & Mahajana Sabha.	By Mahajana Sabha, on the 26th Dec., by "the Progressive Union," 20th Dec., and at a Pub. meeting, Tondiarpett, (Div. 1).
17	"	"	"	Mr. P. V. Krishnaswami Chettiar, B.A., B.L.	Hindu.	Vakil, High Court, Tondiarpett.	do	By Mahajana Sabha, on the 26th Dec., and at a Pub. meetg. Tondiarpett (Div. 1).
18	"	"	"	Rao Saheb R. Balakrishnama Chettiar.	do	Merchant and Ml. Cr.. Tondiarpett.	do	do
19	"	"	"	Mr. Mulla Jaferjee Sahib.	Mussulman.	Merchant.	do	do
20	"	"	"	Mr. Ramakrishniah.	Hindu Brahman.	Banker & Merchant, Black Town.	Madras.	Pub. meetg. on the 12th Dec., Black Town (Div. 2).
21	"	"	"	Mr. K. Krishnama Chariar, B.A., B.L.	do	Vakil, High Court, Black Town.	do	do
22	"	"	"	Mr. R. Sivasankara Pandiya, B.A., F.T.S.	do	Lecturer in English, Pachiappa's College, Guzeratipett.	do	Pub. meetg. on the 23rd Dec. (Divns. 2 and 3).
23	"	"	"	Mr. V. J. Manickavelu Mudaliar.	Hindu.	Printer, publisher, & Propr. Irish Press, Broadway.	do	do
24	"	"	"	Mr. K. Subramanya Iyer, B A.	Hindu Brahman.	Lecturer in History, Pachiappa's College.	do	Pub. meetg. at Black Town on the 23rd Dec. (Div. 3).
25	"	"	"	Mr. C. Nammiah Chettiar, B.A., B.L.	Hindu.	Vakil, High Court, Black Town.	do	do
26	"	"	"	Mr. E. Balasundra Mudaliar, B.A.	do	Secretary to Pachp's Trustees, Black Town	do	do
27	"	"	"	Mr. Arunagiri Nayudu, B.A.	do	Science Asst., Scot. Mission College.	do	do
28	"	"	"	Mr. Waljee Laljee Sait.	Mussulman.	Merchant, Black Town	Madras, & Metal Trading Company	By the Metal Trading Co. and Pub. meetg., Black Town, 23rd Dec., and the 3rd Divn., 1st Dec.

LIST OF DELEGATES.

Number.	Presidency.	Province.	District.	Name in full, with Honorary Titles, Scholastic Degrees, &c.	Religious denomination and caste, if any.	Occupation, Address, &c.	Place or Places or Association, &c., which they represent.	How and when elected.
29	Madras.	Carnatic	Madras City.	Mr. N. Lakshmanasami Mudaliar, B.A.	Hindu	Merchant, Black Town	Madras.	Pub. meetg. at Nungambakkam, 23rd Dec. (Div. 5).
30	„	„	„	Mr. Elayalwar Nayudu.	do	Memb., Dist. Board & Municipal Contractor, Poonamallee Road.	do	do
31	„	„	„	Mir Ansuruddin Sahib Khan Bahadur.	Mussulman.	Retired Presidency, Magistrate, Sydapet.	do	do
32	„	„	„	Mr. Hajee Kadir Moidin Saheb.	do	Land-holder and Merchant, Kodampakkam.	do	do
33	„	„	„	Mr. Desikachariar.	Hindu Brahman.	Retired Tahsildar.	do	do
34	„	„	„	Mr. Narasimhachariar.	do	Schoolmaster, Nungambakkam.	do	do
35	„	„	„	Mr. C. Iyasawmy Pillai.	Hindu.	Landed Proprietor, Komeleswarenpetta.	do	Public meeting at Pudupett, 5th Dec. (Div. 6).
36	„	„	„	Mr. Rajoo Pathur.	Native Christian.	Type-founder, &c., and Agent to Messrs. Figgins & Co., Lond., Pudupett.	do	do
37	„	„	„	Dr. S. Pulney Andy, M.D., M.R.C.S.	do	Medical Practitioner, Editor *Eastern Star*, Egmore.	do	Pub. meetg. at Pudupett 5th Dec. (Div. 6), and Mahajana Sabha, 26th Dec.
38	„	„	„	Mr. R. Sadagopachariar, B.A., B.L.	Hindu Brahman.	Vakil, High Court, Triplicane.	do	Public meeting at Triplicane, 18th Dec. (Div. 7).
39	„	„	„	Rajah Iswaradas Dayawant Bahadur.	Hindu Kshatraya	Landed Proprietor, Triplicane.	do	do
40	„	„	„	Mr. V. Raghava Chariar.	Hindu Brahman.	Land-holder and Dharmakarta, Sri-Parthasaradhi Swami's temple, Triplicane.	do	do
41	„	„	„	Mohamed Abdul Kuddus Badshaw Sahib.	Mussulman.	Merchant, Triplicane.	do	do
42	„	„	„	Hajee Abdul Azeez Sahib.	do	do	do	do
43	„	„	„	Mr. Eardley Norton.	Christian European.	Barrister-at-Law, and Coroner, The Luz.	do	Pub. meetg., 18th Dec., at Triplicane and Tiruvateswarenpetta (Div. 7).
44	„	„	„	Mr. A. C. Parthasaradhi Nayudu Garu.	Hindu	Editor *Andraprakasika*, Tel. Weekly (Cir. 800) Tiruvateswaranpettah.	do	Pub. meetg. at Tiruvateswarenpetta and Pudupakam; also at Triplicane, 18th Dec. (Div. 7).
45	„	„	„	Mr. G. Subramanya Iyer, B.A.	Hindu Brahman.	Editor *The Hindu* (English Tri-Weekly, Cir. 1,400) & *Swadesamitran* (Tamil Bi-Weekly, Cir. 1,000), Triplicane.	Madras & Mahajana Sabha.	Mahajana Sabha, on the 26th Dec., and at a Public meeting at Triplicane (Div. 7), 18th Dec.
46	„	„	„	Mr. M. Viraraghavachariar, B.A.	do	Joint-Editor *The Hindu* and *Swadesamitran*, and Secy., Mahajana Sabha, Triplicane.	do	do
47	„	„	„	Mr. T. R. Ramanadha Iyer, B.A.	do	Master, Pacheappa's High School, Mylapore.	Madras.	Public meeting, 18th Dec., at Mylapore (Div. 8).
48	„	„	„	Mr. T. Swaminadha Mudaliar.	Hindu.	Land-holder, Mylapore.	do	do

LIST OF DELEGATES.

Number.	Presidency.	Province.	District.	Name in full, with Honorary Titles, Scholastic Degrees, &c.	Religious denomination and caste, if any.	Occupation, Address, &c.	Place or Places or Association, &c., which they represent.	How and when elected.
49	Madras.	Carnatic	Madras City.	Mahomed Anvarudeen-khan Bahadur.	Mussulman.	Land-holder & Memb. Anjumani - Mufid - i-Islam, Mylapore.	Madras.	Public meeting at Mylapore, 18th Dec. (Div. 8).
50	"	"	"	Mr. Benjamin Henry Chester, M.A.	Christian Eurasian.	Professor of Mathematics and Phy. Science, Doveton Protestant College, Vepery.	do	At a meeting of the Eurasian and A.-I. Assn. of Southern India, 7th Dec.
51	"	"	"	Mr. Geo. Maddox, B.A.	do	Lecturer, do. Vepery.	do	do
52	"	"	"	Mr. W. S. Gantz.	do	Barrister-at-Law, Vepery.	do	do
53	"	"	"	Mr. B. Lovery.	do	Retired Sheriff, F. Univ., and Ml. Cr., Kilpauk.	do	do
54	"	"	"	Mr. N. Bazely.	do	Public Accountant, 2, Police Commissioner's Office Road, Egmore.	do	do
55	"	"	"	Rao Saheb R. Balaji Rao, B.A., B.L.	Hindu Brahman.	Vakil, High Court and Vice-President, Mahajana Sabha, and Ml. Cr., Mylapore.	Mahajana Sabha, Madras.	General meeting of Mahajana Sabha, and by the Members of the Janopakara Nidhi, Mylapore.
56	"	"	"	Mr. C. Ramachandra Rao, Saheb, B.L.	do	Zemindar, Vakil, High Court, and Vice-President, Mahajana Sabha, The Luz.	do	At a General Meeting of the Mahajana Sabha, on the 26th Dec.
57	"	"	"	Rao Saheb C. V. Cunniah Chetti Garu.	Hindu.	Land-holder, Mercht., and Ml. Cr., Black Town.	do	do
58	"	"	"	Rai Bahadur P. Ananda Charlu, B.L.	Hindu Brahman.	Vakil, High Court; Ml. Cr., and Secy., Mahajana Sabha, Egmore.	do	do
59	"	"	"	Mr. G. Mahadeva Chettiar.	Hindu.	Memb., Dist. Board, Mercht. & Zemindar, Black Town.	do	do
60	"	"	"	Rao Saheb P. Teagaraya Chetti Garu, B.A.	do	Zemindar, Mercht. & Ml. Cr., Tondiarpett.	do	do
61	"	"	"	Rai Bahadur A. Danakoti Mudaliar.	do	do	do	do
62	"	"	"	Rao Saheb W. S. Venkataramanjulu Nayudu Garu.	do	Memb., Dist. and Tal. Bds., Shrotriemdar of Uttukkadu, & Ml. Cr., Komaleswarenpettah.	do	do
63	"	"	"	Rao Saheb C. Yetirajulu Nayudu Garu.	do	Merchant, Secy., Metal Trading Company, and Ml. Cr., Tondiarpett.	do	do
64	"	"	"	Rao Saheb S. Ramaswami Mudaliar, M.A., B.L.	do	Vakil, High Court; F., Uni.; and Ml. Cr., Poonamallee Road.	do	do
65	"	"	"	Mr. T. Namberumal Chetti Garu, B.A.	do	Mercht., Black Town.	do	do
66	"	"	"	Mr. A. Balakrishna Mudaliar.	do	Do, Chulai.	do	do
67	"	"	"	Mr. M. Ramaswami Nayudu Garu.	do	Do, Black Town.	do	do
68	"	"	"	Mr. M. Abboi Nayudu Garu.	do	Do, Tondiarpett.	do	do

LIST OF DELEGATES.

Number.	Presidency.	Province.	District.	Name in full, with Honorary Titles, Scholastic Degrees, &c.	Religious denomination and caste, if any.	Occupation, Address, &c.	Place or Places or Association, &c., which they represent.	How and when elected.
69	Madras.	Carnatic	Madras City.	Mr. P. Murugesa Mudaliar.	Hindu.	Merchant, Poonamallee Road.	M J S Madras.	General meeting, Mahajana Sabha, 26th Dec.
70	"	"	"	Mr. V. Subramiah Chettiar.	do	Do, Black Town.	do	At a general meeting M J S, 26th Dec.
71	"	"	"	Rao Saheb C. Singaravelu Mudaliar.	do	Merchant, and Ml. Cr., Chulai.	do	do
72	"	"	"	Rao Saheb G. Kuppasami Nayudu Garu.	do	Do, Black Town.	do	do
73	"	"	"	Mr. C. Sankara Nair, B.A., B.L.	do	Vakil, High Court, Egmore.	do	do
74	"	"	"	Mr. K. P. Sankara Menon, B.A., B.L.	do	Do, Mylapore.	do, & Cochin Reform Association.	do
75	"	"	"	Mr. Venkatarama Chettiar, B.A., B.L.	do	Do, Black Town.	do	do
76	"	"	"	Mr. K. Narayana Row, B.A., B.L.	Hindu Brahman.	Do, Mylapore.	do	do
77	"	"	"	Mr. C. V. Sundaram Sastri, B.A., B.L.	do	Do, Tondiarpett.	do	do
78	"	"	"	Mr. K. Subba Rao.	do	Asst. Editor, *The Hindu*, Triplicane.	do	do
79	"	"	"	Gulam Dastaghir Sahib.	Mussulman.	Secy., National Mahomedan Assn., Triplicane.	do	do
80	"	"	"	Abdul Razac Hajee Baba Meanee.	do	Merchant.	do	do
81	"	"	"	Hajee Abdus Salam Badsha Sahib.	do	Do, Triplicane.	do	do
82	"	"	"	Mohamed Gouse Sahib.	do	do	do	do
83	"	"	"	Hajee Mahomed Abdul Shakoor Badshaw Sahib.	do	do	Anjumani Mufid - i - Islam.	A meeting of the Executive Committee of Anjumani Mufid - i - Islam, 3rd Dec.
84	"	"	"	Abdul Rahman Hajee Alla Rakha Sajen Sahib.	do	Do, Black Town.	do	do
85	"	"	"	Mr. S. Rangiah Chettiar, B.A.	Hindu.	Prof., Chr. College, Memb. of the Committee of Education, & F. Uni., Black Town.	Graduates' Assn.	By the committee of the Graduates' Association.
86	"	"	"	Mr. T. V. Seshagiri Aiyar, B.A., B.L.	Hindu Brahman.	Vakil, High Court, Triplicane.	Lit. Society Triplicane.	General meeting of Lit. Soc., Triplicane, by ballot.
87	"	"	"	Mr. M. Y. Sri Rangachariar, B.A., B.L.	do	do	do	do
88	"	"	"	Mr. John Adam, M.A.	Christian European.	Principal, Pachiappa's College and F. Univ., Black Town.	Metal Trading Company.	Meeting of the Directors of the Metal Trading Company, 17th Dec.
89	"	"	"	Mr. Hajee Ibrahim Sait.	Mussulman.	Merchant, Black Town.	do	do
90	"	"	"	Mr. C. Batcha Mea Sahib.	do	do	do	do
91	"	"	"	Mr. Krishna Doss, Bala Mookunda Doss.	Hindu.	Banker and Landholder, Sackarpet, Black Town.	do	do
92	"	"	"	Mr. P. Rajam Chetti Garu	do	Mercht., Black Town.	do	do

LIST OF DELEGATES.

Number.	Presidency.	Province.	District.	Name in full, with Honorary Titles, Scholastic Degrees, &c.	Religion, denomination and caste, if any.	Occupation, Address, &c.	Place or Places or Association, &c., which they represent.	How and when elected.
93	Madras.	Carnatic	Madras City.	Mr. C. Mukundu Nayudu Garu.	Hindu.	Mercht., Black Town.	Metal Trading Co	Meeting of the Directors of the Metal Trading Company.
94	"	"	"	Mr. T. V. Appa Rao Pillai.	do	Merchant.	S. India Mercht.Co.	South India Merchants' Co. (Ld.), 22nd Dec.
95	"	"	"	Mr. T Pattabhi Ramiah Nayudu Garu.	do	Secy. S. I. Merchants' Company.	do	do
96	"	"	"	Mr. C. Rangachariar, B.A., B.L.	Hindu Brahman.	Vakil, High Court, Triplicane.	Mutual Impt. Society.	A meeting of the Mutual Improvement Society, Triplicane, 22nd Dec.
97	"	"	"	Mr. M. O. Parthasaradhi Aiyangar, M.A., M.L.	do	Advocate, High Court, Triplicane.	do	do
98	"	"	"	Mr. M. N. Srirangaraja Charya, Pandit, Sathavadhani, Abhinav, Kalidasa.	do	Pandit, Editor, *Lokananda Samaj Patrika*, Triplicane.	Lokananda Samaj.	By the members of Lokananda Samaj, Triplicane, 16th Dec.
99	"	"	"	Mr. C. Ramachandra Rao, B.A., B.L.	do	Vakil, High Court, Triplicane.	Madhva Sabha.	Meeting of the Madhva Sidhantonnahini, 23rd Dec.
100	"	"	"	Mr. T. Venkata Subba Aiyar.	do	No. 231, Tambu Chetti Street, Black Town.	Desa. Sabha.	At a meeting of Desabhimana Sabha, 20th Dec.
101	"	"	"	Mr. P. Singaravelu Mudeliar, B.A.	Hindu.	do	do	do
102	"	"	"	Mr. V. A. Rajaratna Mudaliar.	do	Attorney-at-LawHigh Court, Pursewalkam.	Hindu Nidhi.	The members of the Pursewalkam Hindu S. S. Nidhi, Dec.
103	"	"	"	Mr. Syed Murtuza Sahib Khadri.	Mussulman.	Proprietor and Editor of *Jaridai Rozyar*, (Hindustani Weekly, cir.800), Royapettah.	do	Meeting at Triplicane.
104	"	"	"	Mr. G. J. Solomon Nadar, B.A.	Native Christian.	Black Town.	The Sangam.	Meeting of the Assn. for promoting the political and moral welfare of the Santor race, 17th Dec.
105	"	"	"	Mr. Joseph Satya Nadar, B.A.	do	do	do	do
106	"	"	"	Mr. M. Tangavelu Chetti, B.A.	Hindu.	Tambu Chetti Street, Muttiyalpet	V. Vridhi Sabha.	By the members of Viveka Vridhi Sabha.
107	"	Northern Circas	Ganjam.	Rao Bahadur Venkatarama Pantulu.	Hindu Brahman.	Pleader, Chairman Municipality.	Berhampore.	Public meeting.
108	"	"	"	Rao Saheb P. Venkanna Pantulu.	do	Pleader, Dist. Court, Berhampore, and Ml. Commissioner.	Aska.	Public meeting, Aska.
109	"	"	"	Rao Saheb N. Ramamurti Pantulu, B.A.	do	Pleader, Dist. Court, Ml. Cr. Memb. Local and Tal. Bds. Berhampore.	Berhampore Assn. and the Public.	Meeting of the Assn. and of the merchants, traders and artizans of Berhampore.
110	"	"	"	Mr. M. Venkatanarayana Rao Pantulu	do	Retd. Govt. servant, Berhampore.	Russelcondah.	At a public meeting.
111	"	"	Vizagapatam.	Mr. G. Venkatappa Rao, B.A.	do	Asst. Master Maharajah's College; Editor *Prakasika* (Telugu Fortnightly, cir.300).	Towns and taluks of Gajapati Nagaram, Chipurupally, Palaconda, Parvatipur.	At meetings held at the places stated.
112	"	"	"	Mr. O. Simpachalapati Rao, B.A.	do	Asst. Master Maharajah's College, Viziyanagaram.	Bimlipatam and HinduDeb. Union.	Public meeting, 12th Dec.

LIST OF DELEGATES.

Number.	Presidency.	Province.	District.	Name in full, with Honorary Titles, Scholastic Degrees, &c.	Religious denomination and caste, if any.	Occupation, Address, &c.	Place or Places or Association, &c., which they represent.	How and when elected.
113	Madras	Northern Circars.	Vizagapatam	Rao Saheb Venkatajagannadha Sastri.	Hindu Brahman.	Pleader, Dist. Court, Vizagapatam, and Ml. Cr.	The M.J.S. Vizagapatam.	Special meeting of the Sabha, 1st Nov.
114	„	„	„	Mr. B. Narasimheswara Sarma, B.A.	do	Asst. Master, St. Aloysius School, Vizagapatam.	Do, and Anakapalli Club.	Do do and 1st Dec.
115	„	„	„	Nr. N. V. Chelapati Sastri.	do	Assistant Master, Maharajah's College, and Secy., M. J. S. Viziyanagaram.	M. J. S., Viziyanagaram.	At a special meeting, 29th Nov.
116	„	„	„	Mr. V. Madhava Rao Nayudu, M.A.	Hindu.	Vice-Principal, Maharajah's College, Viziyanagaram & Joint Editor *Telugu Harp.* (English Weekly, cir. 400.)	Viziyanagaram and Vidyabhivardhani Sabha.	By the people of Viziyanagaram.
117	„	„	Godavery	Mir Nalive Ali Khan.	Mussulman.	Mirasidar, Rajamundry.	Godavery Dist.	Public meeting at Rajamundry, 3rd Dec.
118	„	„	„	Mr. V. V. Avadhani Garu, B.A.	Hindu Brahman.	1st Gd. Pleader, Rajamundry.	do	do
119	„	„	Krishna	Srimantu Rajah Yarlagadda Mallikarjuna Prasada Nayudu Bahadur.	Hindu.	Zemindar, Devarakota, or Chellapalli	Masulipatam.	Public meeting, 11th Dec.
120	„	„	„	Mr. K. Krishnama Chariar B.A.	Hindu Brahman.	Hd. Master, Hindu High School, Masulipatam.	do	do
121	„	„	„	Rao Saheb M. B. Venkata Reddi Nayudu Garu.	Hindu.	Ml. Cr., and Propr., Carpet Agency.	do	do
122	„	„	„	Mirza Jamadudin Khan (Nabob's family) Masulipatam.	Mussulman.	Pensioner and Agent to the present Nabob of Masulipatam.	do	do
123	„	Carnatic	Nellore.	Mahomed Abdul Hussain Sahib.	do	Land-holder.	Nellore.	Public meeting, 29th Nov.
124	„	„	„	Mr. D. N. Venkataramayah, B.A.	Hindu Brahman.	1st Asst., F. C. M. School, Nellore.	do	do
125	„	„	„	Mr. M. Ramachandrayah.	Native Christian.	Asst. Teacher, Mission College, Guntur.	M. J. S., & Guntur.	Public meeting, Guntur, 12th December
126	„	„	„	Mr. C. Cotiah Chettair.	Hindu.	Pensioned Deputy Inspector of Schools.	R. P. An., Nellore.	A special meeting, Nellore, 29th Nov., and by members of the Assn., on the 30th Nov.
127	„	„	„	Rao Saheb N. Suryanarain Rao.	Hindu Brahman.	2nd Gd. Pleader, Ongole, Ml. Chairman, Hony. Magte.	Br. M. J. S. Ongole.	At a meeting of the Sabha, 28th Nov.
128	„	„	„	Rao Saheb D. Markandaya Sastri.	do	Banker, Hony. Magte.	do	do
129	„	„	„	Mr. S. Narayanaswami Chetti Garu, B.A.	Hindu.	Dewan to H. H. the Rajah of Venkatagiri.	Venkatagiri.	At a meeting of the Town Hall Committee, 11th Dec., by unanimous vote.
130	„	„	„	Mr. N. Desikachariar.	Hindu Brahman.	Secy., to H. H. the Rajah of Venkatagiri.	do	do
131	„	„	Chingleput	Mr. N. S. Krishnaswami Aiyangar.	Hindu Brahman.	Zemindar, Siranjeri.	Chingleput	Public meeting, 21st Dec.
132	„	„	„	Mr. N. Venkata Rao, B.A.	do	Hd. Master, F. C. M. High School.	do	do

LIST OF DELEGATES.

Number.	Presidency.	Province.	District.	Name in full, with Honorary Titles, Scholastic Degrees, &c.	Religious denomination and caste, if any.	Occupation, Address, &c.	Place or Places or Association, &c., which they represent.	How and when elected.
133	Madras	Carnatic	Chingleput	Rao Saheb V. Srinivasa Raghavachariar.	Hindu Brahman.	Mirasidar, Memb. L.F. Board.	Chingleput	Public meeting, 21st Dec.
134	"	"	"	Rao Saheb T. N. Krishnamachariar.	do	Pleader and Memb., Dist. Bd.	do	do
135	"	"	"	Mr. M. Y. Ramanujachariar.	do	Pleader, Dist. Court.	do	do
136	"	"	"	Mr. M. Kupusami Nayudu.	Hindu.	do	do	do
137	"	"	"	Mr. Ranganadam.	do	Shrotiemdar.	do	do
138	"	"	"	Mr. S. Teagaraja Mudaliar	do	Head Master, Native High School.	do	do
139	"	"	"	Mr. N. Shanmugaraya Mudaliar.	do	Zemindar, Nallathur.	do	do
140	"	"	"	Mr. T. E. Kumara Venkatachariar.	Hindu Brahman.	Pleader, Conjeveram.	Conjeveram.	Public meeting, 12th Dec.
141	"	"	"	Mr. V. Seshiah, B.A.	do	do	do	do
142	"	"	"	Mr. Srinivasachariar.	do	Mirasidar, Conjeveram.	do	do
143	"	"	"	Rao Saheb S. Srinivasa Aiyar.	do	Ml. Cr., & Hd. Master, Pachiappah's High School.	do	do
144	"	"	"	Rao Saheb Sadasivayyah.	do	Ml. Cr., and Head Master, F. C. M. High School.	do	do
145	"	"	"	Rao Saheb Muttu Babu Reddiar.	Hindu.	Zemindar, Kayapakam, Member L.F. Bd.	Maduran-takam.	Public meeting, Dec.
146	"	"	"	Mr. Mutturama Reddiar.	do	Zemindar, Perambakam.	do	do
147	"	"	"	Mr. Narasimha Chariar.	Hindu Brahman.	Land-holder.	do	Public meeting of the Union Club.
148	"	"	"	Mr. Bashyacarlu Nayudu.	Hindu.	Zemindar of Vengal.	do	Public meeting, 21st Dec.
149	"	"	"	Mr. T. Lakshmana Chetti.	do	Merchant.	do	do
150	"	"	"	Rao Saheb Ramanuja Chariar.	Hindu Brahman.	Mirasidar, Damal, and Member, Taluk Bd.	Damal.	do
151	"	"	"	Rao Saheb V. Srinivasa Raghava Chariar.	do	Mirasidar, & Memb., L.F. Bd.	L. Conjeveram.	do
152	"	"	"	Mr. A. Desikachariar.	do	Hd. Master F. C. M. High School.	Trivellore.	By Native Association and Trivellore, 21st Dec.
153	"	"	"	Mr. V. Swami Sastri.	do	Pleader & L. holder.	do	do
154	"	"	"	Mr. J. Dharmaranga Raju.	Hindu Kshatriya.	Agricultural College Society.	Saidapet.	Meeting of the Society at the College.
155	"	"	"	Mr. V. Ramanujachariar.	Hindu Brahman.	Mirasidar, Kannivakam.	Guduvanjeri.	Public meeting.
156	"	"	N. Arcot.	Sriman Seshanna Nayani Varu.	Hindu.	Zemindar.	Chittore, and Native Assn.	Public meeting at Chittore, 15th Dec.
157	"	"	"	Rao Saheb Subramania Reddiar.	do	Land-holder, Vakil, & Member, L. F. Bd.	do	do
158	"	"	"	Mr. Arunachella Mudaliar, B.A., B.L.	do	Vakil.	do	do
159	"	"	"	Mr. C. Srinivasa Chariar, B.A.	Hindu Brahman.	do	do	do
160	"	"	"	Mr. V. Viraraghava Chariar, B.A.	do	Pleader, Dist. Court.	do	do

LIST OF DELEGATES.

Number.	Presidency.	Province.	District.	Name in full, with Honorary Titles, Scholastic Degrees, &c.	Religious denomination and caste, if any.	Occupation, Address, &c.	Place or Places or Association, &c., which they represent.	How and when elected.
161	Madras	Carnatic	North Arcot	Rao Saheb K. Abdul Raiman Bahadur.	Mussulman.	Merchant, & Ml. Cr.	Vellore public.	Public meeting, 14th Dec.
162	"	"	"	Mr. T. A. Arunachala Pillai.	Hindu.	Vice-President, Hindu Medical Union.	do	Elected at Madras, by the Hindu Vydiasangam.
163	"	"	"	Mr. R. M. Thanthoni Pillai.	do	Mirasidar, Mercht. and Secy., Akila Jana Manoramya Sabha.	Kavaripak Kondapuram, & Ramapuram.	General meetings of the people and Sabha.
164	"	"	"	Mr. V. Subba Rao.	Hindu Brahman.	Pleader, Panchayetdar.	Arni.	Public meeting, Nov.
165	"	"	"	Rao Saheb M. G. Visvanatha Sastri.	do	2ndGd. Pleader, Mem. Dist. Bd., & Vice-Presdt. Tal. Bd.	Arni and Polur, and 16 villages.	At several Public meetings, held in Nov. and Dec.
166	"	"	"	Mr. K. Abdul Razak.	Mussulman.	Merchant, trading at Madras.	Kannamanagalam.	Public meeting in Dec.
167	"	"	"	Mr. Chengannah Chettiar.	Hindu.	Vakil, Dasabandhar Lokanathapuram.	Wallajanagar, & Hindu Brethren Assn. Wallaja.	Public meeting on 12th Dec.
168	"	"	"	Mr. A. B. Chikkannah Chettiar.	do	Abkari Contractor.		do
169	"	"	"	Mr. M. Viswanadha Aiyar.	Hindu Brahman.	Tutor to Dewan's son, Kalahasti.	Kalahasti	Public meeting, 11th Dec.
170	"	"	"	Mr. Arunachala Aiyar.	do	Landed Proprietor.	Polur Taluq.	Public meeting 6th and 7th Dec.
171	"	"	"	Mr. A. Kodandapani Mudaliar.	Hindu.	2nd Grade Pleader, Arni.	do	do
172	"	"	S. Arcot.	Mr. V. Sankariah Nayudu.	do	Zemindar, Chinnappanaickan Pallium.	M. J. S. Tirupapulyur.	Public meeting, 21st Dec.
173	"	"	"	Mr. A. Subbarayulu Reddiar, B.A., B.L.	do	Mirasidar and Vakil H. C., Cuddalore.	do	do
174	"	"	"	Mr. M. B. Susay Pillai, M.A.	Native Christian.	Principal, St. Joseph's College.	do	do
175	"	"	"	Mr. S. Sama Rao.	Hindu Brahman.	Pleader, Dist. Court.	do	do
176	"	"	"	Rao Saheb B. Krishnayah, B.A.	do	do	do	do
177	"	"	"	Mr. Desikachariar.	do	Vakil and Agriculturist.	Chidambaram.	Congress Committee.
178	"	"	"	Mr. G. Appasami Aiyar.	do	do	do	do
179	"	"	"	Mr. R. Srinivasa Pillai.	Hindu.	Mirasidar.	do	Tillavadugu and villages.
180	"	"	"	Mr. V. Arunachala Mudaliar.	do	do	do	do
181	"	"	"	Mr. Omaar Khan Saheb.	Mussulman.	do	Villupuram.	Public meeting, 23rd Dec., about 1,000 Mahomedans
182	"	"	"	Mr. V. Kuppusami Aiyar.	Hindu Brahman.	do	Tindivanam.	By the Ryots.
183	"	"	"	Mr. Subramanya Aiyar.	do	Vakil.	Vridhachalm.	do
184	"	"	Tanjore.	Rai Bahadur S. A. Saminada Iyer.	do	Public Prosecutor, Memb., Dist. Bd., Chairman, Tanjore Ml. Council; Presdt. People's Assn.	Tanjore People's Assn.	At a general meeting of the Assn. on the 4th Dec.

LIST OF DELEGATES

Number.	Presidency.	Province.	District.	Name in full, with Honorary Titles, Scholastic Degrees, &c.	Religious denomination and caste, if any.	Occupation, Address, &c.	Place or Places or Association, &c., which they represent.	How and when elected.
185	Madras.	Carnatic	Tanjore	Mr. Krishnasami Aiyar, B.A.	Hindu Brahman.	Head Master Town High School, Kumbakonam.	Tanjore People's Assn.	At a Genl. meeting of the Assn. on the 4th Dec.
186	"	"	"	Mr. K. R. Kodandarama Aiyar.	do	Mirasidar, & 2nd Gd. Pleader, Tiruvalur.	R. Room, and Vic. Jubilee Library.	Public meeting Dec.
187	"	"	"	Mr. R. Ramasami Pillai.	Hindu.	Mirasidar and Tamil Pandit.	Tanjore R. P. Assn.	do
188	"	"	"	Mr. T. V. Kuppusami Sastri, B.A.	Hindu Brahman.	Prof. of Mathematics, St. Joseph's College, Cuddalore.	Jubilee R. Room, Tiruvadi.	Members of the R Room, 17th Dec.
189	"	"	"	Mr. T. Rajagopala Aiyangar, M.A.	do	Hd. Master, Ml. High School.	Mayaveram.	Public meeting, 16th Dec.
190	"	"	"	Rai Bahadur T. A. Alaga Pillai.	Hindu.	L. holder and Chairman, Ml. Council.	do	do
191	"	"	"	Mr. Ibrahim Sahib Ravuther.	Mussulman.	Mirasidar and Village Magte., Kornad.	do	do
192	"	"	"	Mr. A. V. Subramanya Aiyar.	Hindu Brahman.	Mirasidar.	do	do
193	"	"	"	Mr. N. Rajappier.	do	Pleader and Secy., R. Room, Tiruvadamarudur.	do	do
194	"	"	"	Mr. K. Lakshmana Aiyar.	do	1st Grade Pleader, Mayaveram.	Mayaveram, & Dharmapuram.	Sent as delegates by the Dharmapuram Mutt.
195	"	"	"	Mr. Sankaralinga Tambiran.	Hindu.	Kharbar, Dharmapuram Mutt.	Dharmapuram.	Sent as delegates by the Dharmapuram Mutt.
196	"	"	"	Khan Saheb Chinna Marickayar Malumiyar.	Mussulman.	Mercht. Trustee of Nagore Thurga, and Ml. Cr.	Nagore, & Negapatam.	General meeting of the Tanjore People's Assn. 4th Dec., and by the Mahomedan Community, Nagore.
197	"	"	"	Khan Saheb Meera Chinnatambi Marickayar.	do	Merchant and Ml. Cr.	do	do
198	"	"	"	Khan Sahib Janunlabudin Mya.	do	Mercht. and Hony. Magte, Ml. Cr., Thurga Trustees.	do	do
199	"	"	"	Rai Bahadur S. Ratnasabapati Pillai, B.A.	Hindu.	Mirasidar, 1st Grade Pleader, and Ml. Chairman, Negapatam	do	do
200	"	"	"	Mr. K. Mohammed Imam Marickayar.	Mussulman.	Mercht. Street, Nagore	do	do
201	"	"	"	Mr. Meera Meani Marcikayar.	do	Merchant, Hony. Magte., Ship Captain, and Secy., Anjuman Islam.	do	do
202	"	"	"	Mr. Vapakundoo Marcikayar.	do	Mercht. & Mirasidar.	Negapatam.	General meeting at Negapatam, on the 18th Dec.
203	"	"	"	Mr. Meera Lebey Malumiyar.	do	Mirasidar, Honorary, Magte., Mercht., & Ship Captain.	do	do
204	"	"	"	Mr. T. K. Annasami Aiyar.	Hindu Brahman.	1st Grade Pleader.	do	do
205	"	"	"	Mr. Krishnasami Aiyar.	do	Shopkeeper.	Mercht. Assn., Negapatam.	do

LIST OF DELEGATES.

Number.	Presidency.	Province.	District.	Name in full, with Honorary Titles, Scholastic Degrees, &c.	Religious denomination and caste, if any.	Occupation, Address, &c.	Place or Places or Association, &c., which they represent.	How and when elected.
206	Madras.	Carnatic	Tanjore.	Mr. Natukkotai Ramanathan Chettiar.	Hindu.	Merchant.	Merchant Assn., Negapatam.	General meeting at Negapatam, on the 18th Dec.
207	"	"	"	Mr. M. Andapillai Chettiar.	do	Merchant & Mirasidar	do	
208	"	"	"	Mr. Kalifa Syed Meer Mahomed Sahib.	Mussulman.	Durga Kalifa.	Nagore.	do
209	"	"	"	Rao Saheb Nilamega Aiyangar.	Hindu Brahman.	Mirasidar, & Ml. Cr.	Mannargudi.	At a public meeting, 12th Dec.
210	"	"	"	Mr. K. Ramachandra Rao, B.A.		Head Master, Native School, Secy. R. Room.	do	do
211	"	"	"	Mr. S. V. Naganatha Sastri, B.A.	do	Teacher, Town High School, Kumbakonam and Mirasidar.	M. J. S. Tiruvadamarudur.	Meeting of the 11th Dec.
212	"	"	"	Rao Saheb T. M. Mookkanasari.	Hindu.	Iron Mercht. & Ml. Cr.	Artisan Assn., & Kumbakonam.	The Artisans of the Tanjore Dist., 12th Dec.
213	"	"	"	Mr. S. V. Iyasamy Pathar	do	Artisan & Merchant.	do	do
214	"	"	"	Mr. N. Vythilinga Pathar.	do	do	do	do
215	"	"	"	Mr. S. Appu Sastri, B.A.	Hindu Brahman.	Manager & Propr., and Hd. Master, Native High School.	Kumbakonam Club and Sawmimalai, and 30 Villages.	By the Club, 13th Dec., and by the Vidyananda Sabha, Kumbakonam.
216	"	"	"	Mr. V. Nilamega Chariar.	do	Editor *Kudandai Mitran*, Kumbakonam.	Kottayur Sabha.	By the Vidyananda Sabha.
217	"	"	"	Mr. Venkatasami Rowth.	Hindu.	Merchant.	Kumbakonam.	By the Viswa Brahma Panchananattar Sabha, 15th Dec.
218	"	"	"	Rao Saheb T. S. Sivaswami Odayar.	do	Mirasidar.	do	Public meeting, 27th Nov.
219	"	"	"	Rao Saheb A. L. Tiruvengadam Pillai.	do	do	do	do
220	"	"	"	Rao Saheb V. Krishna Aiyar, B.A., B.L.	Hindu Brahman.	Pleader, H. C., Kumbakonam.	do	do
221	"	"	"	Mr. T. A. Sivaramakrishna Sastri, B.A.	do	1st Grade Pleader, Kumbakonam.	The Mutt.	Sent by His Holiness Sri Sankarachariar Swami to represent the Mutt at Kumbakonam, 23rd Dec.
222	"	"	Trichinopoly.	Mr. B. S. Venkataramana Sarma, B.A.	do	Teacher, Native High School.	Trichinopoly Town.	Public meeting, 15th Dec.
223	"	"	"	Srimath S. V. Gurusami Sarma.	do	Secy., Siva Samaj, Trichy. and Teacher Native High School, Satyamangalam.	do	do
224	"	"	"	Mr. Ulagappa Pillai.	Hindu.	Mirasidar, and Propr., *Southern Star* Press.	do	do
225	"	"	"	Rao Saheb B. Nilakanta Aiyar.	Hindu Brahman.	1st Gd. Pleader, and Vice-President, Tal. Bd., Kulitalai.	Trichy. and Kulitalai Public.	Public meetings at Trichy. and Kulitalai, on the 29th Dec.
226	"	"	"	Rao Saheb S. Krishnamachariar, B.A.	do	Govt. Pleader, Dist. Court, Memb. Dist. Bd., and Ml. Cr.	Srirangam	Public meeting, 29th Dec.
227	"	"	"	Khan Sahib Mahomed Sirajuddin.	Mussulman.	Vakil and Ml. Cr.	Trichinopoly.	do

LIST OF DELEGATES.

Number.	Presidency.	Province.	District.	Name in full, with Honorary Titles, Scholastic Degrees, &c.	Religious denomination and caste, if any.	Occupation, Address, &c.	Place or Places or Association, &c., which they represent.	How and when elected.
228	Madras.	Carnatic	Trichinopoly.	Mr. S. Lakshminarasiah Nayudu, B.A.	Hindu.	Prof., S. P. G. College Trichinopoly.	Trichinopoly.	Public meeting, 29th Dec.
229	"	"	"	Rao Saheb Srimantha Prasanna Ragoonatha Dorai.	do	L. holder and Vice-President, R. Room.	Ariyalur.	Public meeting, Ariyalur
230	"	"	"	Mr. J. N. Ramachandra Nayudu.	do	Mirasidar and Presdt. S. J. S. Paripalana Sabha.	Tiruvanakoil.	Meeting of Mirasidars of the place and six adjacent villages on the 15th December.
231	"	"	"	Mr. K. H. Vasudeva Row	Hindu Brahman.	Secy. S. J. S. Sabha, and Mirasidar, Kondiempetta.	do	do
232	"	"	"	Rao Saheb S. Subramanya Sastri, B.A.	do	Prof., S. P. G. College, Trichy., and Ml. Cr.	R. Room	Meeting, 21st December.
233	"	"	"	Mr. N. M. Raghava Aiyangar.	do	1st Gd. Pleader, and Secy. Patriotic Assn. Srirangam.	The Assn., Srirangam Tiruvanakoil and Kondiempetta.	Public meeting, 18th Dec.
234	"	"	"	Mr. S. S. Anantaratnam Aiyar.	do	Mirasidar, Manatatti.	do	do
235	"	South'rn Dist.	Madura.	Rao Saheb R. Ramasubha Aiyar, B.A., B.L.	do	Vakil, H. C. Madura, Presdt. of the Madura Un. Club, Ml. Cr. and Memb. Dist. Bd.	Madura Union Club.	Public meeting, 27th Nov.
236	"	"	"	Rao Saheb G. Subbarayulu Nayudu.	Hindu.	Municipal Councillor.	Madura City.	Public meeting, 23rd Dec.
237	"	"	"	Mr. T. M. Nallasami Pillai, B.A., B.L.	do	High Court Vakil, Madura.	do	do
238	"	"	"	Rao Saheb V. Alagirisami Nayudu.	do	Memb. Dist. & L. Bds., Memb. Devastanam Committee, & Agent to Shivaganga Zemindar.	do	do
239	"	"	"	Mr. P. Narayana Aiyar, B.A., B.L.	Hindu Brahman.	Pleader, High Court, Madura.	Do. & Peramakudi.	Do. and at a Public meeting of Peramakudi.
240	"	"	"	Rao Saheb S. M. Sundaram Aiyar, B.A.	do	L. Propr. and Propr. *Madura Mail* (Eng Weekly, Cir. 250), & Ml. Cr.	do	do
241	"	"	"	Rao Saheb Sri Seshadri Aiyangar.	do	L. Propr. and Memb. Dist. Bd., Madura.	do	do
242	"	"	"	Rao Saheb Geo. Sidney Hickey.	Protestant-Eurasian.	Pleader, Hony. Magte. and Ml. Cr.	Dindigul.	Public meeting, 11th Dec.
243	"	"	"	Mr. A. Atmanatha Aiyar.	Hindu Brahman.	Pleader, Dindigul.	S. J. S., Dindigul.	Do. and surrounding villages, 11th Dec.
244	"	"	"	Mr. K. Annasami Aiyar.	do	Pleader, Shivaganga.	The people of Shivaganga Zemindari.	Public meeting, Dec.
245	"	"	Tinnevelly	Khan Saheb, Mahomed Azimuddin Sahib.	Mussulman.	Pleader, Ml. Cr. and Memb. Tal. Bd.	Tinnevelly.	Public meeting on the 12th Dec.
246	"	"	"	Mr. Peter Paul Pillai.	Protestant Christian (Vellala).	Hd. Master and Manager, C. M. S. School, Srivalliputtur, and Hony. Magte.	S. J. S. and Tinnevelly	Meeting, 16th Dec.
247	"	"	"	Rao Saheb T. Muthier.	Hindu Brahman.	L. Holder, Ml. Cr. and Mercht., Tinnevelly.	Tinnevelly District.	At a Public meeting held 12th Dec.

LIST OF DELEGATES.

Number.	Presidency.	Province.	District.	Name in full, with Honorary Titles, Scholastic Degrees, &c.	Religious denomination and, caste, if any.	Occupation, Address, &c.	Place or Places or Association, &c., which they represent.	How and when elected.
248	Madras.	Southern Dist.	Tinnevelly	Rao Saheb S. Appasami Pillai.	Native Christian (Vellala).	L. Holder, Vakil, Dt. Court and Ml. Cr., Palamcotta.	Tinnevelly District.	At a public meeting, held 12th Dec.
249	"	"	"	Rao Saheb M. R. Ramakrishna Aiyar, B.A., B.L.	Hindu Brahman.	L. Holder, Vakil H.C., Tinnevelly, Memb. Dist. Bd. & Memb. of the Siva Devestanam Committee.	do	do
250	"	"	"	Khan Saheb Mohamed Aji Moidin Sahib.	Mussulman.	L Holder and Ml.Cr., Tinnevelly.	do	do
251	"	"	"	Khan Saheb V. M. Mahomed Kanni Rowthar.	do	L. Holder, Merchant, Memb. Tal. Bd.	Tuticorin Town.	At a public meeting, held in Tuticorin.
252	"	"	"	Mr. N. Padmanabha Aiyar.	Hindu Brahman.	L. Holder, Kalakad village.	Kalakad village.	By the ryots, on the 18th Dec.
253	"	Ceded Districts	Cuddapah.	Rai Bahadur C. Jambulinga Mudaliar, B.A., M.L.	Hindu.	H. C. Vakil, Vice-Presdt. Dist. Bd., Ml. Cr. and Secy. Literary Assn.	Kaddapah Town and Lit. Assn.	Public meeting, Oct., and General meeting.
254	"	"	"	Mr. Venkatasubba Rao.	Hindu Brahman.	Land-holder.	M. J. S. Piler.	At a meeting of the Sabha, 23rd Oct.
255	"	"	"	Mr. Padiki Bara Sahib.	Mussulman.	Agent to Messrs. A. Sabhapati Mudlr & Co., Cotton Agent.	Prodattur.	At a meeting of the Prodattur public, 19th Dec.
256	"	"	"	Mr. Y. Nagiah Garu.	Hindu Brahman.	Pleader.	do	do
257	"	"	"	Mr. T. Narayana Sastri.	do	1st Grade Pleader.	Madanapalli.	At a public meeting, 27th Nov.
258	"	"	Kurnul.	Mr. Hussain Baig.	Mussulman.	Merchant.	Kurnul.	Public meeting, 27th Nov.
259	"	"	"	Mr. Hussain Khan.	do	do	do	do
260	"	"	"	Mirza Hussain Baig.	do	Contractor.	do	do
261	"	"	"	Rao Saheb Subbannah Chettiar.	Hindu.	Banker, Memb. Dist. Bd. and Ml. Cr.	do	do
262	"	"	"	Rao Saheb C. Ramasingh.	do	Contr., Memb. Dist. Bd. and Ml. Cr.	do	do
263	"	"	"	Rao Saheb T. Chidambara Rao, B.A.	Hindu Brahman.	1st Gd. Pleader and Ml. Cr. and Joint Secy. Hindu and Mahomedan Assns.	do	do
264	"	"	"	Mr. Divopaud Syad Sahib.	Mussulman.	Land-holder.	do	do
265	"	"	"	Rao Saheb V. Sunkireddi Garu.	Hindu.	Do, and Memb. Dist. Bd.	do	do
266	"	"	"	Mr. U. Sanjeeva Reddi Garu.	do	Memb. Dist. Bd.	Gudur.	Public meeting, 1st Dec.
267	"	"	"	Mr. S. Pulla Reddi Garu.	do	do	do	do
268	"	"	"	Mr. Khadir Khan.	Mussulman.	do	do	do
269	"	"	"	Mr. M. Balanna Nayudu.	Hindu.	Memb. Dist. Bd. and Abkari Contr.	Nandyal.	Public meeting, 19th Dec.
270	"	"	"	Mr. Khasim Miah Sahib.	Mussulman.	Do, and Hd. Master Mahomedan School.	do	do
271	"	"	"	Mr. C. Vijiya Raghavachariar.	Hindu Brahman.	Pleader.	do	do

LIST OF DELEGATES.

Number.	Presidency.	Province.	District.	Name in full, with Honorary Titles, Scholastic Degrees, &c.	Religious denomination and caste, if any.	Occupation, Address, &c.	Place or Places or Association, &c., which they represent.	How and when elected.
272	Madras	Ceded Districts	Bellary.	Rai Bahadur A. Sabapathy Mudaliar.	Hindu.	Chairman, Municipality, & Merchant.	Bellary Town.	At a public meeting, 19th Dec.
273	"	"	"	Rao Saheb K. Venkata Rao.	do	Merchant.	do	do
274	"	"	"	Mr. S. Venkobachariar, B.A.	Hindu Brahman.	Hd. Master, Wardlaw Institution.	do	do
275	"	"	"	Khan Saheb Ibrahim Sait.	Mussulman.	Hony. Magte., Ml. Cr. and Merchant.	do	do
276	"	"	"	Khan Saheb Anugundi Kadir Batcha Saheb.	do	Merchant.	do	do
277	"	"	"	Rao Saheb G. Kristappah.	Hindu.	do	do	do
278	"	"	"	Rao Saheb S. Nilakantappah.	do	do	do	do
279	"	"	"	Mr. P. Baliah.	do	do	do	do
280	"	"	"	Mr. S. Seenappah.	do	do	do	do
281	"	"	"	Mr. G. Chikka Veerappah.	do	do	do	do
282	"	"	"	Mr. A. Veerabadrappah.	do	do	do	do
283	"	"	"	Mr. T. Humpappaya.	do	do	do	do
284	"	"	"	Rao Saheb C. Hanumantha Goud Garu.	Hindu Brahman.	Mirasidar, Memb. Dis. Bd., Hony. Magte.	Agricul. Assn., Hospet.	Meeting of the Assn., Dec.
285	"	"	"	Mr. S. Dade Sahib.	Mussulman.	Merchant.	People's Assn.	Pub. meetg. 18th Dec. and at a meetg. on 19th Dec.
286	"	"	"	Rao Saheb S. Marisiddappah.	Hindu.	Do and Ml. Cr.	do	do
287	"	"	"	Mr. D. Krishnamacharlu.	Hindu Brahman.	1st Gd. Pleader.	S.V. Sabha Bellary.	Meeting of the Sabha 16th and also at a Pub. meetg. on the 19th Dec.
288	"	"	"	Mr. G. Lakshman Rao.	do	School Master, L. F. M. School.	do	do.
289	"	"	Anantapur	Khan Bahadur Abbas Ali Sahib.	Mussulman.	Mercht. & Memb. Tal. Bd., Gooty.	Gooty, People's Assn.	By the People's Assn. 16th Nov., and at a Public meeting.
290	"	"	"	Rao Saheb P. Kesava Pillai.	Hindu.	Pleader and Memb. Dist. Bd.	do	do
291	"	"	"	Mr. J. Venkatamara Chetti.	do	Mercht., and Memb. Gooty Union.	do	do
292	"	"	"	Rao Saheb J. Srinivasai Rao.	Hindu Brahman.	Presdt. People's Assn. and Vice-Presdt. Tal. Bd.	do	do
293	"	"	"	Mr. V. R. Chakravarti Aiyangar.	do	Pleader, Penukonda.	Penukonda Taluq.	By the ryots of Bukkapatam, and 40 Villages.
294	"	"	"	Mr. P. Sadasiva Reddi Garu.	Hindu.	Reddi of Pandurti.	do	do
295	"	"	"	Mr. A. Ollappah.	do	Ryot.	20 Villages adjoining Buchakarapalli.	By the ryots.
296	"	"	"	Mr. T. Sitaramappah.	do	do	do	do
297	"	Inland Dists.	Coimbatore.	Mr. Khaja Mohamed Sahib.	Mussulman.	Zemindar.	Gobichettipalayam.	Public meeting, 14th Dec.

LIST OF DELEGATES.

Number.	Presidency.	Province.	District.	Name in full, with Honorary Titles, Scholastic Degrees, &c.	Religious denomination and caste, if any.	Occupation, Address, &c.	Place or Places or Association, &c., which they represent.	How and when elected.
298	Madras	Inland Districts	Coimbatore.	Mr. Syed Abdul Razack Sahib.	Mussulman.	Zemindar.	Satyamangalam	Public meeting, 21st Dec.
299	„	„	„	Rao Saheb S. P. Narasimhulu Nayudu Garu.	Hindu.	Editor, *The Crescent*, Hony. Magte. and Memb. Dist. Bd.	Coimbatore and S. D. R. Sabha.	Public meeting, 7th Dec.
300	„	„	„	Rao Saheb B. Bujanga Rao.	Hindu Brahman.	Asst. Master, Coimb. College; Memb. Dist. Bd.; Director, Mercantile Bank.	Coimbatore.	do
301	„	„	„	Mr. Sheik Mohamed Marickayar.	Mussulman.	Merchant.	do	do
302	„	„	„	Mr. N. Rangiah Gownder.	Hindu.	Manager, *Kalanidhi* Newspaper.	do	do
303	„	„	„	Mr. R. Subbrayar.	Hindu Brahman.	Pleader and Landed Proprietor.	M. J. S. Satyamangalam.	Public meeting, 22nd Dec.
304	„	„	„	Rao Saheb S. Rangiah Nayudu.	Hindu.	Member, Tal. Bd.	Coimbatore and Satyamangalam Taluq.	do
305	„	„	„	Rai Bahadur T. Padmanabha Aiyar.	Hindu Brahman.	Pleader & Chairman Karur Municipality.	Karur.	At a public meeting 22nd Dec.
306	„	„	„	Mr. K. Lakshmana Chetti.	Hindu.	Merchant.	do	do
307	„	„	„	Mr. T. R. Ramachandra Aiyar.	Hindu Brahman.	1st Grade Pleader.	do	do
308	„	„	„	Mr. D. Alagirisami Nayudu.	Hindu.	Merchant and Mirasidar.	Dharapuram.	At a public meeting, 14th Dec.
309	„	„	„	Mr. Kandappah Chetti.	do	do	do	do
310	„	„	„	Mr. Syed Murtooza Sahib.	Mussulman.	do	do	do
311	„	„	„	Mr. Kanyur Yegya Aiyar.	Hindu Brahman.	Mirasidar.	Komaralingham & 4 other Villages.	Meeting of the ryots, 6th Dec.
312	„	„	„	Mr. C. S. Siviramakrishna Sarma, B.A.	do	Landed Proprietor.	Udumalapet.	do
313	„	„	„	Mr. K. Narayana Sastri, B.A.	do	do	do	do
314	„	„	„	Mr. C. A. Subbrama Aiyar.	do	do	do	do
315	„	„	„	Mr. S. Kuppusami Sarma, B.A.	do	Teacher, Native High School.	Erode.	Public meeting, 27th Nov.
316	„	„	„	Mr. M. Venkatasami Aiyar.	do	Hd. Master, Hindu School.	do	do
317	„	„	„	Mr. V. Dasappiah.	do	Mirasidar.	do	do
318	„	„	„	Mr. C. V. Seshagiri Aiyar.	do	do	Darapuram Taluq.	Public meeting, 19th Dec.
319	„	„	Salem.	S. Krishnaswami Mudaliar	Hindu.	Zemindar and Hony. Magistrate.	Salem.	Public meeting, 16th Dec.
320	„	„	„	Rao Saheb C. Dharmalinga Chettiar.	do	Mercht. and Hony. Magte., Memb. Tal. Bd. and Ml. Cr.	do	do

LIST OF DELEGATES.

Number.	Presidency.	Province.	District.	Name in full, with Honorary Titles, Scholastic Degrees, &c.	Religious denomination and caste, if any.	Occupation, Address, &c.	Place or Places or Association, &c., which they represent.	How and when elected.
321	Madras	Inland Districts	Salem	Mr. C. Vijiyaraghava Chariar, B.A.	Hindu Brahman.	Vakil.	Salem.	Public meeting, 16th Dec.
322	"	"		Mr. Krishna Doss Sait.	Hindu.	Banker.	do	do
323	"	"		Rao Saheb M. Venkatachalapati Aiyar.	Hindu Brahman.	Merchant and Ml. Cr	do	do
324	"	"	"	Rao Saheb P. T. Subramania Aiyar, B.A., B.L.	do	Member, Tal. Bd.	do	do
325	"	"	"	Rao Saheb P. Narasinga Rao.	do	Shrotriem Pensioner, and Ml. Cr.	do	do
326	"	"	"	Rao Saheb T. Krishna Chettiar.	Hindu.	Merchant and Ml. Cr.	do	do
327	"	"	"	Rao Saheb Ponnusami Chettiar.	do	do	do	do
328	"	"	"	Mr. V. Vythi Aiyar.	Hindu Brahman.	Public Prosecutor	do	do
329	"	"	"	Rao Saheb M. Virasami Aiyar.	do	Pleader and Ml. Cr.	do	do
330	"	"	"	Mr. D. A. Balakrishna Aiyar.	do	Pleader.	do	do
331	"	"	"	Khan Saheb Sheik Moideen Sahib.	Mussulman.	Mercht., Ml.Cr., Member Dist. Bd., Hony. Magte., Presdt. of Anjuman-Islam, & Proprietor *Salem Patriotic Press.*	do	do
332	"	"	"	Mr. Syed Abdul Latiff Sahib.	do	Pleader and Under-Secy., Anjuman-Islam.	do	do
333	"	"	"	Saokar Adam Sahib.	do	Merchant.	do	do
334	"	".	"	Mr. Ameenudin Sahib.	do	do	do	do
335	"	"	"	Mr. S. Sundaram Chettiar.	Hindu.	do	do	do
336	"	"	"	Revd. Muttu.	Christian.	London Mission.	do	do
337	"	"	"	Mr. Chinna Babu Reddiar.	Hindu.	Zemindar, Pottanam.	do	do
338	"	"	"	Mr. Ramaswami Chettiar.	do	Zemindar, Sendamangalam.	do	do
339	"	"	Namakal.	Mr. T. Subbrama Aiyar.	Hindu Brahman.	Pleader.	Namakal.	Public meeting, 1st Dec.
340	"	"	"	Mr. Venkatarama Reddiar.	Hindu.	Zemindar of Eruma-Patti.	do	do
341	"	"	"	Rao Saheb Y. Seshachalam Aiyar.	Hindu Brahman.	Memb., Tal. Bd.	Trichengode.	do
342	"	Western Coast.	Malabar.	Mr. T. Manavikraman.	Hindu.	Zemindar, Elaya Tarumalpad of Nilambur.	Calicut.	At a public meeting at Calicut, 4th Dec.
343	"	"	"	Rao Saheb C. Kunhi Raman Menon, B.A.	do	Editor and Proprietor *Kerala Patrika*, and Ml. Cr.	do	Do and also by the people of Valavanand, at a meeting, 10th Dec.
344	"	"	"	Jehangier D. Mugasett.	Parsi.	Merchant, Messrs. D. Maneckjee & Co.	do	do
345	"	"	"	Rao Saheb C. M. Raricban Muppan.	Hindu	Landed Proprietor and Ml. Cr.	do	do
346	"	"	"	Mr. P. A. Krishna Menon.	do	1st Grade Pleader.	do	do

LIST OF DELEGATES.

Number.	Presidency.	Province.	District.	Name in full, with Honorary Titles, Scholastic Degrees, &c.	Religious denomination and caste, if any.	Occupation, Address, &c.	Place or Places or Association, &c., which they represent.	How and when elected.
347	Madras.	Western Coast.	Malabar.	Mr. Ananta Narayana Pattar.	Hindu.	1st Grade Pleader.	Calicut.	At a pub. meetg. at Calicut and also by the people of Valavanad, at a meeting 10th Dec.
348	"	"	"	Mr. S. Varadaraja Aiyar.	Hindu Brahman.	do	do	do
349	"	"	"	Rao Saheb K. P. Achhutha Menon.	Hindu.	do	S. J. S., Palgahat.	At a meeting of the Sabha, Kerala Sabha, 12th Dec.
350	"	"	"	Mr. V. Vengu Aiyar.	Hindu Brahman.	do	do	do
351	"	"	"	Rao Sahib P. S. Chinnasami Pillai.	Hindu.	Landed Proprietor.	Palghat.	By the townsmen and representative of the Tamil community, 21st Dec.
352	"	"	"	Pandit Parameswara Aiyar.	Hindu Brahman.	Pleader, Dist. Court S. Canara.	Mangalore Union.	At a general meeting, 21st Dec.
353	"	"	"	Mr. T. C. Narayana Kurup, B.A., B.L.	Hindu.	High Court Vakil, Tellicheri.	U. K. Sabha.	At a meeting of the Uttara Kerala, 27th Nov.
354	"	"	"	Mr. J. L. D'Rozario, B.A., B.L.	Christian Eurasian.	do	do	do
355	"	"	"	Mr. V. Ryru Nambiar.	Hindu.	1st Grade Pleader.	do	do
356	"	"	"	Mir Jaffer Ali Sahib.	Mussulman.	Mercht. and Landed-Proprietor.	do	do
357	"	Mysore.	Bangalore (C. and M. Cantonment.)	Rai Bahadur B. Krishna Singh.	Hindu.	Municipal Chairman.	R. P. Assn. and Mahomedan Assn.	Meetings of the Assn., 24th Nov.
358	"	"	Mysore.	Rao Saheb V. Raghava Chariar.	Hindu Brahman.	Advocate, Ml. Cr., Jaghirdar, & Memb. Mysore Representative Assembly.	R. P. Assn. (104), & the citizens of Mysore.	Public meeting.
359	"	"	Chittaldrug.	Mr. Venkataramiah.	do	Pleader.	Chittaldrug.	Public meeting.
360	"	"	"	Mr. Kadappa.	Hindu.	Banker.	do	do
361	"	Deccan.	Secundrabad (British Cantonment.)	Mr. Hajee Sajan Lal.	Mussulman.	Merchant.	The community of Hindus, Mahomedans, Parsis, and Mahboob College.	At a general meeting by votes, Dec.
362	Bombay.	Konkan.	Bombay.	Mr. Budrudin Tyabji.	Mussulman.	Barrister-at-Law, High Court and late Member, Legislative Council.	Bombay, Anjuman, Bombay.	At a general meeting of the Anjuman, President of the Third National Congress.
363	"	"	"	Mr. Veerachand Raghavjee, B.A.	Jain.	Hony. Secy. to The Jain Assn. of India, Articled Clerk to the Govt. Solicitor.	The Jain Assn. India, Bombay.	By the Jain Assn. 15th Dec.
364	"	"	"	Mr. Dayabhai Jaduram.	Hindu.	Solicitor, High Court.	Bombay.	By the Bombay Presidency Association.
365	"	"	"	Mr. V. Atmarama.	do	Merchant.	do	do
366	"	"	"	Mr. V. Purushottamdas.	do	do	do	do
367	"	"	"	Mr. Mathuradas Lilladar.	do	Mill-owner.	do	do
368	"	"	"	Mr. Dharmshjee Sunderdas.	do	do	do	do

LIST OF DELEGATES.

Number.	Presidency.	Province.	District.	Name in full, with Honorary Titles, Scholastic Degrees, &c.	Religious denomination and caste, if any.	Occupation, Address, &c.	Place or Places or Association, &c., which they represent.	How and when elected.
369	Bombay.	Konkan.	Bombay.	Mr. J. A. Wadia.	Parsi.	Mill-owner.	Bombay.	By the B. P. Assn.
370	"	"	"	Mr. Chinnilal Lallubhai Parekh.	Hindu.	Mercht. & Vice-Presdt, Arya Vardhak Gnyan Sabha.	Arya Vardhak Sabha and Samaj Bombay.	By 1st Sabha public meeting, 15th Nov. and the 2nd Sabha public meeting, 18th Dec.
371	"	"	"	Mr. Daji Abaji Khare, B.A., LL.B.	Hindu Brahman.	Pleader, High Court, Bombay & Proprietor *Native Opinion*, of Bombay.	(1) S. J. S. Nasik. (2) Ratnagiri, Ijatpuri. (3) Bombay Pres. Assn.	At public meetings of all the places stated.
372	"	"	"	Mr. Narayen Ganesh Chandravarkar, B.A., LL.B.	Shenawi.	Vakil, H. C. Bombay & Editor *Indu Prakash.*	Bombay.	Bombay Presidency Assn.
373	"	"	"	Dr. Sadashiva Waman Kane, L.M.S.	Hindu Brahman.	Medical Practr., Thakurdwar, Bombay.	do	do
374	"	"	"	Mr. Kashinath Trimbuck Khare.	do	Merchant.	do	Unanimously, by all the Anglo-Vernacular papers of Bombay, 21st Dec.
375	"	"	"	Mr. Kalidas Sankal Chand	Jain.	Editor and Proprietor, *Rajya Bakta* (Guzerati Bi-weekly cir. 500), and *Akmedabad Times* (Guzerati Weekly, cir. 400).	do	do
376	"	"	"	Shamrao M. Rele.	do	High Court Pleader.	do	By the Presidency Assn.
377	"	"	Thana.	Mr. Vasudev Gopal Chitale.	Hindu Brahman.	Muktiar Dahanu.	Bassein Prant Association.	Public meeting, 11th Dec.
378	"	"	"	Mr. Laxman B. Joglekar.	do	Pleader, Thana.	do	do
379	"	"	"	Rao Saheb G. K. Vartak.	do	Pleader, Bassein.	do	do
380	"	Deccan.	Ratnagiri.	Rao Saheb Laxman Dhonddeo Katre.	do	Pleader, Dist. Court.	Ratnagari Dist. Assn.	Public meeting, 18th Nov.
381	"	"	"	Rao Saheb Y. N. Adarkar.	do	Vakil, Vengurla, and Ml. Cr.	Local Sabha.	do
382	"	"	Nasik.	Mr. R. Sadashiva Lele, B.A.	do	Money-leader.	S. J. S., Nasik.	Public meeting, 30th Oct.
383	"	"	"	Rao Saheb J. Raghunath Nimkar.	do	Vakil, Dist. Court and Ml. Cr.	S. J. S., and Nasik City.	do
384	"	"	" (Yeola Taluq).	Mr. P. Damodar Barve.	do	Sirdeshmukha Inamdar and L. Propr.	Local Assn.	Public meeting, 15th Dec.
385	"	"	"	Khan Saheb Soobharjee Kamal.	Mussulman.	Moulvi and Merchant.	do	do
386	"	"	"	Rao Saheb Abdus Sabhan.	do	Merchant.	Nasik.	do
387	"	"	Khandeish	Mr. V. Daji Mutte.	Hindu Brahman.	Mercht. and Banker.	Dhulia and Kandeish.	Public meeting, 1st Dec.
388	"	"	Ahmednagar.	Mr. Mohanlal Hiralal.	Hindu.	Vakil, Dist. Court, and Merchant.	Ahmednagar.	Public meeting.
389	"	"	"	Rao Saheb Haridas Damodarados.	do	Mercht and Ml. Cr.	do	do
390	"	"	Poona.	Rao Saheb Raghunath Daji Nagarkar.	do	Pleader, Ml. Cr., Memb. Sarvajanik Sabha.	Poona.	Public meeting, by Poona S. J. S., 18th Dec.

LIST OF DELEGATES.

Number.	Presidency.	Province.	District.	Name in full, with Honorary Titles, Scholastic Degrees, &c.	Religious denomination and caste, if any.	Occupation, Address, &c.	Place or Places or Association, &c., which they represent.	How and when elected.
391	Bombay	Deccan.	Poona.	Rao Saheb M. B. Nam Joshi.	Hindu.	Schoolmaster and Journalist, an elected Ml. Cr. representing a mercantile Ward of Poona.	Poona.	Public meeting, by Poona S. J. S. 18th Dec.
392	"	"	"	Mr. N. B. Kanitkar.	do	Pleader, Dist. Court.	do	do
393	"	"	"	Mr. V. L. Athawale.	do	Propr. Banking Estab.	do	do
394	"	"	"	Mr. GopālVināyak Joshee.	do		do	do
395	"	"	"	Mr. Ramchandra Ganesh Mundle, B.A., LL.B.	do	Pleader, High Court, Bombay.	Committee of Arbitration Court.	By the Committee, 22nd Dec.
396	"	"	"	Mr. V. B. Ranade.	do	Editor *Dnyan Chakshu* (Marathi weekly, cir. 1,500), and Editor of *Hindu Punch*.	Poona and Thana.	do
397	"	"	"	Mr. Naro Bhaskar Deodhar.	do	Late Asst. Deputy Inspector of School.	Poona Mercantile Assn.	By the Assn. 17th Dec.
398	"	"	Sholapur.	Rao Saheb Sakharam R. Kirloskar, B.A.	do	Pleader and Ml. Cr.	Sholapur & Madha.	Public meeting, 11th Dec.
399	"	"	"	Mr. M. R. Ranade.	do	Medical Practr.	Sholapur.	do
400	"	"	"	Mr. Kashinath V. Natu.	do	Money-lender.	do	do
401	"	"	"	Mr. P. L. Nagpurkar.	do	Pleader.	do	do
402	"	"	"	Rao Saheb Ganesh.	do	Jivaji Kelkar, Pleader, Dist. Court.	do	do
403	"	"	"	Mr. G. N. Kakde.	do	Editor and Propr. *Kalpataru* (Marathi weekly, cir. 225).	Sholapur.	do
404	"	"	"	Mr. Ramchandra Moreshwar Sane.	do	Editor *Dnyan Peshkash*, bi - weekly, A. V. Newspaper.	Do. & Praderpore.	General meeting, 22nd Dec.
405	"	"	"	Mr. Yeshwant Nagesh Ranade, B.A.	do	Editor *English Opinion on India*.	Panderpore.	Public meeting.
406	"	"	Satara.	Rao Bahadur Ganesh Pandurang Agte.	do	Inamdar, Vice-President, Tal. Bd., and Memb. Dist. Bd.; Hony. Magte.; Vice-Pres. S. J. S., Satara.	Satara.	Public meeting, 13th Nov.
407	"	"	"	Rao Saheb Govind Vishnu Ranade.	do	Pleader, Dist. Court, and Ml. Cr.	do	do
408	"	"	"	Rao Saheb Laxman Bulwant Mutalik.	do	Inamdar, Ml. Cr., Memb. Tal.&District Bds., Conciliator, & Hony. Magte.	do	do
409	"	"	"	Rao Saheb B. S. Sahasrabudhe.	do	Pleader, Ml. Cr., Secy. Sarvajanik Sabha.	Do and Karad.	Public meetings, 13th and 15th Nov.
410	"	"	"	Mr. Raghunath Pandurang Karandikar.	do	Vakil, H. C., Satara, and Secy., S. J. S.	do	do
411	"	"	"	Mr. Waman Anant Bhide.	Hindu Brahman.	Genl. Merchant.	Satara.	Council Assn. Satara, 12th Dec.
412	"	"	"	Mr. Ganapatdas Hirachand Devi.	Hindu Guzarati.	Contractor.	do	do
413	"	"	"	Mr. G. H. Gandhi.	Hindu Brahman.	Jeweller.	do	do

LIST OF DELEGATES.

Number.	Presidency.	Province.	District.	Name in full, with Honorary Titles, Scholastic Degrees, &c.	Religious denomination and caste, if any.	Occupation, Address, &c.	Place or Places or Association, &c., which they represent.	How and when elected.
414	Bombay	Deccan.	Satara.	Rao Saheb Govind Dhondev Limaye.	Hindu Brahman.	Vakil, Court Aste: Vice-Presdt., Municipality & Memb. L. Bd.	Satara.	Public meeting, 13th Nov.
415	„	Kanarese Division	Belgaum.	Mr. Syed Haider Saheb Valad Mohidin Sahib.	Mussulman.	Pirjade, Inamdar Sulgi.	Belgaum.	Public meeting, 10th Dec.
416	„	„	„	Mr. Syed Sattar Saheb Valad Mahomed Sahib	do	Pirjade, Inamdar, Honge.	do	Do. 16th Dec.
417	„	„	„	Mr. Mohamed Ibrahim Sahib Valad Hasan Mia Sahib Khatib.	do	Inamdar of Kamarhatte.	do	do
418	„	„	„	Rao Saheb Annajee Vaijanath Bhatkhande.	Hindu Brahman.	Pleader, Dist. Court.	do	Public meeting, 10th Dec.
419	„	„	„	Mr. V. R. Natu, B.A., LL.B.	do	do	do	Public meeting, 16th Dec.
420	„	„	„	Mr. M. Laxman Gadgil.	do	Do and Public Prosecutor.	do	do
421	„	„	„	Mr. B. Gangadhar Deshpande.	do	Do and L. Propr.	do	do
422	„	„	„	Mr. N. Vinayak Velankar.	do	do	do	do
423	„	„	„	Rao Bahadur Hoochrao Achut.	do	Do and Vice-Presdt. Municipality, and Hony. Mgte.	Do and Khanipur.	do and meeting Khanipur.
424	„	„	„	Rao Saheb Raojee Gangadhar Khote.	do	Do and Ml. Cr.	B. P. Assn. (Belgaum Branch) Kanipur.	do do
425	„	„	„	Mr. Anant Mangesh Bidikar.	do	Do and Secy. B. P. Assn.	Do and Nandgad.	do and meeting Nandgad.
426	„	„	„	Mr. D. Jeenappa Setti.	Jain.	Vakil, Dist. Court.	do	do do
427	„	„	„	Rao Saheb S. Balakrishna Bhate, F.S.A.	Hindu Brahman.	Do and Secy. B. P. Assn. and Ml. Cr.	Do. and B. P. Assn.	do and Pres. Assn.
428	„	„	„	Mr. V. Gopal Behere.	do	Pleader, Dist. Court.	do	do do
429	„	„	„	Rao Saheb R. Ganesh Manjraykar.	do	Merchant and Memb. Tal. Bd.	Do and (Chandagad) Merchants.	do and merchants meeting
430	„	„	„	Mr. Syed Gous Saheb Valad Makhteem Sahib.	Mussulman.	Mercht. and Contr.	Belgaum merchants.	do do
431	„	„	Dharwar.	Mr. A. Ramachandra Joglekar.	Hindu Brahman.	Editor *Dharwar Vrit* (Mahratti and Kanarese Weekly, cir. 800).	Dharwar.	Public meeting, 20th Nov.
432	„	„	„	Rao Saheb K. Hanmant.	Hindu.	Inamdar, Vice-Presdt. Dist. Bd., and Ml. Cr.	do	do
433	„	„	„	Rao Saheb A. V. Panendhikar.	do	Memb. Dist. and L. Bd. and Honorary Magistrate.	do	do
434	„	„	„	Mr. G. B. Phatak.	do	Pleader, Dist. Court.	do	do
435	„	„	Bijapur.	Khan Saheb Hajee Ibrahim Sahib.	Mussulman.	Jahagirdar and Muttuvale of Jiganibidri and Ml. Cr. & Memb. L. Bd.	Bijapur.	Public meeting, 12th Dec.
436	„	„	„	Mr. Hanumant Rao Raghavendra Hachehole.	Hindu.	Jahgirdar of Balkundi.	do	do
437	„	„	„	Mr. Shrinivas Krishna Kembhavikar.	do	Pleader and Landed Propr. Akalkot State.	do	do

LIST OF DELEGATES.

Number.	Presidency.	Province.	District.	Name in full, with Honorary Titles, Scholastic Degrees, &c.	Religious denomination and caste, if any.	Occupation, Address, &c.	Place or Places or Association, &c., which they represent.	How and when elected.
438	Bombay	Kanarese Dn.	Bijapur.	Rao Saheb Raghavendra Krishna.	Hindu.	Vakil, Dist. Court, Vice-Presdt. L. Bd.	Bijapur.	Public meeting, 12th Dec.
439	"	"	"	Mr. Seshagiri Rao Rayajee.	do	Pleader, Dist. Court.	do	do
440	"	"	"	Mr. Sitaram Hanmant Nimgaokar.	do	Editor *Ramdoss* (Marathi and Kanarese Weekly, cir. 400.)	do	do
441	"	N. Canara.	Karwar.	Khan Saheb Syed Jaffar Sahib Southagar.	Mussulman.	Merchant and Ml. Cr & Memb. L. F. Bd.	Sirsi Taluq	Public meeting (700 Mahomedans), Dec.
442	"	"	"	Rao Saheb Pundalek Narayan.	Hindu.	Vakil, and Vice-Presd. Ml. Cr. and Memb. K. F. Assn.	do	do
443	"	"	"	Rao Saheb Ananta Putya Nadig.	do	Mercht. and Memb. L. Bd. & Secy., K.F.A.	do	do
444	"	"	"	Mr. A. Venkappa Hegadi.	do	Merchant.	do	do
445	"	"	"	Mr. Venkabhat G. Karki.	do	do	do	do
446	"	Sindh.	Karachi.	Rao Saheb Seth Vishindas Nehalchand.	do	Zemindar and Ml. Cr.	Sindh Sabha, Karachi.	Public meeting, 23rd Nov.
447	"	"	"	Mr. Kesandas Jethmal.	do	Zemindar.	do	do
448	"	"	"	Rao Saheb L. N. Joshi.	Hindu Brahman.	Pensioner.	do	do
449	"	"	"	Dewan Pesumul Jawakiram Samith.	do	Vakil, Court, Shikarpur.	Shikarpur.	Public meeting, 16th Dec. and also by the Sindh Sabha.
450	"	"	"	Rao Saheb Govind Buksh Avatray.	do	do	do	Do. and also by the Sindh Sabha.
451	"	Gujarath.	Ahmedabad.	Prof. P. J. Patshaha.	Parsi.	Professor, Ahmedabad College.	Ahmedabad.	Public meetings, Dec.
452	"	"	Kaira.	Mr. R. B. Harilal Harashadrya Dhruva, B.A., LL.B.	Hindu.	H. C. Vakil & Ml. Cr.	Kaira.	do
453	"	"	Surat.	Mr. Ratiram Durgaram Dave, B.A.	Hindu Brahman.	Articled clerk to Messrs. P. Gilbert & Sayani, Solicitors.	Praja Hit Vardhak Sabha.	By the Sabha, Oct.
454	"	"	Broach.	Mr. Manchashanker Jivanaram, B.A., LL.B.	do	Vakil, High Court.	Broach.	Public meeting and also by the Prajah Vardhak Sabha, Surat.
455	"	Native States.	Sangli.	Rao Saheb Bulvantrao Sakharam Mone.	do	Pensioner.	Sangli.	By the Praja Vardhak Sabha, Surat.
456	"	"	Baroda.	Mr. Dinshaw Dadabhai.	Parsi.	Public Prosecutor.	Nawasari.	Public meeting, 11th Dec.
457	"	"	"	Mr. Mancherji Barjorji.	do	Zemindar, & Memb. Ml. Managing Com.	do	do
458	"	"	"	Mr. S. B. Hejib.	Hindu Brahman.	Vakil, Nawasari.	Do & "Gorakshaka Sabha."	do
459	"	"	"	Mr. Govind Babajee Joshi.	do	Public Lecturer, Baroda State.	Baroda.	Public meeting, 14th Dec.
460	"	"	"	Rao Saheb Gulabadass Bhaidass.	do	Pleader.	Do. & B. P. Assn.	do
461	"	"	Kolapur.	Mr. R. R. Shrigvonkar, B.A., LL.B.	do	do.	Kolapur.	Public meeting, 1st Oct.
462	Bengal.	Central Provs.	Nagpur.	Mr. K. G. Deshpande, M.A.	do	Prof. Morris College, Nagpur, & Mulguzar	Loka Sabha Nagpur.	Public meeting, 22nd Dec.

LIST OF DELEGATES.

Number.	Presidency.	Province.	District.	Name in full, with Honorary Titles, Scholastic Degrees, &c.	Religious denomination and caste, if any.	Occupation, Address, &c.	Place or Places or Association, &c., which they represent.	How and when elected.
463	Bengal.	Central Provs.	Nagpur.	Mr. S. Jairam, B.A.	Hindu Brahman.	Prof. Sanskrit, Hislop College, Nagpur.	Loka sabha Nagpore.	Public meeting, 22nd Dec.
464	"	"	"	Mr. S. Abdul Azeez.	Mussulman.	Pleader, Memb. L. Bd.	Nagpur.	do
465	"	"	Khandwa.	Babu Haridas Chattarjee, M.A., B.L.	Hindu.	Pleader and Ml. Cr.	Khandwa People's Assn., & Burhanpur.	do
466	"	"	Nimar.	Mr. K. Narayan Karwarkar	Hindu Brahman.	Landed Proprietor.	S. J. S., Burhampur.	By the Sabha, 1st Dec.
467	"	"	Raipur.	Mr. Taradas Bannerjee, B.A., B.L.	do	Pleader, Secy. Dist. Council.	Raipur.	By a general meeting, 23rd Oct.
468	"	"	"	Mr. Govind Prasad Dube.	do	Vakil.	do	do
469	"	"	Wardha.	Mr. W. Krishna Abhankar	do	Mulguzar.	Arvi Tahsil	Public meeting, Dec.
470	"	"	"	Mr. M. B. Kolasker.	do		Hinghan Ghaut.	Public meeting, 7th Dec.
471	"	"	"	Mr. L. G. Deuskar.	do	Pleader and Secy. N. G. Library, Arvi.	Wardha.	Public meeting, Arvi, 22nd Dec.
472	"	"	Jubbulpore.	Mr. Behari Lal, B.A.	Hindu Rajput.	1st Asst. C. M. H. School.	(1) Hit Sabha (2) Gorakshan Sabha (3) Arya Samaj (4) Arya K. N. Sabha.	Public meeting, 19th Dec.
473	"	Central India Agency.	Indore.	Mir Ali Mahomed Bhimjee	Mussulman.	Manager, Cotton Press, Indore City.	Central India Assn.	Public meeting, 22nd Dec.
474	"	"	Mhow.	Mr. Mohendranath Chatterjee.	Hindu.	Pleader, Hony. Secy. Central India Assn.	do	do
475	Bengal.	Panjab.	Lahore.	Brahmabadi Satyananda Agnihotri.	Deva Dharmi.	Deva Dharma Mission; Editor, *Dharma Jivan* (Urdu Weekly.)	Lahore & The Indian Assn.	Public meeting held under auspices of the Indian Assn., 28th Nov.
476	"	"	"	Pandit Gopinath.	Hindu Brahman.	Joint-Editor (1) *Akhbar-i-am* (Urdu Tri-Weekly, cir. 2,660). (2) *Mitra vilass* (Hindi Weekly, cir. 350). (3) *People's Journal* (English Weekly, cir 500).	do	do
477	"	"	"	Sirdar Uttam Singh.	Hindu.	Zemindar, Banker, Reis, and Political Pensioner of one of the Darbaris of H. E. The Viceroy.	Do & the Indian Association.	do
478	"	"	"	Lala Hukim Chand.	do	Pleader, Memb. Indian Assn. and of Anjuman, Panjab, & Propr. *Public Advocate Press.*	do	do
479	"	"	"	Mr. Syed Mahomed Shah.	Mussulman.	Pleader.	do	do

LIST OF DELEGATES.

Number.	Presidency.	Province.	District.	Name in full, with Honorary Titles, Scholastic Degrees, &c.	Religious denomination and caste, if any.	Occupation, Address, &c.	Place or Places or Association, &c., which they represent.	How and when elected.
480	Bengal.	Punjab.	Amballa.	Lala Murlidhur.	Hindu.	Pleader, President. Rifa-i-am Assn. and Hindu Sabha, Amballa.	Rifa-i-am Assn. & Hindu Sabha.	By the meetings of the Association and Sabha.
481	"	"	Bannu.	Lala Tansukh Rai.	do	Pleader.	Sukhdaik Sabha and Bannu.	By the Sabha on 19th Oct. People of Bannu, on the 27th Nov.
482	"	"	DeraIsmail Khan.	Mr. Malik Bhugwan Das.	Hindu.	Pleader and Presdt., Bhratre Sabha.	Bhratre Assn Sabha D. I. Khan.	Public meeting.
483	"	"	Kongra.	Mr. Bakshi Jamshi Ram.	do	Pleader, Vice-Presdt., Social Progressive Association.	Kangra & the Assn.	Public meeting, 13th Dec.
484	"	N.-W. P.	Allahabad.	Pandit Beni Madhava Bhattacharya.	Hindu Brahman.	Govt. Pensioner, Ml. Cr. & Hony. Magte., Allahabad.	Madhya Hindu Samaj and Allahabad.	Public meetings, 15th Dec.
485	"	"	"	H. H. Rajah Rampal Singh.	Hindu Kshatria.	Taluqdar Rampur.	Do and Hindu Samaj, Allahabad.	do
486	"	"	"	Pandit M. M. Malaviya, B.A.	Hindu Brahman.	Editor, *Hindustan* (a daily newspaper, cir. 250).	Allahabad Madhya Hindu Samaj.	Public meeting, 15th Dec.
487	"	"	"	Pandit Deokinandan Tivari.	do	Propr. *Pryag Samachar*, and Manager, Vidya Dharma Vardhini Sabha.	Vidya Dharma Vardhini Sabha.	Meeting of the Sabha, 20th Dec.
488	"	"	Ballia.	Munshi Devi Prasad.	Hindu Kayestha.	Pleader, Ml. Cr., Secy., Ballia Institute, Agent to H.H. the Maharajah of Domraon.	Ballia Inste. and Aryadesh opkarni Sabha.	Public meeting, 21st Dec.
489	"	"	Agra.	Mir Mirza Mahomed Ali.	Mussulman.	Vakil, High Court, N.-W. P., Agra.	Agra.	Public meeting Agra, Dec.
490	"	"	"	Mr. Shankar Dayal, B.A.	Hindu Kayestha.	do	do	do
491	"	"	"	Mr. Jumnadas Biswas.	do	Pleader and Editor, *Naseem Agra*, Urdu Weekly.	1. Agra. 2. Arya Samaj.	do
492	"	"	Mainpuri.	Choubay Damri Lal, B.A.	Hindu Brahman.	Vakil.	Mainpuri.	General meeting.
493	"	"	Benares.	Babu Ramakishen.	Hindu Kshatria.	Editor and Propr., *Bharat Jivan*, a Hindu Newspaper.	Benares.	Kashi Sarvajanik Sabha, Dec. General meeting.
494	"	"	"	Babu Bishesar Pande.	Hindu Brahman.	Hd. Master, Jainarain's College.	do	do
495	"	"	"	Babu Ram Kali Chaudhuri.	do	Hony. Magte. and Ml. Cr.	do	do
496	"	"	"	Babu Jogendranath Ghosh B.A.	Hindu Kayestha.	Pleader, Dist. Judge's Court.	do	do
497	"	"	Kumaon.	Pandit Jwala Dutta Joshi.	Hindu.	Vakil, High Court, Naini Tal.	Naini Tal & Almora.	Public meeting, Naini Tal, 5th Dec. and Almora 22nd Dec.
498	"	"	Mirzapur.	Babu Sri Ram.	Hindu Kshatria.	Zemindar, Ml. Cr. and Secy., Arya Samaj.	Mirzapur.	Public meeting, 11th Dec.
499	"	"	"	Munshi Bindheshari Prasada.	Hindu.	Pleader, L. Propr., Ml. Cr. & Memb. Dist. Bd.	do	do

LIST OF DELEGATES.

Number.	Presidency.	Province.	District.	Name in full, with Honorary Titles, Scholastic Degrees, &c.	Religious denomination and caste, if any.	Occupation, Address, &c.	Place or Places or Association, &c., which they represent.	How and when elected.
500	Bengal.	N.-W. P.	Meerut.	Babu Prathad Singh, B.A.	Hindu.	Vakil, High Court N.-W. P. Secy. Ind. Assn.	Meerut City and Deshorpaini Sabha, and Devanagri Sabha.	Meeting held 12th Dec.
501	„	„	„	Choudhuri Durga Singh.	do	Zemindar, Asosah Tahsil.	Hapur.	do
502	„	„	„	Lala Bhawani Prasad.	Hindu.	Banker.	do	do
503	„	„	Cawnpur.	Pandit Patrap Narayan Mishra.	Brahman.	Editor *Brahman*, Hindu monthly.	Inhabitants of Bownpur.	Public meeting held 21st Dec.
504	„	„	Alighur.	Syed Mahomed Maki.	Mussulman.	Zamindar, in Dt. Jaunpur.	Alighur Committee	Public meeting, 2nd Dec.
505	„	„	„	Babu Tota Ram Varma.	Hindu Kayestha.	Zemindar, Vakil, H. Court, Ml.Cr., Editor and Propr. *Bharat Bandhu* (Anglo-Hindu Weekly).	Alighur & Bharrat Varshiya National Assn.	do
506	„	„	„	Babu Ashutosh Bhatta Charya, B.A.	Hindu Brahman.	Pleader, Dist. Court.	do	do
507	„	„	„	Babu Kedernath Chatterjee, B.A.	do	do	do	do
508	„	„	„	Hafiz Mohamed Abdulrahim.	Mussulman.	do and Moulvie	Alighur.	do
509	„	„	Azamgarh.	Pandit Indira Datta Upadhyaya, M.A.	Hindu Brahman.	Zemindar and Asst. Hd. Master, C. M. S. High School.	Azimgarh.	Public meeting, 12th Dec.
510	„	„	„	Mr. Mahomed Hussain Ali, B.A.	Mussulman.	Zemindar, Ahmedpur Asna Pargana Ghosi.	do	do
511	„	„	Basti.	Mr. Bipin Behari Bannerjee.	Hindu Brahman.	2nd Master, C. M. S. H. School.	Jalsa Tahzib.	By the members of the Assn., 16th Dec.
512	„	(Rohilkhand.)	Moradabad.	Pandit Banwari Lal Misra	do	Merchant and Propr. *Sitara-i-Hind.*	Bharat Prakash Club.	Public meeting, 15th Dec.
513	„	Oudh.	Lucknow.	Rao Saheb Babu Gangaprasad Varma.	Hindu Kshatria.	Editor and Proprietor *Hindustani*, Urdu Weekly, Managing Proprietor of *The Advocate*, Ml. Cr., and Secy. Lucknow Standing Congress Committee.	1. Jalsa-Tahzib. 2. Rifa-i-am Assn. 3. B. I. Assn. 4. Anjuman Rifah Gonda. 5. British Ind. Assn., Moradabad. 6. Kheri Institute.	Public meeting, 7th Dec., &c., &c.
514	„	„	„	Babu Biswanath Ray.	Brahmo.	Government Pensioner, President, Brahmo Samaj.	Rifa-i-am Assn.	do
515	„	„	„	Mr. B. M. Ray.	do	Mercht., Proprietor of Messrs. H. C. Ray and Co., Secretary Brahmosamaj, and Director, Tea, Flour, and Oil Mills Co.	do	do

LIST OF DELEGATES.

Number.	Presidency.	Province.	District.	Name in full, with Honorary Titles, Scholastic Degrees, &c.	Religious denomination and caste, if any.	Occupation, Address, &c.	Place or Places or Association, &c., which they represent.	How and when elected.
516	Bengal.	Oudh.	Lucknow.	Pandit Shyam Narayan.	Hindu Brahman.	Rais and Editor *Mirut-ul-Hina* and *Murasila*.	Rifa-i-am Assn. and Kashmir National Club.	Public meeting, 7th Dec &c.
517	„	„	„	Pandit Bishan Naryan Dar.	do	Barrister-at-law, Editor, *The Advocate*, and Secy. Kashmeri National Club.	1. Jalsai-Tahzib. 2. Rifa-i-am Assn. 3. Kashmir National Club.	do
518	„	„	„	Babu Sri Ram, M.A., B.L.	Hindu Kayestha.	Vakil, H. C., Public Prosecutor, Judl. Comr.'s Court, Secy. Rifa-i-am Assn. and Ml. Cr.	(1) Rifa-i-am Assn. (2) Jalsa Tahzib.	do
519	„	„	„	Munshi Hargovind Dayal, M.A.	do	Govt. Pleader, and Vakil, J. C.'s Court, Lucknow & Sitapur.	do	do
520	„	„	„	Babu Bansi Lal Singh.	Hindu Kshatraya.	Vakil, H. Court, N.-W. P. and Zemindar. Chairman, Board of Directors, Upper India Cowper Mills Co.	do	do
521	„	„	„	Mr. Hamid Ali Khan. F.R.A.S., M.R.A.S., (London.)	Mussulman.	Barrister-at-law, and Mooafidar of Amroha Zilla and Vice-President, Rifa-i-am Assn.	do and Bareilly.	Do and meeting at the Bareilly Institute, 18th Dec.
522	„	„	„	Pandit Suraj Narayan Bahadur, B.A.	Hindu Brahman.	Joint-Secy., Jalsa-i-Tahzib.	do	Genl. Meeting.
523	„	„	Nadea and Lucknow.	Babu Ramgopal Vidyaratna.	Hindu.	Asst. Engineer Oudh and Rohilkund Railway, Lucknow, and Director, Upper India Cowper Mills Co.	Santipore &Rifa-i-am Assn.	do
524	„	„	Hardoi.	Swami Shagun Chand.	Hindu Kayestha.	Kayesth Upadeshak, Lucknow & Director, Upper India Couper Mills Co.	Hardoi.	Public meeting, 21st Dec.
525	„	„	Sitapur.	Babu Pitam Roy.	do	Zemindar, Vakil, Jud. Comr.'s Court, Hony Magte. and Vice-Chairman Ml. Bd.	Sitapur.	Public meeting, 16th Dec.
526	„	„	Purtabgarh.	Khan Bahadur Sheikh Ahmed Husain Khan (muzaq.)	Mussalman.	Taluqdar, Puryavan, and Hony. Magte.	do	do
527	„	„	Fyzabad.	Babu Gokul Chand.	Hindu Kshatraya.	Zemindar, Pleader, Hony. Magte., and Vice-Chairman of Ml. Bd.	Anjuman Tahzib and Fyzabad.	Public meeting, 8th Dec.
528	„	„	„	Khan Saheb Sheik Kadir Buksh.	Mussulman.	Mercht, Hony. Magte. and Memb. Ml. Bd.	Anj. Tah. and Mahomedan Assn.	do
529	„	Lower Provinces.	Patna.	Babu Bisweswar Singh.	Hindu Kshatrya.	Zemindar, Pleader, and Joint-Proprietor *Behar Herald and Indian Chronicle*, (English Weekly,) Bankipore.	(1) Patna, (2) Behar People's Assn. (3) Behar L. Propr's Assn. (4) Gaya.	(*a*) Public meetings of the two Associations. (*b*) Authorised by Resolution of Gaya delegates meeting to represent them.

LIST OF DELEGATES.

Number.	Presidency.	Province.	District.	Name in full, with Honorary Titles, Scholastic Degrees, &c.	Religious denomination and caste, if any.	Occupation, Address, &c.	Place or Places or Association, &c., which they represent.	How and when elected.
530	Bengal.	Lower Provs.	Patna.	Babu Gajadhar Prasad.	Hindu Kayestha.	Pleader Ml. Cr. and Memb. District. Bd.	Patna and Behar P. Assn.	Public meeting of the Assn., 18th Nov.
531	"	"	"	Babu Govind Charan, M.A., B.L.	do	Pleader, and Secy. "Behar People's Assn.," Bankipore.	Patna and Behar P. Assn.	Public meeting, 18th Nov.
532	"	"	"	Babu Kuldip Sahai.	do	Pleader, Bankipore.	do	do
533	"	"	"	Babu Guru Prasad Sen, M.A., B.L.	Vaidya Hindu.	Vakil, H. C., Calcutta, practising at Patna, Secy. Behar, L. H. Assn., and Editor, *Behar Herald*.	Behar L. Holders' Assn. and People's Assn,	Do. and Behar Assn., 9th Dec.
534	"	"	Shahabad.	Babu Baijnath Singh.	Hindu Kshatraya.	Zemindar of Kulharia, *via* Kochoor.	East Shahabad.	General meeting of the people.
535	"	"	"	Babu Saligram Singh, B.A., B.L.	do	Vakil, High Court, Hony. Magte. Calcutta, and Zemindar, Shahabad.	(1) Patna (2) Behar P. Assn. (3) Behar L. H. Assn. (4) B. I. Assn. (5) Indian Assn. Calcutta.	By meetings held under the auspices of each of the Assns. & at Patna.
536	"	"	"	Babu Kandhji Sahay, B.A., B.L.	Hindu Kayestha.	Zemindar, and Pleader, Arrah, and Vice-Chairman, Arrah Municipality.	Shahabad.	Meeting at Shahabad, 18th Dec.
537	"	"	"	Babu Syamlananda.	Hindu Kayestha.	Zemindar, Pleader, Ml. Cr. & Memb. Dist. & L. Bds., Shahabad.	Shahabad & B. L. H. Assn.	Meeting, Shahabad. 1st Dec. and Behar Land Holders' Assn. 9th Dec.
538	"	"	Saran.	Babu Bhagwan Sahay, B.A., B.L.	Hindu Brahman.	Zemindar and Vakil, High Court, Calcutta.	District of Saran.	Public meeting, 30th Nov.
539	"	"	"	Babu Taraprasad Mukerjee.	do	Zemindar, Pleader, Dist. Court, Saran; Chairman Revilgunga Municipality. Hony. Bench Magte., Chairman L. Bd. Chupra, and Memb. Dist. Bd. Saran.	do	do
540	"	"	"	Babu Binda Lal.	Hindu Kayestha.	Zemindar, Hony. Magte., Revilgunga. and Pleader, Dist. Court, Saran.	do	do
541	"	"	"	Rao Saheb Bansidhar Gupta.	Hindu.	Pleader, Dist. Court, Hony. Magte., Ml. Cr., and Memb. Dist. and L. Bds.	do	do
542	"	"	Bhagalpore.	Babu Sakhi Chandjee.	Hindu Vaisya.	Zemindar and Banker	Bhagalpore Dist.	Public Meeting, Bhagalpore, 18th Dec.
543	"	"	"	Babu Panch Kari Bannerjee.	Hindu Brahman.	Hd. Master, C. M. S. School.	do	do
544	"	"	"	Babu Saranda Prasad Mukerjee, B.A., B.L.	do	Pleader, Judge's Court.	do	o

LIST OF DELEGATES.

Number.	Presidency.	Province.	District.	Name in full, with Honorary Titles, Scholastic Degrees, &c.	Religious denomination and caste, if any.	Occupation, Address, &c.	Place or Places or Association, &c., which they represent.	How and when elected.
545	Bengal.	Lower Provs.	Calcutta, Midnapur, 24-Pergannahs, Mymensing, and Chittagong.	Maharaj Kumar Neel Krishna Deb Bahadur, J.P.	Summonlik Kayestha (Gostipati)	Zemindar, Sabha Bazaar, Ml. Cr., Pres. Magte, Presidt. Sabha Bazaar Benevolent Soc., Vice-Presdt. P. C.A. Soc., Memb. Indian Assn. for the cultivation of Science, and Memb. Bethune Society.	(1) Ind. Assn., Calcutta. (2) B.N.L. Tamlk Br. (3) B.N.L. Calcutta Br. (4) Agar.parah Assn. (5) Natta Panchgaon, Mukundpore, Nagra. (6) Mymensing Assn. (7) Chittagong Assn	Special Committee meeting, 25th Nov., &c., &c.
546	„		Calcutta & Midnapur.	Maharaj Kumar Binaya Krishna Deb Bahadur.	Summonlik Kayestha (Gostipati).	Zemindar, Sabha Bazaar, Hony. Magte. Sealdah, Calcutta, and Hony. Secy. Benevolent Society, Sabha Bazaar.	(1) I. Assn. Calcutta. (2) Ghatal Ind. Assn. (3) B.N.L. Cal. Br. (4) B.N.L. Tamlk Br.	Special Committee meeting, 25th Nov., and general meeting, 20th Nov.
547	„	„	Calcutta.	Mr. W. C. Bonnerjee.	Hindu Brahman.	Barrister-at-Law, High Court, Standing Counsel to Govt. of India, and F. Uni., Calcutta.	B.N. League and Calcutta.	Public meeting, 20th Nov.
548	„	„	„	Mr. J. Ghosal.	do	Zemindar.	Br. Indian Assn. Ind. Union. B.N.L. Seebpore (Howrah), R.P. Assn.	Public meeting, Dec. and 20th Nov.
549	„	„	„	Babu Jotendranath Tagore.	do	Zemindar.	B. N. L.	General meeting, 20th Nov.
550	„	„	„	Babu Trailokyanath Mitra, M.A., D.L.	do	Pleader, High Court.	Indian Union.	do
551	„	„	„	Babu Surendranath Bannerjee, B.A.	do	Propr. and Editor, *The Bengalee*, an English Weekly, Ml. Counsellor, Honry. Magte., Principal Ripon College.	Ind. Assn. Calcutta, Ranaghaut Ind. Assn., Chinsura.	Public meetings, Joyrampore, 7th Dec., 20th Nov.
552	„	„	„	Babu Jay Govind Shome, M.A., B.L.	Christian.	Vakil, High Court, F. Uni., Calcutta, and Editor *Christian Herald*.	(1) B.N.L. and Calcutta. (2) Shillong.	Public meetings, B. N. League, 20th Nov. and 22nd Dec.
553	„	„	„	Babu Gopal Chandra Mukhopadhyaya.	Hindu Brahman.	Editor *Sungbad Pravakar*, a Bengali Daily, of 57 years' standing, and author of many books.	(1) B.N.L. Cal. Br. (2) Agarparah. Assn., 24 Pergannahs.	20th Nov. do

LIST OF DELEGATES.

Number.	Presidency.	Province.	District.	Name in full, with Honorary Titles, Scholastic Degrees, &c.	Religious denomination and caste, if any.	Occupation, Address, &c.	Place or Places or Association, &c., which they represent.	How and when elected.
554	Bengal.	Lower Provs.	Calcutta.	Babu Dwarakanath Ganguli.	Hindu Brahman.	Asst. Secy. Indian Assn., Calcutta, and Journalist.	(1) I. Assn. (2) Nelphamari H. S. Sabha, Rungpore. (3) Ryots' meeting, Haraich, Rungpore.	By the Assn., 16th Dec. By the meeting.
555	"	"	"	Babu Joginder Chander Ghose, M A., B.L.	Hindu.	Vakil High Court.	Indian Assn.	do
556	"	"	"	Babu Sitanath Roy, B.L.	Hindu.	Mercht. and Secy., National Chamber of Commerce.	(1) Br. Indian A. (2) B.N.L. Ch. of Comce. (3) Et. Bengal Assn.	20th Nov. 11th Dec.
557	"	"	Calcutta & Naddea.	Josoda Nandan Pramanick, M.A., B.L.	do	Vakil, High Court, Calcutta, Chairman Santipore Municipality.	(1) B.N.L., Cal. Br. (2) Santipore.	General meeting, 20th Nov.
558	"	"	Calcutta.	Dr. Ras Behary Ghose, M.A., D.L.	do	Vakil H. C. Calcutta, Fellow Uni.	Indian Union.	General meeting of the Union.
559	"	"	"	Babu Kali Charan Bannerjee, M.A., B.L.	Christian.	do	(1) B.N.L. (2) I. Assn. (3) Christian Conference.	General meeting, 20th Nov., &c.
560	"	"	"	Babu Protab Chunder Moozumdar, L.M.S.	Brahmo.	Independt. Practr.	Ind. Assn. Tumlk Br.	By the Assn., 19th Dec.
561	"	"	"	Babu Bolanath Dhur.	Hindu.	Mercht. and L. Propr.	B. N. Ch. of Comce.	By the Chamber, 20th Dec.
562	"	"	24-Pergannahs.	Rajah Yatindranath Chaudhuri, M.A.	Hindu Kayestha.	Zemindar, Barahnagar.	(1) Taki Ind. Assn. (2) Tripura Hita Sadhini Sabha. (3) Barahnagar cultivators' meeting. (4) Indian Assn., Calcutta.	Public meetings, and committee meetings.
563	"	"	"	Babu Norendranath Sen.	Hindu.	Editor *Indian Mirror*.	24-Pergannahs and Naddea.	By the Central Bengal Union, Oct.
564	"	"	"	Babu Srish Chandra Chaudhuri, M.A., B.L.	Hindu Vaidya.	Vakil H. Court.	(1) B.N.L., S. S. Br. (2) Indian Assn. Midnapur.	General meetings, 30th Nov. and 14th Dec.
565	"	"	Midnapur.	Babu Krishna Lal Muzumdar.	Hindu.	Zemindar, Ml. Cr. and Pleader.	Midnapur Town and Indian Assn., Midnapur Br.	Public meeting, 15th Nov., and meeting, 16th Dec.
566	"	"	"	Babu Eshan Chander Bose	Hindu Kayestha.	Author and Publisher.	Indian Assn., Midnapur Br.	do
567	"	"	Hugli.	Babu Nander Lall Gossain	Hindu Brahman.	Zemindar, Serampur.	(1) B.I. Assn. and (2) R.P.An.	Public meeting, 20th Nov.

LIST OF DELEGATES.

Number.	Presidency.	Province.	District.	Name in full, with Honorary Titles, Scholastic Degrees, &c.	Religious denomination and caste, if any.	Occupation, Address, &c.	Place or Places or Association, &c., which they represent.	How and when elected.
568	Bengal.	Lower Provs.	Hugli.	Kumar Rameswar Maliah Bahadur.	Hindu.	Zemindar & Mercht.	(1) Bengal Congress Committee (2) People's Assn. Ranigange (3) M. J. S. Majdea & Kulna.	Public meetings, 4th Dec. and 12th Dec. and general meetings of the several Assns., &c.
569	"	"	"	Babu Iswari Lal Sircar.	Hindu Brahman.	Zemindar, Serampore and Vakil H. Court.	B. N. League.	do
570	"	"	"	Babu B. M. Ghose.	Brahmo.	Propr. Vict. Press.	Indian Assn., Howrah Br	do
571	"	"	"	Mr. Syed Mahomed Hoshein Ghouse.	Mussulman.	Health officer, Turkish Govt., Bagdad, and Medical Practr.	Chinsurah. & Hugli.	do
572	"	"	Hugli and Balasore.	Babu Romesh Chandra Mandle.	Hindu.	Zemindar & Mercht.	Do, and Balasore National Soc.	do
573	"	"	Howrah.	Babu Narasing Chandra Dutt, B.L.	do	Vakil H. Court, Hony. Magte., Ml. Cr. and Govt. Pleader.	People's Assn., Howrah.	By the Assn., Dec.
574	"	"	Furreedpore.	Babu Ambika Charan Mumzumdar, M.A., B.L.	do	L. Propr., Chairman, Municipality, Memb. Dist. Bd., Hony. Magte. and Secy. People's Assn.	People's Assn., Furreedpore.	Pub. meetings at— (1) Furreedpore. (2) Madaripore. (3) Amgram. (4) Khalia. (5) Gopalgunge. (6) Manikdaha.
575	"	"	Rungpore.	Babu Janaki Bullav Sen.	Hindu. Kayestha.	Zemindar, Mahigunge.	Rungpore.	Meeting of the Ind. Assn. Rungpore Br., 6th Dec. and public meeting of 13th Nov.
576	"	"	"	Babu Pores Chandra Banerjee, M.A., B.L.	Hindu Brahman.	Pleader.	do	do
577	"	"	"	Babu Purna Chandra Maitra, B.A., B.L.	do	do	Dist. Indian Assn., Rungpore Br.	do
578	"	"	Moorshedabad (Berhampore).	Babu Bijay Krishna Maitra, B.A., B.L.	do	Pleader, Berhampore.	Moorshedabad Assn., representing the whole Dist.	By the Assn., Oct
579	"	"	"	Rev. Chandra Nath Banerjee, B.A.	Christian.	L. M. S. Missionary, Berhampore.	do	do
580	"	"	Jessore.	Babu Kalinath Mukerjee, B.A., B.L.	Hindu Brahman.	Vakil Jessore P. O.	Indian Assn., Jessore.	By the Assn., Nov.
581	"	"	"	Babu Umesh Chandra Ghosh, B.A., B.L.	Hindu Kayestha.	Pleader, Ml. Cr., Memb. Dist. Bd., & Vice-Chairman Local Bd.	do	do
582	"	"	"	Babu Ambica Charan Sircar.	Hindu.	L. Propr., Memb. L. Bd. Magurah and Dist. Bd., Jessore, & Hony. Magte.	Magurah People's Assn.	Public meeting, 17th Dec.
583	"	"	Jessore (Narail).	Babu Jogendranath Sen, M.A.	do	Principal Vict. Col. and Vice-President Indian Assn.	Indian Assn. (Br) and the people of Narail.	Public meeting, 17th Dec.

LIST OF DELEGATES.

Number.	Presidency.	Province.	District.	Name in full, with Honorary Titles, Scholastic Degrees, &c.	Religious denomination and caste, if any.	Occupation, Address, &c.	Place or Places or Association, &c., which they represent.	How and when elected.
584	Bengal.	Lower Provs.	Backergunge.	Babu A. K. Dutt.	Hindu.	Ml. Cr., Chairman L. Bd., Memb. Dt. Bd., and Secy. People's Assn.	People's Assn. Bareisal.	Public meeting, 17th Dec.
585	"	"	Rajshahy.	Rajah Kumar Shosisi Khareswar Roy.	Hindu Brahman.	Zemindar, Tahirpur, and Editor *Baisack Tattwa* and *Silpa Krishi Patrika*, both Bengali.	(1) Maldah Dist. Assn. (2) Rajshahy Assn. (3) Mymensing Ryots' Assn.	Public meeting, 9th Dec., 17th. Dec.
586	"	"	"	Babu Kali Prasanna Acharya, B.A., B.L.	do	Pleader, Judge's Court, Beauleah.	Rajshahy Assn.	Meeting of the Assn., 17th Dec.
587	"	"	"	Babu Syam Charan Roy, B.A., B.L.	do	Pleader, Judge's Court, Rampore, Beauleah.	do	do
588	"	"	"	Babu Akshay Kumar Chakravarti.	do	Memb. Agricultural Society.	Agril. Soc., Tahirpur, & Maldah.	By a meeting, 14th Dec.
589	"	"	"	Paramahamsa Gadadharananda—Tirthaswami.	do	Memb. Gorakshini Sabha.	Gorakshini Sabha, Tahirpur.	do
590	"	"	Rajshahy and Maldah.	Mr. Radhesh Chandra Set.	Hindu.	Editor *Hindu Rangini*, Bengali Weekly.	(1) Maldah Assn. Rajhy Br. (2) Agri. Soc. Tahirpore.	Meetings of the Assns., 14th Dec.
591	"	"	Mymensing.	Babu G. C. Acharya Chowdry.	Hindu Brahman.	Zemindar, Muktagocha, and Ml. Cr.	Mymen. Assn. and Muktagocha.	Public meetings, 4th Dec. and 10th Dec.
592	"	"	"	Babu Kalinath Ghoshal.	do	Merchant, Muktagocha.	do	do
593	"	"	"	Babu Srinath Roy, B.L.	Hindu Kayestha.	Pleader, Judge's Court.	Mymensing Assn.	Public meeting, 4th Dec.
594	"	"	Naddea.	Babu Nanda Gopal Bhaduri.	Hindu.	Merchant.	M. J. S. Majdea & Kissengunge.	Special meeting of the Sabha, 3rd Dec.
595	"	"	"	Babu Basanta Kumar Chattopadhyaya, B.A., B.L.	Hindu Brahman.	Pleader and Memb. Dist. Bd.	(1) Krishengung. (2) Indian Assn., Kustia Br. (3) Indian Assn., Joyrampore Br. (4) Sadhupati Assn.	By public meetings at the places, 7th Dec., 9th Dec., etc.
596	"	"	"	Babu Pulin Vihari Lahiri.	do	Pleader.	Krishnaghur.	Public meeting, 14th Dec.
597	"	"	Naddea and Burdwan.	Babu Jagadis Chandra Lahiri.	do	Medical Practr.	(1) M. J. S. Majdea. (2) Kulna. (3) Indian Assn., Calcutta.	By the Sabhas, 4th Dec. and 12th Dec.

LIST OF DELEGATES.

Number.	Presidency.	Province.	District.	Name in full, with Honorary Titles, Scholastic Degrees, &c.	Religious denomination and caste, if any.	Occupation, Address, &c.	Place or Places or Association, &c., which they represent.	How and when elected.
598	Bengal.	Lower provinces.	Nuddea and Burdwan.	Babu Annada Prcsad Banerjee, B.A.	Hindu Brahman.	Zemindar, Kumircola.	Koza Hita Kari Sabha Nuddea Kumircola Ryots Burdwan.	By the Sabha at a general meeting and at public meeting of Ryots.
599	"	"	"	Babu Mohendra Nath Sen.	Hindu Kayestha.	Land-holder.	Russapuglah Improvement Assn.	At a general meeting of the Assn.
600	"	Chota Nagpore	Hazaribagh.	Rai Jodanath Mukerjee, B.L.	Hindu Brahman.	Pleader, Hony. Magte, Secy. Dist. Committee of Public Instruction, Vice-chairman of Hazari Municipality, Presdt. Hazaribagh Assn., & Memb. Dist. Committee.	Hazaribagh Assn. and Ranchi Assn.	By the Assns., 6th Nov. and 4th Dec.
601	"	"	Manbhum	Pandit Prannath Saraswati, M.A., B.L.	Hindu Brahman.	Vakil, H. Court, Calcutta, Vakil Judl. Comr.'s Court, Lucknow, Hony. Magte. for the suburbs of Calcutta, and Ml. Cr. Calcutta.	1. Ind. Union, Calcutta. 2. B. N. League. 3. Pumbiacity.	Committee meetings, and public meeting, 15th Dec.
602	"	Orissa.	Cuttack.	Mr. M. S. Das, M.A., B.L.	Christian.	Vakil, Cuttack.	Orissa Assn.	Special meeting of the Assn., 14th Nov.
603	"	"	"	Babu Gouri Sankar Roy.	Hindu Kayestha.	Editor of an Uriya weekly (cir. 450), & Translator, Judge's Court.	do	do
604	"	Assam.	Sylhet.	Babu Bipin Chandra Pal.	Hindu Brahman.	Journalist, *Tribune*, Lahore, English Bi-weekly.	Sylhet.	Public meeting, 22nd Dec.
605	"	"	Dibrugurh and Tezpur	Babu Radhanath Changkakoti	do	Propr. *Rathanoth Printing Press*, Secy. Upper Assam Assn., Secy. Assam Conference, Ml. Cr. and Member L. Bd. Dibrugurh.	(1) Assam. (2) Assam Conference. (3) U. Assam Assn. (4) Authorised to represent Shillong.	Public meetings of the Conference and Assn. and by wire from Shillong.
606	"	"	Tezpur.	Babu Lakshmi Kant Barkakoti.	do	Supt. Tezpur Mills, and Memb. Tezpur Ryots' Association.	Assam.	By Assam Conference.
607	Madras	Native State Cochin.	Cochin.	V. K. Sankara Menon, B.A.	Nair.	Land-holder.	Cochin.	Public meeting—Cochin Reform Association on 20th November.

Besides these delegates there were present on the platform several distinguished visitors from various parts of India. Also, there were some ladies, Englishmen, and high native officials, numbering a few hundreds, from several remote parts of this Presidency. There came also several officials from the Bombay and Bengal Presidencies to witness the proceedings, among whom the names of Mr. and Mrs. Wadia and Dr. and Mrs. Bose may be mentioned. Among the Zemindars there were present: His Highness the Maharajah of Vizianagaram, K.C.I.E., His Highness the Rajah Shosi Sikhareswar, Roy of Benares, the Rajah of Bobbili, the Zemindar of Ramnad, and Rajah G. N. Gajapathe Row. Besides Mr. and Mrs. A. G. Cardew, Mr. and Mrs. G. H. Stuart, there were Sir Charles Lawson, Messrs. A. T. Arundel, J. C. A. Sim, H. A. Stuart, C Cardoza, J. H. A. Tremenhere, W. S. Meyer, T. Hill, C. M. Barrow, C. G. Underwood, Wilson, Revs. G. M. Rae, J. R. Ellis, W. Joss, Doctors Cook, Quinn, Col. T. E. B. Tennant, Col. G. M. Moore, Col. T. Weldon, and several others. There were present, among others, the following: Dewan Bahadur R. Ragoonath Row (Indore), the Honourable G. M. Ranade (Poona), Justice A. Ramachendra Aiyar (Bangalore), Justice S. Tiruvenkata Chariar (Cochin), Mr. C. Nagam Aiyar, Dewan Peishkar (Trevandrum), Professor Rai Bahadur P. Ranganada Mudaliar, Rai Bahadur P. Rajaruthna Mudaliar, Rajah T. Rama Row, Rai Bahadur V. Bashyam Iyengar, Professor S. Seshiah, N. Vythianatha Iyer, Messrs. S. Sreenevasa Raghava Aiyangar, R. V. Sreenivasa Aiyar, and T. Ganapathy Aiyar.

APPENDIX II.

ENGLISH TRANSLATION OF THE TAMIL CATECHISM

ON THE

INDIAN NATIONAL CONGRESS,

BY

M. VIRARAGHAVA CHARIAR, B.A.

Q.—Which country is India?

A.—India is only another name for the country that is known to many people as Bharta Varsha. It extends over a wide area, from the Himalayas on the north to Cape Comorin, which lies 153 miles S.W. from Ramesaram. The Bay of Bengal and the country of Burmah constitute its eastern boundary. On the west it is bounded by the Arabian Sea and Afghanistan. Its length from north to south is about 1,600 miles, and its breadth from east to west is nearly the same. Its total area is forty-five lakhs of square miles. It has a population of about twenty-five crores and sixty lakhs.

Q.—To whose rule is that country now subject?

A.—This extensive empire of India is now subject to the sovereignty of Englishmen, the natives of a small island to the north-west of Europe. Its area is only about a lakh and a quarter of square miles, and its population only some three and a-half crores.

Q.—What enables the people of such a small country to govern this vast empire? What wonder is this?

A.—That they govern India is no wonder at all. It is the many superior qualities that they possess that make them the most prominent of nations. Though they are only about one-eighth of our number, it is these qualities, and above all their union, which enables them to hold dominion over India. The kings of England are not, like the sovereigns of the East, invested with despotic authority. The people of England firmly believe that the sole end and aim of Government ought to be the good of the people, and accordingly they have constituted a National Assembly known as the Parliament, and this Parliament consists of members chosen by the people as their representatives, and it is the united body of representatives thus elected that conduct the government of the country. The inhabitants of towns and cities in England elect the members in due course in accordance with the established rules. A fresh election must take place every seven years, but in practice Parliaments very rarely last so long, and new elections take place every three or four years, and often at shorter intervals. The members chosen by the people necessarily, as a rule, guide their action mainly in all affairs of State by the views of those who elect them, their Constituents as they are called, for if they did not they would not be re-elected. If you ask how the members of Parliament learn the opinions of the people, the reply is that they are constantly in communication with the leading men amongst their supporters; often go down and hold public meetings of their constituents, and of course study carefully the published resolutions of the meetings held amongst their constituents and of the various associations which exist amongst these, and the articles that appear in the newspapers which their constituents chiefly read. You see, these members of Parliament are only the representatives of certain districts, towns, or groups of towns, or mohullahs or parishes of very large towns, and they must make themselves acquainted with the views and wishes of the majority of the inhabitants of those places, and they must, as a rule, vote in Parliament in accordance with these, as otherwise at the next election that majority would elect some one else who would do this. In England no law can be passed except by Parliament; no tax can under any circumstances be imposed on the people except by Parliament, that is by the representatives of that people. The Ministers of Her Majesty the Queen are strictly responsible to the Parliament for all their actions. In the Government of that country, the Ministers are answerable to the Members of the Parliament and the Members of Parliament to the people. And it is under the control of such a mighty nation that we are prospering.

Q.—If so, why do not they attend to our grievances?

A.—The Members of that grand assembly are no doubt inclined to consider the affairs of our country and promote our happiness; but then firstly they cannot command enough of leisure to study Indian questions. Secondly, even if they had time, they are not aware of our wants. The disabilities under which we labour are never fully realised by them. If our many grievances could only be made clear to their view in their true colours, you may rest assured that they would be gradually redressed. The English nation do not at all understand the real state of affairs here: the two countries are so unlike each other; the climate, customs, habits, food, everything in short is so different, that to understand matters here, an Englishman, who has never lived in India, must make a regular study of the subject. So the English nation as a body has no conception of all the hardships and disadvantages under which we labour under the existing administration here. Nor do the English officials in India ever report to the Members of Parliament what we know to be the true state of this country. In the first place they are not natives of the country and never have that intimate knowledge of its affairs that we possess. In the second place they necessarily believe that all they do is right, and that it is done in the best possible manner, and lastly, they not unnaturally do not desire either a reduction of their salaries or their powers, and this would certainly follow if the English public came really to understand how matters at this present time really stand. So that great English nation never gets to know truly how things go on here, and we, the people of India have not yet been sensible enough as to establish permanently a great Union amongst ourselves and adopt the most effective methods of acquainting the English nation with all our wants and grievances. So how can we expect any material change for the better, and how can we hope for the redress of those grievances?

Q.—What then should we do to inform the English people of our wants and wishes, and obtain justice at their hands?

A—If I am to answer your question fully, it would take me longer than a year. But I shall be brief. Listen to me. Our countrymen should make it a rule to study carefully all public questions and communicate to Government their opinions of them through associations and newspapers. Our countrymen should do their best to establish in India a representative Council similar to the Parliament of Great Britain to consider the questions that relate to our well-being. We should get the permission of the British Parliament to elect the members of that Council. Her Majesty the Queen Empress should make the resolutions of that Council binding upon the Governors-General and Governors. If we succeed in thus establishing one grand representative Council for the whole of India and five or six other smaller Councils, one for each of the more important provinces of the Empire, and if it is enacted that no law be passed or tax imposed except with the express permission of such Councils, we should then have arrived at the commencement of the Political regeneration of India. We should constantly press on the British people the paramount necessity there is for carying into effect the above reforms through the telegraph, associations, newspapers, and delegates. It is only by persisting in the agitation that we can make our grievances heard in England. If the English nation begin to evince interest in the affairs of this country the opposition of the Anglo-Indian officials, who wish to keep matters as they are, will soon cease to be effective.

Q.—Are there any assemblies in India like the Parliament of Great Britain?

A.—The Councils in India resemble the Parliament of England only in name. They are called the Legislative Councils. As at present constituted the Councils are mere shams and have no independent power. Their members are entirely powerless to regulate the expenditure of Government, even to the extent of a single pice, nor could they alter or cancel the laws which the Government resolve to enforce. The Government offer some native gentlemen seats in the Councils merely, it would seem, to lead the people of England into the belief that in the government of this country Native opinion receives due weight.

Q.—But why are these Councils such shams; if there are several of our people on them why don't they fight for us? Why do they not see that justice is done to us?

A.—In the first place the natives who sit in these Councils are not chosen by us, but by Government. If they displease us, we can't turn them out; but if they displease Government, it takes care not to reappoint them after the lapse of the two years for which such gentlemen are appointed. Now men so appointed are entitled to have Honourable put before their names, and it is considered a great honour to be on them, and if they do just what Government likes they are given K.C.S.I.'s, or K.C.I.E.'s, or C.S.I.'s, or C.I.E.'s, all empty titles of no good, but which vain and foolish people set great store by. Then, too, Government mostly chooses not people who will fight for our rights, but more or less foolish big men, who will do just what they are told by Government. So it follows that very few of the natives who have hitherto sat in Council have tried to do good for us. Some, however, have; but the system is such that even if every one of them were clever men and did their very best, they could yet do nothing. For the way is this, they constitute only a small minority in the Council, and the only questions that come before them are new laws. They are not allowed to ask a question even or learn anything about anything else connected with the administration of the country: only when a new law has to be passed they must hear it and may say what they think of it. But no law comes before these Legislative Councils until the Viceroy or Governors have already settled in their Executive Councils, on which there are no natives, what the law is to be; and when they bring it into the Legislative Councils it has been already settled: a few words or clauses may be altered (if such alterations commend themselves to the Viceroy and the members of the Executive Council), but that is all. The poor native members may express their opinion—they may say the law is a very bad one, but they are in a minority and no one minds them. So you see even if our people tried, which only a few ever have done, to fight our battles, they could do nothing, for these Councils are a mere sham.

Q.—How could we, the people of India, ever hope for any redress with the aid of such sham Councils?

A.—Of course we can't hope for anything of the kind. Progress and reform are equally impossible. But if we had the privilege of electing the members, and we had enough members on the Council, it would be very different; for then they would look to please us by whose favour they were elected and might be re-elected. The members who owe their seats in Council to the good will of Government will naturally as a rule vote in their favour. And they dare not fight for the people's cause on pain of never being re-appointed; therefore our countrymen should endeavour to reform the Councils. If we all persevere in insisting on this, and make our case clear, the English nation will certainly accede to our wishes, and improve the constitution of the Legislative Councils, and if these Councils are re-constructed on a representative basis, some of our most serious grievances will begin to disappear one after another.

Q.—If so, why do not all our countrymen unite in endeavouring to reform our Legislative Councils?

A.—It is no doubt true that all our people do not interest themselves in the movement. Till lately our ryots, merchants, and the ordinary run of people entirely neglected public affairs, but their eyes are beginning to be opened now. Many of them now make known their wants through newspapers and public meetings. For the last three years many of the zemindars, merchants, landlords, and men of other professions living in different parts of India, have made it a point to meet once in a year in some Presidency town and discuss public questions of the most vital importance. In 1885 nearly 100 gentlemen assembled together at Bombay from all parts of India, and recorded their opinions on some of the most vital matters of public interest. In 1886 some 440 gentlemen elected for the purpose by various associations, met together in Calcutta for the same purpose. In December, 1887, no less than 604 gentlemen, representing all classes and creeds, and elected by almost all the large towns and associations in the Empire, met together at Madras in the same way, and now in December, 1888, there is to be another and larger gathering at Allahabad. They have given this grand assembly the English appellation of "the Congress." The word Congress means assemblage.

Q.—Will these Congresses be of any help to India?

A.—Yes. The people of this country will at last obtain a hearing. Now the people of this country have no voice in the government of the country. If our countrymen muster strongly in the Annual Congress, and meet year after year, and tell the English Government what they want, that Government will gradually remodel the administration in accordance with the clearly expressed wishes of the whole country. But then if we are to succeed at all quickly, everybody must join; everybody must interest themselves in the matter, and take part in the election of the delegates, and help the work in every way they can; and if some of the local officials be displeased with them they must not be angry with or frightened at this. It is only natural that those amongst the officials who are not highminded should feel annoyed at a movement which will tend to curtail their arbitrary power, and generally to compel them to consult the wishes and feelings of their people a great deal more than they do now. So it is no use being vexed, while it would be foolish to be frightened. Every man should just join and go on with the work good humouredly, not troubling himself what officials or any one else think or say about the matter. They will all come round in a year or two when we have won the day, and will then say it is an excellent thing.

Q.—Then you think the Congress will really be of great use?

A.—Yes, most certainly; for one of the best means of promoting the welfare of India is the establishment of a grand Council on the lines of the English Parliament, and if persevered in and wisely guided and supported by the whole country, the Congress will gradually, when India is fit for this, be converted into an Indian Parliament, which will take the place of the sham Councils of the present day.

Q.—Will the Government recognise the Congress?

A.—Why not? They will certainly recognise it—not this year, or perhaps the next; not till they are satisfied that it is really national and has the whole country at its back; but once you prove this to them, they certainly will recognize and utilize it, and in so doing pave the way for the redress of all our more serious grievances. The English Government is superior to all other Governments in the world, for its fundamental principle is to shape its policy according to the wishes of the people. If the Congress goes on meeting regularly once a year, and working throughout the year, and the whole nation join in electing their delegates to it, and in making plain that they approve and ratify its resolutions, the Government will very soon be obliged by public opinion in England to consider carefully the decisions the Congress arrives at. The present English Parliament in its infant stage resembled in many respects our present Congress, and just as a grand tree grows out of a small seed, so the small temporary gatherings of a former day have now attained the dimensions of the glorious English Parliament.

Q.—When did the first Congress meet, and wha is its history?

A.—The first National Congress met in December, 1885, in the city of Bombay. To partake in that Congress many gentlemen had arrived from the Presidency of Madras, the Presidency of Bengal, the Punjab, North-West Provinces, and other parts of India. All the gentlemen, delegates as they were called, were lodged in one place and discussed together the most important matters connected with the government of the country for three days, and then publicly recorded their opinions, or, as it is termed, passed resolutions in regard to these matters. During the sittings of that Congress each of the delegates learned the views of the others, and all proved to be of one mind, although they had come from parts of the country thousands of miles apart and belonged to different races and castes and creeds. It was one primary object of this Congress to demonstrate, or, if needful, by joint consultation to bring about, this oneness of mind or unanimity of opinion, for unanimity of opinion will produce union among us.

Q.—What are the resolutions passed at the first Congress?

A.—They are as follows: (1) Her Majesty the Queen-Empress should send a Commission to this country, and that Commission should inquire into our grievances. (2) The India Council should be abolished, and a Standing Committee of some of the members of Parliament should be formed for the consideration of Indian questions. (3) The Legislative Councils should be enlarged by the admission of a considerable number of members elected by ourselves, and should be empowered to regulate and control the expenditure, to make laws and to exercise other powers. (4) The Civil Service examination should be conducted not only in England but also in India; the age limit should be raised to 23. (5) That it was unjust for the Government of India to increase the army and consequently the expenditure. (6) The people of this country are already very heavily taxed, and Government should find means to reduce the burden of taxation. (7) As, if Burmah is placed under the control of the Government of India, the latter may not have time at their disposal to attend to Indian affairs, and our money will be wasted in reducing it to order, Her Majesty the Queen should not place the Government of Burmah in the hands of the Indian Government.

Q.—Did the Government pay any attention to any of the above resolutions?

A.—Yes, to a certain extent. Lord Dufferin, our Governor-General, highly eulogised the sixth resolution. He appointed two Commissions to inquire and report in regard to the matters set forth in that and in the fourth resolution. They were known by the names of the Finance Committee and the Public Service Commission. Not only did the Government in India attend to the resolutions, but some of the newspapers in England approved of the work of the first Congress. The then members of the English Ministry, Mr. Gladstone and Mr. Chamberlain, are understood to have spoken favourably of the movement. Is it necessary to add that Lord Ripon and Mr. Slagg, and other avowed friends of India, warmly welcomed the Congress?

Q.—When did the second Congress meet?

A.—It met in December, 1886, at Calcutta.

Q.—Sir, please clearly inform me of the difference between the first and the second Congress.

A.—If I enter into a detailed description of the second Congress, it will occupy a long time. However, I shall give you a brief account of it. Only 78 delegates attended the first Congress at Bombay, while 436 delegates attended the second Congress at Calcutta. The gentlemen that attended the first Congress were not appointed by the people of this country to appear on their behalf. But for the second Congress numbers of the people, at public meetings and through public associations, elected their representatives. In December, 1886, various meetings were held in all parts of India to elect delegates.

While only two Mahomedans attended the first Congress, no less than 33 Mahomedan gentlemen partook in the deliberations of the second Congress. The people generally interested themselves in the second Congress more than they had done in the first. Thirdly, it was not until the second assemblage that the name Congress became familiar to all the people in all parts of the country.

Q.—What are the resolutions of the second Congress?

A.—(1.) A resolution was passed congratulating Her Majesty the Empress on the occasion of the Jubilee and praying for Her Majesty's long life and prosperity.

(2.) It was resolved that in view of the growing poverty of the people of India, representative institutions ought to be established in India, as this would place it within our power to effect those reforms in the administration which we believe to be necessary to relieve that poverty.

(3.) The third resolution of the first Congress about the reconstitution of Legislative Councils was reaffirmed.

(4.) It was further pointed out that it was necessary (*a*) to increase the numerical strength of the Legislative Councils; (*b*) to allow the people to elect half of the total number of members; (*c*) and to invest the members with the right of interpellation.

(5.) That all the associations and public bodies in India should unanimously pray the Viceroy to recommend the Secretary of State to cause the necessary steps to be taken for the establishment of representative Councils

(5.) That as regards the matters under the inquiry of the Public Service Commission, a simultaneous examination should be held in India and England for the Civil Service, that the age limit should be raised to twenty-three, and that no distinction should be made between Europeans and natives in the Civil Service, but that all should be treated alike.

(7.) That the system of trial by jury should be extended, and that the decision of the jury in cases of acquittal should be final.

(8.) That the judicial functions should be separated from the executive.

(9.) That the people of this country should be permitted to enrol themselves as Volunteers in order that they may be able to defend the British Empire in times of war.

Q.—Why should the resolutions passed in the first Congress be re-affirmed in the second?

A.—We re-affirm the resolutions principally to acquaint all the people with our wants and to make our grievances heard in England. It is only when the child cries often that the mother gives it milk. Even so it is only by repeatedly telling the British nation what we are in need of that we can hope for any redress. The Anglo-Indian officials have been for many decades enjoying exceptional rights and privileges, and if these are now to be curtailed will they not oppose us with all their might? If we persevere in our efforts then our hopes will be realised.

Q.—Did the Viceroy take any notice of the Congress?

A.—Yes, he did. The Viceroy and Governor-General invited many of the members of the Congress to his Palace, and had some conversation with them about public affairs. He also honoured the members of the Congress by inviting them to a garden party.

Q.—Was any notice taken in England of the Congress?

A.—Not much as yet, nor can we expect it. The proceedings of the Congress were published in a book, and 5,000 copies of this were distributed in England by Mr. Dadabhai Naorojee, a sincere friend of India, who presided over the second Congress, but what are 5,000 copies, and we had not funds for more, amongst a great nation? Still a few of the newspapers noticed it, and the report was referred to twice in the House of Commons, and several of the leaders of the Liberal Party expressed their approbation of and seem to have been much pleased with the proceedings of the Second Congress. It is impossible at the present time to obtain a hearing for Indian affairs in the English House of Parliament, as its whole time is absorbed by the Irish controversy. But their advice is that we should continue holding our annual Congress year after year till they are in a position to attend to our call. They are further of opinion that we should do our best to make the great mass of the people take an intelligent interest in the subject.

Q.—But, to make so many delegates assemble in one place, to allow them a fitting reception, to print and publish a sufficient number of copies of the report must cost a great deal. Pray, what have the Congresses cost?

A.—Well, the first Congress at Bombay cost only about Rs.3,000, but the second at Calcutta cost something like Rs.16,000. In each case the people of the place and some of the nobility and the gentry of the Province and other friends of the cause subscribed what was needful.

Q.—But you have only told us about the two first Congresses, and you mentioned that there had been a third at Madras, tell us please about that.

A.—Well, that was even grander than the second; at that 604 delegates assembled, and they met in a vast temporary hall specially erected for the purpose. All these delegates had been duly elected either at public meetings in towns or by associations or other public bodies. Indeed, some 700 were elected, but owing to sickness, domestic calamities, and the great distances to be travelled (some had fully 2,000 miles to come), only 604 actually arrived.

Q.—But what kind of people were the delegates?

A.—All kinds of people came as delegates—great men like Rajah Sir T. Madhava Row, and little men like artisans and petty tradesmen. There were a few Europeans, for they are beginning to understand that they are just as much interested as we are in good government, and a number of Eurasians who took an active part, and will year by year take a more and more active part, in the Congress, Parsees, Native Christians, Hindus, Mahomedans and Jains.

Q.—What, Mahomedans? Why, somebody said that the Mahomedans had not joined the Congress. I did not know what the Congress was, and so I did not trouble myself about it, but certainly I heard this.

A.—Well, eighty-three Mahomedans came as delegates, and amongst them were men like the Honble. Mir Humayun Jah Bahadur, the head of the great Mysore family and a member of the Madras Council, and Mr. Budrudin Tyabji, till recently a member of the Bombay Council, who was the President of the third Congress, and many other distinguished and learned Mussalmen. The fact is that one eminent Mahomedan, Sir Syed Ahmed, did not choose to join, for reasons known to himself, and he and his immediate following having been foolish enough to abuse the Congress, have tried to set it about that the Mahomedans generally did not join, whereas the bulk of the intelligent Mahomedans all over the country did join and join heartily.

Q.—I am glad of that; for whatever our religion, we ought all to unite in this work, which I now see is clearly for the good of all. But I should like to know more about these delegates. Were there zemindars, were there ryots, were there Municipal Councillors?

A.—Yes, there were all these, and as you want to know, I will tell you all about it. Out of the 604, there were 61 zemindars, jagirdars, and taluqdars, and there were 95 ryots and other small landholders. Then there were 144 merchants, traders, and shopkeepers, 55 schoolmasters, 206 members of the legal profession, retired judges, barristers, advocates, pleaders, solicitors, &c., 43 editors of newspapers, 19 artizans, 8 doctors, &c.

Then I may tell you that out of these, three were members of Council, 31 were honorary magistrates, 10 were fellows of of one or other university, 103 had seats on municipal boards, and 56 on local fund boards, so that it is difficult to imagine a more truly representative gathering than was this last Congress.

Q.—And what resolutions did this Congress pass?

A.—Well, it first insisted once more on the necessity of two primary reforms that it had advocated at previous sittings, viz., the reconstitution of the Councils on a representative basis and the complete separation of the judicial and executive functions. Then, in view of the universal loyalty of the people, it recorded its opinion that the highest or commissioned ranks in the army should be practically opened to all classes of Her Majesty's Indian subjects, and colleges established whereat our youth may be trained for this career; it advocated the concession to the people of the right to volunteer under such restrictions and conditions as Government might deem necessary, and demanded the material modification of the existing Arms Act.

Further, considering the unsatisfactory working of the income tax, it prayed that the taxable minimum should be raised to Rs.1,000. And lastly, reverting to the growing poverty of the country, it pressed upon Government the necessity of elaborating a practical system of technical education, and of spending more money in buying Indian articles and paying Indian labour, and less in buying English articles and paying English labour.

Q.—All this is very good, and if this were all done India would be a different place; but how can we get the Government to mind what the Congress even says.

A.—No doubt it is difficult, for the bulk of the officials here are prejudiced and think that the system they work under is perfection, and are angry at our saying that it is very defective and at our proposing these changes. But there is no such prejudice amongst the people of England, who are their masters as well as our masters. And if we persevere with these Congresses, and get more and more of the people everywhere to understand them, and take interest in them, and support them, we shall, and that before many years are over, have so strong a voice that even the people of England will hear us, and once they do this as a body (not merely two or three thousands here and there, whom alone, as yet, we have reached), all our reasonable demands will soon be granted.

Q.—But in the meantime it costs a great deal of money, does it not? What may this third Congress have cost?

A.—Well we do not exactly know yet, but probably, including the sending home of 10,000 copies of the report, not less than Rs.30,000, and this of course is exclusive of the very large sum, more than double this amount, which had to be expended by the delegates themselves in journeying to and from the Congress.

Q.—And you said that there was to be yet a fourth Congress at Allahabad? And where is the money for that to come from?

A.—Well, just as the people of Madras, high and low, and sympathisers elsewhere, subscribed and got together Rs.30,000 for the Congress,—for the erection of the meeting hall, the reception and entertainment of the delegates, and the printing and distribution of the report, here and in England,—so must the people of the North-West Provinces subscribe and collect what may be necessary for the Allahabad Congress. And it need not be very difficult, if only the people learn the rights of the matter, and they all begin to take an interest in the matter. One anna from every house would go a long way. But the fact is that this is not all, because it is not sufficient to hold the Congress. We must send to England much larger numbers of the report than we have yet been able to do, from want of funds, and we must send home our own delegates to hold public meetings in England, and there explain fully the nature of the demands that the Congress makes here, and create a knowledge of the circumstances of this country. All this ought to be paid for, not by the one province where the Congress is held, but by the entire country.

We must have a large permanent Congress Fund, the interest from which must be devoted to this work, and while in that province where the Congress is to be held subscriptions must of course be collected for the current expenses of that particular Congress, in all other provinces subscriptions ought to be collected steadily for the permanent fund. It is not large sums that are so much wanted—though we hope to get some such from Rajahs and great people who sympathize with the work, as a very great number do,—but a multitude of small subscriptions from 4 annas, such as you can all give if you choose and can persuade numbers of your fellows to give.

Q.—But to whom are we to give these subscriptions?

A.—In every province there is a Standing Congress Committee, and you are to pay your own subscription, and any subscriptions you can get from others, to that committee and get a receipt for the same. If every one who reads this only tries, we shall very soon have all the money that is required for the work.

Q.—Well, I see it is a good work, and I wish to help and I will do what little I can in the way of getting subscriptions; but is there no other way in which I can help?

A.—Certainly there is. You have read and now understand this: read it to all your friends and see that they understand it; read it to every one in your village and make every one understand the whole question. When every one in your own village understands, make every one in the neighbouring villages understand, and try and persuade every one whom you make understand that it is their duty to go and teach others, and so in a year or two there will be no one left who does not know all about it and is not ready to help, and is not anxious for its success. Let your cry be "*Congress ji ke jai,*" and God will help those who thus prove that they are anxious to help themselves.

APPENDIX III.

A CONVERSATION BETWEEN MOLVI FARID UD DIN, M.A., B.L., VAQUIL (BARRISTER) OF THE HIGH COURT, PRACTISING IN THE ZILLAH COURT OF HAKIKATABAD, AND RAMBAKSH, ONE OF THE MUKADDAMS (CHIEF VILLAGER) OF KAMBAKHTPUR.

(*Scene: The* CHOPAL,* *in Kambakhtpur, Zillah Hakikatabad.*)

Rambaksh: Molvi Sahib, there is a great talk now-a-days of "Re-pre-sen-tation" and "Re-pre-sen-ta-tive Ins-ti-tu-tions," but what does it all mean? Last week a Bengali gentleman was staying for the night at the Sarai, and as many of us were sitting talking round the fire in the gateway, he came and began to talk to us. We told him how bad the times were, and how the police bullied us, and how hard the zemindar and the money-lender were, and how everything seemed going wrong. Then he said it was all our own fault, that if we chose to undergo all this and all the trouble that pervaded the country, that was our look-out; no one could help us if we did not help ourselves. But we said: "How can we help ourselves? Who can oppose the *Sirkar* (Government), and does not the *Sirkar* keep up the police, and do not the Civil Courts of the *Sirkar* support the zemindar and the sahookar (banker) in all their oppression?" He said: "That is true, and obedience to the Government of the time is the duty of all good subjects, but you could, if you chose, so alter the system (*dastur*) of the Government, that it would do the things that are pleasing and beneficial to you, instead of, as now, often doing what you dislike, and what is harmful to you." And we said: "We alter the *Sirkar;* are we Rustams? Are we Devas? This is foolish talk, what can we poor people do?" He said: "By yourselves you are very weak, and can do nothing; you are very ignorant, and can hardly see beyond the ends of your fields; but for all that, if all you ryots all over the country would join those of your countrymen who are better off, and better educated, in calling upon the Government to concede to us 'Representative Institutions,' then the good people in England would insist on these being given to us, and then soon many things would be altered for the better, and many of your causes of complaint would be removed." Now there was a *Sahib* also putting up in the Serai. A *Chota Sahib*, an overseer on the canal, but a good man, and just then he came out and said: "That is all nonsense, Baboo, these poor fellows are mere cattle; what can they understand of such matters, and what good do you think 'Representative Institutions' would do to such as these?" And then the Baboo and he began to argue in English, and we heard nothing more. And indeed I think the *Sahib* was right, and that it was all nonsense. Still we want to know what does "Re-pre-sen-tation" mean? What is it?

Molvi Farid ud din: Well, Rambaksh, I do not know that it is all nonsense. As for "Representation," don't you remember last year, when you and Matadin and Rampershad, and some thirty others of you, had cases against Raja Harbansrai, just about sowing time, and as it was a bad time to be away from the village, and all the cases were quite alike, and you knew all about the matter, and had the best head of the lot, they all chose you out and sent you in, to me, to the *Sudder*† to explain all their cases, and get me to put in petitions for them as well as for yourself? Well, that was "Representation," and you were their "Representative." The words may be new to you but the thing is as old as the soil. Has it not ever been our custom, alike under Emperors or Kings, when any village, or city, or *parganah*,‡ or district, had any favour to ask, or any grievance to complain of, for all the respectable men of the place to have *punchayets*,§ and at these to pick out the wisest and longest-headed men, and the best speakers, and send these to the authority, or *Sirkar*, to make known our prayers? Well, this again was "Representation," and the men so sent to plead the cause of those who deputed them were "Representatives."

Rambaksh: Well, I understand that. As you say, the words are new, and very long, but the thing is old and simple. But what has that to do with Government, and what do "Representative Institutions" mean?

Molvi Farid ud din: There are Governments in all countries; without Government there would be no peace, no security of life or property. Governments are necessary, and, if good, a great blessing. But some Governments are better than others; of course one ruler is a good man and another a bad man; one clever and another a fool or a madman. But I do not mean that; I mean that there are two chief kinds of Government, one of which is better than the other. Now you know Shamshpur, and the good old *Lumberdar* (or senior proprietor) Kour Dharam Singh. There are nearly 200 sharers in that village, but in the five years that I have been a vaquil here, I do not remember a single case coming up from that village, and we all know that there is no more prosperous place in the district.

---

* The raised earthern platform where the villagers congregate to discuss village politics in particular and all things in general. A substitute for a Town Hall.

† The head-quarters of the District.

‡ A Revenue Sub-division.

§ Councils for consultation—originally consisting of five members only any body of men selected to consider and decide any question.

Rambaksh: That is true, and that is because the *Lumberdar*, though he is ten times as rich and as clever as any of the *Hissadars* (co-sharers), never does anything without consulting them. There is not a pie* of village expenses (*gaon khurch*), but what every shareholder has had his say about it; and whatever is to be done it is all talked over on the *chopal*, and if there is any quarrel it is all settled there. Of course there are Jivan Singh and Rajaram and one or two others whom the *Lumberdar* laughingly calls his counsellors (*durbarees*), who have most to say, but that is because they are the leaders of the several *pattis* (main subdivisions of the village), and all their *hissadars* look up to them as the best and wisest men. Ah! that's the way to manage a village. If only ours were like it!

Molvi Farid ud din: Well, I see you understand more than I thought. Now the management of Shamshpur is an example, in a small way, of what we call "Constitutional Government." If a ruler acts like that good *Lumberdar*, and in all he does and orders first consults his subjects, and so manages that the best and wisest of them, on whom the rest rely as their leaders, approve and agree to what is done, then we call that a "constitutional" kind of Government. And this, of course, is the only permanently safe kind of Government, for, as the saying goes, "*Pánch panch mil, kijay kaj —Har jit awai nahin laj*" (Do your work in association with five others, so that, come victory or defeat, you will not stand alone).

Rambaksh: And what kind of Government do you call that of our Rajah Harbansrai? He lives away in the *Sudder*, and he never comes near us, and he never reads any of our petitions, and never consults any of us; indeed, he won't see us, but sends out an order for us to speak to the *Naib*† or the *Gomashtah* (factor) who lives in the Rajah's house here; and as for the *Gomashtah*, he never knows anything about us or the village, for one comes for six months and then goes, and then another comes for a couple of years and then he goes, and then another comes, and so on. And except dear old Rai Sacharam, there has never been a *Naib* or *Gomashtah* here who didn't think he knew more about everything than any of us, or all of us put together. They are all alike, these *Gomashtahs*. "*Jau; Chupraho* (Go away! hold your tongue!); "Do this; Don't do that; Pay this; Pay that!"

Molvi Farid ud din: Well, when a Government behaves as Rajah Harbansrai does, we call it a "Despotic" Government. But how does your village thrive?

Rambaksh: How does it thrive? Why, Molvi Sahib, you know that there is never a day but what there is some case from Kambakhtpur in court; that we are growing poorer and poorer, that land is going out of cultivation, that we have scarcely oxen enough to plough what we still till. Look down the street, why the houses are half of them nearly in ruins, and the two *abkari*‡ shops that the *Sirkar* has set up here are always full. Even this chopal built by our forefathers and so much needed for our meetings and our guests, is now in ruins. Look at Shamshpur; it is twice as populous as this *Bustee* (village), and yet there is no abkari shop there and the *Lumberdar* says there never shall be, and so say they all. Thrive indeed! Of all the miserable places in this whole *zillah*§ Kambakhtlur is nearly one of the worst.

Molvi Farid ud din: I am afraid that is too true. But why is this? Rajah Harbansrai is not a bad man. I live in the *Sudder* and see much of him. He is rather a kind good man, though so occupied with his great big house there and his troops of servants that he has no time to look after his affairs in the Mofussil.

Rambaksh: That's just it. I don't say he is a bad man, but we never see him. We send him petitions but he takes no notice of them. So far as any good to it is concerned he might be dead,—but, for all that he must have his money, and almost every year, more money and more money, till we poor people are almost skin and bone. Ah! if we were only cattle, as the Sahib said, we might perhaps make a rupee or two out of our skins; it is about all we have left.

Molvi Farid ud din: Ah! Rambaksh, I am afraid you say that because you haven't paid me what you owe me for that enhancement case!

Rambaksh: No, Molvi Sahib. You have always been my friend, and I have the money for you safe; have I ever been dishonest? But what I say is too true; we are all very poor now.

Molvi Farid ud din: Well, but how is it? The Rajah no doubt doesn't look after you, but he always keeps his *Naib* or a *Gomashtah* here, and he does seem to me to try to employ good men. I have had many cases for you people against them, but I have found most of them respectable men, far better than the *Naibs* many other Rajahs employ to look after the *Mofussil* villages.

Ramkaksh: That is true enough. They do not take bribes, they do not meddle with our women, they don't drink, but they are city people; they know nothing of the *Mofussil*, they don't understand our village ways; they press in a hurry for rent, and force us to sell our crops below their value when they ought to wait and leave us time to make good bargains; they don't know the difference between a 6-anna and a 16-anna crop,¶ and press in bad times for rent, so that we have to sell our cattle; they don't know who is reliable (*matbir*), and they make advances when none ought to be given, to ne'er-do-weels and lose their money, and then say we are all *budmashes* (bad characters, rogues), and won't even give seed grain to the best of us, when times are such that we really need it.

* The smallest copper coin, value at the present time about one-third of a farthing.
† His deputy or head manager, or agent.
‡ Liquor shops. Public houses.
§ District.
The rural portion of the country as contrasted with the urban portion is called the Mofussil; so again provincial districts as contrasted with the capital are also so designated.
¶ Sixteen annas go to a Rupee. A sixteen-anna crop therefore is a full crop, while a six-anna crop is one which only yields six-sixteenths, or three-eighths of what a full crop would.

And then they are fussy and self-conceited, and won't hear a word from any of us. There was the old tank there, the Soorujkund, that from generation to generation used to irrigate half the village; that burst when I was a boy fifty years ago. Well, we wanted the Rajah to repair this. It wouldn't have cost many hundred rupees and the whole village knew from their forefathers how well it worked. But, no! The *Naib Sahib* knew better; he wouldn't listen to us. "What do you cattle know? Hold your tongues!" He was all for new-fangled plans; he would bring a *kul* (channel) of the *Sirkari* canal to irrigate the village. We told him that canal water is cold; that our lands lay low; that it would not do. But what was the use? "What do you cattle folk know? Hold your tongues;" and so the *kul* was brought, and the first year it overflowed and swamped half the crops, and then, when the water dried up, the canal people came and measured up all the land, and made us pay tax for "one watering." A fine thing, seeing it had ruined our crops. But we had to pay, and now it is bringing the *reh* (a saline efflorescence) all over our best lands. There is that five-bigah field that my ancestors have cultivated for centuries—such a good field; it never gave me less than Rs.50 a year net profits, and now—now it is all white, and it won't pay the rent even. I don't like to give it up; for ages have my forefathers tilled it, but what can I do? I asked the *Gomashtah* to get the rent reduced, and all he said was, "Reduce the rent? You must be a fool, or think me one. Hold your tongue." And so it is in everything. The Rajah pays no heed to us; his *Naibs* understand nothing of our affairs. They order this and order that, press us for money in season and out of season, they know nothing of village matters themselves, and they won't hear a word from us because they think they are all wise and we utter fools—and under such a system (*dastur*), how can a village be otherwise than ruined? What does it matter that the Rajah is not a bad man, or that his *Naibs* don't purposely injure us; nay, at times some of them, after their own fashion, try to help us. It is the bad *dastur* that is ruining us.

Molvi Farid ud din: Ah, Rambaksh, the *Chota Sahib* may think you cattle, but you are wiser than he was. For this evil *dastur* which is ruining you and your neighbours and village is the "Despotic" (*khud muktiar*) *dastur*. And when rulers govern their subjects in this same way we call theirs a "Despotic" Government, and "Despotic" Governments always ruin the countries in which they are carried on for long. They may be necessary in the infancy of a nation; they become crimes when it grows up. Now you have a practical knowledge of both systems; you see how Shamshpur is prospering under a "Constitutional" system, and you know only too thoroughly what Kambakhtpur is coming to under the "Despotic" system, and pray have you any doubts as to which of these two are best?

Rambaksh: Am I an idiot? Who can doubt that the *Lumberdar's bandobast* (administration), which you call the "Constitutional" system, is the best?

Molvi Farid ud din: Well, now, you are only a villager, but you are a thoughtful man; and how would you call our present Sirkar, may its shadow never be less (*dam ikbalahoo!*)? Do you think our Government is a "Constitutional" one, or do you think it is a "Despotic" one? Don't be in a hurry; think before you reply.

Rambaksh: Oh! you must not ask me. What do I know of Governments? I am only a poor ryot!

Molvi Farid ud din: You are only a poor ryot but you nevertheless are not a fool; on the contrary, you are (and you know it and are proud of it) the wisest man in this village. Take the trouble to think it out; compare the management of this country by our present rulers with the management of Shamshpur by Kour Dharam Singh and with that of Kambakhtpur by Rajah Harbansrai and his *Naibs*, and say which does it most resemble.

Rambaksh (after some consideration): Well, there is our good Queen-Empress. She never comes here, certainly, and we never see her, and I hear the people in Hakikatabad sent her a petition last year, and they do say nearly a lakh of people signed it, but she never took any notice of it. But they say she is so busy there, over in *Vallayat* (England), and has so many countries elsewhere belonging to her that she has no time to attend to us Indians. And when I come to think of it, may God long preserve her, but I don't know that it does signify much to us who sits upon the Gaddi* over there in *Vallayat*. I must say that this is all rather like Rajah Harbansrai's *dastur*. Certainly I never heard that she consulted any of us Indians on any point, and as to *gaon khurch* (village expenses)—well, I have heard in Hakikatabad what krores and krores of money are every year spent by the *Sahib log* (Europeans), and without consulting any one! No! This is not at all like the Shamshpur *dastur*.

Molvi Farid ud din: And then look at all the *Naibs* and *Gomashtahs* she sends. Are they not like Raja Harbansrais? Very respectable men, no doubt; they don't take bribes, they don't certainly try to injure us, but what do they know of us and our real wants? Don't they pooh-pooh our old customs and, *har ke amad*† (each who comes) insists on introducing some new-fangled device for improving the condition of the country which, not unfrequently, ends in doing it harm? Do they consult us? Do they ever really talk over anything with us? Do they take care to see that we approve, and agree to everything, nay, to anything they see fit to do? Is it not with them as with your Kambakhtpur *Naibs*? "What do you know, you cattle folk? Hold your tongues." "Do this." "Don't do this." Is this like the Constitutional management of Shamshpur, or like the "Despotic" management of Kambakhtpur?

* *Gaddi*, lit. cushion; equivalent to throne.

† Referring to Saadi's well-known lines "*Har ke amad imarat-i-nau sakht, Raft o manzil ba diger perdakht,*" &c.

Rambaksh: Ah, Molvi Sahib, you are a learned man, but I see now what you mean, and I suppose our Government is what you call a "Despotic" one, and that, perhaps, is why the whole country now is discontented (it never was so when I was a boy), and why everything seems, from all I hear, to be going wrong, and why the Government jumma is always being raised, and with it our rents, and new taxes are imposed and . . . .

Molvi Farid ud din: Yes, certainly, our Government is a "Despotic" one, and a "Despotic" Government is always, when long continued, bad for every country, and we and our country are suffering in a hundred ways on this very account. But don't think I am speaking evil of our Governors, for I know many of them personally, and know that, as a rule, they are good and well-meaning men—men, in many matters, far more highly educated than the best of us. It is not the officers, it is not the members of Government, or the Lieutenant-Governors or Viceroys, that I find fault with. I hate the foolish fault-finding spirit in which some of our newspapers abuse, and wrongly attribute bad motives to, many of these whom I know to be good men. What I condemn and protest against is the system; it is against the system (*dastur*) of the Government, not against the gentlemen who carry on that Government (and who are as much tied down by that system as ourselves), that I complain.

Rambaksh: This is very true, no doubt, Molvi Sahib, and our Collector Sahib is a good man, and in the bad fever here a year ago he came out himself and with his own hands gave quinine to many, and his lady herself helped to nurse my little girl (the one I married this year to Ramrutton's son, you know), and he stopped a whole week here, though it was the rains, and he spoke kindly to all. Yes! he is a good man. But what has ali this to do with "Representative Institutions?"

Molvi Farid ud din: Certainly, Mr. Sidher is a good man, and besides all you know of him, though he does not care to talk much of such things as the officials generally are not favourable to the idea, he in his heart agrees very much with the views we educated natives hold as to those "Representative Institutions" about which you ask. What are these? Well, you have yourself understood that our present form of Government is Despotic, that it resembles the form of management of Kambakhtpur, and that it is a form of Government that entails necessarily much suffering on those subject to it. On the other hand, in Shamshpur you have had an example of "Constitutional" Government, and you have seen how the people have prospered under it, and what we desire is gradually to transform our present "Despotic" into a "Constitutional form of Government."

Rambaksh: But how can you possibly do that?

Molvi Farid ud din: By "Representative Institutions," that is to say, by having "Representatives" of the country, and a considerable number of them, in all the Councils, and thus allowing the country a real share in the administration.

Rambaksh: By "Representatives" you ean, then, men picked out of each town and district who would say to the Government what we want, and how we want it done, and what we don't want, and all that?

Molvi Farid ud din: Yes, but not precisely that; rather the men whom such "Representatives" would pick out from amongst themselves, the wisest and best men (just as your fellow-villagers picked you out to "represent" them in those enhancement cases), who would sit in the Councils and vote upon Government measures, and would have a right to ask the Government questions, and if anything was being done that they considered wrong would be entitled to insist on the Government explaining how the matter stood, or inquiring intc it.

Rambaksh: But I have heard that there were Raeeses and Rajahs in the Council. Why did they not do something good for us?

Molvi Farid ud din: A very proper question. But as a rule, the gentlemen selected by the Government as councillors, under the present despotic system, are not of the class of men who could do any good to the country. They are too generally men of moderate capacity, selected mainly because they are wealthy and always make themselves agreeable to European officials. Some really good men are thus selected, no doubt, but these are a minority. However, even if all were good men they could still, under the present "Despotic" system, do nothing because they are too few in number, and all they are allowed to do is to speak and vote in regard to particular new Acts which the Government has already decided to pass. They may say what they please, they may vote as they like, but the Act never comes before them until the Government has decided to pass it, and pass it the Government does. No doubt they may, and do at times, get a clause altered here and a clause altered there, but as to any real power to influence the action of Government to any useful extent their appointment is a pure farce. What we want is a much larger number of Indian members, and these not mere nominees of Government ready to say "*Bhot Accha*" (very good) or *jo hookum* (as you order) to whatever any official suggests, but the ablest and most independent men in the country, who shall be selected by the people themselves, and who will speak their minds, no matter what any one likes. And this is only a small part of the business. At present the Indian members, as I have already said, have only to vote upon new laws which the Government have decided to pass. But we want our "Representatives" to be consulted as to all public expenditure, and to have what is called the right of "interpellation," that is the right to ask Government questions, and to receive full answers thereon, on all subjects connected with the administration. "Why is this done? Why was that not done? Why is this officer allowed to abuse his authority?" and so on. You surely remember Mr. Zabardast; he was long before my time. But I have heard all about his manner of working the district.

Rambaksh: Remember him. Ram Ram, *uska nam mut lo* (don't mention him), I bear his marks now (where I can't show them to you, Molvi Sahib), though it is twenty years ago. You see his *Lushkur* (camp) came to our village.

That old villain Murtezur Shah (whom you, praise be to God, got transported four years ago in that torture case) was *Tahsildar* (or revenue head of the sub-division). When the Sahib rode in, about ten o'clock, his people complained that there was no grass for the horses. I was standing near. He shouted out, "Where is the Tahsildar?" The Tahsildar came trembling. "Protector of the poor," he said, "it is no fault of mine; it is these *budmashes* (bad characters) here whom I instructed to have every requisite, and who assured my people (I was in attendance on your honour's stirrup) that all was ready." "Whom did you make answerable for the grass?" said the Collector. "This man," said the *Tahsildar*, seizing me by the arm; "he is the *mukaddam*" (or head ryot). "Oh," said the Sahib, striking me with his whip, "you are the son of a pig the misbegotten (*sür ka bacha, haramzada*). I'll teach you how to attend to orders. Here, *khlassi* (tent-pitcher), tie him up and give him thirty *bents* (blows with a cane) on his bottom, and lay it well in." Now the Tahsildar had never spoken a word to me about the matter; it was the year of the drought, and there was not a particle of grass in the place; many of our cattle had died, the rest had been driven away to the dhak jungle beyond Salamabad where Laik Singh allowed them to be grazed. I tried to explain this, but the Sahib hit me over the mouth and face with his whip, shouting out, "Hold your tongue. I'll teach you, tie him up, tie him up, flog his life out." And I was dragged away and flogged till I became insensible. It was a month before I could walk. Yes, he was a bad one; many Collectors have I known—some good, some indifferent, but this was the only real devil.

Molvi Farid ud din: Yes, and I have heard worse things of him than this; far worse. Now do you suppose that if we had real representatives in the local Council that such a Bahadur would have been allowed to retain office for a single month? No! his misdeeds would have been authoritatively forced upon the notice of Government, and his career of oppression and violence cut short. As it was, some years later, Government came to know of some of his misdeeds and he was forced to retire; the Lieutenant-Governor, indeed, I have heard, wanted to dismiss him from the service (for, whatever their faults, not one in one hundred of our higher officials would tolerate such conduct), but he was highly connected, and the Governor-General thought his forced retirement a sufficient punishment. There are no men quite so bad as Mr. Zabardast, I believe, in the service anywhere now-a-days. But still there are in every province many officers who do abuse their official powers, and who are guilty of most unjustifiable acts of high-handedness, and nothing of this kind would be possible under that form of "Representative Institutions" that we advocate. This is only one single branch of the question. In all matters and in all directions the Government would be improved and the country benefited. The great drawback to our present form of Government is that our rulers never know the facts, never really understand the wishes or the wants of the people; our "Representatives" would supply all this, while we should still retain the superior knowledge of methods which the Europeans' greater experience in administration has given them. Don't think I am against Europeans; I have no greater friend than Mr. Sidher; what I want is such a change of system as shall prevent the incompetent and ill-disposed amongst them from doing harm, shall give the good ones a fairer field for the exercise of their talents and virtues, shall utilize for the service of the country the abilities and local knowledge of our own people, and gradually train these up in that work of administration which at present few of them, owing to want of experience, would be competent to carry on wihtout some aid from Europeans.

Rambaksh: Well, Molvi Sabib, it seems all right, but when you talk of picking out the best and wisest men, I don't seem to see my way. For the life of me I shouldn't know who to vote for. Of course, if there was anything to get by it Rajah Harbansrai would want to be elected, and we should all be ordered to vote for him. Not that I would; but I am sure I don't know whom we in this *Tahsil* (revenue sub-division) could select.

Molvi Farid ud din: Now what do you think the people of this whole *Tahsil* would say to Kour Dharam Singh?

Rambaksh.—I forgot. Certainly every man would say he is a wise and good man. Yes, I would vote for him. So would the whole *parganah*. Everybody wants him for *Sarpunch* (President of the Board of Arbitrators) whenever there is any arbitration matter.

Molvi Farid ud din: And what would you say to my Mamun (maternal uncle) Molvi Amanat Ali? Do not the people of Hakikatabad all trust him, and go to him for advice? For thirty years he was a leading pleader in this province—has any one a bad word to say of him?

Rambaksh: I do not myself know him, Molvi Sahib, but I have heard only good of him. Yes, he would be just the man; how he holds his own as elected Chairman of the Municipality! I have heard much good of him.

Molvi Farid ud din: Well, and do you not think that if Kour Dharam Singh and Molvi Amanat Ali and half a dozen others equally good men, equally well known and trusted in the neighbourhoods in which they reside, and almost equally certain to be chosen, were all to meet at the *Sudder* (head-quarters of the district), that they would be able to pick out one man willing and thoroughly fit to speak up for the people of this district, and for all of us Indians in this part of the country? Able and willing to tell Government the truth (which it now never gets) about everything that goes on, about every officer's conduct, about all our troubles and grievances, all our wants and wishes?

Rambaksh: No doubt, no doubt, and the same would be the case in other districts. But if every district sent only one man, there would be quite an army; the Government would never allow so many; they would be too many for them.

Molvi Farid ud din: Very likely, at first, the Government would not allow so many, though we hope to see the day when every district shall send at least two men to our local "Parliament," as they call such Councils in England; but, to begin with, our fifty odd district "Representatives" might meet and select from amongst themselves twelve good men to "represent" them all. And Government, if it allows the thing at all, must allow at least twelve such members in each local Council, as without at least this number it would be impossible to have any adequate "Representation," such as is required in a local Council, of all the many interests involved. Then there is the great Council, the Viceroy's Council, and for this the "Representatives" in the several Provincial Councils would select two, three, or four of their number, as the Government might settle, to "represent" them and their Province with the Government of India.

Rambaksh: This would be all very nice, Molvi Sahib, if ws could only be sure of getting your Mamun Sahib, and Kour Dharam Singh, and the other best men chosen. But people would consider it an honour to be so chosen, and some would fancy to make some profit out of it, and those men like Rajah Harbansrai, and, worse still, Sheikh Zalim, have many villages and tens of thousands of ryots, and they would be sure to order all to vote for them, and though I would not, nor would Matadin, the most of them are poor men, and they would be obliged to do so.

Molvi Farid ud din: Very true, and that is why (although we look forward to a time when every honest ryot shall have a vote for the "Representative" of his *Parganah* or *Tahsil* or *Tappah**), we do not propose in the beginning to give the "Franchise," that means the right to vote for representatives, to any of those classes of people who are unable to understand what a serious business this election is, or are liable to be driven to vote differently to what they think right. No! at first we should give votes to all the educated and well-to-do persons, to members of all local Boards, and all Municipal Committees, to the leading men or Punches of any leading classes, or predominant castes, and so on. In every province the arrangements will very likely have to be somewhat different, and in each district probably some minor special rules will be found necessary. But these are details which can only be worked out when the Government agrees to accept the "Constitutional" in lieu of the "Despotic" system.

Rambaksh: But I don't think much of several of the members of our local Board; and look at the *Choongiwallahs* (literally, Octroi people, *i.e.*, Municipal Commissioners) of Mutteenugger where Ramrattan lives. Why two of them are perfect fools, and as for well-to-do people, why some of them, like Lalla Subkhata Ram, are worse than the police!

Molvi Farid ud din: Certainly in every pod of cotton there are black seeds, and in every collection of men there are some rogues and a good many fools. All five fingers are not equal (*Panchon ungalyan barabar, nehin*). But take the upper and middle, fairly educated classes, and they contain, you well know, a majority of fairly sensible and reasonably honest men. And though even in our district some one or two bad men and some two or three stupids might get selected, the majority would be men whom all their neighbours look up to, like Kour Dharam Singh, and so the one man chosen by these to represent the district would be almost sure to be a good man. And again, if by chance one or two, say even six, of the districts (though this could never really happen) sent up unworthy men, what would these be amongst fifty, and what chance would one of these have of being selected by the majority for the Council? No! even at first starting there would be no serious difficulty, and after a very few years every really suitable man would be known not only in his own district, but throughout the province, and his private life and public acts would be patent to all.

Rambaksh: Yes! I see it is not so difficult as I thought, and I suppose with such Councils that, as time went on, the condition of the country would improve, and things would be done more as we like, and we should be more comfortable. But please tell me what good this would do to us poor men in Kambakhtpur? And this is not quite the worst of the Rajah Sahib's villages. Look at those miserable folks at Sutyanas Kheyra! What could the Council do there? What could they do for Sheikh Zalim's poor folk?

Molvi Farid ud din: Surely you do not suppose that such disgraceful mismanagement, such shameless oppression and roguery, as characterize the dealings of these two persons could go on, for long, unchecked under our new system. No! one or more of the representatives would get up in Council and call the attention of Government to the lamentable state of affairs existing in nearly 100 villages in this district. They would state a series of cases, they would give all the facts, and they would demand an inquiry. All this would be reported in the *akhbárs* (Press), public opinion would be roused against the incapacity in the one case, the wickedness in the other, that was blighting the lives of tens of thousands of poor honest souls. Their own kith and kin would fight shy of them, they would be made by social pressure to turn over a new leaf, and besides this, with full facts authoritatively laid before them, the Government would inquire, and indirectly add their pressure to that of the community, even if they did not find that they could take legal action, which in the Sheikh's case I am pretty sure they could. And mind you that the Government wants to prevent evils of this kind—it really does wish you all to be as happy and comfortable as possible; it is its misfortune that under its existing "Despotic" system, it never knows what is going on, or what ought to be done to attain what it wishes, but, ignorant alike of us and our customs and ways, blunders on trying to do us good, but, not unfrequently, doing us harm instead.

But don't you run away with the idea that when we get "Representation" all injustice and oppression, all poverty and distress, are to cease. This it can never do, unless and until all men are good and kind and wise, and that won't be in our time, Mukkadamji. All we can promise is that the amount of these afflictions will be greatly diminished, and a very great check imposed on the evil omissions or deeds of men like the Rajah Sahib and the Sheikh.

* Different territorial sub-divisions.

Rambaksh: Oh, I understand that. I know that some will be in trouble as long as the world lasts, but there is too much trouble now, and I can quite perceive that with a *bandobast* (arrangement) such as you propose the state of affairs would become a good deal pleasanter. But ah! Molvi Sahib, there is one thing worse than the Rajah Sahib, one thing as bad as the Sheikh, as bad as death, and that is the Police, and what can your new *bandobast* do where that is concerned? No! Parmeshar, the Divinity in heaven has created the tigers to prey upon the deer, and our Government on earth has created the Police to prey upon us.

Molvi Farid ud din: What can our new system do with the Police? Why, reform it: change it from a curse into a blessing. Truly, Rambaksh, you have hit upon one of those national curses for the reform of which, above all things, "Representative Institutions" are essential. You hear much talk about this matter of police; people talk of it as if it were a great difficulty, but really it is the simplest matter in the world. No doubt the police are a curse, but there are just two simple reasons for this. The first is that the police are much more numerous than is necessary, and are not nearly well enough paid. And the second grows partly out of this and partly out of the ignorance of European officers. The police work as enemies of the whole community instead of as friends. And why? First, because, being so ill-paid, they are driven to extort money and take bribes, and to assume a bullying attitude towards every one to frighten them into giving, and this naturally makes the whole community dislike and fear them. And, secondly, because their European officers, men, as a rule, of very moderate capacities, dealing practically only with the dregs of the population, think we are all thieves and scoundrels and deal with us accordingly, and either hate or despise us. I have known many Superintendents of Police, but only one who had not an unreasonably bad opinion of the Indian community. They, as a rule, look upon us all as criminals not yet caught, as enemies to be fought with, as beasts to be kept under, and the only persons they show the least favour to are miserable toadies who poison their minds with lies about all their neighbours. It is not these poor Superintendents' fault so much; it is their misfortune. Very hard many of them work, but it is all in the wrong way, and generally does more harm than good. Mighty careful are they about accoutrements and arms and drill, and all kinds of outside polish (*numaish*), but does one of them try to raise the moral tone of his men, to persuade them to be good, true, and just in all their dealings, to lead them to be kind and conciliatory to all people, to impress upon them that the only chance for real success lies in their having the whole of the non-criminal classes, the great bulk of the population, in fact, with them as friends? No, not one that I have ever seen or heard of; on the contrary, so far as their teachings go, whether by precept or example, they lead the police, already hated by all respectable people for their misdeeds, to look on the whole community as their natural antagonists. The whole question of police reform lies in these two simple matters. The Government don't understand it, nor will it be possible to make them realise it until every council chamber contains a large admixture of independent "representative" Indians, but believe me that within five years of our securing this, the police force of the country would have been entirely reformed, and would have begun to be regarded by the country as their natural protectors and champions.

Rambaksh: Ah! Molvi Sahib, what a thing is learning; rightly do folks say, *bidya bari chiz hai;* all this, now you explain it, is simple and certain, but it would never have occurred to me. Now I know something about it, I am all for "Representation." "Representative Institution" *ke jay** I say. But, oh! Molvi Sahib, you are like one who holds aloft, out of reach, a cup of delicious water to one parched with thirst and fainting for a draught. I see how good a thing it would be. I think if we could get it, that the country might, in time, almost be happy again, as in the old days when I was a boy. But how is it possible to bring about this good thing? Alas! we are poor men, and we cannot help, but you are so clever and so wise, perhaps you and others like you can manage it. Oh! pray try, and we will all bless you and pray for you.

Molvi Farid ud din: No, Rambaksh, I and other educated men are doing our best, but with very little result. It is your help we require, your support, and that of others like you, that is necessary if we are to succeed.

Rambaksh: Our help! What can we feeble beings do? Who cares for us? Don't you remember the saying, *Ghure pai sowen, mahalon ke supne dekhen*? (They sleep on dunghills and dream of palaces).

Molvi Farid ud din: That is a huge bundle of Urher stalks that you have here tied up; it must be very heavy and strong; do you think you could break it over your knee?

Rambaksh: Break it over my knee? No! nor could the Rajah Sahib's *hathi* (elephant) let him try ever so! But what do you mean?

Movil Farid ud din: But I can; see! I pull out one stem, and thus I break it easily over my knee; and now another, and now a third, and a fourth. See! in about ten minutes, though I don't want to spoil your bundle, I could break the whole. Nothing can be weaker or feebler than each single stem, yet see how very strong they become when banded together, each supporting and strengthening the other? Let that teach you that, weak and feeble as you and your fellows are, if once you all unite in good earnest in a good cause you will be so powerful that no Rajah Sahib's *hathi* can break you. (*Sát pánch ki lakri, ek janika bojh.*)

Rambaksh: But surely you don't want us to join together and fight with the Sirkar. If we killed all the Europeans how should we get along? All would be anarchy (*ghader*). You cannot mean this.

Molvi Farid ud din.—God forbid! This would be a sin. Why should we kill the poor Europeans? Many of them are really good men, most of them mean at any rate to do right.

* May it triumph, or May it be victorious.

They are ignorant no doubt of the rights of most matters concerning us; they blunder, they cause us misery, but they do it from ignorance—from an ignorance unavoidable under the system which they work on, and which, even did they wish it, they could not change without our help. Besides, though we of the new generation are growing up able to assist them and to do much for the country, the whole of us put together have not yet sufficient experience and self-reliance to manage the administration entirely without their help. Kill the Europeans! No, Rambaksh, let us say, rather, God bless all of them (and there are many such) who feel kindly towards us in their hearts, and according to their lights mean well towards us, and God forgive those amongst them (and let us hope they are not many) who dislike and despise us, and care nothing what becomes of us.

Rambaksh: That is very good, Molvi Sahib; you are a true *Rishi*, but what then do you mean?

Molvi Farid ud din: It is growing late, and I must be going; but I will try, briefly, to explain this. Although the Government of our country is Despotic, the Government of England is Constitutional and there every respectable man, even the cultivators and artizans, have the Franchise (power to vote for Representatives, you remember); and the people dislike Despotism, and they only allow it to continue here because they do not understand how this country has changed during the last twenty-five years (owing mainly to the education, and railroads, and post offices, and the like that they have given us), and believe us still to be children who must be managed, as a father manages young children, by orders, or in other words "despotically." But if we could once make the English nation at home (who have none of the prejudices on these matters that Europeans who have lived long out here so often insensibly contract) that we are no longer all of us children; that, thanks to their education, numbers of us now are quite fitted by our superior local knowledge, not only to fill a great majority of the posts now held by Europeans, and discharge the duties thereof far more satisfactorily than these by reason of being foreigners possibly can, but even to instruct and advise in most matters of domestic administration, they would at once, through their "representatives," insist upon our association in the work of governing the country on a much larger scale than at present, and on the concession to us of some form of "Representative institutions." To many of the best and highest of them the fact that the Government of India is still what they so greatly dislike, viz., "Despotic," is a source of real regret, and they would gladly accept any reasonable evidence that the continuance of such a system was no longer necessary. Besides this, even those who are less liberal and less high-minded are sensible. Practical common sense is the leading characteristic of the British nation; they know perfectly well that it is better to rule a contented than a discontented people, and one of their own holy texts says that a dinner of herbs where peace is is better than the grandest banquet where there is strife; and if once they saw us all, high and low, banded together and determined to obtain these "Representative Institutions," then they have too much common sense not to allow us to have them. Now, perhaps, you understand what I meant by that bundle of Urher stalks, that Union is strength.

Rambaksh: Well, Molvi Sahib, I am with you altogether, but what must we do, and what are you learned gentlemen doing.

Molvi Farid ud din: The first thing to be done is to make all the more intelligent of your fellows understand all I have explained to you to-day. Let these again teach it to all their friends, and these again to others, till there is not a sensible man in the whole district who does not understand the rights of the case, and does not really, from conviction, desire "Representative Institutions." Other friends are telling the ryots, the shop-keepers, the artisans, the same things in other districts, and if you all bear in mind that this is a matter in which you all, high and low, rich and poor, are in one way or another personally interested, it will not be long before the country as one man is united, in real truth, in their desire for this great reform.

Rambaksh: I see this, and I will do what I can. I will explain it every night on the *chopal* till every one who has any head (and the headless people will do what we tell them) knows it as well as I do, and if some one will put it into a little book, I will make the children read it in the school. Do not fear that in this neighbourhood we shall not all be crying very soon for "Representative Institutions." But what then, and what are you doing?

Molvi Farid ud din: I am founding at Hakikatabad a political association, and later, you and other head ryots, who have brains and honesty, and are not what that *Chota Sahib* thought you, mere cattle, must join it. This association will be a branch of the larger association at the capital, and will work with it. Then in this district, in any place where there are many intelligent ryots like yourself, or clever shop-keepers, or artisans there smaller branches must be formed to work in concert with our Hakikatabad Association.

Now the object of this system of associations, which will soon have spread into every *Parganah* or *Tahsil*, will be two-fold. First, to teach the people what I have this day been teaching you, and give them rational ideas of their rights and duties as free citizens; and, secondly, having brought about a rational agreement on these matters, to make it clear both to the Government here and the English nation, what that agreement and determination is to which we have come. For both purposes a good deal of money is required. We have to print, publish, and distribute books and papers. You want some one to write a little book about these matters I have been talking about? Well, if such a book be written, we should want at least five thousand copies for this district only, for there must be at least one copy for every village and hamlet, and in the larger places there should be 2, 3, 5, 10, 20 copies, according to the size of the place, and that costs money; and this is only one thing, and constantly matters arise about which it is necessary to circulate information. And then we must keep up communication with each other—you in the *mofussil* branches with us at the *Sudder* Station, and we with other district associations and the head-quarters, and the books and pamphlets and papers I have referred to have to be sent about, and to a great extent by post, and this costs a great deal in postage. And then, in connection with other associations, we have to prepare memorials setting forth our views and wishes, and to send people considerable distances to present these to the Viceroy or to the Lieutenant-Governor, and speak on our behalf. And, again, we have the National Congress, which meets yearly, and to which every district ought at least to send one "Representative," and it sometimes happens that the very man we know to be specially fitted for either task cannot, unaided, bear the expense of the long journey. And then, if the truths I have been trying to impress upon your mind are to be imprinted within any reasonable period on the minds of the entire population, merely distributing the books will not do. We must have earnest and clever men to go round from village to village and expound them, and though some of us, whenever we have leisure, do this, such work is intermittent, and we want men who will do nothing else but keep at it every day and all day, and though such men may do it for the love of their country, still they must live; and it is not amongst the rich and happy that we can usually look for such, but rather amongst those who are poor, and have suffered, and can therefore feel for all the suffering so rife amongst us: and for such, of course, we have to provide the necessary funds. And then where the work of an association develops, it becomes necessary to have a paid Secretary to manage the clerical business. None of these are large sums, but still in the aggregate a good deal of money is indispensable to successful work, even of that kind of work which may be called purely provincial. But then again in conjunction with other Associations and Leagues we have national work. We have to get some of our appeals printed and largely circulated in England, circulated not by the hundred but by the hundred thousand. And again it is absolutely essential that we should select able and earnest men like the Delegates we sent not long ago to England, and send them to England not for a week or two, but for a year at a time at least, to go round the country there, to all the larger towns and cities and attend public meetings and speak at them, explaining our grievances, and the remedies we desire to see applied, and generally to educate public opinion there as to the true state of affairs here, and gradually force home upon the minds of the people the conviction that we here have now really made up our minds as a nation that we do want "Representative Institutions." Moreover, it is equally necessary that some of our countrymen should obtain seats in "Parliament," so as to be in a position to advocate authoritatively our country's cause, and to insist on a hearing for our complaints and memorials. And all these things will cost a very great deal of money, and though other Associations will pay most of this, we too ought to give our share. So you see the old saying that "money is the sinews of war" is true even of this bloodless campaign against "Despotic Institutions" that we are undertaking, and money and a good deal of money, we must have.

Rambaksh: And how is it to be got? Of course, there are plenty of rich men who think nothing of giving Rs.10,000 to repair some old tank that nobody wants, or even to build a Racket Court for the *Sahib log*, so as to curry favour with these, and perhaps get their names published in the Gazette. But we shan't get anything from them, for, say what you like Molvi Sahib, the officials won't like all this. I don't say Mr. Sidher, but where is there another like him? But what will the Joint Sahib, Mr. Oonchanak say, and what will Mr. Bahadur, the Judge Sahib, think of it all? No, you won't get much from the rich, and the poor have next to nothing to give, and so, I fear, you will not get that good deal of money you say you must have.

Molvi Farid ud din: Well, as to some of the wealthy, the mean selfish time-servers, whose only thought is for themselves and who care nothing for their country and countrymen, a base herd, but, thank Heaven, not a large one, we shall of course get nothing from them. But there are, despite these miserable exceptions, a great many good men amongst the well-to-do and wealthy who have helped us and who will help us. No doubt, not a few of these consider it inexpedient to join us openly; some think they can do better for us and the country by maintaining friendly relations with the officials, however prejudiced and narrow-minded these may be, by humouring their prejudices and affecting to take no great interest in our movement; some, again, are really afraid of giving offence or of the consequences of this. Well, they give privately; they wish to aid the cause and do so, and we take care that no one knows it at present, and that they get into no trouble about it. But the time will come when the battle has been won, when they will be proud enough to have their names published as early benefactors of the scheme.

Rambaksh: But will these private donations suffice for your needs? I can hardly think so.

Molvi Farid ud din: Certainly not, and our main dependence is on you and your fellows; on the masses. There are twelve lakhs of people in this district, and if only two lakhs out of these gave us each four annas, on an average, during the year, that would yield us Rs.50,000 a year, far more than we could now-a-days require. And you see, what we think is this: that wherever there are good men like yourself who have got the people interested in the matter, they might at the Dusehra, and the Holee, collect a pice or two from each villager for the Association. And then at marriages, the man who is going to spend Rs.20 might resolve to spend only 19 and send in one rupee to the Association. And the tradespeople and the money-dealers, when they make up their accounts yearly, might resolve to set aside a cowrie in the rupee for this work, just as they now set aside a great deal more for other public and sacred purposes. After all, what purpose can be more of a public one, what more sacred, than this which promises to bring about relief and comfort to all classes throughout the empire? Every ryot may give only a pais, but as we say *phui, phui karke, taldo bharta hei.* (Mony a mickle maks a muckle).

Rambaksh: That is a capital plan, and I promise you that you shall have something even from Khambakhtpur at the next Dusehra, and from this day forwards be sure that all the little in my power shall be done to advance this good object. And now you are going, Molvi Sahib, please take this Rs.4-P2 I owe you for stamps and fees in that case you won for me. It ought to be far more for all the trouble you took, but that was what you said in your *Rooqua* (note).

Molvi Farid ud din: Oh! I make those who can afford it pay; we've all got to live. Thanks! Now you owe me nothing, and now I shall enrol you as a Member of our Association, and pay in this money in your name to our slender treasury. One word more, old friend. You said I was a true *Rishi*. I hope, as a good Mahomedan, I am in no way behind a true Brahmin or a true Christian in my love for all that is good, and in my desire to be of service to my fellow-men. Trouble yourself little about what men call themselves, whether Hindu, Moslem, or Christian. Look to what they are, and if good, remember that though they may wear different liveries, they are all humble servants of the one Lord. And may I say this more—"Representative Institutions" we shall get, but if we are to get all the good that is possible out of these, we must not only induce others to do justice to us, but we must do justice to ourselves. It is not merely by political enfranchisement that a people rises; they must grow in goodness as they grow in power, or evil will come of it, and while we band together to struggle against "Despotic Institutions," we must each and all in our inmost hearts resolve, and keep that resolve to live henceforth better lives, to love our fellow-men more, and gradually sink the all-absorbing interest in our own selfish cares, in a wider and nobler interest, in the welfare and the progress of our country and our fellow-countrymen. *Suphal kamai sudh ki jo lagr hur ke het.* ("Blessed are the earnings of the virtuous which go to the service of God.")

N.B.—The plan of the Hall which, in the Indian Edition, is placed at this point and is numbered pp. 215 and 216, will be found facing the inside front cover.

RESOLUTIONS passed at the **Second** *Indian National Congress, composed of Representatives from Calcutta, Madras, Bombay, Poona, Allahabad, Lahore, Lucknow, Agra, Benares, Ahmedabad, Kurrachee, Surat, Veerumgaum, Ganjam, Masulipatam, Chingleput, Tanjore, Combaconum, Madura, Tinnevelly, Coimbatore, Cuddapah, Anantapoor, Bellary, and Umballa, held in Calcutta, on the 27th, 28th, 29th, and 30th December,* **1886.**

RESOLUTIONS.

I.—Proposed by Mr. Rahimatulla Soyani (Bombay), seconded by Lala Murlidhur (Ambala), supported by Mr. G. Subramania Iyer (Madras), and carried by acclamation: "That this Congress of Delegates from all parts of India do humbly offer its dutiful and loyal congratulations to Her Most Gracious Majesty the Queen-Empress, on the approaching completion of the first half century of her memorable, beneficent, and glorious reign, and heartily wish her many, many more, and happy, years of rule over the great British Empire."

II.—Proposed by Mr. Dinshaw Edulji Watcha (Bombay), seconded by the Hon. S. Subramania Iyer (Madras), supported by Pandi Pranath (Lucknow), and carried by a very large majority: "That this Congress regards with the deepest sympathy, and views with grave apprehension, the increasing poverty of vast numbers of the population of India, and (although aware that the Government is not overlooking this matter and is contemplating certain palliatives) desires to record its fixed conviction that the introduction of Representative Institutions will prove one of the most important practical steps towards the amelioration of the condition of the people."

III.—Proposed by Rai Kunia Lall Banerjee Bahadur (Calcutta), seconded by Mr. P. Rangiah Nayudu (Madras), supported by Mr. Ghanasham Nilkanth (Bombay), and carried unanimously: "That this Congress do emphatically re-affirm the 3rd Resolution of the Congress of 1885, and distinctly declare its belief that the reform and expansion of the Council of the Governor-General for making Laws and of the Provincial Legislative Councils, therein suggested, have now become essential alike in the interests of India and England."

IV.—Proposed by Mr. Surendrath Banerjee (Calcutta), seconded by Mr. N. G. Chandavarkar (Bombay), supported by Mr. Sharfuddin (Behar), and carried without a dissentient voice: "That this Congress is of opinion that, in giving practical effect to this essential reform, regard should be had (subject to such modifications as, on a more detailed examination of the question, may commend themselves to the Government) to the principles embodied in the following tentative suggestions:—

(1.)—The number of persons composing the Legislative Councils, both Provincial and of the Governor-General, to be materially increased. Not less than one-half the Members of such enlarged Councils to be elected. Not more than one-fourth to be officials, having seats *ex-officio* in such Councils, and not more than one-fourth to be Members, official or non-official, nominated by Government.

(2.)—The right to elect members to the Provincial Councils to be conferred only on those classes and members of the community, *primâ-facie*, capable of exercising it wisely and independently. In Bengal and Bombay the Councillors may be elected by the members of Municipalities, District Boards, Chambers of Commerce, and the Universities, or an electorate may be constituted of all persons possessing such qualifications, educational and pecuniary, as may be deemed necessary. In Madras, the Councillors may be elected either by District Boards, Municipalities, Chambers of Commerce, and the University, or by Electoral Colleges, composed of members partly elected by these bodies and partly nominated by Government. In the North-West Provinces and Oudh and in the Punjab, Councillors may be elected by an Electoral College, composed of members elected by Municipal and District Boards and nominated, to an extent not exceeding one-sixth of the total number, by Government, it being understood that the same elective system now in force where Municipal Boards are concerned will be applied to District Boards, and the right of electing members to these latter extended to the cultivating class. But whatever system be adopted (and the details must be worked out separately for each province) care must be taken that all sections of the community and all great interests are adequately represented.

(3.)—The elected Members of the Council of the Governor-General for making Laws to be elected by the elected Members of the several Provincial Councils.

(4.)—No elected or nominated Member of any Council to receive any salary or remuneration in virtue of such membership, but any such Member already in receipt of any Government salary or allowance to continue to draw the same unchanged during membership, and all Members to be entitled to be reimbursed any expenses incurred in travelling in connection with their membership.

(5.)—All persons resident in India to be eligible for seats in Council, whether as electees or nominees without distinction of race, creed, caste or colour.

(6.)—All legislative measures and all financial questions, including all Budgets, whether these involve new or enhanced taxation or not, to be necessarily submitted to, and dealt with by, these Councils. In the case of all other branches of the administration, any Member to be at liberty, after due notice, to put any question he sees fit to the *ex-officio* Members (or such one of these as may be specially charged with the supervision of the particular branch concerned), and to be entitled (except as hereinafter provided) to receive a reply to his question, together with copies of any papers requisite for the thorough comprehension of the subject; and, on this reply, the Council to be at liberty to consider and discuss the question, and record thereon such resolution as may appear fitting to the majority. Provided that if the subject in regard to which the inquiry is made involves matters of foreign policy, Military dispositions or strategy, or is otherwise of such a nature that, in the opinion of the Executive, the Public interest would be materially imperilled by the communication of the information asked for, it shall be competent for them to instruct the *ex-officio* Members, or one of them, to reply accordingly and decline to furnish the information asked for.

(7.)—The Executive Government shall possess the power of overruling the decision arrived at by the majority of the Council in every case in which, in its opinion, the public interests would suffer by the acceptance of such decision; but whenever this power is exercised, a full exposition of the grounds on which this has been considered necessary shall be published within one month, and, in the case of local Governments, they shall report the circumstances and explain their action to the Government of India, and, in the case of this latter, it shall report and explain to the Secretary of State; and, in any such case, on a representation made through the Government of India and the Secretary of State by the overruled majority, it shall be competent to the Standing Committee of the House of Commons (recommended in the 3rd Resolution of last year's Congress, which this present Congress has affirmed) to consider the matter, and call for any, and all, papers or information, and hear any persons on behalf of such majority or otherwise, and thereafter, if needful, report thereon to the full House."

V.—Proposed by Mr. N. N. Gupta (Kurrachi), seconded by Mr. M. B. Namjoshi (Poona), supported by Kumar Binay Krishna (Calcutta), and carried unanimously: "That this Congress do invite all Public Bodies and all Associations throughout the country, humbly and earnestly, to entreat His Excellency the Viceroy to obtain the sanction of Her Majesty's Secretary of State for India, to the appointment of a Commission to inquire exhaustively into the best method of introducing such a tentative form of Representative Institutions into India, as has been indicated in Resolutions III. of the past, and IV. of the present, year's Congress.

VI.—Proposed by Mr. Surendra Nath Banerjee (Calcutta); seconded by Mr. M. B. Namjoshi (Poona); supported by Pandit S. Agnihotri (Lahore), and carried unanimously: "That a Committee, composed of the gentlemen named in the margin,* be appointed to consider the Public Service Question and report thereon to this Congress.

*Hon'ble Dadabhai Naoroji (Bombay)
" S. Subramania Iyer (Madras)
" Peary Mohan Mookerjee (Calcutta)
Mr. G. Subramania Iyer (Madras)
Babu Matilal Ghose (Calcutta)
Mr. Surendra Nath Banerjee (Calcutta)
" Gangapershad Varma (Lucknow)
" Ramkali Chaudhuri (Benares)
Mr. Guru Prasad Sen (Patna)
Pundit Prannath (Lucknow)
Munshi Kashipershad (Allahabad)
Nawab Reza Ali Khan (Lucknow)
Mr. Hamid Ali (Lucknow)
Lala Kanhyadal (Amritsar)
Rao Sahib Gungadhar Rao Madhaw Chitnavis (Nagpur)
Mr. Rahimatulla M. Sayani (Bombay)

VII.—Proposed by Mr. Surendra Nath Banerjee (Calcutta), seconded by the Hon. S. Subramania Iyer (Madras), and carried unanimously: "That this Congress approves and adopts the report,* submitted by the Committee appointed by Resolution VI."

VIII.—Proposed by Mr. S. A. Saminada Iyer (Tanjore), seconded by Mr. H. H. Dhruva (Surat), supported by Dr. Trailokyanath Mitter, (Calcutta), and carried unanimously: "That, in the opinion of this Congress, the time has now arrived when the system of trial by jury may be safely extended into many part of the country where it is not at present in force."

IX.—Proposed by Mr. W. C. Bonnerjee (Calcutta), seconded by the Hon. Peary Mohan Mookerjee (Calcutta), supported by Munshi Sadho Lal (Benares), and carried by a very large majority: "That, in the opinion of this Congress, the innovation made in 1872, in the system of trial by jury, depriving the verdicts of juries of all finality, has proved injurious to the country, and that the powers then for the first time vested in Sessions Judges and High Courts, of setting aside verdicts of acquittal, should be at once withdrawn."

X.—Proposed by Mr. Mano Mohan Ghose (Calcutta), seconded by Mr. T. Chidambara Row (Bellary), supported by Khajeh Abdul Aleem, (Dacca), and carried unanimously: "That in the opinion of this Congress, a provision similar to that contained in the Summary Jurisdiction Act of England (under which accused persons in serious cases have the option of demanding a committal to the Sessions Court), should be introduced into the Indian Code of Criminal Procedure, enabling accused persons, in warrant cases, to demand that, instead of being tried by the Magistrate, they be committed to the Court of Sessions."

XI.—Proposed by Mr. Darji Abaji Khare (Bombay), seconded by Munshi Kashipershad (Allahabad), supported by Mr. Sri Ram (Lucknow), and carried unanimously: "That this Congress do place on record an expression of the universal conviction, that a complete separation of executive and judicial functions (such that in no case the two functions shall be combined in the same officer) has become an urgent necessity, and that, in its opinion it behoves the Government to effect this separation without further delay, even though this should, in some Provinces, involve some extra expenditure."

XII.—Proposed by Rajah Rampal Singh (Oudh), seconded by Mr. R. D. Mehta (Calcutta), and carried by acclamation: "That in view to the unsettled state of public affairs in Europe, and the immense assistance that the people of this country, if duly prepared therefor, is capable of rendering to Great Britain in the event of any serious complications arising, this Congress do earnestly appeal to the Government to authorise (under such rules and restrictions as may to it seem fitting), a system of Volunteering for the Indian inhabitants of the country, such as may qualify them to support the Government effectively in any crisis."

XIII.—Proposed by Mr. W. C. Bonnerjee (Calcutta), seconded by Mr. N. G. Chandavarkar (Bombay), and carried unanimously: "That Standing Congress Committees be constituted at all important centres."

XIV.—Proposed by Mr. A. O. Hume (Punjaub), seconded by the Hon. S. Subramania Iyer (Madras), and carried by acclamation: "That the Third Indian National Congress assemble at Madras on the 27th of December, 1887."

XV.—Proposed by Mr. Rangiah Nayudu (Madras), and seconded by Mr. Sorabjee Framjee Patel (Bombay), and carried unanimously; "That copies of these Resolutions be forwarded to His Excellency the Viceroy-in-Council, with the humble request that he will cause the 1st Resolution to be submitted in due course to Her Majesty the Queen-Empress, that he will cause all the Resolutions to be laid before Her Majesty's Secretary of State for India, and that he himself will be graciously pleased, in consultation with his colleagues, to afford them his best consideration."

(Signed) DADABHAI NAOROJI,
President of the Second Indian National Congress.

These Resolutions of the **Second Congress** *were very fully considered and discussed during the year* 1886, *and were unanimously approved and ratified by almost every Political Association (more than one hundred in number) in the Empire, and by Public Meetings at nearly every town in India, so that it is not unreasonable to assume now that they faithfully represent the views of the great bulk of the intelligent classes in British India.*

---

*REPORT.

We, the Members of the Committee appointed by the Congress to submit a statement in connection with the Public Service Question, have the honour to report that the following resolutions were unanimously adopted by us at a meeting held yesterday:—

1.—That the open Competitive Examination be held simultaneously, both in India and in England.

2.—That the simultaneous examinations thus held be equally open to all classes of Her Majesty's subjects.

3.—That the classified list be prepared according to merit.

4.—That the Congress express the hope that the Civil Service Commissioners will give fair consideration to Sanskrit and Arabic among the subjects of examination.

5.—That the age of Candidates eligible for admission to the open Competitive Examination be not less than 19, or, as recommended by Sir C. Aitchison, more than 23 years.

6.—That simultaneous examinations being granted, the Statutory Civil Service be closed for first appointments.

7.—That the appointments in the Statutory Civil Service, under the existing rules, be still left open to the Members of the Uncovenanted Service, and to all professional men of proved merit and ability.

8.—That all appointments requiring educational qualifications, other than covenanted first appointments, be filled by Competitive Examinations held in the different Provinces, and open in each Province to such natural-born subjects of H.M. only as are residents thereof.

These Resolutions, it is hoped, cover the main principles which underlie the questions set by the Public Service Commission. For a more detailed consideration there was no time.

(Signed) DADABHAI NAOROJI,
President of the Committee.

30th December, 1886.

REPORT

OF THE

FOURTH

Indian National Congress,

HELD AT

ALLAHABAD,

On the 26th, 27th, 28th and 29th of December,

1888.

SOME
OF
ENGLAND'S PLEDGES TO INDIA.

ACT OF PARLIAMENT OF 1833.

That no native of the said territories (India) nor any natural-born subject of His Majesty resident therein shall, by reason only of his religion, place of birth, descent, colour, or any of them, be disabled from holding any place, office, or employment under the said Government (Act 3 and 4, Wm. IV., c. 85, s. 87, 1833.)

Her Majesty's Proclamation in 1858.

We hold ourselves bound to the natives of our Indian Territories by the same obligations of duty which bind us to all our other Subjects; and those obligations, by the Blessing of Almighty God, we shall faithfully and conscientiously fulfil.

• • • • •

And it is our further will that, so far as may be, our Subjects, of whatever Race or Creed, be freely and impartially admitted to Offices in our Service, the Duties of which they may be qualified by their education, ability, and integrity, duly to discharge.

Lord Northbrook on Indian affairs.

"There is one simple test which we may apply to all Indian questions: let us never forget that it is our duty to govern India, not for our own profit and advantage, but for the benefit of the Natives of India."

Lord Lytton's Speech at the Delhi Assemblage on 1st January 1877.

"But you, the Natives of India, whatever your race, and whatever your creed, have a recognised claim to share largely with your English fellow-subjects, according to your capacity for the task, in the administration of the country you inhabit. This claim is founded in the highest justice It has been repeatedly affirmed by British and Indian statesmen, and by the Legislation of the Imperial Parliament. It is recognised by the Government of India, as binding on its honour, and consistent with all the aims of its policy."

Lord Ripon in the Viceregal Legislative Council.

The document (Her Majesty's Proclamation) is not a treaty, it is not a diplomatic instrument, it is a declaration of principles of Government which, if it is obligatory at all, is obligatory in respect to all to which it is addressed. The doctrine, therefore, to which Sir Fitzjames Stephen has given the sanction of his authority, I feel bound to repudiate to the utmost of my power. It seems to me to be inconsistent with the character of my Sovereign and with the honour of my country, and if it were once to be received and acted upon by the Government of England, it would do more than anything else could possibly do to strike at the root of our power and to destroy our just influence. Because that power and that influence rests upon the conviction of our good faith more than upon any other foundation, aye, more than upon the valour of our soldiers and the reputation of our arms.

Lord Dufferin's Speech on the occasion of Her Majesty's Jubilee in 1887.

"Glad and happy should I be if, during my sojourn among them, (the people of India), circumstances permitted me to extend, and to place upon a wider and more logical footing, the political status which was so wisely given, a generation ago, by that great statesman, Lord Halifax, to such Indian gentlemen as by their influence, their acquirements and the confidence they inspired in their fellow-countrymen, were marked out as useful adjuncts to our Legislative Councils."

SOME
OF
ENGLAND'S PLEDGES TO INDIA.

ACT OF PARLIAMENT OF 1833.

That no native of the said territories (India) nor any natural-born subject of His Majesty resident therein shall, by reason only of his religion, place of birth, descent, colour or any of them, be disabled from holding any place, office, or employment, under the said Government (Act 3 and 4, Wm. IV, c. 85, s. 87, 1833.)

Her Majesty's Proclamation in 1858.

"We hold ourselves bound to the natives of our Indian territories by the same obligations of duty which bind us to all our other subjects; and those obligations, by the blessing of Almighty God, we shall faithfully and conscientiously fulfil."

* * * *

"And it is our further will that, so far as may be, our subjects, of whatever race or creed, be freely and impartially admitted to offices in our service, the duties of which they may be qualified by their education, ability, and integrity, duly to discharge."

Lord Northbrook on Indian affairs.

"There is one simple test which we may apply to all Indian questions; let us never forget that it is our duty to govern India, not for our own profit and advantage, but for the benefit of the Natives of India."

Lord Lytton's Speech at the Delhi Assemblage on 1st January 1877.

"But you, the natives of India, whatever your race, and whatever your creed, have a recognised claim to share largely with your English fellow-subjects, according to your capacity for the task, in the administration of the country you inhabit. This claim is founded in the highest justice. It has been repeatedly affirmed by British and Indian statesmen and by the legislation of the Imperial Parliament. It is recognised by the Government of India as binding on its honour, and consistent with all the aims of its policy."

Lord Ripon in the Viceregal Legislative Council.

"The document (Her Majesty's Proclamation) is not a treaty, it is not a diplomatic instrument, it is a declaration of principles of Government which, if it is obligatory at all, is obligatory in respect to all to whom it is addressed. The doctrine, therefore, to which Sir Fitzjames Stephen has given the sanction of his authority, I feel bound to repudiate to the utmost of my power. It seems to me to be inconsistent with the character of my Sovereign and with the honour of my country, and if it were once to be received and acted upon by the Government of England, it would do more than anything else could possibly do to strike at the root of our power and to destroy our just influence, because that power and that influence rest upon the conviction of our good faith more than upon any other foundation, aye, more than upon the prowess of our soldiers and the reputation of our arms."

Lord Dufferin's Speech on the occasion of Her Majesty's Jubilee in 1887.

"Glad and happy should I be if, during my sojourn amongst them (the people of India), circumstances permitted me to extend and to place upon a wider and more logical footing, the political status which was so wisely given, a generation ago, by that great statesman, Lord Halifax, to such Indian gentlemen as by their influence, their acquirements and the confidence they inspired in their fellow-countrymen, were marked out as useful adjuncts to our Legislative Councils."

Contents.

CONTENTS

THE FOURTH INDIAN NATIONAL CONGRESS.

"If you go on making your appeal with fairness, courage and moderation to the great English nation, they will assuredly respond to your prayers, for as the harp responds to the harper's touch so does the great deep heart of England respond to every reasonable prayer for justice and freedom."

*(Speech of Pandit Bishen Narayan Dhar.)**

MISUNDERSTOOD, misrepresented and maligned—but ever growing in strength and determination amid the vivifying storms of opposition and abuse—that vast body of Her Majesty's subjects in India, who now support the Congress movement, might well accept the words above quoted as a synthesis of their settled policy.

In the British nation's love of freedom and justice their faith is firm and abiding. They will press their claims by fair and loyal means only, relying solely for success on moral† force. Those claims will always be, not only moderate, but far within the limits of what justice would endorse; no opposition and no persecution will daunt them, but they will go on and on, insisting and insisting, with an ever-growing volume of voice that will and *must*, *some* day, prevail.

The Fourth Indian National Congress was heralded by a tumultuous outbreak of opposition. Ill-informed or prejudiced writers stormed, reviled, and, alike in Indian and English Journals and other publications, distorted every fact and speech. The secret enemies of British rule (too acute not to perceive that the success of the movement means the perpetuation of this rule), and large sections of the official community (too blinded by class bias to catch the faintest glimpse of this cardinal fact), together with their entire train of obsequious followers, laboured ceaselessly to strangle the movement. A Lieutenant-Governor came forward to denounce its methods and ridicule its measures, while a Viceroy—misled, let us hope, by the misrepresentations of adversaries—stood up to condemn its aims and objects in a public speech, characterised by a misconception of facts, unparalleled in any public utterance, of any similarly exalted representative of India's beloved Sovereign.

Yet, despite—or shall we say *in consequence* ‡—of all this frantic opposition, the development of the Congress movement during the year 1888 was simply marvellous, and the Congress which closed the year was not only in every respect greater and grander than any previous one, but was so thoroughly representative of every part of the Empire, and of every class, caste, creed,

* Page 21 of the Detailed Report.

† "Not by violence or noise have the great things of the earth been achieved; not by ambition or self-seeking can a nation's life be regenerated; but by calm indomitable reliance on that moral force which is the supreme reason, and by implanting in all with whom you may come in contact the conviction that you look for eventual triumph to these means, and these only; and that the moral power which has made the English nation glorious throughout an Empire on which it has been well and truly said that the sun never sets, is the power to which you trust for the triumph o those great principles of justice and freedom which you are all here assembled to vindicate and uphold. (*Cheers.* (Mr. Howard's speech on the Separation of the Executive and Judicial functions—*vide* p. 40 of Detailed Report.)

‡ It is a fact that in many parts of the country elderly men, who had almost withdrawn from worldly affairs, an who had never before taken any share in politics, roused by the malignant slanders of the opposition on those whon they knew to be labouring, heart and soul, for the good of the country, for the first time in their lives became politi cians and came forward to support, openly and energetically, the Congress.

community and interest indigenous in that Empire, that further advance in this direction seems, now, to be almost impossible.

During the year the greater part of the country was regularly divided into electoral divisions, and the minimum* number of delegates to be elected by each was settled. These divisions, for the double purpose of the education of the people and the convenience of voters, were re-divided into sub-divisions, and divisional and sub-divisional committees were created in all these, composed either of the delegates to previous Congresses with others whom they co-opted, or, as in Berar for instance, of men specially elected, *ad hoc*, by the people. Hundreds of thousands of tracts, pamphlets, speeches and leaflets were put into circulation in all the languages of India. Thousands of public and semi-public meetings and gatherings were held, not in one province, but in almost every district in the Empire. Hundreds of missionaries of the cause travelled from town to town and village to village, expounding the good tidings of the Congress, and the fiercer the opposition raged and the more persistent the efforts of the adversaries of the movement, the more strenuous became the efforts of its supporters. It resulted that, whereas at the close of 1887 we were unable to assert that more than ten per cent. of the population knew anything of the Congress movement, we can, at the present moment, safely affirm that fully one-third of the population know more or less about, and are distinctly favourable to, the movement. When we say population we refer of course to the adult males thereof, for, except in specially advanced localities,† the women know, as yet, practically, little of the matter, or, if they do, we have no means of ascertaining this. But of the 50 millions of adult males inhabiting British territory, at least one-third are now more or less earnestly on the side of the Congress; and if we exclude from the 50 millions the 10 or 12 millions of adult males, who, utterly poverty-stricken and absolutely without education, can care for nothing beyond that daily food which they so often fail to compass, not very far short of half the remaining 38 millions, the *real* population of the Empire, are this day cognizant of the Congress movement, and, so far as they understand it, its supporters and well-wishers. There are still millions on millions who know nothing about it, but in the entire Empire, including even the Anglo-Indians, there is not half a million even of people in any way opposed to it.

Fully three millions of men (more men than voted at the elections for the present Imperial House of Commons) took a direct ‡ part in the elections for the delegates to the 1888 Congress, either at the final meetings at the divisional head-quarters, or at the minor local meetings, to select representatives to attend these. And this three millions of active supporters, representing fully five times this number of favourers of the movement, and constituting with their women, children and dependents fully 75 millions of the population, is the "microscopic minority" of the Marquis of Dufferin and Ava.

* The education in political work, that a personal participation in these Congresses affords, is so valuable that it was considered inexpedient in 1888 to limit the number of delegates that each division might elect. But some 1,500 (of whom 1,248, at least, actually took their seats at the Congress) were elected in 1888, and there is little doubt that in 1889, if no limits be fixed, 3,000 will be elected. It is felt that these huge numbers are unsuited to a deliberative assembly, and hence it is in contemplation to limit the number to 1,000, which, allowing for death, sickness and other unavoidable causes of absence, would reduce the number of actual sitting members, in future Congresses, to between 800 and 900.

† In Calcutta on the river banks, where tens of thousands of women proceed every morning to bathe, many of them Hindu ladies of the highest families, the *Kangress*, as they call it, was for months the one staple subject of feminine discussion. In Allahabad, native ladies were found to have had serious differences with some few of their old friends, because, as they told their husbands, these old friends were *anti*. But as a rule the women are only now *just* beginning to accept *Kangress* as a household word, and here and there institute a "poojah" or religious observance in its honour.

‡ *Vide* note A, p. lviii.

It may be useful now to compare the constitution, territorially regarded, of the fourth Congress with that of the second and third :—

Presidency or Province.	Number of Delegates.		
	In 1886 in Calcutta.	In 1887 in Madras.	In 1888 in Allahabad.
Madras	47	362	95
Bombay and Sindh	47	99	163
Punjab	17	9	80
North-Western Provinces and Oudh	74	45	583
Central Provinces and Berar	8	13	73
Bengal, Behar, Orissa, and Assam	238	79	254
Total	431	607	1,248

Thus, whilst all the divisions of the country were well represented, the North-West Provinces and Oudh were, so to speak, over represented. This was, to a certain extent, due to the fact that the Congress was held at Allahabad. The expense of the journey and the time occupied in coming and going being much less, the province, in which the Congress is held, always sends the largest number of delegates. It was so at both the second and third Congresses; but a more important reason for the very large attendance from Oudh (and the same cause operated in the North-West Provinces) was well explained by Moulvi Mohamed Hidayut Rasul. He said* :—

'Now, can you say how so many able and distinguished delegates have come to be returned from Oudh and specially from Lucknow? Gentlemen, I will whisper it in your ears. The truth of it is, that all this good result is due to the kindness of our brethren in the Aligurh Camp—the opponents of the Congress. (*Loud cheers.*) I assure you that, if our hostile brethren had not made such a grand show of opposition, the Congress would certainly not have been the success that it has been to-day. (*Cheers.*) To my mind, the National Congress is like the vine, which, the more it is pruned, the more it flourishes. (*Cheers.*) There is no doubt that our kind opponents have spared no pains to prune it out of existence; but still the numerous branches which delight the eyes of spectators in this vast hall to-day are, to no small extent, the outcome of their persistent pruning." (*Cheers.*)

Unquestionably, in the North-West Provinces, the vehement opposition of the officials, and their allies, Sir Syed Ahmed and others of less importance, and their persistent misstatements as to the character and *volume* of the movement, very largely increased the number of the delegates who attended from these provinces. Then came Sir Auckland Colvin's letter, again ludicrously underrating the strength of the party, which not only acted as a stimulant to the people of the provinces over which he rules, but probably doubled the number of delegates from Madras, to the people of which presidency attendance at Allahabad, involving journeys of from three to four thousand miles, was a serious business. Lastly came Lord Dufferin's speech, and this put the finishing touch to the general enthusiasm. Nearly half a vast nation like ours, opposed to adversaries less than one-fiftieth of their number, naturally resented the careless disregard of facts which designated them a microscopic minority; and when in addition to this the highest personage in the land took advantage of a convivial meeting on the eve of his departure—a meeting at which none of them could be present—to ridicule them, and misrepresent in the most grievous manner their aims and aspirations, it is not difficult to

* Page 51 of Detailed Report.

understand how a strong practical protest, in the shape of personal attendance at the much maligned Congress, came to be widely resolved upon. Scores of gentlemen for instance—many of them occupying high positions—candidly avowed that it was Lord Dufferin's speech alone that, almost at the last moment, had decided them to face the sacrifices that attendance at the Congress, in their cases, involved. How powerful was the stimulus afforded may be judged from the very large size of the gathering, notwithstanding the introduction of a new rule (requiring each delegate to pay a fixed fee towards the expenses of the Congress before taking his seat), which was expected materially to reduce the number. But "the fiercer the blast the intenser grows the heat," and, despite this new rule, the raging blasts of calumny and persecution only resulted in 1,248 delegates taking the place, at Allahabad, of the 607 who were present at Madras.

Looking now to the constitution of this very large body of delegates, nothing, as we shall see, could well be more thoroughly representative. If we turn first to creeds and races, we find that there were 965 Hindus,* 221 Mahomedans, 22 Native and 16 European Christians, 11 Jains, 7 Parsees and 6 Sikhs; the comparative paucity of these latter being due, solely, to the fact of there being, as yet, very few Sikhs sufficiently educated to serve advantageously as delegates. If we consider next the positions occupied by these gentlemen, whether hereditary or as public men, we find that there were amongst them 6 Princes, 4 Rajahs, 17 Nawabs, 3 Sardars and 54 members of noble families; again, there were 3 members of Council, 73 Honorary Magistrates, 12 Chairmen, 19 Vice-Chairmen, and 127 Commissioners of Municipalities, 10 Chairmen and Vice-Chairmen and 69 Members of Local and District Boards, 27 Fellows of Universities, 3 Public Prosecutors, 1 Coroner, &c. Lastly, if we consider their occupations and professions, we notice 455 in one branch or other of the legal profession, 42 in the medical profession, 5 engineers, 127 merchants and traders, 85 bankers, 73 editors and journalists, 297 landed proprietors, 102 inferior landholders, 17 ryots or cultivators, 2 artisans, 7 shopkeepers, 31 clergymen, missionaries, priests and religious teachers, 59 educationalists, principals and professors of colleges, masters of schools, and public lecturers, 6 printers, 18 contractors, &c. The numbers of cultivators, artisans and petty shopkeepers are very small, but this was not because these classes did not widely interest themselves in the elections, for they constituted the majority of the electors, but because as a rule† these classes elected men better educated than themselves; often their landlords, where they were on good terms with these; their favourite lawyers, where they were not; or again men known to every one as upholders of the national cause.

Allahabad, the capital of the United Provinces (*i.e.*, the North-Western Provinces and Oudh) was the place at which it was settled, at Madras, that the next Congress should be held. But here it seemed, for a long time, as if it would be impossible to find any suitable site. The authorities, Civil and Military, threw every obstacle in the way of the local Congressmen, whose duty it was

---

* Including members of the Arya and Brahmo Samajes, &c.

† "Whenever any *real* system of representation is introduced into India, the bulk of the representatives here, as in England, will always be drawn from the more highly educated classes. * * * * The Empire of Mind is indestructible, and though clouds may at times, here or there, obstruct their rays, sooner shall the sun cease to give light by day and the moon by night than the more highly educated cease to be chosen as leaders and representatives by their less enlightened brethren." (*Hume's letter to Colvin*, s. 52.)

to prepare for the gathering, and unconstitutionally stretched the large powers vested in them to obstruct, and, if practicable, render impossible the assemblage. As the Hon'ble Pandit Ajoodhia Nath, President of the Reception Committee, remarked* in his opening speech :—

"We were first of all led to believe—I may say distinctly informed—that we should be permitted to occupy the Khusro Bagh for our encampment. But a little later, to our great disappointment, we were told that the requisite permission could not be accorded (*Cries of 'Shame!'*); and no satisfactory reason was assigned for this change of front. In April, after much negotiation, permission was granted to us to pitch our camp on a large plot of waste ground lying between the fort railway station and the fort, on payment of rent. This rent we paid in advance, and we were assured that there would be no further difficulty in the way of our occupying that piece of land. But, Gentlemen, in the month of August—four months later—we were informed that on sanitary grounds we could not be allowed to occupy that place, and the rent money, which we had paid in advance, was returned to us. Then we managed to secure a group of houses belonging to members of the Reception Committee and other friends, not very far away from the office of the *Pioneer*. This was too much for our opponents, and as some of the houses were unfortunately situated within the Cantonment limits, the Military authorities arbitrarily prohibited our utilizing those houses for Congress purposes. ('*Shame!*') No inquiry was made as to the sanitary arrangements we were going to make. It was apparently taken for granted that the Congress Camp—and you have seen what a beautiful and perfectly managed camp ours is—would be the filthiest and most insanitary of all gatherings. ('*Shame!*') It is not too much to say that no other gathering for any other purpose would have been thus barred. Hundreds of thousands of men, poor, ill-clothed, ill-fed, and, I fear, not a few of them far from clean, are allowed to occupy land no further from the fort at the yearly fair—hundreds of thousands who every twelfth year swell to millions—but no authorities, Civil or Military, interfere with *them*. But our gathering of less than 1,500 gentlemen, all well-fed and well-clothed, could not be permitted on sanitary grounds."

At last by a *tour de force* a site was secured. Just seven weeks before the Congress was to be held, without previous notice to any one, a representative of the Reception Committee was quietly despatched to Lucknow, where resided the owner (a Nawab, a Mahomedan gentleman of high rank) of one of the largest houses (surrounded by spacious grounds) in the station—a house which chanced to be then vacant. He took with him a formal lease and adequate funds, and the same night the lease was signed, the rent paid in advance, and on the next day the Reception Committee had taken possession of Lowther Castle, in the very centre of the Civil Station, overlooking the Alfred Park and alongside Government House, and had commenced their preparations there, before the authorities obtained any inkling of the affair.

It was too late to put official pressure on the Nawab; the legal measures had been taken under the guidance of one† of the ablest lawyers in the province. The house was not in cantonments, and the arbitrary power of the Military authorities, so unconstitutionally exerted on the previous occasion, could not this time be brought into play, while as to the Municipality, within whose jurisdiction Lowther Castle lay, its members were, themselves, elected representatives of the people.

Thus, at last, the Congress Dove found rest for the soles of her feet, and, after all, "all's well that ends well," but the incident has been dwelt upon, as happily illustrative of the spirit in which one section of the local Bureaucracy ever seeks to deal with the Indian subjects of Her Majesty,

* Detailed Report, pp: 1, 2. † Pandit Bishamber Nath.

committed to their tender mercies. Well said* Mr. Surendra Nath Banerjee :—

"I must say that it is with a sense of pain that I listened to the statement made by the Hon'ble Pandit Ajoodhia Nath regarding the petty official opposition which the efforts of the Reception Committee encountered at each stage. When the story of this spiteful and unworthy persecution is published in this country, and when it is repeated in England, I am sure there will be one universal feeling of indignation throughout the country, which I hope will teach the local officials a lesson which they have yet to learn." (*Cheers.*)

Amen, and so might it be; but we must say no more, since, in India, as was justly remarked in his memorable speech at Poona by Mr. Caine, M.P., to differ from the authorities, or expose their shortcomings, is held to be rank sedition.†

A site once obtained, the grounds of Lowther Castle were rapidly levelled and studded with long rows of tents, divided off into blocks by broad roads, such as to preclude the possibility of any accidental fires spreading. Dining and meeting halls for each block were created, a splendid hall beautifully decorated interiorly, 150 × 100 feet in length and breadth, capable of accommodating with its galleries 5,000 persons, was erected for the sittings of the Congress, and midway between this and Lowther Castle, where the President, Secretaries and some of the leading delegates and the offices were located, a magnificent *shamianah*, some 100 feet square, kindly lent by His Highness the Maharajah of Durbhungah, was pitched and furnished as a drawing-room, to serve as a general reception room for all delegates and visitors.

Another beautiful *shamianah*, lent by a Mahomedan nobleman, was fitted up as a reading room, and for some days before, during, and some days after the Congress, the tables were supplied with copies of almost every newspaper published in India (except, of course, of some eight or ten Anglo-Indian journals), furnished gratuitously, in token of their good will and sympathy, by their editors and managers.

In one part of the grounds rows of shops were constructed, constituting, a bazar, in which the delegates could obtain every article they could possibly require, from jewellery to fruit, and from kin-khabs to flour and lentils; only spirituous liquors and intoxicants of all kinds were rigidly excluded from the premises—the Congress, though primarily a political body, having also strong temperance and social reform proclivities. Indeed the Congress gatherings were taken advantage of, to hold in the evenings, and, again, on the day immediately following the close of the Congress, large meetings, at which numerous questions of social and moral reform were discussed, and plans of

---

* Detailed Report, p. 18.

† English readers may have heard a good deal of the seditious character of the writings of some of the Congress-men; may even have heard of the proposal by some of the leading Anglo-Indian papers that some of the Europeans of the Congress Party should be summarily deported, and may have, possibly, fancied that there was really something in all this bluster; but they will perhaps appreciate better what weight should be given to Anglo-Indian utterances, when they learn that one of these same organs of the Bureaucracy denounced Mr. Caine as seditious, and insisted on *his* summary deportation, because he ventured to find fault with official arrangements (which are demoralizing the whole country) in regard to intoxicants. The attitude of this section of the Anglo-Indian community was well hit off in one of the Indian comic papers: "B. B. (Blatant Bureaucrat) *loqr.*—Do you consider that we are the sublimest rulers in the universe, that our administration is perfect, and that all we say and do is necessarily right? I. E. (Intelligent Englishman).—Well, no; not exactly—rather the contrary, I fear B. B. (*Angrily*).—Then you're a d—d rebel, and must be summarily deported." Of course there are *many* officials who are *not* B. B.'s, but they are, we fear, in the minority.

operation during the coming year in each of the innumerable sections into which, in social matters, the community is divided by creed, caste, and race, were considered and, in many cases, settled.

Of course all this, and the provision of furniture, lights and food for the delegates during their stay, sanitary arrangements, watch and ward, and fire protection, involved considerable expenditure, and probably when all is settled the Reception Committee's* account will not fall far short of Rs. 45,000. Of this the fees of the delegates furnished about one-fourth, and the rest was raised by subscriptions throughout the Allahabad circle,† supplemented by liberal contributions from the Benares and Oudh circles. The one curious point about the subscriptions was the extreme anxiety felt by a large proportion of the subscribers that the fact of their thus aiding the movement should be kept secret. After dark, men found their way silently into the Congress treasury (in Lowther Castle), and produced bags of money, sent with verbal messages from this or that gentleman, breathing the strongest sympathy with the Congress, but imploring that no hint should be given to any one of their co-operation. Not only did money thus come from nobles and chiefs, supposed to be indifferent to the question, but actually from several gentlemen whose names appear amongst the leaders of the two or three professedly Anti-Congress Associations, got up by the officials.

Whether there is any wisdom in a system of persecution, that, while it stimulates to greater activity in secret, keeps nearly ‡ three-fourths of a movement like the Congress out of sight, we must leave it to others to decide. But this much is certain: The Congress idea has now obtained such a hold upon the mind of the country that no earthly power can extinguish it. If ten thousand of the most prominent Congressmen were deported to-morrow, the idea would still creep on, spreading from mind to mind, till it had seized every man, woman and child amongst the Indian population, ever growing stronger and stronger in every mind which had received the seed. It is essentially beneficent in its character and, in its open growth, instinct with peace and good will to men. Official opposition and persecution will

---

* The Reception Committee consists of all delegates to previous Congresses belonging to the circle in which the Congress is held, together with all the more influential and important residents of the neighbourhood co-opted by these delegates. The Committee, always very large, as soon as constituted, elects office-bearers and a moderate-sized executive council who carry out all the work.

† The Allahabad circle includes the whole of the United Provinces, except Oudh and the Rohilkund and Benares Divisions.

‡ The people are not unnaturally much afraid of the local authorities; they have no hope of being justly dealt with in any such matter by many of these; they fully believe that if they displease the local authorities, by overtly joining a movement which these are pleased to denounce, they will speedily find themselves in trouble. Speaking of the police, Munshi Sajjad Hussain remarked (Detailed Report, p. 45): "Let a man displease them in the slightest, and see the beneficence of our kind police; he may know nothing about it, but there will be a criminal case filed against him, and arrangements made for requiring him to give security for good behaviour, before he can reach his home." (*Loud laughter.*) And the native public, generally, in Upper India, believe that this is equally true in regard to a great many of the district officials. The powers of requiring security to keep the peace and for good behaviour are capable of the most terrible abuse. A native gentleman, of high position, attended the Madras Congress, in defiance of his district officer, a most rabid Anti-Congressman. Shortly after his return he found himself called upon to give Rs. 20,000 security to keep the peace. There was not the smallest real foundation for this demand, but he thought it wisest to comply with the demand and leave his home. He might doubtless have appealed and got the order reversed, but his firm belief was—and, whether well founded or otherwise, it is shared by tens of thousands of other gentlemen—that, had he done so, he would before long have found himself involved hopelessly in some more serious case—an utterly false case, but so got up by the police as to leave him scarcely a chance of escape. (*The discussions on a Reform of the existing Police Systems, Detailed Report, pp. 46-54, should be read.*) In one district of the Punjab, in one year, security for good behaviour, &c., was demanded from between 5,000 and 6,000 people. Free English citizens should realise something of all this before they condemn our poor people too strongly for not having the courage of their convictions.

not only add to its growth, but will operate to convert an open, above-board, constitutional movement, into a secret, underground, and, therefore, unconstitutional one. There was towards the close of Lord Lytton's administration a great deal of secret organization for unavowed, and, probably, even to its originators scarcely understood, purposes : though none who have studied history can doubt in what this would have eventuated. It has been the chief glory of the Congress movement that, aided by the enthusiasm elicited by good Lord Ripon s sympathetic rule, it has swept away all this fungoid undergrowth, and sweetened all political agitation by working it out into the wholesome light of the open day. It will be the fault of the Bureaucracy—and the Bureaucracy alone—if, by the unconstitutional abuse of their authority and powers, they drive a portion of the national energy back into the old, disused and illegitimate channels.

Alike for England and India, whose fortunes are now inextricably interwoven, no more gravely significant question exists at the present day for consideration. If England only invites and welcomes the confidence of India, and receives, with kindly consideration, the loyal suggestions (not necessarily adopting all, but treating them with the respect to which they are entitled) of the Congress which, year by year, more and more thoroughly represents the views of the whole thinking portion of the nation, all will be well for both countries. As a great Indian Prince recently said, after hearing the resolutions passed at the several Congresses: "If only these things be conceded, the rule of the British in India will last for ever." But if Viceroys and other high functionaries are to be permitted to sneer at and misrepresent the aspirations of a great nation, if subordinate officials are to be allowed unconstitutionally to oppose loyal political movements and persecute honest and earnest men for temperately and candidly setting forth what they hold to be their grievances and the best methods of redressing these—if England fancies, in a word, that she can maintain by fear a rule that only love can immortalize, then serious troubles only too probably await both countries.

It is well, however, that it should be clearly said and fully understood that, despite the dislike and distrust with which they regard a section of their present local Anglo-Indian rulers, no nation was ever more loyal to their Sovereign than the Indians now are to our beloved Empress, and no country ever more trustingly and affectionately relied on the justice and good will of another, than does India of the present day on that of Great Britain. But "hope deferred maketh the heart sick," and our best friends may in time, if too long exasperated by our neglect and discourtesy, forget all friendly feelings, and all statesmen should realize that the political concessions that India's altered condition now loudly calls for, should neither be needlessly postponed, nor grudgingly, nor ungraciously yielded.

The first sitting of the fourth Congress took place on the afternoon of the 26th December, 1888, in the grand hall already referred to, when the chair was taken at 2 P.M. by the Hon'ble Pandit Ajoodhia Nath, the Chairman of the Reception Committee, whose duty it was, *ex-officio*, to welcome the delegates.

Over 1,200 delegates and some 5,000 visitors were present. Of these latter, however, a good many were compelled to listen from the outside It may be noted that, unlike other Congresses, the visitors to which were much reduced in number after the first day, at this one, every available seat continued to be occupied throughout the session.

The Hon'ble Pandit commenced his opening speech* by referring to the local opposition with which we have already dealt. He then, alluding to the reckless manner in which accusations of sedition and other equally unfounded charges have been brought against the Congress party by Anglo-Indian journalists and others, who should have known better, went on to say—

"The next reason which induces me to refer to this opposition is the speech of Lord Dufferin, who speaks of the seditious nature of some of our writings and speeches. Some few thoughtless non-official opponents had already, it is true, adopted similar means to discredit us. But I am surprised—I am astonished—to find any sensible man, let alone a gentleman occupying the position of a Viceroy, bringing a charge of disloyalty against us. (*Cheers.*) It is impossible—and I say it with great confidence—to find on the face of this earth a people more loyal than my countrymen. (*Loud cheers.*) We claim the more perfect union of India and England, and yet we are called disloyal. Are we disloyal? (*Loud cries of 'No, no.'*) Some people have gone the length of talking such nonsense as to say that we want the Russians to come into the country. (*Laughter.*) Now, Gentlemen, I ask you, is it not absurd to suppose that the educated natives of India, who have such an admiration for the free and representative institutions of England, could ever wish to be under Russian rule, or become Russian serfs? (*Laughter and cheers.*) History we have read, English education we have received, with Englishmen we have mixed and mixed freely, but we are not credited, it would seem, with even sense enough to realize that the English Government is far better than the Russian or than that of any other European power. The existence of the Congress, the very meetings which we hold annually, are the best proofs of the excellence of the British Government. (*Cheers.*) Where will you find any Government which would allow a foreign country, which it has pleased Providence to place under its charge, to have the same constitutional freedom of speech as the British Government has been pleased to grant to us? (*Cheers.*)

* * * * * *

"If occasion arises, we will prove to our opponents that it is we who are loyal, and not they; it is we who will support the Government and not they; it is we who will be ready with our purses, and not they. (*Cheers*). We fully acknowledge the inestimable blessings conferred upon us by Government. We most gratefully admit the numberless benefits derived by India from the British rule, and all that we now say is this, *viz.*, that there is yet room for improvement; that England can confer still further blessings upon us; and that, therefore, we may properly approach our Most Gracious Empress—approach her most respectfully and loyally—with the prayer that she will cause all those gracious pledges given on her behalf to be now more fully redeemed. (*Cheers.*)

* * * * * *

"Two years ago I gave the subject of the Congress my best consideration, and, after mature deliberation, I arrived at the conclusion that, so far from being dangerous to Government, it embodies the essential germ of the permanency of the British Government. (*Cheers.*) I have since then, in consequence of Sir Auckland Colvin's letter and Lord Dufferin's speech, as a loyal subject of Her Majesty, reconsidered the matter, and believe me, Gentlemen, I have been unable to discover in any of our speeches, publications or proceedings anything which is at all seditious, or which in any way approaches to sedition. You know the multifarious duties of a Viceroy, and you know the heavy work of a Lieutenant-Governor, and I believe that these exalted officials have not had the time to study carefully our pamphlets, but have received their information as to their general purport and bearing at second hand, and you know what the value of that kind of second-hand information is. (*Laughter.*) But this peing so, it is the duty of every loyal subject of the Queen to prove, by his firmness in the cause, and by his moderation, that the charges brought against us by our kind opponents have no foundation in fact.

"These criticisms and this opposition have given rise to certain misapprehensions, the most prominent among these being the idea that the Government means to do injury to those who join the Congress,

* Detailed Report, pp. 2, 3.

Nothing could be more absurd than such a rumour. The great nation on whose possessions the sun never sets—the most advanced of nations, the first to introduce free institutions into this country, and teach us that rulers were created for the good of subjects, not subjects for the pleasure of rulers—the noble nation that has united justice with freedom, will never allow its officers to resort to such unjustifiable and unconstitutional measures. (*Cheers.*) Englishmen, as a nation, are not capable of suppressing any loyal constitutional organization by any arbitrary or unfair means. (*Cheers.*)

* * * * * *

"Then there is an idea that the Congress party is only a microscopic minority. (*Laughter.*) But it is not only natives who have received an English education, and even these may now be numbered by hundreds of thousands, who take part in this movement. I see before me, even in this Congress, numbers of gentlemen, who, though very highly educated and cultured, have not received any so-called English education. I have been to several places in these provinces in connection with the Congress, and wherever I went I found great enthusiasm prevailing amongst all classes of people, and what you will be still more pleased to hear is that we have received contributions from all classes, even from those who profess to be against the Congress. (*Laughter and cheers.*) Nav, from some of those whose names figure high on the list of so-called Anti-Congress Associations. (*Cheers, and cries of 'Name, name.'*) I cannot, of course, disclose their names, for they accompanied their donations with special requests that their names should never be disclosed. I have also received large subscriptions from native noblemen on condition that their names should not be disclosed, because they are afraid of the officials. (*Laughter.*)

"A question was recently put in the House of Commons by a member, in which it was stated that the Native Princes and the Mahomedans as a body were against the Congress. (*'No, no.'*) You have here seated on the platform Sirdar Dayal Singh, the premier Sikh nobleman of the Punjab. Our illustrious friend the Maharajah of Durbhungah, a Brahmin of the Brahmins, the premier nobleman of Bengal, had made arrangements to come here to-day ; but circumstances over which he had no control—a sudden attack of illness—prevented him from being present. Here, too, you have Mahomedans, noblemen of the highest birth, scions of the ex-Royal houses of Delhi and Oudh, and others. Well, who are the Princes that are against us ? The Maharajah of Benares, and he alone ; and, if I understand, Rajah Shiva Persad, who is attending this Congress this year and declares himself to be a delegate, even the Maharajah of Benares is not against the Congress, indeed approves it, but only desires to protest against certain speeches and writings of some Congressmen which he disapproves. (*Laughter.*) But can the Maharajah of Benares represent the Princes of India, or ourselves ? (*Cries of 'No.'*) Has he anything in common with us ? (*'No, no.'*) Then besides the Maharajah of Benares, there are some gentlemen who have the reputation of being the authors of certain Anti-Congress pamphlets and letters to the press. I have the honour of knowing some of them personally, and can tell you that, so far from writing those pamphlets, they are unable to understand them. (*Laughter.*) Since this question was put in the House of Commons, I have tried in vain to ascertain what native Princes were against us.

"Again, I ask you to turn your eyes round this hall and see if it is true that Mahomedans do not sympathize with us. In the last Congress the number of Mussulman delegates was 83 ; now it is more than double this. (*Cries of 'Treble ! treble !'*) The Mahomedans of Oudh have returned at one meeting 57 delegates, including members of the Royal house of Oudh. (*Cheers.*) Some 27 Mahomedan delegates have been returned by the district of Allahabad, and no less than 11 were returned from a place where you might not have believed that even a single one would be elected. (*A voice, 'Aligurh.'**) Yes ! how rightly you have guessed the name. (*Laughter and cheers.*) And now you can appreciate the importance of this so-called opposition which sounds very nicely, but in which there is no reality, as all can see when our opponents are obliged to have recourse to the desperate expedient of putting forward these few titled inanities to show that the Princes of India are against us ; they stand self-condemned and need no further refutation from us ; nor is it my duty now, I am happy to say, to have any fault to find with the Mahomedans, generally, for not joining us, much less for opposing us ; and if any Hindu can claim the honour of enjoying an intimate intercourse with the Mahomedans of this country, I certainly can, and I can assure you that, as a body, they are not against us."

We have quoted at great length from this speech of Pandit Ajoodhia Nath because his words are entitled to great weight. By descent a Cashmeri Brahmin ; a man of large means ; a member of the Legislative Council ; the most distinguished legal practitioner probably in the United Provinces, and unquestionably the leader of his own section of the bar, he is, withal, a most cautious man, deliberating long in every case before he moves. He actually considered over

*Aligurh is the head-quarters of the only Indian Anti-Congressman, at all worthy of a moment's consideration, Sir Syed Ahmed.

our aims and objects and pondered over our methods, for nearly two years before he concluded that he owed it to his country to join our movement. The deliberate utterances of such a man in regard to Indian domestic politics ought to be received with respect by every unbiassed Englishman.

Then Pandit Ajoodhia Nath called upon the assembly to elect a President. The Hon'ble Pheroz Shah Mehta, of the Bombay Council, then proposed Mr. George Yule. He said* :—

"We already boast of an illustrious roll of Presidents of Congress. (*Renewed cheers.*) At the first Congress held in Bombay we had for our Chairman my esteemed and respected friend Mr. W. C. Bonnerjee (*cheers*), a Brahmin gentleman hailing from Bengal, the land of the Baboos, but whom I am proud to be allowed to call one of my oldest and most respected friends. (*Cheers.*) Then at the second National Congress, held in Calcutta, we had for our Chairman a Parsee, that "black man" (*loud laughter and cheers*), Mr. Dadabhai Nowrojee; only a "black man" in the Marquis of Salisbury's estimation, but for all that a man who is admired, esteemed and loved, from one end of India to the other (*renewed and vehement cheers*); and at the last great Congress at Madras we had for our President a Mahomedan gentleman occupying the highest position, and perhaps the most distinguished Mussulman in India, Mr. Budrudin Tyabjee. (*Cheers.*) And now, Gentlemen, I ask you to add to that illustrious roll, the name, as President of this Congress, of Mr. George Yule." (*Loud cheers, which were repeated again and again with the utmost enthusiasm.*)

Sirdar Dayal Singh, Majethia, of the Punjab, seconded, and Sheik Raza Hosain Khan, a Talukdar and President of the *Rifa-i-am*, in supporting the nomination, remarked† :—

"I hear that certain people have given out that the Mahomedans are opposed to the Congress, and that even a member of the British Parliament, long resident in India, who surely might have known better, went so far as to virtually assert this, in the House of Commons. Now I am a Mahomedan, and although I could not take part in any of the preceding Congress meetings, I am proud of the fact that I have all along, since the very first gathering of the Congress, taken a very deep interest in it, and looked upon the movement with a friendly feeling. Much has been said about me, but nobody has doubts about my being a Mahomedan; and, as a Mahomedan, and one not altogether without the means of ascertaining the views of my co-religionists, I can assure you that though certain individual Mahomedans, who are great at talking, profess to be against the Congress, the great bulk of the Mahomedans are in no way against, but rather are favourable to the Congress. This point has been ably treated by the Hon'ble Pandit Ajoodhia Nath, and I need not dwell on it at any greater length. It will be enough for me to say that I have brought with me a Fatwa of the Shamsululma, in which the said dignitary has approved and sanctioned the participation of Mahomedans in these Congresses. This Shamsululma is the spiritual leader of the Suni community of Lucknow, a place noted for learning in the Mahomedan world. He ranks first amongst the Suni Doctors of Law.

"Gentlemen, the secret of the opposition has now been divulged; it is not the Mahomedans, but their official masters, who are opposed to the Congress."

A Madras delegate further spoke in support of the nomination, and no other gentleman having been proposed, Mr. George Yule was elected by acclamation, and received with prolonged and enthusiastic cheers when he took the Presidential seat.

Every word of Mr. Yule's inaugural address (pp. 6—11 of the Detailed Report) should be carefully studied; it constitutes probably the most remarkable political speech ever delivered in India. It dealt mainly with the primary question—that fundamental reform, on which more or less depend all other reforms—of the enlargement, and reconstitution on a partially representative basis, of the Council of the Governor-General and the

* Detailed Report, p. 4.
† Detailed Report, p. 5.

several Provincial Councils. The past history of the British Indian Government, so far as it relates to this question, is tersely epitomized, the unanimous desire of all parties in England in past times, to introduce some representative element into that Government, whenever this should be possible, is shown, and the existing fitness of the India of to-day for such a measure is demonstrated. It is impossible to do justice to this full and closely-reasoned argument without quoting (which our space will not permit) the whole of it, and we must, therefore, again refer our readers to the original (pp. 6-8), but there is one passage in which he shows clearly that the non-official European community ought to be just as deeply interested in this reform as the Indian, which may be advantageously here reproduced. Mr. Yule says :—

"But there are other considerations that add weight to the testimony of the Blue Books. In all the discussions that have taken place in Parliament about the inhabitants of India, there is one section which has never been thought of at all—I mean the British non-official class, to which I belong. I want to make our existence known. We may be known as barristers and solicitors, as bankers, traders, merchants, engineers, editors of newspapers, manufacturers, planters and so forth, but the idea of citizenship, and all that that implies, never seems to have occurred to our rulers in connection with us. I know it has been said that we are already represented. We are English, and the Government is English : therefore we are represented. But that is a false inference and a pure delusion. We have no more power and no more voice in the Government of the country than you Indians have. The Government is no more ours because it is administered by a Secretary of State who is an Englishman, than the bread in a baker's shop is ours because the shop happens to be kept by an Englishman and not by a Native. (*Laughter and cheers.*) We are all alike held to be on the same low level of unfitness and unripeness. The only thing we are the least bit of good for in the country, from the Governmental point of view, is to be taxed. (*Cheers.*) We are ripe enough for that ; ripe enough to come under the sweep of the Board of Revenue sickle, but unripe for the meanest privileges of subjects of a free country. Our number is uncertain. The census tables do not inform us : but, few or many, almost all of us would be voters in England, and I venture to suggest that we would make a passable fraction of a constituency in this country. There is another consideration. There are many thousands of Hindu, Mahomedan, Eurasian, Parsee and other gentlemen in the country, who, if they were to transfer their persons to England for twelve months or more, and pay certain rates, would be qualified to enjoy all the rights and privileges of British subjects. If you and I go to England we are qualified. If we return to India our character changes, and we are not qualified. In England we should be trusted citizens. In India, well, the charitably-minded among our opponents say that we are incipient traitors !" (*Loud and prolonged cheers and laughter.*)

Later, after showing that India is, at the present time, far more fitted for representative institutions than England herself was for hundreds of years after she enjoyed them, and that the actual state of the country would warrant a fundamental change in the form of the administration, he points out how very far short of this, fall the modest and cautious proposals of the Congress, for the introduction of a small representative element, only, into the administration.

Then turning to the late Viceroy's "St. Andrew's Speech," he shows how inaccurate and futile are that nobleman's statements and criticisms, and concludes his refutation of Lord Dufferin's now well-known attack in the following words :—

"Well, the Viceroy having started upon an assumption that is not only incorrect, but is the very opposite of the fact, it follows that his condemnation does not apply to us at all, but to a fanciful piece of workmanship of which we are not the artists. The Viceroy must necessarily depend largely upon his subordinates for correct information about the details of this and other movements, and it looks to me as if one of those compilers of facts had fallen into some grievous error. The authoritative views of the Congress are to be found in its resolutions, and the resolution about the reform of the Councils is the third one of the first meeting of the Congress three years ago, and that resolution has been the one affirmed at the following meetings. We are in no way bound even by any statement or argument that any speaker may make in supporting that resolution, but I say with the greatest confidence that neither in the resolution itself, nor in the speeches of the gentlemen supporting it, is a word to be found that justifies the "ideal authoritatively suggested." There may be some remarks in letters to newspapers, in pamphlets or in speeches made by members of the Congress, that give support to the "ideal." I don't know of them, and, if I did, I should regret them, just as I might regret any of our members having a hump back; but I should feel no responsibility for either his back or speech. If we be charged with encouraging "ideals" on such grounds, we may as logically be charged, in the other event, as a Congress for promoting deformed spines! (*'Hear, hear,' and laughter.*) It is annoying to us, no doubt, that our friends, as I take Lord Dufferin to be, should be deceived by imitations of our ticket; but as we have no Trade Mark Bill to protect our wares, all that we can do is to warn our friends to ask for the real article, and to see that they get it." (*Loud and continued cheers.*)

Finally,* the President called upon the assembly to elect a Committee to settle the subjects that were to be discussed at the sittings to be held during the ensuing three days, as also to frame tentative resolutions in regard to these and select the gentlemen, who were to propose, second, and in the first instance support these.

Accordingly the delegates from each circle elected from amongst themselves a fixed number † of representatives, and a very strong committee of 106 members (*vide* pp. 11 and 12 of Detailed Report) was duly constituted and affirmed by the entire Congress.

Then the Congress adjourned with enthusiastic and prolonged cheers for the Queen-Empress, till next day at 2 P.M., and the Subject Committee began their work, sitting until late that night, and resuming work again next morning, when they sat until 1 P.M.

At 2 P.M. precisely of Thursday, the 27th, the Congress re-assembled; and on the President's taking the chair, one of the delegates, on behalf of a great trader community (the Dasa Porwad Banyas) of Bombay, came forward and presented him with an exquisitely beautiful silver *repoussé* work casket full of new rupees. The President was equal to the occasion, and said ‡ :—

"I have very much pleasure, indeed, in accepting, on behalf of the Congress, the contents of this casket; and as I understand that it is the intention of the donors that, while you (*turning to the Reception Committee*) get the contents, I myself get the casket, I have even greater pleasure in accepting that casket for myself. (*Laughter and cheers.*) Believe me, I shall ever preserve it as a memento of this great and important meeting, and in grateful remembrance of the honour that you have done me in electing me to be its President." (*'Hear, hear,' and cheers.*)

Then one or two of the Standing Congress Committees § laid their annual reports for 1888 on the table; but the majority unfortunately had either prepared no formal reports, or had not had them printed. It was the first year of systematic organization, and so allowances must be made.

---

* Some months previous to the assembling of the Congress, the Reception Committee called upon all the Standing Congress Committees to report the subjects which the people of their respective Circles desired to have brought before the Congress. All those subjects, proposed by more than half the Committees, were then recirculated, with tentative resolutions framed in regard to each, to all the Standing and by them to the Divisional Committees, so that in regard to all these subjects, which comprised the great majority of those actually brought before and discussed by the Congress, the delegates came fully prepared.

† The number was fixed after much previous consultation amongst the leaders of the several circles, partly with reference to the population, wealth, educational status and general importance of the circle, but more especially with regard to limiting the representatives to the smallest number, that would adequately represent all different shades of opinion and views obtaining amongst the delegates of each circle. Thus Madras, politically the most advanced circle, but where opinion is marvellously homogeneous, had fewer representatives on the Committee than the North-Western Provinces, and even the Punjab.

‡ Detailed Report, p. 15.

§ There is one such supreme managing body for each Circle, which controls the Divisional Committees, each of which has charge of one electoral division, and of the several Sub-Committees which manage the several included sub-divisions.

Then rose the Hon'ble Kashinath Trimbuk Telang, member of the Bombay Council, to propose the re-affirmation of the primary resolution passed in 1885, 1886 and 1887, calling for the reform and expansion of the Councils, local and supreme, and the introduction of a representative element into the administration of the country. Of the resolution itself, he said little, for, as he truly remarked, at three previous Congresses the question had been so threshed out as to require no further advocacy from him; but turning to the recent attacks of adversaries, he disposed, good naturedly but effectually, of some of these. His remarks upon Lord Dufferin's ill-advised utterances were so singularly happy that every one regretted that the late Viceroy was not present to profit by them. Mr. Telang said* :—

"I hold in my hand a newspaper report of what his Lordship said at Calcutta, and I think it is desirable to refresh your memory by reading the exact words of His Lordship's remarks in regard to the work of the Congress. 'And now, Gentlemen,' Lord Dufferin said, 'some intelligent, loyal, patriotic and well-meaning men are desirous of taking, I will not say a farther step in advance, but a very big jump into the unknown, by the application to India of democratic methods of government and the adoption of a Parliamentary system which England herself has reached by slow degrees and through the discipline of many centuries. The ideal authoritatively suggested, Gentlemen, as I understand' [mark, please, the qualification implied in, 'as I understand'] 'is the creation of a representative body or bodies in which the official element shall be in a minority, who shall have what is called the power of the purse, and who, through this instrumentality, shall be able to bring the British Executive into subjection to their will.' Before I pass on to another portion of his Lordship's speech, I will pause here for the purpose of pointing out that every one of the statements made here by His Lordship is inaccurate as applied to any proposal that has ever been passed at any previous Congress, or any proposal that you will be asked at this Congress to pass. (*Cheers.*) His Lordship begins by saying that we ask for democratic methods of government for India. You have—all of you, I suppose—read the reports of the three Congresses which have been already held. I myself took part in the first, but was unfortunately unable to attend the second and the third Congresses. I have, however, read the reports, and have failed to find in them anything of which it can be fairly said that either the Congress as a whole, or any individual member of it, has asked for the application of democratic methods of government to India. (*Cheers.*) The next charge is that we are asking for 'the adoption of a Parliamentary system which England herself has only reached by slow degrees, and through the discipline of many centuries of preparation.' I say that precisely the same remark that I made with regard to the first clause is applicable to this. We have asked for no such thing, as will be obvious to those who will consider the precise terms of our resolution, and when Lord Dufferin, so cautious and circumspect a statesman as he is, has been so inaccurate in his observations, I can only conclude that His Lordship has not had time to read our reports, and that he has taken his information at second hand, as indeed is indicated by the qualifying remark, 'as I understand. (*Cheers.*) His Lordship says: 'The idea authoritatively suggested, as I understand, is the creation of a representative body or bodies in which the official element shall be in a minority, who shall have what is called the power of the purse, and who, through this instrumentality, shall be able to bring the British Executive into subjection to their will.' The basis for that statement is our demand that the financial statement shall be brought before the Council for discussion. ('*Hear, hear.*') Not only do I not find in any of the reports any grounds for such a statement, but I find what is actually the reverse of it. (*Cheers.*) It has been said over and over again that the Executive shall have the power of deciding what shall be done, and of absolutely vetoing any proposal emanating from the rest of the Council, and yet in face of such a resolution as this, which we have passed not once, not twice, but three times, such a statement has been made by his Lordship. I can only express my amazement at it, and I cannot believe His Lordship to have been capable of making it except on the assumption that he has lacked the time to study our reports himself. (*Cheers.*) The various charges which His Lordship makes against the Congress are charges which remind me of a certain definition which was once given of a crab, *viz.*, that a crab is a red fish which walks backwards; and the criticism made upon *that* was, that the definition was perfectly correct except that the crab was not a fish, that it was not red, and that it did not walk backwards. (*Laughter.*) Now, I may say that Lord Dufferin's criticism is perfectly correct, except that we have not asked for democratic methods of government, we have not asked for Parliamentary institutions which England has got after many centuries of discipline, we have not asked for the power of the purse, and we have not

* Detailed Report, p. 16.

asked that the British Executive should be brought under subjection to us. (*Laughter and prolongea cheers.*)

"If you permit me, I will go on to the next passage in which he says: 'I am afraid the people of England will not be readily brought to the acceptance of this programme, or to allow such an assembly, or a number of such assemblies either, to interfere with its armies, or to fetter and circumscribe the liberty of action, either of the Provincial Governments, or of the Supreme Executive.' I say this is a programme which is not brought forward officially or unofficially by the Congress. We have never dreamt of or asked for such things as Lord Dufferin supposes. We have—I say we have explicitly—declared that the right of interpellation which we ask for must not extend to questions, military or political. (*Cheers.*) Then again he goes on to say: 'In the first place, the whole scheme is eminently unconstitutional, for the essence of constitutional government is that responsibility and power should remain in the same hands, and the idea of irresponsible Councils whose members could never be called to account for their acts in the way in which an opposition can be called to account in a constitutional country, arresting the march of Indian legislation, or nullifying the policy of the British Executive in India, would be regarded as an impracticable anomaly.' I entirely agree in this view of His Lordship, only I do not see what application it has to anything said by the Congress. We have never asked for a divorce between power and responsibility. We have, on the contrary, distinctly said that the responsibility must rest with the Executive, and that, therefore, they must have the power of rejecting any resolution and vetoing any proposal, even though such should come from a majority of the Council. ('*Hear, hear.*') I need only say, in conclusion, that the criticisms which have been made upon us are criticisms which have no manner of application to the resolutions we have passed, or the proposals we have made, but relate rather to some imaginary scheme which, somehow, seems to have floated through Lord Dufferin's brains, but of which we of the Congress had never even so much as heard, until he enunciated it." (*Prolonged cheers.*)

To him followed Mr. Surendra Nath Bannerjee in a long and eloquent speech. But this matter is an old tale and often told. No rational being, who really understands the facts of the case and the present position of affairs in India, can doubt the urgent necessity of the Reform insisted on in this first resolution, and it will be sufficient if we cull two brief passages from Mr. Bannerjee's speech. In the first he tersely exposes the utter absurdity of the charge of disloyalty and sedition so persistently brought (*faute de mieux*) against the Congress party by its official opponents. He says* :—

"But it is in connection with this charge of sedition, that is, too often, so recklessly brought against us, that I desire, in your name and on your behalf (and in this matter re-echoing the sentiments of the Chairman of the Reception Committee), to enter my most emphatic protest. (*Loud cheers.*) Apart from sentimental considerations—which are no mean considerations with a people so highly sensitive and emotional as we are—is it for one moment to be supposed that we have become so idiotic, and have taken such utter leave of our senses, as not to see that we owe all that we possess—our position and our prestige —to the English connection? (*Cheers.*) Let that connection come to an end, and we lose with it all that we hold most dear in life. Our opponents have charged us with being seditionists, but they have never failed to give us credit for sense. In our case, however, sedition means a measure of folly that is only consistent with idiotcy. The charge can only stand upon the one assumption, that the educated community of India have become demented." (*Laughter.*)

In the second he emphatically and correctly declares (and it is as well that this should be clearly understood, now that rumours of some formal reform in the Councils are afloat) that the country will accept no reform as satisfactory which does not provide for the election, by those sections of the community *primâ facie* qualified to exercise the franchise, of *some* members of all the Councils. His words are† :—

"We have no wish to assume sovereign authority. The supreme power will remain where it is vested at present. We only desire that we may be consulted in its exercise. According to our programme, half the members of the Legislative Councils are to be elected, the rest being nominated by Government. Under the existing law, one-third of the members must at least be non-officials. We pray for an increase in the

* Detailed Report, pp. 18, 19.
† Detailed Report, p. 19.

proportion of non-official members from one-third to one-half, and we further suggest that they should be elected. We attach the utmost importance to the principle of election. A partially elective system is the platform on which we take our stand. That platform we can never quit, and by it we shall judge every system which may be devised for the reform of the Councils.

In a word, the people of India are, at present, neither asking for, nor thinking of, Representative Government, but what they do insist on, is, that an appreciable portion of the *advisers* of Government should be their elected representatives.

Syed Shurf-ud-deen, a well-known Mahomedan Barrister, supported the resolution, and in his speech made some remarks as to the present position of the Congress party and the real attitude in regard to it of the Mahomedan community, that deserve special attention* :—

"Well, Gentlemen, you will remmember perfectly well that in 1885, when the first meeting of the Congress was held at Bombay, it was said by adverse critics that it was a Congress of a few educated native gentlemen. Again you will remember that when the Congress was held in Calcutta in 1886, it was no longer called a Congress of a few native gentlemen, but a Congress of Bengalees ; and in 1887, when the Congress was held in Madras, it was not called a Congress of native gentlemen, or of Bengalees, but a Congress of Hindus. (*Laughter and Cheers*). Now, Gentlemen, here, in 1888, we have got before us not only Hindus, Bengalees and Maharattas, but I am proud to say we have here amongst us to-day more than 200 Mahomedans, including scions of the ex-Royal families of Delhi and of Oudh. (*Loud cheers.*) Now I think I may be right in expressing the hope and opinion that next year, when the reports of the Congress have been published, it will at last be called by its right name, and accepted as an *Indian* Congress. (*Cheers.*) You will remember that in 1885 there were scarcely any Mahomedans. There was an increase at the next Congress, a further increase in 1887, and now I am proud to say that there are more than 200 Mahomedans present. (*Loud cheers and cries of* '*Hear, hear.*') I may tell you that in 1886, when the Congress was held in Calcutta, owing to some local or temporary reasons, the Mahomedans were charged with holding aloof, but I can assure you that, at least in my province of Behar, the Mahomedans have the fullest sympathy with the objects of the Congress. And I can tell you that in my professional capacity I have to travel all over the division, and have been consulted, and have consulted with my friends, many Mahomedans, and they have in every case proved to be in sympathy with and in favour of the Congress. At the same time I do not for a moment deny that there are some, indeed a good many, who, though fully sympathizing with the objects of the Congress, yet for personal and temporary reasons, think it best in their own interests to stay away. Still these gentlemen are with us and help us privately, and when official pressure diminishes will come round publicly. But abstentions of this nature—and they are more numerous amongst Mahomedans than any, except Mahomedans have any idea of—furnish no grounds whatsoever for reckless assertions, such as that recently made in the House of Commons by Mr. Maclean, that the Mahomedans, as a body, are against the Congress, or for designating this latter by any less comprehensive title than that which it righteously bears—The Indian National Congress. (*Loud cheers.*) There are malcontents everywhere—there must always be some who dissent from anything their neighbours approve,—but the great bulk of the Mahomedans, as the great bulk of the Hindus, Jews, Parsees and Indian Christians, are everywhere *for*, and not *against*, the Congress."

Rajah Rampal Singh put the whole case for the reform of the Councils in very few words. He said † :—

"I am afraid I am a very poor speaker ; but I think that every sympathetic Indian, every well-wisher of the country, should say something on the subject before us, however deficient he may be in oratorical powers. We all know that the right of being nominated to the Council has been given us since a long time. But the nomination rests entirely with Government, or rather with a small group of high officials ; and some men entirely ignorant of the English language have been appointed to the Council. (*Cheers.*) They were not the representatives of the people of India, because they were the nominees of Government, and were the proteges of officials. (*Cheers.*) That being the case, the grievances of the country were not properly brought by them to the notice of Government, and, instead of fighting

* Detailed Report, p. 20.
† Detailed Report, pp. 20, 21.

for justice on behalf of the people, they voted blindly with the officials, unless indeed their own personal interests were involved, when, no doubt, they did show some fight on their own behalf. (*Laughter.*) Moreover, the nominated members of Council have always constituted such a microscopic minority, as my kind friend Lord Dufferin would phrase it, that even if they had dissented from the opinion of the officials, and had been bold enough to maintain their views, they would have had no chance of carrying their point. It is for this that we most loyally, constitutionally, and almost pathetically, implore Government to allow us, ourselves, to select half the number of the members of the Legislative Council, and this with the full understanding that supreme authority must always rest with the Executive. With the supremacy of the Executive no Congressman that I have ever met—and I may say that I know a good many of these (*laughter*)—has ever dreamt of interfering ; but we want a good number of our own men in Council, so that the Government here, and the people and Government of England, may hear from their representatives what the people of this country really think and feel and wish about the subjects dealt with by the Government." (*Cheers.*)

Other speakers supported the resolution, and then Lalla Lajpat Rai,* by quotations from Sir Syed Ahmed's own past utterances, demonstrated that that gentleman who *now* poses as the leader of the opponents to the Congress movement, in former years advocated, in the clearest and most emphatic language, those very reforms which he now denounces † :—

"Now" (said Mr. Lajpat Rai in concluding his address), "you will by this time have discovered that here this most loyal of Indian Mahomedans, who now stigmatizes us as traitors, 30 years ago demanded for India reforms of the same character as we, now after 30 years of education and progress, pray for in the resolution which I am supporting, but going far beyond anything in this direction that we have thought it expedient or necessary to ask for." (*Continued cheering.*)

But, perhaps, the most novel and striking point in the debate was that made by Mr. Salem Ramaswami Mudaliar, who, having recently visited relatives at Pondicherry, was able, from personal experience, to contrast British and French modes of dealing with their Indian subjects. He said ‡ :—

"Gentlemen, while we are humbly praying our Government to grant us some small representative element in the Government, we have actually got full-blown representative institutions flourishing in this country under our very noses. I do not know whether you are aware how they are flourishing in Pondicherry and other places which are subject to the French Government. England will not as yet allow us the smallest modicum of representative institutions, but in Pondicherry every man has a right to elect his representative. He enjoys manhood suffrage! Not only that, but the people of Pondicherry have got a member of their own in the Chamber of Deputies and another in the Senate. Then in Pondicherry itself they have got a Council which is called the Council-General, and which meets every year, and this is an elective body, elected by the whole people. Before this Council is placed the Annual Budget (*cheers*), and the Budget is fully discussed by the members. The Budget is there threshed out by that body, and it is not until, after this discussion, it has been approved, that it comes into operation. (*Cheers.*) Gentlemen, it is said that we are not fit for representative institutions, but it is our fellow-countrymen, our relatives in many cases, no better educated, in nowise different from ourselves, whom the French Government has found to be fitted, not only for the small instalment of representative institutions that we ask for, but for fully-developed representative institutions, including manhood suffrage, which none of us ever even dream of demanding. I commend this fact to the careful consideration of our opponents who deny our fitness for even those small reforms we crave.

* * * * * *

"It is indeed an extraordinary thing that the natives of India are in Pondicherry found fitted for representative institutions of an advanced character, while the relatives and brethren of these very men, under British rule, are pronounced unfit for the smallest concession in this direction ; that the French subjects are allowed to discuss and authoritatively deal with their Budget, while nothing is allowed to us but to pay the taxes."

---

* Author of the well-known "Open Letters to Sir Syed Ahmed," which have been so widely and deservedly read and commended.

† Detailed Report, p. 23.

‡ Detailed Report, pp. 23, 24.

Then followed what was perhaps the most remarkable incident of the Congress. Rajah Shiva Prasad is a gentleman who, by official favour, has been gradually raised from a clerk's desk to the cushion of a Rajah. Naturally, in his eyes, the officials are demi-gods, and can do no wrong. He retired years ago from Government service, and has ever since been the chief adviser and master of the ceremonies to the Maharajah of Benares. As soon as the officials declared against the Congress, Rajah Shiva Prasad felt impelled to do the same, and to put forward his patron, the Maharajah of Benares, who is in feeble health, and, really, himself takes no part in politics, as doing "ditto." At the time of the Ilbert Bill the Rajah sided with the Europeans against his countrymen, and was freely burnt in effigy in recognition of this service, and during the six months preceding this late Congress he had been most strenuously exerting himself to misrepresent the views of the Congress party and bring them into disrepute. It had resulted from these and other circumstances in Rajah Shiva Prasad's past history, that no man in the length and breadth of the land, was so universally disliked as this gentleman. It may not have been altogether his own fault, public opinion is capricious as we know, but the fact has to be stated, as without a knowledge of this, the full significance of what occurred cannot be realized. This too must be noted, that, shortly before the Congress, the Rajah had entered into a league with Sir Syed Ahmed to put down the Congress ; but, as happens at times when gentlemen of this sort meet, they fell out, and, after mutual recriminations in the papers and a terrible fiasco at a meeting they tried to hold at Lucknow, Rajah Shiva Prasad returned to Benares, declaring, it was said, that he would join the Congress party. The Congress party, however, would have nothing to say to him, but at a monster public meeting at Benares, after other delegates had been duly elected, a gentleman rose and proposed Rajah Shiva Prasad as a fit and proper representative of the holy city of Benares. One can conceive that if, in older and more jovial times, some light-minded prelate had, at a Synod of cardinals, after the due canonization (despite the *Avocat du diable*) of sundry saints and saintesses, proposed as a new luminary to grace the calendar, St. Diabolus, that some faint murmur of merriment might have crept through the ranks of even that august assembly, and it may, therefore, be well understood with what cheers and roars of laughter the irreverent Plebs of Benares hailed the nomination of Rajah Shiva Prasad. The proposal was simply smothered in the noisy amusement it evoked, and brushed aside as irrelevant, but the proposer, for reasons best known to himself, went off at once and reported to the Chairman of the Standing Congress Committee and to Rajah Shiva Prasad that the latter had been duly elected as a delegate. The Chairman wrote to the Reception Committee at Allahabad, reporting the election and expressing apprehensions as to the result, and Rajah Shiva Prasad took the next train to Allahabad, appeared at the Congress Office, announced himself as a delegate, paid his fees, and obtained his ticket. Ordinarily a formal certificate, duly signed by the Chairman of the meeting, would have been required, but the letter of the Chairman of the Standing Committee and Rajah Shiva Prasad's rank and position and unhesitating declaration that he had been duly elected were accepted as sufficient—nor indeed, *pace* our good friends in Benares, is there the least reason to suspect the Rajah's good faith in this instance; he was the victim of a practical joke, and if any one deserved to be hung, it was the gentleman responsible for this.

Great was, however, the indignation, greater still the wrath of the important body of delegates from the Benares division, when two days later they arrived and discovered who it was who had already enrolled himself as their colleague. At first they were not to be pacified, they would not attend the Congress if he was to be allowed to enter the hall—on the other hand, the Reception Committee felt that, having accepted him as a delegate, to exclude him now would be not only discourteous, he having acted as they believed in good faith, but, looking to his position as one of the two leaders of the Anti-Congress party, possibly open to misconstruction.

If he, after denouncing the Congress 'up hill and down dale,' chose so far to recant, as to join it, declaring himself a duly elected delegate, it seemed desirable on public grounds to allow him to do so.

The public generally, however, inclined to believe that he had obtained admission by a fraud, and a general feeling of exasperation against him prevailed, though the Benares delegates had been partially reconciled by a seat, close under the platform and far away from them,* being assigned to him.

The reader is now in a position to understand something of the sentiments with which Rajah Shiva Prasad was regarded by the entire assemblage, when, immediately after Mr. Salem Ramaswami Mudaliar, he rose to propose, what he was pleased to call, an amendment to the resolution then before the Congress.

He commenced by saying† that he was obliged to the Congress, and was not, as was often supposed, opposed to it, but that self-interested men (and here he looked full at all the Congress leaders on the platform) were circulating pamphlets and inflammatory articles "to excite your minds and lower the Government in your eyes," and he went on to say that before sitting down he would lay on the table an amendment. This he was called on to read, and it proved to be a petition to Government, asking for the addition of further sections to the Penal Code to punish the authors of the Congress pamphlets and leaflets, from which it professed to make quotations. But no one had ever heard the passages quoted (one was shown a few days later in the public press to be a bare-faced forgery, a word in a perfectly innocent passage in the Congress catechism having been altered so as to convert it into a most objectionable one), and as the reading proceeded the cries for the names of the publications from which the pretended extracts had been made became louder and louder.

Then the President interfered; he pointed out that the petition could, under no circumstances, be accepted as an amendment on the resolution, to which it was wholly irrelevant, and that, as the Rajah had already occupied a good deal more time‡ than was allowed by the rules to each speaker, he must now sit down. The Rajah gracefully subsided, and the incident was at an end.

The patience, the forbearance with which he was treated, were simply

---

* The delegates of the several Circles sat in groups, separate blocks, or portions of blocks being assigned to the delegates of each Circle.

† Detailed Report, pp. 24, 25.

‡ Ten minutes were allowed to proposers of resolutions, five minutes to all other speakers. (*Vide*, President's Speech, Detailed Report, p. 15.)

marvellous. In that hall, including delegates, there were at least 5,000 men, who disliked him more than any other living being, and who were, at the moment, specially exasperated against him on account of the trick they held that he had played on the Reception Committee. Yet though he proceeded with the greatest deliberation, he spoke very slowly, to insult—he meant it as an insult, and it was taken as such by all—and misrepresent the entire party, for whole minutes at a time he was listened to in a dead silence, was never, from first to last, interrupted except by calls for the names of the works he professed to be quoting, and finally was permitted to retire with only a few mild hisses. It is not too much to say that nowhere in England, France, or America, would an equally unpopular man have been treated, after such an escapade, with similar courtesy. It has been the custom of adversaries to talk of the excitable character of our Indian population, and to dwell upon this as a reason for withholding from them the privileges—we may say the rights—enjoyed elsewhere by all free men, but the truth of the matter is that the Indians are, at least, as law-abiding and capable of wise self-control as any other people on the face of the earth.

The next speaker was Mr. Mahbub Alum, a Punjabi Mahomedan. His speech was brief, but well worthy of consideration. He said :*—

"It is needless for me to try and explain the innumerable blessings we enjoy under British rule. (*Cheers.*) We do thank God that He has been so good and merciful to us Indians as to place us under such a benign, just, and merciful Sovereign as our Illustrious Queen and Empress Victoria. (*Cheers.*) Long may She and Her Government reign over us. (*Cheers.*)

* * * * * *

"Let me remind you that I am a Mahomedan of the Punjab, of which province the people were, till recently, Anti-Congressists ; but at this moment I assure you their eyes have been opened, and being alive to the true and loyal objects of the National Congress, they are now with us to a man (*loud cheers*) ; and I am pleased to have the opportunity to assure you that the Punjab Anti-Congress movement is a thing of the past. (*Renewed cheers.*)

* * * * * *

"This is a good work, and I feel sure God will help us. (*Cheers.*) Anti-Congressmen accuse us of being disloyal, but I feel inclined to apply the term to them. We openly and truthfully declare our wants, and do not mean to get them by stealth and underhand-work. I am a poor subject, but allow me to advise the Government to mark such men as the Anti-Congressmen, who work by stealth and duplicity. These are the real seditionists ; they do not want the causes of disaffection removed ; they do not want the grievances of the people redressed—they want them to continue to vex and irritate the people till these grow at last as disaffected as themselves. They are the real enemies ; we the real friends and true supporters of the British Government. May God confound their evil schemes, and bless and preserve our Gracious Empress." (*Loud cheers.*)

Other speakers followed, one of them an Allahabad lawyer, Mr. Newal Behari Bajpai, one of Rajah Shiva Prasad's very few well-wishers, made a good point. He said : †—

"I am really sorry if Rajah Shiva Prasad disapproves this resolution, as from the nature of the petition which he seemed to wish us to adopt as an amendment to it, I am led to fear. I am sorry, I say, if this be the case, because I have a high respect for the Rajah, whom I have long known, whom I look upon as a father, nay, whose legal adviser I am at this moment in a certain case. But really my respected and distinguished client should be reasonable. Millions share the prayer embodied in this resolution, but it appears that some two or three men somewhere—who or where I know not—who are also supporters of the Congress, have used words which the Rajah thinks objectionable, nay seditious—

* Detailed Report, p. 25.
† Detailed Report, p. 25.

therefore this resolution is bad, and we ought to drop it. Gentlemen, every year millions look forward hopefully to the rains, and perhaps one or two bad men lose their tempers and use bad language, because the monsoon does not come quite as soon as they want; therefore the rains are bad, and we ought not to have any monsoon. I can't see the argument. What on earth have the objectionable expressions (if any such were ever really used—I at least have never heard of such)—what, I say, have these to do with the prayer set forth in our resolution? Nothing! Simply nothing! And that prayer, let who will have talked nonsense or worse, I support with all my heart."

Then Mr. Golucknath, a Punjabi Christian Barrister (a close connection by marriage with the Rajah of Kapoorthalla), rose and proposed* to modify slightly the terms of the resolution so as to make it explicitly advocate the establishment of a Council for the Punjab, where, as he and his seconder affirmed, such a body was greatly needed. Then Mr. Behari Lall summed up the matter in these words†—

"I heartily support the resolution as amended, and I sincerely hope that the Punjab will soon get its Council, and that all the Councils, Supreme and Provincial, will, before long, be placed upon that sounder and healthier footing that this our resolution suggests. Until this be done, the Government must continue, as now, to be carried on in a more or less haphazard fashion. What men can do, situated as they are, our rulers, I fully believe, do; but they will never be able to do real justice to us or to themselves, to India or to England, until they associate with themselves in their anxious toils those men whom the country knows and trusts, and whom we elect as our representatives."

The amendment was agreed to, and the following resolution was carried by acclamation:—

"RESOLVED—*That this Congress affirms the necessity for the expansion and reform of the Council of the Governor-General for making laws and regulations, and of the existing Provincial Legislative Councils, already set forth in Resolutions III of the Congresses of 1885 and 1886, and Resolution II of the Congress of 1887, (a tentative scheme for which expansion and reform was suggested in Resolution IV of the Congress of 1886) and further urges that a Legislative Council (of the same character as those which have been suggested for provinces where Legislative Councils already exist) be established for the Punjab.*"

As illustrating how infectious enthusiasm is, it may be noted that when this resolution was passed, with loud cheers, by the entire assembly, not only did Rajah Shiva Prasad vote for it—holding up and waving his right arm enthusiastically like all the rest,—but so did the managing proprietor (and the inspirer of all its irrational attacks on the Congress) of the leading local Bureaucratic organ, although being present only as a visitor and reporter, it is *said*, on behalf of Government, he had no right to vote either way. Modern science may ignore magic, but there is something nearly akin to magic in the effects produced upon by-standers by the combined enthusiasm on *any* subject of any really large body of men.

Mr. Eardley-Norton, a leading barrister of Madras, then rose to propose a resolution in regard to the Public Service Question. Soon after the passing of a resolution on this subject at the first Congress, the Government appointed a Commission to enquire into and report upon it. The report of the Commission has been published, and is now under the consideration of Her Majesty's Secretary of State for India, but the recommendations of the Commissioners are universally held to be insufficient, specially because they do not include

* Detailed Report, pp. 25, 26
† Detailed Report, p. 26.

a provision for holding simultaneous examinations for the Civil Service in both India and England. It is felt by every Indian to be a grave injustice that he is debarred from serving his country in any of the higher grades of the service unless he proceeds to England to pass an examination there, the more so that in the case of orthodox Hindus there are still (doubtless they are beginning to disappear) religious objections to crossing the ocean. "What," they reasonably ask, "would the people of Australia and New Zealand feel if they were absolutely precluded from obtaining any of the higher posts in the public service of their own countries unless they had, while still boys, proceeded to England and passed there an English examination?" It was considered by the great bulk of the delegates that it was essential that the country should, before the Secretary of State passed orders on the report, clearly declare that this report was not accepted as altogether satisfactory by the people of India.

At the Congress of 1886 a Committee was appointed to report upon the whole question, and their report, some 20 lines only in length, but tersely embodying the whole pith of the subject, was unanimously adopted by that Congress, and the resolution, of which Mr. Norton was placed in charge, was a re-affirmation of that report. Before touching the special question, Mr. Norton made some remarks in regard to the progress and position of the Congress movement, from which we may extract a few sentences:—

"Your growing representation," he said,* "is the most significant and eloquent testimony to the growing strength and popularity of your cause. (*Cheers.*) You have had many and serious obstacles placed in your path, but you have been nerved by the opposition, and it is a matter of very hopeful and very sincere congratulation that you have manfully met and conquered the impediments in your way. I am glad to think you have successfully withstood the literary assaults of the Rajah of Bhinga.† (*Loud laughter.*) I am glad you have not succumbed to the more polished literary essay of Sir Auckland Colvin. (*Cheers.*) I am glad you have been stimulated and stiffened by the open misrepresentations of Lord Dufferin. (*Loud cheers.*) And I dare say you will even survive the terrible onslaught made upon you to-day by Rajah Shiva Prasad. (*Loud laughter and cheers.*)

* * * * * *

"Our Congress is outside the reach of petty malice. It is increasing day by day in power and extent, pushing aside by its own great weight the opposing forces of envy and of scorn; and while it draws the various peoples of this country into one common fold of mutual sympathy and good will, rises with silent majesty into a future of self-reliance and content. (*Cheers.*)—

Like some tall cliff that rears its awful form,
Swells from the vale, and midway leaves the storm,
Though round its base the gathering clouds may spread,
Eternal sunshine settles on its head." (*Loud cheers.*)

Then turning to the resolution which he proposed, he gave reasons for believing that the recommendations of the Commission were inadequate, and, even if adopted by the Secretary of State, would altogether fail to satisfy the just expectations of the country.

He examined the question historically, and showed the view taken of it

* Detailed Report, p. 26.

† Detailed Report, pp. 27, 28. This is the gentleman whom, rightly or wrongly, his fellow-countrymen, and specially his neighbours in the United Provinces, persist in believing to be incapable, not only of writing, but even of understanding, the letters that have appeared under his signature in the *Times* and other papers.

when it first came before the House of Commons in 1833, quoting, *inter alia*, Sir Robert Peel's memorable words :—

"This is what Sir Robert Peel said : I am glad to be able to shelter myself under his name. Were the words mine, they would be called seditious. (*Laughter.*) 'In a word, to endeavour while we still keep them under British rule, to atone to them for the sufferings they endured, and the wrongs to which they were exposed in being reduced to that rule, and to afford them such advantages and confer on them such benefits as may in some degree console them for the loss of their independence, these, Sir, are considerations which, whatever may be the anxiety to extend British conquest and to maintain the rights of British subjects, must indisputably be entertained in a British Parliament.'" (*Cheers.*)

He passed on to the revision of 1853, showing the noble and generous sentiments entertained by the statesmen of those days as to the rights of the people of India, and England's duties in regard to them, and he then quoted at length the following report of the Departmental Committee of the India Office of 1860 :—

"2. We are, in the first place, unanimously of opinion that it is not only just but expedient that the natives of India shall be employed in the administration of India to as large an extent as possible consistently with the maintenance of British supremacy, and have considered whether any increased facilities can be given in this direction.

"3. It is true that even at present no positive disqualification exists. By Act 3 and 4, William IV, Cap. 85, s. 87, it is enacted 'that no native of the said territories, nor any natural-born subject of His Majesty, resident therein, shall, by reason only of his religion, place of birth, descent, color or any of them, be disabled from holding any place, office or employment under the said Company.' It is obvious, therefore, that when the competitive system was adopted it could not have been intended to exclude natives of India from the Civil Service of India.

"4. Practically, however, they are excluded. The law declares them eligible, but the difficulties opposed to a native living in India and residing in England for a time are so great that, as a general rule, it is almost impossible for a native successfully to compete at the periodical examinations held in England. Were this inequality removed, we should no longer be exposed to the charge of keeping promise to the ear and breaking it to the hope.

"5. Two modes have been suggested by which the object in view might be attained : The first is by allotting a certain portion of the total number of appointments declared in each year, to be competed for in India by natives and by all other natural-born subjects of Her Majesty resident in India. The second is to hold simultaneously two examinatious—one in England and one in India, both being, as far as practicable, identical in their nature, and those who compete in both countries being finally classified in one list according to merit by the Civil Service Commissioners. The Committee have no hesitation in giving preference to the second scheme, as being the fairest and the most in accordance with the principles of a general competition for a common object."

It is, in our opinion, far from creditable to England, that during the, nearly, 30 years that have elapsed since this memorable report, (which precisely embodies the views and wishes of the people of India,) was presented, no single honest attempt has been made to give effect to its recommendations, so that Indians remain to this day excluded from any practical share in the higher branches of the administration. Nor has this been due to any forgetfulness; it is not that the matter has been overlooked; it has been solely owing to the persistent determination of the Indian Bureaucracy, in defiance of the expressed wishes of the people and Parliament of England, to keep for themselves and their class all the loaves and fishes. In 1869 the Duke of Argyll openly condemned the gross breach of faith in which this had involved the nation :—

"With regard, however, to the employment of natives in the Government of their country, in the Covenanted Civil Service formerly of the Company and now of the Crown, *I must say that we have not fulfilled our duty or the promises and engagements which we have made.*"

And that reproach, as Mr. Norton justly remarked, remains as true in 1889 as it was in 1869. Even Lord Lytton—of Press Act and Afghan failures notoriety—in a secret report, which later accidentally saw the light, was compelled to admit that, in this matter of the public service, the people of India had been "*cheated.*"

Nor is it only where the Covenanted Service is concerned, that the people of India are debarred from what their Sovereign, Her Parliament and People have solemnly declared to be their just rights. It is equally the case with all appointments in the Uncovenanted Civil Service that any Englishman can be found to consider worth his acceptance. Mr. Norton put the case clearly. He said* :—

"I wish to touch with brief particularity upon two points in connection with the Public Service Commission: First, as to the excessive cost of the administration of this country. Many people think it ruinous. I agree with them. The only real solution of the difficulty lies in an infusion into the machinery of the country of a large, and yearly larger, element of indigenous Indian talent. ('*Hear, hear.*') What share do you hold to-day in the service of your country? Here are some suggestive figures. Out of 2,357 appointments in the higher Uncovenanted Civil Service, you, Gentlemen of India, hold 188. ('*Shame, shame!*') The non-domiciled Europeans appropriate 1,460 such appointments: the domiciled Europeans 486, Eurasians 223, and the Indians 188! ('*Shame!*') The three first bodies hold 2,169 berths, you only 188! ('*Shame!*') Yes, it is a shame, and it is one you will efface from the history of England's connection with India only by making plain to the people of England your ungenerous and impolitic exclusion from public life in India."

Now the bulk of these 1,460 non-domiciled Europeans are the sons, sons-in-law, brothers, cousins, tutors, proteges or connections of one kind or another of our Indian European officials, civil, military, past or present, and it is certain that fully two-thirds of these gentlemen might be at once replaced by statutory natives of India, on salaries appreciably smaller than those now enjoyed by these flowers of nepotism, with the greatest advantage to the administration of the country.

"I know nothing," said Mr. Norton, "more solemnly beautiful than the language of your Charter from the Queen of England (*loud cheers*), in which are embodied the grand and spontaneous declarations of my own dear island home :—

"'In their prosperity will be our strength, in their contentment our security, and in their gratitude our best reward. And may the God of all power grant to us, and to those in authority under us, strength to carry out these our wishes for the good of our people.'"

But how is India to be prosperous, to be contented, to be grateful, when the people of England, in this and every other matter, allow Her rights to be trampled under foot, and their own most solemn pledges to Her to be persistently and absolutely ignored, in the interests of that *truly* "microscopic minority," the Anglo-Indian officials?

But while, on these points, all thoughtful Indians are of one mind, in regard to one detail of the public service question, a considerable difference of opinion existed, and Mr. John Adam, Principal of the great Patcheappah College at Madras, rose to propose as an amendment the re-affirmation, with some slight additions, of the resolution on this subject

---

* Detailed Report, p. 30.

of the Congress of 1885, instead of, as proposed by Mr. Norton, of the resolution of the Congress of 1886.

Mr. Adam thus explained* the case—

"* * * The latter portion of the amendment is simply Resolution IV of the Bombay Congress of 1885. This, as you will have heard, besides stipulating for simultaneous examinations in England and India, provides that the successful candidates in India shall be sent to England for further study, and be subjected there to such additional tests as may be considered necessary. Now this Resolution of the 1885 Congress was not brought forward in 1886 or 1887. In 1887 the subject was not touched at all because the Public Service Commission had completed their labours, but had not yet issued their report, and the matter was considered to be, as it were, *sub judice*. But in 1886, when the resolution of 1885 might have been re-affirmed, a different resolution, identical with that which has been proposed to you by Mr. Norton, was substituted for it. One reason for this appears to have been that the resolution of 1885 contained a clause, *viz.*, that in regard to successful candidates being sent to England to complete their education, about which great differences of opinion existed. I venture to think that, despite these differences of opinion, it would have been wiser in 1886 to put the original resolution, and have taken the verdict of the Congress upon this point. I myself hold that it is absolutely necessary that successful candidates at examinations in India should be sent to England for two or three years' special training, I urge this upon two grounds—the first, that we must have the best men trained in the most complete manner to administer our laws, and I hold that, however well a man may be trained in this country, he will be greatly improved as a public officer by the additional training which he can obtain in England. The second is, that it is absolutely necessary that Indian gentlemen, who aspire to high official position under the British Government, should have a far more thorough knowledge of English manners, customs and habits of thought than they can possibly acquire in this country. It must be remembered that Indians who rise in the Civil Service will have not only to rule over their own countrymen, but to work in harmony with, and, as time goes on, direct and control the operations of European officials. I think there is nothing more absolutely necessary than that young Indians selected for the Civil Service should go to England, if only to qualify them to maintain later their independence and self-respect in their relations with their European brother-Civilians.

"You will not forget that this question of the Public Service is the one to which the most esteemed of all Indian reformers, Mr. Dadabhai Naoroji (*loud cheers*) has devoted his life and soul; and you will, I am sure, feel that his opinion on this subject is entitled to the very greatest weight. ('*Hear, hear.*') Now the resolution of 1885, which I am asking the Congress to affirm in lieu of the resolution of 1886, which Mr. Norton has proposed to you, was Mr. Dadabhai's own resolution, moved by himself at the first Congress, and I cannot put my case with regard to this disputed question of going to England more strongly than it was put by Mr. Dadabhai at Bombay, whose words I will now quote: 'I say without the least hesitation that the candidate himself, as well as the service, will be vastly benefited by a visit to England. The atmosphere of freedom and high civilization which he will breathe will make him an altered man, in character, in intelligence, in experience, in self-respect, and in appreciation of due respect for others. In short, he will largely increase his fitness and command more respect in his responsible service.' Gentlemen, I venture to hope that you will accept my amendment. To me it seems quite certain that the Government can never concede simultaneous examinations without insisting on the successful candidates expending two or more years in England before they enter on the very responsible duties of an Indian Civilian. Nay more, I am compelled to say that I have doubts whether I could honestly recommend simultaneous examinations unless coupled with such a condition; and I think it would be well if your resolution distinctly set forth your appreciation of its absolute necessity. I am aware that a very large number of you share my views, but are indisposed to press the point, because some others of our brother-delegates object to it, and there is, doubtless, much to be said in favour of the view that, as it is quite certain that if the Government does concede simultaneous examinations, it will necessarily insist upon this condition, it is needless for us to say anything about the matter. But my own view is that the open and straightforward course is the best, and that our cause would gain by our setting forth distinctly, not only the concession that we desire, but the necessary condition to this concession, as one that we are prepared to accept. These, Gentlemen, are the reasons which have led me to submit to you this amendment, which I must now leave to your better judgment."

The amendment was duly seconded, and, evening having closed in, the President adjourned the assembly until next day at 11 A.M.

* Detailed Report, pp. 32, 33.

It will be easily understood that the real question at issue between the two parties, of which Messrs. Norton and Adam were respectively the spokesmen, was, whether the Congress should or should not once more authoritatively re-affirm the recommendation of the first Congress, that, in the event of simultaneous examinations being conceded, successful candidates in India should be required to proceed to England for further training. The younger and more progressive sections were entirely in favour of this, the older and more conservative opposed to it. Naturally, whatever their views as to the desirability of the measure, orthodox Hindus could not, with any regard for consistency, agree to laying down a rule which involved crossing the black waters ; in other words, the breach of what has somehow come to be regarded as a sacred ordinance, and which has not, as yet, been repudiated or abandoned by any general consensus of opinion. Should Government insist on such a condition, public opinion has grown so divided on the subject, that, not impossibly, were their sons successful in a competition, the most orthodox might accept it, but they could not reasonably be expected themselves to join in *inviting* Government to impose it. On the other hand, the party of progress, the social and religious reformers, and all the younger men almost without exception, were intensely anxious to commit the whole Congress to what would virtually have been an authoritative repudiation of what they hold to be a mere superstition in regard to quitting Indian limits.

No Englishman can, perhaps, understand the intense interest felt in the question : to one party it meant the loyal and loving adherence to the faith of their fathers at whatsoever risk to temporal interests ; to the others a notable advance in the upward path of national regeneration. So all that evening and far into the night the camp was alive ; from tent to tent flitted the earnest advocates of the contending parties, arguing, entreating, coaxing ; and again by sunrise the work was recommenced, and to those ignorant of the sweet reasonableness of our people, it really seemed as if the goddess of Discord had, as our adversaries have been so fond of prophesying that she would, at last succeeded in establishing her reign of misrule over the Congress.

At 11 A.M. (Friday, the 28th December) the Congress punctually re-assembled. During the previous day the news of Mr. John Bright's serious illness had been generally disseminated. The great tribune of the people has ever been regarded in India as friendly to her people's cause, and hence a feeling had sprung up amongst delegates from all provinces that it would be well to express, to his family, India's sympathy with them in their sorrow. Accordingly, in response to innumerable suggestions to this effect, the President on taking his seat proposed that a telegram expressive of sympathy should be at once despatched to Mr. Bright's son, a proposal unanimously and enthusiastically accepted by the assembly. The telegram to Mr. John Albert Bright ran as follows* :—

"Congress consisting of 1,200 delegates from all parts of India join in expressing their high appreciation of your father's services to India, their sorrow at his illness, their sympathy with him and his family in his sufferings, and their earnest hope for his complete recovery,"—

---

* Detailed Report, p. 34.

and it was, later, gratifying to all, to know, that this message was duly received and cordially acknowledged.

Then the Public Service debate was resumed by Mr. Ramaswami Mudaliar, who proposed yet another amendment. Mr. Mudaliar had himself been a member of the Public Service Commission, and the gist of his speech was,* that the recommendations of this body, if not all that could be desired, were yet, if adopted in their entirety, likely to be productive of much benefit, and were, at any rate, the best terms that he, and the three other gentlemen who acted with him in the interests of the Indians, a small minority, could extort from the majority. That if they had abandoned the simultaneous examinations, it was partly because the official majority would not listen to the proposal, and partly because, even amongst Indians, differences of opinion existed, both as to the expediency of such simultaneity and as to the conditions that should be attached to it if conceded. He considered that a tolerably fair compromise, on the give-and-take principle, had been arrived at, and that if the Secretary of State accepted this, as it stood, agitation on the subject should cease, for some years at any rate. Therefore, he said, my amendment is to postpone for a year all consideration of the subject.

"At present," he said, "I think we are in a sense bound by the compromise we have made, and this is why I press you to defer further consideration of the subject, until we see what orders the Secretary of State passes on our report. If he accepts it in its entirety, I, for one, think we might be content to drop the subject for some years. If, however, he fails to do this, then I shall be the first to press for further agitation. So all I say now is, *wait and see*—wait another year before you take any further action on the question." (*Cheers.*)

Mr. Telang seconded Mr. Mudaliar's proposal, but the sense of the meeting was not with these gentlemen, and Mr. Mono Mohan Ghose, a distinguished member of the Calcutta Bar, rose and suggested a compromise, which at once satisfied the assembly. He said †:—

"Now, there is one matter as to which we are all agreed, and that is the necessity for holding simultaneous examinations in England and India. I think we are also agreed that we fully appreciate the justice and the propriety of the recommendation made by the Public Service Commission, to raise the limit of age prescribed for the open competition. (*Cheers.*) It would not be right, therefore, to ignore the services rendered to the country by the members of that Commission, who have performed their difficult task in such a manner as to entitle them to the thanks of this Congress. (*Cheers.*) I must confess, however, that, as regards the propriety of taking up this question at all, I at one time entertained considerable doubts. I was at first inclined to believe that the wise course for us would be to follow that suggested by Mr. Mudaliar; but after hearing Mr. Norton, and after mature consideration of the matter, I have come to the conclusion that, if we were not to press our demand on this occasion before the Secretary of State, we might be allowing judgment to go by default. It is our duty to let the Government know what we think on the subject, and I think the Congress will, therefore, agree with me that the best course for us on the present occasion would be the adoption of a resolution which could not possibly cause any difference of opinion in the Congress, and which would explicitly set forth what we mean and wish."

"This, then, is the resolution which I venture to propose for your acceptance :—

'*That this Congress, while appreciating the concessions proposed in the Report of the Public Service Commission, yet feels it necessary to put distinctly on record, its opinion, that full justice will never be done to the people of this country, until the open competitive examination for the Civil Service of India is held simultaneously in England and in India.*'" (*Loud cheers.*)

The original resolution, and both the previous amendments were with-

---

* Detailed Report, pp. 34, 35.
† Detailed Report, p. 37.

drawn, and Mr. Ghose's resolution, which set forth exactly what all were agreed upon, and no more, was passed unanimously.

Is there another country in the world in which a large body of earnest men,—after a debate like that of the previous day, after further most exciting private discussions during half the night and nearly all the morning, after every vote had been canvassed and counted and every man had definitely ranged himself in one of three parties,—would thus unanimously and immediately have abandoned their several positions, which they had been prepared to defend to the last, simply on its being made clear to them that there was yet another position that all might accept without either violence to their own convictions or disrespect to those of their brethren?

It is the "sweet reasonableness" evinced in cases of this nature, and there have been other similar instances at previous Congresses, and the noble self-control exhibited in the incident of Shiva Prasad, that more than anything else, to our mind, conclusively demonstrate the fitness of Indians for a far larger measure of representative institutions than the Congress Party, in their wise caution, have ever yet thought it expedient to suggest.

The next resolution was one reiterating the necessity set forth in similar resolutions at previous Congresses, for the complete separation of judicial and executive functions. No one now is bold enough to deny, openly, that this is a necessary reform. The thing is too clear; but for all that we seem no nearer to it than we were a quarter of a century ago.

As Mr. Yule, in his inaugural address, well remarked *:—

"This was one of the ridiculous proposals, one of those school-boy clamours to start with, but the Viceroy now tells us that 'this is a counsel of perfection to which we are ready to subscribe.' Allow me to congratulate you upon this concession so frankly and handsomely made. All that we want now is to see the concession of the principle reduced into practice."

But this is precisely what our Indian authorities seem resolved not to do. As Mr. Shurf-ud-din, a Punjabi Mahomedan, truly said † :—

"Where a Collector wishes to realise revenue, he does so, not merely by the exercise of those powers conferred on him, on that behalf, by the Legislature, but by the pressure of the authority that he possesses as a Magistrate, conferred on him, not in view to the realisation of land revenue demands, but to enable him to punish offenders against the criminal law."

And this combination they seem to find too convenient to be abandoned. How absolutely indefensible this system of combining all sorts of functions in one and the same official becomes, in some provinces, was clearly set forth by Mr. Devaro Vinayek, a grave and thoughtful legal practitioner of six-and-twenty years' standing, the vice-chairman and moving spirit of one of the best managed municipalities in India. He said ‡ :—

"You will be surprised and startled when you hear from me that in my province, not only the magisterial and police powers are combined in one officer, but also the revenue and civil

* Detailed Report, p. 11.
† Detailed Report, p. 41.
‡ Detailed Report, p. 41.

judicial powers are all combined in one man. (*Cries of 'Shame!'*) There is one head of the district who is the Deputy Commissioner and who is the supreme authority in all matters. He is head of the police—he is the highest local tribunal in criminal matters with powers of sentencing to seven years' imprisonment with hard labour—he is the highest tribunal in all civil cases—he is the chief revenue official, head director, alike, of all fiscal arrangements. In every relation of life you are in the grasp of this one man; if he dislikes you—if he have a prejudice against you—there is no escaping him; it is an absolute despotism. Now, I ask, is this a defensible system? Others have told you, and you yourselves well know what takes place where only police and criminal judicial powers are combined in one officer. You can imagine what might occur in our province. As a matter of fact, serious failures of justice have resulted, and if these have not been more frequent or grievous in our province than elsewhere, it is due solely to the fact that we have had exceptionally good officers who scorned to abuse their powers. But we cannot count upon a continuance of this; the system is susceptible of unlimited abuse and oppression, and against that system I earnestly and unhesitatingly protest, and this, despite the sincere personal respect and esteem in which I hold many of the officers under whom I have lived and worked." (*Cheers.*)

Mr. J. E. Howard, a barrister, was the proposer of the resolution, and he gave several happy illustrations of "the utter confusion to which the existing irrational combination of these two functions, the judicial and the executive, in one official, are apt to give rise."

Two of these may be usefully reproduced :—

"Fourteen years ago," he said,* "I was called upon to defend two persons before the Sessions Judge of Agra, and the evidence against them consisted principally of the statements of policemen who had placed the stolen articles where they were found; so that I had no difficulty in getting the assessors to record a verdict of acquittal. The Sessions Judge, nevertheless, very much to my surprise, convicted the accused persons. I was asked to have tea with the Sessions Judge soon after the trial was over, and he remarked to me that he supposed I was surprised at his having convicted my clients. I confessed I was on the evidence adduced, and he then made the following remarkable observation to me: 'I admit the evidence against them was very weak, but you know *those fellows have a very bad reputation, and Her Majesty's Government must be carried on!!*' (*Laughter.*) That was his notion of exercising judicial functions. As a Magistrate during the previous 20 years of his service, he had always been both head policeman, prosecutor and judge, and when he came to be a Sessions Judge he could not escape the bias thus formed, and when the Magistrate set forth in the committal papers that the accused were very bad characters, he felt bound to convict them, whether there was any sufficient evidence against them or not. As the Judge in question has retired from the service, I will not mention his name, but I will give you the sequel of the case which came in appeal before the High Court of these Provinces. Mr. Justice (afterwards Sir Charles) Turner heard the appeal of the prisoners, Mr. Colvin was my leader, and so flagrantly opposed to common sense and common justice was the conviction, that that eminent Judge (*cheers*) never called upon the counsel for the appellants to say a single word in support of the appeal. Turning to the Government Pleader, who appeared on behalf of the Crown in support of the conviction —as he is a distinguished member of this Congress and present, I may be permitted to mention his name, Mr. Dwarkanath Banerji—(*cheers*)—Mr. Justice Turner said: 'How can you support this conviction, Mr. Banerji? I see the evidence is entirely that of policemen who found the things, which they are accused of having placed where they are said to have found them, and I must confess the case smacks strongly of police manufacture.' Mr. Banerji, with that blandness and frankness which distinguishes him, was forced to admit that the evidence was extremely weak and suspicious, and the men were acquitted on the spot; but observe the result: they had been nearly two months wrongfully in jail, and, as you know, there is no redress for such wrongs. An innocent man, wrongfully convicted or incarcerated, has no compensation of any kind, and it is because of the irreparable nature of the wrong that we should provide every possible safeguard against such abuses.

"The last instance is a comparatively recent one, taken from the most backward of these provinces—Oudh—a non-regulation province as it is called. A few years ago the Judicial Commissioner of Oudh had his judicial soul shocked by finding that a Deputy Commissioner under him, in whom were combined the functions of Revenue Collector and Magistrate, had used his magisterial powers to convict—I forget how many persons (I believe the number was nearly a hundred)—under the Indian Penal Code, for disobeying the lawful order of a public servant, because they had not paid their instalments of revenue in the time within which he had ordered that they should be paid! The Judicial Commissioner sent these

* Detailed Report, p. 39.

cases up to His Honor the Lieutenant-Governor of the North-West Provinces and Chief Commissioner of Oudh, for such notice as His Honor might see fit to take of the matter, and the fines were, I believe, remitted ; but the case illustrates, happily, the utter confusion in regard to the first principles of justice to which the existing irrational combination of these two functions, the judicial and executive, in one official, are apt to give rise."

It is needless to quote further illustrations of the evils to which the existing system everywhere, almost daily, gives rise. Mr. Tahilram Khemchand, of Sind, after quoting an instance which came under his personal experience, truly hit the mark when he said* in conclusion—

"There must be some hundreds of Barristers and Pleaders amongst the twelve hundred and odd delegates here assembled, but I venture to assert that there is not one single one of them who cannot, from his own personal experience, cite many similar cases in which the combination of the two functions, against which this resolution is a protest, has led to the most flagrant miscarriages of justice." (*Loud cheers.*)

The resolution was passed unanimously.

The next resolution brought before the Congress referred to certain other necessary reforms in the existing judicial system, which, though of great practical importance to the people, are not such as to interest greatly the general reader. Those who desire to learn more of the matter, may turn to pages 42-46 of the Detailed Report, but a single speech, that made by Mr. N. Subha Row of Madras in regard to the desirability of extending the system of trial by jury, may, perhaps, be here reproduced with advantage. He said †:—

"This is a matter upon which we are all agreed. ('*Hear, hear.*') We see at present, in several parts of our Presidency, in many important districts, this system of trial by jury in full force. It is a system which is admitted to be an aid to the administration of justice ; it has been in force for a long period with us, and it has worked, and is working, satisfactorily. (*Cheers.*) It is often alleged, as a reason for not further extending the system, that there are not a sufficient number of people of the intelligence required to make men satisfactory jurymen, and that our people are not sufficiently advanced in education to aid Judges as jurors in the discharge of their functions. I must give the most emphatic denial to these allegations so far as my Presidency is concerned. (*Cheers.*) Has not the education of the country been going on for a great number of years? The existence of this assembly is sufficient evidence of that and of the existence of far more than the required number of competent jurors. What town in the Empire, in which Sessions Courts are held, but is represented here by delegates ? (*Cries of 'None, none.'*) What delegate is there in whose election at least fifty educated men, fit to be jurors, to say nothing of the multitudes of the less cultured did not take part ? (*Cries of 'None, none.'*) We are not wanting in men ; men by scores, and hundreds even, in some towns, will willingly come forward and take upon themselves the honorable duties of jurymen. (*Cheers.*) Again it is, at times, alleged that the present system of trial with the aid of assessors is a farce, and that, because that system is a farce, therefore the system of trial by jury would also be a farce. I submit that no more fallacious argument could be advanced. (*Cheers.*) The present system of trials with the aid of assessors may not be quite satisfactory, and if it were, it would be a miracle. For how can you expect really good men to spend a whole day, at times two or three, in working into a case thoroughly, merely to enable a Judge, at the end, to decide perversely without reference, or in direct opposition, to their carefully worked-out opinions ? When assessors are summoned to assist a Judge, they are not, as a rule, consulted in any way. Their presence, in fact, is practically ignored, and they are simply, too often, mere paraphernalia of the Judge's Court, having no more to say to the trial, in which they are supposed to assist, than his inkstand or his chair. Moreover, no efforts are made, in most cases, to secure good men as assessors. When the list of assessors is drawn up, the Judge and the Collector meet and do it in something like five minutes. Nor do they try to see that the better-informed sections of the people are represented on their list, or even to make sure that there are any intelligent people amongst the lot. The most ignorant men, and old people in their dotage, are some-

* Detailed Report, p. 40.
† Detailed Report, pp. 44, 45.

times put on the list. I have known two assessors, who could not read or write, put on in a forgery case, who, when the paper was put into their hands to say if it was forged or genuine, could only say, 'Whichever you please.' (*Laughter.*) This is only one of many instances that I could cite, but I think I have said enough to prove that the not unfrequent failure of the assessor system is absolutely no argument against the success of a properly conducted jury system."

The resolution was unanimously agreed to, and at 1-30 P.M. the Congress adjourned for half an hour. When it re-assembled, the debate was opened by Munshi Sujjad Hussain, a Mahomedan gentleman of Lucknow, the editor of the Lucknow *Punch.* The resolution which he had to propose referred to a reform of the existing police administration, and probably no question came before the Congress in which every individual out of the whole three millions who personally took part in the elections, felt such a lively personal interest as in this one. The iniquities, the atrocities of the present police system, are no new discoveries, yet this was the first occasion on which they have formed the subject of discussion by the Congress. The reason is, that this is one of those matters in which all the educated sections of the community feel that there is little hope of any real reform being effected until the country is largely represented on the Councils. Hence they have never pressed this question, but have rather concentrated their efforts on the reform of the Legislative Councils. This year, however, the intelligent but (according to English ideas) uneducated classes greatly out-numbered the educated at the elections, and so nine-tenths of the delegates came charged with the strictest injunctions from their constituents, to expose and demand a reform of the present police system. No more conclusive evidence of the growing strength of the popular element in the Congress movement could possibly be adduced than this new departure taken this year in regard to the police, which is, *par excellence,* the common-people's grievance.

Munshi Sujjad Hussain is a born orator and a gentleman of infinite humour, and from first to last he kept the assembly in a roar of laughter. His whole speech should be read (pp. 46-48 of Detailed Report), but unfortunately he spoke in Urdu, and the best translation gives but a feeble reflection of the eloquence and humour of the original. He opened the question with the remarks—

"You all know what our good and great and beneficent British Governors have done for our welfare, our protection and advancement; indeed you all probably know more about *this* than I do. (*Laughter.*) Amongst these most excellent works, one is the Police Administration.

* * * * * *

"No Lieutenant-Governor, nor even Viceroy, has such power in regard to my peace and comfort, as a simple *chowkeedar* (village watchman) or His Honor the constable (*saheb bahadur*). (*Cheers and laughter.*) The humblest labourer in the village, the most exalted noble in the city, are equally under the control of these distinguished officials. There is no place, no spot, where their Highnesses of the Police, like the Angel of Death, are not present." (*Cheers.*)

And he went on to show that it was not the people, but the thieves, that the police protected. Great as is the annoyance of being robbed, the police investigation into the robbery is worse.

"On him too they cast the blame of having been careless—of course if he *has* been robbed, which they greatly doubt, it has been solely his *own* fault—and if the thieves have by chance left him anything, this, the poor man's good friends, the police, are always kind enough to accept." (*Loud and continued cheers.*)

The speech should be read, but its conclusion, referring to the futile efforts of secret emissaries of the official party during the Congress to make mischief amongst the delegates, deserves special notice.

"For the last two days I have watched certain men coming into the Congress camp and making friends with the delegates and giving them certain advice, and, without openly opposing our work, doing all they can, in an underhand way, to mislead some of my co-religionists, by holding out to them prospects of the good will of the authorities, and of titles, if they will only leave the camp. Now I cannot help looking upon the friendly advances of these astute individuals as very similar to those made to Adam and Eve by the Devil in Paradise. (*Cheers.*) This is one of the traps of our ingenious and unscrupulous adversaries, who, finding they can do us no harm by their open hostility, seek now to injure us under the guise of friendship. (*Loud cheers.*)

"Let me tell you a little story: There was a certain Moulvi, very learned and pious, who, day and night, was occupied in the praise of God. The Devil was puzzled; said he, 'I can't get hold of this fellow anyhow; really I shall lose him if I don't look out, and, what is worse, people so look up to and revere him, that the whole country here is growing religious, and if I cannot show him up, I shall lose the whole country; it really is deuced hard, and blow me if I know what to do.' One day, however, having put on a wonderful appearance of sanctity, with a beard down to his navel, wearing a huge green turban and a long robe, a rosary in one hand, a staff in the other, and slippers on his feet (*loud laughter*) in the small hours of the night, he appeared before the holy devotee: 'Peace be to you; And to you be peace.' 'May I hope you are well?' 'Whence has your honour come?' The devil said: 'I am Gabriel. Our good friend* God has accepted your devotion and is much pleased with you, and has ordered me to wait upon you and give you his best regards and bring you to the seventh heaven. So here I am, and I have brought the heavenly steed (*Boorak*)†; it is at the door.' Hearing this the devotee was rejoiced beyond bounds, and burst out laughing. Nay, he was in such a hurry that he did not properly perform his ablutions, but combing his beard rapidly and slipping on his robe he announced that he was ready. The devil bound a handkerchief over his eyes and mounted him and took him along with him. Jogging on, when they had got to a certain place on the outskirts of the village, the devil said: 'Highness we have now arrived at the *Sadrat-ul-Muntaha* (*i.e.*, the place beyond which Gabriel could not proceed, when he accompanied Mahomet on his visit to Heaven). I can go no further; from hence other angels will take your worship.' Our devotee, in his enthusiasm about the seventh heaven, remained on the heavenly steed, moving slowly about all night, but no Mr. Angel (*Feristah sahib*) came, nor was the glory of God revealed to him. In the morning, passers-by who saw their much venerated devotee in this condition were greatly astonished and came near him and saw the bandage over his eyes. This they removed, and then the devotee saw that there was neither heaven nor God's throne, nor the Sadrat-ul-Muntaha, nor even the heavenly charger, but there, seated on an ass, he was perched on top of an old brick kiln. (*Prolonged cheers and laughter.*)

* * * * * *

"Now, therefore, it behoves us to weigh carefully the proposals of these enemies of our cause, who come in the guise of friends, and to reckon up well the loss and gain of every thing. Let it not be that unscrupulous people with deceitful stories leading us away from this devotion to our country's cause, and taking us up the mount of flattery, leave us, at last, perched there upon our own folly, to be the laughing-stock of the world." (*Tremendous cheering.*)

After this humourous introduction, the entire question was very ably and fully discussed, and, as it has not been touched on in previous reports, we may quote at some length from the debate.

Mr. Mudholkar said ‡ that this, though a humbler proposition than others that preceded it, was an eminently practical one, which would come, perhaps, more home to the hearts of the masses than any other:—

"It will carry the name of the Congress into every homestead. The policeman's is not a very happy lot, and, as we all know, he is more or less abused all over the world; but in India he is simply execrated from one end of the country to the other. In every village, in every town, amongst all ranks of society, high or low, wherever you go, you will find that there is nowhere any one who has one single

---

* Allah Meah, a kind of familiar way of speaking of God.
† The heavenly charger on which Mahomed rode to heaven.
‡ Detailed Report, pp. 48, 49.

good word to say for the policeman—nay, he is hated and detested—and the reasons are not far to seek. The policeman's duties are such that he ought to be loved by every well-wisher of society. He ought to be the protector of our lives and property, and as such he ought to be almost venerated. But here is the fact; in every village, the person who is most feared—feared even more than the highest official in the district—is the policeman getting Rs. 5 or Rs. 6 per month. The reason is that the law, as it stands at present, invests the policeman with powers so very wide and comprehensive, that it is no wonder that, when exercised by men whose salaries range from £4 to £6 per annum! (Englishmen will, I hope, mark this astounding fact) the result should be so very unsatisfactory. Those powers are in several respects such that they could not safely be entrusted to any set of human beings. There are others which can certainly not be rightly entrusted to any one without proper safeguards and restrictions. And to whom, I ask, are such extraordinary powers entrusted? To men ignorant and illiterate—to men drawn from the lowest ranks of society—men who have no sense of responsibility in regard to their duty (*cheers*), and who are paid the magnificent salary of from £4 to £6 per annum, being actually less than well-to-do people pay their stable assistants, their punka pullers, or their sweepers. Yet any one of these men, if he takes it into his head to insult or annoy you, or to lower you in the public estimation, can do it, and, practically, with impunity. Is it to be wondered if, to make a living, their whole energies are devoted, not to the suppression or detection of crime, but to the extortion, under threats, (of what they will otherwise do) of the means for a luxurious livelihood, out of the rest of the community?

* * * * * *

"Is there one single Indian here present who cannot, from his own personal experiences, narrate a dozen cases of cruelty, oppression and extortion on the part of these wretches? I shall be told by our adversaries that these our oppressors are our own fellow-countrymen, but this attempt to shift the responsibility is futile. When, before Lord Cornwallis' reform, the English Covenanted Civil Service were paid on the same beggarly scale (considering the positions they occupied) as the police now are, they were just as wicked and corrupt as our Indian policemen. The fault lies with Government, and with the Government only. They must restrict the arbitrary powers of the police. They must pay them adequately, and they must put them in charge of officers who care more for truth and justice than for drill and *nakshahs*,* and who really sympathize with and desire truly in their hearts, above all things, the welfare of the people." (*Loud cheers.*)

Some of Mr. Pringle Kennedy's remarks may also be usefully reproduced. He said †:—

"Gentlemen, the resolution which I rise to support to-day is one the importance of which yields to no other or to almost no other of the resolutions before you. (*Cheers.*) In spite of what some people seem to think, a native of India does not spend all his days in the law courts, is not always being tried before a judge, with or without a jury, nor is he continually before the High Court on the Criminal Revision side. But the police, like unto the poor, we have ever with us. There is a French proverb, '*La bouche va toujours*,' which, being translated with its appropriate application, means, '*A policeman is always hungry*.' (*Laughter.*) He is ready for anything—from a pice to a thousand rupees. His mouth is the most elastic of any in the country. A pie ‡ is not too small to escape his notice, and I believe he would not choke even if he swallowed a krore. §

Then holding, as he told us, that an ounce of fact was better than a ton of theory, he gave illustrations of police tactics from his personal experience, and thus concluded his speech:—

"Now I am a microscopic member of a microscopic minority. (*Laughter.*) My experience is limited. It may be that the entire police of the empire do not ill-treat accused persons (*Cries of 'They do; they do'*); that in Bombay and Madras they do not take bribes (*Cries from Madras and Bombay delegates, 'They do, they do'*); and that the stories of ill-treatment by them of persons in the Punjab desiring to attend this Congress are but the figments of an excited imagination (*Cries of 'No, no; they are true!'*); but to the character and conduct of the police in my own part of the country I can speak with confidence, and can boldly assert that it leaves almost everything to be desired. (*Cheers.*)

"We want a commission to inquire into all this. (*Cheers.*) I recognise that it is an extremely difficult problem. The men's pay, as the last speaker remarked, is ridiculously small, their power

---

* *Nakshahs* are printed tabular forms, the multiplicity of which is one of the minor evils of British administration. In India, the word "Nakshahs" is used as the equivalent of the English "Red-Tape."

† Detailed Report, pp. 49, 50.

‡ The ⅓rd of a farthing.

§ One million sterling.

immoderately great, and possibly any alteration in either direction may prove difficult in practice. But I cannot believe that it is beyond the resources of statesmanship, when thoroughly informed as to the facts, which our rulers might be if they appoint a proper Commission. I lay stress on this, for no purely official Commission will be of the least use ; we must have the Commission mixed (*'Hear, hear,' and cheers*), and largely composed of independent non-officials ; otherwise we may be pretty sure that we shall have the old official report, 'Great is Diana of the Ephesians.' (*Cheers.*) We want reform, not a panegyric on existing facts, and if we get the kind of Commission I have suggested, we may then, possibly, also get what the country requires." (*Cheers*)

Mr. Harchandrai Vishnudas, a Sindh lawyer, also spoke * very much to the point :—

"It is the part of a policeman to detect crime, but they ought to catch the criminal, and should not lay hold of the wrong person, as they seem to prefer doing. The cry comes up from all parts of India that the existing police administration in this country is very far from satisfactory. It is true that no institution in this world is capable of absolute perfection, but there are institutions and institutions, and this institution is of such a nature that we must, perforce, if we are to have any peace or comfort in life, try to free it, as much as possible, from the taint of evil and from defects of every kind. The police branch of the service admits of a very great deal of improvement, but the system at present is such that it will hardly lend itself to any of those reforms that we desire. One of its great defects is that the men who constitute the rank and file of the police department are drawn from the very dregs of the community, and are both illiterate and very badly paid. They have not any such sense of duty as can restrain them from those acts of extortion and oppression which they now commit without any scruple of conscience—without, I really believe, in many cases, realizing that they are doing wrong. It would be better if the Government were to raise their pay, and see that they have some education, and some such conscientious feelings as would revolt against gross injustice. It is quite necessary that the continual practice of torture should be put a stop to. There have come within my own observation cases of torture of so revolting and atrocious a nature that I do not like to harrow your feelings by describing them to you. At present men in the lowest grade of the service have no regular promotion to expect. They are kept on the same pay as long as they remain in the service. Not only ought a far higher class of men to be enlisted, not only ought their initial pay to be raised, so that their service may be worth having, which it is not now, unless they extort a good deal of money monthly from the people, but fair chances of promotion ought to be open to all of them, so that they may look forward confidently to both better pay and better positions, and obtain them in the course of time, with certainty, as the reward of real merit." (*'Hear, hear.'*)

Other speakers followed, but we will only quote from one more speech, that of Mr. Parthasaradhy Naidu, of the Madras Presidency :—

"The Police Department," he said,† "constituted as it is at present, consists of men who are in nine cases out of ten utterly uneducated and devoid of all moral sense. Under the false theory that physical strength is the sole necessary qualification, all the roughs and blackguards of our slums are enlisted into the police force ; and, as a matter of fact, they are so badly paid that no good strong able-bodied man, capable of doing a good day's work elsewhere, and whose character was above extortion and corruption, would ever enlist in the force. In my opinion we ought certainly to subordinate physical strength to brains and heart. The police have not always to do pioneer's work, or sepoy's duty. On the contrary, the bulk of their duties require intelligence, judgment, tact, and, above all, integrity. A well-organised police would be more engaged in the prevention than in the detection of crime. The present state of the Department is such that, on the occurrence of a crime, the police spare no pains to bring some man, whether innocent or guilty they seem to care little, into trouble, supplying all the necessary evidence, no matter whether the final result be the conviction of a guilty or an innocent man. They think that the greater the number of the victims they have 'run in' the more efficient will their Department and themselves appear in the eyes of the officials and the public. This, so far as the public is concerned, is a sad and serious mistake, and their villainy, in the long run, renders them quite detestable to every one, and utterly discredits the whole Department. I am, therefore, strongly of opinion that the Police Department must consist of well-paid and educated men, possessing discriminative powers. While we see education spreading everywhere, there is no reason why it should not be more prominently availed of in the Police Department. By so saying I do not mean, for one moment, that feeble, puny men—the victims of over-study—should be enlisted, but the robust amongst the educated should be drafted into this important Department, the

* Detailed Report, p. 50.
† Detailed Report, p. 52.

pay being so raised as to make it worth the while of such men to serve in it. And certainly such men will not only be able to cope with the *wear* and *tear* of the Department, but also will be able to understand that they have not a mere mechanical duty to perform without caution and care, as is now done, and that they are not employed, as our present police seem to fancy, solely to rob and harass the respectable and peaceful sections of the community. In order to induce educated, intelligent and God-fearing men to enlist, the Department must be thoroughly re-organized. Not only must the present emoluments be improved, but the present *uniform* also, and the status of the entire force materially raised. A very large number of matriculates and middle-school youths will then be most willing to join the ranks of the Constabulary, and similarly our B.A.'s, F.A.'s and others will unhesitatingly volunteer for grades like Inspectors and Sub-Inspectors. Unless the Police Department is thus satisfactorily reformed, or, in other words, without an honest and intelligent police force, our life and property will never be safe—no, not even under the benign administration of our beloved and Gracious Imperial Majesty the Queen-Empress." (*Loud cheers.*)

Almost every delegate desired to speak on this subject, but the influence of the leaders of the several circles sufficed to restrain the debate within reasonable limits, and in the end the following resolution was unanimously passed :—

"RESOLVED—*That as it is the general belief of the people of this country that the existing system of police administration in India is highly unsatisfactory in itself and oppressive to them, the Government be respectfully urged to appoint a Commission, consisting of official and non-official members, to investigate the entire question as speedily as possible.*"

Then followed a resolution re-affirming three kindred resolutions, passed at previous Congresses. The first, relative to the establishment of military colleges in India at which young natives of India, as defined by statute,* would be trained for a military career as officers of the Indian Army; the second, pressing the expediency of authorizing (under such rules and restrictions as might seem fitting) a system of volunteering for the people of India; and, the third, praying for a modification of the existing law relating to the possession and use of arms.

All these questions, it may, perhaps, be remembered, were discussed at great length at previous Congresses, and were very fully noticed in the introduction to the Report of the Congress of 1887. Here it may suffice to impress upon the reader the enormous importance of the question involved in these resolutions.

The Empire of the East, the brightest jewel in the diadem of our beloved Queen-Empress, was won, not by England's bayonets, but by India's swords, and by these and these alone can its lustre be maintained undimmed. None of us ignore the glorious achievements of our British troops, for *ours* we now hold them to be, nor the skill and heroism of British officers, but History's pages are no longer sealed to us, and we see that, but for the co-operation, in past times, of India's warriors (inferior though, man for man, these may be held, as compared with the English) Britain's small bands of heroes would have fought, and fallen, in vain. Even in the last great struggle, when a pampered Indian soldiery, false to their allegiance and faithless to their salt, all but wrecked the Empire which a century had nursed to glorious maturity, it was not so much the British soldiery, tardily dribbled into India, as the new Indian soldiery, sprung from the

* Natives of India, as defined by Statute, include pure Natives, Eurasians and domiciled Europeans and Americans.

bosom of the people to uphold their benefactor's cause, who, under British guidance, were instrumental in restoring peace and order. And in the spacious future if, as some forbode, a death struggle with one of the world's greatest Empires for the supremacy in Asia be really impending, it will be by the aid of "India's dusky legions," alone, that England's meteor flag will brave the battle,

"To wave eternal o'er the golden East."

But, unhappily, apparently blind to the true aspect of the case, the Indian Government, like the foolish woodman of the fable, are deliberately sawing through the branch on which they, and England's Empire in India, inevitably depend for support. By the Arms Act, by their refusal to educate our youth as soldiers and to permit volunteering, they are, as Mr. Feroz Shah Mehta phrased it, emasculating the nation. Well said he* :—

"Perhaps a good many of you remember the case of James II., who, when in his hour of peril, appealed to the Duke of Bedford (whose son had been judicially murdered by the king) for help, to whom the old nobleman replied: 'I had once a son whom I could have sent to your assistance. But I have not got him now.' In the same way, in some hour of need, India might have to say something similar to England." (*Cheers.*)

If the present short-sighted policy be persisted in, when next England, in her need, calls upon India, she will call in vain. The martial spirit of her people absolutely extinguished, India will no longer furnish recruits for Britain's armies. With every desire to assist, India's peoples will be powerless, and —to quote Mr. Bhimjee's memorable speech at the Madras Congress—unarmed and helpless, their martial spirit dead, they will have to stand aloof wailing like women, whilst their English friends are massacred by Russian hordes, and they themselves, their fortunes and their families, are left a prey to the ruthless barbarities of the invaders.

Is it at all strange that, under these circumstances, a deep interest is felt in these questions throughout the country? Is it not rather the persistent failure of the British Government to appreciate the vital character of the issues involved, at which we must marvel?

The debate was long, because considerable difference of opinion existed as to the last clause of the resolution, *viz.*, that referring to the Arms Act. In the first place, this was not, perhaps, happily worded; it was more general in its terms than was felt to be necessary, and did not sufficiently clearly emphasize the special reforms in executive procedure which the country really desires; and, in the second place, several of the speakers somewhat misunderstood what the practical effect of this clause would be, and treated this as more sweeping than it was at all likely to be.

The debate may be referred to (pp. 54-60 of Detailed Report), but nothing therein calls for further special notice.

The resolution was carried by a large majority.

The next question that came before the Congress was one which, for the

* Detailed Report, p. 58.

reasons explained when dealing with Police Reform, had never previously been taken up. The evils of the existing systems of Excise and Abkari were universally acknowledged, and the fact that under those systems one of the most sober populations in the world was becoming imbued with a taste for intoxicants, was equally universally deplored. But this was just one of those matters of domestic reform, in regard to which the more highly educated classes, with whom the Congress originated, could see no hopes of effecting anything until a substantial Indian element had been infused into the Councils, and hence it was to secure this latter fundamental reform, out of which all the others might be hoped to flow, that previous Congresses had chiefly directed their efforts. This year, however, the popular element being stronger and the feeling of all classes, (no doubt, to a certain extent, stimulated by Mr. Samuel Smith's crusade in England and Mr. Caine's auspicious visit to India,) very acute on the subject, a great number of the delegates came up pledged to bring it forward. Some sentences may be culled from the speech of Mr. Dinshaw Edulji Watcha, of Bombay. He said * :—

"I congratulate the Congress on this new departure in its programme. Hitherto the resolutions passed by it have had reference to the political welfare of our countrymen, but I take the resolution just read † out to you to be partly political and partly social. It is political so far as it prays the Government to inquire, with the aid of a Commission, which, it is to be hoped, will consist of officials as well as non-officials, into the real condition of the drink traffic, and social so far as it is a practical step in earnest towards the improvement of the masses who contribute largely to the excise revenue. It is not only a general belief, but, I may say, the universal conviction, that the habit of drinking is greatly on the increase ; consequently there is a strong feeling that its further growth should be checked betimes, and, so far as my own Presidency is concerned, I can unhesitatingly say that consumption has greatly increased. It has doubled itself during the last few years. I have also watched the course of the drink revenue in the other provinces, especially in Bengal, Madras and the United Provinces, and I regret to have to say that there, too, intemperance is increasing. The evil must, in a large measure, be attributed to the direct action of the State, or, in other words, to the excise policies of the Imperial and Local Governments.

* * * * * *

"However, the main fact is this : That on the one hand the Government deny that its excise policy is the principal and direct cause of the increased habit of drinking among the people, and on the other the people stoutly maintain that such is the case. I may give credit to the Government for its benevolent intentions to check intemperance and promote sobriety among its subjects. But, all the same, it is not at all able to control the excessive zeal of excise officials to net in a larger and larger drink revenue every year by pushing the drink traffic.

* * * * * *

"What is wanted is not an expansive, but a restrictive, system of Abkari—a system which shall promote sobriety and not one which stimulates intemperance, or puts those who never drank spirits in the way of drinking them. We want a policy which shall really be in practice one of maximum of revenue with minimum of consumption. Unfortunately, as matters now actually stand, there is a maximum of revenue and a maximum of consumption."

Pandit Sattyanand Agnihotri, a leading religious and moral teacher in the Punjab, a man of vast personal experience amongst the peoples of India, spoke very strongly on the subject. He said ‡ :—

"This country is suffering at present from the Abkari plague ; liquor is very cheap, and is everywhere to be had, for Government shops have sprung up everywhere, and the consequence is that habits

* Detailed Report, pp. 60, 61.

† RESOLVED—"That as it is the general belief of the people of this country that the system of Abkari and "Excise now prevailing in India have, despite the well-known benevolent intentions of the Government, permitted, "if they have not directly encouraged, a serious increase in the consumption of intoxicants, the Government be "respectfully urged to investigate the question, and to adopt such an improved system as shall tend to discourage "insobriety."

‡ Detailed Report, pp. 61, 62.

of drunkenness are increasing, and the people, especially the lower classes, are being terribly demoralized. It is in vain that I and others, whose mission it is to labour for the moral elevation of the people, preach and pray and wear our hearts and lives out in the struggle against vice, so long as the existing system—ever tempting to drunkenness and all the sin and wickedness that this brings in its train—is allowed to continue unaltered. It is ruining the country. Thirty years ago, as I know from older men, drunkenness was comparatively rare, and nearly confined to limited, criminal or very low-caste classes. Fifteen years ago—and here I speak from my own knowledge, when I first commenced my labours—the evil was not nearly so great, and liquor was still avoided by all respectable persons. Now, drinking has begun to assume terrible proportions. The Government have no wish to ruin the country; and I feel sure that, when the real state of the case is brought home to them, they will take the matter into their serious consideration, and do their part of the work in remedying this great evil. For our part, we have innumerable societies now all over the country, endeavouring to discourage the use of intoxicants, but it is everywhere the existing evil system of Excise and Abkari that constitutes our greatest difficulty."

* * * * * *

"These associations are doing good, but it is essential that the Government should strengthen them by amending its own ways, which are, I fear, the root of this great social and political evil. Last October, we held in Bengal, as you may remember, a Provincial Congress, and there too a strong resolution, recommending the reform of the existing Abkari system, was unanimously passed by the whole 100 representatives sent up by every district in Bengal. Go where you will, to Madras, Bombay, Guzerat—and I have visited most provinces during the last few years—there is the same complaint everywhere,—the Government system of dealing with the liquor question, by which it is evolving a yearly increasing revenue, is demoralizing the country; and it is not too much to say that, if a radical change be not speedily effected in that system, the national consequences will be most disastrous. Gentlemen, I am at one with you in all your proposals; but my daily personal experiences, for some years now, lead me to be more earnest and to feel more strongly in regard to this resolution, which I with all my heart commend to your acceptance, than in regard to almost any other, and we have the consolation too of knowing that this, at least, is a resolution in which our most unscrupulous and unprincipled adversaries cannot, it seems to me, possibly find anything to cavil at."

But the cautious wording of the original resolution (*vide ante* note, p. xxxvii) did not quite commend itself to the assembly, and Mr. R. D. Mehta of Calcutta, a moderate of the moderates, rose and proposed an amendment in the following words* :—

"Why should we beg the question? Why talk about its being the general belief of the people of this country, &c.? It is not a question of belief, but an established fact, that the consumption of liquor has increased, and is increasing. Then why this talk about benevolent intentions? The intention of the Government is said to be benevolent. Benevolent indeed—not only benevolent, but fruitful—revenue full (*laughter*); very benevolent as far as the Government treasury is concerned, but, as far as the health and morals of the people are concerned, ruinous. (*Cheers.*) The Government has directly encouraged the consumption of drink, and why should we now lay ourselves open to any misconstruction? We do not want any investigations, we have had too many investigations, and the result is merely delay in carrying out the indispensable reforms. I move as an amendment that our resolution on this subject be worded as follows :—

"'*That having regard to the fact that a serious increase in the consumption of intoxicants has taken place under the systems of Abkari and Excise now prevailing in India; the Government be respectfully urged to adopt some such improved system as shall tend to discourage insobriety.*'

"I hope, Gentlemen, that you will accept this amendment. It is shorter and more to the point. and it is not open to the misconstructions which the hesitating tone of the original would be certain to invite. The Government have for a long series of years been stimulating drunkenness; let them now encourage sobriety. This is what we mean, and let this be what we say." (*Cheers.*)

The amended resolution was accepted by the assembly, and, after a few more speeches, passed without a dissentient voice; but before quitting the subject,

* Detailed Report, p 62.

it may be well to reproduce some pregnant remarks by Mr. F. T. Atkins well known as the most active missionary, alike in India and England, of the Anglo-Indian anti-Ilbert Bill agitation, but now, like many others of his then colleagues, a good Congressman. He mentioned that he had been for five years at the head of the largest Teetotal Association in the country—the Independent Order of Good Templars—and that, but for the majority of the members being military men, and thus debarred from participation in political matters, he should have appeared not only as a delegate of the people, but as a representative of the Good Templars. He maintained that the question was a great deal more a political than a social one, and went on to say* :—

"The reason the Good Templars feel so much interest in this liquor question is because the majority of the men in the British Army in India, whose healths are ruined by intemperance, or who are punished for offences committed while under the influence of drink, obtain the liquor from the cheap drinking places, established or maintained under the auspices of the Government Abkari Department, where country liquor is sold. You have already heard from a previous speaker what every English soldier in India costs this country. So you can understand when soldiers fall sick through drink, or their services are lost to the State by their being invalided to England, or in other ways, it means a serious loss of public money, and the amount so lost every year is an enormous sum, which, of course, comes out of the revenues of India, and which ought properly to be set against the revenue that the Government, by its present system of Abkari and Excise, is realizing. I therefore consider that I am quite justified in asserting that this resolution is of great political importance (*Cheers*); and that the question of an improved Abkari system has, even from this single point of view, a grave political significance. I need scarcely add that, amongst the community generally, an increase in drunkenness involves an increase in crime, an increase in the cost of repressive and adjudicative agencies, and an increase in the danger of the lower classes at some time getting out of hand; and so, from whatever side we look at it, whether where the European soldier or the Indian peasant is concerned, it is certainly quite as much, if not more, of a political than a social question." (*Loud cheers.*)

Next came a resolution setting forth the necessity of raising the income-tax taxable minimum. The question is one that has a deep interest for the lower middle classes, multitudes of whom, though in reality only possessing incomes less than the legal minimum, are grievously harassed in consequence of the defective administration of the Act. To very few, if any, of the delegates did it signify personally, whether the minimum remains as now fixed at an income of £34, or is raised, as suggested by the Congress, to £68, because their incomes exceeding largely even the latter sum, their own pockets would be in no way relieved by the change. But even in 1887, the lower middle classes took part in many places in the elections, and during 1888 they did so almost everywhere, and hence the proposed reform, suggested at the Madras Congress, was even more strongly insisted on at that of Allahabad.

Pandit Madan Mohan Malaviya was in charge of the resolution. He commenced by saying † :—

"The Congress will not, I hope, be misunderstood in accepting this resolution. We do not object to the income-tax itself; all that we desire is that the taxable minimum should not be so oppressively low as it is. When Lord Dufferin taunted us in his postprandial oration at St. Andrew's with not representing the country, because we did not ask his Lordship to decuple the income-tax, he quite forgot that the first Congress that met at Bombay distinctly stated that, if the then increasing expenditure could not

---

* Detailed Report, pp. 62, 63.
† Detailed Report, p. 63.

be met by reductions, the necessary additional revenue should be obtained by extending the license-tax to those classes of the community who were till then exempt from its operation. In other words, it was the Congress that first advocated the re-imposition of the income-tax. (*Cheers.*) His Lordship himself complimented the Congress as "that body of intelligent and patriotic men" when he cited their authority in support of his income-tax scheme; but though we approved and desired the imposition of the income-tax on the rich, or those who could afford to pay it, we did not want it to become an engine for harassing the poor; and if only Lord Dufferin knew half as much as we do of the injustice and oppression practised on the poorer classes of the people in connection with this tax, and, Gentlemen, if he knew how wide and deep is the discontent that is consequently spreading in the country, I am sure that, instead of quizzing us, as he did for not proposing an increase in the tax, he would have unhesitatingly raised, as we have advised, the taxable minimum." (*Cheers*),

Then he went on to explain that, though £34 was the legal taxable minimum, in practice, men, with incomes of only some £12 a year, were really made to pay:—

"We do not," he continued, "for a moment insinuate that it is the desire of Government that the poor should be thus oppressed, or that the taxable minimum should in practice be reduced so much below the amount fixed by law. The fault apparently rests on the shoulders of those officers who are entrusted with the duty of assessing and collecting the tax. But, Gentlemen, the very perfunctory manner in which revising officers hear and dismiss appeals, lends colour to the popular belief that the burdensome oppression and injustice that they groan under is practised with the tacit approval of Government. I shall only quote here one instance to show how unbecomingly the tax is administered, and how some Government officials help by their thoughtless conduct to bring our Government into disrepute. Every one knows how poor a man a grain-parcher is. He earns his daily bread by exposing himself to a blazing fire even throughout the hottest months of summer. One would imagine that the tax-collector would pass by such uninviting victims. But that unhappily is not the case. I am sorry to say, and I have it on the best authority, that in some cases the tax has been imposed on even such miserable men as grain-parchers; and what is more painful to have to record is, that the revising officers, instead of exempting such men from payment, have on appeal confirmed the assessment made by their subordinates. In the particular instance that I have just now in my mind, the revising officer ordered the grain-parcher to produce his books and so prove that his income was not what the assessing officer had imagined it to be. Fancy a grain-parcher keeping books! You might as well expect a beggar selling lucifers in the streets of London to keep books! (*Loud cheers.*) But this official would insist upon the books being produced, and that being impossible, as the books had naturally no existence, he compelled the poor man to pay the amount assessed! Tell me, Gentlemen, what can bring Government into greater disrepute than such incidents?"

Mr. T. P. Crowley, a manufacturer and merchant of Allahabad, seconded the resolution, and then in a most humourous speech, which may be read,* prophesied the triumph of the Congress.

*** This is what he said:—**

"Gentlemen, our opponents tell us that the National Congress will never, never succeed. Let me recall to you that when Wilberforce first brought in his Bill for the abolition of the slave trade, all those who reaped the fruits of this accursed traffic swore by all their false gods and said: 'By Heavens, *never*.' But time passed on and right triumphed, and that infamous practice was abolished for ever, and it was *ever* and not *never*, and so will be the success of the Indian National Congress; it will be for *ever* and not *never*. (*Laughter and cheers.*) Then there was the Reform Bill. Have we not read how the old autocrats shook their heads. How they said, Oh, it was outrageous altogether? (*Laughter.*) How they swore that, even if they had to die on the floor of the House, the Bill should never, never pass. But again time ran on and the Bill was passed and passed for *ever*, and so will the triumph of the Congress be for *ever* and not *never*. (*Laughter and cheers.*) Now we come to the repeal of the Corn Laws. It was going to destroy the whole Church and State; it was going to wipe England off from the roll of the nations and usher in a worse than French Revolution. *Never*, so long as one drop of blood remained in their veins, would the landed aristocracy permit it. No, never! (*Loud laughter.*) But again a righteous cause, backed by patience and perseverance, triumphed, and the triumph was for *ever*, and so will be the success of the National Congress for *ever* and not *never*. (*Uproarious laughter and cheers.*) Now we come to the Bill passed by Mr. Gladstone for the Disestablishment of the Church of Ireland. The whole army of Tories and Bigots, all poor Ireland's enemies—and alas! she has too many—declared that though the heavens fell, this awful thing should never be. But the Bill passed and passed for *ever*, and again the right triumphed and was for *ever* and not *never*, and so will the Congress victories be for *ever* and not *never!* (*Renewed laughter and cheers.*) If Lord Salisbury only knew the people of India as I have done for forty years, he would know that he is not worthy to loosen the laces of the shoes of many he seeks to insult by taunting them with their colour. (*Laughter and cheers.*) But do not let us give in to him or those like him, but—let opponents misrepresent and rave as they please—let the Congress be *ever* and *ever* and *ever!*" (*Loud cheers.*)

Mr. K. V. Veshwanadha Iyer, of Madras, followed. He began by saying that he quite agreed with Mr. Crowley that the Congress must be for ever and for ever, but that that was a rather large question, and that the one immediately before them was whether or no the taxable minimum should be raised. He went on to say* :—

"I can tell you without any hesitation that the working of the Act, if the taxable minimum limit be retained at 500 rupees, will continue to be, as now, highly oppressive. (*Cheers.*) Fifty years ago, no doubt, an income of Rs. 500 a year might have been a taxable item. Money went much further, wants were fewer, lives simpler ; but all this is changed now, and what then was competence is now the barest sustenance. It can surely not be desired that, after Government has introduced so many changes by which the conditions of life may be ameliorated and existence made so much fuller, we should now go back to primitive modes of life and be contented with what sufficed us in past times. But that is what is involved in keeping the limit as low as £34, or else it must be admitted that it designedly trenches upon the necessaries of existence which the income-tax is professed *not* to do ! What served us years ago cannot be supposed to serve us now. (*Cheers.*) What were undreamt-of superfluities then are necessaries to-day ; not only do we actually need more for ourselves, but we have other and new demands to meet. For instance, we have to educate our children in a manner unheard of in past times, and the expenses of education are yearly increasing, and Government is throwing more and more of the burthen of this, yearly, on the shoulders of us poorer middle-class men. It is the policy of the Government that we should bear the larger part of these burdens, and that a constantly diminishing share of these expenses should be borne by the State. In all ways, therefore, the men with incomes of Rs. 500, and even considerably more, are becoming practically poorer and poorer and more wholly unfit to be yearly tortured on the income-tax rack. On this ground, amongst others—and there are many others with which I need not trouble you, for they were very fully set forth at the Congress at Madras last year—I support the resolution before you most emphatically."

Other speakers followed. Mr. Boikantha Nath Sen, the eminent pleader of Murshidabad, in an admirable and closely-argued speech, which should be read,† demonstrated the utter futility of the grounds on which, in its late resolution on the subject, the Government assumed that the administration of the income-tax had been satisfactory, while Professor Krishna Row Govind Deshpandye, of the Nagpore College, pointed out that in the Central Provinces, owing to the Pandhri tax, the avowed taxable minimum was only £17. He said‡ :—

"This is an old native tax, and the peculiar blessedness of our position is, that, while the old native taxes are retained, the modern European taxes are superadded to us. Gentlemen, it is, I fear, no use, but I desire by these words to protest respectfully against this Pandhri tax, this special income-tax with a taxable minimum of £17 a year, and to express a hope that when the Government raises the income-tax minimum, as we are praying them by the resolution before us to do, they will be good enough to abolish the Pandhri tax altogether, since, unless they do this, we, poor Central Provincials, alone of all the peoples of this great Empire, will be none the better. However, I support the resolution, and even should we ourselves gain nothing, we are all brothers, and your gain will be our consolation." (*Loud cheers. Cries of* '*Vote, vote.*')

But the night was drawing on apace, the following brief resolution—

"Resolved—*That as the administration of the income-tax, especially as regards incomes below Rs. 1,000, has proved extremely unsatisfactory, it is essential, in the opinion of the Congress, that the taxable minimum be raised to Rs. 1,000*"—

was put and carried unanimously, and the Congress adjourned to the next day at 11 A.M.

---

* Detailed Report, p. 65.
† Detailed Report, pp. 66, 67.
‡ Detailed Report, p. 67.

The first business transacted by the Congress next morning, when it re-assembled, for the last time, was its acceptance of an "Indian National Congress Hall," built and presented, as an office for a Divisional Congress Committee, in the Southern Mahratta country, by one of the delegates, to whom a vote of thanks for his handsome gift was unanimously accorded.

Next the President referred to the mountain of congratulatory telegrams and letters that had accumulated on the table. He said * :—

"We have been receiving simply innumerable telegrams and letters from sympathisers with the Congress,—such as Mr. Budrudin Tyabjee, the Hon'ble Rajah Peary Mohun Mookerjee, Moulvi Haji Mir Jaffir Ali Saheb, the Hon'ble Forbes Adam of Bombay, Dr. Trailokya Nath Mitter, His Highness the Maharajah of Durbungah, the Rajah of Deveracota, Syed Abdul Bari of Dacca, Soobanjee Nanoobhoy and five thousand Mahomedans of Yeola, the Reverend J. P. Mekee, Rajah Rajendra Narain Deb Bahadur, President, Indian Association, the second Rajah of Calicut, &c.,—mostly expressing not only sympathy but regret that unforeseen circumstances prevented their personally taking part in this assembly. Some of these I should have liked to read to you, but the time at our disposal is so very limited that I have decided not to read any. For this same reason—the very little further time now at our disposal—I have to state that I have been receiving. in greater abundance than I at all like, notices of resolutions and amendments to resolutions, and I would ask all those who may be now contemplating sending in any more resolutions, or any more amendments, to have mercy upon me and upon their brother delegates, for I am really afraid that we shall not be able to dispose even of all those that have already been sent in." (*Cheers.*)

Then Mr. John Adam of Madras rose to propose a most important resolution in regard to education. The recent change in the official attitude towards education has been viewed throughout the country with grave disapprobation. Mr. G. Subramania Iyer very tersely explained the dissatisfaction to which the recent change of policy in this matter has given rise. He said † :—

"There is no doubt growing up an idea that the new policy of education is the official reply to the demands of our Congress. (*Cheers.*) That Government finds itself face to face with demands, based upon the principles which it has itself preached, and which, while it is unwilling to concede them, it cannot logically refuse. It thinks, some people fancy, that the people of India are becoming too well-educated to consent to remain any longer in that *statu pupilari* which the Lieutenant-Governor of these Provinces so commends, and it has determined now to do what it can to arrest this growing enlightenment which can only be appeased by reform. Gentlemen, I repudiate any such idea ; it is, I am sure, a slander on our good and wise rulers, and it is moreover an impossibility. Great Britain will never go back from the noble doctrines enunciated in Parliament in 1833, in Lord Stanley's despatch of 1854, in hundreds of State documents, in thousands of public utterances of her noblest and greatest statesmen. If the Government be now acting, as it is, in a way to give colour to such a suspicion in the minds of those incapable of appreciating the greatness and magnanimity of the spirit in which England has ever dealt with India, it is only because the Government, in popular phraseology, is hard up—(*laughter*)—so hard up that it is clutching at every visible straw of retrenchment without stopping to consider anything but the momentary relief ; and I am quite sure that we have only to put the question temperately in its bare light before Government, and to make clear to them what an irreparable and incalculable injury they will do the country, if they really continue to work on this new and indefensible line, for them to retrace their steps and resume their older and wiser policy." (*Cheers.*)

The best and wisest men, no doubt, accept Mr. Subramania Iyer's explanation, but it is to be feared that the suspicions, he so warmly repudiated, find acceptance with a very large proportion of the public, and it seems impossible to deny that they have good *apparent* grounds for the views that they hold.

---

* Detailed Report, p. 68.

† Detailed Report, p. 72.

Very great interest was, therefore, taken in the resolution proposed by Mr. Adam, which ran as follows:—

" *That this Congress being of opinion, that it is the first duty of the British Government in India to foster " and encourage education, general as well as technical, in all its branches, and that the declaration made in the " recent resolution of the Government of India on the subject of education is calculated to encourage the " tendency to reduce Imperial expenditure on education, and to withdraw from the control of it, do respectfully " urge upon Government the extreme importance of increasing, or at any rate of not decreasing, the present " expenditure on education, and of the Government continuing to control the Educational Institutions of all kinds " now existing.*"

Mr. Adam's whole speech may be read, but the following passages are specially deserving of attention, his position as chief of the largest and most flourishing independent educational institution in India, and as founder in this country of what may be designated a system of technical commercial education, entitling his opinions to great weight :—

"Since last Congress," he said,* "a great change has taken place, and Government has not only indicated but adopted a retrograde policy. I have no time at command to prove to you from the note of Government itself that its tendency is what I have indicated. You must take it from me that in the opinion of those who have studied it, the policy marked out is distinctly retrograde. What it will be more useful to do is to prove to you by a concrete instance that the note is not a mere *brutum fulmen*, but that the policy shadowed out is to be enforced through the iniquitous engine of the system of Provincial contracts. We have for long been clamouring in Madras for an increased allotment from Imperial revenues, and this I will say that no Government could be more anxious to foster education and devote to it all the money they can, than our Government, from the Governor downwards. Well, Sir, they told the Director of Public Instruction that he might budget for an extra lakh this year. He did so. He sent in his budget. It came back with a G. O., stating that Government regretted it could not fulfil its promise, and the extra lakh must be cut off. What had happened in the interval between the Government's promise and its failure of performance ? The Hon'ble Mr. Westland† had paid a visit to Madras. You can draw your own conclusion. This is but one example of the way in which the benevolent intentions of local Governments are frustrated by the imperious demands of the Imperial Exchequer. What then are these local Governments compelled to do? As regards higher education, they are compelled to shut up their High Schools and Colleges ; in Madras they have been almost all closed. They commenced with the High Schools. The second grade Colleges have followed suit, and there is no security that the first grade Colleges will not next come. As regards primary education, they are obliged to throw its cost more and more on the local rates. Now, however good it may be, in principle, to look forward to a time when primary education can be supported solely from local funds, that is an ideal of which we can, here, look for the realization only in a distant future.

* * * * * *

"Well, Gentlemen, finally, why should you consider it the duty of Government to foster education ? We are continually told that we Congress-wallahs are only educated men, and represent only an educated minority. Reproach it is intended to be, though I consider it the highest honour ; but, such as it is, remove all grounds for the accusation by striving to turn that minority into a majority. But you have a higher reason for desiring the spread of education. Look back and ask what but education has given you all that amount—and it is no small amount—of liberty which you now possess. Education has brought you here, education has taught you the value of representation, and education has given you men fit to act as your representatives. And why then should Government recognise it as their duty to foster education ? Why, because education, if it has taught you to value liberty, has also taught you the wide gulf that exists between liberty and license ; if it has taught you to know your rights and knowing dare maintain, it has taught you how to use and not abuse them ; if it has taught you to pray for privileges, it has taught you their value, and inspired you with gratitude and loyalty to the giver. It is owing to education that the old India is being rung out and the new India is being rung in, not as in France, in America, aye in England herself, by the tocsin clang heralding revolution and rebellion, but by the silver chimes proclaiming liberty and law. Education is the fairy prince of the beautiful allegory written, as with prophetic prescience of to-day, by the greatest and sagest poet of our time. Education is the fairy prince who with his magic touch

* Detailed Report, p. 69.
† Then officiating Member of the Supreme Council, on a roving retrenchment mission.

has awakened the sleeping liberty of India, and the sleeper awakening, has formed with her deliverer that union which we have to strengthen, more and more, unto the perfect day. How does the poet express it?

And on her lover's arm she leant
And round her waist she felt it fold,
And far across the hills they went,
In that new world which is the old:
And o'er them many a shining star
And many a merry wind was born,
And streamed through many a golden bar.
The twilight brightened into morn."

The Hon'ble Kashinath Trimbak Telang followed in a masterly speech,* which we need scarcely apologize for reproducing, almost in its entirety:—

"Mr. President," he said, "even in the most enlightened countries of Europe—in Germany, for instance, where education has been organized and developed probably more than in any other part of the world,—even in Germany, I say, the Government accepts the duty of fostering and encouraging education, both technical and general, in all its branches. (*Cheers.*) It is only in this country that the doctrine has recently been gaining ground that this duty does not devolve upon the Government. The doctrine is one which, as far as I am concerned, I entirely repudiate. (*Cheers.*) I think it is not only an erroneous doctrine, but it is a fatal doctrine, to be admitted either by the Government or the people. (*Cheers*). I say it is the duty of all Governments, and more of the British Government in India than of any other in the world, to promote education, because here you have a great nation to whom the education most essential to its progress is entirely alien in many respects. It is a kind of education that we in India have never had before; and as it is admitted on all hands that this particular kind of education, and not our own old indigenous type of education, is essential for our proper national development, it is essential for the British Government, whom Providence has made responsible for this, to do all it can to foster it in all its branches. (*Cheers.*) I would also say this, that the doctrine which we enunciate in this resolution of ours is a doctrine which has been traditionally accepted by the British Government in the past. It is only now, under stress of circumstances, which it is not necessary to dwell upon, that a new-fangled doctrine is beginning to be enunciated. I say again that I entirely repudiate this doctrine as an erroneous and disastrous one. ('*Hear, hear.*') In the resolution recently issued by Government, they declare that, as soon as they find local bodies to take over the management of schools, they will themselves withdraw from them. I am not against the Government withdrawing from the direct management of educational institutions. But the limits within which they can, at present, safely or properly carry out the policy of withdrawal are very narrow indeed; and in order that those limits should become wider than they are at present, in order that the field of private management be more extended than it is now, it is necessary that the Government management in some institutions should continue for some considerable time to come (*cheers*); because, I say, except on the footing of model institutions managed by Government and surrounded by institutions under private management, India is not likely to make that progress which we all so much desire, and which the Government ought to desire just as earnestly and strongly as we do. There is one other point to which I would refer before concluding my remarks, and that is with regard to the amount of expenditure which the Imperial Government says it will incur for purposes connected with education. Well, all I can say upon that point is that a Government which finds money for the very varied activities † (*laughter*) in which it is engaged in this country, ought not to say that it has not enough to pay for education, considering especially what a small proportion of revenue is now devoted to education. It is not more than one per cent. of the Imperial revenue. (*Cries of 'Shame!'*) When we remember this insignificant proportion, I cannot but express my amazement that there should be any responsible statesman saying that this is an allowance which we ought not to expect to get hereafter. (*Cheers.*) No reasonable person who understands the position of affairs will ever object to the Government allowance increasing from year to year, by leaps and bounds if necessary, considering what the educational institutions in this country have to deal with. If we only look to the example which England herself has set us in this matter, if we look to the tremendous increase in the grants for education since Forster's Act was passed, I think the Government of India will see that their novel doctrine cannot be sustained for a moment (*cheers*), and is hardly likely to meet the approval of that great British nation to which, as a last resort, we may be compelled to appeal against this threatened systematic scheme for arresting the spread of education and with it the real progress, in the highest sense of the word, of our country and our countrymen." (*Loud cheers.*)

The Editor of the *Hindu*, one of the most moderate and best managed of

* Detailed Report, p. 70.

† Referring to our perpetual wars and expeditions, frontier railways and (so-called) defences, trips to and from the Hills and the like.

all our Indian journals, Mr. G. Subramania Iyer, part of whose speech has been already quoted, then followed, and we shall reproduce the rest of his wise and thoughtful utterances * :—

" Although for special reasons this vast assembly is primarily interested in political reform, still the gentlemen here present are extremely anxious to promote, by all possible efforts, social and moral reform. We have greatly at heart the improvement of the character of our people, the eradication of their old prejudices and crude notions, the modification of our domestic and social institutions, and we want to see many reforms effected in the interest of the moral and material well-being of the people. (*Cheers.*) But how can we expect all this to be done unless the education of our people is continually improved and expanded? (*Cheers.*) It may be said that Government does not intend to discourage the progress of education in this country. It only wishes, for financial reasons, to retire from directly controlling it, and contemplates depending upon private and local efforts to supply its place. But, Gentlemen, though the principle involved may be correct, its application to India at present would be, taking the country as a whole, altogether premature. (*Cheers.*) The condition of this country is not that of European countries, where public spirit has been greatly developed, where there are a large number of wealthy men ready to expend their wealth on altruistic objects where to aid education is a popular and accepted form of public beneficence, and where, lastly, there already exist such a multitude of highly-educated men that high education practically propagates itself in every direction without its being necessary for the State to foster the process. In this country, more especially in Southern India, there is as yet but little real public spirit ; there are comparatively few wealthy men, and those we have, are, too many of them, chiefly intent on keeping their wealth for their own private purposes ; the endowing of schools and colleges is not a popular form of beneficence, and men of high education, though in the aggregate constituting a very large number, form, as compared with our immense population, but a very small percentage. Under such circumstances, private efforts cannot be expected to do one tithe of what is required. There is, no doubt, another agency which, to a certain extent, has taken the place of Government, and during the past few years has done something to aid the progress of education—I mean the Municipal and Local Boards, which have now the entire charge of elementary and secondary education. (*Cheers.*) But the resources of these institutions are extremely limited, and they have so many objects to which they are bound by law to devote their funds that these too are wholly unable to do more than a fraction of the work that is necessary, if England is to redeem her pledges and really do her duty by our people. (*Cheers.*) For just consider these institutions, young and feeble themselves, are responsible for the sanitation, conservancy, communications and hospitals of considerable, often very large, areas, as well as for the education of the inhabitants of these ; and the people are poor, and their revenues small, and of these they can devote at best only a fraction to education : and then in regard to higher education they are helpless, and cannot obviate the evil effects of the policy now newly inaugurated. I shall give an instance. In the district of Madura there has been for many years a Government Second Grade College ; but recently Government resolved to abolish that institution. The people of the place were alarmed, and applied to the local Municipality and District Board to take up the management of the College. They had a meeting, and the result was that the matter was referred to Government. But what did Government do? They said that the Municipal and local funds should be devoted to elementary and secondary education, and that higher education did not come within the scope of their operations. The consequence is the people of the district of Madura have either to go to Madras for their collegiate education, or to have recourse to another college where instruction is given, not commending itself to the religious opinions of the population. Well, that is a real hardship, which is owing to the new policy of parsimony in regard to a matter which should have, more than any other, precedence over mere pecuniary considerations. (*Cheers.*) There is also another point of view in which this subject can be looked at. Our country is in a peculiar position. At the bidding of an allied but widely differently-situated nation, it has to abandon in many matters its old ways, learning, literature, and ideas, and enter upon a new phase of existence. It has to suit itself to the requirements of the latest scientific and artistic developments of European countries, and to remodel all its internal arrangements according to the standards of European civilization ; and I do not see how these stupendous changes are to be effected in a manner altogether wholesome to the people, unless full provision is made for a sound and widespread education permeating every class of society." (*Cheers.*)

Other speakers followed ; Pandit Radha Charan Goswami, a well-known religious teacher, quaintly remarked, speaking in pure Hindee :—

" Mr. President and Gentlemen,—It is a joyful day in which this great Congress, the Fourth Indian National Congress, meets here in this holy city of Prayag.† By your presence here, it has been trans-

* Detailed Report, pp. 71, 72.
† The ancient and sacred name of Allahabad.

formed from a *Tribeni into a *Sahasrabeni*,† the confluence of a thousand streams of learning and patriotism. Safe in this holy region, this blessed Congress has, day by day, conducted its loyal and virtuous work, replete with future prosperity to India and to England."**

But there were absolutely no two opinions on this great question, and the resolution (already given *supra*, p. xliii) was carried unanimously.

A very pleasing incident then diversified the day's proceedings. It had got about, somehow, amongst the delegates, that that day was Mr. Gladstone's birthday, and in response to numerous suggestive slips, sent up to him from all parts of the House, the President now proposed that the Congress should send him a congratulatory telegram. The proposal was received with enthusiasm. None who were then present will ever forget the rapturous and ringing cheers that followed every mention of Mr. Gladstone's venerated name. ‡

The fact is that every Congressman is a firm believer in those principles of Local Self-Government with which Mr. Gladstone's name is identified, and looks forward joyously, but patiently, to the time, distant though it may be, when his children, or, more probably, grand-children, shall be as independent, in the administration of all the internal affairs of the country, as are now the people of the Dominion of Canada. But, whereas, the Canadians thought fit to take up arms, and endeavour to make clear, by violence, the nature of their aspirations, the Congressman, appreciating the great growth of liberal sentiments in Great Britain since 1837, relies implicitly on India obtaining, from time to time, all those successive measures of enfranchisement which the ever-changing condition of her people may demand, by the purely peaceful methods of constitutional agitation.

Next came the following resolution :—

"That, having regard to the poverty of the people, the importance of encouraging indigenous manufactures and the difficulty of practically introducing any general system of technical education with the present imperfect information, Government be moved to delay no longer the appointment of a mixed Commission. to enquire into the present industrial condition of the country."

The rationale of this was well explained by Mr. Ananda Charloo, a leading pleader of Madras, who said § :—

"The problem that is now before us is the practical difficulty of introducing a general system of technical education in this country. This problem is not easy to solve. It will have to be solved with reference to the varying conditions of different parts of the country. What will suit one part may not be found to suit another part. One thing undoubtedly is possible, and that is to open schools ; but that is going very little beyond the first stage. You may teach ever so much, but unless you teach on precisely the practical lines required by the conditions of the time and place you will effect little. You want a good deal of detailed information before there can be an organized effort made in the interests of technical education. You all know, at any rate many of you must know, that in Madras the Jubilee memorial was the creation of an Imperial Institute ('*Hear, hear*'), and the funds collected on that occasion are being mainly applied to technical education. But when we have before us the question of a general system of technical education, it is quite clear that the collection of materials must necessarily precede any effort in that direction, and

---

* *Tribeni*, the confluence of three rivers, *viz.*, the Jumna, Ganges, and Sarasooti, the latter being, in these latter evil days, invisible to human eyes !

† *Sahasra*=a thousand.

‡ And not on this occasion only, but on previous days also. We may quote the following from Mr. Surendra Nath Banerjee's speech (Detailed Report, p. 18) :—

"When a statesman in the position of Mr. Gladstone, long the Prime Minister of England, still the trusted leader of a great party, the hope of Ireland—its future deliverer—holds views such as these, we may say, with confidence, that we are within measurable distance of victory. (*Tremendous cheering for Mr. Gladstone, the audience rising up.*) I hope and trust the mighty voice of a great nation will go forth from this hall and be wafted across mountains, seas and deserts, and reach the ears of Mr. Gladstone, as the expression of our personal regard for him and our sympathy for his labours." (*Cheers.*)

§ Detailed Report, p. 75.

therefore the object of the resolution before you is to ask Government to institute inquiries for the purpose of obtaining all the data and materials that we must have as a foundation on which to base any rational, as opposed to a haphazard, scheme."

A long debate followed;* not because there was any opposition to the resolution, but because some earnest expositors of the alleged wrongs of the emigrant coolies in Assam, desired to combine in it a demand for an enquiry into emigration matters, and because, again, some gentlemen, who distrust Government commissions, wished to add a rider calling upon Government to establish one or more technical schools at once in each Presidency. But Mr. Adam protested against any dovetailing, however neat, of the emigration question into a resolution relating to technical education, a wholly different subject, and Mr. Pheroz Shah Mehta remarked that the rider was inconsistent with the resolution. He said †:—

"The resolution asks for enquiry, because we, as a fact, do not know what class of technical schools to establish, or how to do it, and the rider proposes, with this, to couple a demand for the immediate establishment of technical schools in every province. (*'Hear, hear.'*) You must either abandon the demand for the enquiry, or you must give up the demand for the immediate establishment of the schools in every Presidency. The two demands are inconsistent, and cannot be coupled in one and the same resolution." (*Cheers.*)

So, ultimately, the amendments were withdrawn, and the original resolution adopted unanimously, and we shall only extract from the discussion some general and philosophical remarks that, in its course, fell from the Rev. Ram Chander Bose, and which seem to merit careful consideration. He said ‡:—

"One of the objections advanced against the National Congress is that it peremptorily refuses to discuss and deal with social problems. But the question which is being now discussed is, after all, a social question. Technical education involves a social reform or revolution of gigantic proportions. It will spread correct notions of the dignity of labour—(*'Hear, hear,' and cheers*)—raise the industries of the country from the contempt to which they have been ignorantly consigned, to a position of respectability and influence, and obliterate those of our social distinctions which are fictitious and unnatural. (*Cheers.*) It will cement class to class and create that bond of sympathy which will weld the jarring elements of our national life into a compact, homogeneous whole. (*Cheers.*) It will in this way accomplish a social revolution; nay, it will do something more. It will accomplish a moral revolution of equally gigantic and magnificent proportions. It will effect a salutary change in our national character. Our national character is by no means so dark as it is represented to be by professional detractors. Calm and philosophical observers, like Bishop Heber and Principal Kay, have noticed therein traits which, in their opinion, Christian nations would do well to imitate. (*Cheers.*) But it is a fact, which no one present will call in question, that what preponderates in the national character is quiescence or passivity, the active virtues being thrown in the background or remaining in a state of dormancy. These must be awakened and called into vigorous play before we can march forward alongside of the great nations of Europe and America. The virtues we are sadly deficient in are courage, enterprise, the will to do, and the heart to dare—(*cheers*),—and these, I maintain, will be fostered among us by technical education, and the varied industries that will grow up as the fruits of this. Political questions are inseparably linked to and bound up with social and moral questions. Why? Because life in the first place is a unity. (*'Hear, hear.'*) Our lines of distinction between political, social, and moral life are arbitrarily drawn, as life in its political aspects cannot move forward without causing life in its social and moral aspects to move forward also. Life in one department in motion and in others stationary is an impossibility! In a similar manner progress is an unity, and our distinctions between material and moral progress are fictitious. When true progress is realized in one department of life, the other departments cannot but be affected by it. Progress is, if you will allow the expression, contagious; and when it affects one portion of life, or one of its sides, it spreads over and exercises a restorative influence over the others also. Some of you are friends and champions of social reform, and you are apt to be impatient because social questions are not discussed in the Congress. Let me advise you to be patient. (*'Hear, hear.'*) Social questions in some form or other will come in for discussion, and social reform will emanate from our deliberations. Again, some of you are friends and

* Detailed Report, pp. 73-79.
† Detailed Report, p. 78.
‡ Detailed Report, pp. 78, 79

champions of moral reform, and you are impatient because moral questions are not discussed in Congress. Let me give you the same advice—be patient, and you will by and bye see moral questions discussed here, and a moral influence of the healthiest kind issuing from our association. We have every reason to look forward to the time when the glorious results of our deliberations will be the rectification, not of this solitary evil or that, but of all the varieties of evils under which the country is groaning." (*Cheers.*)

The next matter of importance was Mr. W. C. Bonnerjee's speech proposing the submission of the resolutions, passed by the Congress, to the Governments of India and England. This speech we shall quote in its entirety, it being essential to make clear why the Congress of. 1888 only pressed for a Parliamentary Committee, whilst a previous Congress had insisted on a Royal Commission to enquire into the affairs of India. Mr. Bonnerjee (President of the First Congress and one of the leaders of the Calcutta bar) said* :—

"Mr. President and Gentlemen,—We have hitherto been hewing some of the many stones which are still required to crown the splendid, the unique, the marvellous edifice (*cheers*) which the statesmanship of Great Britain has reared up in this country. (*Cheers.*) It is now necessary that these stones should be submitted by us to the chief superintendent of that edifice in this country, and to his official superior in London, in order that they may consider their merit and fitness. (*Cheers.*) Accordingly I have to present for your acceptance the following resolution :—

"'*That the foregoing Resolutions be submitted for the favourable consideration of His Excellency the Viceroy, and for transmission by him to Her Majesty's Government, with the humble request of this Congress that the reforms suggested in the said Resolutions, based, as most of these are, on Her Gracious Majesty's Proclamation of 1858, may now be effected, and that, should it be deemed necessary, first to institute any enquiry into any of. the matters forming the subjects of these Resolutions, such enquiry may be made as speedily as possible by a Parliamentary Committee.*'

"I may say that this resolution is as of course, and it would not have been necessary for me to detain you a single moment if it had not been for the fact that the concluding portion of it, the portion that is which asks for an enquiry by a Parliamentary Committee, might seem at first sight inconsistent with one of the resolutions which we passed at the Congress of 1885. You will remember that at that Congress we asked that the enquiry into the administration of India which had been promised by the then Secretary of State for India by means of a Parliamentary Committee should be made by a Royal Commission, consisting of representatives both of England and of this country, and taking evidence both in England and India. (*Cheers.*) But, as the late Lord Beaconsfield once said, many things have happened since then. (*Laughter and cheers.*) It has become unnecessary, for the purposes of the resolutions which we have passed here, to ask for a Royal Commission. On this occasion we are only asking that if any of the propositions which we are going to lay before the Government require any further inquiry—in our judgment no inquiry further than what has been already made *is* necessary—then such inquiry may be made by a Parliamentary Committee. A Parliamentary Committee, as you all know, must come to an end with the Parliament that appoints it, and it must conclude its labours before any very long time has expired. On the other hand, a Royal Commission may go on sitting for years and years, hanging up reforms which have been felt, and declared by you all, on behalf of the country, to be absolutely necessary. (*Cheers.*) Many of the resolutions which you have passed deal with matters which may be disposed of in this country by the Government of India, if only the Secretary of State so desires ; and the only thing you have asked for which requires the consideration of Parliament is the expansion of our Legislative Councils. That subject has been before the country now for many years, and it is not necessary that any further inquiry should be made.

"I hope that, should these proceedings come under the eye of Mr. Bradlaugh (*loud and prolonged cheers*), who has so kindly interested himself in matters connected with India, he will see that we are not in any way throwing overboard the notice of motion which he has given, and which he has promised to bring forward at the next sessions of Parliament. We are only asking him to modify his motion to a certain extent. I hope he will not think that, in asking for a Parliamentary Committee, and not for a Royal Commission, we are guilty of any inconsistency, or are in any way unappreciative of his great efforts on our behalf. (*Loud cheers.*) I know I speak the sense of this vast assembly when I say that we are unfeignedly grateful to him for his masterly and able advocacy of our cause (*cheers*) ; and we hope that he will be pleased to help us in the future in the direction of the resolution which I have submitted to you. (*Cheers.*)

* Detailed Report, pp. 80, 81

"The reforms however for which we have pressed in the preceding resolutions are not by any means the only reforms which are essential for the welfare of India. They are perhaps the simplest, and in regard to them the country is now most completely of one mind as to the exact steps that it is necessary for the Government to take. But there are other great and vital reforms which must sooner or later be dealt with if India is to be justly administered, and if even the ultimate interests of the British Empire as a whole are to be considered. Such, for instance, as the reduction of military expenditure, and its re-apportionment on a juster basis between England and India, and various other matters with which I need not trouble you now. These are extremely complicated questions, in regard to most of which we ourselves lack the detailed practical knowledge essential to the suggestion of definite action, and in regard to these we shall have later to press once more for that Royal Commission which we prayed for in 1885. But at the present moment what we first want is that those simple and clear reforms, which are now fully ready for practical embodiment, should be carried out."

The resolution was after all, as the President remarked, a purely formal one, and, after a few more brief speeches, was adopted unanimously, but nothing could be more admirable in its way than Moulvi Mansur Ali's brief speech, which may well be commended to all English readers as fairly illustrative of the feelings which animate the Congress party. He said * :—

"Gentlemen, I also warmly support this resolution and endorse every word spoken by the last speaker. What more can we do, as faithful and loyal subjects, than tell our rulers plainly what those grievances are that make the people dissatisfied and beg them to remove them, if they see fitting, by the measures which we propose to them, if not, by such other measures as their greater wisdom may suggest." (*Cheers.*)

From time to time the efforts of the party of purity in England, to relieve India from the disgrace of a Governmental subvention of prostitution, have attracted notice in this country. The subject has always been felt to be an unsavoury one, and little has been said or written about it, and hence any feeling on the subject is confined to the more highly educated classes. So when in the Subject Committee it was proposed to put on record some expression of sympathy with our English philanthropists, doubts were expressed by many delegates, simply because they knew that the great bulk of their constituents knew absolutely nothing about the matter. However, as the delegates themselves did know, and were agreed to a man on the subject, it was concluded to frame the following resolution :—

"*That this Congress, having watched with interest and sympathy the exertions that are being made in England, for the total abrogation of laws and rules relating to the regulation of prostitution by the State in India, do place on record their appreciation of the services thus rendered to this country, and their desire to co-operate by all means in their power in the attainment of this laudable object.*"

But then arose a difficulty; all were ready to vote for this resolution, none would consent to speak upon it. Indian gentlemen are, perhaps, more reticent on such subjects than Englishmen—who have had greater experience in public matters—and so only three Englishmen and one Indian could be got to bring the subject before the Congress, and the one Indian carefully spoke upon other subjects, confining his remarks on this one to a few words at the very close of his speech.

The whole discussion should be read, but it will suffice to reproduce here a single passage from the eloquent speech of Captain Hearsay, who seconded the resolution. He said † :—

"And, Gentlemen, though the C. D. Acts have been repealed, the rules under the Cantonment Acts,

* Detailed Report, p. 82.
† Detailed Report, p. 84.

under which these evil things are done, are still in full force. There are in India over 2,000 young women, so procured, for the hideous purpose alluded to. If the Government thinks it is a medical necessity for such women to be entertained, why do not they import into India for this purpose the countrywomen of these British soldiers? (*Cheers.*) Why should our poor Indian women be sacrificed on the altar they have erected to lust? Let them import Englishwomen, if they dare, for these vile purposes. Or, what would be much better, allow greater freedom in, and even promote, the marriage of these soldiers. Can any one imagine anything more shocking than this legalized system of prostitution? A body of unfortunate young Indian women kept in a state of moral slavery and annually recruited to supply the supposed carnal wants, not of their own countrymen, whom they can understand, and with whom they have a certain sympathy, for whom it is possible for them to cherish some sort of passion, however degraded, but of the British soldier, whose colour, customs and conduct are all alike repugnant to their natural instincts—a system, which all the better men amongst those soldiers protest against and declare to be a mere incitement to the boys, who now-a-days are sent out in shoals, to sin. Surely it is an astounding thing to find such a system legalized by the rules of a Christian nation. It is, to speak metaphorically, a fearful cancer, and one which requires to be not only firmly cut out, but cauterized, so as to prevent its breaking out in another form, under new laws and rules."

The resolution was carried unanimously. Then followed a resolution embodying a Congress rule of practice, previously agreed to all over India, but which it was deemed expedient to put formally on record. The resolution runs as follows:—

"*That no subject shall be passed for discussion by the Subject Committee or allowed to be discussed at any Congress by the President thereof, to the introduction of which the Hindu or Mahomedan delegates, as a body, object unanimously or nearly unanimously, and that, if, after the discussion of any subject, which has been admitted for discussion, it shall appear that all the Hindu or all the Mahomedan delegates, as a body are unanimously, or nearly unanimously, opposed to the Resolution which it is proposed to pass thereon, such Resolution shall be dropped; provided that this rule shall refer only to subjects in regard to which the Congress has not already definitely pronounced an opinion.*"

And its necessity and objects were thus explained by Mr. Ananda Charloo:—

"Many of you," he said,* "have copies of the Madras Standing Congress Committee's Annual Report. In that report you will find an account explaining how this rule was found to be desirable for our guidance there. I may tell you also that that rule was framed in accordance with the wishes of some of our best Mahomedan friends. (*Cheers.*) Mr. Tyabjee (*cheers*), who was our President last year, in course of conversation told us that a resolution of that kind was considered desirable by many of his co-religionists; and other gentlemen, whose names cannot be mentioned without high praise, Mir Hoomayun Jah Bahadoor of the Mysore Regal house and Hajee Mahomed Abdulla Badshah Thakore Sahib, our Mahomedan Madras Merchant Prince (*cheers*), were a party to this proposition being adopted by the Madras Standing Committee. Then, as you are probably aware, this resolution was sent round to all the other Standing Congress Committees, and after full consideration approved by them. Outsiders may be surprised at this unanimity, but the reason is to be found in the fact that it is in strict accordance with one of the fundamental principles of the Congress, which is that it shall only deal with those subjects on which a substantial agreement has been come to by the great bulk of the intelligent men in the country. Now, of course, if either the Mahomedans or the Hindus as a body object, the subject is clearly not one in regard to which a substantial agreement has yet been come to. Now the resolution consists, as you will see, of two provisions and a rider. The first provision provides for no subject being even considered by the Subject Committee if either Mahomedans or Hindus as a body object to the question being discussed. Thus, if any foolish person were to propose that the question of cow-killing should be considered by the Congress (and there was one such person at Madras), he would be at once silenced under this rule. Then again it may happen that, though no one objects to the discussion of the subject yet, when after that discussion a resolution comes to be framed in regard to it, the conclusion thus arrived at may be distasteful either to the Hindus or the Mahomedans, in which case such resolution would be dropped. You see we want to consult and work together like brothers. (*Loud cheers.*) If we are all agreed on any matter, then we will submit the

* Detailed Report, pp. 85, 86.

universal view to Government ; but if we cannot come to a substantial agreement amongst ourselves, then we drop the subject until we can. But there is a rider. Our resolutions are before the world ; no new comer should join who is not fairly in sympathy with these. Any one who joins us, joins us, broadly, on the basis of these resolutions ; and, though we will allow him to rediscuss them if he likes, and again take the sense of the assembly in regard to them, we cannot allow him, or any one, to block them. With this explanation I commend this resolution, typical as it is of the true Congress spirit, to your hearty concurrence." (*Loud cheers.*)

The whole assembly was absolutely of one mind on this subject, and further quotations from the debate are needless ; but there was one speaker, and a little story he told * that merit special notice.

Swami Alaram, a humble vagrant, a religious and moral preacher, is of the true apostolic type. He takes no thought what he shall eat, or what he shall drink, or wherewithal he shall be clothed. His sole possessions are a single coat and cap (which he wears until their dilapidated condition suggests to some one to give him new ones), a gourd to hold water, a rosary and a staff. Ever on the move—preaching purity, honesty, truthfulness and devotion to the divine—he wanders from village to village, fed by willing hands wherever he halts for the night, and though he has not a farthing in the world (he will not take money), yet even in this dollar-worshipping age, he is loved and respected over a tract of country larger than all England. Quite uneducated, according to English ideas, he is yet very shrewd, and he set forth in broad Hindee the following parable, which our official opponents might advantageously read, mark, learn and inwardly digest :—

" A certain Guru, Lalbujhakar by name, had a large number of disciples (*chelas*). As they were going on their way they saw the footprints of an elephant, which none of them had ever seen before, and they asked their Guru what that was. The Guru laughed at *them*, for not knowing, and cried, because he *himself* did not know, but he said, at last, when pressed :—

Bujhey Lalbujhakar aur nai bujhey koey ;
Peir men chukki band ker hiranna kuda hoey.
(Lalbhujhakar he knows, but no other one knows
A deer has jumped here with millstones on his toes.)

The Anti-Congressists are Lalbujhakars ; one of these is of Benares, and favoured us with his presence here, and another is sitting at Aligurh, and these our would-be Gurus' (teachers') ideas in regard to politics and the present state of our country appear to be about as accurate as Guru Lalbujhakar's ideas in regard to the elephant's footprints ; and mind, that, all over India, those irresistible elephants—education and public spirit—are daily leaving their footprints, and the officials, who are now, we see, the *chelas* of these Gurus, had better get wiser men to tell them what these really mean." (*Loud cheers.*)

Then the question of the permanent settlement was brought forward. A resolution in regard to it had been framed in the Subject Committee, and at an earlier stage of the proceedings (see p. 79 of the Detailed Report) it had been brought forward and then dropped, partly because the gentleman, who by some misunderstanding had been placed in charge of it, began to argue against the resolution he proposed, and partly because the feeling of the assembly in regard to it had not been sufficiently tested. But the landed interests were largely represented in the Congress, and the majority of the constituencies of the South of India are agricultural and intensely interested in this question, and so there was a large body of delegates, who, either on their own account, or on behalf of those they represented, were determined that the subject should not be shelved. So the President having, in response to their reclamations, taken the sense of the

* Detailed Report, pp. 86, 87.

assembly and having ascertained that many were in favour and none opposed to re-opening the question, Mr. Howard, to start the debate, proposed the following resolution* :—

"That in the opinion of this Congress the time has now come for introducing into the major portions of the Madras and Bombay Presidencies, and of the North-Western Provinces and Oudh, and into parts of the Punjab and other Provinces, a permanent settlement of the land revenue demand."

Sheikh Raza Hussein, an Oudh Taluqdar, put the question well. He said † :—

"If the subject of a permanent settlement had not been at all brought before the Indian National Congress, I should have thought that the Congress had not fully performed its duty. The greater part of the population of India is composed of men who have special connection with the tillage of the soil. The main resource of India lies in its agriculture. The best relief for and antidote against the poverty of the people, and the now almost yearly-recurring famines, are to be found in the introduction of a permanent settlement throughout all those portions of the country which have been long settled. I quite admit that there are portions of the country where population is sparse and cultivation in its infancy, where a permanent settlement would be out of place ; but in districts where the population ranges from 500 to 900 per square mile of cultivation, the time has come for fixing the land revenue demand, unless, indeed, in some exceptional localities which railways have not yet approached, and the agricultural value of which we may expect to be materially changed when they do approach it. When I say a permanent settlement, I do not necessarily mean a permanent settlement precisely similar to that in Bengal. In the first place, we are wiser now than we then were. The experience of eighty years has shown us how we can improve on that settlement in many particulars. In the second place, landed tenures vary all over the country, and in each place the permanent settlement must vary accordingly. And again when I say a permanent settlement and speak of a fixity of the Government demand, I do not necessarily mean that that demand should be settled in rupees. On the contrary, I am disposed to believe that it would have to be fixed in terms of quantities of the three or four chief local staples of produce, in regard to which a cash revaluation might be made at intervals of, say, every three, five or seven years, based upon the average local prices of those staples during the preceding period. Thus, if the Government demand in any village were fixed at 50 maunds of wheat, 100 maunds of jowar, 100 maunds of bajra, 50 maunds of gram, and 50 maunds of urher, this would remain the demand for all time, but every three, five, or seven years, the actual number of rupees would be fixed by a calculation based on the average *local* price of these articles during the past three, five, or seven years. I can only say that, unless some such fixity is given to the Government demand in our province, cultivation will never keep up with the growth of population. Grant it, and hundreds of thousands of wells will be dug within the first five years, and millions of acres that now yield only small unirrigated crops would yield double and treble the amounts of far more valuable staples. By one way or another, people would manage to put double the amount of manure they now do into the ground. But no great improvement can take place so long as the people are for ever on the look-out for the recurring swoop of the settlement officer to sweep the fruits of their labours into the official net. Mr. Howard spoke of the 'unearned increment,' which is explained to me to mean, profits that a person has not made for himself, and he tells us that a great political economist tells us this should belong to Government. Well, if this is political economy, our system must be perfection, for at every revision Government appropriates the profits that it never earned, but which the cultivators of the soil have earned. *(Laughter.)*

"Gentlemen, if what I have heard as to the real meaning of the phrase used by Mr. Howard, *viz.*, that it refers to an increased value of lands and produce, owing to the making of railroads and opening out roads and the like is correct, then I say that in the greater part of our provinces no such increased value is any longer to be looked for The country is as fully populated and as much opened out as it can be, and any improvement in the yield of the land will be due to the landlord putting more capital into it, or the cultivator more labour, and neither will ever do this until they get a permanent settlement.

"Now, I am not pretending that I am prepared with any definite scheme. Our resolution does not put forward anything of the kind ; but I do think that the Government should be made aware of the very strong feeling on this subject that pervades the country, and take the matter, which, for some years past, it has, as it were, excluded from the sphere of practical politics, anew into consideration, and into consideration with the view to action, and therefore it is that I consider it imperative to pass the resolution which I have had the honour to second."

* Detailed Report, pp. 88, 89.
† Detailed Report, pp. 89, 90.

Other speakers followed supporting the resolution, Rajah Rampal Singh, remarking, * *inter alia* :—

"I am sure that if the entire population were polled, 70 per cent. would vote for permanence of settlement; and I am also sure that, when we get representative councils, one of the very first, I might say the first thing we should all fight for in all of these, would be the introduction of an equitable permanent settlement into all the thoroughly-cultivated and well-advanced portions of the country. We do not wish to take the Government at a disadvantage; we do not expect them to take immediate action on this resolution; but we desire by it to serve them, as it were, with a notice that we are all thinking of his question, and all fully resolved when other simpler matters, as Mr. Bonnerjee explained, are disposed of, to press for a reform in this matter also. Therefore I desired that this subject should come on for discussion, and therefore it is that I still advocate the passing of this resolution, although I perceive that many, while agreeing with us in principle, consider that any resolution on the subject would be premature."

This last remark exactly defined the attitude of the majority; and Mr. Telang, in a brief but masterly speech, well expressed the general views and wishes on the subject. He said † :—

"The question of a permanent settlement is one of the highest importance, both to the people and the Government. But I do not think that it is one which should be, as it were, rushed through this Congress. (*Cheers.*) On the contrary, I submit that both we—who have assembled in this hall—and those who, though elected as delegates, have not been able to attend here, and lastly our constituents who sent us here, should have an opportunity of maturely and gravely considering the question in all its numerous bearings. Now that the question has been re-opened by the re-admission of the withdrawn resolution, it is for us to consider how we should deal with it. It appears to me that there is a considerable, difference of opinion as to the mode in which we ought now to proceed. I do not want to discuss here the merits of the question of a permanent settlement. It is obvious from the show of hands that there is some difference amongst us even as to whether it should be touched at all, and therefore, I think, it is desirable that any resolution we may now pass on this most important subject should be such that we ourselves may all be satisfied with it, as well as those not present. ('*Hear, hear.*') It appears to me that, looking to the circumstances under which the question has now been raised, no resolution, whatever it might be, that we came to on the merits of the question, whether favourable or unfavourable to a permanent settlement, would be likely to carry much respect or weight. I fully admit the importance of the question, but precisely on that account I submit that no decision should be come to in regard to it, without full previous preparation and detailed discussion of it all over the country. Now many of us, most of us, have had no preparation; it was not one of the 13 subjects circulated over the country before we left our constituents. The question has had no definite practical discussion amongst us in most parts of the country. We have all vague general ideas, probably in most cases favourable to the notion, but very few, if any, of us have really recently studied the question or read up the voluminous literature that exists on a subject which for the last 40 years, at least, has off and on been under discussion alike in India and England. I doubt whether there is one single man of marked ability connected with India who has not written something about this question during the last 50 years. We ought at least to read a good deal of what has been written before expressing definite opinions. By all means let us discuss the question; it is one of first-rate importance, but let the whole country that we represent, and we ourselves, be first properly prepared for the discussion. I therefore suggest an amendment as follows:—

"*That the question of the introduction of a permanent settlement of the land revenue demand into the Madras and Bombay Presidencies and other Provinces be referred to the several Standing Congress Committees, with instructions to report upon the same, in so far as it affects their respective Circles, to the Congress of 1889.*"

This amendment was accepted by every one, and passed unanimously, Sheikh Raza Hussein, only remarking that ‡ :—

"We agriculturists probably know already quite as much, if not more, about the subject than we are ever likely to learn from any official literature, however extensive. For this will be mere theory, whereas we know the practice. At the same time, I agree that the matter is so important that it is well that

* Detailed Report, p. 90.
† Detailed Report, pp. 90, 91.
‡ Detailed Report, p. 91.

anything we say in regard to it should have the appearance of being the result of deep deliberation, and so I am quite willing to accept the amendment. At the same time, if we were to deliberate for 50 years, it would not, in the smallest degree, affect my opinion that in my province a permanent settlement is absolutely required, in the interest alike of landlords and cultivators." (*Cries of 'Vote, vote.'*)

Lastly came the question of the recent enhancement to the salt tax. The President * was somewhat averse, for reasons which he explained, to the passing of any formal resolution on the subject. But all the delegates from Bombay and Madras, Sindh, Berar and the Central Provinces, and not a few of those from other places, were pledged to bring the subject before the Congress, and the assembly unanimously voted for its discussion. Accordingly the following resolution—

"*That this Congress do put on record its disapproval of the recent enhancement of the salt tax as involving a perceptible increase to the burthens of the poorer classes, as also the partial absorption, in a time of peace and plenty, of the only financial reserve of the Empire*"—

was submitted to the assembly.

Mr. Narayan Vishnu Bam, of Poona, took charge of it, and his entire speech merits careful perusal. He said †:—

"Here, in Upper India, you have been used to dear salt, and your people eat much less of it and require less of it than ours in the south, and you can hardly realize the terrible hardship involved to our people in paying, now, a two-rupees-eight-annas duty on salt which costs one anna, and on which, not so very many years ago, we paid a duty of only ten annas. I have heard that in Bengal some gentlemen said they approved of the recent enhancement of the salt tax. (*Cries of 'No, no.'*) I can only say that all over the south of India it has created more discontent than even the income-tax ; and in some parts of the south in the Madras Presidency for instance, this has been aggravated by Government giving a monopoly of the sale to a few men, who have still further artificially raised the price. Gentlemen, the salt tax, which presses proportionally more and more heavily on a man the poorer he is, is altogether a bad tax ; but if kept at a low limit it is bearable. At its present rate, our poor people cry out dreadfully about it. I do not believe that the Government could be right in raising it as they have done, and I think that we shall be ill discharging our duty as representatives of the people if we do not distinctly put on record our disapproval of the measure. Is there any one here who approves it? Do we not all feel it to be a wrong thing to add to the already crushing poverty of the poorest classes? Let them tax articles of luxury—tax them as heavily as is possible without creating smuggling—but do not let them go on raising a tax on the necessaries of life and adding to the burthens of the poor, because it is easy, and they have no voice. Gentlemen, we are the voice of the country, of the poor as much as, nay more than of the rich, for they can speak for themselves, but let us, at any rate, protest on behalf of the poor. Personally there is not one of us here who cares for this increase ; it means to most of us a rupee more a year ; in the largest households, not more than five rupees. But to the very poorest it means eight annas more a year, and let me tell you, Gentlemen, that there are millions on millions to whom that eight annas extra means eight meals less in a year, and that to people who, even before this enhancement, never got more than one meal in the 24 hours. And, Gentlemen, what we all feel is that, had a terrible war with Russia been raging, had there been some great famine, strangling in its deadly grasp huge provinces, there might have been some excuse for this enhancement. But that to do this in normal times, when there were at most only petty wars—and Government always keeps a small stock of these on hand—(*laughter*), and no famine anywhere, was indefensible. We all feel this, and this is what the resolution says, and this being so, I hope you will support this resolution unanimously. I had much more to say, but the President's warning-gong has sounded, and I can only repeat—this is what you mean—this is what you think—then say it, and say it plainly." (*Cheers.*)

Very true and telling were Mr. Girija Shankar Kashiram Dwivedi's brief utterances:—

"We all desire," he said, ‡ "salt to be cheap, for the sake of the poor. We all disapprove the recent increase to the duty. Instead of raising the duty it should have been lowered. Lord Ripon lowered it,

* Detailed Report, p. 92.
† Detailed Report, p. 92.
‡ Detailed Report, p. 93.

and had he remained here he would have reduced it further. But Lord Dufferin, instead of reducing, has raised it because he wanted to annex Burmah, and waste crores up in Afghanistan. Therefore the whole country is displeased with him, and he is displeased with the country and runs down this Congress which Is the voice of the country. Yes, we disapprove this recent increase to the salt tax. We say it was wrong, and that there was no real justification for it, only a justification that Lord Dufferin himself had made by expenditure, which we all disapprove."

These few lines embody, perhaps, the true solution of the otherwise inexplicable attitude assumed by Lord Dufferin towards the Congress, on the eve of his departure from India.

The resolution condemning the recent enhancement of the salt tax was unanimously adopted ; two formal resolutions—one fixing the Bombay Presidency as the scene for the next Congress, the other re-appointing the General Secretary —were passed, and a vote of thanks to the President was enthusiastically carried. The President replied briefly, and after thanking the leading members of the Reception Committee on his own behalf, and that of the delegates at large, declared the Fourth Indian National Congress dissolved.

"There* was much cheering which continued for some time. Then three thundering cheers, repeated again and again, were given for the Queen-Empress, and the vast assembly began to disperse ; but the majority of the delegates went on to give cheers for a variety of people—Mr. Gladstone, Sir William Hunter, Mr. Bradlaugh, Lord Reay, Lord Connemara, &c., until some one proposing a cheer for Lord Dufferin, the assembly, or what was left of it, realising the *reductio ad absurdum*, broke into peals of laughter, and finally dissolved in a state of universal good humour."

Certainly, characteristic as were the self-control, the moderation and the good humour so conspicuously displayed by this late Congress, its most characteristic features were the intense love and loyalty which it displayed towards the Queen-Empress and the thoroughly genuine and hearty desire which it evinced for a permanent and satisfactory union between England and India.

Over the gateway of the Castle was a large medallion of the Queen, the spontaneous effort of a humble local genius. High over the Congress Hall from first to last fluttered and flaunted "the Flag that's braved a thousand years the battle and the breeze." Inside hung pictures of Her Majesty, no part of the original design, but brought thither, at different times, by their owners, unexpected, unsolicited tributes of their loyalty. Great as was the enthusiasm in regard to Mr. Gladstone, it was as nothing to that exhibited in regard to the Queen, every mention of whose name, every allusion even to whom, was uplifted on the cheers of the entire gathering. Nor was this mere lip service, toadyism, or idiotic reverence for a great unknown : it was the heartfelt expression of the genuine love awakened in the entire country by the knowledge that, constitutional Sovereign as she is, fenced in by a thousand traditions and debarred from anything like a free and full expression of her own personal feelings, it was to Her Majesty personally, and not to either of the great English parties, that India owes *her* Magna Charta.

Pandit Madan Mohan Malaviya referred feelingly to this ; he said †:—

"It is not at all surprising to find speaker after speaker, from our worthy President downwards, referring to that great charter of our rights and privileges. This is the keystone of the arch which

* Detailed Report, p. 96.
† Detailed Report, p. 64.

supports all our demands. Therein our gracious Sovereign, under whose benign government we assemble year after year to deliberate upon our common wants and to formulate our common grievances, our gracious Sovereign whose pictures now hang round us, shedding, as it were, some faint reflection of her kindly and motherly influence on our deliberations (*loud cheers*);—therein, Gentlemen, our most noble Queen of England and Empress of India solemnly extended to us pledges, the fulfilment of which we now pray for."

And when he went on, amidst vociferous cheers, to read the Queen's own letter of August the 15th, 1858, (conveying to Lord Derby her instructions as to the tenor of that memorable proclamation, which she in that letter requested him to prepare,) and then to ask what sane man could fail to appreciate the ring of sincerity and beneficence that echoes throughout the sentences, it was the genuine love and gratitude of a nation, face to face, despite all forms and constitutional barriers, with an Empress, whose true heart had felt for and befriended them, that welled up in the flood of cheers in which, for some moments, the debate was drowned.

There was no separatist cry of India for the Indians. "We claim the more perfect union of England and India," said * Pandit Ajoodhia Nath. "How auspicious the meeting," said another speaker, †

"in this sacred city which has from time out of mind been sanctified by the confluence of two sacred rivers, emblematic of the perpetual union between India and England—(*a voice, 'Three cheers for the Union!' and the call was enthusiastically responded to.*)"

We have grave cause for complaint against many of our English officials and even some non-officials; men utterly out of sympathy with our people, never tired of finding fault with and speaking ill of them; incapable of appreciating their many virtues, their high capacities; men enamoured of their own supposed superior wisdom; men whom it would be well, alike for India and England, could they be transplanted once more to bloom in British homesteads, and learn there, anew, those fundamental principles of justice and liberty which are Britain's abiding glory. We have our quarrel with these men, who, to us, seem by no means worthy representatives of the land that gave them birth; but no race feeling mingles in that quarrel on India's part, and her people are still as ready to follow and revere an Englishman like Lord Ripon, who is just and generous to them, as though he were an Indian. Nay, even more ready perhaps, for something of the old hero worship, which arose in days when, if there were fewer Englishmen in India, they were greater and better men, still lingers in the people's hearts.

We have our quarrel with these particular Englishmen; but this has not yet shaken India's reliance in the justice or the generosity of the unprejudiced Englishman or of the English nation as an aggregate.

Conspicuous throughout the debate was the desire manifested by speaker after speaker that the people of England should realise this and should understand that it was equally in the interests of both countries that they lifted up their voices to protest against abuses and entreat for reforms.

---

* Detailed Report, p. 2.
† Pandit Bishen Narayan Dhar. See Detailed Report, p. 21.

Said * Nawab Mahmood Ali Khan :—

"Some people are kind enough to say that we of the Congress are disloyal. If this were indeed so, it would be a bad thing for England and a very bad thing for India, because we of the Congress mean the bulk of the Indians. (*Cheers.*) But it is not so ; we are loyal to the tips of our fingers (*loud cheers*) ; we do not conspire, we do not plot, we do not speak evil in secret, but we come openly forward and say to our rulers, These things we want, these things we do not like : pray give us the former and do away with the latter. We say this in all respect, and we send our prayer home to England, and we say to the English people, These are the promises which our great Empress made to us in 1858 : now please see that these promises are made good, and that our humble prayers, for the redress of our grievances, are attended to. Is this disloyalty ? Is this sedition ? No, Gentlemen, it is the men, be they Indians or Europeans, who are opposing our loyal and constitutional agitation, who, whether they mean it so or not, are really acting disloyally to the interests of both Great Britain and India. (*Cheers.*) May they all soon be wiser, and may the English Government and the English nation come to understand what the real position of affairs is, and do us the kindness and the justice we pray for." (*Cheers.*)

Said † Mr. Tahil Ram Khem Chand :—

"All that we say to Government is—'Do us justice, so that our people may be loyal and contented, so that they may rely implicitly upon you, and hasten to support you in the hour of need.' We ask for justice, because we wish the entire country to be truly loyal in its heart of hearts. If we were sedition-mongers, as some have idly proclaimed, our course would really be quite different. We should sit quiet and let the people brood over their wrongs and the injustice that is too prevalent, and thus allow discontent to grow and spread, and prepare the people for a rising. But we come boldly forward and tell the Government that the system of administration needs to be improved and reformed. We point out to them exactly how this should be done ; and we tell them that, if they want to inspire love and confidence in the people, they must remove those grievances which are now alienating their hearts."

Again ‡ another :—

"The Congress is the noblest movement of the age, and one of its *raisons d'être* is to give us an opportunity of making known to our rulers our grievances in a constitutional and loyal manner. I hail the day on which the Congress first came into existence. It is not only calculated to enable the natives of the soil to protect their rights and privileges, but it is also one of the bulwarks of defence of British rule in India." (*Cheers.*)

Said § Pandit Ajoodhia Nath :—

"I sincerely hope that the members of the two Houses and the people of Great Britain will henceforth commence to take a more lively interest in Indian affairs ; and I hope most sincerely they will never for a moment be misled by the cuckoo cries of our local opponents, who, incapable of refuting our arguments or justifying their frantic and unconstitutional opposition, charge us, and as they well know falsely, with disloyalty. (*Cheers.*)

"This is a charge that we will not submit to Let them call us by any other opprobrious designation they please, and we will treat them with the silent contempt they merit. But if they charge us with disloyalty, we fling back the charge in their teeth, and say, and say truly, that it is they, and not we, who are the real traitors to their country and their Queen." (*Loud cheers.*)

Numerous other passages might be cited, but enough has been said to convince any unbiassed mind of the unaffected loyalty towards the British Sovereign and people, which animates to-day that great and enlightened section of the Nation, which already leads one-third of the entire population, and which will very soon, practically, lead the whole country.

It is well for India and England that this is so ; but no one capable of grasping the situation can fail to realize that the position is not one of stable

* Detailed Report, p. 82.
† Detailed Report, p. 40.
‡ Babu Koilash Chunder Sen. See Detailed Report, p. 53.
§ Detailed Report, p. 4.

equilibrium; that the favour in which England is at present regarded by India partakes somewhat of the character of a *succes d'estime;* and that if this happy state of feeling is to be maintained—and on this India and England's best future hopes depend—there must be *performance* as well as promise on Great Britain's part. The paper credit, of words, must be sustained by the sterling coin of deeds, and it will be doubly well for both Great Britain and our greater India, if English statesmen realize this, and realise it soon, while the tide of sympathy and good will is still high.

One word more: Persistent and disingenuous efforts have been made to saddle the Congress party, as a whole, with a responsibility for every utterance of every supporter of or member of that party. But in reality the Congress party, as a party, repudiates any such responsibility; it is responsible for the formal resolutions passed at its sittings and for nothing else. Day by day, as the movement spreads, men who accept its principles write and publish books, pamphlets, and leaflets, and make speeches, in a dozen languages, here, there and everywhere. For all these productions, the individual authors and orators are alone responsible. The Congress party, as a whole, may or may not agree with what this or that speaker or writer puts forth, but it holds itself RESPONSIBLE *only* for the resolutions it passes; by these it claims to be judged, and by these it must either stand or fall

NOTE A.

Even in parts of the Empire, where the organization was admittedly incomplete, the elections were wonderfully systematically conducted. The following extract from a letter by Mr. Shanker Vinayak Vable, Pleader of the District Court, and Secretary of the Divisional Committee, Ahmednagger, (Dekhan), will serve to illustrate this:—

"One inaccuracy has crept into the statement of delegates called for by you to check the information already furnished during the Congress days. It is this, that not six but seven delegates from this division were present at the Congress. Six were elected at the great public meeting, to which members were returned from every taluqa and important town and village of the district. The seventh, Mr. Ananda Maruti Sangli, was elected at a public meeting of the churches.

"There are about 7,500 Native Christians belonging to the American Mission in this district. They have got 23 churches, who returned 68 members to the Central Union Church Meeting, here, at which Mr. Sangli was elected.

"As regards the method of election generally, the information is given in detail in the Divisional Committee's report which must, by this time, have been submitted to you. From what I have said, I hope you will see that our election was thoroughly constitutional. The Collector of this district has been making all possible enquiries into our movement. He did not anticipate that our election meeting would be so thoroughly representative. It was really a grand success. Over 7,000 people (including numbers of Mahomedans), themselves the delegates of certainly twenty, nay possibly fifty times their own number, attended the final divisional meeting. The Collector has quite satisfied himself that we were *not* "self-constituted delegates."

Yet the Dekhan is only *now* being, what *we* call, thoroughly organised.

SUMMARY OF RESOLUTIONS

PASSED AT THE

FOURTH INDIAN NATIONAL CONGRESS,

Held at Allahabad on the 26th, 27th, 28th & 29th December 1888.

RESOLUTION I.

Resolved—That this Congress affirms the necessity for the expansion and reform of the Council of the Governor-General for making laws and regulations, and of the existing Provincial Legislative Councils, already set forth in Resolutions III of the Congresses of 1885 and 1886, and Resolution II of the Congress of 1887 (a tentative scheme for which expansion and reform was suggested in Resolution IV of the Congress of 1886); and further urges that a Legislative Council (of the same character as those which have been suggested for Provinces where Legislative Councils already exist) be established for the Punjab.

RESOLUTION II.

Resolved—That this Congress, while appreciating the concessions proposed in the Report of the Public Service Commission, yet feels it necessary to put distinctly on record its opinion that full justice will never be done to the people of this country until the open competitive examination for the Civil Service of India is held simultaneously in England and in India.

RESOLUTION III.

Resolved—That this Congress, having read and considered Resolution XI of the Congress of 1886, to wit—

> "That this Congress do place on record an expression of the universal "conviction that a complete separation of executive and judicial functions "(such that in no case the two functions shall be combined in the same "officer) has become an urgent necessity; and that, in its opinion, it "behoves the Government to effect this separation without further delay, "even though this should, in some provinces, involve some extra "expenditure"—

and Resolution III of the Congress of 1887, to the same effect, does now, hereby, affirm the same respectively.

RESOLUTION IV.

Resolved—That this Congress, having read and considered Resolution VIII of the Congress of 1886, to wit—

> "That, in the opinion of this Congress, the time has now arrived when the "system of trial by jury may be safely extended into many parts of the "country where it is not at present in force"—

Resolution IX of the Congress of 1886, to wit—

"That, in the opinion of this Congress, the innovation made in 1872 in the "system of trial by jury, depriving the verdicts of juries of all finality, "has proved injurious to the country, and the powers then for the first time "vested in Sessions Judges and High Courts of setting aside verdicts of "acquittal should be at once withdrawn"—

and Resolution X of the Congress of 1886, to wit—

"That, in the opinion of this Congress, a provision similar to that contained "in the Summary Jurisdiction Act of England (under which accused persons "in serious cases have the option of demanding a committal to the Sessions "Court) should be introduced into the Indian Code of Criminal Procedure, "enabling accused persons, in warrant cases, to demand that, instead of "being tried by the Magistrate, they be committed to the Court of "Sessions"—

does now, hereby, affirm the same respectively.

RESOLUTION V.

Resolved—That, as it is the general belief of the people of this country that the existing system of police administration in India is highly unsatisfactory in itself and oppressive to them, the Government be respectfully urged to appoint a commission, consisting of official and non-official members, to investigate the entire question as speedily as possible.

RESOLUTION VI.

Resolved—That this Congress having read and considered Resolution IV of the Congress of 1887, to wit—

"That in view of the loyalty of Her Majesty's Indian subjects, the Congress "consider it desirable that the Queen's Proclamation should be given "effect to, that the Military services in the higher grades should be practi-"cally opened to the natives of this country, and that the Government "should establish Military Colleges in the country whereat the natives of "India, as defined by Statute, may be educated and trained for a Military "career as officers of the Indian Army;"

Resolution XII of the Congress of 1886, and Resolution V of the Congress of 1887, to wit—

"That in view of the unsettled state of public affairs in Europe, and the immense "assistance that the people of this country, if duly prepared therefor, are "capable of rendering to Great Britain in the event of any serious compli-"cations arising, the Congress once again earnestly appeals to the "Government to authorize (under such rules and restrictions as to it may "seem fitting) a system of volunteering for the Indian inhabitants of the "country, such as may qualify them to support the Government effectually "in any crisis;"

and Resolution VIII of the Congress of 1887, to wit—

"That in view of the loyalty of the people, the hardships which the present Arms "Act (XI of 1878) causes, and the unmerited slur which it casts upon the "people of this country, the Government be moved so to modify the "provisions of Chapter IV, and if necessary other portions of the said "Act, as shall enable all persons to possess and wear Arms unless debarred "therefrom, either as individuals, or members of particular communities "or classes, by the orders of the Government of India, (or any local "authority empowered by the Government of India on that behalf), for "reasons to be recorded in writing and duly published;"

does now, hereby, affirm the same respectively.

RESOLUTION VII.

Resolved—That, having regard to the fact that a serious increase in the consumption of intoxicants has taken place under the systems of Abkari and Excise now prevailing in India, the Government be respectfully urged to adopt some such improved system as shall tend to discourage insobriety.

RESOLUTION VIII.

Resolved—That as the administration of the Income Tax, especially as regards incomes below Rs. 1,000, has proved extremely unsatisfactory, it is essential, in the opinion of the Congress, that the taxable minimum be raised to Rs. 1,000.

RESOLUTION IX.

Resolved—That this Congress being of opinion that it is the first duty of the British Government in India to foster and encourage education, as well general as technical, in all its branches, and that the declaration made in the recent resolution of the Government of India on the subject of education is calculated to encourage the tendency to reduce imperial expenditure on education, and to withdraw from the control of it, respectfully urges upon Government the extreme importance of increasing, or at any rate of not decreasing, the present expenditure on education, and of the Government continuing to control the Educational Institutions of all kinds now existing.

RESOLUTION X.

Resolved—That, having regard to the poverty of the people, the importance of encouraging indigenous manufactures, and the difficulty of practically introducing any general system of technical education with the present imperfect information, Government be moved to delay no longer the appointment of a mixed commission, to enquire into the present industrial condition of the country.

RESOLUTION XI.

Resolved—That the foregoing Resolutions be submitted for the favourable consideration of His Excellency the Viceroy, and for transmission by him to Her Majesty's Government, with the humble request of this Congress that the reforms suggested in the said Resolutions (based as most of these are on Her Gracious Majesty's Proclamation of 1858) may now be effected; and that should it be deemed necessary first to institute any enquiry into any of the matters forming the subjects of these Resolutions, such enquiry may be made, as speedily as possible, by a Parliamentary Committee.

RESOLUTION XII.

Resolved—That this Congress, having watched with interest and sympathy the exertions that are being made in England for the total abrogation of laws and rules relating to the regulation of prostitution by the State in India, places on record its appreciation of the services thus rendered to this country, and its desire to co-operate by all means in its power in the attainment of this laudable object.

RESOLUTION XIII.

Resolved—That no subject shall be passed for discussion by the Subject Committee, or allowed to be discussed at any Congress by the President thereof, to the introduction of which the Hindu or Mahomedan Delegates as a body object, unanimously or nearly unanimously; and that if, after the discussion of any subject which has been admitted for discussion, it shall appear that all the Hindu or all the Mahomedan Delegates as a body are unanimously or nearly unanimously opposed to the Resolution which it is proposed to pass thereon, such Resolution shall be dropped; provided that this rule shall refer only to subjects in regard to which the Congress has not already definitely pronounced an opinion.

RESOLUTION XIV.

Resolved—That the question of the introduction of a Permanent Settlement of the Land Revenue Demand into the Madras and Bombay Presidencies and other provinces be referred to the several standing Congress Committees, with instructions to report upon the same, in so far as it affects their respective circles, to the Congress of 1889.

RESOLUTION XV.

Resolved—That this Congress puts on record its disapproval of the recent enhancement of the Salt Tax, as involving a perceptible increase to the burthens of the poorer classes, as also the partial absorption, in a time of peace and plenty, of the only Financial Reserve of the Empire.

RESOLUTION XVI.

Resolved—That the Fifth Indian National Congress do assemble in the Bombay Presidency (either at Bombay itself or at Poona, as may be settled hereafter) on the 26th of December, 1889.

RESOLUTION XVII.

Resolved—That Mr. A. O. Hume be re-appointed General Secretary for the ensuing year.

GEORGE YULE,

President of the

Fourth Indian National Congress.

ALLAHABAD, *December 31st, 1888.*

DETAILED

REPORT OF THE PROCEEDINGS

OF

THE FOURTH INDIAN NATIONAL CONGRESS

HELD AT

ALLAHABAD

On the 26th, 27th, 28th, and 29th of December, 1888.

FIRST DAY'S PROCEEDINGS.

THE FIRST MEETING OF THE FOURTH CONGRESS took place on the afternoon of the 26th December, 1888, at Allahabad, the capital of the Government of the North-Western Provinces and Oudh, in a vast and splendid temporary Hall, erected for the purpose, in the grounds of Lowther Castle. Lowther Castle lies alongside Government House, and faces and overlooks the Alfred Park. The grounds are very extensive, and were almost completely occupied by rows upon rows of large tents, in which about 800 of the delegates were housed, the rest being accommodated elsewhere.

Some 5,000 visitors, and about 1,200 delegates, had assembled in and around the Congress Hall by 1-30 P.M., and at 2 P.M. precisely the chair was taken by the HON'BLE PANDIT AJOODHIA NATH, Chairman of the Reception Committee, on whom devolved, *ex officio*, the task of welcoming the delegates and calling upon them to elect a President.

1st Day.

Chairman of Reception Committee's Address.

THE HON'BLE PANDIT AJOODHIA NATH—(*North-Western Provinces, No.* 551 *in list*)—rose and said:—

GENTLEMEN,—On behalf of the Reception Committee, I offer you a most hearty welcome. I rejoice to see so many friends and countrymen, many of whom have come long distances and at great personal inconvenience, assembled to try and secure, by all loyal and constitutional means, the amelioration of the political condition of India. (*Cheers.*) It is a matter for great rejoicings that all the leaders of native opinion from all the various provinces, and the representatives of all the different communities of the Empire, have assembled here this day to labour for that *summum bonum*, the greatest good of the greatest number. (*Cheers.*) If Allahabad has not been fortunate enough to be the first to secure the patronage of this great national institution, it may well be proud of being the first place where its organization has arrived at a fair state of perfection. (*Cheers.*) But while our organization has so much improved, I regret to say that our arrangements for your reception have not been, by any means, as satisfactory as they were at either Calcutta or Madras. ('*No, no.*') But, Gentlemen, in consideration of the difficulties thrown in our way by the Civil and Military authorities, we have some claim to your indulgence. We were first of all led to believe—I may say distinctly informed—that we should be permitted to occupy the Khusro Bagh for our encampment. But a little later, to our great disappointment, we were told that the requisite permission could not be accorded (*Cries of* "*Shame!*") ; and no satisfactory reason was assigned for this change of front. In April, after much negotiation, permission was granted to us to pitch our camp on a large plot of waste ground lying between the fort railway station and the fort, on payment of rent. This rent we paid in advance, and we were assured that there would be no further difficulty in the way of our occupying that piece of land. But, Gentlemen, in the month of August—four months later—we were informed that on sanitary grounds we could not be allowed to occupy that place, and the rent money, which we had paid in advance, was returned to us. Then we managed to secure a group of houses belonging to members of the Reception Committee and other friends, not very far away from the office of the *Pioneer*. This was too much for our opponents, and as some of the houses were unfortunately situated within the Cantonment limits, the Military authorities, arbitrarily, prohibited our utilizing those houses for Congress purposes. ("*Shame!*") No inquiry was made as to the sanitary arrangements we were going to make. It was apparently taken for granted that the Congress Camp—and you have seen what a beautiful and perfectly

1st Day.

Chairman of Reception Committee's Address.

managed camp ours is—would be the filthiest and most insanitary of all gatherings. ("*Shame!*") It is not too much to say that no other gathering for any other purpose would have been thus barred. Hundreds of thousands of men, poor, ill-clothed, ill-fed, and I fear not a few of them far from clean, are allowed to occupy land no further from the fort at the yearly fair—hundreds of thousands who every twelfth year swell to millions—but no authorities, Civil or Military, interfere with them. But our gathering of less than 1,500 gentlemen, all well fed and well clothed, could not be permitted on sanitary grounds. Then, as a last resource, we were obliged to rent these premises where we are now assembled. You can, therefore, easily imagine the difficulties with which we have had to contend. We obtained possession of this house and grounds on the 1st November, and had barely six weeks in which to make all the necessary arrangements for housing and feeding over 1,200 delegates. (*Cheers.*) Those friends of ours who have come from Madras will, I hope, remember that the task of providing for the delegates in Allahabad has not been so easy as at Madras, where His Excellency the Governor himself lent them tents, assisted them in many ways, and sympathized with their work. (*Cheers.*) But here I had to dance attendance for an hour at least in the Fort of Allahabad waiting the pleasure of the officers to grant me an audience—officers who not only gave us no assistance, but quite the contrary. (*Laughter, and cries of* "*Shame!*") All this will convince you that we have some claim to your indulgence.

I shall now ask you to elect your own President. But before you proceed with his election, you may perhaps expect me to say a few words about the opposition of other kinds that we have had to encounter. You are now very familiar with the nature of that opposition. You know the strength of that opposition, and you also know that it is fast losing its power for evil, and dying out as all unrighteous things sooner or later die. (*Cheers.*) But I feel it my duty to refer to it in consequence of the letter of Sir Auckland Colvin to our most esteemed, but much abused, friend Mr. Hume. (*Loud cheers.*) Mr. Hume has not only now, but for years past, been working with infinite and unselfish zeal to promote the welfare of India, and we may leave it to time to vindicate his action from the strictures of the Lieutenant-Governor. (*Cheers.*) Again, I am sorry to say that that portion of the Anglo-Indian press which delights in ridiculing and contemning the aspirations of the native community left no stone unturned to bring discredit on Mr. Hume. (*Cheers, and cries of* "*Shame!*") But we are not children. We know the game they are playing; and we mean to stick to Mr. Hume to the last. (*Loud and prolonged cheers.*) His advice to us has always been loyalty and moderation, and yet he has been stigmatized as the most seditious man in India. The next reason which induces me to refer to this opposition is the speech of Lord Dufferin, who speaks of the seditious nature of some of our writings and speeches. Some few thoughtless non-official opponents had already, it is true, adopted similar means to discredit us. But I am surprised, I am astonished, to find any sensible man, let alone a gentleman occupying the position of a Viceroy, bringing a charge of disloyalty against us. (*Cheers.*) It is impossible—and I say it with great confidence—to find on the face of this earth a people more loyal than my countrymen. (*Loud cheers.*) We claim the more perfect union of India and England, and yet we are called disloyal. Are we disloyal? (*Loud cries of* "*No, no.*") Some people have gone the length of talking such nonsense as to say that we want the Russians to come into the country. (*Laughter.*) Now, Gentlemen, I ask you, is it not absurd to suppose that the educated natives of India, who have such an admiration for the free and representative institutions of England, could ever wish to be under Russian rule or become Russian serfs? (*Laughter and cheers.*) History we have read, English education we have received, with Englishmen we have mixed and mixed freely, but we are not credited, it would seem, with even sense enough to realize that the English Government is far better than the Russian or than that of any other European Power. The existence of the Congress, the very meetings which we hold annually, are the best proofs of the excellence of the British Government. (*Cheers.*) Where will you find any Government which would allow a foreign country, which it has pleased Providence to place under its charge, to have the same constitutional freedom of speech as the British Government has been pleased to grant to us? (*Cheers.*) I will only mention to you one instance as a signal proof of our loyalty. When a couple of years ago there was some talk of a Russian invasion, not only our men, but, mark please, also our women, expressed in an unmistakeable manner their wish that the Russians should be kept out of the country by all possible means (*cheers*); and were ready, in some cases, it is said, to sacrifice those jewels, so dear to all females, to provide the necessary funds. (*Loud cheers.*) If occasion arises we will prove to our opponents that it is we who are loyal and not they; it is we who will support the Government and not they; it is we who will be ready with our purses and not they. (*Cheers.*) We fully acknowledge the inestimable blessings conferred upon us by Government; we most gratefully admit the numberless benefits derived by India from British rule, and all that we now say is this, *viz.*, that there is yet room for improvement; that England can confer still further blessings upon us; and that, therefore, we may properly approach our Most Gracious Empress—approach her most respectfully and loyally—with the prayer that she will cause all those gracious pledges given on her behalf to be now more fully redeemed. (*Cheers.*)

England has been the first to introduce free institutions into this country, and we ask Her Majesty now to extend them so far as the circumstances will permit, so that to the end of time the English Government may be held up to all the civilized Governments under the sun, as the very model of perfection. (*Cheers.*) That our prayers will be granted sooner or later I have not the slightest doubt. (*Loud cheers.*)

Two years ago I gave the subject of the Congress my best consideration, and after mature deliberation I arrived at the conclusion that, so far from being dangerous to Government, it embodies the essential germ of the permanency of the British Government. (*Cheers.*) I have since then, in consequence of Sir Auckland Colvin's letter and Lord Dufferin's speech, as a loyal subject of Her Majesty, re-considered the matter, and believe me, Gentlemen, that I have been unable to discover in any of our speeches, publications or proceedings, anything which is at all seditious, or which in any way approaches to sedition. You know the multifarious duties of a Viceroy, and you know the heavy work of a Lieutenant-Governor, and I believe that these exalted officials have not had the time to study carefully our pamphlets, but have received their information as to their general purport and bearing at second hand, and you know what the value of that kind of second hand information is. (*Laughter.*) But this being so, it is the duty of every loyal subject of the Queen to prove, by his firmness in the cause, and by his moderation, that the charges brought against us by our kind opponents have no foundation in fact. These criticisms and this opposition have given rise to certain misapprehensions, the most prominent among these being the idea that the Government means to do injury to those who join the Congress. Nothing could be more absurd than such a rumour. The great nation on whose possessions the sun never sets—the most advanced of nations, the first to introduce free institutions into this country, and teach us that rulers were created for the good of subjects, not subjects for the pleasure of rulers—the noble nation that has united justice with freedom, will never allow its officers to resort to such unjustifiable and unconstitutional measures. (*Cheers.*) Englishmen as a nation are not capable of suppressing any loyal constitutional organization by any arbitrary or unfair means. (*Cheers.*) Having said this much I am obliged to say something more which is not quite so pleasant. News comes to us from district after district that people have been told by their official superiors that they would "come to grief" if they joined, subscribed to, or in any way aided the National Congress. Reports of this nature have reached me from Cawnpore, Etawah, Agra, Aligurh and other places too numerous to mention. I have letters in my office to the effect that in one of the towns in the Aligurh district people held meetings, and were ready not only to elect delegates but to prove unmistakeably the interest they take in the Congress by putting hands deep into their pockets. (*Cheers.*) But down came the news "The district officer will be displeased with you." ("*Shame!*") In Gorakhpore anti-Congress meetings were held, and Government officers took part in them. ("*Shame!*") Important people were forbidden to take part in Congress meetings. Well, Sir, a great many rumours are circulated which are not true, and we will hope that some of these at least may be more or less untrue. (*Laughter*)

Then there is an idea that the Congress party is only a microscopic minority. (*Laughter.*) But it is not only natives who have received an English education, and even these may now be numbered by hundreds of thousands, who take part in this movement. I see before me, even in this Congress, numbers of gentlemen who, though very highly educated and cultured, have not received any so-called English education. I have been to several places in these provinces in connection with the Congress, and wherever I went I found great enthusiasm prevailing amongst all classes of people, and what you will be still more pleased to hear is that we have received contributions from all classes, even from those who profess to be against the Congress. (*Laughter and cheers.*) Nay, from some of those whose names figure high on the list of so-called anti-Congress Associations. (*Cheers, and cries of "Name! name!"*) I cannot, of course, disclose their names, for they accompanied their donations with special requests that their names should never be disclosed. I have also received large subscriptions from native noblemen on condition that their names should not be disclosed because they are afraid of the officials. (*Laughter.*)

A question was recently put in the House of Commons by a member, in which it was stated that the Native Princes and the Mahomedans as a body were against the Congress. ("*No, no.*") You have here seated on the platform Sirdar Dayal Singh, the premier Sikh nobleman of the Punjab. Our illustrious friend the Maharajah of Durbhunga, a Brahmin of the Brahmins, the premier nobleman of Bengal, had made arrangements to come here to-day; but circumstances over which he had no control—a sudden attack of illness—prevented him from being present. Here, too, you have Mahomedans, noblemen of the highest birth, scions of the ex-Royal houses of Delhi and Oudh, and others. Well, who are the Princes that are against us? The Maharajah of Benares, and he alone; and if I understand Rajah Shiva Persad, who is attending this Congress this year and declares himself to be a delegate, even the Maharajah of Benares is not against the Congress, indeed approves it, but only desires to protest against certain speeches

1st Day

Chairman of Reception Committee's Address.

and writings of some Congressmen which he disapproves. (*Laughter.*) But can the Maharajah of Benares represent the Princes of India, or ourselves? (*Cries of "No."*) Has he anything in common with us? ("*No, no.*") Then, besides the Maharajah of Benares, there are some gentlemen who have the reputation of being the authors of certain anti-Congress pamphlets and letters to the press. I have the honor of knowing some of them personally, and can tell you that, so far from writing those pamphlets, they are unable to understand them. (*Laughter.*) Since this question was put in the House of Commons, I have tried in vain to ascertain what native Princes were against us.

Again I ask you to turn your eyes round this hall and see if it is true that Mahomedans do not sympathize with us. In the last Congress the number of Mussulman delegates was 83; now it is more than double this. (*Cries of "Treble! treble!"*) The Mahomedans of Oudh have returned at one meeting 57 delegates, including members of the Royal house of Oudh. (*Cheers.*) Some 27 Mahomedan delegates have been returned by the district of Allahabad, and no less than 11 were returned from a place where you might not have believed that even a single one would be elected. (*A voice, "Aligurh."*) Yes, how rightly you have guessed the name. (*Laughter and cheers.*) And now you can appreciate the importance of this so-called opposition which sounds very nicely, but in which there is no reality, as all can see, when our opponents are obliged to have recourse to the desperate expedient of putting forward these few titled inanities to show that the Princes of India are against us; they stand self-condemned and need no further refutation from us; nor is it my duty now, I am happy to say, to have any fault to find with the Mahomedans, generally, for not joining us, much less for opposing us; and if any Hindu can claim the honour of enjoying an intimate intercourse with the Mahomedans of this country, I certainly can, and I can assure you that, as a body, they are not against us. But, Gentlemen, I am afraid I have detained you too long. (*Cries of "No, no," and "Go on."*) It is enough for me now to say that, so far as I have been able to thresh out this question, persistent efforts in the cause of the Congress are the best and almost the only proofs that you can now-a-days give of true and heartfelt loyalty to our beloved Queen-Empress. (*Loud cheers.*) Our strength has been tried, our firmness has been tested, and our loyalty is unquestionable. Then, Gentlemen, what else is required for our success? One thing, and one thing only, is required. We require—and I say it—to reach the ears and attract the eyes of the people in England; we require only to create a deep interest in Indian affairs in the Houses of Parliament and in the hearts of the British nation. (*Cheers.*) I do not think that, hereafter, you will find the benches of the House of Commons quite so bare as in times past they have ever become as soon as an Indian question was brought before the House. I sincerely hope that the members of the two Houses and the people of Great Britain will henceforth commence to take a more lively interest in Indian affairs; and I hope most sincerely they will never for a moment be misled by the cuckoo cries of our local opponents, who, incapable of refuting our arguments or justifying their frantic and unconstitutional opposition, charge us, and as they well know falsely, with disloyalty. (*Cheers.*)

This is a charge that we will not submit to. Let them call us by any other opprobrious designation they please, and we will treat them with the silent contempt they merit. But if they charge us with disloyalty, we fling back the charge in their teeth, and say, and say truly, that it is they and not we who are the real traitors to their country and their Queen. (*Loud cheers.*) And now, Gentlemen, I have already detained you too long ("*No, no*"), and must now ask you to proceed at once to the election of a President.

Election of President.

THE HON'BLE PHEROZSHAH M. MEHTA—(*Bombay, No. 208 in list*)—then rose and said: GENTLEMEN,—It is my high privilege to-day to propose the election of the President of the Fourth Indian National Congress. (*Cheers.*) We already boast of an illustrious roll of Presidents of Congress. (*Renewed cheers.*) At the first Congress held in Bombay we had for our chairman my esteemed and respected friend Mr. W. C. Bonnerjee (*Cheers*), a Brahmin gentleman hailing from Bengal, the land of the Baboos, but whom I am proud to be allowed to call one of my oldest and most respected friends. (*Cheers.*) Then at the second National Congress, held in Calcutta, we had for our chairman a Parsee, that "black man" (*loud laughter and cheers*) Mr. Dadabhai Nowrojee; only a "black man" in the Marquis of Salisbury's estimation, but for all that a man who is admired, esteemed and loved, from one end of India to the other (*renewed and vehement cheers*); and at the last great Congress at Madras we had for our President a Mahomedan gentleman occupying the highest position, and perhaps the most distinguished Mussulman in India, Mr. Budrudin Tyabjee. (*Cheers.*) And now, Gentlemen, I ask you to add to that illustrious roll, the name, as President of this Congress, of Mr. George Yule. (*Loud cheers, which were renewed again and again with the utmost enthusiasm.*) In the course of my public experience I have heard the names of several public men received with enthusiasm, but the enthusiasm with which you have received the name of Mr. Yule convinces me that I need say but few words in commendation of this gentleman, whom your enthusiastic cheers sufficiently prove that you have already accepted as President of your Congress. (*Renewed cheers.*) Throughout his Indian career he has won the respect, the admiration, and the regard of everybody with whom he has come in contact—Native and European, official and non-official. (*Cheers.*) It is sufficient for me to say that the positions, the high and respected positions, which he has held as leading member of one of those princely mercantile houses which have helped to make British India what she is, as the elected Sheriff of Calcutta, as the President of that Chamber of Commerce which (in common with other Chambers of Commerce of India) has laboured so persistently to bring about the public discussion of the budget; I say the tenure of such positions is a guarantee of the esteem in which he has been held throughout his Indian career. (*Cheers.*) But, Gentlemen, I will mention only one single instance to show how justly founded this esteem has been. I have already told you that Mr. Yule was Sheriff of Calcutta. The fees of this office are going to be abolished now, but in those days they were large; and how did Mr. Yule employ those fees which were intended to be appropriated to his own use by the Sheriff? In supporting Native Schools. (*Loud cheers.*) I say this shows the great, the deep interest, and sympathy with which Mr. Yule has watched the progress and welfare of the people of the country in which his lot is cast. (*Loud cheers.*) In electing Mr. George Yule you will be doing an appropriate and very significant thing in more ways than one. A great deal of criticism and some little abuse have been showered on us, because we have assumed the name of a National Congress; but in doing so I say we are absolutely doing homage to that bond of union which has brought Englishmen and Indians together (*cheers*), paying homage to that civilized British rule of which we are proud to say we are subjects and citizens, subjects and citizens of one great Imperial Majesty. (*Loud cheers.*) Then also in another respect Mr. George Yule's election as Chairman of this Congress is most appropriate. We are giving the most complete guarantee of the loyalty, which not only has marked our proceedings during the preceding three Congresses, but which will animate the proceedings of this and, I can confidently predict, every subsequent Congress. (*Cheers.*) I will not detain you any longer, but will now formally lay before you the proposal that Mr. George Yule be elected President of the Indian National Congress of this year. (*Loud cheers.*)

SIRDAR DYAL SINGH, MAJETHIA—(*Punjab, No.* 341 *in list*)—then said: GENTLEMEN,—I second Mr. Mehta's proposition. We could not possibly have a better President.

SHEIKH RAZA HOSSEIN KHAN—(*Oudh, No.* 439 *in list*)—rose and said, speaking in Oordoo: GENTLEMEN,—I hear that certain people have given out that the Mahomedans are opposed to the Congress, and that even a member of the British Parliament, long resident in India, who surely might have known better, went so far as to, virtually, assert this in the House of Commons. Now I am a Mahomedan, and, although I could not take part in any of the preceding Congress Meetings, I am proud of the fact that I have all along, since the very first gathering of the Congress, taken a very deep interest in it, and looked upon the movement with a friendly feeling. Much has been said about me, but nobody has doubts about my being a Mahomedan; and as a Mahomedan, and one not altogether without the means of ascertaining the views of my co-religionists, I can assure you that though certain individual Mahomedans, who are great at talking, profess to be against the Congress, the great bulk of the Mahomedans are in no way against, but rather are favourable to, the Congress. This point has been ably treated by the Hon'ble Pandit Ajoodhia Nath, and I need not dwell on it at any greater length. It will be enough for me to say that I have brought with me a Fatwa of the Shamsululma, in which the said dignitary has approved and sanctioned the participation of Mahomedans in these Congresses. This Shamsululma is the spiritual leader of the Suni community of Lucknow. a place noted for learning in the Mahomedan world. He ranks first amongst the Suni Doctors of Law.

Gentlemen, the secret of the opposition has now been divulged; it is not the Mahomedans, but their official masters, who are opposed to the Congress, and I need only add that I heartily support the proposal that Mr. Yule, whose great claims on our respect and esteem are well known to you all, be elected the President of this the Fourth Indian National Congress.

RAI BAHADUR SUBHAPATHY MUDELILAR—(*Madras, No.*70 *in list*)—said: GENTLEMEN,—I entirely concur in all that Mr. Mehta has said. It may seem surprising to many of you here—coming as I do from the far south—but as a merchant I have had some dealings with our proposed President, Mr. George Yule. In fact I am one of his oldest constituents. From what I have seen, and from what I have known of his character as a merchant, I support with all my heart the proposition that has been made. In electing this gentleman, we are doing honour to one who has been doing much for the natives of India, and we shall be doing, I fully believe, the very best thing we can for ourselves. Of course I cannot pretend to recapitulate all he has been doing for us in the past, nor does it seem needful, since from the enthusiastic acclamation

1st Day.

Election of President.

with which this Congress has received his name, I can entertain no doubt that you have made up your minds to elect him, and that his election will meet with universal approval. (*Cheers.*)

THE HON'BLE PANDIT AJOODHIA NATH—(*N. W. P., No.* 551 *in list*)—President of the Reception Committee, then said : GENTLEMEN,—No one else having been proposed, and there being no other proposal before you, I now ask you to say whether it is your pleasure that Mr. Yule should be your President ? (*Cries of Yes, yes," and loud and prolonged cheering.*)

Then I declare Mr. Yule duly elected as President of this Congress, and (*suiting the action to his words*) I now thus induct him in the Presidential Chair.

The President's Inaugural Address.

MR. GEORGE YULE, PRESIDENT—(*Calcutta, No.* 1097 *in list*)—who was received with renewed and most enthusiastic cheers, then rose and delivered the following address :—

GENTLEMEN,—When I was asked some time ago to allow myself to be nominated for the position to which you have now elected me, I had some hesitation in giving my assent to the request. It was an unexpected, and with all due deference to the judgment of my too indulgent friends, it was an undeserved compliment. That, however, is a kind of objection which can always and very easily be got over. But I knew your assemblies were very large, and I also know that it is a most desirable quality in the President of such a gathering to have a voice strong enough to reach the remotest listener. I feared I had no such voice. For that reason chiefly, and for others that need not be mentioned, I felt, I hope with unaffected diffidence, that I was scarcely the man to follow those magnificent speakers who had occupied the chair at previous meetings of the Congress. Nevertheless, quickened by my warm sympathies with the main objects of the Congress, I am here at your call, for better or for worse. (*Cheers.*)

And now, Gentlemen, I come at once to the business that lies before us. Why are we here ? What do we want ? What are we striving after ? In the resolutions that are to be submitted to you there are some reforms embodied, which state our wants, which set forth our views, and indicate the direction in which our thoughts are travelling. I think I am right, however, in saying that all these do not occupy exactly the same place in our regards. About one or two of them there is more or less of doubt as to their value or importance. But there is one of them respecting which there is the most complete and perfect unanimity of opinion. I refer to the reform of the Legislative Councils. I myself regard this one as the most important of all. Each of the other reforms begins and ends with itself. The reform of the Councils is not only in itself good, but it has the additional virtue of being the best of all instruments for obtaining other reforms that further experience and our growing wants may lead us to desire. (*Loud cheers.*) With your permission I will confine the observations I have to make to this one question. In doing so, it seems to me to be needful first of all to state some of the facts connected with the origin of the Bill under which the affairs of India are at present administered. When the sole Government of this country was taken over by the Crown in 1858, it fell to the lot of Lord Palmerston, who was then Prime Minister, to introduce into the House of Commons a Bill which was afterwards known as India Bill No. 1. The main provisions of this Bill were, that the Government of India was to vest in a Viceroy and Council in India, and in a Council of eight retired Indian officials presided over by a Secretary of State in London. The proceedings of these two separate bodies, each of whom had certain independent responsibilities, were to be subject to the review and final decision of the House of Commons. The chief objection to this Bill was, that no provision was made for the representation of the people of the country. Mr. Disraeli, who was leader of the Opposition, objected to it on the ground of the insufficient check which it provided ; and he said that with such Councils as those proposed, "you could not be sure that the inhabitants of India would be able to obtain that redress from the grievances under which they suffered, that English protection ought to insure." Almost immediately after the introduction of the Bill, Lord Palmerston was defeated upon a side question, and Lord Derby became Prime Minister with Mr. Disraeli as leader of the House of Commons. No time was lost by the new Ministry in introducing India Bill No. 2. Mr. Disraeli dwelt upon the desirability of having the representative principle applied to the Government of the country, and his scheme was to increase the Council in London, which was proposed by Lord Palmerston, from eight to eighteen Members, half of whom were to be elected and were, in all other respects, to be entirely independent of Government. He regretted that the unsettled state of the country did not admit of a representation of the people in India itself, and all that could be done in the meantime was to approach as near to that form of Government as the circumstances would permit. The provisions of his Bill to effect that purpose were briefly these : Four of the elected half of the Council were to be members of the Indian Civil and Military Services of ten years' standing, and the remaining five must have been engaged in trading with India for at least five years. The constituency electing the four members connected with the services was to consist of all officers of both branches of the

1st Day.

The President's Inaugural Address.

India service, and also of all residents in India owning £2,000 of an Indian railway or £1,000 of Government stock. The five mercantile members were to be elected by the Parliamentary constituencies of London, Belfast, Liverpool, Manchester and Glasgow. So deeply ingrained is this notion of Government by representation in the minds of Englishmen, that, rather than leave it out of sight altogether in dealing with the affairs of India, the Government of that day made the proposals I have stated. Although the intention underlying these proposals was applauded, the scheme itself was felt to be, from the imperfect character of the constituencies, wholly inadequate to secure the check that was desired. It was clear, or rather it soon became clear, that the interests of one set of voters were adverse to the interests of the mass of the people, and that the other set knew absolutely nothing of the country or its wants. Received with favour, at first, the Bill soon became the object of jest and derision on the part of the Opposition, and even its more impartial critics said of it that it was useless offering to the people of India, under the name of bread, what would certainly turn out to be a stone. At the suggestion of Lord John Russell, the Bill was withdrawn, and the House proceeded by way of resolution to construct the frame-work of another Bill. The plan finally adopted was this: the Legislative and Administrative powers were to be entrusted to a Viceroy and a Council in India, and the check upon them was to be a Council of fifteen Members sitting in London. This Council was to be responsible to the Cabinet through a Secretary of State, who was to be responsible in turn to the House of Commons. This arrangement was regarded merely as a provisional one, and the policy to be pursued was to work up to the constitutional standard. Education was to be largely extended and improved, and the natives of the country were to be drafted into the service of Government as they became qualified with the view, among other reasons, to fit them for the anticipated enlargement of their political powers. (“*Hear, hear.*”) The promises made and the prospects held out in the debates in Parliament derived a lustre from the famous proclamation of the Queen,—that half-fulfilled charter of India's rights,—which was first read and published to the people of India in this very city of Allahabad thirty years ago. (*Loud cheers.*) Now, what I wish to impress upon your minds by this brief narrative is the great importance that was attached at that time to some sort of constitutional check. Failing to have it in the form that the English people themselves approved and followed in the management of their own affairs, they devised the substitute with its threefold check that I have mentioned. Parliament itself was full of gushing enthusiasm as to the part it would take in the business. In the absence of a representative body in India, the House of Commons was to play the role of one on our behalf. It was to regard the work as a great and solemn trust committed to it by an all-wise and inscrutable Providence, the duties of which it would faithfully and fully discharge. Such was the style of language employed both in and out of Parliament at the time I allude to. And now what is the actual state of the case? It is summed up in a single sentence. There is no check. The Bill under which our affairs are administered appears, like many other Bills, to be open to more than one interpretation. The interpretation put upon it at the time, and what was probably the intention of Parliament, was this: the Government in India was to have the right of the initiative; the Council in London the right of review; and the Secretary of State, subject to the ultimate judgment of the House of Commons, the right of veto And this was practically the relations of the parties until 1870. In that year the Duke of Argyle was Secretary of State; and in a controversy on this subject with Lord Mayo, who was then Viceroy, he laid down quite another doctrine. He held that the Government in India had no independent power at all, and that the prerogative of the Secretary of State was not limited to a veto of the measures passed in India. “The Government in India,” he maintained, “were merely Executive Officers of the Home Government, who hold the ultimate power of requiring the Governor-General to introduce a measure, and of requiring also all the Official Members of the Council to vote for it.” This power-absorbing Despatch is dated the 24th November, 1870. The supposed powers and privileges of the Council in London have been similarly dealt with, and the Council is now regarded merely as an adjunct of the office of the Secretary of State to furnish him with information or advice when he chooses to ask for it. The present position, then, is this: the Government in India has no power; the Council in London has no power; the House of Commons has the power, but it refuses or neglects to exercise it.

The 650 odd members who were to be the palladium of India's rights and liberties have thrown “the great and solemn trust of an inscrutable Providence” back upon the hands of Providence to be looked after as Providence itself thinks best. (*Laughter.*) The affairs of India, especially in the Financial Department, have passed with no kind of check whatever into the hands of the Secretary of State. I do not blame the present members of the House of Commons for thus abdicating the functions that their predecessors of thirty years ago assumed. The truth is, that they have not time enough to attend to the details of the trust; and on more important matters they can have only one side of every question—the official side—presented to them, and they know from experience that that is not always the whole of the case. (*Laughter.*) As they are not in

1st Day.

The President's Inaugural Address.

a position to judge rightly, they do not attempt to judge at all; and they may fairly come to the conclusion that, if it is not worth our while to demand and agitate for some voice in our own affairs, it is not worth their while to trouble themselves at all about us. If we be satisfied, for example, to have the Budget thrown at our heads like a snow-ball, and a muddy one it is, we deserve to have it in that way. There is a common belief among the European trading community that there are some big leaks in the Store department and in Home charges generally; but we have no means for verifying or disproving the suspicion. Now and again we hear of some facts that confirm it Here is one told me the other day by an authority I would call unimpeachable. The department with which this gentleman is connected indented for an article, and after many weary months it came at last charged six times the price for which, my informant said, he, himself, could have bought it. If we be content with the secresy and the supposed inefficiency of such a system, then I say we deserve no better. Temporary commissions of enquiry into the working of such departments are of little good. The real remedy is a permanent commission in the shape of elected members of Council having the right to look into such matters. (*Cheers.*)

But when we make the demand that the political institutions of the country should be placed on a wider basis, we are not only asking what the Government of thirty years ago avowed was desirable, but also what almost every Viceroy since that time has either promised, or held out as a hope to be indulged in by us. I admit that these promises have been associated with such phrases as "when qualified" or "as far as may be." These words doubtless afford a pretext for shirking the due fulfilment of the promise. Of course, to the antagonistic mind, our qualification will always be in the future; but I am sure I express your conviction when I say that, whatever use the abettors of the present bureaucratic rule may make of these phrases, the distinguished personages who uttered them had far other intentions than to make of them a loop-hole of escape when all other channels of retreat were closed by a reasonable fulfilment of the conditions. Putting aside then this Small Cause Court use of the words (*laughter*), I come to say something on the question of qualification. What does it mean? What was in the minds of the Queen's advisers when these phrases were employed? Can we doubt that they were thinking of the qualifications of ordinary English constituencies at a somewhat more rudimentary stage of their development than they are to-day? Now, if it can be shown that there are considerable numbers of people in this country with attainments and characteristics similar to those of constituencies in Great Britain two or three generations back, the condition as regards them has surely been amply fulfilled. But how is that to be shown? It is not a matter for mere floating opinion to decide, one man saying Yes, and the next saying No, but neither being able to adduce any reason, or state any fact in support of his view. If you want to know the financial resources of a body of men, such as a trading company, you audit their accounts. If you wish to ascertain where a village is in point of education, you don't inquire what Mr. This or Baboo That thinks, but you want to know how many schools there are, how many scholars there are, and what amount of money is being spent upon them. Then you have facts of a kind on which to form an intelligent and reliable judgment. Now, Gentlemen, in the Blue Books published by the Indian Government you have the material, the moral, and the educational state of the country set out in such fulness as to enable us to say where the people are in the scale of humanity as compared with those of other countries. I am not going into an "as-dry-as-dust" analysis of these facts. I simply indicate the method of proof, and I challenge anyone to rise from the study of these books, and give reasonable grounds for denying that there are large bodies of men in this country fitted in every way for the proper discharge of duties connected with a constitutional form of Government. One or two of the facts may be mentioned, however, to illustrate the nature of this evidence. The total foreign trade of India has reached the figure of £150,000,000 a year, which was the extent of the commerce of the United Kingdom in 1837. We are in precisely the same position as regards commerce that England was in fifty years ago, and yet the mercantile community have not an authoritative word to say about the laws and regulations affecting such a prodigious trade. The income of the British Government in 1837 was £47,200,000, not one penny of which was raised or spent without the sanction of the representatives of the people. The Indian Budget of last year shows an income of £77,000,000, and there is not a man in the country outside the Supreme Council who has a vote or a voice in the matter. (*Loud cheers.*) Since 1858, about £20,000,000 have been spent on educational institutions. The number of these institutions at the present time is 122,000, attended by upwards of 3,300,000 students. The number of schools in England in 1821 was only 18,467, and the scholars 650,000. These, however, have rapidly increased during the last twenty years, but it was not till 1881 that they reached the number of the schools and scholars in this country. Now a statesman or a politician would surely be justified in concluding that the country, of which such facts can be stated, must have within it considerable numbers of men of means, intelligence, industry, foresight and moral grit—the very material out of which good representative institutions can be carved. But there are other considerations that add weight to the testimony of the Blue Books. In all

1st Day.

The President's Inaugural Address.

the discussions that have taken place in Parliament about the inhabitants of India, there is one section which has never been thought of at all—I mean the British non-official class to which I belong. I want to make our existence known. ·We may be known as barristers and solicitors, as bankers, traders, merchants, engineers, editors of newspapers, manufacturers, planters and so forth, but the idea of citizenship, and all that that implies, never seems to have occurred to our rulers in connection with us. I know it has been said that we are already represented. We are English and the Government is English therefore we are represented. But that is a false inference and a pure delusion. We have no more power and no more voice in the Government of the country than you Indians have. The Government is no more ours because it is administered by a Secretary of State who is an Englishman, than the bread in a baker's shop is ours because the shop happens to be kept by an Englishman and not by a Native. (*Laughter and cheers.*) We are all alike held to be on the same low level of unfitness and unripeness. The only thing we are the least bit of good for in the country, from the Governmental point of view, is to be taxed. (*Cheers.*) We are ripe enough for that ; ripe enough to come under the sweep of the Board of Revenue sickle, but unripe for the meanest privileges of subjects of a free country Our number is uncertain. The census tables do not inform us : but, few or many, almost all of us would be voters in England, and I venture to suggest that we would make a passable fraction of a constituency in this country. There is another consideration. There are many thousands of Hindu, Mahomedan, Eurasian, Parsee and other gentlemen in the country, who, if they were to transfer their persons to England for twelve months or more and pay certain rates, would be qualified to enjoy all the rights and privileges of British subjects. If you and I go to England we are qualified. If we return to India our character changes, and we are not qualified. In England we should be trusted citizens. In India, well, the charitably-minded among our opponents say that we are incipient traitors ! (*Loud and prolonged cheers and laughter.*)

There is one more consideration. You know that the Government is accustomed to send some of the Bills it has in preparation to all our leading Associations, both Native and European, for the expression of our opinion upon their provisions. If we be qualified to give an opinion outside the Councils, how much more valuable would that opinion be with the fuller knowledge that can be obtained inside the Councils?

I have thus far spoken of the qualification as having an intellectual as well as a material basis, but I may say here that the only qualification ever known to the British constitution has been the possession of a stake, as it is called, in the country. For four hundred years that stake was a forty-shillings freehold. At the present time it is the occupancy of a house and the payment of certain rates. An educational qualification may be implied in these later days, but it has never formed a test of fitness within the British dominions. But assuming it to be so, then, what I find is that India to-day, taking it all over, is in rather a better state in this respect than England was a century ago. At least every ninth man in India can read and write. Now, I will read you a short extract from an excellent little book by Professor Thorold Rogers called the " British Citizen." He says, speaking of England : " I do not believe that 100 years ago more than one man in ten, or one woman in twenty, knew how to read and write. When I was a youth in a Hampshire village hardly one of the peasantry who was over forty years of age knew how to read. It was deemed superfluous to give even a rudimentary education to the peasant." Going another century or two back, the people of England, man and boy, high and low, with the exception of a mere handful, were steeped in the grossest ignorance, and yet there was a House of Commons. But whatever may be deemed to be a proper qualification in England, or here, it is part of our own case that the great majority of the people is quite unfitted for the franchise. There we are at one with our opponents. But then they say that that is a good reason why the minority should wait until the mass be also qualified. There I think they are wrong. Granted that a man is not entitled to a vote any more than he is entitled to drive a steam engine, and that is my own view of this question ; but because the persons in a country capable of managing steam engines are few compared with those who are not, are we, on that account, to debar the capable few from following their vocation ? (*Cheers.*) In like manner, I contend that if there be but a small minority in a country fitted to exercise the useful function of the franchise, it is a mistake to withhold the privilege from them on the ground that others are not fitted. Given increasing means and growing intelligence, and there invariably follows a desire to have a voice in all matters that concern us ; and I hope it is not difficult to believe that such a desire, " the monition of nature," as Carlyle calls it, " and much to be attended to," has been implanted in the human breast for some wise and good purpose. Happy would it be for the world if, instead of thwarting and repressing such a desire, its rulers nourished it and guided it, as it arose, into the proper channels for its due gratification and exercise. (*Loud cheers.*)

Now, the views and facts I have submitted would seem to warrant some important change in the polity of the country ; but the change we do advocate is one of extreme

1st Day.

The President's Inaugural Address.

moderation, and far within the limits that the circumstances of the country, in my own opinion, would justify. We don't seek to begin, as has been asserted, at the point England has reached after many generations of constitutional Government. We don't want the strong meat of full age, but we want to be weaned. We say there are numbers of us who have had the feeding bottle long enough. We desire no sudden snapping of existing ties; we ask only for the loosening of the bonds. We are content to regard ourselves as in the position of the man who has long been confined in a darkened room on account of disordered eyesight. We know that under the skilful treatment of a kindly physician our visual powers have been strengthened. We have sense enough not to demand the full blaze of day to be suddenly let in upon us, but only such a drawing-aside of the curtains as will adjust the light to our powers of vision. But, if the physician, skilful and kindly as we recognise him to be, were to insist upon our remaining in the dark, we should be forced to the unwelcome conclusion that his skill was resultless and abortive, or that the unlovable side of his character had manifested itself in that he wished to keep us in the dark for some unworthy purpose of his own. If under such treatment we became discontented with his services, the blame of it would be with the physician and not with the patient. (*Cheers.*)

Now, Gentlemen, I will state more definitely the change we desire. We want the Legislative Councils to be expanded to an extent that will admit of the representation of the various interests in the country, as far as that may be practicable. We want half the Councils to be elected, the other half to be in the appointment of Government, and we are willing that the right of veto should be with the Executive. We also want the right of interpellation. These are the substance of our wants. We propose that the constituencies should consist of Members of Municipalities, Chambers of Commerce, Trades Associations; associations like the British Indian Association, and, generally, all persons possessing such qualifications, educational and pecuniary, as may be deemed necessary. We should have to go far back in the history of England to find a parallel to the limited privileges we should be content with,—to the time, at all events, of Edward the First, 600 years ago, when Barons and Commons sat together, and when King and Barons held the sway. We are not wedded even to these proposals. The principle of election frankly accepted, there would be little difficulty in satisfying us in the matter of the constituencies, or as to the size of the Councils. The devising of a suitable elective body might well be left to the Government, or better still, by way of a preliminary, to the final judgment of the Government, to a small Commission which could easily be rendered acceptable to the whole community. Happily there is no scarcity of men in the country, both among the official and non-official classes, abundantly qualified for such a work. I should like to mention the names of half-a-dozen such men chiefly for the purpose of dissipating the fears of those who seem to think we have some revolutionary scheme in view, and not because they only are competent for such an undertaking. If you were willing to commit the working-out of the practical details of the reform we ask for to the men I wish to name, we ought to hear the last of the reckless charges that are made against us. The first I have in my mind's eye is that wary, sagacious Scotchman who has just closed a long and honorable career of worthy service among us, Sir Charles Aitchison. The second is an Englishman, no less qualified by experience and by endowment of head and heart for the task, Sir Steuart Bayley. The next is the veteran statesman from the Southern Provinces, Sir Madhava Rao. The next is a Mahomedan of tried legislative ability from the Bombay side of the peninsula, Budrudin Tyabjee. The next is a gentleman from Bengal whose character and talents have placed him in the front rank of his profession, W. C. Bonnerjee. These five men presided over, and the balance held even between them, by such an one as the Governor of Bombay or Madras would, I believe, produce a scheme which would secure the approval of the Government, allay the fears of the timid, and satisfy the aspiring ones among us for a generation at least. (*Loud cheers.*)

I fear I have occupied your time to an unreasonable length, but I wish to trespass on your indulgence for a short time longer for the purpose of making a few remarks on the speech of the ex-Viceroy at the Scotch Dinner in Calcutta. All movements of the kind in which we are concerned pass through several phases as they run their course. The first is one of ridicule. That is followed, as the movement progresses, by one of abuse, which is usually succeeded by partial concession and misapprehension of aim, accompanied by warnings against taking "big jumps into the unknown." The final stage of all is a substantial adoption of the object of the movement with some expression of surprise that it was not adopted before. These various phases overlap each other, but between the first and last the distinction is complete.

Well, we are out and away from the comical aspect of the movement. It has become too serious for that, and we are midway between the abusive and misapprehensive stages. In the speech of our ex-Viceroy we have, as might be expected, none of the coarser instruments of attack—indeed, I find a vein of sympathy with us running through his speech—and we have partial concession, misapprehension regarding some of our

1st Day.

The President's Inaugural Address.

demands, and, in consequence, the usual warning voice. The concession I refer to is as regards the separation of the Executive and Judicial functions. This was one of the ridiculous proposals, one of those school-boy clamours to start with. but the Viceroy now tells us that "this is a counsel of perfection to which we are ready to subscribe." Allow me to congratulate you upon this concession so frankly and handsomely made. All that we want now is to see the concession of the principle reduced into practice. ("*Hear, hear.*") The misapprehension is contained in the following sentence: "The ideal authoritatively suggested, as I understand, is the creation of a representative body or bodies, in which the official element shall be in a minority, who shall have what is called the power of the purse, and who through this instrumentality shall be able to bring the British Executive into subjection to their will." Now, Gentlemen, if there be one thing more than another that we have tried to make clear, it is that the British Executive should continue to be paramount in the Councils. We have made it as clear as the English language is capable of expressing thought, that the utmost we want is that half of the Councils be elected; the other half to be wholly in the nomination of the Government. These may be all officials or not, just as the Government pleases, and we have made it equally clear, in addition, that the Government should have the right to veto all adverse votes. Such an arrangement guarantees the supremacy of the Executive under all circumstances, aye, even if their own side vote against them. But, is it to be assumed that the elected members are all to vote adversely? Is it to be supposed that any measure of the Executive will be such as to be condemned by every section of the community? I hope no British Executive will ever take leaps into the dark to lead to such a result. Well, the Viceroy having started upon an assumption that is not only incorrect, but is the very opposite of the fact, it follows that his condemnation does not apply to us at all, but to a fanciful piece of workmanship of which we are not the artists. The Viceroy must necessarily depend largely upon his subordinates for correct information about the details of this and other movements, and it looks to me as if one of those compilers of facts had fallen into some grievous error. The authoritative views of the Congress are to be found in its resolutions, and the resolution about the reform of the Councils is the third one of the first meeting of the Congress three years ago, and that resolution has been the one affirmed at the following meetings. We are in no way bound even by any statement or argument that any speaker may make in supporting that resolution; but I say with the greatest confidence that, neither in the resolution itself, nor in the speeches of the gentlemen supporting it, is a word to be found that justifies the "ideal authoritatively suggested." There may be some remarks in letters to newspapers, in pamphlets, or in speeches made by members of the Congress that give support to the "ideal." I don't know of them, and if I did, I should regret them, just as I might regret any of our members having a hump back; but I should feel no responsibility for either his back or speech. If we be charged with encouraging "ideals" on such grounds, we may as logically be charged, in the other event, as a Congress for promoting deformed spines! ("*Hear hear,*" *and laughter.*) It is annoying to us, no doubt, that our friends, as I take Lord Dufferin to be, should be deceived by imitations of our ticket; but as we have no Trade Mark Bill to protect our wares, all that we can do is to warn our friends to ask for the real article and to see that they get it. (*Loud and continued cheers.*)

And now, Gentlemen, I wish to say, in conclusion, that I have a strong faith that our limited enfranchisement is in the near and not in the distant future. No rational mind can believe that the present system can go on for ever,—that it is the last will and dying testament of Providence regarding us. (*Laughter.*) We are, I trust, the heirs of a better hope. A careful reading of the speeches and writings of our leading officials leads me to believe that they would be glad to see this matter settled; and I do not exclude Sir Auckland Colvin from this category. His objection seems to be to some of the bye-play and not to the general drift of the drama. The great difficulty hitherto has been to find the time to deal with the subject. Lord Dufferin had his thoughts too fully occupied with the troubles on the frontier and in Burmah to give adequate attention to this question, which is apparent in the mistake he has fallen into regarding our demands. And I for one regret that it has not fallen to his lot to add a new lustre to his name, and to establish a further claim upon our regard by promoting a measure such as we advocate,—a measure which any statesman might well be proud to be the instrument of carrying; for it is one which (while going a long way, if not the whole way, in calming the present agitation) would draw into closer connection the two extreme branches of the Aryan race, the common subjects of the Queen-Empress: a measure which would unite England and India, not by the hard and brittle bonds of arbitrary rule which may snap in a moment, but by the flexible and more enduring ligaments of common interests promoted, common duties discharged, by means of a common service, chosen with some regard to the principles of representative Government.

(*Here the President had to pause for a time, to allow the prolonged storm of applause and cheering which greeted the conclusion of his address to wear itself out. Then he resumed as follows.*)

1st Day.

The President's Inaugural Address

And now, Gentlemen, I will ask you before we separate to appoint a Subject Committee, who will discuss the subjects to be brought before the Congress to-morrow and on the subsequent days, frame tentative resolutions on these subjects, and settle the names of the gentlemen who are to be invited to propose, second and support these Resolutions.

Now, it is extremely desirable that this Subject Committee should not be too large and unwieldy, but after consulting the leading delegates, from every Province, it seems agreed that it is impossible, if its representative character is to be preserved, to reduce the number of the members of this committee below 106.

The numbers to be allotted to each circle have been most carefully considered in consultation with a great number of delegates, and I will ask you to accept these as now settled, *viz.* :—

For the Calcutta Circle, *viz*, Lower Bengal, Orissa and Assam	18
For the Behar Circle, *viz.*, the Patna, Bhagulpur and Hazaribagh Divisions ...	7
For the Benares and N.-W. Provinces Circles	16
For the Oudh Circle	8
For the Punjab and Delhi Circles	17
For the Sindh Circle	3
For the Guzerat Circle	4
For the Bombay Circle	4
For the Poona Circle	6
For the Berar Circle	3
For the Nagpur Circle, *viz.*, the Central Provinces	8
For the Madras Circle	12

Election of the Subject Committee.

I will now ask the delegates from each circle to elect from amongst themselves the number of delegates that I have just mentioned for their respective circles, to represent them on the Subject Committee.

The following gentlemen were then elected to be members of the Subject Committee, *viz.* :—

CALCUTTA CIRCLE (*Lower Bengal, Orissa and Assam*).

ISWAR CHANDRA DAS (Dacca). No. 1223.
BAIKUNTHA NATH SEN (Berhampur). No. 1192.
NUFER CHANDER PAL CHOWDHRY (Krishnagur). No. 1174.
ANATH BANDHU GUHA (Mymensingh). No. 1240.
NILMONI CHOWDHRY (Rajshahye). No 1211.
MOHESH CHANDER CHOWDHRY (Burdwan). No. 1101.
BEPIN CHANDRA PAL (Assam). No. 1245.
AMBIKA CHARAN MAZUMDAR (Furridpur). No. 1210.
MOULVI MAHOMED HAFIZ (Burrisal). No. 1204.
MOTI LAL GHOSE (Jessore). No. 1112.
NARENDRA NATH SEN (Calcutta). No. 1106.
RAJKUMAR SARVADHIKARI (ditto). No. 1099.
KALI CHARAN BANERJEE (ditto). No. 1135.
SURENDRA NATH BANERJEE (ditto). No. 1128.
MANOMOHUN GHOSE, ESQ. (ditto). No. 1111.
W. C. BONNERJEE, ESQ. (ditto). No. 1098.
J. GHOSAL, ESQ. (ditto). No. 1100.
18 MOHAMED ALTAHAR (Orissa). No. 1244.

BEHAR CIRCLE (*Patna, Bhagalpur and Hazaribagh Divisions*).

BABOO SALIG RAM SINGH (Patna Division). No. 1104.
„ GURU PRASAD SEN (ditto). No. 1016.
MR. SHARF-UD-DIN (ditto). No. 1083.
MR. PRINGLE KENNEDY (ditto). No. 1049.
BABOO TARINI PRASAD (Bhagalpur Division). No. 1090.
MOULVI ABDUL RAHMAN (ditto). No. 1032.
7 RAI JADU NATH MOOKERJI (Hazaribagh Division). No. 1028.

N.-W. P. AND BENARES CIRCLES.

THE HON BLE PANDIT AJOODHIA NATH (Allahabad). No. 551.
PANDIT BISHAMBHER NATH (ditto). No. 552.
RAJA RAMPAL SINGH (ditto). No. 571.
MR. J. E. HOWARD, Barrister-at-Law (ditto). No. 573.
PANDIT MADAN MOHAN MALAVIYA, B.A.(ditto). No. 569.
MOULVI ABDUL JALIL (Cawnpur). No. 720.
RAJAH LUCHMAN SINGH (Agra). No. 707.
BABOO JAMNA DAS BISWAS (Agra). No. 687.
HAFIZ ABDUR RAHIM (Aligurh). No. 797.
MR. PYARI LAL, Barrister-at-Law (Meerut). No. 768.
BABOO RAMKALI CHOWDHRY (Benares). No. 872.
MR. W. DIGBY, C.I.E. (Allahabad). No, 631.
SHEIKH NASIR-UD-DIN (Benares). No. 880.
MIR WAHID ALI (Rohilkhund). No. 526.
PANDIT JWALADATT JOSHI (Almora). No. 840.
16 MR. GOPI NATH (Ajmere). No. 992.

1st Day.

Election of Subject Committee.

OUDH CIRCLE ...		SHEIKH RAZA HOSSEIN KHAN (Lucknow). No. 439.
		MUNSHI GANGA PRASAD VARMA (ditto). No. 471.
		MR. HAMID ALI KHAN, Barrister-at-Law (Lucknow). No. 435.
		„ GOKUL CHAND (Faizabad). No. 482.
		MUNSHI SAJJAD HUSEIN (Lucknow) No. 434.
		CAPTAIN HEARSAY (Lucknow). No. 841.
		MR. ALI MOHAMED BHIMJEE (Lucknow). No. 455.
	8	„ BISHAN NARAYAN DAR, Barrister-at-Law (Lucknow). No. 437.
PUNJAB AND DELHI CIRCLES.		SIRDAR DYAL SINGH MAJETHIA (Lahore). No. 341.
		LALA KANHAIYA LAL (Lahore). No. 342.
		PANDIT SHEO NARAYAN (Jullundhur). No. 370.
		„ S. M. AGNIHOTRI (Lahore). No. 344.
		MR. C. GOLAKNATH, Barrister-at-Law (Lahore). No. 340.
		„ J. C. BASU (Lahore). No. 346.
		„ K. P. ROY (ditto). No. 337.
		LALA MURLIDHAR (Umballa). No. 376.
		SHEIKH UMR BAKSH (Hoshiarpur). No. 361.
		LALA GIRDHARILAL (Delhi). No. 393.
		„ LAJPAT RAI (Hissar). No. 348.
		SYED SARDAR ALI SAHIB (Ludhiana). No. 381.
		UMRAO MIRZA HAIRAT (Delhi). No. 397.
		MOULVI MAHBUB ALAM (Gujranwala). No. 367.
		CAPTAIN BANON (Dharamsala). No. 374.
		MOULVI MANSUR ALI (Delhi). No. 411.
	17	SHEIKH SHARF-UD-DIN (Ludhiana). No. 383.
SINDH CIRCLE ...		RAO BAHADUR GOVIND BUKSH AWATRAI (Sukkur). No. 238.
		RAO SAHIB TAHILRAM KHEMCHAND (Karachi). No. 241.
	3	MR. N. GUPTA (Karachi). No. 239.
GUZERAT CIRCLE ...		MR. S. N. PANDIT, Barrister-at-Law (Rajkot). No. 257.
		„ YUSAF ALI JEMADAR, B.A. (Kaira) No. 244.
		RAO SAHIB KESHAVLAL MOTILAL (Ahmedabad). No. 245.
	4	RAO SAHIB MOHANLAL RANCHODDAS (Surat). No 248.
BOMBAY CIRCLE ...		THE HON'BLE KASHINATH TRIMBAK TELANG, M.A., LL.B., C.I.E. (Bombay). No. 201.
		THE HON'BLE PHEROZSHAH M. MEHTA, Barrister-at-Law (Bombay). No. 208.
		MR N. G. CHANDAVARKAR, B.A., LL.B. (Bombay). No. 203.
	4	MR. D. E. WACHA. No. 204.
POONA CIRCLE ...		RAO BAHADUR V. M. BHIDE (Poona). No. 96.
		MR. M. B. NAMJOSHI (ditto.). No. 101.
		„ K. V. PATWARDHAN (Ahmednagar). No. 150.
		„ S. R. KIRLOSKAR, B.A. (Sholapur). No. 168.
		„ SADASIVA BOLKRISHNA BHATE (Belgaum). No. 170.
	6	„ FRAMJI MANCHERJEE (Satara). No. 140.
BERAR CIRCLE ...		RAO SAHIB DEVARAO VINAYEK (Akola). No. 273.
		R. N. MUDHOLKAR, B.A., LL.B. (Amraoti). No. 259.
	3	MR. P. N. JOG, B.A., LL.B. (ditto). No. 275.
CENTRAL PROVINCES CIRCLE.		MR. JAGANNATH PRASAD (Hoshangabad). No. 304.
		„ BEPIN KRISHA BOSE, M.A., B.L. (Nagpur). No. 285.
		„ BAPU RAO DADA, M.A. (ditto). No. 290.
		„ SADA SHIVA R. C. PATWARDHAN (Harda). No. 325.
		„ HARI DASS CHATTERJI, M.A., B.L. (Khundwa). No. 313.
		„ HARIVAMAN KELKAR, B.A., B.L. (Wardha). No. 322.
		„ K. G. DESHPANDE, M.A. (Nagpur). No. 291.
	8	„ BIHARI LAL, B.A. (Jubulpore). No. 298.
MADRAS CIRCLE ...		M. R. RY. S. RAMASWAMI MUDALIAR, M.A., B.L., F.M.U. No. 15.
		RAI BAHADUR A. SABAPATHY MUDELLIAR (Bellary). No. 70.
		C. VIJIARAGHAVA CHARIAR, ESQ., B.A. (Salem). No. 90.
		EARDLEY NORTON, ESQ., Barrister-at-Law (Madras). No. 19.
		JOHN ADAM, ESQ., M.A., F.M.U. (ditto). No. 2.
		M. R. RY. G. SUBRAMANIA IYER, ESQ., B.A. (ditto). No. 20.
		M. R. RY. M. VIRARAGHAVA CHARIAR, B.A. (ditto). No. 21.
		M. R. RY. C. SANKARA NAIR, B.A., B.L., F.M.U. (Malabar). No. 17.

1st Day.

Election of Subject Committee.

MADRAS CIRCLE (*contd.*) ABDUL RAHIMAN SAHIB, ESQ. (Coimbatore). No. 87.
M. R. RY. C. JAMBULINGA MUDALIAR, B.A., M.L. (Cuddapah). No. 58.
M. R. RY. N. SUBBA RAO, B.A., B.L. (Godavari). No. 38,
M. R. RY. M. G. AROKIASWAMI PILLAI, B.A. (Coimbatore).
12 No. 86.

Adjournment.

The elections having been completed and announced by the President and ratified unanimously by all the delegates, cheers were called for, simultaneously, by at least a score of delegates, for Her Majesty the Queen-Empress, and these having been enthusiastically given, over and over again, the President at about 5 P.M. notified the adjournment of the assembly till next day, and the meeting commenced to disperse. But some considerable time elapsed before the last cheers for Her Majesty were given, and the Subject Committee was able to gather together on the President's platform and commence work.

The Subject Committee sat till late that night and resumed work next morning sitting till 1 P.M.

SECOND DAY'S PROCEEDINGS.

Thursday, December 27th, 1888.

2nd Day.

Presentation of Casket, Report, &c., &c.

THE Congress re-assembled at 2 P.M. of the 27th. Immediately on the President's taking his seat—

MR. JUGMOHUNDAS VANDRAVANDAS—(*Bombay, No. 225 in list*)—rose and said: Sir, as spokesman and representative of my community—the Dasa Porwad Banya community of Bombay—I rise to present to you this humble token of our sympathy in the cause of the Congress, and our respect, Sir, for you as President. It is a silver casket containing Rs. 175, and we desire that these Rs. 175 may be taken as our mite towards the expenses of this great gathering, and that you, Sir, may be pleased, yourself, to retain the casket as a memento alike of this Congress and of the respect and good will with which we, all, here regard you. (*Loud cheers.*)

THE PRESIDENT in reply said: I have very much pleasure, indeed, in accepting, on behalf of the Congress, the contents of this casket; and, as I understand that it is the intention of the donors that, while you get the contents, I myself get the casket, I have even greater pleasure in accepting that casket for myself. (*Laughter and cheers.*) Believe me, I shall ever preserve it as a memento of this great and important meeting, and in grateful remembrance of the honor that you have done me in electing me to be its President. ("*Hear, hear,*" *and cheers*). And now, Gentlemen, we must proceed to business, and I have to submit to you one or two small regulations by which I propose to guide my Presidential action. The first rule that I desire to observe is this: Proposers of resolutions will be allowed ten minutes in which to set forth their motions (and this, I believe, is in accordance with the precedents of previous Congresses); while seconders of resolutions and all other speakers will be restricted to five minutes. In the case of amendments I see no necessity for further law, and I propose to allow the movers and the seconders of such only the same five minutes allowed to other speakers. The other regulation or suggestion—for it scarcely amounts to a rule—is that all speakers able to speak in English should speak in that language, because a far larger proportion of the delegates understand English than any other language; and it is hence the most appropriate for our debates. No departure from this rule will be allowed except in the cases of those delegates who are *bonâ fide* unable to address an audience in English. (*Cheers and cries of* "*Quite right.*")

MR. EARDLEY NORTON—(*Madras, No. 19 in list*)—rose, and, laying a printed report on the table, said: Sir, on behalf of the Madras Standing Congress Committee, I have the honour of laying on your table a report drawn up of the work done by our Committee during the past year under the resolutions passed at last Congress.

MR R. N. MUDHOLKAR—(*Berar, No. in 259 list*)—next presented a report to the President and said: Sir, on behalf of the Berar Standing Congress Committee, of which I am the Secretary, I beg to present this report of the work done by our Committee in 1888, and lay it on the table for the information of those members of the Congress who may care to read it.

MR. VISHNU MORESHWAR BHIDE—(*Poona, No. 96 in list*)—next rose, and presenting a report said: Sir, I beg to present a report of the proceedings of the Provincial Conference held at Poona, at the invitation of our Standing Congress Committee, in connection with the work of the Congress, and lay it on the table for the information of the members.

Res. I

Reform of the Legislative Councils.

THE HON. K. T. TELANG—(*Bombay, No. 201 in list*)—then addressed the assembly as follows: Mr. President and brother delegates,—I have the honour to move the first resolution, which runs as follows:—

"*That this Congress do affirm the necessity for the expansion and reform of the Council of the Governor-General for making laws and regulations, and the Provincial Legislative Councils, already set forth in Resolutions III of the Congresses of 1885 and 1886, and Resolution II of the Congress of 1887, a tentative scheme for which expansion and reform was suggested in Resolution IV of the Congress of 1886.*"

I think you will see from the terms of the resolution that its substance hardly requires much explanation or much in the way of remark to commend it to the acceptance of the delegates here assembled from all parts of the Empire. The subject-

2nd Day.

Res. I., Reform of the Legislative Councils.

matter of that resolution has been considered by each of the three Congresses which have been held in Bombay, Calcutta and Madras, and this Congress is to be asked to re-affirm the proposition which was passed by those Congresses. It would, therefore, be pure surplusage if I were to address any lengthened remarks to the Congress in support of the subject-matter of this resolution. The subject to which the resolution refers has not only been fully discussed and debated by the three Congresses which have been already held, but has also been debated and discussed outside these, both in the public press and at innumerable public meetings. And it has been discussed not only by those who sympathize with the Congress, but also by other bodies and individuals throughout the Empire; and the conclusions at which they have all, as a rule, arrived have been in full accord with the resolutions which the various Congresses have already passed. (*Cheers.*) After all this threshing out of the matter dealt with in this resolution, it would be unpardonable were I now to inflict on the Congress any lengthened dissertation on the main question at issue. But there are certain points in connection with this resolution which have been raised in recent controversies, and brought forward by gentlemen who are authorities upon Indian questions, and whose remarks, observations and suggestions are unquestionably entitled to the greatest attention, to which I am constrained to refer.

One of our critics who, in this particular part of the Empire, will easily be identified—I mean the Lieutenant-Governor of these provinces—has said that the Congress, in putting forward this suggestion about the expansion and reform of the Legislative Councils, has not suggested anything of a very novel or original character; that the thing which the Congress has been asking for is one which has been considered long before the Congress was dreamt of. And he has made this observation as though this fact might be supposed to throw some discredit on the work of the Congress. (*"Hear, hear."*) Perhaps discredit is a stronger word than should be used; but the remark has been made at any rate in a depreciatory sense. Now, speaking for myself, I must say that I consider that remark as by no means one to which we need object. When a scheme does not issue forth in full panoply, as it were, from the brain of a single author, but is the synthesis of the best thoughts of many brains during a long period, it is considered in practical politics as rather a merit than a defect; and therefore when Sir Auckland tells us that our suggestion is one which has been put forward long before this Congress came into existence, I welcome that remark as one of the certificates to the work of the Congress (*cheers*), and I consider it rather satisfactory than the reverse. (*Cheers.*)

But, Gentlemen, we have had criticism from another quarter, about which also it is necessary to speak, though not in any great detail. We have all read Lord Dufferin's speech at the St. Andrew's Dinner at Calcutta, and in this too we have seen some criticisms upon our work, which similarly deserve some passing notice. For my own part, I am prepared to treat Lord Dufferin's criticism as on the whole friendly criticism, and as a piece of warning and advice coming from a friendly quarter which deserves all the attention which can be bestowed upon it. But while I am prepared to welcome His Lordship's deliverances from that point of view, I think it my duty to point out from my place here that some of his Lordship's criticisms and statements have been based upon a complete misapprehension of the actual facts of the case. (*"Hear, hear," and cheers.*)

I hold in my hand a newspaper report of what his Lordship said at Calcutta, and I think it is desirable to refresh your memory by reading the exact words of His Lordship's remarks in regard to the work of the Congress. "And now, Gentlemen," Lord Dufferin said, "some intelligent, loyal, patriotic and well-meaning men are desirous of taking, I will not say a further step in advance, but a very big jump into the unknown, by the application to India of democratic methods of Government and the adoption of a Parliamentary system which England herself has reached by slow degrees and through the discipline of many centuries. The ideal authoritatively suggested, gentlemen, as I understand" [mark, please, the qualification implied in, "as I understand"] "is the creation of a representative body or bodies in which the official element shall be in a minority, who shall have what is called the power of the purse, and who, through this instrumentality, shall be able to bring the British Executive into subjection to their will." Before I pass on to another portion of his Lordship's speech, I will pause here for the purpose of pointing out that every one of the statements made here by his Lordship is inaccurate as applied to any proposal that has ever been passed, at any previous Congress or any proposal that you will be asked at this Congress to pass. (*Cheers.*) His Lordship begins by saying that we ask for democratic methods of Government for India. You have all of you, I suppose, read the reports of the three Congresses which have been already held. I myself took part in the first, but was unfortunately unable to attend the second and the third Congresses. I have, however, read the reports, and have failed to find in them anything of which it can be fairly said that either the Congress as a whole, or any individual member of it, has asked for the application of democratic methods of Government to India. (*Cheers.*) The next charge is that we are asking for "the adoption of a Parliamentary system which England herself has only reached by slow degrees, and through the discipline of many centuries of preparation." I say that precisely the same remark that I made with regard to the first clause is applicable to this. We have asked for no such thing, as will be obvious to those who will consider the precise terms of our resolution; and when Lord Dufferin, so cautious and circumspect a statesman as he is, has been so inaccurate in his observations, I can only conclude that His Lordship has not had time to read our reports, and that he has taken his information at second hand, as indeed is indicated by the qualifying remark, "as I understand." (*Cheers.*) His Lordship says: "The idea authoritatively suggested, as I understand, is the creation of a representative body or bodies in which the official element shall be in a minority, who shall have what is called the power of the purse, and who, through this instrumentality, shall be able to bring the British Executive into subjection to their will." The basis for that statement is our demand that the financial statement shall be brought before the Council for discussion. ("*Hear, hear.*") Not only do I not find in any of the reports any grounds for such a statement, but I find what is actually the reverse of it. (*Cheers.*) It has been said over and over again that the Executive shall have the power of deciding what shall be done, and of absolutely vetoing any proposal emanating from the rest of the Council; and yet in face of such a resolution as this, which we have passed not once, not twice, but three times, such a statement has been made by his Lordship. I can only express my amazement at it, and I cannot believe His Lordship to have been capable of making it, except on the assumption that he has lacked the time to study our reports himself. (*Cheers.*) The various charges which His Lordship makes against the Congress are charges which remind me of a certain definition which was once given of a crab, *viz.*, that a crab is a red fish which walks backwards; and the criticism made upon that was that the definition was perfectly correct, except that the crab was not a fish, that it was not red, and that it did not walk backwards. (*Laughter.*) Now, I may say that Lord Dufferin's criticism is perfectly correct; except that we have not asked for democratic methods of Government; we have not asked for Parliamentary institutions which England has got after many centuries of discipline; we have not asked for the power of the purse; and we have not asked that the British Executive should be brought under subjection to us. (*Laughter and prolonged cheers.*)

If you permit me, I will go on to the next passage in which he says: "I am afraid the people of England will not be readily brought to the acceptance of this programme, or to allow such an assembly, or a number of such assemblies, either to interfere with its armies, or to fetter and circumscribe the liberty of action, either of the Provincial Governments, or of the Supreme Executive." I say this is a programme which is not brought forward officially or unofficially by the Congress. We have never dreamt of or asked for such things as Lord Dufferin supposes. We have—I say we have explicitly—declared that the right of interpellation which we ask for must not extend to questions military or political. (*Cheers.*) Then again he goes on to say: "In the first place, the whole scheme is eminently unconstitutional; for the essence of constitutional Government is that responsibility and power should remain in the same hands, and the idea of irresponsible Councils, whose members could never be called to account for their acts in the way in which an opposition can be called to account in a constitutional country, arresting the march of Indian legislation, or nullifying the policy of the British Executive in India, would be regarded as an impracticable anomaly." I entirely agree in this view of His Lordship, only I do not see what application it has to anything said by the Congress. We have never asked for a divorce between power and responsibility. We have, on the contrary, distinctly said that the responsibility must rest with the Executive, and that, therefore, they must have the power of rejecting any resolution and vetoing any proposal, even though such should come from a majority of the Council. ("*Hear, hear.*") I need only say, in conclusion, that the criticisms which have been made upon us by the late Viceroy are criticisms which have no manner of application to the resolutions we have passed, or the proposals we have made, but relate rather to some imaginary scheme which somehow seems to have floated through Lord Dufferin's brains, but of which we of the Congress had never even so much as heard, until he enunciated it. (*Prolonged cheers.*)

BABU SURENDRANATH BANERJEE—(*Bengal, No.* 1128 *in list*)—in seconding the resolution on the expansion of the Legislative Councils, spoke as follows: Brother-Delegates,—I cannot shut my eyes to the grave responsibility which I incur, in common with my leader, in having to speak to this resolution. It is the most important resolution in your programme. (*Cheers.*) You have chosen to put it in the forefront among the topics to be discussed by this Congress. Round it have gathered that mass of misconceptions which the organs of your public opinion have been at so much pains to dispel. It has been the chief theme of controversy and of complaint. It is the one point in your armour against which your opponents have hurled their sharpest darts with merciless severity and with unflagging steadiness. For my part, I may say that I welcome this opposition. I rejoice at it, and I thank God with all my heart that it has pleased Him in His inscrutable Providence to subject us to this ordeal and to the chastening influence of this severe discipline. Nothing but good can come out of it. (*Cheers.*) Causes the noblest, the most beneficent, the most far-reaching in their consequences for good have never prospered or triumphed except under the stress of adverse criticism. (*Cheers.*) Comparing great things with small, I may say that

2nd Day.

Res. I., Reform of the Legislative Councils.

the noblest page of Christian history has always appeared to me to be that which records the triumphant sufferings and is ensanguined with the blood of the martyrs of early Christianity. ("*Hear, hear.*") There is nothing more attractive in Moslem annals than that which describes Mohamed as flying from the hands of his persecuting relatives, seeking a home and an asylum at Medina, and there installlng himself as king, prophet, priest, the deliverer of his people. So in our case, the opposition will do nothing bnt good. It will put us on our mettle and bring out all that is good in us. Lord Dufferin has done us a service, the magnitude of which it is impossible to exaggerate, and for which we should be truly grateful. (*Loud cheers.*) He has done for you by his speech at St. Andrew's Dinner what you could not have done for yourselves by twenty years of persistent agitation. By one great bound—a big jump into the unknown—the National Congress has taken its place among the foremost topics of discussion in English political circles, and has arrested the attention of leading English politicians. (*Cheers.*) The National Congress and the expansion of your Legislative Councils are now being discussed by the fire-sides of English homes, around the tables of English Clubs, and upon the platforms of English public meetings. Not the least valuable of your acquisitions has been that of Mr. Gladstone. Only three months ago, in a conversation with the Nawab Mohsin-ul-Mulk of Hyderabad, he professed ignorance of the programme of the Congress, and thought that it was associated in some way with Mr. Malabari's agitation. But mark what he said only the other day in his Lime-house speech. He spoke in terms of strong sympathy with the National Congress. (*Loud cheers.*) He observed: "It will not do for us to treat with contempt or even with indifference the rising aspirations of this great people." (*Loud cheers.*) When a statesman in the position of Mr. Gladstone, long the Prime Minister of England, still the trusted leader of a great party, the hope of Ireland —its future deliverer—holds views such as these, we may say with confidence that we are within measurable distance of victory. (*Tremendous cheering for Mr. Gladstone, the audience rising up.*) I hope and trust the mighty voice of a great nation will go forth from this hall and be wafted across mountains, seas and deserts, and reach the ears of Mr. Gladstone as the expression of our personal regard for him and of our sympathy for his labours. (*Cheers.*)

I must say that it is with a sense of pain that I listened to the statement made by the Hon'ble Pandit Ajoodhia Nath regarding the petty official opposition which the efforts of the Reception Committee encountered at each stage. When the story of this spiteful and unworthy persecution is published in this country, and when it is repeated in England, I am sure there will be one universal feeling of indignation throughout the country, which I hope will teach the local officials a lesson which they have yet to learn. (*Cheers.*) I must say that it seems to me a marvel that there should be any misconception with regard to the nature of our demands. "Demands," do I say? We have really made none. We have put forth some tentative suggestions regarding the reform and expansion of the Legislative Councils. We pin our faith to no particular system, to no special programme. We say so in terms as clear as the resources of the English language can supply. We say (and I quote the very words of the Resolution of 1886), "whatever may be the scheme that may be adopted, care should be taken that all sections of the community and all great interests are adequately represented." (*Cheers.*) All that we pray for—all that the Congress has ever asked for—is the acceptance, in a modified form, of the representative principle in the constitution of the Legislative Councils, with a due regard for the interests of all sections of the community. I will not hesitate to say that it seems to me inexplicable that there should be any misconception with regard to our programme. There is a singular vein of inconsistency running through much of what has been said and written on the subject by our official critics. Sir Auckland Colvin says in that letter, with which we are all so familiar, and of which I desire to speak with the utmost possible respect, that he saw nothing to object to in the programme of the first Congress, nothing to object to in the proceedings of the second Congress. But then there came a reaction in his mind when he read the Report of the third Congress. If there was nothing to object to in the proceedings of the first and the second Congresses, does it stand to reason that he should take exception to the third, which re-affirmed the most important Resolutions of the second Congress? (*Cheers.*) But then he goes beyond the limits of the Congress programme; there are the conversations and catechisms which have upset the official classes, and account for this change of feeling. I am not here to defend these conversations and catechisms. (*Laughter and cheers.*) I see the distinguished authors of these productions on this platform, and they are quite able to take care of themselves. (*Renewed lauhgter.*) But it is in connection with this charge of sedition, that is too often so recklessly brought against us, that I desire, in your name and on your behalf (and in this matter re-echoing the sentiments of the Chairman of the Reception Committee), to enter my most emphatic protest. (*Loud cheers.*) Apart from sentimental considerations —which are no mean considerations with a people so highly sensitive and emotional as we are—is it for one moment to be supposed that we have become so idiotic and have taken such utter leave of our senses as not to see that we owe all that we possess—our position and our prestige—to the English connection? (*Cheers.*) Let that connection come to an end, and we lose with it all that we hold most dear in life. Our opponents have charged us with being seditionists, but they have never failed to give us credit for sense. In our case, however, sedition means a measure of folly that is only consistent with idiotcy. The charge can only stand upon the one assumption, that the educated community of India have become demented. (*Laughter.*) For my part I may say—and I believe that in this matter I express the sense of this great Congress—that I regard the connection between England and India as Providential, and that England is here for one of the noblest purposes of history. (*Loud cheers.*) I can find nothing more glorious in the matchless record of England's fame than that under her influence this mighty national awakening should take place which finds its highest expression in this great and historical gathering of the National Congress. (*Cheers.*)

Our programme for the expansion and reform of the Legislative Councils which we are called upon to re-affirm by this Resolution is extremely moderate. It is neither a Parliamentary system, nor representative Government, nor the application of democratic methods to Indian institutions that we seek for. Our demand is much more moderate than that. All that we want is to rescue the present Legislative Councils from their character as monstrous shams, and convert them into useful consultative assemblies which may help the Government in the difficult task which Providence has assigned to it ; and in India, more than in any other country, is such a step necessary where there are so many races and nationalities and such diversified interests. Therefore even for administrative purposes if for nothing else, the reconstitution of the Councils has become a necessity. (*Cheers.*) We desire to place non-official opinion on an organized footing for purposes of consultation by the Government. Non-official opinion is consulted now. We say it should be consulted in a more formal and methodical manner. We have no wish to assume sovereign authority. The supreme power will remain where it is vested at present. We only desire that we may be consulted in its exercise. According to our programme, half the members of the Legislative Councils are to be elected, the rest being nominated by Government. Under the existing law, one-third of the members must at least be non-officials. We pray for an increase in the proportion of non-official members from one-third to one-half, and we further suggest that they should be elected. We attach the utmost importance to the principle of election. A partially elective system is the platform on which we take our stand. That platform we can never quit, and by it we shall judge every system which may be devised for the reform of the Councils. The next point in our programme is that the Budgets should be discussed in Council ; and in this respect we only want a partial extension of a principle already admitted and acted upon. The Budget is now discussed in the Supreme Council, but only when a new measure of taxation is proposed. The Congress suggests that the Budgets should be discussed on all occasions in the Provincial as well as in the Supreme Council, and whether a new scheme of taxation is proposed or not. There is a singular unanimity of opinion in connection with this part of the programme of the Congress. The Chambers of Commerce throughout the country have repeated the same demand and with marked persistency. Intimately connected with this part of our programme is the right of interpellation. The discussion of the Budget would become a meaningless and empty form unless the members had the right of asking questions or calling for papers with regard to items entered in the accounts. (*Cheers.*) Thus, even for the satisfactory discussion of the Budget, the right of interpellation is needed. But let it be noted that we want the right to be confined purely to domestic matters. It is therefore a marvel how Lord Dufferin could fall into the mistake that we are anxious to claim authority over military arrangements.

Such, in short, is our programme for the reform and expansion of the Legislative Councils. But we suffer from misconception. A formidable opposition has been organized against us. The victory, however, is ours, if we be only true to ourselves. The signs of a great national awakening are visible on all sides. (*Cheers.*) It may be a portent for good ; or it may be a portent for evil. God grant that it may be the harbinger of countless blessings to our country! God grant that it may deepen our loyalty, stimulate our patriotism, and consolidate our imperial connection with England. It is for us to lead it into fruitful channels pregnant with good to the people. We shall not be wanting in our duty. Let us press our claims ; let us not sleep over the matter ; but rather let us agitate, pray and supplicate ; and England, too, will not be wanting in her duty by us. England, the home of the brave, the sanctuary of the free, the asylum of persecuted freedom, will not refuse to extend to us, in part at least, those institutions which have upreared her own greatness and have built up the fabric of her immortal renown. (*Loud cheers.*) Then will England have enthroned herself in the hearts of our people, and will have cemented her connection with India by bonds of love and gratitude which no change of circumstances and no stroke of untoward fate will ever suffice to sever. (*Loud and prolonged cheers.*)

MR. SYED SHARF-UD-DIN—(*Behar, No.* 1083 *in list*)—in supporting the resolution, said: Mr. President and Brother-delegates,—You can perfectly well understand the importance of this the most important of all the resolutions in the business at this Congress It is unnecessary for me to dwell on its importance, because this has already been set forth in the eloquent speeches of the two gentlemen who have preceded me. There is

2nd Day. Res. I., Reform of the Legislative Councils.

one point, however, to which, if I may be allowed, I should like to make some reference. In the resolution we claim the right of interpellation. Might I be permitted to recall to you one fact in regard to this right of interpellation. In the year 1854—so long ago as that—under the administration of Lord Dalhousie, it was laid down—if I am right—at the first meeting of the Legislative Council that the right of interpellation was to be conceded to all members of Council. Well, may I be allowed to ask you why a right granted us so far back as 1854 should be withheld in 1888? (*Cheers.*) In regard to the general question of introducing some representative element into the Government of the country, I need not say much, as the sentiments of the entire assemblage on this point have been faithfully expressed by the two able speakers who have preceded me, and it only remains, Gentlemen, for me to bring to your notice the fact that I am a Mahomedan. (*Loud cheers.*) Well, Gentlemen, you will remember perfectly well that in 1885, when the first meeting of the Congress was held at Bombay, it was said by adverse critics that it was a Congress of a few educated native gentlemen. Again you will remember that when the Congress was held in Calcutta in 1886, it was no longer called a Congress of a few native gentlemen, but a Congress of Bengalees; and in 1887, when the Congress was held in Madras, it was not called a Congress of native gentlemen, or of Bengalees, but a Congress of Hindus. (*Laughter and cheers.*) Now, Gentlemen, here in 1888, we have got before us not only Hindus, Bengalees and Mahrattas, but I am proud to say we have here amongst us to-day more than 200 Mahomedans, including scions of the ex-royal families of Delhi and of Oudh. (*Loud cheers.*) Now I think I may be right in expressing the hope and opinion that next year, when the reports of the Congress have been published, it will at last be called by its right name, and accepted as an *Indian* Congress. (*Cheers.*) You will remember that in 1885 there were scarcely any Mahomedans. There was an increase at the next Congress, a further increase in 1887, and now I am proud to say that there are more than 200 Mahomedans present. (*Loud cheers and cries of "Hear, hear."*) I may tell you that in 1886, when the Congress was held in Calcutta, owing to some local or temporary reasons, the Mahomedans were charged with holding aloof, but I can assure you that at least in my province of Behar the Mahomedans have the fullest sympathy with the objects of the Congress. And I can tell you that in my professional capacity I have to travel all over the division, and have been consulted, and have consulted with my freinds, many Mahomedans, and they have in every case proved to be in sympathy with and in favour of the Congress. At the same time I do not for a moment deny that there are some, indeed a good many, who, though fully sympathising with the objects of the Congress, yet for personal and temporary reasons think it best in their own interests to stay away. Still these gentlemen are with us and help us privately, and, when official pressure diminishes, will come round publicly. But abstentions of this nature—and they are more numerous amongst Mahomedans than any, except Mahomedans, have any idea of—furnish no grounds whatsoever for reckless assertions, such as that recently made in the House of Commons by Mr. Maclean, that the Mahomedans as a body are against the Congress, or for designating this latter by any less comprehensive title than that which it righteously bears—The Indian National Congress. (*Loud cheers.*) There are malcontents everywhere; there must always be some who dissent from anything their neighbours approve, but the great bulk of the Mahomedans, as the great bulk of the Hindus, Jews, Parsees and Indian Christians, are everywhere *for* and not against the Congress.

RAJAH RAMPAL SINGH—(*Allahabad, No. 571 in list*)—said: I am afraid I am a very poor speaker; but I think that every sympathetic Indian, every well-wisher of the country, should say something on the subject before us, however deficient he may be in oratorical powers. We all know that the right of being nominated to the Council has been given us since a long time. But the nomination rests entirely with Government, or rather with a small group of high officials; and some men entirely ignorant of the English language have been appointed to the Council. (*Cheers.*) They were not the representatives of the people of India, because they were the nominees of Government, and were the proteges of officials. (*Cheers.*) That being the case, the grievances of the country were not properly brought by them to the notice of Government; and, instead of fighting for justice on behalf of the people, they voted blindly with officials, unless indeed their own personal interests were involved, when, no doubt, they did show some fight on their own behalf. (*Laughter.*) Moreover, the nominated members of Council have always constituted such a microscopic minority, as my kind friend Lord Dufferin would phrase it, that even if they had dissented from the opinion of the officials, and had been bold enough to maintain their views, they would have had no chance of carrying their point. It is for this that we most loyally, constitutionally, and almost pathetically implore Government to allow us ourselves to select half the number of the members of the Legislative Council, and this with the full understanding that supreme authority must always rest with the Executive. With the supremacy of the Executive no Congress man that I have ever met—and I may say that I know a good many of these (*laughter*)—has ever dreamt of interfering; but we want a good number of our own men in Council, so that the Government here, and the people and Government of England, may hear from their representatives what the people of this country really think, and feel, and wish, about the subjects dealt with by the Government. (*Cheers.*)

2nd Day.

Res. I., Reform of the Legislative Councils.

PANDIT BISHAN NARAYAN DAR—(*Oudh, No.* 437 *in list*)—said: It is a matter of great pleasure to me to find that we are going to re-affirm this, the most important of all the resolutions of the National Congress. In this city, which will always be famous as the place where that great Proclamation of 1858 was first published—in this sacred city which has from time out of mind been sanctified by the confluence of two sacred rivers, emblematic of the perpetual union between India and England—(*a voice "Three cheers for the Union," and the call was enthusiastically responded to*)—it is a matter of great pleasure to me to find that you are going to re-affirm the resolution about the reform and extension of the Legislative Councils. I consider it as the keystone of all our political progress; it is the pivot on which will turn the political fortunes of this country. (*Cheers.*)

The principal objections which are advanced against our demands for the introduction of a representative element into the Legislative Councils is that it would weaken the hands of the Government; and that the methods by which we are seeking to obtain this reform are objectionable. Now my own meagre knowledge of history does not permit me to arrive at any such conclusions. The little knowledge of modern history that I possess leads me to the contrary conclusion, and to a conviction that the concession of local autonomy within certain limits and safeguards can only add to the strength and stability of the British Empire. (*Cheers.*) Let me take an instance from the history of the British Colonies. Take the Dominion of Canada. I do not wish to say that the analogy between India and the English Colonies is at all perfect; but I think there are a great many points in the history of Canada which might furnish very instructive lessons to our Government in its dealings with India. Canada is divided into two parts—Upper and Lower Canada. Upper Canada is English, and Lower is French. Now, some time ago, both the Canadas were governed separately by a Government and Council, who were not at all responsible to the people of Canada, and were removeable only by the Home Government of England. These Canadians had not even the semblance of self-government; but they so bitterly resented the system, and they became so disaffected to the Home Government that in 1837, when Queen Victoria came to the throne and *Te Deums* were sung in the churches in honour of the event, the congregations left their seats and walked out, and signs of rebellion soon became visible everywhere. The assembly of Canada forwarded their national grievances in the form of ninety resolutions to the British Government, who replied by placing the country under military control. While these things were occurring in Canada, you will be surprised to hear that the British public knew nothing about them. It was only when some Canadians, under sentence of transportation, were landed in England that they at all realized what had been going on. Then the conscience of the British public was touched, their indignation against the existing authorities was aroused, and such a cry was raised that the prisoners were at last released. (*Cheers.*) That event rivetted the attention of the British public upon the Canadian question, and as soon as the mist of ignorance was dispelled from the minds of the British nation in regard to Canadian affairs, the demands of Canada were at once conceded. Ever since Canada has obtained responsible Government, she has become more and more loyal and attached to the British Government. The history of Canada teaches us three lessons—first, that the concession of autonomy within certain limits and safeguards is good for the strength of the Imperial unity; secondly, that the English nation is always ready to do justice to every class, and that, if it sometimes fails do so, it is simply for want of accurate knowledge and information (*cheers*); and, thirdly, that we should go on agitating in the most loyal and consititutional manner, and supply the great British nation with all information we can as to our present position and aspirations. If you go on in this way, I am sure your appeal will not be made in vain. (*Cheers.*)

Who will solve the great problem of Indian politics if the English were to give it up? I have great faith in the English nation, and I assure you that I feel the full weight of responsibility which I believe everybody feels here who rises to address this august assembly. But knowing full well that every word uttered here will be carefully scrutinized by the public outside, that every sentiment expressed here will be considered, and justly considered, the voice of India's sons, whose voice never through any other channel reaches English ears, I have yet ventured on this occasion to stand before you, my countrymen, and tell you that if you go on making your appeal with fairness, courage and moderation to the great English nation, they will assuredly respond to your prayers, for as the harp responds to the harper's touch, so does the great deep heart of England respond to every reasonable prayer for justice and freedom. (*Loud cheers.*)

2nd Day.

Res. I, Reform of the Legislative Councils.

Mr. Umrao Mirza Hairat—(*Delhi, No.* 397 *in list*)—who spoke in Urdu, then said: Gentlemen,—I am here as a delegate from the Punjab, and I am a Mahomedan. I am at a loss, in the presence of such able men as have preceded me, to express myself worthily before this noble meeting; but my feelings, both national and religious, prompt me to address a few words to you. (*Cheers.*) As regards the resolution asking permission to elect natives of this country as members of Council, I can but say that it is the mainspring of this movement, in connection with which we are here assembled; and it is only when we are properly represented in the Councils that this country will obtain what it actually needs, for it is we who know our wants and how to represent them. It is a known fact that the two hundred and fifty millions of subjects depend solely on the Council for the remedy of their grievances (*cheers*); and it is essentially necessary that the members of the Council should be thoroughly conversant with the innumerable wants of the people, high and low, which it is next to impossible to expect from the Council as it now stands, composed of members never moving with, but diligently avoiding, the people. Hence the necessity, as we all see, that we should be more truly represented. Members elected would carefully avoid anything that would create religious or caste prejudices, and their views would be such as not to hurt the feelings of the various classes of the people, who depend on them for securing their safety and comfort. It is my opinion that the people should elect the members, as only such members will ever be fully aware of the actual wants of the people (*cheers*); and the House of Commons should take this into its earnest consideration. It is a sad fact that the present native members even are, as a rule, quite ignorant of our wants, and such opinions as they express, when they are asked to deal with or legislate on any question, are received by them from officials as much estranged from and unknown to the people as themselves (*cheers*); therefore I beg that the House of Commons will add to the many blessings this country enjoys by granting this earnest and not unreasonable prayer of the people and by permitting us to elect members to represent the Indian people on the Council. We are fully and gratefully impressed with the justice of British rule, with which may God long continue to bless us. (*Cheers.*)

Lala Lajpat Rai—(*Punjab, No.* 348 *in list*)—said: It is with a feeling of exultation and pride that I address this splendid assembly—splendid on account of its loyalty to the Crown, splendid on account of its sincere attachment to our great Queen-Empress. You might think it audacious on my part to address this vast assembly; but I come here for a special purpose. I come here to tell you why we want to have the right of interpellation. A few days ago a high and responsible officer of Government visited one of the towns of the Punjab. The inhabitants of the town, including the Vice-President of its Municipality and its leading men, waited on the high officer for redress of grievances in relation to a certain department. Can you guess what the reply of that officer was? It was practically to this effect, *viz.*, that the Government of India had its own interests to consult, and did not care for the people. (*Cries of "Impossible," "Name," and "Shame."*) Gentlemen, the fact is as I have stated, incredible as it may seem, and those of our opponents who say that we are spreading disaffection should know this incident, and consider whether it is we who are spreading disaffection or officers like these. (*Cheers.*) This is no exaggeration, Gentlemen; I repeat that it is a fact to which a thousand citizens of that town can testify. I therefore support this proposition with all my heart. I support it in the words of the Mahomedan who is said to be the leader of the opponents of the Congress. I will speak to you in the words of no less an authority than Sir Syed Ahmed. (*Hisses and cheers.*) That exalted personage, addressing a body of gentlemen at the laying of the foundation stone of the new Ghazipore, now the Victoria College, pretty well endorsed all our claims.

I will begin, however, with his book on the "Causes of the Indian Revolt," which was written in 1858, and translated and published in English in the year 1873. It may be worth while to note here that the translators of this were no other than Sir Auckland Colvin, the present Lieutenant-Governor of these Provinces, and Lieutenant-Colonel Graham, the writer of Sir Syed Ahmed's biography. In this book, after trying to prove that the Mutiny of 1857 was no "religious war," nor the result of a preconcerted conspiracy, he says that "most men, I believe, agree in thinking that it is highly conducive to the welfare and prosperity of the Government, indeed that it is essential to its stability, that the people should have a voice in its Councils. It is from the voice of the people that Government can learn whether its projects are likely to be well received; the voice of the people can check errors in the bud, and warn us of dangers before they burst upon and destroy us." To make the matter more clear, he went on saying that "this voice, however, can never he heard, and this security never acquired, unless the people are allowed a share in the consultations of Government. The security of a Government, it will be remembered, is founded on its knowledge of the character of the governed as well as on its careful observance of their rights and privileges." These are noble words nobly spoken—words of sterling honesty and independence of spirit. Can they have any other meaning than what attaches to this resolution of our National Congress, which prays for the introduction of a representative element into the constitution of our Legislative Councils? Pray tell me how can the people have a voice in the Councils of Government if not by representation? How can the people of a country have their voice constantly heard if not through their representatives? But, to leave no doubt on the subject, I will go on giving further quotations from the writings of the same great opponent of the National Congress. He once advocated the introduction of the representative element into the Legislative Councils of India in these words: "The evils which came to India from the non-admission of natives into the Legislative Councils of India were various. * * * * It (*i.e.*, the Government) could never hear, as it ought to have heard, the voice of the people on the laws and regulations which it passed." Again he says: "But the greatest mischief lay in this, that the people misunderstood the views and the intentions of the Government. They misapprehended every Act." Further on he says that, "if Hindustanees had been in the Legislative Councils, they would have explained everything to their countrymen, and thus these evils which have happened to us would have been averted." In his opinion, as expressed in his writings, this non-representation of the voice of the governed in the Legislative Council of the realm is stated to have been the "one great cause," and the "origin of all small causes of dissatisfaction." He further went to the length of saying that our own countrymen should be selected, to form an assembly like the English Parliament, which demand at the time he advanced it was certainly more premature than it now is, though the National Congress, with all the advantages that the country has had of education and enlightenment since the year 1858, only advocates the partial introduction of a representative element into the Legislative Councils. (*Loud cheers.*)

With your permission, Gentlemen, I shall quote a little more from the writings of Sir Syed. He says: "I do not wish to enter here into the question as to how the ignorant and uneducated natives of Hindustan could be allowed a share in the deliberations of the Legislative Councils, or as to how they should be selected to form an assembly like the English Parliament. These are knotty points. All I wish to prove here is that such a step is not only advisable but absolutely necessary, and that the disturbances are due to the neglect of such a measure." Could clearer words be used than what I have just quoted? Is there any doubt as to their meaning? Because, if so, I shall be obliged to quote the exact Hindustani words used by him to express the ideas propounded in the above lines. No; I do not suppose you can feel any doubt on that point, as the English rendering was undertaken, as I have already mentioned, by no other than Sir Auckland Colvin and Lieutenant-Colonel Graham, the former of whom, at least, has now declared himself to be hostile to the National Congress. Now you will by this time have discovered that here this most loyal of Indian Mahomedans, who now stigmatizes us as traitors, 30 years ago demanded for India reforms of the same character as we now after 30 years of education and progress pray for in the resolution which I am supporting, but going far beyond anything in this direction that we have thought it expedient or necessary to ask for. (*Continued cheering.*)

MR. SALEM RAMASWAMI MUDALIAR—(*Madras, No.* 15 *in list*)—also supported the resolution. He said: It is with great pleasure I now rise to support the proposition which has been so eloquently seconded and supported, but I do not think many words of mine or of any one else's are needed to induce you to re-affirm this resolution, which has been so often and so fully discussed and accepted at previous Congresses. I do not propose therefore to repeat those arguments which have been so forcibly urged, not only on the present occasion, but on all previous occasions, in support of this proposition; but I simply wish to place before you some facts which it may interest you to know, and which will enable you to judge whether the resolution placed before you involves quite so great a leap in the dark as some people seem to suppose. (*Cheers.*) Gentlemen, while we are humbly praying our Government to grant us some small representative element in the Government, we have actually got full blown representative institutions flourishing in this country under our very noses. I do not know whether you are aware how they are flourishing in Pondicherry and other places which are subject to the French Government. England will not as yet allow us the smallest modicum of representative institutions, but in Pondicherry every man has a right to elect his representative. He enjoys manhood suffrage! Not only that, but the people of Pondicherry have got a member of their own in the Chamber of Deputies and another in the Senate. Then in Pondicherry itself they have got a Council which is called the Council-General, and which meets every year, and this is an elective body elected by the whole people. Before this Council is placed the Annual Budget (*cheers*), and the Budget is fully discussed by the members. The Budget is there threshed out by that body, and it is not until, after this discussion, it has been approved that it comes into operation. (*Cheers.*) Gentlemen, it is said that we are not fit for representative institutions, but it is our fellow-countrymen, our relatives in many cases, no better educated than, and in nowise different from ourselves, whom the French Government has found to be fitted, not only for the small instalment of representative institutions that we ask for, but for fully-developed representative institutions, including manhood suffrage, which none of us ever even dream of demanding. I commend this fact to the careful consideration of our opponents who deny our fitness for even those small reforms we crave; and

2nd Day.

Res. I., Reform of the Legislative Councils

I say further to them, read the constitutional history of England. There was a time when the members who were elected for the English Parliament felt most unwilling to attend Parliament, because the meaning of the summons was that they were sent for to be taxed. That was in the earlier period of representative institutions in England. And we, at any rate, have passed beyond that stage. Now take the state of affairs in this country. We are certainly not now in a flourishing condition so far as finances are concerned. We are even now approaching a great crisis, and, when we ask for representative institutions, we know full well that the earliest duty we may have to discharge may be to tax ourselves and countrymen even more heavily than they are now taxed. I have simply to tell you that a further fall in the exchange to the extent of only one penny means that we should have to pay a crore more than we now pay ; and yet, so far from wishing to shirk our duty in this matter, as the Commons in England did in former times, it is we who urge our right to share the burthen of devising additional taxation in such ways as shall be least injurious to the country, and it is the Government who refuses to allow us any share in anything but the *payment* of the taxes that they, with a very imperfect knowledge of our country and ourselves, see fit in their wisdom to impose. It is indeed an extraordinary thing that the natives of India are in Pondicherry found fitted for representative institutions of an advanced character, while the relatives and brethren of these very men, under British rule, are pronounced unfit for the smallest concession in this direction ; that the French subjects are allowed to discuss and authoritatively deal with their Budget, while nothing is allowed to us but to pay the taxes. I may note in this connection that all people do not share the views of the authorities in this matter, but that the Madras Chamber of Commerce has addressed an important letter to Government, urging the advisability of extending to the people of India the principles of Representative Government. Sir, India can never be properly governed without these representative institutions, but I do not want to take up more of your time, because so much has been already said, and said so well and powerfully on this head, that if any man, either in England or India, is not now convinced that the time has come for extending some form of representative institutions to India, that man is beyond the scope of argument, and will *never* be convinced. (*Loud cheers.*)

RAJA SIVA PRASAD—(*Vide note at end of list p.* 157.)—next addressed the Congress. He said : We all feel obliged to the Congress, and I myself am not, as is often supposed, opposed to the Congress itself. But some unthoughtful people or self-interested men have been publishing pamphlets and inflammatory articles in the newspapers (*cries of "Not true" and "No, no"*) to excite your minds and to lower the Government in your eyes. The nobility and gentry of Oudh have applied to Government to have a law to stop such proceedings. My sole object is to clear the Congress from such a stigma (*cheers*) which prevents many from joining the Congress. With reference to the Legislative Council, we know that the matter has been for long before Government. The difficulties are great and numerous. I think we should have faith in the Government and wait. I can take my oath that India is now more prosperous than it has ever been in the past, and no country in the world is more happy ; but the distribution of copies of inflammatory pamphlets and speeches (*cries of "Where are they ? We have seen none such"*) is calculated to stir up the ignorant against Government. Before sitting down, I would, therefore, propose that the Congress do approve and adopt the amendment which I place on the table. (*Loud cries of "Read it."*)

The Rajah then began to read a document which proved to be a draft of a petition * *to the Lieutenant-Governor in the following terms :—*

"We, the undersigned nobility and gentry of the United Provinces of the North-West and Oudh, approach your Honour with the view of representing our sense of the political danger which, in our humble opinion, threatens to disturb the peaceful condition of the Empire. The growing and mischievous practice of communicating to the weak and unlettered masses ideas tending to create distrust against the existing order of Government (*here there was an interruption*) by means of speeches delivered in the midst of large concourses of people, or by the publication and extensive distribution of newspaper articles and pamphlets in towns and villages, both in the language of the people, and containing matter eminently calculated to unsettle the mind of the ignorant and unthinking portion of our countrymen, should not, we respectfully submit, be any longer ignored. We feel it to be our duty to condemn the practice of men of position and influence laying before large audiences of the people a statement of the misgovernment of the Empire—(*loud cries of dissent*)—naturally, involved in such inflammatory language as "to what condition the nation has been reduced" and "how distressed she feels." "In what calamity the nation has fallen ?" "Is she alive or dead ?" To declare the value of the "principles of democracy," and that "England owes its greatness to it ;"

* It has since been pointed out in the public Press that one at any rate of the so-called quotations in this petition is a barefaced forgery, a word having been so altered as to change a perfectly innocent into a very objectionable phrase.

to hold up to admiration the "Republican form of government in France;" to show that "in the Colonies even the negroes enjoy the same rights as the British-born subjects," implying thereby that the condition of the negroes is better than that of the people of India—(*interruption and hissing*)—to denounce "the annexation of Burma;" to represent the conduct of the authorities as arbitrary, "doing whatever they like," that "people are regarded as nobody," that "our business is to bow down and not to murmur," that the reforms in the European army will remove the necessity for imposing taxes," that "we are dying by paying the taxes, and the authorities in England do not care a bit," demanding "the formation of an Imperial Council, two-thirds of the members of which shall be elected by the people."

(*Here the Rajah was interrupted by many delegates, who demanded the names of the publications from which he professed to quote, as no one knew of these passages.*)

THE PRESIDENT, having called the assembly to order, said: Rajah Siva Prasad,—I allowed you to go on speaking, though a good deal of what you said seemed to me scarcely relevant to the question actually before this meeting, and when you said you had an amendment to propose, I readily allowed you to read it; but having heard you thus far, I have no hesitation in saying that this petition is in no sense an amendment on the resolution now under consideration, and must be rejected as irrelevant. I will ask you now, sir, (you have occupied a good deal more than the allotted time) to sit down. (*Loud and enthusiastic cheering, which was mingled with hisses as the Rajah retired.*)

MR. MUHAMMED MAHBUB ALAM—(*Punjab, No. 367 in list*)—then spoke in Urdu, as follows: Gentlemen,—It is needless for me to try and explain the innumerable blessings we enjoy under British rule. (*Cheers.*) We do thank God that he has been so good and merciful to us Indians as to place us under such a benign, just, and merciful Sovereign as our illustrious Queen and Empress Victoria. (*Cheers.*) Long may she and her Government reign over us. (*Cheers.*) I support the proposals of those of my friends who have just addressed you. A sick man once asked Sugra Hakim what safe cure there was for a severe illness, and he replied: "When you recover from your illness, then you will know what is the safe cure." (*Laughter.*) When the sick man knows his ailments, he knows his cure, and he has faith and hope that the remedy applied will cure. (*Cheers.*) The remedy for our cure is in the hands of the benevolent British Government, and we are sure it will not withhold it when it is so earnestly prayed for by us. Let me remind you that I am a Mahomedan of the Punjab, of which province the people were, till recently, anti-Congressists; but at this moment I assure you their eyes have been opened, and, being alive to the true and loyal objects of the National Congress, they are now with us to a man (*loud cheers*); and I am pleased to have the opportunity to assure you that the Punjab anti-Congress movement is a thing of the past. (*Renewed cheers.*) As I have been assured and persuaded, so allow me to assure you that we cannot fail to obtain our wants as represented by the National Congress. This is a good work, and I feel sure God will help us. (*Cheers.*) Anti-Congressmen accuse us of being disloyal, but I feel inclined to apply the term to them. We openly and truthfully declare our wants, and do not mean to get them by stealth and underhand work. I am a poor subject, but allow me to advise the Government to mark such men as the anti-Congressmen, who work by stealth and duplicity. These are the real seditionists; they do not want the causes of disaffection removed; they do not want the grievances of the people redressed—they want them to continue to vex and irritate the people till these grow at last as disaffected as themselves. They are the real enemies; we the real friends and true supporters of the British Government. May God confound their evil schemes, and bless and preserve our gracious Empress. (*Loud cheers.*)

MR. S. B. BHATE—(*Poona, No. 170 in list*)—then said: Sir,—I only wish to remark that I have seen and heard a good deal of the Congress agitation, and have read a good deal of the Congress literature, and all I can say is that I have never heard or seen a single word in connection with the movement that any rational being could characterize as disloyal. Had there been any taint, however slight, of disloyalty in the matter, I would have had no hand in it; but, as it is, I am an earnest Congressman, all the more earnest because I am loyal to the core. (*Cheers.*)

MR. NAWAL BEHARI BAJPAI—(*Allahabad, No. 559 in list*)—then rose and said: Gentlemen,—I support this resolution—the most essential of all the resolutions which are to be placed before you. I am really sorry if Rajah Siva Prasad disapproves this resolution, as from the nature of the petition which he seemed to wish us to adopt as an amendment to it, I am led to fear. I am sorry I say if this be the case, because I have a high respect for the Rajah, whom I have long known, whom I look upon as a father, nay whose legal adviser I am at this moment in a certain case. But really my respected and distinguished client should be reasonable. Millions share the prayer embodied in this

2nd Day.

Res. I., Reform of the Legislative Councils.

resolution, but it appears that some two or three men somewhere—who or where I know not—who are also supporters of the Congress, have used words which the Rajah thinks objectionable, nay seditious—therefore this resolution is bad and we ought to drop it. Gentlemen, every year millions look forward hopefully to the rains, and perhaps one or two bad men lose their tempers and use bad language, because the monsoon does not come quite as soon as they want; therefore the rains are bad and we ought not to have any monsoon. I can't see the argument. What on earth have the objectionable expressions (if any such were ever really used—I at least have never heard of such)—what, I say, have these to do with the prayer set forth in our resolution? Nothing! simply nothing; and that prayer, let who will have talked nonsense or worse, I support with all my heart.

MR. CHARLES GOLAKNATH—(*Punjab, No. 340 in list*)—rose and said: Sir,—I am entirely in sympathy with the resolution so far as it goes, but I desire to suggest a small addition to it. You will remember that, when at the first Congress a resolution on this subject was passed, it embodied a prayer that Councils should be created for both the North-Western Provinces and the Punjab. Well, the N.-W. Provinces have since had a Council granted for them, and you, Gentlemen, seem to have been so satisfied with that result that ever since then you have neglected our claims and left us, poor Punjabees, out in the cold; but I can assure you that we need a Council quite as much as these Provinces, and so I hope you will agree to add a few words to the resolution now before you, advocating our claims. (*Cries of "Yes, yes!"*) Well, my definite proposition is, that in the third line of the resolution you insert before the word "*provincial*" the word "*existing*," and that at the end of the resolution you add the words:

"*And do further urge that a Legislative Council (of the same character as those which have been suggested for Provinces where Legislative Councils already exist) be established for the Punjab.*" (*Loud cheers.*)

I see that you have kindly accepted my additions, and I need not therefore, I think, take up your time by any further remarks on the subject.

MR. JADU NATH MAZUMDAR—(*Bengal, No. 1187 in list*)—said: I beg to second this proposal. Though now coming from Bengal, I was until recently a resident and a worker in the Punjab as a journalist, and I can tell you from long personal experience that there is no province in India in which the authorities are so completely a law unto themselves, and in which a Council, partly composed of independent and representative men, is so urgently needed.

The proposer and seconder of the original resolution now signified their acceptance of the amendment.

MR. BEHARI LALL—(*N.-W. Provinces, No. in list*)—said: I heartily support the resolution as amended, and I sincerely hope that the Punjab will soon get its Council, and that all the Councils, Supreme and Provincial, will, before long, be placed upon that sounder and healthier footing that this our resolution suggests. Until this be done the Government must continue, as now, to be carried on in a more or less haphazard fashion. What men can do, situated as they are, our rulers I fully believe do, but they will never be able to do real justice to us or to themselves, to India or to England, until they associate with themselves in their anxious toils those men whom the country knows and trusts, and whom we elect as our representatives.

MR. SADHO LAL—(*Benares, No. 884 in list*)—then said: This is a day of joy when we consider what difficulties and oppositions we have had to contend with which at one time threatened the success of this, the Fourth Congress; but it is the will of God, the Just, that justice be shown and dealt out to us, and He has ruled that we do meet here to-day from all parts of this vast Empire ruled over by our gracious Queen Victoria. (*Cheers.*) The regulation appointing certain Indian members to the Legislative Council of India has been passed and is in force, but yet it is not as we would wish for the benefit of the millions. Members appointed should be those elected by the people, whose wants they know and can represent. We are aware that Her Gracious Majesty, the Empress Victoria, cares for us as a mother does for her children, and as such, while forgiving our many little faults, she grieves to know that we are sufferers in any way, and will, we are sure, grant our wants which we meet here to express, so that they may reach her tender heart. We do and shall continue to enjoy the blessings of liberty of speech, and therefore feel sure our cries will reach Her Gracious Majesty, who, I feel certain, will grant our request. (*Cheers.*)

Other delegates rose to speak, but were interrupted by cries of "Vote, vote."

THE PRESIDENT.—Is there any gentleman who wishes to speak against this resolution? (*Cries of "None, none."*) Do you wish the debate to be further prolonged? (*"No, no." "Vote, vote."*) Then I shall put the resolution which will, as amended, stand thus:—

2nd Day.

Res. I., Reform of the Legislative Councils.

RESOLVED—" *That this Congress affirms the necessity for the expansion and reform of the Council of the Governor-General for making laws and regulations, and of the existing Provincial Legislative Councils, already set forth in Resolutions III of the Congresses of 1885 and 1886, and Resolution II of the Congress of 1887 (a tentative scheme for which expansion and reform was suggested in Resolution IV of the Congress of 1886), and further urges that a Legislative Council (of the same character as those which have been suggested for provinces where Legislative Councils already exist) be established for the Punjab.*"

THE PRESIDENT then put the Resolution, which was carried by acclamation.

Res. II., Public Service Question.

MR. EARDLEY NORTON—(*Madras, No. 19 in list*)—who was received with enthusiastic and long-continued cheering, then rose and said: Gentlemen,—With your permission, I will first read out to you the important though rather lengthy resolution which I am to have the honour of proposing for your acceptance. It runs as follows :—

" *That this Congress, having read and considered the report of the Committee appointed "by the Congress of 1886 to submit a statement in connection with the Public Service Ques-" tion, do approve and adopt the said report, to wit—*

" 1. ' *That the open competitive examination be held simultaneously in India and in England.*

" 2. ' *That the simultaneous examination thus held be equally open to all classes of Her Majesty's " ' subjects.*

" 3. ' *That the classified list be prepared according to merit.*

" 4. ' *That the Congress express the hope that the Civil Service Commissioners will give fair con-" ' sideration to Sanskrit and Arabic among the subjects of examination.*

" 5. ' *That the age of candidates eligible for admission to the open competitive examination be not " ' less than nineteen, nor, as recommended by Sir Charles Aitchison, more than twenty-three years.*

" 6. ' *That simultaneous examinations being granted, the Statutory Civil Service be closed for first " ' appointments.*

" 7. ' *That the appointments in the Statutory Civil Service, under the existing rules, be still left " ' open to the Members of the Uncovenanted Service and to professional men of proved merit and ability.*

" 8. ' *That all appointments requiring educational qualifications, other than covenanted first appoint-" ' ments, be filled by competitive examinations held in the different provinces, and open in each province to " ' such natural-born subjects of Her Majesty only as are residents thereof, and declare that nothing short " ' of the reforms therein suggested will satisfy the people of this country.*' "

Gentlemen, it is just one year since we met in Madras ; and, before I proceed to deal with the resolution which has been entrusted to my care, and which I have just read to you, I should like to take this, possibly my first and last, opportunity of saying a few words upon the Congress at large. You will recollect that when we met in Bombay in 1885 we numbered only 70 delegates. (*Cheers.*) At the end of one year we met again in Calcutta, and then in 1886 our numbers had increased to 407. (*Cheers.*) At Madras in 1887 you raised that total to 608. (*Cheers.*) And now I am glad and proud to know that, in spite of grave impediments, official and otherwise, you have doubled that representation, and stand to-day an aggregate of 1,200 delegates. (*Loud cheers and cries of " More than that.*") Yes, more than 1,200. (*Cheers.*) I trust that you will still further progress, and that at our next Congress you may double your number of to-day. (*Loud cheers.*) Your growing representation is the most significant and eloquent testimony to the growing strength and popularity of your cause. (*Cheers.*) You have had many and serious obstacles placed in your path, but you have been nerved by the opposition, and it is matter of very hopeful and very sincere congratulation that you have manfully met and conquered the impediments in your way. I am glad to think you have successfully withstood the literary assaults of the Rajah of Bhinga. (*Loud laughter.*) I am glad you have not succumbed to the more polished literary essay of Sir Auckland Colvin. (*Cheers.*) I am glad you have been stimulated and stiffened by the open misrepresentations of Lord Dufferin. (*Loud cheers.*) And I dare say you will even survive the terrible onslaught made upon you to-day by Rajah Siva Persad (*cheers*), who has been safely brought to bed in the public view of a speech and a petition, which I think we may safely assume to be a speech and petition for a K. C. S. I. (*Loud laughter and cheers.*) Gentlemen, you and I will grant, and cheerfully grant, to every delegate the most complete freedom of speech. Every man is entitled not merely to hold but to publish his opinions. But I leave it to Rajah Siva Persad to settle accounts with his own conscience (*cheers*), and to justify, if he can, to himself and the world, that line of action which has permitted him to enter this assembly as a delegate of the people and simultaneously to attack it upon the very principle of its existence. (*Loud cheers.*)

I pass on to the matter confided to my charge, with the expression only of this hope that you will not give way to the opposition arrayed against you ; that you will not be frightened by the number or the rank of those who are combined to intimidate, to insult, and to delay you. (*Cheers.*) We can point to this meeting, both in its quantity and quality, as evidence of the most re-assuring of beliefs that the *morale* of the country is expanding

2nd Day.

Res. II., Public Service Question.

and solidifying under the vivifying effect of abusive opposition. (*Cheers.*) And it is gratifying also to know that among this audience there is at any rate one gentleman, a member of Parliament (*cheers*), who will be able to tell the people of England what he has seen and what he has heard; and who—though I know not what his opinions are—will speak with the weight which is due to personal familiarity with the subject of which he talks. (*Cheers.*) He has been in both camps. He has spoken at first hand with Sir Syed Ahmed; he has been tickled with the seductive oratory of Mr. Beck (*laughter*), and I for one am not afraid of the result of any comparison he may draw between them and ourselves. (*Cheers.*) There is nothing they can teach which will not benefit us. (*Cheers.*) Our Congress is outside the reach of petty malice. It is increasing day by day in power and extent, pushing aside by its own great weight the opposing forces of envy and of scorn; and while it draws the various peoples of the country into one common fold of mutual sympathy and good will, rises with silent majesty into a future of self-reliance and content. (*Cheers.*)

Like some tall cliff that rears its awful form,
Swells from the vale, and midway leaves the storm,
Though round its base the gathering clouds may spread,
Eternal sunshine settles on its head. (*Loud cheers.*)

Next to the question of the reconstitution of the Legislative Councils, the most important, in my opinion, is the resolution which has been entrusted to my advocacy. This refers to the labours of the Public Service Commission which, you will recollect, travelled round the country. Its labours have fructified into a report. That report, I believe, is under the consideration of the Secretary of State in Council,—such consideration, that is, as he ever gives to subjects which are Indian (*laughter*), and I daresay we shall, in the course of a few years, have some expression of opinion from that august individual. (*Laughter.*) Meanwhile it seems to me extremely desirable that you should take a strong and natural interest in the question how far you shall share in the public service of your country. It seems desirable that you should, in your own interests, endeavour to strengthen the Secretary of State's hands, and to bring to his notice the opinions you in this country hold. ("*Hear hear.*") I am sorry to think that on this question I shall not be supported from my own Presidency of Madras with unanimity. Mr. Salem Ramaswamy Mudeliar will ask you to defer further consideration of the report of the Service Commission for the period of one year. He wishes to await the decision of the India Office. He is stronger than I am in the faith which he holds with respect to the relief which the Secretary of State will give us. (*Laughter.*) I am one of those who are of opinion that you will get nothing at all unless you ask for it, and unless you go on asking for it. ("*Hear, hear.*")

Mr. Ramaswamy Mudeliar was one, and by no means the least distinguished, of the dissentient Indian gentlemen who sat upon the Commission. His and their views, I believe, are entirely in accord with the spirit and the letter of the resolution which I have read to you. The report of the Committee was not a unanimous one in one sense, and from that report three Indian gentlemen dissented, although they agreed in the opinions which received the signatures of the entire Commission. I am sure we shall be all unanimous that Mr. Ramaswamy Mudeliar and his Indian colleagues honestly did their best on your behalf (*cheers*), and that they laboured courageously and conscientiously to press your views upon the majority (*cheers*), and in anything I say I wish, absolutely, to cast no shadow of reflection upon their efforts. But you will be told that these gentlemen upon the Commission were your representatives, and that you are bound to support them at all cost to the whole extent of their considerations. The answer to that is that they were not your representatives, for the simple reason that you had no voice in their election (*laughter and "Hear, hear"*), and are not therefore bound by their decision or their views. ("*Hear, hear.*") With all respect for the judgment of Mr. Ramaswamy and his colleagues, I cannot help thinking that in surrendering, not a detail, but a principle, he and his friends will be found not to have done the best for the people of India. (*Cheers.*) I cannot suppress the belief that if Mr. Ramaswamy and his co-adjutors, instead of signing the report, had written a dissentient minute with that force and perspicuity of which he and Mr. Justice Mitter are such masters, you would have been in a far stronger position with respect to your memorial to the Secretary of State than you are now. (*Cheers.*)

Let me shortly tell you the history of this measure. In 1833 the question first came before Parliament. It was discussed and supported by men of such eminence and distinction as Sir Robert Peel, Lord Lansdowne, the grandfather of the present Viceroy (*cheers*), and I trust heartily that the grandson will show himself worthy of his grandfather (*loud cheers*), and Mr. Charles Grant. These are names of some historic moment, of some intellectual worth. (*Cheers.*) They will compare not unfavourably with Lord Dufferin and Sir Auckland Colvin (*cheers*), with the Rajah of Bhinga (*laughter*), and Mr. Beck. (*Laughter.*) This is what Sir Robert Peel said. I am glad to be able to shelter myself under his name. Were the words mine, they would be called seditious. (*Laughter.*) "In a word, to endeavour while we still keep them under British rule, to atone to them for the sufferings they endured, and the wrongs to which they were exposed in being reduced to that rule, and to afford them such advantages and confer on

2nd Day: Res. II., Public Service Question.

them such benefits as may in some degree console them for the loss of their independence. These, Sir, are considerations which, whatever may be the anxiety to extend British conquest and to maintain the rights of British subjects, must indisputably be entertained in a British Parliament." (*Cheers.*) Listen to Mr. Charles Grant: "Convinced as he was of the necessity of admitting Europeans to India, he would not consent to remove a single restriction on their admission unless it was consistent with the interests of the natives." (*Cheers.*) "Provide for their protection," Mr. Grant said, "and then throw open wide the doors of those magnificent regions, and admit British subjects there—not as aliens, not as culprits, but as friends." (*Loud cheering.*) "In spite of the differences between the two people, in spite of the difference of their religions, there was a sympathy which he was persuaded would unite them, and he looked forward with hope and eagerness to the rich harvest of blessings which he trusted would flow from the present measure." (*Cheers.*) Twenty years elapsed, and in 1853 the matter came before Parliament again. And on this second revision, men of the stamp of Lord Stanley and Lord Monteagle, Lord Granville, and he the great tribune of the people John Bright (*loud and prolonged cheering, the audience rising and giving Mr. Bright's name three cheers*) re-affirmed the principles expressed in 1833. Then in 1858 our Queen gave you your great Charter, unasked (*loud cheers*), with wondrous and sagacious magnanimity, thus affording a signal and illustrious example of how to invest a gift with a deep and abiding value. (*Cheers.*) Hers is the spirit in which concession should be made. How I wish our rulers in India would act upon her lesson, and not force us, by their attitude, into the belief that we must wring, by years of acrimonious toil the faintest semblance of reform, yielded at length only with ungracious reluctance. (*Cheers.*) Where are the brave and generous sentiments of thirty years ago; where the men to lend their aid and sympathy to the cause of Indian liberty and Indian reform? (*Cheers.*) What a vast and sorrowful difference between our rulers of 1850 and of 1888! (*Loud cheers.*)

Lastly, in 1860, a Departmental Committee of the India Office thus reported :—

"2. We are, in the first place, unanimously of opinion that it is not only just but expedient that the natives of India shall be employed in the administration of India to as large an extent as possible consistently with the maintenance of British supremacy, and have considered whether any increased facilities can be given in this direction.

"3. It is true that even at present no positive disqualification exists. By Acts 3 and 4, Wm. IV, Chap. 85, s. 87, it is enacted 'that no natives of the said territories, nor any natural-born subject of His Majesty resident therein, shall, by reason only of his religion, place of birth, descent, colour or any of them, be disabled from holding any place, office or employment under the said Company. It is obvious, therefore, that when the competitive system was adopted it could not have been intended to exclude natives of India from the Civil Service of India.

"4. Practically, however, they are excluded. The law declares them eligible, but the difficulties opposed to a native living in India and residing in England for a time are so great that, as a general rule, it is almost impossible for a native successfully to compete at the periodical examinations held in England. Were this inequality removed we should no longer be exposed to the charge of keeping promise to the ear and breaking it to the hope.

"5. Two modes have been suggested, by which the object in view might be attained. The first is by allotting a certain portion of the total number of appointments declared in each year, to be competed for in India, by natives and by all other natural-born subjects of Her Majesty resident in India. The second is to hold simultaneously two examinations—one in England and one in India, both being, as far as practicable, identical in their nature, and those who compete in both countries being finally classified in one list according to merit by the Civil Service Commissioners. The Committee have no hesitation in giving preference to the second scheme, as being the fairest and the most in accordance with the principles of a general competition for a common object."

Such is the history of the pledges made to you. What as to their fulfilment? This is what the Duke of Argyll said in 1869: "With regard, however, to the employment of natives in the Government of their country, in the Covenanted Civil Service formerly of the Company and now of the Crown, *I must say that we have not fulfilled our duty, or the promises and engagements which we have made.*" (*Cheers.*) The reproach is as true in 1888 as it was in 1869. (*Cheers.*) That is an admission which as an Englishman it shames me to have to record. I like to believe that my countrymen not merely make, but redeem, their promises. (*Cheers.*) It pains me when I see them lack the courage of their convictions. (*Cheers.*) Let me call one more witness to the point He shall be a former Viceroy. I will examine Lord Lytton. (*Laughter.*) I should be afraid to use his language as my own, lest I should be indicted for high treason. (*Laughter.*) But a Viceroy can do no wrong. (*Laughter.*) Lord Lytton in a secret report, which accidentally came to light, in terms told the authorities in England that the people of this country had been "cheated"—I am quoting, Gentlemen (*laughter*)—of their hopes. (*Cheers.*) So much for the manner and extent of England's redemption of her vows.

2nd Day.

Res. II., Public Service Question.

I wish to touch with brief particularity upon two points in connection with the Public Service Commission: First, as to the excessive cost of the administration of this country. Many people think it ruinous. I agree with them. The only real solution of the difficulty lies in an infusion into the machinery of the country of a large, and yearly larger, element of indigenous Indian talent. (" *Hear, hear.*") What share do you hold to-day in the service of your country? Here are some suggestive figures. Out of 2,357 appointments in the higher Uncovenanted Civil Service you, gentlemen of India, hold 188. ("*Shame, shame.*") The non-domiciled Europeans appropriate 1,460 such appointments: the domiciled Europeans 486, Eurasians 223, and the Indians 188! (" *Shame.*") The three first bodies hold 2,169 berths, you only 188! (" *Shame.*") Yes, it is a shame, and it is one you will efface from the history of England's connection with India only by making plain to the people of England your ungenerous and impolitic exclusion from public life in India. (*Cheers.*) Here is an interesting analysis of your position in this country :—

* Name of Department.	Non-domiciled Europeans.	Domiciled Europeans.	Eurasians.	Indians.	Remarks.
Accounts Department	25	8	3	6	* The number of " domiciled Europeans " in the superior branch and of Native Sub-Assistants and Rangers not given.
Customs	13	60	117	12	
Forest	5	25*	13	2	
Jails	60	15	13	16	
Opium	49	13	8	1	
Postal	33	59	9	39	
Police	315	33	5	17	
Public Works	810	119†	...	86	† "Domiciled" Europeans include Eurasians.
Registration	7	1	1	...	
Salt	35	32	16	7	
Survey	108	103	38	2	
Total ...	1,460	486	223	188	

I can add little, gentlemen, to the story that this tells.

My second point is one which you will find for yourselves hidden away in the dark recesses of the Commission's Report. I quote from the report itself. Paragraph 47 of that report says: "The strength of the Covenanted Civil Service in the several provinces (including Statutory Officers, Junior Civil Servants and officers absent on leave) is about 940 officers." Paragraph 77 of the same report tells us that "the effect of these proposals is to remove about 108 appointments from the list of appointments reserved in the schedule, and by the orders of the Secretary of State, a number in excess of the proportion of one-sixth of the same appointments thrown open under the statutory rules." The case, therefore, stands thus: At present the Covenanted Civilians hold 940 appointments. To one-sixth of those appointments Statutory Civilians are eligible. One-sixth of 940 is 156. If, therefore, the Statutory Civil Service, as at present In existence, is not abolished, Indians may look forward to securing for themselves 156 appointments in the course of an official generation. But the Public Service Commission proposes to abolish the Statutory Civil Service. With that abolition will disappear your 156 appointments in the Civil Service, and by way of compensation you will receive 108 appointments. (*Cheers.*) You lose 48 appointments! And this is the *razinamah* or compromise which is so beneficial to you that you are to be asked to endorse the action of Mr. Ramswamy Mudeliar and his colleagues! (*wheers.*) I ask you to accept of no suggestion for further delay (*cheers*), but to let the Secretary of State for India know plainly that you are not satisfied with the recommendations of the Public Service Commission, and that you cannot fairly be expected to receive with a sense of gratitude any scheme which does not honestly meet your just wants by raising the age of the candidate (*cheers*), and permitting you to compete upon fair and equal terms by the establishment of a simultaneous examination in India. (*Loud cheers.*) These are the two great principles for which you are contending. (*Cheers.*) To these you are entitled, and, please God, we shall live to see you in the full enjoyment of both. (*wheers.*) The question of age is one which concerns not merely the Indians; it is of equal moment to the Englishman. We cannot too earnestly condemn a system which pushes young English boys into positions of grave trust and serious responsibility, at a time of life when, without the safeguard of any previous training, they have not discarded, and cannot discard, the frailties of precocious youth. (*Cheers.*)

* Taken from a pamphlet on "Indian Civil Service Reform," by Mr. Parbati Churn Roy, B.A. Fisher Unwin: London.

2nd Day.

Res. II., Public Service Question.

You will be asked to await the Secretary of State's decision. Be advised, gentlemen, and do not. (*Cheers.*) You will find yourselves in a very awkward predicament if you stay your hand and await the final pronouncement of judgment on your claims. How can you then turn round and, being silent now, express your discontent? Be honest and avow your conviction now (*cheers*), and by your action not merely strengthen the efforts of your many friends in England, but assist the Secretary of State to a right decision by a clear and manly exposition of your views. If you are inclined to accept that very modest instalment of reform to which my friend Mr. Ramswamy Mudeliar has accorded his consent, I admit that I have formed a very mistaken estimate of your character and your claims. (*Cheers.*)

I have in a previous portion of my speech expressed my regret at the seeming alteration in the sentiments and sympathies of my fellow-countymen. Let me appeal to them in all sincerity and in all earnestness to let their actions be guided by that larger, that nobler, that wiser liberalism which a quarter of a century ago characterized our views of India's wants and our own relations to our Indian fellow-subjects, which bound us together in a closer and truer bond of mutual esteem and fellow-feeling. (*Cheers.*) I would ask them to act in the spirit, and on the lines of those magnificent words—I say magnificent, for I know nothing more solemnly beautiful than the language of your Charter from the Queen of England (*loud cheexs*)—in which are embodied the grand and spontaneous declarations of my own dear island home:

"In their prosperity will be our strength, in their contentment our security, and in their gratitude our best reward. And may the God of all power grant to us, and to those in authority under us, strength to carry out these our wishes for the good of our people." (*Loud and long-sustained applause.*)

THE HON'BLE MR. PHEROZSHAH M. MEHTA—(*Bombay, No. 208 in list*)—Gentlemen,—I mean to set the best of examples, and will put an end to my oratorical existence within the period of five minutes allowed by that guillotine.* (*Laughter.*) I will take one minute of the five to make one observation which has suggested itself to me by an incident which took place to-day. Some of you, gentlemen, were disposed to be rather angry with the gentleman who wished to propose an amendment to the first proposition. You will remember the words of wisdom which fell from the President in the course of one of the most remarkable speeches I have ever heard. (*Cheers.*) He told us that all such agitations passed through three stages—hostility, partial acquiescence, and misapprehension, and finally complete surrender. Now, I say we should be glad that we find the Rajah Shiva Prasad, who is in the Congress to-day, in the second stage of preparation. (*Cheers and laughter.*) His hostility to the Congress has ceased, and he comes here to-day to do you an act of homage by moving an amendment. (*Laughter.*) That act of homage means that he subscribes to the great and sacred principles on which this Congress is founded. (*Cheers.*) And I think I shall prove a very safe prophet when I say that by the time the next great Congress is held, the Rajah will have reached the last stage of transformation, and that is one of complete surrender. (*Laughter and cheers.*) Now I pass on to the task which has been entrusted to me, a very difficult task indeed, when I remember that I was preceded by Mr. Eardley Norton, who has placed before you the proposition in his charge in one of the most able and eloquent speeches that I have ever heard. (*Cheers.*) I will therefore confine myself to a few observations on the proposition. It is said that we want to enter the Civil Service of India, because the educated classes of this country aspire to it. It is said that the admission is demanded for the purpose of satisfying what are called the legitimate aspirations of the educated classes of this country. That may be one way of putting the matter. But I would ask you to put it on a simpler and broader basis. The reason why the Congress is so earnest about securing the equal admission of the natives of this country into the public Civil Service rests upon a two-fold foundation. Mr. Dadabhai Naoroji has over and over again pointed out to us that the question rests upon economic necessity. It is necessary on economic grounds that natives should be largely employed in the administration of the country. But there is a necessity even greater than that, and that is a political necessity. (*Cheres.*) I say that when the time came to settle the principles on which British rule in India was to be carried on, it was clearly recognised by those sober statesmen who guided the destinies of England at that time, that even for Orientals an absolute despotism was an impossible creed in practical politics. (*Cheers.*) It was clearly recognised that even the most benevolent and the most paternal despotism must, if it wants to be stable and permanent, place its roots in the country in which it carries on that rule; and this principle was soberly, though eloquently, enunciated by Lord Macaulay in 1833, when he said that, for the sake of English honour and English wisdom, it was absolutely imperative that the natives of this country should have an equal share in the administration. (*Cheers.*)

* Pointing to the somewhat guillotine-like frame, in which hung the President's gong, one tap on which warned the speaker that he must draw to a close, while two peremptorily closed his harangue.

2nd Day. Res. II., "Public Service Question."

I would press these two grounds on the Government, I would press them on the Secretary of State, and I would press them on the people of England, because I am one of those who wish that the British rule in India should be a stable and permanent rule. (*Cheers.*) Now, I will say a word about the question of age. It is not only necessary for Indian candidates to get into the Civil Service, but it is equally necessary for the right and better administration of the country, as Mr. E. Norton has so well pointed out, that the limit of age should be increased. What does the present limit of age mean? It means that for our Magistrates and Deputy Collectors we have mere boys of 22 and 24. I know too well from the experience I have acquired in my professional capacity what it is to have first class magisterial and administrative powers placed in the hands of youths. However good they may be, they are only youths, inexperienced, unripe youths. (*Cheers.*) I say, therefore, that this is a most important question. Do not be carried away by the great importance of the first resolution, and think that the one now before you is of a subordinate importance. It is, on the contrary, in the eyes of many of our most advanced thinkers, *par excellence*, the question of the day, and I earnestly hope and trust that this Congress will energetically raise their united voices in this matter to the powers that be, as the question really, most vitally, affects the best interests and the future progress and welfare of the country. (*Loud cheers.*)

MR. JOHN ADAM—(*Madras, No. 2 in list*)—said: Sir,—I rise to propose an amendment. I am entirely at one with the mover and seconder of the original resolution, in desiring that full justice should be done to the people of India in the matter of thoroughly opening to them, to the fullest extent, the door of admission to all branches of the Public Service. But the form of the resolution as proposed does not commend itself to my mind, nor to those of many of my friends, and it appears to me in some respects defective; and I therefore desire to propose for your consideration a resolution essentially to the same purpose, but differently worded. This resolution, that I would propose for your consideration, runs as follows:—

"*That this Congress, while acknowledging that the proposals of the Public Service Com-*
"*mission would, if adopted in their entirety, be a great improvement upon the present system of*
"*admission to the various branches of the Public Service, declares that no system will be*
"*satisfactory to the country which does not also provide for a selection examination in India,*
"*and therefore affirms Resolution IV of the Congress of 1885, namely—*

"'*That the Competitive Examinations now held in England for first appointments in various Civil*
"'*departments of the Public Service should henceforth, in accordance with the views of the India Office*
"'*Committee of 1860, be held simultaneously, one in England and one in India, both being as far as*
"'*practicable identical in their nature, and those who compete in both countries being finally classified*
"'*in one list according to merit, and that the successful candidates in India should be sent to England*
"'*for further study, and subjected there to such further examinations as may seem needful. Further, that*
"'*all other first appointments (excluding peonships and the like) should be filled by competitive examina-*
"'*tions held in India under conditions calculated to secure such intellectual, moral and physical qualifica-*
"'*tions as may be decided by Government to be necessary. Lastly, that the maximum age of candi-*
"'*dates for entrance into the Covenanted Civil Service be raised to not less than 23 years.*'"

Now it might at first hearing appear as though this resolution which I have just read to you (and what I shall have to say in regard to it) were in some way opposed to what previous speakers have contended for; but you will find that my amendment does not in the smallest degree militate against the privileges which you are demanding. There is no more earnest advocate than I am for holding simultaneous examinations in both countries and for increasing the limit of the age. (*Cheers.*) On this latter point especially my opinion is extremely decided. I know English young men well, and for the last four years I have had considerable experience of Indian young men also, and I must say I think it utterly absurd and ridiculous to take English boys, of the ages at which they now often come to this country, and place them in such positions of responsibility as they now habitually occupy. ("*Hear, hear.*") I know many members of the present Civil Service. No doubt after a few years' experience they become able and efficient, but I maintain that the experience which they require should not be acquired in independent positions at the expense of the people of India. (*Cheers.*) The amendment I propose commences by acknowledging that the recommendations of the Public Service Commission would, if adopted in their entirety, prove a great improvement on the present system, and it goes on to declare that no system would be satisfactory to the country which does not also provide for selection and examination in India. In fact, the latter portion of the amendment is simply Resolution IV of the Bombay Congress of 1885. This, as you will have heard, besides stipulating for simultaneous examinations in England and India, provides that the successful candidates in India shall be sent to England for further study, and be subjected, there, to such additional test as may be considered necessary. Now this resolution of the 1885 Congress was not brought forward in 1886 or 1887. In 1887 the subject was not touched at all, because the Public Service Commission had completed their labours but had not yet issued their report, and the matter was considered to be, as it were, *sub judice*. But in 1886, when the resolution of 1885 might have been re-affirmed, a

2nd Day.

Res. II., Public Service Question.

different resolution, identical with that which has been proposed to you by Mr. Norton, was substituted for it. One reason for this appears to have been that the resolution of 1885 contained a clause, *viz.*, that in regard to successful candidates being sent to England to complete their education, about which great differences of opinion existed. I venture to think that, despite these differences of opinion, it would have been wiser in 1886 to put the original resolution, and have taken the verdict of the Congress upon this point. I myself hold that it is absolutely necessary that successful candidates at examinations in India should be sent to England for two or three years' special training. I urge this upon two grounds—the first, that we must have the best men trained in the most complete manner to administer our laws; and I hold that, however well a man may be trained in this country, he will be greatly improved as a public officer by the additional training which he can obtain in England. The second is, that it is absolutely necessary that Indian gentlemen, who aspire to high official position under the British Government, should have a far more thorough knowledge of English manners, customs and habits of thought than they can possibly acquire in this country. It must be remembered that Indians who rise in the Civil Service will have not only to rule over their own countrymen, but to work in harmony with, and, as time goes on, direct and control the operations of European officials. I think there is nothing more absolutely necessary than that young Indians selected for the Civil Service should go to England, if only to qualify them to maintain later their independence and self-respect in their relations with their European brother-Civilians.

You will not forget that this question of the Public Service is the one to which the most esteemed of all Indian reformers, Mr. Dadabhai Naoroji (*loud cheers*) has devoted his life and soul; and you will, I am sure, feel that his opinion on this subject is entitled to the very greatest weight. ("*Hear, hear.*") Now the resolution of 1885, which I am asking the Congress to affirm, in lieu of the resolution of 1886 which Mr. Norton has proposed to you, was Mr. Dadabhai's own resolution, moved by himself at the first Congress, and I cannot put my case with regard to this disputed question of going to England more strongly than it was put by Mr. Dadabhai at Bombay, whose words I will now quote: "I say, without the least hesitation, that the candidate himself, as well as the Service, will be vastly benefited by a visit to England. The atmosphere of freedom and high civilization which he will breathe will make him an altered man, in character, in intelligence, in experience, in self-respect and in appreciation of due respect for others. In short, he will largely increase his fitness, and command more respect in his responsible service." Gentlemen, I venture to hope that you will accept my amendment. To me it seems quite certain that the Government can never concede simultaneous examinations without insisting on the successful candidates residing two or more years in England before they enter on the very responsible duties of an Indian Civilian. Nay more, I am compelled to say that I have doubts whether I could honestly recommend simultaneous examinations unless coupled with such a condition; and I think it would be well if your resolution distinctly set forth your appreciation of its absolute necessity. I am aware that a very large number of you share my views, but are indisposed to press the point, because some others of our brother-delegates object to it, and there is doubtless much to be said in favour of the view that, as it is quite certain that if the Government does concede simultaneous examinations, it will necessarily insist upon this condition, it is needless for us to say anything about the matter. But my own view is that the open and straightforward course is the best, and that our cause would gain by our setting forth distinctly, not only the concession that we desire, but the necessary condition to this concession, as one that we are prepared to accept. These, Gentlemen, are the reasons which have led me to submit to you this amendment, which I must now leave to your better judgment.

MR. SANKARA MENON—(*Madras, No. 28 in list*)—said: Sir,—I beg to second my friend Mr. Adam's resolution. I do not know what the view may now be in other provinces, but I know that even in Madras a great many of the ablest men who gave their evidence before the Public Service Commission agreed that, even if simultaneous examinations in India and England were conceded, it would still be necessary for successful candidates in India to go to and spend at least two years in England, mixing with the English people, learning their methods of administration, and acquiring those habits of independence and self-reliance which in India, situated as we now are, we rarely acquire. In this view I wholly concur, and this is why I support this amendment, which has been so fully explained by my leader, that I need trouble you now no further.

It being now nearly dark, the PRESIDENT adjourned the meeting till next day at 11 A.M.

The Subject Committee re-assembled and again sat until late.

THIRD DAY'S PROCEEDINGS.

Friday, the 28th December, 1888.

3rd Day.

Telegram to Mr. Bright.

THE Congress re-assembled punctually at 11 A.M. As soon as all were seated the PRESIDENT rose and said: Gentlemen,—I have to ask your attention to a special subject this morning, and I will be very brief in my remarks. You know that Mr. John Bright is now lying seriously ill, and, recognising the interest he has always taken in the welfare of this country (*cheers*), it is proposed to send a telegram to him, or to his son, expressing sympathy with him in his affliction. (*Cheers.*) The terms of the proposed telegram are these:—

"TO JOHN ALBERT BRIGHT,"—that is, his son,—"FROM THE PRESIDENT OF THE INDIAN NATIONAL CONGRESS, ALLAHABAD.

"*Congress, consisting of* 1,200 *delegates* (cheers) *from all parts of India, join in expressing their high appreciation of your father's services to India* (cheers), *their sorrow at his illness, their sympathy with him and his family in his sufferings, and their earnest hope for his complete recovery.*" (Cheers.)

Is it your desire that this telegram should be despatched? (*Loud cheers and cries of "Yes, yes; all, all.*")

PANDIT AJOODHIANATH then read the telegram in Urdu for the benefit of non-English-speaking delegates, who also warmly approved of the proposal.

Res. II., Public Service Question.

MR. RAMASWAMI MUDALIAR—(*Madras, No. 15 in list*)—then, resuming the debate on the second Resolution, said: I intimated yesterday to our President that I was going to move another amendment upon the Resolution that has been placed before you, and which was proposed by my friend Mr. Norton and seconded by Mr. Mehta. You have all heard that Resolution, and the amendment I am going to propose is—

"*That the further consideration of the questions dealt with by the Public Service Commission be postponed to the next Congress.*"

Before taking this step of proposing the postponement for a whole year of this important question, I have weighed in my own mind my duty, and, after giving it my best consideration, I am convinced that I should not be acting like an honourable man if I did not come forward here and explain to you what it was that was done by the Public Service Commission in its report, and ask you to look into that question carefully before committing yourselves to any definite opinion against it. I was one of the members of that Commission, and I accepted the position because I felt that it involved the performance of an important duty towards my fellow-countrymen. (*Cheers.*) In all that we did there—and I speak out boldly, not so much on my own account as because I am concerned about the reputation of my absent friends who acted with me on that Commission—we were actuated by one sole desire, that of doing justice to our countrymen as a whole. (*Cheers.*) With that resolve we took our seats, and from beginning to end our attitude was one, in no way sympathetic with the attitude of the official members, but directly opposed to this. We took evidence in the North-West Provinces and in the Central Provinces also, and indeed all over the country, and after taking the evidence of all who had anything to say upon this most important question, we came to the conclusion that it was perfectly hopeless to find any unanimity of opinion upon it. You are all aware that the essential point in the propositions brought before you, alike by Mr. Norton and Mr. Adam, is that there should be a simultaneous examination in England and India for admission to the Civil Service. (*Cheers.*) Now I am entirely in favour of this, but then I am also a strong advocate of the condition that the men who may be selected in India must be sent to England to complete their education. ("*Hear, hear,*" *and cheers.*) I held that opinion when I entered the Commission, and I hold it at this moment. After deliberate consideration, I came to the conclusion that I must merge my own opinions, so far as the Commission was concerned, in the opinions held by the majority of my countrymen whom I virtually represented; and, after much evidence had been taken, we found that the majority of the Mahomedans on the one hand, and of the Hindus on the other, were not quite of one mind as to what they wanted. Most of the Mahomedans said, "We do not want simultaneous examinations for some years to come," while the Hindus said, "But we want them *now*"—at the same time, they would not say upon what terms and subject to what conditions they desired this concession. The fact was that some were agreed that they would send selected men to England, while others said this could not be done. Now I am very much mistaken if, in case you should take the sense of this assembly on this point, you would not find opinions, even now, almost equally divided on this point. At all events, the minority (and I cannot guess on which side the minority would be) would be so powerful a minority, that you would not be doing your duty unless you took into consideration the opinions expressed by that minority. (*Cheers.*) Now, finding this irreconcileable difference of opinion in connection with the question, we had to see also what Government had to say upon the matter. The Government said they were prepared to concede a great deal, and they accepted the view that the Indians had the right to demand a fair share in the Government of the country; but, that if we asked them to take a step which might exclude all Englishmen from the service—and this some supposed might be the result of holding simultaneous examinations in India and England—they were not prepared to accede to that. That was the view taken by Government. Of course, as a fact, we were not, in pressing for simultaneous examinations, asking them to take a step which could possibly lead to such a result. But they said, We, who are responsible for the good government of the country cannot take a leap like that into the dark. (*Cheers.*) It is for you to devise some scheme which we may safely accept. (*Laughter.*) But I felt that there was little chance of surmounting this difficulty or overcoming their objections in any such way. I knew that they held the reins, and that we had to submit. So it only remained to us to get the best terms we could, and to see if we could effect a compromise, whereby the children of the soil might have as large a share as they would concede to us in the government of the country, and no offices be kept apart for the ruling classes (*cheers*), and no natives excluded from any office by reason of caste or colour. (*Cheers.*) The terms of the compromise were that Government would give us one-third of the whole of the appointments of the judicial service throughout India, in which it was distinctly established and admitted that we were really doing our work as well as the Europeans. But it was difficult, they alleged, to say whether we possessed the necessary qualifications for the Executive branches, and therefore for the present they would give us only one-tenth of the appointments in these. They admitted that the men who held High Court Judgeships had done their work as well as Europeans, and they were willing to give us one-third of all judicial appointments. There was also no reason, they conceded, why natives should not be appointed to be members of the Executive Council, but these were in the gift of the Crown and did not fall within the scope of our enquiries. But as regards Executive appointments generally, our official colleagues, that is to say Government, felt, they said, no certainty that we were qualified, and therefore one-tenth of these was the most that we could get conceded. They were also ready to raise the age limit, and there were also minor points well known to all, in which the report, as adopted, would improve our position. But the question of simultaneous examinations was one that the rest of the Commission would not entertain. Now we were only four—Mr. D. S. White, Mr. Justice Mitter, Mr. Nulkar, and myself—and what we had to consider was, Should we hold out as irreconcileables, as impracticable men who, though much was being conceded to them, refused to accept anything short of the whole, and recorded dissents because we could not get everything we wanted; or were we rather, like reasonable men, to try to meet our colleagues half way, and in our turn give up something? Especially, was it worth while making such a stand in regard to a concession which the Mahomedans did not want, and in regard to the terms of which the Hindus, who did want it, were diametrically opposed to each other? It was our unanimous opinion that, under the circumstances, we must abstain from pressing this point and join our colleagues in their report, favourable as, in our opinion, this is in many respects to us; but we did this under the condition, which we put in writing, that the report was to be adopted in its entirety. If this be done, then I do not think we should at present agitate further on this subject. If it be not done, then I shall consider myself free to re-open the whole question. But at present I think we are in a sense bound by the compromise we have made, and this is why I press you to defer further consideration of the subject, until we see what orders the Secretary of State passes on our report. If he accepts it in its entirety, I, for one, think that we might be content to drop the subject for some years. If, however, he fails to do this, then I shall be the first to press for further agitation. So all I say now, is, *wait and see*—wait another year before you take any further action on the question. (*Cheers.*)

THE HON'BLE K. T. TELANG—(*Bombay, No. 201 in list*)—said: I rise for the purpose of expressing my concurrence, to a certain extent, in the remarks which the last speaker has addressed to the Congress in support of the amendment that he has moved. The way in which the question strikes me is this: The Congress has already stated what it considers to be an appropriate solution of this question, and has also stated that that solution requires that there should be a simultaneous examination for the Indian Civil Service held both in England and India. The Congress has stated that the limit of age for admission to that examination should be from 19 to 23. The Congress has also made other demands in reference to the examinations. They are on the records of the proceedings of the Congress. I accept them entirely, and in the evidence I gave before the Public Service Commission I stated my opinion to be in entire accordance with the proposals of the Congress. Therefore, if I now rise for the purpose of asking the Congress not to pass the resolution which has been moved by Mr. Norton, or even Mr. Adam's amendment, it is not because I do not accept the principle of Mr. Norton's resolution, nor because I consider that circumstances have occurred since

3rd Day.

Res. II., Public Service Question.

that Resolution was first passed which have in any way altered the condition of the case, but because I consider it a prudential measure to accept Mr. Ramaswamy's amendment. The reason is that the circumstances under which we now meet require that we should wait and be quiet a little, rather than that we should, by re-opening the question, perhaps sacrifice all that we might otherwise get under the report. Let us wait for the present and see what attitude the Government takes in the matter, and then begin to fight anew if it is necessary to do so. Having put on record what we have done, having never receded from the position we have taken, we are not now called upon to do anything more. We have made our claim, and Government, who has to decide on that claim, appointed a Commission for the purpose of advising as to how that claim should be satisfied. The Government has received this advice, and it has now to pass judgment on it. When that tribunal has given its decision, it would be for us to go, if necessary, to a higher tribunal, and you will remember that, after all, the Secretary of State for India is not the final tribunal in this matter. There is one other remark I wish to make, and that is with reference to the figures mentioned by Mr. Norton to the Congress yesterday. I had myself worked out the figures some months ago, and I had come to a conclusion very similar to what he did ; but there is a certain miscalculation in those figures which I am not at present in a position to explain. However, one remark I should like to make. Mr. Norton made a comparison of what we get under the system of the Statutory Civil Service with what we should get under the compromise effected by the Public Service Commission ; and he said that under the Statutory Civil Service we get a good many more appointments than we should get under the compromise recommended by the Commission. For my part, I have always held that the appointments obtained under the Statute were not worth having (*cheers*) ; and therefore, even if we were to lose a few places, what we should obtain under the circumstances recommended by the Public Service Commission would be a clear gain. I hold that the appointments obtained under the Statutory Civil Service arrangements are not only useless, but mischievous, because they have a tendency in them to demoralize the community, and we can get rid of that demoralization at very little cost indeed, by accepting the compromise suggested by the Commission. (*Cheers.*)

Mr. Monomohun Ghose—(*Calcutta, No. 1111 in list*)—then said : I did not intend, when I came to Allahabad, to intrude myself upon your attention on this occasion ; and the importance of the subject now before you is my only justification for abandoning my original intention, and appearing before you with a third amendment. The subject is one which has engrossed my attention during the last 25 years of my life, and you will readily understand that, as the result of the consideration which I have been able to give to the subject, I have formed definite and very strong opinions upon various points connected with it. I had hoped that it might not have been necessary for me to express any of those opinions, but Mr. R. S. Mudaliar's remarks make it impossible for me to abstain from doing so. Indeed, it would be needless affectation on my part to attempt to conceal my views, which I have already publicly expressed in my evidence before the Public Service Commission. (*Cheers.*) I will, therefore, state at the outset that these views are in entire accord with what has fallen from the mover of the first amendment, Mr. Adam ; and I have the satisfaction of feeling that I am supported in this respect, as I have ascertained, by almost the entire body of delegates from Bombay and Madras, and the majority of those who have come from Bengal. I have long felt that there could not have been a greater misfortune to the people of this country than the traditional idea, which has prevailed for centuries, to the effect that it is a sin and a pollution to cross the geographical boundaries of Hindustan, and that any person who commits such a sin must be regarded as an alien and a foreigner. I believe the days when such an idea was prevalent are gone, never to return. (*Cheers.*) I believe that it is absolutely necessary that the men of our own nationality, who are to be our rulers and administrators, should receive precisely the same training as the European Covenanted Servants of the Crown. I believe it is essential and exceedingly important that the Covenanted Civil Servants in this country should be men imbued with Western ideas and Western culture, or, in other words, that they should have a competent knowledge of the social and political institutions of England, which cannot be acquired without a residence in that country, and without familiar association with Englishmen in their own homes. I also believe that it would be idle to expect that the Government would permit simultaneous examinations in England and in India unless we were prepared to send our young men to be trained in England. ("*Hear, hear.*") Nevertheless, I feel, and I must acknowledge, that there is a section of our countrymen, and an influential section too, who think somewhat differently on the subject. It may be that in the Congress the representatives of that section are in a minority, and that, if called upon to vote, the majority of us will probably support the amendment proposed by Mr Adam. (*Cheers.*) But we must remember that the opinions of those who differ from us in this respect are entitled to our respectful and even indulgent consideration (*cheers*) ; and I am therefore not prepared to say that we should be acting wisely if we were to invite discussion upon points on which any difference of opinion might prove disastrous to our best interests. (*Cheers.*) I think we must try to avoid, in regard to questions of this sort, any substantial difference of opinion, and, above all, heated discussions which are not likely to lead to any useful result or secure any good object. (*Cheers.*) What we ought to aim at, in such matters, is to secure, as far as possible, unanimity of opinion. (*Cheers.*) With this view I will submit for your consideration a resolution which, I have no doubt, will meet with general approval. Now, there is one matter as to which we are all agreed, and that is the necessity for holding simultaneous examinations in England and India. I think we are also agreed that we fully appreciate the justice and the propriety of the recommendations, made by the Public Service Commission, to raise the limit of age prescribed for the open competition. (*Cheers.*) It would not be right, therefore, to ignore the services rendered to the country by the members of that Commission, who have performed their difficult task in such a manner as to entitle them to the thanks of this Congress. (*Cheers.*) I must confess, however, that, as regards the propriety of taking up this question at all, I at one time entertained considerable doubts. I was at first inclined to believe that the wise course for us would be to follow that suggested by Mr. Mudaliar ; but, after hearing Mr. Norton, and after mature consideration of the matter, I have come to the conclusion that, if we were not to press our demand on this occasion before the Secretary of State, we might be allowing judgment to go by default. It is our duty to let the Government know what we think on the subject, and I think the Congress will, therefore, agree with me that the best course for us on the present occasion would be the adoption of a resolution which could not possibly cause any difference of opinion in the Congress, and which would explicitly set forth what we mean and wish.

This then is the resolution which I venture to propose for your acceptance :—

" *That this Congress, while appreciating the concessions proposed in the Report of the Public Service Commission, yet feels it necessary to put distinctly on record its opinion that full justice will never be done to the people of this country, until the open competitive examination for the Civil Service of India is held simultaneously in England and in India.*" (*Loud cheers.*)

I do not think, Gentlemen, that I need say more upon this amendment, which I now leave in your hands.

MR. N. G. CHANDAVARKAR—(*Bombay, No. 203, in list*)—said : I have great pleasure in seconding this amendment. We have saved ourselves, I hope, from presenting to the outside world the spectacle of a house divided against itself; and I hope that, for the sake of unanimity, we shall avoid touching on points on which any difference of opinion exists among ourselves. The mission of the Congress is to deal with those questions on which we are all substantially agreed, not those on which we differ. When we get all that we all agree to be necessary, it will be time to take up questions on which we are not agreed. Now we are all agreed to a man as to the point set forth in this amendment, and I hope we shall pass it by acclamation. If I were to express my own convictions on the subjects touched upon in the speeches, lying outside this amendment, I should have to say that my views are quite in accord with those of Mr. M. Ghose. (*Cheers.*)

MR. EARDLEY NORTON—(*Madras, No. 19, in list*)—said : Sir,—So far as I am concerned, I shall be quite willing to withdraw my motion in favour of that proposed by my friend Mr. Monomohun Ghose. (*Loud cheers.*)

THE HON'BLE MR. PHEROZSHAH MEHTA—(*Bombay, No 208, in list*)—said : Sir,—As seconder of the original Resolution, I gladly follow my leader in withdrawing it in favour of Mr. Ghose's motion. (*Cheers.*)

MR. JOHN ADAM—(*Madras, No. 2, in list*)—said: Gentlemen,—I entirely concur in Mr. Ghose's amendment so far as it goes, and it has the advantage of meeting every body's views to this extent, and I have therefore no hesitation in withdrawing my amendment, which, with my seconder, Mr. Sankara Menon's concurrence, I now do. (*Cheers.*)

MR. RAMASWAMY MUDALIAR—(*Madras, No. 15, in list*)—said : Gentlemen,—I suppose it is expected of me that I too should make a recantation and withdraw my amendment. Well, Gentlemen, I cannot exactly do that, but I will abstain from pressing it. (*Laughter and cheers.*)

THE HON'BLE K. T. TELANG—(*Bombay, No. 201, in list*)—said : Sir,—To make the recantation of my friend Mr. Mudaliar complete, I, as the seconder of his amendment, declare my concurrence in its withdrawal in favour of Mr. Ghose's amendment. (*Cheers*

3rd Day.

Res. II., Public Service Question.

and cries of " Vote, vote.") One or two delegates rose to speak, but the assembly insisted on the vote being taken, it having been ascertained that no one wanted to speak against the amendment.

THE PRESIDENT : Then, Gentlemen, shall I put Mr. Ghose's amendment, which, by the withdrawal of the original Resolution and the other amendments, has now become the substantive resolution ? *(Cries of " Yes, yes ;" " Vote, vote.")* It will stand thus :—

RESOLVED—" *That this Congress, while appreciating the concessions proposed in the Report of the Public Service Commission, yet feels it necessary to put distinctly on record its opinion that full justice will never be done to the people of this country until the open competitive examination for the Civil Service of India is held simultaneously in England and in India.*"

The resolution was then put and carried unanimously.

Res. III., Separation of Judicial and Executive Functions.

MR. J. E. HOWARD—*(Allahabad, No. 573, in list)*—who was in charge of the third resolution, did not appear for a minute or two. Then hastily entering the hall he said : Mr. President and Gentlemen,—I must apologise to you for being rather late for to-day's proceedings, but I did not expect to be required so early. However, I am glad to see that the warning voice of your wise and practical President has been heard, and that you have got through your business earlier to-day than I anticipated from the great differences of opinion that appeared to exist at the close of yesterday evening's proceedings. The resolution I have to propose runs as follows :—

" *That this Congress having read and considered Resolution XI of the Congress of* " ' *1886, to wit—*

" ' *That this Congress do place on record an expression of the universal conviction that a complete* " ' *separation of executive and judicial functions (such that in no case the two functions shall be combined* " ' *in the same officer) has become an urgent necessity, and that, in its opinion, it behoves the Government* " ' *to effect this separation without further delay, even though this should, in some provinces, involve some* " ' *extra expenditure,'—*

" *and Resolution III of the Congress of 1887, to the same effect, do now, hereby, affirm the* " *same respectively.*"

Well, Gentlemen, in moving this resolution I find myself in a happier position than many others who have had to move other resolutions covering more debateable ground ; and, before I come to my point, you will permit me to say a few words by way of introduction as to the Congress itself, and what I have heard as to the Princes and Chiefs who have *not*, and of the people who *have*, joined this movement. Gentlemen, I should not be standing here to-day associated with this movement if I did not believe it to be essentially a middle-class movement representing the independence and intelligence of the country, and thus the interests of the various peoples of this land. So much has been said about the Proclamation of the Queen in 1858 that I must tell you that I heard that Proclamation myself, having laboured in this place in various capacities ever since then for the period of thirty years. If I have no other qualification for the task that has been entrusted to me, at least I have the one of having seen the various phases through which this country has passed during that time. I trust that you will pardon my giving you three instances, taken from my own experience, to illustrate those phases. We have no quarrel, Gentlemen, with the Executive power. Eventual power must reside somewhere, and authority must be obeyed in the last resort for the welfare of the people ; but it is in the nature of Executive authority that its orders must be obeyed, and no judicial officer can discharge his duties impartially or with that moral effect which is necessary to the administration of justice, save in absolute independence and according to his conscience. As you are aware, in 1860, the first Penal Code was passed for India, and shortly after this there was a trial in these parts of a person of some consequence, accused of treason and waging war against the Queen. In those days we had no legal profession in these provinces, and that blessed peace reigned which, in the opinion of many persons, is only disturbed now by the presence of lawyers, who are regarded as the scourge of the country. *(Laughter.)* The accused person had, therefore, to get a solicitor of some distinction from Calcutta to defend him, and a remark was heard by me in a railway carriage in which an official was told of the arrival of the legal gentleman from Calcutta. When he heard of this he said, " What a scoundrel the fellow " (meaning the legal gentleman) " must be ! " *(Cries of Shame ! shame !")* No, Gentlemen, there is no shame except in conscious wrongdoing. That unfortunate gentleman only spoke according to his lights, and we know what notions of justice prevailed in those days from the ignorance which he displayed. It is our justification for existence that such ignorance must be dispelled, and it is the glory of our nation that we have, by the highest legislative authority of this land, disseminated a notion of the people's rights by the various laws enacted from time to time for their benefit. *(Cheers.)* Well, Gentlemen, the next instance illustrates the evils arising from a combination of judicial and executive ideas in the same person, which is a necessary result of the two functions being habitually combined in one official. Fourteen years ago I was called upon to defend two persons before the Sessions Judge of Agra, and the evidence against them consisted principally of the statements of policemen who had placed the stolen articles where they were found; so that I had no difficulty in getting the assessors to record a verdict of acquittal. The Sessions Judge, nevertheless, very much to my surprise, convicted the accused persons. I was asked to have tea with the Sessions Judge soon after the trial was over, and he remarked to me that he supposed I was surprised at his having convicted my clients. I confessed I was on the evidence adduced, and he then made the following remarkable observation to me: "I admit the evidence against them was very weak, but you know *those fellows have a very bad reputation, and Her Majesty's Government must be carried on!!" (Laughter.)* That was his notion of exercising judicial functions. As a Magistrate during the previous 20 years of his service, he had always been both head policeman, prosecutor and judge, and when he came to be a Sessions Judge he could not escape the bias thus formed, and when the Magistrate set forth in the committal papers that the accused were very bad characters, he felt bound to convict them, whether there was any sufficient evidence against them or not. As the Judge in question has retired from the Service, I will not mention his name, but I will give you the sequel of the case which came in appeal before the High Court of these Provinces. Mr. Justice (afterwards Sir Charles) Turner heard the appeal of the prisoners. Mr. Colvin was my leader, and so flagrantly opposed to common sense and common justice was the conviction that that eminent Judge (*cheers*) never called upon the counsel for the appellants to say a single word in support of the appeal. Turning to the Government Pleader, who appeared on behalf of the Crown in support of the conviction—as he is a distinguished member of this Congress and present, I may be permitted to mention his name, Mr. Dwarkanath Banerji—(*cheers*)—Mr. Justice Turner said: "How can you support this conviction, Mr. Banerji? I see the evidence is entirely that of policemen who found the things, which they are accused of having placed where they are said to have found them, and I must confess the case smacks strongly of police manufacture." Mr. Banerji, with that blandness and frankness which distinguishes him, was forced to admit that the evidence was extremely weak and suspicious, and the men were acquitted on the spot. But observe the result: They had been nearly two months wrongfully in jail, and, as you know, there is no redress for such wrongs. An innocent man, wrongfully convicted or incarcerated, has no compensation of any kind, and it is because of the irreparable nature of the wrong that we should provide every possible safeguard against such abuses. The last instance is a comparatively recent one, taken from the most backward of these provinces—Oudh—a non-regulation Province as it is called. A few years ago the Judicial Commissioner of Oudh had his judicial soul shocked by finding that a Deputy Commissioner under him, in whom were combined the functions of Revenue Collector and Magistrate, had used his magisterial powers to convict—I forget how many persons (I believe the number was nearly a hundred)—under the Indian Penal Code, for disobeying the lawful order of a public servant, because they had not paid their instalments of revenue in the time within which he had ordered that they should be paid! The Judicial Commissioner sent these cases up to His Honor the Lieutenant-Governor of the N.-W. P. and Chief Commissioner of Oudh, for such notice as His Honor might see fit to take of the matter, and the fines were, I believe, remitted; but the case illustrates, happily, the utter confusion in regard to the first principles of justice to which the existing irrational combination of these two functions, the judicial and executive, in one official, are apt to give rise.

Gentlemen, this and similar cases (of which all of you present could doubtless cite many) are evils resulting from an imperfect conception of what justice really means, and we must not be too indignant with the men who thus err, but rather with the system which permits, nay, rather, naturally leads up to such things, and it is against this faulty system that the resolution, which I have had the honour to propose to you, is specially directed. I do not, for a moment, pretend that this is the only defect of our existing judicial system, but human nature being what it is, we must not wonder that the system of sublime impartiality, gradually attained in England by purifying the judicial system there until it represents the most exalted ideal conceivable for giving a man a fair trial, should not yet be fully understood here, except by men especially trained in the more advanced English conceptions of justice. The profession to which I have the honour to belong, after generations of effort in England, has attained to a practice of independence and fairness which stands unrivalled throughout Europe; and I would ask you to remember that it is only by patience and perseverance and long effort that all this has come about, and to entreat you, yourselves, to emulate that patience and that perseverance.

The triumph of moral force, which the existing system of jurisprudence in Great Britain so aptly demonstrates, is one more proof that right must ever prevail in the end; and I would ask you, not only in the matter of this special reform, which it has been my duty this day to advocate, but in the case of all those other reforms which we know to be essential to the well-being of ourselves and our countrymen, to find no fault with your

3rd Day.

Res. III., Separation of Judicial and Executive Functions.

opponents, to resort to no angry declamation and no heated remonstrance, but to be patient, persistent and true to yourselves. Not by violence or noise have the great things of the earth been achieved ; not by ambition or self-seeking can a nation's life be regenerated ; but by calm indomitable reliance on that moral force which is the supreme reason, and by implanting in all with whom you may come in contact the conviction that you look for eventual triumph to these means, and these only ; and that the moral power which has made the English nation glorious throughout an empire, on which it has been well and truly said that the sun never sets, is the power to which you trust for the triumph of those great principles of justice and freedom which you are all here assembled to vindicate and uphold (*Cheers.*)

MR. TAHILRAM KHEMCHAND—(*Sindh, No. 241, in list*)—said : Gentlemen,—I second the Resolution. All that we say to Government is—" Do us justice, so that our people may be loyal and contented; so that they may rely implicitly upon you, and hasten to support you in the hour of need." We ask for justice, because we wish the entire country to be truly loyal in its heart of hearts. If we were sedition-mongers, as some have idly proclaimed, our course would really be quite different. We should sit quiet and let the people brood over their wrongs and the injustice that is too prevalent, and thus allow discontent to grow and spread, and prepare the people for a rising. But we come boldly forward and tell the Government that the system of administration needs to be improved and reformed. We point out to them exactly how this should be done ; and we tell them that, if they want to inspire love and confidence in the people, they must remove those grievances which are now alienating their hearts. Now it is quite certain that the existing combination of judicial and executive functions is a very fruitful source of dissatisfaction; and I will give you an instance which occurred in my province, to illustrate the evil of combining these two divergent functions in one official. A man was charged by the police with a certain offence before a second-class Magistrate. The Magistrate made inquiries and found that there was no valid ground for the police suspecting the man, and that the police had apprehended him to satisfy some grudge that they had against him. The Magistrate reported the circumstances of the case to his official superior, stating in his report that he had discovered that the police had made some alterations in their diary in order to substantiate the false charge. The matter being brought to the notice of the next higher authority, a native first-class Magistrate, a prosecution was directed against the policeman who had made the false entry in the diary. The District Superintendent of Police interested himself on behalf of the policeman who was concerned in the offence, and got the case transferred from the Court of a first-class Magistrate, who was a native, to that of an European first-class Magistrate in whom the two functions were combined. The injured man who had been falsely accused was not represented by a Pleader, and not being prepared to go on with the case elsewhere without a legal adviser, he applied for a postponement. But his application was summarily disallowed and the Magistrate took advantage of his unavoidable unpreparedness to dismiss the case, entirely ignoring the fact that it was on the State, and not the individual sufferer, that, when the case had reached this stage, rested the onus of causing the facts of the case to be investigated.

There must be some hundreds of Barristers and Pleaders amongst the twelve hundred and odd delegates here assembled, but I venture to assert that there is not one single one of them who cannot, from his own personal experience, cite many similar cases in which the combination of the two functions, against which this resolution is a protest, has led to the most flagrant miscarriages of justice. (*Loud cheers.*)

MR. DEVARAO VINAYEK—(*Berar, No. 273, in list*)—rose and said : I am here to speak a few words in support of this resolution. I do not stand here because there is anything of great importance left unsaid by my predecessors, or because I desire to exhibit powers of oratory which, unfortunately, I do not possess, but solely because I feel very strongly upon this subject, and desire to corroborate what has been alleged as to the evils of combining the judicial and executive functions in one officer, by my own experience, during the six and twenty years that I have practised as a Pleader. I come from Berar. The name of our little province may be perhaps scarcely known to many of my brother-delegates (*laughter*), but I can assure them that even in this little out-of-the-way tract of country the evils of this unholy union of functions, that can never be joined in lawful matrimony, are as apparent as elsewhere. (*Cheers.*)

But the question has been discussed, not only in this Congress, but at several of the previous Congresses, and the universal opinion is that the severance of the executive and judicial functions is a necessity, and that the Government is bound to effect that severance without any further delay. Of course I might give instances as my predecessors did—aye any number you please—of failures of justice due to this unconstitutional combination, but really it would be simply taking up your time in vain, and as it were slaying the already dead.

3rd Day.

Res. III, Separation of Judicial and Executive Functions.

But there is one point that I may properly touch on. You have a resolution here before you, and if I understand that proposition, or rather resolution, properly, its object is to disconnect the magisterial or criminal judicial powers from the police or executive powers. But you will be surprised and startled when you hear from me that in my province, not only the magisterial and police powers are combined in one officer, but also the revenue and civil judicial powers are all combined in one man. (*Cries of "Shame."*) There is one head of the district who is the Deputy Commissioner and who is the supreme authority in all matters. He is head of the police—he is the highest local tribunal in criminal matters with powers of sentencing to seven years' imprisonment with hard labour—he is the highest tribunal in all civil cases—he is the chief revenue official, head director, alike, of all fiscal arrangements. In every relation of life you are in the grasp of this one man ; if he dislikes you—if he have a prejudice against you—there is no escaping him ; it is an absolute despotism. Now, I ask, is this a defensible system ? Others have told you, and you yourselves well know what takes place where only police and criminal judicial powers are combined in one officer. You can imagine what might occur in our province. As a matter of fact, serious failures of justice have resulted, and if these have not been more frequent or grievous in our province than elsewhere, it is due solely to the fact that we have had exceptionally good officers, who scorned to abuse their powers. But we cannot count upon a continuance of this ; the system is susceptible of unlimited abuse and oppression ; and against that system I earnestly and unhesitatingly protest, and this, despite the sincere personal respect and esteem in which I hold many of the officers under whom I have lived and worked. (*Cheers.*)

BABOO TARINI PRASAD—(*Behar, No. 1090, in list*)—said : I have been asked to support the resolution which has been proposed by Mr. Howard. My duty is simple enough. The resolution deals with a subject which has been thoroughly discussed both at the Congress of 1886 at Calcutta and at the Congress of 1887 at Madras. I respectfully ask you to say whether there were any differences of opinion on either of these occasions upon this subject. I submit that there can be no hesitation in saying that there were really no two opinions on this question. (*Cheers.*) All I need say here, therefore, is that my experience for the last twenty-five years, as a member of the legal profession, has convinced me, as it must have convinced all of you, that the evils which flow from the combination of the executive and of the judicial functions are too numerous to dwell upon, and too serious to be overlooked, and that the sooner they are done away with, by what I suppose Mr. Vinayek would designate a divorce *a vinculo* (*laughter*), the better. With these words I would commend the resolution to your acceptance. (*Cheers.*)

MR. SHARF-UD-DIN—(*Punjab, No. 383, in list*)—said, speaking in Oordoo : Gentlemen, This resolution which we now have to dispose of concerns the existing powers of district officers, in which are amalgamated judicial, executive and revenue powers—a combination which is a source of great suffering to people who have the misfortune to have dealings with our trinitarian authorities, three officers in one. For instance, where a Collector wishes to realise revenue, he does so not merely by the exercise of those powers conferred on him on that behalf by the legislature, but by the pressure of the authority that he possesses as a Magistrate, conferred on him, not in view to the realisation of land revenue demands, but to enable him to punish offenders against the criminal law. What we now pray for is the immediate discontinuance of this anomalous combination of various functions in one individual. The need for this reform is urgent and well known to you, and has been already so repeatedly and clearly set forth that I need not, I think, dwell upon it at any great length. You all know the doubts we one and all entertain, when under trial before such compound officials, of getting any real justice meted out to us. The Magistrate ought to be our refuge against unlawful and arbitrary acts of the Collector, but the two men are one, and so far from the one acting as a check on the other, the two offices being combined in one, we have practically no redress. Thus a man is brought up for arrears and non-payment of rent before the Collector, and, though he feels that he is being unjustly dealt with, he has to keep his mouth closed and bear his hard lot, whatever it may be, with patience, because he knows that if he protests or fights against the Collector's order, the Collector, who is also a Magistrate, will either commit him for contempt of court or fine him for disobedience of lawful order, or in some other way bring the criminal law to bear upon him. Officials, who are Revenue Collectors, Civil Judges, and also Magistrates, as they are in many places, not unfrequently seem to think it their duty to superadd a criminal charge to the revenue or civil case before them. In a civil suit, when books and accounts and deeds are presented to establish a claim, an officer whose temper is ruffled takes it into his head that there is some cheating or forgery, orders an investigation by the police of which he is the head—the police whose oppressions are only too well known to all of you, and who at once bring them into play to obtain the conviction of an innocent man for their own exaltation in the eyes of their superior—and then tries and convicts the man himself. This is only a single instance of the kind of injustice and oppression to which this combination of

3rd Day.

Res. III., Separation of Judicial and Executive Functions.

functions, the complete separation of which we are now praying for, continually leads. I have myself seen instances in the Punjab of officers, sitting as Civil Judges, letting their temper get the better of them, and exercising magisterial powers to commit unoffending witnesses, in civil suits before them, to the *Havalat* * and trial, for unknown or imaginary faults. The system leads to all kinds of abuses, and I cannot doubt that, if we press our request for a separation of the two functions, it will be granted to us, for it is a just and righteous one. (*Cheers and cries of " Vote, vote."*)

THE PRESIDENT : Does any one wish to oppose this resolution ? (*None, none.*) Do you wish the discussion to be prolonged ? (*No, no, vote, vote.*) Then I will now put the resolution as follows :—

RESOLVED—" *That this Congress having read and considered Resolution XI of the " Congress of 1886, to wit—*

" ' *That this Congress do place on record an expression of the universal conviction, that a complete " ' separation of executive and judicia functions (such that in no case the two functions shall be combined in the " ' same officer) has become an urgent necessity, and that, in its opinion, it behoves the Government to effect this " ' separation without further delay, even though this should, in some provinces, involve some extra " ' expenditure'—*

" *and Resolution III of the Congress of 1887, to the same effect, does now, hereby, affirm the " same respectively.*"

The resolution was then put and carried unanimously.

Res. IV., Extension of Trial by Jury—Finality of Juries' Verdicts—Option to be given to accused of committal to the Sessions.

MR. KALI CHARAN BANERJEE—(*Bengal, No. 1135, in list*)—The terms of the resolution which I have the honour to propose are as follows :—

" *That this Congress having read and considered Resolution VIII of the Congress of " 1886, to wit—*

" ' *That, in the opinion of this Congress, the time has now arrived when the system of trial by jury " ' may be safely extended into many parts of the country where it is not at present in force'—*

" *Resolution IX of the Congress of 1886, to wit—*

" ' *That, in the opinion of this Congress the innovation made in 1872 in the system of trial by jury, " ' depriving the verdicts of juries of all finality, has proved injurious to the country, and the powers " ' then, for the first time, vested in Sessions Judges and High Courts, of setting aside verdicts of acquittal, " ' should be at once withdrawn'—*

" *and Resolution X of the Congress of 1886, to wit—*

" ' *That in the opinion of this Congress, a provision, similar to that contained in the Summary " ' Jurisdiction Act of England, under which accused persons in serious cases have the option of demand- " ' ing a committal to the Sessions Court should be introduced into the Indian Code of Criminal Procedure " ' enabling accused persons, in warrant cases, to demand that, instead of being tried by the Magistrate " ' they be committed to the Court of Sessions'—*

" *do now, hereby, affirm the same respectively.*"

This tri-partite resolution is cognate to the resolution which you have just adopted. Sir Richard Garth, late Chief Justice of Calcutta, puts it so, and not only puts it so, but plainly tells us that the posture of affairs which necessitates the separation of judicial and executive functions, is the very posture of affairs which necessitates the carrying out of the principle underlying this resolution. This is a resolution in the interests of the administration of justice, and is framed upon lines tried, and adopted, and effectuated in England. As regards the first of these resolutions, which refers to the extension of the system of trial by jury into many parts of the country where it is not at present in force, I need say but little. Indeed, if we were to consider the principle which underlies this institution—the principle, namely, that the accused person should have the benefit of a trial at the hands of his peers—it is impossible to conceive that there should be any district in India which would be found backward. Everywhere it must be possible for the accused person to find peers at whose hands he might claim to be tried. But our resolution does not go so far. We demand simply that the system of trial by jury be further extended ; and is it possible for any one, having regard to the districts represented in this Congress, to say that such of them, for example, as did not enjoy the privileges, would be found too backward for the experiment ? There is the alternative system of trial with the aid of assessors. If in a district there are persons whose opinion taken individually is worth taking, surely in that district there must be persons whose opinion taken collectively should be worth taking, with the further incident of being binding on the Court. I come now to the second resolution, and in speaking to it I must confess that at one time I had the perversity of intellect to be taken in by the phrase " perverse verdicts." I congratulate myself on the fact that I am in a position to-day to tell you that I have been exorcised of the delusion, and the great exorcists are present here. If it is open to a judge to speak of the verdict of a jury as perverse,

* *i.e.*, the Lock-up.

3rd Day.

Res. IV., Extension of Trial by Jury—Finality of Juries' Verdicts—Option to be given to accused of committal to the Sessions.

jurors accustomed to call things, as viewed by them, by their proper names, may be permitted to retort and say that there may as well be a perverse reference from their verdicts, and a perverse reversal of them. With regard to this reference section, you will be pleased to remember that there is a still further sting about it. If an accused person is convicted by the Sessions Court in a trial by jury, he has a right of appeal to the High Court, but his appeal must be based on grounds of law; whereas if a reference is made by the Sessions Judge from the verdict of a jury, the whole case is re-opened by the High Court, and not only are legal grounds taken into consideration, but the evidence is also looked into. We must also always remember that, as far as the system of trial by jury is concerned, it is not only a system good for administrative purposes, but it is likewise well fitted to develop the political education of the country, and the reference section, suspended like the sword of Damocles over the heads of jurors, cannot fail to have a demoralising effect. I will now pass on to what I consider a still more important resolution, and that is the third. Your attention has just been drawn to the evil consequences of combining judicial and executive functions in the same hands. The necessity for separating these functions is admitted by Government, but in order to carry out the principle, there is *said* to be need for funds, and funds may not be forthcoming. As far as the third resolution is concerned, it is a resolution to which effect may be given at once; at any rate, it is a resolution to which Government may be pressed to give effect, so long as funds are not forthcoming for the separation of judicial and executive functions. We complain of injustice being done at the hands of officers in whom we find a combination of these functions, and this resolution asks that the accused person should have the right of demanding in serious cases a committal to the Court of Sessions. The Sessions Judge of the present day has, as a rule, no executive weaknesses; you may not be prepared to accept that proposition after what has fallen from the lips of Mr. Howard, but, still, as a rule, we may take it that the Sessions Judge is not affected with any such weakness, and so we ask that the accused person should in certain cases have the right of demanding a sessions trial. In pressing this resolution, we should remember that this was a matter submitted to the consideration of the Government of Lord Ripon, and that in respect to it the Government of Lord Ripon recorded a strong minute, and the Select Committee entrusted with the Criminal Procedure Bill recorded it as their opinion that it was a matter well worthy of being considered when the Criminal Procedure Code came next to be amended. Sir Auckland Colvin was on that Select Committee. We may press this resolution on Government with such credentials in our favour. It may be said that the result of this change would be that the Sessions Judge would find his file much heavier than it is now, but this option would not be exercised in every case. It would often be the interest of the accused person not to be committed to the Sessions. He would not think of exercising the option, except when he had grave apprehensions of a failure of justice. Then you must remember that if the case goes direct to the Sessions Court, you have, it is true, more sessions cases; but then, on the other hand, you have fewer appeals. At any rate, here is a necessity arising from the fact that justice suffers from the combination of judicial and executive functions. Justice should not only be done, but the machinery should be such as to justify that justice to the sense of the country.

MR. N. G. CHANDAVARKAR—(*Bombay, No. 203, in list*)—rose and said: I do not think I could recommend this resolution to your approval better than by simply saying that it is eminently more reasonable, more liberal, and more in accordance with true British citizenship than that other resolution suggested yesterday by our old friend Rajah Shiva Prasad, which our worthy President was good enough to decline with thanks. (*Laughter and cheers.*) Rajah Shiva Prasad is so charmed with the existing criminal laws of the country that he would have the rigours of these laws increased. The Rajah is so anxious to be governed by the principles of British justice that he wishes to be rid of that, as he views it, objectionable regard to the rights of free speech and private opinion, which apparently in his opinion disgrace and discredit the existing criminal laws. (*Laughter and cheers.*) Rajah Shiva Prasad suggests that we ought to introduce into the criminal laws of this country a provision for what he pleases to call seditious libel. Well, though this combination of words is not unknown to legal experts in England, I confess that I have never thoroughly been able to realize its meaning. I can understand what sedition is, and what libel is, but I find it hard to realize what we are to understand by that jumble of words, seditious libel. (*Laughter and cheers.*) Believe me, we ought to have no faith in such nostrums as he places before you. Gentlemen, the question which is involved, alike in the Rajah's suggestion to increase the rigours of the criminal law and in the proposition before you to amend the existing law, is simply this: Are we to be ruled in accordance with the principles enunciated by such men as Sir James Stephen (*hisses*), or to be ruled in accordance with the principles of that august Sovereign of ours who in 1857 so impressed upon Lord Stanley that every Indian was not to be treated as a rebel, but, on the contrary, that every native inhabitant in this country was to be assured that Her most anxious desire was

3rd Day.

Res. IV., Extension of Trial by Jury—Finality of Juries' Verdicts—Option to be given to accused of committal to the Sessions.

to see the people of India happy and contented and flourishing. (*Cheers.*) I see, Gentlemen, that the response of this Congress will be that you are anxious to be ruled in accordance with the sentiments of our august Sovereign rather than by those of Sir James FitzJames Stephen. (*Cheers.*) If any Ministry ventured to propose any such laws in England, as Shiva Prasad and his friends suggest for India, they would be out of power within the week. (*Cheers.*) Nay more; if any Ministry were to propose to insert in the criminal law of England a provision such as that against which we protest in the second clause of our resolution, they would speedily find themselves on the Opposition Benches. Is it because we belong to what Lord Salisbury was once pleased to call the colored millions of India, that such an objectionable provision has been inserted into our Criminal Procedure Act? But further discussion is needless, and I shall only add that, in passing this resolution, we are demanding to be ruled in accordance with the principles of those who have been approved by time as the worthiest statesmen of England, and conformably to the express wish of our august and beloved Sovereign. (*Loud cheers.*)

SHEIKH UMR BAKSH—(*Punjab, No. 361, in list*)—then spoke. He said: I am called to support this resolution, the importance of which has been clearly set forth by the gentlemen who have preceded me. I have specially risen to support this resolution because I am a Mahomedan, and it is well to show that we Mahomedans are not behind the followers of any other creed in our desire to secure, by combined action, the welfare of the entire country. (*Cheers.*) In passing this resolution, we shall not be evincing any ill-feeling towards Englishmen, who already enjoy the right of trial by jury; but just as we have asked for other things, we ask for this also as a matter to which we may lay claim under that Charter of Liberty granted us in 1858. (*Cheers.*) If this resolution be accepted by the British Government, this Congress will gain the thanks of the whole country. But this is just one of the resolutions which will be most likely to be granted by the Government, and the country will then come to realize fully that the Congress has done a good many things for their countrymen. (*Cheers.*) It is said, I know, by some men that this system of trial by jury will fail in some parts of this country; that the country is not everywhere prepared for it. There is, perhaps, some truth in this, but in the first place there is no measure but fails in some points at first, and in the second we are not blindly pressing for the extension to every district of this system. No doubt there are places where the people are too backward, and where it *would* be difficult to secure a sufficient number of sufficiently good men to act as jurors. But we do not pray for its extension to such backward places, but only to those numerous districts in which good jurors can certainly be obtained in large numbers. As in all other cases, our prayers are moderate. At present we only want trial by jury extended to places clearly fit to receive this boon, but as time goes on there is no doubt that it will have to be further and further extended, and that in the long run it will succeed here as it has done in all other places where it has been introduced. (*Cheers.*) In regard to the other two clauses of the resolution, I need hardly speak, for the most captious critic can, it seems to me, find nothing to cavil at in these. (*Cheers.*)

MR. N. SUBBA RAO—(*Madras, No. 38, in list*)—said: This is a matter upon which we are all agreed. ("*Hear, hear.*") We see at present, in several parts of our Presidency, in many important districts, this system of trial by jury in full force. It is a system which is admitted to be an aid to the administration of justice; it has been in force for a long period with us, and it has worked, and is working, satisfactorily. (*Cheers.*) It is often alleged, as a reason for not further extending the system, that there are not a sufficient number of people of the intelligence required to make men satisfactory jurymen, and that our people are not sufficiently advanced in education to aid Judges as jurors in the discharge of their functions. I must give the most emphatic denial to these allegations so far as my Presidency is concerned. (*Cheers.*) Has not the education of the country been going on for a great number of years? The existence of this assembly is sufficient evidence of that and of the existence of far more than the required number of competent jurors. What town in the Empire, in which Sessions Courts are held, but is represented here by delegates? (*Cries of* "*None, none!*") What delegate is there in whose election at least fifty educated men, fit to be jurors, (to say nothing of the multitudes of the less cultured) did not take part? (*Cries of* "*None, none!*") We are not wanting in men; men by scores, and hundreds even, in some towns, will willingly come forward and take upon themselves the honourable duties of jurymen. (*Cheers.*) Again it is, at times, alleged that the present system of trial with the aid of assessors is a farce, and that, because that system is a farce, therefore the system of trial by jury would also be a farce. I submit that no more fallacious argument could be advanced. (*Cheers.*) The present system of trials with the aid of assessors may not be quite satisfactory, and if it were it would be a miracle. For how can you expect really good men to spend a whole day, at times two or three, in working into a case thoroughly, merely to enable a Judge, at the end, to decide

3rd Day.

Res. IV., Extension of Trial by Jury—Finality of Juries' Verdicts—Option to be given to accused of committal to the Sessions.

perversely without reference, or in direct opposition, to their carefully worked-out opinions? When assessors are summoned to assist a Judge, they are not, as a rule, consulted in any way. Their presence, in fact, is practically ignored, and they are simply, too often, mere paraphernalia of the Judge's Court, having no more to say to the trial, in which they are supposed to assist, than his inkstand or his chair. Moreover, no efforts are made, in most cases, to secure good men as assessors. When the list of assessors is drawn up, the Judge and the Collector meet and do it in something like five minutes. Nor do they try to see that the better-informed sections of the people are represented on their list, or even to make sure that there are any intelligent people amongst the lot. The most ignorant men, and old people in their dotage, are sometimes put on the list. I have known two assessors, who could not read or write, put on in a forgery case, who, when the paper was put into their hands, to say if it was forged or genuine, could only say "Whichever you please." (*Laughter.*) This is only one of many instances that I could cite, but I think I have said enough to prove that the not unfrequent failure of the assessor system is absolutely no argument against the success of a properly-conducted jury system.

MOULVI ABDUL JALIL—(*Cawnpur, No. 720 in list*)—spoke in Urdu and said: As regards the resolution now before you, I have only a very few words to say. Previous speakers have insisted on the necessity of an extension of the jury system, and you all realize the disadvantages under which we Indians suffer by reason of this system being in most places denied to us. So on this head I need say no more. But the sufferings and oppression undergone too often by accused persons in criminal cases, while their cases are pending in the lower or magistrate's courts, are so real and serious that, for my part, the section of the resolution which I would most earnestly press for is the last, which would entitle accused persons in warrant cases to demand that they be at once committed to the sessions instead of being tried by the magistrate. This would be quite as great a boon to the country in its way as trial by jury in another way, and I think we cannot too earnestly press this on the consideration of Government.

RAJAH RAMPAL SINGH—(*Allahabad, No. 571 in list*)—rose and said: Gentlemen,—These questions relating to the improvement of our judicial system have been very ably discussed throughout the debate, but there is one small point which has been missed. That bears upon and is an argument in favour of the separation of the judicial and executive functions. In that you have virtually assured our overworked officials that you desire to relieve them by taking a portion of their work off their shoulders. The officers who are overwhelmed with all those varied functions, to whose combination we object, are worked from morning to night like a horse. (*Laughter.*) Therefore if these gentlemen are allowed the same pay, and by being relieved of some of their now too multifarious functions, have less work to do, they will, or at least ought to, be much obliged to you. (*Renewed laughter.*) So these gentlemen in whom these many irreconcileable functions are jointly vested, and who have very much too much work upon their hands, will probably be as greatly benefited by the change we recommend as the people of this country. (*Cheers.*) And, if they have any gratitude in them, they ought to applaud and not condemn us. (*Laughter.*) And now I want to pay a compliment to a gentleman to whom I may perhaps have been thought to do scant justice on a former occasion (*laughter*), Sir Drigbijhai Singh. Now he practically tested the merits of the jury system, for he introduced what we call the *panchyet* system into his State, which was, in fact, nothing but a trial by jury; and though there had been, previous to that time, constant litigation in his State, after the system came once into force, he never was troubled in that way. All cases were settled by juries.

On a former occasion I made the remark that this gentleman held up his hand to signify assent in the Governor-General's Council, although he did not understand a word of what was going on; but his conduct in this matter of the jury system shows that although, perhaps, he knew no English, he understood well the practical side of good administration. Now I have finished. I wanted to mention this fact, because without it my remarks would have been too one-sided, failing to recognize merits though I had pointed out defects. (*Cheers. Persistent cries of "Vote, vote." We are all agreed," &c.*)

THE PRESIDENT: Gentlemen,—Does any one oppose this resolution? (*Cries of "No, no."*) Do you want any more speeches on the subject? (*Deafening cries of "No, no."*) Then, Gentlemen, I will put the resolution, which will stand thus:—

RESOLVED—"*That this Congress having read and considered Resolution VIII of the "Congress of 1886, to wit—*

"'*That, in the opinion of this Congress, the time has now arrived when the system of trial by jury may "'be safely extended into many parts of the country where it is not at present in force'—*

3rd Day.

Res. IV., Extension of Trial by Jury—Finality of Juries' Verdicts—Option to be given to accused of committal to the Sessions.

" *Resolution IX of the Congress of 1886, to wit—*

" '*That, in the opinion of this Congress, the innovation made in 1872 in the system of trial by jury, " 'depriving the verdicts of juries of all finality, has proved injurious to the country, and the powers then, " 'for the first time, vested in Sessions Judges and High Courts, of setting aside verdicts of acquittal, should be " 'at once withdrawn,'—*

" *and Resolution X of the Congress of 1886, to wit—*

" '*That, in the opinion of this Congress, a provision, similar to that contained in the Summary Jurisdic- " 'tion Act of England (under which accused persons in serious cases have the option of demanding com- " 'mittal to the Sessions Court), should be introduced into the Indian Code of Criminal Procedure, enabling " 'accused persons, in warrant cases, to demand that, instead of being tried by the Magistrate, they be commit- " 'ted to the Court of Sessions,'—*

" *does now, hereby, affirm the same respectively.*"

The resolution was then put and carried unanimously; and it being then 1-15 P.M., the President adjourned the assembly to 2 P.M.

Res. V, Reform of the Police Administration.

The Congress re-assembled at 2 P.M., when MUNSHI SAJJAD HOSEIN—(*Lucknow, No. 434 in list*)—rose and said, speaking in Urdu*: This is the first time that I have had the honour of attending this great National Assembly, the Indian National Congress; and when I find that this Assembly, which in 1885 numbered some 70 delegates only, now consists of over 1,200, I feel tempted to express, at some length, my great gratification at this astounding success. But the magnitude of the task, the vast number of abler speakers, and above all the shortness of the time allotted to each speaker, lead me to hurry on at once to the subject allotted to me, and acting on the words of the Persian Poet—

" Time is short, work much we see,
Brief and few our words should be—"

say only just a few words, and on one single question only.

You all know what our good and great and beneficent British Governors have done for our welfare, our protection and advancement; indeed you all probably know more about *this* than I do. (*Laughter.*) Amongst these most excellent works, one is the Police Administration, which we, at all places, at all times, and under all conditions greatly need in order that our property and lives may be fully protected from the long arms of thieves and budmashes, and in order that under the shadow of our subject-projecting English Government, we may repose, without a care, in peace and safety. Just as for our bodily life, air, water and food are necessary, and on their purity depends our health, so is the safety and comfort of the people dependent on the Police, and on its good administration rests the public welfare. Hence, probably, it is that the ocean of their powers is shoreless, and that its expanse is such that nowhere any coast is visible. No Lieutenant-Governor, nor even Viceroy, has such power in regard to my peace and comfort, as a simple chowkeedar (village watchman) or His Honour the constable (*saheb bahadur*). (*Cheers and laughter.*) The humblest labourer in the village, the most exalted noble in the city, are equally under the control of these distinguished officials. There is no place, no spot, where Their Highnesses of the Police, like the Angel of Death are not present. (*Cheers.*) Let a man displease them in the slightest, and see the beneficence of our kind Police. He may know nothing about it, but there will be a criminal case filed against him, and arrangements made for requiring him to give security for good behaviour, before he can reach his home. (*Loud laughter.*)

Gentlemen, you will remember that in this Assembly a notorious Rajah was pleased to *say* that now-a-days pamphlets and speeches were going about which did not fall short of seditious libels, and to *present* a petition for signature in which the Lieutenant-Governor was requested to introduce into the Criminal Code sections for the punishment of this offence. Gentlemen, this new invented crime is beyond the scope of my limited intellect; but this I will say, that I have carefully studied all that has been written and said by the Congress party in the various papers in which from time to time these have appeared, and I have seen pamphlets and speeches, calculated to promote the welfare and prosperity of the country, issued by its truest well-wishers and friends (*loud cheers*); and, as far as I can make out, these are the very pamphlets and speeches referred to by that fifty-per-cent.-above-proof, trebly-distilled-quintessence of loyalty, the Rajah aforesaid (*loud laughter*), and I want you to reflect what new additional scope for our good Police's energy there will be, if even things like these are to be repressed by law, and to consider what amount of comfort this Police, with its already vast powers, in practice confers upon us.

I do not deny those blessings conferred on us by the Police department, but I cannot forget that it is not at present so managed as to be in any way reassuring to the public. (*Cheers.*) It is a department for looking after thieves and budmashes, but experience shows

---

* Great pains have been taken with this translation, and as a translation it is exact, but it altogether fails to give any idea of the eloquence, the happy turns of expression, and the quaint verbal quips and quirks that characterized the original, which throughout its delivery kept the audience in a roar of laughter.

that the way it does this is by petting and protecting them. ("*Hear, hear.*") Is there one man, be he ruler or ruled, who will this day say one word in praise of the Police? The people complain bitterly of their oppression and extortion, the officials are disgusted at their systematic getting up of false cases, and involving of innocent men in serious charges. The Police doubtless investigate closely and exert themselves greatly, but the budmashes and disturbers of the peace, in virtue of presents, and sucking up to them, and giving them information, and filling their fists with cash, get off Scot-free, and the whole weight of their persecutions falls upon those unfortunate well-conducted people, to protect whom these Police are appointed. I daily see, in whomsoever's house a theft occurs, the Police forget all about recovering the property and tracing out the thieves, and think first and only of what they can get for themselves in the way of entertainment and bribes, so that, often besides the loss by the theft, the poor man has to bear also the cost of lavishly entertaining and feeing the Police. On him too they cast the blame of having been careless—of course if he *has* been robbed, which they greatly doubt, it has been solely his *own* fault—and if the thieves have by chance left him anything, this the poor man's good friends, the Police, are always kind enough to accept. (*Loud and continued cheers.*)

Once a European friend asked me, joking, "What is the meaning of cholera pills?" I said, "Why, of course, pills to cure cholera"; he replied, "Why, of *course?* cholera pills don't mean, *necessarily*, that they will *cure cholera*, it may mean that they will *cause* it." So our Police, too, are just such cholera pills; for when they were first established they were supposed to have the first meaning and to cure crime, but now experience shows that they have the second, and cause crime. (*Loud cheers.*)

And now let others advocate the reform of the Legislative Councils, the separation of judicial functions, and what not; but, as for me, what I want to see is a thorough reform of the Police, so this is the resolution which I have to propose to you, and to which I would invite your most earnest consideration, *viz.:—*

"*That, as it is the general belief of the people of this country that the existing system of Police administration in India is highly unsatisfactory in itself and oppressive to them, the Government be respectfully urged to appoint a Commission, consisting of official and non-official members, to investigate the entire question as speedily as possible.*"

It is not improbable that our kind friends of the Police,* whom I see listening carefully to all that is going on (*laughter*), or others of them who may hear of this resolution that I have ventured to propose, will cry out that "these Congress fellows are indeed great scoundrels. (*Laughter.*) They are always finding fault—now here, now there, and now they want to lay their hands on the Police. Hitherto we have, in a casual way, made inquiries about them at the instigation of this or that officer, but *now we we'll show* them what comes of meddling with US! Amongst them no doubt there are very wealthy and learned barristers and vaquils, but what does that signify? Just let Mr. Eardley-Norton from Madras visit some village of Oudh, or Mr. Howard, or the Hon'ble Pundit Ajoodhia Nath of Allahabad appear in some town in the Punjab, and we'll be even with them! At the very least we can always arrest them on suspicion, and bundle them in, handcuffed, to the sudder station." (*Loud laughter.*) But let me respectfully say to Their Highnesses the Police—yes, my friends, truly you possess just these powers, and you are well practised in playing such tricks. All this kind of thing you can easily do; but, if you will consider carefully, you will see that this resolution is calculated to be of great service to you also. I know that sometimes, on account of not catching thieves or by reason of an insufficient number of cases being sent up from your circle, your superior officers pitch into you, and you, to lift the load off your own heads, seize upon any one that you can lay your hands on and force him to carry it, and so make up a false case. But do you suppose that this improper pressure on you by your officers will not be dealt with by the Commission? This is true that, by the limitation of your powers, there is some danger of the belly of that bottomless pit† of a pocket of yours remaining empty, but increased salary, providing a certain and more respectable income, will make amends for this. So you need not cut up rough with us, but ought rather to be grateful. (*Laughter and cheers.*)

Now the fixed time has passed, and indeed I have finished my speech ("*Go on, go on*"); but, as you insist on my going on, I will just say a few words more in reference to this Congress. For the last two days I have watched certain men coming into the Congress camp and making friends with the delegates and giving them certain advice, and, without openly opposing our work, doing all they can, in an underhand way, to mislead some of my co-religionists, by holding out to them prospects of the good will of the authorities, and of titles, if they will only leave the camp. Now I cannot help looking upon the friendly advances of these astute individuals as very similar to those made to Adam and Eve by the Devil in Paradise. (*Cheers.*) This is one of the traps of our ingenious and unscrupulous adversaries, who, finding they can do us no harm by their open hostility, seek now to injure us under the guise of friendship. (*Loud cheers.*)

---

* A number of Policemen were watching the Proceedings.

† Lit., "Devil's eye." A thing without limit of length or depth is a "Devil's eye."

3rd Day.

Res. V., Reform of the Police Administration.

Let me tell you a little story: There was a certain Moulvi, very learned and pious, who, day and night, was occupied in the praise of God. The Devil was puzzled. Said he, "I can't get hold of this fellow anyhow. Really I shall lose him if I don't look out, and, what is worse, people so look up to and revere him, that the whole country here is growing religious, and, if I cannot show him up, I shall lose the whole country. It really is deuced hard, and, blow me! if I know what to do." One day, however, having put on a wonderful appearance of sanctity, with a beard down to his navel, wearing a huge green turban and a long robe, a rosary in one hand, a staff in the other, and slippers on his feet (*loud laughter*), in the small hours of the night he appeared before the holy devotee: "Peace be to you;" "And to you be peace." "May I hope you are well?" "Whence has your honour come?" The Devil said: "I am Gabriel; our good friend * God has accepted your devotion and is much pleased with you, and has ordered me to wait upon you and give you his best regards and bring you to the seventh heaven. So here I am, and I have brought the heavenly steed (*Boorak*) †; it is at the door." Hearing this, the devotee was rejoiced beyond bounds, and burst out laughing. Nay, he was in such a hurry that he did not properly perform his ablutions, but, combing his beard rapidly and slipping on his robe, he announced that he was ready. The Devil bound a handkerchief over his eyes and mounted him and took him along with him. Jogging on, when they had got to a certain place on the outskirts of the village, the Devil said: "Highness, we have now arrived at the *Sadrat-ul-Muntaha* (*i.e.*, the place beyond which Gabriel could not proceed, when he accompanied Mahomet on his visit to Heaven). I can go no further; from hence other angels will take your worship." Our devotee, in his enthusiasm about the seventh heaven, remained on the heavenly steed, moving slowly about all night, but no Mr. Angel (*Feristah sahib*) came, nor was the glory of God revealed to him. In the morning passers-by who saw their much-venerated devotee in this condition were greatly astonished, and came near him and saw the bandage over his eyes. This they removed, and then the devotee saw that there was neither heaven nor God's throne, nor the *Sadrat-ul-Muntaha*, nor even the heavenly charger, but there, seated on an ass, he was perched on top of an old brick kiln. (*Prolonged cheers and laughter.*)

Friends, this folly on the part of the devotee was solely due to his desire for a visit to heaven being so great that he never stopped to consider that in these days such a visit is impossible. If he had really used his wits, it would have been impossible for the Devil's trick to have succeeded, or for him to have been made such a fool of.

Now, therefore, it behoves us to weigh carefully the proposals of these enemies of our cause, who come in the guise of friends, and to reckon up well the loss and gain of everything. Let it not be that unscrupulous people with deceitful stories leading us away from this devotion to our country's cause, and taking us up the mount of flattery, leave us, at last, perched there upon our own folly, to be the laughing-stock of the world. (*Tremendous cheering.*)

MR. R. N. MUDHOLKAR—(*Berar, No. 259 in list*)—said: Sir,—This is a much humbler proposition than some of those which have preceded it; but it is an eminently practical one, which will come perhaps more immediately home to the hearts of the masses of the people than any other. It will carry the name of the Congress into every homestead. The policeman's is not a very happy lot, and, as we all know, he is more or less abused all over the world; but in India he is simply execrated from one end of the country to the other. In every village, in every town, amongst all ranks of society, high or low, wherever you go, you will find that there is nowhere anyone who has one single good word to say for the policeman—nay, he is hated and detested,—and the reasons are not far to seek. The policeman's duties are such that he ought to be loved by every well-wisher of society. He ought to be the protector of our lives and property, and as such he ought to be almost venerated. But here is the fact: In every village, the person who is most feared—feared even more than the highest official in the district—is the policeman getting Rs. 5 or Rs. 6 per month. The reason is that the law, as it stands at present, invests the policeman with powers so very wide and comprehensive that it is no wonder that, when exercised by men whose salaries range from £4 to £6 per annum! (Englishmen will, I hope, mark this astounding fact) the result should be so very unsatisfactory. Those powers are in several respects such that they could not safely be entrusted to any set of human beings. There are others which can certainly not be rightly entrusted to anyone without proper safeguards and restrictions. And to whom, I ask, are such extraordinary powers entrusted? To men ignorant and illiterate—to men drawn from the lowest ranks of society—men who have no sense of responsibility in regard to their duty (*cheers*), and who are paid the magnificent salary of from £4 to £6 per annum, being actually less than well-to-do people pay their stable assistants,

* Allah Meah, a kind of familiar way of speaking of God.
† The heavenly charger on which Mahomed rode to heaven.

3rd Day.

Res. V., Reform of the Police Administration.

their punka-pullers, or their sweepers. Yet any one of these men, if he takes it into his head to insult or annoy you, or to lower you in the public estimation, can do it, and, practically, with impunity. Is it to be wondered, if, to make a living, their whole energies are devoted, not to the suppression or detection of crime, but to the extortion, under threats, (of what they will otherwise do) of the means for a luxurious livelihood, out of the rest of the community? Some years ago a native gentleman, a very high officer of Government, was dragged from his house in Bombay and walked bareheaded through the streets on his way from his house to the police station, simply because he would not bribe the police to permit him to proceed in a more suitable manner. ("*Hear, hear.*") Many such instances of police iniquity occur almost daily in every part of the country, and during my eight years' experience, as a lawyer in the districts, I have come across cases of police oppression and violence which have made my blood boil within me, and my hair stand on end. I know of cases in which persons have been convicted and sentenced under a wholly trumped-up charge, and the truth only discovered when it was too late. ("*Shame.*") Is there one single Indian here present who cannot, from his own personal experiences, narrate a dozen cases of cruelty, oppression and extortion on the part of these wretches? I shall be told by our adversaries that these our oppressors are our own fellow-countrymen, but this attempt to shift the responsibility is futile. When, before Lord Cornwallis' reform, the English Covenanted Civil Service were paid on the same beggarly scale (considering the positions they occupied) as the Police now are, they were just as wicked and corrupt as our Indian policemen. The fault lies with Government, and with the Government only. They must restrict the arbitrary powers of the Police. They must pay them adequately, and they must put them in charge of officers who care more for truth and justice than for drill and *nakshahs*,* and who really sympathize with and desire truly in their hearts, above all things, the welfare of the people. (*Loud cheers.*)

MR. PRINGLE KENNEDY—(*Behar, No. 1049 in list*)—rose and said: Gentlemen,—The resolution which I rise to support to-day is one, the importance of which yields to no other or to almost no other of the resolutions before you. (*Cheers.*) In spite of what some people seem to think, a native of India does not spend all his days in the law courts, is not always being tried before a judge, with or without a jury, nor is he continually before the High Court on the Criminal Revision side. But the police, like unto the poor, we have ever with us. There is a French proverb, "*La bouche va toujours*," which being translated with its appropriate application means: "*A policeman is always hungry.*" (*Laughter.*) He is ready for anything—from a pice to a thousand rupees. His mouth is the most elastic of any in the country. A pie† is not too small to escape his notice, and I believe he would not choke even if he swallowed a krore.‡ (*Laughter.*) Now, as it has been remarked, an ounce of fact is worth a ton of theory. So, to illustrate that, let me give you two stories. The first is concerning a case in which a richer man was accused of a criminal offence by a poorer man. The complainant asked the District Superintendent of Police to investigate the case himself, but he not only declined, but refused to permit first one and then another subordinate to take up the case on the ground that he could not trust them. At last the most honest Sub-Inspector in the division, as he was said to be, was sent to conduct the investigation; and what do you think this most honest man did? Why, after sitting for a few days, and taking a pretty considerable mass of evidence, he sent word to the rich man that he wanted 5,000 rupees; and on this being refused, he asked for less and less, until he came down to 500 rupees; and, when this, too, was refused, he being too lazy to write a fresh report, simply added to it a page, saying that the case was true, though it was difficult to get evidence. (*Laughter.*) Some time after, the Collector of the district told me that he believed the case to be a perfectly true one, as the Sub-Inspector had told him so, but had also added that the rich man had bribed and won over all the witnesses! Then here is another case. Some little time ago I was engaged in a case in which the question arose as to the abandonment of a new-born infant. The mother of the child was dwelling in the house, in the garden of which the infant was found. And you would hardly believe that it took four days before the mother could be found, although she was not a purda-nashin, and although several policemen were in the search, one of them known as a literate policeman, a Mr. Dogberry, and the others illiterate. These latter may well be deemed relations of Mr. Verges. And while these things occur, violent death after violent death occurs in our part of the country, and no one is brought to justice, inasmuch as the Police, instead of detecting crime, cannot get up any case without bringing into it a quantity of false evidence. And then we see, sometimes, the scandal of an Under-Secretary, as was seen two years ago, scolding the High Court, inasmuch as it did not punish crime. Is it any wonder, then, that the policeman is considered, not as a watch-dog, but rather as an animal—I will not name which—that has not the reputation of wisdom, or as another animal, whose cunning is its most conspicuous feature? (*Cheers.*)

* Red tape.
† The ⅓rd of a farthing.
‡ One million sterling.

3rd Day.

Res. V., Reform of the Police Administration.

Now I am a microscopic member of a microscopic minority. (*Laughter.*) My experience is limited. It may be that the entire police of the empire do not ill-treat accused persons (*Cries of "They do, they do"*); that in Bombay and Madras they do not take bribes (*Cries from Madras and Bombay delegates, "They do, they do"*); and that the stories of ill treatment by them of persons in the Punjab desiring to attend this Congress are but the figments of an excited imagination (*Cries of "No, no; they are true!"*); but to the character and conduct of the Police in my own part of the country I can speak with confidence, and can boldly assert that it leaves almost everything to be desired. (*Cheers.*)

We want a Commission to inquire into all this. (*Cheers.*) I recognise that it is an extremely difficult problem The men's pay, as the last speaker remarked, is ridiculously small, their powers immoderately great, and possibly any alteration in either direction may prove difficult in practice. But I cannot believe that it is beyond the resources of statesmanship, when thoroughly informed as to the facts, which our rulers might be if they appoint a proper Commission. I lay stress on this, for no purely official commission will be of the least use; we must have the Commission mixed (*"Hear, hear," and cheers*) and largely composed of independent non-officials. Otherwise we may be pretty sure that we shall have the old official report, "Great is Diana of the Ephesians." (*Cheers.*) We want reform, not a panegyric on existing facts, and if we get the kind of Commission I have suggested we may then, possibly, also get what the country requires. (*Cheers.*)

LALLA JAISHI RAM—(*Punjab, No. 373 in list*)—speaking in Urdu, said: Mr. President and Gentlemen,—After the able speeches of the gentlemen who proposed, seconded and supported this resolution, it is almost superfluous for me to make any remarks on the subject. The Police vagaries and abuses are, however, so notorious that one can hardly avoid making some observations thereon. The law on the police administration is defective, the rules made in accordance therewith are faulty, and the working of the system is highly unsatisfactory. It is not at all uncommon, quite the reverse, to find Police officers grossly abusing their authority. We often meet with instances in which Police officers have fabricated evidence and got up false cases against poor innocent persons. The security, of the people vests in them, but, instead of enhancing that security, it is the Police themselves who are the chief source of the present insecurity of both persons and property.

The Police system is, broadly speaking, an unmistakeable failure, and in support of this assertion I may note that the report of the Public Service Commission which recently met, furnishes important evidence.

With these observations I support the resolution put before the meeting.

MR. HARCHANDRAI VISHNUDAS—(*Sind, No. 242 in list*)—said: It is the part of a policeman to detect crime, but they ought to catch the criminal, and should not lay hold of the wrong person, as they seem to prefer doing. The cry comes up from all parts of India that the existing Police administration in this country is very far from satisfactory. It is true that no institution in this world is capable of absolute perfection, but there are institutions and institutions, and this institution is of such a nature that we must perforce, if we are to have any peace or comfort in life, try to free it, as much as possible, from the taint of evil and from defects of every kind. The Police branch of the service admits of a very great deal of improvement, but the system at present is such that it will hardly lend itself to any of those reforms that we desire. One of its great defects is that the men who constitute the rank and file of the Police department are drawn from the very dregs of the community, and are both illiterate and very badly paid. They have not any such sense of duty as can restrain them from those acts of extortion and oppression which they now commit without any scruple of conscience—without, I really believe, in many cases, realizing that they are doing wrong. It would be better if the Government were to raise their pay, and see that they have some education and some such conscientious feelings as would revolt against gross injustice. It is quite necessary that the continual practice of torture should be put a stop to. There have come within my own observation cases of torture of so revolting and atrocious a nature that I do not like to harrow your feelings by describing them to you. At present, men in the lowest grade of the service have no regular promotion to expect. They are kept on the same pay as long as they remain in the service. Not only ought a far higher class of men to be enlisted, not only ought their initial pay to be raised, so that their service may be worth having which it is not, now unless they extort a good deal of money monthly from the people but fair chances of promotion ought to be open to all of them, so that they may look forward confidently to both better pay and better positions, and obtain them in the course of time, with certainty, as the reward of real merit. ("*Hear, hear.*")

MR. MAHOMED HIDAYAT RASUL—(*Lucknow, No. 466 in list*)—in seconding the resolution, said, speaking in Urdu: Mr. Chairman and brother delegates,—

"All the evils of the world are due to disunion,
But this our grand union here is the gift of Destiny."

Gentlemen, this couplet, full of moral meaning, is the production of my able friend Mirza Machcha Beg, Sitamzarif, who is present here in the capacity of a delegate. (*Cheers.*) The *Aujuman-i-Islam*, which has delegated the Mirza Sahib and my humble self that comprehensive and venerable association which bears more than 400 members on its rolls, has deputed thirty distinguished delegates, including three Princes Royal, grandsons of the late lamented Mahomed Ali Shah III. of Oudh—Sheikh Raza Husain Khan Saheb, Taluqdar, Mr. Ali Mahomed Bhimjee, and others—to take part in the proceedings of this Congress (*loud cheers*) ; and no less than seventy Mahomedan delegates represent at this meeting our own province of Oudh. (*Loud cheers.*) Now, can you say how so many able and distinguished delegates have come to be returned from Oudh, and specially from Lucknow ? Gentlemen, I will whisper it in your ears. The truth of it is, that all this good result is due to the kindness of our brethren in the Alighur camp—the opponents of the Congress. (*Loud cheers.*) I assure you that, if our hostile brethren had not made such a grand show of opposition, the Congress would certainly not have been the success that it has been to-day. (*Cheers.*) To my mind, the National Congress is like the vine, which, the more it is pruned, the more it flourishes. (*Cheers.*) There is no doubt that our kind opponents have spared no pains to prune it out of existence ; but still the numerous branches which delight the eyes of spectators in this vast hall to-day are, to no small extent, the outcome of their persistent pruning. (*Cheers.*) You do not know how much opposition was raised against the Congress in Lucknow, and you will be sorry to hear what shameful tactics were employed against it. In the first place, the people of Lucknow are, as you know, famous for their intelligence, and no doubt they are intelligent; then, again, there was the "loyal" Rajah Siva Prasad bent on still further developing that abnormal intelligence; and to crown all, there was the co-operation of Sir Syed Ahmed, the evil genius of Mahomedans. (*Loud cheers.*) You can well understand now that, under such a combination, no tactics would be considered too mean to adopt. The first act of faithfulness was the issuing of the notice to the effect that the Hon'ble Pandit Ajoodhianath had insulted the Mahomedan faith in his speech. Of course, this was the spark designed to set the hearts of the general mass of Mahomedans on fire. There was not a single individual who did not for the time feel a sort of excitement, and this was made the ground for a meeting at the Kaisarbagh, to which all our hawkers of vegetables and butchers were specially invited. But the fun of it was that in that meeting neither the merits of Islam were explained (*Cries of "Shame, shame!"*), nor was it proposed to hang Pandit Ajoodhianath for six months* (*loud laughter*), nor yet were the audience metamorphosed from human beings into—*naturias* (the followers of Sir Syed Ahmed, with their coats, pantaloons, and red Turkish caps). (*Laughter.*) What then, you would ask, was done there ? Nothing. Those who attended the meeting found themselves in the position depicted in the well-known colloquy: "Where did you go ?" "Nowhere." "What did you bring ?" "Nothing." (*Tremendous cheering.*) Of course, the Government was praised in the usual way for introducing telegraphs and railways into the country. And nothing else. (*Cheers.*) Say, Gentlemen, where is the wretch who has ever denied this ? (*Cheers.*) Well, this meeting produced two results : On the one hand, the Mahomedans, having seen through their grandly got-up but empty proceedings, became disgusted with the promoters of the meeting; on the other hand, a message was wired to the Sage of Alighur,—"We congratulate you in that, like the Punjab, Lucknow also has, in all faith, come within the circle of your disciples." (*Loudlaughter.*) And this was the "natural" mistake that tempted the Sage to come again to Lucknow. (*Loud laughter.*) But alas ! the second meeting disclosed the true state of things, in which, despite the strongest endeavours, not even three persons and a half could be brought together (*loud cheers*), and the few that assembled fell out amongst themselves, as a providential punishment for their evil actions, and a natural sequence of their traitorship to the country. (*Loud cheers.*) (*Here the President touched the gong.*)

3rd Day.

Res. V., Reform of the Police Administration.

I regret that the time allotted to me is over. (*Cries of "Go on, go on."*) Gentlemen, our opponents may be justly compared to a false witness (*cheers*), in whose heart there still shines the divine light (conscience), but whose lips give utterance to those words only that he has been paid to speak. (*Loud cheers.*) You have heard the narrative of the opposition. Hear for a moment now of the effect it has produced upon us. You will laugh to hear that where there was one Congressman before, there, there are now ten. (*Loud cheers.*) Nay, even our opponents themselves are now secretly in sympathy with us ; because, when the fruits of our endeavours begin to ripen, these gentlemen will be the first to stretch forth their hands. (*Vociferous cheers.*) It is for this reason that I have compared them to mercenary witnesses. (*Loud cheers.*) Gentlemen, have delegates from any other part of India been started on their journey amidst the same outburst of enthusiasm and patriotic feeling, with music-playing and flags fluttering in the air, amid shouts of "*Jai Hume Sahib*," *and* "*Jai Congress*" ("Victory to Hume Sahib" and "Success to the Congress")—as were the delegates from Lucknow ? You will yourself say No. (*Cheers.*) Then why were they so started ? Because of the good services of the opposition. (*Laughter.*) I

* A colloquialism.

3rd Day.

Res. V., Reform of the Police Administration.

cannot here refrain from giving this much praise to the heroes of Lucknow, that from the position which they took up in their own peculiar plucky style in the matter of the Congress, they have never swerved one hair's breadth, despite the virulence and violence of the stupid opposition. (*Loud cheers.*) I have through your indulgence taken so much of your time that I cannot expect more, or else I would have shown that it is not merely deception, but sheer dishonesty to claim for Sir Syed Ahmed the leadership of the Mahomedans. It is very strange that, while all the learned Mahomedans of India, Arabia and Persia unite in denouncing him as an unbeliever, Sir Syed, in his own vanity, should still consider himself the leader of the Mahomedans. As the Persian proverb says, "How bold is the thief who carries a light in his hand?" (*Loud cheers.*)

I will now say a few words in the discharge of my duty of seconding the resolution moved by my able friend, Munshi Mahommad Sajjad Hussain. I fully concur with my able friend in all that he has said about the Police. By ill luck, our own misdeeds, incarnate in the shape of the Police, rule over us. (*Loud cheers.*) No more "faithful" body of men than that could be found in the whole world, who openly fly at the throats of their employers. (*Cries of "Shame! shame!"*) You know whence the Police are paid. From Municipal funds and other miscellaneous sources of revenue. Yet while we ourselves are robbed, our own kith and kin are implicated and disgraced; while those near and dear to us are killed and wounded, we have to provide rich and delicious dishes for the relentless Police. (*Cries of "Shame! shame!"*) You will never hear of any great theft being traced out, but, of course, petty thieves are hunted up. Now, say, in whose greedy maw are buried those big sums; and why are petty thefts of a penny or half-penny belched out? (*Cheers.*) I will not disclose the reason of it. You must guess it for yourselves. (*Laughter.*) In my opinion, investigations are made simply that there may be no mistake in apportioning the shares. (*Vociferous cheers.*) In short, the troubles that the country at large, and specially the gentry, suffer at the hands of the police, are too numerous to be described in such a short time. It is one of those serious evils that admits of no remedy, except a radical reform. In my opinion, Police oppression by itself fully weighs against all our other grievances. I say, and say openly, that the existing Police is a source of great disrepute to Government, and it loudly calls for reform. And now, Gentlemen, I bring my poor discourse to an end, and make room for those able and learned gentlemen, whose eloquent speeches I myself long to hear. (*Cheers.*)

MR. PARTHASARADHI NAIDU—(*Madras, No. 26 in list*)—spoke in Telegu. He said: Mr. Chairman and Brother Delegates,—It is with great pleasure I have come forward to support this very important resolution—a resolution, in my humble opinion, almost more important than all the resolutions that have already been proposed, or any of those that will be proposed, hereafter. In short, this resolution is so important because it concerns all classes, and all creeds and both the rich and the poor amongst these. The dread of the policeman's high-handed oppression is a terror to the young and old, and all alike. Previous speakers have cited instances that have come under their observation to substantiate the statement that the Police department is rotten to the core, and have urged the necessity of urgent reform. I shall just mention two little incidents to illustrate Mr. Kennedy's remark that nothing is too small and nothing too large for them in the way of extortion. A second class police constable of the Madras Reserve Police Force once called on me at my office and asked me for some charity to remove an unclaimed corpse, and I gave him eight annas, believing his statement to be true. Some time after, *i.e.*, on the 28th November last, he called on me again and asked me to help him with four annas to enable him to engage a carriage to go and arrest a thief who had absconded, against whom he said he had a warrant. I refused to give him this, seeing that it was a public duty, and directed him to the Inspector of Police. Subsequently I reported the matter to the Commissioner of Police, and from inquiries instituted many similar cases cropped up against him, with the result that, for having cheated and attempted to cheat me and others by false representations, he was sentenced to seven months' hard labour. This is only an instance of Mr. Kennedy's "hungry men," who constitute the Police force. I will mention another specimen of our good Police's tricks that occurred just before I left Madras. At a great festival in a big temple in Madras, a golden necklace, worth Rs. 700, was snatched away from the person of a native lady in the crowd by some-one who remains unknown. A poor man who chanced to be close by was however arrested, dragged to the station, and every possible search was made by the Station House Officer and others, and yet the lost jewel was not found with the suspected party. The next day the Divisional Inspector called at the station, entered into a room with the suspected party, bolting the door from inside, and in a few minutes came out with the lost jewel, exclaiming exultingly at the top of his voice "Look here, you rascals, here is the necklace which you have not been able to trace out." The Station House Officer and others, who had searched the man beforehand, were simply lost in amazement at this, as it were, *theosophic mystery*. The case was sent up before the Magistrate, who, of course, acquitted the man; and how the Inspector became possessed of the

3rd Day.

Res. V., Reform of the Police Administration.

necklace is still a matter of inquiry. The ever-itching-palmy police-wallahs in the case in question had induced the lady that lost the necklace to give them in writing a promise of Rs. 200 in case the necklace was recovered. Such cases are but samples of what may be seen and heard in the Magisterial Courts everywhere. Most of the murder cases appealed to the High Court reveal startling facts of police oppression, high handedness and torture, and not unfrequently these professional preservers of the peace are sent to the School of Correction. To what is all this owing? The answer is as clear as daylight. The Police Department, constituted as it is at present, consists of men who are, in nine cases out of ten, utterly uneducated and devoid of all moral sense Under the false theory that physical strength is the sole necessary qualification, all the roughs and blackguards of our slums are enlisted into the police force; and, as a matter of fact, they are so badly paid that no good strong able-bodied man, capable of doing a good day's work elsewhere, and whose character was above extortion and corruption, would ever enlist in the force. In my opinion we ought certainly to subordinate physical strength to brains and heart. The police have not always to do pioneer's work, or sepoy's duty. On the contrary, the bulk of their duties requires intelligence, judgment, tact, and above all integrity A well-organised police would be more engaged in the prevention than in the detection of crime. The present state of the Department is such that, on the occurrence of a crime, the police spare no pains to bring some man, whether innocent or guilty they seem to care little, into trouble, supplying all the necessary evidence, no matter whether the final result be the conviction of a guilty or an innocent man. They think that the greater the number of the victims they have "run in" the more efficient will their Department and themselves appear in the eyes of the officials and the public. This, so far as the public is concerned, is a sad and serious mistake, and their villainy, in the long run, renders them quite detestable to every one, and utterly discredits the whole Department. I am therefore strongly of opinion that the Police Department must consist of well-paid and educated men, possessing discriminative powers. While we see education spreading everywhere, there is no reason why it should not be more prominently availed of in the Police Department. By so saying I do not mean, for one moment, that feeble, puny men—the victims of over-study—should be enlisted, but the robust amongst the educated should be drafted into this important Department, the pay being so raised as to make it worth the while of such men to serve in it. And certainly such men will not only be able to cope with the *wear* and *tear* of the Department, but also will be able to understand that they have not a mechanical duty to perform without caution and care, as is now done, and that they are not employed, as our present police seem to fancy, solely to rob and harass the respectable and peaceful sections of the community. In order to induce educated, intelligent and God-fearing men to enlist, the Department must be thoroughly re-organized Not only must the present emoluments be improved, but the present *uniform* also, and the status of the entire force materially raised. A very large number of matriculates and middle-school youths will then be most willing to join the ranks of the Constabulary, and similarly our B.A.'s, F.A.'s and others will unhesitatingly volunteer for grades like Inspectors, Sub-Inspectors. Unless the Police Department is thus satisfactorily reformed, or. in other words, without an honest and intelligent police force, our life and property will never be safe—no not even under the benign administration of our beloved and Gracious Imperial Majesty, the Queen-Empress. (*Loud cheers.*)

BABOO KAILASH CHUNDRA SEN—(*Dacca, No.* 1132 *in list*)—next rose and said: Mr. President and Brother Delegates,—I come from Eastern Bengal, and, had it not been my desire to place before you certain painful cases of police oppression in certain districts of Eastern Bengal, of which I am a resident, I would not have risen to speak to-day. The Congress is the noblest movement of the age, and one of its *raisons d'être* is to give us an opportunity of making known to our rulers our grievances in a constitutional and loyal manner. I hail the day on which the Congress first came into existence. It is not only calculated to enable the natives of the soil to protect their rights and privileges, but it is also one of the bulwarks of defence of British rule in India. (*Cheers.*) Although many able speakers who spoke before me on the police reform did full justice to the subject, still I thought you would be desirous of knowing something about the state of affairs in connection with the police administration in Eastern Bengal, and this is my justification, Gentlemen, in asking your indulgent attention to my few observations on the unsatisfactory state of police administration in our country.

This is a resolution which concerns the masses, who should be allowed to protect their rights, liberties and properties from being encroached upon by police officers, who, having gradually grown corrupt, have become powerful engines of oppression in Eastern Bengal. In order to cite some examples I would draw your attention to a painful case in which I defended the accused, a girl of eighteen, who was accused of having murdered her husband. The case was, with the aid of assessors, tried by the then Sessions Judge of Backergunge, Mr. L. R. Tottenham, who is now one of the Judges

3rd Day.

Res. V., Reform of the Police Administration.

of Her Majesty's High Court in Calcutta. You will be startled to hear, Gentlemen, that the girl was about to be convicted on her own confession which was extorted from her by the police. It was a confession made partly under a threat of ill-treatment and beating held out by the police officers, and partly under an assurance given her by a Sub-Inspector of Police that she would not get into any trouble of any kind if she would only say what they told her to say.

It was a confession containing long stories as to how she, the accused, alleged that she had committed the murder. Yet when the witnesses for the prosecution were subjected to a sharp cross-examination they were totally broken down, and circumstances of a harrowing character came to light, clearly shewing that the confession was extorted by the Police, and that the charge against her was wholly unfounded.

Some of the circumstances which gave the lie to the confession and proved it to have been extorted were that the wound inflicted on the throat was deeper than the cutting instrument (called a *dhao* in our part of the country) by which it was alleged to have been inflicted, was long ; the curtain within which the accused was alleged to have been asleep when the foul deed of murder was committed did not bear any marks of blood. The man had been murdered somewhere else, and the police officer, instead of bringing the charge home to the real murderer, when he found a difficulty in doing this, charged the poor wife of the deceased with the foul deed. For his credit's sake he had to convict someone, but who he cared not. The result was that the woman's confession was found to have been extorted by the police, and she was acquitted and the police officer suspended. But in how many cases do such fabricated cases pass undetected, and how often are the innocent punished instead of the guilty ? There are many other painful cases of police oppression in Eastern Bengal which I could bring to your notice, but, as the time allowed me to speak has expired, I finish my remarks with the earnest request that you will all carry this resolution with acclamation and pray to Government for the appointment of a Commission to institute a searching enquiry into the manner in which the police officers in the different provinces of India are discharging their duties, and to consider whether it is not essentially necessary to remodel entirely the system of filling up the higher appointments, especially in the Police Department, so as to get the best and thoroughly upright men in the police force. (*Cheers.*) (*Cries of " No more speaking. Vote, vote."*)

THE PRESIDENT : There appears to be no difference of opinion on this question. Shall I now put the resolution ? Are you all agreed ? (*Cries of " Yes, yes ; all, all."*) Then, Gentlemen, the resolution stands as follows :—

RESOLVED—" *That as it is the general belief of the people of this country that the existing system of Police administration in India is highly unsatisfactory in itself and oppressive to them, the Government be respectfully urged to appoint a Commission, consisting of official and non-official members, to investigate the entire question as speedily as possibe.*"

The resolution was then put and carried unanimously.

Res. VI, Establishment of Military Colleges—Volunteering—Modification of Arms Act.

MEER WAHID ALI—(*Rohilcund, No.* 526 *in list*)—who spoke in Urdu, proposed the resolution as follows :—

He said : The resolution that I have to propose runs as follows :—

" *That the Congress having read and considered Resolution IV of the Congress of 1887,* " *to wit—*

" ' *That in view of the loyalty of Her Majesty's Indian subjects, the Congress considers it desirable that the* " ' *Queen's Proclamation should be given effect to, that the Military services in the higher grades should be* " ' *practically opened to the natives of this country, and that the Government should establish Military Colleges* " ' *in the country whereat the natives of India, as defined by Statute, may be educated and trained for a* " ' *Military career as officers of the Indian Army;* '

" *and Resolution XII of the Congress of 1886, and Resolution V of the Congress of 1887,* " *to wit—*

" ' *That, in view of the unsettled state of public affairs in Europe, and the immense assistance* " ' *that the people of this country, if duly prepared therefor, are capable of rendering to Great Britain in the* " ' *event of any serious complications arising, the Congress once again earnestly appeals to the Government* " ' *to authorize (under such rules and restrictions as to it may seem fitting) a system of volunteering for the* " ' *Indian inhabitants of the country such as may qualify them to support the Government, effectually, in any* " ' *crisis ;* '

" *and Resolution VIII of the Congress of 1887, to wit—*

" ' *That, in view of the loyalty of the people, the hardships which the present Arms Act (XI of 1878)* " ' *causes, and the unmerited slur which it casts upon the people of this country, the Government be moved* " ' *so to modify the provisions of Chapter IV, and, if necessary, other portions of the said Act, as shall* " ' *enable all persons to possess, and wear Arms, unless debarred therefrom, either as individuals or members* " ' *of particular communities or classes, by the orders of the Government of India (or any local authority*

Res. VI., Establishment of Military Colleges—Volunteering—Modification of Arms Act.

"'*empowered by the Government of India on that behalf) for reasons to be recorded in writing and duly*
"'*published*'—
"*do now, hereby, affirm the same respectively.*"

Now there can be no doubt about the advisability, as well as the justice, of admitting native gentlemen to the higher ranks of the Indian Army. Properly trained, they would unquestionably be just as fit for these posts as the European gentlemen who now monopolize them. I do not think I need say more about this. As to volunteering, I think that the people of the country, at any rate the better classes, ought to be permitted to prepare themselves to defend and protect their country and their possessions against any possible foreign invasion. When, too, we reflect upon the enormous cost of each European soldier to the country, something like Rs. 800 yearly for each man, I think the Government might well consider whether they could not, by encouraging volunteering, make the country as safe, if not safer than now, at much smaller cost. Twenty thoroughly effective Indian volunteers, drawn from the fighting races, could be had at the cost of one European soldier, and I believe I am not unreasonable in thinking that ten such volunteers might safely take the place of one European soldier, at any rate to the extent of one-fourth of the British troops now in India. As to the Arms Act, it undoubtedly produces much heart-burning and involves many annoyances, enormous loss of crops, and in some places very considerable loss of life also. Something must be done to mitigate existing evils, and, though I have not thought much about it, I recognize that what is proposed, if it can be practically carried out, would have this effect. I need not, I think, say more. (*Cheers.*) I commend the resolution to your favourable consideration. (*Cheers.*)

MR. ALI MAHOMED BHIMJEE—(*Lucknow, No.* 455 *in list*)—said: In regard to the question of establishing military colleges, I should like to refer you to the Secretary of State's despatch, dated 26th January, 1886, in which his Lordship says:—

"The position of India in relation to taxation and the sources of the public revenues is very peculiar, not merely from the habits of the people and their strong aversion to change, which is more specially exhibited to new forms of taxation, but likewise from the character of the Government, which is in the hands of foreigners, who hold all the principal administrative offices *and form so large a part of the army*. The impatience of new taxation, which would have to be borne, wholly as a consequence of the foreign rule imposed on the country, and virtually to meet additions to charges arising outside of the country, *would constitute a political danger*, the real magnitude of which, it is to be feared, is not at all appreciated by persons who have no knowledge of or concern in the government of India, but which those responsible for that government have long regarded as of *the most serious order*."

Now, one of the means by which the political danger referred to in this despatch can be removed is the establishment of military colleges and the admission of natives to high military offices; therefore the National Congress, by asking for the establishment of military colleges in this country, will be showing a method of partially removing one of those serious causes of political danger on which the Secretary of State lays so much stress.

I have compared the cost of soldiers in four countries—France, Germany, England and India; and the following is the result, according to an official return published in 1880. No doubt the figures will have slightly varied since then, but it will be found that the cost of our European soldiers in India is even more disproportionately large, now, than it was then. The average cost per soldier in France, with an army of 900,000, was Rs. 185; in Germany, with an army of 1,200,000, it was Rs. 145; in England it was Rs. 277; and in India the average cost of a soldier was Rs. 775. (*Cries of "Shame."*) Now, Gentlemen, if we were to have military colleges and training schools established in India, and if our own men were to receive the education necessary to render them fit for military service—the less competent in the lower grades, the most able in high military posts—not only would the cost per head be greatly reduced, but the number of imported soldiers might also be greatly reduced. On economic grounds, as well as for the purpose of minimizing that political danger referred to by the Secretary of State, it is necessary, nay imperative, that we should have military educational establishments to qualify our young men for all, alike the higher and the lower, military posts. A native of India, under the present system, may serve for fifty years, and yet he can only rise to be a subadar-major on a paltry salary of Rs. 200 per month, whereas a young sub-lieutenant, coming out straight from England, immediately steps into a salary of over Rs. 300.

The second part of this resolution is that we should be allowed to become volunteers. Is there anything wrong in asking the Government to allow us arms for the purpose of defending our own country and the honour of our families? (*Cheers.*) Then why should this privilege or right, which has been granted or conceded, take it in which light you will, to Englishmen, be peremptorily denied to us? (*Cheers.*) We should go on demanding this concession till Doomsday, if necessary, though I hope it will not be necessary to wait *quite*

3rd Day.

Res. VI., Establishment of Military Colleges—Volunteering—Modification of Arms Act.

so long. (*Laughter.*) I have confidence in the justice of the English nation and the English Government, and as sure as this Congress is a success and perseveres you will get it. (*Cheers*) If we are given arms, we will prove, when the time comes, to the Government that we are all loyal and ready to make a brave stand for the defence of the country and English rule.

The last clause of this resolution refers to the Arms Act. Some people really seem to think that we want arms to run amuck, pell-mell, and commit havoc. But we are not madcaps. We do not want arms in order to cause bloodshed. It is simply for the purpose of removing the slur which is cast upon our loyalty, and the invidious distinctions that have been made, that many of us who live in towns ask for this concession. A native of the West Indies, who may very likely be my own servant, may carry arms. But I, his master, may not, because I am a native of India. (*Laughter.*) Surely our good Government will see that this is not only unjust and unreasonable, but necessarily repugnant to our national pride and our best feelings of self-respect. (*Cheers.*)

MR. JADUNATH MAZUMDAR—(*Bengal, No.* 1187 *in list*)—then rose and spoke, but he was not clearly understood, and none of the reporters took down his speech. He desired such an amendment of the third clause of the resolution as should provide that people should be debarred from the use of arms, not at the discretion of any authority but under fixed rules. He handed in before sitting down the following amendment to be read in place of the third clause: "That, in view of the loyalty of the people and the hardships which the present Arms Act (XI of 1878) entails, the Government be moved so to modify the rules for issuing licenses to possess and wear arms as shall enable all persons to obtain them, unless declared by Government as debarred from possessing and wearing arms for reasons to be specified in the rules and not left to the discretion of the officers issuing them."

But he did not read his amendment, and the assembly, unable to understand what he was talking about, grew impatient, and finally after seven minutes had elapsed, the PRESIDENT asked him to sit down, which he did, expressing dissatisfaction (he subsequently by letter apologized for this). No one seconded his proposal.

DEWAN RAN BIJAY BAHADUR—(*Oudh, No.* 519 *in list*)—said: Mr. President and Brother Delegates,—It is with great diffidence and hesitation that I rise at this late hour to propose an amendment to the resolution that has been so ably moved and seconded. I hail from the land of the Baboos. You may consider that, because I belong to the Baboo race, I am unwilling to wear arms or to let my children be trained in a military college. But wait a moment. It is certainly my desire to see my countrymen allowed to wear arms, to see my countrymen being trained for a military career, or for the protection of our homes, whenever an emergency may occur. (*Cheers.*) But I wish to point out that this Congress meeting should proceed like practical men, and not ask too much at once, and not by so doing allow it to be said that we are demanding arms simply to depose the English people from their government of the country. (*Cries of* "*No, no.*") No one in this assembly has the smallest desire to subvert the British power, so let us be extra-cautious not to give any opportunity, by asking too much at once, to any one to impute any such madness to us. So, now, what I say, is, stick to the military colleges and drop the Volunteering and Arms Act for the present. (*Cries of* "*No, no; never.*") Well, Gentlemen, this is my view, and I propose an amendment. I think it is wise to be on the safe side and not ask too much. Drop the Arms Act, drop Volunteering. (*Cries of* "*No, no,*" *and some confusion, during which some few further words of the speaker were lost.*)

MR. EARDLEY NORTON—(*Madras, No.* 19 *in list*)—rose and addressing the speaker said: May I be allowed to ask you, Sir, to be good enough to read out to us your amendment, and let us know exactly what it proposes.

The speaker then handed his amendment to the President, at whose request

PUNDIT AJOODHIA NATH—(*Allahabad, No.* 551 *in list*)—then read the amendment as follows:—

Proposed that clauses 2 and 3 of the Resolution, now under consideration, referring to Volunteering and to the Arms Act, be omitted."

DEWAN RAN BIJAY BAHADUR—(*Oudh, No.* 519 *in list*)—then again resumed speaking, this time repeating, most of what he had already said in English, in Urdu.

Finally he asked if any one would second his proposal, but, no one coming forward, and he being answered by loud cries of ("*None, none*") he sat down.

After this, however, several delegates rose, and, addressing the Chair, begged that the amendment might be explained to them as they did not quite understand it.

THE PRESIDENT, in explanation, said: You know what the resolution is. This gentleman simply wants to have the second and third clauses deleted from the resolution. He wants to drop the questions of the Arms Act and Volunteering altogether for the present, and so he desires that the resolution now before you may conclude at the word "army," which is the last word of the first part of the resolution. Now, does any gentleman wish to second this proposal? (*Cries of "No, no."*) (After a pause, and turning to the late speaker): Then, Sir, I fear that your proposal must be dropped. (*Loud cheers.*)

MR. PRINGLE KENNEDY—(*Behar, No.* 1049 *in list*)—then rose and said: I, too, have got an amendment to propose, somewhat similar to that which you have just heard, but less extensive in its scope. I propose to leave out the last part only of the resolution, *viz.*, that about the Arms Act. If the resolution had been put in parts, I would have voted against the third altogether. As regards the first part, I look upon a national army as a necessity. India is a continental power, and the country will never be safe until the flower of her youth are able to defend her. (*Cheers*) As to the volunteers, I would go further. I would make all our young men volunteers, whether they liked it or not. (*Laughter and cheers.*) I would teach them to obey as a necessary preliminary to command (*Cheers.*) As to the third point, I am thoroughly against it. I believe it is purely a sentimental grievance. (*Cries of "No."*) To ask the Government to repeal the Arms Act because it is a slur on your loyalty is about as unreasonable as to ask to have the sections of the Penal Code, relating to theft, repealed because it is a slur on the honesty of the people. The whole course of modern civilization is against any man wearing arms, except when there is absolute necessity for using them. It has been tried in the army, and a great amount of the crime in the army is simply because they have had arms near them. I do not think that, except for practical purposes, any man should have arms to wear. I should like to say this also in the matter, *viz.*, that if there is any desire for equality, I would rather see Europeans put on the same level as the natives, and be compelled to take out licenses in the same way. Speaking for my own part of the country, if Government were to grant this request, the only consequence would be that, instead of men being charged for hurts and assaults, there would be a great many cases of homicide in the land fights that take place so often. I think I correctly represent the views of my own fellow delegates from Behar (*cheers*) when I say that it is extremely undesirable to allow men generally the use of arms. I have heard the bearing arms talked of as if it were a right. I say it is a right which no man can possibly possess as such. If you can get a better form of magistracy, you will get a better administration of licenses. (*Cheers.*) But if we say that we wish the Arms Act to be removed, we can only say that we desire it on purely sentimental grounds, and I may mention one fact. No one can say that the Marquis of Ripon, though a good friend to India, ever took the slightest step towards removing the Arms Act. You will make people think that you are acting from other motives if you persist in passing this resolution about the Arms Act. (*Cheers.*)

THE HON'BLE MR. K. T. TELANG—(*Bombay, No.* 201 *in list*)—said: I beg to second the amendment. I entirely agree with Mr. Kennedy in thinking that those of us who ask for this modification in the Arms Act do so for perfectly innocent, and indeed justifiable, purposes. (*"Hear, hear."*) Upon that point I have no manner of doubt whatever. At the same time, I think it cannot be denied that we are asking for it mainly on sentimental grounds. (*"Hear, hear."*) But as a practical body of men dealing with practical affairs of administration, we should not be governed merely by sentimental considerations. You cannot deny that there are some classes of people in the country who are turbulent, and, under the terms of this resolution, as it is framed, by which everybody would be entitled to wear arms, unless specially debarred, it is quite possible that weapons might go into the hands of the turbulent classes, in which case peaceful people might not find themselves in such a position of security as at present. (*"Hear, hear."*) Secondly, the resolution affirms that when the Government does issue an order that certain individuals, or classes of individuals, are not to have arms, they shall state in writing and publish to the world the reasons for withholding them. I cannot agree to throw this burden of stating their reasons upon the responsible executive. It will be found, on further consideration, that the real practical difficulty in regard to the administration of the Act is one which is not created by the Act itself, but by its practical maladministration by individual officers; and the real difficulty in regard to it is not to be met by a general resolution addressed to the Imperial Government, but by special representations to Local Governments in regard to the shortcomings of individual officers to whom the duty is entrusted by Government. (*"Hear, hear."*)

THE HON. P. M. MEHTA—(*Bombay, No.* 208 *in list*)—said: It is always with the greatest regret that I differ from any view which is taken by my friend Mr. Telang. (*Cheers.*) But I wish to state before the delegates in this Congress assembled the reason why I

3rd Day.

Res. VI., Establishment of Military Colleges—Volunteering—Modification of Arms Act.

steadfastly support the original resolution placed before you. (*Cheers.*) It is said that the proposition is placed before you simply on sentimental grounds. Perhaps it is so to a certain extent, if you look to the wording of the resolution. But the reason why I support that resolution is a different one. It is not sentimental, but eminently practical, and one of the most vital importance. That consideration is that you cannot, and ought not, to emasculate a whole nation. (*Cheers.*) It may be said that the time may come in future when these restrictions will be removed. But remember that when once the Indian people become emasculated, it will be a very long time indeed before you can get them to recover their manliness and their vigour. (*Cheers.*) That is my ground for supporting the proposition; and I say it is a practical ground. Perhaps, a good many of you remember the case of James II., who, when in his hour of peril, appealed to the Duke of Bedford (whose son had been judicially murdered by the king) for help, to whom the old nobleman replied: "I had once a son whom I could have sent to your assistance. But I have not got him now." In the same way, in some hour of need, India might have to say something similar to England. (*Cheers.*) I entirely recognize all the reasonable, and to a certain extent alarming, difficulties which have been raised, but I say that, if you strive to follow a really far-sighted policy, you will realize from the lessons of History that it can never be wise to emasculate a nation. (*Cheers.*)

RAJAH LUCHMAN SINGH—(*Agra, No.* 707 *in list*)—then spoke in Urdu. He said: Mr. President and Gentlemen,—The young men of almost every class in this country are certainly anxious that the law which prevents them from wearing arms should be entirely repealed; but such does not seem to me to be the desire of their elders. The Rajputs are a warlike race and lovers of arms, yet even these men, I am sure, do not wish an entire repeal of the Arms Act, but, like sensible men, would join us in requesting only the amendment of certain clauses, which, I feel sure, the Government, assured as it is of our loyalty, will grant, if we put our case properly before them.

I will only add that I cannot accept that English gentleman's* statement that the Indians might as well declare the sections of the Penal Code relating to theft, to be a slur upon their honesty, as the rules laid down under the Arms Act, a slur on their loyalty. Were those sections of the Code made applicable only to us Hindus and Mahomedans, and were all Europeans, Eurasians and other non-Indian men expressly exempted from their operation, then perhaps even that gentleman would agree that they constituted a slur upon the honesty of Indians. It is precisely because those sections apply to everyone, without distinction of nationality or creed, that no one considers them a slur upon our honesty; it is precisely because the Arms Act restrictions apply to nobody, but only to us, that many consider them to involve a slur upon our loyalty. (*Cheers.*)

CAPTAIN HEARSEY—(*N.-W. Provinces, No.* 841 *in list*)—said: Gentlemen,—I desire to put before you, in plain terms, the danger you are incurring. It is a danger to your homes, a danger to your wives, a danger to your families. This is a proposition of young men who have not seen the difficulties in which this country was involved 30 years ago. There are not perhaps a hundred among you who can remember the troubles that befel this country in 1857. I have done or tried to do my duty here for the last 35 years, and I have shed here my blood for my country and for India (*cheers*), and am willing to do so again, although I am getting old. (*Renewed cheers.*) But that is neither here nor there.

The point is this,—the danger lies in arms being distributed indiscriminately. As Mr. Telang has very justly said, they will get into the hands of the wrong kind of people. Remember what a small thing it was in 1857 that created the disturbance it did. This country—I say it in all kindness, and without any desire to say one word against you—may be likened to a barrel of gunpowder requiring but a spark to ignite it, and then we might have all the trouble over again. (*Cries of "No, no," and "Never."*) I do not say it is likely, but I say there is still a danger, and we ought to keep well on the right and safe side. But I would put it in this way—I would choose rather the lesser evil. I would have the law of licenses applicable to every man in India, whether European or native. (*Cheers.*) I should be a sufferer thereby, for all my family shoot, and I should require to pay for licenses for them. Very well, I am quite willing to do that, rather than there should be any danger to the country. I ask you again, for the sake of generations to come, for the sake of your children and children's children, not to do anything hastily in this matter, but to think the matter carefully over in your minds. (*Cheers.*) Abuses in the administration of the Arms Act there are: injustice to you is no doubt involved in some of the present rules; but are you sure that the resolution you propose is the only or the best way, even, of protesting against what is wrong? Far better drop it at present, and let the subject be more thoroughly threshed out. (*Cheers.*)

---

* Mr. P. Kennedy.

MR. SURENDRANATH BANERJEE—(*Bengal, No.* 1128 *in list*)—rose and said: Sir,—There seems to me to be a fatality connected with my having to come upon the Congress platform for the purpose of replying to objections brought against the passing of this resolution in regard to the Arms Act. Last year at the Madras Congress this question was most carefully threshed out and discussed, and, as the result of these deliberations, we arrived at the resolution we are now asked to re-affirm. Now, I ask, what has happened since then that we should modify, or withdraw from, that position which we occupied at the last Madras Congress? (*Cheers.*) Nothing except a reference made in a speech of the Viceroy, where, replying to our so-called demand for representative Government, he also thought it necessary to condemn the Volunteer movement and the request for the modification (repeal he seems to have fancied· of the Arms Act. Repeated reference has been made to sentimental considerations but sentimental considerations are considerations of the greatest moment to us. (*Cneers.*) We are a sentimental people. (*Cheers.*) The world is governed by sentiment. (*Renewed cheers.*) The greatest events in European and American history have been shaped, and moulded, and guided by sentimental considerations, and it will not be for me to ask you to come down from the lofty pedestal of sentiment to a mere matter-of-fact existence in this world. *Cheers and cries of* "*Oh! oh!*") But it is not merely a sentimental grievance. It is a grievance which is complained of, which is denounced, because it is keenly felt by every peasant and artisan, and every man who desires to protect his life or his property. (*Cheers.*) 'In the year 1885, when the Conference was held in Calcutta,. one of the speakers who delivered an address on this subject, said that in his immediate neighbourhood hundreds of acres of land remained uncultivated in consequence of the depredations of wild beasts, and the question was asked, Why do not your people go in for licenses? But look at the difficulties by which the acquisition of licenses is surrounded. It necessitates a man's absenting himself from his work for days in order to give his attendance at the Courts of Law, and it necessitates the payment, not only of fees, but of douceurs to all kinds of people. And, after all, the license only lasts for one year. This tedious and expensive process has to be repeated again and again. These are not sentimental considerations. (*Cheers.*) Brother delegates, you may not feel it yourselves, but you are here, not only to represent yourselves, but the dumb voiceless millions—not only on your own behalf, but on behalf of the voiceless agricultural community,—and what is your next resolution? It is a resolution for raising the minimum of the income tax. You have undertaken to defend the poor and oppressed, and in their name and on their behalf I ask you to support the resolution which has been proposed and seconded. (*Cheers.*) Mr. Kennedy was pleased to say Lord Ripon did not do anything in the matter of the Arms Act I venture to question Mr. Kennedy's assertion. The Marquis of Ripon did his best to improve the administration of the Act. (*Cheers.*) And we have been confronted with the dark days of the Indian Mutiny. But is not India now completely changed since the Indian Mutiny? Instead of suspicion and distrust, there is this Congress teeming with loyalty, teeming with devotion to our Queen, teeming with patriotism. (*Cheers.*) The times have changed. India of to-day is not the India of the Mutiny. The experiences of the Mutiny are not applicable to the experiences of the present hour; and in the name of our new India of changed circumstances, and of our poor down-trodden countrymen, I ask you to support the resolution. (*Cheers.*)

RAJAH RAMPAL SINGH—(*Allahabad, No.* 571 *in list*)—then said: Sir,—In rising to address this assembly, I must first express my great regret that I am here to oppose the resolution, and not to support it. Of course it is a very painful duty for me to be compelled to come forward and oppose a resolution. But I think it is a mistaken measure, and one which I think will be fraught with danger to the objects of the Congress. I would heartily support a resolution to grant us the privilege of becoming volunteers; but I, at the same time, with the greatest regret, oppose the third part of the resolution, in which you ask Government to allow you to use arms without any check. (*Cheers.*) It has been said that, for the sake of the dumb millions, we should ask Government to grant us this; but for the sake of these same dumb millions I think that you should not ask it. (*Cheers.*) Really you are making a great mistake. It will rouse the suspicions of the English people, and prevent the promotion of your cause in England. I have always been under that impression, and I strongly support the statements made by the honourable gentleman from Bombay, Mr. Telang. You may amend the Arms Act, but India does not need nor want it repealed. (*Cheers and cries of* "*We don't want it repealed, we only want it amended.*")

THE PRESIDENT then asked for a show of hands as to whether or not the subject had been sufficiently discussed, and, on the vote being taken, he announced that it appeared that even now there was a desire to discuss the resolution further. There were, he said, eight more resolutions to come before them, and ten persons had already spoken on the one before them. He then took another vote as to whether the question should be put, and, receiving an affirmative answer, Mr. Kennedy's amendment was put and lost.

3rd Day.

Res. VI., Establishment of Military Colleges—Volunteering—Modification of Arms Act.

THE PRESIDENT: Then, Gentlemen, I shall now put the original resolution, which will stand as follows :—

RESOLVED—"*That this Congress, having read and considered Resolution IV of the "Congress of 1887, to wit—*

"'*That, in view of the loyalty of Her Majesty's Indian subjects, the Congress considers it desirable "'that the Queen's Proclamation should be given effect to, that the Military services in the higher "'grades should be practically opened to the natives of this country, and that the Government "'should establish Military Colleges in the country whereat the natives of India, as defined by "'Statute, may be educated and trained for a Military career as officers of the Indian Army;'*

"*Resolution XII of the Congress of 1886, and Resolution V of the Congress of 1887, to wit—*

"'*That, in view of the unsettled state of public affairs in Europe, and the immense assistance that "'the people of this country, if duly prepared therefor, are capable of rendering to Great Britain "'in the event of any serious complications arising, the Congress once again earnestly appeals to "'the Government to authorize (under such rules and restrictions as to it may seem fitting) a "'system of Volunteering for the Indian inhabitants of the country such as may qualify them to "'support the Government effectually in any crisis;'*

and Resolution VIII of the Congress of 1887, to wit—

"'*That, in view of the loyalty of the people, the hardships which the present Arms Act (XI of "'1878) causes, and the unmerited slur which it casts upon the people of this country, the "'Government be moved so to modify the provisions of Chapter IV, and if necessary, other "'portions of the said Act, as shall enable all persons to possess and wear arms unless debarred "'therefrom, either as individuals or members of particular communities or classes, by the orders "'of the Government of India (or any local authority empowered by the Government of India "'on that behalf) for reasons to be recorded in writing and duly published;'*

"*does now, hereby, affirm the same respectively.*"

The resolution was then put and carried by a very large majority.

Res. VII., Reform of the Excise and Abkari Systems.

MR. D. E. WACHA—(*Bombay, No. 204 in list*)—then rose and said: Gentlemen,—The resolution that has been entrusted to me to propose runs as follows :—

"*That, as it is the general belief of the people of this country that the systems of Abkari and Excise now prevailing in India have, despite the well-known benevolent intentions of the Government, permitted, if they have not directly encouraged, a serious increase in the consumption of intoxicants, the Government be respectfully urged to investigate the question, and to adopt such an improved system as shall tend to discourage insobriety.*"

I congratulate the Congress on this new departure in its programme. Hitherto the resolutions passed by it have had reference to the political welfare of our countrymen, but I take the resolution just read out to you to be partly political and partly social. It is political so far as it prays the Government to inquire, with the aid of a Commission, which, it is to be hoped, will consist of officials as well as non-officials, into the real condition of the drink traffic, and social so far as it is a practical step in earnest towards the improvement of the masses who contribute largely to the excise revenue. It is not only a general belief, but, I may say, the universal conviction, that the habit of drinking is greatly on the increase; consequently there is a strong feeling that its further growth should be checked betimes, and, so far as my own Presidency is concerned, I can unhesitatingly say that consumption has greatly increased. It has doubled itself during the last few years. I have also watched the course of the drink revenue in the other provinces, especially in Bengal, Madras and the United Provinces, and I regret to have to say that there, too, intemperance is increasing. The evil must, in a large measure, be attributed to the direct action of the State, or, in other words, to the excise policies of the Imperial and Local Governments.

Many of you are, no doubt, aware that the fact of the increase of intemperance in this country was last year brought to the notice of the House of Commons by Mr. Samuel Smith, a well-known friend, who has evinced great interest in the condition of India, and whose sympathies are for the true welfare of us Indians. (*Cheers.*) Mr. Smith, you may be further aware, is a member who is most careful of the correctness of his facts, so that he was stating the bare truth when he observed in Parliament that the Government of India was pushing on the drink traffic with the view of augmenting the revenue, and his facts were ably supported by the statement of the Revd. M. Evans, a gentleman well known, at least in Bengal, where he has watched the Abkari administration for the last 20 years, and who is now acting as Private Secretary to a distinguished member of Parliament who has been most active in the temperance movement at home, and who has lately been paying attention to the same question in this country, and who is just now sitting among us here. (*Continued cheers for Mr. Caine.*) It is superfluous to refer further to Mr. Smith's inquiry, in which he was vigorously supported by all the temperance organisations and societies in England, headed by the Bishop of London. Neither is it necessary to refer to that other, now well known, debate on the subject in the early part of this year; suffice it to say Mr. Smith's agitation in the House of Commons virtually obliged the Secretary of State for India to direct the Indian Government to enquire into the allegation brought against it, that it was pushing on the drink traffic with the object of increasing the excise revenue. After a prolonged inquiry through the various Local Governments, that Government forwarded a despatch to the Secretary of State in June, 1887, in which it vainly tried to combat the allegation. It was a most unsatisfactory State document, full of gross misstatements and otherwise imperfect in information. But for its unsatisfactory character, I believe that the necessity for the resolution that I have moved might have been obviated. Having given considerable attention to the study of the Abkari administration, I was constrained to criticise that despatch in the form of a pamphlet, a copy of which was officially forwarded to the Secretary of State. The reply was that it was not his province to investigate the two statements of the Bombay Government, on which I had laid special stress, and that I should open communications with that Government, a reply which I considered to be simply fatuous. However, the main fact is this: that on the one hand the Government deny that its excise policy is the principal and direct cause of the increased habit of drinking among the people, and on the other the people stoutly maintain that such is the case. I may give credit to the Government for its benevolent intentions to check intemperance and promote sobriety among its subjects. But all the same it is not at all able to control the excessive zeal of excise officials to net in a larger and larger drink revenue every year by pushing the drink traffic. Under the circumstances, it is needful that the truth should be sifted to the bottom, and the best way to do this is by the appointment of an impartial and unbiassed Commission. What is wanted is not an expansive but a restrictive system of Abkari—a system which shall promote sobriety, and not one which stimulates, intemperance or puts those who never drank spirits in the way of drinking them. We want a policy which shall really be in practice one of maximum of revenue with minimum of consumption. Unfortunately, as matters now actually stand, there is a maximum of revenue and a maximum of consumption. With these few observations I now beg to move the resolution which I have already read to you. (*Cheers.*)

PANDIT SATTYANAND AGNIHOTRI—(*Lahore, No.* 344 *in list*)—then rose and said, speaking in Urdu: Brother Delegates,—I rise with the greatest pleasure to second the resolution proposed by Mr. Watcha. This country is suffering at present from the Abkari plague; liquor is very cheap, and is everywhere to be had, for Government shops have sprung up everywhere, and the consequence is that habits of drunkenness are increasing, and the people, especially the lower classes, are being terribly demoralized. It is in vain that I and others, * whose mission it is to labour for the moral elevation of the people, preach and pray and wear our hearts and lives out in the struggle against vice, so long as the existing system—ever tempting to drunkenness and all the sin and wickedness that this brings in its train—is allowed to continue unaltered. It is ruining the country. Thirty years ago, as I know from older men, drunkenness was comparatively rare, and nearly confined to limited, criminal or very low-caste classes. Fifteen years ago—and here I speak from my own knowledge—when I first commenced my labours, the evil was not nearly so great, and liquor was still avoided by all respectable persons. Now drinking has begun to assume terrible proportions. The Government have no wish to ruin the country; and I feel sure that, when the real state of the case is brought home to them, they will take the matter into their serious consideration, and do their part of the work in remedying this great evil. For our part, we have innumerable societies now all over the country endeavouring to discourage the use of intoxicants, but it is everywhere the existing evil system of excise and Abkari that constitutes our greatest difficulty. I may mention that Lahore had a strong association for combating the spread of drunkenness, which has been still further strengthened by the advice and recent visit of our friend Mr. Caine, whom I see present here now. (*Cheers.*) These associations are doing good; but it is essential that the Government should strengthen them by amending its own ways, which are, I fear, the root of this great social and political evil. Last October we held in Bengal, as you may remember, a Provincial Congress, and there too a strong resolution, recommending the reform of the existing Abkari system was unanimously passed by the whole 100 representatives sent up by every district in Bengal. Go where you will, to Madras, Bombay, Guzerat—and I have visited most provinces during the last few years—there is the same complaint everywhere,—the Government system of dealing with the liquor question, by which it is evolving a yearly increasing revenue, is demoralizing the country; and it is not too much to say that, if a radical change be not speedily effected in that system, the national consequences will be most disastrous. Gentlemen, I am at one with you in all your proposals,

*** He is a well-known Brahmo Missionary—a leading religious and moral reformer in the Punjab.**

3rd Day.

Res. VII., Reform of the Excise and Abkari Systems.

but my daily personal experiences for some years now lead me to be more earnest and to feel more strongly in regard to this resolution, which I with all my heart commend to your acceptance, than in regard to almost any other, and we have the consolation too of knowing that this, at least, is a resolution, in which our most unscrupulous and unprincipled adversaries cannot, it seems to me, possibly find anything to cavil at.

MR. R. D. MEHTA—(*Calcutta, No.* 1139 *in list*)—said : Gentlemen,—I am not going to make a speech of any length, but I will tell you that, although the resolution has my entire sympathy and concurrence, I think the wording of it should be modified, and modified in such a manner as to leave no doubt as to its meaning, and in a way that it could be placed before the British public by the Member of Parliament who is with us to-day. Why should we beg the question ? Why talk about its being the general belief of the people of this country, &c. ? It is not a question of belief, but an established fact, that the consumption of liquor has increased and is increasing. Then why this talk about benevolent intentions ? The intention of the Government is said to be benevolent. Benevolent indeed—not only benevolent, but fruitful—revenue-full (*laughter*) ; very benevolent as far as the Government treasury is concerned, but, as far as the health and morals of the people is concerned, ruinous. (*Cheers.*) The Government has directly encouraged the consumption of drink, and why should we now lay ourselves open to any misconstruction ? We do not want any investigation. We have had too many investigations, and the result is merely delay in carrying out the indispensable reforms. I move, as an amendment, that our resolution on this subject be worded as follows :—

" *That, having regard to the fact that a serious increase in the consumption of intoxicants has taken place under the systems of Abkari and excise now prevailing in India, the Government be respectfully urged to adopt some such improved system as shall tend to discourage insobriety.*"

I hope, Gentlemen, that you will accept this amendment. It is shorter and more to the point, and it is not open to the misconstructions which the hesitating tone of the original would be certain to invite. The Government have for a long series of years been stimulating drunkenness ; let them now encourage sobriety. This is what we mean, and let this be what we say. (*Cheers.*)

MR. J. E. HOWARD—(*Allahabad, No.* 573 *in list*)—then said : Gentlemen,—I have great pleasure in supporting Mr. Mehta's amendment. I agree with him that the question is one in regard to which we may well be as explicit as possible. I am quite sure that the Government has never designedly encouraged the spread of drunkenness ; on the contrary, I believe it has always held before its eyes the principle of " the maximum of revenue with the minimum of drinking." But no impartial man can pretend that hitherto it has been successful so far as the latter clause is concerned ; nay, there is reason to fear that we are fast progressing towards a state in which with, *possibly*, a maximum of revenue there will also be a maximum of insobriety. I cordially join Mr. Mehta in desiring to press clearly upon Government the necessity of reform in these matters.

THE PRESIDENT : Gentlemen,—I have great pleasure in informing you that both the proposer and seconder of the original resolution have signified to me their acceptance of Mr. R. D. Mehta's amendment, which has therefore now become the substantive resolution before the assembly.

MR. ATKINS—(*Allahabad, No.* 579 *in list*)—then said : I am very glad to have an opportunity of addressing you upon this subject. The proposer of the resolution has said that it is partly political and partly social. Perhaps I may be able to prove to you that it is a great deal more a political than a social question. I may perhaps take the liberty of informing you that for five years I was at the head of the largest teetotal association in this country—the Independent Order of Good Templars ; and that body feels very great interest in this resolution, so much so that, were the majority of the members not military men, and therefore unable to take part in this Congress movement, I should have had the honour of appearing at the Congress, not only as a delegate of the people, but also as the representative of this great Temperance Association, which might however well have found a far abler representative. (*Cries of* " *No !* " *and cheers.*) The reason the Good Templars feel so much interest in this liquor question is because the majority of the men in the British Army in India, whose healths are ruined by intemperance, or who are punished for offences committed while under the influence of drink, obtain the liquor from the cheap drinking places, established or maintained under the auspices of the Government Abkari Department, where country liquor is sold. You have already heard from a previous speaker what every English soldier in India costs this country, so you can understand, when soldiers fall sick through drink, or their services

Res. VII., Reform of the Excise and Abkari Systems.

are lost to the State by their being invalided to England, or in other ways, it means a serious loss of public money; and the amount so lost every year is an enormous sum, which of course comes out of the revenues of India, and which ought properly to be set against the revenue that the Government, by its present system of Abkari and excise, is realizing. I therefore consider that I am quite justified in asserting that this resolution is of great political importance (*cheers*); and that the question of an improved Abkari system has even, from this single point of view, a grave political significance. I need scarcely add that, amongst the community generally, an increase in drunkenness involves an increase in crime, an increase in the cost of repressive and adjudicative agencies, and an increase in the danger of the lower classes at some time getting out of hand; and so, from whatever side we look at it, whether where the European soldier or the Indian peasant is concerned, it is certainly quite as much, if not more, of a political than a social question. (*Loud cheers.*)

MR. SABAPATHY MUDALIAR—(*Madras, No. 70 in list*)—said: Mr. President,—I have the greatest pleasure in supporting this resolution. For ten years I was myself an Abkari contractor, but I gave up this business for the sake of my brethren. (*Cheers*) So you must give me credit for knowing, perhaps better than most people, the evils entailed upon this country by the excessive drunkenness which is increasing every day ("*Hear, hear,*" *and cheers*) under our existing Abkari system. I cannot, however, state clear facts so as to show directly how this excessive drunkenness is being brought about. It may be due in some measure to our own social customs, and to the want of effective moral training amongst our lower classes, and by no means exclusively to the wrong principles upon which the traffic is conducted by Government. I cannot, with all my experience, speak positively on this point. But, in the resolution, Government is urged to adopt all such measures as lie in their power to relieve their administration from any share it may now have in producing the evil consequences we deplore, and we, on our own part, by temperance associations and by the education of our poorer brethren, will do our best to remove any other causes, if there be such independent of the system in force, of this great and growing curse to the country. I do not think that I need add more to what has already been said, but simply once more commend to your acceptance this resolution. (*Cheers.*)

THE PRESIDENT: Gentlemen,—As no one else seems to wish to address you, I will, if you approve, now put the amended resolution. (*Cries of "Yes, yes, Vote, vote."*) Very good. Then the resolution will stand thus:—

RESOLVED—"*That, having regard to the fact that a serious increase in the consumption of intoxicants has taken place under the systems of Abkari and excise now prevailing in India, the Government be respectfully urged to adopt some such improved system as shall tend to discourage insobriety.*"

The resolution was then put and carried without a single dissentient voice.

Res. VIII., Income-tax—Taxable minimum to be raised.

PANDIT MADAN MOHAN MALAVIYA—(*Allahabad, No. 569 in list*)—then rose and said: Mr. Chairman and Gentlemen,—I rise to propose the eighth resolution, which runs thus:—

"*That as the administration of the income-tax, especially as regards incomes below Rs. 1,000, has proved extremely unsatisfactory, it is essential, in the opinion of the Congress, that the taxable minimum be raised to Rs. 1,000.*"

I think, Gentlemen, I need hardly say much to commend this resolution to your acceptance. This is, as you all know, specially the respectable poor man's resolution. The other and larger reforms that we are seeking will no doubt conduce as much to the welfare of the poor as of the rich. But the effect of this measure, if the Government would only accept it, would be to relieve immediately a large number of poor but respectable people from injustice and oppression. The Congress will not, I hope, be misunderstood in accepting this resolution. We do not object to the income-tax itself; all that we desire is that the taxable minimum should not be so oppressively low as it is. When Lord Dufferin taunted us, in his postprandial oration at St. Andrew's, with not representing the country, because we did not ask his Lordship to decuple the income-tax, he quite forgot that the first Congress that met at Bombay distinctly stated that, if the then increasing expenditure could not be met by reductions, the necessary additional revenue should be obtained by extending the license-tax to those classes of the community who were till then exempt from its operation. In other words, it was the Congress that first advocated the re-imposition of the income-tax. (*Cheers.*) His Lordship himself complimented the Congress as "that body of intelligent and patriotic men" when he cited their authority in support of his income-tax scheme; but, though we approved and desired the imposition of the income-tax on the rich, or those who could afford to pay it, we did not want it to become an engine for harassing the poor; and if only Lord Dufferin knew half as much as we do of the injustice and oppression practised on the poorer classes of the people in connection with

3rd Day.

Res. VIII., Income-tax—Taxable minimum to be raised.

this tax, and, Gentlemen, if he knew how wide and deep is the discontent that is consequently spreading in the country, I am sure that, instead of quizzing us as he did for not proposing an increase in the tax, he would have unhesitatingly raised, as we have advised, the taxable minimum to Rs. 1,000. (*Cheers.*)

The taxable minimum at present is, as you very well know, Rs. 500 (£34), *i.e.*, less than one-fourth of what it is in England (£150). But, as if this were not a sufficient ground for complaint, in actual practice, people whose incomes do not go beyond Rs. 15 a month, or say Rs. 180 (£12) per annum, are often enough taxed as though their incomes reached the legal minimum of Rs. 500. Official apologists may deny that this is a true representation of facts. But I am confident, Gentlemen, that if an honest, independent inquiry were instituted, and the evidence of non-official gentlemen obtained, my assertions would be amply borne out by their testimony. We do not for a moment insinuate that it is the desire of Government that the poor should be thus oppressed, or that the taxable minimum should in practice be reduced so much below the amount fixed by law. The fault apparently rests on the shoulders of those officers who are entrusted with the duty of assessing and collecting the tax. But, Gentlemen, the very perfunctory manner in which revising officers hear and dismiss appeals lends colour to the popular belief that the burdensome oppression and injustice that they groan under is practised with the tacit approval of Government. I shall only quote here one instance to show how unbecomingly the tax is administered, and how some Government officials help, by their thoughtless conduct, to bring our Government into disrepute. Every one knows how poor a man a grain-parcher is. He earns his daily bread by exposing himself to a blazing fire even throughout the hottest months of summer. One would imagine that the tax-collector would pass by such uninviting victims. But that unhappily is not the case. I am sorry to say, and I have it on the best authority, that in some cases the tax has been imposed on even such miserable men as grain-parchers ; and what is more painful to have to record is, that the revising officers, instead of exempting such men from payment, have on appeal confirmed the assessment made by their subordinates. In the particular instance that I have just now in my mind, the revising officer ordered the grain-parcher to produce his books, and so prove that his income was not what the assessing officer had imagined it to be. Fancy a grain-parcher keeping books ! You might as well expect a beggar selling lucifers in the streets of London to keep books ! (*Loud cheers.*) But this official would insist upon the books being produced, and, that being impossible, as the books had naturally no existence, he compelled the poor man to pay the amount assessed ! Tell me, Gentlemen, what can bring Government into greater disrepute than such incidents ? And what we therefore pray to Government is, that it may raise the taxable minimum to Rs. 1,000, so that at least persons whose incomes fall *below* Rs. 500 may be removed sufficiently far from the pale of the tax-collector's harassment. This we urge, Gentlemen, primarily out of regard for the sufferings of the poor, but also in vindication of the good name of Government. (*Cheers.*) It is needless for me to dilate further on this resolution. I have no doubt that it will meet with your ready approval and, I venture to hope, with the favourable consideration of Government. (*Cheers.*)

And now, Gentlemen, before I resume my seat, permit me to refer for a moment to a subject which, though not connected with the one entrusted to my humble advocacy, is yet of such vital importance as to justify a momentary digression—I mean the Proclamation of 1858. It is not at all surprising to find speaker after speaker, from our worthy President downwards, referring to that great charter of our rights and privileges. This is the keystone of the arch which supports all our demands. Therein our gracious Sovereign, under whose benign government we assemble year after year to deliberate upon our common wants and to formulate our common grievances,—our gracious Sovereign whose pictures now hang round us, shedding, as it were, some faint reflection of her kindly and motherly influence on our deliberations (*loud cheers*) ;—therein, Gentlemen, our most noble Queen of England and Empress of India solemnly extended to us pledges the fulfilment of which we now pray for. I refer to it here simply to denounce with all the strength I can command the false and foolish utterance of a high official that the promises therein made were made more as a matter of policy than in honest good faith. I hold in my hand an extract from Her Majesty's private letter, dated Babelsburg, August 15, 1858, in which Her Majesty gave instructions to Lord Derby to draft that Proclamation, and I will, with your permission, read it to you. (*Loud cheers.*) It runs thus :—

"The Queen would be glad if Lord Derby would write it (the Proclamation) himself in his own excellent language, bearing in mind that it is a female Sovereign who speaks to more than a hundred millions of Eastern people on assuming the direct government over them, and after a bloody civil war giving them pledges which her future reign is to redeem, and explaining the principles of her government. Such a document should breathe feelings of generosity, benevolence, and religious toleration, and point out the privileges which the Indians will receive in being placed on an equality with the subjects of the British Crown and the prosperity following in the train of civilization." (*Loud and continued cheers.*)

Who in his senses, Gentlemen, could fail to be struck with the ring of sincerity and beneficence that echoes throughout these sentences? *(prolonged cheering)* and yet we find some exalted personages foolish enough to cast a doubt on the sincerity of Her Majesty's promises. Well, Gentlemen, perhaps it was to give the lie to such faithless men that the Queen-Empress reiterated her solemn pledges on the memorable occasion of her Jubilee. *(Cheers.)* In responding to the Bombay Jubilee Address, Her Majesty was pleased to say that 'it had always been and would be her earnest desire to maintain unswervingly the principles laid down in the Proclamation published on her assumption of the direct controls of the Government of India." *(Cheers.)* And, Gentlemen, when we ask for an increased share in the administration of our affairs, whether it be as members of the Legislative Councils or of the Public Service, Civil or Military, what more do we want than that the pledges so graciously given should be as graciously redeemed? And we hope and trust they will be soon redeemed. *(Cheers.)*

With this slight digression, Gentlemen, for which I need scarcely apologise to you, considering the universal importance of the subject, I beg to invite your acceptance of the resolution that I have had the honour to lay before you. *(Cheers.)*

MR. T. P. CROWLEY—*(Allahabad, No.* 555 *in list)*—said: I have the greatest pleasure in seconding this resolution. Beyond that, I cannot say more on the income-tax. Against the income-tax itself I have no quarrel; but, if it be so adjusted that it involves the harassment of the poor, its incidence must be altered, as is proposed by this resolution. There is no more to be said on this head; but, if the President will give me a few minutes, I will allude to certain past occurrences which may help to encourage us in the great work undertaken by the Indian National Congress. *(Cheers and cries of "To the point.")* Well, Gentlemen, our opponents tell us that the National Congress will never, never succeed. Let me recall to you that when Wilberforce first brought in his Bill for the abolition of the slave trade, all those who reaped the fruits of this accursed traffic swore by all their false gods and said: "By Heavens, *never.*" But time passed on, and right triumphed, and that infamous practice was abolished for ever, and it was *ever* and not *never*, and so will be the success of the Indian National Congress; it will be for *ever* and not *never*. *(Laughter and cheers.)* Then there was the Reform Bill. Have we not read how the old autocrats shook their heads. How they said, Oh, it was outrageous altogether? *(Laughter.)* How they swore that, even if they had to die on the floor of the House, the Bill should never, never pass. But again time ran on, and the Bill was passed and passed for *ever*, and so will the triumph of the Congress be for *ever* and not *never*. *(Laughter and cheers.)* Now we come to the repeal of the Corn Laws. It was going to destroy the whole Church and State; it was going to wipe England off from the roll of the nations, and usher in a worse than French Revolution. *Never*, so long as one drop of blood remained in their veins, would the landed aristocracy permit it. No, never! *(Loud laughter.)* But again a righteous cause, backed by patience and perseverance, triumphed, and the triumph was for *ever*, and so will be the success of the National Congress for *ever* and not *never*. *(Uproarious laughter and cheers.)* Now we come to the Bill passed by Mr. Gladstone for the Disestablishment of the Church of Ireland. The whole army of Tories and Bigots, all poor Ireland's enemies—and alas! she has too many—declared that, though the heavens fell, this awful thing should never be. But the Bill passed and passed for *ever*, and again the right triumphed and was for ever and not never, and so will the Congress' victories be for *ever*, and not *never!* *(Renewed laughter and cheers.)* If Lord Salisbury only knew the people of India as I have done for forty years, he would know that he is not worthy to loosen the laces of the shoes of many whom he seeks to insult, by taunting them with their colour. *(Laughter and cheers.)* But don't let us give in to him or those like him, but—let opponents misrepresent and rave as they please—let the Congress be *ever* and *ever* and *ever!* *(Loud cheers.)*

MR. K. P. VISWANADHA IYER—*(Madras, No.* 4 *in list)*—said: I have completely to endorse everything that has been so eloquently said by previous speakers about the income-tax. I agree also with Mr. Crowley that the Congress must be *ever*, and that we must persevere in the face of all opposition!—for ever and ever if need be. But this is a large question, and the question at present immediately before us is whether the minimum taxable limit under the income-tax arrangement should be raised from 500 rupees to 1,000 rupees, or stand at 500 rupees. I may, before proceeding further, point out that the raising of the taxable limit from 500 to 1,000 rupees means practically, at the existing rate of exchange, raising it from £34 to £68. I can tell you without any hesitation that the working of the Act, if the taxable minimum limit be retained at 500 rupees, will continue to be, as now, highly oppressive. *(Cheers.)* Fifty years ago, no doubt, an income of Rs. 500 a year might have been a taxable item. Money went much further, wants were fewer, lives simpler; but all this is changed now, and what then was competence is now the barest sustenance. It can surely not be desired that, after Government has introduced so many changes by which the

3rd Day.

Res. VIII., Income-tax—Taxable minimum to be raised.

conditions of life may be ameliorated and existence made so much fuller, we should now go back to primitive modes of life and be contented with what sufficed us in past times. But that is what is involved in keeping the limit as low as £34, or else it must be admitted that it designedly trenches upon the necessaries of existence which the income-tax is professed *not* to do! What served us years ago cannot be supposed to serve us now. (*Cheers.*) What were undreamt-of superfluities then are necessaries to-day; not only too do we actually need more for ourselves, but we have other and new demands to meet. For instance, we have to educate our children in a manner unheard of in past times, and the expenses of education are yearly increasing, and Government is throwing more and more of the burthen of this, yearly, on the shoulders of us poorer middle-class men. It is the policy of the Government that we should bear the larger part of these burdens, and that a constantly diminishing share of these expenses should be borne by the State. In all ways, therefore, the men with incomes of Rs. 500, and even considerably more, are becoming practically poorer and poorer, and more wholly unfit to be yearly tortured on the income-tax rack. On this ground, amongst others, and there are many others with which I need not trouble you, for they were very fully set forth at the Congress at Madras last year, I support the resolution before you most emphatically.

MR. BAIKUNTHA NATH SEN—(*Bengal, No.* 1192 *in list*)—next spoke. He said: Mr. President and Brother Delegates,—A resolution which seeks to raise the income tax taxable minimum, and thus lighten the burthens of the poorest, most hardly worked, and most struggling sections of the middle classes, carries to us—who know the difficulties which beset these unhappy sections of the community—too far advanced to live as the poorer peasants do, too poor to do what they feel to be the simplest justice to their children,—carries, I say, to us its own commendation, and should not require any elaborate arguments to support it. But as I have been called upon by our respected President technically to "*support*" it, I will endeavour to do so in a few words.

The resolution as drawn sets forth the opinion of the Congress, that the administration of the income-tax is extremely unsatisfactory. But the last Government resolution on the subject in a manner declares it to have been satisfactory. So here we have a conflict of opinions, and I deem it my duty therefore to submit to you a few observations on this point. With every respect for this Government enunciation, and with the greatest deference to the official who drew it up, I am compelled to submit that it has been based on insufficient and inaccurate data. I regret that I have not the resolution at hand to quote the exact words, but I may say that the main grounds on which the Government seem to have inferred the satisfactory character of the income-tax administration were the small number of appeals against assessments, the small number of warrants issued, and the small number of sales carried out foı the realization of the tax.

Now the number of appeals preferred is worthless as a criterion of the merits of the administration—firstly, because the expenses of an appeal are almost equal in amount to the tax assessed; secondly, because of the extremely uncertain and, as a rule, discouraging character of the results of such appeals; thirdly, because of the existing universal indisposition to allow the real facts of incomes to be known to the public, which they always must become when appeals are made; and fourthly, because people are afraid of prosecutions under the Stamp Act. As to this latter point, I may note that when, in appeals, books are produced to prove income, these are carefully scrutinized and if in them any transactions can be unearthed in which, under the strictest reading of the law, stamped documents ought to have been used, but by some oversight or failure to realize some special point they have not been used, a criminal prosecution is at once set on foot. In the course of my professional work I have come to know of a large number of criminal prosecutions for alleged evasion of stamp duty, under the Stamp Act, resulting from investigations into income-tax appeals. These four reasons sufficiently explain the great paucity of income-tax appeals, and this paucity therefore furnishes no reason for believing the administration of the tax to have been satisfactory, nay, rightly considered, to those who understand the country and the people it is a significant sign of its utter rottenness. If it were at all healthy, there *would* be lots of appeals, and that no matter how perfect (humanly speaking) the assessment might be.

As regards the warrants, their smallness in number is equally no proof of the goodness of an assessment. The assessee knows that he will have to pay the costs of the warrant as well as the tax, and therefore of course, at any sacrifice, endeavours to find the money required before a warrant is issued. Moreover, the issue of a warrant lowers a man in the estimation of his fellow-citizens, and this consideration alone makes even the poorest of respectable men anxious to pay up—even if he sells his household utensils—before this indignity can be offered to him. We are very thin-skinned in these matters; but you all know it is a fact, and, being so, the talk about a limited issue of warrants proving anything in favour of the administration is futile.

3rd Day.

Res. VIII., Income-tax—Taxable minimum to be raised.

Lastly, as to the small number of sales. The inference drawn is almost impudently fallacious. If there be a single sale for the realization of the tax, this is sufficient to condemn the administration. Think only what a sale means, you who know how things are managed amongst us. It means that a tax has been imposed upon a man so heavy as to exceed not only all his available means, but all his borrowing powers. What single man amongst us, if he can beg or borrow the money anywhere, will allow his property to be sold in such a case?—sold always for less than half that it will cost him to replace it. Who, if he can by any device avoid it, will add, to his other troubles, the heavy official costs of attachment and sale, and the disgrace before his fellows of these ultimate punitive proceedings? Poor men of good family have committed suicide in such cases, unable to show their faces or again hold up their heads before their fellows after such public dishonour. We know better, perhaps, in big towns, now, but in the mofussil the old ideas still linger.

Few sales, indeed, a criterion of good administration! Every single sale is a record of cruelty and oppression. Every single sale signifies an assessment, not only even a 50 per cent. assessment on the victim's means, but an assessment involving in one fell swoop more than all that he has, or can beg or borrow. (*The gong here sounded.*) But the President gives the warning—the fatal guillotine, as Mr. Mehta says,* has been adjusted to the throat of my poor discourse; another moment and it will cease to be, and I will now therefore only add that, had Fate, in the shape of our President, been willing to prolong my oratorical existence for only a few more minutes, I would have passed on to the positive side of the question, and shown to you very clearly how, in a dozen different ways, the existing administration of the income-tax is not only unsatisfactory, but in many of its practical details unjustifiable and wholly unworthy of our enlightened and civilized Government. (*Loud cheers.*)

MR. KRISHNA RAO GOVIND DESHPANDE—(*C. Provinces, No.* 291 *in list*)—rose and said: Gentlemen,—I heartily support the resolution before us, but, instead of reiterating the arguments of the able speakers who have preceded me, I will ask you for one moment to consider our position in the Central Provinces. It is, I know, a provincial question which the Congress cannot take up, but still it is a fact that I wish you all to know, because it may be a sort of consolation to all of you to realize that, bad as may be the state of affairs, in this matter of the income-tax, in the rest of India which you inhabit, it is just exactly twice as bad in our poor "*Mummalik Mutawasit*,"† as we are officially designated in your North-Western Provinces vernacular. You feel compassion for the poor folks amongst yourselves who are taxed down to incomes of £34 a year, but we groan under a supplementary income-tax, called the Pandhri tax, which taxes all incomes between £17 and £34. This is an old native tax, and the peculiar blessedness of our position is, that, while the old native taxes are retained, the modern European taxes are superadded to us. Gentlemen, it is I fear no use, but I desire by these words to protest respectfully against this Pandhri tax, this special income-tax with a taxable miminum of £17 a year, and to express a hope that when the Government raises the income-tax minimum, as we are praying them by the resolution before us to do, they will be good enough to abolish the Pandhri tax altogether, since, unless they do this, we poor Central Provincials, alone of all the peoples of this great Empire, will be none the better. However, I support the resolution, and even should we ourselves gain nothing, we are all brothers, and your gain will be our consolation. (*Loud cheers; cries of "Vote, vote."*)

THE PRESIDENT: I think I may now put the resolution, which stands thus:—

RESOLVED—"*That as the administration of the income-tax, especially as regards incomes below Rs. 1,000, has proved extremely unsatisfactory, it is essential, in the opinion of the Congress, that the taxable minimum be raised to Rs. 1,000.*"

The resolution was then put and unanimously carried. The assembly then adjourned to 11 A.M. of the next day.

---

* *Vide ante*, p. 31.

† *i.e.*, Central Provinces, in Urdu. The speaker is a Mahratta.

FOURTH DAY'S PROCEEDINGS

Saturday, the 29th December, 1888.

4th Day.

The Congress re-assembled at 11 A.M. precisely.

Dedication of a Hall to the Congress.

THE PRESIDENT said: Gentlemen,—The first thing I have to inform you is that we have to-day received an offer from one of our delegates, Mr. Ram Chundra Bahdeva Apte, of a large hall forty feet by twenty-six which he has erected at Ichalkarngi, in the Southern Mahratta country, as a permanent home for the Divisional Congress Committee, which he proposes now to dedicate formally to the National Congress. (*Cheers.*) If at any time the National Congress itself will take up its abode for a week or for a month or a year at that place, the hall will be placed entirely at the disposal of the Congress. (*Cheers.*) In the meantime it will be the home of the Divisional Committee. I am afraid that the hall is in a part of the country which the Congress as a body is not likely to visit. Nevertheless it is an evidence of the kindly feeling which animates the donor, and it will be locally useful, and I may add that the donor, who asks your permission to name it the "INDIAN NATIONAL CONGRESS HALL, ICHALKARNGI," undertakes to retain charge of it and keep it in repair until such time, if ever, as you may deem it expedient to take it under your own direct charge. (*Loud and continued cheering.*)

PANDIT AJOODHIA NATH—(*Allahabad, No.* 551 *in list*)—then read the donor's letter to the above effect.

THE PRESIDENT: Is it now your pleasure that this gentleman's kind offer be accepted? (*Loud cries of "Yes, yes," and enthusiastic cheers.*) Then, Sir (turning to Mr. Ram Chundra), I now, on behalf of this Congress, place you in charge of the Ichalkarngi Indian National Congress Hall.

THE PRESIDENT then proposed a vote of thanks to Mr. Ram Chundra for his handsome gift, which was responded to by long-continued cheering.

Letters and Telegrams expressing sympathy with the Congress.

THE PRESIDENT then said: The next matter I have to mention is this. We have been receiving simply innumerable telegrams and letters from sympathisers with the Congress, such as Mr. Budrudin Tyabjee, the Hon'ble Raja Peary Mohun Mookerjee, Moulvi Haji Mir Jaffir Ali Saheb, the Hon'ble Forbes Adam of Bombay, Dr. Trailokya Nath Mitter, His Highness the Maharajah of Durbungah, the Rajah of Deveracota, Syed Abdul Bari of Dacca, Soobanjee Nanoobhoy and five thousand Mahomedans of Yeola, the Reverend J. P. Mekee, Rajah Rajendra Narain Deb Bahadur, President, Indian Association, the second Rajah of Calicut, &c., mostly expressing not only sympathy but regret that unforeseen circumstances prevented their personally taking part in this assembly. Some of these I should have liked to read to you, but the time at our disposal is so very limited that I have decided not to read any. For this same reason—the very little further time now at our disposal—I have to state that I have been receiving, in greater abundance than I at all like, notices of resolutions and amendments to resolutions, and I would ask all those who may be now contemplating sending in any more resolutions, or any more amendments, to have mercy upon me and upon their brother delegates, for I am really afraid that we shall not be able to dispose even of all those that have already been sent in. (*Cheers.*)

Res. IX., Education.

MR. ADAM—(*Madras, No.* 2 *in list*)—then rose and said: Gentlemen,—The resolution I have to submit to you is one affecting that special subject, Education, in which I am perhaps more interested than in any other that has come before this Congress. The resolution runs thus:—

"*That this Congress being of opinion that it is the first duty of the British Government in India to foster and encourage education, as well general as technical, in all its branches, and that the declaration made in the recent resolution of the Government of India on the subject of education is calculated to encourage the tendency to reduce Imperial expenditure on education, and to withdraw from the control of it, do respectfully urge upon Government the extreme importance of increasing, or at any rate of not decreasing, the present expenditure on education, and of the Government continuing to control the Educational Institutions of all kinds now existing.*"

Gentlemen, this resolution, that I propose, is so very far-reaching that it would be impossible for me, in the limited time at my disposal, to treat it in any detail, and I can therefore only submit to you a few general observations on the subject.

The first point to which I would call your attention is that we urge on Government the desirability of encouraging all branches of education, general as well as technical. The drift of Government policy has hitherto been to divert money granted in support of education into two divergent streams—one flowing towards primary education, the other towards collegiate education. The practical result—I do not say the intended policy, for there seems to have been no policy—has been to leave secondary education very much to chance. It has been either unassisted or assisted in a haphazard way, without reference to any recognised system. I desire next to point out that we desire education to be fostered in all its branches. I impress this on you, because some seem to think the claims of one particular branch of education cannot be urged without a desire to injure some other branch. Those, for example, who are pressing for technical education have not the remotest wish to discourage collegiate education, as I endeavoured to prove to you at some length last year at Madras. What we desire is to extend primary education, to broaden secondary education, and to maintain at the highest now possible, and an ever rising, level, higher education. (*Loud cheers.*)

4th Day.

Res. IX., Education.

The next clause contains the reason why this resolution is introduced in its present form this year. Since last Congress a great change has taken place, and Government has not only indicated, but adopted, a retrograde policy. I have no time at command to prove to you from the note of Government itself that its tendency is what I have indicated. You must take it from me that, in the opinion of those who have studied it, the policy marked out is distinctly retrograde. What it will be more useful to do is to prove to you, by a concrete instance, that the note is not a mere *brutum fulmen*, but that the policy shadowed out is to be enforced through the iniquitous engine of the system of Provincial contracts. We have for long been clamouring in Madras for an increased allotment from Imperial revenues, and this I will say that no Government could be more anxious to foster education and devote to it all the money they can than our Government, from the Governor downwards. Well, Sir, they told the Director of Public Instruction that he might budget for an extra lakh this year. He did so. He sent in his budget. It came back with a G. O., stating that Government regretted that it could not fulfil its promise, and the extra lakh must be cut off. What had happened in the interval between the Government's promise and its failure of performance? The Hon. Mr. Westland had paid a visit to Madras. You can draw your own conclusion. This is but one example of the way in which the benevolent intentions of local Governments are frustrated by the imperious demands of the Imperial Exchequer. What then are these local Governments compelled to do? As regards higher education, they are compelled to shut up their High Schools and Colleges; in Madras they have been almost all closed. They commenced with the High Schools. The second grade Colleges have followed suit, and there is no security that the first grade Colleges will not next come. As regards primary education, they are obliged to throw its cost more and more on the local rates. Now, however good it may be, in principle, to look forward to a time when primary education can be supported solely from local funds, that is an ideal of which we can, here, look for the realization only in a distant future.

With regard to the last clause, I desire to point out that it is not, of course, desired that Government should force its control on independent institutions—they are few enough—able to support and control themselves. What is contemplated is that Government should not cease to support and control institutions which without that support and control could not continue to exist, and whose place, if they ceased to exist, could not be supplied by private or local agencies.

Well, Gentlemen, finally, why should you consider it the duty of Government to foster education? We are continually told that we Congress-wallahs are only educated men, and represent only an educated minority. Reproach it is intended to be, though I consider it the highest honour, but, such as it is, remove all grounds for the accusation, by striving to turn that minority into a majority. But you have a higher reason for desiring the spread of education. Look back and ask what but education has given you all that amount—and it is no small amount—of liberty which you now possess. Education has brought you here, education has taught you the value of representation, and education has given you men fit to act as your representatives. And why, then, should Government recognise it as their duty to foster education? Why, because education, if it has taught you to value liberty, has also taught you the wide gulf that exists between liberty and license; if it has taught you to know your rights, and, knowing, dare maintain, it has taught you how to use and not abuse them; if it has taught you to pray for privileges, it has taught you their value, and inspired you with gratitude and loyalty to the giver. It is owing to education that the old India is being rung out and the new India is being rung in, not as in France, in America, aye in England herself, by the tocsin clang heralding revolution and rebellion, but by the silver chimes proclaiming liberty and law. Education is the fairy prince of the beautiful allegory written, as with prophetic prescience of to-day, by the greatest and sagest poet of our time. Education is the fairy prince who, with his magic touch, has awakened

4th Day.

Res. IX., Education.

the sleeping liberty of India, and, the sleeper awaking, has formed with her deliverer that union which we have to strengthen, more and more, unto the perfect day. How does the poet express it?

And on her lover's arm she leant,
And round her waist she felt it fold,
And far across the hills they went,
In that new world which is the old,
And o'er them many a shining star
And many a merry wind was born,
And streamed through many a golden bar,
The twilight brightened into morn. *(Loud cheers.)*

THE HON. K. T. TELANG—(*Bombay*, *No.* 201 *in list*)—said: In rising to second this resolution, I may congratulate the meeting upon Mr. Adam having been able to keep his voice * till the end of his eloquent speech. (*Cheers.*) I may say that I entirely agree with Mr. Adam in the great importance which he attaches to this resolution, and, although I had the honour of moving the first resolution which has been called the most important one, I, for my part, am prepared to give precedence to the one which has just been moved by Mr. Adam. (*Cheers.*) The reason is, that I consider that, if the Legislative Councils were reformed and expanded in the way we wish them to be, the *sine qua non* for their proper and satisfactory working is the dissemination of that education which, just now, does not seem to have very good prospects before it. I hope Government will agree with us in thinking that it is its duty to foster and encourage education to the best of its power. (*Cheers.*) Mr. President, even in the most enlightened countries of Europe, in Germany for instance, where education has been organized and developed, probably, more than in any other part of the world, even in Germany, I say, the Government accepts the duty of fostering and encouraging education, both technical and general, in all its branches. (*Cheers.*) It is only in this country that the doctrine has recently been gaining ground that this duty does not devolve upon the Government. The doctrine is one which, as far as I am concerned, I entirely repudiate. (*Cheers.*) I think it is not only an erroneous doctrine, but it is a fatal doctrine to be admitted either by the Government or the people. (*Cheers.*) I say it is the duty of all Governments, and more of the British Government in India than of any other in the world, to promote education, because here you have a great nation to whom the education most essential to its progress is entirely alien in many respects. It is a kind of education that we in India have never had before, and, as it is admitted on all hands that this particular kind of education, and not our own old indigenous type of education, is essential for our proper national development, it is essential for the British Government, whom Providence has made responsible for this, to do all it can to foster it in all its branches. (*Cheers.*) I would also say this, that the doctrine which we enunciate in this resolution of ours is a doctrine which has been traditionally accepted by the British Government in the past. It is only now, under stress of circumstances, which it is not necessary to dwell upon, that a new-fangled doctrine is beginning to be enunciated. I say again that I entirely repudiate this doctrine as an erroneous and disastrous one. ("*Hear, hear.*") In the resolution recently issued by Government they declare that, as soon as they find local bodies to take over the management of schools, they will themselves withdraw from them. I am not against the Government withdrawing from the direct management of educational institutions; but the limits within which they can at present safely or properly carry out the policy of withdrawal are very narrow indeed. And in order that those limits should become wider than they are at present, in order that the field of private management be more extended than it is now, it is necessary that the Government management in some institutions should continue for some considerable time to come (*cheers*), because, I say, except on the footing of model institutions managed by Government and surrounded by institutions under private management, India is not likely to make that progress which we all so much desire, and which the Government ought to desire just as earnestly and strongly as we do. There is one other point to which I would refer before concluding my remarks, and that is with regard to the amount of expenditure which the Imperial Government says it will incur for purposes connected with education. Well, all I can say upon that point is, that a Government, which finds money for the very varied activities† (*laughter*) in which it is engaged in this country, ought not to say that it has not enough to pay for education, considering, especially, what a small proportion of revenue is now devoted to education. It is not more than one per cent. of the Imperial revenue. (*Cries of "shame!"*) When we remember this insignificant proportion, I cannot but express my amazement that there should be any responsible statesman saying that this is an allowance which we ought not to expect to get hereafter. (*Cheers.*) No reasonable person who

* Mr. Adam was suffering from a very severe attack of bronchitis, and at one period of his speech everyone feared that he would be unable to complete his address. As it was, he said far less than he had, it is believed, intended to say.

† Referring to our perpetual wars and expeditions, Frontier railways and (so-called) defences, trips to and from the Hills and the like.

understands the position of affairs will ever object to the Government allowance increasing from year to year, by leaps and bounds if necessary, considering what the educational institutions in this country have to deal with. If we only look to the example which England herself has set us in this matter, if we look to the tremendous increase in the grants for education since Forster's Act was passed, I think the Government of India will see that their novel doctrine cannot be sustained for a moment (*cheers*), and is hardly likely to meet the approval of that great British nation to which, as a last resort, we may be compelled to appeal against this threatened systematic scheme for arresting the spread of education, and with it the real progress, in the highest sense of the word, of our country and our countrymen. (*Loud cheers.*)

MR. G. SUBRAMANIA IYER—(*Madras, No.* 20 *in list*)—said : I have much pleasure in supporting this resolution, and in doing so I would only say a few words. Although for special reasons this vast assembly is primarily interested in political reform, still the gentlemen here present are extremely anxious to promote, by all possible efforts, social and moral reform. We have greatly at heart the improvement of the character of our people, the eradication of their old prejudices and crude notions, the modification of our domestic and social institutions, and we want to see many reforms effected in the interest of the moral and material well-being of the people. (*Cheers.*) But how can we expect all this to be done unless the education of our people is continually improved and expanded? (*Cheers.*) It may be said that Government does not intend to discourage the progress of education in this country. It only wishes, for financial reasons, to retire from directly controlling it, and contemplates depending upon private and local efforts to supply its place. But, Gentlemen, though the principle involved may be correct, its application to India at present would be, taking the country as a whole, altogether premature. (*Cheers.*) The condition of this country is not that of European countries, where public spirit has been greatly developed, where there are a large number of wealthy men ready to expend their wealth on altruistic objects, where to aid education is a popular and accepted form of public beneficence, and where, lastly, there already exist such a multitude of highly-educated men that high education practically propagates itself in every direction without its being necessary for the State to foster the process. In this country, more especially in Southern India, there is as yet but little real public spirit ; there are comparatively few wealthy men, and those we have are too many of them chiefly intent on keeping their wealth for their own private purposes ; the endowing of schools and colleges is not a popular form of beneficence, and men of high education, though in the aggregate constituting a very large number, form, as compared with our immense population, but a very small percentage. Under such circumstances, private efforts cannot be expected to do one tithe of what is required. There is, no doubt, another agency which, to a certain extent, has taken the place of Government, and during the past few years has done something to aid the progress of education—I mean the municipal and local boards, which have now the entire charge of elementary and secondary education. (*Cheers.*) But the resources of these institutions are extremely limited, and they have so many objects to which they are bound by law to devote their funds that these too are wholly unable to do more than a fraction of the work that is necessary, if England is to redeem her pledges and really do her duty by our people. (*Cheers.*) For just consider these institutions, young and feeble themselves, are responsible for the sanitation, conservancy, communications and hospitals of considerable, often very large, areas, as well as for the education of the inhabitants of these ; and the people are poor, and their revenues small, and of these they can devote at best only a fraction to education : and then in regard to higher education they are helpless, and cannot obviate the evil effects of the policy now newly inaugurated. I shall give an instance. In the district of Madura there has been for many years a Government Second Grade College ; but recently Government resolved to abolish that institution. The people of the place were alarmed, and applied to the local Municipality and District Board to take up the management of the College. They had a meeting, and the result was that the matter was referred to Government. But what did Government do? They said that the municipal and local funds should be devoted to elementary and secondary education, and that higher education did not come within the scope of their operations. The consequence is, the people of the district of Madura have either to go to Madras for their collegiate education, or to have recourse to another college where instruction is given, not commending itself to the religious opinions of the population. Well, that is a real hardship, which is owing to the new policy of parsimony in regard to a matter which should have, more than any other, precedence over mere pecuniary considerations. (*Cheers.*) There is also another point of view in which this subject can be looked at. Our country is in a peculiar position. At the bidding of an allied but widely differently situated nation, it has to abandon in many matters its old ways, learning, literature, and ideas, and enter upon a new phase of existence. It has to suit itself to the requirements of the latest scientific and artistic developments of European countries, and to remodel all its internal arrangements according to the standards of European civilization ;

4th Day

Res. IX., Education.

and I do not see how these stupendous changes are to be effected in a manner altogether wholesome to the people, unless full provision is made for a sound and widespread education permeating every class of society. (*Cheers.*) There is, no doubt growing up an idea that the new policy of education is the official reply to the demands of our Congress. (*Cheers.*) That Government finds itself face to face with demands, based upon the principles which it has itself preached, and which, while it is unwilling to concede them, it cannot logically refuse. It thinks, some people fancy, that the people of India are becoming too well-educated to consent to remain any longer in that *statu pupilari* which the Lieutenant-Governor of these Provinces so commends, and it has determined now to do what it can to arrest this growing enlightenment which can only be appeased by reform. Gentlemen, I repudiate any such idea ; it is, I am sure, a slander on our good and wise rulers, and it is moreover an impossibility. Great Britain will never go back from the noble doctrines enunciated in Parliament in 1833, in Lord Stanley's despatch of 1854, in hundreds of State documents, in thousands of public utterances of her noblest and greatest statesmen. If the Government be now acting, as it is, in a way to give colour to such a suspicion in the minds of those incapable of appreciating the greatness and magnanimity of the spirit in which England has ever dealt with India, it is only because the Government, in popular phraseology, is hard up (*laughter*)—so hard up, that it is clutching at every visible straw of retrenchment without stopping to consider anything but the momentary relief. And I am quite sure that we have only to put the question temperately in its bare light before Government, and to make clear to them what an irreparable and incalculable injury they will do the country, if they really continue to work on this new and indefensible line, for them to retrace their steps and resume their older and wiser policy. (*Cheers.*) With these words I again express my hearty concurrence in the resolution now before you. (*Cheers.*)

PANDIT SHEO NARAYAN—(*Punjab, No.* 370 *in list*): I rise to support this resolution, but my remarks must refer chiefly to the Punjab. (*Cheers.*) In the Punjab, as you are well aware, the Delhi College was abolished, so that at the present moment there is only one College for higher education in the province. The officials of the Department of Public Instruction are adverse to having anything to do with practical education. They fear that by Colleges and higher education they will convert a military race into baboos. (*Laughter*) But they forget that the people of the Punjab are by no means of a too peaceful character, and that a higher education without, as Mr. Mehta would say, emasculating our people, would render them more reliable and useful subjects. At the same time, a more healthy public opinion is being every day created, and the people are beginning to find out what are the rights as well as the duties of citizenship, and are beginning to agitate for their rights, in this matter of education as well as in other matters. This, however, is what some of the officials do not quite like. (*Laughter.*) You are well aware that there was a time in the Punjab when the Punjab University College was going to be raised to the status of a University. At one city the movement was started by a powerful but limited clique ; but, on the other hand, there was the whole body of educated society to oppose it. Ultimately, the University was constituted in such a manner that a fair compromise was arrived at, and higher English education was not dropped altogether, as certain persons desired ; so that, although we do not boast of many colleges and schools, we have graduates evolved every year in the Punjab. (*Cheers.*) Still there is only one Government College, and only one self-supporting institution of a high class now existing in the Punjab, and these are utterly inadequate for our provincial educational wants. Like every other part of India, education is being stunted in the Punjab. I may also note that education and schools have in the Punjab, also in certain municipalities, been entrusted entirely to the local and municipal boards ; but in these cases, as in Madras, the means available are quite inadequate, and we have so very few educated men as yet that the schools are not well looked after. If anything like justice were to be done to the Punjab, backward as it now is, the Government expenditure on education there ought to be at least doubled. In supporting this resolution, I desire, therefore, to urge that my province will perhaps suffer more than any other if the, as it is utterly inadequate, existing expenditure is to be further curtailed.

PANDIT R. C. GOSWAMI—(*North-Western Provinces, No.* 822 *in list*)—then spoke in Hindee. He said : Mr. President and Gentlemen,—It is a joyful day in which this great Congress, the Fourth Indian National Congress, meets here in this holy city of Prayag.* By your presence here, it has been transformed from a *Tribeni* † into a *Sahasrabeni*,‡ the confluence of a thousand streams of learning and patriotism. Safe

* The ancient and sacred name of Allahabad.

† *Tribeni* the confluence of three rivers, *viz.*, the Jumna, Ganges, and Sarasooti, the latter being, in these latter evil days, invisible to human eyes !

‡ *Sahasra* = a thousand.

in this holy region, this blessed Congress has, day by day, conducted its loyal and virtuous work, replete with future prosperity to India and to England.

4th Day.

Res. IX., Education.

The two prime movers in that Anti-Congress clique are a Hindu and a Mahomedan, whose names, as you know them, I will not trouble myself with repeating, the more so that by this time they are probably quite ashamed of the failure of their efforts to annoy us, and of our success, proved as this is by this vast meeting of 1,000—yes and far more than 1,000—delegates, Hindus, Mahomedans, Christians, Parsees, Sikhs, Jains,—yes, people of all creeds and all colours from every part of the country.

We regret Sir Auckland Colvin's absence from Allahabad and from this great assembly, whose proceedings, had he watched them, would, I am sure, have convinced him not only of our loyalty, but that we are really representatives of all the peoples and races of India.

Last year at Madras we proposed a resolution very similar to that we are dealing with now, which urges the importance of Government aid to, and control over, all existing educational institutions, and the necessity of its increasing and not decreasing the contribution from Imperial funds towards our educational necessities. I cordially support this resolution, for, as ignorance is the root of all evil, so education and true knowledge are the sources of all individual and national advancement. (*Cheers from the N.-W., Oudh and Punjab.*)

THE PRESIDENT: Gentlemen,—Time is passing. We are all agreed, and, if you permit me, I will now put the resolution. (*Cries of "Yes, yes."*) Well, then, the resolution will stand thus :—

RESOLVED—"*That as this Congress is of opinion that it is the first duty of the British Government in India to foster and encourage education, as well general as technical, in all its branches, and as the declaration made in the recent resolution of the Government of India on the subject of education is calculated to encourage the tendency to reduce imperial expenditure on education, and to withdraw from the control of it, this Congress now respectfully urges upon Government the extreme importance of increasing, or at any rate of not decreasing, the present expenditure on education, and of the Government continuing to control the Educational Institutions of all kinds now existing.*"

The resolution was then put and carried unanimously.

Birthday Congratulatory Telegram to Mr. Gladstone.

THE PRESIDENT then said: Some of the delegates have just remembered that this is the birthday of William Ewart Gladstone—(*loud cheers, all rising to their feet, waving hats and handkerchiefs and shouting "Long live Mr. Gladstone," and "Hip, hip, hurrah!"*)—and it is proposed to send to him the following congratulatory telegram ("*Hear, hear,*" *and renewed cheers*) :—

"To W. E. Gladstone, M.P., Hawarden Castle, from the President of the Indian National Congress.

"*Congress assembled at Allahabad from all parts of India, consisting of 1,200 delegates, heartily congratulates you on your birthday, and trusts that you may, by the blessing of God, enjoy many happy returns of the day.*" (*Renewed cheering.*)

I take it that it is your pleasure that this telegram should be despatched. (*Cries of "Yes" and "At once," and renewed cheering.*)

Res. X., Industrial Survey in view to Technical Education

RAI TEJ NARAYAN SINGH BAHADUR—(*Bhagalpur, No.* 1091 *in list*)—then rose and said: It is with the greatest pleasure I move this resolution, which runs as follows:—

"*That, having regard to the poverty of the people, the importance of encouraging indigenous manufactures, and the difficulty of practically introducing any general system of technical education with the present imperfect information, Government be moved to delay no longer the appointment of a mixed Commission, to inquire into the present industrial condition of the country.*"

The resolution I offer for your acceptance is one that touches the material interests of the country, and as such calls for immediate support from all classes of the people. (*Cheers.*) It is a subject in regard to which there can be no possible divergence of opinion between one sect or another, or between rulers and ruled. (*Cheers.*) In fact, it is a subject which has already met with some consideration at the hands of the Government. I am, I fear, hardly qualified to deal adequately with so vast a subject in the short time allotted to us, but I have already carefully noted down and arranged my thoughts in regard to it, and I will endeavour to do my best, trusting to your indulgence to supply my shortcomings. (*Cheers.*)

Technical education, Gentlemen, in whichever of its various aspects we may consider it—whether as giving an impetus to the cultivation of art which forms the mainspring

4th Day.

Res. X., Industrial Survey in view to Technical Education.

of civilization, or as creating habits of activity, industry, and self-reliance in a nation, or as opening various departments of business in which people may occupy themselves— constitutes a most useful and vitally important branch of education. This mode of training has evolved in most of the countries of Europe, in America, China and recently in Japan, stupendous industries, which at once mark the stage of high civilization to which each of these countries has attained. In India, Gentlemen, with its educated members by hundreds, sitting quite idle for want of occupation, with many of its avenues leading to honour and distinction, blocked up against the children of the soil, with manufacture at its lowest level—in India, without commerce or trade on any extensive scale, except what is carried on by Europeans ; without credit and without capital—in India, with its ever-increasing population depending entirely upon foreign countries for the ordinary decencies of life—in India, with its starving millions that can procure no labour—technical education, if systematically introduced into every province of the land, will be salvation to the people. It will in time stop the ruinous influx of foreign goods into the country, marring the industry of the natives of the soil ; it will send the capital of the country to its proper use, that of raising the status of trade and manufacture in the land ; it will create a spirit of emulation and enterprise among the people ; and indirectly it will serve to improve the moral tone of the people by curing them of their sedentary habits, and that spirit of listlessness and quietism which characterise and form the curse of all Orientals. (*Cheers.*)

National greatness, Gentlemen, depends upon the character of the individuals of which the nation consists. In proportion as the individuals are active and industrious, the nation will rise in wealth and importance. National character takes its bent to a great extent from the nature of the education that the people receive. Thus education constitutes an important factor in problems involving questions of national greatness and importance. The practical nature of the training that obtains in England and Belgium, and in a less degree in other countries of Europe, has raised these countries during the course of three centuries only to their present pitch of power and prosperity ; while India, with its long standing civilization and with its modern advantages of Western education, is a long way behind them in point of national industry and advancement. The reason lies on the surface. The greatness of modern Europe, I may make bold to say, is the outcome of the grand Baconian philosophy which for the first time formulated the doctrine that the end of all knowledge ought to be the promotion of human comfort. Thus it is that, while the system of philosophy perfected in India thousands of years ago has only led the intellectual energies of the people to exhaust themselves in spinning out cobwebs of fine and intricate reasonings and in aiming at things unattainable, at least by ordinary mortals, the grand revolution in philosophy, heralded by that great genius Bacon into England, has during a short period carried the Europeans farthest in the race of social progress and civilization. This utilitarian principle was understood among the Chinese alone of all the Asiatics even before Bacon came into existence, and the Chinese are yet a flourishing people. This ought to convince us that, wherever this principle is followed, it will effect changes for the better, and the experiment as to how it would work in India needs but be given a fair trial, and its success will go beyond our most sanguine expectations. (*Cheers.*)

Gentlemen, knowledge is power when it is applied to practical purposes. For a people to flourish it is not only necessary that they should possess knowledge, but that they should know the right method of using it. Our close contact with the enlightened people of the West has developed the national intellect in an unusual degree, has made us familiar with Western science, has stocked us with ideas of what conduces to the national welfare and prosperity. But the education that we are receiving must be utilised in order that we may derive benefit from it. Our thoughts must be reduced to action ; the science that we have imported must be made to go hand in hand with art. What is as yet only theory must be turned into practice. India protected from external aggression by the strong hands of British authority—enjoying as it does profound peace and tranquillity under the beneficent British administration, with its various races living in perfect harmony among themselves—is in a fit condition to prosper and to improve. The introduction of technical education at this favourable opportunity will lend a powerful stimulus to the latent energy of the people to burst forth in splendid and glorious action. The alarm that now spreads through the length and breadth of the land, that the country is on the very brink of ruin, will subside so soon as it is perceived that the trades and manufactures of the country, which now seem to be at their last gasp, are in a fair way to flourish again. The cry for bread and murmurs of discontent that now prevail will soon give place to the clinking of hammers and anvils—the sure signs of national prosperity.

Now, Gentlemen, it lies with you to set this grand engine in motion, that is, to work out all these important and salutary changes, and I leave it to you, Gentlemen, to consider whether it is not worth the labour of the great Hercules, to whom this Congress has so often been likened both by friends and foes. Our enterprising Parsee brethren have taken the bull by the horns and have made some steps towards the solution of the question by founding an institution to impart training of a technical character to the youthful members of their community. They are entitled to full credit for their pluck, and the example set by them will doubtless be followed. I shall only beg leave to suggest, Gentlemen, that to render the scheme of introducing technical education into the country, with a view to promoting its welfare, a complete success, funds will have sooner or later to be raised for the support of a band of promising youths of this country in England for a term of years to enable them to perfect themselves in every branch of industry and industrial art after the European methods, so as to be fully able to carry on the arduous task, that will have to be entrusted to them, of reviving art and manufacture in the land. (*Cheers.*)

At the same time I fully recognize that, with our existing imperfect knowledge of the exact state of all our declining and perishing indigenous industries, the first practical step must be to ascertain this precisely, so that in our new departure we may utilize to the fullest extent all the materials already in existence. Therefore, Gentlemen, it is that I press on your acceptance the resolution that I have already read to you. (*Loud cheers.*)

MR. ANANDA CHARLU—(*Madras, No.* 16 *in list*)—seconded the proposition. He said: Everything that has been said by Professor Adams in support of the resolution which he moved, and by every speaker who has since followed him, forms part of what might be said in commending the motion now before you to your acceptance. The premises having been fully explained to you, the grounds for those premises having also been placed before you, your own mind will readily draw conclusion, and I am here only to announce that conclusion in the terms of this proposition. The proposition commences with an axiom, establishes a postulate, and ends with a problem. (*Cheers.*) It is an axiom known to every one here that the people of this country are poor. I suppose it is assumed by every one, as a thing which cannot be denied, that the indigenous manufactures should be encouraged. That postulate having been admitted, the problem that is now before us is the practical difficulty of introducing a general system of technical education in this country. This problem is not easy to solve. It will have to be solved with reference to the varying conditions of different parts of the country. What will suit one part may not be found to suit another part. One thing undoubtedly is possible, and that is to open schools; but that is going very little beyond the first stage. You may teach ever so much, but, unless you teach on precisely the practical lines required by the conditions of the time and place, you will effect little. You want a good deal of detailed information before there can be an organized effort made in the interests of technical education. You all know, at any rate many of you must know, that in Madras the Jubilee memorial was the creation of an Imperial Institute ("*Hear, hear*"), and the funds collected on that occasion are being mainly applied to technical education. But when we have before us the question of a general system of technical education, it is quite clear that the collection of materials must necessarily precede any effort in that direction, and therefore the object of the resolution before you is to ask Government to institute inquiries for the purpose of obtaining all the data and materials that we must have as a foundation on which to base any rational, as opposed to a haphazard, scheme. (*Cheers.*)

BABOO BEPIN CHANDRA PAL—(*Assam, No.* 1245 *in list*)—then rose and said: Mr. President, Brother Delegates,—Coming as a delegate from a part of Bengal, I had, partly from moral considerations and partly from physical necessity, imposed upon myself the golden rule of silence, but I am compelled by force of circumstances to break it now. I feel it to be my honest duty to move an amendment to this resolution—a duty which I owe to myself, to my constituents and to the institution which, under the direction of a benign and overruling Providence, and under the protection of the benign Government whom that Providence has placed over us, has brought together so many of my educated and illustrious countrymen from the most distant parts of the country, in this magnificent hall. But I must, first of all, read out to you the amendment which I want to propose, lest I come to grief like the gentleman who yesterday spoke for full seven minutes (and had, therefore, then to go back to his seat) without telling us what the amendment, which he wished to place before us, really was. This is my amendment:—

"*That, having regard to the poverty of the people, the importance of encouraging indigenous manufactures and the migration of population from the congested parts of the country, and the difficulty of practically introducing any general systems of technical education and emigration suited to the requirements of the country with the present imperfect information, Government be moved to delay no longer the appointment of a mixed Commission to enquire into the present industrial condition of the country, and to consider the question of emigration especially in relation to the working of the existing Acts bearing on the subject.*"

And, Gentlemen, I owe it to myself to move this amendment, because I feel that, holding the opinions that I do on this subject, it would simply be an act of sheer intellectual recklessness on my part if I were to vote for a resolution which professes to deal

4th Day.

Res. X., Industrial Survey in view to Technical Education.

with the poverty question, and yet leaves out of consideration the main cause of this poverty, namely, agricultural depression, caused by the congestion of the agricultural populations in large portions of a pre-eminently agricultural country. I owe it to my constituents in Assam, because ever since I had the honour of first representing them in the Congress, they have, year after year, asked me to press this question upon the attention of my brother delegates; and I owe it to this Congress to move this amendment, because since we met last the Government of India has published a long and exceedingly important resolution, which I hold here in my hand, on this subject of emigration as a means, as a principal and most effective means, for removing agricultural distress; and the late Viceroy, in his speech at St. Andrew's Dinner, having called the attention of the Congress to this subject, it would be wrong, and a serious neglect of duty on our part, if we were not to pass some opinion on it. It will lead our opponents to say what they have so often said without valid, reasons, that "you men of the Congress run after grand ideas and high sentiments, but neglect things nearer home—things which require sound and practical knowledge—things with regard to which the Government is willing and anxious to receive your help and your advice." You are bound, Gentlemen, to take Lord Dufferin at his word; you are bound to take the Government of India, whose opinions the late Viceroy expressed in this matter, at their word, and declare what your opinions and ideas are on this subject. Lord Dufferin having thrown the gauntlet direct at your face, you are bound in duty and in honour to take it up. My friend, Mr. Ananda Charlu, has told you that the poverty of the people of this country is an axiomatic truth; so it is, and so is also the fact that this poverty has been brought about mainly, if not wholly, by the depression of agriculture caused by a congestion of population in the more fertile parts of the country. In Bengal, for instance, in eight districts the average population is 802·66 per square mile of cultivated area; in the North-Western Provinces and Oudh it is 700; in the Punjab it ranges from three to four hundred, and it is said, that even with this comparatively moderate population, "in the most populous districts the capacity of the soil to support the agricultural population has been strained to the utmost." In Madras, out of twenty-one districts, in eighteen, the population ranges from 910 to 877 to each square mile of cultivated area. In Bombay, we are told, "the density of normal population nowhere reached a high figure; but the census taken in that Presidency indicated that in some districts the struggle for subsistence was severe," and the situation in the most fertile districts of the country, it has been declared even by a habitually optimist Government, "must be perilous." I admit—we are all bound to admit—that the situation is perilous; and we are also bound to admit that emigration is, perhaps, the one remedy for this evil, and we are ready to help the Government in this matter. But what has the Government themselves done to help emigration? There are four kinds of emigration: (1) to the Colonies, (2) to Burma, (3) Inland emigration to Assam, (4) Inland emigration without Government supervision. With regard to Colonial emigration, considering the large areas of culturable land still awaiting in India the hand of the ploughman to bring out an abundant harvest, I do not think it is much needed, and it can never, even if pushed to its extremest limits, afford relief to an even perceptible percentage of our poor. Mr. Ilbert, the late Law Member, said the policy of the Government in this matter of Colonial emigration should be one of "benevolent neutrality." They should neither foster it nor obstruct it. Such was also the opinion of Sir A. Lyall, the late Lieutenant-Governor of these provinces, and I think it is just the position that should be taken by us also in this matter. With regard to Inland emigration (time is passing and I am obliged to hurry on,) under Act I of 1882, which has sent out during the last ten years some 300,000 men and women from Behar, the North-West Provinces, Oudh and Bengal to the tea districts of Assam, it has been described by a Government official—Mr. Porteous, the late Sub-Divisional Officer of Karimganj in Sylhet—as a system that reduces free men and women to a condition of quasi-slavery. The evils that attend this system, the defects in the law that regulates it, and the shameful manner in which even the few benevolent provisions of this law are worked, are too numerous to be mentioned here. The President has already given me warning that my time is up, and I am not going to allow him to deal the fatal double stroke on the gong, but will immediately disappear, only asking others who know the evils of the present systems of emigration, and who feel for the emigrant coolies, to come forward and lay their case before you; and I hope and trust, in the interest of justice and humanity, that you will all accept this amendment and give it your heartiest support. (*Cheers.*)

MR. ALI MAHOMED BHIMJEE—(*Oudh, No.* 455 *in list*)—said: Sir,—Although this resolution of my friend, Mr. Pal, can hardly be called an amendment, it being in fact a new resolution compounded out of the original one, and a different one which Mr. Pal desires to have dealt with, still the subject which he thus includes for our consideration is a very serious one, and deserves our careful consideration. From the reports we have read of the condition of the people who are taken away to other parts of the country, I think that, in the interests of these units of our dumb millions, we should take some action on this subject; and I think that I shall be only doing my duty to the dumb hundreds and thousands of people who are led away from their homes, on false representations, if, without saying anything further, I second Mr. Pal's proposal and solicit for this proposed resolution your most careful consideration. (*Cheers.*)

MR. ADAM—(*Madras, No.* 2 *in list*)—said: As Mr. Bhimjee has himself admitted, this is no amendment at all. I admit fully, and I am sure all the members of this Congress admit, the immense importance of the subject of emigration. It was most fully discussed by the Subject Committee, and, considering the immense mass of subjects before them, and the general ignorance in regard to this question that prevails amongst us, it was decided that it should not be put forward as the subject of one of their resolutions by the Committee. If, however, the mover of this compound resolution chooses, he may bring forward the emigration portion of it as an independent resolution after all the other resolutions have been disposed of. I do not know the facts, but, supposing all the statements regarding coolie emigration are such as they have been stated by the mover to be, the Commission proposed in my motion could have nothing whatever to do with that subject. (*Cheers.*) The two subjects are not at all akin, and we must have two Commissions—for the class of men who should sit upon the one Commission will be quite different from the class of men who should sit upon the other. If, therefore, you lump together both the question of emigration and technical education as is done in the so-called amendment, you will never be able to get on, and it is on this ground, primarily, that I oppose the amendment, without depreciating, in the slightest degree, the importance of the subject which it is framed to bring before us. As Mr. Budrudeen Tyabji, the President of the last Congress, urged at the time, you must not go on moving such amendments to resolutions as would make the resolutions perfectly ridiculous, and it would be ridiculous to ask Government to appoint one Commission to investigate two such utterly distinct questions. If the emigration portions of the amendment are brought forward as a separate motion at the end of the proceedings, and if the Congress decides that it should be discussed and voted upon, then, for my part, I shall not oppose it. But we must not, on any account, mix up the two questions. (*Cheers.*) I may add that the wording of the latter part of Mr. Pal's resolution, and the peroration of his eloquent speech alike indicate that what he really wants to have investigated is the alleged ill-treatment of the emigrants to Assam. But this is a subject on which we delegates from other parts of India know absolutely nothing, and in regard to which we all, as was urged by an immense majority of the Subject Committee, should feel great hesitation in voting either way. Mr. Pal's resolution was negatived by the Subject Committee, and I must protest against his endeavouring to reintroduce it, by dovetailing it, however neatly, into my resolution on a totally different subject. I repeat the two subjects must be kept distinct. (*Cheers.*)

MR. ATKINS—(*Allahabad, No.* 579 *in list*)—said: Mr. President,—I wish to enquire whether this so-called amendment is not out of order?

THE PRESIDENT: I suppose we must accept it as an amendment.

MR. ATKINS: Well, I was in some doubt as to whether it was an amendment or not. But since you have ruled it to be so, I must accept your ruling. Well, in the original resolution, you ask the Government "to delay no longer the appointment of a mixed Commission to inquire into the present industrial condition of the country." But do you think any good will come of that inquiry? The rider I have to propose is this—

"That the Government be moved to delay no longer the appointment of a mixed Commission to inquire into the present industrial condition of the country, *and to establish one or more technical schools in each Presidency.*"

The mover of the resolution has agreed to that rider. May I obtain the permission of the seconder to it?

MR. ADAM—(*Madras, No.* 2 *in list*): No; certainly not.

MR. ATKINS: Well, I am very sorry indeed. There is no doubt technical schools are largely needed in this country. The advantages to be derived from technical schools cannot be over-estimated. There may be a difference of opinion as to the best manner to work them, so as to produce the best results, but that difference of opinion should not operate to prevent their establishment. An academical education is a very excellent thing, but that alone is not sufficient to give a nation wealth and power. The Germans are essentially a very practical people, and that they are so is due to the training they receive. The Universities and Colleges in Germany are very old institutions, for the Continent was the home of learning in the fifteenth century, but it is only since the establishment of technical schools that the Germans as a nation have made any great progress, and so it will

4th Day.

Res. X., Industrial Survey in view to Technical Education.

be with India. The scholastic institutions in this country will go on turning out students who will have nothing to which they can turn their hands. With the establishment of technical schools, our youths will have an opportunity of acquiring a degree of skill that will serve them in after life and make them better men. If you merely ask for a Commission, the report thereof might possibly be pigeon-holed (*laughter*), but if you ask for something in a definite manner, you, then, may hope to get a definite reply and secure some definite advance. (*Cheers.*)

MR. HOWARD—(*Allahabad, No.* 573 *in list*)—said: This is a very simple measure before you at this moment, and in seconding Mr. Atkins' rider I will not take two minutes. I wish to press upon you that the additional words which Mr. Atkins has suggested should be added to the resolution, as the subject of technical education is of great practical importance. Mr. Atkins has been a practical man all his life, and knows the urgent need there is for the additional words, because inquiry without action would do no good. What is the use of an indefinite postponement of some measure of practical relief when India's greatest need at the present moment is the teaching of handicrafts? In addition to what Mr. Atkins has said about the importance the German nation attached to the teaching of technical skill in all the arts by which the German nation is fast spreading its commerce all over the world, the Prince Consort, the late husband of the Queen-Empress, taught all his children, the Prince of Wales and all his brothers and sisters, handicrafts of some description or other (*cheers*), and what Germans found it advisable to teach their Princes is surely necessary in case of men who have to earn their livelihood. (*Cheers.*) Nor will you become better citizens without having the knowledge of some trade, and even if you do not require to use it for a living, the knowledge would at least keep idle hands from mischief during leisure hours. *Cheers.*) I therefore warmly second the rider, as I am certain no resolution of the Congress would go more home to the heart of the Sovereign of our country. (*Cheers.*)

THE HON'BLE MR. P. M. MEHTA—(*Bombay, No.* 208 *in list*)—then said: I would point out that the essence of the rider is already included in Resolution IX, which asks for the fostering and encouraging of education, as well general as technical, and that, further than this, we are really not in a position to go. The rider seems to me inconsistent with the resolution. The resolution asks for enquiry, because we, as a fact, do not know what class of technical schools to establish or how to do it, and the rider proposes, with this, to couple a demand for the immediate establishment of technical schools in every province. ("*Hear, hear.*") You must either abandon the demand for the enquiry, or you must give up the demand for the immediate establishment of the schools in every Presidency. The two demands are inconsistent, and cannot be coupled in one and the same resolution. (*Cheers.*)

THE REV. RAMCHANDER BOSE—(*Oudh, No.* 450 *in list*)—then said: Mr. President and Gentlemen,—In support of the resolution under discussion I have a few observations to make on its theoretical rather than practical bearing. One of the objections advanced against the National Congress is that it peremptorily refuses to discuss and deal with social problems. But the question which is being now discussed is, after all, a social question. Technical education involves a social reform or revolution of gigantic proportions. It will spread correct notions of the dignity of labour—("*Hear, hear,*" *and cheers*)—raise the industries of the country, from the contempt to which they have been ignorantly consigned, to a position of respectability and influence, and obliterate those of our social distinctions which are fictitious and unnatural. (*Cheers.*) It will cement class to class, and create that bond of sympathy which will weld the jarring elements of our national life into a compact, homogeneous whole. (*Cheers*) It will in this way accomplish a social revolution; nay, it will do something more. It will accomplish a moral revolution of equally gigantic and magnificent proportions. It will effect a salutary change in our national character. Our national character is by no means so dark as it is represented to be by professional detractors. Calm and philosophical observers like Bishop Heber and Principal Kay have noticed therein traits which, in their opinion, Christian nations would do well to imitate. (*Cheers.*) But it is a fact, which no one present will call in question, that what preponderates in the national character is quiescence or passivity, the active virtues being thrown into the background or remaining in a state of dormancy. These must be awakened and called into vigorous play before we can march forward alongside of the great nations of Europe and America. The virtues we are sadly deficient in are courage, enterprise, the will to do, and the heart to dare—(*cheers*),—and these, I maintain, will be fostered among us by technical education, and the varied industries that will grow up as the fruits of this. Political questions are inseparably linked to and bound up with social and moral questions. Why? Because life in the first place is a unity. ("*Hear, hear.*") Our lines of distinction between political, social, and moral life are arbitrarily drawn, as life in its political aspects cannot move forward without causing life in its social and moral aspects to move forward also. Life in one department in motion and in others stationary is an impossibility! In a similar manner progress is an unity, and our distinctions between material and moral progress are fictitious. When true progress is realized in one department of life, the other departments cannot but be affected by it. Progress is, if you will allow the expression, contagious ; and when it affects one portion of life, or one of its sides, it spreads over and exercises a restorative influence over the others also. Some of you are friends and champions of social reform, and you are apt to be impatient because social questions are not discussed in the Congress. Let me advise you to be patient. ("*Hear, hear.*") Social questions, in some form or other, will come in for discussion, and social reform will emanate from our deliberations. Again, some of you are friends and champions of moral reform, and you are impatient because moral questions are not discussed in Congress. Let me give you the same advice—be patient, and you will by and bye see moral questions discussed here, and a moral influence of the healthiest kind issuing from our association. We have every reason to look forward to the time when the glorious results of our deliberations will be the rectification, not of this solitary evil or that, but of all the varieties of evils under which the country is groaning. (*Cheers.*)

4th Day.

Res X., Industrial Survey in view to Technical Education.

BABOO BEPIN CHANDRA PAL—(*Assam, No.* 1245 *in list*)—then said : Gentlemen,—As I believe that it is in accordance with the general wish of the meeting, I withdraw my amendment with the permission of the President. (*Cheers.*)

THE PRESIDENT (addressing Mr. Atkins) : Sir,—I would ask you to consider whether you might not withdraw your rider, as the essential principle involved in it has been substantially carried before, while your concrete development of this seems to be considered premature.

MR. ATKINS : If you, Sir, think it is premature I will withdraw it, with the consent of my seconder.

MR. HOWARD (addressing the President) : Out of deference to you, Sir, I agree to the withdrawal.

THE PRESIDENT : I have, then, only to ask you to vote upon the original resolution, which will run thus :—

RESOLVED—" *That, having regard to the poverty of the people, the importance of encouraging indigenous manufactures, and the difficulty of practically introducing any general system of technical education with the present imperfect information, Government be moved to delay no longer the appointment of a mixed Commission, to enquire into the present industrial condition of the country.*".

The resolution was then put and carried unanimously.

Proposition in regard to Permanent Settlements.

MR. V. M. BHIDE—(*Poona, No.* 96 *in list*)—then rose and said : Sir, Gentlemen,—The resolution that I have been asked to propose runs as follows :—

" *That, in the opinion of this Congress, the time has now come for extending to the major portions of the Madras and Bombay Presidencies, and of the North-Western Provinces and Oudh, and to parts of the Punjab and other provinces, a permanent settlement of the land revenue demand.*"

I must now ask permission, owing to failing health and age, for the remarks which I have committed to writing being read by a friend of mine.

THE PRESIDENT : Under the circumstances I have no objection.

MR. PATWARDHAN—(*Poona, No.* 150 *in list*)—then commenced to read Mr. Bhide's remarks, when it at once became apparent that Mr. Bhide did not want the resolution he had proposed, but something different. The assembly objected that a gentleman having proposed a resolution could not go on to argue *against it* and for something quite different, ahd Mr. Patwardhan's voice was drowned in the universal laughter that greeted this novel mode of proposing a resolution.

THE HON'BLE KASHINATH T. TELANG—(*Bombay, No.* 201 *in list*)—then rose and said : Gentlemen,—I propose that the consideration of this subject be deferred to next year.

MR. V. M. BHIDE—(*Poona, No.* 96 *in list*)—said: Gentlemen,—I have no objection. (*Loud laughter.*)

4th Day.

Proposition in regard to Permanent Settlements.

DR. WAZIR ALI—(*Behar, No.* 1034 *in list*)—said: Well, I was to have seconded this resolution, but as the proposer has cut the ground from under my feet and left me no *locus standi*, I suppose I must accept the situation. (*Cries of "no, no; go on, go on."*)

THE PRESIDENT: Order. Gentlemen,—As I understand, this resolution has been withdrawn by the proposer, who has agreed to its consideration being postponed to next year, and who, so far as I can gather, does not himself wholly approve it; we must now go on to the next resolution which I will ask Mr. W. C. Bonnerjee to propose.

(A good deal of noise ensued, a large section of the delegates, as it later appeared, being dissatisfied with this ruling, but this was immediately drowned in the storm of applause that greeted the next speaker when he appeared on the platform.)

Res. XI. Submission of the Resolutions to the Governments of India and England.

MR. W. C. BONNERJEE—(*Calcutta, No.* 1098 *in list*)—said: Mr. President and Gentlemen,—We have hitherto been hewing some of the many stones which are still required to crown the splendid, the unique, the marvellous edifice (*cheers*) which the statesmanship of Great Britain has reared up in this country. (*Cheers.*) It is now necessary that these stones should be submitted by us to the chief superintendent of that edifice in this country, and to his official superior in London, in order that they may consider their merit and fitness. (*Cheers.*) Accordingly I have to present for your acceptance the following resolution:—

"*That the foregoing resolutions be submitted for the favourable consideration of His Excellency the Viceroy, and for transmission by him to Her Majesty's Government, with the humble request of this Congress that the reforms suggested in the said resolutions, based as most of these are on Her Gracious Majesty's Proclamation of 1858, may now be effected, and that, should it be deemed necessary first to institute any enquiry into any of the matters forming the subjects of these Resolutions, such enquiry may be made as speedily as possible by a Parliamentary Committee.*"

I may say, that this resolution is as of course, and it would not have been necessary for me to detain you a single moment if it had not been for the fact that the concluding portion of it, the portion that is which asks for an enquiry by a Parliamentary Committee, might seem at first sight inconsistent with one of the resolutions which we passed at the Congress of 1885. You will remember that at that Congress we asked that the enquiry into the administration of India, which had been promised by the then Secretary of State for India by means of a Parliamentary Committee, should be made by a Royal Commission consisting of representatives both of England and of this country, and taking evidence both in England and India. (*Cheers.*) But, as the late Lord Beaconsfield once said, many things have happened since then. (*Laughter and cheers.*) It has become unnecessary for the purposes of the resolutions which we have passed here to ask for a Royal Commission. On this occasion we are only asking that if any of the propositions which we are going to lay before the Government requires any further inquiry—in our judgment no inquiry further than what has been already made *is* necessary—then such inquiry may be made by a Parliamentary Committee. A Parliamentary Committee, as you all know, must come to an end with the Parliament that appoints it, and it must conclude its labours before any very long time has expired. On the other hand, a Royal Commission may go on sitting for years and years, hanging up reforms which have been felt, and declared by you all on behalf of the country, to be absolutely necessary. (*Cheers.*) Many of the resolutions which you have passed deal with matters which may be disposed of in this country by the Government of India, if only the Secretary of State so desires; and the only thing you have asked for which requires the consideration of Parliament is the expansion of our Legislative Councils. That subject has been before the country now for many years, and it is not necessary that any further inquiry should be made.

I hope that, should these proceedings come under the eye of Mr. Bradlaugh (*loud and prolonged cheers*), who has so kindly interested himself in matters connected with India, he will see that we are not in any way throwing overboard the notice of motion which he has given, and which he has promised to bring forward at the next sessions of Parliament. We are only asking him to modify his motion to a certain extent. I hope he will not think that, in asking for a Parliamentary Committee, and not for a Royal Commission, we are guilty of any inconsistency, or are in any way unappreciative of his great efforts on our behalf. (*Loud cheers.*) I know I speak the sense of this vast assembly when I say that we are unfeignedly grateful to him for his masterly and able advocacy of our cause (*cheers*); and we hope that he will be pleased to help us in the future in the direction of the resolution which I have submitted to you. (*Cheers.*)

The reforms, however, for which we have pressed in the preceding resolutions are not by any means the only reforms which are essential for the welfare of India. They are perhaps the simplest, and in regard to them the country is now, most completely, of one mind as to the exact steps that it is necessary for the Government to take. But there are other great and vital reforms which will sooner or later have to be dealt with if India is to be justly administered, and if even the ultimate interests of the British Empire, as a whole, are to be considered. Such, for instance, as the reduction of military expenditure, and its re-apportionment on a juster basis between England and India, and various other matters with which I need not trouble you now. These are extremely complicated questions, in regard to most of which we, ourselves, lack the detailed practical knowledge essential to the suggestion of definite action, and in regard to these we shall have later to press once more for that Royal Commission which we prayed for in 1885. But at the present moment what we first want is that those simple and clear reforms, which are now fully ready for practical embodiment, should be carried out.

Now, Brother Delegates, one word more and I have done. Do not be cast down do not be disheartened, if immediately you put forward a request it is not granted by those who are responsible for the good government of the country. (*Cheers.*) Be patient, be moderate, be true to your cause and to yourselves. Remember that even now there are many reforms about which large majorities are agreed, which the English people are themselves asking for and which they have not yet got. ("*Hear, hear.*") If you are true to yourselves, if you are moderate, if you are reasonable in your demands, and if you go on agitating, agitating and agitating, loyally and constitutionally, believing that the British public—and in that public I include our Anglo-Indian friends in this country—is a truth-loving and a justice-loving public, you will be sure to get what you are asking for in the end. (*Cheers.*) Give a long pull, a strong pull, and a pull altogether, and you will reach the shores of victory in no time. (*Loud cheers.*)

PANDIT BISHAMBHER NATH—(*Allahabad, No.* 552, *in list*)—who seconded the motion, said: Mr. President and Gentlemen,—Though I appear before you after a long and bright array of brilliant speakers, and at rather a late stage of the proceedings, I have at least the great satisfaction and honour of holding a junior brief, together with so highly distinguished and eminent a senior from the Bar of the Presidency Court as Mr. Bonnerjee. (*Laughter and applause.*) I do not know whether the conjunction is happy or otherwise, but the conjoint appearance of two persons on the same side, one from the metropolis of India and the other from the North-West, obviously shows that the bonds of mutual union are being drawn closer and tighter by the combined efforts of the promoters of the reform party. Our critics might, perhaps, have said that some of the preceding resolutions, summed up and expressed in this resolution, are the outcome of the heated imaginations of a few spoilt children of British rule; but their adverse criticism will hardly be of much value in the face of the request, expressed in the concluding part of this resolution, for an enquiry by a Parliamentary Committee. Such a constitutional course will be no innovation; on the contrary, it will be quite consistent with the precedent and practice established and recognised on several previous occasions. Such a procedure, if adopted and effectively carried out, will enable the Government to test the legitimate character of the several aspirations of the Congress Party, which I believe to be, with scarcely any exception, fair, reasonable, and well-founded; many of them, resting in a great measure, upon that bulwark of our liberty, our great *Magna Charta*—I mean the Proclamation of Her Gracious Majesty the Queen-Empress of India,—which has been so often referred to here by the speakers who have preceded me. The proposed enquiry will, it is to be hoped, help,to close the mouths of our opponents and demonstrate that their assertions, that the reform party are bent upon the subversion of constituted authority, are as groundless as they are malicious. Our honourable chief, the Lieutenant-Governor, Sir Auckland Colvin, has, in his now historical letter, referring to the supposed impossibility of the creation of a healthy tone of independence in India, been pleased to employ certain figures of speech. Two of them are that an elephant would be out of his element in the mists of Scotland, and that a banyan tree could not grow in Parliament-street. I do not attach much value as arguments to these figures of speech. I think a case that has to be bolstered up by such illustrations very unlikely to secure a verdict, and anyhow had His Honour graciously condescended to honour this vast temple of the People with a visit for a while, he would have possibly been satisfied, by what he witnessed, that the sentiments expressed, in this and other resolutions, are the natural fruits of that noble and healthy spirit of independence by which the peoples assembled here are animated—a spirit developing hand in hand with the most enthusiastic feelings of loyalty and devotion towards Her Gracious Majesty's throne. (*Applause.*) Having made these few remarks, no further display of words by me is, I think, necessary, as my duty here is principally to "ditto to Edmund Burke." I therefore beg to recommend to you the propriety of adopting the resolution which I have had the honour to second. (*Laughter.*) And, Gentlemen, as I am a bit of lawyer, I retire without transgressing the provisions of the Limitation Act so stringently enforced by our worthy President, and wish you all, sincerely and from the bottom of my heart, God-speed and the compliments of the season. (*Laughter and applause.*)

4th Day.

Res. XI., Submission of the Resolutions to the Governments of India and England.

NAWAB MAHMOOD ALI KHAN—(*Oudh, No.* 421 *in list*)—then rose and said, speaking in Urdu: I support this resolution. Some people are kind enough to say that we of the Congress are disloyal. If this were indeed so, it would be a bad thing for England and a very bad thing for India, because we of the Congress mean the bulk of the Indians. (*Cheers.*) But it is not so; we are loyal to the tips of our fingers (*loud cheers*); we do not conspire, we do not plot, we do not speak evil in secret, but we come openly forward and say to our rulers, These things we want, these things we do not like: pray give us the former and do away with the latter. We say this in all respect and we send our prayer home to England, and we say to the English people, These are the promises which our great Empress made to us in 1858: now please see that these promises are made good, and that our humble prayers, for the redress of our grievances, are attended to. Is this disloyalty? Is this sedition? No, Gentlemen, it is the men, be they Indians or Europeans, who are opposing our loyal and constitutional agitation, who, whether they mean it so or not, are really acting disloyally to the interests of both Great Britain and India. (*Cheers.*) May they all soon be wiser, and may the English Government and the English nation come to understand what the real position of affairs is, and do us the kindness and the justice we pray for. (*Cheers.*)

MR. KARANDIKAR—(*Poona, No.* 137 *in list*)—said: It is with the greatest pleasure that I support this resolution. Since Her Gracious Majesty's Proclamation in 1858 there has been a lapse of 30 years, which is surely a long enough period of development to warrant our expecting that these gracious promises should now bear fruit. When they were first uttered, India hardly realized their magnanimity and beneficence. It is the changes that have occurred during this long interval that impel us now to ask for their fulfilment, and to place these resolutions indicating how we wish them fulfilled before Her Majesty's Government, with the fervent hope that the suggestions therein made may meet with their approval and that of the great British nation generally. (*Cheers.*)

MOULVI MANSUR ALI—(*Delhi No.* 411 *in list*)—who spoke in Urdu, then said: Gentlemen,—I also warmly support this resolution and endorse every word spoken by the last speaker. What more can we do, as faithful and loyal subjects, than tell our rulers plainly what those grievances are that make the people dissatisfied and beg them to remove them, if they see fitting, by the measures which we propose to them; if not, by such other measures as their greater wisdom may suggest. (*Cheers.*)

MUNSHI SADRUDDIN AHMAD—(*Allahabad, No.* 586 *in list*)—said, speaking in Urdu: Gentlemen,—I cannot too strongly support the proposal that the resolutions passed by this the Fourth National Congress be submitted to His Excellency the Viceroy for his favourable consideration and for transmission by him to Her Majesty's Government, with the humble prayer of this Congress that the reforms and amendments suggested may be accepted, and that, if necessary, enquiries may be made by Parliament as early as possible. As regards the Anti-Congress movement, whose leaders most falsely call our movement seditious, I would urge on the Government to note as a fact that numbers of the nominal members of that movement are at heart with us, but, fearing the displeasure of the Government and subordinate officials, and thereby loss of favour, join that body. (*Cheers.*) The time at my disposal is not sufficient to allow me to enter into a detailed examination of the objections of our real opponents, yet so much would I say that their arguments are weak and their reasonings fallacious. It may, however, be asked why some few more or less important and titled men have taken upon themselves the unprofitable task of carrying on the opposition. To this I would simply reply by saying that some really misunderstand the question, being old men unable to move with the times, while some are actuated by the vain desire of pleasing the more narrow-minded section of the official classes, and the rest are hankering after titles—Rai Bahadurs, Khan Bahadurs and C. I. E.s, &c., which they fancy they will obtain by posing as earnest upholders of existing conditions, and as loyal men, who believe that everything is precisely as it should be. (*Cheers.*)

THE PRESIDENT: Gentlemen,—This is a merely formal resolution, and may now I think be put, without further discussion. (*Cries of "yes, yes; put it."*) It will stand thus:—

RESOLVED—"*That the foregoing Resolutions be submitted for the favorable consideration of His Excellency the Viceroy, and for transmission by him to Her Majesty's Government, with the humble request of this Congress that the reforms suggested in the said Resolutions, based as most of these are, on Her Gracious Majesty's Proclamation of 1858, may now be effected, and that, should it be deemed necessary, first to institute any enquiry into any of the matters forming the subjects of these resolutions, such enquiry may be made, as speedily as possible, by a Parliamentary Committee.*"

The resolution was then put and carried unanimously.

4th Day.

Res. XII., Abrogation of Laws and Rules for the regulation of Prostitution.

CAPTAIN BANON—(*Punjab, No. 374 in list*)—then rose and said : Mr. President and Gentlemen,—I shall commence by reading to you the resolution which I have been invited to propose. It is as follows :—

" *That this Congress, having watched with interest and sympathy the exertions that are being made in England, for the total abrogation of laws and rules relating to the regulation of prostitution by the State in India, do place on record their appreciation of the services thus rendered to this country, and their desire to co-operate by all means in their power in the attainment of this laudable object.*"

Gentlemen of this Meeting,—It is needless to say much on this resolution. It is one on which you are asked to pronounce your verdict, whether you approve or disapprove of the steps taken in England to remove a great reproach from the administration of the government of India. In no other country, calling itself civilized, in this Eastern hemisphere are such regulations, for the demoralization of the military, in force, and it is a matter of shame that we should have to talk even on such subjects. The matter appeals so broadly and strikingly to everyone's sense of right and wrong that few words are needed. You know that in England, in the English House of Commons, the Members passed a resolution, without any attempt at debate or objection, condemning these Government regulations, and it is to strengthen the hands of those in England, working for the great moral laws of the land, that you are asked to pass any resolution at all on the subject. It is for you to say, therefore, whether you wish this shameful practice continued by which men become degraded and women suffer insult. (*Cheers.*)

As this resolution is considered an unsavoury one by our critics, I shall not say much concerning it, nor do I think that much need be said to commend it to your hearty acceptance ; but our critics assert that in these Congresses we are totally neglecting all social subjects : this resolution, then, will conclusively prove that such is not the case. Although we cannot take up every social subject, we cannot avoid taking up this matter, as it is a burning question of the day both in England and India, and one affecting all classes of the Indian community. ("*Hear, hear.*") The brightest and purest intellects of England and India have spoken in no uncertain tones regarding it, and have denounced it in unqualified terms, and their opinion has been ratified, without one dissentient voice, by the entire English House of Commons. It would be a matter of extreme regret if, after this sweeping condemnation by enlightened public opinion, this infamous system were allowed any longer to disgrace and pollute our administration. (*Cheers.*) Our critics also taunt us with neglecting to raise our Indian women to their proper position, and with wishing to consign them to one of degrading inferiority. But we deny these sweeping assertions with all the scorn that such falsehoods merit ; for in every respectable Indian home* our Indian women are treated with all the respect and tender consideration due to their loving and gentle natures. Although, perhaps, we may have failed to satisfy our critics, and may not even have done as much as we ourselves could wish to educate and refine them, still, at least, we can protest as one man with all the earnestness and warmth of our hearts, and minds, and souls, against the systematic degradation by the authorities of numbers of our Indian women to a state of existence revolting to our common humanity. ("*Hear, hear,*" *and cheers.*) It is said that these infamous regulations are absolutely necessary for the health and welfare of our European Army in India. As a soldier of many years' service, I emphatically deny this. ("*Hear, hear.*") To advance this argument would be to degrade the European soldier below the level of his Indian brother-in-arms, for whom no such arrangements are made, and for whom no such arrangements are considered necessary, although they are compelled to lead the same celibate lives. I myself have borne Her Most Gracious Majesty's commission for many years, and I do not hesitate to say that these infamous regulations are neither necessary nor even desired by the European soldier himself. To assert the contrary is to cast a vile aspersion and foul calumny on one who is in many cases a model of all that a man should be in his moral relations, and who is in no way inferior to his brother in civil life. (*Loud cheers.*)

CAPTAIN HEARSAY—(*N.-W. P. No.* 841 *in list*)—in seconding said : With regard to the important resolution that I have been called upon to second (for, important it is, as it is for the protection and well-being of our Indian countrywomen), insomuch as it protests against the social evil, as it appears in its most offensive form in this country, I give it my most earnest and heartfelt support. Nothing can be worse than the laws and rules now still in force, despite the pretence of repealing the C. D. Acts, for, so to say, legalizing in India this leprosy of modern times and of all civilized countries. The social evil is bad enough, as it is, without the legalizing force given to it by the Government of this country, by issuing instructions to their Civil Officers to hunt up eligible prostitutes. I see highly-placed English gentlemen compelled to turn procurers and devote their energies to securing healthy, young and good-looking native women to supply and renew each of the Regimental bazaars of each British Regiment or Company of Artillery, in this country.

* Captain Banon is himself married to a Brahmin lady.

4th Day.

Res. XII., Abrogation of Laws and Rules for the regulation of Prostitution.

("*Shame, shame:*") I know that when it was reported to Parliament that such a state of things existed, it was disbelieved and denied by the Under-Secretary of State for India, until by clear demonstration it was found to be only too fearfully true. And, Gentlemen, though the C. D. Acts have been repealed, the rules under the Cantonment Acts under which these evil things are done, are still in full force. There are in India over 2,000 young women, so procured, for the hideous purpose alluded to. If the Government thinks it is a medical necessity for such women to be entertained, why do not they import into India for this purpose the countrywomen of these British soldiers? (*Cheers.*) Why should our poor Indian women be sacrificed on the altar they have erected to lust? Let them import Englishwomen, if they dare, for these vile purposes. Or, what would be much better, allow greater freedom in, and even promote, the marriage of these soldiers. Can anyone imagine anything more shocking than this legalized system of prostitution? A body of unfortunate young Indian women kept in a state of moral slavery and annually recruited to supply the supposed carnal wants, not of their own countrymen, whom they can understand, and with whom they have a certain sympathy, for whom it is possible for them to cherish some sort of passion, however degraded, but of the British soldier, whose colour, customs and conduct are all alike repugnant to their natural instincts—a system which all the better men amongst those soldiers protest against and declare to be a mere incitement to the boys, who now-a-days are sent out in shoals, to sin. Surely it is an astounding thing to find such a system legalized by the rules of a Christian nation. It is, to speak metaphorically, a fearful cancer, and one which requires to be not only firmly cut out, but cauterized, so as to prevent its breaking out in another form, under new laws and rules. I believe, through the assistance of our noble Parliament, although that assistance has been impeded by the opposition of the Council of the Secretary of State for India, we shall yet succeed. (*Cheers.*)

I have, in concluding, to point out that it is only by acting on the perfectly legal and constitutional lines which we are at present following, that any real reforms can be effected. The process is slow but sure, and believe me that the voice of this great Council of the whole Indian nation, this National Congress, must eventually find an echo in the hearts of the people of England and gain an impartial hearing from our fellow-subjects, the natives of the British Isles, of our great Colonies, of the whole British Empire. (*Cheers.*)

The well-known distitch applies to India in its present phase:—

For freedom's battle once begun,
Tho' baffled oft is ever won.

Then to this goal, I say, distant though it yet may seem, advance old Hindustan; close well your ranks! Union masters everything. God save the Queen! (*Loud and continued cheering.*)

MR. HOWARD—(*Allahabad, No.* 573 *in list*)—then addressed the meeting in Urdu. He said: Gentlemen,—I have been asked to say a few words to you in regard to this resolution relating to the regulation of prostitution by the State. I want you to understand that such an immoral procedure is approved by none of us educated Christians, European or Eurasian, though, it may be, that some military men persuade themselves that it is a good thing for the soldiers. But it is not, it never can be, if ultimate consequences and general results are fairly weighed against momentary gains and particular instances. It is wrong, and a wrong can never bear aught but evil fruit. Nothing can prosper but right. The wages of sin are death, and the outcome of such wicked regulations can be only misery and death. The subject is a shameful one—one difficult even to speak of in a public assembly, and I hope therefore you will pardon my now saying nothing further than this, that I hope you will to a man vote for this resolution.

MOULVI MAHOMED HAFIZ—(*Bengal, No.* 1204 *in list*)—then spoke in Urdu. He said: Gentlemen,—I am a Mahomedan from Backergunge, a Mahomedan district in Bengal. I bring with me the views of the Mahomedans of that district who were pleased to return me, along with certain Hindu brethren, at no less than twelve meetings held in different parts of that district. Before I support this motion, allow me to make one or two general observations in regard to the attitude of some of the Mahomedans towards the Congress. It will take only a minute to do so. This is the first time that I see the Congress. This imposing sight of so many nationalities being knit together, under the auspices of a beneficent Government, by the sweetest bonds of brotherhood in the noblest work that has ever been given to man to do, overwhelms me with a feeling which it would be impossible for me to describe. If at any time, any sort of misgiving has found any place in my mind, I can assure you, Gentlemen, that misgiving has now vanished, thoroughly vanished for ever, and I shall be glad to labour at this glorious work as long as I live. I wish my Anti-Congress brother Mussulmans of Bengal (and there are some such, though they are far fewer than has been supposed) were here to-day; this august spectacle (and the unselfish unsectarian spirit that pervades this assembly) would be sufficient answers to all their doubts and difficulties. Gentlemen, some of them are afraid the majority of Hindus will interfere with our religious customs and observances. I, for one, cannot understand what this Congress has to do with our religion or any religion whatever; it is a purely secular association. Then some are afraid of the reconstitution of the Legislative Councils; they say the majority of Hindu members will upset the Mahomedans. May I ask them, will the Government retire as soon as the Councils are reformed, or strike off from its lines of policy the principle of religious toleration which is the sure foundation on which it has been built? Will it strike off this principle, simply to pander to the caprices of Hindus? It cannot, it will not; the executive under our scheme will always possess the right of veto, and be sure they would exercise it if we tried to be unjust to the Hindus, or they to us. But besides all this, I am not so foolish as to suppose that our Hindu brethren will ever seek to meddle with our religion; they are the most tolerant of people, and they never have done so in the past. Are they now, as the result of Western Christian education, to begin it in these latter days, when all bigotry is fast fading away?

Res. XII., Abrogation of Laws and Rules for the regulation of Prostitution.

Now, Gentlemen, as to this motion, we must most sincerely thank those good people in and out of Parliament for having led the latter to pass their well-timed resolution of June 5th, against State prostitution in India. There cannot be any difference of opinion as to the propriety of this resolution. The action of the House, once the facts became known, was inevitable. The principle of purity will ever triumph over vice, and I doubt not India, noted in the history of the world for its regard for such purity, will heartily co-operate with the effort, which is being made in England, for the abolition of the Governmental subvention of prostitution. With these remarks I heartily support this motion. (*Cries of "Vote, vote; enough! enough!"*)

THE PRESIDENT: Then, Gentlemen, I submit to you the resolution:—

RESOLVED—"*That this Congress, having watched with interest and sympathy the exertions that are being made in England for the total abrogation of laws and rules relating to the regulation of prostitution by the State in India, places on record its appreciation of the services thus rendered to this country and its desire to co-operate by all means in its power in the attainment of this laudable object.*"

The resolution was then put and carried unanimously.

Res. XIII., Subjects or Resolutions objected to by Mahomedans or Hindus as a body.

MR. ANANDA CHARLU—(*Madras, No. 16 in list*)—next rose and said: The resolution which you have now to deal with, and which I have the honour to propose, is a very necessary one, and I will tell you how it is necessary. But first I had better read it out to you, so that you may more readily follow me in my remarks:

"*That no subject shall be passed for discussion by the Subject Committee or allowed to be discussed at any Congress by the President thereof, to the introduction of which the Hindu or Mahomedan Delegates, as a body, object, unanimously or nearly unanimously, and that, if, after the discussion of any subject, which has been admitted for discussion, it shall appear that all the Hindu or all the Mahomedan Delegates, as a body, are unanimously, or nearly unanimously, opposed to the resolution which it is proposed to pass thereon, such resolution shall be dropped; provided that this rule shall refer only to subjects in regard to which the Congress has not already definitely pronounced an opinion.*"

Many of you have copies of the Madras Standing Congress Committee's Annual Report. In that report you will find an account explaining how this rule was found to be desirable for our guidance there. I may tell you also that that rule was framed in accordance with the wishes of some of our best Mahomedan friends. (*Cheers.*) Mr. Tyabjee (*cheers*), who was our President last year, in course of conversation told us that a resolution of that kind was considered desirable by many of his co-religionists; and other gentlemen, whose names cannot be mentioned without high praise. Mir Hoomayun Jah Bahadoor of the Mysore Regal House and Hajee Mahomed Abdulla Badshah Thakore Sahib, our Mahomedan Madras Merchant Prince (*cheers*), were a party to this proposition being adopted by the Madras Standing Committee. Then, as you are probably aware, this resolution was sent round to all the other Standing Congress Committees, and after full consideration approved by them. Outsiders may be surprised at this unanimity, but the reason is to be found in the fact that it is in strict accordance with one of the fundamental principles of the Congress, which is that it shall only deal with those subjects on which a substantial agreement has been come to by the great bulk of the intelligent men in the country. Now of course if either the Mahomedans or the Hindus as a body object, the subject is clearly not one in regard to which a substantial agreement has yet been come to. Now the resolution consists, as you will see, of two provisions and a rider. The first provision provides for no subject being even considered by the Subject Committee if either Mahomedans or Hindus as a body object to the question being discussed. Thus, if any foolish person were to propose that the question of cow-killing should be considered by the Congress (and there *was* one such person at

4th Day.

Res. XIII. Subjects or Resolutions objected to by Mahomedans or Hindus as a body.

Madras), he would be at once silenced under this rule. Then again it may happen that, though no one objects to the discussion of the subject, yet, when, after that discussion, a resolution comes to be framed in regard to it, the conclusion thus arrived at may be distasteful either to the Hindus or the Mahomedans, in which case such resolution would be dropped. You see we want to consult and work together like brothers. (*Loud cheers.*) If we are all agreed on any matter, then we will submit the universal view to Government ; but if we cannot come to a substantial agreement amongst ourselves, then we drop the subject until we can. But there is a rider. Our resolutions are before the world ; no new comer should join who is not fairly in sympathy with these. Any one who joins us, joins us, broadly, on the basis of these resolutions ; and, though we will allow him to rediscuss them if he likes and again take the sense of the assembly in regard to them, we cannot allow him, or any one, to block them. With this explanation I commend this resolution, typical as it is of the true Congress spirit, to your hearty concurrence. (*Loud cheers.*)

THE HON'BLE PANDIT AJOODHIA NATH—(*Allahabad, No.* 551 *in list*)—then said: It affords me sincere pleasure to second this proposition. A more pleasant duty could not have been afforded me. (*Cheers.*) It is especially for the satisfaction of those with whom I have spent the greater portion of my life, and with whom I am wholly in sympathy (*cheers*), that this resolution is designed. Hindu and Brahmin as I am, I think so highly of Mussulmans that, were I convinced that I ought to be a Mahomedan, I should be proud to become one. (*Cheers.*) A nobler race I have not seen, a more intelligent people I have not met with. It has ever seemed to me a thousand pities that there should be differences between the Professors of India's two great creeds. For this reason, if for nothing else, I was extremely sorry that so important an element as the Mahomedan should be in any measure lost to us, in our work of considering the question of political reform. (*Cheers.*) If you look at the history of the world, you will find that the sciences and arts of modern Europe have been borrowed largely, or at least were mainly derived, from the Mahomedans. It is sheer nonsense to say the Mahomedans are behind other Indian communities in the field of science and art. I find colleges established and institutions springing up for the welfare of the Mahomedans all over the Empire from one end to the other, yet there are some people who pretend that, in the battle for prominence, the Mahomedans will be behind the other races of India. The Mahomedans are a brave race, a braver than whom could not be found in the world. They have never been found to turn their backs to their enemies. (*Cheers.*) My advice to the Mahomedans is advance, and advance, and advance ; excel, and excel, and excel ; and go on educating your children, and do not listen to those who in the guise of friends are your worst enemies. (*Cheers.*) Come forward and shake hands with us as friends, and be convinced that we are prepared to meet you *more* than half way. It is with this desire that we have laid this resolution before you. Let us away with old foolish creed differences ; as practical men, let us work shoulder to shoulder in those secular matters in which our interests are really identical. It is part of the mission of the Congress to heal all old wounds and bind together all the races of this great empire in one homogeneous brotherhood. Do not keep aloof, be not deceived by false friends who seek their own advantage, Oh ! my Mahomedan brethren, in keeping you apart from us, to our and your loss equally ; join us—join the Congress in earnest, and see in this resolution a type of the spirit in which we are prepared to requite your trust. (*Prolonged cheering.*)

SWAMI ALARAM—(*Allahabad, No.* 591 *in list*)—then spoke in Hindee : Gentlemen, —Praise be to Almighty God and our Most Gracious Queen-Empress Victoria that a vast number of people from the various presidencies of all the various castes and creeds are here assembled, unanimous, of one mind, seeking only to do good to their fellows and benefit their country. Differences of opinion, particularly in political matters, is like a cholera plague, and this Congress is the hospital for patients suffering thus, under the able supervision of Mr. Hume, as its doctor. This Congress does not confine its aims to any particular grievance, or religious sect or body, but does and shall continue to represent all reasonable grievances of any class—Hindu, Mahomedan or Parsee. As this is Tribani or city of three rivers, so also are the three religious bodies of this nation represented here to-day. One day I attended an Anti-Congress meeting, when a Syed said to me : "Your Congress is the right movement, but prematurely put forward by Mr. Hume." I ask you if a sick man will refrain from sending for and obtaining medical advice or postpone calling the medical man till he is too far gone. Will a doctor refuse or postpone his treatment when called ? We are the sick men, and call on our doctor, Mr. Hume, to treat us for our ailments ; and I am sure nobody will say that we have been unwise in calling him so early. His remedies we know are slow but sure. The Anti-Congress people say we are working against the Government. Now I am reminded of a story which allow me to quote : A certain guru, Lalbujhakar by name, had a large number of disciples (*chelas*). As they were going on their way they saw the footprints of an elephant, which none of them had ever seen before, and they asked their guru what that was. The guru laughed at *them*, for not knowing, and cried, because he *himself* did not know, but he said, at last, when pressed :—

Res. XIII., Subjects or Resolutions objected to by Mahomedans or Hindus as a body.

> Bujhey Lalbujhakar aur nai bujhey koey ;
> Peir men chukki band ker hiranna kuda hoey.
> (Lalbujhakar he knows, but no other one knows ;
> A deer has jumped here with millstones on his toes.)

The Anti-Congressists are Lalbujhakars ; one of these is of Benares, and favoured us with his presence here, and another is sitting at Alighur, and these our would-be Gurus' (teachers') ideas in regard to politics and the present state of our country appear to be about as accurate as Guru Lalbujhakar's ideas in regard to the elephant's footprints ; and mind, that, all over India, those irresistible elephants' Education and Public spirit are daily leaving their footprints, and the officials, who are now, we see, the *chelas* of these gurus, had better get wiser men to tell them what these really mean. (*Loud cheers.*)

PANDIT SHAM NARAYAN—(*Lucknow, No.* 436 *in list*)—then spoke in Urdu and said : Mr. Chairman and Gentlemen,—I am glad to support the resolution which has just been moved by my friend Mr. Ananda Charloo, and seconded by my friend Pandit Ajoodhia Nath. The purport of this resolution is that, when the Mahomedan delegates as a body, or the Hindu delegates as a body object to any subject or resolution, that subject shall not be allowed to be discussed by the National Congress, and that resolution shall be dropped. For instance, if twelve hundred Hindu delegates assembled in this Congress desire to discuss any topic, or pass any resolution, and if three hundred Mahomedan delegates object to its being discussed or passed, then that topic or resolution shall be dropped. That is to say, the minority, when composed of all, or nearly all, the representatives of one community, shall have an equal voice with the majority.

The opponents of the Congress, or rather the ill-wishers of the Government, say that, as the number of the Mahomedans is small, the introduction of repesentative institutions would make the Hindus all-powerful in the country, and the Mahomedan interests would consequently suffer. Now these critics, who are so fond of vaunting their knowledge of history, do not see that history gives a most emphatic contradiction to their baseless and mischievous statements. At one time Scotland and England were politically divided. When the union between the two countries took place, one of the main conditions of the union was that the British Parliament should pass no laws for the sole good of England which would in any way be prejudicial to Scotland, and that the purely Scotch legislation should be carried on with the advice, not of the majority of the House of Commons, but of the majority of the Scotch members. If the majority of the Scotch members did not approve of any Scotch measure, that measure could not be forced upon Scotland by the adverse vote of the House of Commons. In the same way, it is possible to devise some method by which purely Mahomedan interests (supposing that they do really exist) may be guarded against the adverse vote of a Hindu majority.

But I do not believe that any such safeguards will ever be needed in India. Hindus and Mahomedans have become one nation, and I am proud to say that Lucknow is the place where the bond of unity beteewn the two nationalities is probably the strongest. In support of my statement, I may be allowed to refer to the riots on the occasion of the *Mohurrum* and the *Ram Lila* in recent years. These riots took place in a good many of the principal towns of the country. But in Lucknow everything passed off quietly and with perfect harmony. There the Hindus and Mahomedans left the whole thing to the arbitration of Nawab Aga Ali Khan and Sah Kirpa Dayal, and while the Hindus accepted the decision of the Mahomedan Nawab, the Mahomedans agreed to the terms dictated to them by the Hindu Sah. Again, when Nawab Aga Ali Khan of Lucknow executed his will, he made a Hindu gentleman, in preference to any of his Mahomedan relations or friends, his executor. These are instances, I could give dozens of similar ones, which serve to show that in all serious affairs, whether of a private or a public nature, Hindus and Mahomedans repose an amount of confidence in each other incompatible with what is alleged, by some unscrupulous critics, as to the non-existence of a real unity between these two communities.

The Anti-Congresswallahs have been very busy in sowing the seeds of dissension between Hindus and Mahomedans by telling the latter that the former are seeking their selfish ends at their cost, and that if they join the Congress-movement they will be set down as rebels and seditionists. Thanks to the quick intelligence and the robust manliness of the Mahomedans, they have detected the snares and tricks of their false friends and repudiated them, and have come forward to stand shoulder to shoulder with their Hindu friends, to support and advance a movement which, more than anything else, teaches us to trust to the efficacy of constitutional methods and to the justice, the good sense, and the benevolence of the British nation. (*Loud and prolonged cheering.*)

MUNSHI NASIRUDDIN—(*Benares, No.* 880 *in list*)—then spoke in Urdu as follows: Mr. President and Gentlemen,—I am extremely grateful to you, my countrymen,

4th Day.

Res. XIII., Subjects or Resolutions objected to by Mahomedans or Hindus as a body.

Hindus, Mahomedans and Parsees, for your kindness in favouring us with your presence at this Congress, and permitting me to be of the number. I would ask you to remember Pandit Ajoodha Nath's late speech at Lucknow, the truths of which are clearly before you here to-day. The Mahomedans with the aid of the Hindus ruled over this land for 700 years. Since the reign of Aurungzeb, the oppressor of Hindus, the feelings of the two, Hindus and Mahomedans, have been somewhat estranged towards each other, but the Congress comes to unite us altogether as brothers once more as we were in the good old days before Aurungzeb. (*Cheers.*) I was elected a delegate at Benares, but I must confess to you that before this I was at one time among those unfortunates, the Anti-Congressmen, but I swear to you I have nothing to do with that body now, but am entirely with you. (*Cheers.*) Ill winds rose from Aligurh and Benares, and blew over the country, but have subsided and dispersed by this resolution, and I think you feel assured with me that this Congress is on strong foundations and indestructible. (*Cheers.*)

I welcome this resolution now before us, not because I think it was really needed, not because any educated Mahomedan believes that in secular and political matters our interests can be otherwise than identical with those of our Sikh, Hindu and Parsee brethren, but because, with this resolution in hand, we can convert and reassure many ignorant Mahomedans, who really believe, or half believe, the falsehoods circulated by those who think fit to oppose the Congress. I am sure you will all accept this wise resolution. (*Cries of " Vote, vote."*)

THE PRESIDENT: There does not seem to be any objection raised by any one to this resolution. ("*No, no, none ; vote.*") So then I will put the resolution, which runs thus :—

RESOLVED :—" *That no subject shall be passed for discussion by the Subject Committee or allowed to be discussed at any Congress by the President thereof, to the introduction of which the Hindu or Mahomedan Delegates, as a body, object, unanimously or nearly unanimously, and that, if after the discussion of any subject which has been admitted for discussion, it shall appear that all the Hindu or all the Mahomedan Delegates, as a body, are unanimously, or nearly unanimously, opposed to the resolution which it is proposed to pass thereon, such resolution shall be dropped: provided that this rule shall refer only to subjects in regard to which the Congress has not already definitely pronounced an opinion.*'

The resolution was then passed unanimously and with acclamations.

Res. XIV., Question of a Permanent Settlement.

THE PRESIDENT said : Gentlemen,—I find myself in a difficulty about a resolution, *viz.*, that about the permanent settlement, which was withdrawn. I understand that there is a large number of the delegates here who contend that, because the mover or seconder of a resolution, approved by the Subject Committee, chooses to withdraw it, that does not commit the whole meeting to the withdrawal. Whether it does or does not, the fact of keeping silence at the time the proposition was withdrawn puts aside, it seems to me, any claim to resuscitate it. It has, however, been asserted that the withdrawal did not receive the assent of the meeting. I now therefore propose to take a show of hands on the question as to whether this resolution should be re-opened or not.

A large number of hands having been raised in favour of re-opening the resolution, and none against it—

THE PRESIDENT said : As it seems to be your pleasure that this resolution should be again placed before you, I would ask one of those delegates who concurs in the resolution and wants *it* to be passed and not something different (*laughter*) now to propose it. (*Cheers.*)

MR. J. E. HOWARD—(*Allahabad, No. 573 in list*)—then moved the resolution. He said : Gentlemen,—I have great pleasure in moving this resolution, to which our respected friend Mr. Bhide proved so unkind a sponsor. It runs thus :—

" *That, in the opinion of this Congress, the time has now come for introducing into the major portions of the Madras and Bombay Presidencies, and of the N.-W. P. and Oudh, and into parts of the Panjab and other Provinces, a permanent settlement of the land revenue demand.*"

You know perfectly well that in Bengal there is a permanent settlement, whereas in other parts of India they revise the settlement every thirty years, and in some parts the period is even less than that. Those of you who know what a permanent settlement means —and there has been one in Bengal for more than two or three generations—will be able to tell whether it has worked for good or for evil. The question, however, is one of the greatest difficulty. I do not know much about it myself ; and I leave it to the delegates to say whether, looking at the question from a comprehensive point of view, it would be advisable that this resolution should be carried. I must confess that it is a question bristling with difficulties. If the effect of making a permanent settlement is to be a reduction of

4th Day.

Res. XIV., Question of Permanent Settlement.

revenue, it will be for the Government of this country to devise other taxes to make up for any deficiency in the land revenue. You may at the same time remember the great maxim of John S. Mill, that the unearned increment of land should not go to individual proprietors, but should belong to the whole people. (*Cheers.*) It is now for you to consider, with all the wisdom you can bring to bear upon this great question, whether it is wise and proper that this resolution should be carried just now, with such imperfect information as is at present at our command, or at any rate at the command of some of us; or whether it is more expedient that it should be postponed for further consideration. My object in moving this resolution is simply to start a discussion that may throw some light on the subject, and perhaps I have not sufficiently fulfilled the conditions of our respected President, who wanted a mover, who wished to see the resolution passed and did not wish for something different; for; though I cannot say I wish for anything different, neither can I, as at present informed, or rather, wanting in information on the subject as I am, honestly say that I wish to see this resolution passed. But perhaps some one who does really understand the question will, in seconding my motion (which I made merely to secure some discussion of the subject), explain more fully its bearings and the grounds on which the present is fixed upon as an appropriate time for commencing action upon it.

SHEIKH RAZA HOSSEIN KHAN—(*Oudh, No.* 439 *in list*)—then said, speaking in Urdu: Mr. President and Gentlemen,—I rise to second this resolution. If the subject of a permanent settlement had not been at all brought before the Indian National Congress, I should have thought that the Congress had not fully performed its duty. The greater part of the population of India is composed of men who have special connection with the tillage of the soil. The main resource of India lies in its agriculture. The best relief for and antidote against the poverty of the people, and the now almost yearly recurring famines are to be found in the introduction of a permanent settlement throughout all those portions of the country which have been long settled. I quite admit that there are portions of the country where population is sparse and cultivation in its infancy, where a permanent settlement would be out of place; but in districts where the population ranges from 500 to 900 per square mile of cultivation, the time has come for fixing the land revenue demand, unless, indeed, in some exceptional localities which railways have not yet approached, and the agricultural value of which we may expect to be materially changed when they do approach it. When I say a permanent settlement, I do not necessarily mean a permanent settlement precisely similar to that in Bengal. In the first place, we are wiser now than we then were. The experience of eighty years has shown us how we can improve on that settlement in many particulars. In the second place, landed tenures vary all over the country, and in each place the permanent settlement must vary accordingly. And again when I say a permanent settlement and speak of a fixity of the Government demand, I do not necessarily mean that that demand should be settled in rupees. On the contrary, I am disposed to believe that it would have to be fixed in terms of quantities of the three or four chief local staples of produce, in regard to which a cash revaluation might be made at intervals of, say, every three, five or seven years, based upon the average local prices of those staples during the preceding period. Thus, if the Government demand in any village were fixed at 50 mds. of wheat, 100 mds. of jowar, 100 mds. of bajra, 50 mds. of gram, and 50 mds. of urher, this would remain the demand for all time, but every three, five, or seven years, the actual number of rupees would be fixed by a calculation based on the average *local* price of these articles during the past three, five, or seven years. I can only say that, unless some such fixity is given to the Government demand in our province, cultivation will never keep up with the growth of population. Grant it, and hundreds of thousands of wells will be dug within the first five years, and millions of acres that now yield only small unirrigated crops would yield double and treble the amounts of far more valuable staples. By one way or another, people would manage to put double the amount of manure they now do into the ground. But no great improvement can take place so long as the people are for ever on the look-out for the recurring swoop of the settlement officer to sweep the fruits of their labours into the official net. Mr. Howard spoke of the "unearned increment," which is explained to me to mean, profits that a person has not made for himself, and he tells us that a great political economist tells us this should belong to Government. Well, if this is political economy, our system must be perfection, for at every revision Government appropriates the profits that it never earned, but which the cultivators of the soil have earned. (*Laughter.*)

Gentlemen, if what I have heard as to the real meaning of the phrase used by Mr. Howard, *viz.*, that it refers to an increased value of lands and produce, owing to the making of railroads and opening out roads and the like is correct, then I say that in the greater part of our provinces no such increased value is any longer to be looked for. The country is as fully populated and as much opened out as it can be, and any improvement in the yield of the land will be due to the landlord putting more capital into it,

4th Day.

Res. XIV., Question of Permanent Settlement.

or the cultivator more labour and neither will ever do this until they get a permanent settlement.

Now I am not pretending that I am prepared with any definite scheme. Our resolution does not put forward anything of the kind; but I do think that the Government should be made aware of the very strong feeling on this subject that pervades the country, and take the matter, which, for some years past it has, as it were, excluded from the sphere of practical politics, anew into consideration, and into consideration with the view to action, and therefore it is that I consider it imperative to pass the resolution which I have had the honour to second.

MUNSHI SHEIKH HUSSEN—(*Bombay, No.* 109 *in list*)—said: I cordially endorse all that my friend Sheikh Raza Hosein Khan said. As in Oudh so in the Bombay Presidency, a fixity of the land revenue demand has become a necessity. The revision of settlement has thrown back the country for years, and until we get a permanent settlement of some kind, and the ryots feel that they will really enjoy, or that their children will enjoy, the fruits of any sacrifices they make for the land, the land will never yield half what it might, and there will never be any real improvement in agriculture—no, not if Government has a model farm in every village.

RAJAH RAMPAL SINGH—(*Allahabad, No.* 571 *in list*): I am requested by some of my friends to say something on this important question, and I stand here once more before you in obedience to their request. Gentlemen from Bengal, who have got a permanent settlement, do not know what difficulties we have to face and what oppression we are suffering by being subjected to a thirty years' settlement. (*Cheers.*) The object of the Congress is to unite all gentlemen assembled here in a feeling of mutual sympathy and on grounds of common interests. But if this resolution had been withdrawn without discussion, it would have been the drowning of the voice of a very large number of delegates, simply because they happen to be in the minority. (*Cheers.*) Owing to the system under which the land tax is increased every thirty years, people do not improve their land from fear that the benefit of the improvement will be only reaped by the State. The Proclamation of Her Majesty said that all her subjects in this country would be treated in the same way as Her Majesty's subjects in England. But no land is taxed in England. I had to pay very little for the leasehold of a house in England. The intention of Government is to improve the condition of the people, but the condition of the agriculturists, who constitute the majority of the people, cannot improve so long as there is no permanent settlement, which will not only be advantageous to the landowner, but also, if proper arrangements be made, to his tenants who are really the backbone of the country. (*Cheers.*) I am sure that if the entire population were polled, 70 per cent. would vote for permanence of settlement; and I am also sure that, when we get representative Councils, one of the very first, I might say the first, thing we should all fight for, in all of these, would be the introduction of an equitable permanent settlement into all the thoroughly cultivated and well-advanced portions of the country. We do not wish to take the Government at a disadvantage; we do not expect them to take immediate action on this resolution; but we desire by it to serve them, as it were, with a notice that we are all thinking of this question, and all fully resolved when other simpler matters, as Mr. Bonnerjee explained, are disposed of, to press for a reform in this matter also. Therefore I desired that this subject should come on for discussion, and therefore it is that I still advocate the passing of this resolution, although I perceive that many, while agreeing with us in principle, consider that any resolution on the subject would be premature.

THE HON'BLE MR. TELANG—(*Bombay, No.* 201 *in list*)—then said: The question of a permanent settlement is one of the highest importance, both to the people and the Government. But I do not think that it is one which should be, as it were, rushed through this Congress. (*Cheers.*) On the contrary, I submit that both we who have assembled in this hall and those who, though elected as delegates, have not been able to attend here, and lastly our constituents who sent us here, should have an opportunity of maturely and gravely considering the question in all its numerous bearings. Now that the question has been reopened by the readmission of the withdrawn resolution, it is for us to consider how we should deal with it. It appears to me that there is a considerable difference of opinion as to the mode in which we ought now to proceed. I do not want to discuss here the merits of the question of a permanent settlement. It is obvious from the show of hands that there is some difference amongst us even as to whether it should be touched at all, and therefore I think it is desirable that any resolution we may now pass on this most important subject should be such that we ourselves may all be satisfied with it, as well as those not present. ("*Hear, hear.*") It appears to me that, looking to the circumstances under which the question has now been raised, no resolution, whatever it might be, that we came to on the merits of the question, whether favourable or unfavourable to a permanent settlement, would be likely to carry much respect or weight. I fully admit the importance of the question,

4th Day.

Res. XIV., Question of Permanent Settlement.

but precisely on that account I submit that no decision should be come to in regard to it, without full previous preparation and detailed discussion of it all over the country. Now many of us, most of us, have had no preparation: it was not one of the 13 subjects circulated over the country before we left our constituents. The question has had no definite practical discussion amongst us in most parts of the country. We have all vague general ideas, probably in most cases favourable to the notion, but very few if any of us have really recently studied the question or read up the voluminous literature that exists on a subject which, for the last 40 years, at least, has off and on been under discussion, alike in India and England. I doubt whether there is one single man of marked ability connected with India who has not written something about this question during the last 50 years. We ought at least to read a good deal of what has been written before expressing definite opinions. By all means let us discuss the question; it is one of first-rate importance, but let the whole country that we represent, and we ourselves, be first properly prepared for the discussion. I therefore suggest an amendment as follows :—

" *That the question of the introduction of a permanent settlement of the land revenue demand into the Madras and Bombay Presidencies and other Provinces be referred to the several Standing Congress Committees, with instructions to report upon the same, in so far as it affects their respective Circles, to the Congress of 1889.*"

Then this question can be brought before the Congress in due form for consideration next year. (*Cheers.*) Although I am myself a citizen of Bombay, I happen to know something about the visits, not always very welcome, of the survey officer; and, if I may be permitted to mention a personal circumstance, I may state that in the Council of the Government of Bombay I have myself taken some part in the fight for obtaining some fixity of tenure for the ryots of Bombay. (*Cheers.*) My own inclinations, if you permit me to say so, are in favour of a certain class of permanent settlement. At the same time I admit that there are opposing considerations of the greatest moment to be taken into account, and I am not at present prepared to say that, taking the balance of all those considerations as a whole, the weight, certainly, clearly preponderates on one side or the other ; and I desire that any resolution we may come to on this great question should be one which, if I may borrow a phrase of Lord Brougham's, should proceed from this Congress with authority, and be received outside with respect. It should not go out without authority and be returned to the Congress without respect. (*Cheers.*) When we meet again with the reports of all the Standing Committees before us, after having in the meantime ourselves carefully studied all that others have before written on the subject, we shall be in a much better position to decide upon the question, and I have no doubt that any decision which we shall then come to will be loyally accepted by the minority, (*cheers*) should it then prove, which I venture to doubt, that we are unable to arrive at a perfectly unanimous conclusion.

RAJAH RAMPAL SINGH—(*Allahabad, No.* 571 *in list*)—then said : I have great pleasure in seconding this amendment. (*Loud cheers.*) The question has been too long overlooked by the Congress, and therefore it was that I wished it brought before this assembly. But after Sheikh Raza Husein's eloquent speech, and the discussion that has taken place, I think that the proposed amendment will do all that is required, that is to say, bring the subject definitely within the sphere of our practical politics.

MR. HOWARD—(*Allahabad, No.* 573 *in list*) : Sir, —I am quite prepared to withdraw my motion in favour of Mr. Telang's amendment. I never professed to know much about the question, and, as I explained in moving the original resolution, I merely did so to secure attention to and obtain some discussion of a subject which, however imperfect may be our knowledge of its details, we all realize to be one of the first magnitude.

SHEIKH RAZA HOSSEIN—(*Oudh, No.* 439 *in list*)—speaking in Urdu, said: We agriculturists probably know already quite as much, if not more, about the subject, than we are ever likely to learn from any official literature, however extensive. For this will be mere theory, whereas we know the practice. At the same time, I agree that the matter is so important that it is well that anything we say in regard to it should have the appearance of being the result of deep deliberation, and so I am quite willing to accept the amendment. At the same time, if we were to deliberate for 50 years, it would not, in the smallest degree, affect my opinion that in my province a permanent settlement is absolutely required, in the interest alike of landlords and cultivators. (*Cries of " Vote, vote.*")

THE PRESIDENT : I shall now put the amendment, which has become the substantive resolution before us by the formal withdrawal (I hope there is no mistake about it this time) (*cries of " No, no ; it's all right*") of the original resolution. It will stand thus :—

4th Day.

Res. XIV., Question of Permanent Settlement.

RESOLVED—"*That the question of the introduction of a permanent settlement of the land revenue demand into the Madras and Bombay Presidencies and other provinces be referred to the several Standing Congress Committees, with instructions to report upon the same, in so far as it affects their respective Circles, to the Congress of 1889.*"

The resolution was then put and carried unanimously.

Res. XV., Disapproval of the recent enhancement of the Salt Tax.

THE PRESIDENT : Another resolution, which has been sent in to me supported by a great many names runs as follows :—

"*That this Congress do put on record its disapproval of the recent enhancement of the salt tax as involving a perceptible increase to the burthens of the poorer classes, as also the "partial absorption, in a time of peace and plenty, of the only financial reserve of the Empire.*"

Before this resolution is proposed, I wish to state that it came before the Subject Committee and was fully dealt with, and the majority, if not the whole, of the Subject Committee seemed to feel that the question had been dealt with so recently by the Government that it was useless on our part to put it before them for repeal, knowing the circumstances in which the Government are now placed. It is for the consideration of our friends from Madras, at whose instance mainly this resolution is put before the meeting, whether under such circumstances they should do more than merely mention the matter as a grievance. (*Cheers.*)

The Madras Delegates then, amidst loud cheering, expressed a wish that the discussion of the question should proceed.

THE PRESIDENT : Then I will put it to the assembly. Do you wish this resolution discussed ? (*Loud cries of " Yes, yes ; all, all.*") Very well, then I will ask the gentleman who has been noted as proposer to proceed.

MR. NARAYAN VISHNU BAM—(*Poona, No. in list,*)—said in the vernacular : Mr. President and Gentlemen,—I beg to propose the resolution that our good President has read to you. Here, in Upper India, you have been used to dear salt, and your people eat much less of it and require less of it than ours in the south, and you can hardly realize the terrible hardship involved to our people in paying, now, a two rupees eight annas duty on salt which costs one anna, and on which, not so very many years ago, we paid a duty of only ten annas. I have heard that in Bengal some gentlemen said they approved of the recent enhancement of the salt tax. (*Cries of "No, no.*") I can only say that all over the south of India it has created more discontent than even the income tax ; and in some parts of the south, in the Madras Presidency for instance, this has been aggravated by Government giving a monopoly of the sale to a few men, who have still further artificially raised the price. Gentlemen, the salt tax which presses proportionally more and more heavily on a man the poorer he is, is altogether a bad tax ; but if kept at a low limit it is bearable. At its present rate, our poor people cry out dreadfully about it. I do not believe that the Government could be right in raising it as they have done, and I think that we shall be ill discharging our duty as representatives of the people if we do not distinctly put on record our disapproval of the measure. Is there any one here who approves it ? Do we not all feel it to be a wrong thing to add to the already crushing poverty of the poorest classes ? Let them tax articles of luxury—tax them as heavily as is possible without creating smuggling, but do not let them go on raising a tax on the necessaries of life and adding to the burthens of the poor, because it is easy, and they have no voice. Gentlemen, we are the voice of the country, of the poor as much as, nay more than of the rich, for they can speak for themselves ; but let us, at any rate, protest on behalf of the poor. Personally there is not one of us here who cares for this increase ; it means to most of us a rupee more a year ; in the largest households not more than five rupees. But to the very poorest it means eight annas more a year ; and let me tell you, Gentlemen, that there are millions on millions to whom that eight annas extra means eight meals less in a year, and that, to people who, even before this enhancement, never got more than one meal in the 24 hours. And, Gentlemen, what we all feel is that, had a terrible war with Russia been raging, had there been some great famine strangling in its deadly grasp huge provinces, there might have been some excuse for this enhancement. But that to do this in normal times, when there were at most only petty wars—and Government always keeps a small stock of these on hand—(*laughter*), and no famine anywhere, was indefensible. We all feel this, and this is what the resolution says, and this being so, I hope you will support this resolution unanimously. I had much more to say, but the President's warning gong has sounded, and I can only repeat—this is what you mean—this is what you think—then say it, and say it plainly. (*Cheers.*)

4th Day.

Res. XV., Disapproval of the recent enhancement of the Salt Tax.

MR. LAKSHMAN DHUNDEV KATRE—*(Bombay, No.* 230 *in list)*—then said : Mr. President and Gentlemen,—I come to second and to address you upon the resolution, that has been read by our worthy President, on behalf of the Ratnagari District of the Bombay Presidency. It is a very poor district, the poorest of the whole of the districts in the Bombay Presidency. There the people are all suffering from the great hardship which is caused by the recent enhancement of the salt duty by the Government of India. The people are groaning under the burden, so much so that by the enhancement of the salt tax, that has been made by the Government of India, even the salt that they require for salting their fishes is denied them. The people are groaning, their misery is great, and it is for the Congress to say whether they have some regard for the condition of this people, and pray for the reduction of the duty made by the Government of India. The resolution does not mean the total repeal of the salt tax. We do not at all expect that. The Marquis of Ripon reduced the salt tax, but our late Viceroy, Lord Dufferin, has raised it more and more. Therefore, the present resolution has been submitted to your approval, and in it I heartily concur, though I should have liked to add to it a distinct prayer to Government to reduce the tax and bring it again to what it was at the end of the reign of the Marquis of Ripon. *(Cheers.)* I was appointed a delegate to this Congress for this special purpose, *viz.*, to submit to you the resolution which has been read just now by our worthy President. *(Cheers.)*

MR. GIRIJA SHANKAR KASHIRAM DWIVEDI—*(Bombay, No.* 223 *in list)*—then spoke in Urdu. He said : Brother Delegates,—We all desire salt to be cheap, for the sake of the poor. We all disapprove the recent increase to the duty. Instead of raising the duty, it should have been lowered. Lord Ripon lowered it, and had he remained here he would have reduced it further. But Lord Dufferin instead of reducing has raised it, because he wanted to annex Burmah, and waste crores up in Afghanistan. Therefore, the whole country is displeased with him, and he is displeased with the country and runs down this Congress, which is the voice of the country. Yes, we disapprove this recent increase to the salt tax. We say it was wrong, and that there was no real justification for it—only a justification that Lord Dufferin himself had made by expenditure which we all disapprove.

Several other delegates then spoke in rapid succession very short speeches, in various vernaculars, all denouncing the recent enhancement of the salt tax ; but their names were not recorded, and even the native reporters failed to report them at all, and they have furnished no translation of their speeches, and so there is no record of what they said beyond this, that one and all said they supported the resolution.

All this time loud cries of " *Vote, vote* ;" " *We are all agreed, &c.*," were going on.

THE PRESIDENT, addressing several gentlemen who had appeared on the platform: Do you wish to oppose the resolution ? (" *No, no," from these Delegates.*) Addressing the assembly : Does any one wish to oppose the resolution ? *(Loud cries of " None, none." " Vote, vote.")* Then I shall put the resolution as follows :—

RESOLVED—" *That this Congress puts on record its disapproval of the recent enhancement of the Salt Tax, as involving a perceptible increase to the burthens of the poorer classes, as also the partial absorption, in a time of peace and plenty, of the only financial reserve of the Empire.*"

The resolution was then put and carried without a dissentient voice.

Res. XVI., Next or 5th Congress to meet in the Bombay Presidency.

MR. A. O. HUME—*(Allahabad, No.* 6 *in list)*—who on rising was received with vociferous cheers, again and again renewed, said : I am extremely obliged to you for the very kind manner in which you have received me, and I am only sorry that after all this tremendous fuss I should have only a very small resolution to propose for your acceptance. *(Laughter.)* Ever since the commencement of the Congress it has fallen to my lot, each year, to move a small formal resolution in regard to the next meeting of the Congress. I may tell you that our friends in the Punjab were extremely anxious to have the Congress next year at Lahore. They were so anxious that the Punjab Delegates here present, some 70 only in number, actually subscribed among themselves Rs. 15,000 last evening as the nucleus of a fund for defraying the expenses of the Congress. *(Loud cheers.)* It is a sure sign of a man's earnestness when he puts his hand in his pocket *(cheers)*, and Rs. 15,000 is no small sum for only about seventy delegates to subscribe among themselves. *(Cheers.)* We should have been very pleased to oblige them ; but then we have to look all round the country, and consult the convenience of people residing in all parts of India. This year the Bombay and Madras delegates had to undertake a long journey to be present here. If we go to Lahore next year, the journey will be longer by nearly 1,000 miles for the delegates from the Southern Presidencies. We must deal fairly in this matter with all parts of the Empire, so we have made up our minds to hold the next Congress in the Bombay Presidency, leaving

4th Day.

Res. XVI., Next or 5th Congress to meet in the Bombay Presidency.

it to the gentlemen of Bombay and Poona to settle among themselves in which of the two places the meeting should take place. I therefore move that the Fifth Indian National Congress—you see we have got to the *Fifth*—(*Loud cheers and laughter*)—

"*That the Fifth Indian National Congress do assemble in the Bombay Presidency (either at Bombay itself or at Poona, as may be settled hereafter) on the 26th of December, 1889.*" (*Loud cheers.*)

I see that you have accepted our proposal and need therefore trouble you no longer. (*Renewed cheers.*)

THE HON'BLE P. M. MEHTA—(*Bombay, No.* 208 *in list*)—rose and said: I second the motion. I have only one remark to make, and that is, that if it falls to the lot of Bombay to receive the delegates, we shall welcome them in that place right cordially. Remember, Gentlemen, that in coming to Bombay you will be coming to the birthplace on the Congress. (*Cheers.*)

MR. M. B. NAMJOSHI—(*Poona, No.* 101 *in list*)—said: On behalf of the people of Poona I am authorized to say that, if it be arranged to hold the Congress in Poona, they will be only too delighted to receive you in that city. (*Cheers.*) For myself I say, don't go to Bombay; you have been there once, but come to Poona, which was to and would have been the birthplace of the Congress, but for a slight miscarriage. (*Renewed cheers.*)

(A delegate here called for three cheers for the Punjab and Sirdar Dayal Singh, a call which was very heartily responded to.)

MR. LAJPATRAI—(*Punjab, No.* 348 *in list*)—then rose and said: Gentlemen,—We do not, of course, desire to dispute the decision arrived at by the executive. But I am here to state distinctly on behalf of ourselves, the Punjab delegates, and of our countrymen of the Punjab, that however poor we may be, both in intellect and wealth, we would have received you with open arms, and given you a royal welcome had you decided to come to us next year. (*Cheers.*) For your sakes, for the sake of the Congress, and for the sake of our common country, if it had been decided to hold the next meeting in Lahore, we should have given you the most hearty and enthusiastic reception, and should have done our best to make you forget the hospitality of Allahabad, Madras and Calcutta in the affectionate entertainment we should have provided for you; and we desire to say this, further, that whenever you choose to throw upon us the responsibllity of receiving you, we shall most willingly accept, and unanimously glory in it. (*Cheers.*)

BABA NARAIN SINGH—(*Punjab, No.* 356 *in list*)—then spoke to the same effect in Urdu.

A voice: "Three cheers for the Punjab," and the meeting responded to the call very cordially.

THE PRESIDENT: It is agreed, then, that we meet next year in the Bombay Presidency? ("*Yes, yes.*") Well, then, I formally put the resolution :—

RESOLVED.—"*That the Fifth Indian National Congress do assemble in the Bombay Presidency (either at Bombay itself or at Poona, as may be settled hereafter) on the 26th of December, 1889.*"

The proposition was then carried unanimously and by acclamation.

Res. XVII., Reappointment of Mr. Hume as General Secretary.

MR. W. C. BONNERJEE—(*Calcutta, No.* 1098 *in list*)—then rose and said: Mr. President and Brother Delegates,—I, too, have to submit to you a resolution which is formal in its nature. It is that our respected friend and universal leader, Mr. A. O. Hume, (*vociferous cheers again and again repeated*) be re-appointed General Secretary of the Congress for the year 1889. From the manner in which you have received Mr. Hume's name, it is, I see, absolutely unnecessary for me to say one word in support of my proposition. I will only say this of Mr. Hume, that, notwithstanding the attacks which have been made upon him in the past, and despite any attacks which may be made on him in the future, he possesses, and will continue to possess, our unabated confidence. (*Loud cheers.*) We owe him a debt of immense and endless gratitude. (*Loud and prolonged cheering.*) It is a privilege to have Mr. Hume as our General Secretary. (*Loud cheers.*)

The proposition was received by the vast assembly with the utmost enthusiasm, every one vociferously cheered, and "three cheers for Mr. Hume" were called for by a delegate, and the assembly responded to the invitation right heartily. It was some time before quiet was restored, and then Mr. Telang rose to second the proposition.

4th Day

Res. XVII., Reappointment of Mr. Hume as General Secretary.

HON'BLE K. T. TELANG—*(Bombay, No. 201 in list)*—rose and said : I have the very greatest pleasure in seconding the resolution which has just now been moved by Mr. Bonnerjee. All the members of the Congress having already expressed their feeling in reference to this resolution, it is unnecessary to say more than this, that it is a great advantage and a privilege to us all to have Mr. Hume as our Secretary. Attacks have been made upon Mr. Hume from high quarters as well as low quarters *(cheers and laughter)*, but in spite of those attacks our confidence in and regard for Mr. Hume continue unabated. *(Loud cheers.)*

MR. ANANDA CHARLU—*(Madras No. 16 in list)*—rose and said : I support this resolution with all my heart ; Mr. Telang has said, *in spite* of all the attacks that have been made upon Mr. Hume *(cheers)*, but I regard these attacks as the highest homage that could be paid to him *(cheers)* ; it is the only tribute our adversaries could consistently pay to our old friend. *(Loud cheers.)*

A Punjab Delegate having also supported the resolution in Urdu, it was carried by acclamation amidst continued cheering.

Vote of thanks to Mr. Yule, the President.

THE HON'BLE PANDIT AJOODHIA NATH—*(Allahabad, No. 551 in list)*—said : Gentlemen, I hold myself to be a fortunate man in several respects. I am fortunate in that the pleasant duty of receiving you all in Allahabad has devolved upon the Committee over which I have the great, and I fear unmerited, honour to preside. I am again fortunate because the duty of seconding the 14th resolution, which was most congenial to my feelings, devolved upon me, and I am still more fortunate, in that it is now reserved for me to propose a vote of thanks to our honoured President. *(An outburst of cheering, which lasted for some time.)* Gentlemen, you who, for the last four days, have been witnesses of the good temper and tact, the striking ability and marked kindliness, and the entire self-devotion and forgetfulness of self, which have characterised our respected President's discharge of the arduous duty, which the hourly, almost momentary, governance and guidance of a vast assembly like this has entailed, will feel with me that no vote of thanks that we can pass can at all adequately represent the deep obligations under which Mr. George Yule has, during the past week, laid not only all of us here, but the entire country. Still, Gentlemen, this is unfortunately all that we can do at this moment to testify our gratitude, and I shall therefore now ask you to pass this vote of thanks by acclamation and at once.

The whole assembly then rose and carried the resolution by acclamation and with many cheers for "our worthy President."

President's Concluding Address.

THE PRESIDENT, who was obviously deeply moved by the extreme cordiality with which the vote of thanks had been passed, then rose and said : I must first unburden myself of the duty which I owe to several gentlemen who have sent me certain applications to allow them to do certain things at the Congress. I am, indeed, very sorry that I have been unable to comply with their requests, not because I thought that there was anything in them improper in themselves, but because it seemed to me that it would be irregular to allow them. For example, there is one gentleman who, in the course of the proceedings, desired to have an opportunity of reciting to you all some verses of his own composition. *(Laughter.)* I have no doubt that these verses would be well worth listening to. But it would be departing from the order of public meetings to allow such a thing to be done. I hope that that gentleman and others, amongst our visitors, anxious to disburthen themselves, for your benefit, of various kinds of literary productions, will not think me uncourteous for refusing their requests. *(Cries of "No, no.")*. There are other Delegates who have made other applications of a similarly harmless nature, but, yet, as I may phrase it, "out of order," which also I have been reluctantly obliged to refuse.

Now, Gentlemen, I have to thank you all for the very handsome way in which you have received and carried the resolution which has been proposed by my friend on the left. *(Cheers.)* It is not always easy to express one's feelings on such occasions, and I sometimes think it is best not to attempt to do so, but simply to adopt the old but simple form of returning thanks, "Gentlemen, I thank you from the very bottom of my heart" *(loud cheers)*, and this I do, now, in all sincerity and truth. I am very glad, indeed, to have rendered any service to the cause of the National Congress. *(Cheers.)* I believe the principles upon which it is founded are just, good and true ; and that in due time its aims will be accomplished. *(Loud cheers.)* There are many grievances in the country under the present system of government, and these multiply and deepen, for the simple reason that there has been no channel through which they could be adequately represented to the authorities. *(Cheers.)* In this respect the Congress offers great advantages, and I have paid a good deal of time and attention to the question on which I addressed you in my opening speech, namely, the reform of the Legislative Councils, as being the best of all outlets for the grievances that are scattered over the whole country. *(Cheers.)* I do not only esteem it to be a proper thing to attach myself to such a Congress, but I also

4th Day.

President's Concluding Address.

esteem it as an honour. (*Cheers.*) I am sure that, in course of a year or two, or perhaps even before that, the main principles on which the Congress is based will be recognized, not by you and me alone, but by the highest authorities in the land. (*Loud and prolonged cheers.*) X

But now to turn to another subject. Our thanks, the best thanks of the Congress, are due to the Reception Committee. You all know what they have done for us, and how well and kindly and lovingly they have done it. Where there have been so many gentlemen rendering such efficient and willing service, it is difficult to specify any names without running the risk of doing some injustice to the others. But there are two or three who have placed themselves in the forefront of the battle; and I may take it, as is usually taken under the circumstances that, when the leaders are thanked, the rank and file are also included in it. (*Cheers.*) First, there is the Hon'ble Pandit Ajoodhia Nath who, assisted by Pandit Bishumber Nath, has worked, night and day, driving the entire train. (*Cheers.*) Then there is Baboo Charoo Chandra Mitter. "Charoo Baboo" must be, by this time, a household word to all of you (*cheers*); but whether to liken him to the fireman or the boiler (*laughter*) I know not; but this I know, that he always has the steam up, let him be called for when he may. (*Loud cheers.*) Next we have Lala Ram Charan, and he, I am sure, has been our wise and courteous guard, taking care, in kindly fashion, of everyone and everything. (*Cheers.*) Lastly there is our good old friend always smiling, always pleasant—I mean Raja Rampal Singh—who is either a first-class passenger or the station master (*laughter*), whichever he and you please (*cheers*), though I am inclined to think he is both! (*Loud cheers.*) The other gentlemen whom I should name are Captain Banon and Pandit Muddun Mohun. (*Cheers.*) I have nothing more to say to you, and I now announce that the fourth sitting of the Indian National Congress is dissolved.

There was much cheering, which continued for some time. Then, three thundering cheers, repeated again and again, were given for the Queen-Empress, and the vast assembly began to disperse; but the majority of the Delegates went on to give cheers, for a variety of people—Mr. Gladstone, Sir William Hunter, Mr. Bradlaugh, Mr. Hume, Lord Reay, Lord Connemara, &c.—until someone proposing a cheer for Lord Dufferin, the assembly, or what was left of it, realising the *reductio ad absurdum*, broke into peals of laughter, and finally dissolved, in a state of universal good humour.

APPENDIX I.

LIST OF DELEGATES

WHO ATTENDED THE

FOURTH INDIAN NATIONAL CONGRESS,

HELD AT ALLAHABAD, DECEMBER, 1888.

Number.	Presidency or Government.	Congress Circle.	Electoral* Division.	Names in full of Delegates with honorary titles, scholastic degrees, etc.	Race, Religious denomination, and Caste, if any.	Occupation and Address.	Other Places or Associations for which they were also elected.	How and when elected.
1	Madras	Madras	Black Town 1st Metropolitan.	Mr. A. Sambamurthy Iyer, B.A., B.L.	Hindu, Brahmin.	Vakil, High Court	......	Public Meeting, 18th December, held at Pachiapa's Hall.
2	"	"	"	Mr. John Adam, M.A. ...	Christian, European.	Principal, Pachiappa's College, and Fellow, Madras University, Black Town.	......	do.
3	"	"	"	Rao Saheb Salla Gurusami Chetty, B.A., B.L.	Hindu	Merchant and Municipal Commissioner, Black Town.	......	do.
4	"	"	"	Mr. K. P. Viswanatha Iyer, B.A., B.L.	Hindu, Brahmin.	Vakil, High Court, Tondiarpett.	......	do.
5	"	"	"	Mr. E. Balasundra Mudelliar, B.A.	Hindu.	Secretary, Pachiappa's Charity, and Editor of the "Suguna Bodhini."	......	do.
6	"	"	"	Mr. A. O. Hume ...	Christian, European	Retired Civil Servant, Simla. General Secretary, Indian National Congress. Fellow, Calcutta University.	Allahabad & Calcutta.	Public Meeting, 18th December, held at Pachiappa's Hall, Public Meeting, Kayestha Patsala, 10th November, and at a Public Meeting held at Sobhabazar Rajbati, 21st October, 1888.
7	"	"	"	Mr. M. Ramaswamy Naidu	Hindu.	Manager, Tanjore Rama Naidu's Charity; Merchant and Contractor, Black Town.	......	Public Meeting, 18th December, held at Pachiappa's Hall.
8	"	"	"	Mr. T. Kanaya Naidu ...	do.	Dubash of Messrs. Arbuthnot & Co., Tondiarpett.	......	do.
9	"	"	"	Mr. V. J. Manickavalu Mudaliar.	do.	Printer and Publisher, Black Town.	......	do.
10	"	"	"	Mr. T. V. Apparow Naidu	do.	Merchant and Trustee of the Southern India Merchants Company (Limited), Black Town.	......	do.
11	"	"	"	Mr. G. Bakthavachulu Naidu.	do.	Dubash, Messrs. Walker & Co., Madras.	......	do.
12	"	"	"	Mr. N. Appalraju Garu	do.	Merchant, Black Town.	......	do.
13	"	"	"	Mr. K. Nathamuni Naidu	do.	do.	......	do.
14	"	"	"	Mr. C. Kristnaswamy Pillai.	do.	do.	......	do.
15	"	"	Egmore 2nd Metropolitan.	Rai Bahadur Salem Ramaswamy Mudaliar, M.A., B.L.	Hindu.	Vakil, High Court, Poonamallee Road, Municipal Commissioner, and Fellow, Madras University.	......	Public Meeting, Egmore.

* Electoral Divisions are of two kinds, 1st TERRITORIAL, as in England, and 2nd (to secure the representation of Minorities), SECTIONAL, each including a specia community, or an Association, Sabha, or Samaj, representing such.

Number.	Presidency or Government.	Congress Circle.	Electoral Division.	Names in full of Delegates with honorary titles, scholastic degrees, etc.	Race, Religious denomination, and Caste, if any.	Occupation and Address.	Other Places or Associations for which they were also elected.	How and when elected.
16	Madras	Madras	Egmore, 2nd Metropolitan.	Rai Bahadur P. Anandacharlu, B.L.	Hindu, Brahmin.	Vakil, High Court, and Municipal Commissioner, Poonamallee Road.	Mahajana Sabha, Madras.	Public Meeting, Egmore, and at a General Meeting of the Mahajana Sabha.
17	„	„	„	Mr. C. Sankara Nair, B.A., B.L.	Hindu.	Vakil, High Court, Egmore, Madras; Fellow, Madras University.	......	Public Meeting, Egmore.
18	„	„	„	Mr. P. Rajagopalacharlu, B.A., B.L.	Hindu, Brahmin.	Vakil, High Court, Egmore.	......	do.
19	„	„	Triplicane 3rd Metropolitan.	Mr. Eardley Norton, B.A.	Christian, European.	Barrister-at-Law and Coroner of Madras, Dunmore House, The Luz.	Triplicane Literary Society.	Public Meeting, 14th December, and at the Literary Society's Meeting, 17th December, 1888.
20	„	„	„	Mr. G. Subramania Iyer, B.A.	Hindu, Brahmin.	Editor, "The Hindu" (English), daily and "Swadesa Mitran" (Tamil bi-weekly), Triplicane.	......	Public Meeting, 14th December.
21	„	„	„	Mr. M. Viraraghavachariar, B.A.	do.	Joint Editor, "The Hindu" and "Swadesa Mitran," and Secretary, Mahajana Sabha, Triplicane.	The Mahajana Sabha, Madras.	Do. and at a Meeting of the Mahajana Sabha, 20th December.
22	„	„	„	Mr. S. Subramania Iyer, B.A., B.L.	do.	Vakil, High Court, Triplicane.	Triplicane Literary Society.	Public Meeting, 14th December, and at the Meeting of the Literary Society, 17th December.
23	„	„	„	Mr. T. V. Seshagiri Iyer, B.A., B.L.	do.	do. ...	......	Public Meeting, 14th December.
24	„	„	„	Mr. T. P. Kodandarama Iyer, B.A.	do.	Head Master, A. V. High School, Triplicane.	Triplicane Literary Society.	Do. and Meeting of the Literary Society, 17th December.
25	„	„	„	Mr. S. Varadachariar ...	do.	Printer and Bookseller, Triplicane.		Public Meeting, 14th December.
26	„	„	„	Mr. A. C. Parthasaradhi Naidu.	Hindu.	Editor, "Andhraprakasika," Hindu Press, Mount Road.	The S. I. Brahmo Samaj.	Do., and at a Meeting of the S. I. Brahmo Somaj.
27	„	„	„	Mr. W. Utham Chand Lall.	do.	Landed Proprietor, Triplicane.	Madras Kayestha Sabha of the Triplicane Association.	Public Meeting, 14th December, 1888, and at the Meeting of the Kayestha Sabha.
28	„	„	Mylapore 4th Metropolitan.	Mr. K. P. Sankara Menon, B.A., B.L.	do.	Vakil, High Court, Mylapore.	......	Public Meeting.
29	„	„	Madras Mahajana Sabha.	Mr. M. A. Singrachariar	Hindu, Brahmin.	Cashier, Bank of Madras, Triplicane.	......	At the General Meeting of the Mahajana Sabha, 20th December.
30	„	„	„	Mr. K. Sanku Wariyar, B.A.	Hindu.	Landholder, Calicut.	......	do.
31	„	„	„	Mr. Chandragiri Gopala Kristnama Naidu.	do.	Merchant. ...	......	do.
32	„	„	Triplicane Association	Mr. T. Balakristna Doss	do.	Landed Proprietor, Triplicane.	Madras Kayestha Sabha of the Triplicane Association.	At the General Meeting of the Kayestha Sabha.

Number.	Presidency or Government.	Congress Circle.	Electoral Division.	Names in full of Delegates with honorary titles, scholastic degrees, etc.	Race, Religious denomination, and Caste, if any.	Occupation and Address.	Other Places or Associations for which they were also elected.	How and when elected.
33	Madras	Madras	Triplicane Association	Mr. S. A. Raja Aiyar ...	Hindu, Brahmin.	Member, Triplicane Literary Society, Triplicane.	......	At the General Meeting of the Literary Society, 17th December, 1888.
34	,,	,,	,,	Mr. T. Rup Lall ...	Hindu.	Landholder, Triplicane.	Madras Kayestha Sabha of the Triplicane Association.	At the General Meeting of the Kayestha Sabha.
35	,,	,,	Vizagapatam.	Mr. Ram Dass Naidu Garu.	do.	Landholder and Merchant, Vizagapatam.	......	Public Meeting, 9th December.
36	,,	,,	,,	Mr. Jagannadha Sastri, B. A.	Hindu, Brahmin.	Pleader, District Court, and Secretary, Mahajana Sabha, Vizagapatam.	Mahajana Sabha of Vizagapatam.	Public Meeting, 9th December, and General Meeting, Mahajana Sabha.
37	,,	,,	Vizianagaram.	Rao Saheb Vijapurappa Anunta Row Puntulu Garu.	do.	Cashier, Bank of Madras, Bimlipatam ; President, Sub-Division Congress Committee ; and Chairman of M. C.	Bimlipatam.	Public Meeting, November, 1888, Bimlipatam.
38	,,	,,	Rajahmundry.	Rao Saheb N. Subba Rao Puntulu Garu, B.A., B.L.	do.	Vakil, High Court, and Municipal Councillor, Rajahmundry.	Cocanada and Ellore.	Public Meetings.
39	,,	,,	,,	Mr. D. Kasi Viswanadham.	Hindu, Komali.	Merchant, Rajahmundry.	......	Public Meeting.
40	,,	,,	Nellore	Mr. M. Venkatasulbiah Chetty.	Hindu	Municipal Councillor, Contractor and Merchant, Nellore.	Venkatagiri Town Hall, and Kavaly Literary Society, and Nellore Young Men's Literary Association.	Public Meetings.
41	,,	,,	,,	Mr. T. V. Venkatarama Iyer, B.A., B.L.	Hindu, Brahmin.	High Court Vakil, and District Board Member, Nellore.	do.	do.
42	,,	,,	Chingleput.	Mr. C. R. Chakrapani Iyengar.	do.	1st Grade Pleader, Chingleput.	......	Public Meeting.
43	,,	,,	Chittore (N. Arcot).	Mr. K. Devoo Mudelliar	Hindu.	Merchant and Mirasidar, Kaveripauk, Chittore.	Sri Agilajana Manoramia Sabha, Kaveripauk.	General Meeting of the S. A. M. Sabha, Kaveripauk, 20th December.
44	,,	,,	,,	Mr. T. A. Narasimhachariar.	Hindu, Brahmin.	Pleader, Chittore ...	The North Palar Division & the Chittore Native Association.	Public Meeting of the people of North Palar and at the General Meeting of the Chittore Native Association.
45	,,	,,	,,	Rao Saheb A. Subba Row.	do.	1st Grade Pleader, Municipal Councillor, District Board Member, and Secy., Hindu and Mahomedan Association, Kurnool.	Madhva Sabha, Tirupati.	General Meeting of the Madhva Sabha, Tirupati.
46	,,	,,	Cuddalore (S. Arcot).	Mr. T. N. Desikachariar	Hindu, Brahmin.	2nd Grade Pleader, Chedambaram (S. Arcot).	Chedambaram.	Public Meeting.
47	,,	,,	,,	Mr. V. Desikachariar ...	do.	do. ...	do.	do.
48	,,	,,	,,	Mr. M. Parthasarathy Raju	Hindu, Kshatriya.	Landholder, Member of the Madras M. J. Sabha, President of the Panrutti Public Association, and President, Panrutti Congress Committee, Panrutti, Cuddalore.	Panrutti Hindu Union Association & M. J. D. Society, Vathireddipalayam.	Public and Special Meetings.

Number.	Presidency or Government.	Congress Circle.	Electoral Division.	Names in full of Delegates with honorary titles, scholastic degrees, etc.	Race, Religious denomination, and Caste, if any.	Occupation and Address.	Other Places or Associations for which they were also elected.	How and when elected.
49	Madras	Madras	Tanjore	Mr. V. Neelamagachariar	Hindu, Brahmin.	Editor, "Jana Mitran," Kumbakonam.	......	Public Meeting and by a large body of electors appointed by the people, 2nd December, Kumbakonam.
50	„	„	„	Mr. T. M. Mookkanachari	Hindu.	Merchant, Kumbakonam.	......	do.
51	„	„	Negapatam.	Mr. Batta Sree C. R. Naraina Sastrial.	Hindu, Brahmin.	Sanskrit Pandit, Chedambaram.	......	Public Meeting, 19th December.
52	„	„	Trichinopoly.	Mr. Sundara Vaidianatha Gurusami Sarma.	do.	Lecturer in Trichinopoly.	Srirangam	Public Meetings at both places, 2nd December.
53	„	„	„	Mr. P. T. Streenivasa Iyengar, M.A.	do.	Professor, St. Joseph's College, Trichinopoly.	......	By an electoral College of 48 electors, 2nd December, 1888.
54	„	„	Madura	Mr. L. Narasimhachariar	do.	1st Grade Pleader and Sub-Divisional Zemindar, Madura.	Madura Union Class.	Public Meeting, 9th November.
55	„	„	Dindigal	Mr. P. N. Subramania Iyer.	do.	Pleader, Planter, and Secretary, Congress Committee, Dindigal.	......	Public Meeting convened by the District Congress Committee on the 25th November, 1888.
56	„	„	Tinnevelly	Mr. Peter Paul Pilla ...	Native Protestant Christian, Vellala.	Agent, Landholders Association, Madras Presidency, Hony. Magistrate, Srivilliputtur, Tinnevelly District.	Srivilliputtur.	Elected at Public Meeting, Tinnevelly, 10th December, and at Srivilliputtur, 29th November.
57	„	„	„	Mr. M. S. Sankara Iyer, B.A.	Hindu, Brahmin.	Head Master, Hindu High School, Srivilliputtur.	Sivakasi Srivilliputtur Viraduputti, Watrap, Rajapalayam, Sivagiri & Sankaranainar Coil	Public Meetings, Tinnevelly Sivakasi, Srivilliputtur, Viradupatti, Watrap, Rajapalayam, Sivagiri and Sankaranainar Coil, November, 1888.
58	„	„	Cuddapah	Rai Bahadur C. Jambulinga Mudaliar, B.A., M.L.	Hindu.	Vakil, High Court; Vice-President, District Board; and Municipal Councillor, Cuddapah.	......	Public Meeting, 28th November, 1888.
59	„	„	„	Rao Saheb Bellary Bujanga Row.	Hindu, Brahmin.	Mirasidar and District Board Member, Vayalpad.	Vayalpad	do.
60	„	„	„	Mr. Rayachoti Giri Row, B.A.	do.	Head Master, Congress High School, Madanapallee.	Madanapallee Debating Society.	do., and Meeting of the M. D. S. on the 29th November.
61	„	„	„	Mr. Varnasi Thimwa Reddy Garu.	Hindu, Sudra.	Landholder and Abkari Contractor, Piler.	Piler Division.	Public Meeting on the 30th November, 1888.
62	„	„	„	Mudupula Kemula Pellavelu Obul Reddy Garu.	do.	Landholder, Piler ...	do.	do.
63	„	„	„	Sreeman Nallan Chackravarti Vijia Raghava Charlu.	Hindu, Brahmin.	Priest, Piler ...	do.	do.
64	„	„	„	Mr. O. Lakshmana Sarma	Hindu, Brahmin.	Pleader, Madanapallee, and President of the Congress High School Committee, Madanapallee, Cuddapah.	Madanapallee Debating Society.	Public Meeting, 28th November, and Meeting of the M. D. S., 29th November, 1888.

Number.	Presidency or Government.	Congress Circle.	Electoral Division.	Names in full of Delegates with honorary titles, scholastic degrees, etc.	Race, Religious denomination, and Caste, if any.	Occupation and Address.	Other Places or Associations for which they were also elected.	How and when elected.
65	Madras	Madras	Kurnool	Mr. Midutur Rama Reddy	Hindu, Brahmin.	Landholder ...	......	Public Meeting, 30th November, 1888.
66	„	„	„	Mr. Chanugondla Hussain Reddy.	Mahomedan.	do. ...	......	do.
67	„	„	„	Rao Saheb T. Chedambara Row, B.A.	Hindu.	1st Grade Pleader, Kurnool; Municipal Councillor; President, Desàbhinani Sabha; President, Sanskrit School; Joint Secretary, Hindu and Mahomedan Association; and Secretary, Congress Committee, Kurnool.	......	do.
68	„	„	„	Mr. O. Burandin Sahib...	Mahomedan.	Manager, Municipal Office, Kurnool.	......	do.
69	„	„	„	Mr. Chanugondla Gokari Sahib.	do.	Landholder, Kurnool	......	do.
70	„	„	Bellary	Rai Bahadur A. Sabapathy Mudelliar.	Hindu.	Merchant, Landholder, and Chairman, Municipal Board, Bellary.	......	Public Meeting, 5th December.
71	„	„	„	Rao Saheb K. Venkata Row.	Hindu, Brahmin.	Municipal Councillor, 1st Grade Pleader, and Landholder, Bellary.	......	do.
72	„	„	„	Rao Sahib R. Rama Row, B.A.	do.	1st Grade Pleader, Bellary.	......	do.
73	„	„	„	Mr. R. Runga Row ...	do.	1st Grade Pleader and Landholder, Bellary.	......	do.
74	„	„	„	Mr. Thanakunty Humpayya.	Hindu, Weaver.	Cloth Merchant, Bellary.	......	Public Meeting, 9th December, 1888.
75	„	„	„	Mr. Kotra Kanda Runga Row.	Hindu, Brahmin.	1st Grade Pleader and Landholder, Bellary.	......	do.
76	„	„	„	Mr. Penukonda Rama Row.	do.	Pleader, District Court, and Municipal Councillor, Bellary.	S. M. S. A. Sabha, Triplicane, Madras.	Public Meeting and at the Meeting of the Madhva Brahmins.
77	„	„	Bellary Peoples' Association.	Mr. Sindigi Mariaidappa	Hindu.	Merchant, Bellary ...	......	At a General Meeting, 5th December.
78	„	„	„	Mr. Golaconda Kristnappa	Hindu, Komati.	do. ...	......	do.
79	„	„	„	Mr. Geriappa ...	Hindu.	do. ...	......	do.
80	„	„	Gooty	Rao Saheb P. Kesaya Pillai.	Hindu.	Pleader, Gooty. ...	Gooty People's Association, People of Anuntapur, Gooty, Tadputry, Pamidy, and Kistapad.	At a General Public Meeting, and at a Meeting of the people of Gooty and 40 adjacent villages, presided over by Revd. W. Stephenson, London Missionary, Gooty.
81	„	„	„	Rao Saheb J. Sreenivasa Row.	Hindu, Brahmin.	Vice-President of the Taluq Board, President of the Gooty Peoples' Association, and Landholder, Gooty.	do.	do.

Number.	Presidency or Government.	Congress Circle.	Electoral Division.	Names in full of Delegates with honorary titles, scholastic degrees, etc.	Race, Religious denomination, and Caste if any.	Occupation and Address.	Other Places or Associations for which they were also elected.	How and when elected.
82	Madras	Madras	Gooty	Mr. R. Seshiah ...	Hindu, Brahmin.	Chairman of Gooty Minor Panchayet, Gooty.	Gooty People's Association People of Anuntapur, Gooty, Tadputry, Pamidy, & Kistapad.	At a General Public Meeting, and at a Meeting of the people of Gooty and 40 adjacent villages, presided over by Revd. W. Stephenson, London Missionary, Gooty.
83	"	"	"	Mr. Chemulnagapallee Chenna Reddy Garu.	do.	Reddy of Chemulnagapallee, Taluq Board Member, and Ryot of Tadputry Taluq.	do.	do.
84	"	"	"	Mr. Jutur Naraina Reddy Garu.	do.	Reddy of Jutur, Tadputry Taluq.	do.	do.
85	"	"	Coimbatore	Mr. K. Naraina Sastriar, B.A., B.L.	Hindu, Brahmin.	Landholder, Mylapore, Madras.	Amravathi Mahajana Sabha, Kanyoor.	Meeting of the Members at Kadatur on the 29th November, 1888, and at a Public Meeting held at Coimbatore, December.
86	"	"	"	Mr. M. G. Arokiaswamy Pillai.	Native Christian.	Pleader, District Court, Coimbatore.	......	Public Meeting, 17th December.
87	"	"	"	Mr. Abdul Rahiman Sahib	Mahomedan.	Head Master, Mahomedan School, Satiamangalam.	......	do.
88	"	"	"	Mr. S. Kasturi Ranga Iyengar, B.A., B.L.	Hindu, Brahmin.	Vakil, High Court, Coimbatore.	......	do.
89	"	"	Salem	Rao Saheb Kadathoor Venkatachariar.	do.	Landholder and Member of the District Board, Salem.	......	Public Meeting, 25th November.
90	"	"	"	Mr. C. Vijiaraghavachariar, B.A.	do.	Pleader, Salem ...	....	do.
91	"	"	"	Mr. Pandit Gopala Iyengar.	do.	Sanskrit Pandit, Salem College.	......	do.
92	"	"	North Malabar.	Mr. Kolieth Ramuni ...	Hindu.	1st Grade Pleader, North Malabar, Tellicherry.	Kerala Sabha.	General Meeting of the Sabha.
93	"	"	Calicut Branch, Mahajana Sabha.	Mr. P. Govinda Menon...	do.	Landlord, Calicut ...	......	General Meeting of the Mahajana Sabha, Branch Calicut.
94	Govt. of India.	"	Secunderabad.	Mr. P. Ramachendra Pillai.	do.	Public Prosecutor, Secunderabad.	......	Public Meeting.
95	"	"	"	Mr. Mahomed Yusuf ...	Mahomedan.	Merchant ...	Koterugiri	do.
96	Bombay	Poona	Poona	Rao Bahadoor Vishnu Moreshwar Bhide.	Hindu, Brahmin.	Honorary Magistrate, Chairman, Poona Sarvajanik Sabha, & 1st class Pensioned Sub-Judge, Poona.	Poona Sarvajanik Sobha.	At a Public Meeting of the Inhabitants of the City and Cantonments of Poona, held on the 9th December, 1888.
97	"	"	"	R. S. Damodhur Vydyadhar Gokhale.	do.	Municipal Commissioner, Member, Sarvajanik Sabha, and Pleader, District Court, Poona.	......	do.
98	"	"	"	Mr. Narain Bapuji Kanitkar.	do.	Pleader, District Court, Poona.	......	do.
99	"	"	"	Mr. Vasudeo Laxuman Athavale.	do.	Banker and Member, Sarvajanik Sabha, Poona.	......	do.
100	"	"	"	Mr. Shivaram Hari Sathi	do.	Secretary, Poona Sarvajanik Sabha, Poona.	......	do.

Number.	Presidency or Government.	Congress Circle.	Electoral Division.	Names in full of Delegates with honorary titles, scholastic degrees, etc.	Race, Religious denomination, and Caste if any.	Occupation and Address.	Other Places or Associations for which they were also elected.	How and when elected.
101	Bombay	Poona	Poona	Row Sahib Mahadeo Ballal Namjoshi.	Hindu, Brahmin.	Journalist, Municipal Commissioner. Secretary, Provincial Conference, and Member, Deccan Education Society, Poona.	......	At a Public Meeting of the Inhabitants of the City and Cantonments of Poona, held on the 9th December, 1888.
102	,,	,,	,,	Mr. Balvant Anunt Deva	do.	Member, Sarvajanik Sabha, Poona.	......	do.
103	,,	,,	,,	Mr. Vishnu Venkatesh Behare.	do.	Inamdar, Poona ...	......	do.
104	,,	,,	,,	Mr. Vaman Balkrishna Ranade.	do.	Editor, "Dnyana Chokshu," Poona.	......	do.
105	,,	,,	,,	Mr. Balkrishna Narain Chitale, B.A., LL.B.	do.	do. ...	......	do.
106	,,	,,	,,	Mr. R. S. Gunput Rao Krishna Bavdekar, B.A.	do.	Member, Arbitration Court, Poona.	Arbitration Court.	do. and at a Meeting held on the 14th December, 1888.
107	,,	,,	,,	Mr. Krishna Rao Bapu Mande.	do.	Editor, Shivaji Press, and Member. Sarvajanik Sabha, Poona.	......	do.
108	,,	,,	,,	R. S. Amrit Shripat Nagpoorker.	do.	1st Class Honorary Magistrate, Concillator and Secretary, Poona, Arbitration Court, Poona.	......	do.
109	,,	,,	Junnar (Poona.)	Munshi Sheikh Hussen *Walad* Shaik Chand.	Mahomedan.	Public Lecturer, Junnar.	......	At a Public Meeting held at Junnar in December, 1888.
110	,,	,,	Narayangaum (Poona.)	Mr. Anunt Vaman Barvi.	Hindu.	Editor, "Ktakoha," Poona.	......	At a Public Meeting.
111	,,	,,	Talegaum (Poona.)	Mr. Gopal Vinayek Joshi.	do.	......	......	At a Public Meeting.
112	,,	,,	Mercantile Association (Poona.)	Mr. Vinayak Narain Apte.	do.	Merchant, Poona ...	......	At a Meeting of the Association held on the 2nd December, 1888.
113	,,	,,	Nasik	Mr. Vasudeo Balkrishna Takalkar.	do.	Municipal Commissioner, Honorary 2nd Class Magistrate, Nasik, Punchwal, Member of District Nasik Local Board and Taluqa L. B. of Niphad.	......	By a Public Meeting held on the 25th November, 1888.
114	,,	,,	,,	Mr. Sitaram Damoder Bhonde.	do.	Merchant ...	......	do.
115	,,	,,	,,	Mr. Laxman Rai Ramdas.	do.	Jahagirdar of Satuna and Assessor.	......	do.
116	,,	,,	,,	Mr. Raghoji Trimbuk Sanag.	do.	Municipal Commissioner, Nasik.	......	do.
117	,,	,,	,,	Mr. Sridhor Annaji Chandhore.	Brahmin.	Mukatiar, Vakil and Assessor.	......	do.
118	,,	,,	,,	Mr. Gonesh Pandurang Paranjpi.	do.	Pleader, District Court, Nasik.	......	do.
119	,,	,,	,,	Mr. Purshotam Sadashiv Matonge.	do.	do., and Municipal Commissioner.	......	do.
120	,,	,,	,,	Mr. Gangadhar Narsingh Ketkar.	do.	Municipal Commissioner and Secretary, Sarvajanik Sabha.	......	do.
121	,,	,,	,,	Mr. Kachardas Magaram Marwadi.	Hindu, Marwadi.	Merchant, Banker and Municipal Commissioner.	......	do.

Number.	Presidency or Government.	Congress Circle.	Electoral Division.	Names in full of Delegates with honorary titles, scholastic degrees, etc.	Race, Religious denomination, and Caste if any.	Occupation and Address.	Other Places or Associations for which they were also elected.	How and when elected.
122	Bombay	Poona	Nasik	Mr. Sridhar Gopal Patekar,	Brahmin,	Hindu, Missionary	......	By a Public Meeting held on the 25th November, 1888.
123	"	"	"	Mr. Janardan Raghunath Nimkar.	do.	District Pleader, Municipal Commissioner, Chairman, School Board and Health Committee.	......	do.
124	"	"	"	Mr. Ram Chandra Gonesh Mundle, B.A., LL.B.,	Hindu, Brahmin.	High Court Pleader, Bombay.	......	do.
125	"	"	"	Mr. Waman Rao Mahadeo.	Parbhu, Hindu.	Municipal Commissioner, Sinar; District Local Board; Pleader, Sub-Judge's Court, & Taluqa Local Board Member.	......	do.
126	"	"	"	Mr. Kashinath Gopal Deshapande.	Brahmin.	Member of Sinar Municipality.	......	do.
127	"	"	"	Mr. Anunt Raoji Kawale.	do.	Agriculturist and Vakil.	......	do.
128	"	"	"	Mr. Vittal Bhikaji Bhide.	do.	Pleader, Sub-Judge's Court, Pinpalgaon.	......	do.
129	"	"	"	Mr. Ganesh Raoji xirsagar.	do.	Pleader, Sub-Judge's Court, Satara and Member of Nasik.	......	do.
130	"	"	"	Mr. Ramakant Balvant thale.	do.	Pleader, Sub-Judge's Court, Yeola.	......	do.
131	"	"	"	Mr. Parshotam Damoder Barve.	do.	Sirdesham Kha and Member of Yeola Arya Somaj.	......	do.
132	"	"	"	Mr. Kacheshwar Sakharam Despande.	do.	Mukatiar and Member of Nasik District, Local Board and Taluka Local Board.	......	do.
133	"	"	"	Mr. Krishno Rao Trimbuk Marathi.	do.	Pleader, Sub-Judge's Court, Yeola, and Member of Yeola Municipality.	......	do.
134	"	"	"	Mr. Kabiroodin Bahar ...	Mahomedan.	do. ...	......	do.
135	"	"	Satara	Mr. R. B. Ganesh Pandurang.	Hindu, Brahmin,	Honorary Magistrate, Vice-President, Municipality, Satara.	......	By a Public Meeting held on the 9th December, 1888.
136	"	"	"	Mr. R. S. Balvant Shreedhar Saha.	do.	Municipal Commissioner, Satara, Pleader, Secretary, Sarvajanik Sabha.	......	do.
137	"	"	"	Mr. Raghunath Pandurang Karandikar.	do.	Pleader, and Secretary, Sarvajanik Sabha.	......	do.
138	"	"	"	R. S. Laxuman Balvant Mutalik.	do.	Honorary Magistrate, Municipal Commissioner, Inamdar.	......	do.
139	"	"	"	Mr. Mir Mohamed Roshan.	Mahomedan.	Teacher, Satara. ...	......	do.
140	"	"	Parsee Community Satara.	Mr. K. S. Framji Mancherji.	Parsee.	Merchant. ...	......	do.
141	"	"	Ashte Taluka Valve.	R. S. Govind Dhondeo Limaye.	Hindu, Brahmin.	do. ...	......	By a Public Meeting held on the 25th November, 1888.

Number.	Presidency or Government.	Congress Circle.	Electoral Division.	Names in full of Delegates with honorary titles, scholastic degrees, etc.	Race, Religious denomination, and Caste. if any.	Occupation and Address.	Other Places or Associations for which they were also elected.	How and when elected.
142	Bombay	Poona	Ashte Taluka Valve.	Mr. Balvant Narain Tagare.	Brahmin.	Merchant. ...	......	By a Public Meeting held on the 25th November, 1888.
143	,,	,,	,,	Mr. Moorarji Chopadi Sinde.	Maratha.	do.	......	do.
144	,,	,,	Karhad (Satara.)	Row Sahib Bhaskar Gopal Savarkar.	Hindu, Brahmin.	Municipal Commissioner, Satara. ...	......	By a Public Meeting held at Karodee on the 31st October, 1888.
145	,,	,,	,,	Mr. Mohamed Yusaff ...	Mohamedan.	Trader, Satara. ...	......	do.
146	,,	,,	,,	Mr. Hari Purshotam Kelkar.	Hindu, Brahmin.	Pleader. ...	......	By a Public Meeting on the 1st November, 1888.
147	,,	,,	,,	Mr. Jaganath Balaji ...	do.	Editor "Chitrogupta."	......	do.
148	,,	,,	Tasgaum (Satara.)	Row Sahib Ganapat Rao Yeshwant Joga.	do.	Banker. ...	......	By a Public Meeting held at Tasgaum.
149	,,	,,	,,	Mr. Anunt Narain Koulgikar.	do.	Editor. ...	......	do.
150	,,	,,	Ahmednagar	Row Sahib Keshava Vishwa Nath Patwardhan, B.A.	do.	Pleader, District Court, Municipal Commissioner and Chairman, Sarvajanik Sabha, Ahmednagar.	Ahmednagar Sarvajanik Sabha.	By a Public Meeting held at Ahmednagar on the 25th November, 1888, and by a Meeting of the Sabha
151	,,	,,	,,	Row Sahib Kashinath Balvant Lunaye.	do.	Editor and Proprietor, "Jagodadarsha" newspaper, Municipal Commissioner and Member of the Education Society, Ahmednagar.	......	do.
152	,,	,,	,,	Mr. Mohun Lal Hiralal...	Hindu, Kayest.	Pleader, & Merchant, Ahmednagar.	......	do.
153	,,	,,	,,	Mr. Shankar Vinayek Vabhale Kalkarani.	Hindu, Brahmin.	Pleader, District Court, Shopkeeper, Valandar, Kulkarni and Secretary, Sarvajanik Sabha.	......	do.
154	,,	,,	,,	Mr. Shivaram Ekanath Bharde.	do.	Teacher, Native Institution and Inamdar, Ahmednagar.	......	do.
155	,,	,,	,,	Mr. Shaharao Ram Krishna Moduk.	Christian.	Evangelist ...	The Naga Christian community.	Do. and special Meeting of the Churches.
156	,,	,,	,,	Mr. Anondorao Maroti Sangle.	do.	do., and Editor, "Dnyanodaya."	......	do.
157	,,	,,	Julgaum	Mr. Abaji Ragho Mhalasa	Hindu, Brahmin.	Pleader, Member of the Municipality and Chairman of School Board.	......	By a Public Meeting held on the 26th October, 1888.
158	,,	,,	Bhusawal	Mr. Chintamon Bapuji Maregaumkar.	do.	Pleader and the Vice-President of the Bhusawal Municipality.	......	By a Public Meeting held at Bhusawal on the 25th October, 1888.
159	,,	,,	Dhulia	Mr. Sukharam Ganesh ...	do.	Pleader and Member of the Municipality.	......	By a Meeting held on the 16th December, 1888.
160	,,	,,	,,	Mr. Vamon Vishun Athavale.	do.	do. ...	......	do.
161	,,	,,	,,	Mr. Balkrishna Hanmant.	do.	do. ...	......	do.
162	,,	,,	,,	Sheikh Chand, *Walad* Sheikh Bullan Munjaver.	Mahomedan.	Jagirdar. ...	......	do.
163	,,	,,	Amulner (Khandesh)	Mr. Wassudeo Daji Mathe.	Hindu, Brahmin.	Merchant, Landholder and Banker.	......	By a Public Meeting.

Number.	Presidency or Government.	Congress Circle.	Electoral Division.	Name in full of Delegates with honorary titles and scholastic degrees, &c.	Race, Religious denomination, or Caste, if any.	Occupation and Address.	Other Places or Associations for which they were also elected.	How and when elected.
164	Bombay	Poona	Amulner (Khandesh)	Mr. Ahmed Nurja ...	Mahomedan.	Landholder. ...	......	By a Public Meeting.
165	"	"	Sholapur	Mr. Mahadeo Ram Chandra Ranade.	Hindu, Brahmin.	Medical Practitioner, Sholapore.	......	By a Public Meeting held at Sholapur on the 28th October, 1888.
166	"	"	"	Mr. Kashinath Vasudeo Natu.	do.	Banker, Sholapore.	......	do.
167	"	"	"	Khan Saheb Haji Kazi Sultan Dost Mohamed.	Mahomedan.	Kazi City, Sholapore	Barsi	do. and at a Public Meeting held at Barsi on the 12th November, 1888.
168	"	"	"	Row Bahadur Sakharam Ram Chandra Kirloskar, B.A.	Hindu, Brahmin.	Vakil, High Court and Pleader, Sholapore, Bijapore District and President of the Sholapore Municipality.	do. and Bijapore.	do. and at a Meeting held at Bijapore on the 23rd December, 1888.
169	"	"	Pandharpore (Sholapore)	Mr. Narain Apaji Dixit.	do.	Secretary to the Pandharpore Municipality.	......	By a Public Meeting held at Pandharpore on the 21st October, 1888
170	"	"	Belgaum	Rao Saheb Sadasiva Balkrishna Bhate.	do.	Pleader, Belgaum ...	......	By a Public Meeting on the 2nd December, 1888.
171	"	"	"	Mr. Ellapa Virappa Jadhava.	Hindu.	do. ...	......	do.
172	"	"	"	Mr. Shripat Anunt Chatre.	do.	Pleader and Secretary, A. Nyaya Sabha.	......	do.
173	"	"	"	Mr. Anunt Mungesh ...	do.	Pleader, Belgaum ...	......	do.
174	"	"	"	Mr. Balkrishna Gangadhar Deshpande.	do.	do. ...	......	do.
175	"	"	"	Mr. Syed Shamsudin, *Walad* Bhukhareo.	Mahomedan.	Inamdar, Kolapore...	......	do.
176	"	"	"	Mr. Rahiman Saheb, *Walad* Abdoola Saheb.	do.	do. ...	......	do.
177	"	"	"	Mr. Syed Goushheb, *Walad* Makhtumsaheb.	do.	General Merchant ...	......	do.
178	"	"	"	Mr. Abdul Rahman, *Walad* Dostgeer Saheb Bashvan Peer Zade.	do.	Inamdar, Bastwad ...	......	do.
179	"	"	"	Mr. Ibrahim Saheb, *Walad* Hasan Mirja Khateeb.	do.	Honorary Magistrate and Inamdar, Sangli.	......	do.
180	"	"	"	Mr. Mahamadally, *Walad* Avaliya Saheb.	do.	Inamdar, Kamkarhatthi.	......	do.
181	"	"	"	Mr. Abdul Rahman, *Walad* Mohamed Kareem.	do.	Merchant. ...	......	do.
182	"	"	"	Mr. Fatehulmulk, *Walad* Asarkhan Sherkan-wala.	do.	do. ...	......	do.
183	"	"	Khanapore (Belgaum.)	Rao Saheb Krishnajee Chitamberdao Despande.	Hindu, Brahmin.	Inamdar and Member of D. L. Board.	......	By a Public Meeting at Khanapore.
184	"	"	Sankeswar (Belgaum.)	Mr. Vaman Kalkarni ...	do.	Landholder. ...	......	By a Public Meeting on the 18th December, 1888.
185	"	"	Sirsi	Mr. Pandappa Rampai ...	Saraswet Brahmin.	Merchant and Local Board Member.	......	By a Public Meeting held on the 4th December, 1888.
186	"	"	"	Mr. Anant Narayen Ranade	Brahmin.	Municipal Commissioner.	......	do.
187	"	"	"	Sitaram Hegde Ramai Hegde.	do.	Rayat.	......	do.
188	"	"	"	Vyankabhatta Venkabhatta Shante.	do.	do. ...	......	do.

Number.	Presidency or Government.	Congress Circle.	Electoral Division.	Names in full of Delegates with honorary titles and scholastic degrees, &c.	Race, Religious denomination, or Caste, if any.	Occupation and Address.	Other Places or Associations for which they were also elected.	How and when elected.
189	Bombay	Poona	Sirsi	Subbabhatta Deverbhatta.	Brahmin.	Rayat.	......	By a Public Meeting held on the 4th December, 1888.
190	,,	,,	,,	Bhavani Venkabhat Gonapbhatta.	do.	do. ...	......	do.
191	,,	,,	,,	Rudrappa Veerappa.	do.	Arshikeri. ...	......	do.
192	,,	,,	Wai Sarvajanik Sabha.	Mr. Ram Krishna Madheo Rao Vaidya.	do.	Secretary to the Sarvajanik Sabha, Wai Concilliator and Inamdar.	......	At a General Meeting of the Association held on the 4th August, 1888.
193	,,	,,	,,	Mr. Ram Chandra Krishna Kothawale.	do.	Member, District L. Board, Satara, Merchant.	......	do.
194	,,	,,	,,	Mr. Vinayak Amrit Pant Despande.	do.	Inamdar and Member L. Board.	......	do.
195	,,	,,	Inchalkaranjee.	Ramchandra Bahdeva Apte.	do.	Vakil and a Member of the Local A. V. School Committee.	......	At a Public Meeting held on the 16th November, 1888.
196	,,	,,	Hubli (Dharwar).	Syed Mahomed Saheb ...	Mahomedan.	... ...	......	By a Public Meeting held at Hubli.
197	,,	,,	,,	Munshi Hidayatulla ...	do.	... ...	......	do.
198	,,	,,	Bijapur	Sitaram Hanmantrao ...	Hindu, Brahmin.	Publisher ...	......	At a Public Meeting held on the 16th December, 1888.
199	,,	,,	,,	Khansaheb Haji Ibrahim Mutwalle.	Mahomedan.	Jahagirdar, Member, District and Local Board, Bijapur.	......	do.
200	,,	,,	,,	Row Sahib Sheshgir Rayajee.	Hindu, Brahmin.	Pleader and Member, Local Board Bijapur.	......	do.
201	Bombay	Bombay	Bombay Presidency Association.	The Hon'ble K. T. Telang, M.A., LL.B., C.I.E.	Hindu, Brahmin.	Member Bombay Legislative Council Advocate, Professor of Law. Fellow of the B. U.	Graduates' Association	At a Meeting of the Presidency Association on the 13th December, 1888, and at a General Meeting of the Graduates' Association.
202	,,	,,	,,	Mr. Hari Sitaram Dikshit, B.A., LL.B.	do.	Solicitor, Bombay, High Court, No. 2, Church Gate Street, Fort, Bombay.	do.	do.
203	,,	,,	,,	Mr. N. G. Chandavarkar, B.A., LL.B.	Hindu, Brahmin.	Pleader and Journalist	......	At a Meeting of the Bombay Presidency Association held on the 13th December, 1888
204	,,	,,	,,	Mr. Dinsha Eduljee Wacha, B.A.	Parsee.	Merchant. ...	......	do.
205	,,	,,	,,	Mr. Gonesh Ram Chundra Kirloskar, M.A., LL. B.	Hindu, Brahmin.	Vakil, High Court, Bombay.	......	do.
206	,,	,,	,,	Mr. T. Tookaram Tatya	Maharatta	Merchant. ...	......	do.
207	,,	,,	,,	Mr. Sadanand Trimbak Bhandare.	Hindu, Brahmin.	Head Salesman, Messrs. Wallace & Co.	......	do.
208	,,	,,	,,	The Hon'ble Pherozshah M. Mehta, M.A., LL. B.	Parsee.	Barrister-at-Law, Member, Bombay Legislative Council.	......	do.
209	,,	,,	,,	Mr. Dhondu Maraba, Sanzgiri, B.A., LL.B.	Gaud, Brahmin.	Vakil, No. 677, Girgaum, Bombay.	......	do.
210	,,	,,	,,	Mr. Gobordhan Dass ...	Hindu, Bhatia.	Mill-owner & Chairman to the Khatan Macconji.	......	do.
211	,,	,,	,,	Mr. Mathura Das Lila Dhur, Shamji, Jadavji Raghuji.	do.	Mill-owner. ...	......	do.
212	,,	,,	,,	Dr. Sadashiva Waman Kane, L.M.S.	Hindu, Konkonsth Brahmin.	Doctor, Plough Road Market Post, Bombay.	......	do.

Number.	Presidency or Government.	Congress Circle.	Electoral Division.	Names in full of Delegates with honorary titles and scholastic degrees, &c.	Race, Religious denomination, or Caste, if any.	Occupation and Address.	Other Places or Associations for which they were also elected.	How and when elected.
213	Bombay	Bombay	Bombay Presidency Association.	Mr. Lalla Bhai Ambalal Desai.	Hindu, Brahmin.	Pleader, Rajkot ...	Rajkot.	At a Meeting of the Bombay Presidency Association held on the 13th December, 1888, and by a Public Meeting.
214	"	"	Graduates Association, Bombay.	Mr. Ganesh Krishna Desmukh, B.A., LL.B.	do.	Do., High Court, Land-holder and Zemindar and Editor, "Native Opinion," Bombay.	Ratnagiri, Bassein & Prant Association.	At the Meetings of the Associations and at a Public Meeting of Ratnagiri on 11th November, 1888.
215	"	"	Bombay Dasa Shriwali Bania, Community	Mr. Ramdin Das Keshwaji	Hindu, Bania.	Doctor, Pellow Road, Market Post, Bombay.	Bombay Presidency Association	At the Meeting of the Community and at the Meeting of the Association on the 13th December, 1888.
216	"	"	"	Mr. Ardeshir Kavasjee Setna.	Parsee.	Barrister-at-Law, Ahmedabad.	Do., and Ahmedabad.	At a Meeting at Ahmedabad and at the Meetings of the Community and of the Bombay Presidency Association on the 13th December, 1888.
217	"	"	"	Mr. Dinsha D. Davor ...	do.	Barrister-at-Law ...	Bombay Presidency Association and Bombay Graduates' Association	At the Meetings of the Bombay Presidency Association on 13th December, 1888, and at Bombay Graduates' Association and Bania Community.
218	"	"	"	Mr. Rustam K. R. Cama, B A., LL.B.	do.	Solicitor ...	do.	do.
219	"	"	Jain Association.	Mr. Wirchand Raghobji Gandi, B.A.	Jain.	Honorary Secretary to the Jain Association, India, and Articled Clerk to the Government Solicitor.	Bombay Presidency Association	At the Meeting of the Bombay Presidency Association on the 13th December, and at the Public Meeting of Jain Association on 9th December, 1888.
220	"	"	Jain Association.	Fakir Chand Prem Chand Rai Chand.	do.	Exchange Broker ...	.....	By the Meeting of the Jain Association on 9th December, 1888.
221	"	"	"	Manik Lal Ghelloybhoy Javeri.	do.	Jeweller ...	.....	do.
222	"	"	Arya Gannavardhok Sabha, Bombay.	Mr. Chuni Lal Lalubhai Parekh.	Hindu, Bania.	Merchant, Withal Dadi, No. 2. Bombay; Vice-President, Gannavardhok Sabha, Bombay.	Bombay Presidency Association, and Ahmedabad Viramgaum, Lhasna (Kaina).	At the Meeting of Bombay Presidency Association on 13th December, 1888, and at the Meetings of Gannavardhok Sabha, Ahmedabad, Viramgaum and Lhasna.
223	"	"	Audichhy Hitachhoo Sabha, Bombay.	Mr. Girija Shankar Kashiram Dwivedi.	Hindu, Brahmin.	Editor, "Rajya Bhukta" and "Swadhu Misthi," Bombay.	Bombay Presidency Association Audichhy Hitachhoo Sabha, Ahmedabad, Dhocka, Loonawada and Bhavnagore.	At the Meeting of Bombay Presidency Association on 13th December, 1888, and at the Meetings of Audichhy Hitacchhoo Sabha, Ahmedabad, Dhocka, Loonawada and Bhavnagore.
224	"	"	Bombay	Mr. Fatehulmulk	Mahomedan.	Inamdar.	......	By a Public Meeting.
225	"	"	Jambusar (Bombay.)	Seth Jugmohun Das Vandravan Das.	Hindu, Porwad Bania.	Banker, Bombay, the Head of the "Dasa Purwad Bania Community."	Bombay Presidency Association Purwad Bania Community	At the Meeting of Pesidency Association on 13th December, 1888, and at the Public Meetings of Jambusur and Purwad Bania Community.
226	"	"	Thana	Mr. Damodor Kashinath Vartak.	Hindu, Brahmin.	Subordinate, Government Pleader, Bassein, Thana District.	Bassein Mahim, Dahaun Association	By Public Meetings held at Bassein, Mahim and Dahaun in the District on the 18th November, 1888, and at a Meeting of the Thana Association on 2nd December, 1888.

Number.	Presidency or Government.	Congress Circle.	Electoral Division.	Names in full of Delegates with honorary titles and scholastic degrees, &c.	Race, Religious denomination, or Caste, if any.	Occupation and Address.	Other Places or Associations for which they were also elected.	How and when elected.
227	Bombay	Bombay	Thana	Mr. Govinda Rao Babaji Sendi.	Hindu, Brahmin.	Missionary. ...	Bassein Mahim, Dahaun Association	By Public Meetings held at Bassein, Mahim and Dahaun in the District on the 18th November, 1888, and at a Meeting of the Thana Association on 2nd December, 1888.
228	"	"	Ratnagiri	Mr. Woman Vinayok Showche.	do.	Pensioner, Chairman, City Municipality, Ratnagiri.	......	By a Public Meeting held at Ratnagiri on 11th November, 1888.
229	"	"	"	Mr. Govind Shastri Bin Ram Chundra Shastri Shewde.	do.	Landlord ...	......	do.
230	"	"	"	Rao Saheb Lakshman Dhonduv Katre.	do.	Pleader, District Court, Ratnagiri; Municipal Commissioner and Member of the District Local Board.	......	do.
231	"	"	"	Mr. Dhondo Mahadeo Barve.	do.	Pleader, Sub-Judge's Court, Dapoli, District Ratnagiri, and Member of the Taloka Local Board, Dapoli.	......	do.
232	"	"	"	Mr. Mohamed Isub, *walad* Abdool Karim Lalla.	Mahomedan.	Merchant, Municipal Commissioner and Member of the Local Board.	......	do.
233	"	"	Kolaba	Mr. Rawji Hari Athaolay.	Hindu, Brahmin	Editor, "Satyasadhan Newspaper," Alibag.	......	At a Meeting held at Kolaba on the 16th December, 1888.
234	"	"	"	Mr. Sukhram Parsharam. Ghaisas.	do.	Sheristadar, Sir Yyayadhist Janjira.	......	do.
235	"	"	"	Mr. Vinayak Vasudeo Barve.	Hindu, Brahmin.	District Pleader ...	......	do.
236	"	"	"	Mr. Vinayak Shevarao Dharkar.	Hindu, Kyastha.	Zemindar Khot and Merchant.	......	do.
237	"	"	"	Mr. Waman Bapuji Deva.	Hindu, Brahmin.	Landholder & Merchant, Kolaba.	......	do.
238	"	Kurrachee.	Sindh Sabha.	Rao Bahadoor Govindbuksh Awatrai.	Hindu, Khetri.	Pleader, Assistant Public Prosecutor, Zemindar, Vice-President. Sukkur Municipality and Member. District Board, Shikarpur.	......	At a Meeting of the Sabha in November, 1888.
239	"	"	"	Mr. N. Gupta. ...	Hindu.	Editor and Proprietor of the Phœnix, and Municipal Commissioner, Kurrachi.	......	do.
240	"	"	"	Rao Saheb Pesumul Zokiram.	do.	Pleader and Municipal Commissioner, Sukkur.	......	do.
241	"	"	"	Rao Saheb Tahilram Khemchand, B.A., LL.B.	do.	Pleader and Municipal Commissioner, Kurrachi.	......	do.
242	"	"	"	Rao Saheb Harchandrai Vishnudas, B.A., LL.B.	do.	Pleader and Municipai Commissioner, Kurrachi and Member, Taluk Local Board, Kotri, Kurrachi District.	......	do.
243	"	"	Sukker	Mr. Mulraj Sujan Singh.	do.	Zemindar. ...	......	At a Public Meeting.
244	"	Guzerat	Kaira and Panch-Mahal.	Khan Saheb Jemadar Yasuf Ali Yacoob Ali, B.A.	Mahomedan.	Landholder, Naosar (Native Place Tharda, Kaira Division.	Neriad Association.	Public Meetings held on 16th December and 22nd November, 1888.

Number.	Presidency or Government.	Congress Circle.	Electoral Division.	Names in full of Delegates with honorary titles, scholastic degrees, &c.	Race, Religious denomination, and Caste, if any.	Occupation and Address.	Other Places or Associations for which they were also elected.	How and when elected.
245	Bombay	Guzerat	Ahmedabad.	Rao Sahib Keshavlal Motilal.	Hindu	District Pleader and Municipal Commissioner, Ahmedabad.	Neriad Association.	By two separate Public Meetings held on the 22nd November, 1888.
246	"	"	"	Mr. Kalidas Sankal Chand.	Jain.	Editor and Proprietor of the "Ahmedabad Times."	......	By a Meeting held on the 22d November, 1888.
247	"	"	"	Mr. Desai Jivanlal Veaj Rai.	Hindu.	......	......	do.
248	"	"	Prija Hitabardhuk Sabha, Surat.	Rao Saheb Mohanlal Runchhod Das Jhaviri.	do.	Government Pensioner, Deputy Educational Inspector & Chairman, Congress Committee, Surat.	......	At the Meeting of the Association on the 9th December, 1888.
249	"	"	"	Mr. Balwant Rao Tripurashunkur Dave.	do.	District Pleader, Surat.	.. ...	do.
250	"	"	"	Rao Saheb Mancharam Bhagvanjee.	do.	Landholder ...	Broach.	do. and at a Public Meeting on the 25th November, 1888.
251	"	"	Broach	Mr. Hiralal Ichalal Moozoomdar.	do.	Zemindar, Broach ...	......	By a Public Meeting on 25th November, 1888.
252	"	"	"	Rao Saheb Keshavram Kasiram.	do.	Government Sub-Pleader. Aukleshur. Chairman, Aukleshur Municipality and Secretary, Congress Sub-Divisional Committee, Aukleshur.	Aukleshur.	By Public Meetings on the 24th and 25th November, 1888.
253	"	"	Gannodoya Sabha, Broach.	Mr. Anupram Mithalal Deenbandhu.	Hindu, Brahmin.	Secretary, "Gonnodhya Sabha."	Jambusor.	By a Public Meeting on the 25th November, 1888.
254	"	"	"	Dr. Manilal Mohunlal Jhaviri.	Hindu, Bania.	President, "Ganno doya Sabha," Medical Officer in charge, Kundla Dispensary.	......	do.
255	"	"	"	Mr. Mahomed Ali Ahmed Ali.	Mahomedan.	Artist and Photographer.	......	do.
256	"	"	Kattywar	Mr. Vinayakrao Ganapatrao Kolhare.	Hindu, Prabhu.	Barrister-at-law, Rajkot.	Rajkot.	By a Public Meeting on 16th December, 1888.
257	"	"	"	Mr. Sitaram Neelkanta Pundit.	Hindu, Dakshini. Brahmin.	do.	do.	do.
258	"	"	"	Mr. Ghanesham Neelkanta Pundit, B.A., LL.B.	do.	High Court Pleader, Rajkot.	do.	do.
259	Govt. of India.	Berar.	Amraoti	Mr. Rangnath Narasing Mudholkar, B.A., LL.B.	Hindu, Brahmin.	High Court Pleader, Amraoti.	......	At a Public Meeting held on the 25th November, 1888.
260	"	"	"	Mr. Antaji Govind Keskar	do.	do.	......	do.
261	"	"	"	Mr. Wasudev Narain Jog.	do.	do.	......	do.
262	"	"	"	Mr. Balkrishna Hari Karandikar.	do.	do.	......	do.
263	"	"	"	Mr. Vishwanath Kashinath Kale.	do.	......	......	do.
264	"	"	"	Mr Rama Chandra Narasinh Mudholkar, L.M.S.	do.	Medical Practitioner,	......	do.
265	"	"	Ellichpur	Mr. Moro Vishuanath Joshi, B.A., LL.B.	do.	High Court Pleader and Municipal Commissioner, Amraoti.	......	At a Public Meeting held on the 23rd October, 1888.
266	"	"	"	Mr. Narayan Keshav Deshapande.	do.	Special Magistrate ...	......	do.
267	"	"	Bassein	Mr. Yashavant Vamba Digha.	do.	Pleader, Bassein. ...	......	At a Public Meeting.

Number.	Presidency or Government.	Congress Circle.	Electoral Division.	Names in full of Delegates with honorary titles and scholastic degrees, &c.	Race, Religious denomination, or Caste if any.	Occupation and Address.	Other Places or Associations for which they were also elected.	How and when elected.
268	Govt. of India.	Berar.	Mangrul (Bassein).	Mr. Laxman Atmaram Mahajan.	Hindu, Brahmin.	Merchant. ...	......	At a Public Meeting at Mangrul, on the 2nd December, 1888.
269	"	"	Pershah Taluk (Bassein).	Mr. Raja Udaram Shankar Rao.	do.	Jaghirdar. ...	......	At a Public Meeting.
270	"	"	Baldana	Mr. Gopal Waman Bapat, B.A.	do.	......	... ..	At a Public Meeting held at at Baldana on the 1st September, 1888.
271	"	"	"	Mr. Dattatraya Vishnu Bhagabat, LL.B.	do.	Pleader, High Court, Akola.	......	do.
272	"	"	"	Mr. Gulam Ahmad Soudagar.	Mahomedan.	Merchant. ...	......	do.
273	"	"	Akola	Mr. Rao Saheb Devarao Vinayak.	Hindu, Brahmin.	Pleader, Akola and Vice-President, Akola Municipality.	......	At a Public Meeting, 16th October, 1888.
274	"	"	"	Mr. Shankar Govind ...	do.	Pleader, Akola. ...	......	do.
275	"	"	Berar, Sarvajanik Sobha.	Mr. Pralhad Narayan Jog, B.A., LL.B.	do.	Pleader, High Court	......	At a Public Meeting of the Sabha held on the 28th October, 1888.
276	"	"	"	Mr. Yashavant Govind Keskar.	do.	Editor, "Pramode Sindhu," Amraoti.	......	do.
277	"	"	"	Mr. Vyankatesh Ramchundra Mudholkar.	do.	Editor, "Vaidarbha of Kola."	......	do.
278	Central Provinces.	Nagpore	Mandla	Mr. Jagannath Pershad Choudhari.	Kalar. ...	Zemindar, Maharajpore, C. P., Mandla.	......	By a Public Meeting, 3rd November, 1888.
279	"	"	"	Mr. Gopal Das ...	Brahmin.	Contractor. ...	......	do.
280	"	"	"	Mr. Chowdhari Jagan Nath.	Hindu....	Landlord. ...	......	do.
281	"	"	"	Mr. Seth Chedilal ...	Agarwala.	Municipal Commissioner, and Banker.	......	do.
282	"	"	Narsingpore Dharam Sabha.	Mr. Ganesh Ram Mantri	Hindu, Brahmin.	Zemindar, and Honorary Magistrate.	......	Meeting of Dharam Sabha, 24th December, 1888.
283	"	"	"	Munshi Jiwan Lal ...	Hindu....	Legal Practitioner ...	......	do.
284	"	"	"	Mr. Baliram Narayan Deshmookh, B.A.	do.	Landlord. ...	Malguzari Sabha.	do. and Meeting of the Malguzari Sabha of 12th December.
285	"	"	Nagpore	Babu Bipin Krishna Bose, M.A., B.L.	do.	Advocate, Municipal Member; and Member, Loka Sabha.	Loka Sabha, Nagpore.	By a Public Meeting held in December, and by a Meeting of the Managing Committee, Loka Sabha, Nagpore.
286	"	"	"	Mr. Sham Rao Krishnaji Jackate.	do.	Pleader... ...	Malguzari Sabha.	Public Meeting of 3rd December, and by the Managing Committee Meeting, 12th December, 1888.
287	"	"	"	Mr. Sada Shiva Jairam, B.A.	Hindu, Brahmin.	Professor, Hislop College, Nagpore.	......	By a Public Meeting held on the 3rd December, 1888.
288	"	"	"	Mr. Bhagiratha Prosad, B.A.	Hindustani Kalar, Hinduism.	Professor of Mathematics, Hislop College, Nagpore; Municipal Member, Nagpore; Member, Loka Sabha, Central Provinces; Member and Treasurer, Temperance Association.	......	do.

Number.	Presidency or Government.	Congress Circle.	Electoral Division.	Names in full of Delegates with honorary titles, scholastic degrees, &c.	Race, Religious denomination and Caste, if any.	Occupation and Address.	Other Places or Associations for which they were also elected.	How and when elected
289	Central Provinces.	Nagpore	Nagpore	Mr. Martand Bapooji Waikar	Hindu, Brahmin.	Pleader and Member, Loka Sabha, Nagpore.	......	By a Public Meeting held on the 3rd December, 1888.
290	"	"	"	Pandit Bapu Rao Dada, M.A.	Mahratta, Brahmin.	Pleader: Secretary, Loka Sabha; Municipal Commissioner; and Landlord.	......	do.
291	"	"	"	Pandit Krishna Rao Govind Deshpande, M.A.	do.	Professor, Morris College; and Member, Loka Sabha.	......	do.
292	"	"	"	Mr. Raghoba Rattiram ...	Hindu.	Landlord; Municipal Commissioner, Saoner, District Nagpore.	......	do.
293	"	"	Jubbulpore	Baboo Kali Charan Bose	Bengali, Kayasth.	Head Master, Hitkarni School; Editor, "Shubh Chintaka," Weekly Anglo-Hindi Paper.	......	At a Public Meeting of the inhabitants of the town, consisting of Mahajans, Zemindars, Pleaders & men of other professions and trades, 23rd November.
294	"	"	"	Lala Jankee Prasad ...	Kaistha.	Pleader. ...	......	do.
295	"	"	"	Baboo Debi Prasad Chobey	Hindu, Brahmin.	Malguzar and Banker, Jubbulpore.	......	do.
296	"	"	"	Mr. Gungadhur Chintaman Mandape.	Mahratta Brahmin.	Head Clerk, District Engineer's Office, G. I. P. Railway.	......	Elected at a Public Meeting, 23rd November.
297	"	"	"	Mr. D. Raghubar Prasad	Brahmin.	School Master. ...	......	do., and at a General Meeting held on 5th December, 1888.
298	"	"	"	Mr. Bihari Lal, B.A. ...	do.	do. ...	......	By a Public Meeting, 23rd November.
299	"	"	"	Mr. Lakshmi Narayan Agnihotri.	do.	do. ...	......	do.
300	"	"	"	Baboo Purna Chandra Mukerjee	Hindu.	Pleader...	......	do.
301	"	"	"	Rajah Aman Singh ...	do.	Landlord. ...	......	do.
302	"	"	Hoshangabad.	Mr. Prag Chand Chowdhury	do.	Zemindar. ...	......	By a Public Meeting on 9th October.
303	"	"	"	Pandit Sukhdeo Prasad...	Brahmin.	Pleader, Hoshangabad.	......	do.
304	"	"	"	Mr. Jagan Nath Prasad	do.	Pleader, Hoshangabad; Member, District Council; and Secretary. Loka Sabha and Bipro Sabha.	......	do.
305	"	"	"	Baboo Hari Dass Gosh, M.A., B.L.	Hindu, Kyastha.	Pleader. ...	......	At a Meeting on the 16th December, 1888.
306	"	"	"	Babu Kalli Dass Chowdhury, B.A.	Hindu....	Pleader, Landholder; Secretary, Standing Congress Committee and Branch Loka Sabha.	Harda.	Do., and Meeting on the 6th November, 1888
307	"	"	Sohagpore.	Mr. Kashi Ram Tiwari...	do.	Landlord.	......	By a Public Meeting on 18th December, 1888.
308	"	"	Burhanpore (Nimar.)	Mr. Luxmon Moreshewar	Hindu, Brahmin.	Public Preacher; Agent, Berar Agricultural Association.	......	do.
309	"	"	"	Mr. Ram Chandra Bapuji	Hindu...	Malguzar; Member, Loka Sabha.	......	do.

Number.	Presidency or Government.	Congress Circle.	Electoral Division.	Names in full of Delegates with honorary titles, scholastic degrees, &c.	Race, Religious denomination, and Caste, if any.	Occupation and Address.	Other Places or Associations for which they were also elected.	How and when elected.
310	Central Provinces.	Nagpore	Dungargarh.	Mr. Purshotum Mudhro Rao Rajalwar.	Brahmin.	......	......	At a Meeting, 9th December, 1888.
311	"	"	"	Mr. Govind Rao Hari Mankeshwar.	do.	Contractor and Pleader, Khairgarh State, Dungargarh.	......	do.
312	"	"	Rajnundgaon (Raipur.)	Mr. V. Sarangpani Moodliar	Hindu.	Contractor; Manager, Bolaram Dass' Press.	......	At a Public Meeting.
313	"	"	Khandwa	Babu Hari Dass Chatterji, M.A., B.L.	Brahmin.	Pleader; Secretary, Branch Loka Sabha and Branch Standing Congress Committee.	Burhanpore.	At Meetings held 22nd and 29th November.
314	"	"	Saugor	Seth Mohan Lall ...	Hindu.	Banker and Mahajan Tahsil Khurai	......	By a Meeting held on the 12th December, 1888.
315	"	"	"	Seth Luchmi Chund ...	do.	do.	......	do.
316	"	"	"	Mr. Gopal Lakshmana Shrikhande.	do.	Legal Practitioner ...	......	By a Meeting held on 6th November, 1888.
317	"	"	"	Baboo Kali Prossono Mookerji, B.A., B.L.	Brahmin.	Pleader and Member, District Council, Saugor.	......	do.
318	"	"	"	Baboo Tara Prassanna Sen, B.A., B.L.	Hindu, Vaidya.	Pleader, Saugor, and Vakil, High Court, Calcutta, and Hony. Magistrate, Howrah.	Saugor Hita Sabha.	Public Meeting held on the 6th November, 1888, and Meeting of the Hita Sabha.
319	"	"	Wardha	Mr. Wasdeo Krishna Abhyankar.	Hindu Mahratta, Brahmin.	Malguzar; Cultivator; and Secretary, Local Board.	.	By a Public Meeting of voters elected by three Tahsils of Wardha District, 20th December.
320	"	"	"	Mr. Keshavrao Mahadev Kavle	do.	Pleader, Member of Municipality and District Council, & Vice-Chairman of District Council, Wardha.	......	do.
321	"	"	"	Mr. Luxman Govind Deuskar.	do.	Cultivator and Pleader, Member of Municipality of Arvi District, Wardha; Member of District Council.	......	do.
322	"	"	"	Mr. Hari Vaman Kelkar, B.A., LL.B.	do.	Pleader, Member of Municipality.	......	do.
323	"	"	"	Mr. Washudeo Rao Pranjpe	Hindu. ...	Pleader, Wardha ...	......	do.
324	"	"	Harda	Pundit Narayan Rao Govind Paroolkar.	Brahmin.	Zemindar, Honorary Magistrate; President, Harda Municipality, and Vice-President, Loka Sabha, Nagpore.	......	By a General Meeting, 6th November, 1888.
325	"	"	"	Pandit Sadashiva Ram Chandra Patwardhan.	do.	Pleader, Proprietor and Editor of the "Nyayoaodha," Zemindar and a Member of Municipality, Harda.	......	do.
326	"	"	"	Pandit Bhikaji Vinayak Naik.	do.	Zemindar; Secretary, Harda Branch of Loka Sabha, Nagpore.	......	do.
327	"	"	"	Pandit Raghu Nath Rao Vama Kakera.	do.	do.	......	do.

Number.	Presidency or Government.	Congress Circle.	Electoral Division.	Names in full of Delegates with honorary titles, scholastic degrees, etc.	Race, Religious denomination, and Caste, if any.	Occupation and Address.	Other Places or Associations for which they were also elected.	How and when elected.
328	Central Provinces.	Nagpore	Harda	Pandit Balwant Rao Ganesh Naik,	Brahmin.	Zemindar ; Secretary, Harda Branch of Loka Sabha, Nagpore.	......	By a General Meeting 6th November, 1888.
329	Govt. of India.	„	Central India Association, Mhow.	Babu Mohendro Nath Chatterjee.	Hindu, Brahmin.	Pleader, Mhow, Central India.	.....	By a General Meeting held on the 20th December, 1888.
330	„	„	„	Kesho Sakhram Bapat ...	do.	Teacher, 1st Assistant. Khan Bahadoor. Edulji Pestonji's School, Mhow.	.. ...	do.
331	„	„	C. I. Association, Indore.	Lala Dharama Chandra ...	Jain.	Photographer, Indore	......	do.
332	Punjab	Lahore	Lahore	Mr. Golak Nath Chatterjie, B.A.	Christian	Professor, Govt. College.	Indian Christian Association of Lahore.	Elected 23rd Nov., 1888, and 17th Dec., 1888, respectively.
333	„	„	„	Lala Narain Dass ...	Abloowalya.	Pleader, Hoshiarpur	......	do.
334	„	„	„	Mr. I. C. Sarkar, C.E. ...	Christian	Landholder in Oudh ; Retired Executive Engineer, S. P. D.	......	At a Public Meeting, 21st Dec., 1888.
335	„	„	„	Mr. Sangam Lall, LL. ...	Hindu.	Pleader, Lahore ...	......	Public Meeting held on 23rd Nov., 1888.
336	„	„	„	Mr. Nund Lall ...	do.	Cloth Merchant Lahore.	......	do.
337	„	„	„	Baboo Kali Prosonno Roy, M.A., B.L.	Hindu.	Pleader, Chief Court	Lahore Indian Association.	Do., and by a Meeting of the Association.
338	„	„	„	Mr. Bhagat Ram ...	do.	Barrister-at-Law, Lahore.	do.	do.
339	„	„	„	Mr. Lakhsmi Narain, M.R.A.S., F.S.A.	Hindu, Kayesth.	do. ...	do.	do.
340	„	„	„	Mr. Charles Golak Nath, B.A., LL.B.	Punjabi, Christian.	do. ...	do.	do.
341	„	„	„	Sirdar Dyal Singh Majethia.	Sikh.	Jageerdar, Lahore ; Amritsar; President, Indian Association, Lahore.	do.	do.
342	„	„	„	Lala Kanhaiya Lall ...	Hindu, Bhatta.	Pleader, Chief Court	do.	do.
543	„	„	„	Mr. Nathu Ram ...	Agarwalla.	Editor ...	......	Public Meeting, 23rd Nov., 1888.
344	„	„	„	Pundit Sattya Nand Agnihotri.	Devo Dhurmo.	Editor, and Missionary of the Devo Dhurmo Mission.	......	do.
345	„	„	„	Dr. Permanund ...	Khetri, Arya.	Surgeon-Dentist, Lahore.	......	do.
346	„	„	„	Baboo Jogendro Chandra Basu, M.A., B.L.	Hindu.	Pleader, Chief Court, Lahore ; Vice-President, Indian Association.	......	do.
347	„	„	„	Mr. Balmokund ...	Khetri	Merchant, Lahore ...	......	do.
348	„	„	Hissar	Lala Lajpat Rai ...	Hindu, Bania.	Pleader, Hissar ...	......	By a Public Meeting on the 12th Dec., 1888.
349	„	„	„	Lalla Chhahil Dass ...	do.	Banker, Hissar ...	......	do.
350	„	„	„	Lalla Gauri Sankar ...	do.	Rais, Hissar ...	......	do.
351	„	„	„	Lalla Churamoni ...	do.	Pleader, Hissar ...	......	do.
352	„	„	Ferozepore	Lalla Dindial ...	Kaystha, Aryan.	Pleader, Ferozepone	......	23rd Dec., 1888, at a Public Meeting.

Number.	Presidency or Government.	Congress Circle.	Electoral Division.	Names in full of Delegates with honorary titles, scholastic degrees, etc.	Race, Religious denomination, and Caste, if any.	Occupation and Address.	Other Places or Associations for which they were also elected.	How and when elected.
353	Punjab	Lahore	Ferozepore	Pandit Moolraj ...	Brahmin, Aryan.	Pleader, Ferozepore; and Municipal Commissioner.	......	23rd Dec., 1888, at a Public Meeting.
354	"	"	Amritsar.	Lala Shahoo Nath ...	Hindu, Khetri.	Merchant, Amritsar, Punjab.	......	Public Meeting, Dec. 12th, 1888.
355	"	"	"	Bhai Harnam Singh ...	Sikh.	Private Service ...	......	do.
356	"	"	"	Bhai Narain Singh ...	do.	Pleader, Amritsar; Municipal Commissioner; Inspector, and Indian Law Publisher.	......	do.
357	"	"	"	Mr. Balmakund ...	Hindu, Khetri.	Private Service, care of Veroo Mull Kapoor, Kutra Churt Singh, Amritsar, Punjab.	......	do.
358	"	"	"	Mr. Govind Singh ...	do.	Shawl Merchant ...	......	do.
359	"	"	Gurdaspur	Mr. Ram Saran Dass ...	do.	Gurdaspur, Pleader	......	By Public Meeting on the 2nd Nov., 1888.
360	"	"	"	Mr. Guru Charan Dass ...	do.	Pleader; President, Gurdaspur Municipality.	......	do.
361	"	"	Hoshiarpur	Shaik Umr Baksh, B.A. H.A.	Mahomedan.	Pleader. ...	......	Elected at a Public Meeting, 15th Dec., 1888.
362	"	"	"	Mr. Davee Dial ...	Agurwala, Bania, Bishnoo faith.	Pleader, Hoshiarpur.	......	do.
363	"	"	Gujranwala.	Lala Dhuni Ram, B.A. ...	Khanna, Khetri.	Govt. College, Lahore.	......	By a Public Meeting held on the 9th December, 1888.
364	"	"	"	Mr. Kahan Chand ...	Hindu.	Pleader, Gujranwala.	......	do.
365	"	"	"	Mr. Chuni Lall ...	do.	Mukhtar, Gujranwala.	......	do.
366	"	"	"	Mr. Jivan Kishen ...	do.	Pleader, Gujranwala.	......	do.
367	"	"	"	Moulvi Muhammed Mahbub Alam	Mahommedan.	Editor, "Vaisa Akbar"	......	do.
368	"	"	"	Mr. Sardari Mal ...	Hindu. ...	Pleader, Gujranwala.	"Aror Bans" of Gujranwala.	Do., and at a Meeting of the Aror Bans of Gujranwala held on the 22nd Dec., 1888.
369	"	"	Jullundur	Bakshi Sohan Lal ...	Hindu. ...	Pleader. ...	......	At a Public Meeting on the 2nd December, 1888.
370	"	"	"	Pundit Sheo Narayan ...	Brahmin Pundit, Kashmiri.	Pleader, Chief Court, Punjab.	......	do.
371	"	"	"	Pundit Devi Chund ...	Brahmin.	Pleader, Chief Court.	......	do.
372	"	"	"	Mr. Madan Gopal ...	Hindu, Khetri.	Pleader, Chief Court, Punjab.	......	do.
373	"	"	Dharamsala.	Bakhshi Jaishi Ram ...	Hindu.	Pleader, Chief Court, and Zemindar.	......	At a Public Meeting held on the 1st December, 1888.
374	"	"	"	Captain A. T. Banon ...	English, Christian.	Zemindar, Kooloo-Kangra, and late Bengal Staff Corps.	......	Public Meeting held on the 1st December, 1888.
375	"	"	"	Lala Thakoor Dass ...	Abloowalay.	Pleader, Chief Court, Dharamsala, Kangra.	......	do.
376	"	"	Umballa	Lala Murli Dhar ..	Hindu.	Pleader. ...	......	At a Public Meeting.

Number.	Presidency or Government.	Congress Circle.	Electoral Division.	Names in full of Delegates with honorary titles, scholastic degrees, etc.	Race, Religious denomination, and Caste, if any.	Occupation and Address.	Other Places or Associations for which they were also elected.	How and when elected.
377	Punjab	Lahore	Umballa	Lala Than Singh ...	Hindu.	Contractor. ...	......	At a Public Meeting.
378	"	"	Ludhiana	Khoaja Abad Shah ...	Mahomedan.	Merchant. ...	......	By Public Meeting held on the 12th December, 1888.
379	"	"	"	Sheikh Ahmadjan ...	do.	do. ...	......	do.
380	"	"	"	Mr. Durga Dat ...	Hindu, Agarwalla.	Pleader, Jullundur. ...	......	do.
381	"	"	"	Syed Sardar Ali Sahib	Mahomedan.	Zemindar, Municipal Commissioner.	......	do.
382	"	"	"	Syed Jati Shah Sahib ..	do.	do. ...		do.
383	"	"	"	Sheik Sharfuddin ...	Mahomedan.	Journalist, Editor and Managing Proprietor, "Moshiri Hindi" Press, Ludhiana.		do.
384	"	"	Dera-Ismail-Khan.	Mr. Jhinda Ram ...	Hindu, Khetri.	Pleader, Chief Court, Dera-Ismail-Khan, and Secy., Congress Committee, Dera-Ismail-Khan.	......	Public Meeting held on the 19th Dec.
385	"	"	"	Mr. Hira Nand ...	Arya.	Mukhtar. ...	......	do.
386	"	"	"	Mr. Assa Nand ...	do.	Mukhtar of a Rais ...	......	do.
387	"	"	"	Kazi Abdul Ghofoor ...	Mahomedan.	...	......	do.
388	"	"	Multan	Baba Parduman Singh ...	Sikh.	Pleader, Multan ...	......	In a Public Meeting on 7th Dec., 1888.
389	"	"	"	Mr. Chetan Anand, B.A.	Arya.	Pleader, Municipal Commissioner.	......	do.
390	"	"	"	Pandit Jamayat Rai ...	Brahmin.	Priest and Municipal Commissioner.	......	do.
391	"	"	Rawalpindi.	Mr. Hans Raj Sawhuij ...	Khetri, Arya.	Pleader, Chief Court, Rawalpindi.	Rawalpindi Association, Rawalpindi Sukhvaik Sabha.	By Public Meeting on 14th Dec., 1888, and Meetings of the Associations.
392	"	Delhi	Delhi	Lala Gopal Rao ...	Hindu, Agarwal.	Banker. ...	......	By a Public Meeting held on the 2nd December, 1888.
393	"	"	"	Lala Girdhari Lal ...	Hindu, Vaish.	Pleader and Municipal Commissioner.	......	do.
394	"	"	"	Lala Pyare Lal ...	Jain.	Vakil, High Court...	......	do.
395	"	"	"	Lala Jugal Kishore ...	Hindu, Kayesth.	Pleader, Chief Court	......	do.
396	"	"	"	Babu Hem Chunder Sen, L.M.S.	Hindu.	Medical Practitioner, Delhi.	......	do.
397	"	"	"	Mr. Umrao Mirza Hairat.	Mahomedan.	Author of several vernacular books.	......	do.
398	"	"	"	Moulvi Sayad Moulana Abu Mansur, Imam-i-fani Manazra (order of Mejdi.)	Mahomedan	Author of several religious books.	......	do.
399	"	"	"	Mr. Mohammad Ismail	Mahomedan.	Proprietor of landed property, Delhi.	......	do.
400	"	"	"	Moulvi Syad Nasrat Ali...	Mahomedan, Syad.	Editor of " Nasrutul-Akbar," Delhi.	......	do.
401	"	"	"	Mr. Kedar Nath ...	Hindu, Vaish.	Pleader, Delhi. ...	......	do.

Number.	Presidency or Government.	Congress Circle.	Electoral Division.	Names in full of Delegates with honorary titles, scholastic degrees, &c.	Race, Religious denomination, and Caste, if any.	Occupation and Address.	Other Places or Associations for which they were also elected.	How and when elected.
402	Punjab	Delhi	Delhi	Lala Girdhari Lal ...	Hindu, Khettry.	Pleader, Chief Court.	......	By a Public Meeting on the 19th December, 1888.
403	„	„	„	Mr. P. C. Mukerji, M.A.	Hindu, Brahmin.	Professor of Physical Science, St. Stephen's College, Delhi.	......	do.
404	„	„	„	Kanvar Badhri Krishen...	Hindu.	Rais and Pleader ...	......	do.
405	„	„	„	Mir Yakub Ali ...	Mahomedan.	Special Pleader and Proprietor of landed property, Faridabad, Delhi District.	......	do.
406	„	„	„	Lala Durga Prasad ...	Hindu, Vaish.	Banker ...	......	do.
407	„	„	„	Lala Shambhoo Dial ...	Hindu.	Merchant, Delhi. ...	......	do.
408	„	„	„	Lala Sanwal Das ...	do.	Cloth Agent, Chandni Chowk.	......	do.
409	„	„	„	Lala Ramsur Das ...	do.	Pleader, Gurudaspore	......	do.
410	„	„	„	Lala Damodar Das, B.A.	Hindu, Vaish.	Banker	......	do.
411	„	„	„	Moulvi Mansur Ali ...	Mahomedan.	Proprietor of the Nasrut-ul-Akbar.	......	do.
412	N.-W. P. & Oudh.	Lucknow.	Lucknow.	Pundit Luchman Prosad	Brahmo.	Preacher. ...	......	do.
413	„	„	„	Mr. Thaker Prosad ...	Hindu, Kayastha.	Pleader. ...	......	do.
414	„	„	„	Munshi Mahomed Ibrahim.	Mahomedan.	Draftsman. ...	Unjuman Mohamadi.	do.
415	„	„	„	Hakim Mahomed Askari	do.	Physician. ...	......	do.
416	„	„	„	Lala Surjoo Prosad ...	Hindu.	Service. ...	......	do.
417	„	„	„	Babu Bissonath Rai ...	do.	Government Pensioner and House Proprietor.	......	do.
418	„	„	„	Babu Kali Dass Sircar ...	do.	Do. ...	......	do.
419	„	„	„	Nawab Kasim Ali Khan	Mahomedan.	Wasikadar, & Rais.	Unjuman Mohamadi.	do.
420	„	„	„	Mirza Abbas Hossein ...	do.	Rais. ...	......	do.
421	„	„	„	Nawab Mahmood Ali Khan Bahadoor.	do.	Rais, Rampore, uncle of the present Chief.	......	do.
422	„	„	„	Sheikh Ashgar Ali ...	do.	Merchant. ...	......	do.
423	„	„	„	Babu Ishri Doyal ...	Hindu, Kayastha.	Vakil. ...	......	do.
424	„	„	„	Pundit Sree Kissen ...	Hindu, Brahmin.	Rais. ...	......	do.
425	„	„	„	Nawab Ahmud Hossen Khan.	Mahomedan.	Wasikadar, & Rais...	......	do.
426	„	„	„	Munshi Abdool Rahman	do.	Trader. ...	......	do.
427	„	„	„	Munshi Ashraf Ali ...	do.	Rais. ...	......	do.
428	„	„	„	Babu Bhuban Mohan Banerjee, B.A.	Hindu. Brahmin.	Professor of Science and Mathematics, Christian College.	......	do.
429	„	„	„	Babu Bepin Behary Bose, M.A.	Hindu.	Vakil, High Court....	Refa-i-am Association	do., and a Meeting of the Association.

Number.	Presidency or Government.	Congress Circle.	Electoral Division.	Name in full of Delegates with honorary titles and scholastic degrees, &c.	Race, Religious denomination, or Caste, if any.	Occupation and Address.	Other Places or Associations for which they were also elected.	How and when elected.
430	N.-W. P. & Oudh.	Lucknow.	Lucknow	Babu Bhubon Mohun Roy	Hindu.	Merchant, Secretary, Brahmo Samaj.	Refa-i-am Association.	At a Public Meeting held on the 19th December, and a Meeting of the Association.
431	"	"	"	Babu Sreeram, M.A., B.L.	do.	Zemindar, Vakil, High Court; Public Prosecutor, Oudh, Judicial Commissioner's Court; Secretary, Refa-i-am Association; & Mucipal Commissioner.	do.	do.
432	"	"	"	Babu Ram Gopal Vidyanta.	do.	Assistant Engineer, Oudh and Rohilkhund Railway, and Director, Upper India Couper Mills Company, Limited.	do.	do.
433	"	"	"	Babu Bansi Lall Singh ...	do.	Zemindar, Vakil, High Court; Chairman of the Board of Directors of Upper India Couper Mills Company, Limited.	Refa-i-am Association, and Khetri and Saratswati Sabha.	Do., and at a Meeting of the Khetrio and Saratswati Sabha.
434	"	"	Refa-i-am Association, Lucknow.	Munshi Mahomed Sajjad Hosein.	Mahomedan.	Zemindar, Editor & Proprietor, "Oudh Punch."	Jalsa Tehzeeb.	By a Meeting of the Association.
435	"	"	"	Mr. Hamid Ali Khan, F.R.A.S., M.R.A.S.	do.	Barrister-at-law, Mafidar, Amroha District, Vice-President, Refai-am Association, and Municipal Commissioner.	......	do.
436	"	"	"	Pundit Sham Narayan Musladan.	Hindu.	Zemindar ...	......	do.
437	"	"	"	Pundit Bishan Narayan Dar.	do.	Barrister-at-law and Secretary, Kashmiri National Club.	......	do.
438	"	"	"	Nawab Ahamad Ali Khan	Mahomedan.	Wasikadar, & Rais...	......	do.
439	"	"	"	Sheikh Raza Hossein Khan.	do.	Ellakadar, Municipal Commissioner, Life President, Refa-i-am Association.	......	do.
440	"	"	"	Mir Sadik Hossein ...	do.	Rais. ...	......	do.
441	"	"	"	Munshi Mahomed Mirza Jan.	do.	do. ...	......	do.
412	"	"	"	Mirza Nadir Hossein *alias* Munnay Aga.	do.	do. ...	......	do.
443	"	"	"	Sheikh Mahomed Ahsan Hossain Khan.	do.	do. ...	......	do.
444	"	"	"	Sheik Mahomed Yusuf Hossain Khan.	do.	do. ...	......	do.
445	"	"	"	Maulvi Mohamed Serajuddin.	do.	do. ...	......	do.
446	"	"	"	Nawab Hashmut Hossein Khan.	do.	Wasikadar, & Rais...	......	do.
447	"	"	"	Syed Hadi Hossain Khan	do.	do. ...	......	do.
448	"	"	"	Mr. Yusuf Ali Khan ...	do.	do. ...	......	do.
449	"	"	"	Munshi Mahomed Abdool Baseer.	do.	Assistant Secretary, Refa-i-am Association.	......	do.

Number.	Presidency or Government.	Congress Circle.	Electoral Division.	Name in full of Delegates with honorary titles and scholastic degrees, &c.	Race, Religious denomination, or Caste, if any.	Occupation and Address.	Other Places or Associations for which they were also elected.	How and when elected.
450	N.-W. P. & Oudh.	Lucknow.	Rafai-am Association, Lucknow.	Rev. Ram Chander Bose, M.A.	Christian, Protestant.	Missionary, Methodist Mission, Lucknow.	Bengal Christian Conference and Bengal Christian Alliance.	At the Meeting of the Rafa-i-am Association, and at the Meetings of the Bengal Christian Conference and Bengal Christian Alliance.
451	"	"	"	Nawab Mahomed Mirza	Mahomedan.	Rais. ..	...	By a Meeting of the Association on the 19th December, 1888.
452	"	"	"	Nawab Baker Mirza ...	do.	do. ...	......	do.
453	"	"	"	Nawab Mahomed Taki Ali Saheb.	do.	do. ..	......	do.
454	"	"	"	Mirza Mahomed Kasim...	do.	do. ...		do.
455	"	"	Aujuman Mahamadi, Lucknow.	Khuaja Ali Mahomed Bhimjee.	do.	Late Manager, Indore Cotton Press.	......	By a Meeting of the Anjuman on the 23rd December, 1888.
456	"	"	"	Munshi Mohamed Amir Ahmed.	do.	Secretary, Anjuman Mahamdai, Lucknow.	......	do.
457	"	"	"	Nawab Baker Mirza ...	do.	Rais. ...	......	do.
458	"	"	"	Prince Alijah Mirza Mahomed Hossein Ali Khan Bahadoor.	do.	Wasikadar. ...	......	do.
459	"	"	"	Prince Sikundar Hadur Mirza Mahomed Ahmed Ali Bahadoor.	do.	do. ...	......	do.
460	"	"	"	Prince Nawab Jafer Ali Khan Bahadoor.	do.	do. ...	......	do.
461	"	"	"	Nawab Mobarak Hossain Khan.	do.	do. ...	......	do.
462	"	"	"	Nawab Valayet Hossain Khan	do.	do. ...	......	do.
463	"	"	"	Nawab Ali Mahommed Khan.	do.	do. and President, Anjuman Mahamadi.	......	do.
464	"	"	"	Mirza Masum Ali ...	do.	Wasikadar. ...	......	do.
465	"	"	"	Mirza Mahomed Murteza *alias* Machu Beg	do.	Rais. ...	......	do.
466	"	"	"	Munshi Mahomed Hidayat Rasul.	do.	do. ...	......	do.
467	"	"	"	Moulvi Golam Mahomed Mohadis.	do.	do. ...	......	do.
468	"	"	"	Khuaja Syud Fareedudin.	do.	do. ...	......	do.
469	"	"	"	Sheikh Husammuddin	do.	do. ...	......	do.
470	"	"	"	Aga Syud Mehdi Raza ...	do.	do. ...	......	do.
471	"	"	Khetrio & Saratswati Sabha, Lucknow.	Munshi Gunga Prasad Varma.	Hindu.	Editor and Proprietor, "Hindustani," Managing Proprietor of the "Advocate," Municipal Commissioner and Secretary, Oudh Standing Congress Committee.	......	By a Meeting of the Khetrio and Saratswati Sabha.
472	"	"	"	Mr. Kedar Nath ...	Hindu, Khetry.	Vakil, N.-W. P., High Court.	......	Do., and at a Public Meeting.
473	"	"	"	Mr. Luchmon Dass ...	do.	do. ...	......	do.

Number.	Presidency or Government.	Congress Circle.	Electoral Division.	Name in full of Delegates with honorary titles and scholastic degrees, &c.	Race, Religious denomination, or Caste, if any.	Occupation and Address.	Other Places or Associations for which they were also elected.	How and when elected.
474	N.-W. P. & Oudh.	Lucknow.	Khetrio & Saratswati Sobha, Lucknow.	Mr. Ram Dass Varma	Hindu, Khetry.	Banker, Zemindar, Editor, "Dinkar Prakash."	......	By a Meeting of the Khetrio and Saratswati Sobha, and at a Public Meeting.
475	"	"	"	Mr. Raja Ram Varma ...	do.	Banker, Treasurer, Oudh and Rohilkhund Railway	......	do.
476	"	"	"	Pundit Gyaneshwarjee ...	Hindu, Brahmin.	Priest and President, Khetrio and Saratswati Sabha.	......	do.
477	"	"	"	Pundit Shew Nath Misser	do.	Do., and Assistant Secretary, Khetrio and Saratswati Sabha.	......	do.
478	"	"	Jalsa Tahzib, Lucknow.	Pundit Jagat Narain Mulloh, B. A.	do.	Pleader, Vice-Chairman.	......	By a Public Meeting and Meeting of the Association.
479	"	"	"	Pundit Suraj Narain Bahadoor.	do.	Secretary, Jalsa Tahzib.	......	do.
480	"	"	Youngman's Association, Lucknow.	Mr. L. B. Bose	Christian.	President, Youngmen's Association, Lucknow,	......	Do. and Meeting of the Association.
481	"	"	(Kakari), Lucknow.	Munshi Hamiduddeen ...	Mahomedan.	Rais Kakari. ...	......	By a Public Meeting.
482	"	"	Fyzabad	Mr. Gokul Chand ...	Hindu, Khetry.	Zemindar, Pleader, Honorary Magistrate, Vice-Chairman of Municipal and District Board.	.. ...	do.
483	"	"	"	Mr. Hari Singh ...	Hindu, Vaish.	Banker, Zemindar and Municipal Commissioner.	......	do.
484	"	"	"	Babu Ram Saran Dass, M.A., M.A.S., and Fellow, Allahabad University.	Hindu, Kayastha.	Zemindar and Secretary, Oudh Commercial Bank ; President, Anjuman Tahzib ; Municipal Commissioner and Honorary Magistrate.	......	do.
485	,	"	"	Munshi Salig Ram, B.A.	do.	Zemindar & Pleader.	......	do.
486	"	"	"	Munshi Baluk Ram ...	do.	do.	......	do.
487	"	"	"	Mr. Rughu Nundun Bajpai.	Hindu, Brahmin.	Government Pensioner.	......	do.
488	"	"	"	Sheikh Kedar Bux ...	Mahomedan.	Merchant, Honorary Magistrate, Vice-Chairman, District Board, and Municipal Commissioner.	......	do.
489	"	"	"	Munshi Imtiaz Ali, B.A....	do.	Pleader.	......	do.
490	"	"	"	Sardar Salig Singa ...	Sikh.	Talukdar.	......	do.
491	"	"	"	Mr. Monohur Lall Manocha.	Hindu.	Pleader, Secretary, Municipal Board.	......	do.
492	"	"	"	Pundit Bisseswar Nath Hangel.	do.	Pleader and Zemindar, Akbarpur.	......	do.
493	"	"	Bara Banki	Moulvi Mahomed Nasim, B.A.	Mahomedan.	Pleader. ...	......	do.
494	"	"	"	Mr. Panna Lall ...	Hindu, Khetry.	do. ...	......	do.
495	"	"	"	Pundit Purmeshiri Dass	Hindu, Brahmin.	do., and Honorary Magistrate and Municipal Commissioner.	......	do.

Number.	Presidency or Government.	Congress Circle.	Electoral Division.	Name in full of Delegates with honorary titles and scholastic degrees, &c.	Race, Religious denomination, or Caste, if any.	Occupation and Address.	Other Places or Associations for which they were also elected.	How and when elected.
496	N.-W. P. & Oudh.	Lucknow.	Bara Banki	Mr. Brij Mohun Lal ...	Hindu, Kayastha.	Pleader. ...	......	By a Public Meeting.
497	"	"	Sitapur	Munshi Murli Dhur ...	do.	do. and Municipal Member.	......	do.
498	"	"	"	Pundit Makhun Lal ...	Hindu, Brahmin.	Pleader. ...	......	do.
499	"	"	"	Mr. Hur Gobinda Doyal, M.A.	Hindu, Kayastha.	Govt. Pleader. ...	......	do.
500	"	"	"	Mr. Buldeo Prosad ...	Hindu, Khetry.	Vakil, High Court, and Hony. Magte.	......	do.
501	"	"	"	Seth Changa Mall ...	do.	Banker. ...	......	do.
502	"	"	"	Mr. Kanhya Lall ...	Hindu, Vaish.	Pleader. ...	......	do.
503	"	"	"	Pundit Suraj Prosada ...	Hindu, Brahmin.	Religious Teacher....	......	do.
504	"	"	"	Mr. Pitam Roy ...	Hindu, Kayastha.	Zemindar, Honorary Magistrate, and Vice-Chairman, Municipal Board.	......	do.
505	"	"	"	Mr. Chotey Lall, M.A. ...	do.	Vakil, Secretary, Municipal Board and Hony. Magistrate.	......	do.
506	"	"	"	Pundit Hurshai ...	Hindu, Brahmin.	Pensioned Sub-Judge.	......	do.
507	"	"	Kheri	Syed Mahomed Ibrahim Khan.	Mahomedan.	Talookdar. ...	......	do.
508	"	"	"	Hafiz Syad Jamaluddin...	do.	Muafidar. ...	......	do.
509	"	"	"	Kazi Zamin Ali ...	do.	Zemindar. ...	......	do.
510	"	"	"	Sheikh Mahomed Hossain	do.	Merchant. ...	......	do.
511	"	"	"	Pundit Burma Nand ...	Hindu, Brahmin.	Banker. ...	......	do.
512	"	"	"	Seth Dwarka Dass ...	Hindu, Khaitria.	Do. and Zemindar and Municipal Member.	......	do.
513	"	"	"	Mr. Sheo Bux Roy ...	Hindu, Vaish.	Pleader and Zemindar.	......	do.
514	"	"	"	Pundit Lalta Prosad ...	Hindu, Brahmin.	Pleader. ...	......	do.
515	"	"	"	Babu Kumar Chunder Bhuttacharjee.	do.	do. ...	......	do.
516	"	"	Partabgarh	Raghubans Sahai ...	Hindu, Kayastha.	Pleader, Partabgarh, Oudh.	......	By a Public Meeting held on the 7th December, 1888.
517	"	"	"	Syed Alim Saheb ...	Mahomedan.	do. ...	......	do.
518	"	"	"	Syed Moulvi Mir Mahomed Saheb.	do.	do. ...	......	do.
519	"	"	"	Dewan Ran Bijay Bahadur Singa.	Hindu, Chattre.	Talookdar, Koodhora.	......	do.
520	"	"	"	Bakshee Uday Bham ...	Hindu, Kayastha.	Service, Partabgarh.	......	do.
521	"	"	Rampore	Lala Ramdial ...	do.	Zemindar and Karinda to His Highness Raja Rampal Singh Bahadoor.	.....	By a Public Meeting.
522	"	"	"	Munshi Jumna Prosad Saheb.	Hindu.	Zemindar. ...	Partabgarh.	Do., and by a Public Meeting held at Partabgarh on the 7th December, 1888.

Number.	Presidency or Government.	Congress Circle.	Electoral Division.	Name in full of Delegates with honorary titles and scholastic degrees, &c.	Race, Religious denomination, or Caste, if any.	Occupation and Address.	Other Places or Associations for which they were also elected.	How and when elected.
523	N.-W. P. & Oudh.	Lucknow.	Kalakanker	Pundit Ram Lal Munshi	Hindu.	Karinda to His Highness Raja Rampul Singh Bahadoor and Zemindar.	......	By a Public Meeting on the 9th December, 1888.
524	„	„	Rai Bareli	Meer Khadim Hossain ...	Mahomedan.	Zemindar, Rai Bareli.	......	By a Public Meeting.
525	„	„	Ajodhia	Babu Charu Chunder Ghosh.	Hindu, Kayastha.	Private Medical Practioner and Municipal Member.	Anjumani Tahzib.	Do., and at a Meeting of the Association.
526	„	„	Moradabad	Meer Wahid Ali Rizwi...	Mahomedan.	Zemindar. ...	......	By a Public Meeting on the 19th December, 1888.
527	„	„	„	Moulvi Sahebuddin Khan	do.	Service. ...	......	do.
528	„	„	„	Pundit Banwari Lal Misra.	Hindu.	Proprietor, "Sitara Hind" Newspaper.	......	do.
529	„	„	„	Mr. Amba Pershad ...	do.	Editor, Jama-ul-ulam.	......	do.
530	„	„	„	Babu Narendra Chunder Bose.	do.	Vakil. ...	......	do.
531	„	„	„	Lala Kunj Behari Lal ...	do.	Editor, "Churpooz" Newspaper.	......	do.
532	„	„	„	Pundit Pertab Kishen Aga	do.	Proprietor and Editor. "Rabber" Newspaper, Moradabad.	......	do.
533	„	„	Arya Somaj, Bijnour.	Pundit Radha Kishen ...	do.	President, Arya Somaj.	......	At a Meeting of the Somaj on the 18th December, 1888.
534	„	„	Bijnour	Jairaj Singh ...	do.	Pleader, Zemindar and Municipal Commissioner.	......	By a Special Meeting held on the 29th December, 1888.
535	„	„	Bareilly	Mr. Badri Nath Chaturvedy, M.A.	Brahmin.	Professor, Mathematics and Physical Science, Ramsay College, Almora, Kumaon.	......	At a Public Meeting held at the Town Hall on the 6th December, 1888.
536	„	„	„	Lala Narain Dass ...	Agarwala.	Banker. ...	......	At a Public Meeting held on the 5th December, 1888.
537	„	„	„	Munshi Thakur Pershad	Hindu, Kayastha.	Zemindar, Editor, "Dubdubai Kuisri," & Municipal Commissioner.	......	do.
538	„	„	„	Babu Preo Nath Bannerjee.	Hindu, Brahmin.	Pleader, High Court, N.-W. P.	......	do.
539	„	„	„	Pundit Chedda Lal, B.A.	do.	Zemindar.	......	do.
540	„	„	„	Mr. Seeta Ram	Hindu, Kayastha.	Contractor, Firm of Messrs. Seetaram and Co.	......	do.
541	„	„	„	Mr. Tribani Sahai ...	do.	Pleader. ...	......	At a Public Meeting held in the Institution.
542	„	„	„	Babu Baldeo Pershad ...	do.	do. ..	......	do.
543	„	„	„	Mr. Behary Lal Mookerjee.	Hindu, Brahmin.	......	......	do.
544	„	„	„	Babu Kali Prosonno Banerjee.	do.	Vakil. ...	......	At a Public Meeting held at the Town Hall on the 6th December, 1888.
545	„	„	Shahjehanpur.	Babu Baiconto Nath Sircar.	Hindu.	Pleader, Judge's Court, Shahjehanpur.	......	By a Public Meeting held on the 18th December, 1888.
546	„	„	„	Pundit Bisheshur Nath Bham.	do.	Vakil. ...	......	do.

Number.	Presidency or Government.	Congress Circle.	Electoral Division.	Name in full of Delegates with honorary titles and scholastic degrees, &c.	Race, Religious denomination, or Caste, if any.	Occupation and Address.	Other Places or Associations for which they were also elected.	How and when elected.
547	N.-W.-P. & Oudh.	Lucknow.	Shahjehanpur.	Munshi Bukhtawar Singh	Hindu.	Zemindar, Printer and Publisher and Editor, "Arya Durpan" & "Ayna Riazi."	......	By a Public Meeting held on the 18th December, 1888.
548	"	"	"	Babu Hur Govind Bannerjee.	do.	Retired Deputy Collector.	......	do,
549	"	"	"	Lala Seeta Ram ...	do.	Contractor. ...	......	do.
550	"	"	Faridpore	Mr. Augan Lal ...	do.	Zemindar. ...	......	At a Public Meeting held on the 6th December, 1888.
551	N.-W. P.	Allahabad.	Allahabad	The Hon'ble Pundit Ajoodhianath.	Hindu, Brahmin.	Vakil, High Court, N.-W. P., Member, Legislative Council, N.-W. P. & Oudh, Vice-President, N.-W. P. & Oudh Association, President, Congress Reception Committee, and Fellow, Calcutta and Allahabad Universities.	N.-W. P. & Oudh Association	By a Public Meeting held at Kayastha Patshala on the 10th November, 1888, and at a General Meeting of the N.-W. P. and Oudh Association on the 22nd December, 1888.
552	"	"	"	Pundit Bishambher Nath	do.	Vakil, High Court, N.-W. P., President, N.-W. P. and Oudh Association and Vice-President, Congress Reception Committee,	do.	do.
553	"	"	"	Revd. David Mohun ...	Christian.	Pastor, Muirabad, Vice-President, N.-W. P. and Oudh Association.	do.	do.
554	"	"	"	Mr. D. Banerjee ...	Hindu, Brahmin.	Barrister-at-Law. ...	do.	do.
555	"	"	"	Mr. T. P. Crowley ...	European, Christian.	Of the firm, Messrs. Crowley and Co., Mechanical Engineers & Contractors, and Member, Municipal Board.	do.	do.
556	"	"	"	Pundit Mati Lal ...	Hindu, Brahmin.	Vakil, High Court, N.-W.P., Secretary, N.-W. P. and Oudh Association.	do.	do.
557	"	"	"	Munshi Jwala Prosad ...	Hindu, Kyasth.	Vakil, High Court, N.-W. P. and Zemindar.	do.	do.
558	"	"	"	Pundit Sundar Lal, B A.	Hindu, Brahmin.	Vakil, High Court, N.-W. P. & Fellow, Allahabad University.	do.	do.
559	"	"	"	" Nawal Behari Bajpai.	do.	Vakil, High Court, N.-W. P.	do.	do.
560	"	"	"	Mr. Roohun Lal ...	Hindu, Kyasth.	Barrister-at-Law. ..	do.	do.
561	"	"	"	" T. N. Ghose ...	do.	Pleader, Member, Municipal Board, and Secretary, Allahabad Jubilee Club.	do.	do.
562	"	"	"	Pundit Joy Krishna Vyas	Hindu, Brahmin.	Medical Practitioner.	do.	At a Ward Meeting at Ahiapur in the Town of Allahabad on the 21st December, 1888.
563	"	"	"	Babu Durga Charan Banerji, B.A.	do.	Vakil, High Court, N.-W. P.	do.	do.
564	"	"	"	Lala Bhowani Prosad ...	Hindu. Khettri.	Banker. ...	......	do.
565	"	"	"	" Giridhari Lal, B.A.	do.	Licensed Translator, High Court, N.-W. P.	......	do.

Number.	Presidency or Government.	Congress Circle.	Electoral Division.	Names in full of Delegates with honorary titles and scholastic degrees, &c.	Race, Religious denomination, or Caste, if any.	Occupation and Address.	Other Places or Associations for which they were also elected.	How and when elected.
566	N.-W. P.	Allahabad.	Allahabad	Munshi Kashi Prosad ...	Hindu, Kyasth.	Vakil, High Court, N.-W. P., Secretary, Madhya Hindu Samaj and N.-W. P. and Oudh Association.	N.-W. P. & Oudh Association, and the Madhya Hindu Somaj.	By a Public Meeting held at Kayastha Patshala on the 10th November 1888, and at a General Meeting of the N.-W. P. & Oudh Association on the 22nd December, 1888, and at the Meeting of the M. Hindu Somaj on the 27th November, 1888.
567	"	"	"	Pundit Lakshmi Narain Vyasa.	Hindu, Brahmin.	Vaidya; President, Hindu Samaj, Allahabad.	do.	do.
568	"	"	"	Munshi Madhava Prosad	Hindu, Kyasth.	Vakil, High Court, N.-W. P. and Zemindar.	do.	do.
569	"	"	"	Pundit Madan Mohan Malaviya, B.A.	Hindu, Brahmin.	Editor of the "Hindustani," Joint Secretary, Congress Reception Committee, Allahabad.	do.	do.
570	"	"	"	Babu Charoo Chundra Mittra.	Hindu, Kyasth.	Pleader, Zemindar, Senior Vice-Chairman, Municipal Board, Allahabad, and Secretary, N.-W. P. and Oudh Association.	do.	do.
571	"	"	"	Rajah Rampal Singh ...	Hindu, Khetri.	Rajah of Rampore, Oudh, Honorary Magistrate, Member, Municipal Board, Vice-President, Madhya Hindu Somaj, and Secretary, Reception Committee.	Do., and Partabgarh	Do., and at a Meeting held at Partabgarh.
572	"	"	"	Dr. S. P. Roy, M.B., M.R.C.S.	Hindu, Brahmin.	Medical Practitioner and Chemical Examiner, Municipal Board, Allahabad.	N.-W. P. & Oudh Association, and Rajshahye.	By a Public Meeting held at the Kayastha Patshala on the 10th November, 1888, and at the General Meeting of the Association on the 22nd December, 1888, and by a Public Meeting held at Beaulia in Rajshahye.
573	"	"	"	Mr. J. E. Howard, F.S.S., L. & A.	European, Christian.	Barrister-at-Law, President, Anglo-Indian and Eurasian Association, Allahabad.	......	By a Public Meeting held at Kayastha Patshala on the 10th November, 1888.
574	"	"	"	Lala Ram Charn Das ...	Hindu, Khetry,	Banker, Landholder, Honorary Magistrate, and Junior Vice-Chairman, Municipal Board, Allahabad.	......	do.
575	"	"	"	Mirza Nowazish Hosein	Mahomedan.	Zemindar and Mill Owner.	......	do.
576	"	"	"	Mir Fazal Ali Khan ...	do.	Ilaqidar. ...	......	do.
577	"	"	"	Moulvi Mahomed Hosein	do.	Moulvi. ...	......	do.
578	"	"	"	Mr. R. A. Fairlie ...	European, Christian.	Agent, Uncovenanted Service Bank, and Member, Municipal Board, Allahabad.	......	do.
579	"	"	"	Mr. F. T. Atkins ...	European, Christian.	Managing Director of the Railway Service Press, and the "Morning Post," and President, United Railway and Government Servants Association.	......	do.

Number.	Presidency or Government.	Congress Circle.	Electoral Division.	Names in full of Delegates with honorary titles and scholastic degrees, &c.	Race, Religious denomination, or caste, if any.	Occupation and Address.	Other Places or Associations for which they were also elected.	How and when elected.
580	N. W. P.	Allahabad.	Allahabad	Lala Ganesh Prosad ...	Hindu, Vaishya.	Banker & Zemindar	......	By a Public Meeting held at Kayastha Patshala on the 10th November, 1888.
581	"	"	"	Lala Raja Ram ...	do.	Do., Zemindar and Member, Municipal Board.	......	do.
582	"	"	"	Mr. Khushwaqt Rai ...	Hindu.	Barrister-at-Law. ...	......	do.
583	"	"	"	Dr. Abinash Chandra Banerji, L.M.S.	do.	Medical Practitioner.	......	do.
584	"	"	"	Mr. H. P. Niblett ..	European, Christian.	Vakil, High Court, N.-W. P.	......	do.
585	"	"	"	Lala Raj Bahadoor ...	Hindu, Kyastha.	Pleader. ...	......	do.
586	"	"	"	Munshi Sadruddin Ahmed.	Mahomedan.	Zemindar. ...	......	Public Meeting.
587	"	"	"	Pundit Ram Prassanna Achari.	Hindu, Brahmin.	Religious Teacher ...	......	Public Meeting, 22nd December, 1888.
588	"	"	"	Lala Kanhya Lal ...	Hindu, Agarwalla.	Banker. ...	......	Ward Meeting at Sawaldas-ka-Kacha, 21st December, 1888.
589	"	"	"	Lala Doorga Prosad ...	Hindu, Khetry.	Cloth Merchant. ...	......	do.
590	"	"	"	Lala Raghu Nandan Lal	Hindu.	Mahajan, Ward No. 5	......	Ward Meeting at Matiganj, held at Gokuldas Tejpal Dharmsala on the 10th December, 1888.
591	"	"	"	Swami Ala Ram ...	do.	Religious Teacher, Ward No. 5.	......	do.
592	"	"	"	Lala Jaggonath Prosad ...	do.	Mahajan, Ward No. 5	......	do.
593	"	"	"	Ramlal Pragwal ...	Hindu, Brahmin.	Priest, Ward No. 5	......	do.
594	"	"	"	Lala Mathura Prosad ...	Hindu, Bania.	Chowdhuri and Landowner, Ward No. 5.	......	do.
595	"	"	"	Lala Ganga Prosad ...	do.	Banker & Zemindar, Ward No. 5.	......	do.
596	"	"	"	Sitaram Pragwal ...	Hindu, Brahmin.	Priest, Ward No. 5...	......	do.
597	"	"	"	Babu Ashutosh Mookerji	do.	Contractor and Member, Municipal Board, Ward No. 5.	......	do.
598	"	"	"	Moulvi Mazher Ali ...	Mahomedan.	Muktear, Ward No. 5	......	do.
599	"	"	"	Lala Suraj Prosad ...	Hindu, Kyastha.	Pleader, Ward No. 6	......	Ward Meeting held at Daragunj, on the 9th December, 1888.
600	"	"	"	Pundit Madhoram Tiwary	Hindu, Brahmin.	Pundit, Ward No. 6	......	do.
601	"	"	"	Mohunt Janki Dass ...	Hindu, Byragi.	Mohunt, Ward No. 6	......	do.
602	"	"	"	Lala Gonesh Dass ...	Hindu, Bania.	Banker, Ward No. 2	......	Ward Meeting held at Katra, on the 23rd December, 1888.
603	"	"	"	Pundit Raj Nath ...	Hindu, Brahmin.	Munsarim (Jeypore) Ward No. 2.	......	do.
604	"	"	"	Babu Gopal Chandra Bose.	Hindu, Kyastha.	Government Pensioner, Ward No. 2.	......	do.
605	"	"	"	Munshi Bunk Behari Lal, B.A.	do.	Licensed Translator and Vakil, High Court, N.-W. P. Member of Municipal Board.	......	do.

Number.	Presidency or Government.	Congress Circle.	Electoral Division.	Names in full of Delegates with honorary titles and scholastic degrees, &c.	Race, Religious denomination, or Caste, if any.	Occupation and Address.	Other Places or Associations for which they were also elected.	How and when elected.
606	N.-W. P.	Allahabad.	Allahabad	Lala Ramdhan Lal ...	Hindu, Kyastha.	Muktear, Ward No. 2	......	Ward Meeting held at Katra on on the 23rd December 1888.
607	"	"	"	Babu Ambica Charan Mozoomdar, B.A.	do.	Teacher, Ward No. 2	......	do.
608	"	"	"	Lala Mata Doyal ...	do.	Muktear, Ward No. 2	......	do.
609	"	"	"	Babu Basanto Behary Ghosal.	Hindu, Brahmin.	House Owner, Ward No. 2.	......	do.
610	"	"	"	Mr. Joel David ...	Christian.	Superintendent, Bible and Tract Depository, Allahabad, Ward No. 2.	......	do.
611	"	"	"	M. Rabhir Hosein Khan	Mahomedan.	Zemindar, Duriabad, Allahabad.	......	By a Meeting held at Duriabad, in Allahabad, on the 15th December, 1888.
612	"	"	"	M. Mahomed Hosein Khan.	do.	do. ...	......	do.
613	"	"	"	M. Ali Muhammad Khan	do.	do. ...	......	do.
614	"	"	"	M. Nazar Hossein Khan	do.	do. ...	......	do.
615	"	"	"	M. Salamat Khan ...	do.	do. ...	......	do.
616	"	"	"	M. Ali Naki Khan ...	do.	do. ...	......	do.
617	"	"	"	Syed Mazher Hossein Khan.	do.	do. ...	......	no.
618	"	"	"	M. Nadad Hossein Khan	do.	do. ...	.. ...	do.
619	"	"	Allahabad City.	Lalla Munni Lal Kapur	Hindu, Khetry.	Mahajan, Ward No. 4	......	Ward Meeting held at Gangodas-ki-Chowk on the 16th December, 1888.
620	"	"	"	" Mahadeo Prosad Kapur.	do.	do. ...	......	do.
621	"	"	"	" Shital Prosad ...	do.	Muktear and Zemindar, Ward No. 4.	......	do.
622	"	"	"	" Mahadeo Prosad ...	do.	Tent Merchant, Ward No. 4.	......	do.
623	"	"	"	Pundit Ram Narain Proha.	Hindu, Brahmin.	Priest, Ward No. 4	......	do.
624	"	"	"	Pundit Sheo Narain ...	do.	do. ...	......	do.
625	"	"	"	Lala Mohun Lal Tandan	Hindu, Khetry.	Contractor, Ward No. 4	......	do.
626	"	"	"	Pundit Brojo Mohun Dube.	Hindu, Brahmin.	Cloth Merchant and Zemindar, Ward No. 4.	......	do.
627	"	"	"	Pundit Balmukund Bhatt	do.	Trader, Ward No. 4	.....	do.
628	"	"	"	Lala Chunni Lal ...	Hindu, Khetry.	Banker, Ward No. 4	......	do.
629	"	"	"	Rai Bhagwati Narain ...	do.	Zemindar, Ward No. 4.	......	do.
630	"	"	N.-W. P. and Oudh Association	Babu Ratan Chand, B.A.	Jain.	Vakil, High Court, President, Graduate Association, N.-W. P. and Oudh,	......	By the General Meeting of the Association held on the 22nd December, 1888.
631	"	"	"	Mr. William Digby ...	European, Christian.	Journalist, Indian Political Agency, 25, Craven Street, London.	....	do.
632	"	"	"	Babu Jogendra Nath Chowdhuri, M.A., B.L.	Hindu, Kyastha.	Vakil, High Court, N.-W. P,	......	do.
633	"	"	"	Pundit Baldeo Ram Dave	Hindu, Brahmin.	Pleader ...	......	do.

Number.	Presidency or Government.	Congress Circle.	Electoral Division.	Names in full of Delegates with honorary titles and scholastic degrees, &c.	Race, Religious denomination, or Caste if any.	Occupation and Address.	Other Places or Associations for which they were also elected.	How and when elected.
634	N.-W. P.	Allahabad.	N.-W. P. and Oudh Association	Babu Ram Kishore Lal	Hindu, Kyastha.	Honorary Magistrate, Retired Moonsiff.	......	By the General Meeting of the Association held on the 22nd December, 1888.
635	,,	,,	,,	Munshi Mathura Prosad	do.	Pleader & Zemindar	......	do.
636	,,	,,	,,	Lala Datti Lal, B.A. ...	Hindu, Khetry.	Vakil, High Court, N.-W. P.	......	do.
637	,,	,,	Madhya Hindu Somaj.	Pundit Balkrishno Bhatt	Hindu, Brahmin.	Editor, "Hindu Pradipa."	......	By a General Meeting of the Somaj held on the 27th November, 1888.
638	,,	,,	,,	Mr. Gokul Prosad, M.A.	Hindu, Kyastha.	Rais. ...	......	do.
639	,,	,,	,,	Babu Shama Charan Mookerji.	Hindu, Brahmin.	Pleader. ...	....	do.
640	,,	,,	,,	Pundit Deoki Nandan Tewari.	do.	Proprietor & Editor, "Pryag Somachar."	....	do.
641	,,	,,	,,	Mr. Mohesh Prosad ...	Hindu, Kyastha.	Pleader. ...	......	do.
642	,,	,,	,,	Babu Parbutty Charan Chatterji, C.E.	Hindu, Brahmin.	Do., and Civil Engineer.	....	do.
643	,,	,,	,,	Mr. Narayan Moreshivar Same, M.A.	do.	Private Tutor. ...	......	do.
644	,,	,,	,,	Lala Mulraj ...	Hindu, Kyastha.	Pleader. ...	......	do.
645	,,	,,	,,	Pundit Gungadhor Rao Goray.	Hindu, Brahmin.	Service. ...	......	do.
646	,,	,,	,,	Babu Hari Mohun Roy, B.A.	do.	Vakil, High Court, N.-W. P.	......	do.
647	,,	,,	,,	Dr. Brojendra Nath Banerji, L.M.S.	do.	Medical Practitioner.	......	do.
648	,,	,,	,,	Pundit Bany Madhub Bhuttacharji.	do.	Government Pensioner, Honorary Magistrate, and Member, Municipal Board.	......	do., and at the Meeting held at Kayastha Patshala on the 10th November, 1888.
649	,,	,,	,,	Srimant Swami ...	Hindu.	Religious Teacher. ..	......	do.
650	,,	,,	Peoples' Association	Munshi Mule Narain ...	Hindu, Khetri.	Rais and Zemindar...	......	By a General Meeting of the Association held on the 23rd December, 1888.
651	,,	,,	,,	Babu Annoda Prosad Banerji.	Hindu, Brahmin.	Pleader, and Secretary, Peoples' Association.	......	do.
652	,,	,,	,,	Dr. Tincouree Mukerji, L.M.S.	do.	Medical Practitioner.	......	do.
653	,,	,,	,,	Mr. Lal Behary Lal ...	Hindu, Khetri.	Head Accountant, Allahabad Bank, and Chairman, Peoples' Association.	......	do.
654	,,	,,	,,	,, Govind Prosad ...	do.	Deshi Tejarut Company.	......	do.
655	,,	,,	,,	,, Madho Prosad ...	do.	Pleader. ...	......	do.
656	,,	,,	,,	Mr. Nadir Hossein Khan.	Mahomedan.	Landowner. ...	......	do.
657	,,	,,	,,	Pandit Kripa Sanker ...	Hindu, Brahmin.	Pleader. ...	......	do.
658	,,	,,	Reform Association.	,, Suraj Nath ...	do.	Talookdar. ...	......	By a General Meeting of the Association held on the 20th December, 1888.
659	,,	,,	Native Christian Community.	Mr. Jacob Simeon ...	Christian.	Vakil, High Court, N.-W. P.	......	At a General Meeting of the Community held in Divinity School on the 29th December, 1888.

Number.	Presidency or Government.	Congress Circle.	Electoral Division.	Names in full of Delegates with honorary titles, scholastic degrees, etc.	Race, Religious denomination, and Caste, if any.	Occupation and Address.	Other Places or Associations for which they were also elected.	How and when elected.
660	N.-W. P.	Allahabad.	Medara, (Allahabad.)	Munshi Ahmed Hossein	Mahomedan.	Zemindar. ...	......	By a Public Meeting held on the 18th December, 1888.
661	"	"	"	Sheikh Mahomed Fazil ...	do.	do.	......	do.
662	"	"	"	" Raziuddin	do.	do.	......	do.
663	"	"	"	Hafiz Kumruddin ...	do.	do.	......	do.
664	"	"	"	Chowdhiri Rashiuddin ...	do.	do.	......	do.
665	"	"	"	Sheikh Zahiruddin ...	do.	do.	......	do.
666	"	"	"	Hafiz Amir Hasan ...	do.	do.	......	do.
667	"	"	"	Hafiz Sajjad Hossein ...	do.	Darvesh. ...	......	do.
668	"	"	Cotiva, (Allahabad.)	Thakur Jagut Bahadur Singh.	Hindu, Chattri.	Zemindar. ...	......	By a Public Meeting held on the 11th December, 1888.
669	"	"	"	Thakur Anant Bahadur Singh.	do.	do.	......	do.
670	"	"	Alamchand, (Allahabad).	Mir Abul Hossein ...	Mahomedan.	do.	......	By a Public Meeting held on the 17th December, 1888.
671	"	"	Kara (Allahabad).	Mir Nur-ul Hossein ...	do.	Service & do.	......	By Public Meeting, 14th December, 1888.
672	"	"	"	Shah Mahomed Naki ...	do.	Zemindar. ...	......	do.
673	"	"	"	Syed Mahomed Taki ...	do.	do.	......	do.
674	"	"	"	Mir Golam Mustafa ...	do.	Service & do.	......	do.
675	"	"	Ujjehini, (Allahabad).	Mir Mahomed Hadi ...	do.	Muafidar ...	......	By Public Meeting, 16th December, 1888.
676	"	"	"	Mir Golam Mahomed ...	do.	Zemindar. ...	......	do.
677	"	"	"	Hakim Gazaffir Hasan ...	do.	Service & do.	......	do.
678	"	"	"	Shah Mahomed Yunus	do.	Zemindar. ...	......	do.
679	"	"	Janka (Allahabad).	Hafiz Amiruddin ...	do.	Trader. ...	......	Public Meeting, 19th December, 1888.
680	"	"	Kon (Allahabad).	Sheikh Abdul Rahim ...	do.	Service and Zemindar.	......	Public Meeting, 18th December, 1888.
681	"	"	Hasseinpur (Allahabad).	Haji Abdul Rahim ...	do.	Zemindar. ...	......	Public Meeting, 17th December, 1888.
682	"	"	Kyhatta (Allahabad).	Munshi Bhyrava Sinha Varma.	Hindu, Chettri.	Service. ...	......	Public Meeting, 23rd December, 1888.
683	"	"	Agra.	Pandit Kanta Proshad ...	Hindu, Brahmin.	Pleader, Agra. ...	......	At a Public Meeting held on the 16th December, 1888
684	"	"	"	Thakur Umrao Singh ...	Hindu, Rajput.	Zemindar, Agra. ...	......	do.
685	"	"	"	Pandit Chotey Lall Sarma, M.A.	Hindu, Brahmin.	Professor, Guzrat College, Ahmedabad, Kalachin ghât, Agra.	......	do.
686	"	"	"	Mr. Ganga Proshad ...	Hindu, Kyastha.	Pleader, District Court, Agra.	......	do.
687	"	"	"	Babu Jumna Das Biswas	Hindu.	Pleader, Editor of the "Nasim Agra" and Municipal Commissioner.	......	do.

Number.	Presidency or Government.	Congress Circle.	Electoral Division.	Names in full of Delegates with honorary titles and scholastic degrees, &c.	Race, Religious denomination. or Caste, if any	Occupation and Address.	Other Places or Associations for which they were also elected.	How and when elected.
688	N.-W. P.	Allahabad.	Agra.	Lala Mathura Das Chowdhury.	Hindu. Chettry.	Teacher, Municipal Commissioner, and Director of Agra Mill Company, Limited.	......	At a Public Meeting held on the 16th December, 1888.
689	„	„	„	Thakur Zaher Singh ...	Hindu, Rajput.	Landholder, Rais, Vazarpur, Agra.	......	do.
690	„	„	„	Lala Shanker Dyal, B.A.	Hindu, Kyastha.	Vakil, High Court, N.-W. P., Agra.	......	do.
691	„	„	„	Lala Nehal Chand ...	Hindu, Khettry.	Accountant Unconvenanted Service Bank, Municipal Commissioner and Vice-President, Khetry, Hitkari, Sabha, Agra.	......	do.
692	„	„	„	Hakim Mushraff Hossein.	Mahomedan.	Physician, Agra. ...	......	do.
693	„	„	„	Mir Ezzat Ally ...	do.	Muktear, Agra. ...	......	do.
694	„	„	„	Nawab Mahomed Ali Mirza.	do.	Rais, Agra. ...	......	do.
695	„	„	„	Nawab Nanna Mirza ...	do.	do. ...	......	do.
696	„	„	„	Lalla Harnarayan ...	Hindu.	Bankar and Jeweller.	......	do.
697	„	„	„	Meah Kanja Buksh ...	Mahomedan.	Proprietor of a press, at Mandhi, Agra.	......	do.
698	„	„	„	Pandit Jaggan Nath ...	Hindu.	Rais and Vakil. ...	......	do.
699	„	„	„	Lalla Dwarka Das ...	do.	Vakil, Municipal Commissioner, and Manager, Bidya Dharam Varthani Patshala, Agra.	......	do.
700	„	„	„	Sheikh Mahomed Ali ...	Mahomedan.	Mukhtear, Reasut Ava, Agra.	......	do.
701	„	„	„	Rai Sohan Lall ...	Hindu, Kyastha.	Rais and Zemindar, Agra.	......	do.
702	„	„	„	Swamy Nangal Giri ...	Hindu.	Religious Teacher ...	......	do.
703	„	„	„	Lalla Kuar Pal ...	do.	Banker and Trader.	......	do.
704	„	„	„	Lalla Punna Lal ...	do.	Landholder. ...	......	do.
705	„	„	„	Munshi Shafatulla ...	Mahomedan.	Rais, Agra. ...	......	do.
706	„	„	Agra City.	Pandit Kashi Nath Chaturvedi.	Hindu.	Agra College. ...	......	do.
707	„	„	„	Rajah Luchman Singh.	Hindu, Rajput.	Zemindar, Rais and Retired Deputy Collector, Agra.	......	do.
708	„	„	„	Munshi Mahomed Golam Sarver Khan.	Mahomedan.	Muktear, Agra. ...	......	do.
709	„	„	„	Pandit Gopi Nath. ...	Hindu.	... ...	......	do.
710	„	„	„	Thomas Carr Morton. ...	European, Christian.	Pleader, Civil lines, Agra.	Muttra.	do., and at Muttra.
711	„	„	Agra Khetry Hitkary, Community.	Mr. Murlidhar. ...	Hindu.	Head Master, Victoria College, Agra and President, Khetry Hitkary Community, Agra.	......	By a Meeting of the Community, held on the 16th December, 1888.

Number.	Presidency or Government.	Congress Circle.	Electoral Division.	Names in full of Delegates with honorary titles, scholastic degrees, etc.	Race, Religious denomination. and Caste, if any.	Occupation and Address.	Other Places or Associations for which they were also elected.	How and when elected.
712	N.-W. P.	Allahabad.	Bah, Shamsabad, Iradat Nagur, Agra.	Mr. Ramprashad, B.A.	Hindu, Arya, Vaisya.	Pleader, Civil Court, Agra.	......	By Public Meeting.
713	"	"	"	Pundit Hurra Dhar. ...	Brahmin.	Pleader. ...	......	do.
714	"	"	"	Mirza Valayat Ali Beg.	Mahomedan.	Rais, Zemindar and Pensioner.	......	do.
715	"	"	Cawnpur.	Babu Tryloknath Bannerjee.	Hindu, Brahmin.	Pleader and Municipal Commissioner.	......	By a Public Meeting held on the 23rd December, 1888.
716	"	"	"	Sheik Ali Ahmed. ...	Mahomedan.	Merchant. ...	......	do.
717	"	"	"	Moulvi Mahammad Nabeh.	do.	Pleader. ...	......	do.
718	"	"	"	Syed Ali Hossein Moulvi.	do.	Service. ...	......	do.
719	"	"	"	Moulvi Jamilooddin. ...	do.	Pleader. ...	......	do.
720	"	"	"	Moulvi Abdul Jalil. ...	do.	Do., and Merchant.	......	do.
721	"	"	"	Hakim Fakharool Hosain.	do.	Physician. ...	......	do.
722	"	"	"	Munshi Tasaddooq Hosain	do.	Merchant. ...	......	do.
723	"	"	"	Moulvi Karim Dadkhan.	do.	Teacher. ...	......	do.
724	"	"	"	Moulvi Aboo Said Khan	do.	Priest. ...	......	do.
725	"	"	"	Moulvi Mahomed Sanauddin.	do.	Merchant. ...	......	do.
726	"	"	"	Mr. Bansi Dhar. ...	Hindu.	Rais. ...	......	do.
727	"	"	"	" Nanak Chand. ...	do.	do. ...	......	do.
728	"	"	"	Lala Shib Narain. ...	do.	do., and Merchant.	......	do.
729	"	"	"	Mr. Shib Prasad. ...	do.	Merchant. ..	......	do.
730	"	"	"	Babu Khetter Nath Ghose.	do.	Government Pensioner and Pleader.	......	do.
731	"	"	"	Sheik Karim Bux Hafiz.	Mahomedan.	Merchant. ...	......	do.
732	"	"	"	Dr. Mandhar Pershad Tewari, L. M.S.	Brahmin Kanoujea.	Medical Practitioner.	......	do.
733	"	"	"	Dr. Mohendra Nath Ganguli. L. M.S.	Hindu, Brahmin.	Medical Practitioner and Vice-Chairman, Municipal Board.	......	do.
734	"	"	"	Pundit Pratap Narain Misra.	do.	Editor of the "Brahman."	......	do.
735	"	"	"	Pundit Hirdenarain ...	Hindu, Kashmiri.	Pleader, Secretary, Hindu Somaj.	......	do.
736	"	"	"	Pundit Prithi Nath. ...	do.	Vakil and Vice-Chairman, Municipal Board.	......	do.
737	"	"	"	Pundit Janki Nath ...	Hindu, Brahmin.	Pleader and Zemindar.	......	By a Public Meeting held on the 24th December, 1888.
738	"	"	"	Lala Pirbhu Diyal ...	Bhargava.	Proprietor and Editor "Shoola Toor."	......	do.
739	"	"	"	Lala Shew Ram Marwari	Hindu, Bania.	Proprietor of the Firm of Narva Ram Seva Ram.	......	do.

Number.	Presidency or Government.	Congress Circle.	Electoral Division.	Names in full of Delegates with honorary titles and scholastic degrees, &c.	Race, Religious denomination, or Caste, if any	Occupation and Address.	Other Places or Associations for which they were also elected.	How and when elected.
740	N.-W. P.	Allahabad.	Cawnpore	Rai Chedi Lal Bahadoor	Hindu.	Rais	......	By a Public Meeting held on the 24th December, 1888.
741	,,	,,	,,	Mr. Bisheshwar Nath	do.	Zemindar. ...	......	do.
742	,,	,,	,,	Lala Gaya Pershad ...	do.	Rais, Banker, Municipal Commissioner.	......	do.
743	,,	,,	,,	Moulvi Mahomed Ashraf	Mahomedan.	Pleader and Zemindar.	......	do.
744	,,	,,	,,	Pundit Dharam Narain	Hindu.	Banker and Zemindar.	......	do.
745	,,	,,	,,	Munshi Bhup Narain ...	do.	Country Produce Merchant and Proprietor of "The Merchant."	......	do.
746	,,	,,	,,	Shahzada Mirza Farrukh Shah	Mahomedan.	Wasikadar, Rais ...	......	do.
747	,,	,,	National League, Cawnpur.	Mr. Ram Chandra, B.A.	Hindu.	Pleader and Banker.	......	By a Meeting of the League.
748	,,	,,	Bithoor	Pundit Gur Baksh Singh	do.	Zemindar and Editor, "Bharatvarsa"	......	By a Public Meeting held on the 6th December, 1888.
749	,,	,,	,,	Pundit Ram Narain Bajpai	do.	Zemindar and Manager "Bharatvarsa."	......	do.
750	,,	,,	Saharanpur.	Munshi Ram Chandra, M.A.	Hindu, Kaystha.	Resident, Saharanpur.	......	At a Public Meeting held on the 2nd December, 1888.
751	,,	,,	,,	Lala Madan Mohan Lal, B.A.	Hindu, Agarwala.	Teacher. ...	......	do.
752	,,	,,	,,	Mr. Dharm Das Suri	Khatri, Theist.	Pleader, Saharanpur.	......	do.
753	,,	,,	,,	,, Joti Pershad ...	Hindu, Bhargava.	Judge's Court Pleader.	......	do.
754	,,	,,	,,	Lala Moorari Lal ...	Khutri.	General Agent. ...	......	do.
755	,,	,,	,,	Munshi Nazir Hasan ...	Mahomedan.	Zemindar. ...	......	do.
756	,,	,,	Etah	Seth Kishan Lal ...	Hindu, Brahmin.	Banker, Sakit, District, Etah.	......	By a Public Meeting.
757	,,	,,	Etawah	Pundit Baldeo Prasad ...	do.	Physician ...	......	do.
758	,,	,,	,,	Pundit Kashi Nath ...	do.	do. ...	......	do.
759	,,	,,	Mainpuri	Babu Krishna Gopal Sanyal, B.A., B.L.	do.	Pleader, Mainpuri, and Vice President, District Board, Mainpuri.	......	By a Public Meeting, held on the 16th December, 1888.
760	,,	,,	,,	Pundit Dammi Lal Choubey, B.A.	do.	Vakil, High Court, and Member, Municipal Board, Mainpuri.	......	do.
761	,,	,,	,,	Babu Noni Lal Bannerjee	do.	Pleader, Mainpuri ...	......	do.
762	,,	,,	Meerut	Mr. Prahlad Singh ...	Hindu.	Zemindar and Vakil, High Court, N.-W. P.	......	By a Public Meeting held at Meerut on the 16th December, 1888.
763	,,	,,	,,	Lala Govinda Prashad ...	do.	Pleader. ...	......	do.
764	,,	,,	,,	Lala Badri Prashad ...	do.	do. ...	......	do.
765	,,	,,	,,	Mohant Brimha Atal ...	do.	Zemindar. ...	......	do.
766	,,	,,	,,	Chowbey Radhe Lal ...	do.	Pleader. ...	......	do.
767	,,	,,	,,	Dr. Guruprosonna Ray, M.B.	Hindu, Kyastha.	Medical Practitioner.	......	do.

Number.	Presidency or Government.	Congress Circle.	Electoral Division.	Names in full of Delegates with honorary titles, scholastic degrees, etc.	Race, Religious denomination, and Caste, if any.	Occupation and Address.	Other Places or Associations for which they were also elected.	How and when elected.
768	N.-W. P.	Allahabad.	Meerut	Mr. Pyari Lal ...	Jain.	Barrister-at-Law. ...	......	By a Public Meeting held at Meerut on the 16th December, 1888.
769	,,	,,	,,	Lala Jia Lal ...	do.	Banker. ...	......	do.
770	,,	,,	,,	Qazi Mohamed Ismail ...	Mahomedan.	Imam Musjid. ...	......	do.
771	,,	,,	,,	Moulvi Ahmed Hasan Shankat	do.	Editor and Proprietor of "Shahna Hind," Meerut.	......	do.
772	,,	,,	,,	Mr. Raghubir Saran ...	Hindu.	Pleader and Zemindar.	Hassur.	do., and at a Public Meeting at Hassur.
773	,,	,,	,,	Chaudhari Dorga Sing ...	do.	Zemindar. ...	do.	do.
774	,,	,,	,,	Mr. Mallu Mal ...	do.	Pleader. ...	do.	do.
775	,,	,,	,,	Mr. Shimbhu Nath Bhargo, B.A.	do.	Vakil, High Court...	do.	do.
776	,,	,,	,,	Pundit Mathura Das ...	do.	Zemindar. ...	do.	do.
777	,,	,,	,,	Lala Mahtab Rai ...	do.	do. ...	do.	do.
778	,,	,,	,,	Seth Govind Prashad ...	do.	do. ...	do.	do.
779	,,	,,	,,	Pundit Ram Prashad, M.A.	do.	Pleader. ...	Deshmiti Sabha.	do., and by a General Meeting of the Sabha.
780	,,	,,	,,	Munshi Ajudhya Prashad	do.	do. ...	......	do.
781	,,	,,	Farakhabad.	Lala Durga Pershad Rastogy.	do.	Land-holder, Municipal Commissioner.	......	By a Public Meeting held on the 12th December, 1888.
782	,,	,,	,,	Pandit Gopal Rao Hari Chaturvedi.	do.	Secretary Vaidic Somaj.	......	do.
783	,,	,,	,,	Pandit Ram Narain Missr.	do.	Stores Clerk, District Traffic Superintendent's Office.	......	do.
784	,,	,,	,,	Chowbay Makhan Lall	do.	Pleader, Chhabra Mao.	......	do.
785	,,	,,	,,	Mr. Suraj Pershad ...	do.	Contractor and General Merchant.	......	do.
786	,,	,,	,,	Mr. Badri Pershad ...	do.	Head Clerk, District Traffic Superintendent's Office.	......	do.
787	,,	,,	,,	Pandit Soonder Narain Mushram.	do.	Banker.	......	do.
788	,,	,,	,,	Pundit Mudun Lall ...	do.	Private service Muhullah Khotramba.	......	do.
789	,,	,,	Vaidic Somaj, Farakhabad.	Munshi Chintaman ...	do.	Bookseller.	......	By a General Meeting of the Somaj on the 12th December, 1888.
790	,,	,,	,,	Seth Sawa Ram ...	do.	Banker, Member Municipal Board, and Hon. Treasurer, Vaidic Somaj.	......	do.
791	,,	,,	Chhabra Mao (Farakhabad.)	Pandit Ajudhia Pershad	do.	Pleader, Zemindar and Member, Local Board.	......	By a Public Meeting held on the 13th December, 1888.
792	,,	,,	Kanoj (Farakhabad.)	Munshi Mahomed Mashuk Ali.	Mahomedan.	Zemindar.	......	do.
793	,,	,,	,,	Munshi Mahomed Alam	do.	do. and Vakil and Member, Local Board.	......	do,
794	,,	,,	Fategarh (Farakhabad.)	Lalla Sarup Narain ..	Hindu.	Pleader, District Court Fatehgarh.	Kanoj and Farakhabad.	do. and Meeting held 16th December.

Number.	Presidency or Government.	Congress Circle.	Electoral Division.	Names in full of Delegates with honorary titles and scholastic degrees, &c.	Race, Religious denomination or Caste, if any.	Occupation and Address.	Other places or Association for which they were also elected.	How and when elected.
795	N.-W. P.	Allahabad.	Pilakhana (Farakhabad.)	Pundit Sohan Singh Chaturvedi	Brahmin.	Zemindar.	......	By a Public Meeting.
796	,,	,,	Aligurh.	Choudheri Faiz Bux ...	Mahomedan.	Zemindar Mouza Jamka Tahsil Khair	......	do.
797	,,	,,	,,	Hafiz Mahomed Abdurrahim.	do.	Pleader.	......	do.
798	,,	,,	,,	Sheik Nemat Hossein Mutwali.	do.	Muafidar.	......	do.
799	,,	,,	,,	Moulvi Mahomed Yakub Khan.	do.	Zemindar, Kasgunj.	......	do.
800	,,	,,	,,	Moulvi Mahomed Nurrullah Khan.	do.	do.	......	do.
801	,,	,,	,,	Babu Ashutos Bhattacharji, B.A.	Hindu, Brahmin.	Pleader.	......	By a Public Meeting held on the 20th December, 1888.
802	,,	,,	,,	Babu Jwala Pershad Chatterji, B.A.	do.	do.	......	do.
803	,,	,,	,,	Babu Jogendra Nath Chatterjee.	do.	Vakil, High Court.	.....	do.
804	,,	,,	,,	Munshi Tota Ram ..	Hindu, Vaisya.	Pleader.	......	do.
805	,,	,,	,,	Mr. Kuber Nath ...	Hindu, do.	Contractor and Zemindar.	......	do.
806	,,	,,	,,	Thakur Makhan Singh.	Rajput.	Zemindar.	......	do.
807	,,	,,	,,	Babu Kalyan Singh ...	do.	do.	......	
808	,,	,,	,,	Sheik Banda Ali ...	Mahomedan.	Service.	......	do.
809	,,	,,	,,	Munshi Gouri Shunker Sahai.	Hindu.	Pleader.		do.
810	,,	,,	,,	Mr. Jani Ballabh Shunker	do.	Banker, Zemindar and Municipal Commissioner.	......	do.
811	,,	,,	,,	,, Jani Chandra Shunker.	do.	Banker and Zemindar.	......	do.
812	,,	,,	,,	,, Lajja Shunker	do.	do.	......	do.
813	,,	,,	,,	,, Pacholi Gunga Shunker.	do.	Banker.	......	do.
814	,,	,,	,,	Lala Radhica Proshad ...	do.	Lace Manufacturer.	......	do.
815	,,	,,	,,	Babu Kedar Nath Chatterjee, B.A.	do.	Pleader.	......	do.
816	,,	,,	Muttra	Rev. J. E. Scott, P.H.D.	American, Christian.	Representing the American Methodist Mission.	......	By a Public Meeting held on the 16th December, 1888.
817	,,	,,	,,	Mr. R. A. Morton .	do.	Pleader. ...	......	do.
818	,,	,,	,,	Lala Jagannath Prosad.	Hindu..	do., and Indigo Merchant, Muttra.	......	do.
819	,,	,,	,,	Lala Jagannath Prosad Bhargobha.	do.	Indigo Merchant and Zemindar.	......	do.
820	,,	,,	,,	Pundit Bishambher Nath	do.	Trader. ...	......	do.
821	,,	,,	,,	Munshi Tribhuban Nath	do.	Landholder and Merchant.	......	do.
822	,,	,,	Brindabun	Pundit Radha Charan Goswami.	Hindu, Brahmin.	Shebait of a Brindabun Temple, Religious Teacher.	Muttra ...	do., and at Brindabun on the 21st December, 1888.

Number.	Presidency or Government.	Congress Circle.	Electoral Division.	Names in full of Delegates with honorary titles and scholastic degrees, &c.	Race, Religious denomination or Caste, if any.	Occupation and Address.	Other Places or Associations for which they were also elected.	How and when elected.
823	N.-W. P.	Allahabad.	Brindabun	Babu Satya Chandra Mukerjee, M.A.	Hindu, Brahmin.	Vakil, High Court, N. W. P., Southern Suburbs, Calcutta.	Muttra.	By a Public Meeting held at Brindabun, on the 21st December, 1888.
824	,,	,,	,,	Pundit Thakur Proshad.	do.	Trader. ...	do.	do.
825	,,	,,	,,	Pundit Radhe Lal Swarma Jyotishi.	do.	Religious Teacher ...	......	do.
826	,,	,,	Banda ...	Seth Shiam Karan ...	Hindu, Guzrati Bania.	Honorary Magistrate, Municipal Commissioner, and Member, District Board, Banker and Landholder.	......	By a Public Meeting held on the 25th November, 1888.
827	,,	,,	,,	Dube Chandi Din ...	do.	Honorary Magistrate, Senior Vice-Chairman, Municipality Banda, Member of Agricultural and Commercial Department, and Member of District Board, and Land Owner.	......	do.
828	,,	,,	,,	Chowdhari Mohesiri Din	do.	Municipal Commissioner, Member, District Board, Landlord, Banda.	......	do.
829	,,	,,	,,	Awasthi Sundar Lal ...	do.	Landlord, Municipal Commissioner. Banda.	......	do.
830	,,	,,	,,	Hafiz Alayar Khan ...	Mahomedan.	Pensioner, Tahsildar, Sub-Registrar, Honorary Magistrate, and Zemindar.	......	do.
831	,,	,,	,,	Munshi Mata Prashad ...	Hindu Kyasth.	Muktear, Secretary, Municipal Board, Superintendent, Kayestha Sabha, Banda, Secretary, Bar Association, Municipal Commissioner, Zemindar.	......	do.
832	,,	,,	Umaria...	Dr. Damri Lal Tewari ...	Hindu, Bramin.	Assistant Surgeon. ...	......	By a Public Meeting held at Umaria, on the 10th December, 1888. The Rajah of Chandia presided.
833	,,	,,	Jhansi ...	Behary Lal Mahore ...	Hindu. ...	2nd Teacher, City High School.	......	By a Public Meeting held at Jhansi on the 19th December, 1888.
834	,,	,,	,,	Shankar Sahai	do.	Pleader. ...	......	do.
835	,,	,,	,,	Pundit Prayag Das ...	do.	Zemindar and Mooktar.	......	do.
836	,,	,,	,,	Pundit Deoki Nandan ...	do.	Contractor. ...	......	do.
837	,,	,,	,,	Gopi Singh ...	do.	do. and Zemindar, and Banker.	......	do.
838	,,	,,	Kumaon (Almora).	Pandit Bachaspati Pant...	Hindu, Brahmin.	Pleader, Almora. ...	......	By a Public Meeting held on the 20th December, 1888.
839	,,	,,	,,	Sheikh Manulla ...	Mahomedan.	General Merchant. ...	......	do.
840	,,	,,	Nainital...	Pundit Jwala Dutt Joshi	Hindu. ...	Vakil, High Court, N.-W. P.	Almora...	do., and at Nainital, on the 14th December, 1888.

Number.	Presidency or Government.	Congress Circle.	Electoral Division.	Names in full of Delegates with honorary titles, scholastic degrees, etc.	Race, Religious denomination, and Caste, if any.	Occupation and Address.	Other Places or Associations for which they were also elected.	How and when elected.
841	N.-W. P.	Allahabad.	Dehradun	Captain Andrew William Hearsey.	European, Christian.	Retired Officer, H. M. S., Kheri, Lakhanpore, Oudh.	Kheri ...	By a Meeting held at Dehradun on the 17th December, 1888, and at a Meeting held at Kheri.
842	"	"	"	Lala Gopal Krishna ...	Hindu, Khetri.	Jeweller. ...	......	By a Public Meeting held on the 17th December, 1888.
843	"	"	"	Pandit Jyotis Swarupa ...	Arya. Kyasth.	Pleader, District Court, Dehradun.	......	do.
844	"	"	"	Lala Radhe Lal ...	Hindu, Vaisya.	Banker and Zemindar	......	do.
845	"	"	"	Pundit Anand Narain ...	Kashmiri.	Pleader, Dehradun ...	......	do.
846	"	"	"	Mr. V. A. Chety ...	Hindu, Vaisya.	......	......	do.
847	"	"	Chakrata (Dehradun)	Babu Raghuvor Dyal Sundhel.	Hindu, Brahmin.	Rais.	......	By a Public Meeting held on 21st December, 1888.
848	"	"	Bulandshahar.	Pundit Ratan Lal ...	Hindu, Brahmin.	Pleader, Bulandshahar.	......	By a Public Meeting.
849	"	"	"	Thakur Mahabeer Singh	Hindu, Khetri.	Zemindar, Chandooh, Jahangirabad, Bulandshahar.	......	do.
850	"	"	Jahangirabad, Gerruhobami Sabha, Bulandshahar.	Lalla Bishan Singh ...	Hindu.	do. ...	......	By a Meeting of the Sabha on the 18th December, 1888.
851	"	"	"	" Pirbho Lal ...	do.	do. ...	......	do.
852	"	Benares	Benares	Vindhya Nath Jha, B.A. ...	Hindu, Brahmin.	Zemindar, Durbhanga District.	......	By a Public Meeting held on the 16th December 1888.
853	"	"	"	Mr. Govind Narayan Singha.	do.	Talukdar, Gazipur and Rais, Benares.	......	do.
854	"	"	"	" Brijraton Dass ...	Guzrati Bania.	Banker, Chowkhunba, Benares.	......	do.
855	"	"	"	Pundit Vishwanath Misra	Hindu, Brahmin.	Land-holder, Benares.	......	do.
856	"	"	"	Mr. Kandhya Singh ...	Sikh.	Merchant. ...	......	do.
857	"	"	"	" Hari Das ...	Hindu, Khetri.	do. ...	......	do.
858	"	"	"	Mr. A. T. Mudalier ...	Hindu.	......		do.
859	"	"	"	Revd. Kashi Nath Datta	Christian.	Missionary and Head Master, L. M. College.	......	do.
860	"	"	"	Babu Abinashi Lal ...	Hindu, Khetri.	Zemindar and Banker.	......	do.
861	"	"	"	Pundit Ram Chundra Naik Kalia.	Hindu, Brahmin.	Banker and Zemindar. Dasaswamedh, Benares.	......	do.
862	"	"	"	Mr. Bunsidhar ...	Hindu, Khetri.	Banker, Benares. ...	......	do.
863	"	"	"	" Chottey Lal ...	Hindu. Vyasa.	Merchant, Benare s.	......	do.
864	"	"	"	" Madho Dass ...	do.	Banker and Zemindar and Hony. Magistrate, Benares.	......	do.
865	"	"	"	" Ram Narayan Dass	do.	Zemindar, and Government Pensioner, Benares.	......	do.

Number.	Presidency or Government.	Congress Circle.	Electoral Division.	Names in full of Delegates with honorary titles and scholastic degrees, &c.	Race, Religious denomination, or Caste, if any.	Occupation and Address.	Other Places or Associations for which they were also elected.	How and when elected.
866	N.-W. P.	Benares	Benares	Dr. Shiyam Kishan Singh, L.M.S.	Hindu, Vyasa.	Medical Practitioner, Benares.	.....	By Public Meeting held on the 16th December, 1888.
867	"	"	"	Pundit Uma Shanker Dubey.	Hindu, Brahmin.	Land-holder, Benares	.....	do.
868	"	"	"	Babu Upendra Nath Basu, B.A.	Hindu, Kyastha.	Pleader and Zemindar, Benares.	......	do.
869	"	"	"	Mr. Kanaya Lal Das, B.A.	do.	Trader and Landholder, Benares.	......	do.
870	"	"	"	" Dawlut Chund ...	Jain.	Banker and Jeweller, Benares.	......	do.
871	"	"	"	" Faquir Chand ...	do.	do. ...	......	do.
872	"	"	"	Babu Ram Kali Chowdhry.	Hindu, Brahmin.	Pensioner, Municipal Commissioner and Hony. Magistrate, Benares.		do.
873	"	"	"	" Lakshman Das ...	Hindu, Vyasa.	Zemindar, Banker and Hony. Magistrate, Benares.	....	do.
874	"	"	"	Chowdry Ram Prasad ...	do.	Banker and Zemindar, Benares.	......	do.
875	"	"	"	Syed Nazir Ali ...	Mahomedan.	Pleader, Benares ...		do.
876	"	"	"	Mir Imdad Hossein ...	do.	Teacher, Benares ...	......	do.
877	"	"	"	Nawab Syed Hossein Askari Khan.	do.	Rais, Benares	......	do.
878	"	"	"	Shaik Gaus Ally	do.	Pleader and Zemindar, Benares.		do.
879	"	"	"	Lala Vendheswari, B.A....	Hindu, Kyastha.	Vakil and Zemindar, Benares.	......	do.
880	"	"	"	Shaik Nasir Uddin	Mahomedan.	Pleader, Benares ...	......	do.
881	"	"	"	Pundit Kailash Nath Sukla.	Hindu.	Late Private Secretary to H. H. the Maharaja of Balrampur, K.C.S.I., now Pensioner.	......	do.
882	"	"	"	Shaik Altaf Hossein Rangin.	Mahomedan.	Zemindar and Merchant and Proprietor of the Rais-i-Azam, Benares.	......	do.
883	"	"	"	Munshi Roghunundun Proshad, B.A.	Hindu Kyastha.	Pleader, Hony. Secretary, District Board, Municipal Commissioner and Landholder, Benares.	.....	do.
884	"	"	"	Munshi Sadho Lal	Hindu.	Banker, Zemindar, Municipal Commissioner and Hony. Magistrate.	......	do.
885	"	"	"	Dr. Chunnee Lal ...	do.	Medical Practitioner.	......	do.
886	"	"	"	Thakur Sampat Ram ...	do.	Landholder and Banker.	......	do.
887	"	"	"	Pundit Vidyaput Tewari	Hindu, Brahmin.	Zemindar.	......	do.
888	"	"	"	Thakur Basant Ram ...	do.	Banker. ...	......	do.
889	"	"	"	Rai Sham Kishen ...	Hindu, Vyasa.	Rais, Zemindar, Banker and Hony. Magistrate, Benares.		do.

Number.	Presidency or Government.	Congress Circle.	Electoral Division.	Names in full of Delegates with honorary titles, scholastic degrees, etc.	Race, Religious denomination, and Caste, if any.	Occupation and Address.	Other Places or Associations for which they were also elected.	How and when elected.
890	N.-W. P.	Benares	Benares	Mr. Shunker Lal ..	Hindu, Brahmin.	Zemindar, Benares ...	......	By a Public Meeting held on the 16th December, 1888.
891	"	"	"	Babu Mukshada Dass Mitter.	Hindu, Kyastha.	Zemindar and Rais, Benares.	Bengalitola Association.	Do., and at a Meeting of the Association on the 21st December, 1888.
892	"	"	"	Mr. Bisseswar Pandya	Hindu, Brahmin.	Land-holder, Jeweller, Benares.	do.	do.
893	"	"	"	Babu Niranjon Mookerjee	do.	Ex.-Minister, Rewah, Benares.	do.	do.
894	"	"	"	" Annoda Charan Dutt, B.A.	Hindu, Kyastha.	Pleader, Naradaghat, Benares.	do.	do.
895	"	"	"	Pundit Chowan Lal Jyotishi	Hindu, Brahmin.	Pleader, District Court, Benares.	Sujan Samaj.	At a Public Meeting on the 16th December 1888. and by a General Meeting of Samaj on the 23rd December 1888.
896	"	"	"	Mr. Joykissen Dass ...	Hindu.	Banker and Zemindar, Bulanala, Benares.	do.	do.
897	"	"	"	" Bishun Pant Rajwade.	Hindu, Brahmin.	Teacher, Benares ...	do.	do.
898	"	"	"	" Damodar Dass, B.A.	Hindu.	Vakil, High Court, Benares.	do.	do.
899	"	"	"	" Brindabon Behary	Hindu, Khattri.	Pleader and Landholder, Benares.	do.	do.
900	"	"	"	" Behari Lal ...	do.	Merchant, Benares ...	do.	do.
901	"	"	"	Pundit Beni Ram ...	Hindu, Brahmin.	Pleader, Benares ...	do.	do.
902	"	"	"	" Mangalram	do.	Banker.	do.	do.
903	"	"	"	Babu Jogendra Nath Ghose, B.A.	Hindu, Kyastha.	Pleader ...	do., and Allahabad Modhya Hindu Samaj.	do., and at a General Meeting of the Samaj on the 23rd December, 1888.
904	"	"	"	Pundit Ranga Nath Row	Hindu, Brahmin.	Manager, Kanara Swami Mat, Katha-ra-ghat, and Assistant School Master, Town High School, Benares.	Kumba conum.	By Public Meetings held on the 16th and 21st December, 1888 and at Kumbaconum on the 18th December, 1888.
905	"	"	"	Mr. Shama Dass ...	Hindu.	Banker and Zemindar, Benares.	......	By a Public Meeting held on the 21st December, 1888.
906	"	"	"	Lala Narsingh Dass	do.	Pleader, Benares ..	......	do.
907	"	"	"	Pundit Munna Lal ...	do.	do. ...	......	do.
908	"	"	"	" Vijaya Nandji. ...	do.	Pundit, Benares ...	......	do.
909	"	"	"	Babu Ram Krishna Varma	do.	Editor and Proprietor, "Barat Jewan," Benares.	......	do.
910	"	"	"	Pundit Jagat Narain ...	do.	Religious Teacher, Benares.	......	do.
911	"	"	"	" Ganga Dhar Upadhya.	do.	Banker, Benares.	......	do.
912	"	"	"	" A. Krishna Swamy Aiyar.	do.	Landholder and Pundit, Benares.	....	do.
913	"	"	"	Chowdhry Mohammad Resa Khan.	Mahomedan.	Zemindar, Benares...	......	do.
914	"	"	"	Kazi Syed Jawad Hossain	do.	do. ...	.....	do.

Number.	Presidency or Government.	Congress Circle.	Electoral Division.	Names in full of Delegates with honorary titles and scholastic degrees, &c.	Race, Religious denomination, or Caste, if any.	Occupation and Address.	Other Places or Associations for which they were also elected.	How and when elected.
915	N.-W. P.	Benares	Benares	Sheik Nisar Ali ...	Mahomedan.	Zemindar, Benares ...	......	By a Public Meeting held on the 21st December, 1888.
916	„	„	„	Mir Nasir Ali ...	do.	Teacher, Shiwala, Benares.	......	do.
917	„	„	„	„ Akbar Ali ...	do.	Zemindar, Benares...	....	do.
918	„	„	„	Shaik Qasim Ali ...	do.	Legal Practitioner and Landholder, Benares.	......	do.
919	„	„	„	Syed Muzafar Hussein ...	do.	Muafidar, Benares ...	......	do.
920	„	„	„	Moulvi Zair Hussein ...	do.	Teacher, Benares ...	....	do.
921	„	„	„	Mirza Hossain Ali Beg.	do.	Physician, Benares.	......	do.
922	„	„	„	Babu Kailas Nath Mookerjee.	Hindu, Brahmin.	Pensioner, Benares.	......	do.
923	„	„	„	Hakim Wali Mahomed...	Mahomedan.	Physician ...	......	do.
924	„	„	„	Babu Bhuvon Mohun Sen	Hindu.	Homœopathic Practitioner, Benares.	.....	do.
925	„	„	„	„ Chintaman Mookerjee, B.A.	Hindu, Brahmin.	Teacher, T. College. Panday-ke-Houly at Benares.	Bengalitola Association.	do. and at a Meeting of the Association held same day.
926	„	„	„	„ Ram Mohun Day, B.A.	Hindu, Kyastha.	Pleader, Gurrooreswar.	Bengalitola Association, Benares.	do.
927	„	„	„	Munshi Mahomed Karim Khan.	Mahomedan.	Landholder, Benares.	......	By Public Meeting of 21st December, 1888.
928	„	„	„	Prince Mirza Mahomed Abid Bukht Bahadoor.	do.	Prince, Mogul Imperial Family, Pensioner, Benares.	......	By a Public Meeting on 23rd December, 1888.
929	„	„	„	Panda Jokhuram ...	Hindu.	Priest, Benares ...	......	do.
930	„	„	„	Prince Mirza Farkhimda Bukht Bahadoor.	Mahomedan.	Prince, Mogal Imperial Family, Pensioner, Benares.	......	do.
931	„	„	„	Syed Laakut Ali ...	do.	Service. ...	......	By a Public Meeting on the 22nd December, 1888.
932	„	„	Taluka Surujpore, Benares.	Mr. Basdeo Narain Singh.	Hindu	Taluqdar, Surujpore, Benares.	......	By a Public Meeting in November, 1888.
933	„	„	„	„ Mukhteshwar Roy	do.	Pleader and Zemindar, Surujpore, Benares.	AryaSamaj, Azimgarh.	Do. and at a Meeting of the Samaj.
934	„	„	„	„ Gauri Shanker Singh.	do.	do. ...	do.	do.
935	„	„	„	Munshi Hira Lal ...	do.	do. ...	do.	do.
936	„	„	„	„ Basdeo Sahai ...	do.	Second Master, C. M. School, Azimgarh.	Do. and Madhya Hindu Samaj, Allahbad.	Do. and at a Meeting of the M. H. Samaj on the 23rd December, 1888.
937	„	„	Gorakhpur	Gorakh Prosad ...	Hindu, Kyastha.	District Court, Pleader, Gorakhpur.	......	By a Public Meeting held on the 13th November, 1888.
938	„	„	„	Lalla Modhuvan Dass ...	do.	do.	......	do.
939	„	„	„	Pandit Chunder Sikhar Dhar Misra.	do.	Zemindar, Ratnawala. Post Office, Bagha, District Champarun.	......	do.

Number.	Presidency or Government.	Congress Circle.	Electoral Division.	Names in full of Delegates with honorary titles, scholastic degrees, etc.	Race, Religious denomination, and Caste, if any.	Occupation and Address.	Other Places or Associations for which they were also elected.	How and when elected.
940	N.-W.P.	Benares	Gorakhpur	Mr. Tara Pershad, M.A.	Hindu, Kyastha.	Pleader, Gorakpur.	......	By a Public Meeting held on the 13th November, 1888.
941	"	"	"	" Lachhmi Charan ...	do.	Vakil, High Court, and Member of the Municipal Committee, Gorakpur.	......	do.
942	"	"	"	" Chhutu Lal ...	do.	Pleader and Landholder, Gorukpur.	......	do.
943	"	"	"	" Bishun Singh ...	Hindu, Kshatriya.	Barhi Post Office, Landholder, Gorakpur.	......	do.
944	"	"	Balna Bidyadharam Bardhini Sabha.	Pundit Ram Charitra ...	Hindu, Brahmin	Zemindar, Balna, Post Office, Rigauli.	......	By a Meeting of the Sabha on the 29th November, 1888.
945	"	"	Ghazipur.	Munshi Oodit Narain Lal	Hindu.	Zemindar, Pleader, Ghazipur.	......	By a Public Meeting held on the 2nd December, 1888.
946	"	"	"	Pundit Kawaleshwar Prasad Misra.	Hindu, Brahmin.	Pleader, Ghazipur.	......	do.
947	"	"	"	Mohamed Usmani Khan	Mahomedan.	Pleader and Landholder, Ghazipur.	......	do.
948	"	"	"	Babu Devendra Nath Sen, B.A.	Hindu	Pleader, Judge's Court, Ghazipur.	......	do.
949	"	"	"	" Jagat Narain Sinha	do.	Taluqdar and Rais, Ghazipur.	......	do.
950	"	"	"	Pundit Shri Nath Dube...	Hindu, Brahmin.	Taluqdar and Municipal Commissioner, Ghazipur.	......	do.
951		"	"	Babu Sital Singh ...	Hindu, Khetri.	Pleader, Ghazipur, Landholder and Member, District Board.	......	do.
952	,	"	"	Haji Abdulmoghani ...	Mahomedan.	Landholder, Indigo Planter, Member, District Board and Municipal Commissioner.	......	do.
953			"	Pundit Arjun Pandey ...	Hindu	Agriculturist and Pleader.	......	do.
954		"	"	Babu Bhola Nath Rai, B.A. ...	do.	Landholder and Pleader.	......	do.
955	"	"	"	Mahomed Quasim ...	Mahomedan.	Pleader, Ghazipur ...	......	do.
956	"	"	Ballia.	Mr. Nandan Prasad ...	Hindu, Kyastha.	Pleader, Ballia, and Agriculturist.	.....	By a Public Meeting held on the 21st December, 1888.
957	"	"	"	" Ram Kumar Lal	do.	Pleader and Zemindar, Ballia.	......	do.
958	"	"	"	" Parameswari Dayal	do.	Pleader and Zemindar and Agriculturist, Ballia.	......	do.
959	"	"	"	" Devi Prasad ...	do.	Pleader, Ballia, and Municipal Commissioner.	......	do.
960	"	"	Doaba (Ballia.)	" Radha Mohun Prasad, Pande, Rais Bairya.	Hindu	Zemindar, Bairya, Ballia.	......	By a Public Meeting held on the 22nd November, 1888.
961	"		Azimgarh City.	Moulvi Abdulghafoor ...	Mahomedan.	Pleader, Surajpore ...	.....	By a Public Meeting.

Number.	Presidency or Government.	Congress Circle.	Electoral Division.	Name in full of Delegates with honorary titles and scholastic degrees, &c.	Race, Religious denomination, or Caste, if any.	Occupation and Address.	Other Places or Associations for which they were also elected.	How and when elected.
962	N.-W. P.	Benares	Azimgarh City.	Moulvi Tawajuh Hussein	Mahomedan.	Pleader and Zemindar, Azimgarh.	......	By a Public Meeting.
963	,,	,,	,,	,, Mahomed Hussein	do.	Muktear and Zemindar, Azimgarh.	.....	do.
964	,,	,,	Arya Samaj, Azimgarh.	Munshi Lallan Prosad	Hindu, Kyasth.	Pleader and Zemindar, Surajpore.	......	By a General Meeting of the Samaj in December, 1888.
965	,,	,,	,,	,, Shamboo Nath ...	do.	do. ...	.....	do.
966	,,	,,	Taluqa Amila	,, Mohanlal ...	do.	Head Master, National School, Azimgarh.	Arya Somaj, Azimgarh.	By a Public Meeting and at a Meeting at the Samaj.
967	,,	,,	Basti.	Babu Adhar Chunder Bannerjee	Hindu, Brahmin.	Pleader. ...	....	By a Public Meeting on the 27th November, 1888.
968	,,	,,	,,	,, Bepin Behary Banerjee ...	do.	2nd Teacher, C. M. H School.	.....	do.
969	,,	,,		Mir Jharat Hussein ...	Mahomedad.	Pleader and Zemindar.	......	do.
970	,,	,,	Mirzapur.	Lala Bindeswari Prosad	Hindu, Kyastha.	Pleader, Member, district and Municipal Boards.	......	By a Public Meeting held on 17th December, 1888.
971	,,	,,	,,	Mr. Sri Ram	Hindu. Khettri.	Zemindar, Banker and Member, Municipal Board.	......	do.
972	,,	,,	,,	,, Beni Prosad	do.	Contractor, Carpet Manufacturer, Zemindar and Member, District and Municipal Boards.	......	do.
973	,,	,,	,,	Munshi Abduljabbar	Mahomedan.	Pleader and Member, District and Municipal Boards.	......	do.
974	,,	,,	,,	Lala Beni Prasad	Hindu, Kyastha.	Pleader and Agriculturist.	......	do.
975	,,	,,	,,	Mr. Sultan Singh	do.	Banker.		do.
976	,,	,,	,,	Pundit Shewsampat ...	Hindu, Brahmin.	Zemindar.		do.
977	,,	,,	,,	,, Kandhya Ram ...	Hindu.	do. ...		do.
978	,,	,,	,,	Lala Hera Lal	do.	Banker. ...		do.
979	,,	,,	,,	,, Luchman Das	do.	do., and Zemindar	......	do.
980	,,	,,	,,	,, Bishumbhar Das ...	do.	Banker.		do.
981	,,	,,	,,	Babu Bhola Nath Chowdhary.	do.	Zemindar.		do.
982	,,	,,	,,	Babu Budri Narayn Chowdhary	do.	Zemindar and Editor "Annud Kudambani," and Member, Municipal Board.	......	do.
983	,,	,,	,,	Mr. Kashi Nath Baroah	Christian.	3rd Master, L. M. School.	......	do.
984	,,	,,	,,	Babu Beni Kant Dutt, B.A.	Hindu.	2nd Master, L. M. School.	......	do.
985	,,	,,	,,	,, Kedar Nath Bhattacharjee, B.A.	do.	Pleader. ...	......	do.
986	,,	,,	,,	Mr. Gungadeen Anusthi...	Brahmin, Hindu.	Medical Practitioner	......	do.
987	,,	,,	,,	,, Jodu Nath Singh ...	do.	Zemindar.	Pargana Korh.	do., and at a Public Meeting on 14th December, 1888.
988	,,	,,	,,	Lala Bhagwan Prosad ...	do.	Pleader. ...	Korh Kayestha Sabha.	By a Public Meeting held on the 17th December, 1888, and at a Meeting of the Sabha on the 14th December, 1888.
989	,,	,,	,,	,, Ganga Prosad ...	do.	do. ...	do.	do.

Number.	Presidency or Government.	Congress Circle.	Electoral Division.	Name in full with honorary titles and scholastic degretes &c.	Race Religious denomination, or Caste if any.	Occupation and Address.	Other Places or Associations for which they were also elected.	How and when elected.
990	Govt. of India.	Allahabad.	Ajmere & Bandiqui.	Rev. Tara Chand ...	Christian.	Missionary, Ajmere	......	By a Public Meeting held on the 27th October, 1888.
991	"	"	"	Lalla Kishen Dass ...	Hindu. Agarwal.	Teacher and Vice-President, Agarwal Sabha, Ajmere.	......	do.
992	"	"	"	Lalla Gopi Nath ...	Hindu, Kayasth.	Secretary, Kayasth Sabha, Ajmere.	......	do.
993	"	"	Railway Association.	Babu Moona Lal Gupta	Hindu.	R. M. Railway, Delhi	Arya Samaj, Kankulej Mondul.	By a Public Meeting and a Meeting of the Association.
994	"	"	"	Babu Hari Dayal Sircar	do.	Clerk, R. M. Railway, Bandiqui.	......	do.
995	Bengal.	*Behar	Bankipur.	Mirza Golam Hyder ...	Mahomedan.	Bank Manager, Patna City, Bankipur.	......	By a Public Meeting held on the 5th December, 1888.
996	"	"	"	Babu Parmeswari Sahai	Hindu, Kyasth.	Municipal Commissioner, Honorary Magistrate, Member, District Board, Patna, and Zemindar, Sultangunj, Bankipur.	......	do.
997	"	"	"	Moulvi Taffazool Hossain Khan.	Mahomedan.	Zemindar, Honorary Magistrate, Member, District Board, Patna, Bankipur.	......	do.
998	"	"	"	Babu Bhubanashari Sahai, B.A., B.L.	Hindu Kyasth.	Junior Government Pleader, Bankipur and Zemindar of Garibputty, Saran.	......	do.
999	"	"	"	Babu Mohesh Narain ...	do.	Joint Editor, "Behar Herald" & "Indian Chronicle."	......	do.
1000	"	"	"	Babu Sreekishen Lall ...	do.	Pleader, Bankipur.	......	do.
1001	"	"	"	Babu Prayag Singh ...	Hindu.	Zemindar, Behar.	.....	do.
1002	"	"	"	Babu Adit Prosad Singh	do.	Zemindar, Sultangunj Bankipur.	......	do.
1003	"	"	"	Babu Edul Singh ..	do.	Zemindar, Rani Digha, Behar.	.....	do.
1004	"	"	"	" Baij Nath Singh ...	do.	Zemindar, Amawan, Behar.	......	do.
1005	"	"	"	Sayad Amir Hyder ...	Mahomedan.	Zemindar and Pleader, Bankipore.	......	do.
1006	"	"	"	Babu Raghu Nandan Prosad.	Hindu.	Municipal Commissioner, Zemindar, Gulzarbagh.	......	do. do.
1007	"	"	"	Babu Govinda Charan, M. A., B. L.	do.	Secretary, Behar People's Association, Zemindar, and Pleader, Bankipur.	Behar Peoples' Association.	do. and at the Meeting of the Association on the 2nd December, 1888.
1008	"	"	"	Babu Bisseswar Singh ...	Rajput.	Zemindar and Pleader, Bankipore.	do.	do.
1009	"	"	"	Babu Brojonandan Singh, B.A.	Hindu, Kyasth.	Pleader, and Secretary, Behar Standing Congress Committee.	do,	do.
1010	"	"	"	" Abinash Chundra Ghose, M.A., B.L.	do.	Vakil, Bankipore	do.	do.
1011	"	"	"	Babu Gujjadhar Prosad	do.	Zemindar, Member, District Board, Municipal Commissioner and Pleader, Bankipur.	do.	do.

* Behar has since been divided into three congress circles with standing C. C.'s at Bankipore for the Patna Division, and at Hazaribagh and Bhagulpore, for the divisions of these names.

Number.	Presidency or Government.	Congress Circle.	Electoral Division.	Name in full of Delegates with honorary titles and scholastic degrees, &c.	Race, Religious denomination, or Caste, if any.	Occupation and Address.	Other Places or Associations for which they were also elected.	How and when elected.
1012	Bengal	Behar	Bankipur.	Babu Shew Shunkur Sahai.	Hindn Kyastha.	Pleader and Zemindar, Bankipur.	Behar Peoples' Association	By a Public Meeting of the 5th Dec. and at the Meeting of the Association on the 2nd December, 1888.
1013	„	„	„	Babu Purnendu Narain Singh, M.A., B.L.	do.	Pleader, Bankipore.	do.	do,
1014	„	„	„	Pandit Joy Narain Bajpai	Hindu, Brahmin.	Banker and Zemindar, Patna City.	do.	do.
1015	„	„	„	Babu Narain Prosad, B.A., B.L.	Hindu, Khettriya.	Vakil and Municipal Commissioner.	do. and Patna City.	do. and at a Meeting held at Patna City on the 9th December, 1888.
1016	„	„	„	Babu Guru Prasad Sen, M.A., B.L.	Hindu, Vaidya.	Zemindar, Municipal Commissioner Editor, "Behar Herald," Vakil, Bankipur.	do. and Vicrampur.	do. and at a Meeting at Vicrampore.
1017	„	„	„	Babu Bishembhar Singh	Hindu.	Zemindar and Cultivator, Chintamun Chock, Mokamah, Zillah Patna.	Mokamah.	Public Meetings held at Bankipore on the 5th and at Mokamah on the 7th December, 1888.
1018	„	„	Suniti Sancharini Sabha, Bankipore.	Babu Anupnarain, B.A.	Hindu Kyastha.	Zemindar and Secretary "Sunity Sancharini Sabha," Bankipore.	......	At a Meeting of the Sabha on the 2nd December, 1888.
1019	„	„	Behar Arya Samaj.	„ Akhouri Luxminarayan, B.A.	do.	Zemindar and Secretary "Arya Samaj," Bankipore.	......	At a Meeting of the Samaj in November 1888.
1020	„	„	The Progress Club, Bankipore.	„ Thakur Prosad, B.A.	do.	Banker and Zemindar, Gya.	......	At a Meeting of the Club held on the 6th December, 1888.
1021	„	„	Patna City	Babu Gopal Chand Choubey.	Hindu, Brahmin.	Zemindar and Mahajan.	......	At a Public Meeting held at Patna on the 9th December, 1888.
1022	„	„	„	Dr. Mohendra Nath Chakrabutty.	do.	Doctor, Zemindar and Municipal Commissioner, Patna City.	......	do.
1023	„	„	„	Babu Raja Ram ...	Hindu, Agarwalla.	Zemindar, Banker, and Indigo Planter, Patna City.	Bankipur.	Do., and at Bankipur on the 5th December, 1888.
1024	„	„	„	„ Grijaput Sahai ...	Hindu, Kyastha.	Zemindar, Honorary Magistrate and Member, District Board, Patna City.	do.	do.
1025	„	„	Mokameh Peoples' Association.	„ Sital Prosad Singh.	Hindu, Bhavan.	Zemindar and Secretary, Mokameh Peoples' Association.	do.	At a General Meeting of the Association on the 7th December 1888, and at Bankipur on the 5th December 1888.
1026	„	„	Hazaribagh.	Mirza Imdad Ali ...	Mahomedan.	Landholder, Honorary Magistrate, Municipal Commissioner, Hazaribagh.	Hazaribagh Association	By a Public Meeting held at Hazaribag on the 7th November, 1888, and at a General Meeting of the Association.
1027	„	„	„	Munshi Golab Chand ...	Hindu, Kyastha.	Pleader, Landholder, Honorary Magistrate Municipal Commissioner, Member, District Committee, Education Committee; Vice-President, Hazaribagh Association, Hazaribagh.	do.	do.

Number.	Presidency or Government.	Congress Circle.	Electoral Division.	Names in full of Delegates with honorary titles, scholastic degrees, etc.	Race, Religious denomination, and Caste, if any.	Occupation and Address.	Other Places or Associations for which they were also elected	How and when elected.
1028	Bengal	Behar	Hazaribagh.	Rai Jadu Nath Mookerji, B.L.	Hindu, Brahmin.	Vakil, Honorary Magistrate, Vice-Chairman, Municipality, Member, District Committee, Member, Education Committee, President, Hazaribagh Association, Hazaribagh.	Hazaribagh Association	By a Public Meeting held at Hazaribag on the 7th November, 1888, and at a General Meeting of the Association.
1029	"	"	"	Babu Hari Churn Mittra, M.A., B.L.	Hindu, Kyastha.	Vakil, Honorary Magistrate, Municipal Commissioner, Vice-Cha rman, District Committee, Member, Education Committee, Vice-President, Hazaribagh Association, Hazaribagh.	do.	do.
1030	"	"	Giridi, Hazaribagh.	Munshi Gowri Prashad.	do.	Manager, Raj Palgunj, Giridi, E.I.R.	......	By a Meeting held at Giridi on the 23rd October, 1888.
1031	"	"	Monghir.	Babu Shewnunden Prosad Singh.	Hindu.	Zemindar, Monghir.	......	By a Public Meeting held at Monghir on the 19th December, 1888.
1032	"	"	"	Moulvi Abdul Rahman Khan.	Mahomedan.	do.	......	do.
1033	"	"	Jamalpore Association (Monghir.)	Babu Harendra Chundra Talookdar, B.L.	Hindu Kyastha.	Pleader, Jamalpore.	......	By a Public Meeting held on the 10th December, 1888.
1034	"	"	Gya.	Mahomed Wazir Ali Khan Lodi, L.M.S., F.S.S.	Mahomedan.	Private Medical Practitioner, Secretary Rate-payers' Association, Member of Gya Gorakhini Sabha.	......	By a Public Meeting held at Gya on the 25th November, 1888.
1035	"	"	"	Kazi Maqbool Ali.	do.	Zemindar, Honorary Magistrate, M. L. Board, Gya.	......	do.
1036	"	"	"	Babu Drigpal Lal.	Hindu.	Zemindar and Banker, Gya.	......	do.
1037	"	"	Tikari (Gya.)	Babu Bhagwat Sahai, B.A.	do.	Head Master Tikari School, Tikari, Gya.	......	At a Public Meeting held on the 5th December, 1888.
1038	"	"	"	Babu Nundo Kishore ...	do.	Zemindar, Tikari, Gya.	......	do.
1039	"	"	"	Pundit Shew Narain Bajpai.	Hindu, Brahmin.	Medical Practitioner, Tikari, Gya.	......	do.
1040	"	"	Baidyanath (Deoghur.)	Babu Jogendra Nath Bose	Hindu, Kyastha.	Journalist.	......	At a Public Meeting held at Baidyanath on the 27th October, 1888.
1041	"	"	Chupra	Babu Bunsidhur Gupta ...	Hindu, Vaidya.	Pleader, Honorary Magistrate, Member, District and Local Boards, Municipal Commissioner.	......	By a Public Meeting held o the 4th December, 1888.
1042	"	"	"	Babu Raghu Nath Prosad	Hindu.	Zemindar, Chupra. ...	......	do.
1043	"	"	"	Moulvi Syed Mahomed Nagy	Mahomemedan.	do ...	......	do
1044	"	"	"	Babu Choob Lall ...	Hindu.	Do., and Pleader, Chupra.	Behar Arya Samaj	Do., and at the Meeting of the Samaj.
1045	"	"	"	Babu Raghubans Sahai B.A., B.L.	do.	do. ...	Arrah.	By a Public Meeting held at Chupra on the 4th December, 1888, and at a Public Meeting at Arrah.
1046	"	"	Rivelgunj (Sarun).	Lala Januki Prosad ...	do.	Cultivator ...	......	By a Public Meeting in December, 1888.

Number.	Presidency or Government.	Congress Circle.	Electoral Division.	Names in full of Delegates with honorary titles and scholastic degrees, &c.	Race, Religious denomination or Caste, if any.	Occupation and Address.	Other Places or Associations for which they were also elected.	How and when elected.
1047	Bengal	Behar	Rivelgunj (Sarun).	Babu Tara Kanta Chakrabutty.	Hindu, Brahmin.	Cultivator ...	......	By a Public Meeting in December, 1888.
1048	„	„	„	Sheik Abdool Hossein ...	Mahomedan.	Zemindar ...	......	do.
1049	„	„	Muzafarpur	Mr. P. Kennedy, M.A., B.L.	European, Christian.	Pleader, Muzafarpur, and Editor, "Tirhoot Courier,' and Roy Chand and Prem Chand Scholar.	......	At a Public Meeting on the 9th December, 1888.
1050	„	„	„	Babu Ishri Prosad ...	Hindu.	Banker and Zemindar	......	do.
1051	„	„	„	Babu Jogodis Kumar Mookerjee.	do.	Zemindar and Honorary Magistrate, Muzafarpur.	......	do.
1052	„	„	„	Moulvi Syed Ahmed Hossein.	Mahomedan.	Zemindar & Pleader	......	do.
1053	„	„	„	Babu Urjoon Dass	Hindu.	Merchant, Muzafarpur.	......	do.
1054	„	„	„	„ Kunj Lal ...	do.	Zemindar, Honorary Magistrate and Banker.	......	do.
1055	„	„	„	„ Rameshwar Narain Mahtha.	do.	Do., do., do. Municipal Commissioner, and Proprietor of the "Tirhoot Courier."	......	do.
1056	„	„	„	Moulvi Zahiruddin Ahmed	Mahomedan.	Pleader and Zemindar	......	do.
1057	„	„	„	Syed Afzul Hossein ...	do.	Muktar and Manager, "Tirhoot Courier."	......	do.
1058	„	„	„	Babu Sorashi Churn Mitter, B.L.	Hindu.	Pleader ...	......	do.
1059	„	„	„	Babu Mungul Prasad ...	do.	Zemindar ..	......	do.
1060	„	„	„	„ Hari Har Prasad ...	do.	do.	......	do.
1061	„	„	„	„ Jogesshur Prosad Singh.	do.	Do., and Member, Sooniti Sancharini Sabha.	Sooniti Sancharini Sabha.	do., and at a Meeting of the Sabha on the 2nd December, 1888.
1062	„	„	Shahabad	„ Baij Nath Singh ...	Hindu, Khetriya.	Zemindar and Member, District Board, Shahabad.	......	At a Public Meeting on the 2nd December, 1888.
1063	„	„	„	„ Chaturbhuj Sahai ...	Hindu, Kyastha.	Pleader, Judge's Court, Arrah, and Zemindar.	......	do.
1064	„	„	„	„ Kandhji Sahai, B.A., B.L.	do.	Pleader, Arrah, Vice-Chairman, Arrah Board, Zemindar and Member, District Board.	......	do.
1065	„	„	„	„ Shyamolanand	do.	Pleader, Arrah, Landholder, Municipal Commissioner, Member, Local Board, Arrah, and Member, District Board, Shahabad.	......	do.
1066	„	„	„	„ Ramjanun Singh ...	Hindu, Rajput.	Zemindar and Merchant, Arrah.	......	do.
1067	„	„	„	„ Jadubans Sahai ...	Hindu, Kyastha.	Zemindar, Municipal Commissioner, and Pleader, Arrah.	......	do.
1068	„	„	„	Mr. W. M. Reid ...	European, Christian.	Zemindar, Arrah ...	......	do.
1069	„	„	„	Babu Thakur Prosad Sinha.	Hindu.	Zemindar & Banker, Arrah.	Ghazipur	do., and at a Meeting held at Ghazipur on the 5th December, 1888.

Number.	Presidency or Government.	Congress Circle.	Electoral Division.	Names in full of Delegates with honorary titles, scholastic degrees, etc.	Race, Religious denomination, and Caste, if any.	Occupation and Address.	Other Places or Associations for which they were also elected.	How and when elected.
1070	Bengal	Behar.	Buxar (Shahabad)	Baboo Hurdhyan Singh ...	Hindu.	Zemindar, Pleader, Member, Local Board, Buxar.	......	At a Meeting held at Buxar.
1071	"	"	"	" Raghu Nandan Prosad.	Hindu, Kyastha.	Vakil, High Court, Calcutta.	......	do.
1072	"	"	Dumraon (Shahabad).	" Brojendra Kumar Bose.	do.	Head Master, Domraon School.	......	By a Public Meeting on the 23rd December, 1888.
1073	"	"	"	" Radha Kishun Lal	do.	Muktear, Domraon...	......	do.
1074	"	"	"	Mr. Omrao Ali ...	Mahomedan.	Inspector, Raj Schools, Domraon Division.	......	do.
1075	"	"	Durbhunga.	Babu Mitterlal Chowdhari	Hindu.	Zemindar, Durbhunga	......	Public Meeting held at Durbhunga on the 9th December, 1888.
1076	"	"	"	Qazi Farasatali ...	Mahomedan.	do. ...	......	do.
1077	"	"	"	Moulvi Mahammad Ishaque Khan.	do.	Zemindar, and Honorary Magistrate, Durbhunga.	......	do.
1078	"	"	"	Shah Wazarat Ali ...	do.	Zemindar, Durbhunga	......	do.
1079	"	"	"	Moulvi Ally Hossain ...	do.	do. ...	......	do.
1080	"	"	"	Shamsul Huq ...	do.	do. ...	......	do.
1081	"	"	Dinapore	Babu Madho Lal ...	Aryan, Vedic Religion.	Merchant, Municipal Commissioner, Dinapore.	......	By a Public Meeting on the 4th December, 1888.
1082	"	"	"	Roy Lakshmi Narayan Siuba.	Aryan Kyastha.	Zemindar and Secretary, Congress Committee.	......	do.
1083	"	"	"	Syed Sharfuddin ...	Mahomedan.	Barrister-at-Law, Zemindar, Municipal Commissioner, Vice-Chairman, District Board, Chairman, Local Board, Dinapore, Bankipur.	Bankipore.	do., and at Bankipore on the 5th December, 1888.
1084	"	"	"	Sayad Abdool Hamid, B.A., B.L.	do.	Zemindar, Member, District Board, Vice-Chairman, Local Board. Chairman, Municipality, Khagaul. Pleader, Bankipore.	do.	do.
1085	"	"	Bhagulpore	Babu Ladhi Mohan Ghose	Hindu.	Medical Practitioner, Bhagulpore.	.. ...	At a Public Meeting held on the 15th December, 1888.
1086	"	"	"	" Soshi Bhusan Mookerjee.	do.	Pleader, Bhagulpore.	......	do.
1087	"	"	"	" Moti Lal Misser ...	do.	do. ...	......	do.
1088	"	"	"	Munshi Elahi Buksh ...	Mahomedan.	Zemindar, Bhagulpore	......	do.
1089	"	"	"	Babu Upendra Chandra Singh.	Hindu.	Zemindar, Naga House, Chaunpong, Bhagulpore.	......	do.
1090	"	"	"	" Tarini Prasad ...	do.	Pleader, Bhagulpore, Member, District Board, Municipal Commissioner, and Honorary Magistrate.	......	do.
1091	"	"	"	Rai Tej Narayan Singh, Bahadoor.	do.	Zemindar, Honorary Magistrate, and Merchant, Bhagulpore, and 9, Ripon Street, Calcutta.	National Chamber of Commerce, Calcutta.	do., and at a Meeting of the Chamber of Commerce.

Number.	Presidency or Government.	Congress Circle.	Electoral Division.	Names in full of Delegates with honorary titles and scholastic degrees, &c.	Race, Religious denomination, or Caste, if any.	Occupation and Address.	Other Places or Associations for which they were also elected.	How and when elected.
1092	Bengal	Behar.	Purneah	Babu Nanak Prasad ...	Hindu.	Zemindar, Pleader, Vice-Chairman, Purneah Municipality & Secretary, Congress Committee, Purneah and Member, District Board.	Kishengunj.	At a Public Meeting held at Purneah on the 1st December, 1888, and at Kishengunj on the 27th November, 1888.
1093	„	„	„	„ Parbutty Churn Dass.	do.	Pleader, Purneah, Member, District Board, and Municipal Commissioner, Purneah.	do.	do.
1094	„	„	„	„ Sheo Prasad ...	do.	Zemindar, Purneah...	Brarea.	At a Public Meeting at Purneah on the 1st December, 1888, and at a Meeting at Brarea.
1095	„	„	„	„ Jogendra Nath Mookerjee, M.A., B.L.	do.	Pleader, Purneah ...	do.	do.
1096	„	„	„	Mir Jowhar Ali ...	Mahomedan.	Zemindar, Purneah District.	do.	do.
1097	„	Calcutta	Southern Suburbs of Calcutta.	Mr. George Yule ...	Englishman, Christian.	Merchant, 7, Clive Row, Calcutta.	Indian Association.	By a Public Meeting of the residents of the Suburbs held at Bhawanipore on the 1st December, 1888, and by a General Meeting of the Association.
1098	„	„	Bengal National League.	Mr. W. C. Bonnerjee ...	Hindu, Brahmin.	Barrister-at-Law, Fellow, Calcutta University, 6 Park Street, Calcutta.	......	By a Public Meeting held at Shobhabazar Rajbati on the 21st October, 1888.
1099	„	„	British Indian Association.	Babu Rajkumar Sarvadhikari, B.L.	Hindu. ...	27, Mott's Lane, Calcutta. Editor, "Hindu Patriot." Fellow, Calcutta University.	......	At a Committee Meeting of the Association held on the 12th December 1888.
1100	„	„	„	Mr. J. Ghosal ...	Hindu, Brahmin.	Zemindar and Honorary Magistrate, Municipal Commissioner, Kashia Bagan Garden House, Upper Circular Road, Calcutta.	Bengal National League, and Joyrampore, Association.	do., and at a Public Meeting held at Shobhabazar Rajbati on the 21st October, 1888, and also at a Meeting of the Joyrampore Association on the 20th October, 1888.
1101	„	„	„	Babu Mohesh Chander Chowdhry.	Do. Vaidya.	Zemindar, Merchant, and Pleader, Fellow Calcutta University, High Court, 10, Harrington Street, Calcutta.	Bengal National League.	At a Committee Meeting of the Association on the 12th December, 1888, and at a Public Meeting held at Shobhabazar Rajbati on the 21st October, 1888.
1102	„	„	„	Rai Parvati Shunker Chowdhury.	do.	Zemindar, Post Teota, *via*, Shivalya, 50, Durmahatta Street, Calcutta.	Manickgunge.	At a Committee Meeting of the Association on the 12th December, 1888, and at a Meeting held at Manickgunge.
1103	„	„	„	Babu Nobin Chand Bural	Hindu. ...	Solicitor, 10, Old Post Office Street, Calcutta.	......	At a Committee Meeting of the Association on the 12th December, 1888.
1104	„	„	„	„ Saligram Singh, B.L.	Hindu, Rajput.	Vakil, High Court, Presidency Magistrate, and Zemindar, Calcutta.	Bankipore.	Do., and at a Public Meeting held at Bankipore, on the 5th December 1888.
1105	„	„	„	„ Jogendra Chandra Ghose ...	Do. Kyastha.	Zemindar, 14, Pudma Pooker Street, Kidderpore, Calcutta.	Southern Suburbs of Calcutta.	At a Committee Meeting of the Association held on the 12th December, 1888, and at a Public Meeting held at London Missionary Institution, Bhowanipore, on the 1st December 1888

Number.	Presidency or Government.	Congress Circle.	Electoral Division.	Names in full of Delegates with honorary titles and scholastic degrees, &c.	Race, Religious denominations or Caste, if any.	Occupation and Address.	Other Places or Associations for which they were also elected.	How and when elected.
1106	Bengal	Calcutta	Bengal National League.	Babu Narendra Nath Sen	Hindu, Vadya.	Proprietor, and Editor, "Indian Mirror," Attorney-at-Law, & Honorary Presidency Magistrate, and Municipal Commissioner, 74, Dhurmotollah Street, Calcutta.	Indian Association and Central Bengal Union.	At a Public Meeting held at Shobhabazar Rajbati, on the 21st October, 1888, and at a Meeting of the Indian Association, and also at a Meeting of the Central Bengal Union.
1107	,,	,,	,,	Maharaj Kumar Neelkrishna Deb Bahadoor.	Hindu, Kyastha.	Zemindar, Shobhabazar Rajbati, Calcutta, Honry. Magistrate.	Indian Association and its Tamlook Branch, Agarparah Association, Ichapur Reform Association, Najra Natra Ustica Gopalpur, Joynagore, Ratepayers' Association, Bharot Barsa Arya Dharmo Procharinу Sabha, Chittagong Association, Khirpai.	At a Public Meeting held at Shobhabazar Rajbati, on the 21st October, 1888, at a Meeting of the Indian Association, Tamlook Branch, Indian Association, on the 25th December, 1888, at a Meeting of the Agarparah Association, on the 2nd December, 1888, at a Meeting of the Ichapur Reform Association, on the 9th December, 1888, at a Meeting of the Najra Natra Ustica, Meeting of Gopalpur, and Joynagoro Ratepayers' Association Meeting, at a Meeting of the Bharat Barsa Arya Dharmo Procharini Sabha, on the 12th December, 1888, at a Meeting of the Chittagong Association, and also at a Meeting of Khirpai, on the 14th November, 1888.
1108	,,	,,	,,	Maharaj Kumar Benoya Krishna Deb Bahadoor.	do.	Zemindar and Municipal Commissioner.	do.	do.
1109	,,	,,	,,	Babu Gopal Chandra Mukerji.	Hindu, Brahmin.	Editor, "Songbad Probhakor," 40, Sankor Halder's Lane, Ahiritolla, Calcutta.	Agarparah Association, and Ichapore Reform Association.	By a Public Meeting held at Shobhabazar Rajbati, on the 21st October, 1888, and at a Public Meeting at Agarparah Association, on the 2nd December, 1888, and also at a Meeting of the Ichapore Reform Association held on the 19th December, 1888.
1110	,,	,,	,,	,, Bijoy Lall Dutt ...	Hindu, Kyastha.	Zemindar, Bhowanipore, Calcutta, Arbalia, 24-Purgunnahs.	Arbalia Bikashini Sabha.	At a Meeting held at Shobhabazar Rajbati, on the 21st October, 1888, and at a Meeting of the Arbalia Bikashini Sabha.
1111	,,	,,	,,	Mr. Mono Mohun Ghose	do.	Barrister-at-Law, 4, Theatre Road, Calcutta.	Joyrampore Association.	By a Public Meeting held at Shobhabazar Rajbati, on the 21st October, 1888, and at a Meeting of the Association on the 20th October 1888.
1112	,,	,,	,,	Babu Moti Lal Ghose ...	do.	Editor, "Amrita Bazar Patrika," &c, Zemindar, and Member, District Board, Calcutta, 2, Anonda Chandra Chatterjee's Lane, Bagbazar, Calcutta.	......	By a Public Meeting held at Shobhabazar Rajbati on the 21st October 1888.
1113	,,	,,	,,	,, Pasupati Nath Bose	do.	Zemindar, 65, Bagbazar Street, Calcutta.	......	do.

Number.	Presidency or Government.	Congress Circle.	Electoral Division.	Names in full of Delegates with honorary titles, scholastic degrees, etc.	Race, Religious dinomination, or Caste, if any.	Occupation and Address.	Other Places or Associations for which they were also elected.	How and when elected.
1114	Bengal	Calcutta	Bengal National League.	Mr. Nagendra Nath Ghose.	Hindu, Kyastha.	Editor, "Indian Nation," Barrister-at-Law, Municipal Commr. & Honorary Magistrate, 43, Bancharam Aukoor's lane, Calcutta.	......	By a Public Meeting held at Sobhabazar Rajbati on the 21st October, 1888.
1115	,,	,,	,,	Babu Bhupendra Nath Bose, M.A., B.L.	do.	Attorney-at-Law, 14 Balaram Ghose's Street, Calcutta.	......	do.
1116	,,	,,	,,	,, Nolin Behary Sarkar	do.	Merchant, Secretary, India Club, 21, Beadon Street, Calcutta.	......	do.
1117	,,	,,	,,	,, Poolin Behary Sarkar.	do.	Merchant, 21, Beadon Street, Calcutta.	......	do.
1118	,,	,,	,,	,, Jogendra Chandra Bose, B.A.	do.	Editor, "Shurobhi and Potaka," 33, Bechoo Chatterjee's Street, Calcutta.	......	do.
1119	,,	,,	,,	,, Mohini Mohun Chatterjee, M.A., B.L.	Hindu, Brahmin.	Attorney-at-Law, 10, Old Post Office Street, Calcutta.	......	do.
1120	,,	,,	,,	,, Radha Ramon Kar	Hindu, Kyastha.	Contractor and Trader, 10, Shambazar Street, Calcutta.	......	do.
1121	,,	,,	,,	,, Jogendra Krishna Bose.	do.	35-1, Raja Novokrishna's Street, Calcutta.	......	do.
1122	,,	,,	,,	,, Radha Govind Kar, L.R.C.P., etc.	do.	Medical Practitioner, 107, Shambazar Street, Calcutta.	......	do.
1123	,,	,,	Indian Association.	Kumar Satyabadi Ghosal	Hindu, Brahmin.	Zemindar, Bhukailash	......	At a General Meeting of the Association.
1124	,,	,,	,,	Babu Upendra Nath Mookerjee, B.A., B.L.	do.	Pleader, 31 Sitaram Ghose's Street, Calcutta.	......	do.
1125	,,	,,	,,	Babu Debendra Chandra Ghose, B.A., B.L.	Hindu, Kyastha.	Senior, Government Pleader, Honorary Magistrate, 24 Pergunnas, Bhowanipore, Calcutta.	......	do.
1126	,,	,,	,,	Babu Khetra Mohun Das	Christian.	Pleader, 16 Simla, Street, Calcutta.	......	do.
1127	,,	,,	,,	Mr. Ananda Mohun Bose, M.A.	Hindu.	Barrister-at-Law, Fairy Hall, Dum-Dum, 24 Pergunnas.	Rohora Branch, India Association, Mymensingh Association, Noakhali.	do., and at a General Meeting of the Rohara Branch, Indian Association, on the 18th November, 1888, and at a General Meeting of the Mymensingh Association, on the 9th December, 1888, and at a Public Meeting held at Noakhali.
1128	,,	,,	,,	Babu Surendra Nath Banerjee, B.A.	Hindu, Brahmin.	Editor of the "Bengali" and Principal, Ripon College, Honorary Magistrate and Municipal Commissioner, and Secretary, Indian Association, Calcutta.	Moulvibazar, Sylhet, Dhubri, Rohora Branch, Indian Association.	At a General Meeting of the Association, and at Public Meetings held at Moulvibazar, Sylhet, Dhubri, and also at a General Meeting of the Rohora Branch, Indian Association.

Number.	Presidency or Government.	Congress Circle.	Electoral Division.	Names in full of Delegates with honorary titles, scholastic degrees, etc.	Race, Religious denomination, and Caste if any.	Occupation and Address.	Other Places or Associations for which they were also elected.	How and when elected.
1129	Bengal	Calcutta	Indian Association	Babu Krishna Kumar Mittra, B.A.	Hindu.	Editor, "Sanjibani." 4, College Square, Calcutta.	Mymensingh Association, Tangail Association, Sankrail. Hitsadhini Sabha, Krishnaghar Indian Association.	At a General Meeting of the Association, and at a Meeting held at Mymensing Association on the 9th December. 1888, and at Sankrail Hitsadhini Sabha on the 16th December, 1888, Krishnaghar Indian Association on the 26th December, 1888, and also at a Meeting of the Tangail Association.
1130	,,	,,	,,	Babu Umesh Chandra Dutt, B.A.	Hindu, Kyastha.	Principal, City College, 13 Mirzapore Street, Calcutta.	Central Bengal Union, Joynagore Association.	At General Meetings of the Indian Association, Central Bengal Union and Joynagore Association.
1131	,,	,,	,,	Babu Dwarka Nath Gangooly.	Hindu.	Assistant Secretary, Indian Association, 62, Bowbazar Street, Calcutta.	Bikrampore (Dacca) and Tezpore Ryots' Association.	At a General Meeting of the Association and at a Meeting held at Bikrampore on the 15th December, 1888, and at a General Meeting of the Tezpore Ryots' Association.
1132	,,	,,	,,	Babu Kailash Chandra Sen, L.L.	Hindu, Vadya.	Pleader, 24-Purgunnas, Zemindar, Dacca. 164-3 Maniktolla Street, Calcutta.	Bikrampore Association.	At a General Meeting of the Association and at a Meet- of the Bikrampore Association held on the 15th December, 1888.
1133	,,	,,	,,	Babu Jagodis Chandra Lahiri.	Hindu, Brahmin.	Medical Practitioner, 101, College Street, Calcutta.	Majdia Mahajany Sabha, Kissengunj Indian Association.	At a General Meeting of the Association and at Meetings held at the Majdia Mahajany Sabha and Kissengunj Indian Association.
1134	,,	,,	,,	Rai Jotindra Nath Chowdhury, M.A., B L.	Hindu, Kyastha.	Zemindar, Taki. 24-Purgunnas, Buranagore.	Taki Branch, Indian Association, Baranagore and Kassipore Sreepore Hitsadhony.	At a General Meeting of the Association, and at Meetings of the Taki Branch Indian Association and of the Buranagore, Kassipore and Sreepore Hitshadhony.
1135	,,	,,	Bengal Christian, Alliance.	Babu Kali Charan Banerjee, M.A., B.L.	Christian	Vakil. High Court. 81, Baranasy Ghose's Street, Calcutta.	Indian Association and Bengal Christian Conference.	At a General Meeting of the Alliance on the 14th December, 1888, and at a General Meeting of the Indian Association and at a Meeting of the Bengal Christian Conference.
1136	,,	,,	,,	Dr. K. G. Sarkar, M.B., L.R.C.P.	do.	Physician, 19 Mott's Lane, Calcutta.	......	do.
1137	,,	,,	Bengal, Christian Conference.	Babu Joy Gobind Shome, M.A., B.L.	do.	Vakil, High Court. 16, Simla Street, Calcutta.	Indian Association.	At a General Meeting of the Bengal Christian Conference, and at a General Meeting of the Association.
1138	,,	,,	Students' Association.	Babu Tara Prosonna Mittra.	Hindu, Kyastha.	Secretary, Ripon College. Bhowanipore, Calcutta.	Rajpore Improvement Assotion.	By a General Meeting of the Student's Association, and at a Meetinng of the Rajpore Improvement Association.
1139	,,	,,	Bengal National, Chamber of Commerce.	Mr. R. D. Mehta ...	Parsee	Merchant, 55, Canning Street, Calcutta, Honorary Magistrate.	Indian Association.	By General Meetings of the National Chamber of Commerce and of the Indian Association.

Number.	Presidency or Government.	Congress Circle.	Electoral Division.	Names in full of Delegates with honorary titles, scholastic degrees, etc.	Race, Religious denomination, and Caste, if any.	Occupation and Address.	Other Places or Associations for which they were also elected.	How and when elected.
1140	Bengal	Calcutta	Bengal National Chamber of Commerce.	Kumar Rameswar Malia	Hindu, Brahmin.	Zemindar and Colliery Proprietor.	Howrah and Ranigunj Peoples' Associations.	By a General Meeting of the National Chamber of Commerce, and by a Meeting of the Howrah Peoples' Association and also of the Ranigunj Peoples' Association on the 1st December, 1888.
1141	,,	,,		Babu Janki Nath Roy ...	Hindu.	Banker and Zemindar. Vice-President. National Chamber of Commerce.	......	By a General Meeting of the National Chamber of Commerce.
1142	,,	,,	Metropolitan Union, Bengal, Calcutta.	Babu Amrit Lal Dass ...	Hindu.	Landholder, Sub-Editor, "Shomeprokash" 12, Guruprasad Chowdhury's Lane, Calcutta.	......	By a General Meeting of the union on the 29th November, 1888.
1143	,,	,,	Police Court Pleaders' Association, Calcutta	Mr. J. K. Bose ...	do.	Pleader, High Court, 5, Mohendro Bose's Lane, Calcutta.	Ichapore Reform Association.	By a General Meeting of the Ichapore Reform Association on the 9th December, 1888, and by a General Meeting of the Pleaders' Association.
1144	,,	,,	East Bengal Association, Calcutta.	Babu Kassy Kinkor Sen, L.L.	Hindu, Vaidya.	Talookdar, District Dacca.	......	By a General Meeting of the Association in December, 1888.
1145	,,	,,	Bar Association Sealdah, Suburb of Calcutta.	Babu Nil Moni Dhor, B.A., B.L.	Hindu.	Pleader, Sealdah, 94, Serpentine Lane, Calcutta.	......	By a Meeting of the Association on the 19th December, 1888.
1146	,,	,,	South Suburbs of Calcutta.	Pundit Pran Nath Saraswati, M.A., B.L.	Hindu, Brahmin.	Vakil, High Court, Calcutta. Municipal Commissioner.	......	By a Public Meeting of the Residents of the South Suburbs on the 1st December, 1888.
1147	,,	,,	,,	Babu Umakally Mukerji	do.	Do., 12, Pudma Pooker Street, Calcutta.	......	do.
1148	,,	,,	,,	Babu Benod Lal Sen ...	Hindu, Vaidya.	Native Physician, 10, Kallighat Road, Bhowanipore, Calcutta.	......	do.
1149	,,	,,	,,	Babu Tarapado Ghose ...	Hindu. Kyastha.	Zemindar, 14. Pudma pooker Street, Kidderpore, Calcutta.	......	do.
1150	,,	,,	,,	Babu Mohendra Lal Sen	do.	Land Proprietor, Rushapagla, *viâ* Taligunj P. O., Calcutta.	Rushapagla Improvement Association.	Do. and at a General Meeting of the Association on the 6th November, 1888.
1151	,,	,,	,,	Babu Biprodas Banerji ...	Hindu, Brahmin.	Pleader, Honorary Magistrate, and Editor, "Sohochur."	Barasat and Chittagong.	At a Meeting of the residents of the South Suburbs on the 1st December, 1888, and at a Meeting of the Barasat Public, and also at a Meeting held at Chittagong on the 4th December, 1888.
1152	,,	,,	Northern Suburbs of Calcutta.	Babu Kiron Chandra Ray	Hindu, Kyastha.	Zemindar, Narail, Cassipore.	Branch Indian Association, Narail.	By a Public Meeting of the Inhabitants of the Northern Suburbs of Calcutta in November and by a Meeting of the Association in December.
1153	,,	,,	do., and (Nynan.)	Babu Hari Dass Bose ...	do.	Jute Merchant, Mohunbagan, Calcutta.	......	Workmen's Meeting at Nynan.

Number.	Presidency or Government.	Congress Circle.	Electoral Division.	Names in full of Delegates with honorary titles, scholastic degrees, etc.	Race, Religious denomination, and Caste, if any.	Occupation and Address.	Other Places or Associations for which they were also elected.	How and when elected.
1154	Bengal	Calcutta	Dum-Dum and the adjoining villages in the 24 Pergunnas District	Babu Mon Motho Nath Mookerji	Hindu, Brahmin.	Kadihati, Dum-Dum, Calcutta.	......	By a large Public Meeting of the Villagers on the 16th December, 1888.
1155	"	"	Taki, Branch, Indian Association.	Babu Mohit Chunder Bose M.A., B.L.	do.	Vakil, High Court, Calcutta, and now Resident of Baranagur.	......	By a General Meeting of the Association on the 18th November.
1156	"	"	Howrah Branch Indian Association.	Babu Monmotho Nath Banerji	Hindu, Brahmin.	Landholder, Shibpore, Howrah.	......	By a Meeting of the Association.
1157	"	"	Howrah Pleaders' Association.	Babu Hari Mohun Mookerji.	do.	Pleader, Howrah.	......	do.
1158	"	"	"	Babu Ramdoy Malia, L.L.	do.	do. ...	......	do.
1159	"	"	Howrah Peoples' Association.	Babu Narasina Datta, B.L.	Hindu, Kyastha.	Vakil, High Court, Notary Public, Honorary Magistrate and Municipal Commissioner, Howrah, Punchanuntola.	......	By a General Meeting of the Association on the 1st December, 1888.
1160	"	"	"	Babu Upendra Nath Mittra, B.L.	do.	Vakil, High Court, Notary Public, Honorary Magistrate and Municipal Commissioner.	......	do.
1161	"	"	"	Babu Umbica Charan Ghosal.	Hindu.	Law Agent ...	......	do.
1162	"	"	Hooghly	Babu Amoy Nath Bose	Hindu.	Landholder, Khulsini, British Chandernagore, District Hooghly.	......	By a Public Meeting 10th December, 1888.
1163	"	"	"	Babu Romesh Chandra Mandal.	do.	Zemindar, Honorary Magistrate, Chinsura	Balasore National Society and Well-wishing Club, Chinsurah.	do., and by a Meeting of the National Society on the 23rd November, 1888, and by a Meeting of the Well-wishing Club.
1164	"	"	"	Babu Mohendra Nath Ray, M.A., B.L.	do.	Vakil, Calcutta High Court, and Honorary Magistrate, Howrah.	Howrah Peoples' Association.	By a Public Meeting held on the 10th December, 1888, and by a Meeting of the Association on the 1st December, 1888.
1165	"	"	"	Doctor Syud Mahomed Hashun Gouse.	Mahomedan.	Hakim. Chinsurah, Hooghly, 70, Bentinck Street, Calcutta.	Well-wishing Club, Chinsurah.	By a Public Meeting held on the 10th December, and by a Meeting of the Club.
1166	"	"	Parwasthali, (Burdwan.)	Babu Mohima Nath Ray	Hindu.	Inspector, Pikeparah Estate, Parwasthali, Burdwan.	......	By a Public Meeting held at Parwasthali in December, 1888.
1167	"	"	Calna Branch, Indian Association, (Burdwan.)	Babu Bisnu Charan Banerji.	do.	Merchant, Calna Street, Burdwan, Municipal Commissioner.	......	At a General Meeting of the Association.
1168	"	"	Ahmedpore, (Burdwan.)	Babu Srish Chunder Chowdhury, M.A., B.L.	do.	Pleader, Landholder, Bhowanipore, Calcutta.	Indian Association, Tamlook.	By a Public Meeting at Ahamedpore and General Meeting of Tamlook Association.
1169	"	"	"	Babu Sree Pada Chowdhury.	do.	Landholder ...	......	By a Public Meeting held at Ahmedpore.
1170	"	"	Nuddea	Babu Akhoy Kumar Mukerji, B.L.	Hindu, Brahmin.	Pleader. Krishnaghur, Municipal Commissioner, Krishnaghur.	......	At a Public Meeting held the 19th December, 1888.

Number.	Presidency or Government.	Congress Circle.	Electoral Division.	Names in full of Delegates with honorary titles, scholastic degrees, etc.	Race, Religious denomination, and Caste, if any.	Occupation and Address.	Other Places or Associations for which they were also elected.	How and when elected.
1171	Bengal	Calcutta	Krishnaghar, (Nuddea.)	Babu Jadu Nath Chatterji, B.L.	Hindu, Brahmin.	Pleader, Zemindar, Honorary Magistrate and V. C. Municipality, Krishnaghar	......	At a Public Meeting held at Krishnaghar, on the 26th December, 1888.
1172	"	"	"	Babu Prasanna Chunder Rai, M.A., B.L.	Hindu, Chettri.	Zemindar and Indigo Planter, Kuralgachi, P. O., Chundipore *Viâ* Kissengunj.	......	do.
1173	"	"	"	Babu Abhoya Nund Rai	Hindu, Brahmin.	Zemindar, Municipal Commissioner, Honorary Magistrate, and Member, Local Board, Krishnaghar.	......	do.
1174	"	"	"	Babu Nafer Chander Pal Chowdhry.	do.	Zemindar, Merchant. Indigo Planter and Tea Planter, Natudoha.	Chooadangah and Meherpore.	do., and at the Public Meetings held at Chooadanga, and at Meherpore.
1175	"	"	"	Babu Basanta Kumar Chatterji, B.L.	Hindu, Brahmin.	Pleader, Judge's Court, Krishnaghar and Member Nuddea District Board.	Khustia Branch Indian Association, Poradaha Branch, Indian Association, and Joyrampore B. I. Association.	By a Public Meeting held at Krishnaghar on the 26th December, 1888, at the General Meeting of the Kushtia B. I. Association, on the 23rd November, 1888, at a General Meeting of the Poradaha B. I. Association, and also at a General Meeting of the Joyrampore Association on the 20th October, 1888.
1176	"	"	Ranaghat. (Nuddea.)	Babu Banku Behary Singh	Hindu,	Merchant, Habibpore, Ranaghat Sub-Division, Nuddea.	Kissengunj Mahajani Sabha.	By a Public Meeting held at Ranaghat on the 2nd December, 1888, and at a General Meeting of the Sabha.
1177	"	"	"	Babu Bepro Das Mukerji	Hindu, Brahmin.	Vakil, High Court, Calcutta.	Branch Indian Association, Ranaghat.	By a Public Meeting held at Ranaghat on the 2nd December, 1888, and at a General Meeting of the Association.
1178	"	"	"	Babu Akshai Kumar Ghose.	Hindu, Kyastha.	Assistant Sale Master Messrs. Graham & Co., Calcutta.	do.	do.
1179	"	"	Chagdoha (Nuddea.)	Babu Karuna Nidhan Ghose.	do.	Contractor and Secretary. Ranaghat Shuhrid Library, Ranaghat.	......	At a Public Meeting held at Chagdoha on the 9th December, 1888.
1180	"	"	"	Babu Akshai Kumar Mitter.	do.	Talookdar, Jasra, Chagdoha.	Ranaghat.	do., and at a Public Meeting held at Ranaghat on the 2nd December, 1888.
1181	"	"	Majdeah, (Nuddea.)	Babu Nanda Gopal Bhaduri.	Hindu, Brahmin.	Landholder and Merchant.	Kissengunj Mahajani Sabha.	At a Public Meeting held at Majdeah and by a General Meeting of the Sabha.
1182	"	"	"	Babu Pulin Behary Lahiri	do.	Pleader, Krishnaghar.	do.	do.
1183	"	"	Katdoha Association (Nuddea.)	Babu Nitya Nand Bose, B.A.	Hindu, Kyastha.	Teacher, Katdoha School, Paradoha P. O., Nuddea.	......	At a Meeting of the Association on the 8th December, 1888.
1184	"	"	Kushtia Branch, Indian Association, (Nuddea.)	Babu Chand Mohun Moitra.	Hindu, Brahmin.	Government Pensioner, Hizlabut, Kushtia, Nuddea.	......	By a Meeting of the Association on the 23rd November, 1888.
1185	"	"	Moheshpore, (Nuddea.)	Babu Jadu Bhuban Bhaduri, B.A.	do.	Head Master, Higher Class English School, Jessore.	......	By a Public Meeting held at Moheshpore.

Number.	Presidency or Government.	Congress Circle.	Electoral Division.	Names in full of Delegates with honorary titles, scholastic degrees, etc.	Race, Religious denomination, and Caste, if any.	Occupation and Address.	Other Places or Associations for which they were also elected.	How and when elected.
1186	Bengal	Calcutta	Indian Association, Jessore.	Babu Kali Nath Mookerji, B.A., B.L.	Hindu.	Vakil Landholder, and Honorary Magistrate, Jessore.	......	At a General Meeting of the Association on the 9th December, 1888.
1187	"	"	"	Babu Jadu Nath Mazumdar, M.A., B.L.	do.	Vakil and Talookdar, Jessore.	......	do.
1188	"	"	"	Babu Preo Shanker Ghose	do.	Landholder ...	......	do.
1189	"	"	Indian Association, Magurah, (Jessore.)	Babu Ambica Charan Sarkar.	do.	Vice-Chairman, Local Board, Magurah. Member, District Board, Jessore, and Honorary Magistrate, Magurah.	......	At a General Meeting of the Association on the 16th November, 1888.
1190	"	"	"	Babu Bhubanananda Chakrabutty.	do.	Medical Practitioner, Member Local Board, and Honorary Magistrate, Magurah.	......	do.
1191	"	"	Jingergacha Ryots' Association, (Jessore.)	Babu Neel Kumal Dass	do.	Assistant Auditor, E. I. Railway, 32, Raja Rajbullab's Street, Calcutta.	......	At a Committee Meeting of the Association.
1192	"	"	Moorshedabad Association.	Babu Baikuntha Nath Sen, B.L.	do.	Vakil, Zemindar Berhampore, Moorshedabad, Chairman, Berhampore Municipality, Honorary Magistrate and Chairman, Moorshedabad Association.	......	By a Committee Meeting of the Association.
1193	"	"	"	Babu Hamendra Nath Sen, B.L.	do.	Pleader, Berhampore	......	do.
1194	"	"	"	Babu Prosanna Kumar Gupta, B.L.	do.	Pleader and Municipal Commissioner.	......	do.
1195	"	"	"	Babu Sree Nath Pal, B.L.	do.	do., and Zemindar, Berhampore.	......	do.
1196	"	"	"	Babu Mirtonjoy Bhuttacherjie.	do.	Assistant Engineer, Berhampore, Moorshedabad.	......	do.
1197	"	"	"	Babu Bijoy Krishna Maitra, B.L.	do.	Pleader, Honorary Magistrate, Berhampore, Moorshedabad.	......	do.
1198	"	"	"	Revd. C. N. Banerjee, B.A.	Christian.	Missionary of the London Missionary Society, Municipal Commissioner, President, Berhampore Total Abstinence Society, Berhampore, Moorshedabad.	......	do.
1199	"	"	Birbhoom	Babu Chandra Nath Chatterji, B.L.	Hindu.	Vakil, Zemindar, Vice-Chairman, District Board, Birbhoom.	......	By a Public Meeting.
1200	"	"	"	Babu Dhono Krishen Ghose, M.A., B.L.	do.	Vakil, Zemindar, Chairman, Municipality, Suri, Birbhoom.	......	do.
1201	"	"	Rungpore Branch, Indian Association.	Babu Janaki Balluv Sen	do.	Zemindar, Municipal Commissioner, Member, District Board.	......	By a General Meeting of the Association held on the 26th November, 1888.
1202	"	"	"	Babu Hem Chandra Mitter, B.L.	do.	Pleader, Judge's Court and Secretary Ratepayers' Association, Rungpore.	Rungpore Ratepayers' Association.	do., and at the Meeting of the Rate payers' Association on the 18th November, 1888.

Number.	Presidency or Government.	Congress Circle.	Electoral Division.	Names in full of Delegates with honorary titles, scholastic degrees, etc.	Race, Religious denomination, and Caste, if any.	Occupation and Address.	Other Places or Associations for which they were also elected.	How and when elected.
1203	Bengal	Calcutta	Saidpore (Rungpore.)	Babu Biroja Mohon Chowdhury.	Hindu.	Zemindar, Kamarpookur, Rungpore, and Member, District Board.	Nelphamari.	By a Public Meeting held at Saidpore on the 28th November, 1888. and at Nelphamari on the 25th November, 1888.
1204	,,	,,	Backergunge.	Moulvi Mahomed Hafiz...	Mohamedan.	Zemindar ...	......	At a Public Meeting held at Backergunge on the 9th December, 1888.
1205	,,	,,	,,	Babu Hari Kant Sen ...	Hindu.	Secretary to the Loan Office, Secretary to the Peoples' Association, Barisal.	......	do.
1206	,,	,,	Barisal Peoples' Association (Backergunge.)	Aswani Kumar Dutt, M.A., B.L.	do.	Landholder, Barisal, Chairman, Barisal Local Board, V. C. Barisal Municipality, Member, Backergunge District Board, and Secretary Barisal Peoples' Association.	(1.) Pherozepore. (2.) Bhola Sub-division. (3.) Patuakhali Sub-division. (4.) Haibutpore. (5.) Lata. (6.) Rahmutpur. (7.) Goda. (8.) Keara. (9.) Jhalokati. (10.) Baesan. (11.) Backergunge.	(1.) At a General Meeting of the Barisal Peoples' Association on the 16th December, 1888. (2.) By a Public Meeting at Pherozepore on the 16th December, 1888. (3.) By a Public Meeting of the people of the Bhola Sub-division on the 13th December, 1888. (4.) do. of the Patuakhali Sub-division on the 13th December, 1888. (5.) By a Meeting at Haibutpur on the 16th December, 1888. (6.) By a Meeting at Lata on the 15th December, 1888. (7.) By a Public Meeting at Rahmutpur on the 16th December 1888. (8.) By a Public Meeting at Goda on the 18th December, 1888. (9.) By a Meeting at Keara on the 14th December, 1888. (10.) By a Public Meeting at Jhalokati on the 16th December, 1888. (11.) By a Public Meeting at Baesan on the 19th December, 1888. (12.) By a Public Meeting of the residents of Backergunge held at Barisal on the 9th December, 1888.
1207	,,	,,	Farridpore Peoples' Association.	Babu Pyari Lal Roy, B.L.	Hindu.	Vakil, Barisal and Zemindar, Farridpur, Honorary Magistrate, and Municipal Commissioner, Barisal.	Backergunge.	At a Public Meeting of Backergunge held in Barisal on the 9th December, 1888, and at a General Meeting of the Farridpore Peoples' Association.
1208	,,	,,	,,	Babu Girija Sunker Mazoomdar.	do.	Zemindar and Pleader, High Court, Calcutta.	Arkandi and Rooderca.	(1.) By a General Meeting of the Peoples' Association. (2.) By a Public Meeting at Arkandi. (3.) By a Public Meeting at Rooderca.
1209	,,	,,	Madaripore Peoples' Association.	Babu Amrit Lal Ray Chowdhury.	do.	Zemindar, Madaripore.	......	By a General Meeting of the Association on the 27th November, 1888.
1210	,,	,,	Farridpore.	Babu Ambica Charan Mazumdar, M.A., B.L.	do.	Zemindar and Pleader, Chairman, Municipality, Member, District Board and Honorary Magistrate.	(1.) Madaripore. (2.) Bhatsa (3.) Rudrapore. (4.) Pinjon. (5) Amgram.	(1.) By a Public Meeting held at Farridpore on the 14th December, 1888. (2.) By a Public Meeting held at Madaripore on the 27th November, 1888. (3.) By a Public Meeting held at Rudrapore on the 5th December, 1888.

Number.	Presidency or Government.	Congress Circle.	Electoral Division.	Names in full of Delegates, with honorary titles, scholastic degrees, etc.	Race, Religious denomination, and Caste, if any	Occupation and Address.	Other Places or Associations for which they were also elected.	How and when elected.
	Bengal	Calcutta	Farridpore				(6,) Farridpore Peoples' Association. (7.) Manikdoha Hitshadhoni Sabha. (8.) Furridpore Suhrid Sabha, (9) Bhanga Peoples Association. (10.) Gopalgunj Association.	(4.) By a Public Meeting held at Pinjon on the 29th November, 1888. (5.) By a Public Meeting held at Amgram on the 11th December, 1888. (6.) At a General Meeting of the Farridpore Peoples' Association on the 14th November, 1888. (7.) At a General Meeting of the Sabha on the 2nd December, 1888. (8.) At a General Meeting of the Suhrid Sabha. (9.) At a General Meeting of the Bhanga Peoples' Association on the 9th December, 1888. (10.) At a General Meeting of the Gopalgunj Association.
1211	,,	,,	Rajshahye	Babu Nil Moni Chowdhry.	Hindu.	Superintendent and Agent, India General, Steam Navigation Company, Honorary Magistrate.	......	By a Public Meeting held on the 2nd December, 1888.
1212	,,	,,	,,	Abdur Rahman, B.A. ...	Mahomedan.	Teacher, Madrassa, Member of Municipal and Local Board.	......	do.
1213	,,	,,	,,	Rajah Shoshi Shekorashwar Roy.	Hindu.	3, Manicktolla Street, Zemindar of Tahirpore, Rajshahye.	......	do.
1214	,,	,,	Pubna	Mr. A. Chowdhury, B.A., LL.B. (Cantab) M.A., (C.U.)	do.	Barrister-at-Law, Calcutta and Zemindar, Pubna.	......	At a Public Meeting held at Pubna.
1215	,,	,,	Pubna Branch, Indian Association.	Babu Mohini Mohun Chukerbutty, M.A., B.L.	do.	Pleader, District Court, Pubna.	Rungpore Branch, Indian Association.	By a General Meeting of the Association held on the 16th December, 1888, and at a Meeting held at Rungpore Branch I. Association on the 25th November, 1888.
1216	,,	,,	Bagirhat (Khulna.)	Babu Bepin Behary Roy	do.	Pleader, Bagirhat, Khulna District.	......	By a Public Meeting held on the 14th December, 1888.
1217	,,	,,	Khulna	Babu Ambica Charan Sen, B.L.	do.	Pleader, Khulna, Municipal Commissioner, Member, District Board and Chairman, Local Board, Khulna.	Khulna Peoples' Association, Bagirhat Peoples' Association, Senhati Peoples' Association.	By a General Meeting of the Khulna Peoples' Association. By a General Meeting of the Bagirhat Peoples' Association on the 14th December. By a General Meeting of the Senhati Peoples' Association.
1218	,,	,,	Bogra Peoples' Association.	Babu Pyaree Sunker Das Gupta, L.M.S.	do.	Medical Practitioner, Bogra, Municipal Commissioner and Honorary Magistrate.	......	By a General Meeting of the Association.
1219	,,	,,	Dacca	Babu Brojendra Kumar Roy Chowdhury.	do.	Zemindar, Banker, Balihati, Dacca, Municipal Commissioner, and President Peoples' Association, Dacca.	......	By a Public Meeting.
1220	,,	,,	,,	Babu Sarat Chandra Gupta.	do.	Pleader, District Judge's Court, Dacca, Chairman, Local Board, Naraingunge, and Member, District Board, Dacca.	......	do.

Number.	Presidency or Government.	Congress Circle.	Electoral Division.	Names in full of Delegates, with honorary titles, scholastic degrees, etc.	Race, Religious denomination, and Caste, if any.	Occupation and Address.	Other Places or Associations for which they were also elected.	How and when elected.
1221	Bengal	Calcutta	Dacca Bar Association.	Babu Ishwar Chandra Ghose, B.A., B.L.	Hindu.	Pleader, Judge's Court, Dacca.	......	By a General Meeting of the Association.
1222	,,	,,	,,	Babu Trilokya Nath Bose, B.A., B.L.	do.	do. ...	......	do. and at a Public Meeting held at Dacca.
1223	,,	,,	Vicrampore (Dacca.)	Babu Ishwar Chundra Das, B.L.	do.	do., Chairman Dacca Municipality, Honorary Magistrate, Member, District Board, Secretary to the Peoples' Association, Dacca.	......	o.
1224	,,	,,	Midnapore.	Babu Navokumar Mittra	Hindu.	Pleader, Judge's Court, and Member, District Board, Midnapore.	......	By a Public Meeting on the 2nd December, 1888.
1225	,,	,,	,,	Chowdhury Jogendra Nath Mallick.	do.	Zemindar, Midnapore	......	do.
1226	,,	,,	,,	Babu Bhuboneshwar Mitter.	do.	Medical Practitioner, 12, Radha Nath Bose's Lane, Goabagan, Calcutta.	......	do.
1227	,,	,,	,,	Babu Ishan Chandra Bose	do.	Rent-free Landholder, Midnapore.	......	do.
1228	,,	,,	,,	Babu Ashutosh Ghose ...	do.	Zemindar, Raj Villore, Pingla P. O., Midnapore.	......	do.
1229	,,	,,	,	Babu Narain Prasad Dutt	do.	Pleader, Ghatal, Honorary Magistrate, Municipal Chairman & Secretary to the Indian Association, Ghatal.	......	do.
1230	,,	,,	Khirpai Indian Association (Midnapore.)	Babu Rameshwar Mandal, B.A., B.L.	do.	Pleader, 164, Upper Circular Road, Calcutta.	......	By a General Meeting of the Association on the 19th December, 1888.
1231	,,	,,	,,	Babu Raghu Nath Dass, M.A., B.L.	do.	Pleader and V. C. Municipality, Midnapore.	......	do.
1232	,,	,,	Chittagong Association.	Babu Aunada Charan Dhur, B.A.	do.	Zemindar, Chandanparah, Chittagong town.	......	By a General Meeting of the Association on the 4th December, 1888.
1233	,,	,,	,,	Babu Tara Charan Mukerji.	do.	Native Physician ...	......	do
1234	,,	,,	Chandpore (Tipperah.)	Babu Kritanto Kumar Bose, M.A., B.L.	do.	Vakil, High Court, Calcutta.	......	By a Public Meeting held in November.
1235	,,	,,	Commillah Peoples' Association (Tipperah.)	Babu Shiv Nath Misser	do.	Banker, Commillah.	......	By a General Meeting of the Association.
1236	,,	,,	,,	Babu Annunda Chandra Roy.	do.	Zemindar, Honorary Magistrate and Municipal Commissioner, Tipperah.	Moradnagore.	do., and at a Public Meeting held at Moradnagore.
1237	,,	,,	Muktagacha (Mymensingh.)	Babu Kally Nath Ghosal	Hindu.	Municipal Commissioner, Muktagacha.	......	By a Public Meeting held on the 16th December, 1888.
1238	,,	,,	,,	Babu Sreenath Roy, B.L.	do.	Pleader, Judge's Court, Mymensingh.	......	do.

Number.	Presidency or Government.	Congress Circle.	Electoral Division.	Names in full of Delegates with honorary titles, scholastic degrees, etc.	Race, Religious denomination, and Caste, if any.	Occupation and Address.	Other Places or Associations for which they were also elected.	How and when elected.
1239	Bengal	Calcutta	Mymensingh Association.	Babu Radha Ballabh Chowdhury.	Hindu.	Zemindar, Sherpore, Vice-Chairman, Local Board, Member Mymensingh District Board, Secretary, Sherpore Landholders' Association, and Secretary, Victoria Academy, Sherpore, Mymensingh.	Landholders' Association, Sherpore.	By a General Meeting of the Association on the 9th December, 1888, and at a General Meeting of the Landholders' Association on the 4th December, 1888.
1240	,,	,,	,,	Babu Anath Bandhu Guha B. A., B.L.	do.	Pleader, Talukdar, Honorary Magistrate and Secretary, Mymensingh Association, Mymensingh.	Tangail	By a General Meeting of the Association on the 9th December, 1888, and at a Public Meeting held at Tangail.
1241	,,	,,	Hossanpore Association (Mymensingh.)	Babu Harihar Chukerbutty B.A., B.L.	do.	Vakil and Zemindar, Mymensingh, and Member, District Board, Mymensingh.	Mymensingh Association	By a Public Meeting of the Hassanpore Association on the 12th December, 1888, and at a Meeting of the Mymensingh Association on the 9th December, 1888.
1242	,,	,,	Sherpore Landholders' Association (Mymensingh.)	Babu Kailas Chunder Nag	do.	Talukdar and Vice-Chairman, Sherpore Municipal Board.	......	By a General Meeting of the Association.
1243	,,	,,	Orissa Association Cuttack (Orissa.)	Mr. Sampson Rout ...	Christian.	Municipal Commissioner, and Member, Orissa Association.	......	By a Special Meeting of the Orissa Association held on the 16th December, 1888.
1244	,,	,,	,,	Mahomed Altahar ...	Mahomedan.	do. ..	......	do.
1245	,,	,,	Sylhet (Assam.)	Babu Bepin Chandra Pal	do.	Journalist, 13, Cornwallis Street, Calcutta.	Shillong	By Public Meetings at both places.
1246	,,	,,	Nowgong Ryots' Association (Assam.)	Babu Gonesham Baruah	do.	Nowgong, Assam, Cultivator.	......	By a General Meeting of the Association.
1247	,,	,,	Dhubri (Assam)	Babu Horendra Narain Singh Chowdhury.	Hindu.	Zemindar, Bugribari, Dhubri.	......	By a Public Meeting.
1248	,,	,,	Shillong (Assam.)	Babu Ram Chandra ...	do.	Merchant, Shillong ...	......	By a Public Meeting on the 15th December, 1888.

[The subnoted gentleman also sat as a delegate, but was not really elected, see p. xviii of introductory article: Rajah Siva Prasad, C.S.I., &c., &c., of Benares.]

Although great pains have been taken to make this list complete, there is no doubt that some names will prove to have been unintentionally omitted, in consequence of several delegates having failed to register their names in due form at the Congress. On the other hand several names have been intentionally omitted of gentlemen who did register, because, on enquiry from the local Standing and Divisional Committees, it did not appear that these gentlemen had been duly elected. Of all the 1,248 delegates entered in the list the election was duly verified, but one of these, No. 370, Pandit Shiv Narayan, wrote subsequently a letter to the papers saying that he was a self-constituted delegate. How he came to this conclusion it is difficult to say. As was pointed out in the *Tribune* of the 6th March, he at the Congress recorded himself in the register as elected at a public meeting at Jullundur on the 2nd of December, 1888, and further he held a regular certificate, signed by Pandit Devi Chand, the President of that meeting, that he had been duly elected. He had probably forgotten these facts when he wrote.

It has to be noticed that the same names will be found spelt in several different ways. This is due to the fact that people are beginning to spell their names—family names especially—differently, to distinguish themselves from members of other branches of the family. Thus Bannerjee will be found spelt Bannerjee, Banerjea, Bonnerjee, Bonarjee, &c.; Iyer is spelt Aiyer, Ayer, &c.; Pershad is spelt also Prosad, Proshad, Prasad, &c. Where gentlemen recorded their own names their own spelling has been followed; in other cases the spelling given the lists of the Standing and Divisional Committees has been adopted.

In the list many gentlemen who are Municipal Commissioners, members of District or Local Boards, Honorary Magistrates, Fellows and Graduates of the Universities, &c., &c., are not entered as such, simply because they themselves in recording their names, &c., failed to note these particulars, and it has been found impossible to supply these omissions.

APPENDIX II.

SUMMARY OF RESOLUTIONS

PASSED AT THE

FIRST, SECOND & THIRD CONGRESSES.

RESOLUTIONS PASSED AT THE FIRST CONGRESS.

RESOLUTION I.

Resolved—That this Congress earnestly recommends that the promised inquiry into the working of Indian Administration, here and in England, should be entrusted to a Royal Commission, the people of India being adequately represented thereon, and evidence taken both in India and in England.

[Proposed by Mr. G. Subramania Iyer *(Madras)* ; seconded by Mr. P. M. Mehta (*Bombay*) ; and supported by Mr. Norendronath Sen (*Calcutta*).]

RESOLUTION II.

Resolved—That this Congress considers the abolition of the Council of the Secretary of State for India, as at present constituted, the necessary preliminary to all other reforms.

[Proposed by Mr. S. H. Chiplonkar (*Poona*) ; seconded by Mr. P. Ananda Charlu (*Madras*) ; and supported by Mr. J. Ghosal (*Allahabad*).]

RESOLUTION III.

Resolved—That this Congress considers the reform and expansion of the Supreme and existing Local Legislative Councils, by the admission of a considerable proportion of elected members (and the creation of similar Councils for the North-Western Provinces and Oudh, and also for the Punjab) essential ; and holds that all Budgets should be referred to these Councils for consideration, their members being moreover empowered to interpellate the Executive in regard to all branches of the administration ; and that a Standing Committee of the House of Commons should be constituted to receive and consider any formal protests that may be recorded by majorities of such Councils against the exercise by the Executive of the power, which would be vested in it, of overruling the decisions of such majorities.

[Proposed by the Hon'ble K. T. Telang, C.I.E. (*Bombay*) ; seconded by the Hon'ble S. Subramania Iyer (*Madras*) ; and supported by the Hon'ble Dadabhai Naoroji (*Bombay*).]

RESOLUTION. IV.

Resolved—That in the opinion of this Congress the competitive examinations now held in England, for first appointments in various civil departments of the public service, should henceforth, in accordance with the views of the India Office Committee of 1860, "be held simultaneously, one in England and one in India, both being as far as practicable identical in their nature, and those who compete in both countries being finally classified in one list according to merit," and that the successful candidates in India should be sent to England for further study, and subjected there to such further examinations as may seem needful. Further, that all other first appointments (excluding peonships, and the like) should be filled by competitive examinations held in India, under conditions calculated to secure such intellectual, moral, and physical qualifications as may be decided by Government to be necessary. Lastly, that the maximum age of candidates for entrance into the Covenanted Civil Service be raised to not less than 23 years.

[Proposed by the Hon'ble Dadabhai Naoroji (*Bombay*) ; seconded by Mr. Vira Raghavacharya (*Madras*) ; and supported by Mr. D. S. White (*Madras*).]

RESOLUTION V.

Resolved—That in the opinion of this Congress the proposed increase in the military expenditure of the empire is unnecessary, and regard being had to the revenues of the empire and the existing circumstances of the country, excessive.

[Proposed by Mr. Rangaya Nayadu (*Madras*) ; seconded by Mr. Dinsha Edaljee Wacha (*Bombay*) ; and supported by Mr. Dayaram Jethmul (*Karachi*).]

RESOLUTION VI.

Resolved—That in the opinion of this Congress, if the increased demands for military expenditure are not to be, as they ought to be, met by retrenchment, they ought to be met, firstly, by the re-imposition of the Customs duties ; and, secondly, by the extension of the license-tax to those classes of the community, official and non-official, at present exempted from it, care being taken that in the case of all classes a sufficiently high taxable minimum be maintained. And, further, that this Congress is of opinion that Great Britain should extend an imperial guarantee to the Indian debt.

[Proposed by Mr. J. U. Yajnik (*Bombay*) ; seconded by Mr. S. A. Swaminath Iyer (*Tanjore*) ; supported by Rao Saheb S. Venkata Subbarayudu Pantulu (*Masulipatam*).]

RESOLUTION VII.

Resolved—That this Congress deprecates the annexation of Upper Burmah, and considers that if the Government unfortunately decide on annexation, the entire country of Burmah should be separated from the Indian Viceroyalty and constituted a Crown Colony, as distinct in all matters from the Government of this country as is Ceylon.

[Proposed by Mr. P. M. Mehta (*Bombay*) ; seconded by Rao Bahadur Krishanji Laxman Nulkar (*Poona*).]

RESOLUTION VIII.

Resolved—That the resolutions passed by this Congress be communicated to the Political Associations in each province, and that these Associations be requested, with the help of similar bodies and other agencies within their respective provinces, to adopt such measures as they may consider calculated to advance the settlement of the various questions dealt with in these resolutions.

[Proposed by Mr. Murlidhar (*Umballa*); seconded by Mr. H. H. Dhruba (*Surat*).]

RESOLUTION IX.

Resolved—That the Indian National Congress re-assemble next year in Calcutta, and sit on Tuesday, the 28th of December, 1886, and the next succeeding days.

[Proposed by Mr. A. O Hume (*Bengal*) ; seconded by the Hon'ble S. Subramania Iyer (*Madras*).]

RESOLUTIONS PASSED AT THE SECOND CONGRESS.

RESOLUTION I.

Resolved—That this Congress of delegates from all parts of India do humbly offer its dutiful and loyal congratulations to Her Most Gracious Majesty, the Queen-Empress, on the approaching completion of the first half century of her memorable, beneficent and glorious reign, and heartily wish her many, many more, and happy years of rule, over the great British Empire.

[Proposed by Mr. Rahimatulla M. Sayani (*Bombay*) ; seconded by Lala Murlidhur (*Ambala*) ; supported by Mr. G. Subramania Iyer (*Madras*), and carried by acclamation.]

RESOLUTION II.

Resolved—That this Congress regards with the deepest sympathy, and views with grave apprehension, the increasing poverty of vast numbers of the population of India, and (although aware that the Government is not overlooking this matter and is contemplating certain palliatives) desires to record its fixed conviction that the introduction of Representative Institutions will prove one of the most important practical steps towards the amelioration of the condition of the people.

Proposed by Mr. Dinshaw Edulji Wacha (*Bombay*) ; seconded by the Hon'ble S. Subramania Iyer (*Madras*) ; supported by Pandit Prannath (*Lucknow*), and carried by a very large majority.]

RESOLUTION III.

Resolved—That this Congress do, emphatically, re-affirm the 3rd Resolution of the Congress of 1885, and distinctly declare its belief that the reform and expansion of the Council of the Governor-General for making Laws and of the Provincial Legislative Councils, therein suggested, have now become essential alike in the interests of India and England.

[Proposed by Rai Kunja Lall Banerjee, Bahadur (*Calcutta*); seconded by Mr. P. Rangiah Naidu (*Madras*); supported by Mr. Ghanasham Nilkanth (*Bombay*), and carried unanimously.]

RESOLUTION IV.

Resolved—That this Congress is of opinion that in giving practical effect to this essential reform, regard should be had (subject to such modifications as, on a more detailed examination of the question, may commend themselves to the Government) to the principles embodied in the following tentative suggestions :—

(1.)—The number of persons composing the Legislative Councils, both Provincial and of the Governor-General, to be materially increased. Not less than one-half the Members of such enlarged Councils to be elected. Not more than one-fourth to be officials having seats *ex-officio* in such Councils, and not more than one-fourth to be Members, official or non-official, nominated by Government.

(2.)—The right to elect Members to the Provincial Councils to be conferred only on those classes and members of the community, *primâ facie*, capable of exercising it wisely and independently. In Bengal and Bombay the Councillors may be elected by the Members of Municipalities, District Boards, Chambers of Commerce and the Universities, or an electorate may be constituted of all persons possessing such qualifications, educational and pecuniary, as may be deemed necessary. In Madras, the Councillors may be elected either by District Boards, Municipalities, Chambers of Commerce and the University, or by Electoral Colleges composed of Members partly elected by these bodies and partly nominated by Government. In the North-West Provinces and Oudh and in the Punjab, Councillors may be elected by an Electoral College composed of Members elected by Municipal and District Boards, and nominated, to an extent not exceeding one-sixth of the total number, by Government, it being understood that the same elective system now in force where Municipal Boards are concerned will be applied to District Boards, and the right of electing Members to these latter extended to the cultivating class. But whatever system be adopted (and the details must be worked out separately for each province) care must be taken that all sections of the community, and all great interests, are adequately represented.

(3.)—The elected Members of the Council of the Governor-General for making Laws, to be elected by the elected Members of the several Provincial Councils.

(4.)—No elected or nominated Member of any Council, to receive any salary or remuneration in virtue of such Membership, but any such Member, already in receipt of any Government salary or allowance, to continue to draw the same unchanged during Membership, and all Members to be entitled to be reimbursed any expenses incurred in travelling in connection with their Membership.

(5).—All persons, resident in India, to be eligible for seats in Council, whether as electees or nominees, without distinction of race, creed, caste or colour.

(6).—All legislative measures and all financial questions, including all budgets, whether these involve new or enhanced taxation or not, to be necessarily submitted to and dealt with by these Councils. In the case of all other branches of the administration, any Member to be at liberty, after due notice, to put any question he sees fit to the *ex-officio* Members (or such one of these as may be specially charged with the supervision of the particular branch concerned) and to be entitled (except as hereinafter provided) to receive reply to his question, together with copies of any papers requisite for the thorough comprehension of the subject, and on this reply the Council to be at liberty to consider and discuss the question, and record thereon such resolution as may appear fitting to the majority. Provided that, if the subject in regard to which the inquiry is made involves matters of Foreign policy, Military dispositions or strategy, or is otherwise of such a nature that, in the opinion of the Executive, the Public interests would be materially imperilled by the communication of the information asked for, it shall be competent for them to instruct the *ex-officio* Members, or one of them, to reply accordingly, and decline to furnish the information asked for.

(7.)—The Executive Government shall possess the power of overruling the decision arrived at by the majority of the Council, in every case in which, in its opinion, the public interests would suffer by the acceptance of such decision; but whenever this power is exercised, a full exposition of the grounds on which this has been considered necessary, shall be published within one month, and in the case of local Governments they shall report the circumstances and explain their action to the Government of India, and in the case of this latter, it shall report and explain to the Secretary of State; and in any such case on a representation made through the Government of India and the Secretary of State by the overruled majority, it shall be competent to the Standing Committee of the House of Commons (recommended in the 3rd Resolution of last year's Congress which this present Congress has affirmed) to consider the matter, and call for any and all papers or information, and hear any persons on behalf of such majority or otherwise, and thereafter, if needful, report thereon to the full House.

[Proposed by Mr. Surendra Nath Banerjee (*Calcutta*); seconded by Mr. N. G. Chandavarkar (*Bombay*); supported by Mr. Sharfuddin (*Behar*), and carried without a dissentient voice.]

RESOLUTION V.

Resolved—That this Congress do invite all Public Bodies and all Associations throughout the Country, humbly and earnestly, to entreat His Excellency the Viceroy to obtain the sanction of Her Majesty's Secretary of State for India, to the appointment of a Commission, to enquire exhaustively into the best method of introducing such a tentative form of Representative Institutions into India, as has been indicated in Resolutions III of the past, and IV of the present year's Congress.

[Proposed by Mr. N. N. Gupta (*Karrachi*); seconded by Mr. M. B. Namjoshi (*Poona*); supported by Kumar Binay Krishna (*Calcutta*), and carried unanimously.]

RESOLUTION VI.

Resolved—That a Committee composed of the gentlemen named in the margin* be appointed to consider the Public Service Question and report thereon to this Congress.

*Hon'ble Dadabhai Naoroji (*Bombay*).
,, S. Subramania Iyer (*Madras.*)
,, Peary Mohun Mookerjee (*Calcutta*).
Mr. G. Subramania Iyer (*Madras*).
Babu Matilal Ghose (*Calcutta*).
Mr. Surendra Nath Banerjee (*Calcutta*).
,, Gungapershad Varma (*Lucknow*).
,, Ramkali Chaudhuri (*Benares*).
Mr. Guru Prasad Sen (*Patna*).
Pundit Prannath (*Lucknow*).
Munshi Kashipershad (*Allahabad*).
Nawab Reza Ali Khan (*Lucknow*).
Mr. Hamid Ali (*Lucknow*).
Lala Kanhyalal (*Amritsar*).
Rao Sahib Gungadhar Rao Madhaw Chitnavis (*Nagpur*).
Mr. Rahimatulla M. Sayani (*Bombay*).

[Proposed by Mr. Surendra Nath Banerjee (*Calcutta*); seconded by Mr. M. B. Namjoshi (*Poona*); supported by Pandit S. Agnihorti (*Lahore*), and carried unanimously.]

RESOLUTION VII.

Resolved—That this Congress approves and adopts the report* submitted by the Committee appointed by Resolution VI.

[Proposed by Mr. Surendra Nath Banerjee (*Calcutta*); seconded by the Hon'ble S. Subramania Iyer (*Madras*), and carried unanimously.]

RESOLUTION VIII.

Resolved—That, in the opinion of this Congress, the time has now arrived when the system of trial by jury may be safely extended into many parts of the country where it is not at present in force.

[Proposed by Mr. S. A. Saminada Iyer (*Tanjore*); seconded by Mr. H. H. Dhruva (*Surat*); supported by Dr. Trailokyanath Mitter (*Calcutta*), and carried unanimously.]

RESOLUTION IX.

Resolved—That, in the opinion of this Congress, the innovation made in 1872 in the system of trial by jury, depriving the verdicts of juries of all finality, has proved injurious to the country, and that the powers then, for the first time, vested in Sessions Judges and High Courts, of setting aside verdicts of acquittal, should be at once withdrawn.

[Proposed by Mr. W. C. Bonerjee (*Calcutta*); seconded by the Hon'ble Peary Mohan Mookerjee (*Calcutta*); supported by Munshi Sadho Lal (*Benares*), and carried by a very large majority.]

RESOLUTION X

Resolved—That, in the opinion of this Congress, a provision, similar to that contained in the Summary Jurisdiction Act of England (under which accused persons in serious cases have the option of demanding a committal to the Sessions Court), should be introduced into the Indian Code of Criminal Procedure, enabling accused persons, in warrant

---

* REPORT.

We, the Members of the Committee appointed by the Congress to submit a statement in connection with the Public Service Question, have the honor to report that the following resolutions were unanimously adopted by us at a meeting held yesterday:—

1.—That the open Competitive Examination be held simultaneously both in India and in England.

2.—That the simultaneous examinations thus held be equally open to all classes of Her Majesty's subjects.

3.—That the classified lists be prepared according to merit.

4.—That the Congress express the hope that the Civil Service Commissioners will give fair consideration to Sanskrit and Arabic among the subjects of examination.

5.—That the age of candidates eligible for admission to the open Competitive Examination be not less than 19, or, as recommended by Sir C. Aitchison, more than 23 years.

6.—That simultaneous examinations being granted, the Statutory Civil Service be closed for first appointments.

7.—That the appointments in the Statutory Civil Service, under the existing rules, be still left open to the Members of the Uncovenanted Service and to professional men of proved merit and ability.

8.—That all appointments requiring educational qualifications, other than covenanted first appointments, be filled by Competitive Examinations held in the different Provinces, and open in each Province to such natural-born subjects of H. M. only as are residents thereof.

These Resolutions, it is hoped, cover the main principles which underlie the questions set by the Public Service Commission. For a more detailed consideration there was no time.

(Sd.) DADABHAI NAOROJI,
President of the Committee.

30th December, 1886.

cases, to demand that, instead of being tried by the Magistrate, they be committed to the Court of Sessions.

[Proposed by Mr. Mano Mohan Ghose (*Calcutta*); seconded by Mr. T. Chidambara Row (*Bellary*); supported by Khajeh Abdul Aleem (*Dacca*); and carried unanimously.]

RESOLUTION XI.

Resolved—That this Congress do place on record an expression of the universal conviction, that a complete separation of executive and judicial functions (such that in no case the two functions shall be combined in the same officer) has become an urgent necessity, and that, in its opinion, it behoves the Government to effect this separation without further delay, even though this should, in some Provinces, involve some extra expenditure.

[Proposed by Mr. Daji Abaji Khare (*Bombay*); seconded by Munshi Kashi Pershad (*Allahabad*); supported by Mr. Sri Ram (*Lucknow*), and carried unanimously.]

RESOLUTION XII.

Resolved—That in view of the unsettled state of public affairs in Europe, and the immense assistance that the people of this country, if duly prepared therefor, is capable of rendering to Great Britain in the event of any serious complications arising, this Congress do earnestly appeal to the Government to authorise (under such rules and restrictions as may to it seem fitting) a system of Volunteering for the Indian inhabitants of the country, such as may qualify them to support the Government, effectively, in any crisis.

[Proposed by Rajah Rampal Singh (*Oudh*); seconded by Mr. R. D. Mehta (*Calcutta*), and carried by acclamation]

RESOLUTION XIII.

Resolved—That Standing Congress-Committees be constituted at all important centres.

[Proposed by Mr. W. C. Bonnerjee (*Calcutta*); seconded by Mr. N. G. Chandavarkar (*Bombay*), and carried unanimously.]

RESOLUTION XIV.

Resolved—That the third Indian National Congress assemble at Madras on the 27th of December, 1887.

[Proposed by Mr. A. O. Hume (*Punjab*); seconded by the Hon'ble S. Subramania Iyer (*Madras*), and carried by acclamation.]

RESOLUTION XV.

Resolved—That copies of these Resolutions be forwarded to His Excellency the Viceroy in Council, with the humble requests, that he will cause the 1st Resolution to be submitted in due course to Her Majesty the Queen-Empress, that he will cause all the Resolutions to be laid before Her Majesty's Secretary of State for India, and that he himself will be graciously pleased, in consultation with his colleagues, to accord them his best consideration.

[Proposed by Mr. Rangiah Naidu (*Madras*); seconded by Mr. Sorabjee Framjee Patel (*Bombay*), and carried unanimously.]

(*Signed*) DADABHAI NAOROJI,
President of the Second Indian National Congress.

RESOLUTIONS PASSED AT THE THIRD CONGRESS.

RESOLUTION I.

Resolved—That a Committee is appointed, consisting of the gentlemen (marginally enumerated*), to consider what rules, if any, may now be usefully framed in regard to the constitution and working of the Congress, with instructions to report thereon to the Congress, on the 30th instant.

* Messrs. Namjoshi, Chandavarkar, Mir Humayun Jah Bahadur, Hajee Mahomed Abdul Shakoor Badshaw Sahib, S. Subramania Iyer, W. S. Gantz, Rangiah Naidu, Surendranath Bannerjee, Trailokhyanath Mitra, Kali Charan Bannerjee, Guru Prasad Sen, Saligram Singh, Ram Kali Chaudhuri, Hafiz Abdul Rahim, Rampal Singh, Pandit Madan Mohun, Ganga Prasad Varma, Bishan Narayen Dar, Hamid Ali, Murlidhur, Satyanand Agnihotri, H. H. Dhruva, W. C. Bonnerjee, Norendranath Sen, Eardley Norton, Joy Govind Shome, Iswari Lal Sircar, G. Subramania Iyer, D. A. Khare, S. A. Saminada Iyer, Sabapathy Mudaliar, A. O. Hume, C. Vigiya Raghava Chariar, Govind Buksh, Karandikar.

[Proposed by Dr. Trailokhyanath Mitra (*Bengal*); seconded by Mr. Hamid Ali (*Oudh*); supported by Mr. W. S. Gantz (*Madras*), and carried unanimously.]

RESOLUTION II.

Resolved—That this Congress re-affirms the necessity for the expansion and reform of the Council of the Governor-General for making Laws, and the Provincial Legislative Councils, already set forth in Resolutions III of the Congresses of 1885 and 1886, and expresses the earnest hope that the Government will no longer delay action in the direction of this essential reform.

[Proposed by Mr. Surendranath Bannerjee (*Bengal*); seconded by Raja Sir T. Madava Rao, K.C.S.I. (*Madras*); supported by M. R. Ry. P. Somasundaram Chettiar (*Madras*), and carried unanimously.]

RESOLUTION III.

Resolved—That this Congress once again places on record an expression of the universal conviction, that a complete separation of the Executive and Judicial functions (such that in no case the two functions shall be combined in the same officer) has become an urgent necessity, and declares that, in its opinion, it behoves the Government to effect this separation, without further delay, even though this should, in some provinces, involve some extra expenditure.

[Proposed by Mr. N. Subramaniem (*Madras*); seconded by Babu Kali Charan Bannerjee (*Bengal*); supported by Mr. Hafiz Abdul Rahim (*N.-W. Provinces*), and carried unanimously.]

RESOLUTION IV.

Resolved—That in view of the loyalty of Her Majesty's Indian subjects, this Congress considers it desirable that the Queen's Proclamation should be given effect to; that the Military Service in its higher grades should be practically opened to the natives of this country; and that the Government of India should establish Military Colleges in this country, whereat the natives of India, as defined by Statute, may be educated and trained for a military career as officers of the Indian Army.

[Proposed by Babu Norendranath Sen (*Bengal*); seconded by Babu Saligram Singh (*Behar*); supported by Mr. Eardley Norton; (*Madras*); and carried unanimously.]

RESOLUTION V.

Resolved—That in view of the unsettled state of public affairs in Europe, and the immense assistance that the people of this country, if duly prepared therefor, are capable of rendering to Great Britain in the event of any serious complications arising, this Congress once again earnestly appeals to the Government to authorize (under such rules and restrictions as may to it seem fitting,) a system of volunteering for the Indian inhabitants of the country, such as may qualify them to support the Government, effectively, in any crisis.

[Proposed by C. Sankara Nair (*Madras*); seconded by Khan Bahadur Sheikh Ahmed Hussain Khan (*Oudh*); supported by Rajah Rampal Singh (*N.-W. Provinces*), and carried unanimously.]

RESOLUTION VI.

Resolved—That as the administration of the Income-Tax, especially, as regards incomes below Rs. 1,000, has proved extremely unsatisfactory, it is essential, in the opinion of the Congress, that the taxable minimum be raised to Rs. 1,000, the loss of revenue thus involved, being made good, and further financial difficulties, if any, met, by reductions in the existing public expenditure, or, should this prove impossible, by the re-imposition of an import duty on the finer classes of cotton goods.

[Proposed by Babu Guru Prasad Sen (*Behar*); seconded by Babu Jogender Chander Ghose (*Bengal*), and carried unanimously.]

RESOLUTION VII.

Resolved—That having regard to the poverty of the people, it is desirable that the Government be moved to elaborate a system of Technical Education, suitable to the condition of the country, to encourage indigenous manufactures by a more strict observance of the orders, already existing, in regard to utilizing such manufactures for State purposes, and to employ more extensively, than at present, the skill and talents of the people of the country.

[Proposed by Sir S. Ramasawmi Mudaliar, C.I.E., (*Madras*); seconded by Mr. John Adam (*Madras*); supported by Sheikh Kadir Buksh (*Oudh*), and carried unanimously.]

RESOLUTION VIII.

Resolved—That in view of the loyalty of the people, the hardships which the present Arms' Act (XI of 1878) causes, and the unmerited slur which it casts upon the people of this country, the Government be moved so to modify the provisions of Chapter IV and, if necessary, other portions of the said Act, as shall enable all persons to possess and wear arms, unless debarred therefrom, either as individuals or members of particular communities or classes, by the orders of the Government of India (or any local authority empowered by the Government of India on that behalf), for reasons to be recorded in writing and duly published.

[Proposed by Rao Bahadur Sabapathy Mudaliar (*Madras*) ; seconded by Babu Bipin Chandra Pal (*Bengal*), and carried unanimously.]

RESOLUTION IX.

Resolved—That the rules drafted by the Committee appointed under Resolution I, stand over for consideration till next Congress, but that, in the meantime, copies be circulated to all Standing Congress Committees, with the request that they will, during the coming year, act in accordance with these rules, so far as this may seem to them possible and desirable, and report thereon to the next Congress, with such further suggestions as to them may seem meet.

[Proposed by Mr. A. O. Hume (*Madras*) ; seconded by Dr. Trailokyanath Mitra (*Bengal*), and carried unanimously.]

RESOLUTION X.

Resolved—That the Fourth Indian National Congress assemble at Allahabad on the 26th December, 1888.

[Proposed by Mr. A. O. Hume (*Madras*) ; seconded by Rajah Rampal Singh (*N.-W. Provinces*), and carried by acclamation.]

RESOLUTION XI.

Resolved—That copies of these Resolutions be forwarded to His Excellency the Viceroy-in-Council, with the humble request that he will cause all the Resolutions to be laid before Her Majesty's Secretary of State for India, and that he himself will be graciously pleased, in consultation with his colleagues, to accord them his best consideration.

[Proposed by Rajah Yatindranath Chaudhuri (*Bengal*) ; seconded by Babu Jotendra Nath Tagore (*Bengal*), and carried unanimously.]

(Signed) BUDRUDIN TYABJI,

President of the Third Indian National Congress.

REPORT

OF THE

FIFTH

Indian

National Congress,

HELD AT

BOMBAY,

On the 26th, 27th and 28th of December,

1889.

Contents.

THE FIFTH INDIAN NATIONAL CONGRESS.

"Now I venture to submit, that what occurred yesterday and to-day is truly typical of the action of this Congress movement, throughout this great Empire. By bringing men of all creeds and classes together on a common platform, and by enabling them to discuss face to face all those questions of domestic politics, which are closest to the lives and hearts of our people, it first brings out into clear relief all differences and doubts that underlaid the old, mutual, class-distrust, that has in the past been India's curse, and then it composes those differences and sets at rest for ever those doubts—except in the minds of perhaps one or two isolated fanatics whose own brethren disown them,—not by an authoritative enactment, not by the power of numbers, but by the arguments of reason and by appeals to that deep-seated, brotherly feeling which we all (when our lower and selfish natures are held in check) which we all, I say, be we Mahomedans, Hindus or what not, do truly cherish in our heart of hearts for all who, born on India's sacred soil, claim India, like ourselves, as their home, their hope, their motherland. (*Loud and continued applause.*)"

(*Speech of the Honorable Pandit Ajoodhianath.*)

IT is pleasant, after the senseless opposition that, in past years, we have had to surmount, to be able to record that the fifth session of the Indian National Congress commenced and ended under the happiest auspices, no man, practically, hindering or molesting it. Naturally there were, here and there, a sprinkling of irreconcilables—an Anglo-Indian newspaper or two had their customary, though very subdued and dispirited, jeers, and that paragon of veracity, the Calcutta Correspondent of the *Times*, telegraphed his accustomed batches of fiction—but these were only *rari nantes, in gurgite vasto,* in the full tide of public opinion wholly favourable to the Congress.

After all, a good cause is safe to win all the world over, and marvellous as is the change that a single year has wrought in the position of the Congress, it is only what, sooner or later, was certain to ensue. Still, it is gratifying to know that the tables *have* been turned, and that save "a microscopic minority" none of our follow-subjects now believe us to be "seditionists" or doubt that our great Congress is working towards the good, alike, of India and England.

Bombay, where the first Congress t work for the common welfare, was once more the scene of this reat gathering. Sir Albert Sassoon, Bart., the head of the Jewish community in India, gave the site, and Mr. Makund's genius, reared on it a vast* temporary hall, intended to accommodate 4,600 persons, but into which some 6,000 people, somehow, succeeded in bestowing themselves. A hall, the quaint

* Including the verandahs or open corridors on two sides, it measured 220 feet by 150 feet and covered 33,000 square feet.

picturesque beauty of which has seldom been equalled and which, when crowded by the brightly clad representatives of all India's multitudinous clans and peoples, presented a spectacle that, for breadth and brilliancy of colouring, has certainly never been surpassed.

Unquestionably Mr. Bradlaugh's kindly presence had contributed in no small degree to the greatness of the gathering, both of Delegates and Visitors. This was his first visit to India—to the Indians, he was still only a name—and yet millions of hearts throbbed with pride and pleasure, when the news was first flashed all over the country that he intended to be present at the then coming Congress. Again, no Englishman living is more trusted or more respected throughout India, than is Sir William Wedderburn, and the news that he had consented to come out to India to preside over the assembly, undoubtedly gave a further stimulus to the country which, having crushed all serious opposition was, to tell the truth, a little lazily inclined. Partly owing to these favouring influences and partly to the great spread during the past year of the Congress idea throughout the country, this last Congress proved to be by far the greatest and grandest assembly yet witnessed—greater and grander, perhaps, than will ever again occur, in our times at least—for the physical difficulties and great expense attending, in India, the transport over the huge distances covered by the Empire of these large numbers of Delegates, and of providing for them a sufficiently large meeting Hall, accommodation, furniture, food, lights, and what not, are so great,* that the Congress was compelled to pass this time a rule (*vide* Resolution XIII. Cl. *a.*) limiting for the future the number of Delegates from each circle to five per million of the population represented, or in fact, to about 1,000, in all.

The elections commenced rather late, and less care, we regret to say, was taken to collect statistics than in the previous year. Of a great deal of the work, no reliable record could be obtained, as it was done in a very quiet and unobtrusive fashion. Although open opposition had ceased, a considerable section of the European official community and of the Police, who take their cues from this community, were still credited by the people, unjustly as we hope, with nourishing in secret hostile feelings towards the Congress, and the lower classes, especially, thought it prudent to attract as little attention as possible. No groups of delegat [illegible] were gathered at provincial centres and despatched to the [illegible] ing and bands playing amidst the cheers of enormou [illegible] former occasions—probably, three times as many meetings were actually held, but there were fewer, rather than more,

* The brunt of the work on the present occasion devolved upon Mr. Dinsha Eduljee Wacha, the Secretary of the Reception Committee. The Provision Committee also did their work, which was very heavy, both well and economically, and they more especially deserve commendation because they did it, *themselves*, whereas in Bombay the accepted method of doing anything, is to give *some one else* a contract to do it. Many others also in Bombay, like Messrs. Daji Abaji Khare and Motilal M. Munshi, chief of the warders, really did exert themselves when the time came, but our thanks are especially due to two gentlemen from other parts of the country, and therefore in no way bound so to exert themselves. Mr. Ghosal, the Secretary of the Calcutta Standing Congress Committee, who had charge of the Delegates' Registry Office and prepared the voluminous roll of Delegates appended to this report, and Capt. Banon, a delegate from Kangra.

great public meetings, with elaborate speeches and more or less enthusiastic demonstrations. Independent of the fact that amongst the lower classes, at any rate, it was held inexpedient to do anything to excite the supposed latent hostility of the officials, it was felt, amongst the better classes, that anything capable of being construed as a crowing over fallen foes would be inconsistent with our principles. *Debellare superbos, parcere subjectis* is our motto, and while always ready to fight vigorously and hit hard at those who attack us, our chief desire is to live in peace and amity with all men, whether they agree with us, or, have not, as yet, come to grace.

So it resulted that elections at which over 2,500 delegates (over 1,900 of whom duly took their seats at the Congress) were elected, were carried through with a rapidity and noiselessness, that misled the few Anglo-Indian journalists, with whom the wish was father to the thought, into the idea, (which they industriously disseminated and which we saw no object in contradicting, knowing well what time would bring forth,) that the Congress movement was dying away. They did not reflect—do they ever seriously reflect on *anything*, these good people?—that a train when starting makes a good deal of noise and fuss, but runs along smoothly and noiselessly enough when steam has once been got up and the necessary momentum acquired!

In thousands of villages one or two elders were selected by the people and quietly sent off to meet similar representatives at some neighbouring fair or market, where these again selected two or three from amongst themselves, to attend a sub-divisional meeting, where sometimes delegates were elected but, more often, a few men were picked out to attend a larger and more public meeting. The consequence was that almost everywhere these meetings consisted not, as in past times they mostly did, of all the local inhabitants who could be got together, but to a large extent of people elected as their representatives by the people, or by the representatives of these. As a matter of fact, practically no opposition, worthy the name, was anywhere experienced from the officials. Amongst the people themselves one or two individuals tried to persuade the Parsees, that they were going to hold aloof from the Congress, with the result that they attended in five times greater strength than they had ever previously done, in fact, in numbers quite disproportionate to the size of the very enlightened and wealthy, but still small community that they represented. A venerable Kazi, too, who doubtless in a past historical period did not seem to lag so conspicuously behind his co-religionists in education and intelligence, held a small meeting, of persons, who declared their determination (a wise one, considering what is now-a-days required of Delegates) of not attending the Congress—in reply to which the ablest and most learned Moulvi in Bombay, held a large meeting at which some 500 of the Mahomedans of light and leading in the place attended and elected some score or more of their co-religionists. It was noticed that, although the first meeting was trumpeted over the country and telegraphed immediately to England, the latter—which really had some little importance, though both of them were mere drops in the ocean—somehow escaped the attention of Anglo-Indian journalists!

Fortunate is the nation, it has been said, that has no history, and fortunate may our Congress be esteemed, that has no more serious, in fact, no other hostile incidents to chronicle in its past year's history than these little episodes. The movement swam on noiselessly, swelling softly like a summer's tide—

> " A tide that moving seemed to sleep
> Too full for sound or foam."

If now the bulk of our quondam, doubtless honest—if at times somewhat captious—critics and opponents, convinced alike of the universal and the beneficial character of the movement, will only join us and aid us, by their advice and example, to make good, better, we, on our side, are equally ready to ignore the past and welcome them with open arms to a share in the good work. A real beginning has been made in this direction; important men like Rajah T. Rama Rao (for six years a member of the Madras Council), the Rev. Mr. Evans, and others, once gravely distrustful of the Congress, having this year appeared amongst its warmest supporters, and our adversaries having disbanded their forces, we on our part have been able to assume that more pacific and unobtrusive attitude which best befits a movement, whose sole object is the common weal. This is all as it should be, but this change of tactics, however delectable, brings with it this disadvantage to the chronicler, that the widespread substitution of private gatherings of representatives for public meetings of the people, leaves him without the requisite data for gauging numerically the extent to which the population took part in the work. Last year we had fairly reliable statistics to show that at least three millions of men, voted, at one stage or other of the proceedings, for the delegates who were elected; this year we can only assert that a *much* larger number took part in the elections; but, whether that number really rose to close on ten millions, as sanguine Congress men, founding their calculations on the facts of their own particular districts, have asserted, or whether it materially exceeded the five millions at which we are inclined to estimate it, no one can certainly say.

Nor indeed, to us here, does it much signify; for assuredly, out of the 40 millions of intelligent, non-starving males, of which the India of the present day is the home—fully 35 millions, whether they voted or whether they remained passive, are with the Congress. Whatever it has been in past days, the movement has now become truly national, and only ignorance (very possibly honest, *bonâfide,* ignorance) of the facts of the *day*, can lead any *truthful* man, to deny that it is so.

This being the case, necessarily, the Congress was a compendium of all the races, castes, creeds, professions, trades and occupations included in the Empire, and it may seem superfluous to discuss in detail its composition. Still a few words on this subject may not be devoid of interest. The subjoined table will give some idea of how the movement, and with it the number of the representatives, have grown.

Presidency or Province.	Number of Delegates. In Bombay in 1885.	In Calcutta in 1886.	In Madras in 1887.	In Allahabad in 1888.	In Bombay in 1889.
Madras	21	47	362	95	366
Bombay and Sindh	38	48	99	163	821
Punjab	3	17	9	80	62
N.-W. Provinces and Oudh..............	7	74	45	583	261
Central Provinces and Berar	...	10	13	73	214
Bengal, Behar, Orissa and Assam	3	240	79	254	165
* Total......	72	436	607	1,248	1,889

The great distances† that have to be travelled constitute our greatest obstacles, and so it is always the provinces nearest to the Congress site that send the greatest number of delegates. When the Congress first met in Bombay, 38 out of 72 delegates were from the Bombay Presidency ; when it met in Calcutta 240 out of the 436 belonged to Bengal ; in Madras, 362 out of 607 belonged to that Presidency ; in Allahabad 583 out of 1,248 belonged to the United Provinces, and now in Bombay, again, 821 out of 1,889 belonged to the Bombay Presidency. It was *partly* to avoid this disproportion in representation, which—if the country at any time ceased to be as unanimous, as it at present is, on all essentials—might operate inequitably, though chiefly on account of the enormous size to which the assembly was growing, that the Congress has this year decided that in future, each circle is only to send delegates to the number of five per million of the total population included in it.

* These are the numbers of which names and full particulars were in each case recorded. But at each Congress the names of a few delegates escaped record, and at this last Congress 24 more delegates took tickets and paid their fees, than we have recorded in the list.

† An ingenious and pains-taking friend has calculated the actual total distance travelled by the 1889 recorded delegates in coming to and returning from this fifth Congress. Incredible as it may seem, it slightly exceeds two millions of miles ! We on a rough calculation of averages (366 from Madras travelled 794 miles each way in all cases, 112 from the Central Provinces 520, 175 from N.-W. Provinces 844, 53 from Oudh 884, 33 from the Benares circle 937, 22 from the Dehli circle 890, 42 from the Lahore circle 1,138, 21 from Behar 1,050, 144 from Lower Bengal and Assam 1,400, &c., &c. each way in all cases) made it only 1,894,000, but his account which calculates the exact distance for each individual is doubtless correct.

As it was, as will be seen from the table given in the note,* the number of delegates per million, though it averaged 9·5 for the entire country, varied from 96·1, and 52·3 in the cases of the Bombay and Poona circles, to 0·9 in Rajshaye, which, besides being very inaccessible, is very backward. Berar, which is not only comparatively close, but traversed from end to end by the G. I. P. Ry. running straight into Bombay, was, so to say, over represented with 37·3 per million--but the province is perhaps richer as regards its agricultural population than any in the Empire. Madras, the Central Provinces, the N.-W. Provinces and the Dehli circles were all fully represented—the rest somewhat inadequately so.

Turning to creeds and religions we find that the representation was more catholic than ever, as the subjoined little table will show :--

Congress of	Delegates.									
	Hindus.	Mahomedans.	Christians.		Jains.	Sikhs.	Jews.	Parsees.		Total.
			Europeans and Eurasians.	Indians.						
1885...............	58	2	1	2	1	...	...	8		72
1886...............	387	33	1	5	2	2	...	6		436
1887...............	492	81	10	15	4	...	...	5		607
1888...............	965	221	16	22	11	6	...	7		1,248
1889...............	1,502	254	23	31	31	3	1	44		1,889

Studying this, the philosophical reader may be inclined to remark--" See, my friends, with what little regard to veracity journalism is conducted." The English Press published numerous telegrams, commenting on the entire absence of Parsees ; as a matter of fact they were five times more numerous than at any previous gathering, included the majority of the most cultured and enlightened men in the community, and, the total number of Parsees being only 85,000, they were represented at the rate of 529 to the million !

* Circle.	* Population in millions.	Numbers of Delegates sent.	Number of Delegates per million.
Calcutta (*including the Presidency, Burdwan and Chittagong Division Assam and Orissa.*)	28·6	102	3·5
Dacca	8·7	15	1·7
Rajshaye	7·7	7	0·9
Bhagulpore	8·1	14	1·7
Chota Nagpore	4·4	6	1·4
Behar	15·1	21	1·4
Benares	9·8	83	8·4
Allahabad	22·9	175	7·5
Oudh	12·2	53	4·3
Delhi .. .. — ..	2·0	22	11·0
Lahore	17·0	42	3·0
Kurrachi	2·4	12	5·0
Guzerat	2·9	85	29·3
Bombay	3·1	298	96·1
Poona	8·1	425	52·3
Amraoti	2·7	101	37·3
Nagpore	11·5	112	9·7
Madras	32·0	366	11·4
	198·9	1889	9·5

* Excluding Native States and allowing for increase of population since the last census, where there are reasons to believe that this has occurred,

Then, again, we were informed by the English papers—we here had not discovered the fact—that the Mahomedans were abstaining from the Congress; whereas we not only had a larger number than at any previous gathering, but, if the circumstances of the case are considered, a far larger proportion of Musalmans than at any other time.

True, at Allahabad we had 221 Mahomedans out of a total of 1,248, or nearly 18 per cent., whereas this year out of a total of 1,889 we have 254, or only 13½ per cent. But then it has to be remembered, that at Allahabad, the populations of Bengal, the United Provinces and the Panjab furnished 917 out of 1,248 delegates, and those populations include 42 millions of our Mahomedans, whereas, this year, the populations of Madras, Bombay, the Central Provinces and Berar, furnished 1,401 out of the 1,889 delegates, and these populations only include 6 millions of Musalmans. In fact, at Allahabad three-fourths of the delegates came from provinces including six-sevenths of the Mahomedans of India, while this year three-fourths came from provinces only including one-seventh of our Musalmans. So that the wonder is, not that we had only 254 this year as against 221 last year, but that, despite the very small proportion of Mahomedans in the populations that chiefly made up this Congress, we had so unexpectedly large a number as 254; a sufficient indication, if any were wanted, of that growing *rapprochement* between the two communities which has ever been one of the objects of the Congress.

It may be added that the lamentable poverty of such a very large proportion of our Musalmans, is an almost insuperable bar to large numbers of them attending, as delegates, at any Congress distant from their homes. This poverty is directly and indirectly due, in a great measure, to their having too much despised Western education, which, whatever its shortcomings, is, in practice, at this present day, one important factor in material progress. Not only are the Mahomedan leaders, therefore, doing their best to dissemminate education amongst their co-religionists, not only do the better classes of Hindus in no wise grudge any special facilities for education that Government may afford to the Mahomedans, but amongst the most advanced Hindus it is being seriously considered how the Hindus can best co-operate to place their Musalman brethren on a better footing.

"India," said a distinguished Hindu recently, "has only two real legs on which to stand, the Musalmans and the Hindus. It is no use developing the muscles of one leg only—you will progress none the more rapidly—both must be strengthened and trained at the same time. This is why I—a Hindu, no doubt, but an Indian before all things—am at this present moment more anxious about Musalman education than that of Hindus. This is why I always rejoice at any special encouragement being given to them, such as Syed Ameer Ali's elevation to the High Court. Very likely there are a dozen English and Hindu barristers and pleaders in Calcutta who would have made better Judges, but neither the English nor we Hindus now require any stimulus to education—the Mahomedans do—and they should get it. We Hindus are as much interested in their progress as they themselves *can be*—more, I believe, than they, as a rule, actually *are*." And these wise and kindly feelings are shared and reciprocated by all the educated Mahomedans—all their real leaders of the present day—and yet it is these Hindus and Mahomedans, who, the veracious English writers on these topics endeavour to persuade the British public, are ready to rush at each other's throats and would destroy each other but for the wise interposition of British rule !

Of course there are bad characters in every country, and, though we have probably fewer than other nations, we are not exempt from these universal pests, and the fact that now and again some little group of these in some corner of an empire, nearly as large as Europe, get up some trumpery disturbance, in no way affects the simple fact, that broadly speaking the Hindus and Mahomedans are extremely good friends and—realizing that both pay the same taxes, both share in all the good or evil that fate may bring and, in a word, that both stand on the same platform in regard to all secular matters—trouble themselves very little about religious distinctions. Indeed, long before the country was as enlightened as it now is, when the kindly Pax Britanica gave place to the sepoy war, we never heard that the Hindus and Mahomedans flew at each other, but on the contrary we know, that whether they sided with the British or with the king of Dehli and the Nawab of Oudh, they fought side by side, shoulder to shoulder, and stuck to their comrades like true men, without giving a thought to differences of creed.

We have dwelt somewhat at length upon this point, because no more imposing Bogey has ever been evolved from the lurid imagination of the Anti-Indian party, than this purely fictitious scare as to the deadly animosity of Musalmans and Hindus. When all other arguments against conceding to us some modicum of the rights or privileges enjoyed by British subjects elsewhere, fail, as fail they must in the strong light of honest English public opinion, these Black Magicians at once conjure up the spectre of religious antagonism. It is well that all our English friends, and we believe that they are to be counted by the million, should realize, once for all, that this spectre is only a " Pepper's Ghost," amusing as a display of perverted ingenuity, but wholly devoid of any reality.

It remains to say a few words as to the composition of this last Congress, so far as the positions, professions, and occupations of the delegates are concerned. And first we must notice that no less than ten lady delegates graced the assembly, one elected by men at a public meeting, the others by various ladies' associations, the Women's Christian Temperance Union, the Bengal Ladies' Association, and the Arya Mohila Samaj. They included European and Native Christians, a Parsee, an orthodox Hindu, and three Brahmo Samaj ladies. With one exception they were ladies who have for years done good work for India. It is sufficient to mention Pandita Ramabai's name, which—as well as the good work she is so zealously carrying on—is, we believe, as well known in Europe and America as in India. Miss S. Manockjee Cursetjee, the lady directress of the well known Alexandra Girls' School, whose distinguished grandfather's statue is amongst the ornaments of Bombay, is one of our foremost educationalists. Mrs. Ghosal, better known by her maiden title of Sreemati Swarna Kumari Devi, the grand-daughter of Dwarkanath Tagore, and sister of Bengal's most thoughtful poet, has been for years the editress and chief writer in the *Bharati*, a Bengali magazine for ladies, which has done much to expand the minds and raise the mental standard of our fair sisters in that province. An accomplished English scholar, she has yet preferred to write only in the vernacular, and in that create a suitable literature for her less advanced and non-English educated sisters. The happy wife of Mr. J. Ghosal, than whom a more earnest, indefatigable and self-devoted, if modest and unassuming labourer in the cause of the Congress, all India cannot boast, she ever gratefully acknowledges how much of the high culture she enjoys, she owes to his kindly encouragement and guidance. Miss Jessie Royce Carleton, M.D., a young lady doctor, has realized in practice the Christian Idyl, and is the idol of the people of Umballa, amongst whom she lives and labours, untiringly, by her own choice on the barest pittance, in the purest spirit of Christian love and self-abnegation. Mrs. Gangooli (*née* Kadamini Bose) is the most distinguished lady graduate that has as yet passed out of the Calcutta University. Mrs. Emma Brainerd Ryder, M.D.—who, travelling for health, came to India with Pandita Ramabai—is the organizer of the Sorosis Club, a literary and artistic association for young Indian ladies, which is already doing much good. She has also formed a Woman's Technical Education Association to give some kind of industrial training to young native females, who, left widows and unprovided for, (and who, brought up at Orphanages, or from other causes, have no homes to which to return,) would, (and *do*), in default of some occupation by which to earn an honest livelihood, drift into evil courses. Mrs. Trimbuck (Shevantlibai) Canaran has, with her worthy husband, devoted her entire life to the cause of education, and beginning in an unassuming way now directs, with the happiest results, a whole congeries of schools, day, night and Sunday schools. This lady, though a Christian, as was her father, is of pure Brahmin descent, and, alike physically and mentally, exemplifies the highest type of Aryan. Mrs. Kashibai Kanitkar, an orthodox Hindu lady, is the authoress of the well known Mahrattee life of the late lamented Dr. Anandibai Joshi. She is also joint editress with her husband, Mr. Kanitkar, of the Mahratti magazine the *Manoranjan*, which is doing to a great extent for the Deccan what the *Bharati* is for Lower Bengal, and she is admittedly one of the two most highly cultured ladies in her province. Mrs. Nikambe, of Hindu parentage, the Christian wife of an active and well known minister, has also specially interested herself in and devoted much of her time to the practical work of education, both secular and religious.

But we must pause nor "further seek their merits to disclose," as these ladies will, we fear, hardly forgive us for having made such public mention of their private affairs ; a liberty on which we should not have ventured were it not essential that the world should realize what manner of women these are who now lead that devoted band of India's daughters, who, at their country's call, are rallying around the standard of the Congress.

As regards the male section of the assembly, it truly included "all sorts and conditions of men." There were seven Princes ; a like number of Sirdars and Chiefs, 2 Rajahs, 10 Nawabs, and 8 Members of Council, past or present. Besides these 269 are recorded as chairmen or members of Municipalities, 185 as chairmen or members of district and local boards, 50 as honorary Magistrates,* a dozen as Fellows of Universities, and 250 odd as graduates of some University ; but a great many delegates entitled to be classed in one or more of these divisions, failed to record the same in their rolls, and so are not included in these numbers. Then as regards professions, there were 23 barristers and advocates, 582 pleaders, 23 attorneys and solicitors, 541 land-holders (*a great* many of them ryots cultivating, under the ryotwari system, their own lands, and so entitled to be classed as Land-*holders*), 41 cultivators, *pur et simple*, 147 bankers and money dealers, 417 merchants, traders, brokers and shop-keepers, 56 belonging to the medical profession, 8 engineers, 9 Christian clergymen and missionaries, 19 non-Christian religious teachers and priests, 104 educationalists, 88 journalists, 10 printers and publishers, and 2 working artizans. It is difficult to conceive any possible body of men more thoroughly representative of the higher, middle and upper lower classes of the Indian community than was this last assemblage.

At 2 p.m. on Thursday the 26th of December, the Congress met, Mr. Pherozshah Mehta, the Chairman of the Reception Committee, and late a member of the Bombay Legislative Council, taking the chair. He welcomed the delegates in an eloquent speech from which we may reproduce a few sentences. He said † :—

"It would be at all times a high pleasure and privilege to receive and welcome so many and such distinguished guests from all parts of the country. But when I remember that, though you may not be the chosen of the people by any scientific mode of election, you virtually and substantially represent them, their wants, wishes, sentiments and aspirations, in all the various ways in which representation manifests and works itself out in the early stages of its progressive development, that pleasure and that privilege are infinitely enhanced. (*Cheers.*) There is, besides, a peculiar zest in our welcome of you ; for in welcoming the Congress to Bombay, we welcome it back to ' its own native land. (*Cheers.*) I well remember the day, this time four years ago, when, anxiously but hopefully, we launched the Congress on its enterprise, not of supplanting the existing rulers of the country, but of supplementing the endeavours of the best and most sagacious among them by proposing modifications and developments based on our peculiar and native knowledge and information,

* Equivalent to J. P., in England.

† Pages 1-3 of the Detailed Report.

and suggested, gratefully, by that enlightenment and education, which is one of the most precious gifts bestowed upon us by British rule. (*Loud and prolonged cheering.*)"

* * * * *

"Even the indirect political gains of the Congress have not been inconsiderable. It has brought vividly into clear and emphatic recognition that most important fact of the growth of the national idea amongst us. Despite social and religious differences, we have all begun earnestly to realize that we are fairly on the way to a common national existence, united and bound together by the common political ties of an equal, impartial and enlightened rule."

* * * * *

"Gentlemen, in a country so vast and varied as India, it would be impossible, it would be unnatural, to expect perfect and absolute unanimity. (*Hear, hear.*) It is no wonder that we have our halt, our lame, and our blind, and that they should hobble off to what I may call the Indian political cave of Adullam."

* * * * *

"We in this Presidency, have also our halt, our lame, and our blind. We also have had our little cave of Adullam. (*Laughter and cheers.*) But I am glad to be able to inform you that we have taken the infection very mildly, and that there is every hope of a speedy and complete recovery. (*Laughter and cheers.*)"

Then referring to the ridiculous charges of disloyalty and sedition brought against the Congress party in its earlier days, and commenting on the utter collapse of these misrepresentations he said :—

"The Congress has, however, emerged unscathed even from this trial. Never was a greater truth uttered than that to which our esteemed friend Mr. Caine gave utterance, that we of the Congress are more loyal than Anglo-Indians themselves. (*Loud cheers.*) If by loyalty is meant a keen solicitude for the safety and permanence of the Empire, in which, we are firmly persuaded, lie implanted the roots of the welfare, the prosperity, and the good government of the country, then we are certainly more loyal than Anglo-Indians, who do not hesitate, frequently, to subordinate the interests of that safety and that permanence to the seductions of conquest and vainglory, or to the immediate gains and temptations of commercial enterprise. (*Hear, hear, and cheers.*)"

"Therefore it is that all our greetings of welcome go forth to you, and with a full heart we wish you God-speed in your labours. Those labours have for their aim and object measures of which the central idea has been recently admirably summarized by one of the most sober and sagacious of modern politicians, Sir Charles Dilke, when he said that the time had now arrived when it was neither safe nor expedient to continue to carry on the administration of the country by the hands of a secret and irresponsible bureaucracy, and that working on lines already laid down, a distinct step in advance should now be made. The policy of the Congress is thus a policy, not seditious or revolutionary, but 'conservative of the public welfare, strengthening the just authority of the British Government, and adding day by day fresh lustre and dignity to the Imperial Crown.' (*Loud cheers.*) I do not know whether we are doomed to failure or destined to succeed ; but the blessing which rests upon all high and honest endeavour will surely rest upon a mission imposed by duty, sanctified by patriotism and guided by loyalty. (*Cheers.*)"

Then turning to our honoured visitor, Mr. Bradlaugh, he went on :—

"It has always seemed to me that English strength and greatness consist in nothing so much as in the lofty conception of moral and political duty which illumines the life and career of many an illustrious Englishman. We still mourn the loss of that great and good man whose heart was always with us, and whose voice was always raised for us, during many a long and eventful year. The memory of John Bright is reverently enshrined in our hearts. His place was filled by one whose life has a singular charm for all who prize sober simplicity and nobility of character above rank and riches. I mean Professor Fawcett. (*Cheers.*) The mantle has now descended upon Mr. Bradlaugh. (*Renewed cries of cheers for Mr. Bradlaugh.*) We sincerely and unaffectedly joined in the general grief at his recent illness, not simply out of selfish fears of losing our chosen champion, but out of that single-hearted feeling of sorrow which all men feel, when peril threatens a life devoted to high and unselfish ends. I know I am not employing the language of exaggeration when I say that our hearts are unutterably stirred within us at his presence among us to-day, restored to health and usefulness. (*Cheers.*) With no particular thoughts of the Congress in our minds, let us wish him that simple welcome which is in all our hearts and the hearts of people all over the country."

He then called upon the assembly to elect their President. Mr. W. C. Bonnerjee, one of the leaders of the Calcutta Bar, proposed Sir W. Wedderburn (whose name was received with great enthusiasm), remarking* :—

"If you look back to the Presidents that we have had from 1885, you will see that the selection of Sir William Wedderburn has been arrived at by a sort of logical process. The first Congress in 1885, was comparatively an insignificant one, and you were presided over on that occasion by an equally insignificant individual.† (*Loud cries of 'No, no.'*) The second Congress had the honour of being presided over by one who has devoted the whole of his life to the cause of his country, and who, even in his old age, is at the present moment. appealing to the electors of one of the constituencies of England in order that, if returned to the House of Commons, he may be able still more effectively to serve that country. Can I name Dadabhai Naoroji without calling from you enthusiastic applause? (*Long and loud cheers.*) The third Congress was presided over by a gentleman of the Mahomedan persuasion, who, having distinguished himself at the bar and in public life, was thought to be the fittest man to contradict the rumours that had been sedulously cast abroad that this was a Hindu Congress and that Mahomedan gentlemen had no sympathy with it. The next President ought, according to the process which we followed, to have been a gentleman belonging to the Eurasian community ; but at the time when it became necessary to select a President *the* man amongst the Eurasian community whom the whole of this country would have hailed with one voice as President of the Congress, Mr. D. S. White, was lying ill in bed ; and while he was in that condition it would have been improper for us to ask any other Eurasian gentleman to take his place. Now, unfortunately, he is no more ; and India has lost one of her brightest sons and best patriots in Mr. D. S. White. (*Prolonged cheers.*) Failing Mr. White, we had to go to that other community in India, the Anglo-Indian community, and there we found our late respected President Mr. George Yule. (*Loud cheers.*) Of him I need say no more than this; that having retired to England he is still devoting his time and his money to the furtherance of the cause of the Congress. (*Cheers.*) From the non-official European community to the official European community is but a slight descent (*laughter*), but unfortunately it is impossible for us to get a gentleman at the time actually belonging to the official classes to guide our deliberations. However sympathetic they may be, however much they may wish success to the Congress, the rules of the service to which they belong prevent their publicly joining us and taking a prominent part in our proceedings. But ex-officials do not occupy such a restricted position : they are able to exercise their judgment in matters political. And we have in Sir William Wedderburn an ex-official who has throughout his career in this country, extending over 25 years, shown the deepest sympathy with the aspirations of the people of this country, and who is one of the few men in the service who have had the eye to see and the heart to feel that the Government of India, conducted though it may be upon generous principles, is not all that is required for the best interests of the country, and that its institutions require to be liberalized in order that they may harmonize with the conditions of the present day. (*Cheers.*)"

Seconding the proposal, the Honorable Pandit Ajodhianath, of the United Provinces Council, said‡ :—

"Permit me to refer to a matter to which my learned leader has referred, namely the unity of the different races and classes of the country. I am a living evidence of that. I am returned not only by Allahabad, but I come before you as one of the representatives—will you guess of whom ?—

* Page 3 of the Detailed Report. † Namely himself. ‡ Page 4 of the Detailed Report.

of the Mahomedans of Bombay. (*Cheers.*) A meeting which has just been held at no great distance from this place, under the presidency of a Mahomedan Moulvi, who is well known for his ability, his knowledge of Mahomedan law and piety, elected me unanimously as one of its delegates. You may take it from me that that meeting was convened by Mahomedans and for Mahomedans only."

Sir William Wedderburn, having been declared to have been duly elected, then delivered his inaugural address. At the very outset he struck a true note when he said*:—

"I will mention this one fact, that I have passed a quarter of a century among you, and during that period of time I have not known what it was to suffer an unkindness from a native of India. During that period I have been in the service of the people of India, and have eaten their salt. (*Loud and continued cheering.*) And I hope to devote to their service what still remains to me of active life."

It is amusing to remark, how often our anti-Indian journalists suggest that Sir W. Wedderburn, Mr. Hume, and other retired Civilians, ought to give up or be deprived of their so-called pensions, because these Reformers contend that the existing Government of India is capable of very material improvement. It seems to be overlooked that, in the first place, these so-called pensions are annuities for which the recipients have paid with their own money, and that, in the second place, even if any part of these came out of the public funds, the duty of these gentlemen, as pensioners, would be to the people of India, to whom these funds belong, and not to any Government who are merely servants employed to administer these funds on behalf of that people.

He then defined and vindicated succinctly the origin, objects and methods of the Congress :—

"I have watched," he said, "from its commencement the movement which has now culminated in the National Indian Congress. And in my humble judgment the movement is unmitigated good, in its origin, its objects, and its methods. As regards its historical origin, we know that it is the direct result of the noblest efforts of British statesmanship : the natural and healthy fruit of higher education and free institutions freely granted to the people of India. Again, what are the practical objects of the Congress movement ? They are, to revive the National life, and to increase the material prosperity of the country ; and what better objects could we have before us ? Lastly, as regards our methods, they are open and constitutional, and based solely on India's reliance upon British justice and love of fair play. Looking back to the history of the movement, there was one critical time in its development : that was about ten years ago. The leaven was then actually at work, though the purposes of the movement were not then so well defined, and it was unwisely sought to deal with it by a policy of repression. The results might have been disastrous. But happily that time of tribulation was cut short by the arrival of the greatest and best of all our Viceroys, the Marquis of Ripon. (*Loud cheers.*) By his wise and sympathetic policy Lord Ripon met and fulfilled the aspirations of the national movement. And on their side the people of India recognised that a government conducted in such a spirit could not be regarded as an alien rule. This was the meaning of the passionate demonstrations at the time of Lord Ripon's departure. You, gentlemen, will correct me if I am wrong in saying that those demonstrations were a popular declaration that on such terms British rule could be accepted as the national Government of the Indian people. (*Long and enthusiastic cheers.*)"

He next summarised admirably the case as it now practically stands between England and India. He remarked†:—

"The case of India in England is really a simple one. The Crown and Parliament of Great Britain have laid down certain broad and liberal principles for the administration of India, and have

* Page 5 of the Detailed Report. † Page 6 of the Detailed Report.

solemnly pledged themselves that these shall be acted on. With those principles the people of India are fully satisfied. But the difficulty is in the practice. For owing to the necessity of the case the actual administration has to be entrusted to official agents in India. And the problem is, how, under the circumstances, can an effectual control be exercised from England so as to ensure these principles being carried out and these pledges fulfilled ? Unfortunately there is one very serious fact which much enhances the difficulty of this problem, and it is this, that in certain important particulars the professional interests of our official administrators in India are in antagonism with the interests of the Indian tax-payer whose affairs they administer. This is a somewhat delicate matter, but it is an important one, and I feel it my duty to speak out clearly. Perhaps also it is easier for me than for most people to speak freely regarding the Indian official class, and that for two reasons. First, because I am deeply interested personally in the honor of that class. (*Hear, hear.*) The Indian Civil Service has been a sort of hereditary calling in our family since the beginning of the century. My father entered the Civil Service in 1807 ; and my eldest brother followed him, until he lost his life in the Bengal mutinies. I came out shortly afterwards so that we are identified with what may be called the Indian official caste. The other reason is, because my complaint is against the system ; not against the men who carry it out. On the contrary, it is my deliberate belief that the Indian Civil and Military services have never been surpassed for honest hard work and unselfish devotion to duty. (*Cheers.*) Such being the case, I have no hesitation in repeating that the interests of the Indian services are in great measure antagonistic to the interests of the Indian tax-payer. The main interests of the Indian tax-payer are peace, economy, and reform. But all those are necessarily distasteful to the civil and military classes. A spirited and well-equipped army naturally desires, not peace, but active service. And who can reasonably expect officials to love economy, which means reduction of their own salaries ; or reform, which means restriction of their authority ? (*Cheers and laughter.*) It cannot be expected that as a class our official administrators in India will work for peace, economy, and reform. But this very fact makes all the more urgent the necessity for a control in England which shall be both vigilant and effectual."

He proceeded to show that, as a matter of fact and practice, no control whatsoever now existed in England ; and he explained how, by the transfer of the Government of the country from the East India Company to the Crown, the whole of such control as then existed, and which even a hundred years ago, Burke and Fox had denounced as inadequate, had disappeared, and happily illustrated, by two typical instances, how injuriously to India's interests the existing system operates. The whole passage, which is too long for reproduction here, should be studied in the original.*

Then reviewing our modern organizations, the Congress itself, the English Congress Agency, with its Committee (including men of all parties), the nucleus of an Indian Parliamentary party, he augured favourably of their combined efforts and commended the resolve of the Congress to send to England certain chosen representatives to plead India's cause.

"You will know," he said† "well how to address those great audiences, appealing fearlessly to the highest motives, and calling on the people of England to perform their trust and duty towards the unrepresented millions of India : appeals to unselfishness, to justice, and to humanity will ever find a sure response from the great heart of the British people. (*Cheers.*)"

Lastly, he appealed to the English in India, too many of whom, united by race bias with the Bureaucracy, are out of sympathy with the movement.

"In conclusion, I would like to address a few words to those of our English friends who distrust the Congress movement. The promoters of the Congress profess strong attachment to British rule. And I would ask, is there any reason to doubt this profession ? (*'No, no.'*) Have

---

* Pages 6, 7 of the Detailed Report. † Page 8 of the Detailed Report.

those men any interests antagonistic to our rule ? ('*No, no.*') Remember that the originators of this movement are educated men, trained up by us in a love of freedom and free institutions. Is it likely that these men should wish to exchange the rule of England, the freest and the most enlightened country in the world, for that of Russia, which is one of the most barbarous and retrograde ? (*Cheers.*) I remember being much struck with the remark of a native friend of mine with reference to Russian advances. He said to me, 'If India is lost, we are the chief losers ; you can go to your ships and will be safe in your distant homes. We, on the other hand, should lose all : our country, our liberties, and our hopes for the regeneration of our race.' Perhaps some of our doubting English friends will say, 'We attach more importance to deeds than to words.' I think we can point also to deeds. It is well known that in all schemes for the invasion of India the Russian Generals depend for success on a hoped-for rising of the native population. In 1885 they appear to have put this idea to the test by a pretended advance. Had this move been followed by any signs of sympathy, or even by an ominous silence of expectancy throughout India, Russia would have rejoiced, and we should have felt our position weakened. But India does not treat England's difficulty as her opportunity. On the contrary, there went up on all sides a patriotic cry, led by the native press, calling on all to join with men and money, and make common cause against the common foe. (*Cheers.*) I think also the action of the Congress, when calmly viewed, will be seen to point in the same direction. *The man who points out the rocks and shoals towards which the ship is moving, is the friend of the captain, not the enemy.** And that is the light in which the Government should regard the criticisms of the Congress. The moderate reforms proposed by the Congress will all tend to make the people of India more prosperous and more contented, and will thereby strengthen the foundations of British rule. (*Cheers.*) And here I would specially invite our English commercial friends to join with us in our efforts to increase the material prosperity of the country. At present owing to the poverty of the people the trade is nothing in comparison with what it ought to be. This is an argument which has been effectively pressed by our veteran leader Dadabhai Naoroji. He has pointed out that our Australian Colonies take English goods at the rate of £17 or £18 per head per annum, whereas poor India can only take at the rate of eighteen pence a head. If, by releasing him from his bonds of debt, and placing him in a position to exercise his industry, we could make the ryot moderately prosperous, how great would be the benefit to English trade ! If the Indian customer could take even £1 a head, the exports to India would exceed the exports to all the rest of the world put together. I would therefore say to our mercantile friends, help us to make the ryot prosperous, and your commercial business will soon increase by leaps and bounds."

The address concluded amidst a storm of applause, rarely witnessed even in our Congress, where people express very freely both their approbation and the reverse, and then the Hon'ble Pundit Ajoodhianath, on behalf of the Allahabad Standing Congress Committee, tendered a donation to the funds of the Bombay Reception Committee, and a silver Cutch work salver to the President, as a memento of his "presidency of this Fifth Indian National Congress." Following him, Mr. Nagpurkar presented a copy of his last novel, "The Old Palace," to the President, and the profits, thus far derived from its sale, to the English Agency Fund, and—finally—the Subjects Committee was elected.

This is a most important body, for with it, it rests to decide not only what subjects shall primarily be brought before the Congress, but the exact wording of the resolutions in regard to these, which are to be submitted to the Congress. Its members are elected by all the delegates ; all those from each Congress circle, electing a sufficient number to represent fully the views of all its various sections. Long prior to the Congress the several Standing Congress Committees after consulting their divisional Com-

* The italics are ours.

mittees, communicate to the Reception Committee, the subjects that, in their respective circles, the people desire should be discussed, and the Reception Committee, compile all these suggestions into a programme, including all those subjects of which several Committees have advocated the discussion, and send it round again to all the Standing Congress Committees, who thus come fully prepared for the greater portion, at any rate, of the work likely to be taken up. This programme, though of course a good deal modified, and at times materially added to in the Subjects Committee, constitutes the basis of their discussions. The Committee varies a little in size from year to year, and this year, including the President and General Secretary, who sit on it, *ex-officio,* consisted of 109 members.

The Committee having been elected, the President adjourned the assembly till 1 p.m. of the following day, and the audience, dispersing, left the Committee to their deliberations which, we may mention, were carried on until late in that evening, and again the next morning until a few minutes before the Congress re-assembled.

Next day, the first business on the list was a proposal that the President, should, on behalf of the entire Congress, present an address to Mr. Bradlaugh. Mr. Mehta thus explained* the matter :—

" I think I truly represented the public feeling, yesterday, when I spoke in the terms I did about Mr. Charles Bradlaugh. (*Loud cheers.*) Telegrams and addresses have been pouring in from all parts of the country, from every nook and corner, with requests that we should present them to him. I think, gentlemen, you will agree with me that it would be a matter of physical impossibility to present all those addresses to Mr. Bradlaugh. It would occupy us I think, I may say, at least a week, if not a fortnight. (*Laughter.*) It has occurred to many of the leading delegates that instead of pretending to present to him all these hundreds of addresses, separately, they should all be laid together on a large table and taken as read, and that at the time when those addresses are thus laid before Mr. Bradlaugh, one brief address on behalf of this Congress, representing as it does the public opinion of the whole country, should be read and presented to him."

The proposal was unanimously agreed to, and the address was, after the close of the Congress, duly presented.†

Then the President introduced the subject of the Reform the Legislative Councils. He said ‡:—

" As you are aware, a draft Bill has been prepared by Mr. Bradlaugh (*cheers*), and has been circulated throughout the whole of India. We have all seen it, and I think we have all read it. That Bill embodies in legal form what was believed to be the view of the Congress, so far as its opinion had been expressed up to the time that this draft was prepared. Mr. Bradlaugh's wish was to ascertain, upon certain important points, the still more mature opinion of the people of India. I think I may say on his behalf that none of the provisions introduced into the Bill were introduced because he personally wished those provisions to be contained in it. [Mr. BRADLAUGH: *Hear, hear.*] The Bill was only drafted to put into a clear and tangible form what was supposed to be the general wishes of the people. In dealing with the subject, therefore, it is not now proposed to bring forward draft sections or draft clauses prepared in legal phraseology—that is not what is required—but to state in particular and general terms certain important principles which it is desired should be embodied in the Bill."

* Pages 12, 13 of the Detailed Report. † *Vide* p. 85 of the Detailed Report. ‡ Page 13 of the Detailed Report.

Mr. Bradlaugh's Bill had been most earnestly considered and discussed all over the country—perhaps more earnestly than any other document ever was—it had been translated into many vernaculars and every section and every clause had been jealously scrutinized. With the greater part of the Bill, based as it was on the resolutions of earlier Congresses, every one was agreed. But on one important point, the opinion of the Congress, as a whole, was no longer what it had been three years previously. The reason is not far to seek. The principle of allowing the members of the Legislative Councils to be elected by the members of Municipalities, Local Boards, Chambers of Commerce, Trades and Planters' Associations, and similar organizations, Graduates of Universities, &c., which the Bill embodied, and which had been prominently put forward at the Calcutta Congress, when the Congress party consisted largely of these, had gradually ceased to be generally acceptable as more and more of the entire population became absorbed in the party. The whole question had been re-discussed, and, taking the empire as a whole, an immense majority were of opinion that a different and wider basis must be adopted for our electoral system. Accordingly, the following skeleton scheme*, for the reorganization of the Councils on an elective basis, had been worked out, to indicate the leading principles on which the election of members to the Councils should be based.

"(1.) *The Imperial and Provincial Legislative Councils to consist respectively of members not less than one-half of whom are to be elected, not more than one-fourth to sit ex-officio and the rest to be nominated by Government.*

"(2.) *Revenue districts to constitute, ordinarily, territorial units, for electoral purposes.*

"(3.) *All male British subjects above 21 years of age possessing certain qualifications and not subject to certain disqualifications (both of which will be settled later) to be voters.*

"(4.) *Voters in each district to elect representatives to one or more electoral bodies, according to local circumstances, at the rate of 12 per million of the total populatian of the district, such representatives to possess certain qualifications, and not to be subject to certain disqualifications, both of which will be settled later.*

"(5.) *All the representatives thus elected by all the districts included in the jurisdiction of each electoral body, to elect members to the Imperial Legislature at the rate of 1 per every five millions of the total population of the electoral jurisdiction, and to their own Provincial Legislature at the rate of one per million of the said total population, in such wise that whenever the Parsees, Christians, Mahomedans or Hindus are in a minority, the total number of Parsees, Christians, Mahomedans or Hindus, as the case may be, elected to the Provincial Legislature, shall not, so far as may be possible, bear a less proportion to the total number of members elected thereto, than the total number of Parsees, Christians, Hindus or Mahomedans, as the case may be, in such electoral jurisdiction, bears to its total population. Members of both legislatures to possess certain qualifications and not to be subject to certain disqualifications, both of which will be settled later.*

"(6.) *All elections to be by ballot.*"

The scheme is extremely simple. In each district all male British subjects of 21 years of age and upwards, possessing certain qualifications and not subject to certain disqualifications, will elect by ballot a certain

* Pages 13, 14 of the Detailed Scheme.

number of men to represent that district. The number will depend on the size of the district ; if it contains a population of a quarter of a million, they will elect three, if half a million six, and so on. The Representatives thus elected, by all the districts in any circle, province or presidency, as Government may arrange, will meet together and elect members for their Provincial Council and for the Imperial Council, in such wise that for every million of population that these Representatives represent, they will elect one member to their Provincial Council, and for every five millions, one to the Imperial Council. These Representatives must necessarily be a body of picked men—the average voter may not be a good judge as to who would make the best member of Council, but he knows well who the men in his own district are who bear the highest characters for ability, public spirit and rectitude of conduct, and he will assuredly, in nine cases out of ten, elect these. The Representatives will therefore include all the best men in the circle, and these may, with absolute safety, be trusted to pick out for the Councils the men who will there most truly and effectively represent the views and wishes of the people of the Province. Some presidencies, like Bengal, are very large—some like Bombay (with Sindh) very scattered—and it may, in practice, prove inconvenient to make *all* the Representatives of the entire Presidency assemble in one place ; and, so, a provision is made by which in such cases Government can divide the territory into two or more circles, and allow the representatives of each to meet separately and elect their due proportion of members. Of course this is only a skeleton, and therefore the provisions which would appear in the Act, as to the treatment of fractional parts of millions, and five millions, &c., &c., are omitted. So, too, though they were separately discussed and settled, are the qualifications requisite for, and the disqualifications which should debar from, becoming Voters, Representatives and Members of the Provincial and Imperial Councils respectively. These are, after all, only matters of detail ; what the country thinks on these points will be embodied in Mr. Bradlaugh's Bill, but if in England it be held that in any case the qualifications are pitched too high, or too low, or that the disqualifications are unnecessary or insufficient, the needful modifications can be made without affecting the principle of the Bill.

Two more points of principle, however, are embodied in the scheme: one, that all elections are to be by ballot ; the other that, for the protection of minorities, wherever Hindus, Mahomedans, Christians or Parsees are in a minority, they shall be entitled to have at least as many members on the Provincial Council, as they are entitled to by their numerical strength. The best men, Christians, Mahomedans, and Parsees, and Hindus in the Punjab where these latter are in a minority, attached no great importance to this clause, believing, and as we think correctly, that the best men will be elected without any reference to caste or creed, but the general sense of the country is in favour of the rule, and it is conceivable, though improbable, that occasions might arise when it would prove really useful.

This then was the scheme which Mr. Eardley Norton had been deputed to propose, which he did in a long and eloquent speech, which should be read *in extenso*,* though we will here reproduce from it one or two passages.

"To-day," he remarked, on rising, "I speak to you as an accredited representative of the people addressing nearly two thousand other accredited representatives of the country. We have lived to see the great elective principle, at least in its inception, being slowly carried out in the fruition of time, until, year after year, from the original number of 72, with which I believe the Congress began in this very city, we are assembled to-day in numbers which, I think, I may fairly say, defy criticism. (*Hear, hear.*) We have been told† that we have come back to the birth-place of this institution a discredited and a hopeless set of men. (*Loud cheers and laughter.*) It does not truly look much like this; a grander, a more enthusiastic assemblage, I venture to say that none here have ever witnessed either in India or Europe."

He next gracefully referred to our honoured visitor.

"I am speaking," he said, "in the presence of another gentleman, a Member of that House of Commons to whose intervention we look, and possibly to whose intervention alone we look, for reform and for assistance. (*Cheers.*) He is a man of the people speaking for the people, who comes to us with all that immense dignity and with all that immense power which lie behind the suffrages of the English nation. (*Cheers.*) And we are proud, as our address will hereafter show, to think that we have, as our Champion in the House of Commons, a man who, by a dauntless and unconquerable Championship of the truth, has earned the position which he holds alike in their affections and in ours. (*Loud cheers.*)

Reviewing the main features of the scheme he dwelt upon the importance of the elective system.

"The first section incorporates the great living principle for which, for the last six or seven years, we, the voiceless people of India, Europeans and Natives alike, have been contending; I mean the great living principle of election. I would ask you to believe in and to hold fast to that principle, and to take care that nothing is introduced into this Bill (it certainly will not be introduced by Mr. Bradlaugh) which in any way interferes with or improperly limits the operation of this great living principle."

* * *

"Gentlemen, provided you religiously adhere to that essential principle; provided you are never seduced into departing from it; provided that no matter what proportion is given to you of the election in your respective Councils, you stand and insist upon the right to have your own share in it absolutely free (*cheers*); provided you insist that there shall be no Government manipulation in your one-half—that Government shall not touch it, either directly or indirectly, undisguised or disguised—so long as you do that, you will be certain, in the long run of years, to work out for yourselves your own political emancipation."

* * * *

"Looking round wherever you will either at the Supreme Council at Calcutta or at those bodies of men who are designated, I don't know why, the Legislative Councils in the Provincial Jurisdictions—(*laughter and cheers*)—looking wherever you will, I think we are all agreed that, so far at any rate as the real wants of the people are concerned, they are practically, absolutely useless, and are mere shams. (*Cheers.*) Into such bodies of men we wish to introduce the quickening principle of election by the people, and all that we ask for is that, whatever may be the total number, hereafter of the members of the Imperial Council at Calcutta or of the Local Provincial Councils elsewhere, we shall have one-half of such bodies to do with as we choose. Now, gentlemen, if that is conceded to us—and I regret that there has been a recent departure from the more liberal principles which were enunciated by our late Viceroy upon this question—if that principle be conceded to us,

* *Vide* Detailed Report, pp. 13-18.

† By the *Pioneer*, an anti-Indian organ of the official classes, published at Allahabad.

I think we may safely expect that the peoples of this country will take a new departure, certainly in their moral, probably in their physical happiness. We shall have the right, to control ourselves ; we shall have the right, to a certain extent, to control our taxation ; we shall have the right, to criticise the Budget ; and last, but not least, we shall have the glorious privilege of interpellation. (*Cheers.*) A right which, if properly applied, will inure to the enormous benefit both of the rulers and of the ruled. (*Cheers.*)"

He explained the adoption of an indirect form of Representation to the Councils, saying*:—

"Having disposed of the principle of election in the first clause, the resolution goes on to deal with the question of who shall be the voters, in other words the original electors, and the scheme which has eventually, I am glad to say, received the unanimous acceptance of the whole Congress Committee, is shortly this. Representation direct from the people into the Council, is no doubt theoretically right and it is a sort of representation which we, who are Europeans, and you who have been brought up in the traditions of the English people, would, alike, be glad to receive. (*Cheers.*) But, gentlemen, we must limit our desires and our requests by the circumstances amidst which we find ourselves placed ; and we have heard, in that informal Committee which met a few days before the Congress assembled, from the lips of one who speaks upon this point with a peculiar emphasis, that any such proposal emanating from the Congress in India, asking the people of England to give us direct representation from the people, is sure to meet with an absolute and flat denial. Under such circumstances it would be useless for us to persist in that scheme, and I am glad therefore to think—although possibly some enthusiast may hereafter rise to propose an amendment, on this point, to my resolution—that the scheme has been abandoned—for the time being only, remember—because, as I have suggested, we shall have got the thin end of the wedge in. (*Cheers.*) In the course of years the time will come when no man, and no living set of men, shall any longer deny us that right. (*Cheers.*) But, for the time being, we have elected to abandon it and I am glad to think that this resolution will practically meet with the unanimous consent of all. (*Cheers.*)

Incidentally he referred to the scheme which had in the earlier Congresses found favour in the eyes of many, but which, when carefully examined, had been almost universally abandoned, viz., of allowing the members of Municipalities and Local and District Boards to elect the members of the Councils. As public opinion now stands, the country would prefer to have no reform in the Councils, to one based on any such deceptive system. We say deceptive, because, as a matter of fact, taking the country as a whole, fully three-fourths of these gentlemen are either Government nominees or are elected by such, and because the Government has, in each of the acts under which these bodies are constituted in the several provinces, reserved to itself power to abolish summarily any or all of them, without assigning any reasons, by a simple notification in the *Government Gazette.* "So that," as Mr. Norton remarked, "this sort of thing may happen,"

"If, once, one of us were elected, say for some particular district by some particular Municipal Board, and if in the course of two years he made himself obnoxious to the Government because he always advocated the rights of the people as against the exceptional privileges of the officials, on coming up at the end of that time for re-election such a one might find his constituency absolutely vanished ; and in answer to the query 'What has become of my constituency ?' The only response would be this, probably from the lately deceased Chairman, 'Sir, we have expired in consequence of a notification in the *Government Gazette.*' (*Laughter and cheers.*) Surely that is not the sort of electorate, to which it is either right or advisable that we should entrust our franchise."

* Page 16 of the Detailed Report.

Moreover the constituencies thus formed would be so limited in numbers that official pressure could easily be brought to bear on them and the entire object of the reform defeated.

In conclusion referring to the scheme as a whole, he said * :—

" We claim for it two merits which nothing can take from it, the merit that it is a scheme which has taken two great principles into consideration, and purposes to embody these two great principles in an Act of Parliament, namely, first, the great principle that we are to introduce for the first time in Indian political history the principle of election by the people, and, secondly, that we have taken into consideration and respected the question of the representation of the minorities of this country. (*Cheers.*)"

In seconding the question, the Honorable Pandit Ajoodhianath remarked† in reference to the happy change that has taken place in our position :—

" In those days we were, it was alleged, a set of rebels. Stuff and nonsense, (*Laughter and cheers.*) We are the most loyal people on the face of the earth. (*Renewed cheers.*) We are those who have ever been worshippers of our Sovereign ! Our friends knew well the hollowness of this libel on us, and they have now, I fancy, dropped it. They know that we have always said that the British Government was a very good Government. All that we added was that if it were a little more open to conviction, a little less distrustful of the people and a little less expensive (*laughter*) it would be still better. (*Cheers.*) This, we then thought, this we still think, and therefore desire to effect a distinct improvement in the administration of the country by associating in it our best men, who really do understand, which even our best rulers do not, how and where, exactly, the shoe pinches."

He went on to " set before " the Congress

" Three facts which almost mathematically demonstrate the necessity of this primary reform that we are seeking. I shall first take the Viceregal Council ; under the Indian Council's Act, by virtue of which these Councils are constituted, every member, official and non-official, has the right and privilege of introducing any Bill that he pleases into the Council. It may be thrown out by the votes of the majority, or, it may be vetoed by Her Majesty's Government ; but no one under the British House of Parliament, you would have thought, would venture to interfere with this privilege of a British subject explicitly conferred by an Act of Parliament. But I am sorry to say that the authority of Parliament does not, it would seem, go for much in India. There is a rule—you may take it from me—that before any Bill is introduced into the Council of the Viceroy the subject of the proposed Bill must be communicated to the Secretary of State for India (' *shame !* ') , even after this communication the poor Bill cannot be introduced unless the Secretary of State and the Government, here, both say ' yes,' or do not say ' no,' to it, within a certain period ; I believe two months. [A DELEGATE : Six months.] Some one says six months but I believe the time is not so long as that. When you come to realize that there are commonly, on an average, only 14 meetings of the Viceregal Council held in Calcutta, you can very well imagine the result of this restriction. That is fact Number one. (I do not believe in generalities, but I believe in facts.) The next fact is that for the greater part of the year the Viceroy's Council sits at Simla, and that at Simla no non-official member as a rule is present, because of the trifling allowance, some six hundred pounds I think, allowed to each non-official member each season, and which the Government cannot, it says, afford to give twice in the year so as to secure the attendance of the non-official members at the Simla Session also. Would you be surprised to learn that during this greater part of the year legislation is carried on without any non-official members in much the same way as if the Council were sitting in Calcutta with its full legal complement of non-officials ? The third fact is that for the last two years no single meeting of the United Provinces' Council has been held at Allahabad. In thinking of that, no milder word has occurred to me to describe our supposed Government by Councils than that of

* Page 18 of the Detailed Report.

† Page 18 of the Detailed Report.

'farce ;' my friend Mr. Norton says it is a 'sham,' but English is a foreign language to me (*laughter*), and I am not quite sure of the difference between a '*sham*,' and 'a *shame*,' and I will adhere to my own epithet 'a farce ;' and, truly, for India a melancholy one ! "

Pandit Bishan Narayan Dar followed in a very plain-spoken speech, which, by the sustained applause it elicited, manifestly found an echo in the hearts of the entire audience. The speech was short, and we reproduce the greater portion of it :--

"Gentlemen," he said,* " I am glad that this year the National Congress is going to deal in a practical spirit with the scheme for the reformation of the Legislative Councils—I believe that that is the most important question that could be brought before us ; and upon the settlement of this great question, upon the lines that have just been indicated by Mr. Norton, depend not only the success of India's just demands but also the permanence of the British Indian Empire. (*Loud cheers.*)"

* * * * *

" We have been appealing to our Government here, and Government has up to this time turned a deaf ear to our appeals. But in England rest assured, gentlemen, that if the English people and the English Parliament are in full possession of the facts, they will grant to you readily, promptly and cheerfully a concession which will be simply an act of justice and the redemption of a sacred pledge given long ago by our Sovereign to the people of this country. (*Prolonged cheers.*) We hear that there is a scheme in contemplation by the Indian Office on the lines suggested by Lord Dufferin or even less liberal ones. That scheme involves the expansion of the Councils, but upon the basis of nomination. Well, gentlemen, I think that we are all agreed that no reformed Councils are worth having which are founded on such a basis. The chief plank of the Congress platform, is the *elective* principle, and we are not going to be satisfied with a thing that will be a snare, a mockery and a delusion, leading men to believe that they have something which they do not really possess. What we want is not sham, but reality ; not shadow, but substance ; not nomination which is another name for deception, but representation which is the essence of political reform. (*Prolonged cheers.*) The time at my disposal is very short, and there are many points in connection with this subject that it is impossible for me to deal with. ('*Go on.*') I remember a remark of Sidney-Smith's to the effect that of all ingenious instruments of despotism, he most commended a popular assembly in which the majority of members were paid, and by their free speeches made the people believe that they were a free people. I believe this remark is peculiarly applicable to the Indian Legislative Councils wherein the majority of the members are undoubtedly the paid servants of the State, and in which a set of nominated Indian members (entirely at the mercy, so far as their seats are concerned of the Government) are allowed to make a pretence of free speeches and free criticisms and take up quasi independant attitudes in order to make the people believe that they are free, and that their voice is listened to in all matters affecting their welfare. Now I think, gentlemen, that if the Government is going to settle this question it ought to settle it in an honest and straighforward manner. If the Government really means what it so often and so loudly professes, viz., that in all matters of our country's legislation it desires to consult the people of the country, then I think the principle of election is the only principle upon which any reform worthy of the name can be based. But if the Government despite its professions, really in its heart means ' No, we do not at all want to consult in anything the views of the people, we wish to do exactly what we like, and yet keep them quiet' if it thinks that it can legislate for us and base the foundations of secure government in this country upon popular mistrust, upon suspcion and upon fear, then I must say that the system of nomination is a most ingenious instrument for carrying out that design (*cheers*), and all I would add is, *Respice finem !* (*Loud cheers.*)"

Next came the Rev. Ramchander Bose, for the reproduction of whose admirable little address no apology is needed :--

"Allow one," said he,† " whose knowledge of politics is below zero to make a few general remarks on the Resolution under consideration. The Resolution is, I maintain, a complete and triumphant reply to all the objections that have ever been advanced or ventilated by the opponents of the

* *Vide* Detailed Report, p. 19 † *Vide* Detailed Report, p. 20.

Congress. The Resolution in the first place shows that we are not doctrinaries or manipulators of impracticable theories and romantic or quixotic notions. We have again and again been charged with the folly of elaborating an ideal scheme of Government without the slightest regard to the conditions of life in India, and of striving to force it upon the acceptance of responsible officers. The Resolution before you gives the lie to this accusation inasmuch as it proposes only such moderate expansion of the existing machinery of State as is absolutely demanded by the altered state of the country. (*Cheers.*) In the second place the Resolution proves that we are not revolutionists, for it shows plainly that evolution not revolution is our object. (*Loud cheers.*) The Resolution proves that we are not demagogues, that we are not flattering the masses of our countrymen with an idea of their importance, disproportionate to their present state of culture, or inspiring amongst them hopes that cannot possibly be realized without ruining the country. Our object is their gradual elevation by means of the best type of political culture. (*Hear, hear.*) In the last place, we are accused of being conceited and being ridiculously self-assertive, of being impatient of sound counsel, and lastly of being unwilling to be led. The Resolution shows that we are being led by superiors. The framer of the Bill on which the Resolution is mainly based is an Englishman ; our illustrious President is an Englishman, and he who is the heart and soul of the movement, our General Secretary, is also an Englishman. (*Prolonged cheers.*) We have our own strong irrepressible yearnings for a freer and higher political life, but as to the best and wisest modes of attaining this, we have committed ourselves to their guidance, believing that they will conduct us safely, in due time, to the green pastures of political emancipation. (*Loud cheers.*)

" One more objection I shall take notice of before I conclude. It has been said ' you are mad after the politics of the country, but you leave the morals of the country untouched.' Do we leave the morals of the country untouched ? (*Loud and prolonged cries of ' No, no.'*) That is just the question. Neither the sphere of sociology, nor the sphere of morals has been left unaffected by the Congress. This year we have received applications from ladies for permission to appear as delegates ; and they have been elected and are here now to grace our assembly ; this shows that even the cloistered chambers of the Zenana have been thrilled by the Congress idea, and, that we, as a nation, are awakening to broader views of woman's capacities and woman's mission. Nor has the region of morals been left untouched by the Congress. The civic virtues to which ancient Rome owed her ascendency and world-wide domination are being matured amongst us ; and that virtue, sir, which is the parent of all virtues, from which every virtue emanates and into which every virtue may be resolved—I mean the virtue of self-sacrifice--is being generated amongst us. (*Cheers.*) Bombay had never distinguished itself, by such a splendid display (a display of outlay of money, of energy and of time), as we see around us to-day, for a national cause. This ancient land of religious pilgrimages, this land of religious self-denial, has never witnessed so many streams of self-sacrificing pilgrims, coming from so many centres of influence and covering such distances, as have united here in a volume of homage to the National Congress movement. (*Loud cheers.*)

" The activity of the movement has left its mark on the surface, so to speak, of every department of life ; and I have only to repeat what I said last year, viz., that partial reform, such as is directly aimed at by the Congress, is sure to effloresce or expand into universal reform. (*Prolonged cheers.*)"

Mr. G. Subramania Iyer, the editor-in-chief of the *Hindu*, a daily and also weekly paper, published in Madras, and one of the most thoughtful, earnest and moderate of Indian journals, next rose to support the scheme. He said* :—

" First of all, sir, the principle that was most predominant in our minds was this, that, whatever we may ultimately arrive at, no measure that we might now put forward, before the Congress, should be obnoxious to the criticism that it aimed—even to any slight extent—at transferring the power of ultimate control from the Government of India, representing Great Britain, to the hands of the native community of this country. The next principle we had in mind was this, that it must be a feasible, a practical, and a simple measure ; it must be one that could be worked out

* Page 21 of the Detailed Report.

without detriment to the interests of the country, and without detriment to the supremacy of British power in this country. There is another principle which we bore in mind, and it was this, that it should be a measure which would give to a large section of the people—a large number of our countrymen—a substantial measure of political power."

* * * * *

"You will remember that according to the Bill framed by Mr. Bradlaugh (and which, except in those few points in which it is at variance with our present scheme, the country has unanimously accepted), the Supreme Government in this country has had reserved to it full power of contro over half the number of the members in the Council ; this half will consist of either its servants or its nominees, the other half alone is to be elected by the people : and although the Council will be expanded, and the elected members of Council will exercise some influence in the financial arrangements, and also enjoy the right of interpellation, still the Governor-General in Council will retain the absolute power of vetoing any or every decision arrived at even by the majority of the Council. This is considered necessary in order to secure our first principle that the representatives of the nation shall not in any degree take away from the Government of India the final power of control. At the same time we are anxious that this measure should not be a sham, and result in giving no additional political influence to the people. Therefore we have insisted on the principle of election as the essential feature of our scheme."

* * * * *

"The chief feature of the measure is the institution of an intermediate electorate between the people and the Government. I think that that kind of intermediate electorate is most desirable, if not necessary, under the circumstances of the country. The Congress, as my predecessors have said, think that if any system of direct representation could be allowed, under any reasonable conditions, direct representation would have constituted the best basis possible for our scheme ; but I am not sure that even amongst our own countrymen there are not many who would disapprove of any scheme which would give the power of direct election, by ordinary voters, to seats in Council. But when besides this we were told that any measure of direct representation would certainly be unacceptable to the English Parliament, our duty clearly was to leave that out of consideration and see what else could be substituted for it. Now our present proposal, while doing away with that bugbear of direct representation and proposing a more moderate measure, also gives the people I think more substantial political advantages. It provides for the education of a large number of people in the affairs of the country. If we had direct representation we should have had only voters, who, no more than in England, could be expected to be profound politicians, and an hundred or so members of Council. But under our present scheme we shall have some thousands of representatives between the voters and the members of Council, who must necessarily train themselves in public affairs and create year by year a wider field from which the members of Council can be selected."

* * * * *

"It must be borne in mind, too, that our scheme has this great advantage that it provides for the members of the Council being elected by a picked body of gentlemen who will be the leaders of the native community in every district. That provides a guarantee that the members elected to the Council will be members who owe their position to their intelligence, integrity, and social position and influence in the native community, and not to mere demagogic gifts."

An Assam delegate, Mr. Bepin Chunder Pal, after thanking* Mr. Bradlaugh on behalf of his constituents for his exertions in championing "the down trodden slave† population" of his province, and remarking that he exemplified in his life the lines,

"I live for the cause that lacks assistance,
I live for the wrong that needs resistance
I live for the future in the distance
And the good, that I can do."

---

* Page 22 of the Detailed Report.

† These words are much too strong, but the condition of the coolies in Assam is one calling for early action by the Government. Unhappily in this as in numbers of other vitally important, provincial and even imperial questions, there is very little hope of any effective or equitable action until the people of India are *really* represented on her Councils.

concluded his speech, supporting the scheme, in the following words :—

"I should like to say is that the scheme submitted here before you is, it seems to me, in some senses even more perfect than the system of Parliamentary representation in England. Of course, I speak subject to correction, but I scrutinized the rolls of the electors of Great Britain and Ireland, and I found, it seemed to me, that more than one-fourth of the general population were unrepresented : and there is absolutely nothing in the British constitution that provides for the representation and protection of the interests of this large and influential minority. But we have done so, in our scheme, in a double way, both by leaving the Government to provide for it by nomination, and by the minority clause of the scheme laid before you. With these words I support the resolution and I hope you will carry it unanimously. (*Applause.*)"

A Panjab delegate, Lalla Lajpat Rai of Hissar, also supported the scheme and remarked* :—

"I may say that in accepting this resolution, you will have the gratification of precisely giving effect to the words and wishes of Sir Syed Ahmed, who in 1864 looked hopefully forward to the time when the Legislative Councils of India would include representatives from every district and division. (*Cheers.*) There is one other point to which I wish to refer, and that is the protection of the interests of Mahomedans in the measure now before us. In 1884 when Sir Syed Ahmed went to Lahore, he delivered a speech in which he defined the word Hindu as including both Hindus and Mahomedans, and said that he would make no distinction between Hindus and Mahomedans so far as political privileges were concerned (*cheers*), because we required no such distinction. But though we concur in his sentiments, though we hold that, we are *all*, Hindus, Parsees or Mahomedans, equally truly represented, be our elected members Mahomedans, Parsees or Hindus, because we are all one people and one nation, still we fear lest in some cases, minorities, in whom this feeling of Indian brotherhood is not yet as fully developed as it will be a few years hence, might have doubts, and think themselves unrepresented, if men of their own special section did not sit upon the Councils and so, though in reality the thing is not needed (for we are all one), we have specially provided so that all such minorities shall necessarily be represented by men of their own particular sections. This will show how sincere we are in guarding not only the real interests but even the possible prejudices of our Mahomedan brethren, and how careful we are to look to the interests of all minorities in every part of the country. I am a Hindu ; in the Panjab the Hindus are in a minority and so far as I am concerned, I should be quite content to be represented by any good Mahomedan or Sikh member—but others may not share this view—and hence the minority clause in that scheme which has been laid before you, and which I commend to your acceptance from the bottom of my heart. (*Cheers.*)"

Then followed Pandit Madan Mohan Malaviya, who first pointing out that of the *four points* for which the Congress has been contending, the Government had virtually admitted the propriety of conceding, partially at least, three, viz., the expansion of the Councils, the discussion of the Budget and the right of interpellation, went on to say† :—

"The only vital point of difference between us and Government now, therefore, is with regard to the manner of appointing members to the Council. The Government wish to nominate all the members, and we ask for the privilege of electing half of them. How evidently simple and just our prayer ! How utterly indefensible the unwillingness of Government to grant it ! (*Cheers.*) You know, gentlemen, that in the reformed Councils the Government will be exactly what they now are, the final arbiters of all questions that may be brought before the Council. Even in cases where the majority of the members are opposed to any measure and vote against it, the Government will still possess the power to veto their decision, and carry things entirely according to their own will and pleasure. In other words, they will occupy the position of a judge in deciding all questions affecting our purses, our character, in fact our whole well-being. The sole privilege which we are praying for is to be allowed to choose our own counsels to represent our case and condition fully before them.

* Detailed Report, p. 23.

† *Vide* pp. 23, 24, 25, of the Detailed Report.

And the Government seem unwilling to allow us even that ! (*Shame.*) They say they will appoint counsels of their own choice to plead our cause. Now, gentlemen, we thank them for this overflow of kindness towards us (*laughter*), but we feel, and we have good reasons to feel, that we should be much better off if they allowed us to exercise our own discretion in the choice of the counsels, who are to plead our cause, defend our rights, and protect our interests. (*Cheers.*) The Legislative Council is the great tribunal before which measures of the greatest possible moment, affecting not only ourselves, but even our posterity, are continually coming up for decision, and justice requires that before the Council passes its final judgment upon them, we should be allowed to have our say with regard to them through our chosen and accredited representatives. We do feel, gentlemen, and feel strongly that we should no longer be debarred from exercising this simple and rightful privilege. The privilege of selecting one's own counsel is not denied even to the most abandoned of criminals under the British rule. Why then should it be denied to the loyal and intelligent subjects of Her Gracious Majesty ? When a jury is being empanelled, the judge asks the person whose fate is to be decided by that jury, to say if he has any objection to any person composing it, and in case he has any such objection that person is removed from the panel. But the Government of India and our Secretary of State—if the reports published in the newspapers represent their views faithfully—seem unwilling to allow the vast millions of Her Majesty's subjects in this country any voice whatever in the appointment of persons who decide questions which concern not merely any one man or any set of men amongst them, but the entire nation of them and their posterity. Could there be anything more in conflict with reason and justice ? (*Loud cheers.*)

" If, gentlemen, the choice of Government in the selection of non-official members had, even generally, been exercised in a manner tending to promote the interests of the people we might not have been so anxious to burden ourselves with the responsibility of electing our representatives ourselves. But unhappily, as you know, in a large majority of cases, their choice has been exercised in favour of persons who have proved to be the least qualified or willing to advocate the interests, and plead fearlessly for the rights, of the people, nay, not unfrequently, in favour of persons whose presence in the Council has helped to contribute to the miseries of the people. We would much rather that there were no non-official members at all on the Councils than that there should be members who are not in the least in touch with the people (*hear, hear*), and who being ignorant of their true conditions and requirements, betray a cruel want of sympathy with them in heedlessly supporting measures which tend to increase suffering and discontent among them.

" I will recall to your mind only two instances to illustrate what I have said. A couple of years ago, you remember, the Government was driven by reason of its excessive and, as we think, wasteful military expenditure to find some fresh means of increasing its revenue and it resolved upon drawing the required money from the poor, the class least able to offer any resistance or protest. (*Shame.*) The question come up before the Legislative Council and unofficial honorable members, the so-called representatives of our people, so far from protesting against the proposal, gave their ready consent to it. Some of these gentlemen even went the length of declaring that the enhancement of the duty on salt would not inflict any hardship on the poorer classes of the people. (*Shame.*) Now, gentlemen, these big honourable gentlemen enjoying private incomes and drawing huge salaries may find it hard to believe that the addition of a few annas every year to the burdens of the poor, can cause any serious hardship to them. But those who know in what abject misery and pinching poverty our poorer classes generally exist, know how painfully the slightest increase in their burdens presses upon them. But these honorable members were pleased to say 'the people will not feel the increase in the tax.' (*Shame.*)

" I will remind you of only one more case. You remember a few months ago the Government again found itself badly in want of money. Those who regulate their income by their expenditure, and not their expenditure by their income, must frequently find themselves in that unhappy position. It became necessary to raise more revenue and after misappropriating the Famine Insurance Fund, and mulcting the provincial Governments (thereby starving education and arresting progress in all directions) Government, then resolved again on squeezing something more out of the poor. It resolved to reimpose the Patwari Cess on the ryots of the North-West Provinces and Oudh. Now you may know that when the Government of our good Lord Ripon had (*cheers*), by a cessation of war and warlike operations (*hear, hear*), effected a saving in the public expenditure; and desired to give relief to those who most needed it they found after inquiry that the Ryots of the North-Western Provinces and Oudh stood most especially in need of some relief, and they remitted the Patwari Cess to the extent of 20 lakhs. But the Government of Lord Lansdowne has this year reimposed that same Cess upon them! See, I beseech you, gentlemen, what gross injustice has been perpetrated in the reimposition of this Patwari Cess? The Patwari Cess was remitted seven years ago, but the poor ryots have had to pay it, it seems all the same, year after year. (*Shame.*) It was said that the Cess had been amalgamated with other taxes and could not be separated from them. If the money had had to go to the coffers of the Government, such a plea would never have been listened to for a moment. (*Hear, hear.*) But it was the poor ryot who was concerned, the plea was allowed to hold good, the Talukdars and Zemindars were thus allowed to enjoy the entire benefit of the measure which the Government of Lord Ripon had passed in the interests of the ryots; and it is now on this very plea that the remission of this Cess did not benefit the ryot, that the Patwari Cess has been reimposed, not on the Zemindars, but on the poor ryot, whereby he is now compelled to pay the Cess twice over, for no other fault of his than that he is poor and helpless. (*Loud cheers and cries of 'Shame, shame.'*)

"The Hon'ble Mr. Quinton, who represented the Government of Sir Auckland Colvin at the Viceroy's Council, said in his speech on the subject that the consent of the Talukdars of Oudh had been obtained to the measure. Fancy, gentlemen, the justice of adding to the burthens of the ryot on the strength of the consent of the Zemindar! But that was not all. There were other honourable members present in the Council, who said that the reimposition of the Cess would not add much more than about 12 annas a year to the load of taxation on the ryot, and they said it was so slight a sum that the ryot would not feel the pressure at all. Well, gentlemen, it is sinful to desire unhappiness to any one. But when I hear these honourable members assert with cruel levity of heart that the addition of a few annas a year to the burthens of the insufficiently fed and clothed poor, whether it be in the shape of the Salt Tax or the Patwari Cess, will not increase their wretchedness and misery, I feel tempted to exclaim with old Lear :—

'Take physic pomp,
Expose thyself to feel what wretches feel
That thou may'st shake the superflux to them
And show the heavens more just.

If these gentlemen had to live, even for a day or two, on that coarse unpalatable diet which is the best our poor, often starving, can command in the brightest times, and if they had to brave the cold of our up-country winters without all those warm and soft clothings, they themselves luxuriate in, they would understand what hardship the enhancement of the Salt Tax and the reimposition of the Patwari Cess entails upon the people. (*Prolonged cheers.*) There are hundreds of thousands of ryots at this moment in the North-West Provinces and Oudh who cannot buy sufficient cloth to cover even the upper half of their bodies properly, to protect themselves and their children from the piercing chill and cold of our northern winter nights; and remember, you gentlemen of the south, that the times are far more relentlessly severe with us there than with you here. (*Hear, hear.*) These miserable people cover themselves, their wives and children, when the season becomes very severe, with grass at night, and when the intensity of the cold drives away sleep, they warm themselves by burning some of this very grass. And even that is now and then taken away from them for feeding the cattle of the officials on tour. (*Shame.*) Such is the condition of the people to whom the honorable member of the Viceroy's Council said that an increase of 12 annas a year in their burthens would not mean any serious hardship! Do you think, gentlemen, such members would be appointed to the Council if the people were allowed any voice in their selection? (*'No, no, never!'*) And even if they were, by some mistake, once appointed, would they not be scornfully rejected at the next election? (*'Yes, yes.'*) But such men *are* appointed at present to the great disgust of the people, and the people are forced to submit to their legislatorship. (*Prolonged cheering.*)"

No apology seems requisite for this lengthy quotation, for certainly no speech from first to last, more truly, if simply, expressed the universal feelings of the middle classes, throughout the empire, on all the various topics touched upon. It could boast no rhetorical graces—it was no impassioned

burst of oratory—it was a simple matter of fact statement, but one that so entirely coincided with the opinions of the audience that it was received throughout with tokens of assent and approval such as greeted only a few of the other addresses.

Of these few the very next was one, but Mr. Surendranath Banerjee is a practised orator and ever carries his hearers along with him. He said* :—

" SISTER AND BROTHER DELEGATES,—I think it will be admitted on all hands that we, the supporters of the Indian National Congress, are now entering upon what may be regarded as the most important stage in the history of the Congress movement. (*Hear, hear.*) The storm of opposition by which we were so fiercely assailed a year ago has now disappeared, and has dissolved itself into those primitive elements of isolated hate and individual despair which originally gave rise to it. The atmosphere around us is now clearer and serener. (*Cheers.*) We are now passing from the critical into what may be called the constructive stage in the history of the Congress movement. And Mr. Bradlaugh's draft Bill is at once the token, the symbol, and the herald of the new epoch which is dawning upon us. (*Cheers.*) I rejoice to note that you have resolved to devote your attention, this time, principally to this great question of the reform of the Legislative Councils. The reform of the Councils lies at the root of all other reforms. If you get that, you get everything else. On it depends in one sense the entire future of the country and the future of our administrative system. (*Hear, hear.*)

" There is nothing which we so heartily deplore, nothing which we so strongly condemn, nothing which seems to us to be in such utter conflict with the fundamental principles of political economy, the maxims of common sense, and even the ordinary considerations of prudence and righteous administration, as the enhancement of the salt duties. (*Loud and prolonged cheers.*) Is it conceivable that, if the people of this country had the slightest control over the deliberations of the Supreme Council, if the Council had even affected to be guided by the semblance of public opinion, a law of this kind could have been passed to the prejudice of the voiceless peasantry of the country ? (*'No, no,' and applause.*) Now, I would appeal to my brother delegates, especially those who come from Bombay, and I would ask them to say whether if they had the smallest representation of the wealth, the culture, and the intelligence of this great Presidency in the Supreme Legislative Council, the Mamlatdars' Bill would have been passed in the way that it was passed. (*Loud applause.*) Turning to my brother journalists (*hear, hear, and cheers*) who are present here, I would ask them if the Official Secrets' Act would have been smuggled through the Legislative Council in the way that it was done, if they had any influence over the deliberations of that body ? (*'No, no,' and loud applause.*) Gentlemen, our Legislative Councils are so many farces (*'Yes, yes,' and cheers*) ; magnificent nonentities, gilded shams which may delude children, but cannot deceive sensible men like ourselves, who have grown into the adolescence of vigorous manhood. (*Loud applause.*) India, sir, is now changing, and we are changing with the times (*'Yes, yes,' and loud cheers*), and the new-born circumstances of modern India demand that our Legislative Councils should be adapted to our present needs and wants.

"Gentlemen, you must have all read the minute of Lord Dufferin on the expansion and reform of the Legislative Councils. At that time there was no Official Secrets' Act (*laughter*), and the Despatch was accordingly published.† I wish to speak of Lord Dufferin with the utmost possible show of consideration. (*Laughter and applause.*) I remember, very well remember, the time when my distinguished friend (Mr. A. O. Hume) behind me (*loud cheers*) with a faltering hand and a trembling heart sketched out the faint and meagre outlines of a scheme for the reform of our Councils. (*Loud applause.*) It was a dream, the Old Man's Hope‡ (*hear, hear*), but it is now about to be realized, to his great and undying glory, and the happiness of the countless millions of my own countrymen. (*Loud applause.*) The question has indeed reached a practical stage. It is no

---

* Pages 25 and 26 of the Detailed Report.

† In Mr. Surendranath's own paper, "THE BENGALEE."

‡ "THE OLD MAN'S HOPE" is the name of a pamphlet which helped, *inter alia*, to inaugurate the Congress movement.

longer in the region of vague and nebulous abstractions. I mean no disrespect to the late Viceroy when I say that he was no friend of the Congress movement, and that he was not sympathetic towards the aspirations which it represents. But even he, such as he was, was so influenced by the growing efflux of public opinion, that he felt himself called upon, as much in the interests of the people of this country as for the credit and good name of the English Government (*hear, hear,*) to recommend the reform and the reconstitution of the Councils. He suggested the expansion of the Legislative Councils, and the reconstitution of the Provincial Councils upon a partially elective basis. (*Hear, hear.*) Then came Lord Lansdowne, and I need hardly say that I desire to speak with the utmost possible respect and deference of the august representative of her most gracious Majesty the Queen-Empress, our Sovereign. Lord Lansdowne declared from his place in the Vice-regal Council that he was prepared to reform the Councils, to widen and to extend their functions. (*Hear, hear.*) But unfortunately, there is a rift in the lute. (*Loud laughter and cheers.*) His Excellency is ominously silent with regard to the recognition of the elective system in the constitution of the Councils. (*Laughter.*) I desire to repeat what has been so eloquently said here on this platform by my friend, Mr. Bishan Narayen Dar, that no reform of the Councils will ever be regarded by the country as satisfactory which does not provide for a truly representative element in their constitution. (*Loud applause.*) Nothing indeed, has been done, so far as we are aware, to give effect to Lord Lansdowne's declaration or to the recommendations of Lord Dufferin. All Governments, whether Liberal or Conservative, are slow to move in the path of reform. *Quieta non movere,* is their motto. (*Laughter and cheers.*) They will let things alone. They will not move except under the irresistible pressure of public opinion. (*Loud applause.*) If our Government will not move, we can at any rate do so. (*Hear, hear, and loud applause.*) Our champion on this platform (*cheers*) has already taken the first step in this direction by his draft Bill. (*Loud cheers.*)"

Then touching lightly on the more prominent features of the scheme, he concluded, amidst a perfect storm of applause, with the following words* :—

"Such is our scheme, and such are our proposals. And we commend them to the care of our friend on the platform (*hear, hear*), the Champion of Indian interests in the House of Commons. (*Loud and prolonged cheers.*) We wish him 'God-speed' in his noble work for the good of India. (*Loud applause.*) The prayers of a nation attend him to his Western home. (*Loud cheers.*) Illustrious, indeed, is the muster-roll of those great Englishmen who, having consecrated their lives to the cause of India, have won an undying place in the grateful recollections of our people. (*Loud and prolonged cheers.*) Fawcett and Bright are dead and gone (*cheers*), but their names are embalmed in our memories (*loud cheers*), and will be bequeathed as pious legacies to after-generations. (*Loud and continued applause.*) And, sir, if I am permitted to take a glance into the future and to anticipate the verdict of history, this I will say with confidence that in the coming times no English name will occupy a higher, a worthier, a more affectionate place in our grateful recollections than that of Charles Bradlaugh. (*Loud cheers that continued for some minutes.*) We have great confidence in him. (*Applause.*) We have great confidence in the justice and generosity of the English people (*loud cheers*), and above all we rely with abounding faith upon the liberty-loving instincts of the greatest representative assembly in the world (*cheers*), the palladium of English liberty, the sanctuary of the free and the brave—the British House of Commons. (*Loud and prolonged applause.*) When before such an assembly our prayer is pressed by such a man (*cheers*), there can come but one response which, I am confident, will be in accord with the great traditions of the English people, and will serve to consolidate the foundations of British rule in India and to broad-base it upon the affections of a happy, prosperous, and contented people. (*Loud applause which continued for several minutes.*)"

Thus far no dissentient voice had been raised, but now objections and amendments, good signs of the healthy character of the discussion, began to pour in. The first to come forward was a gentleman, who having married

---

* *Vide* p. 27 of the Detailed Report.

the most distinguished lady graduate of the Calcutta University, has apparently forgotten that all our Indian women do not, unfortunately, occupy quite so high a platform. He proposed the omission of the word male from the 3rd Clause, the effect of which would have been to confer the franchise on many millions of women. Even our staunchest Conservatives had no serious objection to the admission to the Congress, as delegates, of some of those distinguished ladies who by their labours of love have endeared themselves to many hearts and by their strenuous efforts for the people's good are already casting a reflex glory on our country, but even the most advanced of our Radicals feels and knows that the great bulk of our women, at least 99,999 in every hundred thousand, are as yet, unhappily, owing partly to want of education and most especially to the secluded lives they lead, wholly unfitted to exercise the franchise, intelligently or usefully, and the amendment was therefore, practically, unanimously negatived. There was a strong feeling that some of our most eminent lady workers, whose capacities have been demonstrated by their works, ought to be associated in our Congress, and might, possibly, hereafter be usefully elected, in some special cases, as members of Council, but this was a widely different thing from conferring the franchise, generally, on several millions of women, not one in a hundred thousand of whom could possibly, in consequence of the wholly secluded lives they lead, exercise it to any real advantage. Rambuksh, the fairly well-to-do cultivator, S. Pillay, the artizan, and Chandideen, the petty shopkeeper, thanks to the recent great diffusion of elementary political education, know, just as well as our worthy President, that peace, reform and economy are what the country and they, as units of that country's population, need, and will vote straight enough for those whom they believe will advocate and make a fight for these, but, as yet, the spouses of these good men know only of the "Kangress" as a newly discovered divinity to whom the occasional offering of a few flowers may not be inexpedient.

The next amendment was proposed by Mr. Tilak* on behalf of the great and educated Deccan community. Their view was that instead of allowing the electoral bodies to elect both the members of the Provincial and the members of the Imperial Council, they should elect the former only, and leave these to select the latter amongst themselves. The amendment was ably moved† and seconded, but it in no way commended itself to the bulk of the delegates and was emphatically negatived.

Mr. Kaliprasanna Kavyabisharad, an agnostic, then proposed that for the word "*Christians*" in Cl. 5, the words "*Europeans, Eurasians, and Native Christians*" should be substituted. This gentleman's contention, so far as could be gathered from his very brief speech, was that there might "be‡ people amongst Europeans, for instance, who are not at

* Mr. Tilak is one of some ten devoted gentlemen, connected with the Fergusson College of Poona, who deliberately putting aside the prizes that the learned professions offer to such men, have settled down on the smallest pittances on which they can support themselves and their families to promote by their personal exertions the education of their countrymen.

† *Vide* pp. 28, 29 of the Detailed Report.

‡ See p. 29 of the Detailed Report.

all Christians," and that these ought to have fair play. Whether he contemplated having members in Council specially to represent the 20 or 30 Europeans, who amongst a population of 200 millions "are not at all Christians" he omitted to explain. His seconder, however, Mr. N. Subramanyam, an Indian Christian, put it on different grounds.

"I can," he said,* "without enumerating them, imagine—and I think you can imagine—that the interests of Europeans, Eurasians, and Native Christians may not in all cases be precisely the same ; on that account alone I will second the amendment which has been proposed."

This amendment met the same fate as its predecessors amidst a great deal of, politely suppressed, laughter.

The Rev. R. A. Hume then proposed that the minority clause should be omitted, the interests of minorities being left to be protected by the Government to whom the nomination of one-fourth of the members of the Councils, was by the scheme, reserved. Mr. Hume is the much loved and respected pastor of the large Christian community of Ahmednagger, where he was elected. In proposing the amendment he admitted that he was in doubt whether the time had quite come for this, but said that as his constituency was unanimous on this question, he felt bound to bring forward the amendment on which they laid much stress "the more so because it represents the principle that must more and more dominate this movement, namely, that it is safe to trust the people." He went on to say† :—

"In a country with the past history of India, with its divisions caused by language, by race, by religion, and other things, it is most natural that those communities which are in a minority should fear lest, if this power of representation were given to the entire community, they might be overlooked. This is a reasonable fear ; at the same time if we have in a large sense the right and the qualifications for asking the Government to endow us with the privilege of electing representatives, we ought to be able—and I verily believe that in a considerable measure we are able—to take care that even as regards minorities we are properly represented, without such safe-guards as are attempted in the original Resolution. It is a pleasure to one who like myself comes from another part of the world for a particular purpose, to say that I have always found it safe to trust the people. (*Hear, hear.*) I for one should always expect that to be true, and so to my mind the wisest policy ever *is* to trust the people. Even if in a particular case at a particular time I, or those in whom I am especially interested, may not get the full representation to which in our judgment we are entitled, yet on the whole we ought to secure it by our public spirit, by our freedom from prejudice, our freedom from all restrictions, and we should be ready even to take less, than we might otherwise be entitled to, in order to set a good example, in order to emphasize a righteous principle and help on this great cause. However, I think we can hardly expect that this large Congress of communities, in its present position, should be prepared entirely to accept this proposition, yet I feel it a pleasure to follow the request of my brother delegates and to say that I believe, that certainly in such parts of the country as I live in, it is safe and it is right, without such safe-guards, to trust the people to give even the minorities a fair representation ; and when they are not fairly represented, as may sometimes be the case, to trust the wise Government under which we live to make up such deficiencies by nomination and not further seek to emphasize and keep alive distinctions which ought not, longer, to exist. (*Cheers.*)"

He was ably seconded by Mr. Hardeoram Haridas, a Hindu of Bombay, who referring to what Mr. Norton had said in his opening speech, remarked‡ :—

"I quite agree with Mr. Norton that minorities should be represented. At the same time I beg to differ from him, inasmuch as I do not agree with him that minorities are not represented if

* See p. 29 of the Detailed Report. † See p. 30 of the Detailed Report. ‡ Detailed Report, p. 31.

the principle, of insisting on the same proportion of Parsees, Hindus, Musalmans, amongst the members, that exists in the population they represent, is disallowed. To recognise such a principle would be very bad policy. We do not want sectional differences in the Legislature; we do not want a Legislature for Parsees separately, for Hindus separately, for Jews separately, for Mahomedans or for Christians separately. The business of the Legislative Council has nothing to do with these matters. I do not see how the question of a man being a Mahomedan or a Hindu has any relation to the question of the Salt Tax for example. For my part I would rather be represented by a European like Mr. Bradlaugh, by a European like Sir William Wedderburn, or any other equally good and able gentleman, than by nine-tenths of my Hindu brethren. If we make these divisions in caste or religion I do not know where they will land us. There are so many sections amongst the Hindus themselves, and we may have to look to the several creeds existing amongst them ; and then the Jains would want to be represented separately, the Sivites would want to be represented separately, the Jews would want to be represented separately, and I do not know where we should be carried. By allowing these caste or creed representatives to be brought into the Legislature you will be strengthening the hands of our opponents. Again, the spirit of the Congress as shown in its literature has been from the beginning against any such distinctions of caste and creed. (*Cheers.*)"

Mr. Eardley Norton, as the original proposer of the section, replied. He contended that the minority clause was a necessity :—

"It is impossible," he argued,* "to shut our eyes to the fact that not merely does a racial distinction exist, to a marked degree, but that here, also, are very great differences of opinion on matters theologic. Now I would put aside for one moment the question of theological disputes. But imagine this amendment accepted ; imagine the safe-guard as to minorities withdrawn, and imagine, as may well be, that some great wave of a political crisis should sweep over the country when Mahomedans would stand on the one side and Hindus on the other. What would then become of the Mahomedans ? With all the best and most Christian-like intentions on the part of the Hindus, human passion would assert itself ; and when you came to the question of counting heads or hands, the Hindus would forget all about this theoretical universal brotherhood and make it a point to see that no Mahomedan should be returned. (*'No, no.'*) Perhaps it may not be so in your opinion, but it is so in mine. I put it upon no grounds of theological dislike ; but in these great crises men loose their heads and, in their effort to obtain some particular object which they desire, they sacrifice, rightly or wrongly, everything else. Such a state of things may well arise here, and if it does, I think you will agree with me that it would be most deplorable indeed, if the proposed safe-guard should be taken away and Mahomedans and Parsees and Europeans should find themselves without the power of getting into Council. We have been discussing this matter on the grounds of the elective principle, and we have said that we intend to have that principle, pure and undiluted ; but my reverend friend's amendment cuts it away, because it says that if a sufficient number of Mahomedans are not returned the deficiencies are to be filled up—by whom ?—not by the people but by the Government. I beg his pardon ! The Government, I understand, are to use their nominations to fill up these so-called vacancies or deficiencies. The Government will not have sufficient nominations at their disposal. The time might arrive when the Hindus might reject all these various communities and Government would not then have enough seats to represent all classes other than the Hindus. (*Cries of* '*No, no, never.*') Lastly, I am satisfied that no measure which does not contain such a proposal as this contains, will commend itself either to the Government here or the Government at home. No ; let us insist upon proportional representation, leaving it to Government to strengthen this from its nominations in the case of any section where this seems, to it, needful."

It was the last argument that, we believe, carried the day. As far as could be judged, the majority alike of Christians, Parsees, Hindus and Mahomedans attached very little importance to the minority clause, and would (as was stated very distinctly later, when a subsequent amendment was being discussed) gladly have dispensed with it ; but it was felt uni-

* *Vide* pp. 31, 32 of the Detailed Report.

versally that if the Governments of India and England attached weight to it, it ought certainly to be adopted. No one objected to it except as tending to the possible revivification of those divided counsels that have, to a great extent, disappeared, but it was felt to be superfluous, and alien to the spirit of union now abroad in the country. Still all were agreed that if its retention would tend to satisfy any doubts that the authorities entertained, it would be preferable to retain it, and so the amendment was negatived.

Then ensued one of the most interesting episodes in the day's debate, a Mahomedan gentleman rising to propose, that instead of the population proportion minority clause, it should be laid down that in all the Councils there should always be as many Musalman as Hindu members.

This amendment was put forward in a very aggressive and defiant speech, and commended itself, broadly speaking, to no one, Mahomedans or Hindus. A considerable number of the Mahomedans were disposed to go with the speaker so far as the matter went, but, except one other gentleman, no one sympathized in the manner. It must, however, be borne in mind that amongst our Mahomedans we have still a few men who, living wholly in the glories of the past, honestly believe the Mahomedans to be, not merely the equals, which with education they certainly might be, of all the other races in the world, but greatly their superiors. Also amongst our Mahomedans we have a certain number of jingoes, and Munshi Hidayet Rasul, who proposed the amendment, in a marvellously eloquent and aggressive Urdu speech (to which his English translation,* very much toning down the vehemence of his expressions, does but scant justice) is both a jingo and a firm believer in the vast intrinsic superiority of the Musalmans.

It was a remarkable proof of the sprit of tolerance that animated the Congress, that from the moment this amendment was proposed, no Hindu, Parsee or Christian, despite the violence of the speaker's tone, took any part in the debate. It seemed to be felt that it was a matter chiefly affecting the Mahomedans,and that these had best be left to argue it out amongst themselves. Absurd and unreasonable as the proposal was, considering that the Hindus are at least three times as numerous as the Mahomedans, there is little doubt that had these latter as a body, asserted its justice or propriety, the rest of the Congress, in deference to their views and believing that Hindus may be just as well represented by good Mahomedans as by good Hindus, would have accepted the proposal. But the great bulk of the educated Musalmans, and necessarily it is those who chiefly attend our Congresses, are quite on the same level as the educated men of other races, and hence as a body the Mahomedans would have none of this amendment.

Mr. Syed Hamid Ali, a Musalman barrister, at once rose to repudiate it, and the whole question at issue is so ably and succinctly dealt with by him, that we may advantageously reproduce the greater part of his

---

* Pages 32, 33 of the Detailed Report.

speech. He began to explain that he himself though elected by the Mahomedan community of Lucknow, had also been elected by and was "in an equal degree a trusted representative of the Hindu community."

"Before I proceed," he* continued, "to consider the amendment and point out the fact that it is based upon a mistaken notion of the principles which ought to and do guide our scheme of representation, permit me to say that we are all endeavouring to create an United India and to form ourselves into one nation so far, at the least, as our political rights and wants are concerned. We do not come here to spread disunion and disagreement as this amendment, which implies a want of confidence in our Hindu brethren, is certainly calculated to do, especially when brought forward in speeches of the tone to which we have listened. I do not wish to call in question the motive of the gentleman who moved the amendment. However indiscreet and unbecoming his language (*hear, hear*), I trust that it has been with the best of motives that he has taken this step. I am willing to assume that he has been actuated by a sincere and honest desire to protect, as he understands them, the interests of the Mahomedans, and benefit them by his advocacy. Let none think, my Mahomedan brethren, that I myself am impelled by any other desire, when I tell you that I honestly believe that while no good can come out of demanding or even obtaining an equal number of Musalman members on the Legislative Councils, you will necessarily rouse suspicion regarding your relations with and intentions towards your Hindu brethren, by attempting thus, without any just cause or reason, to violate the principle of population on which our entire scheme of representation has been based, in furtherance of, what some of you suppose to be, your own special class interests. (*Hear, hear.*)

"Moreover, you directly incite other communities, who are now perfectly satisfied with the scheme as propounded, to make similar preposterous claims. If you disregard the population standard—if you say no matter if the Hindus number fifteen crores and we only five, we will have as many members in the Councils as they—why, by a parity of reason, or unreason, should not the Parsees, the Jains, the Sikhs, the Europeans, the Eurasians, each and all claim to have as many members in the Councils as you or the Hindus? Gentlemen, the thing is absurd. (*Cheers.*) You must adopt some standard as a basis for a scheme of representation and on the whole that of population is the fairest for all and certainly the most favourable to us. If instead of population, property or education were selected as the basis, we should be far worse off—but one of these three must be adopted, and adhered to, or the absurd result I have just indicated to you is arrived at.

"But the fact is that the amendment is based upon a wholly mistaken and baseless fear, that if the Hindus exceed the Mahomedans in Council they will carry all before them and injure Musalman interests. Now in the first place—as has been said at least an hundred times since this Congress first met—there is no such a thing in the ordinary secular matters that come before the Councils, as Hindu interests and Mahomedan interests—our interests in all such matters are absolutely one and undivided. But even if there were separate Mahomedan interests,—and I, as a Mahomedan, truly wonder what they can be—how could the Hindus in the Council, even if they were 5 to 1, as compared with the Mahomedans, and even if they wished it—which long experience has convinced me that they do not—how could they injure these interests? Are there not to be European and Eurasian members, amongst those elected, besides Sikhs and Parsees in some Provinces? Are not one-fourth of the members to be officials who sit *ex-officio* and one-fourth to be nominees of Government, amongst whom probably there would be some Mahomedans? Are all these going to combine with the Hindus to deal unjustly with the Mahomedans? It is absolutely absurd—in the first place the educated Hindus have never—and all history is my witness—attempted in any way to injure the Mahomedans—and you will only have educated Hindus elected to the Council—men of light and leading—and in the second place even if they wished it ever so, our legislative scheme renders it absolutely impossible for them to do anything of the kind. (*Loud cheers.*)

"This amendment then is calculated to create disunion and breed mutual distrust, it is absolutely illogical and leads, if accepted, to a palpable absurdity, and it is based upon a purely

** Vide* Detailed Report, pp. 34, 35.

mistaken fear, ungenerous and unreasonable in itself and originating in an inexcusable ignorance of what is, and is not, possible under our scheme for the reform of the Legislative Councils which has now been, in all essentials, before the country for the last four years. I trust therefore that you will unanimously reject it. (*Loud cheers.*)

This seemed fairly conclusive, but it in no way satisfied Syed Wahid Ali Rizwi, from Moradabad, who instinct with all the fire and eloquence of the old Arab blood, rose, as he said, to carry the matter a step or two further. When he commenced, out Heroding Herod, the general idea was that he was merely burlesquing with the view of showing up the ridiculous side of Munshi Hidayet Rasul's amendment, but it soon appeared that he was entirely in earnest, and his speech is so characteristic of the, now daily diminishing, section of our Musalman brethren to which he belongs, that we reproduce* it, *in extenso*, interruptions and all; for human nature is human nature all the world over, and even Hindus with all their tolerance, and love of hearing both sides of every question, will not quite cheerfully sit quiet under contemptuous and disparaging remarks.

"I do not rise now," said this gentlemen, "to second or support the amendment proposed by Munshi Hidayet Rasul, which stipulates for an equal number of Mahomedans and Hindus, on all the Councils, but to go a step or two beyond his contention. To my mind his contention that the number of Mahomedans should only equal that of the Hindus is far from satisfactory and by no means what a due regard for Mahomedan interests and the interests of the country demand.

"Taking this Congress as a whole, I can hardly allow to it the title of National—('*Why, why?*') It is much more of a Hindu than a Mahomedan Congress; whereas if it is to be truly national and adequately represent the best portion of the nation, it ought to be far more Mahomedan than Hindu. (*Cries of 'No, no, nonsense—why?' and considerable interruption.*)

"THE PRESIDENT—Gentlemen, silence please. One of the things we want to show the world is that we are able to hear the other side. ('*Quite so, but he must be decorous—he must not insult us.*') Well, well, gentlemen, the more disagreeable are the things said, the more patiently let us listen—I am sure this gentleman has something he wishes to say, even though he may not put it with much consideration for the feelings of others—and you will, I am sure, set him a better example, by letting him say what he has to say without interruption.

"SYED WAHID ALI RIZWI, resuming: As I was saying, to be truly national, this Congress ought to be far more Mahomedan than Hindu, and indeed, had the Mahomedans, as a whole, taken to the Congress as the Hindus have there would this day be present more Mahomedans than Hindus—for the Mahomedans are far more independent, energetic, and self-helpful than the Hindus, and if their 50 millions believed in and supported the Congress as the 200 millions of Hindus do, you would have here this day, believe me, many more Mahomedans than Hindus, whereas I do not believe that we have here even one Mahomedan to every five Hindus.

"Mr. President, the design of the Congress is doubtless good enough—I have no quarrel with its fundamental idea, which is to give scope for the full expression of the views and wishes, the wants and aspirations of the Indian Nation—but what I say is that despite all the efforts of the Hindus, to raise aloft and decorate and glorify this great work, it yet remains, and must remain, until the Musalmans fully espouse the cause, a mere dead body—it will be for the Musalmans to breathe life into it, and they must constitute its main-spring if success is to attend its career.

"Gentlemen, I must emphatically assert that without the hearty support of those true Musalmans, who represent the generations and dynasties of the old Islamite conquerors, and who are mainly now to be found in the North-West Provinces, Oudh and the Punjab, the Congress will come to nothing, now or hereafter; but if these descendants of our great warriors of the past once side, in earnest, with the Congress, then undoubtedly this will triumph. For it is on these that the British Government relies—never has that Government ceased to understand how much it owes to these

* *Vide* pp. 35, 36 of the Detailed Report.

loyal, statesmen soldiers, the true supporters of its widespread Indian Empire. Not only has it ever sympathized with these, but it has sacrificed its own interests to uphold these brave hands who fight for Britain's Empire in every moment of need and peril.

" The support of these high class Mahomedans will lift the Congress, to something like that high position that the Mahomedans occupy on the platform of the world's nationalties, where they stand elevated to a dignity and grandeur to which the Hindus have never had any pretensions since they were conquered by the Mahomedans, and were thus so reduced and lowered that they are now naturally unfit to execute higher duties and perform the greater works of the present day. *(Cries of ' No, no—bosh ! !' Nonsense !")*

" Mr. PRESIDENT—If now you ask how I prove the great superiority of the high-class Mahomedans over the Hindus, my reply is simple. In the total population only one-fifth are Mahomedans, and amongst the Mahomedans so-called, only one-fifth are of the real blood, the pure descendants of the Arabs, Moguls and Afghans. So that of the typical Musalman, there are but ten millions against two hundred and forty millions of the rest of the population, and yet this ten millions furnishes more officers in the higher grades of the Political, Military and Civil branches of the Administration than the whole of the rest of the population—in other words every true high-class Mahomedan is as valuable to the State as any 25 of other races, castes and creeds. *(Laughter.)*

" Now if India is to be represented let her be represented by her best and not by her inferior races, and in accordance with these views and out of regard to the past glories of our great and ancient race, I call upon this Congress to rule, not that there shall always be as many Mahomedans as Hindus in Council, but that there shall always be *three* times as many Musalman as Hindu members. *(Laughter and cries of ' Ten, ten. ')* "

Before he concluded, the humour of this marvellous self-assertion had quite mastered the greater portion of the Congress, and from having been rather annoyed at the studied insolence of the speaker's remarks, they appeared, before he sat down, to have quite accepted the thing as a real bit of fun.

Many of the Mahomedan delegates, however, felt apparently annoyed that any of their co-religionists should put forward such demands, and especially in such a tone. Syed Mir-uddeen Ahmed Balki gravely condemned the amendment, and we may quote the following passage from his speech. He said*:—

" Gentlemen, if I allowed my natural impulses to guide my actions, or selfishness to enter my head and heart, then of course I should support this amendment,—nay, I might even go the length of proposing with the last speaker that there should be three times as many Mahomedans as Hindus on the Councils, or go a step further and insist that none but genuine Mahomedans should be returned to the Councils ; that Mahomedans only should legislate for the whole of India ; and that all the Indian subjects of Her Majesty should be bound to observe such laws. But, gentlemen, are such natural impulses and such selfishness justifiable under the present circumstances of the country ? Or does the Mahomedan sense of justice prompt us to entertain such unworthy thoughts ? No ! We Mahomedans of India are the subjects of the same British Government under whose paternal care Hindus, Mahomedans, Parsees, Christians and all the various castes and communities of the country thrive alike. And just as our rights and privileges are inseparably connected with the country and the Government, so are those of the Hindus, Parsees, Christians and all the rest of our fellow-subjects. Then does our Mahomedan sense of justice make us ignore everybody's rights save our own ? Every creed and caste has the same immutable right of representation on the Council that we Mahomedans have. And in my judgment nothing can be more just and fair than the principle of election according to numerical proportion. O ! my Mahomedan brethren, I quite endorse what you say as to our unimpeachable loyalty to the Government and that we will stand by it through thick and thin. Undoubtedly we Mahomedans are bound by our religious tenets to obey and submit to our sovereign. It is our duty absolutely to obey the ruling power of the day. But, O

* See pp. 36, 37 of the Detailed Report.

my co-religionist brethren, you are now assembled in the *National Congress* : you are praying the Government jointly to give us all those political rights and privileges which you respectfully ask for. It is not that the Hindus, Mahomedans, Christians and Parsees are going to ask for these privileges separately, each for himself. We have assembled here for one common object, and that object is a secular and not a religious one. We standing here on a common political platform appeal to the British nation's sense of justice to permit us, their Indian follow-subjects, to enjoy something of the rights and privileges which have made them what they are. On such an occasion Mahomedans cannot call themselves Mahomedans ; nor Hindus, Hindus ; but rather forgetting all differences of creed, caste and colour we should call ourselves *Indians.* Undoubtedly every one present seems to feel so, or else why should he be here in this national assembly ? And on an occasion like this any vaunting of our own particular merits any ostentatious display of our own loyalty, as if we only were loyal, seems to be absolutely out of place ; though it might be proper when we go to ask the Government for anything concerning the Mahomedans only."

Munshi Naseeruddin Ahmed followed, very frankly rebuking the proposers of the two amendments. He remarked* :—

" I regret that Mr. Hidayet Rasul and Mr. Wahid Ali should have put their amendments before you with such violence and with such a lack of common courtesy. The amendment is opposed to the first principles of our scheme of representation, for why should five crores of ourselves have the same number of representatives as fifteen crores of Hindus ? But the proposal itself was a fair enough subject to submit quietly to the Congress for calm consideration, not to be thundered out at its head, with denunciations and empty vaunts. (*Cheers.*)

" Mr. Hidayet Rasul has talked much of the honour of our nation. I only know one nation in India, the Indians—all in fact who are born and bred there—and in this too I have the countenance of Sir Syed Ahmed, who though he may not, at one time, have favoured the Congress, knew well what he was speaking of when he laid this down distinctly, that here in India there was only one nation, the Indians, let them be Mahomedans or Hindus. (*Cheers.*) But if by our nation, Mr. Hidayet Rasul means our co-religionists, then let me tell him that it is not by vain boastings, or loud swaggerings about our valour, that our honour is to be preserved, but by showing that we are at least as reasonable, earnest and considerate of the feelings of others as the professors of other creeds and faiths.

" He has told us that five crores of Musalmans think precisely as he does—for the honour of my people I am bound to say that there are not five lakhs who think as he does and certainly not five thousand educated Mahomedans, in the whole Empire, who would have put forward *any* proposition, let alone this amendment, in the same unseemly and unbecoming manner. And now, gentlemen, as regards the merits of the amendment, I can tell you that not one in ten of the Mahomedans here present, believe in it one bit—mind, I do not say we should not like it—if you kindly chose to concede it to us, we should doubtless be very pleased and grateful—just as if I were partner of a one-fourth share in a village and my co-sharer who owned three-fourths were to say, 'never mind, let us share the profits equally.' Of course, I should be glad—of course I should think him a very liberal and good friend—but I should never presume to ask for such a thing—never delude myself with the belief that I had any right to it. So here, we Musalmans shall rejoice if, as a mark of your confidence in and love for us, you were to concede to us an equal number of representatives in the Council—but none of us, at least who are sane and in the possession of our full senses, are going to pretend that we have any right to this. We shall certainly not vote against it—why should we prevent your making us this concession of you like—but neither shall we, I believe, with very few exceptions, vote for it.

" The whole thing lies in small compass—there are brave Hindus and wise Hindus, as well as brave Musalmans and wise Musalmans, and I as a Mahomedan am certainly not going to say that we are so much better than the Hindus, that they with fifteen crores to represent shall, necessarily, have only as many representatives as we with five crores to represent. (*Cheers.*) It is the whole nation that elects—not a particular community—and the election of representatives is not based upon the majority or minority of a particular community in any particular province. I myself would con-

* *Vide* pp. 37 and 38 of the Detailed Report.

tentedly have left out the minority clause, being certain that, in the long run, when the system comes to be thoroughly understood, the best men, those who will strive most earnestly for the good of the people, will be elected, no matter whether they are Mahomedans or Hindus or members of any other of the smaller communities. But the Congress, as is well known, out of deference to the views, of some of my co-religionists, have inserted this clause so as to make sure that, even at the first, Musalmans, despite the fact that they are somewhat backward in English and general education, shall always be in the Councils, in at least as large a proportion to, the total number, as the population they may be supposed to represent especially, bears to the total population. What can be fairer? Other far smaller communities, Parsees, Christians, Jains, Sikhs, Jews, here represented, are quite content with this. What grounds have we Mahomedans for complaining? (*Cheers.*)

The rest of his speech, too, is excellent and may be read with profit. The last sentence was vigorous :—

"I utterly oppose this amendment—and to you two or three men who are pressing it on, at whose instigation you best know, I say that this assembly is not so foolish as to scatter this nosegay of union, which has been bound by the threads of love and common interests and sympathy by all the races of this land, simply to gratify the arrogance, or worse, of men whose action is founded not on reason, but impulse, not on a regard for the welfare of the whole country, but on a narrow and selfish view of what they mistakenly fancy are their own class interests. (*Loud cheers.*)"

It elicited a rejoinder on the following day from Munshi Hydayet Rasul, clever enough in its way, but in a style that is not appreciated in the Indian National Congress. Several other Musalman delegates also spoke. Mr. Cumroodin Furrukhai, expressed* disagreement with Syed Wahid Ali, but recommended the adoption of Hidayet Rasul's amendment, as a graceful concession by the Hindus which, looking to the backwardness of the Mahomedans in English education, would not, he conceived, be unfair to either party. Munshi Sheikh Hussein, in a voice of marvellous power (he is a public preacher), preached the doctrine of good-will between all classes and creeds most eloquently, but in the end was understood to recommend the Hindus to concede, what he thought would re-assure and please so many of his co-religionists. Mr. Hidayet Buksh, of Dacca, strongly opposed the amendment. This latter was then put to the Mahomedans only, when out of 254, only 39 voted either way, 16 for and 23 against the amendment. It was then put to the whole Congress, and the amendment negatived by an overwhelming majority, most of the Mahomedan delegates this time voting against it. We may add, though we shall refer to it again, in due course, later, that next day, after having discussed it amongst themselves during the evening, all the Mahomedans, except Munshi Hidyet Rasul and Syed Wahid Ali, had come round to the view that the minority clause, as framed, was perfectly fair, and that even these two, while saying that their private convictions remained unchanged, declared that in deference to the opinions of their co-religionists, they also accepted it.

The Resolution as a whole, as orginally proposed, was passed, and the Congress adjourned to the next day.

---

* See his speech, p. 39 of the Detailed Report.

When the Congress re-assembled, on the morning of the 3rd day, the first business dealt with was an Omnibus resolution, as it was called, reiterating the conclusions, on a number of points, of previous Congresses. There are a number of questions in regard to which public opinion, throughout India, is now absolutely unanimous. These questions have been brought up in Congress, time after time, and there discussed and re-discussed; they have been canvassed at thousands of public meetings and speechified upon till they have become positively threadbare; they have been taken up in hundreds upon hundreds of newspapers, published in all the vernaculars of India, and threshed out to the last grain, and there is scarcely a hamlet, in most parts of this country, in which the grey beards have not talked them over, night after night, till they have become, even for the youngsters, household words. Some of the more important of these questions were thus summarised in the Resolution laid before the Congress :—

" RESOLVED : *That this present Congress does hereby ratify and confirm the resolutions passed by previous Congresses as to*

" *(a) the urgent necessity for the complete separation of executive and judicial functions, such that, in no case, shall the two functions be combined in the same officer ;*

" *(b) the expediency of extending into many parts of the country, where it is not at present in force, the system of trial by jury ;*

" *(c) the necessity of withdrawing from the High Courts, the powers, first vested in them in* 1872, *of setting aside verdicts of acquittal by juries ;*

" *(d) the necessity of introducing, into the Code of Criminal Procedure, a provision enabling accused persons, in warrant cases, to demand that instead of being tried by the Magistrate, they be committed to the Court of Sessions ;*

" *(e) the highly unsatisfactory character of the existing system of Police Administration in India, and the absolute necessity of a fundamental reform therein ;*

" *(f) the expediency of both, establishing Military Colleges in India, whereat the Natives of India, as defined by statute, may be educated and trained for a military career as officers of the Indian Army, and of authorising, under such rules and restrictions as may seem necessary, such a system of volunteering for the Indian inhabitants of the country, as may qualify them to support the Government in any crisis ;*

" *(g) the extremely unsatisfactory character of the Income Tax Administration, especially as regards incomes below rupees one thousand, and the expediency of raising the taxable minimum to this amount ;*

" *(h) the extreme importance of increasing, instead of diminishing, as the present tendency appears to be, the public expenditure on education in all its branches, and the necessity, in view to the promotion of one of the most essential of these branches, the technical, of the appointment of a mixed commission to enquire into the present industrial condition of the country ;*

" *(i) the impolicy and injustice involved in the late increase of the Salt Tax in a time of profound peace, and the urgent necessity for an immediate reduction of this tax, and the reimposition, to balance the deficit thus caused, of light ad valorem import duties ;*

" *(j) the necessity for the reduction of, instead of the continual increase to, the military expenditure of the country.*"

No arguments, even plausible, traversing these propositions, have ever been put forward. We believe that the Government is just as well aware of their truth as we are—but the fact remains, as a forcible but none the less lamentable illustration of the inertness of our bureaucratic administration, that despite much writing and talking on these subjects, for many years, they have not yet taken one single practical step towards the removal of the gross abuses and grave evils against which this resolution protests. Encrusted, as is the bureaucracy, by routine and official and class bias, and sustained, as it is, superior to all criticism, by a pious conviction of its own infallibility, our prayers, our protests, our arguments, might with equal efficacy be addressed to the man in the moon or the irresponsive spirits of the vasty deep. Our worthy rulers need absolutely some special stimulus to rouse them into action. If there are new lucrative appointments to be created, if a neighbour's house is to be broken into and his property ruthlessly appropriated, as recently in Burmah—or if polyliteral stars twinkle ever so faintly on the horizon, our sleepers in the Council caves are at once on the *qui vive.* Or, again, if the House of Commons, glancing for once at India's unhappy condition, passes a resolution, as in regard to the drink question, condemning their inactivity, they do, for a time, grudgingly and grumblingly do *some* thing. And it is not that this administration, helpless for any good work as it seems, contains no good men and true—it can boast many such—and not a few men who, if made dictators for a single year, would do more to make crooked ways straight, and render India and her people prosperous and happy, than the Government as a whole can, or will, in a century. It is the system, which operates to give a predominance to the dull, heavy, safe men—the men safe never to do any good to any, but themselves. It is the utter absence of any popular element, which, while asking nothing better than to be led by the good and wise, would as ruthlessly push aside from *their* paths the selfish dullards, as these now combine to push aside all consideration of our just claims and grievances. Here in India we are hopeless of securing any improvement in the administration as at present constituted; hopeless of being able in any way, unaided by the people of England, to transfuse new life into the moribund organization; and this is why, in despair at the blindness and deafness of those, here, who should be our chief friends and allies, the Congress, representing the feelings of the entire country, insists so strongly upon the reform of the Councils on a partially elective basis, and why turning from the half lazy and half contemptuous *non possumus*, which meets us at every step here, it has resolved to seek upon the footsteps of the Throne and from the hearts of our British fellow-subjects, that redress of wrongs, that justice, that rational freedom, which nought that we can, here, do or say, avails one whit to secure for us.

But to return. Each of the points embodied in the omnibus resolution, having been thoroughly and repeatedly discussed in the reports of previous Congresses, nothing need be said about them here. The Resolution was proposed in a brief and telling speech* by Mr. Kalicharan Bannerjee, the eloquent and well-known Christian preacher. His speech should be

---

* *Vide* Detailed Report, pp. 41, 42.

read, but one passage in it deserves special prominence. Referring to a late oracular dictum condemnatory of the Congress he said :—

"The passage ran something like this : 'The Congress has the educational department for its father, the law for its mother, and the missionary bodies for its sponsors.' Perhaps it was intended, as I have said, for a crushing aphorism ; but, speaking for myself as a member of this Congress, I am proud of the parentage, and I am certainly not ashamed of my sponsors. (*Cheers.*)"

It is a remarkable fact that while the Government chaplains, true to their official character, are many of them far from friendly to the Congress, the great bulk of the real missionaries, the men who live amongst and for the people, are with us, and many of them zealous workers for the cause ; and were it not that the Congress falls at Christmas, when their religious duties to their flocks are paramount, instead of the few missionaries who were able to join us, we should, as their letters show, have had more than fifty of the most earnest and active men of this devoted body in our assembly. It is the custom in some circles to sneer politely at missionaries, and ask how many converts they have made,* but to thinking men, whatever their creed, it should be a powerful argument in favour of the Congress, that its sponsors really are, to a considerable extent, the very cream of that devoted body who, of all Europeans, live most closely in contact with our people, and know most of their sorrows and sufferings.

The next Resolution referred to the reform of the Abkari and Excise systems ; it tendered thanks to Messrs. Caine, Smith, and other members of Parliament who had voted in the House for the Resolution of the 30th April 1889 on this subject (condemnatory of the inaction of the Indian Government), and while acknowledging that in some Provinces, something had been done to improve the state of affairs, expressed a hope that no further time might be lost in giving full effect to the Resolution of the House of Commons. The Rev. Mr. Cobban, who proposed the Resolution, gave expression to the general feeling when he remarked.†

"In the first place, in pressing a resolution upon this subject, I should like all, our Government especially, to understand that we are doing it intelligently. (*Cheers.*) I should like them further to understand that while we press this resolution and continue to press it substantially in one form or another, we are not without a due appreciation of the extremely difficult and delicate questions which it involves. (*Hear, hear, and loud cheers.*)

The Rev. R. A. Hume, the pastor, as already noticed, of the great Christian community which his father-in-law the Rev. Mr. Fairbank so much contributed to create in Ahmednuggar, made a very appropriate quotation from his father's old papers. He said‡ :—

"The main thing which I have to say is that a few days ago, looking over the papers of my father, who was a missionary in this city from 1850 to 1854, I found a memorial that was presented by him on behalf of the citizens of this city to the Right Honourable Lord Falkland, Governor and President in Council at that time, regarding the spread of intemperance among the native op ulation of Western India. This memorial, which I hold in my hand, has, as you see, been p iddled by white ants, and worse still, the vice to which it refers has since those days eaten deep

* If they have not made many formal converts, they have at any rate breathed into tens of thousands of hearts conceptions of higher and altruistic lives, which their own examples have illustrated and enforced.

† Page 44 of the Detailed Report.

‡ Detailed Report, p. 45.

into the vitals of the country, through the continued spread of that intemperance, the earlier stages of which so alarmed my father and his co-labourers. One paragraph alone I care to read. Let me just say that I heartily believe in all that Mr. Cobban has said about the difficulty of any practical solution, but there is one paragraph in this memorial, which should commend our importunity on the subject, even to the Government. 'We believe,' runs the memorial, 'that it is a lamentable fact in the history of British India, that the transfer of any new territory to the English Government has generally been followed by a speedy and marked increase in the number of liquor shops and a removal of the restraints on the spread of intemperance amongst the people. If we mistake not, the revenue from this source and the prevalence of intemperance have generally at once increased many-fold, and it can hardly be doubted that in this respect the territories still under native rule would compare most favourably with the English territories.' Gentlemen, this is as true, I fear, to-day as it was forty years ago."

And the Rev. Mr. Evans clinched the nail, saying * :—

"Let me just point out how this traffic has been progressing. Under the Mahomedan rule the excise revenue of India was not twenty lakhs of rupees, and then it was imposed as a fine, as a restriction to try and keep the people from drinking. When the King of Oudh was Lord and Master in his country, there was no grogshop in Lucknow within ten miles of the city, but now we have over 100 grogshops in Lucknow, under British rules. When that wicked man—I suppose I should not call him by a better name—God have mercy on him ! King Theebaw of Burmah was sitting upon his throne, there was not a grogshop in Upper Burmah. But the English have taken possession of the country, and last year the excise revenue in Upper Burmah was over two lakhs. (*Shame !*) Thus, you see, gentlemen, it is going on. When the Honourable East India Company came to an end in 1858, the revenue from the excise of India was 50 lakhs of rupees, to-day it is nearly 500 lakhs of rupees. (*Shame !*)

The whole debate may be read,† but this question is another of those in regard to which no difference of opinion is possible, amongst those who know the country and the people as they *now* are, *at this present day*, and in which all that is requisite is energetic, systematic and sustained action by the authorities, and so we need not dwell upon it further.

The next Resolution was a very important one. For some time past nothing has caused so much dissatisfaction as the recent orders of the Secretary of State on the Public Service Commission's Report. There is an official theory that only a couple of million, or so, of educated men care anything about this and kindred questions. It would be a revelation to some people, perhaps, could they realize how deep and widespread are the disappointment, we fear we must say bitterness, that these orders have provoked. Had they emanated from the Government of India, they would not have created quite the same effect‡. No one expects either justice or fairplay from the Government of India, as ordinarily constituted, in cases like this in which the rights of the people are more or less antagonistic to the privileges of the Bureaucracy. But India looks for better things from Her Majesty's Secretary of State; other previous Secretaries of State have been emphatically our friends, where this very question has been concerned and have stood up boldly for equality of rights for and justice to our people, whereas these present orders are characterised by a distinctly opposite tendency. The Resolution (which was passed later unanimously) runs as follows :—

"RESOLVED : *That this Congress, while thanking Her Majesty's Government for raising the age for the Indian Civil Service Competitive Examination from 19 to 23, does hereby put on record*

* Detailed Report, p. 46.

† *Vide* pp. 44-48 of the Detailed Report.

‡ Though this is absolutely true as a general proposition, it would be unjust not to notice, that in this particular matter and two or three others Lord Dufferin showed himself to be distinctly more liberal in his views than Lord Cross.

an emphatic expression of the universal disappointment which has been created by the rest of that Government's orders in regard to the Public Service Question (the net result of which orders is to place the people of India in a worse position than they previously held), and reiterates the national conviction that no real justice will be done to India, in this matter, until the simultaneous holding in India and in England, of all Examinations, for all Civil branches of the Public Service in India, at present held only in England, be conceded."

The question is one of great importance, not only intrinsically but in consequence of the excessive soreness which it has created, and we shall therefore quote largely from the discussions. It is necessary that people, especially people in England, should realize something of what the Indians think, and feel, and say even, (and our people ever say far less than they think) of the manner in which they have been treated.

Mr. S. R. Mudaliar (who was himself one of the members of Commission) proposed the Resolution. Last year he opposed the passing of any Resolution on the subject. contending that the Secretary of State would do us justice. This year he congratulated his audience on having on that occasion declined to accept his optimistic views. He is not the only man, who firm, originally, in his belief that justice was certain at the hands of a Minister of the Crown, is beginning to lose heart and doubt. The change is one to be most gravely deprecated, but if it spreads, and becomes universal, it will not be due to any fault on the part of the people of India.

He said* :—

"Let me first say a few words on each of the clauses into which this proposition can be resolved. The first part proposes to thank the Secretary of State for having conceded to us the boon of raising the age for admission to the Civil Service. Well, thanks cost little, and I have no objection to thanking the Secretary of State for this concession, but, if you will calmly examine the matter, you will find that it was not so much a concession to the natives, as an act of policy, an act of self-protection ; an act which was found necessary, and the withholding of which would have led to disastrous results. Up to 1854 the age that was fixed for admission was 21. In that year a Committee known as Lord Macaulay's Committee recommended that the age should be raised to 23. That age remained the maximum for about five or six years. In 1860 the age was reduced to 22, and in 1866 it was reduced to 21, an arrangement which subsisted until 1878 when it was proposed to reduce the maximum to 19. When this was proposed there was a strong consensus of opinion in India, even the officials being nearly unanimous on this point, that if the age was reduced it would lead to disastrous results. But in spite of that opposition the Secretary of State, for reasons best known to himself, did reduce the age to 19. When the Commission was appointed it gave an opportunity to all the officials in the Local Governments to express their opinion that the reduction of age was a great mistake, because the men sent out were, as they were called, 'boy magistrates.' It was more, I believe, in deference to that opinion than from any wish to grant any concession to the natives, that the age was again raised. But all the same we are thankful for what was done, and we shall not pause to enquire into the motive. It *is* a concession and a boon, and as such we thank the Secretary of State for what he has done.

"The second part of the resolution expresses the opinion (which at first sight appears most startling) that the net result of what the Secretary of State has done is to place us in a worse position than we occupied when the Public Service Commission was appointed. And that, I regret to say, is a fact which cannot be denied. In a matter like this I do not wish to rely upon my own words, and I have therefore copied what the Secretary of State in his despatch says on this point. I have not an authorised copy, and must therefore rely upon the public papers. Perhaps the Secretary of State, feeling that he had treated the Public Service Commission so shabbily, was

* Pages 47-49 of the Detailed Report.

ashamed to send a copy to the members; anyhow he ought to have been ashamed and anyhow he did send no copies to us members. (*Laughter.*) Well, here is what the Secretary of State himself says :—

" ' I have no desire to extend the practical application of that principle further than political necessity requires. It is, in fact, based on the same considerations of fitness in the broadest sense which regulate the admission of Natives of India to the higher public offices of every kind ; but it justifies on indisputable grounds of public expediency the necessity of maintaining the special reservations which have hitherto existed in regard to a particular class of executive offices. No share of these offices (among which I include that of chief executive officers of a district, as well as that of Commissioner of a division and the administrative offices of still higher rank) could, without a violation of that principle, be formally excluded from statutory reservation and transferred to a Provincial Service. I do not suggest that the reservation of these offices to the Covenanted Civil Service should be so absolute as to exclude from them military officers in the Non-Regulation Provinces or that in special circumstances a member of the Provincial Service might not be appointed to one of them on grounds of proved individual fitness. What I desire to establish is that the transfer of a definite portion of them to the Provincial Service is inappropriate.'

" That is the first point that struck me when I read the despatch. When the Act of 1870 was passed, it was passed without any such reservation. It simply provided that if Government found that there was a native, who by his distinguished services, his merit and ability, had proved that he had a capacity to discharge the duties of his office, he should be appointed to any of those offices which were reserved for the English Covenanted Civilians. That Act was general in its wording, but when the rules under the Act were framed an attempt was made to exclude these executive offices from the sphere of the Statutory Service. In the rules sent by the Government of India that was one of the clauses ; but the then Secretary of State thought that it was a most improper thing to do, and he struck out the rule. So that, gentlemen, who were admitted into the Statutory Service in 1879, and subsequently, were distinctly, encouraged to hope that if they proved themselves worthy they might fairly aspire to those higher posts which are now distinctly barred to all branches of the service save the Covenanted. I say that in that respect we have been placed in a worse position than we were in at the time when the Commission was appointed.

" The second point in which our position has been changed for the worse relates to the disgraceful way in which the Statutory Civil Servants have been treated. When evidence was taken, no doubt it was found that the natives who gave evidence expressed the opinion that better selections could have been made—that the selections actually made by the Government were not the best that could have been made ; but not one went the length of saying that these men were not fit for admission. You will find that the Government accepted the statement that these selections were on the whole satisfactory. Yet look at the way in which they have been treated. They have been told that either they should be satisfied with the positions they at the moment occupy (which means with the particular office that they occupy now) or that they should become members of the Provincial Service, the members of which are excluded from all the higher executive appointments—such as Collectorships, Divisional Commissionerships, Memberships of Council, and others ; thus distinctly placing the Indian community in a worse position than it occupied before this Commission was appointed.

" The third point in which we are worse off has reference to the claims of the members of the English Covenanted Service. At the time when the statute of 1870 was passed, strong objections were raised to it—there was almost a storm one might say—and strong disapproval was expressed by the service of the view which found expression in the Act. The Civilians then said, ' we have vested interests, and these will be destroyed by the introduction of this Act.' But their protests, essentially selfish and disregardful of the higher interests of the country, were overruled, and the Act was passed, though, no doubt, no real effect was given to it till 1879. The Public Service Commission suggested that the claims of those who had entered the service previous to 1870, *i.e.*, previous to the passing of the Act, should be respected, but nobody pretended that after the Act was once passed any new European members of the service had any grounds for complaint on the score of the admission of natives. They entered the service knowing this to be the rule. But I find that the Secretary of State in his despatch says that those who entered the service up to 1880, *i. e.*

ten years later, have a prior claim to the natives of India as regards these appointments. If there were time to go on discussing this matter in all its details I could show how in many other respects the Secretary of State has deliberately placed us in a worse position than we occupied before. We are therefore fully justified in stating as *our* deliberate opinion that the Secretary of State by the orders embodied in his despatch has placed us in a worse position than we formerly occupied.

"Last year I referred to the remedy which, in our opinion, is the only remedy for these evils and that remedy is an equal competitive examination. At present, there is no equality of competition, no fair play, no 'careers open to talent.' As regards appointments made from England, there is a competitive examination, but it is held away in a distant corner of the world seven thousand miles from India, so that ninety-nine out of every hundred Indians competent to hold these posts, are virtually debarred from competing for them, by the great distances to be traversed, the large expenditure and the difficulties, about caste, involved. As regards appointments made in India, there is no fair play ; if a man seeks to get one, he must first '*poojah**' the authorities, and if he flatters and toadies enough, and makes things agreeable enough to those in whose gift the appointment lies, and those who have influence with those officials, he does get in, and then this man having got in and reached to higher office is able, to keep out far more deserving men, who scorn to make influence by such questionable means, and to let in all his relatives, friends and dependents.

"What we want is for all—Indian or English—a fair field and no favour. (*Loud cheers.*) So that the country may get the best possible men for its money (*cheers*) ; and the only way to secure this is to have open competitive examinations in India for all civil branches of the Public Service. (*Hear, hear.*) We have no objection whatsoever to identical simultaneous examinations being held in Great Britain for any branches which Europeans think it worth their while to enter. We want the best men we can get, and if the Europeans can beat the Indians in a fair competition, let them do so. (*Cheers.*) And we don't want to reproduce in their case, the gross injustice under which we are now suffering. ('*No, no.*') We don't want to drag *them* 7,000 miles on the chance of passing an examination. ('*No, certainly not.*') Let them have an examination in *their* own homes, as we claim one for ourselves in our homes. (*Prolonged cheers.*) Surely, gentlemen, no one, not wilfully blind to the dictates of common-sense and common justice, could refuse this simple demand. (*Cheers.*)"

We commend this last paragraph to the best consideration of our readers. Though the speaker is an Indian, it has a real old English ring about it, and it tells, better than any academical honours can, what English education is doing for our people. But if that love of fair play which was once Britain's chief glory is not wholly dead within her people's hearts, how can they remain deaf to such appeals? Nay, if common-sense, the other chief characteristic of the English nation, has not deserted them, how can they fail to realize that men so anxious that others, and their rivals, should have fair play, will assuredly insist, on getting it, for themselves?

Said Mr. Gokhale†:—

"Fifty-six years have come and gone since the promise was first made that no distinction of race or creed or color should be allowed to stand in the way of the prospects of preferment of any native of India. That noble promise then made—a promise worthy of the highest and most generous attitude of England towards any of the countries with which she has ever come into contact—was reiterated in yet stronger terms in the proclamation of 1858. The terms of the enactment of 1833 and of the proclamation of 1858 are so explicit that those who now try to withhold from us the privileges then assured to us must be prepared to face the painful dilemma of hypocrisy or treachery—must be prepared to admit that England was insincere when she made those promises, or that she is prepared to break faith with us now."

* "Worship" or "prostrate himself before."

† *Vide* p. 50 of the Detailed Report.

And it is impossible to traverse his assertion for, as correctly remarked by the same speaker, "great as has been the breach of faith on the part of the Government where the Bombay Mamlatdars were concerned, the breach of faith implied in the present orders of the Secretary of State is infinitely greater."

Many speakers followed, Mr. Khaparde, amongst others reiterating Mr. Mudaliar's manly statement of the case.

"Some few of our people," he said,* "overcoming innumerable difficulties have been to England and have passed the Civil Service Examination, although they were under the double disadvantage of having to go to a far distant country when very young, and of having to compete with Englishmen, in English, which to our youths is a foreign language. Notwithstanding this some of our people have passed and have since been a credit to the service. All that we want now is to do away with one of these disadvantages by the holding of this examination, in which we have shown ourselves qualified to compete, simultaneously, here and in England. This is the real watchword, and I heartily support what previous speakers have said in regard to this matter. I hope that all of you will concentrate your minds on this one great point that we are fighting for now. We do not ask for any favour, for any partiality, for any number of places to be reserved for us ; all we want is to have an equal chance in the examinations and to be then classed, be we English or Indian, according to our merits. If we take higher marks, let us go up, if not let us go down ; we want fair play and no favours. I ask you to support this proposition, and to set yourselves against every idea of reserving to ourselves any place whatever. If we desire to compete, by all means let us do so but on perfectly fair terms ; if we cannot succeed, then it is best, in every way, that we should not have appointments. All that we ask is that, so far as locality of examination is concerned, we and our English fellow-subject should compete on equal terms. If more of us pass, it will be creditable to us ; if more of them pass, it will be creditable to them. We are willing to admit that they are our superiors, so far as they can prove this, only let us have a fair competition and no favour (*cheers*), and then, *palmam qui meruit ferat !* (*Loud cheers.*)

We can only afford space for a single further quotation in which the speaker gives a clue, by references to the past, to the origin of that suspicion which is now, we fear, beginning to gain ground in India, that England's policy towards us is changing and is no longer actuated by quite those same noble and lofty motives that, in bygone† days, threw a halo around the British name.

"We must devote our attention," remarked‡ Mr. Ali Mahomed Bhimjee, "mainly to securing simultaneous examinations. You will remember that we are supported by the Parliamentary Commission which reported in 1860. On that Commission were Sir J. P. Willoughby, Mr. Mangles, Mr. Arbuthnot, Mr. MacNaughten, and Sir Erskine Perry. The report is dated 26th January 1860, and the fifth paragraph of it says 'two modes have been suggested by which the object in view might be attained. The first is by letting a certain portion of the total number of appointments declared in each year be competed for India. The second is to hold two examinations simultaneously, one in England and one in India, both being as far as practicable, identical in their nature, and those who compete in both countries being finally classified in one list according to merit by the Civil Service Commissioners. The Committee have no hesitation in giving the preference to the second scheme as being the fairest and the most in accordance with the principles of a general competition for a common object.' Now, gentlemen, let me briefly quote a few words in support of this view. How did they arrive at this view ? How did they come to support the second scheme ? Lord Stanley said, 'he could not refrain from expressing his conviction that in refusing to carry on examinations in India as well as in England, a thing that was easily practicable, the Government were in fact negativing that which they had declared to be one of the principal objects of their Bill and confining the Civil Service as heretofore to Englishmen. The result was unjust, and he believed it would be most pernicious.' Then again Lord Stanley further said, 'let them suppose, for instance, that

* See pp. 51, 52 of the Detailed Report.

† *Vide, inter alia,* the memorable debates in the House of Commons, in 1833. ‡ Detailed Report, p. 52.

instead of holding these examinations here in London, they were to be held in Calcutta ; well, how many Englishmen would go there, or how many would send their sons perhaps to spend two or three years in the country, on the chance of obtaining an appointment ? Nevertheless that was exactly the course proposed to be adopted towards the natives of India.' These are the opinions that were expressed at the time, when the Commissioners came to the conclusion that simultaneous examinations should be held in India, and we are asking nothing more nor less than what they decided in 1860 ; and now 29 years have gone by and the prospects then held out to us by one of England's wisest statesman and endorsed by a Parliamentary Commission, prospects based upon our Gracious Queen-Empress's solemn promises, have not yet been realized. I know that men have been found base enough—men traitors alike to their Queen and country—to assert that our beloved Empress's words were no promises, merely emotional utterances never intended to be acted upon. But how did an honest English statesman treat this dastardly stuff ? What did Lord Ripon say ? 'The document (Her Majesty's Proclamation) is not a treaty, it is not a diplomatic instrument, it is a declaration of principles of Government, which if it is obligatory at all, is obligatory in respect to all to whom it is addressed. The doctrine, therefore, to which Sir Fitzjames Stephen has given the sanction of his authority, I feel bound to repudiate to the utmost of my power. It seems to me to be inconsistent with the character of my sovereign and with the honour of my country, and if it were once to be received and acted upon by the Government of England, it would do more than anything else could possibly do to strike at the root of our power and to destroy our just influence.' (*Hear, hear, and loud cheers.*)"

Never did Lord Ripon utter truer words than these, but even he probably could hardly realize, for the India of to-day is widely different from that India which only six short years ago, bid him a sorrowing farewell, even he, we say, could perhaps scarcely realize the depth and breadth of that indignation which our present Secretary of State's orders, based essentially on that very doctrine which he, Lord Ripon, so earnestly repudiated, have everywhere generated.

The next Resolution was one in regard to the Arms Act. This Act, as now administered, not only offends against the natural and reasonable self-respect of the Indians, but is productive of very serious hardships and loss to the people. All this has been well shown at former Congresses : only, unfortunately, at these, the Resolutions passed, were wanting in explicitness and were capable of being construed as going further than the people really wished. The Resolution passed this year is open to neither of these objections, it is perfectly clear and explicit, it sets forth exactly what the country wants, neither more nor less, and is not open, we believe, to any reasonable objection. It runs as follows :—

"RESOLVED : *That in view of the loyalty of the people, the hardships that the Arms Act (XI. of* 1878*), as at present administered, entails and the unmerited slur which it casts upon them, the Government be moved so to modify the rules made under this Act, that all restrictions as to the possession and bearing of arms shall apply equally, to all persons residing in or visiting India ; that licenses to possess and bear arms shall be liberally and generally distributed wherever wild animals habitually destroy human life, cattle or crops, and that these and all licenses issued under the rules shall be granted once for all, shall operate throughout the provincial jurisdiction within which they are issued, be only revocable on proof of misuse, and shall not require yearly or half-yearly renewals.*"

It was proposed by Mr. J. Adam, M.A., the Principal of the great Patcheappah, college and schools, at Madras, and our first pioneer in the cause of technical education. We may quote a few paragraphs from his speech. He remarked*:—

"You will observe that we begin with the preamble which states that the Act, as at present administered, entails certain hardships upon various classes of the people, and we ask Government

* Pages 53, 54 of the Detailed Report.

to modify the rules framed under the Act. First, we say that in the modifications of these rules, they should be made to apply equally to all persons in India, not only to those who are residing in India, but to persons visiting India. With reference to persons visiting India I would simply call your attention to this. It has been said that it would be a great hardship to require European or American gentlemen coming here for a little shooting, to go through the process of taking out a license. I do not think that it would be a very great hardship ; but visitors are not included in our resolution for the purpose of paying especial attention to these few Western travellers, English and American, who may come here. It must not be overlooked that there are a large number of visitors to India, not at all of the pacific nature of English and American gentlemen. I will only call your attention to two or three instances. In the Subjects Committee a friend, from the Punjab, mentioned the case of the Northern Frontier, where there are Afghans and other tribes who frequently come into this province, and, not being British subjects, are allowed to bear arms without restriction. And then again in many sea-ports, in Bombay and along the Western Coast, sailors, negroes from Zanzibar, and other parts of Africa, come walking in the streets, swaggering about fully armed, while the inhabitants have no arms to protect themselves. The resolution refers not only to European visitors, but to all people coming into the country, and it is proposed that if there are to be, as there should be, restrictions on the indiscriminate carrying arms, they should apply equally to all persons, residing in or visiting India. I do not think it could justly be considered any hardship by those people who will be put under such a disability, if it be a disability.

" With regard to the second point of the resolution I do not think I need to emphasize it. I will only remark that statistics show that the destruction of cattle by wild animals is going on very rapidly. I do not know whether it is *propter hoc* or only *post hoc*, but it is curious that a very large increase has taken place since the time when the Act was first introduced. Sir William Hunter in his little book, published ten years ago, with reference to what England has done for India, has a very eloquent chapter upon the state of the country owing to wild beasts, robbers and others during the last century, and he points out how much that state of affairs had been modified at the time in which he was writing. He gives statistics with reference to deaths from wild beasts. I have looked over the last statistical abstract published, and I find that in 1878 (the year which Sir W. Hunter referred to, the year of the passing of the Act), the registered number of cattle killed by tigers and leopards in India was 32,000. In 1887, which is the last year for which the statistics are available, the number had risen to 52,000. Of course, you all know that these numbers do not at all represent the numbers which are really killed, they are the number reported to the police, and the proportion reported probably gets smaller, yearly, as the people realize, more and more clearly, that to report anything to the police means only further loss and annoyance to themselves, but they are the numbers which are acknowledged by the Government. The real increase is therefore, probably, much greater.

" The next point has reference to the great hardships involved by the frequent renewals which are required of the licenses. We say that whenever a license has been granted to a man, presumably of good character, so long as he does nothing to forfeit that character, he shall be allowed to retain his license without coming up every half-year and having to renew his license. If he has once been passed as having a good character, and being fit to be trusted with arms and has obtained a license, let him keep it ; of course, if he does anything wrong so as to render him unfit, for the privilege, let it be taken from him. The fourth point is the great hardship entailed by the fact that the present licenses only run in the particular district, in which they are issued. We say that the licenses that are granted should run throughout the whole jurisdiction, that is throughout the Presidency or the Province as the case may be ; that a license in any province, shall hold good throughout that province and that the holder shall be entitled to keep it, without asking for a renewal, unless he has done something to forfeit his privilege. Those are the principal points ; we do not in our resolution attempt to go into minor questions as to the forms of the licenses, the fees to be paid and so on. We leave that to Government. It is only with the vital points of principle upon which we consider that the working of the Arms Act should be amended that we deal. The proposal is straightforward, plain, simple, not extravagant, and extremely pacific ; it will not do harm to anything, and I hope I am not doing too much when I ask you all to accept this proposition that I have brought before you. (*Cheers.*)"

Referring to the inequitable distinction made under the existing rules between Europeans and Indians, Lalla Bhugwan Das very pertinently remarked* :—

"In order to insure the unity of all the races in India it is necessary that the interests of all should be the same, that is, there should be no distinction between one class and another. Our laws and regulations, as far as possible, ought to be such that they may tend to unite all classes of Her Majesty's subjects in India,—Europeans, Eurasians, Hindus, Mahomedans, Parsees, and everybody else,—and any law or regulation which serves to perpetuate class or race distinctions, tends to divide one class from another, and to diversify instead of unifying their interests, a course which is not desirable for any section of the community."

To him followed the Musalman orator, Mr. Hidayet Rasul, who on the previous day had so vehemently opposed the terms of the minority clause. He began by retaliating on those of his co-religionists who had, on the previous day, condemned his per-fervid utterances.

"We cannot agree," he said,† "with those unmeaning utterances that two-thirds of our Musalman brethren (in name only) made yesterday. They had no reasonable reply to our arguments, and their yesterday's speeches showed that they had made them simply to be loudly cheered by our Hindu brethren. (*'No, no.'*) For instance, now Munshi Nasirud-din Saheb Benarsi did not know why he had got on to the platform and what he should say. (*Cries of 'Order.'*) He had brought his rotten rope of union with him simply to hang liberty therewith. If such is an average Musalman I can assure you that none is worse than a Musalman. (*'Order, order.'*) I may say frankly that if I should have to choose between such a Musalman and a Hindu I would elect the latter.‡ (*'Question, question.'*)

He then stated that while retaining his own conviction, he withdrew his opposition to the measure passed on the previous day finding that the great majority of his co-religionists were opposed to him. He warmly supported the present resolution. He said§ :—

"You might have observed how my to-day's speech as compared with that of yesterday is dull, although I am standing to support the resolution regarding the Arms Act. It is expected that a person who undertakes to speak about arms should be vehement in his speech, but the fact is that yesterday Islam's excitement, which does not require arms to make it keener, had taken possession of me. Yesterday's fury was the fury of that nation whose deeds of valour have thrown the world into confusion. To-day the circle of speech is larger and a circle (on a liquid) the larger it becomes the less it is perceptible. This is the reason ; all our brethren the Hindus, Parsees, Jews, and Christians are agreed with us, and it is clear why my to-day's speech is dull as compared with that of yesterday. The second reason is that we are now qualified only to be loquacious as I showed you yesterday. To-day, that I am called upon to use arms, you find me rather less furious. Truly, by reason of our being disarmed we have not only lost our courage, but we are actually become women. If you duly consider the matter you will find that our nature is altogether changed. Even if we are now allowed to procure arms freely, it will be a long time before we learn their use. We do not see what good our liberal and humane Government means to reap out of this, and God knows the reward of emancipating how many slaves it will earn by its crushing the natural propensities of crores of God's creatures. (*'Order, order.'*)"

* * * * * *

"We think that the Arms Act should be greatly amended."

* * * * * *

"If this is not done, I wish to impress upon your mind that while at present we have no recourse but to part with our money when faced by robbers and dacoits, the critical time is nigh when

---

* Detailed Report, pp. 54, 55. † Detailed Report, p. 55.

‡ Munshi Nasirud-din replied to this, again, briefly, when speaking on the Permanent settlement. He said—see p. 63 of the Detailed Report. "As for Munshi Hidayat Rasul's personal remarks in regard to me I do not think them worth notice. He tried to create disunion and has failed, as I hope all such efforts ever will fail."

§ Detailed Report, pp. 55, 56.

we will seeiour houses set on fire in front of us and we will be unable to help ourselves and all this through the kindness of our Government. (*'Order, order'*)"

But, though he spoke with his usual eloquence, and strenuously supported the movement, there were points in his utterances which did not commend themselves to any portion of his audience, and he was more than once called to order.

Syed Wahid Ali, who spoke later, took much the same line as regards the previous day's disagreement, but his speech, brief as it is, is so perfectly characteristic of the feelings of a certain, but daily diminishing, section of our Musalman brethren, to whom the facts of the present day are as nothing and the glories of the past everything, that we shall reproduce it *in extenso*. He said*:—

"Mr. PRESIDENT, Gentlemen of the Congress,—I know something of politics, and I wish to say some few further words in regard to what fell from me yesterday. Then you seemed all surprised at finding me a zealous Mahomedan fighting for my race and creed brethren, and waving the crescent flag of our national and ancestral glory high in the heavens. But to-day it is otherwise, the fiery spirit has subsided, and I am willing to throw in my vote with that of the majority of the Musalmans, rather than continue to hold aloof from what the bulk of my co-religionists approve. (*Cheers.*)

"United we stand ; divided we fall," is the maxim by which I am this day governed.

"My Mahomedan brethren from Behar, Bombay and other places, are pleased to hold that the numerical superiority of the Hindus in the Provincial and Imperial Councils could never under any circumstances prove prejudicial to Mahomedan interests. How they have convinced themselves of this, is certainly a thing which I am quite unable to understand, and which it seems to me no leader or philosopher amongst the Musalmans would ever have agreed to. Well, I am master of my own ideas, and retain in my heart my conviction unchanged, but I am quite willing to waive my personal views, and vote for the view which has commended itself to the Congress as a whole, and specially which has been approved by the great majority of my learned and high-minded co-religionists here—for the very basis of all our success has been union.

"Mr. PRESIDENT: All the world knows, that mainly in virtue of this same *union*, my illustrious and brave nation, the Arabs, conquered all the countries of the Eastern Hemisphere in past ages, in an incredibly short space of time and held them for full 500 years, without check or interruption.

"From the great wall of China to the rocky fastnesses of Gibraltar, from the icy plains of Kazin to the burning deserts of Africa, the whole world rejoiced under their wise and beneficent rule. The followers of Islam, in every capacity and respect, whether as rulers or warriors, or even in numerical strength, are on the world's national platform, far in advance of other nations, and are respected and feared throughout the world. The Mahomedan laws, alike for secular and spiritual guidance, are unequalled and may truly be designated, the golden code of progress, and the footprints of our great Musalman rulers remain behind for all ages, to point to rulers and law-givers of every clime, the only safe and perfect path. But I no longer oppose the resolution passed yesterday—nay, retaining my own personal views I yet assent to it—because division leads to shipwreck in the deep, wide ocean of human affairs. (*Loud cheers and laughter.*)"

Whatever else, of Syed Wahid Ali's claims (put forward in sober earnest, and with an eloquence, to which the above translation, though made under his personal supervision, in no way does justice), the modern world may be willing to concede, no one who, thoroughly understanding the language in which they spoke, listened to the many Musalman speakers during these two days' debates, will, for an instant, deny the marvellous fire and

* *Vide* p. 57 of the Dtailed Report.

eloquence, which many of these seem to have inherited from their far-off Arab ancestors. Intoning the first few of their measured, rythmical sentences, as though chaunting a song of battle, and lashing themselves into real, or well simulated, fury, they pour out a torrent of fiery oratory such as is almost unknown among other races. Hearing some of these it becomes no longer difficult to understand how half the world fell captive at the feet of leaders who could both fight and *speak* as these men's progenitors did.

Far soberer in style, but yet perhaps not less effective in its own way, was the speech in which the Honorable Pandit Ajoodhianath summed up the incident and which (although its eloquent peroration already heads this article) we quote *in extenso* here, as a contrast to the foregoing, as essentially western in *its* character as that was eastern. He said* :—

" I am happy to support the resolution which has been placed before you, because in my humble judgment, it is calculated to bring into closer union the different classes and races now living in India under one common Sovereign. Fate has brought us together, and it is most desirable that we should all live together here on the most friendly terms, until time blends all differences into one perfect national unity. The one consideration which more especially induced me, after the most deliberate consideration for two years, to join the Congress was that in my opinion, it was the most likely institution to promote friendly feeling and an ever developing unity between the different races domiciled in the country. Yesterday I was a little disappointed, for the attitude taken by some of my Mahomedan friends was not reasonable, but, gentlemen, you can imagine my feelings when I find, to-day, that my opinion was perfectly correct. The gentlemen who came here yesterday to propose an amendment were, I am sure, actuated solely by the honest desire to place before you their own convictions and uphold what they considered were the rights of their co-religionists, but after leaving this hall they tell me that they met together again, in the place provided as quarters for the Mahomedan delegates, and discussed the whole matter amongst themselves, and after full and mature deliberation, these gentlemen inform me that they and others arrived at the conclusion that the resolution was a fair and just one and requires no amendment. (*Cheers.*) No one can be more pleased than I at that conclusion. If there is a Hindu who has been associated on terms of perfect friendship with Mahomedans, it is I. I can count among their number, gentlemen, with whom I am on the most friendly terms, and who regard me as amongst their best friends. It was a matter of deep regret to a staunch friend of Mahomedans, like myself, to see them yesterday led away more by feeling than by judgment, and proposing a really indefensible amendment, but I find to my great satisfaction that better counsels have prevailed, that judgment has now got the better of their emotional impulses; and that they, of their own accord, abandon their suggested amendment. This should be a new era in the unity of the different races of the country. (*Applause.*)

" Now I venture to submit, that what occurred yesterday and to-day is truly typical of the action of this Congress movement, throughout this great Empire. By bringing men of all creeds and classes together on a common platform and by enabling them to discuss, face to face, all those questions of domestic politics, which are the closest to the lives and hearts of our people, it first brings out into clear relief all differences and doubts that underlaid the old, mutual, class-distrust that has, in the past, been India's curse, and then it composes those differences and sets at rest for ever those doubts—except in the minds of perhaps one or two isolated fanatics whose own brethren disown them,—not by an authoritative enactment, not by the power of numbers, but by the arguments of reason and by appeals to that deep-seated, brotherly feeling which we all (when our lower and selfish natures are held in check) which we all I say, be we Mahomedans, Hindus or what not, do truly cherish in our heart of hearts for all who, born on India's sacred soil, claim India, like ourselves, as their home, their hope, their motherland. (*Loud and continued applause.*)

---

* Pages 56 and 57 of the Detailed Report.

The sequel we may quote from the Detailed Report.

"The resolution was then put and carried unanimously.

"A HINDU DELEGATE—Let us have three cheers for the Mahomedan gentleman. (*Loud cheers.*)"

"A MAHOMEDAN DELEGATE—Let us return the compliment, and have three cheers for the Hindus. (*Loud and prolonged cheers.*)"

"The Congress then adjourned for half-an-hour."

Next followed a subject which, for the last two or three years, has been greatly agitating the minds of the agricultural classes (and that means four-fifths of the entire population) throughout the greater portion of the Empire, and that is the necessity of substituting a permanent settlement, for the temporary ones which now (except in Lower Bengal and the Benares Division of the United Provinces) harrass, and as they maintain, impoverish the people.

The Resolution proposed was a very guarded one, for no one ignores the difficulties involved. As Mr. Baikunth Nath Sen said in proposing it, "its importance is only commensurate with the difficulties that beset the question." It was only intended as a declaration of principle, as the proposer said* :—

"It is not that this is to be considered once for all. We have this time simply to consider the question of principle. It will perhaps be considered at the next Congress, and perhaps repeated and re-discussed at the succeeding Congress, and so on until we attain our object."

Still the discussion† was a most interesting and instructive one, from which we shall quote freely. The Resolution ran as follows:—

"RESOLVED : *That the Government be urged to take the subject of a Permanent Settlement once more under consideration in view to practical action thereon, such that fixity and permanency may be given to the Government Land Revenue demand without further delay at any rate, in all fully populated and well cultivated tracts of country.*"

Mr. Baikunth Nath Sen, after proposing it, went on to say :—

"You all know how the Permament Settlement of Bengal was obtained. In 1770 there was a famine in Bengal. Government was induced to take action in 1783 which led to the Permanent Settlement in 1793. That Permament Settlement has worked in Bengal about a century. Agriculture forms the principal and staple industry of the country. Our agriculturists in Bengal are, comparatively speaking, better off than their brethren in the sister Presidencies or Provinces. And what is this owing to if not chiefly, or solely, to the Permanent Settlement in Bengal ? (*Cheers.*) The Permanent Settlement spoken of in the resolution contemplates the fixity of the Government demand. It also involves and implies that the rights and titles of the different classes of landholders and occupiers should be defined. Just after the introduction of the Permanent Settlement in Bengal the rights as between the superior landholders and the inferior landholders were gradually developed and defined by several enactments, and their present condition is attributable, as I have said, if not solely, chiefly, to the Permanent Settlement prevailing in Bengal. In 1837 the North-West Provinces were visited with a famine, followed by another famine in 1860. That led to the appointment of a Commission which took evidence and submitted their report. They set forth the expediency of fixing for ever the public demand on land. This was supported by the Governor-General in Council. It was Lord Canning's administration. In this state of things the matter went before the Secretary of State in Council, and, after the review of the whole matter there was a

* Detailed Report, p. 58. † *Vide* pp. 58-67 of the Detailed Report.

despatch in 1862. In this despatch the advantages which were expected to accrue by the concession of the Permanent Settlement were considered sufficiently great to justify the risk of a prospective loss of increment, in the Government revenue on land. It was considered in that despatch that the security of title and the permanence of the Government demand on land (these being the two principal incidents of Permanent Settlement) were important factors in the acceleration of the development of the resources of the country, leading to the general welfare and contentment of all Her Majesty's subjects in British India. (*Cheers.*) This was the enunciation of the principle in 1862. Practical effect, however, has not been given to it, and although a quarter of a century has quietly passed away, we do not yet find any symptoms or indications of any active measures being adopted by the Government. The question now before you is whether or not the time has arrived for moving the Government to take active measures to give practical effect to the policy indicated in the despatch of 1862, on the lines formulated in that despatch ; or, in other words, whether the territories which will be affected by this are, or are not, ripe for receiving this Permament Settlement. That is the main question.)"

* * * * *

"Every temporary arrangement, or temporary settlement as it is called, in contradistinction to a Permanent Settlement, with its concomitant evils, if not oppressions, effectually retards the progress of the development of the natural resources of the soil by discouraging the investment of capital ; and the sooner this state of things becomes a matter of history the better for the Government as well as for all concerned. (*Cheers.*) We ought not to lose sight of or ignore the interests of Government, because the Government as representing the country at large has enormous interests at stake, and these are of a nature somewhat conflicting with those of the agriculturists, at any rate at first sight ; for what is lost by Government as representative of the entire nation, is so much gained by the agricultural section of that nation. We cannot expect that Government should part with lands which have not been for a sufficient period under its direct control, to enable it to gauge, as trustees for the nation, their true value. Land must be for a certain period under its direct management to enable it to form accurate notions as to its actual produce and its capacities. I think that in the North-West Provinces, Oudh and parts of the Punjab and the greater portions of Madras and Bombay, sufficient time has passed, and we ought to consider that the Government is now in possession of those materials which are necessary to form a definite opinion as to the actual capacities of the soil and also the produce of the land. (*Cheers.*)

" A few statistics perhaps may be enough. Let us take the accounts of the *last* ten years from 1879 to 1888 ; you will find from these that the Government revenue on land averages 19 millions sterling (I am speaking of the net revenue exclusive of the charges of collection.) The net revenue from the North-Western Provinces varies from five crores, to something less than that in 1888; in Madras, from four crores to something less ; in Bombay from three crores to a little more. In Bombay there is a tendency to improve ; in the North-West Provinces and in Madras there is a tendency to decrease. So that, if these last ten years be taken as a test, the Government cannot expect to receive any very large increase to its land revenue in those Provinces and Presidencies within the *next* ten years or more. A few years ago an estimate was submitted to Government, and it was reported by an efficient and responsible officer that if the Permanent Settlement be withheld the Government might expect a prospective gain of about £200,000 or about 30 lakhs of rupees. Now this is not a very large amount after all; it is not a very appreciable figure, compared with the total revenue of the Empire, and we all know that if a Permanent Settlement be effected the resources of the country will develope in other respects, and whatever the loss on this point may be it will, I hope, be more than recouped by increased income from those other sources. The best wealth of the Government, can be found in the growing wealth of the nation. (*Cheers.*)"

* * * * *

" I do not take up vexed questions like those of proprietary rights, or the ' unearned increment,' or the rights and privileges as between landowners of different degrees and classes ; those are questions of detail ; I am contending simply now for this broad principle ; that in fully developed tracts of the country the permanence of the land revenue demand is desirable alike in the interests of the agriculturists and the nation as a whole."

Mr. S. Subramania Iyer, late a member of the Madras Legislative Council, also spoke* at length on the subject :—

" This question of Permanent Settlement I have considered from the time when I first became a landholder more than 15 years ago. In an inconsiderate moment, about that time, I invested the savings of a laborious professional career in the purchase of land in the well-watered plains of Tanjore, having left my own district, which had the misfortune of being, from time to time, visited by drought and famine. At the time that I invested these savings it was understood, on official authority, that the well-to-do province of Tanjore was to be left free from the blighting influences of a revision of assessment. The fact that the Province was to be let alone on the principle of 'let well alone' induced me to invest my savings in that district ; but, to my surprise, a few years after the purchase of these lands, I found that the authorities had made up their minds to revise the settlement of Tanjore. By that time I had spent a very considerable amount of money in the improvement of the property which I had purchased. Now, the important difficulty in connection with settlement operations is that they do not really, in practice, whatever they may profess in theory, make any allowance for the improvements effected by the ryot. I admit, and the authorities proclaim as loudly as they can, that they do not intend to tax the improvements of the ryot ; but the question is whether in practice this is not done, whether under the circumstances and the rules which are enforced they can possibly avoid doing this ? I assure you, gentlemen, as far as my experience goes, it is impossible for any proper allowance to be made for the improvements, or for these improvements to escape taxation. Of course that is a matter upon which we can only give our testimony. The authorities will assert on the one hand that they are not taxing improvements ; the ryot on the other hand *knows* and asserts that the improvements are being taxed. But whatever be the exact truth in this matter, the feeling that the improvements of the ryot *are* taxed is most detrimental to agriculture in this country.

" Gentlemen, there is no tribunal before which you can go and contest the position taken by the authorities in dealing with the land which is going to be settled. Their operations are in secret, their decisions are pronounced in such a way that it is impossible for you to attack their propriety. That character inherently belongs to the determinations of the executive in a proceeding not subject to any correction under process of law. The only facts therefore that have to be noted are these ; does the ryot feel that his improvements are certain to be taxed, or does he feel that the authorities are *not* likely to tax improvements, and therefore go on investing his money upon them ? Gentlemen, I have received an English education, I have practised nearly twenty years before the Courts, and have constantly had occasion to come before the authorities, and I therefore know their position now. If my feeling in regard to this matter is that my improvements *are* likely to be taxed, I ask you to consider what will be the ideas of the ryots, and whether they are likely to say, 'We will put a child-like faith in the justice of the authorities, we will take it that they will not tax our improvements, therefore we will go on making improvements in the expectation that they will not tax them,' or whether they, like myself, will feel that improvements never do, in practice, escape assessment and say 'we won't spend our money on improvements merely to put more money into the pockets of Government ?' From the moment it was announced that the Tanjore Settlement was going to be revised, I gave strict orders to my agent that not a single rupee should be spent upon the improvement of the land. From that moment I have not bought one acre of land, under a temporary settlement.

" That single fact, I submit to you, is of great importance in the determination of the question. I think therefore that the operation of the Settlement Department cannot but be taken to have a disturbing influence in regard to improvements in land, nay, in my belief, almost to the extent of preventing them altogether. The necessity of a Permanent Settlement, therefore, will appear to you as plain as daylight. (*Cheers.*)

" Upon the question of what sort of a Permanent Settlement the various parts of the country should get there may be a difference of opinion. All are not as fortunate as Bengal. They happened to get their Permanent Settlement at the end of the last century, we cannot hope to get a Permanent Settlement on the same terms. If we are so fortunate, well and good ; but I for one do

* *Vide* pp. 60, 61 of the Detailed Report.

not expect that we shall get such a settlement as they have. But it does not matter whether we get it on the same terms as Bengal; it is sufficient for our purposes to get a Permanent Settlement of some kind or other ; a Permanent Settlement which would instil sufficient confidence in the ryot to induce him to make improvements and which would enable him, even if certain kinds of revisions were still insisted on, to make sure that in such revisions the increased profits due to his improvements could not, and would not, be taxed. The expression 'Permanent Settlement' is somewhat ambiguous ; the authorities that have written upon it have given to it different meanings but they all agree that the feeling of security, which the settlement gives, is the essence of the thing. Therefore the resolution which simply says that a Permanent Settlement should be given to the other provinces is a resolution which I think you may confidently adopt. As I have said, the question as to the method to be adopted in the various Provinces will have to be dealt with by and by. To my mind, the one essential circumstance that requires to be provided against is this. Without binding down the Government for ever from demanding from the tenant a just share in the improvement which may be effected in the country, in the course of time, by means other than his own, such safe-guards and provisions should be adopted as would enable the tenant to obtain absolute security and immunity from further taxation in regard to all that improvement which is due to his means, to his labour, skill and capital. Mind it would be almost sufficient if the revision of the Settlement were to be effected under the sanction of law, and under the protection of the Courts. I do not care to say that for many years to come I would have the land settled in such a way that no Government could touch it. It is quite sufficient for my purpose that the tenant may feel that he can protect himself in the Courts against the secret, and at present irresponsible, orders of the Settlement Department. A Permanent Settlement, on the footing which was recommended some time back in the Madras Presidency, would be quite effective under one condition that it shall not rest with the Government in its executive capacity to determine whether a revision shall take place. If circumstances should arise which would justly entitle the State to make a further demand, on the holders of land and an enactment were passed and machinery created for the purpose of assessing this increase, such that every person liable to the increased tax would have a right to appear before a properly constituted tribunal and there obtain, in open daylight, a clear judicial decision as to his increased liabilities (the enhanced tax not being imposed as now by a stroke of the pen behind the back of the tenant), the Madras Presidency would look upon that arrangement as possessing most of the essential characters of a Permanent Settlement, and would be content to accept it."

It is the absolutely arbitrary character of modern settlements and the inferior calibre of the officials often, now-a-days, deputed to effect them that constitute important factors in the growing dissatisfaction with temporary settlements, and one speaker made rather a hit, by referring to a well known story. He said* :—

" I now come to the question of the demarcation of boundaries. Well, a certain Settlement Officer, still holding a high position in the North-West Provinces, used to say that the place where his horse stopped marked the true boundary of the village. Times are so changed, gentlemen, that matters which officials of a previous generation used to settle after making long and patient inquiries and with the help of arbitrators are now settled only by the capricious halting of a horse ! (*Shame.*) Verily, gentlemen, if in ancient times the dog of the Seven Sleepers of the Cave, had by long association with the virtuous acquired the disposition of man, the *horse* of a, by no means wide-awake, English official might well acquire the abilities demanded of a Settlement Officer, in these days of progress and advancement ! (*Laughter.*)"

He then quoted passage after passage to show that in the past, all grades of authorities, from the Secretary of State downwards, had admitted the expediency of a Permanent Settlement, and had even ordered it, and he concluded with these words :—

" For these reasons, gentlemen, I am of opinion that the introduction of a Permanent Settle-

* Page 60 of the Detailed Report.

ment is not only very desirable, but that the time has come when it should no longer be deferred. (*Cheers.*) Let the Government only act up to its own excellent published intentions. (*Loud cheers.*)"

But this lands us in *the* difficulty of all difficulties. Broadly speaking the Government never does, in India, act up to its excellent published intentions. Never was there such an immaculate administration so far as words go, and it certainly is too bad of the people of India, that they are rapidly, and visibly, becoming tired of these charming professions, and are audibly, it still *sotto voce*, grumbling at the lack of corresponding performance.

Mr. Nasiruddin Ahmed handled the question very intelligently. He said*:—

" There is no doubt that the time has now come to give greater fixity to the Government demand in many parts of India. By its repeated settlements, and re-settlements, valuations and re-valuations of lands, classifications and re-classifications of soils, statistics of produce and what not, operations which have cost the country the ransom of many kings, without bringing emancipation to a single peasant, the Government *must* have come by this time to know as much of the capacities of those parts of the country as it ever will or can know. Moreover, by its meritorious exertions, and through the good services and energies of its officers, Roads, Railways, Canals and Markets have been everywhere opened out, leaving no room to hope for any material further development in these directions. This all being so, and the greatest authorities in Europe being unanimous in regard to the necessity (if the agriculture of any country is to be fully developed) of investing the holders or cultivators of the soil with some fixity of tenure—so that, feeling a real security therein, they may give their best of labour or capital to the improvement of the land—it seems difficult to understand why, now for many years, the Government have gone to sleep, as it were, over the matter of extending the Permanent Settlement, and that, too, after they had, or the Secretary of State had, publicly announced the determination of conceding such a settlement.

" One thing is certain, and that is, that, in the temporarily settled districts, the zemindars and cultivators, greatly dreading the plague of the Settlement Officers, do nothing whatever to improve the lands permanently, but only struggle to get as much as they possibly can out of it, and bring it down to its lowest level before the next revision. All the poor ryot looks to, or can look to, is how to fill, if possible, his belly. And, gentlemen, looking to the state of the country in all your parts, if all that this resolution meant was that the existing Settlement, with all its evils and injustice, and, in many cases, bitter severity, was to be made permanent, I could not at all sympathise with it. For that is not at all what I want to see, but a widely different and really just Permanent Settlement—just to the country—just to the ryot—not a Settlement made merely to please the ryot and necessitating the recourse by Government to Income Taxes and other hateful forms of direct taxation, but a settlement securing to the country a proper return on the land, which is *her* capital, and to the ryot a proper return on his labour, which is *his* capital—not a Settlement stereotyping the evils and iniquities of your existing arrangements, but one securing the real rights, for ever, of all classes interested in the land, from the state which holds it in trust for all of us, down to the cultivator who actually tills it ; and moreover securing to each class the full future profits of all improvements that they severally or individually may make in the land. This is what is required, and this I believe is what your proposed Resolution means and, in this belief, I support and recommend it to your acceptance. (*Cheers.*)"

Very much to the point, too, was Munshi Mahomed Sakhawat Husain's speech†, which we subjoin :—

" GENTLEMEN,—If the material prosperity of the country is to increase at all in proportion with the growth of the population, the Government Land Revenue demand, must be given permanence and fixity, must be settled once for all, in all fully cultivated and well peopled portions of the country and that right soon. Every one here knows how the masses are becoming poorer

* Page 63 of the Detailed Report.

† Pages 64, 65 of the Detailed Report.

decade by decade—there may be an increase in the wealth of the higher classes (and this only intensifies the peril of the position), but the condition of the masses is steadily deteriorating. The land does not produce more, but markedly less, as the Ayeen Akhbari show us, than it did in Akhbar's time, and yet there are now more than three men dependent on the same land which in his time had to support only two ; and before many years are over there will be four. Doubtless, emigration, and the development, slow though it be, of manufacturing industries, the establishment of cotton, woollen, paper, soap, silk and other mills and the great extension of public works do offer certain, relatively tiny, channels by which somewhat of the surplus population may drain off the people-flooded land, but all these taken together afford a comparatively insignificant relief, and if the country is not to be utterly swamped in its seething and ever augmenting millions of paupers, it must be by developing the agriculture of the country. (*Loud cheers.*) At present the perpetual recurrence of Settlements is an ever present blight on agricultural progress. (*Cheers.*)

" As for the zemindars and Government they prowl about like a wolf and a sheep—the sheep ever seeking to graze up the entire pasture, and the wolf seeking to devour the sheep. (*Laughter.*)

" Will the zemindar try to improve the land—to increase its yield ? Certainly not ; an increase in the Government demand is ever before his eyes—nay, years before each revision is due, he purposely lets land fall out of cultivation and he causes false village papers to be prepared both as to the land tilled and the rents paid, and he harasses the cultivators to make them look as wretched as possible, and in fact so far from trying to improve his land, in his short-sighted policy (short-sighted, for he rarely succeeds in hood-winking the trained Settlement Officials though he may bribe their subordinates) he does his best to reduce its condition.

" But, indeed, did he wish to improve it, where can he now get the money ? As it stands, it might be good security for a loan of a thousand rupees, but who will advance half this sum on it now, when a few years hence a revision of Settlement may have reduced its value by more than half ?

" Or if he be in debt and wish to sell a part, who will give him half its value, when there is no saying but what, after the next re-settlement, it may hardly have any value at all to any proprietor who does not himself cultivate.

" Then as to the cultivators ; rights of occupancy are good things in theory, but—with bad seasons ever and anon—what real security do they afford ? Is the cultivator, who can barely keep his family and himself alive, likely to spend one farthing on the land, or give it one atom more labour than is just necessary to get the ordinary crops out of it ? No, the zemindar is here the wolf and the cultivator the sheep, and just as the Government is ever seeking to squeeze more and more out of the zemindar, so he in turn, and in absolute self-defence, is ever seeking, to squeeze more out of the ryot. All the ryot can, as a rule, possibly do is to keep himself and his children alive—and now-a-days, famines are more common than in our father's times—for the lands are in worse condition, and less of the crops are stored, and more people have to be fed—and in bad seasons he very often don't succeed even in that one thing. (*Shame.*)

" All round it is a bad system ; the Government officials do, I think, their best, but under this perpetual change of Settlements, under this constant fear of increased demands for Land Revenue, the Agriculture of the country, on whose development, we mainly depend to avert the most serious calamities, instead of developing is deteriorating. Relieve the Agriculturists of this bane, and the necessities of an increasing population will soon largely improve our agriculture and increase our produce. (*Prolonged cheers.*)

The debate was closed by a very long and able speech* by Rao Sahib Janardan Ragunath Nimbkar, a Mahratta landholder, who explained from his personal experiences, why the recurrent settlements at present in vogue are creating such bitter discontent, and then boldly grappled with that

* See pp. 65-67 of the Detailed Report.

plausible official fallacy, that the Land Revenue under the present administration is lighter than under former rulers.

" I must be brief," he remarked, " though the subject is long at the briefest—Look to what a member of Council said the other day in the light-hearted fashion, in which people speak of sufferings which they do not share. 'Our Survey Assessments have been lower than those of former rulers.' True in one sense, utterly false in reality, just as a clothier might urge that he charged less than a former dealer, because he only asked Rs. 2 for a suit and the other asked Rs. 3. But when you look into it and find that for Rs. 3 the former man, supplied, not merely coat and trousers, but pagree, waist-belt, over-cloth, shoes, and that the new man now charges Re. 1 extra for each of these over and above the Rs. 2 for the coat and trousers, you don't think much of his pretended liberality and fair dealings. (*Laughter.*) Now that is just our case, and if Mr. Peile did not know it, he ought to have known it. A particular number* may be pointed out which pays a lower assessment than it did under former rulers, though I doubt even this, but if you take the landholders, the cultivators as a body, you will find that with no more land to live on—and it is the land and the land only on which they live—they are made to pay, one way and another, at least four times what they ever paid under any previous rulers, no matter how grasping and unmerciful. Take my own lands in Ratnagiri, they have been assessed at the late survey at not less than ten times what they were assessed at under the Arba Saman survey under the Mahomedan Government.

" People may ask why are we now pressing for a Permanent Settlement,—why did we never ask for it in former times ? I will tell you, gentlemen, it is because in former times, we could easily pay for the suit ; even a little more than what is now nominally asked for it ; for in those former days we got the shoes, and the puggree and the kummerbund and the over-cloth and everything else free, and *now* we have to pay separately for everything and heavily for everything. Our means of subsistence, *i.e.*, the produce of the land, is the same, or even less, there is the same amount of water in the pot, but there are now six holes by which it runs out, when before there was but one. (*Cheers.*)

" Gentlemen, we got our salt, life's first necessary, at a nominal price—for ourselves and for our cattle. Now it is so dear that the latter cannot have it at all. (*Cheers.*)

" We had our cattle in plenty, lots of grazing free and salt to keep them healthy—now the land is all taken up by the Forest Department and we have no grazing, and if the starving herds stray where there is food, they are run into the pound and we are fined (*cheers*) ; and, day by day, cattle, the first necessity of agriculture, are decreasing in number and deteriorating in quality. (*Loud cheers.*)

" We had plenty of fuel free, both for our own purposes and to make the rab, or ash manure, without which our rice will not grow—but the forests have absorbed all the woodlands, and our Warkas lands are assessed, and we must buy our fuel and buy it dear. (*Cheers.*)

" We had plenty of wood for our houses, our ploughs, for every agricultural purpose, now it is all under the lock and key of the Forest Department, and if we touch it without leave we are run in, and if we want a stick we have a week's running about from one official to another before we get it, and we have to pay, pay, pay ! (*Loud cheers.*)

" We had arms, and we could shoot or destroy the wild beasts that ravage our crops, but now we have an Arms Act that allows a basket full of arms to every Negro rascal who lands on our shores, but takes good care that we poor cultivators, who need them to protect our subsistence from wild animals, are practically debarred from any. (*Cheers.*)

" We had such simple liquor as our people absolutely needed, at the cost of making it. But now a grand system has been introduced which, while it makes the population drunken, involves

* Every field under the Bombay system has its official number, and so the fields themselves are spoken of as numbers. The speaker here simply means by "number," "field" or "plot of land."

considerable expenditure, and that for a hurtful mixture, to provide what our cultivators, in the damp low-lying lands of Rutnagiri, really require for their health in the way of stimulus.

"We could borrow money on reasonable terms, for the land and the crops could not run away and people were willing to trust us—there was profit in those days in the land—and we could get what we wanted for seed or what not—but now when the next turn of the screw may so reduce the value of the land that the surplus may be, as it already is in many places, *nil*, no one will give credit except for very short periods at very high interest ; for the usurers care nothing for the welfare of the people, all they care for is to exact interest at a penal rate—and yet, gentlemen, Mr. Francis' Assessment, which was a fair one, and one that men could pay and live, when all these advantages were ours, has now been largely enhanced when not one of them remains to us.

"The Deccan Agricultural Relief Act, the reports of Collectors, of the Agricultural Department, all show what the real position of our cultivators is—why do they not abandon the hopeless task ? Because, unfortunately, they must either cultivate on, they and their families half-starving, or die themselves at once with their wives and little ones. Every one here knows that outside the Presidency towns where the mills and other works give some relief, our cultivators and labouring classes can barely provide sustenance for themselves and families, even in the most hand to mouth fashion —and most assuredly one of the main causes for this is the unreasonable and recurring increases to the Land Revenue Assessment, and the absence of a Permanent Settlement. (*Loud cheers.*)

"I think I have said enough to secure your acceptance of this proposition. May it please God to grant us a Permanent Settlement and with it a permament alleviation of the miseries of our poor ryots, and thus lay the foundation of the long-looked-for material prosperity of India. At present, as the proverb has it, we are told to eat, but our mouths are forcibly closed. This is not fair play. (*Loud and prolonged cheers.*)"

It is perhaps needless to say that the Resolution was unanimously carried.

Next came a Resolution calling for the abolition of the plate duties and the transformation of the obligatory Hall marking system into a voluntary institution. In the course of the remarks which fell from the speakers, a well merited tribute was paid to the memory of the late Mr. Slagg, for the interest which he had so persistently evinced in this and other Indian questions. But there is really no difference of opinion upon this plate duty and Hall-marking question, *any where.* Everybody, official and non-official, is of one mind where this is concerned, and we need not dwell further on the matter.

The next Resolution dealt both with a recent change in the rules of the House of Commons, and with a *not recent*, we regret to say, but altogether confirmed, practice of that august assembly, whereby the interests of the people of India are most gravely prejudiced.

The Resolution runs as follows :—

Resolved : *That this Congress respectfully expresses the earnest hope that, in the interests of the people of India, the House of Commons will forthwith restore the right, formerly possessed by members of that Honourable House, of stating to Parliament any matter of grievance of the natives of India, before Mr. Speaker leaves the chair, for the presentation in Committee of the Indian Budget statement, and earnestly trusts that the House of Commons will, in future, take into consideration the Annual Indian Budget statement at such a date as will ensure its full and adequate discussion, and further authorises the President, Sir William Wedderburn, Bart., to sign a petition in the name and on behalf of this Congress, for presentation to the House of Commons, in accordance with the terms of this Resolution.*

Mr. W. C. Bonnerjee, our earliest President, in moving the Resolution fully and clearly explained the position. He said.*

" You, sir, pointed out to us in your excellent address yesterday, that a great many checks which existed, in connection with the House of Commons, upon the Government of India, have been removed by the Act of 1858 ; I am sorry to say that one of the checks which existed for us even after the Act of 1858, was by a resolution, which was not intended to have that effect, taken away in the year 1888. You are all aware, that in the House of Commons, discussions with regard to grievances, take place when there is a motion for Mr. Speaker to leave the chair. Formerly when any motion that the speaker do leave the chair was made in the House of Commons, in anticipation of the House going into Committee to discuss Financial Statements or to discuss supply, it was open to any member to bring any subject of grievance to the notice of the House, Mr. Speaker sitting in the chair of the House.

" By the rule to which I have alluded, it is not now necessary to put the motion to the House that Mr. Speaker do leave the chair. The Speaker himself announces that he is about to leave the chair, and he is allowed to leave the chair without any discussion of any description, and the grievances that might have been formerly brought forward are not allowed to be brought forward at all. The House of Commons when it passed this rule had no idea how it would operate with regard to the people of this country. Formerly whenever a motion was made that the Speaker should leave the chair, in order that the House might get into Committee, to consider the Indian Financial Statement, any member of the House could get up and bring any grievances of the people of India to the notice of the House, and through that notice, to the notice of the people of Great Britain.

" But last year the rule above referred to operated in this way. When the Speakers said that he would leave the chair, he left the chair, and no opportunity was allowed to Mr. Bradlaugh to bring forward our motion with regard to the appointment of a Royal Commission to consider the administration of the Government of India, and he was therefore obliged, as a last resource, when speaking upon the Budget Statement made by Sir John Gorst, to bring to notice in an indirect and, for practical purposes, unsatisfactory way some of our grievances. (*Cheers.*) You see, therefore, that this rule operates in a very detrimental manner to our interests. It was not the intention of the House of Commons that it should have that effect, and consequently, if we from this Congress, send up this humble petition to the House, that House, justice-loving as it is, will, I have no doubt, grant us the relief which we seek. (*Cheers.*) There is another matter; you are aware that the Indian Budget Statement is not presented to the House, until about a day or two before it rises for the Session. Most of the influential members have then gone away from London to all parts of the world, and you have the Budget Statement made to a House consisting only nominally of 40 members, no more than half-a-dozen of whom remain present when the statement is actually made. (*Shame.*) If the statement could be brought forward at an earlier date, many of the most influential members, who take an interest in Indian affairs, would remain in London and take part in the discussion, but at present it is impossible that it should be so. I remember when I was present in the House last year, to listen to the Budget Statement, there was a time when the only members present were the Chairman of Committee, Mr. Courteney and Sir R. Lethbridge, who was addressing the empty benches of the House. (*Laughter.*) There was not another soul present, Mr. Bradlaugh having withdrawn for two or three minutes to the smoking-room. This state of things operates very detrimentally to India, and I think, if we from this Congress, send up a petition to the House asking them to consider this prayer of ours, it will be granted. I accordingly ask you to adopt this proposition and empower our President to sign and present to Parliament a petition, on our behalf, pointing out how seriously we suffer, from the change of rules and deprecating earnestly the late date at which the Budget is introduced. (*Cheers.*)

There is no doubt that the, apparently heartless, neglect of the British House of Commons, where Indian matters are concerned, is producing a very undesirable feeling in the minds of some of our people, and it may be

---

* *Vide* pp. 69, 70 of the Detailed Report.

well, therefore, to quote a portion of Pandit Madan Mohan Malaviya's speech on this Resolution, the more so that every sentence was received by his audience in a manner which showed how correctly he was expressing the universal feeling. He said* :—

" You will remember that two years ago when we met at Madras, we expressed our deep regret at the fact that the English Parliament did not devote that attention to our affairs which we had a right to expect of it. But now we regret still more to find that during the period that has since elapsed, matters have gone from bad to worse. Till recently, when the Indian Budget was laid before the House of Commons such of the members, as felt any interest in our affairs, were given an opportunity of saying whatever they thought necessary to say on our behalf. We complained that the opportunity thus afforded was very inadequate for anything like a fair consideration of the affairs of this vast country, and we prayed that more time might be given to the consideration of those affairs. (*Hear, hear.*) But so far from that reasonable request being granted we find, gentlemen, that even the little opportunity that had hitherto been allowed for the discussion of Indian questions has been circumscribed within still narrower bounds. The new rules of the House have, in a way, practically shut out all discussion bearing on the welfare of the 250 millions of Her Majesty's subjects in India. (*Shame, shame.*) I cannot properly express the regret and disappointment which this has created amongst us.

"Mr. Bonnerjee has very ably pointed out how injuriously to us this new rule of the House of Commons operates. The British Parliament, as representing the British people, is the one power to whom we look for the redress of our grievances. They it is who are really responsible for the good or bad Government of this country. (*Hear, hear.*) And if they refuse or neglect to pay proper attention to our affairs, the result must be entirely injurious to the interests of our people. (*Cheers.*)

"The importance and necessity of Parliamentary control over the Indian administration, especially in matters of finance has always been recognised. But it is even more important and necessary now than perhaps it ever was before ; for our finances are unfortunately getting more and more embarrassed day by day. And yet it is at this very critical time that Parliament has partly withdrawn even that little attention which it hitherto has been wont to bestow upon Indian questions. The evil results of this diminution of control are already visible. Hitherto when complaints were made of the excessive increase of expenditure in India the member of the Government in charge has grudgingly admitted that there was room for economy and retrenchment. In the year 1883, the House of Commons passed a resolution to the effect that in the opinion of that House it is necessary that early steps be taken to reduce the expenditure of India. Lord Kimberley, our then Secretary of State, in his despatch, dated the 8th of June 1883, urged the Government of India to take the subject of the reduction of expenditure into their earliest consideration. Lord Randolph Churchill, our next Secretary of State, later on, said that 'the financial position of India was very grave indeed, and required the most careful consideration, and the exercise of the most rigid economy was necessary, in his opinion, in order to avoid bankruptcy.' But the withdrawal of Parliamentary control seems to have emboldened the present Under-Secretary to take up a very different attitude. When complaints were made on the occasion of the last debate on the Indian Budget in the House of Commons, of the ever-growing increase of expenditure in India, Sir John Gorst met them boldly by saying that 'expenditure has increased, it ought to increase, and it ought not to be diminished,' (*Shame, shame.*) And he tried to justify this view by asserting that the wealth and prosperity of the country was increasing.

" Now, gentlemen, no one would be more delighted than ourselves to know that the country was really growing in wealth and prosperity. (*Cheers.*) But unhappily the stern reality of facts forbids us from consoling ourselves with such pleasing fancies. We look wistfully in all directions ; we go deep into the Mofussil, we see our brethren in their homes and huts as they actually live ; and far from seeing any indications of that increasing prosperity which Sir J. Gorst said he discerned at that distance, we find the people growing poorer and less able to maintain themselves, their wives

* See pp. 70, 72 of the Detailed Report.

and children, than they were before. *(Cries of 'Hear, hear', and cheers.)* And we therefore say, gentlemen, that the increase of expenditure is under existing circumstances not only unjustifiable, but positively sinful. *(Prolonged cheers.)*

"The increase of public expenditure would undoubtedly be welcome if it followed upon an increase of wealth and prosperity among the people. There has been a large increase of revenue in England during the past quarter of a century. But it has followed an enormous growth of wealth and commerce in England, and no one complains much of it. But in India public expenditure goes on increasing while the condition of the people is deteriorating day by day. *(Hear, hear.)* One simple but incontrovertible proof of this lies in the fact that almost all the recent additions to the revenue of the Government have been screwed out of the first necessities of the Indian people. To take only the most recent instances, increased expenditure has been met by enhancing the duty on salt, a thing necessary alike to man and cattle ; by taxing the poor man's oil, as petroleum has rightly been called, by imposing a double tax on the famishing ryots of the North-Western Provinces and Oudh, and by misappropriating the Famine Insurance Fund *(shame!)*, a fund especially created and promised by three Viceroys to be religiously set apart for meeting difficulties in times of scarcity and famine. *(Shame!)*

"This ceaseless growth of expenditure is, gentlemen, an evil of alarming magnitude and deserves the most earnest consideration of Parliament. *(Cheers.)* Look ! only to your military expenditure. In 1857 with an army numbering about 254,000 men, the total military expenditure amounted to 11½ millions a year. But now with an army smaller by not less than 40,000 men, your military expenditure stands at the high figure of 20 millions sterling a year ! And you know how it is met. It is met, as I have told you, by making salt and petroleum dear to the masses, and by making men starve and die in times of scarcity and famine. *(Cries of 'Shame!')*"

The Resolution having been passed, Mr. Javerilal Umiashankar Yajnik, ex-Sheriff of Bombay, rose to propose a special vote of thanks to His Excellency Lord Reay, whose term of office was about to expire. No such vote had ever previously been passed by the Congress, for the simple reason that since our good Lord Ripon left us, there has been no Viceroy, or Governor, except Lord Reay, who has extended a single hearted and unremitting sympathy to the efforts and aspirations of the people of India. Mistakes may no doubt have occurred under Lord Reay's administration. It is so hard, so impossible at times, for one man, to struggle successfully, almost single handed, against that great conservative section* of the bureaucracy, into whose clutches almost all Viceroys and Governors, sooner or later, fall, becoming (unknown to themselves, and while still believing hugely in their own independence,) merely their puppets. This latter Lord Reay certainly never did become, although some people hold that, in more than one matter, the official classes succeeded in leading him astray; but as Mr. Hormasjee A. Wadia, the well-known barrister in Kathiawar, remarked†:—

"What I wish to say is that if you regard the position in which the Governor of a Presidency is placed—if you see how he is surrounded, if you see what little means he has of knowing our wishes and our wants,—the surprise is not that Lord Reay has made, as some think, a mistake, here and there, but that his mistakes have been so few and so slight.' *(Cheers.)*

"When a Governor comes to this country all the surroundings, political, social, public and private, influence him in one direction. We have no means at our command to redress the balance ; we have no organized means of letting him know the way in which we regard the questions of importance that come before him ; and if under these circumstances he makes a mistake the fault is not in the Governor, but in the system. The fact that Lord Reay has been such a successful Governor is

* We say section, advisedly, because though the majority of the officials are strongly hostile to Indian claims, there are everywhere a few good and wise men, who share Lord Reay's views and do what little they can for us.
† Page 74 of the Detailed Report.

due to the high sense of duty, to the lofty conception which he had of England's mission, and above all to the singular rectitude of purpose which has always guided him in everything that he has done for us. Of course he could not satisfy every interest, he could not satisfy every want and wish of the community over which he rules. In this respect I would remind you that the Governor of a Presidency is not a free agent. He, too, has to obey imperial behests, he has to shape his policy according to imperial demands ; and we have to remember the demands made upon the Provincial Government during Lord Reay's regime. You remember the late edict in which the Governor was told, 'Let your sick and suffering be without hospitals, let your uneducated poor remain without education, let no provision be made against famine, because we want all your money and all your taxes in order to indulge in annexation on the one hand and in creating frontier defences on the other.' I am afraid those frontier defences may prove the harbingers of further annexations in a more difficult and dangerous quarter. But this apart. In spite of these demands let us see what Lord Reay has done for us in this Presidency. He has created institutions, he has laid the foundations broad and deep for edifices that will rise hereafter to be the homes of industries, of arts, of sciences, such as never existed before in this country, and which I trust when they thrive and when they are properly supported, will remain for all time the mighty monuments of Lord Reay's wise, sympathetic and sagacious rule. These are remarks which refer perhaps locally to Bombay. I will only make one remark more which may be more in harmony with the feeling prevalent on this occasion ; I refer to Lord Reay's attitude to our aspirations and our demands. My friend Javerilal spoke of the members of Council whom Lord Reay had chosen ; and it is a remarkable fact that of his Councillors two have been Presidents of this Congress, and among the remainder you have no less than five, Messrs. Pherozshah Mehta, Nulkar, Dayaram Jethmul, Telang and Ranade, who have ever been leaders and pilots of the Congress movement on this side of India. (*Prolonged cheers.*)"

No doubt Lord Reay has had his detractors. The mere facts of his having persistently tried to do justice to the Indians and of his having sympathized with their aspirations were sufficient to condemn him in the eyes of that section of the Anglo-Indian community that reads and supports the *Pioneer* and similar papers. But we, at any rate, have never been misled, and he reaps in the love and gratitude of India's people an ample compensation for the sneers and calumnies with which the official journalistic organs have, from time to time, assailed him.

Thus runs the Resolution :—

RESOLVED : *That in view to his approaching departure, this Congress puts on record an expression of the high sense entertained not only in the Bombay Presidency, but throughout India, of the ability, integrity, and impartiality that have characterised Lord Reay's administration, as also of the gratitude which the whole country feels to be his due for the sympathy that he has ever extended to Indian aspirations and efforts.*

From all Presidencies Madras, Bombay, Bengal, the Panjab—from all classes, Hindus, Mahomedans, Parsees, men rose to support it, and that too with a delicacy of feeling that should not pass unnoticed. Every man felt that one of Lord Reay's strongest claims to our gratitude was the determined effort that he had made to purify the higher ranks of the bureaucracy, but none even alluded to this matter, feeling that it would be ungenerous to hurl a stone at the fallen. Said Mr. Yajnik* :—

" Gentlemen, it will thus be seen that there is hardly an important province or an important interest which has been left unrepresented in the Legislative Council of Lord Reay ; Bombay, the Deccan, Gujarat, the Konkan, Sind, the Southern Maratha Country, and even the remote Canarese Districts, have all had their representatives, and these, in almost every case, the very Representatives that the people would themselves have selected."

* * * * *

" The only question which Lord Reay's nominations to the Legislative Council suggests is that though these have been good, exceptionally good nominations, what is the guarantee that under a

* Detailed Report, p. 73.

system which leaves the nomination of so-called representative men to the individual opinion of the head of the Government, equal discrimination will be shown at other times, in the selection of genuinely representative and able men? It is just because equal wisdom and impartiality never has anywhere else been shown in similar selections, that we insist so strongly on the right to elect these our, at present nominal, representatives ourselves, and it is just for this reason too that we desire to put clearly on record an expression, of the respect, admiration and gratitude which we feel to be Lord Reay's simple due."

Mr. A. M. Dharamsey, a well-known Musalman Solicitor, remarked* :—

"If there has been one thing, more than another, which has characterized Lord Reay's administration, it has been his anxious desire to deal in a spirit of fairness, and justice, equality and impartiality, with the varied interests committed to his care among the various sections of the community with which he has to deal. At the same time Lord Reay has not been unmindful of the special wants of the backward units; and as a member of the Mahomedan community I can assure you that Lord Reay has always given a willing ear to our demands, and, so far as lay in his power, has tried to meet our real wants. (*Cheers.*) The selections made by Lord Reay have marked a new era, a new departure in the nominations to our Legislative Council. Some of our best University men who had never before been appointed to the Council were appointed by Lord Reay; and I trust that the days of appointing as our so-called representatives, men who did not in any way represent the people of India, are gone by for ever, and that Lord Reay has rendered impossible a return of those old evil days. One remark more, and I have done. You have heard from my friend Mr. Wadia that Lord Reay has been a sympathiser with our just aspirations. I venture to say that next after the name of our late beloved Viceroy, Lord Ripon (*cheers*), the name of Lord Reay will be enshrined in our memories (*cheers*) and our hearts. (*Loud cheers.*)"

Nothing, however, was more striking than the address, brief as it was, of the Punjab Delegate.†

"LALA MURLIDHAR ascended the platform, and, raising his joined hands, said :—Brothers, that God may bless the country which has given to us such a just and conscientious Governor as Lord Reay, is the heartfelt prayer of the people of the Punjab. (*Loud and prolonged cheers.*)"

Finally the President said‡ :—

"Now, are you all agreed? (*'Yes, yes; all, all! loud and prolonged cheering.'*) Gentlemen, that Resolution has been carried by acclamation, and permit me to say, that in thus honouring Lord Reay you have equally done honour to yourselves. (*Cheers.*)"

The greater portion of the subsequent proceedings were more or less formal or referred to the internal affairs of the Congress itself. By a technical oversight the Subjects Committee had been allowed to expire, *re infecta*, and had to be resuscitated.§ The General Secretary had to be re-elected and a Joint Secretary appointed to carry on work during his absence in England. Some check had to be put on the large and ever growing number of delegates that throng our Congresses, and it was settled that in future the several jurisdictions were not to send more than five delegates for each million of the population they include, thus limiting future Congresses to some 1,000 members, Messrs. W. S. Caine, W. S. Bright Maclaren, J. E. Ellis, M.P.'s, Sir W. Wedderburn, Messrs. George Yule, and Dadabhai Naoroji, had to be formally constituted, a London Committee, "to guide and direct the operations and control the expenditure of the National Congress Agency in England." Messrs. G. Yule, A. O. Hume, J. Adam, E. Norton, J E. Howard, P. Mehta, S. Banerjee, M. M. Ghose, Sharfuddin,

* Detailed Report, p. 75.
† Detailed Report, p. 75.
‡ Detailed Report, p. 75.
§ Pages 75, 76 of the Detailed Report.

R. N. Mudholkar, and W. C. Bonerjee, had to be appointed a deputation, "to represent in England the views of the Congress, and press upon the British public the political reforms which it has advocated." And, lastly, money had to be voted for Congress work in England and India. Mr. Surendranath's eloquent speech may be read (pp. 76-78), as also Mr. Norton's, who succeeded him, but we need not quote from either, though both, together with Mr. Murlidhar's deposition on the table of a huge pile of rupees, contributed to the memorable scene that ensued.

It must be noted that a few months previously, the General Secretary finding that the contributions promised for the English Agency were not being sent home, found it necessary to send round a pretty smart reminder.

The country with its customary good temper and good sense at once woke up and despatched the necessary remittances. But though marked conspicuously "strictly private and confidential," some rascal (we have no Congress Secrets Act) stole a copy somewhere, and published it in one of the papers. Thereupon, the Anglo-Indian organs, and the *Time's* bright particular Calcutta Star, waxed jubilant, hailed this *ad interim* motion as the final verdict, and declared the Congress bankrupt in character and purse. Of course these poor people had never heard of a whip being sent round--nor did they realize, that great movements, like great poets, *quandoque dormitant*--so at last they were happy, and the Congress Hydra, was, according to them, finally trampled under foot. Well, this hurt no one, and nobody took any notice of their pæans of triumph, but a feeling grew up, throughout the country, that it would be well to reply to these by deeds and not words.

Hence no sooner had Mr. Norton announced donations (Mr. Sabapathy Mudaliar's and his own) of Rs. 2,000 and Mr. Murlidhar had poured his Rs. 555 on to the table, than this was literally besieged by donors. Such a sight has rarely been witnessed—the platform was fairly stormed by people desirous of adding their contributions* to the fund, and although the required amount voted by the Congress was only Rs. 45,000, in less than half an hour, over Rs. 9,000 had been heaped upon the table in coin and notes, and written promises for over Rs. 56,000, had been given in; in all Rs. 65,400, or nearly half as much again as had been asked for! Much more would undoubtedly have been collected, as many were still struggling through the vast crowd towards the table, but the presentation of addresses to Mr. Bradlaugh, after the close of the Congress, had been arranged for an hour, which was fast approaching.† The hall had to be cleared and rearranged, and all the addresses and their beautiful caskets had to be laid out on the table and platform, and so the President was compelled to call the assembly to order, make all resume their seats, (which they promptly did in obedience to his call, with that marvellous respect for constituted authority which

* One little incident may be noted. Our old friend, Swami Alaram, was at the Congress as usual, and when others were piling their money on the table, he ascended the platform and said :—" For thirty years, no money has ever defiled my hands, so I have none to give, but I give you my blessing and my only worldly possession." So saying, he placed upon the table his large red blanket, which constituted his chief article of attire, and departed.

† And a largenumber of the European community who hria not attended the Congress were, it] was known, coming to hear Mr. Bradlaugh speak, and it was not thoughtght dto risk keeping them waiting.

17

is one of the best characteristics of Indian audiences,) and proceed to complete the business the Congress still had to dispose of. Accordingly the Resolution then before the Congress, relating mainly to its own affairs, another fixing Bengal as the locality for the next Congress, and a third, embodying a very special vote of thanks to our universally respected President (which he duly replied to in his own modest, kindly fashion), were all passed unanimously or by acclamation, and then, to quote the report once more.

"The PRESIDENT said—The pleasing duty now remains to me of tendering our best thanks to the gentlemen of the Bombay Reception Committee and the Bombay Presidency generally for the magnificent reception accorded to us. (*Loud cheers.*) I now declare this Congress dissolved with three cheers for Her Gracious Majesty the Queen. (*Loud and enthusiastic cheers for Her Majesty, intermingled with cries of 'God bless our Empress,' were accordingly given, and repeated again and again.*)"

"The proceedings of the Congress then terminated."

Thus, with ringing and manifestly heartfelt cheers, and blessings on our beloved Sovereign Lady, closed the Fifth Indian National Congress, an assemblage of which every Indian and every true Briton may be justly, and equally, proud.

With two exceptions, all the speeches, throughout the long discussions, were characterised by common-sense, courtesy, and consideration for the views of others, to a degree rarely met with in deliberative assemblies in any part of the world. The ability, the earnestness and the sincere sympathy for the sufferings of the poorer classes, evinced by many of the speakers were sufficient, without other evidence, to indicate the moral progress which this great movement is promoting. How the civic virtues of self-denial and self-sacrifice are being evolved, the enormous and almost incredible distance, in the aggregate, traversed by the nineteen hundred odd delegates, in journeying to and from the Congress, and the enthusiasm with which, for the first time in India, a gathering, mainly composed of the middle classes, subscribed in less than half an hour over Rs. 65,000 towards the furtherance of the Reforms they had advocated, sufficiently show.

Nothing, again, could be more encouraging than the manner in which the Mahomedan delegates, after thoroughly talking over the matter amongst themselves, came round and frankly admitted the fairness of a resolution passed by the Congress, from which many of them, at the time, had dissented.

The presence of lady delegates, few in number, but all women who in one field or another have justly earned distinction, is a grateful indication of the awakening that is going on, throughout the country, to higher and better things.

---

* Page 84 of the Detailed Report.

Any man's heart (at least if that man truly loved either India or England) might well have been glad within him as he watched the proceedings of that grand assembly—three times as large as the House of Commons, and giving, as the President playfully remarked, three times as little trouble to manage—watched them to their triumphant close and realized all that they signified and the enormous and healthy growth of National life that they symbolized.

One thing, only, remains and that is for the people of Great Britain to justify and strengthen by righteous deeds the high and loving estimation in which they are held by their Indian fellow-subjects. "We have great confidence," said Mr. Surendranath Banerjee, amidst the thundrous applause of assenting thousands, "in the justice and generosity of the English people, and above all we rely with abounding faith upon the liberty-loving instincts of the greatest Representative assembly in the world--the palladium of English liberty, the sanctuary of the free and brave--the British House of Commons." From that assembly, he went on to say "can come but one response to our prayers which, I am confident, will be in accord with the great traditions of the English people and will serve to consolidate the foundations of British Rule in India and to broad-base it upon the affections of a happy, prosperous and contented people."

Let Britain only heartily reciprocate (as all her best and noblest surely will) these generous and appreciative sentiments, and a brighter era dawning alike for England and for India, will amply repay her for her magnanimity, and *us*, for all our labours.

SUMMARY OF RESOLUTIONS

PASSED AT THE

FIFTH INDIAN NATIONAL CONGRESS,

Held at Bombay on the 26th, 27th, and 28th December 1889.

RESOLUTION I.

Resolved—That an address be presented to Mr. Charles Bradlaugh, M.P., on behalf of this Congress here assembled, and that Messrs. Adam, Pherozshah Mehta, and W. C. Bonnerjee are appointed a Committee to settle the wording of the said address.

RESOLUTION II.

Resolved—That the following skeleton scheme for the reform and reconstitution of the Council of the Governor-General for making Laws and Regulations, and the Provincial Legislative Councils, is adopted, and that the President of this Congress do submit the same to Charles Bradlaugh, Esq., M.P., with the respectful request of this Congress that he may be pleased to cause a Bill to be drafted on the lines indicated in this skeleton scheme and introduce the same in the British House of Commons :—

SCHEME.

(1) The Imperial and Provincial Legislative Councils to consist respectively of Members not less than one half of whom are to be elected, not more than one-fourth to sit *ex-officio* and the rest to be nominated by Government.

(2) Revenue districts to constitute ordinarily territorial units, for electoral purposes.

(3) All male British subjects above 21 years of age possessing certain qualifications and not subject to certain disqualifications (both of which will be settled later) to be voters.

(4) Voters in each district to elect representatives to one or more electoral bodies, according to local circumstances, at the rate of 12 per million of the total population of the district, such representatives to possess certain qualifications and not to be subject to certain disqualifications, both of which will be settled later.

(5) All the representatives thus elected by all the districts included in the jurisdiction of each electoral body, to elect members to the Imperial Legislature at the rate of 1 per every five millions of the total population of the electoral jurisdiction, and to their own Provincial Legislature at the rate of 1 per million of the said total population, in such wise that whenever the Parsees, Christians, Mahomedans or Hindus are in a minority, the total number of Parsees, Christians, Mahomedans or Hindus, as the case may be, elected to the Provincial Legislature, shall not, so far as may be possible, bear a less proportion to the total number of members elected thereto, than the total number of Parsees, Christians, Hindus or Mahomedans, as the case may be, in such electoral jurisdiction, bears to its total population. Members of both legislatures to possess certain qualifications and not to be subject to certain disqualifications both of which will be settled later.

(6) All elections to be by ballot.

RESOLUTION III.

Resolved—That this present Congress does hereby ratify and confirm the resolutions passed by previous Congresses as to

(*a*) the urgent necessity for the complete separation of executive and judicial functions, such that, in no case, shall the two functions be combined in the same officer ;

(*b*) the expediency of extending into many parts of the country, where it is not at present in force, the system of trial by jury ;

(*c*) the necessity of withdrawing from the High Courts, the powers, first vested in them in 1872, of setting aside verdicts of acquittal by juries ;

(*d*) the necessity of introducing, into the Code of Criminal Procedure, a provision enabling accused persons, in warrant cases, to demand that instead of being tried by the Magistrate, they be committed to the Court of Sessions ;

(*e*) the highly unsatisfactory character of the existing system of Police Administration in India, and the absolute necessity of a fundamental reform therein ;

(*f*) the expediency of both, establishing Military Colleges in India, whereat the Natives of India, as defined by statute, may be educated and trained for a military career as officers of the Indian Army, and of authorising, under such rules and restrictions as may seem necessary, such a system of volunteering for the Indian inhabitants of the country, as may qualify them to support the Government in any crisis ;

(*g*) the extremely unsatisfactory character of the Income Tax Administration, especially as regards incomes below Rupees one thousand, and the expediency of raising the taxable minimum to this amount ;

(*h*) the extreme importance of increasing, instead of diminishing, as the present tendency appears to be, the public expenditure on education in all its branches, and the necessity, in view to the promotion of one of the most essential of these branches, the technical, of the appointment of a mixed commission to enquire into the present industrial condition of the country ;

(*i*) the impolicy and injustice involved in the late increase of the Salt Tax in a time of profound peace, and the urgent necessity for an immediate reduction of this tax, and the reimposition, to balance the deficit thus caused, of light *ad valorem* import duties ;

(*j*) the necessity for the reduction of, instead of the continual increase to, the military expenditure of the country.

RESOLUTION IV.

Resolved—That this Congress hereby tenders its sincere thanks to Messrs. Caine and Smith, and the members who voted with them, in connection with the debate on the Indian Excise Question in the House of Commons ; and while fully appreciating what has been done by some of the local Governments towards the improvement of their systems of Excise and Abkari, desires to express the earnest hope that no further time may be lost in giving full effect to the Resolution of the House of Commons.

RESOLUTION V.

Resolved—That this Congress, while thanking Her Majesty's Government for raising the age for the Indian Civil Service Competitive Examination from 19 to 23, does hereby put on record an emphatic expression of the universal disappointment which has been created by the rest of that Government's orders in regard to the Public Service Question, (the net result of which orders is to place the people of India in a worse position than they previously held), and reiterates the national conviction that no real justice will be done to India, in this matter, until the simultaneous holding in India, and in England, of all Examinations, for all Civil branches of the Public Service in India, at present held only in England, be conceded.

RESOLUTION VI.

Resolved—That in view of the loyalty of the people, the hardships that the Arms Act, (XI. of 1878), as at present administered, entails, and the unmerited slur which it casts, upon them, the Government be moved so to modify the rules made under this Act that all restrictions as to the possession and bearing of arms shall apply equally, to all persons residing in or visiting India; that licenses to possess and bear arms shall be liberally and generally distributed wherever wild animals habitually destroy human life, cattle or crops, and that these and all licenses issued under the rules shall be granted once for all, shall operate throughout the Provincial jurisdiction within which they are issued, be only revocable on proof of misuse, and shall not require yearly or half-yearly renewals.

RESOLUTION VII.

Resolved—That the Government be urged to take the subject of a Permanent Settlement once more under consideration in view to practical action thereon, such that fixity and permanency may be given to the Government Land Revenue demand without further delay, at any rate in all fully populated and well cultivated tracts of country.

RESOLUTION VIII.

Resolved—That in view of the fall that has already occurred in the price of silver and in the exchange value of the Indian Rupee, it is impolitic on the part of the British Government to maintain any hinderances whatever to the consumption of silver for manufacturing purposes; and that this Congress strongly urges upon Her Majesty's Government that, not only as an act of justice to India (a matter which has been repeatedly brought to the notice of Her Majesty's Ministers), but also as an act of expediency in the interests of Her Majesty's British as well as Indian subjects, the plate duties should be immediately abolished, and Hall marking be made a voluntary institution.

RESOLUTION IX.

Resolved—That this Congress respectfully expresses the earnest hope that, in the interest of the people of India, the House of Commons will forthwith restore the right, formerly possessed by members of that Honourable House, of stating to Parliament any matter of grievance of the natives of India, before Mr. Speaker leaves the Chair, for the presentation in Committee of the Indian Budget statement, and earnestly trusts that the House of Commons will, in future, take into consideration the Annual Indian Budget statement at such a date as will ensure its full and adequate discussion, and further authorizes the President, Sir William Wedderburn, Bart., to sign a Petition in the name and on behalf of this Congress for presentation to the House of Commons in accordance with the terms of this Resolution.

RESOLUTION X.

Resolved—That in view to his approaching departure, this Congress puts on record an expression of the high sense entertained, not only in the Bombay Presidency, but throughout India, of the ability, integrity and impartiality that have characterised Lord Reay's administration, as also of the gratitude which the whole country feels to be his due for the sympathy that he has ever extended to Indian aspirations and efforts.

RESOLUTION XI.

Resolved—That the Subjects Committee be instructed to settle the questions, (left open in the skeleton scheme for the reconstruction of the councils, embodied in resolution II.), of the qualifications requisite for, and the disqualifications which should debar from, becoming

(*a*) a Voter ;

(*b*) a Representative ;

(*c*) a Member of a Provincial Legislative Council and

(*d*) a Member of the Imperial Legislative Council ;

and to submit their Report thereon to Charles Bradlaugh, Esq., M.P., for the purposes of the Bill which he has been requested to have drawn.

RESOLUTION XII.

Resolved—That Mr. A. O. Hume, C.B., be re-elected General Secretary of the National Indian Congress for the ensuing year.

RESOLUTION XIII.

Resolved—

(*a*) That, in view of the large number of delegates this year assembled and the probability, arising from past experience, of their number continuing to increase year by year, henceforth the number of delegates to be allowed from each Congress circle be limited to five per million of the total population of the circle: the Standing Committee of each circle allotting the number which their jurisdiction, as a whole, is entitled to elect, amongst their several electoral divisions, as may seem most expedient.

(*b*) That from the date of Mr. Hume's departure for England, the Hon'ble Pundit Ajoodhianath be appointed Joint General Secretary, and that Rs. 5,000 be assigned for the payment by him of such Assistant Secretaries as he may find it necessary to employ, clerical assistance, postage, telegraphs, and printing, and further that Mr. W. C. Bonnerjee be appointed Standing Counsel for Bengal, Mr. Pherozshah Mehta, Standing Counsel for Bombay, and Mr. Ananda Charlu, Standing Counsel for Madras, to the Joint General Secretary.

(c) That the tentative rules for the constitution and working of the Congress which were first considered at Madras, and in regard to which various addenda have from time to time been circulated, be thoroughly considered during the coming year by the several Standing Congress Committees, and definitely dealt with by the Congress at its next session.

(d) That this Congress does hereby confirm the appointment of Sir W. Wedderburn, Bart., and Messrs. W. S. Caine, M.P., W. S. Bright Maclaren, M.P., J. E. Ellis, M.P., Dadabhai Naoroji and George Yule, as a Committee (with power to add to their number) to guide and direct the operations and control the expenditure of the National Congress Agency in England, and does further tender its sincere thanks to these gentlemen, and to Mr. W. Digby, C.I.E., the Secretary, for the service which they are rendering to India.

(e) That this Congress does formally appoint Mr. George Yule, Mr. A. O. Hume, Mr. Adam, Mr. Eardley Norton, Mr. J. E. Howard,* Mr. Pherozshah Mehta, Mr. Surendranath Banerjee, Mr. Mono Mohan Ghose, Mr. Shurfuddin, Mr. R. N. Mudholker, and Mr. W. C. Bonnerjee to represent its views in England and press upon the consideration of the British Public the political reforms which the Congress has advocated.

(f) That a sum of Rs. 45,000 be raised for the expenses of the Congress Work in this country and in England during the ensuing year, and that the different Standing Committees do send their respective apportioned amounts to the General Secretary, the one half in three, and the balance in six months.

RESOLUTION XIV.

Resolved—That the Sixth Indian National Congress do assemble at some City in Bengal, the exact place to be fixed hereafter, on the 26th of December, 1890.

RESOLUTION XV.

Resolved—That the Fifth Indian National Congress hereby tenders its heart-felt thanks to its President, Sir William Wedderburn, as well for his ready sacrifice of personal and political considerations involved by his journey from England to India, as for that courtesy, impartiality and never failing sympathy which, characteristics of his long and honourable career as an official of this country, have marked his control of the proceedings of this assembly.

WILLIAM WEDDERBURN,

President of the

Fifth Indian National Congress.

BOMBAY, *December* 31*st*, 1889.

* By some oversight, this gentleman's name was omitted, when the Resolution was read to the Congress—the error has been rectified with the consent of the several Standing Congress Committees.

DETAILED
REPORT OF THE PROCEEDINGS
OF THE
FIFTH INDIAN NATIONAL CONGRESS,
HELD AT
BOMBAY
ON THE 26th, 27th, AND 28th OF DECEMBER 1889.

FIRST DAY'S PROCEEDINGS.

1st Day.

THE FIRST MEETING OF THE FIFTH CONGRESS took place on the afternoon of the 26th December 1889, in a magnificent temporary Hall, 200 feet in length by 130 feet in breadth, and with a very broad verandah, outside this again, running along its Southern and Western faces. The Hall was erected,* by the kind permission of Sir ALBERT SASSOON, Bart., on a large open space, enclosed by handsome iron railings, adjoining his Mansion, Sans-souci, and now his property. Suitable sites are extremely difficult to procure in Bombay and the Congress are greatly indebted to Sir Albert, for his kindly loan of this excellent and peculiarly centrically situated plot.

Seats had been provided for over 2,000 delegates and some 2,500 visitors, but, as far as could be ascertained, some four thousand of the latter succeeded in finding, at least standing room in the hall, and fully half as many more, thronged the Waiting Hall (80 feet square), the verandahs and all the approaches to the Hall.

At 2 P.M. the chair was taken by Mr. PHEROZSHA M. MEHTA, (late member of the Bombay Council), the Chairman of the Reception Committee, to whom pertained, *ex-officio*, the duty of opening the Congress, and calling upon the delegates to elect a President.

MR. PHEROZSHA M. MEHTA (*Bombay, No.* 967, *in list*) rose and said :—

Chairman of Reception Committee's Address.

LADIES AND GENTLEMEN,†—On behalf of the Reception Committee, I beg to tender to you all, Delegates of the Fifth Indian National Congress, a cordial, sincere, and earnest welcome. (*Cheers.*) It would be at all times a high pleasure and privilege to receive and welcome so many and such distinguished guests from all parts of the country. But when I remember that, though you may not be the chosen of the people by any scientific mode of election, you virtually and substantially represent them, their wants, wishes, sentiments and aspirations, in all the various ways in which representation manifests and works itself out in the early stages of its progressive development, that pleasure and that privilege are infinitely enhanced. (*Cheers.*) There is, besides, a peculiar zest in our welcome of you ; for in welcoming the Congress to Bombay, we welcome it back to " its own native land." (*Cheers.*) I well remember the day, this time four years ago, when, anxiously but hopefully, we launched the Congress on its enterprise, not of supplanting the existing rulers of the country, but of supplementing the endeavours of the best and most sagacious among them by proposing modifications and developments based on our peculiar and native knowledge and information, and suggested, gratefully, by that enlightenment and education, which is one of the most precious gifts bestowed upon us by British rule. (*Loud and prolonged cheering.*) The young enthusiast, whom we thus started, has now come back to us, robust and manly, broadened and strengthened, with a record of achievement of which we may be justly proud. (*Renewed cheering.*) Even the indirect political gains of the Congress have not been inconsiderable. It has brought vividly into clear and emphatic recognition that most important fact of the growth of the national idea amongst us. Despite social and religious differences, we have all begun earnestly to realize that we are

---

* To Mr. Makoond, a well known Engineer here, and a staunch Congress man, is due the entire credit for this remarkably effective and thoroughly satisfactory erection.

† To Mr. Thos. Reid, the eminent English shorthand writer, who came out to Bombay specially to report the proceedings of the Congress, we are indebted for the extreme accuracy, hitherto rarely, if ever, attained in India, of this present report.

fairly on the way to a common national existence, united and bound together by the common political ties of an equal, impartial and enlightened rule, just as the United States have raised up the American Nation on the basis of an infinite diversity of races and creeds. When we call the Congress national, we give expression to this nationalizing tendency which is now so powerfully leavening New India. (*Hear, hear, and cheers.*) Instead of being jealously resented and angrily denounced, this free and frank acknowledgment of the grandest outcome of British rule ought to be welcomed as a sure token of our rational and discerning loyalty (*cheers*), at least by those who are always so mightily distressed that we do not set up a perpetual hallelujah in praise of it, in season and out of season. (*Renewed cheers.*) Then, gentlemen, the labours of the Congress have contributed to do that which is a necessary prelude to all reform, a thorough sifting and searching of some of the most vital of Indian political problems. Nothing that passion or prejudice or malice could urge has been left unsaid. And now that the proposals of the Congress have bravely stood the test, our opponents have recourse to the familiar device, which is so often employed to cover retreat, and they are lost in wonder that we are making so much fuss about things which have nothing new in them and which have been long contemplated by many an Anglo-Indian statesman at the head of affairs. Now, gentlemen, we are quite ready at once to plead guilty to this not very dreadful impeachment. (*Laughter.*) But though it may not be said of these statesmen what was once said of the Anti-Reform party in England, and can certainly be said of some Anglo-Indians, that they never have anything kind or generous to say of the Indian people, this may surely be said of them, that though they do sometimes have something generous to say of the Indians, they have never shown the slightest disposition to confer upon them any portion of political rights. If the Congress has done nothing more than quicken into action these political *yogis*, so long lost in contemplation, it will not have laboured in vain. (*Hear, hear, and cheers.*)

Laden with these and other gains, the Congress has now come back to us, but not without undergoing trials and ordeals, two of which have been of exceptional severity. The first device employed by our opponents was to create disunion and dissension among ourselves. (*Cries of "Shame."*) Well, gentlemen, in a country so vast and varied as India, it would be impossible, it would be unnatural, to expect perfect and absolute unanimity. (*Hear, hear.*) It is no wonder that we have our halt, our lame, and our blind, and that they should hobble off to what I may call the Indian political cave of Adullam at the call of Sir Syed Ahmed and Rajah Shiva Prasad. But when two gentlemen, so amiable, so patriotic, so anxious to display their loyalty, were united together in one party, and formed the Anti-Congress United Patriotic Association, the same difficulty arose that was described by Mr. Bright, from whom I have borrowed my illustration, as having arisen in the case of the Anti-reform Adullamites. They were too like the traditional Scotch terrier, who was so covered with hair, that you could not tell which was the head or which was the tail of it. (*Laughter and cheers.*) Sir Syed Ahmed pulled vigorously one way, Rajah Shiva Prasad as vigorously the other ; and they so pulled between them the poor popinjay they had set up—that it burst, and poured out—to the amazement of a few, and the amusement of us all,—not the real patriotic stuff with which it had been announced to be filled, but the whitest and the purest saw-dust. (*Renewed laughter and cheers.*) The utter collapse of this vaunted Patriotic Association has taught our opponents a significant lesson. Every blandishment had been employed to lure prince and peasant ; but prince and peasant alike would have none of it. It would be difficult to gather a more convincing, if passive and indirect, proof that the heart of the country is with us, and that it understands and appreciates the honesty, the loyalty, and the propriety of the movement. (*Cheers.*)

I should like to say here one word to the delegates from Bengal and the North-West Provinces, lest they should imagine that I have referred to these events, which pertain more particularly to their Provinces, with the object of indirectly boasting of our own immunity from human frailty. (*Cries of "No, no."*) Let me at once proceed to assure them that we in this Presidency, have also our halt, our lame, and our blind. We also have had our little cave of Adullam. (*Laughter and cheers.*) But I am glad to be able to inform you that we have taken the infection very mildly, and that there is every hope of a speedy and complete recovery. (*Laughter and cheers.*)

Baffled in the attempt to disunite us, our opponents had recourse to a measure of extraordinary virulence. They raised against us a cry as terrible as the cry of heresy which was sometimes raised in the old days of the Inquisition to crush an obnoxious personage, otherwise unimpeachable and invulnerable. They raised against us the cry of sedition and disloyalty. (*Cries of "Shame."*) It was a cry well calculated to create alarm and uneasiness even among persons otherwise well disposed towards us. The Congress has, however, met the charge firmly and boldly (*cheers*) by a steadfast appeal to the authoritative record of our words, thoughts, and deeds, and to the personalities of the members composing it year after year. (*Renewed cheers.*) It was conclusively shown that the charge was founded on calumnies, lies, and misrepresentations. (*Renewed cheers.*) Then, gentlemen, something like the old story of the wolf and the lamb enacted itself. True, you may not be disloyal yourselves, said the wolf, that does not matter at all ; it is quite enough that your great-grandfathers were, and your great-grand-children might be. The Congress has, however, emerged unscathed even from this trial. Never was a greater truth uttered than that to which our esteemed friend Mr. Caine gave utterance, that we of the Congress are more loyal than Anglo-Indians themselves. (*Loud cheers.*) If by loyalty is meant a keen solicitude for the safety and permanence of the Empire, in which, we are firmly persuaded, lie implanted the roots of the welfare, the prosperity, and the good government of the country, then we are certainly more loyal than Anglo-Indians, who do not hesitate frequently to subordinate the interests of that safety and that permanence to the seductions of conquest and vainglory, or to the immediate gains and temptations of commercial enterprise. (*Hear, hear, and cheers.*)

1st Day.

Chairman of Reception Committee's Address.

Therefore it is that all our greetings of welcome go forth to you, and with a full heart we wish you God-speed in your labours. Those labours have for their aim and object measures of which the central idea has been recently admirably summarized by one of the most sober and sagacious of modern politicians, Sir Charles Dilke, when he said that the time had now arrived when it was neither safe nor expedient to continue to carry on the administration of the country by the hands of a secret and irresponsible bureaucracy, and that working on lines already laid down, a distinct step in advance should now be made. The policy of the Congress is thus a policy, not seditious or revolutionary, but " conservative of the public welfare, strengthening the just authority of the British Government, and adding day by day fresh lustre and dignity to the Imperial Crown." (*Loud cheers.*) I do not know whether we are doomed to failure or destined to succeed ; but the blessing which rests upon all high and honest endeavour will surely rest upon a mission imposed by duty, sanctified by patriotism and guided by loyalty. (*Cheers.*)

And now, gentlemen, I know you will not allow me to conclude without giving utterance to the deep thankfulness which we feel at the presence among us to-day of one whom we have learned to hail as the Member for India in the British House of Commons. (*Loud cheers and cries of " Cheers for Mr. Bradlaugh."*) The strength and greatness of the English character has been proudly sung by one of their most charming poets in lines with which we are familiar :—

> Pride in their port, defiance in their eye,
> I see the lords of human kind pass by.

But it has always seemed to me that English strength and greatness consist in nothing so much as in the lofty conception of moral and political duty which illumines the life and career of many an illustrious Englishman. We still mourn the loss of that great and good man whose heart was always with us, and whose voice was always raised for us, during many a long and eventful year. The memory of John Bright is reverently enshrined in our hearts. His place was filled by one whose life has a singular charm for all who prize sober simplicity and nobility of character above rank and riches. I mean Professor Fawcett. (*Cheers.*) The mantle has now descended upon Mr. Bradlaugh. (*Renewed cries of " Cheers for Mr. Bradlaugh."*) We sincerely and unaffectedly joined in the general grief at his recent illness, not simply out of selfish fears of losing our chosen champion, but out of that single-hearted feeling of sorrow which all men feel, when peril threatens a life devoted to high and unselfish ends. I know I am not employing the language of exaggeration when I say that our hearts are unutterably stirred within us at his presence among us to-day, restored to health and usefulness. (*Cheers.*) With no particular thoughts of the Congress in our minds, let us wish him that simple welcome which is in all our hearts and the hearts of people all over the country.

Having now delivered to you my message of welcome, I invite you to proceed to elect your president. (*Loud and prolonged cheers.*)

Election of President.

Mr. W. C. Bonnerjee proposes Sir W. Wedderburn.

MR. W. C. BONNERJEE (*Calcutta, No.* 1788, *in list*) rose amidst loud cheering and said :—MR. CHAIRMAN AND FELLOW DELEGATES,—Following the precedent of former Congresses, our first business is to proceed to the election of a President, and it is my privilege to place before you the name of one who is already well-known to you all, and who, if you approve of my nomination, will preside over this assembly. I mean Sir William Wedderburn. (*Prolonged cheers.*) If you look back to the Presidents that we have had from 1885, you will see that the selection of Sir William Wedderburn has been arrived at by a sort of logical process. The first Congress in 1885, was comparatively an insignificant one, and you were presided over on that occasion by an equally insignificant individual.* (*Loud cries of "No, no."*) The second Congress had the honor of being presided over by one who has devoted the whole of his life to the cause of his country, and who, even in his old age, is at the present moment, appealing to the electors of one of the constituencies of England in order that, if returned to the House of Commons, he may be able still more effectively to

* Namely himself.

1st Day.

Election of President.

Mr. W. C. Bonnerjee proposes Sir W. Wedderburn.

serve that country. Can I name Dadabhai Naoroji without calling from you enthusiastic applause. (*Long and loud cheers.*) The third Congress was presided over by a gentleman of the Mahomedan persuasion, who, having distinguished himself at the bar and in public life, was thought to be the fittest man to contradict the rumours that had been sedulously cast abroad that this was a Hindu Congress and that Mahomedan gentlemen had no sympathy with it. The next President ought, according to the process which we followed, to have been a gentleman belonging to the Eurasian community ; but at the time when it became necessary to select a President *the* man amongst the Eurasian community whom the whole of this country would have hailed with one voice as President of the Congress, Mr. D. S. White, was lying ill in bed ; and while he was in that condition it would have been improper for us to ask any other Eurasian gentleman to take his place. Now, unfortunately, he is no more ; and India has lost one of her brightest sons and best patriots in Mr. D. S. White. (*Prolonged cheers.*) Failing Mr. White, we had to go to that other community in India, the Anglo-Indian community, and there we found our late respected President Mr. George Yule. (*Loud cheers.*) Of him I need say no more than this, that having retired to England he is still devoting his time and his money to the furtherance of the cause of the Congress. (*Cheers.*) From the non-official European community to the official European community is but a slight descent(*laughter*),but unfortunately it is impossible for us to get a gentleman at the time actually belonging to the official classes to guide our deliberations. However sympathetic they may be, however much they may wish success to the Congress, the rules of the service to which they belong prevent their publicly joining us and taking a prominent part in our proceedings. But ex-officials do not occupy such a restricted position : they are able to exercise their judgment in matters political. And we have in Sir William Wedderburn an ex-official who has throughout his career in this country, extending over 25 years, shown the deepest sympathy with the aspirations of the people of this country, and who is one of the few men in the service who have had the eye to see and the heart to feel that the Government of India, conducted though it may be upon generous principles, is not all that is required for the best interests of the country, and that its institutions require to be liberalized in order that they may harmonize with the conditions of the present day. (*Cheers.*) Speaking in Bombay, in the chief city of the presidency, where Sir William Wedderburn has passed almost the whole of his official life, I need not detain you by enumerating the many services which he has rendered to the country. If I may venture so to speak, the greatest service which he could render to the cause of the country is that which at great personal sacrifice he is now rendering. He is, as you are aware, contesting the seat of North Ayrshire in the House of Commons ; and those of you who know anything of English politics know how essential it is to work day after day and month after month, and so keep persistently before your constituents as to make certain of their voices when the right moment comes. Sir William Wedderburn has unhesitatingly, left that, his own work, for the purpose of devoting himself to this our work for which, relying on his love to India and her people, we have summoned him to India. Let us hope that his being amongst us will not in any degree prejudice his chances in North Ayrshire. Let us from this Congress Hall send up the united voice of India praying the electors of North Ayrshire to do themselves the honor of electing Sir William Wedderburn as their representative (*cheers*) so that, while looking as he assuredly will, closely after the interests of his own constituency, he may be able also to devote himself to the cause of India which we know is ever near his heart. (*Loud cheers.*)

The Hon'ble Pundit Ajoodhianath Seconds.

THE HON'BLE PUNDIT AJOODHIANATH (*North-West Provinces, No.* 1517, *in list*)—MR. CHAIRMAN AND FELLOW DELEGATES,—It affords me sincere pleasure to second the proposition that has just been laid before you. With long and varied experience Sir William Wedderburn unites in himself a deep interest in the amelioration of the political condition of the country ; and he has availed himself of every opportunity to do all that he can for the good of India, and that at great personal sacrifice. We only wish that there were many more Englishmen like Sir William Wedderburn and Mr. Bradlaugh. I am happy indeed to think that their number is increasing. India feels that she cannot pay her debt of gratitude to gentlemen like these ; but she appreciates their kindness all the same (*Cheers.*) I do not wish to inflict a long speech upon you on this occasion. But permit me to refer to a matter to which my learned leader has referred, namely the unity of the different races and classes of the country. I am a living evidence of that. I am returned not only by Allahabad, but I come before you as one of the representatives—will you guess of whom ?—of the Mahomedans of Bombay. (*Cheers.*) A meeting which has just been held at no great distance from this place, under the presidency of a Mahomedan Moulvi, who is well known for his ability, his knowledge of Mahomedan law and his piety, elected me unanimously as one of its delegates. You may take it from me that that meeting was convened by Mahomedans and for Mahomedans only. Let Sir Syed Ahmed now sit in mourning for a fortnight. (*Cheers and laughter.*) And let us, gentlemen, most joyfully adopt the proposition now before the meeting. (*Cheers.*)

1st Day.

Election of President.

Rajah Rama Rao Supports.

RAJAH T. RAMA RAO (*late member of Council, Madras, No.* 43, *in list.*)—GENTLEMEN, I have the honour to support the proposition which has been so ably proposed, namely, to ask Sir William Wedderburn to be President of our fifth National Congress. I have great pleasure in supporting the motion that Sir William Wedderburn, an Englishman of first-rate capacity, do take the chair, and I would ask him to observe carefully how two thousand Indians assembled from every town and district in the Empire can meet and discuss the most important national questions. Gentlemen, in Bombay it is needless for me to recall the claims of Sir William Wedderburn to your gratitude. As a Madrassee let me say that his liberal views and advanced sentiments have not passed unnoticed in the sister Presidency. Remember also that we are under the eyes of an able debater, of a careful speaker, an attentive observer, a friend of India, and a champion of her rights. (*Cheers.*) Gentlemen, let him go back to his native country with the happiest recollections of what he has seen in this large meeting, and let him take home with him the impression, nay, the conviction, that we can manfully uphold our rights, and that we are not merely empty babblers. (*Cheers.*) Gentlemen, let us all join together and request Sir William Wedderburn to take the chair. (*Cheers.*)

Sir W. Wedderburn declared Elected.

MR. PHEROZSHA M. MEHTA (*Bombay, No.* 967, *in list*)—GENTLEMEN,—No other name has been proposed and you have received Sir William's with enthusiasm ; I now ask you if you are unanimous in desiring that he should be your President ? (*Cries of " Yes, yes ; all, all."*) Then I declare Sir William Wedderburn to be duly elected as President of this Congress and I will ask you, Sir (*turning to Sir William Wedderburn*), kindly to take the chair.

SIR WILLIAM WEDDERBURN, PRESIDENT (*Calcutta, No.* 1825, *in list*), then took the chair amidst a perfect storm of applause, the entire assembly rising and hailing him with prolonged and deafening cheers. When this great ovation had a little subsided, he rose and said :—

The President's Inaugural Address.

I thank you, gentlemen, from the bottom of my heart, for the great honor you have conferred upon me. I beg leave also to offer my acknowledgments to the mover, the seconder and the supporter of this resolution for the gracious terms in which they have referred to my past connection with India. After our long acquaintance it seems hardly necessary that I should assure you of my feelings of good-will towards the people of India. (*Cheers.*) But I will mention this one fact, that I have passed a quarter of a century among you, and during that period of time I have not known what it was to suffer an unkindness from a native of India. During that period I have been in the service of the people of India, and have eaten their salt. (*Loud and continued cheering.*) And I hope to devote to their service what still remains to me of active life. I take this chair to-day with much pleasure and pride. It warms my heart to receive this mark of confidence from the Indian people. And I rejoice to take part in a movement so well calculated to promote the best interests of India and of England. (*Cheers.*)

I have watched from its commencement the movement which has now culminated in the National Indian Congress. And in my humble judgment the movement is unmitigated good, in its origin, its objects, and its methods. As regards its historical origin, we know that it is the direct result of the noblest efforts of British statesmanship : the natural and healthy fruit of higher education and free institutions freely granted to the people of India. Again, what are the practical objects of the Congress movement ? They are, to revive the National life, and to increase the material prosperity of the country ; and what better objects could we have before us ? Lastly as regards our methods, they are open and constitutional, and based solely on India's reliance upon British justice and love of fair-play. Looking back to the history of the movement, there was one critical time in its development : that was about ten years ago. The leaven was then actually at work, though the purposes of the movement were not then so well defined, and it was unwisely sought to deal with it by a policy of repression. The results might have been disastrous. But happily that time of tribulation was cut short by the arrival of the greatest and best of all our Viceroys, the Marquis of Ripon. (*Loud cheers.*) By his wise and sympathetic policy Lord Ripon met and fulfilled the aspirations of the national movement. And on their side the people of India recognised that a government conducted in such a spirit could not be regarded as an alien rule. This was the meaning of the passionate demonstrations at the time of Lord Ripon's departure. You, gentlemen, will correct me if I am wrong in saying that those demonstrations were a popular declaration that on such terms British rule could be accepted as the national Government of the Indian people. (*Long and enthusiastic cheers.*)

But, gentlemen, you know all this as well as I do, and better. I think what you want to hear from me is not so much about your affairs in India as about your affairs in England. I have been nearly three years away from you, and have been studying English politics with special reference to Indian interests. And you would like to know what are the

1st Day.

The President's Inaugural Address.

results. You will naturally ask me, what are the prospects of the Congress movement in England? What are the obstacles which we have to overcome? And what are the practical objects to which our activity can best be directed? To these inquiries I would reply generally that our hopes depend entirely upon the degree to which the British people can be induced to exert their power with reference to India. Our one great ultimate question is that of a Parliamentary control over Indian affairs. If that can be obtained, all will be well. The case of India in England is really a simple one. The Crown and Parliament of Great Britain have laid down certain broad and liberal principles for the administration of India, and have solemnly pledged themselves that these shall be acted on. With those principles the people of India are fully satisfied. But the difficulty is in the practice. For owing to the necessity of the case the actual administration has to be entrusted to official agents in India. And the problem is, how under the circumstances can an effectual control be exercised from England so as to ensure these principles being carried out and these pledges fulfilled? Unfortunately there is one very serious fact which much enhances the difficulty of this problem, and it is this, that in certain important particulars the professional interests of our official administrators in India are in antagonism with the interests of the Indian tax-payer whose affairs they administer. This is a somewhat delicate matter, but it is an important one, and I feel it my duty to speak out clearly. Perhaps also it is easier for me than for most people to speak freely regarding the Indian official class, and that for two reasons. First, because I am deeply interested personally in the honor of that class. (*Hear, hear.*) The Indian Civil Service has been a sort of hereditary calling in our family since the beginning of the century. My father entered the Civil Service in 1807; and my eldest brother followed him, until he lost his life in the Bengal mutinies. I came out shortly afterwards so that we are identified with what may be called the Indian official caste. The other reason is, because my complaint is against the system; not against the men who carry it out. On the contrary, it is my deliberate belief that the Indian Civil and Military services have never been surpassed for honest hard work and unselfish devotion to duty. (*Cheers.*) Such being the case, I have no hesitation in repeating that the interests of the Indian services are in great measure antagonistic to the interests of the Indian tax-payer. The main interests of the Indian tax-payer are peace, economy and reform. But all those are necessarily distasteful to the civil and military classes. A spirited and well equipped army naturally desires, not peace, but active service. And who can reasonably expect officials to love economy, which means reduction of their own salaries; or reform, which means restriction of their authority? (*Cheers and laughter.*) It cannot be expected that as a class our official administrators in India will work for peace, economy and reform. But this very fact makes all the more urgent the necessity for a control in England which shall be both vigilant and effectual. We have therefore now to see what is the state of that control. Is it strong, vigilant, and effectual? I am sorry to say that the answer to this question is highly unsatisfactory. A brief historical review will, I fear, show that, in the matter of Parliamentary control, things have gone from bad to worse, until they are now about as bad as can be. It is now more than a hundred years ago since Edmund Burke (*cheers*) pointed out the crying need for a strong impartial control in England over Indian affairs. And Mr. Fox's Indian Bill would have provided an organized machinery for exercising this control. But unhappily, owing to party struggles unconnected with India, this bill fell through, "India's Magna Charta," as Burke called it, and never since has a similar attempt been made. But although no remedy was then applied, things were not so bad until the passing of the Government of India Act in 1858, which transferred the Government from the Company to the Crown. It is from that Act that I date our principal misfortunes. Till then we had two important safe-guards. The first was the wholesome jealousy felt by Parliament towards the East India Company as a privileged Corporation. The other was the necessity for the renewal of the Company's charter at the end of every 30 years. At each of those renewals the Company's official administration had to justify its existence; there was a searching inquiry into grievances: and there never was a renewal without the grant to the public of important reforms and concessions suited to the progressive condition of Indian affairs. (*Cheers.*) Now unfortunately both those safe-guards are lost. The official administrators, who used to be viewed with jealousy, have now been admitted into the innermost sanctum of authority; and, as Council to the Secretary of State, form a secret Court of appeal for the hearing of all Indian complaints. They first decide all matters in India, and then retire to the Indian Council at Westminster to sit in appeal on their own decisions. Such a method of control is a mockery, a snare and a delusion. This evil is very far reaching, for when a decision is passed at the India Office the Secretary of State becomes committed to it, so that if an independent member tries to take up the case in the House of Commons, he finds himself confronted, not by a discredited company, but by the full power of the Treasury Bench. But the loss of the periodical inquiry once at least in 30 years, is perhaps a still more serious disaster. There is now no day of reckoning. And Indian reformers find all their efforts exhausted in the vain attempt to obtain a Parliamentary inquiry, such as was before provided, without demand and without effort. At the present moment such an inquiry is much over due. The last periodical inquiry was held in 1854, so that under the old system a Parliamentary inquiry would have been begun five years ago. But although such an inquiry has been constantly asked for, and has been promised, it has never been granted. No doubt, we shall manage to get it in the end, but it will be at the cost of much wasted energy.

I think, gentlemen, I have shown that the last state of our control is worse than the first. On the one hand, we have been deprived of our periodical inquiry into grievances, while on the other hand, all complaints are calmly referred for disposal to the very officials against whom the complaints are made. (*Hear, hear.*) I should like, by way of illustration, to give a couple of instances to show how this system works in practice. The first case I will take is that which was well known, at the time, as the Break of Gauge controversy. In that matter General Strachey, as Public Work member of the Viceroy's Council, held his own against the whole united public opinion of India, European and Native, official and unofficial; and the railway gauge was fixed in the way he wished it. Later on the question came in appeal to the Secretary of State. But by that time General Strachey had retired from his position in India, and had been appointed to the Indian Council (*laughter*), where he was the official adviser of the Secretary of State in matters relative to railways and public works. When therefore the public fancied they were appealing from the Government of India to the Secretary of State, they were really enjoying an appeal from General Strachey to himself. (*Laughter.*) This instance shows how the system of the Indian Council is even worse in fact than in theory. One might perhaps suppose that there being 15 members of the Council, one's grievance might come before those not personally affected. But such is not the case. Each member is considered as an expert as regards his particular province or department, and is allowed to ride his own hobby, provided he allows his colleagues also to ride their own hobbies in the way they choose. The other instance is taken from my own experience, and has reference to Agricultural Banks. We cherish the idea that if he had fair play, the Ryot might develop into a substantial Yeoman instead of being the starveling he is. With a fertile soil, a glorious sun, and abundance of highly skilled labour, there is no reason why India should not become a garden if the Ryot were not crushed by his debts. The only thing that is required is capital, in order to settle these old debts and make advances to the Ryots on reasonable terms, so that they may be supplied with water for irrigation and manure. As you know, we prepared a practical scheme, founded on the German system of peasant Banks, and got all the parties concerned to agree to it. The Bombay Government approved of the experiment, which was to be on a very limited scale; and the scheme was forwarded for sanction to the Secretary of State by Lord Ripon's Government, Sir Evelyn Baring as Finance Minister having agreed to advance 5 lakhs of rupees for the settlement of the old debts. In England the scheme was well received. Mr. John Bright took the chair at a meeting in Exeter Hall in furtherance of the project, and each of the leading London daily papers expressed approval. The Manchester Chamber of Commerce also memorialized the Secretary of State in its favor. Well, gentlemen, this scheme entered the portals of the India Office, and never left it alive. (*"Shame!"*) It was stabbed in the dark, no one knows by what hand or for what reason. Not long ago our friend Mr. Samuel Smith asked a question about it in the House of Commons; he inquired why the experiment recommended by Lord Ripon's Government was not allowed; and he was informed by Sir John Gorst that the scheme was not considered "practicable." Not practicable indeed! I wonder whether Sir J. Gorst is aware that in Germany alone there are 2,000 such Agricultural Banks in active working, and that throughout the continent of Europe it is admitted that without such financial institutions the peasant proprietor is absolutely unable to maintain himself without falling into the clutches of the village usurer. I think I may say with confidence that the India Office has not yet heard the last word on the subject of Agricultural Banks in India. (*Cheers.*)

I fear, therefore, that in reviewing the situation in England, we must admit that the organized forces are in the hands of our opponents. The India Office is strong against us, together with the influence of the services and of society. The London Press is not favourable to us. And those members of Parliament who have Indian experience rank themselves mostly on the official side. On the other hand, we need not lose hope; for the spirit of the age is on our side. The forces of the new democracy are in favour of national aspirations; and wherever meetings of working men are addressed they are found willing, nay, eager, that justice should be done to India. (*Cheers.*) My friend has referred to the constituency of North Ayrshire which has been good enough on the liberal side to choose me as its candidate; and he hoped that my invitation to come out here would not in any way damage my chances. I am very glad to assure you that so far from damaging my chances it has very much raised me in their estimation. (*Loud cheers.*) As soon as my supporters in North Ayrshire learned that I had been invited to preside at this Congress, they were highly gratified, and resolutions were passed expressing strong sympathy with the Indian people. Nor is it on

1st Day.

The President's Inaugural Address.

the liberal side only that India has active sympathisers. She has many good friends among Conservatives; and to those I think we may reasonably appeal in the matter of parliamentary control over Indian affairs. It is sometimes said that conservatives walk in the footsteps of good reformers; that is, they stand now in the position that good reformers stood in perhaps 50 years ago. If this is so, we may well ask their help to carry through the reforms that commended themselves to Burke and to Fox; and still more to restore that 30 years periodical inquiry which was originally secured to us by the wisdom of our ancestors. (*Cheers.*)

And if the older organizations are against us, we have younger organizations which are making good and healthy growth. First and foremost, the Indian National Congress, is becoming a household word in England; and it will become a power in the State, if you continue patient, persistent, moderate. Then again, you have done well and wisely to establish organization No 2, a Congress Agency in London. In the Indian National Congress the people of India, hitherto dumb, have found a voice. But the distance to England is great, and the agency is needed, like a telephone, to carry the voice of the people of India to the ear of the people of England. It seems to me that the agency, under your indefatigable Secretary, Mr. William Digby (*loud cheers*), is simply invaluable in bringing India in contact with her friends in England, and in briefing those friends when they take up Indian subjects either in Parliament or before the public. Also the agency, with the Committee which supervises its working, will, we hope, be the nucleus round which an Indian party will gradually gather itself This will be our organization No. 3, the Indian Parliamentary party, consisting of men who, however different their views may be on other subjects, are willing to co-operate on the basis of a just and sympathetic policy towards India. The meeting three weeks ago, at the National Liberal Club, under the presidency of our valued friend Mr. George Yule, was the first movement towards the formation of such a party. Strong sympathy was then expressed with the objects of the Congress; and it is hoped that when Parliament meets arrangements will be made to secure joint action in matters affecting Indian interests. But, gentlemen, I have not come to the end of our list of activities on behalf of India. I rejoice to learn that a group of Indian speakers of weight and experience are about to proceed to England, in company with our General Secretary (*loud cheers*) for the purpose of initiating a systematic propaganda by addressing popular audiences at the great centres of population throughout Great Britain. You will know well how to address those great audiences, appealing fearlessly to the highest motives, and calling on the people of England to perform their trust and duty towards the unrepresented millions of India: appeals to unselfishness, to justice, and to humanity will ever find a sure response from the great heart of the British people. (*Cheers.*)

In conclusion, I would like to address a few words to those of our English friends who distrust the Congress movement. The promoters of the Congress profess strong attachment to British rule. And I would ask, is there any reason to doubt this profession? (*" No, no."*) Have those men any interests antagonistic to our rule? (*" No, no."*) Remember that the originators of this movement are educated men, trained up by us in a love of freedom and free institutions. Is it likely that these men should wish to exchange the rule of England, the freest and the most enlightened country in the world, for that of Russia which is one of the most barbarous and retrograde? (*Cheers.*) I remember being much struck with the remark of a native friend of mine with reference to Russian advances. He said to me, " If India is lost we are the chief losers, you can go to your ships and will be safe in your distant homes. We, on the other hand, should lose all: our country, our liberties, and our hopes for the regeneration of our race." Perhaps some of our doubting English friends will say, " We attach more importance to deeds than to words." I think we can point also to deeds. It is well known that in all schemes for the invasion of India the Russian Generals depend for success on a hoped-for rising of the native population. In 1885 they appear to have put this idea to the test by a pretended advance. Had this move been followed by any signs of sympathy, or even by an ominous silence of expectancy throughout India, Russia would have rejoiced, and we should have felt our position weakened. But India does not treat England's difficulty as her opportunity. On the contrary, there went up on all sides a patriotic cry, led by the native press, calling on all to join with men and money, and make common cause against the common foe. (*Cheers.*) I think also the action of the Congress, when calmly viewed, will be seen to point in the same direction. The man who points out the rocks and shoals towards which the ship is moving, is the friend of the captain, not the enemy. And that is the light in which the government should regard the criticisms of the Congress. The moderate reforms proposed by the Congress will all tend to make the people of India more prosperous and more contented, and will thereby strengthen the foundations of British rule. (*Cheers.*) And here I would specially invite our English commercial friends to join with us in our efforts to increase the material prosperity

The President's Inaugural Address.

of the country. At present owing to the poverty of the people the trade is nothing in comparison with what it ought to be. This is an argument which has been effectively pressed by our veteran leader Dadabhai Naoroji. He has pointed out that our Australian Colonies take English goods at the rate of £17 or £18 per head per annum, whereas poor India can only take at the rate of eighteen pence a head. If, by releasing him from his bonds of debt, and placing him in a position to exercise his industry, we could make the Ryot moderately prosperous, how great would be the benefit to English trade! If the Indian customer could take even £1 a head, the exports to India would exceed the exports to all the rest of the world put together. I would therefore say to our mercantile friends, help us to make the ryot prosperous, and your commercial business will soon increase by leaps and bounds.

Gentlemen, I have now concluded my preliminary remarks, and I thank you for the patience with which you have heard me, and have now to invite you to attack, with good appetite, the substantial bill of fare which will be placed before you. I will not in any way anticipate your proceedings, but I may perhaps express a hope that you will give early and earnest attention to the Bill for the Reform of the Legislative Council. And in connection with this Bill I would take the opportunity to congratulate you on the presence here to-day of a very distinguished visitor—one whose name is a synonym for independence, for strength, and for success. I think poor India is very fortunate in securing such a champion as Mr. Charles Bradlaugh (*loud and continued cheers*), a very Charles Martel of these latter days, whose sledge-hammer blows have often shaken to their foundations the citadels of prejudice, of ignorance and of oppression.

To-day there only remains to appoint, as usual, a Subjects Committee, and I will ask you to do this before we separate.

Gentlemen, I will not detain you longer, but will only express my earnest hope that your labors may prosper, and that your deliberations may effectually promote "the safety, honor and welfare of Her Majesty and her dominions." (*Loud and long continued cheers, followed by a general rising and waving of handkerchiefs and a final "One cheer more!"*)

Presentation of donation to Committee and of Salver to President.

The Hon'ble Pandit Ajoodhianath (*North-West Provinces, No.* 1517, *in list*)—Addressing the President said: Sir, the members of the Congress Committee at Allahabad desire me to ask you to be pleased to receive this Rs. 150 (*resting on a silver salver of fine Cutch workmanship*), as a small donation towards the expenses of the Reception Committee here, and as a slight mark of the interest we take in the Indian National Congress, whether it be held in or out of our province, and as a token of our good-will to our fellow-subjects and fellow-workers here, and of our appreciation of their hospitality. This salver we trust that you will be graciously pleased yourself to accept in memory of your tenure of the presidency of this fifth Indian National Congress. (*Loud cheers.*)

The President—On behalf of the Reception Committee permit me to say that we return to the Allahabad Committee our very best thanks. I feel quite ashamed that I should receive the lion's share of this gracious offering in the shape of this beautiful salver; and I regret to say that I have not proper words to express my thanks to you for your kindness. I will only say that it has been a very great pleasure and honor to me to come among you on this occasion, to meet old friends whom I have left for a short time, and shake hands with them again.

Mr. Alli Mahomed Bhimjee (*Bombay, No.* 892, *in list*)—I have the honor to make a presentation on behalf of Mr. P. L. Nagpurkar of Sholapur (Deccan). He has written and published a novel in Mahrattee, called "The Old Palace," in which Bajee Row and other old-time Poona worthies figure. From the sale of this novel he has already netted Rs. 150, as profits, which he has requested me to hand to you as a donation either to the Indian National Congress Fund or to the Agency in England, as the General Secretary may think best. You will be good enough to convey this amount to the Congress Committee, and to accept this presentation copy of the novel. (*Cheers.*)

The President—Here again I am extremely happy to accept alike the money for Congress work and the book for myself, and I hope you will convey our best thanks for both to Mr. Nagpurkar.

Election of a Subjects Committee.

Mr. A. O. Hume, General Secretary (*Lahore, No.* 1402, *in list*)—I will now ask the Secretaries of the several Standing Congress Committees to hand in the lists of the names of those gentlemen, who have been elected, by the assembled delegates from each circle, to represent them on the Subjects Committee.

The lists having been given in they were read out, and approved by the entire assembly.

1st Day.

Election of a Subjects Committee.

The following were the delegates elected to the Subjects Committee :—

CALCUTTA CIRCLE, (*includes the Presidency and Burdwan Divisions, Orissa, Assam, Sylhet, and Cachar*).	1.	W. C. BONNERJEE	No. 1788, (Calcutta).
	2.	SURENDRANATH BANERJEE	No. 1816, (do.).
	3.	J. GHOSAL	No. 1789, (do.)
	4.	KALICHARAN BANERJEE	No. 1827, (do.).
	5.	MOTILAL GHOSE	No. 1867, (do.).
	6.	PRANNATH PANDIT	No. 1889, (do.).
	7.	NANDOLAL BOSE	No. 1809, (do.).
	8.	H. C. MOITRA	No. 1829, (do.).
	9.	BAIKUNTNATH SEN	No. 1873, (Murshedabad).
	10.	REV. C. N. BANERJEE	No. 1875, (do.).
	11.	NUFFER CHANDRA PAL CHOWDHRY	No. 1853, (Nuddia).
	12.	AMBICA CHARAN SEN	No. 1885, (Khulna).
	13.	KALI SHANKER SUKUL	No. 1866, (Jessore).
	14.	DR. ATAR ALLI	No. 1855, (Nuddia).
	15.	AKSHOY CHANDER DAS	No. 1845, (Howrah).
	16.	RUGHUNATH DAS	No. 1881, (Midnapur).
	17.	JOGENDRA CHANDRA ROY	No. 1878, (do.).
	18.	BISHNUPADA CHATTERJEE	No. 1848, (Hoogly).
	19.	BIPIN CHUNDRA PAL	No. 1888, (Assam).
DACCA CIRCLE, (*includes the Dacca and Chitagong Divisions*).	1.	SARAT CHANDER GUPTA	No. 1774, (Dacca).
	2.	AMBICA CHARAN MUZUMDAR	No. 1785, (Faridpur).
	3.	ASWINI KUMAR DUTT	No. 1782, (Barisal).
	4.	ANATH BUNDHOO GUHA	No. 1778, (Mymensingh).
	5.	ANANDA MOHAN BOSE	No. 1825, (Chitagong).
	6.	MOHENDRA CHANDER DEV	No. 1787, (Tipperah).
RAJSHAYE CIRCLE, (*includes the Rajshaye Division*).	1.	PRASANNO NARAYEN CHOUDHURY	No. 1772, (Rungpur).
BHAGULPUR CIRCLE, (*includes the Bhagalpur Division*).	1.	LADLI MOHAN GHOSE	No. 1752, (Bhagulpur).
	2.	PARBUTI CHARAN DASS	No. 1762, (Purnea).
CHOTA NAGPOOR CIRCLE, (*includes the Chota Nagpoor Division*).	1.	HARI CHARAN MITRA	No. 1750, (Hazaribagh).
BEHAR CIRCLE, (*includes the entire Behar Division*).	1.	SYED SHARF-UD-DIN	No. 1736, (Dinapore).
	2.	GURU PERSHAD SEN	No. 1732, (Bankipur).
	3.	SALIGRAM SINGH	No. 1791, (do.)
	4.	SHAROSHI CHARAN MITTER	No. 1727, (Mozufferpore).
	5.	MOULVI ABDULLA FYAZ	No. 1739, (Dinapore).
	6.	ABDUL HAMID	No. 1737, (do.)
	7.	AHMED HOOSSEIN	No. 1729, (Mozufferpore).
	8.	BADERUL HOOSSEIN	No. 1735, (Patna).
BENARES CIRCLE, (*includes the Benares Division*).	1.	SHEIKH NASEER-UD-DIN	No. 1693, (Benares).
	2.	BHOLANATH ROY	No. 1724, (Ghazipore).
	3.	JOGENDRANATH GHOSE	No. 1705, (Benares).
	4.	BINDESERI PERSHAD	No. 1712, (Mirzapur).
N. W. PCES. CIRCLE, (*includes whole N. W. Pces. except the Benares Division*).	1.	PANDIT AJOODHIANATH	No. 1517, (Allahabad).
	2.	HAFIZ ABDUR RAHMAN	No. 1633, (Aligarh).
	3.	MUNSHI SAKHAWAT HOOSSEIN	No. 1674, (Shahjehanpur).
	4.	PANDIT MADAN MOHAN MALAVIYA	No. 1520, (Allahabad).
	5.	„ PRITHINATH	No. 1572, (Cawnpur).
	6.	„ JWALADATTA JOSHI	No. 1688, (Almora).
	7.	„ BADRINATH	No. 1663, (Bareilly).
	8.	LALLA BIJAY BAHADUR	No. 1560, (Futtehpur).
	9.	PRAHLAD SINGH	No. 1643, (Meerut).
	10.	CHAUBE DAMMI LAL	No. 1616, (Mainpuri).
	11.	MOULVI FAZL AHMED	No. 1653, (Muzaffarnagar).

1st Day.

Election of a Subjects Committee.

OUDH CIRCLE, *(includes the entire Province of Oudh).*	1.	HAMID ALI KHAN	No. 1494, (Lucknow).
	2.	BISHEN NARAYAN DAR	No. 1491, (do.).
	3.	GOKUL CHAND	No. 1552, (Fyzabad).
	4.	MURLIDHAR	No. 1513, (Sitapore).
	5.	GANGAPRASAD VARMA	No. 1501, (Lucknow).
	6.	BANSILAL SINGH	No. 1499, (do.).
	7.	REV. R. C. BOSE	No. 1507, (do.).
	8.	NAWAB ALI MAHOMED KHAN	No. 1469, (Anjuman Mahomedi.
	9.	PRINCE ALI JAH MAHOMED HUSSAIN ALI	No. 1466 (do.)
LAHORE AND DEHLI CIRCLES, *(include the entire Panjab).*	1.	RAJAH NIAMUT ULLAH KHAN	No. 1416, (Kangra).
	2.	JOGENDRA CHANDRA BOSE	No. 1406, (Lahore).
	3.	KANIHYA LAL	No. 1404, (do.).
	4.	MURLIDHAR	No. 1422, (Amballa).
	5.	LAJPAT RAI	No. 1437, (Hissar).
	6.	HARBHAGWANDAS	No. 1440, (Jhelam).
	7.	GUR CHARANDAS	No. 1434, (Gurdaspur).
	8.	GIRDHARI LALL	No. 1445, (Dehli).
	9.	CAP. A. BANON	No. 1417, (Kangra).
	10.	SHEIKH OOMAR BAKSH	No. 1442, (Hoshiapur).
SINDH CIRCLE, *(includes the entire Province of Sindh).*	1.	HARCHANDRAI VISHINDAS	No. 878, (Karachi).
GUZERAT CIRCLE, *(includes Guzerat, Cutch, Kathyawar and Panch Mahals).*	1.	DR. NAROTAMDAS INDRAJIT VAISHNAV	No. 851, (Surat).
	2.	M. D. DADY SETT	No. 830, (Surat).
	3.	RANCHORELAL CHOTELAL	No. 792, (Ahmedabad).
	4.	HORMASJEE A. WADIA	No. 855, (Rajkot).
BOMBAY CIRCLE, *(includes Bombay and the Thana, Colaba and Ratnagiri districts).*	1.	PHEROZSHAH M. MEHTA	No. 967, (Bombay).
	2.	DINSHA EDULJEE WACHA	No. 908, (do.)
	3.	JAVERILAL UMIASHANKER YAJNIK	No. 932, (Bombay).
	4.	N. G. CHANDAVARKAR	No. 962, (Bombay).
	5.	ABDULLA M. DHARAMSI	No. 891, (do.).
	6.	DAJI ABAJI KHARE	No. 906, (do.).
	7.	AMEERUDDIN TYABJI	No. 894, (do.).
	8.	MOULVI HIDAYET ULLAH	No. 1032, (do.).
DECCAN CIRCLE, *(includes the Deccan, N. Kanara, and Khandeish).*	1.	G. V. PATWARDHAN	No. 442, (Sholapur).
	2.	B. S. SAHASRABUDDHE	No. 644, (Satara).
	3.	REV. R. A. HUME	No. 486, (Ahmednuggur).
	4.	K. L. NULKAR	No. 391, (Poona).
	5.	B. G. TILAK	No. 401, (do.).
	6.	M. B. NAMJOSHI	No. 369, (do.).
	7.	M. N. JOGALEKAR	No. 723, (Belgaum).
BERAR CIRCLE, *(includes the entire Province of Berar).*	1.	DEORAO VINAYAK	No. 1332, (Akola).
	2.	R. N. MUDHOLKAR	No. 1303, (Amraoti).
	3.	GANESH S. KHAPARDE	No. 1379, (Ellichpur).
CENTRAL PROVINCES CIRCLE, *(includes the whole of the C. Pces).*	1.	ALFRED NUNDY	No. 1268, (Jubbalpore).
	2.	GOVIND PRASAD	No. 1275, (Raipur).
	3.	NARAYANSWAMI NAYADU	No. 1211, (Nagpur).
	4.	KALIDAS CHOWDHRY	No. 1840, (Hoshangabad).
	5.	BAPU RAO DADA	No. 1190, (Nagpur).
	6.	SADASHIVARAO PATWARDHAN	No. 1259, (Hurda).
MADRAS CIRCLE, *(includes the entire Madras Presidency).*	1.	RAJAH T. RAMA RAO	No. 43, (Madras).
	2.	S. SUBRAMANIA IYER	No. 73, (do.).
	3.	N. SUBRAMANYAM	No. 75, (do.).
	4.	SALEM RAMASWAMY MUDALIAR	No. 29, (Madras).
	5.	C. SANKARA NAIR	No. 74, (do.).
	6.	EARDLEY NORTON	No. 44, (do.).
	7.	W. S. GANTZ	No. 86, (do.).
	8.	J. ADAM	No. 1, (do.).

1st Day.

Election of a Subjects Committee.

MADRAS CIRCLE (*contd.*)	9.	P. RANGAIAH NAIDU	No. 32, (Madras).
	10.	G. SUBRAMANIA IYER	No. 50, (do.).
	11.	C. JAMBULINGA MUDALIAR	No. 219, (Cuddapah).
	12.	V. MAHOMED SHERIF.	No. 36, (Madras).
	13.	G. VENCATARATNAM	No. 100, (Coconada).
	14.	C. VIGIARAGHAVA CHARRIAR	No. 312, (Salem).
	15.	REV. G. M. COBBAN	No. 2, (Madras).
	16.	P. ANANTA CHARLU	No. 31, (Madras).
	17.	N. SHIVA ROW	No. 351, (Mangalore).

Thus this Committee, including the President and General Secretary, who sit on it *ex-officio,* consisted of 109 members, elected by the 1,900 odd delegates present, to represent their views in, deciding what subjects should come before the Congress, preparing draft resolutions on those subjects for submission to the Congress, and fixing on the gentlemen, who were to be asked to propose, second and support these Resolutions.

Adjournment of the Assembly.

THE PRESIDENT said—The Subjects Committee having now been duly elected and the election formally ratified by the Congress, I wish before adjourning to remind you of the rule which has been adopted by my predecessors in office and to which I propose to adhere, viz., that in the discussions that will take place at our further Meetings, only ten minutes will be allowed to the proposers of Resolutions, and only five minutes to all other speakers. And now having said this I declare this assemblage adjourned until 1 P.M., to-morrow.

Immediately after this the Subjects Committee met and sat until late. It met again next morning at 10 A.M., and sat until 1 P.M., appointing before it separated a Special Sub-Committee to settle the terms of a Resolution (*vide* Resolution XIII.), in regard to certain matters connected with the future Administration of the Congress.

SECOND DAY'S PROCEEDINGS.

Friday, 27th December 1889.

2nd Day.

Presentation of the Madras Report.

THE PRESIDENT took his seat at 1-30 P.M., and MR. P. SOMASUNDRUM (*Madras, No.* 87, *in list*), accompanied by MR. EARDLEY NORTON (*Madras, No.* 44, *in list*), appeared on the Platform.

MR. EARDLEY NORTON (*Madras, No.* 44, *in list*)—SIR,—In accordance with the rules of the Congress, we are here to submit to you, and the Congress generally, the Annual Report of the Standing Committee of the Madras Circle.

THE PRESIDENT—Has any other Standing Committee of the Congress its report to present ? If so, now is the time.

No other report was presented.

Res. I. Address to Mr. Bradlaugh.

MR. PHEROZSHAH MEHTA (*Bombay, No.* 967, *in list*) then rose and said—MR. PRESIDENT,—Gentlemen, I have a very short motion to lay before the assembly. I think I truly represented the public feeling, yesterday, when I spoke in the terms I did about Mr. Charles Bradlaugh. (*Loud cheers.*) Telegrams and addresses have been pouring in from all parts of the country, from every nook and corner, with requests that we should present them to him. I think, gentlemen, you will agree with me that it would be a matter of physical impossibility to present all those addresses to Mr. Bradlaugh. It would occupy us I think, I may say, at least a week, if not a fortnight. (*Laughter.*) It has occurred to many of the leading delegates that instead of pretending to present to him all these hundreds of addresses, separately, they should all be laid together on a large table and taken as read, and that at the time when those addresses are thus laid before Mr. Bradlaugh, one brief address on behalf of this Congress, representing as it does the public opinion of the whole country, should be read and presented to him. I beg therefore to propose that an address be presented to Mr. Charles Bradlaugh, M.P., on behalf of the Fifth Indian National Congress. (*Cheers.*) I further propose that the following Committee be appointed for the purpose of framing this address, *viz.*, Mr. W. C. Bonnerjee, Mr. Adam and myself. (*Cheers.*) I am sorry to add my own name, but it is not at my own instance that I do so.

2nd Day.

Res. I. Address to Mr. Bradlaugh.

THE HON'BLE PUNDIT AJOODHIANATH (*North-West Provinces, No.* 1517, *in list*)—It affords me great pleasure to second this proposition. A more pleasant duty could hardly have devolved upon me; and I have no doubt that you will carry the proposition by acclamation. It will stand thus.

PROPOSED: *That an address be presented to Mr. Charles Bradlaugh, M.P., on behalf of this Congress here assembled, and that Messrs. Adam, Pherozshah Mehta, and W. C. Bonnerjee be appointed a Committee to settle the wording of the said address.*

MR. JOHN ADAM (*Madras, No.* 1, *in list*)—Although I am in the same position as Mr. Pherozshah Mehta in having my name placed on the Committee, not at my own suggestion, I have very great pleasure in supporting, on behalf of Madras, the resolution which has been proposed by Mr. Mehta and seconded by Pundit Ajoodhianath. I am perfectly sure that you will approve it (no words of mine therefore are required to support it), and that it will be carried by acclamation. (*Cheers.*)

THE PRESIDENT—Are you all agreed ? (*Cries of " Yes, yes; all, all," and loud cheers.*) Our first Resolution then will stand;

RESOLVED: *That an address be presented to Mr. Charles Bradlaugh, M.P., on behalf of this Congress here assembled, and that Messrs. Adam, Pherozshah Mehta, and W. C. Bonnerjee are appointed a Committee to settle the wording of the said address.* (*Renewed cheers.*)

Res. II. Expansion and Reform of Legislative Councils.

THE PRESIDENT—Gentlemen, the first business—and it is a very important one—that will be brought before you to-day will be the scheme for the reform of the Legislative Councils. (*Cheers.*) As you are aware, a Draft Bill has been prepared by Mr. Bradlaugh (*cheers*) and has been circulated throughout the whole of India. We have all seen it, and I think we have all read it. That Bill embodies in legal form what was believed to be the view of the Congress, so far as its opinion had been expressed up to the time that this draft was prepared. Mr. Bradlaugh's wish was to ascertain, upon certain important points, the still more mature opinion of the people of India. I think I may say on his behalf that none of the provisions introduced into the Bill were introduced because he personally wished those provisions to be contained in it. [MR. BRADLAUGH: *Hear, hear.*] The Bill was only drafted to put into a clear and tangible form what was supposed to be the general wishes of the people. In dealing with the subject, therefore, it is not now proposed to bring forward draft sections or draft clauses prepared in legal phraseology—that is not what is required—but to state in particular and general terms certain important principles which it is desired should be embodied in the Bill. Therefore, after consultation, certain proposals have been prepared, and will now be laid before you for your judgment. I will call upon Mr. Eardley Norton to move the first resolution.

MR. EARDLEY NORTON (*Madras, No.* 44, *in list*)—Gentlemen,—I had better begin by reading to you the proposition which I have been charged to lay before you. It runs thus:

PROPOSED: *That the following skeleton scheme for the reform and reconstitution of the Council of the Governor-General for making Laws and Regulations, and the Provincial Legislative Councils, be adopted, and that the President of this Congress do submit the same to Charles Bradlaugh, Esq., M.P., with the respectful request, of this Congress, that he may be pleased to cause a Bill to be drafted, on the lines indicated in this skeleton scheme, and introduce the same in the British House of Commons:—*

SCHEME.

(1.) ***The Imperial and Provincial Legislative Councils to consist respectively of Members, not less than one-half of whom are to be elected, not more than one-fourth to sit ex-officio and the rest to be nominated by Government.***

(2.) ***Revenue districts to constitute, ordinarily, territorial units, for electoral purposes.***

2nd Day.

Res. II. Expansion and Reform of Legislative Councils.

(3.) *All male British subjects above 21 years of age, possessing certain qualifications and not subject to certain disqualifications (both of which will be settled later), to be voters.*

(4.) *Voters in each district to elect representatives to one or more electoral bodies, according to local circumstances, at the rate of 12 per million of the total population of the district, such representatives to possess certain qualifications, and not to be subject to certain disqualifications, both of which will be settled later.*

(5.) *All the representatives thus elected by all the districts included in the jurisdiction of each electoral body, to elect members to the Imperial Legislature at the rate of 1 per every five millions of the total population of the electoral jurisdiction, and to their own Provincial Legislature at the rate of 1 per million of the said total population, in such wise that whenever the Parsees, Christians, Mahomedans or Hindus are in a minority, the total number of Parsees, Christians, Mahomedans or Hindus, as the case may be, elected to the Provincial Legislature, shall not, so far as may be possible, bear a less proportion to the total number of members elected thereto, than the total number of Parsees, Christians, Hindus or Mahomedans, as the case may be, in such electoral jurisdiction, bears to its total population. Members of both legislatures to possess certain qualifications and not to be subject to certain disqualifications both of which will be settled later.*

(6.) *All elections to be by ballot.*

Mr. Chairman and Brother Delegates,—When, in the after years of my life, I look back upon my Indian career, the proudest and most cherished recollection in it will be my memory of to-day ; for to-day I speak to you as an accredited representative of the people addressing nearly two thousand other accredited representatives of the country. We have lived to see the great elective principle, at least in its inception, being slowly carried out in the fruition of time, until, year after year, from the original number of 72, with which I believe the Congress began in this very city, we are assembled to-day in numbers which, I think, I may fairly say, defy criticism. (*Hear, hear.*) We have been told that we have come back to the birth place of this institution a discredited and a hopeless set of men. (*Loud cheers and laughter.*) It does not, truly, look much like this ; a grander, a more enthusiastic assemblage, I venture to say that none here have ever witnessed either in India or Europe, and I think if we look back upon the record of our career we shall be able to point to works which we have carried out, and which give the most complete refutation to any such statement. (*Hear, hear.*)

But now let us turn to the business of the day, and first and foremost stands, and must stand, the question of the reconstitution of the Legislative Councils ; because, gentlemen, when we stand with the dignity (limited perhaps) and the authority of the chosen of the people, we shall make the Governments of the various Provinces in India listen, in a manner in which they will not listen to-day, to our various wants. (*Hear, hear.*) And I am proud to think that I have been entrusted with this resolution to-day in the presence of two new additions to our ranks, with whose names the Bombay Congress of 1889 will be inseparably connected. (*Cheers.*) I am glad to think that there has come to us our venerated friend Sir William Wedderburn (*cheers*), of whose connection with Bombay and through Bombay with all India, I need not say anything, for his actions are written so that all men can read, and we who live in other Presidencies are as grateful to him as you in Bombay can be. (*Cheers.*) I am speaking in the presence of another gentleman, a Member of that House of Commons to whose intervention we look, and possibly to whose intervention alone we look, for reform and for assistance. (*Cheers.*) He is a man of the people speaking for the people, who comes to us with all that immense dignity and with all that immense power which lie behind the suffrages of the English nation. (*Cheers.*) And we are proud, as our address will hereafter show, to think that we have, as our Champion in the House of Commons, a man who, by a dauntless and unconquerable Championship of the truth, has earned the position which he holds alike in their affections and in ours. (*Loud cheers.*)

Gentlemen, it lies with me now to propose formally this resolution which I have just read. Its history has been shortly placed before you by Sir William Wedderburn, and we know that we have not, now, to deal with any details or particulars, but that we are dealing solely with the main principles of this Bill. The first section incorporates the great living principle for which, for the last six or seven years, we, the voiceless people of India, Europeans and natives alike, have been contending ; I mean the great living principle of election. I would ask you to believe in and to hold fast to that principle, and to take care that nothing is introduced into this Bill (it certainly will not be introduced by Mr. Bradlaugh) which in any way interferes with or improperly limits the operation of this great living principle. The resolution points therefore to the necessity that the Imperial and Provincial Legislatures of this country should consist of members not less than half of whom are to be elected, and not less than one-fourth of whom are to sit *ex-officio*, the remaining one-fourth being nominated either by the Governor-General or by the local Provincial authorities in their respective Councils. Now, gentlemen, provided you religiously adhere to that essential principle; provided you are never seduced into departing from it; provided that no matter what proportion is given to you of the election in your respective Councils, you stand and insist upon the right to have your own share in it absolutely free (*cheers*); provided you insist that there shall be no Government manipulation in your one-half—that Government shall not touch it, either directly or indirectly, undisguised or disguised—so long as you do that, you will be certain, in the long run of years, to work out for yourselves your own political emancipation. Because we all know that if this Bill is passed we shall have introduced the thin end of the wedge. (*Cheers.*)

The second section says that the Revenue Districts are to constitute, ordinarily, the territorial units for electoral purposes. The third section says that all male British subjects above twenty-one years of age, and possessing certain qualifications and not subject to certain disqualifications—which qualifications and disqualifications are to be settled hereafter—are to be voters. Then the fourth section says: Voters in each district to elect representatives to one or more electoral bodies, according to the local circumstances, at the rate of twelve per million of the total population of the district. Such representatives to possess certain qualifications and not to be subject to certain disqualifications which are to be settled hereafter. Section five says that all representatives thus elected by all the districts included in the jurisdiction of each electoral body are to elect members to the imperial legislature at the rate of one for every five millions of the total population and to their own provincial councils at the rate of one member per million of the said total population, in such wise (now we come to the great point wherein this bill proposes to afford protection for the representation of minorities), " that when Parsees, Christians, Mahomedans, or Hindoos are in a minority, the total number of Parsees, Christians, Hindus or Mahomedans, as the case may be, elected to the provincial legislatures shall not, so far as may be possible, bear a less proportion to the total number of members elected thereto, than the total number of Parsees, Christians, Hindus or Mahomedans, as the case may be, in such electoral jurisdiction, bear to its total population." The members of both Legislatures to possess certain qualifications and not to be subject to certain disqualifications both of which are to be settled hereafter. And lastly the elections are to be made by ballot. This is the scheme which you are asked to accept and you are asked to accept it in the following phraseology. " That the following skeleton scheme for the reform and reconstitution of the Council of the Governor-General for making laws and regulations, and the Provincial Legislative Councils be adopted, and that the President of this Congress do submit the same to Mr. Charles Bradlaugh, M.P., with the respectful request, of this Congress, that he may be pleased to cause a Bill to be drafted on the lines indicated in this skeleton scheme, and introduce the same in the British House of Commons."

I am much afraid, gentlemen, that a good deal of my apportioned ten minutes has been taken up in reading the resolution, so that if by any means I trespass upon your patience for a little longer period than ten minutes you will forgive me. (*Cries of " Go on."*) That is the scheme you are asked to adopt and in plain language it comes to this, that the declarations constitute a practical proposal, and if you hold on to it always, it will remain the Magna Charta of the liberties of the people of this country. Looking round, wherever you will, either at the Supreme Council at Calcutta or at those bodies of men who are designated, I don't know why, the Legislative Councils in the Provincial Jurisdictions—(*laughter and cheers*)—looking wherever you will, I think we are all agreed that, so far at any rate as the real wants of the people are concerned, they are practically, absolutely useless, and are mere shams. (*Cheers.*) Into such bodies of men we wish to introduce the quickening principle of election by the people, and all that we ask for is that, whatever may be the total number, hereafter of the members of the Imperial Council at Calcutta or of the Local Provincial Councils elsewhere, we shall have one-half of such bodies to do with as we choose. Now, gentlemen, if that is conceded to us—and I regret that there has been a recent departure from the more liberal principles which were enunciated by our late Viceroy upon this question—if that principle be conceded to us, I think we may safely expect that the peoples of this country will take a new departure, certainly in their moral, probably in their physical happiness. We shall have the right, to control ourselves; we shall have the right, to a certain extent, to control our taxation; we shall have the right to criticise the Budget; and last but not least we shall have the glorious privilege of interpellation. (*Cheers.*) A right which, if properly applied, will inure to the enormous benefit both of the rulers and of the ruled. (*Cheers.*)

The right of interpellation, gentlemen, is a point on which I feel very strongly, and on which, though not included in this skeleton resolution, the great majority of you, my co-delegates, feel, I know, equally strongly. You will recollect that in the Bill submitted to us by Mr. Bradlaugh, following the previous resolution of the Congress, certain subjects were excluded from the operation of the right of interpellation. Amongst those things was taken away the right of scrutiny by the representatives of the people in respect of all questions touching the foreign policy of this country. When we come to consider that question hereafter whatever may be your opinions now—and I know perfectly well that there is probably a not uninfluential section of you against me upon this point—I trust that when the time comes for us to consider what matters may fairly be held to be included within that very elastic phrase, Foreign Policy, you will agree with me that one class of questions, which certainly ought not to be brought within the category of Foreign Policy, is that relating to the Native States of India. (*Cheers.*) What I mean is this, that whereas by this Bill the power will be conceded to us to criticise the conduct of any official under the British Government residing in British India, whether it be some unfortunate youngster fresh from home or whether it be the Governor himself, it will probably be contended, by those who are endeavouring to constitute themselves the arbiters of our political aspirations, that we are not to have the right to criticise the conduct of British officials in Native States. Now those who are in any way acquainted, as I take it a large majority of us are, with the vagaries of many of our British officials, must surely agree with me that the limitation which would debar us from criticising the public actions of those public officials is a limitation which is neither just nor even rational. Therefore when the time comes, we who know what has been going on in Kashmir and Bhopal, we who know what is going on in Travancore, and in other Native States—amongst others Hyderabad—due, in a measure, either to the misconduct, the apathy or the interference of our own officials,—we who know these things, should in the interests of our own privileges, in the interest of the millions of natives who have no voice, firmly stand upon our rights, and insist that we shall be permitted to criticise these gentlemen's conduct.

Now permit me to say a few more words upon the other parts of the Bill. The resolution itself is so worded that anybody can follow it with great ease. It is very simple, and the remaining clauses of it practically deal with this question. Having disposed of the principle of election in the first clause, the resolution goes on to deal with the question of who shall be the voters, in other words the original electors; and the scheme which has eventually, I am glad to say, received the unanimous acceptance of the whole Congress Committee, is shortly this. Representation direct from the people into the Council, is no doubt theoretically right and it is a sort of representation which we, who are Europeans, and you who have been brought up in the traditions of the English people, would, alike, be glad to receive. (*Cheers.*) But, gentlemen, we must limit our desires and our requests by the circumstances amidst which we find ourselves placed; and we have heard, in that informal Committee which met a few days before the Congress assembled, from the lips of one who speaks upon this point with a peculiar emphasis, that any such proposal emanating from the Congress in India, asking the people of England to give us direct representation from the people, is sure to meet with an absolute and flat denial. Under such circumstances it would be useless for us to persist in that scheme, and I am glad therefore to think, —although possibly some enthusiast may hereafter rise to propose an amendment, on this point, to my resolution—that the scheme has been abandoned—for the time being only, remember—because, as I have suggested, we shall have got the thin end of the wedge in. (*Cheers.*) In the course of years the time will come when no man, and no living set of men, shall any longer deny us that right. (*Cheers.*) But, for the time being, we have elected to abandon it and I am glad to think that this resolution will practically meet with the unanimous consent of all. (*Cheers.*)

There is a second scheme, which is also dead, and which I simply refer to because without it the historical sketch of this resolution would be incomplete. It was suggested, by persons for whose opinions we all entertain the most absolute respect, that, instead of accepting the scheme as it now stands, the power to elect members, as well to the Provincial as to the Imperial Legislatures should be given over to Corporations, such as Municipal Bodies, Taluk Boards, Universities, Chambers of Commerce, and other kindred institutions. But that has been abandoned now, because careful scrutiny of the constitution of the Municipal and District Boards has revealed the fact that their constitution has placed them absolutely at the mercy of the Government. (*Hear, hear.*) And I suppose we are all agreed that the one thing for which we have been fighting, and for which we are fighting to-day, is to have full and undiluted, and absolutely to ourselves, that scource of political power to which we shall be able to turn and find it always there pure and stable. (*Cheers.*) Now, gentlemen, the proposition suggested—and I speak with respect for those who differ from me on this point—that we should hand over our electoral franchise into the keeping of such bodies of men was, practically, a proposition that meant this, that you were going to hand over to the Government, in the velvet-glove disguise of these various Corporations, the power to do absolutely what they wished with your electorate (*cheers*) and for this short and simple reason that all these Corporations, as you ought to know, are the creations of the

Government. They were created by Legislative Acts of the various Presidencies and—I think it was denied last night—the same power which creates these Municipalities reserves to itself the right of absolutely extinguishing them, without assigning any reason, by a notification in the *Government Gazette*, without consultation with anyone except the members of Council, if consultation that can be called. So that this sort of thing may happen. If, once, one of us were elected, say for some particular district by some particular Municipal Board, and if in the course of two years he made himself obnoxious to the Government because he always advocated the rights of the people as against the exceptional privileges of the officials, on coming up at the end of that time for re-election such a one might find his constituency absolutely vanished ; and in answer to the query "What has become of my constituency ?" the only response would be this, probably from the lately deceased Chairman, "Sir, we have expired in consequence of a notification in the *Government Gazette*." (*Laughter and Cheers.*) Surely that is not the sort of electorate, to which it is either right or advisable that we should entrust our franchise.

Now, gentlemen, living as we do amongst such vast varieties of creeds and men of different races, it would not be acceptable I think to the Government of this country nor to the Government of England, nor to the peoples of England or India, if a scheme should be submitted which did not take into consideration and provide for the absolute protection of the minorities of this country. (*Cheers.*) I dare say in years to come when travel and education shall have rubbed off the angularities which at present separate Hindus from Mahomedans, and Mahomedans from Eurasians—when we are all permeated by that theoretical Christian spirit which shall enable us to treat every man exactly as a brother and nothing less—when that time has arrived we shall be ready for the repeal of this clause of our scheme which for the present provides especially for the protection of the rights of minorities. (*Cheers.*) But recollecting as we do the practical conditions under which we live, recollecting the differences of caste, of custom and of creed that prevail in India, it is absolutely essential that any scheme which is to receive the sympathy of the people of England should bear upon its face clear proof that it takes into cognizance and protects the interests of minorities. Now, gentlemen, in that respect there cannot be any well founded criticism of the measure which I have had the honour to move, because legislative protection of minorities is expressly therein provided and not left to the varying discretion or the varying passions of the human breast. Our scheme sets forth explicitly that the Electoral College, when it elects, shall necessarily, no option being left in this matter, elect a certain minimum percentage of Christians or Mahomedans, or Hindoos to their respective Legislative Councils. So that at any rate the members of Council, when elected, will fairly represent, in the ratio of the populations to which they belong, their various interests. (*Cheers.*) And now, gentlemen, the scheme which has been accepted is shortly this that though we have not direct representation in so many words, we try to have it in another way. We interpose, that is, between the people and the Legislative Councils, a body of men whom we call the electoral body, which body derives its inspiration and its being from the popular suffrage. We summon—the number hereafter will be fixed—say, in the Madras Presidency, 500 persons who are to sit as the Electoral body. These 500 persons will be elected from all the twenty-two districts of Madras, freely, by the people of these districts and absolutely outside the control or the interference of the Government. Those 500 persons will then meet either in one, or more cities of their local jurisdiction and will then proceed to elect, either from amongst themselves or from those who may choose to offer themselves as candidates for the Imperial and local Councils, such persons as, in their opinion, are best qualified to represent the wants and wishes of the people. Now whatever may be the demerits of this scheme—and I do not for an instant profess to say that it is perfect—it has this great merit which ought to recommend it to you : that though it is not a direct representation from the people, still it is a representation undefiled from the people. (*Cheers.*) That therefore, gentlemen, is the best, the highest qualification which we can claim for the Electoral bodies. If you adopt this resolution subject to that, all other matters are mere matters of detail. Questions of the qualifications of voters, questions of the qualifications of those Representatives that the voters are to elect, questions of the qualifications of members of the Imperial Council or of the local Councils are questions as to which we shall not quarrel. These are mere matters of detail which any person, with an ordinary amount of brains, can hammer out for himself, but which of course must receive the approval of the Congress or its Representatives. But subject to that, provided you accept this one principle of the present resolution, you will have built up for yourselves a new Magna Charta in the land, even more powerful and more enduring than the great Magna Charta of 1858 which your Queen (*cheers*) unasked gave you.

I do not think there is anything left for me to say which I can say in the allotted period. I have already trespassed on your good nature. (*Cheers and go on.*) There are a large number of people who wish to speak, and I have no wish to stand between aspiring

2nd Day.

Res. II. Expansion and Reform of Legislative Councils.

ambition and its fruition; so that I consider my task fulfilled when I have finished the remarks with which I find it necessary to preface this particular resolution. When my voice is silent, when I am no longer here and able to protect its interests, you will recollect, if anything is said against this resolution which touches its details, that we claim for it two merits which nothing can take from it, the merit that it is a scheme which has taken two great principles into consideration, and proposes to embody these two great principles in an Act of Parliament, namely, first, the great principle that we are to introduce for the first time in Indian political history, the principle of election by the people, and, secondly, that we have taken into consideration and respected the question of the representation of the minorities of this country. (*Cheers.*) With these principles—you may disagree as you like over the details—I think I may depart in the assurance that we are absolutely and unanimously agreed. (*Loud Cheers.*)

THE HON'BLE PANDIT AJOODHIANATH: (*North-West Provinces, No.* 1517, *in list.*)—Then rose and said:—MR. PRESIDENT and FELLOW DELEGATES,—It is now my privilege and duty to second this proposition, and I am proud to follow an eminent leader like Mr. Norton. You in general, and those of my brethren who come from the North-West Provinces, and Oudh in particular, are well aware of the storm of opposition which was raised against us last year, especially in connection with this resolution. I said to you, *then*, that that opposition was bound soon to die out. Pardon me for saying that that proved me to be somewhat of a prophet. There is now really no opposition worthy of the name (*hear, hear,*) although a Government official, here and there, makes the best of any opportunity which he may have of using his official influence to prevent the people of his district taking part in this Congress. (*Shame.*)

In those days we were, it was alleged, a set of rebels. Stuff and nonsense! (*Laughter and Cheers.*) We are the most loyal people on the face of the earth. (*Renewed Cheers.*) We are those who have ever been worshippers of our Sovereign! Our friends knew well the hollowness of this libel on us, and they have now, I fancy, dropped it. They know that we have always said that the British Government was a very good Government. All that we added was that if it were a little more open to conviction, a little less distrustful of the people and a little less expensive (*laughter*) it would be still better. (*Cheers.*) This, we then thought, this we still think, and therefore desire to effect a distinct improvement in the administration of the country by associating in it our best men, who really do understand, which even our best rulers do not, how and where, exactly, the shoe pinches.

Let me, in the short time allotted to me, set before you three facts which almost mathematically demonstrate the necessity of this primary reform that we are seeking. I shall first take the Viceregal Council; under the Indian Councils Act, by virtue of which these Councils are constituted, every member, official and non-official, has the right and privilege of introducing any Bill that he pleases into the Council. It may be thrown out by the votes of the majority, or, it may be vetoed by Her Majesty's Government; but no one under the British House of Parliament, you would have thought, would venture to interfere with this privilege of a British subject explicitly conferred by an act of Parliament. But I am sorry to say that the authority of Parliament does not, it would seem, go for much in India. There is a rule—you may take it from me—that before any Bill is introduced into the Council of the Viceroy the subject of the proposed Bill must be communicated to the Secretary of State for India, ("*shame*!") even after this communication the poor Bill cannot be introduced unless the Secretary of State and the Government here both say yes or do not say "no," to it within a certain period; I believe two months.

[A DELEGATE: Six months.] Some one says six months, but I believe the time is not so long as that. When you come to realize that there are commonly, on an average, only 14 meetings of the Viceregal Council held in Calcutta you can very well imagine the result of this restriction. That is fact Number one. (I do not believe in generalities, but I believe in facts.) The next fact is that for the greater part of the year the Viceroy's Council sits at Simla, and that at Simla no non-official member as a rule is present, because of the trifling allowance, some six hundred pounds I think, allowed to each non-official member each season, and which the Government cannot, it says, afford to give twice in the year so as to secure the attendance of the non-official members at the Simla Session also. Would you be surprised to learn that during this greater part of the year legislation is carried on without any non-official members in much the same way as if the Council were sitting in Calcutta with its full legal complement of non-officials? The third fact is that for the last two years no single meeting of the United Provinces' Council has been held at Allahabad. In thinking of that no milder word has occurred to me to describe our supposed Government by Councils than that of "farce;" my friend Mr. Norton says it is a "sham," but English is a foreign language to me (*laughter,*) and I am not quite sure of the difference between "a *sham*," and "a *shame*" and I will adhere to my own epithet "a farce;" and, truly, for India a melancholy one!

Now if the President will allow me to mention only one other fact I shall be much obliged. (*Cries of " go on."*) We know that Government at times is not over wise (*laughter.*) In October this year, I went down to Calcutta, and it was reported to the police authorities that so-and-so had come with so many servants, had put up in such a house, and remained so long. Now yesterday in this compound was seen a head constable, whose name is Mansab Alli, who has come from Allahabad (where I came from) and he was making close inquiries as to what persons have come from the North-West Provinces, especially Government officials. (*Shame.*)

I hope you will carry this resolution by acclamation. (*Cheers.*)

Mr. Eardley Norton : (*Madras, No.* 44, *in list.*)—Gentlemen : The Punditjee has just told you the story of how one head constable from Allahabad is watching the delegates from the North-Western Provinces. I wish to tell you that Colonel Weldon, our Madras Commissioner of Police is here in charge of all the delegates from Madras (*" Shame and laughter."*) A delegate.—And Colonel Henderson, the head of the Thuggy and Dacoity Department and of the Secret Police of all India, is, by a strange coincidence, also sniffing round our Premises. (*Laughter and Cheers.*)

Pundit Bishan Narayandar : (*Oudh, No.* 1491, *in list.*)—Then said :—I am extremely sorry that I have been unexpectedly asked to speak upon this very important subject ; and I am sorry for more than one reason. In the first place, the resolution is so important that I think every speaker should have time to think out thoroughly his speech before venturing to address you in regard to it. In the second place I have to follow two able speakers who have, it seems, really left me little to say. And in the third place I have to speak on behalf of Oudh, the people of which cannot hope for more, from me, than a very imperfect and inadequate expression of their views (*" No, no."*) Well, gentlemen, I am glad that this year the National Congress is going to deal in a practical spirit with the scheme for the reformation of the Legislative Councils—I believe that that is the most important question that could be brought before us ; and upon the settlement of this great question, upon the lines that have just been indicated by Mr. Norton, depends not only the success of India's just demands but also the permanence of the British Empire. (*Loud Cheers.*)

Gentlemen, it is a matter of congratulation and joy to us all that in this question we have the support and sympathy of a man whose perseverance has triumphed over every obstacle, a statesman whose indomitable courage, whose independence of character and whose broad human sympathies command the admiration of thinking and honest men of all shades of political opinion. (*Loud Cheers.*) And I am glad that the scene of this controversy is now going to be shifted from this country to England ; because after the scheme is passed by the Congress it will be pressed upon the notice of the House of Commons by Mr. Bradlaugh. We have been appealing to our Government here, and Government has up to this time turned a deaf ear to our appeals. But in England rest assured, gentlemen, that if the English people and the English Parliament are in full possession of the facts, they will grant to you readily, promptly and cheerfully, a concession which will be simply an act of justice and the redemption of a sacred pledge given long ago by our Sovereign to the people of this country. (*Prolonged cheers.*) We hear that there is a scheme in contemplation by the Indian Office on the lines suggested by Lord Dufferin or even less liberal ones. That scheme involves the expansion of the Councils, but upon the basis of nomination. Well, gentlemen, I think that we are all agreed that no reformed Councils are worth having which are founded on such a basis. The chief plank of the Congress platform, is the *elective* principle, and we are not going to be satisfied with a thing that will be a snare, a mockery and a delusion, leading men to believe that they have something which they do not really possess. What we want is not sham, but reality ; not shadow, but substance ; not nomination which is another name for deception, but representation which is the essence of political reform. (*Prolonged cheers.*) The time at my disposal is very short, and there are many points in connection with this subject that it is impossible for me to deal with (*" go on."*) I remember a remark of Sidney-Smith's to the effect that of all ingenious instruments of despotism, he most commended a popular assembly in which the majority of members were paid, and by their free speeches made the people believe that they were a free people. I believe this remark is peculiarly applicable to the Indian Legislative Councils wherein the majority of the members are undoubtedly the paid servants of the State, and in which a set of nominated Indian members (entirely at the mercy so far as their seats are concerned of the Government) are allowed to make a pretence of free speeches and free criticisms and take up quasi independant attitudes in order to make the people believe that they are free, and that their voice is listened to in all matters affecting their welfare. Now I think, gentlemen, that if the Government is going to settle this question it ought to settle it in an honest and straightforward manner. If the Government really means what it so often and so loudly professes, viz : that in all matters of our country's legislation it desires to consult the people of the country, then I think the principle of election is the only principle upon which any reform worthy of the name can be based. But if the Government despite its professions, really in its heart means "No, we do not at all want to consult in anything the views of the people, we wish to do exactly what we like, and yet keep them quiet" if it thinks that it can legislate for us and base the foundations of secure government in this country upon popular mistrust, upon suspicion and upon fear, then I must say that the system of nomination is a most ingenious instrument for carrying out that design. (*Cheers.*) And all I would add is *Respice finem.* (*Loud Cheers.*)

THE REV. MR. RAMCHANDER BOSE: (*Oudh, No.* 1507, *in list*).—Rose and said:—MR. PRESIDENT, LADIES AND GENTLEMEN,—Allow one whose knowledge of politics is below Zero to make a few general remarks on the Resolution under consideration. The Resolution is I maintain a complete and triumphant reply to all the objections that have ever been advanced or ventilated by the opponents of the Congress. The Resolution in the first place shows that we are not doctrinaires or manipulators of impracticable theories and romantic or Quixotic notions. We have again and again been charged with the folly of elaborating an ideal scheme of Government without the slightest regard to the conditions of life in India, and of striving to force it upon the acceptance of responsible officers. The Resolution before you gives the lie to this accusation inasmuch as it proposes only such moderate expansion of the existing machinery of State as is absolutely demanded by the altered state of the country. (*Cheers.*) In the second place the Resolution proves that we are not revolutionists for it shows plainly that evolution not revolution is our object. (*Loud Cheers.*) The Resolution proves that we are not demagogues, that we are not flattering the masses of our countrymen with an idea of their importance, disproportionate to their present state of culture, or inspiring amongst them hopes that cannot possibly be realized without ruining the country. Our object is their gradual elevation by means of the best type of political culture. (*Hear, Hear.*) In the last place, we are accused of being conceited and being ridiculously self-assertive, of being impatient of sound counsel, and lastly of being unwilling to be led. The Resolution shows that we are being led by superiors. The framer of the Bill on which the Resolution is mainly based is an Englishman; our illustrious President is an Englishman, and he who is the heart and soul of the movement, our General Secretary, is also an Englishman. (*Prolonged cheers.*) We have our own strong irrepressible yearnings for a freer and higher political life, but as to the best and wisest modes of attaining this we have committed ourselves to their guidance believing that they will conduct us safely, in due time, to the green pastures of political emancipation. (*Loud cheers.*)

One more objection I shall take notice of before I conclude. It has been said "you are mad after the politics of the country, but you leave the morals of the country untouched." Do we leave the morals of the country untouched? (*Loud and prolonged cries of "No, no."*) That is just the question. Neither the sphere of sociology, nor the sphere of morals has been left unaffected by the Congress. This year we have received applications from ladies for permission to appear as delegates; and they have been elected and are here now to grace our assembly; this shows that even the cloistered chambers of the Zenana have been thrilled by the Congress idea, and, that we, as a nation, are awakening to broader views of woman's capacities and woman's mission. Nor has the region of morals been left untouched by the Congress. The civic virtues to which ancient Rome owed her ascendency and world wide domination are being matured amongst us; and that virtue, Sir, which is the parent of all virtues, from which every virtue emanates and into which every virtue may be resolved—I mean the virtue of self-sacrifice—is being generated amongst us. (*Cheers.*) Bombay had never distinguished itself, by such a splendid display, (a display of outlay of money, of energy and of time) as we see around us to-day, for a national cause. This ancient land of religious pilgrimages, this land of religious self-denial, has never witnessed so many streams of self-sacrificing pilgrims coming from so many centres of influence and covering such distances as have united here in a volume of homage to the National Congress movement. (*Loud Cheers.*)

The activity of the movement has left its mark on the surface, so to speak, of every department of life; and I have only to repeat what I said last year, *viz.*, that partial reform, such as is directly aimed at by the Congress, is sure to efflouresce or expand into universal reform. (*Prolonged cheers.*)

MR. G. SUBRAMANIA IYER: (*Madras, No.* 50, *in list.*)—Said:—MR. PRESIDENT AND GENTLEMEN OF THE CONGRESS,—The measure which I have been called upon to join Mr. Norton and others in recommending to your approbation, is a measure of the utmost importance and a measure beset by difficulties of practise and of principles. Well, sir, I am glad to say that this measure which is now submitted for your consideration, is only a slight modification of the measure recently propounded by the Madras Standing Committee and I think I know, and all of us know, that any measure which might be proposed for the reconstitution of the Legislative Councils, by one Presidency must—however well matured however carefully thought out—require the fullest criticism and at least some modifications by the country as a whole, to make it in all ways worthy of acceptance.

Still I hope that the Madras Standing Committee's scheme, as now slightly modified by the Subjects Committee, which represents *all* the Standing Congress Committees, is now really worthy of national acceptance. Our Committee sat many many times thoroughly thrashing out the measure, of which the resolution before you embodies the most salient features, and it considered, I may add, the various details (into which our present resolution does not enter) with the greatest care and deliberation. The Committee bore in mind certain leading principles in working out their scheme, and I shall crave your indulgence for a few minutes whilst I refer to those principles.

First of all, Sir, the principle that was most predominant in our minds was this, that, whatever we may ultimately arrive at, no measure that we might now put forward before the Congress should be obnoxious to the criticism that it aimed—even to any slight extent,—at transferring the power of ultimate control from the Government of India, representing Great Britain, to the hands of the native community of this country. The next principle we had in mind was this, that it must be a feasible, a practical, and a simple measure; it must be one that could be worked out without detriment to the interests of the country, and without detriment to the supremacy of British power in this country. There is another principle which we bore in mind, and it was this, that it should be a measure which would give to a large section of the people—a large number of our countrymen—a substantial measure of political power. These were the principles we had in our minds; and taking the resolutions of previous Congresses as our basis, we went on at different meetings maturing this scheme. And after certain modifications that struck most of us to be necessary, when we came to Bombay, this measure is placed before you for your consideration. We shall presently see how these principles apply to the measure before us. You will remember that according to the Bill framed by Mr. Bradlaugh, (and which, except in those few points in which it is at variance with our present scheme, the country has unanimously accepted) the Supreme Government in this country has had reserved to it full power of control over half the number of the members in the Council; this half will consist of either its servants or its nominees, the other half alone is to be elected by the people: and although the Council will be expanded, and the elected members of Council will exercise some influence in the financial arrangements, and also enjoy the right of interpellation, still the Governor-General in Council will retain the absolute power of vetoing any or every decision arrived at even by the majority of the Council. This is considered necessary in order to secure our first principle that the representatives of the nation shall not in any degree take away from the Government of India the final power of control. At the same time we are anxious that this measure should not be a sham, and result in giving no additional political influence to the people. Therefore we have insisted on the principle of election as the essential feature of our scheme. This is the point about which most differences exist. Various schemes have been put forward, but we consider that all the requisite conditions have been satisfied by the measure now proposed and placed before you for your consideration. The chief feature of the measure is the institution of an intermediate electorate between the people and the Government. I think that that kind of intermediate electorate is most desirable, if not necessary, under the circumstances of the country. The Congress, as my predecessors have said, think that if any system of direct representation could be allowed under any reasonable conditions, direct representation would have constituted the best basis possible for our scheme; but I am not sure that even amongst our own countrymen there are not many who would disapprove of any scheme which would give the power of direct election, by ordinary voters, to seats in Council. But when besides this we were told that any measure of direct representation would certainly be unacceptable to the English Parliament, our duty clearly was to leave that out of consideration and see what else could be substituted for it. Now our present proposal, while doing away with that bugbear of direct representation and proposing a more moderate measure, also gives the people I think more substantial political advantages. It provides for the education of a large number of people in the affairs of the country. If we had direct representation we should have had only the voters, who, no more than in England, could be expected to be profound politicians, and an hundred or so members of Council. But under our present scheme we shall have some thousands of representatives between the voters and the members of Council, who must necessarily train themselves in public affairs and create year by year a wider field from which the members of Council can be selected. Nay I think that according to the scheme which is now before you it will be possible to collect a considerable number of people in every district, throughout the whole Empire, who will be compelled to educate and interest themselves in the public affairs of the country. Of course the mere voter does not exercise the power of electing members to the Council; he will merely elect the representatives who are to sit for his district on that grand electoral body who will elect to the Councils. And so far the great interest which the people might naturally feel in electing members direct to the Legislature might be diminished. But under the circumstances of our country that cannot be helped; and it is by no means certain that after all the

2nd Day.

Res. II. Expansion and Reform of Legislative Councils.

ordinary elector will not take an even greater interest in the election of twelve representatives all people of his own district and personally known to him, than in that of one member of Council who thus far has only been a name to him. People in some out-of-the-way districts may not perhaps take as much interest, at first, in electing representatives to the electoral body as they would take in electing members to the Council; but probably, as time runs on, these local elections, with their immediate practical local results will engage even more of the popular interest. It must be borne in mind too that our scheme has this great advantage that it provides for the members of the Council being elected by a picked body of gentlemen who will be the leaders of the native community in every district. That provides a guarantee that the members elected to the Council will be Members who owe their position to their intelligence, integrity, and social position and influence in the native community and not to mere demagogic gifts.

Well these are some of the recommendations that the scheme possesses. I may mention that after we came here one or two alternative schemes were placed before us. I might refer to one scheme which was recommended by our friends from Poona. That scheme was, in purport, that the election to the Council should be direct, and that the voters who should exercise the power of election, should consist of members of Municipal and Local Boards and persons included in the panel of Assessors, graduates and members of one or two professions and of certain political Associations and other public bodies. That is a system of direct representation, and that system is open to the same objections as every other system of direct representation. Our friends in England have distinctly discouraged us from presenting such a scheme for the consideration of the people in that country. There is also another defect in the scheme: as far as Madras is concerned, with its local institutions, that system could not work. I dare to say that in every other part of the country also, the proposed system will prove defective as giving no guarantee that the gentlemen thus elected to the Council, would be true and properly qualified representatives of the people. But I have already exceeded the time allotted to me and I must now only say in conclusion that I strongly recommend to your acceptance the scheme now before you, which is the only one, that can be placed with any hopes of success before the British Parliament, that will in any measure satisfy the just aspirations and claims of the people of this country.

MR. BEPIN CHUNDER PAL: (*Assam, No.* 1888, *in list.*)—Then rose and said:—MR. PRESIDENT, LADIES AND GENTLEMEN,—I hope you will not take it amiss, if I turn from you just for a moment, and address a few words on my own behalf, on behalf of my constituents in Assam, and on behalf of the wretched and down-trodden slave population of that province, to our distinguished guest, who has so bravely championed the cause of the Assam coolies in Parliament, and who seems to have adopted as the motto of his life those beautiful lines of the poet who says:

I live for the cause that lacks assistance,
I live for the cause that needs resistance;
I live for the future in the distance
And the good that that I can do. (*Loud Cheers.*)

Accept, Sir, our sincere thanks for your labours on our behalf, and kindly convey our best thanks to your constituents in Northampton, and to the working people of England, generally, who have in the past expended their money and their blood in removing the shackles of the slaves in every part of the world.

Coming, gentlemen, now to the resolution before me, the first thing that I should like to mention regards that oft repeated charge—that we are seditionists. (*Cries of no, no.*) Yes, I know you do indignantly repudiate that charge but considering that we have with us members of Parliament and tried, trusted and distinguished ex-officials of Government, this charge does not only carry its own condemnation with it, but also the condemnation of the existing state of things, which must be bad indeed to convert members of Parliament and faithful servants of the Crown into seditionists if, in truth, we are seditionists.

The next thing that I should like to say is that the scheme submitted here before you is, it seems to me, in some senses even more perfect than the system of Parliamentary representation in England. Of course, I speak subject to correction, but I scrutinized the rolls of the electors of Great Britain and Ireland, and I found, it seemed to me, that more than one-fourth of the general population were unrepresented; and there is absolutely nothing in the British constitution that provides for the representation and protection of the interests of this large and influential minority. But we have done so, in our scheme, in a double way, both by leaving the Government to provide for it by nomination, and by the minority clause of the scheme laid before you. With these words I support the resolution and I hope you will carry it unanimously. (*Applause.*)

LALA LAJPUT RAI: (*Punjab, No.* 1437, *in list.*)—BROTHER DELEGATES,—I do not think I shall be fulfilling my duty to my province if I do not tender the heart-felt gratitude of that province to the gentleman who does himself the honour of championing the cause of the poor and the oppressed. I, belonging to a province that is poor, both intellectually and materially, have a right to say (*Cries of " Question.*")

MR. PHEROZSHAH M. MEHTA: (*Bombay, No.* 967, *in list.*)—Rose here and said :—I wish to rise to a point of order. Speakers ought to confine themselves to the proposition before the Congress.

THE PRESIDENT: It is necessary to keep to the question of the resolution that has been placed before the meeting.

LALA LAJPUT RAI: (*Punjab, No.* 1437, *in list.*)—Resuming said :—Well turning to the special question before us I may say that in accepting this resolution, you will have the gratification of precisely giving effect to the words and wishes of Sir Syed Ahmed, who in 1864 looked hopefully forward to the time when the Legislative Councils of India, would include representatives from every district and division. (*Cheers.*) There is one other point to which I wish to refer, and that is the protection of the interests of Mahomedans in the measure now before us. In 1884 when Sir Syed Ahmed went to Lahore, he delivered a speech in which he defined the word Hindu as including both Hindus and Mahomedans, and said that he would make no distinction between Hindus and Mahomedans so far as political privileges were concerned (*cheers*), because we required no such distinction. But though we concur in his sentiments, though we hold that, we are *oll*, Hindus, Parsees or Mahomedans, equally truly represented, be our elected members Mahomedans, Parsees or Hindus, because we are all one people and one nation, still we fear lest in some cases, minorities, in whom this feeling of Indian brotherhood is not yet as fully developed as it will be a few years hence, might have doubts, and think themselves unrepresented, if men of their own special section did not sit upon the Councils and so, though in reality the thing is not needed, (for we are all one) we have specially provided so that all such minorities shall necessarily be represented by men of their own particular sections. This will show how sincere we are in guarding not only the real interests but even the possible prejudices of our Mahomedan brethren, and how careful we are to look to the interests of all minorities in every part of the country. I am a Hindu ; in the Punjab the Hindus are in a minority and so far as I am concerned, I should be quite content to be represented by any good Mahomedan or Sikh member—but others may not share this view—and hence the minority clause in that scheme which has been laid before you, and which I commend to your acceptance from the bottom of my heart. (*Cheers.*)

PANDIT MADAN MOHAN MALAVIYA: (*North-West Provinces, No.* 1520, *in list.*)—Said :—MR. PRESIDENT, LADIES AND GENTLEMEN,—I am happy to find that we are to-day discussing the leading features of the scheme for the reform and expansion of the Legislative Councils. You know since we met last, our position has somewhat improved in this matter, and the difference between us and Government is not now quite so great as it was a year ago. The four principal points which the Congress has been urging on the Government in relation to the reform of the Councils have been, 1st that the number of members on the Council should be increased ; 2ndly that the privilege of electing at least half of these members should be given to the people ; 3rdly that the Budget should be laid every year before the Council ; 4thly that the members should have the right to interpellate the executive on questions of public concern. Of these, gentlemen, His Excellency the Viceroy assured us in his speech on the occasion of the last discussion of the Budget in his Council, that Her Majesty's Government had decided to grant us three, viz., the enlargement of the Councils ; the presentation to them of the Budget every year, whether there be any new tax to be imposed or not ; and the right to interpellate the Government in regard to any branch of the administration. Of course there are some limitations to be put upon the exercise of this latter right ; but His Excellency's words made it perfectly clear that the right itself will be conceded.

The only vital point of difference between us and Government now, therefore, is with regard to the manner of appointing members to the Council. The Government wish to nominate all the members and we ask for the privilege of electing half of them. How evidently simple and just our prayer ! How utterly indefensible the unwillingness of Government to grant it ? (*Cheers.*) You know, gentlemen, that in the reformed Councils the Government will be exactly what they now are, the final arbiter of all questions that may be brought before the Council. Even in cases where the majority of the members are opposed to any measure and vote against it, the Government will still possess the power to veto their decision, and carry things entirely according to their own will and pleasure. In other words, they will occupy the position of a judge in deciding all questions affecting

2nd Day.

Res. II. Expansion and Reform of Legislative Councils.

our purses, our character, in fact our whole well-being. The sole privilege which we are praying for is to be allowed to choose our own Counsels to represent our case and condition fully before them. And the Government seem unwilling to allow us even that ! (*Shame.*) They say they will appoint Counsels of their own choice to plead our cause. Now, gentlemen, we thank them for this overflow of kindness towards us, (*laughter*) but we feel and we have good reasons to feel, that we should be much better off if they allowed us to exercise our own discretion in the choice of the Counsels, who are to plead our cause, defend our rights, and protect our interests.(*Cheers.*) The Legislative Council is the great tribunal before which measures of the greatest possible moment, affecting not only ourselves, but even our posterity, are continually coming up for decision, and justice requires that before the Council passes its final judgment upon them, we should be allowed to have our say with regard to them through our chosen and accredited representatives. We do feel, gentlemen, and feel strongly that we should no longer be debarred from exercising this simple and rightful privilege. The privilege of selecting one's own Counsel is not denied even to the most abandoned of criminals under the British rule. Why then should it be denied to the loyal and intelligent subjects of Her Gracious Majesty ? When a jury is being empanelled, the judge asks the person whose fate is to be decided by that jury, to say if he has any objection to any person composing it and in case he has any such objection that person is removed from the panel. But the Government of India and our Secretary of State—if the reports published in the newspapers represent their views faithfully—seem unwilling to allow the vast millions of Her Majesty's subjects in this country any voice whatever in the appointment of persons who decide questions which concern not merely any one man or any set of men amongst them, but the entire nation of them and their posterity. Could there be anything more in conflict with reason and justice ? (*Loud cheers.*)

If, gentlemen, the choice of Government in the selection of non-official members had, even generally, been exercised in a manner tending to promote the interests of the people we might not have been so anxious to burden ourselves with the responsibility of electing our representatives ourselves. But unhappily, as you know, in a large majority of cases, their choice has been exercised in favor of persons who have proved to be the least qualified or willing to advocate the interests, and plead fearlessly for the rights, of the people, nay, not unfrequently, in favour of persons whose presence in the Council has helped to contribute to the miseries of the people. We would much rather that there were no non-official members at all on the Councils than that there should be members who are not in the least in touch with the people, (*hear, hear,*) and who being ignorant of their true conditions and requirements, betray a cruel want of sympathy with them in heedlessly supporting measures which tend to increase suffering and discontent among them.

I will recall to your mind only two instances to illustrate what I have said. A couple of years ago, you remember, the Government was driven by reason of its excessive and, as we think, wasteful military expenditure to find some fresh means of increasing its revenue and it resolved upon drawing the required money from the poor, the class least able to offer any resistance or protest. (*Shame.*) The question came up before the Legislative Council and unofficial honorable members, the so called representatives of our people, so far from protesting against the proposal, gave their ready consent to it. Some of these gentlemen even went the length of declaring that the enhancement of the duty on salt would not inflict any hardship on the poorer classes of the people. (*Shame.*) Now, gentlemen, these big honorable gentlemen enjoying private incomes and drawing huge salaries may find it hard to believe that the addition of a few annas every year to the burdens of the poor, can cause any serious hardship to them. But those who know in what abject misery and pinching poverty our poorer classes generally exist, know how painfully the slightest increase in their burdens presses upon them. But these honorable members were pleased to say " the people will not feel the increase in the tax." (*Shame.*)

I will remind you of only one more case. You remember a few months ago the Government again found itself badly in want of money. Those who regulate their income by their expenditure, and not their expenditure by their income, must frequently find themselves in that unhappy position. It became necessary to raise more revenue and after misappropriating the Famine Insurance Fund, and mulcting the Provincial Governments (thereby starving education and arresting progress in all directions,) Government then resolved again on squeezing something more out of the poor. It resolved to reimpose the Patwari Cess on the ryots of the North-West Provinces and Oudh. Now you may know that when the Government of our good Lord Ripon had, (*cheers*) by a cessation of war and warlike operations, (*hear, hear,*) effected a saving in the public expenditure, and desired to give relief to those who most needed it, they found after inquiry that the Ryots of the North-Western Provinces and Oudh stood most especially in need of some relief, and they remitted the Patwari Cess to the extent of 20 lakhs. But the Government of Lord Landsdowne has this year reimposed that same Cess upon them! See I beseech you, gentlemen, what gross injustice has been perpetrated in the reimposition of this Patwari Cess? The Patwari Cess was remitted seven years ago, but the poor ryots have had to pay it, it seems, all the same, year after year. (*Shame.*) It was said that the Cess had been amalgamated with other taxes and could not be separated from them. If the money had had to go to the coffers of the Government, such a plea would never have been listened to for a moment. (*Hear, hear.*) But it was the poor ryot who was concerned, the plea was allowed to hold good, the Talukdars and Zemindars were thus allowed to enjoy the entire benefit of the measure which the Government of Lord Ripon had passed in the interests of the ryots; and it is now on this very plea that the remission of the Cess did not benefit the ryot, that the Patwari Cess has been reimposed, not on the Zemindars, but on the poor ryot, whereby he is now compelled to pay the Cess twice over, for no other fault of his than that he is poor and helpless. (*Loud cheers and cries of "Shame, shame.*)

The Hon'ble Mr. Quinton who represented the Government of Sir Auckland Colvin at the Viceroy's Council, said in his speech on the subject that the consent of the Talukdars of Oudh had been obtained to the measure. Fancy, gentlemen, the justice of adding to the burthens of the ryot on the strength of the consent of the Zemindar! But that was not all. There were other honorable members present in the Council, who said that the reimposition of the Cess would not add much more than about 12 annas a year to the load of taxation on the ryot, and they said it was so slight a sum that the ryot would not feel the pressure at all. Well, gentlemen, it is sinful to desire unhappiness to any one. But when I hear these honorable members assert with cruel levity of heart that the addition of a few annas a year to the burthens of the insufficiently fed and clothed poor, whether it be in the shape of the Salt Tax or the Patwari Cess will not increase their wretchedness and misery. I feel tempted to exclaim with old Lear:

> "Take physic pomp,
> Expose thyself to feel what wretches feel
> That thou may'st shake the superflux to them
> And show the heavens more just."

If these gentlemen had to live, even for a day or two, on that coarse unpalatable diet which is the best our poor, often starving, can command in the brightest times, and if they had to brave the cold of our up-country winters without all those warm and soft clothings, they themselves luxuriate in, they would understand what hardship the enhancement of the Salt Tax and the reimposition of the Patwari Cess entails upon the people. (*Prolonged cheers.*) There are hundreds of thousands of ryots at this moment in the North-West Provinces and Oudh who cannot buy sufficient cloth to cover even the upper half of their bodies properly, to protect themselves and their children from the piercing chill and cold of our northern winter nights; and remember, you gentlemen of the south, that the times are far more relentlessly severe with us there than with you here. (*Hear, hear.*) These miserable people cover themselves, their wives and children, when the season becomes very severe, with grass at night, and when the intensity of the cold drives away sleep, they warm themselves by burning some of this very grass. And even that is now and then taken away from them for feeding the cattle of the officials on tour. (*Shame.*) Such is the condition of the people to whom the honorable member of the Viceroy's Council said that an increase of 12 annas a year in their burthens would not mean any serious hardship! Do you think, gentlemen, such members would be appointed to the Council if the people were allowed any voice in their selection? (*No, no, never!*) And even if they were, by some mistake, once appointed, would they not be scornfully rejected at the next election? (*Yes, yes.*) But such men *are* appointed at present to the great disgust of the people, and the people are forced to submit to their legislatorship. (*Prolonged cheering.*)

I fear, gentlemen, I have taken up too much of your time, and I won't detain you any longer. I hope I have made it clear why we pray the Government to allow the people the privilege of electing at least half of the members of the Council, men whom the people esteem and confide in by reason of their loving sympathy with them in all their sorrows and joys. And I earnestly hope the Government will no longer delay granting us this simple rightful privilege, which while conducing greatly to our happiness, will not fail to add to the strength and glory of British rule in India. Gentlemen, I heartily support this resolution.

MR. SURENDRANATH BANERJEE: (*Bengal, No.* 1816, *in list.*)—Then rose and said:—SISTER AND BROTHER DELEGATES,—I think it will be admitted on all hands that we, the supporters of the Indian National Congress, are now entering upon what may be regarded as the most important stage in the history of the Congress movement. (*Hear, hear.*) The storm of opposition by which we were so fiercely assailed a year ago has now disappeared, and has dissolved itself into those primitive elements of isolated hate and individual despair which originally gave rise to it. The atmosphere around us is now clearer and serener. (*Cheers.*) We are now passing from the critical into what may be called the constructive stage in the history of the Congress movement. And Mr. Bradlaugh's Draft Bill is at once the token, the

2nd Day.

Res. II. Expansion and Reform of Legislative Councils.

symbol, and the herald of the new epoch which is dawning upon us. (*Cheers.*) I rejoice to note that you have resolved to devote your attention, this time, principally to this great question of the reform of the Legislative Councils. The reform of the Councils lies at the root of all other reforms. If you get that, you get everything else. On it depends in one sense the entire future of the country and the future of our administrative system. (*Hear, hear.*) There is nothing which we so heartily deplore, nothing which we so strongly condemn, nothing which seems to us to be in such utter conflict with the fundamental principles of political economy, the maxims of common sense, and even the ordinary considerations of prudence and righteous administration, as the enhancement of the salt duties. (*Loud and prolonged cheers.*) Is it conceivable that, if the people of this country had the slightest control over the deliberations of the Supreme Council, if the Council had even affected to be guided by the semblance of public opinion, a law of this kind could have been passed to the prejudice of the voiceless peasantry of the country? (*No, no, and applause.*) Now, I would appeal to my brother delegates, especially those who come from Bombay, and I would ask them to say whether if they had the smallest representation of the wealth, the culture, and the intelligence of this great Presidency in the Supreme Legislative Council, the Mamlatdars' Bill would have been passed in the way that it was passed. (*Loud applause.*) Turning to my brother journalists (*Hear, hear and cheers*) who are present here, I would ask them if the Officials Secrets' Act would have been smuggled through the Legislative Council in the way that it was done, if they had any influence over the deliberations of the body? (*No, no, and loud applause.*) Gentlemen, our Legislative Councils are so many farces (*Yes, yes, and cheers*); magnificent nonentities, gilded shams which may delude children, but cannot deceive sensible men like ourselves, who have grown into the adolescence of vigorous manhood. (*Loud applause.*) India, Sir, is now changing, and we are changing with the times (*Yes, yes, and loud cheers*) and the new-born circumstances of modern India demand that our Legislative Councils should be adapted to our present needs and wants. Gentlemen, you must have all read the minute of Lord Dufferin on the expansion and reform of the Legislative Councils. At that time there was no Official Secrets' Act (*laughter*) and the Despatch was accordingly published.* I wish to speak of Lord Dufferin with the utmost possible show of consideration. (*Laughter and applause.*) I remember,—very well remember—the time when my distinguished friend (Mr. A. O. Hume) behind me (*loud cheers*) with a faltering hand and a trembling heart sketched out the faint and meagre outlines of a scheme for the reform of our Councils. (*Loud applause.*) It was a dream, the Old Man's Hope† (*hear, hear*), but it is now about to be realized, to his great and undying glory, and the happiness of the countless millions of my own countrymen. (*Loud Applause.*) The question has indeed reached a practical stage. It is no longer in the region of vague and nebulous abstractions. I mean no disrespect to the late Viceroy when I say that he was no friend of the Congress movement, and that he was not sympathetic towards the aspirations which it represents. But even he, such as he was, was so influenced by the growing efflux of public opinion, that he felt himself called upon, as much in the interests of the people of this country as for the credit and good name of the English Government (*hear, hear*) to recommend the reform and the reconstitution of the Councils. He suggested the expansion of the Legislative Councils, and the reconstitution of the Provincial Councils upon a partially elective basis. (*Hear, hear.*) Then came Lord Lansdowne and I need hardly say that I desire to speak with the utmost possible respect and deference of the august representative of her most gracious Majesty the Queen-Empress, our Sovereign. Lord Lansdowne declared from his place in the Viceregal Council that he was prepared to reform the Councils, to widen and to extend their functions. (*Hear, hear.*) But unfortunately, there is a rift in the lute. (*Loud laughter and cheers.*) His Excellency is ominously silent with regard to the recognition of the elective system in the constitution of the Councils. (*Laughter.*) I desire to repeat what has been so eloquently said here on this platform by my friend, Mr. Bishan Narayen Dar, that no reform of the Councils will ever be regarded by the country as satisfactory which does not provide for a truly representative element in their constitution. (*Loud applause.*) Nothing indeed, has been done so far as we are aware, to give effect to Lord Lansdowne's declaration or to the recommendations of Lord Dufferin. All Governments, whether Liberal or Conservative, are slow to move in the path of reform. *Quieta non movere* is their motto. (*Laughter and cheers.*) They will let things alone. They will not move except under the irresistible pressure of public opinion. (*Loud applause.*) If our Government will not move, we can at any rate do so. (*Hear, hear, and loud applause.*) Our champion on this platform (*cheers*) has already taken the first step in this direction by his Draft Bill. (*Loud cheers.*)

The most important question that we have now to consider is undoubtedly that of the electorate. What is to be the constituency? What is to be the body that should return our members to the Legislative Councils? Direct representation is

* In Mr. Surendranath's own paper, "THE BENGALEE."

† "THE OLD MAN'S HOPE" is the name of a pamphlet, which helped, *inter alia*, to inaugurate the Congress movement.

altogether out of the question. However much we may wish it, any claims that we may urge in this direction would be considered inadmissible by the British public. We must, therefore, turn to our local bodies, our Municipal and District Boards, or we must adopt the suggestion of an intermediate electoral body which has been put forward by the Madras Committee. In this connection I cannot help referring to the onslaught that has been made upon Municipalities in general by my friend Mr. Norton. I cannot join him in those strictures. (*Laughter.*) Mr. Norton has no faith in Municipal institutions, although he is a distinguished ornament of one of the greatest Municipalities in the Indian Empire. (*Laughter and loud applause.*) I have myself been now for fifteen years a Municipal Commissioner—pardon me for this personal reference—and have come to have some faith in Municipal institutions. As far as Bengal is concerned, Local Self-Government has on the whole been a success (*yes, yes, and applause*), and if we say that it has not been so, we cut away the ground from underneath our feet. If we have not been successful in the matter of Local-Self Government we have no right to aspire to higher political privileges. (*Hear, hear, and cheers.*) But there can be no doubt that the local bodies, taken by themselves, would afford a constituency that would be extremely limited in its character. Even in Bengal some of the most distinguished men, of whom we are justly proud, are not members of our Municipalities (*hear, hear*), and would have no chance of being returned as members to the Legislative Councils, if the Municipalities alone were to form the constituency. My friend behind me, Mr. W. C. Bonnerjee, (*loud applause*), my friends opposite. Mr. Ananda Mohun Bose, and Babu Kalicharan Bannerjee are not connected with any Municipality ; and yet I am sure no Legislative Council would be complete without them. (*No, no, it won't.*) The local bodies thus forming a far too limited constituency, we must look elsewhere for a suitable electorate ; and the process that has been suggested is the formation of an intermediate body—of representatives—for the purpose of electing members to the Legislative Councils. The voters in the first instance, are to elect the Representatives who are to compose the electorate who in their turn are to return members to the Council. Thus by a process of what may be called double distillation, we provide a suitable machinery, at once independent and popular, for the election of members to the Councils.

Such is our scheme, and such are our proposals. And we commend them to the care of our friend on the platform (*hear, hear*), the Champion of Indian interests in the House of Commons. (*Loud and prolonged cheers.*) We wish him " God-speed " in his noble work for the good of India. (*Loud applause.*) The prayers of a nation attend him to his Western home. (*Loud cheers.*) Illustrious, indeed, is the muster-roll of those great Englishmen who, having consecrated their lives to the cause of India, have won an undying place in the grateful recollections of our people. (*Loud and prolonged cheers.*) Fawcett and Bright are dead and gone (*cheers*), but their names are embalmed in our memories (*loud cheers*), and will be bequeathed as pious legacies to after-generations. (*Loud and continued applause.*) And, sir, if I am permitted to take a glance into the future and to anticipate the verdict of history, this I will say with confidence that in the coming times no English name will occupy a higher, a worthier, a more affectionate place in our grateful recollections than that of Charles Bradlaugh. (*Loud cheers that continued for some minutes.*) We have great confidence in him. (*Applause.*) We have great confidence in the justice and generosity of the English people (*loud cheers*), and above all we rely with abounding faith upon the liberty-loving instincts of the greatest representative assembly in the world, (*cheers*), the palladium of English liberty, the sanctuary of the free and the brave—the British House of Commons. (*Loud and prolonged applause.*) When before such an assembly our prayer is pressed by such a man (*cheers*), there can come but one response which, I am confident, will be in accord with the great traditions of the English people, and will serve to consolidate the foundations of British rule in India and to broad-base it upon the affections of a happy, prosperous, and contented people. (*Loud applause which continued for several minutes.*)

The President : Gentlemen, you have heard the resolution proposed, seconded and supported. I now propose to put it clause by clause ; and if any gentleman wishes to move an amendment he can move it upon the particular clause which he wishes to amend. Is there any amendment upon clause 1 ? (" *No, no.*")

Clause 1 was put and agreed to.

Clause 2 was put and agreed to.

On clause 3 being put,

Mr. Dwarkanath Ganguli : (*Bengal, No.* 1828, *in list.*)—Rose and said:—I have an amendment to propose, *viz.*, that the word " *male*" preceding " British Subjects," in this clause, be omitted. In proposing the amendment I am fully aware that it will not be accepted by the British public. But I wish to draw your attention to this fact, *viz.*, that in certain respects we are somewhat in advance of the English people. You know that we have opened

2nd Day.

Res. II. Expansion and Reform of Legislative Councils.

all our Universities to our women; but, with the exception of the University of London, none of the English Universities have been really opened to women, though there are ladies Colleges at both Oxford and Cambridge. I would also draw attention to another fact. You have admitted to this deliberative assembly some distinguished ladies to represent, I presume, the women of this country; and you will, I venture to submit, be scarcely consistent if you do not accept my amendment. The English public have not yet allowed the privilege of voting to English women; but if we are to be consistent I would ask you to accept my amendment. It would be inconsistent in us not to allow women to vote while we allow other persons less competent to be voters. With these few remarks I propose the amendment.

Mr. N. Subramanyam: (*Madras, No.* 75, *in list*).—I second the amendment with great pleasure. I understand that the general qualifications for electors are to be the ability to read and write, the possession of property, and the payment of revenue to Government, or the payment of rent to a certain amount; and if men having these qualifications have the right to vote, I do not see why ladies having the same qualifications should not vote.

The amendment was put and lost. The clause was then put and agreed to.

Clause 4 was put and agreed to.

Clause 5 was read, and was further translated into Hindustani by Pandit Ajoodhia Nath.

Mr. B. G. Tilak: (*Deccan, No.* 401, *in list*).—I beg to propose as an amendment that instead of asking the different electoral bodies to elect members to the Imperial Legislature, the elected members of the Provincial Legislative Council should constitute the body to elect members to the Imperial Council. As I have moved this amendment more from a sense of duty to my province than from any confidence in my own oratorical powers I shall not trouble you with any platitudes about this National Congress. What I have to do is to place before you the reasons that induce us to come forward with this amendment, although we know there is very little chance of its being accepted by other provinces. You have been told that Bombay is opposed to the general scheme of the Legislative Council proposed by other provinces; and the position that we took has been represented to you in a rather misleading light. What I suggest is this, that we from Bombay have been opposed to the Madras Scheme, not on the ground that it is not based upon Local Boards and Municipalities. The opposition was not between Local Boards and Municipalities on the one hand and electoral bodies on the other, but whether we should have one electoral body or more than one, and I am glad to say to the Bombay delegates that this point, to which there was no real opposition, has been conceded. The next question is, having more than one electoral body, in some presidencies at any rate, will it be convenient to authorize each of these electoral bodies to send their own members to the Imperial Legislative Council, or will it be more convenient to invest elected members of the Provincial Council with that authority? Now, having, as I hope, shown that the Supreme Legislative Council must have on it representatives from the different presidencies, and not from districts* or divisions, I think it will be more in accordance with this principle to allow representations to each presidency than to a sub-division of each. It is not each division that has to elect a representative to the Imperial Council, but it is each presidency that has to do it; and if that is so, I place it before you whether, having several centres, each electoral body is to be allowed a representation in the Imperial Legislative Council. Then there is another objection which I would call objection No. 2. If you look to logical sequence you will find that the amendment I propose comes in its proper order. I will explain a little. You have adopted indirect representation; that is, the members of the Council are not to be directly sent by the voters but through the medium of electoral bodies. So then, having adopted the principle of indirect representation for the election of the Provincial Council, the natural sequence is that the Provincial Council should elect the Imperial Council. It follows in the same order. Then there is a third objection. You have been told that Municipalities and Local Boards are not allowed representation direct because Municipalities and Local Boards have not the best of your men. No such objection can be urged against our system of double election. You have the best men in your Provincial Councils, and if you entrust the best men thus selected with the task of selecting men to the Imperial Council I am sure you will not be placing the power in the wrong hands. The last objection I have to urge to the proposed system is that it is cumbrous every time to ask an electoral division to send members to the Provincial Council and also to the Imperial Council. It would be too cumbrous to be carried into practice. The time is short, and I can only summarize what I have to say. If you

* It has never, any where, it is believed, been contemplated to have separate electoral bodies for districts or any lesser tract than a province. Thus even in Bombay, where the question of having more than one electoral body in a Presidency was most strongly pressed, no one suggested more than four, viz: one for Sindh, one for Guzerat, one for Bombay and the Concan, one for the Deccan and Khandesh. In Madras the people are unanimously in favour of having only one electoral body for the whole Presidency.

will consider the logical sequence of the proposal, and the local circumstances of the several presidencies, especially that of Bombay, where there will be several electoral bodies—if you will consider that it is the Provincial interest that you have to represent, and not the divisional interest, in the Imperial Council, you will find that the amendment is at least more in conformity with the view you have already adopted than is the resolution as it now stands. With these few words I propose the amendment which will run thus :

PROPOSED : *"That elections to the Imperial Legislature shall be made by the elected members of the Provincial Councils."*

MR. GOKHALE : (*Deccan, No.* 418, *in list.*)—MR. PRESIDENT AND FELLOW DELEGATES,—I come before you with great reluctance and greater diffidence to second the proposal which has been placed before you by my friend Mr. Tilak. I will briefly state the various reasons for which I am in favour of the amendment, as opposed to the original proposition. I should not have troubled you, but I believe that the scheme proposed in the amendment would work better that the one in the original proposal. I will merely enumerate the various points, and say a little in explanation of each. My first point is that there would be unnecessary trouble. You have already election at two stages, and what we want you to do is to go a little further and have election at three stages ; thereby all the cumbrousness of the original method would be avoided, and the thing would be reduced to a simple principle. The presumption is that all the best men will be in the Provincial Council and, if they are there, I do not see why they should not, from their own body, depute two, three or four persons to the Supreme Council. My third point is that there was already an objection to the Local Boards and Municipalities electing representatives to the Provincial Councils. It was said that the persons elected on Local Boards and Municipalities are elected for a different function, and that the persons to be elected on the Legislative Councils have to discharge different functions. No such objection can be raised to the amendment placed before you. The functions of members of the Provincial and of the Supreme Councils are not greatly dis-similar. The objection with regard to Municipalities and Local Boards does not apply in the present case. As my friend who has placed this proposition before you has said, the system proposed in the resolution is very cumbrous. Whenever there is a vacancy you will have to go through the whole form and there will be a great deal of unnecessary labor. I therefore ask you to accept this principle of election at three stages instead of two.

RAJAH T. RAMA ROW : (*Madras, No.* 43, *in list.*)—Gentlemen, I have a few words to say against this amendment. My reasons are these. We have found it impracticable, under present circumstances to give the direct principle of election to the people, we therefore abandoned the project and said that there should be an intermediate body who should have the right of electing members to the Legislative Councils. This electoral body directly represents the people ; and to allow the members elected to the Provincial Council by this electoral body to elect members to the Supreme Council would be delegating the functions entrusted to the electoral body in the first instance to another body, which is illegal and illogical. We should have only one electoral body, if possible, in Madras ; but with regard to the other presidencies, let them have one or more in order to suit the conveniences of the time being.

The amendment was put and lost.

THE PRESIDENT : Is there any other amendment ?

MR. KALIPRASANNA KAVYABISHARAD : (*Bengal, No.* 1834, *in list.*)—GENTLEMEN AND BROTHER DELEGATES,—I beg to propose that for the word "Christian," in the resolution, you "substitute Europeans, Eurasians and Native Christians." There may be people amongst the Europeans, for instance, who are not at all Christians. This is my proposal which I submit to your kind consideration. I have no capacity for addressing such a huge audience, and I am not going to inflict a speech upon you.

THE PRESIDENT : Does any one second the amendment ?

MR. N. SUBRAMANYAM : (*Madras, No.* 75, *in list.*)—MR. PRESIDENT : I second the amendment and I wish to say a few words with regard to it. Although Europeans, Eurasians and Native Christians may all be Christians in general, yet their interests are not identical. Some of those interests which would naturally come before the Legislative Council are interests not affecting so much their religion, because the policy of the Government of India is that of neutrality so far as religious tenets are concerned, but their rights as different sections of the community. And I can, without enumerating them, imagine—and I think you can imagine—that the interests of Europeans, Eurasians and Native Christians may not in all cases be precisely the same ; on that account alone I will second the amendment which has been proposed.

2nd Day.

Res. II. Expansion and Reform of Legislative Councils.

The amendment was then put to the meeting and lost.

Mr. N. Subramanien : Gentlemen, I thank you still. (*Laughter.*)

Rev. R. A. Hume : (*Deccan, No.* 486, *in list.*)—Mr. President, Ladies and Gentlemen, Since I came here this morning I have been over-urged, by my fellow delegates from the Deccan, to propose an amendment with reference to the most sensitive and delicate part of this entire proposition, viz., that which relates to the representation of minorities. I have the greatest hesitation in taking this action, first because I am confident that even a large proportion of those who are interested in these minorities will be slow to accept any modification which is proposed ; and in the second place I am myself somewhat in doubt whether the time has come for it ; but as I believe I was elected a representative by the voices of the people of my district, and as I am requested by them to present this proposition, it has become my duty to do so, the more so because it represents the principle which will more and more dominate this movement ; namely, that it is safe to trust the people. It is not necessary to give minorities the safeguard which is attempted by this clause, it is better to depend upon another safe-guard which is secured by the nomination of one-fourth of the members by the Government. My amendment therefore is this, to omit the sentence in the fifth clause from the words " In such-wise that the total number of Europeans, Christians, Hindus and Mahomedans respectively," to the end of the sentence, and substitute there for the following :—" *Whereas with a view to make up deficiencies in elections, the power to make nominations has been reserved to Government, it is undesirable to make any other special provision for the protection of minorities.*"

In support of this amendment I have one word to say. In a country with the past history of India, with its divisions caused by language, by race, by religion, and other things, it is most natural that those communities which are in a minority should fear lest if this power of representation were given to the entire community they might be over-looked. This is a reasonable fear ; at the same time if we have in a large sense the right and the qualifications for asking the Government to endow us with the privilege of electing representatives we ought to be able—and I verily believe that in a considerable measure we are able—to take care that even as regards minorities we are properly represented, without such safeguards as are attempted in the original Resolution. It is a pleasure to one who like myself comes from another part of the world for a particular purpose, to say that I have always found it safe to trust the people. (*Hear, hear.*) I for one should always expect that to be true, and so to my mind the wisest policy ever *is* to trust the people. Even if in a particular case at a particular time I, or those in whom I am specially interested, may not get the full representation to which in our judgment we are entitled, yet on the whole we ought to secure it by our public spirit, by our freedom from prejudice, our freedom from all restrictions, and we should be ready even to take less, than we might otherwise be entitled to, in order to set a good example, in order to emphasise a righteous principle and help on this great cause. However I think we can hardly expect that this large Congress of communities, in its present position, should be prepared entirely to accept this proposition, yet I feel it a pleasure to follow the request of my brother delegates and to say that I believe, that certainly in such parts of the country as I live in, it is safe and it is right, without such safe guards, to trust the people to give even the minorities a fair representation ; and when they are not fairly represented, as may sometimes be the case, to trust the wise Government under which we live to make up such deficiencies by nomination and not further seek to emphasise and keep alive distinctions which ought not, longer, to exist. (*Cheers.*)

Mr. Samuel G. Lee Pillai : (*Deccan, No.* 487, *in list.*)—Mr. President, Ladies and Gentlemen,—I second the amendment. Before proposing to trouble you I wrote to the Secretary, but unfortunately I have not been able to bring on this point earlier. I am glad that I have now the opportunity of presenting my remarks in defence of my countrymen. I adopt the country of India though I am not born in India. I am a Singalese, and I am your servant in the cause of education. I have very great pleasure in seeing so large an audience assembled here for the benefit of India, (" *Question.*") The great point which we have to bring before the British Parliament in such a way that we may realize our political aspirations is (" *Question.*")

This amendment has been brought forward by the Revd. Mr. Hume (a man of great experience and wisdom, a man who knows the whole history of the Deccan), and it is with great pleasure I support it. You may want to know the reason why I support it ? I think you will remember with great pleasure the visit of Mr. Caine, M. P., the great Champion of the temperance cause in India (*Question.*) Mr. Caine, told us at a meeting in connection with this very Bill that Parliament would be very glad to give the very privilege for which we are fighting to-day, under suitable conditions and restrictions, and he especially referred to one point, *viz.,* that we should be careful about safe-guarding the interests of our minorities. You know what takes place in England with regard to constituencies there. You know how the Irish people are governed because they are in the minority. (" *Question.*") You know what suffering there has been. They have no members of Parliament (*nonsense, nonsense*) simply because they are in the minority. We should take fairly into consideration the question of minorities. Parsees, Mahomedans, Christians and all.

The President : I think that the gentleman who has just spoken has made a little mistake. He told us that he was going to second the amendment, but in reality he wishes to oppose it ; however there is another gentleman who has come forward to second it.

Mr. Hardeoram N. Haridas : (*Guzerat, No.* 827, *in list.*)—Ladies and Gentlemen,—I quite agree with Mr. Norton that minorities should be represented. At the same time I beg to differ from him, in as much as I do not agree with him that minorities are not represented if the principle, of insisting on the same proportion of Parsees, Hindus, Musalmans, amongst the members, that exists in the population they represent, is disallowed. To recognise such a principle would be very bad policy. We do not want sectional differences in the Legislature ; we do not want a Legislature for Parsees separately, for Hindus separately, for Jews separately, for Mahomedans or for Christians separately. The business of the Legislative Council has nothing to do with these matters. I do not see how the question of a man being a Mahomedan or a Hindu has any relation to the question of the Salt Tax for example. For my part I would rather be represented by a European like Mr. Bradlaugh, by a European like Sir William Wedderburn, or any other equally good and able gentleman, than by nine-tenths of my Hindu brethren. If we make these divisions in caste or religion I do not know where they will land us. There are so many sections amongst the Hindus themselves, and we may have to look to the several creeds existing amongst them ; and then the Jains would want to be represented separately, the Sivites would want to be represented separately, the Jews would want to be represented separately, and I do not know where we should be carried. By allowing these caste or creed representatives to be brought into the Legislature you will be strengthening the hands of our opponents. Again, the spirit of the Congress, as shown in its literature, has been from the beginning against any such distinctions of caste and creed. (*Cheers.*)

The President : Does any one wish to speak in support of this amendment ?

Mr. Eardley Norton : (*Madras, No.* 44, *in list.*)—As the original proposer of this Resolution I should like to say a few words in defence of the section as it stands. The amendment which has been moved by my reverend friend Mr. R. Hume has been moved in a spirit with which I thoroughly and fully sympathise. I am perfectly certain that there is no Lady or Gentleman inside the walls of this Congress Hall who does not fully appreciate the sincerity of Mr. Hume's motives in coming forward to make this proposition. But, gentlemen, I hope the Rev. Mr. Hume will forgive me when I say that I cannot help thinking that his amendment is somewhat Utopian. I quite understand, in theory, that perfect equality of Christianity which recognises only all that is good in man and leaves out all that is bad ; but gentleman, I rarely find that theory carried out into practice, (*laughter*) and however willing I may be to believe that the time will come when we may be able to trust the people, in the way Mr. Hume desires us to trust them, I am perfectly convinced that that time has not yet come. But there are two very grave objections to the amendment to which I would particularly direct your attention. The first objection is that it would take away absolutely the safe-guard of minorities. No reliance can be placed on inductions drawn from England or any other European country and attempted to be applied to the conditions under which we ourselves are placed. In England the people are homogeneous ; here in India the very converse is true. It is impossible to shut our eyes to the fact that not merely does a racial distinction exist, to a marked degree, but that here, also, are very great differences of opinion on matters theologic. Now I would put aside for one moment the question of theological disputes. But imagine this amendment accepted : imagine the safe-guard as to minorities withdrawn, and imagine, as may well be, that some great wave of a political crisis should sweep over the country when Mahomedans would stand on the one side and Hindus on the other. What would then become of the Mahomedans ? With all the best and most Christian-like intentions on the part of the Hindus, human passion would assert itself ; and when you came to the question of counting heads or hands, the Hindus would forget all about this theoretical universal brotherhood and make it a point to see that no Mahomedan should be returned (*no, no.*) Perhaps it may not be so in your opinion but it is so in mine. I put it upon no grounds of theological dislike ; but in these great crises men loose their heads and, in their effort to obtain some particular object which they desire, they sacrifice, rightly or wrongly, everything else. Such a state of things may well arise here, and if it does I think you will agree with me that it would be

2nd Day.

Res. II. Expansion and Reform of Legislative Councils.

most deplorable indeed, if the proposed safe-guard should be taken away and Mahomedans and Parsees and Europeans should find themselves without the power of getting into the Council. We have been discussing this matter on the grounds of the elective principle and we have said that we intend to have that principle, pure and undiluted ; but my reverend friend's amendment cuts it away, because it says that if a sufficient number of Mahomedans are not returned the deficiencies are to be filled up—by whom ?—not by the people but by the Government. I beg his pardon ! The Government I understand are to use their nomination to fill up these so called vacancies or deficiencies. The Government will not have sufficient nominations at their disposal. The time might arrive when the Hindus might reject all these various communities and Government would not then have enough seats to represent all classes other than the Hindus. (*Cries of No, no, never.*) Lastly I am satified that no measure which does not contain such a proposal as this contains, will commend itself either to the Government here or the Government at home. No ! let us insist upon proportional representation, leaving it to Government to strenghten this from its nominations in the case of any section where this seems, to it, needful ; with these few remarks I leave the matter to your discretion,

The amendment was then put to the meeting and lost.

MUNSHI HIDAYET RASUL : (*Oudh, No.* 1477, *in list.*)—Addressed the meeting in Urdu as follows* :—MR. CHAIRMAN and Brother Delegates. To-day on seeing my fierce aspect, you might have thought that I was some great enemy of the Congress. But indeed it is not so. (*Cheers.*) Probably you have not forgotten what we did for the Congress movement last year. We have borne hateful taunts and great hardship for the Congress. (*Cries of no, no.*) But as they were all suffered at the hands of our Musalman brethren, we do not wish to narrate them before this great assembly. Again when we duly consider the views of those opponents, we find that they are not our enemies in the least. Our Musalman brethren will look at us with wrathful eyes only so long as they think that we, in a league with the Hindus, are the ill-wishers of the Musalmans and injurers of their National Honour. For I want you to bear in mind that those brave brethren of ours have a certain characteristic by virtue of which they will not advance a step until they have fully considered the consequences. But having advanced once, if it please God, they will never retreat. (*Cheers.*) In view of these facts should we look upon them as our enemies and should we so behave towards them as to make them our enemies in reality ? Nay, instead of widening the gulf of separation, it is advisable for us to show them, nay, to the whole world, that we are not the people to agree to anything without proper consideration as some persons have thought us to be. We are not come here for the sake of any person and we are not come here to prejudice the rights and injure the National Honour of the Musalmans by any underhand means. (*Order, order.*) And rather than that any harm be caused to Islam (*a Mahomedan Delegate—who wants to injure Islam? You, I think—cries of order*) or to the people who profess it, at our hands or tongue, we ask God to let death overpower us. By Musalmans I do not mean those who are atheists at heart, nor does any Musalman think them to be his co-religionists, so these people are outside the holy circle. (*Loud cries of order, order.*)

You can understand under what difficulties we few persons, (*cries of, more than* 250) who are supposed to be representatives of 5 crores of Musalmans, are placed. Firstly, petty officers of the different districts frown at us ; secondly, Government is looking askance at us to see how we conduct ourselves ; thirdly our nation is adverse to the Congress movement (*cries of no, no, it is not*) and fourthly the anxiety for the preservation of their honour and their rights is constantly preying upon our minds. Under these circumstances is it advisable that we remain dumb and quietly bear the adverse criticism that is being made against us ? We look upon those delegates who have come here simply to enjoy themselves and to say 'ay' to everything proposed as faithless and murderers of their brethren. (*Order, order.*) Perhaps my language is unpleasant to some improvident persons but we ought not to care for them in the least. We have not joined the Congress movement to sell our freedom of speech. We will support this movement only so long as our National Honour is not injured. None should expect more from us. We have told you before that we have no right to urge our personal views. Being taken for representatives we must speak in the same capacity and for this reason I want you to believethat the views I urge are the views of 5 crores of Musalmans. (*No, no, they are not—are you the only Musalman here ?*) We Musalmans are opposed to the several proposals made in this matter. We have been frequently told that the number of Musalman Councillors will not be less than that of the Hindu Members. (*Never, never.*) At the Allahabad Congress the Honourable

---

*** This is this gentleman's own translation of his speech,**

Pandit Ajoodhianath distinctly stated that the four hundred* Musalman Delegates at that Congress were equal in importance to thirteen hundred Hindu Delegates that were present there. This falls in with our view. We assure you that out of 5 crores of Musalmans there will be found hardly five thousand of them who will agree that the number of seats for the Musalmans be less than those for the Hindus in the various Councils. Upon a calm consideration you will find that this is a legitimate aspiration. In support of this fact I will mention two or three arguments; 1. (*a*) Up to this time the Government has not treated us in any manner less favourably than the Hindus. (*b*) The Government has given us an equal share with them in every department of public service, nay, in some departments, even a larger share; so far as I know in the North-Western Provinces and Oudh, nay, if I do not make a mistake in Bengal and Behar, Musalmans are employed in all grades of the public service from Tahsildarships to the office of a Judge. If by accident any of such offices is withheld, our press at once takes up the matter and Government immediately replies that Musalmans also shall have them and indeed it does fulfil its promises. Then why do Hindus, in forgetfulness of their claims of brotherhood, want to deprive us of that honourable position which Government has always accorded us? I do not understand why Musalmans should join this Congress if the forfeiture of that position be demanded by the Hindus or if such loss should prove to be the result of it. If we apprehend such a consequence we must clearly bid *salam* to this movement. You must understand that the Musalmans will not be the worse for keeping aloof from the Congress. You may try while we shall pray that you may succeed. In that case we shall have the advantage of sharing your reward without having had to share your toils. It is impossible that there will be Hindu members in the Councils to the exclusion of the Musalmans. (*No one proposed this.*) Nay, if it please God we shall not have a smaller number of Councillors. Now tell me who will be such a fool as to join the Congress movement in the face of these facts and bear to see his National Honour injured. 2. I say that if our Hindu Brethren are proud of their advancement in English education, we are proud of our religious zeal and our valorous instincts. If they can by their pen help the Government in administering the internal affairs of the country, we can by submitting our necks to the sharp glittering swords of the enemies and by pursuing them to their very guns protect the Government against foreign invasions. And the time is nigh when Government will, with due appreciation, avail itself of these our valuable instincts. Because when that powerful enemy which is at the gate of India advances a step further, you will see that the people who will with a firm resolve first come forward to assist the Government, will be those whom our Hindu brethren call Musalmans, and of whom a division has already put up its fortifications in the plains of Afghanistan. (*Loud cheers.*) We can say unhesitatingly that our nation can give soldiers in numbers far exceeding those in which you exceed us. 3. I do not know of any Hindu Consuls in foreign countries. In this department, therefore, we totally exclude you. Then is it not unjust that you should try to mar our such high position as a nation? Is it the result of our joining the Congress movement that our Hindu brethren do not regard us as their useful comrades in times of need, and grant us an equal number of seats in the various Councils. And if Hindus have no mind to do this, then it is a pity. I am fully sensible that my defiant speech may be appearing unpleasant to you, but if it please God, and you agree with our demand, you will reap a rich harvest in future. I also tell you frankly that though it is the business of both, the Hindus and the Musalmans, to sow the seed of this movement, yet for a long time, by reason of their advancement in English education, it will be the lot of the former only to enjoy the fruits. But we do not envy you. We regard the welfare of the country as our own. But, brethren, you cannot clap hands without using both of them. Take you something and leave something for us. In conclusion I promise you that if you accept this principle of equality you will have on your side 90 per cent. of Musalmans from to-morrow and the remaining 10 per cent. from the day after to-morrow. (*Cheers.*)

MR. ALI MAHOMED BHIMJEE: (*Bombay, No.* 892, *in list.*)—MR. PRESIDENT, LADY DELEGATES AND BROTHER DELEGATES.—The speaker who preceded me, speaking in Urdu, has proposed an amendment. It has reference to the minority section in the fifth clause. He wants to omit the mention of Mahomedans and to add the following :—

"*Provided that the number of Mahomedan members shall always be equal to that of the Hindus, in both the Imperial and Provincial Councils.*"

The amendment has not been proposed with any distrust towards the Hindu majority, but it is put forward relying on your spirit of tolerance. In the same spirit which actuated you to come forward and embrace all the Mahomedans as brother delegates—with the same intentions and the same feelings this amendment has been placed before you. You

---

* As a matter of fact, the Mahomedans at Allahabad numbered 221, the Hindus (including members of the Arya and Brahmo Samajes, &c.,) 965.

know the condition of the Mahomedans, you know their ignorance, you know that in number they are not equal to the Hindus, you know that in intellectual power and English education they are not equal to the Hindus but in physical power they are equal or more than equal to the Hindus. As my friend says Russia is now knocking at our doors, and if Government were to treat us more liberally and have confidence in us we would certainly give it our heads. I will not take up your time for I have lost my voice and I am not audible. I have spoken those few words and leave the matter to your generosity and humanity. And I beg you will be actuated by the same feelings of friendship that you at present exhibit towards the Mahomedans, aud allow this amendment to be carried with acclamation.

Mr. Hamid Ali Khan : (*Oudh, No.* 1494, *in list.*)—Gentlemen, you perhaps do not know who I am, and perhaps there is nothing in my appearance to tell you, (except the pin which I wear, with a crescent and a star,) that I am a Mahomedan. I may as well explain that though a Mahomedan I do not represent the Mahomedan Community alone, but I also have in my pocket a certificate showing that I am in an equal degree a trusted representative of the Hindu Community. I had now better speak in Urdu. So that all my co-religionists several of whom I see do not understand English thoroughly, may the better follow me.

He then spoke as follows in Urdu. Before I proceed to consider the amendment and point out the fact that it is based upon a mistaken notion of the principles which ought to and do guide our scheme of representation, permit me to say that we are all endeavouring to create an United India and to form ourselves into one nation so far, at the least, as our political rights and wants are concerned. We do not come here to spread disunion and disagreement as this amendment, which implies a want of confidence in our Hindu Brethren, is certainly calculated to do, especially when brought forward in speeches of the tone to which we have listened. I do not wish to call in question the motive of the gentleman who moved the amendment. However indiscreet and unbecoming his language. (*Hear, hear.*) I trust that it has been with the best of motives that he has taken this step. I am willing to assume that he has been actuated by a sincere and honest desire to protect, as he understands them, the interests of the Mahomedans, and benefit them by his advocacy. Let none think, my Mahomedan brethren, that I myself am impelled by any other desire, when I tell you that I honestly believe that while no good can come out of demanding or even obtaining an equal numbers of Musalman members on the Legislative Councils, you will necessarily rouse suspicion regarding your relations with and intentions towards your Hindu brethren, by attempting thus, without any just cause or reason, to violate the principle of population on which our entire scheme of representation has been based, in furtherance of what some of you suppose to be your own special class interests. (*Hear, hear.*)

Moreover you directly incite other communities, who are now perfectly satisfied with the scheme as propounded, to make similar preposterous claims. If you disregard the population standard—if you say no matter if the Hindus number 15 crores and we only five, we will have as many members in the Councils as they—why, by a parity of reason or unreason, should not the Parsees, the Jains, the Sikhs, the Europeans, the Eurasians each and all claim to have as many members in the Councils as you or the Hindus?—Gentlemen, the thing is absurd. (*Cheers.*) You must adopt some standard as a basis for a scheme of representation and on the whole that of population is the fairest for all and certainly the most favourable to us. If instead of population, property or education were selected as the basis; we should be far worse off—but one of these three must be adopted, and adhered to, or the absurd result I have just indicated to you is arrived at.

But the fact is that the amendment is based upon a wholly mistaken and baseless fear, that if the Hindus exceed the Mahomedans in Council they will carry all before them and injure Musalman interests. Now in the first place as has been said at least an hundred times since this Congress first met—there is no such a thing in the ordinary secular matters that come before the Councils, as Hindu interests and Mahomedan interests—our interests in all such matters are absolutely one and undivided. But even if there were separate Mahomedan interests,—and I as a Mahomedan, truly wonder what they can be—how could the Hindus in the Council, even if they were 5 to 1, as compared with the Mahomedans, and even if they wished it—which long experience has convinced me that they do not—how could they injure these interests? Are there not to be European and Eurasian members, amongst those elected, besides Sikhs and Parsees in some Provinces? Are not one fourth of the members to be officials who sit *ex-officio*, and one fourth to be nominees of Government, amongst whom probably there would be some Mahomedans? Are all these going to combine with the Hindus to deal unjustly with the Mahomedans? It is absolutely absurd—in the first place the educated Hindus have never—and all history is my witness—attempted in any way to injure the Mahomedans—and you will only have educated Hindus elected to the Council—men of light and leading—and in the second place even if they wished it ever so, our legislative scheme renders it absolutely impossible for them to do anything of the kind. (*Loud cheers.*)

This amendment then is calculated to create disunion and breed mutual distrust, it is absolutely illogical and leads, if accepted, to a palpable absurdity and it is based upon a purely mistaken fear, ungenerous and unreasonable in itself and originating in an inexcusable ignorance of what is, and is not, possible under our scheme for the reform of the Legislative Councils which has now been, in all essentials, before the country for the last four years. I trust therefore that you will unanimously reject it. (*Loud cheers.*)

Syed Wahid Ali Rizwi : (*North-West Provinces, No.* 1686, *in list.*)—From Moradabad in Rohilkhand)—then spoke in Urdu, he said :

Mr. President and Brother Delegates, I do not rise now to second or support the amendment proposed by Munshi Hidayet Rasul, which stipulates for an equal number of Mahomedans and Hindus, on all the Councils, but to go a step or two beyond his contention. To my mind his contention that the number of Mahomedans should only equal that of the Hindus is far from satisfactory and by no means what a due regard for Mahomedan interests and the interests of the country demand.

Taking this Congress as a whole, I can hardly allow to it the title of National—(*why, why ?*) It is much more of a Hindu than a Mahomedan Congress ; whereas if it is to be truly national and adequately represent the best portion of the nation, it ought to be far more Mahomedan than Hindu (*cries of no, no, nonsense—why ? and considerable interruption.*)

The President : Gentlemen, silence please. One of the things we want to show the world is that we are able to hear the other side. (*Quite so, but he must be decorous—he must not insult us.*) Well, well gentlemen, the more disagreeable are the things said, the more patiently let us listen—I am sure this gentlemen has something he wishes to say even though he may not put it with much consideration for the feelings of others—and you will I am sure set him a better example, by letting him say what he has to say without interruption.

Syed Wahid Ali Rizwi, resuming : As I was saying, to be truly national, this Congress ought to be far more Mahomedan than Hindu, and indeed, had the Mahomedans, as a whole, taken to the Congress as the Hindus have, there would this day be present more Mahomedans than Hindus—for the Mahomedans are far more independent, energetic, and self-helpful than the Hindus, and if their 50 millions believed in and supported the Congress as the 200 millions of Hindus do, you would have here this day, believe me, many more Mahomedans than Hindus, whereas I do not believe that we have here even one Mahomedan to every 5 Hindus.

Mr. President, the design of the Congress is doubtless good enough—I have no quarrel with its fundamental idea, which is to give scope for the full expression of the views and wishes, the wants and aspirations of the Indian Nation—but what I say is that despite all the efforts of the Hindus, to raise aloft and decorate and glorify this great work, it yet remains and must remain until the Musalmans fully espouse the cause, a mere dead body—It will be for the Musalmans to breathe life unto it, and they must constitute its main-spring if success is to attend its career.

Gentlemen, I must emphatically assert that without the hearty support of those true Musalmans, who represent the generations and dynasties of the old Islamite conquerors, and who are mainly now to be found in the North-West Provinces, Oudh and the Punjab, the Congress will come to nothing, now or hereafter, but if these descendants of our great warriors of the past once side, in earnest, with the Congress, then undoubtedly this will triumph. For it is on these that the British Government relies—never has that Government ceased to understand how much it owes to these loyal, statesmen-soldiers, the true supporters of its wide-spread Indian Empire. Not only has it ever sympathized with these, but it has sacrificed its own interests to uphold these brave hands who fight for Britain's Empire in every moment of need and peril.

The support of these high class Mahomedans will lift the Congress to something like that high position that the Mahomedans occupy on the platform of the world's nationalities, where they stand elevated to a dignity and grandeur to which the Hindus have never had

2nd Day.

Res. II. Expansion and Reform of Legislative Councils.

any pretensions since they were conquered by the Mahomedans, and were thus so reduced and lowered that they are now naturally unfit to execute higher duties and perform the greater works of the present day. (*Cries of no, no—bosh! Nonsense!*)

Mr. President: If now you ask how I prove the great superiority of the high class Mahomedans over the Hindus, my reply is simple. In the total population only one-fifth are Mahomedans, and amongst the Mahomedans so-called, only one-fifth are of the real blood, the pure descendants of the Arabs, Moguls and Afghans. So that of the typical Musalman, there are but ten millions against two hundred and forty millions of the rest of the population and yet this ten millions furnishes more officers in the higher grades of the Political, Military and Civil branches of the Administration than the whole of the rest of the population—in other words every true high class Mahomedan is as valuable to the State as any 25 of other races, castes and creeds. (*Laughter.*)

Now if India is to be represented let her be represented by her best and not by her inferior races, and in accordance with these views and out of regard to the past glories of our great and ancient race, I call upon this Congress to rule, not that there shall always be as many Mahomedans as Hindus in Council, but that there shall always be *three* times as many Musalman as Hindu members. (*Laughter and cries of ten, ten.*)

Syed Mir-uddin Ahmed Balkhi: (*Behar No.* 1734, *in list.*)—Rose and spoke in Urdu as follows:—Mr. President and Brother Delegates,—Although it was never my intention to speak on a political theme in an assembly like this, where the ablest and best men from all quarters of India are entertaining the audience with their charming eloquence; yet since some Mahomedan delegates have expressed conflicting opinions on one of the most difficult problems before us, and as I think such diversity of opinions might cause some harm to the whole country in future; I believe it to be my duty to speak out my thoughts on this question, even though I lack the ability of doing so effectually.

Gentleman, Mr. Norton has proposed for your acceptance a resolution which requires that half the members of the Legislative Councils should be *elected* and that among those so elected the numerical strength of Hindus, Mahomedans, Christians, and Parsee should be, so far as may be practicable, in proportion to their respective populations. On the other hand sone Mahomedan gentlemen have brought forward an amendment to this effect,—viz.: that the number of Mahomedans in the Council should be equal to that of the Hindus and it is in connection with this amendment that I beg leave of you to say a few words.

Gentlemen, if I allowed my natural impulses to guide my actions, or selfishness to enter my head and heart; then of course I should support this amendment,—nay, I might even go the length of proposing with the last speaker that there should be three times as many Mahomedans as Hindus on the Councils or go a step further and insist that none but genuine Mahomedans should be returned to the Councils; that Mahomedans only should legislate for the whole of India; and that all the Indian subjects of Her Majesty should be bound to observe such laws. But gentlemen, are such natural impulses and such selfishness justifiable under the present circumstances of the country? Or does the Mahomedan sense of justice prompt us to entertain such unworthy thoughts? No. We Mahomedans of India are the subjects of the same British Government under whose paternal care Hindus, Mahomedans, Parsees, Christians and all the various castes and communities of the country thrive alike. And just as our rights and privileges are inseparably connected with the country and the Government; so are those of the Hindus, Parsees, Christians and all the rest of our fellow-subjects. Then does our Mahomedan sense of justice make us ignore everybody's rights save our own? Every creed and caste has the same immutable right of representation on the Council that we Mahomedans have. And in my judgment nothing can be more just and fair than the principle of election according to numerical proportion. Oh! my Mahomedan brethren. I quite endorse what you say as to our unimpeachable loyalty to the Government and that we will stand by it through thick and thin. Undoubtedly we Mahomedans are bound by our religious tenets to obey and submit to our Sovereign. It is our duty absolutely to obey the ruling power of the day. But oh my co-religionist brethren, you are now assembled in the *National Congress*; you are praying the Government jointly to give us all those political rights and privileges which you respectfully ask for. It is not that the Hindus, Mahomedans, Christians and Parsees are going to ask for these privileges separately, each for himself. We have assembled here for one common object, and that object is a secular and not a religious one. We standing here on a common political platform appeal to the British nation's sense of justice to permit us, their Indian fellow-subjects, to enjoy something of the rights and privileges which have made them what they are. On such an occasion Mahomedans cannot call themselves Mahomedans; nor Hindus, Hindus; but rather forgetting all differences of creed, caste and colour we should call ourselves *Indians*. Undoubtedly every one present seems to feel so, or else why should he be here in this national assembly? And on an occasion like this any vaunting of our own particular merits, any ostentatious display of our own loyalty, as if we only were loyal, seems to be absolutely out of place; though it might be proper when we go to ask the Government for anything concerning the Mahomedans only.

Gentlemen, I am extremely conservative in religious matters, but in things political and social I am perfectly liberal. In point of religion a Mahomedan is a Mahomedan when he is praying in his mosque, a Hindu is a Hindu when he is worshipping in his temple; a Parsee is a Parsee when offering incense to his sacred fire; and a Christian is a Christian when he is kneeling down in his church; in short one can be called to belong to a particular religion only so long as he is engaged in its work. But in the political world I strongly object to distinguishing people or communities on account of religious differences as if they constituted different nationalities. Generally the distinction of nationalities is made in consideration of the countries inhabited; *e. g.* the people of England are called the English nation and the people of India, the Indian nation. When you call the English people collectively the English nation then you do not mean to say that you include in that term only the Protestants and exclude the Catholics or only the Christians and exclude the Jews, the free-thinkers or people of any other religious belief. Consequently there appears to be no reason why we people of India should not be called the Indian nation irrespective of our religious differences. O, my Mahomedan brethren remember well that unless you entertain free and liberal views in matters political you will make no progress in the world. Personally I was for striking out those words from the original resolution which point to the restriction of castes and creed, the minorities clause in fact, and of leaving the principle of election free from all such encumbrances; and I would have proposed that; but since the field of our liberty is circumscribed within rather narrow bounds, and we are assured that in England some protection of minorities will be insisted on, I for the present quite agree with the resolution as it stands.

O ye people of the Indian nation, whether in point of religion you be Hindus or Mahomedans, Parsees or Christian or of any other denomination whatsoever; remember that if you ever give room to feelings of religious bigotry and difference in your heart, you will never be entitled to receive those free British institutions which you are so eagerly praying for. God be praised that the time has come when we begin to feel the genial warmth of mutual sympathy and fellow-feeling; for, were it not so, it would have been impossible for so many Hindus, Mahomedans, Parsees and Christians thus lovingly to come together this day.

After these few remarks I hope gentlemen you will kindly accept the original resolution as proposed by Mr. Norton.

MUNSHI NASIRUDDIN AHMED: (*Benares, No.* 1694, *in list.*)—Then spoke in Urdu as follows:—MR. PRESIDENT AND GENTLEMEN, I am a Mahomedan delegate from Benares. I regret that Mr. Hidayet Rasul and Mr. Wahid Alli, should have put their amendments before you with such violence and with such a lack of common courtesy. The amendment is opposed to the first principles of our scheme of representation, for why should five crores of ourselves have the same number of representatives as fifteen crores of Hindus? But the proposal itself was a fair enough subject to submit quietly to the Congress for calm consideration, not to be thundered out at its head, with denunciations and empty vaunts. (*Cheers.*)

Mr. Hidayet Rasul has talked much of the honour of our nation. I only know one nation in India, the Indians—all in fact who are born and bred there—and in this too I have the countenance of Sir Syed Ahmed, who though he may not, at one time, have favoured the Congress, knew well what he was speaking of when he laid this down distinctly, that here in India there was only one nation, the Indians, let them be Mahomedans or Hindus. (*Cheers.*) But if by our nation, Mr. Hidayet Rasul means our co-religionists, then let me tell him that it is not by vain boastings, or loud swaggerings about our valour, that our honour is to be preserved, but by showing that we are at least as reasonable, earnest and considerate of the feelings of others as the professors of other creeds and faiths.

He has told us that five crores of Musalmans think precisely as he does—for the honour of my people I am bound to say that there are not five lakhs who think as he does and certainly not five thousand, educated Mahomedans, in the whole Empire, who would have put forward *any* proposition, let alone this amendment, in the same unseemly and unbecoming manner. And now, gentlemen, as regards the merits of the amendment, I can tell you that not one in ten of the Mahomedans here present, believe in it one bit—mind, I do not say we should not like it—if you kindly chose to concede it to us, we should doubtless be very pleased and grateful—just as if I were partner of a one-fourths share in a village and my co-sharer who owned three-fourths were to say, "never mind let us share the profits equally." Of course, I should be glad—of course I should think him a very liberal and good friend—but I should never presume to ask for such a thing—never delude myself with the belief that I had any right to it. So here, we Musalmans shall rejoice if, as a mark of your confidence in and love for us, you were to concede to us an equal number of representatives in the Council—but none of us, at least who are sane and in the possession of our full senses, are going to pretend that we have any right to this. We shall certainly not vote against it—why should we prevent your making us this concession of you like—but neither shall we, I believe, with very few exceptions, vote for it.

The whole thing lies in small compass—there are brave Hindus and wise Hindus, as well as brave Musalmans and wise Musalmans, and I as a Mahomedan am certainly not going to say that we are so much better than the Hindus, that they with fifteen crores to represent shall, necessarily, have only as many representatives as we with five crores to represent. (*Cheers.*) It is the whole nation that elects—not a particular community—and the election of representatives is not based upon the majority or minority of a particular community in any particular province. I myself would contentedly have left out the minority clause—being certain that in the long run, when the system comes to be thoroughly understood, the best men, those who will strive most earnestly for the good of the people, will be elected, no matter whether they are Mahomedans or Hindus or members of any other of the smaller communities. But the Congress, as is well known out of deference to the views of some of my co-religionists, have inserted this clause so as to make sure that, even at the first, Musalmans, despite the fact that they are somewhat backward in English and general education, shall always be in the Councils, in at least as large a proportion to the total number, as the population they may be supposed to represent specially, bears to the total population—what can be fairer? Other far smaller communities, Parsees, Christians, Jains, Sikhs, Jews, here represented, are quite content with this. What grounds have we Mahomedans for complaining? (*Cheers.*)

It looks to me like an attempt to stir up religious and race feelings, and weaken our union—gentlemen, this assembly is not a religious but a secular one—it consists not of one caste or creed—but of all castes and creeds—its object is not the special grievances of this or that community, but the good of all, the welfare of the entire nation. (*Loud cheers.*) I am proud to feel this and to realize that our leaders setting aside the prejudices and religious differences, which have in the past so distracted the country (and still at times give sad trouble amongst the ignorant, when these are egged on by fanatics) have laboured faithfully to unite us in one national whole and have taught us the beauty and wisdom of union. It is not by Hindus grudging Mahomedans, or Mahomedans grudging Hindus seats in Council, or anything else, but by all, let them profess what creed they may, pushing on our best men, *let them* profess what creed *they* may, to the highest places, that we shall all rise and all benefit (*cheers*) and for my part, I see no cause whatsoever for any anxiety in regard to my co-religionists. As a matter of equity and perhaps looking to the fact that hitherto we Musalmans have been somewhat backward in English education, this minority clause, which is all that we could claim, has been inserted, but I see no reason to *fear* that we may not as time goes on, get in the natural course of things, and that legitimately as the result of our proved deserts, even more than this clause ensures to us. I do not forget that though we may be numerically in the minority, that yet it was this minority that diffused anew in the darkest ages the light of learning, arts and civilization in Europe, Africa and Asia; this minority which still rules the land from which our forefathers sprung, this minority that ruled and on the whole ably ruled India for seven hundred years, this minority that at all times and places has ever stood firm in words and deeds, and to me it seems pusillanimous or still worse a treason to ourselves, to accept the view that we are unable by our own merits to make good our claim to full representation which this amendment, trying to secure by law an equal number of the memberships, involves. The most we can justly claim under a rule of law, is a proportional number—if we stickle for more than this, it can only be because we doubt our capacity to hold our own. I do not doubt it. Let us get by all means an equal share in the Councils—let us get a preponderance if it may be—but let us get it not by an act of the legislature, but by proving to the whole country that we make better representatives. Then indeed we might be proud, but if we are to sit in larger numbers than our stake in the country warrants, by law, and not by the verdict of our countrymen, then would it be humiliation rather than a source of pride. I utterly oppose this amendment—and to you two or three men who are pressing it on, at whose instigation you best know, I say that this assembly is not so foolish as to scatter this nosegay of union, which has been bound by the threads of love and common interests and sympathy by all the races of this land, simply to gratify the arrogance or worse of men whose action is founded not on reason, but impulse, not on a regard for the welfare of the whole country, but a narrow and selfish view of what they mistakenly fancy are their own class interests. (*Loud cheers.*)

SHAIKH CUMROODIN FURRUKHAI : (*Bombay, No.* 1002, *in list.*)—Then spoke in Urdu as follows :—I disagree with Syed Wahid Ali Rizwi, but I most strongly second the amendment proposed by Mr. Hidayet Rasul, and on the following grounds.

I would not have seconded the amendment had I any reason to believe that the Mahomedan Community can at present keep pace with others, viz. : Hindus, Parsees, &c., in point of English education, and so I ask you brother delegates, most humbly, to concede to us the privilege of having the same number of our people in the Imperial and Provincial Councils, as the Hindus. By our educational attainments we shall not at present be able to compete on even terms ; give us the advantage of more members than we are entitled to as a matter of proportional calculation.

Although my predecessors (Messrs. Hamid Alli and Nassiruddin) are quite able to compete with members of other communities yet with every honour and respect to them, I think that feeling this and without previously minutely considering the conditions of the Mahomedans, in point of English education, they have opposed the amendment. In doing so they have hardly, I think, had sufficiently at heart the good interests of their co-religionists as a body. Therefore, gentlemen, it is my earnest request to you that, as an encouragement to the Mahomedans, you will kindly grant us this concession, which no doubt may appear to be an unjust one from the point of view of the numerical strength of the two creeds, but which, looking to the present condition of the Mahomedans in regard to English education, would not, I conceive, be in reality unfair to either party.

I now propose a simple compromise to the effect that, with the permission of the President, a meeting consisting only of the Mahomedans who have come here as delegates from different parts of the country be called, to discuss the matter and decide whether or not the Mahomedan delegates can give their consent to the original proposal.

MUNSHI SHEIK-HUSSEIN *v.* SHEIKH CHAND : (*Deccan, No.* 433, *in list.*)—Then spoke in Urdu. (*This gentleman has failed to supply either a copy of his speech or a translation thereof, and, hence, no report of his speech can be given, there having been no reporters for vernacular speeches.*)

MR. HIDAYET BUKSH : (*Dacca, No.* 1775, *in list.*)—Then spoke in Urdu. (*Of this gentleman's speech there is, for the reasons stated in the case of the preceding speaker, no report. He strongly opposed the amendment.*)

The PRESIDENT : I will now ask the meeting whether it is prepared to vote upon this amendment without further discussion ?

The proposition was carried in the affirmative. The amendment, after having been again explained in Urdu was then put. A show of hands of Mahomedans only was first taken, and the result was, for the amendment 16 ; against 23. The great bulk of the Mahomedans did not vote at all. As explained by many of them, later, they could not vote for what they felt to be unreasonable—neither did they like to oppose, what was so vehemently urged, by several of their co-religionists and was, if it could be conceded, so manifestly complimentary to their community.

The amendment was then put to the whole Congress and negatived by an overwhelming majority, most of the Mahomedans this time voting against it. The result was greeted by prolonged cheers.

Clause 5 was then adopted.

Clause 6 was passed without amendment or discussion.

The preamble was then put and agreed to.

The PRESIDENT : You have now passed the entire proposition and our second Resolution will stand as follows :—

RESOLVED : *That the following skeleton scheme for the reform and reconstitution of the Council of the Governor-General for making Laws and Regulations, and the Provincial Legislative Councils, is adopted, and that the President of this Congress do submit the same to*

2nd Day.

Res. II. Expansion and Reform of Legislative Councils.

Charles Bradlaugh, Esq., M.P., with the respectful request of this Congress that he may be pleased to cause a Bill to be drafted on the lines indicated in this skeleton scheme and introduce the same in the British House of Commons :—

(1.) *The Imperial and Provincial Legislative Councils to consist respectively of Members, not less than one half of whom are to be elected, not more than one-fourth to sit ex officio and the rest to be nominated by Government.*

(2.) *Revenue districts to constitute ordinarily territorial units for electoral purposes.*

(3.) *All male British subjects above 21 years of age possessing certain qualifications and not subject to certain disqualifications (both of which will be settled later) to be voters.*

(4.) *Voters in each district to elect representatives to one or more electoral bodies, according to local circumstances, at the rate of 12 per million of the total population of the district; such representatives to possess certain qualifications, and not to be subject to certain disqualifications, both of which will be settled later.*

(5.) *All the representatives thus elected by all the districts included in the jurisdiction of each electoral body, to elect members to the Imperial Legislature at the rate of 1 per every five millions of the total population of the electoral jurisdiction, and to their own Provincial Legislature at the rate of 1 per million of the said total population, in such wise that whenever the Parsees, Christians, Mahomedans or Hindus are in a minority, the total number of Parsees, Christians, Mahomedans or Hindus, as the case may be, elected to the Provincial Legislature, shall not, so far as may be possible, bear a less proportion to the total number of members elected thereto, than the total number of Parsees, Christians, Hindus or Mahomedans, as the case may be, in such electoral jurisdiction, bears to its total population. Members of both legislatures to possess certain qualifications and not to be subject to certain disqualifications both of which will be settled later.*

(6.) *All elections to be by ballot.*

And now, gentlemen, I declare this Congress adjourned until 11 A.M. to-morrow.

The assembly then dispersed with loud cheers.

THIRD DAY'S PROCEEDINGS.

Saturday, the 28th December 1889.

THE Congress re-assembled at 11 A.M.

3rd Day.

THE PRESIDENT said :—Gentlemen, we have a great deal of business to get through to-day, and I think we must begin without any further delay. In the first place, we have to deal with what has been called an Omnibus resolution which combines within itself the decisions which have already been arrived at by the Congress upon a variety of important matters. With regard to this omnibus resolution I do not think that there will be much difference of opinion. We have then, to follow, a variety of resolutions, upon which the judgment of the Congress is required, with regard to certain other practical questions that have not yet been finally disposed of by the Congress. Of course upon these questions we shall be glad to have the opinion of speakers, but I would mention that we are to have a speech from Mr. Bradlaugh at half-past six o'clock, and in order to have all the preparations ready it is necessary that we should close our proceedings by five o'clock. I hope therefore that gentlemen will bear this in mind, and, where they are in accord with the resolutions, will, if they speak at all, make their remarks as brief and as pointed as possible. There remains a third set of subjects also of great importance having reference to the future administration of the affairs of this Indian National Congress. These are matters to which your special attention will be called, and we must do our best to get through the other questions and bring ourselves fresh to deal with these. We will now proceed to business.

3rd Day.

Res. III. Confirmation of Resolutions passed at previous Congresses in re, Judicial and Police Reforms, Military Colleges, Volunteering, Income Tax, Salt Tax, Technical Education, and Reduction of Expenditure.

Mr. Kalicharan Banerjee (*Bengal, No.* 1827, *in list*) rose and said :—Mr. President, Sister and Brother Delegates, the proposition which I am about to present for your adoption has been, as it might well be, described as an Omnibus resolution. Let not the announcement however alarm you. When I have read it to you I shall only have to appeal to your instincts of heredity which must be well pronounced, I believe, in the fifth generation. (*Hear, hear.*) These are the terms of my proposition :—

Proposed : *That this present Congress do ratify and confirm the resolutions passed by previous Congresses as to*

(*a*) *the urgent necessity for the complete separation of executive and judicial functions, such that, in no case, shall the two functions be combined in the same officer ;*

(*b*) *the expediency of extending into many parts of the country, where it is not at present in force, the system of trial by jury ;*

(*c*) *the necessity of withdrawing from the High Courts, the powers, first vested in them in* 1872, *of setting aside verdicts of acquittal by juries ;*

(*d*) *the necessity of introducing into the Code of Criminal Procedure, a provision enabling accused persons, in warrant cases, to demand that, instead of being tried by the Magistrate, they be committed to the Court of Sessions ;*

(*e*) *the highly unsatisfactory character of the existing system of Police Administration in India, and the absolute necessity of a fundamental reform therein ;*

(*f*) *the expediency of both, establishing Military Colleges in India, whereat the Natives of India, as defined by statute, may be educated and trained for a military career as officers of the Indian Army, and of authorising, under such rules and restrictions as may seem necessary, such a system of volunteering for the Indian inhabitants of the country, as may qualify them to support the Government in any crisis ;*

(*g*) *the extremely unsatisfactory character of the Income Tax Administration, especially as regards incomes below Rupees one thousand, and the expediency of raising the taxable minimum to this amount ;*

(*h*) *the extreme importance of increasing, instead of diminishing, as the present tendency appears to be, the public expenditure on education in all its branches, and the necessity in view to the promotion of one of the most essential of these branches, the technical, of the appointment of a mixed commission to enquire into the present industrial condition of the country ;*

(*i*) *the impolicy and injustice involved in the late increase of the Salt Tax in a time of profound peace, and the urgent necessity for an immediate reduction of this tax, and the reimposition, to balance the deficit thus caused, of light ad valorem import duties ;*

(*j*) *the necessity for the reduction of, instead of the continual increase to, the military expenditure of the country.*

It must be superfluous for me to speak to each of these ten clauses, each embodying a resolution in regard to which the entire country has long since become unanimous. If I say a few words it will only be by way of helping you to bear in mind the several resolutions as you proceed to adopt them. The other night I overheard a friend of mine read out a passage from some paper, which I am not just now in a position to name, which sounded like a crushing aphorism. The passage ran something like this : "The Congress has the educational department for its father, the law for its mother, and the Missionary bodies for its sponsors." Perhaps it was intended, as I have said, for a crushing aphorism ; but, speaking for myself, as a member of this Congress, I am proud of the parentage, and I am certainly not ashamed of my sponsors. (*Cheers.*) When I call your attention to these ten resolutions, you will find that in the first place we deal with certain resolutions which clearly indicate that we are here to-day to stand up for the honour and glory of our mother. (*Cheers.*) The glory of the law consists in this, that offences should be duly prevented, that offences should be duly detected, and that offences should be duly dealt with. In the first five resolutions referred to in this Omnibus resolution you find one having regard to the reform of the police, and another relating to the separation of the judicial and executive functions. Then you have three resolutions relating to the system of trial by jury with a view of extending the system to parts of the country where it is not at present in force, of securing a finality for the verdicts of juries ; and of extending the system of trial by jury to certain cases which are not at present tried with the help of a jury. There we stand up for the glory of our mother. (*Cheers.*) Then you have a resolution which refers to education. Well, we stand up there for the glory of our father. (*Cheers.*) We wish that the interests of high education should be promoted, and while we seek education for ourselves, we do not overlook the interests of what I may describe as the education of our motherly environments ; that is to say, we are anxious at the same time to secure the development of the material resources of the country, and as a preparative for that development, we desire a proper system of technical education. It follows therefore, that as a Congress we are neither irrational nor lawless ;

3rd Day.

Res. III. Confirmation of Resolutions passed at, previous Congresses, in re, Judicial and Police Reforms, Military Colleges, Volunteering, Income Tax, Salt Tax, Technical Education, and Reduction of Expenditure.

and as we desire that we should have our bodies in an efficient condition so that we may cope with the movements into which we may enter with our heads and our hearts ; we also desire that something should be done in connection with the taxation of the country, so that the burdens we may have to bear, in the interests of Government, may be as little oppressive as possible. And so the Omnibus resolution calls your attention to direct taxation and seeks to remove from some of the incidents of that taxation, whatever has proved oppressive hitherto. Then when a reference is made also to indirect taxation we seek to secure that taxation should be directed more against luxuries of life than against the necessaries of life. (*Cheers.*) You have a reference in these resolutions to the salt tax. That matter was referred to most forcibly by our dear friend Pundit Madan Mohun yesterday. I will only say that we, the Congress, are the true salt ; only if we are true to ourselves let not our salt be taxed. (*Laughter.*) Then lastly, if we have this education, and if we have a state of affairs secured in which all shall be done according to law, and if we are able to sustain ourselves in the flesh so as to promote the movements which we take in hand, we want to go still further and qualify ourselves both to defend these blessings and the Government itself, should its authority be ever threatened in any crisis. So one of these resolutions relates to the military education of the natives of India and also to the securing of the benefits of the Volunteering system. In that connection we demand that the military expenditure of the country should be reduced. We are prepared to supply the Government with the sinews of war, not in the shape of money, but in the shape of ourselves. (*Cheers.*) We will supply them with men qualified to act as the soldiery of the country, so that, if there should come a crisis, (which God forbid !) we Indians, may be prepared to help the Government with our blood in maintaining the cause of British rule. (*Cheers.*) With these few remarks, I would present this proposition for your adoption.

MR. N. G. CHANDAVARKAR (*Bombay, No.* 962, *in list*)—MR. PRESIDENT, Lady Delegates, and Brother Delegates, I am entrusted with the duty of seconding this resolution : which means that I am to speak on ten subjects in the course of five minutes. But as that is not possible I shall merely indicate some general features of the resolution which has been submitted for your approval. If you carefully examine the resolution you will find that it comprises within itself two classes of subjects. The first class consists of those on which official opinion, which it is said is proverbially slow to move onwards, has pronounced itself in favor of the reforms suggested by the Congress. I say suggested by the Congress : but do not let me be misunderstood. I do not think that the Congress claims for itself anything like originality in any of its proposals. As my distinguished friend, who was at one time a member of the Congress, but who is no longer privileged to be with us (I refer to the Hon. Mr. Justice Telang) (*cheers*), said at the last meeting, originality in matters of practical politics is always dangerous. Now, gentlemen, it has been officially acknowledged that it is necessary to separate the judicial and executive functions, and that it is also necessary to reform the police administration of the country. These are subjects on which it is no longer necessary to re-state our facts or our arguments, because we have discussed them over and over again, and when even officials have acknowledged that reform is necessary all that we have to do is to re-affirm our old resolutions. Then again with regard to military colleges, some of the highest military authorities are declared to be in favor of the establishment of an Indian Sandhurst. For instance, it has been stated on reliable authority that the Commander-in-Chief of Bombay, H. R. H. the Duke of Connaught, is in favour of that scheme. And as to volunteering it was only very recently that the Hon. Mr. Justice Bailey, who commands the Bombay Volunteer Corps, said that natives ought to be admitted as Volunteers. (*Cheers.*) There again we have nothing more to do than to re-affirm our own resolution. The second class of subjects comprised within this resolution, consists of those upon which, although official opinion has not declared itself to be in favour of the reforms suggested by the Congress, yet it has not been able to deny our facts or to meet our arguments with anything like cogency. For instance, gentlemen, it is admitted by everybody—in fact no official has had the boldness to deny the fact—that salt is a necessary of life in India. It is as much, or even more, a necessary of life in India than are tea, sugar, cocoa, necessaries of life in England. Now, no English Chancellor of the Exchequer will ever venture to enhance the duty on these articles, but the Government of India with one stroke of the pen enhances the duty on salt at one sitting of the Legislative Council. As to military expenditure the state of things is discreditable, for this reason that while the expenditure has gone on increasing from £16,000,000 to £20,000,000 in two years, the Government has been reduced to the necessity of starting a famine insurance and afterwards using it for another purpose, ultimately denying that such a fund was ever created or existed. Let me simply say further, because I do not wish to trespass upon you beyond the allotted time, that this resolution deserves your best sympathy, and especially for this reason, that most of the subjects comprised within the resolution affect, most deeply, the interests of the masses, even more than they affect those of the classes, in this country ; I therefore call it the poor man's resolution and if the reforms suggested herein become accomplished facts, you, the delegates to this Congress, will become the means of securing to the poorer classes of the country, especially the blessings of a light and equable taxation, the blessings of spotless justice, and, last but not least, the blessings of education which, in my humble opinion, constitute the highest moral claim of England to the Government of India. (*Cheers.*)

3rd Day.

Res. III. Confirmation of Resolutions passed at, previous Congresses, in re, Judicial and Police Reforms, Military Colleges, Volunteering, Income Tax, Salt Tax, Technical Education, and Reduction of Expenditure.

Mr. S. B. Senkaram (*Madras, No. 98, in list*)—then spoke as follows:—Mr. President, Lady Delegates and Gentlemen, you will all be surprised to learn that I am a Brahmin of the Northern Circars belonging to the priestly class. (*Hear, hear.*) Fortunately for me, and to the credit of the Officers, and the Eurasian members of the Corps, I have had the privilege of becoming a volunteer. (*Hear, hear, and cheers.*) I joined the Vizagapatam Rifle Volunteer Corps two years ago as a private. (*Hear, hear, and laughter.*) A Brahmin of the priestly class has been ever looked upon, in our part of India, as being unfit to become a soldier. But let me tell you that I have risen above the rank of a private. (*Hear, hear, and laughter.*) I am a Non-Commissioned Officer (*hear, hear*), and I have been recommended for the post of the Quarter Master Sergeant of the Corps. (*Renewed laughter.*) I now bear a certificate which, however, I am prohibited from producing before you. This certificate shows that I can superintend at target practice, that I can drill a company in close and extended order, and that I can command a company in the field. (*Cheers and laughter.*) That certificate was granted me not by the officers of my own Corps but by a military Board that came over from Madras to inspect our Corps. There are other members of the Brahmin caste, who have won the badges of marksmen in the Corps. When such is the case, and when a Brahmin is able within a short period so to distinguish himself (*great laughter and cheers*)—pardon me for the word—is it not gross misrepresentation to pretend that our Non.-Brahmins, who are descended from long lines of warriors, are not eligible to be officers as well as soldiers ! (*Cheers.*)

The President—Every single point embraced in this proposition has been discussed and rediscussed at previous Congresses and, so far as I know, there is absolutely no difference of opinion in regard to any one of them. Is it necessary that there should be any further discussion now on any of these points (*no, no*) shall I then put it ? (*Yes, yes.*) Then our third resolution will stand thus :—

Resolved : *That this present Congress does hereby ratify and confirm the resolutions passed by previous Congresses as to*

(*a*) *the urgent necessity for the complete separation of executive and judicial functions, such that, in no case, shall the two functions be combined in the same officer ;*

(*b*) *the expediency of extending into many parts of the country, where it is not at present in force, the system of trial by jury ;*

(*c*) *the necessity of withdrawing from the High Courts, the powers, first vested in them in 1872, of setting aside verdicts of acquittal by juries ;*

(*d*) *the necessity of introducing, into the Code of Criminal Procedure, a provision enabling accused persons, in warrant cases, to demand that, instead of being tried by the Magistrate, they be committed to the Court of Sessions ;*

(*e*) *the highly unsatisfactory character of the existing system of Police Administration in India, and the absolute necessity of a fundamental reform therein ;*

(*f*) *the expediency of both, establishing Military Colleges in India, whereat the Natives of India, as defined by statute, may be educated and trained for a military career as officers of the Indian Army, and of authorising, under such rules and restrictions as may seem necessary, such a system of volunteering for the Indian inhabitants of the country, as may qualify them to support the Government in any crisis ;*

(*g*) *the extremely unsatisfactory character of the Income Tax Administration, especially as regards incomes below Rupees one thousand, and the expediency of raising the taxable minimum to this amount ;*

(*h*) *the extreme importance of increasing, instead of diminishing, as the present tendency appears to be, the public expenditure on education in all its branches, and the necessity, in view to the promotion of one of the most essential of these branches, the technical, of the appointment of a mixed commission to enquire into the present industrial condition of the country ;*

(*i*) *the impolicy and injustice involved in the late increase of the Salt Tax in a time of profound peace, and the urgent necessity for an immediate reduction of this tax, and the reimposition, to balance the deficit thus caused, of light ad valorem import duties ;*

(*j*) *the necessity for the reduction of, instead of the continual increase to, the military expenditure of the country.*

I now put the resolution—are you all agreed ? (*All, all.*)

The resolution is then passed unanimously.

3rd Day.

Res. IV. Reform of the Abkari and Excise System.

THE REV. G. M. COBBAN (*Madras, No.* 2, *in list*)—MR. PRESIDENT, the proposition which I have to move runs as follows :—

PROPOSED : *That this Congress do tender its sincere thanks to Messrs. Caine and Smith, and the members who voted with them, in connection with the debate on the Indian Excise Question in the House of Commons; and while fully appreciating what has been done by some of the local Governments towards the improvement of their systems of Excise and Abkari, do express the earnest hope that no further time may be lost in giving full effect to the Resolution of the House of Commons.* (*Loud cheers.*)

I can see by the reception which the text of the proposition has already met with that you are all prepared heartily to vote for its adoption. (*Cheers.*) When I remember that, during the past few years, at our successive Congress meetings this question of the Abkari, has been fully discussed, and is now come, I suppose, to be intelligently understood by us all, I feel that very few words are necessary from me on this occasion to recommend the proposition to your acceptance; yet, permit me to say a word or two. In the first place, in pressing a resolution upon this subject, I should like all, our Government especially, to understand that we are doing it intelligently. (*Cheers.*) I should like them further to understand that while we press this resolution and continue to press it substantially in one form or another, we are not without a due appreciation of the extremely difficult and delicate questions which it involves. (*Hear, hear, and loud cheers.*) We feel, I am sure, great sympathy with our Governments in the very difficult task, that has devolved upon them, of regulating such a very knotty business—if I may be allowed such an expression—as the business of drinking. The fact is that the habit of drinking is not new. It is old; and remember that there have always been, and I suppose will be, for a long time in India, certain classes who, for one reason or another, will continue to drink. The practice of drinking cannot be all at once suppressed; but what we ask in these resolutions is, that while Government regulates it and while Government compels the man who drinks to be perforce a philanthropist, *in a way*, by contributing to the benefit of his fellow-subjects (*laughter*)—while this is so, we desire that the Government should derive as little profit as possible from such an unhallowed traffic. (*Cheers.*)

Coming, as I do, from the Madras Presidency, in which I have been accustomed to move among the masses of Hindus for many years, I know pretty well the effect of the excise system in that Presidency, and here, as a witness, I cannot but bear testimony to this, that in many villages its effects have been most demoralising; that in villages where drinking was formerly comparatively unknown, now that drinking has been introduced, the people are not only reduced to poverty, but are deeply in debt and without education. (*Hear, hear.*) And when I see such things, with the heart of a man in me, how can I help protesting from my very soul, against such a system? (*Cheers.*) I find also that this practice of drinking is not only extending amongst the middle classes, for which I am very sorry, but among the lowest class especially it is a fruitful source of all ills. A few months ago, in those terrible months when palmyra toddy is abundant, I happened to be in a non-caste village and I took some pains to ascertain how much was money expended in that non-caste village in a month for the purchase of toddy. I am sure you cannot guess the amount. The village has only about 120 families; it is a village of low castes most of whom, however, are pattadars, and I found that they actually drank at least a thousand rupees worth of toddy, in that month. Why, brother delegates, if in every non-caste village we could get drinking of this kind suppressed, how these low caste people might be lifted up, and how education might flourish! We cannot have our Government supported by the demoralisation of any class. (*Hear, hear.*)

My resolution says that we express thanks to Messrs. Caine and Smith and other members in England. I am sure we owe much to them. Here in India, the members of the Congress will continue to do their duty, and supplemented and encouraged as we are by the help of earnest and hearty friends at home, I doubt not but that as the years pass, with increased vigilance and activity, on our part, with that confidence that the best shall be the strongest in the end, which we all possess, we shall see this cause triumph and India by God's help shall be a sober country enlightened and blessed and happy. I have every confidence in leaving this resolution in your hands. (*Cheers.*)

MR. DINSHA EDULJEE WACHA (*Bombay, No.* 908, *in list*)—MR. CHAIRMAN, Ladies and Gentlemen, I was entrusted with this excise resolution at the last Congress, and I then took some pains to explain to the delegates what were the defects in the existing excise system. Since then we have to congratulate ourselves on the effect that the Congress resolution has produced. Thanks to the efforts of Mr. Caine and Mr. Smith, since the last Congress was held, the House has passed (on the 30th April,) a resolution directing the Government of India to modify their excise regulations in harmony with the wishes of the people. Gentlemen, this first step gained is the first fruit of the Congress exertions towards the practical solution of this question. (*Hear, hear.*) I need not go over the whole ground which the resolution has covered. The evils of increasing drinking are now admitted, and it is therefore no use further dilating on the more immediate aspect of the matter. Let us now only go to the practical part of the question. Let us go on knocking at the door of the Government, so to control their excise revenue as to bring about in every part of the country a diminution in the consumption of ardent spirits. That is the practical point on which we must now concentrate our attention. The resolution now before you is a sort of incentive to quicken the action of the Government of India and make it move a little faster than it has done in this respect. The resolution of the House of Commons was dated the 30th April. We are now at the close of the year; nine months have passed away but yet there are no signs from the Government of India that they are really doing anything in the matter. That is the very reason why this Congress should further avail themselves of the assistance of Mr. Caine, and other gentlemen interested in the question, in getting the Government of India to expedite their scheme for the reform of the Indian Abkari Administration. There is no time to say more, and really there remains nothing to be said to you, who all understand the vital import of this sad question as well as, or better even than, I do myself. (*Loud cheers.*)

REV. R. A. HUME: (*Deccan, No.* 486, *in list.*)—MR. PRESIDENT, Ladies and Gentlemen, The main thing which I have to say is that a few days ago, looking over the papers of my father, who was a Missionary in this city from 1850 to 1854, I found a memorial that was presented by him on behalf of the citizens of this city to the Right Honourable Lord Falkland, Governor and President in Council at that time, regarding the spread of intemperance among the native population of Western India. This memorial, which I hold in my hand has, as you see, been riddled by white ants, and worse still, the vice to which it refers has since those days eaten deep into the vitals of the country, through the continued spread of that intemperance, the earlier stages of which so alarmed my father and his co-labourers. One paragraph alone I care to read. Let me just say that I heartily believe in all that Mr. Cobban has said about the difficulty of any practical solution, but there is one paragraph in this memorial, which should commend our importunity on the subject, even to the Government. "We believe" runs the memorial "that it is a lamentable fact in the history of British India, that the transfer of any new territory to the English Government has generally been followed by a speedy and marked increase in the number of liquor shops and a removal of the restraints on the spread of intemperance amongst the people. If we mistake not, the revenue from this source and the prevalence of intemperance have generally at once increased many-fold, and it can hardly be doubted that in this respect the territories still under native rule would compare most favourably with the English territories." Gentlemen, this is as true I fear to-day as it was forty years ago. Still I doubt if it can be said that in any other respect, the territory under the administration of the British People and the British Government unfavourably contrasts with that under native rule, save in this one great point. Take the case of Burmah. We understand the fact to be that the liquor revenue has more than doubled since we occupied Upper Burmah. It is certainly time for all of us who are interested in the people of this country, without dictating particular measures, to beg the Government to do its utmost to inaugurate some fundamental and sweeping reforms in its excise administration. (*Cheers.*)

REV. MR. THOMAS EVANS: (*Bengal, No.* 1835, *in list.*)—MR. PRESIDENT, and Gentlemen, My first pleasing duty to-day is to convey to you all the kind compliments and sympathy of my friend and your friend Mr. Caine (*cheers*), and I may add to that name the name of Mr. Samuel Smith, (*Hear, hear*), as well as of the members of the Anglo-Indian Temperance Association. I am glad and thankful, Sir, that this National Indian Congress has been established, is progressing and has bright prospects before it. There was a time when I doubted the movement, and some doubt it still. I have been thinking over it for some years. I have not rushed into the conflict without thought, but I have acted upon my own experience and upon the advice of my friends. Last night, Mr. Kalicharan Bannerjee, at a Christian meeting, said to all "Come and see and judge for yourselves," and all who have ever done so, as I did last year, have, I feel sure, had all their doubts as to the Congress removed.

This Congress, Sir, has performed a mighty task. It has, in a very large measure, unified the diversified interests of the people of India. India before consisted of units, but not of union; it consisted of sections but not of society, it consisted of nations but had not a nationality. (*Cheers.*) I am therefore glad, Sir, of the existence and progress of the National Congress. (*Hear, hear.*) I am, however, especially glad that this question of the Abkari has been brought so prominently before it. One of the reflections cast upon the National Congress has been this, that you educated gentlemen only care for your own promotion, that you wish to obtain political power for yourselves, and that you care nothing for the social regeneration of the people. I say it is not so. (*Hear, hear.*) The very fact that this resolution on the question of the Indian excise has been so persistently brought before you

3rd Day.

Res. IV. Reform of the Abkari and Excise System.

is a proof that it is not so. Mr. President, we need and sadly need reform in this matter. The evil is growing and growing rapidly. We are told sometimes that India was a drunken country before the English came here. I deny it, I most positively deny it. I know there were people here who drank, but they were comparatively few and not people of any social importance, but almost exclusively low caste people ; now, however, I am sorry to say, Mr. President, that our Brahmins even are taking to drinking (*Shame !*) and they are so ashamed of it that in many places they drink brandy under the name of kerosine oil. (*Laughter.*)

Gentlemen, I wish I had half an hour to address you, but I have not and therefore my words must be few. (*Cries of go on.*) Let me just point out how this traffic has been progressing. Under the Mahomedan rule the excise revenue of India was not twenty lakhs of rupees, and then it was imposed as a fine, as a restriction to try and keep the people from drinking. When the King of Oudh was Lord and Master in his country, there was no grogshop in Lucknow within ten miles of the city, but now we have over 100 grogshops in Lucknow under British rules. When that wicked man—I suppose I should not call him by a better name—God have mercy on him ! King Theebaw of Burmah was sitting upon his throne, there was not a grogshop in Upper Burmah. But the English have taken possession of the country, and last year the excise revenue in Upper Burmah was over two lakhs. (*Shame !*) Thus you see, gentlemen, it is going on. When the Honourable East India Company came to an end in 1858, the revenue from the excise of India was 50 lakhs of rupees, to-day it is nearly 500 lakhs of rupees. (*Shame !*) What is to be done ? Some repressive measures must be resorted to. I am glad to say that the Government is moving ; let us give them all the praise due to them. Our friend, Mr. Wacha, said that nothing has been done—I suppose not in Bombay. A great deal has been done in Bengal. I had an interview with the Excise Commissioner the other day in Calcutta and he said to me " Mr. Evans, I hope you are satisfied now. " I said " No, I am not." (*Laughter.*) He said " We have done a great deal." I replied " Precious little. " (*Laughter.*) " But this year, " he said, " we lose nine lakhs." I said " Next year I hope you will lose twenty,"—and so they will. Thank God, a large number of these fountains of corruption, the out-stills, have been shut up in Bengal, and I may tell you that in one division 750 out-stills are to be shut up next April ; which means that the Bengal Government at any rate *is* moving, and we are very thankful. But then what moved the Government ? The House of Commons. (*Cheers.*) Gentlemen, that is the place to appeal to, to the faithful hearts in the House of Commons. Mr. Caine and Mr. Smith obtained the passing of a resolution reproaching the Government of India for its Abkari Administration, and the Secretary of State was bound to move ; he moved the Viceroy of India, and the Viceroy moved the Lieutenant-Governor of Bengal, so that the thing is still moving. We want to keep it moving. Thank God, India is no longer to be seen in units. We have now a four-fold cord ; we have Hindus, we have Mahomedans, we have Christians, we have Parsees. These form a strong rope bound together, and if we will only join together heartily, with " a long pull, and a strong pull and a pull altogether," we shall drive this accursed drink out of India. (*Cheers.*) What do we want to get ? A great many things, but I have only time to dwell briefly upon one thing ; we want to get local option and that is a thing which Government is not prepared to give us. (*Shame !*) At Calcutta I pressed this matter upon Mr. Westmacott, the Excise Commissioner. I asked " Do you not approve of local option ? " " No " he said " I do not. " I know why : local option would shut up the shops and diminish the revenue. But we want to get it and we will get it, God helping us. It is in accordance with the laws of the British Government in India. Is there not a law that if a man sets up a nuisance near your house, you can appeal and have it removed ? Now what is a grogshop but a nuisance ? It is more than a nuisance. It is a foul temptation corrupting, degrading, and demoralising your children, and your fellow countrymen.

Then, gentlemen, we can appeal on another ground. It is in accord not only with the laws of India, but with the traditions and religion of India. We have been told sometimes that the Vedas and Shastras sanctioned the use of strong drink (" *no, no.*") I say they did not. " *Mpi Mdi Magrahajam.*" You know what that means. It means " intoxicant drinks do not give, do not take." This is in accordance with the laws of Manu and the laws of the Shastras. A Brahmin who drinks is a Brahmin no longer, and a Mahomedan who drinks is a Mahomedan no longer (*cheers*) so says the Koran. This practice then is in the teeth of, and against the religion of the people. Now when Hindus and Mahomedans, according to their Shastras and Koran are dead against drink, if our Government puts the drink under their noses, they are interfering with their religion. (*Cheers.*)

But I am afraid that my time is more than up. (" *Go on.*") What shall I say ? It is an easy matter to find fault with the Government and when the Government is wrong let us do it. I maintain that the people who speak out are the loyal people, not the people who keep a thing close under their waistcoats and say " *Han-*

jee ; Hanjee " (Yes, Sir ; Yes, Sir.) (*Laughter.*) We know lots of gentlemen in India who may be called "*ghoulam hazirs*"* (your slave is in attendance), but we, here, of the Congress are not made of such stuff. We have a little courage and independence, and when we see our beloved Government in the wrong we are not afraid to tell it so. Yet we love it. It is the best Government that India has ever seen and the best Government perhaps that India ever will see. (*Cheers.*) And that is why we want to *improve* it, gentlemen. (*Cheers and laughter.*) But then what of us ? How many of you are total abstainers ("*a good many.*") You can boycott the Government in the matter of liquor to-morrow if you will. The power is in your own hands. You have only to do two things—shut up your mouths and shut up your purses ; that is what you have to do. (*Laughter.*) Some one may say. "But Mr. Evans, I take it medicinally, I am weak and feeble and cannot get on without it." That is an European excuse. (*Laughter.*) They say that India "is *so* hot," but when they go to England they say it "is *so* cold !" One reason why Indian gentlemen take to the use of strong drink is that they think it is English-like to drink. I am sorry to confess that many Englishmen do drink, but many Englishmen do not. (*Hear, hear.*) We have 5,000,000 total abstainers in England. We have thirty total abstainers in the House of Commons, and we have total abstainers in the House of Lords. In England, as in our own case here, misery and degradation has followed this course and from this, good men in England want to save India. But we also want to save ourselves. Do not imitate the English in their faults ; imitate them in their virtues. (*Cheers.*) They have noble excellencies. They are independent, they are truth-speaking, they are faithful ; imitate them in these things, but do not imitate their faults and failings. And remember, that in this case especially, prevention is better than cure.

3rd Day.

Res. IV. Reform of the Abkari and Excise System.

What does the religion of the Hindus say ? "It is the son who saves the father from Hell." Yet how many of you allow your boys, almost children, to take to drink and die of delirium tremens before the age of thirty. I was told in Calcutta by the late Keshab Chunder Sen that many of the under-graduates of the University of Calcutta died of delirium tremens before they were thirty. I therefore, appeal to you by your affection for your own children and your own homes, to take the pledge and get others to do the same. (*Cheers.*)

The President : After this earnest and eloquent appeal, I am sure you all wish to vote and I will therefore put what will be our fourth resolution and which will stand as follows :—

Resolved—*That this Congress hereby tenders its sincere thanks to Messrs. Caine and Smith, and the members who voted with them, in connection with the debate on the Indian Excise Question in the House of Commons ; and while fully appreciating what has been done by some of the local Governments towards the improvement of their systems of Excise and Abkari, desires to express the earnest hope that no further time may be lost in giving full effect to the Resolution of the House of Commons.*

Are you all agreed ? (*Yes, yes ; All, all.*)

The resolution is carried unanimously, and I will now call upon Mr. R. S. Mudeliar to bring forward the next proposition.

Mr. Salem Ramaswamy Mudaliar : (*Madras, No. 29, in list.*)—I have been asked to bring forward this proposition.

Res. V. Universal Dissatisfaction created by Secretary of State's orders on the Public Service Commission's Report.

Proposed—*That this Congress, while thanking her Majesty's Government for raising the age for the Indian Civil Service Competitive Examination from 19 to 23, do put on record an emphatic expression of the universal disappointment which has been created by the rest of that Government's orders in regard to the Public Service Question, (the net result of which orders is to place the people of India in a worse position than they previously held), and reiterate the national conviction that no real justice will be done to India, in this matter, until the simultaneous holding in India, and in England, of all Examinations, for all Civil branches of the Public Service in India, at present held only in England, be conceded.*

And I have great pleasure in so doing. When, about this time last year, a similar proposition was brought forward I was anxious that we should postpone the consideration of the subject for one year; but luckily wiser counsels prevailed, and I am glad to think that I was beaten on the point, and that we did take up the question last year and pass a resolution respecting it. This year I appear before you to express my regret that I should have thought that any good could have come out of a delay in the consideration of the question. The Secretary of State has sent his despatch ; and what a despatch it is ! But before I proceed to discuss it let me first say a few words on each of the clauses into which this proposition can be

* **Or your slave is ready to do anything you wish—a common sycophantic reply to superiors in India.**

3rd Day.

Res. V. Universal Dissatisfaction created by Secretary of State's order on the Public Service Commission's Report.

resolved. The first part proposes to thank the Secretary of State for having conceded to us the boon of raising the age for admission to the Civil Service—well, thanks cost little, and I have no objection to thanking the Secretary of State for this concession, but, if you will calmly examine the matter, you will find that it was not so much a concession to the natives, as an act of policy, an act of self-protection ; an act which was found necessary, and the withholding of which would have led to disastrous results. Up to 1854 the age that was fixed for admission was 21. In that year a Committee known as Lord Macaulay's Committee recommended that the age should be raised to 23. That age remained the maximum for about five or six years. In 1860 the age was reduced to 22, and in 1866 it was reduced to 21, an arrangement which subsisted until 1878 when it was proposed to reduce the maximum to 19. When this was proposed there was a strong consensus of opinion in India, even the officials being nearly unanimous on this point, that if the age was reduced it would lead to disastrous results. But in spite of that opposition the Secretary of State, for reasons best known to himself, did reduce the age to 19. When the Commission was appointed it gave an opportunity to all the officials in the Local Governments to express their opinion that the reduction of age was a great mistake, because the mensent out were, as they were called, " boy magistrates. " It was more, I believe, in deference to that opinion than from any wish to grant any concession to the natives, that the age was again raised. But all the same we are thankful for what was done, and we shall not pause to enquire into the motive. It *is* a concession and a boon, and as such we thank the Secretary of State for what he has done.

The second part of the resolution expresses the opinion (which at first sight appears most startling) that the net result of what the Secretary of State has done is to place us in a worse position than we occupied when the Public Service Commission was appointed. And that, I regret to say, is a fact which cannot be denied. In a matter like this I do not wish to rely upon my own words, and I have therefore copied what the Secretary of State in his dispatch says on this point. I have not an authorised copy, and must therefore rely upon the public papers. Perhaps the Secretary of State, feeling that he had treated the Public Service Commission so shabbily, was ashamed to send a copy to the members, anyhow he ought to have been ashamed and any how he did send no copies to us members. (*Laughter*) Well, here is what the Secretary of State himself says :—

" I have no desire to extend the practical application of that principle further than political necessity requires. It is, in fact, based on the same considerations of fitness in the broadest sense which regulate the admission of Natives of India to the higher public offices of every kind ; but it justifies on indisputable grounds of public expediency the necessity of maintaining the special reservations which have hitherto existed in regard to a particular class of executive offices. No share of these offices (among which I include that of chief executive officers of a district, as well as that of Commissioner of a division and the administrative offices of still higher rank) could, without a violation of that principle, be formally excluded from statutory reservation and transferred to a Provincial Service. I do not suggest that the reservation of these offices to the Covenanted Civil Service should be so absolute as to exclude from them military officers in the Non-Regulation Provinces or that in special circumstances a member of the Provincial Service might not be appointed to one of them on grounds of proved individual fitness. What I desire to establish is that the transfer of a definite portion of them to the Provincial Service is inappropriate."

That is the first point that struck me when I read the despatch. When the Act of 1870 was passed, it was passed without any such reservation. It simply provided that if Government found that there was a native who, by his distinguished services, his merit and ability, had proved that he had a capacity to discharge the duties of his office, he should be appointed to any of those offices which were reserved for the English Covenanted Civilians. That Act was general in its wording, but when the rules under the Act were framed an attempt was made to exclude these executive officers from the sphere of the Statutory Service. In the rules sent by the Government of India that was one of the clauses ; but the then Secretary of State thought that it was a most improper thing to do, and he struck out the rule. So that gentlemen who were admitted into the Statutory Service in 1879, and subsequently, were distinctly encouraged to hope that if they proved themselves worthy they might fairly aspire to those higher posts which are now distinctly barred to all branches of the service save the Covenanted. I say that in that respect we have been placed in a worse position than we were in at the time when the Commission was appointed.

The second point in which our position has been changed for the worse relates to the disgraceful way in which the Statutory Civil Servants have been treated. When evidence was taken, no doubt it was found that the natives who gave evidence expressed the opinion that better selections could have been made—that the selections actually made by the Government were not the best that could have been made ; but not

3rd Day.

Res. V. Universal Dissatisfaction created by Secretary of State's orders on the Public Service Commission's Report.

one went the length of saying that these men were not fit for admission. You will find that the Government accepted the statement that these selections were on the whole satisfactory. Yet look at the way in which they have been treated. They have been told that either they should be satisfied with the positions they at the moment occupy (which means with the particular office that they occupy now) or that they should become members of the Provincial Service, the members of which are excluded from all the higher executive appointments—such as Collectorships, Divisional Commissionerships, Memberships of Council, and others; thus distinctly placing the Indian Community in a worse position than it occupied before this Commission was appointed.

The third point in which we are worse off has reference to the claims of the members of the English Covenanted Service. At the time when the statute of 1870 was passed, strong objections were raised to it—there was almost a storm one might say—and strong disapproval was expressed by the service of the view which found expression in the Act. The Civilians then said "we have vested interests, and these will be destroyed by the introduction of this Act." But their protests, essentially selfish and disregardful of the higher interest of the country, were overruled, and the Act was passed, though no doubt no real effect was given to it till 1879. The Public Service Commission suggested that the claims of those who had entered the service previous to 1870, *i.e.*, previous to the passing of the Act, should be respected but nobody pretended that after the Act was once passed any new European members of the service had any grounds for complaint on the score of the admission of natives. They entered the service knowing this to be the rule. But I find that the Secretary of State in his despatch says that those who entered the service up to 1880 *i.e.* ten years later, have a prior claim to the natives of India as regards these appointments. If there were time to go on discussing this matter in all its details I could show how in many other respects the Secretary of State has deliberately placed us in a worse position than we occupied before. We are therefore fully justified in stating as our deliberate opinion that the Secretary of State by the orders embodied in his despatch has placed us in a worse position than we formerly occupied.

Last year I referred to the remedy which, in our opinion, is the only remedy for these evils and that remedy is an equal competitive examination. At present, there is no equality of competition, no fair play, no "careers open to talent." As regards appointments made from England, there is a competitive examination, but it is held away in a distant corner of the world seven thousand miles from India, so that ninety-nine out of every hundred Indians competent to hold these posts, are virtually debarred from competing for them, by the great distances to be traversed, the large expenditure and the difficulties, about caste, involved. As regards appointments made in India, there is no fair play; if a man seeks to get one, he must first "*poojah* *" the authorities, and if he flatters and toadies enough, and makes things agreeable enough to those in whose gift the appointment lies, and those who have influence with those officials, he does get in, and then this man having got in and reached to higher office is able to keep out far more deserving men, who scorn to make influence by such questionable means, and to let in all his relatives, friends and dependents.

What we want is for all—Indian or English—a fair field and no favour. (*Loud cheers.*) So that the country may get the best possible men for its money; (*cheers*) and the only way to secure this is to have open competitive examinations in India for all civil branches of the Public Service. (*Hear, hear.*) We have no objection whatsoever to identical simultaneous examinations being held in Great Britain for any branches which Europeans think it worth their while to enter. We want the best men we can get, and if the Europeans can beat the Indians in a fair competition, let them do so. (*Cheers.*) And we don't want to reproduce in their case the gross injustice under which we are now suffering. (*No, no.*) We don't want to drag *them* 7,000 miles on the chance of passing an examination. (*No, certainly not.*) Let them have an examination in *their* own homes, as we claim one for ourselves in our homes. (*Prolonged cheers.*) Surely, gentlemen, no one, not wilfully blind to the dictates of common sense and common justice, could refuse this simple demand. (*Cheers.*)

But, gentlemen, the PRESIDENT warns me that I am exceeding the allotted period and though I could say much more, I think I have said enough to justify, thoroughly, both to you and to the world, the proposition that I have had the honour to introduce and recommend to your acceptance. (*Loud cheers.*)

MR. G. K. GOKHALE: (*Poona, No.* 418, *in list.*)—Then said:—MR. PRESIDENT and Fellow Delegates,—I have great pleasure in seconding the proposal which has been placed before you by Mr. Mudaliar. I may mention a fact, of which you may perhaps be aware, that Mr. Mudaliar was himself a member of the Public Service Commission, on the report of which the Secretary of State has passed the orders now under discussion; and I believe that the very

* "Worship" or "prostrate himself before."

3rd Day

Res. V. Universal Dissatisfaction created by Secretary of State's, orders on the Public Service Commission's, Report.

fact that Mr. Mudaliar himself is dissatisfied with the orders of the Secretary of State is most eloquent testimony to the view that we present before you, that the Secretary of State has placed us in a worse position than we previously occupied. The vast majority of us were not satisfied with the report of the Public Service Commission itself, and now that one of the gentlemen who signed the report is, himself, dissatisfied with what the Secretary of State has done on that report, it necessarily follows that the Secretary of State has done something worse than the Commission recommended.

I will only make a few observations on this subject, the time at my disposal being very short, although I have much to say with regard to it. First, I will ask you to remember the message which has been sent to us from England by the London correspondent of the *Hindu* of Madras. Mr. Dadhabhai Naoroji says, that great as has been the breach of faith of the Government where the Bombay Mamlatdars are concerned the breach of faith implied in the present orders of the Secretary of State is infinitely greater. Perhaps some of you may think that this is the language of exaggeration, but I can assure you that it is not so. In the first place, Mr. Dadhabhai Naoroji is not a gentleman who delights to indulge in the language of exaggeration; and secondly, you can easily satisfy yourselves of the absolute truth of what he has said. Fifty-six years have come and gone since the promise was first made that no distinction of race or creed or color should be allowed to stand in the way of the prospects of preferment of any native of India. That noble promise then made—a promise worthy of the highest and most generous attitude of England towards any of the countries with which she has ever come into contact—was reiterated in yet stronger terms in the proclamation of 1858. The terms of the enactment of 1833 and of the proclamation of 1858 are so explicit that those who now try to withhold from us the privileges then assured to us must be prepared to face the painful dilemma of hypocrisy or treachery—must be prepared to admit that England was insincere when she made those promises, or that she is prepared to break faith with us now.

Gentlemen, you may be aware that an English Judge famous (or infamous) in a way, did not scruple to accept this latter position and propound the preposterous doctrine that the proclamation of 1858 was never meant to be seriously taken. (*"Shame!"*) I hope however that there are not many Englishmen of that kind. With these noble promises of 1833 and 1858 before us, I ask you, are we not entitled to say that the least we expect from our English rulers is that they should always show a steadily progressive tendency towards the fulfilment of these promises?

I had intended to review the whole question, but time is short, and I am afraid of abusing the almost fatherly indulgence of the President. My point is two-fold. First, the Commission which was appointed with such a flourish of trumpets left us in a worse position than we were in before; and secondly, the Secretary of State has left us in a worse position a great deal than did the Commissions Report. I want to draw your attention to three points. First, there were competitive examinations before the Commission sat and before the Secretary of State issued his orders. Secondly, there was a Statutory System whereby one-sixth of the posts reserved by the enactment of 1861 for the Covenanted Service were to be given to us Indians. Thirdly, what is called the Provincial Service, or the Uncovenanted Service, was, theoretically at least, almost exclusively ours—the natives of India. With regard to these points let me tell you what the Commission did and what the Secretary of State has done. The Commission has rejected the almost unanimous prayer of the whole nation for simultaneous examination in England and India. This is no more than an equitable demand. *For posts in our own country, if we are not to be examined in our own country, I do not know what justice and equity are.* (*Loud and prolonged cheers.*) The Secretary of State was only too glad to endorse the judgment of the Commission on this point. The second point refers to the number of places reserved for us by the rules of 1879 framed under the statute of 1870. The Commission proposed that 108 posts should be taken out of the Schedule of 1861, and should be gradually incorporated with the higher branch of the Uncovenanted Service, to which they gave a new nomenclature, calling it the Provincial Service. This was retrograde. There are 941 posts reserved for the Covenanted Service of India. One-sixth were to be ours by the Statutory Rules of 1879; that means 158. We were therefore entitled to 158 of these posts. The Commissioners however recommended that only 108 posts should be given to us. The Secretary of State however did something worse than this, for he changed the word to "May," and said that we *may* be given 108 places, leaving it to the discretion of the Government; and we know what that means. For every one of these 108 places that we shall have, half a dozen will go to the European official class. (*"Shame."*) As to the simultaneous question there can be no difficulty or doubt; or if there are any difficulties the day is not far distant when these will have to be removed. Students of Roman history are aware that the present struggle between the Indians and Anglo-Indians is something like that between the patricians and the plebeians. (*"Cries of no, no. and time."*) Something like the struggle that has been going on in England, but which is in reality nearly won now, between the classes and the masses, and it needs no prophet to foretell to which side victory must, in the long run, incline. (*Loud cheers.*)

Res. V. Universal Dissatisfaction created by Secretary of State's orders on the Public Service Commission's Report.

MR. J. ADAM: (*Madras, No. 1, in list.*)—Then said:—I can assure you that I shall not exceed the allotted five minutes, because on this occasion, I do not intend to go into any details. I wish rather to call the attention of the delegates to what I consider is the most important point in the resolution. I may compare it with the resolution which we succeeded in passing, so harmoniously, yesterday with reference to the Legislative Councils. In that we sank a great deal of detail, but made up our minds to stick most thoroughly to one great principle, the principle of electing our representatives. So in reference to this question I think there is a great deal of detail which, on an occasion like this, we may put on one side. It is not necessary to enter into a discussion on very minute points; we should rather seek for one great principle, which over-rides all the others, and make it our watchword on this question. And I consider that in this matter the great point which we should make our watchword is "simultaneous examination." (*Cheers.*) It is all very well to enter into elaborate discussions as to reserved appointments, the proportions of appointments, and other questions of that kind which are referred to in the Report and in the Secretary of State's despatch. If you get the simultaneous examination, you will really get everything. Just as if we once get the system of election for our representatives, though there may be differences of detail and we may not get it so fully or widely as we wish, still we shall be content to wait, a little while, till we can get something further; so in this matter, if we can once get the principle of simultaneous examination practically recognized, even though it may be clogged with certain restrictions, or there may be details which may not satisfy us at present, still if it is recognized that every young man from our Colleges can be examined here in view to entering the service on an equal footing with young men from Colleges in England, you will get everything, and all these questions as to reserved appointments, statutory appointments, and all the other paraphernalia, which are mere shams and blinds, will soon disappear altogether. (*Cheers.*) Let me call your attention to a fact which has not hitherto been noticed. This resolution refers not only to the Civil Service but to other examinations—examinations for various branches of the service many of which are called Uncovenanted,—examinations for the Engineering, Medical, Forest and other Departments, which are now held solely in England. In many of these branches it would not be desirable or necessary that the students, after passing the examination here, should go to England; in some it would be desirable: but these are points with which we need not now trouble ourselves.

Let us fight for this one great pr nciple of simultaneous examination. I have dwelt upon this point because I have some share in educating some of our young men of India, and there is nothing that makes me more annoyed than to hear people say, with a sneer, that these young men care for nothing but to get into the Government service. It is a very honorable desire to try and get into the service of the country. If it is considered in England one of the blue ribbons of the Public Schools to get pupils passed into the Civil Service and sent to govern a distant country like India, it should be all the more a blue ribbon for our Colleges to be able to pass our young men in to help to govern their own country. I therefore appeal to you, without going into any elaborate discussion as to small details, to stick fast to the principle which is put prominently forward in the resolution—to insist upon, and fight until you get them—of simultaneous examinations in India. (*Prolonged cheers.*)

MR. G. S. K. KHAPARDE: (*Berar, No. 1379, in list.*)—Ladies and Gentlemen, I rise to support this proposition, which I am sure you are all prepared heartily to accept. As has been already well said by Mr. Adam, this subject of the Service Commission and the Secretary of State's orders thereon, is no little akin to the subject that we discussed yesterday. We were fighting yesterday, to have some part in the deliberations of our country, some share in the Councils which decide on the various measures on which depend all our well being. To-day we are fighting to secure an adequate share in that great executive to which the carrying out of these measures is entrusted. The question for us now to consider is "are we to take part in this business?" I answer "yes." How? Is there any nation more loyal than you? Is there any nation that has shown greater aptitude or that has shown a more law-abiding nature than you yourselves possess? We serve the country, we serve our masters, we serve the British alone; we have served in the Military and all the Civil Departments. In some of these where opportunities have been given us, such as the accounts branch, we have so made our mark that it has become a common thing, to say "this is a class of account which the natives can manage best and cheapest; it is so intricate, leave it to them." We have served in all kinds of departments, and wheresoever we have been tried we have proved our fitness, and all that we now ask is to go on a step higher and be allowed a fair chance of proving our capacities in more responsible positions. This higher step, this fair chance has been often promised, as has been already said. We have already secured a minute portion of it. Some few of our people overcoming innumerable difficulties have been to England

3rd Day.

Res. V. Universal Dissatisfaction created by Secretary of State's orders on the Public Service Commission's Report.

and have passed the Civil Service Examination, although they were under the double disadvantage of having to go to a far distant country when very young, and of having to compete with Englishmen, in English, which to our youths is a foreign language. Notwithstanding this some of our people have passed and have since been a credit to the service. All that we want now is to do away with one of these disadvantages by the holding of this examination, in which we have shown ourselves qualified to compete, simultaneously, here and in England. This is the real watchword and I heartily support what previous speakers have said in regard to this matter. I hope that all of you will concentrate your minds on this one great point that we are fighting for now. We do not ask for any favour, for any partiality, for any number of places to be reserved for us; all we want is to have an equal chance in the examinations and to be then classed, be we English or Indian, according to our merits. If we take higher marks, let us go up, if not let us go down; we want fair play and no favours. I ask you to support this proposition, and to set yourselves against every idea of reserving to ourselves any place whatever. If we desire to compete, by all means let us do so but on perfectly fair terms; if we cannot succeed, then it is best, in every way, that we should not have appointments. All that we ask is that, so far as locality of examination is concerned, we and our English fellow subjects should compete on equal terms. If more of us pass it will be creditable to us; if more of them pass it will be creditable to them. We are willing to admit that they are our superiors, so far as they can prove this, only let us have a fair competition and no favour (*Cheers*), and then, *palmam qui meruit ferat*! (*Loud cheers.*)

MR. ALI MAHOMED BHIMJEE: (*Bombay, No.* 892, *in list.*)—MR. PRESIDENT, Lady Delegates and Brother Delegates, I have very great pleasure in supporting the resolution that has been brought forward. I am of the same mind as Mr. Adam. We must devote our attention mainly to securing simultaneous examinations. You will remember that we are supported by the Parliamentary Commission which reported in 1860. On that Commission were Sir. J. P. Willoughby, Mr. Mangles, Mr. Arbuthnot, Mr. MacNaughten and Sir Erskine Perry. The report is dated 26th January 1860, and the fifth paragraph of it says "two modes have been suggested by which the object in view might be attained. The first is by letting a certain portion of the total number of appointments declared in each year be competed for in India. The second is to hold two examinations simultaneously, one in England and one in India, both being as far as practicable, identical in their nature, and those who compete in both countries being finally classified in one list according to merit by the Civil Service Commissioners. The Committee have no hesitation in giving the preference to the second scheme as being the fairest and the most in accordance with the principles of a general competition for a common object." Now gentlemen, let me briefly quote a few words in support of this view. How did they arrive at this view? How did they come to support the second scheme? Lord Stanley said "he could not refrain from expressing his conviction that in refusing to carry on examinations in India as well as in England, a thing that was easily practicable, the Government were in fact negativing that which they had declared to be one of the principal objects of their Bill and confining the Civil Service as heretofore to Englishmen. The result was unjust and he believed it would be most pernicious." Then again Lord Stanley further said, "let them suppose for instance, that instead of holding these examinations here in London, they were to be held in Calcutta; well how many Englishmen would go there, or how many would send their sons perhaps to spend two or three years in the country, on the chance of obtaining an appointment? Nevertheless that was exactly the course proposed to be adopted towards the natives of India." These are the opinions that were expressed at the time, when the Commissioners came to the conclusion that simultaneous examinations should be held in India, and we are asking nothing more nor less than what they decided in 1860; and now 29 years have gone by and the prospects then held out to us by one of England's wisest Statesmen and endorsed by a Parliamentary Commission, prospects based upon our Gracious Queen-Empress's solemn promises, have not yet been realized. I know that men have been found base enough —men traitors alike to their Queen and country—to assert that our beloved Empress's words were no promises, merely emotional utterances never intended to be acted upon. But how did an honest English Statesman treat this dastardly stuff? What did Lord Ripon say? "The document (Her Majesty's Proclamation) is not a Treaty, it is not a diplomatic instrument, it is a declaration of principles of Government, if it is obligatory at all, is obligatory in respect to all to whom it is addressed. The doctrine, therefore, to which Sir James Stephen has given the sanction of his authority, I feel bound to repudiate to the utmost of my power. It seems to me to be inconsistent with the character of my Sovereign and with the honour of my country, and if it were once to be received and acted upon by the Government of England, it would do more than anything else could possibly do to strike at the root of our power and to destroy our just influence." (*Hear, hear, and loud cheers.*) But the gong warns me—my friends, stick to this one point, insist on simultaneous examinations, and if you secure these then you will secure everything, for which you are really fit. I hope you will support this resolution as one man. (*Loud cheers and cries of vote, vote.*)

Res. V. Universal Dissatisfaction created by Secretary of State's orders on the Public Service Commission's Report.

THE PRESIDENT—Shall I now put the Resolution? (*Yes, yes, vote, vote.*) Then our fifth Resolution will run thus :—

RESOLVED : *That this Congress, while thanking Her Majesty's Government for raising the age for the Indian Civil Service Competitive Examination from 19 to 23, does hereby put on record an emphatic expression of the universal disappointment which has been created by the rest of that Government's orders in regard to the Public Service Question, (the net result of which orders is to place the people of India in a worse position than they previously held), and reiterates the national conviction that no real justice will be done to India, in this matter, until the simultaneous holding in India and in England, of all Examinations, for all Civil branches of the Public Service in India, at present held only in England, be conceded.*

Now are you all agreed ?—(*All! all!*) I declare this Resolution to be passed unanimously.

Res. VI. Reform in the administration of the Arms Act.

MR. J. ADAM (*Madras, No. 1, in list*)—MR. PRESIDENT,—The proposition which I have been asked to lay before you is one relating to a subject, which has always proved, if I may so express it, a nasty corn on the Congress foot, but I hope, upon the present occasion, we shall be able to dispose of it satisfactorily, and a good deal more quickly that we have succeeded in doing upon previous occasions. It refers to the Arms Act.

I have been requested to move it on two grounds. The first is that several gentlemen considered it is desirable that some one should put forward this proposition, who in accordance with its terms will be thereby placed under certain disabilities, to which he is not now subjected. Well I do not feel at all offended at having to be subjected to certain disabilities, and if it is thought better that a representative of the class, on whom certain restrictions are to be imposed, should move the resolution, I am happy to do it. It was also suggested that it would be as well for some very pacific person to move it. I am very much flattered at being considered so very pacific as to be entrusted with this motion. And I only hope that in being pacific, I shall not meet with the fate that I met with when in Madras, at the hand of my friend, Mr. Surendranath Banerjee, who turned upon me and rent me in the ardour of his patriotic proclivities because I *was* so very pacific. (*Laughter.*) I trust you will treat me better than I was treated on that occasion.

It seems to me that the mistake that we made on previous occasions, in discussing the question of the Arms Act, was in attempting to go too much into detail, that is, instead of expressing our opinion upon two or three leading principles, we really attempted to do the duty of the Executive. It is a very difficult thing to introduce regulations, which are really executive regulations, into a general resolution. The present resolution takes up I think the four important points which are really considered hardships in connection with the Arms Act ; and although I am afraid that the resolution, and my support of it, will have the effect, (I know that some of my friends will not altogether agree with it) of pulling down this resolution from the pedestal of sentiment to the level of plain common sense, at the same time, I think that this common sense resolution will commend itself to you and not only to you, but to the public outside, who have to consider what we are dealing with here. Now my proposition runs as follows :—

PROPOSED : *That in view of the loyalty of the people, the hardships that the Arms Act, (XI. of 1878), as at present administered, entails, and the unmerited slur which it casts upon them, the Government be moved so to modify the rules made under this Act that all restrictions as to the possession and bearing of arms shall apply equally, to all persons residing in or visiting India ; that licenses to possess and bear arms shall be liberally and generally distributed wherever wild animals habitually destroy human life, cattle or crops, and that these and all licenses issued under the rules shall be granted once for all, shall operate throughout the Provincial jurisdiction within which they are issued, be only revocable on proof of misuse, and shall not reguire yearly or half-yearly renewals.*

You will observe that we begin with the preamble which states that the Act, as at present administered, entails certain hardships upon various classes of the people, and we ask Government, to modify the rules framed under the Act. First we say that in the modifications of these rules, they should be made to apply equally to all persons in India, not only to those who are residing in India, but to persons visiting India. With reference to persons visiting India I would simply call your attention to this. It has been said that it would be a great hardship to require European or American gentlemen coming here for a little shooting, to go through the process of taking out a license. I do not think that it would be a very great hardship ; but visitors are not included in our resolution for the purpose of paying especial attention to these few Western travellers, English and American, who may come here. It must not be

3rd Day.

Res. VI. Reform in the Administration of the Arms Act.

overlooked that there are a large number of visitors to India, not at all of the pacific nature of English and American gentlemen. I will only call your attention to two or three instances. In the Subjects Committee a friend, from the Punjab, mentioned the case of the Northern Frontier, where there are Afghans and other tribes who frequently come into this Province, and, not being British Subjects, are allowed to bear arms without restriction. And then again in many sea-ports, in Bombay and along the Western Coast, sailors, negroes from Zanzibar, and other parts of Africa, come walking in the streets, swaggering about fully armed, while the inhabitants have no arms to protect themselves. The resolution refers not only to European visitors, but to all people coming into the country, and it is proposed that if there are to be, as there should be, restrictions on the indiscriminate carrying arms, they should apply equally to all persons, residing in or visiting India. I do not think it could justly be considered any hardship by those people who will be put under such a disability, if it be a disability.

With regard to the second point of the resolution I do not think I need to emphasize it. I will only remark that statistics show that the destruction of cattle by wild animals is going on very rapidly. I do not know whether it is *propter hoc* or only *post hoc*, but it is curious that a very large increase has taken place since the time when the Act was first introduced. Sir William Hunter in his little book, published ten years ago, with reference to what England has done for India, has a very eloquent chapter upon the state of the country owing to wild beasts, robbers and others during the last century, and he points out how much that state of affairs had been modified at the time in which he was writing. He gives statistics with reference to deaths from wild beasts. I have looked over the last statistical abstract published, and I find that in 1878 (the year which Sir W. Hunter refered to, the year of the passing of the Act,) the registered number of cattle killed by tigers and leopards in India was 32,000. In 1887, which is the last year for which the statistics are available, the number had risen to 52,000. Of course, you all know that these numbers do not at all represent the numbers which are really killed, they are the number reported to the Police, and the proportion reported probably gets smaller yearly as the people realize, more and more clearly, that to report anything to the Police means only further loss and annoyance to themselves, but they are the numbers which are acknowledged by the Government. The real increase is therefore, probably, much greater.

The next point has reference to the great hardships involved by the frequent renewals, which are required of the licences. We say that whenever a license has been granted to a man, presumably of good character, so long as he does nothing to forfeit that character, he shall be allowed to retain his license without coming up every half year and having to renew his license. If he has once been passed as having a good character, and being fit to be trusted with arms and has obtained a license, let him keep it; of course, if he does anything wrong so as to render him unfit for the privilege, let it be taken from him. The fourth point is the great hardship entailed by the fact that the present licenses only run in the particular district, in which they are issued. We say that the licenses that are granted should run throughout the whole jurisdiction, that is throughout the Presidency or the Province as the case may be; that a license in any Province, shall hold good throughout that Province and that the holder shall be entitled to keep it, without asking for a renewal, unless he has done something to forfeit his privilege. Those are the principle points; we do not in our resolution attempt to go into minor questions as to the forms of the licenses, the fees to be paid and so on. We leave that to Government. It is only with the vital points of principle upon which we consider that the working of the Arms Act should be amended that we deal. The proposal is straightforward, plain, simple, not extravagant, and extremely pacific; it will not do harm to anything, and I hope I am not doing too much when I ask you all to accept this proposition that I have brought before you. (*Cheers.*)

LALLA HARBHAGWAN DAS (*Punjab, No.* 1440, *in list*)—MR. PRESIDENT and Brother Delegates, I am a Punjabee and therefore you will not expect any eloquence from me. I have simply come to state certain facts which I think will induce you to give ready assent to the proposition that has been brought before you for your acceptance. First I admit to you that the Arms Act as at present administered is an unnecessary slur upon the loyalty of the people. The British Government has existed in our country and has been ruling us for a sufficiently long time to be able to judge that we are thoroughly loyal, and that having received the benefits that we have from the Government, civilisation, education and many others, it may now be perfectly sure that, if it deals reasonably and fairly with us, we will stick to it through thick and thin. It is, therefore, quite unnecessary to keep up any such distinction as the practical working of the Arms Act as at present administered involves. (*Hear, hear.*) Then there is another objection which I think is more specific than that. In order to insure the unity of all the races in India it is necessary that the interests of all should be the same, that is there should be no distinction between one class and another. Our laws and regulations as far as possible ought to be such that they may tend to unite all classes of

Her Majesty's subjects in India,—Europeans, Eurasians, Hindus, Mahomedans, Parsees and everybody else,—and any law or regulation which serves to perpetuate class or race distinctions, tends to divide one class from another, and to diversify instead of unifying their interests, a course which is not desirable for any section of the community. In order to be more specific, let me say that under the Arms Act, the two classes of our resident community, which are exempted from the operation of the Act are those of the Europeans and Eurasians. Now, gentlemen, as you have heard from the gentleman who moved this resolution, many of the members of these very communities are of opinion that their interests are so identical with our own, that they themselves are ready to give up any such special exemption in their favour. And when we find them willing to do that, I think that Government should have no hesitation in doing away with this invidious distinction in the administration of the Act. I would submit to your attention that we have not only a wise Government, to look after our interests, but we have a strong Government to protect our lives and property. And that Government has given us laws, which on the whole are probably second to none in the world ; still we hope that the Government will not only still further improve these laws but improve their administration. The Government which is sufficiently strong to protect the lives and property of 250,000,000 subjects, is presumably sufficiently strong to protect the lives and property of our Eurasian brothers, who live with us in this country, and it is certainly not for their interest that any such distinction should be maintained and the masses thereby taught to look upon them as aliens, if not possible enemies. By this I mean that they not only derive no particular benefit from it, but may be injured thereby, by the loss of the sympathy of the people generally, while doing away with this distinction would remove doubts as to their interests being identical with ours would make us feel that they were one with us and still further strengthen the bond of union, which has now been inaugurated. (*Cheers.*)

Munshi Hidayet Rasul (*Oudh, No.* 1477, *in list*) then spoke in Urdu. He said : —

* Brethren, there are times when we are pleased and times when we are displeased. Probably you will be surprised to find me the most earnest of your supporters to-day because I am the same man who was yesterday the firmest of your opponents. But you must bear in mind that neither was my yesterday's opposition with the object of displeasing any person, nor is to-day's support to please you. Rather, if you duly consider, you will find that both my opposition and my support are meant to advance the cause of justice. We Musalmans can co-operate with you only so long as Our National Honour is not injured ; since we few hundred delegates are taken to represent five crores of Musalmans, we can only urge those views that are entertained by the said five crores of Musalmans unanimously. (*Loud cries from Mahomedan delegates of "No, no, it is not so."*) We cannot agree with those unmeaning utterances that two-thirds of our Musalman brethren (in name only) made yesterday. They had no reasonable reply to our arguments and their yesterday's speeches showed that they had made them simply to be loudly cheered by our Hindu brethren. (*No, no.*) For instance, now Munshi Nasirud-din Saheb Benarsi did not know why he had got on to the platform and what he should say. (*Cries of order.*) He had brought his rotten rope of union with him simply to hang liberty therewith. If such is an average Musalman I can assure you that none is worse than a Musalman. (*Order, order.*) I may say frankly that if I should have to choose between such a Musalman and a Hindu I would elect the latter. (***Question, question.***)

So I told you yesterday what the unanimous opinion of the Musalmans is in the matter. (*Cries of " No, no—it is not."*) Although I have not changed my mind nor can I, in view of such unanimous opinion as I have above described, do so, yet I may inform you that last night all our Musalman delegates met together to discuss the subject of election, and I must confess that the majority of those assembled gave an adverse opinion. As I do not like perverseness nor am I an enemy of the Congress, I, in deference to the majority, for the present give up the contest until I consult those who have sent me as their delegate.

Although my sharp language may be hurting you, but it is my duty that I should not in the least care either for your pleasure or for your displeasure. We are not such fools that you will be able to impose upon us. (*Order.*)

You might have observed how my to-day's speech as compared with that of yesterday is dull although I am standing to support the resolution regarding the Arms Act. It is expected that a person who undertakes to speak about Arms should be vehement in his speech, but the fact is that yesterday Islam's excitement, which does not require Arms to make it keener, had taken possession of me. Yesterday's fury was the fury of that nation whose deeds of valour have thrown the world into confusion. To-day the circle of speech is larger, and

*** This is this gentleman's own translation of his speech.**

3rd Day.

Res. VI. Reform in the Administration of the Arms Act.

a circle (on a liquid) the larger it becomes the less it is perceptible. This is the reason, all our brethren the Hindus, Parsees, Jews and Christians are agreed with us and it is clear why my to-day's speech is dull as compared with that of yesterday. The second reason is that we are now qualified only to be loquacious, as I showed you yesterday. To-day that I am called upon to use Arms, you find me rather less furious. Truly, by reason of our being disarmed we have not only lost our courage, but we are actually become women. If you duly consider the matter you will find that our nature is altogether changed. Even if we are now allowed to procure Arms freely, it will be a long time before we learn their use. We do not see what good our liberal and humane Government means to reap out of this, and God knows the reward of emancipating how many slaves it will earn by its crushing the natural propensities of crores of God's creatures. (*Order, order.*) I am sincerely of opinion that if Government allows us to bear Arms in the same manner as the people of England are allowed to do, our co-operation will be very valuable to it in time of need. (*Cheers.*) As I said yesterday, and probably you have not forgotten it, that no nation can afford to give a larger number of persons to die than ours, and by this number I do not mean the number of persons dying from cholera. Nay, this number is to the number of dying persons of any other community of India as ten is to one. (*No, no.*) We learn from you that a powerful enemy of our Government is knocking at the gate of India. Can we in this helpless state save our poor country from that tyrant? Are we in this helpless state supposed to be equal to the task of (if not of assisting the Government) saving the honour of our own families? (*Never!*) Well then, do you think that this stain of causing us to be killed like so many sheep will ever be effaced from the brow of Government? (*Cries of "Order, order."*) Suppose Government gives us Arms at the last hour. Of what use will they be then? We, in the first instance, do not know whether a rifle is loaded from its mouth or from its tail. We, Musalmans, are enemies of the hated Russians not only because it is an enemy of our Government, but also because it is an enemy of our Sultan of Turkey and an enemy of Islam. We can never consent that so long as we live, it should advance a step beyond its proper boundaries and may it not please God that, in our life time, we should see five crores more of Musalmans under its sway. But this desire can be fulfilled only when we have Arms with us, and it is impossible for us (Musalmans) even to consent to die in this helpless state. We think that the Arms Act should be greatly amended. For the present I propose as follows:—(1) The licence to bear Arms should be freely given to all, *i.e.*, Hindus, Musalmans, Christians and Parsees: (2) that the licence once taken should remain in force the whole life time: (3) the absurd rule that a licence taken in one Collectorate should be renewed in another ought to be abolished. If this is not done I wish to impress upon your mind that while at present we have no recourse but to part with our money when faced by robbers and dacoits, the critical time is nigh when we will see our houses set on fire in front of us and we will be unable to help ourselves and all this through the kindness of our Government. (*Order, order.*)

THE HON'BLE PUNDIT AJOODHIANATH (*North-West Provinces, No.* 1517, *in list*)—MR. PRESIDENT and Fellow Delegates, I am happy to support the resolution which has been placed before you, because in my humble judgment, it is calculated to bring into closer union the different classes and races now living in India under one common Sovereign. Fate has brought us together and it is most desirable that we should all live together here on the most friendly terms, until time blends all differences into one perfect national unity. The one consideration which more especially induced me, after the most deliberate consideration for two years, to join the Congress was that in my opinion, it was the most likely institution to promote friendly feeling and an ever developing unity between the different races domiciled in the country. Yesterday I was a little disappointed, for the attitude taken by some of my Mahomedan friends was not reasonable, but, gentlemen, you can imagine my feelings when I find, to-day, that my opinion was perfectly correct. The gentlemen who came here yesterday to propose an amendment were, I am sure, actuated solely by the honest desire to place before you their own convictions and uphold what they considered were the rights of their co-religionists, but after leaving this hall they tell me that they met together again, in the place provided as quarters for the Mahomedan delegates, and discussed the whole matter amongst themselves, and after full and mature deliberation, these gentlemen inform me that they and others arrived at the conclusion that the resolution was a fair and just one and requires no amendment. (*Cheers.*) No one can be more pleased than I at that conclusion. If there is a Hindu who has been associated on terms of perfect friendship with Mahomedans, it is I. I can count among their number, gentlemen, with whom I am on the most friendly terms, and who regard me as amongst their best friends. It was a matter of deep regret to a staunch friend of Mahomedans, like myself, to see them yesterday led away more by feeling than by judgment, and proposing a really indefensible amendment, but I find to my great satisfaction that better counsels have prevailed, that judgment has now got the better of their emotional impulses, and that they of their own accord, abandon their suggested amendment. This should be a new era in the unity of the different races of the country. (*Applause.*) Now I venture to submit, that what occurred yesterday and to-day is truly typical of the

3rd Day.

Res. VI. Reform in the Administration of the Arms Act.

action of this Congress movement, throughout this great Empire. By bringing men of all creeds and classes together on a common platform and by enabling them to discuss face to face all those questions of domestic politics, which are closest to the lives and hearts of our people, it first brings out into clear relief all differences and doubts that underlaid, the old, mutual, class-distrust, that has, in the past, been India's curse, and then it composes those differences and sets at rest for ever those doubts—except in the minds of perhaps one or two isolated fanatics whose own brethren disown them,—not by an authoritative enactment, not by the power of numbers, but by the arguments of reason and by appeals to that deep-seated, brotherly feeling which we all (when our lower and selfish natures are held in check) which we all I say, be we Mahomedans, Hindus or what not, do truly cherish in our heart of hearts for all who, born on India's sacred soil, claim India, like ourselves, as their home, their hope, their motherland. (*Loud and continued applause.*)

SYED WAHID ALI RIZWI (*North-Western Provinces, No.* 1686, *in list*) then spoke in Urdu. He said: Mr. PRESIDENT, Gentlemen of the Congress, I know something of politics and I wish to say some few further words in regard to what fell from me yesterday. Then you seemed all surprised at finding me a zealous Mahomedan fighting for my race and creed brethren, and waving the crescent flag of our national and ancestral glory high in the heavens. But to-day it is otherwise, the fiery spirit has subsided, and I am willing to throw in my vote with that of the majority of the Musalmans, rather than continue to hold aloof from what the bulk of my co-religionists approve. (*Cheers.*)

"United we stand; divided we fall," is the maxim by which I am this day governed.

My Mahomedan brethren from Behar, Bombay and other places, are pleased to hold that the numerical superiority of the Hindus in the Provincial and Imperial Councils could never under any circumstances prove prejudicial to Mahomedan interests. How they have convinced themselves of this is certainly a thing which I am quite unable to understand, and which it seems to me no leader or philosopher amongst the Musalmans, would ever have agreed to. Well, I am master of my own ideas, and retain in my heart my conviction unchanged, but I am quite willing to waive my personal views, and vote for the view which has commended itself to the Congress as a whole, and specially which has been approved by the great majority of my learned and high-minded co-religionists here—for the very basis of all our success has been union.

MR. PRESIDENT: All the world knows, that mainly in virtue of this same *union*, my illustrious, and brave nation, the Arabs, conquered all the countries of the Eastern Hemisphere in past ages, in an incredibly short space of time and held them for full 500 years, without check or interruption. From the great wall of China to the rocky fastnesses of Gibraltar, from the icy plains of Kazin to the burning deserts of Africa, the whole world rejoiced under their wise and beneficent rule. The followers of Islam, in every capacity and respect, whether as rulers or warriors or even in numerical strength, are on the world's national platform, far in advance of other nations, and are respected and feared throughout the world. The Mahomedan laws, alike for secular and spiritual guidance, are unequalled and may truly be designated, the golden code of progress, and the foot-prints of our great Musalman rulers remain behind for all ages, to point to rulers and law-givers of every clime, the only safe and perfect path. But I no longer oppose the Resolution passed yesterday—nay, retaining my own personal views I yet assent to it—because division leads to ship wreck in the deep, wide ocean of human affairs. (*Loud cheers and laughter.*)

THE PRESIDENT—Every one seems to be agreed about the Resolution now before us and complete harmony has been restored, even as regards that one small point on which yesterday differences occurred. We have still a great deal of work to get through and I will put the Resolution without further discussion, if you approve. (*Yes, yes—vote, vote.*) Our sixth Resolution then will run.

RESOLVED: *That in view of the loyalty of the people, the hardships that the Arms Act,* (*XI. of* 1878), *as at present administered, entails and the unmerited slur which it casts, upon them, the Government be moved so to modify the rules made under this Act, that all restrictions as to the possession and bearing of Arms shall apply equally, to all persons residing in or visiting India; that licenses to possess and bear Arms shall be liberally and generally distributed wherever wild animals habitually destroy human life, cattle or crops, and that these and all licenses issued under the rules shall be granted once for all, shall operate throughout the Provincial jurisdiction within which they are issued be only revocable on proof of misuse, and shall not require yearly or half-yearly renewals.*

[The resolution was then put and carried unanimously.]

A HINDU DELEGATE—"Let us have three cheers for the Mahomedan gentlemen." (*Loud cheers.*)

A MAHOMEDAN DELEGATE—Let us return the compliment, and have three cheers for the Hindus." (*Loud and prolonged cheers.*)

The Congress then adjourned for half-an-hour.

3rd Day.

Res. VII. Extension of the Permanent Settlement.

Mr. Baikunth Nath Sen (*Bengal, No.* 1873, *in list*), on the re-assembling of the Congress, said :—

Mr. President and Fellow Delegates, it has devolved upon me to lay before you a proposition regarding the extension of the permanent settlement to Provinces and Districts where it has not yet been conceded; I will simply say as a prefactory remark, that I come from Bengal. The proposition runs as follows :—

Proposed : *That the Government be urged to take the subject of a Permanent Settlement once more under consideration in view to practical action thereon, such that fixity and permanency may be given to the Government Land Revenue demand without further delay, at any rate in all fully populated and well cultivated tracts of country.*

The question is one of vital interest to all concerned : its importance is only commensurate with the difficulties that beset the question. It is also rather a delicate subject as it in one sense goes to affect the Imperial Exchequer. The limited time allotted does not permit of any elaborate discussion of the subject. I will confine myself therefore simply to placing before you certain facts of an important nature to pave the way, as it were, to the consideration of the question in a quiet manner, and then I will ask you to adopt the proposition.

It is necessary in the first instance to make a few observations by way of explanation or justification of the introduction of this proposition, in view of the 13th resolution adopted last year by the Congress at Allahabad. That resolution is to the effect that the question of Permanent Settlement be referred to the Standing Congress Committees for submission of reports. Those reports have not come in. It is therefore necessary to explain why, notwithstanding the non-receipt of these reports, this proposition is being placed before you. Those present at Allahabad are expected to know something about the genesis of that resolution. The proposition was submitted at a very late stage of the proceedings, and it was considered advisable that the question should be deferred for a year. The Hon. Mr. Telang moved an amendment, which was adopted. The object was simply to obtain time. The reports were not so essential as the time. Now time has been obtained. A year has passed, and the National Congress feels itself justified in again raising this question. It is not that this is to be considered once for all. We have this time simply to consider the question of principle. It will perhaps be considered at the next Congress, and perhaps repeated and rediscussed at the succeeding Congress, and so on until we attain our object. With these remarks I proceed in as few words as possible to explain the leading features of the case.

You all know how the Permanent Settlement of Bengal was obtained. In 1770 there was a famine in Bengal. Government was induced to take action in 1783 which led to the Permanent Settlement in 1793. That Permanent Settlement has worked in Bengal about a century. Agriculture forms the principal and staple industry of the country. Our agriculturists in Bengal are, comparatively speaking, better off than their brethren in the Sister Presidencies or Provinces. And what is this owing to if not chiefly, or solely, to the Permanent Settlement in Bengal ? (*Cheers.*) The Permanent Settlement spoken of in the resolution contemplates the fixity of the Government demand. It also involves and implies that the rights and titles of the different classes of landholders and occupiers should be defined. Just after the introduction of the Permanent Settlement in Bengal the rights as between the superior landholders and the inferior landholders were gradually developed and defined by several enactments, and their present condition is attributable, as I have said, if not solely, chiefly, to the Permanent Settlement prevailing in Bengal. In 1837 the North-Western Provinces were visited with a famine, followed by another famine in 1860. That led to the appointment of a Commission which took evidence and submitted their report. They set forth the expediency of fixing for ever the public demand on land. This was supported by the Governor-General in Council. It was Lord Canning's administration. In this state of things the matter went before the Secretary of State in Council, and, after the review of the whole matter there was a despatch in 1862. In this despatch the advantages which were expected to accrue by the concession of the Permanent Settlement were considered sufficiently great to justify the risk of a prospective loss of increment, in the Government revenue on land. It was considered in that despatch that the security of title and the permanence of the Government demand on land (these being the two principal incidents of Permanent Settlement) were important factors in the acceleration of the development of the resources of the country, leading to the general welfare and contentment of all Her Majesty's subjects in British India. (*Cheers.*) This was the enunciation of the principle in 1862. Practical effect, however, has not been given to it, and although a quarter of a century has quietly passed away, we do not yet find any symptoms or indications of any active measures being adopted by the Government. The question now before you is whether or not the time has arrived for moving the Government to take active measures to give practical effect to the policy indicated in the despatch of 1862, on the lines formulated in that despatch ; or, in other words, whether the territories which will be affected by this are, or are not, ripe for receiving this Permanent Settlement. That is the main question.

I must also bring to your notice that it was expected that certain conditions should be fulfilled before the Government could think it proper to give a Permanent Settlement; one of the prominent conditions being that at least four-fifths of the cultivable area should be actually redeemed and brought into cultivation. Now it is to be hoped that these conditions have been fulfilled; and I dare say that the gentlemen from Madras and Bombay, who are likely to follow me, will be able to furnish materials and data from which you will be able to judge whether or not the actual conditions have been fulfilled.

Every temporary arrangement, or temporary settlement as it is called, in contradistinction to a Permanent Settlement, with its concomitant evils, if not oppressions, effectually retards the progress of the development of the natural resources of the soil by discouraging the investment of capital; and the sooner this state of things becomes a matter of history the better for the Government as well as for all concerned. (*Cheers.*) We ought not to lose sight of or ignore the interests of Government, because the Government as representing the country at large has enormous interests at stake, and these are of a nature somewhat conflicting with those of the agriculturists, at any rate at first sight; for what is lost by Government as representative of the entire nation, is so much gained by the agricultural section of that nation. We cannot expect that Government should part with lands which have not been for a sufficient period under its direct control, to enable it to gauge, as trustees for the nation, their true value. Land must be for a certain period under its direct management to enable it to form accurate notions as to its actual produce and its capacities. I think that in the North-West Provinces, Oudh and parts of the Punjab, and the greater portions of Madras and Bombay sufficient time has passed, and we ought to consider that the Government is now in possession of those materials which are necessary to form a definite opinion as to the actual capacities of the soil and also the produce of the land. (*Cheers.*)

A few statistics perhaps may be enough. Let us take the accounts of the *last* ten years from 1879 to 1888; you will find from these that the Government revenue on land averages 19 millions sterling (I am speaking of the net revenue exclusive of the charges of collection.) The net revenue from the North-Western Provinces varies from five crores, to something less than that in 1888, in Madras, from four crores to something less; in Bombay from three crores to a little more. In Bombay there is a tendency to improve; in the North-West Provinces and in Madras there is a tendency to decrease. So that, if these last ten years be taken as a test, the Government cannot expect to receive any very large increase to its land revenue in those Provinces and Presidencies within the *next* ten years or more. A few years ago an estimate was submitted to Government, and it was reported by an efficient and responsible officer that if the Permanent Settlement be withheld the Government might expect a prospective gain of about £200,000 or about 30 lakhs of rupees. Now this is not a very large amount after all; it is not a very appreciable figure, compared with the total revenue of the Empire, and we all know that if a Permanent Settlement be effected the resources of the country will develope in other respects, and whatever the loss on this point may be it will, I hope, be more than recouped by increased income from those other sources. The best wealth of the Government, can be found in the growing wealth of the nation. (*Cheers.*) So I think, gentlemen, that does not stand in our way—my time perhaps is up. (*" Go on."*) I thank you for those expressions, but in deference to the chair I must beg you to excuse me if I only occupy another minute. I do not take up vexed questions like those of proprietary rights, or the "unearned increment," or the rights and privileges as between landowners of different degrees and classes; those are questions of detail; I am contending simply now for this broad principle; that in fully developed tracts of the country the permanence of the land revenue demand is desirable alike in the interests of the agriculturists and the nation as a whole. With these remarks I place this proposition before you for adoption. (*Cheers.*)

Mr. Hamid Ali (*Oudh, No.* 1494, *in list*) then read the resolution in Urdu and explained fully its purport in that language.

Mr. S. Subramania Iyer (*late Member of Council, Madras, No.* 73, *in list*) then spoke:—Mr. President, Ladies and Gentlemen, on the occasion of the discussion of this proposition before the Allahabad Congress the Hon'ble Mr. Telang stated that any resolution adopted upon this important question should be of such an authoritative character that it would be received outside with respect. How, within the short space of the five minutes, allowed to speakers upon any question, you are to thresh out such an important question in such a way that the decisions we come to may be received, outside, with authority, is at first difficult to understand. But, gentlemen, the learned speaker who moved this proposition has explained to you that the matter will come on for discussion, over and over again, until the matter has been sufficiently thrashed out, and can be placed before the Government in such a way that they will be compelled to pay attention to the resolutions of this Congress on the subject. Considering therefore the limited time at my disposal I shall try to be as brief as possible.

3rd Day.

Res. VII. Extension of the Permanent Settlement.

This question of Permanent Settlement I have considered from the time when I first became a landholder more than 15 years ago. In an inconsiderate moment, about that time, I invested the savings of a laborious professional career in the purchase of land in the well-watered plains of Tanjore, having left my own district, which had the misfortune of being, from time to time, visited by drought and famine. At the time that I invested these savings it was understood, on official authority, that the well-to-do province of Tanjore was to be left free from the blighting influences of a revision of assessment. The fact that the Province was to be let alone on the principle of "let well alone" induced me to invest my savings in that district; but, to my surprise, a few years after the purchase of these lands, I found that the authorities had made up their minds to revise the settlement of Tanjore. By that time I had spent a very considerable amount of money in the improvement of the property which I had purchased. Now, the important difficulty in connection with settlement operations is that they do not really, in practice, whatever they may profess in theory, make any allowance for the improvements effected by the ryot. I admit, and the authorities proclaim as loudly as they can, that they do not intend to tax the improvements of the ryot; but the question is whether in practice this is not done, whether under the circumstances and the rules which are enforced they can possibly avoid doing this? I assure you, gentlemen, as far as my experience goes, it is impossible for any proper allowance to be made for the improvements, or for these improvements to escape taxation. Of course that is a matter upon which we can only give our testimony. The authorities will assert on the one hand that they are not taxing improvements; the ryot on the other hand *knows* and asserts that the improvements are being taxed. But whatever be the exact truth in this matter, the feeling that the improvements of the ryot *are* taxed is most detrimental to agriculture in this country.

Gentlemen, there is no tribunal before which you can go and contest the position taken by the authorities in dealing with the land which is going to be settled. Their operations are in secret, their decisions are pronounced in such a way that it is impossible for you to attack their propriety. That character inherently belongs to the determinations of the executive in a proceeding not subject to any correction under process of law. The only facts therefore that have to be noted are these; does the ryot feel that his improvements are certain to be taxed, or does he feel that the authorities are *not* likely to tax improvements, and therefore go on investing his money upon them? Gentlemen, I have received an English education I have practised nearly twenty years before the Courts, and have constantly had occasion to come before the authorities, and I therefore know their position now. If my feeling in regard to this matter is that my improvements *are* likely to be taxed, I ask you to consider what will be the ideas of the ryots, and whether they are likely to say, "We will put a child-like faith in the justice of the authorities, we will take it that they will not tax our improvements, therefore we will go on making improvements in the expectation that they will not tax them" or whether they, like myself, will feel that improvements never do, in practice, escape assessment and say "we won't spend our money on improvements merely to put more money into the pockets of Government?" From the moment it was announced that the Tanjore Settlement was going to be revised, I gave strict orders to my agent that not a single rupee should be spent upon the improvement of the land. From that moment I have not bought one acre of land, under a temporary settlement.

That single fact I submit to you, is of great importance in the determination of the question. I think therefore that the operation of the Settlement Department cannot but be taken to have a disturbing influence in regard to improvements in land, nay, in my belief, almost to the extent of preventing them altogether. The necessity of a Permanent Settlement, therefore, will appear to you as plain as daylight. (*Cheers.*)

Upon the question of what sort of a Permanent Settlement the various parts of the country should get there may be a difference of opinion. All are not as fortunate as Bengal. They happened to get their Permanent Settlement at the end of last century, we cannot hope to get a Permanent Settlement on the same terms. If we are so fortunate, well and good; but I for one do not expect that we shall get such a settlement as they have. But it does not matter whether we get it on the same terms as Bengal; it is sufficient for our purposes to get a permanent Settlement of some kind or other; a Permanent Settlement which would instil sufficient confidence in the ryot to induce him to make improvements and which would enable him, even if certain kinds of revisions were still insisted on, to make sure that in such revisions the increased profits due to his improvements could not, and would not, be taxed. The expression "Permanent Settlement" is somewhat ambiguous; the authorities that have written upon it have given to it different meanings, but they all agree that the feeling of security which the settlement gives is the essence of the thing. Therefore the resolution which simply says that a Permanent Settlement should be given to the other Provinces is a resolution which I think you may confidently adopt. As I have said, the question as to the method to be adopted in the various Provinces will have to be dealt with by and by. To my mind, the one essential circumstance that requires to be provided against is this. Without binding down the Government for ever from demanding from the tenant a just share in the improvement which may be effected in the country, in the course of time, by means other than his own, such safe-guards and provisions should be adopted as would enable the tenant to obtain absolute security and immunity from further taxation in regard to all that improvement which is due to his means, to his labour, skill and capital. Mind it would be almost sufficient if the revision of the settlement were to be effected under the sanction of law, and under the protection of the Courts. I do not care to say that for many years to come I would have the land settled in such a way that no Government could touch it. It is quite sufficient for my purpose that the tenant may feel that he can protect himself in the Courts against the secret and at present irresponsible orders of the Settlement Department. A Permanent Settlement on the footing which was recommended some time back in the Madras Presidency would be quite effective under one condition, that it shall not rest with the Governent in its executive capacity to determine whether a revision shall take place. If circumstances should arise which would justly entitle the State to make a further demand, on the holders of land and an enactment were passed and machinery created for the purpose of assessing this increase, such that every person liable to the increased tax would have a right to appear before a properly constituted tribunal and there obtain, in open daylight, a clear judicial decision as to his increased liabilities, (the enhanced tax not being imposed as now by a stroke of the pen behind the back of the tenant), the Madras Presidency would look upon that arrangement as possessing most of the essential characters of a Permanent Settlement, and would be content to accept it. They will not be so foolish as to say, "If you will not give us such a Settlement as has been made in Bengal—a fixed money rent never to be interfered with for all time—we shall not accept any other as a permanent settlement." They will be quite content with a settlement say for 50 or 100 years, (founded if need be on a crop valuation basis) and only liable to be revised under a special legislative enactment and in open daylight. (*Cheers.*)

Munshi Sadarudin Ahmed: (*North-West Provinces, No.* 1527, *in list.*)—Then spoke in Urdu as follows:—Gentlemen, as I rise to support the proposition that in future a Permanent Settlement of the land revenue should take the place of periodical settlements, I think it advisable first to say something about the evils of the latter system and then something in regard to the necessity and advantages of the former. The most important and necessary points in settlement operations are first—the Assessment of the Government Revenue; Second—the preparation of the Record of Rights; Third—the Demarcation of Boundaries; and Fourth—the assuring the Ryots of the kindness and goodwill of Government by considerate treatment.

Till the year 1846, men of great experience, clear judgment and affable disposition were, as a rule, appointed settlement officers to effect these objects and both the Government and the people reposed confidence in them. But the old order of things has now changed. Without any regard being had to their experience and local knowledge, young officers of one district are now appointed as Settlement Officers in another district, entirely new to them. I shall refer here to some only of the evils—they are many and various—that result from such a state of things, and shall quote instances to show how little justice is done to the four principal points mentioned above.

I shall first give you an example of how the assessment of revenue is made, a work which requires the exercise of the greatest care and judgment, and for which directions are given in Section 47 of the Settlement Manual. When the district of Allahabad was under settlement last time, the Government Revenue assessed on the village 'Paras' in the Pargana of Kara exceeded the total gross proceeds of that village (*Shame*). You are surprised to hear this and you seem curious to know who it was that made such an iniquitous assessment. Gentlemen, the Settlement Officer who did this was no other than Sir Auckland Colvin (*Shame*)—who by the grace of fortune now occupies the exalted position of the Lieutenant-Governor of the North-West Provinces and Oudh. The poor Zemindar of Paras, vehemently protested against this assessment, but it was to no purpose. Finding himself helpless and driven to despair the Zemindar presented a petition to Mr. Colvin to the effect that his aged father had before his death foretold that ere long there would come a Settlement Officer, in whose time the people would be so miserable and poverty-stricken that in their homes would neither be heard the sound of the grinding mill nor the glimmer of the lamp be seen, and that when this came to pass the best thing that he could do, would be to give up all his rights and interests in his village to the Government and become a Mendicant, and, the petitioner went on to say, that he accordingly prayed that the name of Mr. Colvin as representing Government be substituted for his name in all the Revenue papers. Mr. Colvin, of course, did not accept the offer, but in consequence of this petition he made a slight reduction in the excessive assessment which he had at first proposed—a reduction that was so slight that it left the

3rd Day.

Res. VII. Extension of the Permanent Settlement.

poor Zemindar little better off than before (*Shame*). If, gentlemen, only a few more Zemindars had come forward boldly and made over their Zemindaries to Mr. Colvin to relieve themselves of the burden of his excessive assessment (and I do not mean to say that he was a bit more hasty or less competent, than the majority of modern Settlement Officers—perhaps quite the contrary) Sir Auckland Colvin would not perhaps so soon have lost all recollection of the cruel thoughtlessness of officers in disposing of questions which affect the very existence of the people, and would not perhaps have so attacked Mr. Hume about the Congress. (*Cheers.*)

Well, to give you an illustration of the careful way in which the record of rights is prepared, I will only mention that in the *Wajibularz* (Record of Rights) of a certain village was found a Statement to this effect :—

" In this village the co-sharers are Pathans, Brahmins and Rajpoots, who all eat and drink together." Now, gentlemen, the absurdity of such a statement must be patent to you all, for in this, the Settlement Officers claim to have brought about what monarchs like Akbar could not do, *i.e.*, to have made Hindus and Mahomedans all eat and drink together. (*Laughter.*) This shews with what care the record of rights is prepared.

I now come to the question of the demarcation of boundaries. Well, a certain Settlement Officer, still holding a high position in the North-West Provinces, used to say that the place where his horse stopped marked the true boundary of the village. Times are so changed, gentlemen, that matters which officials of a previous generation used to settle after making long and patient inquiries and with the help of arbitrators are now settled only by the capricious halting of a horse ! (*Shame.*) Verily, gentlemen, if in ancient times the dog of the Seven Sleepers of the Cave, had by long association with the virtuous acquired the disposition of man, the *horse* of a, by no means wide-awake, English official might well acquire the abilities demanded of a Settlement Officer, in these days of progress and advancement ! (*Laughter.*)

I will now say a few words about the treatment of the *ryots*. An official, still living, was once comparing the Rent Roll and Field List with the *Patwari*, of course in the presence of all the cultivators. Being hasty and inexperienced, the officer did not understand the *Patwari* on a particular point, and getting angry at this he struck the *Patwari* so hard in the face that three of his teeth were knocked out. (*Shame.*) Every human being can understand what impression such violent and unbecoming behaviour on the part of the Settlement Officer must have produced, on the minds of the poor ryots, as to the kindness and good will of Government towards them.

Besides all these and several other similar evils, are the expenses to which the Zemindars are put and which are so many and so heavy that a Zemindar weighed down by the expenses of one Settlement does not begin to get his head once more above water until the next Settlement. The proverb is well known which says that where the revenue is Rs. 2-8, the other expenses amount to Rs. 36-0-0.

As the time is very short, I will now very briefly draw your attention to the advantages and the necessity of a Permanent Settlement. It is plain that by a Permanent Settlement the land-owners will be relieved from the fear of enhancement after every 30 years, will be sure of a fairly stable and reliable income and will have reasonable hopes of future prosperity (*cheers*). They will attend far more, than they do now, to populating their villages, and will find greater inducements to dig wells and tanks and to throw up embankments. Farmers of the classes of *Jats, Kachis, Ahirs*, &c.; who now from fear of enhancement of rent, do not devote themselves heartily to the improvement of their land, and are growing more and more lax in their efforts every day, will once more begin to work harder and more cheerfully. Cultivation will improve, the value of the land will increase and the out-turn of food will be greatly enhanced. (*Cheers.*)

It has always been the intention of Government to extend the system of a Permanent Settlement when the time should come for it, so that the ryots may be happy and contented and the land-owners prosperous. This statement of mine is corroborated by despatches No. 14, dated July 9th, 1862, and No. 11, dated the 24th March 1865, from the Secretary of State for India to the Governor-General of India. The rules of Settlement, prepared by a Member of the Viceregal Council, and published under date January 22nd, 1867, also support the view I have expressed above. I might cite many more official authorities in support of my position. For instance, Section 9, of Circular No. 24, dated the 27th November 1867, says :—

3rd Day.

Res. VII. Extension of the Permanent Settlement.

* "When it has been proved that 80 per cent. of the culturable area is under cultivation, then that *Mahal* (Parish) should be entered in the list of lands which should be settled permanently." Again, Circular No. 10, of the Board of Revenue, dated 26th July 1865, issued in compliance with the orders of the Government of India, dated 19th June 1865, and the Despatch of the Secretary of State, No. 11 of 24th March 1865, says :—

* Section 2. "In those districts in the *Mahals* (parishes) of which cultivation has reached a high degree and the produce is ample the Settlement of Revenue should be permanent."

Section 4. "All those *Mahals* (parishes) in which the proportion of the land under cultivation to the whole land paying revenue to Government is as 80 to 100, should be permanently settled."

* Section 5. "Under all circumstances, it is generally accepted that in those *Mahals* (parishes) in which 80 per cent. of the cultivable area is actually under cultivation, it should be understood that all the requisite conditions of Permanent Settlement exist in them, and they have reached the stage when they should be settled permanently."

* Again in Section 8. "It is the opinion of Sir William Muir (then Mr. Muir) Member of the Board of Revenue, that in those tracts whereof the land under cultivation is 80 per cent. of the whole culturable area, agreements for a Permanent Settlement of the land should, at once, be asked for from the Zemindars," and it is not necessary for me to tell you, gentlemen, that cultivation has reached such a high degree now, everywhere, that you would not find a single village except some veritable "*Kambakhtpur*," (*Laughter.*) where the land, actually under cultivation, is not 80 per cent. of the whole culturable area. But the fact is that here as in so many other cases, our rulers make indeed good rules but somehow do not at all act upon or abide by them. For these reasons, gentlemen, I am of opinion that the introduction of a Permanent Settlement is not only very desirable, but that the time has come when it should no longer be deferred (*Cheers*). Let the Government only act up to its own excellent published intentions. (*Loud cheers.*)

MR. NASIRUDDIN AHMAD : (*Benares, No. 1694, in list.*)—Also spoke in Urdu and said : —MR. PRESIDENT, Gentlemen,—I am, I regret to say, the same Mahomedan delegate, who felt compelled to detain you all so long yesterday when arguing with some of my Brother Mahomedans as to the unreasonable demands which they made for a numerical equality in the Councils with the Hindus, though our Musalman members will only have to represent less than one-third of the population that the Hindu members will have to represent. I am sure I heartily apologize to all for my long-windedness yesterday and will only further add my congratulations to that of other previous speakers on the fact of all my co-religionists, with the exception of perhaps one or, at most, two, irreconcileables having subsequently come round to realize the essential fairness, to all creeds and castes, of the terms of the minority clause which we passed yesterday. (*Cheers.*) As for Munshi Hidayat Rasul's personal remarks in regard to me I do not think them worth notice. He tried to create disunion and has failed, as I hope all such efforts ever will fail. (*Loud cheers.*)

Really, gentlemen, I am at a loss to understand why I have been one of those selected for the honour of supporting this proposition in regard to that most important question now before you, the fixation or giving of permanence to the Land Revenue demand. My native Province, Benares, no doubt, like the greater part of Bengal, enjoys the blessings of a Permanent Settlement, and I am therefore able fully to appreciate and sympathize with the aspirations of the people of Madras, Bombay, the North-West Provinces and the unhappy Province of Oudh, where agricultural development is impossible under the ever impending dread of the perpetually recurrent visit of the Settlement Department.

There is no doubt that the time has now come to give greater fixity to the Government demand in many parts of India. By its repeated settlements and re-settlements, valuations and re-valuations of lands, classifications and re-classifications of soils, statistics of produce and what not, operations which have cost the country, the ransom of many kings, without bringing emancipation to a single peasant, the Government *must* have come by this time to know as much of the capacities of those parts of the country as it ever will or can know. Moreover, by its meritorious exertions, and through the good services and energies of its officers, Roads, Railways, Canals and Markets have been everywhere opened out leaving no room to hope for any material further development in these directions. This all being so, and the greatest authorities in Europe being unanimous in regard to the necessity (if the agriculture of any country is to be fully developed) of investing the holders or cultivators of the soil with

* These extracts are not taken from the originals, but have been literally translated from the Urdu of the speech.

3rd Day.

Res. VII. Extension of the Permanent Settlement.

some fixity of tenure—so that, feeling a real security therein, they may give their best of labour or capital to the improvement of the land,—it seems difficult to understand why, now for many years, the Government have gone to sleep, as it were, over the matter of extending the Permanent Settlement and that, too, after they had, or the Secretary of State had, publicly announced the determination of conceding such a Settlement.

One thing is certain and that is, that, in the temporarily settled districts, the zemindars and cultivators, greatly dreading the plague of the Settlement Officers, do nothing whatever to improve the lands permanently, but only struggle to get as much as they possibly can out of it, and bring it down to its lowest level before the next revision—all the poor Ryot looks to or can look to is how to fill, if possible, his belly. And, gentlemen, looking to the state of the country in your parts, if all that this resolution meant was that the existing Settlement, with all its evils and injustice and, in many cases, bitter severity was to be made permanent, I could not at all sympathize with it. For that is not at all what I want to see, but a widely different and really just Permanent Settlement—just to the country—just to the Ryot—not a Settlement made merely to please the Ryot and necessitating the recourse by Government to Income Taxes and other hateful forms of direct taxation, but a Settlement securing to the country a proper return on the land, which is *her* capital, and to the Ryot a proper return on his labour, which is *his* capital—not a Settlement stereotyping the evils and iniquities of your existing arrangements but one securing the real rights, for ever, of all classes interested in the land, from the state which holds it in trust for all of us, down to the cultivator who actually tills it; and moreover securing to each class the full future profits of all improvements that they severally or individually may make in the land. This is what is required and this I believe is what your proposed Resolution means and, in this belief, I support it and recommend it to your acceptance. (*Cheers.*)

MUNSHI MUHAMMAD SAKHAWAT HUSAIN: (*N.-W. Provinces, No. 1674, in list.*)—Spoke in Urdu and said:—Gentlemen,—If the material prosperity of the country is to increase at all in proportion with the growth of the populations, the Government Land Revenue demand must be given permanence and fixity, must be settled once for all, in all fully cultivated and well peopled portions of the country and that right soon. Every one here knows how the masses are becoming poorer decade by decade—there may be an increase in the wealth of the higher classes (and this only intensifies the peril of the position) but the condition of the masses is steadily deteriorating. The land does not produce more, but markedly less, as the Ayeen Akhbari show us, than it did in Akhbar's time and yet there are now more than three men dependant on the same land which in his time had to support only two; and before many years are over there will be four,—doubtless, emigration, and the development, slow though it be of manufacturing industries, the establishment of cotton, woollen, paper, soap, silk and other Mills and the great extension of public works do offer certain relatively tiny channels by which somewhat of the surplus population may drain off the people-flooded land, but all these taken together afford a comparatively insignificant relief and if the country is not to be utterly swamped in its seething and ever augmenting millions of paupers, it must be by developing the agriculture of the country. (*Loud cheers.*) At present the perpetual recurrence of Settlements is an ever present blight on agricultural progress. (*Cheers.*)

As for the Zemindars and Government they prowl about like a wolf and a sheep—the sheep ever seeking to graze up the entire pasture and the wolf seeking to devour the sheep. (*Laughter.*)

Will the Zemindar try to improve the land—to increase its yield? Certainly not; an increase in the Government demand is ever before his eyes—nay, years before each revision is due, he purposely lets land fall out of cultivation and he causes false village papers to be prepared both as to the land tilled and the rents paid, and he harasses the cultivators to make them look as wretched as possible, and in fact so far from trying to improve his land, in his short-sighted policy (short sighted for he rarely succeeds in hood-winking the trained Settlement Officials though he may bribe their subordinates) he does his best to reduce its condition.

But indeed, did he wish to improve it, where can he now get the money? As it stands it might be good security for a loan of a thousand rupees, but who will advance half this sum on it now, when a few years hence a revision of Settlement may have reduced its value by more than half?

Or if he be in debt and wish to sell a part, who will give him half its value, when there is no saying but what, after the next re-settlement, it may hardly have any value at all to any proprietor who does not himself cultivate?

3rd Day.

Res. VII. Extension of the Permanent Settlement.

Then as to the cultivators; rights of occupancy are good things in theory but—with bad seasons ever and anon—what real security do they afford? Is the cultivator, who can barely keep his family and himself alive, likely to spend one farthing on the land, or give it one atom more labour than is just necessary to get the ordinary crops out of it? No, the Zemindar is here the wolf and the cultivator the sheep, and just as the Government is ever seeking to squeeze more and more out of the Zemindar, so he in turn, and in absolute self-defence, is ever seeking, to squeeze more out of the Ryot. All the ryot can, as a rule, possibly do is to keep himself and his children alive—and now-a-days, famines are more common than in our father's times—for the lands are in worse condition, and less of the crops are stored, and more people have to be fed—and in bad seasons he very often don't succeed even in that one thing. (*Shame.*)

All round it is a bad system; the Government Officials do, I think, their best, but under this perpetual change of Settlements, under this constant fear of increased demands for Land Revenue, the Agriculture of the country, on whose development, we mainly depend to avert the most serious calamities, instead of developing is deteriorating. Relieve the Agriculturalists of this bane, and the necessities of an increasing population will soon largely improve our agriculture and increase our produce. (*Prolonged cheers.*) I heartily recommend this proposition to your most cordial acceptance. (*Cheers.*)

Rao Saheb Janardan Raghunath Nimbkar (*Deccan, No.* 542, *in list*) spoke in Maharatti. He said :—Mr. President, Ladies and Gentlemen, I have the greater pleasure in supporting this resolution that I am a landholder myself. You will know, gentlemen, that such a vast subject as this cannot be dealt with, in the short time allotted me, as it should be. I will confine myself therefore to a few striking facts for your speedy enlightenment. I have studied the subject very carefully, but it will be needless on this present occasion to inflict facts and figures on you. Every one knows what practical experience has shown every cultivator, that a Permanent Settlement, is alike the most advantageous for them and for the entire country. What need to cite theoretical proofs when we have the practical proof before us of the Permanent Settlement in Lower Bengal which, incomplete and faulty as it doubtless was, has yet made Bengal the richest Province in the Empire. (*Cheers.*)

Every one knows that the material prosperity of a country depends most of all on its agriculture; trades and professions occupy but a secondary place. Notwithstanding a beneficent rule, and the spread of Education, Railways, and Public Works, the condition of our agricultural classes becomes worse, day by day. Why should this be so? Absence of fixity in the Government Land Revenue demand, whereby the landholder's heart is deterred from ever truly doing his best with his land, is the natural and true reply—not that other causes are not at work, but that this is the great underlying cause out of which all other causes either spring or draw their importance. Who will seek to improve lands, of which he cannot be truly called the owner, and in regard to which he knows that the more he does for them, the more he will have to pay for them. And this enhancement has no bounds. No one has ever seen the land grow one inch, but the Government Assessment grows day by day. And in such an arbitrary way. When a new Survey and Assessment is ordered no reasons are ever given. The Survey Department must find work for itself or how could it keep its large salaries, and with reason or without reason, it always manages to satisfy Government that it is right—and then of course with reason or without reason it must run up the Assessment. The poor cultivator may protest against the enhanced rates—but he might save himself the trouble, his application is summarily dismissed without so much as a hearing. No Civil Suit will lie—there is no remedy and no justice. I myself have been a victim and I know what it feels like. In 1888 my land was cruelly over assessed, and I begged the Survey Superintendent then in charge of the Karjah Talooka to visit my fields and hear me on the spot; as without seeing the lands, their poverty and drawbacks could not be realized. But that gentleman was good enough to say that it was quite impossible to examine every field just to please the holders—he had no time for that sort of thing. No, they have no time, for anything but to extort money out of the poor. Look at the case of that entire Karjah Talooka. They screwed up and up, but they could not screw the Revenue up to the amount they had set their hearts upon, and so they had recourse to this ingenious novelty. They took a walk along the river running past our fields and laid down a new rule, that these riverside lands, which have never been cultivated, nor assessed, since earth first came under man's plough, should in future be assessed as Kharif Land at an average rate of Rs. 2 per acre. Probably the next time they will assess the rocks in the River, or the river's surface itself and make us pay the Assessment. These River-bank lands have been unassessed from time immemorial, because though not cultivated, they are needed for the cultivation of rice land. One acre of assessed rice land requires three acres of unassessed Warkas land to furnish the ash manure (*rab*) required for the rice. You cannot grow rice without such Warkas land—any more than you can live in a house which has no right of way to it through some adjoining piece of

3rd Day.

Res. VII. Extension of the Permanent Settlement.

land. But they have increased the Assessment on the rice land, and also put a ment on the immemorially rent free Warkas Lands. Was the Talooqua rich ? A thriving ? No, far from it, but the Settlement Department to justify its existe screw the Revenue up to a certain pitch, and it did it. The actual detail work up is done by ignorant clerks and what they do is just confirmed as a matter o the Mabap (father and mother) official in charge, under the plea that the details a tudinous to permit of his going into them.

Nor are these unjust and injurious changes confined to the 30 years' re take place equally, though on a smaller scale, upon the yearly sub-survey by t clerks under the Mamlatdar.

Have you ever, gentleman, heard of a more self-evident fact than that the railway improves the quality of land ? (*Laughter.*) Your old established mar only a couple of miles away, but a railway which has no station within five mil side passes near your field and so the field has, say the Settlement Departr more valuable and, whether or no, you must *pay* more.

I must be brief, though the subject is long at the briefest—Look to what Council said the other day in the light-hearted fashion, in which people speak which they do not share. " Our Survey Assessments have been lower than tho rulers." True in one sense, utterly false in reality, just as a clothier might charged less than a former dealer, because he only asked Rs. 2 for a suit ar asked Rs. 3. But when you look into it and find that for Rs. 3 the supplied, not merely coat and trousers, but pagree, waist belt, over-cloth, sh the new man now charges Re. 1 extra for each of these over and above the coat and trousers, you don't think much of his pretended liberality and fair deali Now that is just our case and if Mr. Peile did not know it, he ought to hav A particular number* may be pointed out which pays a lower Assessment than former rulers, though I doubt even this, but if you take the landholders, th as a body, you will find that with no more land to live on—and it is the land a only on which they live—they are made to pay one way and another at leas what they ever paid under any previous rulers, no matter how grasping an Take my own lands in Ratnagiri, they have been assessed at the late survey at ten times what they were assessed at under the Arba Saman survey under the Government.

People may ask why are we now pressing for a Permanent Settlement,- never ask for it in former times ? I will tell you, gentlemen, it is because in we could easily pay for the suit ; even a little more than what is now nomin it ; for in those former days we got the shoes, and the pugree and the kummer over-cloth and everything else free, and *now* we have to pay separately for ev heavily for everything. Our means of subsistence, *i.e.*, the produce of the lan or even less, there is the same amount of water in the pot, but there are now which it runs out, when before there was but one. (*Cheers.*)

Gentlemen, we got our salt, life's first necessary, at a nominal price—for for our cattle. Now it is so dear that the latter cannot have it at all. (*Cheers*

We had our cattle in plenty, lots of grazing free and salt to keep them the land is all taken up by the Forest Department and we have no grazin starving herds stray where there is food, they are run into the pound an (*cheers*) ; and day by day cattle, the first necessity of agriculture here, are decre ber and deteriorating in quality. (*Loud cheers.*)

We had plenty of fuel free, both for our own purposes and to make th manure without which our rice will not grow—but the forests have abso woodlands and our Warkas lands are assessed, and we must buy our fuel and (*Cheers.*)

We had plenty of wood for our houses, our ploughs, for every agricult now it is all under the lock and key of the Forest Department, and if we tou leave we are run in, and if we want a stick we have a week's running about fro to another before we get it, and we have to pay, pay, pay ! (*Loud cheers.*)

We had arms, and we could shoot or destroy the wild beasts that ravage now we have an Arms Act that allows a basket full of arms to every Negro ras on our shores, but takes good care that we poor cultivators who need them subsistence from wild animals are practically debarred from any. (*Cheers.*)

* Every field under the Bombay system, has its official number, and so the fields themse of as numbers. The speaker here simply means, by " number " " field " or " plot of land."

Res. VII. Extension of the Permanent Settlement.

We had such simple liquor as our people absolutely needed, at the cost of making it. But now a grand system has been introduced which, while it makes the population drunken, involves considerable expenditure, and that for a hurtful mixture, to provide what our cultivators, in the damp low-lying lands of Rutnagiri, really require for their health in the way of stimulus.

We could borrow money on reasonable terms, for the land and the crops could not run away and people were willing to trust us—there was profit in those days in the land—and we could get what we wanted for seed or what not—but now when the next turn of the screw may so reduce the value of the land that the surplus may be, as it already is in many places, *nil*, no one will give credit except for very short periods at very high interest; for the usurers care nothing for the welfare of the people, all they care for is to exact interest at a penal rate—and yet, gentlemen, Mr. Francis' Assessment which was a fair one and one that men could pay and live, when all these advantages were ours, has now been largely enhanced when not one of them remains to us.

The Deccan Agricultural Relief Act, the reports of Collectors, of the Agricultural Department, all show what the real position of our cultivators is—why do they not abandon the hopeless task ? Because unfortunately they must either cultivate on, they and their families half-starving, or die themselves at once with their wives and little ones. Every one here knows that outside the Presidency towns where the mills and other works give some relief, our cultivators and labouring classes can barely provide sustenance for themselves and families, even in the most hand to mouth fashion—and most assuredly one of the main causes for this is the unreasonable and recurring increases to the Land Revenue Assessment, and the absence of a Permanent Settlement. (*Loud cheers.*)

I think I have said enough to secure your acceptance of this proposition. May it please God to grant us a Permanent Settlement and with it a Permanent alleviation of the miseries of our poor Ryots and thus lay the foundation of the long-looked-for material prosperity of India. At present, as the proverb has it, we are told to eat, but our mouths are forcibly closed. This is not fair play. (*Loud and prolonged cheers.*)

The President—Gentlemen, so far as I can discover, all of you are of one mind as to this question. Is it your pleasure to allow further discussion ? (*Cries of " No, no, vote, vote."*) Then I shall put the question; our 7th Resolution will then be as follows :—

Resolved : *That the Government be urged to take the subject of a Permanent Settlement once more under consideration in view to practical action thereon, such that fixity and permanency may be given to the Government Land Revenue demand without further delay, at any rate, in all fully populated and well cultivated tracts of country.*

The Resolution was then put and carried unanimously.

The President—I shall now call upon Mr. Wacha to bring forward the next proposition.

Res VIII. Abolition of the Plate Duties.

Mr. Dinsha E. Wacha (*Bombay, No.* 908, *in list*)—Mr. President and Gentlemen, the proposition entrusted to me runs as follow :—

Proposed : *That in view of the fall that has already occurred in the price of silver and in the exchange value of the Indian Rupee, it seems impolitic on the part of the British Government to maintain any hinderances whatever to the consumption of silver for manufacturing purposes; and that this Congress do therefore strongly urge upon Her Majesty's Government that, not only as an act of justice to India (a matter which has been repeatedly brought to the notice of Her Majesty's Ministers) but also as an act of expediency in the interests of Her Majesty's British as well as Indian subjects, the plate duties should be immediately abolished, and Hall marking be made a voluntary institution.*

This is a resolution which I dare say will be passed with acclamation. It refers to one of the few Indian subjects on which there may be said to be absolute unanimity of opinion. The Government of India and the Government of England alike are now agreed that the duties are oppressive and ought to go. The Government of India, be it said to its credit, has been fighting for the repeal of these duties for the last 5 years. It has during this period addressed five despatches to the Secretary of State, and have so far succeeded in its efforts as to force the " My lords " of the British Treasury into recognising the justice of our grievance against the duty. And it is satisfactory to observe that our former Viceroy, the Earl of Northbrook, has ably supported our Government in the House of Lords. Again, last year, the late Mr. Slagg brought forward a motion on the subject in the House of Commons which was all that could be wished. It is a matter of deep regret to us all that this very able member of Parliament—so well versed in Indian economic questions, on whom the mantle

3rd Day.

Res. VIII. Abolition of the Plate Duties.

of the late Mr. Fawcett had worthily fallen—has been prematurely lost to us. In him we have indeed lost a most valued friend and sympathiser with our cause and I take this opportunity to express all India's deep regret at the death of that esteemed friend—a regret shared, I am sure, by all the delegates here assembled. (*Hear, hear.*) Since Mr. Slagg brought forward his motion last year this question has advanced a stage, which is very hopeful. The Right Hon'ble the Chancellor of the Exchequer, in bringing up the English Budget the other day distinctly assured the House of Commons that the duty should go, and if there be a substantial surplus next year he promised that the relief which we have been seeking for years past would be afforded. At the same time he thought there might be some difficulty as to the drawback on plate which may be on hand and on which duty may have been paid. He observed that there always remains a large quantity of silver plate in the hands of manufacturers in bond, particularly with the Goldsmith Company. These may incur a great loss. The Silver Commission, however, have thoroughly gone into the question and have suggested to the British Treasury that the drawback difficulty could be satisfactorily solved in this way. That the duty might be abolished gradually, say within the next three years.

The duty, as you, gentlemen, may not be unaware, is 1*s.* 6*d.* So that if 6d. is taken off the first year, 6d. the second year and 6d. the third year, all interests would be protected and the ultimate objécts would be gained without prejudice to any rights; the powerful guild, known as the Goldsmith Company, will be satisfied, and India will receive a great stimulus to her present silver industries.

It is expedient in the interests both of England and of India that the duty should go. It is owing to the oppressive, or as Mr. Slagg characterised it, barbarous duty, for it is a relic of mediæval finance, that the manufacture of silver plate has immensely gone down in England. In 1875 there were a million ounces of silver manufactured; whereas the quantity manufactured last year was only 600,000 ounces, a reduction of 30 per cent. Thus, while England herself has suffered in the industry by her own suicidal policy, the Continent and the United States have greatly increased it. What is therefore wanted both in England and here is that these industries should be stimulated; and the abolition of the duty is the only thing necessary to bring about so desirable a result. In a way it would perceptibly improve the Indian exchange—a change which from even the financial point of view is, you will admit, much to be desiderated. (*Cheers.*)

Mr. Hamid Ali (*Oudh, No.* 1494, *in list*) translated the proposition into Urdu and briefly explained its bearing and purport.

Mr. Ranchore Lal Chothe Lal (*Guzerat, No.* 792, *in list*) said :—Mr. President, Ladies and Gentlemen, I am very glad to second this proposition, because I think it is very just, very moderate, and very temperate, and because in addition to the other grounds that have been mentioned, I say that we are entitled to have these duties removed in England, in consideration of our heavy sacrifice in abolishing the duties on English goods. We used to levy duties on articles manufactured in England, but now all these have been abolished. Why? In the interests of free-trade. Therefore in these same interests it is nothing but just that English duties on Indian manufactured articles should be similarly abolished.

In connection with this subject I want to say a few words if time permits. It is not only England, but we might also add other countries of Europe, such as Germany, Russia, and France, which have laid heavy if not prohibitive duties on our manufactures. I know from my own experience that if we were to send yarn from India to Germany, it would sell well there, but for the prohibitive duty which they levy on Indian manufactured articles, amounting to ten or fifteen per cent. But for that duty we could find better markets for our Indian goods. We could find a market in Germany, in Russia, in America; but they all stop it by their prohibitive import duties. Now I want to suggest one thing to the Congress. We feel that the English should treat our goods in the same way as we treat theirs. With regard to France, to Germany, to America, who tax our goods so heavily, why should we not ask them to repeal these duties? And if they do not do so, I think our Government should be asked to put some import duty upon their goods which come to us. It is nothing but just that we should treat them as they treat us. You are in want of money. We say we want to reduce the Income Tax and the Salt Tax. Where is the money to come from? You must get it from somewhere. Now I say why should not the goods from these foreign countries expect to be taxed moderately by us when they tax ours so heavily. Here is a matter for the Indian Government to consider. It would not affect the British trade, it would not affect the Indian trade in any way, and we should be benefitted to a certain extent. I think, the Congress might, next year, take this point into consideration. If you have read the returns you will have noticed, that the quantity of goods imported from foreign European countries and America are increasing every year. Why?

Because British goods being here exempted from duty all others are exempted, and we get no benefit. Then again, our goods go to Afghanistan and Central Asia, and there Russia puts on prohibitive duties, yet their goods come into India and we allow them to come in free. I do not see much fairness in that. Let us ask them to remove all obstructions to our goods, and if they do not we can treat theirs in the same way. (*Cheers.*)

3rd Day.

Res. VIII. Abolition of the Plate Duties.

The President : I think our friend Mr. Ranchorelal Chothelal is a favourer of the Fair Trade heresy, but the points he has raised are beside the actual proposition before you, which is so simple and so universally agreed to, that with your permission I will put it at once without further discussion. (*Yes, yes.*) Then our 8th Resolution will stand.

Resolved—*That in view of the fall that has already occurred in the price of silver and in the exchange value of the Indian Rupee, it is impolitic on the part of the British Government to maintain any hindrances whatever to the consumption of silver for manufacturing purposes; and that this Congress strongly urges upon Her Majesty's Government that, not only as an act of justice to India (a matter which has been repeatedly brought to the notice of Her Majesty's Ministers), but also as an act of expediency in the interests of Her Majesty's British as well as Indian subjects, the plate duties should be immediately abolished, and Hall marking be made a voluntary institution.*

Are you all agreed ? (*Yes, yes.*) Then that resolution is passed unanimously.

Mr. W. C. Bonnerjee : (*Calcutta, No.* 1788, *in list.*)—Who was received with loud and continued cheering, said :—

Res. IX. Modifications of the Rules and practice of the H. of C., in regard to Indian Grievances and Budgets.

Mr. President, Ladies and Gentlemen, at this late hour of the day, it is not necessary for me to detain you by any long preliminary observations in connection with the proposition which I have the honour to place before you and which reads thus :—

Proposed—*That this Congress do respectfully express the earnest hope that, in the interests of the people of India, the House of Commons will forthwith restore the right, formerly possessed by members of that Honourable House, of stating to Parliament any matter of grievance of the natives of India, before Mr. Speaker leaves the Chair, for the presentation in Committee of the Indian Budget statement, and the earnest trust that the House of Commons will, in future, take into consideration the Annual Indian Budget statement at such a date as will ensure its full and adequate discussion, and do further authorize the President, Sir William Wedderburn, Bart., to sign a Petition in the name and on behalf of this Congress for presentation to the House of Commons in accordance with the terms of this Resolution.*

You, Sir, pointed out to us in your excellent address yesterday, that a great many checks which existed, in connection with the House of Commons, upon the Government of India, have been removed by the Act of 1858; I am sorry to say that one of the checks which existed for us even after the Act of 1858, was by a resolution, which was not intended to have that effect, taken away in the year 1888. You are all aware, that in the House of Commons, discussions with regard to grievances, take place when there is a motion for Mr. Speaker to leave the chair. Formerly when any motion that the speaker do leave the chair was made in the House of Commons, in anticipation of the House going into Committee to discuss Financial Statements or to discuss supply, it was open to any member to bring any subject of grievance to the notice of the House, Mr. Speaker sitting in the chair of the House.

By the rule to which I have alluded, it is not now necessary to put the motion to the House that Mr. Speaker do leave the chair. The speaker himself announces that he is about to leave the chair and he is allowed to leave the chair without any discussion of any description, and the grievances that might have been formerly brought forward are not allowed to be brought forward at all. The House of Commons when it passed this rule had no idea how it would operate with regard to the people of this country. Formerly whenever a motion was made that the speaker should leave the chair, in order that the House might get into Committee, to consider the Indian Financial Statement, any member of the House could get up and bring any grievances of the people of India to the notice of the House, and through that notice, to the notice of the people of Great Britain.

But last year the rule above referred to operated in this way. When the speaker said that he would leave the chair, he left the chair, and no opportunity was allowed to Mr. Bradlaugh to bring forward our motion with regard to the appointment of a Royal Commission to consider the administration of the Government of India, and he was therefore obliged, as a last resource, when speaking upon the Budget Statement made by Sir John Gorst, to bring to notice in an indirect and, for practical purposes, unsatisfactory way some of our grievances. (*Cheers.*) You see therefore that this rule operates in a very detrimental manner to our interests. It was not the intention of the House of Commons that it should have that effect, and consequently, if we from this Congress, send up this humble petition, to

3rd Day.

Res. IX. Modifications of the Rules and practice of the H. of C., in regard to Indian Grievances and Budgets.

the House, that House, justice-loving as it is, will, I have no doubt, grant us the relief which we seek (*cheers*). There is another matter; you are aware that the Indian Budget Statement, is not presented to the House, until about a day or two before it rises for the Session. Most of the influential members have then gone away from London to all parts of the world, and you have the Budget Statement made to a House consisting only nominally of 40 members, no more than half-a-dozen of whom remain present when the Statement is actually made. (*Shame.*) If the statement could be brought forward at an earlier date, many of the most influential members who take an interest in Indian affairs, would remain in London and take part in the discussion, but at present it is impossible that it should be so. I remember when I was present in the House last year, to listen to the Budget Statement, there was a time when the only members present were the Chairman of Committee, Mr. Courteney and Sir R. Lethbridge, who was addressing the empty benches of the House. (*Laughter.*) There was not another soul present, Mr. Bradlaugh having withdrawn for two or three minutes to the smoking-room. This state of things operates very detrimentally to India and I think, if we from this Congress, send up a petition to the House asking them to consider this prayer of ours, it will be granted. I accordingly ask you to adopt this proposition and empower our President to sign and present to Parliament a petition, on our behalf, pointing out how seriously we suffer, from the change of rules and deprecating earnestly the late date at which the Budget is introduced. (*Cheers.*)

Mr. Shurfuddin: (*Behar, No.* 1736, *in list.*)—Mr. President and Brother Delegates, After my learned senior's able speech, with regard to this resolution, you cannot expect me to inflict a long speech upon you; moreover I am suffering from a bad cold and cannot speak loud enough, I fear, to make myself heard. With regard to the resolution itself I cannot say any more than this, that it has been already shown to you by Mr. Bonnerjee, that the effect of the rule in question has operated very injuriously for India's interests. The English people and the English Parliament understand as well as we do that India is the most precious jewel in the English Crown, and when we in a body from this great Congress, which truly represents all that is best and worthiest in India, raise as one man our united voices in respectful remonstrance to the House against this rule which has so prejudiced our cause, I am certain that the House will not reject our prayer without full consideration. I hope now that you will excuse my saying any more. I have however been asked to translate the proposition into Hindustani for the benefit of such of our friends as do not sufficiently understand English to realize the real purport of the technical part of this proposition. (The Speaker then translated the proposition into Hindustani and explained what the practical bearing of the first part of it was.)

Pandit Madan Mohan Malaviya: (*North-Western Provinces, No.* 1520, *in list.*)—Then rose and said:—Mr. President, Ladies and Gentlemen, I have very great pleasure in supporting this Resolution, and I hope you will listen with kind patience to the few remarks that I have to address to you on this important subject. You will remember that two years ago when we met at Madras, we expressed our deep regret at the fact that the English Parliament did not devote that attention to our affairs which we had a right to expect of it. But now we regret still more to find that during the period that has since elapsed, matters have gone from bad to worse. Till recently, when the Indian Budget was laid before the House of Commons such of the members, as felt any interest in our affairs, were given an opportunity of saying whatever they thought necessary to say on our behalf. We complained that the opportunity thus afforded was very inadequate for anything like a fair consideration of the affairs of this vast country, and we prayed that more time might be given to the consideration of those affairs. (*Hear, hear.*) But so far from that reasonable request being granted we find, gentlemen, that even the little opportunity that had hitherto been allowed for the discussion of Indian questions has been circumscribed within still narrower bounds. The new rules of the House have, in a way, practically shut out all discussion bearing on the welfare of the 250 millions of Her Majesty's subjects in India. (*Shame, shame.*) I cannot properly express the regret and disappointment which this has created amongst us. Mr. Bonnerjee has very ably pointed out how injuriously to us this new rule of the House of Commons operates. The British Parliament, as representing the British people, is the one power to whom we look for the redress of our grievances. They it is who are really responsible for the good or bad Government of this country. (*Hear, hear.*) And if they refuse or neglect to pay proper attention to our affairs, the result must be entirely injurious to the interests of our people. (*Cheers*). The importance and necessity of Parliamentary control over the Indian administration, especially in matters of Finance has always been recognised. But it is even more important and necessary now than perhaps it ever was before; for our finances are unfortunately getting more and more embarrassed day by day. And yet it is at this very critical time that Parliament has partly withdrawn even that little attention which it hitherto has been wont to bestow upon Indian questions. The evil results of this diminution of control are already visible. Hitherto when complaints were made of the excessive increase of expenditure in India the member of the Government in charge has grudgingly admitted that there was room for economy and retrenchment. In the year 1883, the House of Commons passed a resolution to the effect that in the opinion of that House it is necessary that early steps be taken to reduce the expenditure of India. Lord Kimberley, our then Secretary of State, in his despatch, dated the 8th of June 1883, urged the Government of India to take the subject of the reduction of expenditure into their earliest consideration. Lord Randolph Churchill, our next Secretary of State, later on, said that "the financial position of India was very grave indeed, and required the most careful consideration, and the exercise of the most rigid economy was necessary, in his opinion, in order to avoid bankruptcy." But the withdrawal of Parliamentary control seems to have emboldened the present Under-Secretary to take up a very different attitude. When complaints were made on the occasion of the last debate on the Indian Budget in the House of Commons, of the ever-growing increase of expenditure in India, Sir John Gorst met them boldly by saying that "expenditure has increased, it ought to increase, and it ought not to be diminished." (*Shame, shame.*) And he tried to justify this view by asserting that the wealth and prosperity of the country was increasing. Now, gentlemen, no one would be more delighted than ourselves to know that the country was really growing in wealth and prosperity. (*Cheers.*) But unhappily the stern reality of facts forbids us from consoling ourselves with such pleasing fancies. We look wistfully in all directions ; we go deep into the Mofussil, we see our brethren in their homes and huts as they actually live ; and far from seeing any indications of that increasing prosperity which Sir J. Gorst said he discerned at that distance, we find the people growing poorer and less and less able to maintain themselves, their wives and children, than they were before. (*Hear, hear, and cheers.*) And we therefore say, gentlemen, that the increase of expenditure is under existing circumstances not only unjustifiable, but positively sinful. (*Prolonged cheers.*) The increase of public expenditure would undoubtedly be welcome if it followed upon an increase of wealth and prosperity among the people. There has been a large increase of revenue in England during the past quarter of a century. But it has followed an enormous growth of wealth and commerce in England and no one complains much of it. But in India public expenditure goes on increasing while the condition of the people is deteriorating day by day. (*Hear, hear.*) One simple but incontrovertible proof of this lies in the fact that almost all the recent additions to the revenue of the Government have been screwed out of the first necessities of the Indian people. To take only the most recent instances, increased expenditure has been met by enhancing the duty on salt, a thing necessary alike to man and cattle ; by taxing the poor man's oil, as petroleum has rightly been called, by imposing a double tax on the famishing ryots of the North-Western Provinces and Oudh and by misappropriating the Famine Insurance Fund (*shame !*), a fund especially created and promised by three Viceroys to be religiously set apart for meeting difficulties in times of scarcity and famine. (*Shame !*)

3rd Day.

Res. IX. Modifications of the Rules and practice of the H. of C., in regard to Indian Grievances and Budgets.

This ceaseless growth of expenditure is, gentlemen, an evil of alarming magnitude and deserves the most earnest consideration of Parliament. (*Cheers.*) Look only to your military expenditure. In 1857 with an army numbering about 254,000 men, the total military expenditure amounted to 11½ millions a year. But now with an army smaller by not less tham 40,000 men, your military expediture stands at the high figure of 20 million sterling a year ! And you know how it is met ! It is met, as I have told you, by making salt and petroleum dear to the masses and by making men starve and die in times of scarcity and famine. (*Cries of shame !*)

I have no wish, gentlemen, to take up much more of your time. But allow me just a moment more to enable me to point out how dreadfully serious the financial situation in India has become and how urgently necessary it is, in consequence, to check and curtail this overgrown military expenditure. Taxation has reached its utmost limit in India. There is no margin left for the Government to fall back upon in the hour of necessity. Sir E. Baring, our former Finance Minister, said in his evidence before the Royal Commission, in July last, that when Finance Minister in India he "was very much struck with the weakness of the financial position by reason of the absence of any financial reserve." He said he had publicly declared in his Budget Statement of 1882 that the duty on salt was lowered with the view to constituting a financial reserve, and that he had intended to bring down the duty, in the course of years, to a rupee a maund in order that it might constitute a real reserve. But far from that wise course being persisted in, the duty on salt has, as you know, been again raised to Rs. 2-8 a maund, and the financial position is weaker than it ever was before. If unfortunately a war breaks out to-morrow, which God forbid, Government have no means of raising the necessary amount of money except by borrowing ("*Question !*") I do not know what the gentleman behind means by the word "Question." If he questions the validity of my statement I am willing to quote official authorities in support of what I say. But I don't wish to detain you any longer. All that I say, I say to show the great necessity of Parlia-

3rd Day.

Res. IX. Modification of the Rules and practice of the H. of C., in regard to Indian Grievances and Budgets.

ment exercising a constant control over the Indian expenditure, and by cutting down all that is unnecessary or extravagant in it, rescue the finances of India from that sorrowful embarrassment into which they are at present plunged. (*Cheers.*)

It is sad and strange, gentlemen, that the new rules of the House of which we are complaining have been brought into force during the Premiership of the Marquis of Salisbury. His Lordship, when Secretary of State for India, very emphatically expressed the opinion, in his evidence before the Parliamentary Committee on Indian finance, that the most effectual way of securing financial justice for India was for the House of Commons to be constantly watchful on our behalf. His Lordship said that in order to save India from being oppressed, the House of Commons should keep a sufficiently sharp eye over matters concerning India. And yet it is in his time that these new rules have been passed, whereby the House is precluded from exercising even that little watchfulness over Indian matters which it hitherto used to do. But, gentlemen, as has been explained to you, this has been an unforeseen result of the rules. I hope with confidence that the rules will soon be amended, and that not only will our old privilege be restored to us, but that the Hon'ble House will fix such a date for the consideration of the Indian Budget as will allow of a fair and full discussion of questions affecting the welfare of the 200 millions of people entrusted by providence to their care. (*Cheers and loud cries of Vote.*)

THE PRESIDENT: Then gentlemen, I proceed to put the proposition—our 9th Resolution it will be and will stand thus:—

RESOLVED—*That this Congress respectfully expresses the earnest hope that, in the interest of the people of India, the House of Commons will forthwith restore the right, formerly possessed by members of that Honourable House, of stating to Parliament any matter of grievance of the natives of India, before Mr. Speaker leaves the Chair, for the presentation in Committee of the Indian Budget statement, and earnestly trusts that the House of Commons will, in future, take into consideration the Annual Indian Budget statement at such a date as will ensure its full and adequate discussion, and further authorizes the President, Sir William Wedderburn, Bart., to sign a Petition in the name and on behalf of this Congress for presentation to the House of Commons in accordance with the terms of this Resolution.*

Those who are in favour of this Resolution will please hold up their hands, (*all, all.*) Those who are against it (*none, none*). The Resolution is therefore passed unanimously.

Res. X. Conveying the thanks of India to Lord Reay.

MR. JAVERILAL UMIASHUNKAR YAJNIK (*Ex-Sheriff of Bombay, No. 932, in list*) said:—Gentlemen, The proposition which it is my pleasing duty to lay before you runs as follows:—

PROPOSED—*That, in view to his approaching departure, this Congress do put on record an expression of the high sense entertained, not only in the Bombay Presidency, but throughout India, of the ability, integrity and impartiality that have characterised Lord Reay's administration, as also of the gratitude, which the whole country feels to be his due, for the sympathy that he has ever extended to Indian aspirations and efforts.*

I think, gentlemen, that truly, as has been said therein, the feeling in regard to Lord Reay which this resolution expresses is the feeling not merely of Bombay but the universal feeling of India. (*Yes, yes, and loud and continued cheers.*) Though Governor of the Bombay Presidency, Lord Reay has made friends and has numerous admirers in all parts of India. His liberal policy and his enlightened administration, his habitual courtesy and kindness have been appreciated as well in the north, east, and south, as in the west of India. I am sure, therefore, that by passing this resolution on the eve of his retirement from the Government of this Presidency, the Congress, as an exponent of the national feeling of the country, will place on record its emphatic approval of his administration and the high sense it entertains of the ability, integrity and impartiality which have distingushed it. By this resolution, the Congress only anticipates the action which, I am sure, Bombay will take at no distant date in recognizing his valuable services. Gentlemen, I need scarcely say, that one of the ways by which England can best do its duty to India is by giving her good rulers,—good Viceroys and good Governors. And who can say,—hostile critics apart,—that Lord Reay has not proved himself to be as good, as conscientious and as sympathetic a Governor as any that this Presidency has seen since the time of Mountstuart Elphinstone? Before Lord Reay came among us, his reputation for ability and statesmanship had preceded him, and I think I express the sense of the whole of this assembly when I say that he will leave us with a still higher reputation for those qualities. It is difficult, within the short time at my disposal, to do justice to any of his public measures during the last five years. But there is one point on which one can speak with tolerable accuracy. This is about his selection of men to sit in the Legislative Council. These selections have at all times received public approbation. In his appointments, Lord Reay has tried to carry out practically, as

3rd Day.

Res. X. Conveying the thanks of India to Lord Reay.

far as in him lay, the principle of representation. One of his earliest appointments made after his assumption of office was that of our honoured and distinguished friend, Rao Bahadur Mahadev Govind Ranade. This was followed by the appointment of our venerable colleague, Mr. Dadabhai Naoroji—a martyr to India's cause. His re-appointment for two successive terms of our learned and valued friend, the Hon'ble Mr. Kashinath Trimbak Telang, was a well-merited recognition of that gentleman's high character and ability. Then followed the appointments of Messrs. Dayaram Jethmul, Kazi Shahabuddin, R. M. Sayani and of our worthy friend who now adorns the chair of the President of the Recepition Committee,—Mr. P. M. Mehta. The latest nomination is that of my friend, the Hon'ble Mr. Krishnaji Lakshaman Nulkar, than whom perhaps there is hardly a better representative of all that is good and noble in the Deccan community. Gujarat is represented by Hon. Mr. Behecherdas Viharidas. Gentlemen, it will thus be seen that there is hardly an important Province or an important interest which has been left unrepresented in the Legislative Council of Lord Reay; Bombay, the Deccan, Gujarat, the Konkan, Sind, the Southern Maratha Country and even the remote Canarese Districts have all had their representative and these in almost every case, the very Representatives that the people would themselves have selected. Coming to the great English mercantile interest in Bombay, I think that a better representative of this interest could not be found than the Hon'ble Mr. F. Forbes Adam, C.I.E., Chairman of the Bombay Chamber of Commerce—a gentleman who, to a wide knowledge of fiscal and economic problems adds an intimate knowledge of Bombay. The only question which Lord Reay's nominations to the Legislative Council suggests is that though these have been good, exceptionally good nominations, what is the guarantee that under a system which leaves the nomination of so-called representative men to the individual opinion of the head of the Government, equal discrimination will be shown at other times in the selection of genuinely representative and able men? It is just because equal wisdom and impartiality never has anywhere else been shown in similar selections, that we insist so strongly on the right to elect these our, at present nominal, representatives ourselves, and it is just for this reason too that we desire to put clearly on record an expression, of the respect, admiration and gratitude which we feel to be Lord Reay's simple due. For these and other reasons too numerous to mention, I am sure you will carry this resolution by acclamation. *(Loud and prolonged cheers.)*

MR. NUFFER CHUNDER PAL CHOWDHRY (*No.* 1853, *in list*)—MR. PRESIDENT, Lady Delegates and Brother Delegates,—It is a pleasant duty to me to second this Resolution. Although I belong to the Province of Bengal and have not had the opportunity of being under his Lordship's rule, his Lordship's reputation has spread so far that we can unhesitatingly say that we wholly approve this resolution. This is not the time to discuss the details of his Lordship's administration; suffice it to say, that we in Bengal, to a man, approve of this proposition with all our hearts. (*Cheers.*)

The Resolution was translated into Urdu.

THE HON. C. SANKARA NAIR (*Madras, No.* 74, *in list*)—I have very great pleasure in supporting the proposal. Our friend the Bombay Delegate has already told you the grounds on which this proposition is brought forward for your acceptance. I have only to add on behalf of the delegates from Madras that we fully agree with him and the delegates from the other Presidencies in considering that the fearlessness in the cause of justice and the sympathy with native aspirations displayed by Lord Reay fully deserve our thanks. The delegates from Madras will not easily forget the incidents in the career of another and very different Governor who refused to inquire into charges to enforce respect to constituted authority, and with that rememberance before them they will join the other delegates in thanking Lord Reay, and in heartily praying that Bombay, after his departure and other presidencies also, may be blessed with Governors like himself to preside over their administration. With these observations I commend this proposition to your kind acceptance. *(Loud cheers.)*

MR. HORMASJI A. WADIA (*Rajkote, No.* 855, *in list*)—MR. PRESIDENT and Brother Delegates,—In considering the present proposition and listening to the remarks of my friend who preceded me, I could not help feeling a wish that Lord Reay had been rather a Conservative than a Liberal. I am afraid you will not quite like that wish because you would not like Lord Reay to be lost to the liberal fold; but my wish was rather a personal one, because we do not look at what party a Governor belongs to in England but to what he does for *us* here in India. Our Governors and Viceroys come to us, and we accept them not as representatives of any party in British politics, but as representatives of our Sovereign in the first instance, and in the next of the Great British people; and if there is any policy or if there are any principles which we ask of them, those principles and that policy are the principles and policy which the united wisdom of Parliament has proclaimed for us, and which have been given to us in the words of a great Conservative Prime Minister, and which likewise have this one additional merit for us, that they also represent the personal wishes and feelings of the Sovereign Lady in whose name

3rd Day.

Res. X. Conveying the thanks of India to Lord Reay.

they were proclaimed. (*Cheers.*) Sir, if our Conservative friends have any doubt as to this profession on our part, I would invite them to come and test us. I would invite our Governor designate, who is a Conservative, if these proceedings arrest his attention, to come and do likewise. If he proves to us as good a Governor as Lord Reay has been, we shall feel for him the same gratitude, the same devotion, and we shall not be the less ready to acknowledge our obligation to him because in English politics he happened to be a follower of Lord Salisbury and not of Mr. Gladstone. One point more about this proposition. It will be urged that Lord Reay has made some mistakes. I am not here to deny that mistakes may have been made, these are a good deal matters of opinion, but what I wish to say is that if you regard the position in which the Governor of a presidency is placed—if you see how he is surrounded, if you see what little means he has of knowing our wishes and our wants,—the surprise is not that Lord Reay has made, as some think, a mistake, here and there, but that his mistakes have been so few and so slight. (*Cheers.*)

When a Governor comes to this country all the surroundings, political, social, public and private, influence him in one direction. We have no means at our command to redress the balance ; we have no organized means of letting him know the way in which we regard the questions of importance that come before him ; and if under these circumstances he makes a mistake the fault is not in the Governor, but in the system. The fact that Lord Reay has been such a successful Governor is due to the high sense of duty, to the lofty conception which he had of England's mission, and above all to the singular rectitude of purpose which has always guided him in everything that he has done for us. Of course he could not satisfy every interest, he could not satisfy every want and wish of the community over which he rules. In this respect I would remind you that the Governor of a presidency is not a free agent. He too has to obey imperial behests, he has to shape his policy according to imperial demands ; and we have to remember the demands made upon the Provincial Government during Lord Reay's regime. You remember the late edict in which the Governor was told, "Let your sick and suffering be without hospitals, let your uneducated poor remain without education, let no provision be made against famine, because we want all your money and all your taxes in order to indulge in annexation on the one hand and in creating frontier defences on the other." I am afraid those frontier defences may prove the harbingers of further annexations in a more difficult and dangerous quarter. But this apart. In spite of these demands let us see what Lord Reay has done for us in this presidency. He has created institutions, he has laid the foundations broad and deep for edifices that will rise hereafter to be the homes of industries, of arts, of sciences such as never existed before in this country, and which I trust, when they thrive and when they are properly supported, will remain for all time the mighty monuments of Lord Reay's wise, sympathetic and sagacious rule. These are remarks which refer perhaps locally to Bombay. I will only make one remark more which may be more in harmony with the feeling prevalent on this occasion ; I refer to Lord Reay's attitude to our aspirations and our demands. My friend Javerilal spoke of the members of Council whom Lord Reay had chosen ; and it is a remarkable fact that of his Councillors two have been Presidents of this Congress, and among the remainder you have no less than five, Messrs. Ferozshah Mehta, Nulkar, Dayaram Jethmul, Telang and Ranade, who have ever been leaders and pilots of the Congress movement on this side of India. (*Prolonged cheers.*)

Well, Bombay must be, I am sure, grateful to her Sister Presidencies and Provinces for their help and co-operation without which this unique demonstration in Lord Reay's favor would not have been possible. We are sure, first, that you share our regret at Lord Reay's departure ; we are equally sure you will join with us in our wish, and thus give it not only greater volume but greater weight, that when Lord Reay retires from his Governorship, and when he has taken such rest as may be necessary for one who has toiled so hard and so unremittingly he may place himself in the ranks of the Indian party of the formation of which you, sir, brought the glad tidings, side by side, and shoulder to shoulder with that great nobleman, our noblest, our never-to-be forgotten Viceroy, whose legitimate successor in India, to the admiration, the attachment and grateful affection of the people of India, Lord Reay has proved himself. (*Cheers.*) One word more, and I have done. If in consideration of Lord Reay's services to the State (for he who serves India's cause serves one of Britain's greatest causes) it should please our gracious Sovereign to send him back to us in another and more exalted character (*hear, hear*), we shall hail and welcome him as no Sovereign representative ever was welcomed before in India ; for we believe, and we will cherish the faith, that what Lord Reay has done, as Governor, is but the earnest of what Lord Reay would do, as Viceroy. (*Loud cheers.*)

Mr. A. M. Dharamsey (*Bombay, No.* 891, *in list*)—Mr. President, Ladies and Gentlemen, I have very great pleasure indeed in supporting the proposition that has been so ably laid before you by my friend Javerilal and so ably supported by my friend Mr. Wadia. After the remarks that have fallen from these gentlemen, I feel that I

3rd Day.

Res. X. Conveying the thanks of India to Lord Reay.

am not called upon to make any lengthened observations or to detain you by going over the same ground which my friends have traversed. If there has been one thing, more than another, which has characterized Lord Reay's administration, it has been his anxious desire to deal in a spirit of fairness, and justice, equality and impartiality, with the varied interests committed to his care among the various sections of the community with which he has to deal. At the same time Lord Reay has not been unmindful of the special wants of the backward units; and as a member of the Mahomedan Community I can assure you that Lord Reay has always given a willing ear to our demands, and, so far as lay in his power, has tried to meet our real wants. (*Cheers.*) The selections made by Lord Reay have marked a new era, a new departure in the nominations to our Legislative Council. Some of our best university men who had never before been appointed to the Council were appointed by Lord Reay; and I trust that the days of appointing, as our so-called representatives, men who did not in any way represent the people of India, are gone by for ever, and that Lord Reay has rendered impossible a return of those old evil days. One remark more, and I have done. You have heard from my friend Mr. Wadia that Lord Reay has been a sympathiser with our just aspirations. I venture to say that next after the name of our late beloved Viceroy, Lord Ripon (*cheers*), the name of Lord Reay will be enshrined in our memories (*cheers*) and our hearts. (*Loud cheers.*)

A DELEGATE—I think that a Punjabee should be heard on this subject.

LALA MURLIDHAR (*Punjab, No.* 1422, *in list*) ascended the platform and raising his joined hands, said:—BROTHERS! that God may bless the country which has given to us such a just and conscientious Governor as Lord Reay is the heartfelt prayer of the people of the Punjab. (*Loud and prolonged cheers.*)

THE PRESIDENT—It is quite clear that there are no two opinions on this subject. Shall I not put the resolution at once? (*Cries of " Yes, yes."*) Then our tenth Resolution will stand.

RESOLVED: *That in view to his approaching departure, this Congress puts on record an expression of the high sense entertained not only in the Bombay Presidency, but throughout India, of the ability, integrity, and impartiality that have characterised Lord Reay's administration, as also of the gratitude which the whole country feels to be his due for the sympathy that he has ever extended to Indian aspirations and efforts.*

Now, are you all agreed? (*Yes, yes, all, all!—loud and prolonged cheering.*) Gentlemen, that Resolution has been carried by acclamation, and permit me to say, that in thus honouring Lord Reay you have equally done honour to yourselves. (*Cheers.*)

Res. XI. Qualifications and Disqualifications in electoral Scheme.

MR. EARDLEY NORTON (*Madras, No.* 44, *in list*)—MR. PRESIDENT and Gentlemen, the proposition I have to move is a purely technical one. You recollect that at the beginning of the Congress you appointed a Subjects Committee to consider certain matters delegated to them by the Congress. Yesterday that Committee, in considering the matter of the Legislative Councils elected to leave over until another day the question of the qualifications and disqualifications of the various sections of the electorate. By some of our friends it is believed that that Subjects Committee is now, strictly speaking, dead. I have been asked to invite you to resuscitate it, and it is merely in that behalf, inasmuch as we require your authority to recall that body into being, that I rise to move this proposition:—

PROPOSED: *That the Subjects Committee be instructed to settle the questions, (left open in the skeleton scheme for the reconstruction of the Councils, embodied in Resolution II.) of the qualifications requisite for, and the disqualifications which should debar from, becoming*

(*a*) *a Voter;*
(*b*) *a Representative;*
(*c*) *a Member of a Provincial Legislative Council, and*
(*d*) *a Member of the Imperial Legislative Council;*

and to submit their Report thereon to Charles Bradlaugh, Esq., M.P., for the purposes of the Bill which he has been requested to have drawn.

I have only to say this much, that a great deal of thought has already been devoted to the consideration of the scheme which was laid before you yesterday with respect to Legislative Councils, and it certainly was always intended that the scheme should be handed over to Mr. Bradlaugh, perfect, so far as any scheme can be perfected by the introduction of these qualifications. The omission to keep the Subjects Committee alive by adjourning it, was accidental, and I ask you to repair it by resuscitating this Committee, so that we may complete our work and enable Mr. Bradlaugh to know exactly what the feeling, of the Congress as a whole, is upon these matters which though in one sense matters of detail are yet of very essential and vital importance. (*Cheers.*)

3rd Day.

Res. XI. Qualifications and Disqualifications in electoral Scheme.

MR. W. C. BONNERJEE (*Calcutta, No. 1788, in list*)—I have great pleasure in seconding this Resolution. You will remember that in the scheme you adopted you have the words "qualifications and disqualifications" "which will be settled later" alike in clauses 3, 4, and 5.

It is necessary that this Congress should settle these qualifications and disqualifications before they can be introduced into the Bill, and for that reason it is necessary that this matter should come before the Congress's duly-elected representatives, the subjects Committee, once again. Perhaps, Mr. President, you will now put the Resolution which is a purely formal one. (*Cries of "Yes, yes."*)

THE PRESIDENT—Very well, then our 11th Resolution is this.

RESOLVED : *That the Subjects Committee be instructed to settle the questions, (left open in the skeleton scheme for the reconstruction of the Councils, embodied in Resolution II.), of the qualifications requisite for, and the disqualifications which should debar from, becoming*

(*a*) *a Voter;*
(*b*) *a Representative;*
(*c*) *a Member of a Provincial Legislative Council, and*
(*d*) *a Member of the Imperial Legislative Council;*

and to submit their Report thereon to Charles Bradlaugh, Esq., M.P., for the purposes of the Bill which he has been requested to have drawn.

Those in favour of this Resolution will please hold up their hands—those against it—the Resolution is passed unanimously.

Res. XII. Re-appointment of Mr A. O. Hume as General Secretary.

Mr. W. C. BONNERJEE (*Calcutta, No. 1788, in list*)—Gentlemen,—I now rise to propose that Resolution which is never seconded but which is always carried with the greatest enthusiasm, I mean the resolution re-appointing our old friend and leader Mr. Hume as General Secretary. (*Loud and continued cheers and waving of handkerchiefs.*)

THE PRESIDENT—It is hardly necessary to tell you that this, our twelfth Resolution.

RESOLVED : *That Mr. A. O. Hume, C.B., be re-elected General Secretary of the National Indian Congress for the ensuing year,*

has been carried by acclamation. (*Renewed cheers.*)

I will now call upon Mr. Surendranath Banerjee to move the next proposition which relates to many matters affecting the administrative arrangements of the Congress during the coming year. Our movement is expanding and entering upon a wider sphere of activity and it is necessary that our administrative arrangements should be constantly re-adjusted in conformity with external changes. (*Cheers.*)

Res. XIII. Regulation of certain matters pertaining to the Congress.

MR. SURENDRANATH BANERJEE (*Calcutta, No. 1816, in list*) said :—Brother Delegates,—I rise to move certain more or less formal propositions which relate to the constitution of the Congress, and certain arrangements which it will be necessary for us to make, consequent upon certain changes which are likely to take place in the course of the year. I will place this proposition at once before you, and I am sure it will be carried with acclamation. It will constitute a sort of omnibus resolution in its own way.

PROPOSED :—

(*a*) *That, in view of the large number of delegates this year assembled and the probability, arising from past experience, of their number continuing to increase year by year, henceforth the number of delegates to be allowed from each Congress circle be limited to five per million of the total population of the circle: the Standing Committee of each circle allotting the number which their jurisdiction as a whole is entitled to elect, amongst their several electoral divisions, as may seem most expedient.*

(*b*) *That from the date of Mr. Hume's departure for England, the Hon'ble Pundit Ajoodhianath be appointed Joint General Secretary, and that Rs. 5,000 be assigned for the payment by him of such Assistant Secretaries as he may find it necessary to employ, clerical assistance, postage, telegraphs, and printing, and further that Mr. W. C. Bonnerjee be appointed Standing Counsel for Bengal, Mr. Pherozshah Mehta, Standing Counsel for Bombay, and Mr. Ananda Charlu, Standing Counsel for Madras, to the Joint General Secretary.*

(*c*) *That the tentative rules for the constitution and working of the Congress which were first considered at Madras, and in regard to which various addenda have from time to time been circulated, be thoroughly considered during the coming year by the several Standing Congress Committees, and definitely dealt with by the Congress at its next session.*

(*d*) *That this Congress do hereby confirm the appointment of Sir W. Wedderburn, Bart., and Messrs. W. S. Caine, M.P., W. S. Bright Maclaren, M.P., J. E. Ellis, M.P., Dadabhai Naoroji and George Yule, as a Committee (with power to add to their*

3rd Day.

Res. XIII. Regulation of certain matters pertaining to the Congress.

number) to guide and direct the operations and control the expenditure of the National Congress Agency in England, and do further tender its sincere thanks to these gentlemen, and to Mr W. Digby, C.I.E., the Secretary, for the service which they are rendering to India.

(e) *That this Congress do formally appoint Mr. George Yule, Mr. A. O. Hume, Mr. J. Adam, Mr. Eardley Norton, Mr. Pherozshah Mehta, Mr. Surendranath Banerjee, Mr. Mono Mohan Ghose, Mr. Shurfuddin, Mr. R. N. Mudholker, and Mr. W. C. Bonnerjee,* to represent its views in England and press upon the consideration of the British Public the political reforms which the Congress has advocated.*

(f) *That a sum of Rs. 45,000 be raised for the expenses of the Congress Work, in this country and in England, during the ensuing year, and that the different Standing Committees do send their respective apportioned amounts to the General Secretary, the one half in three, and the balance in six months.*

I will now make a few remarks on this series of propositions. It will not require many words from me to recommend them to your unanimous, I was going to say, enthusiastic acceptance.

The first clause refers to the fixing of the number of delegates, and I think it is important that the number should now be fixed. We have already shown what we can do in respect of organisation. We have abundantly made clear the life and vitality which animates the whole of the Congress movement. In the first year of the Congress there were 70 delegates present in Bombay, in the next year the number came up to 400 in Calcutta; in Madras the number again doubled itself to 800; at Allahabad the number reached 1,200; and in this fifth year of the National Congress we have something like 1,900 delegates. If this state of things were to be allowed to go on the largest hall which we can erect would not accommodate the delegates, who would be thronging from all parts of the Empire. We have shown our capacity and our powers of organisation. The vitality of the movement is manifest and now I think it is time that we should so organise the Congress that it will be available for the practical purposes of deliberation and business. And therefore it has been resolved to fix the number at about one thousand.

Then we have the appointment of a joint General Secretary in the person of my distinguished friend behind me. Mr. Hume is going to England. What for? Not for pleasure, not for enjoyment, not for recreation, not for the purpose even of recruiting his health: he goes as the trusted leader of the Congress movement (*Loud cheers*) to guide and instruct that deputation that will accompany him to England. You have done your part upon Indian platforms, you have done your work in this country, and now you must appeal to the instincts of the English nation, not merely to the voice of the English friends who are always ready and willing to assist us, but through your own countrymen who will plead your cause in English Halls and upon English platforms. (*Cheers.*) I think this will be the realization of one of the grandest ideals that ever flashed across the minds of any patriot or philanthrophist; India standing before the bar of English Public opinion, and there through her own accredited delegates, chosen by the representatives of the nation in this august assembly, pleading her cause and demanding the redress of her grievances; no finer, no nobler, no grander spectacle has ever been presented to the gaze of mankind. (*Cheers.*) Rome, Greece, America, the greatest nations in the world, have nothing to show equal to this spectacle in magnitude, in solemnity and in majestic grandeur. (*Loud cheers.*)

Next comes the question of our Indian Political Agency. It cannot be doubted that this agency has rendered most memorable service to the people of this country. If there is at the present moment an awakening of interest in the minds of Englishmen in reference to Indian matters, it is due, in no small degree, to the indefatigable labors of that Political Agency controlled and guided by our distinguished Chairman and his colleagues; it is therefore our duty to support that Agency. It is not enough to vote thanks—that we can do easily enough; it is necessary that we should follow this vote of gratitude to the English gentlemen who have been enlisting themselves in our cause by a substantial mark of our interest. (*Cheers.*) You are therefore called upon to pay—very little indeed, considering the magnitude of the work and the vastness of the Indian population. I call upon you to pay according to the measure of your ability and the measure of your self-sacrifice. You are two hundred millions of people. If every individual member of that two hundred millions were to pay but one pice you would have thirty lakhs of rupees to send in. Can we not all pay a pice (*Yes, yes*). Are we so wanting in the capacity for self-sacrifice as to be incapable of a paltry effort of this kind? Yes, we may so orgainize the Congress that it may be possible to go to the humblest cottager and demand of him his contribution in aid of this grand national movement. It is not right that from year to year your distinguished Secretary should pay ten or fifteen thousand rupees out of his own pocket. I think it scarcely creditable to the patriotism of my countrymen that this should be repeated from year to

* To these names was subsequently added, the name of Mr. J. E. Howard, inadvertently omitted. *Vide ante*—Summary of Resolutions. Foot note last page.

3rd Day.

Res. XIII. Regulation of certain matters pertaining to the Congress.

year. I therefore hope and trust that from this time forth there will be no difficulty whatever in raising the necessary contributions for the support of the Indian Political Agency. I would make an earnest appeal to you in this connection. Gentlemen, we must learn the lesson of self-sacrifice. It is not enough to make long speeches, to pass resolutions in this Congress; we must learn to sacrifice ourselves for the good of the country and in furtherance of the great cause to which we have consecrated ourselves. England paid twenty million pounds for the enfranchisement of Negro slaves. Will you not pay fifty thousand rupees, not for Emancipation of foreign slaves but for your own political redemption? (*Cheers.*) If you are not able to do that, the National Congress is a meaningless demonstration which cannot lead to those great results that have been expected of it. But I hope and trust there will be no difficulty. Let us organise and then let us raise the necessary funds and the National Congress will have fulfilled the noble mission which belongs to it in the political reorganisation of this country. (*Loud and continued cheering.*)

Mr. Eardley Norton: (*Madras, No. 44, in list.*)—Mr. President and Gentlemen, I have been called upon at a moment's notice to perform a most difficult task—to follow Mr. Surendranath Banerjee. I do not pretend for one second that I have such qualifications as his to rivet your attention or enchain your admiration; but I will not yield even to him in the feeling I entertain with regard to the aspirations which the people of this country cherish. In our respective spheres and with our different capacities we both alike labor humbly but energetically on your behalf, and I am not prepared to give the palm, in that respect, to my friend from Calcutta. It would be strange indeed if, trained as I have been by the inheritance which I have received from my father, I did not also take the deep and solemn interest which I do, in the legitimate aspirations of the people of this country (*Cheers.*) I think I scarcely need assure you in words—because I have endeavoured, at any rate, throughout my very short career in this country, to let my words be followed by deeds, so that all men could plainly read from the Governor-General downwards—I need hardly assure you, I say, that if I go home I shall go gladly as your servant, and doubly gladly in this sense, since whereas last year we were told that we were speaking as the unaccredited agents of the millions of this country, on this occasion we shall produce our certificates from the Congress of Bombay. (*Cheers.*) For many years I have been endeavourng to rivet the attention of the people of Madras, my own Presidency, on this great fact, *viz.*, that redress you will not get from the authorities in India, and that no reform will come to you which is not given to you by the people of England. In that view, gentlemen, you cannot over-estimate the wonderful importance of the Congress Agency in London; and although his name has not been previously referred to, though it is included in the resolution moved by Mr. Surendranath Banerjee,—believe me that you owe to Mr. Digby a deep debt of gratitude. (*Cheers.*) We have been fortunate indeed in having him as our right hand man in London and, aided by the advice of gentlemen better qualified than himself by age and experience, our agency, as a whole, is an organization of which we may be proud, and believe me, gentlemen, that no man is more entitled, by reason of his industry, his assiduity and single-mindedness of purpose, to our confidence and respect, than is our agent in London, Mr. William Digby. (*Cheers.*) We shall go to England all of us and possibly by this time next year we may return as glad harbingers of tidings even more important than our President brought us on this present occasion. Possibly the Bill which Mr. Bradlaugh shall have moved will have advanced at any rate one stage towards completion, but I warn you not to look for the complete fruition of your desires within the short space of twelve months.

If, with us who go home to plead your cause, you will not merely speak but put your hands in your pockets and pay—if only you will do that and supply us with the sinews of war, take it from us an absolute fact incapable of contradiction that your cause will progress at ten times its present speed. (*Cheers.*) My belief always has been that action is better than words. I have to announce to you—I will not mention the name, because he shall come forward and say it for himself—that one at any rate of the Madras delegates has been so moved by the oratory of Mr. Surendranath Banerjee that he is prepared to give Rs. 1,000 towards this movement. (*Cheers.*) And as it is desirable that the contagion should spread I shall be happy to make that 1,000, 2,000 (*Cheers*). That will only leave Rs. 43,000 to subscribe, and I trust you will do it at once.

The President: I think I may now put the resolution.

A Delegate: Take the money, and then put the resolution.

On this Mr. Murlidhar of the Punjab, led off by depositing Rs. 555 on the table, and then faster than could be recorded or announced, notes, silver and copper coins and promises to pay poured in. Mr. Hume's and Sir W. Wedderburn's and other prominent gentlemen's hats were seized and carried round and round coming back each time full of silver and copper. The time was running short, Mr. Bradlaugh was to arrive shortly to receive addresses and the flow of money had to be arrested, all the money and promises being locked and sealed up and taken charge of.

When, later on in the evening, the money could be counted and the promises classified, it appeared that Rs. 9,179-11-7 had been paid in, in cash, as follows :—

3rd Day.

Res. XIII. Regulation of certain matters, pertaining to the Congress.

Subscriptions Paid in.

No.	Names of Subscribers.	Amount.			Total.
	Paid in Cash.	Rs.	a.	p.	
1	Lala Murlidhar from Loodhiana people	555	0	0	
2	Midnapur Congress Committee (Bengal)	300	0	0	
3	Munshi Sakawat Hussain of Shajahanpur	100	0	0	
4	A. Nundi for Jubbulpore people (part payment)	350	0	0	
5	Anonymous	10	0	0	
6	Atmaji Ramchunder Hardikar	5	0	0	
7	Madras Delegates	50	0	0	
8	V. Srinivasa of South Arcot	25	0	0	
9	Govind Gopal Tipnis of Poonah	5	0	0	
10	Nursing Dutt of Howrah (Bengal)	50	0	0	
11	F. G. S., Berar	10	0	0	
12	Lala Durgaprasad, Allahabad	15	0	0	
13	O. L Sarma, Madras	20	0	0	
14	Lala Thansing, Umballa	50	0	0	
15	M. Vasudeva Naidu Pillay, Madras	100	0	0	
16	Shibchunder Seal, Bengal	100	0	0	
17	Amreli, Kattyawar	150	0	0	
18	Delegate, Chidumbrum	10	0	0	
19	Gopal Ramkristna, Central Provinces	10	0	0	
20	Lukshman Atmaram, Basim, Berar	25	0	0	
21	L. C. Baput, Yeotmal, Berar	50	0	0	
22	Bengal Delegates	20	0	0	
23	J. R. Nimbkar, Nasick	10	0	0	
24	Allahabad and Benares Standing Congress Committees, through Hon'ble Pundit Ajoodhianath	3,000	0	0	
25	Anonymous	10	6	0	
26	Anonymous	7	0	0	
27	Gungadhur	10	0	0	
28	Keshava Bapuji	20	0	0	
29	Pundit Prithinath, Cawnpur	500	0	0	
30	Gungaram	100	0	0	
31	Gungaram Bhau Moske	100	0	0	
32	Rambhajan Tripatuk	100	0	0	
33	Itaria Pillay	100	0	0	
34	Balkrishna Pillay	50	0	0	
35	Baranasi Rameswar Reddy	50	0	0	
36	Panwell Taluka	30	0	0	
37	Sriram of Mirzapore, N.-W. Provinces	200	0	0	
38	Balwant Vyankaji Khot of Amraoti, Berar	50	0	0	
39	Ramchandra N. Mudholkar, Amraoti, Berar	10	0	0	
40	People of Ichulkuranji	100	0	0	
41	Jotindranath Mullick of Midnapur, Bengal	100	0	0	
42	Dhone Kristo Ghose on behalf of Beerbhom Distoict, Bengal	100	0	0	
43	S. P. M., through Mr. Sirkar	500	0	0	
44	Friends do do	69	0	0	
45	Deviprasad Vaid	12	0	0	
46	K. P. Banarjee, for Bareilly City	8	0	0	
47	Manikdah Hitashadhani Sabha, through Baroda Khant Joarda	27	0	0	
48	Anonymous	20	0	0	
49	Hat collections in the Congress Meeting and donations, the donors of which have not been recorded.	507	13	7	
50	Rai Bahadur Sabaputty Mudaliar	1,000	0	0	
51	Standing Congress Committee, Pandharpur District Sholapur, through Messrs. Keskar and Dharurkar	100	0	0	
52	Bali Shadharam Sabha	16	0	0	
53	Secretary Congress Committee Vridhachellam, South Arcot	15	0	0	
54	Bhasker Vittul Jaminis, Secretary, Congress Committee Mulkapur, Kolapur	35	0	0	
55	P. K. T. Sinwan, Muzaffargarh	5	0	0	
56	Dwarkanath Moitra, Secretary, Nattore Divisional Congress Committee	50	0	0	
57	P, K. T. Sinwan, Muzaffargarh (second payment)	2	8	0	
58	Kandjhi Sahye, Shahabad	150	0	0	
59	Sunt Sing Salutry and Rungnarain Bajpai, Shwebo, Upper Burmah	5	0	0	
	Total paid in Cash...	....			9 179 11 7

3rd Day.

Res. XIII. Regulation of certain matters pertaining to the Congress.

Subscriptions promised.

Moreover, written promises of contributions to the further extent of Rs. 56,226 had been given, as follows :—

No.	Names of Subscribers.	Amount.			Total.		
	Promised.	Rs.	a.	p.	Rs.	a.	p.
60	Seokatan Sing, Berar	20	0	0			
61	P. N. Mitter, Calcutta	3,000	0	0			
62	Bunko Behary Sing, Bengal	100	0	0			
63	Krishnaghur Standing Congress Committee	150	0	0			
64	Chogdah do. do. do.	50	0	0			
65	Bapuji Ramchand Pandit, Pleader, Poonah	100	0	0			
66	Balkrishna Ramchund do. do.	100	0	0			
67	Narayan Bapujee Kelatkar do. do.	100	0	0			
68	Tanjore Congress Committee, per Swaminada Iyer	1,000	0	0			
69	Swaminada Iyer	200	0	0			
70	Secunderabad Congress Committee	1,000	0	0			
71	Vasudeva Rao of Warda, C. P.	50	0	0			
72	Rati Kant Bose, Katdah, Nuddea	100	0	0			
73	Guzerat Delegates	75	0	0			
74	Russapugla Improvement Society	25	0	0			
75	Dinanath Gui, Ghatal Congress Committee	200	0	0			
76	Ganesh Vinayek Patwurdhan, Sholapur	25	0	0			
77	Mullapa Warid do.	200	0	0			
78	Bapuji Parasram do.	25	0	0			
79	Dinkar Bulal do.	25	0	0			
80	Mulkarjun Sidramappa Pasare do.	25	0	0			
81	Lala Kunhaya Lal, Pleader, Chief Court, Punjab	300	0	0			
82	R. Vinkaya, Vellore	150	0	0			
83	Mohendra Chundra Deb, Tipperah	50	0	0			
84	Khattry Sabha, per Pundit Durga Prasad	100	0	0			
85	Hoshungabad Congress Committee, per Kalidas Chaudhri	150	0	0			
86	Khandwa Congress Committee, per Haridas Chatterji	100	0	0			
87	Antaji Govind, Amraoti, Berar	25	0	0			
88	B. H. Karandikar, do. do.	25	0	0			
89	Shunker Govind, Akola, do.	50	0	0			
90	Popat Lal Purushottam, Balapur, Berar	100	0	0			
91	Venkata Rao Hunmant Rao Deshmuk, Elichpur, Berar	100	0	0			
92	Pandu Wd. Nundajee, Akola, Berar	25	0	0			
93	Rao Saheb Deo Rao Vinayek, Akola, Berar	500	0	0			
94	R. N. Mudholker, Amraoti, Berar	500	0	0			
95	G. S. Kaparde, do. do.	500	0	0			
96	P. N. Jog, do. do.	500	0	0			
97	Trimbak Keshut Vaidya and Sons	150	0	0			
98	Kanitkar and Co., Deccan Dramatic Company	200	0	0			
99	Hon'ble S. Subramania Iyer, C.I.E.	1,000	0	0			
100	Prahladji Deo Shunkkur	20	0	0			
101	Golabdas Bhaidas, Surat	2,000	0	0			
102	Hariprasad Santukhram Desai	1,000	0	0			
103	Sunker Naik, Wagle, Ahmednuggur	500	0	0			
104	Goburdhandas Goculdas Tejpal	1,000	0	0			
105	Baikuntha Nath Sen, Murshidabad	1,000	0	0			
106	Srinath Pal, do.	1,000	0	0			
107	Nuffer Chunder Pal Chowdhry, Nuddea	1,000	0	0			
108	Mohadeb Chetty, Madras	1,000	0	0			
109	Eardley Norton, do.	1,500	0	0			
110	P. Soomasoondram, do.	500	0	0			
111	Narayan Vishnu Pranjabai, Khandala	50	0	0			
112	Bijapur District, per Kesava Ramjee	500	0	0			
113	Thakoordas Atmaram and Vijbhukundas Atmaram	1,000	0	0			
114	Dr. Bhalchundra Krishna Bhatvadkar, Bombay	200	0	0			
115	Keshub Chunder Sadhu, Hooghly	150	0	0			
116	Vandravandas Purushotamdas, Bombay	500	0	0			
117	Makshadas Mitter Benares	300	0	0			
118	Bombay Central Students' Union, per Bhowani Bapuji ...	20	0	0			
119	Virchand Dipchund, Bombay,	1,275	0	0			
120	Narayandas Kaliandas and Dhierdas Hari Ballabhdass	250	0	0			
	Carried forward	....			25,860	0	0

3rd Day.

Res. XIII. Regulation of certain matters pertaining to the Congress.

Subscriptions promised.

No.	Names of Subscribers.	Amount.	Total.
		Rs. a. p.	Rs. a. p.
	Brought forward......		25,860 0 0
121	Hiralal Tribhuvandas Parekh	25 0 0	
122	Sadasiva Balkrishna Bhate, Pleader, Belgaum	300 0 0	
123	Sanmilani Sabha, Nilphamari, per Biraja Mohan Choudhri	5 0 0	
124	Lala Chandika Prasad	25 0 0	
125	Lala Rajaram Bhargava, Banker, Allahabad	250 0 0	
126	Lala Bhowani Prasad Brijmohunlal, Banker, Allahabad	100 0 0	
127	Pundit Motilal Nehru, Vakil, N.-W. Provinces	100 0 0	
128	Balkrishna Gopal Sanyal, B.A., B L., Manipuri	100 0 0	
129	Gya Congress Committee, per Dr. M. Wazir Ali Khan Lodi	300 0 0	
130	Chota Nagpur Congress Committee, per Hari Charan Mitter	200 0 0	
131	Pesumal, Pleader, Sukker, Scinde	100 0 0	
132	Venkatesh Ganesh Sasi Hital, Pleader, Honore, Canara	25 0 0	
133	Shivaram Shoobrao, Pleader, Karwar	25 0 0	
134	Fureedpore People's Association	100 0 0	
135	Ambica Churn Sen, Pleader, Khulna	50 0 0	
136	Norendra Chundra Bose, Pleader, Moradabad	100 0 0	
137	Tribani Sahai, Pleader, Bareilly	100 0 0	
138	Anonymous, per Shivaram Hari Sathe	100 0 0	
139	Dr. Sada Siva W. Kane, Bombay	100 0 0	
140	S. H. Nimbhgarkar, Bijapur Kine Defence Society	50 0 0	
141	V. K. Juglekar Kirajgee, Dharwar	50 0 0	
142	Lukshman Ramrao Sukenkar, Jahghirdar, Nasik	200 0 0	
143	Bulwant Shridhur Sahasra Buddhe, Satara	100 0 0	
144	R. P. Karandikar do.	100 0 0	
145	Kondha Dipaji Poulkar, Manager, Jain Temple, Shirpur, Berar	51 0 0	
146	Lahiri and Co., 101, College Street, Calcutta	50 0 0	
147	Madhavdas Gokuldas Pasta	250 0 0	
148	Biraj Mohun Choudhri, Rungpore	50 0 0	
149	Pareshnath Choudhri	25 0 0	
150	Tukaram Puddamjee Deshmuk, Jarud, Berar	200 0 0	
151	Narahur Bugwant Deshpande, Elichpur, do	200 0 0	
152	Balkrishna Mahadev Patel, Warud, do.	100 0 0	
153	Govindrao Deshpande, Anjansingi, do.	100 0 0	
154	Krishnarao Raghav, Budnera, do.	50 0 0	
155	Damaji Vaghaji, Patel, Basim, do.	50 0 0	
156	Yeswant Vaman Dighe, do. do.	25 0 0	
157	Hurchandrao Vishnarao, Sindh	200 0 0	
158	Govind Narayan Kane, Amraoti, Berar	25 0 0	
159	Narayandas Purshottamdas	200 0 0	
160	Ishverdas Shri, Surat	100 0 0	
161	Amritrao Manicklal Desai	50 0 0	
162	Jiwandas Mulji, Bombay	125 0 0	
163	Narayanrao Vasudev Kharkar, Tansa	100 0 0	
164	A. Nundi, Jubbulpore	150 0 0	
165	Kursundas Bhugudia	100 0 0	
166	Narayan Rao Govind, Hardah	100 0 0	
167	Krishnarao Rajaram	100 0 0	
168	Bulwunt Kashinath	100 0 0	
169	Raghunathrao Vaman	100 0 0	
170	Moro Vishvanath Joshi, Amraoti, Berar	1,000 0 0	
171	Bhagirath Prasad, Hislop College, Nagpur	150 9 0	
172	Lakshman Govind and Keshavrao, Kandwali, Warda	5,000 0 0	
173	Vishnu Narain Apte, in memory of his late brother Chintamun Narain Apte	100 0 0	
174	Jagadish Kumar Mukerji	50 0 0	
175	District Association, Belgaum	1,000 0 0	
176	Hubli Congress Committee, per Gurunath Balajee, Morab, Dharwar	200 0 0	
177	Rajkote Delegates per Hormusjee Ardashir Wadia	1,500 0 0	14,206 0 0
	Carried forward......	....	40,066 0 0

3rd Day.

Res. XIII. Regulation of certain matters pertaining to the Congress.

Subscriptions promised.

No.	Names of Subscribers.	Amount.	Total.
		Rs. a. p.	Rs. a. p.
	Brought forward......	....	40,066 0 0
178	The Desai of Gundevi..	200 0 0	
179	Tookaram Tatya, 17, Tamarind Lane, Bombay	200 0 0	
180	Tribhuvan Malvi, Solicitor, Bombay	100 0 0	
181	Proprietor, Nyaya Shuddha Press, Harda	100 0 0	
182	Narayan Balkrishna N. Atreya, do.	25 0 0	
183	P. Narain Swami Naidu (Resident of Nagpur)	1,000 0 0	
184	Mhow Association, Per Hyder Ali	150 0 0	
185	Sylhet Coolies, per Beppin Chander Pal	200 0 0	
186	Kondo Vithul Godbole, Sangli	25 0 0	
187	Sheikh Nasirrudin, Benares	100 0 0	
188	Badrinath Chaturvedi, Bareilly	10 0 0	
189	Barisal People's Association, per Akshini Kumar Dutt. ...	300 0 0	
190	Howrah Congress Committee	200 0 0	
191	Hubli Delegates, per Shivarao Bepati	1,200 0 0	
192	Motilal D. Desai	50 0 0	
193	Tumluk Indian Association	100 0 0	
194	Poonah Committee, per M. B. Namjoshi.....................	2,000 0 0	
195	Bhan Dandallyk, Mahim	25 0 0	
196	Madras Standing Congress Committee......	5,000 0 0	
197	Waman Bepare Dene (Residents of Pen).....................	50 0 0	
198	Manickavaloo Moodliar	10 0 0	
199	Vinayekrao Vaman Duraskar (Junior branch), Diwas, C.P.	5 0 0	
200	Calcutta Northern Metropolitan Electoral Division........	2,000 0 0	
201	"Sanjibani" (Calcutta Newspaper)	100 0 0	
202	Delhi Congress Committee..	500 0 0	
203	Lala Dassondhe Ram, Pleader, Chief Court, Lahore	500 0 0	
204	Hissar Congress Committee	250 0 0	
205	Babu K. P. Roy, Pleader, Chief Court, Lahore	100 0 0	
206	Lahore, per Babu Jogendra Chandra Bose	395 0 0	
207	K. Timar Reddy (Ryots of Perote)	50 0 0	
208	Ramchander Keshav Limaye.....................................	100 0 0	
209	Pandurang Bapuji	15 0 0	
210	Bhikajee Anandram, Baramoti, Poonah	100 0 0	
211	The people of Cawnpore per Secretary	1,000 0 0	16,160 0 0
	Total Promised	......	56,226 0 0
	Total Paid (*vide ante*)	......	9,179 11 7
	Grand Total......	......	65,405 11 7

Thus, in less than half an hour, no less a sum than Rs. 65,400 was subscribed for Congress work.]

The President—Really, gentlemen, we must go on with our business and finish it. I shall put our 13th Resolution, as follows :—

Resolved:—

(*a*) *That, in view of the large number of delegates this year assembled and the probability arising from past experience, of their number continuing to increase year by year, henceforth the number of delegates to be allowed from each Congress circle be limited to five per million of the total population of the circle: the Standing Committee of each circle allotting the number which their jurisdiction, as a whole, is entitled to elect, amongst their several electoral divisions, as may seem most expedient.*

(*b*) *That from the date of Mr. Hume's departure for England, the Hon'ble Pundit Ajoodhianath be appointed Joint General Secretary, and that Rs. 5,000 be assigned for the payment by him of such Assistant Secretaries as he may find it necessary to employ, clerical assistance, postage, telegraphs, and printing, and further that Mr. W. C. Bonnerjee be appointed Standing Counsel for Bengal, Mr. Pherozshah Mehta, Standing Counsel for Bombay, and Mr. Ananda Charlu, Standing Counsel for Madras, to the Joint General Secretary.*

(*c*) *That the tentative rules for the constitution and working of the Congress which were first considered at Madras, and in regard to which various addenda have from time to time been circulated, be thoroughly considered during the coming year by the several Standing Congress Committees, and definitely dealt with by the Congress at its next session.*

3rd Day.

Res. XIII. Regulation of certain matters pertaining to the Congress.

(*d*) *That this Congress does hereby confirm the appointment of Sir W. Wedderburn, Bart., and Messrs. W. S. Caine, M.P., W. S. Bright Maclaren, M.P., J. E. Ellis, M.P., Dadabhai Naoroji and George Yule, as a Committee (with power to add to their number) to guide and direct the operations and control the expenditure of the National Congress Agency in England, and does further tender its sincere thanks to these gentlemen, and to Mr. W. Digby, C.I.E., the Secretary, for the service which they are rendering to India.*

(*e*) *That this Congress does formally appoint Mr. George Yule, Mr. A. O. Hume, Mr. Adam, Mr. Eardley Norton, Mr. Pherozshah Mehta, Mr. Surrendranath Bannerjee, Mr. Mono Mohan Ghose, Mr. Shurfuddin, Mr. R. N. Mudholker, and Mr. W. C. Bonnerjee to represent its views in England and press upon the consideration of the British Public the political reforms which the Congress has advocated.*

(*f*) *That a sum of Rs. 45,000 be raised for the expenses of the Congress Work in this country and in England during the ensuing year, and that the different Standing Committees do send their respective apportioned amounts to the General Secretary the one half in three, and the balance in six months.*

Now is this all agreed to? (*Yes, yes.*) Has any one any alteration to suggest? (*No, no, we are all agreed.*) Then I declare this Resolution to have been passed unanimously.

Res. XIV. 6th Congress to Meet in Bengal.

MR. A. O. HUME (*Punjab, No. 1402, in list*), who was received with prolonged and enthusiastic cheers—when the storm of welcome had somewhat subsided—said:—Gentlemen, I have my one little customary annual resolution to submit to you; but before I read it I must really thank you all extremely for the very noble and generous manner in which you have hailed me. If I have worked hard on your behalf—and I really have worked hard—if I have labored for you, if I have loved you, I am sure that by this spontaneous and enthusiastic demonstration you have amply repaid me. (*Renewed cheers and cries of "No, no."*) Well, gentlemen, we will not argue the question: we are all brethren together; and as the time is passing, and passing rapidly, and this Hall has to be prepared for the reception of Mr. Bradlaugh and the presentation of the addresses, I shall content myself with reading the proposition: "*That the Sixth Indian National Congress assemble at some city in Bengal, the exact place to be fixed hereafter, on the 26th December* 1890." I do not think it needs seconding, and feel sure that you will carry it by acclamation. (*Deafening cheers and shouts of approval.*)

THE PRESIDENT—Then I record this as our 14th Resolution.

RESOLVED: *That the Sixth Indian National Congress do assemble at some City in Bengal, the exact place to be fixed hereafter, on the 26th of December* 1890.

Res. XV. Special vote of thanks to Sir W. Wedderburn.

MR. ANANTA CHARLU (*Madras, No. 31, in list*)—Sisters and Brothers, I appear before you now that you are brimming over with patriotism and enthusiasm. I am sure that the mighty waves of eloquence that have rolled and thundered over you during this last hour must still be re-echoing in your ears, and I am equally sure that you are anxiously waiting for further floods of eloquence of a similarly overwhelming and heart-stirring character. This is not the time, truly, when any one like your humble servant should come forward in the vain hope of engaging your attention or satisfying your excited imaginations. But I, weak and humble as I am, and you know what a meek creature I am (*loud cheers and laughter*), have my own strength that makes me bold enough to face you and address you, strength of a tremendous kind, for I am going to ask you to pass a special vote of thanks to our distinguished Chairman, Sir William Wedderburn. (*Tremendous cheers.*) Now my proposition is this:—

PROPOSED: *That the Fifth Indian National Congress do tender its heart-felt thanks to its President, Sir William Wedderburn, as well for his ready sacrifice of personal and political considerations involved by his journey from England to India, as for that courtesy, impartiality and never failing sympathy which, characteristics of his long and honourable career as an official of this country, have marked his control of the proceedings of this assembly.*

This is not the time for a long speech, but one remark I will make, *viz.*, that if the 5th Indian National Congress is a greater success than any which has preceded it, it is due in a very great measure to the fact that Sir William Wedderburn consented to preside over it. (*Cheers.*) I am not surprised that he cheerfully consented to sacrifice all personal and other considerations because I, who have known him through a great portion of his career,

3rd Day.

Res. XV. Special Vote of thanks to Sir W. Wedderburn.

know perfectly well that he has thus given but one more proof of that sympathy and interest which he has felt for this country during his whole life. (*Cheers.*) As Sir William Wedderburn cannot put this resolution to the vote, I will ask you to carry it by acclamation. (*Loud and prolonged cheering.*)

THE GENERAL SECRETARY—Then I have much pleasure in recording that this our 15th Resolution has been carried by acclamation :—

RESOLVED : *That the Fifth Indian National Congress hereby tenders its heart-felt thanks to its President, Sir William Wedderburn, as well for his ready sacrifice of personal and political considerations involved by his journey from England to India, as for that courtesy, impartiality and never-failing sympathy which, characteristics of his long and honourable career as an official of this country, have marked his control of the proceedings of this assembly.*

THE PRESIDENT—Ladies and Gentlemen, I thank you most sincerely for the very kind things you say and think of me. My only difficulty is that I do not think I ought to receive your thanks ; I should rather express my thanks to you ("*No, no,*") for your kind welcome on coming back almost to my own home, and for the grand sight that I have enjoyed during these three days of your deliberations. I must say that the closing scene was to me a most interesting one—the storming of the platform by people desirous of contributing to the public good was such a sight as I have never before witnessed. I wish also to thank this great assembly for the wonderful support they have given me in the fulfilment of my duties as Chairman. This assembly is three times as large as the House of Commons, and gives three times as little trouble to manage. (*Laughter.*) I should also like to take the opportunity of expressing thanks for the numberless kind letters and telegrams which I have received from distant friends during the sitting of the Congress expressive not only of great kindness to myself but full of sympathy with the objects of the Congress. I think this Congress will be a memorable one in many ways. It has swollen to such proportions that you yourselves have been forced, on account of physical difficulties, to reduce the number to manageable proportions. Secondly, I think we may consider this meeting specially interesting because for the first time it has been graced by the presence of lady delegates. And thirdly, I do not think the most hardened opponents of the movement will now deny that we have entered into the domain of practical politics when our programme has been taken up by a public man of the firmness of character of Mr. Charles Bradlaugh. (*Long and loud cheers.*) Gentlemen, I have not only had the opportunity of addressing you at the commencement but I have had the pleasure of speaking to you a good deal during the course of our proceedings. I will not therefore further trespass upon your indulgence. I will only say that, as long as I live, I shall ever retain the proud memory of having presided over the 5th Indian National Congress. (*Loud and prolonged cheering, towards the close of which*)

MR. W. C. BONNERJEE (*Calcutta, No.* 1788, *in list*) rose and said :—Before this Congress is dissolved I beg in the name of my brethren of Bengal to give you a most cordial invitation to come next year to some place in Bengal which will be notified to you long before the date of the meeting. (*Cheers.*)

Dissolution of the Congress.

THE PRESIDENT—The pleasing duty now remains to me of tendering our best thanks to the gentlemen of the Bombay Reception Committee, and the Bombay Presidency generally, for the magnificent reception accorded to us. (*Loud cheers.*) I now declare this Congress dissolved with three cheers for Her Gracious Majesty the Queen. (*Loud and enthusiastic cheers for Her Majesty intermingled with cries of, "God bless our Empress," were accordingly given, and repeated, again and again.*)

The proceedings of the Congress then terminated.

(*Although Mr. Bradlaugh only attended the Congress as a visitor and although the presentation to him of addresses by the Congress and by bodies and Associations belonging to all parts of the Empire, and his speech in acknowledgment of these, formed no part of the Congress proceedings, the Congress having been dissolved before the presentation of the addresses commenced ; still, in accordance with the universal wish of the Delegates, a brief report of the proceedings in connection with the addresses, is subjoined.*)

Presentation of Addresses to Mr. C. Bradlaugh, M.P.

At about 7 p.m. a very large crowd assembled in the Congress Hall to witness the presentation of addresses to Mr. Bradlaugh. All the delegates were, we believe, present and fully four thousand other persons amongst whom were a very considerable number of the European community of Bombay who had not thus far honoured the Congress by their presence in force, at its sittings. All the other races and classes of India were of course as fully represented as they had been throughout the Congress.

Presentation of Addresses to Mr. C. Bradlaugh, M.P.

The large table on the platform (some 18 feet by 4½ feet) which served during the Congress as the President's table, was crowded from end to end, and piled up, with rugs, mats, and similar Indian offerings and with endless addresses many of them in very beautiful silver and gold and silver and carved ebony, and sandal-wood cases.

Mr. Bradlaugh had declined to receive any presents of value, such as the beautiful shawl which had been sent down from Cashmir, but accepted small rugs, mats, wood carvings, &c., of little or no intrinsic value, but interesting not only for the spirit in which hundreds of poor men had travelled hundreds of miles to present them, but as illustrative of indigenous Manufactures in out-of-the-way nooks and corners of this great Empire.

Mr. Pherozshah M. Mehta (who had been Chairman of the Congress Reception Committee) was voted to the chair, and having at last succeeded in obtaining something like silence amidst the vast, eager and enthusiastic crowd that filled every portion of the great hall, addressed them as follows :—

Ladies and Gentlemen,—I stand here to-night in the proud position—I think I can truly say, in the proud position—of being the spokesman of the peoples of India, in formally giving their welcome to our illustrious guest, Mr. Charles Bradlaugh. (*Cheers.*) Many and various have been the ways in which greeting and welcome have poured in from all parts of the country ; but we are met here to join in one formal welcome the whole voice of the country. (*Cheers.*) Gentlemen, if you ask me for my credentials I will point to the hundreds of meetings which have been held all over the country, to the telegrams which we have been receiving in shoals, day after day, to the addresses which have poured in upon us from every nook and corner of this vast and various country. And, I think, gentlemen, I can say that I truly represented the feeling of the country the other day, when I said that our hearts were unutterably stirred within us, at finding amongst us Mr. Charles Bradlaugh, restored to health and usefulness. (*Cheers.*) Ladies and Gentlemen, I need not tell you—the people assembled here to-day—what it is that promotes this simple and heartfelt welcome to Mr. Bradlaugh. The country, deeply grateful, enthusiastically appreciates the high and unselfish endeavours, by a gentleman who never saw us before and on whom we have no peculiar claim, to promote its welfare, its prosperity, and its best interests. I am not going to give you a long address to-day. I shall be short, for the simple reason that Mr. Bradlaugh may have time to be long. There is a ceremony to be performed. It is impossible, as I have said already, that all the addresses which have poured in upon us, should be read or presented. The utmost that can be done to-night is, that an address representing the joint united feelings of the country, through the mouths of the numerous representatives that have assembled in this city for the purpose of sitting in the Fifth Indian National Congress, be read. Then all that we can do is to ask the representatives of some of the principal addresses to come up and present them to Mr. Bradlaugh. After that all the other addresses will be taken as having been read and presented.

I will now call upon the much-beloved President of the late Congress, Sir William Wedderburn, to present the address on behalf of the Congress. (*Cheers.*)

Sir William Wedderburn, who was most cordially received, then read the following address :—

To Charles Bradlaugh, Esq., Member for Northampton in the Parliament of Great Britain and Ireland.

Sir,—On behalf of the Fifth Indian National Congress, assembled at Bombay, we beg to offer you our united and most heartfelt welcome and through you we desire to convey our thanks to the electors of Northampton who have permitted you to espouse the cause of India. (*Cheers.*)

Presentation of Addresses to Mr. C. Bradlaugh, M.P.

You come to us a stranger in person, not repute. For your disinterested advocacy of the claims, (founded on the unanswerable demands of human progress and the solemn promises of their Queen) preferred by millions—whose appeals for justice have evoked a widespread response since you aroused the people of Great Britain into a sympathetic recognition of India's needs—will enshrine your name for all time in the proudest and most imperishable of human homes, the hearts and traditions of a loving and a grateful race. (*Cheers.*)

Brilliant as was the tribute of national respect which your illness elicited from the fellow-countrymen who for long years had been the daily spectators of your labours and your triumphs in England, you have won, sir, in the mental distress and prayerful anxiety with which the population of India followed you in the tribulation of your sickness, a homage the more unique and tender that it is not matched in the recorded history of any living statesman. (*Cheers.*) They have appreciated the unflinching courage with which, throughout your political career, you have confronted error and have championed truth. You have enchained their admiration by your inalienable fidelity to the popular cause. (*Cheers.*)

Proud in your possession of such qualities, and thankful for your efforts in our cause, we trust that you may be spared to complete the great work you have begun (*cheers*), and to read the vindication of your generous interpretation of our political aspirations, as well in the ever closer union of India and of England, as in the quickened vigour and expanding energies of a country regenerated by the partial redemption of pledges too long permitted to remain unfulfilled. (*Loud cheers*).—We have, &c.

In reply, Mr. Bradlaugh said :—Sir William, and Delegates of the Indian National Congress, I thank you not so much for myself, for I have not yet deserved the tribute you pay me. I thank you for my Electors without whom I should not have the right to do all the work I do. And in their name and because I believe that their example will be followed by other constituencies (*cheers*), I feel grateful to you and only do not translate my gratitude into words because no words can express what I feel. (*Loud cheers.*)

Then followed the presentation of a few of the articles and addresses with which the table was piled—some forty or fifty of the larger and more beautiful caskets containing addresses, were touched or lifted and the names of the places presenting them were mentioned and one or two small articles of native manufacture were formally given over, and then all the addresses were taken as read and all presentations as made. This was unavoidable. Mr. Bradlaugh's health was still delicate. Even this little show of presenting addresses occupied fully one hour. The heat, owing to the excessive crowding of the hall and the numbers of lamps and lights of various kinds burning, was getting, despite the lateness of the hour, trying. There was scarcely a town of any size in the Empire of India proper (we exclude Burmah) from which there was not at least one address, while many of these, like that of the Madras city had attached to them scores of addresses from smaller places, and from local Societies, Associations, Guilds and Professions. If one was to be read, all must be read. The thing was out of the question and all that could be done, was, as *was* done, just to mention the names of the places, from which the most striking or beautiful caskets came, and assume the function completed.

Silence having been again secured (for the people kept cheering as each address was referred to) Mr. Bradlaugh, still as all grieved to see, somewhat enfeebled by his recent severe illness, rose and addressed the assembly.

Mr. Bradlaugh said :—Friends, fellow-subjects, and fellow-citizens ! I address you as friends, for the greeting you have given me entitles me to use the same language to you as I would use to those at home, and you have made me feel since I have been in Bombay that the word home has a wider significance than I had given it. I have learned that if I have only a little home, I have a larger one in your sympathies and in your affections, and, as I trust, to deserve by future work, in your love. I address you as fellow-subjects ; we are here loyal to one rule with the best of loyalty. (*Cheers.*) That is no real loyalty which is only blind submission. (*Cheers.*) Real loyalty means that the governed help the governors by leaving little for the Government to do. Real loyalty means that the claim of right is made with the consciousness of duty ; and I feel proud to be a fellow-subject with you in the hope that the phrase fellow-citizens may grow into a reality even before my life-time ends. (*Cheers.*) I pray your indulgence to-night, for it is the first speech I have made since I looked into the blackness of the grave, and I am not sure how far I can trust my tongue to interpret what I would wish to say. Of one thing I am sure, you have overrated alike my work and my ability. (*No, no.*) I pray you, be as indulgent to me as you have been generous ; and if you disagree with what I say let me say it in my own poor

Presentation of Addresses to Mr. C. Bradlaugh, M.P.

fashion, so that you may find at least my meaning clear to you. I am only here as a visitor by your courtesy, a member of a great assembly, the mother of Parliaments in the world, of which I am one of the poorest members; and as to any force that I may have had in advocating the cause of those to whom I belong at home, let me say I was sorry to hear that I was thanked for my work in the popular cause. For whom should I work if not for the people? Born of the people, trusted by the people, I will die of the people. (*Cheers.*) And I know no geographical or race limitations. If the nationality—pardon the word—to which I am proud to belong has raised its Empire, the rule carries with it the duty on the part of every citizen to recognise that which I recognise in you, lawful constitutional association for the assertion of your just claims and for the advancement of your homes and interests. (*Cheers.*)

I will ask you not to expect too much. One man is only a water drop in the ocean of human life: you are the breeze driving the water drop on the western side of the seas, and by your encouragement, adding others to it, and giving it a force that shall wash it into the old rock of prejudice that hindered; you will make those on the other side hear, as I have heard, the clear English sounds which show that you share our language, our traditions, and our hopes, and are willing to work with us and to make common cause with us. (*Cheers.*)

Not only do not expect too much, but do not expect all at once. Great as this assembly is in its suggestiveness, by its delegates travelling hundreds and thousands of miles, you are yet only the water drop of the two hundred and ten millions whom you number under our Empire, yours and mine—not mine against yours, not English against Indian, but our common Empire for common purposes. (*Cheers.*) Don't be disappointed if of a just claim only some thing is conceded. It is new but shall be every day coming; it is new but you have those who stand in the House of Commons to plead for you; not I alone, but members as devoted to you as I can possibly be; and I hope soon to see added to their ranks, with the authority of his knowledge and of the position which his presiding here has given him—Sir William Wedderburn. (*Cheers.*) I would remind you, as an encouragement to you to be patient, that in England great reforms have always been slowly won. Those who first enterprised them were called seditious, and sometimes sent to jail as criminals; but the speech and thought live on. No imprisonment can crush a truth; it may hinder it for the moment, it may delay it for an hour, but it gets an electric elasticity inside the dungeon walls, and it grows, and moves the whole world when it comes out. (*Cheers.*) Your presence here to-day confutes and answers in anticipation one sneer that I have heard spoken within the walls of Parliament. It is said, "There is no Indian Nation, there can be no Indian National Congress; there is no Indian people, there are only two hundred millions of diverse races and diverse creeds." The lesson I read here is that this Congress movement is an educational movement hammering upon the anvil of millions of men's brains until it welds into one common whole men whose desire for political and social reforms is greater than all distinctions of race and creed. (*Cheers.*)

It will be my duty, as it is my right, to present to Parliament directly I get back, on the very day of its opening, the claim you make to have the Bill considered. On the second day the Bill will be introduced. For so much I can answer; but I can answer for nothing more. I think it is possible the Government may introduce some Bill itself. If they do it will take precedence of, but it will not avoid the one you have charged me with; because the Government Bill, in Committee, will come to the discussion of Parliament on every one of the propositions that you desire in the Bill you have charged me with. It is not easy work. There are differences; and I have been glad to see that you can meet and discuss differences as you have done. You have shown that you can meet together and listen to one another, and that you are worthy of public trust and the right of electing and being elected to help to make the laws which you so discuss.

Then you may take it that in your own Bill or the Government Bill this decision of the House of Commons will be taken. You can help that decision; you have a constitutional right, not of coming into the House and being heard yourselves, but of sending your petitions there from every division, from far off Sind, from every part, and I would ask you, if you want to make me really your mouth-piece in that house, send signatures to petitions which you understand, by the thousand, by the hundred thousand, by the million if you can, so that India's people may kneel—and there is no shame in kneeling—on the threshold where the mother of Parliaments sits, and ask that she may do the same justice to those six, seven or eight thousand miles away that she has done to those who can assemble and make themselves heard with the living voice. (*Cheers.*)

Presentation of Addresses to Mr. C. Bradlaugh, M.P.

We—you will permit me to say "we" although I am only a guest—are here engaged in no seditious movement. We are not even seeking (though if we did there would be no great crime in the high endeavour) to transplant the democratic Institutions of England to this land. We are only seeking in the hill which is hard to climb, to carve, steps in which the strongest may stand and through coming generations help the weaker brethren to higher posts. (*Cheers.*) It is said that there are many who stand aloof from this movement. I, looking at you, wonder that in its infancy so many have joined in it. It is said that there are influential men of this party and of that who have not yet come. Oh! but the sun's rays grow as the sun rises. You are the dawn, I see the day, and I do not count the rays which are yet below the horizon, but I take account of the gilding of the clouds that I see from the rays. (*Cheers.*)

I feel that I should like to have the title that some have given me in sneer and some in hearty meaning of "Member for India." (*Cheers.*) Dead men, whose measure I cannot hope to cope with, have partly held that title. But I should love to hold it not simply by great efforts made on great occasions, but by simple doings whenever there is injustice to be touched. I know how little, one can do, but *little* though one man can do, I will tell you *what* he can do. When after rain and storm the waters have gathered, one man may make a little boring through which the water begins to percolate, that washes all away; and I will try and be that one man, leaving greater ones than I can ever be, to swim on the tide when the water flows. (*Cheers.*)

I am here because I believe you loyal (*cheers*) to the law which I am bound to support. (*Cheers.*) I am here because I believe you wish, as we in England have done, to win within the limits of the constitution the most perfect equality and right for all. (*Cheers.*) I have no right to offer advice to you; but if I had and if I dared, I would say to you, men from lands almost as separate, although within your own continent, as England is from you, I would say to you, men with race traditions and caste views and religious differences, that in a great Empire like ours all we have the right to is equality before the law for all, equality of opportunity for all, equality of expression for all, penalty on none, favoritism to none, and I believe that in this great Congress I see the germ of that which may be as fruitful as the most hopeful tree that grows under your sun. (*Cheers.*)

I am glad to see that you have women amongst you; glad, although they are few; glad for they are your mothers and teach your children; glad for in our land the wives may count through their husbands, and great thoughts and great endeavours are not made less because the man turns to the woman for counsel in his hour of need and thus makes the woman stronger than the man.

I fear I have already spoken to you too long (*no, no*) if not for you at any rate for myself. (*Laughter.*) I beg you—the most eloquent whom I have heard among you—to put into your own words and your own thoughts what you would have me say of hope for you; and let that be said. (*Cheers.*) One thing be sure of, I will only advocate the right. I must judge the right I advocate, and I may not always judge it as you do; but as long as you let me speak for you I will only speak that which seems to me to be right and true. (*Cheers.*) In this movement no force save the force of brain: no secret union; all open frank before the Law. So far as one man may and so far as one man's speech can do, English liberty shall put itself on the side of yours. (*Cheers.*) This is the first and it may be the last speech that I may ever make to you (*no, no,*) but let me beg of you to think, and let me think, that you are listening and that if I do rightly you will be generous with me in your judgment, and that even if I do not always plead with the voice that you would speak with, you will believe that I have done my best and that I meant my best to be, greater happiness for India's people, greater peace for Britain's rule, greater comfort for the whole of Britain's subjects. (*Loud and long continued cheering and waving of handkerchiefs.*)

The proceedings then terminated and the great assembly slowly, and as it were grudgingly, separated and dispersed.

APPENDIX I.

LIST OF DELEGATES

WHO ATTENDED THE

FIFTH INDIAN NATIONAL CONGRESS,

HELD AT BOMBAY, DECEMBER, 1889.

Number.	Presidency or Government.	Congress Circle.	Electoral Division.	Names in full of Delegates with honorary titles, scholastic degrees, etc.	Race, Religious denomination, and Caste, if any.	Occupation and Address.	How and when elected.
1	Madras	Madras	1st City, Electoral Division.	Mr. John Adam, M.A. ...	Christian, European.	Principal, Pacheappah's College, and Fellow, Madras University, Black Town.	At a Public Meeting, 13th December 1889, held at Pacheappah's Hall.
2	"	"	"	Rev. Mr. G. M. Cobban ...	do.	Missionary, Madras.	do.
3	"	"	"	Row Saheb S. Guruswami Chetty, B.A., B.L.	Hindu Vysia.	Vakil, High Court, and Municipal Commissioner, Black Town.	do.
4	"	"	"	Mr. T. Numberumal Chetty, B.A.	do.	Merchant, Madras	do.
5	"	"	"	Row Saheb S. Ramiah Chetty.	do.	Merchant, and Member District Board, Cuddappah.	do.
6	"	"	"	Mr. M. Rangaswamy Iyengar.	Hindu Brahmin.	Barrister-at-Law, Madras ...	Do. and at Pursapakam, Madras, on the 15th December, 1889.
7	"	"	"	Sait Lalji Valji	Mahomedan.	Merchant, Black Town ...	Public Meeting held at Pacheappah's Hall, on the 13th December, 1889.
8	"	"	"	Mr. P. K. A. Komarappa Chetty.	Hindu Nattukkotai Chetty.	Proprietor, P. K. A. Money Trading Co., Madras.	Do. and at meetings of City Merchants' Association, and Chetty's Association, Kunnaccudy, on 19th and 5th December, respectively.
9	"	"	"	Mr. N. Appusundram Pillay.	Hindu Vellala.	Assistant Cashier, C. M. Bank, Madras, & Landed Proprietor.	By a Public Meeting, held at Pacheappah's Hall, on the 13th December, 1889.
10	"	"	"	Mr. K. Etharaja Pillay ...	Hindu.	Contractor, Blacktown... ...	do.
11	"	"	"	Mr. Kalavai Annadurai Iyer.	Hindu Brahmin.	1st Grade Pleader and Law Books Publisher, Madras.	do.
12	"	"	"	Mr. C. Ponnuswamy Mudaliar.	Hindu Vellala.	Landed Proprietor	do.
13	"	"	"	Mr. D. Narasiah	Hindu Brahmin.	Editor, "People's Friend," Madras.	do.
14	"	"	"	Thakur Alwarpet R. Balaji Singh.	Hindu Kshatriya.	Contractor, Blacktown... ...	At a Public Meeting, held by the "Black Town Progressive Union" on the 15th December, 1889.
15	"	"	"	Mr. Kolapanjeri Kalianasundram Mudaliar.	Hindu Vellala.	Blacktown	Public Meeting, held at Pacheappah's Hall on the 13th December, 1889.
16	"	"	"	Mr. Arcot Lokanatha Mudaliar.	do.	Merchant, Blacktown	do.
17	"	"	"	Mr. Oratoor Krishnaswamy Pillay.	Hindu.	Contractor and Merchant, Blacktown.	do.
18	"	"	"	Mr. I. J. Sriramaloo Naidu.	do.	Merchant, Blacktown	do.
19	"	"	"	Mr. Kolapenjeri Appadurai Mudaliar.	Hindu Vellala.	Contractor and Merchant ...	do.
20	"	"	"	Mr. Mylapore Thiruvengadaswamy Naick.	Hindu.	Do. ...	do.
21	"	"	"	Mr. Conjevaram Singaravelu Ekambara Mudaliar.	do.	Assistant Dubash, Blacktown...	do.
22	"	"	"	Mr. Mallisetti Krishnaswamy Naidu.	do.	Dubash, Blacktown ...	do.
23	"	"	"	Mr. N. Appalraju Naidu....	do.	Merchant, Blacktown ...	do.
24	"	"	"	Mr. P. M. Sivagnana Mudaliar, B.A., B.L.	Brahmin.	High Court Vakil, Madras ...	do.

Number.	Presidency or Government.	Congress Circle.	Electoral Division.	Names in full of Delegates with honorary titles, scholastic degrees, etc.	Race, Religious denomination, and Caste, if any.	Occupation and Address.	How and when elected.
25	Madras.	Madras.	Blacktown 1st City, Electoral Division.	Mr. M. Ramaswamy Naidu.	Hindu.	Merchant, Contractor, and Manager, Tanjore Rama Naick's Charities, Madras.	Public Meeting, held at Pacheappah's Hall, on the 19th December, 1889.
26	"	"	"	Mr. V. J. Manickavalu Mudaliar.	do.	Printer and Publisher, Black Town, Madras.	do.
27	"	"	"	Mr. Kayar Chakravarti Srinivasachariar.	Hindu Brahmin.	Govt. Pensioner and Salt Agent to Messrs. Arbuthnot & Co., Madras.	do.
28	"	"	"	Mr. R. Sivasankara Pandiyaji, B.A., F.T.S.	Hindu Brahmin.	Head Master, "The Hindu Theological High School," Madras.	At a Public Meeting, held by the Sowcarpet Literary Association, on the 22nd December, 1889.
29	"	"	Egmore 2nd City, Electoral Division.	Rai Bahadur S. Ramaswamy Mudaliar, M.A., B.L.	Hindu.	High Court Vakil, Mittadar and Municipal Commissioner, and Fellow, Madras University, Poonamallee Road, Madras.	Public Meeting, held at Pursapakam, on the 13th Dec. 1889, and by the Mahajana Sabha, on the 17th.
30	"	"	"	Rao Saheb D. V. Srinivasa Raghavachariar.	Hindu Brahmin.	Landholder, Conjevaram Taluq, Chingleput District.	Public Meeting, held at Pursapakam, on 15th December, 1889.
31	"	"	"	Rai Bahadur P. Ananta Charlu, B.L.	do.	High Court Vakil, Madras, and Municipal Commissioner, Madras.	Public Meeting, held at Pursapakam, on 13th December 1889, and by the Mahajana Sabha, on 17th December, 1889.
32	"	"	"	Rao Saheb P. Rangiah Naidu, B.L.	Hindu.	High Court Vakil, Zamindar, and Municipal Commissioner, Madras, Member, District and Taluq Boards, Chingleput, and President, Mahajana Sabha, Madras.	Public Meeting, held at Purasapakam, on the 15th December 1889. and by the Mahajana Sabha, on the 17th December, 1889.
33	"	"	"	Mr. P. Thanikachala Naikar	Hindu.	Merchant and Land-holder, Partner, P. S. Chetty & Co.	Public Meeting, held at Pursapakam, on 13th December, 1889.
34	"	"	"	Mr. V. Arunagiri Naidu ...	do.	Indian and Colonial Merchants, Madras.	do.
35	"	"	"	Mr. Meah Husain Shah...	Mahomedan Syed.	Hide and Indigo Merchant ...	do.
36	"	"	"	V. Mohamed Sherif Saheb Bahadur.	Mahomedan.	Merchant and Member, Harbour Trust Board.	Public Meeting, held at Pursapakam, on 15th December, 1889.
37	"	"	"	Mr. Bhaktavatsalu Naidu.	Hindu.	Merchant, Madras	Do., and also at that held at Pacheappah's Hall, on 13th December, 1889.
38	"	"	"	Mr. C. S. Theagaraya Mudaliar.	do.	do. ...	Public Meeting, held at Pursapakam, on the 15th December, 1889.
39	"	"	"	Mr. N. Krishnaswamy Naidu, B.A., and B.L.	do.	Vakil, High Court, Madras ...	do.
40	"	"	"	Mr. T. Seshachella Row, B.A.	Hindu Brahmin.	Landholder	do.
41	"	"	"	Mr. P. Narayanaswamy Naidu.	Hindu.	Landlord and Merchant, Egmore.	do.
42	"	"	"	Mr. M. Lakshmanaswamy Mudaliar.	do.	Tutor in Biology, Madras Christian College.	Public Meeting, held at Pursapakam, on the 13th December, 1889.
43	"	"	Triplicane 3rd City, Electoral Division.	Rajah T. Rama Rao, B.A., B.L.	Hindu Brahmin.	High Court Vakil, Fellow, Madras University, and Member Legislative Council (1881-87), Madras.	Public Meeting, held at Triplicane, on the 8th December, 1889.
44	"	"	"	Mr. Eardley Norton, B.A...	Christian European.	Barrister-at-Law and Municipal Commissioner, "The Luz," Mylapore, Madras.	do.
45	"	"	"	Mr. M. O. Parthasaradhi Iyengar, M.A., M.L.	Hindu Brahmin.	Advocate, High Court, Madras.	Do. and at a Special Meeting of "Triplicane Literary Society," on the 7th December, 1889.

Number.	Presidency or Government.	Congress Circle.	Electoral Division.	Names in full of Deligates with honorary titles, scholastic degrees, etc.	Race, Religious denomination, and Caste, if any.	Occupation and address.	How and when elected.
46	Madras.	Madras.	Triplicane 3rd City, Electoral Division.	Mr. T. V. Sashaghery Iyer, B.A., B.L.	Hindu Brahmin.	Vakil, High Court, Madras ...	Public Meeting, held at Triplicane, on the 8th December, 1889.
47	"	"	"	Mr. T. P. Kothandarama Iyer, B.A., B.L.	do.	do. ...	Do. and at a Special Meeting of the "Triplicane Literary Society," on the 7th December 1889.
48	"	"	"	Mr. R. Shadagopa Chariar, B.A., B.L.	do.	do. ...	Public Meeting, held at Triplicane, on the 8th December, 1889.
49	"	"	"	Mr. R. Venkata Subba Row, B.A., B.L.	do.	do. ...	do.
50	"	"	"	Mr. G. Subramania Iyer, B.A.	do.	Editor, "The Hindu," Madras...	do.
51	"	"	"	Mr. C. Srinivasa Chariar ...	do.	Merchant, Printer and Publisher, Madras.	do.
52	"	"	"	Mr. A. C. Parthasarady Naidu.	Hindu.	Editor, "Aundra Prakasika," Madras.	do.
53	"	"	"	Mr. M. Viraraghava Chariar B.A.	Hindu Brahmin.	Joint Editor, "The Hindu," Madras.	do.
54	"	"	"	Mr. G. Krishnamachary ...	do.	Merchant, Triplicane	do.
55	"	"	"	Mr. S. Viraraghavacharry.	do.	do. ...	do.
56	"	"	"	Mr. M. Kuppuswamy Chetty.	Hindu.	Salt Merchant	do.
57	"	"	"	Mr. G. Ramaswamy Naidu	do.	Merchant and Contractor, Triplicane.	do.
58	"	"	"	Mr. K. V. Subramania Iyer	Hindu Brahmin.	Editor, "Tharangani Nesan."...	Public Meeting of the "Triplicane Association" on the 22nd December, 1889.
59	"	"	"	Mr. S. Siva Subramania Iyer.	do.	Mirasdar, Triplicane	do.
60	"	"	"	Mr. Alagadda Lokiah Raju.	Hindu Kshatriya.	Pensioner Triplicane	Public Meeting, held at Triplicane, on the 8th December, 1889.
61	"	"	"	Mr. V. Viswanatha Sastri.	Hindu Brahmin.	Landholder, Triplicane ...	do.
62	"	"	"	Mr. P. N. Muthuswami Iyer, B.A., B.L.	Hindu Brahmin.	Vakil, High Court, Madras, Triplicane.	At a Public Meeting, held by the "Young Men's Association," Madras, in December, 1889.
63	"	"	"	Mr. M. A. Parthasarady Iyengar, B.A.	do.	Joint Secretary, "Triplicane Literary Society," Madras.	At a Public Meeting held at Triplicane, on 8th December, 1889.
64	"	"	"	Mr. T. Venkatrangachary.	do.	Land-holder, No. 64, Banakadai Street, High Road, Triplicane, Madras.	At a General Meeting of the "Triplicane Literary Society," held in December, 1889.
65	"	"	"	Mr. M. K. Lakshmanachariar, F.H. F.A.	do.	Agent, Oriental Government Security Life Assurance Company, Bombay, Limited; Triplicane, Madras.	By a Public Meeting, held at Triplicane, on the 8th December, 1889.
66	"	"	"	Mr. Kuppuswamy Sarma, B.A., B.L.	do.	Vakil, High Court, Madras ...	Do. and at a Special Meeting of the "Triplicane Literary Society," on the 7th December, 1889, and at a Public Meeting, held at Srivarangam, Trichinopoly District, on the 13th December, 1889.
67	"	"	Piler, Cuddapah District.	Mr. Varanasi Ramasawmy Reddy.	Hindu.	Abkari Contractor	By a Public Meeting, held at Piler in December, 1889.
68	"	"	Srivilliputtur, Tinnevelly Dist.	Mr. Peter Paul Pillai ...	Christian.	Agriculturist	By a Public Meeting held at Srivilliputtur on the 3rd November, 1889.
69	"	"	Triplicane 3rd City, Electoral Division.	Mr. Sreshtalur Viraraghvachariar.	Hindu Brahmin.	Merchant, Mount Road, Madras.	By a Public Meeting, held at Triplicane, 8th December, 1889.
70	"	"	"	Mr. P. T. Srinivasa Iyengar	do.	Pleader, District Court, Chingleput, No. 26, Tolasingaperumal Street, Triplicane.	do.
71	"	"	"	Mr. C. Gopal Rao, B.A. ...	do.	Teacher, Pacheappah's College, Madras.	do.

Number.	Presidency or Government.	Congress Circle.	Electoral Division.	Names in full of Delegates with honorary titles, scholastic degrees, etc.	Race, Religious denomination, and Caste, if any.	Occupation and Address.	How and when elected.
72	Madras.	Madras.	4th City, Electoral Division.	C. Ramachendra Row Saheb, B.L.	Hindu Brahmin.	Vakil, High Court, Madras ...	By a Public Meeting, held at Mylapore, on the 14th December, 1889.
73	"	"	"	Rai Bahadur S. Subramania Iyer, B.L., C.I.E.	do.	do. ...	Do., and by that of "The Mahajana Sabha," on the 17th December, 1889.
74	"	"	"	The Hon'ble C. Sankara Nair, B.A., B.L.	Hindu.	Do., and Member, Legislative Council, Madras.	By a Public Meeting, held at Mylapore, on the 14th December, 1889.
75	"	"	"	Mr. N. Subramanyam ...	Christian Indian.	Barrister-at-Law, "The Luz," Mylapur.	do.
76	"	"	"	Mr. K. P. Sankara Menon, B.A., B.L.	Hindu.	High Court Vakil, Madras ...	do.
77	"	"	"	Mr. K. Narayana Row, B.A., B.L.	Hindu Brahmin.	do. ...	Do., and by the Mahajana Sabha, on the 17th December, 1889.
78	"	"	"	Mr. K. P. Govinda Menon, B.A., B.L.	Hindu.	do. ...	By a Public Meeting, held at Mylapore, on the 14th December, 1889.
79	"	"	"	Mr. R. Renga Row, B.A., B.L.	Hindu Brahmin.	do. ...	do.
80	"	"	"	Mr. V. Krishnaswamy Iyer, B.A., B.L.	do.	do. ...	do.
81	"	"	"	Mr. P. R. Sundara Iyer, B.A., B.L.	do.	do. ...	do.
82	"	"	"	Mr. M. Venugopaul Pillay.	Hindu.	Retired Government Servant.	do.
83	"	"	"	Mr. P. Subramanya Iyer.	Hindu Brahmin.	Attorney-at-Law, High Court, Madras, Mylapur.	do.
84	"	"	"	Mr. D. V. Narasimha Chariar, B.A.	do.	Landholder, Conjevaram Taluq, Chingleput District.	Public Meeting, held at Mylapore, on the 8th December, 1889.
85	"	"	"	Mr. V. Rangachariar, B.A., B.L.	do.	Vakil, High Court, Madras ...	By a Public Meeting, held at Mylapore, on the 14th December, 1889.
86	"	"	"	Mr. W. S. Gantz	Christian Eurasian.	Barrister-at-Law and President, Eurasian and Anglo-Indian Association, Madras.	do.
87	"	"	Mahajana Sabha, Madras.	Mr. P. Somasundrum Chettiar.	Hindu.	Merchant, and Trustee, Town Hall, Madras.	By a Meeting of the Sabha, on the 17th December, 1889.
88	"	"	"	Rao Saheb G. Mahadeva Chettiar.	do.	Merchant, and Member, District Board, Chingleput.	do.
89	"	"	"	Mr. C. V. Ganappiah	Hindu Brahmin.	Zemindar, Kassergode... ...	do.
90	"	"	"	Mr. J. Krishna Rao, B.A....	do.	Teacher, Madras Christian College.	do.
91	"	"	"	Mr. K. Srinivasa Rao, B.A.	do.	Pleader, Bellary	do.
92	"	"	"	Mr. K. S. Krishnamachariar.	do.	Assistant Master, A. V. School, Triplicane.	do.
93	"	"	"	Saheb Bahadur A. Azeemudin.	Mahomedan.	Merchant	do.
94	"	"	"	Mr. K. P. Padmanabha Menon, B.L.	Hindu.	High Court Vakil, Madras ...	do.
95	"	"	Vizianagaram.	Mr. J. Syama Sundara Rao Pantulu.	Hindu Brahmin.	Landlord	Public Meeting, held at the Maharajah's College, Vizianagaram, on 1st December, 1889.
96	"	"	"	Rao Saheb J. V. Narasimha Raju.	Hindu Kshatriya.	Landed proprietor	do.
97	"	"	Vizagapatam.	Mr. Venkata Jagga Row...	Hindu.	do. ...	Public Meeting, held on the 15th December, 1889.
98	"	"	"	Mr. S. B. Senkaram, Pantulu.	Hindu Brahmin.	2nd Grade Pleader, Vizagapatam, and Land-holder.	do.
99	"	"	Coconada (Godaveri District.)	Mr. D. Subramaniem	do.	Pleader	Public Meetings held in Coconada, on the 16th November, 1889, and in Ellore, on the 21st December, 1889.
100	"	"	"	Mr. G. Venkatratnam Garu	Hindu Brahmin.	1st Grade Pleader	do.
101	"	"	Rajamundry (Godavery District.)	Mr. Ramabrahmam Chetty	Hindu.	Pleader, Secretary, Godavery Association.	Public Meeting held in Rajamundry, on the 10th November, 1889.
102	"	"	"	Mr. S. Sambasiva Row ...	Hindu Branmin.	Pleader, Rajamundry	Do., and at that held in Ellore, on the 21st December, 1889.

Number.	Presidency or Government.	Congress Circle.	Electoral Division.	Names in full of Delegates with honorary titles, scholastic degrees, etc.	Race, Religious denomination, and Caste, if any.	Occupation and Address.	How and when elected.
103	Madras.	Madras.	Rajamundry (Godaveri District.)	Mr. T. S. Muthuswamy Sastri.	Hindu Brahmin.	Head Master, Mahratta High School, Rajamundry.	Public Meeting, held in Rajamundry, on the 10th November, 1889.
104	"	"	"	Khaja Ahmedulla Khan Saheb.	Mohamedan.	Municipal Councillor	do.
105	"	"	Ellore (Godaveri District.)	Mr. D. Venkata Nageswara Sastri.	Hindu Brahmin.	Pleader, Senior Assistant Agent's Court.	Public Meeting, held in Ellore, on the 21st December, 1889.
106	"	"	Tanuku (Godaveri District.)	Mr. I. Sangamiah... ...	do.	Pleader	Do., and at that held in Tanuku, on the 20th December, 1889.
107	"	"	Masulipatam (Krishna District.)	Rao Saheb K. Krishnamachariar, B.A.	do.	Head Master, Hindu High School, and Member, District and Taluq Boards, Masulipatam.	By a Public Meeting, held on the 17th November, 1889.
108	"	"	"	Mr. V. V. S. Avadhani, B.A.	do.	Pleader, District Court ...	By Public Meetings, held in Masulipatam and Gudivada, on the 17th and 24th November, 1889.
109	"	"	"	Mr. D. Venkatappiah Garu, B.A.	do.	Government Pleader	By a Public Meeting, held in Masulipatam, on the 17th November, 1889.
110	"	"	"	Mr. P. Gaurinatha Sastri, B.A., B.L.	do.	Assistant Master, Hindu High School, Masulipatam.	Do., and by a Public Meeting, held in Kollur, on the 16th November, 1889.
111	"	"	"	Mr.M. Venkataratnam Pantulu, B.A., B.L.	do.	Pleader, District Court ...	By a Public Meeting, held on the 17th November 1889.
112	"	"	"	Mr. C. Purushothamiah Pantulu.	do.	Editor, "Union Desabhimani," Landholder and Secretary, "Native Theological School."	By a Public Meeting, held on the 19th November, 1889.
113	"	"	"	Mr. M. Kalyan Nagabhushana Naidu.	Hindu.	Merchant.	By a Public Meeting, held on the 17th November, 1889.
114	"	"	"	Rao Saheb M. Bitchi Venkatareddi Naidu.	do.	Carpet Merchant and Municipal Commissioner.	do.
115	"	"	Karempudy (Krishna District.)	Mr. N. Anjeneyulu ...	do.	Pleader	By a Public Meeting, held on the 13th December, 1889.
116	"	"	Guntoor (Krishna District).	Mr. V. Bhavanachary, F.T.S.	Hindu Brahmin.	Pleader, Vice-President, Mahajana Sabha Branch, and Sanscrit High School Committee, and Honorary Magistrate, Guntur.	By a Public Meeting, held in Guntur, on the 4th December, 1889, and that of Vidwan Manoranjani Sabha, on the 7th December, 1889.
117	"	"	Ongole (Nellore District.)	Mr. K. Ramakrishnamachary.	do.	Teacher, Baptist Mission School, Ongole.	By a Public Meeting, held on the 5th December, 1889.
118	"	"	Nellore.	Rao Saheb C. Kotiah Chettiar.	Hindu.	Pensioned Deputy Inspector of Schools.	By a Public Meeting, held on the 3rd December, 1889.
119	"	"	"	Mr. I. Venkatramaniah.....	do.	Merchant.	do.
120	"	"	"	Mr. K. Chenchiah Chetty..	do.	do. ...	do.
121	"	"	"	Rao Saheb A. Venkiah Garu.	Hindu Brahmin.	Pleader, District Court, and Municipal Councillor.	By Public Meetings, held in Nellore and Venkatagiri, on the 3rd and 9th December, 1889.
122	"	"	"	Mr. P. Lakshminarasu Pantulu.	do.	Government Pleader, Nellore...	By a Public Meeting, held in Nellore, on the 3rd December, 1889.
123	"	"	"	Rao Saheb T. V. Venkatramier, B.A., B.L.	do.	High Court Vakil, Municipal Councillor and Member, District Board, Nellore.	Do., and by Public Meetings, held in Ongole and Venkatagiri, on the 5th Nov. and 9th Dec., respectively.
124	"	"	"	Rao Saheb N. Suryanarayana Row.	do.	Pleader, District Court, Nellore, and Municipal Commissioner, Ongole.	By a Public Meeting, held in Nellore, on the 3rd December, 1889.
125	"	"	"	Mr. R. Jaggannath Rao Garu.	do.	Pleader	do.
126	"	"	"	Mr. Mohamed Abdul Husson.	Mohamedan.	Shrotriemdar	do.
127	"	"	"	Mr. I. Venkatasubbiah ...	Hindu.	Merchant	do.

Number.	Presidency or Government.	Congress Circle.	Electoral Division.	Names in full of Delegates with honorary titles, scholastic degrees, etc.	Race, Religious denomination, and Caste, if any.	Occupation and Address.	How and when elected.
128	Madras.	Madras.	Nellore.	Mr. N. Venkatramacharlu.	Hindu Brahmin.	Pleader	By a Public Meeting, held in Nellore, on the 3rd December, 1889.
129	"	"	"	Mr. N. Srinivasachari ...	do.	Landholder	do.
130	"	"	"	Mr. Mohamed Abdul Kadir Saheb.	Mahomedan.	do.	do.
131	"	"	"	Mr. M. Venkataramanuja Row.	Hindu Brahmin.	do.	do.
132	"	"	"	Mr. M. Venkatasubba Row	do.	Pleader...	do.
133	"	"	Vadayur (Chingleput Dist.)	Mr. C. Venkata Subramania Iyer.	do.	Zemindar, Trivellore	By a Public Meeting, held at Vadayur, in December, 1889.
134	"	"	Trivellore (Chingleput Dist).	Mr. M. Bhashyam Iyengar	do.	Mirasdar and Pleader	By a Public Meeting, held in December, 1889.
135	"	"	Conjevaram (Chingleput Dist.)	Rao Saheb D. A. Ramanujachariar.	do.	Landholder, Conjevaram Taluq, Chingleput District, and Member, District Board.	By a Public Meeting, held at Conjevaram, on the 23rd December, 1889.
136	"	"	"	Mr. T. E. Kumara Venkatacharyar.	do.	Pleader and Landholder, Chingleput.	do.
137	"	"	Kaveripak (N. Arcot Dist.)	Mr. K. Deva Mudaliar ...	Hindu.	Mirasdar and Merchant ...	By a Public Meeting of the S. A. M. R. Sabha, held on the 22nd December, 1889.
138	"	"	"	Mr. S. Krishna Shastri ...	Hindu Brahmin.	Teacher and Mirasdar... ...	do.
139	"	"	"	Mr. K. Muniswamy Iyer...	do.	Mirasdar	do.
140	"	"	"	Mr. A. Lokanatha Naick...	Hindu.	Toddy-renter	do.
141	"	"	Tirupati (N. Arcot Dist.)	Mr. Vembakam V. Rangachary, B.A.	do.	Pleader, Tirupati	By a Public Meeting, held 18th December, 1889.
142	"	"	Chittore (N. Arcot Dist.)	Mr. N. Srinivasa Varadachary.	do.	1st Grade Pleader, Chittore. ...	By a Public Meeting, held on the 8th December, 1889.
143	"	"	"	Mr. D. V. Rajagopalachariar.	do.	1st Grade Pleader and Landholder, Chittore.	do.
144	"	"	"	Mr. C. V. Srinivasa Charlu, B.A.	Hindu Brahmin.	Pleader and Honorary Magistrate.	do.
145	"	"	"	Mr. T. A. Narsimhachariar, B.A., B L.	do.	Vakil, Chittore	do.
146	"	"	Tirukoilore (S. Arcot District.)	Mr. V. Srinivasa Row ...	Hindu Brahmin.	Shrotriemdar, 1st Grade Pleader, and Member, Taluq Board.	By a Public Meeting of the Mahajana Sabha Branch, held on the 1st December, 1889.
147	"	"	"	Mr. V. Khrishnaswamiah..	do.	Mirasdar, Tirukoilore	do.
148	"	"	Chidambaram (S. Arcot District.)	Mr. T. N. Desikachariar....	do.	Mirasdar and 2nd Grade Pleader.	By a Public Meeting of the Mahajana Sabha, on the 23rd November, 1889.
149	"	"	"	Rao Saheb T. V. Desikachariar.	do.	Municipal Councillor and 2nd Grade Pleader, Chidambaram.	do.
150	"	"	Cuddalore.	Mr. A. Rama Row ...	do.	First Grade Pleader, Cuddalore.	By a Public Meeting of the Goddalore Mahajana Sabha, in November, 1889.
151	"	"	"	Mr. M. Coomaraswamy Pillay.	Hindu.	do.	do.
152	"	"	"	Mr. P. T. Shadagopachariar.	Hindu Brahmin.	Editor, "Desabhimani." ...	By a Public Meeting of the Mahajana Sabha, at (New Town) Cuddalore, on the 22nd December, 1889.
153	"	"	"	Mr. J. P. Kotilingam, M.A...	Christian Indian.	Principal, Cuddalore College ...	do.
154	"	"	Nannilam (Tanjore District.)	Mr. S. A. Raja	Hindu Brahmin.	Landholder	By a Public Meeting of the Mirasdars' Association, Nannilam, held on the 24th November, 1889.
155	"	"	"	Mr. D. Natesa Aiyar ...	do.	do.	do.
156	"	"	Mayavaram (Tanjore District.)	Mr. P. Krishnaswamiah....	do.	Agent, Oriental Life Assurance Company, Mayavaram, and Dharmapuram Adhinam, Tanjore.	By a Public Meeting, held on the 22nd December, 1889.
157	"	"	"	Mr. N. P. Krishnaswamy Iyer.	do.	Mirasdar, and 1st Assistant, High School, Mayavaram.	By a Public Meeting, held at Mayavaram, on the 17th November, 1889, and also deputed by His Holiness The Thiruvaduthorai, Pandara Sannidhi.

Number.	Presidency or Government.	Congress Circle.	Electoral Division.	Names in full of Delegates with honorary titles, scholastic degrees, etc.	Race, Religious denomination, and Caste, if any.	Occupation and Address.	How and when elected.
158	Madras.	Madras.	Mayavaram (Tanjore District).	Mr. M. Chinnaswamy Sastri.	Hindu Brahmin.	Landholder	By a Public Meeting, held at Mayaveram, on th. 17th November, 1889.
159	,,	,,	,,	Mr. T. Subramanya Iyer...	do.	Mirasdar, Mayaveram... ...	do.
160	,,	,,	Kumbaconum (Tanjore District).	Mr. Y. Sankaranarayana Sastri, B.A., B.L.	do.	1st Grade Pleader, Kumbaconum.	By a Public Meeting, held at Kumbaconum, on the 21st November, 1889.
161	,,	,,	,,	Mr. Maruthakkudy Sambasiva Sastri.	do.	Landholder and Member, Tanjore People's Association.	do.
162	,,	,,	Negapatam (Tanjore District).	Rao Bahadur P. Rathnasabapathy Pillay, B.A.	Hindu.	1st Grade Pleader, Landholder, Chairman, Municipal Council, Negapatam, Member, District and Taluq Boards, Tanjore.	By a Public Meeting, held at Negapatam, on the 14th November, 1889.
163	,,	,,	Tanjore.	Rao Bahadur S. A. Swaminatha Iyer.	Hindu Brahmin.	Government Pleader, Landed Proprietor, Secretary, Raja Mirasdar Hospital Committee, Chairman, Municipal Council, Member, District Board, Tanjore, and Temple Committee, Kumbaconum.	By a Public Meeting, held at Tanjore and Shyalli, on the 19th November, and 23rd December, 1889.
164	,,	,,	,,	Mr. V. Neelamegachariar .	do.	Editor, "Tanjai Jana Mithran."	By a Public Meeting, held by the Tanjore People's Association, on the 1st December, 1889.
165	,,	,,	,,	Mr. Kotur Krishnaswamy Mudaliar.	Hindu.	Landed-proprietor, and Member, District Board, Tanjore.	do.
166	,,	,,	,,	Mr. P. V. Ramachendra Iyer.	Hindu Brahmin.	Editor, "The Southern Star," Tanjore.	By a Public Meeting, held at Tanjore, on the 19th November 1889.
167	,,	,,	,,	Mr. S. A. Swaminatha Sastri, B.A., B.L.	do.	Pleader and Secretary, Law Library, Tanjore.	do.
168	,,	,,	,,	Mr. Kotur Rengaswamy Mudaliar.	Hindu.	Mirasdar, and Member, Local Fund and Taluq Boards, Tanjore.	By a Public Meeting of the Tanjore People's Association, on the 1st December, 1889.
169	,,	,,	Shyalli (Tanjore District).	Mr. S. Vadamalai Pillay....	do.	Landholder, and Member, District Board, Tanjore.	By a Public Meeting, held at Shyalli, on the 24th December, 1889.
170	,,	,,	Trichinopoly.	Srimath, S. V. Guruswamy Sarma Avl.	Hindu Brahmin.	Headmaster, Hindu High School, Trichoor, (Cochin); Missionary, Religious, Political and Social; President-Founder, "Temperance Associations," South Madras; and Lecturer, Swadarmachara Samrakshana Sabha, Trichoor.	By Public Meetings, held at Trichinopoly Town Hall, Srirangam, and Trichoor, on 8th, 11th, and 18th December, respectively.
171	,,	,,	,,	Rao Saheb B. Nilakantiah.	do.	1st Grade Pleader, Kulithali, Trichinopoly.	By a Public Meeting, held at Kulithalai, on the 15th December, 1889.
172	,,	,,	Madura.	Rao Saheb Sashadri Iyengar.	do.	Zemindar	By a Public Meeting, held at Madura, on the 17th November, 1889.
173	,,	,,	,,	Rao Saheb G. Srinivasa Rao, B.A.	do.	Landholder, Pleader, and Member, District Board, Madura.	do.
174	,,	,,	,,	Mr. J. M. Nallaswamy Pillay, B.A., B.L.	Hindu.	High Court Vakil, Madura ...	By a Public Meeting, held on the 17th November, 1889.
175	,,	,,	,,	Mr. P. Narayana Iyer, B.A., B.L.	Hindu Brahmin.	do. ...	do.
176	,,	,,	,,	Mr. S. M. Sundara Iyer, B.A.	do.	Editor and Proprietor, "Madura Mail" and Member, District Board.	do.
177	,,	,,	,,	Mr. A. Rajaram Iyer, B.A.	do.	1st Assistant, Native College, Madura.	By a Meeting of the Union Club, on the 24th November 1889.
178	,,	,,	Sivagunga (Madura District).	Mr. Peer Mohamed Saheb.	Mahomedan.	Village Munsiff, Tripatore ...	By a Public Meeting, held at Tripatore, in November 1889.
179	,,	,,	,,	Mr. Muthuvadagu Pillay *alias* Chinnaswamy Pillay.	Hindu.	Landed-proprietor	By Public Meetings, held at Sivagunga and Tirukostiyur in November, 1889, and at Tripatore and Knunakkudy, in December, 1889.
180	,,	,,	,,	Mr. Ramaswamy Pillay ...	do.	do. ...	By Public Meeting, held at Sivagunga, in November, 1889.

Number.	Presidency or Government.	Congress Circle.	Electoral Division.	Names in full of Delegates with honorary titles, scholastic degrees. etc.	Race, Religious denomination, and Caste, if any.	Occupation and Address.	How and when elected.
181	Madras	Madras	Sivagunga (Madura District).	Mr. V. Viswanatha Iyer ...	Hindu Brahmin.	2nd Grade Pleader, Sivagunga.	By a Public Meeting, held at Sivagunga, in November 1889.
182	"	"	"	Mr. Anantanarayana Iyer.	do.	do. ...	do.
183	"	"	"	Mr. K. Annaswamy Iyer...	do.	Agent to the Zemindar of Sivagunga.	do.
184	"	"	"	Mr. V. Subba Iyer ...	do.	2nd Grade Pleader, Sivagunga.	do.
185	"	"	"	Mr. M. G. Sankaranarayana Iyer.	do.	do. ...	do.
186	"	"	"	Mr. M. S. Sankara Iyer, B.A.	do.	Head Master, Zemindar High School, Sivagunga.	do.
187	"	"	Dindigul (Madura District).	Mr. N. Elumalai Chettiar.	Hindu.	Merchant and Municipal Commissioner.	By a Public Meeting, held on the 28th November, 1889.
188	"	"	"	Mr. Vadagiri Pillay	do.	Merchant	do.
189	"	"	"	Mr. P. R. Narayana Iyer.	Hindu Brahmin.	Pleader	do.
190	"	"	"	Mr. V. P. Rajam Iyer ...	do.	do.	do.
191	"	"	"	Mr. R. Sundaram Iyer ...	do.	Head Master, Hindu High School, Dindigul.	do.
192	"	"	"	Mr. T. Ponnambala Mudaliar.	Hindu.	Mirasdar	do.
193	"	"	"	Mr. R. Vengu Iyer ...	Hindu Brahmin.	Pleader	do.
194	"	"	"	Mr. P. M. Ramier...	do.	do.	do.
195	"	"	"	Mr. Karuppan Chettiar ...	Hindu.	Cultivator and Merchant ...	do.
196	"	"	"	Mr. Atmanatha Iyer ...	Hindu Brahmin.	Pleader and Municipal Councillor.	do.
197	"	"	"	Mr. P. N. Subramania Iyer.	do.	Pleader	do.
198	"	"	"	Mr. T. Rajagopaul Naidoo.	Hindu.	do.	do.
199	"	"	Kalakkad (Tinnevelly District).	Mr. D. A. Pichumani Iyer.	Hindu Brahmin.	Mirasdar	By a Public Meeting, held at Kalakkad in December, 1889.
200	"	"	Tinnevelly.	Mr. A. S. Appaswamy Pillay.	Hindu.	Pleader, Palamcottah	By a Public Meeting, held on the 9th December, 1889.
201	"	"	"	Mr. G. Chandrasekara Iyer	Hindu Brahmin.	Pleader, District Court, Viraraghavapuram.	do.
202	"	"	"	Mr. M. R. Ramakrishna Iyer, B.A., B.L.	do.	High Court Vakil, Tinnevelly...	By a Public Meeting, held on the 9th December 1889.
203	"	"	"	Mr. P. N. Venkatachellam Iyer, B.A.	do.	Pleader	do.
204	"	"	"	Mr. Roche Victoria ...	Christian Indian.	Merchant, Tuticorin	do.
205	"	"	"	Mr. N. S. Appaswamy Pillay.	do.	Pleader, District Court, Tinnevelly	do.
206	"	"	"	Mr. Mahomed Ally Taraganar.	Mahomedan.	Landholder and Merchant ...	do.
207	"	"	"	Mr. A. Krishnaswamy Iyer.	Hindu Brahmin.	Pleader, District Court, Kailasapuram	do.
208	"	"	"	Mr. N. Sundaram Iyer ...	do.	Pleader, Shenkottai	By a Public Meeting, held in Thenkasi, on the 14th December, 1889.
209	"	"	"	Mr. R. M. Chithambara Iyer.	do.	2nd Grade Pleader	By a Public Meeting, held at Srivallipputtoor, on the 3rd November, 1889.
210	"	"	Madanapalle (Cuddapah District).	Mr. Seshagiri Row ...	do.	Assistant Master, Congress High School.	By a Public Meeting, held on the 3rd November, 1889.
211	"	"	"	Mr. M. K. Subba Row ...	do.	1st Grade Pleader	By a Public Meeting, held on the 10th November, 1889.
212	"	"	"	Mr. R. Giri Row, B.A. ...	do.	Head Master, Congress High School.	do.
213	"	"	"	Mr. O. Lakshmana Sarma.	do.	Pleader	do.
214	"	"	Vayalpad (Cuddapah District).	Mr. T. Narayana Sastri ...	do.	1st Grade Pleader	By a Public Meeting, held on the 3rd November, 1889.

Number.	Presidency or Government.	Congress Circle.	Electoral Division.	Names in full of Delegates with honorary titles, scholastic degrees, &c.	Race, Religious denomination. and Caste, if any.	Occupation and Address.	How and when elected.
215	Madras.	Madras.	Vayalpad (Cuddapah District).	Mr. P. C. Venkatramiah Chetty.	Hindu.	Landholder and Money-lender.	By a Public Meeting, held on the 3rd Nov. 1889.
216	"	"	"	Mr. G. Sambhoo Row ...	Hindu Brahmin.	Law Agent, and Member, Vayalpad Union Punchayet.	do.
217	"	"	"	Mr. Bhujanga Row ...	do.	Landholder	do.
218	"	"	Prodatur (Cuddapah District).	Mr. K. Thimmappa Chetty.	Hindu.	Pleader and Landholder ...	By a Public Meeting, held on the 4th Dec. 1889.
219	"	"	Cuddapah.	Rao Bahadur C. Jambulinga Mudaliar, B.A., M.L..	do.	High Court Vakil, and Vice-President, District Board, Cuddapah.	By a Public Meeting, held in November, 1889.
220	"	"	"	Mr. C. Ruthnam Mudaliar..	do.	Merchant	do.
221	"	"	"	Mr. A. Nunjundappah, B.A., B.L.	Hindu Brahmin.	Vakil, Cuddapah	do.
222	"	"	Kurnool.	Mr. C. Buddappah ...	Hindu.	Merchant	By a Public Meeting, held on the 23rd Nov., 1889.
223	"	"	"	Mr. K. Peda Alpurappah...	do.	do.	do.
224	"	"	"	Mr. C. Tippannah	do.	do.	do.
225	"	"	"	Seth Matangappah ...	do.	do.	do.
226	"	"	"	Mr. C. Coidaiah ...	do.	do.	do.
227	"	"	"	Mr. A. Baliah Chetty ...	do.	do.	do.
228	"	"	"	Mr. I. Krishnaswamy Chetty.	do.	do.	do.
229	"	"	"	Mr. J. Chelamiah Chetty ..	do.	do.	do.
230	"	"	"	Mr. B. Seshachella Chetty.	do.	do.	do.
231	"	"	"	Mr. A. Subbannah Chetty.	do.	Merchant, Nandyal	do.
232	"	"	"	Rao Saheb Adoni Subba Row.	Hindu, Brahmin.	1st Grade Pleader; Municipal Councillor; Member, District Board; and President "Kurnool Union Club," Kurnool.	do.
233	"	"	"	Mr. P. Ramanna Chetty...	Hindu.	Merchant	do.
234	"	"	"	Mr. Sheik Burandin Saheb.	Mahomedan.	Manager, Municipal Commissioner's Office.	do.
235	"	"	"	Mr. Misrikhan Khalibkhan Saheb.	do.	Merchant, Kurnool	do.
236	"	"	"	Mr. Kodumur Dade Saheb, Khan Saheb.	do.	do.	do.
237	"	"	"	Mr. Nawazeish Ally Khan Khalib.	do.	do.	do.
238	"	"	"	Mr. Shikarkhana Ahmed Saheb.	do.	do.	do.
239	"	"	"	Rao Saheb Tumucherla Chidambara Rao, B.A.	Hindu, Brahmin.	Municipal Councillor; Secretary, Union Club; 1st Grade Pleader; President, Desabhimani Sabha, and Sanscrit School, Kurnool	do.
240	"	"	"	Rao Bahadur Atmakur Venkoba Row.	do.	1st Grade Pleader, Public Prosecutor and Chairman, Municipal Council, Kurnool.	do.
241	"	"	"	Mr. Kodumur Lakshmanacharlu	do.	2nd Grade Pleader, and Vice-President, Sanscrit School, and Desabhimani Sabha, Kurnool.	do.
242	"	"	"	Rao Saheb Bavanchikar Row.	do.	2nd Grade Pleader, and Member, Taluq Board, Nandyal.	do.
243	"	"	"	Mr. Meloor Srinivasa Row, M.A.	do.	Head Master, Municipal High School, Kurnool.	By a Meeting of the Kurnool Desabhimani Sabha, on the 29th Dec. 1889.
244	"	"	Bellary.	Rao Bahadur K. Venkat Row.	do.	1st Grade Pleader and Chairman, Municipal Council, Bellary.	By a Public Meeting, held on the 24th November, 1889.
245	"	"	"	Mr. C. Doraiswamy Naidu.	Hindu.	Attorney-at-Law	do.
246	"	"	"	Mr. B. Janardanam Pillay.	do.	Railway Contractor	do.
247	"	"	"	Mr. A. Moonniah	Hindu, Brahmin.	Contractor and Money-lender...	do.
248	"	"	"	Mr. B. Puttiah Chetty ...	Hindu.	Merchant	do.

Number.	Presidency or Government.	Congress Circle.	Electoral Division.	Names in full of Delegates with honorary titles, scholastic degrees, etc.	Race, Religious denomination, and Caste, if any.	Occupation and Address.	How and when elected.
249	Madras.	Madras.	Bellary.	Mr. G. Venkatannah ...	Hindu.	Merchant	By a Public Meeting, held on the 24th November, 1889.
250	"	"	"	Mr. N. Govindappah ...	do.	do.	do.
251	"	"	"	Mr. V. Seshappah ...	do.	do.	do.
252	"	"	"	Rao Saheb C. H. Gowd ...	Hindu Brahmin.	Landlord and Municipal Commissioner.	do.
253	"	"	"	Rao Saheb M. Vasudeva Naidu.	Hindu.	1st Grade Pleader and Contractor.	do.
254	"	"	"	Mr. C. Annamalai Mudaliar	do.	Agricultural Agent, Bellary. Graduate of the College of Agriculture.	do.
255	"	"	"	Mr. H. Pampanna Gowd...	Hindu.	Landholder	do.
256	"	"	"	Rao Saheb D. Krishnamacharlu.	do.	1st Grade Pleader and Municipal Commissioner.	do.
257	"	"	"	Mr. K. Renga Row ...	Hindu Brahmin.	1st Grade Pleader and Landholder.	do.
258	"	"	"	Mr. V. Krishna Row.	do.	Money-lender, Hospet... ...	do.
259	"	"	"	Mr. D. Venkatramanacharlu.	do.	Landholder	do.
260	"	"	"	Rao Bahadur A. Sabapathy Mudaliar.	Hindu.	Landholder, Merchant, Member, District Board, and Municipal Commissioner.	do.
261	"	"	"	Mr. A. Narasimhalu ...	Hindu Brahmin.	Telugu Pandit, Municipal High School.	do.
262	"	"	"	Mr. G. Krishnam Chetty...	Hindu.	Cashier, Bank of Madras, Bellary.	do.
263	"	"	"	Mr. M. Ramanjulu Naidoo.	do.	Railway Contracter	do
264	"	"	"	Mr. R. Venkatanarasiah...	do.	Manager, Spinning and Weaving Mill.	do.
265	"	"	"	Mr. C. Lakshmana Row ...	Hindu Brahmin.	Head Master, Wardlaw Institution.	do.
266	"	"	"	Mr. H. Seenappah	Hindu.	Karnam Mirasdar	By a Meeting of the Sanmarga Samaj, in December, 1889.
267	"	"	"	Mr. V. Krishnama Chetty.	do.	Private Service in the "Sabapathy Press."	do.
268	"	"	"	Mr. R. V. Krishniah ...	Hindu Brahmin.	Money-lender	do.
269	"	"	"	Mr. D. Virupaksha Row ...	do.	Private Service... ...	do.
270	"	"	"	Mr. Swamy Chetty ...	Hindu.	Merchant	By a Public Meeting, held at Hospet, Bellary, in December, 1889.
271	"	"	"	Mr. K. Raghavacharlu ...	Hindu Brahmin.	Landholder and Priest ...	do.
272	"	"	"	Mr. D. Gopalacharlu ...	do.	2nd Grade Pleader	do.
273	"	"	"	Mr. D. Rajhavendra Naick	do.	Merchant and Landholder ...	do.
274	"	"	"	Mr. Virupakshi Mari ...	Hindu.	Do., and Honorary Magistrate.	do.
275	"	"	"	Mr. G. Karigangappah ...	do.	Merchant and Honorary Magistrate.	do.
276	"	"	"	Mr. A. C. P. Iyer... ...	Hindu Brahmin.	Landholder	At a Meeting of the "Hindu Club," in December, 1889.
277	"	"	"	Mr. Subba Sastrulu ...	do.	Inamdar...	At a General Meeting of the D. J. Sabha, in December, 1889.
278	"	"	"	Mr. K. Sashagiri Row ...	do.	Contractor	do.
279	"	"	"	Mr. V. Chandriah... ...	Hindu.	Merchant	At a Meeting of the Cowl Bazaar People's Association, in December, 1889.
280	"	"	Coimbatore.	Mr. K. S. Venkatrama Sastri.	Hindu Brahmin.	Mirasdar, Kadathore Kanyur ; and Member, Taluq Board.	By a Public Meeting, held at Coimbatore, in the 15th December, 1889.
281	"	"	"	Mr. T. S. Balakrishna Iyer, B.A., B.L.	do.	High Court Vakil, Coimbatore..	do.
282	"	"	"	Mr. C. M. Padmanabhachar, B.A., B.L.	do.	do.	do.

Number.	Presidency or Government.	Congress Circle.	Electoral Division.	Names in full of Delegates with honorary titles, scholastic degrees, etc.	Race, Religious denomination, and Caste, if any.	Occupation and Address.	How and when elected.
283	Madras.	Madras.	Coimbatore	Mr. N. Kolanthaivelu Pillay.	Hindu.	Merchant and Municipal Councillor.	By a Public Meeting, held on the 16th November, 1889.
284	"	"	Kanyur (Coimbatore District).	Mr. Yagnier	Hindu Brahmin.	Mirasdar Kanyur	By a Public Meeting, held at Kanyur, on the 20th November, 1889.
285	"	"	"	Mr. C. A. Subramanya Iyer.	do.	do.	do.
286	"	"	"	Rao Saheb Venkatrama Sastri, B.A.	do.	Proprietor, Amravati High School, and Member, District Board.	do.
287	"	"	"	Mr. K. Narayana Sastri, B.A., B.L.	do.	High Court Vakil, and Member Taluq Board, Pollachi.	do.
288	"	"	"	Mr. C. S. Anantakrishnier.	do.	Mirasdar, Komaralingam. ...	do.
289	"	"	"	Mr. K. Ramaswamy Iyer.	do.	do. ...	do. and by that held at Coimbatore, on the 15th December, 1889.
290	"	"	"	Mr. K. Venkatakrishna Iyer.	do.	Mirasdar and Member, Devasthanam Committee.	do.
291	"	"	"	Mr. V. S. Ramaswamy Iyer.	do.	Vakil, Udumalapet	By a Public Meeting, held at Kanyur, on the 20th November, 1889.
292	"	"	Gooty (Anantapur District).	Mr. P. Balakrishna Pillay.	do.	Contractor	By a Public Meeting, held at Gooty, on the 9th November, 1889.
293	"	"	"	Rao Saheb P. Kesava Pillay.	do.	Pleader and Member, District Board.	do.
294	"	"	"	Mr. M. Nagesa Row ...	Hindu Brahmin.	Pleader	do.
295	"	"	"	Rao Saheb J. Srinivasa Row.	do.	Pleader and Vice-President, Taluq Board.	do.
296	"	"	"	Mr. R. Seshiah	do.	Pleader, Honorary Chairman, Gooty Major Union.	do.
297	"	"	"	Mr. Mudiem Nagesa Row.	do.	2nd Grade Pleader, Gooty ...	do.
298	"	"	Penukonda (Anantapur District).	Mr. Venkata Renganada Chakravarti Iyengar.	do.	Pleader, Ceded Districts ...	By a Public Meeting, held on the 13th November, 1889.
299	"	"	Pamdurti (Anantapur District).	Mr. P. Venkata Reddi ...	Hindu.	do. ...	do.
300	"	"	Anantapur	Rao Saheb S. Vedaji Row.	Hindu Brahmin.	Pleader, Member, District and Taluq Boards and Municipal Councillor.	By a Public Meeting, held on the 12th December 1889.
301	"	"	Salem.	Mr. B. A. Ratnaswami Pillay.	Christian Indian.	Mirasdar and Contractor ...	By a Public Meeting, held on the 8th December, 1889.
302	"	"	"	Mr. T. S. Ayakannu Chettiar.	Hindu.	Merchant, Tirupatur	do.
303	"	"	"	Rao Saheb S. A. Kutti Chettiar.	do.	Money-lender and Municipal Commissioner.	do.
304	"	"	"	Rao Saheb C. Renganada Mudaliar.	do.	1st Grade Pleader and Member, L. F. B., Tirupatur.	do.
305	"	"	"	Mr. T. Muthialu Chettiar.	do.	Merchant	do.
306	"	"	"	Rao Saheb T. Narasinga Row.	Hindu Brahmin.	Shrotriem Pensioner and Municipal Councillor.	do.
307	"	"	"	Mr. Subrama Iyer ...	do.	Pleader, Namkal	do.
308	"	"	"	Mr. Velappa Kowndar ...	Hindu.	Zemindar, Velakurichi ...	do.
309	"	"	"	Mr. T. V. Raghavachariar.	Hindu Brahmin.	1st Grade Pleader	do.
310	"	"	"	Mr. C. Venkatachariar ...	do.	Mirasdar and Member, L. F. B.	do.
311	"	"	"	Mr. P. Sundram, B.A. ...	Christian Indian.	Head Master, L. M. High School.	do.
312	"	"	"	Mr. C. Vijiaraghavachary.	Hindu Brahmin.	Pleader, Salem.	do.
313	"	"	"	Mr. V. Vythi Iyer ...	do.	Government Pleader, Salem ...	do.
314	"	"	"	Mr. S. V. Mohamed Meera. Hassain Rowthar	Mahomedan.	Merchant, Shevapet, Salem ...	do.
315	"	"	"	Mr. Mohamed E. P. Madar Saheb.	do.	Merchant, Vaniembady, Salem.	do.

Number.	Presidency or Government.	Congress Circle.	Electoral Division.	Names in full of Delegates with honorary titles, scholastic degrees, etc.	Race, Religious denomination, and Caste, if any.	Occupation and Address.	How and when elected.
316	Madras.	Madras.	Salem.	Mr. Feerzada Syed Allauddin Saheb.	Mahomedan.	Jaghirdar, Ammapalayam, Salem.	By a Public Meeting, held on the 8th December, 1889.
317	„	„	„	Mr. Feerzada Syed Shah Mirdeen Saheb, Shutari.	do.	do.	do.
318	„	„	„	Mr. V. Raghavachariar ...	Hindu Brahmin.	1st Grade Pleader, Salem ...	do., and by the Madras Mahajana Sabha, on the 17th Dec., 1889.
319	„	„	„	Mr. Y. Seshachellam Iyer.	do.	Mirasdar and Secretary to Lord Ripon Excelsior Institute, Trichengode.	By Public Meetings, held at Salem and Trichengode, in December, 1889.
320	„	„	Tellicheri (N. Malabar District).	Mr. Thomas Richmond ...	Christian.	1st Grade Pleader and Municipal Commissioner.	By a Public Meeting, held on the 8th December, 1889.
321	„	„	„	Mr. V. Ryen Nambiar, B.A., B.L.	Hindu.	High Court Vakil	do.
322	„	„	„	Mr. Raman Nayanar ...	do.	Landholder	do.
323	„	„	„	Mr. T. C. Narayana Kurup, B.A., B.L.	do.	High Court Vakil and Municipal Councillor.	do.
324	„	„	„	Mr. M. Gopala Menon ...	do.	1st Grade Pleader and Municipal Councillor.	do.
325	„	„	Calicut (N. Malabar District).	Mr. S. Anantanarayana Putter.	Hindu Brahmin.	Government Pleader	By a Public Meeting, held on the 23rd November, 1889.
326	„	„	„	Mr. K. R. Ramaswamy Iyer.	do.	1st Grade Pleader and Municipal Councillor.	do.
327	„	„	„	Mr. C. Kunji Raman Menon, B.A.	Hindu.	Editor, "Kevala Patrika," and Member, District Board.	do.
328	„	„	Palghat (N. Malabar District).	Mr. S. Ramachendra Iyer..	Hindu Brahmin.	1st Grade Pleader	By a Public Meeting, held on the 29th November, 1889.
329	„	„	„	Mr. P. T. Chinnaswamy Pillay.	Hindu.	Municipal Councillor and Member, District Board.	do.
330	„	„	„	Mr. K. P. Achyutha Menon.	do.	1st Grade Pleader and Municipal Councillor.	do.
331	„	„	„	Mr. K. Raman Unni Mupil Nair.	do.	Landlord	do.
332	„	„	„	Mr. V. Raman Nair, B.A....	do.	Landed-proprietor ...	do.
333	„	„	„	Mr. V. Vengu Iyer	Hindu Brahmin.	1st Grade Pleader	do.
334	„	„	„	Mr. S. Ramakrishna Iyer..	do.	do.	do.
335	„	„	„	Mr. S. Viraraghava Iyer...	do.	Landed-proprietor and Municipal Councillor.	do.
336	„	„	Kasergode (S. Canara District.)	Mr. N. Krishna Row	do.	Private Gentleman	By a Public Meeting, held at Kesergode, on December, 1889.
337	„	„	„	Mr. N. Srinivasa Row ...	do.	Merchant	do.
338	„	„	„	Rao Saheb D. Venkata Row.	do.	do., and Zemindar... ...	By a Public Meeting, held at Kundapur, in December, 1889.
339	„	„	„	Mr. N. Raghavendra Row.	do.	Zemindar	do.
340	„	„	Mangalore (S.Canara).	Mr. T. Bhavani Row ...	do.	Vakil, District Court	By a Public Meeting, held in December, 1889.
341	„	„	„	Mr. B. A. Brito ...	Christian.	Merchant	do.
342	„	„	„	Mr. Narasiah Prabhu ...	Hindu Brahmin.	do.	do.
343	„	„	„	Mr. Krishna Prabhu ...	do.	Merchant and Zemindar ...	do.
344	„	„	„	Mr. M. Narasiah Shanbog.	do.	Landlord	do.
345	„	„	„	Mr. K. Narayen Shatti ...	Hindu.	do.	do.
346	„	„	„	Mr. George Vas ...	Christian.	Private Gentleman ...	do.
347	„	„	„	Mr. M. Subba Row ...	Hindu Brahmin.	Vakil, District Court	do.
348	„	„	„	Mr. J. N. Coelho ...	Christian.	Merchant	do.
349	„	„	„	Mr. J. T. D'Souza, B.A. ...	do.	Pleader, District Court ...	do.
350	„	„	„	Mr. N. Subba Row ...	Hindu Brahmin.	Zemindar	do.
351	„	„	„	Rao Bahadur N. Shiva Row	do.	Vakil and Zemindar	do.

Number.	Presidency or Government.	Congress Circle.	Electoral Division.	Names in full of Delegates with honorary titles, scholastic degrees, etc.	Race, Religious denomination, and Caste, if any.	Occupation and Address.	How and when elected.
352	Madras.	Madras.	Mangalore (S. Canara.)	Mr. K. Deva Row... ...	Hindu Brahmin.	Vakil, District Court	By a Public Meeting, held in December 1889.
353	„	„	„	Mr. N. Krishna Bhattar, B.A. and B.L.	do.	High Court Vakil and Municipal Councillor.	do.
354	„	„	„	Mr. M. Subraya Shastri ...	do.	Retired District Court Vakil and Landholder.	do.
355	„	„	„	Mr. H. Madappiah ...	do.	Landlord	do.
356	„	„	Mangeswar.	Mr. M. Ramakrishna Row.	do.	Zemindar	By a Public Meeting, held at Mangeswar.
357	„	„	„	Mr. M. Rengappah ...	do.	do.	do.
358	„	„	Puttoor.	Mr. Kallianpur Narayana Row.	do.	Merchant and Zemindar ...	By a Public Meeting, held at Puttoor.
359	Govt. of India.	„	Secundrabad.	Mr. K. Edulji	Parsi.	Pleader, Secunderabad ...	By a Public Meeting, held on the 27th November, 1889.
360	„	„	„	Mr. C. Rungiah	Hindu.	Merchant and Banker... ...	do.
361	„	„	„	Mr. R. M. Ramannah ...	do.	Merchant	do.
362	„	„	„	Mr. Shaik Sunnah ...	Mahomedan.	do.	do.
363	„	„	„	Mr. D. Krishtamiah ...	Hindu.	do. and Banker	do.
364	„	„	„	Mr. P. Ramachendra Pillay.	do.	Pleader, Hydrabad and Berar, Secundrabad.	do.
365	„	„	„	Mr. B. Krishna Iyengar, F.T.S.	Hindu Brahmin.	Attorney-at-Law, Madras High Court; Advocate, Mysore Chief Court and the High Court, Hydrabad and Member, Local Fund Committee—Residency Bazaar, Chudderghat, Hyderabad (Deccan).	do.
366	„	„	Bangalore.	Dr. J. Sausman, M.D. ...	Eurasian.	Retired Surgeon, Bangalore ...	By a Meeting of the Eurasian Association, Bangalore.
367	Bombay.	Deccan.	Poona.	Mr. Raghunath Bajirao Potnis.	Purbhu Hindu.	Jahagirdar	Public Meeting at Poona, 15th December, 1889.
368	„	„	„	Mr. Gopal Gunesh Agarkar, M.A.	Brahmin.	Teacher and Journalist. Professor, Fergusson College, Editor, Sudharak.	do.
369	„	„	„	Mr. Mahadev Ballal Namjoshi.	do.	Municipal Commissioner, Journalist, Secretary, Provincial Conference, Bombay, Secretary. Standing Congress Committee. Deccan, Editor, Shilpa Kala Viduana.	do.
370	„	„	„	Mr. Vasudev Harihar Pandit, alias, Shri Baba Maharaj.	do.	1st Class Sirdar of the Deccan, Spiritual priest to H. H. the Maharaj of Kolhapur.	do.
371	„	„	„	Rao Bahadur Gopalrao Hari Deshmukh, Ex-Member of the Legislative Council.	Hindu Maratha Brahmin.	First Class Sirdar of the Deccan, Fellow of the University of Bombay; Justice of the Peace for the Town and Island of Bombay, President, Aryasamaj.	do.
372	„	„	„	R. B. Narayen Bhai Dandekar.	Hindu.	Late D. P. Instruction... ...	do.
373	„	„	„	Mr. Ganesh Narayen Ghotwadekar.	Hindu Brahmin.	Proprietor, Shetkari Press, and Secretary to the Agricultural Association, Umraoti.	do.
374	„	„	„	Mr. Bhimrao Madhavrao Potnis.	Hindu.	Inamdar, Poona, and 1st Class Sirdar.	do.
375	„	„	„	R. S Ramnaryan Ameerchand.	do.	Merchant and Municipal Commissioner.	do.
376	„	„	„	R. S. Gangaram Bhaoo, Mhuske.	Maratha.	Pleader, and Member S. Sabha.	do.

Number.	Presidency or Government.	Congress Circle.	Electoral Division.	Names in full of Delegates with honorary titles, scholastic degrees, etc.	Race, Religious denomination, and Caste, if any.	Occupation and Address.	How and when elected.
377	Bombay.	Deccan.	Poona.	Mr. Narayen Krishna Dharap, B.A.	Brahmin.	Teacher, New English School, Poona.	Public Meeting at Poona 15th December, 1889.
378	"	"	"	R. S. Sitaram Hari Chiplonker.	do.	Editor, "Dyana Prakash," Member S. Sabha.	do.
379	"	"	"	Mr. Govind Mahadeo Gadre.	do.	Pleader, Member, Sarvajanik Sabha.	do.
380	"	"	"	Mr. Krishnarow Bapoojee Mande.	do.	Editor, "Shri Shiwajee" ...	do.
381	"	"	"	Mr. Keshevrow Pandurang Godbole.	do.	Schoolmaster	do.
382	"	"	"	Rao Bahadoor Dajee Nilkant Nagarkar.	do.	Late Professor Engineering College, Poona, Fellow of the Bombay University, and Land-lord.	do.
383	"	"	"	Mr. Naro Bhaskar Devdher.	do.	Inamdar, Poona Shanwar Peit...	do.
384	"	"	"	Mr. Chintaman Ballal Gharpure.	do.	Sowkar, Poona	do.
385	"	"	"	Mr. Vishnudas Harikisandas.	Gujarati Hindu.	Merchant, Poona, and Sarpanch Guzerathi Committee.	do.
386	"	"	"	Mr. Vasudev Lakshuman Athavale.	Brahmin.	Money lender, Poona City Narayen Pait House No. 464.	By a Public Meeting, held at Poona, under the auspicies of P. S. Sabha, and by the Mercantile Association, Poona, on the 17th of December, 1889.
387	"	"	"	Rao Saheb Marutishet Damodhar Malwalkar.	Namdeosimpi, Hindu.	Merchant, Municipal Commissioner.	Public Meeting, Poona, 15th December, 1889.
388	"	"	"	Mr. Balaji Babaji Godbole.	Brahmin.	Medical Practitioner	do.
389	"	"	"	Rao Saheb Kashinath Govind Natu.	do.	Pleader, District Court, Poona, and Municipal Commissioner.	do.
390	"	"	"	Mr. Bapurao Ramchander Pandit.	do.	Merchant and Sowkar... ...	do.
391	"	"	"	The Hon'ble Rao Bahadur Krishnaji Luxman Nulkar, C.I.E.	Hindu Brahmin.	Late Dewan of Cutch, Member of the Viceroy's Legislative Council, and also of the Legislative Council, Bombay.	do.
392	"	"	"	Mr. Banaji Krishna Parasnis.	Brahmin.	Jahagirdar of Temple	do.
393	"	"	"	Mr. Narayan Bapuji Kanitkar.	Hindu Brahmin.	Pleader, District Court, Poona.	do.
394	"	"	"	Rao Saheb Damodar Vidyadhar Gokhále.	Brahmin.	Asst. Government Prosecutor and Municipal Commissioner.	do.
395	"	"	"	Mr. Vishnu Narayen Apte.	do.	Assistant Manager and Accountant of the Deccan Paper Mills Company, Limited. Honorary Secretary of the Poona Mercantile Association, Honorary Secretary of the Poona Sanskrit Pathshala.	do.
396	"	"	"	Mr. Rajuna Lingoo ...	Telugu.	Pleader	do.
397	"	"	"	Mr. Dalpat Manchund ...	Gujarathi Hindu.	Merchant	do.
398	"	"	"	Rao Bahadur Vasudev Bapuji Kanitkar.	Hindu Brahmin.	Justice of the Peace and Fellow of the Bombay University, Pensioned Executive Engineer.	do.
399	"	"	"	Mr. Abraham David Ezekiel.	Jew.	Merchant, Synagoge Street ...	do.
400	"	"	"	Dr. Ganesh Krishna Garde, L.M. and S.	Brahmin.	Medical Practitioner	do.
401	"	"	"	Mr. Bal Gangadhar Tilak, B.A., LL.B.	Hindu Brahmin.	Professor, Fergusson College, and Journalist.	do.
402	"	"	"	Mr. Vamanrao Balkrishna Ranade.	Brahmin.	Editor, "Dnyan Chakshu." ...	do.
403	"	"	"	Mr. Vishnu Govind Chinapatnum.	do.	Merchant	do.
404	"	"	"	Khan Bahadur Adarji Dorabji Ghaswalla.	Parsee.	Merchant	do.
405	"	"	"	Rao Saheb Daji Shripat Nagpurkar.	Brahmin.	Municipal Commissioner	do.
406	"	"	"	Mr. Ramji Bhor	Maratha Christian.	......	do.
407	"	"	"	Rao Saheb Coopsawami Mudliar.	Telugu.	Municipal Commissioner ...	do.

Number.	Presidency or Government.	Congress Circle.	Electoral Division.	Names in full of Delegates with honorary titles, scholastic degrees, etc.	Race, Religious denomination, and Caste, if any.	Occupation and Address.	How and when elected.
408	Bombay.	Deccan.	Poona.	Mr. Ravaji Shridhar Gondhalekar.	Brahmin.	Proprietor, Jagadhitechu Press.	Public Meeting Poona, 15th December, 1889.
409	"	"	"	Rao Saheb Mudu Krishna Mudliar.	Telugu.	Municipal Commissioner ...	do.
410	"	"	"	Dr. Narayan Vinayak Chhatre, B.A., L.M. & S.	Brahmin.	Medical Practitioner	do.
411	"	"	"	Mr. Ramchandra Keshev Limaye.	do.	Pleader, Peit Sadashiv, Poona.	do.
412	"	"	"	Rao Saheb Sadashivarao Raghunath Medadkar.	do.	Inamdar, 11 Shunwar Peit, Poona; Member, Poona Sarvajanik Sabha, and Honorary Magistrate, Poona.	do.
413	"	"	"	Mr. Balkrishna Ramchander Vaidya.	Brahmin.	Pleader, D. C., Poona	16th December, Pleaders' Association.
414	"	"	"	Mr. Vaman Ganesh Ghanekar.	do.	do.	do.
415	"	"	"	Rao Saheb Pandurang Buchaji Baholikar.	Hindu Brahmin.	Pleader D. C., Poona, Municipal Commissioner.	do.
416	"	"	"	Mr. Luxman Krishna Nulkar, B.A., L.L.B.	do.	Pleader	do.
417	"	"	"	Mr. Ganpatrao Krishna Bavdekar, B.A.	do.	District Pleader, Poona Shanwar Peit, Bavdekar's house.	Elected by the General Meeting of the Poona Arbitration Court on the 19th December, 1889.
418	"	"	"	Mr. GopalKrishna Gokhale, B.A.	Brahmin.	Teacher and Professor, Fergusson College, Joint Secretary, Provincial Conference, Joint Editor, Sudharuk, Editor, Quarterly Journal Sarvajanik Subha.	Public Meeting, Poona and Sarvajanik Subha, on the 15th December, 1889.
419	"	"	"	R. B. Vishnoo Moreshwur Bhide.	Hindu Brahmin.	Chairman, Poona Sarvajanik Sabha and First Class Honorary Magistrate. Pensioned Sub-Judge.	do.
420	"	"	"	R. S. Chintamanrao Vishwanath Natu, Sirdar.	Brahmin.	Inamdar, Member, Local Board, Poona, and Member, Poona Sarvajanik Sabha, Chairman, Poona, Mercantile Association Landlord, Resident, Shanwar Peith, Poona.	do.
421	"	"	"	Rao Saheb Raghunath Daji Nagarkar.	Hindu Brahmin.	Pleader, Member, Poona Municipal Corporation, Member, District Local Board, Inamdar, Landlord and Member, Poona Sarvajanik Sabha, Secretary, Poona Mercantile Association, Resident Poona Raviwar Peit.	do.
422	"	"	"	Mr. Shivram Hari Sathe ...	do.	Secretary, P. S. S., and Editor, Nyayashraya Monthly Magazine.	do.
423	"	"	"	Rao Saheb Vaman Prabhaker Bhave.	Brahmin.	Principal, Poona Native Institution, Municipal Commmissioner, and Member, Poona Sarvajanik Sabha.	do.
424	"	"	"	Mr. Waman Shivaram Apte, M.A.	Brahman.	Principal, Fergusson College, Poona, Member, Poona Sarvajanik Sabha.	21st December, 1889, Sarvajanik Sabha.
425	"	"	"	Mr. Vinayak Ramchandra Jalnapurker.	Brahmin.	Science Lecturer, Poona Native Institution, and Member, Poona Sarvajanika Sabha.	Elected on the 15th and 21st December, 1889, by a Public Meeting, held in Poona and by the Poona Sarvajanik Sabha.
426	"	"	"	Mr. Bapurao Narayan Natekar.	Hindu.	Pleader, District Court, Poona...	Poona, 15th December, 1889, Dinbundhu Sarvajanik Sabha.
427	"	"	"	Mr. Khanderao Narayen Vaidya,	Hindu Brahmin.	Native Physician Poona, Boodwar Peit, Arya Owshadey, Sangrahalaya.	On 17th Decenber, by Merchants' Association.
428	"	"	"	Shet Haridas Nanubhai.	Guzerati.	Banker	do.

Number.	Presidency or Government.	Congress Circle.	Electoral Division.	Names in full of Delegates with honorary titles, scholastic degrees, etc.	Race, Religious denomination, and Caste, if any.	Occupation and Address.	How and when elected.
429	Bombay.	Deccan.	Poona.	Mr. Lachmandass Rughoonathdass.	Hindu Guzerati.	Poona Soogandhi	On 17th December by Merchants' Association.
430	"	"	"	Mr. Narayen Babaji Joshi, L.C.E	Brahmin.	Pensioner and Merchant ...	do.
431	"	"	"	Mr. Vinayak Narayen Apte.	do.	Merchant	do.
432	"	"	"	Mr. Vasudeva Ganesh Joshi	do.	Manager, Chitra Shala Press ...	do.
433	"	"	Junnar (District, Poona.)	Munshi Shaik Hussen, Vallad Shaikh Chand.	Mahomedan.	Public Preacher, Islam, Village Munsiff, Municipal Commissioner, Local Board, Commissioner.	Public Meeting, Junnar, 30th November, 1889.
434	"	"	Baramati (Poona District.)	Rao Saheb, Bhikaji Anandrao Deshpande.	Brahmin.	Pleader, Inamdar, Chairman of the Baramati Municipality and a Local Board Member of the Bhimthadi Taluka.	Public Meeting, Baramati, in the Poona District, 13th December, 1889.
435	"	"	Supa (District, Poona.)	Rao Saheb Lakshman Anandrao Deshpande.	Brahmin.	A member of the Local Board Taluka Bhimthadi, in the Poona District, and an Inamdar.	Public Meeting, Supa in the Poona District, 25th November, 1889.
436	"	"	"	Mr. Raojirao Bhimrao Chavan Deshmukh.	Maratha.	Khote and Zamindar, Member of the Local Board. Taluka Bhimthadi District, Poona.	do.
437	"	"	Saswad, (District, Poona.)	Mr. Maruti Antoba Nirgude	Shimpi.	Merchant	Public Meeting, Saswad, 20th November, 1889.
438	"	"	"	Mr. Gunpat Mahadev Badhe.	Mahratta.	Agriculturist	do.
439	"	"	Bagewadi.	Mr. Bhimrao Ramaji Guttikar	Hindu Brahmin.	Pleader	Public Meeting at Bagewadi, 3rd Nov. 1889.
440	"	"	Indapur Taluka, (District, Poona.)	Mr. Vamanrao Vishnu Lele	Brahmin.	Pleader District Court, Poona, and Member Puna Sarvajanika Sabha, Member Poona Arbitration Court.	Public Meeting at Indapur District, Poona, 16th December, 1889.
441	"	"	Sholapur.	Mr. Ramchandra Sakharam	Gujar.	Merchant and Agriculturist ...	Public Meeting, held at Sholapur, on 6th December, 1889.
442	"	"	"	Mr. Ganesh Venayak Patwardhan.	Brahmin.	District Pleader	do.
443	"	"	"	Mr. Bhagwandas Rajaram.	Nagar.	Merchant	do.
444	"	"	"	Mr. Govind Balkrishna ...	Brahmin.	District Pleader	do.
445	"	"	"	Mr. Narayanrao	do.	Contractor	do.
446	"	"	"	Mr. Dinkar Ballal Chakrade.	do.	District Pleader	do.
447	"	"	"	Mr. Prabhaker Balaji Keskar.	Christian.	Medical Practitioner ...	do.
448	"	"	"	Mr. Anna Anandrao ...	Lingayet.	District Pleader	do.
449	"	"	"	Mr. Balasahib Deshmukh	Maratha.	Agriculturist	do.
450	"	"	"	Mr. Malkarjunapa Sidramappa Pasare.	Vishaiva Lingayet Brahmin.	Merchant	do.
451	"	"	"	Mr. Sakharam Nemchand.	Gujar, Hindu.	Merchant	do.
452	"	"	"	Mr. Ramchandra Motichand Shaha.	do.	Merchant	do.
453	"	"	"	Mr. Nanchand Fattechand.	Gujar.	Merchant	do.
454	"	"	"	Mr. Bapuji Parashram Phadke	Brahmin.	District Pleader	do.
455	"	"	"	Mr. Prabhakar Laxuman Nagpurkar.	do.	District Pleader	do.
456	"	"	"	Mr. Narayan Pandharinath Kavathekar.	Komta.	Merchant	do.

Number.	Presidency or Government.	Congress Circle.	Electoral Division.	Names in full of Delegates with honorary titles, scholastic degrees, etc.	Race, Religious denomination, and Caste, if any.	Occupation and Address.	How and when elected.
457	Bombay.	Deccan.	Sholapur.	Mr. Lachmee Narayan Sardar.	Marwadi.	Merchant	Public Meeting, held at Sholapur, on 6t December 1889.
458	"	"	"	Mr. Mahadeo Ramchundra Ranade.	Brahmin.	Medical Practitioner, Sholapur.	do.
459	"	"	"	Mr. Shidram Appa Jamma.	Lingayet.	Agriculturist and Artisan ...	do.
460	"	"	"	Rao Bahadur Narayen Govind Deshmukh.	Brahmin.	Pleader, District Court, Sholapur-Bejapur.	do.
461	"	"	"	Rao Bahadur Sakharam Ramchander Kirloskur, B.A.	do.	Pleader, District Court, Sholapur, President Sholapur Municipality.	do.
462	"	"	"	Rao Saheb Mallappa Basappa, Warad.	Wani Lingayet.	Merchant, Municipal Commissioner, Sholapur.	do.
463	"	"	"	Mr. Sitaram Vishnu Bhave.	Brahmin.	District Pleader...	do.
464	"	"	"	Mr. Panchappa Umbarjee.	Bania Lingayet.	Merchant	do.
465	"	"	"	Mr. Heerachand Nemchand Guzar.	Guzerathi Hindu.	Sowkar, Sholapur, and Municipal Commissioner.	do.
466	"	"	"	Rao Saheb Ganputdass Khushal.	Guzerathi Hindu.	Municipal Commissioner and Merchant.	do.
467	"	"	"	Mr. Chinabupsapa Boramain.	Lingayet.	Merchant	do.
468	"	"	"	Mr. Chinabupsapa Chawan.	do.	do.	do.
469	"	"	"	Mr. Y. N. Ranade, B.A., LL.B.	Brahmin.	Pleader, Sholapur, Bijapur, and Editor, "English Opinion on India."	do.
470	"	"	"	Khan Saheb Kazi Sultan...	Mahomedan.	Municipal Commissioner, Sholapur.	do.
471	"	"	"	Khan Saheb Kazi Abdul Kadar.	do.	Municipal Commissioner ...	do.
472	"	"	Pandhurpur (District Sholapur.)	Mr. Ganesh Rajaram Keshakar.	Brahmin.	Pleader at Pundharpur ...	By a Public Meeting, held on the 5th December, 1889, and at a Meeting of the Sholapur People's Association, 6th December 1889.
473	"	"	"	Mr. Ramchandra Narayan Karandikar.	do.	Vakil at Pandhurpur, Conciliator, Municipal Commissioner.	do.
474	"	"	"	Mr. Ganesh Daji Dharurker.	do.	Merchant at Pundhurpur Municipal Commissioner, Taluka Local Board and District Local Board Member.	do.
475	"	"	Barsi (Sholapur.)	Mr. Kallyanji Khemji ...	Guzar Hindu.	Merchant	Public Meeting, Barsi, 6th December 1889.
476	"	"	"	Mr. Sunder Malhar ...	Brahmin.	Agriculturist	do.
477	"	"	"	Mr. Abasahib Panse ...	do.	do.	do.
478	"	"	"	Mr. Visanji Viraji ...	Guzar Hindu.	Merchant	do.
479	"	"	"	Mr. Parushram Jugganath Pardeshi	Rajput Hindu.	do.	do.
480	"	"	"	Mr. Balkrishna Pandurang Kasid.	Kasid Hindu.	do.	do.
481	"	"	Akuj (Sholapur.)	Mr. Gulabechanda Lakhamichand.	Guzar.	Merchant, Akluj Taluka, Malshiras, Zilla Sholapur.	do.
482	"	"	Velapur (Sholapur.)	Mr. Dutto Balvant Agnihotri.	Brahmin.	Inamdar	Public Meeting, Velapur Malshiras, 5th December, 1889.
483	"	"	Sangola (Sholapur.)	Mr. Vishwanath Vithoba Patne.	Lingayet.	Merchant, Member, Sangola Municipality.	Public Meeting, in November 1889.
484	"	"	Nevri (Sholapur.)	Mr. Haibatrao Malhar ...	Brahmin.	Inamdar...	Public Meeting, Nevri Taluka Malshiras.
485	"	"	Ahmednagar.	Mr. Vithuram Nandram ...	Marvari.	Money-lender	Public Meeting, Ahmednagar, 3rd Dec., 1889.
486	"	"	"	Rev. Mr. R. A. Hume, M.A.	Christian American.	American Missionary	do.

Number.	Presidency or Government.	Congress Circle.	Electoral Division.	Names in full of Delegates with honorary titles, scholastic degrees, etc.	Race, Religious denomination, and Caste, if any.	Occupation and Address.	How and when elected.
487	Bombay.	Deccan.	Ahmadnagar.	Mr. Samuel G. Lee Pillai	Protestant Christian (Vellala Caste).	Professor of Mathematics and Logic, Ahmednagar College Graduate, Jaffna College, Ceylon.	Public Meeting, held at Ahmednagar, on 3rd December 1889.
488	"	"	"	Mr. Kondo Kanji	Hindu.	Vakil	do.
489	"	"	"	Sirdar Rao Bahadur Yeshwantrao T. Mirikar.	Brahmin.	Jahagirdar Miri, Exercising Civil and Criminal Powers.	do.
490	"	"	"	Mr. Mahadev Keshav Rishi	do.	Money-lender	do.
491	"	"	"	Rao Saheb Sahadu Ravji Bagde.	Hindu.	Merchant, Municipal Commissioner.	do.
492	"	"	"	Mr. Krishnaji Rantuji Tangle.	Christian.	Pundit and Preacher	do.
493	"	"	"	Kaji Shirajo Din Saheb Bahodin Saheb.	Mahomedan.	Municipal Commissioner, Sangamner.	do.
494	"	"	"	Rao Saheb Davalutram Hambirmal.	Marwari Jain.	Merchant, Ahmednagar, Sowkar and Municipal Commissioner, Member, Ahmednagar Educational Society.	do.
495	"	"	"	Mr. Surajmal Nemidas Khothare.	Marwari.	Merchant and Landholder ...	do.
496	"	"	"	Mr. Vaman Moreshvar Potdar, B.A.	Brahmin.	Teacher, Ahmednagar... ...	do.
497	"	"	"	Mr. Kashinath Bapurao Limaye.	Brahmin Hindu.	Editor of Jagadadarshi, Ahmednagar.	do.
498	"	"	"	Mr. Shankar Vinayek Vable.	do.	Pleader, District Court, Ahmednagar.	do.
499	"	"	"	Mr. Narayanrao Keshao.	Brahmin.	Merchant, Pleader, and Municipal Member.	do.
500	"	"	"	Mr. Kondaji Madhavrao Bhagure.	Maratha.	Merchant and Banker... ...	do.
501	"	"	"	Rao Saheb Trimbuck Krishna Joshi.	Brahmin.	Vakil, Sub-Judge's Court, Newasa, Local Board Member.	do.
502	"	"	"	Rao Saheb Bapu Narhar Sohani.	do.	General Merchant, Conciliator, Money-lender.	do.
503	"	"	"	Mr. Yamaji Bin Bapuji Chandagude.	Maratha.	Agricuturist, Patel of Chass, T. Kopargaon District, Ahmednagar.	do.
504	"	"	"	Mr. Kisandass Navalmall.	Jain Marwari.	Banker	do.
505	"	"	"	Rao Saheb Mohonlal Hiralal.	Kayesth.	Municipal Commissioner, Pleader and Merchant, Member, Ahmednagar Education Society.	do.
506	"	"	"	Mr. Ramchandra Govind Shaligram.	Brahmin.	Kulkarni, Sowkar Agriculturist, Taluka, Akola.	do.
507	"	"	"	Mr. Shitaram Ganesh Deodhar.	do.	Teacher, American Mission High School.	do.
508	"	"	"	Mr. Balkrishna Trimbuck Pornarak.	do.	Sowkar and Trader	do.
509	"	"	"	Mr. Hari Ramchandra Saraph.	do.	Pleader, District Court, Ahmednagar.	do.
510	"	"	"	Mr. Vasudeo Vishnu Ketkar.	do.	Vakil, Sub-Judge's Court ...	do.
511	"	"	"	Mr. Vinayek Balwant Chaukar.	do.	Secretary, Ahmednagar Education Society, Pleader, Ahmednagur.	do.
512	"	"	"	Mr. Sadashiv Vyankatesh Jog.	do.	Pleader, District Court, Ahmednagar.	do.
513	"	"	"	Mr. Vaman Vishwanath Mahajan.	do.	Private Medical Practitioner ...	do.
514	"	"	"	Rao Saheb Haridas Damodhardas.	Vaishnava Nagar Bania.	Sowkar and Municipal Commissioner, Ahmednagar.	do.
515	"	"	"	Mr. Martand Ramchandra Deshmukh.	Brahmin	Trader and Sowkar, Ahmednagar, Inamdar.	do.
516	"	"	"	Mr. Bhaskar Anant Kunti.	do.	Private Teacher	do.
517	"	"	"	Mr. Ramchander Mahadeo Despande.	do.	Kohilay	do.

Number.	Presidency or Government.	Congress Circle.	Electoral Division.	Names in full of Delegates with honorary titles, scholastic degrees, etc.	Race, Religious denomination, and Caste, if any.	Occupation and Address.	How and when elected.
518	Bombay.	Deccan.	Ahmednagar.	Rao Saheb Ragunathrao Govind Jinsiwale.	Brahmin.	Local Board Member, Banker and Municipal Commissioner.	By a Public Meeting, held at Ahmednagar on 3rd December 1889.
519	„	„	„	Mr. Vithal Mahadeo Bhate.	do.	Banker, Member Taluka Local Board.	do.
520	„	„	„	Mr. Madhavrao Gungadhar	do.	Subordinate Government Pleader, Akola, Member, Local Board.	do.
521	„	„	„	Mr. Vaman Trimbak Godbole.	do.	Vakil, Local Board, Member, Parner.	do.
522	„	„	„	Rao Saheb Keshav Bapuji.	do.	Member, Municipality, Sangamnair and Vakil, Chairman, School Board.	do.
523	„	„	„	Mr. Krishnaji Keshev Gharpurey.	do.	Khot, Ahmednagar, New Peit.	do.
524	„	„	„	Rao Saheb Babaji Ganesh Deshpande.	Hindu Brahmin.	Government Pleader, and Municipal Commissioner.	do.
525	„	„	„	Rao Saheb Gajanan Daji Nisal.	Brahmin.	District Local Board Member and Sowkar, Member of Educational Society, Ahmednagar.	do.
526	„	„	„	Sardar Rao Saheb Vasudev Shivrao Shastri.	do.	Jahagirdar of Baku Pimpalgaon Toka Taluka, Nevasa. Member, District Local Board.	do.
527	„	„	„	Mr. Keshev Vishwanath Patwardhan, B.A.	do.	Vakil, Ahmednagar District ...	do.
528	„	„	„	Rao Saheb Sawliaram Dinanath.	Hindu Pardeshi.	Member, District Local Board, and Pleader.	do.
529	„	„	„	Mr. Chandrarao Eknath, Dharmadhikari.	Hindu Brahmin.	Agriculturist	do.
530	„	„	„	Mr. Hasankhan Amirkhan, Pathan.	Mahomedan.	Contractor	do
531	„	„	„	Sirdar Rao Saheb Moro Krishna Dabholkar.	Brahmin.	Jahagirdar of Akolner, Exercising Civil and Criminal Powers, Member of the District Local Board and a Sardar of the Deccan.	do.
532	„	„	„	Mr. Ganesh Krishna Dabholkar.	do.	Jahagirdar of Akolner.	do.
533	„	„	Sangamner (Ahmednagar District).	Mr. Balaji Yeshwant Gatve	do.	Pleader, District Court, Ahmednagar and Village Munsiff.	do.
534	„	„	„	Mr. Shanker Rao Deshpande.	do.	Agriculturist	do.
535	„	„	Nasik.	Mr. Shankarrao Daji Kanade.	Hindu. Lingayat.	Banker, Malegaon, Nasik District.	Elected by the Nasik Sarvajanik Sabha, on 1st December 1889.
536	„	„	„	Rao Saheb Mahadeo Janardan Palnitkar.	Hindu Brahmin.	Pleader, District Court, Nasik, Municipal Commissioner.	do.
537	„	„	„	Mr. Gopal Anant Kulkarni.	Brahmin.	District Pleader, Satana, Nasik.	do.
538	„	„	„	Mr. Ballajee Narayan Vaidya.	do.	Pleader, Sub-Judge's Court, Malegaon City.	do.
539	„	„	„	Mr. Parsharam Vishnoo Yogee.	do.	Pleader, District Court, Nasik City.	do.
540	„	„	„	Mr. Balkrishna Hari Kale.	do.	Merchant and Manager, Nasik Vritta, Press.	do.
541	„	„	„	Mr. Ambadas Ramchandra Pimpaladker.	do.	Jahagirdar, Monje Pimpalad Taluka, Chandwad, Nasik.	do.
542	„	„	„	Rao Saheb Janardan Raghunath Nimbkar.	do.	Pleader District Court, Nasik City, Chandwadkar's Alli, and Municipal Commissioner.	do.
543	„	„	„	Mr. Daji Vishnoo Ketkar.	Hindu Brahmin.	Pleader, District Court ...	do.
544	„	„	„	Mr. Shridhar Annaji Chawdhari.	do.	Vakil	do.
545	„	„	„	Shrimant Ganpatrao Damodar alias Abasaheb Chandwadker.	do.	Banker	do.

Number.	Presidency or Government.	Congress Circle.	Electoral Division.	Names in full of Delegates with honorary titles, scholastic degrees, etc.	Race, Religious denomination, and Caste, if any.	Occupation and Address.	How and when elected.
546	Bombay	Deccan.	Nasik.	Shrimant Damodarrao Krishna Hingre.	Brahmin.	Jahagirdar of Chandore, 2nd Class Sardar.	Elected by the Nasik Sarvajanik Sabha, on 1st December 1889.
547	"	"	"	Mr. Shitaram Damoder Bhonde.	Hindu Brahmin.	Merchant and District Local Board Commissioner.	do.
548	"	"	"	Mr. Ragho Narotum ...	Pardeshi.	Pleader, Sub-Judge's Court, Satana.	do.
549	"	"	"	Mr. Hari Kashinath Kelkar	Hindu Brahmin.	Pleader, Sub-Judge's Court, Satana.	do.
550	"	"	"	Rao Saheb Ganesh Raoji Kshirsagar.	do.	Pleader, Sub-Judge's Court, Satana, Municipal Commissioner, District Local Board Member.	do.
551	"	"	"	Rao Saheb Balaji Narayan Vaidya.	Brahmin.	Pleader, Sub-Judge's Court, Malegaum, Municipal Commissioner.	do.
552	"	"	"	Rao Saheb Gangadhar Narshive Ketkar.	Hindu Brahmin.	District Pleader, Municipal Commissioner, Nasik.	do,
553	"	"	"	Rao Saheb Kachardas Mayam.	Marwadi.	Merchant and Municipal Commissioner.	do.
554	"	"	"	Mr. Vishnu Vinayek Sathaye.	Hindu Brahmin.	Teacher and Proprietor of Yeshavant English School.	do.
555	"	"	"	Mr. Krishnarao Jairam Gupte.	Purbhu.	Pleader, Sub-Judge's Court, Malegaon.	do.
556	"	"	"	Rao Saheb Ganesh Pandurang.	Brahmin.	Government Pleader Nasik, Chairman, Nasik Municipality, and a Member of the Local District Board.	do.
557	"	"	"	Mr. Nayansukha Kevalchand.	Jain Marwari.	Merchant	do.
558	"	"	"	Mr. Sitaram Vishnoo Vaidya.	Hindu Brahmin.	Vakil	do.
559	"	"	"	Mr. Vithal Bhikaji Bhide.	do.	Pleader of the Sub-Judge's Court at Pimpalgaon, Baswant.	do.
560	"	"	"	Shrimant Lakshamanrao Ramarao alias Dada Saheb Sukenkar.	do.	Jahgirdar of Satana ...	do.
561	"	"	"	Mr. Trimbak Ganesh Takle.	do.	Merchant	do.
562	"	"	"	Rao Saheb Wasudev Rao Balkrishna Takleskar.	do.	Jahagirdar, Municipal Commissioner, Local Board Member Nighed and Nasik Taluka District Local Board Member and Honorary Magistrate, Panchawati, Nasik.	do.
563	"	"	"	Shrimant Ramchandra Rajaram alias Daji Saheb.	Brahmin.	Jahagirdar	do.
564	"	"	"	Mr. Ramachandra Ballal Godbole.	do.	Superintendent, Yeshwantrao Maharaj English School.	do.
565	"	"	"	Mr. Jairam Abaji Joshi ...	Hindu Brahmin.	Pleader, District Court, Nasik.	do.
566	"	"	"	Mr. Vishnu Hari Kale ...	Brahmin.	Banker, Nasik	do.
567	"	"	"	Mr. Vishwanath Sitaram Takale.	Hindu Brahmin	Merchant	do.
568	"	"	"	Mr. Shivaram Govind Phalke.	Brahmin.	Teacher, Trimbak	do.
569	"	"	"	Mr. Ramchandra Vishwanat Patwardhan.	do.	District Pleader	do.
570	"	"	"	Mr. Shunker Luxuman Date.	Brahmin.	Pleader, District Court, Nasik.	Public Meeting, Nasik, 1st December 1889.
571	"	"	"	Mr. Hiralal Ramdin	Jain Marwari.	Merchant and Sowkar... ...	do.
572	"	"	"	Mr. Anant Waman Joshi...	Brahmin.	Merchant	do.
573	"	"	"	Mr. Chunilal Ravatmal ...	Marwari.	Merchant	do.

Number.	Presidency or Government.	Congress Circle.	Electoral Division.	Names in full of Delegates with honorary titles, scholastic degrees, etc.	Race, Religious denomination, and Caste, if any.	Occupation and Address.	How and when elected.
574	Bombay.	Deccan.	Nasik.	Sirdar Shrimant Ramrao, Krishna alias Baba Saheb Vinchurkar.	Brahmin.	Jahagirdar of Vinchur... ...	Public Meeting, held in Nasik, on the 1st December, 1889.
575	,,	,,	,,	Mr. Ramchandra Gunesh Mundle, B.A., LL.B.	do.	High Court Pleader	do.
576	,,	,,	Manamad (Nasik.)	Mr. Sakharam Chhajmal.	Jain Marwari.	Merchant and Cultivator ...	do.
577	,,	,,	Yeola (Nasik.)	Rao Saheb Khemachanda Dajiba Shet.	Hindu Brahmin.	General Merchant, Cultivator, Municipal Commissioner, Member, Arya Samaj.	Public Meeting, held at Yeola, on the 17th November, 1889.
578	,,	,,	,,	Rao Saheb Shankar Narhar Dhande.	Brahmin.	Municipal Commissioner ...	do.
579	,,	,,	,,	Mr. Krishnarao Trimbuk.	do. Maratha	Pleader and Inamdar	do.
580	,,	,,	,,	Rao Saheb Purshotam Damodar Barve.	Hindu Brahmin.	Landlord, Yeola, Zilla Nasik, Sir Deshmukha, Political Pensioner, Municipal Commissioner and Member, Arya Samaj.	do.
581	,,	,,	,,	Rao Saheb Keshav Nandram, Marwadi.	Hindu Jain.	Cultivator and Merchant, Member, Local Board, Yeola.	do.
582	,,	,,	,,	Rao Saheb Ramkant B. Thathe.	Hindu Brahmin.	Pleader, Yeola, Zilla Nasik, and Member of the Municipal and Local Boards.	do.
583	,,	,,	,,	Shet Jagjivan Khemchandra Gurothi.	Hindu Guzar.	General Merchant and Cultivator, Member, Arya Samaj.	do.
584	,,	,,	,,	Mr. Damodar Narayen.	Hindu Guzeratti.	General Merchant and Banker, Member, Arya Samaj, Yeola.	do.
585	,,	,,	,,	Shrimant Murlidhur Nathubhai.	Hindu Guzar.	Banker, Cultivator and General Merchant.	do.
586	,,	,,	,,	Shet Balmukand	Hindu Guzeratti.	Merchant, Agriculturist, Yeola..	do.
587	,,	,,	,,	Rao Saheb Damodhar Mohanlal.	do.	General Merchant, Municipal Commissioner.	do.
588	,,	,,	,,	Mr. Raoji Parasharam Jogalekar.	Hindu Brahmin.	Mukhtiar	Yeola "Arya Samaja."
589	,,	,,	Sinnar (Nasik.)	Rao Saheb Sakharam Dhondeo.	do.	Sowkar Vavi Taluka Sinnar, Nasik District, Landlord, General Merchant, and a Member of the Taluka Local Board.	Elected by a Public Meeting, on the 6th December, 1889.
590	,,	,,	,,	Rao Saheb Anant Raoji Kavale.	do.	Pleader, Sinnar, Zilla Nasik, Municipal Commissioner and Chairman of the Sanitation Committee.	do.
591	,,	,,	,,	Mr. Parasharam Jayaram Gupte.	Hindu Purbhu.	Vakil and Secretary of the Native General Library, Shemur.	do.
592	,,	,,	,,	Rao Saheb Vamanrao Mahadeo Pradhan.	do.	Government Pleader, Member of the District Local Board, Municipal Commissioner and Chairman.	do.
593	,,	,,	,,	Rao Saheb Kashiraja Gopal Deshpande.	Hindu Brahmin.	Landlord, Sinnar, Nasik District, Member of the Local Board, Municipal Commissioner.	do.
594	,,	,,	,,	Mr. Balvant Gunesh Novle.	Hindu.	Merchant	do.
595	,,	,,	,,	Mr. Trimbuck Kasheeram Shet.	Shimpee.	Landlord and General Merchant, Vadeengule, Sinnar Taluka, Nasik District.	do.
596	,,	,,	,,	Mr. Waman Bapuji Pradhan alias Appasaheb.	Hindu Purbhu.	Pleader, Sub-Judge's Court, Pimpalgaon, Baswant.	do.
597	,,	,,	Khandesh.	Mr. Ganoo Bhica... ...	Hindu Marathi.	Merchant, Municipal Commissioner.	By Public Meeting, on 16th November, 1889.
598	,,	,,	,,	Rao Saheb Chintaman Bapuji.	Brahmin.	Pleader and Vice-President, Municipality.	do.

Number.	Presidency or Government.	Congress Circle.	Electoral Division.	Names in full of Delegates with honorary titles, scholastic degrees, etc.	Race, Religious denomination, and Caste, if any.	Occupation and Address.	How and when elected.
599	Bombay.	Deccan.	Khandesh.	Mr. Janardhan Bhicajee Khare.	Brahmin.	Pleader, District Court, Dhulia, Municipal Commissioner.	Public Meeting, 17th November, 1889.
600	"	"	"	Mr. Damodar Laxman Deshpande, B.A., LL.B.	do.	Pleader, District, Khandesh ...	do.
601	"	"	"	Shaik Sandumiya Walad, Shaik Bulan.	Mahomedan.	Money Lender and Agriculturist	At a Public Meeting, on the 24th November, 1889.
602	"	"	"	Rao Saheb Martand Luxmon Harat.	Hindu. Maratha.	Inami Jahagirdar, Member of the Taluka and District Local Board and Municipal Commissioner.	Community of Dhulia and Taluka, on the 17th November, 1889.
603	"	"	Dhulia (Khandesh)	Mr. Madhowrao Narayen Gudre.	Hindu Brahmin.	Government Pleader, Vice-President of Taluka Local Board, Dhulia, and Municipal Commissioner.	Public Meeting, Dhulia, 25th November, 1889.
604	"	"	"	Mr. Krishna Dhanaji ...	Nhavi.	Medical Practitioner.	At a Meeting, held at Dhulia, on 17th November, 1889.
605	"	"	"	Mr. Yadav Vyanktesh Niphadkar.	Brahmin.	District Pleader and Municipal Commissioner.	do.
606	"	"	"	Rao Bahadur Govindrao Ramchundra Garud.	do.	District Pleader, Vice-President, District Local Board and Municipality, Dhulia, Khandesh.	do.
607	"	"	"	Mr. Tukaram Arjun, Maistry.	Hindu.	Municipal Commissioner, and Merchant.	do.
608	"	"	"	Mr. Sakharam Dulab Das..	Jain.	Municipal Member	do.
609	"	"	Jalgaon (Khandesh)	Mr. Abaji Ragho Mhalas..	Hindu Brahmin.	Pleader, Jalgaon, Khandesh ...	Elected by a Public Meeting, on the 17th November, 1889.
610	"	"	"	Rao Saheb Sitaram Mahadeo Barve.	do.	Pleader and Member of the District Local Board, Landlord and Khote.	do.
611	"	"	Bhusawal.	Mr. Sakharam Ganesh Patankar.	Brahmin.	Municipal Member, Bhusawal, and Pleader.	Bhusawal, Khandesh, 16th November, 1889.
612	"	"	"	Mr. Vithal Govind ...	do.	Pleader	do.
613	"	"	"	Mr. Keshav Ballal ...	do.	Contractor and Municipal Commissioner.	do.
614	"	"	Amalnere.	Mr. Rupchand Magandas...	Guzerathi Jain.	Merchant	Public Meeting, Amalnere, 24th November, 1889.
615	"	"	"	Mr. Dhondo Sadashive Panwalkar.	Brahmin.	Vakil, Amalnere	do.
616	"	"	"	Mr. Narayen Vishnu Parajpe.	do.	Vakil, Sub-Judge's Court, Amalnere, Vice-President, Taluka, Local Board, and Municipal Commissioner.	do.
617	"	"	"	Mr. Wasudeo Daji Mwthe.	Hindu Brahmin.	Member, Taluka Local Board, Municipal Commissioner and Sowkar.	do.
618	"	"	Yawal (Khandesh)	Mr. Baburao Moreshwar Halbe.	Brahmin.	Pleader, District Court, Yawal, Zilla Khandesh.	Public Meeting, 17th November, 1889.
619	"	"	"	Rao Saheb Dhondoo Bhawji Deshmukh.	Kunbi.	Merchant, Member, Municipality, Yawal, and District Local Board, Khandesh.	do.
620	"	"	"	Rao Saheb Ghanasham Khushal.	Lingayet.	Government Pleader, Sub-Judge's Court, Vice-President, Municipality, Yawal, and Taluka Local Board, Sowda, Khandesh.	do.
621	"	"	"	Mr. Gangadher Narayan Late.	Brahmin.	Pleader, and Member, Municipality, Yawal, Taluka Sowda, Khandesh.	do.
622	"	"	"	Mr. Sakharam Pandurang Gupte.	Hindu Parbhu.	Pleader	do.
623	"	"	Jamner (Khandesh)	Mr. Waman Ganesh Sathe.	Hindu Brahmin.	Merchant, Money-lender, and Landlord.	Elected by a Meeting, on the 14th December.
624	"	"	Thalnar (Khandesh)	Mr. Hari Ramdas... ...	Hindu Wani.	Member, Local Board, Merchant, and Landlord.	Public Meeting, Thulner, 1st December, 1889.

Number.	Presidency or Government.	Congress Circle.	Electoral Division.	Names in full of Delegates with honorary titles, scholastic degrees, etc.	Race, Religious denomination, and Caste, if any.	Occupation and Address.	How and when elected.
625	Bombay.	Deccan.	Shirpur (Khandesh District).	Rao Saheb Ramchandra Chintaman Khare.	Brahmin.	Pleader at Shirpur, Khandesh District, Vice-President, Municipality of Shirpur, Chairman, Taluka Local Board, Shirpur.	Elected 1st December, 1889, at a Public Meeting in Shirpur.
626	"	"	"	Mr. Wasudev Vinayek Karundikar.	Hindu Brahmin.	Pleader	Public Meeting, Shirpur, in Khandesh, 17th November, 1889.
627	"	"	Erandol Taluka (Khandesh District.)	Rao Saheb Bhikaji Dhondev Nigudkar.	Brahmin.	Member, District Local Board, Pleader, and Chairman, School Committee, Erandol.	Public Meeting at Erandol, 30th November, 1889.
628	"	"	Sawada (Khandesh Taluka.)	Mr. Tarachand Amarchund Nahatta.	Jain Oswal Marwari.	Banker, and Member Local, Board.	Public Meeting, at Bamanod, Sowada Talooka, 10th December, 1889.
629	"	"	Raver (Khandesh)	Mr. Dayaldas Kunjalal.	Marwari.	Sowkar	Raver, Khandesh, 12th December, 1889.
630	"	"	"	Mr. Devidas Devlal ...	do.	do.	do.
631	"	"	"	Mr. Mahadev Vishnu Bhalerao.	Brahmin.	do.	do.
632	"	"	"	Shrimant Raje Raghunathrao Jaykrishnarao.	do.	Deshmukh Deshpande, Member, District Local Board, and Jahagirdar.	do.
633	"	"	Tasgaon (Satara.)	Mr. Anant Narayan Kaulgikar.	do.	Editor, Chandansha	Public Meeting, at Tasgaon 20th November, 1889.
634	"	"	"	Mr. Vinayak Daji,. Kaulgikar.	do.	Inamdar...	do.
635	"	"	"	Mr. Vinayak Ragunath Mahiskar.	do.	Inamdar and Merchant ...	do.
636	"	"	"	Mr. Vinayak Wishwanath Huprikar.	do.	Municipal Commissioner, Tasgaon.	do.
637	"	"	"	Mr. Shriniwas Laksman Chipade.	do.	Pleader, Tasgaon	do.
638	"	"	"	Rao Saheb Anantrao ...	Maratha Hindu.	Saran Inamdar, Tasgaon, Satara, and Zilla Local Board Member.	do.
639	"	"	"	Mr. Ababhai W. Shirajibhai Momin.	Mahomedan.	Trader	do.
640	"	"	"	Mr. Datatraya Shewram, Sidhore.	Brahmin.	Pleader, Tasgaon, Satara ...	do.
641	"	"	Satara.	Mr. Lakshman Dadaji Pathak.	Hindu. Brahmin.	Pleader and Inamdar	Satara, Public Meeting 17th November, 1889.
642	"	"	"	Shrimant Sakharam Nilkanth Kanhere.	do.	Inamdar	do.
643	"	"	"	Mr. Krishnarao Sakharam.	do.	Mahajani Inamdar	do.
644	"	"	"	Rao Saheb Balvant Shridhar Sahasrabuddhe.	do.	Pleader, Municipal Commissioner, and Secretary, Sarvajanik Sabha.	do.
645	"	"	"	Rao Bahadur Ganesh Pandurang Agte.	do.	Inamdar, Vice-President, Satara Municipality, Vice-President, District and Taluka Local Boards, Honorary Bench Magistrate and Chairman, School Board.	do.
646	"	"	"	Rao Saheb Pandurang Nilkanth Bhadkamkar.	do.	Assistant Government Pleader, District Court, Municipal Commissioner, and Inamdar, Satara.	do.
647	"	"	"	Rao Saheb Vaman Ganesh Phadnis.	do.	Inamdar and Municipal Commissioner, Satara, and Member, Taluka Local Board, Satara.	do.

Number.	Presidency or Government.	Congress Circle.	Electoral Division.	Names in full of Delegates with honorary titles, scholastic degrees, etc.	Race, Religious denomination, and Caste, if any.	Occupation and Address.	How and when elected.
648	Bombay.	Deccan.	Satara.	Mr. Raghunath Pandurang Karandikar.	Hindu Brahmin.	High Court Pleader, Secretary, Sarvajanik Sabha.	Satara, Public Meeting, 17th November, 1889.
649	„	„	„	Rao Saheb Malhar Khanderao Chitnis, B.A., LL.B.	Hindu Parbhu.	Municipal Commissioner, High Court Pleader, and Inamdar.	do.
650	„	„	„	Rao Saheb Laxman Balvant Mutalik.	Hindu Brahmin.	Inamdar, Municipal Commissioner, Member, Taluka and District Local Boards, Honorary Bench Magistrate and Conciliator under the Deccan Agriculturist Act.	do.
651	„	„	„	Rao Saheb Vishnu Laxman Rangole.	Hindu Kasar.	Trader, Municipal Commissioner, Member, Taluka Local Board, and Honorary Bench Magistrate.	do.
652	„	„	„	Mr. Gokuldas Shitaram Gandhi.	Hindu Gujar.	Trader	do.
653	„	„	„	Rev. Mr. Kasambhai Muhmud.	Christian.	Preacher	do.
654	„	„	„	Rao Saheb Govind Vishnu Ranade.	Hindu Brahmin.	Pleader	do.
655	„	„	„	Mr. Ganpatdas Hirachand Devi.	Gujarati.	Contractor and General Merchant.	do.
656	„	„	„	Mr. Dattatraya Balwant, Parasnis.	Hindu Brahmin.	Proprietor, "Maharashtra Kokil."	do.
657	„	„	„	Mr. Shuaodin Haji Ababsaly.	Mahomedan.	General Merchant ...	Anjumane Ahbab, Khademutubh, Satara, 20th November, 1889.
658	„	„	„	Mr. Vaman Anant Bhide...	Hindu Brahmin.	Trader	Traders' Association, Satara, 15th December, 1889.
659	„	„	„	Mr. Narayan Pandurang Agte.	Hindu Brahmin.	Trader	do.
660	„	„	„	Mr. Krishnaji Ramchandra Ranbhor.	do.	Pleader	do.
661	„	„	„	Mr. Rango Ramchandra Ranbhor.	do.	Trader	Satara, Public Meeting, Ashta, 24th November, 1889.
662	„	„	„	Mr. Anu Jinapa	Hindu Jain.	Agriculturist and Money-lender.	do.
663	„	„	„	Rao Saheb Govind Dhondadeo Limaye.	Hindu Brahmin.	Pleader and Merchant, Member, Local Board, Satara, Vice-President, Taluk Local Board, Chairman, and Vice-President, Municipality.	do.
664	„	„	„	Mr. Ganapatrao Vithalrao Deshamukh.	Hindu Lingayat.	Member, Local Board and Inamdar.	do.
665	„	„	„	Mr. Pandurang Vaman Chitnis.	Hindu Porbhu.	Inamdar...	do.
666	„	„	„	Mr. Murori Chopadi Shinde	Hindu Maratha.	Cultivator and Money-lender ...	do.
667	„	„	„	Mr. Rudrapa Guru Lingapa.	Hindu Lingayat.	Trade	do.
668	„	„	„	Rao Saheb Hari Ramkrishna Hardikar.	Hindu Brahmin.	Agriculturist, Money-lender, Member, Local Board, Walwa.	do.
669	„	„	Walwa (Satara).	Mr. Krishnaji Luxman Desai.	do.	Pleader	do.
670	„	„	„	Mr. Hari Krishna Talvadkar.	Hindu.	do.	do.
671	„	„	„	Mr. Balaji Damodar Hasamnis.	Hindu Brahmin.	Agriculturist and Money-lender.	do.
672	„	„	„	Mr. Balaji Venktesh Hasamnis.	do.	Agriculturist	do.
673	„	„	„	Mr. Ganesh Vishnu Hasamnis.	do.	do.	do.
674	„	„	„	Mr. Vanaji Hukmaji ...	Hindu Marwari.	Trader and Money-lender ...	do.
675	„	„	„	Mr. Narayan Bhaw, Patel.	Hindu Maratha.	do.	do.

Number.	Presidency or Government.	Congress Circle.	Electoral Division.	Names in full of Delegates with honorary titles, scholastic degrees, etc.	Race, Religious denomination, and Caste, if any.	Occupation and Address.	How and when elected.
676	Bombay.	Deccan.	Walva (Satara)	Rao Saheb Sambhu Ranu Patel.	Hindu Maratha.	Agriculturist, Money-lender, Chairman, Municipality, Walwa, Vice-President, Municipality, and Village Moonsiff.	By a Public Meeting, 24th November, 1889.
677	"	"	"	Mr. Keshev Raghunath Fadke.	Hindu Brahmin.	Pleader	do.
678	"	"	"	Mr. Balvant Narayen Tagare.	do.	Money-lender, and Municipal Chairman.	do.
679	"	"	Taluka Karhad (District Satara.)	Rao Saheb Bhasker Gopal Savarkar.	do.	Government Pleader, Sub-Judge'sCourt, Karhad District, Satara, and President of the Karhad Municipality, and Vice-President of the Taluk Local Board, Karhad.	By Public Meeting, on 19th November, 1889.
680	"	"	"	Rao Saheb Vaman Narayan Kirane.	do.	Member of the District Local Board, Satara.	do.
681	"	"	"	Rao Saheb Ganesh Chintaman Bhate.	do.	Pleader, Sub-Judge's Court, Karhad District, Satara.	do.
682	"	"	"	Rao Saheb Vitthal Mahipat Supanekar.	do.	Do. and Member of the Taluq Local Board, Karhad.	do.
683	"	"	"	Naro Vitthal Ghate ...	Brahmin.	Inamdar and Local Board Member, and Municipal Commissioner, Karad District, Satara.	Karhad, 2nd December, 1889.
684	"	"	"	Mr. Ganesh Gopal Kelkar.	Hindu Brahmin.	Pleader	Public Meeting held at Karhad, on 19th November, 1889.
685	"	"	"	Mr. Gangadhar Ramkrishna Kirane, L.C.E.	Brahmin Karhada.	Money-dealer and Farmer ...	do.
686	"	"	"	Khan Saheb Chandsha Manesha.	Mahomedan	Kazi, Inamdar, Member, Taluka Local Board, and Municipal Commissioner.	Karhad, Public Meeting, 2nd December, 1889.
687	"	"	Wai Taluka (Satara District.)	Rao Saheb Ramchandra Krishna Kothavale.	Hindu Brahmin.	Inamdar, Member of the Satara District Local Board and Municipal Commissioner, Wai Municipality.	Public Meeting, Wai, 17th November, 1889.
688	"	"	"	Mr. Sudashiv Ramchandra Bakhle.	do.	Merchant	do.
689	"	"	Taluka Rahimutpoor (Satara District)	Mr. Sitaram Anant Bhide, Pleader.	do.	Pleader, Sub-Judge's Court, Rahimatpoor Taluq, Koregaon.	Elected by the Rahimatpur Congress Sub-Committee on 24th November, 1889.
690	"	"	"	Mr. Mahadev Khando Vaidya.	Hindu Brahmin.	Pleader, Rahimatpoor Taluq, Koregaon.	do.
691	"	"	Khanapur (Satara District.)	Rao Saheb Gopal Keshava Limaye.	do.	Pleader, and Chairman, Vita Municipality.	Vita Khanapur, Public Meeting, 10th December, 1889.
692	"	"	"	Mr. Gopal Vishnu Ranade.	do.	Inamdar, and Trader	do.
693	"	"	"	Mr. Shankarrao Ragunnath Agashe.	do.	Sawkar, Taluka, Patan District, Satara.	Public Meeting, 20th November, 1889.
694	"	"	"	Rao Saheb Krishnarao Ramchandra Garvare.	do.	Inamdar, Trader, and Member, District, Local, and Taluka Board.	Vita Khanapur, Public Meeting, 10th December, 1889.
695	"	"	"	Rao Saheb Vaman Shridhar.	do.	Pleader, Vice-President, Taluka Local Board, and Member of the District Local Board.	do.
696	"	"	Bijapur.	Rao Saheb Raghabedra Krishna.	do.	Landholder and Pleader, Vice-President, District Local Board, Bijapur, and Municipal Commissioner.	Public Meeting at Bijapur, 10th November, 1889.

Number.	Presidency or Government.	Congress Circle.	Electoral Division.	Names in full of Delegates with honorary titles, scholastic degrees, etc.	Race, Religious denomination, and Caste, if any.	Occupation and Address.	How and when elected.
697	Bombay.	Deccan.	Bijapur.	Rao Saheb Sheshjirao Rayaji.	Hindu Brahmin.	Pleader, Chairman, Municipality, Bijapur, and Vice-President, Taluka Local Board.	Public Meeting at Bijapur, 10th November, 1889.
698	"	"	"	Mr. Balwantrao Moreshwar Joshi.	do.	Merchant	do.
699	"	"	"	Rao Saheb Narharrao Ramchandra.	do.	Landholder, Vakil, Municipal Commissioner, Bijapur, and Member, District Local Board.	do.
700	"	"	"	Khan Saheb Haji Ibrahim Mahomed Goshmirasahib, Mutuwally.	Mahomedan.	Jahagirdar, and Member, District Local Board.	do.
701	"	"	"	Khan Saheb Mahomedsaheb.	do.	do.	do.
702	"	"	Bagalcote (District Bijapur.)	Azum Virbhudruppe, late Bhadmshetti.	Lingayat.	Merchant	Public Meeting, held on the 3rd of December, 1889, at Bagalcote Town.
703	"	"	"	Mr. Bulwantrao Bhimrao Jambhekar.	Brahmin.	Citizen of the Town of Bagalcote.	do.
704	"	"	"	Mr. Dhondidas Gunneshdas.	Guzerati Wanee.	Banker, Bagalcote	do.
705	"	"	"	Mr. Sitaram Hanmantrao Nimbgamkar.	Brahmin.	Journalist, Proprietor of the Shri-Ramdas Press at Bijapur, and the Kumind Punch, Bagalcote.	do.
706	"	"	"	Mr. Venkatidas Tukaidas.	Hindu Gujar.	Merchant	Public Meeting at Bagalcote, 10th Dec. 1889.
707	"	"	"	Azum Rukmuddin Saheb, Jubbur.	Mahomedan.	Merchant and Municipal Commissioner, Bagalcote.	Meeting held on the 3rd of December, 1889.
708	"	"	"	Mr. Nuhne Saheb Jamadar.	do.	Land-holder	do.
709	"	"	Indi (District Bijapur)	Mr. Sadashiva Laxman Kalekar.	Hindu Shudra.	Merchant and Land-holder ...	Public Meeting at Indi, 14th December, 1889.
710	"	"	Mudebihal (Bijapur.)	Mr. Venkatrao Appaji Gothe.	Hindu Brahmin.	Pleader at Mudebihal	Public Meeting, Mudebihal, 12th December, 1889.
711	"	"	Belgaum.	Mr. Anandrao Sidoji Mane.	Maratha.	Honorary Magistrate, Banker, and Cloth Merchant.	Public Meeting, Belgaum District, 8th December, 1889.
712	"	"	"	Mr. Bhimrao Shrinivasrao Pridi.	Brahmin.	Land-holder	do.
713	"	"	"	Mr. Shripad Anant Chhattre.	do.	Pleader	do.
714	"	"	"	Mr. Shankar Raghunath Patherpekar Pili.	Maratha.	1st Assistant Master, London Mission High School.	do.
715	"	"	"	Mr. Vaman Vithal Kulkarni.	Brahmin.	Land-owner, and Vatandar, Sankeshvar, Belgaum District.	do
716	"	"	"	Mr. Rao Saheb Appaya Dhamagi.	Lingayat.	Merchant and Municipal Commissioner.	do.
717	"	"	"	Mr. Bhimrao Apaji Mahajan.	Brahmin.	Pleader, Chikodee, Land-owner, Gokak, Belgaum.	do.
718	"	"	"	Mr. Anant Mangesh Birdikar.	Goad Brahmin.	District Pleader, Land-holder, Joint Secretary, District Association, Belgaum, Khanapore.	do.
719	"	"	"	Mr. Vaman Govind Palekar	Guzerati Brahmin.	Pleader, Belgaum	do.
720	"	"	"	Mr. Narayan Vinayak Velankar.	Brahmin.	do.	do.
721	"	"	"	Mr. Vishnu Raghunath Natu, B.A., LL.B.	do.	District Pleader and Secretary, Belgaum District Association.	do.
722	"	"	"	Mr. Maheshvar Lakshman Gadgil.	do.	Pleader	do.
723	"	"	"	Rao Bahadur Mahdevrao Narayan Jogalekar.	do.	Vice-President, Municipality, Belgaum.	do.
724	"	"	"	Khan Saheb Ibrahim Saheb Khateb, Inamdar, Khamkarhatti.	Musalman.	Honorary Magistrate, Municipal Commissioner, Member of the District Local Board, Member, Agricultural Committee, Contract Association.	do.
725	"	"	"	Rao Saheb Appaya Basling Appa Halagi.	Ligayat.	Merchant, and Municipal Commissioner.	do.

Number.	Presidency or Government.	Congress Circle.	Electoral Division.	Names in full of delegates with honorary titles, scholastic degrees, etc.	Race, Religious denomination, and Caste, if any.	Occupation and Address.	How and when elected.
726	Bombay.	Deccan.	Belgaum.	Mr. Abdul Rahiman Saheb.	Mahomedan.	Inamdar, Khateb, Belgaum ...	By Public Meeting, 8th December, 1889.
727	"	"	"	Mr. Mukdoom Saheb Arcot.	do.	Merchant	do.
728	"	"	"	Mr. Golam Hoosen Saheb.	do.	Sarnur Moulvi	do.
729	"	"	"	Mr. Raoji Gangadhar Khot.	Goad Brahmin.	Pleader, Belgaum	do.
730	"	"	"	Mr. Burjorjee Framjee ...	Parsee.	Land-owner, and Contractor ...	do.
731	"	"	"	Mr. Vyankatarao Krishna Mahajan.	Hindu Brahmin.	Pleader	do.
732	"	"	"	Mr. Hanamant Dattatraya Kulkarni.	do.	Landholder and Contractor ...	Public Meeting, 24th November, 1889.
733	"	"	"	Mr. Ramchandra Dhondo Kulkarni.	do.	Landholder and Sowkar ...	do.
734	"	"	Sankeswar (Belgaum.)	Mr. Keshev Abaji Kulkarni.	Brahmin.	Village Accountant	Public Meeting, Sankeswar, Belgaum District, 19th December, 1889.
735	"	"	Chikodi (Belgaum.)	Rao Saheb Sadashiv Balkrishna Bhate.	do.	Chairman, Schools Committee, Belgaum Municipality and District Court Pleader.	Public Meeting, Chikodi, 24th November, 1889.
736	"	"	Dharwar.	Rao Saheb Ramchandra Swamirao, Malapur.	Hindu Brahmin.	Pleader, District Court, Dharwar, Member of the Local Board (District and Taluka).	In Public Meeting, 16th August, 1889.
737	"	"	"	Mr. Hari Bhimrao Jambhekar, B.A.	do.	Head Master, Victoria High School, Dharwar.	do.
738	"	"	"	Rao Saheb Anant Vyankatesh Panindikar.	Hindu Saraswat.	Pleader, District Court, Dharwar, Honorary Magistrate, and Member District Local Board.	do.
739	"	"	"	Mr. Krishnarao Hanmant.	Brahmin.	Pleader and Honorary Magistrate.	do.
740	"	"	"	Mr. Govind Appa Krisnaappa Konaraddi.	Hindu Raddi Caste.	Land-holder and Merchant, Dharwar.	do.
741	"	"	"	Mr. Antaji Ramchandra Joglekar.	Brahmin.	Editor "Dharwar Vritta" Newspaper.	Public Meeting, Dharwar, 21st July, 1889.
742	"	"	Hubli (District Dharwar)	Mr. Gururao Babaji Morah.	do.	Pleader	Public Meeting, 13th August, 1889.
743	"	"	"	Mr. Krishnarao Raghavendra Valeekar.	Hindu Brahmin.	do.	Public Meeting, Hubli, held on 8th October, 1889.
744	"	"	"	Mr. Sitaram Narayen Guttal.	do.	do.	do.
745	"	"	"	Mr. Narayenrao Shrinewas Chitgupi.	do.	Merchant	do.
746	"	"	"	Rao Saheb Subrao Ramchandra Behatti.	Brahmin.	Pleader, District Court, Dharwar, Chairman, Municipality, and Member Local Board.	do.
747	"	"	Gadag (District Dharwar.)	Mr. Subrao Sheshoo ...	do.	Pleader, Sub-Judge's Court, Gadag.	Public Meeting, held on the 15th December, 1889.
748	"	"	"	Mr. Vyankatrao Narayen Arur.	do.	Pleader, District Court, Dharwar.	do.
749	"	"	"	Rao Saheb Raghavendra Rao Krishna Mulgundhakar.	do.	Pleader, Sub-Judge's Court, Gadag, Member, Local Board.	do.
750	"	"	"	Mr. Vasudevdas Venkatidos	Guzeratti.	Sowkar Merchant, and Chairman, Gadag Municipality.	do.
751	"	"	"	Mr. Gopaldas Govindas ...	do.	Sowkar Merchant, Gadag ...	do.
752	"	"	"	Mr. Venkatesh Ganesh Sashihital.	Brahmin.	Pleader	do.
753	"	"	"	Mr. Nasarwanji Hormasji Padsha.	Parsee.	Agent, Framjee & Co.	do.
754	"	"	Karajagi (Dharwar.)	Mr. Hari Sakharam Jogalekar.	Hindu Brahmin.	Sowkar Landholder, and Honorary Magistrate, Karajagi, Dharwar.	Elected at Public Meeting, held at Karajgi, 27th September, 1889.
755	"	"	"	Mr. Vishwanath Keshav Joglekar.	Brahmin.	Merchant, and Vice-President, Local Board.	do.

Number.	Presidency or Government.	Congress Circle.	Electoral Division.	Names in full of delegates with honorary titles, scholastic degrees, etc.	Race, Religious denomination, and Caste, if any.	Occupation and Address.	How and when elected.
756	Bombay	Deccan.	Karwar (Kanara)	Rao Saheb Shanker Wenktesh Take.	Brahmin.	Member, District Local Board and Municipal Commissioner.	Public Meeting, held on 17th November, 1889.
757	"	"	"	Rao Saheb Subrao Nangappa Wagle.	do.	Landholder, and Municipal Commissioner.	do.
758	"	"	"	Mr. Atmaram Hari Suktankar.	do.	Medical Practitioner ...	do.
759	"	"	"	Mr. Narayan Anant Vinekar.	Hindu Brahmin.	Pleader, District Court, Karwar.	do.
760	"	"	"	Rao Saheb Shivaram Subrao Nagarkathe.	do.	Member, District Local Board, Kanara, and Pleader, District Court, Karwar.	do.
761	"	"	"	Mr. Subrao Narayen Kamat.	do.	Landholder	do.
762	"	"	Gokarna (Kanara.)	Mr. Narshiava Ganesh Bhut.	Brahmin.	Native Doctor	Public Meeting, 29th October, 1889.
763	"	"	"	Mr. Hosmani Nageshrao Shantaya Gokarnakar.	Hindu Saraswata.	Landholder, Gokarna	do.
764	"	"	Kumta (District Kanara.)	Mr. Nannji Bhanjee Shet.	Hindu Thakkar.	Merchant.	Kumta Town, 3rd November, 1889.
765	"	"	"	Sayad Kassim Sayad Mahomed.	Mahomedan.	Merchant	do.
766	"	"	"	Rao Saheb Haji Sayad Hoosein Sayad Yasoofalli Perjade.	do.	Merchant, Landholder and Municipal Commissioner.	do.
767	"	"	Ankola (District Kanara.)	Mr. Damodar Pandurang Prabhu.	Hindu Brahmin.	Landholder	Public Meeting, Ankola, September 1889.
768	"	"	Sirsi (District Kanara.)	Mr. Mahableshwar Bhat Bhadrabhat Gopi.	Dravid Hindu Brahmin.	District Pleader, Kanara, President, Kanara Vanadukha, Nivarini Sabha.	Sirsi, Public Meeting, 19th November, 1889.
769	"	"	"	Mr. Pundlik Narayan ...	Hindu Brahmin.	Municipal Commissioner, Vice-President, Kanara, Vanadukha Nivarini Sabha and District Pleader.	do.
770	"	"	"	Mr. Devar Hegde Devappa Hegde.	do.	Landholder	do.
771	"	"	"	Mr. Motensar Manjappa Hegde bin Paramaya Hedge.	do.	Merchant and Zemindar ...	do.
772	"	"	"	Mr. Anappa Hegde Venkappa Hegde.	do.	do. ...	do.
773	"	"	"	Mr. Ramaya Hegde, Paramaya Hegde.	Dravid Hindu Brahmin.	Zemindar	do.
774	"	"	"	Mr. Narayan Appa Hegde Permaya Hegde.	Havik Brahmin.	Agriculturist	do.
775	"	"	Sangali State.	Mr. Dattatraya Ramchandra Tilvi.	Goad Brahmin.	Superintendent, Dhundiraji Printing Press, Shahapur.	At a Public Meeting held on 16th December, 1889.
776	"	"	Miraj.	Mr. Gangadhur Amrit Joshi.	Brahmin.	Pleader	Public Meeting, 8th December.
777	"	"	Sangali	Mr. Anant Ramchandra Patkar.	do.	Pleader and Public Prosecutor.	Public Meeting, at Dighraj, Sangali State, 29th November, 1889.
778	"	"	"	Mr. Govind Balwant Garde	Hindu Brahmin.	Pleader at Sangali ...	Public Meeting 9th October 1889.
779	"	"	"	Mr. Atmaram Balwant Khandekar.		Pleader	do.
780	"	"	"	Mr. Yeshwant Balkrishna Lagu.	Hindu Brahmin.	Inamdar...	do.
781	"	"	"	Mr. Kondo Vittal Godbole.	do.	Sangali, S.M.Country, Merchant	do.
782	"	"	"	Mr. Keshava Narayen Bakhle.	do.	do. Agricularist.	do.
783	"	"	Mangal Wedhe.	Mr. Gunesh Laxman Page.	Brahmin.	do. Landholder and Merchant.	Public Meeting, 9th December, 1889.
784	"	"	Kolhapur.	Mr. Ramchandra Narshinh Kulkarni.	do.	School Master, Kolhapur	Public Meeting, 24th November, 1889, at Kolhapur.
785	"	"	"	Mr. Govind Krishna Sohoni, B.A., LLB.	do.	Pleader and Landholder, Kolhapur.	do.
786	"	"	"	Mr. Kallapa Anna Ashtekar.	Jain.	Pleader	do.

Number.	Presidency or Government.	Congress Circle.	Electoral Division.	Names in full of Delegates with honorary titles, scholastic degrees, etc.	Race, Religious denomination, and Caste, if any.	Occupation and Address.	How and when elected.
787	Bombay.	Deccan.	Ajara (Kolhapur.)	Mr. Chintaman Hari Sohoni	Brahmin.	Pleader and Inamdar	Ajara Public Meeting 24th November, 1889.
788	"	"	Gad Ingalaj (Kolhapur.)	Mr. Shriniwas Vyankatesh Deshpande.	do.	Inamdar...	Gad Ingalaj, Kolhapur.
789	"	"	Kurundwad (Kolhapur.)	Mr. Krishnaji Ballal Godbole.	Hindu Brahmin	Superintendent Bhannana Press, Kurandwad, S. M. Country.	By Public Meeting held at Kurundwad on the 4th December 1889.
790	"	"	Inchalkaranji (Kolhapur.)	Mr. Keshav Ganesh Sabins, B.A., LL.B.	Brahmin.	District Pleader, Belgaum, Pleader, Miraj, Kurundwad and Sangli States.	Public Meeting, 22nd November 1889, Indian National Congress Hall, Inchalkaranji.
791	"	"	"	Mr. Ramchandra Bobdeo Apte.	do.	Pleader, Member, A. V. School Committee, Inchalkaranji ...	do.
792	"	Guzerat.	Ahmedabad	Rao Bahadur Ranchorelal Chotelal, C.I.E.	Hindu Nagar Brahmin.	Manager of a Cotton Mill and Municipal President.	Public Meeting, 4th December, 1889.
793	"	"	"	Mr. Behecherlal Nathooram Bhat.	Hindu Brahmin.	Manager, Vag Bhatt Vaidaka Grantha Bhashantar, Member of Swadesha Vatsal Society.	At a Meeting held at Ahmedabad of the Swadesha Vatsal Society on the 17th December 1889.
794	"	"	"	Mr. Purnanand Mahanand Bhatt.	Rayakwal Hindu Brahmin.	Late Naib Dewan to His Highness Sir Shri Keshrisingjee, K.C.S.I., Maharaja of Idar, Mahikanta Agency.	do.
795	"	"	"	Seth Manibhai Premabhai.	Jain Bania.	Banker	Public Meeting, 4th December, 1889.
796	"	"	"	Mr. Dalsukhram Hargovind	Hindu Kunbi.	Merchant	do.
797	"	"	"	Mr. Sakalchand Ratanchand Vohora.	Jain Bania.	Pleader	do.
798	"	"	"	Mr. Narbheram Raghunathdas.	Hindu Kshatri.	Government Pleader	do.
799	"	"	"	Rao Saheb Chunilal Raghunathdas.	do.	Pleader and Municipal Commissioner.	do.
800	"	"	"	Rao Saheb Vrijrai Sakarlal.	do.	Do. do. ...	do.
801	"	"	"	Rao Saheb Chunilal Kapurchand.	Hindu Bania.	Pleader and Assistant Public Prosecutor, Ahmedabad, and Municipal Commissioner.	do.
802	"	"	"	Rao Saheb Keshavlal Motilal.	do.	Pleader and Municipal Commissioner.	do.
803	"	"	"	Rao Saheb Trikamlal Vadilal.	Jain Bania.	Banker and Municipal Commissioner.	do.
804	"	"	"	Rao Saheb Someshvar Narayenji Trivadi.	Hindu Brahmin.	Government Pleader 1 Punch Mahals.	do.
805	"	"	"	Rao Saheb Desaibhai Kalidas.	do.	Government Pleader and Municipal Commissioner.	do.
806	"	"	"	Khan Saheb Cowasji Mancherji Karanjawalla.	Parsee.	Merchant and Municipal Commissioner.	do.
807	"	"	"	Mr. Krishnalal Lullubhai Mehta.	Hindu Nagar Brahmin.	District Court Pleader... ...	do.
808	"	"	Broach.	Mr. Pranshankar Narottum.	Hindu Brahmin.	District Pleader	do.
809	"	"	"	Mr. Ratanram Amrutram Thanki.	Hindu Brahmin.	Head Master, Loka Hitechhu Sabha's School, Broach.	At a Public Meeting, of the Zilla, at Broach, and the Loka Hitechhu Sabha, on the 1st of December, 1889.
810	"	"	"	Mr. Madhavram Narbheram	do.	Judge Sirdar Court, Baroda ...	1st December, 1889, at a Public Meeting, of the Zilla, Broach.
811	"	"	"	Mr. Motilal Jamnadas Shroff.	Hindu Bania.	Shroff	do.
812	"	"	"	Mr. Mohuulal Manaklal ...	Vishlad Hindu Bania.	Pleader, Municipal Commissioner and Chairman, School Board.	do.
813	"	"	"	Mr. Kanayalal Maneklal Desai.	Hindu Kshatri.	Zamindar	do.
814	,	"	"	Mr. Acharatlal Govinddas Ihanvi.	Hindu Bania.	District Pleader	do.
815	"	"	"	Mr. Tiludhur Ramchander.	Baj Khedaval Hindu Bania.	Money-lender and Landholder, Municipal Commissioner.	do.

Number.	Presidency or Government.	Congress Circle.	Electoral Division.	Names in full of Delegates with honorary titles, scholastic degrees, etc.	Race, Religious denomination, and Caste, if any.	Occupation and Address.	How and when elected.
816	Bombay.	Guzerat.	Broach.	Mr. Manmohundas Ranchordas Javeri.	Hindu Bania.	Banker and Zamindar, President, Prarthna Samaj.	1st December 1889, at a Public Meeting of the Zilla, held at Broach.
817	"	"	"	Mr. Subhrai Ramchander..	Khedaval Hindu Brahmin.	Land-holder and Pleader, Vice-President, Taluq Board, Member, District Local Board.	do.
818	"	"	"	Mr. Anupram Mithalal Din Bundhw.	Hindu Brahmin.	Land-owner, Bahadur Buraj, Secretary, Gnanadaya Sabha.	do.
819	"	"	"	Mr. Sukerlal Purmodrai ...	Brahmin Kshatri Hindu.	Pleader and Land-holder, Member of the Taluq Board, Vagra.	do.
820	"	"	"	Mr. Nathubhai Shunkerdas	Mohod Bania Hindu.	Shroff	do.
821	"	"	"	Mr. Itchalal Parmanand Munshi.	Hindu Bania.	Member, Bombay Presidency Association, and Secretary Khaduta Educational Fund.	do.
822	"	"	"	Mr. Mugerrelal Mohanlal Javeri.	Hindu Mohod Bania.	Land-holder.	do.
823	"	"	"	Mr. Dayabhai Dalpatbhai Dalal.	Hindu Jain Visha Shrimali Shravik.	Assistant Master, Loka Hitechhu Sabha, English School.	By a Public Meeting, of the Jain Community of Broach, held on 20th November, 1889, of the Lokh Hitechhu Sabha, and at Broach on 1st December, 1889.
824	"	"	"	Mr. Damodhar Rao Dadaji Dalpate.	Hindu Purbhu or Pathare Kshatri Somwashi.	District Pleader and Medical Practitioner, Ankleswar.	Ankleswar Taluka, Public Meeting, 3rd November, 1889, Broach Zillah, Public Meeting, 18th December, 1889.
825	"	"	"	Mr. Motilal Dalpatram Desai, B.A., LL.B.	Hindu Bania.	Solicitor High Court, Bombay, Member Guzerat Social Union, Member, Hindu Club, Bombay.	Broach Zillah, Public Meeting, 15th December, 1889.
826		"	Anklesh-war.	Khan Saheb Jamsetji Nusserwanji Gunwalla.	Parsee.	Abkari Contractor, Cotton Merchant, Member, Municipal and Local Boards of Ankleshwar, Joint Secretary Sub-divisional Congress Committee, Ankleshwar.	At a Meeting, held at Ankleshwar and Broach, on the 30th November, 1889.
827	"	"	Surat.	Mr. Hardeoram Nanabhai Haridas.	Hindu Kayastha.	Landowner	Public Meeting at Surat, 8th December, 1889.
828	"	"	"	Mr. Mansukhlal Hiralal Nagar.	do.	Merchant	do.
829	"	"	"	Mr. Harilal Harshadai Dhruva, B.A., LL.B. (Bombay) D.L.A. (Sweden) M.R.A.S. (Great Britain and Ireland).	Nagar Brahmin Hindu.	President, Prajahit Vardhak Sabha, Surat, Member, Gujerat Vernacular Society, Ahmedabad, Member, Authropological Society, Bombay, Member, Royal Asiatic Society of Great Britain and Ireland.	At a Public Meeting, Ahmedabad, 5th December, 1889, and at Surat, 8th December, 1889. Withdrew after assemblage of Congress under orders of the Baroda Government whose servant he is.
830	"	"	"	Mr. M. D. Dadysett ...	Parsi.	Barrister-at-Law, Municipal Commissioner.	Public Meeting at Surat, 8th December, 1889.
831	"	"	"	Rao Saheb Narbheram Mansookram.	Hindu Bisnagra Nagar Brahmin.	Contractor and Municipal Commissioner.	do.
832	"	"	"	Mr. Bulram Motiram Munshi.	Nagar Hindu Brahmin.	District Pleader	do.
833	"	"	"	Mr. Motabhai Motilal Desai	do.	High Court Pleader, Surat ...	do.
834	"	"	"	Mr. Gulebdas Bhaidas ...	Hindu Brahmin.	Vakil, and Municipal Commissioner.	do.
835	"	"	"	Mr. Jamietram Jivanram, B.A.	do.	......	do.
836	"	"	"	Rao Saheb Gulabdas Purshotamdas.	Hindu Bania.	Banker	do.
837	"	"	"	Mr. Manchershaw Pallonji Kaikobad.	Parsee.	Head Master, Mission High School, Surat.	do.
838	"	"	"	Mr. Naraindas Parsotamdas	Hindu Bania.	Merchant	do.

Number.	Presidency or Government.	Congress Circle.	Electoral Division.	Names in full of Delegates with honorary titles, scholastic degrees, etc.	Race, Religious denomination, and Caste, if any.	Occupation and Address.	How and when elected.
839	Bombay.	Guzerat.	Surat.	Mr. Anoopram Kirparam.	Hindu Anavla Brahmin.	Secretary to Nawab Mir Goolam Babu Khan Bahadur of Surat, and Vakil.	At a Public Meeting held at Surat, on 8th December, 1889.
840	"	"	"	Mr. Hargovind Harnarayen Vyas.	Hindu Brahmin.	Pleader	do.
841	"	"	"	Mr. Mohanlal Ranchhordas	Hindu Bania.	Educational Inspector, Pensioner.	do.
842	"	"	"	Mr. Motilal Moogutlal, Munshi.	Hindu.	Pleader, High Court	do.
843	"	"	"	Mr. Ishwardas Jugjivandas Store.	do.	Shroff and Municipal Commissioner.	do.
844	"	"	"	Mr. Ratiram Durgaram Dave, B.A.	Hindu Nagar Brahmin.	Articled Clerk	do.
845	"	"	"	Mr. Maharaj Vallabhadas Dwarikadas.	Hindu.	Shroff and Landed Proprietor...	Public Meeting, on 13th December, 1889.
846	"	"	"	Mr. Desaiji Harraiji Bapubhai.	Hindu Anavla Brahmin.	Jaghirdar	8th December, Surat, 12th December, Bulsar and Navsari.
847	"	"	"	Mr. Manchhashankar Jivrnram, B.A. & LL.B.	Brahmin.	Vakil, High Court, Bombay ...	At a Meeting of the Praju Hitvardhak Sabha of Surat.
848	"	"	"	Mr. Hormasji Fardunji Doctor.	Parsee	Teacher, Mission High School.	do.
849	"	"	"	Mr. M. B. Bhatt ...	Hindu.	Landed Proprietor	Public Meeting at Mandvi District, Surat, on 13th December, 1889.
850	"	"	"	Mr. Rustomji Jamasji Garda.	Parsee.	Landlord, Rustom Bag, Jalalpore, Nowsaree.	Elected by a Public Meeting at Bulsar, on 12th December, 1889, and at Jalalpore, on 13th Deber, 1889.
851	"	"	"	Mr. Narotamdas Indrajit Vaishnav, M.B.B S.	Nagar Brahmin.	Medical Practitioner, Junagadh.	Pruja Hathvarthak Sabha's Meeting.
852	"	"	Rajkot (Katiawar.)	Mr. Ghanasham Narayan Pandit, B.A., LL.B.	Hindu Brahmin.	Pleader, Rajkot...	Public Meeting, Rajkot, 20th December, 1889.
853	"	"	"	Mr. Lakshmichand Pitambar Adulja.	Hindu Bania.	Pleader, High Court, Translator, Katthiawad Political Agency.	do.
854	"	"	"	Mr. Haridas Wakhatchand Vora.	do.	Pleader. High Court, Banker, and Millowner.	do.
855	"	"	"	Mr. Hormasji Ardeshir Wadia.	Parsee.	Barrister-at-Law, Civil Station, Rajkot.	do.
856	"	"	"	Mr. Virpal Daya Parekh...	Hindu Bania.	Merchant, Rajkot	do.
857	"	"	"	Mr. Damodardas Gordhandas Thakur.	Hindu Luoana.	Printer and Publisher	do.
858	"	"	"	Mr. Abubaker Jamal ...	Mahomedan	Merchant	do.
859	"	"	"	Mr. Gulam Mahomed B. Munshee.	do.	Judge, Sudder Adalat, Junaghur, Kathiawar, Barrister-at-Law.	do.
860	"	"	Amreli (Kathiawar)	Mr. Verji Shivdas... ...	Kunbi Hindu.	Landed Proprietor and District Pleader, Amreli.	By a Public Meeting, held at Amreli, 21st Dec. 1889.
861	"	"	"	Mr. Jasraj Rupsi	Kapole BaniaHindu	Japtedar Harmaduja	do.
862	"	"	Kaira.	Mr. Goverdanram Madhavram Tripathi, B.A., LL.B.	Hindu Brahmin.	Pleader, High Court	In a Public Meeting, 8th December, 1889.
863	"	"	"	Mr. Girdhardas Mangaldas.	Patidar Kunbi.	Desai of Nadiad...	do.
864	"	"	"	Mr. Harilal Kirparam Pandia.	Hindu Vadanagara Nagar Brahmin.	Pleader, High Court	do.
865	"	"	"	Mr. Manilal Nabhubhai Dwivedi, B.A.	Hindu Brahmin.	State Service and late Professor of Sanskrit, Jamaldas College.	do.
866	"	"	Balsar.	Mr. Goolabhai Vassanjee Desai, B.A.	Hindu.	Private Service, Bulsar ...	By a Public Meeting, held on the 12th December, 1889.
867	"	"	"	Mr. Vasanty D. Desai, G.M.A.E.	do.	Landholder, Chikhli, Surat ...	do.
868	"	"	"	Mr. Jivanji Haribhai ...	Hindu Anavla Brahmin.	District Pleader	do.
869	"	"	"	Mr. Jivanji Gulabhai Desai.	do.	do.	do.
870	"	"	Thasra.	Rao Saheb Amritlal Maneklal Desai.	Hindu Nagar Brahman.	Zemindar, Thasra District, Kaira, Vice-President, Taluka Board.	Public Meeting, held on the 17th November, 1889.

Number.	Presidency or Government.	Congress Circle.	Electoral Division.	Names in full of delegates with honorary titles, scholastic degrees, etc.	Race, Religious denomination, and Caste, if any.	Occupation and Address.	How and when elected.
871	Bombay.	Guzerat.	Thasra and Dakor.	Mr. Chunilal Lallubhai Parekh.	Hindu Nagar Brahmin.	Merchant and Vakil, Balasinor State.	Elected by Public Meetings at Thasra, on the 17th November, and at Dakor, on the 18th November, 1889.
872	"	"	Gogo.	Mr. Parmanand Jeewandas	Hindu Bania.	Landlord, Municipal Commissioner, Vice-President, Taluka Board.	14th December, 1889, Public Meeting.
873	"	"	Guzerat.	Mr. Ratanbhudra Manikbhudra, L.M. & S.	Hindu Nagar Brahmin Guzerat.	Civil Surgeon, Amreli	Elected by the Sankir Swami of Jotirwat, 13th December, 1889.
874	"	"	Wadhwan.	Mr. Vanayakrao Ganpatrao Kothare.	Prabhu Hindu.	Barrister-at-Law, Rajkot ...	At a Public Meeting, held on the 23rd December, 1889.
875	"		Nariad.	Mr. Jamadar Yusufali Yakubali, B.A.	Mahomedan.	Service, Navsari	By a Public Meeting at Nariad.
876	"		"	Mr. Ganpatram Nanalal Bhatta.	Hindu.	Late Tutor to the Kumar Saheb of Porbander.	Alukchatra Nager Association.
877	"	Sind.	Karachi.	Mr. N. Gupta	Hindu Vaidya.	Proprietor and Editor, *The Phœnix*, Karachi, Municipal Commissioner, Member, Cantonment Committee.	8th December, 1889, Sind Sabha Meeting, Karachi.
878	"	"	"	Mr. Harchandrai Vishindas, B.A., LL.B.	Hindu.	Pleader, Karachi, Municipal Commissioner, Member, Taluka Board, Kotri.	do.
879	"	"	"	Mr. Hiranand Showkiram Advani, B.A.	Hindu Brahmo.	Head Master, Union Academy, Hyderabad (Sind), Honorary Secretary, Countess Dufferin Fund, Hydrabad Broach, Honorary Superintendent Girls' School, Hyderabad.	do.
880	"	"	"	Mr. Faiz Mahomed Futtehali.	Mahomedan.	Merchant	do.
881	"	"	"	Seth Vishindas Fatehchand.	Hindu.	do.	do.
882	"	"	"	Mr. Wadhumal Belaram ...	Hindu Amil.	Pleader	do.
883	"	"	"	Mr. Manghanmal Kundanmal Advani.	do.	Pleader and Municipal Commissioner.	do.
884	"	"	"	Mr. Balchand Kundunmal.	do.	Pleader	do.
885	"	"	Sukkur.	Rao Saheb Pesumal Towkiram.	Hindu.	Pleader and Municipal Commissioner, Member, Taluka Local Board.	do.
886	"	"	"	Rao Saheb Dhunrajmal ...	do.	Pleader and Municipal Commissioner.	do.
887	"	"	"	Rao Saheb Chetanram Awatrai Malkani.	do.	do. ...	do.
888	"	"	"	Rao Bahadur Govindhur Awatrai.	do.	Pleader and Zemindar, Vice-President, Sukkur Municipality, Member, District Local Board, Member, Sind Arts College Board.	do.
889	"	Bombay.	Bombay Presidency Association.	Dr. A. D. Mody, L.M. & S.	Parsi.	Medical Practitioner, Grant Road.	At the Meeting of the Council of the Bombay Presidency Association, on 17th December, 1889.
890	"	"	"	Mr. Allibhoy Cassam Soomar.	Mahomedan.	do. ...	do.
891	"	"	"	Mr. Abdulla M. Dharamsey, M.A., LL.B.	do.	Solicitor, High Court, Pedder Road, Member, Municipal Corporation.	do.
892	"	"	"	Mr. Ali Mahomed Bhimjee.	do.	Contractor...	do.
893	"	"	"	Atmaram Pandurang, G.G.M.C.	Hindu.	Medical Practitioner, Chowpatty.	do.
894	"	"	"	Mr. Ameerudin Tyabji ...	Mahomedan.	Khetwady, Member, Municipal Corporation.	do.
895	"	"	"	Mr. A. P. Cama, L.M. & S.	Parsi.	Medical Practitioner, Gowalia Tank Road.	do.
896	"	"	"	Mr. Bhalchandra K. Bhatavadekar, L.M. and S.	Hindu.	Medical Practitioner, Girgaum.	do.
897	"	"	"	Mr. Bhaishankar Nanabhai	do.	Solicitor, High Court, Girgaum.	do.
898	"	"	"	Mr. Byramji D. Panday ...	Parsi.	Assistant, Ritchie Steuart, & Co.	do.

Number.	Presidency or Government.	Congress Circle.	Electoral Division.	Names in full of Delegates with honorary titles, scholastic degrees, etc.	Race, Religious denomination, and Caste, if any.	Occupation and Address.	How and when elected.
899	Bombay.	Bombay.	Bombay Presidency Association.	Mr. Carsondas Vallabhdas.	Hindu.	Millowner, Bazaar Gate Street..	At the Meeting of the Council of the Bombay Presidency Association, on 17th December, 1889.
900	"	"	"	Mr. Cowasji Hormusji, G.G.M.C.	Parsi.	Medical Practitioner, Member, Municipal Corporation, Chira Bazaar.	do.
901	"	"	"	Mr. Chutoorbhooj Morarji.	Hindu.	Merchant, Mandevi.	do.
902	"	"	"	Mr. Damodar Gokuldas ...	do.	do. Cloth Bazaar. ...	do.
903	"	"	"	Mr. Dinsha D. Davar ...	Parsi.	Barrister-at-Law, Eldon Road.	do.
904	"	"	"	Mr. Dayabhai Jaduram, B.A., LL.B.	Hindu.	Solicitor, High Court, Apollo Street.	do.
905	"	"	"	Mr. D. F. Cama	Parsi.	Lower Colaba	do.
906	"	"	"	Mr. Daji Abaji Khare, B.A., LL.B.	Hindu.	Pleader, High Court, Girgaum.	do.
907	"	"	"	Mr. Dhondo Shamrao Garud, B.A., LL.B.	do.	Solicitor do. do.	do.
908	"	"	"	Mr. Dinsha Eduljee Wacha.	Parsi.	Mill Agent, Member, Municipal Corporation, Secretary, Bombay Presidency Association, Mody Street.	do.
909	"	"	"	Mr. Devidas Harivallabhdas.	Hindu.	Merchant	do.
910	"	"	"	Mr. Dharamsey Moorarji Goculdas.	do.	Millowner, Girgaum.	do.
911	"	"	"	Dorabji C. Shroff ...	Parsi.	do. Hornby Row. ...	do.
912	"	"	"	Mr. Damodar Thakersey Mulji.	Hindu.	do. Member, Municipal Corporation, Hanuman Lane.	do.
913	"	"	"	Mr. Dharamsey Sunderdas.	do.	Millowner, Hanuman Lane ...	do.
914	"	"	"	Mr. Ellapa Balaram ...	do.	Contractor	do.
915	"	"	"	Fattehalli Shaik Ahmed...	Mahomedan.	Merchant, Khetwadi	do.
916	"	"	"	Fazulbhoy Cassam Gangji.	do.	do. do. ...	do.
917	"	"	"	Mr. Fakirchand Premchand Raychand.	Jain.	Broker, Kalbadevi	do.
918	"	"	"	Mr. Furdunji M. Banaji ...	Parsi.	Secretary, Manekji Petit Mills, Malabar Hill.	do.
919	"	"	"	Mr. Gordhandas K. Makanji.	Hindu.	Millowner, Malabar Hill ...	do.
920	"	"	"	Mr. Gordhandas Goculdas Tejpal.	do.	do. do. ...	do.
921	"	"	"	Mr. Goculdas K. Parekh, M.A., LL.B.	do.	Pleader, High Court, Girgaum.	do.
922	"	"	"	Mr. Ganput Sadashiv Rao, M.A., LL.B.	do.	do. Kalbadevi Road.	do.
923	"	"	"	Mr. Ganesh Krishna Deshmukh, B.A., LL.B.	do.	do. Girgaum...	do.
924	"	"	"	Mr. Ghanasham Nilkanth, B.A., LL.B.	do.	do. Girgaum...	do.
925	"	"	"	Mr. Ganesh R. Kirloskar, M.A., LL.B.	do.	do. do. ...	do.
926	"	"	"	Mr. Hariprasad Santookram.	do.	Merchant and Banker, Kalbadevi.	do.
927	"	"	"	Mr. Hari Shitaram Discit.	do.	Solicitor	do.
928	"	"	"	Mr. Hiralal Tribhuwandas.	do.	Merchant	do.
929	"	"	"	Mr. Haji Essaka Sob ...	Mahomedan.	do.	do.
930	"	"	"	Mr. Jivaji Dinshaw Gandy, B.A., LL.B.	Parsi.	Solicitor, Breach Candy ...	do.
931	"	"	"	Mr. Dhala Jairaj	Mahomedan.	Juma Musjid Street	do.
932	"	"	"	Mr. Javerilal Ú. Yajnik ...	Hindu.	Merchant, Member, Municipal Corporation, and Sheriff of Bombay, Cowasji Patel Tank Road.	do.
933	"	"	"	Mr. Jamsetji Cursetji Jamsetji.	Parsi.	Mazagon Castle...	do.
934	"	"	"	Mr. Jehanghir B. Marzban.	do.	Proprietor, *Advocate of India* and *Jam-e-Jamshed* Press, Gowalia Tank Road.	do.
935	"	"	"	Mr. Jeejeebhoy Pestonjee Mistri, M.A.	do.	Articled Clerk, Fort	do.

Number.	Presidency or Government.	Congress Circle.	Electoral Division.	Names in full of Delegates with honorary titles, scholastic degrees, etc.	Race, Religious denomination, and Caste, if any.	Occupation and Address.	How and when elected.
936	Bombay.	Bombay.	Bombay Presidency Association.	Mr. Jagmohandas Vandrawandas.	Hindu.	Merchant	At the Meeting of the Council of the Bombay Presidency Association, on 17th December 1889.
937	"	"	"	Mr. Jamsetjee Ardashir Wadia.	Parsi.	Millowner, Chinchpoogly ...	do.
938	"	"	"	Mr. Jivandas Mulji ...	Hindu.	do. Fort	do.
939	"	"	"	Mr. Jamsetji Cursetji Cama	Parsi.	Solicitor, High Court, Mount Road.	do.
940	"	"	"	Dr. K. B. Bullel, L. M. & S.	Hindu.	Medical Practitioner	do.
941	"	"	"	Mr. Karimbhoy Nensey ...	Mahomedan.	Merchant, Malabar Hill ...	do.
942	"	"	"	Mr. K. M. Shroff ...	Parsi.	Proprietor, *Advocate of India* and Bombay *Jam-e-Jamshed*, Member, Municipal Corporation.	do.
943	"	"	"	Mr. Noormahomed Jairaj Peerbhoy.	Mahomedan.	Merchant, Breach Candy ...	do.
944	"	"	"	Mr. Khimji Jeva	Hindu.	Iron Merchant, Mandevi ...	do.
945	"	"	"	Mr. Lilladhar Jairam Naranji	do.	Millowner, do. ...	do.
846	"	"	"	Mr. Lilladhar Shamji ...	do.	do. Waudby Road ...	do.
947	"	"	"	Mr. Mansukram Surajram.	do.	Girgaum	do.
948	"	"	"	Mr. Makund Ramchandra, C.E.	do.	Retired, Government Engineering Dept., Officer, Kandewady.	do.
949	"	"	"	Mr. Manchashankar Jaishanker.	do.	do.	do.
950	"	"	"	Mr. Lakhmedas Khemji ...	do.	Millowner, Malabar Hill ...	do.
951	"	"	"	Mr. Mathurdas Liladhar Shamji.	do.	do. Wandy Road ...	do.
952	"	"	"	Mr. Fuzulbhai Joomabhai Lalji.	Mahomedan.	Merchant, Breach Candy ...	do.
953	"	"	"	Mr. Manekji Burjorji ...	Parsee.	Proprietor and Editor, *Bombay Samachar*, Frere Road.	do.
954	"	"	"	Mr. Maniksha Jahangirsha, M.A., LL.B.	do.	Pleader, High Court, Chowpaty	do.
955	"	"	"	Mr. Mulji Bhawanidas Barbhaya.	Hindu.	Solicitor, High Court, Member, Municipal Corporation, Hornby Row.	do.
956	"	"	"	Mr. Mancherji Nowraji Banaji.	Parsee.	Millowner, Member, Municipal Corporation, Mazagon.	do.
957	"	"	"	Mr. Motilal Jamnadas Shroff.	Hindu.	Merchant, Kalbadavie	do.
958	"	"	"	Mr. Nanabhoy R. Ranina...	Parsee.	Proprietor, Union Press, Chandanwady.	do.
959	"	"	"	Mr. Narayen Vishnu Gokhle. B.A., LL.B.	Hindu.	Pleader, High Court, Kandawady.	do.
960	"	"	"	Mr. Nazir Mahomed Fattehalli.	Mahomedan.	Merchant	do.
961	"	"	"	Mr. Narotam Gordhandas...	Hindu.	Merchant, Member, Municipal Corporation.	do.
962	"	"	"	Mr. Narayen Ganesh Chandavarkar, B.A., LL.B.	do.	Pleader, High Court, Girgaum..	do.
963	"	"	"	Mr. N. N. Katruck, L.M.&S.	Parsee.	Medical Practitioner, Fort ...	do.
964	"	"	"	Mr. Nasirbhoy Abdulla ...	Mahomedan.	Merchant	do.
965	"	"	"	Mr. Najmuddin Tyabji ...	do.	do.	do.
966	"	"	"	Mr. Nenseybhoy Peeroomahomed	do.	Merchant, Malabar Hill ...	do.
967	"	"	"	Mr. Pherozesha M. Mehta, M.A.	Parsee.	Barrister-at-Law, Member, Municipal Corporation.	do.
968	"	"	"	Mr. Pestonji Byramji Dantara.	do.	3rd Marine Line Street ...	do.
969	"	"	"	Mr. N. D. Setna, B.A., LL.B.	Parsi.	Barrister-at-Law, Chinchpoogly.	do.
970	"	"	"	Mr. Purshotam P. Khare, B.A., LL.B.	do.	High Court Pleader, Thakordwar.	do.
971	"	"	"	Mr. Premchand Roychand.	do.	Broker, Kalbadevi	do.
972	"	"	"	Mr. Rustom K. R. Cama, M.A., LL.B.	Parsee.	Solicitor, High Court, Breach Candy.	do.
973	"	"	"	Dr. R. N. Khory, L.M. & S.	do.	Medical Practitioner, Malabar Hill.	do.

Number.	Presidency or Government.	Congress Circle.	Electoral Division.	Names in full of Delegates with honorary titles, scholastic degrees, etc.	Race, Religious denomination, and Caste, if any.	Occupation and Address.	How and when elected.
974	Bombay.	Bombay.	Bombay Presidency Association.	Mr. Ramchandra V. Madgavkar.	Hindu.	Salesman, Graham & Co., Chowpatty.	At the Meeting of the Council of the Bombay Presidency Association, on 17th December 1889.
975	"	"	"	Mr. Ramchandra Hemraj...	do.	Secretary, Jewraj Baloo Mill Company, Bazaar Gate Street.	do.
976	"	"	"	Mr. Raoji V. J. Shankarsett.	do.	Girgaum...	do.
977	"	"	"	Mr. Rattonsey Mulji ...	do.	Merchant	do.
978	"	"	"	Mr. Shivji Dharmaji ...	do.	Contractor	do.
979	"	"	"	Mr. Shaik Ahmed bin Essa Khalifa.	Mahomedan.	Pearl Merchant, Foras Road ...	do.
980	"	"	"	Mr. Sorabji Dadabhoy Bastavala, B.A.	Parsee.	Articled Clerk, Mody Street ...	do.
981	"	"	"	Mr. Sorabji Kavasji Khambatta.	do.	Journalist, Girgaum	do.
982	"	"	"	Mr. Shamrao M. Rele ...	Hindu.	Pleader, High Court, Girgaum..	do.
983	"	"	"	Dr. Sadashiv Vaman Kane.	do.	Medical Practitioner	do.
984	"	"	"	Mr. Shivram V. Bhandarkar B.A., LL.B.	do.	Pleader, High Court	do.
985	"	"	"	Mr. Sadanand T. Bhendare.	do.	Assistant, Wallace & Co., Apollo Street.	do.
986	"	"	"	Mr. Shamrao Vithal ...	do.	Pleader, High Court, Girgaum .	do.
987	"	"	"	Mr. Shantaram Narayen ...	do.	Govt., High Court Pleader ...	do.
988	"	"	"	Mr. Sorabji Edulji Warden.	Parsee.	Merchant, Hornby Row ...	do.
989	"	"	"	Mr. S. Burjorji Bharucha.	do.	Broker, Fort	do.
990	"	"	"	Mr. Sorabji M. Kanga, M.A., LL.B.	do.	Solicitor, High Court	do.
991	"	"	"	Mr. T. Tukaram Tatia ...	Hindu.	Merchant, Bandora	do.
992	"	"	"	Mr. Nagindas Jamnadas Shroff.	do.	Merchant, Bhuleshwar... ...	do.
993	"	"	"	Mr. Veerchand Deepchand.	do.	Millowner, do. ...	do.
994	"	"	"	Mr. Vasudev Gopal Bhandarkar, B.A., LL.B.	do.	Pleader, High Court	do.
995	"	"	"	Mr. Veerchand Raghoji Ghandy, B.A.	do.	Articled Clerk, Love Lane ...	do.
996	"	"	"	Mr. Vishnu Krishna Bhatardekar, B.A., LL.B.	do.	Pleader, High Court, Editor, *Indu Prakash*, Girgaum.	do.
997	"	"	"	Mr. Vijbhukandas Atmaram.	do.	Merchant, Cowasji Patel Tank Road.	do.
998	"	"	"	Mr. Vandravandas Purshotumdas.	do.	Merchant, Member, Municipal Corporation, Malabar Hill.	do.
999	"	"	"	Mr. V. K. Dhairyawan ...	do.	Barrister-at-Law	do.
1000	"	"	"	Mr. Vasudeo Jagonnath Kirtikar.	do.	Pleader, High Court, Girgaum.	do.
1001	"	"	"	Mr. Vasanji Khimji ...	do.	Merchant, Mandvie	do.
1002	"	"	Bombay Mahomedan Community.	Shaik Cumroodin Furrukhai.	Mahomedan Sooni.	22, Bellasis Junction Road ...	Elected at a Meeting of Mahomedans on 22nd Dec., 1889, when 500 Mahomedans were present, Moulvi Hidaytulla presiding.
1003	"	"	"	Moulvi Burkuttulla ...	do.	Grant Road	do.
1004	"	"	"	Mr. Ahmedbhai Somejee...	Khoja Mahomedan.	Agent, Cotton Ginning Factory at Dhallisgaum, Samuel Street.	do.
1005	"	"	"	Mr. Abdullabhai Laljee ...	do.	Merchant, Samuel Street ...	do.
1006	"	"	"	Mr. Esmailbhai Abdoola ...	do.	do. ...	do.
1007	"	"	"	Mr. Bandalibhai Hajeebhoy	do.	do. ...	do.
1008	"	"	"	Munshi Mahomed Baker..	Mahomedan Sooni.	Secretary to the Turkish Consul General, Temkar Mohla, New Nagpada.	do.
1009	"	"	"	Mr. Ebrahim R. Dhurumsey.	Khoja Mahomedan.	Merchant, Mahaluxmi	do.

Number.	Presidency or Government.	Congress Circle.	Electoral Division.	Names in full of Delegates with honorary titles, scholastic degrees, etc.	Race, Religious denomination, and Caste, if any.	Occupation and Address.	How and when elected.
1010	Bombay.	Bombay.	Bombay Mahomedan Community.	Mr. Peerbhai Kasambhai...	Mahomedan Khoja.	Furniture Merchant	Elected at a Meeting of Mahomedans, on 22nd Dec., 1889, when 500 Mahomedans were present, Moulvi Hidayetullah presiding.
1011	"	"	"	Mr. Abedin Peerbhai Damji	do.	Merchant	do.
1012	"	"	"	Mr. Casumbhai Ahmedbhai.	Khoja Sooni Mahomedan.	Merchant, Dungri Street ...	do.
1013	"	"	"	Mr. Rahimtoola Noor Mahomed.	do.	Commission Agent, Dungri St.	do.
1014	"	"	"	Mr. Bandalibhoy Sewjee ...	Khoja Mahomedan.	Merchant, Samual Street ...	do.
1015	"	"	"	Syed Kuthoodin Edroos ...	Mahomedan.	Medical Department, Byculla...	do.
1016	"	"	"	Munshi Mahomed Ismail Mackba.	do.	Landholder, Parel Road ...	do.
1017	"	"	"	Mr. Mahomed Eusuf Khat Khate.	do.	do. Old Kazi Street...	do.
1018	"	"	"	Mr. Abdul Kadar Khat Khate.	do.	do. do. ...	do.
1019	"	"	"	Mr. Abdul Rahman Mackba	do.	do. Parel Road ...	do.
1020	"	"	"	Mr. Mahomed Ebrahim Mackba.	do.	do. do. ...	do.
1021	"	"	"	Mr. Jafferbhai Sochedina...	Khoja Mahomedan.	Merchant, Juma Musjid ...	do.
1022	"	"	"	Mr. Salay Mahomed Noor Mahomed.	do.	do. do. ...	do.
1023	"	"	"	Mr. Moloobhai Nanji ...	do.	do. Chukla ...	do.
1024	"	"	"	Mr. Ahmedbhai Kurim ...	do.	do. do. ...	do.
1025	"	"	"	Mr. Dholabhai Jairaj ...	do.	do. Juma Musjid ...	do.
1026	"	"	"	Hakim Abdul Husain Abdul Kadar.	Mahomedan Bohra.	Native Doctor, Foolgally, Parel, Road.	do.
1027	"	"	"	Mr. Fazulbhai Mahomed Dama.	Khoja Sooni Mahomedan.	Merchant, Pydhoni Road ...	do.
1028	"	"	"	Mr. Peerbhai Khaki Pudamsi	Khoja Mahomedan.	Merchant, Khadak	do.
1029	"	"	"	Mr. Goolam Hussain Mooljeebhai Jewraj.	do.	do.	do.
1030	"	"	"	Mr. Zamilbhai Ahmedbhai.	Mahomedan Bohra.	Merchant, Modikhana	do.
1031	"	"	"	Munshi Mahomed Alahuddin Khatib.	Mahomedan.	Mootwali of Juma Musjid, Kazi Street.	do.
1032	"	"	"	Moulvi Hidayetullah ...	Mahomedan Sooni.	Religious Preceptor	do.
1033	"	"	"	Mr. Ahmedbhoy Kassumbhoy Mooljeebhoy Jewraj.	Khoja Mahomedan.	Merchant, Khaduck	do.
1034	"	"	"	Mr. Talibali Shamsuddin Nazir.	Mahomedan Bohra.	Proprietor, "Alavi" Press, Bombay.	At a Meeting, held on the 23rd December 1889, at Bombay.
1035	"	"	"	Mr. Abdoolla R. Hubbibhoy.	Khoja Mahomedan.	Merchant	do.
1036	"	"	"	Mr. Nainselbhoy Peroo ...	do.	do. Crawford Market.	do.
1037	"	"	"	Mr. Ali Mahomed Nainsey.	do.	do. do. ...	do.
1038	"	"	"	Mr. Hajee Rahimtulla Hajee Dawood.	Mahomedan Memon.	do. do. ...	do.
1039	"	"	"	Mr. Jafferbhai Ladha Chuttu.	Khoja Mahomedan.	do. Khoja Mola ...	do.
1040	"	"	"	Mr. Mahomedbhai Dosabhai.	do.	do. Old Nagpada ...	do.
1041	"	"	"	Mr. Fazulbhai Ebrahim Uttunvala.	Mahomedan.	do.	Dada Meekha's Bungalow, on the 24th Nov. 1889.

Number.	Presidency or Government.	Congress Circle.	Electoral Division.	Names in full of Delegates with honorary titles, scholastic degrees, etc.	Race, Religious denomination, and Caste, if any.	Occupation and Address.	How and when elected.
1042	Bombay.	Bombay.	Bombay.	Mr. Rangildas Bhukhandas.	Hindu.	Merchant, No. 23, Church Gate Street.	Public Meeting of China Traders, held on 24th December, 1889.
1043	"	"	"	Mr. Doolabdas Vallabdas...	Bania.	Banker	do.
1044	"	"	"	Mr. Maneklal Chukoobhoy.	Hindu.	Merchant and China Broker, Balaji Samset Street.	do.
1045	"	"	"	Mr. Goculdas Madhewji ...	Bhatia.	Cotton Merchant	17th December, 1889, Meeting of the Cotton Merchants' Association.
1046	"	"	The Jain Association of India, Bombay.	Mr. Talakchand Manekchand.	Jain.	Merchant, Khara Koona, Bombay.	At a Public Meeting of the Jain Association, on the 24th November, 1889.
1047	"	"	"	Dr. Jumnadas Premchand, L. M. & S.	do.	Doctor, Bhooleshwar, Bombay.	do.
1048	"	"	"	Mr. Maganlal Dalputram...	Hindu Jain.	Mukadum, Vithalvadi, Bombay.	do.
1049	"	"	"	Mr. Mohanlall Maganbhai.	Jain.	Jeweller	do.
1050	"	"	Jain Union Club.	Mr. Amarchund P. Parmar.	do.	General Merchant and Commission Agent, Pydownee.	At a Meeting, held on 9th December, 1889, in the Hall of the Jain Union Club, Pydownee.
1051	"	"	"	Mr. Mohanlal Hemchund.	do.	Broker, Tambakanta, Honorary Secretary to the Jain Union Club.	do.
1052	"	"	Mandvie Bunder, Bombay.	Mr. P. Nemchand Vussonjee.	do.	Merchant and Commission Agent.	At a Meeting of the Community, held on 16th December, 1889, at Mandvie Bunder.
1053	"	"	"	Mr. Dewjee Purbat ...	Hindu Shravak Bania.	Cotton Merchant	do.
1054	"	"	"	Mr. Maneckial Atmaram Tunksally.	Hindu.	Assistant Secretary, Bombay Pinjrapole Charitable Institution and Honorary Assistant Secretary, the Bombay Native Cotton Merchants' Association.	do.
1055	"	"	"	Mr. Shamji Mulji ...	Hindu Bania.	Cotton Merchant	do.
1056	"	"	"	Mr. Oomersey Nagsey	do.	do. ...	do.
1057	"	"	"	Mr. Callyanji Narayanji ...	Bhattia.	General Merchant	At a Public Meeting, on the 24th December, 1889, by the Merchants, Brokers and Residents of Mandvi Bunder.
1058	"	"	"	Mr. Mathuradas Goculdas.	do.	Cotton Merchant	do.
1059	"	"	"	Mr. Raghavji Jayakrishna, B.A., LL.B.	Brahmin	Articled Clerk to Messrs. Jefferson, Bhaishanker, Dinshaw & Kanga.	do.
1060	"	"	Nagpada, Bombay.	Mr. Keshaw Vaman Pethe..	Hindu Brahmin.	Teacher and Landholder, Gopinath's Chal.	New Nagpada General Meeting, 1st Dec., 1889.
1061	"	"	"	Mr. Anant Vaman Barve..	Hindu.	Author, Jagadiswar Press, Kandewadi, Editor Kutumb Shiksaka.	do.
1062	"	"	"	Mr. Anna Janardan Despande.	do.	Sub-Manager, No. 46, Khataralee, Landholder and Sub-Manager, I. P. Press.	do.
1063	"	"	"	Mr. Govind Ballal Deval.	Hindu Brahmin.	Author, and Passed Agricultural Pupil, Shantaram's Chal, Kandevadi.	do.
1064	"	"	Mitra Mandali Sabha, Bombay.	Mr. Damodar Chhabaram Bhatt.	do.	Secretary, The Oriental Oil and Flour Manufacturing Co., Ld.	At a Meeting of the "Mitra Mandali Sabha," held at Bombay, on the 28th December, 1889.
1065	"	"	Swadesh Mitrotejaek Mandalee, Bombay.	Mr. Moreshwar Babulji Pane.	Hindu (Purbhu.)	Merchant, 371, Palow Road, Bombay, Market Post, President, Swadesh Mitrotejack Mandali.	Swadesh Mitrotejack Mandalee's General Meeting, 22nd December, 1889.
1066	"	"	"	Mr. Narayen Ramchandra Senjit.	do.	Merchant, 70, Jamboolwady, Kalkadevi Road, Bombay, Honorary Secretary, P. M. Mandalee.	do.

Number.	Presidency or Government.	Congress Circle.	Electoral Division.	Names in full of Delegates with honorary titles, scholastic degrees, etc.	Race, Religious denomination, and Caste, if any.	Occupation and Address.	How and when elected.
1067	Bombay.	Bombay.	Lad Samaj Bombay.	Mr. Choonilal Motilal ...	Vishnav.	Stock Merchant...	Bombay Meeting, held on 15th December.
1068	"	"	"	Mr. Motilal Hurkisondas Dalal.	do.	Doctor	do.
1069	"	"	Shiva-Dharma-Nishta Sabha, Bombay.	Mr. Mangaldas Jamnadas...	Hindu.	Shroff	23rd November, by a Meeting held in Bombay.
1070	"	"	"	Shastri Shamji Valji ...	Vishnav.	Shastri and Editor	do.
1071	"	"	"	Mr. Manmohandas Treebhovandas.	do.	Service, Anant Rishi Oart, No. 31.	do.
1072	"	"	Veda Dharma Sabha.	Mr. Vishvanath Prabhuram.	Brahmin.	Land-owner, 29, Portuguese Church Street, Bhuleshwar, Bombay.	At a Meeting of Vade Dharma Sabhá, held on the 1st of December, 1889.
1073	"	"	"	Mr. Purbhuram Jivanram Vaidya.	do.	Native Physician do.	do.
1074	"	"	Ayarveda Shodhaka Mandali, Bombay.	Mr. Trimbuklal Tribhuvandas.	Guzerati.	Native Physician, Ayurvedeshodheka Mandali, President Barbhai Mohla, Bombay.	Elected at the Meeting, held of the said Mandali, on 25th December, 1889.
1075	"	"		Mr. Govind Krishna Nimbkar.	Brahmin.	Native Physician, Ayurvedeshodhak Mandali, Secretary, Thakurdwar Line, Jitekar's Chal, Bombay.	do.
1076	"	"	Calcutta Merchants' Association, Bombay.	Mr. Mowjee Madhavjee.	Hindu Bhatia.	Rice Merchant, Secretary, Calcutta Merchants' Association.	At a Meeting, held on 24th December, 1889, at Gokuldas Madhavji's Firm.
1077	"	"	"	Mr. Hunsraj Soorjee ...	do.	General Merchant, Cazee Syed Street.	do.
1078	"	"	Cutchhi Dushashrimali Caste Bombay.	Mr. Panachand Anandjee Parekh, F.T.S.	Hindu.	Merchant and American Commission Agent, 49, Hornby Row, Fort, Bombay.	Cutchhi Dashashrimali Caste, Meeting on the 18th December, 1889.
1079	"	"	"	Mr. Meolraj Panachand Parekh.	do.	49, Hornby Row, Fort, Bombay.	do.
1080	"	"	Kutchhi Oswal Community, Bombay.	Mr. Sha Champsey Purbat.	Jaimsin.	Cotton Merchant	At a Meeting, held on the 16th December, 1889, of the Kutchhi Oswal Community.
1081	"	"	Dasa Porward Bania Caste, Bombay.	Mr. Ranchoddas Valabhai.	Dasa Porwad Bania.	Banker and Landowner ...	By a Caste Meeting, in December, 1889.
1082	"	"	"	Mr. Hurgowandas Cooberdas.	Dasa Porwad Caste Hindu.	Banker	do.
1083	"	"	"	Mr. Tribhuvandas Veerji Gandhi.	Hindu.	Merchant	At a Meeting of the Caste, held on 24th December, 1889.
1084	"	"	"	Mr. Ramdas Keshowji ...	do.	do.	do.
1085	"	"	"	Mr. Mody Tribhovandas Ruttonji.	do.	do.	do.
1086	"	"	Arya Gnyan Vurdhuk Subha, Bombay.	Seth Luxmidas Khimjee...	Bhatia.	Millowner	At a Meeting of the 7th December, Arya Gnyan Vurdhuk Subha, at the Meeting of the Council of the Bombay Presidency Association.
1087	"	"	"	Mr. Nagurdas Jamnadas...	Hindu.	Shroff	do., and at a Meeting of the Lad Samaj, held on 15th December, 1889.
1088	"	"	"	Mr. Prahaladji Davshanker.	Brahmin.	Service, Fort, Holichakla, Shamji Ladha's House.	At the General-Meeting of the Sabha, held on 12th December, 1889.
1089	"	"	"	Mr. Jagonnath Ichharam...	do.	Surat	do.
1090	"	"	"	Mr. Kalianji Naranji ...	do.	Head Clerk, Greaves, Cotton & Co.	do.

Number.	Presidency or Government.	Congress Circle.	Electoral Division.	Names in full of Delegates with honorary titles, scholastic degrees, etc.	Race, Religious denomination, and Caste, if any.	Occupation and Address.	How and when elected.
1091	Bombay.	Bombay.	Bombay.	Mr. Girijashanker Kashiram Dunivedy.	Brahmin.	Editor and Proprietor "Rajyabhakta," Umarkhadi Post, Bombay.	By the General Meeting of the Sabha, held on 12th December, 1889.
1092	,,	,,	,,	Mr. Ramshanker Iswar Viyas.	do.	Service, Fort, Gorjirs's House, Holichakla.	do.
1093	,,	,,	,,	Mr. Utamram Jivanram ...	do.	Native Doctor, Loowarchal ...	do.
1094	,,	,,	Arya Mohila Samaj, Bombay.	Pundita Ramabai	Christian.	Teacher	Women's Christian Temperance Union Meeting on the
1095	,,	,,	,,	Miss Serene Manock Cursetjee	Parsi.	Lady Superintendent Alexandra Girls' School.	Meeting of the Arya Mohila Somaj on the
1096	,,	,,	Women's Christian Temperance Union.	Mrs. Ryder	Christian.	Physician	Women's Christian Temperance Union Meeting on the
1097	,,	,,	,,	Mrs. Trimbak	do.	Superintendent of School ...	do.
1098	,,	,,	,,	Mrs. Nikambi	do.	Teacher	do.
1099	,,	,,	Arya Mohila Samaj, Bombay.	Mrs. Kanitkar	Hindu.	Journalist	Meeting of the Arya Mohila Samaj on the
1100	,,	,,	,,	Mrs. Ghosal	do.	do. and Author...	do.
1101	,,	,,	,,	Mrs. G. N. Dass	do.	44, Mulungasain, Calcutta ...	do.
1102	,,	,,	Thana District Association.	Mr. Namdeo Vithal Samant, B.A., LL.B.	Hindu Brahmin.	Pleader, High Court, Bombay, Banker and Landed Proprietor.	At a Public Meeting, held at Thana, on 1st December, 1889.
1103	,,	,,	,,	Mr. Narayan Bajee Thosar	do.	Pleader, Landholder and Jahagirdar.	do.
1104	,,	,,	,,	Mr. John Joseph D'Almeida	East Indian Catholic Christian.	Member of the Thana Local Board, Landed Proprietor, Bandra.	do.
1105	,,	,,	,,	Mr. Domingos Francis D'Almeida.	do.	Member of the Thana District, Local Board, Landed Proprietor, Condotun near Marol, Salsett.	do.
1106	,,	,,	,,	Mr. Damodar Kisandas ...	Visalad Vani.	Pleader, Bassein	do.
1107	,,	,,	,,	Mr. Ramchandra Krishna Subnis.	Brahmin.	do. Kalyan	do.
1108	,,	,,	,,	Mr. Sakharam Keshav Bhagvat, B.A., LL.B.	Hindu Brahmin.	do. District Court, Thana..	do.
1109	,,	,,	,,	Mr. Raghunath Moroba Raikar.	Khsatriya Somawansi.	Municipal Commissioner and Member, Taluka Local Board, Bassein, Landholder.	do.
1110	,,	,,	,,	Mr. Janardan Dhondev Karandikar.	Hindu Brahmin.	Landed Proprietor	do.
1111	,,	,,	,,	Mr. Balkrishna Vamanaji.	Brahmin.	Landholder, Bassein, Member of Local Board.	do.
1112	,,	,,	,,	Mr. Waman Ganesh Dandekar.	Hindu Brahmin.	MunicipalCommissioner, Mahim, Landlord.	do.
1113	,,	,,	,,	Mr. Motilal Hurgowandas..	Vani.	Merchant, Banker and Landlord.	do.
1114	,,	,,	,,	Mr. Bapooji Cowasji Divecha.	Parsee.	Contractor	do.
1115	,,	,,	,,	Mr. Gangadhar Moreswar Dandekar.	Brahmin.	Banker, Landholder, Merchant, K. Mahim.	do.
1116	,,	,,	,,	Mr. Balkrishna Appaji Valavalkar.	do.	Landholder and Contractor ...	do.
1117	,,	,,	,,	Mr. Bhau Rughoonath Thakur.	do.	do. ...	do.
1118	,,	,,	,,	Mr. Balavant Govind Godbole.	do.	Pleader, Bandra...	do.
1119	,,	,,	,,	Shet Mangaldas Devidas...	Hindu Vani.	Municipal Commissioner, Thana, General Merchant, Banker, Landlord.	do.
1120	,,	,,	,,	Mr. Vinayek Balwant Shaligram.	Hindu Brahmin.	District Court Pleader, Municipal Commissioner and Landlord.	do.
1121	,,	,,	,,	Mr. Krishnaji Hari Kirkire, B.A., LL.B.	do.	Vakil, District Court, Thana ...	do.
1122	,,	,,	,,	Mr. Atmaram Vithal Kharkar.	Prabhu.	Landholder	do.

Number.	Presidency or Government.	Congress Circle.	Electoral Division.	Names in full of Delegates with honorary titles, scholastic degrees, etc.	Race, Religious denomination, and Caste, if any.	Occupation and Address.	How and when elected.
1123	Bombay.	Bombay.	Thana.	Mr. Hari Atmaram Mohile, B.A., LL.B.	Hindu Parbhu.	Vakil, High Court	At a Meeting, held on 1st December, 1889, of the Thana Association.
1124	"	"	"	Mr. Narayen Daji Gupte ...	Parbhu.	Pleader, Thana	do.
1125	"	"	"	Mr. Mahadeva Ramchandra Nadkarni.	Brahmin.	do.	do.
1126	"	"	"	Mr. Luxuman Ballal Joglekar.	do.	do.	do.
1127	"	"	"	Mr. Shankar Damodar Gupte.	Parbhu.	do. Bassein	do.
1128	"	"	Bandra Rate Payers' Association (Thana.)	Mr. Vincent Almeida ...	Catholic East Indian.	Bandra	November 24th, 1889, at a General Meeting, held for that purpose.
1129	"	"	Ratnagiri.	Mr. Shivram Khrishnarao Dalvi.	Hindu Kshatriya Maratha.	Government Pensioner and Landlord, Deogad.	Rutnagiri, elected by the Congress Committee, 10th November, 1889.
1130	"	"	"	Rao Saheb Shivram Mahadeo Namjoshi.	Hindu Brahmin.	Pleader, District Court, Member of the District Local Board, and Member of the Ratnagiri Municipality, &c.	do.
1131	"	"	"	Mr. Anant Mahadeo Damale, B.A., LL.B.	do.	do. ...	do.
1132	"	"	"	Mr. Govind Balkrishna Ranade.	do.	Landlord	do.
1133	"	"	"	Mr. Narayen Rao Babaji.	Brahmin.	Pleader, Sub-Judge's Court, Rajapur.	do.
1134	"	"	"	Mr. Govind Motiram Saple.	Maratha Hindu Bania.	Merchant, Rajapur, Rutnagiri District.	do.
1135	"	"	"	Mr. Dhondo Mahadeo Barve.	Hindu Brahmin.	Pleader, Sub-Judge's Court, Dapoli District, Rutnagiri, Khot Landlord, Municipal Commissioner, Town Municipality, Dapoli, and Member of the Taluka Local Board, Dapoli.	do.
1136	"	"	"	Mr. Narayan Ramchandra Gogte.	do.	Manager of the Western India Arrowroot Plantation, Dapoli District, Rutnagiri.	do.
1137	"	"	"	Rao Saheb Vishnu Hari Barve.	do.	Banker, Khot, Landlord, Inamdar, President, Town Municipality, Dapoli, Member, District Local Board, Rutnagiri.	do.
1138	"	"	"	Mr. Gangadhar Luxuman Oka.	do.	Landlord and Sowcar, Palgad Taluka, Dapoli Zilla, Rutnagiri.	do.
1139	"	"	"	Rao Saheb Gangadhar Bhicaji Bapat.	do.	Pleader, Sub-Judge's Court, Deogad, Member, District Local Board, Rutnagiri.	do.
1140	"	"	"	Mr. Waman Bhaskar Kelkar.	do.	Pleader, Sub-Judge's Court, Deogad, Rutnagiri District.	do.
1141	"	"	"	Mr. Krishnajee Hari Desai.	do.	Vatundar, Landlord	do.
1142	"	"	"	Mr. Ganesh Dinkar Bapat.	do.	Pleader, Sub-Judge's Court, Chiplun.	do.
1143	"	"	"	Mr. Janardan Hari Athale.	do.	Editor and Proprietor of the Jaghunmitra Newspaper, Landlord, Inamdar.	do.
1144	"	"	"	Mr. Abdool Kadir Valad Shaik Enoos Kalsekar.	Mahomedan.	Merchant, Khot, Landlord, Dasur Taluka, Rajapoor, Rutnagiri District.	do.
1145	"	"	"	Shaik Ahmed alias Dada Saheb Tambe.	do.	Landlord, Khot, Merchant and Member of the Talooka Local Board, Khed, Rutnagiri District.	do.
1149	"	"	"	Kaji Shirajudeen Valad Kaji Gulam Ahmed Parkar.	do.	Landlord and Inamdar, at Bankot Taluka, Dapoli District, Rutnagiri.	do.

Number.	Presidency or Government.	Congress Circle.	Electoral Division.	Names in full of Delegates with honorary titles, scholastic degrees, etc.	Race, Religious denomination, and Caste, if any.	Occupation and Address.	How and when elected.
1147	Bombay.	Bombay.	Ratnagiri.	Rao Saheb Luxman Dhondeo Katre.	Hindu.	Pleader, District Court, Rutnagiri, Member, Ratnagiri City Municipality, Member of the District Local Board, Ratnagiri, Secretary.	At a Public Meeting, 10th November, 1889.
1148	"	"	"	Mr. Govind Keshavshet Shet.	Hindu Bania.	Rutnagiri, Merchant, Agent, B. I. S. N. Co.	do.
1149	"	"	"	Rao Bahadur Bhasker Vishnu Phadke.	Hindu.	Sowkar, President, Ratnagiri Municipality, Vice-President, District Local Board,Ratnagiri Town.	do.
1150	"	"	"	Mr. Krishnarao Balwant Paranjpe.	Hindu Brahmin.	Landlord, Member, Taluka Local Board, Dapoli.	do.
1151	"	"	"	Mr. Ganesh Raghunath Patwardhan.	Hindu.	Rutnagiri.	do.
1152	"	"	"	Mr. Ramchandra Saji Dhond, B.A.	Hindu Gowd Brahmin.	do.	do.
1153	"	"	"	Rao Saheb Narayen Bapuji Samant.	do.	Landlord, Member of the District Local Board, Ratnagiri, Member, Taluka Board, Matwan, Late Secretary and Engineer, District Local Board, Ratnagiri, &c.	do.
1154	"	"	"	Mr. Hari Narayan Limaye.	Hindu.	Editor, Satya Shodhak Press, Member, Rutnagiri City Municipality.	do.
1155	"	"	"	Mr. Balaji Udho Joshi ...	do.	Head Master, Tedford New English School, Member, Rutnagiri Municipality, Member, Taluka Local Board, Rutnagiri.	do.
1156	"	"	"	Mr. Yeshwunt Narayan Adarkar.	Hindu Brahmin.	Pleader, Sub-Judge's Court, Vengorla.	Do., and Vengorla, 12th October, elected by the Hitachintak Sabha, Vengorla, and a Public Meeting.
1157	"	"	Murud (Ratnagiri)	Mr. Narhar Balkrishna Joshi, B.A.	Maratha Brahmin.	Teacher	At a General Meeting of Murud Survajanik Sabha, 23rd December, 1889.
1158	"	"	"	Mr. Dhondo Keshav Karve, B.A.	do.	Proprietor of High School ...	do.
1159	"	"	Mahad (Kolaba District.)	Rao Saheb Chimnaji Narayen Bhate.	Brahmin.	Pleader, Sub-Judge's Court, Mahad, Chairman, Municipality, Mahad.	Elected at a Public Meeting at Mahad, on 1st December, 1889.
1160	"	"	"	Khan Saheb Ismail Khan Sale Khan, Deshmukh.	Mahomedan.	Municipal Commissioner, Mahad, Member, District Local Board, Kolaba, Vatandar Deshmuk, Mahad, Kolaba.	do.
1161	"	"	"	Mr. Hutaji Chintaman Damale.	Brahmin.	Head Master, 2nd Grade Anglo-Vernacular School, Mahad.	do.
1162	"	"	"	Mr. Antaji Ramchandra Hardikar.	do.	Secretary, Municipality, and Member, Taluka Local Board, Mahad.	do.
1163	"	"	"	Rao Saheb Krishnaji Laxuman Ambekar.	do.	Chairman, Talook Local Board, Mahad, and Inamdar.	do.
1164	"	"	"	Mr. Mahadev Govind Bhuskute.	do.	Member, Taluka Local Board, Mahad, and Money-lender.	do.
1165	"	"	Pen (District, Kolaba.)	Mr. Narayen Krishna Ghanekar.	do.	Money-lender, Pen District, Kolaba.	At a Public Meeting, on the 17th of November, 1889, in Pen District, Kolaba.
1166	"	"	"	Mr. Waman Bapuji Deva...	Hindu Brahmin.	Landholder and Merchant ...	do.
1167	"	"	"	Mr. Sitaram Babajishet Namoshi.	Vaishya Vani.	Merchant	do.

Number.	Presidency or Government.	Congress Circle.	Electoral Division.	Names in full of Delegates with honorary titles, scholastic degrees, etc.	Race, Religious denomination, and Caste, if any.	Occupation and Address.	How and when elected.
1168	Bombay.	Bombay.	Pen (District, Kolaba.)	Mr. Sakharam Sadashiv Agashe.	Hindu Brahmin.	Head Master, Municipal English School, Pen District, Kolaba.	At a Public Meeting, held on 17th November, 1889, in Pen District, Kolaba.
1169	"	"	"	Mr. Vinayak Vasudev Barve.	Brahmin.	District Pleader, Kolaba, Municipal Commissioner, Pen.	do.
1170	"	"	"	Mr. Vinayak Shivarao Dharkar.	Hindu Kayast Parbhu.	Zamindar, Khot, Merchant, Pen, Kolaba District.	do.
1171	"	"	"	Mr. Luxuman Govind Agarkar.	Hindu Brahmin.	Land-holder and Merchant. ...	do.
1172	"	"	"	Mr. Narayen Ganesha Mandlik.	do.	Land-holder, Editor, and Municipal Commissioner.	do.
1173	"	"	"	Mr. Vinayakrao Waman Dighe.	Hindu Parbhu.	Jahagirdar	Elected at a Public Meeting, held on 15th of December, of Kayestha Parbhu Community of Pen.
1174	"	"	"	Mr. Shankar Rao Keshav Gandhe.	Hindu Brahmin.	Jahagirdar	do.
1175	"	"	Roha (Kolaba District.)	Mr. T. S. Charles, B.A. ...	Christian.	Head Master, American Mission School, Roha.	Elected at a Public Meeting in Roha, on 7th December, 1889.
1176	"	"	"	Mr. Vasudevi Setharam Paradkar.	Hindu Brahmin.	Teacher	do.
1177	"	"	Goregaon (Kolaba District.)	Mr. Hari Luxuman Adhikari.	do.	Merchant and Trader, Goregaon.	Elected at a Meeting, held at Goregaon, on 10th November, 1889.
1178	"	"	"	Mr. Govind Luxuman Ranade.	do.	do. ...	do.
1879	"	"	Tala Taluka, Mangaum, (Kolaba District.)	Mr. Govind Narayen Sathe	do.	Vakil, Tala Taluka, Mangaum, Kolaba District.	At a Meeting, held at Tala, under the Presidency of Abaji Parshoram Bhat, on the 24th December, 1889.
1180	"	"	Mangaum (Kolaba District.)	Rao Saheb Anund Rao Putlaji.	Puthuren Purbhu.	Kuvilwuhul, Mangaum Taluka.	By a Public Meeting, 12th December, 1889, at Mangaum.
1181	"	"	Panvel (Kolaba District.)	Mr. Jagannath Bhikaji Dapke.	Hindu Brahmin.	Merchant	General Meeting, 15th December, 1889.
1182	"	"	"	Mr. Luxuman Bapuji Dongre.	do.	do.	do.
1183	"	"	"	Mr. Krishnaji Kashinath Patwardhan.	do.	District Pleader...	do.
1184	"	"	"	Mr. Antaji Bhikaji Patwardhan.	do.	Landholder	do.
1185	"	"	"	Mr. Wasudeva Mahadeva Karandikar.	do.	District Pleader, Panwel ...	do.
1186	"	"	"	Mr. Khanderao Bhikaji Belsar.	do.	School Master, English School, Panwel.	do.
1187	"	"	"	Mr. Krishnaji Shamrao Keskar.	do.	Merchant	do.
1188	Central Provinces.	Nagpur.	Nagpur	Mr. Gangadhar Rao Madhav Chitnavis.	Hindu.	Rais, Sowkar and Landlord, Honorary Magistrate, President, District Council, President, Loka Sabha, C. P., Member, Municipality.	Elected at a Public Meeting, held at Nagpur, on the 28th of October, 1889, and at a Meeting of the Loka Sabha.
1189	"	"	"	Seth Ramchandra... ...	Hindu Marwari.	General Merchant, Malguzar and Sowcar.	do.
1190	"	"	"	Mr. Bapu Rao Dada, M.A...	Hindu Brahmin.	Pleader, Secretary, Loka Sabha, Municipal Commissioner.	do.
1191	"	"	"	Mr. Gopal Hari Bhide ...	do.	Pleader, Municipal Commissioner, Secretary, Gorakshini Sabha.	do.
1192	"	"	"	Mr. Govind Meghasham Budkas.	do.	Pleader	do.
1193	"	"	"	Mr. Sadasiva Ganpat Rao Subhedar, B.A.	do.	Rais and Landlord	do.
1194	"	"	"	Mr. Keshava Gopal Tamhan, B.A.	do.	Officiating Principal and Professor of Sanscrit, Morris College, Nagpur.	do.
1195	"	"	"	Mr. Diwakar Janardan Waze.	do.	Assistant Master, City Aided High School, Nagpur.	do.
1196	"	"	"	Mr. Balkrishna Jairam Ratnaparkhy.	do.	Pleader	do.
1197	"	"	"	Mr. Atmaram Bhagwant...	do.	do. and Malguzar, Nagpur.	do.
1198	"	"	"	Mr. Rambhaoo Raghunath Bobade,	do.	do. and Landlord	do.

Number.	Presidency or Government.	Congress Circle.	Electoral Division.	Names in full of Delegates with honorary titles, scholastic degrees, etc.	Race, Religious denomination, and Caste, if any.	Occupation and Address.	How and when elected.
1199	Central Provinces.	Nagpur.	Nagpur.	Mr. Sadasiva Jairam Dehadrai, B.A.	Hindu Brahmin.	Professor of Sanscrit, Hislop College, Nagpur.	Elected at a Public Meeting, held at Nagpur, on the 24th of October, 1889.
1200	"	"	"	Mr. Laxman Ganesh Sonak	do.	Malguzar...	do.
1201	"	"	"	Mr. Balamakunda Ramchandra.	Hindu Guzerati Bania.	Contractor	do.
1202	"	"	"	Mr. Visnu Pandita ...	Hindu Maharastra Brahmin.	Nagpur	do.
1203	"	"	"	Mr. Vithal Balkrishna Date, L.C.E.	Hindu Brahmin.	Contractor	do.
1204	"	"	"	Mr. Gopal Ramkrishna Waradfande.	Brahmin.	Landholder and Private Service.	do.
1205	"	"	"	Seth Narayendas Patbisad.	Hindu Bania.	do.	do.
1206	"	"	"	Seth Ram Narain	Hindu Marwari.	Sowkar and Malguzar, Merchant.	do.
1207	"	"	"	Mr. Lakhshman Prabhakar Panchkhede.	Hindu Brahmin.	Landholder	do.
1208	"	"	"	Mr. Ramkrishna Puree Pademe Puree.	Gosavi.	Sowkar and Malguzar	do.
1209	"	"	"	Mr. Bapu Khem Patel ...	Hindu Brahmin.	Malguzar	do.
1210	"	"	"	Mr. Bhagiratha Prasada, B.A.	Hindu Kalara.	Professor of Mathematics, Hislop College, Nagpur, Municipal Member, Nagpur City, Member, Loka Sabha, Nagpur.	Elected to represent Loka Sabha, Nagpur, (for the Central Provinces), at a Meeting of the Managing Committee, held on 23rd November 1889.
1211	"	"	"	Mr. Narainswami Nayadu..	Hindu Nayadu.	Pleader and President, Municipal Committee, Nagpur.	do.
1212	"	"	"	Mr. Tatya Balkrishna Ksheersagar, B.A.	Hindu Brahmin.	Landowner, Member of Loka Sabaha.	do.
1213	"	"	"	Mr. Rajaram Sitaram Dixit.	do.	Contractor	do.
1214	"	"	"	Pandit A. Krishnaswamy Aiyer.	do.	Pandit......	do.
1215	"	"	"	Mr. Raghunath Narayen	Brahmin.	Malguzar	At a Public Meeting, held on the 18th October, 1889.
1216	"	"	Malguzari Association, Nagpur.	Mr. Shamrao Kishnaji ...	do.	Pleader and Malguzar	At a Meeting, of the Malguzar Association, Nagpur, 21st December 1889.
1217	"	"	"	Mr. Lakshman Rao Rajeshwar Chitnis.	Hindu. Parbhu.	Malguzar...	do.
1218	"	"	"	Mr. Krishnarao Narayan Deshmuk.	Hindu Brahmin.	Do.	do.
1219	"	"	"	Mr. Tukaram Kashinath ...	do.	Malguzar and Secretary, Malguzari, Association.	do.
1220	"	"	"	Mr. Ramchandra Ganesh Narale.	do.	Pleader and Malguzar	do.
1221	"	"	"	Mr. Gopal Anajee	Maratha Brahmin.	Sowkar and Teacher, Free Church Institution, Nagpur.	do.
1222	"	"	"	Mr. Ganpat Rao Gopal Ghatate.	Hindu Brahmin.	Malguzar and Sowkar, President Malgazari Association, Central Provinces, Nagpur.	do.
1223	"	"	"	Mr. Raghoba Ratiram ...	do.	Sowkar, Vice-President, Municipal Committee, Saoner.	do.
1224	"	"	Katol.	Mr. Govindrao Deshmukh..	Kunbi Hindu.	Malguzar	do.
1225	"	"	Wardha.	Mr. Hari Vaman Kelkar, B.A., LL.B.	Hindu Brahmin.	Pleader, Member, Municipality.	Elected at a Meeting, held at Wardha, on the 8th of December 1889.
1226	"	"	"	Mr. Keshav Mahadeo Kavle	do.	Pleader and Malguzar, Vice-President, Municipality.	do.
1227	"	"	"	Mr. Jayakrishna Ramchandra.	do.	Malguzar and Cultivator, Member, Local Board.	do.
1228	"	"	"	Mr. Sheo Rao Chintaman Deshmuk.	do.	Malguzar and Cultivator ...	do.
1229	"	"	"	Mr. Purushottam Vithal Gole.	do.	Inamdar...	do.
1230	"	"	"	Mr. Narayan Shripat Ingolay.	Kunbi Hindu.	Malguzar and Banker, Takli ...	do.
1231	"	"	"	Mr. Pralhad Bhaskar Deshpande.	Hindu Brahmin.	Agent and Malguzar	do.
1232	"	"	"	Mr. Balkrishna Pandurang Kaliyan.	do.	Do.	do.

Number.	Presidency or Government.	Congress Circle.	Electoral Division.	Names in full of Delegates with honorary titles, scholastic degrees, etc.	Race, Religious denomination, and Caste, if any.	Occupation and Address.	How and when elected.
1233	Central Provinces.	Nagpur.	Wardha.	Mr. Yadow Rao Pandurang Kalyani.	Hindu Brahmin.	Malguzar Sonegam	Elected at a Meeting, held at Wardha, on the 8th of December 1889.
1234	"	"	"	Mr. Baliram Chanaji Ingolay.	Hindu Kunbi.	do. and Banker, Takli ...	do.
1235	"	"	"	Mr. Tukaram Patel ...	do.	do. of Asta ...	do.
1236	"	"	"	Mr. Gunpatrao Kashinath Malguzar.	do.	do. and Banker, Takli ...	do.
1237	"	"	"	Mr. Damudar Nilkante Khare, B.A., LL.B.	Hindu Brahmin.	Pleader	do.
1238	"	"	"	Mr. Balwant Keshav Bhowalkar.	do.	Technical Institute, Bombay ...	do.
1239	"	"	"	Mr. Purshotum Atmaram Palkar.	do.	Trader	do.
1240	"	"	"	Mr. Nilkant Damodar Tale Tulee.	do.	Malguzar and Banker, Sudi ...	do.
1241	"	"	"	Mr. Vasudev Vinayek Paranjpe.	do.	Pleader and Vice-President, Municipality, Secretary, District Council.	do.
1242	"	"	"	Mr. Datto Vinayek Gokhale	do.	Contractor, Sitabuldi	do.
1243	"	"	"	Mr. Amritrao Madhavrao Meghay.	Hindu Kunbi.	Malguzar and Banker	do.
1244	"	"	"	Mr. Madhav Sadashiv Soman.	Hindu Brahmin.	Pleader	do.
1245	"	"	"	Mr. Laxaman Govind Deoskar.	do.	Pleader, Member of Municipality and District Council, Wardha.	do.
1246	"	"	"	Mr. Gunpatrao Madhowji...	Hindu Kunbi.	Malguzar and Banker	do.
1247	"	"	"	Mr. Dada Patel	do.	do. do. ...	do.
1248	"	"	"	Mr. Ramkrishna Punjaji Bhat.	Bhat Hindu	Agent and Malguzar	do.
1249	"	"	"	Mr. Apliman Patel ...	Hindu Kunbi.	do.	do.
1250	"	"	"	Mr. Maroti Ramchandra...	Brahmin.	Pleader	do.
1251	"	"	"	Mr. M. Gupta, Barrister-at-Law, LL.B. (London).	Hindu.	do.	do.
1252	"	"	"	Mr. Ramkrishna Ramchundra Bande.	Hindu Brahmin.	Cultivator	do.
1253	"	"	"	Mr. Vasudev Krishna ...	do.	Secretary, Local Board, Malguzar and Cultivator.	do.
1254	"	"	"	Mr. Gunpat Rao Keshev Deshunton.	do.	Honorary Magistrate, Malguzar and Member, Local Board.	do.
1255	"	"	Harda.	Mr. Narayan Rao Govind Paroolkar.	Brahmin Mahratta.	Zemindar, Honorary Magistrate, and President, Harda Municipality.	At a Public Meeting, held on 17th November 1889.
1256	"	"	"	Mr. Mahomed Chandkhan Naik Kazi.	Mahomedan.	Law-Agent	do.
1257	"	"	"	Mr. Raghunath Rao Waman Kekre.	Hindu Brahmin.	Zemindar	do.
1258	"	"	"	Mr. Krishna Rao Narayana Raigay.	do.	Jagirdar and Zamindar ...	do.
1259	"	"	"	Mr. Sadasheo Ramchandra Patwardhan.	do.	Zamindar, Pleader, Honorary Magistrate, Municipal Member, Editor and Proprietor, Nyaya Sudha.	do.
1260	"	"	"	Mr. Gulzarimal Choubey...	Hindu Chouby.	Pleader, Banker and Landlord...	do.
1261	"	"	"	Mr. Ramchandra Shamrao Kekre.	Brahmin.	Zemindar	do.
1262	"	"	"	Mr. Balvant Rao Kashinath Agnihotri.	do.	Zemindar, Secretary's Branch, Loka Sabha Harda.	do.
1263	"	"	"	Mr. Narayen Balkrishna Nakhre Atreya.	do.	Sub Editor Nyaya Sudha, Harda.	do.
1264	"	"	Jabbalpore.	Pandit Gangadhur Chintaman.	do.	Clerk in Railway Department...	At a Public Meeting at Jubbalpur, 23rd Nov. 1889.
1265	"	"	"	Mr. Pandit Ganesh Wasudeo	do.	Contractor	do.
1266	"	"	"	Abdul Hussain Suleman ...	Mahomedan.	Merchant	do.
1267	"	"	"	Mr. R. Narayen Rao ...	Christian.	Head Master, Mission School...	do.
1268	"	"	"	Mr. Alfred Nundy... ...	do.	Barrister-at-Law, and Municipal Commissioner, Jubbalpore.	do.

Number.	Presidency or Government.	Congress Circle.	Electoral Division.	Names in full of Delegates with honorary titles, scholastic degrees, etc.	Race, Religious denomination, and Caste, if any.	Occupation and Address.	How and when elected.
1269	Central Provinces.	Nagpur.	Jubbalpore.	Mr. Gajadhur Shakool ...	Hindu Brahmin.	Manager, Cotton Mill	At a Public Meeting, held on 17th November 1889.
1270	"	"	"	Mr. Purnachandra Mukerjia, B.A., B.L.	do.	Pleader	do.
1271	"	"	Burhanpur.	Mr. Govindrao Ramchandra	do.	Malguzar	Public Meeting, held at Burhanpur, 12th Dec. 1889.
1272	"	"	"	Mr. Gunpatrao Vithal ...	do.	do.	do.
1273	"	"	"	Mr. Raghunath Balkrishna Bhide.	do.	Proprietor of the Arya Vaidhaw Press.	do.
1274	"	"	Raipur.	Mr. Tukaram Vishnu Gosawi.	do.	Pleader	Raipur, 8th December 1889.
1275	"	"	"	Mr. Govinda Prasada Dube.	do.	do.	do.
1276	"	"	"	Mr. Ramchandra Rao Lakhay.	do.	Malguzar and Banker	do.
1277	"	"	Khandwa.	Mr. Vithal Waman Page...	Hindu Brahmin.	Pleader	At a Public Meeting of the inhabitants of Khandwa, held on 24th November 1889.
1278	"	"	"	Mr. Hormusjee Dhunjeebhoy.	Parsi.	Contractor	do.
1279	"	"	"	Munshi Said Mahomed ...	Mahomedan.	Clerk and Petition Writer ...	do.
1280	"	"	"	Seth Herallal Bondrusa ...	Hindu Mahajan Jain.	Banker and Trader	do.
1281	"	"	"	Mr. Haridas Chatterjee, M.A., B.L.	Hindu Brahmin.	Pleader, Secretary, District Council, Honorary Magistrate and Municipal Commissioner.	do., and also at Burhanpur, on 12th December 1889.
1282	"	"	Bhandara.	Mr. Govind Balwant ...	do.	Pleader	At a Public Meeting held at Bhandara, on the 10th November 1889.
1283	"	"	"	Mr. Vishawanath Nelkant Pandit.	do.	do.	do.
1284	"	"	"	Mr. Sakharam Sitaram Wazalwar.	do.	do.	do.
1285	"	"	Raj Nandgaon.	Mr. V. Sarangapany Moodliar.	Hindu Vysia Madrasi.	Contractor and Manager, Balram Press, and Praja Hithyshi, Member, Municipality.	At a Public Meeting of the inhabitants of Raj Nandgaon, held on 1st December 1889.
1286	"	"	"	Mr. Ganesh Kasinath Khare.	Hindu Maharashtra Brahmin.	Contractor, Member, Municipality.	do.
1287	"	"	Saugor.	Mr. Behari Lal... ...	Hindu Vaishya.	Manager to the Estate of the Rajah of Pitehra.	At a Public Meeting, 1st December 1889.
1288	"	"	"	Mr. Jugganath Pershad ...	Hindu Brahmin.	Munshi	do.
1289	"	"	"	Mr. Gopal Lakshamana Shrikhande.	Maratha Brahmin.	Municipal Commissioner and Legal Practitioner.	do.
1290	"	"	Narsinghpur.	Mr. P. Khubchandra Gudhowlia.	Brahmin.	Zemindar and Malguzar ...	Elected at Narsinghpur, 5th December, 1889, by the Local Arya Samaj.
1291	"	"	"	Mr. Jiwan Lall	Hindu Kaisth.	Pleader	do.
1292	Govt. of India.	"	Mhow.	Mr. Sadashivrao Ganesh Dighe.	Hindu Brahmin.	Jahagirdar	Public Meeting, Indore, 17th December 1889.
1293	"	"	"	Mr. Kedarnath	Hindu.	Head Master, Khan Bahadur Eduljee Pestonjee's High School, Mhow.	Meeting held at the Central India Association, Mhow, on the 17th December 1889.
1294	"	"	"	Mr. Balmokund	do.	Merchant	do.
1295	"	"	"	Mr. Hyder Ali Rosulbhai...	Mahomedan.	Merchant, Mhow	do.
1296	"	"	"	Mr. Peer Bux	do.	Contractor, Mhow	do.
1297	"	"	"	Mr. Gangaram Choonilal	Hindu.	Banker, Mhow	do.
1298	"	"	"	Kazi Hafiz Arum	Mahomedan.	Kazi, Mhow	do.
1299	"	"	"	Mr. Mohendranath Chatterjee.	Hindu.	Pleader, Mhow, Central India, Honorary Secretary, Central India Association, Mhow, Editor, *Eastern Herald*.	do.

Number.	Presidency or Government.	Congress Circle.	Electoral Division.	Names in full of Delegates with honorary titles, scholastic degrees, etc.	Race, Religious denomination, and Caste, if any.	Occupation and Address.	How and when elected.
1300	Government of India.	Berar.	Berar Sarvajanik Sabha.	Mr. Moro Vishwanath Joshi, B.A. LL.B.	Hindu Maharastra Brahmin.	High Court Pleader, Municipal Commissioner and Vice-Chairman, Amraoti Municipality.	At a General Meeting of the Berar Sarvajanik Sabha, held at Amraoti, on 1st of December 1889.
1301	"	"	"	Mr. Yeshwant Govind Keskar.	do.	Proprietor and Editor, Pramoda Sindhu, Amraoti, Municipal Commissioner, Amraoti.	do.
1302	"	"	Amraoti	Mr. Prahlad Narayen Jog, B.A., LL.B.	Brahmin Hindu.	High Court Pleader, Banker, Municipal Commissioner, Amraoti.	At a Public Meeting held at Amraoti, on the 24th of November 1889.
1303	"	"	"	Mr. Rangnath Narsinh Mudholkar, B.A., LL.B.	Hindu Maharastra Brahmin.	High Court Pleader, Municipal Commissioner, Amraoti.	do.
1304	"	"	"	Mr. Balkrishna Jairam Pendke.	do.	Banker, Municipal Commissioner, Amraoti.	do.
1305	"	"	"	Mr. Devji Damodar Amalia	Hindu Bhatia.	Agent, Empress Sabhapathy Mudeliar and Co.'s Amraoti Branch.	do.
1306	"	"	"	Mr. Tukaram Padmaji......	Hindu Kunbi.	Deshmukh, Banker and Landholder, Jarood in Morsi Taluk, Amraoti District.	do.
1307	"	"	"	Mr. Balkrishna Hari Karandikar.	Hindu Maratha Brahmin.	Pleader, Amraoti	do.
1308	"	"	"	Mr. Khrishnarao Raghav..	Hindu Maharastra Brahmin.	Deshpande, Banker, Landholder, Member, and Honorary Secretary of the Local Committee, Badneira.	do.
1309	"	"	"	Mr. Wasudev Narayan Jog.	Brahmin Hindu.	Pleader	do.
1310	"	"	"	Mr. Balkrishna Madhav	Hindu Maharastra Brahmin.	Banker, Landholder and Patel, Varood in Morsi Taluk, Amraoti District.	do.
1311	"	"	"	Mr. Janardan Narayan Toke Pravara Sangamkar.	do.	Pleader, Jahagirdar of Mhalapur, Ahmednagar District and Municipal Commissioner, Amraoti.	do.
1312	"	"	"	Mr. Antaji Govind Keskar.	Hindu Brahmin.	Pleader, and Municipal Commissioner, Amraoti.	do.
1313	"	"	"	Mr. Narayan Govind Ketkar.	Hindu Maharastra Brahmin.	Pleader and Municipal Commissioner, Amraoti.	do.
1314	"	"	"	Mr. Ramchandra Narasinh Mudholkar, L.M. and S.	Hindu Brahmin.	Medical Practitioner, Municipal Commissioner, and Honorary Secretary of Amraoti Municipality.	do.
1315	"	"	"	Mr. Govind Narayan Kane.	Christian.	Pleader, Amraoti ...	do.
1316	"	"	"	Mr. Bhaskar Sakharam Thatte.	Hindu Brahmin.	Overseer, Amraoti Municipality, and Landholder.	do.
1317	"	"	"	Mr. Vishvanath Kashinath Kale.	do.	Amraoti....	do.
1318	"	"	"	Mr. Balwant Venkajee Khot.	Hindu Brahmin.	Landholder, Municipal Commissioner, Amraoti, Head Clerk of Messrs. Gaddum, Bythell and Co's. Amraoti Branch.	do.
1319	"	"	"	Mr. Narhar Bhagwant......	Hindu Maharastra Brahmin.	Deshpande, Jahagirdar, Patel and Pandit in Elichpur and Kholapur Amraoti Districts.	do.
1320	"	"	"	Mr. Vyankatrao Hanmantrao.	do.	Jagirdar, Deshmukh and Landholder of Elichpur.	do.
1321	"	"	"	Mr. Govind Anant Deshpande	do.	Deshpande, Landholder and Trader of Anjau Singi Taluk, Chandur, Amraoti District.	do.
1322	"	"	"	Mr. Krishnaji Bapuji Kide.	do.	Banker, Landholder, Member and Honorary Secretary of the Local Committee, Karanja.	do.
1323	"	"	"	Mr. Nicholas Godfrey ...	Christian European.	Pleader and Honorary Secretary of the Amraoti Camp, Municipality.	do.
1324	"	"	"	Mr. Sakharam Chimnaji Gole.	Hindu Maharastra Brahmin.	Secretary, Berar Agricultural Association, Landholder, Editor of the "Shetkari Amraoti."	do.
1325	"	"	"	Mr. Shivram Walad Awachitji Patel.	Hindu Kunbi.	Landholder	do.
1326	"	"	"	Mr. Ramkisan Sakharam Pethe.	Hindu Kalal.	Landholder and trader of Morsi.	do.
1327	"	"	"	Mr. Bapoo Mahadev Pendse	Hindu Maharastra Brahmin.	Pleader Berar Court, Ellichpur..	do.

Number.	Presidency or Government.	Congress Circle.	Electoral Division.	Names in full of Delegates with honorary titles, scholastic degrees, etc.	Race, Religious denomination, and Caste, if any.	Occupation and Address.	How and when elected.
1328	Government of India.	Berar.	Amraoti.	Mr. Keshav Balwant Deshpande.	Hindu Maharastra Brahmin.	Banker, Landholder	At a Public Meeting, held at Amraoti, on 24th November 1889.
1329	"	"	"	Mr. Ramchandra Renko ...	do.	Banker, Member of the District Local Board, and Landholder, Amraoti.	do.
1330	"	"	Berar Agricultural Association.	Mr. Sitaram W. Suryabhan Rund.	Hindu Kunbi.	Patel, Landholder	At a Meeting, of the Association held at Amraoti on the 22nd of December 1889.
1331	"	"	"	Mr. Sakharam Narayan Jog	Hindu Brahmin.	Money-lender	do.
1332	"	"	Akola.	Rao Saheb Deorao Vinayak.	Hindu Deccan Brahmin.	High Court Pleader, Municipal Commissioner, Akola.	At a Public Meeting held at Akola, on 1st December 1889.
1333	"	"	"	Mr. Dattatraya Vishnu Bhagvat, B.A., LL.B.	Hindu Mahratta Brahmin.	High Court Pleader, Vice-Chairman of the Akola Municipality, and Vice-Chairman of the Akola District Board.	do.
1334	"	"	"	Mr. Puran Shamlal ...	Hindu Jain.	Banker and Special Magistrate, Khamgam.	do.
1335	"	"	"	Mr. Nyamatkhan Wd. Belankhan.	Mahomedan.	Abkari Contractor, Balapur ...	do.
1336	"	"	"	Mr. Poputlal Parusram ...	Hindu Gujarati Jain.	Banker and Member of District Board, Akola.	do.
1337	"	"	"	Mr. Vyankatesh Ramchandra Mudholkar.	Hindu Maharastra Brahmin.	Editor of Vaidarbha, Akola ...	do.
1338	"	"	"	Mr. Panachand Nathoosawat.	Hindu Gujarati Jain.	Banker, Balapur	do.
1339	"	"	"	Mr. Anant Vishnoo Bhag.	Maharastra Brahmin.	Pleader, Telhara	do.
1340	"	"	"	Mr. Gopal Govind Ghosal...	Brahmin.	Cotton Merchant and Municipal Member, Shegaon.	do.
1341	"	"	"	Mr. Pandu Walad Nandaji..	Kunbi.	Money-lender and Agriculturist.	do.
1342	"	"	"	Mr. Shankar Govind ...	Hindu Maharastra Brahmin.	Pleader and Municipal Commissioner, Akola.	do.
1343	"	"	"	Mr. Hari Ramachandra Anvikar.	Hindu Krishna Pakshi.	Editor of "Shudha Varhadi," Newspaper.	do.
1344	"	"	"	Mr. Pandurang Bapuji Rajandekar.	Hindu Brahmin.	Merchant, Vice-Chairman of Akola, Taluka Board, and Member of Akola District Board.	do.
1345	"	"	"	Mr. Gopaldas Naraindas ...	Hindu Gujarathi.	Banker	do.
1346	"	"	"	Mr. Vyankatesh Krishna Desai.	Hindu Deccan Brahmin.	Pleader	do.
1347	"	"	"	Mr. Yeshwantrao Govind Hoondiwale.	Hindu Brahmin.	Landholder and Member of Taluk Board, Balapoor.	do.
1348	"	"	"	Mr. Govind Vishvanath	do.	Deshpande, Landholder and Pleader, Akola.	do.
1349	"	"	"	Mr. Madharao Ramchandra Tipnis.	Parbhu Hindu.	Pleader, Telhara	do.
1350	"	"	"	Mr. Mugoot Rao Balwant Rao.	Hindu Mahratta.	Landholder, Deshmukh Patel, and Member of Akola District Board.	do.
1351	"	"	"	Mr. Hari Sakharam ...	Kunbi.	Patel and Landholder	do.
1352	"	"	"	Mr. Mukundrao Nandaji...	do.	Patel, Mundgaon, Akola District.	do.
1353	"	"	"	Mr. Dattu Walad Gambhir	Hindu Maratha.	Patel Landholder	do.
1354	"	"	"	Mr. Narayan Dinaji Patel...	Hindu Kunbi.	do.	do.
1355	"	"	"	Mr. Govind Rao Luxman. Rao	Hindu Maratha.	Deshmukh Patel, Member of Akola Taluk and District Board.	do.
1356	"	"	"	Mr. Fakirchand Nowlaji...	do.	Patel and Landholder	do.
1357	"	"	"	Mr. Anand Rao Harsing ...	do.	Deshmukh, Patel, Patwari and Member of Akola Taluk Board and Landholder.	do.

Number.	Presidency or Government.	Congress Circle.	Electoral Division.	Names in full of Delegates with honorary titles, scholastic degrees, etc.	Race, Religious denomination, and Caste, if any.	Occupation and Address.	How and when elected.
1358	Government of India.	Berar.	Akola.	Mr. Bapu Balkrishna ...	Hindu Brahmin.	Kulkarni, Akola, Member of Taluk Board, Money-lender and Agriculturist.	At a Meeting held at Akola, on the 1st of December 1889.
1359	"	"		Mr. Jayawat Rao Sunderji.	Hindu Mahratha.	Deshmukh Patel, Kulkarni, Member of Akola Taluk Board and Agriculturist.	do.
1360	"	"	"	Mr. Vithal Gangaram ...	Hindu Brahmin.	Pleader, Telhara	do.
1361	"	"	"	Mr. Krishna Rao Ganesh...	Hindu Parbhu.	do.	do.
1362	"	"	"	Mr. Namdev Visram ...	Hindu Mahratha Kunbi.	Patel, Agriculturist and Banker.	do.
1363	"	"	"	Mr. Sadashiv Oodebhan ...	Hindu Mahratha.	do. ...	do.
1364	"	"	"	Mr. Amritrao Akaram ...	do.	Patel and Agriculturist... ...	do.
1365	"	"	"	Mr. Gopal Ganesh ...	Hindu Brahmin.	Member of Taluk, Jalgaon, and Akola District Board, Agriculturist and Money-lender.	do
1366	"	"	"	Mr. Maruti Balwant Pande.	do.	Kulkarni, Agriculturist and Money-lender.	do.
1367	"	"	"	Mr. Sonaji Bhawani ...	do.	Putwari, Member of Akola District Board and Vice-Chairman of Khamgaum, Taluka Board.	do.
1368	"	"	Buldana.	Mr. Damodar Hari Ranade.	Hindu Brahmin.	Vakil, Malkapur	At a Public Meeting held at Buldana, on 14th November 1889.
1369	"	"	"	Mr. Gulam Amed Khan ...	Mahomedan.	Merchant and Landholder ...	At a Public Meeting held at Malkapur, on 30th November 1889.
1370	"	"	"	Mr. Gopal Narayan Deshpande.	Hindu Brahmin.	Deshpande and Landholder ...	At a Public Meeting held at Buldana, on 14th November 1889.
1371	"	"	"	Mr. Waman Renko	do.	Pleader	do.
1372	"	"	"	Mr. Vishnusa Gopalsa Savaji.	Hindu Lada.	Banker of Chikhali, Buldana District.	do.
1373	"	"	"	Mr. Trimbak Mairal	Hindu Brahmin.	Vakil Malkapur...	do.
1374	"	"	"	Mr. Kashinath Bhikaji ...	do.	Pleader and Landholder ...	do.
1375	"	"	"	Mr. Jankiram Wasudev ...	do.	Patwari	do.
1376	"	"	"	Mr. Raoji Raghav...	do.	Pleader, Malkapur	do.
1377	"	"	"	Mr. Keshav Wasudev Soman.	do.	do.	do.
1378	"	"	"	Sampatrao Parwatrao Deshmukh.	Hindu Mahratha.	Deshmukh and Landholder, Malkapur.	do.
1379	"	"	Ellichpur.	Mr. Ganesh Shri Krishna Khaparde, B.A., LL.B.	Brahmin Hindu.	High Court Pleader, Member of the District Board, Amraoti, Landholder and Malguzar in Central Provinces, Amraoti.	At a Public Meeting held at Ellichpur, on the 5th of November 1889.
1380	"	"	"	Mr. Ganesh Nagesh	do.	Pleader, Ellichpur	do.
1381	"	"	"	Mr. Gangadhar Narayan Jaydule.	do.	District Court Pleader... ...	do.
1382	"	"	"	Mr. Shriput Mahadeo Keskar.	do.	do. ...	do.
1383	"	"	"	Mr. Ramrao Sadashiv Sadhu	Hindu Mahratha. Brahmin.	Landholder and General Agent.	do.
1384	"	"	"	Mr. Gangaram Dewaman Kavitkar.	Hindu Mali.	Landholder, Ellichpur... ...	do.
1385	"	"	Wun.	Mr. Lakshman Chintaman Bapat.	Hindu Brahmin.	Pleader, Yeotmal	At Public Meeting at Yeotmal the 26th November 1889.
1386	"	"	"	Mr. Mahadeo Govind Damale, B.A.	do.	District Pleader, Yeotmal ...	do.
1387	"	"	"	Mr. Sitaram Bavraji.	Hindu Kunbi.	Ijardar and Sowkar, Patel of Venikota in Yeotmal Taluk, Wun District.	do.
1388	"	"	"	Mr. Dadoo Bajirao Hore Patel.	do.	Landholder, Wun District, Malguzar, C. P.	do.
1389	"	"	"	Mr. Gopal Narayan Bhat...	Hindu Brahmin.	Pleader, Ijardar, Yeotmal ...	do.

Number.	Presidency or Government.	Congress Circle.	Electoral Division.	Names in full of Delegates with honorary titles, scholastic degrees, etc.	Race, Religious denomination, and Caste, if any.	Occupation and Address.	How and when elected.
1390	Government of India.	Berar.	Ellichpur.	Mr. Krishnaji Bhikaji Palnitkar.	Hindu Maratha Brahmin.	Landholder, Yeotmal... ...	At a Public Meeting held at Yeotmal, on the 26th November 1889.
1391	„	„	„	Mr. Jairam Ganesh ...	Hindu Parbhu.	Pleader and Ijardar	do.
1392	„	„	Basim.	Mr. Yeshwant Vaman Dighe	Hindu Parbu.	Pleader, Member and Honorary Secretary of Basim Municipality, Basim.	At a Public Meeting held at Basim, on the 23rd November 1889.
1393	„	„	„	Baba Shivaratansing Mahasing.	Arya Samajist Khsatriya.	Landholder and Money-lender.	do.
1394	„	„	„	Mr. Daji Dipaji Palkar ...	Hindu Maratha.	Manager of the Jain Temple of Shirpur (Basim District).	do.
1395	„	„	„	Mr. Trimbukrao Vithalrao.	Hindu Brahmin.	Deshmukh, Basim, Berar ...	do.
1396	„	„	„	Mr. Seshrao Raghunath Havaldar.	do.	Pleader, Basim...	do.
1397	„	„	„	Mr. Balkrishna Vyankatesh Bhaye.	do.	Agent, Basim, Berar	do.
1398	„	„	„	Mr. Laxuman Atmaram Mahajan.	do.	General Merchant, Mangrul Pir, Member, District Board, Basim, and Chairman, Taluq Board, Mangrul Pir.	General Meeting held at Pusad on 19th November, and at a General Meeting held at Mangrul Pir on 10th December 1889.
1399	„	„	„	Mr. Ramaji Vagaji Patel...	Hindu Kunbi.	Merchant, Vice-Chairman, Taluq Board, Mangrul Poti, Mangrul Pir.	General Meeting held at Mangrul Pir, on 10th December 1889.
1400	„	„	„	Mr. Devising Balaram ...	Hindu Raghuvanshy Rajput.	Sowkar, Mangrul Pir	do.
1401	„	„	„	Mr. Rafiuddin Gulamohiddin.	Mahomedan.	Merchant, Pusad, Basim District, Berar.	General Meeting held at Pusad on 19th Nov., 1889.
1402	Punjab.	Lahore.	Lahore.	Mr. A. O. Hume, C.B. ...	European Christian.	Retired Civilian, Resident at Simla, Fellow of the Calcutta University.	By a Public Meeting at Lahore, 8th December, 1889.
1403	„	„	„	Moulvi Mir Nisar Ali Shohrat.	Mahomedan.	Editor of "Rozana Punjab." ...	do.
1404	„	„	„	Mr. Kanihya Lal	Hindu Bhatia.	Pleader, Chief Court ...	do.
1405	„	„	„	Bawa Surmirkh Das ...	Sikh.	Sadhu, Bhai	do.
1406	„	„	„	Mr. Jogendra Chandra Bose, M.A., B.L.	Hindu.	Pleader, High Court, Lahore ...	do.
1407	„	„	„	Mr. Kali Prosonno Roy, M.A., B.L.	do.	Pleader, High Court, Fellow of Punjab University.	do.
1408	„	„	„	Lala Daswandee Ram.	Rajput.	Pleader, Chief Court, Punjab, and Landholder.	do.
1409	„	„	„	Mr. Parmanand	Arya.	Surgeon Dentist	do.
1410	„	„	„	Lala Sangam Lal, L.L. ...	Arya Khsatriya.	Pleader	do.
1411	„	„	„	Pandit S. N. Agnihotri ...	Deva Dharma.	Editor, Missionary Deva Dharma Mission.	do.
1412	„	„	„	Lala Gia Lal	Jain.	Banker	do.
1413	„	„	„	Mr. Dharm Das Suri ...	Khsatriya. Theist.	Vakil, High Court	do.
1414	„	„	„	Mr. Lachman Prasada ...	Brahmin.	Missionary Brahmo Samaj ...	do.
1415	„	„	The Indian Association Lahore.	Mr. I. C. Sarkar, C. E. ...	Christian.	Engineer and Landholder ...	At a Meeting of the Committee of the Indian Association, held on 4th December, 1889.
1416	„	„	Kangra.	Raja Niamat Ullah Khan...	Mahomedan.	Jaghirdar, Rehloo, Honorary Magistrate and Civil Judge, President, Local Board, Kangra, Vice President, District Board, Kangra.	Public Meeting, 1st December, 1889.
1417	„	„	„	Captain A. T. Banon ...	Christian European.	Zemindar, Kooloo, late Bengal Staff Corps.	do.
1418	„	„	„	Lala Sukhdial, LL. ...	Hindu Arya.	Pleader	do.
1419	„	„	„	Mr. K. Moti Lal	do.	Mukhtar, Tea Planter and Landholder.	do.
1420	„	„	„	Mr. Sohan Lal	do.	Pleader and Zemindar... ...	do.
1421	„	„	Umballa.	Lalla Than Singh ...	Hindu Agrawalla Vaishya.	Contractor	Public Meeting, held on 15th December 1889.
1422	„	„	„	Lala Murlidhar	do.	Pleader and Proprietor Hume Press and Khair Andesh.	do.

Number.	Presidency or Government.	Congress Circle.	Electoral Division.	Names in full of Delegates with honorary titles, scholastic degrees, etc.	Race, Religious denomination, and Caste, if any.	Occupation and Address.	How and when elected.
1423	Panjab.	Lahore.	Umballa.	Chaudhri Ganga Ram ...	Hindu Rajput.	Zemindar and Lumberdar ...	Public Meeting held on 15th December 1889.
1424	"	"	"	Miss Jessie Royce Carleton.	American Christian.	Physician	do.
1425	"	"	"	Lala Dwarka Parshad ...	Hindu Kshatrya.	Cloth Merchant	do.
1426	"	"	"	Pandit Brij Mohan Dattatrya.	Hindu Brahmin.	Editor, "Khair Andesh," Urdu Weekly.	do.
1427	"	"	Rawalpindi.	Lala Hansraj Sahai ...	Aryan Khsatri.	Pleader, Chief Court and Landholder.	Public Meeting, held on 23rd November 1889.
1428	"	"	"	Lalla Maya Das Sahai ...	do.	do. and Landholder.	do.
1429	"	"	"	Lala Radhu Kishen Seth...	do.	Banker and Merchant... ...	do.
1430	"	"	"	Mr. Hem Chunder Mookerjee, LL.	Christian.	Pleader	do.
1431	"	"	Amritsar.	Bawa Narain Singh ...	Sikh.	do. and Publisher, Law Reports.	Elected at the Public Meeting, held Dec. 1889.
1432	"	"	"	Lala Balmokund	Hindu Khsatriya.	Agent, Law Publication and Private Service.	do.
1433	"	"	"	Mr. Gangadin	Behari Arya.	Homeopathic Physician and Surgeon.	do.
1434	"	"	Gurdaspur.	Mr. Gurcharan Das, M.C. ...	Hindu Bhatia.	Pleader and President, Municipal Committee.	At a Public Meeting held on the 4th Dec. 1889.
1435	"	"	"	Lala Amrao Singh	Hindu.	Merchant	do.
1436	"	"	"	Lala Ram Saran Das	Hindu Ahlewaleya.	Pleader and Landholder ...	do.
1437	"	"	Hissar.	Lala Lajpat Rai, LL.	Arya Vaish.	do. and Municipal Commissioner.	Public Meeting held on 3rd December 1889.
1438	"	"	"	Mr. Chura Mani, L.L.	Arya.	Pleader, Hissar	do.
1439	"	"	"	Lala Gauri Shankar	Hindu Vaish.	Landholder	do.
1440	"	"	Jhelam.	Lala Harbhagwan Das, L.L.	Arya Khatri.	Pleader, Chief Court	Public Meeting, 8th December 1889.
1441	"	"	"	Lala Fatah-Chand, L.L. ...	Hindu Khsatriya.	do.	do.
1442	"	"	Hoshiarpur.	Sheikh Oomar Baksh, B.A.	Mahomedan Shaikh.	do. and Landholder.	At a Public Meeting held on 30th November.
1443	"	"	Gujarat.	Mr. Niranjan Das... ...	Khsatriya. Vedic. Religion.	Pleader	At a Public Meeting, on the 10th December 1889.
1444	"	Delhi	Delhi.	Lala Girdhari Lal...	Hindu Khuttri.	do.	Elected at a General Meeting held on 24th November 1889.
1445	"	"	"	Lala Girdhari Lal...	Hindu Vaish.	do. and Municipal Commissioner, President, Arya Samaj, &c.	do.
1446	"	"	"	Mr. Mohammed Fakhruddin	Mahomedan.	Editor, *Delhi Review*	do.
1447	"	"	"	Mr. Mohammed Shahaleud-din, Sugib.	do.	Service	do.
1448	"	"	"	Moulvi Nusrat Ali ...	do.	do.	do.
1449	"	"	"	Mr. Nur-ud-din Ahmed ...	do.	Landed Proprietor	do.
1450	"	"	"	Shaikh Mohammed Ismail.	do.	do.	do.
1451	"	"	"	Sayed Ali	do.	do.	do.
1452				Moulvi Sayed Moulana Abu Mansur Ali (Order of Majidi) Imam Manaziru Ahl-i-Kitab.	do.	Author of several books and Proprietor of Nusrat-ul-Akhbar.	do.
1453	"	"	"	Lala Piyari Lal ...	Hindu Jain.	Pleader, High Court	do.
1454	"	"	"	Mr. Kedar Nath ...	Hindu Kayesth.	Pleader	do.
1455	"	"	"	Lala Ramsaran Das ...	Hindu Vaish.	Banker	do.
1456	"	"	"	Lala Gunesh Lall ...	Hindu Khatri.	Merchant	do.
1457	"	"	"	Lala Ram Narain Kapur ...	do.	Landholder	do.
1458	"	"	"	Lala Chhuttan Lal	do.	Merchant	do.
1459	"	"	"	Mr. Rang Lal, B.A. ...	Hindu Jain.	Barrister-at-Law	do.

Number.	Presidency or Government.	Congress Circle.	Electoral Division.	Names in full of Delegates with honorary titles, scholastic degrees, etc.	Race, Religious denomination, and Caste, if any.	Occupation and Address.	How and when elected.
1460	Punjab.	Delhi.	Delhi.	Lala Daulat Ram	Hindu Khsatri.	Banker and Wholesale Cloth Merchant.	Elected at a General Meeting, held on 24th November 1889.
1461	„	„	„	Lala Narain Das	Hindu Vaish.	Banker	do.
1462	„	„	„	Lala Chhung Mal... ...	do.	do	Elected at a General Meeting, held on the 15th December 1889.
1463	„	„	„	Lala Bansidhar	Hindu Khsatriya.	Wholesale Cloth Merchant ...	Elected at a Special Meeting of Delegates and other Members of Congress, held on the 1st December 1889, Delhi.
1464	N.-W. P. & Oudh.	Lucknow.	Anjuman Mahomedi.	Nawab Mirza Abu Talibkhan Bahadur.	Mahomedan.	Wasikadar, Zamindar	At a General Meeting of the Anjuman Mahomedi on 12th December 1889.
1465	„	„	„	Mirza Mahomed Abas Hussain "Hosh"	do.	Secretary, Anjuman Mahomedi..	do.
1466	„	„	„	Prince Alijah Mahomed Hussain Ali Bahadur.	do.	Wasikadar	do.
1467	„	„	„	Nawab Mahomed Taki Khan.	do.	do.	do.
1468	„	„	„	Nawab Mahomed Askari...	do.	do.	do.
1469	„	„	„	Nawab Ali Mahomed Khan.	do.	do.	do.
1470	„	„	„	Nawab Baker Mirza Saheb.	do.	do.	do.
1471	„	„	„	Nawab Aga Mehdi Raza Khan.	do.	do.	do.
1472	„	„	„	Mahomed Faqurudin ...	do.	Merchant	do.
1473	„	„	„	Sikandar Kadir Prince Mirza Mahomed Ahmed Ali Bahadur.	do.	Wasika-holder	do.
1474	„	„	„	Munshi Hissam Ali ...	do.	Merchant	do.
1475	„	„	„	Mirza Ali Hussain ...	do.	Mukhtar	do.
1476	„	„	„	Syed Bakir Hussain ...	do.	Wasika-holder	do.
1477	„	„	„	Munshi Hidayet Rasul ...	do.	Service	do.
1478	„	„	„	Nawab Mirza Zulfikar Bahadur Khan.	do.	Wasika-holder and Zemindar...	Do. at a Meeting of the Rifa-i-am Association held on the 13th December 1889.
1479	„	„	„	Shamsuddowla Mumtaz-ul-Mulk Nawab Ali Hussain Khan Bahadur Mustakim Jung.	do.	Wasika-holder	do.
1480	„	„	„	Nawab Aga Sujjad Ali Khan.	do.	Reis	do.
1481	„	„	„	Munshi Ahmed Hussain ...	do.	Mukhtar	do.
1482	„	„	„	Nawab Tasuddak Hussain Khan.	do.	Reis	do.
1483	„	„	Lucknow.	Mr. Ali Ahmed Yar Meer Hussain.	do.	Merchant	Public Meeting at the Rafa-i-am Hall, 14th instant.
1484	„	„	„	Mr. Bhuban Mohan Roy...	Brahmo.	Merchant and Secretary, Lucknow Brahmo Samaj.	do.
1485	„	„	„	Mr. Sri Ram, M.A., B.L. ...	Hindu Kayastha.	Zemindar and Vakil, High Court. Vice Chairman of Municipality.	do.
1486	„	„	„	Mr. Bhuhan Mohan Banerji, B.A., F.R.H.S., F.S. Sc. (London), and Member, London Dialectical Society.	Bengali Hindu Brahmin.	Professor of Science and Mathematics, Lucknow Christian College.	do.
1487	„	„	„	Munshi Ashrufali... ...	Mahomedan.	Pension-holder and Translator...	do.
1488	„	„	„	Munshi Mahommed Ibrahim.	do.	Service	do.

Number.	Presidency or Government.	Congress Circle.	Electoral Division.	Names in full of Delegates with honorary titles, scholastic degrees, etc.	Race, Religious denomination, and Caste, if any.	Occupation and Address.	How and when elected.
1489	N.-W. P. & Oudh.	Lucknow	Lucknow.	Munshi Amjad Alli ...	Mahomedan.	Service	Public Meeting at the Rifa-i-am Hall, 14th instant.
1490	"	"	"	Munshi Furhat Alli ...	do.	do.	do.
1491	"	"	"	Pandit Bishan Narayan Dar.	Kashmiri Brahmin.	Lucknow, Barrister-at-Law	do.
1492	"	"	"	Mr. Kalidas Sircar ...	Hindu.	Lucknow	do.
1493	"	"	"	M. Suraj-ul-Hussein ...	Mahomedan.	Reis	do.
1494	"	"	"	Mr. Hamid Ali Khan ...	do.	Barrister-at Law, Moafidar and Municipal Commissioner.	do.
1495	"	"	"	Meer Hoossein Ali ...	do.	Reis	do.
1496	"	"	"	Khuaja Mohamed Yusuf...	do.	do.	do.
1497	"	"	"	Meer Mohamed Hussain...	do.	do.	do.
1498	"	"	"	Pandit Shyam Narayan Masaldan.	Kashmiri Brahmin.	Zamindar and Municipal Commissioner, Lucknow.	do. and Rifa-i-am Association, on the 19th instant.
1499	"	"	"	Mr. Bansi Lal Singh ...	Hindu Kshatrya.	Vakil, Landlord, Chairman of U. I. C. Paper Mill Company, Lucknow and Municipal Commissioner.	do.
1500	"	"	"	Mr. Kedar Nath ...	Hindu.	High Court, Pleader	do.
1501	"	"	"	Munshi Gangaprasad Varma.	do.	Proprietor of the Advocate and Hindustani, Municipal Commissioner and Secretary, Lucknow, Standing Congress Committee.	do.
1502	"	"	"	Munshi Sufder Hussain ...	Mahomedan.	Reis	do.
1503	"	"	"	Sheikh Asgar Ali...	do.	Merchant and Reis	do.
1504	"	"	"	Khwaja Fariduddin ...	do.	Zemindar and Reis	do.
1505	"	"	"	Munshi Ahmed Ali ...	do.	Reis	do.
1506	"	"	"	Bhaiya Rudra Pershad ...	Hindu Kayastha.	Manager, Kaistha Akhbar ...	do.
1507	"	"	"	Rev. Mr. Ram Chandra Bose, M.A.	Christian Indian.	Missionary (Local Preacher), Lucknow.	By the Bengal Christian Conference, December 6th, 1889.
1508	"	"	Lucknow Jalsa Tahzib.	Pandit Suraj Narayan Bahadur, B.A.	Kashmiri Brahmin.	Secretary, Jalsa Tahzib ...	At a General Meeting of Jalsa Tahzib, Lucknow.
1509	"	"	Fyzabad.	Munshi Lala Pershad ...	Hindu Kayastha.	Zemindar	Public Meeting, on the 7th December.
1510	"	"	"	" Saligram, B.A. ...	do.	Pleader and Zemindar... ...	do.
1511	"	"	"	" Balak Ram ...	do.	do. ...	do.
1512	"	"	"	Mr. Gokul Chund	Kshatriya.	do. Honorary Magistrate ; Vice-Chairman, Municipality and District Board.	do.
1513	"	"	Sitapore.	Munshi Murlidhar ...	Kayastha.	Pleader and Municipal Commissioner.	do.
1514	"	"	"	Mr. Buldeo Pershad ...	Hindu Kshatriya.	Pleader, Zemindar and Honorary Magistrate.	do.
1515	"	"	Khiree.	Seth Dwarka Dass ...	do.	Banker, Zemindar, Municipal Commissioner and Honorary Magistrate.	do. on the 18th December.
1516	"	"	"	Mr. Sheo Buksh Rai ...	Hindu Vaisya.	Pleader and Zemindar... ...	do.
1517	North Western Provinces.	Allahabad.	Allahabad.	The Hon'ble Pandit Ajoodhianath.	Hindu Kashmeri Brahmin.	Member of the Legislative Council, N. W. P. and Oudh, Vakil High Court, N. W. P., President of the Allahabad Standing Congress Committee, Member of the Royal Asiatic Society of Bengal, Fellow of the Calcutta and Allahabad Universities.	Public meeting, at the Kayastha Pathshala, Allahabad, November 16th, 1889, and also at a Public Meeting of the Mahomedans of Bombay, 22nd December, 1889.
1518	"	"	"	Mr. Ratan Chand, B.A. ...	Jain.	Vakil High Court, N. W. P. and President Graduates Association, N. W. P. and Oudh.	Public Meeting at the Kayastha Pathshala, November 16th, 1889.
1519	"	"	"	Pandit Motilal Nehru ...	Hindu Kashmeri Brahmin.	Vakil High Court, N. W. P. ...	do.

Number.	Presidency or Government.	Congress Circle.	Electoral Division.	Names in full of Delegates, with honorary titles, scholastic degrees, etc.	Race, Religious denomination, and Caste, if any.	Occupation and Address.	How and when elected.
1520	North Western Provinces.	Allahabad.	Allahabad.	Pandit Madan Mohan Malaviya, B.A.	Hindu Brahmin.	Editor, "Hindustan," Joint Secretary, Congress Committee, Allahabad.	Public Meeting at the Kayasth Pathshala November 16th and at a General Meeting, of the Hindu Samaj, 15th Dec. 1889.
1521	„	„	„	Mr. Ganesh Prasad ...	Hindu Vaishya.	Banker and Zemindar	Public Meeting, Kayastha Pathshala, November 16th, 1889.
1522	„	„	„	Mr. Raja Ram, Bhargava...	Hindu Bhargava.	Banker and Zemindar, Member Municipal Board.	do.
1523	„	„	„	Mr. Bhavani Prasad ...	Hindu Khattri.	Banker and Zemindar	do.
1524	„	„	„	Mr. Dayal Das	do.	Merchant	Public Meeting, Gangadaska Chowky, 17th December 1889.
1525	„	„	„	Mr. Durga Prasad... ...	do.	do.	do.
1526	„	„	„	Mr. Durga Charan Banerjea, B.A.	Hindu Brahmin.	Vakil, High Court, N. W.-P. ...	Public meeting, Kayastha Pathshala, November 16th 1889, and also at a General Meeting of the Hindu Samaj, 15th Dec., 1889.
1527	„	„	„	Munshi Sadarudin Ahmed.	Mahomedan.	Zemindar	Public Meeting, Kayastha Pathshala Nov. 16th, 1889.
1528	„	„	„	Pandit Balkrishna Bhatta...	Hindu Brahmin.	Editor "Hindi Pradip" ...	do.
1529	„	„	„	Mr. Balmakund Bhatta ...	do.	Merchant	do.
1530	„	„	„	Mr. Mohanlal Tandan ...	Hindu Khattri.	do.	Public Meeting, at Gangadaska Chowky, 17th December 1889.
1531	„	„	„	Mr. Hafiz Kumroodin ...	Mahomedan.	Zemindar	Public Meeting, at Maydara, 10th December 1889.
1532	„	„	„	Mr. Mir Mahomed Hadi ...	do.	do.	Public Meeting, at Ujihni 11th December 1889.
1533	„	„	„	Sayad Noorool Hussain ...	do.	Munshi	Public Meeting, at Kara, 13th December 1889.
1534	„	„	„	Mr. Mir Nowroze Ali ...	do.	Zemindar	do.
1535	„	„	„	Shaik Zahirooddeen ...	do.	do.	Public Meeting, at Maydara, 10th December 1889.
1536	„	„	„	Shaikh Mahomed Zaki ...	do.	do.	do.
1537	„	„	„	Munshi Ahmed Hussain ...	do.	do.	do.
1538	„	„	„	Shah Sultan Hussain ...	do.	Durbaish	Public Meeting, at Ujihni, 11th December 1889.
1539	„	„	„	Shaikh Ashruf Ali ...	do.	Zemindar	Public Meeting, at Maydara, 10th December 1889.
1540	„	„	„	Mr. Chail Biharilal, B.A. ...	Hindu Kayastha.	Head Master, Kayastha Pathshala Allahabad.	Public Meeting, at Gangadaska Chowky, 17th December 1889.
1541	„	„	„	Mr. T. N. Ghose	do.	Pleader	Public Meeting, at the Kayasha Pathshala, November 16th, 1889.
1542	„	„	„	Pandit Deokinandan Tivari.	Hindu Brahmin.	Proprietor and Editor "Prayag Samachar."	do.
1543	„	„	„	Mirza Tufail Ali Beg ...	Mahomedan.	Zemindar	Public Meeting, at Gungadaska Chowky, 17th Dec. 1889.
1544	„	„	„	Syed Mir Jan	do.	do.	do.
1545	„	„	„	Mir Mahdi Ali	do.	do.	do.
1546	„	„	„	Moulvi Mahomed Ali ...	do.	do.	Public Meeting at Kara, 13th December 1889.
1547	„	„	„	Mir Nazim Hussain ...	do.	do.	Public Meeting held at Karari, 12th Dec. 1889.
1548	„	„	„	Sheikh Abdul Aziz ...	do.	do.	Public Meeting held at Samuhi, 13th Dec. 1889.
1549	„	„	„	Mir Bagar Hussain ...	do.	do.	Public Meeting at Janka, 15th December 1889.
1550	„	„	„	Mir Haidar Hussain ...	do.	do.	Public Meeting at Kara, 13th December 1889.
1551	„	„	„	Sheikh Ali Hussain ...	do.	Trader	Public Meeting at Gungadaska Chowky, 17th Dec. 1889.
1552	„	„	„	Moulvi Mahomed Ishag ...	do.	Zemindar	do.
1553	„	„	„	Syed Faqruddin	do.	do.	Public Meeting at Janka, 15th December 1889.

Number.	Presidency or Government.	Congress Circle	Electoral Division.	Names in full of Delegates with honorary titles, scholastic degrees, etc.	Race, Religious denomination, and Caste, if any.	Occupation and Address.	How and when elected.
1554	N.-W. Provinces.	Allahabad.	Hindu Samaj, Allahabad.	Mr. Mahadeva Prasad Chaddhe.	Hindu Khattri.	Merchant	At a General Meeting, of the Hindu Samaj, 15th December 1889.
1555	"	"	"	Mr. Sital Prasad	do.	Pleader	Public Meeting, at Gangadaska Chowky, December 17th, 1889.
1556	"	"	"	Swamy Ala Ram	Hindu.	Anchorite	Public Meeting, at the Kayastha Pathashala, November 16th, 1889.
1557	"	"	"	Mr. L. Tracy	Christian European.	Journalist	do.
1558	"	"	"	Sayed Mahomed Tata ...	Mahomedan.	Zemindar	Public Meeting, at Kara Allahabad, December 13th, 1889.
1559	"	"	"	Sayed Fakhrullah... ...	do.	do.	Public Meeting, at Janka on December 13th, 1889.
1560	"	"	Fatehpur Hanswa.	Mr. Bijay Bahadur ...	Hindu Kayastha.	Taluqdar, Reis, Member, Local Board.	Public Meeting, 15th December 1889.
1561	"	"	"	Sayad Mahomed Amiruddin.	Mahomedan.	Reis and Zemindar	do.
1562	"	"	Banda.	Mr. Dubey Chandi Din ...	Hindu Brahmin.	Zemindar, Magistrate, Senior Vice-Chairman, Municipal Board, Member of the Agricultural and Commercial Department, Member, District Board, Banda.	Public Meeting, held on the 24th December 1889.
1563	"	"	"	Mr. Bisheshwar Chaudhri.	Arya Brahmin.	Junior Vice-President of the Banda Municipality.	do.
1564	"	"	"	Mr. Raghubar Dayal ...	Hindu Kayastha.	Legal Practitioner, Secretary, Kayastha Sabha.	do.
1565	"	"	"	Mr. D. N. Banerji... ...	Christian.	Municipal Commissioner ...	do.
1566	"	"	Jhansi.	Mr. Sitaram	Arya Vaishya.	Landlord, Merchant, Printer, Member, Municipal Board.	Bublic Meeting at Jhansi, Ist December 1889.
1567	"	"	"	Mr. Shankar Sahai ...	Arya Khayastha.	Pleader, Secretary Arya Samaj.	do.
1568	"	"	"	Pandit Pragdass	Arya Brahmin.	Mukhtar, Zemindar	do.
1569	"	"	"	Mr. Sivapada Ghose ...	Hindu Kayastha.	Pleader	do.
1570	"	"	"	Mr. Basanta Kumar Sanyal.	Hindu Brahmin.	do.	do.
1571	"	"	"	Mr. Mahendra Nath Niogi.	Hindu Vaishya.	Proprietor, Progressive Medical Hall.	do.
1572	"	"	Cawnpore.	Pandit Prithinath... ...	Cashmire Brahmin.	Vakil High Court, N.-W.P. ...	Public Meeting, 8th December 1889.
1573	"	"	"	Moulvi Abdul Jalil ...	Mahomedan.	do. ...	do.
1574	"	"	"	Mr. Gaya Prasad ...	Hindu Khatri.	Banker and Zemindar, Proprietor Cotton Ginning Factory.	do.
1575	"	"	"	Mr. Nanak Chand... ...	Hindu Vaisya.	Reis and Banker	do.
1576	"	"	"	Mr. Sheonarayan	Hindu Maheshri Bania.	Banker	do.
1577	"	"	"	Mr. Narain Singh... ...	Hindu Khatri.	Service	do.
1578	"	"	"	Mr. Gangadyal	do.	Pleader	do.
1579	"	"	"	Bhai Harnam Singh ...	Sikh.	Late Sowar 3rd Regiment Sind Horse, Book seller "Arya Samaj" Cawnpore.	do.
1580	"	"	"	Mr. Govindprasad... ...	Hindu Khatri.	Merchant and Contractor ...	do.
1581	"	"	"	Sheikh Ahmed Hussain ...	Mahomedan.	Merchant	Public Meeting, 15th December 1889.
1582	"	"	"	Mr. Hafiz Abdulahad Khan.	do.	Zemindar	do.
1583	"	"	"	Hakim Fakhral Hussain ...	do.	Physician	Public Meeting, 8th December 1889.
1584	"	"	"	Moulvi Mahomed Nabeel ...	do.	Pleader	Public Meeting, 15th December 1889.
1585	"	"	"	Mr. Pirbhu Dayal	Hindu Bhargava.	Proprietor of Shola Toor Press.	Public Meeting, 8th December 1889.
1586	"	"	"	Pandit Jankinath	Cashmire Brahmin.	Pleader and Zemindar... ...	do.
1587	"	"	"	Mr. Kali Khan	Mahomedan.	Pleader	Public Meeting, 15th December 1889.

Number.	Presidency or Government.	Congress Circle.	Electoral Division.	Names in full of Delegates, with honorary titles, scholastic degrees, etc.	Race, Religious denomination, and Caste, if any.	Occupation and Address.	How and when elected.
1588	North Western Provinces.	Allahabad.	Cawnpore.	Mr. Bansidhar	Hindu Maheshri.	Reis	Public Meeting, 8th December 1889.
1589	"	"	"	Moulvi Latapat Hussain ...	Mahomedan.	Zemindar	Public Meeting, 15th December 1889.
1590	"	"	"	Mr. Kareemdad Khan ...	do.	Service	do.
1591	"	"	"	Sheikh Karam Ilahi ...	do.	Merchant	do.
1592	"	"	"	Mr. Khurshed Bahadur ...	Hindu Kayastha.	Reis	do.
1593	"	"	"	Mr. Brij Mohan Lal ...	Hindu Khatri.	Merchant	do.
1594	"	"	"	Mr. Bhai Madho	do.	Banker, Proprietor of the Cotton Ginning Mill.	do.
1595	"	"	"	Mr. Gajadhar Pershad ...	Hindu Kavi.	Kavi	Public Meeting, 8th December 1889.
1596	"	"	"	Mr. Chandrika Prasad ...	Hindu Vaisya.	Merchant	do.
1597	"	"	"	Mr. Daulatram	Hindu Kayasth.	Pleader	do.
1598	"	"	"	Mr. Madhavchand Khanna.	Hindu Khatri.	Merchant	do.
1599	"	"	"	Mr. Hardyal	Hindu Vaisya.	Proprietor of the Firm of Shree Hardyal, Merchants.	do.
1600	"	"	"	Pandit Hirdayal Narayan...	Hindu Brahmin.	Pleader and Zemindar... ...	do.
1601	"	"	"	Mr. Ramsingh Bhargava ...	Hindu Bhargava.	Pleader and Municipal Commissioner.	do.
1602	"	"	"	Mr. Bharoo Pershad ...	Hindu Khatri.	Merchant, of the Firm of Permashree Dass.	do.
1603	"	"	"	Mr. Lalta Pershad... ...	do.	Merchant and Indigo Broker ...	do.
1604	"	"	"	Sheik Azizul Haq... ...	Mahomedan.	Service	do.
1605	"	"	"	Mr. Baichoo Lal	Khatri.	Merchant	do.
1606	"	"	"	Moulvi Ahsan Ali	Mahomedan.	Landlord	do.
1607	"	"	Farrakhabad.	Mr. Abdul Ghani	do.	Shopkeeper	Public Meeting, held at Farrakhabad on 30th November 1889.
1608	"	"	"	Mr. Bashratullah	do.	do.	do.
1609	"	"	"	Mr. Amanatullah	do.	do.	do.
1610	"	"	"	Mr. Ahmad Hussain ...	do.	do.	do.
1611	"	"	"	Mr. Abdullah	do.	do.	do.
1612	"	"	"	Mr. Abdul Karim	do.	do.	do.
1613	"	"	"	Mr. Dilawar Beg	do.	Land-owner	do.
1614	"	"	"	Mr. Amir Khan	do.	do.	do.
1615	"	"	"	Pandit Gopalrao Hari ...	Brahmin.	Secretary, Vedic Samaj ...	do.
1616	"	"	Mainpuri.	Chaube Dammilal, B.A. ...	Hindu Brahmin.	Vakil, High Court, N.-W. P., and Member, Municipal Board	Public Meeting at Mainpuri, 8th December 1889.
1617	"	"	"	Mr. Krishna Gopal Sanyal, B.A., B.L.	do.	Pleader, Vice-President, District Board.	do.
1618	"	"	"	Kumar Des Raj Singh ...	Hindu Rajput.	Zemindar, Tidoli ...	do.
1619	"	"	"	Mr. Nani Lal Banerjee	Hindu Brahmin Kashmiri.	Pleader	do.
1620	"	"	Agra.	Pandit Jagannath... ...	Brahmin.	do.	At a Public Meeting, held at Agra on 18th December 1889.
1621	"	"	"	Thakur Durjun Lal	Jat.	Pleader and Zemindar...	do.
1622	"	"	"	Thakur Zahir Sinh ...	Rajput.	Zemindar	do.
1623	"	"	"	Sheik Rahim-uddin ...	Mahomedan.	Reis, Pleader, District Court ...	do.
1624	"	"	"	Hakim Mahomed Salem Khan.	do.	Reis and Physician ...	do.

Number.	Presidency or Government.	Congress Circle.	Electoral Division.	Names in full of Delegates, with honorary titles, scholastic degrees, etc.	Race, Religious denomination, and Caste, if any.	Occupation and Address.	How and when elected.
1625	N.-W. Provinces.	Allahabad.	Agra.	Hakim Mohammed Ghaffar Khan.	Mohamedan.	Reis and Physician	At a Public Meeting held at Agra on 18th December 1889.
1626	"	"	"	Mr. Mohamed Mian Jan Khan.	do.	Bohrah and Reis	do.
1627	"	"	"	Mr. Mohamed Munir Khan.	do.	Merchant	do.
1628	"	"	"	Mr. Jamnadas Biswas ...	Hindu.	Pleader and Municipal Commissioner; Proprietor "Nasim Agra."	do.
1629	"	"	"	Mr. Muttra Das Choudry ...	Hindu Kshatriya.	Municipal Commissioner and Director of Spinning and Weaving Mills Company. Teacher and Secretary, St. John's College, Agra.	do.
1630	"	"	"	Mr. Murli Dhar	do.	Head Master, Victoria College; Municipal Commissioner.	do.
1631	"	"	"	Sheikh Rahim Baksh ...	Mahomedan.	Reis and Mukhtyar-i-am of Sett Pectam Mull.	do.
1632	"	"	"	Sheikh Fyaz-u-din	do.	Reis	do.
1633	"	"	Aligarh.	Hafiz Abdurrahim	do.	Pleader and Zemindar... ...	At a Public Meeting held on the 4th December 1889.
1634	"	"	"	Mr. Shukr Ullah Khan ...	do.	Zemindar	do.
1635	"	"	"	Sheikh Barkat Ali ...	do.	do.	do.
1636	"	"	"	Mr. Kalyan Singh ...	Hindu Rajput.	do.	do.
1637	"	"	"	Mr. Mahomed Zakharyah Khan.	Mahomedan.	Pleader and Zemindar... ...	At a Public Meeting held on the 22nd of December 1889.
1638	"	"	"	Syad Sarfraz Ali	do.	do. ...	do.
1639	"	"	"	Mr. Jagendro Nath Chatterjee.	Hindu Brahmin.	Vakil, H. C., Professor of Law, Mahomedan Anglo-Oriental College, Aligarh.	Public Meeting, 4th December 1889.
1640	"	"	"	Mr. Mahomed Sarfraz Khan.	Mahomedan.	Zemindar	do.
1641	"	"	"	Mr. Mustajab Ullah Khan..	do.	Zemindar, and Indigo Merchant.	do.
1642	"	"	Bulandshahar.	Thakur Ram Prasad Singh.	Hindu Rajput.	Pleader and Zemindar	Public Meeting.
1643	"	"	Meerut.	Mr. Prahlad Singh ...	Hindu Vaisha.	Vakil, High Court, N.-W. P., Zemindar and Municipal Commissioner.	Public Meeting at the Meerut Association Rooms, 1st December 1889.
1644	"	"	"	Mr. Choube Radhe Lal ...	Hindu Brahmin.	Pleader and Zemindar... ...	do.
1645	"	"	"	Choudhry Durga Singh ...	Hindu.	Zemindar, Asora, and Member of the District Board.	do.
1646	"	"	"	Moulvi Ahmad Hasan Shoukah.	Mahomedan.	Editor and Proprietor "Shanai Hind."	do.
1647	"	"	"	Hafiz Mahommed Qazi Ismail.	do.	Reis	do.
1648	"	"	"	Mr. Mahommed Mohsin ...	do.	Contractor and House-owner ...	Public Meeting, held on the 15th of December 1889.
1649	"	"	"	Mr. B. D. Kapur	Hindu.	Reis and Zemindar	do.
1650	"	"	"	Mr. H. C. Roy	do.	Merchant	Public Meeting, December 1st, 1889.
1651	"	"	"	Mr. M. Muzaffar Ali	Mahomedan.	Teacher	Public Meeting, on the 15th of December 1889.
1652	"	"	"	Mr. Mahomed Yaseem Khan.	do.	Zemindar	do.
1653	"	"	Muzaffarnagar.	Moulvi Fazl Ahmed	do.	Reis of Pur and Pleader ...	Special Public Meeting, December 17th, 1889.
1654	"	"	"	Pandit Indar Prasad ...	Kashmiri Brahmin.	Pleader and Reis, Delhi ...	do.
1655	"	"	"	Mr. Ackhoy Chandra Bhattacharjee.	Christian.	Pleader	do.
1656	"	"	"	Sheik Zakir Ali	Mahomedan.	Reis, Pur, and Pleader... ...	do.
1657	"	"	Saharanpur.	Munshi Nazir Husein ...	do.	Zemindar	Public Meeting, December 3rd, 1889.
1658	"	"	Dehra Dun.	Mr. Radhe Lal	Hindu Vaishya.	Zemindar, Banker, and Municipal Commissioner.	Public Meeting at the Training School, 14th December 1889.
1659	"	"	"	Pandit Anand Narayan ...	Kashmiri Brahmin Arya.	Pleader and Municipal Commissioner.	do.

Number.	Presidency or Government.	Congress Circle.	Electoral Division.	Names in full of Delegates with honorary titles, scholastic degrees, etc.	Race, Religious denomination, and Caste, if any.	Occupation and Address.	How and when elected.
1660	North-Western Provinces.	Allahabad.	Dehra Dun.	Choudri Pratap Singh ...	Rajput.	Zemindar	Public Meeting at the Training School, on 10th December 1889.
1661	"	"	"	Mr. Bhuban Mohan Bose...	Christian.	Late Head Master, Mission School; Pastor, Reformed Presbyterian Church.	do.
1662	"	"	"	Mr. Kali Kanto Sen ...	Brahmo.	Head Master, Training School, Dehra Dun.	do.
1663	"	Rohilkhund.	Bareilly.	Pandit Badri Nath Chaturvedy, M.A.	Hindu Brahmin.	Zemindar and Reis	Public Meeting held on the 6th of December 1889.
1664	"	"	"	Mr. Tirbeni Sahay ...	Hindu Kayastha.	Vakil, High Court, N. W. P. ...	do.
1665	"	"	"	Mr. Baldeo Prasad ...	do.	Pleader	do.
1666	"	"	"	Mr. Haji Lutfullah Khan...	Mahomedan.	Zemindar	do.
1667	"	"	"	Moulvi Rahat Ali... ...	do.	Merchant	do.
1668	"	"	"	Mr. Baij Nath	Hindu Vaisya.	Law Agent	Special Meeting held on the 14th December 1889.
1669	"	"	"	Mr. Choube Bihari Lal ...	Brahmin.	Physician	do.
1670	"	"	"	Pandit Daya Shanker	do.	Private Service...	do.
1671	"	"	"	Pandit Hori Lal	do.	Reis and Zemindar	do.
1672	"	"	"	Mr. M. Sadik Ali	Mahomedan.	Merchant	do.
1673	"	"	"	Hafiz Ahmad Yar Khan ...	do.	Mukhtar and Zemindar ...	do.
1674	"	"	Shahjahanpur.	Munshi Muhammad Sakhawat Husain.	do.	Pleader and Zemindar, Member, Municipal Board	Public Meeting, on the 7th December 1889.
1675	"	"	"	Malik Barkat Ullah Khan.	do.	Zemindar	do.
1676	"	"	"	Sayed Irshad Ali... ...	do.	Cazi of the City	do.
1677	"	"	"	Mirza Ahmad Ullah Beg...	do.	Zemindar	do.
1678	"	"	"	Mr. Kalka Prasada ...	Hindu Khatri.	Zemindar and Merchant ...	do.
1679	"	"	"	Mr. Bakhtawer Sing ...	Hindu Vaishya.	Editor and Proprietor "Arya Darpan."	do.
1680	"	"	"	Mr. Mohammed Muzaffar Ali Khan.	Mahomedan.	Zemindar	do.
1681	"	"	"	Mirza Mansur Ali Beg ...	do.	do.	do.
1682	"	"	"	Sayed Muhammad Ibrahim.	do.	do.	do.
1683	"	"	"	Pandit Ram Bhajan Tripathi.	Brahmin.	Zemindar and Contractor ...	do.
1684	"	"	Moradabad.	Mr. Brij Bullabh Das ...	Hindu Vaishya.	Pleader, Judge's Court... ...	Public Meeting, at Moradabad, 12th December 1889.
1685	"	"	"	Mr. Norender Chunder Bose.	Kayasth Hindu.	Pleader and Member Local Board.	do.
1686	"	"	"	Syed Wahid Ali Rizwi ...	Mahomedan.	Zemindar	do.
1687	"	"	"	Mr. Hari Das	Hindu Vaishya.	do.	do.
1688	"	"	Almora (Kumaon.)	Pandit Jwaladatta Joshi ...	Hindu Brahmin.	Vakil, High Court, N. W. P. ...	Public Meeting at Almora 15th of December 1889.
1689	"	Allahabad.	Ajmere.	Mr. K. B. Bose	Christian.	Editor "Rajputana Herald." ...	At a Public Meeting, November 30th, 1889.
1690	"	"	Bandiqui.	Mr. Fouji Singh ...	Aryan Rajput.	......	At a Public Meeting, Kankulee, Mondy, and also at a General Meeting of the Arya Samaj, 20th December 1889.
1691	"	"	do.	Mr. Dwarka Nath...	do.	......	do.
1692	"	Benares.	Benares.	Mr. Govind Narain Sing ...	Hindu Brahmin.	Zemindar, Taluqdar and Indigo Planter Municipal Commissioner.	Public Meeting on 8th December 1889.
1693	"	"	"	Mr. Jagat Narain Sing ...	do.	Zemindar, Taluqdar, Indigo Planter.	do.
1694	"	"	"	Sheikh Nasiruddin Ahmad.	Mahomedan.	Legal Practitioner	do.
1695	"	"	"	Mr. Mohamed Karim Khan	do.	Land-holder Nadesar	do.

Number.	Presidency or Government.	Congress Circle.	Electoral Division.	Names in full of Delegates with honorary titles, scholastic degrees, etc.	Race, Religious denomination, and Caste, if any.	Occupation and Address.	How and when elected.
1696	N.-W. Provinces.	Benares.	Benares.	Mr. Chunnoolal, L.M.S. ...	Hindu Brahmin.	Medical Practitioner	Public Meeting, 8th December 1889.
1697	"	"	"	Mr. Bisesar Pandya ...	do.	Service in the Native States ...	do.
1698	"	"	"	Pandit Umashankar Dubey.	do.	Landholder	do.
1699	"	"	"	Mr. Ram Narayan Vyasa...	do.	Banker	do.
1700	"	"	"	Gossain Ramcharan Puri...	Hindu.	Zemindar and Banker	do.
1701	"	"	"	Gossain Jang Bahadur Puri.	do.	do.	do.
1702	"	"	"	Mr. Upendra Nath Bose, B.A.	do.	Pleader District Court	do.
1703	"	"	"	Rana Tej Bahadur ...	Hindu Gurkha.	Jagirdar, Grandson of the Late Subadar Major Kharg Sinha Rana Sirdar Bahadur, Member of the order of Valour of 44th G. L. Infantry.	do. and by Kasi Sajan Samaj, on the 14th December 1889.
1704	"	"	"	Mr. Makshada Das Mittra...	Hindu.	Zemindar and Banker... ...	do.
1705	"	"	"	Mr. Jogendranath Ghosh, B.A.	do.	Pleader, District Court ...	do.
1706	"	"	"	Mr. Vishnu Panth Rajwade	Hindu Brahmin.	Teacher	do.
1707	"	"	"	Mr. Lukshmi Narayan Gupta.	Hindu Agarwala.	Zemindar and Banker	14th December, by Sajan Samaj.
1708	"	"	"	Mr. Vishwanath Sing ...	Hindu Brahmin.	Taluqdar	do.
1709	"	"	Mirzapur.	Mr. Sri Ram ...	Khatri Hindu (Arya).	Zemindar and Banker, and Proprietor of Hydraulic Cotton Press and Municipal Commissioner.	Public Meeting, 8th December 1889.
1710	"	"	"	Pandit Mathura Prasad Choudhry, B.A.	Hindu Brahmin.	Zemindar	do.
1711	"	"	"	Mr. Beni Prasad	Hindu Bhargava.	Honorary Magistrate, Contractor, Carpet Manufacturer and Landholder, Municipal Commissioner and Member, District Board.	do.
1712	"	"	"	Mr. Bindeshari Prasad	Hindu (Arya) Kayestha.	Pleader, Landholder and Moneylender, Municipal Commissioner, Member, District Board.	do.
1713	"	"	"	Sadh Sultan Sing... ...	Hindu Sadh.	Banker, Municipal Commissioner and Member, District Board.	do.
1714	"	"	"	Sadh Mathura Das ...	do.	Merchant	do.
1715	"	"	"	Pandit Kanahya Ram Pathak.	Hindu Brahmin.	Zemindar	do.
1716	"	"	"	Pandit Damodar Datt ...	do.	Priest	do.
1717	"	"	"	Munshi Sohan Lal ...	Hindu Kayestha.	Service	do.
1718	"	"	"	Kazi Ashghar Ali... ...	Mahomedan.	Landholder	do.
1719	"	"	"	Moulvie Abdul Aziz ...	do. Syud.	Physician	Public Meeting, 21st December 1889.
1720	"	"	"	Qazi Mahamed Farogh ...	do.	Contractor	do.
1721	"	"	"	Mr. Basdeo Sahai... ...	Hindu Kayestha.	2nd Master, C. M. School, Azamgurh.	do.
1722	"	"	"	Mr. Abdul Salam... ...	Mahomedan.	Head Master, National School.	do.
1723	"	"	"	Mr. Basdeo Narain Singh.	Hindu Brahmin.	Talukdar, Member, District Board.	do.
1724	"	"	Ghazipur.	Mr. Bholanath Ray, B.A. ...	do.	Landholder and Pleader High Court, Municipal Commissioner, Vice-Chairman, District Board.	By a General Meeting, held at Ghazipur, on the 24th November 1889.
1725	Bengal.	Behar.	Mozaffurpore.	Mr. Jagadish Kumar Mukherjee.	do.	Zemindar, Hony. Magistrate and Proprietor Mukherjee's Seminary.	At a Public Meeting, held at Mozaffurpore, on the 24th November 1889.
1726	"	"	"	Syed Ali Nawab ...	Mahomedan.	Zemindar and Banker	do.
1727	"	"	"	Mr. Shorashi Charan Mitra, B.L.	Hindu Kayestha.	Pleader and Journalist... ...	do.

Number.	Presidency or Government.	Congress Circle.	Electoral Division.	Names in full of Delegates with honorary titles, scholastic degrees, etc.	Race, Religious denomination, and Caste, if any.	Occupation and Address.	How and when elected.
1728	Bengal.	Behar.	Mozaffurpore.	Mr. Bhavacharan Mookerji, B.L.	Hindu Brahmin.	Pleader, District Court... ...	At a Public Meeting held at Mozaffurpore, on the 24th November 1889.
1729	"	"	"	Moulvi Syed Ahmed Hussain, B.A., B.L.	Mahomedan.	Pleader and Zemindar... ...	do.
1730	"	"	Bankipur.	Moulvi Basharat Hussain...	do.	Zemindar	At a Meeting held at Bankipur, on the 25th November 1889.
1731	"	"	"	Syed Ali Rashid	do.	do.	do.
1732	"	"	"	Mr. Guru Proshad Sen ...	Hindu Vaidhya.	Zemindar, Vakil, High Court, Editor "Behar Herald," and "Indian Chronicle," President, Behar People's Association, Bankipur.	do.
1733	"	"	"	Mr. Biseswar Singh ...	Hindu Rajput.	Pleader and Zemindar... ...	do.
1734	"	"	Patna.	Syed Miruddin Ahmed Balkhi.	Mahomedan.	Pleader and Zemindar, Municipal Commissioner.	At a Meeting held at Patna City, on the 1st December 1889.
1735	"	"	"	Syed Badrool Hussain ...	do.	Zemindar, Vice Chairman, Patna Local Board and Member, Patna Municipality.	do.
1736	"	"	Dinapore.	Syed Shurfuddin	do.	Barrister-at-Law, and Zemindar, Municipal Commissioner, Vice-Chairman Patna District Board, Chairman, Dinapur Local Board.	At a Meeting held at Dinapore on the 1st December 1889.
1737	"	"	"	Moulvi Abdul Hamid, B.A., B.L.	do.	Zemindar and Pleader, Chairman, Khagole Municipality, Member, Patna District Board, Vice-Chaircman, Dinapore Loal Board.	do.
1738	"	"	"	Moulvi Ali Hussain ...	do.	Zemindar	do.
1739	"	"	"	Moulvi Abdullah Fyaz ...	do.	Pleader and Zemindar, Vice-Chairman, Dinapore Municipality.	do.
1740	"	"	Durbhanga.	Moulvi Moonir Alam ...	do.	Zemindar and Mukhtar ...	At a Meeting at Dhurbhanga, on the 20th December 1889.
1741	"	"	"	Mr. Sardar Lal Sing ...	Hindu.	Zemindar	do.
1742	"	"	Shahabad.	Mr. Baijnath Singh ...	Hindu Rajput.	Zemindar, Member, Arrah Local Board.	By a Meeting at Arrah.
1743	"	"	Gya.	Dr. Mahomed Wazir Ali Khan Lodi, L.M.S., F.T.S.	Mahomedan Lodi Afghan.	Medical Practitioner, Municipal Commissioner, Secretary, Anjuman Islamiya.	Public Meeting, Gya 24th November 1889.
1744	"	"	Mokameh.	Mr. Sital Prosad Sing ...	Hindu Bhimistrar Brahmin.	Zemindar, Member, Local Board Barh, Secretary, Peoples Association, Mokameh.	At a public Meeting. held at Mokameh on 30th November 1889.
1745	"	"	Baidyanath Deoghur.	Mr. Jogindranath Bose ...	Hindu Kayestha.	Journalist	At a Public Meeting held in the Courtyard of the Baidyanath Temple, on the 23rd November 1889.
1746	"	Chotanagpur.	Hazaribagh.	Mr. Biswambhar Nath Pandit, B.A.	Hindu Kashimiri Brahmin.	Articled Clerk	Elected at a Public Meeting held at Purulia, on the 17th December 1889.
1747	"	"	"	Mr. Aukshay Kumar Gupta.	Hindu Vaidya.	Contractor, Hazaribagh ...	At a General Meeting of the Hazaribagh Association and the Residents of Hazaribagh Ichak Hibeir Suburbs, on the 8th December 1889.
1748	"	"	"	Mr. Narendra Nath Mukherjee.	Hindu Brahmin.	Landholder, Government Pleader Hazaribagh.	do.
1749	"	"	"	Mr. Rukbal Das Tah ...	Hindu.	Coal Mine Proprietor, Giridi ...	do.
1750	"	"	"	Mr. Hari Charan Mitra, M.A., B.L.	Hindu Kayestha.	Vakil, Honorary Magistrate, Municipal Commissioner, Vice-Chairman, District Committee, &c.	do.
1751	"	"	"	Mr. M. L. Mitter ...	Christian.	Hotel Proprietor and Honorary Magistrate, Hazaribagh.	do.
1752	"	Bhagulpur.	Bhagulpur.	Dr. Ladli Mohan Ghosh ...	Hindu Kayestha.	Medical Practitioner, Honorary Magistrate, Municipal Commissioner, Secretary, T. N. Jubilee College.	By Public Meeting 30th November 1889.

Number.	Presidency or Government.	Congress Circle.	Electoral Division.	Names in full of Delegates with honorary titles, scholastic degrees, etc.	Race, Religious denomination, and Caste, if any.	Occupation and Address.	How and when elected.
1753	Bengal	Bhagulpur.	Bhagulpur.	Mr. Jnanendra Chandra Bandopadhyay, B.L.	Brahmin.	Pleader, Judge's Court, Bhagalpur.	By Public Meeting, 30th November 1889.
1754	"	"	"	Mr. Tilokdheri Lal ...	Hindu Kaisa Bania.	Zemindar and Banker, Bhagalpur,	do.
1755	"	"	"	Mr. Isan Chandra Misra, M.A.	Brahmin.	Professor, T. N. Jubilee College, Bhagalpur.	do.
1756	"	"	"	Mr. Mukund Lal	Hindu.	Zemindar, Honorary Magistrate and Municipal Commissioner, Bhagalpur.	do.
1757	"	"	"	Mr. Harendra Lal Roy, B.L.	Brahmin.	Pleader, Judge's Court, Bhagalpur.	do.
1758	"	"	"	Mr. Mahipat Sing... ...	do.	Zemindar, Bhagalpur	do.
1759	"	"	"	Mr. Avinash Chunder Bose, B.L.	Hindu Kayestha.	Pleader, Bhagalpur, Judge's Court.	do.
1760	"	"	"	Mr. Rash Behary Lal Mandal.	Hindu Sudra.	Zemindar, Member, Local Board.	do.
1761	"	"	Purnea.	Mr. Jogendranath Mukherjee, M.A., B.L.	Hindu Brahmin.	Pleader, Judge's Court, Purnea.	Public Meeting, Purnea, on the 25th November 1889.
1762	"	"	"	Mr. Parbutty Charan Das, B.L.	Brahmo.	Municipal Commissioner, Member, Local Board and Pleader, Judge's Court, Purnea.	do.
1763	"	"	"	Mr. Siva Prasad	Hindu Nanackpanthi Kayestha.	Landholder and Mukhtear ...	do
1764	"	"	"	Mr. Birnaryan Roy ...	Hindu Brahmin.	Zemindar, Purnea	do.
1765	"	"	"	Mr. Cheyt Narayan Singh.	Hindu Kayestha Chitra Gupta Bansi.	Muktear and Municipal Commissioner.	do.
1766	"	Rajshahye.	Rajshahye Association.	Mr. Trailakyanath Maitra, B.L.	Hindu Brahmin.	Pleader, Rampore Beaulia ...	At a Meeting of the Association, 21st Dec. 1889.
1767	"	"	"	Mr. Chandranath Choudry, L.M.S.	Hindu.	Medical Practitioner, Beaulia and Honorary Magistrate, Rajshahye Bengal.	Do. and by Public Meeting of the Rajshahye people at Rampur Beaulia, 14th November 1889.
1768	"	"	Rungpur and Nelphamary.	Mr. Biroja Mohun Choudhury.	do.	Zemindar Kamarpukur, Rungpur, Honorary Magistrate, Independent Bench Nelphamary, Vice-Chairman, Nelphamary Local Board and Member Rungpore, District Board	By General Meeting of the Branch Indian Association of Rungpur, held on 24th November 1889 at a Meeting of Nelphamary Sanmilan Sabha, 12th December 1889.
1769	"	"	Rungpur.	Mr. Prasannanath Choudhury, L.L.	Hindu Brahmin.	Pleader, District Court, Rungpur. Vice Chairman, Rungpur Municipality.	do.
1770	"	"	"	Mr. Hem Chandra Mitra, B.L.	Hindu Kayestha.	do. ...	do.
1771	"	"	Branch Indian Association, Pabna.	Mr. Mohini Mohan Chukrayarti, M.A., B.L.	Hindu Brahmin.	Pleader, District Court, Pabna...	At a Meeting of the Pabna Branch Indian Association, on 17th Nov. 1889, at the Town Hall, Pabna.
1772	"	"	"	Mr. Prasanna Narayen Choudhury, B.A. and B.L.	do.	do. ...	do.
1773	"	Dacca.	Dacca.	Syed Karim Ullah ...	Mahomedan.	Dacca, Zemindar and Municipal Commissioner.	28th September 1889, Public Meeting, Dacca.
1774	"	"	"	Mr. Sarat Chundra Gupta.	Hindu.	Honorary Magistrate, Municipal Commissioner, Chairman, Local Board, Member, District Board, Dacca, Landholder.	do.
1775	"	"	"	Shaikh Hidayet Buksh	Mahomedan.	Talukdar and Merchant, Secy, Dacca Anjumani Islamia.	do.
1776	"	"	"	Mr. Adinath Das	Hindu.	Pleader	do.
1777	"	"	"	Mr. Satish Chundra Ghosh.	Hindu Kayestha.	Journalist, School Master ...	(1) At a Public Meeting of the People's Association, held 28th September, (2) at a Meeting of the Parjore Association, dated 20th November, & (3) at a Meeting, Hoosainpore Branch, Indian Association, Mymensing, 25th Nov. 1889.
1778	"	"	Mymensing.	Mr. Anath Bandhu Guha, B.L.	do.	Taluqdar, Pleader, Honorary Magistrate, Mymensing.	(1) Public Meeting at Mymensing 18th December, (2) Jamalpur, dated 3rd December, and (3) Tangail, dated 12th Dec. 1889.

Number.	Presidency or Government.	Congress Circle.	Electoral Division.	Names in full of Delegates with honorary titles, scholastic degrees, etc.	Race, Religious denomination, and Caste, if any.	Occupation and Address.	How and when elected.
1779	Bengal.	Dacca.	Mymensing.	Mr. Koylash Chundra Nag.	Hindu Kayestha.	Taluqdar, Vice-Chairman, Sherepore Municipality Sherepore Town, Mymensing.	(1) Mymensing Association, dated 18th December, 1889 and (2) Sherepore Landholder's Association.
1780	"	"	"	Mr. Amur Chandra Dutt...	Brahmo.	Editor, Chara Varta Town, Sherepore, Mymensing.	By the Mymensing Association, 18th Dec. 1889.
1781	"	"	..	Mr. Prasanna Kumar Basu.	do.	Talukdar, Alisakanda, Tangail, Mymensing.	At a Public Meeting of the Tangail Association, 12th December 1889.
1782	"	"	Backergunge.	Mr. Aswini Kumar Datta, M.A., B.L.	Hindu Kayestha.	Landholder and Pleader, Chairman, Burrisal Local Board, Vice-Chairman, Barrisal Municipality, Member, Backergunge District Board, Secretary, Barrisal People's Association.	(1) By a Meeting of Burrisal People's Association held on the 24th November; (2) a Public Meeting of the Residents of Backergunge held at Burrisal, on the 15th December; (3) a Meeting of the Rahamatpur People's Association, on 11th December; (4) Barapaika Subhadaini Sabha, on 9th December; (5) Hanua Hitasadhini Sabha on 7th December; (6) Siddhakathi Hitaishini Sabha on 5th December; (7) Habibpur Sammilani, on 8th December; (8) Public Meeting of the Residents of Lota, on 4th December; (9) Banaripara People's Association, on 8th December; (10) Teradarun Sammilani, on 8th December; (11) Ramchandrapur, Public Meeting, 3rd December; (12) Mahilara People's Association, 27th November; (13) Meeting of the Noakhali People's Association, on 15th December 1889.
1783	"	"	"	Mr. Harakanta Sen ...	Hindu Vaidya.	Secretary to the Barrisal Loan Office and Assistant Secretary, Barrisal People's Association.	(1) By a Public Meeting of the Residents of Backergunge, on 17th November; (2) Burrisal People's Association, on 24th November; (3) Rahamatpur People's Association, 11th December; (4) Purva Dulladi Electoral Meeting, on 1st December; (5) Maijaraddi Electoral Meeting, 30th November; (6) Lakhirdia Hitaishini Sabha, 2nd December; (7) Bakal, Public Meeting; (8) Sahaspur Hitaishini, 14th December; (9) Goila, Public Meeting, 17th Agrahaon; (10) Lota, Public Meeting, 4th December; (11) Khanjapur, Public Meeting, 2nd December; (12) Batajore, Public Meeting, 28th November; (13) Patuakhali, 8th December; (14) Dehergati, Public Meeting, 26th November; (15) Ramchandrapur, Public Meeting, 3rd December; (16) Samudaykathi, 2nd December; (17) Khalisakotha Hitasadhini, 30th November; (18) Bamrail Village Association, 2nd Dec. 1889.

Number.	Presidency or Government.	Congress Circle.	Electoral Division.	Names in full of Delegates with honorary titles, scholastic degrees, etc.	Race, Religious denomination, and Caste, if any.	Occupation and Address.	How and when elected.
1784	Bengal.	Dacca.	Backergunge.	Mr. Govra Chand Das, B.A., B.L.	Hindu.	Vakil, Barrisal	(1) By a Public Meeting of the Residents of Backergunge, held on 17th November; (2) Barisal, Public Association, on 24th November; (3) Faridpur, Public Association, 8th December; (4) Hasamdia Public Meeting, 11th December; (5) Hahipur Sanmilani Sabha, 8th December; (6) Lota Sarva Sadharan's Sabha, 4th December; (7) Kharyapur, Sadharan's Sabha, 2nd December; (8) Bavanipur Branch, P. A., 8th December; (9) Batapore, Sarvasadham Sabha, 28th November; (10) Ramchunderpur, Sarvasadhani Sabha, 3rd December; (11) Mahilarajana Sadhani Sabha, 27th November; (12) Sahashpur, Hitaisani Sabha, 14th December; (13) Bakal, Sarvashadan Sabha, 25th Kartik, 1296; (14) Lukhirda Hitaisini Sabha, 2nd December; (15) Bawpika Hundu Samprodoy, 9th Dec., 1889.
1785	„	„	Furreedpore.	Mr. Ambika Charan Muzumdar, M.A., B.L.	Hindu Vaidya.	Zemindar and Pleader, Chairman, Furreedpore Municipality, Honorary Magistrate, Member District Board.	Elected by Public Meeting, held at Fureedpore, on the 8th December; at Manikdaha, on the 2nd November; at Madaripore, on the 7th November; at Nurpoor, on the 4th December; at Amgram, on the 6th December; at Siladharcher, on the 8th December; by the Furreedpore Surhid Sabha, on the 3rd December 1889.
1786	„	Calcutta.	Tipperah People's Association.	Mr. Shib Nath Misser ...	Hindu Brahmin.	Money-lender, Commillah, Tipperah.	At a Public Meeting, held at Commillah, on 16th November, 1889.
1787	„	„	Tipperah.	Mr. Mohendra Chandra Dev, B.L.,	Hindu Baidya.	Pleader, Judge's Court, Tipperah.	By Tipperah, People's Association and Muradnagore, People's Association.
1788	„	„	Bali Sadharni Sabha (Bengal).	Mr. W. C. Bonnerjee ...	Hindu Brahmin.	Barrister-at-Law	By Bali Sadharni Sabha Meeting, 15th Dec. 1889, and at a Public Meeting, held at Albert Hall Calcutta, on the 6th Dec. 1889.
1789	„	„	British Indian Association, Calcutta.	Mr. J. Ghosal	do.	Zemindar, Merchant, Municipal Commissioner, Honorary Magistrate, Member, Government Committee of Management of Bethune Female School and College, Kasheabagun Garden House, Upper Circular Road.	Committee Meeting British Indian Association on the 21st December, 1889.
1790	„	„	„	Mr. Dwipendra Nath Tagore.	do.	Zemindar	Do. and at a Public Meeting, held at the Albert Hall, on the 6th December 1889.
1791	„	„	„	Mr. Saligram Sing, B.A., B.L.	Hindu Rajput.	Vakil, High Court, Calcutta, Zemindar, Member, British Indian Association.	At a Committee Meeting of the British Indian Association, on the 21st December 1889, and at a Meeting, at Bankipore on the 25th Nov. 1889.
1792	„	„	Northern Metropolitan Electoral Division.	Mr. J. C. Dutt, M.A., B.L....	Christian.	Pleader, 171, Manictola Street, Calcutta.	Public Meeting, held at the Albert Hall, on the 6th December 1889.

Number.	Presidency or Government.	Congress Circle.	Electoral Division.	Names in full of Delegates with honorary titles, scholastic degrees, etc.	Race, Religious denomination, and Caste, if any.	Occupation and Address.	How and when elected.
1793	Bengal.	Calcutta.	Northern Metropolitan Electoral Division.	Mr. N. C. Bose	Hindu.	Solicitor, High Court, 3, Hastings Street, Calcutta.	Public Meeting held at the Albert Hall, on the 6th December 1889.
1794	„	„	„	Mr. S. C. Biswas	Hindu Kayestha.	Barrister-at-Law, 34, Beadon Street, Calcutta.	do.
1795	„	„	„	Mr. P. N. Mitter	do.	Proprietor, Oshcroft Jute Press, Chitpore and Landholder, Oshcroft Hall, Bagbazar.	do.
1796	„	„	„	Mr. Prandhone Mitter ...	do.	10, Lower Circular Road, Calcutta.	do.
1797	„	„	„	Mr. Narendranath Sen ...	Hindu Vaidya.	Solicitor, High Court, Editor *Indian Mirror*, 24, Motts Lane.	do.
1798	„	„	„	Mr. Ganendra Narayen Dutt, B.L.	Hindu Kayestha.	Zemindar, Bachu Chatterjee's Street, Calcutta.	do.
1799	„	„	„	Mr. Amoy Nath Bose ...	do.	Landowner, 13, College Square, Calcutta.	do.
1800	„	„	„	Pandit Durga Prosad ...	Hindu Brahmin.	Landholder, Editor and Proprietor of "Uchit Bakta," 65, Cross Street, Calcutta.	do.
1801	„	„	„	Dr. Shashi Bhusan Dey, M.B.	Hindu Kayestha.	Medical Practioner, 13, College Square, Calcutta.	do.
1802	„	„	„	Mr. Girindranath Bhose ...	do.	Zemindar, 15, Shamacharan Dey's Lane, Calcutta.	do.
1803	„	„	„	Mr. Benodebehary Bose, B.A.	do.	Zemindar, 65, Bagbazar Street, Calcutta.	do.
1804	„	„	„	Mr. Jogendra Krishna Bose	do.	Service, Calcutta, 35/1 Raja Nabakissen's Street.	do.
1805	„	„	„	Mr. Radharaman Kar ...	Hindu Kayestha.	Contractor and Jute Trader, 107, Shambazar Street, Calcutta.	do.
1806	„	„	„	Mr. Upendra Kison Raichaudhuri, B.A.	Brahmo.	Zemindar, 13, Cornwallis, Street, Calcutta.	do.
1807	„	„	„	Pandit Siva Nath Sastri, M.A.	do.	Brahmo Missionary, 13, Cornwallis Street.	do.
1808	„	„	„	Dr. R. G. Kar, L.R C.P., (Edin).	Hindu Kayestha.	Medical Practitioner	do.
1809	„	„	„	Mr. Nandolal Bose ...	do.	Zemindar, 65, Bagbazar Street..	do.
1810	„	„	„	Mr. Pashupati Nath Bose...	do.	do. ...	do.
1811	„	„	„	Rai Bipin Behary Mittra ...	do.	Zemindar, 226, Upper Circular Road, Calcutta.	do.
1812	„	„	„	Mr. Baroda Kanta Mitra...	do.	Zemindar, 2/4 Rajah Naba Kissen's Street, Calcutta.	do.
1813	„	„	„	Mr. Jagadish Chunder Lahury.	Hindu Brahmin.	Medical Practitioner, 101, College Street, Calcutta.	At a Public Meeting held at the Albert Hall on 6th December 1889. By the Committee of the Indian Association, on the 15th November. At a Meeting held at Kissengunge on the 17th Dec. 1889.
1814	„	„	„	Mr. Bhupendra Nath Basu, M.A., B.L.	Hindu Kayestha.	Attorney-at-Law and Vakil, High Court, 14, Bolaram Ghoshe's Street, Calcutta.	At a Public Meeting, held at the Albert Hall, on the 6th December. At a Committee Meeting of the Indian Association on the 15th November 1889.
1815	„	„	„	Mr. Arunendra Nath Tagore.	Hindu Brahmin.	Zemindar, 6, Dwarkanath Tagore's Lane, Calcutta.	At a Public Meeting held at the Albert Hall, on the 6th December 1889; also at a Meeting, held at Pabna Town Hall, on the 17th November 1889.
1816	„	„	„	Mr. Surendra Nath Banerjee, B.A.	do.	Honorary Secretary, Indian Association, Editor Bengalee, Principal Ripon College, Honorary Presidency Magistrate, Municipal Commissioner, 33, Neogy pooker, East Lane, Calcutta.	At a Public Meeting, held at the Albert Hall on the 6th December, 1889. At a Meeting of the Committee of the Indian Association held on November 15th 1889.
1817	„	„	„	Mr. Bepin Beharee Maitra, M.B.	Hindu Brahmin.	Medical Practitioner, Address Santipore, District Nuddia, Bengal.	At a Public Meeting held at Santipur on the 14th of October 1889, and at a Public Meeting, held at the Albert Hall, on the 6th of December 1889.

Number.	Presidency or Government.	Congress Circle.	Electoral Division.	Names in full of Delegates with honorary titles, scholastic degrees, etc.	Race, Religious denomination, and Caste, if any.	Occupation and Address.	How and when elected.
1818	Bengal.	Calcutta.	Northern Metropolitan Electoral Division.	Mr. Narendra Nath Mullick.	Hindu Kayestha.	Zemindar, 92, Upper Circular Road, Calcutta.	At a General Meeting of the Committee, held at 3, Hastings Street, on the 18th December 1889.
1819	"	"	"	Mr. Gnanendra Chundra Das, M.A., B.L.	Hindu.	Vakil, High Court, Editor "Samoy" Sreenath Das's Lane, Calcutta.	do.
1820	"	"	"	Mr. Gopalchandra Mittra...	Hindu Kayestha.	Landholder, 41, Bonomali Sarkar's Street, Calcutta.	do.
1821	"	"	"	Mr. Nebaran Chandra Ghosh.	do.	Landowner, 226, Upper Circular Road, Calcutta.	do.
1822	"	"	"	Mr. Chandi Charan Sen...	do.	Landowner, 44, Ramkanti Bose's Street, Calcutta.	do.
1823	"	"	"	Mr. Nibaran Chander Dutt.	do.	Landholder, 83, Muktaram Babu's Street, Calcutta.	do.
1824	"	"	"	Mr. Jogini Mohan Chatterji, B.A.	Hindu Brahmin.	53, Masjidbaree Street... ...	do.
1825	"	"		Sir William Wedderburn, Barrister.	European Christian.	Retired Civilian...	do. and at Poona on the 15th December 1889.
1826	"	"	Calcutta Indian Association	Mr. Ananda Mohan Bose, M.A.	Brahmo.	Zemindar, Chairman, South Dum Dum, Municipality, Fellow of the Calcutta University, Barrister-at-Law, Honorary Magistrate, Fairy Hall, Dum Dum.	(1) At a Committee Meeting of the Indian Association, dated 15th November 1889; (2) Chittagong; (3) Jalpaiguri; (4) Noakhali, (5) Barrisal.
1827	"	"	"	Mr. Kali Charan Banerjee, M.A., B.L.	Bengali Christian.	Pleader, High Court, Calcutta, 81, Baranasi Ghosh's Street, Calcutta.	By Indian Association, 15th November 1889, by Northern Electoral Division, Calcutta, 6th December, 1889, by Bengal Christian Conference, 6th December 1889.
1828	"	"	"	Mr. Dwarkanath Ganguli...	Brahmo.	Assistant Secretary to the Indian Association, Calcutta Journalist.	At a Public Meeting and by the Indian Association, on the 15th Nov. 1889.
1829	"	"	"	Mr. Heramba Chandra Maitra, M.A.	Hindu Brahmin.	Professor of English Literature, City College.	By the Indian Association, on Nov. 15th 1889, and by the Northern Metropolitan Electoral Division.
1830	"	"	"	Mr. Krishnakumar Mitra, B.A.	Bengali Brahmo.	Editor Sanjibani, 4, College Square.	Indian Association and Tangail Association, on the 15th November and 12th December 1889.
1831	"	"	Bengal Ladies Association.	Mrs. D. N. Ganguli, B.A.G.M.L.B.	Brahmo.	Lady Doctor	At a Meeting by the Bengal Ladies Association.
1832	"	"	Bengal Christian Conference (Calcutta).	Mr. Khettar Mohan Das...	Christian.	Merchant, Calcutta	By Bengal Christian Conference, on 6th December 1889.
1833	"	"	Kumastoli Ghedenti Association (Calcutta).	Mr. Suruthnath Mullick ...	Hindu Kayestha.	Medical Practitioner and Manager, Co-operative Pharmacy Company, Limited, 28, Nundo Ram Sen's Street.	At a Meeting held by the Kumartoli Students Association, on the 8th December 1889.
1834	"	"	Southern Metropolitan Electoral Division.	Pundit Kaliprasanna Kavyabisharad.	Agnostic.	Journalist, Proprietor, Secular Press, Bhowanipore, &c., &c., 69 & 70, Baloram Bose's Ghat Road, Bhowanipore, Calcutta.	Elected at a Public Meeting held at Bhowanipore, on the 7th December 1889.
1835	"	"	"	Rev. Mr. Thomas Evans...	Christian European.	Missionary	do.
1836	"	"	"	Mr. Benode Lal Sen. ...	Hindu Vaidya.	Kabiraj, 146, Lower Chitpore Road.	At a Public Meeting held at the London Missionary Institute on the 7th December 1889.
1837	"	"	"	Mr. Behari Lal Bose ...	Hindu Kayestha.	Zemindar and Merchant, 56, Puddopooker Street, Bhowanipore, Calcutta.	do.
1838	"	"	"	Mr. Mohendra Nath Sen...	do.	Zemindar, Vice Chairman, South Suburban Municipality, Russapagla, Via Tally Gange, P. O., Calcutta.	At a Meeting held at the London Missionary Institution, dated 7th December. Russapagla Improvement Association, dated 8th December 1889.
1839	"	"	Nehadhia Peoples Association (24 Parganas)	Mr. Nilratan Banerji ...	Hindu Brahmin.	Zemindar Nehadhia	At a Public Meeting held at Nehadhia, on 14th December 1889.

Number.	Presidency or Government.	Congress Circle.	Electoral Division.	Names in full of Delegates with honorary titles, scholastic degrees, etc.	Race, Religious denomination, and Caste, if any.	Occupation and Address.	How and when elected.
1840	Bengal.	Calcutta.	Rohora Branch Indian Association.	Mr. Kalidas Chowdhry, B.A.	Hindu Brahmin.	Pleader and Malguzar, Hoshangabad, Member, District Council, Vakil, High Court, North Western Provinces.	Elected by Branch Indian Association, Rohora, on 15th December 1889; and by a General Meeting at Hoshungabad, on 10th November 1889.
1841	"	"	Barahanagar, (24 Parganas.)	Mr. Haridas Mookerjee ...	do.	Zemindar, Barahanagar, North Suburbs of Calcutta.	At a Public Meeting held at Barahanagar, on the 29th September 1889.
1842	"	"	"	Mr. Mohit Chunder Bose, M.A., B.L.	Hindu Kayestha.	Vakil, High Court, and Taluqdar.	do.
1843	"	"	Howrah.	Mr. Hari Mohun Mukerjee..	Hindu Brahmin.	Pleader	Elected on the 9th of November 1889 at a Public Meeting, held at the Howrah Town Hall.
1844	"	"	"	Mr. Upendra Chandra Mitra, B.L.	Hindu Kayastha.	Vakil, High Court, Calcutta, Notary Public, Howrah, Municipal Commissioner and Honorary Magistrate, Howrah.	Elected on the 9th of November 1889, at a Public Meeting held at Howrah Town Hall as well as by the Howrah People's Association.
1845	"	"	"	Mr. Akshoy Charan Das, B.L.	Hindu Kaibutta.	First Grade Pleader	do.
1846	"	"	"	Mr. Nara Sinha Dutta, B.L.	Hindu Sabarna Bania.	Vakil, High Court, Notary Public, Howrah, Honorary Magistrate, Municipal Commissioner, Howrah.	do.
1847	"	"	Chinsurah (Hooghly District.)	Mr. Hem Chandra Rai. M.A., B.L.	Hindu Vaidya.	Pleader, Judge's Court, Alipore, 12, Nebutala, Bowbazar, Calcutta.	Public Meeting held at Ranaghat on December 1st, 1889, at Chinsurah on the 24th August 1889, and at Manikgung, October 6th, 1889.
1848	"	"	"	Mr. Bishnupada Chatterjee M.A., B.L.	Hindu Brahmin.	Pleader, Judge's Court, Hooghly, Municipal Commissioner and Chinsurah Municipality.	Elected by a Public Meeting, held at Chinsurah on 15th September 1889.
1849	"	"	"	Mr. Kesava Chandra Sadhu	Hindu.	Merchant	do.
1850	"	"	"	Mr. Shil Chandra Seal ...	do.	Banker	do.
1851	"	"	Chogdah (Nuddea).	Mr. Akshay Kumar Mitra.	Hindu Kayestha.	Talukdar, Chogdah Municipal Commissioner.	(1) At a Public Meeting held at Chogdah, on the 27th November; (2) do. Ranaghat, on the 1st December; and (3) at a Meeting of the Jessore Indian Association, held on the 24th November 1889.
1852	"	"	"	Mr. Karuna Nidhan Ghosh.	do.	Contractor, Ranaghat	At a Public Meeting held at Chogdah, on the 27th November 1889.
1853	"	"	Krishnagore (Nuddea.)	Mr. Nuffer Chunder Pal Chowdhry.	Hindu.	Zemindar, Indigo Planter, Tea Planter, Mahajan, Member of District and Local Board, Kishnaghore, Member of Indian Association, Calcutta, Hon. Magistrate.	Elected at a Public Meeting at Kishnaghore on the 10th November 1889.
1854	"	"	Nuddea.	Mr. Ratikanta Bose ...	Hindu Kayestha.	Zemindar, Poradah, P. O., E. B. S. R.	Katdah Association, dated 23rd November 1889.
1855	"	"	"	Dr. Atar Alli... ...	Mahomedan.	Medical Practitioner and Zeminder, Chuadangah, Nuddea.	Elected by a Public Meeting held at Krishenghur, on the 10th November 1889.
1856	"	"	"	Biswambhar Ray, B.L.,	Hindu Kayestha.	Pleader, District Court, Nuddea, Krishenghur, Bengal. Member, District Board, Nuddea, Chairman, Local Board, Kooshtia.	do

Number.	Presidency or Government.	Congress Circle.	Electoral Division.	Names in full of Delegates with honorary titles, scholastic degrees, etc.	Race, Religious denomination, and Caste, if any.	Occupation and Address.	How and when elected.
1857	Bengal.	Calcutta.	Nuddea.	Mr. Sabdar Ali	Mahomedan.	Pleader and Zemindar. Chuadangah (Nuddea)	Elected by a Public Meeting held at Krishnagore, on the 10th November 1889.
1858	"	"	"	Mr. Basanta Kumar Chatterjee, B.L.	Hindu.	Pleader, Judge's Court, and Member, District Board, Nuddea.	do.
1859	"	"	"	Mr. Judunath Chatturgy, B.A., B.L.	Hindu Brahmin.	Zemindar, Pleader, Krishnagore.	do.
1860	"	"	"	Mr. Nalinaskhya Dutta.	Hindu.	Zemindar, Member of Local Board, Krishnaghur.	do.
1861	"	"	"	Mr. Nanda Gopal Bhaduri.	Hindu Brahmin.	Merchant, Majdia, Kessengunge, Bengal.	Public Meeting held at Krishnagore, dated 10th November, and Meeting held at Kessengunge, on the 17th December 1889.
1862	"	"	Ranaghat (Nuddea.)	Mr. Banka Behari Singha.	Hindu Tamli.	Merchant, Honorary Magistrate, Member of the District Board, Krishnaghore, and Vice-Chairman of the Local Board.	Ranaghat, Public Meeting held on 1st December, Krishnaghore, 10th November, Majdia, Kessengunge, 17th December 1889.
1863	"	"	"	Mr. Bacharan Ghatak ...	Hindu Brahmin.	Merchant and Broker, Ranaghat.	Ranaghat, Public Meeting held on 1st December 1889.
1864	"	"	Kushtia (Nuddea).	Mr. Puna Chandra Ray,	do.	Talukdar, Kushtia, Vice-Chairman, Kushtea Local Board.	At a Public Meeting of the inhabitants of Kushtea Sub-division, held on the 23rd November 1889.
1865	"	"	Hitkari Sabha Koya Kushtia (Nuddea).	Mr. Brojo Nath Rakhit ...	Hindu.	Merchant, Kissengunge ...	At Koya, Meeting held on 10th November 1889.
1866	"	"	Narail, (Jessore District.)	Mr. Kali Shankar Sukul, M.A.	Brahmo.	Principal, Victoria College, Narail.	At a Public Meeting held in Narail, on the 8th of December 1889.
1867	"	"	Jessore Indian Association.	Babu Motilal Ghosh ...	Hindu Kayestha.	Editor "Amrita Bazar Patrika." Member, District Board.	At a Meeting of Jessore Indian Association, held on the 15th December 1889, and at a Meeting held at the Albert Hall, Calcutta, on the 6th December 1889.
1868	"	"	Branch Indian Association, Magurah, (Jessore.)	Mr. Ambica Charan, Sarkar.	Hindu.	Landholder, Magurah, Vice-Chairman, Local Board, Magurah, Member, District Board, Jessore, Honorary Magistrate.	26th November 1889, Magurah Branch Indian Association.
1869	"	"	"	Mr. Basantu Cumar Bose.	Hindu Kayestha.	Pleader, Magurah	do.
1870	"	"	Moorshidabad.	Mr. Mrityunjay Bhattacharya, C.E.	Hindu Brahmin.	Engineer in Private Service, Saidabad Khagra P. O., Bengal.	At a Public Meeting of the Moorshidabad Association, held on the 30th November 1889 at Berhampore.
1871	"	"		Mr. Hemendra Nath Sen, B.L.	Hindu Baidya.	Pleader, Berhampore, Bengal...	do.
1872	"	"	"	Mr. Aughore Nath Sen ...	do.	Private Service Saidabad, Khagra P. O., Bengal.	do.
1873	"	"	"	Mr. Baikunth Nath Sen, B.L.	do.	Vakil, Berhampore, Chairman, Berhampore Municipality, President, Murshedabad Association, Bengal.	do.
1874	"	"	"	Mr. Sri Nath Pal, B.L. ...	Hindu Tili.	Honorary Magistrate	do.
1875	"	"	"	Rev. Mr. C. N. Banerjee, B.A.	Bengali Christian.	Missionary, Berhampore, Municipal Commissioner.	do. and also by the Bengal Christian Conference, at Calcutta on 6th December 1889.

Number.	Presidency or Government.	Congress Circle.	Electoral Division.	Names in full of Delegates with honorary titles, scholastic degrees, etc.	Race, Religious denomination, and Caste, if any.	Occupation and Address.	How and when elected.
1876	Bengal.	Calcutta.	Midnapur.	Mr. Trailokya Nath Pal ...	Hindu Satgope.	Pleader, Sangat Bazar, and Member of the Sudder Local Board.	Meeting of the Midnapur Public, 19th November 1889.
1877	„	„	„	Mr. Jyotindra Nath Mullick.	Hindu Tamli.	Zemindar, Shib Bazar, Midnapore.	do.
1878	„	„	„	Mr. Jogendra Chunder Roy.	Hindu Brahmin.	Zemindar and Pleader, Judge's Court, Midnapore.	do.
1879	„	„	„	Mr. Saroda Persad Chatterjee.	do.	Pleader, Judge's Court, Midnapore.	do.
1880	„	„	Tumluk (Midnapur)	Mr. Doorgaram Bose, B.L.	Hindu Kayestha.	Pleader at Tamluk, Vakil High Court, Municipal Commissioner.	Elected on the 24th November 1889, by a Meeting of the people of Tumluk.
1881	„	„	„	Mr. Raghunath Das, M.A., B.L.	Hindu Karan.	Vakil, Vice-Chairman, Midnapore Municipality, Vice-Chairman, Sudder Local Board, and Member of District Board, Midnapore, Colonelgola, Midnapore.	(1) 19th November 1889, at a Public Meeting held at Midnapur; and (2) 24th November 1889, by the Tumluk Indian Association.
1882	„	„	Ghattal, (Midnapur)	Mr. Deno Nath Gui ...	Hindu Tantee.	Merchant	Elected on the 14th of December 1889, by a Public Meeting held at Ghatal.
1883	„	„	Cutwa (Burdwan).	Mr. Brajendra Nath Sen, L.M. & S.	Hindu Baidya.	Medical Practitioner, Cutwa, District Burdwan, Chairman, Cutwa Local Board, Honorary Magistrate, 2nd Class.	At a Public Meeting held at Cutwa, on the 19th December 1889.
1884	„	„	Burdwan.	Mr. Sarat Chandra Basu, B.L.	Hindu Kayestha.	Pleader, District Court, Burdwan.	Elected by the Burdwan Association, at a Meeting held in the Burdwan Municipal School.
1885	„	„	Khulna.	Mr. Ambica Charan Sen, B.L.	Hindu Vaidya.	Pleader, Land holder, Khulna, Member, District Board, Chairman, Local Board, Municipal Commissioner, Khulna.	(1) By a Public Meeting of the Khulna People's Association, on the 16th November; (2) at a Meeting of the Senhat People's Association, on the 1st December; and (3) at a Meeting of the Bagirhat People's Association, on the 10th December 1889.
1886	„	„	Dibrugarh.	Mr. Haridas Roy	Hindu.	Cultivator, Dibrugarh, late Agent, I. M. Railway.	Public Meeting ... ...
1887	„	„	Sylhet.	Mr. Jay Govind Shome, M.A., B.L.	Christian.	Vakil, High Court, and Editor "Indian Christian Herald."	Public Meeting, Sylhet, and India Association and Bengali Christian Conference, on 15th and 16th December 1889.
1888	„	„	Shillong.	Mr. Bipin Chundra Pal ...	Brahmo.	Journalist and Landholder ...	At a Public Meeting held at Sylhet and Shillong, on the 28th December 1889.
1889	„	„	Northern Metropolitan.	Pandit Prannath	Hindu.	H. C. Pleader, Municipal Commissioner, Honorary Magistrate.	Public Meeting, Albert Hall, 6th December 1889.

(NOTE.—As a matter of fact over 1,900 delegates were present—but of some 24 delegates who took tickets and paid their fees, the rolls and certificates are not forthcoming—as some 2,500 delegates were elected, it is hopeless to attempt to discover, now, in time for insertion in this report, which particular 24 out of the 600 or so Gentlemen, who, tho' elected, do not seem to have attended, really *did* attend.)

(In the above List, the very same names will be found spelt in different ways. This is because people, in spelling their names, adopt different systems of transliteration from the various vernaculars into English. We have, in all cases, followed the spelling adopted in the Nomination Rolls, filed by the Delegates, themselves.)

APPENDIX II.

SUMMARY OF RESOLUTIONS

PASSED AT THE

FIRST, SECOND, THIRD & FOURTH CONGRESSES.

RESOLUTIONS PASSED AT THE FIRST CONGRESS.

RESOLUTION I.

Resolved—That this Congress earnestly recommends that the promised inquiry into the working of the Indian Administration, here and in England, should be entrusted to a Royal Commission, the people of India being adequately represented thereon, and evidence taken both in India and in England.

RESOLUTION II.

Resolved—That this Congress considers the abolition of the Council of the Secretary of State for India, as at present constituted, the necessary preliminary to all other reforms.

RESOLUTION III.

Resolved—That this Congress considers the reform and expansion of the Supreme and existing Local Legislative Councils, by the admission of a considerable proportion of elected members (and the creation of similar Councils for the North-Western Provinces and Oudh, and also for the Punjab) essential; and holds that all Budgets should be referred to these Councils for consideration, their members being moreover empowered to interpellate the Executive in regard to all branches of the administration; and that a Standing Committee of the House of Commons should be constituted to receive and consider any formal protests that may be recorded by majorities of such Councils against the exercise by the Executive of the power, which would be vested in it, of overruling the decisions of such majorities.

RESOLUTION IV.

Resolved—That in the opinion of this Congress the competitive examinations now held in England, for first appointments in various civil departments of the public service, should henceforth, in accordance with the views of the India Office Committee of 1860, "be held simultaneously, one in England and one in India, both being as far as practicable identical in their nature, and those who compete in both countries being finally classified in one list according to merit," and that the successful candidates in India should be sent to England for further study, and subjected there to such further examinations as may seem needful. Further, that all other first appointments (excluding peonships, and the like) should be filled by competitive examinations held in India, under conditions calculated to secure such intellectual, moral, and physical qualifications as may be decided by Government to be necessary. Lastly, that the maximum age of candidates for entrance into the Covenanted Civil Service be raised to not less than 23 years.

RESOLUTION V.

Resolved—That in the opinion of this Congress the proposed increase in the military expenditure of the empire is unnecessary, and, regard being had to the revenues of the empire and the existing circumstances of the country, excessive.

RESOLUTION VI.

Resolved—That in the opinion of this Congress, if the increased demands for military expenditure are not to be, as they ought to be, met by retrenchment, they ought to be met, firstly, by the re-imposition of the Customs duties; and, secondly, by the extension of the license-tax to those classes of the community, official and non-official, at present exempted from it, care being taken that in the case of all classes a sufficiently high taxable minimum be maintained. And, further, that this Congress is of opinion that Great Britain should extend an imperial guarantee to the Indian debt.

RESOLUTION VII.

Resolved—That this Congress deprecates the annexation of Upper Burmah, and considers that if the Government unfortunately decide on annexation, the entire country of Burmah should be separated from the Indian Viceroyalty and constituted a Crown Colony, as distinct in all matters from the Government of the country as is Ceylon.

RESOLUTION VIII.

Resolved—That the resolutions passed by this Congress be communicated to the Political Associations in each province, and that these Associations be requested, with the help of similar bodies and other agencies within their respective provinces, to adopt such measures as they may consider calculated to advance the settlement of the various questions dealt with in these resolutions.

RESOLUTION IX.

Resolved—That the Indian National Congress re-assemble next year in Calcutta and sit on Tuesday, the 28th of December, 1886, and the next succeeding days.

RESOLUTIONS PASSED AT THE SECOND CONGRESS.

RESOLUTION I.

Resolved—That this Congress of delegates from all parts of India, do humbly offer its dutiful and loyal congratulations to Her Most Gracious Majesty, the Queen-Empress, on the approaching completion of the first half century of her memorable, beneficent and glorious reign, and heartily wish her many, many more, and happy years of rule, over the great British Empire.

RESOLUTION II.

Resolved—That this Congress regards with the deepest sympathy, and views with grave apprehension, the increasing poverty of vast numbers of the population of India, and (although aware that the Government is not overlooking this matter and is contemplating certain palliatives) desires to record its fixed conviction that the introduction of Representative Institutions will prove one of the most important practical steps towards the amelioration of the condition of the people.

RESOLUTION III.

Resolved—That this Congress do, emphatically, re-affirm the 3rd Resolution of the Congress of 1885, and distinctly declare its belief that the reform and expansion of the Council of the Governor-General for making Laws and of the Provincial Legislative Councils, therein suggested, have now become essential alike in the interests of India and England.

RESOLUTION IV.

Resolved—That this Congress is of opinion that in giving practical effect to this essential reform, regard should be had (subject to such modifications as, on a more detailed examination of the question, may commend themselves to the Government) to the principles embodied in the following tentative suggestions :—

(1.)—The number of persons composing the Legislative Councils, both Provincial and of the Governor-General, to be materially increased. Not less than one-half the Members of such enlarged Councils to be elected. Not more than one-fourth to be officials having seats *ex-officio* in such Councils, and not more than one-fourth to be Members, official or non-official, nominated by Government.

(2.)—The right to elect Members to the Provincial Councils to be conferred only on those classes and members of the community, *primâ facie*, capable of exercising it wisely and independently. In Bengal and Bombay the Councillors may be elected by the Members of Municipalities, District Boards, Chambers of Commerce and the Universities, or an electorate may be constituted of all persons possessing such qualifications, educational and pecuniary, as may be deemed necessary. In Madras, the Councillors may be elected either by District Boards, Municipalities, Chambers of Commerce and the University, or by Electoral Colleges composed of Members partly elected by these bodies and partly nominated by Government. In the North-West Provinces and Oudh and in the Punjab, Councillors may be elected by an Electoral College composed of Members elected by Municipal and District Boards, and nominated, to an extent not exceeding one-sixth of the total number, by Government, it being understood that the same elective system now in force where Municipal Boards are concerned will be applied to District Boards, and the right of electing Members to these latter extended to the cultivating class. But whatever system be adopted (and the details must be worked out separately for each province) care must be taken that all sections of the community, and all great interests, are adequately represented.

(3.)—The elected Members of the Council of the Governor-General for making Laws, to be elected by the elected Members of the several Provincial Councils.

(4.)—No elected or nominated Member of any Council to receive any salary or remuneration in virtue of such Membership, but any such Member, already in receipt of any Government salary or allowance, to continue to draw the same unchanged during Membership, and all Members to be entitled to be reimbursed any expenses incurred in travelling in connection with their Membership.

(5.)—All persons, resident in India, to be eligible for seats in Council, whether as electees or nominees, without distinction of race, creed, caste or colour.

(6.)—All legislative measures and all financial questions, including all budgets, whether these involve new or enhanced taxation or not, to be necessarily submitted to and dealt with by these Councils. In the case of all other branches of the administration, any Member to be at liberty, after due notice, to put any question he sees fit to the *ex-officio* Members (or such one of these as may be specially charged with the supervision of the particular branch concerned) and to be entitled (except as hereinafter provided) to receive a reply to his question, together with copies of any papers requisite for the thorough comprehension of the subject, and on this reply the Council to be at liberty to consider and discuss the question, and record thereon such resolution as may appear fitting to the majority. Provided that, if the subject in regard to which the inquiry is made involves matters of Foreign policy, Military dispositions or strategy, or is otherwise of such a nature that, in the opinion of the Executive, the Public interests would be materially imperilled by the communication of the information asked for, it shall be competent for them to instruct the *ex-officio* Members, or one of them, to reply accordingly, and decline to furnish the information asked for.

(7.)—The Executive Government shall possess the power of overruling the decision arrived at by the majority of the Council, in every case in which, in its opinion, the public interests would suffer by the acceptance of such decision ; but whenever this power is exercised a full exposition of the grounds on which this has been considered necessary, shall be published within one month, and in the case of local Governments they shall report the circumstances and explain their action to the Government of India, and in the case of this latter, it shall report and explain to the Secretary of State ; and in any such case on a representation made through the Government of India and the Secretary of State by the overruled majority, it shall be competent to the Standing Committee of the House of Commons (recommended in the 3rd Resolution of last year's Congress which this present Congress has affirmed) to consider the matter, and call for any and all papers or information, and hear any persons on behalf of such majority or otherwise, and thereafter, if needful, report thereon to the full House.

RESOLUTION V.

Resolved—That this Congress do invite all Public Bodies and all Associations throughout the Country, humbly and earnestly, to entreat His Excellency the Viceroy to obtain the sanction of Her Majesty's Secretary of State for India, to the appointment of a Commission, to enquire exhaustively into the best method of introducing such a tentative form of Representative Institutions into India, as has been indicated in Resolutions III. of the past, and IV. of the present year's Congress.

RESOLUTION VI.

Resolved—That a Committee composed of the gentlemen named in the margin* be appointed to consider the Public Service Question and report thereon to this Congress.

*Hon'ble Dadabhai Naoroji *(Bombay)*.
" S. Subramania Iyer *(Madras)*.
" Peary Mohun Mookerjee *(Calcutta)*.
Mr. G. Subramania Iyer *(Madras)*.
Babu Motilal Ghose *(Calcutta)*.
Mr. Surendra Nath Banerjee *(Calcutta)*.
" Gungapershad Varma *(Lucknow)*.
" Ramkali Chaudhuri *(Benares)*.
Mr. Guru Prasad Sen *(Patna)*.
Pundit Prannath *(Lucknow)*.
Munshi Kashipershad *(Allahabad)*.
Nawab Reza Ali Khan *(Lucknow)*.
Mr. Hamid Ali *(Lucknow)*.
Lala Kanhyalal *(Amritsar)*.
Rao Sahib Gungadhar Rao Madhaw Chitnavis *(Nagpur)*.
Mr. Rahimatulla M. Sayani *(Bombay)*.

RESOLUTION VII.

Resolved—That this Congress approves and adopts the report* submitted by the Committee appointed by Resolution VI.

---

* REPORT.

We, the Members of the Committee appointed by the Congress to submit a statement in connection with the Public Service Question, have the honor to report that the following resolutions were unanimously adopted by us at a meeting held yesterday:—

1.—That the open Competitive Examination be held simultaneously both in India and in England.

2.—That the simultaneous examinations thus held be equally open to all classes of Her Majesty's subjects.

3.—That the classified lists be prepared according to merit.

4.—That the Congress express the hope that the Civil Service Commissioners will give fair consideration to Sanskrit and Arabic among the subjects of examination.

5.—That the age of candidates eligible for admission to the open Competitive Examination be not less than 19, nor, as recommended by Sir C. Aitchison, more than 23 years.

6.—That simultaneous examinations being granted, the Statutory Civil Service be closed for first appointments.

7.—That the appointments in the Statutory Civil Service, under the existing rules, be still left open to the Members of the Uncovenanted Service and to professional men of proved merit and ability.

8.—That all appointments requiring educational qualifications, other than covenanted first appointments, be filled by Competitive examinations held in the different Provinces, and open in each Province to such natural-born subjects of H. M. only as are residents thereof.

These Resolutions, it is hoped, cover the main principles which underlie the questions set by the Public Service Commission. For a more detailed consideration there was no time.

(Sd.) DADABHAI NAOROJI,
President of the Committee.

30th *December*, 1886.

RESOLUTION VIII

Resolved—That, in the opinion of this Congress, the time has now arrived when the system of trial by jury, may be safely extended into many parts of the country where it is not at present in force.

RESOLUTION IX.

Resolved—That, in the opinion of this Congress, the innovation made in 1872 in the system of trial by jury, depriving the verdicts of juries of all finality, has proved injurious to the country, and that the powers then, for the first time, vested in Sessions Judges and High Courts, of setting aside verdicts of acquittal, should be at once withdrawn.

RESOLUTION X.

Resolved—That, in the opinion of this Congress, a provision, similar to that contained in the Summary Jurisdiction Act of England (under which accused persons in serious cases have the option of demanding a committal to the Sessions Court), should be introduced into the Indian Code of Criminal Procedure, enabling accused persons, in warrant cases, to demand that, instead of being tried by the Magistrate, they be committed to the Court of Sessions.

RESOLUTION XI.

Resolved—That this Congress do place on record an expression of the universal conviction, that a complete separation of executive and judicial functions (such that in no case the two functions shall be combined in the same officer) has become an urgent necessity, and that, in its opinion, it behoves the Government to effect this separation without further delay, even though this should, in some Provinces, involve some extra expenditure.

RESOLUTION XII.

Resolved—That in view of the unsettled state of public affairs in Europe, and the immense assistance that the people of this country, if duly prepared there for, is capable of rendering to Great Britain in the event of any serious complications arising, this Congress do earnestly appeal to the Government to authorise (under such rules and restrictions, as may to it seem fitting) a system of Volunteering for the Indian inhabitants of the country, such as may qualify them to support the Government, effectively, in any crisis.

RESOLUTION XIII.

Resolved—That Standing Congress-Committees be constituted at all important centres.

RESOLUTION XIV.

Resolved—That the third Indian National Congress assemble at Madras on the 27th of December, 1887.

RESOLUTION XV.

Resolved—That copies of these Resolutions be forwarded to His Excellency the Viceroy in Council, with the humble requests, that he will cause the 1st Resolution to be submitted in due course to Her Majesty the Queen-Empress, that he will cause all the Resolutions to be laid before Her Majesty's Secretary of State for India, and that he himself will be graciously pleased, in consultation with his colleagues, to accord them his best consideration.

RESOLUTIONS PASSED AT THE THIRD CONGRESS.

RESOLUTION I.

Resolved—That a Committee is appointed, consisting of the gentlemen (marginally enumerated*), to consider what rules, if any, may-now be usefully framed in regard to the constitution and working of the Congress, with instructions to report thereon to the Congress, on the 30th instant.

* Messrs. Namjoshi, Chandavarkar, Mir Humayun Jah Bahadur, Hajee Mahomed Abdul Shakoor Badshaw Sahib, S. Subramania Iyer, W. S. Gantz, Rangiah Naidu, Surendranath Bannerjee, Trailokhyanath Mitra, Kali Charan Bannerjee, Guru Prasad Sen, Saligram Singh, Ram Kali Chaudhuri, Hafiz Abdul Rahim, Rampal Singh, Pandit Madan Mohun, Ganga Prasad Varma, Bishan Narayen Dar, Hamid Ali. Murlidhur, Satyanand Agnihotri, H. H. Dhrnva, W. C. Bonnerjee, Norendranath Sen, Eardley Norton, Joy Govind Shome, Iswari Lal Sircar, G. Subramania Iyer, D. A. Khare, S. A. Saminada Iyer, Sabapathy Mudaliar, A. O. Hume, C. Vigiya Raghava Chariar, Govind Buksh, Karardikar.

RESOLUTION II.

Resolved—That this Congress re-affirms the necessity for the expansion and reform of the Council of the Governor-General for making Laws, and the Provincial Legislative Councils, already set forth in Resolutions III. of the Congress of 1885 and 1886, and expresses the earnest hope that the Government will no longer delay action in the direction of this essential reform.

RESOLUTION III.

Resolved—That this Congress once again places on record an expression of the universal conviction, that a complete separation of the Executive and Judicial functions (such that in no case the two functions shall be combined in the same officer) has become an urgent necessity, and declares that, in its opinion, it behoves the Government to effect this separation, without further delay, even though this should, in some provinces, involve some extra expenditure.

RESOLUTION IV.

Resolved—That in view of the loyalty of Her Majesty's Indian subjects, this Congress considers it desirable that the Queen's proclamation should be given effect to; that the Military Service in its higher grades should be practically opened to the natives of this country; and that the Government of India should establish Military Colleges in this country, whereat the natives of India, as defined by Statute, may be educated and trained for a military career as officers of the Indian Army.

RESOLUTION V.

Resolved—That in view of the unsettled state of public affairs in Europe, and the immense assistance that the people of this country, if duly prepared there for, are capable of rendering to Great Britain in the event of any serious complications arising, this Congress once again earnestly appeals to the Government to authorize (under such rules and restrictions as may to it seem fitting,) a system of volunteering for the Indian inhabitants of the country, such as may qualify them to support the Government, effectively, in any crises.

RESOLUTION VI.

Resolved—That as the administration of the Income-Tax, especially, as regards incomes below Rs. 1,000, has proved extremely unsatisfactory, it is essential, in the opinion of the Congress, that the taxable minimum be raised to Rs. 1,000, the loss of revenue thus involved, being made good, and further financial difficulties, if any, met, by reductions in the existing public expenditure, or, should this prove impossible, by the re-imposition of an import duty on the finer classes of cotton goods.

RESOLUTION VII.

Resolved—That having regard to the poverty of the people, it is desirable that the Government be moved to elaborate a system of Technical Education, suitable to the condition of the country, to encourage indigenous manufactures by a more strict observance of the orders, already existing, in regard to utilizing such manufactures for State purposes, and to employ more extensively, than at present, the skill and talents of the people of the country.

RESOLUTION VIII.

Resolved—That in view of the loyalty of the people, the hardships which the present Arms' Act (XI. of 1878) causes, and the unmerited slur which it casts upon the people of this country, the Government be moved so to modify the provisions of Chapter IV. and if necessary, other portions of the said Act, as shall enable all persons to possess and wear arms, unless debarred therefrom, either as individuals or members of particular communities or classes, by the orders of the Government of India (or any local authority empowered by the Government of India on that behalf), for reasons to be recorded in writing and duly published.

RESOLUTION IX.

Resolved—That the rules drafted by the Committee appointed under Resolution I., stand over for consideration till next Congress, but that, in the meantime, copies be circulated to all Standing Congress Committees, with the request that they will, during the coming year, act in accordance with these rules, so far as this may seem to them possible and desirable, and report thereon to the next Congress, with such further suggestions as to them may seem meet.

RESOLUTION X.

Resolved—That the Fourth Indian National Congress assemble at Allahabad on the 26th December, 1888.

RESOLUTION XI.

Resolved—That copies of these Resolutions be forwarded to His Excellency the Viceroy-in-Council, with the humble request that he will cause all the Resolutions to be laid before Her Majesty's Secretary of State for India, and that he himself will be graciously pleased, in consultation with his colleagues, to accord them his best consideration.

RESOLUTIONS PASSED AT THE FOURTH CONGRESS.

RESOLUTION I.

Resolved—That this Congress affirms the necessity for the expansion and reform of the Council of the Governor-General for making laws and regulations, and of the existing Provincial Legislative Councils, already set forth in Resolutions III. of the Congress of 1885 and 1886, and Resolution II. of the Congress of 1887 (a tentative scheme for which expansion and reform was suggested in Resolution IV. of the Congress of 1886); and further urges that a Legislative Council (of the same character as those which have been suggested for Provinces where Legislative Councils already exist) be established for the Punjab.

RESOLUTION II.

Resolved—That this Congress, while appreciating the concessions proposed in the Report of the Public Service Commission, yet feels it necessary to put distinctly on record its opinion that full justice will never be done to the people of this country until the open competitive examination for the Civil Service of India is held simultaneously in England and in India.

RESOLUTION III.

Resolved—That this Congress, having read and considered Resolution XI. of the Congress of 1886, to wit—

> " That this Congress do place on record an expression of the universal conviction that a complete separation " of executive and judicial functions (such that in no case the two functions shall be combined in the " same officer) has become an urgent necessity ; and that, in its opinion, it behoves the Government " to effect this separation without further delay, even though this should, in some provinces, involve " some extra expenditure "—

and Resolution III. of the Congress of 1887, to the same effect, does now, hereby, affirm the same respectively.

RESOLUTION IV

Resolved—That this Congress, having read and considered Resolution VIII. of the Congress of 1886, to wit—

"That, in the opinion of this Congress, the time has now arrived when the system of trial by jury may "be safely extended into many parts of the country where it is not at present in force"—

Resolution IX. of the Congress of 1886, to wit—

"That, in the opinion of this Congress, the innovation made in 1872 in the system of trial by jury, "depriving the verdicts of juries of all finality, has proved injurious to the country, and the powers "then for the first time vested in Sessions Judges and High Courts of setting aside verdicts of "acquittal should be at once withdrawn"—

and Resolution X. of the Congress of 1886, to wit—

"That, in the opinion of this Congress, a provision similar to that contained in the Summary Jurisdiction "Act of England (under which accused persons in serious cases have the option of demanding a "committal to the Sessions Court) should be introduced into the Indian Code of Criminal Procedure, "enabling accused persons, in warrant cases, to demand that, instead of being tried by the Magistrate, "they be committed to the Court of Sessions"—

does now, hereby, affirm the same respectively.

RESOLUTION V.

Resolved—That, as it is the general belief of the people of this country that the existing system of police administration in India is highly unsatisfactory in itself and oppressive to them, the Government be respectfully urged to appoint a commission, consisting of official and non-official members, to investigate the entire question as speedily as possible.

RESOLUTION VI.

Resolved—That this Congress having read and considered Resolution IV. of the Congress of 1887, to wit—

"That in view of the loyalty of Her Majesty's Indian subjects, the Congress consider it desirable that the "Queen's Proclamation should be given effect to, that the Military services in the higher grades should "be practically opened to the natives of this country, and that the Government should establish Military "Colleges in the country whereat the natives of India, as defined by Statute, may be educated and "trained for a Military career as officers of the Indian Army;"

Resolution XII. of the Congress of 1886, and Resolution V. of the Congress of 1887, to wit—

"That in view of the unsettled state of public affairs in Europe, and the immense assistance that the "people of this country, if duly prepared there for, are capable of rendering to Great Britain in the "event of any serious complications arising, the Congress once again earnestly appeals to the Govern- "ment to authorize (under such rules and restrictions as to it may seem fitting) a system of "volunteering for the Indian inhabitants of the country, such as may qualify them to support the "Government effectually in any crises;"

and Resolution VIII. of the Congress of 1887, to wit—

"That in view of the loyalty of the people, the hardships which the present Arms Act (XI. of 1878) causes "and the unmerited slur which it casts upon the people of this country, the Government be moved "so to modify the provisions of Chapter IV., and if necessary other portions of the said Act, as shall "enable all persons to possess and wear Arms unless debarred therefrom, either as individuals, or "members of particular communities or classes, by the orders of the Government of India, (or any "local authority empowered by the Government of India on that behalf), for reasons to be recorded "in writing and duly published;"

does now, hereby, affirm the same respectively.

RESOLUTION VII.

Resolved—That, having regard to the fact that a serious increase in the consumption of intoxicants has taken place under the systems of Abkari and Excise now prevailing in India, the Government be respectfully urged to adopt some such improved system as shall tend to discourage insobriety.

RESOLUTION VIII.

Resolved—That as the administration of the Income Tax, especially as regards incomes below Rs. 1,000, has proved extremely unsatisfactory, it is essential, in the opinion of the Congress, that the taxable minimum be raised to Rs. 1,000.

RESOLUTION IX.

Resolved—That this Congress being of opinion that it is the first duty of the British Government in India to foster and encourage education, as well general as technical, in all its branches, and that the declaration made in the recent resolution of the Government of India on the subject of education is calculated to encourage the tendency to reduce imperial expenditure on education, and to withdraw from the control of it, respectfully urges upon Government the extreme importance of increasing, or at any rate of not decreasing, the present expenditure on education, and of the Government continuing to control the Educational Institutions of all kinds now existing.

RESOLUTION X.

Resolved—That, having regard to the poverty of the people, the importance of encouraging indigenous manufactures, and the difficulty of practically introducing any general system of technical education with the present imperfect information, Government be moved to delay no longer the appointment of a mixed commission, to enquire into the present industrial condition of the country.

RESOLUTION XI.

Resolved—That the foregoing Resolutions be submitted for the favourable consideration of His Excellency the Viceroy, and for transmission by him to Her Majesty's Government, with the humble request of this Congress that the reforms suggested in the said Resolutions (based as most of these are on Her Gracious Majesty's Proclamation of 1858) may now be effected ; and that should it be deemed necessary first to institute any enquiry into any of the matters forming the subjects of these Resolutions, such enquiry may be made, as speedily as possible, by a Parliamentary Committee.

RESOLUTION XII.

Resolved—That this Congress, having watched with interest and sympathy the exertions that are being made in England for the total abrogation of laws and rules relating to the regulation of prostitution by the State in India, places on record its appreciation of the services thus rendered to this country, and its desire to co-operate by all means in its power in the attainment of this laudable object.

RESOLUTION XIII.

Resolved—That no subject shall be passed for discussion by the Subjects Committee or allowed to be discussed at any Congress by the President thereof, to the introduction of which the Hindu or Mahomedan Delegates as a body object, unanimously or nearly unanimously ; and that if, after the discussion of any subject which has been admitted for discussion, it shall appear that all the Hindu or all the Mahomedan Delegates, as a body, are unanimously or nearly unanimously opposed to the Resolution which it is proposed to pass thereon, such Resolution shall be dropped ; provided that this rule shall refer only to subjects in regard to which the Congress has not already definitely pronounced an opinion.

RESOLUTION XIV.

Resolved—That the question of the introduction of a Permanent Settlement of the Land Revenue Demand into the Madras and Bombay Presidencies and other provinces be referred to the several standing Congress Committees, with instructions to report upon the same, in so far as it affects their respective circles, to the Congress of 1889.

RESOLUTION XV.

Resolved—That this Congress puts on record its disapproval of the recent enhancement of the Salt Tax, as involving a perceptible increase to the burthens of the poorer classes, as also the partial absorbtion, in a time of peace and plenty, of the only Financial Reserve of the Empire.

RESOLUTION XVI.

Resolved—That the Fifth Indian National Congress do assemble in the Bombay Presidency (either at Bombay itself or at Poona, as may be settled hereafter) on the 26th of December, 1889.

RESOLUTION XVII.

Resolved—That Mr. A. O. Hume be re-appointed General Secretary for the ensuing year.

RESOLUTION IX.

Resolved—That this Congress, being of opinion that it is the first duty of the British Government in India to foster and encourage education, as well general as technical, in all its branches, and that the declaration made in the recent resolution of the Government of India on the subject of education is calculated to encourage the tendency to reduce imperial expenditure on education and to withdraw from the control of it, respectfully urges upon Government the extreme importance of increasing, or at all events of not decreasing, the present expenditure on education, and of the Government continuing to control the educational institutions of all kinds now existing.

RESOLUTION X.

Resolved—That, having regard to the poverty of the people, the importance of encouraging indigenous manufactures, and the difficulty of practically introducing any general system of technical education with the present imperfect information, Government be moved to delay no longer the appointment of a mixed commission, to enquire into the present industrial condition of the country.

RESOLUTION XI.

Resolved—That the foregoing Resolutions be submitted for the favourable consideration of His Excellency the Viceroy, and for transmission by him to Her Majesty's Government, with the humble request of this Congress that the reforms suggested in the said Resolutions (based as most of these are on Her Gracious Majesty's Proclamation of 1858) may now be effected; and that should it be deemed necessary first to institute any enquiry into any of the matters forming the subjects of these Resolutions, such enquiry may be made, as speedily as possible, by a Parliamentary Committee.

RESOLUTION XII.

Resolved—That this Congress, having watched with interest and sympathy the exertions that are being made in England for the total abolition of State regulation of vice in India, places on record its appreciation of the services rendered to this country, and its desire to co-operate by all means in its power in the eradication of this loathsome evil.

RESOLUTION XIII.

Resolved—That no subject shall be passed for discussion by the Subjects Committee, or allowed to be discussed at any Congress by the President thereof, to the introduction of which the Hindu or Mahomedan Delegates as a body object, unanimously or nearly unanimously; and that if, after the discussion of any subject which has been admitted for discussion, it shall appear that all the Hindu or all the Mahomedan Delegates as a body are unanimously or nearly unanimously opposed to the Resolution which it is proposed to pass thereon, such Resolution shall be dropped; provided that this rule shall refer only to subjects in regard to which the Congress has not already definitely pronounced an opinion.

RESOLUTION XIV.

Resolved—That the question of the introduction of a Permanent Settlement of the Land Revenue Demand into the Madras and Bombay Presidencies and other provinces [illegible] in their bearing on the circumstances of their respective provinces, to the Congress of 1889.

RESOLUTION XV.

Resolved—That this Congress puts on record its disapproval of the recent enhancement of the Salt Tax, as involving a perceptible increase to the burdens of the poorer classes, as also the partial absorption, in a time of peace and plenty, of the only financial Reserve of the Empire.

RESOLUTION XVI.

Resolved—That the Fifth Indian National Congress do assemble in the Bombay Presidency (at Bombay or such other place as may be decided upon) on the 26th December 1889.

RESOLUTION XVII.

Resolved—That Mr. A. O. Hume be re-appointed General Secretary for the ensuing year.

LIST OF CONGRESS PUBLICATIONS

To be obtained at

THE OFFICE OF THE ADVOCATE, LUCKNOW.

BIOGRAPHY OF Mr. CHARLES BRADLAUGH M. P.—By Mr. Andelophe S. Headlingey with his Photo. Price Rs. 1, postage one anna.

INDIA IN ENGLAND, Vol. II.—Contents :—The introductory Essay.—Some Historial Analogies to the National Congress ; Reuter's Telegrams on the Congress ; Comments of the Press ; Sir Edward Watkin interviewed ; Mr. A. O. Hume on Sir Edward Watkin's attack, Mr. Bradlaugh Libelled ; Mr. William Digby on Sir E. Watkin's attack ; Memorandum of Indian Political Agency on the Reform of Councils ; Mr. Bradlaugh interviewed ; Two letters ot Mr. William Digby to the Secretary of State on the report of the Public Service Commission ; Mr. William Digby's interview with Right Hon. William E. Gladstone ; Nottingham liberals and Indian Reform; The Hull Radical Club and the Congress; Mr. J. Dacosta's Notes on the Assesment and Collection of the Land Revenue in India ; Mr. C. W. Whish on the Congress ; Mr. Frederick Pincott on the Congress ; Mr. Robert Brown on the Indian Financial Statement 1889-90 ; The Queen Empress's Promises : how they are broken ; Work of the Indian Political Agency ; India Awake ; Mr. Charless Bradlaugh at Newcastle ; Mr. Dadabahi Nowroji at Loughborough ; India neglected in the Queen's speech ; the Congress Catechism in Parliament ; Memo by Sir William Wedderburn ; Mr. C. Bradlaugh at Home ; Mr. Bradlaugh's Good Services for India ; Mr. Bradlaugh on the Indian Uncovenanted Service ; Mr. Bradlaugh on the Indian Budget ; The Liverpool demonstration ; Mr. W. S. B. MacLaren at Crew. Price Re. 1 Postage two annas.

INDIA IN ENGLAND, Vol. I.—Contents :—Introduction ; Recent movements of India ; Mr. Dadabhai Naoroji at Islington Club ; Mr. Caine M. P. on the Congress ; The Indian Political and General Agency ; Circular letter ; Placards ; Sir W. W. Hunter's articles in the *Times* ; Cuttings from the English Press ; Garth's "A few Plain Truths about India ;" Mr. W. C. Bonnerji at Wainfleet ; Mr. Eardley Norton and Mr. W. C. Bonnerji at Bensham grove Gateshead ; Statement prepared by the English Agency for the information of the members of Parliament ; Indian Budget in the Parliament ; Great meeting in Northampton ; The present Problem in India ; Mr. W. C. Bonnerji at Wood Hall Spa ; Mr. W. C. Bonnerji at Tetford ; Mr. W. C. Bonnerji at Spalding ; Mr. W. C. Bonnerji at Lincoln ; Mr. Bradlaugh's speech on our Indian Empire ; Sir William Wedderburn's Lecture on our duty to Iudia ; Sir J. B. Phear on the Congress ; Mr. William Digby on Sir Auckland Colvin ; Letters and articles of the opponents; Letters of Mr. Eardlev Norton to the *Hindu* of Madras.

PUBLIC SERVICE COMMISSION AND ITS RESULT—Contains conclusions and suggestions of the Commission, Government of India and Lord Cross's dispatches. Price 8 annas, postage 6 pies.

REPORT OF THE FIRST NATIONAL CONGRESS.—A reprint of the First Report on the size of other reports. Price 8 annas, postage half anna.

LORD SALISBURY'S "BLACKMAN."—Containing cuttings from some 200 English papers bearing on the incident ; also speeches of the Hon'ble Dadabhai Nowrojee, Lord Ripon, Mr. W. Hunter, M. P. and other English politicians at the National Liberal Club meeting, with full reports of all other sympathetic public meetings held in England in honor of Mr. Nowroji with several wood cuts. Price 8 annas, postage half anna.

INDIA AS SEEN BY MR. CAINE.—Mr. W. S. Caine's ten letters, which he addressed to the English papers from India and which were reprinted by the Indian papers only in parts. Price annas 8, postage half anna.

THE DRINK QUESTION IN PARLIAMENT.—Contains the full report of the speeches of Mr. S. Smith, Mr. W. S. Caine, Sir R. Lethbridge, Sir Richard Temple, Sir John Gorst, Sir W. Harcourt, and other speakers. Price annas 2, postage half anna.

MR. E. NORTON *versus* LORD DUFFERIN.—A pamphlet containing Lord Dufferin's St. Andrews Dinner speech, and Mr. E. Norton's Open letter to his Lordship. Price annas 2, postage half anna.

TWO MEMORABLE SPEECHES.—Delivered by Mr. E. Norton at Pacheapaha's Hall, Madras, giving a full account of his English travels. Price 1 anna and 6 pies, postage half anna.

	Price.			*Postage.*		
Audi Altrem Partem	0	3	0	0	0	6
Third Congress Report	1	0	0	0	3	0
Fourth Congress Report	1	0	0	0	3	0
Fifth Congress Report	1	0	0	0	3	0
Mr. Hume's Allahabad speech		free		0	0	6
Babu Surendra Nath Bannerji on present problem of India...		free		0	0	6
Mr. George Yule's Inaugural address ...		free		0	0	6
Open letters to Sir Syed Ahmad Khan ...		free		0	0	6
Congress edition of the *Advocate,* contains the detailed account of the fifth Congress	0	2	0	0	0	6

URDU.

Second Congress Report	1	0	0	0	2	0
Third Congress Report	1	0	0	0	2	0
Fourth Congress Report	1	0	0	0	2	0
Fifth Congress Report (will be out in March)	1	0	0	0	2	0
Conversation of Moulvi Farid-ud-din and Ram Baksh ...	0	0	6	0	0	6
Catechism	0	0	3	0	0	6
Short History of English Constitution ...	0	8	0	0	0	6
Mr. Hume's Allahabad speech	0	0	6	0	0	6
Sir W. W. Hunter's article in the *Times* and short account of English Agency	0	1	6	0	0	6
Lord Dufferin's St. Andrews Dinner speech and Mr. Eardley Norton's Open letter	0	1	6	0	0	6
Letters of Mr. Hume and Sir Auckland Colvin	0	3	0	0	0	6
Nakkara Islam—a Poem	0	0	6	0	0	6
Lucknow speech of Hon'ble Pandit Ayodhia Nath ...	0	1	0	0	0	6

HINDI.

Fourth Congress Report	1	0	0	0	3	0
Fifth Congress Report (will be out in April)	1	0	0	0	3	0
Short History of English Constitution	0	8	0	0	0	6
Catechism		free		0	0	6

☞ ***All books or pamphlets, ordered will be sent by Value Payable Post unless the price as noted above plus postage is sent with order.***

Professor Mushirul Hasan is an internationally renowned historian, prolific author and former Vice-Chancellor of Jamia Millia Islamia University, Delhi. Professor Hasan has also authored *Partners in Freedom, Jamia Millia Islamia* (Niyogi Books, 2006); *Moving Memories* (Niyogi Books, 2009) and *The Avadh Punch: Wit and Humour in Colonial North India* (2007) and *Wit and Wisdom: Pickings from the Avadh Punch* (2012) as part of the Avadh series brought out by Niyogi Books.

He has written extensively on the Partition of India, on communalism and on the histories of Islam in South Asia. Professor Hasan was the elected President of the Indian History Congress in 2002. In 2007, he was awarded the Padma Shri by the Government of India and in 2010 the Ordre des Palmes Académiques was conferred upon him by the French Government. He is presently the Director General of the National Archives of India.

Professor Mushirul Hasan is an internationally renowned historian, prolific author and former Vice-Chancellor of Jamia Milia Islamia University, Delhi. Professor Hasan has also authored *Partners in Freedom: Jamia Milia Islamia* (Niyogi Books, 2006); *Mutiny Memoirs* (Niyogi Books, 2009); and *The Avadh Punch: Wit and Humour in Colonial North India* (2007) and *Wit and Wisdom: Pickings from the Parsee Punch* (2012) as part of the Punch series brought out by Niyogi Books.

He has written extensively on the Partition of India, on communalism and on the histories of Islam in South Asia. Professor Hasan was the elected President of the Indian History Congress in 2002. In 2007, he was awarded the Padma Shri by the Government of India and in 2010 the Ordre des Palmes Académiques was conferred upon him by the French Government. He is presently the Director General of the National Archives of India.